Brill's
New Pauly

ANTIQUITY
VOLUME 6

HAT-JUS

Brill's New Pauly

Brill's

Encyclopaedia of the Ancient World

New Pauly

Edited by
Hubert Cancik and
Helmuth Schneider

English Edition
Managing Editor *Christine F. Salazar*

Assistant Editors *Simon Buck, Tina Chronopoulos,*
Susanne E. Hakenbeck, Tina Jerke, Ingrid Rosa Kitzberger,
Claudia Kunze, Sebastiaan R. van der Mije, Astrid Möller,
Antonia Ruppel, Reinhard Selinger and *Ernest Suyver*

ANTIQUITY
VOLUME 6

HAT-JUS

BRILL
LEIDEN · BOSTON
2005

© Copyright 2005 by Koninklijke Brill NV,
Leiden, The Netherlands

Koninklijke Brill NV incorporates the imprints
Brill Academic Publishers, Martinus Nijhoff
Publishers and VSP.

Originally published in German as DER NEUE
PAULY. Enzyklopädie der Antike. Herausgegeben
von Hubert Cancik und Helmuth Schneider.
Copyright © J.B. Metzlersche Verlagsbuch-
handlung und Carl Ernst Poeschel Verlag
GmbH 1996ff./1999ff. Stuttgart/Weimar

Cover design: TopicA (Antoinette Hanekuyk)
Front: Delphi, temple area
Spine: Tabula Peutingeriana

Translation by protext TRANSLATIONS B.V.

Data structuring and typesetting:
pagina GmbH, Tübingen, Germany

The publication of this work was supported
by a grant from the GOETHE-INSTITUT INTER
NATIONES.

ISBN (volume) 90 04 12269 9
ISBN (set) 90 04 12259 1

Table of Contents

Notes to the User

Arrangement of Entries

The entries are arranged alphabetically and, if applicable, placed in chronological order. In the case of alternative forms or sub-entries, cross-references will lead to the respective main entry. Composite entries can be found in more than one place (e.g. *a commentariis* refers to *commentariis, a*).

Identical entries are differentiated by numbering. Identical Greek and Oriental names are arranged chronologically without consideration of people's nicknames. Roman names are ordered alphabetically, first according to the *gentilicium* or *nomen* (family name), then the *cognomen* (literally 'additional name' or nickname) and finally the *praenomen* or 'fore-name' (e.g. *M. Aemilius Scaurus* is found under *Aemilius*, not *Scaurus*).

However, well-known classical authors are lemmatized according to their conventional names in English; this group of persons is not found under the family name, but under their *cognomen* (e.g. Cicero, not Tullius). In large entries the Republic and the Imperial period are treated separately.

Spelling of Entries

Greek words and names are as a rule latinized, following the predominant practice of reference works in the English language, with the notable exception of technical terms. Institutions and places (cities, rivers, islands, countries etc.) often have their conventional English names (e.g. *Rome* not *Roma*). The latinized versions of Greek names and words are generally followed by the Greek and the literal transliteration in brackets, e.g. *Aeschylus* (Αἰσχύλος; *Aischýlos*).

Oriental proper names are usually spelled according to the 'Tübinger Atlas des Vorderen Orients' (TAVO), but again conventional names in English are also used. In the maps, the names of cities, rivers, islands, countries etc. follow ancient spelling and are transliterated fully to allow for differences in time, e.g. both Καππαδόκια and *Cappadocia* can be found. The transliteration of non-Latin scripts can be found in the 'List of Transliterations'.

Latin and transliterated Greek words are italicized in the article text. However, where Greek transliterations do not follow immediately upon a word written in Greek, they will generally appear in italics, but without accents or makra.

Abbreviations

All abbreviations can be found in the 'List of Abbreviations' in the first volume. Collections of inscriptions, coins and papyri are listed under their *sigla*.

Bibliographies

Most entries have bibliographies, consisting of numbered and/or alphabetically organized references. References within the text to the numbered bibliographic items are in square brackets (e.g. [1.5 n.23] refers to the first title of the bibliography, page 5, note 23). The abbreviations within the bibliographies follow the rules of the 'List of Abbreviations'.

Maps

Texts and maps are closely linked and complementary, but some maps also treat problems outside the text. The authors of the maps are listed in the 'List of Maps'.

Cross-references

Articles are linked through a system of cross-references with an arrow → before the entry that is being referred to.

Cross-references to related entries are given at the end of an article, generally before the bibliographic notes. If reference is made to a homonymous entry, the respective number is also added.

Cross-references to entries in the *Classical Tradition* volumes are added in small capitals.

It can occur that in a cross-reference a name is spelled differently from the surrounding text: e.g., a cross-reference to Mark Antony has to be to Marcus → Antonius, as his name will be found in a list of other names containing the component 'Antonius'.

List of Transliterations

Transliteration of ancient Greek

α	a	alpha
αι	ai	
αυ	au	
β	b	beta
γ	g	gamma; γ before γ, κ, ξ, χ: n
δ	d	delta
ε	e	epsilon
ει	ei	
ευ	eu	
ζ	z	z(d)eta
η	ē	eta
ηυ	ēu	
θ	th	theta
ι	i	iota
κ	k	kappa
λ	l	la(m)bda
μ	m	mu
ν	n	nu
ξ	x	xi
ο	o	omicron
οι	oi	
ου	ou	
π	p	pi
ϱ	r	rho
σ, ς	s	sigma
τ	t	tau
υ	y	upsilon
φ	ph	phi
χ	ch	chi
ψ	ps	psi
ω	ō	omega
ʽ	h	spiritus asper
ᾳ	ai	iota subscriptum (similarly ῃ, ῳ)

In transliterated Greek the accents are retained (acute ´, grave `, and circumflex ^). Long vowels with the circumflex accent have no separate indication of vowel length (makron).

Transliteration of Hebrew

א	a	alef
ב	b	bet
ג	g	gimel
ד	d	dalet
ה	h	he
ו	w	vav
ז	z	zayin
ח	ḥ	khet
ט	ṭ	tet
י	y	yod
כ	k	kaf
ל	l	lamed
מ	m	mem
נ	n	nun
ס	s	samek
ע	ʿ	ayin
פ	p/f	pe
צ	ṣ	tsade
ק	q	qof
ר	r	resh
שׂ	ś	sin
שׁ	š	shin
ת	t	tav

Pronunciation of Turkish

Turkish uses Latin script since 1928. Pronunciation and spelling generally follow the same rules as European languages. Phonology according to G. Lewis, Turkish Grammar, 2000.

A	a	French a in *avoir*
B	b	b
C	c	j in *jam*
Ç	ç	ch in *church*
D	d	d
E	e	French ê in *être*
F	f	f
G	g	g in *gate* or in *angular*
Ğ	ğ	lengthens preceding vowel
H	h	h in *have*
I	ı	i in *cousin*
İ	i	French i in *si*
J	j	French j
K	k	c in *cat* or in *cure*
L	l	l in *list* or in *wool*
M	m	m

N	n	n
O	o	French o in *note*
Ö	ö	German ö
P	p	p
R	r	r
S	s	s in *sit*
Ş	ş	sh in *shape*
T	t	t
U	u	u in *put*
Ü	ü	German ü
V	v	v
Y	y	y in *yet*
Z	z	z

Transliteration of Arabic, Persian, and Ottoman Turkish

ء, ا	ʾ, ā	ʾ	ʾ	hamza, alif
ب	b	b	b	bāʾ
پ	–	p	p	pe
ت	t	t	t	tāʾ
ث	t̲	s̱	s̱	t̲āʾ
ج	ǧ	ǧ	ǧ	ǧīm
چ	–	č	č	čim
ح	ḥ	ḥ	ḥ	ḥāʾ
خ	ḫ	ḫ	ḫ	ḫāʾ
د	d	d	d	dāl
ذ	d̲	z̲	z̲	d̲āl
ر	r	r	r	rāʾ
ز	z	z	z	zāy
ژ	–	ž	ž	že
س	s	s	s	sīn
ش	š	š	š	šīn
ص	ṣ	ṣ	ṣ	ṣād
ض	ḍ	ḍ	ḍ	ḍād
ط	ṭ	ṭ	ṭ	ṭāʾ
ظ	ẓ	ẓ	ẓ	ẓāʾ
ع	ʿ	ʿ	ʿ	ʿain
غ	ġ	ġ	ġ	ġain
ف	f	f	f	fāʾ
ق	q	q	q, k	qāf
ك	k	k	k, g, ñ	kāf
گ	–	g	g, ñ	gāf
ل	l	l	l	lām
م	m	m	m	mīm
ن	n	n	n	nūn
ه	h	h	h	hāʾ
و	w, ū	v	v	wāw
ى	y, ī	y	y	yāʾ

Transliteration of other languages

Akkadian (Assyrian-Babylonian), Hittite and Sumerian are transliterated according to the rules of RLA and TAVO. For Egyptian the rules of the Lexikon der Ägyptologie are used. The transliteration of Indo-European follows Rix, HGG. The transliteration of Old Indian is after M. Mayrhofer, Etymologisches Wörterbuch des Altindoarischen, 1992ff. Avestian is done according to K. Hoffmann, B. Forssman, Avestische Laut- und Flexionslehre, 1996. Old Persian follows R.G. Kent, Old Persian, ²1953 (additions from K. Hoffmann, Aufsätze zur Indoiranistik vol. 2, 1976, 622ff.); other Iranian languages are after R. Schmitt, Compendium linguarum Iranicarum, 1989, and after D.N. MacKenzie, A Concise Pahlavi Dictionary, ³1990. For Armenian the rules of R. Schmitt, Grammatik des Klassisch-Armenischen, 1981, and of the Revue des études arméniennes, apply. The languages of Asia Minor are transliterated according to HbdOr. For Mycenean, Cyprian see Heubeck and Masson; for Italic scripts and Etruscan see Vetter and ET.

List of Illustrations and Maps

Illustrations are found in the corresponding entries.
ND means redrawing following the instructions of the
author or after the listed materials.
RP means reproduction with minor changes.

Some of the maps serve to visualize the subject matter
and to complement the articles. In such cases, there will
be a reference to the corresponding entry. Only literature that was used exclusively for the maps is listed.

Lemma Title AUTHORS Bibliography

Ḫattusa
Hattusa: archaeological site-plan (period of the Hit-
tite Empire)
ND: J. SEEHER (after P. NEVE, Die Ausgrabungen in
Bogazköy/Hattusa 1993, in: AA 1994, 290 Fig. 1)
Summary of Hittite kings and queens
ND after originals by F. STARKE
Political map of the Hittite Empire: 'Ḫattusa' (13th
cent. BC)
ND: F. STARKE

Headgear
Greek headgear
Sakkos
ND after: H. Blanck, Einführung in das Privatleben
der Griechen und Römer, 1976, 62, fig. 14 K
Kekryphalos
ND after: same, fig. 14 M
Tholia
ND after: H. Kühnel, Bildwörterbuch der Kleidung
und Rüstung, 1992, 262
Petasos
ND after: same, 52
Pilos
ND after: P. Paris, s.v. Pileus, DS 4.1.479, fig. 5670
Kausia
ND after: L. Heuzey, s.v. Causia, DS 1.2, 975, fig.
1259
Phrygian cap
ND after: G. Seiterle, Die Urform de phrygischen
Mütze, in: Antike Welt 16.3, 1985, 15, fig. 9
Roman headgear
Ricinium
ND after: U. Scharf, Straßenbekleidung der römi-
schen Frau, 1994, 123, fig. 23
Suffibulum
ND after: same, 127, fig. 24

Heating
Hypocaust
ND after an original by H.-O. LAMPRECHT

Hellenistic states
The Hellenistic world in the 3rd. cent. BC
ND: W. EDER/EDITORIAL TEAM TÜBINGEN (after:
H. WALDMANN, Vorderer Orient. Die hellenistische
Staatenwelt im 3. Jh. v. Chr., TAVO B V 3, 1983.
© Dr. Ludwig Reichert Verlag, Wiesbaden)
The Hellenistic world in the 2nd. cent. BC
ND: W. EDER/EDITORIAL TEAM TÜBINGEN (after:
H. WALDMANN, Vorderer Orient. Die hellenistische
Staatenwelt im 2. Jh. v. Chr., TAVO B V 4, 1985.
© Dr. Ludwig Reichert Verlag, Wiesbaden)

Helmet
Ancient Helmets
ND after: A. BOTTINI (Ed.), Antike Helme. Collec-
tion Lipperheide et al., exhibition catalogue Staatl.
Mus. Preuss. Kulturbesitz, Antikenmuseum Berlin,
1988
Mycenaean boar's tusk helmet: 192 fig. 9
Oriental pointed helmet: 192, fig. 9
Oriental caterpillar-crested helmet: 192, fig. 9
Cypriot helmet: 33, fig. 7
Geometric conical helmet: 21, fig. 10A
Illyrian helmet: 43, fig. 1
Corinthian helmet (early): 91, fig. 32
Corinthian helmet (middle): 77, fig. 77
Corinthian helmet (late): 91, fig. 32
Chalcidian helmet: 138, fig. 2
Pilos type helmet: app. 1 nr. 3
Attic helmet: app. 1 nr. 17
Phrygian helmet: app. 1 nr. 9
Helmet with transverse crest: 192, fig. 9
Negau type helmet: 269, fig. 44
Helmet with fluted front part and cut-outs for the
ears: 281, fig. 8
Hagenau type helmet: app. 2 nr. 4
Weisenau type helmet: app. 2 nr. 9
Face helmet: app. 2 nr. 35
Gladiator's helmet: 368, fig. 5

Herculaneum
Herculaneum: site-map
ND: CH. HÖCKER/EDITORIAL TEAM TÜBINGEN

Herodes
Stemma
ND: K. BRINGMANN

Heuneburg
The 'princely seat' of the Heuneburg (Hallstatt pe-
riod, 6th cent. BC)
ND: V. PINGEL

List of Authors

Aigner-Foresti, Luciana, Vienna	L.A.-F.	Daverio Rocchi, Giovanna, Milan	G.D.R.
Albiani, Maria Grazia, Bologna	M.G.A.	De Francesco, Giuliana, Genova	G.d.F.
Ambühl, Annemarie, Basle	A.A.	de Libero, Loretana, Hamburg	L.d.L.
Ameling, Walter, Jena	W.A.	Decker, Wolfgang, Cologne	W.D.
Bäbler, Balbina, Göttingen	B.BÄ.	Di Marco, Massimo, Fondi (Latina)	M.D.MA.
Badian, Ernst, Cambridge, MA	E.B.	Diefenbach, Steffen, Erfurt	ST.D.
Baltes, Matthias, Münster	M.BA.	Dietz, Karlheinz, Würzburg	K.DI.
Bär, Jürgen, Berlin	J.BÄ.	Docter, Roald Frithjof, Gent	R.D.
Barceló, Pedro, Potsdam	P.B.	Domhardt, Yvonne, Zürich	Y.D.
Baudy, Dorothea, Konstanz	D.B.	Donohue, Alice A., Bryn Mawr	A.A.D.
Baudy, Gerhard, Konstanz	G.B.	Dorandi, Tiziano, Paris	T.D.
Beck, Hans, Cologne	HA.BE.	Döring, Klaus, Bamberg	K.D.
Belke, Klaus, Vienna	K.BE.	Doyen-Higuet, Anne-Marie, Ciney	A.D.-H.
Bendlin, Andreas, Erfurt	A.BEN.	Dräger, Paul, Trier	P.D.
Berger, Albrecht, Berlin	AL.B.	Drew-Bear, Thomas, Lyon	T.D.-B.
Betegh, Gábor, Budapest	G.BE.	Drexhage, Hans-Joachim, Marburg/Lahn	H.-J.D.
Bieberstein, Klaus, Fribourg	K.B.	Dreyer, Boris, Göttingen	BO.D.
Binder, Gerhard, Bochum	G.BI.	Ebner, Constanze, Innsbruck	C.E.
Binder, Vera, Gießen	V.BI.	Eck, Werner, Cologne	W.E.
Birley, A.R., Düsseldorf	A.B.	Eder, Walter, Bochum	W.ED.
Bleckmann, Bruno, Bern	B.BL.	Ego, Beate, Osnabrück	B.E.
Bloch, René, Princeton, NJ	R.B.	Eigler, Ulrich, Trier	U.E.
Blume, Horst-Dieter, Münster	H.-D.B.	Eleuteri, Paolo, Venice	P.E.
Böttrich, Christfried, Leipzig	CHR.B.	Elvers, Karl-Ludwig, Bochum	K.-L.E.
Bowie, Ewen, Oxford	E.BO.	Engels, Johannes, Cologne	J.E.
von Bredow, Iris, Stuttgart	I.v.B.	Englund, Robert K., Berlin	R.K.E.
Bremmer, Jan N., Groningen	J.B.	Erler, Michael, Würzburg	M.ER.
Brentjes, Burchard, Berlin	B.B.	Errington, Robert Malcolm, Marburg/Lahn	MA.ER.
Breuer, Stefan, Bonn	ST.B.	Euskirchen, Marion, Bonn	M.E.
Bringmann, Klaus, Frankfurt/Main	K.BR.	Falco, Giulia, Athens	GI.F.
Brisson, Luc, Paris	L.BR.	Fantuzzi, Marco, Florence	M.FA.
Brock, Sebastian P., Oxford	S.BR.	Felber, Heinz, Leipzig	HE.FE.
Brodersen, Kai, Newcastle and Mannheim	K.BRO.	Fell, Martin, Münster	M.FE.
Buonocore, Marco, Rome	M.BU.	Folkerts, Menso, Munich	M.F.
Burchard, Christoph, Göttingen	CH.BU.	Forgó, Nikolaus, Vienna	N.F.
Burckhardt, Leonhard, Basle	LE.BU.	Fornaro, Sotera, Sassari	S.FO.
Burian, Jan, Prague	J.BU.	Forssman, Bernhard, Erlangen	B.F.
Cabanes, Pierre, Clermont-Ferrand	PI.CA.	Frahm, Eckart, Heidelberg	E.FRA.
Calboli, Gualtiero, Bologna	G.C.	Franke, Thomas, Bochum	T.F.
Calmeyer-Seidl, Ursula, Berlin	U.SE.	Freitag, Klaus, Münster	K.F.
Camassa, Giorgio, Udine	G.CA.	Frey, Jörg, Stuttgart	J.FR.
Campbell, J.Brian, Belfast	J.CA.	Freyburger, Gérard, Mulhouse	G.F.
Cancik, Hubert, Tübingen	HU.C.	Frigo, Thomas, Bonn	T.FR.
Cancik-Lindemaier, Hildegard, Tübingen	H.C.-L.	Fröhlich, Roland, Tübingen	RO.F.
Carmichael, Calum M., Ithaca, NY	C.M.C.	Fuhrer, Therese, Zürich	T.FU.
Cartledge, Paul A., Cambridge	P.C.	Fündling, Jörg, Bonn	JÖ.F.
Chantraine, Heinrich, Mannheim	HE.C.	Funke, Peter, Münster	P.F.
Christmann, Eckhard, Heidelberg	E.C.	Furley, William D., Heidelberg	W.D.F.
Cobet, Justus, Essen	J.CO.	Fusillo, Massimo, L'Aquila	M.FU.
Colpe, Carsten, Berlin	C.C.	Galli, Lucia, Florence	L.G.
Courtney, Edward, Charlottesville, VA	ED.C.	Galsterer, Hartmut, Bonn	H.GA.

Galter, Hannes D., Graz	HA. G.	Kaletsch, Hans, Regensburg	H. KA.
Gamauf, Richard, Vienna	R. GA.	Käppel, Lutz, Kiel	L. K.
García-Ramón, José Luis, Cologne	J. G.-R.	Karttunen, Klaus, Helsinki	K. K.
Gatti, Paolo, Triento	P. G.	Kaster, Robert A., Princeton	R. A. K.
Gehrke, Hans-Joachim, Freiburg	H.-J. G.	Kaufmann, Helen, Basle	HE. KA.
Geppert, Karin, Tübingen	KA. GE.	Kehne, Peter, Hannover	P. KE.
Giaro, Tomasz, Frankfurt/Main	T. G.	Kessler, Karlheinz, Emskirchen	K. KE.
Gippert, Jost, Frankfurt/Main	J. G.	Kierdorf, Wilhelm, Cologne	W. K.
Gizewski, Christian, Berlin	C. G.	King, Helen, Reading	H. K.
Gödde, Susanne, Münster	S. G.	Klinger, Jörg, Bochum	J. KL.
Görgemanns, Herwig, Heidelberg	H. GÖ.	Klodt, Claudia, Hamburg	CL. K.
Gottschalk, Hans, Leeds	H. G.	Klose, Dietrich, Munich	DI. K.
Goulet-Cazé, Marie-Odile, Antony	M. G.-C.	Knauf, Ernst Axel, Bern	E. A. K.
Graf, Fritz, Princeton, NJ	F. G.	Knell, Heiner, Darmstadt	H. KN.
Graßl, Herbert, Salzburg	H. GR.	Köckert, Matthias, Berlin	M. K.
Green, Anthony, Berlin	A. GR.	Kohler, Christoph, Bad Krozingen	C. KO.
Grieshammer, Reinhard, Heidelberg	R. GR.	Kramolisch, Herwig, Eppelheim	HE. KR.
Groß-Albenhausen, Kirsten, Frankfurt/Main	K. G.-A.	Krause, Jens-Uwe, Munich	J. K.
Gschnitzer, Fritz, Heidelberg	F. GSCH.	Kuhrt, Amélie, London	A. KU.
Gundel, Hans Georg, Gießen	H. G. G.	Kunz, Heike, Tübingen	HE. K.
Gundert, Beate, London, Ontario	BE. GU.	Kytzler, Bernhard, Durban	B. KY.
Günther, Linda-Marie, Bochum	L.-M. G.	Lafond, Yves, Bochum	Y. L.
Gutsfeld, Andreas, Münster	A. G.	Lakmann, Marie-Luise, Münster	M.-L. L.
Haase, Mareile, Erfurt	M. HAA.	Lamprecht, Heinz-Otto, Cologne	H.-O. L.
Haase, Richard, Leonberg	RI. H.	Latacz, Joachim, Basle	J. L.
Hadot, Ilsetraut, Limours	I. H.	Le Bohec, Yann, Lyon	Y. L. B.
Hadot, Pierre, Limours	P. HA.	Leisten, Thomas, Princeton, NJ	T. L.
Haebler, Claus, Münster	C. H.	Leonhardt, Jürgen, Marburg/Lahn	J. LE.
Halbwachs, Verena Tiziana, Vienna	V. T. H.	Leppin, Hartmut, Frankfurt/Main	H. L.
Harder, Ruth Elisabeth, Zürich	R. HA.	Ley, Anne, Xanten	A. L.
Hartmann, Elke, Berlin	E. HA.	Liebermann, Wolf-Lüder, Bielefeld	W.-L. L.
Hauser, Stefan R., Berlin	S. HA.	Lienau, Cay, Münster	C. L.
Heeßel, Nils, Heidelberg	NI. HE.	von Lieven, Alexandra, Berlin	A. v. L.
Heider, Ulrich, Cologne	U. HE.	Liwak, Rüdiger, Berlin	R. L.
Heimgartner, Martin, Basle	M. HE.	Lohmann, Hans, Bochum	H. LO.
Heinze, Theodor, Geneva	T. H.	Löhr, Winrich Alfried, Cambridge	W. LÖ.
Herzhoff, Bernhard, Trier	B. HE.	Lombardo, Mario, Lecce	M. L.
Heyworth, Stephen, Oxford	S. H.	Losemann, Volker, Marburg/Lahn	V. L.
Hidber, Thomas, Göttingen	T. HI.	Maaß, Michael, Karlsruhe	MI. MA.
Hild, Friedrich, Vienna	F. H.	Manganaro, Giacomo, Sant' Agata li Battiata	GI. MA.
Hitzl, Konrad, Tübingen	K. H.	Manthe, Ulrich, Passau	U. M.
Höcker, Christoph, Zürich	C. HÖ.	Markschies, Christoph, Heidelberg	C. M.
Höckmann, Olaf, Mainz	O. H.	Mastrocinque, Attilio, Verona	A. MAS.
Hoesch, Nicola, Munich	N. H.	Mehl, Andreas, Halle/Saale	A. ME.
Högemann, Peter, Tübingen	PE. HÖ.	Meier, Mischa, Bielefeld	M. MEI.
Holzhausen, Jens, Berlin	J. HO.	Meiser, Gerhard, Halle/Saale	GE. ME.
Hose, Martin, Munich	MA. HO.	Meißner, Burkhard, Halle/Saale	B. M.
Hübner, Wolfgang, Münster	W. H.	Meissel, Franz-Stefan, Vienna	F. ME.
Hünemörder, Christian, Hamburg	C. HÜ.	Meister, Klaus, Berlin	K. MEI.
Hunger, Hermann, Vienna	H. HU.	Meloni, Piero, Cagliari	P. M.
Hunter, Richard, Cambridge	R. HU.	Menci, Giovanna, Florence	G. M.
Hurschmann, Rolf, Hamburg	R. H.	Meyer-Schwelling, Stefan, Tübingen	S. M.-S.
Huß, Werner, Munich	W. HU.	Michel, Simone, Hamburg	S. MI.
Inwood, Brad, Toronto, ON	B. I.	Miller, Martin, Berlin	M. M.
Jansen-Winkeln, Karl, Berlin	K. J.-W.	Mlasowsky, Alexander, Hannover	A. M.
Johne, Klaus-Peter, Berlin	K. P. J.	Mommsen, Heide, Stuttgart	H. M.
Johnston, Sarah Iles, Columbus	S. I. J.	Montanari, Franco, Pisa	F. M.
Kalcyk, Hansjörg, Petershausen	H. KAL.	Montanari, Ornella, Bologna	O. M.

Most, Glenn W., Pisa	G.W.M.	Sallmann, Klaus, Mainz	KL.SA.
Müller, Christian, Bochum	C.MÜ.	Sancisi-Weerdenburg, Helen, Utrecht	H.S.-W.
Müller-Kessler, Christa, Emskirchen	C.K.	Santi Amantini, Luigi, Genova	L.S.A.
Nadig, Peter C., Duisburg	P.N.	Šašel Kos, Marjeta, Ljubljana	M.Š.K.
Narcy, Michel, Paris	MI.NA.	Sauer, Vera, Stuttgart	V.S.
Neschke, Ada, Lausanne	A.NE.	Savvidis, Kyriakos, Bochum	K.SA.
Nesselrath, Heinz-Günther, Göttingen	H.-G.NE.	Schaffner, Brigitte, Basle	B.SCH.
Neudecker, Richard, Rome	R.N.	Schaller, Bernd, Göttingen	BE.SCH.
Neumann, Günter, Münster	G.N.	Schanbacher, Dietmar, Dresden	D.SCH.
Neumann, Hans, Berlin	H.N.	Scheibler, Ingeborg, Krefeld	I.S.
Niehoff, Johannes, Budapest	J.N.	Scheid, John, Paris	J.S.
Niehr, Herbert, Tübingen	H.NI.	Scherf, Johannes, Tübingen	JO.S.
Niemeyer, Hans Georg, Hamburg	H.G.N.	Schiemann, Gottfried, Tübingen	G.S.
Nissen, Hans Jörg, Berlin	H.J.N.	Schmidt, Peter Lebrecht, Konstanz	P.L.S.
Nünlist, René, Providence, RI	RE.N.	Schmitt-Pantel, Pauline, Paris	P.S.-P.
Nutton, Vivian, London	V.N.	Schmitz, Winfried, Bielefeld	W.S.
Oakley, John H., Williamsburg, VA	J.O.	Schneider, Helmuth, Kassel	H.SCHN.
Oelsner, Joachim, Leipzig	J.OE.	Schön, Franz, Regensburg	F.SCH.
Oettinger, Norbert, Augsburg	N.O.	Schönig, Hanne, Halle/Saale	H.SCHÖ.
Olshausen, Eckart, Stuttgart	E.O.	Schottky, Martin, Pretzfeld	M.SCH.
Osborne, Robin, Oxford	R.O.	Schulte-Altedorneburg, Jörg, Marburg/Lahn	J.S.-A.
Osing, Jürgen, Berlin	J.OS.	Schulze, Christian, Bochum	CH.S.
Pahlitzsch, Johannes, Berlin	J.P.	Schulzki, Heinz-Joachim, Freudenstadt	H.-J.S.
Pappalardo, Umberto, Naples	U.PA.	Schwertheim, Elmar, Münster	E.SCH.
Patzek, Barbara, Essen	B.P.	Seeher, Jürgen, Istanbul	J.SE.
Paulus, Christoph Georg, Berlin	C.PA.	Seidlmayer, Stephan Johannes, Berlin	S.S.
Peschlow-Bindokat, Anneliese, Berlin	A.PE.	Senff, Reinhard, Bochum	R.SE.
Peter, Ulrike, Berlin	U.P.	Siebert, Anne Viola, Hannover	A.V.S.
Pingel, Volker, Bochum	V.P.	Sievertsen, Uwe, Tübingen	U.S.
Plath, Robert, Erlangen	R.P.	Siewert, Peter, Vienna	P.SI.
Plontke-Lüning, Annegret, Jena	A.P.-L.	Simon, Dietrich, Jena	DI.S.
Podella, Thomas, Lübeck	TH.PO.	Sonnabend, Holger, Stuttgart	H.SO.
Portmann, Werner, Berlin	W.P.	Spickermann, Wolfgang, Bochum	W.SP.
Potter, Paul, London, Ontario	P.PO.	Spitzbart, Günter, Herscheid	G.SP.
Prayon, Friedhelm, Tübingen	F.PR.	Stanzel, Karl-Heinz, Tübingen	K.-H.S.
Prescendi, Francesca, Geneva	FR.P.	Starke, Frank, Tübingen	F.S.
Pressler, Frank, Freiburg	F.P.	Stegemann, Ekkehard, Basle	E.STE.
Raber, Fritz, Innsbruck	FR.R.	Stegmann, Helena, Bonn	H.S.
Radke, Gerhard, Berlin	G.RA.	Stein-Hölkeskamp, Elke, Cologne	E.S.-H.
Raepsaet, Georges, Brussels	G.R.	Steinbauer, Dieter, Regensburg	D.ST.
Rathbone, Dominic, London	D.R.	Steinhart, Matthias, Freiburg	M.ST.
von Reden, Sitta, Bristol	S.v.R.	Stoevesandt, Magdalene, Basle	MA.ST.
Redies, Michael, Berlin	M.R.	Storch, Helmut, Tübingen	H.ST.
Renger, Johannes, Berlin	J.RE.	Strauch, Daniel, Berlin	D.S.
Rhodes, Peter J., Durham	P.J.R.	Strobel, Karl, Klagenfurt	K.ST.
Riederer, Josef, Berlin	JO.R.	Strothmann, Meret, Bochum	ME.STR.
Riedweg, Christoph, Zürich	C.RI.	von Stuckrad, Kocku, Erfurt	K.v.S.
Rieker, Jörg, Trier	JÖ.RI.	Stumpf, Gerd, Munich	GE.S.
Rist, Josef, Würzburg	J.RI.	Szlezák, Thomas A., Tübingen	T.A.S.
Robbins, Emmet, Toronto, ON	E.R.	Takacs, Sarolta A., Cambridge, MA	S.TA.
Roberts, Michael, Middletown	M.RO.	Tardieu, Michel, Joigny	MI.TA.
Röllig, Wolfgang, Tübingen	W.R.	Temporini – Gräfin Vitzthum, Hildegard, Tübingen	
Rosen, Klaus, Bonn	K.R.		H.T.-V.
Rosenberger, Veit, Augsburg	V.RO.	Thür, Gerhard, Graz	G.T.
Rottler, Christoph, Tübingen	C.R.	Tinnefeld, Franz, Munich	F.T.
Runia, David T., Parkville	D.T.R.	Todd, Malcolm, Exeter	M.TO.
Rüpke, Jörg, Erfurt	J.R.	Tomaschitz, Kurt, Vienna	K.T.
Sallaberger, Walther, Leipzig	WA.SA.	Toral-Niehoff, Isabel, Freiburg	I.T.-N.

Tosi, Renzo, Bologna	R. T.	Weiß, Peter, Kiel	P. W.
Touwaide, Alain, Madrid	A. TO.	Weißenberger, Michael, Greifswald	M. W.
Treidler, Hans, Berlin	H. T.	Welwei, Karl-Wilhelm, Bochum	K.-W. WEL.
Uggeri, Giovanni, Florence	G. U.	Wiegels, Rainer, Osnabrück	RA. WI.
von Ungern-Sternberg, Jürgen, Basle	J. v. U.-S.	Wiesehöfer, Josef, Kiel	J. W.
Untermann, Jürgen, Pulheim	J. U.	Wilhelm, Gernot, Würzburg	GE. W.
Visser, Edzard, Basle	E. V.	Will, Wolfgang, Bonn	W. W.
Völkl, Artur, Innsbruck	A. VÖ.	Willi, Andreas, Basle	AN. W.
Wachter, Rudolf, Heidelberg	R. WA.	Wilson, Nigel, Oxford	N. W.
Wagner-Hasel, Beate, Darmstadt	B. W.-H.	Wirbelauer, Eckhard, Freiburg	E. W.
Walde, Christine, Basle	C. W.	Wiseman, Timothy Peter, Exeter	T. W.
Waldner, Katharina, Erfurt	K. WA.	Zaminer, Frieder, Berlin	F. Z.
Walser †, Gerold, Basle	G. W.	Zhmud, Leonid, St. Petersburg	L. ZH.
Walter, Uwe, Cologne	U. WAL.	Zimmermann, Bernhard, Freiburg	B. Z.
Wandrey, Irina, Berlin	I. WA.	Zingg, Reto, Basle	RE. ZI.
Wartke, Ralf-B., Berlin	R. W.		

Hat see → Clothing; → Headgear

Haterius

[1] Mentioned by Cic. Fam. 9,18,3 in the year 46 BC; possibly identical with the proscript of the same name in App. B Civ. 4,29.

[2] **Q. H.** Possibly descendant of H. [1], from a senatorial family. If he died in AD 26 at almost 90 years of age, he must have been born in c. 65 BC. Through his wife, he was related to the house of Augustus. Cos. suff. in 5 BC, i.e. at an advanced age. Mentioned several times by Tacitus in the context of negotiations of the Senate under Tiberius. He appears as a model of rash candour and flattery (Tac. Ann. 1,13,4; 3,57; 59). He was famous for his spontaneous eloquence (PIR² H 24). Perhaps the grave that stood on the *via Nomentana* [1. vol. 2, 340] can be attributed to him. If so, CIL VI 1426 (cf. Additamenta CIL VI pars VIII ad 1426) refers to him. The offices mentioned are probably just a selection, but they possibly refer to a son.

[3] **D. H. Agrippa.** Son or grandson of H. [2]. In the year AD 15 *tr. pl.*, by-elected as praetor in 17, supported by Germanicus and Drusus. As *cos. des.*, he proposed the death penalty against Clutorius Priscus. In the year 22 *cos. ord.* In the year 32, unsuccessful charge against the consuls of the year 31. PIR² H 25.

[4] **Q. H. Antoninus.** Probably son of H. [3]. Cos. ord. in AD 53. Nero granted him an annual financial support because he had squandered his paternal fortune. PIR² H 26.

[5] **T. H. Nepos.** *Eques*, father of H. [6]. From AD 119 to 124, he was *praefectus Aegypti* [2. 284]. Usually, the equestrian *cursus* in CIL XI 5213 = ILS 1338 from Fulginiae is attributed to him (PFLAUM I 217ff., PIR² H 29). Then, however, he would have taken on five equestrian offices from AD 114 to 119. It is more likely that the latter was an unknown *eques* [cf. 3. 485f.].

[6] **T. H. Nepos Atinas Probus Publicius Matenianus.** Son of H. [5] originating from Fulginiae. *Frater Arvalis* probably since AD 118; praetorian legate of Arabia c. 130 until at least 133, perhaps until 135 [4. 23, 25, 26]. Cos. suff. in 134; consular governor of Pannonia superior c. 137–140. Last known senator to receive the *ornamenta triumphalia*, presumably at the end of his governorship in Arabia in his battle with the rebellious Jews under Bar Kochba.

> CIL XI 5212 = ILS 1058; W. ECK, in: Chiron 13, 1983, 167ff., 182ff.; PIR² H 30.

[7] **Ti. H. Saturninus.** Praetorian governor of Pannonia inferior c. AD 161–164 (THOMASSON Lat. I 113); cos. suff. in 164 (CIL XVI 185; RMD I 64). PIR² H 32.

> 1 NASH   2 G. BASTIANINI, in: ZPE 17, 1975   3 R. SAB-LAYROLLES, Libertinus miles, 1996   4 N. LEWIS (ed.), The Documents from the Bar Kokhba Period in the Cave of Letters, 1989, no. 23, 25, 26.   W.E.

Hathor (Egyptian Ḥw.t-ḥrw, 'house of Horus'; Greek Ἀθωρ/*Áthōr* [4]). The Egyptian goddess H. – in human or cow shape – is regarded as the daughter of → Re and as the mother of the music god Ihy. She is often matched with → Horus of Edfu as a partner. H.'s areas of competence cover love, music, as well as the realm of the dead. In the → *interpretatio* [2] *Graeca* she is identified with → Aphrodite [4]. At birth, seven H.s determine the baby's destiny [5. 41 f.]. As an aspect of the 'dangerous goddess', H. usually represents the appeased side, while the angered 'dangerous goddess' turns into → Sachmet. She is also often connected to → Isis, for instance in the inscriptions of → Dendara. It is to Isis also that she hands her typical crown of cow horns and a disc. Important symbols are → sistrum and menit, a beaded collar with a counterweight that can be used as a rattle. Similar to the form of the *naos* sistrum are the H. columns which show the face of H. and are typical of temples of female deities. Cult centres were → Dendara and the west bank of Thebes, among others.

> 1 S. ALLAM, Beiträge zum H.-Kult, 1963   2 C. J. BLEE-KER, H. and Thot, 1973   3 PH. DERCHAIN, H. Quadrifrons, 1972   4 É. DRIOTON, Notes diverses 12. Aphrodite Anadyomène invoquée comme H., in: Annales du service des antiquités de l'Égypte 45, 1947, 82 f.   5 D. MEEKS, Génies, anges et démons (Sources Orientales, vol. 8), 1971, 17–84.   A. v. L.

Hatra

[1] Trading centre in north Mesopotamia, founded middle of the 1st cent. AD. Expanded to a fortified round city (c. 2 km diameter) in the mid 2nd cent., H. was an important sanctuary of the sun god → Šamaš and capital of a 'kingdom of the Arabs' starting c. 166, at the same time an Arsacid border province. The city was besieged in vain by Trajan (AD 116) and Septimius Severus (196 and 198). After the end of the Arsacid dynasty, it was briefly allied with Rome against the Sassanids, but was conquered AD 240/1 and afterwards abandoned.

> H. J. DRIJVERS, H., Palmyra und Edessa, in: ANRW II 8, 799–906; S. R. HAUSER, H. und das Königreich der Araber, in: J. WIESEHÖFER (ed.), Das Partherreich und seine Zeugnisse (Historia Einzelschriften 122), 1998, 493–528.   S. HA.

[2] The language of H. belongs to the east dialect group of → Aramaic and is handed down in a few hundred inscriptions (1st–3rd cent. AD). Language and script resemble that on inscriptions of the same time from → Assur and are also found in other places between Euphrates, Tigris and Ḫābūr (Ǧadala, aṣ-Ṣaʿadiya, Takrīt, → Dura-Europus, Tall Šaiḫ Ḥamad). From the mainly brief, rarely dated, commemorative, votive and grave inscriptions, as well as from graffiti, it is possible to reconstruct the city pantheon with → Šamaš, the triad Maran, Martan and Barmaren, as well as Bēl

(→ Baal) and Nišar. Apart from many Arabic and a few Iranian personal names, the onomasticon is primarily Aramaic.

→ Palmyrenian

S. ABBADI, Die Personennamen der Inschriften aus Ḥ., 1983; B. AGGOULA, Inventaire des inscriptions Hatréennes, 1991; R. BERTOLINO, La cronologia di H., 1995; F. VATTIONI, H., 1994.   C.K.

Hatshepsut (*Ḥꜣ.t-šps.wt*, 'first among noble women').

Daughter of → Thutmosis [1] I, wife of Thutmosis [2] II; after his death she assumed the rulership for her underage stepson and nephew Thutmosis [3] III. Soon thereafter, she had herself crowned → Pharaoh and was depicted as a man. Her reign (*c.* 1490–1469 BC) was marked by an important building programme. Aside from extensions to the Imperial temple in Karnak (→ Thebes), H.'s architectonically unique temple of the dead in ad-Dair al-Baḥrī deserves special mention. Among many enterprises, she undertook campaigns to Nubia and Palestine and an expedition to → Punt [1]. H. regarded herself as an ideological successor to the Middle Kingdom kings and as the true liberator from the foreign rule of the → Hyksos. H.'s rule appears to have remained unchallenged during her lifetime. Not until *c.* 20 years after her death, her names and depictions were destroyed on the orders of Thutmosis III [1. 46–65]. However, the reference to her name in the 21st Dynasty suggests that she was neither completely forgotten nor judged entirely negatively [2. 52].

→ Rulers, female

1 P. F. DORMAN, The Monuments of Senenmut, 1988 2 A. VON LIEVEN, Kleine Beiträge zur Vergöttlichung Amenophis' I., II. Der Amenophis-Kult nach dem Ende des NR, in: ZÄS 128, 2001, 41–64   3 S. RATIÉ, La reine Hatchepsout. Sources et problèmes, 1979.   A. v. L.

Hatti see → Ḥattusa

Hattic Only the essential features of the agglutinative, probably non-ergative linguistic structure of the still mostly enigmatic Hattic are understood. The features that are recognized include an extreme prefixation of the verb, a strongly reduced case morphology of the noun, the differentiation of two genders (masculine and feminine), and the function of various particles. Most of the lexemes are unknown, therefore the monolingual texts remain generally obscure. The few and also mostly badly preserved Hattic-Hittite → bilingual inscriptions are dominated by mythologems, which are still a fixed component of rituals, and thus have not yet become independent. The Hattians, originally living in central Anatolia and north to the Black Sea, in many ways influenced the Hittite culture, which developed in the course of the 1st half of the 2nd millennium, so that a series of terms with Hatti origins found their way into Hittite; an example of this would be the titles *tabarna*, *tawananna* and *tuḫkanti*, which were borne by the reigning Hittite king, his wife and the designated heir to the throne.

The overwhelming portion of the Hattic texts may be assigned to the cultic-religious area, which is also suggested by the recitations and songs in descriptions of rituals in the Hittite language. Knowledge of Hattic was evidently already lost in the course of Hittite history, so that the texts in more recent copies often prove to be imperfect.

→ Anatolian languages; → Ḥattusa

J. KLINGER, Untersuchungen zur Rekonstruktion der hattischen Kultschicht, 1996.   J. KL.

Ḥattusa

I. CITY, ARCHAEOLOGICAL   II. STATE AND EMPIRE OF THE HITTITES

I. CITY, ARCHAEOLOGICAL

Capital of the Hittites in central Asia Minor near Boğazkale (earlier Boğazköy), province Çorum, *c.* 150 km east of Ankara, Turkey. Sporadically settled since the Chalcolithic (6th millennium BC), Ḥ. was the location of an Assyrian trading colony (*kārum*; → Kaneš) next to a native Hatti settlement in the 19th/18th cents. BC. The city was destroyed around 1700 BC; from Ḥattusili I (around 1600 BC), it was the seat of the Hittite kings and imperial capital. Under Ḥattusili III and his sons Tudḫaliya IV and Suppiluliuma II, Ḥ.'s townscape was redesigned and the central cult centre extended: reconstruction of the residence on Büyükkale, erection of the Great Temple, at the same time the expansion of the city to more than twice the size through the inclusion of the southern upper city; construction there of a temple quarter (29 temple structures identified, cf. map col. 5/6); development of the rock sanctuary of → Yazılıkaya. Shortly after 1200 BC, the city was destroyed again (fall of the Hittite Empire). Ḥ. is the find spot of a large archive of → cuneiform tablets.

Following a 'Dark Age', a prolonged Phrygian occupation from the 9th to the 5th cent. BC can be proven; East Greek and Achaemenid influences are occasionally recognizable. The identification of the site with the Pteria of the Medes named by Herodotus (1,76; 79) has been recently called into question in favour of Kerkenes Dağı, which lies approximately 60 km south-east. Traces of settlement stem from the Galatian-Hellenistic era and the Roman Imperial period, above all in the area of the former Hittite old town. A new fortification of Büyükkale (2 km east of the Roman road Tavium-Amasea) has been detected. Rural farms and church and monastic complexes from the early and middle Byzantine periods have been found. After the subsequent settlement gap came the settlement at the end of the 17th cent. of a Turkmen group of the Dulkadiroğlu.

K. BITTEL, Ḥ., Hauptstadt der Hethiter, 1983; P. NEVE, Ḥ., Stadt der Götter und Tempel, ²1996; Id., Die Ausgrabungen in Boğazköy/Ḥattuša 1993, in: AA 1994, 290 fig. 1 (city map).   J. SE.

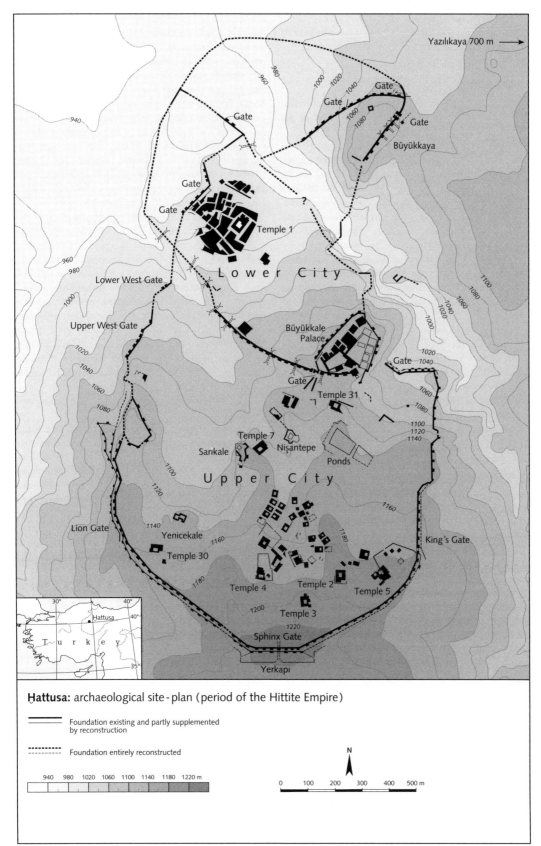

Ḫattusa: archaeological site-plan (period of the Hittite Empire)

——————— Foundation existing and partly supplemented by reconstruction

- - - - - - - Foundation entirely reconstructed

940   980   1020   1060   1100   1140   1180   1220 m

N

0   100   200   300   400   500 m

II. State and Empire of the Hittites
A. Introduction B. Essential Features of the Political History C. Constitution
D. State and Religion

A. Introduction
Since the 16th cent. BC-Ḫattusa (after the capital of the same name), or more completely 'Land of Ḫ.' (*Ḫattusas utnē*; akkadograph. KUR ^{URU}ḪATTI [1. 96¹]), is the Hittite name for the state of the Hittites which had already formed in central Asia Minor at the end of the 18th cent., as well as for the Hittite empire which existed from the 14th cent. until shortly after 1200, finally encompassing almost all of Asia Minor, northern Syria and a part of northern Mesopotamia, which depicts itself as a confederatively organized state (Hittite core state and treaty-bound vassal states).

The term 'Ḫatti', still often found in the secondary literature, is based on the Akkadian name form *Ḫatti*, which serves in the Hittite texts as the logogram for *Ḫattusa*. This made its way into all non-Anatolian languages of the Ancient Orient, however, and after the collapse of the Hittite empire was also used as the general term for the (Luwian speaking) Hittite successor states in Asia Minor and northern Syria of the 1st millennium BC, who themselves never used the name *Ḫatti* [2]. Correspondingly, Neo-Assyrian *Ḫattû/Ḫattaja*, Hebr. *Ḥittîm* 'Hittites' cover the inhabitants of these successor states, while the Hittite *Ḫattusumen* 'Hittites' stands for the members of the state/empire-leading royal clan, to which vassal kings in the 14th/13th cents. also belonged. Hittite nationality was denoted by 'man/people/prince (etc.) of the Land of Ḫ.'.

B. Essential Features of the Political History
1. Prehistory and Beginnings of the Hittite State (3rd millennium – 18th cent.)
2. Ḫattusa in the 16th–14th cents. 3. The Empire of Ḫattusa (14th–13th cent.) 4. The Collapse of the Empire and its Successors

1. Prehistory and Beginnings of the Hittite State (3rd millennium – 18th cent.)
Of the Indo-European Anatolian speakers (→ Anatolian languages) who were already resident in Asia Minor in the 3rd millennium, the Hittites settled inside the arc of the Halys, where they encountered an autochthonous population whose own language (→ Hatti) was, however, superseded in the 18th–16th cents. at the latest by → Hittite.

At the beginning of the 2nd millennium, when the Assyrians set up their trading settlements with the centre Kaneš (Hittite *Nēsa-*) in Asia Minor, this area was politically splintered into competing small kingdoms. At the end of the 18th cent., however, King Anitta (also attested in Old Assyrian texts; his father Pitḫāna, king of Kussara, conquered Nēsa and made it

his residence), according to his own report handed down in a 16th cent. copy [3], succeeded with Nēsa as his base, in becoming Great King by bringing down, in particular, the important kingdoms Zalpa, Ḫ. and Purusḫanda and thus forming a central Anatolian territorial state that stretched from the Black Sea to the Mediterranean (cf. [4. § 1–4], where by the supposed personal name Labarna only Anitta can be meant as founder of the state [5. 111]). The specifically Hittite organization of rule, with the king and royal clan bearing equal political responsibility, was already characteristic for this state [6. 81–83, 114]. Despite the *c.* 130-year hiatus in written records after Anitta's rule, it may have continued essentially into the 16th cent.

2. Ḫattusa in the 16th–14th cents.
Ḫattusili I (*c.* 1565–1540), under whom Ḫ. is now documented as the capital (known Hittite history begins here), certainly descended from the narrow circle of the old royal clan, although not in direct succession from Anitta, according to his self-description as 'Kussarian' and as 'nephew of the *tau̯annanna* (reigning queen)'. Under him the Hittite policy of expansion was resumed, which was now directed toward western Asia Minor (→ Arzawa) and in particular towards gaining supremacy in Syria over the great kingdom of Ḫalpa (→ Aleppo), and which peaked under Mursili I in the conquest of Ḫalpa and finally even Babylon (1531 [middle chronology: 1595]; end of the Ḫammurapi dynasty).

After initial tensions in the royal clan as early as the time of Ḫattusili I, a bloody intradynastic power struggle, which would last until *c.* 1500, broke out openly with the murder of Mursili I, and soon led not only to the loss of all conquered areas – which prepared the way for the supremacy of → Mittani (Hittite *Mittanna-*) in northern Syria – but also aided the incursion of the → Kaskans (at the time of Ḫantili I) in the Pontic region, from which grew a continuing threat to the core Hittite territory and the capital that would last into the 13th cent.

The end of this internal and external political decline was marked by the formal constitution established under Telibinu (from *c.* 1500), which returned to the old fundamental political values of the royal clan (loyalty, unity, sense of responsibility) [4]; among other things, it regulated the succession and the powers of the king and royal clan, and became the starting-point of numerous legislative measures concerning administration, cult and military affairs ('orders'/'instructions'; until the time of Arnuwanda I, *c.* 1400–1375. In foreign policy, the change from the previous policy of simple conquest and incorporation to the – from then on decisive – policy of alliance is characterized by the → international treaties concluded since Telibinu (first with → Kizzuwatna). This was dictated by national good sense, because the royal clan would hardly have had enough resources to manage all conquered areas themselves.

Summary of Hittite kings and queens

Dates	Kings	Queens
late 18th cent.	a) Kings of Nēsa	
	Pitḫāna of Kussara	
	Anitta [son of Pitḫānas], Great King	
	(After Anitta, there is a roughly 130-year gap in transmission.)	
	b) Great Kings of Ḫattusa	
c. 1565–1540	1. Ḫattusili I. ['Kussarian', 'nephew of *taɥannanna*']	Kaddusi
c. 1540–1530	2. Mursili I. [son of 1]	Kali
after c. 1530	3. Ḫantili I. [brother-in-law of 2]	Ḫarapsegi
	4. Zidanta I. [son-in-law of 3]	?
	5. Ammuna [son of 4]	?
	6. Ḫuzzija I. [family relationship unclear]	?
after c. 1500	7. Telibinu [son of 5?, brother-in-law of 6]	Istabarija
	8. Taḫurwaili [position 8 uncertain, family relationship unclear]	
	9. Alluwamna [son-in-law of 7]	Ḫarapsili
	10. Ḫantili II. [probably son of 9]	?
	11. Zidanta II. [probably son of 10]	Ijaja
	12. Ḫuzzija II. [probably son of 11]	Summiri
		Katteshabi
	13. Muwattalli I. [son/brother of 12?]	Katteshabi?
c. 1420–1400	14. Tudḫalija I. [son of 12]	Nigalmadi
c. 1400–1375	15. Arnuwanda I. [son-in-law and adoptive son of 14]	Asmunigal
c. 1375–1355	16. Tudḫalija II. [son of 15]	Taduḫeba
c. 1355–1320	17. Suppiluliuma I. [son of 16]	Taduḫeba
		Ḫenti
		Malnigal
c. 1320–1318	18. Arnuwanda II. [son of 17]	Malnigal
c. 1318–1290	19. Mursili II. [son of 17]	Malnigal
		Gassulawija
		Tanuḫeba
c. 1290–1272	20. Muwattalli II. [son of 19]	Tanuḫeba
c. 1272–1265	21. Mursili III. – Urḫitesub [son of 20]	
	(mentioned as late as 1245, in exile in Egypt)	Tanuḫeba
c. 1265–1240	22. Ḫattusili II. (= previously 'III'!) [son of 19]	Puduḫeba
c. 1240–1215	23. Tudḫalija III. (= previously 'IV'!) [son of 22]	Puduḫeba
c. 1220–?	24. Kurunta von Tarḫuntassa [son of 20.]	?
after c. 1215	25. Arnuwanda III. [son of 23]	?
	26. Suppiluliuma II. [son of 23]	?
	The first Great Kings of the kingdoms resulting from the collapse of the Hittite Empire.	
about 1200	a. *Secundogeniture of Karkamis:*	
	Kuzitesub [great-great-great-grandson of 17], Great King	
	b. *Secundogeniture of Tarḫuntassa:*	
	Ḫartapu [son of Mursili = probably 21], Great King	
	c. *Vassal state of Mirā:*	
	Masḫuitta [great-great-grandson of Masḫuiluwas of Arzawa/Mirā and the daughter of 17], Great King	

Under Tudḫaliya I (*c.* 1420–1400), the struggle with Mittani for the recovery of supremacy in Syria began (campaign to → Isuwa, destruction of Ḫalpa). At the same time, all of western Asia Minor came into the focus of Hittite politics through the strengthening of Arzawa in the 15th cent. (campaigns as far as Āssuwa/Mysia) [7; 8. 455–456]; however, the intensification of the Kaskan danger at the time of Arnuwanda I and esp. Tudḫaliya II (*c.* 1375–1355, plundering of the city of Ḫ.) made it necessary to first of all concentrate forces to secure the core territory [9; 10].

3. THE EMPIRE OF ḪATTUSA (14TH–13TH CENT.)

The rise of Ḫ. to empire and the third great power of the Middle East, after Egypt and Babylonia, occurred under Suppiluliuma I (*c.* 1355–1320); aided by succession disputes in Mittani and the Egyptian inactivity in regard to foreign policy (Amenophis III/IV) in Syria, he was able, in a single campaign, to conquer or draw to his side without a fight first Isuwa, then all Mittani-controlled small states between the Euphrates and the Mediterranean (among others → Alalaḫ (Hittite *Alalḫa*-), → Ugarit (Hittite *Ugaritta*-), Nuḫašše (Hittite *Nuḫassa*-)) as well as, in Egyptian territory, especially → Amurru (Hittite *Amurra*-). As Azzi-Ḫajasa before in north-eastern Asia Minor, he was able to bind these small states and finally even the politically collapsed core state of Mittani itself by treaty to Ḫ. as (internally autonomous) vassal states. Furthermore, to consolidate this system of indirect rule, the secundogenitures of Ḫalpa and – far more significantly as political centre for all Syrian affairs – Karkamis (Hittite *Karkamissa*-; → Karkemiš) were established.

Through the destruction of Arzawa, which had represented a serious threat to Ḫ. since the beginning of the 14th cent. as a result of several advances into the 'lower land' (*katteran utnē*), as well as through the formation of the Arzawan vassal states → Mirā (core territory of Arzawa with its capital at Abasa/Ephesus), Ḫaballa and Sēḫa, Mursili II (*c.* 1318–1290) was then able to extend the imperial territory as far as the Aegean coast (including Lazba/Lesbos and other offshore islands). Thus, in the 13th cent., after Wilusa (Troad) was also added to the Arzawan vassal states in the time of Muwattalli II, all of western Asia Minor – apart from Māsa, → Lukkā and Millawa(n)da (→ Miletus), which had belonged to → Ahhiyawa (Greece) since the 14th cent. – found itself in Hittite hands [8. 450–455]. Under Muwattalli II the reconquest of the Kaskan region, already pursued by Suppiluliuma I and esp. Mursili II, between Plā and the 'upper land' (*srazzi utnē*), was probably to a large extent completed (recovery of the cult city Nerikka), and in Syria the expansionism of Ramses II (temporary secession of Amurru to Egypt) was successfully stopped in the battle of → Qadesh (Kadeš; Hittite *Kinza*-) in 1275.

Domestically, however, the unilaterally promoted (to the point of ceding sovereign rights) career of Muwattalli's brother Ḫattusili, as well as some disput-ed decisions (such as the temporary transfer of the capital to Tarḫuntassa) evoked the first tensions and factions within the royal clan [11], which led to the usurpation of the throne by Ḫattusili II ('III') under Mursili III-Urḫitesub (flight of Urḫitesub into Egyptian exile). However, the threatening division of the royal clan could at first be averted by the creation of the secundogeniture of Tarḫuntassa for Kurunta (the second son of Muwatalli II, adopted by Ḫattusili II, who was actually the legitimate claimant to the Hittite throne after Urḫitesub) and by the peace treaty with Ramses II (1259; recognition of the dynastic line of Ḫattusili II [12. § 10]), which established a continuing, close Egyptian-Hittite friendship (dynastic connection 1246) [13]. The good relations with Egypt (and Babylonia) at the time of Ḫattusili II stood in contrast to the increasingly deteriorating relationship with the Assyrians (Salmanassar I), who were expanding in the direction of northern Mesopotamia (Mittani, Assyrian Ḫanigalbat) and the Euphrates. In the west, the political and military actions of the Arzawan prince Piyamaradu [8. 453–454], who was operating out of Millawanda, against Mirā and Sēḫa led to an exchange of diplomatic notes with Ahhiyawa (Tawaglawa letter) and to campaigns in Lukkā and Millawanda.

For Tudḫaliya III ('IV', *c.* 1240–1215; cf. the biographical sketch [14]), who was named as successor after the demotion of an 'older brother' (probably Kurunta), the problem of the division in the royal clan intensified when he took power. Meanwhile, concessions to the secundogeniture of Tarḫuntassa (esp. granting Kurunta a protocolary status equal to that of the king of Karkamis as third man in the empire after the Great King and crown prince) [15] and urgent appeals to the loyalty and unity of the royal clan could not prevent an at least temporarily successful coup d'état by Kurunta [16. 62]. Additional strains arose for the empire through, among other things, the military confrontation with Assyria (Tukulti-Ninurta I; Hittite defeat at Niḫirija).

4. THE COLLAPSE OF THE EMPIRE AND ITS SUCCESSORS

After the brief reign of Arnuwanda III (after 1215), Suppiluliuma II became the last Hittite Great King under the omen of greatest domestic unease. Apart from campaigns to Māsa and Lukkā (in connection with a naval battle at → Alaschia, Hittite *Alasija*-), a military operation against Tarḫuntassa points to the outbreak of 'civil war' [16. 57–65]. Even if the final collapse of the empire is still not clear in all its details, today it is certain that it did not occur through invading → Sea Peoples, but rather from within, and that, at the beginning of the 12th cent., in the east and south the secundogenitures of Karkamis and Tarḫuntassa succeeded immediately as great kingdoms [16. 64; 17]. Moreover, in the west, the most important Arzawan vassal state, Mirā, appears to have already gained the status of great kingdoms in the time of Suppiluliuma II [18]. At the same time, these new great kingdoms

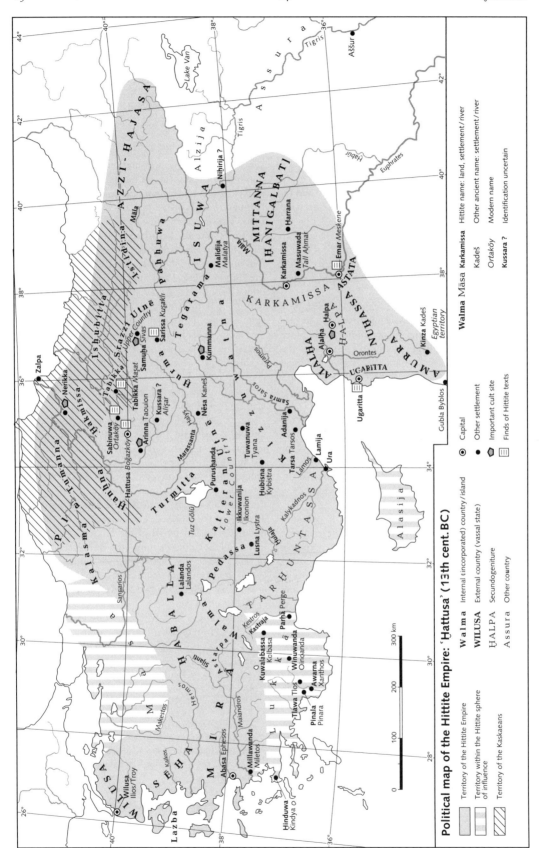

Political map of the Hittite Empire: 'Ḫattusa' (13th cent. BC)

Territory of the Hittite Empire

Territory within the Hittite sphere of influence

Territory of the Kaskaeans

Walma Internal (uncorporated) country/island

WILUSA External country (vassal state)

ḪALPA Secundogeniture

Assura Other country

● Capital

● Other settlement

● Important cult site

▣ Finds of Hittite texts

Walma Māsa Karkamissa Hittite name: land, settlement/river

Kadeš Other ancient name: settlement/river

Ortaköy Modern name

Kussara ? Identification uncertain

formed the prerequisite for what is today termed the 'Dark Ages' for historical continuity in Asia Minor down to the 8th/7th cents., which can be followed directly in southern and south-eastern Asia Minor (incl. northern Syria) and is probably perceptible to some extent in the west (→ Asia Minor).

C. CONSTITUTION

From its beginnings, the Hittite state, whose constitution can probably best be characterized as aristocratic with a monarchical leadership, saw itself as a political body (ḫassuuas tuuekka-, 'body of the king', i.e. the public or national body) with the king as head and the members of the royal clan (in the 14th/13th cents. widely branched), the 'lords', as its authoritative limbs (for the administrative composition in the 13th cent. cf. [19]). It was the ethical obligation of the royal clan to maintain, expand and increase the prosperity of the land of Ḫ., which belonged to the weather god and was entrusted to the king to govern.

The royal clan, to which one belonged through birth or (e.g. in the case of the vassal kings) marriage, formed a political organ, the bangu- ('community [of the State/Empire]'), which the king summoned to 'assembly' (tuliia-) for all fundamental political questions. The inner circle of the royal clan, the members of the royal family ('princes'), also if they came from the secundogenitures, provided the 'Great' (in the 13th cent.: 'Foremost'), the holders of the highest court positions ('Great leader of the bodyguard/scribes/cupbearers' etc.), who formed the government as advisers and executive organs (ambassadors, military commanders) together with the king [20]. Princes also administered the 'internal (incorporated) lands' of the core state ('foreign lands' = vassal states) as' sovereigns' (utniiashes).

Even if he ruled in the legal sense, the king had to ensure, to a large extent, the agreement of the royal clan for his decisions, whose members were in turn expected to be loyal to the king and the land of Ḫ. (loyalty oaths). Pragmatism, emphasis on the responsibility of each individual for the state or empire, argumentative disputes from the viewpoint of the opposition, and persuasiveness were thus essential elements of political thought and action which become visible particularly in Hittite → historiography and international treaties. The kingship was hereditary; however, in the absence of male descendants of the first and (from a concubine) second rank, the dynastic line could also be continued through the (adopted) husband of a first-ranking princess (e.g. Arnuwanda I); the heir to the throne, determined by the king, required the recognition of the bangu-, which on its part swore an oath of loyalty to the designated heir [21].

Besides the kingship, there was an institutionalized queenship, granted for life, which the chief wife of the king, at first crown princess, only took over with the death of her predecessor. The queen played an active role in political life, as is documented in particular for Puduḫeba, the wife of Ḫattusili II ('III') [22].

D. STATE AND RELIGION

The interdependence of state and religion, based on the ethical responsibility towards the gods, esp. the → weather god and sun goddess, which is noticeable, i.a. in the royal prayers (since the 15th cent.) as a venue for political reflection [23], found its most important political expression in the festivals which were held in various cult centres during the course of the year; they often lasted several days and were accompanied by a complex liturgy (sacrifices, cult meal, recitation, music, song, dance, dramatic presentations). Here the king and queen performed their cult functions, which were prescribed in detail, as highest priests, along with the members of the royal clan, particularly holders of court positions. The state cult, into which the gods of conquered territories were also absorbed, were initially under Hattian, in the 15th–13th cents. increasingly under Hurrian influence (→ Hurrians, → Yazılıkaya). The will of the gods in political and military questions was determined through varying oracular means (→ Divination). In order to be in harmony with the will of the gods, the state activities in the civil and military areas required the execution of numerous, mostly cathartic rituals (for military rituals see [24]). These also served as defence against magic, which, despite the ban in the Telibinu constitution [4. § 50], was a weapon often used in the internal disputes, esp. by female members of the royal clan [25] (→ Magic).

The royal ritual for the dead (also conducted for queens) is based on a distinction between the king as natural person (body natural) and as representative of the kingdom, who never dies, but rather 'becomes god' (body politic) that is unique in the Ancient Orient; in the ritual the body natural was burned immediately, and the following 13 day rite de passage was carried out on an effigy of the deceased. The same is true for the comparatively modest burial of the body natural on one hand, and the cultic worship of the immortal body politic on the other, to which, in the 13th cent., a memorial (ḫēgur, for its political significance see [26. 27–35]) was erected as well [20. 174[145], 181[164]; 27]; see also → Dead, cult of the.

→ Hittite law; → Asia Minor; → Literature (Hittite); → Seal; → HITTITOLOGY

1 A. GOETZE, Kleinasien, ²1957   2 J. D. HAWKINS, s.v. Ḫatti, RLA 4, 152–159   3 E. NEU, Der Anitta-Text, 1974   4 I. HOFFMANN, Der Erlaß Telipinus, 1984   5 F. STARKE, Der Erlaß Telipinus, in: WO 16, 1985, 100–113   6 Id., Ḫalmašuit im Anitta-Text und die hethit. Ideologie vom Königtum, in: ZA 69, 1979, 47–120   7 ST. DE MARTINO, L'Anatolia occidentale nel medio regno ittita (Eothen 5), 1996   8 F. STARKE, Troia im Kontext des histor.-polit. und sprachlichen Umfeldes Kleinasiens im 2. Jt., in: Studia Troica 7, 1997, 447–487   9 S. ALP, Hethit. Briefe aus Maşat-Höyük, 1991   10 J. KLINGER, Das Corpus der Maşat-Briefe und seine Beziehungen zu den Texten aus Ḫattuša, in: ZA 85, 1995, 74–108   11 PH. HOUWINK TEN CATE, Urhi-Tessub Revisited, in: Bibliotheca Orientalis 51, 1994, 234–260   12 E. EDEL, Der Vertrag zw. Ramses II. von Äg. und Hattusili III. von Hatti, 1997   13 Id., Die äg.-hethit. Korrespondenz aus Boghazköi,

1994   14 H. KLENGEL, Tuthalija IV. von Hatti, in: Alt-oriental. Forsch. 18, 1991, 224–238   15 H. OTTEN, Die Bronzetafel aus Boğazköy, Ein Staatsvertrag Tuthali-jas IV., 1988   16 J. D. HAWKINS, The Hieroglyphic In-scription of the Sacred Pool Complex at Hattusa, 1995   17 D. SÜRENHAGEN, Polit. Niedergang und kulturelles Nachleben des hethit. Großreiches, in: U. MAGEN, M. RAS-HAD (ed.), FS Th. Beran, 1996, 283–293   18 J. D. HAWKINS, Tarkasnawa King of Mira, "Tarkondemos", Boğazköy Sealings and Karabel, in: Anatolian Studies 48, 1998, 1–31   19 TH. VAN DEN HOUT, Der Ulmitešub-Vertrag, 1995   20 F. STARKE, Zur "Regierung" des he-thit. Staates, in: Zschr. für Altoriental. und Biblische Rechtsgesch. 2, 1996, 140–182   21 G. BECKMAN, Inher-itance and Royal Succession Among the Hittites, in: H. A. HOFFNER, G. M. BECKMAN (ed.), FS H.G. Güterbock, 1986, 13–31   22 H. OTTEN, Puduhepa, 1975   23 R. LE-BRUN, Hymnes et prières hittites, 1980   24 R. H. BEAL, Hittite Military Rituals, in: M. MEYER, P. MIRECKI (ed.), Ancient Magic and Ritual Power, 1995, 63–92   25 M. HUTTER, Bemerkungen zur Verwendung mag. Rituale in mittelhethit. Zeit, in: Altoriental. Forsch. 18, 1991, 32–43   26 H. OTTEN, Die 1986 in Boğazköy gefun-dene Bronzetafel, 1989   27 TH. VAN DEN HOUT, Death as a Privilege, The Hittite Royal Funerary Ritual, in: J. M. BREMER et al. (ed.), Hidden Futures, 1994, 37–75.

R. H. BEAL, The Organization of the Hittite Military, 1992; T. BRYCE, The Kingdom of the Hittites, 1998; V. HAAS, Gesch. der hethit. Rel., 1994; E. v. SCHULER, Die Kaškäer, 1965; G. WALSER (ed.), Neuere Hethiterforsch., 1964.
MAPS: O. GURNEY, Hittite Geography, in: H. OTTEN et al. (ed.), FS S. Alp, 1992, 213–221; F. STARKE, Troia im Kon-text des histor.-polit. und sprachlichen Umfeldes Klein-asiens im 2. Jt., in: Studia Troica 7, 1997, fig. 1.; TAVO B III 6.   F.S.

Hawthorn Greek κράταιγος/*krátaigos* or κραταιγῶν/*krataigôn*, Lat. *spina alba* are names for various thorny plants (cf. Plin. HN 24,108; Columella 3,11,5; 7,7,2 and 7,9,6); in Plin. HN 21,68 *spina alba*, for instance, obviously means the edible Carline thistle (*Carlina*). This also includes ὄα/*óa* or ὄη/*óē*, Lat. *sorbus*, the mountain ash. An exact identification of what is meant in ancient texts with *crataegus* and *sorbus* is not pos-sible. In Theophr. Hist. pl. 3,15,6, the Azarole/Crete hawthorn (*Crataegus azarolus*) is probably being de-scribed, which Plin. HN 27,63 incorrectly translates as *aquifolium* (possibly holly, *Ilex aquifolium L.*). Of the four types mentioned at Plin. HN 15,85, three might be determined as follows: 1. common hawthorn (*Cratae-gus oxyacantha L.*), which Dioscorides 1,93 WELL-MANN = 1,122 BERENDES probably referred to as ἡ ὀξυάκανθα/*oxyákantha*; 2. service tree (*sorba* or *sorva*; *Sorbus domestica L.*); 3. wild service tree (*torminale*; *Sorbus torminalis Crantz*); the latter was used as an astringent medicinal herb (Celsus, Artes 4,26,6). On the other hand the root of *C. oxyacantha* is supposed to have lead to premature births. The Romans attached hawthorn rods to doors and windows on the kalends of June to keep harm away from people (Ov. Fast. 6,129 ff.). The fruits of the service tree were eaten pre-served – as with pears – in must (*sapa*; Cato Agr. 7,4 and 143,3; Pall. Agric. 3,25,10) or also dried (cf. Varro, Rust. 1,58). According to Verg. G. 3,380 Scythians pro-duced an alcoholic beverage by fermenting the service tree.

→ Intoxicating substances

M. SCHUSTER, s.v. Weißdorn, RE 8 A, 610–612.   C.HÜ.

Hazel The genus *Corylus L.* of the Betulaceae family is represented in Europe especially by the widespread, bush-forming (cf. Verg. Ecl. 1,14) common or shrub hazel *Corylus avellana* (already *abellana* in Cato Agr. 8,2; *corylus*: hazel wood for the wine press lid ibid. 18,9; *corulus* Columella 7,9,6). In the Mediterranean region the Turkish hazel *C. colurna L.*, which grows up to 20 m tall and has a range from Asia Minor to the Balkans, *C. pontica Koch* and the giant filbert *C. maxima Mill.* (= *tubulosa Willdenow*; perhaps = *nuces calvae*, Cato Agr. 8,2 = *galbae* Plin. HN 15,90) are also found. Theophr. Hist. pl. 3,15,1f. combines these three species as *Hērakleōtikè karýa*. Hazels, which Diosco-rides (1,125,3 WELLMANN = 1,179 BERENDES) calls *karýa Pontikḗ* (= Plin. HN 15,88, cf. Macrob. Sat. 3,18,6), were cultivated in several varieties on the Black Sea and were taken from there to southern Italy (espe-cially to Abella/Avellino in Campania), France and southern Germany. The Latin name *nux abellana* in Plin. HN 15,88 refers to the varied use of these oil-rich nuts in food despite the negative opinion on their dietary value (Dioscurides ibid. = Plin. HN 23,150) and as a medication against coughs and catarrh. In Verg. G. 2,299 (with Servius loc.cit.) the hazel is considered the enemy of the vine. Germans, Celts and Slavs preferred the nuts but also used wild hazel rods to search for water and as a symbol of life. Many place names are derived from *coruletum*, *colurnum* etc. or from Old High German *hasal*, e.g., Coleri, Glurns, Haseldorf and Haslach.

→ Walnut   C.HÜ.

Headgear plays only a minor role in myth and history. One case in point is Hades' helmet of invisibility which Athena uses (κυνέη Ἄϊδος/*kynéē Áïdos*, Hom. Il. 5,844 f.) and then hands to → Perseus [1]. → Midas hides his donkey ears under a turban (→ Tiara), Ov. Met. 11,180 f. A hat (→ *pilleus*) was taken from → Lucumo (→ Tarquinius [11] Priscus) by an eagle and then brought back, which was seen as a positive omen for the future, Liv. 1,34; a wind blows → Alexander [4] the Great's → *kausia* off his head (Arr. Anab. 7,22,2 f.).

Greek and Roman men went bareheaded in every-day life, unless bad weather forced them to protect themselves from the rain with parts of their coat or → toga, or with a hood.

Greek and Roman women showed themselves out-doors only with headgear (Val. Max. 6,3,10; Tac. Ann. 13,45; Tert. De pallio 4). It was enough for the Greek woman to cover her head with the *himation* (→ Pal-

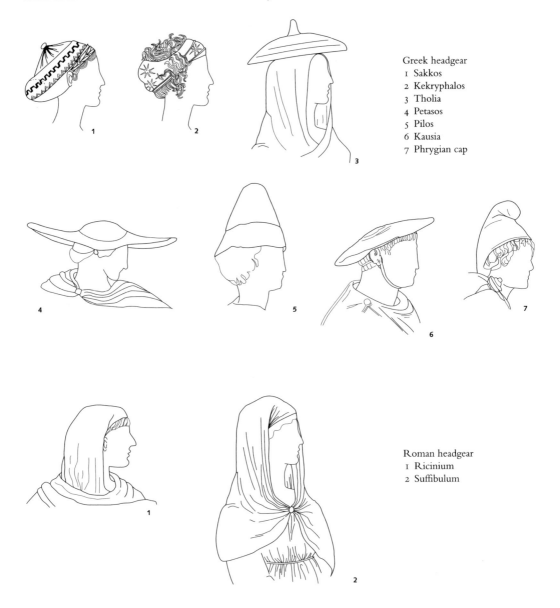

Greek headgear
1 Sakkos
2 Kekryphalos
3 Tholia
4 Petasos
5 Pilos
6 Kausia
7 Phrygian cap

Roman headgear
1 Ricinium
2 Suffibulum

lium) or with a fold of the → *peplos* [1]; for this, the Roman woman used the *palla* (→ *pallium*) or special head scarfs such as the *ricula* (Isid. Orig. 19,31,5) or the *mavors* (also *mafors*, *maforte*; Isid. Orig. 19,25,4). The *palliolum*, on the other hand, was worn by men and women alike (Mart. 11,27,8). In the 4th cent. BC, the *tholia* became fashionable for Greek women – a round hat with a protruding brim and conical top, depicted primarily on the clay figurines from → Tanagra (→ Terracottas III. C.). Otherwise, Greek women only gathered their hair with the → *kekryphalos*, the → *sakkos*, or ribbons. Nightcaps apparently existed too (Aristoph. Thesm. 257).

There was also headgear for special occasions: while travelling, Greek women and men protected themselves from the sun with the → *petasos*, while a brimless, conical headgear (→ *pilos*) was the mark of craftsmen,

boatmen, or labourers. The Romans adopted *petasos*, *pilos* (→ *pilleus*) and → *kausia* from the Greeks. In times of → mourning, Roman women wore the *ricinium*. At → sacrifices, priests and → vestals covered their heads with the *suffibulum*, while the participants in the sacrifices used the toga or *palla* to do the same (*capite velato*). The so-called Phrygian cap served to identify orientals (→ Amazones, → Aeneas [1], → Ganymede, → Attis etc.), a tall, brimless hat with the top bent frontwards (cf. → Tiara).

→ Diadema; → Helmet; → Clothing; → Wreath, Garland; → Kredemnon; → Mitra [1]; → Taenia [1]; → Mourning dress

L. BONFANTE, Etruscan Dress, 1975, 67–80; U. SCHARF, Straßenkleidung der röm. Frau, 1994, 78–82, 112–123; I. KRISELEIT (ed.), Bürgerwelten. Hell. Tonfiguren und Nachschöpfungen im 19. Jh., exposition Berlin 1994, no. 1, 5, 12 f., 17, 42, 46, 62, 90.   R.H.

Healing Deities, Healing Cults
I. INTRODUCTION   II. MESOPOTAMIA AND SYRIA
III. EGYPT   IV. GREECE AND ROME

I. INTRODUCTION
The healing of illness is, in principle, within the province of any deity or hero in possession of superhuman powers of assistance. But in the reality of cult practice, the healing function came to be concentrated in certain deities and heroes whose powers were particularly strong [1].

1 W. A. JAYNE, The Healing Gods of Ancient Civilizations, 1925.   F.G.

II. MESOPOTAMIA AND SYRIA
In Mesopotamia, a series of deities were associated with healing powers through names, epithets, and references in medical texts. The significance of the healing goddesses was far greater than that of their male counterparts. The various healing goddesses in evidence as early as the Fara period (middle of the 3rd millennium) became consolidated in the figure of Gula at the latest by the Ancient Babylonian era (1st half of the 2nd millennium) [1. 101–106]. The main centre of her cult was the city of Isin [3]. Healing functions were also ascribed in epithets to the major gods → Marduk and Ea.

In Syria, → Ešmūn, who was equated with Asclepius, and Šadrapa (etymologized as *šd-rpʾ* 'Šed, 'healing'') were known as healing gods in to the middle of the 1st millennium BC [2. 286f.]. In Asia Minor, healing gods did not play a significant role.

1 H. AVALOS, Illness and Health Care in the Ancient Near East, 1995, 99–231   2 H. W. HAUSSIG (ed.), WB der Myth., 1. Abt., vol. 1: Götter und Mythen im Vorderen Orient, 1965   3 B. HROUDA, Isin 1, 1977.   NI.HE.

III. EGYPT
All Egyptian deities can, in principle, be called upon as healers. → Amun or → Min, for instance, were described as physicians in prayers; → Thot or → Horus were also regarded as physicians to the gods. In the Late Period, Horus frequently appears as a child god in magical statues ('Horus stelai') that were chiefly thought to cure snake bites and scorpion stings. As the mistress of magic, → Isis is particularly well-suited to healing the sick; as the mother of Horus, she is responsible specifically for curing childhood illnesses. Gods who are known to cause illnesses – such as the scorpion goddess → Selcis or Sachmet, who spreads pestilence through her arrows and 'messengers' – are also responsible for their healing and are considered to be the patrons of physicians. In the Late Period, especially in the Ptolemaic and Roman eras, the deified scholars and master architects Imhotep (→ Imuthes) and Amenhotep were worshipped as healers and saviors. The cult of Amenhotep is limited to Thebes, but Imhotep was incorporated in the Egyptian pantheon as the 'son of Ptah' and worshipped throughout the land from the time of the Ptolemaic period. The Greeks identified him with → Asclepius.

H. BRUNNER, s.v. Götter, Heil-, LÄ 2, 645–647; D. WILDUNG, Imhotep und Amenhotep, 1977.   K.J.-W.

IV. GREECE AND ROME
A. THE DEITIES   1. EARLY GREECE   2. GREECE AND ROME FROM THE 5TH CENT.   3. LATER DEVELOPMENTS   B. THE CULT   1. INDIVIDUAL CULT FORMS   2. INCUBATION

A. THE DEITIES
A distinction must be made between those possessing exceptional technical skill and those with exceptional powers of healing; in accordance with the ambivalence of divine and heroic action, the latter could also be the bringers of disease. With the progress of medical knowledge and the achievements of medical science, the function of healing deities became increasingly limited to illnesses with no successful medical treatment and somatic dysfunctions – among which sexual and reproductive difficulties were particularly prominent, as evidenced by anatomical votives (→ Votive offerings). Broad areas of medical practice acquired a scientific basis, as a further consequence of which ritual healing practices that took place outside of institutional healing cults were relegated to the realm of healing → magic. However, though the ancient perception is often clouded by rivalries between physicians and ritual healers, it discriminates in far fewer cases than modern scholarship would have it.

1. EARLY GREECE
In early Greece, the supreme healing god is → Apollo. In the first book of the *Iliad*, Apollo uses his pestilent arrows (a motif from the Ancient Orient) to unleash a great plague, which he takes away again after the Greeks have placated him with ritual offerings. This double function continued well into the Imperial period, in which the Clarian Oracle (→ Clarus) advised several cities in Asia Minor to erect statues of Apollo shooting arrows as protection against the great plague of AD 165/6 – probably referring to the Homeric image as well [1]. A widespread epiclesis of the healer Apollo in the post-Homeric period is → Paean – also the name of the ritual songs and dances to appease the god in Hom. Il. 1,467–474. This epiclesis takes up the name of *Paiawon* (Knossos: [2. 164f.]), who was the object of a Mycenaean cult and also appears in Homer as the healer of wounds and an authority on cures (Hom. Il. 5,401; Od. 4,232). However, the identification with Apollo here is uncertain. Later, the functional epiclesis *Iatrós*, 'physician' becomes widespread and is incorporated into the cult of Apollo Medicus, occasioned probably by an epidemic in Rome. In response to an outbreak of the plague in 433 BC, the cult was provided with a temple (Liv. 4,25,3. 29,7).

In Homer, the god who can cure the medically incurable plague is joined by the healing hero → Machaon, son of → Asclepius, whose technical craft heals the wounds of the warriors (Hom. Il. 5,193–219), but who is also a capable fighter in his own right (Hom. Il. 11,504–520). In the Epic Cycle, the same role is also given to his brother → Podalirius (Quint. Smyrn. 4,396–404): The surgeons of historical reality were reflected, in the fictional world of epic, in these brothers. In the time after Homer, they were worshipped as healing heroes not only within the cult of Asclepius, but also individually (or both together) in their own cults (Machaon's grave and shrine in Gerenia, Paus. 3,26,9; his son Polemocrates in Eua, Paus. 2,38,6; his sons in Pharae, Paus. 4,30,3; Daunian heroon of Podalirius, Str. 6,3,9). First aid is also given by other epic heroes: in the *Odyssey*, the uncles of Odysseus use a powerful incantation, *epaoidé*, in order to staunch the flow of blood from the wound in his thigh (Hom. Od. 19,457f.) – a problem that could still be considered the domain of 'magical' medicine as late as the modern era.

2. GREECE AND ROME FROM THE 5TH CENT.

In the classical and post-classical eras, the central body of evidence for healing cults, in Greece [3] as well as Italy [4; 5], is formed by votives – especially anatomical votives. They demonstrate which deities were worshipped as healers, and which problems were particularly pressing for which sex; and they provide insight into medical pathology [6]. The figures that emerge on this evidence as especially significant in the Greek world (aside from the widely established → Asclepius), are, on the one hand, → Hercules and → Zeus (most particularly, the Oriental Zeus → Hypsistos of the Imperial era on the Athenian Pnyx); and on the other hand, a series of female deities (→ Demeter, → Eileithyia, → Artemis). In the case of Hercules, this is the result of the widespread protective and healing functions of the hero (with the very popular epiclesis *Alexíkakos*, 'averter of evil'), which were especially important in late antiquity. For the female deities, the healing function arises out of their continued concern with → birth and the care of children (→ Kourotrophos). One atypical area of specialization is Demeter's healing of eye maladies, which may have grown out of the role of seeing in the Eleusinian mysteries [7]. In addition, there are the numerous → hero cults, particularly well attested to in Attica [8] – such as the multiply documented one of → Iatros, of → Amynus ('averter'), and of Pancrates ('all-powerful'), who was worshipped together with Hercules, or as a form of the latter [9].

The Italic healing cults of the Republican era confirmed by the existence of anatomical votives are more widely scattered, though in some cases they are no longer identifiable. Female cults played a particularly large role here as well. The finds from Latium do not differ significantly from those of Etruria, except that the Etruscan healing cults, which are documented only by archaeological deposits, remain, as a rule, anonymous [10]. What is significant and well-documented is the healing power of the → springs and the deities associated with them (Frontin. Aq. 1,4). The presence of → Aesculapius (large sanctuary in Fregellae, architectonically based on the one in Kos [11]) in central Italy is documented from the mid-Hellenistic period. After his introduction to Rome in 293 BC, he gradually eclipsed Apollo Medicus. Another particularly important figure is → Minerva, who was worshipped from the 3rd cent. BC in Lavinium and, as Minerva Medica, in a temple on the Esquiline in Rome (Cic. Div. 2,123; Ov. Fast. 3,827f.; CIL VI 10133). In addition, there are also → Juno (Lucina) and the spring- and birth-goddess → Carmentis. In the late Hellenic period, in Greece as well as in Italy, → Isis becomes important as a healing deity, taking up a function she already had in Egypt. At the same time, it belongs to her increasingly significant role as the all-powerful protectress of her worshippers and cannot be limited to any one specific area (Diod. Sic. 1,25,2–5); her circle also includes the healers Hermes-Thot and Imuthes-Asclepius [12. 199–209].

3. LATER DEVELOPMENTS

In the sphere of Celtic mythology, a significant role is played by → spring deities, in particular, deities of thermal springs. Many of these were identified in the Roman era with Apollo (very widespread, Apollo → Grannus); the goddess Sul in the British town of Bath was identified with Minerva [13; 14]. In the New Testament tradition, Christ himself is a healer of otherwise hopeless maladies (possession, bleeding). For that reason, → exorcisms to cure possession, as well as amulets to ward off illness, make use of his name. The true successors of the pagan healing deities and heroes were the numerous saints in whose *vitae* healing miracles in emulation of Jesus played an important role, helping to form the cult of the saints and shaping expectations of them.

B. THE CULT

1. INDIVIDUAL CULT FORMS

The forms of the healing cults are as diverse as their deities. Healing may be sought through the usual forms of ancient cult worship, i.e., through prayer and sacrifice. The Greeks of the *Iliad* already engaged in this practice, organizing a large sacrificial festival with a great feast followed by dancing and singing of paeans in order to ward off the plague. Many votive offerings have been preserved; they are the result of a prayer that contains a vow to offer the appropriate gift if a cure is effected. Cathartic rites are employed in the case of illnesses that were understood as possession or punishment, such as → epilepsy or psychological disorders (*manía*, 'insanity'). The nature of such rites was oriented to the specific deity considered to be the cause of the illness (Hippoc. De morbo sacro 2f.; Pl. Resp. 2,364bd).

A separate category consists in the so-called confession inscriptions – an extensive group of inscribed stelai from north-western Lydia that were erected in local sanctuaries (particularly those of Men and Meter). The inscriptions related a religious offence (perpetrated either knowingly or unwittingly), together with the otherwise inexplicable illness the offence brought on as a punishment. Through the public and permanent confession of the inscription, the confessor regained his health [15].

2. INCUBATION

The most common ritual method of healing is of course, sleeping in the temple – the → incubation. This is a ritual method of communing with the deity directly and sharing in his/her superior wisdom. Incubation is institutionalized not only in the cults of → Asclepius and of Isis – who usually comes to one's aid in dreams anyway; rather, it is found in a great number of healing cults. The dreamer's requests and the contents of the dream's messages, however, are nowhere limited to healing, in accordance with the general divinational function of dreaming (→ Dreams, Interpretation of dreams). The tradition of incubation continues into the modern era with the Christian cult of saints (→ Saints, Veneration of saints) [16]. In Greece and Rome, the practice described in modern times as 'magical' medicine [17] employed incantations (epoidaí, carmina) – documented since Homer – in conjunction with often peculiar ingredients and rites. Such methods were employed in the treatment of maladies that medicine found difficult or impossible to comprehend (head- and toothaches, but also luxations, Cato Agr. 160; Plin. HN 28,21). The importance of healing for magic – at least in the later period – is demonstrated in the history of magic sketched out in Plin. HN 30,1, where medicine is one of the sources for magic. This function is also apparent in the formulas of the Graeco-Egyptian → magic papyri, which also made use of magical dream requests as a non-institutional form of incubation for the purposes of healing.

→ Hero cult; → Incubation; → Medicine; → Magic; → Votive offerings

1 H. W. PARKE, The Oracles of Apollo in Asia Minor, 1985, 150–158   2 M. GÉRARD-ROUSSEAU, Les mentions religieuses dans les tablettes mycéniennes, 1968 3 B. FORSÉN, Griech. Gliederweihungen. Eine Unt. zu ihrer Typologie und ihrer religions- und sozialgesch. Bed., 1996   4 M. TABANELLI, Gli ex-voto poliviscerali etruschi e romani. Storia, ritrovamenti, interpretazioni, 1962 5 A. COMELLA, Tipologia e diffusione dei complessi votivi in Italia in epoca medio- e tardo-repubblicana, in: MEFRA 93, 1981, 717–810   6 J. M. TURFA, Anatomical Votives and Italian Medical Traditions, in: J. P. SMALL, R. D. DE PUMA (ed.), Murlo and the Etruscans. Art and society in ancient Etruria, 1994, 224–240   7 O. RUBENSOHN, Demeter als Heilgottheit, in: MDAI(A) 20, 1895, 360–367   8 F. KUTSCH, Attische Heilgötter und Heilheroen, 1913   9 E. VIKELA, Die Weihreliefs aus dem Athener Pankrates-Heiligtum am Ilissos. Religionsgesch. Bed. und Typologie, 1994   10 PFIFFIG, 269–271 11 F. COARELLI (ed.), Fregellae 2. Il santuario di Esculapio, 1986   12 R. MERKELBACH, Isis Regina – Zeus Sarapis. Die griech.-ägypt. Rel. nach den Quellen dargestellt, 1995   13 C. LANDES (ed.), Dieux Guérisseurs en Gaule romaine, 1992   14 A. ROUSELLE, Croire et guérir. La foi en Gaule dans l'antiquité tardive, 1990   15 G. PETZL, Die Beichtinschr. Westkleinasiens, 1994   16 M. F. G. PARMENTIER, Incubatie in de antieke hagiografie, in: A. HILHORST (ed.), De heiligenverering in de eerste eeuwen van het christendom, 1988, 27–40   17 G. LANATA, Medicina magica e religione popolare in Grecia fino all'età di Ippocrate, 1967.   F.G.

Hearth (ἐσχάρα/eschára, ἑστία/hestía, Lat. focus, ara, lar, cf. also → Altar). Greeks and Romans honour the hearth and hearth fire especially (→ Hestia, → Lares, → Penates, → Vesta, → Fire), since these are the places of worship and the seats of the household gods. It was also the place in the house where the family would meet for meals, as well as a source of light and warmth; thus hearth came to be synonymous with house. During the wedding (→ Wedding customs) the bride is led into the bridegroom's house and around the hearth, and the katachýsmata are poured over her, cf. the amphidrómia of the newborn child (Aristoph. Lys. 757; schol. in Pl. Tht. 160e). In Rome the bride additionally laid an as on the hearth (Non. 531,8); it would be one of her responsibilities in the future, to keep the hearth clean and to sweep it every evening (Cato Agr. 143,2–4). In Greece it was also possible to swear by the hearth (e.g. Hom. Od. 14,159), in the same way that someone who sought protection found refuge here (Hom. Od. 7,153.248; Thuc. 1,136,3; Plut. Themistocles 24,4–6, cf. Plin. HN 36,70).

The central function of the hearth or the fireplace in the → house (see also → Megaron) is already shown by the round hearth of the Mycenaean palaces in Pylos, Mycenae, etc. Houses of the second millennium BC also show fixed stone hearth places, in part with a smoke outlet. There were also portable hearths and firepans. The tradition of the fixed as well as the portable hearth continues in the geometrical, archaic as well as in the classical period. Open hearth places on packed clay floors were also used (cf. the houses in Olynthus, also the temple of Apollo of Drerus). The pots were placed on stands (tripods etc.) or on a surface above a fireplace.

According to tradition the hearth was originally in the → atrium of a Roman house (Ov. Fast. 6,301), a custom that continued later at least in rural areas (Hor. Sat. 2,6, 65–67). But already the early Roman houses and certainly the later large residences (house of the Faun in Pompeii; house on the Palatine; houses of Cosa) have cooking places or a separate kitchen with a hearth (→ Culina), so that the place in the atrium was not used and became occupied by a square stone table (cartibulum). Especially from the houses of Pompeii both fixed hearths (free-standing or set against a wall) as well as portable hearths are preserved, which are made from bronze or iron and variously shaped; the smoke was cleared through openings in the wall or chimneys.

Whether or not one can conclude from Prop. 4,5,26 that different types of hearth with respective names existed is still debated. The lighting of fuel on the hearth is often mentioned but never described in detail; there was always a small fire burning or glowing on the hearth, which could be ignited again by blowing or with a → fan (ῥιπίς; rhipís, Anth. Pal. 6,306; Aristoph. Ach. 669; 888; Hsch. s.v. ῥιπίς; [1]). If necessary, a flint

(πυρίτης; *pyrítēs*, Αἰθιοπικός λίθος; *Aithiopikós líthos*,
Plin. HN 36,137), tinder fungus (ἀγαρικόν; *agarikón*),
tinder and wood (Plin. HN 16,207) etc. could be used.

On the religious-cultic aspects of the hearth → Altar;
→ Fire.

1 V. TRAN TAM TINH, Le culte des divinités orientales à
Herculaneum (EPRO 17), 1971, pl. 27,40.

F. E. BROWN, Cosa. The making of a Roman town, 1980,
64–65; G. BRUHNS, Küchenwesen und Mahlzeiten, Arch.
Hom. Q, 1970, 2–6, 31; M. CHRISTOFANI (ed.), La grande
Roma dei Tarquini, exhibition catalogue Rome 1990,
97–99; G. DITMAR-TRAUTH, Das galloröm. Haus. Zu
Wesen und Verbreitung des Wohnhauses der galloröm.
Bevölkerung im Imperium Romanum, 1995, 83–87, 108–
109; H. DRERUP, Griech. Baukunst in geom. Zeit, Arch.
Hom. II O, 1969; R. J. FORBES, Stud. in ancient technol-
ogy 6, 1958, 1–35, 57–86; V. GASSNER, Die Kaufläden in
Pompeji, 1986, 40–41; W. HOEPFNER, E. L. SCHWAND-
NER, Haus und Stadt im klass. Griechenland, ²1994, 353,
s.v. Haus; s.v. Hestia; J. K. PAPADOPOULOS, Lasana,
tuyère and kiln firing supports, in: Hesperia 61, 1992,
203–221; C. SCHEFFER, Cooking and cooking stands in
Italy 1400–400 B.C., Acquarossa II 1, 1981.   R.H.

Heating

A. GENERAL B. TYPES OF HEATING C. HEATING
EFFECT

A. GENERAL

All Mediterranean countries have freezing temperatures in the winter (average minimum temperature:
Rome −9° C; central Turkey −18° C; southern France
−11° C; Sicily −3° C; northern Algeria −2° C). Heat
sources in residences were originally the hearthfire,
wood or charcoal braziers of various kinds, which were
made of metal; in Greek antiquity there were occasionally also permanently installed hearths that sometimes
resembled fireplaces (e.g. Cassope, 'marketbuilding',
[2. 128]). These required that the partially poisonous
smoke gases escape, and a cold floor had to be taken
into account. On the other hand, these heating methods
were easy to regulate; water could be heated on the
→ hearth as well as in the → baths in metal containers or
stone basins over wood or charcoal fires.

A developmental leap occurred with the invention of
the principle of a room heated through the floor from a
central heat source (underfloor-heating, Greek
ὑπόκαυστον, Lat. *hypocaustum*, [3. 161f.]). According
to Plin. HN 9,168 and Val. Max. 9,1,1 C. Sergius Orata
from Puteoli is considered the 'inventor' of hypocaust
heating around 80 BC, who, in order to accelerate the
growth of his fish and shellfish had the pools built over
a hollow cavity so that they could be heated from
below. Meanwhile, however, it has become certain that
at least the baths in → Gortys were already equipped
with similarly designed underground heating systems in
the 3rd cent. BC (→ Baths, with fig.). In the enormous
→ thermal baths of the Roman imperial period heatable
pools increased to gigantic proportions; the thermal

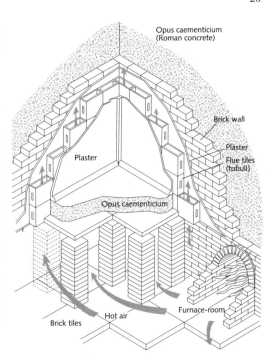

Schematic representation of hypocaust heating with wall flues.

baths of Barbara in Trier (→ Augusta [6] Treverorum)
contained two heated pools with an area of 13 × 23 m
each; the thermal baths of Augustus in Ankara have one
pool *c.* 50 m long. In the late 1st cent. BC this form of
heating spread throughout the entire Roman Empire in
the construction of houses and villas.

Living comfort depends on the temperature of the air
and the walls, as well as the movement, humidity and
purity of the air. Heat can be transmitted by radiation
(modern example: underfloor heating) and convection
(the air is heated up by hot objects; modern example:
heaters). Radiant heating does not create draughts and
thus always feels better than convection heating. Up to
2/3 of ancient heating systems worked through radiant
heat; today convection heating is far more common.
Above all → wood served as fuel, which was especially
in Roman antiquity required in large quantities for the
operation of the numerous thermal baths (this resulted
in large areas of erosion around the Mediterranean that
exist until today); more effective but also more costly
was heating using charcoal.

B. TYPES OF HEATING

1. *Hypocaust method* (from 3rd/2nd cents. BC): air
was heated in a heating chamber that was controlled
from outside (*praefurnium*) and it flowed through the
hollow spaces between small pillars (mostly made of
quadratic or round tiles, mortared with clay or lime
mortar), on which the floortiles rested. The air warmed
the pillars as well as the floor, escaped upwards through
vertical canals (mostly) in the corners of the rooms and

then outside. Vitruvius (5,10) gave a detailed description of this form of heating in the 1st cent. BC.

2. *Hypocaust wall heating* (from the 1st cent. AD): the heating effect was clearly improved when additional tracks of hollow bricks (*tubuli*) were built into the walls. Thus the hot air could warm the walls as well and then escape outside through an upper heating channel.

3. *Air heating* (from the 1st cent. AD): both of the previously mentioned constructions were also used for an air heating system. Here the ability of massive pillars and thick floors, walls and ceilings to store heat was utilized. After these were heated up the fire was allowed to go out, the smoke to escape and fresh air to flow into the rooms through the heating chamber. Modern experiments showed that the residual flue gases proved to be only a minor inconvenience for people, especially when compared to open fires.

4. *Channel heating* (from the 2nd cent. AD): it was used above all as an 'economical building method' in the cold northern provinces of the Roman Empire; it consisted mostly of a covered, horizontal heating channel under the floor which was heated from outside and which led into the center of the room. From there channels ran to the four corners and met vertical tracks of hollow bricks that led outside at the top. The minimal effort required to construct the system and the ease handling were an advantage, but the low effectivity was a disadvantage, which could nevertheless be balanced out by combining the system with a small hypocaust.

C. HEATING EFFECT

Heating experiments in wintry temperatures were carried out repeatedly in reconstructed Roman → thermal baths in Germany [1]. Temperatures on the floors were between 20° and 50° C and on the walls between 18° and 30° C. Usually the *caldarium* of the thermal baths, the room for warm bathing, had air temperatures of about 32° C, humidity of 100%, and the *sudatorium* even had air temperatures of 37° and water temperatures of about 48° C at the inlet (the warm water had to be mixed here with cold water). The negative energy balance of ancient hypocaust heating was increased by its poor adjustability; large facilities were open at all hours (24 hours a day).

1 D. BAATZ, Heizversuch an einer rekonstruierten Kanal-H. in der Saalburg, in: Saalburg-Jb. 36, 1979, 31–44   2 W. HOEPFNER, E. L. SCHWANDNER, Haus und Stadt im klassischen Griechenland, ²1994   3 I. NIELSEN, Thermae et Balnea, ²1993.

J. BECKER et al. (ed.), Gesundes Wohnen, 1986, 36–104; E. W. BLACK, Hypocaust Heating in Domestic Rooms in Roman Britain, in: Oxford Journal of Archaeology 4, 1985, 77–92; E. BRÖDNER, Die römischen Thermen und das antike Badewesen, 1983, 155–162; ID., Wohnen in der Antike, 1989, 119–124; H. in der röm. Architektur. Berichte zum 3. Augster Symposion 1980, Jahresber. aus Augst und Kaiseraugst 3, 1983; H.-O. LAMPRECHT, Opus Caementitium, ⁵1996, 126–137; W. MÜLLER-WIENER, Griech. Bauwesen in der Antike, 1986, 169–170; H. J. SCHALLES et al. (ed.), Colonia Ulpia Traiana: Die röm. Bäder, 1989, 21–42.   H.-O.L.

Heavenly cycles see → Kykloi

Heba (Magliano) The Roman colony H., established in the 3rd or 2nd cent. BC, lay on a hill south-east of Magliano. The equation with the H. mentioned by Ptol. 3,1,43 and Plin. HN 3,52 is confirmed on the basis of an inscription on a → cippus. A previous Etruscan settlement is assumed only because of necropoleis which are documented from the late 7th cent. BC and were esp. wealthy in the 6th cent. A lead plate of the 5th–4th cents. BC found in the area of the ancient city, on which is scratched a spiral-shaped Etruscan text containing instructions for sacrifice, is important.

M. MICHELUCCI, Caltra, Καλουσιον, H. Indagini sugli insediamenti etruschi nella bassa valle dell'Albegna, in: Studi di antichità in onore di G. Maetzke, 1984, 377–392; A. MINTO, Per la topografia di Heba etrusca nel territorio di Magliano in Toscana, in: SE 9, 1935, 11–59.   M.M.

Hebdomas see → Week

Hebe (Ἥβη; *Hḗbē*) – the name stands for 'Youth', personification of the beauty of youth. Cults were dedicated to her in Mantinea (Paus. 8,9,3), in Cos together with Hercules (Cornutus 31), and esp. in Argos with Hera (Paus. 2,17,5). She is better documented in mythological poetry, as the daughter of Zeus and Hera, than in cult (Hes. Theog. 922; 950–952; Apollod. 1,13). She was given to → Hercules as his wife after his death (Pind. Nem. 1,69–72). Among the gods she appears as helper (Hom. Il. 4,2; 5,722; 905), in choral poetry as dancer (H. Hom. 3,195). Iconography: the (non-extant) statue of Naucydes in Argos; in vase painting often depicted as cupbearer [1]. In Rome cf. → Iuventas(us).

1 A. F. LAURENS, s.v. H. 1, LIMC 4.1, 458–464.   RE.ZI.

Hebrew The name of the Hebrew language is derived from the *nomen gentile*, also called 'Hebrew'. This language belongs to the → Canaanite branch of Semitic languages. The 22 symbols of the epigraphical Old Hebrew alphabet developed from the proto-Canaanite → alphabet. The later Hebrew → square script was used only as a book hand. Hebrew developed over several linguistic stages, of which spoken Classical Hebrew, also defined as Old Hebrew, is preserved in inscriptions (10th–6th cents. BC) on stone, ostraka, papyri and metal and in the oldest parts of the OT (11th–6th cents. BC) such as Judg 5, Gn, Ex, Lv, Nm, Dt, Jos, Sam and Kg. It is followed by the Exile (Is, Jer, Ez and the 'lesser prophets') and the post-Exile period of the late OT books (Dan, Ezra, Est, Song, Ecc, Neh, Chr) and the Apocrypha (6th–2nd cents. BC), which closes with the Biblical and non-Biblical writings from → Qumran and Judea (1st cent. BC–2nd cent. AD). This is followed by Middle Hebrew (2nd–3rd cents. AD) of the Mishna (legal part of the Talmud) and other → rabbinical literature (Tosephta, Halakhic Midrashim), which heavily borrowed

words from Aramaic, Greek and Latin. New Hebrew
was used only as a scholarly language by later scholars.
Modern Hebrew (Ivrit) was created in the 19th cent.
from this artificial branch and became the official language of the state of Israel since 1948.
→ Bible; → Inscriptions; → Judaism

C. BROCKELMANN, Das Hebräische (HbdOr III,1), 1953,
59–132; J. RENZ, W. RÖLLIG, Hdb. der Althebr. Epigraphik, 1–3, 1995.   C.K.

Hebron Canaanite *hæbrōn* ('place of alliance' or 'junction', the same semantics are at work in the more recent
(!) name *Qiryat 'Arba'*, 'four-town', sc. the four clans or
tribes named in 1 Sam 25:3; 27:10; 30:26–31); Greek
Χεβρων (LXX), Ἑβρών, Γιβρών, Ναβρόν, Χεβρών etc.
(Jos passim); *ha-barûk* ('the blessed' = Abraham, Gen
14,19) in → Qumran (DJD III 298, DJD II 160); Arab.
al-Halīl ar-Rahmān ('the friend [= Abraham, see e.g. Is
41,8] of the merciful [= Allah]'). Central city in the
Judaean mountains, 30 km south of Jerusalem on the
old road from Bethel to Beerseba, or on the old transit
connections to Egypt and Arabia. The location on the
border between fertile agricultural land and the steppe
region of the Negev made H. a trade centre for farmers
and livestock breeders.

Significant in the 18th–16th cents. BC (with cyclo-
pean city walls, Num 13:22; 28; 33), the city was
abandoned in the 15th–13th cents. in favour of → Jerusalem. H. experienced a new upswing in settlement in
the 12th cent. BC, when it became the centre of the
Calebites (Jos 14:12–15; 15:13f.; Judg 1:20). The Abraham clan, who according to Gen 18 were greeted by the
gods of H., must have settled near H. at around the
same time. In the first half of the 10th cent. BC, H. was
the capital of the tribal kingdom of Judah for 7 years,
which the Philistine vassal → David [1] had founded
from Judaeans, Kenites and Jerahmeelites at the cost of
the Calebites (war report 2 Sam 2:1–4) and from which
he gained the kingship over Israel (2 Sam 5:1–5). Still
under David, H. was again abandoned in favour of
Jerusalem, not without resistance, however (1 Sam
15:7; 9). Literary-sociological considerations suggest
that H. was the centre of the countryside-based Judaean
opposition to the capital Jerusalem.

Between 597 and 582, Judah lost control over H.,
and the city became Edomite/Idumaean. In the
6th/5th cents. BC, at the Abraham sanctuary, which
was about to move from → Mamre to H. (Gn 23), there
was obviously a simultaneous Jewish-Idumaean-Arabic
cult (Gn 25:9; 35:29), like the one in Mamre (*Ramet
al-Halil*, 'Cave of the Friend'), in the 4th/5th cents. AD,
according to Sozomenus. Herod the Great already had
a temenos built there on the remains of a Hasmonaean
building, whose ruins Hadrian reused for a sanctuary
for Hermes-Mercury; in the east of the temenos the
remains of a Constantinian basilica are still found (cf.
Euseb. Vita Const. 3,51ff.), which did not survive the
invasion of the Sassanids in AD 614. A Jewish settle-

ment in Idumaean H. is also cited in Neh 11:25. After
the Idumaeans 129/8 BC had been forcibly Judaized
and, following that, an Idumaean, Herod the Great,
ascended to the newly established throne in Jerusalem
(37–34 BC), he monumentally embellished the Graves
of the Patriarchs (cave of Machpela), located on the
eastern hill in the *Haram al-Halīl* (perimeter wall
extant). The graves were further elaborated under Byzantine, early Arabic, Crusader and Ayyubid rule and
were an important pilgrimage destination for Jews and
Christians in the Byzantine era and, from the Arab conquest in 639 on, for Muslims as well. In the north-west
of the Haram, Justinian had a basilica set up; in the
south-east is a church built in the Crusader period
which was converted into a mosque. In AD 1165, H.
was the seat of a bishopric under the name St. Abraham.
→ Edom; → Judah and Israel

O. KEEL, M. KÜCHLER, Orte und Landschaften der Bibel
2, 1982, 670–696; E. A. KNAUF, Die Umwelt des AT,
1994, 235–237; A. Ofer, NEAEHL 2, 606–609.
M.K. and E.A.K.

Hebrus (Ἕβρος; *Hébros*). Southern Thracian river,
modern Bulgarian Marica, Byzantine/Modern Greek
Εὖρος, longest river after the Danube on the Balkan
peninsula. According to Ps.-Plutarchus (De fluviis 3), its
earlier name is supposed to have been Rhombus. Its
headwaters lie in the Rila mountains (Thuc. 2,96,4).
From there, it flows in an easterly direction through the
fertile Thracian plain to → Hadrianopolis, where it is
joined by the Tonzos, then turns toward the south and
empties into the Aegean through two arms near Aenus
(Str. 7, fr. 52). The banks were swampy on the lower
course (Aristid. 24,59B). The H. was navigable from
Hadrianopolis; according to Str. 7, fr. 48, ships could
easily sail as far as Philippopolis. Thus it was one of the
most important traffic routes to the interior of
→ Thrace. Besides Philippopolis and Hadrianopolis, a
series of other cities lay on its course, e.g. Cypsela,
Aenus and Doriscus (Trajanopolis), partly on locations
of older Hallstatt settlements. Important roads crossed
the H.: the *via Egnatia* near Cypsela, the Singidunum-
Naissus-Serdica-Byzantium road near Philippopolis
and Hadrianopolis. The representation of the river god
H. often appears on the coin images of these cities.

G. KAZAROV, Antični izvestija za reka Marica, in: FS Mit-
ropolit Maxim, 1931, 81–86; C. DANOV, Zu den histor.
Umrissen Altthrakiens 1, 1944.   I.v.B.

Hebryzelmis (Ἑβρύζελμις; *Hebrýzelmis*).
[1] On coins ΕΒΡΥΤΕΛΜΙΟΣ or ΕΒΡΥ. King of the
Odrysians in the 80s of the 4th cent. BC (IG II/III² 31;
Syll.³ 1,138; TOD 117) [1. 18]; perhaps a son of Seuthes
II [4]. Some scholars identify H. with Ἀβροζέλμης (*Ab-
rozélmēs*), the interpreter of Seuthes II, who negotiated
with Xenophon (An. 7,6,43) [5]. H. minted several
types of bronze coins [2. 106–112].

1 C.L. Lawton, Attic Document Reliefs, 1995
2 U. Peter, Die Münzen der thrakischen Dynasten, 1996
3 A. Höck, Der Odrysenkönig Hebrytelmis, in: Hermes 26, 1891, 453–462   4 V. Velkov, Der thrakische König Hebryzelmis und seine Herkunft, in: Thracia 11, 1995, 299f.   5 K. Vlahov, Zur Frage der Gräzisierung thrakischer Personennamen, in: Živa antika 15/1, 1965, 39–44.   U.P.

[2] One of the four sons of Seuthes III and Berenice (IGBulg 3,1731).   U.P.

Hecabe (Ἑκάβη/*Hekábē*, Lat. Hecuba). Wife of the Trojan king → Priamus, mother of numerous children (Hom. Il. 24,496; Eur. Hec. 421), among them → Hector, → Paris/Alexander, → Cassandra, → Polyxene and → Troilus. Her parentage is unclear, in Hom. Il. 16,718f. she is the daughter of king → Dymas [1], in Eur. Hec. 3 of king Cisseus (cf. also Hyg. Fab. 91; 111; 243), and in Apollod. 3,148 of Sangarius. Her mother is mentioned in Suet. Tib. 70,3. In Homer, at Hector's urging, she goes to Athena's temple to pray and bearing a → peplos (Hom. Il. 6,269–311), and tries to keep him from battle with → Achilles (Hom. Il. 22,79–83). Later she prepared a libation to Zeus for Priamus when, despite her objection, he wants to go to Achilles to ask for the return of Hector's body (Hom. Il. 24,193–216; 283–321). H. leads the lamentation for Hector (Hom. Il. 22,430; 24,747–760). The dream of H. before the birth of Paris/Alexander, that she would give birth to a torch, and the exposure of the newborn seem already to be a theme of the → *Cypria* (Pind. Paean fr. 8a 17–20, with variations Apollod. 3,148; Enn. Scaen. 35–46). At the conquest of Troy according to Stesich. fr. 198 PMG, H. is carried away by Apollo to Lycia, probably in connection with the version of the myth that Hector was supposed to be a son of H. and Apollo (Stesich. fr. 224 PMG; Ibycus fr. 295 PMG).

Lyric poets and tragedians give H. a prominent role in the depiction of the fate of the vanquished: she witnesses the murder of her husband and her daughter Polyxene (Soph. Polyxena; Eur. Hec. 518–570; Eur. Tro. 482f.), sinks into mourning for her dead relatives (Eur. Tro. 1250), tries in vain to convince → Menelaus to punish → Helena (Eur. Tro. 890), and finally avenges the murder of her son Polydorus on his murderer Polymestor, by blinding him and killing his children (Eur. Hec. 1116–1121); here Euripides either incorporates a local myth into his tragedy, or else he has newly created the figure of Polymestor and connected it to the fate of Polydorus. H. escapes the lot of having to serve her archenemy → Odysseus as a slave (Eur. Tro. 277) by throwing herself into the sea from one of the Greek ships near the Thracian Chersonesus, while transforming into a dog, whereupon a monument is erected to her on land (κυνὸς σῆμα, *kynòs sêma*; Eur. Hec. 1265), which serves sailors as a point of orientation (Str. 13,1,28; Diod. Sic. 13,40,6; Ov. Met. 13,565–575; Sen. Ag. 705–709; Suda s.v. H.). This is probably also a local

myth, which was put to use in the Polymestor story. According to some authors, H. has already transformed into a dog in Troy (Quint. Smyrn. 14,346–351; Triphiodorus, Ilii excidium 401f.), or this occurs after her stoning by the Greeks (Lycoph. 330–334). This transformation points to the goddess → Hecate, to whom the dog is attributed and with whom H. can be connected through her revenge on Polymestor for his abuse of hospitality [1. 154–155]. With H., Euripides has created one of the most impressive female figures in his tragedies, which was taken up by the Roman tragedians and epic poets (Ennius, Accius: *Hecuba*; Pacuvius, *Iliona*; Verg. Aen. 2,524–558; Seneca, *Troades*). In pictorial representation, H. is an example for the collective fate of the Trojan royal family; her revenge on Polymestor is rarely depicted. She appears in the handing over of the peplos by the Trojan women to Athena, as a spectator at the battle between Achilles and Hector, at Hector's burial, and as prominent victim at the conquest of Troy by the Greeks. For later representations in literature, and art cf. [2].

1 D. Lyons, Gender and Immortality. Heroines in Ancient Greek Myth and Cult, 1997   2 Hunger, Mythologie, 149–150.

BIBLIOGRAPHY: R.E. Harder, Die Frauenrollen bei Euripides, 1993; A.-F. Laurens, s.v. H., LIMC 4.1, 473–474; N. Loraux, Matrem nudam. Quelques versions grecques, in: L' Ecrit du Temps 11, 1986, 90–102; J. Mossman, Wild Justice. A Study of Euripides' Hecuba, 1995; Ch. Segal, Euripides and the Poetics of Sorrow: Art, Gender, and Commemoration in Alcestis, Hippolytus and Hecuba, 1993, 157–213; E. Sittig, s.v. H., RE 7, 2652–2662; F. Zeitlin, Euripides' Hecuba and the Somatics of Dionysiac drama, in: Ramus 20, 1991, 53–94.
FIG.: A.-F. Laurens, s.v. H., LIMC 4.2, 280–283.   R.HA.

Hecademus see → Academus

Hecale (Ἑκάλη; *Hekálē*).
[1] Heroine of the like-named Attic deme on Pentelicon, who takes in → Theseus, who has been surprised by a storm on his way to fight the Bull of Marathon, very hospitably despite her poverty. As he returns after his victory, he finds her dead and out of gratitude establishes a cult to her and → Zeus Hekal(ei)os, at which the surrounding demes meet for an annual sacrifice. → Callimachus (Hecale fr. 230–377) and Plut. Thes. 14,6b-c (= Philochorus FGrH 328 F 109) fall back on older atthidographers in their representations. Callimachus, in turn, influenced the development of individual themes in later authors (e.g. the hospitality: Ov. Met. 8,626–724; Nonnus, Dion. 17,32–86).

BIBLIOGRAPHY: P. Friedländer, s.v. H., RE 7, 2665f.; A.S. Hollis, Callimachus, H., 1990, 5–10, 26–35, 341–354; E. Simon, s.v. H., LIMC 4.1, 481.
FIGURES: E. Simon, s.v. H., LIMC 4.2, 283.   R.HA.

[2] Attic Mesogeia deme of the phyle Leontis, from 224/3 BC of Ptolemaïs, with one *bouleutes*. For its exact location on the way from Athens to Marathon (Plut. Thes. 14 after Philochorus, FGrH 328 F 109; [1]), the collected finds at the monastery Kukunar(t)i (among other things cult calendar of the deme Marathon: IG II² 1258 [2; 3. 128⁴⁴, 173, 185, 384 no. 76]) or at the early Christian church of Mygdaleza (= Anacaea? [2]) prove little. The fragment of a decree ibid. allots H. [3. 386f. no. 97] to Plothea. Several demes around H. participated in the cult of Zeus Hekaleios, which is explicitly confirmed as located in H. [3. 210f.].

> 1 D.M. LEWIS, Cleisthenes and Attica, in: Historia 12, 1963, 22–40   2 J.S. TRAILL, Demos and Trittys, 1986, 131 with n. 24   3 WHITEHEAD, Index s.v. H.
>
> E. SIMON, s.v. H., LIMC 4.1, 481; TRAILL, Attica, 6, 8, 19, 46, 62, 69, 110 no. 53, table 4, 13.   H.I.O.

Hecamede (Ἑκαμήδη; *Hekamḗde*). Daughter of Arsinous of Tenedus. H. was taken as booty by → Achilles, who destroyed Tenedus, and later given to Nestor as a gift of honour (Hom. Il. 11,624; 14,6; Suda, s.v.).

> H.W. STOLL, s.v. H., Roscher 1, 1885.   K.WA.

Hecataeus (Ἑκαταῖος; *Hekataîos*).
[1] Tyrant of → Cardia, kept in office by → Alexander [4] although → Eumenes [1] made an effort to free the city (Plut. Eumenes 3). In the Lamian War, he supported → Antipater [1] (Diod. Sic. 18,14,4).
[2] One of the → hetairoi of Alexander [4], entrusted by him in 336 BC with the removal of → Attalus [1], whom he murdered (Diod. Sic. 17,2,5; 5,2).

> BERVE 2, no. 292 (not identical with no. 293).   E.B.

[3] **H. of Miletus.** Son of Hegesander, *c.* 560–480 BC, first 'logographer' (using the term – current since FR. CREUTZER, but somewhat incorrect – for the prose authors before Herodotus), from whom numerous fragments exist (*c.* 370 in the collection of the FGrH 1). H. is of utmost significance for the development of Greek geography and historiography. According to ancient tradition (T 3 in Str. 14,1,7), he was a student of → Anaximander. This is hardly possible chronologically, but in any case Anaximander had a lasting influence on H.: his cosmogony, his representation of the development of life forms and humans, as well as the map of the world he created, inspired H. to works in which he often reported and expanded on the views and ideas of his predecessor (see esp. [1. 409ff.]). In 500, H. advised in vain against the → Ionian Revolt, noting the size of the Persian Empire and the military potential of the Great King; his suggestion for building a fleet also met with no response (Hdt. 5,36). After the failure of the revolt, he allegedly pleaded for the mild treatment of the Ionians with the satrap Artaphernes (Diod. Sic. 10,25,4). To what extent he experienced the Persian Wars is uncertain. H. was a 'widely travelled man' (Aga-

tharchides Geography 1,1) and, among other things, spent a long time in Egypt (Hdt. 2,143).

Works: 1. 'Map of the World' (FGrH F 36). H. improved the map of Anaximander 'in an admirable fashion' (T 12a). An idea of this map is given by the anonymous criticism of Herodotus (4,36), which is generally believed to be aimed at H. (cf. F 36b): According to this, H. considered the Earth to be a circular disc, with the Ocean flowing around it and composed of two equally sized continents: Europe and Asia. The border between the two was an east-west line running from the Mediterranean to the Black Sea, which together with a north-south line stretching from the Danube to the Nile divided the Earth into four quadrants of the same size. According to H., even the individual countries had the shape of geometric figures, e.g. circles, squares, rectangles and trapezoids. Furthermore, he was the first to distinguish zones and belts and was thus the predecessor of → Eudoxus of Cnidus, who created the division into degrees of latitude and longitude.

2. *Periḗgēsis* or *Períodos gês*, 'Description of the Earth' (F 37–369). The description of the Earth annotated and illustrated the world map and consisted of 2 books with the titles 'Europe' and 'Asia' (the latter erroneously declared a fake by Callimachus, cf. T 15). Following the → periplus literature in terms of form and content, H. generally followed the coasts, but occasionally penetrated into the interior, sometimes even to the edge of the world. Starting from Spain, he described Europe, Asia, Egypt and Libya and then returned to the 'Pillars of Hercules'. The materially rich, literarily unpretentious work gave a current general view of the knowledge of the Earth and its inhabitants, however, without the intention of immediately practical use, as with the peripli. Listed were peoples, tribes, borders, cities, rivers, mountains, etc. The relative location of the places to one another was often determined by giving distances and directions (cf. e.g. F 100, 108, 144, 207). It was not lacking in notes on the customs of the inhabitants (F 154, 287, 323, 358), the nature of the country (F 291, 292, 299) as well as the flora and fauna (F 291). Mythological entries and foundation legends were also not uncommon (F 31, 32, 119, 120, 140, 302); in contrast, historical notes remained an exception (F 74, 119).

Of the *c.* 330 existing fragments, almost 80 % come from the geographical lexicon of Stephanus of Byzantium (6th cent. AD) and therefore contain mostly only the bare enumeration of cities together with terse entries on location (cf. e.g. F 38–101). Additional material from H. can be gained from Herodotus: H. is the only one of his sources he cites by name (2,143,1; 6,137,1); according to ancient judgement (F 324a), his information in the Egyptian logos on the phoenix (2,73), the hippopotamus (2,71) and the crocodile hunt (2,70), among other things, was taken from H. (cf. F 324b = Hdt. 2,70–73); cf. also the concordance between Hdt. 2,156,1 and F 305. The Libyan logos of Herodotus (4,168–199) is also essentially based on H., as

[2. 2728ff.] has shown on the basis of the conformity of 4,186,1 and 4,191,1 with F 335.

3. *Genealogíai* = 'Genealogies' (also cited (F 1–35) as *Historíai* or *Hērōología*). The central theme of this work of 4 books was the *Hērōología*, i.e. the 'history' of the heroes and demigods. Still extant is the programmatic introductory sentence (F 1a in Demetrius, De elocutione 12): 'Hecataeus of Miletus proclaimed the following: I write this, as it appears to be true to me. For the tales of the Greeks are many and ridiculous, or so they seem to me at any rate.' H. correspondingly sought to systematize the 'many', that is the disordered and disconnected tales of the Heroic Age, to link them to one another and integrate them into a chronological system, similarly to what Hesiod had already done for the world of the gods in the 'Theogony' (which H. paid no attention to). The chronology took Hercules as its starting-point and was based on the calculation of the generations [1. 70]. He furthermore subjected the 'ridiculous' stories of the myths to a rationalistic criticism and stripped them of the fantastic and supernatural. Particularly instructive examples of this are F 1, 6, 19, 26. The subsequent use of this principle is underestimated by [3. 418,10a], overrated by [1. 48ff.], on the other hand [cf. 4. 23].

In research, H. was often criticized for 'unsuitable subjects and unsuitable methods' (W. SPOERRI). In reality, his critical attitude toward tradition can be considered as the 'nucleus of Greek historiography' [5]. H. wrote in an archaic style of charming simplicity (cf. T 16–20).

1 K. VON FRITZ, Griech. Geschichtsschreibung 1, 1967 2 F. JACOBY, s.v. H. (3), RE 7, 2667–2750 3 H. STRASBURGER, Die Entdeckung der polit. Gesch. durch Thukydides, in: H. HERTER (ed.), Thukydides, 1968, 412–476 4 K. MEISTER, Die griech. Geschichtsschreibung, 1990 5 O. LENDLE, Einführung in die griech. Geschichtsschreibung, 1992, 10ff.

FRAGMENTS: FGrH 1; G. NENCI, Hecataei Milesii Fragmenta, 1954.
BIBLIOGRAPHY: T.S. BROWN, The Greek Historians, 1973, 7ff.; F. JACOBY, Griech. Historiker, 1956, 186–237 (fundamental, first: cf. n. 2); E. MOSCARELLI, Ecateo: verifiche e proposte, in: Atti dell' Accademia Pontaniana 42, 1993, 129–146; L. PEARSON, Early Ionian Historians, 1939, ch. 2; P. TOZZI, Studi su Ecateo di Mileto I–V, in: Athenaeum 41–45, 1963–67; B. UHDE, Die Krise der Gegensätze, in: Tijdschrift voor Philosophie 33, 1971, 559–571; ST. WEST, Herodotus' Portrait of Hecataeus, in: JHS 111, 1991, 144–160.   K. MEI.

[4] H. of Abdera. 4th cent. BC; born in Abdera or Teos; philosopher and historian who lived at the time of Alexander the Great and Ptolemy I (Jos. Ap. 1,22). He was a student of the sceptic Pyrrho and probably held an official post under → Ptolemy I Soter, which took him to Sparta (Plut. Lycurgus 20,2). H.'s works are only preserved in fragments: 'On the Hyperboreans' (Περὶ Ὑπερβορέων; Diod. Sic. 2,47) and a history of Egypt (Αἰγυπτιακά, [6. 61–78], Diod. Sic. 1). The Suda also

names a work on Homer and Hesiod (Περὶ τῆς ποιήσεως Ὁμήρου καὶ Ἡσιόδου) which has not survived and was also mentioned nowhere else. In the 'History of Egypt', the Jews are described in a non-polemic fashion. This is why the work 'On the Jews' (Περὶ Ἰουδαίων) was ascribed to H. This pseudepigraphic work (Pseudo-Hecataeus I) was probably written by a Hellenized Jew; citations are found in Jos. (Ap. 1, 183–214; 2, 43) and a mention in Origenes (contra Celsum 1,15) [1; 7. 146–148; 6. 78–91]. The work 'On Abraham and the Egyptians' (Κατ' Ἄβραμον καὶ τοὺς Αἰγυπτίους; title in Clem. Al. Strom. 5,113) is another which is ascribed to H. (Ps.-Hecataeus II), but probably stems from a third author [7. 149–151].

EDITIONS: 1 FGrH 264, F 1–14; F 21–24 2 M. STERN, Greek and Latin Authors on Jews and Judaism, vol. 1, 22–24; 26–44 (Ps.-H.).
BIBLIOGRAPHY: 3 B. SCHALLER, H. von Abdera, Über die Juden. Zur Frage der Echtheit und der Datierung, in: ZNTW 54, 1963, 15–31 4 SCHÜRER, 671–677 5 W. SPOERRI, s.v. H. von Abdera, RAC 14, 1988, 275–310 6 G.E. STERLING, Historiography and Self-Definition. Josephos, Luke-Acts and Apologetic Historiography, 1992, 55–91 7 N. WALTER, Fragmente jüd.-hell. Historiker, 1976, 144–153.   I.WA.

[5] H. of Thasos. (Ἑκαταῖος Θάσιος; *Hekataîos Thásios*). Epigrammarian; otherwise unknown. The *Anthologia Palatina* assigns to him (or to Dioscorides) the epitaph of an 18-year-old, who died at the birth of her child which itself only lived for 20 days (7,167). His affiliation with the Wreath of Meleager is uncertain.

GA I,2,270.   M.G.A.

Hecate (Ἑκάτη; *Hekátē*). Into the modern age, the goddess H. has been known as the mistress of ghosts, as the demonic mediator *par excellence* between above and below. In this function, she is closely associated with → magic in which the 'use' of the spirits of the dead plays an important role (Eur. Med. 397; Hor. Sat. 1,8,33). H. probably stems from Caria and came to Greece around the archaic age, from where her worship spread to the entire Graeco-Roman world. Her cult in Caria (above all in Lagina) and other places in Asia Minor remained significant into the Imperial period [5. 11–56, 166–168; 6; 7. 257–259]. The family tree of H., usually depicted as a virgin, remains unclear: the most important source, Hesiod (Theog. 409–411), makes her the daughter of the Titans → Asteria [2] and → Perses and therefore a cousin of → Artemis and → Apollo (cf. Schol. Apoll. Rhod. 3,467). Her name is probably related to Apollo's epithets Hekatos and Hekatobolos; however, a convincing etymology is missing. H.'s role as mistress of ghosts has been emphasized in literature since the classical period (Adespota 375 TrGF; Eur. Hel. 569f.). Particularly in later antiquity, she is herself regarded as a fearsome, ghostly figure (PGM P4, 2520–2611).

Other sources, however, show that she could also always be seen as a normal, even kind, deity. The H. hymn in Hesiod (Theog. 404–492) praises her as a mighty goddess who aided various groups of people, among them mothers, kings and fishermen. Pindar describes her as a 'friendly virgin' (Paean 2,73–77). The iconography – except on magical gems and lead tablets [4. 1010f., no. 291–322] from late antiquity – represents her without any terrifying features: an Attic votive statuette of the late 6th cent. BC shows her sitting, dressed no differently than other goddesses ([4. no. 105], with IG I 2, 836); Attic vase images in which she carries wedding torches show her as a girlish figure in a → peplos [4. 993, no. 44–46 with comm.].

H.'s connection to spectral beings can partially be derived from her function in the premarital rites of transition for women (Hes. Theog. 450; 452; Aesch. Supp. 676; Eur. Tro. 323; Vita Homeri 30; Schol. Aristoph. Vesp. 804; more on this [1. ch. 6]): unmarried girls and childless women who died thus, according to Greek ideas, unsuccessfully, could become menacing ghosts who went about in the entourage of H., probably because she was responsible for their lot. In this context, her identification with → Iphigenia can also be seen (Hes. Fr. 23b; Procl. Summ. Cypr. 55–64; [1. ch. 6]). Another important myth, which may possibly be traced back to Euripides, connects H. with → Persephone, who came to the underworld as a virgin (Hom. H. 2,24f.; 52–59; 438–440 with comm. by [8]; Callim. Fr. 466; Orph. Fr. 41; [4. 989–991; 1013, no. 1–17]).

Another fact which contributed to H.'s depiction as the mistress of ghosts was her role as guardian of entrances and other liminal public and private places where ghosts were imagined to be ([1. ch. 3; 3]; Aesch. Fr. 388; Aristoph. Vesp. 802–804). Shrines or statuettes of H. (hekataía) protected entrances and crossroads ('triple ways', tríodoi); meals (deípna) were laid out for H. and the ghosts at the crossroads, above all on the night of the new moon (Aristoph. Plut. 594 with schol.; Dem. Or. 54,39; Plut. Mor. 708f; Apollod. FGrH 244 F 110). Also deposited there and not to be confused with the H. meals were the remnants [3] of domestic purification rituals (Plut. Mor. 280c; 290d; Lucian, Dial. Mort. 1,1; Suda, Phot. and EM s.v. κάθαρμα). H.'s close relationship with crossroads is reflected in the Greek epithet Trioditis, the Roman name Trivia and the frequent sculptural representations of the goddess since classical times with three heads or even as three goddesses [4. 998–1004, no. 112–215; 5. 84–165]. In the course of time, other epithets were added to express the triple figure; Chariclides (fr. 1) provides a not entirely serious collection.

H.'s connection with the dog and dog sacrifices (Eur. fr. 968 TGF; Aristoph. fr. 608 PCG; Schol. Aristoph. Pax 276) probably resulted, on the one hand, from her role as birth goddess (→ Eilithyia, → Genita Mana, → Genetyllis), on the other hand, at the end of the classical era, the dog was connected with H.'s appearances as mistress of ghosts, accompanied on her nightly wan-

derings by packs of howling dogs that were seen as the souls of the dead, or whose coming was announced by the howling of dogs (Theoc. 2,12f.; 35f.; Verg. Aen. 6,255–258 [2. ch. 9]). The souls of the dead in H.'s entourage caused madness or night terrors (Hippoc. De morbo sacro 6 p. 342 LITTRÉ), which explains H.'s role in mystery cults, which among other things promised healing from madness (Aristoph. Vesp. 122; Paus. 2,30,2; Dion. Chrys. Or. 4,90; Aristot. Mir. 173; [1. ch. 4]).

In cult, myth and iconography, H. was identified with various goddesses, above all with → Artemis (Aesch. Supp. 676; IG XIII 383,125–127; [4; 5. 11–23; 7. 228–231]), with whom she shared the interest in girls' initiations and births as well as the representation with two torches; furthermore with → Selene (Plut. Mor. 416e-f, [2. 29–38]) and with Enodia, a Thessalian goddess (Soph. fr. 535), who was also brought into connection with births and the protection of entrances (IG IX 2, 575; 577; [1. ch. 6; 5. 57–83]). In the → magic papyri, H. is often combined with → Kore/Persephone (e.g. PGM PIV, 1403–1405; 2745–2747) and with Ereshkigal, the Sumerian mistress of the Underworld (e.g. PGM P4 1417; LXX 4–25). In late antiquity, her connection with births and the protection of liminal places also led to her role as tutelary divinity of → theurgy, where she was identified with the Platonic cosmic soul, which separates the (earthly) world of matter from the (heavenly) world of the *nous*; she enables the passage of individual souls down into embodiment and up to union with the divine [2].

→ Ahorus; → Apollo; → Artemis; → Demons; → Eilithyia; → Genetyllis; → Genita Mana; → Hecabe; → Iphigenia; → Kore/Persephone; → Lagina; → Magic; → Nekydaimon; → Selene; → Theurgy; → Magic papyri

1 S. I. JOHNSTON, Restless Dead, 1999   2 Id., H. Soteira, 1990   3 Id., Crossroads, in: ZPE 88, 1991, 217–224   4 H. SARIEN, s.v. H., LIMC 6.1, 985–1018   5 TH. KRAUS, H., 1960   6 A. LAUMONIER, Les cults indigènes en Carie, 1958, 344–425   7 GRAF   8 N. J. RICHARDSON, The Homeric Hymn to Demeter, 1974.

J. HECKENBACH, s.v. H., RE 7, 2769; NILSSON, Feste 394–401; M. L. WEST, Hesiod Theogony, 1966, 276–290.

S.I.J.

Hecatomb (ἑκατόμβη; *hekatómbē*). In Homeric epic, a frequent term ([2]: 38 instances) for a large sacrifice. The derivation that had already become common in antiquity (100 heads of cattle: *hekatón boûs*) is not certain ([1] considers a paraetymological formation). In any case, in Homer, *hecatomb* is already divorced from its literal meaning, functioning as a general term for large sacrifice, which is often clarified by additional information about the number and kind of the sacrificed animals [2]. Even the earliest instance of *hecatomb* in an inscription involves only three sacrificial animals (450/49 BC., Miletus: LSAM no. 50,18 f.). The month *Hekatombaión* (see → Months, names of the) can be traced back to the period prior to the Ionian migration

[4. 31–34] (→ Colonization II.); there is no connection to the *hecatomb* at the → *Panathénaia* (see [3]). *Heka-tómbai* as large sacrifices appear occasionally in the Euergetes inscriptions of the Imperial period (IG IV 602; OGIS 533). The restoration policies of → Iulianus [11] referred back to the venerable old notion of the *hecatomb* (Julian Ep. 26,415C), significantly in an archaizing literal sense of the 'sacrifice of a 100 head of cattle' (Amm. Marc.22,12,6).

→ Sacrifices

1 E. Campanile, Riflessioni su ἑκατόμβη, in: Studia linguistica E. Evangelisti, 1991, 149–154   2 H. W. Nord-heider, s.v. ἑκατόμβη, LFE 2, 1991, 500–502   3 V. J. Rosivach, IG 2² 334 and the Panathenaic H., in: PdP 46, 1991, 430–442   4 C. Trümpy, Untersuchungen zu den altgriechischen Monatsnamen und Monatsfolgen, 1997.

                                       ST.D.

Hecatombaeum (Ἑκατόμβαιον; *Hekatómbaion*). Sanctuary near → Dyme [1], where Cleomenes III gained a victory over the Achaeans in 226 BC (Pol. 2,51,3; Plut. Cleomenes 14,2, Aratus 39,1). The exact location is unknown; the location is dependent on the interpretation of Cleomenes' campaign route.

M. Osanna, Santuari e culti dell'Acaia antica, 1996, 42f.

                                       Y.L.

Hecatomnos (Ἑκατόμνως; *Hekatómnōs*). Carian dynast from Mylasa (Syll.³ 167; 168). Son of Hyssaldomos. Appointed satrap of the newly founded satrapy of Caria by Artaxerxes II in 392/1 BC (Diod. 14,98,3). H. was supposed to lead the war against the renegade → Evagoras [1] I of Salamis on Cyprus together with the satrap Autophradates of Lydia (115 Theopompus FGrH F 103). The war at sea started unsuccessfully in 391 because H. secretly supported Evagoras with money (Diod. Sic. 14,98,3 with 15,2,3). H. probably planned a secession on his part (Isoc. Or. 4,162), but did not carry it out. Death of H. and accession of his son → Maussollos in 377/6 (calculated according to Diod. Sic. 16,36,?).

S. Hornblower, Mausolus, 1982, 29–39.   PE.HÖ.

Hecatompylus According to Appianus (Syr. 57,298, Ἑκατόμπολις/*Hekatómpolis*), a new foundation of Seleucus I in Comisene; according to Pliny (HN 6,17,44), 133 miles from the Caspian Gates. Probably the modern Šahr-e Qūmes near → Damghan. After brief Arsacid occupation at the beginning of the 2nd cent. BC, it became Parthian capital. Excavation has brought to light abundant evidence from the Parthian period, including – besides palace architecture, ceramics and seal impressions – two Parthian ostraca with name lists, the second of which is probably datable to the year 170 of the Arsacid Era = 78 BC.

A. D. H. Bivar, The Second Parthian Ostracon from Qūmis, in: Iran 19, 1981, 81–84; M. A. R. Colledge, Parthian Art, 1977, s.v. H.   J.W.

Hecaton of Rhodes. Pupil of → Panaetius and influential Stoic of the 1st cent. BC. → Diogenes [17] Laertius used H.'s writings for his account of Stoic ethics. The views of H. he cites correspond to old Stoic orthodoxy. Among the (mostly extensive) works often quoted by Diogenes are the *Chreíai* (which he draws on as the source for biographical and anecdotal information about Stoics and Cynics), and the treatises 'Final Ends', 'Virtues', 'Goods', 'Emotions', 'Stoic Paradoxes'. Cicero mentions at least 6 books of 'On duty' (περὶ καθήκοντος), which were dedicated to Quintus Aelius Tubero (Off. 3,63 and 89). Seneca also used H.'s writings in *De beneficiis* and in his letters. In his treatment of the virtues, H. differentiates between qualities that are based on theoretical considerations (such as prudence/*phrónēsis*, self-control and justice) and those that are not intellectually based (such as strength and health). In this he follows the orthodox Stoic and Socratic view, according to which the moral virtues are forms of knowledge. According to Cicero (Off. 3,63,89ff.), H. placed considerable weight on self-interest when deciding on the appropriate behaviour in difficult cases. In this respect, he gave the approach of → Diogenes [15] of Babylon preference over that of → Antipater [10] of Tarsus (Off. 3,51–55).

→ Panaetius

H. Gomoll, Der stoische Philosoph H., 1933; M. Pohlenz, Die Stoa, 1955, 123–4.   B.I.

Hecatonnesi (Ἑκατόννησοι; *Hekatónnēsoi*). Archipelago in the north of the eastern strait which divides Lesbos from the mainland of Asia Minor, modern Moschonisia; its largest island was Pordoselene or Nasos, modern Moschonisi. The inhabitants were known as *Nēsiôtai* (Hdt. 1,151; Diod. Sic. 13,77; Str. 13,2,5; Plin. HN 5,137; Ptol. 5,2,5; Ael. NA 2,6; Hsch. s.v. H.; Steph. Byz. s.v. Ἑκατόννησοι and Σελήνης πόλις). The city *Selénēs pólis* was probably founded, like Mytilene, by the Aeolians, on whom it was long dependent culturally and politically. H. was a member of the → Delian League. Coins ΠΟΡΔΟΣΙΛ from the 5th–3rd cents. BC, ΠΟΡΟΣΕΛΗΝΕΙΤΩΝ in the Roman Imperial period.

HN 563; Kirsten/Kraiker, 532.   H.KAL.

Hector (Ἕκτωρ/*Héktōr*; Lat. *Hector*). Son of the Trojan royal couple → Priamus and → Hecabe, husband of → Andromache and father of → Astyanax. As the strongest fighter of Priamus' sons, H. (and not Paris, who is to blame for the war) is responsible for the defence of the besieged city in *The Iliad*. He is most successful on the third day of battle: after Agamemnon's wounding (Hom. Il. 11,200ff.), H. breaks through the Achaean wall (12,445ff.), and – despite a set-back (14,409ff.) – he pushes them back to their ships and sets one of them on fire; he kills → Patroclus (16,787ff.) who is rushing to the Greeks' aid in → Achilles' place

(16,112ff.) and takes Achilles' armour off him (17,122). In so doing, H. induces Achilles to end the combat boycott. On the fourth day of battle, H. is defeated by Achilles in a duel (bk. 22). His dead body is defiled by Achilles and finally handed over to the aged Priamus only after divine intervention (bk. 24). *The Iliad* ends with the burial of H.'s body.

One characteristic of H. is his fighting nature, but just as important is his relationship with his parents, wife and son, characterized by his love, care and sense of responsibility (esp. evident in the famous farewell scene in Hom. Il. 6,392ff. [1]). He is further characterized by: a) his repeated reasoning that despite the bleak prospects, his responsibility for the common good left him no choice than to defend the city (e.g. 6,441ff.; 22,99ff.); b) his repeated references to the assessment of his deeds by posterity (6,461f.; 6,479; 7,87–91; 7,300–302; 22,106f.); c) his occasionally too optimistic appraisal of the situation (e.g. in Zeus' prophecy of his success he 'overhears' that this is limited to the third day of combat: 11,208f. in contrast to 18,293f.); this is in tune with his disregard for warnings, above all those of → Polydamas, born on the same day as he (12,210ff.; 18,243ff.; cf. also 13,725ff.), who is correct with his more pessimistic appraisal of the situation, as H. must recognize when it is too late (22,100–103); he reacts in a similarly dismissive fashion in response to Patroclus' announcement that his death by Achilles' hand is imminent (16,844–862). In contrast to Achilles, H. is of human descent (consistently emphasized by the gods who are favourable to the Greeks, e.g. 24,56ff.). It is this very same 'human nature' that contributes considerably to the fact that H., despite (or perhaps even because of) his faults is a figure of identification. In general, H. appears in Homer's representation of the Trojans (i.e. the opponents!) as a figure who apparently has earned the sympathies of poet and audience alike in no small measure.

According to a plausible supposition, Homer enhanced H.'s importance within the Troy narration and staged him as the actual opponent of Achilles (but it cannot be proven that he invented him [2. 182–185]). H. represents the (in the epic likely traditional) figure of the defender of a besieged city. The name H. is already documented in the Mycenaean [3] and is telling (connected with ἔχειν/*échein*, originally likely 'conqueror', 'victor' [4]; interpreted by Homer as 'keeper', 'defender': Il. 24,730).

Homer's representation of H. is formative for the entire later literature and is supplemented or modified only in details [5. 476–480]: Stesichorus (fr. 224 PMGF), Ibycus (fr. 295 PMGF), Euphorion (fr. 56 POWELL) and Lycophron (Alexandra 265) make him the son of Apollo (likely due to a misinterpretation of Hom. Il. 24,258–259). Sappho (fr. 44 VOIGT) describes the wedding of H. and Andromache. The Trojan who kills the first Greek jumping onto land (Protesilaus) remains anonymous in Homer (Il. 2,701). The *Cypria* (argumentum p. 42 BERNABÉ) typically fill this 'gap' and identify him with H. (cf. Soph. fr. 497 RADT).

The dominating influence of *The Iliad* is clearly apparent also in the pictorial representations of H. [5. 480; 6]. They show H. above all, a) in arming scenes, b) in a farewell, c) in combat scenes; and d) the defilement and e) the handing over of his body.

1 W. SCHADEWALDT, Von Homers Welt und Werk, ⁴1965, 207–233 2 W. KULLMANN, Die Quellen der Ilias, 1960 3 DMic s.v. e-ko-to 4 M. MEIER, ἔχω und seine Bedeutung im Frühgriech., in: MH 33, 1976, 180–181 5 P. WATHELET, Dictionnaire des Troyens de l'Iliade 1, 1988, 466–506 6 O. TOUCHEFEU, s.v. H., LIMC 4.1, 482–498.

W. SCHADEWALDT, H. in der Ilias, in: WS 69, 1956, 5–25; H. ERBSE, H. in der Ilias, in: Id., Ausgewählte Schriften zur Klass. Philol., 1979, 1–18; J. REDFIELD, Nature and Culture in the Iliad, ²1994; J. DE ROMILLY, Hector, 1997. RE.N.

Hectoridas Sculptor, listed in the accounts for the sculptures of a gable of the temple of Asclepius at → Epidaurus, which was finished around 370 BC. Therefore, the fragments of an original *Iliupersis* are to be ascribed to him and must be considered as an independent work and not – as often presumed – as copies in the fashion of models of → Timotheus. In addition, H. provided models for the painting of lionhead gargoyles. His signature is also to be found on the base of a lost statue in Epidaurus.

A. BURFORD, The Greek temple builders at Epidauros, 1969; LIPPOLD, 220; N. YALOURIS, Die Skulpturen des Asklepiostempels in Epidauros, 1992. R.N.

Hedgehog (ἐχῖνος χερσαῖος/*echînos chersaîos*, Lat. *ericius*, *ire-* or *erinaceus*, seldom *echinus*), *Erinaceus europaeus* L., a mammal from the order of insectivores. Its typical characteristics are described by Aristotle and other authors: the spines (Aristot. Hist. an. 1,6,490b 29 and 3,11,517b 24, cf. Emp. fr. 83 DIELS/KRANZ; Aristoph. Pax 1086), the position of the testicles within the body (Aristot. Hist. an. 3,1,509b 9) and its mating in an upright position, stomach to stomach (ibid. 5,2,540a 3f.; Plin. HN 10,174). Its spiny skin was used to comb woven fabric (Plin. HN 8,135), and therefore it was hunted (Nemes. Cynegetica 48). It was said to destroy its fur with its supposedly poisonous urine as soon as it becomes the target of a hunt; therefore it was hanged (Plin. HN 8,134 and 30,65; Anth. Pal. 6,45 and 169). That it collects fruit and grapes (Plin. HN 8,133; Plut. De sollertia animalium 16 = Mor. 971e-f), is of course an oft repeated folk-tale. The meat of the hedgehog was eaten (Plin. HN 30,65), but it was first and foremost prescribed as a medicine: i.a. for dropsy (Plin. HN 30,105) and urinating problems (Plin. HN 30,65), as well as spasms (Plin. HN 30,110), ulcers and scars. The hedgehog's ashes were used against hair loss (Plin. HN 29,107). The hedgehog was kept from early times as a domestic animal to exterminate snakes (cf. Aristot. Hist. an. 8(9),612b 6) and it was admired for its clever behaviour of stockpiling (Plin. HN 8,133; Plut. loc. cit. 16 = Mor. 971 e-f), as a weather prophet (Aristot. Hist. an. 8(9),6,612b 4–10) and for its form of self-defence by 'curling up into a ball' (Archilochus 118 BURCK = 103 DIEHL; Lycoph. 1093; Plin. HN 8,133; Ael. NA 6,54). An old Corinthian vase [1. 1,19; fig. 2,279] depicts it with other animals as prophets of bad tidings at → Amphiaraus' departure. The hedgehog was used against insanity in analogous magic (Plin. HN 30,95). In the Christian period, the impure hyrax mentioned in Lv 11:5 and Dt 14:7 (*choerogryllus*) was often interpreted as a → hare or as a hedgehog.

1 KELLER.   C.HÜ.

Hedna (ἕδνα/*hédna*, ep. ἔεδνα/*éedna*). Common only in the collective plural, in Homer they are the bridegroom's → presents to the bride's father (idea of the 'purchase marriage') or to the bride herself (similar to the Germanic jointure). Differently to Hom. Od. 1,277 and 2,196: endowing of the bride by her father (related to the → *parápherna* or the → *phernḗ*), sometimes also to be interpreted as a 'dowry' (→ *proíx*). Unclear: Od. 2,53 (verb); Il. 13,382 (deverbative noun). Presumably, the *hedna* is based on the archaic idea of arranging social relationships by means of gifts and counter-gifts.

R. KÖSTLER, Raub- und Kaufehe bei den Hellenen, in: Id., Homer. Recht, 1950, 29–48; Id., H., ibid. 49–64; M. SCHMIDT, s.v. H., LFE 2, 1991, 396f.   G.T.

Hedone see → Pleasure

Hedyla (Ἡδύλη; *Hēdýlē*). According to Ath. 297a, the daughter of the Attic female iambic Moschine and the mother of → Hedylus. This means that she wrote in the early 3rd cent. BC [1]. Athenaeus allocates to H. five elegiac verses (and one word of a sixth) that stem from a poem with the title *Skýlla*. In it → Glaucus [2] brings his beloved → Scylla maritime presents, presumably before her monstrous metamorphosis, in Sicily or southern Italy (cf. Ov. Met. 13, 904ff.; Hyg. Fab. 199).

1 GA I,2, 289.

SH 456; U.v. WILAMOWITZ-MOELLENDORFF, Lesefrüchte, in: Hermes 60, 1925, 302 (= Id., KS 4, 390).   E.BO.

Hedylus (Ἥδυλος; *Hédylos*). Epigrammatist of the Garland of Meleager (Anth. Pal. 4,1,45), son of the female elegiac poet → Hedyle, lived on Samos and under Ptolemy II in Alexandria (283/282–243 BC). Of his poems (dedicatory, funerary, epideictic, sympotic and derisive epigrams) eight are passed down in Athenaeus and five in the *Anthologia Palatina* (Anth. Pal. 11,123 and 414 are probably not authentic; 5,161 is perhaps from → Asclepiades [1]; cf. Ath. 7,297a; Str. 14,683; EM 72,16 for other possible works in verse and prose). These few epigrams suffice to recognize a poetic

personality of the first order who feels an intensive connection between life and inspiration (cf. epigrams 5 and 6 GOW-PAGE). There was probably an anthology compiled by H. of works by Asclepiades, Posidippus and himself (cf. → Anthology).

SH 457–460; GA I,1, 100–103; I,2, 289–298; I.G. GALLI CALDERINI, Su alcuni epigrammi dell' Anthologia Palatina..., in: Atti dell' Accademia Pontiana N.S. 31, 1982, 239–280; Id., Edilo epigrammista, in: ibid. N.S. 32, 1983, 363–376; Id., Gli epigrammi di Edilo..., in: ibid. N.S. 33, 1985, 79–118.   M.G.A.

Hegelochus (Ἡγέλοχος; *Hēgélochos*).
[1] Son of Hippostratus, officer under → Alexander [4]. Initially commander of the vanguard cavalry, he was commissioned to form a Macedonian fleet from ships collected from Greek cities in the summer of 333 BC (Arr. Anab. 2,2,3; inexact Curt. 3,1,19f.; Amphoterus was his subordinate, not his colleague). After the death of → Memnon his fleet dominated the Hellespont, where he i.a. stopped an Athenian grain fleet (Ps.-Dem. Or. 17,20). He conquered Tenedos, Chios, Lesbos and Cos. The Persian admiral → Pharnabazus was taken prisoner, but escaped. H. handed over the captive friends of the Persians from the islands to Alexander in Egypt. He fell in action at → Gaugamela (Curt. 6,11,22), where he was ilarch (→ Cavalry) of the → Hetairoi (Arr. Anab. 3,11,8). According to → Philotas' information during interrogation under torture, he is supposed to have conspired with Philotas and → Parmenion against Alexander (Curt. 6,11,21–33). That is contested by Curtius and is an invention to justify the murder of Parmenion.

J.E. ATKINSON, A Commentary on Q. Curtius Rufus... Books 5–7,2, 1994, 242–244 (for the 'conspiracy'); BERVE 1, 160f.; 2, no. 341.   E.B.

[2] According to Diodorus (34/5,20), a *strategos* who defeated an army of Alexandrians for Ptolemy VIII (124 BC) rather than for Ptolemy IX (110/108).

PP 1, 151; 2, 2162; F. WALTON, Notes on Diodorus, in: AJPh 77, 1956, 408–414, esp. 409ff.   W.A.

Hegemon (Ἡγέμων; *Hēgémōn*).
[1] of Thasos. Poet of the Old Comedy (preserved is a fragment of the *Philínna*, cf. PCG V 547) and first professional parodist (παρῳδός/*parōidós*, Aristot. Poet. 1448a 12f.). Parodizing literature became a literary genre through him, a funny appendix at the rhapsode games, similar to the satyr play at the tragedy agons (cf. [1]). In the only preserved fragment, H., known by the nickname 'Lentil' (φακῆ; *phakê*), recalls with humour the difficult beginnings of his own career (42–44 BRANDT). Later, in 415 BC, he had a glowing success with the *Gigantomachía* (Chamaileon fr. 44 WEHRLI). Only the title is preserved from a similarly hexametric *Deîpnon* (perhaps the earliest example of → gastrono-

mical poetry). Append. Peor. Bodl. II 65 suggests that there may have been other than just hexametric parodies.

1 E. DEGANI, Studi su Ipponatte, 1984, 187f.

P. BRANDT, Corpusculum poesis epicae Graecae ludibundae I, 1888, 37–49; E. DEGANI, Poesia parodica greca, 1983, 17–24; R. GLEI, Aristoteles über Linsenbrei, in: Philologus 136, 1992, 42–54; V. TAMMARO, Note al frammento parodico di Egemone, in: Mousa. Scritti in onore di G. Morelli, 1997, 123–126.   O.M.

[2] Author of a funerary epigram stemming from the Garland of Meleager that praises the heroism of the Spartans who had fallen in action at → Thermopylae, without turning their backs to their enemy (ἀστρεπτεί; astreptei, a hapax legomenon) (Anth. Pal. 7,436; on the philolaconism esp. of the Hellenistic epigram, cf. → Epigram E.). The identification of the epigrammatist with the epic poet H. of Alexandria ('Ηγήμων; Hēgémōn), who celebrated the defeat of the Spartans at Leuctra (in 371 BC) in verse, is unlikely.

GA I,1, 103; I,2,298f.   M.G.A.

Hegemonia (ἡγεμονία, 'leading position'). An important basic feature of international relations in Greece was the formation of alliances in which one of the members took up a prominent position as hēgemón ('leader'). The earliest example was a group of alliance agreements through which Sparta secured its position in the 6th cent. BC in the Peloponnese and which solidified into the → Peloponnesian League: therefore, Cleomenes I was therefore able 'to collect an army from the entire Peloponnese' in 506 (Hdt. 5,74,1), and in 432 the Spartans decided to go to war against Athens before they summoned their allies to a congress in order to vote about it (Thuc. 1,87,4; 118,3). Presumably, the formal duty of the allies consisted of 'following wherever Sparta wanted to lead them (hēgeîsthai)' ([1. 108–110]; cf. SEG 28, 408 = ML [1988] 67 bis). Sparta was also the hēgemón of the Greeks who united in resistance to the Persian invasion of 480. Argus and Syracuse supposedly distanced themselves from the alliance because they were not granted any participation in the hegemonia (Hdt. 7,148–152; 157–162). After the Persian War, the unpopularity of Pausanias led to the 'takeover of hegemonia' by the Athenians and to the founding of the → Delian League (Thuc. 1,95f.), in which they not only provided the military leaders, but also the treasurers (hellēnotamíai) and other functionaries. In the → Corinthian League, which Philip II established after the battle of Chaeronea in 338 BC, he held the title hēgemón (IG II² 236 = TOD 177). Later the Antigonids (→ Antigonus) also used this term in the alliance organizations founded by them (302: Plut. Demetrius 25,3; 224: Pol. 2,54,4).

1 G. E. M. DE STE. CROIX, The Origins of the Peloponnesian War, 1972   2 V. EHRENBERG, Der Staat der Griechen, ²1965, 137–147.   P.J.R.

Hegemonius Alleged author, otherwise unknown, of a powerfully effective anti-Manichaean (→ Mani, Manichaeism) polemical treatise, recorded in its entirety only in Latin translation and known as the Acta Archelai (CPG 3570).

Despite an indication of a Syrian source (Jer. Vir. ill. 72), the basis of the Latin translation from the 1st half of the 5th cent. could well have been a Greek original created between 330 and 348 [1. 136–140]. Information beyond any doubt regarding the author – H. names himself as author (Acta 68: ego scripsi; in the sense of 'scribe', 'editor'?) – and the place of origin cannot be ascertained.

Embedded in a fictitious framework of numerous meetings between the Mesopotamian bishop Archelaus and Mani, the Acta attempt to refute the central doctrines of Manichaeism, esp. their anti-Christian polemics. In the course of the narration, action is taken against Mani three times: after a previous interrogation of Turbo, a messenger of Mani, about him and his doctrine (chs. 7–13), Archelaus twice defeats Mani, whom he invited to Carchar (likely Carrhae or Ḥarrān, cf. [1. 140–145]), in a public disputation before pagan representatives of the city (chs. 43 and 61), and in a third confrontation makes the person and the doctrines of the self-appointed paraclete look ridiculous (chs. 61–66). Mani's flight and death in Persia complete the Christian triumph.

Taking into consideration their underlying polemical, distorting tendency, the Acta, regarded as the main source for Manichaeism until the 19th cent., offer in a broad outline a reliable picture of contemporary Manichaeistic mission and propaganda [1. 152], particularly for the biographical information concerning Mani (chs. 62–66, trans. [2. 220–223]). A catalogue of heretics added to the Acta may well have been drawn up around 400 in Rome (Ps.-H.: CCL 9, 325–329).

EDITIONS: CH. H. BEESON (ed.), GCS 16, 1906.
BIBLIOGRAPHY: 1 S. N. C. LIEU, Fact and Fiction in the Acta Archelai, in: Id., Manichaeism in Mesopotamia and the Roman East, 1994, 132–152   2 M. SCOPELLO, Vérités et contre-vérités: la vie de Mani selon les Actes Archelai, in: Apocrypha 6, 1995, 203–234.   J.RI.

Hegesander

[1] Athenian rhetor, son of Hegesias from the deme Sunium and brother of → Hegesippus [1], in 361/60 BC treasurer (Aeschin. In Tim. 55f.; 95) of the strategos Timomachus and despite the latter's sentence for bribery shortly afterwards → tamias of Athena (Aeschin. In Tim. 110f. and schol.), implying that he was a rich man. In the trial against Timocrates → Aeschines [2] most likely slanderously accused him of illegal enrichment. H. was considered an opponent of Aristophon of Azenia, a friend of Diopeithes [3] (Aeschin. In Tim. 63f.) and a follower of → Demosthenes [2]. In 357/6 he proposed a decree in the Social War (IG II² 123 = TOD, 156) about the garrison on Andros and defended Timarchus against Aeschines in 345 (Aeschin. In Tim. 64; 71).
→ Rhetoric

DAVIES, 209; DEVELIN, no. 1350; PA 6307; TRAILL, PAA 480930.   J.E.

[2] H. of Delphi [1], 2nd cent. AD, author of *Hypomnémata* in at least six books, a collection of entertaining and piquant curiosities and anecdotes with historical background, probably ordered according to criteria based on content (one book Περὶ ἀνδριάντων καὶ ἀγαλμάτων, 'On Statues of Men and Gods' appears to have been a systematically laid out catalogue of votive articles in Delphi), with digs at Athens and interest in the Macedonian ruling house [4]; H. draws from anecdotal collections of the same type, but also from historical works (→ Mnesiptolemus; → Pythermus). The main source for the fragments (collected in [2]) is Athenaeus, who personally made excerpts of his works [3].

1 G. DAUX, Notes de lecture, in: BCH 81, 1957, 391   2 FHG IV, 412–422   3 F. JACOBY, s.v. H., RE 7, 2600–2602   4 L. PRANDI, Perché "guerra cremonidea"? Egesandro di Delfi (FGH, IV, p. 415, frg. 9) e la fortuna di un nome, in: Aevum 12, 1989, 24–29   5 F. SUSEMIHL, Gesch. der griech. Litt. in der Alexandrinerzeit, I, 1891, 489–491.   S.FO.

Hegesaretus (Ἡγησάρετος; *Hēgēsáretos*). Thessalian from Larissa, described as *princeps civitatis* by Cicero in a letter of recommendation from the year 46 BC (Fam. 13,25). Leader of the Pompeian *factio* in Thessaly (Caes. B Civ. 3,35,2). Presumably pardoned by Caesar.   W.W.

Hegesianax of Alexandria (Troad). Lived under Antiochus III of Antioch (222–187 BC) and became the king's 'friend' (*phílos*, SH 464) when he gave him his poetry. In 197 and 193 he was the Seleucid ambassador at the Roman Senate and in 196 with T. Quinctius Flamininus in Corinth. Grammarian, author of the work 'On the Style of Democritus' and 'On the Poetic Style' as well as astronomical-mythological poetry (*Phainómena*, SH fr. 465–467; in total five hexameters have been passed down, but the allocation is uncertain; cf. [7. 734°], with bibliography). H. is the oldest known author of the 'Trojan histories' (*Trōïká*), perhaps also cited under the name *Historíai* (but cf. [6. 48–49] with further bibliographical references) that were published under the fictitious name Cephalon (or Cephalium) of Gergis; it is one of the first works that historicized the Homeric tales in the form of a mythological novel on the basis of supposed epigraphical or literary documents. H. shows himself to be friendly to Rome; for the political intentions of the work and the possible relationships to diplomatic activity of the author, cf. [7] with rich bibliography; [5].

1 SH 464–470   2 FGrH I A: 45   3 CollAlex 8–9   4 I.C. CUNNINGHAM, The Hexameter of Fragmentary Hellenistic Poets, in: Quaderni urbinati di cultura classica 25, 1977, 95–100   5 J. G. FARROW, Aeneas and Rome: pseudoepigrapha and politics, in: CJ 87, 1991–1992, 339–359   6 S. MERKLE, Die Ephemeris belli Troiani des Dictys von Kreta, 1989, 48–49 (with bibliography)   7 E. PACK,

Antiochia, in: G. CAMBIANO, L. CANFORA, D. LANZA (ed.), Lo spazio letterario della Grecia antica I/2, 1993, 733–736   8 F. SUSEMIHL, Gesch. der griech. Litt. in der Alexandrinerzeit 2, 1892, 31–33.   S.FO.

Hegesias (Ἡγησίας; *Hēgēsías*).

[1] → Cyrenaic, lived in the decades before and after 300 BC. Due to the modifications that he (presumably in dialogue with → Epicurus) made on the original Cyrenaic doctrine of pleasure, some ancient philosophical historians have a new phase in the history of the Cyrenaics begin with him. H. assessed the view that one could succeed in achieving → pleasure and avoiding pain much more pessimistically than the original Cyrenaics. He based this on the numerous complaints which afflict the body and the chance occurrences of life. What matters first and foremost, therefore, is to avoid painful sensations and feelings. Correspondingly, he did not set the goal (*télos*) to be pleasure (*hēdonē*) like the original Cyrenaics, but rather to be free of physical and psychological pain. H. spelled out these views and those derived from them that life does not have a value of its own in a treatise entitled 'The Hunger Suicide' (Ἀποκαρτερῶν; *Apokarterôn*). His pessimistic world view brought H. the epithet Πεισιθάνατος (*Peisithánatos*, 'death-persuader'). Ptolemy I Soter is supposed to have forbidden H. to spread his teachings because they could lead numerous people to commit suicide. Most important sources: Diog. Laert. 2,85–86; 93–96 and Cic. Tusc. 1,83–84.

SSR IV F; K. DÖRING, s.v. H., in: GGPh² 2.1, 1998, § 19 B.   K.D.

[2] Greek rhetor and historian of the 4th and 3rd cents. BC., from Magnesia at the Sipylus; a few fragments of his epideictic speeches (→ Epideixis) and his history of Alexander (FGrH 142) have been passed down, mostly cited in a polemic context (e.g. Dion. Hal. Comp. 18,125–27 USENER-RADERMACHER; without evaluation: Str. 9,1,16); although H. considered himself as one who continued the Attic rhetoric (Cic. Brut. 286), from the 1st cent. BC he was regarded as the main representative of the more and more scorned → Asianism (Cic. Orat. 226; 230; Ps.-Longinus, De sublimitate 3,2); his style, marked by short, strongly rhythmicized cola and bold metaphors, overladen with paronomasias and homoioteleuta, which Cicero parodied (Cic. Att. 12,6,1), was however admired by Varro (who was also criticized for his style: Quint. Inst. 10,1,95; Aug. Civ. 6,2) (Cic. Att. 12,6,1).

G. KENNEDY, The art of persuasion in Greece, 1963, 301–303; NORDEN, Kunstprosa vol. 1, 134–139; L. PIOTROWICZ, De Hegesia Magnete rerum gestarum scriptore, 1915; E. SPINELLI, Il racconto di un racconto, in: Vichiana 18, 1989, 333–340; A. TRAGLIA, Elementi stilistici nel De lingua Latina di Varrone, in: ASNP 12, 1982, 481–511.   M.W.

Hegesicles see → Agesicles

Hegesidamus (Ἡγησίδαμος; *Hēgēsídamos*). In the Suda s.v. Ἱππίας/*Hippías* named as the teacher of → Hippias of Elis.   M.MEI.

Hegesileos (Ἡγησίλεως; *Hēgēsíleōs*). Relative of Eubulus of Probalinthus (Dem. Or. 19,290), → *strategos* of the Athenian troops in the battle of Mantinea in 362 BC (Xen. Vect. 3,7; Ephoros FGrH 70 F 85; Diod. Sic. 15,84,2) and probably in 349/8 again *strategos* of the Athenian reinforcements for the tyrant Plutarchus of Eretria. In agreement with the latter he was convicted of deceiving the people in an → *eisangelia* law-suit (Dem. Or. 19,290 with schol.).

DEVELIN, no. 1358; PA 6339; TRAILL, PAA 481385.   J.E.

Hegesilochus (Ἡγεσίλοχος; *Hēgesílochos*).
[1] Rhodian, exploited the conflict between Rhodes and Athens (→ Social Wars [1]) in 356/5 BC, in order to take over power in Rhodes at the head of an oligarchical clique with the support of → Maussollos of Caria.

R.M. BERTHOLD, Rhodes in the Hellenistic Age, 1984, 31, with n. 41 (sources and bibliography).   M.MEI.

[2] (also: Ἀγησίλοχος; *Agesílochos*). Son of Hagesias, Rhodian, moderate friend of Rome, who as *prytanis* (172/1 BC) and as envoy to Rome (in the summer of 169) in the spring of 168 to L. → Aemilius [I 32] Paullus supported Rome against → Perseus (Pol. 27,3,3; 28,2; 16; Liv. 42,45) [1. 139f., 144f.; 2. 185–190].

1 H.H. SCHMITT, Rom und Rhodos, 1957
2 J. DEININGER, Der polit. Widerstand gegen Rom in Griechenland, 1971.   L.-M.G.

Hegesinus (Ἡγησίνους; *Hēgēsínous*).
[1] H. of Pergamum, 1st half of the 2nd cent. BC, likely identical with Hegesilaus in Clem. Al. strom. 1,64,1. He took over the direction of the Academy from Evander (Diog. Laert. 4,60). H., the last representative of the Middle Academy (Galen hist. phil. 3 = DIELS, DG 599f.; Clem. Al. ibid.), was the teacher of Carneades (Cic. Acad. 2,16), his later (before 155 BC) successor in the scholarchate. The name H. turns up only in succession lists; information going beyond mention of the name is lacking.
→ Academy   K.-H.S.
[2] Epic poet, from whose work *Atthís* Paus. 9,29,1 cites four hexameters about the founding of Ascra by Oioklos [1]. Pausanias' source is → Callippus of Corinth, who probably invented the name H.

1 J. ZWICKER, s.v. Oioklos, RE 17, 2283.

PEG I, 143–144 (with bibliography); EpGF 166; FGrH III B: 331 (commentary: 609–610).   S.FO.

Hegesippus (Ἡγήσιππος; *Hēgésippos*).
[1] Son of Hegesias from Sunium, Athenian rhetor and envoy from a wealthy family. In 357/6 BC he spoke in the *ekklesia* as a champion of aid for Eretria (IG II² 125 = TOD, 154), in 356/5 of the Athenian symmachy with Phocis (Aeschin. In Ctes. 118; Dem. Or. 19,72–74 with schol.) and between 346 and 340 of further decrees for foreign policy (Dem. Or. 18,75). In the year 345 he defended Timarchus against → Aeschines [2] (Aeschin. In Tim. 71) together with his brother Hegesander [1]. At the time of the delegation of Python, he opposed a revision of the Peace of Philocrates, was unsuccessful himself as the envoy to → Philippus II in the dispute over Halonessos (cf. the speech of H.: Ps.-Dem. Or. 7) and in 343/2, together with → Demosthenes [2], Polyeuctus and Lycurgus, he attempted to actively oppose the influence of Philip in the Peloponnese (Dem. Or. 9,72). In 338/7 he proposed decrees in honour of the Acarnanians and about Phormion and Carphinas (IG II² 237 = TOD, 178), in c. 333/2 he perhaps gave the speech 'On the Treaties with Alexander' (schol. to Dem. Or. 17 p. 195 DILTS). In 325/4, he redeemed a surety he had made in 341/40 for triremes for the expedition to Chalcis (IG II² 1623, 185 and 1629, 543), this being the last information on his life.
→ Rhetoric

DAVIES, 209f.; DEVELIN, no. 1360; PA 6351; TRAILL, PAA 481555.   J.E.

[2] Poet of the New Comedy. Athenaeus cites 30 verses from the 'Brothers' (Ἀδελφοί; *Adelphoí*) with the boastful self-recommendation as a cook (fr. 1), as well as six verses from 'Those who love their companions' (Φιλέταιροι; *Philétairoi*) with a dialogue fragment, in which speaker B joyfully refers → Epicurus' maxim (Ἐπίκουρος ὁ σοφός; *Epíkouros ho sophós*) that the highest good is pleasure (ἡδονή; *hēdoné*), represented by speaker A, to eating. Due to this quote, H. is likely to be dated to the 3rd cent. (perhaps after the death of the philosopher in 271/0 BC).

1 PCG V, 548–551.   T.HI.

[3] Epigrammatic poet in the Garland of Meleager, who describes his muse as μαινὰς βότρυς (*mainàs bótrys*; 'raving grape') (Anth. Pal. 4,1,25), yet the extant eight poems (dedicatory and funerary epigrams) really have nothing 'raving' about them: they are (not word-for-word) imitations especially of Anyte, Nicias, Callimachus and Leonidas of Tarent (Anth. Pal. 7,276, this one however very uncertain). The metric combination of two epigrams (ibid. 6,266 and 13,12), that appears verifiable for the 3rd cent. BC, suggests H.'s lifetime to be around the middle of this cent.

GA I,1, 104–106; I,2, 299–304; A. CAMERON, The Greek Anthology from Meleager to Planudes, 1993, 3f.   M.G.A.

[4] H. from Mecyberna near Olynthus, author of *Palleniaká*, likely around 300 BC. The only known older

local history of Chalcidic cities in Thrace, of which a few fragments relating to the legendary period are preserved. The supposed *Milēsiaká* of H. are likely based on a verbal corruption.

EDITIONS: FGrH 391.
BIBLIOGRAPHY: F.JACOBY, s.v. H. (4), RE 7,2, 2610f.
K.MEI.

[5] H. is described as 'one of the first successors of the apostles' by → Eusebius [7] (Euseb. Hist. eccl. 2,23,3), but judging from a fragment handed down by Eusebius himself (Euseb. Hist. eccl. 4,22,3) he is more likely to have been active literarily between AD 174 and 189. He wrote five bks. of *Hypomnémata* (Euseb. Hist. eccl. 4,22,1), fragments of which are handed down mainly by Eusebius, but also by Philippus Sidetes and the anthologist Stephanus Gobarus (6th cent., Photius, Bibliotheke cod. 232 p. 288b 10–16) (CPG 1, 1302; however, MSS of the text possibly still existed up into the 17th cent.). Topics include: James, the brother of Jesus (Euseb. Hist. eccl. 2,23,3–19), the Jerusalem bishops (Hist. eccl. 3,11 and 32,1–8 as well as 4,22,4), Palestinian local tradition about the family of Jesus (Hist. eccl. 3,20,1–6) and a genealogy of the heresies (Hist. eccl. 4,22,5–6). H. is not the first witness for the theologoumenon of a personal continuity regarding the transmission of the special spiritual gifts of teaching authority and church leadership ('apostolic succession'); rather, Eusebius interprets a passage of H. about the unbroken continuity of teaching of the apostolic faith in the Roman congregation (Hist. eccl. 4,22,3) in view of this idea which arose late and was first documented by → Irenaeus [2] of Lyon (cf. Hist. eccl. 4,11,7). From the fact that H. quoted from Aramaic and Hebrew texts Eusebius concluded that he had converted from Judaism to Christianity; he also supposedly reported from the 'unwritten Jewish tradition' (Hist. eccl. 4,22,8), which could indicate that he was trained as a scribe. The allocation of H. to Jewish-Christianity is just as controversial as the category itself; what might argue for it is i.a. his special interest in the early Jerusalem church and its bishop James as well as the anti-Paulinism of the fragment passed down by Photius. H. himself mentions a journey to Rome (Euseb. Hist. eccl. 4,22,2).

EDITIONS: TH. ZAHN, Apostel und Apostelschüler in der Provinz Asien (Forsch. zur Gesch. des nt. Kanons 6/1), 1900, 228–249; L.ABRAMOWSKI, ΔΙΑΔΟΧΗ und ΌΡΘΟΣ ΛΟΓΟΣ bei Hegesipp, in: ZKG 87, 1976, 321–327; E.CASPAR, Die älteste röm. Bischofsliste (Schriften der Königsberger Gelehrten Ges., Geisteswiss. Klasse 4), 1926 (repr. 1975), 447–451; A.v. HARNACK, Die Chronologie der altchristl. Litteratur 1, 1897, 311–313; N.HYLDAHL, Hegesipps Hypomnemata, in: Studia Theologica 14, 1960, 70–113.
C.M.

[6] H. of Tarent see → Cookery books

Hegesipyle (Ἡγησιπύλη; *Hēgēsipýlē*). Daughter of King Olorus of Thrace. Married → Miltiades [2] in *c.* 515–513 BC and bore him a child → Cimon (Hdt. 6,39,2; Plut. Cimon 4,1).

C.FERETTO, Milziade ed Egesipile. Un matrimonio d'interesse, in: Serta Historica Antiqua [1], 1986, 77–83.
U.P.

Hegesistratus (Ἡγησίστρατος; *Hēgēsístratos*).
[1] Son of → Peisistratus and the Argive Timonassa (Hdt. 5,94; Aristot. Ath. Pol. 17,3). Installed as tyrant of Sigeum by his father around 530 BC, he defended the city as a colony of the Peisistratids against the Mytilenaeans (Hdt. loc. cit.).
→ Tyrannis

DAVIES 11793,VI (B); M.STAHL, Aristokraten und Tyrannen, 1987, 220f.; TRAILL, PAA 481600.

[2] H. of Elis, son of Tellias. Fled from Spartan captivity and became a seer in the army of → Mardonius. After the battle of Plataeae (479 BC) he was recaptured by the Spartans and executed (Hdt. 9,37f.).
[3] Samian, son of Aristagoras, in the 5th cent. BC leader of a delegation to the Spartan king → Leotychidas whom H. – in view of the retreat of the Phoenicians from Samos (Hdt. 9,90–92) – asked to take action against the Persians in Ionia.

J.HEINRICHS, Ionien nach Salamis, 1989, 46–55.   HA.BE.

[4] Under → Darius [3] in 334 BC commander of Miletus, wanted initially to hand over the city to → Alexander [4] but then defended it and fell during the storming of the city (Arr. Anab. 1,18,4; 19,4).   E.B.
[5] In 262/1 BC as envoy of Ptolemy II brought a letter to Miletus, without being able to make concrete promises (IMilet I 3, 139). A short while later the city rebelled against Ptolemy.   W.A.

Hegetor Alexandrian doctor, lived between the time of Herophilus (330/320–260/250 BC), whose successor he was, and Apollonius (1st cent. BC), by whom he is cited; generally he is placed in the 2nd cent. BC because of his polemics against the → Empiricists and their views on aetiology.

Of his works only indirect citations are extant, of which three bear his name, and the last (Gal. Def. med. 220 = 19,448f. K.) was merely attributed to him [1. 73 n. 44; 137 n. 183; 2]. Fragment 3 comes from a work *Perì aitíōn* ('On the causes') in which H. refutes the aetiological nihilism of the Empiricists; he defends research into the causes of the pathological facts that combines anatomical studies and clinical research. In this way he contributes to the definition of an epistemology that is characterized by rationalism. Fragments 1 and 2 concern sphygmology and contain a definition and theory of the pulse. Fragment 4 concerns heart rhythm and again takes up the definition suggested by the Herophilean → Zeno (1st half of the 2nd cent. BC) replacing the concept of *schésis* with that of *táxis*.

All these elements indicate that H. continued the teachings of Herophilus as they are known from other sources.

1 J. KOLLESCH, Untersuchungen zu den pseudogalenischen Definitiones medicae, 1973   2 STADEN.   A.TO.

Hegetorides (Ἡγητορίδης; *Hēgētorídēs*). Respected citizen of Cos. The story of his daughter who was abducted by the Persians and who, as a suppliant, is said to have been freed by the Spartan ruler → Pausanias after the battle of Plataeae (479 BC), is one of Herodotus' examples of the moral superiority of the Greeks (Hdt. 9,76; cf. Paus. 3,4,9).   E.S.-H.

Hegias (Ἡγίας; *Hēgías*).
[1] Sculptor who signed the base of a lost bronze statue on the Acropolis in Athens that must be dated around 490–480 BC. He is mentioned by Pausanias (8,42,10), Pliny (HN 34,49) and Dio Chrysostom (55,1) as a late archaic artist, a contemporary of → Critius and Nesiotes, → Onatas, → Ageladas and → Calon, and as a teacher of → Phidias. Quintilian (Inst. 12,10,7) and Lucian (Rhetorum praeceptor 9) describe his style as still archaic and call him by his full name Hegesias. Pliny (HN 34,78) saw Dioscuri and an Athena by him in Rome, but created confusion by also attributing to him a *Pyrrhus rex* and *pueri celetizontes* and in addition dated him (HN 34,49) to the 83rd Olympiad (448–444 BC). There is no need to trace for those subjects a later artist of the same name as the 'riding boys' are unknown to us, and moreover it is probably an oversight by Pliny who, in another passage (HN 34,80), mentions a Hygieia and Minerva by the sculptor → Pyrrhus.

H. BRUNN, Gesch. der griechischen Künstler 1, 1857, 101–102; LIPPOLD, 108; P. ORLANDINI, s.v. H. (1), EAA 3, 1960, 1128–1130; OVERBECK, no. 420, 422, 452–456 (sources); A. E. RAUBITSCHEK, Dedications from the Athenian Agora, 1949, no. 94; B. S. RIDGWAY, The Severe Style in Greek Sculpture, 1970, 89.   R.N.

[2] When Seleucus, son of Antiochus III, advanced on Phocaea in 190 BC, H., who was a pro-Roman member of a partially pro-Seleucid delegation, was unable to convince him to recognize the temporary neutrality of his hometown Phocaea (Pol. 21,6,2ff.).   A.ME.

[3] Athenian sculptor from the early Imperial period. Together with Philathenaeus he signed the statue of Claudius as Zeus that was erected for the ruler cult in the Metroon of Olympia.

K. HITZL, Die kaiserzeitliche Statuenausstattung des Metroon, in: OlF 19, 1991; LOEWY, no. 332.   R.N.

[4] Son of Asclepigeneia (daughter of Achiadas and Plutarche) and of Theagenes, a member of the family of → Plutarchus [3] of Athens. Despite his youth, H. was admitted by the Neoplatonist Proclus (AD 412–485) to his classes on the *Oracula Chaldaica* (Marinus, Vita Procli 26; Damascius, Vita Isidori 351 ZINTZEN), but he was also a pupil of → Isidorus [4] of Alexandria (Damascius, Vita Isidori 230 ZINTZEN). He became a teacher at the Neoplatonist school (→ Neoplatonism) but was more interested in → theurgy than in philosophical considerations, bringing the school into disrepute (ibid. 221). His teacher Isidorus constantly tried to reason with him (ibid. 227). As a fanatical pagan he made enemies amongst the Christians (ibid. 351). His two sons Eupeithius and Archiadas had no interest in philosophy (Suda s.v. Ἡγίας, 2,550,3–24 ADLER; s.v. Εὐπείθιος καὶ Ἀρχιάδας, 2,464,20–465,9).   L.BR.

Heidelberg Painter see → Little-master cups

Heimarmene see → Fate

Heircte (Εἰρκτή/*Heirktḗ*, Pol. 1,56,3; Ἐρκτή/*Erktḗ*, Diod. Sic. 22,10,4). Extensive mountain massif hard to access near Panormus, in 278/7 BC captured from the Carthaginians by Pyrrhus, in 248 won back again by them and defended for three years against Roman attacks (Pol. 1,56f.; Diod. Sic. 33,20). It clearly refers to Monte Pellegrino (606 m) north of Palermo.

BTCGI 7, 1989, 343.   GI.MA.

Heiress see → Epikleros

Heius Latin proper name (SCHULZE 459).
H., C. Around 75 BC a respected and rich citizen of the Sicilian city of Messana. Of his possessions → Verres stole four famous Greek statues and valuable carpets (Cic. Verr. 2,4,3–19; 27). In spite of this, in 70, on behalf of his community, he appeared in Rome for Verres as a witness for the defence but incriminated him in the cross-examination by Cicero (Verr. 2,2,13; 4,15–19; 150; 5,47).   K.-L.E.

Hejira (*hiǧra*). Emigration, movement of the prophet → Muhammad and some of his followers from → Mecca to → Medina in AD 622 after tribal difficulties (withdrawal of the clan protection on the part of his tribe Quraiš); beginning of the Islamic calendar. Only with the *hejira* did Mohammed's work as a statesman begin; it also marked the starting-point of the actual spread of → Islam (initially through a policy of alliances).

A. NOTH, Die Hiǧra, in: U. HAARMANN (ed.), Geschichte der arabischen Welt, 1987, 11–57.   H.SCHÖ.

Hekaerge (Ἑκαέργη).
[1] Epithet of → Artemis (Clem. Al. Strom. 5,8,48,4f.; EpGr 460,6).
[2] A mythical maiden named Aspalis Ameilete H., from the city of Melite in Thessaly, active in the cult of

→ Artemis. Because she hanged herself in order to escape being raped by the tyrant Tartarus, the virgins made an annual sacrifice to her by hanging a young goat (Nikander in Antoninus Liberalis 13).

[3] A *kore* from the island of Ceos, analogous to → Cydippe, who was abducted from a temple of Artemis and died in childbirth. In cult worship, she was known by the names Aphrodite Ktesylla and Ktesylla H. (Nikander in Antoninus Liberalis 1).

> NILSSON, Feste, 207ff.; O. JESSEN, E. NEUSTADT, s.v. H. (1–3), RE 7, 2662f.　　　　　　　　　　G.B.

[4] One of the Hyperboreans (→ Hyperborei) whose graves were honoured in cult worship on → Delos. Her name is derived from the epicleses of Artemis (see [1]) and Apollo (→ Hekaergos). H. appears as a variant of Arge. According to Hdt. 4,35, Arge, along with → Opis, was the first of the Hyperboreans to come to Delos 'together with the gods', and was celebrated in a hymn by → Olen. Paus. 5,7,8 mentions a hymn by Melanopus to Opis and H. In Callim. H. 4,292f., Oupis, H., and → Loxo, the daughters of → Boreas, appear as the bringers of the first sacrificial offering, and it is to them that the girls of Delos sacrifice locks of hair before their wedding (cf. Paus. 1,43,4). These are functions originally fulfilled by the second Hyperborean pair, Hyperoche and Laodice (Hdt. 4,33f.). According to Pl. Ax. 371a, Opis and H. (or Hekaergus; cf. Serv. Aen. 11,532; 858) brought with them bronze tablets with mystical content. Later, H. was regarded as one of the companions of Artemis (Claud. Carm. 24,253; Nonnus, Dion. 5,491; 48,332).

> W. SALE, The Hyperborean Maidens on Delos, in: Harvard Theological Review 54, 1961, 75–89.　　　A.A.

Hekaergos

Hekaergos (Ἑκάεργος; *Hekáergos*). Epithet of → Apollo and → Artemis (→ Hekaerge), mostly interpreted as *Ϝέκα (cf. ἑκών) + Ϝέργον, 'working of his own free will', connected by the poets, however, with ἑκάς, ἕκαθεν: 'working from afar'.

> W. BECK, s.v. H., LFE 2, 493–494.　　　　　RE.N.

Hekatompedos

Hekatompedos (Ἑκατόμπεδος; *Hekatómpedos*). Probably a *c.* 32 m wide street in Syracusae near the Hexapylon gate (Plut. Dion 45,5, cf. Diod. Sic. 16,20,2.　GI.MA.

Hekatoncheires

Hekatoncheires (Ἑκατόγχειρες, *centimani* = 'hundred-handed'). Briareus (also called Aegaeon: Hom. Il. 1,403f.), Cottus and Gy(g)es (for the name forms see [1]) are powerful monsters (hundred arms, fifty heads: Hes. Theog. 147ff.), offspring of → Uranus and → Gaia. They were chained by their father and thrown into Tartarus (617ff.). Zeus frees them and, on account of their hundred arms, makes them allies in the battle with the → Titans (626ff.). The belief that the H. later guarded the defeated Titans in Tartarus (Apollod. 1,2,7) is probably due to a misinterpretation of Hes. Theog. 734f.

Occasionally the H. also appear individually (the group name 'H.' first appears in the late mythographers): with the support of Briareus, → Thetis thwarts an attack on Zeus (Hom. Il. 1,401ff.). According to Eumelus (Titanomachy fr. 3 BERNABÉ), Briareus alone took part in the → Titanomachy, but on the side of the Titans (cf. Verg. Aen. 10,565ff.).

Their similar external appearance as primordial creatures may be the reason that individual H. are occasionally described as → giants (e.g. Callim. H. 4,142). Their identification in pictorial representations is correspondingly difficult [2].

> 1 M. L. WEST, Hesiod. Theogony, 1966, 209　2 E. SIMON, s.v. H., LIMC 4.1, 481–482.　　　　RE.N.

Hekatoste

Hekatoste (ἑκατοστή; *hekatosté*). In antiquity → taxes of 1% were called *hekatoste*:

1. There were numerous forms of *hekatoste* in Athens (Aristoph. Vesp. 658), like the ἑκατοστὴ ἡ ἐν Πειραιεῖ (*hekatosté hē en Peiraiei*) mentioned in Ps.-Xen. Ath. pol. 1,17, and the port customs duty documented in IG I³ 182 l.15. According to Theophrast (F 650 FORTENBAUGH; Stob. 44,20 WACHSMUTH-HENSE) the buyer of a piece of land had to pay a 1% sales tax. Ancient and Byzantine lexica mention 'certain *hekatoste*' among the sales taxes (ἐπώνια; *epónia*) (Anecd. Bekk. I 255,1). Three fragmentary inscriptions from the time around 330–310 BC document a 1% sales tax on real estate, which the seller or the lessor had to pay (IG II² 1594–1603; SEG 42,130 bis). This *hekatoste* flowed into the coffers of Athena's treasurers (cf. IG II² 1471 l.10–13; SEG 38,138).

2. In Chalcedon a *hekatoste* is documented as addition to the selling price for the office of a priest (Syll.³ 1009,19: around 200 BC).

3. In Chios a *hekatoste* was levied on harvests in the 4th cent. BC, in Carian Pidasa on grain harvests in the 2nd cent. BC.

4. In Ptolemaic Egypt the *hekatoste* has been documented as port customs duty, customs on wine trade and taxes on the sale of land, in imperial Egypt as an additional fee on shipments of grain, as toll and sales tax as well as property tax on sums of more than 20,000 sesterces.

5. In Berytus a *hekatoste* has been documented in an inscription as a market tax for the 5th–7th cents. AD (SEG 39,1575–1577).

> 1 BUSOLT/SWOBODA　2 M. CORSARO, Tassazione regia e tassazione cittadina dagli Achemenidi ai re ellenistici, in: REA 87, 1985, 73–95　3 M. FARAGUNA, Atene nell' età di Alessandro, in: Atti della accademia nazionale dei Lincei 389. Memorie 9,2,2, 1992, 167–445　4 K. HALLOF, Der Verkauf konfiszierten Vermögens vor den Poleten in Athen, in: Klio 72, 1990, 402–426　5 B.R. MACDONALD, The Phanosthenes Decree, in: Hesperia 50, 1981, 141–146　6 PRÉAUX, 186; 334f.; 379　7 V. J. ROSIVACH, The rationes centesimarum, in: Eirene 28, 1992, 49–61　8 ROSTOVTZEFF, Hellenistic World　9 S. L. WALLACE, Taxation in Egypt from Augustus to Diocletian, 1938, 39; 231f.; 268ff.; 278.　　　　　W.S.

Hekebolos (Ἑκηβόλος; *Hekēbólos*). Epic epithet for → Apollo in his role as an archer (Hom. Il. 1,14 et passim), for → Artemis in early Greek texts only attested in the Nikandre inscription (SEG 19, 507 5); later with a considerably widened field of reference. In antiquity understood as 'hitting far away into the distance' (for ἑκάς and βάλλειν) (schol. T for Hom. Il. 1,14; cf. Aesch. Eum. 628: τόξοις ἑκηβόλοισιν), more probable is a derivation from ἑκών (roughly: 'hitting at will').

FRISK, s.v. H.; CHANTRAINE, s.v. H. E.V.

Hekhalot Literature Hekhalot literature (HL), to which belong, as the most important types, *Hekaloth Rabbati* ('the great palaces'), *Hekaloth zuṭarti* ('the small palaces'), *Ma'ase Merkabah* ('the work of the throne chariot'), *Merkabah Rabbah* ('the great throne chariot'), *Re'uyyot Yeḥeqkel* ('the visions of Ezechiel'), *Massekhet Hekaloth* ('treatise of the palaces') and the 3rd Henoch, is a testimony to early Jewish mysticism constituted by an 'experimental knowledge of God won through lively experience' [4. 4]. One of the most significant motifs is the ascent to heaven of a pious person: after perilous disputes with the angels of God who do not want to allow any human being access to the heavenly world ('threat motif') the pious person crosses, with the help of divine protection, the seven heavenly palaces (Hebrew *Hekhalot*), in the inside of which God resides on his throne chariot (*Merkabah*) as king of the world, and can finally participate in the service taking place there and in the praise of the angels. In this overall context, spells that should avert the destructive power of the angels as well as highly poetic hymns with which God is praised by his retinue play an important role. The traditions of HL also contain magic formulae with the help of which the initiate can acquire full knowledge of the Torah and protect himself from forgetting the Torah. In this way the mystic is in direct contrast with the ideal of Rabbinic Judaism that attempts to deduce insight into God and interpretation of the world through constant, often painstaking learning of the Torah. HL probably arose in the late or post-Talmudic period (*c.* 6th–7th cents. AD) by absorbing older traditions. With reference to the representation of the heavenly service, there are however remarkable parallels with texts from → Qumran (cf. particularly the Sabbath songs of sacrifice, 4Q Shirot 'Olat-ha-Shabbat) as well as with the New Testament (cf. 2 Cor 12,1–4; Hebr 13,22; Apc 4). Presumably these different traditions draw from common sources.

1 J.DAN, The Ancient Jewish Mysticism, 1993 2 P. SCHÄFER, Der verborgene und offenbare Gott. Hauptthemen der frühen jüd. Mystik, 1991 3 Id. (ed.), Übersetzung der H. 1–4, 1987–1994 4 G. SCHOLEM, Die jüd. Mystik in ihren Hauptströmungen, 1967, 43–78.
B.E.

Hekte (ἕκτη; *hékte*). Greek term for the sixth of a unit. Nominal term for the electrum staters (→ Stater) of Cyzicus (inscription IG I² 199; 203), Mytilene and Phocaea made of a gold-silver alloy. In addition, series from the 7th to the 5th cents. BC have been found from indeterminate minting sites of Asia Minor that were launched according to the Milesian, Phocaean and Samian-Euboean standard [3. 7–17]. The coins of Mytilene and Phocaea made in the gold-silver ratio of 1:13$^1/_3$ [1. 55] as joint mintings according to the coinage agreement of 394 BC [2. 29] correspond as sixth staters (average weight 2.55 g) to 4 Attic → drachmai or 20 Aeginetan → oboli [1. 56]. Hemi-hecte ($^1/_{12}$ stater), obolos ($^1/_{24}$ stater), hemiobolos ($^1/_{48}$ stater) and tartemorion ($^1/_{96}$ stater) appear as partial pieces.
→ Electron

1 F. BODENSTEDT, Phokäisches Elektron-Geld von 600–326 v.Chr., 1976 2 Id., Die Elektronmünzen von Phokaia und Mytilene, 1981 3 Monnaies Grecques de Haute Epoque – Collection Jonathan P. Rosen. Venté Publique Monnaies et Medailles S.A.Bâle No. 72, 1987.

H. CHANTRAINE, s.v. H., KlP 2, 986; L. WEIDAUER, Probleme der frühen Elektronprägung, 1975; N. M. WAGGONER, Early Greek Coins from the Jonathan P. Rosen Collection, 1983. H.-J.S.

Hektemoroi (ἑκτήμοροι; *hektémoroi*) were tenants on agricultural land in Attica; their impoverishment was one of the most important manifestations of the social and economic crisis that → Solon as mediator (διαλλακτής, *diallaktés*) and archon was meant to settle. The spelling of the term (ἑκτήμορος in Aristot. Ath. Pol. 2,2 and in most lexicographers; ἑκτημόριος in Plutarch) was discussed in antiquity just as much as its meaning. According to Plutarch (Solon 13,4f.), the *hektemoroi* kept five-sixths of the yield from the land worked by them and had to give one sixth as rent, whilst the Byzantine scholar Eustathius (*Commentarius ad Homeri Odysseam* 19,28) maintains that the *hektemoroi* had to pay five-sixths. In modern research it is considered that contributions of one-sixth of the yield were more probable. In view of such a low burden, however, a serious economic crisis could only have been caused by population growth or a reduction in the fertility of the soil to an utterly improbable extent; for this reason we must assume that the resolute rejection of social dependency relationships was just as important a factor in the crisis as economic need.

Although *hektemoroi* were later connected exclusively with the reforms of Solon, the term *hektemoroi* cannot be demonstrated in any text of Solon; it therefore also remains unclear whether Solon had officially abolished the rank of the *hektemoroi* or whether, as a result of other reform measures, it gradually disappeared. Solon himself boasted that he had eliminated the → *hóroi* (boundary stones) that 'had made the black earth into a slave' (Aristot. Ath. Pol. 12,4), and it is highly probable that the status of the *hektemoroi* was also affected by this revocation of the burden of debt based on the soil. Under what circumstances and at what point in time the obligation to pay the tax of the *hektemoroi* arose in Attica and was regulated is impossible to discern at present; it likewise remains unclear how large a part of the population of Athens belonged to the *hektemoroi* in the 7th cent. BC. Archaeological excavations in Attica have not been able to date to determine any fundamental change in settlement structure around 600 BC.

→ Seisachtheia

1 RHODES, 90–97.   R.O.

Hekteus (ἑκτεύς; *hekteús*). Greek term for a dry measure, mainly for grain, in volume ¹/₆ → *medimnos*, corresponding to 8 → *choinikes* and 32 → *kotylai*. According to [1], the *hekteus* depends on the region and amounts to 8.75 litres (Attica) or 12.12 litres (Aegina) [1. 504–506]. In the Ptolemaic period the *hekteus* corresponded to 13.13 litres [1. 623]. According to [3], the Attic *hekteus* passed through the stages of 4.56, 5.84, 6.56, 8.75, 10.21, 10.94 litres, the Aeginetan-Lakonian *hekteus* corresponded to 9.12 litres. According to [6], the Solonian *hekteus* amounted to 8.64 litres, the younger Attic to 9.82 litres, the Aeginetan to 12.33 litres, the Sicilian to 8.73 litres. [7] calculates the Attic *hekteus* as 7.248 litres, the Sicilian as 9.06 litres and the Ptolemaic with 10.87 litres.

→ Hollow measures (Greece and Rome)

1 F. HULTSCH, Griech. und röm. Metrologie, ²1882 2 H. CHANTRAINE, s.v. H., KlP 2, 987 3 O. VIEDEBANTT, s.v. H., RE 7, 2803–2806 4 Id., Forsch. zur Metrologie des Alt., 1917, repr. 1974 5 Id., in: H.v. PETRIKOVITS (ed.), FS für A. Oxé, 1938, 135–146 6 H. NISSEN, Griech. und röm. Metrologie, HdbA I², 842f. 7 A. OXÉ, in: BJ 147, 1942, 91–216.   H.-J.S.

Helcias

[1] Relative and friend of King → Herodes [1] Agrippa I (Jos. Ant. Iud. 19,9,1; 20,7,1), in AD 40 a member of the deputation to the Syrian governor P. Petronius (ibid. 18,8,4), which achieved its goal of stopping Caligula's statue from being erected in the Temple; after that he probably took over the position of commander-in-chief of the army from Silas (ibid. 19,6,3; 7,1), whom he had killed after Agrippa's death in AD 44 (ibid. 19,8,3).

[2] Temple treasurer (γαζοφύλαξ; *gazophýlax*) in Jerusalem. As a member of a deputation of the → synhedrion in AD 61 or 62, he went to Rome where he was informed by Nero that a wall that blocked Agrippa II's view into the temple was to remain standing. The future empress Poppaea Sabina kept H. in Rome (Jos. Ant. Iud. 20,8,11), probably so that he could instruct her in the Jewish religion.   C.C.

Heleius (Ἕλειος; *Héleios*). Youngest son of → Perseus (Apollod. 2,49; Paus. 3,20,6); eponym of the city of Helus in Laconia, which he is said to have founded after taking part in the campaign against the Taphians (Apollod. 2,59; Str. 8,5,2).   J.S.-A.

Helellum (Tab. Peut. 3,4; *Alaia*, Geogr. Rav. 26). Roman *vicus* of the Triboci in Upper Alsace (not identical to → Helvetum) on the Argentovaria-Argentoratum route at the crossing of the Ill near modern Ehl-Benfeld, Département Bas-Rhin [1]; a late La Tène period settlement was followed in the late Augustan period by the Gallo-Roman *vicus* that ultimately developed *c.* 100 m on both sides of the main road over a length of *c.* 1,000 m. A necropolis (3rd/4th cents. AD) is located south of H. Despite the minor artisan businesses, H. was primarily a trading centre. The *vicus*, which was also guaranteed through a station of *beneficiarii*, remained inhabited right through to the 4th cent. in spite of being destroyed several times.

1 H. STEGER, *Regula*/Riegel am Kaiserstuhl – Helvetum?, in: Römer und Alamannen im Breisgau (Arch. und Gesch. 6), 1994, 233–361.

E. KERN, Benfeld-Ehl (Bas-Rhin), in: Atlas des agglomérations secondaires de la Gaule, 1994, 148f.; F. PETRY, Observations sur les vici explorés en Alsace, in: Caesarodunum 11, 1976, 273–295.   F.SCH.

Helena (Ἑλένη; *Helénē*, Lat. *Helena*).

[1] Goddess who was worshipped at various cult sites in and around Sparta, especially in the Menelaion in → Therapne (Hdt. 6,61; Paus. 3,15,3; Hsch. s.v. Ἐλένεια, [1]). In → Rhodes she had a cult as H. Dendritis (Paus. 3,19,10), in → Cenchreae and → Chios she is attested as a deity of springs (Paus. 2,2,3; Steph. Byz. s.v. Ἑλένη). There is no completely reliable etymology for her name [2. 63–80]. For evidence of her cult in historical times cf. [1]; on the rites described by Theoc. 18 and the function they have in the coming-of-age of women, cf. [3. vol.1, 281–285, 333–350]. H. is associated with the → Dioscuri by evidence that describes how she appears to sailors as a flame that can be a good or a bad omen (Eur. Or. 1637; Plin. HN 2,37,101; on a joint cult in Athens cf. Eust. 1425,62–63 ad Hom. Od. 1,399; attempts at interpretation in [2. 48–53] and [4. 190–193]). H. later played an important role in → Gnosticism [5. 345–355].

In the epic tradition → Zeus is regarded as H.'s father (Hom. Il. 3,418; Od. 4,184; 219; 227), while → Nemesis (Cypria fr. 9,1 PEG I) is named as her mother. Nemesis gives birth to an egg, which is brought to → Leda, the wife of Tyndareus or which she finds and out of which H. is born (Sappho fr. 166f. VOIGT; Cratinus fr. 115 PCG IV = Ath. 9,373e; Hyg. Poet. Astr. 2,8; Apollod. 3,127–128). Leda as her mother is first mentioned by Eur. Hel. 18f. (then Paus. 3,16,1). The Dioscuri are regarded as her brothers (Hom. Il. 3,236–238). In Hes. Cat. fr. 24 H. is the daughter of → Oceanus. → Theseus abducts H. together with → Peirithous and takes her to Aphidna, from where the Dioscuri bring her back again. It is unclear how old H. was at this time (Alcm. fr. 21 PMG; Hellanicus FGrH 4 F 168b; Hyg. Fab. 79). According to some sources H. is supposed to have given birth to → Iphigenia by Theseus

(Stesich. fr. 191 PMG = Paus. 2,22,7). When numerous suitors came to Tyndareus wishing to marry H., he made them (Hes. Cat. fr. 196–200; 202; 204; Hyg. Fab. 81) swear an oath to support the future husband of H. in battles over her (Stesich. fr. 190 PMG). With her husband → Menelaus she had a daughter, → Hermione (Hom. Od. 4,12–14; Eur. Or. 107–112).

H.'s great beauty was praised and is already a *topos* in antiquity (e.g. Hom. Il. 3,154–158; in Ov. Met. 15,232f. the elderly H. complains of the loss of her beauty). Aphrodite (Hom. Il. 3,399–420), or → Paris (Hom. Il. 13,626f.), with whom she eloped to Troy, were blamed for the judgement of Paris which triggered the Trojan War (Sappho fr. 16 Voigt; Alc. fr. 283 Voigt; Alcm. fr. 77 PMG; Hyg. Fab. 92). After Paris' death H. married → Deiphobus, who was slain by Menelaus after the conquest of Troy (Hom. Od. 8,517; Ilias parva fr. 4 PEG I; Apollod. Epit. 5,22). After the fall of Troy Menelaus forgave her and returned with her to Greece (Ilias parva fr. 19 PEG I; Iliupersis Argumentum PEG I).

Criticism of H. and her role as the trigger for the Trojan War existed from an early age (Alc. fr. 42 Voigt); Stesichorus (fr. 192 PMG) retracted his negative representation, by having only an *eídōlon* ('phantom') of H. taken to Troy with Paris, while H. herself was removed to Egypt (Hdt. 2,113–115 with a slight variation), where she lived until Menelaus found her there on his return from Troy and took her back to Greece (Eur. Hel.). Gorgias (*Enkōmion Helénēs*, 'Praise of Helena') and Isocrates (Or. 10) also defend H. She is a very popular figure in drama (Aesch. Ag. 403–408; 737–749; Soph. fr. 176–184 TrGF; Cratinus fr. 39–51 PCG IV), H's beauty becoming an important topic (Eur. Tro. 991f.; Eur. Andr. 627–631; Aristoph. Lys. 155f.). In Eur. Or. 1625–1642 she is attacked by → Orestes and rescued by Apollo. Another version of the myth has her becoming the wife of → Achilles on the island of Leuce after her death (Paus. 3,19,11; 13). In Latin literature she is frequently portrayed in a negative light (Verg. Aen. 2,567–587; 6,494–530; Hor. Epod. 17,42; Sat. 1,3,107; Sen. Tro.; Dares Phrygius; Dictys, Ephemeris belli Troiani; Ov. Epist. 16, 17 stands out against this and describes H.'s moral scruples in considering her relationship with Paris). In pictorial representation of H. a few scenes from her life dominate: her birth, her abductions and re-encounter with Menelaus. On her afterlife in literature and art cf. the summary in [6].

1 H. W. Catling, H. Cavanagh, Two Inscribed Bronzes from the Menelaion, Sparta, in: Kadmos 15.2, 1976, 145–157   2 L. L. Clader, H. The Evolution from Divine to Heroic in Greek Epic Tradition, 1976   3 C. Calame, Les chœurs de jeunes filles en Grèce archaïque, 2 vol., 1977   4 O. Skutsch, H., her Name and Nature, in: JHS 107, 1987, 188–193   5 J. Fossum, G. Quispel, s.v. H. (1), RAC 14, 338–355   6 Hunger, Mythologie, 154–156.

BIBLIOGRAPHY: N. Austin, H. of Troy and her Shameless Phantom, 1994; K. Bassi, H. and the Discourse of Denial in Stesichorus' Palinode, in: Arethusa 26, 1993, 51–75; E. Bethe, s.v. H., RE 7, 2824–2835; L. Braun, Die

schöne H., wie Gorgias und Isokrates sie sehen, in: Hermes 110, 1982, 158–174; O. Carbonero, La figura di Elena di Troia nei poeti latini da Lucrezio a Ovidio, in: Orpheus 10, 1989, 378–391; F. Charpouthier, Les Dioscures au service d'une déesse, 1935; L. Kahil, Les enlèvements et le retour d'H. dans les textes et les documents figurés, 1955; Id., N. Icard, s.v. H., LIMC 4.1, 498–563; D. Lyons, Gender and Immortality, Heroines in Ancient Greek Myth and Cult, 1997, 134–135, 138–141, 148–149, 158–159, 161–162; H. Pelliccia, Sappho 16, Gorgias' H. and the Preface to Herodotus' Histories, in: YClS 29, 1992, 63–84; J. I. Porter, The Seductions of Gorgias, in: Classical Antiquity 12, 1993, 267–293; G. B. Schmid, Die Beurteilung der H. in der frühgriech. Lit., 1982; M. Suzuki, Metamorphoses of H. Authority, Difference, and the Epic, 1989.

FIG.: L. Kahil, N. Icard, s.v. H., LIMC 4.2, 291–358.

R.HA.

[2] Wife or concubine of → Constantius [1], mother of Constantine the Great [1] (→ Constantinus [1] with the stemma). The renaming of Drepana into → Helenopolis under Constantine can be explained by her particular devotion to the martyr Lucianus rather than suggesting Bithynian origins. She was presumably from the area of the Balkans, perhaps from Naissus, where Constantine was born. During the first years of her son's rule her role at court is difficult to determine; apparently she was brought to Christianity through him (Euseb. vita Const. 3,47,2). In November AD 324 she was elevated to Augusta together with → Fausta. This brought with it certain honours and rights (e.g. the minting of gold coins for H., cf. Euseb. op. cit. 3,47,2), and also the possibility of falling back upon the imperial treasure for supporting the building of churches in the Holy Land (Euseb. op. cit. 3,47,3), without justifying the assumption that H. was co-regent. Later legend gives her a special role in the finding of the 'True Cross', because of which she is venerated as a saint together with Constantine in the Orthodox Church (feast: 21 May). There is an authentic core to this legend: the striving for relics that was customary among pilgrims (→ Pilgrimage) of the period, and that appears to have in fact led to the presumed discovery of the 'True Cross' under Constantine's rule.

J. W. Drijvers, Helena Augusta, 1992.

[3] Daughter of Constantine [1], was married in AD 355 to the recently elevated Caesar → Iulianus [5], her cousin, at the wish of Constantius [2] II. She died in 360/1 and was buried by the *via Nomentana* (Amm. Marc. 21,1,5).

B.BL.

[4] Painter from Egypt. (Alexandria?); her father Timon was also a painter (Phot. 190,481). Her activity can be dated to the 2nd half of the 4th cent. BC, as she is said to have created a contemporary, non-extant, painting of Alexander's battle at Issus, which was exhibited in the *templum pacis* in Rome at the time of Vespasian's reign. Research has sometimes discussed H. in connection with the mosaic copy of the painting (→ Alexander Mosaic, handed down in Pompeii); authorship was refuted,

alluding to the inability of women to attain 'artistic achievements of this level' (*sic!*), not to any lack of other evidence. [1. 2837].

1 E. Pfuhl, s.v. H. (7), RE 7.

A. COHEN, The Alexander Mosaic, 1996, 139–143; L. FORTI, s.v. H., EAA 3, 1134f.   N.H.

[5] Narrow rocky island of *c.* 12 km in length (height 281 m above sea-level) off the east coast of Attica (Str. 9,1,22; 9,5,3), also *Mákris* (Μάκρις, Steph. Byz. s.v. Ἑ.; Eur. Hel. 1673ff.; Mela 2,7,10; Plin. HN 4,62; [1; 2]). Prehistoric finds: [3; 4; 5].

1 W. KOLBE, L. BÜRCHNER, s.v. H. (1), RE 7, 2823f. 2 L. BÜRCHNER, s.v. Μάκρις, ἡ, RE 14, 814   3 N. LAMBERT, Vestiges préhistoriques dans l'île de Makronissos, in: BCH 96, 1972, 873–881   4 Id., Vestiges préhistoriques dans l'île de Macronisos, in: AAA 6, 1973, 1–12 5 P. SPITAELS, Provatsa on Makronissos, in: AAA 15, 1982, 155–158.   H.LO.

Helenium

Helenium (ἐλένιον; *helénion, helenium*). According to Plin. HN 21,59 and 159, the name is derived from the tears of Helena (rather differently Ael. NA. 9,21). Roman authors meant by the *(h)enula* or *inula* in general the elecampane (*Inula helenium L.*), a large *Composita* growing in western Asia and eastern Europe. Since late antiquity it had been grown in gardens as a medicinal plant (cf. Columella 11,3,17 and 35). In particular the bitter root (description of how to preserve it with sweet additives: Columella 12,48,1–5; Plin. HN 19,91; Hor. Sat. 2,8,51) was supposed (Dioscorides 1,28 WELLMANN = 1,27 BERENDES; Plin. HN 20,38) to help e.g. against flatulence, coughs, cramps and stomach upsets (Plin. HN 19,92; Hor. Sat. 2,2,44) and bites by wild animals. For Plin. HN 21,159, *helenium* was a women's cosmetic. Theophrastus (Hist. pl. 2,1,3; 6,6,2) and others also used it to designate labiates such as *Calamintha incana* or *Satureia thymbra L.* (probably = *tragoríganos* in Dioscorides 3,30 WELLMANN = 3,32 BERENDES). In the 17th cent. the name was adopted for American *Compositae* of the genus *Helianthus L.* (*Helenium indicum C. Bauhin*, sunflower) and *Helenium L.*

R. STADLER, s.v. H., RE 7, 2838–2840.

Helenius Acron

Helenius Acron Roman grammarian, especially commentator. His partial commentary on Terence (*Adelphoe* and *Eunuchus*) is taken into account in grammatical tradition; traces of his more famous commentary on Horace ([3. 1,3] puts him above Porphyry and Modestus) are to be found in the various reviews of the scholia, in particular in → Porphyry. As Gellius appears not to know H., yet H. is used by Porphyry (on Hor. Sat. 1,8,25) and Iulius Romanus (Charisius, Gramm. p. 250,11ff. BARWICK) dating to the later 2nd cent. AD is likely. H. as the name of the author of a humanist strand of the Horace scholia [3; 6] is completely unwarranted.

FRAGMENTS: 1 P. WESSNER, Aemilius Asper, 1905, 16ff. 2 A. LANGENHORST, De scholiis Horatianis quae Acronis nomine feruntur quaestiones selectae, 1908, 6ff. EDITIONS: 3 Pseudacronis schol. in Hor. vetustiora, ed. O. KELLER, 2 vols., 1902–1904. BIBLIOGRAPHY: 4 P. GRAFFUNDER, Entstehungszeit ... der akronischen Horazschol., in: RhM 60, 1905, 128–143 5 G. NOSKE, Quaestiones Pseudacroneae, 1969, 220ff.; 236ff.   6 C. VILLA, I manoscritti di Orazio III, in: Aevum 68, 1994, 129–134   7 P. L. SCHMIDT, in: HLL, § 444.
                                                                                                              P.L.S.

Helenopolis

Helenopolis Place at the exit of the Gulf of Astacus in Bithynia, originally Drepanon, modern Altinova. Birthplace of → Helena [2], elevated to a city in her honour by Constantine [1] and extended by Justinian (Amm. Marc. 26,8,1; Procop. Aed. 5,2).

R. JANIN, Les églises et les monastères des grands centres byzantins, 1975, 97f.; W. RUGE, s.v. Drepanon (4), RE 5, 1687.   K.ST.

Helenus

Helenus (Ἕλενος; *Hélenos*).
[1] One of the great early seers, more important in the epic *kyklos* than in Homer; son of → Priamus and → Hecabe (Hom. Il. 6,76; 7,44; Soph. Phil. 605f.; Apollod. 3,151; P Oxy. 56,3829), twin brother of → Cassandra (Anticlides FGrH 140 F 17; P Oxy. 56,3830). According to a probably archaic tradition, H. received his gift of prophecy when he was still a child in the temple of Apollo Thymbraeus, where he and Cassandra had fallen asleep. When their parents returned the next morning, they saw the sacred snakes cleaning the 'entrances to their sensory organs' with their tongues (Anticlides loc. cit.; rationalized in Arrianus FGrH 156 F 102); this association with Apollo can also be seen on an Apulian volute-krater of *c.* 330 BC, where H. is represented with a wreath and branch of laurel in his hand [1]. In Homer H. advises and encourages Hector, since he is 'the best interpreter of bird flight by far', (Hom. Il. 6,76) and hears 'the voice of the gods' (Hom. Il. 7,53). Like other archaic Greek seers [2] he fights on the battlefield (Hom. Il. 12,94f.; 13,576–600) and belongs to the highest aristocracy [3. add. PKöln VI, 245].

According to the *Cypria*, H. prophesied misfortune before → Paris left for Sparta. Later he took part in the funeral games after his alleged death (Hyg. Fab. 273,12) and with Deiphobus asked for the hand of the 'widow' → Helene [1] in marriage. After his failure he withdrew to the Ida mountains. There Odysseus took him prisoner in an ambush; H. foretold him that Troy could be captured with the aid of Hercules' bow, which the latter had given to → Philoctetes (Ilias parva; Bacchyl. fr. 7; Soph. Phil. 604–616; 1337–1341; P Oxy. 27,2455 fr. 17,254–259 = hypothesis of Euripides' *Philoctetes*); later sources cite as fatal 'talismans' for Troy → Pelops' bones (Apollod. 5,9; Tzetz. schol. Lycoph. 911), the Trojan horse or the acquisition of the → Palladium (Conon FGrH 26 F 1,34; Quint. Smyrn. 10,343–361). According to other later sources H. went over to the Greeks voluntarily (Triphiodorus 45–50) or begged Priam to be allowed to go to the Molossians (Dion. Chrys. 11,137; 142), a version, clearly influenced by Euripides' *Andromache*(1233–45; Verg. Aen. 3,295–297); he is even supposed to have had a child, Cestrinus, by → Andromache (Paus. 1,11,1).

1 N. ICARD-GIANOLTO, s.v. H., LIMC 8.1, 613f., no. 1
2 J. N. BREMMER, The Status and Symbolic Capital of the Seer, in: R. HÄGG (ed.), The Role of Rel. in the Early Greek Polis, 1996, 97–109   3 P. WATHELET, Dictionnaire des Troyens de l'Iliade, 1988, no. 109.   J.B.

[2] Son of Apollonius (?) of Cyrene; father of Thaubarion (PP 3/9, 5139). In 134 BC in Diospolis as representative of the king; from *c.* 120 worked in various capacities in Cyprus (cf. also SEG 41, 1479), from 117/16 until the appointment of Ptolemy IX *strategos* of the island (συγγενής, στρατηγὸς καὶ ἀρχιερεὺς καὶ ἀρχικυνηγός), between 116 and 114/13 τροφεύς (*tropheús*) of Ptolemy X Alexander. After the latter was proclaimed king, H. became *stratēgós* of Cyprus under him from 114 to 106/5; from 107/6 H. was also an admiral and γραμματεὺς τοῦ ναυτικοῦ (not confined to Cyprus); in that year he is attested as a priest of Cleopatra III for life.
→ Court titles

PP 3/9, 5112; 6, 15041; E. VAN'T DACK, Apollodôros et Helenos, in: Sacris erudiri 31, 1989/90, 429–441, esp. 431ff.   W.A.

[3] Freedman of Octavian of Greek origin. In 40 BC he occupied Sardinia for Octavian, but was there driven out (App. B Civ. 5,277), captured, and sent back to Octavian by Menodorus (Cass. Dio 48,30,1; 48,45,5). In his honour ILS 6267 (= CIL X 5808).   ME.STR.

Helepolis The *helepolis* (ἑλέπολις; *helépolis*, literally 'city-taker') was a large mobile siege tower, fitted with wheels, designed to bring up soldiers and catapults to the walls of a besieged city. The term is first attested for a tower built by Posidonius for Alexander the Great (Biton 52f. WESCHER; cf. for the siege of Tyre, Arr. Anab. 2,18–24), *helepoleis* were probably also already used by → Dionysius [1] I of Syracuse (Diod. Sic. 14,51,1). They may be of oriental or Carthaginian origin (Diod. Sic. 13,55). The *helepoleis* used by → Demetrius [2] Poliorcetes for the sieges of Salamis on Cyprus in 307 BC (Diod. Sic. 20,48,2f.) and Rhodes in 304 BC (Diod. Sic. 20,91,2f.; Plut. Demetrius 21,1f.) were already famous in antiquity. The latter was built by Epimachus of Athens (Athenaeus Mechanicus 27W, → Athenaeus [5]; Vitr. De arch. 10,16,4). It had nine storeys, a side length of over 20 m and a height of approximately 50 m. *Helepoleis* were cumbersome and as wooden structures easily damaged, in spite of a protective covering of metal or leather; moreover, to use them it was necessary for the ground to be flat and solid.
→ Siegecraft

1 KROMAYER/VEITH, 70, 219, 226, 236   2 O. LENDLE, Texte und Untersuchungen zum technischen Bereich der antiken Poliorketik, 1983, 36–106   3 E. W. MARSDEN, Greek and Roman Artillery. Technical Treatises, 1971, 84f.   LE.BU.

Heliadae (Ἡλιάδαι; *Hēliádai*). The sons of → Helios and Rhodos (Rhode: Hellanicus FGrH 4 F 137; schol. Hom. Od. 17,208 confused with Clymene, mother of Heliades [1]): Ochimus, Cercaphus, Actis, Macar(us) (Macareus), Candalus, Triopas and Phaethon (= Tenages: Pind. Ol. 7,71–73; cf. schol. 131a-c, 132a). According to a Rhodian local myth in Pind. Ol. 7,34–55 [2. 2849] Helios advised the H. to be the first to sacrifice to Athena after her birth. In their haste, however, they forgot the fire for the sacrifice (ἄπυρα ἱερά: aition for a Rhodian custom, Pind. Ol. schol. 71b; 73; Diod. Sic. 5,56). According to Zeno FGrH 523 F 1, four of the brothers killed Tenages out of jealousy and therefore emigrated: Macar to Lesbos, Candalus to Cos, Actis to Egypt, Triopas to Caria. However, the heroes were obviously adopted from there.

1 U. VON WILAMOWITZ-MÖLLENDORFF, Phaethon, in: Id., KS, vol. I, 1935, 110–148   2 L. MALTEN, s.v. H., RE 7, 2849–2852.   T.H.

Heliades (Ἡλιάδης; *Hēliádēs*).
[1] Officer of → Alexander [13] Balas, whom he betrayed after the defeat he suffered in 145 BC at Oenoparas at the hands of Ptolemy VI and → Demetrius [8] II (Jos. Ant. Iud. 13,4,8), with another officer and a north Syrian Bedouin sheikh, in exchange for securities offered by the victors, and helped to murder (Diod. Sic. 32,10,1).   C.C.
[2] see → Helios

Heliaia (ἡλιαία; *heliaía*). 1. Derived from ἁλίζω (*halízō*, 'assemble'), *heliaia* originally means simply 'assembly'. In the Doric area this expression survived for the public assembly [1. 32ff.] and in Arcadia for a committee, of probably fifty people, which made political and legal decisions (IG V 2,6A 24 and 27; 3,20 = IPArc nos. 2 and 3, both from Tegea [2. 36f]).

2. In Athens, according to Aristot. Ath. Pol. 9,1 (cf. on this [3. 160]), in opposition to judicial decisions by the archons, Solon introduced the → *ephesis* to the *heliaia*, at that time either the entire public assembly as a legal community [3. 160] or a smaller lawcourt determined by lot [4. 30], which is supported also by the parallel from Tegea. In later sources the *heliaia* is definitely a court, synonymous with → *dikastérion*, in the 4th cent. BC manned by at least 1,000 jurors [4. 191]. *Heliaia*, like *dikastérion*, was a catchword for the system of jurisdiction by jurors of democratic Athens [5. 4] Every → *dikastés* had to swear the 'heliast oath' [4. 182f.].

3. In Athens *heliaia*, as the site of the court, ultimately designated the place at which the *heliaia* convened. It

was located on the Agora. The following hypothesis exists [5]: in the 5th cent. *heliaia* (also called *mētiocheíon* or *meízon*) was the rectangular peribolus at the south-west corner of the Agora, and in the 4th cent. building A was the forerunner of the quadratic peristyle construction in the north-east of the Agora, which at the time of Aristotle's *Athenaion politeia* housed the *dikastéria* together with the *heliaia* as an overall complex.

1 M. WÖRRLE, Unt. zur Verfassungsgesch. von Argos, 1964 2 G. THÜR, H. TAEUBER, Prozeßrechtliche Inschr. der griech. Poleis. Arkadien, 1994 3 RHODES 4 M. H. HANSEN, The Athenian Democracy in the Age of Demosthenes, 1991 5 A. L. BOEGEHOLD, The Lawcourts at Athens (Ath. Agora vol. XXVIII), 1995. G.T.

Helicaon (Ἑλικάων; *Helikáōn*). Son of → Antenor [1], husband of Priam's daughter Laodice (Hom. Il. 3,123). During the conquest of Troy he was saved by Odysseus (Paus. 10,26,8). With Antenor (Verg. Aen. 1,247) and his brother Polydamas (Serv. Aen. 1,242) H. founded Patavium (Mart. 10,93). RE.ZI.

Helice (Ἑλίκη; *Helíkē*).
[1] City on the plain of Aegium in Achaea between the mouths of the Selinus and the Cerynitis (modern Buphusia) with the famous sanctuary of Poseidon Helikonios. H. took part in the Ionian and wider Greek colonization (founding of Sybaris, Str. 6,1,13–15) and in the classical period was the main headquarters of the Achaean League with the league sanctuary of Homarion. In 373 BC H. was destroyed by an earthquake and a tidal wave during the night and sank into the sea. The exact location of H. is unknown. Evidence: Hom. Il. 2,575; Hdt. 1,145; Pol. 2,41,7; Diod. Sic. 15,48f.; Str. 8,7,2; Paus. 7,24,5–25,4.

Y. LAFOND, Die Katastrophe von 373 v.Chr. und das Verschwinden der Stadt H. in Achaia, in: E. OLSHAUSEN, H. SONNABEND (ed.), Naturkatastrophen in der ant. Welt (Geographica Historica 10), 1998, 118–123. Y.L.

[2] see → Constellations

Helicon (Ἑλικών; *Helikṓn*).
[1] Mountain range in central Greece, dividing the Copais Basin and the upper Cephissos Valley from the Gulf of Corinth (cf. Str. 9,2,25; Paus. 9,28,1–31,7). The western part of the H. belonged to Phocis and the eastern part to Boeotia. The highest elevation is the peak of the Palaiovouno (1,748 m). Few passes lead over the H., which is rich in springs and forests and was famed for its herbs. The H. has large areas that were used in antiquity for agriculture and cattle pasture. The H. was well known for its cults. On its eastern foothills, on the peak of the Zagora, were a Zeus sanctuary and below it the → Hippocrene. In the valley of a brook, south of Ascra, was the cult site of the Muses, which was part of Thespiae. Whether the cult of Poseidon Helikonios attested in Hom. H. ad Venerem 22,3 can be related to H. is uncertain.

A. HURST, A. SCHACHTER (ed.), La montagne des Muses (Recherches et rencontres 7), 1996. K.F.

[2] **H. of Cyzicus.** Mathematician and astronomer from the circle of Plato, → Eudoxus [1] and → Isocrates. H. predicted the eclipse of the sun of 12 May 361 BC (Plut. Dion 19) and was involved with Eudoxus in solving the problem of the → duplication of the cube (Plut. Mor. 579C).

F. BOLL, s.v. H. (2), RE 8, 7–8. M.F.

[3] According to Ath. 2,48b, H. and his father Acesas were famous weavers from Salamis in Cyprus. Together they allegedly created the first → *peplos* of Athena Polias for the Panathenaea. A cloak that the Rhodians later gave to Alexander the Great and that he is said to have worn in the battle of Gaugamela (Plut. Alexander 32) is thought to be the work of H. An epigram names H. and Acesas jointly as the creators of a work in Delphi (Ath. 2,48b). The expression Ἀκέσεως καὶ Ἑλικῶνος ἔργα ('a work as if by Acesas and Helicon') was proverbial for particularly admirable works of weaving (→ Textile art).

G. CRESSEDI, s.v. H., EAA 3, 1135. R.H.

[4] see → Music

Heliconius (Ἑλικώνιος; *Helikṓnios*). From Byzantium, chronicler, known only from the Suda, wrote a χρονικὴ ἐπιτομή (*chronikè epitomé*) from Adam up to emperor Theodosius I (Suda E 851). The Suda (A 3215 and 3868) quotes one note each from the chronicle on the lives of Apion and Arrian.

PLRE 1, 411 [Heliconius]; G. WIRTH, Helikonios der Sophist, in: Historia 13, 1964, 506–509. F.T.

Heliocles (called *Díkaios*, Middle Indian *Heliyakriya*). Greek king of Bactria in the 2nd cent. BC, attested only by his coins. According to TARN [1] son of Eucratides I and the last Greek king of Bactria, overthrown by nomads in 141/128. NARAIN [2] and BOPEARACHCHI [3] differentiate between two H.s on numismatic grounds. The second was supposedly a son of the first and ruled in the south of the Hindu Kush.

1 W. W. TARN, The Greeks in Bactria and India, ²1951 2 A. K. NARAIN, The Indo-Greeks, 1958 3 BOPEARACHCHI, 74–76, 222–225 (H. I.), 97–99, 281–285 (H. II.). K.K.

Heliodorus (Ἡλιόδωρος; *Heliódōros*).
[1] Son of Aeschylus of Antioch on the Orontes, was educated with Seleucus IV and was a courtier (τῶν περὶ τὴν αὐλήν) and well-respected chancellor (ὁ ἐπὶ τῶν πραγμάτων τεταγμένος) under him in 187–175 BC (IG XI 4,1112–1114, or OGIS 247; App. Syr. 45). When financial difficulties after the defeat of Seleucus' father Antiochus III against the Romans (190/188), in conjunction with internal Jewish intrigues, had led to spe-

cial tax demands on the Jews and H. had met with opposition when collecting them on the orders of his king, he murdered Seleucus IV in 175 and took on the guardianship of his son Antiochus. However, he was very soon driven out by the murdered man's brother and new king, Antiochus IV, and his helpers Eumenes II and Attalus II (2 Macc 3,4ff.; App. Syr. 45; Hieron. in Dan 11,20, without mention of H.). As JACOBY showed, there is no reason to conclude from FGrH 373 F 8 that H. wrote a work of memoirs.

A. BOUCHÉ-LECLERCQ, Histoire des Séleucides (323–64 avant J.-C.), 1913/1914, 238–242, 580–582, 627; GRUEN, Rome, 646f.; O. MØRKHOLM, Antiochus IV of Syria, 1966, Index s.v.; H.H. SCHMITT, Untersuchungen zur Geschichte Antiochos' d. Gr. und seiner Zeit, 1964, 20; WILL, 33, 36, 41, 44, 46f., 49, 104, 136f.   A.ME.

[2] Periegetic; a mention by Antiochus [6] Epiphanes (reign 175–164 BC) in a convincingly attributed (Athenaeus 2,45C) fragment gives for H. a dating *terminus post quem*. Pliny (HN 1,34,35) ascribes to him a treatise on the *anathēmata* of the Athenians; Harpocration (s.v. Νίκη Ἀθηνᾶ) and Athenaeus (9,406D) call H. ὁ Περιηγητής ('the Periegetic'), while Athenaeus (6,229E) calls him an Athenian and mentions a work Περὶ Ἀκροπόλεως ('On the Acropolis') in 15 bks. Harpocration once recorded (s.v. Προπύλαια ταῦτα) the extended title Περὶ τῆς Ἀθήνησιν ἀκροπόλεως ('On the Acropolis in Athens') and quotes, likewise once (s.v. Ὀνήτωρ), περὶ τῶν Ἀθήνησιν τριπόδων ('On the tripods in Athens'), the latter normally interpreted as an excerpt from a larger work. The few fragments reveal topographical organisation and portrayal in enormous detail.

FGrH 373.   A.A.D.

[3] Sculptor from Rhodes. Pliny (HN 36,35) wrongly calls a famous symplegma by H., which stood in Rome in the Porticus Octaviae, 'Pan and Olympus'. Identification with an often copied group of Pan and Daphnis is considered secure. It is dubious whether H. is identical to a H. attested in Halicarnassus and Rhodes in the late 2nd cent. BC or to a H. whom Pliny recorded in the catalogue at HN 34,91. Stylistically the work is dated to the period around 100 BC.

M. BIEBER, The Sculpture of the Hellenistic Age, 1961, 147, fig. 628; LIPPOLD, 323–324; LOEWY, no. 403; N. MARQUARDT, Pan in der hell. und kaiserzeitlichen Plastik, 1995, 195–206; OVERBECK, no. 2096, 2097 (sources).   R.N.

[4] H. of Athens (TrGF I 209); otherwise unknown tragedian, mentioned in Galen (De antidotis XIV p. 144 KÜHN), probably also the author of a work in the paradoxographical tradition *Apolytiká* ('Medicines').

A. A. M. ESSER, Zur Frage der Lebenszeit Heliodors von Athen, in: Gymnasium 54/55, 1943/4, 114–117.   B.Z.

[5] Greek surgeon from Egypt (?). The period in which he lived is concluded from a mention in Juvenal (Sat.

6,370–373); he was therefore seen as a contemporary of the satirist, but he was also dated to the Hellenistic period. He is said to have practised in Rome and was regarded as a Pneumatist.

Four treatises are known to us: a 'Surgery' in five bks., describing surgical operations in the arrangement *a capite ad calcem* and giving evidence of the efforts made to ensure safe methods of treatment [1. 114–116, 121]; 'On luxations'; 'On the joints'; 'On bandages'. Only fragments of the first-mentioned work are extant, directly through a single papyrus [1; 2] and indirectly through quotations in Oribasius.

Several Greek [3] and Latin [4] works circulated under H.'s name, including the *Cirurgia Eliodori*, the Latin translation of a questionnaire from the Hellenistic period [5]. Several papyrus texts have been attributed to him [6; 7; 8; 9. 164f.]), doubtless because of the high regard H. enjoyed from antiquity to the Renaissance [9. 165].

→ Pneumatist school

1 M.-H. MARGANNE, Un témoignage unique sur l'incontinence intestinale: P. Monac. 2. 23, in: D. GOUREVITCH (ed.), FS M.D. Grmek, 1992, 109–121   2 D. MANETTI, P.Coln. inv. 339, in: A. CARILE, Die Pap. der Bayerischen Staatsbibliothek München, 1986, 19–25   3 H. DIELS, ADAW 1906, 41f.   4 G. SABBAH et al., Bibliogr. des textes médicaux latins, 1987, 93f.   5 M.-H. MARGANNE, La Cirurgia Eliodori et le P. Genève inv. 111, in: Etudes de lettres 1968/1, 65–73   6 MARGANNE, no. 75, 77, 87, 103, 153, 168   7 I. ANDORLINI-MARCONE, L'apporto dei papiri alla conoscenza della scienza medica antica, in: ANRW II 37.1, no. 9, 54, 57, 70, 75, 98   8 D. FAUSTI (ed.), P. Strasb. inv. gr. 1187, in: Annali della facoltà di lettere e filosofia di Siena 10, 1989, 157–169   9 M.-H. MARGANNE, L'ophtalmologie dans l'Egypte grécoromaine d'après les papyrus littéraires grecs, 1994.

M.-H. MARGANNE, Le chirurgien Héliodore. Trad. directe et indirecte, in: Etudes de médecine romaine, 1989, 107–111.   A.TO.

[6] Metrician of the 1st cent. AD, tutor of → Irenaeus [1], author of an edition of the comedies of Aristophanes, in which the text was divided into *stíchoi* and *kóla*. Colometric symbols drew attention to rhythmic and metric phenomena and referred to a continuous commentary dealing almost exclusively with questions of metre. The entries differentiate the verses according to length (ἐν ἐκθέσει/ἐν εἰσθέσει). The fragments handed down in the corpus of the scholia of Aristophanes were collected in [7], then in [8. 396–421]. On H.'s critical terminology cf. [5]. H. applied an already known method of editing to Aristophanes [1]. He also wrote a treatise on metre 'for those who want to have access to the main terms of metric theory' (Choeroboscus in Heph. 181, 9–11 CONSBRUCH), which according to Longinus (in Heph. 81,13 C.) began with the 'definition of the metres' (ἀπὸ τοῦ μέτρων ὅρου); Hephaestion polemicized against the elementary character of the presentation [2. 49].

H. was an advocate of the doctrine of the (according to him eight) 'original metres' (μέτρα πρωτότυπα, → Hephaestion; → Philoxenus; → the art of verse) and also enlisted the theory of the formation of new metres by omitting and adding one or more syllables at the beginning of the colon (ἐπιπλοκή/*epiplokḗ*; cf. [2. 97–99]). → Juba of Mauretania used him as a source.

→ Metre

1 C. QUESTA, L'antichissima edizione dei cantica di Plauto, in: RFIC 102, 1974, 183–186   2 B. M. PALUMBO STRACCA, La teoria antica degli asinarteti, 1979   3 O. HENSE, Heliodoreische Unt., 1870   4 Id., s.v. H. (16), RE 8, 28–40   5 D. HOLWERDA, De Heliodori commentario metrico in Aristophanem, in: Mnemosyne 17, 1964, 113–139 and 20, 1967, 247–272   6 R. PFEIFFER, History of Classical Scholarship, 1968, 189, 196   7 O. THIEMANN, Heliodori colometriae Aristophaneae quantum superest, 1864   8 J. W. WHITE, The Verse of Greek Comedy, 1912 (repr. 1969), 384–395.   S.FO.

[7] **H. Arabius.** Sophist, around AD 210–235, according to Philostratus from Arabia (Philostr. Soph. 2,32), unlikely to be identical to T. Aurelius H. of Palmyra (IGR 1,43–45) or the author of novels H. [8] from Emesa. When in 213 as ambassador he had to represent the interests of his fatherland single-handedly, the emperor Caracalla, impressed, allowed him to give an impromptu lecture and appointed him *advocatus fisci* and made him and his sons *equites equo publico*. After Caracalla's death H. was exiled and later acquitted of a charge of murder; he lived in Rome during the creative period of Philostratus.

→ Philostratus; → Second Sophistic

F. G. B. MILLAR, The Emperor in the Roman World, 1977, 234; 281f.; PIR H 54.   E.BO.

[8] Author of the novel *Aithiopiká*. The only certain information on his life emerges from a *sphragís* at a point in the novel which would today be designated as the 'paratext': H., as a 'Phoenician from the city of Emesa, from the house of the descendants of Helios, as son of Theodosius, called himself Heliodorus'. The name H. may be an appropriate pseudonym for an author whose work praises the god Helios, yet the personal statement must surely be correct. The chronology is controversial: ROHDE dates the work to the reign of the emperor Aurelian (AD 270–275), who declared the cult of Sol a state religion [1. 496–7]. Others date him earlier, but not before the death of Elagabalus (who came from Emesa), and equate H. with the Arabian sophist H. [7], who died in 240 and is mentioned by Philostratus (Soph. 2,32) [2]; this possible dating produces a connection with the latter's 'Life of Apollonius of Tyana' and the neo-Pythagorean circle of → Iulia Domna. A further dating to the 4th cent. AD is based on the similarity between the Syene episode in the 9th book of the *Aithiopiká* and the account of the siege of Nisibis in the year 350 by the later emperor → Iulianus (Julian Or. 1 and 3) [3]. However it is not ruled out that, as a notorious novel reader, he imitates H. here (the prob-

lem is exacerbated by the existence of further Greek and Syrian sources) [4]. This last dating fits in with the statements of the historian Socrates, according to whom H. was bishop of Tricca and wrote the *Aithiopiká* in his youth (Socr. 5,22).

Whichever dating is correct, the *Aithiopiká* are the latest ancient Greek novel. H. worked in a popular genre, which he refined by means of a complex narrative architecture and regenerated in philosophical tone (which compares in mirror image to the ironic pastiche of → Achilles Tatius [1]). With a direct borrowing from the Odyssey – beginning of *medias in res* and repetition of the past history in the inner narrative – the typical structure of the Greek novel is remodelled. The other novels tell a circular story in linear form, beginning and ending in the home city of the protagonists, while the *Aithiopiká* tells a linear story in circular form: the return of the Ethiopian princess Chariclea to her home. The mysterious initial scene of the novel is similar to a film setting: an abduction typical of a novel is told from the perspective of a band of robbers, who do not understand what is happening. Gradually the reader understands that the two protagonists Chariclea and Theagenes are the victims; they are handed over to Cnemon, a young man from Athens, who tells them his life story – a version in novel form of the myth of Phaedra (I). Only after the feigned death of Chariclea and the parting of the three does Cnemon discover the past history of the couple from the Egyptian priest Calasiris (II): how they fell in love in Delphi (III), how Chariclea's origin became known through the message of her mother, the Ethiopian queen Persinna, written on a strip of material, how the couple fled from Delphi (IV) and fought with pirates and rivals (V). At this point the main narrator, standing outside the action, intervenes again and makes Calasiris and Chariclea, disguised as beggars, search for Theagenes (VI); this is followed by a long 'Persian' episode, set in Memphis, in which Calasiris dies after rediscovering his children, and Theagenes becomes the object of the desire of Arsace, the sister of the Great King (VII–VIII). The novel concludes with the victory of the Ethiopian king Hydaspes over the Persians at Syene (IX); the royal couple finally recognize their daughter Chariclea, dedicate the two protagonists to Helios and Selene and thereby abolish human sacrifice (X).

H.'s sophisticated narrative technique always has a thematic function. The exciting beginning already shows the theme running through the novel: the deciphering of truth and the divine as a circumstantial process in which readers and the characters of the novel are confronted with signs which are difficult to interpret [5]. The metadiegetic narrative also becomes a metaliterary process; a quasi-maieutic relationship develops between the narrator and those addressed by the narrative: Calasiris (who reflects the role of the author) urges Cnemon (who on his part represents the typical reader of romantic novels) to comprehend the deeper meaning of the story; the naive 'reader reaction' of Cnemon, who particularly likes digressions and spectacular descriptions, is only partial, however. The narrative polyphony transports various cultures into the field of vision by an intensification culminating in the wisdom of the → gymnosophists. No uniform theological system is recognizable (in spite of attempts at allegorical interpretation even in antiquity); there is a strong Neoplatonic influence (e.g. in the motif of love at first sight, relating to the Platonic 'Phaedrus'). The mutual love of the two protagonists has sacred value for H. and is contrasted with the erotic promiscuity of the hetaerae Thisbe and Arsace (even though the latter invites readers to identify with her [6. 3f.]). Virginity (differently from Achilles Tatius) is praised even in men in tones almost redolent of Christianity (the idea of sexuality as a sin is alien to the novel, however). The equal ranking of the couple is emphasized, yet the heroine of the novel leaves the undoubtedly stronger impression, not only because of her beauty and purity, but also because of her pragmatic capabilities, whose exquisitely Odyssean nature is unmistakable.

The novel was very popular in the Byzantine period and was imitated by Theodoros Prodromos *i.a.* It turned up again in the Renaissance (*editio princeps*: Basle 1534) and had its greatest success in the baroque era, because it concurred with the poetry of the period. The *Aithiopiká* were translated into all the main languages and put on an equal level with Homer and Virgil by later writers, and much imitated and used as models (e.g. by Cervantes in the *Trabajos de Persiles y Sigismonda*, Racine and Shakespeare). Calderón and others dramatized them, Basile presented a free verse version in the *Teagene*. The last echo of their rich legacy must be Verdi's opera *Aida* [7].
→ Novel; → NOVEL

1 E. ROHDE, Der griech. Roman und seine Vorläufer, ²1914   2 F. ALTHEIM, Helios und H. von Emesa, 1942   3 M. VAN DER WALK, Remarques sur la date des Éthiopiques, in: Mnemosyne 9, 1941, 97–100   4 T. SZEPESSY, Die Neudatierung des Heliodoros und die Belagerung von Nisibis, in: Acta XII Eirene 1975, 279–87   5 J. WINKLER, The Mendacity of Kalasiris and the Narrative Strategy of Heliodoros's 'Aithiopika', in: YClS 27, 1982, 93–158   6 M. FUSILLO, Il romanzo greco, 1989   7 O. WEINREICH, Der griech. Liebesroman, 1962.

J. R. Morgan, H., in: G. SCHMELING (ed.), The Novel in the Ancient World, 1996; P. PAULSEN, Inszenierung des Schicksals, 1992; S. SANDY, Heliodorus, 1982; S. SZEPESSY, Die Aithiopika des Heliodoros und der griech. sophistische Liebesroman, in: H. GÄRTNER (ed.), Beiträge zum griech. Liebesroman, 1984, 432–450.   M.FU.

[9] 7th-cent. AD; author of a commentary on the *Téchnē grammatikē* of → Dionysius [17] Thrax [2], which is also drawn on in the scholia to this; the beginning of the work, which is handed down anonymously, is missing in Cod. Oxoniensis Baroccianus 116 (14th cent.); the extracts of Georgius → Choiroboskos supply the *terminus ante quem* for the dating.

EDITIONS: 1 GG I,3, 67–106.
BIBLIOGRAPHY: 2 A. HILGARD, Praefatio in GG I,3, XIV–XVIII (with older literature)   3 R.R. H. ROBINS, The Byzantine Grammarians, 1993, 77–86   4 J.E. SANDYS, A History of Classical Scholarship I, 1958, 139.
S.FO.

Heliogabalus see → Elagabalus

Helion *Comes* and *magister officiorum* AD 414–427. The effect of his work is attested by numerous laws in the Codex Theodosianus. In 422, on the orders of Theodosius II, he made a peace treaty with the Persians (Socr. 7,20) and in 425 he brought Valentinian III the news of his elevation to Caesar (Olympiodorus fr. 43 BLOCKLEY).   M.R.

Heliopolis, Heliupolis

[1] Egyptian *Jwnw*, Hebrew *'ôn*, modern Matarije. City on the eastern edge of the southern tip of the Nile delta axis (today a suburb of Cairo), metropolis of the 13th Lower Egyptian district and from the Old Kingdom the most important cult centre of the sun god in his forms → Aton and Re-Harachte (→ Re). H. was of central theological significance in a myth of creation which in the generational model of the 'Ennead of H.' (Aton – Geb – Nut – Shu – Tefnut – Osiris – Isis – Seth – Nephthys), starting from the sun, parallels the development of the world and the world of the gods. In the Greek and Roman period H. was visited by travellers as the centre of all wisdom (Hdt. 2,3; Str. 17,1,29), yet the significance of the site lessened and its monuments (obelisks) were removed to other cities of the Delta and even as far as Italy. H. has still scarcely been investigated archaeologically; there is an obelisk of Sesostris I *in situ* at the site.
[2] see → Baalbek

D. RAUE, Prosopographie von H. im NR, 1998.   S.S.

Heliopolitanus The chief god of the Biqāʿ Plain, in which the Arabian kingdom of the Ituraeans (→ Ituraea) had been established from the 2nd cent. BC, had been since the pre-Arabian period the 'Lord of the Biqāʿ' (*bʿl bqʿ*). Under the name of Zeus Helios or Juppiter (Optimus Maximus) H., he was worshipped in Roman times in → Baalbek (= Heliopolis), where his main temple was erected on older remains. His solarisation must have been the result of Ptolemaic influence. Well attested iconographically and epigraphically, this god is a → weather god, rain dispenser, lord of the springs, oracle god, highest god and cosmocrator. Pictorial depictions show him as a young man on a plinth flanked by two bulls. In his right hand he is holding a sheaf of corn and in his left hand a whip. On his head, which at times was encircled by a shining wreath, he wears a → kalathos or an Egyptian crown. His garment is decorated with astral symbols. The popular opinion, according to which the chief god of Baalbek was worshipped jointly with Venus and Mercury as a triad, is much questioned in more recent research [4].

1 P. Haiser et al. (ed.), Religionsgesch. Syriens, 1996, 198–210 2 Y. Hajjar, Baalbek, grand centre religieux sous l'Empire, in: ANRW II 18.4, 2458–2508 3 G. H. Halsberghe, The Cult of Sol Invictus, 1972 4 Millar, Near East, 281–285. H.NI.

Helios see → Sol

Helisson (Ἑλισσών; *Helissṓn*).
[1] River in Arcadia with abundant water at all seasons, tributary of the Alpheius [1], rises on the north-west slope of the Maenalum range, firstly flows south, then, turning west, in a narrow gorge penetrates the central mountains of Arcadia, composed of lime, flows through the Megalopolis Basin and flows out to the west of this into the Alpheius (Paus. 5,7,1; 8,29,5; 30,1f.). An important connecting route to northern Arcadia (today the Tripolis-Vitina road) runs through the upper valley of the H.

Philippson/Kirsten 3, 261ff.

[2] River in the west of Sicyon, which flows out into the Gulf of Corinth near Kiato (Paus. 2,12,2; Stat. Theb. 4,52).

Philippson/Kirsten 3, 161. C.L. and E.O.

[3] Settlement of the Maenalii in the source region of the river of the same name [H. 1] near Mantinea, but separated from it by the Mainalon mountains. At the beginning of the 4th cent. BC *kṓmē* of Mantinea, later incorporated with all the surrounding countryside into Megalopolis. Evidence: Diod. Sic. 16,39,5; Paus. 8,3,3; 27,3; 27,7; 30,1.

M. Jost, Villages de l'Arcadie antique, in: Ktema 11, 1986 (1990), 150–155. Y.L.

Heliupolis see → Heliopolis

Helixus (Ἕλιξος; *Hélixos*). *Strategos* from Megara. In 411 BC, H. led a fleet contingent of the → Peloponnesian League, which caused Byzantium to break away from Athens (Thuc. 8,80). When the city was later besieged by the Athenians, H. defended it until it capitulated in the winter of 409/8 (Xen. Hell. 1,3,15; 17; 21). E.S.-H.

Helladius (Ἑλλάδιος; *Helládios*).
[1] H. of Antinupolis in Egypt. Grammarian of the 4th cent. AD, author of a *Chrēstomatheía* ('Things worth knowing') in iambic trimeters. Photius, the only biographical source, took extracts from it (Cod. 279, 529b 25–536a 22), but also knew of a prose epitome (cf. [4. 99; 6. 16]). The encyclopaedic work includes grammatical, etymological, historical and mythological information; on the literary genre cf. [6. 24–26]. Neither a criterion for the arrangement nor a model of the commentary are recognizable – though Phrynichus is not considered to be the main source (for [6], against [2]). There is no question of dependency on Aristophanes of Byzantium [3]. Photius also hands down titles of other lost works in iambic trimeters.

1 A. Cameron, Pap. Ant. III 115 and the Iambic Prologue, in: CQ 20, 1970, 120 2 E. Fischer, Die Ekloge des Phrynichos (SGLG 1), 1974, 48 3 W. J. Slater, Aristophanis Byz. Fragmenta (SGLG 6), 1986, XVIII and 19, n. 4 4 A. Gudeman, s.v. H. (2), RE 8, 98–102 5 M. Haupt, Opuscula II, 1876, 421–427 6 H. Heimannsfeld, De Helladii Chrestomathia quaestiones selectae, 1911 7 Id., Zum Text des H. bei Photius (cod. 279), in: RhM 69, 1914, 570–574 8 R. A. Kaster, Guardians of Language, 1988, 411–412 9 P. Maas, Review of [6], in: ByzZ 21, 1912, 269–270 10 E. Orth, Photiana, 1928, 68–69. S.FO.

[2] H. of Alexandria. Grammarian, priest of Zeus in Alexandria, fled to Constantinople in AD 391 (Socr. 5,16,1–14). He worked under Theodosius II (404–450) (Suda ε 732) and received the *comitiva primi ordinis* (Cod. Theod. 6,21,1; cf. [1]), probably on 15 March 425. The eulogy of Theodosius, quoted by the Suda together with other titles of epideictic speeches or perhaps poems, may relate to this event. H. was also the author of a lexicon comprising 7 bks. (Λεξικὸν κατὰ στοιχεῖον), the alphabetic arrangement of which was confined to the first syllable. It was 'the most comprehensive' of the lexicons known to Photius (Cod. 145,98b 40–99a 12) and is named by the Suda (praef.) as one of its sources.

1 A. Cameron, The Empress and the Poet, in: YClS 27, 1982, 286.

A. Cameron, Wandering Poets, in: Historia 14, 1965, 470–509 (repr. see [1]) 3 A. Gudeman, s.v. H. (3), RE 8, 102–103 4 R. A. Kaster, Guardians of Language, 1988, 411–412 5 O. Seeck, s.v. H. (8), RE 8, 103. S.FO.

[3] Otherwise unknown author of a short satirical epigram (Anth. Pal. 11,423), which hits out at a dyer (βαφεύς) who has the ability to change his own poverty into wealth by means of dyes. It probably belongs to the epigram collection of Diogenianus [2] of Heraclea; H. can therefore be dated approximately to the period of Hadrian (1st half of the 2nd cent. AD). M.G.A.

Hellana Staging-post in Etruria on the *via Cassia* between Florentia (*c.* 27 km away) and Pistoriae (*c.* 9 km away; Tab. Peut. 4,2; Geogr. Rav. 4,36); in AD 848 attested as Alina (MGH, Diplomata Karolina 3,242, no. 102) and therefore to be identified with Agliana (Pistoia).

S. Pieri, Toponomastica della Valle dell'Arno, 1919, 114; M. Lopes Pegna, Itineraria Etruriae, in: SE 21, 1950/1, 407–443, esp. 426. G.U.

Hellanicus (Ἑλλάνιχος; *Hellánikos*).

[1] H. of Mytilene. (T 1). Contrary to ancient tradition, which sometimes puts his birth date towards the end of the 6th cent. (T 4), sometimes at the beginning of the 5th cent. (T 3) and sometimes in the year 480/479 BC (T 1 and 6), younger rather than older contemporary of → Herodotus. At any rate the datable works belong to the last third of the 5th cent.

H. analyzed the Herodotean collection of topics into individual components by a series of monographs and, reverting to → Hecataeus [3], even added new themes. This gave rise to writings on mythography, ethnography and chronology, based less on independent research than on earlier authors, e.g. Hecataeus, Acusilaus of Argus (T 18), Herodotus (F 72) and Damastes of Sigeum (F 72), which were quite frequently of a compilatory nature. H. is the first prolific writer of Greek literature. The titles of 23 works have been handed down, though all have been lost apart from *c.* 200 fragments.

In his mythographical works *Deukalōneía, Phoronís, Asōpís* and *Atlantís* (each comprising two bks., with the exception of the one-volume *Asōpís*) H. reduced the genealogies of early Greek history to four forefathers, systematized and linked them by means of synchronisms, structures and speculations and in so doing made them into a uniform whole. Most of the genealogies dealt with were entered in the *Trōïká*. This gave rise to 'a self-contained overall picture of early Greek history' [1].

Ethnographic works: H. wrote general portrayals, e.g. on 'customs of barbarians', 'the history of the foundation of peoples and cities', 'on peoples', 'names of peoples' (the three latter-named titles perhaps designate one and the same work). He additionally wrote monographs on foreign peoples, including *Aigyptiaká, Lydiaká, Persiká, Skythiká*, and on Greek tribes and landscapes, e.g. *Aioliká, Lesbiká, Argoliká, Boiōtiká, Thessaliká*. To this series also belongs the *Atthís*, comprising two bks. (F 163–172), which appeared after 407/6 (F 171 and 172) and marks the start of Atthidography (→ Atthis). H. describes Athenian history from the mythological beginnings up to the time of the Peloponnesian War. For this purpose he drew up a list of the Athenian kings and completed the list of archons to the point where it linked up to the period of the kings. Thucydides (1,97,2) criticizes the imprecise chronology of the → *pentekontaetía* in H.

Chronographical works: two works by H. mark the beginning of Greek chronography. These are the 'Hera priestesses of Argus' (F 74–84) and the *Karneoníkai* = 'victors at the Carnean Games' (F 85f.). Here an attempt was made to erect a basic chronological framework for the whole of Greek history (cf. F 79, 84), using the duration of rule of the Argive priestesses or the victors of the Spartan festival.

In research H., who wrote in archaizing style, is thought of simply as the 'end of older Greek historiography' [2]; in reality he also marks a new beginning,

above all as the 'first Greek universal historian' [1] and bold innovator in the domain of chronology.

1 O. LENDLE, Einführung in die griech. Geschichtsschreibung, 1992, 63ff.   2 F. JACOBY, s.v. H. (7), RE 8.1, 104–153 (fundamental).

FRAGMENTS: FGrH 4, 323a, 608a; F. JACOBY, FGrH III C, Fasc. I; CH. W. FORNARA, Commentary on Nos. 608a–608, 1994; J. J. CAEROLS PÉREZ (ed. and transl.), Hélanico de Lesbos. Fragmentos, 1991.

BIBLIOGRAPHY: D. AMBAGLIO, Per la cronologia di Ellanico di Lesbo, in: RAL 32, 1977, 389–398; Id., L'opera storiografica di Ellanico di Lesbo, in: Ricerche di storiografia antica 2, 1980, 9–192; R. DREWS, The Greek Accounts of Eastern History, 1973, 97ff.; K. VON FRITZ, Die griech. Geschichtsschreibung 1, 1967, 476ff.; F. JACOBY, Atthis, 1949; R. J. LENARDON, Thucydides and Hellanicus, in: Classical Contributions. Studies in Honour of M.F. McGregor, 1981, 59–70; K. MEISTER, Die griech. Geschichtsschreibung, 1990, 41f.; J. H. SCHREINER, Historical Methods, Hellanikos and the Era of Kimon, in: Opuscula Atheniensia 15, 1984, 169–171; Id., Hellanikos, Thucydides and the Era of Kimon, 1997; J. D. SMART, Thucydides and Hellanicus, in: J. S. MOXON, J. D. SMART, A. J. WOODMAN (ed.), Past Perspectives, 1986, 19–35.
                                                              K.MEI.

[2] Alexandrian grammarian around 200 BC (cf. Suda s.v. Πτολεμαῖος ὁ Ἐπιθέτης), one of the most important representatives of the → Chorizontes (Procl. Vita Homeri, p. 102,3 ALLEN). His doctrines are identifiable only in small remains on the critical comments of → Aristarchus [4] of Samothrace and his pupils in the scholia to Homer (schol. Hom. Il. 5,269; 15,651; 19,90; schol. Hom. Od. 2,185). He also seems to have concerned himself with Herodotus (schol. Soph. Phil. 201).

→ Xeno

F. MONTANARI, H., in: SGLG 7, 1988, 43–73; Id., Un misconosciuto frammento di Ellanico di Lesbo (e piccole note su frammenti meno dubbi), in: Studi Classici e Orientali 37, 1987, 183–189.   F.M.

Hellanodikai (Ἑλλανοδίκαι; *Hellanodíkai*, also Ἑλληνοδίκαι; *Hellēnodíkai*), the supervisors and judges at the competitions of Olympia, Nemea (IG IV 587) and the Asclepiea in Epidaurus (IG IV 946; 1508). The *hellanodikai* of the Olympic Games were chosen in Elis from the local aristocracy for one festival in each case. The office (official oath: Paus. 5,24,10), the sacred components of which are still reflected in a cleansing ritual of the *hellenodikai* (Paus. 5,16,8), probably involved large financial outlays. The number of *hellenodikai* was initially restricted to one or two, but at the latest from the mid 4th cent. BC ten became the norm, though at times up to twelve *hellenodikai* are attested (Paus. 5,9,4–6; Philostr. VA 3,30; schol. Pind. Ol. 3,22). At the games they were accorded virtually unrestricted authority, symbolized by a crimson garment (EM s.v. *hellenodikai*). After they had been instructed in the rules for ten months by *nomophylakes* (Paus. 6,24,3), it was their duty to check the rights to compete, the qualifications of the athletes, and their responsibilities included the power of arbitration, the allocation of prizes and the keeping of lists of victors; however, they were not allowed to interfere in the code of rules. They additionally had the right to punish and flog athletes [1. 111–120]. Pausanias (6,24,1–3) testifies to an official building for the *hellenodikai* (*hellanodikaíōn*) (6,24,1–3).

An office of *hellenodikai* with a judicial function in Sparta is mentioned by Xenophon (Lac. pol. 13,11).

1 M. I. FINLEY, H. W. PLEKET, Die olympischen Spiele der Antike, 1976.   M.MEI.

Hellas

[1] H., Hellenes. (Ἑλλάς; *Hellás*, Ἕλληνες; *Héllēnes*). The Hellenes (Homeric Ἕλλανες, Ionic-Attic Ἕλληνες) were a tribe in southern Thessaly at the time of Homer, more precisely, or at the most, confined to the area around the river Spercheus, the country named Hellas (Ἑλλάς) after them, adjacent to the territory of Phthia (Hom. Il. 2,683f.; 9,395, 447, 478; 16,595; Hom. Od. 11,496). Ancient and modern speculation that the Hellenes had originally settled around → Dodona are based on the unprovable assumption of a connection with the Hellopes (→ Hellopia) and the Dodonian dynasty of priests of the Helloi or Selloi (Hom. Il. 16,234).

Bipartite expressions for describing the Greeks and the whole of Greece are found in the catalogue of ships in the *Iliad* and in the *Odyssey, Hellás* and *Pan-héllēnes* ('the Hellenes in general') evidently referring to mainland Greece and *Árgos* and *Achaioí* to the Peloponnese (Hom. Il. 2,530; Hom. Od. 1,344; 4,726, 816; 15,80). The H. must therefore at times have held a leading position in north and central Greece, about which we otherwise know nothing. By reducing the bipartite expression to the second element, from Hesiod the name of Hellenes then became the customary name for all Greeks. The country name H. at first referred to all areas inhabited by Greeks, even to the colonies, but then in general linguistic usage became restricted to a self-contained geographical region, the Greek motherland, sometimes even to the mainland, even excluding the Peloponnes (Dem. Or. 19,303; Plin. HN 4,23; Ptol. 3,14,1). In general the northern boundary of Greece was drawn, without consideration of the linguistic circumstances, from the Ambracian Gulf over the Pindus to Olympus and to the Tempe Valley. This was already confirmed in the *Iliad* and also in the 5th cent. by the geographer Phileas of Athens (in Dionysius Calliphontis 31ff., GGM I p. 239) and also by Strabo (1st cent. BC/1st cent. AD) in the 8th to 10th books. The peoples on the far side of this boundary, Epirotes (→ Epirus) and Macedonians, were thought of as barbarians until well into the classical period and later as Greeks.

When, in the wake of the great processes of → Hellenization, the outer boundaries of the Greek domain became unclear and under Roman rule the Greeks increasingly forfeited their independent political life, and when ultimately, as holders of the empire now reduced to the east, they felt themselves to be 'Romans', the name Hellenes gradually lost its classical meaning, especially as it was contaminated with the specific Jewish and Christian meaning of 'heathen'. The Greeks in the Byzantine and Ottoman empires were called *Rhōmaíoi* or *Rūmī*. The liberation and restoration movement from the 18th cent., with the revival of the names *Héllēnes* and *Hellás,* signified a return to the great traditions of antiquity.

W. WILL, H. KLEIN, s.v. Hellenen, RAC 14, 375–445 (with lit.).   F.GSCH.

[2] Wife of Gongylus of Eretria, mother of Gongylus III, in 399 BC gave Xenophon a hospitable reception in Pergamon on his return from Asia Minor (Xen. An. 7,8,8).

G. FOGAZZA, Sui Gongilidi di Eretria, in: PdP 27, 1972, 129f.   PE.HÖ.

Helle (Ἕλλη; *Héllē*). Daughter of → Athamas and → Nephele, fled with her brother → Phrixus on a golden ram from her stepmother Ino and drowned in the sea, which from then on has been called → Hellespont (Pind. fr. 189; Aesch. Pers. 69f.) (Apollod. 180–182; Ov. Fast. 3,851–876; Hyg. Fab. 1–3; her tomb on the Chersonesus: Hdt. 7,58,2). Valerius Flaccus (5,476ff.; 2,611) associates H. and Phrixus more closely with the → Argonauts, by making Athamas the son of → Cretheus, rather than his brother, and therefore Phrixus and H. his grandchildren; another of his inventions is that H. also appears to → Pelias in a dream and rises from the sea as a Nereid during the voyage of the Argo (1,50; 2,587ff. [1. 333ff.]). H. has perhaps come into mythology through the 'brother-and-sister' type of folk tale.

1 P. DRÄGER, Argo pasimelousa I, 1993.

PH. BRUNEAU, s.v. Phrixos et H., LIMC 7.1, 398–404; P. FRIEDLÄNDER, s.v. H., RE 8, 159–163; U. v. WILAMOWITZ-MOELLENDORF, Hell. Dichtung, ²1962, 2, 244 n. 1.   P.D.

Hellebic(h)us Bearer of a Germanic name; attested as *comes et magister utriusque militiae per Orientem* from AD 383 to 387; a proponent of euergetism in Antioch. Together with → Caesarius [3], in 387 conducted the investigations after the Antioch statue revolt. → Libanius thanked him with a panegyric for having achieved lenient actions (Or. 22). H. corresponded with Libanius (Ep. 2; 868; 884; 898; 925) and → Gregorius [3] of Nazianzus (Ep. 225). Probably a Christian [1]. (PLRE 1,277f.).

1 v. HAEHLING 265–267.   H.L.

Hellebore (ἐλλέβορος; *helléboros, helleborus*). The name refers to poisonous plants of various families: 1) the Ranunculacea *Helleborus L.* (ἐλλέβορος μέλας in Theophr. Hist. pl. 9,14,4, etc., = *H. cyclophyllus Boissier*, not *H. niger L.* (the Christmas rose); Dioscorides 4,162 WELLMANN = 4,149 BERENDES; Paus. 10,36,7). The root, in particular, (Plin. HN 25,48). 2), of the Liliacea *Veratrum album L.* (ἐλλέβορος λευκός, *Helleborus candidus*, white hellebore: Hippoc. De victu 1,35 [1. 292]; Theophr. Hist. pl. 9,10,1–4 with many local forms; Dioscorides 4,148 WELLMANN and BERENDES) was used as a laxative. This is a dietetic emetic and abortifacient, which is difficult to dose (Paus. 10,36,7). In Phocis Hercules is supposed to have been cured of madness with black hellebore. In spite of a poor description in Pliny (HN 13,114 and 27,76), the *helleborínē* or *epipaktís* of Dioscorides (4,108 WELLMANN = 4,107 BERENDES), applied internally to counteract poisons and liver complaints, is interpreted as the orchid species *Helleborine Miller* or the rupturewort *Herniaria glabra L.*

1 W. H. S. JONES (ed.), Hippocrates, De victu, vol. 4, 1931, repr. 1992, 292. C.HÜ.

Hellen (Ἕλλην; *Héllēn*). Eponymous progenitor of the Hellenes, therefore of the entirety of the inhabitants of Greece; the individual tribes took their names from H.'s sons and grandsons → Dorus, → Xuthus (father of → Ion and → Achaeus [1]) and → Aeolus [1]. → Pyrrha and either → Deucalion (Hes. fr. 2; schol. Hes. Op. 158a; Thuc. 1,3,12; Diod. Sic. 4,60,2) or Zeus (schol. Pl. Symp. 208d; Apollod. 1,49) are named as H.'s parents. In the Homeric catalogue of ships the Hellenes inhabit only a small region of Greece (Spercheus region); according to this the structure is a reflection of an older situation, whereas in post-Homeric documents the status of the 7th cent. BC (H. as forefather of *all* Greeks) is the basis.

→ Hellas

G. A. CADUFF, Ant. Sintflutsagen, 1986, 84–87; E. VISSER, Homers Katalog der Schiffe, 1997, 650–659. E.V.

Hellenica Oxyrhynchia Two series of papyrus fragments, both 2nd cent. AD.: P Oxy. 842 = PLond., year of discovery 1906, ed. by GRENFELL and HUNT (who called the anonymous author P. = Papyrus) and PSI 1304 = PFlor., year of discovery 1942, belonging to one and the same work of history from the first half of the 4th cent. BC and comprising a total of *c*. 20 pages of Greek history (with gaps!). There is also possibly another new fragment, cf. [1].

Contents: events in the Ionian-Decelean war (→ Decelea), particularly the naval battle of Notium in 407/6 (= PFlor.). Political atmosphere in Greece in 397/6, the naval war between Athenians under → Conon and Spartans, disputes between Thebes and Phocis (with an excursus on the administration of the Boeotian League)

and → Agesilaus' [2] campaigns in Asia Minor (= PLond.).

The Hellenica Oxyrhynchia form a valuable and independent parallel tradition to Xen. Hell. bks. 1 and 2, and via Ephorus form the basis of Diodorus' description in bks. 13 and 14. The author is close in time to the events described and works on the basis of autopsy and personal research. The presentation is objective and the style unpretentious, without direct speeches but with frequent excursus. The author, like Thucydides (quoted in ch. 2 of the PFlor.), arranges the work according to summers and winters and, like him, uses an epoch year, in other words 403/2 (= take-over of the hegemony by the Spartans). He accordingly continued Thucydides' work for the period from 411 until at least 395 and wrote after the King's Peace in 387/6 (cf. 11,2) and before the end of the Sacred War in 346 (13,3).

On the question of authorship, numerous studies have led to the following identifications: Ephorus (WALKER, GELZER), Theopompus (ED. MEYER, LAQUEUR, RUSCHENBUSCH, LEHMANN, REBUFFAT), Androtion (MOMIGLIANO, CANFORA), Daemachus (JACOBY), Cratippus (BREITENBACH, ACCAME, HARDING); exact literary references in [2. 65ff.].

However, the argument against this thesis is that Ephorus and Theopompus are not primary sources. Ephorus also writes *katá génos* ('according to subject areas'), furthermore, the author is not a universal historian. Style, ethos and presentation ought to rule out Theopompus. Neither was the author an Atthidographer: Androtion arranges his material by archons. The Boeotian local writer Daemachus is eliminated because the author shows no sympathy for the politics of Thebes (cf. 12,4–5, even though he had a good knowledge of Boeotia and the Boeotian League). Detailed knowledge of circumstances in Athens, sympathy for Conon and the close continuation of Thucydides suggest an Athenian author and – in line with what was stated above – someone who followed on from Thucydides. The most likely candidate is → Cratippus of Athens (FGrH 64), who was unjustly called by JACOBY a 'late fraud', but was actually an important historian: in particular the agreement of the list of contents and the basic tendency of Cratippus' work in Plutarch (Mor. 345C-E) with Ephorus in Diod. Sic. (bks. 13 and 14) makes this identification likely [cf. 3].

→ Cratippus (further bibliography)

1 G. A. LEHMANN, Ein neues Frg. der H.O., in: ZPE 26, 1977, 181–191 2 K. MEISTER, Die griech. Geschichtsschreibung, 1990 3 S. ACCAME, Ricerche sulle Elleniche di Ossirinco, in: Miscellanea greca e romana 6, 1978, 125–183.

FRAGMENTS: FGrH 66; M. CHAMBERS (ed.), H.O., 1993 (after V. BARTOLETTI, 1959); P. R. MCKECHNIE, S. J. KERN (ed., transl., comm.), H.O., 1988; J. A. BRUCE, A Historical Commentary on the H.O., 1967.
BIBLIOGRAPHY: G. BONAMENTE, Studi sulle Elleniche di Ossirinco, 1973; H. R. BREITENBACH, s.v. H.O., RE Suppl. 12, 383–426 (fundamental); P. HARDING, The Authorship of the H.O., in: The Ancient History Bull. 1,

1987, 101–110; E. REBUFFAT, Teopompo e le Elleniche di Ossirinco, in: Orpheus 14, 1993, 109–124.   K.MEI.

Hellenism (hellēnismós).

In antiquity from the time of Aristotle or his pupil → Theophrastus, this was the name for the correct use of the Greek language (hellēnízein = 'speaking Greek'), but it is not attested as a term until the 2nd cent. BC (2 Macc 4,13) and there designates the Greek way of life, disapproved of from a Jewish point of view. Based on the meaning of Hellenism, originating among Alexandrian scholars at almost the same time, as 'Greek spiritual world', Christian writers then use Hellenism in the sense of 'paganism' and in late antiquity also to designate heretical trends within Christianity [1. 5–22] (→ Heresy). Hellenism is not found in antiquity as the name for a chronologically distinguishable historical epoch.

Since the 17th cent. the adjective 'Hellenistic' has designated the particular language, interspersed with non-Greek elements, of Biblical Greek, but the noun Hellenism until well into the 19th cent. designated the Greek way of life and spiritual world as an expression of the Greek 'genius'. 'Hellenism' has survived in this meaning to the present day in French, whereas in the Anglo-Saxon language area intense preoccupation with Greek language and culture is also referred to as Hellenism ('Hellenist' as a term for 'Greek scholar').

As well as this, starting from Germany under the influence of the work of J. G. DROYSEN [2] and his successors, the term Hellenism took on the nature of a term for an epoch. The decisive criterion for qualification of the period approximately between Alexander the Great and Augustus as a historical epoch is for DROYSEN the fusing of Greek civilization with the culture of oriental peoples (with clear dominance of Greek), which finally made possible the development of Christianity. However, as the term Hellenism in DROYSEN is also characterized by other criteria (for instance the development of the rational spirit within Greek civilization or the change in political structure of the Greeks by the 'Hellenistic monarchy'), obvious chronological and spatial restriction of Hellenism resulting from DROYSEN is not possible, especially as on the one hand he has Hellenism starting with Alexander only in the 2nd edition [3] and in a large-scale plan of a history of Hellenism intends to go as far as the beginnings of Islam [1. 91f.], and on the other hand has in mind in his definition of Hellenism the eastern Mediterranean and the Near East, but also involves Carthage, Sicily and Rome in his representation. The still customary restriction of Hellenism from Alexander (334 BC) to Augustus is therefore based on a thoroughly well-founded convention [4. 1–3, 129–131], which, at the moment, though, is often deconstructed with equally good reasons (beginning of 360 BC: [5. 299]). More recently there is a strong tendency to let the epoch of Hellenism start only after the death of Alexander in 323 BC (for instance [6], [7], [8], [9]). The end of Hellenism (contrary to DROYSEN, who ultimately wanted to go as far as Caesar [1. 91f.]), is

today almost universally equated with the victory of Augustus over Antony and Cleopatra at Actium (31 BC) or the amalgamation of Egypt into the Roman empire (30 BC).

→ Periods, division into; → EPOCHS, CONCEPTS OF; → HELLENISM

1 R. BICHLER, "H.", 1983   2 J. G. DROYSEN, Gesch. des H. 1. Theil, Gesch. der Nachfolger Alexanders, 1836   3 Id., Gesch. des H., 1. Theil, Gesch. Alexanders d. Gr., ²1877   4 H. J. GEHRKE, Gesch. des H., 1990   5 H. BENGTSON, Griech. Gesch., ⁵1977   6 C. PRÉAUX, Le monde hellénistique, 1978   7 WILL   8 CAH 7.1, 1984   9 P. GREEN, From Alexander to Actium, 1990.   W.ED.

Hellenistic poetry

A. GENERAL   B. DRAMATIC POETRY   C. SATIRICAL AND IAMBIC POETRY   D. HEXAMETER AND ELEGIAC DISTICH

A. GENERAL

From the period between Alexander's death in 323 BC and Octavian's victory over Cleopatra in 31 BC, Greek poetry is characterized by a great variety of themes and a deep richness of forms. Unfortunately, only very little is known of the poetry of the late 2nd and early 1st cents. BC that must have been so important for the Roman → Neoteric poets. While the 5th cent. was dominated by Attic comedy and tragedy, other regions produced significant poetry, as early as the 4th cent., especially in the Aegean and in the East (→ Antimachus [3] of Colophon, → Erinna, → Philitas), whose works anticipated important milestones of Hellenistic poetry (HP) and to a large extent stood more in the Ionian than in the Attic tradition. Changes in the political situation in the 4th and 3rd cents. led to the concentration of great power in the hands of a few significant ruling houses (the Ptolemies in Alexandria, the Antigonids in Pella, the Seleucids in Antioch) and thus also to a pronounced system of patronage. A large proportion of HP is linked to one or other of these courts (→ Hellenistic states; → Court).

The first Ptolemies created institutions in which philosophical scholarship could develop (the → Mouseion, the royal → Library), and Antiochus III followed suit. A few poets were significant scholars as well (→ Aratus [4], → Callimachus, → Eratosthenes [2], → Euphorion [3], → Philitas), and this was reflected in their poetry (→ Philology). Far more important, however, is the fact that the circulation of texts in book form, the separation of poetic texts from the context of (stage) performance for which they had been originally intended (cf. below), and the gradual separation of an elite from popular culture, all led to poets writing for a reading public. The nature of poetry was strongly shaped by that process. The origin of → books of poetry, which were later to become so important for Roman poets, probably dates back to the 3rd cent. The fact that there was so much continuing interest in reworkings of earlier works, especially Homer's, and in

the history and aetiology of Greek cults and institutions, does not simply illustrate the scholarship of Hellenistic poets but also reflects their interest in the continuity of Greek cultural heritage. It also expresses the
acknowledgement of a break and a turning-point.

B. Dramatic poetry

Tragedies and satyr plays continued to be written
and the Dionysiac *technitai* ('Artisans of Dionysus')
staged plays throughout the Greek world. Both genres
flourished in Alexandria (at least some tragic poets of
the so-called 'Pleiad' wrote there), but many tragedies
were probably written just for publication (and in that
perhaps already point the way to → Seneca). Traditional but also less conventional themes were treated, including contemporary history, but in staging and costume tragedy continued to separate itself from other
dramatic forms and moved further away from them.
Even when it comes to metre, the avoidance of resolution in iambic trimeter marks tragedy as remote from
colloquial speech (so also → Lycophron's 'Alexandra').
Comedy spread beyond Athens and became an important element in Hellenistic culture. New Comedy, the
greatest writers of which were → Menander, → Diphilus and → Philemon, treated the private lives of well-to-
do citizens and their dependents. It was no longer
bound up with public life in Athens, as had been the
case with Old Comedy. It was almost entirely spoken;
the → Chorus no longer played any role in the play itself
but simply marked the division into five acts. The moralizing aspect of New Comedy probably influenced
popular ethics in the Hellenistic period.

Tragedy, like comedy, influenced other poetic forms
that were not strictly dramatic. Lycophron's 'Alexandra' is a long account to Priam of Cassandra's prophecies, Machon's *Chreíai* is an iambic version of anecdotal literature, which was very widespread in the 4th
cent. The folk tradition of the → *mimos* was especially
important; only scanty papyrus fragments of the
'scripts' of these often obscene presentations have survived. Literary adaptations of these vernacular forms
can be seen in → Theocritus (Eidyllia 2; 3; 14; 15) and in
the choliambic mimiambs of → Hero(n)das.

C. Satirical and iambic poetry

The aggressive tradition of the archaic iambus and
Attic Old Comedy were continued in a remarkable
range of poetic forms. In his mixed collection of 13
iambic and lyrical *Íamboi*,→ Callimachus, like Herodas, took Hipponax as his point of reference. In his
learned *Sílloi* ('squinting verses') in hexameters,
→ Timon poked fun at the zeal and ambition of philosophers. Apart from → Sotades of Maronea, mockery of
powerful political figures was rarely expressed in
formal verse. The moralizing character of HP can also
be noted in the 'cynical' *Melíamboi* of → Cercidas of
Megalopolis (short lyrical poems denouncing greed and
presumption) and the choliambs of → Phoenix of Colophon.

D. Hexameter and elegiac distich

The domination of the so-called epic as a metric
form (by which is meant both the hexameter and the
elegiac distich) is one of the most striking features of
Hellenistic literature. The heroic-monumental epic in
the Homeric tradition lives on, although it was modified, in form and content (including the concept of heroism), from at least as early as → Apollonius [2] Rhodius
and possibly from the time of → Rhianus. Nothing can
be said, however, about the mythological epics of some
other authors who are difficult to date, and by the same
token we cannot simply assume that their works had
monumental dimensions to them. The historical or
mythological-historical → epic flourished in the Hellenistic period, as did the encomiastic epic. It is difficult to
assess how substantial the encomiastic 'epics' were, but
the better-known of these are all very short and are at
most the size of archaic hymns (to which tradition they
are linked).

The Hellenistic hexameter hymns, like Callimachus'
hymns and Theocritus' 22, contain a stronger aetiological component than the 'Homeric' hymns, even
though the latter had placed more emphasis on → aetiology than any other genre of archaic poetry. The strong
mimetic component particularly evident in Callim. H.
2, 5 and 6 perhaps plays out a possibility in hexametrical form that the lyrical → hymn and other hieratical
lyrical genres had already practised extensively. Other
Hellenistic hymns that were actually intended for sacral
functions preserve the lyric metres of the archaic hieratic hymns (→ Aristonus [4] of Corinth, → Isyllus of
Epidaurus, Philodamus of Scarphea). By contrast, the
hymns of → Philicus of Corcyra and → Castorion of Soli
experiment – quite explicitly (SH 310,3 and 677) – with
metre.

The didactic epic of Hellenism can at times make
universalistic claims, even in the Hesiodic tradition
(→ Aratus [4]), but generally selects very technical subjects in which the author does not necessarily have to be
competent (for the most part he merely puts into verse
manuals already available in prose. There are poems
about astronomy: → Aratus [4]; paradoxography: Philostephanus of Cyrene and Archelaus of Chersonesus;
geography: Callimachus the Younger; fishing: → Numenius of Heraclea, → Nicander; agriculture and apiculture: Nicander; medicine: Aratus, Heliodorus of
Athens, Philo of Tarsus. The metric innovation of a
didactic poem (→ Didactic poetry) in iambic trimeters
seems to originate with Apollodorus [7] of Athens
(chronography) and to have established itself especially
between the 2nd and 1st cents. BC. in works of descriptive geography (Scymnus, Dionysius [26], son of Calli-
phon; Apollodorus).

Mythological catalogues in hexameters go back at
least to → Hesiod ('Catalogue of women'); Antimachus
[3] (*Lýdē*), for one, had composed some in elegiac form.
The *Aítia* of Callimachus, for example, select from the
preceding mythological tradition (from that of 4th-
cent. local historians writing in prose much more than

from that of earlier poets) precisely the aspect (aetiology) and quality ('small' myths) most likely to appeal to the new aesthetic taste. → Hermesianax' poem *Leóntion* and the catalogue of women of Nicaenetus of Samos represent mythological love stories in the Hesiodic tradition – but also, at least in the case of Hermesianax, love stories of historical figures like Socrates; other novelties are the *Érōtes è kaloí* ('love stories or handsome boys') of → Phanocles and the *Ehoíoi* of Sostratus or Sosicrates of Phanagorea, which treat mythological stories of homosexual love. *Araí* ('curses'; → *defixiones*; cf. Moiro, papyrus Brux. II,22; Call. *Íbis*; Euphorion of Chalcis, *Poterioklépt̄es*/'cup-thief', *Chiliádes*) are a specific form of catalogue.

At the heart of even the bucolic poetry (→ Bucolics) of → Theocritus there is a mindset of primitive escapism and an idealization of rustic life that may have some connection with everyday life in the new urban reality.

In terms of the *Iliad-Odyssey* epic tradition, the → epyllion is an innovation but has precursors in the ps.-Hesiodic *Aspís* and the narrative core of the archaic epic in hymnal or catalogue form.

→ Catalogue B. Poetry; → Comedy; → Didactic poetry; → Epic; → Hellenism; → Literary activity; → Satyr play; → Tragedy

P.BING, The Well-Read Muse: Present and Past in Callimachus and the Hellenistic Poets, 1988; A.CAMERON, Callimachus and his Critics, 1995; G.CAMBIANO, L.CANFORA, D.LANZA (ed.), Lo spazio letterario della Grecia antica, 1.2, 1993; B.EFFE, Dichtung und Lehre: Unt. zur Typologie des ant. Lehrgedichts, 1977; P.M.FRASER, Ptolemaic Alexandria, 1972; R.HUNTER, The New Comedy of Greece and Rome, 1985; Id., Theocritus and the Archaeology of Greek Poetry, 1996; G.O.HUTCHINSON, Hellenistic Poetry, 1988; R.KASSEL, Die Abgrenzung des Hell. in der griech. Literaturgesch., 1987; A.KÖRTE, P.HÄNDEL, Die hell. Dichtung, ²1960; F.SUSEMIHL, Gesch. der griech. Lit. in der Alexandrinerzeit, 1891–92; G.WEBER, Dichtung und höfische Ges., 1993; U. VON WILAMOWITZ-MOELLENDORFF, Hell. Dichtung in der Zeit des Kallimachos, 1924; K.ZIEGLER, Das hell. Epos, ²1966 (Ital. transl. 1988, with an overview of the testimonia on the Epici minores); G.ZANKER, Realism in Alexandrian Poetry, 1987.　　　　　M.FA. and R.HU.

Hellenistic politics see → Hellenistic states

Hellenistic states
A. HISTORICAL DEVELOPMENT　B. INTER-STATE
RELATIONS　C. INTRA-STATE ORGANIZATION

A. HISTORICAL DEVELOPMENT
Hellenistic states (HS) evolved from the collapse of → Alexander [4] the Great's empire in the eastern Mediterranean and Near Asia, and from the imitation by individual rulers in Sicily and southern Italy (→ Agathocles [2], → Hieron [2] II) of Hellenistic government and administrative institutions. After the death of the 32–year old Alexander, who left behind no heirs competent to govern nor any solid imperial administration,

the empire's unity was at risk: its component parts were linked exclusively to the person of Alexander (King of the Macedonians, leader of the → Corinthian League, Great King of the Persians, Pharaoh in Egypt), and with him there had developed a new legitimization of the Hellenistic kingdom, founded on conquest ('acquisition at the point of a spear'), that was soon employed by his generals, too. In the period of the → Wars of the Diadochi independent royal dynasties had been establishing themselves from 305 BC in Egypt (Ptolemy), Thrace and Asia Minor (Lysimachus) as well as in northern Syria and Babylonia (Seleucus), were confirmed after the death of Antigonus [1] in the battle of Ipsus (301 BC) and finally consolidated after the defeat of Lysimachus (at Curupedion, in 281). When after decades of chaos Antigonus [2] Gonatas was able to establish himself in Macedonia in 276, following a defensive victory over the Celts, the fragmentation of the Alexandrian empire essentially came to an end and only minor changes took place over the next 200 years or so:

a) the kingdom of the Ptolemies (Lagids; → Ptolemaeus), with Egypt at its heart (centre: → Alexandria) and extensive (but fluctuating) external possessions in Cyrene, Syria Coele and Palestine, Cyprus, the Aegean and western Asia Minor. Despite strong Roman influence from the beginning of the 2nd cent. BC, the kingdom remained independent even after the loss of its external possessions. After Octavian's (→ Augustus) victory over Antony [I 9] and Cleopatra in 30 BC it was incorporated into the Roman Empire as a 'personal province' of the emperor's.

b) the kingdom of the → Seleucids, with northern Syria and Babylonia at its heart (several centres: e.g. Antioch on the Orontes, Sardis, Seleucea on the Tigris) and a heavily fluctuating territory that around 303 extended from the eastern edge of the Mediterranean to India. From the middle of the 3rd cent. it steadily declined in size, with the loss of Bactria, the growing power of the Parthians, conflict within the dynasty and wars with Egypt and Rome. From 129 it was limited to northern Syria. In 63 BC it was turned into the Roman province of Syria by Pompey.

c) the kingdom of the Antigonids (→ Antigonus), in the old heartland of Macedonia (centre: Pella) with Thrace, Thessaly and parts of Greece that from the start had to fight off incursions into Greece by the Ptolemies and later the Seleucids. By a policy of restraint toward the Greek *poleis* that were intent on autonomy, coupled with military pressure applied from 'the shackles of Greece' Demetrias, Chalcis, and Corinth, the Antigonids succeeded in holding on to their kingdom, despite expansionist efforts by Sparta (→ Agis [4]) and the Achaean and Aetolian Leagues. After three Macedonian wars it was broken up by the Romans in 168 BC (→ Perseus) and the territory became the Roman province of Macedonia in 148.

d) As well as those three great monarchies, there arose in the 3rd cent., principally at the expense of the Seleucids, a number of sometimes short-lived autocratic

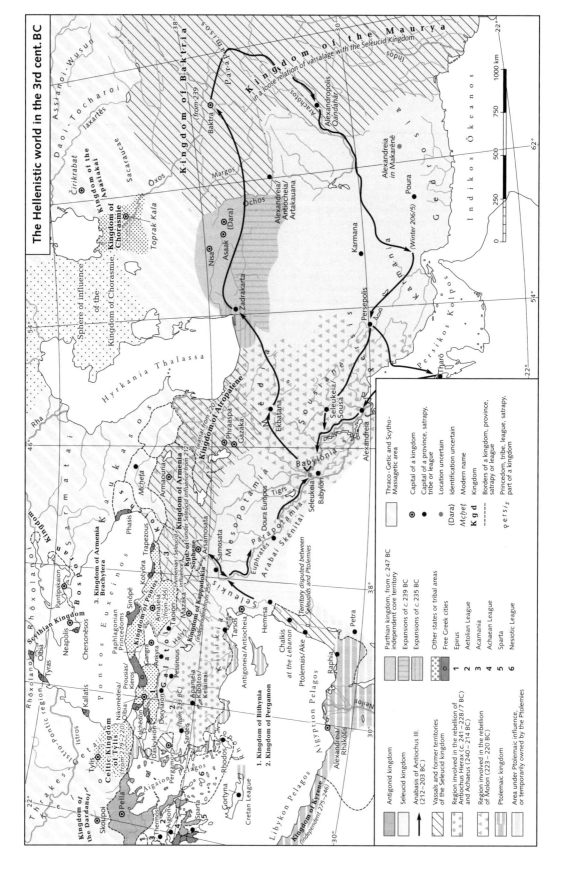

The Hellenistic world in the 3rd cent. BC

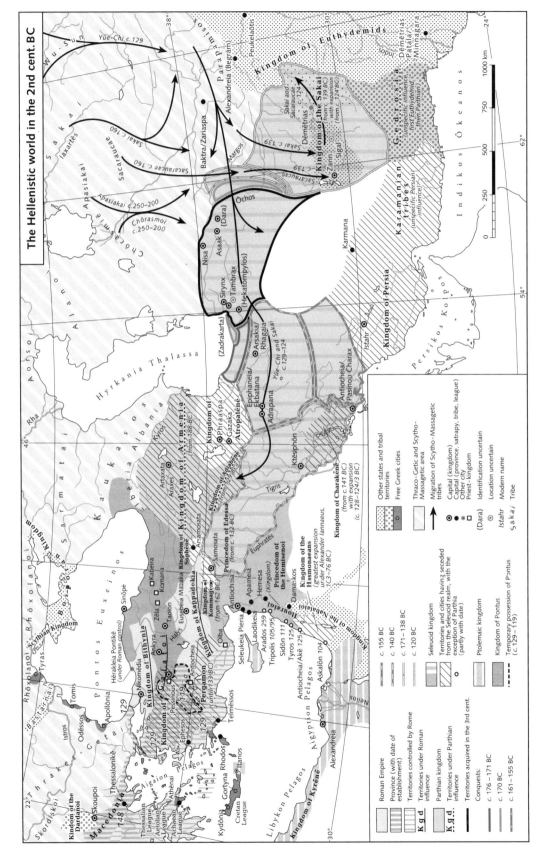

The Hellenistic world in the 2nd cent. BC

regimes (Antiochus Hierax and Achaeus [5] in Asia Minor; Molon in Iran), but also enduring dynasties as in Bithynia (Zipoetes, from 297), the Pontus (Mithridates, from 297/281) or Cappadocia (Ariarathes, from c. 255). The most significant of these dynasties was that of the Attalids of Pergamum: in the civil war between Seleucus II and Antiochus Hierax, → Attalus [4] I assumed the kingly title after defeating the Galatians, who were allied to Hierax, and extended his territory to the Taurus. Despite some territorial setbacks, good relations with Rome made the Attalid kingdom the greatest power in Asia Minor from 188 BC (peace of Apamea), until Attalus III bequeathed it to the Romans in his will in 133 BC.

B. INTER-STATE RELATIONS

Relations between the larger Hellenistic states were determined by the specific legitimation of the Hellenistic monarchy that Alexander had helped shape, based on personal (military and organizational) achievement and requiring constant demonstration of success (→ Basileus E.). Despite the practice of dynastic marriages between the royal houses, as well as individual treaties and territorial agreements, no state 'system' based on constitutional relationships evolved. The individual monarch was instead forced to expand continuously, with the ultimate goal of universal monarchy. Stability depended solely on the individual ruler's inability to conquer any of the others' territories by himself. This urge to expand lay behind the attempt by Lysimachus to set out against Macedonia, and behind the anti-Ptolemaic alliances of the Seleucid Antiochus [2] I with Antigonus Gonatas and Magas of Cyrene. Even the 'Syrian wars' (280–253) of Ptolemy II, extending far beyond Syria, against the Seleucids and his policy of 'liberation' in Greece that was aimed against Antigonus (→ Chremonidean War), have hegemonic features in common with the Asian campaign of Ptolemy III (246/45) during the 'Laodicean War' (3rd Syrian War) and especially the 'Anabasis' of Antiochus [5] III into eastern Iran, his efforts to realign the boundaries in Syria Coele, Asia Minor and Thrace, and his invasion of Greece. The latter resulted in Rome's massive incursion into the HS and, with it, the effective end of any independent policy on the part of a Hellenistic monarchy.

C. INTRA-STATE ORGANIZATION

As the political and ethnic diversity of Alexander's empire continued in the HS, there arose quite differing tasks of administration and government. In the Antigonid kingdom with its very homogeneous population the king had to respect the basic, traditional customary rights of the people, especially of the army and the aristocracy. He thus never acquired the same level of power as the Ptolemies, Seleucids and Attalids, whose word was law. In their case the king embodied the State, whose affairs were regarded as his 'concern' (ta prágmata). As the very idea of including local authorities in the conduct of the State perished with Alexander, a thin upper stratum of Macedonians and Greeks who enjoyed the king's confidence was formed in Asia and Egypt (→ Court; → Court titles; → Hellenization). This functional élite was – not least in order to avoid communication problems – grafted on top of the lower level of the existing system of administration (particularly evident in Egypt but also attested amongst the Seleucids and Attalids), so that the duties involved in collecting new taxes and traditional tributes were performed by locals.

Although Hellenistic kings regarded the country as their own private property and (generally) passed it on to their eldest sons, they did not much intervene nor did they pursue any deliberate policy of → Hellenization. In allocating estates to high officials, in settling cleruch farmers (in Egypt) or in establishing new cities (in the case of the Seleucids), they used old domain land or newly developed regions and even respected the rights of temples and temple states. Not until the 2nd cent. BC, when financial pressures led to the seizure of temple treasures, were there any significant tensions contributing to an erosion of royal authority and thus to the internal weakening of the monarchies. Special relationships existed with Greek cities within their territories and beyond, as these formed a recruiting pool for the highest levels of administration and for the mercenary armies that were used in all Hellenistic monarchies.

As self-contained, self-administering bodies, the poleis fulfilled subsidiary tasks of administration, particularly in the Seleucid empire, which conducted its policy of founding new cities with Greek settlers for more than just military reasons. The kings observed the autonomy of the cities, acted as benefactors (→ Euergetes) and were in return elevated to the cult rank of a divinely protected person. The real patterns of power were revealed only in the case of conflict. This 'balance' between monarchy and polis was promoted by an increasing 'plutocratization' of the poleis, whose wealthiest citizens took over the highest offices of the city and, as royal confidants, were frequently able to gain privileges for 'their' city. With some justification we can speak of a second phase of prosperity of the polis; it survived the decline of the HS and played an important political, economic and cultural role until late antiquity.

→ Diadochi; → Hellenization; → Hellenism

BIBLIOGRAPHY: → Hellenism; Hellenization I.   W.ED.

MAPS: H. WALDMANN, Die hell. Staatenwelt im 3. Jh. v.Chr., TAVO B V 3, 1983; Id., Die hell. Staatenwelt im 2. Jh. v.Chr., TAVO B V 4, 1985.

Hellenization
I. HISTORY II. LANGUAGE

I. HISTORY
A. TERM B. HISTORICAL DEVELOPMENT C. ART AND ARCHITECTURE D. SUMMARY

A. TERM

Hellenization is understood here to be a complex acculturation phenomenon composed of different processes operating on several levels. In addition to the area of language and literature, Greek ideas and forms of expression were also adopted in architecture, fine arts, as well as in religion and cult; non-Greek patterns of sociopolitical organization were also adapted to fit the Greek model (polis state, forms of organizations and associations, → gymnasium). All of these changes often had wide-reaching effects on the cultural and ethnic identity of the societies involved. Hellenization led, in various degrees, to a break with the past. We must differentiate however not only between the cultures, but also according to the social groups within each culture area. Special cases of Hellenization were those societies in which the indigenous cultural patterns determined to a large extent what would be taken from Greek cultural skills as usable for their own purposes, or without risk to their own identity, including Rome, the Jews, Parthian-Sassanid Iran, and Carthage, where despite extensive Hellenization processes the native identity could survive in an unbroken line of tradition, altered certainly but also strengthened. Recourse to a – real or idealized – pre-Greek past here consciously served also as the demarcation from the encroaching Greek culture.

We will consider here those cultural spaces, primarily in the eastern Mediterranean and Near East, which in the period between the campaign of Alexander and the Arab-Islamic conquest, were under the political control of Greek or other power centres culturally and mentally close to Hellenism and came under the lasting rule of Rome. There is also a question of the causes and factors of the acculturation processes, whether they can be explained by the characteristics of Greek culture itself, by the native desire for self-Hellenization, or even by pressure from Greek or philhellenic power elites. There are two points of view: Greek culture itself was a historically variable quantity, that is in describing Hellenization, the yard-stick does not remain the same. Moreover, with the Imperial period two additional acculturation processes, → Romanization and Christianization, began, overlapping with Hellenization, sometimes furthering and sometimes hindering it.

B. HISTORICAL DEVELOPMENT
1. PRE-HELLENISTIC PERIOD 2. HELLENISM
3. IMPERIAL PERIOD 4. LATE ANTIQUITY

1. PRE-HELLENISTIC PERIOD

With the exception of Etruria, the cultural spread of the early Greek colonies was primarily limited to the immediate hinterland. Only from the 5th cent. BC were Greek cultural skills and specialists in greater demand with non-Greeks (artistic styles, coinage, military technology with Persians, Phoenicians, Etruscans and others). Further-reaching consequences arose in the course of the 4th cent. in some coastal regions of Asia Minor (Caria, Lycia, Pamphylia). In addition to the adoption of Greek art and architecture, the transformation of native settlement centres and political units according to the pattern of the Greek community state (→ polis) began there. In Caria the philhellene princes of the Hecatomnid dynasty (primarily → Maussollus, 377–353 BC) played a leading role. In Lycia and Pamphylia the initiative probably came more from the political communities themselves. A similar process occurred in the west with the Siculi in Sicily. The northern provinces of Macedonia and Epirus represented a borderline case: despite their great closeness to Greek civilization, their inhabitants could be categorized as 'barbarians', particularly because of the different political and social structures (central role of the kingship and its aristocratic followers). At first, only the ruling families demanded recognition of their Greek identity and massively adopted elements of Greek culture. Another special case was Cyprus, where Greeks and Phoenicians settled next to and influenced one another. The role of the city princedoms in Cypriot poleis, which for Greek history were uncommonly stable, can hardly be explained without reference to the close contact with their Phoenician neighbours.

2. HELLENISM

As a result of Alexander's campaign (→ Alexander [4], with map) and the wars of the → Diadochi, numerous Greeks and Macedonians reached the more remote areas of non-Greek population and culture for the first time. The new arrivals occupied the core of the power apparatus of the developing Hellenistic monarchies in the army and administration, served the interests of the administration as businessmen, merchants, artists and craftsmen, or satisfied the needs of their countrymen in strange surroundings. The Macedonian rulers themselves organized their more immediate environment, court society, according to their native pattern as entourage (→ *hetairía*, → *hetaíroi*; → court) with the associated forms of expression (e.g. symposium, → banquet). Alexander's attempt to use as a model the structures of the Persian court, which more strongly marked the king off from his surroundings, found no imitators. The main concentrations of the Graeco-Macedonian settlement were Lydia, Caria, parts of Phrygia and Cilicia, in the Levant, northern Syria (so-called → 'Tetrapolis': Antioch [1], Seleucea, Apamea [3], and Laodicea) and the area of the later → Dekapolis in Trans-Jordan, in the east of the northwestern Iranian area in the hinterland of the metropolis Seleucia on the Tigris, in Egyptian Alexandria and the middle Egyptian → Faiyum. In the Seleucid area, the closed settlement dominated in poleis or polis-like military settlements (→ *kátoikos*), while in Ptolemaic Egypt, the military set-

tlers (→ *klêroûchoi*) often established themselves within native villages.

The Hellenization potential, which grew considerably owing to all these precedents, remained, however,
mostly unexploited in the proper Hellenistic epoch.
Two factors acted as obstacles: on the one hand, the
rulers themselves had only limited interest in promoting
Hellenizing processes among the native populations,
and showed little readiness to accept assimilated people
as new social climbers with equal rights in the ethnically
and culturally restricted power elite. This was particularly true in the 3rd cent. BC, but remained crucial up to
the time of Roman rule. The number of leading men of
non-Greek origin close to the kings (particularly Iranians) declined sharply after the first decades. At the lower level, it was the natives close to the Greek and Macedonian settlers who were mostly tied to those of private
means in a clearly hierarchical manner; acceptance into
the privileged society was at first difficult.

The lack of promotion of Hellenization corresponded, on the other hand, to the targeted support of traditional native organization forms and cultural patterns
by the middle and lower levels of the government. As a
result it was unnecessary for the local elite to assimilate
to the culture of the new rulers in order to keep power.
The backdrop to this was the existing organizational
structure, primarily in the Persian tradition, of the Hellenistic kingdoms. As before, the greatest part of the
government was, in regionally varying concentrations,
under the control of royal officials. The lowest level was
local units of native character, which could be dependent on the centre to varying degrees: individual village
communities or groups, 'private' and royal domains,
temple principalities, tribally organized mountain peoples, in Palestine the Jewish Temple state under the leadership of the high priests, the Phoenician city states
under the leadership of their kings and aristocracies,
and in Babylonia the cities jointly led by the priesthood,
community assembly and native city leaders. The Graeco-Macedonian settlements, together with the surrounding areas directly under their control, merely
formed pockets within a different territorial structure.
They were, therefore, not the only administrative and
organizational centres, rather they probably served primarily as supply and recruitment bases for the core
areas of the royal governing apparatus.

Symptomatic of the limitations of Hellenization is
the relatively low number of native communities without a core of Greek settlers which during the course of
Hellenism became poleis or were confirmed in this status. The behaviour of → Antiochus [6] IV Epiphanes
(175–164 BC), which was contrary to this rule, is attributable to fiscal interests rather than to a cultural sense
of mission. His policy aimed at the conversion of Jewish
worship can probably only be understood in terms of
the specific local context. It was primarily non-Greek,
'philhellenically' oriented princes who converted native
communities into Greek poleis: the Bithynian and Cappadocian kings, the kings of Commagene, and at the

end of the epoch the Jewish rulers of the Herodian dynasty (→ Herod). Greek culture served here as a status
symbol, in order to be able to rise to the level of the
Macedonian rulers.

Besides this, there was active self-Hellenization by
native populations in those areas of western, southwestern, and southern Asia Minor where these changes
had already begun before the Hellenistic era: in Caria,
Lycia, and Pamphylia the process of polis formation
was completed; Greek culture conquered new territory
only in parts of Lydia and Pisidia. In the Levant, the
Phoenician city states distinguished themselves: in the
1st half of the 3rd cent. the old city kingdoms came to
an end, followed at first by an organizational form in
the native tradition under the leadership of *shophetim*
('judges'). Characteristically, the Phoenician cities
finally became poleis at the time of the decline of the
Seleucid kingdom, after the middle of the 2nd cent. BC.
As proof of the new ethnic and cultural alignment came
the participation of the citizens in the Greek → festival
culture and the interpretation of their own prehistory
within Greek mythology (myth of → Cadmus). The
same is true for the Phoenicians in Cyprus, where, on
the other hand, the Greeks joined the mainstream of
Greek cultural development (e.g. the abandonment of
the city principalities and the old syllabic script, → Cy-
pro-Minoan scripts). The growing mercantile orientation of the Phoenicians in the Aegean area appears to
have been a central factor in these transformations. In
this way, the urban centres of the Levantine coast, together with the afore-mentioned parts of Asia Minor
and the regions of early Hellenic settlement listed
above, became new centres of Greekness, in addition to
the old Greek settlement areas, just like the inhabitants
of Epirus and Macedonia, who were now indisputably
regarded as Greeks and were living in poleis.

However, such a comprehensive form of Hellenization, with its consequences for the local identity, remained the exception until the arrival of Rome in the
East. Particularly in Babylonia, Egypt, and Judaea, the
native cultural, religious, and political traditions continued only slightly altered. These regions also offer the
clearest example of continuous native literacy and literary production in the vernacular.

3. IMPERIAL PERIOD

A) ADMINISTRATION

With the spread of the Roman provincial system in
the eastern Mediterranean from the last third of the
2nd cent. BC, it was in fact a non-Greek power which
eliminated previous hindrances to more extensive Hellenization. The new supremacy of Rome had itself
emerged from a communal state and in the Imperial
period remained in some respects marked by this tradition. Emperor, Senate, and governor were accustomed to dealing with local Italian units, which were
limited to an urban centre and its surroundings, constituted by a citizen community led by a city-dwelling
land-owning elite analogous to the Roman senatorial

aristocracy. In the east this expectation corresponded best to a Greek polis. In addition, the Romans were familiar with a series of central Greek cultural patterns which they themselves had adapted and considered their own. The Republic had dissolved the intermediate levels of royal territorial administration in the areas that they had annexed, or allowed them to decline. The Roman governor was therefore in direct contact with the local units of the cities, tribes, sanctuaries, and villages which were subordinate to him. Furthermore, a possible unification of the organization of these units according to the familiar model of the polis also had practical advantages. To this structurally necessary, increased goodwill of the new power towards native desires for Hellenization corresponded a growing interest precisely among the local elites. On the one hand, Rome's fixation on the polis model and the associated forms of communication brought about an increased effort to achieve this legal status, because the subjects wanted the best possible contact with their rulers. On the other hand, from the last third of the 1st cent. AD members of the local upper classes in the east were also being accepted in greater numbers into the imperial aristocracy of the senatorial and equestrian classes, for which Greek culture and education became an admission ticket.

Through this combination of promotion from above and desire for self-Hellenization by the provincials, a process of fundamental territorial and structural transformation was set in motion. At its end in the early 4th cent. AD the eastern part of the Roman empire consisted primarily of polis territories, now forming a continuous administrative network, with between them isolated imperial domains, private estates and village communities directly subject to the governor. The situation of Hellenization had therefore reversed. Only in Egypt was the Ptolemaic tradition of royal administration reaching down as far as the villages continued. However, the organization of the capitals of the Egyptian districts (*nomoi*) was increasingly aligned with the image of the Greek polis, until in the 4th cent. the situation even here was not much different from that of other regions of the empire.

B) CULTURE

These administrative and political changes were the framework and prerequisite for further-reaching cultural and mental processes. The spread of the polis organization brought extensive Hellenization of the local elites; with that the 'high-cultural' variants of the respective regional cultures broke down: the central sanctuaries were 'rededicated' according to the → *interpretatio Graeca*, Greek art and architecture were the model, literary production now occurred only in Greek and in Greek forms. Foundation myths giving each city a 'Greek' pre-history were acquired. In addition, communication between the elite and ordinary people changed (→ Euergetism, festival culture, → theatre and → spectacles, → rhetoric). Even the rural population was affected: although in many places the pre-Greek

traditions of the folk culture survived, particularly in a religious context, and the native colloquial language continued to dominate in extensive regions, nevertheless from the beginning of the Imperial period Greek forms of community increasingly found their way into the villages. Particularly in Syria and Asia Minor, village communities were often composed according to the pattern of the polis, with their own treasuries and council and a founding upper class. In many rural areas, a culture of Greek inscriptions appeared, associated with a new monumentalizing rural architecture on the model of Greek forms. An unbroken continuation of pre-Greek traditions was no longer possible.

C) EXCEPTIONS

A partial exception – apart from Judaism – is again Egypt, where in many temples the old cult traditions were maintained, and priests and scribes kept producing literature in the demotic script and Egyptian language into the 3rd cent. AD. An interesting departure is represented by the cultures which arose in the border regions of the Syrian-Mesopotamian desert steppe after the end of the 2nd cent. BC (→ Nabataei, → Palmyra, → Edessa, → Hatra). They are each distinguished by their own individual synthesis of Greek and non-Greek elements, as well as by written Aramaic. However, this is not simply a matter of continuation of old traditions, but of new developments, the results of the increasing settlement of nomadic population groups on the edges of the civilized world. As a result, these groups found themselves simultaneously in the area of influence of the peasant folk cultures of their long-settled neighbours and in that of the Hellenized centres.

D) ROMANIZED HELLENISM

Besides Hellenization, in the east there was also to some extent the phenomenon of Romanization. The influence of the few Roman settlement colonies was limited – their Roman/Latin character did not survive the 3rd cent. – however, the Roman cultural patterns increasingly flowed in indirectly. It was the rise of members of the urban elites into the imperial aristocracy which resulted in a convergence of the Greek and Roman urban cultures (construction forms and technologies, clientele structures, name forms, loan-words from Latin, gladiatorial games and animal hunts, → *munera*, urban offices and institutions). To a more limited extent the sometimes massive presence of the army in the border regions from the 2nd cent. AD also worked in this direction. The result was a Romanized Hellenization.

4. LATE ANTIQUITY

Hellenization in the east, during the period from the early 4th to late 6th cents. AD, was fundamentally characterized by continuity. Still extant gaps in the territorial distribution pattern of Greek-style cities were closed, the culture of Greek inscriptions and monuments in the countryside spread farther, particularly in Syria. In Asia Minor the native languages were by then spoken only by a minority, even in the Anatolian highlands. On the other hand, new contradictions arose. An important factor was the Christianization of the majority of the inhabitants of the empire by the 6th cent. → Christianity first developed in the Graeco-Hellenic centres of the eastern Mediterranean, and was therefore strongly characterized by Greek influences. On the other hand, the Christians considered themselves a 'new people', neither Greeks nor barbarians, and were inclined to equate the term 'Hellenes' ("Ελληνες) with paganism. In the 5th cent., this, together with the spread of an imperial identity particularly among the upper class, led to a break in identity, while at the same time the culture continued: instead of 'Greeks' the usual self-description was now 'Christians' or 'Romans', or both.

Furthermore, Christianity, as a revealed and preached religion based on canonical texts, depended on promoting its message also in the non-Greek colloquial languages. In 4th-cent. Egypt and Mesopotamia this led to the establishment of a Christian literature in the Coptic (Egyptian) and Syriac (Aramaic) languages. However, this is not a matter of a conscious movement against the Greek culture as such. On the one hand, the sphere of influence of both literatures remained limited prior to the Islamic conquest. In Egypt Greek literature continued to dominate, the so-called Syrian literature was hardly able to gain a footing west of the Euphrates, and there was nothing at all comparable in Roman Asia Minor. On the other hand, both literatures were strongly dependent in form and content on the Greek Christian literature. Also lacking was a positive reference to their 'own' pre-Hellenic past, which was also a pre-Christian one. The only literary memory of a time before the campaign of Alexander relating to the collective self was the history of salvation, oriented towards Israelite-Jewish history. Neither the pharaohs nor the old Aramaic kings could therefore offer starting-points for separate 'anti-Greek' or 'anti-imperial' awareness. Polemics against 'Greekness' were here a rejection of paganism, even if the latter showed non-Greek traits.

Extensive political and social changes between the 4th and 6th cents. also increasingly blurred the difference between Greek and non-Greek forms of organization: e.g. the dissolution of the polis as a community of citizens, which led in the 6th cent. to municipalities characterized by bishops, imperial officers, and local notables, and the growing social authority, in town and country among Greeks and non-Greeks, of charismatic outsider groups thought to be closely associated with the divine (monks, ascetics).

C. Art and Architecture
Since the Archaic period, it had been the aesthetic forms of expression of Greek culture that had been most willingly accepted by non-Greeks. This was the case in Etruria in the 6th cent. BC, then in the 5th and 4th cents. in Caria and Lycia, where the native dynasts used Greek forms, particularly in the area of tomb representations (→ Funerary architecture). In the Hellenistic period, Greek art also had an effect in milieus which

were hardly affected structurally by Hellenization. There arose, particularly in the Iranian sphere, idiosyncratic syntheses of native and Greek art and architecture. The new Graeco-Macedonian settlements naturally had primary monuments everywhere in pure Greek style, although it is the main centres of Alexandria, Antioch on the Orontes, and Seleucia on the Tigris that we know very little about as yet. But particularly in Egypt and Babylonia, the native building and artistic traditions also continued to exist, almost unchanged. The Imperial period brought expansion and standardization to this area too: in Egypt art was rarely produced in a purely native tradition, and from the 2nd cent. AD a unified Greek 'imperial art' extended by western influences, asserted itself everywhere, and mixed forms were suppressed. Only in the new cultural areas of the Syrian-Mesopotamian desert steppe did they exist into the 3rd cent. In late antiquity, on the one hand, the trend towards homogeneity continued, on the other, strong local distinctive features developed once more, though now on a unified basis and without the tie to the imperial art of the large centres being severed anywhere.

D. Summary
The often repeated judgment that the Hellenization of the Near East between Alexander and → Muhammad was a cultural veneer over a deep substratum of pre-Hellenic continuity supported only by a small elite, misses the complexity of the phenomenon. On the contrary, at the end of a thousand-year development in the eastern Roman empire there was a provincial culture similar everywhere in its basic features, which had assimilated, according to regional shading, varying contributions of Greek, Roman, and pre-Greek origin. Greek culture offered a kind of accepted 'common language' for the expression even of regional identities and for the purpose of communication between the individual regions of the empire and with the centre. There no longer was a truly unbroken pre-Greek tradition. In the most extreme case a complete break in identity resulted; people were perceived by themselves and others as Greek, and the remains of the pre-Greek cultural context acted as 'local colour'. This situation can probably be assumed for the greater part of the urban population, as well as for many rural areas of Asia Minor, and in parts of Syria, Phoenicia, and Palestine. There was a fluid transition to a situation where only the elite were affected by this radical break, but a primarily oral, native folk culture handed down through cult forms persisted. However, these too were not unaffected by the changes of Hellenization and the end of their 'high-cultural' variants. This was probably the case in late antiquity for the greater parts of the rural areas in Syria-Palestine and Egypt. Finally, we also find the development of a new cultural synthesis from the break (areas of Coptic and Syrian literature). The early Islamic culture was heir to this complex cultural mix. It also continued the central Greek tradition, and so does not simply rep-

resent the completion of a process often incorrectly called 're-orientalization'.

→ Hellenism; → Hellenistic politics; → Romanization

R.S. Bagnall, Egypt in Late Antiquity, 1993; G.W. Bowersock, Hellenism in Late Antiquity, 1990; A.K. Bowman, Egypt after the Pharaohs, 1986; P.Bilde et al. (ed.), Religion and Religious Practice in the Seleucid Kingdom, 1990; J.-M.Dentzer, W.Ortmann, Archéologie et histoire de la Syrie II, 1989; B.Funck (ed.), Hellenismus. Beitr. zur Erforschung von Akkulturation und politischer Ordnung in den Staaten des hellenistischen Zeitalters. Akten des Internat. Hellenismus-Kolloquiums 9.–14. März 1994 in Berlin, 1996; A.H.M. Jones, The Cities of the Eastern Roman Provinces 2, 1971 (repr. 1983); A.Kuhrt, S.Sherwin-White (ed.), Hellenism in the East. The Interaction of Greek and non-Greek Civilizations from Syria to Central Asia after Alexander, 1987; H.Lauter, Die Architektur des Hellenismus, 1986; F.G. B. Millar, The Phoenician cities: a case-study of hellenisation, in: PCPhS 209, 1983, 55–71; Id., Empire, community and culture in the Roman Near East: Greeks, Syrians, Jews and Arabs, in: Journal of Jewish Studies 38/2, 1987, 143–164; Id., The Roman Near East. 31 BC-AD 337, 1993; M.Sartre, L'orient romain. Provinces et sociétés provinciales en Méditerranée orientale d'Auguste aux Sévères (31 avant J.-C.-235 après J.-C.), 1991; Id., L'Asie mineure et l'Anatolie d'Alexandre à Dioclétien, 1996; D.Schlumberger, Der hellenisierte Orient. Die griech. und nachgriech. Kunst außerhalb des Mittelmeerraumes, 1969; F.R. Trombley, Hellenic Religion and Christianization c. 370–529, 2 vols., 1993.   J.G.

II. Language
A. General B. Egypt, Asia Minor, Syria
C. Hellenization and Latin

A. General

With Greek → colonization, pockets of Greek, whose linguistic influence can still be discerned today, had formed outside the 'mother country', in e.g. northern Africa (Cyrene), lower Italy, Sicily and southern France. One of the most significant events in the history of the Greek language, however, was the decision by Philip to make Greek the language of the Macedonian court chancellery, as with the conquests of → Alexander [4] the Great (with map) and Diadochi kingdoms (→ Diadochi, with map) the Greek language, in the form of the *koiné*, spread far beyond the original Greek linguistic area. Indigenous languages lost partially, at first, their status as written languages (where they had had it) and died out. Others were subject to Greek linguistic influences, particularly in vocabulary, still others lost their rank as official languages, but survived, e.g. Aramaic. However, a language can survive as a spoken language long after the end of its epigraphical documentation: after the 4th cent. BC, there are no more Lycian inscriptions; nevertheless, according to the witness of Acts 14,11, it was still spoken in Lystra at least into the 1st cent. AD.

With the establishment particularly of the Ptolemaic and Seleucid kingdoms and the founding of Greek cities, Greek came into contact with a variety of languages. This only rarely led to foreign vocabulary entering Greek (e.g. βάιον 'palm branch' from the Egyptian *b'j*, cf. Modern Greek τα βάγια 'Palm Sunday'; the Semitic loan-words in Greek mostly date from much earlier times, some are even already demonstrable in Mycenaean such as χιτών), more frequently to the borrowing of Greek words into other languages (because of the prestige of Greek as the language of the rulers).

Greek inscriptions have been found as far away as the Indian language area (an inscription by Aśoka in Kandahar is written in Greek and Aramaic). The Seleucids also made use of Greek, in continuation of the Achaemenid use of Aramaic (e.g. there is a bilingual Greek-Aramaic milestone from Pasargadae dated *c.* 280 BC). At the court of the Parthian king Hyrodes tragedies by Euripides (Plut. Crassus 33) were performed. Even under the first Sassanids Greek versions were added to middle Persian inscriptions.

B. Egypt, Asia Minor, Syria

In the Ptolemaic kingdom, Greek was the official and administrative language; in multilingual inscriptions the Greek version is the original. Because Egypt is the only country from which Greek → *papyri* are preserved in large numbers, they are the most important non-literary source for Hellenistic and Greek Imperial uses. The linguistic peculiarities of the papyri can mostly be explained from Greek linguistic history, without having the influence of the Coptic substrate to trouble about. In Alexandria, there was also a Hellenized Judaism (Hebrew names were often converted into Greek; particularly popular were names which happened to be the same or similar in both languages, such as Simeon/Simon or Joshua/Jason), whose initiative was the origin of the → Septuagint, which, however, quickly became authoritative even in Palestine.

As for Asia Minor, the Carian queen → Artemisia [2] had held a Greek rhetoric agon as early as 353 BC. However, native languages survived into late antiquity: New Phrygian inscriptions (in the Greek alphabet, often bilingual) reach into the 4th cent. AD, and according to a statement of Jerome, Celtic was still spoken in Asia Minor in his time. How strong the influence of Greek was here, for example on vocabulary, cannot be estimated because of the lack of documentation. It can therefore be assumed that, in the Byzantine period, Asia Minor used to be a closed Greek language area, and that the circumstances changed only with the immigration of the Turkic peoples.

Greek linguistic influence and Greek inscription finds in a Jewish context are also considerable in Syria and Palestine. A Hellenized Judaism existed there as well – after all, the Gospels were written in Greek and moreover *not* in a specifically Jewish Greek (the Semitic Gospel theory has generally been dropped). Even → Bar Kochba wrote his letters partly in Greek. It is precisely this region which produced specifically Greek writers (→ Lucianus of Samosata, → Iamblichus).

C. Hellenization and Latin

The Hellenization of Latin has been particularly well researched: Latin literature begins with a translation from Greek (→ Livius Andronicus), Roman literary genres have Greek models (exception: → satire), and Latin has many Greek loan-words, which is not only a matter of 'educated vocabulary' such as *philosophia*, but rather everyday vocabulary, terms for trade goods (an old example is *ampulla* from the Greek ἀμφορεύς), for plants (*malum* < Doric μᾶλον) and even swear-words (*malacus*, Plaut. < Greek μαλακός). There was also a whole series of Greek words in the Latin vernacular (cf. French *jambe* < Greek καμπή). The Latin-Greek linguistic contact is a special case, because Latin, as the language of the Roman empire, succeeded in influencing Greek as well. This is reflected in a large number of Latin words in Greek, not only in the areas of administration, military, and law, and can even be shown today in Modern Greek (σπίτι 'house' < Latin *hospitium*). In literarily ambitious works, however, Latin words are avoided. Yet the mutual influence extended so far that the linguistic development of Latin into the Romance languages on the one hand and of Ancient Greek into Modern Greek on the other run in parallel, so that it is possible to speak of a Latin-Greek language union (Kramer).

The Romans scarcely conducted an active linguistic policy, rather they maintained Greek as the official language in the East (Latin loanwords e.g. in Aramaic, Hebrew, Arabic, Syrian, Coptic, were passed on through Greek). This led to a continuation of the linguistic Hellenization in the East in the Roman era, which even gained new impetus with Christianization (the southernmost Greek inscription is that of the Nubian king Silko from the middle of the 6th cent. AD). In the Latin language area Christian terms often have Greek origins (French *église* < ἐκκλησία) and they passed into other languages, such as German, through Latin. However, Christianization also led to a series of languages being written in a new way or for the first time (first texts are mostly translations of NT writings) such as Syrian, Coptic, Ethiopian, Gothic, Armenian, and Georgian. The fact that these languages became written languages of Christianity early on probably contributed to their survival: Coptic succumbed only to Arabic, and an Aramaic enclave still exists in Syria today. Gothic survived in the Crimea into the 16th cent. AD. The influences of the Greek language can be seen in all of these languages. For example, the number of Greek loanwords in Coptic is estimated to be about 20% (even particles such as ἀλλά and γάρ). Many Greek words are preserved also in Armenian and Georgian, but only those Latin words which are also documented in Greek.

F. Altheim, Die Weltgeltung der griech. Spr., in: E.C. Welskopf (ed.), Neue Beiträge zur Gesch. der Alten Welt. I: Alter Orient und Griechenland, 1964, 315–332; F. Biville, Les emprunts du latin au grec. Approche phonétique, 1990; A. Böhlig, Die griech. Lehnwörter im sahidischen und bohairischen Neue Testament (= Stud. zur Erforschung des christl. Äg. 2), 1953; R. Browning, Me-

dieval and Modern Greek, ²1983; S. Daris, Il lessico latino nel greco d'Egitto ²1991; A. Debrunner, A. Scherer, Gesch. der griech. Sprache II. Grundfragen und Grundzüge des nachklassischen Griech., 1969; G. Deeters, Die kaukasischen Sprachen III Wortschatz, in: G. Deeters, G. Solta, V. Inglisi (ed.), Armenisch und kaukasische Sprache (HbdOr I.7), 1963, 33–46; W. Dietrich, Griech. und Romanisch. Parallelen und Divergenzen in Entwicklung, Variation und Strukturen (= Münstersche Beitr. zur Roman. Philol. 11), 1995; H. Hübschmann, Armenische Grammatik. 1. Teil Armenische Etym., 1897 (repr. 1962); A. Jeffery, The Foreign Vocabulary of the Qurʾān, 1935; S. Kapsomenos, Das Griech. in Ägypten, in: MH 10, 1953, 247–262; G. Narr (ed.), Griech. und Romanisch (= Tübinger Beitr. zur Linguistik 16), 1971; G. Neumann, J. Untermann (ed.), Die Sprache im röm. Reich der Kaiserzeit (Kolloquium vom 8.–10. April 1974), 1980; A. Thumb, Die griech. Sprache im Zeitalter des Hellenismus, 1901; J. Kramer, Der kaiserzeitliche griech.-lat. Sprachbund, in: N. Reiter (ed.), Ziele und Wege der Balkanlinguistik (Beitr. zur Tagung vom 2.–6. März 1981 in Berlin), 1983, 115–131 (= Balkanologische Veröffentlichungen 8); R. Schmitt, Die Sprachverhältnisse in den östlichen Provinzen des röm. Reiches, in: ANRW II 29.2, 554–586; D. Sperber, A Dictionary of Greek and Latin Legal Terms in Rabbinic Literature, 1984; W. von Wartburg, Die griech. Kolonisation in Südgallien und ihre sprachlichen Zeugen im Westroman., in: Zschr. für roman. Philol. 68, 1952, 1–48.

V.BI.

Hellenotamiai (ἑλληνοταμίαι). The title Hellenotamiai ('Stewards of Greece') was borne by the treasurers of the → Delian League. The exchequer they managed, originally located on Delos, was probably transferred to Athens in the year 454/3 BC (Thuc. 1,96,2; Plut. Aristides 25,3; Pericles 12,1; cf. IG I³ 259 = ATL List 1), because the annually elected boards were numbered in a continuous sequence starting in 454/3. From the beginning, however, the Hellenotamiai were Athenians, were appointed by Athens (Thuc. ibid., cf. [1. 44f., 235–237]), and constituted a committee of ten, one member from each phyle. They received the contributions from the allies, and from 453 paid into the treasury of Athena $^1/_{60}$ of the amount from each state as *aparché* ('first fruit'). On the instruction of the assembly they made payments, primarily to the generals for the conduct of war, but also at times for other purposes such as construction on the Acropolis (Parthenon: IG I³ 439; Propylaea: IG I³ 465 = ML 60). In 411 BC or shortly before, an expanded committee of 20 Hellenotamiai was granted responsibility for the treasuries of both the League and the polis of Athens ('future' constitution in Ps.-Aristot. Ath. Pol. 30,2; IG I³ 375 = ML 84; cf. [3. 391–393]).

1 R. Meiggs, The Athenian Empire, 1972 2 ATL; jüngste Edition der Listen: IG I³ 259–290 3 Rhodes 4 A. G. Woodhead, The Institution of the Hellenotamiae, in: JHS 79, 1959, 149–152. P.J.R.

Hellespontus (Ἑλλήσποντος; *Helléspontos*, Dardanelles, Turkish Çanakkale Boğazı). Strait, formed from a river valley during the glacial epoch, between the Propontis in the north and the → Aegean Sea in the south, the Thracian peninsula Chersonesus [1] in the west (Europe) and the Troad in the east (Asia; cf. Plin. HN 4,49), *c.* 65 km long, between 1.2 km (between Sestus and Abydus [1]) and 7.5 km wide, between 57 m and 103 m deep. As in the → Bosporus [1], a strong (maximum 5 knots; cf. Hom. Il. 2,845; 12,30; Hsch. s.v. Ἐ.; Aristot. Mete. 2,8; Avien. 3,466), cool (Theophr. Perì ichthýōn 5; Ath. 7,317f.) surface current flows southwest out of the Propontis and a warmer, salt water bottom current to the northwest. In the bends and bays along the H. countercurrents form on the surface making sailing and rowing to the northeast easier [1. 69f.]. The Hellespontias, a cold wind that often blew from the east-northeast for weeks during the summer (cf. Hdt. 7,188; Aristot. Mete. 2,6,364b 19; Plin. HN 2,121), caused many problems for navigation in addition to the difficulties due to the currents (cf. Pol. 16,29,9). Originally the H. did not exclusively describe the strait as in later authors (such as Pol. 16,29; Str. 1,2,39; Plin. HN 2,202; 205; 4,75) but also bordering areas of the Propontis and the Aegean (cf. Hdt. 6,33; Thuc. 2,9; Xen. Hell. 6,8,31 [2. 324]). For the wealth of fish in the H. cf. Hom. Il. 9,360; Ath. 1,9d; 3,105a; d; 4,157b; Avien. 3,34; 717. Menecrates of Elaea, a pupil of Xenocrates, devoted a monograph to the H. about 300 BC (*Períodos Hellespontiaké*, cf. Str. 12,3,22; FHG 2,342).

The mythological etymology of the name H. is that Helle, the daughter of Athamas, is supposed to have died in the H. (cf. the legend of the Golden Fleece: Pind. Fr. 51; 189; Aesch. Pers. 68; Eur. Med. 1284). The myth of Hero and Leander is also located here (Ov. Epist. 17f.).

The H. represented a significant traffic node, which both separated and joined; the shipping route between the Black Sea and the Aegean was, for example, vital for providing the Athenians with grain from the Crimea, yet it could easily be blocked (cf. Pol. 4,50,6; 27,7,5). Those who wanted to cross the H. in a west-east or east-west direction had to contend with the depth and current of the water, but possibly also with opponents on the opposite shore seeking to prevent the crossing. The H. was crossed, for example, by → Darius [1] I in his Scythian campaign 513/2 BC (Hdt. 4,85; 87), similarly → Xerxes 480 BC (Hdt. 7,33–36; 54–57), → Alexander [4] the Great in spring 334 BC from Elaeum to Ilium (Arr. Anab. 1,11,6), and both Scipios 190 BC (Liv. 37,33,4). To secure this shipping route, the Aeolians/→ Aeoles (Sestus, Assus) and → Ionians (Cyzicus, Lampsacus, Abydus, Elaeus [1]) founded colonies on both shores in the 8th/7th cents. BC.

1 W.-D. HÜTTEROTH, Türkei, 1982 2 W. SIEGLIN, Die Ausdehnung des Hellespontes bei den antiken Geographen, in: FS H. Kiepert, 1898, 323–331.

G. JACHMANN, H. als geogr. Terminus, in: Athenaeum 33, 1955, 93–111; G. STRASBURGER, s.v. H., Lex. zur frühgriech. Gesch., 1984, 169f. E.O.

Hellopia (Ἑλλοπία; *Hellopía*) is the name in the early Archaic period for the area around → Dodona and the modern Ioannina (Hes. Cat. 240), later a region in northern Euboea (Hdt. 8,23,2; Str. 10,1,3f.), a city of the → Dolopians and a valley near Thespiae in → Boeotia (Steph. Byz. s.v. Ἐ.). The Aetolian town of Hellopium (Pol. 11,7,4) can perhaps be equated with the H. of the Dolopians. These names are evidence of the settlings and wanderings of the Hellopes, a lost tribe, named only by Plin. HN 4,2 among the people of → Epirus, probably based on scholarly reconstruction.

F.GSCH.

Hellotis (Ἑλλωτίς; *Hellōtís*). Epiclesis of → Athena in Marathon and Corinth, as well as the name of a goddess in Crete identified with → Europe [2]. In Marathon a sanctuary (Ath. 15,22,678b; schol. Pind. Ol. 13,56ad) and sacrifices (LSCG 20) are attested; the epithet is derived from a local swamp (Greek *hélos*). In Corinth the festival of Hellotia is celebrated for Athena H. with an agon (Pind. Ol. 13,40, according to schol. ad loc. a torch race of young men); the aetion derives the cult either from Athena capturing Pegasus (Greek *heleín*) and bridling him here – more commonly as aetion for the Corinthian cult of Athena Chalinitis (from Greek *chálinos*, 'Bridle') – or from the girl H. dying with her sister (Chryse or Eurytion) in the temple of Athena in a fire, either because both commit suicide or because the temple is set alight by the Heraclids (→ Heraclidae) in the conquest of the Peloponnese; in both cases the festival is endowed as a ritual of atonement (schol. Pind. Ol. 13,56).

On Crete – mentioned by name is Gortyn that was originally called H. (Steph. Byz. s.v. Gortys) – H. is also the name of a large wreath of myrtle twigs that is carried in the procession of the Hellotia and which supposedly contained the bones of Europe (Seleucus in Ath. 15,678ab); probably for this reason H. is considered to be the old name of Europe (EM s.v. H.). Here too (as in Corinth) the festival and deity are connected with the death of a young woman; the link reminds us especially of the cult and myth of → Ariadne.

NILSSON, Feste, 94–96; P. STENGEL, s.v. Hellotia, RE 8, 197; F. WEICKER, s.v. H., RE 8, 197f.; W. BURKERT, Homo necans, 1972. F.G.

Hellusii In Tac. Germ. 46,4, the name of a fantastic people with a human face and a body the shape of an animal. An etymology that goes back to an animal name is therefore assumed; a Germanic equivalent with Greek ἑλλός, Armenian *eln*, Lithuanian *élnis* 'deer (fawn)' [1. 534–537] has been suggested. Whether this fantastic people bears witness to Scandinavian peoples or rather to seals with a face resembling that of a human remains to be seen [1. 537]. They should certainly not be linked with the Helisii, part of a tribe of Lugians (Tac. Germ. 43,2).

1 R. MUCH, Die Germania des Tacitus, ³1967. JO.S.

Helmet

A. GENERAL B. EARLY EVIDENCE C. CYPRUS AND
HISTORIC GREECE D. ITALY AND ROME
E. CELTO-GERMANIC REGION

A. GENERAL

Helmets protect and impress. Their design therefore
mostly went beyond purely purposeful weapon engineering (→ Weapons). Individual decoration served as
insignia of rank and standard decoration as a sign of
collective power. The representation emerged in magnificent parade helmets as an exclusive aspect, likewise
in copies made of clay used as burial objects [1]. The
leather cap (e.g. late Roman [2. K 120, 121]) was timeless; the words κυνέη (kynéē) and galea (both with the
meaning 'dog's coat') bear witness to this. The protective function was reinforced by means of small squares
stuck on, e.g. in the Homeric boar-tooth helmet. Disc-
shaped appliqués (φάλοι, pháloi) are known from
Homer and from statuettes from the Geometric period
[3]. The most common other Greek names for helmet
are κράνος (krános), περικεφαλαία (perikephalaía),
πήληξ (pélēx).

The protective effect is based on elastic or malleable
distortion, whether it be of the shell, the padding or the
supportive bracing. Some Italian helmets show that the
lining on the calotte was attached in a tight-fitting
manner [4. fig. 3 and 4]; however on the Sosias Cup
(Berlin, SM) the wounded Patroclus has removed his
helmet but is still wearing a leather cap. In the case of
tight-fitting armour, the lining could cushion the blows
(shin pad lining made of sponge: Aristot. Hist. an. 548b
1); better protection was provided by fitted lining not
touching the helmet shell so that blows could only have
an indirect effect. A helmet made with two shells shows
that this principle was put into practice using metal
[4. 240, fig. 18]. Narrowed helmet edges also show that
the shell was kept at a protective distance from the
head. The properties of the helmet shell were also decisive; metal brittle from beating that is not reannealed
provides less fracture resistance than annealed metal
which with its toughness can absorb greater energy before it cracks [5]. On some helmets and armour from
the 5th and 4th cents. BC from Italy, moulding of the
workpieces through casting and not through beating
could be demonstrated [6].

B. EARLY EVIDENCE

The oldest helmets in the Orient are known only
from pictorial representations [7]. In Greece, the helmets from the Minoan and Mycenaean era – that are
mostly likewise known from pictorial representations –
show oriental influences. These are the so-called spiked
and pointed helmets and the characteristic comb-
shaped and caterpillar-shaped crests [2. 11ff.; 8]. Numerous neo-Assyrian and Urartian helmets are dated by
means of royal inscriptions; they mostly consist of
bronze, occasionally also of iron [9]. Their decoration
was admired in Greece [10]. In Egypt, helmets first ap-

peared from the Amarna period as equipment of foreign
mercenaries [11].

C. CYPRUS AND HISTORIC GREECE

The shapes of Cypriot helmets occupy a middle position; Oriental influence is shown by the pointed calottes
crowned with knobs, eastern Greek on the other hand
by the cheek-piece forms [2. 27]. Greek helmets, the
earliest from about the middle of the 8th cent. BC, are
known to us as pieces from finds and from pictorial
representations. Common to the different types is a development from stereometric to organic design. Helmet
panaches and beaten, chased or appliqued decorations
are not connected with certain types of helmets but are
combined freely. Of the helmet shapes from the 8th
cent. BC the conical helmet and the Illyrian helmet with
the round calotte and rectangular facial cut-out can be
seen to be linked with oriental models. The latter probably appeared in the Peloponnese and was particularly
widespread in Illyria and Thrace [2. 42ff.].

The Corinthian helmet (Hdt. 4,180) that surrounds
the head apart from the eye openings and slits between
the nose protection and the cheek-pieces stands on its
own. The oldest representations and examples come
from the period from about 730 to 700 BC. The so-
called Chalcidic [12] and Attic helmets are distinguished from the Corinthian particularly by the shapes
of the browband and the cheek-pieces; from the 5th
cent. onwards other helmet-shapes, e.g. in the form of
Phrygian or pointed caps, became more significant;
protection for the nape of the neck became more important. The Boeotian helmet has not been identified with
certainty (κράνος βοιωτιουργές, Xen. Hipp. 12,3). The
preferred material for the manufacture of helmets was
bronze; among the few extant examples made of iron is
the helmet from the royal tomb of Vergina.

D. ITALY AND ROME

The crested helmets (9th cent. BC) [2. 195ff.] from
the Villanova period show links with the central European Urnfield culture. Characteristic of the 7th to the
5th cents. BC are hat-shaped helmets with a brim
[2. 222ff.]. Their best known form is the 'Negau type',
named after the place where they were found in Slove-
nia. There and in the central Alpine area local traditions
of this form of helmet were maintained right through to
the 1st cent. BC. Related are the helmets of the 5th and
4th cents. BC with the peak, ear cut-outs and a relatively large concave neck-guard that are indicative of
stronger Greek influences.

From the 4th to the 1st cent. the conical helmets with
a knob for the top of the head and a narrow neck protection were prevalent among the Romans, Etruscans
and Italians. The equipment of the Imperial period
troops [2. 293ff.] used the helmets of Italian (Hagenau
type) and Celtic (Weisenau type) tradition, while forms
from the eastern Mediterranean also occur. Characteristic features are round calottes, an emphasis on neck
protection, attached cheek-pieces and browband. The

Ancient Aegean and Ancient Near East

Greece

1 Mycenaean boar's tusk helmet, 2 Oriental pointed helmet, 3 Oriental caterpillar-crested helmet, 4 Cypriot helmet,

5 Geometric conical helmet, 6 Illyrian helmet, 7 Corinthian helmet (c. 700 BC), 8 Corinthian helmet (c. 600 BC), 9 Corinthian helmet (c. 500 BC), 10 Chalcidian helmet, 11 Pilos type helmet, 12 Attic helmet, 13 Phrygian helmet,

Etruscan and Italic

14 Helmet with transverse crest, 15 Negau type helmet, 16 Helmet with fluted front part and cut-outs for the ears,

Roman Empire

17 Hagenau type helmet, 18 Weisenau type helmet, 19 Face helmet, 20 Gladiator's helmet.

bowls are smooth or bear a knob, a crest-box or a plume-holder. Parade facial helmets with rich iconographic decoration were used for combat games [2. 327ff.]; their aristocratic nature differentiates them from the gladiator's helmets which with their bizarre visor forms were calculated to produce an effect in the arena [2. 365ff.].

1 O.-H. Frey, Ein tönerner Kammhelm aus Populonia. Überlegungen zur Verbreitung früher H. in It., in: GS J. Driehaus, 1990, 225–235   2 A. Bottini et al., Ant. Helme. Slg. Lipperheide und andere Bestände des Antikenmus. Berlin, 1988 (bibl.)   3 A. Lebessi, Zum Phalos des homer. H., MDAI(A) 107, 1992, 1–10   4 M. Egg, Ital. H. Stud. zu den ältereisenzeitlichen H. Italiens und der Alpen, 1986   5 P. H. Blyth, Metallurgy of Bronze

Armour, in: Πρακτικὰ τοῦ XII διεθνοῦς συνεδρίου ἀρχαιο-λογίας, Congr. Athens 1983, 1988, vol. 3, 293–296 6 H. BORN, Ant. Herstellungstechniken. Gegossene Brust-panzer und H. aus It., in: Acta praehistorica et archaeo-logica 21, 1989, 989–1013 7 P. CALMEYER, s.v. H., RLA 4, 313–316 8 J. BORCHARDT, Helme, in: H. G. BUCH-HOLZ, J. WIESNER (ed.), Kriegswesen 1, (ArchHom, E 1), 1977, 57–74 9 T. DEZSÖ, Assyrian Iron Helmets from Nimrud now in the British Museum, in: Iraq 53, 1991, 105–126, pl. 16–20 10 S.-G. GRÖSCHEL, Der goldene H. der Athena (Ilias 5,743/4), in: AMI 19, 1986 (1988), 43–78 11 R. KRAUSS, s.v. H., LÄ 2, 1114f. 12 E. KUNZE, Chalkidische H., Olympiaber. 9, 1994, 29ff.

M. FEUGERE, Casques antiques. Les visage de la guerre de Mycènes à la fin de l'Empire romain, 1994.   MI.MA.

E. CELTO-GERMANIC REGION
From the late Bronze Age to the end of the Iron Age (around the birth of Christ) the helmet plays a signifi-cant part in the ancients finds. Mostly these are metal helmets or preserved metal parts of helmets that tend preferably to be magnificent representative objects and frequently show links with Mediterranean helmets.

The bronze helmets of the late Bronze Age (→ Urn-field culture, 13th–8th cents. BC) are of various shapes (crested, horned, bonnet-shaped helmets, etc.) and are partly equipped with moveable cheek-pieces. They often come from rivers and bogs as votive offerings. In the Celtic → Hallstatt culture (8th–5th cents. BC) the helmets (double-crested helmets, bowl-shaped helmets, Negau type helmets, etc.) are burial objects from richly furnished warrior graves from the eastern Hallstatt region. Helmetted warriors are also depicted on the toreutic work of the 'situla circle' (→ Situla) in the east-ern Alpine and Upper Italian area.

In the Celtic → La Tène culture (5th–1st cents. BC) iron helmets are also known; these, as well as the bronze helmets, are often richly decorated with metal crests (bird figure in Ciumeşti/Romania) or gilding, as on magnificent helmets in France.

In the Germanic culture of the cents. around the birth of Christ there is hardly any archaeological evi-dence for the helmet and it is not until the period of the migration of peoples (5th–7th cents. AD) that richly decorated magnificent helmets (Spangenhelm) which ultimately come from late Roman-Byzantine work-shops appear again scattered across Europe.
→ Germanic archaeology; → Celtic archaeology; → To-reutics

K. BÖHNER, Die früh-ma. Spangen-H. und die nordischen H. der Vendelzeit, in: JRGZ 41, 1994 (1996), 471–549 H. BORN, L. D. NEBELSICK, Ein brn. Prunk-H. der Hall-stattzeit, 1991 A. BOTTINI et al., Ant. Helme. Slg. Lip-perheide und andere Bestände des Antikenmus. Berlin, 1988, 181–364 H. HENCKEN, The Earliest European Helmets, 1971 M. RUSU, Das kelt. Fürstengrab von Ciu-meşti in Rumänien, in: BRGK 50, 1969 (1971), 267–300 P. SCHAUER, Urnenfelderzeitl. H.- Formen und ihre Vor-bilder, in: Fund-Ber. Hessen 19/20, 1979/80, 521–543.
V.P.

Heloris (Ἔλωρις; *Hélōris*). Syracusan, close friend, perhaps even the adoptive father of the older → Dio-nysius [1] (Diod. Sic. 14,8,5). During an uprising of the Syracusans against the tyrant in 404/3 BC he uttered, according to Diodorus (loc. cit.), the remark that was quoted right through to late antiquity: 'Tyranny is a beautiful shroud' (*kalòn entáphiòn estin hē tyrannís*). Later banished for unknown reasons, he fought in 394 in Rhegium against Dionysius, laid siege to Messana in vain in 393 and defended Rhegium successfully in 392 against the tyrant (Diod. Sic. 14,87,1f.; 90,4f.). In 388, as commander of the Italiot League, he fell in battle fighting against Dionysius [1] I with the advance guard of his army on the Elleporus (Diod. Sic. 14,103,5–104,3).

H. BERVE, Die Tyrannis bei den Griechen, 1, 1967, 222, 226, 234.   K.MEI.

Helorus (Ἔλωρος; *Hélōros*).
[1] Son of the river god Ister and brother of Actaeus; as an ally of the Trojan → Telephus, he fell in the battle of the Mysians against the Achaeans (Philostr. Heroicus 23,13f.,157).

A. BETTINI, s.v. Aktaios II, LIMC 1.1, 470f.   J.S.-A.

[2] River in eastern Sicily, modern Tellaro. It has its origin near Palazzolo and flows into the *mare Ionium* 20 km north of the southern tip of the island. Often mentioned because of the battle in which → Hippocra-tes [4] defeated Syracuse there in 493/2 BC (Hdt. 7,154), and because of the disastrous retreat route of the Athenians in 413 BC (so-called Ἑλωρινὴ ὁδός, *Helōrinè hodós*, Thuc. 6,66,3; 6,70,4; 7,80,5).   GI.F.
[3] Small town on Sicily at the mouth of the river of the same name (Scyl. 13; Plin. HN 32,16), in the peace treaty of 263 BC promised by the Romans to Hieron II (Diod. Sic. 23,4,1), conquered in 214 by Marcellus (Liv. 24,35,1), plundered by Verres (Cic. Verr. 2,3,103; 129; 4,59; 5,90f.). The town was already settled from the 8th cent. BC. From the archaic to the Hellenistic periods come fortifications, agora (?) with porticoes, roads, residential dwellings; Koreion outside the town, Ascle-pieum (?), a sanctuary of Demeter, theatre (4th cent. BC). From the Byzantine period: basilica. C. 1 km north of the town is a gigantic Hellenistic burial complex ('La Pizzuta'), 2.5 km south-west is a peristyle villa from the late Imperial period with polychromatic floor mosaics.

G. VOZA, M. T. LANZA, s.v. Eloro, EAA² 3, 1995, 462f.; R. J. WILSON, Sicily under the Roman Empire, 1990.   GI.F.

Helots
I. Definition II. The origins of Helotia
III. The treatment of the Helots IV. The
role of the Helots in Sparta

I. Definition
The numerous literary sources regarding the history
of the H. are often contradictory and inaccurate. In general the H. (εἵλωτες, εἱλῶται, *heílōtes, heilôtai*) are called
by the usual Greek term for bonded persons, δοῦλοι
(*doûloi*), but there is no agreement about the form of
their dependency. Now and then the H. are compared
with other likewise dependent population groups, for
instance with the → Penestae of Thessaly (Pl. Leg.
776cd; Aristot. Pol. 1269a 36–39). According to Pollux
(3,83), the H. were between ἐλεύθεροι (*eleútheroi*, 'free
persons') and *doûloi*; Strabo (8,5,4) called them 'public
slaves in a certain manner' (τρόπον τινὰ δημόσιοι δοῦλοι), according to Pausanias (3,20,6), on the other
hand, they were slaves of the Spartan *koinón* ('Community'). In modern research too there is no agreement
about the status of the H.; it is however incontestable
that the H. as a collective group were public slaves of
the Spartan community and could not be the private
possession of individual Spartans, as is also indicated by
the official term δουλεία ('servitude'; Thuc. 5,23,3) as a
term for the H.

II. The origins of Helotia
In the 5th cent. BC most H. were Messenians (Thuc.
1,101). We should however assume that Helotia arose
in Laconia during the 'Dark Ages' and in the 8th/7th
cents. BC was transferred to → Messenia as a result of
the Spartan conquest. The ancient authors were convinced that the H. were the original population of Laconia who had been defeated in the war and enslaved. The
etymology of the word *heilôtai* from ἑλ- (*hel*-, 'to take
captive') appears to confirm this view; however there is
also an additional ancient derivative of the term from
→ Helus, a town in the southern part of the valley of the
Eurotas (Paus. 3,20,6). The Spartans treated the H. in
any case as a conquered people.

III. The treatment of the Helots
According to the judgement of ancient authors, the
H. and in particular the Messenians were a bonded
population whose correct treatment was very hard (Pl.
Leg.776c; 777bc; Aristot. Pol. 1269a 36–b 12; Theopompus, FGrH 115 F 13). As early as the 7th cent. BC
Tyrtaeus vividly described the situation of the Messenians: 'Like donkeys under great burdens they exhaus-
tedly bring to their masters, obedient to harsh duress,
half the fruits of the soil' (fr. 6; Paus. 4,14,5). This text
comes from the period of the first great uprising of the
Messenians; further uprisings followed, probably in
490 BC, 465 BC and finally successfully in 370/369 BC.
The H. of Sparta took part in the revolt of 465 BC; they
were however less ready to resist than the Messenians,
for on the one hand they could be controlled more easily

because of the geographical situation, and on the other
hand they lacked a sense of a common bond and a self-
assurance, such as were probably possessed by the Messenians.

Soon after taking up office, the ephors (→ *éphoroi*)
declared war officially on the H. every year (Plut.
Lycurgus 28), in order in this way to release from their
blood guilt Spartans who had killed H. The H. had to
wear clothing that equated them symbolically with animals (Myron, FGrH 106 F 2), and they were forced to
get themselves utterly drunk and were put on show in
this way at *syssitia* (→ Banquet) (Plut. Lycurgus 28). On
the other hand there were possibilities for them to be set
free (Theopompus, FGrH 115 F 176; Myron, FGrH
106 F 1) that however required a public ceremonial act
from the Spartan people's assembly. The most important group of freed H. were the νεοδαμώδεις (*neodamôdeis*). Thucydides tells of the Spartans, intent on
their own security, offering the H. freedom for services
in the war against Athens and then secretly killing 2,000
H. who had reported to them (Thuc. 4,80,3f.; Diod. Sic.
12,67,4; Plut. Lycurgus 28). This policy was clearly
unsuccessful for it intensified the hatred of the H., who
according to Xenophon would 'most like to eat the
Spartiates raw' (Xen. Hell. 3,3,6); according to Aristotle, the H. waited like enemies only for the misfortune
of the Spartans (Aristot. Pol. 1269a 37ff.). Nevertheless
this system existed for over 500 years and contributed
to Sparta becoming a great power in Greece.

IV. The role of the Helots in Sparta
H. and freed H. (*neodamôdeis*) were used by the
Spartans as hoplites (→ *hoplítai*), lightly armed soldiers
as well as oarsmen in the war (Hdt. 6,80f.; 9,28f.;
9,80,1; 9,85; Thuc. 4,80; Xen. Hell. 6,5,28f.; 7,1,12f.).
In Sparta female and male H. were servants in Spartiate
households (Hdt. 6,63; Xen. Hell. 5,4,28; Xen. Lac.
7,5; Plut. Agesilaus 3,2), and male H. were also watch-
men (Hdt. 6,75,2), grooms (Hdt. 6,68,2) and servants
who waited at table (Critias 88 B 33 DK).

As the Spartans themselves did not do any economically productive work, commerce, mining and trades
were the job of the → Perioikoi; the H. performed the
agricultural work. The Spartans relied on the agricultural products as they were obligated to supply barley,
wine, olive oil and pork for the *syssitia*, upon which in
turn rested their status as citizens (Tyrtaeus fr. 6; Aristot. Pol. 1264a 32–36; Plut. Lycurgus 8,7; Plut. Mor.
239de). The H., who cultivated the land with their
family, each worked only for a single Spartan but were
obligated to also place horses, dogs or provisions for a
journey at the disposal of other Spartans (Xen. Lac. 6,3;
Aristot. Pol. 1263a 35–37).

Modern research saw in helotage in many cases the
cause of the development and achievement of the characteristic social and political system of Sparta; it was
consequently the fear of H. that induced the Spartans to
transform their city into a military camp and to wage a
kind of permanent war against the H. On the other

hand, the view was however also held that the threat from the H. was overestimated both in antiquity and in modern research. It is clear, however, that Sparta, with the loss of Messenia in 369 BC, also irrevocably forfeited its position of power. Strabo (8,5,4) was of the opinion that helotage still continued to exist right through to the Roman conquest of Greece. Probably, however, Cleomenes III (235–222 BC) and Nabis (207–192 BC) had already freed many of the H. in order to use them as soldiers in the last attempt to defend Sparta's independence, initially against Macedonia, then against Rome. → Slavery; → Sparta

1 P. CARTLEDGE, Agesilaos and the Crisis of Sparta, 1987 2 Id., Serfdom in Classical Greece, in: L. J. ARCHER (ed.), Slavery and Other Forms of Unfree Labour, 1988, 33–42 3 Id., Sparta and Lakonia, 1979 4 P. CARTLEDGE, A. SPAWFORTH, Hellenistic and Roman Sparta, 1989 5 J. DUCAT, Les Hilotes, 1990 6 J. DUCAT, Les Pénestes de Thessalie, 1994 7 M. I. FINLEY, The Servile Statuses of Ancient Greece, in: Id., Economy, 133–149 8 Y. GARLAN, Slavery in ancient Greece, 1988 9 S. HODKINSON, Sharecropping and Sparta's Economic Exploitation of the Helots, in: J. M. SANDERS, H. W. CATLING (ed.), ΦΙΛΟΛΑΚΩΝ, FS H. W. Catling, 1992, 123–134 10 H. KLEES, Die Beurteilung der Helotie im hist. und polit. Denken der Griechen im 5. und 4. Jh. v.Chr., in: Laverna 2, 1991, 27–52; 3, 1992, 1–31 11 D. LOTZE, Μεταξὺ ἐλευθέρων καὶ δούλων, 1959 12 P. OLIVA, Sparta and her Social Problems, 1971 13 A. PARDISO, Forme di dependenza nel mondo greco, 1991 14 G. DE STE. CROIX, The Class Struggle in Ancient Greece, 1981 15 R. TALBERT, The Role of the Helots in the Class Struggle at Sparta, in: Historia 38, 1989, 22–40 16 K.-W. WELWEI, Unfreie im ant. Kriegsdienst I, 1974 17 M. WHITBY, Two Shadows: Images of Spartans and Helots, in: A. POWELL, S. HODKINSON (ed.), The Shadow of Sparta, 1994, 87–126. P.C.

Helpidius

[1] In AD 321–324 vicarius urbis Romae (Cod. Theod. 2,8,1; 16,2,5; 13,5,4; Cod. Iust. 8,10,6 calls him agens vicem praefectorum praetorio). In 329 he was still the recipient of laws (Cod. Theod. 9,21,4; 13,5,4); as such a long period in office as a vicarius would have been unusual, we should assume that he held a higher office in the meantime, perhaps that he was praefectus praetorio Italiae. PLRE 1, 413 (H. 1).
[2] Claudius H. Paphlagonian of lowly origin, Christian (he visited the hermit Antonius [5]), began his career as notarius, was then praeses Mauretaniae Sitif. (after AD 337), consularis Pannoniae (353), praefectus praetorio Orientis (360–361); he was unpopular with the soldiers and only the intervention of Julian prevented his murder. After the death of the emperor he tried nevertheless to slander the latter. He died soon afterwards (363). PLRE 1, 414 (H. 4).
[3] Supporter of Julian, brother-in-law of Libanius, born before AD 331 in Antioch; he was already highly respected at court under Constantius II; under the emperor Julian, who persuaded him to renounce Christianity, he was comes rei privatae as he was sent to

Antioch in 358/9, probably to take up the inheritance of Gallus for Julian. In 363 he took part in the Persian campaign, in 364 he was proconsul Asiae; he was involved in the uprising of Procopius, which is why he was taken prisoner by Valens and his assets were confiscated. PLRE 1, 415 (H. 6). K.G.-A.

Helus (Ἕλος; Hélos, 'swamp, marshland').

[1] Town in the area of rule of → Nestor (Hom. Il. 2,594); the geographical position was already the subject of debate in antiquity (Str. 8,3,25).

B. MADER, s.v. H., LFE. J.S.-A.

[2] Town, the location of which has not been pinpointed precisely, in the eastern plain surrounding the mouth of the → Eurotas (Pol. 5,19f.), one of the richest agricultural regions in Laconia. The name of the Spartan Helots is said to be derived from H. (Str. 8,5,4; Paus. 3,20,6), which is however not possible phonetically [1]. Probably already a fleet centre in the Bronze Age (Hom. Il. 2,584). However, river deposits made the harbour unusable and as early as the 2nd cent. BC H. declined. In the time of Pausanias H. was in ruins (Paus. 3,22,3). Evidence: Thuc. 4,54,4; Xen. Hell. 6,5,32; Str. 8,3,12; 3,24; 5,2; Paus. 3,20,6f.

1 CHANTRAINE, s.v. H.

H. WATERHOUSE, R. HOPE SIMPSON, Prehistoric Laconia, in: ABSA, 55, 1960, 87–103; 56, 1961, 173. Y.L.

Helvecones

Aside from the → Harii, Manimi, Halisiones and Nahanarvali, a powerful partial tribe of the Vandali-Lugii (Tac. Germ. 43,2); probably identical to the Elouaíōnes (Ἐλουαίωνες, Ptol. 2,11,9), although they do not have the addition Loûg[i]oi (Λοῦγ[ι]οι) and their location is pinpointed as between Rhoutíkleioi (Ῥουτίκλειοι) and Burgundiones (Βουργοῦντες). In this case they would be the most northerly Lugii. K.DI.

Helvetii

Celtic tribe of people who settled in the area of modern Switzerland in the Roman Imperial period. Borders of the settlement area: to the north of Rhine, only between the mouth of the Aare and Stein am Rhein (so-called Tabular Jura between Basle and Brugg) is the region of the Raurici; to the west the Folded Jura between Basle and Geneva; to the south Lake Geneva without the area of the colonia Equestris (Nyon); in the east the border towards Raetia is on a line from the eastern bank of Lake Geneva to Pfyn-Frauenfeld. The H. were subdivided into tribal districts (according to Caes. B Gall. 1,12,4 four pagi; according to Posid. in Str. 4,3,3 three pagi). Earlier places where the H. lived in south-western Germany can be deduced from Ptol. 2,11,2 (Ἐλουητίων ἔρημος). Individual sections were involved in the campaign of the Cimbri (Caes. B Gall. 1,12,5); the remainder of them settled in the eastern Alps; from them come the devotional inscriptions for the family of Augustus on the Magdalensberg [1. 70–74]. The internal Celtic battles in 60/58 BC, in which mercenary troops from the right bank of the Rhine were recruited, gave Caesar the excuse he wanted to intervene in independent Gaul. Based on the model that he had successfully used as *propraetor* in Spain, he declared an internal tribal movement to be a *casus belli* [2]. The outbreak of war in 58 BC has been packaged as a fiction of Caesar acting correctly according to international law as a result of his skills of portrayal and despite diverse criticism is still considered today to be the historical truth. The military historian HANS DELBRÜCK and others a long time ago demonstrated the implausibility of Caesar's details in relation to the Helvetian population statistics, the nature of the exodus and the alleged goal of the expedition. What was in reality a limited military exodus of the H. to assist the Haedui against Ariovistus was reinterpreted by Caesar as a dangerous Gallic civil war which justified Roman intervention.

After the defeat of the expedition corps at Bibracte, the H. continued to live in their old tribal area and also took part in the revolt of Vercingetorix. At the end of his life Caesar had the Roman traffic routes into the region of the H. secured by establishing two *coloniae*, the Colonia Iulia Equestris (Nyon: road over the Great St. Bernhard to Geneva) and the *Colonia Raurica* (Augst in the region of the Raurici, Jura border road from Geneva to the Upper Rhine). The Romans did not take possession of the H. region until the alpine war of Augustus (15 BC). The territory became a peregrine *civitas* with the capital city of Aventicum although the internal organization is not known precisely. When the army of Vitellius marched through at the beginning of AD 69, Aventicum was in danger of being plundered (Tac. Hist. 1,67–70). Through Vespasianus, whose father had carried out banking business among the H., the city was accorded the rank of a *colonia* (Suet. Vesp. 1,3): *Colonia Pia Flavia Constans Emerita Helvetiorum Foederata*. It is a matter of debate to which period the *foedus* between Rome and the H. belongs.

From the Flavian period onwards the city developed enormously (city wall with five gates and 73 towers, amphitheatre, scenic theatre, baths, temple, association houses, so-called *scholae*). From Domitian the region of the H. belonged to the province of Germania superior, and the neo-Romans were registered in the *tribus Quirina*. Some of them were recruited into Roman legions whilst a larger number of those left in the status of *perigrini* entered the *auxilia* (*cohortes Helvetiorum*). In AD 259/260 the estates and the capital city suffered under the invasions of the Alemanni. After the fall of the German *limes*, the new provincial classification of Diocletian (small province of *Maxima Sequanorum*) also no longer protected the romanized H. Around AD 400 the Roman troops withdrew, and the slow immigration of the Burgundian and Alemannic *foederati* began. The diocese of Aventicum survived the end of the Roman empire in Lausanne.

1 J. ŠAŠEL, Huldigung norischer Stämme am Magdalensberg in Kärnten, in: Historia 16, 1967, 70–74 2 W.

WIMMEL, Caesar und die Helvetier, in: RhM 123, 1980, 126–137; 125, 1982, 59–66.

H. DELBRÜCK, Gesch. der Kriegskunst I, 1900, 423–442; W. DRACK, R. FELLMANN, Die Römer in der Schweiz, 1988; G. FERRERO, Grandezza e decadenza di Roma, German: Größe und Niedergang Roms 2, ²1914, 1–30; R. FREI-STOLBA, Die röm. Schweiz, in: ANRW II 5.1, 1976, 288–403; E. HOWALD, E. MEYER, Die röm. Schweiz, 1940; P. HUBER, Die Glaubwürdigkeit Caesars in seinem Ber. über den gall. Krieg, ²1931; E. MEYER, Röm. Zeit, in: Hdb. der Schweizer Gesch. I, 1980, 55–92; F. STAEHELIN, Die Schweiz in röm. Zeit, ³1948; G. WALSER, Röm. Inschr. in der Schweiz I–III, 1979–1980; Id., Zu Caesars Tendenz in der geogr. Beschreibung Galliens, in: Klio 77, 1995, 217–223; Id., Bellum Helveticum. Stud. zum Beginn der caesarischen Eroberung von Gallien (Historia Einzelschrift 118), 1998.   G.W.

Helvetum (It. Ant. 252; 350; ᾿Ελκηβος; *Élkēbos*, Ptol. 2,9,18). Previously often equated with → Helellum (Tab. Peut. 3,4) or Alaea (Geogr. Rav. 26) and already confused with this in It. Ant. 354, but its location should not be pinpointed as near Ehl in the Alsace but as being on the right bank of the Rhine on the Mons Brisiacus–Argentoratus route near modern Riegel, district of Emmendingen [1]. Forts from the Claudian and Vespasian periods, which as a continuation of the series of forts on the Upper Danube secured the link with the Rhine. After the conquest of the → *Decumates agri*, loss of military strategic importance. The *cannabae* (camp villages) developed into a larger → *vicus* with artisan businesses, potters' workshops, brickworks and a cult district with a Mithraeum. According to recent investigations, the name Riegel (derived from *regula, a functional description for a regional legal and administrative district [1]) suggests Roman continuity after the penetration of the *limes* in 260.

1 H. STEGER, *Regula/Riegel am Kaiserstuhl – Helvetum?, in: Römer und Alamannen im Breisgau, (Archäologie und Geschichte 6), 1994, 233–361.

G. FINGERLIN, Riegel, in: P. FILTZINGER et al., Die Römer in Baden-Württemberg, ³1986, 504–508.   F.SCH.

Helvia

[1] Mother of Cicero, never mentioned by him, described by his brother as a painstaking housewife (Cic. Fam. 16,26,2), led a blameless life (Plut. Cicero 1,1).

[2] Wife of Seneca the Elder whom she lost in AD 40 (Sen. Dial. 12,2,4; 19,4). → Seneca the Younger, one of her three sons, wrote for her in exile the consolatory discourse Ad Helviam. PIR² H 78.

[3] Elder sister of H. [2]. Her husband → Galerius [1] died in AD 31 on the return journey to Rome from Egypt (Sen. Dial. 12,19). PIR² H 79.   ME.STR.

[4] **H. Procula.** Daughter of the Tiberian senator T. Helvius [II 2] Basila, whom she honoured posthumously in Antium (CIL X 5056 = ILS 977). Probably identical with the wife of the Spanish senator C. Dillius

Vocula, who died in AD 70 in Germania (CIL VI 1402 = ILS 983). PIR² H 82. w.e.

Helvidius

[1] **C.H. Priscus.** Came from Cluviae. His father had been → primipilus. Entry to the Senate before AD 49. Quaestor Achaiae at the latest in 49/50; his companion was P. → Celerius of Histonium (IEph 7, 1, 3043/4 = [1. 67ff.]). Legionary legate in Syria as quaestorian in 51. During this period he married Fannia, the daughter of → Clodius [II 15] Thrasea Paetus. People's tribune in 56; then no other office under Nero, a consequence of the link with his father-in-law and the Stoic-influenced circles in Rome. When Thrasea Paetus had to kill himself in 66, H. was exiled. Return under Galba, praetor in 70. In the Senate he attacked senatorial collaborators of the Neronian period, particularly Eprius Marcellus; in the process he also supported the autonomy of the Senate alongside the princeps vis-à-vis Vespasian. Later he was exiled for this and finally executed against the will of the princeps. A biography of H. was written by → Herennius [II 11] Senecio [2.; 3]

> 1 W. ECK, in: Splendidissima Civitas. Etudes ... à Fr. Jacques, 1996, 67ff. 2 SYME, RP VII, 568ff. 3 PIR² H 59.

[2] **H. (Priscus)** Son of H. [1] from his first marriage; therefore he was born before AD 51. Senator who in spite of his father attained the suffect consulate; the year is unknown; either in 87 at the latest or not until 93 (which could be supported by the age). At the end of 93 allegedly condemned and executed because of a play containing allusions to Domitian; presumably bitter rivalries between opposing groups in the Senate were the cause. In 97 Pliny attacked Publicius Certus as the prosecutor; his speech De Helvidii ultione was published later. Married to → Antea [2]; the name was passed on via two daughters.

> SYME, RP VII, 568ff.; W. ECK, in: Kölnische Jbb. 26, 1993, 449; PIR² H 60. w.e.

Helvii (Elvii, Elvi or Ilvi, Caes. B Civ. 1,35; Ἐλουοί, Str. 4,2,1). Celtic tribe of people whose area (modern Dép. Ardèche) on the right bank of the Rhône in the north bordered on the Segusiavi, in the west on the Vellavii and Gabali and in the south on the Volcae Arecomici. The Cevennes separated them from the Arverni (Caes. B Gall. 7,8). In 52 BC in the war against Vercingetorix they were on the side of Caesar. In the new division of the province under Augustus they were attached to Aquitania (Str. loc.cit.) but soon afterwards (Plin. HN 3,36) belonged to Gallia Narbonensis with the capital city of Alba Augusta Helviorum. Under Diocletian the civitas Albensis was allocated to the provincia Viennensis. In the 6th cent. AD Vivarium (modern Viviers) was its capital city. Y.L.

Helvius Roman proper name, possibly derived from the first name Helvus.

SCHULZE 82; 421; HOLDER, 1, 1430f.

I. REPUBLICAN PERIOD II. IMPERIAL PERIOD

I. REPUBLICAN PERIOD

[I 1] **H., C.** In 199 BC plebeian aedile, in 198 praetor in Gallia Cisalpina (Liv. 32,7,13), in 189 legate of Cn. → Manlius Vulso in the campaign against the Galatians of Asia Minor (Pol. 21,34,2–4; Liv. 38,14,4f. etc.). MRR 1,327; 330; 364.

[I 2] **H., M.** In 198 plebeian aedile, in 197 praetor in Hispania citerior. Kept there until 195 because of an illness, he defeated the Celtiberians on the return march at Illiturgis on the Baetis and received an ovatio (Liv. 34,10,1–5; InscrIt 13,1,79). K.-L.E.

[I 3] **H. Cinna, C.** Probably comes from Brixen in Gallia Transpadana (fr. 9 COURTNEY: Genumana per salicta). The Helvii were a respected, long-established family there [1. 46f.]; H.'s date of birth is unknown. He could be identical to the Cinna, who bought the poet → Parthenius of Nicaea at the end of the Mithridatic War as a slave and gave him his freedom because of his erudition (Suda s.v. Parthenius). – H.'s own writing comprised epigrams (Non. 124L), a → propemptikon for Asinius [I 5] Pollio (Char. 158B = 124K) and the small epic Zmyrna (Catull. 95, fr. 6–8 COURTNEY). Like Parthenius' writing, H.'s writing was extraordinarily erudite: comm. were written on his propemptikon by Iulius → Hyginus [1] and on the Zmyrna by → Crassicius Pansa (Char. 171B = 134K, Suet. Gram. 18,2). As a close friend of → Catullus (95; cf. 10,30; 113,1), he was probably a leading member of the writers' group which Cicero criticized in 45 BC as 'singers of Euphorion'.

H. was a friend (Plut. Brutus 20; Caesar 68; Dio 44,50,4) and relative (Val. Max. 9,9,1) of Caesar. After the Transpadanians were granted citizenship he apparently became a member of the Senate in 49 BC. As tribune he suggested in 44 (Suet. Iul. 52,3) the dismissal of his colleagues in office, the opponents of Caesar, Epidius Marullus and Caesetius Flavus (Cass. Dio 44,10,3). Despite an ominous dream, he attended Caesar's funeral on 20 March 44, where the rabble – spurred on by Antony's speech and in the belief that he was the praetor L. Cornelius Cinna, who had condoned the murder, – seized him and tore him to pieces (Plut. ibid.; Val. Max. 9,9,1; Suet. Iul. 85; App. B Civ. 2,147; Cass. Dio 44,50,4; Zon. 10,12). Ovid's allusion to his death (Ov. Ib. 539f.) confirms Plutarch's identification of the writer as the tribune [3].

H. was revered by the poets of the following generation (Verg. Ecl. 9,35f.; Valgius fr. 2 COURTNEY; Ov. Tr. 2,435), and his Zmyrna was critically incorporated by Ovid in Met. 10,298–502 [4]; nevertheless his erudition rich in allusions was not to everyone's taste (Mart. 10,21). He is quoted by antiquarians and grammarians up to → Isidorus [9] (Orig. 6,12,2; 19,2,9; 19,4,7).

1 T. P. WISEMAN, C. the Poet, 1974 2 COURTNEY, 1993
3 J. D. MORGAN, The Death of C. the Poet, in: CQ 40,
1990, 558f. 4 G. BRUGNOLI, Ovidi Zmyrna, in: Rivista
di cultura classica e medioevale 24, 1982, 47–52.

H. DAHLMANN, Über H.Cinna (AAWM 8), 1977; R. O. A.
M. LYNE, The Neoteric Poets, in: CQ 28, 1978, 167–187;
R. F. THOMAS, C., Calvus and the Ciris, in: CQ 31, 1981,
371–374; L. C. WATSON, C. and Euphorion, in: SIFC 54,
1982, 93–110.   T.W.

[I 4] H. Mancia. Son of a freedman from Formiae,
known because of his mockery (for instance regarding
the censor Marcus Antonius [I 7], Cic. De or. 2,274)
and himself the victim of mockery by C. Iulius [I 5]
Caesar Strabo because of his ugliness (before 87 BC,
Cic. De or. 2,266; Quint. Inst. 6,3,8). In old age (probably in 55 BC) he denounced L. Scribonius Libo to the
censors and in the process passionately attacked his defence counsel Pompey (Val. Max. 6,2,8).   K.-L.E.

II. IMPERIAL PERIOD

[II 1] L.H. Agrippa. Senator of Baetica. In AD 68/9 proconsul of Sardinia. Perhaps identical with the pontifex
who died under Domitian during the investigation of
sexual misdemeanours of Vestals. PIR² H 64.

[II 2] T.H. Basila. Senator who had property in Atina at
least. Praetorian career, perhaps identical with the proconsul of Achaia in AE 1949, 90. Governor of Galatia
probably in c. AD 37/8. [1]. His daughter was Helvia
Procula. PIR² H 67; 82.

1 S. ŞAHIN, in: EA 25, 1995, 25ff.   W.E.

[II 3] P.H. Pertinax. see → Pertinax
[II 4] P.H. Pertinax. Born around AD 175, son of the
emperor → Pertinax and of Flavia Titiana (CIL XIII
4323; III 14149,35+38; BGU 2,646; Cass. Dio 37,7).
He was not brought up at court but together with his
sister at the house of his grandfather Flavius Sulpicianus
and against the will of his father he bore the titles
Caesar and *princeps iuventutis* (Cass. Dio 73,7,3; Hdn.
2,4,9; [1]). After the death of his father he was given the
priestly office of *flamen* of the deified Pertinax (SHA
Pert. 15,3). Around 212 he held the suffect consulate
and was killed in office by Caracalla (SHA Carac. 4,8;
Hdn. 4,6,3).

1 H. COHEN, Monnaies sous l'empire romain, repr. 1955,
vol. 3, 397.

PIR² H 74; DEGRASSI, FCIR 59; KIENAST², 153; LEUNIS-
SEN, 166f.   T.F.

[II 5] H. Successus. The freedman and textile dealer (in
SHA Pert. 1; *lignariam* is probably a mistake) was the
father of the emperor H. → Pertinax (SHA Pert. 1;
3,3f.), who was born in the Ligurian Apennines near
Albae Pompeiae on the estate of his mother, the wife of
Successus (Cass. Dio 73,3,1). PIR² H 77.   T.F.

Hemerologion (ἡμερολόγιον; *hēmerológion*) is a text
arranged according to the days of the year. The ancient
spectrum of meaning ranges from → calendar (Plut.
Caesar 59) to diary (Cosmas Indicopleustes, Topogra-
phia christiana PG 88,276A, 6th cent. AD) and is still
used in the specialized Latin of the 19th cent. in this
way. In modern scientific language *hemerologion* is
used to describe two quite different objects. In Egyptology and the study of the Ancient Orient, *hemerologion*
refers to lists with a divinatory (and as a corresponding
frame of reference – cosmological) interest: because of
the theological qualification of a day (that does not
always have to be explained) a certain action is allo-
wed/forbidden ('day-selection calendar'); in individual
cases that can also lead to lists that are no longer organized according to the calendar, but according to their
subject matter. In their systematic interest, the → parapegma and (later) Christian sanctilogia that compile
saints for each day present a comparable type of text. –
With reference to Graeco-Roman antiquity, *hemerologion* describes a group of texts that are first attested in
medieval MSS but can certainly be traced back to the
Imperial period: synopses of various local calendars
that allow for the conversion of the days of the month of
a calendar into other calendar systems.

R. LABAT, Hémérologies et ménologies d'Assur, 1939;
P. VERNUS, Omina calendériques et théorie médicale dans
l'Egypte ancienne, in: RHR 199, 1982, 246f.; L. TROY,
Have a Nice Day!, in: Boreas 20, 1989, 127–147;
C. LEITZ, Tagewählerei. Das Buch ḥȝt nhḥ ph.wy dt und
verwandte Texte, 2 vols., 1994; W. KUBITSCHEK, Die
Kalenderbücher von Florenz, Rom und Leyden (= Denk-
schriften der kaiserlichen Akad. Wiss. Wien, phil.-hist. Kl.
57,3), 1915 (with ed.); A. E. SAMUEL, Greek and Roman
Chronology, 1972, 171–178.   J.R.

Hemerology

I. SYSTEMATICS   II. HEMEROLOGY ACCORDING TO
THE CALENDAR   III. COMPLEX CALENDAR AND
LUNATIONS   IV. ASTROLOGICAL HEMEROLOGY

I. SYSTEMATICS

The term hemerology denotes the cultural practice
of connecting the success or failure of actions with favourable or unfavourable days defined by the calendar
(= cal.). The assumption that days are fixed not only
quantitatively but also qualitatively was common to all
ancient cultures and led to its own genre, the → hemerologion. The concept of hemerology meanwhile goes
beyond this genre and must be seen in connection with
→ calendar, → divination and → astrology. Further to
be noted is the fact that despite the common basic
assumption, both the divinatory rationality and the
concrete forms – often due to religious charging –
varied.

II. Hemerology according to the calendar

The need to differentiate favourable from unfavourable days is ascertainable quite early. The simplest solution to this existed in linking to the calendar. The earliest sources in this regard stem from Mesopotamia, where a rich omen literature forms the background [15. 156; 14. 13–16; 19; 27], and from Greece, where two Mycenaean documents contain data about the quality of days ordered by date ([6. 311, no. 207] = V 280, cf. also [6. 311, no. 172] = KN 02; [17]). Egypt was also familiar with hemerology according to the cal. which was further differentiated in association with the decan gods of the days and hours and not least was known to the Greeks via Plato's student Eudoxus [1] of Cnidus (see Plut. De Is. et Os. 52; cf. [10; 2. 35; 16]).

In Rome the term *dies religiosi* was familiar to denote those days that were unfavourable for ventures, on which activities as a whole were limited (Gell. NA 4,9,5 f.; 5,17,1; Macrob. Sat. 1,16,21–27; Fest. 348,22–30; Ov. Fast. 1,57 f.; Non. 73,30; 379,1; Liv. 6,1,12; CIL I², 231) and which at the same time were marked by cultic acts. *Dies religiosi* were further subdivided, e.g. into *dies atri* ('black days' or *dies postriduani*), i.e. next-days of the monthly orientation days of Kalends, Nones and Ides (Macrob. Sat. 1,16,21), on which nothing new was to be undertaken (Macrob. Sat. 1,15,22; Varro, Ling. 6,29 with the beginnings of a catarchic astrology; → *fasti*). The reasons for such a social and cultural determination of time qualities lie not only in the religious-cultic area, but also in political interests since orientation days standardized the cultural memory and also allowed for the influencing of religious actions and for systematizations [21. 563–575].

The most widespread form of cal. hemerology consisted however in the simple analogy between days of the week and planet rulers. Whether it deals with the 7-day week that came from Mesopotamia and influenced Judaism and later also the Roman calendar, or with differing Roman week countings – the quality of a day was consistently interpreted in accordance with the respective planet gods (→ Planets II; first naming of Saturnus as a weekday god at Tib. 1,3,18; cf. Juv. 6,569–576; Babrius latinus 2154 in [22. fig. 8–12] according to the → Chronographer of 354 with hour rulers; cf. [4. 476–484; 7; 18. 162; 8; 20]).

III. Complex Calendar and Lunations

In keeping with its nature, the divinatory sophistication of a simple cal. hemerology is minor. In order to come to more complex statements, the counting of weeks was frequently combined with other determining units, either with further cal. intervals or with astronomically based values. An example of the former is the combination of the 7-day planet week with the 8-day rhythm of the Roman → *nundinae*, which despite its handiness led to an expansion of the day determinations [21. 588]; a typical representative for this is the Chronographer of 354 [22]. The priestly cultic-theo-logical → Henoch-astronomy in the Jewish calendar shows how complicated this type of technique can become: By extending rhythms of 7 to year cycles, yovel or jubilee (49 years), deca-jubilees etc. while at the same time combining these with the Jerusalem priestly service cycles resulted in an exact salvation-historical meaning for each day of world history, which became central for apocalyptic calculations ([1; 24. 160–222, 316–365] (examine the material from Qumran, but cf. also Jos. BI 6,249 f. *et passim*). The salvation-historical designation of certain days play a part also in early Christianity, as the discussions around the date of Jesus' death and Parousia as well as the 'correct' calendar demonstrate [23].

In connection with the combination with astronomically based values, the observation of the course of the moon became particularly significant (→ Lunaria). Not only the respective moon phase was important for lunation (for instance in the compilation of the moon calendar and other calendars), but above all the position of the → moon in certain zodiacal signs, which allotted its special quality to each day or time of day. The moon-prophecy books or zodiacal lunaria form a separate genre of ancient literature and were circulated in all cultural areas [25; 9. 5; 29; 11. 77 ff.; 12. 263–269].

IV. Astrological Hemerology

The most sophisticated form of hemerology consisted in the application of different astrological teachings on the qualitative determination of days and time intervals. Already the Babylonians dedicated special attention to the supposed west-to-east movement and reverse phase of the planetary orbits as well as their respective turning points [28. 172–203; 26]; in the Graeco-Roman period such phase qualifications were further expanded; the retrograde phases of the planets were seen as weak periods of the respective principle (Ptol. Apotelesmatika 1,23, Epilogue; rationale ibid. 1,8; cf. [4. 110–121]), now and then also as days of danger (Dorotheus Sidonius, Carm. astrologicum 1,6,7 Pingree; cf. [12. 117–121; 13. 38]). Further sophistication was achieved when planet and zodiacal rulers were alloted to individual hours of the day [4. 206–215]. Corresponding teachings of the *chronokrátores* (rulers over time periods) were also fostered in Christianity (for instance by Bardesanes, De libro legum regionum 524 Nau), in Judaism (see the discussion around the *mazzal*, the birth ruler, or planet of fate, in bSchab 156ab [24. 470–473]) and in Manichaeism (Kephalaia 25,15–19).

A separate discipline for the ascertainment of favourable and unfavourable days existed in catarchic astrology (*katarchaí / electiones*, beginnings [sc. of undertakings]) that not only calculated the rulers of days and hours, ascendants (*horoskópos*) etc., but also prepared separate horoscopes for possible undertakings such as journeys by sea and the sowing of fields (Ptol. Apotelesmatika 1,3) or the founding of cities (Ptol. ibid. 2,5), cf. also Hephaestion of Thebes, Apotelesmatika 3,2–5;

Vettius Valens 2,29 – attributed there to Abraham –, Manil. 3,510–513; Firm. Mat. 2,26–28 KROLL (see [4. 458–511]). Precursors in this regard are to be found in Greek fragments that were ascribed to → Orpheus or other authorities (verifications at [12. 69]).

→ Astrology; → Divination; → Calendar; → Omen

1 M. ALBANI, Astronomie und Schöpfungsglaube, Untersuchungen zum astronomischen Henoch-Buch, 1994 2 J. ASSMANN, Zeit und Ewigkeit im alten Ägypten, 1975 3 T. BARTON, Ancient Astrology, 1994 4 A. BOUCHÉ-LECLERCQ, L'astrologie grecque, 1899 5 A. CAQUOT, M. LEIBOVICI (ed.), La divination, 2 vols., 1968 6 J. CHADWICK, Documents in Mycenaean Greek, ²1973 7 F. H. COLSON, The Week, 1926 8 S. ERIKSSON, Wochentagsgötter, Mond und Tierkreis. Laienastrologie in der römischen Kaiserzeit, 1956 9 M. FÖRSTER, Vom Fortleben antiker Sammellunare im Englischen und in anderen Volkssprachen, in: Anglia 67/68, 1944, 1–170 10 W. GUNDEL, Dekane und Dekanherrscher. Ein Beitrag zur Geschichte der Sternbilder der Kulturvölker, 1936 11 Id., Sternglaube, Sternreligion und Sternorakel, ²1959 12 Id., H. G. GUNDEL, Astrologumena. Die astrologische Literatur in der Antike und ihre Geschichte, 1966 13 J. H. HOLDEN, A History of Horoscopic Astrology, 1996 14 R. LABAT, Hémérologies et ménologies d'Assur, 1939 15 S. LANGDON, Babylonian Menologies and the Semitic Calendars, 1935 16 C. LEITZ, T. Das Buch ḥ3t nhh ph.wy dt und verwandte Texte, 1994 17 J. D. MIKALSON, The Sacred and Civil Calendar of the Athenian Year, 1975 18 O. NEUGEBAUER, The Exact Sciences in Antiquity, 1951 19 L. OPPENHEIM, Divination and Celestial Observation in the Last Assyrian Empire, in: Centaurus 14, 1969, 97–135 20 G. RADKE, Fasti Romani, 1990 21 J. RÜPKE, Kalender und Öffentlichkeit. Die Geschichte der Repräsentation und religiösen Qualifikation von Zeit in Rom, 1995 22 M. R. SALZMAN, On Roman Time: The Codex-Calendar of 354 and the Rhythms of Urban Life in Late Antiquity, 1990 23 A. STROBEL, Ursprung und Geschichte des frühchristlichen Osterkalenders, 1977 24 K. VON STUCKRAD, Das Ringen um die Astrologie. Jüdische und christliche Beiträge zum antiken Zeitverständnis, 2000 25 E. SVENBERG, De Latinska Lunaria, thesis 1936 26 N. M. SWERDLOW (ed.), The Babylonian Theory of the Planets, 1998 27 Id. (ed.), Ancient Astronomy and Celestial Divination, 2000 28 B. L. VAN DER WAERDEN, Die Anfänge der Astronomie, 1968 29 E. WIFSTRAND, Lunariastudien, 1944. K. V. S.

Hemina (*emina*). Latin term adopted from the Greek (ἡμίνα; *hēmína*) for a measure of volume for liquids and dry goods in the volume of $^1/_{96}$ → amphora, $^1/_{32}$ → modius, $^1/_2$ → sextarius, corresponding to 2 → quartarii, 4 → acetabula, 6 → cyathi. It corresponds to 0.273 l; calibrated in relation to water, there are 10 ounces to 1 *hemina*. Widespread as a measurement for drinks – comparable with 'half a pint' in comedy and in other writers [1. 2602–2604] as well as a quantity indicator in recipes in Caelius Apicius [2. 99–100; 3. 143]. As an oil measure, *hemina* describes by the name λιτραῖον κέρας (horn holding one *lítra*) a vessel made of horn for measuring oil with a scale of 12 measurement strokes.

→ Measures (Greece and Rome)

1 ThlL VI 3.   2 I. STRIEGAN-KEUNTJE, Concordantia et Index in Apicium, 1992.   3 A. URBÁN, Concordantia Apiciana, 1995.

F. HULTSCH, Griech. und röm. Metrologie, ²1882; O. VIEDEBANTT, s.v. H., RE 8, 248–249; H. CHANTRAINE, s.v. Uncia, RE 9 A, 659–662; Id., s.v. H., KlP 2, 1020. H.-J.S.

Hemiobolion (ἡμιωβόλιον; *hēmiōbólion* or ἡμιωβέλιον; *hēmiōbélion*). Coin with the value of half an → obolos. On silver coins of the Peloponnese the abbreviated value indication HM, H or E is often found. In Corinth the head of Pegasus was the symbol of the *hemiobolion* from the 5th cent. BC onwards [1. 400f.], in Athens in the 4th cent. BC it was the owl instead of the crescent moon common on the obolos and $^1/_4$ obolos [1. 374]. The weight of the *hemiobolion* depended on the standards of → coinage of the minting places.

On bronze coins from Aegae/Achaia in Roman times there is the nominal description HMIOBEΛIN [1. 413]. → Obolos; → Coinage, standards of

1 HN.

SCHRÖTTER, s.v. Hemiobol, 262. GE.S.

Hemiolion (ἡμιόλιον; *hēmiólion*), literally 'one and a half times'. *Hemiolion* refers to a supplementary charge of 50% of a monetary or goods service (calculated by multiplying the basic amount by one and a half). In the Hellenistic and Roman periods the *hemiolion* stereotypically appeared in the penalty clauses of private contracts as a fine for non-fulfilment (frequently in addition to interest), both in the papyri of Egypt and in the few documents extant elsewhere. The *hemiolion* had replaced the *diploûn* (διπλοῦν, double) of the older contractual clauses, as is well illustrated by building contracts extant in inscriptions (cf. Pl. Leg. 921d). The public administration of Egypt too used the *hemiolion*, e.g. for failure to pay taxes.

A. BERGER, Die Strafklauseln in den Papyrusurkunden, 1911; G. THÜR, Bemerkungen zum altgriech. Werkvertrag, in: FS Biscardi 5, 1984, 510; H.-A. RUPPRECHT, Einführung in die Papyruskunde, 1994, 114, 118. G.T.

Hemisphairion (ἡμισφαίριον; *hēmisphaírion*). The term refers to a 'hemisphere' a) in stereometry as a geometrical body, b) in astronomical cosmology as half a celestial sphere on both sides of one of the large celestial circles (→ Kykloi), mostly of the horizon, i.e. outwards from the earth that was thought to be central, the upper, visible celestial hollow sphere and the bottom, invisible half of the sky, then also c) the convex hemisphere of the earth on both sides of the horizon that was only deduced in antiquity. Furthermore human artefacts were also called *hemisphairion*: on a large scale d) a domed vault – Greek also → *thólos* – (Varro, Vitruvius), or e) the shape of the Greek amphitheatre (Cassiodorus), on a small scale f) the concave hollow of a certain type of sundial and then synecdochically the latter itself (= σκάφη; → Clock; Vitruvius 9,8,1 distinguishes *hemicy-*

clium excavatum from this), as well as g) quite late also in the Latinized form *duo semisphaeria* (= μαγάδεις) of a double semicircle-shaped device for tensioning the string of a monochord (Boeth. De institutione musicae 4,18 with fig. in FRIEDLEIN).

H. DEGERING, s.v. H., RE 8, 253f.; H.H. GROTH, s.v. H., ThlL VI 3, 2604f.   W.H.

Hemithea (Ἡμιθέα; *Hēmithéa*, 'demigoddess'). Name of a healing goddess in Castabus on the Carian Chersonnese. Her sanctuary, whose archaeological traces go back to the late 7th cent. BC at the earliest, was expanded under Rhodian hegemony and achieved more than regional fame until the decline of Rhodes after 167 BC. In the sanctuary, patients received healing dreams through → incubation (*klísis*, 'incubation (room)' in an inscription from *c.* 150 BC, SEG 14,690); H. also aided women in childbirth (Diod. Sic. 5,63). The cult forbade the use of wine and the sacrifice or any other use of pigs.

The aetiology of the cult derives the goddess from → Molpadia, the daughter of Dionysus' son → Staphylus and sister of → Rhoeo and → Parthenos (Diod. Sic. 5,62f.). Molpadia and Parthenos were to guard the newly discovered wine but they fall asleep; a pig smashes the wine jug. The sisters flee, Parthenos is taken to Bubastus by Apollo, Molpadia to Castabus, where she is worshipped as H.

H. is also the sister of → Ten(n)es, the son of → Cycnus, in the foundation myth of Tenedus, which probably goes back to the → *Cypria*. In this, Tenes is accused of rape by his stepmother, who he had rejected. Cycnus sets both adrift in a chest which washes ashore on Tenedus. H. has no function here; on Tenedus she is pursued by Achilles, who kills Tenes (main passages: Apollod. Epit. 3,24f.; Conon FGrH 16 F 1,28; Plut. Quaest. Graec. 28; Paus. 10,14,2–4).

Staphylus and his daughters H. and Rhoeo also play a role in a myth told by Parthenius 1 (according to Nicaenetus and Apollonius Rhodius). In this, Lyrcus and his father-in-law Aebialus, ruler of Caunus in Caria, stayed with Staphylus after visiting the oracle of Didyma. Lyrcus was childless, and the oracle had prophesied that the first woman Lyrcus slept with would bear his son – so, Staphylus places H., who is pregnant, in his bed and her son becomes the next ruler of Caunus.

A. LAUMONIER, Les cultes indigènes en Carie, 1958, 664–667; J. M. COOK, W. H. PLOMMER, The Sanctuary of H. at Kastabos, 1966; H. A. CAHN, s.v. Ten(n)es, LIMC 7, 892.
F.G.

Hemitomos see → Vessels, shapes and types

Hemlock (Greek κώνειον/*kṓneion* due to its conical ovary κῶνος; *kônos*, Lat. *cicuta*, other names were derived from its poisonous effect, e.g. in Dioscorides 4,78 WELLMANN = 4,79 BERENDES), the umbellifer which grows wild in Europe in two species (the spotted hemlock, *Conium maculatum* and water hemlock, *Cicuta*

virosa). Theophrastus (Hist. pl. 1,5,3) mentions the fleshy and hollow (ibid. 6,2,9) stem of the plant which is similar to devil's dung (*Ferula asafoetida*) (→ Narthex [1]). The root, when brewed, leaves a residue stronger than that of the umbel (differing: Plin. HN 25,151), and, as a (narcotic) additive to other poisonous plants, causes a more rapid death (Theophr. Hist. pl. 9,8,3). This recipe is said to have been invented by a Thrasyas from Mantinea (ibid. 9,16,8). The best description of the effect of hemlock can be found in Dioscorides (4,78 WELLMANN = 4,79 BERENDES), who recommended the juice pressed from the unripe umbel mixed with wine (regarded as an antidote) as an analgesic, and for suppressing the sexual drive during puberty. Pliny (HN 25,151–154) confirms this, and mentions that the main use of the juice, applied externally, was to stem the flow of tears and to relieve eye pain; the effect was explained with a cooling of the limbs and a thickening of the blood (thus also Ael. NA 4.23). Plato offers a detailed description of → Socrates' slow death after drinking a cup of hemlock in the year 399 BC (Phdr. 117a–118). Many executions (→ Capital punishment), esp. in Athens, and many murders by poison in antiquity were carried out with the use of hemlock.

→ Poisons

H. GOSSEN, s.v. Schierling, RE Suppl. 8,706–710.   C.HÜ.

Hemmoor (Cuxhaven district). Cremation burial fields of the early Imperial era (2nd/3rd cents. AD) with bronze or brass vessels that were used as urns. The finding-place gave its name to the typical Hemmoor buckets, some of which have richly decorated rims and attachments; They come from Roman workshops in the Rhineland.

→ Germanic archaeology; → Urna

M. ERDRICH, Zu den Messingeimern vom Hemmoorer Typ, in: R. BUSCH (ed.), Rom an der Niederelbe, 1995, 71–80; H. WILLERS, Die röm. Bronzeeimer von H., 1901.
V.P.

Hemp The dioecious (with smaller male form) fibrous plant *Cannabis sativa* L. (κάνναβις/-ος/*kánnabis/-os*, *cannabis/-us*) is from the *Urticaceae* family, 2–4 m tall with finger-shaped long-stemmed leaves. Around 500 BC hemp probably grew in the area from the Caspian Sea to China. The Scythians are said to have used the seeds, which both grew wild and were cultivated, for ritual sweat baths and ecstatic states of intoxication (Hdt. 4,74f.). This suggests hashish, which is won from the subspecies *Cannabis Indica* (cf. Hsch. s.v. κάνναβις). The Thracians are said to have used the bast fibres to make linen-like fabrics. Hemp was later cultivated in Greece (for instance in Elis, Paus. 6,26,6); Pers. 5,146 and Gell. NA 17,3,4 mention the cultivation in Italy. Hieron II of Syracuse imported ship's ropes made of hemp from the Rhône in the 3rd cent. BC (Ath. 5,206f); this has been documented for the city of Athens as well (Xen. Ath. pol. 2). Hemp ropes were known already to the Roman satirist Lucilius (fr. 1325 M.; cf. Varro, Rust. 1,23,6).

Hemp seeds are planted outdoors from the end of February in well-fertilized soil (Columella 2,10,21; Pall. Agric. 3,5); Plin. HN 19,173f. describes the treatment of various kinds of ripe seeds and fibres after the harvest in the autumn. Ropes that could be used under water were made of the Spanish halfa grass (*spartum*; Plin. HN 19,29). It was believed that the oil-rich seeds of the wild (in Dioscorides 3,148 WELLMANN = 3,155 BERENDES: cultivated) hemp would make men sterile, its juice would drive worms and other creatures out of one's ears, and that the boiled root would help as a topical remedy for gout and burns (Plin. HN 20,259). Hemp was confused, among others by Dioscorides (3,149 WELLMANN = 3,156 BERENDES), with the hemp-leaf mallow (*Malvaceae*; *Althaea cannabina* L.).
→ Linen

1 V. HEHN, O. SCHRADER, Kulturpflanzen und Haustiere, [8]1911, repr. 1963, 190–193   2 F. ORTH, s.v. H., RE 7, 2313–2316.   C.HÜ.

Henbane Knowledge of *Hyoscyamus* L., a member of the *Solanacaea* family (ὑοσκύαμος; *hyoskýamos*, named after cramps which pigs apparently get from eating the poisonous herb), can be demonstrated in Dioscorides 4,68 [1. 224ff.; 2. 402f.]. According to Plin. HN 25,35, Hercules discovered the plant. According to Dioscorides, of the varieties found in Greece, the first two *Hyoscyamus niger* (ὑοσκύαμος μέλας) and *aureus* (ὑοσκύαμος λευκός), are not usable due to their poisonous nature. A juice pressed from the plant or seeds of the third, *Hyoscyamus albus*, a ruderal plant, was used in preparing pain-relieving medications. The leaves were also used topically because of their alkaloid content. *Hyoscyamus reticulatus* L. was also mentioned. Pall. Agric. 1,35,5 uses the juice together with vinegar against 'fleas' on cabbage. In the Middle Ages *iusquiamus* was used often after the publication of the 'Lorscher Arzneibuch' [3].
→ Poisonous herbs

1 M. WELLMANN (ed.), Pedanii Dioscuridis de materia medica, 2, 1906, repr. 1958   2 J. BERENDES (ed.), Des Pedanios Dioskurides Arzneimittellehre übers. und mit Erl. versehen, 1902, repr. 1970   3 U. STOLL (ed.), Das "Lorscher Arzneibuch", 1992.   C.HÜ.

Hendeka, hoi (οἱ ἕνδεκα; *hoi héndeka*). The 'Eleven', an office of eleven men, were in charge of the prison in Athens and of the execution of prisoners who had been sentenced to death. They executed ordinary criminals (*kakoûrgoi*) or exiles who were apprehended in Athens and turned over to them by means of the → *apagōgḗ*, without a trial if the prisoner confessed, or they presided over the trial if the prisoner denied his guilt. They also presided over trials that were instituted by means of → *éndeixis* and over cases that were meant to force the confiscation of land (Ps.-Aristot. Ath. Pol. 52,1).

The office appears to have existed already at the time of Solon (ibid. 7,3). The ones who held the office under the oligarchy of the Thirty were seen as being connected to the government for the most part, so that they were counted among those who were subject to the → *eúthynai* if they wanted to live in the restored democracy (loc. cit. 35,1; 39,6).

1 A. R. W. HARRISON, The Law of Athens, 1971, 17f.
2 J. H. LIPSIUS, Das attische Recht und Rechtsverfahren, vol. 1, 1905–1915, 74–81.   P.J.R.

Hendiadyoin see → Figures I

Hengist and Horsa ('stallion and steed'). The brothers H. and H., sons of the Jute (Danish) Wihtgil, were said to be the leaders of Anglo-Saxon warriors recruited by the southern British king Vortigern in AD 449 to help him repel the Scots and Picts. After a few years, a conflict developed between the Britons and their Germanic allies. In the battle of Aylesford (455) Horsa is said to have died on the Germanic side, and Vortigern's son Categirn, on the British. According to the *Anglo-Saxon Chronicle*, Hengist founded the kingdom of Kent in the same year. Hengist and his son Oisc (Aesc) are said to have fought against the Britons at Crayford in 457, at Wippedsfleot in 465, and at an unknown location in 473. Hengist died in 488 and left his kingdom to Oisc, after whom the later kings of Kent were named 'Oiscingas'. Whether or not Oisc was a blood descendant of Hengist is debatable, Bede's testimony (Historia ecclesiastica 2,5) notwithstanding. Also questionable are the (somewhat lengthy) time-spans given in the *Anglo-Saxon Chronicle* that on the basis of British (Nennius, *Historia Brittonum*) and continental sources should probably be reduced by about 20 years.

C. AHRENS (ed.), Sachsen und Angelsachsen, 1978; J. MORRIS, The Age of Arthur, [2]1977; Id., Studies in Dark-Age History, 1995; K. SCHREINER, Die Sage von Hengist und Horsa, 1921, repr. 1967   M.SCH.

Henioche (Ἡνιόχη/*Hēnióchē*, 'Holder of the reins').
[1] Epithet of Hera in Boeotian Lebadea, where sacrifices were made to, e.g., Zeus Basileus, Demeter and H. before consulting the Trophonius-oracle (Paus. 9,39,5); Hera is also a chariot driver in the *Iliad* (Hom. Il. 8,392).

SCHACHTER 1, 240f.   AN.W.

[2] According to Ps.-Hes. Sc. 83, the wife of → Creon (Soph. Ant. 1180: Eurydice, cf. schol.).
[3] Daughter of Creon (Paus. 9,10,3).
[4] Daughter of → Pittheus of Troezen, wife of Canethus, mother of → Sciron, of → Sinis according to others (Plut. Thes. 25,6).
[5] Daughter of Armenius, wife of Andropompus, mother of → Melanthus, (Hellanicus FGrH 323a F 23), eponymous heroine of the → Heniochi.

[6] Val. Fl. 5,357 called Medea's otherwise nameless wet-nurse H., possibly after the Heniochi.

G. Weicker, s.v. H. (1–6), RE 8, 258.   T.H.

Heniochi (Ἡνίοχοι/*Heníochoi*, Ps.-Scyl. 71). In the 5th cent. BC, a large group of tribes on the Caucasian coast of the Pontus – then a densely wooded area with many inlets – between the Zygi and the Achaeans in the north and the San(n)igae in the south. → Pityus/Picunda was founded in the territory of the H. The H. raised cattle and engaged in piracy with light boats (Str. 11,2,14) and were subjugated towards the end of the 4th cent. BC by the Bosporan king → Eumelus [4], who campaigned against piracy on the Pontus (Diod. Sic. 20,25,2). In the 1st cents. BC and AD, a large migratory movement took place in which the H. settled in an area that stretched from the Pontian Alps to the sources of the → Cyrus (Plin. HN 6,26; 6,30) and were under Roman suzerainty at least in the Hadrianic period (Arr. Peripl. p. eux. 15).

W. E. D. Allen, Ex Ponto III, in: Bedi Kartlisa 32/33, 1959, 28–35; E. Kiessling, s.v. Ἡνίοχοι, RE 8, 259–280.
                                                        A.P.-L.

Heniochus (Ἡνίοχος; *Hēníochos*). Writer of Middle Comedy, of whose work the Suda still mentions eight titles: Τροχίλος ('Trochílos'), Ἐπίκληρος ('The daughter heiress'), Γοργόνες ('The Gorgons'), Πολυπράγμων ('The Busybody'), Θωρύκιον ('Thōrýkion'), Πολύευκτος ('Polýeuktos'), Φιλέταιρος ('Philhétairos'), Δὶς ἐξαπατώμενος ('The Twice Deceived') [1. test. 1]. Apart from the scanty remains of these plays preserved by Athenaeus (at least the dithyrambizing language of fr. 1 [2. 262] is noteworthy), Strobaeus transmits 17 verses (probably from the prologue) of a political comedy. Strobaeus does not provide a title, and the comedy remains difficult to date (fr. 5).

1 PCG V, 552–557   2 H. G. Nesselrath, Die att. mittlere Komödie, 1990.   T.HI.

Henna (Ἔννα/*Henna*, Ἔννα/*Énna*).
[1] Well-fortified city of the Siculi (Cic. Verr. 2,4,107; Diod. Sic. 5,3,2; though possibly founded by Syracuse, Steph. Byz. s.v. H., cf. [1. 74²⁴; 2. 395]) on a steep, almost 1,000 m high mountain in the centre of Sicily, Hellenized from the 5th cent., besieged for a short time in 403, then on a long-term basis from 396 by Dionysius I (Diod. Sic. 14,14,6–8; 78,7), defected from Agathocles in 309 (Diod. Sic. 20,31,5). H. was fought over in the 1st Punic War (Diod. Sic. 23,9,4f.; Pol. 1,24,12, who includes it among the πολισμάτια, 'little cities') and was heavily punished in 214 for its attempt to defect to the Carthaginians (Liv. 24,37–39; Frontin. Str. 4,7,22; Polyaenus, Strat. 8,21; CIL I 530). In the Great Slave War, which began in H. in 136, it was the residence of Eunus (for his coin-minting: [2. 416ff.]),

and was captured only in 132 after being starved out after a longer siege. According to Cicero (Verr. 2,3,100; 4,106–115), the *mun(icipium) Hennae* (thus on coins) was also a victim of the machinations of Verres.

H. is mentioned in Byzantine accounts of the Arab invasion, to which the city eventually succumbed in 859 AD. The medieval name Castrogiovanni (from *Castrum Hennae* through the Arabic *Qaṣr Ǧanna*) was changed to Enna in 1927. Ancient finds in the Museo Alessi. Inscriptions: SEG 30,1123 (decree of appreciation from → Entella for help received from H.). Coins: HN 136f. [3. 173ff.].

1 G. Manganaro, Mondo religioso greco e mondo "indigeno" in Sicilia, in: C. Antonetti (ed.), Il dinamismo della colonizzazione greca, 1997   2 Id., Metoikismos, in: ASNP 20, 1990, 391–408   3 V. Cammarta, H., Tra storia e arte, 1990.

BTCGI 7, 1989, 189ff.   GI.MA.

[2] The blossoms of the oriental shrub *Lawsonia inermis*, described by Dioscorides (1,95 Wellmann = 1,124 Berendes) as κύπρος/*kýpros* (*cypros*, Plin. HN 12,109 *et passim*), known as coming from Ascalon (Palestine) and Canopus (Lower Egypt) and resembling privet, provide the orange-yellow colouring material used today, e.g. for tinting nails and hair. Preparation of henna unguent (κύπρινον ἔλαιον), recommended for nervous disorders, is likewise to be found in Dioscorides 1,55 Wellmann = 1,65 Berendes.   C.HÜ.

Henoch (Enoch) During the Jewish exile (6th cent. BC), the figure of the Biblical patriarch H. attracted various traditions from Babylonian antiquarians or cultural carriers. Even the short reference in Gen 5,21–24 makes probable the background of such a tradition, which is then further developed in Jewish literature between the 3rd BC and the 1st cent. AD. The central notion is that H. did not die but was translated into heaven while he was still alive. At the same time his age of 365 years indicates an awareness of astronomical-calendrical theories. The earliest Aramaic MSS (e.g. 'Book of Watchers', 'Book of the Similitudes', 'Book of Astronomical Writings', 'Book of Dreams', 'Epistle of H.') were editorially comprised in the so-called Ethiopian Book of H. (originally Greek, 1st cent. AD), in that it is dominated by interest in the myth of fallen angels and by an apocalyptical interpretation of history. The so-called Slavonic Book of H. (originally Greek, 1st cent. AD) builds on this circle of writings but recounts anew the story of H. in a strict sequence of ascent to heaven, admonitions, and cult establishments, in which wisdom sayings and paraenetic themes take prominence. A so-called Hebrew Book of H. (5th–6th cents. AD), which fits into the context of → Hekhalot literature of Jewish mysticism, shows H. as the highest-ranking angel and leader of the adept on the ascent to the world of God's throne.

In those three writings H. is presented as a revealer of cosmological and eschatological secrets, a leader of humanity, a scribe at the eschatological court, an intercessor, prophet, and God's designated plenipotentiary, and becomes a model of wisdom and justice. Numerous allusions to this are to be found in early Jewish literature – e.g. Sir 44,16; 49,14; Jub 4,16–26 *et passim*; LibAnt 1,13–17; TestAbrB 11,3–9; PsEupol F I 1,9; ApcEsdr 5,22; TestXII. The H. interpretation by Philo contains some original features – e.g. Mut 38; Abr 23–24; Praem 15–21. In the NT, Jud 14 refers to Ethiopian Hen 1,9; Hebr 11,5 emphasizes H.'s beliefs. The Church Fathers (→ Clemens [3] of Alexandria, → Origenes, → Tertullianus etc.) and chronographers (→ Syncellus) refer to H. and quote his writings. Rabbinic texts attempt to qualify H.'s moral integrity. Later independent adaptions of the material can be found in a fragmentarily preserved Christian apocryphon (Coptic, 5th cent. AD) that shows H. as brother of the → Sibyl, and also in a Jewish → Midrash (Hebr., *c.* 11th cent.), in which H. appears as a model ascetic and primeval king of peace. Together with → Elias [1], as one of the two witnesses from Apc 11, H. is to be found in Christian apocalyptic writing down to the beginning of the modern era.

J. T. Milik, The Books of Enoch. Aramaic Fragments of Qumran Cave 4, 1976; S. Uhlig, Das äthiop. H.buch (Jüd. Schriften aus hell.-röm. Zeit V/6), 1984, 459–780; Ch. Böttrich, Das slav. H.buch (Jüd. Schriften aus hell.-röm. Zeit V/7), 1996, 781–1040; P. Schäfer, K. Herrmann (ed.), Übers. der Hekhalot-Lit. I [= so-called Hebrew book of H.] (Texte und Studien zum ant. Judentum 46), 1995; Ch. Böttrich, Beobachtungen zum Midrasch vom "Leben Henochs", in: Mitt. und Beitr. der Forschungsstelle Judentum Leipzig, 10–11, 1996, 44–83; K. Berger, s.v. H., RAC 14, 473–545; J. C. VanderKam, Enoch. A Man for All Generations, 1995.   CHR.B.

Henotikon (Ἑνωτικόν; *Henōtikón*). Aimed at the churches of Egypt, Libya and the Pentapolis, on the occasion of patriarch Petrus Mongus' assumption of office, the H., promulgated in AD 482 by the East Roman emperor → Zeno, with the influential collaboration of patriarch Acacius of Constantinople (CPG III, 5999; originally Ἥδικτον Ζήνωνος, 'edict of Zeno', named H. since Zacharias Rhetor, Historia ecclesiastica 5,8; cf. Evagrius, Hist. eccl. 3,13f.), sought to restore the unity of belief and empire, endangered after the AD 451 Council of → Calchedon, on the basis of the Symbolum Nicaeno-Constantinopolitanum and Cyrillic Christology. Rome's refusal (Synod 484 under Felix III [II]) led to the Acacian (→ Acacius [4]) Schism (until 519).

EDITIONS: E. Schwartz, Cod. Vaticanus gr. 1431, 1927, no. 75, 52–54.
BIBLIOGRAPHY: A. Grillmeier, Jesus der Christus im Glauben der Kirche 2/1, 1986, 279–358 (transl.: 285–287).   J.RI.

Heosphoros see → Phosphoros

Hepatoscopy see → Divination; → Haruspices

Hephaestion (Ἡφαιστίων; *Hēphaistíōn*).
[1] H. of Pella, friend and probably lover of → Alexander [4]. Their relationship was soon likened to that of → Patroclus and → Achilles [1] and correspondingly embellished. It is doubtful whether he was a childhood friend of Alexander (Curt. 3,12,16), as he was not banished by → Philippus II in 337 BC. The wreath offered to Patroclus at Troy and the scene described in the vulgate version (→ Alexander historians) of the confusion of H. and Alexander by → Sisygambis (Arr. Anab. 1,12,1; 2,12,6) are highlighted as fictitious.

After minor missions, he appears at → Gaugamela, where he was wounded, as the 'leader of the → Somatophylakes' (Diod. Sic. 17,61,3). This hardly means that he was in command of the → Hetairoi bodyguards ('among the Somatophylakes' is how H. is later attested: 'leader' was probably added by Diodorus. Arr. Anab. 3,15,2 gives no rank). At the trial of → Philotas, he took part in the arrest and torture. As a reward, he took over the command of the Hetairoi with → Cleitus. He is hardly mentioned in → Bactria and → Sogdiana, particularly surprisingly at the death of Cleitus, and as accuser of → Callisthenes only in Plutarch (Alexander 55,1), from an unidentifiable source. Only in the Indian campaign, and particularly after the mutiny at the → Hyphasis, does he appear in leading roles. At → Patala and in the battle with the → Oreitae he carried out important missions and from → Carmania he led the main body of the army and the baggage train to → Susa. At the weddings in Susa, he married a sister of Alexander's royal bride → Statira. There he was probably made → *chiliarchos*. He died in → Ecbatana in the winter of 324/3, primarily from excessive wine consumption. Alexander had H.'s doctor executed, burned H.'s body on a royal pyre, set up a hero cult to him with the permission of → Ammon [1] and had the Persian royal fires extinguished (which was interpreted as an omen of his own death). The 'Lion of Hamadan' may be his memorial.

H. was a competent general, but not as outstanding as other officers, and Alexander knew it. As a spiteful intriguer, he did not get along with many of the courtiers and generals, but Alexander (partly even because of this) trusted him completely. He is supposed to have said that H. would have been nothing without him (Plut. Alexander 47,11).

BERVE 2, no. 357; HECKEL, 65–90.   E.B.

[2] Sculptor from Athens, son of Myron and father of → Eutychides (also sculptors). Based on nine extant pedestal inscriptions on Delos, his creative period can be limited to between 124 BC and the beginning of the 1st cent. BC. Some of his works were portrait statues, two of them, on the basis of traces on their pedestals, bronze.

V. C. Goodlett, Rhodian sculpture workshops, in: AJA 95, 1991, 672; Loewy, no. 252-255; J. Marcadé, Recueil des signatures de sculpteurs grecs, 2, 1957, 58-62; Id., Au musée de Délos, 1969, 59, 65-66; Overbeck, no. 2245-2247 (sources).   R.N.

[3] Son of Thrasyllus, was *syngenès kai epistratēgós* (συγγενὴς καὶ ἐπιστρατηγός) of Thebes before 62 BC and acted as → *dioikētés*, probably for the whole country. He was then promoted into the office itself, and was also *pròs tō idíōi lógōi kaì pròs procheírois* (πρὸς τῷ ἰδίῳ λόγῳ καὶ πρὸς προχείροις), from 60 to 57.
→ Court titles

> PP 1/8, 30a; 31.; L. Mooren, Aulic Titulature in Ptolemaic Egypt, 1975, 96 no. 060; 138f. no. 0173; J. D. Thomas, The Epistrategos in Ptolemaic and Roman Egypt 1, 1975, 105 no. X; E. van 't Dack, Ptolemaica Selecta, 1988, 295f.   W.A.

[4] Alexandrian metrician of the 2nd cent. AD perhaps teacher of the emperor Lucius Verus (cf. SHA Verus 2,5). The most significant work of this author of 'many works' (according to Suda η 659) was a treatise on metrics. This was originally composed of 48 books, but was abridged by H. himself first to 11, then to 3 books, and finally to the 'little handbook' (*Encheirídion*; 181,11-16 Consbruch) which still exists today (Suda η 659). The summary is schematic, if rich in examples from lost works; evidently H. did not wish to address beginners as → Heliodorus [3] did [5. 49-50]. At the end of the *Encheirídion* there are two fragmentary sections of a work 'On Poetry' (Περὶ ποιήματος) (an analysis of poetic texts according to their metrical structures) authorship, as well as a short treatise on diacritical marks showing metrical peculiarities (Περὶ σημείων).

H. is a follower of the theory of the *métra prōtótypa*, according to which all verses are formed from a few fundamental (*prōtótypa*) metres. These metres, in turn, are formed from the combination of short elements with one time unit (˘), and long elements with two time units (¯). After an introduction on prosody, where H. also covers the phenomenon of *synekphṓnēsis* (synizesis), H. dedicates one chapter to each of his nine *métra prōtótypa*: the iamb (˘¯), the trochee (¯˘), the dactyl (¯˘˘), the anapaest (˘˘¯), the choriamb (¯˘˘¯), the antispast (˘¯¯˘), the major Ionic (¯¯˘˘), the minor Ionic (˘˘¯¯), the cretic or amphimacer (¯˘¯). The 'uniform' verses were formed from them, i.e. they have the same rhythm throughout (iambic, trochaic, etc.) and appear in complete form (acatalectic), or they are missing their last one or two syllables (catalectic, brachycatalectic). However, the verses could also be 'mixed', i.e. composed of metres with varying rhythms, in particular: a) mixed from related or 'similar' (ὁμοιοειδῆ) metres, b) 'contrastingly' mixed (κατ' ἀντιπάθειαν) as in the Sapphic hendecasyllabic, c) asynartetic, 'not connected to one another', that is without homogeneous rhythmic structure (cf. [3; 5; 7]), d) polyschematic. Lastly H. deals with 'unclear' (συγκεχυμένα) verses (schol. Her-

mog. 78,1-2 C.). The teachings of H. agree with the metric-rhythmic system in the first book of → Aristides [7] Quintilianus [3; 4]. H.'s fragment 2 = 77,4-17 C., where the mutual 'relationship' (συγγένεια) of the metres is discussed, also seems to contain the other fundamental theories of Greek metrics, according to which all verses can be derived from dactylic hexameter and iambic trimeter [5. 380].

H.'s handbook represents the foundation for metrics in the Byzantine school and was annotated by → Longinus and → Choiroboskos, provided with scholia and later organized into a compendium (excerpts from these texts in [2. 79-334]). It also influenced the medieval tradition of poetic texts (cf. [1]). John → Tzetzes wrote a poetic version of the *Encheirídion*. Indeed, H.'s theory has had strong influence down to the modern descriptions of metrics: P. Masqueray's textbook of 1899 still follows it.
→ Phonetics; → Metrics; → Philoxenus

> 1 J. Irigoin, Les scholies métriques de Pindar, 1958, 93-106.
> Editions: 2 M. Consbruch, 1906.
> Bibliography: 3 B. Gentili, L'asinarteto nella teoria metrico-ritmica degli antichi, in: P. Händel, W. Meid (ed.), FS Robert Muth, 1983, 135-143 4 J. M. van Ophuijsen, H. on Metre. A translation and commentary, 1987 5 B. M. Palumbo Stracca, La teoria antica degli asinarteti, 1979 (trans. and comm. on 43,5-56,3 C.) 6 R. Pretagostini, Le teorie metrico-ritmiche degli antichi, in: G. Cambiano et al. (ed.), Lo spazio letterario della Grecia antica, I,2, 373-379 7 L. E. Rossi, Teoria e storia degli asinarteti dagli arcaici agli alessandrini, in: Miscellanea filologica. Problemi di metrica classica, 1978, 29-48.   S.FO.

[5] H. of Thebes. wrote an astrological work in 3 books in about AD 381: 1. Basic concepts, 2. Forecasts for newborns, 3. Times for beginning actions (*katarchaí*). In it H. quoted long passages of older literature (almost) literally: → Nechepso, → Dorotheus [5] (partially translated into prose) and → Ptolemaeus. Four different epitomes have been preserved.
→ Astrology

> D. Pingree (Ed.), Hephaestionis Thebani apotelesmaticorum libri tres, 1973-1974; W. and H. G. Gundel, Astrologumena, 1966, 241-244.   W.H.

Hephaestus (Ἥφαιστος; *Héphaistos*).
I. Myth   II. Cult   III. Iconography

I. Myth

H., the son of → Hera, is the Greek god of fire, the smithy and of craftsmen; the name's etymology is unknown.

H. is not documented in the Minoan-Mycenaean texts, even if a theophoric name appears in Mycenaean Knossos (*apaitijo*, KN L 588; [1. 34f.]). In Homer, H. is closely connected with his element, → fire. He possesses fire, which is stereotyped as φλὸξ Ἡφαιστοίο ('flame of

H.'; Hom. Il. 9,468 etc.), and his name is used as a metonym for fire (Hom. Il. 2,426 etc., formula); at Hera's request he uses fire to intervene in Achilles' battle against Scamander (Hom. Il. 21,328–382). But above all he is, in his capacity as master of the fire, the divine smith. He fashions the new shield for Achilles, creates a series of wondrous automata for himself and for others, self-propelled tripods (Hom. Il. 18,373–379), golden maidservants (ibid. 417–421), bronze dogs as guards for King Alcinous (Hom. Od. 7,91–94, an ancient Oriental motif [2]); in Hes. Op. 70f. he works together with Athena on the creation of → Pandora.

He is an outsider in the society of the 'easy-living' Homeric gods: He works and sweats (Hom. Il. 18,372); at the meal of the gods (which, like the human symposium, displays different social roles) he tries his hand at the role of → Ganymede [1] and reaps only laughter (Hom. Il. 1,571–600); in his marriage to → Aphrodite he is deceived by his brother → Ares (Hom. Od. 8,267–366). He does not have the physical perfection of the other gods either: he has crippled feet (archaic pictures on vases mostly portray them as being backwards). While Homer calls → Zeus his father (Hom. Il. 1,578; 14,388; Hom. Od. 8,312), in Hesiod Hera gave birth to him parthenogenetically (Theog. 927), just as she gives birth to the monster Typhaon (Hom. H. Apoll. 305–355, as a reaction to the birth of Athena) or the outsider Ares (Ov. Fast. 5,229–258); in Hesiod, this birth is the consequence of a quarrel with Zeus, who reacts with his affair with → Metis and the motherless birth of Athena out of his head (Hes. fr. 343, cf. Theog. 886–900). When Hera sees the crippled child, she angrily throws it out of Olympus into the sea, where Eurynome and → Thetis raise it (Hom. Il. 18,395–405; similarly Hom. h. Apoll. 316–320); or Zeus is angry with H., because he takes Hera's side against Zeus, and throws him out of Olympus to earth, where he lands on the island of → Lemnos and is cared for by the Sinties (Hom. Il. 1,590–594).

But one should not underestimate H.: He not only creates wonderful automata and is socially skilled enough to deliberately provoke the gods to laughter in order to cheer them up; he takes revenge on the adulterers Aphrodite and Ares with the help of his sophisticated art, making them an object of laughter in their turn (Hom. Od. 8,267–366), and on his mother Hera (Alcaeus fr. 349 L.-P.). In this way the epic traces the position which the smith held in an early aristocratic society: indispensable because of his art, highly valued and at the same time secretly feared. Similar conditions are found in other societies [3].

Apart from developments in Athens, this picture continues without fundamental changes. From the 5th cent. BC his technical capabilities make him into a bearer of culture, who made fundamental changes in the beast-like life of human beings (a sophistic theme; H. Hom. 20). His workshop, which was only vaguely located in the epic, is situated on or under active volcanoes (Aetna: Aesch. PV 365f., or Hiera, one of the Lipari Islands: Thuc. 3,88,3), where he also has a cult (Ael. NA 11,3; Str. 6,2,10); the → Cyclopes, who produce thunder and lightning for Zeus (Hes. Theog. 141), are given to him as workers. In the same way he is connected to other natural fires, like the ones on Lycian Olympus (Sen. Ep. 79,3) or the region of Pozzuoli ('agora of H.', Str. 5,4,6 – where it is impossible to separate him from → Volcanus).

II. CULT

Lemnos, where myth had him live after the fall from Olympus, is especially important among the cult centres of H.; fire and the production of weapons are supposed to have been invented here (Hellanicus, FGrH 4 F 71; Tzetz. Lycoph. 227). One of the island's two towns is called Hephaestia (Steph. Byz. s.v.), after a sanctuary of H., whose eponymous priest had a one-year charge. H. is connected with the local mysteries of the → Cabiri, whose father he is (Hdt. 3,37; Str. 10,3,20f. connects this with Samothrace) [4]. This connection appears to have derived from archaic leagues of smiths. Non- and pre-Greek elements are in the background: The Sinties are considered to be pre-Greek Thracians (Steph. Byz. s.v. Lemnos) or Etruscans (schol. Apoll. Rhod. 1,608). But one cannot conclude from this and the numerous coins and theophoric personal names in Asia Minor that his origins are outside of Greece (in spite of the overwhelming majority of earlier researchers who derived him from Asia Minor, maybe from Lycia [5. 1–3]). Rather, the connection to Lemnos is part of H.'s marginal position, and the (late) documentation from Asia Minor point to the → Interpretatio Graeca with an indigenous deity.

The cult in Athens is better known, where H. is closely connected to → Athena as the patroness of crafts and goddess of practical wisdom; craftsmen can be understood to be 'dedicated to H. and Athena' (Pl. Leg. 11,920d, cf. Solon, fr. 13,49f.). In the city's main H. sanctuary on the hill between Ceramicus and Agora, the so-called 'Theseium', a creation of → Alcamenes [2] from the year 421/0 BC (Cic. Nat. D. 1,83; cf. Val. Max. 8,11 ext. 3; Paus. 1,14,6; [5. 75–90]) the cult statues of H. and Athena (Hephaestia: Hsch. s.v.) stood next to each other. Along with the temple, the festival of the Hephaestia was reorganized in 429/428 as a penteteric festival (festival celebrated every four years) in honour of the two deities, with a torch race and large sacrifices (Aristot. Ath. Pol. 54,7; the sacred law LSCG 13). This reflects the importance of craftsmen in the Athenian democracy; the torch race is reminiscent of the theme of new fire, which is also important for Lemnos and which accompanies H.'s role as the bearer of culture [6; 7]. The festival of the Chalkeia ('Festival of the Smiths'), in which the craftsmen walked in a procession through the city (Soph. fr. 844) is equally important for H. and Athena. At the phratria festival of the → Apatouria the participants, in their best clothes and carrying a torch, sang a hymn to H. at the end and sacrificed to him

(Istrus, FGrH 334 F 2). The Athenian myth of H.'s attempt to do violence to Athena is connected to this ritual: In the attempt his sperm fell to the ground and produced the child → Erichthonius [1], the autochthonous ancestor of the Athenian phratries [8].

H. was identified with the Egyptian Ptah in Memphis (Hdt. 2,2.99), the Etruscan Sethlans and the Roman → Volcanus – the latter already in the late 6th cent. BC, according to a black-figured vase with H.'s return home, which was found at the Volcanal on the Forum Romanum [9].

1 M. GÉRARD-ROUSSEAU, Les mentions religieuses dans les tablettes mycéniennes, 1968   2 C. FARAONE, Hephaestus the Magician and Near Eastern Parallels to Alcinous's Watchdogs, in: GRBS 28, 1987, 257–280   3 M. ELIADE, Forgerons et alchimistes, 1977   4 B. HEMBERG, Die Kabiren, 1950   5 F. BROMMER, H. Der Schmiedegott in der antiken Kunst, 1978   6 DEUBNER, 212f.   7 W. BURKERT, Iason, Hypsipyle and new fire on Lemnos. A study in myth and ritual, in: CQ 20, 1970, 1–16   8 N. LORAUX, Les enfants d'Athéna. Idées athéniennes sur la citoyenneté et la divison des sexes, 1981   9 F. COARELLI, Il Foro Romano. Periodo Arcaico, 1983, 177.

M. DELCOURT, Héphaistos ou la légende du magicien, 1957 (repr. 1982); A. BURFORD, Craftmanship in Greek and Roman Society, 1979; A. HERMARY, A. JACQUEMIN, s.v. H., LIMC 4, 257–280.   F.G.

III. ICONOGRAPHY

The earliest pictures of H. on Corinthian and Attic ware since the 2nd quarter of the 6th cent. BC show the god at the birth of Athena, the wedding of Peleus and above all at his return to Olympus (François Vase, Florence, MA, 570/560 BC). He is portrayed with or without a beard, at first without headgear, from the early 5th cent. BC with a → pilos, occasionally also with a → petasos; his crippled feet are portrayed on a few archaic vases. His attributes change according to his portrayed occupation: ax or double hammer, from the end of the 6th cent. BC smith's tools (hammer and – often red-hot – tongs), which like bellows and firebrands also serve as weapons. Pausanias describes 5,19,8 H. handing over his weapons to Thetis on the → Cypselus Chest in Olympia (around 600 BC) and 3,18,13 H. pursuing Athena on the 'throne' of Apollo in Amyclae (2nd half of the 6th cent. BC). H.'s presence at the creation of Pandora is to be expected on the relief base of the statue of Athena Parthenos (447/6–439/8 BC; Paus. 1,24,7; Plin. HN 36,18.; cf. the Praenestine cista in London, BM, the original dates to the late 4th cent. BC). H. was portrayed at the birth of Athena on the east pediment of the → Parthenon on the Athenian Acropolis (438–432 BC), the eastern frieze shows H. among the assembled gods (around 440 BC). The northern frieze of the Siphnian Treasury in Delphi (around 525 BC) shows H. in the battle against the giants. The first freestanding representation of the god is the no longer extant cult image of → Alcamenes [2], which stood together with Athena in the Hephaesteum of Athens (421/20–417/6 BC).

Numerous statuettes of → Volcanus, the Roman counterpart of H., have been preserved (among others the large marble statuette from the Baths of Mithras in Ostia, 2nd cent. AD, as well as bronze statuettes mainly from the Imperial period); he appears in workshop scenes, often accompanied by the → Cyclopes who assist him in his work, on sarcophagi of the 2nd–3rd cents. AD, Pompeiian frescoes and (a few) mosaics (for example Tunis, Bardo Museum, from Dougga; cf. Volcanus as the sign for the month of September: so-called mosaic of Monnus, Trier, Rheinisches Landesmuseum, about AD 300). The god of the smithy has been portrayed on reliefs of representations of the twelve gods (Dōdekátheoi/Dei → consentes: 'Ara Borghese', Paris, LV, early Imperial period?), and, as far as the north-western provinces of the Roman Empire are concerned, especially on votive reliefs and → four-sided columns with reliefs of gods on each side of the 1st–3rd cents. AD; representations on coins from Asia Minor are relatively numerous, mostly 3rd cent. AD.

T. H. CARPENTER, Dionysian imagery in archaic Greek art, 1986; A. HERMARY, A. JAQUEMIN, s.v. H., LIMC 4, 627–654 (with older bibliography); A. SCHÖNE, Der Thiasos. Eine ikonographische Untersuchung über das Gefolge des Dionysos in der attischen Vasenmalerei des 6. und 5. Jh. v. Chr., 1987; E. SIMON, G. BAUCHHENSS, s.v. Vulcanus, LIMC 8, 283–298 (with older bibliography).   A.L.

Hephthalites According to R. GÖBL's classification ([1], cf. [2]), → Iran experienced four successive 'waves' of invading Hunnic peoples from the 4th cent. AD. While the first three groups of these 'Iranian Huns' (Kidarites, Alchon, Nezak) have left few traces in the literary sources, the H. in the 5th/6th cents. AD belonged to the most prominent and dangerous eastern neighbours of the Persians. They are first explicitly attested at the time of King Perozes and were vividly described by Procopius (BP 1,3). According to his report, the *Ephthalitai* were a Hunnic people, also known as 'White Huns'. He stresses, however, that they did not intermingle with other known Huns, were distinguished from them in appearance and way of life, and lived separately from the others north of the Persians. The H. were also not nomadic, they had a king and an ordered state. At the time of Perozes and his son Cavades I, the H. had a strong influence on the Sassanid empire, until their power was broken by combined actions of the western Turks and the Sassanids under → Chosroes I in about 560.

1 R. GÖBL, Antike Numismatik, vol. 2, 1978, 107f. 2 F. ALTHEIM, R. STIEHL, Gesch. Mittelasiens im Altertum, 1970, 690–698.

M. ALRAM, Die Gesch. Ostirans ... bis zu den iranischen Hunnen, in: W. SEIPEL (ed.), Weihrauch und Seide, 1996, 119–140; M. SCHOTTKY, s.v. Huns, EncIr (in print).   M.SCH.

Heptanomia Administrative unit set up by Augustus before AD 11/12 in Egypt, comprising the area between the Delta and Thebes. Its seven districts were Memphites, Heracleopolites, Aphroditopolites, Oxyrhynchites, Cynopolites, Hermopolites, and perhaps Letopolites. From the beginning the Arsinoites and often also the small Oasis were included. Its expansion to 11 districts under Marcus Aurelius and Commodus is attested, but its composition cannot currently be clearly determined. The Heptanomia was subordinate to an *epistrategos* with the rank of *procurator Augusti*.

J. D. THOMAS, The Epistrategos in Ptolemaic and Roman Egypt 2, 1982, 19ff.　　　　　　　　　　　　　　W.A.

Heptateuch poet This name was given to the author of a hexameter version of the first 7 books of the Bible, which was falsely ascribed to → Cyprianus in a 9th-cent. manuscript. The poem, probably written in Gaul in the early 5th cent., is the longest (over 5,700 verses) of the Biblical epics from late antiquity. An exception to this metre consists in three hendecasyllablic sections, which correspond to Biblical *cantica*. Originally, the poem was significantly longer than its current form and included all historical books of the OT (manuscript catalogues refer to other books, extant today only in fragments). The H. was read and cited by the Anglo-Saxon authors Aldhelm and → Bede, copied and excerpted in the Carolingian period, but afterwards to a large extent forgotten.

→ Biblical poetry

R. PEIPER, CSEL 23,1–211 (ed.); R. HERZOG, Die Bibelepik der lat. Spätantike, 1975, 53–60, 99–154.　　M.RO.

Hera (Ἥρα/*Héra*, Ἥρη/*Hérē*, Mycenaean *e-ra*).
I. CULT AND MYTH　　II. ICONOGRAPHY

I. CULT AND MYTH

H. is the daughter of → Kronos and → Rhea and wife of → Zeus. On the one hand, she is associated with the world of the early polis (esp. with young warlike men), on the other and primarily, she is the tutelary goddess of marriage, her marriage to Zeus representing the prototype.

Her cultic (and probably also mythic) association with Zeus can already be seen in Linear B documents, where she is attested in Pylos (PY Tn 316, with Zeus and *dirimijo* = Drimios, son of Zeus [1. 94–96]) and Thebes (TH Of 28). In Homer and later she is the wife of Zeus, in an often strained relationship (also reflecting the perception of marriage in Homeric society). While Zeus must be impartial in the *Iliad*, H. resolutely takes the side of the Greeks, to the point of deceiving her husband (Hom. Il. 14, cf. 20,30–33). The male children of this marriage reflect these tensions (Catalogue in Hes. Theog. 921–923). While their daughter → Hebe, as goddess of the bloom of youth, is the prerequisite, and their daughter → Eileithyia, as goddess of birth, is the natural consequence of marriage, → Ares and → Hephaestus (described as their joint son by Homer but not by Hesiod) are problematic outsiders. H. bore Hephaestus by parthenogenesis according to Hes. Theog. 927. A similar ambivalence of the goddess appears in her (however ultimately resolved) enmity towards Zeus' son → Heracles and in that she is the mother or foster-mother of monsters (Typhon: Hom. Hymn Apoll. 305–355; the Hydra and the Nemean Lion: Hes. Theog. 313f.; 327f.). In later philosophical → allegoresis H. is regularly identified with the air. This is derived from the metathesis of the letters in her name (HPA → AHP), and from the Homeric story of her punishment by Zeus: he hangs her from the heavens (= aether) on a golden chain, with two anvils (= water and earth) attached to her feet (Hom. Il. 15,18–21; Heraclitus, Allegoriae Homericae 40 [2]).

H.'s sanctuaries are among the earliest, distinguished by large, often monumental, temple structures: this holds for Perachora, Argos, Samos, as well as the large Heraea of southern Italy (Metapontum, Croton, Paestum). These sanctuaries generally lie clearly outside the settlements, which is often the case with particular cult forms [3]. The role of the temple and the fact that models of temples were often dedicated in Heraea point to the significance that H. had for the archaic political community [4].

The cult of H. involved both her aspects, that of protector of cities, in particular their young men, and that of protector of marriages, wives, and children. The duality of political divinity and goddess of women reflects the role of the woman citizen in the polis and is repeated in the Roman → Juno, who was identified with her at an early stage. In the course of her development, the political aspects visibly take second place to those of the goddess of weddings, marriage and motherhood.

As a goddess whose mythical biography reflects the regular life of women, H. can simultaneously be called 'Maiden' (*Paîs*), 'Wife' (*Téleia*), 'Widow' (*Chéra*) (Paus. 8,22,2), bear the epithet 'Bride' (*Nympheuoménē*) (image in the temple of H. Teleia in Plataeae, Paus. 9,2,7) or even ritually regain her virginity (Paus. 3,28,2). As goddess of marriage, she is consistently called Teleia (*télos*, 'completion' denoting marriage), more rarely Zygia. As H. Teleia, she is invoked together with Zeus Teleios in the wedding ritual (Aesch. Eum. 214f. and fr. 383; cf. Aristoph. Thesm. 973–976). Isolated festivals are associated with the mythical wedding between Zeus and H., particularly the Attic festival of the Theogamia (→ *hieros gamos*) and an unknown Cretan festival regarded as 'emulation' of this wedding (Diod. Sic. 5,72,4) [5]. As receiver of a sacrifice called 'childbed' (*lechérna*) in Argos (Hsch. s.v.), she is directly, and as mother of → Eileithyia indirectly, associated with birth, and dedications from individual Heraea identify her as → Kourotrophos [6; 7]. Other rites associate her with growing children (Hera Acraea in Corinth: schol. Eur. Med. 264; [8]), particularly girls (Foce del Sele).

The large cult centres mirror this double aspect in the extant documentation, at least in part. In the *Iliad*, H.'s favourite cities are Argos, Mycenae, and Sparta (Hom. Il. 4,51f.). While the cults in Sparta [9. 46] and Mycenae remain vague, the Heraeum of → Argos was her primary cult centre for the whole of antiquity, besides those of → Samos and the lower Italian Heraea of Croton and Paestum (Foce del Sele).

The central Argive festival was the Heraia, also called Hekatombaia after the main sacrifice. Its main ritual was the sacrificial procession out to the sanctuary far outside the city, where the polis of Argos was represented and symbolically constituted under H.'s protection: in this procession the hundred cows, whose sacrificial meat was divided among the citizens, were driven, the eponymous priestess rode on an ox-cart (Hdt. 1,31), and selected young men carried the sacred shield of the goddess, which had been dedicated by the first king → Danaus and carried by his successors since → Lynceus [10]. The theme of the marriage to Zeus is addressed through the myth of the seduction of H. by Zeus in the form of a cuckoo: the myth is located on the Argive Cuckoo Mountain (with a Zeus sanctuary) and a cuckoo crowned H.'s sceptre in the Argive cult image (Paus. 2,36,1f.; schol. Theoc. 15, 64; [9. 42–45]). H's role as birth goddess is mirrored in the Argive → epiclesis of Eileithyia (Hsch. s.v.).

The Samian sanctuary, which is connected with Argos according to the myth that the very ancient cult image (*brétas*) came from there (Menodotus, FGrH 541 F 1; Paus. 7,4,4), is the centre of the state representation in the Archaic era. The main festival, the Toneia, (according to the better manuscripts) enacts an exceptional ritual, in which people lay on beds of *lygos* twigs (a *lygos* tree is the centre of the sanctuary) ritually searched for the cult image which had disappeared from the temple, then found it, washed it and dressed it in new clothes (Menodotus). The details do not point, as earlier researchers (since Varro) thought, to a marriage ritual but rather a New Year's ritual in which the normally chained cult image was set free [11; 12].

According to detailed ancient descriptions (Plut. fr. 157; Paus. 9,3,3–8), the inhabitants of Plataeae and a considerable number of surrounding Boeotian towns acted out a marriage ritual in the Daidala – celebrated every seven years (Little) and every sixty years (Great) – in which wooden dolls adorned like brides were brought in a procession to the peak of → Cithaeron and burned there on a pyre. The myth considers the creation and exhibition of the dolls as a remembrance of a trick by Zeus to reconcile himself with the jealous H. More important than the marriage aspect is that of violent destruction in an enormous fire, which has numerous parallels, and the role of the cities, which all participate with the sacrifice of a cow for H. and a bull for Zeus.

1 M. GÉRARD-ROUSSEAU, Les mentions religieuses dans les tablettes mycéniennes, 1968   2 P. LÉVÊCQUE, Aurea catena Homeri, 1959   3 F. GRAF, Culti e credenze nella Magna Grecia, in: Megale Hellas. Nome e immagine (Atti del Convegno di Studi sulla Magna Grecia 21, 1982), 157–185   4 F. DE POLIGNAC, La naissance de la cité grecque. Culte, espace et société, VIIIe-VIIe siècles av. J.-C., 1984   5 J.C. BERMEJO BARRERA, Zeus, H. y el matrimonio sagrado, in: Quaderni di Storia 15, 1989, 133–156   6 T.H. PRICE, Kourotrophos, 1978, 138–146   7 S.I. JOHNSTON, Corinthian Medea and the Cult of Hera Akraia, in: J. CLAUSS, S.I. JOHNSTON (ed.), Medea, 1997, 44–70   8 A. BRELICH, I figli di Medeia, in: Studi e materiali di storia delle religioni 30, 1959, 213–254   9 NILSSON, Feste   10 W. BURKERT, Homo necans, 1972, 163f.   11 G. KIPP, Zum H.-Kult auf Samos, in: F. HAMPL, I. WEILER (ed.), Kritische und vergleichende Studien 18, 1974, 157–208   12 GRAF, 93–96   13 M. CREMER, Hieros Gamos im Orient und in Griechenland, in: ZPE 48, 1982, 283–290.

NILSSON, 427–433; PH. E. SLATER, The Glory of H. Greek Mythology and the Greek Family, 1968; K. KERÉNYI, Zeus und H. Urbild des Vaters, des Gatten und der Frau, 1972; W. PÖTSCHER, H. Eine Strukturanalyse im Vergleich mit Athena, 1987; D. Q. ADAMS, Hêrôs and Hêrê, in: Glotta 65, 1987, 171–178; A. KOSSATZ-DEISSMANN, s.v. H., LIMC 4.1, 659–719; B. M. FRIDH-HANESON, H.'s Wedding on Samos. A Change of Paradigm, in: R. HÄGG, N. MARINATOS, G. C. NORDQUIST (ed.), Early Greek Cult Practice, 1988, 205–213; J. V. O'BRIEN, The Transformation of H. A Study of Ritual, Hero, and the Goddess in the Iliad, 1993; R. HÄUSSLER, H. und Juno. Wandlungen und Beharrung einer Göttin, 1995.   F.G.

II. ICONOGRAPHY

Individual representations of the goddess H. are certain in only a few traditions. In a mythological group, she is more clearly recognizable, particularly as the companion of Zeus, dressed as a bride; in images of courtship and the → *hieros gamos* as a matronal hieratic divinity. Her characteristic iconography includes the → *peplos* and *himation*, usually pulled over her head like a veil, → *polos* or *stephane*, and the attributes of sceptre, → *phiale*, and pomegranate. As cult goddess she was particularly important in the Dorian-Achaean region. Her cult images, however, appearing on coins (from the 5th cent. BC, but mainly from the Imperial period) and cited in written sources, have mostly not survived.

Pausanias provides descriptions e.g. from Argos of the famous enthroned H. of → Polyclitus made of gold and ivory (late 5th cent. BC, Paus. 2. 17,4, cf. representation on Argive bronze coins) and of the older xoanon (Paus. 2,17,5), of the cult group in Olympia with enthroned H. and standing Zeus (Paus. 5,17,1), and of the cult group of → Praxiteles in Mantinea with enthroned H. and standing Athena and Hebe (around the mid 4th cent. BC, Paus. 8, 9, 3). The cult image by → Alcamenes [2] in the H. temple near Athens (430/400 BC, Paus. 1,1,5, 10,35,2) was recognized in copies of various *peplophoroi* of the 5th cent. BC (attempted identification with the Hestia Giustiniani, Rome, VA) and seems to be depicted in documentary reliefs (treaty between Athens and Samos, Athens, AM, 403/2 BC). A wooden statuette from the → Heraeum on Samos

(Vathy, Mus., third quarter of the 7th cent. BC) probably represents H., as do the marble statue from the late 4th cent. BC (Berlin, SM) salvaged there and the monumental statue from around 210/160 BC (Pythagoreum, Samos), while the H. statue dedicated by Cheramyes also in the Samian Heraeum (Paris, LV; 570/550 BC) can also be seen as a *kore*. Copies of classical statues connected to H. may also be applied to Demeter (Demeter Cherchel), Aphrodite (H. Borghese), and others.

Early traditions of the *hieros gamos* group are presumably on a relief pithos from Crete (second quarter of the 7th cent. BC, Basle, AM), a wooden relief from Samos (lost, around 620/610 BC), a terracotta group from the Heraeum of Foce del Sele near → Paestum (archaic), and on metopes from Temple E in Selinunte dated about 470 BC. Numerous vase images record the divine couple in assemblies of the gods, cf. H. and Zeus also in the eastern frieze of the Parthenon (about 440 BC), treasury of the Siphnians in Delphi, eastern frieze (about 525 BC). Various terracottas from Heraea quite probably depict the goddess (from the 7th and particularly in the 6th cent. BC).

Among mythological representations featuring H. are the Judgment of Paris, a widespread theme from early times (pot by → Chigi Painter, Rome, VG, about 630 BC) and the return of Hephaestus to Olympus to free H., from the first half of the 6th cent. BC. The François Crater (Florence, MA, 570/560 BC) may possibly show H. chained. Relatively few representations show H. with Hercules: at the introduction of the hero to Olympus, Hercules protecting H. from satyrs pursuing her (bowl by → Brygus Painter in London, BM, 490/480 BC), and H. at the wedding of Hercules and Hebe in her role as mother of the bride. As a warrior goddess H. takes part in the battle with the → giants: treasury of the Siphnians in Delphi, northern frieze (about 525 BC), Parthenon, eastern metope (about 440 BC), eastern frieze of the Pergamon Altar (about 160 BC), Hecataeum of → Lagina, western frieze (second half of the 2nd cent. BC).

A. DELIVORRIAS, Der statuarische Typus der sog. H. Borghese, in: H. BECK, P.C. BOL (ed.), Polykletforschung, 1993, 221–252; A. KOSSATZ-DEISSMANN, s.v. H., LIMC IV, 659–719 (with bibliography of older literature); W. PÖTSCHER, H. Eine Strukturanalyse im Vergleich mit Athena, 1987.   A.L.

Heraclas Before his conversion to the Christian faith H. took lessons from the Platonic philosopher → Ammonius [9] Saccas (Euseb. Hist. eccl. 6,19,13) with his brother Plutarchus, who later died a martyr's death. After five years of instruction he met → Origenes there as a fellow student and then visited his class in Alexandria (Euseb. Hist. eccl. 6,3,2). At a certain point Origen made H. responsible for the beginning students (Euseb. Hist. eccl. 6,15).

H. himself was a celebrated teacher (Euseb. Hist. eccl. 6,31,2) and apparently belonged to the presbyters who were responsible for driving Origen out of Alex-

andria; perhaps one can even call him the 'head of the anti-Origenists' [1]. H. then took over the direction of the Christian classes; from 231 until 247 he was the bishop of Alexandria. As a late source shows, H. reacted very strongly to Origen appearing at a worship service in the Nile delta, even long after Origen had moved to → Caesarea [2] (Palaestina) (Photius, Interrogationes decem 9, PG 104, 1219–1232).

1 W. A. BIENERT, Dionysius von Alexandrien, 1978, 100–104   2 P. NAUTIN, Origène. Sa vie et son œuvre, 1977   3 C. SCHOLTEN, Die alexandrinische Katechetenschule, in: JbAC 38, 1995, 16–37.   C.M.

Heraclea (Ἡράκλεια; *Hērákleia*).
[1] **H. Trachinia** (Ἡράκλεια ἡ Τραχινία; *H. hē Trachinía*). City on a rock to the left of and above the exit of the gorge of the → Asopus [1] into the Spercheus plain, separated from Oete (→ Oetaei, Oete) on the southern and western flanks by deep streambeds, where the Trachinian rocks rise up with their numerous tomb caves. The lower city has vanished without trace. H. was founded in 426 BC by the Spartans, who had been asked for help by Trachis against the Oetaei, c. 7 km west of Thermopylae near → Trachis (Thuc. 3,92). In 371, Jason of Pherae conquered the colony (Xen. Hell. 6,4,27), which was hated by its neighbours, and gave it to the → Malieis and Oetaei (Diod. Sic. 15,57,2). Hieromnemones (delegates to the Amphictyonic council) from H. appeared from that time as representatives of the Malieis in Delphi. H. belonged to the Aetolian League from 280 (Paus. 10,20,9) and enjoyed its greatest prosperity after expansion into Trachis – this city had long since fallen into decline – as the site of the League's assembly (Liv. 28,5,13). In 191, H. was plundered by → Acilius [I 10] after a dramatic siege. From 167, H. was the capital of the newly founded autonomous tribal state of the Oetaei, who were united with the Thessalian Phthiotis by the future Augustus about 30 BC. Justinian had the fortifications renewed in the 6th cent. (Procop. Aed. 4,2,17–21). A little later, H. was finally abandoned.

Y. BÉQUIGNON, La vallée du Spercheios, 1937, 243ff.; G. DAUX, Sosthenis, in: BCH 58, 1934, 156ff.; PRITCHETT 1, 81f.; F. STÄHLIN, s.v. H. (4), RE 8, 424ff.; Id., Das hellenistische Thessalien, 1924, 205ff. (sources); TIB 1, 1976, 172.   HE.KR.

[2] **H. Lyncestis** (Ἡράκλεια Λύγκου; *H. Lýnkou*). Most important town of upper Macedonia, modern Bitola. Possibly founded by Philip II. Flourished in the Roman era (*provincia Macedonia*) owing to its position on the via Egnatia and the intersecting road to Stobi. Meeting-place of Pompey with the envoy of the Dacian king → Burebista in 48 BC (Syll.³ 762). Following the Roman civil wars the number of Roman citizens living here, who played a large part in the flourishing municipal life of the Imperial period, increased. In the 3rd cent. AD, H. was granted the title *Septimia Aurelia Heraclea* [1. 162] and was a see before the Council of Serdica

(343) at the latest. Devastated in the 5th cent. by the Goths under Theodemir (Iord. Get. 285) and Theoderic (Malchus, fr. 20 BLOCKLEY), H. was last mentioned at the Council of Constantinople in 553. In the Byzantine period the bishop of H. was also responsible for Pelagonia and this has occasionally led to confusion with Pelagonia.

> 1 F. PAPAZOGLOU, Septimia Aurelia Heraclea, in: BCH 85, 1961, 162–175.   2 Id., Les villes de Macédoine, 1988, 258–268.   MA.ER.

[3] Town in the eastern Macedonian Sintica on the → Strymon (Str. 7 fr. 36). Not located, perhaps to be found near Neo Petritsi. Probably a foundation of Philip II, annexed by the Romans in 167 BC to *Macedonia I* (Liv. 45,29,6; Diod. Sic. 31,8,8). H. still existed in the 6th cent. AD (Hierocles, Synekdemos 639,9).

> F. PAPAZOGLOU, Les villes de Macédoine, 1988, 258–268.
> MA.ER.

[4] Island (19 km²) south of Naxos with a fortified settlement and Meter shrine (Plin. HN 4,70; → Mater Magna, → Cybele), today part of the lesser Cyclades (formerly Erimonisia).

> PHILIPPSON/KIRSTEN 4, 13; L. ROSS, Reisen auf den griech. Inseln des ägäischen Meeres 2, 1834, 34ff.   H.KAL.

[5] City in Caria on the southern slope of Mount Latmus, successor to the Carian settlement of Latmus. With its position on the innermost corner of the Latmian Gulf (modern Bafa Gölü), it was an important port of reshipment for east-west trade. Founded in about 300 BC by Pleistarchus, the brother of Cassander, as a residence (Steph. Byz. s.v. Πλειστάρχεια), H. was insignificant in the Roman era (Str. 14,2,22). A see from the early Christian period. With orthogonal street grid: public and sacred buildings around the agora, and the residential city primarily on the slope. Enormous defensive ring from the time of Pleistarchus. Extensive necropolis outside the city walls. Temple of Athena Latmia (3rd cent. BC). Bouleuterion, agora, gymnasium, theatre, temple of Endymion from the 3rd/2nd cents.

> F. KRISCHEN, Die Befestigungen von H. am Latmos, 1922; L. BÜRCHNER, s.v. H. am Latmos, RE 8, 431ff.; K. WULZINGER, Das Rathaus von H. am Latmos, in: F. KRISCHEN, Antike Rathäuser, 1941, 22ff.; P. ROMANELLI, s.v. Eraclea, in: EAA 3, 1960, 390–392; M. WÖRRLE, Inschr. von H. am Latmos I: Antiochos III., Zeuxis und H., in: Chiron 18, 1988, 421ff.; Id., Inschr. von H. am Latmos II: Das Pristertum der Athena Latmia, in: Chiron 20, 1990, 19ff.; A. PESCHLOW-BINDOKAT, Der Latmos, 1996, 29ff.   A.PE.

[6] **H. Salbace.** (Σαλβάκη; *Salbákē*). City in eastern Caria (modern Vakıf) in the border region of Phrygia and Pisidia, on the northern edge of the plain of → Tabae in the southeastern foothills of the Salbacus (Babadağ). The inhabitants are called Ἡρακλεῶται ἀπὸ Σαλβάκης in inscriptions (cf. also Ptol. 5,2,15; Steph.

Byz. s.v. H.; Hierocles 688). Foundation date unknown. After a visit by Trajan in AD 113, which was arranged by the emperor's personal physician, the historian T. → Statilius Criton, who was the most significant of doctors originating from H., the city was given the epithet *Ulpia* for a short time at the beginning of the 2nd cent. AD. Inscriptions document the usual city officials and the classification of the population by age groups. Coins from Augustus to Macrinus (217/8). Hercules, as the city eponym, was the chief god.

The remains of city walls and stadium as well as blocks with figurative reliefs from a sanctuary (?) north and east of the village have been dispersed to a large extent.

> J. BENEDUM, s.v. Kriton, RE Suppl. 14, 216ff.; L. ROBERT, J. ROBERT, La Carie 2, 1954, 153–230, pl. LXV (map); MAMA 6, 33ff. no. 87ff.; SNG Copenhagen no. 391ff.; SNG v. Aulock no. 2542ff.   H.KA.

[7] **H.** (*Heraclea Pontica*). City founded *c.* 560 BC by Megara with Boeotian participation, with Dorian characteristics (Xen. An. 6,2,1; Ephor. fr. 44a; Arr. Peripl. p. eux. 18) on the south shore of the Pontus Euxinus, with excellent natural harbour and economically significant hinterland as far as Akçakoca Dağları, modern Ereğli. Colonial foundations: Panelus (location?), Callatis (550/525 BC), Calpe, Cierus, the island of Thynias or Daphne, Chersonesus on the Crimea (*c.* 422/1). The native Mariandyni were partially subjugated (status similar to the Helots or Penestae; cf. Str. 12,3,4). The economy was originally strongly agrarian, increasing significance in Black Sea trade after the middle of the 5th cent. BC (430/420 beginning of coin minting), economic prosperity in the 4th cent., decline in the export economy after 300. Oligarchic rule was abolished in 364/3 by Clearchus, a pupil of Plato, who set up a tyranny. After his murder in 352, he was succeeded by his brother Satyrus, Clearchus' sons Timotheus (*c.* 345–338/7) and Dionysius (338/7–305), who took the title of king in 306/5. He was succeeded by his widow → Amastris [3]. Absolute power was increasingly accepted. The kingdom ultimately comprised the coastal region of the eastern part of Thynias (eastern Hypius) to Cotyrus in the east. After a brief marriage to → Lysimachus, Amastris lived in → Amastris [4], which she had founded, and was probably murdered by her sons. In 284 Lysimachus ended their rule and occupied the city, which he then presented to his wife → Arsinoe [II 3] (loss of autonomy). The kingdom of H. was dissolved. H. was a significant naval base and mint for Lysimachus. In 281 H. got rid of its governor Arsinoe, entered into conflict over the Seleucid claim to power, and initiated the Northern League [1. 188ff.]. After the Bithynian king joined this, his conquests Cierus and Tius returned to the hegemony of H. Both cities were lost to → Prusias I in 196/190. In 190 diplomatic contact began with Rome; after 188 treaties of friendship and alliance. At the end of 47 BC as a *civitas libera*, H. was affected by the organization of the Roman province Bi-

thynia and the associated customs law for Asia and Bithynia. In the year 73 the town supported → Mithridates VI and proceeded violently against the Roman *publicani*. In 72, H. became part of the Pontic kingdom. In 72/1–70 siege, conquest, and destruction by → Aurelius [11]. From 65/4, H. was part of the province of Pontus and from 46/5 a Roman *colonia*. In *c.* 40, Antony gave the Greek sector of the city and territory to the Galatian prince Adiatorix, who in 32/31 had the Romans murdered (Str. 12,3,6). After his removal in 31/30, H. was part of the province → Bithynia et Pontus. From AD 384/387, the city belonged to the province of Honoria. Documented as a suffragan diocese since 431.

→ Bithynia; → Bithynia et Pontus

1 K. STROBEL, Die Galater I, 1996.

D. ASHERI, Über die Frühgesch. von H., in: Forsch. an der Nordküste Kleinasiens I (ETAM 5), 1972, 9–34; A. AVRAM, Bemerkungen zu den Mariandynern von H., in: Studii Clasici 22, 1984, 19–28; K. BELKE, Paphlagonien und Honorias, 1996, 208–216; A. BITTNER, Eine Polis zwischen Tyrannis und Selbstverwaltung: Gesellschaft und Wirtschaft in H., 1998; S. M. BURSTEIN, Outpost of Hellenism. The Emergence of H., 1976; P. DESIDERI, Cultura Eracleotica, in: Pontica 1, 1991, 7–24; W. HOEPFNER, H.-Ereğli. Eine baugesch. Unt., in: Forschung an der Nordküste Kleinasiens (ETAM 2.1), 1966, 3–37; Id., Top. Forschung (ETAM 5), 1972, 37–60; L. JONNES, W. AMELING, The Inscriptions of H. (IK 47), 1994; W. LESCHHORN, Antike Ären, 1993, 195ff.; S. J. SAPRYKIN, Heracleia Pontica and Tauric Chersonnesus before Roman Domination IV.–I. c. B.C., 1996.   K.ST.

[8] City founded by Dorieus with Lacedaemonian settlers on the foot of Mount → Eryx [1] (Sicily) about 510 BC, destroyed not much later by Carthage and Segesta. Documentary evidence: Hdt. 5,46; Diod. Sic. 4,23,3; Paus. 3,16,4f.

BTCGI 7, 1989, 229f.   GI.MA.

[9] City on the south coast of Sicily, 25 km west of Acragas, east of the mouth of the Halycus, modern Eraclea Minoa. Founded by Selinus (so after 628 BC) on the site of a pre-Greek settlement attributed to Minos and therefore called Minoa (Μινώα; *Minóia*). Occupied in about 505 by Euryleon and renamed (or additionally named) H. (Hdt. 5,46; Diod. Sic. 4,79,1; 4,79,5; 16,9,5). The place name H. Minoa appears only rarely in the sources, more often Minoa, but mostly H. There can, however, be no doubt about the identity of the location. As a result of its location in the Graeco-Carthaginian border region, the city changed rulers several times: in the year 357 it was Carthaginian (Diod. Sic. 16,9,4; Plut. Dion 25), in the time of Timoleon Greek, in 314 Carthaginian (Diod. Sic. 19,71,1). After that under the rule of → Agathocles [2] (Diod. Sic. 20,56,3), after his death, and a brief spell under Pyrrhus (Diod. Sic. 22,10,2), it was expanded as a naval base by the Carthaginians. After the fall of Acragas in 262 under

Roman rule. In the second Punic War, after the death of Hiero (214), H. seceded from Rome and became Roman once more only after Acragas fell again (210) becoming a *civitas decumana* (Cic. Verr. 2,3,103). After the great slave war in 132, H. took in Roman settlers (Cic. Verr. 2,2,125). Plundered by Verres, H. took part in the lawsuit against him.

In Eraclea Minoa, remains from prehistoric (late Neolithic and early Bronze Age settlement [1]), Greek [2] (first settlement phase, mid 4th cent. to the second half of the 2nd cent. BC, with elegant houses, fortifications, theatre with sanctuary; second settlement phase, end of the 2nd cent. to end of 1st cent. BC, with modest houses in the western part of the plain; necropolis used in the Archaic and Hellenistic eras [2. 17]) and early Christian eras [3] (cemetery basilica with necropoleis, in use from the 4th cent. AD at the latest, coins of Constans [2] II; settlement in the 3rd cent., coins of Gallienus [3. 729ff.]).

1 D. GULLÌ, Primi dati sull'insedamento preistorico di Eraclea Minoa, in: Quaderni dell'Istituto di Archeologia dell'Università di Messina 9, 1993   2 G. FIORENTINI, Eraclea Minoa. Necropoli arcaica, in: BCA Sicilia 9–10/3, 1988/9   3 Id., Attività di indagini archeologiche della Soprintendenza di Agrigento, in: Kokalos 1993/4, 39f.; 717–733.

E. DE MIRO, Eraclea Minoa, 1958; Id., La fondazione di Agrigento e l'ellenizzazione del territorio fra il Salso e il Platani, in: Kokalos 8, 1962, 144.   GI.F.

[10] → *Apoikía* founded in the year 433/2 BC (Diod. Sic. 12,36,4) between Aciris and Siris (Plin. HN 3,97) near Policoro by Tarentum and Thurii. The settlement of Siris at the mouth of the River Siris on the Mediterranean served as its maritime trading site. H. took its name from the Tarentine Hercules cult (Str. 6,1,14). In the 4th cent. BC, H. was the centre of the alliance founded by the Greek cities of lower Italy against the Lucani (Str. 6,3,4). In 280 BC the battle between → Pyrrhus and the Romans was fought at H. (Plut. Pyrrhus 16; Liv. 22,59,8). At that time, H. had a *prope singulare foedus* ('an almost unique alliance') with Rome (Cic. Arch. 50). The lease found in H. dates to the end of the 4th or the beginning of the 3rd cent. BC and is important for our understanding of the organization and agricultural utilization of the territory of H. (IG XIV 645). H. was *municipium, tribus Menenia*. Mentioned in the Imperial period only in the *itineraria*. Archaeological excavations have uncovered a sanctuary to Demeter with many votive gifts, as well as a Hephaestus sanctuary. The painter → Zeuxis and the Orphic poet → Zopyrus were probably citizens of H.

B. NEUTSCH (ed.), Herakleiastudien (Arch. Forschung in Lukanien 2), 1967; L. QUILICI, Siris-Heraclea, 1967; A. UGUZZONI, F. GHINATTI, Le tavole greche di Eraclea, 1968; Studi su Siris-Eraclea, 1989; G. CAMASSA, I culti delle poleis italiote, in: Storia del Mezzogiorno, I/1, 1991, 467–471, 493f.; M. OSANNA, Chorai coloniali da Taranto a Locri, 1992, 97–114; B. OTTO (ed.), H. in Lukanien und das Quellheiligtum der Demeter, 1996 (with extensive

bibliography); A. Muggia, L'area di rispetto nelle colonie magno-greche e siceliote, 1997, 105–108 *et passim*.
G.CA.

[11] Town in Acarnania on the south shore of the Ambracian Gulf, the exact location is unknown. Documentary evidence: Plin. HN 4,5; Steph. Byz. s.v. ʿH.

Pritchett 8, 97–101.   D.S.

Heracleianus Physician and anatomist from Alexandria, active *c.* AD 152, the son of the anatomist and teacher → Numisianus. He compiled an extract of his father's works (Gal. De musculorum dissectione 18 B, 926, 935 K.), demonstrating his own considerable knowledge (Gal. Admin. anat. 16,1). He had a conversation with → Galen, when the latter arrived in Alexandria in *c.* AD 151, and Galen initially followed his anatomical lectures with benevolence (CMG V,9,1, p. 70). However, when Galen later requested to see the works by H.'s late father, their relationship cooled considerably. H.'s refusal to show them eventually gave rise to the rumour that he had burned his father's works shortly before his death to prevent others from access to his discoveries (Gal. Admin. anat. 16,1).   V.N.

Heracleon (ʿΗρακλέων; *Hērakléōn*).
[1] from Beroea, a favourite of Antiochus [10] VIII, caused the latter's death in 96 BC during a plot to become king, but was foiled by the succession of Seleucus VI to the throne. H.'s son Dionysius ruled parts of northern Syria incl. Bambyce, Beroea and Heraclea (Pomp. Trog. prologus 39; Str. 16,2; 7; Jos. Ant. Iud. 13,365; Ath. 4,153b).   A.ME.
[2] Pirate leader, defeated the fleet of Syracuse in 72 BC (→ Heraclius [2]) and penetrated with four ships into the city's Great Harbour (Cic. Verr. 5,90f.; 97–100). He was driven out in 70 by L. Caecilius [I 13] Metellus, the successor of Verres.   K.MEI.
[3] from Ephesus. Grammarian, author of an Atticist lexicon that is quoted six times by → Athenaeus [3] (2,52b; 3,76a; 7,303b; 7,308f; 11,503a; 14,647b); perhaps it is the one of which → Didymus [3] Claudius made an epitome (which would provide a *terminus ante quem* for its date: [1]; by contrast [2]).
→ Lexicography

1 A. Gudeman, s.v. Herakleon (5), RE 8, 513
2 M. Schmidt, Didymi Chalcenteri fragmenta, 1854, 3.

F. Susemihl, Geschichte der griechischen Literatur in der Alexandrinerzeit, II, 1892, 22 and 190.

[4] H. of Tilotis (Egypt). Grammarian, presumably of the Augustan period, taught in Rome (Suda η 455). Author of a commentary on Homer κατὰ ῥαψῳδίαν (*katà rhapsōidían*; book by book) in 48 books, and on the lyricists; the fragments of the first work preserved in the scholia on Homer and Apollonius Rhodius [1] show that H. was interested in all aspects of the text (grammar, etymology, topography) and occasionally contradicted the views of Aristarchus [4] of Samothrace; he

occasionally tended towards exegesis ([2]; by contrast [5]).

1 R. Berndt, Die Fragmente des Homererklärers Heracleo, 1913   2 Diels, DG, 1929², 91–93   3 M. Schmidt, Didymi Chalcenteri Fragmenta, 1854, 47
4 H. Schrader, Porphyrii Quaestiones Homericae, I, 1880, 406   5 F. Susemihl, Geschichte der griechischen Literatur in der Alexandrinerzeit, II, 1892, 20–22
6 M. van der Valk, Researches on the Text and Scholia of the Iliad I, 1963, 110–111; 436–437.   S.FO.

Heracleopolis magna (Egyptian *Nn-njswt*, modern Ihnāsiyat al-madīna). Town on the western bank of the Nile near the entrance of the → Faiyum; metropolis of the 20th Upper Egyptian nome; cult site of the ram god Harsaphes who was equated with → Heracles, and place of origin of the Heracleopolitan 9th/10th Dynasties in the First Intermediate Period. The archaeological remains (grave fields and temples) extend back to the First Intermediate Period or the Middle Kingdom (1st half of the 2nd millennium BC).

F. Gomaà, s.v. H.m., LÄ 2, 1124–1127 (with map); M. C. Perez-Die, P. Vernus, Excavaciones en Ehnasya el Medina, 1992.   S.S.

Heracles (ʿΗρακλῆς; *Hēraklês*).
[1] The most prominent Greek hero (→ Hero cult) in myth and cult. In his myths, which have not resulted in any outstanding work of poetry that is focussed on him, he is connected especially to Thebes, Argos and the countryside around Trachis; in the cult he is honoured almost panhellenically, without any place being able to display a hero's grave.

I. Cult and Myth   II. Iconography

I. Cult and Myth
A. Name   B. Myth   C. Cult   D. Identification
E. Teaching on Virtue

A. Name
His name was connected with → Hera's already in antiquity: it follows the customary formation of Greek anthroponyms like Patro-kles ('he who brings his father fame') or Dio-kles/Zeno-kles ('he who brings Zeus fame'). But the relationship to Hera is problematical: she is H.'s bitter opponent out of anger at H.'s mother, her rival → Alcmene (since Hom. Il. 15,25–28; 18,119); the ancient explanation of the name (since Pind. fr. 291), that H. came to fame through Hera's challenge, tries to understand this paradox. This is all the more urgent since (since Pind. fr. 291) the opinion has been documented that H. was originally called Alcides (or Alcaeus, Diod. Sic. 1,24,2) and received his second name because of Hera; this misunderstands the patronymic Alcides, which marks H. as the grandson of Alcaeus the son of Perseus, the father of Amphitryon (Apollod. 2,47).

More radical but very hypothetical are a few modern attempts to bring the name together with *hḗrōs* in the sense of 'young man' [1].

B. MYTH

Myths about H. are almost too numerous to be counted [2]. Although numerous poets have composed H.-epics from archaic times, which are devoted to his complete biography (especially → Peisander of Rhodes and → Panyassis of Halicarnassus) or single episodes (conquest of Oechalia, → Creophilus of Samos; H. on Cos, → Meropis), no poetry has organized and canonized the myths, and only few tragedies are about him (death: Soph. Trach.; madness: Eur. HF); summarizing representations are preserved first by Diodorus (4,8–39) and Apollodorus (2,57–166), who refer back to older reports, especially by → Herodorus (FGrH 31 F 13–37) and → Pherecydes of Athens (FGrH 3, Book 2 and 3 of the Historiai).

H. is the son of Zeus and → Alcmene (Hom. Il. 14,323f.), the wife of the Theban king → Amphitryon (Hom. Od. 11,266–268, cf. Il. 5,392), by whom she gives birth to H.'s half-brother Iphicles, the father of H.'s comrade at arms → Iolaus. He gives a first proof of his divine origins when he strangles two snakes that Hera sent into his cradle (Pind. Nem. 1,39–59).

In the centre of his myths are the twelve labours which he performed at Hera's command in the service of → Eurystheus of Argus; this service with its numerous labours (*áthloi*), bringing Cerberus up out of Hades and Athena's support are already assumed by the *Iliad* (Hom. Il. 8,362–369; 15,639; 19,132f., cf. Od. 11,621–626), his final transfer into heaven and the marriage to Zeus' daughter → Hebe are assumed by the *Odyssey* (11,601–604). The deeds (called the 'Dodekathlos' in modern scholastic diction) were canonized in their entirety and in their order of occurrence only at the end of the archaic period (Pind. fr. 169; metopes of the temple of Zeus in Olympia, [3. no. 1705]), while earlier cycles also describe adventures that do not belong to the later cycles ([3. no. 1698–1703], cf. Eur. HF 359–435). Always certain was the fight with the Nemean lion as a youthful adventure, in which H. obtains the invulnerable lionskin as protection that is typical for the iconography (cf. Stesich. fr. 52). The canonical order of the killing of the Lernaean Hydra, the Erymanthean boar, the Cerynthian hind, the Stymphalian birds and cleaning the stables of → Augias follow, and they all take place in the Peloponnese. The Cretan bull (south of the Peloponnese), the man-eating horses of the Thracian Diomedes (north), capturing the belt of the Amazon (east) and the cattle of → Geryoneus (west) reach out into the four cardinal directions; bringing up Cerberus leads into the Underworld, the apple of the Hesperids to the (western) edge of the world, where heaven and earth meet (→ Atlas [2]). These adventures have all been recorded individually in archaic literature and art: Homer mentions Cerberus (Hom. Il. 8,367f.; Hom. Od. 11,623–626), Hesiod mentions Geryoneus, the Hydra and the lion of Nemea (Hes. Theog. 287–294; 313–318; 327–332); the Nemean lion, the Hydra, the hind, the birds and Geryoneus are attested (fr. 2–5) for the epic *Herakleia* of → Peisander (7th cent.); → Stesichorus composed a *Geryonëíd* and a *Kérberos*.

Not taken up in this list of twelve labours but connected from an early stage are the conflicts with the → Centaurs (Peisander, Stesichorus), with → Antaeus, the son of → Gaia (Peisander), the conquest of Troy under → Laomedon, a generation before the Trojan War (Hom. Il. 5,640–651) – which since Pindar was connected with the campaign against the Amazons, later also with H.'s participation in the → Argonaut journey (Pind. Nem. 3,36f., cf. Hellanicus FGrH 4 F 26; Diod. Sic. 4,32) – and the battle against the Meropes, the original inhabitants of Cos, which is described in detail in a local late archaic epic, the *Meropís* ([4], cf. Hom. Il. 15,25–28; Pind. Isthm. 1,31).

The large majority of these tales show H. in battle with wild, monstrous and dangerous animals (a giant boar, man-eating horses) or monstrous people (the triple-bodied Geryoneus, the virago Amazons, the invulnerable Antaeus); H.'s mission to civilize was read into this at an early point already, and this becomes clear in the story of his murder of the Egyptian king → Busiris [3] and the termination of his human sacrifices (Hdt. 2,45; Isoc. Or. 11,45; [5]). Behind many of these stories is traditional and partially ancient story material, which can be traced into the Indo-European, and even Stone Age past [6; 7; 8]; there are also clear narrative parallels to the Near East and to the Egyptian ideology of kings (summarizing [9. 458–472]).

The complex of myths around H.'s battle against the → Minyae of Orchomenus and their king → Erginus is closely connected to Thebes. H. gets the Theban king's daughter → Megara as a reward, with whom he has several sons. Struck mad by Hera, he kills (the mother and) his sons. This narrative, which exists in several, strongly divergent versions, is tied to the Theban cult of H. (Pind. Isth. 4,80–86); the definitive description is from Eur. Heraclid. (cf. Sen. Herc. f.).

Another wife of H. is → Deianira, the daughter of King Oeneus of Calydon and the sister of → Meleager; H. fights for her against his rival suitor → Achelous [2] and wins her (Archil. fr. 286; Pind. fr. 249a; Bacchyl. 5,165). While crossing a river, the Centaur → Nessus, who is supposed to be carrying Deianira, assaults her; when H. shoots him with an arrow poisoned with the Hydra's blood, the dying Centaur advises her to keep his blood as a love-charm. When Deianira uses it to defend herself against her rival → Iole, she kills H. (in detail Soph. Trach.; on the religious background [10]). → Hyllus is a son from this relationship, and the eponym of the Doric Hylleis.

The story of Iole is integrated into a complex plot, which connects the conquest of the city → Oechalia in Trachis (north-east Greece) with the service to Omphale in Lydia and the final immolation on the Oeta, the highest mountain near Trachis. Iole is the daughter of → Eurytus [1] and the sister of → Iphitus from Oechalia; H. takes her as his concubine, killing her father and brother – in the best-known story, because he wins Iole in an archery competition, but is sent away without her; he takes revenge by murdering Eurytus and Iphitus (differently Hom. Od. 21,13–37, where H. kills Iphitus because of his twelve mares, even though he was his host). Because of the murder he is overtaken by a disease, about which he tries to get information in Delphi, but the Pythia does not want to answer the murderer. So he steals the tripod, and Apollo resists (often portrayed since Attic black-figured vase painting, [3. no. 2947–3071]), until Zeus intervenes. Slave labour for → Omphale in Lydia brings healing; with her he has the son Acheles, eponym for the Lydian river Acheles, whose waters heal him (Panyassis fr. 20). The identification of H. with the Lydian hero Masnes might be behind this [11]. Another son is → Tyrsenus, eponym for the Etruscans (Dion. Hal. Ant. Rom. 1,28,1; Paus. 2,21,3); the genealogy – which competes with others since Hdt. 1,94 – is an expression of the Lydian descent of the Etruscans.

In the *vulgata*, which is attested since Soph. Trach., H. conquers Oechalia after his service with Omphale and brings the young Iole back; in order to win back his affections Deianira sends H. a robe that is smeared with Nessus' blood. It eats its way into his body; the pain can only be stopped by H. letting himself be burned alive on the peak of Mount Oeta. This self-immolation is later understood as a means of apotheosis (Cic. Tusc. 2,20), but it is the aition of a fire cult with the sacrifice of a bull and agons on the peak of Oeta, which has been archaeologically located [12; 13].

In countless local myths H. also appears as the founder of a royal genealogy. This is well developed for the Spartan kingship, whose role is substantiated with the story about the return of the Heraclids, but it may apply to the Lydian or Macedonian kings as well (Hdt. 1,7,2; 8,137f.); in this respect the Egyptian royal legend about the fathering of the Pharaoh by the most supreme god is taken over and is the starting-point for the story of → Amphitryon (especially exploited from stage since the Middle Comedy and Plautus).

C. CULT

H. is included in a large number of cults in the entire Greek world (his cult is rare in Crete). The cult forms vary and hardly differ from the divine cults; for this reason Pindar can call him *hérōs theós* ('hero god') (Nem. 3,22). Next to the fire cult on Oeta there is a similar cult in Thebes, which is dedicated to his children (for this reason one version of the myth has them die in fire, Pherecydes FGrH 3 F 14), and was included in the annual festival of H. as hero sacrifice (*enágisma*)[14]; the structure of the festival is reminiscent of the hero sacrifices that precede a divine cult (→ Hero cult).

H. had an important sanctuary, which was central for the entire polis (Thasios, LSCG 63), on Thasos; the cult is connected to cultic meals (maybe by clans, which

is why it is called Patroios) and the awarding of weapons to the sons of the war dead (LSCG Suppl. 64) [15]. The connection to young men in military training is characteristic of the eastern Greek cult of H. [16], and in general for H. to the subgroups of the polis. In Attica a large number of small sanctuaries that are connected to cult societies are a characteristic of H. [17]; for this reason the Athenian Comedy (but also Eur. Alc.) made him to be a great eater and drinker. The connection to the ephebes and the → gymnasium is also widespread (→ Ephebeia); in Athens H. receives a libation from the young men, the *oinistéria*, and in many places he is the protector of the gymnasium along with Hermes.

Especially from Hellenistic times his role as protector in all sorts of perils is widespread; as such he is called Alexikakos ('defender against evil'), and Kallinikos ('who brings beautiful victory'); an epigrammatical prayer to H. Kallinikos, which is widespread in the entire Greek-speaking Mediterranean area (and transformed into Christian form), above the house doors is supposed to protect the house [18].

D. IDENTIFICATION

H. is identified with a large number of non-Greek gods and heroes; he was taken over as → Hercle by the Etruscans, as → Hercules by the Romans. The identification with the Tyrian Melqart, present already in Herodotus, is important (central cult centre is Gades in south-west Spain); but the fact that individual Heraclea of the Greek (Thasos, Erythrae) and Roman world (Ara Maxima) continue a cult of → Melqart is improbable [19; 20]. Of more local nature is the equating of H. with the Lydian Masnes and the god → Sandon from Asia Minor who is especially honoured in Tarsus [21]; it is unclear how far his popularity in Italy and his role as protector of Italian shepherds continue an indigenous, no longer clear figure.

E. TEACHING ON VIRTUE

H. entered into moral philosophy early as an example of the person who gains immortality through his forbearing efforts. The starting-point is the story composed by Prodicus about H. at a crossroads, where the youthful hero has to decide between (the personifications of) happy sensual enjoyment (*Eudaimonía, Voluptas*) and efficiency (*Areté, Virtus;* Xen. Mem. 2,1,21–34); it was told often in antiquity and was often portrayed visually in the Renaissance and Baroque [22; 23]. Allegoresis generally exploited the myths of H. in this sense and passed them on to the post-classical world [24]. More specifically, since Alexander the Great H. is the model of the ruler's virtue; this was adopted by, e.g., the Roman emperor → Commodus or even still by Charles V. (in his motto *Plus Ultra*, which claims to go beyond the Pillars of Hercules) [25].
→ Hercules

1 W. PÖTSCHER, Heros und Hera, in: RhM 104, 1961, 302–355 2 PRELLER/ROBERT II 2, 421–675 3 J. BOARDMAN et al., s.v. H., LIMC 4, 728–838. 5, 1–192

4 H. LLOYD-JONES, The Meropis (SH 903 A), in: Id. (ed.), Greek Epic, Lyric, and Tragedy. The Academic Papers of Sir Hugh Lloyd-Jones, 1990, 21–29 (1984) 5 A.-F. LAURENS, s.v. Bousiris, LIMC 3, 147–152 6 L. RADERMACHER, Mythos und Sage bei den Griechen, 1943 7 F. BADER, De la préhistoire à l'idéologie tripartite. Les travaux d'H., in: R. BLOCH (ed.), D'H. à Poséidon. Mythologie et protohistoire, 1985, 9–124 8 W. BURKERT, Structure and History in Greek Mythology and Ritual, 1979, 78–98 9 M. L. WEST, The East Face of Helicon, 1997, 458–472 10 C. A. FARAONE, Deianira's Mistake and the Demise of Heracles. Erotic Magic in Sophocles' Trachiniae, in: Helios 21, 1994, 115–136 11 G. M. A. HANFMANN, Lydiaka II. Tylos and Masnes, in: HSPh 63, 1958, 68–88 12 M. P. NILSSON, Der Flammentod des H. auf dem Oite, in: ARW 21, 1922, 310–316 13 Y. BÉQUIGNON, La vallée du Spercheios, 1937, 204–231 14 SCHACHTER 2, 14–30 15 B. BERGQUIST, H. on Thasos. The Archaeological, Literary and Epigraphic Evidence for his Sanctuary, Status and Cult Reconsidered, 1973 16 GRAF, 98f. 17 S. WOODFORD, Cults of Heracles in Attica, in: Studies G.M.A. Hanfmann, 1971, 211–225 18 R. MERKELBACH, Weg mit dir, H., in die Feuershölle!, in: ZPE 86, 1991, 41–43 19 D. VAN BERCHEM, Sanctuaires d'Hercule- Melqart, in: Syria 444, 1967, 73–109; 307–336 20 C. BONNET, Melqart. Cultes et mythes de l'Héraclès tyrien en Méditerranée, 1988 21 H. GOLDMAN, Sandon and H., in: Hesperia Suppl. 8, 1949, 164–174 22 M. KUNTZ, The Prodikean "Choice of H.". A Reshaping of Myth, in: CJ 89, 1994, 163–181 23 E. PANOFSKY, Herkules am Scheidewege und andere ant. Bildstoffe in der neueren Kunst, 1930 24 W. SPARN, Hercules Christianus. Mythographie und Theologie in der frühen Neuzeit, in: Wolfenbütteler Forschungen 27, 1984, 73–107 25 W. DERICHS, H. Vorbild des Herrschers, 1950. F.G.

II. Iconography

Among the earliest pictorial records of the hero is a bronze clasp with H. and the Hydra that dates to around 700 BC. The pictures on vases from the late 7th cent. BC with all important H.-scenes are numerous: H. feasting (Eurytus Krater, Paris, LV, 7th/6th cents. BC), H. introduced into Olympus by Athena (bowl by the → Phrynus Painter, London, BM, 550/530 BC), his deeds and adventures. In 6th-cent. Attica the hero is painted more often than any other mythological figure, especially in the times of the Peisistratids, whose influence on the figure of H. cannot be proven with certainty however (but cf. the procession of → Peisistratus, which is reminiscent of H.'s entry into Olympus). In earlier representation H. mostly appears bearded, towards the end of the 6th cent. BC more often beardless. His weapons are the club or bow, sometimes a sword, he points a harpoon at the Hydra. He is often portrayed naked or with a short → chiton, with the lionskin, above all, from the end of the 6th cent. BC.

The western poros pediment of the old temple of Athena on the Athenian Acropolis (1st half of the 6th cent. BC) shows H. battling the fish-bodied old man of the sea Nereus or Triton, in the eastern pediment of the Siphnian Treasury in Delphi is the battle between H. and Apollo for the Delphic tripod (around 525 BC); H. appears as an archer with a lion's head helmet in the eastern pediment of the temple of Aphaia on → Aegina (around 490 BC). Various series of metopes have preserved H.'s cycle of labours: the Athenian Treasury in Delphi (north and west metopes; around 490 BC), the Temple of Zeus of Olympia (around 460 BC), the Hephaesteum in Athens (450/440 BC). His decisive participation in the battles of the → Giants are described on the Parthenon in Athens (east metope 11, 442–432 BC) and on the Pergamum Altar, eastern frieze (around 160 BC). H. appears almost without exception with Athena on document-reliefs – as the eponymus (of Heraclea, Thebes) or as the patron of the honoured person.

Single portrayals of H. have been passed down from about the middle of the 6th cent. BC (especially bronze statuettes). H. Cherchel (possibly after a bronze original of the 2nd quarter of the 5th cent. BC) characterizes the bearded H. standing with his weight on his right leg; cf. H. Farnese (Naples, MN, early 3rd cent. AD after an original of the 3rd quarter of the 4th cent. BC, ascribed to → Lysippus); the youthful. H. from the Baths of Caracalla in Rome, (TM, 1st/2nd cents. AD, original around 430 BC) is presumably Polycletic; the not extant colossal seated statue of the hero in Tarentum (cf. funerary relief of the Haterii, Rome, MV, beginning of the 2nd cent. AD; Byzantine ivory box in Xanten) is by Lyssipus. The Heracliscus motif of the snake-strangling child H. has been repeated from early classical times. The H. figure takes a unique pose in the legitimation of ruling dynasties and the efforts of various poleis to expand, in particular from the 4th cent. BC.

The Italian Hercules, honoured latest from the early Republican times at the Ara Maxima on the Forum Boarium (→ Roma), has been recorded on numerous frescoes and mosaics, often on cameos. Small bronzes show, among others, H. *bibax* (new find from the *burgus* of Lich, presumably motif from the 4th cent. BC). His image was part of the statuary outfit of the Villa dei Papiri in Herculaneum. Sarcophagus reliefs of the 2nd–3rd cents. AD almost always show his deeds. H. can be seen in Roman state art from Republican times (Victory monument of Bocchus on the Capitol, Rome, Palace of the Conservatori, 91 BC), from Trajan again stronger in representations of imperial politics (Trajan's Arch at Beneventum, AD 114) and especially popular with the army.

L. J. BALMASEDA, s.v. H./Hercules, LIMC V, 253–262 (with older lit.); J. BOARDMAN et al., s.v. H., LIMC IV, 728–838; LIMC V, 1–192 (with older lit.); P. GROS, Hercule à Glanum, in: Gallia 52, 1995, 311–331; U. HUTTNER, Die polit. Rolle der H.-Gestalt im griech. Herrschertum, 1997; P. F. B. JONGSTE, The Twelve Labours of Hercules on Roman Sarcophagi, 1992; H. KLOFT, H. als Vorbild. Funktion eines griech. Mythos, 1994; S. RITTER, Hercules in der röm. Kunst – Von den Anfängen bis Augustus, 1995; E. TAGALIDOU, Weihreliefs an H. aus klass. Zeit, 1993; R. VOLLKOMMER, H. in the Art of Classical Greece, 1988; S.R. WOLF, H. beim Gelage, 1993.

A.L.

[2] Son of → Alexander [4] and his lover → Barsine, never acknowledged as legitimate by his father. Born 327 BC (Diod. Sic. 20,20,1), he is not mentioned during Alexander's life and lived with his mother in Pergamum. His uncle's → Nearchus suggestion to take him into consideration as successor after Alexander's death (323) was not taken seriously (Curt. 10,6,10–12). After eliminating → Alexander [5], → Polyperchon called H. to himself in order to use him as a weapon against → Cassander. But he preferred to unite with Cassander and had H. killed in 309 (Diod. Sic. 20,28; Plut. Mor. 530).

P.A. BRUNT, Alexander, Barsine and Heracles, in: RFIC 103, 1975, 22–34.   E.B.

Heracles coinage A joint minting by some cities (Rhodes, Cnidus, Iasus, Ephesus, Samos, Byzantium, Cyzicus and Lampsacus) with local ethnika and representations on the reverse, ΣΥΝ (for Symmachia) and the young snake-strangling Hercules on the obverse. The coins were generally seen as the expression of an alliance not documented by other sources, which is mostly dated in the time immediately after 394 BC (defeat of the Spartans off Cnidus).

H.A. CAHN, Knidos, 1970, 173f.; G.L. CAWKWELL, A Note on the Heracles Coinage Alliance of 394 B.C., in: NC 1956, 69–75; S. KARWIESE, Lysander as Herakliskos-Drakonopnignon, in: NC 1980, 1–27; E. SCHÖNERT, Die Münzprägung von Byzantion I, 1970, 31–35.   Dl.K.

Heracleum (Ἡράκλειον; *Hērákleion*).
[1] Town on Crete's northern coast, modern Iraklion. In a legal support agreement with Miletus (259/250 BC) H. appears as a sovereign town allied with → Knossos (Stv III 482 I) [1]. H. was in the 1st cent. BC, probably in succession to Amnisus, the port town of Knossos (Str. 10,4,7f.) and probably subject to it (cf. Str. 10,5,1). Based on Plin. HN 4,59, it was presumed that H. also bore the name Mation [2]. However, the consensus is that Pliny misunderstood his Greek source (πολισμάτιον Ἡ.; *polismátion H.*, 'the little town of Heraclion') [3]. Because the list of Cretan towns in Pliny (and presumably also his source) does not differentiate elsewhere between large and small towns, the existence of a settlement by the name of Mation near H. cannot be ruled out (cf. also Plin. HN 4,61: the island of Dia, which is located *contra Matium*). Ancient ruins are virtually non-existent in H., with the exception of some Roman graves and remains of an early Byzantine town wall between Odos Khandakos and Odos Daidalos [4].

1 A. CHANIOTIS, Die Verträge zw. kret. Poleis in der hell. Zeit, 1996, 448f., no. 78 2 C. BURSIAN, Geogr. von Griechenland 2, 1872, 560f. 3 N. PLATON, Δύο ὀνόματα ἀνυπάρκτων Κρητικῶν πόλεων, in: Kretika Chronika 1, 1947, 14–21 4 I.F. SANDERS, Roman Crete, 1982, 152.

H.SO.

[2] Southernmost town in Macedonian Pieria (Ps.-Scyl. 66) near modern Platamon. Mentioned in the Athenian tribute quota lists of 425/4 and 422/1 (IG I³ 71; 77); boundary dispute with → Gonni in the 3rd cent. BC. [1]; conquered by the Romans in the 3rd Macedonian War (171–168 BC; Liv. 44,8,8f.). Probably absorbed into the Roman colony of Dion [II 2].

1 B. HELLY, Gonnoi II, 1973, no. 93.

F. PAPAZOGLOU, Les villes de Macédoine, 1988, 114.

MA.ER.

[3] Greek settlement in the eastern Crimea on the south bank of the Maeotis (Ptol. 3,6,4), according to Str. 11,2,6 between Myrmecium and Parthenium.

[4] Two promontories on the Caucasian Black Sea coast: *ákra* H. at the mouth of the Nesis (Arr. Peripl. p. eux. 9v46 DILLER) and *akrōtérion* H., which was called *tà Érēma* (τὰ Ἔρημα, l.c. 1014,4) in Arrian's time, on the river Achaius.   I.v.B.

Heraclianus Western Roman usurper in the year AD 413. He murdered → Stilicho in Ravenna in 408 and was rewarded for this by being named *comes Africae* (Zos. 5,37,6). In spite of the despotism he practiced there he was made consul in 413 (Oros. 7,42,10), but he revolted against → Honorius [3] and landed near Rome with a large fleet. He was defeated and condemned to death on the 3rd of August 413 (Cod. Theod. 15,14,13). He fled to Carthage, where he was killed (Oros. 7,42,14; Zos. 6,7ff.; Chron. min. 1,467, 654; 2,18,71 MOMMSEN).

PLRE 2, 539f.; A. DEMANDT, Die Spätantike, 1989, 148; St. I. OOST, The Revolt of Heraclian, in: CPh 61, 1966, 236–242.   K.P.J.

Heraclidae (Ἡρακλεῖδαι; *Hērakleîdai*). Every descendant of → Hercules may be called *Herakleídēs* (see below). The narrower sense of the myth, which appears to have originated in the 7th cent. (Tyrteus fr. 2 WEST) and was developed by the 5th cent. at the latest, of the 'return of the H. to the Peloponnese' refers to Hercules' son → Hyllus and his descendants until the fourth generation (main sources: (Ps.-) Apollod. 2,167–180, Diod. Sic. 4, 57–58; as well as papyrus finds of → Euripides *Temenos*, *Temenidai*, *Kresphontes*, *Archelaos*).

While fleeing from Eurystheus after Hercules' death, the H. are first taken in at Trachis, then in → Athens (Paus. 1,32,6; (Ps.-)Apollod. 2,167–168) or the Attic Tetrapolis (Pherecydes FGrH 3F84). After Hyllus killed Eurystheus with the help of the Athenians, the Delphic Oracle advises him to wait for the third fruit before returning. Hyllus marched into the Peloponnese three years later and fell in single combat with → Echemus [1] of Tegea. Then, according to an agreement, the H. renounced for 50 years any attempt to return and withdrew in part into the Attic Tetrapolis, in part into the Doris to → Aegimius [1] (Diod. Sic. 4,37,3–4; Ps.-

Apollod. 2,154). Only after interpreting the saying of the third fruit as the third generation do the H. succeed in entering the Peloponnese under the leadership of → Oxylus.

After building three altars for Zeus Patroos in the casting of lots for the peninsula, → Temenos receives Argus, the sons of Aristodemus, Procles and Eurysthenes, Lacedaemon (aition for the Spartan double monarchy: Hdt. 7,204; 8,131,2; [1. 175]), → Cresphontes Messenia.

In the light of new evaluations of archaeological finds the myth can be interpreted only in a limited sense as a reflection of the → Doric migration, if at all (but cf. [2; 3; 5]). Rather its function as a 'charter myth' for the division of the Peloponnese among the Dorian states and the founding of the Spartan hegemony is clearly recognizable. Beyond that the legend closes the gap between mythical and historical time (cf. Isoc. Or. 4,54, Ephoros FGrH 70 T8; differently Thuc. 1,12).

The legend of the taking in of the H. developed in Athens especially in rhetoric (for example Lys. 2,11–16) and tragedy (Eur. Heracl., possibly already Aesch. Heracl.), as a counterweight to the Peloponnesian myth (cf. Hdt. 9,26–27). The cult of H. has been documented in the Attic demes Erchia (SEG 21.541 = LSCG 18, B42–43; c. 375/50 BC) and Aixone (IG II/III² 1199, 23–25; c. 325–24 BC), in Porto Rafti (IG II/III² 4977; 4th–3rd cents. BC) and possibly also in Thoricus ([9]; 1st half 4th cent. BC).

Mostly with propagandistic intentions, H. are mythical colonizers already early on (→ Tlepolemus; → Thessalus; Rhopalus founded Phaestus: Paus. 2,6,6–7), or ruling dynasties call themselves H. (Tylonids and Mermnads: Hdt. 1,7; Bacchiads and others in Corinth: Diod. Sic. 7,9, Paus. 2,4,3, → Hippotes; the Macedonian ruling house: Hdt. 8,137–139, Hyg. Fab. 219, cf. the freely invented derivation in Eur. Archelaus; the Attalids, via → Telephus, cf. [4]).

The sons of → Hercules and → Megara are also H.

1 C. CALAME, Spartan Genealogies, in: J. BREMMER (ed.), Interpretations of Greek Mythology, 1987, 153–186 2 R. DREWS, The Coming of the Greeks, 1988, 203–225 3 J. CHADWICK, I Dori e la creazione dei dialetti greci, in: D. MUSTI (ed.), Le origini dei greci. Dori e mondo egeo, ²1986, 3–12 4 T.S. SCHEER, Myth. Vorväter. Zur Bed. griech. Heroenmythen im Selbstverständnis kleinasiat. Städte, 1993, 71–152 5 C. BRILLANTE, Il ritorno degli Eraclidi, in: Id., La leggenda eroica e la civiltà micenea, 1981, 149–182 6 O. CARRUBA, L'arrivo dei Greci, le migrazioni indoeuropee e il "ritorno" degli Eraclidi, in: Athenaeum 83, 1995, 5–44 7 F. KIECHLE, Die Ausprägung der Sage von der Rückkehr der H., in: Helikon 6, 1966, 493–517 8 M.A. LEVI, Studi Spartani, 1: Dori ed Eraclidi, in: RIL 96, 1962, 479–499 9 R. PARKER, The H. at Thorikos, in: ZPE 57, 1984, 59 10 F. PRINZ, Gründungsmythen und Sagenchronologie, 1979 11 J.S. RUSTEN, The Return of the H., in: ZPE 40, 1980, 39–42 12 B. SERGENT, Le partage du Péloponnèse entre les H., in: RHR 192, 1977, 121–136; 193; 1978, 3–25.

T.H.

Heraclidas Sculptor from Atrax in Thessaly, active in the 4th cent. BC. Together with Hippocrates he signed a victory votive of the Pharsalians in Delphi, where it was set up in the mid 4th cent. BC. Because of the measures at the base, it may have been the bronze group of Achilles on horseback and Patroclus, which Pausanias (10,13,5) describes. However, because the base bears a rededication to Claudius there can be no certainty. Pausanias may not have seen the original work.

G. DAUX, Pausanias à Delphes, 1936, 141–143; J. MARCADÉ, Recueil des signatures de sculpteurs grecs, 1, 1953, 35; H. POMTOW, Das Anathem der Pharsalier in Delphi, in: Philologus 7, 1921, 194–199. R.N.

Heraclides (Ἡρακλείδης; *Hērakleídēs*). Famous persons: the politician and writer H. [19] Lembus, the philosopher H. [16] Ponticus the Younger, the doctor H. [27] of Tarentum.

I. POLITICAL FIGURES   II. LITERARY FIGURES
III. DOCTORS   IV. ARTISTS

I. POLITICAL FIGURES

[1] H. of Clazomenae (cf. Pl. Ion 541d) was in the service of the Persians and probably called *basileús* for that reason. Thus, he was able to perform valuable services for Athens at the Persian court in 423 BC for which he received Attic citizenship soon after moving there (after 400, Syll.³ 118). To move the Athenians to stronger participation in the *ekklesia*, he had the payment to each participant increased from one obol to two (Aristot. Ath. Pol. 41,3), which was in Aristotle's opinion a (radical) democratic measure (Aristot. Pol. 1297a 35–38).

M.H. HANSEN, Die athenische Demokratie im Zeitalter des Demosthenes, 1995, 155. PE.HÖ.

[2] Syracusan, the son of Lysimachus. In 415 BC he was chosen as the general for the campaign against the Athenians (Thuc. 6,73,1; Diod. Sic. 13,4,1), but was already deposed after setbacks in the next year (Thuc. 6,103,4).
[3] Syracusan, the son of Aristogenes. One of the leaders of the Syracusan relief squadron for conducting the naval war on the west coast of Asia Minor, where he arrived in 410 BC (Xen. Hell. 1,2,8). K.MEI.
[4] H. of Aenus. In 360/359 BC he and his brother → Python murdered the Odrysian King → Cotys I. He had been encouraged by theories of his teacher Plato regarding tyrannicide (Diog. Laert. 3,46; Plut. Mor. 1126C). The Athenians honoured him with citizenship and a golden wreath for this action (Dem. Or. 23,119; Aristot. Pol 5, 10, 12, 1311b 21; Plut. Mor. 542f, 816e).

K. TRAMPEDACH, Platon, die Akademie und die zeitgenössische Politik, 1994, 90–92. J.E.

[5] Prominent Syracusan, mercenary commander under → Dionysius [2] II, friend of → Dion [I 1]. Fled to Greece in 361/360 BC and set up the return to Sicily in 357 with Dion, but only followed him a year later with 20 warships and 1,500 men (Diod. Sic. 16,16,2). An

alleged estrangement of the two even at that time cannot be assumed (thus, Plut. Dion 32,4). The separate advance was probably based on a strategic plan. Only the naval victory of H., who was appointed nauarch, over Philistus, the admiral of Dionysius II, led to an increased rivalry. H. also enjoyed great popularity with the *demos* while Dion was suspected of striving for a tyrannis. As a result H. was elected into the college of *strategoi* while Dion thought it necessary to leave the town. When Dion regained the rule over Syracuse after a victory over the troops of Dionysius II, he spared H. However, when the latter repeatedly opposed Dion at the head of the *demos* – for example, he even contacted Dionysius II through the Spartan Phares – Dion insti-gated his murder in 354 (Plut. Dion 53). This finally undermined Dion's authority among the people and soon resulted in his violent death. Sources: Plato, Letter 7 and 8, and Plutarch's *vita* of Dion, which was based on Timonides of Leucas (FGrH 651), who was a member of the Academy and participant in the expedi-tion (Plut. Dion, 22,4; 30,10; 35,4), are very positive towards Dion (who allegedly wanted to make real the ideal Platonic state in Syracuse) and very hostile towards H. (who is described as an uninhibited dema-gogue). Diodorus 16,9–20 (mostly based on Ephorus) is more objective.

H. BERVE, Dion, in: AAWM, 1956, no. 19; M. SORDI, in: E. GABBA, G. VALLET (ed.), La Sicilia antica 2.1, 1980, 237ff.; H. D. WESTLAKE, in: CAH ²1994, 698ff.   K.MEI.

[6] Son of Agathocles, participated in the African cam-paign of 310 BC and stayed with Ophellas of Cyrene to make the latter feel safe. He was even adopted by Ophellas (Just. Epit. 22,7,6; Polyaenus, Strat. 5,3,4) but then was killed by his soldiers after Agathocles' secret escape from Africa in 307 (Diod. Sic. 20,69,3).

K. MEISTER, Agathocles, in: CAH 7,1, ²1984, 384–411, esp. 393ff.   K.MEI.

[7] Macedonian officer from Bottiaea. In the Balkan war of → Alexander [4] the Great (335 BC) and at → Gaugamela, he led one of the *ilai* (→ Cavalry) of the → *hetairoi* (Arr. Anab. 1,2,5; 3,11,8).
[8] After the death of → Hephaestion [1] assigned by → Alexander [4] in 324 BC with building a fleet in → Hyrcania and sailing around the Caspian Sea. Alex-ander's death probably prevented the order from being completed.

BERVE 2, no. 348.

[9] H. of Chalcedon, sent as an emissary to → Darius [3] and remained in his company until his death (330 BC). Captured by → Alexander [4] but released unharmed (Arr. Anab. 3,24,5).   E.B.
[10] As commander of the garrison of king → Deme-trius [2] Poliorcetes, which still controlled the Muny-chia and Piraeus in 287 BC, he fended off an attack by the Athenians in 287/6 (Polyaenus, Strat. 5,17,1; Paus. 1,29,10).

HABICHT, 129f.   J.E.

[11] H. of Tarentum, portrayed very negatively by Poly-bius (13,4; cf. Diod. Sic. 28,2): because he was suspect-ed of high treason by the Tarantines and the Romans, he went to Macedonia in about 210 BC, where he gained the confidence of Philip V. As an agent of Philip in 204 he started a fire in the Rhodian naval arsenal (Pol. 13,5; Polyaenus, Strat. 5,17,2) and in the 2nd Macedonian War he commanded the king's navy (Liv. 31,16,3; 46,8) until Philip deposed him in 199/8, probably at the request of the Macedonian war council (Liv. 32,5,7; Diod. Sic. 28,9) [1. 108f.].

1 S. LE BOHEC, Les "philoi" des rois Antigonides, in: REG 98, 1985, 93–124.

[12] H. of Gyrton, Thessalian functionary of Philip V (and friend of the king?) in 208 BC (Syll.³ 552). He commanded the Thessalian cavalry in 197 at Cynosce-phalae (Pol. 18,22,2).   L.-M.G.
[13] H. of Byzantium. In 190 BC after the defeat of Antiochus [5] III at Myonnesus he attempted in vain as a negotiator to persuade the Roman general L. Corne-lius [I 72] and his brother P. Cornelius [I 71] Scipio, with territorial and financial concessions as well as pri-vate offers from his king, to make peace (Pol. 21,13ff.; Diod. Sic. 29,7f.; Liv. 37,34ff.; App. Syr. 29; Just. Epit. 31,7,4ff.).   A.ME.
[13a] H. of Miletus Under the → Seleucid → Antiochus [6] IV, H. rose to the office of *ho epì tôn prosódōn* (roughly equivalent to 'finance minister'), and served the king as his envoy to Rome. After Antiochus' death, he supported the pretender → Alexander [13] Balas in 158 BC.

J. D. GRAINGER, A Seleukid Prosopography and Gazet-teer, 1997, 92, s. v. H. (2); P. HERRMANN, Milesier am Seleukidenhof, in: Chiron 17, 1987, 183–188.   JÖ. GE.

[14] *Tôn archisōmatophylákōn, epistátēs, epì tôn pro-sódōn* (Τῶν ἀρχισωματοφυλάκων, ἐπιστάτης, ἐπὶ τῶν προσόδων); *epistates* of the Perithebas district in 117/6 BC.

L. MOOREN, The Aulic Titulature of Ptolemaic Egypt, 1975, 129 no. 0142; E. VAN'T DACK, Ptolemaica Selecta, 1988, 291, 355.   W.A.

II. LITERARY FIGURES

[15] Two authors of Syracusan origin (presumably in the 4th cent. BC) who wrote treatises on cooking seem to have borne this name (Ath. 516c), but nothing is known of their lives. Only → Athenaeus [3] mentions them, one as the author of the *Opsartytiká* ('Treatise on the Art of Cooking') in connection with eggs (58b), cake (114a), fish (105c; 328d) and cookery that is un-suited for a slave (661e). The other is mentioned as the author of the work *Perì Thesmôn* ('On Customs') in association with a sesame-honey cake in the form of female genitals, which was used in the ritual of the → *Thesmophória* in Syracuse (647a).   P.S.-P.

[16] H. Ponticus the Elder
A. The person B. Works C. Teachings

A. The person

Born about 390 in Heraclea [7] on the Pontus, died after 322 BC. About 365 H., who is always mentioned among those who heard Plato's lectures 'On the Good' (F 7 and 8, cf. F 42 Wehrli), entered the Platonic Academy (→ Academy) and was its deputy head during Plato's third Sicilian voyage (361/60). After the death of Speusippus (339/8), who was close to him, he applied for his succession in the scholarchate, but narrowly lost out to Xenocrates, whereupon he retreated to Heraclea to found his own school. Although H. never officially belonged to the → Peripatos, Sotion (2nd cent. BC) – and following him Diogenes [17] Laertius – assigned him to this school. In any case, H. shared many interests with the representatives of the Peripatos (cf. Plut., Adversus Colotem XIV, 1115a = F 68 W.) [on this 1. 60f.; 2. 523, 527]. He owed his alternative epithet pompikós (cf. F 3 W.) to his appearance and behaviour.

B. Works

An (incomplete) catalogue of his voluminous oeuvre is contained in Diog. Laert. 5,86–88 (a brief and instructive summary of individual works is contained in [2. 524–527]). H.' chosen format was the dialogue, which he preferred to set in the past and drew out with respect to the setting and the circumstances of the conversation. Cicero referred to this when he spoke of herakleídeia ('dialogue in the manner of H.', F 27a-f W.; regarding interpretation [3. 10–12]).

C. Teachings

H. is remarkable for his unique linkage of Platonic positions with new (especially Pythagorean) thought. Also remarkable is, in physics, the assumption of extremely small particles that still admit change (ἄναρμοι ὄγκοι; ánarmoi ónkoi, 'non-solid mass parts') that are not identical with the θραύσματα (thraúsmata 'fragments', F 121 W.), the actual atoms (on its relationship and links to the Platonic 'Timaeus' [4. 89f.] → Atomism). The doctor → Asclepiades [6] of Bithynia (1st cent. BC) develops his corpuscular theory from this particular atomic theory. In psychology H. differs from Plato in assuming a physical structure of the soul; at the same time, the qualification of the soul as light-like (φωτοειδής; phōtoeidés) or as light is unmistakably influenced by the thought of the Academy. Problems of the theory of the soul, especially the relationship of the soul to the body, are the topic of the only dialogue that can be constructed in outline, 'On Apparent Death', in the centre of which stood the awakening of an apparently dead woman by Empedocles [1] of Acragas and Empedocles' subsequent divine departure (in detail regarding this dialogue [3. 13–36]).

From a modern perspective, H.'s true significance lies in his theses on → astronomy and → cosmology, since he seems to have preceded later theories in assuming a revolution of the earth around its axis (H. appears to have priority over Ecphantus [2], to whom a similar theory was ascribed) and an annual rotation of the earth around the centre of the universe to explain apparent anomalies in the annual path of the sun. However, a positive appreciation of H.'s scientific achievement is rendered difficult by several fantastic speculations that are encountered in his fragments (Cicero already spoke of pueriles fabulae, 'children's tales': Nat. D. 1,13,34 = F 111 W.).

1 Wehrli, Schule (H. 7: H. Pontikos; Sammlung und Komm. der Frg.) 2 F. Wehrli, H. Pontikos, in: GGPh² 3, 523–529 3 H.P. Gottschalk, H. of Pontus, 1980 4 H.J. Krämer, H. Pontikos, in: GGPh² 3, 1983, 88–102. K.-H.S.

In his musical treatise ([1] fr. 157–163), which contains a mythical and historical genealogy of musicians (157–160), H. (163) affirmed the superiority of harmonies (harmoníai) named Dorian, Aeolian, Ionian after Hellenic tribes and differentiated by their ethos over the barbarian ones of the Phrygians and Lydians. It is not certain beyond doubt that a much discussed quote on sound theory (→ Acoustics) (Porph. in Ptol. Harm. 30f.) is from this H. [1. 113].

1 Wehrli, Schule, H. 7. F.Z.

[17] Poet of the Middle Comedy who is known from the great didaskalia inscription [1. test. 1] to have come third at the Dionysia or Lenea after Alexis and before Theopilus in the mid 4th cent. An untitled fragment is preserved in which Adaeus, a general of Philip II of Macedonia, is mocked with the nickname 'Rooster'.

1 PCG V, 558f. B.BÄ.

[18] H. Creticus/Criticus. Greek periegete of the 3rd cent. BC, author of the treatise Perì tôn en têi Helládi póleōn ('On the Towns of Greece'), which describes a journey through central and northern Greece according to the following scheme: distance, road and region, description of the town, local products and inhabitants. Three anonymous excerpts for Attica, Boeotia, Euboea and Thessaly are extant. They are valuable because of the quality of their prose [1. 199–219], the interspersed poetic quotations, mostly from comedies of the 4th/3rd cents., and especially their vividness, which was probably based on autopsia. The work has usually been attributed since its first edition by H. Stephanus in 1589 to → Dicaearchus, but a note in the paradoxographer Apollonius [2. 120–142 § 19] (2nd cent. BC?) attests author and title.

1 G. Pasquali, Die schriftstellerische Form des Pausanias, in: Hermes 48, 1913, 161–223 2 A. Giannini, Paradoxographorum Graecorum Reliquiae, 1965.

FHG II 254–264; GGM I 97–110; F. Pfister, Die Reisebilder des Herakleides, in: SAWW 227.2, 1951 (ed., transl., comm.); E. Perrin, Héracleidès le Crétois à Athènes, in: REG 107, 1994, 192–202. K.BRO.

[19] H. Lembus. Hellenistic statesman and writer. According to Diog. Laert. 5,94 born in Callatis (Pontus) and later a citizen of Alexandria. Because of his (otherwise unknown) *Lembeutikòs lógos* he was nicknamed Lembos ('little boat'). However, the short biography in the Suda s.v. claims Oxyrhynchus as his birth place (less probable) and mentions that he participated in successful diplomatic negotiations between → Ptolemy VI Philometor (180–145 BC) and → Antiochus Epiphanes. Agatharchides [6] of Cnidus was his reader and secretary (Phot. Bibl. 213).

H.'s literary activity seems to have consisted mostly of compilation and popularization. Fragments of, and evidence for, the following works are preserved: (1) The 'Histories' (*Historíai*) in at least 37 books (only five fragments, almost all by Athenaeus). (2) An epitome of the *Bíoi* by → Satyrus. (3) An epitome of the *Diadochaí* by → Sotion. Diogenes Laertius frequently refers to the last two works and their valuable information on Hellenistic philosophy (regarding this succession literature: → Doxography). (4) Epitomes of → Hermippus' three works 'On Legislators', 'On the Seven Wise Men', 'On Pythagoras' (POxy. 1367). (5) Short excerpts from the 'Constitutions' (*Politeíai*) and 'Barbarous Customs' (*Nómima barbariká*) of Aristotle, which are preserved in manuscripts. H. continued the themes of peripatetic research in the Alexandrian environment of the 2nd cent. BC.

→ Doxography

EDITIONS: FHG 3, 167–171 (a new collection of fragments is outstanding; not in FGrH); M. DILTS, Heraclidis Lembi excerpta Politiarum, 1971.
BIBLIOGRAPHY: H. BLOCH, H. Lembos and his *Epitome* of Aristotle's *Politiae*, in: TAPhA 71, 1940, 27–39 (on the excerpts); P.M. FRAZER, Ptolemaic Alexandria, 1972, 514f., 741ff.; J. MEJER, Diogenes Laërtius and His Hellenistic Background, 1978, 40–42, 62ff. D.T.R.

[20] H. of Athens (TrGF I 166), 1st cent. BC; victory of his satyr play at the Amphiaraea and Romaea established by Sulla in Oropus shortly after 85 BC (TrGF I: DID A 6,1). B.Z.

[21] H. Ponticus the Younger. Grammarian of the 1st cent. AD, student of → Didymus [1] Chalcenterus, taught under Claudius and Nero in Rome (Suda η 463; α 2634 [1]) and defended his teacher against the attacks of the Aristarchian Aper [2] in three books of 'Conversations' (Λέσχαι), which were composed in Sapphic hendecasyllables and earned him the nickname *Leschēneutḗs* ('Blabbermouth': Ath. 14,649c). This learned work was perhaps organized as a dialogue and was compared because of its obscurity that required a commentary (Et. Gud. 297,50) with the works of Lycophron and Parthenius (Artem. 4,63).

According to the Suda, H. also wrote epic poetry and 'weapon dances' (πυρρίχαι). He is probably also the author of a grammatical treatise on δεῖ and χρή (EM s.v. δοῦλος) and a work on etymologies, which has often been attributed [4] to H. [16] and was used for the lexicon of Orion.

1 M. SCHMIDT, Didymi Chalcenteri Fragmenta, 1854, 5; 8–10 2 L. COHN, s.v. Aper (6), RE 1, 2697 3 H. DAEBRITZ, G. FUNAIOLI, s.v. H. (49), RE 8, 487–488 4 A.R. DYCK, New Light on Greek Authors from Grammatical Texts, in: MH 46, 1989, 5–6 5 E. HEITSCH, Die griech. Dichterfragmente der röm. Kaiserzeit, II, 1964, 41 6 A. MEINEKE, Analecta Alexandrina, 1843, 377–381 7 H. SCHRADER, Heraclidea, in: Philologus 44, 1885, 238 n. 3.

[22] H. Milesius. Grammarian, about AD 100 (he quotes → Aristonicus [5] and in turn is quoted by → Apollonius [11] Dyscolus); the epithet occurs in Hdn. 2,60,24 LENZ. Author of a treatise 'On Accents' (Περὶ καθολικῆς προσῳδίας), probably the first comprehensive discussion of the subject before → Herodianus, who uses him in his work of the same title but does not always provide a citation. His treatise 'On Irregular Words' (Περὶ δυσκλίτων ῥημάτων) was referred to by → Eustathius, the lexicographers (→ Lexicography) and Byzantine works on this subject. An edition of the fragments in [1]; H. also appears to have been an adherent of → analogy (see [2]). He is an important source for the history of dialects.

Bibliography: 1 L. COHN, De Heraclide Milesio grammatico, in: Berliner Studien für Klass. Philol. 1.2, 1884, 609–717 2 W. FRYE, De Heraclidae Milesii studiis homericis, in: Leipziger Studien zur class. Philol. 6, 1883, 93–188. S.FO.

[23] Sophist from Lycia, who became the *archiereús* (high priest) of the cult of the Emperor there (Philostr. VS 2,26). A student of → Hadrianus [1] and → Chrestus in Athens, where he held the imperial teaching chair about 193 to 209 [1], although his tax freedom (*atéleia*) was forfeit after he lost his train of thought before emperor Septimius Severus in a rhetorical competition against Apollonius of Athens about 202 (VS 2,20,601; 26,614). The adherents of Apollonius of Naucratis violently drove him from his teaching chair and he then taught in Smyrna, where he exercized an eponymous *stephanēphoría*. He was over 80 when he died and was buried in Lycia.

→ Philostratus; → Second Sophistic

1 I. AVOTINS, The Holders of the Chairs of Rhetoric at Athens, in: HSPh 79, 1975, 322–324 2 PIR H 87. E.BO.

[24] H. of Sinope. (Σινωπεύς; *Sinōpeús*). Author of an epigram in the Garland of Philippus. Tlesimenes, who drowned at sea, asks his parents in a prayer to set up a cenotaph for him (Anth. Pal. 7,392). The *Anthologia Palatina* attributes another epitaph (7,281) to H. (without the ethnicon), which is also of a high quality, but not positioned in the alphabetical sequence of the Garland. Perhaps these are two different poets. Diog. Laert. 5,94 may be referring to H. when he lists among 14 persons of this name a 'musical poet of epigrams'.

GA II,1,266f.; II,2,300f. M.G.A.

III. DOCTORS

[25] **H. of Cos.** Doctor, the father of → Hippocrates [6] (Soranus, Vita Hippocratis ch. 1), *fl. c.* 440 BC. The claim that he was considered by some the author of the 'Aphorisms' and the 'Prognostikon' [1], is based on a misunderstanding of the Greek text in Galen (18A,678 K.), which explicitly ascribes both works to Hippocrates.

1 H. GOSSEN, s.v. H. (53), RE 8, 493. V.N.

[26] **H. of Erythrae.** Active in the late 1st cent. BC as a Herophilean doctor (Str. 645C). He wrote a work with the title 'On the School of Herophilus' in at least 7 books (Gal. 8,746 K.). When describing the pulse as a dilatation and contraction of the heart and arteries he emphasized the special significance of the pneuma (Gal. 8,743f. K.). Galen considered H.'s detailed commentaries on the 'Epidemics', books 2, 3 and 6 in the *Corpus Hippocraticum* particularly noteworthy (fr. 4–10 VON STADEN). H. departed from orthodox Herophilean interpretative practice when he agreed with the empiricists in the assumption that the acronymous symbols added to individual case descriptions were later additions. Galen accuses him of false interpretations and long-windedness but admits that he normally wrote nothing nonsensical (CMG V,10,2,2, p. 378).
→ Herophilus V.N.

[27] **H. of Tarentum.** The most important → Empiricist physician of antiquity between 100 and 65 BC. As a pupil of the Herophilean → Mantias, probably in Egypt, he became an Empiricist and wrote a detailed account of this school and its theories (fr. 1 DEICHGRÄBER). Diogenes Laertius (9,115 = fr. 9) wrote of a H., who was a student of the sceptical philosopher Ptolemy of Cyrene and teacher of → Aenesidemus, but identification with H. of Tarentum is not convincing. Only fragments of H.'s works are preserved. He wrote pharmacological treatises (fr. 208–210), at least one dietetic treatise (fr. 241–246, cf. fr. 187) and a large work dedicated to the female doctor → Antiochis [2] (fr. 203–207). His comments on the pulse as representing a visible movement of the heart and arteries (fr. 172) and on the peritoneum (fr. 185) indicate experience in dissection or rather the practice of surgery. His most important therapeutic treatises are the four books on external (frs. 174–178) and internal ailments (frs. 179–191). He demonstrated that he had mastered a wide range of therapeutical methods that included general surgery, eye surgery and especially pharmacological therapy for physical and mental disorders. In his works H. explained the theories of the empiricist school and declared experience the foundation of medicine, but did not wholly reject causal explanations. His explanations earned him the approval of Galen, who praised his precision and love of truth (fr. 175).

H. also played an important role in the history of interpreting Hippocrates. He commented on all Hippocratic works that he considered genuine. As one of the first he examined the 'Aphorisms' (fr. 365) and *De offi-cina* (fr. 319); his commentary on the fourth book of the 'Epidemics' in at least two books (fr. 348) was extraordinary for his time.

H.'s broad range of interest and his logical argumentation are only accessible in fragments but make the loss of his work appear all the more painful. He was appreciated even by medical authors who did not share his theoretical perception, e.g., Galen, Soranus, Caelius Aurelianus and Statilius Criton, who took up some of H.' prescription in his *Kosmētiká* (fr. 234–240). H. is among the pharmacologists depicted on the title page of the 6th-cent. Vienna Dioscurides codex (Vienna, Cod. med. gr. 1, folio 2). Similar pictures of his person were also adopted by the Muslim world. In the Latin west nothing more than H.'s name remained by the 6th cent. (fr. 7; Agnellus, Comm. in Gal. De sectis, p. 22 WESTERINK).
→ Empiricists

EDITION/FRAGMENTS: DEICHGRÄBER, 172–202, 220–249; A. GUARDASOLE, Eraclide di Taranto, Frammenti, 1997.
BIBLIOGRAPHY: H. GOSSEN, s.v. H. (54), RE 8, 493–496. V.N.

IV. ARTISTS

[28] Greek painter, named in an epigraphical wage account preserved at the proscenium of the Hellenistic theatre in Delos. According to it he painted two tablets for 200 drachmas in the early 3rd cent. BC. Probably they were exchangeable backdrop images as were customary in the → stage decoration of that period.

H. BULLE, Unt. an griech. Theatern (ABAW 33), 1928; EAA 3, s.v. H (2), 1149. N.H.

[29] Sculptor, son of Agavus of Ephesus. His signature and that of Harmatius are on a statue worked under Trajan found near Naples, now located in Paris (Louvre) and amended as Mars. It probably represents a portrait of the hip-mantle type. The reading of all names is disputed but in any case indicate a well-known Ephesian sculptor family.

T. ASHBY, Thomas Jenkins in Rome, in: PBSR 6, 1913, 500; CLARAC, pl. 313, no. 1439; G. CRESSEDI, s.v. H. (8), EAA 3, 1960, 1150; LOEWY, no. 293; OVERBECK, no. 2279 (sources). R.N.

[30] Greek painter from Macedonia, active about the mid 2nd cent. BC, perhaps as a court painter. He moved to Athens after the overthrow of King Perseus following the battle of Pydna (168 BC). H., who was described as 'famous' (Plin. HN 35,135; 146), began either as a decorator of ships or as a painter of illusionistic paintings. Neither career is out of the ordinary in Greek → painting. If the latter is correct, the appearance of the ship images remains speculation because his work is unknown.

L. FORTI, s.v. H. (6), EAA 3, 1150; E. PFUHL, s.v. H. (62), RE 8, 497. N.H.

(Ps.-)Heraclitean letters A corpus of nine pseudo-epigraphic letters of the 1st cent. and the 1st half of the 2nd cent. AD, of which two were attributed to the Persian King → Darius [1] and seven to the philosopher → Heraclitus. The topics are political. The first two letters are also recorded by Diog. Laert. 9,13–14. The four letters to → Hermodorus (4; 7–9) are about the addressee's exile, as is the preceding letter 3, in which Darius accuses the Ephesians of having sent the best man in all Ionia into exile. Thus, in letter 4 Heraclitus attempts to comfort his friend, who is living in exile, by noting that he himself was recently accused of godlessness (asébeia) in his native town. In letter 7 Heraclitus informs his friend that the Ephesians had passed a law against him that threatened 'every man who did not laugh and was a misanthrope' with immediate banishment (a longer version of this letter is found in Pap. Geneva 271). In letters 5 and 6 to his friend Amphidamas, Heraclitus writes about his dropsy and assails doctors. The Ps.-Heraclitean letters contain several items familiar as popular cynical and stoic ethical topoi. According to [3] letters 4, 7 and 9 indicate a Jewish author, but this opinion is much disputed among scholars.

EDITIONS: 1 H.W. ATTRIDGE, First-Century Cynicism in the Epistles of Heraclitus (Harvard Theological Studies 29), 1976 (introduction, Greek text with Engl. transl.) 2 V.MARTIN, Un recueil de diatribes cyniques. Pap. Genev. inv. 271, in: MH 16, 1959, 77–115 3 J.BERNAYS, Die Heraklitischen Briefe. Ein Beitrag zur philos. und religionsgesch. Litt., 1869 4 L.TARÁN, Lettere Pseudo-Eraclitee, in: R.MONDOLFO, L.TARÁN, Eraclito. Testimonianze e imitazioni. Introduzione, traduzione e commento (Biblioteca di studi superiori 59), 1972, 279–359 BIBLIOGRAPHY: 5 I.HEINEMANN, s.v. Briefe des Herakleitos (16a), RE Suppl. 5, 228–232. M.G.-C.

Heracliteans The Ionian philosopher → Heraclitus [1] was considered one of the 'scattered' (οἱ σποράδην; oi sporádēn) philosophers in antiquity, i.e. as one who had no place in the successive sequences of teachers and students.

Tradition mentions no students in the strict sense but speaks of followers of Heraclitus. A Heraclitean could be anyone who was philosophically dependent on Heraclitus in some manner (cf. → Democriteans). Some of the 'Heraclitizing' thinkers (Ἡρακλειτίζοντες; Hērakleitízontes), of whom → Cratylus is usually the only one named, seem to have carried Heraclitus' theory of the flow of the physical world to an extreme and denied every form of stability or identity of the self. On this basis they also considered knowledge of the world an impossibility (Aristot. Metaph. 5,1010a 7ff.).

However, Aristotle ascribes to some (other?) followers of Heraclitus certain physical and physiological teachings. These teachings appear to be applications of a theory of 'emanation' onto various phenomena that may have originated with Heraclitus (Aristot. Pr. 908a 30; 934b 34).

Diogenes Laertius also speaks of 'H.' (Ἡρακλείτειοι; Hērakleíteioi, 9,6), among whom he names a certain Antisthenes (6,19), and of a certain Pausanias as a 'Heraclitist' (Ἡρακλειτιστής; Hērakleitistés, 9,15). The first term possibly refers to followers, the second possibly to commentators on Heraclitus.
→ Heraclitus

S.MOURAVIEV, Heraclitea II. A.1 Héraclite d'Éphese – La tradition antique et médiévale I. D' Épicharme à Platon et Héraclide le Pontique, 1993. G.BE.

Heraclitus (Ἡράκλειτος; Hērákleitos).
[1] H. of Ephesus Son of Bloson, outstanding personality within Ionian philosophy.
A. THE PERSON B. LANGUAGE C. PHILOSOPHY D. LATER RECEPTION

A. THE PERSON
H.'s main period of activity is estimated to have been about 503–500 BC (Diog. Laert. 9,1). He belonged to a leading family in the public life of Ephesus. The doxographic tradition records several anecdotes of H.'s arrogance and contempt for his fellow citizens and humanity in general, which are mostly based on fragments of H.

B. LANGUAGE
In antiquity H. was known for his darkness, which brought him the epithets 'the Dark ' (σκοτεινός; skoteinós, e.g., Str. 14,25) and 'the Riddler' (αἰνίκτης; ainíktēs, Timon of Phlius in Diog. Laert. 9,6). H. deliberately uses cryptic language for his philosophical reflections: instead of a continuous argument, the text offers a structured series of enigmatic and aphoristic statements using a broad spectrum of poetic and rhetorical devices – from parallelism and chiasmus (22 B 1 DK; B 5; B 10 etc.) to word play (B 48; B 114) and riddles (B 56, B 34). The meaning develops in a two-fold process: through the skilful use of language individual statements have several levels of meaning while the aphoristic phrases are integrated into an intermeshed system of cross-references and overlays through repeating formulas and structures [1. 87–95; 2].

C. PHILOSOPHY
H. takes a special place among the Ionian philosophers because the fundamental question of his philosophy is not the structure of the physical universe but how to understand this world: reflections on the world, the nature of possible knowledge of the world, and the means to express this knowledge are closely interrelated. A central aspect of his teachings is the idea that a universal, all-penetrating logos structures and governs the cosmos (B 1; B 2; B 72 etc.). It is difficult to define the exact meaning of the term → logos (λόγος) because H. deliberately exploits the entire range of the word's meaning ('Language', 'Accountability', 'Measure', 'Proportion', 'Principle', 'Law', 'Cause' and 'Rational-

ity'). Because the Logos is the most comprehensive principle of the cosmos, it should be the objective in human efforts to achieve true knowledge. Although the Logos is common to all people (ξυνός; *xynós*) and manifest in all phenomena of the world, people are not aware of it (B 2; B 72). They do not grasp the essence (φύσις, *phýsis*), the deeper structure of the experienced world, in the same way that a speech is just meaningless noise for those who do not know the language (B. 107; B 17; B 34; B. 56). H. sees an extensive analogy and even identity between the understanding of the world and the understanding of the meaning of a statement that expresses something with regard to it. The Logos is not beyond reach: it requires special attentiveness and a conscious hermeneutic effort comparable with the understanding of a divine message in the form of an oracle (B 18; B 35; B 86; B 93; B 113; B 115; B 116). Furthermore, everyone must seek true understanding on their own (B 50; B 101a).

H.'s theory of the Logos is related to his use of pairs of opposites: he presents contrasting pairs, alternating phases of a process constitute contrasting qualities (B 57; B 88; B 126 etc.), a single object or phenomenon may exhibit opposite characteristics (B 48; B 59; B 60 etc.), but different observers may ascribe opposite qualities to the same object (B 61; B 83). H. does not deny the existence of opposites in the pairs but understands them as synthetically forming parts of the whole and, finally, as *the* whole, as the cosmos itself (B 8; B 10). Just as the bow has to be drawn into two opposite directions, things can only function based on the never-ending tension and confrontation between opposites and the world will never loose its dynamic. Furthermore, the Logos guarantees at all times that the flow of the world is harmonic and the confrontation of opposites remains productive.

The physical aspect of the force organizing the cosmos is evident in → fire. It is considered the highest and purest divine form of matter. As the basic substance of the world that maintains its nature through all changes and transformations, it represents the material side of the world's unity. The regularity and proportionality of the changes of fire guarantees that the universe remains an orderly whole (B 30; B 31). However, it is problematic that fire is declared the archetypal form of matter and the principle controlling all physical processes in some fragments, but in others it appears equal to the other two elements (water and earth). H. explicitly denies the possibility of an absolute origin of the world (B 30), but it is unclear if the thesis of a permanent cosmic order can be reconciled with the theory of a periodic world fire (as it was ascribed to H. by Aristotle and the Stoics).

The mutual relationship of the epistemic and the physical is also apparent in H.'s theory of the soul. The cosmic fire, which is rational and alive, is equated with the soul (Aristot. An. 405a25). The soul in turn participates in the cosmic process as fire (B 36). Man can participate in cosmic rationality through fire: the more

fiery the soul of a person, the more intelligent it is (B 1 17, B 1 18) and, therefore, the more capable it is of grasping the divine principle of the cosmos.

D. LATER RECEPTION

Although → Plato's knowledge of H. was limited, the Heraclitean theory of flow had a fundamental influence on his description of the physical world as something that is in a state of change (cf. Pl. Tht. 152d ff.). This thesis was further developed by → Aristotle (cf. Aristot. Metaph. Γ 3; 7; 8). Many central theses of the Stoics (→ Stoicism) reveal a Heraclitean influence. The most important is probably the assumption that the Logos is an actively governing principle of the cosmos. → Zeno and → Cleanthes also followed H. in assuming that fire is the physical aspect of the Logos. The Sceptic → Aenesidemus once again puts H. centre stage by believing that the Sceptic's path would lead to Heraclitean philosophy (Sext. Emp. P.H. 1,210ff.).

→ Heracliteans; → Heraclitean Letters; → PRE-SOCRATICS

1 CH. H. KAHN, The Art and Thought of Heraclitus, 1979 2 R. MONDOLFO, The evidence of Plato and Aristotle relating to the ekpyrosis in Heraclitus, in: Phronesis 3, 1958, 75–82.

FRAGMENTS: M. MARCOVICH, Heraclitus, 1967; S. MOURAVIEV, New readings of three Heraclitean fragments (B 23, B 28, B 26), in: Hermes 101, 1973, 114–127; R. MONDOLFO, L. TARÁN, Eraclito, testimonianze e imitazione, 1972.
BIBLIOGRAPHY: W. K. C. GUTHRIE, A History of Greek Philosophy I, 1962, 403–492; M. MARKOVICH, s.v. H., RE Suppl 10, 246–320; K. REINHARDT, Heraklits Lehre vom Feuer, in: Hermes 77, 1942, 1–17; B. SNELL, Die Sprache Heraklits, in: Hermes 61, 1926, 353–381; J. BOLLACK, H. WISMANN, Héraclite ou la séparation, 1972; E. HUSSEY, s.v. Héraclite, in: J. BRUNSCHWIG, G. E. R. LLOYD (ed.), Le savoir grec, 1996.　　　G.BE.

[2] Ath. 12,538f mentions H. of Tarentum, who acted as kithara-player at Alexander the Great's wedding in 324 at Susa, with a quote of Chares [2] of Mytilene (FGrH 125 F 4). Ath. 1,20a likewise knew a H. of Mytilene, a magician at Alexander's court who had also performed at the wedding in Susa (Ath. 12,538e). Diog. Laert. 9,17 assembled the homonyms of the philosopher H., among them a court jester who had been a kithara-player previously. However, Diogenes, by assuming two phases in the court jester's career, may have merged the two persons at Alexander's court named by Athenaeus.　　　E.R.

[3] **H. of Halicarnassus.** Poet of epigrams, identifiable as the elegiac poet in Diog. Laert. 9,17 (ἐλεγείας ποιητὴς Ἁλικαρνασσεύς; *elegeías poiētès Halikarnasseús*) and friend of Callimachus, who mourns his death with a remarkable poem (Anth. Pal. 7,80). A unique funerary epigram by H. is preserved in the Garland of Meleager (7,465) and was imitated by Antipater [8] of Sidon (7,464); his traditional theme (a young woman who died in childbirth) is treated with great originality and elegance.

GA I,1,106.; I,2,304f.; R. HUNTER, Callimachus and Heraclitus, in: Materiali e discussioni 28, 1992, 113–123.

M.G.A.

[4] Comedy writer of unknown date. The title of the play Ξενίζων (*Xenízōn*; 'The Host') is preserved. It mocks a gluttonous woman by the name of Helena (PCG V, 560).

B.BÄ.

[5] Otherwise unknown mythographer, under whose name the Cod. Vaticanus Graecus 305 (cf.: [1. LII–LIII]) preserves 39 excerpts from a collection of marvellous things entitled 'Refutation or Cure of Myths with Unnatural Phenomena ' (ἀνασκευὴ ἢ θεραπεία μύθων τῶν παρὰ φύσιν παραδεδομένων; *anaskeuè è therapeía mýthōn tôn parà phýsin paradedoménōn*). The myths are rationalistically explained (as in the work of → Palaephatus). H. must not be equated with the author of the 'Homeric allegories' [2; 3].

> Editions: 1 N. FESTA (ed.), Mythographi Graeci, Vol. III, Fasc. II, 1902, 73–87.
> BIBLIOGRAPHY: 2 F. BUFFIERE, Les mythes d'Homère et la pensée grecque, 1956, 232–233 3 ID. (ed.), Héraclite. Allégories d' Homère, 1962, VIII–IX. S.FO.

[6] **H. of Rhodiapolis.** (Lycia). Doctor and writer, 1st–2nd cents. AD, the 'Homer of medical poetry', author of medical and philosophical writings. Because his works, of which he made copies available, the Alexandrians, Rhodians and Athenians, and the Epicurean philosophers honoured him, as did the Areopagus. His native city honoured him with a statue and a detailed inscription because of his donations, including especially the dedication of games in honour of Asclepius (TAM II,2,910), which represents the only preserved information on this productive and well-travelled thinker.

V.N.

[7] see → Paradoxographi

[8] In AD 193/4, Septimius Severus ordered H. to secure rulership over Britain for him (SHA Sev. 6,10; SHA Pescennius 5,2 incorrectly names Bithynia) and possibly to offer the title of Caesar to Clodius Albinus (Cass. Dio 73,15,1; Hdn. 2,15,4). He may be identical with the *legatus of the legio VI Ferrata* H. of the year 196 (PIR² H 89; IGR 3,1107) or with H. [2] (PIR² H 88). T.F.

[9] Held the office of a *procurator publici portorii vectigalis Illyrici* in AD 201, when he received a rescript from Septimius Severus and Caracalla on the tax exemption of the city of Tyras on the Djnstr (CIL III 781, cf. p. 1009f. and no. 1209). He could be identical with M. Aurelius H., the presidial procurator of Dacia Malvensis between AD 198 and 209 (AE 1944, 100). Afterwards he apparently functioned as *praeses* of the province of Mauretania Caesariensis (AE 1927, 24, 25). It is rather improbable that he in turn could be identified with Aurelius Septimius H., *praefectus Aegypti* in the year 215 (BGU II 362 col. VII 8f, 20f.).

PIR² H 90; FPD 1, 91, n. 41; PFLAUM, 684ff., no. 253.

T.F.

Heraclius (Ἡράκλειος; *Hērákleios*). Two prominent Sicilians known from the trial of → Verres in 70 BC:

[1] The son of a certain Hieron, a wealthy citizen of Syracuse. In 73 BC he inherited from a homonymous relative a magnificent house including furnishings and 3 million sesterces (Cic. Verr. 2,14,35). Because of the machinations of Verres, who contested the will, H. lost his wealth and the inheritance. The real estate was returned to him by L. Caecilius [I 13] Metellus, the successor of Verres (Cic. Verr. 2,19,47–50; 25,62).

[2] H. of Egesta, captain of a ship in the Syracusan fleet that was captured by pirates while he was ill. At the instigation of Verres he was sentenced and executed (Cic. Verr. 5,44,115–45,120).

K.MEI.

[3] A Cynic. The emperor → Iulianus [11] wrote the speech 'Against the Cynic H. regarding the correct practice of Cynicism and the question if it is appropriate for a 'dog' to invent myths' in March AD 362. As a Peripatetic philosopher, H. expounded with the outspokenness of the Cynics especially upon the teachings of religions that ran counter to Julian's programme of restoring Hellenism. Julian denies H. the right to invoke → Diogenes [14] of Sinope (Julian Or. 223c), faults him for being godless (204c – 205a) having a deficient education (7,235a), and finally accuses him of spreading his works in the army and even the imperial palace (224d).

→ Cynicism

> G. ROCHEFORT, Discours de Julien l'Empereur II 1, texte établi et traduit. Collection des Universités de France, 1963, 34–90; L. PAQUET, Les cyniques grecs. Fragments et témoignages, ²1988, 271–294. M.G.-C.

[4] Otherwise unknown author of a short epigram from the Imperial period that was found near Thebes in Egypt: the poet considers the tomb associated with the name of the mythical Memnon the most incomparable of royal tombs (σύριγγες; *sýringes*).

> EpGr 1018; Anth. Pal. app. I 195 COUGNY; J.A. LETRONNE, Recueil des inscriptions grecques et latines de l'Égypte, 2, 1848 (repr. 1974), 265f. M.G.A.

[5] Court eunuch of emperor → Valentinianus III, in AD 454/5 *primicerius sacri cubiculi*, enemy of the imperial general → Aetius [2], whose murder in 454 was instigated by him; soon after he was killed together with the emperor (Iohannes Antiochenus fr. 201 FHG IV 614f.; Chron. min. 1,303,483f.; 2,86 MOMMSEN; Iord. Rom. 334).

> PLRE 2, 541; A. DEMANDT, Die Spätantike 1989, 155f. K.P.J.

[6] **H. of Edessa.** Roman general under emperors → Leo I and → Zeno, successfully fought in 468–470 against the Vandals. As *magister militum per Thracias* he became a prisoner of the Ostrogoths in 474. He was ransomed by Zeno but on the way to Constantinople fell victim to a Gothic attack. PLRE 2, 541f. (Heraclius 4).

[7] East Roman emperor in AD 610–641, born about 575, son of the homonymous general and exarch of Carthage. In 610 he overthrew the usurper → Phocas and founded a dynasty that governed until 711. He inherited the war with the Sassanid Persians and the Avars from his predecessors. Many details of the conflict are disputed because of the confused state of the sources [cf. 2], e.g. the course of the Avar siege of Constantinople (together with the Persians and Slavs?) in 626 during an absence of H., which ended with a defeat of the enemy that was interpreted as a miracle, as well as the events that led to the peace with the Persians in 628 and the return of the True Cross, which had been captured in Jerusalem in 614. After about 634 the advances of Islamic Arabs put H.'s successes against the Persians into doubt already during his lifetime.

He made a significant contribution to streamlining the imperial administration [1], but he was not the founder of the empire's division into themes (θέματα; *thémata*, military provinces), as was once supposed; they gradually formed at a later stage. In 615 he introduced a silver coin of 6 Roman grams (= 6.81 g; ἐξάγραμμα; *hexágramma*), which essentially replaced the large copper follis. H. was the first emperor to call himself → *basileus* in an official document.

His attempt to settle the dispute over Christ having one or two energies in 638 with the so-called Ekthesis in favour of → Monotheletism was rejected by adherents of the dogma of Chalcedon.

After his death in February 641, his instruction to share the power between his son from his first marriage, Constantinus [3] III, his second wife Martina and his son with her, → Heraclonas, resulted in conflicts. When Constantinus died in September 641, the Senate awarded the succession to his eleven-year old son Constans [2] II.

1 J. F. HALDON, Byzantium in the Seventh Century, 1990 2 P. SPECK, Das geteilte Dossier, 1988 3 A. N. STRATOS, Byzantium in the Seventh Century, vol. 1: 602–634, 1968; vol. 2: 634–641, 1972.

PLRE 3, 586f. (Heraclius 4); ODB 2, 916f.; LMA 4, 2140f.   F.T.

[8] H. the Younger East Roman emperor (January/February–20 April? 641), son of the emperor → Heraclius [7] by his first wife Fabia Eudocia, born in Constantinople on 3 May 612, Augustus since 22 January 613; in memory of Constantinus [1] I the Great also called Νέος Κωνσταντῖνος/*Néos Kōnstántinos* (Lat. *Novus Constantinus*; for the meaning of this epithet, see [3. 1–9]), and for that reason also counted as Constantine III (→ Constantinus [3]) by modern historians, thus distinguishing him from a usurper in the west of the empire. After the death of his father, H. inherited the imperial throne, together with his half-brother → Heraclonas. The latter's mother, Martina, second wife of H. [7], rejected him, considering him a rival to her son. However, it cannot be proven that she brought about his early death by poisoning him; he probably died of

tuberculosis. His short rule was overshadowed by the dismal state of the empire at the time when Islam spread to the eastern provinces of the empire.

1 W. E. KAEGI, A. KAZHDAN, s. v. Herakleios Constantine, ODB 2, 917 2 PLRE 3, 349–351 (Heraclius 38) 3 P. MAGDALINO (ed.), New Constantines, 1994.   F. T.

Heraclonas (Ἡρακλωνᾶς; *Hēraklōnâs*). Son of the emperor → Heraclius [5] and his second wife Martina, born *c.* AD 626. After his father's death in 641, he was to assume the succession as a minor represented by his mother together with Heraclius' oldest son Constantinus III, but was already deposed and exiled with his mother in Sept. 641 at the instigation of the Senate.

PLRE 3, 587f.; ODB 2, 918.   F.T.

Heraea (Ἡραία; *Hēraía*). Western Arcadian city on the right bank of the central course of the Alpheius, shortly before the mouth of the Ladon, with extensive territory, comprising a number of fortified settlements. H. was of strategic importance because of its location on a major road, linking Elis, Arcadia, and the Argolid. According to Paus. 8,26,1, the city was located on a plateau, rising gently from the banks of the Alpheius (minor remains near the modern Hagios Ioannis). There is documentary evidence for an alliance with Elis in the 6th cent. (IvOl 9; SGDI I, 1149; Syll.³ 9). In the 6th cent., H. began to mint its own coins. From the 6th to the 4th cents., several victors at the Olympic Games hailed from H. In the classical period, the city was allied with Sparta (Thuc. 5,67,1). According to Str. 8,3,2, at the time of the battle of Leuctra (371 BC), the Spartans initiated the foundation in H. of a synoecism of nine villages (Xen. Hell. 6,5,11; 22). H. was a member of the Arcadian League (IG V,2,1 = Syll.³ 183), and 236 BC of the Achaean League (Polyaenus, Strat. 2,36; Aen. Tact. 18,8ff.). In 227 BC, the city was occupied by Cleomenes III (Plut. Cleomenes 7,3), in 222/1 by Antigonus [3] Doson (Pol. 2,54,12f.), and in the winter of 219/8 captured by Philip V (Pol. 4,77,5ff.). It was returned to the Achaean League in 196 (Pol. 18,47,10; Liv. 33,34,9). Coins are evident into the 3rd cent. AD (HN 418; 447ff.; cf. also Str. 8,8,2; Paus. 5,7,1; 8,25,12; 26,1–3).

JOST, 70–77; E. MEYER, Peloponnes. Wanderungen, 1939, 100–106; Id., Neue peloponnesische Wanderungen, 1957, 20f.; M. MOGGI, I sinecismi interstatali greci, 1976, 256–262; A. PHILADELPHEUS, Ἀνασκαφαὶ Ἡραάς, in: AD 14, 1931/2 (1935), 57–70.   Y.L.

Heraeum (Ἡραιον; *Hēraion*).
[1] General term for sanctuaries of the goddess → Hera; more important Heraea are found, among others, in → Argos, → Olympia, → Paestum, Perachora and on the island of → Samos.   C.HÖ.
[2] The outermost cape (today Cape Melangavi) of the peninsula that is formed by the foothills of the Geraneia opposite Corinth with a settlement, fort and sanctuary

of Hera Akraia and Limenia (rich finds from the 9th cent. BC onwards) on a small bay on the south side of the cape (Xen. Hell. 4,5,5ff.; Xen. Ages. 2,18f.; Str. 8,6,22; Plut. Cleomenes 20,3; Liv. 32,23,10).

H. PAYNE et al. (ed.), The Sanctuaries of Hera Akraia and Limenia, 2 vols., 1940/1962. C.L. and E.O.

Heraïscus (Ἡραΐσκος; *Hēraḯskos*). Neoplatonist from Alexandria (5th cent. AD). Under the Monophysite patriarchate of Peter III Mongus (AD 482–489), H. was an important person of the Greek party (Zacharias, Vita Severi 16,22 KUGENER) although he was 'not a strong warrior for the cause of truth' (Damascius, Vita Isidori fr. 182 ZINTZEN), i.e. for paganism. H. was a student of → Proclus in Athens (§ 107 ZINTZEN) and a teacher of → Isidorus (§ 37, fr. 160). He was very experienced in religious rites (fr. 162,174) and the oracles (§ 112–114), and distinguished by his ability in soothsaying (fr. 171,317). In contrast, he lacked experience in dialectics (fr. 163). Following the Orphic ideal (cf. Pl. Phd. 69c-d), he became a 'Bacchant' through strict ascetic handling of his Titanic nature (i.e., the body; Βάκχος; fr. 172) and was considered 'god-like' (θεοειδής; fr. 161). As a member of the Egyptian priesthood, he received a burial from his older brother Asclepiades (fr. 173) according to the appropriate rite. Proclus considered him more learned than himself (Damascius Vita Isidori § 107), and Damascius called him a philosopher because of his lifestyle (Damascius Vita Isidori fr. 163).

M. TARDIEU, Le "Livre de Moïse sur le Nom" et les théologes égyptiennes d'Héraïscus et d'Asclépiade, in: Annuaire de l'École Pratique des Hautes Etudes – Sciences Religieuses 97, 1988–89, 317–319; Id., Formes et justifications de la fusion des dieux, in: Annuaire du Collège de France 92, 1991–92, 501–506. MI.TA.

Heras Greek doctor from Cappadocia who practiced in Rome. He explained his medication-based therapy, dated to between 100 BC and AD 40, in a treatise that has been dated [1. 242–246] to between 20 BC and AD 20. The recipes, which characteristically tend to be composite, indicate a late date. H.'s origin and the classicism of his medical material suggest an association with the 'School of Tarsus' [2], as it may be called, or at least permit classification with the current that it represents.

Apart from a papyrus fragment [3], we have 25 quotes in Galen, of which 20 appear to be direct [1. 184–185]. These are recipes of medications and their indications. Several quotes are from one work, which is described as the 'Book of Medications' and entitled the 'Narthex' or 'Book of Properties'; others are taken from a book entitled the *bíblos pharmakîtis* ('Pharmaceutical Book') that is equated with the former. The recipes are classified according to the relevant body parts or types. The materia medica, which consists of substances from the three realms (fauna, flora and minerals), is distinguished by its classicism, as are the recipes even though the term *antídotos* appears among them, which remains limited to a toxicological context. → Galen

1 C. FABRICIUS, Galens Exzerpte aus älteren Pharmakologen, 1972 2 V. NUTTON, J. SCARBOROUGH, The "Preface" of Dioscorides' "Materia Medica": Introduction, Translation, and Commentary, in: Transactions and Studies of the College of Physicians of Philadelphia Series 5, vol. 4, 1982, 187–227 3 I. ANDORLINI MARCONE, L'apporto dei papiri alla conoscenza della scienza medica antica, in: ANRW II,37,1, num. 10.

ID., Ricette mediche nei papiri, in: Atti e Memorie dell'Accademia Toscana di Scienze e Lettere "La Colombaria" 46, 1981, 41–45 and n. 36f.; MARGANNE, 134f. A.TO.

Herbessus (Ἑρβησσός; *Herbēssós*). Sicilian town, modern Montagna di Marzo near Piazza Armerina (Sicily), clearly identified through bronze coins and silver *litrai*. Literary references: Diod. Sic. 14,7,6–8 (404 BC); 78,7 (396 BC); 20,31,5 (309 BC); 23,8,1; Pol. 1,18,9 (attests, in the report on 262 BC, the geographical proximity of H. to Acragas). Other references: coin hoards of 214–212 BC from M. di Marzo; inscriptions in the Siculian language and script; Greek graffiti; a new, onomastically interesting type of clay *glandes*.

G. MANGANARO, Montagna di Marzo – H., in: Sikelika 1990; BTCGI 7, 1989, 278–282. GI.MA.

Herbita (Ἕρβιτα; *Hérbita*, Ἑρβίτα; *Herbíta*). Landlocked Siculian town. Archonides I of H. was a cofounder of Cale Acte (Diod. Sic. 12,8,2; 447/6 BC); Archonides II founded Halaesa after a fight and reconciliation with Dionysius I in 403 BC (Diod. Sic. 14,15,1; 14,16,1–4; 14,78,7). Other records: Cic. Verr. *passim*; decree of Entella (SEG 30, 1117); coins from M. Alburchia near Gangi [1].

1 L. DUBOIS, Inscriptions grecques dialectales de Sicile, 1989, 254f., no. 204 2 G. SCIBONA, Epigraphica Italaesina I (Schede 1970), in: Kokalos 17, 1971, 5f. 3 C. BÖHRINGER, Herbita, in: Numismatica e antichità classiche 10, 1981, 95ff. 4 BTCGI 7, 1989, 283–289 5 G. MANGANARO, Alla ricerca di poleis mikrai della Sicilia centro-orientale, in: Orbis Terrarum 2, 1996, 130 n. 9. GI.MA.

Hercle In addition to the most often substantiated form H., *Hercles, Heracle, Hercele, Herchle* and *Herkle* are known in Etruscan inscriptions as Etruscanized forms of the Greek name → Heracles [1] since the beginning of the 5th cent. BC [1. vol. 1, 114f.]. *H. calanice* corresponds to the Greek *Hēraklēs kallínikos* ('the glorious victor') (Archil. fr. 324 IEG). For the Etruscans, the cult of H. especially belongs to the private sphere – as does the Heracles cult for the Greeks; he is mainly portrayed on small works of art (mirrors and cameos), which were mostly used in the burial cult.

In spite of similar names and attributes (club and lion skin), H. and Heracles differ from one another: H., in contrast to the Greek hero, was considered to be more a god than a hero [1. vol. 2, 329 Pa 4.2,29]. The Etruscan iconography, which has been documented as well as that of the Greeks, portrays him as a clean-shaven, curly-haired youth [2. vol. 2,131; 3. fig. 21; 22]. The myth of H., who lifts up the beautiful Mlukukh from the ground [2. vol. 4, 344; 3. Fig. 14], is also Etruscan. The theme of H. on a raft of empty amphorae with a frame on top and a lion skin raised as a sail [2. vol. 4, 398] is not Greek and generally Italic. Local and Greek myths gradually blended together: H. reconciles himself with Uni and is adopted by her with a non-Greek rite [2. vol. 5, 59; 60; 3. fig. 19f.; 1. vol. 2, 352 VT S.2]. However, the joint representation of the two friends H. and Vile (→ Iolaus) [2. vol. 1, 128; 3. fig. 15] is of Greek origin. H. only performs those actions of the Greek hero, which can be interpreted as vanquishing death, e.g. the defeat of Cerberus, the journey (on the raft?) to the garden of the → Hesperids. Because of this interpretation, his popularity also reaches beyond Etruria far into the Alps [4].

H. appears in the visual arts of the Etruscans at the end of the 6th cent. BC [5; 6]. The note by Pliny (HN 35,157), that the artist Vulca [7] created a *Hercules fictilis* ('out of clay') for Veii also refers to this time.

1 ET   2 E. GERHARD, G. KÖRTE, Etruskische Spiegel, 1884–1897   3 A. J. PFIFFIG, Herakles in der Bilderwelt der etr. Spiegel, 1980   4 E. WALDE-PSENNER, Die vorröm. und röm. Bronzestatuetten aus Südtirol, in: Arch.-histor. Forsch. in Tirol 6, 1979, no. 11–14   5 W. DRÄYER, M. HÜRLIMANN, Etr. Kunst, 1955, fig. 56   6 G. COLONNA, An Etruscan Inscription from Acquarossa, in: OpRom 16.1, 1987, 7ff.   7 M. PALLOTTINO, La scuola di Vulca, 1945.

PFIFFIG; S. SCHWARZ, s.v. Herakles/H., LIMC 5.1, 196–253; E. SIMON, Etr. Kultgottheiten, in: M. CRISTOFANI (ed.), Die Etrusker, 1995, 158ff.   L.A.-F.

Herculanean Papyri

A. DEFINITION   B. TYPOLOGY OF SCROLLS
C. SCRIPT

A. DEFINITION

Papyri with Latin and Greek texts found during the Bourbon excavations in the middle of the 18th cent. in a villa near → Herculaneum (with site map). These were part of the library of the poet and philosopher → Philodemus of Gadara, who had gone from Athens to Italia during the period 80–70 BC and maintained a friendly relationship there with L. → Calpurnius [I 19] Piso Caesoninus, the owner of the villa in Herculaneum. In this luxurious villa, Philodemus collected an extensive library of Epicurean philosophers (→ Epicurus), their opponents' schools, copies of his own numerous works, as well as a Latin section (the most famous text is the anonymous *Carmen de bello Actiaco*, PHerc. 817)

The Herculanean papyri (HP) are of inestimable value for the knowledge of Hellenistic philosophy; at the same time, they afford an important contribution to the

typology of prose scrolls, as well as to Greek and Latin palaeography. The papyri were largely written in the villa itself, the remainder mostly outside of Egypt; they are an important source for the debate on whether the Greek script in the Mediterranean area had developed everywhere uniformly or with regional differences.

B. TYPOLOGY OF SCROLLS

The HP are important for technical questions, because they support the Roman-Italian MSS practice alongside the Egyptian and other Greek finds. Papyrus scrolls and books constantly correspond to each other in the case of the HP: a scroll does not contain any more than a book; very long works were copied onto two scrolls (PHerc. 1423 and 1007/1673; PHerc. 1538). The standard length of a scroll amounts to c. 10 m (sometimes slightly more). The identification of the joints (*kollēseis*) in the script of the respective columns (*sélides*) confirms that the HP were produced in such a way that the single sheets of papyrus (*kollēmata*) were glued together to obtain a strip in a standard length on which the text was written. The ratio of written area to empty space maintains the usual criteria found in the Graeco-Egyptian area. Many scrolls, however, have an empty final sheet (*ágraphon*; e.g. PHerc. 1675), that is not found in the Graeco-Egyptian papyri: this sheet was always glued onto the papyrus strips in a vertical direction. The ancient papyrus scrolls were evidently generally provided with an initial sheet and an empty final sheet. There are also scrolls with writing on both sides, containing the same work copied on both sides (PHerc. 1021; 1670).

The stichometry is more difficult to define: it is certain that at least towards the end of the 1st cent. BC, the Attic system of acrophonic numbering was still used. The titles were written at the end of the scroll, often in a → display script. Diacritical marks are used in large numbers.

C. SCRIPT

The different types of script can be divided into seventeen groups, which are classified by the letters A to R in alphabetical order and can be ascribed to at least 34 anonymous scribes of the 3rd to 1st cents. BC. However, Philodemus' personal handwriting is missing; visible interventions and corrections are each time by scribes or the professional proof-reader (*diorthōtēs*), and not by Philodemus himself. Differences from comparable Greek → papyri from Egypt manifest themselves in the more numerous use of diacritical marks and by the use of the → display script for the title at the end of the scroll. This can be explained by the different origins: the Greek papyri of Egypt come from frontier areas, the HP in contrast from the great cultural centres of Hellenism amongst other regions. The graphic analysis of the scrolls PHerc. 255, 418, 1084, 1091 and 1112 shows similarities to the documents from the Zeno archive (3rd cent. BC). PHerc. 1044 and 1746 have been written in the typical 'epsilon-theta style', which was very common in Egypt. The scrolls of groups A and I are the oldest and show similarities with Ptolemaic scripts of the middle of the 3rd cent. BC or later (2nd or 2nd/1st cents. BC). Group K can be dated to the 2nd cent. BC. Groups B and C (2nd cent. BC, writings of → Demetrius Lakon) show stylistic characteristics of Greece or the Mediterranean area of Asia Minor, where he worked and where these scrolls may also have been written. Groups F, G and H contain works by Philodemus and can thus be dated to the 1st cent. BC. Later scripts from the time between the 1st cent. BC and 1st cent. AD have also been preserved. Interestingly enough, several papyri of group Q show some influence of the Latin → capital scripts (PHerc. 380; 362). The question of whether the scribes at work in 1st-cent. BC Herculaneum could write both Greek and Latin and whether Latin capital script influenced the Greek scribes, cannot be answered at the present stage of research. Nevertheless, the script of some of the Latin papyri of the Philodemus Library shows definite similarities with, and influences of, Greek script (PHerc. 817; 1067; 1475).

> T. DORANDI, La "Villa dei Papiri" a Ercolano e la sua biblioteca, in: CPh 90, 1995, 168–182; G. CAVALLO, Libri scritture scribi a Ercolano, 1983 (also in: Scrittura e Civiltà 8, 1984, 5–30); K. KLEVE, An approach to the Latin papyri from Herculaneum, in: Studi M. Gigante, 1994, 313–320.   T.D.

Herculaneum Campanian coastal town between Neapolis and Pompeii on a height between two rivers (Sisenna, HRR fr. 53; Str. 5,4,8). *Municipium* of the *regio I*, *tribus Menenia*. H. was struck by an earthquake in AD 62 and possible aftershocks before being buried by the eruption of Vesuvius in AD 79.

From 1709 looting by prince E. D'ELBŒUF; systematic research only began with R. J. DE ALCUBIERRE (1738–1756) who used shafts and tunnels; excavations in 1927–1958 by A. MAIURI. In 1961–1977 excavations at the palaestra and decumanus maximus: basilica, curia, college of Augustales.

Stratigraphic studies revised the views on the processes of its burial in AD 79: H. was first buried under a hot, liquid pyroclastic flow (that effected extensive conservation of wood); later, light volcanic material was deposited on it (deposits from the fire cloud), so that the ancient settlement was buried under as much as 20 m of volcanic materials. The two *fluviae* (Sisenna loc. cit.) disappeared and the coastline advanced into the sea. People who fled to the water sought refuge in fishermen's storage buildings. So far about 300 skeletons have been found.

In 1982 an armoured statue of M. Nonius Balbus, the *patronus* of H., was found on the beach. His funerary monument had been found in 1942 on the terrace in front of the baths in the suburbs. In 1988 three archaic reliefs of Athena, Hermes and Hephaestus were recovered from the beach section opposite the sanctuary

district. After the exact location of the Villa dei Papiri had been determined, the *villa* was initially examined using the tunnels of the Bourbon period; the subsequent orderly excavation is not yet complete. Numerous inscriptions that have in part been torn from their original location by the lava flows have been found. Recently, interest has focused primarily on the publication of the papyri from the Villa dei Papiri (→ Herculanean papyri).

→ Pompeii

> L. FRANCHI DELL'ORTE (ed.), Ercolano 1738–1988, 1993; U. PAPPALARDO, s.v. Ercolano, EAA², Suppl. 2, 1994, 484–489; I. C. MCILWAINE, H., 1988 (with suppl. in: CE 20, 1990, 87–128); E. RENNA, Vesuvius Mons, 1992; E. LEPORE, Origini e strutture della Campania antica, 1989, 243–263; G. CAMODECA, La ricostruzione dell'élite municipale ercolanese negli anni 50–70, in: Cahiers G. Glotz 7, 1996, 167–178; T. BUDETTA, Ercolano, in: Rivista Studi Pompeiani N.S. 3, 1989, 266 fig. 45; H. SIGURDSSON et al., The Eruption of Vesuvius in A.D. 79, in: National Geographic Research 1, 1985, 332–387; U. PAPPALARDO, L'eruzione pliniana del Vesuvio nel 79 d.C., in: Volcanologie et Arch., 1990, 198–215; Id., Osservazioni su un secondo grande terremoto a Pompei, in: Arch. und Seismologie, 1995, 191–194; G. GUADAGNO, Documenti epigrafici ercolanesi relativi ad un terremoto, in: Arch. und Seismologie, 1995, 119–128; S. C. BISEL, Human Bones at Herculaneum, in: Rivista Studi Pompeiani N.S. 1, 1987, 123–129; D. MODESTI, Ercolano, in: Rivista Studi Pompeiani N.S. 1, 1987, 199f.; S. ADAMO MUSCETTOLA, Nuove letture borboniche, in: Prospettiva 28, 1982, 2–16; M. PAGANO, Il teatro di Ercolano, in: CE 23, 1993, 121–156; Id., La nuova pianta della città e alcuni edifici pubblici di Ercolano, in: CE 26, 1996, 229–248; U. PAPPALARDO, Nuove testimonianze su Marco Nonio Balbo ad Ercolano, in: MDAI(R) 104, 1997, 285–297; C. KNIGHT, A. JORIO, L'ubicazione della Villa Ercolanese dei Papiri, in: Rendiconti Napoli 55, 1980, 51–65, fig. 1–19; M. GIGANTE (ed.), La Villa dei Papiri, 1983; A. DE SIMONE et al., Ercolano 1992–1997, in: CE 28, 1998; M. GIGANTE, Catalogo dei Papiri Ercolanesi, 1979; M. CAPASSO, Storia fotografica dell'Officina dei Papiri Ercolanesi, 1983; Id., Manuale di papirologia ercolanese, 1991.
> MAPS: E. KIRSTEN, Süditalienkunde 1. vol. Campanien und seine Nachbarlandschaften, 1975, 289–312, fig. 28–30a; M. PAGANO, Ercolano, 1997, esp. 8, 21; U. PAPPALARDO, s.v. Ercolano, EAA Suppl. 2, 1994, 484–489, esp. 485.   U.PA.

Herculaneus rivus Branch of the *aqua Marcia* in Rome behind the *horti Pallantiani* (Frontin. Aq. 19,8) south of the *porta Tiburtina*, which supplied the *regiones I, XI* and *XII* via the *Caelius mons* and the *Porta Capena*. The association of a *Herculaneus rivus* (HR) with the *aqua Virgo* in Plin. HN 31,42 is probably due to a mistake. Another HR was the permanent spring that supplied the *Anio novus* 38 miles east of Rome at the *via Sublacensis* (Frontin. Aq. 15,4f.).

> RICHARDSON, 17f.; D. CATTOLINI, s.v. H.r., LTUR 1, 1993, 69.   G.U.

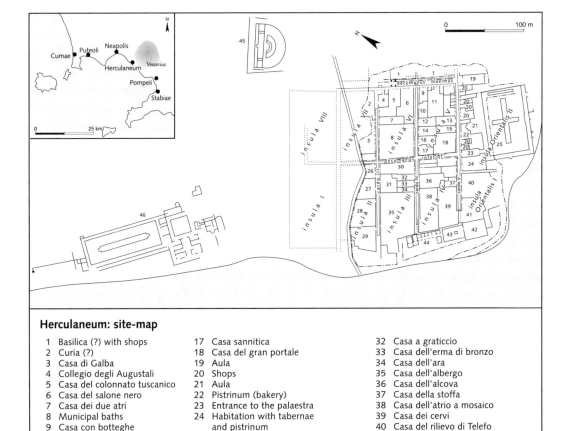

Herculaneum: site-map

1	Basilica (?) with shops	17	Casa sannitica	32	Casa a graticcio
2	Curia (?)	18	Casa del gran portale	33	Casa dell'erma di bronzo
3	Casa di Galba	19	Aula	34	Casa dell'ara
4	Collegio degli Augustali	20	Shops	35	Casa dell'albergo
5	Casa del colonnato tuscanico	21	Aula	36	Casa dell'alcova
6	Casa del salone nero	22	Pistrinum (bakery)	37	Casa della stoffa
7	Casa dei due atri	23	Entrance to the palaestra	38	Casa dell'atrio a mosaico
8	Municipal baths	24	Habitation with tabernae	39	Casa dei cervi
9	Casa con botteghe		and pistrinum	40	Casa del rilievo di Telefo
10	Casa del bel cortile	25	Palaestra	41	Casa della gemma
11	Casa del bicentenario	26	Casa con botteghe	42	Suburban baths
12	Casa di Nettuno e Anfitrite	27	Casa del Genio	43	Ara of M. Nonius Balbus
13	Casa dell'atrio corinzio	28	Casa di Argo	44	Sacred precinct
14	Casa del mobilio carbonizzato	29	Casa di Aristide	45	Theatre
15	Casa del sacello di legno	30	Casa del tramezzo di legno	46	Villa dei Papiri (villa of Piso)
16	Casa del telaio	31	Casa dello scheletro	—·—·—	Excavated area

Herculanius (Ἐρκουλιανός; *Herkoulaniós*). Neoplatonist philosopher, died about AD 408. Only known from letters that his friend → Synesius wrote to him (137–146 GARYZA). They lived together in Alexandria. Both attended lectures by → Hypatia, who introduced them to the works of Plotinus, Porphyrius and Iamblichus.

CH. LACOMBRADE, Synésios de Cyrène, Hellène et Chrétien, 1951, 50–63, 72–73.   L.BR.

Herculem, ad Station in Etruria on the *via Aemilia Scauri* between Vada Volaterrana and Pisae (It. Ant. 293).

M. SORDI, La via Aurelia da Vada a Pisa, in: Athenaeum 59, 1971, 302–312.   G.U.

Hercules

A. NAME B. CATTLE BREEDING C. SPRINGS
D. FOUNDER OF CITIES AND PEOPLES E. INITIATION CULTS F. MANTICISM G. COMMERCE
H. TRIUMPH

A. NAME

H. is the Roman form of the Greek → Heracles (Ἡρακλῆς; *Hēraklês*), Old Latin Hercle and Hercoles, Latin Hercules, Oscan Her(e)cleis/clos, Etruscan → Hercle.

B. CATTLE BREEDING

The theft of → Geryoneus' cattle, which the oldest witnesses of the H. legend in Etruria (*c.* 600 BC) refer to, was the most important of H's. heroic deeds in Italy. The Roman myth relates that H. killed → Cacus, who had stolen some of his cattle, and in memory of this, together with → Evander [1] and the Arcadians, he made sacrifices and a ritual meal at the Ara Maxima in Rome (Verg. Aen. 8,193–272; Dion. Hal. Ant. Rom.

1,39f.; Liv. 1,7, cf. Str. 5,3,3; Ov. Fast. 1,543–584; Prop. 4,9). In the euhemeristic version (Dion. Hal. Ant. Rom. 1,42; Solin. 1,8) H. was made a commander who defeated Cacus. The myths and cults of H. in Rome were located in the Forum Boarium, where a bronze bull stood in his memory (cf. Tac. Ann. 12,24). H. was also the divine giver of salt, which was used to conserve meat (Columella 10,135; CIL IX 3961); accordingly he lived near the *salinae* in the southern part of the Forum Boarium (Solin. 1,8).

C. Springs

Springs, especially hot ones, were sacred to H. (Ath. 12,512f; Aristid. 5,35; Suda s.v. Ἡράκλεια λουτρά). Among the Sabellian peoples statuettes of H. were sacrificed near springs. The epithets Salutaris and Salutifer (for example CIL VI 237) refer to H. as the god of healing waters. There were hot springs of H. for instance at the Oracle of the → Palici (Diod. Sic. 4,23,5), in the Iapygian foothills (Aristot. Mir. 97), at Allifae (CIL IX 2338), Caere (Liv. 22,1,10), fons Aponi (Suet. Tib. 14; Claud. Carm. 26,23–26) and at the mouth of the Timavus [1], also in Dacia near Mehadia (CIL III 1566) and in many places in Gaul, where he was often identified with Borvo.

D. Founder of Cities and Peoples

H.'s deeds which led to the founding of cultures often link him to the first local kings. He often fathered a son with the daughter of a local king, who became the → eponym of a city or progenitor of a people. In Rome, Pallas (Dion. Hal. Ant. Rom. 1,43,1), Aventinus (Verg. Aen. 7,655–663, cf. Lydus, Mag. 1,34), → Latinus (Dion. Hal. Ant. Rom. 1,43,1), the first Fabius (Fest. 77; Sil. Pun. 6,633ff., cf. Ov. Fast. 2,237) and the first Antonius (Plut. Antonius 917c) were born to him.

E. Initiation cults

Some of H.'s cults have an old background in initiation rites. H. was often honoured by → collegia iuvenum (for example CIL IX 1681; 3578). Women were excluded from his rites. In the wedding ritual the bridegroom loosed the *nodus Herculaneus* on his bride's belt as an expression of the wish for many children (Fest. 55).

F. Manticism

In the legend of → Acca Larentia H. cast dice; in the oracle of → Geryoneus at the fons Aponi one used dice and lots (*sortes*) (Suet. Tib. 14); there were H.-oracles in several Italian cities with *sortes* [2] (Ostia: [3]; Tibur: Stat. Silv. 1,3,79; Caere: Liv. 22,1,10; Manliana: CIL VIII 9610). In a dream H. gave Larentia a prophecy (Plut. Quaest. Rom. 35,273ab; Aug. Civ. 6,7,2), and he was honoured as *somnialis* ('H. of the dream', CIL XI 1449). Faunus and H. were called *incubones* as the gods of erotic dreams (Porph. Hor. comm. sermo 2,6,12; → incubo).

G. Commerce

H. was also the god of commerce, oaths, law, purchasing contracts and of personal property in Italy. It was customary in Rome (at the Ara Maxima) and in all of Italy, to dedicate the tithe to H. after successful business transactions and war campaigns (*pars Herculanea*: Plaut. Bacch. 666; Fest. 237; Plut. Quaest. Rom. 18,267f; Diod. Sic. 4,21,3f.; Macrob. Sat. 3,6,11). Generous feasts (Serv. Auct. Aen. 8,278; Dion. Hal. Ant. Rom. 1,40) were held for the masses from this income – but women (Plut. Quaest. Rom. 60,278f) or slaves and freedmen (Serv. Aen. 8,179) were excluded. Many times a scant third of the tithe (Tert. Apol. 14,1), the *polluctum*, was burned on the altar; the rest was distributed among the people (*profanatum*: Varro, Ling. 6,54). The praetor offered the sacrifice (on the 12th of August with his head uncovered: *aperto capite* and *ritu Graeco*), maybe in the presence of the → Salii (Verg. Aen. 8,285ff.) The entire cult was with the Potitii and Pinarii in the beginning; in the year 312 BC the state took over control of the H. cult, and slaves of the state (*servi publici*) were put in the place of the Potitii (Liv. 9,29,9). Oaths in H.'s name were sworn outdoors (Plut. Quaest. Rom. 28,271bd); H. was called Dius Fidius or (Semo) Sancus (changed to Sanctus) as the god of oaths (Varro, Ling. 5,66; Prop. 4,9,73f.). As an international god H. was the ultimate supervisor of treaties between states. Beyond that the figure of H. took on many of the characteristics of → Faunus in the traditions.

H. Triumph

Already for the Tarquinii and other Etruscan nobility, but especially for Roman commanders and emperors (Scipio Africanus, Commodus), H. became the model of a human who was deified through his victorious deeds. This found expression in the ritual of the → triumph: An old statue of H. Triumphalis in the Forum Boarium was dressed with the *habitus triumphalis* during the *triumphi* (Plin. HN 34,16,33), and the meal during a *triumphus* was called *hērakleōtikós* (Ath. 4,153c).

H. was sometimes honoured as a deified human in the Lararia or dressed up as Lar (→ Lares) [5; 6]. His efforts for suffering humanity and his deification made the comparison with Christ (→ Hercules Oetaeus) possible later. On iconography cf. → Heracles [1] II.

1 G. Cuscito, Revisione delle epigrafi di età romana rinvenute intorno al Timavo, in: Antichità altoadriatiche 10, 1976, 51   2 J. Champeaux, Sors oraculi. Les oracles en Italie sous la république et l'empire, in: MEFRA 102, 1990, 271–302   3 D. Biolchi, L'erma di Ercole del Teatro Ampiternino, in: BCAR 67, 1939, 37ff. 4 M. Guarducci, Graffiti parietali nel santuario di Ercole Curino presso Sulmona, in: L. Gasperini (ed.), Scritti in memoria di F. Grosso, 1981, 225ff.   5 M. Floriani Squarciapino, L'ara dei Lari di Ostia, in: ArchCl 4, 1952, 204ff.   6 O. de Cazanove, Plastique votive et imagerie Dionysiaque, in: MEFRA 98, 1986, 21ff.

J. Bayet, Les origines de l'Hercule romain, 1926; Id., Hercle, 1926; C. Jourdain-Annequin, Héraclès aux portes du soir, 1989; Id., Ercole in Occidente, 1993; Id., Héraclès, 1992; A. MASTROCINQUE, Romolo, 1993; Id., Héraclès. Les femmes et le féminin, 1996; M. SIMON, Hercule et le Christianisme, 1955.   A.MAS.

Hercules Oetaeus Roman tragedy by an unknown author, handed down in the corpus of → Seneca's tragedies. This drama, the longest in antiquity (1996 v.), has been subject to highly controversial assessments, mostly depending on whether Seneca's authorship is accepted or rejected (extremes [1] and [2], mediating [3]). The subject, the events leading up to the death of Hercules and his apotheosis, is treated originally, despite artistic and intelligent → intertextuality with Soph. Trach., Ovid (Epist. 9 and Met. 9) and to Seneca's *Hercules Furens*. The stylization of Hercules as saviour of the world and an almost Christ-like figure of martyrdom as well as the exultant tone, owing much to rhetoric, is typical of the literature of the late 1st cent. AD. Despite the impressiveness with which Hercules is depicted, *Hercules Oetaeus* is not to be interpreted as either a philosophical or a religious didactic drama: the intertextuality and desire to create effect take precedence over any ideological statement.
→ Seneca, Tragedy, Hercules

1 F. LEO, Observationes Criticae, 1872, 48ff.   2 O. REGENBOGEN, Schmerz und Tod in den Trag. Senecas, 1927 (repr. 1963)   3 C. WALDE, Herculeus labor. Stud. zum Pseudosenecanischen Hercules Oetaeus, 1992.   C.W.

Herculis portus Ports of this name existed 1. on the Ligurian coast (in Ptol. 3,1,2 different from Monaco, maybe the bay of Villafranca east of Nice), 2. at Monte Argentario west of → Cosa (Str. 5,2,8; Rut. Namat. 1,293; Tab. Peut. 4,4; modern Port'Ercole), 3. on the west Bruttian coast near Cape Vaticano (Str. 6,1,5; Plin. HN 3,73), and 4. on the south coast of Sardinia (Ptol. 3,3,3). The best-known is 5. Herculis Monoeci portus, already mentioned in Hecat. FGrH 1 F 57 (Str. 4,5,6; Plin. HN 3,47; Verg. Aen. 6,830; Sil. Pun. 1,585f.; Luc. 1,405f.; Tac. Hist. 3,42; Amm. Marc. 15,10,9); the town was supposedly founded by Hercules on his return from → Geryoneus (modern Monaco).   Y.L.

Herculius
[1] Praefectus praetorio Illyrici from AD 408 to 410 (Cod. Theod. 12,1,172; 15,1,49), in whose honour the Sophists erected statues in Athens and Megara (IG II² 4224f.; VII 93). → Iohannes Chrysostomos sent him epist. 201. PLRE 2, 545.   K.P.J.
[2] see → Maximianus

Hercyna (Ἕρκυνα; *Hérkyna*). River in Boeotia, whose powerful, in part lukewarm springs originate in → Lebadea at the mouth of a rock canyon (cave sanctuary and temple) and were closely connected to the cult of the neighbouring oracle of → Trophonius. References: Paus. 9,39,2–8; Plin. HN 31,15; Plut. Mor. 771f; Philostr. VA 8,19.

F. BÖLTE, s.v. H., RE 8, 690f.; H. G. LOLLING, Reisenotizen aus Griechenland (1876 und 1877), 1989, 609–614; N. D. PAPACHATZIS, Παυσανίου Ἑλλάδος Περιήγησις 5, ²1981, 244–250; PHILIPPSON/KIRSTEN 1, 445–448.   P.F.

Hercynia silva
I. GEOGRAPHY   II. THE HERCYNIAN BIRDS

I. GEOGRAPHY
Collective term for the central European low mountain ranges, first mentioned in Aristot. Mete. 1,13. It took nine days to cross it from north to south (Caes. B Gall. 6,25–28; interpolated according to [1]), and 60 from west to east; the forest, abundant with unknown wild beasts, extended from the borders of the Helvetii, Nemetes, and Rauraci along the Danube to the border region (*fines*) of the Dacians and Anartes (further source references easily accessible through the indices in [2]). Even though the Roman occupation and discovery of the North led to more specific knowledge (e.g. → Abnoba mons), the elementary notions of central European geography, gained from the experience with the Cimbrii, remained dominant [3].

1 G. GÖTTE, Die Frage der geogr. Itp. in Caesars Bellum Gallicum, thesis Marburg 1964, 197–205, 215–222, 270–303, 337–361   2 J. HERRMANN (ed.), Griech. und lat. Quellen zur Frühgesch. Mitteleuropas bis zur Mitte des 1. Jt. unserer Zeit, 1988ff.   3 D. TIMPE, s.v. Entdeckungsgesch., RGA 7, 307–389, esp. 342.

F. BECKMANN, Geogr. und Ethnographie in Caesars Bellum Gallicum, 1930, 86–103, 158–161, 169–171.   K.DI.

II. THE HERCYNIAN BIRDS
The legendary Hercynian birds with feathers that glow brightly at night were first mentioned in Pliny (HN 10,132) and introduced to the Middle Ages by Solin. 20,3. They were erroneously located by Honorius Augustodunensis in Hyrcania (Imago mundi 1,18 [1. 58]), thus spawning a further tradition. Thomas of Cantimpré (5,75; [2. 213]) knew them under their original name, and also (after the *Liber rerum*) as *lucidii aves* [3].

1 V. I. J. FLINT (ed.), Honorius Augustodunensis Imago mundi, in: Archives d'histoire doctrinale et littéraire du moyen age 49, 1983, 7–153   2 H. BOESE (ed.), Thomas Cantimpratensis Liber de natura rerum, 1973   3 C. HÜNEMÖRDER, Hercyniae aves, in: RhM 110, 1967, 371–384.   C.HÜ.

Herdoniae (also *Herdonia*: Str. 6,3,7; Sil. Pun. 8,567; App. Hann. 48; Ptol. 3,1,72; *Herdonea*: Liv. 25,21,1; 27,1,6). City in Apulia (*regio* II: Plin. HN 3,105; CIL IX 689f.; 1156; It. Ant. 116,2), modern Ordona, on the *via Minucia* (Str. 6,3,7; Plin. HN 2,244), starting-point of the roads to Beneventum, Aeclanum, and Ausculum. After the battle of Cannae (216 BC), H. switched allegiance to Hannibal, and until 210 BC, it was frequently involved in the disputes of the Second Punic War. Hannibal pre-empted H.'s threatened secession in 210 BC with the destruction of the city and the deportation of its inhabitants (Liv. 27,1,14). Later, H. experienced a moderate urban bloom as a *municipium*, still evident in some surviving buildings. For the 1st cent. BC, the number of inhabitants is estimated at 7,500 [1].

1 J.MERTENS, Alba Fucens et Herdonia, in: E. OLSHAUSEN, H. SONNABEND (ed.), Stuttgarter Kolloquium zur histor. Geogr. des Alt. 2/1984 und 3/1987 (Geographica Historica 5) 1991, 425.

NISSEN 2, 847; J.MERTENS, Ordona 1978–1986, in: Ordona 8, 1988, 7–67.   H.SO.

Herdonius

[1] Appius H. A Sabine who in 460 BC seized the Capitol with the help of 2,500 exiles and slaves (Liv. 3,15,5–18,11; according to Dion. Hal. Ant. Rom. 10,14,1–17,1 with 4,000 clients and servants). He died in the battle against the troops of consul Valerius and L. Mamilius, the dictator of Tusculum. This story, modelled on the conspiracy of → Catilina, might be a possible indication of ethnic tensions in early Republican Rome.

P. M. MARTIN, Des tentatives de tyrannies à Rome, in: EDER, Staat, 49–72, esp. 60f.

[2] Turnus H. Latinian from Aricia, who turned against → Tarquinius Superbus during a meeting of the Latini with the latter. Based on Tarquinius' false suspicions that H. planned a conspiracy against himself and leading Latini, H. was executed by the Latini (Liv. 1,50,3–51,9; Dion. Hal. Ant. Rom. 4,45,3–48,3). In Rome, this episode was probably the origin myth for a ritual execution by drowning.

C. AMPOLO, Un supplicio arcaico: L'uccisione di Turnus Herdonius, in: Du châtiment dans la cité (Coll. École française de Rome, 79), 1984, 91–96.   W.ED.

Hereas (Ἡρέας; *Hēréas*). From Megara, author of *Megariká*, evidently more recent than Dieuchidas. The current view is that the fragments in Plutarch's *Theseus* and *Solon* derive ultimately from the *Megariká* (via Ister and Hermippus!) or another (anti-Athenian) work by H. He is probably identical with the *theoros* mentioned in IG VII 39 (beginning of 3 BC), but highly unlikely to be Heragoras, another author of *Megariká* as has been commonly assumed since [1.8].

1 U. VON WILAMOWITZ-MOELLENDORFF, Comm. gramm. 1880/1881.

FRAGMENTS: FGrH 486.
BIBLIOGRAPHY: L. PICCIRILLI, Megariká, Testimonianze e Frammenti, 1975, 51ff.   K.MEI.

Heredium In the language of the XII Tables (7,3) the farmstead measuring two *iugera* (0.5 ha.; Plin. HN 19,4,50), consisting of a *hortus* (farm with garden, Paul Fest. 91,12 L.) and *ager* (agricultural land). Tradition has it that Romulus assigned to each citizen an inalienable *heredium*, which was passed on to the respective heir (*heres*) (Varro Rust. 1,10,2); the XII Tables already allowed the entire property to be sold and inherited (6,1; 5,3), this therefore included the *heredium*. As a *heredium* was insufficient to sustain a large family with servants, MOMMSEN's assumption, [1], that the *heredium* was only the private parcel of land next to collectively used agricultural land, is a reasonable one. In later language use *heredium* is a not very technical description of a very small estate (Paul Fest. 89,1 L.).
→ Agrarian structure [2]; → Limitation

1 MOMMSEN, Staatsrecht, vol. 3, 23ff.   U.M.

Herennianus The younger son of → Odaenathus and → Zenobia (SHA Gall. 13,2; SHA Tyr. Trig. 15,2; 17,2; 24,4; 27; 28; 30). Following the death of his father he and his elder brother Timolaus received the *ornamenta imperatoria*, while their mother ruled on behalf of the under-age children (SHA Tyr. Trig. 27,1; 30,2; SHA Aurel. 22,1; 38,1). Later, however, her third son → Vaballathus assumed power. H. was probably killed by Aurelian (SHA Tyr. Trig. 27,1f.).

PIR² H 95; PLRE 1, 421 (H. 1).   T.F.

Herennius Common Italian proper name (associated with the praenomen *Herennus* that is often confused with H.), which however is not documented as a surname among the Roman upper class until the 1st cent. BC. It frequently appears with epithets showing place of origin (*Etruscus, Gallus, Picens, Siculus*). In the Imperial period it is the name of Caesar Q.H. [II 3] Etruscus, son of emperor → Decius [II 1], of the historian H. → Dexippus [2], and of the jurist H. → Modestinus.

SALOMIES 73f.; SCHULZE 82; 282.   K.-L.E.

I REPUBLICAN PERIOD

[I 1] H. Centurio, who at the end of 43 BC murdered → Cicero near his villa at Formiae and – mutilated the body under instruction from M. Antonius [I 9] (Plut. Cicero 48,1f.). In Jer. Chron. Ol. 184,2 (= Suet. De oratoribus, p. 81 REIFFERSCHEID) Popilius, according to Plutarch H.'s superior military tribune, is the main culprit.   T.FR.

[I 2] H., C. In 116 BC, following the election of C. → Marius to the position of praetor, he refused to testify against Marius, who was accused of obtaining office by devious means, arguing that he was Marius' patron. Whereupon Marius declared that this relationship of clientela with H. had ceased following his election (Plut. Marius 5,7f.).

[I 3] H., C. Otherwise unknown relative and friend of the anonymous author of the so-called → *Rhetorica ad Herennium*, which was dedicated to him around 85 BC (1,1; 4,69).

[I 4] H., C. In 80 BC, in his capacity as plebeian tribune, he prevented a law proposed by Sulla on the return and triumph of Cn. → Pompeius Magnus (Sall. Hist. 2,21M; [1. 194–196]). He may be identical with the senatorial juror who was convicted of corruption after 80 (Cic. Verr. 1,39) and with the legate of Q. → Sertorius who died in 76 or 75 in the battle against Pompey in Spain (Sall. Hist. 2,98,6M; Plut. Pompeius 18,3).

1 P. McGushin, Sallust: The Histories 1, 1992.

MRR 3, 101.　　　　　　　　　　　　　　K.-L.E.

[I 5] H., C. People's tribune 60 BC; his support of P. Clodius [I 4] Pulcher's plan to assume plebeian status failed on the intercession of fellow tribunes (Cic. Att. 1,18,4; 19,5) and the resistance of consul Q. Caecilius [I 22] Metellus (Cic. Att. 2,1,5). It is not clear whether he was also responsible for proposing that the office of people's tribune be made generally accessible to patricians (Cass. Dio 37,51,1).　　　　　　　　　　T.FR.

[I 6] H., M. Although he only came from an insignificant senatorial family and was just an average orator, he was praetor not later than 96 BC and consul 93 (Cic. Mur. 36; Brut. 166; MRR 2,14); possibly mint master 108–107 (RRC 308).　　　　　　　　　　　K.-L.E.

[I 7] H., M. Councillor (decurio) in Pompeii, who was struck dead by lightning from a clear sky in 63 BC (Plin. HN 2,137). Cicero (Div. 1,18) counts the event among the omens preceding the Catilinarian turmoil (The name Vargunteius, borne by the victim in Obseq. 61, is not substantiated in Pompeii).

P. Castrén, Ordo Populusque Pompeianus, 1975, 174f., no. 191.　　　　　　　　　　　　　　T.FR.

[I 8] H. (Picens ?), M. Cos. suff. 34 BC; father of H. [II 6]. (PIR² H 118; MRR 3, 101f.).　　　　　　K.-L.E.

[I 9] H. Balbus, L. 56 BC one of the prosecutors in the trial against M. Caelius Rufus, who was defended by Cicero (Cic. Cael. 25; 27; 49; 53; 56). In 52, in the trial of the murderers of Clodius [I 4], H. found himself once more on the opposing side to Milo and Cicero (Ascon. 34 CLARK), who generally, however, regarded H. as his friend (Cael. 25).

[I 10] H. Siculus. Diviner (haruspex), probably from Sicily (Catane?) (but cf. Vell. Pat. 2,7,2: haruspex Tuscus), follower of C. → Sempronius Gracchus. In 121 he was imprisoned as part of the reprisals against the sympathisers of the Gracchi and committed suicide, by smashing his skull against a post in his dungeon (Val. Max. 9,12,6). The minting on the coin of his possible descendent H. [I 6] probably alludes to H's intransigence and loyalty to his political ideals (RRC 308).　　　　　　　　　　　　　　　　　T.FR.

II Imperial period

[II 1] C. H. Caecilianus. From Verona, accepted into the Senate under Hadrian, mentioned in s.c. Beguense in AD 138. An equestrian statue of him was erected on a property at Sirmione.

W. Eck, Tra epigrafia, prosopografia e archeologia, 1996, 306f.; PIR² H 102.

[II 1a] C. H. Capella Suffect consul in AD 119, together with L. Coelius Rufus. Named in the records of the Arvales (CIL VI 2080 = [1]) as well as in several military certificates [2].

1 J. Scheid (ed.), Commentarii fratrum Arvalium qui supersunt, 1998, 210, no. 69　2 W. Eck et al., Neue Diplome für Auxiliartruppen in den dakischen Prov., in: Acta Musei Napocensis 39, 2002.　　　　　　W. E.

[II 2] C. H. Capito. Knight from Teate Marrucinorum, who, following a military career, became patrimonial procurator of Livia, Tiberius and Caligula in Jamnia in Judaea (AE 1941, 105). According to Philo he was hostile to the Jews, whom he plundered. He demanded money for the patrimonial finances from Agrippa II; when this was not forthcoming he instituted legal proceedings before Tiberius.

PIR² H 103; Devijver, H 13.　　　　　　　　W.E.

[II 3] Q. H. Etruscus Messius Decius. The elder son of emperor → Decius [II 1] and of Herennia Etruscilla, born between AD 220 and 230 in Pannonia (Aur. Vict. Caes. 29; Ps.-Aur. Vict. Epit. Caes. 29; Amm. Marc 31,5,16; Eutr. 9,4; Oros. 7,21,3). Elevated to the rank of Caesar and Princeps iuventutis (CIL II 4058; XIII 6115; 9123; Cod. Iust. 5,12,9; AE 1942/3, 55) in May 250; in May 251 he was cos. ord. (CIL VI 1100f.; XI 3088; Chron. min. 1, 521,39 Mommsen) and received the title Augustus (CIL VI 31129 [1. 215ff., no. 7,16, 18,19,30,37,41]). During his and his father's attempt, to block the plundering Goths' retreat across the Danube, under their leader Cniva, there was a battle at Abrittus (now Razgrad, Bulgaria), in which H. died even before his father from an arrow (Aur. Vict. Caes. 29,4; Iord. Get. 18; Chron. min. 1, 521,39); his name and memory were erased in accordance with the process of damnatio memoriae.

1 H. Cohen, Monnaies sous l'empire romain, repr. 1955, vol. 5.

PIR² H 106; Kienast² 206f.; M. Peachin, Roman Imperial Titulature and Chronology, 1990, 32f.　　　　T.F.

[II 4] M. H. Faustus Ti. Iulius Clemens Tadius Flaccus. Senator of the Trajan-Hadrianic period, who was i.a. legionary legate in Apulum and, probably in AD 121, became cos. suff. He probably accompanied Hadrian to Egypt in the year 130.

PIR² H 107; , FPD 214ff.

[II 5] H. Gallus. Legate of legio I in Bonna in AD 69/70. His battles against the insurgent Batavians were unsuccessful. In 70 he was murdered by his own soldiers. PIR² H. 108.

[II 6] M. H. Picens. Cos. suff. in AD 1; it is either he or his father, cos. ord. 34 BC, who was proconsul of Asia under Augustus (Thomasson, Laterculi I 209). He financed public buildings in Veii. PIR² H 118.

[II 7] P. H. Pollio. Cos. suff. in the year AD 85, father of H. [II 8].

AE 1975, 21; W. Eck, s.v. H. (35b), RE Suppl. 14, 197.

[II 8] **M. Annius H. Pollio.** Together with his father (H. [II 7]) *cos. suff.* in the year 85 (AE 1975, 21; VIDMAN, FO² 44, 79). Under Trajan he brought charges in the Senate against the proconsul of Pontus-Bithynia, → Iulius [II 28] Bassus. PIR² H. 119.

[II 9] **H. Rufinus.** Citizen of Oea in Africa. Father-in-law of Sicinius Pontianus, the stepson of Apuleius. He instigated the charges of magic against Apuleius. PIR² H. 123.

[II 10] **L. H. Saturninus.** Proconsul of Achaia in AD 98, *cos. suff.* 100, consular governor of Moesia superior *c.* 104–106 [1. 330, 340ff.]. Plutarch dedicated his work against the Epicureans to him. PIR² H. 126.

1 W. ECK, in: Chiron 12, 1982, 281–362.

[II 11] **H. Senecio.** Originating from Baetica; senator who only made it to the rank of quaestor; together with Pliny he brought charges of *repetundae* against Baebius Massa in AD 93. Supposedly because of his book on → Helvidius [1] Priscus he was accused in the Senate by Mettius Carus and killed by Domitian. PIR² H. 128.

[II 12] **P. H. Severus.** Spanish senator, perhaps became a suffect consul under Hadrian; possibly identical with the *vir doctissimus* named by Plin. Ep. 4,28,1. PIR² H. 130.

CABALLOS, Senadores I, 156f. W.E.

Herennius Philo
A. PERSON B. WORKS

A. PERSON
H. was an antiquarian and grammarian in the second half of the 1st cent. AD (main source for the biography: Suda s.v. Φίλων Βύβλιος, φ 447, where the text, however, is problematic). His original name was *Phílōn*, the ethnicon *Býblios* (after the town Byblos in Phoenicia), the *praenomen* H. perhaps taken over from Herennius Severus Plin. Ep. 4,28 [4]. He was the teacher of → Hermippus of Berytus.

B. WORKS
(FGrH 790): Historical and antiquarian works: 1) The 'Phoenician History' (Φοινικικὴ ἱστορία or Φοινικικά), according to Eusebius in nine books, curiously not mentioned in the Suda. Longer fragments have been handed down by Eusebius (Pr. Ev.). H. claimed he had translated a treatise by the ancient Phoenician scholar → Sanchuniathon, who according to H. lived in about 1000 BC and under whose name a counterfeit work was actually published in 1837 [8]. Even though the fragments have fundamental significance as a source of knowledge about the myths and religion of the Phoenicians [17], which H. claims had been distorted by the Greeks, the authenticity of the material from the 2nd millennium in its entirety is unlikely (as was thought from 1929 onwards following the publication of texts from Ugarit and Ḫattuša, cf. especially [7] with bibliography, regarding status of research [11. 357–358]). However, the work exhibits characteristics of Greek historiography (euhemerism, world history, nationalistic perspectives, the deduction made from a 'revelation': cf. [13]).

2) 'On the Jews' (Περὶ Ἰουδαίων) [11]. 3) 'On Phoenician Letters' or 'On Phoenician Elements' (Περὶ τῶν Φοινίκων στοιχείων). 4) *Hypomnémata Ethōthíōn* (Ὑπομνήματα Ἐθωθ(ι)ῶν); the title is puzzling [3. 256]. 5) The 'Paradoxical History', (Παράδοξος ἱστορία) in 3 books, in which the 'disharmony' (διαφωνία) between the various myths handed down by the Greeks was investigated. 6) 'On Cities and their Famous Citizens' (Περὶ πόλεων καὶ οὓς ἑκάστη αὐτῶν ἐνδόξους ἤνεγκε) in 30 books, summarized by Aelius Serenus. The work, probably ordered alphabetically in books, covered the whole Greek world. It was cited by → Stephanus of Byzantium, → Hesychius and other → lexicographers. 7) 'On Owning and Selecting of Books' (Περὶ κτήσεως καὶ ἐκλογῆς βιβλίων) in 12 books, structured according to the various fields of knowledge. 8) 'On Physicians' (Περὶ ἰατρῶν). 9) 'On things worth knowing' (Περὶ χρηστομαθείας). 10) 'On the Reign of Hadrian' (Περὶ τῆς βασιλείας Ἀδριανοῦ): this title handed down in the Suda helps to provide more accurate dating for H.

Works relating to linguistics and grammar: 11) 'On Nomina Deverbativa' (Τὰ ῥηματικά). 12) 'On the Dialect of Rome' (Περὶ Ῥωμαίων διαλέκτου). 13) a dictionary of synonyms (→ Lexicography), from which some Byzantine excerpts are preserved. The most extensive work, however, is 'On Synonyms and Antonyms' (Περὶ ὁμοίων καὶ διαφόρων λέξεων), attributed to → Ammonius [4], the title of which could also have been the original title of H.'s dictionary.

Epigrams in 4 books.

1 H. W. ATTRIDGE, R. A. ODEN, The Phoenician history: Introduction, crit. text, translation and notes, 1981 2 J. BARR, Philo of Byblos and his 'Phoenicean History', in: Bull. of the John Rylands Library 57, 1974, 17–68 3 A. I. BAUMGARTEN, The Phoenician History of Philo of Byblos. A commentary, 1981 4 J. CHRISTES, Sklaven und Freigelassene als Grammatiker und Philologen im antiken Rom, 1979, 105–106; 137–139 5 J. EBACH, Weltentstehung und Kulturentwicklung bei Philo von Byblos, 1979 6 M. J. EDWARDS, Philo or Sanchuniathon? A Phoenicean cosmogony, in: CQ 41, 1991, 213–220 7 O. EISSFELDT, s.v. Philo Byblius, RGG³ 5, 346–347; s.v. Sanchunjaton, RGG³ 5, 1361 8 S. FALLER, Der "neue" Sanchuniathon oder Die Anatomie einer Fälschung, in: T. BAIER, F. SCHIMANN (ed.), Fabrica. Studien zur antiken Literatur und ihrer Rezeption, 1997, 165–178 9 A. GUDEMAN, s.v. H. Philon (2), RE 8, 650–661 10 E. LIPIŃSKI, The Phoenician History of Philo of Byblos, in: Bibliotheca Orientalis, 1983, 305–310 11 A. MOMIGLIANO, La storiografia greca, 1982, 357–362 12 K. NICKAU, Ammonius. De adfinium vocabulorum differentia, 1966, LXVII. 13 R. A. ODEN, Philo of Byblos and Hellenistic History, in: Palestine Exploration Quarterly 110, 1978, 115–126 14 V. PALMIERI, 'Eranius' Philo, De differentia significationis, in: Revue d'Histoire des Textes 11, 1981, 47–80 15 Id., Herennius Philo. De diversis verborum significationibus, ²1988 16 Id., Anonimo 'Excerptum Casanatense', in: Bolletino dei classici III, 5,

1984, 150–168   17 S. Ribichini, Poenus advena. Gli dei fenici e l'interpretazione classica, 1985   18 Id., Taautos et l'invention de l'écriture chez Philon de Byblos, in: Cl. Baurain, C. Bonnet, V. Krings, Phoinikeia grammata, 1991, 201–213   19 L. Troiani, L'opera storiografica di Filone da Byblos, 1974.   S.FO.

Heresiology The term heresiologists refers to several early Christian authors, who enumerate past as well as contemporary → heresies in one or more of their works in an effort to describe and repudiate them. In the first three cents., this so-called antiheretical corpus (on the problems inherent in the concept of heresy cf. [1. 290–295]) focused on the disputes with → Gnosticism, → Montanism, and Jewish-Christian groups.

→ Iustinus provided a first collection of various heresies, tracing them back successively to their origin in Simon Magus (*Sýntagma*; lost, content reconstruction in [3. 21–30]). A fundamental work for all later authors is the work *Adversus haereses* by Irenaeus of Lyons (→ Irenaeus [2]), which, for the most part, argues against Valentinianus' Gnosticism. Written around 180, it chronicles the historical development of Gnosticism and in five bks presents a systematic refutation of Valentinianus' teachings based on Church theology, and with a wealth of source material. Further treatises are based on → Hippolytus of Rome (*Refutatio omnium haeresium*) and → Tertullianus (fundamental work: *De praescriptione haereticorum*; treatises against particular heresies: *Adversus Marcionem*, etc.).

Building on these writings, later heresiologies are characterized by a tendency to give a schematic presentation of the various religious fallacies and their originators ('catalogues of heretics'). A high point is → Epiphanius [1] of Salamis (d. 403), who presents 80 types of heresies incl. 20 pre-Christian forms in his *Panárion* ('medicine chest'). Other relevant authors include: → Theodoretus of Cyrrhus (*Haereticarum fabularum compendium*), Philastrius from Brescia (*Diversarum haereseon liber*), → Augustinus (*De haeresibus*, unfinished), → Iohannes of Damascus (*Perì hairéseōn* as the second part of his main work *Pēgè gnóseōs*).

→ Apologists; → Polemics

1 N. Brox, s.v. Häresie, RAC 13, 248–297   2 Eresia ed eresiologia nella Chiesa antica: XIII Incontro di Studiosi dell'Antichità Cristiana, 1985 (Augustinianum 25/3, 583–903)   3 A. Hilgenfeld, Die Ketzergesch. des Urchristentums, urkundlich dargestellt, 1884 (repr. 1963)   4 A. Schindler, s.v. Häresie II., TRE 14, 318–341, esp. 322–326.   J.RI.

Heresy
I. Christian   II. Islamic

I. Christian
Term used to delineate unwelcome religious teachings divergent from orthodoxy. In Pre-Christian and non-Christian contexts, the Greek term → *haíresis* (αἵρεσις, Latin *haeresis* [5]) was still entirely value-free:

the basic meaning 'to take', 'to choose' evolves into 'religious or philosophical school of thought', 'school perspective', as well as 'member of a school of thought', '(fragmentation into) parties', 'sect', cf. for example the titles in Lucian, *Hermótimos è perì hairéseōn*; Antipater of Tarsus, *Katà tôn hairéseōn*; Varro, *Perì hairéseōn* (Menippean satire). Furthermore, cf. Lucian Hermotimus 48; Convivium 10; Vita Demonacis 13; Plot. 2,9,6; Diog. Laert. 1,18–21; 2,87f.; Diod. Sic. 2,29,6; Epict. 2,19,20f.; Pol. 5,93,8 etc.; Sext. Emp. P.H. 1,16f. 34. 185. 212. 236f. 241; 2,6; 3,218 [1. 6]. Josephus uses the term to refer to the three (inner-) Jewish religious groups (the Sadducees, Pharisees, and Essenes), cf. Jos. AI 7,347; 13,171. 288. 293; Jos. BI 2,118. 122. 137. 142. 162; Euseb. Hist. eccl. 10,5,2 (cf. Jos. BI 2,119. 124. 141 *hairetistḗs*, 'member of a party') [7].

In the NT, the noun *haíresis* appears nine times: in the Acts, it refers exclusively to (inner-) Jewish groups (5,17: Sadducees; 15,5; 26,5: Pharisees; 24,5. 14; 28,22: but also 'Nazoraeans' = Christians); in the Acts, therefore, Christianity still appears to be both a form of Jewish *haíresis*, as well as 'orthodox' in the Christian sense, although, for Jewish ears, the word *haíresis* already carried pejorative undertones (Acts 24,5). In Paul, we find the first indication of its future meaning: Gal 5,20 and 1 Cor 11,18f. address diverging Christian *hairéseis* within the community, here already branded as unwelcome tendencies. In the post-Apostolic period, the term *haíresis* refers to the 'heresy' that diverges from the author's 'right' doctrine (Tit 3,10; cf. 2 Petr 2,1 etc.); from the 2nd cent. AD onwards, the negative sense of the term is firmly established (Ignatius to the Ephesians 6,2; Id. to the Trallians 6,1; Justin. Apol. 1,26,8; Justin. Dial. 35,3; 51,2 etc.). It is finally used throughout in the sense of the heresiologist *terminus technicus* beginning with → Irenaeus and → Tertullianus [1. 2. 3. 4.].

It is impossible to create a historical summary of Christian heresy due to fundamental problems: within the inner-Christian dispute surrounding the true doctrine, the reproach of heresy is always aimed at the opponent. An academic history of heresy not engaged in Christian → heresiology would have to accept a certain line in the transmission as the orthodox line. Modern Church history therefore operates with the idea that the 'lack of historical success' of a certain school is a criterion for its designation as heresy [8. 318]. Heretics discussed by ancient heresiologists are, for instance, → Simon Magus, → Marcion, → Valentinus, → Arius [3]. Augustine primarily discusses the following heresies: → Gnosticism; → Manichaeism; Donatism; Pelagianism (→ Pelagius) [8. 320–326].

Following Constantine's transformation and unification of the Church, the state began combating heretics: exile, book-burnings, and prohibition of assembly were common punishments for heretics beginning in the 4th cent., capital punishment still remaining an exception. From the 13th cent., the violence against heretics intensified (Inquisition). In the wake of the Reformation, a movement towards greater tolerance finally emerged, which continues until this day (cf. [8. 326–341]).

→ Heresiology; → Canon; → HERESY

1 LSJ s.v. αἵρεσις B II. 2   2 BAUER/ALAND, s.v. αἵρεσις 3 H. SCHLIER, s.v. αἱρέομαι etc., ThWB 1, 179–184 4 G. BAUMBACH, s.v. αἵρεσις, Exegetisches Wörterbuch zum Neuen Testament 1, 1978, 96f.   5 ThlL 6, 3, 250f. 6 J. GLUCKER, Antiochos and the Late Academy, 1978 7 M. SIMON, From Greek Hairesis to Christian Heresy: Early Christian Literature and the Classical Intellectual Tradition, in: FS R.M. Grant, 1979, 101–116 = Id., Le christianisme antique et son contexte religieux, Scripta varia II, 1981, 821–836   8 A. SCHINDLER, s.v. H. II, TRE 14, 318–341.

W. BAUER, Rechtgläubigkeit und Ketzerei im älteren Christentum, hrsg. von G. STRECKER, ²1964; M. DESJARDINS, Bauer and Beyond: On Recent Scholarly Discussion of Hairesis in the Early Christian Era, in: The Second Century 8, 1991, 68–82.   L.K.

II. ISLAMIC

In early Islam, the Manichaeans are accused of heresy (*zandaqa*) [2]. However, the term – no exact Arabic translation exists [1. 51–63] – soon sees a broadening of its meaning and refers to any kind of heresy, religious attitude, or behaviour diverging from the (orthodox) norm that could threaten the Islamic state, thus, ultimately, to any kind of free thinking. What began as an accusation of heresy directed at certain writers resulted in the inquisitorial persecution and stigmatization of the accused from the 2nd half of the 8th cent. on. At times, heresy was punished by death.

→ Kalam; → Manus

1 B. LEWIS, Some Observations on the Significance of Heresy in the History of Islam, in: Studia Islamica 1, 1953, 43–63   2 G. VAJDA, Les zindîqs en pays d'islam au début de la période abbaside, in: Rivista degli Studi Orientali 17, 1938, 173–229.

L. MASSIGNON, s.v. zindīk, EI 4, 1228a–1229a.   H.SCHÖ.

Heretics, baptism of As is evident in → Tertullianus [2] (De baptismo 15), the African Church only recognized its own → baptism. Christians baptized by separate groups (→ Heresy I; → Schism) were rebaptized when changing to the mainstream Church. Under bishop → Cyprianus [2], a conflict arose in Carthage with the Roman bishop → Stephanus [6] (254–257) (known to historiography as the controversy about the 'baptism of heretics') because Rome accepted the baptisms performed by separate groups (notably the Novatians and Marcionites; → Novatianus; → Marcion) as valid (Cypr. Epist. 67; 69; 70; 72; 75). After Cyprian's death, the differing positions were mutually recognized. The African Church was only won for the Roman position in 314 during the conflict with the Donatists (→ Donatus [1]). However, the definitive breakthrough came with → Augustinus' teachings on sacraments, which differentiated between the validity and effectiveness of the sacraments.

A. SCHINDLER, s. v. Afrika I., TRE 1, 1977, 640–700, esp. 648–650; 688 f.; L. PIÉTRI, G. GOTTLIEB, Christenverfolgungen zwischen Decius und Diocletian, in: C. and L. PIÉTRI (ed.), Das Entstehen der einen Christenheit: 250–430 (Die Geschichte des Christentums 2), 1996, 156–190, esp. 166 f.   M. HE.

Hergetium (Ἐργέτιον; *Hērgétion*). Small town in the interior of Sicily, near Grammichele, and north of → Hybla [1] Heraea; it is mentioned in the Delphian list of the *theōrodókoi* (col. IV 106; cf. [1. 434f.] with a suggested localization in Ferla, [2. 133ff.³²]), and also in an oracle of Dodona [4. 85f.], as well as in Steph. Byz. s.v. Segesta. For the ethnicon cf. bronze coins from Syracuse [3. 203].

1 G. MANGANARO, Città di Sicilia e santuari panellenici nel III e II sec. a.C., in: Historia 13, 1964, 414–439   2 Id., Alla ricerca di poleis mikrai della Sicilia centro-orientale, in: Orbis Terrarum 2, 1996, 129–144   3 R. CALCIATI (ed.), Corpus nummorum Siculorum 3, 1987   4 J. VOKOTOPOULOU, in: A. STAZIO (ed.), La Magna Grecia e i Grandi Santuari della Madrepatria. Atti XXXI Conv. Studi Magna Grecia, 1991, 62–90.

M. GIANGIULIO, s.v. Ergezio, BTCGI 7, 1989, 344ff.   GI.MA.

Herillus (Ἥριλλος; *Hérillos*) of Carthage (Calchedon). Stoic philosopher of the 3rd cent. BC, a student of → Zeno of Citium. He developed a form of → Stoicism that resembled that of Ariston of Chios because of its emphasis on ethics. After the tendency represented by Cleanthes and Chrysippus had prevailed in this school, H.'s approach was considered to differ from Zeno's. Diogenes Laertius' biography of H. contains a list of work titles, which mostly appear to refer to ethical themes (However, only assumptions are possible about the content of his Dialogues, and the works 'Hermes' and 'Medea'). The treatise 'On Assumptions' (περὶ ὑπολήψεως) presumably discusses the supreme objective (→ *télos*), which according to H. was 'knowledge', 'i.e., a lifestyle that directed all efforts towards gaining scientific insight and did not allow itself to be misguided by ignorance' (Diog. Laert. 7,165). H. was credited with the opinion that there was no definite *télos* but only one that depended on the circumstances. In this respect he also approached → Ariston [7] of Chios, who held the opinion that the wise man knows how to act in a given situation, and denied that there are universal guidelines for action. H. differentiated the actual supreme goal (*télos*) that the wise strive for from subordinate goals (*hypótelis*) that are accessible to the unwise.

→ Stoicism

SVF 1, 91–93; A.M. IOPPLO, Aristone di Chio e lo stoicismo antico, 1980, 176–179.   B.I.

Herineus River in Sicily along the *via Elorina*, mentioned by Thucydides (7,80,6; 82,3) in conjunction with the retreat of the Athenians in 413 BC, possibly identical with the Cavallata north of the Assinarus.

> G. MANGANARO, Alla ricerca di poleis mikrai della Sicilia centro-orientale, in: Orbis Terrarum 2, 1996, 139 with fn. 50; L. ROBERT, Noms indigènes de l'Asie Mineure gréco-romaine, 1963, 37f.   GI.MA.

Herippidas (Ἐριππίδας; *Herippídas*). A Spartiate, who after 400 BC belonged to the inner circle of Sparta's political leaders [1. 154]; in 399, he suppressed an uprising in Heraclea Trachinia (Diod. Sic. 14,38,4–5) [2. 120f., 154]. 395 saw him as an influential adviser to Agesilaus [2] during the latter's campaign in Asia Minor, when he also commanded the Cyreans, who in 394 were once again under his command at Coronea (Xen. Hell. 3,4,20; 4,1,11–14; 20–28; 4,3,15). Following the death of the *nauarchos* Podanemus, he temporarily assumed command of the navy in the Corinthian Gulf in 392/1, despite his lack of experience in naval warfare (Xen. Hell. 4,8,11). As one of the three *harmostai* of the Spartan occupation force in Thebes, he was unable to prevent Thebes being liberated by Pelopidas in 379/8, in consequence, he was sentenced to death in Sparta (Plut. Pel. 13).

> 1 P. CARTLEDGE, Agesilaos and the Crisis of Sparta, 1987
> 2 CH. D. HAMILTON, Sparta's Bitter Victories, 1979.
>   K.-W.WEL.

Herm( ) Perhaps a *dioiketes* in Alexandria, at any rate a high ranking official; on 5 March 112 BC, he sent a letter to his subordinate Asclepiades, *ho epì tôn prosódōn* (ὁ ἐπὶ τῶν προσόδων) in Fayoum, regarding the preparations for the reception of the Roman senator L. Memmius (cf. [1], who also rejects the extension of the name to Herm(ias)).

> 1 MITTEIS/WILCKEN I 3.
> E. OLSHAUSEN, Rom und Ägypten von 116 bis 51 v.Chr., Diss. 1963, 6f.   W.A.

Hermaeus (Ἑρμαῖος; *Hermaîos*).
[1] **H. Soter.** (Middle Indian *Heramaya*). The last of the Indo-Greek kings in Paropamisadai (modern south-east Afghanistan) in the 1st cent. BC, perhaps a son of Amyntas [8]. Like so many of the Indo-Greek kings, he is only known through his coins, a large amount of which were issued postumously by Indo-Scythians from Bactria, who had removed him (according to [1] after 30, according to [2] around 50, according to [3] around 70 BC). He was married to → Calliope.

> 1 W. W. TARN, The Greeks in Bactria and India, 1951
> 2 A. K. NARAIN, The Indo-Greeks, 1958   3 BOPEA-
> RACHCHI, 112–125, 325–343.   K.K.

[2] Perhaps 1st cent. BC, the author of at least two bks. 'On the Egyptians', only quoted by Plutarch ('Isis and Osiris'). It is possible that he was the father of the grammarian Nicanor.

> FR.: FGrH 620.
> BIBLIOGRAPHY: F. JACOBY, s.v. H. (4), RE 8, 712.
>   K.MEI.

Hermagoras (Ἑρμαγόρας; *Hermagóras*).
[1] Greek orator from Temnus (Str. 13,3,5 = 621; Suda, s.v. H.), probably active in the 2nd half of the 2nd cent. BC (earlier than Molon, cf. Quint. Inst. 3,1,16). Except for his main work, texts written by him were already lost in antiquity (ibid. 3,5,14). His main work was probably titled *Téchnai rhētorikaí*, comprising 6 bks. (according to the Suda). Its content can be partially reconstructed from Cic. Inv., Quint. Inst. (esp. bk. 5) and Aug. De rhetorica. H. exerted an authoritative influence on the development of the rhetorical system: he established the terminology of the theory of *stáseis* (→ Rhetoric), the beginnings of which can be traced back to the 4th cent. In the process, he is claimed to have added a fourth *stásis* (μετάληψις, *metálēpsis*) – which examines the validity of the proceedings per se (Cic. Inv. 1,16) – and to have subsumed the symbouleutic and epideictic types of speech under the ποιότης (*poiótēs*), the issue concerned with the quality of the action (ibid. 1,12). Furthermore, H. is said to have claimed both *hypóthesis* (a specific conclusion, usually tied to an individual case) and the more general *thésis* (a major premis) as legitimate subjects of rhetoric, thus disputing philosophy's claim on them (Quint. Inst. 3,5,12–16; cf. Cic. De or. 3,107f.). H.'s theory did much to accommodate the needs of oratorical eloquence in Republican Rome. For this reason, and on account of their clear structure, the *Téchnai* became the basis of rhetorical teaching in Rome; not even the criticism that the work was overly complicated in its terminology (Quint. Inst. 3,11,21f.) and extremely dry in style (Cic. Brut. 263; Tac. Dial. 19,3) could change this.

> EDITIONS: D. MATTHES, 1962.
> RESEARCH REPORT: Id., H. von Temnos, in: Lustrum 3, 1958, 58–214.
> BIBLIOGRAPHY: K. BARWICK, Augustins Schrift de rhetorica und H. von Temnos, in: Philologus 105, 1961, 97–110; Id., Zur Erklärung und Gesch. der Stasislehre des H. von Temnos, in: Philologus 108, 1964, 80–101; Id., Zur Rekonstruktion der Rhet. des H. von Temnos, in: Philologus 109, 1965, 186–218; A. C. BRAET, Das Krinomenonschema und die Einseitigkeit des Begriffes στάσις von H. von Temnos, in: Mnemosyne 41, 1988, 299–317; Id., Variationen zur Statuslehre bei Cicero, in: Rhetorica 7, 1989, 239–259; R. NADEAU, Classical Systems of Stases in Greek, in: GRBS 2, 1959, 51–71; E. SCHÜTRUMPF, H. v.T. and the Classification of Aristotle's Work in the Neoplatonic Commentaries, in: Mnemosyne 44, 1991, 96–105; W. N. THOMPSON, Stasis in Aristotle's Rhetoric, in: Quarterly Journal of Speech 58, 1972, 134–141.

[2] Greek rhetor from the 1st cents. BC and AD. Like Tiberius, he was a student of → Theodorus of Gadara just like the emperor Tiberius, although H. must have outlived the emperor by many years (cf. Quint. Inst. 3,1,18). Later, he was a teacher of rhetoric in Rome. The Suda (s.v. H.) mixes pieces of information about H. [1] of Temnus with others about Theodorus' student. It is highly likely that some of the texts attributed there to the former were probably actually written by the latter (Περὶ πρέποντος, *Perì prépontos*: on the appropriate expression; Περὶ σχημάτων, *Perì schēmátōn*: on the theory of figures; Περὶ φράσεως, *Perì phráseōs*: on *elocutio*; Περὶ ἐξεργασίας, *Perì exergasías*: on composition), since they are not documented for H. [1] elsewhere (this may also apply to a piece which argues for the exclusion of the *théseis* from rhetoric, cf. Quint. Inst. 3,5,12–16). Seneca praises H. frequently for his unpretentious yet striking aphorisms (Controv. 1,1,25; 2,1,39; 2,3,22; 7, Praef. 5; 7,5,14f.; 10,1,15).

EDITIONS: D. MATTHES, 1962, 56–59.
BIBLIOGRAPHY: Id., H. von Temnos, in: Lustrum 3, 1958, 79.

[3] Greek orator from the 1st half of the 2nd cent. AD, referred to as ὁ νεώτερος ('the Younger') in order to distinguish him from H. [2] (Maximus Planudes in WALZ 5,337,23). The dating is based on Sopater, who places H. after Lollianus and prior to Minucianus and Hermogenes (WALZ 5,8,20). H. composed a monograph about the στάσις πραγματική (*stásis pragmatikḗ*), the decision question of whether or not an action is possible in the future should take place (sub-category of *poiótēs*, cf. Hermog. De statibus 2,12), a work frequently mentioned and still used in the Byzantine period. H. may also have written a textbook on rhetoric (cf. the definition transmitted in the schol. Hermog.: WALZ 4,63,9–14; also 2,683,25–27).

EDITIONS: D. MATTHES, 1962, 59–65.
BIBLIOGRAPHY: Id., H. von Temnos, in: Lustrum 3, 1958, 79–81. M.W.

Hermai see → Herms

Hermaphroditus (Ἑρμαφρόδιτος; *Hermaphróditos*). Androgynous figure which, like that of Priapus (cf. Diod. Sic. 4,6; [6. 76–79]), did not appear before the 4th cent. BC. Though androgynous gods of the Orient like → Astarte, 'dual-sexuality' gods like Aphrodite-Aphroditus on Cyprus, joint cults of Hermes and Aphrodite (see below) have rites involving changing gender roles and the exchange of clothing, as well as a background of myths of successive (→ Caeneus, → Teiresias) and simultaneous (e.g. Pl. Symp. 189d–192d) bisexuality, its origin remain somewhat unclear [6. 69].

The name is not, like Hermathena etc., as documented beginning with Cicero, a combination of *hérma* (ἕρμα) and the goddess' name, but can be explained, due to the combination of → Hermes and → Aphrodite,

as being a rare twin form analogous to *andrógynos*, *arrhenóthelys* ('man-womanly') (Ov. Met. 4,384).

The only extant mythological story (possibly of oriental origin) is Ov. Met. 4,274–388: when H., son of Hermes and Aphrodite (first mention Diod. Sic. 4,6,5), bathes in a fountain, the nymph Salmacis merges with him into an androgynous body (aition of the androgyny of H.); thereupon H. requests from his parents that those bathing there be made effeminate (aition of the characteristic attributed to the fountain). Vitr. De arch. 2,8,11–12 mentions a Temple of Mercury and Venus near the fountain, located at Halicarnassus, of which however nothing has survived.

Sources documenting a cult can be listed, with varying levels of confidence, as follows: 1. a votive inscription from Hymettus in the deme of Anagyrus (385 BC); 2. possibly Theophr. Char. 16,10: depending on our reading of the corrupt MS, the superstitious man crowned with wreaths on the 4th and 7th of the month (the 4th was sanctified as wedding day of Hermes and Aphrodite: Hes. Op. 800) either H. or herms; 3. a private altar (Cos, 3rd cent. BC), on which H. is named in an inscription with other gods; 4. possibly Alci. 2,35: depending on interpretation, a woman makes an offering of an → *eiresione* to H. in the deme Alopece (MS), or to a person named H. or even to the pile of stones (*hérma*) of Phaedrias.

The fact that H.'s presence is most strongly felt in iconography (starting in the last quarter of the 4th cent. BC [3. 283]; overview [3; 4. 659–661; 5; 6. 83–103]) is not entirely coincidental. Along with Cicero, it was the main source for later adaptations. In the H. of the alchemists we find influences of the Ovidian allegory and other ancient androgynous archetypes.

1 J. KIRCHNER, ST. DOW, in: MDAI(A) 62, 1937, 7–8, fig. 4–5 2 R. G. USSHER, The Characters of Theophrastus, 1960, l.c. 3 A. AJOOTIAN, s.v. H., LIMC 5.1, 268–285; 5.2, 190–198 4 M. DELCOURT, K. HOHEISEL, s.v. H., RAC 14, 650–682 5 M. DELCOURT, Hermaphroditea. Recherches sur l'être double promoteur de fertilité dans le monde classique, 1966 6 Id., Hermaphrodite. Mythes et rites de la Bisexualité dans l'Antiquité classique, 1958 7 J. JESSEN, s.v. H., RE 7, 714–721. T.H.

Hermarchus (Ἕρμαρχος; *Hérmarchos*). Born in Mytilene on Lesbos, a contemporary of → Epicurus. In his youth he was trained in rhetoric and encountered Epicurus in Mytilene in about 310 BC. H. did not immediately turn to philosophy, but only followed his teacher Epicurus to Athens after he had founded a school (306 BC). From 290 to 270 BC he went to Lampsacus to visit the Epicurean school there. Before his death in 270 BC, Epicurus transferred the leadership of the Athenian school to H. despite his being a metic. H. died in old age, of paralysis; his successor as head of the school was Polystratus.

Diogenes Laertius (10,25 = [1. fr. 25]) records the titles of the following works: 'Treatises in the Form of Letters' (Ἐπιστολικά); 'Against Empedocles in 22

Books' (Πρὸς Ἐμπεδόκλεα, εἴκοσι καὶ δύο); 'On Science' (Περὶ μαθημάτων); 'Against Plato' (Πρὸς Πλάτωνα); 'Against Aristotle' (Πρὸς Ἀριστοτέλην). There are also two maxims attributed to H. [1. fr. 23, 24], several letters [1. fr. 40–42] as well as some statements on ethical topics to which Philodemus and later authors attest [1. fr. 43–48]. A work entitled Ἐπιστολικὰ περὶ Ἐμπεδοκλέος ('Letters Regarding Empedocles') was not written by H. It consists of two separate works of which the second is entitled Πρὸς Ἐμπεδόκλεα ('Against Empedocles') [1. 33; 3].

Its dating [1. fr. 27–34] is uncertain. It is evident from Philodemus [1. fr. 29] that his last book was written before the 12th book of Epicurus' *De natura* (written before 301 BC). It is uncertain if the work is directed against Empedocles' *Katharmoí*. The largest fragment is found in Porphyrius' *De abstinentia* [1. fr. 34]; it is about the origin of law in primitive society. Other fragments treat theological questions [1. fr. 27 and 29–32]. Possibly, some fragments dealing with demons (*daímones*) [1. fr. 50], miracles (*térata*) [1. fr. 51] of Empedocles and the migration of souls [1. fr. 52] are attributable to 'Against Empedocles'. The assumption that Epicurus' maxims 31–40 are derived from H.'s 'Against Empedocles' is untenable.

A 'letter' dated precisely to 267/6 BC from the Ἐπιστολικά ('Treatises in the Form of Letters') to an otherwise unknown Theophides is contained in Philodemus' 'Rhetoric' [1. fr. 35; 36; cf. fr. 37–39]. It contains a polemic against the Megarian → Alexinus of Elis, in which H., similar to Epicurus and Metrodorus, espouses the opinion that only Sophist rhetoric should be granted the status of an art (τέχνη). A passage about the usefulness of prayer in Proclus [1. fr. 48] refers to his work 'Against Plato' (Πρὸς Πλάτωνα).

Nothing is preserved of the other works. Still, statements by H. on anger [1. fr. 43], flattery [1. fr. 44], friendship [1. fr. 45] and the necessity of a frugal life [1. fr. 47] are found in ancient sources. There is also evidence of a correspondence [1. fr. 40–42].

→ Epicurus; → Epicurean School

1 F. LONGO, Ermarco. Frammenti, 1988   2 M. ERLER, GGPh² 4.1, 227–234   3 D. OBBINK, H., Against Empedocles, in: CQ 38, 1988, 428–435.   T.D.

Hermas, Hermae Pastor

Hermas, Hermae Pastor The work 'The shepherd of H.' (Greek only Ποιμήν; *Poimén*, Latin *Liber pastoris nuntii paenitentiae* or *Liber Hermae prophetae*) is a Christian prophetic script with the stylistic character of an → apocalypse but not wholly corresponding to this genre. The work places H. among the → Apostolic Fathers. The title 'Shepherd' (Ποιμήν) for the entire work appeared in the *Canon Muratori*, a substantial index of canons (more likely dated end of the 2nd cent. than the 4th cent.: l. 74), but it refers only to the second part of the work (visio 5 to similitudo 10) in which an angel of repentance, protection, and retribution appears in the form of a shepherd as vehicle of revelation. The text

may have been written in Rome. Facing a new wave of persecution, the author instructs the reader to do penance and preaches that sins may be forgiven once more after baptism (at the time still controversial among theologians) (mand. 4,3,1).

The book is divided by the author himself into five ὁράσεις (*visiones*), twelve ἐντολαί (*mandata*) and ten παραβολαί (*similitudines*) (vis. 5). The author receives the first four *visiones* in a field by the road to Cumae from an old woman, whom he takes to be a Sibyl but who introduces herself as Church (vis. 2,4,1). In the remainder of the book a shepherd appears. The *mandata* contain ethical instructions, the *similitudines* parables.

Despite various controversies and literary divisions, theories that various authors wrote the entire work have not prevailed. Currently, a gradual formation of the text at the hand of *one* author is usually assumed. According to BROX [1. 27–29] the earlier *visiones* 1–4 are editorially (vis. 5) linked to the later 'Shepherd Book' (mand. and sim. 1–8).

The author of the text calls himself H. (vis. 1,1,4; 2,2,2) and claims to have been sold by his foster father (θρέψας) and owner in Rome to a certain Rhodian (vis. 1,1,1). At the time of composition he evidently lived there as a freed businessman and styles himself a sinner requiring penance. According to the *Canon Muratori* he was a brother of Pius, who is anachronistically described as 'Bishop of Rome' (l. 73–77) and whose office is dated by a later Roman list of bishops as AD 140–155. According to Origen (commentary in epistulam ad Romanos 10,31, PG 14, 1282. Euseb. Hist. eccl. 3,3,6 is more discerning), the H. mentioned in Paul's Romans 16,14 was meant. None of these sources can be taken at face value as historical information, because they served literary and theological interests or have their origin in scholarly speculation. It is certain that the author represents a very (also linguistically) simple, but hence all the more interesting, 'lay theology', which presumably corresponds more to the thinking of a wide circle of people in the Roman community than to the theology of educated Christians such as → Iustinus Martyr.

The text of 'The Shepherd', which was one of the most popular books of Christian antiquity and evidently was even read by individual congregations during services, has been fully attested in Greek only since 1855 by two (albeit incomplete) MSS [3. IX–XII] and by a large number of papyruses (cf. [4; 5]). Also of importance for a reconstruction of the text are the old translations (e.g. Latin: *Versio Vulgata*, 2nd cent., *Versio Palatina*, 4th/5th cents., also Ethiopic and fragmentary Coptic versions). A new edition of the text taking all fragments into account is needed.

1 N. BROX, Der Hirt des Hermas, übersetzt und erklärt (Komm. zu den apostolischen Vätern 7), 1991   2 A. CARLINI (ed.), Erma: Il Pastore (Ia–IIIa visione) Papyrus Bodmer XXXVIII, 1991   3 M. WHITTAKER (ed.), Der Hirt des Hermas (GCS 48), ²1956   4 A. GIACCONE, Papyrus Bodmer XXXVIII, 1991   5 K. ALAND†, H.-U. RO-

SENBAUM, Repertorium der griech. christlichen Papyri (Patristische Texte und Stud. 42), 1995, 232–311: KV 29–43. C.M.

Hermathena, Hermeracles Cicero called the → Herms of Athena and Hercules, which Atticus had obtained in 67–65 BC for Cicero's Tusculanum (Cic. Att. 1,1; 4; 8; 9; 10), Hermathena and Hermeracles. The bronze heads were set on marble pillars and were considered an appropriate *ornamentum* for his peristyle, which was compared to the *Academia* and a gymnasium. These terms are Cicero's creation. Setting up Herms of this type in the gardens of Roman villas became a common practice.

R. NEUDECKER, Die Skulpturenausstattung röm. Villen in Italien, 1988, 11–18; H. WREDE, Die ant. Herme, 1986, 59f. R.N.

Hermeias (Ἑρμείας; *Hermeías*) see also Hermias (Ἑρμίας; *Hermías*).
[1] of Methymna. Probably 4th cent. BC. First 'foreign' author of *Sikeliká*, comprising 10 or 12 bks and covering the period up to 376/5 (Diod. Sic. 15,37,3). As only a single fragment is extant, he hardly seems to have influenced the subsequent tradition.

FR.: FGrH 558.
BIBLIOGRAPHY: K. MEISTER, Die griech. Geschichtsschreibung, 1990, 69. K.MEI.

[2] of Curium, iambic poet of the Hellenistic period. Ath. 13,563d-e (= CollAlex. p. 237) transmits five of his choliambs, harshly criticizing the Stoics for their way of life, which he claimed stood in such marked contrast with their teachings. He is perhaps identical with the author of a verse consisting of four cretics, quoted in Heph. περὶ ποιημάτων 3,5, p. 65 CONSBRUCH (= SH 484). M.D.MA.

[3] of Alexandria Neoplatonist philosopher of the 5th cent. AD. H. was (like → Proclus) a student of → Syrianus in Athens, whose lectures on Plato's 'Phaedrus' [1; 2] he recorded and to whom he was related through his wife Aidesia. His sons were → Ammonius [12] and Heliodorus. H. taught in Alexandria [1]. Damascius (Vita Isidori 74) did not consider him a sharp-witted and creative thinker. H.'s teachings apparently did not deviate from those of Syrianus.
→ Neoplatonism

1 H. BERNARD (ed.), H. von Alexandrien, Komm. zu Platons Phaidros, 1997 (with German transl.)
2 P. COUVREUR, Hermias Alexandrinus in platonischen Scholia, 1901 (²1971) 3 ZELLER 2, 890–892. A. LA.

Hermenericus
[1] see → Ermanaric
[2] Youngest son of Flavius Ardabur [2] Aspar (Candidus FHG 4, 135), *cos.* AD 465 (Chron. min. 3,535

MOMMSEN). When his father was murdered, he was able to save himself, possibly with the help of Zeno, whose daughter he married, by fleeing to Constantinople. He later returned (Theophanes a. 5964). PLRE 2,549 (Herminericus). ME.STR.

Hermeneutics If understood in the sense of everyday, unreflected experience of the interpretation of texts, hermeneutics existed in antiquity no less than it did later; however, hermeneutics taken as the systematic elaboration of a set of rules to control and guide the interpretation was not created until early modern times [5]. Originally, the semantic field ἑρμηνεύειν (*hermēneúein*) means 'to express, translate' [17], and only acquires the metaphorical meaning 'to interpret' in Plato [12]. Aristotle's Περὶ ἑρμηνείας (*Perì hermēneías*, *De interpretatione*) is a theory of expression, not of interpretation.

Ancient attempts at a systematic theory of interpretation are scarce and late; with few exceptions, hermeneutics remains the domain not of the theoretical philosopher, but of the less respected practical grammarian [18] until late antiquity. Ancient hermeneutics remained limited to implicit tendencies rather than developed systems [10], lacking the conditions that favoured the birth of modern hermeneutics in the 17th cent., i.e. an increasingly acute awareness of history, the resulting problemizing of the discrepancies between sacred text and altered circumstances, the refutation of allegoresis, which had been developed for the elimination of these very discrepancies, the institutionalization and standardization of a respected caste of exegetes, and modernity's trust in sets of rules.

The most important trend in ancient hermeneutics is → allegoresis, which collapses the time difference between text and recipient by means of an allegedly perpetually valid philosophical ὑπόνοια (*hypónoia*, 'under-sense' or underlying meaning) or ἀλληγορία (*allēgoría*, 'other saying') [2. 16]. Beginnings of allegoresis are present as early as Homer [14], but as a literary genre it is created only as a reaction to counteract the gradually increasing literality, and therefore unchangeability, of the Homeric epics (→ Theagenes of Rhegium), remaining an effective means, beyond the end of antiquity, for harnessing the prestige of well-known poets for maxims that might otherwise be doubted [13]. In the late 5th cent. BC → Anaxagoras and → Metrodorus of Lampsacus, as well as the author of the so-called Derveni Papyrus [15], pursued allegoresis of Homer and Orpheus; subsequently all ancient philosophical sects (excepting the Epicureans and the Middle Academy) subscribed to allegoresis, which had its high point, important for its later reception, in Neoplatonism [6].

Three other trends were of rather sporadic importance. (1) Biographism: Aristophanes already used literary texts to comical purpose by drawing malicious conclusions about the author's personality. The serious development of these beginnings, in particular in Peripatetic literary history, as well as in Hellenistic and Imperial Roman biography [1], led to many an absurdity preserved in medieval poets' biographies (and influential until fairly recently [7]).

(2) Historicizing: among the many pointers towards a solution for the objections against Homer collected in Aristotle's 'Poetics', ch.25, is the emphasis on the peculiar conditions of heroic times ('things that people say and think'; 60b 10; 61a2; 'this was their custom', 1461a2) as an excuse for certain questionable details. This style of historicizing tends to be alien to ancient hermeneutics, with the important exception of → Aristarchus [4] of Samothrace, who justified his principle of 'explaining Homer through Homer' by assuming a homogeneous heroic age [19].

(3) Formalism: the microscopical and macroscopical analysis of the formal elements of poetry goes back to the sophists, but Plato's objections made it to a large extent out of bounds for ancient philosophy, leaving it to grammar [11]. Study of the scarce traces of these beginnings in the ancient scholia has begun [9], but the grammarians remain largely unresearched. It was only in the philosophical schools of Imperial Rome (led by the Platonic-Aristotelian) that various factors led to the creation of a rudimentary form of hermeneutics [3. 4]: the canonicity of a limited corpus of texts of considerable interpretive difficulty; the long succession of masters who, while revering their predecessors, emend them at the same time, and are themselves legitimated by the interpretation of the same basic texts; a tendency towards philosophical systematization and didactic reglementation. Some prolegomena (e.g. Anon. Prolegomena in Plat. Phil. 3,13–10,26, p. 25–49 WESTERINK; Olympiodori Prolegomena = CAG 12.1, p. 6.6–14.11 BUSSE) and proems to individual commentaries (Ammonii in Cat. Prooemium = CAG 4.4, p. 3.20–8.19 BUSSE; Simplicii in Cat. Prooemium = CAG 8, p. 3.18–9.31 KALBFLEISCH; Eliae in Cat. Prooemium = CAG 18.1, p. 113.17–129.3 BUSSE) list and explain in schoolmasterly fashion the themes of all interpretation of philosophical writings. For Plato these are: writings, dialogue form, characters, time, place, style, method, titles, subdivision of works, form of representation, topic, order of dialogues, authenticity; for Aristotle: arrangement of the Corpus, literary genre, order of works, purpose, attributes of the appropriate student and interpreter, form of representation, opacity, goals of the interpretation, authenticity [8].

1 G. ARRIGHETTI, Poeti, eruditi e biografi. Momenti della riflessione dei greci sulla letteratura, 1987   2 F. BUFFIÈRE, Les mythes d'Homère et la pensée grecque, 1956   3 J. COULTER, The Literary Microcosm. Theories of Interpretation of the Later Neoplatonists, 1976   4 D. DAWSON, Allegorical Readers and Cultural Revision in Ancient Alexandria, 1992   5 H. G. GADAMER, Wahrheit und Methode, 1960   6 R. LAMBERTON, Homer the Theologian. Neoplatonist Allegorical Reading and the Growth of the Epic Tradition, 1986   7 M. LEFKOWITZ, The Lives of the Greek Poets, 1981   8 J. MANSFELD, Prolegomena. Questions to be Settled before the Study of an Author, or a

Text, 1994   9 R. MEIJERING, Literary and Rhetorical Theories in Greek Scholia, 1987   10 G. W. MOST, Rhet. und H.: Zur Konstitution der Neuzeitlichkeit, in: A&A; 30, 1984, 62–79   11 Id., Sophistique et hermeneutique, in: B. CASSIN (ed.), Positions de la Sophistique. Colloque de Cérisy, 1986, 233–45   12 Id., Pindar, O. 2.83–90, in: CQ 36, 1986, 308–311   13 Id., Cornutus and Stoic Allegoresis: A Preliminary Report, in: ANRW II 36.3, 2014–2065   14 Id., Die früheste erh. griech. Dichterallegorese, in: RhM 136, 1993, 209–212   15 Id., The Fire Next Time. Cosmology, Allegoresis, and Salvation in the Derveni Papyrus, in: JHS 117, 1997, 117–135   16 J. PÉPIN, Mythe et allégorie. Les origines grecques et les contestations judéochrétiennes, ²1976   17 Id., L'herméneutique ancienne. Les mots et les idées, in: Poétique 23, 1973, 291–300   18 R. PFEIFFER, History of Classical Scholarship from the Beginnings to the End of the Hellenistic Age, 1968   19 M. SCHMIDT, Die Erklärungen zum Weltbild Homers und zur Kultur der Heroenzeit in den bT-Scholien zur Ilias, 1976.   G.W.M.

Hermericus AD 419–438 king of the Suebi, who in 419 fought unsuccessfully against the Vandals in Spain (Hydatius Lemiensis 71). After pillaging Gallaecia in 430 and 433 (ibid. 91; 100), he made peace. In 438, already suffering from illness, he handed his throne to his son Rechila; he died in 441 (ibid. 114; 122). PLRE 2,546f.

ME.STR.

Hermes (Ἑρμῆς/*Hermês*, in epic, also Ἑρμείας/*Hermeías*, Ἑρμείης/*Hermeíēs*, Ἑρμάων/*Hermáōn*)
I. CULT AND MYTHOLOGY   II. ICONOGRAPHY

I. CULT AND MYTHOLOGY
A. PROFILE   B. GOD OF THE HERM   C. GOD OF THE SHEPHERDS   D. GOD OF MESSENGERS AND HERALDS   E. HERMES AS GOD OF THE MYSTERIES

A. PROFILE
According to mythological tradition, a god native to Arcadia. He was, however, worshipped throughout Greece. Evidence of his name appears in Linear B as early as the Mycenaean era [1. 285f.]. A bringer of culture with a special relationship to shepherds, he belongs to the ethnological category of the trickster. In epic poetry he functioned as the messenger and herald of Zeus. Ultimately, he was considered to be a god endowed with universal wisdom and extensive powers of communication, offering aid and protection to tradesmen and merchants and legitimation to mystagogues and authors of esoteric literature. He is identified with the Roman → Mercurius.

B. GOD OF THE HERM
As his name suggests, H. is the god of the herm (→ Herms; see also below, II.), a partially anthropomorphic stone pillar used in Greece to mark the entryways of houses (Thuc. 6,27; Ath. 10,437b), as well as private property borders (e.g., Anth. Pal. 9,314) and city limits (Paus. 2,38,7; 3,10,6; 8,34,6) [2; 1. 299–306

no. 58, 75, 76, 78, 79, 81, 87, 92–179]. In this context, he also took on the function of travel guide (Suda, s.v. ἑρμαῖον). The desired effect of the boundary stone as a signal of the unrelenting vigilance of the territory's owner was reinforced [4] with imposing markers of virility – i.e., bearded face and erect phallus [3]. The sacralization of the herm protected the provocative border markers from attacks, although it could certainly come to that in times of political tension: prior to the Sicilian Expedition, herms throughout the city of Athens were mutilated (Thuc. 6,27) [5] (→ Herms, mutilation of the).

In the countryside, wanderers threw stones at the herms; the cairn of stones that collected around the pillars was called *hermaion* (Cornutus 16; Eust. ad Hom. Od. 16,471 [6. 48]). The custom had the pragmatic function of clearing stones from the road. At the same time, it allowed for an act of controlled aggression aimed against the challenge of the apotropaic sign. Ultimately, this did not call the function of the boundary marker into question, but instead reinforced it. According to the aetiological myth, the *hermaion* was the result of a symbolic stoning: for fear of provoking Zeus' anger, the gods did not dare to condemn H. for his killing of → Argos [I 5] and threw their voting-stones at his feet (schol. Hom. Od. 16,471). As a cultic marker on the border between gardens and uncultivated land, herms were resting-places (Anth. Pal. 9,314) where owners of gardens left fruit and shepherds left milk in sacrificial offering to H. (Anth. Pal. 9,316; 318). The provisions were available to anyone who stopped to rest there; therefore, this trove was also called *hermaion*, which came to mean any unexpected gain as such (Suda, s.v. ἑρμαῖον). The tribute of food undoubtedly prevented plundering. It was meant to keep passers-by from venturing uninvited onto private property and helping themselves to the fruit and cattle.

C. God of the shepherds
1. Relationship to shepherd life 2. The myth of the cattle raid 3. The origin of culture and the rites of initiation
4. Saturnalian Hermes festivals

1. Relationship to shepherd life
The herms separated cultivated land from the uncultivated pastures grazed by the herds. Thus H., as the god of the border stone, became the patron in particular of the male youths who had to watch the cattle and keep them away from crop fields [6. 48]. H. is regularly represented as a youth in poetry, and in the iconographic tradition from the classical era. As the god of the shepherds, he was responsible for the protection (Anth. Pal. 6,334; 16,190), flourishing and reproduction of the herds (Hom. Il. 14,490f.; Hes. Theog. 444; H. Hom. 4,567–573). Herdsmen honoured him through sacrifices – as did the swineherd Eumaeus in the Homeric epic (Hom. Od. 14,435). H. was therefore also linked to shepherd festivals and their aesthetic forms. In a myth

from the island of Cos, he punishes farmers who stay away from the shepherd feast by transforming them into birds (Antoninus Liberalis 15). The Arcadian shepherd god → Pan was considered to be the son of H. (H. Hom. 19,1), as was the shepherd youth → Daphnis [1], who was revered in Sicily as the inventor of pastoral music (Stesich. fr. 102 PMG; Timaeus FGrH 566 F 83; Diod. Sic. 4,84,2).

2. The myth of the cattle raid
The oldest version of the myth of the cattle raid appears in the Homeric Hymn to H. (also treated, e.g., by Alcaeus, according to Paus. 7,20,4; Apollod. 3,112–115). It may be read as the mythical origin of animal husbandry and some of the technical skills involved in herding. H., the son of → Zeus and → Maia, is born in an Arcadian cave. Soon after, he climbs out of the winnowing-basket which serves as his cradle (H. Hom. 4,18ff.); he then makes his way to Thessaly, where he steals a herd of cattle (which were immortal until then) belonging to his older half-brother → Apollo and drives them to the Peloponnese, cunningly covering his traces. There, he hides the animals in a cave, except for two that he slaughters and roasts – for which purpose he specifically invents the trick of rubbing kindling sticks to start a fire (108ff.). He does not eat any of the meat on the spit, but instead divides it into twelve portions (*moîrai*, H. Hom. 4,128): an aition of the sacrifice to the Twelve Gods as it was practised in Olympia, where H. shared an altar with Apollo (Paus. 5,14,8; schol. Pind. Ol. 5,10; [7]). Zeus commands H. to return the stolen cows to Apollo. But when Apollo attempts to bind the overpowered thief with withes of willow, the branches miraculously begin to grow, taking root in the ground, twining around one another and completely encircling the cattle (H. Hom. 4,409ff.). Thus, H.'s demonstration of his maintained claim to ownership gives rise to the mythical prototype of the fence, which will henceforth make possible the practices of pasture farming and cattle breeding [8. 1ff.].

H. succeeds in persuading his half-brother to leave him the herds in exchange for the seven-stringed lyre and the theogonic song he first strikes up to its accompaniment at that time (H. Hom. 4,425ff.). He had constructed the lyre earlier by stringing the sinews of the sacrificed animals across a tortoise shell (47ff.; according to this source, the strings came from sheep, but in other versions they come from the cattle: Apollod. 3,113). Aside from the cattle herd, Apollo also gives H. the tools of the herdsman, the whip and the staff, as well as a rural oracle (H. Hom. 4,496ff.). Thus, the younger brother becomes the successor to the office of the herdsman, which Apollo himself – on the cusp of adulthood – has now vacated.

3. The origin of culture and the rites of initiation
On the archetypal level of the myth of the gods, the biography of H. contains in germinal form the early phases of cultural development before the rise of agriculture and the cities (→ Origin myths): as the inventor

of fire and blood sacrifice, the shepherd H. is a rival of the trickster → Prometheus; as the creator of the string instrument and the theogonic song he strikes up to its music, H. appears as the initiator of an aesthetic framework for rituals which marked a change in social status. Like Apollo, the 'minstrel' → Amphion [1] – also a young shepherd – was also said to have received his lyre from H. He is supposed to have erected the walls of seven-gated Thebes merely by playing on its strings (Paus. 9,5,7f.). This should be understood as the reflection of a social ritual staging the origin of cities, by means of which adolescent shepherds were taken up into the community of citizens. That this is the case is demonstrated by an analogous cult in the Boeotian city of Tanagra, which worshipped H. Kriophorus ('Rambearer'). On the god's feast day, the most beautiful ephebe of the city carried a lamb around the city walls. This was done as a ritual repetition of a mythical, originary event: in order to prevent a plague, the shepherd god himself had once carried a ram around Tanagra's walls (Paus. 9,22,1). The tour, which traced the city borders anew, thus periodically restaged the overcoming of an imaginary, life-threatening crisis.

H. was here also linked to the transitional phase of adolescence in another way: he was said to have once led the ephebes of Tanagra in battle against the Eritreans, joining in the fight himself armed with a scraper. Because he helped the Tanagraeans achieve victory, H. was also worshipped there under the epithet Promachos ('champion') (Paus. 9,22,2). According to a record referring to the same mythical battle, the city had a cult image of the god called the 'White Hermes'. Supposedly, the statue was erected to commemorate a youth and a maiden who were sacrificed on the command of the oracle (Tzetz. schol. Lycophr. 680): it reflects a symbolic death anchored in the H. festival, suffered by young people of both genders as representatives of their age group. The aetiological reference to a war shows H. as a divine paradigm of male youths, who, upon completion of their time as shepherds, were to be incorporated into the defence community of the adults before they officially belonged to it. It is for this reason that H. does not fight with the weapons of the → Hoplites, but rather with the scraper instrument of the athlete – a symbolic reference to the institutional context of the agonistic exercises that prepared male youths for later military service. H. takes his place next to → Heracles, the ephebe hero, as the patron god of palaestrae and gymnasia [9].

4. SATURNALIAN HERMES FESTIVALS

As a youthful shepherd, H. stands outside the normative system associated with agriculture and adult life. His mythical cattle theft was the paradigm of a behaviour that was, at best, tolerated only prior to the rite of initiation – as in Sparta, for instance, where juveniles were expressly given license to steal (Plut. Lycurgus 17,50ef; cf. 28,56e on the Krypteia). This also explains why Saturnalia-style festivals, which suspended or inverted the social order, were occasionally

dedicated to H. Samos had a sacrificial feast for H. Charidotes, during which everyone was permitted to steal. Allegedly, this was to commemorate a decade-long exile of the Samians to Mycale in Caria, during which they lived by robbery. In the end, the exiles were able to reconquer their island (Plut. Quaest. Graec. 55). This myth takes the period of licence in the shepherd phase of the life-cycle and projects it onto national history – for the initiates apparently performed the transition into adulthood in the knowledge of walking in the footsteps of their forefathers, who had reconquered Samos. It is unclear whether the slaves who were served at table by their masters during a H. festival in Crete (Ath. 14,639b) were shepherds. If so, the question is whether there were freeborn youths among them who were nominally considered as slaves during their time as shepherds, and whether participation in the festival implied a change in social status for these youths.

D. GOD OF MESSENGERS AND HERALDS

The messenger role given to H. in epic poetry may be derived from the secondary service functions that the young, mobile shepherds could be called upon to fulfil. Zeus sends him to other gods and to men in order to deliver instructions (Hom. Il. 24,333ff.; Od. 5,29f.). Mediating between heaven and earth, the Underworld and the world above, H. becomes the divine prototype of the interpreter and herald (Pl. Crat. 408ab). The authority-giving staff of the herald, which he holds in his hand, is a shepherd's staff endowed with new symbolic content. The ability to traverse great distances is given iconographic expression in the winged sandals that H. wears (see below, II). The function of the messenger who can travel across borders goes hand in hand with that of the guide who knows the roads. Just as H. leads the cattle, so does he provide escort for the heroes entrusted to him (Hom. Il. 24,336ff.; Aesch. Eum. 90–94): he brings the infant → Dionysus to Aristaeus or the nymphs (Apollod. 3,28; [1. 365ff.]) and → Pandora to Epimetheus (Hes. Op. 84f.); as psychopomp, he leads the souls of the dead to the Underworld, driving them with his golden shepherd's staff (Hom. Od. 24,1ff.); conversely, he also guides privileged figures such as → Heracles (Hom. Od. 11,626) or → Kore (H. Hom. 2,335ff.) back out of the realm of the dead again.

E. HERMES AS GOD OF THE MYSTERIES

As the god of transition and the mediator between gods and men, H. was the mythical prefiguration of the cult functionaries who organized the rites of the Mysteries. The Eleusinian priest family of the Kerykes ('heralds') traced itself to H. and Aglaurus [2], daughter of Cecrops (Paus. 1,38,3). In Samothrace, H. was equated with → Cadmus-Cadmillus, the mythical prototype of a cult servant assisting in the rites of initiation (schol. Lycoph. 162). Two ithyphallic statues of H. (Hippolytus, Refutatio omnium haeresium 5,8,10) here evoke the unspeakable symbolic acts performed in the inner sanctum of the temple (Hdt. 2,51; Cic. Nat. D. 3,56).

Prenuptial rites of sexual initiation are reflected in a great number of myths in which the god conceives children with nymphs (H. Hom. 5,262f.) or mortal girls (Hom. Il. 16,181ff.)

Anchored in the rites of puberty, the function of H. as → *mystagogos* in turn predestined the god to emerge as the *archegetes* of the secret documents circulated under his name in the Hellenistic period and late antiquity. Known as H. Trismegistus, he is equated with the Egyptian → Thot, and figures as the pseudonymous author of the esoteric literature now designated as hermetic (→ Hermetic writings). These writings are concerned with transmitting a totalizing cosmic vision and the path to redemption that depends upon it. In the first programmatic text of the → Corpus Hermeticum, the *Poemandres*, H., the future master of initiation, still occupies the prototypical role of the initiate, personally instructed by the *Nous*. The hermetic world view is, essentially, that of Plato's *Timaeus*: the seven planetary spheres separate the human spirit from its true home, which lies beyond the sphere of the fixed stars. → Eratosthenes [2] interpreted the seven-stringed lyre of H. as a symbol of the harmony of the spheres and portrayed H. as overcoming the distance between heaven and earth with his music (fr. 13 CollAlex). Does the ritual background of the hermetic visionary literature perhaps come to the fore here? The same Egyptian and Greek traditions are presupposed by the → magic papyri of late antiquity, which contain, e.g., instructions for rituals involving ecstatic visions of the gods and heavenly journeys. In the texts, H. is invoked as the mediator of cosmic knowledge (PGM 5,401ff.). In this respect, H. Trismegistus rivals the mythical → Zoroaster, the Iranian forefather of the sorcereres (→ Magic [10]).

1 G. Siebert, s.v. H., LIMC 5.1, 285–387   2 S. Eitrem, s.v. Hermai, RE 15, 696–708   3 D. Fehling, Ethnologische Überlegungen auf dem Gebiet der Altertumskunde, 1974, 7ff.   4 D. Furley, Andokides and the Herms, 1996   5 M. W. de Visser, Die nicht menschengestaltigen Götter der Griechen, 1903, 102f.   6 A. Athanassakis, From the Phallic Cairn to Shepherd God and Divine Herald, in: Eranos 87, 1989, 33–49   7 W. Burkert, Sacrificio-sacrilegio: il "trickster" fondatore, in: Studi Storici 25, 1984, 835–845   8 D. Baudy, Das Keuschlamm-Wunder des H., in: Grazer Beiträge 16, 1989, 1–28   9 Burkert, 247   10 G. Fowden, The Egyptian H., 1986.

G. Costa, H., dio delle iniziazioni, in: Civiltà classica e christiana 3, 1982, 277–295; J. Duchemin, La houlette et la lyre, 1960; L. Kahn, Hermès passe ou les ambiguités de la communication, 1978; K. Kerényi, H. der Seelenführer, 1944; Nilsson, Feste, 392–394; J. P. Vernant, Hestia-Hermès. Sur l'expression religieuse de l'espace et du mouvement chez les Grecs, in: Id., Mythe et pensée chez les Grecs I, (1965) 1980, 124–170; P. Walcot, Cattle Raiding, Heroic Tradition, and Ritual: The Greek Evidence, in: HR 18, 1979, 326–351.   G.B.

II. Iconography

In early vase images, H. appears almost exclusively as the messenger and escort of the gods. He wears a long robe or a short → chiton and a → chlamys that is often draped with fur, also the → petasos, and frequently winged sandals as well (François Krater, Florence, MA, 570/560 BC.). He is represented with or without a beard until the middle of the 5th cent. BC, when the youthful type becomes generally established. His characteristic attributes are the herald's staff (*kērýkeion/ caduceus*) and wings, either on his hat or his sandals. Animals that most often accompany his image are the cock, the dog, the goat, and the ram – as the Ram-bearer, H. Kriophoros (e.g., bronze statuette from Sparta, Boston, MFA, 510/500 BC). As psychopomp, H. leads the deceased to the Underworld (vase images, a few reliefs; also the statue of H. Andros-Farnese, London, BM and Athens, NM, after original of 350 BC). H. is the leader of the goddesses at the judgment of Paris (vase by the → Chigi Painter in Rome, VG, 640/630 BC). In many vase images, H. escorts the heroes Perseus, Theseus, Hercules, and Triptolemus. The assembly of the gods on the east frieze of the → Parthenon (442/438 BC) shows him together with Dionysus, in whose circle H. usually appears on vases of the 6th–5th cents. BC. H. takes part as a fighter in the → Gigantomachy (Siphnian Treasury in Delphi, ca. 525 BC; Parthenon in Athens, east metope 1, 447–441 BC).

Surviving sculptures include the Ludovisi H. (Rom, NM, 2nd cent. BC, after original of 450/440 BC; perhaps the oldest large-scale, sculptural representation of the god; Phidias?); the H. with the infant Dionysius (Polyclitus, *c.* 440–430 BC), probably the Boboli sculpture (Florence, formerly Giardino Boboli, 2nd cent. AD; cf. bronze statuette from Annecy, Paris, Petit Palais, 1st cent. BC–1st cent. AD); in the Polyclitan tradition, the Richelieu H. (Paris, LV, Antonine copy, orig. *c.* 360 BC); the H. of → Praxiteles from Olympia, also with the infant Dionysus (marble original?, *c.* 340/330 BC); the H. tying his sandals by → Lysippus (Copenhagen/ Paris, LV; attribution to Lysippus probable; *c.* 310/300 BC?); the seated H. by Lysippus (bronze, Naples, NM; after original, *c.* 330/320 BC?).

The → Herm pillars named after the god are in evidence from the late 6th cent. BC until well into the Roman Empire; → Alcamenes [2] sculpted the bearded H. Propylaios (end of 5th cent. BC: copy from Ephesus, Izmir Mus., Basmahane, 2nd half of 2nd cent. AD; Pergamum type, Istanbul, AM, copy, 2nd cent. AD). In the Hellenistic and Roman periods, the image of the god often served as a model for the representation of Hellenistic rulers and Roman dignitaries (cf. statue of the Numidian king Ptolemy in Rabat, Mus., early 1st cent. AD). The Roman H. (→ Mercurius) is represented as a youthful herald and escort; as the god of commerce and trade, he holds a → purse (*marsupium*); the *caduceus* adopted from H. has been considered a symbol of peace since the time of the Roman Republic.

J. FLOREN, Der H. des Polyklet, in: H. BECK, P. C. BOL (ed.), Polykletforsch., 1993, 57–72; J. İNAN, Der Sandalenbindende H., in: Ant. Plastik 22, 1993, 105–116; H. P. LAUBSCHER, Ein Ptolemäer als H., in: H. FRONING et al. (ed.), Kotinos. FS für E. Simon, 1992, 317–322; C. MADERNA, Juppiter, Diomedes und Merkur als Vorbilder für röm. Bildnisstatuen, 1988; H. OGGIANO-BITAR, Typologie de Mercure en Gaule. Akt. der 10. Internationalen Tagung über ant. Bronzen, 1994, 311–318; G. SIEBERT, s.v. H., LIMC 5, 285–387 (with older literature); E. SIMON, G. BAUCHHENSS, s.v. Mercurius, LIMC 6, 500–554 (with older literature).   A.L.

Hermesianax (Ἑρμησιάναξ; *Hermēsiánax*). Elegiac poet from Colophon, friend and pupil of → Philitas (schol. Nic. Ther. 3 = fr. 12 POWELL). He published an elegiac poem in three books, with the name of the woman he loved, Leontion, as title. In it, he recounted the experiences of famous people in love, drawing on myth and history. From the third volume 98 verses are preserved by Ath. 13,597b (= fr. 7 POWELL), showing how love conquered both poets (Orpheus, Musaeus, Hesiod, Homer, Mimnermus, Antimachus, Alcaeus, Anacreon, Sophocles, Euripides, Philoxenus, Philitas) and philosophers (Pythagoras, Socrates, Aristippus) and led them to make great sacrifices. The work, which was very probably modelled on the *Lýdē* by → Antimachus [3] of Colophon, can be categorized as catalogue verse based on the epic-Hesiodic model. At the same time the chronological order of the examples and the allocation of the poets to literary genres clearly demonstrates the influence of biographic-literary studies of the Peripatetic school. Some of the stories are highly improbable, pure inventions or fictitious connections: e.g. Homer is said to have fallen in love with Penelope, Hesiod with Eoia (!), both Alcaeus and Anacreon are supposed to have courted Sappho. This prompted the hypothesis [4] that H. was attempting to caricature the tendency of contemporary biography to deduce unfounded information from the texts and then use it to construct completely arbitrary interpretations. The influence of H. on subsequent Alexandrian catalogue verse seems to have been considerable.

Recently it has been suggested [3] that fragments of an elegy of the *araí* (→ Curse) genre, whose author threatens to tattoo on his enemy images of horrible mythological punishments (PSorb. inv. 2254 and PBrux. inv. E 8934) should be attributed to H.: the work treats, e.g., the myth of Eurytion, who, as Paus. 7,18,1 testifies, was also the subject of H.'s elegies (= fr. 9 POWELL).

1 O. ELLENBERGER, Quaestiones Hermesianacteae, thesis Gießen 1907   2 J. S. HEIBGES, s.v. H (2), RE 8, 823–28   3 M. HUYS, Le poème élégiaque hellénistique P. Brux. inv. E 8934 et P. Sorb. inv. 2254, 1991   4 P. BING, The Biostradition and Poet's Lives in Hellenistic Poetry, in: R. M. ROSEN, J. FARRELL (ed.), Nomodeiktes. Greek Studies in Honor of M. Ostwald, 1993, 619–31   5 A. HARDIE, Philitas and the Plane Tree, in: ZPE 119, 1997, 21–36.

CollAlex. p. 96–106.   M.D.MA.

Hermetic writings Hermetic writings (HW; the terminus is modern) are Graeco-Egyptian texts, whose author is supposed to have been the Egyptian god Thot, Greekified as Hermes Trismegistus. His epithet ('the thrice great H.'), which has only existed since the Imperial period, derives from the thrice repeated call to Hermes-Thot as 'the greatest' (which is already documented in Hellenistic Demotic and Greek sources). Clemens [3] of Alexandria (Strom. 6,4,35) describes a procession, in which 42 fundamental writings of Hermes on Egyptian religion were displayed, comprising hymns, astrology, cosmography, geography, medicine, ritual regulations and theology. Clearly, from a contemporary Graeco-Roman perspective, Egyptian religion is in part seen as an occult philosophy. The so-called → *Corpus Hermeticum*, 17 Greek writings which have been passed down complete in only two MSS and comprised theological-philosophical writings, has been preserved. Their background is mostly a 'vulgar Platonism', common among the educated especially in the Imperial period. An Egyptocentric, xenophobic attitude is very rare – astrology, alchemy and magic are only marginally important. The same applies to the Latin *Asclepius*, which is passed down in the corpus of the writings of the Platonist Apuleius [III], and to the 40 Greek texts and textual fragments in → Stobaeus and the three Coptic HW among the texts from → Nag Hammadi. Aside from this more or less closed field there are astrological, astrological-medical and alchemistical writings, which research [6] tends to ascribe to a 'popular' Hermetism. The collection of the *Kyranídes*, which describes the occult characteristics of stones, plants and animals, also claims to have been revealed by Hermes Trismegistus. Finally, Hermes Trismegistus is mentioned in the Greek and Demotic → magic papyri as a powerful deity knowledgeable in magic and a source of magical prescriptions. Whether or not the traditional separation between philosophy and popular HW is legitimate is under discussion. In any event, the collection of the *Corpus Hermeticum* that has been handed down to us is probably a Byzantine selection, edited by Christian scholars.

Augustine rejected the wisdom of Hermes with sustained success (Civ. 8,23). The ideas of the HW reached the High Middle Ages through Arab transmission and the pseudo-Apuleian *Asclepius* (school of Chartres, John of Salisbury), but it was only the interest in all things Platonic of Florentine Humanism that really brought the corpus into the European consciousness: In 1463 FICINO translated a Greek MS with 14 of the 17 treatises (Pimander, printed 1471); followed by the complete works (Patrizi 1591) and commentaries (Lefèvre d'Etaples, 1494), which led to a regular 'Hermolatry' in the 16th and early 17th cents., until Isaac CASAUBON exposed the supposedly ancient writings as dating from late antiquity (1614). Modern research started in the early 20th cent. with Richard REITZENSTEIN [5].

→ OCCULTISM

EDITIONS: 1 W. Scott, Hermetica, 1–4, 1924–1936
2 A. D. Nock, A.-J. Festugière, Corpus Hermeticum 1–4,
1945–1954   3 B. O. Copenhaver, Hermetica. The
Greek Corpus Hermeticum and the Latin Asclepius in a
New English Translation, 1992   4 J. Holzhausen,
Corpus Hermeticum, 1–2, 1993.
BIBLIOGRAPHY: 5 R. Reitzenstein, Poimandres. Stu-
dien zur griech.-ägypt. und frühchristl. Lit., 1904   6 A.-
J. Festugière, Hermétisme et mystique païenne, 1967
7 J. Doresse, L'Hérmetisme égyptisant, in: H.-C. Puech,
Histoire des religions 2, 1972, 430–497   8 G. Fowden,
The Egyptian Hermes. A Historical Approach to the Late
Pagan Mind, 1986.   F.G.

Hermias (Ἑρμίας; Hermías).

[1] (or Hermeias) Around 350 BC successor of Eubulus
as tyrant over → Atarneus and → Assos (Diog. Laert.
5,3), possibly pupil of Plato (Str. 13,1,57; Theopomp.
FGrH 115 F 250; by contrast Pl. Ep. 6,322e). Along
with other philosophers he brought Aristotle to the
court and married him to his niece → Pythias. After the
Persians had reconquered Egypt in 343/342, H. considered his region to be under threat and contacted → Philippus II (Dem. Or 10,31f. with schol.). For this reason,
Darius [3] III probably had him arrested and executed
in 341 (Diod.Sic. 16,52,1ff.). Callisthenes and Aristoteles praise his philosophical education and exemplary
conduct as ruler and during his execution (cf. Callisthenes FGrH 124 F 2; Aristot. fr. 674f. Rose), while
Theopompus criticized the life of H. in the form of a
moral didactic play in the Philippiká (FGrH 115 F 291).
A defensive alliance between 'H. and his companions
(ἑταῖροι)' and the Erythraeans (Tod, 165 = Stv 322)
points to the unusual regime of a hetairia or a collective
tyrannis. Didymus and Philodemus saw H. was an example of a Platonic Philosopher King. In Athenaeus he
is not listed among the students of Plato who became
tyrants. Hermippus of Smyrna, however, mentions him
in his writings on philosophers who became rulers.

H. Berve, Die Tyrannis bei den Griechen, 1967, vol. 2,
688f.; K. Trampedach, Platon, die Akademie und die
zeitgenössische Politik, 1994, 66–79.   J.E.

[2] Ptolemaic nesiarch (from Halicarnassus?), successor
of → Bacchon, founded the festival of Philadelphia on
Delos, where he is mentioned in the inventories from
267 BC.

PP 6,15042 (= 14915?); Ph. Bruneau, Recherches sur les
cultes de Délos, 1970, 528ff.; I. Merker, The Ptolemaic
Officials and the League of the Islanders, in: Historia 19,
1970, 141–160, esp. 153; R. Bagnall, The Administration of the Ptolemaic Possessions Outside Egypt, 1976,
138.

[3] Prior to 125/4 BC recorded as epistátēs (ἐπιστάτης)
of the Egyptian district of Perithebas, from 125/4 to
117/6 as stratēgós kai nomárchēs (στρατηγὸς καὶ
νομάρχης) of the districts Perithebas, Pathyrites, Latopolites; before April 119 he was promoted from the
rank of a tôn homotímōn toîs syngenési (τῶν ὁμοτίμων

τοῖς συγγενέσι) to syngenés (συγγενής) (→ Court titles
B 2).

L. Mooren, The Aulic Titulature in Ptolemaic Egypt,
1975, 116f., no. 0122.

[4] Son of an officer named Ptolemaeus (Perses), who
around 200 BC fled from the rebelling Thebans to
Ombi, where he remained even after the revolt was suppressed. H. is a soldier and officer in Ombi, tôn perì
aulēn diadóchōn kai hēgemṑn ep' andrôn (τῶν περὶ
αὐλὴν διαδόχων καὶ ἡγεμὼν ἐπ' ἀνδρῶν). A house in
Thebes vacated by Ptolemy had been in the possession
of a family of Theban Choachytes for most of the time
since 153: H. took legal action to have the property
returned (the files from the case before the various instances are in UPZ II 160ff.). H. lost the case, which
lasted from May/June 125 until December 117, as his
deeds of ownership had evidently been lost during the
flight.

P. W. Pestman, Il processo di Hermias e altri Documenti
dell'archivio dei Choachiti, 1992; Id., The Archive of the
Theban Choachytes, 1993.

[5] Epì tôn prosódōn (ἐπὶ τῶν προσόδων) in the Fayum
113 BC; PP 1,978.
[6] As tôn diadóchōn kaì epimelētés (τῶν διαδόχων καὶ
ἐπιμελητής) in Pathyrites c. 130/120 BC, epì tôn prosódōn (ἐπὶ τῶν προσόδων) in the Perithebas, Pathyrites
and Latopolites districts 112–108.

L. Mooren, The Aulic Titulature in Ptolemaic Egypt,
1975, 144, no. 0187.   W.A.

[7] Unknown, probably Christian author of a short
work deriding the teachings of the Greek philosophers
in 19 chs. (Διασυρμὸς τῶν ἔξω [φιλο]σόφων, CPG
1113). Committed to the doxographic tradition
(→ Doxography), H. represents various received opinions in a humorous way. In consequence, he rejects philosophy as a falsehood, the origins of which he sees in
the Fall of the Angels from God (1,4f.) At present the
work, which exhibits links to texts from the 2nd/3rd
cents. (cf. [1. 23]), is generally dated at around AD 200
[1. 67; 4. 811].

1 R.P. C. Hanson, D. Joussot, H. (SChr 388), 1993
(with summary 85–87, 94)   2 J. Leitl, A. Di Pauli, BKV
14 (Apologeten 2), 1913, 115–122 (Ger. trans.)   3 A. Di
Pauli, Die Irrisio des H., 1907   4 J.H. Waszink, s.v. H.,
RAC 14, 808–815.   J.RI.

Herminafrid
King of the Thuringians c. AD 507/511–
531/2. Around 510 he married → Amalaberga, the
niece of the king of the Ostrogoths → Theoderic the
Great, and thus became involved in his policy of alliances (Anon. Vales. 12,70; Cassiod. Var. 4,1; Iord. Get.
299; Procop. Goth. 5,12,22). H. initially ruled with his
brothers Baderic and Berthar. After their murder, he
was sole ruler until he was overthrown by the king of
the Franks → Theoderic c. 531/2. He died shortly afterwards. His territory became part of Franconia (Greg.

Tur. Franc. 3,4–8; Procop. Goth. 5,13,1f.). The Rodelinda, who married the King of the Lombards, → Audoin, may have been H.'s daughter (Procop. Goth. 8,25,11f.). PLRE 2,549f.   M.MEI.

Herminius Nomen gentile of a Roman family of Etruscan origin. After the expulsion of the Etruscan king at the beginning of the republic, it produced two consuls but then disappeared from history like most Etruscan families from the middle of the 5th cent. BC. The consul of 506 (T.H. Aquilinus) is mentioned, partly with his colleague Sp. Larcius (likewise of Etruscan origin), in the battle against the Etruscans and Latins (Liv. 2,10,6f.; 11,7–10; 20,8f.; Dion. Hal. Ant. Rom. 5,22,5; 23,2 and 4; 24,1; 6,1,3). The consul of 448, Lar(s) H. Coritinesanus (in Liv. the first name is Sp.), perhaps the son or grandson of H. Aquilinus, is attested in inscriptions (InscrIt 13,1,366f.), but is only known by his name (Dion. Hal. Ant. Rom. 11,51). MRR 1, 6 (T.H.) and 1, 50 (Lar H.).   W.ED.

Herminones H., → Ingaevones and → Istaevones are Germanic names for the original Germanic tribes traced back to the three sons of Mannus in the ancient mythological ethnogony of the Germans, based on an indigenous core, (Mannus genealogy) that was probably introduced to ancient literature by Posidonius and was gradually expanded under the influence of the Roman discovery of the north (Mela 3,32; Plin. HN 4,99f.; Tac. Germ. 2,2). Ethnically, spatially and socially the myth remains without context, and although the Roman conquerors did not find the tribal groups where they were actually to be expected, the Mannus pattern, adjusted to reality, lived on: according to Plin. l.c., the H., who included the Suebi, the → Hermunduri, the → Chatti and the → Cherusci, settled in the interior of Germania.

D. TIMPE, Romano-Germanica, 1995, 1–60.   K.DI.

Herminus (Ἑρμῖνος; *Herminos*). Peripatetic of the 2nd cent. AD, student of → Aspasius [1] whose view on the movement of the stars he quoted, and teacher of → Alexander [26] of Aphrodisias. Fragments of his commentaries on Aristotle's *Categoriae*, *Analytica Priora*, *De interpretatione* and *Topica*, and two comments on *De Caelo* are extant. His assumption that the eternity of the movements of the stars was caused by a heavenly soul probably goes back to Aristotle (Cael. 2,12).
→ Aristotle, commentators on; → Aristotelianism

H. SCHMIDT, De H. Peripatetico, 1907; MORAUX II, 361–398; H.B. GOTTSCHALK, Aristotelian Philosophy in the Roman World from the Time of Cicero to the End of the Second Century AD, in: ANRW II 36.2, 1158f.   H.G.

Hermion(e) (epigraphically and literarily Ἑρμιών; *Hermión* and Ἑρμιόνη; *Hermióne*, ethnikon Ἑρμιονεῖς; *Hermioneîs*). Town in the eastern area of the Argolid, modern Ermioni, whose territory comprised the south-

east of the area of Cape Thermisi 6 km east of H. to Cape Iri south of the Bedeni stream. H. owed its importance to the two well-protected harbours, separated by narrow, elongated foothills, the area of the old town. In Roman times H. was moved *c.* 700 m north-west to the eastern slope of the Pron mountain on which the acropolis was located (Paus. 2,34,10–11). Parts of the city wall, temple foundations, a theatre, baths and a large necropolis are preserved. Another necropolis proves that the town, mentioned also in Hom. Il. 2,560, already existed in Mycenaean times. H. was a member of the old → Amphiktyonia of Calaureia (Str. 8,6,14), but stood out little in the historical period. The original inhabitants are said to have been Dryopes (Hdt. 8,43; 73,2; Diod. Sic. 4,37,2; Str. 8,6,13). H. sent three ships to Salamis in 480 BC (Hdt. 8,43) and 300 men to Plataeae in 479 BC (Hdt. 9,28,4; Paus. 5,23,2; Syll.³ 31,15). In the Peloponnesian War, H. was allied with Sparta (Thuc. 1,27,2; 2,56,5; 8,3,2; Xen. Hell. 4,2,16; 6,2,3; 7,2,2), in 229 BC it was a member of the Achaean League (Pol. 2,44,6; Str. 8,7,3), temporarily allied with Cleomenes III (Pol. 2,52,2). It was plundered by pirates (Plut. Pompeius 24). Purple snail fishing is attested (Scyl. 51; Str. 8,6,11–14; Paus. 2,34,4–36,3; Ptol. 3,14,33).

M.H. JAMESON, Inscriptions of the Peloponnesos, in: Hesperia 22, 1953, 160–167; M.H. McALLISTER, A Temple at H., in: Hesperia 38, 1969, 169–173; P. LEVI (trans.), Pausanias. Guide to Greece, 1, 213–218; N. PHARAKLAS, Ἑρμιονίς – Ἁλιάς (Ancient Greek Cities 19), 1972.   Y.L.

Hermione (Ἑρμιόνη; *Hermióne*). Daughter of → Helene and → Menelaus (Hom. Od. 4,12ff.), sister of Nicostratus (Hes. fr. 175 M-W). According to one version of the myth, Menelaus promises her to → Neoptolemus outside the gates of Troy (Hom. Od. 4,3ff.), in another version she is promised to → Orestes before the war (Soph. Hermione TrGF 4, 192f.; Eur. Andr. 966ff.; Ov. Epist. 8, slightly different in Eur. Or. 1653ff.). Neoptolemus abducts her but is killed by Orestes (Eur. Andr. 993ff.; 1085ff.; Hyg. Fab. 122f.). Eur. Andr. makes the competition between the childless H. and the prisoner of war → Andromache, who has borne Neoptolemus a child, Molossus, his subject.

BIBLIOGRAPHY: L. KAHIL, s.v. H., LIMC 5.1, 388; W. OTTO, s.v. H., RE 8, 841–844.
FIG.: L. KAHIL, s.v. H., LIMC 5.2, 284.   R.HA.

Hermippus (Ἕρμιππος; *Hérmippos*).
[1] Writer of Attic Old Comedy, brother of the comedian → Myrtilus. Active probably around 440 BC: a Dionysian victory is attested for 435 BC [1. test. 3], on the epigraphical list of Dionysian victors H. ranks after → Pherecrates and before → Aristophanes [1] and → Eupolis [1. test. 4], and on the list of Lenaean victors after → Cratinus and Pherecrates and before → Phrynichus, Myrtilus and Eupolis [1. test. 5]. Apart from the

Dionysian victory a total of four Lenaean victories are recorded [1. test 5]; a total of ten titles of plays are extant. Apart from comedies, iambs [1. test. 8] and Παρῳδίαι/*Parōidíai* [1. test. 7] have also been attributed to H. Among the extant titles of plays, five refer to a parody of a myth (Ἀθηνᾶς γοναί; *Athēnâs gonaí*/'The Birth of Athene', the oldest attested comedy with the motif of a divine birth [2. 12–14]; Εὐρώπη/ *Európē*, Θεοί/*Theoí*: 'The Gods', Κέρκωπες/*Kérkōpes*: 'The Cercopes') or a tragedy (Ἀγαμέμνων/*Agamémnōn*), in the others H. proves himself to be a typical writer of the Old Comedy with a lot of political invective: in the 'Moirae' (Μοῖραι/*Moîrai*) of 430 BC against Pericles, who is accused of doing nothing in the face of the Spartan invasions of Attica (fr. 42; 47), and in the 'Female Bakers' (Ἀρτοπώλιδες/*Artopólides*) written soon after 421 (cf. Aristoph. Nub. 551–559 and [1. Ἀρτοπ. test.]) against Hyperbolus; an alleged attack by H. on Pericles' wife Aspasia should probably likewise be reinterpreted as a stage invective [1. test. 2 n.]. The 'Soldiers' (Στρατιῶται/ *Stratiôtai*) (or Στρατιώτιδες, 'The Female Soldiers'?) and the 'Basket Carriers' (Φορμοφόροι/ *Phormophóroi*) written before 424 (cf. fr. 63,7) of which fr. 63 offers a long and much-quoted hexameter passage (introduced by a parodistic invocation of the Muses) refer to the situation of Athens in the Archidamian War (431–421 BC).

1 PCG V, 561–604 2 H.-G. NESSELRATH, Myth, Parody and Comic Plots: The Birth of Gods and Middle Comedy, in: G. W. DOBROV (ed.), Beyond Aristophanes: Transition and Diversity in Greek Comedy, 1995, 1–27.   H.-G.NE.

[2] H. of Smyrna.

(Ath. 7,327c). Greek grammarian and biographer of the 3rd cent. BC, called 'the Callimachean' (ὁ Καλλιμάχειος; *ho Kallimácheios*, Ath. 2,58f; 5,213f), also 'the Peripatetic' (περιπατητικός; *peripatētikós*) – in this period the epithet describes a scholar in the field of literature and biography without necessarily containing a link with Peripatos. As H. reports on the death of → Chrysippus [2] (208/204 BC: Diog. Laert. 7,184), he must have lived approximately up to the end of the cent. As far as we know, he dedicated himself mainly to biography for which he used material and results from the library of Alexandria (→ Philology). H.'s comprehensive collection of *Bíoi* of famous men probably followed the *Pínakes* of his teacher → Callimachus, whose work he probably continued and completed. The extensive material appears to have been frequently used in the later biographical tradition (of → Plutarch, → Diogenes [17] Laertius, etc.): H.'s influence can also be seen from the fact that → Heraclides [19] Lembus wrote an epitome in the 2nd cent. (a fragment in POxy. 1367). The work was divided into sections and individual biographies: 'On the Legislators' (Περὶ νομοθετῶν; *Perì nomothetôn*) and 'On the Seven Wise Men' (Περὶ τῶν ἑπτὰ σοφῶν; *Perì tôn heptà sophôn*) are attested in Ath. 14,619b, Diog. Laert. 1,42 and POxy. 1367. 'On Pythagoras', 'On Aristotle', 'On Gorgias', 'On Hipponax', 'On Isocrates'. The credibil-ity of these writings, however, is questioned as the anecdotes are clearly an invention (cf. H.'s special interest in the circumstances of the deaths of the famous men). These, however, should be regarded as a literary genre feature for the characterization of the respective persons, but not as signs of a questionable approach with an emphasis on imagination. Finally H. wrote a (lost) astrological poem.

EDITIONS: FHG III, 35–54; WEHRLI, Schule, Suppl. I; SH, 245–46 (no. 485–90); CPF I 1**, 249–67 (no. 59).
BIBLIOGRAPHY: A. H. CHROUST, The Vita Aristotelis of Diogenes Laertius, in: AC 34, 1965, 97–129; Id., Aristotle's alleged revolt against Plato, in: JHPh 11, 1973, 91–94; I. DÜRING, Ariston or Hermippus? A note on the Catalogue of Aristotle's writings, in: Classica et Mediaevalia 17, 1956, 11–21; Id., Aristotle in the Ancient Biographical Tradition, 1957, 464ff.; J. ENGELS, Der Michigan-Pap. über Theramenes und die Ausbildung des "Theramenes-Mythos", in: ZPE 99, 1993, 125–55; C. FRIES, Zu H. von Alexandria, Wochenschrift für klass. Philol. 21, 1904, 1043ff.; I. GALLO, in: CPF I 1, 249–257; J. S. HEIBGES, s.v. H. (6), RE 8, 845–852; F. LEO, Die griech.-röm. Biographie, 1901, 124ff.; A. MOMIGLIANO, The Development of Greek Biography, ²1993; F. MONTANARI, in: CPF I 1, 258–265; P. MORAUX, Les listes anciennes des ouvrages d'Aristote, 1951, 221–222; P. VON DER MÜHLL, Ant. Historismus in Plutarchs Biographie des Solon, in: Klio 35, 1942, 89–102; G. E. PESELY, The origin and value of the Theramenes Papyrus, in: Ancient History Bull. 3, 1989, 29–35; PFEIFFER, KP I, 125, 163, 188–89, 301; F. SUSEMIHL, Gesch. der griech. Lit. in der Alexandrinerzeit, 1891–1892, I, 492–495.

[3] H. of Berytus

(a village in the interior of Phoenicia, not from the town on the Mediterranean Sea), Greek grammarian from the Hadrianic period (Suda ε 3045, s.v. Ἕρμιππος; ν 375, s.v. Νικάνωρ; ι 706, s.v. Ἴστρος; α 97, s.v. Ἄβρων; etymology with 118,14, s.v. Ἀπάμεια). The child of slaves and later freed, H. was a student of → Herennius Philon of Byblus and thus gained access to the circle around the Roman politician → Herennius [II 12] Severus. Of his works only a few fragments are extant (in some cases the question of attributing the works to him or to H. [2] of Smyrna is still unresolved): important and famous in antiquity was his biographical work (influenced by his teacher) 'On the Different Education of Slaves' (Περὶ τῶν ἐν παιδείᾳ διαπρεψάντων δούλων; *Perì tôn en paidía diaprepsántōn doúlōn*).

SCHMID/STÄHLIN II, 2, 805, 868; FHG III, 35–36, 51–52; J. S. HEIBGES, s.v. H. (8), RE 8, 853–54; S. MAZZARINO, Il pensiero storico classico, II/2, 134–35, 173, 177–79; F. SARTORI, Ermippo di Berito, schiavo e storiografo, in: Index 10, 1981, 260–70; WEHRLI, Schule, Suppl. I, 106.   F.M.

Hermochares

(Ἑρμοχάρης; *Hermochárēs*). Nicander (Heteroieumena 3 = Antoninus Liberalis 1) applies – in a parallel to, or an adaptation (1, 2 with [1. 71 A11]) of the tale of Acontius and → Cydippe (Call. Aitia fr. 65–75) – the motif of throwing an apple to H. of Athens and Ctesylla, the daughter of Alcidamas of Iulis on Ceos;

finally the two flee together to Athens. After the death and disappearance (*aphanismós*) of Ktesylla in the form of a dove (in Carthaea: Ov. Met. 7,368–370, cf. [1. 72 A20; 2]), an oracle instructs H. to establish a sanctuary in Iulis (aetion for the cult of an Aphrodite Ktesylla or Ktesylla Hekaerge: cf. [1. 72 A22] with a reference to the parallels in Antoninus Liberalis 23: Aspalis).

1 M.PAPATHOMOPOULOS (ed.), Antoninus Liberalis, Les Métamorphoses, 1968　2 F.BÖMER, P. Ovidius Naso, Metamorphosen, Komm. zu B. VI–VII, 1976.　　　　T.H.

Hermocles (Ἑρμοκλῆς; *Hermoklês*).

[1] From Cyzicus. Around 300 BC author of → paeans on → Antigonus I and → Demetrius [2] Poliorcetes [4] (lost) and an ithyphallos on the latter [1; 2] (fully extant). Addressing traditional religious poetry no longer only to gods but also to rulers was in keeping with the general common practice of the Hellenistic ruler cult [3].

EDITIONS: 1 CollAlex 173–175　2 D.EBENER, Griech. Lyrik, ²1980, 426 (Ger. trans.).
BIBLIOGRAPHY: 3 C.HABICHT, Gottmenschentum und griech. Städte (Zetemata 14), ²1970, 148, 232f. 4 L.KÄPPEL, Paian, 1992, Test. 7.　　　　L.K.

[2] Bronze sculptor of Rhodes. According to Lucian, H. created for Seleucus Nicator (312–285 BC), in the Hera sanctuary of Hierapolis, a statue of → Combabus, the first gallos (→ Cybele, → Syria Dea), who was represented as a woman dressed in men's clothing.

OVERBECK, no. 2044 (sources).　　　　R.N.

Hermocrates (Ἑρμοκράτης; *Hermokrátēs*).

[1] Syracusan statesman and general. Became prominent for the first time at the peace conference of Gela in 424 BC and successfully invited the Sicilian Greeks with the slogan 'Sicily to the Siceliots' to settle the internal disputes (Thuc. 4,58–64). In 415 he recommended the formation of a coalition against Athens reaching beyond Sicily (Thuc. 6,32,3–34). Initially chosen as one of three authorized *strategoi*, but soon, like his colleagues, deposed because of his lack of success (Thuc. 6,73,1; 103,4), he then became the most important assistant and adviser of → Gylippus and had a decisive part in the victory over the Athenians. Against Diocles he stood up in vain for lenient treatment of the Athenian prisoners (Diod. Sic. 13,19,4–6). In 412, when sent as admiral to Asia Minor, he was exiled in his absence by the radical democrats after the loss of his ships in the naval battle of Cyzicus (Xen. Hell. 1,1,18). In 408 he returned to Sicily and successfully operated in the Carthaginian epicracy, but was suspected of tyrannical ambitions and therefore was not recalled to Syracuse (Diod. Sic. 13,63). In a failed surprise attack on Syracuse in which Dionysius [1] was also involved, he fell in the street battle in 407 (Diod. Sic. 13,75). Praised by Thucydides (4,58–64; 7,73) and Xenophon (Hell. 1,1,30f.) as a statesman and patriot.

A.ANDREWES, The Peace of Nicias, in: CAH 5, ²1992, 433–463, esp. 446ff.; D.ASHERI, Sicily, in: CAH 5, ²1992, 147–170; B.CAVEN, Dionysius I., 1990, 21ff.; G.MADDOLI, in: E.GABBA, G.VALLET (ed.), La Sicilia antica, vol. 2.1, 1980, 74ff.; H.D.WESTLAKE, H. the Syracusan, in: Bull. John Rylands Library 41, 1958, 239–268 = Id., Essays on the Greek Historians and Greek History, 1969, 174ff.　　　　K.MEI.

[2] **L. Flavius H.** Sophist from Phocaea, around AD 200, great-grandson of → Polemon. Philostratus praises his talents (VS 2,25,608), partly to criticize H.' teacher Claudius Rufinus (Rufinus IK 24,1,602), his appearance and his ποικιλία (*poikilía*; diversity), but condemns his extravagant lifestyle (ibid. 610). Emperor Septimius Severus, who admired his speech, once gave him 50 talents of incense, but also forced him into a marriage that was only short-lived (195 or 197–199) to an ugly daughter of Antipater of Hierapolis, with whom he took part in Caracalla's → *consilium* between 200 and 205 (IK 16,2026). Prior to his death at the age of 25 or 28 he was honoured in the Asclepieum of Pergamum as an *archiereús* and philosopher [1; 2].
→ Philostratus; → Second Sophistic

1 Altertümer von Pergamon 8.3,76–79 no. 34　2 PIR F 285.　　　　E.BO.

[3] *Syngenēs, stratēgós* (συγγενής, στρατηγός) and *epistratēgós* (ἐπιστρατηγός) of the Thebaid in 116/5 BC.

L.MOOREN, The Aulic Titulature of Ptolemaic Egypt, 1975, 94, no. 057.　　　　W.A.

[4] H. of Miletus. Son of Alexander, tragedian. According to DID A 6,1b he was once victorious at the Amphiaraea/Rhomaea in Oropus after 85 BC.

METTE, 56; TrGF 167.　　　　F.P.

Hermocreon

[1] Greek architect of the 3rd cent. BC; according to Str. 10,5,7 and 13,1,13, he built a state altar, 1 stadium long (→ Measures), from the material of an abandoned temple near Parium; it is presumably depicted on coins (London, BM) and could be compared with the Hieronian monumental altar of → Syracusae.

OVERBECK, 2086–2087 (sources); G.A.MANSUELLI, s.v. H., EAA 4, 1961, 13 (with fig. 18).　　　　C.HÖ.

[2] Epigrammatist whose existence cannot be proven with certainty; two poems are attributed to him which, on the basis of their style and content, can be dated to the 3rd cent. BC; the attribution by Anth. Pal. 9,327 (a dedication of gifts that a certain H. offers to the Nymphs originating from the 'Garland' of Meleager), however, can be derived from the poem, whilst 16,11 (about a statue of Hermes) is attributed to Plato by *Sylloge Euphemiana*.

GA I 1, 106; 2, 305f.　　　　M.G.A.

Hermodamas (Ἑρμοδάμας; *Hermodámas*). Descendant of the Homerid Creophylus of Samos (cf. [1]), probably 6th cent. BC. Is said to have been the teacher of Pythagoras in old age (Neanthes FGrH 84 F 29 = Porph. vita Pythagorae 1; Antonius Diogenes p. 136 STEPHENS-WINKLER = Porph. ibid. 15; Diog. Laert. 8,2; cf. Apul. Flor. 15; Iambl. VP 9 and 11; [2]).
→ Homerids; → Creophylus; → Pythagoras

1 W. BURKERT, Die Leistung eines Kreophylos, in: MH 29, 1972, 77f. 2 M. DETIENNE, Homère, Hésiode et Pythagore, 1962, 13f. C.RI.

Hermodorus (Ἑρμόδωρος; *Hermódoros*).
[1] In a fragment of the philosopher → Heraclitus [1] of Ephesus, the latter criticizes his fellow citizens because they had banished H., the 'most estimable man' among them, with the justification that among them 'no one should be the most estimable' (DIELS/KRANZ 22,121 = Str. 14,1,25; Cic. Tusc. 5,105). According to later tradition, H., who went into exile in Italy, was involved in the drawing up of the Twelve Table Laws (→ Tabulae duodecim). For Pliny it was this H. whose statue was on the Comitium (Plin. HN 34,21).

K.-J. HÖLKESKAMP, Schiedsrichter, Gesetzgeber und Gesetzgebung im archa. Griechenland, 1999, 102ff.
E.S.-H.

[2] **H. of Syracuse.** Student of Plato and author of one of the first biographical works, 'On Plato' (Philod. Academicorum index 6,6–10, according to Timaeus), which Diogenes Laertius also cites (2,106 and 3,6). H. furthermore offers a testimony for the Platonic lecture 'On the Nature of the Good' (cf. Testimonium Platonicum 31 GAISER) that is independent of the notes of Aristotle. He sold the dialogues of Plato in Sicily (Philod. ibid.; also Zenobius 5,6 = 1, 116 LEUTSCH-SCHNEIDEWIN); hence the comic verse λόγοισιν Ἑρμόδωρος ἐμπορεύεται ('H. makes profit with the dialogues (sc. of Plato)'; on this Cic. Att. 13,21,4).

EDITIONS: M. ISNARDI PARENTE, Senocrate – Ermodoro. Frammenti, 1982. K.-H.S.

[3] Syrian epigrammatist from the 'Garland' of Meleager (Anth. Pal. 4,1,43f.). Only one poem which is attributed to him by Planudes is extant (ibid. 16,170; the epigram 9,77, the one that is attributed to him by the latter as an alternative to → Ariston [6], is not by him): two distichs in which the Cnidian Aphrodite of Praxiteles is compared unfavourably with the Athenian Pallas of Phidias. It is hard to decide whether the poem is a variation or a model of the anonymous epigram 16,169.

GA I 1, 107; 2, 306f. M.G.A.

[4] Greek architect of the 2nd cent. BC; according to Vitruvius (3,2,6), he built the temple of Jupiter Stator in Rome in the Porticus Metelli and with it perhaps the very first Roman marble temple (cf. Vell. Pat. 1,11,3 and 5).

E. FABRICIUS, s.v. H. (8), RE 8, 861f. (sources); P. GROS, H. et Vitruve, in: MEFRA 85, 1973, 137–161; M. B. MARZANI, s.v. H., EAA 4, 1961, 11. C.HÖ.

Hermogenes (Ἑρμογένης; *Hermogénēs*).
[1] Athenian, son of Hipponicus, brother of Callias, appears on many occasions in the Socratic writings of Plato and Xenophon as the companion of → Socrates. Together with the eponymous character, H. is the dialogue partner of Socrates in Plato's *Cratylus*.

1 SSR VI B 71–77 2 DAVIES, 269–270. K.D.

[2] H. from Aspendus. In the struggle of Antiochus [2] I (died in 261 BC) to regain territories in Asia Minor after the murder of his father Seleucus I he campaigned against towns in northern Asia Minor as an assistant commander of Patrocles, and he made a treaty with Heraclea on the Pontus. In the subsequent campaign against Bithynia he was ambushed and perished together with his army (FGrH 434 F 1,9,1–2).
[3] One of the commanders of Antiochus III in 219 BC in the siege of Seleucea in Pieria (Pol. 5,60,4). A.ME.
[4] According to Vitruvius (3,2,6), a Hellenistic → architect from Alabanda; an inscription found in Priene could be the reason why he is assumed to have come from this town [2]. Questions of dating connected with his work are contested. The periods after 220 BC and 130 BC provide key figures for discussion [9]. An inscription found in 1963 gives clear indications for an early dating [4]. The most important source on H. is → Vitruvius who refers repeatedly to H. According to him, H. designed the temple of Artemis in → Magnesia on the Maeander (Vitr. De arch. 3,2,6) whose beauty is emphasized by Strabo (14,647), and the temple of Liber Pater in → Teos (Vitr. 3,3,8). H. wrote about both buildings (Vitr. De arch. 7, praef. 12). He is said to have invented the → pseudodipteros with the temple of Artemis and to have realized eustyle → proportions in the temple in Teos in the peripteros described as hexastyle. However Vitruvius (7, praef. 12) describes this building as a → monopteros whose type he (4,8,1) defines as a baldachin-like circular building without cella so that the typological characterization of the temple in Teos as hexastyle remains hard to understand. Regarding the temple of Liber Pater in Teos (Vitr. De arch. 4,3,1–2), it is also said that H. had the material already prepared for a temple of the Doric order reworked later because of the problems with the triglyph frieze (→ Angle triglyph problem) and constructed a building in the Ionic order. Probably this supposed process should not be understood too literally [7], although the tale is best suited to characterizing H. as a master builder who was a patron of the Ionic building order.

As both the temple in Teos [11] and the one in Magnesia [6] are in principle well known, the ideals claimed for H. can be compared with concrete traditions. The findings uncovered in Teos, which to a large extent go back to a Roman imperial revival, appear, however, in a rather sceptical light. It is indeed a hexastylos of the Ionic order but by no means a building whose intercolumniations, at a ratio of 2¼ of the column diameter, correspond to eustyle proportions. Instead, the plan is so close to that of the temple of Athena designed by → Pytheus in → Priene that – if the temple that has become well known in Teos were actually to go back to a design of H. – the building would rather raise the question of whether H. could not on the contrary have come from the tradition of Pytheus. The temple of Artemis in Magnesia can be connected with H. with greater certainty. Its dating to the period of H. is likewise debatable, as is its pseudodipteral type. However, with this building H. would have had to dispense with the eustyle pillar arrangement that was advocated by him. Instead, such proportions could be found in the small temple of Zeus Sosipolis on the agora of Magnesia [3].

The tradition, in accordance with which H. is said to have invented the pseudodipteros, does not bear critical examination, for temples with large roof spans were already known in ancient times [5. 2f.]. It appears to be more accurate that after the architecture of the classical period had obviously made no use of this type variant, it was revived again in Hellenism and systematized by H. Apparently this temple shape was particularly in keeping with contemporary taste: shadows used to striking effect and strong contrasts emphasize the width of the peripteros accented to provide effect [1]. Column bases and the entablature with the frieze show that the great temple in Magnesia was also enriched with atticisms [10]. The eustyle column arrangement too need not have been an ideal of architecture produced for the first time and individually by H. Such proportions can have come from a further development of design concepts that already arose in a previous period [8]. In this respect H. probably stands out less for his new architectonic solutions than for the unerring development of formulas by which diverse models and sources could be updated according to the contemporary style [5. 10–16]. In the writings which allow us to understand H. as a pioneer of → architectural theory, he seems to have included the sum of his knowledge and his experiences in order to pave the way for particular architectural ideals.

1 H. DRERUP, Zum Artemistempel in Magnesia, in: MarbWPr 1964, 13–22   2 P. GROS, Le dossier vitruvien d'Hermogénès, in: MEFRA 90, 1978, 697–700   3 G. GRUBEN, Die Tempel der Griechen, ³1980, 388f. 4 P. HERRMANN, Antiochos der Große und Teos, in: Anatolica 9, 1965, 29–33   5 W. HOEPFNER, Bauten und Bed. des H., in: W. HOEPFNER, E. L. SCHWANDNER (ed.), H. und die hochhell. Architektur, 1990, 1–34   6 C. HUMANN et al., Magnesia am Mäander, 1904, 39–83 7 H. KNELL, Die H.-Anekdote und das E. des dor. Ringhallentempels, in: Vitruv-Kolloquium des Dt. Archäologenverbandes, 1984, 41–64   8 Id., Der jüngere Tempel des Apollon Patroos auf der Athener Agora, in: JDAI 109, 1994, 228   9 M. KREEB, H. Quellen- und Datierungsprobleme, in: W. HOEPFNER, E. L. SCHWANDNER (ed.), H. und die hochhell. Architektur, 1990, 103–113 10 U. SCHÄDLER, Attizismen an ion. Tempeln Kleinasiens,

in: MDAI(Ist) 41, 1991, 301–312   11 D. M. UTZ, The Temple of Dionysos at Teos, in: W. HOEPFNER, E. L. SCHWANDNER (ed.), H. und die hochhell. Architektur, 1990, 51–61.

G. DE BONFILS, H., in: Index 9, 1980, 183–192; E. FABRICIUS, s.v. H. (29), RE 8, 879–881; W. HOEPFNER, E. L. SCHWANDNER (ed.), H. und die hochhell. Architektur, 1990; W. MÜLLER, Architekten in der Welt der Ant., 1989, 160f.; F. W. SCHLIKKER, Hell. Vorstellungen von der Schönheit des Bauwerks nach Vitruv, 1940, 22–26; B. WESENBERG, Beitr. zur Rekonstruktion griech. Architektur nach lit. Quellen, 9. Beih. MDAI(A), 1983, 95–100.
                                                              H.KN.

[5] Sculptor from Cythera. On the agora of Corinth, Pausanias (2,2,8) saw an Aphrodite by H. that was perhaps reproduced on coin images and that corresponds to the type of the armed Aphrodite of Cythera.

H. BRUNN, Gesch. der griech. Künstler, 1, 1857, 522; J. FLEMBERG, Venus armata. Stud. zur bewaffneten Aphrodite in der griech.-röm. Kunst, 1991, 102–104; OVERBECK, no. 2074 (sources); C. K. WILLIAMS II, Corinth and the cult of Aphrodite, in: Corinthiaca, 1986, 15–18.   R.N.

[6] Painter from Antioch who worked between AD 175 and 205 in Carthage. According to Tertullian (Adversus Hermogenem 1) the bad way of life of the womanizer H. was reflected in the tasteless content of his paintings. The actual reason for this tendentiously negative criticism was probably the opposing views of the Stoic heretic who was to be defamed as a bad Christian.

M. DURST, s.v. H., LThK³ 5, 12; J. H. WASZINK, Tertullian: The Treatise against H., 1956.   N.H.

[7] H. of Tarsus. Greek rhetor, c. AD 160–230; reliable reports about his life are provided only by Philostratus (VS 2,7 = 577f.; cf. Syrian in WALZ 4,30, n. 101), all other details are based on speculation, invention and mistakes from the Byzantine period (cf. [9. 868]). At the age of 15 he had already achieved such mastery of the art of oratory that he aroused the admiration of the emperor Marcus Aurelius with his declamations and improvized lectures. However, as an adult, he was no longer active as an orator for reasons unknown, which made him the object of mockery by his contemporaries. When he died in old age, he enjoyed neither fame nor popularity.

Five pieces of writing under his name have been passed down to us.: 1) Περὶ ἰδεῶν (Perì ideôn), his most important work and the most sophisticated treatise from antiquity on the systematic recording and evaluation of stylistic characteristics. H. replaces the Peripatetic concept of the three types of style (→ genera dicendi) by a categorization of characteristic stylistic expressions (idéai); by means of a fine subdivision he arrives at a total of 18–20 (depending on the means of counting). Each idéa is systematically described and documented with rich material, mostly from Demosthenes. Stylistic mastery, he says, arises through accomplished mixing of the *idéai*, which in Demosthenes reaches a perfection not seen elsewhere.

2) Περὶ τῶν στάσεων (*Perì tôn stáseōn*): H. varies and refines the *stasis* theory defined by → Hermagoras [1]: especially through subtle subdivision of the question of quality (*poiótēs*), he distinguishes 13 types of → status that are not geared to oratorical practice but exclusively to fictitious contentious matters of the rhetoric school. The degree of dependence on earlier theoreticians and hence the extent of H.' independent achievement cannot be determined here for certain as in *Perí ideôn*, however the latter has been emphasized in recent research.

3) Περὶ εὑρέσεως (*Perì heuréseōs*), a work divided into four main parts (proemium, narration, evidence, figures of speech) that in its present form certainly does not go back to H. but was probably designed by an editor in the Byzantine period. Perhaps the same person also compiled the three works 1)–3) clearly designed as individual writings under the title passed down to us of *Téchnē rhētorikē*.

4/5) Experts agree today that the two writings Προγυμνάσματα (*Progymnásmata*) and Περὶ μεθόδου δεινότητος (*Perì methódou deinótētos*) are not by H., but were written in about his period.

The work of H., which did not initially receive much attention (however, the rhetor → Menander wrote a commentary as early as the 3rd cent.), had a far-reaching effect from late antiquity onwards (commentary of Syranus, Sopater, etc.) and progressed in the Byzantine age to become a widespread, often commentated (Maximus Planudes, Gregorius of Corinth, et al.) and important standard work for schools. In western Europe too the stylistic theory of H. in particular has been received intensively since Humanism.

1 E. Bürgi, Ist die dem H. zugeschriebene Schrift Περὶ μεθόδου δεινότητος echt?, in: WS 48, 1930, 187–197 und 49, 1931, 40–69   2 D. Hagedorn, Zur Ideenlehre des H., 1964   3 G. A. Kennedy, Greek Rhetoric under the Christian Emperors, 1983, 96ff.   4 G. L. Kustas, Stud. in Byzantine Rhetoric, 1973, 5–62; 127–199   5 G. Lindberg, Stud. in H. and Eustathios, 1977   6 M. Patillon, La théorie du discours chez H. le rhéteur, 1988   7 A. M. Patterson, H. and the Renaissance, 1970   8 L. Pernot, Anecdota rhetorica. Un résumé d'H. et d'Aphthonios, in: Révue d'Histoire des Textes 10, 1980, 55–73   9 L. Radermacher, s.v. H. (22), RE 8, 865–877   10 I. Rutherford, Inverting the Canon: On Literature, in: HSPh 94, 1992, 355–378   11 B. Schouler, La classification des personnes et des faits chez H. et ses commentateurs, in: Rhetorica 8, 1990, 229–254   12 B. P. Wallach, Ps.-H. and the Characterizing Oath, in: GRBS 22, 1981, 257–267   13 C. W. Wooten, Dionysius of Halicarnassus and H. on the Style of Demosthenes, in: AJPh 110, 1989, 576–588.

Editions: H. Rabe, 1913 (repr. 1985).

Transl. and comm.: M. Heath, H. on Issues, 1995; M. D. Reche Martinez, Téon, H., Aftonio, Ejercicios de retórica, 1991; C. Ruiz Montero, H., sobre las formas de estilo, 1993; C. Wooten, H. Tarsensis – On Types of Style, 1987.   M.W.

[8] **Aurelius H.** Proconsul of Asia between AD 286 and 305 (CIL III 7069), 30 October 309 – 8 October 310 city prefect of Rome (Chron. min. 1, 67 Mommsen).   B.BL.

[9] *Magister equitum* under Constantius II (Amm. Marc. 14,10,2; Sozom. Hist. eccl. 3,7,6), probably from Tyre (Lib. Ep. 828), Arian. In the winter of AD 341/2 he was given a command in Thrace and simultaneously the order to banish the Nicene bishop of Constantinople, Paulus. The Nicene townspeople however opposed imperial control, supported their bishop, set H.'s house on fire and killed him (Socr. 2,13; Sozom Hist. eccl. 3,7; Lib. Or. 59,94ff.; Jer. Chron. 235 Helm; Historia acephala 1,4 Martin). H. had a son, Herculanus (Amm. Marc ibid.). PLRE 1, 422f. (H. 1).

[10] Born in Pontus, not a Christian, possibly began his career as a page of Licinius (Himerius Or. 48,18 Colonna). After studying philosophy he became an imperial adviser, later probably *quaestor sacri palatii* under Constantine [1] the Great (Himerius or. 48,28ff.). Probably appointed *proconsul Achaeae* after AD 337. He is possibly identical to the city prefect of Rome of 349/350 (Chron. min. 1,68f. Mommsen). In 358 H. was elevated to the rank of *praefectus praetorio Orientis* (Lib. Or. 1,115f.; Cod. Theod. 1,7,1). Ammianus and Libanius, who were his friends, praise his gentleness (Amm. Marc. 19,12,6; Lib. ibid.). In winter 359/360 he resigned from office (Lib. Ep. 138) and died in 361 (Amm. Marc. 21,6,9). PLRE 1, 423ff. (H. 3, see also H. 2 and H. 9).   M.R.

[11] see → Little-master cups

Hermogenianus Jurist from the Hellenistic east of the Roman empire, from AD 293 to 295 *magister libellorum* (head of the petition office) of Diocletian [1; 3], published in AD 295 the *Codex Hermogenianus*, a semi-official collection of rescripts of Diocletian from 293 and 294. Excerpts were taken from the collection in the → *Fragmenta Vaticana*, in the → *Collatio legum Mosaicarum et Romanarum* and in the → *Consultatio* and adopted by the *Codex Justinianus* (Haec, pr.; Summa § 1). H. also wrote the legal breviary *Juris epitomae* (6 bks.; re [2]) from which excerpts were taken probably at the latest in the Digests of Justinian.

1 PLRE I, 425f.   2 D. Liebs, Hermogenians Iuris epitomae. Zum Stand der röm. Jurisprudenz im Zeitalter Diocletians, 1964   3 Id., Recht und Rechtslit., in: HLL 5, 62ff.   T.G.

Hermolaus (Ἑρμόλαος; *Hermólaos*).
[1] Son of Sopolis, page (→ Basilikoi paides) of → Alexander [4], pre-empted the king in the slaying of a wild boar and was humiliatingly punished by him (327 BC). In revenge he hatched a conspiracy among the pages but it failed and was betrayed to the king. The accused, after being tortured, were sentenced to death and stoned with the consent of the army. → Callisthenes, hated by Alexander as an opponent of → proskynesis, was suspected of incitement because he was the teacher of the

pages. Although he was not accused by any of the boys he was arrested somewhat later (Plut. Alexander 55).

Berve 2, no. 305.   E.B.

[2] Sculptor whose period of creativity is unknown and whose works were used to decorate the imperial palace on the → Mons Palatinus; he worked together with Polydeuces.

Overbeck, no. 2300 (sources).   R.N.

Hermolochus (Ἑρμόλοχος; *Hermólochos*). Author of several lines regarding the imponderables and hopes of life. In Stob. 4,34,66 (also in Phot. Bibl. 167) he is called H. in two MSS, and Hermolaus in one MS. [1. 637] attributes this fragment to a Hermodotus and rearranges two verses; [2] maintains the attribution to H. but slightly changes the colometry. The dactyloepitritic verses show traces of the Doric in Stobaeus. Modern editors have made further conjectures with regard to the Doric elements.

1 Th. Bergk, Poetae Lyrici Graeci III, ⁴1882   2 PMG 846
3 SH 491–493.   E.R.

Hermon
[1] Mountain massif (maximum height 2,814 m) south of the Antilebanon; Hebrew *Ḥærmôn* (from *ḥrm* 'ban, taboo'), Greek Ἀερμών; *Aermón*, Latin *Hermon*, modern *Ǧabal aš-Šaiḫ*, 'mountain of the white-haired man' /*Ǧabal aṯ-Ṯalǧ*, 'snow mountain'. Dt 3:9 equates H. with Phoenician *Siriōn* and Amorite *Senīr*, hence H. would be found as *Šryn* in Ugaritic, *Šarijana* in Hittite and *Saniru* in Assyrian. Biblical tradition considers H. to be the northern border of the land conquered by Moses and Joshua east of the Jordan (Jos 11:17; Dt 3:8). From the biblical references it is not clear whether H. describes the whole Antilebanon (→ Antilibanus) or only its northern and southern foothills. Josephus (Ant. Iud. 5,3,1) does not speak of H. but only of 'Mount Lebanon' (→ Libanus); Eusebius (On. 20,12) describes only the southern foothills as H. On the south-western summit are the remains of an ancient temple facility (Qasr-ʿAntar) from the 1st–4th cents. AD. A Greek inscription found there was directed at anyone who did not refrain from coming closer in spite of a curse. A total of over twenty temple compounds, which correspond typologically with Canaanite open-air sanctuaries, were found within the H. area. In the Bible the H. was already considered to be the dwelling-place of the god Baʿal Ḥærmôn (Judg. 3:3; 1 Chr 5:23) (→ Baal). In the 1st cent. AD, temples of the classical building type were added. In the Hellenistic period H. belonged to the kingdom of the Ituraeans of Chalcis (→ Ituraea).

R. Arav, s.v. H., The Anchor Bible Dictionary 3, 1992, 158–159; Sh. Dar, s.v. H., NEAEHL 2, 616–617.
TH.PO.

[2] Athenian; in 411 BC he took part in the revolt of the taxiarch → Aristocrates [2] against the Rule of the Four

Hundred as a commander of the army of occupation in Munichia (Thuc. 8,92,5). The idea that he killed the oligarch → Phrynichus in 411 is based on a misunderstanding of Plutarch (Alcibiades 25,14). In 410/409 he was the commander in Pylus (IG I³ 375,10).
[3] from Megara, helmsman (κυβερνήτης; *kybernétēs*) on the ship of the Spartan fleet commander → Callicratidas in the battle at the Arginusae in 406 BC (Xen. Hell. 1,6,32) and on the ship of → Lysander at Aegospotamoi in 405 BC (Dem. Or. 23,212; cf. Xen. Oec. 4,20); honoured with a statue in the group of Lysander in Delphi (Paus. 10,9,7f.).   W.S.
[4] from Delos. From the Hellenistic period, between 319 and 167 BC [1], he is mentioned by Porphyrius, appears to have written poetry about bird omens (schol. bT ad Il. K 274–5 Erbse, III, 57–58; Porph. Quaestiones Homericae 1,154,23 Schrader = CollAlex 251–252) and on divination from lightning (Porph. ibid. 1,39,7 where, however, Ἕρμων ὁ Δήλιος [*Hérmōn ho Délios*] is a correction of Meinecke).

1 U. v. Wilamowitz-Moellendorff, Euripides: Herakles, vol. II, 1889, 135f.   S.FO.

Hermonaktos kome (Ἑρμώνακτος κώμη; *Hermónaktos kómē*). Settlement at the mouth of the → Tyras (Str. 7,3,16) or at a distance of *c.* 16.5 km from it (Ptol. Geog. 3,10,7). Perhaps identical with the remains of an ancient settlement near modern Kosovka.

M. V. Arbunov, K voprosu o lokalizacii bašni Neoptolema u Germonaktovoj derevni [On the problem of locating the tower of Neoptolemos and H.K.], in: VDI 1, 1978, 43–51.   I.v.B.

Hermonassa (Ἑρμώνασσα; *Hermónassa*).
[1] Greek port on the Asiatic bank of the Cimmerian → Bosporus [2], on the southern coast of the Bay of Taman, founded as a colony of Ionians and Aeolians before the middle of the 6th cent. BC. Imports and coins attest to lively trade. H. was situated in the tribal area of the Sindi (Str. 11,2,10) whose upper class also lived in H. (rich kurgans). Main cults: Apollo Ietros, Delphinius, Artemis, Aphrodite (Ps.-Scymn. 886–889; Arr. Peripl. p. eux. 60 and others).

V. F. Gaidukevič, Das Bosporanische Reich, 1971, 221–225.   I.v.B.

[2] Greek trading-post on the southern coast of the → Pontus Euxinus west of Trapezus, possibly near Akçaabat (formerly Polathane), 'medium-sized colony' (κατοικία μετρία; *katoikía metría*, Str. 12,3,17), tentatively identified by [1] with Liviopolis (Plin. HN 6,4,11).

1 W. J. Hamilton, Reisen in Kleinasien 1, 1843, 233.

Olshausen/Biller/Wagner, 135; C. Marek, Stadt, Ära und Territorium in Pontus-Bithynia und Nord-Galatia (IstForsch 39), 1993, 19.   E.O.

Hermonax

[1] Attic red-figure vase painter whose signature is to be found on 10 of the *c.* 200 vases attributed to him by scholarship. He worked between 475 and 450 BC and was a pupil of the → Berlin Painter. Of the vessel shapes, he preferred stamnoi, pelikai, neck amphorae, lutrophoroi and cups, with the latter particularly showing the influence of → Macron. The inside of a cup in Brauron (Archaeolog. Mus. A. 39) is decorated in white-ground technique. H. preferred scenes of pursuit, komos and Dionysian scenes; on some of his vases rather rare themes are also to be found, for instance Philoctetes being bitten by a snake (Paris, LV G 413). The signed vases come from the first half of his period of creativity, later works are less careful and show less variation. Although he was technically very experienced, H. produced no paintings of the creative quality for which his teacher is famous. A pelike from London (BM E 410) that was regarded previously as his most valuable work is today considered to be the name-giving piece of his important successor, the 'Painter of the Birth of Athena'.

BEAZLEY, ARV², 483–492; 1655–1656; 1706; BEAZLEY, Paralipomena, 379f.; 512; C. ISLER-KERÉNYI, The H. in Zürich I, II, III, in: AK 26, 1983, 127–135; AK 27, 1984, 54–57; 154–165; F. P. JOHNSON, The Late Vases of H., in: AJA 49, 1945, 491–502; Id., The Career of H., in: AJA 51, 1947, 233–247; H. E. LANGENFASS, Unt. zur Chronologie, PhD thesis München 1972; N. WEILL, Un cratère d'H., in: BCH 86, 1962, 64–94.   J.O.

[2] of Delos. Writer of 'Cretan glosses', consulted by Ath. 3,81f and 6,267c (both times quoted under the name *Hérmōn*, to whom a register of synonyms perhaps also goes back (cf. Ath. 11,480f) [1].

1 E. DEGANI, Hipponax. Testimonia et fragmenta, 1983, 186   2 A. GUDEMAN, s.v. H. (3), RE VIII 1, 899–900.
                                                          S.FO.

Hermonthis

Town on the western bank of the Nile, 20 km south of Luxor, capital of the 4th Upper Egyptian district, Egyptian *jwnj* or *jwnj šm'j*, 'Upper Egyptian → Heliopolis', or *jwnw mnṯw*, the 'Heliopolis of Month', Greek H. The chief god is Month, household and royal god of the rulers of the 11th dynasty (20th cent. BC); his temple is attested from that time, was destroyed in the Persian period and restored in the 30th dynasty. The worship of the bull Buchis with its own necropolis (Bucheum) is significant. After the decline between the 3rd and 1st cents. BC, H. is again the capital city of the district in the Roman Imperial period; in the Coptic period it is a bishop's seat.

A. EGGEBRECHT, s.v. Armant, LÄ 1, 435–441; R. MOND, O. H. MYERS, Temples of Armant, 1937; Id., The Bucheum, 1934.   R.GR.

Hermotimus

[1] Prisoner of war from Pedasa, who, according to Hdt. 8,104f., as a eunuch, had become one of the closest confidants of → Xerxes I and is said to have taken his revenge on the slave trader Panionius (Ath. 6,266e attests that the story was well known).

→ Eunuchs

1 P. BRIANT, Histoire de l'empire perse de Cyrus à Alexandre, 1996, 283–288   2 P. GUYOT, Eunuchen als Sklaven und Freigelassene, 1980, Register s.v.   J.W.

[2] of Colophon, mathematician. He continued (according to Eudemus) the study of → Eudoxus [1] and Theaetetus and found many theorems contained in the 'Elements' and several τόποι (*tópoi, loci geometrici*) (Procl. in Euc. I p.67, 20–23 FRIEDLEIN).

T. L. HEATH, History of Greek Mathematics, vol. 1, 1921, 320f.   M.F.

Herms

Hermai (ἕρμαι/*hérmai*, 'Hermes heads'), also *hermádion* ('small Hermes'), *schêma tetrágōnon*, *tetráglōchis*, describes in Graeco-Roman art a special form of anthropoid freestanding sculpture. The herm consists of a pillar with a head, mostly with wooden lateral beam stumps instead of arms (*cheîres, cunei*) and a male sexual organ attached at the front that is always ithyphallic in early herms. Double herms bear two heads turned away from each other. Three- and fourfold herms on one pillar are also to be found. In Arcadian herms up to five pillars are connected and placed next to each other. The human form is more extensively executed in foot herms, shoulder herms, hip herms and full-body herms on which the body mostly grows with the abdomen out of the shaft, more rarely already on the thighs. Garment herms, in which the transition from pillar to body is left unclear are frequently used for female herms.

Herms are derived from aniconic stone monuments that were erected from pre-classical times on crossroads, borders, entrances and tombs for → Hermes as the god of transition. The canonical form was created in Attica when Hipparchus had 130 herms with epigrams erected on the roads (522–514 BC). Their rapid spread is documented through vase painting. The Hermes herms that were initially always bearded were to be found from the 5th cent. BC in Athens in sanctuaries (Hermes Propylaios of → Alcamenes [2]) and they were used on the Agora to record documents and in gymnasia as Hermes Logios for conveying an educational ideal. Their religious importance is proven by the Hermokopidai scandal (→ Herms, mutilation of the) of 415 BC. From the 4th cent. BC the circle of gods and mythological beings represented by means of herms is increasingly widened, but the fertility symbolism of the phallic herms is preserved by the limitation to the Dionysian-Aphrodisian circle. Theseus and Hercules follow the Hermes Logios of the gymnasia. Priapus herms arose from wooden posts and are therefore shaped as head herms with a shaft tapering downwards. In Hellenistic landscape and sacred reliefs herms are an ever-present feature of a place. Accordingly herms also appear as supporting figures on Dionysian-Aphrodisian statues.

The use of herms for contemporary portraiture starts with Roman sculpture in the 1st cent. BC, encouraged by the tradition of Italian head cippi (→ *cippus*). Whether they should initially be interpreted as an indication of the fertility of the → genius of the person painted in the portrait is debatable. Soon herms become a cost-saving practice for the erecting of portraits which is probably why portraits of emperors are not created as herms before late antiquity. With historical portraits mostly of spiritual heroes from the 1st cent. BC the function of the Greek gymnasium herms is transferred to the garden décor (→ Garden) of villas (Villa dei papiri [1]). By creating lines of herms, galleries of them arose that could be connected into railings. In late antique herm-galleries, the form became independent with a selection of whatever head was desired (Welschbillig [2]) so that they could also be put up in a Christian ambience.

A functional spread of herms in Roman times brought their use in architecture as supports, railing parts, fountain courses or on a small scale in furniture. → Hermathena; → Wood; → Cult image

1 R. NEUDECKER, Die Skulpturenausstattung röm. Villen in Italien, 1988, 65–67, 105–114   2 H. WREDE, Die spätantike Hermengalerie von Welschbillig, 1972.

J. L. KEITH, Herms of Egypt, 1975; R. LULLIES, Die Typen der griech. Herme, 1931; P. MINGAZZINI, s.v. erma, EAA 3, 1960, 420–421; A. STÄHLI, Ornamentum Academiae. Kopien griech. Bildnisse in Hermenform, in: Acta Hyperboraea 4, 1992, 147–172; H. WREDE, Die antike Herme, 1986; Id., Die spätantike Herme, in: JbAC 30, 1987, 118–148.   R.N.

Herms, mutilation of the In summer 415 BC, shortly before the Sicilian expedition, all → Herms in Athens were damaged in one night. The citizens saw in this a bad omen for the enterprise. The posting of high rewards for informers led to the discovery of a further religious heinous deed: the desecration of the Eleusinian Mysteries (→ Mysteria) in the private houses of some rich citizens. → Alcibiades [3], initiator of the Sicilian expedition, was accused of participating in both crimes. In the 'witch hunt' that followed there were ever new denunciations, arrests and executions. Whilst the Mutilation of the Herms in older research is often dismissed as a 'boyish prank', modern interpreters again follow the assessment of Thucydides and see in the attack on the ever-present herms that were considered typically Athenian a purposeful raid of an oligarchic → *hetairia* on traditional religion and the democratic order. Sources: Thuc. 6,27–29; 53; 60f.; And. 1.

W. D. FURLEY, Andokides and the Herms, 1996; G. A. LEHMANN, Überlegungen zur Krise der attischen Demokratie im Peloponnesischen Krieg, in: ZPE 69, 1987, 33–73; R. OSBORNE, The Erection and Mutilation of the Hermai, in: PCPhS 211, 1985, 47–73.   E.S.-H.

Hermunduri The Germanic combat unit that was probably based on fealty, together with Suebi and Semnones in the mythical original tribe of the → Herminones (Plin. HN 4,100), pinpointed in the Augustan period as being located at the Elbe (Str. 7,1,3; Vell. 2,106,2), had possibly already lost its political and organizational connection at that time. H., searching for land, were settled by → Domitius [II 2] in 6/1 BC in the former Marcomannis (Cass. Dio 55,10a,2), possibly as a strategic help against the Suebian fluctuation that had increased through Roman occupation and was directed towards Bohemia and southern Germany (cannot be limited to Franconia: [1]). Under Vibilius the northern H. drove out → Catualda in AD 19 (Tac. Ann. 2,62f.) and overthrew Vannius around 50 (ibid. 12,29f.); shortly afterwards they defeated the → Chatti in the battle for the salt of the border river (ibid. 13,57; [2]). The *Hermundurorum civitas* (cf. CIL III 14359,4) neighbouring Raetia had *commercium* and free access to the province of Raetia (Tac. Germ. 41; [3; 4. 80–82; 5]). In the Marcomanni Wars the H. were opponents of Rome (SHA Aur. 22,1; 27,10). The central German H. were probably decisive for the ethnogenesis of the Thuringians [6; 7. 475], whilst the southern H. probably merged with the fighting units of the → Iuthungi [8. 234, 236f.].

1 D. TIMPE, Erwägungen zur histor. Einordnung des augusteischen Truppenlagers von Marktbreit, in: BRGK 72, 1991, 315f.   2 J. HERRMANN (ed.), Griech. und lat. Quellen zur Frühgesch. Mitteleuropas bis zur Mitte des 1. Jt. u. Z., III, 1991, 531f.   3 G. PERL, Tacitus, Germania, 1990, 240–242   4 R. WOLTERS, Der Waren- und Dienstleistungsaustausch zw. dem Röm. Reich und dem Freien Germanien, in: Münstersche Beitr. zur antiken Handelsgesch. 10, 1991, 78–132   5 K. DIETZ, in: W. CZYSZ, K. DIETZ, T. FISCHER, H.-J. KELLNER (ed.), Die Römer in Bayern, 1995, 202f.   6 K. PESCHEL, Die Thüringer der Völkerwanderungszeit zw. Arch. und Gesch., in: Wiss. Zschr. Jena (Gesellschafts- und sprachwiss. Reihe) 35, 1986, 561–574   7 B. SCHMIDT, Das Königreich der Thüringer und seine Prov., in: W. MENGHIN (ed.), Germanen, Hunnen und Awaren, 1988, 471–480   8 T. STICKLER, Iuthungi sive Semnones, in: Bayerische Vorgeschichtsblätter 60, 1995, 231–249.   K.DI.

Hermupolis magna 300 km south of Cairo on the western bank of the Nile, Egyptian Ḥmnw, 'Town of the eight', after a group of four pairs of ancient gods, modern al-Ašmunein, Greek Hermupolis magna (HM) after → Hermes Trismegistus, who was worshipped there and was equated with the town god → Thot. In the sacred precinct there are remains of the temples of the Pantheon of HM from the middle kingdom to the Roman Imperial period. Under the Ptolemies and Romans HM again experienced a period of flourishing. From the Coptic period, remains of a settlement and a basilica (5th cent. AD) are preserved.

D. KESSLER, s.v. H., LÄ 2, 1137–1147.   R.GR.

Hermus (Ἑρμός; *Hermós*).
[1] Attic *asty* deme of the phyle Acamantis, with two *bouleutaí*. Position: on the 'Sacred Road' to Eleusis at the entrance to the pass near modern Daphni, modern Chaidari; there is the tomb of Pythionice, the wife of Harpalus (Plut. Phoc. 22,2; Paus. 1,37,5; [1]). Near Daphni there are funerary inscriptions of *Hermeioi*: IG II² 6072.

> 1 N.D. PAPACHATZIS, Παυσανίου Ἑλλάδος Περιήγησις. Ἀττικά, 1974, 468 with n. 6.

> W. KOLBE, s.v. H., RE VIII 1, 903; TRAILL, Attica, 47, 69, 110 no. 54 table 5. H.LO.

[2] River in western Asia Minor, modern Gediz nehri or çayı, has its origin in the Dindymus (modern Murat Dağı), forms flood plains in the valley of the central and lower reaches with tributaries and branches (→ Kurupedion), flows north past → Sardeis and → Magnesia on the Sipylus and has its mouth, often with displaced branches, in the bay of Smyrna (in antiquity *Hérmeios kólpos*, 'H. bay'); advancing delta surrounding the mouth with spits of land there (the Myrmekes Cliffs, i.e. 'Ant' Cliffs, which had been offshore in antiquity). Evidence: cf. Hom. Il. 20,392; Hes. Theog. 343; Hdt. 1,55; 80; 5,101; Scyl. 98,4; Str. 12,3,27; Plin. HN 5,119 [1. 237]; Arr. Anab. 1,17,4; 5,6,4; 7; Ptol. 5,2,5 ('H. of Aeolis').

Because of the threat that the bay could silt up, the mouth branch is today again being directed further north to the west to the outer bay (canal linking it to the ancient river bed built in 1886 near Menemen) where in ancient times the mouth of the H. lay south of Phocaea and Larisa, once further upstream near Temnos (Hdt.; Plin. loc.cit.). The river god H. is represented on coins from Magnesia on the Sipylus and other towns on the H.

> 1 G. WINKLER, R. KÖNIG, C. Plinius Secundus d.Ä., Naturkunde (Lat.-Ger.), vol. 5, 1993 (comm.).

> travel map Türkiye-Türkei, Turkish Ministry of Defence/ Kartograph. Verlag Ryborsch, Obertshausen near Frankfurt/M., 1994, sheet 2; W. M. RAMSAY, The Historical Geography of Asia Minor, 1890, 59f., 108; W.-D. HÜTTEROTH, Türkei, 1982, 65f. H.KA.

Hernac (Ἡρνᾶς; *Érnâs*, Ἡρνάχ; *Érnách*). Youngest son of Attila (Priscus fr. 8 = FHG 4, 93), after the defeat of the Huns in AD 455 settled with his retinue in the north of the province of Scythia (Iord. Get. 266). Because of a peace treaty, in 466/7 he and → Dengizich sent envoys to Leon I (Priscus fr. 36 = FHG 4, 107). PLRE 2, 400f. (Ernach). ME.STR.

Hernici Italian people in Latium on the → Liris and its tributary Trerus or Tolerus (modern Sacco); here lay Anagnia, Ferentinum and Frusino on the *via Latina*, and further inland Verulae, Aletrium and Capitulum Hernicum. Possibly attested from the beginning of the Iron Age, they appear to have been the oldest Italian

people who immigrated to Latium, possibly in connection with the migrations of the Sabini (Serv. Aen. 7,684) or Marsi (Paul Fest. 89 L.). Laevus Cispius of Anagnia supported Tullus Hostilius against Alba Longa and gave the mountain Cispius its name. The H. were temporarily members of the Latin League (Liv. 2,40). They were subjugated by Rome in 306 (Liv. 9,43,23). From the time of Augustus in the *regio I* (Plin. HN 3,63f.). Their settlement area was the modern Ciociaria. Iron Age settlement near Colleferro, sanctuaries below Anagnia (8th–5th cent.) and in Osteria della Fontana near *compitum Anagninum*, where the *lucus Dianae* was probably located near the *circus Maritimus*, the centre of the H. (Liv. 9,42,11; 27,4,12).

> M. MAZZOLANI, Anagnia, 1969; C. LETTA, I Marsi, 1973; S. GATTI, A. ASCENZI (ed.), Dives Anagnia, 1993. G.U.

Hero (Ἡρώ; *Hērō̄*). Priestess of Aphrodite in Sestus, mistress of Leander. As H.'s parents stand in the way of marriage, Leander swims the Hellespont each night from Abydus to Sestus where H. awaits him in a tower. When the torch that shows the way goes out on one occasion, he drowns. H. throws herself off her tower when she catches sight of the body of her lover. The tale has been passed down coherently for the first time in a small epic of → Musaeus from the 5th cent. AD. A further version is provided by Ov. Epist. 18 and 19. There are also mentions in Verg. G. 3,358ff.; Str. 13,1,22; Ov. Ars am. 2,249f.; Ov. Tr. 3,10,41f. On a papyrus there are 10 lines from an adaptation of the material [1]. A Hellenistic elegy is assumed to be the common source. The motif also appears in art for the first time from the 1st cent. BC.

> 1 H. LLOYD-JONES, P. PARSON (ed.), Supplementum Hellenisticum, 1983, fr. 951.

> H. FÄRBER, H. und Leander: Musaios und die weiteren antiken Zeugnisse, 1961; A. KOSSATZ-DEISSMANN, s.v. H. und Leander, LIMC 8.1 (Suppl.), 619–622; G. SCHOTT, H. und Leander bei Musaios und Ovid, PhD thesis Köln 1956; E. SITTIG, s.v. H., RE VIII 1, 909–916; K. VOLK, H. und Leander in Ovids Doppelbriefen (epist. 18 und 19), in: Gymnasium 103, 1996, 95–106. K.WA.

Hero (Ἥρων; *Hérōn*).
A. LIFE B. WORKS C. AFTER-EFFECT

A. LIFE
H. of Alexandria, mathematician and engineer. No details of his life are known. He lived after → Archimedes [1], whom he quotes, and before → Pappus, who quotes him. In the *Dioptra*, ch. 35, H. describes a method for determining the time difference between Rome and Alexandria by observing the same eclipse of the moon at both locations. It is quite likely that this eclipse occurred in AD 62 and that H. probably observed it himself in Alexandria [10. 21–24].

B. Works

H. wrote numerous works on mechanics, pneumatics, surveying and the production of machines. The authorship of many of the documents is uncertain and some may well be revised textbooks from the Byzantine period. H. is not very original. His significance lies in the way he summarizes existing knowledge in the form of a handbook.

1) H. wrote a commentary on the 'Elements' by Euclid [3], of which Greek fragments have been handed down in Proclus (In Euc. I) and Arabic fragments in the commentary on Euclid by an-Nairīzī. In this H. examined, among other things, the meaning of the axioms and presented alternative proofs and generalizations of theorems [8. 310–314].

2) The 'Definitions' (Ὅροι/Hóroi; ed. [1. vol. 4, 1–169]), which present 133 explanations of geometrical terms – partly going beyond Euclid – are preserved as part of a Byzantine collection of mathematical principles. Units of measurements are also converted. The extant text is probably a later adaptation.

3) The Metrica (Μετρικά, 3 bks.; ed. [1. vol. 3, 1–185] and [3]), unknown until 1896, contain directions for measuring plane and curved surfaces (bk. 1), and bodies (bk. 2), and for dividing surfaces and bodies (bk. 3). Practical arithmetical rules with numeric examples alternate with strict geometric proofs, which are very concise. The document contains, among other things, the formula for the area of a triangle (1,8), named after H., but already known to Archimedes.

4) Several collections handed down in H.'s name, but probably compiled later, are based on the Metrica: the Geometrica (equivalent to Metrica, bk. 1; ed. [1. vol. 4, 171–449]) and Stereometrica (equivalent to Metrica, bk. 2; ed. [1. vol. 5, 1–162]) contain practical examples which are calculated as a template. De mensuris (Περὶ μέτρων/Perì métrōn, 'On Measures'; ed. [1. vol. 5, 163–219]) is an inferior compilation of geometrical rules. The collection entitled Geodaesia (Γεωδαισία/Geōdaisía; ed. [1. vol. 5, LXX–XCIII]) contains excerpts from the geometric sections of the Metrica.

5) The Dioptra (Περὶ διόπτρας/Perì dióptras; ed. [1. vol. 3, 187–315]) describes competently a complicated sighting instrument, a kind of theodolyte, which can be used in a variety of ways by surveyors, astronomers and engineers, e.g. for land surveys, canal and tunnel constructions and for determining distances in the sky. Attached is the description of an automatic road measuring device.

6) A 'Catoptrics' (ed. [1. vol. 2, 301–365]), handed down in the name of Ptolemy, probably originates from H. This work, known only in the Latin translation by Wilhelm von Moerbeke, illustrates the basic principles of reflection on plane, convex and concave mirrors and also arrangements of distorting mirrors, which are reminiscent of H.'s 'Automata' (see no. 9).

7) The 'Mechanics' (Μηχανικά/Mēchaniká) (3 bks.), which (apart from fragments) is known only from the Arabic translation by Qustā ibn Lūqā (ed. in [1. vol. 2, 1–299]), is addressed to engineers and architects. Bk. 1 deals with the construction of a winch with toothed gearing (βαρουλκός/baroulkós), geometric principles of similar figures, the production of instruments for representing plane and three-dimensional figures true to scale, and elementary principles of statics. Bk. 2 contains the theory of the five simple machines (→ Winch, lever, block and pulley, cf. → lifting devices, wedge, screw) and further principles of statics. Bk. 3 gives instructions on the construction, use and operation of machines of daily usage.

8) The 'Pneumatics' (Πνευματικά/Pneumatiká, 2 bks.; ed. in [1. vol.1, 1–333]), H.'s most comprehensive work, has links with → Ctesibios and → Philo of Byzantium. It could be the preliminary stage for a textbook, of which only the beginning was finalized. Here, the compression and suction of air and water are employed to drive utility objects or to produce devices for spectacular demonstrations. In the introduction the existence of the vacuum is discussed. H.'s conception of matter ranges between Aristotle and the Atomists.

9) In the work on producing automata (Περὶ αὐτοματοποιητικῆς/Perì automatopoiētikês, 2 bk.; ed. [1. vol. 1, 335–453]) two kinds of automata are described: mobile ones, which are imitations of processional vehicles, and stationary ones in a display cabinet. Both are driven by weights which turn shafts by means of cords. On the principle of water clocks an even course is achieved by placing the driving weight on a filling of sand or grain, which gradually runs out, thus defining the course of the movement (cf. → Automata with fig.).

10) The Belopoiika (Βελοποιικά/Belopoiiká; ed. [2]) deal with the individual parts and the production of artillery weapons (→ Catapults), comprising bow-type weapons, heavy hand weapons, as well as arrow and stone catapults. The work ends with formulae, based on experience, for the ratio between the weight or length of the projectile and the calibre.

11) Extant only as fragments are: Baroulkós (Βαρουλκός/Baroulkós), probably just the special title of a section of the 'Mechanics' (see [1. vol. 2, XXIII–XXV; ed. [1. vol. 2, 256–267]); it describes a machine for lifting heavy loads. The Cheirobalistra (Χειροβαλίστρας κατασκευή/cheirobalístras kataskeué) deals with the individual parts of a projectile machine. Works by H. on water clocks and vault construction are lost.

C. After-effect

Many rules for calculating surfaces and volumes found in H. and already known in a similar fashion to the Egyptians and the Babylonians were also used by the Roman agrimensori and, through their writings, were widespread in the west throughout the Middle Ages. H.'s works were also well known among the Arabs, especially the works on mechanics, but also the Metrica, which were used by an-Nairīzī and al-Ḫwārizmī et al. The 'Heronic Formula of the Triangle', among others, was again accessible in the west from the 12th cent. [4. 635–657] through the translations from Arabic. H.'s works were very popular in the Renaissance, especially the 'Pneumatics' and the 'Automata', which served as the inspiration for similar works of art. → Euclides [3]

EDITIONS: 1 W. SCHMIDT, L. NIX, H. SCHÖNE, J. L. HEIBERG, Heronis Alexandrini opera quae supersunt omnia, 5 vols. in 6 parts, 1899–1914 (Greek-Arabic-German) 2 H. DIELS, E. SCHRAMM, Herons Belopoiika (Schrift vom Geschützbau), 1918 (Greek-German) 3 E. M. BRUINS, Codex Constantinopolitanus Palatii Veteris no.1, 3 vols., 1964.
BIBLIOGRAPHY: 4 M. CLAGETT, Archimedes in the Middle Ages, vol. 1, 1964 5 A. G. DRACHMANN, Ktesibios, Philon and Heron. A study in ancient pneumatics, 1948 6 Id., The mechanical technology of Greek and Roman antiquity, 1963 7 Id., M. S. MAHONEY, Hero of Alexandria, in: GILLISPIE, vol. 6, 1972, 310–315 8 T.L. HEATH, History of Greek Mathematics, vol. 2, 1921, 298–354 9 J. MAU, s.v. H., KlP 2, 1106–1109 10 O. NEUGEBAUER, Über eine Methode zur Distanzbestimmung Alexandria-Rom bei Heron, 1938–1939 11 SEZGIN, vol. 5, 151–154 12 C. R. TITTEL, s.v. H. (5), RE 8, 992–1080.
M.F.

Hero cult

Hero cult (HC) is the cult worship of a particular group of superhuman beings whom the Greeks describe as heroes from the time of Homer (ἥρωες, hḗrōes); the etymology of the word is unclear, and the modern link with → Hera is problematical [1]. The HC uses both the form of the common Olympian sacrifice as well as more specific cult forms. In the course of the development of Greek religion, various groups have been subsumed under the category of heroes, from original gods to real deceased people [2].
A. THE MYTHS   B. THE CULT   C. THE INTERPRETATIONS

A. THE MYTHS

In Bronze Age Greece, heroes are perhaps presupposed by the ti-rise-ro-e ('three times hero', PY Tn 316) who could be understood like the later → Tritopatores as an ancestor worshipped in cult [3]. In Homer hḗrōes always designate the human protagonists of the epic, not cult figures, but this is epic stylization: the Homeric warriors are radically separated from the present time of the narrator and tombs where HC was practiced are sometimes mentioned. The fact that a historical and essential distance to the person of Homer's own time is implied is shown in Hesiod's myth of the World Ages (→ Period), where the group of hḗrōes interrupts the descending series of metals (adopted from the Middle East) from gold to iron: the heroes, the fourth of fifth races, are better than the third bronze race, they are demigods (hēmítheoi) who fought in the epic battles for Thebes and Troy and whom Zeus placed on the Islands of the Blessed (Hes. Op. 156–173). In this way they are indeed mortal but have taken up an abode between

gods and men and are semi-divine; this remains the common Greek view that is only modified by the Platonic introduction of the daímones (→ Demons) as lower interim beings. In the genealogies of the pseudo-Hesiodic 'Catalogues' ('Ehoiai', see Hesiod [1]) all the heroes live between Deucalion's Flood (→ Deucalion) and a generation after the end of the Trojan War; at the beginning of each genealogical line there is the link between a god and a heroine.

As deceased humans, most heroes not only have a biography but also a story about their death and a tomb, and they are far more ambivalent than the gods. Their place of residence is thought to be the depths of the earth from which they send blessings as well as punishment for offenders (Aristoph. Heroes [4]) and sometimes also appear themselves to bring help (Theseus and Marathon on Polygnotus' painting of the battle, Paus. 1,15,3). Well before the Imperial period, when they are invoked in magic, heroes can be sinister and dangerous dead; the hero of Temesa in lower Italy had to be pacified each year by the deflowering of a girl (Paus. 6,6,4–11), and the Boeotian hero Actaeon had to be depicted chained (Paus. 9,38,5). From the 5th cent. BC at the latest, historical persons can become heroes and be accorded a cult; during Hellenistic times this spread to such an extent that older scholarship considered that the term had been totally devalued. This is hardly tenable because the decisive feature always remains that the dead person understood as a hero suffered a remarkable death (for instance he died young) and an influence beyond the grave develops that is greater than that of other deceased (in this way he can have a special protective function or also appear only in dreams) [5].

The archaeological material has always shown more clearly that HC, to the extent that it is archaeologically provable, does not start until the 8th cent. BC. In many cases the worship of epic heroes was probably linked with previously anonymous graves from the Mycenaean period whose owners had long been forgotten. The renaissance of the 8th cent. thus provides itself with a past rooted in epic storytelling and only imagined continuity with the Bronze Age past [6; 7]. The same is repeated in the subsequent period again and again and also spreads to Italy; in this way in the 4th cent. the cult of → Aeneas [1] in Lavinium is linked with a grave from the 7th cent. [8], even though Roman religion does not know the category of the hero but speaks continuously of gods (dei) and often equates epic heroes with old gods (Aeneas with → Indigenes and Romulus Quirinus). In addition individual poleis or their subcategories (for instance the Athenian → phyles reformed by Cleisthenes) give themselves mythical or historical founding heroes or construct their past in other ways through HC [9; 10; 11]; this continues for a long time into the Imperial period in the political discourse of Greek towns. Moreover heroes, i.e. former humans, are often closer to the individual with his worries than the gods. That is why we find numerous cults in which heroes are active as bestowers of blessings, especially as healers for the individual; often such heroes are not called by their proper name in the cult but only by a function title (*hérōs iatrós*, 'healing hero'; *dexíōn*; *euergétēs*, 'benefactor').

The so-called Thracian horseman-hero represents a special case. He is attested in numerous inscriptions, mostly on votive reliefs with the typical iconography of a young mounted hunter (often with a dog) by a tree around which a snake is curling. His main area of distribution is the Balkan region between the western Black Sea Coast and the northern Adriatic, but reliefs are also found in Italy and Egypt [18]. The Greek and Latin dedications are preserved in the dative case. *Heroi* or (more rarely) *Heroni* (where the /n/ form should be understood as a subsidiary form of the /s/r root). This hero never bears an individual name, but probably occasionally a local epiclesis and he can also be addressed as *theòs Hérō(n)/deus Hero(n)*. In each case it has to be a matter of (also Romanized) *interpretatio Graeca* of an indigenous cult figure.

B. THE CULT

In keeping with the heroes' nature as (imagined or historic) dead, most HC have local affiliations: heroes have tombs that focus their worship. Epic heroes can of course have a tomb or cult in several places (Menelaus for instance in Therapnae and Tarentum, Agamemnon in Mycenae and Tarentum) and some special heroes are accorded a Panhellenic cult by which they are definitely brought close to gods (→ Heracles as *hérōs theós*, Pind. Nem. 3,22; the → Dioscuri) or even become gods (→ Asclepius). The tombs of the heroes can be situated outside settlements, both Mycenaean tumuli (tomb of Agamemnon in Mycenae, tomb of the Seven against Thebes in Eleusis) and real tombs. In many cases they are situated on the boundary of the settlement and in this way protect it (the tomb of Iolaus in Thebes at a city gate, Paus. 9,23,1; tomb of an unknown nobleman made into a hero at a gate in Eretria [12]; the tomb of a hero at the city wall on Naxos [13]). In numerous cases, however, they are located inside the settlement: the tombs of founding heroes are mostly on the Agora and are the centre of a cult that has as its theme the identity of the polis.

Very often the tombs of heroes with their cults are also associated with a sanctuary of an Olympian deity: the tomb of Pelops in the Zeus sanctuary of Olympia, that of Pyrrhus-Neoptolemus with the sanctuary of Apollo in Delphi, that of Iphigenia with the Artemisium in Brauron. Frequently the cults of the hero and the god are constructed as antithetic, with libations by night or burnt sacrifices for the hero without this necessarily corresponding to the modern pattern of 'Olympian versus chthonic' (→ Chthonic deities). Just as often, however, the cults of the heroes are not arranged differently from those of the gods through animal sacrifices with joint meals that are in many cases connected with agones; sacrificial laws can set common conditions for gods and heroes (for instance the law of Salaminii,

LSCG, Suppl 19) [14]. As dead worshipped in a cult, heroes contrary to the gods are also accorded cult forms that are oriented towards rites for the dead or generally inter-human social rites. Crying and wailing are often attested (which would be impossible in rituals for the gods where there are already lesser deviations from the norm, for instance the lack of the flute or of the wreath are understood as a sign of unusual mourning), likewise banquets that are eaten together with the hero; that is why the most common iconography represents the hero lying down at the meal (mostly together with a heroine and a cup-bearer) [15]. Occasionally the preparation of a bath is attested as a further sociomorphic ritual.

The heroines are more vague than the heroes: this corresponds with the sociomorphic idea when an (often nameless) heroine is very often assigned to a local hero as his wife or even a family is constructed, as for Asclepius. If heroines stand alone, they are mostly linked with cults of women (e.g. → Iphigenia in Brauron); only quite rarely have they attained supralocal importance (→ Helena [1]) [16].

C. THE INTERPRETATIONS

In contrast with ancient opinion that continuously understood heroes as dead ancestors, modern research mostly emphasizes the complex genesis and attempts to provide various categorizations; the most widespread is the pragmatic-descriptive categorization of FARNELL [2]. Some heroes can be understood as earlier local deities (Helene), others have arisen from local ancestor cults; numerous ones have originated in the epic (without the prehistory being clear in each case), whilst still others have been freely constructed as eponymous founders (the previous prejudice that understood such cults as less religious does not any longer holds true in the face of the cult material). The theory of NILSSON, according to which HC continues the Mycenaean ancestor cult, has not been confirmed by any means, and the view (only sketched in outline) of BRELICH who links the HC with initiatory themes is also too monocausal [17].

Modern terminology understands heroes not just in their religious sense but also in the literary sense; this goes back to the adoption of the word from Homeric use into that of the Latin epic by Vergil and Ovid.

1 D. O. ADAMS, Hera and Heros. Of Men and Heroes in Greek and Indo-European, in: Glotta 65, 1987, 171–178 2 L. R. FARNELL, Greek Hero Cult and Ideas of Immortality, 1921 3 M. GÉRARD-ROUSSEAU, Les mentions religieuses dans les tablettes mycéniennes, 1968, 222–224 4 TH. GELZER, Zur Versreihe der "Heroes" aus der Alten Komödie (Pap. Mich. Inv. 3690), in: ZPE 4, 1969, 123–133 5 GRAF, 127–137 6 A. M. SNODGRASS, The Archaeology of the Hero, in: AION, 10, 1988, 19–26 7 C. M. ANTONACCIO, An Archaeology of Ancestors. Tomb Cult and Hero Cult in Early Greece, 1995 8 G. DURY-MOYAERS, Enée et Lavinium. A propos des découvertes archéologiques récentes, 1981 9 S. E. ALCOCK, Tomb Cult and the Post-classical Polis, in: AJA 95, 1991, 447–467 10 T. S. SCHEER, Mythische Vorväter. Zur Bedeutung griech. Heroenmythen im Selbstver-

ständnis kleinasiatischer Städte, 1993   11 U. KRON, Die zehn attischen Phylenheroen. Gesch., Mythos, Kult und Darstellung, 1976   12 C. BÉRARD, L'Héroon à la Porte de l'Ouest (Eretria 3), 1970   13 V. K. LAMBRINOUDAKIS, Veneration of Ancestors in Geometric Naxos, in: R. HÄGG, N. MARINATOS, G. C. NORDQUIST (ed.), Early Greek Cult Practice, 1988, 235–246   14 A. D. NOCK, The Cult of Heroes, in: A. D. NOCK, Z. STEWART (ed.), Essays on Rel. and the Ancient World, 1972, 575–602 (1944)   15 J.-M. DENTZER, Le motif du banquet couché dans le Proche-Orient et le monde grec du VIIe au IVe siècle avant J.-C., 1982   16 J. LARSON, Greek Heroine Cults, 1995   17 A. BRELICH, Gli Eroi Greci. Un Problema Storico-Religioso, 1958   18 E. WILL, Le relief cultuel gréco-romain, 1955.   F.G.

Herodas, Herondas (originally probably Ἡρώιδας (*Hērōídas*), later Ἡρώδας (*Hērṓdas*); Ἡρώνδας (*Hērṓndas*) only in Ath. 3,86b).
A. ON THE PERSON B. WORKS C. ACKNOWLEDGEMENT D. INFLUENCE

A. ON THE PERSON

The Hellenistic author wrote dramatic verse sketches in the choliambic metre (→ Metre). He lived, according to contemporary allusions in his poems, in the 1st half of the 3rd cent. BC and was a contemporary of → Theocritus and → Callimachus (1,30: 'twin temple' of Ptolemy II Philadelphus and his sister Arsinoë [II 3]; 1,31: Museion in Alexandria; 4,23–26: the sons of Praxiteles; 4,76–78: Apelles; 2,16: Ake in Phoenicia, before 260 renamed Ptolemais). According to the background of the poems (2 and perhaps 4 on Cos; 6–7 in Asia Minor) and the praise of Egypt in the 1st *mimos*, they were probably created in a town or island of the Ionian coast of Asia Minor or Alexandria itself. Only in 8,75–79 does H. speak of himself, announcing that he wanted to take up the literary heritage of → Hipponax (2nd half of the 6th cent. BC).

B. WORKS

The work of H. had been lost and forgotten from antiquity until the publication of a papyrus acquired by the British Museum that contains seven mimiambi almost complete and two additional ones in fragmentary form (London, BM Pap. 135). There is also POxy. 22,2326 that reproduces 8,67–75. They are miniature dramas, scenes from everyday life that are written in literary dialect (Ionian) for one or more 'voices'. The mimiambus (= m.) as a form represents the connection between a type of street theatre (*mîmos*) on the one hand – whereby the artist 'mimics' one or more character types through voice and gestures without a mask on a small stage, in prose – and the choliamb of Hipponax of Ephesus on the other hand, who used this form for sharp criticism of contemporary ills. Similar miniature dramas in poem form are to be found in Theocr. 2 (*Pharmakeútria*) and 15 (*Adoniázousai*), choliamb and mimetic form in → Phoinix of Colophon, *Korōnistaí* [1]. Before H. the *mimos* achieved a literary level only in

→ Sophron of Syracuse (end of the 5th cent. BC) whose (lost) prose works are said to have impressed Plato. From the point of view of content, the m. are similar to the 'Characters' of → Theophrastus; otherwise they have – apart from dialect and metre – most in common with Attic → Comedy [2].

Whether the m. were performed by several actors, recited in a mimic manner by one actor or were only read privately remains a matter for debate. The following factors should be taken into consideration: the mimic was in an earlier period a single artist who mimicked several figures; the 8th m. of H. only makes sense if it is presented by the author himself; among the m. two voices are the rule, four the maximum. Probably the m. were dramatically performed in an individual presentation in front of few listeners (stage, symposium) with the artist making the individual 'roles' clear through supporting gestures and by changing the voice. MASTROMARCO [4] decisively opposes the hypothesis that the m. were pure book poetry [3]. In Plut. Mor. 712e two forms of *mimos* (*hypothéseis, paígnia*) are attested as entertainment at the symposium. The fact that the m. were also meant for presentation at the royal court is suggested by praise of the achievements of Alexandrian culture in the 1st m. Whether the droll scenes of many m. that border on the obscene tended to have an offensive or stimulating effect on the aristocratic audience is an open question.

1. *Prokyklís* or *Mastropós* ('Female matchmaker') depicts the visit of a matchmaker to a middle-class woman whose husband has already been absent for a long time. The matchmaker suggests a meeting with a handsome man. 2. *Pornoboskós* ('Pimp') is the – parodistically understood – court speech of a pimp who is sueing a ship's captain for compensation for damages for wilful destruction of his property and abduction of a prostitute. 3. *Didáskalos* ('School teacher') depicts the caning by a teacher of a lazy boy for persistent truancy. 4. 'Women who bring and sacrifice a gift to Asclepius' contains the dialogue between two women who go on a pilgrimage to the sanctuary of Asclepius (on Cos?) where they admire the artworks displayed there [5] and then finally make a sacrifice to the god. Parallels with a play by → Sophron, Θάμεναι τὰ Ἴσθμια (*Thámenai tà Ísthmia*), 'Women Attending the Isthmia' are clear. 5. *Zēlótypos* ('The Jealous Woman') depicts a jealous mistress who is indignant about the infidelity of her lover, a slave. The jealousy motif is comparable both with Theocr. 2 (*Pharmakeútria*) and with the anonymous 'Poisoner Mimos' ([12. 47–52] = POxy. 413, col. 1–3). 6. *Philiázousai* or *Idiázousai* ('Loving Women' or 'Women among each other') contains the private conversation between two women about the merits of a *baubón* (artificial phallus) that one has acquired. 7. *Skyteús* ('Cobbler') is thematically linked with 6: the women present themselves to the shoemaker who makes the *baubónes* and they admire his shoes. 8. *Enhýpnion* ('Dream'; text very incomplete, interpretation debatable): H. tells how in a dream he took part in a rural

Dionysian festival in which he competed with an old man in the → *askōliasmós* dance; as an interpretation of his dream, H. indicates that he was embarking on the literary legacy of the 'old' Hipponax by writing 'crooked poems for Ionians' (τὰ κύλλ' ἀείδειν Ξουθίδης) [6]. 9. *Aponestizómenai* ('Women after Fasting'). Only the first lines are extant. The names of two other m., *Molpínos* and *Synergazómenai* ('Women at Work'), are passed down in Stobaeus.

C. ACKNOWLEDGEMENT

The papyrus probably represents a selection of H.'s works. The low social milieu of the characters depicted does not correspond in all probability with that of the intended audience which had to be capable of acknowledging the literary art work produced by H. as a revival of an extinct literary form. CUNNINGHAM [11] therefore decisively opposes the hypothesis that H. was a 'realist'; his language was very far removed from everyday language. Various scenes are depicted with many being purely 'women's *mimoi*' (Suda s.v. Sophron divides into women's *mimoi* and men's *mimoi*) and many being mixed gender. From the sly shoemaker who promotes his wares to the naive admiration of the 'Women Sacrificing to Asclepius' – everywhere H. allows the reader to perceive a particular life situation through the eyes of a character who is indeed drawn with sympathy but also with an ironic distance. The form, plot, characters and feelings in H. are all a reductive form of the Attic comedy. The humour comes from the absurdity of the situation treated, the discernible character weaknesses of the persons in the plot as well as the aesthetic contrast between the language of literary art and everyday content. In his predilection for glosses that appear to stem from special lexica rather than the dialect of the lower class, H.'s works seem very Hellenistic. The obscenity of many passages is also comparable with Aristophanes.

D. INFLUENCE

The younger Pliny praises the m. of Arrius Antoninus as equal or even superior to a H. or Callimachus (Plin. Ep. 4,3,3). Otherwise scholia, lexicon entries and ancient comm. attest to knowledge of m. right through to the Byzantine period. H. should be regarded as a model of Roman mimiambography, otherwise his influence is very limited: between Byzantium and the modern age he is completely forgotten. The extensive comm. by HEADLAM-KNOX [9] attests to the value of the m. for the scholar as a treasure trove of rare concepts and sayings: the judgement of CUNNINGHAM [11] that H. deserves attention not least because otherwise only a few Hellenistic writers are extant does not do justice to the author. The fact that the m. did not attain the general fame that H. hoped for (8,75–79) perhaps lies partly with the modest claim of the poems themselves and partly with their lexical difficulties, but certainly not with any lack of ability on the part of the author to depict or to empathize.

→ Hellenistic poetry; → Mimos

1 W.D. FURLEY, Apollo humbled: Phoenix' Koronisma in its Hellenistic literary setting, in: Materiali e Discussioni per l'analisi dei testi classici, 33, 1994, 9–31   2 H. KRAKERT, H. in mimiambis quatenus comoediam graecam respexisse videatur, PhD thesis Freiburg/Leipzig 1902   3 G. PASQUALI, Se i mimiambi di Eroda fossero destinati alla recitazione, in: Xenia Romana, 1907, 15–27   4 G. MASTROMARCO, The Public of Herondas (London Studies in Classical Philology vol. 11), 1984   5 T. GELZER, Mimus und Kunsttheorie bei Herondas, Mim. 4, in: C. SCHÄUBLIN (ed.), Katalepton. FS B. Wyss, 1985, 96–116   6 R. M. ROSEN, Mixing of Genres and Literary Program in H. 8, in: HSPh 94, 1992, 205–216.

EDITIONS: 7 F. G. KENYON, London 1891   8 O. CRUSIUS, Leipzig 1892 (Teubner)   9 W. HEADLAM, A. D. KNOX, Cambridge 1922   10 P. GROENEBOOM, Groningen 1922 (only I–VI)   11 I. C. CUNNINGHAM, Oxford 1971 (edition with comm. = 1)   12 Id., Leipzig 1987 (Teubner, cum appendice fragmentorum mimorum papyraceorum = 2)   13 B. G. MANDILARAS, Athens 1986 (with photographs of the papyrus).

BIBLIOGRAPHY: 14 O. CRUSIUS, Unt. zu den Mimiamben des H., 1892   15 F.-J. SIMON, Τὰ Κύλλ' Ἀείδειν, Interpretationen zu den Mimiamben des H., 1991   16 R. G. USSHER, The Mimiamboi of H., in: Hermathena 129, 1980, 65–76   17 Id., The mimic tradition of "character" in H., in: Quaderni urbinati di cultura classica 50, 1985, 45–68.   W.D.F.

Herodes (Ἡρῴδης; *Hēróidēs*).

[1] H. I.; Herod the Great. Born in *c.* 73 BC, son of → Antipater [4] and the Arabian woman Cyprus. In 47 appointed *strategos* of Galilaea, he came into conflict with the Sanhedrin of Jerusalem because of the execution on his own authority of persons involved in a revolt. The Roman governor of Syria Sex. → Iulius [I 11] Caesar made him the *strategos* of Coilesyria and Samaria. In 43 he proved himself to be indispensable to one of the murderers of Caesar, C. → Cassius [I 10], in the exploitation of the land, likewise in 41 after the battle of Philippi he proved indispensable to the triumvir Marcus → Antonius [I 9] who elevated him and his brother Phasael to the rank of tetrachs. H. fled – from the Parthians and the king and high priest → Antigonus [5] appointed by them – to Rome where the Senate appointed him as the rival claimant to the throne at the end of 40. Returning with Roman help, in 37 he married the Hasmonean woman Mariamme. Antony's gifts of land to → Cleopatra VII affected H.'s kingdom as well: aside from the access to the sea, in 34 the balm-tree plantations of Jericho were also lost. The transition to Octavian/Augustus after the battle of → Actium ensured H. royal status and the enlargement of his kingdom: in 30 he obtained – aside from Jericho – Gadara, Hippus, Samaria, Gaza, Anthedon, Joppa and Straton's Tower on the coast, in 23/22 the districts of Trachonitis, Batanaea and Auranitis as well as in 20 the territory of Zenodorus north and north-west of Lake Genezareth to the sources of the Jordan. H. united with the Jewish heartland the areas on the periphery where there were serious problems caused by Jews and non-Jews living

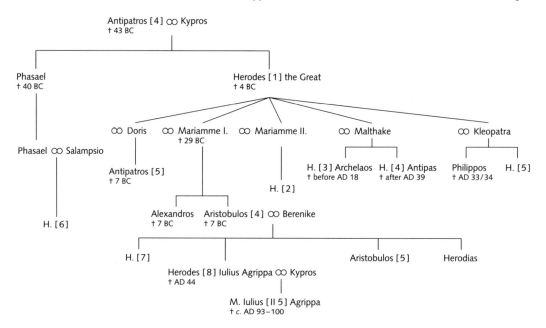

together. The violent efficiency with which he exercised his rule recommended H. to the Roman overlord, as did as his unconditional loyalty. In this way he ruled thanks to imperial favour over a kingdom whose size matched that of King David's.

H. was one of the great building sponsor of the ancient world. As a city founder, benefactor (→ *euergétēs*) of the Hellenistic world and patron of Greek culture he proved himself, as also in his rule, to be a person who continued the Hellenistic kingdom. Of his great buildings and the cities he founded, the following should be emphasized: in Jerusalem the theatre, amphitheatre, royal palace and from 20/19 onwards the rebuilding of the Temple, the reconstruction of → Samaria as a town of Augustus = Sebaste, the founding of the port of Caesarea (22–10/9), the building of the fortress Herodium close to Bethlehem, the rebuilding of the destroyed Hasmonean fortresses of Alexandria and Hyrcania as well as the extension of Machaerus and Masada. In the non-Jewish parts of his kingdom and in Syria he established temples for the imperial cult, supported the extension of the city of Nicopolis/Actium established by Augustus and among other things set up a foundation for the Olympic Games.

Although H. respected the religious law and the influence of the → Pharisees in the Jewish heartland, some of his innovations awakened the indignation of the pious, particularly the construction of the theatre and amphitheatre in Jerusalem as well as the placement of an eagle at the entrance to the Temple. High priests and Sanhedrin lost their traditional power. He met all threats to his rule, whether they were caused by the priestly aristocracy, social protest and national religious expectations or dynastic conflicts, with brutal severity. His marriage to Mariamme and the rivalry be-

tween Herodians and → Hasmoneans resulted in the bloody drama of dynastic murders and executions: in 35 H. had the high priest → Aristobulus [3], the brother of Mariamme, murdered, in 30 the former high priest and ethnarch → Hyrcanus [3] II executed, and in 29/28 followed Mariamme and her mother Alexandra, in 27 his brother-in-law Kostabar and the last surviving Hasmoneans hidden by him. The conflict between H. and his sons by Mariamme, Aristobulus [4] and Alexander, ended in 7 with their execution, and Antipater who was chosen as his successor was also executed in 4 BC a few days before H.'s death when he was found guilty of conspiracy. In his last will and testament he appointed H. [3] Archelaus as king and the latter's brother H. [4] Antipas and their half-brother Philippus as tetrarch. Main sources: Jos. BI 1,181–673; Jos. Ant. Iud. 14,121–17,199. For the other sources see the literature.

The Biblical report on the slaughter of the innocents at Bethlehem (Mt 2,16) has no historical basis.
→ Judaism

SCHÜRER, vol. 1; H. OTTO, s.v. H. I., RE Suppl. 2, 1–158; A.H.M. JONES, The Herods of Judaea, ²1967, 39–152; A. SCHALIT, König H., 1969; P. RICHARDSON, H., King of the Jews and Friend of the Romans, 1997.

[2] Born in 22 BC, married to Herodias, the daughter of his half-brother → Aristobulus [4] before she entered into a second marriage to H. [4] Antipas. Designated as the successor to the crown temporarily, he was passed over by his father in the final line of succession to the throne. He was probably one of the sons of H. who under → Pontius Pilatus and emperor Tiberius were opposed to the fastening of golden votive tables in their names to the royal palace of Jerusalem (Phil. Legatio ad Gaium 38,300; Jos. BI 1,557; 573; 588; 600; Ant. Iud. 17,14; 19; 78; 18,109f.; 136).

[3] **H. Archelaus.** Born around 23 BC, named as king in his father's will, he travelled to Rome in 4 BC after putting down a revolt in Jerusalem in order to attain from Augustus the confirmation of this decree against the claims of his brother H. [4] Antipas. During his absence a new rebellion broke out, which was put down through the intervention of the governor of Syria, P. → Quinctilius Varus. Envoys of the priestly aristocracy demanded in vain that none of the Herodians should attain the rule but that the theocracy of the high priests should be restored. Augustus decreed that the kingdom should be divided. H. received, with Judea, Samaria and Idumaea, the heartland of the kingdom and the title of Tetrarch. His violent regime caused the Jewish and Samaritan aristocracy to demand that he be deposed. In AD 6 Augustus exiled him to Vienna in Gaul. His kingdom became an imperial province and in Jerusalem theocracy was restored under Roman supervision (Jos. BI 1,562–2,116; Ant. Iud. 17,20; 188–355; Str. 16,765).

[4] **H. Antipas.** In 4 BC tetrarch of Galilaea and Peraea by the last will of his father H. [1], in AD 17 H. founded on Lake Genezareth the new capital city Tiberias named after Augustus' successor. His second marriage to Herodias, his sister-in-law and niece, gave reason for criticism – for instance, from John the Baptist (Mk 6,14–29) whom H. had executed as a potential troublemaker – and entangled him in a war with his father-in-law from his first marriage → Aretas [4] IV, the king of the Nabataean kingdom. The attempt initiated by Herodias to obtain the kingship for him instead of his brother H. [8] Agrippa failed and caused in 39 his exile to Lugdunum by the emperor Caligula (Jos. BI 1,646; 2,20–183; Ant. Iud. 17,146; 17,224–18256; Str. 16,765; Cass. Dio. 55,27,6).

[5] Younger brother of the tetrarch Philippus, was not considered by H. [1] the Great in his testamentary disposition regarding his successors. No further details are known (Jos. BI 1,562; Jos. Ant. Iud. 17,21).

[6] Son of Phasael, the nephew of H. [1] the Great, and of Salampsio, the daughter of H. the Great by the Hasmonean Mariamme (Jos. Ant. Iud. 18,130).

[7] **H. (II.)** Born between 15 and 11 BC, son of → Aristobulus [4]. Emperor Claudius granted him Chalcis ad Libanum in AD 41, i.e. the remainder of the Ituraean kingdom, with the royal title (Jos. BI 2,217). As a Jewish client king and Roman citizen with praetorian rank (Cass. Dio 60,8,3) he supported the rights of the Jews of Alexandria and in 44 after the death of (H.) [8] Agrippa attained the right to appoint the high priests. After his death his kingdom was forfeited in 48 and transferred to his nephew → Iulius [II 5] Agrippa II (Jos. Ant. Iud. 19,279; 288; 20,15f.; 103).

[8] **(H.) Iulius Agrippa I.** Born in 10 BC, son of → Aristobulus [4], grew up in Rome with close relationships with the imperial family. In AD 37, after an eventful life and greatly in debt, he received from emperor Caligula the tetrarchy of → Philippus, the Gaulanitis, the Trachonitis, Batanaea and Panias with Caesarea [2] as well as the royal title, in 39 also the tetrarchy of H. [4]

Antipas. Emperor Claudius, in whose elevation to the position of emperor he played a role, distinguished him in 41 with consular rank and transferred to him the Roman province of Judea (Cass. Dio 60,8,2) so that he ruled over the restored kingdom of H. I. He appeared to the Jews to be an admirer of the Jewish religion and outside the borders of his kingdom as well as in Caesarea [1] he was regarded as a generous supporter of non-Jewish Hellenistic culture. His attempts to expand his political scope through developing the fortification of Jerusalem and through calling a conference of eastern client kings to Tiberias – were ruined through the intervention of the governor of Syria, C. → Vibius Marsus. After his death his kingdom was forfeited in 44 (Jos. BI 2,178–220; Jos. Ant. Iud. 18,126–366).

[9] Son of → Aristobulus [6] and Salome (Jos. Ant. Iud. 18,137). No further details have been passed down to us.

SCHÜRER, vol. 1; A. H. M. JONES, The Herods of Judaea, [2]1967.

[10] **H. ben Miar.** and

[11] **H. ben Gamala.** Aristocratic citizens of Tiberias who in AD 66 at the outbreak of the great Jewish uprising maintained loyalty to Rome and King → Iulius [II 5] Agrippa II (Jos. Vit. 33f.).

[12] Son of Aumus, in the service of King Iulius Agrippa II, military commander in the Trachonitis (OGIS 425).

K.BR.

[13] *Dioikētḗs* (διοικητής) in Alexandria, letters of October 164 BC to the subordinates Dorion, Onias [1] and Theon on the interpretation of the royal *próstagma* (πρόσταγμα) are extant: SB XVI 12821, UPZ I 110.

1 V. A. TCHERIKOVER, A. FUKS (Ed.), Corpus Papyrorum Iudaicorum 1, 1957, no. 132   2 D. THOMPSON, Memphis under the Ptolemies, 1988, 254f.

[14] Son of Demophon of Pergamum, citizen of Ptolemais in the phyle of Ptolemais and deme of Bereniceus. Between 152 and 145 BC *tôn diadóchōn, hēgemṑn ep' andrôn* (τῶν διαδόχων, ἡγεμὼν ἐπ' ἀνδρῶν), phrourarch in Syene, *gerrhophýlax* (γερροφύλαξ), and governor of *ánō tópoi* (ἄνω τόποι); at the same time prophet of Chnubis and *archistolístēs* (ἀρχιστολίστης) of the temples in Philae, Abaton and Elephantine, before 143/2 governor of the Dodekaschoinos. Also attested as *epistátēs tôn metállōn* (ἐπιστάτης τῶν μετάλλων); in 144/2 becomes *archisōmatophýlax* (ἀρχισωματοφύλαξ) and *strategos* of the Thebaid.

PP 2/8,2059; E. VAN'T DACK, Ptolemaica Selecta, 1988, 343ff.   W.A.

[15] Of Marathon, prominent Athenian, ancestor of H. [16] Atticus, archon in 60/59 BC and four-time *strategos*, friend of Cicero and T. Pomponius Atticus. In 50 he obtained from Caesar the endowment of 50 talents for Athens (Cic. Att. 6,1,25), in 45/44 Cicero approached him about keeping the philosopher Cratippus in Athens (Plut. Cicero 24,7f.), in 44 BC he was the

mentor of → Cicero's son M. Tullius Cicero (Cic. Att. 14,16,3 and others).

HABICHT, Index s.v. H.; RAWSON, Culture, 444–449.
K.-L.E.

[16] L. Vibullius Hipparchus Ti. Claudius Atticus Herodes.

c. AD 101/103–177, richest Athenian of his time who combined a Roman career with activities as a sophist and politician in Athens. His father, Ti. → Claudius [II 10] Atticus, was the first Greek from Achaea to become *cos. suff.* (probably in 108). H. was educated partly in Rome by P. → Calvisius [10] Tullus Ruso (Fronto I, 60 HAINES), learnt rhetoric (Philostr. VS 2,1, 564) with → Scopelianus (a house guest during the time of H.'s youth, ibid. 1,21,521), → Favorinus and Secundus; he did not hear → Polemon until *c.* 134 (ibid. 1,25, 537). His career began early, probably with a delegation to Hadrian in 117/118 (at which he became agitated and lost his nerve, ibid. 2,1,565). He then became 'market overseer' (*agoranómos*; ?124/5) and *árchōn* (126/7) of his home town as well as 'organizer of the games' (*agonothétēs*) of the Panhellenia, probably as first archon of the Panhellenium in 133–137, and of the → Panathenaea in 140 (ibid. 549–50); later *archiereús*. In his Roman career he was *quaestor candidatus Caesaris* (129?), *tr. pl.*, *praetor* (?133), in *c.* 134 special legate for the order of the towns in the province of Asia, and in 143 *cos. ord.*

Within the framework of his spectacular programme of beneficient building enterprises (cf. Philostr. VS 2,1,551), H. rebuilt for his Panathenaea the stadium in Athens (ibid. 550) out of Pentelic marble (Paus. 1,19,6). Further buildings were as follows [1]: the stadium in Delphi (Paus. 10,32,1); the Nymphaeum in Olympia, officially opened by his wife Regilla (*c.* 149–153 [1]); the Odeum in Athens, dedicated to her memory (Paus. 7,20,6); reconstruction of an Odeum in Corinth; statues on the Isthmus and in Olympia (Paus. 2,1,7; 6,21,4); support for Oricon in Epirus and many towns in Achaea; aqueduct for Canusium and – with a donation from his father of about 4 million drachmas – an aqueduct and (probably) baths for Alexandria Troas in *c.* 134 (Philostr. VS 2,1,548). H.'s wealth was also visible because of his possessions in Cephisia, Marathon (his *démos*), Corinth, Cynuria and on the *via Appia* close to Rome where he constructed a temple to Faustina just before 143 and had poems by → Marcellus of Side recorded in inscriptions that celebrated his wife after her death (late 150s).

Such a high position caused conflicts: supposedly with Antoninus Pius during the period of his proconsulate in Asia in 134/5 (ibid. 554–555); with the brother of his late wife; with the Quintilii brothers while they were administering Achaea (as special legates) around 174 (ibid. 559); with the freedmen of the family; with Athenians, especially with other magnates (Ti. Claudius) Demostratus, Mamertinus and Praxagoras (ibid. 559) – which led to a court proceeding before the emperor Marcus Aurelius in Sirmium (*c.* 174) and exile to

Oricon. Marcus' intervention in favour of reconciliation of H. with Athens (as previously with Fronto), documented by a long inscription [2], effected H.'s return (*c.* 175) which was welcomed by ephebes with an effusive elegiac hymn (IG II² 3606).

Of four children by Regilla, only Regillus Atticus (*cos.* in 185) survived H.; the others and his wife and foster children (*tróphimoi*) Polydeucio, Achilles, Memnon and Aethiops were ostentatiously mourned by him.

→ Gellius (especially 19,12,1) and Philostratus praise H. as outstanding in the area of oratory (cf. Lucian, De morte Peregrini 19). Emperor Antoninus Pius appointed him teacher of his sons Marcus Aurelius and L. Verus (Cass. Dio 72,35,1). Among his students in Rome were → Aristocles and in Athens Gellius, → Chrestus, Ptolemy of Naucratis, Onomarchus, Theodotus and possibly Aelius → Aristides. A closer circle (called the 'water-clock', *klepsýdrion*) that enjoyed special regard comprised → Hadrianus of Tyrre, Pausanias of Caesarea and Amphicles of Chalcis. H.'s rhetorical style was distinguished by its rich simplicity and in this way was reminiscent of his model Critias. Philostratus (VS 2,1,564) lists speeches, letters, diaries and an anthology as works of H. However, the only works still extant are the Latin translation of a fable that originated in a criticism of the Stoic ideal of the absence of passion (*apátheia*) (Gell. NA 19,12), a speech that addresses problems in classical Thessaly ([3], attributed to Critias by [4]), as well as several poems [5].
→ Philostratus; → Second Sophistic

1 K.W. ARAFAT, Pausanias' Greece, 1996, 37–8, 111, 195–201   2 Hesperia, Suppl. 13, 1970   3 U. ALBINI (ed.), Περὶ Πολιτείας, 1968   4 H.T. WADE-GERY, Kritias and H, in: CQ 39, 1945, 19ff.   5 E.L. BOWIE, Greek sophists and Greek poetry in the second sophistic, in: ANRW II 33.1, 231–235.

P. GRAINDOR, Un milliardaire antique. Hérode Atticus et sa famille, 1930; A. STEIN, PIR² C 802; W. AMELING, H. Atticus, 2 vols., 1983; J. TOBIN, H. Attikos and the city of Athens, 1997.   E.BO.

Herodianus (Ἡρωδιανός; Hērōdianós).

[1] Aelius H. (Αἴλιος Ἡρωδιανός; Aílios Hērōdianós), of Alexandria, one of the most important Greek grammarians, lived in the 2nd cent. AD; son of → Apollonius [11] Dyscolus and his worthy student and successor. For a time he lived in Rome and dedicated his main work, the Καθολικὴ προσῳδία (Katholikḕ prosōidía) to the emperor Marcus Aurelius (161–180). He is justifiably not seen as a brilliant but as a careful and precise grammarian, the great heir and systematician of the Alexandrian tradition of studies on language and of rational analysis of linguistic phenomena. The epithet ὁ τεχνικός (ho technikós) is not given just to him so that it cannot be considered to be a description for the grammarian *par excellence*: his writings were famous, however, and were often consulted in scholarly circles (not only by grammarians but also in scholia, etymologica

and lexica). The original works are lost so that our knowledge of his teaching can only be based on these middlemen. The collection and reconstruction endeavours of Lentz (for 33 works) are fundamental; these have, despite their known great weaknesses, errors and defects, not been overhauled in their entirety and form the starting-point for dealing with the Herodianic material: papyrus fragments and particularly the text published by Hunger have expanded our knowledge with important information (see Dyck 1993).

The main work by H. was the *Katholikè prosōidía* in 20 bks., fruit of a tireless collection of examples (over 60,000 words) with a rigorous formulation of the rules. The greatest part concerned the general theory of accenting but the term *prosōidía* also comprises all diacritical symbols for the correct reading of words: accents; breathings; symbols for length or shortness of the dichronic vowels; symbols for elision, linkage or separation between syllables. Bks. 1–19 treated accenting: 1–13 nouns; 14 monosyllables; 15 numerals and other; 16 verbs ending in –ω and –μι; 17 composite verbs and participles; 18–19 the other types of words; bk. 20 contained the quantities of the dichronic vowels and the breathings (one problem consists in its relationship to the short treatise Περὶ διχρόνων, which is transmitted separately; it is however probably put together from excerpts from the larger work); finally H. himself appears to have added a type of supplement about words as parts of a sentence, of which an excerpt about enclitics is extant.

Further (probably earlier) works concerned the *prosōidía* of specific linguistic environments. We have only a little of the 'Attic Prosody' (Ἀττικὴ προσῳδία; *Attikè prosōidía*), whereas there are extensive fragments of the 'Prosody of the Iliad' (Ἰλιακὴ προσῳδία; *Iliakè prosōidía*) and (less) of the 'Prosody of the Odyssey' (Ὀδυσσειακὴ προσῳδία; *Odysseiakè prosōidía*) that are dedicated to Homeric language: of the latter we have extracts in the scholia to the *Iliad* and the *Odyssey*, as an unknown grammarian of late antiquity (siglum VMK = Four-Man Commentary) wrote a commentary on Homer by compiling writings from Aristonicus [5], Didymus [1] of Alexandria, Nicanor and H. whose material went into Byzantine scholia and lexicographical collections.

H. also wrote a large number of works on grammatical questions: the 'Pathology' – a term that relates to the enormous and inadequately defined area of πάθη τοῦ λόγου (*páthē toû lógou*), i.e. to all phenomena of phonetic, morphological and dialectal change in words, taking as the starting-point the base form; 'Orthography' (Περὶ ὀρθογραφίας; *Perì orthographías*), noun and verb inflection, word formation, phonology and still more. The only completely extant work is the treatise Περὶ μονήρους λέξεως (*Perì monérous léxeōs*, on words that are distinguished by their strangeness from a morphological point of view.

His fame favoured the attribution to H. of dubious or clearly inauthentic texts: we know a total of about 20

(that were not edited by Lentz). The best-known is the short Atticist encyclopaedia Φιλέταιρος (*Philétairos*), additional ones are Περὶ ἀκυρολογίας (*Perì akyrologías*); Περὶ σχημάτων (*Perì schēmátōn*); Ἐπιμερισμοί (*Epimerismoí*).

EDITIONS: A. Lentz (Ed.), Herodiani Technici reliquiae, in: GG 3; Scholia Il. (*Iliakè prosōidía*); A. Ludwich, Herodiani Technici Reliquiarium supplementum, 1890 (Addenda to *Odysseiakè prosōidía*); K. Lehrs, Herodiani scripta tria emendatiora, 1848; A. Dain, Le Philetairos attribué à Hérodien, 1954 (*Philétairos*); K. Hajdú, SGLG 8, 1998 (*Perì schēmátōn* (more information: Schultz RE (see below) and Dyck 1993).
BIBLIOGRAPHY: D. Blank, Ancient Philosophy and Grammar. The Syntax of Apollonius Dyscolus, 1982, 24–25; U. Criscuolo, Per la tradizione bizantina dei lessici atticisti, in: Bollettino della Badia greca di Grottaferrata, n.s. 26, 1972, 143–156; A. R. Dyck, Herodian über die Etym. von ἴφθιμος, in: Glotta 55, 1977, 225–227; Id., Notes on the Epimerismoi attributed to Herodian, in: Hermes 109, 1981, 225–235; Id., Notes on Greek grammarians, in: RhM 124, 1981, 50–54; Id., Aelius Herodian: Recent Studies and Prospects for Future Research, in: ANRW II 34.1, 772–794 (very useful research overview incl. bibliography); P. Egenolff, Zu Lentz' Herodian, I–III, in: Philologus 59, 1900, 238–255; 61, 1902, 77–132, 540–576; 62, 1903, 39–63; H. Erbse, Zu Herodian π. παθῶν, in: Philologus 97, 1948, 192; Id., Beiträge zur Überlieferung der Iliasscholien (Zetemata 24), 1960, 344–406; K. Hajdú, SGLG 8, 1998 (see above); H. Hunger, Palimpsest-Frg. aus Herodians Καθολικὴ προσῳδία, Buch 5–7 (cod. Vindob. Hist. gr. 10), in: Jb. der österr. Byz. Ges. 16, 1967, 1–33; D. J. Jakob, Herakleides oder Herodian?, in: Hermes 113, 1985, 495–497; Lehrs 1848, (see above); R. Reitzenstein, Gesch. der griech. Etymologika, 1897, 299–312; Schmid/Stählin II, 887–888; M. Schmidt, Die Erklärungen zum Weltbild Homers und zur Kultur der Heroenzeit in den bT-Scholien zur Ilias (Zetemata 62), 1976, 32–35; H. Schultz, s.v. H. (4), RE VIII 1, 959–973; H. Stephan, De Herodiani Technici dialectologia, PhD thesis Straßburg 1889; Ch. Theodoridis, Zur Schreibernotiz im Etymologicum Genuinum (s.v. ᾖχι), in: RhM 132, 1989, 409–410; M. van der Valk, Researches on the Text and Scholia of the Iliad, 1963–64, I, 592–602; A. Wouters, The Grammatical Papyri from Graeco-Roman Egypt, 1979, 216–224, 231–236 *et passim*.   F.M.

[2] Born in *c.* AD 178/180, was possibly a freedman or *eques* in subordinate positions of the imperial or state service. His origin and family circumstances are uncertain; perhaps he came from Alexandria or from Syrian Antioch. He wrote a history of Rome from the death of Marcus Aurelius to the sole rule of Gordianus III (AD 180–238) in eight bks. ('History of the Empire after Marcus Aurelius'), divided up according to the periods of government of the emperors (of a biographical-historiographic nature), in the Greek language. The work, written in a down-to-earth, easily comprehensible and fluid style was published after 240.

His statements betray slight or no experience in matters of high politics or the conduct of war. As he said himself (1,2,5), his concern was contemporary history, but this probably only applies to the last bks. It is not known which sources were used by H.; methodical source criticism is unknown to him. His work was used as a model by the → Historia Augusta on many occasions and had a great influence on Eutropius, Aurelius Victor, Ammianus Marcellinus and Iohannes Antiochenus among others and was praised by ancient and Byzantine authors because of the pleasing style. Whilst H.'s work was unfavourably judged by the older research on the basis of its obvious historiographical defects, it is evaluated in modern times more positively again and seen as an important, although not defect-free source, with indispensable information on the history of the 1st half of the 3rd cent. AD.

DIHLE, 356f.; F. L. MÜLLER, Herodian, 1996, 7–26.   T.F.

[3] *Comes*, assistant commander in the Byzantine Italian campaign against the Ostrogoths, in AD 535–540 under Belisarius, from 542 under Maximinus. In 545 he delivered Spoleto into the hands of the Goths. From then on in the service of the Gothic king Totila, he helped the latter in 546 in the conquest of Rome and from 552 he guarded his treasure in Cumae (→ Cyme). His fate after the conquest of Cumae in 553 by Byzantine troops is unknown. PLRE 3, 593–595.   F.T.

Herodias Daughter of → Aristobulus [4], a son of Herod the Great. Married in her first marriage to the latter's half-brother Herodes Philippus, H. left her husband to enter into wedlock with → Herodes Antipas, the Tetrarch of Galilaea and Peraea who for his part got a divorce from his wife, a daughter of the king of the Nabataeans, Aretas. This led to a war with the Nabataean kingdom that ended with the defeat of Antipas in AD 36. H. was probably also involved in the execution of → Iohannes the Baptist who criticized her unlawful marriage. When Antipas at her instigation requested from Caligula the title of king for himself, he was deposed in AD 39 and banished to Gaul. H. followed her husband into exile.

→ DECADENCE; → FIN DE SIÈCLE

P. SCHÄFER, Geschichte der Juden in der Antike, 1983.   J.P.

Herodicus
[1] *Paidotribés* from Megara who settled in Selymbria, contemporary of Protagoras. His birth was estimated to around 500 BC [2. 200f.] and his death in old age to around 430–420 [5. 53].

After Plato had attributed to him the development of a new form of therapy, he was regarded as the author of a small work [1. 979, l. 21f.] despite the absence of any evidence that he had written anything at all or even, despite Anon. Londiniensis IX, 20–36, that he had an explicit, elaborated theory. Plato attributes to him two types of treatment in contrast to each other: an aggressive treatment consisting of walks (Phdr. 227d 3–4) and a treatment involving waiting to see how things turn out (Resp. 406a-d), with constant observation and the

maintenance of a condition that Plato describes as 'frail'. The attention that H. dedicates to dietetics has led to his being regarded – certainly unjustifiably [3. 12–14, 16 with n. 3] – as the author of the Hippocratic treatise 'On Diet'. Although the → Anonymus Londiniensis attributes a differentiated theory to him, it is probably more to the point to attribute great interest in the diet of athletes to him. He is supposed to have recognized its applicability to medicine [5. 42–57]. Subsequently the assertion was made that he had been the teacher of Hippocrates [4. 10] and had even established dietetics [5. 42–57].

→ Dietetics; → Hippocrates

1 H. GOSSEN, s.v. H. (2), RE VIII 1, 978–9.   2 H. GRENSEMANN, Knidische Medizin, I, 1975   3 R. JOLY, Hippocrate, Du régime, 1967   4 J. RUBIN-PINAULT, Hippocratic Lives and Legends, 1992   5 G. WÖHRLE, Stud. zur Theorie der antiken Gesundheitslehre, 1990.

[2] Physician (?) from Cnidus; dating to around 400 cannot be justified conclusively. The only explicit testimony is made by the Anon. Lond. (IV,40–V,35), who links him with → Euryphon but without making him his pupil.

In the aetiology H. like Euryphon traced the reason for diseases back to digestive remains; but differently from the latter, he thought that these *perissómata* dissolve into two fluids (sour and bitter) that cause various illnesses. If the allocation of the references in Galen and Caelius Aurelianus to this H. is correct, he noticed the therapeutic qualities of mother's milk (Gal. 6,775; 7,701; 10,474f.) and in addition recommended vomiting as a dietetic measure for which he is said to have described several ways and means (Caelius Aurelius, Tard. pass. 3,8,139).

His theory about the lack of physical exercise encouraged confusion with H. [1] of Selymbria, likewise the type of aetiology that is attributed to the latter by the Anon. Lond.   A.TO.

Herodorus ('Ηρόδωρος; *Heródōros*) from Heraclea on the Pontus. Mythographer, father of → Bryson of the Megarian School, wrote in Ionian dialect around 400 BC, often cited in the MSS as → Herodotus. Monographs on individual mythical figures (Heracles in at least 17 bks., Pelops, Oedipus) or groups (*Argonaútai*, *Orphéōs kaì Musaíou historía* = 'Orpheus and Musaeus'), of which a few fragments are extant (FGrH 31), are conceivable in the titles. Accordingly H. adopted the mythical traditions especially of → Hellanicus and → Pherecydes of Athens. The selection of handed-down material is less independent than their use as a framework for all possible geographical and natural history reports – for instance F 2 on Iberia, F 22 on the vulture, F 21 on the lunar world. The myths are rationalized (F 57: the gilded ram of Atreus is in reality a golden dish) and allegorized (F 13: Hercules learns astronomy from Atlas); contradictions in the tradition are solved through the formulation of homonyms (F 42: two

Orpheuses, F 14: several Herculeses). In this way H. stands on the threshold of later mythography that was to break free from tradition more strongly.

F. JACOBY, s.v. H. (4), RE VIII 1, 980–987; P. DESIDERIO, Cultura eracleota. Da Erodoro a Eraclide Pontico, in: R. BERNARD (ed.), Pontica I. Recherches sur l'histoire du Pont dans l'antiquité, 1991, 7–24.   F.G.

Herodotus (Ἡρόδοτος; Heródotos).

[1] The historian Herodotus.
A. LIFE   B. STRUCTURE OF HIS WORK   C. GENESIS OF HIS WORK   D. SOURCES AND HISTORICAL METHODS   E. BIAS AND CREDIBILITY   F. WORLD VIEW AND VIEW OF HISTORY   G. HERODOTUS AS NARRATIVE WRITER   H. LANGUAGE AND STYLE I. INFLUENCE

A. LIFE

Sources on the life of H., the 'father of history' (Cic. Leg. 1,1,5), c. 485–424 BC (fundamental for all of the following: [1]) are, apart from the information he provided himself in particular, the Suda s.v. H. or s.v. Panyassis. H. came from Halicarnassus (modern Bodrum) in the south-west of Asia Minor. The names of his father, Lyxes, and his uncle, Panyassis, a famous epic poet, point to Carian origin. Because of a failed attempt to overthrow the tyrant → Lygdamis, H. fled for some time to Samos; after returning home, he was involved in the final overthrow of Lygdamis before 454. Because of differences with his fellow citizens, he later left his homeland forever and emigrated to the panhellenic colony of Thurii founded in 444. According to Eusebius (Chronica Arm. 83), H. held public readings from his work in 445/4 in Athens and was given a large fee for it (cf. Diyllus FGrH 73 F 3). In Athens he was also introduced to the circle of → Pericles and made friends with → Sophocles who wrote an ode to H. (Anthologia Lyrica Graeca I³ 79 DIEHL) and on several occasions made reference to the work of H. (cf. especially Soph. Ant. 903ff. with Hdt. 3,119; further passages. [2. 318³] and [3. 2ff.]). On the other hand, a lasting influence of tragedy on H. is noticeable, e.g. in the story of Adrastus (Hdt. 1,34ff.) or the portrayal of Xerxes (bks. 7 and 8). According to Apollodorus (FGrH 244 F 7), H. was 53 years old at the outbreak of the Peloponnesian War: the date of birth resulting from this – 484 – should be about accurate. H. still experienced the first years of the Peloponnesian War (cf. Hdt. 6,91; 7,137; 233; 9,73). In 424 his historical work was available, as several passages from it were parodied in the 'Acharnians' of Aristophanes (cf. e.g. Aristoph. Ach. 523ff. with Hdt. 1,4; [4. 210¹⁴] lists scholars who support a later date of publication). He probably died a little later.

H. went on extended journeys whose chronology is uncertain [5. 128ff.; 6; 7. XVff.]: 1. to the Black Sea region, base at Olbia (Hdt. 4,17), from there up the Hypanis to the land of the Scythians (4,81). In the process H. probably also got to know the southern Black Sea coast, Thrace and Macedonia. 2. to Egypt up to Elephantine and the first cataract of the Nile. In total about a four-month stay after the battle of Papremis 460/459 (cf. 3,12); from Egypt probably a detour to Cyrene (cf. 2,32f.; 181). 3. to the Near East, to Tyre (2,44), to the Euphrates (1,185) and to Babylon (1,178ff.), but not to actual Persia. 4. to the whole Greek settlement area, among others to the motherland (locations of battles in the Persian War!), Asia Minor, Magna Graecia and Sicily.

B. STRUCTURE OF HIS WORK

H.'s work is completely extant; the classification into nine books (cf. Diod. 11,37,6) probably goes back to the Alexandrian philologist Aristarchus [4] of Samothrace who also wrote a commentary on H. The proem states: 'This is the presentation of the investigation (historíēs apódexis) of H. of Halicarnassus, so that what happened among humans shall not fade with time nor shall great deeds, some the work of Hellens, some of → barbarians, or lose their fame, particularly however, for whatever blame or cause (aitíē) they waged war upon each other' (on the proem most recently [8. 234ff.] with literature). H. brushes aside the mythological conflicts between Greeks and 'Barbarians' (1,1–5) and turns immediately to the historical period, i.e. the recent past, namely the Lydian king → Croesus (c. 560–547) 'of whom I know that he started the injustices against the Greeks.' Thus, the sequence of the 'barbarian kings' who wanted to subjugate the Greeks becomes the leitmotif of the portrayal: Croesus (1,6–94), Cyrus (1,141–214), Cambyses (2,1–3; 70), Darius (3,61–7,4), Xerxes (7,5–8 end) (on the structure of the work cf. especially [1. 288ff.] and [9; 10. 47ff.]).

To this single-stranded main narration H. adds an immense wealth of geographical, ethnographical and historical material in the form of shorter and longer excursuses (lógoi), at whose ends the main narration is continued where it was interrupted. The individual peoples (country and people, history, etc.) are always introduced where they first come into contact with the conquering power Persia. Examples: 1,178–200 (Babylonians); 1,201–216 (Massagetians); 2,2–182 (Egyptians); 3,20–24 (Ethiopians); 4,5–82 (Scythians); 1,142–151 (Ionians); 3,39–60; 120–149 (Samians). The history of the Greek motherland, especially of Athens and Sparta, however, is presented in several parts that are correlated with each other (Athens: 1,59–64; 5,55–96; 6,121ff.; Sparta: 1,65–68; 5,39–48; 6,51–84). In the → Ionian Revolt (5,28ff.) the Persian and the Greek narrative threads are united: H. describes the great → Persian War with a technique of parallel narration, in which the events are represented alternately from one side or the other up to the clash of the two powers. The expedition of Darius that fails at Marathon (6,102ff.) is followed by the great campaign of Xerxes, from the decision to go to war (7,5ff.) through the mustering of his armies (7,59ff.), the battles of Thermopylae (7,198–239), of Artemisium (8,1–23) and of Salamis (8,40–96) to the victories at Plataeae (9,19–89) and Mycale (9,90–

107). The work ends with the capture of Sestus in 479 which marks the Greeks' transition from being on the defensive to being on the offensive. Whether it is complete or not in its present form is contested (cf. the research review in [1. 152]; on this problem most recently [12. 47ff.]).

C. GENESIS OF HIS WORK

Characteristic is on the one hand the extraordinarily wide exposition with a great amount of ethnographical and geographical material, and on the other hand a density of representation that increases as the work develops and that narrates the history of the Persian Wars in an essentially cohesive way in the last three books. This discrepancy is interpreted biographically by numerous scholars (this so-called analytical trend was initiated by [1. 205ff., 467ff.] and further developed especially by [5. 442]; cf. also [13. 36–68]): H. is said to have originally been a geographer and ethnographer like → Hecataeus [3] and in this capacity to have written the great ethnographic *lógoi* that were originally independent constructs. Only under the influence of Periclean Athens did he become a historian and decided to portray the Persian Wars, the great glorious feat of the Athenians. Accordingly a range of very heterogeneous material went into his work and was combined into a whole after a fashion. In fact there is, however, much to support the view that H. planned and wrote his work in the present form from the outset (supporters of the unitarian faction are among others [14; 15. 360ff.; 4. 32ff.]).

D. SOURCES AND HISTORICAL METHODS

In the ethnographical-geographical parts, H. now and then uses literary sources, for instance Hecataeus [3], who forms the basis for i.a. 2,70–73 (FGrH 324a); on the other hand there is almost a total lack of written sources for the historical parts: H. occasionally uses poetry like the 'Persians' of Aeschylus, and he also uses inscriptions (e.g. the Snake Column of Delphi, cf. ML 27 with Hdt. 8,82) and collections of oracles, but neither notable historical works nor local chronicles, nor lists of officials and victors were available to him. The ancient Oriental and Egyptian records remained incomprehensible to him. His method of working was essentially as follows (cf. 2,99; in this regard in particular [16; 17; 4. 35ff.; 13. 44f.]): in the ethnographical-geographical parts he mainly worked on the basis of autopsy (his own observation) and his own experience [18], in the historical sections on the basis of oral tradition (cf. the treatises mentioned in [4. 211³⁴]) that he collected from 'knowledgeable' people, either individuals (2,28,1; 125,6; 4,76,6; 8,65,6), professional groups ('the priests') or anonymous inhabitants of countries ('the Egyptians', 'the Scythians', 'the Carthaginians') and cities ('the Athenians', 'the Corinthians', 'the Cyrenians' etc.) [13. 44].

The assumption that H. 'quite freely invented' the virtually unbelievable wealth of such citations and should be regarded as a mere 'arm-chair scholar' who only feigned his journeys, his personal observation and his sources, is an aberration on the part of modern research (this research faction was established by [19] and still has numerous adherents, e.g. [20; 21; 22 and 23], but on [23] cf. individually the essays quoted and critically discussed by [35. 234–285]) that actually require no serious refutation ([24] is fully justified in opposing the scholars mentioned in the previous note who consider the historical work of H. to be a 'great compilation of lies'). In fact H.'s unique 'scholarly' achievement lies in his crystallization – from the welter, the diversity, the conflicting oral information that he drew from numerous persons in the most varied of places – of the history of the Persian Wars as a unity in its form that has become classical, which he achieved without notable written sources.

H.'s methodological basic principle is: 'I am obligated to report that which is reported, but I am not obligated to believe everything; and these words shall apply to my entire representation' (7,152) [4. 34ff.]. This maxim results in the rendering of divergent and partly contradicting traditions, according to the tendency and view of the respective informants, without H. supporting the correctness of one version or the other. Thus, for example, an Alcmeonid and a Philaid tradition in Athens, a tradition for and against Demaratus in Sparta, a Spartan, Tegeatic and Athenian tradition regarding the battle of Plataeae, exist equally side by side.

E. BIAS AND CREDIBILITY

With regard to the great thematic framework, it can be noted that H. often acknowledges the superiority of 'barbarians', especially the Egyptians, to the Greeks (cf. 2,4; 32; 50; 58; 77; 82) and always describes the customs and way of life of non-Greeks with great objectivity. His reports about foreign peoples, e.g. Egyptians, Babylonians, Scythians and Massagetians, also prove to be reliable to a large extent (cf. [4. 211³⁶]; most recent [25; 26]). With regard to the main topic, H., similar to Aeschylus, regards the Persian Wars as a battle between freedom and slavery, democracy and despotism, frugality and luxury, individual competence and the anonymous mass (cf. especially the dialogue between Xerxes and Demaratus in 7,101–104) [27. 215ff.], but he should by no means be regarded as a panegyrist of the 'National War': in his view the Persian Wars under Darius, Xerxes and Artaxerxes rather brought greater disaster to Hellas then all the previous 20 generations together (6,98). H. also mentions the mistakes and weaknesses of the Greeks by name, e.g. their lack of unity, their particularism, their reciprocal rivalries and disputes, the way in which numerous poleis sided with the Persians, and the shortcomings of the Greeks of Asia Minor in the Ionian Revolt [2. 565f.]. He does indeed admire the *nómos* ('law and customs') and the bravery of the Spartans very much (cf. 7,101–104), but in the passage about Athens (7,139) he regards the Athenians as actual 'saviours of Greece'. Certainly his admiration for Athens is generally not unlimited, his work must therefore by no means be considered to be pro-Athenian in its bias (first demonstrated by [28. 474ff.]; cf. in this regard most recently [29]). In the chronological field H.'s achievements were also considerable (on this cf. [30]).

F. World view and view of history

The transitory nature of all earthly things is a leitmotif in the entire presentation (1,5), and the 'cycle of human things' is mentioned throughout, especially in the *logos* about Solon and Croesus (1,207). Despite occasional rationalism a religious world view predominates that is manifested in a fateful predestination of events, the idea of the gods' envy and → *némesis* (retribution) and the punishment of human hubris by 'the divine' (cf. e.g. 1,30–33: Croesus; 3,39ff.: Polycrates of Samos; 7,35: Xerxes) (cf. [31. 368ff.]). Divine agency is expressed in omens, dreams, oracles and the voices of warners, but human motivations and decisions are not unimportant either [32].

G. Herodotus as narrative writer

Since Cicero (Leg. 1,1,5) H. has been considered to be not only the first historian but also the first narrative writer of the West. From the wealth of anecdotes, novellas and stories the following can be emphasized: the picaresque deed of Rhampsinitus (2,121), the ring of Polycrates (3,40–45), the recklessness of Hippocleides (6,126ff.), and the horror meal of Harpagus (1,117ff.). Such tales are not an end in themselves but contain *in nuce* the elements of Herodotus' world view; the same applies to conversations, dialogues, and direct speeches that can often be found in his works [31; 33].

H. Language and style

Ancient stylistic criticism (Dion. Hal. Ad Pompeium 3,11 and De Thucydide 23) already emphasized the *poikilía* ('vividness') of H.'s language that reflects the great wealth of content. Colloquial-style narrative, matter-of-fact reporting style, the linguistic means of the epic, the tragedy and of Sophistic are the main factors in his stylistic synthesis that as a whole, however, has a character *sui generis*. [34].

I. Influence

H. had an enormous influence on all subsequent Greek and Roman historiography; on this [3; 4. 40f.]. He prompted the writing of historical specialized literature (e.g. works of Hellanicus, Antiochus), whilst → Thucydides (1,22) formulated his historical method in dialogue with H. (who is not mentioned by name). The shaping of rhetorical, dramatic or pragmatic historiography took place only in the Hellenistic period but it is already present, at an embryonic stage, in the work of H. The commentary of Aristarchus of Samothrace (PAmherst II 12, 1901) shows H., to be a recognized classic work, and also Plutarch's writing 'On the malice of Herodotus' attests to his great authority. In the Middle Ages two textual recensions existed; in Humanism and in the Renaissance H. was known through the Latin translation of Lorenzo Valla (1452–1456) but well into the 20th cent. he was still regarded as an unreliable inventor of stories. Only in recent times has H. begun to emerge from the shadow of Thucydides. The universal historical concept of his work, the breadth of his idea of history, the detailed consideration of the anthropological dimension as well as the heuristic principle 'report what is reported' among other things contributed to this [4. 41].

→ Historiography

1 F. Jacoby, s.v. H., RE Suppl. 2, 205–520 = Griech. Historiker, 1956, 7–164   2 Schmid/Stählin I 2   3 K.-A. Riemann, Das herodoteische Geschichtswerk in der Antike, diss. 1967   4 K. Meister, Die griech. Geschichtsschreibung, 1990   5 K. von Fritz, Die griech. Geschichtsschreibung, 1967   6 R. P. Lisler, The Travels of Herodotus, 1980   7 D. Asheri, Erodoto, Le storie, libro 1, 1988   8 K. Meister, Die Interpretation histor. Quellen, vol. 1, 1997   9 H. Wood, The Histories of Herodotus, 1972   10 K. H. Waters, Herodotus, the Historian, 1985   11 H. Bengtson, Griech. Geschichte, ⁵1977   12 R. Oswald, Gedankliche und thematische Linien in Herodots Werk, in: Grazer Beiträge 21, 1995, 47–59   13 O. Lendle, Einführung in die griech. Geschichtsschreibung, 1992   14 J. Cobet, Herodots Exkurse und die Frage der Einheit seines Werkes, 1971   15 Chr. Meier, Die Entstehung des Politischen bei den Griechen, 1980   16 K. Verdin, De historisch-kritische methode van Herodotus, 1971   17 D. Lateiner, The Historical Method of Herodotus, 1984   18 G. Schepens, L' autopsie dans la méthode des historiens grecs du Vᵉ siècle avant J.-C., 1980   19 D. Fehling, Die Quellenangaben bei Herodot, 1971 (Eng. transl. 1989)   20 S. West, Herodotus' Epigraphical Interests, in: CQ 79, 1985, 278–305   21 F. Hartog, The Mirror of Herodotus, 1988   22 E. Hall, Inventing the Barbarian, 1989   23 O. K. Armayor, Herodotus' Autopsy of the Fayoum, 1985   24 W. K. Pritchett, The Liar School of Herodotus, 1993   25 Hérodote et les peuples non grecs, Entretiens 35, 1988   26 R. Rollinger, Herodots babylonischer Logos (Innsbrucker Beiträge zur Kulturwissenschaft, Sonderheft 84), 1993   27 W. Schadewaldt, Die Anfänge der Geschichtsschreibung bei den Griechen, 1982   28 H. Strasburger, Herodot und das perikleische Athen, in: W. Marg (ed.), Herodot, ³1982, 574–608   29 M. Ostwald, Herodotus and Athens, in: Illinois Classical Studies 16, 1991, 137–148   30 H. Strasburger, Herodots Zeitrechnung, in: W. Marg (ed.), Herodot, ³1982, 688–736   31 Lesky   32 L. Huber, Rel. und polit. Beweggründe in der Geschichtsschreibung des Herodot, diss. 1965   33 M. Lang, Herodotean Narrative and Discourse, 1984   34 W. Schadewaldt, Die Anfänge der Geschichtsschreibung bei den Griechen, in: Antike 10, 1934, 144–168, esp. 158   35 W. K. Pritchett, Studies in Ancient Greek Topography, vol. 4, 1982.

Editions: J. Feix, 2 vols. (Heimeran) ⁵1995; A. D. Godley, 4 vols. (Loeb), 1922–1938; K. Hude, 2 vols. (Oxford), 1926/7; Ph.-E. Legrand, 10 vols. (Budé), 1946–1954; H. B. Rosen, 2 vols. (Teubner), 1987 and 1997. Commentaries: D. Asheri et al. (Mondadori) 1988ff. (Ital.), one book respectively; W. W. How, J. Wells, 2 vols., ²1928; H. Stein, 5 vols., ⁴⁻⁶1893–1908; On book 2:

A.B. LLOYD, 2 vols., 1975–1987.
LEXICA: J.E. POWELL, 1938.
BIBLIOGRAPHY: Most recent FR. BUBEL, Herodot-Bibliographie 1980–1988, 1991.
GERMAN TRANSLATIONS: TH. BRAUN, H. BARTH, 2 vols., ²1985; A. HORNEFFER, ⁴1971; W. MARG, 2 vols., ³1980; H. STEIN, W. STAMMLER, 1984.
BIBLIOGRAPHY: T.S. BROWN, The Greek Historians, 1973, 25ff.; A. CORCELLA, Erodoto e l'analogia, 1984; H. DREXLER, Herodot-Studien, 1972; H. ERBSE, Studien zum Verständnis Herodots, 1992; Id., Histories apodexis bei Herodot, in: Glotta 73, 1995/96, 64ff.; J.A. EVANS, Herodotus, 1982; Id., Herodotus, Explorer of the Past, 1991; K.J. GOULD, Herodotus, 1989; Id., Herodotus and Religion, in: S. HORNBLOWER (ed.), Greek Historiography, 1994, 91–106; F. HARTOG, Herodotus and the Invention of History, 1987 (= Arethusa, vol. 20); V. HUNTER, Past and Process in Herodotus and Thucydides, 1982; H.R. IMMERWAHR, Form and Thought in Herodotus, 1966; T.J. LUCE, The Greek Historians, 1997, 15ff.; W. MARG (ed.), Herodot, ³1982 (WdF 26); D. MÜLLER, Topographischer Bildkommentar zu den Historien Herodots, 1987; B. SHIMRON, Politics and Belief in Herodotus, 1989.   K.MEI.

[2] Student and addressee of a letter from → Epicurus about the principles of physics (extant in Diog. Laert. 10,29–83). Presumably this letter can be equated with the 'little epitome to H.' about which Epicurus speaks in his letter to Pythocles (Diog. Laert. 10,85: ἐν τῇ μικρᾷ ἐπιτομῇ πρὸς Ἡρόδοτον; cf. also 10,35 without an addressee). H. is mentioned, together with → Timocrates, as the author of a book Περὶ Ἐπικούρου ἐφηβείας (Perì Epikoúrou ephēbeías; 'On the youth of Epicurus') (Diog. Laert. 10,4).

H. v. ARNIM, s.v. H. (10), RE 8, 990.   T.D.

[3] Greek physician of the 1st/2nd cents. AD who practised in Rome (Gal. 8,750–751). He is identified without conclusive evidence with the teacher of → Sextus Empiricus, is said to have been born in Tarsus as the son of a certain Arius and was a student of the Pneumatist → Agathinus and the Empiricist → Menodotus (Diog. Laert. 10,116). He was critical of all medical schools apart from that of the → Pneumatists (Gal. 11,432).

Apart from his statement that takes into consideration an aetiological nihilism at least with regard to fever ([Gal.] 19,343), he seems to have worked particularly on therapeutics, namely in a way that shows similarities with the school of Tarsus; this link is even more likely since → Galen links him with → Pedanius Dioscorides (11,443) in a criticism of his interpretation of a therapeutic activity.

→ Oribasius (CMG, 4,330–331 s.v.) cited fragments that all tend towards therapeutics: mechanical remedies, laxatives and external remedies. Although attempts were made to attribute all the known quotations to what was considered one single treatise those in Galen appear to belong rather to one work or several works that possibly dealt with simple and composite remedies.

→ Anonymus Parisinus   A.TO.

[4] Sculptor from Olynthus. Tatian (Ad Graecos 33) attributes to him the statues of the prostitutes Phryne and → Glycera [1] as well as of the musician Argea. While the fundamental unreliability of this source is proven, on the basis of a lost signature on the statue of a hetaera in Rome the existence of H. cannot be excluded.

A. KALKMANN, Tatians Nachr. über Kunstwerke, in: RhM 42, 1887, 489–524; LOEWY, no. 541; OVERBECK, no. 1590–1591 (sources).   R.N.

Heron (ἐρῳδιός/erōidiós, in MSS frequently ἐρωδιός/erōdiós, also ἀρωδιός/arōdiós, ῥωδιός/rhōdiós, ἐρωγάς/erōgás, ἐδωλιός/edōliós; Latin ardea and ardeola) of the Ardeidae family with several species of birds. Interpretation of the erōdión (Hom. Il. 10,274) that flew past Odysseus at night as a heron is disputed today (in spite of Ael. NA 10,37). The following species are identifiable [1. 38f.]: 1) the grey heron (Ardea cinerea): ὁ πέλλος ἐρῳδιός/ho péllos erōidiós (Aristot. Hist. an. 8(9),1,609b 22–25 and 8(9), 18,616b 33–617a 1 = Plin. HN 10,164: pelion); 2.) the great white heron (Egretta alba): ὁ λευκὸς ἐρῳδιός/ho leukòs erōidiós. (Aristot. Hist. an. 8(9),1,609b 22 and 8(9),18,617a 2–5 = Plin. HN 10,164: leucon, reputedly with only one eye); 3.) the spoonbill (Platalea leucorodia), also interpreted as a → pelican, with a long, wide beak: λευκερωδιός/leukerōdiós (Aristot. Hist. an. 7(8),3,593b 2–3), Latin platea (Plin. HN 10,115) or platalea (Cic. Nat. D. 2,124), which lives on pre-digested shells ([1. 182], among other things; cf. Ael. NA 5,35; Plut. Mor. 967c-d et al.); 4) the great bittern (Botaurus stellaris): ὁ ἀστερίας/ho asterías, also called the 'lethargic' bittern (ὄκνος/óknos) (Aristot. Hist. an. 8(9),1,609b 22f. and 8(9),18,617a 5–7 = Plin. HN 10,164: asterias). No further names can be assigned to the other European species such as purple heron, glossy ibis, night heron and little egret.

According to Aristot. Hist. an. 7(8),3,593b 1 f, grey herons and spoonbills live on lakes and rivers. Ath. 9,398d transmits the designation, coined by Epicharmus (fr. 49), of the heron lying in wait for fish – e.g. eels – (Semonides, fr. 8(9) DIEHL) as 'long curved neck' (μακροκαμπυλαύχην/makrokampylaúchēn). When it flies, the heron – like the → purple swamphen (πορφυρίων/porphyríōn) – does not steer with its tail, but with its outstretched legs (Aristot. De incessu animalium 10,710a 11–15). Elements of the description, such as the crest of feathers on its head (Dionysius, Ixeuticon 2,9: [2. 31]), are rare. The grey heron is supposed to live in enmity with the eagle, the fox and the crested lark (κόρυδος/kórydos) (Aristot. Hist. an. 8(9),1, 609a 25–28), also with the woodpecker (πίπος/pípos, ibid. 609a 30f.), but is friendly with the crow (κορώνη/korónē) (ibid. 610a 8; Ael. NA 5,48; Plin. HN 10,207). The seagull (λάρος/láros, Ael. NA 4,5) and the shrew were also thought to be its enemies (sorex, Plin. HN 10,204).

A heron flying inland and calling out was regarded as an omen of storm and winter (Aristot. fr. 253,2;

Theophr. De signis 28; Arat. 913, cf. 972), as was a bird flying above the clouds (Verg. G. 1,363 f.), but also one standing on the sand and looking sad (Plin. HN 18,363).

The heron was sacred to Poseidon (Alexander Myndius fr. 15). In mantic terms it almost always meant something positive (Plin. HN 11,140; Callim. Aet. 2 fr. 43,62 PFEIFFER; [3]). In Antoninus Liberalis 7,7 three men were transformed into herons. According to Aesch. fr. 478 METTE, the heron was responsible for the death of Odysseus. Aesop. 156 PERRY recounts the fable of the wolf, from whose throat the heron removes a bone without receiving any thanks. Fine representations (on this [6. 204 f.]) are found on ancient coins [4. pl. 6,5 and 8–9] and gems [4. pl. 22,6 and 9–11, possibly 14], and also on a Pompeian mural [5. 234] and e.g. a mosaic from Tabgha (including a grey heron with a snake [5. 234 and pl. 118]).

1 LEITNER   2 A. GARZYA (ed.), Dionysii Ixeuticon, 1963   3 W. EHLERS, Die Gründung von Zankle, thesis, Berlin 1933, 37 ff.   4 F. IMHOOF-BLUMER, O. KELLER, Tier- und Pflanzenbilder auf Mz. und Gemmen des klass. Alt., 1889 (repr. 1972)   5 TOYNBEE, Tierwelt   6 KELLER 2, 202–207.

D' ARCY W. THOMPSON, A Glossary of Greek Birds, 1936 (repr. 1966), 102–104.   C.HÜ.

Heroninus Archive The Heroninus Archive (HA) consists of over 1,000 Greek papyri, mostly letters, balance sheets and receipts from the middle of the 3rd cent. AD. They are in fact documents relating to the administration of the large estates, located in the *Arsinoîtēs nomós* (Fayum/Egypt; → Arsinoe [III 2]), of Aurelius Appianus, who belonged to the council of Alexandria. Appianus' central administration had its seat in Ptolemais Euergetis, the capital of the *nomós*, and was conducted by councillors from the region. At the head of the administration stood Alypius, himself a large estate-holder and imperial procurator. Appianus' estates were made up of scattered fields, vineyards and other lands. The whole property was divided into administrative units known as φροντίδες (*phrontídes*). Each *phrontís* was controlled by an administrator usually termed *phrontistḗs*. The archive comes from the village of Theadelphia and is named after Heroninus, who was administrator of the *phrontís* there from AD 249–268. The HA is not an orderly collection of documents but rather represents the chance remnants of Heroninus' administrative papers. It nevertheless offers important information on the administration of Appianus' estates.

The most important objective of the estate's administration was the production of olives (for oil) and wine for the market, as well as the estate's own needs. The property had a centrally directed transport system that used donkeys, oxen and camels for agricultural work and for transporting the harvest and goods that were needed on the estates. This transport system enabled the *phrontídes* to share agricultural tools and implements and to specialize in specific products. This guaranteed

speedy communication and, in addition, centralized control over the sale of all products, while at the same time providing the basis for Appianus' estates to become a true economic unity. Although some fields and facilities were leased, most of the estates were cultivated under their own management. All workers employed on the estate seem to have had the status of freedmen: the *oikétai* and *metrēmatiaîoi* worked on the estates a longer time; they received board as well as a monthly payment in cash, sometimes even lodging and payment of their taxes (this arrangement may have been the precursor of the colonate). Day labourers were also employed, though on a short-term basis.

Economic management was organized on a monetary basis and used various forms of credit and transactions through banks, as well as maintaining accounts for the workers showing credit for wage payments and a debit for expenses and tax contributions. The *phrontistaí* kept detailed accounts of employment of the workers, the receipt and expenditure of money, the harvest yield and the sale of products, etc. They had to record these individual items in a standardized annual balance sheet, divided into months, and submit it to the estate's central administration. These monthly statements contained entries for purchases and sales in the columns for money and provisions, giving continuous balances for cash and stock. They enabled the central administration to assess the agricultural productivity of each *phrontís* and perhaps also to estimate its profitability. With its highly developed book-keeping, the HA calls into question the widely held current view that property administration in antiquity was uniformly 'primitive' and 'not economically rational'.

→ Colonatus; → Large estates / Latifundia

1 D. W. RATHBONE, Economic Rationalism and Rural Society in Third-Century A.D. Egypt: The Heroninos Archive and the Appianus Estate, 1991.   D.R.

Heroon see → Funerary architecture; → Hero cult

Herophilus (Ἡρόφιλος; *Hēróphilos*)
[1]
A. LIFE   B. WORK   C. HISTORY OF SCIENCE
D. EFFECT

A. LIFE
Greek physician from Chalcedon, about 330/320 to 260/250 BC [5. 43–50]. Apart from his training with Praxagoras, with a Hippocratic orientation, he spent the majority of his active career under Ptolemy I and II in Alexandria. However, he does not appear to have worked in the → Mouseion, nor was he a court physician [5. 26f.].

B. WORK
Of the eleven works attributed to H. six are almost certainly genuine: 'Anatomy', 'On the Pulse', 'Obstetrics', 'Dietetics', 'Therapeutics' and 'Against Common

Opinions'. The seventh, 'On the Eyes', belongs to him without doubt. The eight (a refutation of the *Prognō-stikón* attributed to Hippocrates) may perhaps be assigned to him. The last three are pseudepigrapha: the 'Commentary on the Hippocratic Aphorisms', the work 'On Nutrition' and the medieval *Epistula ad regem Antiochum* [1].

C. HISTORY OF SCIENCE

H. worked in all areas of medicine, which he conceived of as a unity and divided in a new fashion into three epistemic areas: 'things relating to the state of health' (anatomy and physiology), 'relating to the state of disease' and relating to a state introduced by him, the 'neutral' state (comprising medicinal therapeutics, surgery and therapeutic dietetics), according to a model sometimes designated as Peripatetic [5. 100], sometimes as Stoic [6. 205]. In terms of methodology he is reputed to have introduced a new heuristic method in anatomy: he is said to have carried out not only autopsies on human bodies, but also vivisection, which he performed on prisoners.

In the area of 'things relating to health', and more specifically in anatomy, H. examined many organs and created a descriptive nomenclature, which has been partly retained. H. apparently examined physiology in the context of the humoral system [5. 246] and identified the functions of various organs (nerves, lungs, cardiovascular system) and physical mechanisms (pulse). Even though H. attempted to explain the reason for ill-health primarily by symptoms, he defined disease simply as 'that which is difficult to resolve, the reason for which is to be found in the humours,' or as 'that which is resolved in time' [5. 301]; thus a time factor is involved in relation to disease and undoubtedly also to health.

Among the 'neutral things' he used medicines largely according to an allopathic principle and in an aggressive manner, as single or combined medicines; regarding their effect they were directed towards the 'instrumental' parts of the body and not at its components and were called by H. 'the hand of the gods' [5. 400]. H.'s surgical practice does not seem to have benefited from his anatomical discoveries and probably consisted principally of obstetric operations. He is said to have practised bloodletting widely and in conjunction with administering medicines.

In addition to H.'s technical work, there was also his theoretical work: the exegesis of Hippocratic texts and medical lexicography [5. 427–442].

H., who was esteemed because of his anatomical discoveries and who was called the 'father of anatomy' or 'forerunner of A. Vesalius', has been regarded as a Sceptic [3]. In fact he made efforts to extend and clearly illustrate Hippocratic knowledge. His work on the texts shows a pragmatism not dependent on authority, yet without being empiricism [2. 48–52]. This orientation (in particular the practice of autopsy, which was traditionally ascribed to contact with Egyptian culture and mummification), has recently [5. 1–31] been attributed to the situation in the Alexandrian world 'on the margins' of cultures and societies.

The entire body of H.'s work has been called an 'unfinished epistemological revolution' [4. 89] and was probably aimed at transforming pre-Alexandrian knowledge according to the Euclidean paradigm of science and its relation to evidence [4].

D. EFFECT

H.'s work marked the beginning of a 'school', to which belonged in particular → Andreas [1], → Mantias and → Apollonius [17] Mys in pharmacology, and Bacchius in medical lexicology. It was made widely known by the debates of later epochs, especially by the Empiricist school founded by → Philinus, a pupil of H., and by the Pneumatist 'school'. After Galen H.'s work remained unknown until it was rediscovered in the Renaissance, however only to face competition right away from the innovative works of A. VÉSALE.

→ Anatomy; → Galen; → Hippocrates; → Praxagoras

1 K.D. FISCHER, H. VON STADEN, Der angebliche Brief des H. an König Antiochus, in: AGM 80, 1996, 86–98 2 M.D. GRMEK, Il calderone di Medea, 1996 3 F. KUDLIEN, H. und der Beginn der medizinischen Skepsis, in: Gesnerus 21, 1964, 1–13 4 M. VEGETTI, La scienza ellenistica, in: M.D. GRMEK (ed.), Storia del pensiero medico occidentale 1, 1993, 73–120 5 STADEN 6 G. WÖHRLE, Stud. zur Theorie der ant. Gesundheitslehre, 1990.

A.TO.

[2] Gem-cutter of the Imperial period, son of → Dioscorides [8], the name by which he also signed; extant: blue glass cameo with portrait, discussed as being Tiberius, Augustus or Drusus I.
→ Dioscorides [8], Hyllus, Eutyches [1], Gem-cutting

ZAZOFF, AG, 316 n. 58 (bibliography), pl. 91,1. S.MI.

Heros see → Hero cult

Herostratus (Ἡρόστρατος; *Hēróstratos*). Arsonist, of unknown origin, involved in the destruction of the Temple of Artemis at → Ephesus in 356 BC. Under torture he confessed that he had been motivated by a thirst for glory, whereupon the Ephesians decided that his name should never again be mentioned. According to Valerius Maximus (8,14 ext. 5), only Theopompus did not abide by that (Ael. NA 6,40; Solin. 40,2–5; Str. 14,1,22 are based on him). In fact, other sources (collected in [1. 262ff.]) do not give any name. Synchronization of the fire with the birth of Alexander [4] the Great is fictitious.

1 FiE 1 2 ST. KARWIESE, Groß ist die Artemis von Ephesos, 1995, 57–59. M.MEI.

Herpyllis (Ἑρπυλλίς; *Herpyllís*). Life companion (first as slave, then freed, but probably not second wife) of Aristotle [6] (died 322 BC), in whose will she was lavished with money, servants, and the right of residence in the philosopher's estates in Chalcis and Stageira because of her excellent care of him (ὅτι σπουδαία περὶ ἐμὲ ἐγένετο). In case of a future marriage, the executors were to take care that she would not be given to someone unworthy of her (Diog. Laert. 5,13). It is impossible to prove that H. was the mother of Nicomachus, one of the sons of Aristotle; it could have been made up by Timaeus (FGrH 566 F 157; cf. Ath. 13,589c).   M.MEI.

Herpyllis fragment The name of a work well known because of a papyrus fragment (PDubl. inv. C3; early 2nd cent. AD), which almost [3] all scholars acknowledge to be a novel. A narrator portrays how he and a woman, after a painful separation, board two different ships. Then follows the detailed, rhetorically virtuoso description of a storm (a typical theme for a novel). The text breaks off with the appearance of St Elmo's fire. The name of the woman is usually read as Herpyllis but it has been surmised [2. 159; 4] that it could be amended to read Dercyllis and the fragment could, therefore, be ascribed to the novel by → Antonius [3] Diogenes.
→ Novel

EDITIONS: 1 R. KUSSL, Papyrusfragmente griech. Romane, 1991, 103–140   2 S. A. STEPHENS, J. J. WINKLER (ed.), Ancient Greek Novels. The Fragments, 1995, 158–172.
BIBLIOGRAPHY: 3 O. CRUSIUS, Die neuesten Papyrusfunde, Beilage zur Allgemeinen Zeitung 145 (3. Juli), 1897, 1–2   4 C. GALLAVOTTI, Frammento di Antonio Diogene?, in: SIFC n.s. 8, 1930, 257.   M. FU. and L.G.

Herse (Ἕρση; *Hérsē*). Daughter of → Cecrops and → Aglaurus [2] (or Agraulus) (Paus. 1,2,6; Apollod. 3,14,2). In Athens, H. and her sisters Aglaurus (or Agraulos) and → Pandrosus constitute the Cecropids. Despite the prohibition of Athena, who had entrusted it to them, they open a basket containing the new-born → Erichthonius [1]. Then in madness H. and Aglaurus hurl themselves from the Acropolis (Eur. Ion, 268 274; Paus. 1,18,2; cf. 1,2,6; 27,2; Apollod. 3,14,6; Ov. Met. 2,552–561). H. and her lover Hermes bring into the world Cephalus (Apollod. 3,14,3) and Ceryx (IG XIV 1389, I, 32; 54). In Alcman (fr. 67 PMG) there is a H. who is the daughter of Zeus and → Selene. H. means 'dew' (ἕρση, epic ἐέρση).
→ Arrhephoroi

G. J. BAUDY, Der Heros in der Kiste. Der Erichthonios-Mythos als Aition athenischer Feste, in: A&A; 38, 1992, 1–47; D. BOEDEKER, Descent from Heaven: Images of Dew in Greek Poetry and Rel., 1984; U. KRON, s.v. Aglauros, LIMC 1.1, 283–286; E. SITTIG, s.v. H., RE 8, 1146–1149.   K. WA.

Hersilia Daughter of the noble Sabine Hersilius (Dion. Hal. Ant. Rom. 3,1). During the rape of the Sabine women, she is the only married woman who is abducted (Cass. Dio 56,5,5 is a reflection of this: H. teaches the Roman women *tà gamiká*, 'what forms part of mar-

riage'), she stays with her daughter, who was also abducted (Dion. Hal. Ant. Rom. 2,45; Macrob. Sat. 1,6,16), and marries, according to some sources, a certain Hostilius in Rome and so becomes the grandmother of King Tullus → Hostilius (Dion. Hal. Ant. Rom. 3,1; Plut. Romulus 18,29a). More frequently, however, she appears as the wife of → Romulus (Sil. Pun. 13,812–815; Liv. 1,11,2; Serv. Aen. 8,638). This may well have originated with Zenodotus of Troezen (FHG IV 531 = Plut. Romulus 14,26a; here there are also a Prima as daughter of the couple and a son Aollius, later called Avillius). A mention that Romulus gave her to Hostilius in marriage (Macrob. Sat. 1,6,16) sounds like an attempt to balance the two versions. H. acts as spokeswoman for the women in the peace negotiations between the Romans and the Sabines (Plut. Romulus 19,29d-f; Cn. Gellius in Gell. NA 13,23,13). In Ov. Met. 14,829–851 it is only after the death of her husband Romulus that she is identified with Hora, the cult companion of Quirinus [1. 156].

1 G. WISSOWA, Rel. und Kultus der Römer, ²1912
2 F. BÖMER, P. Ovidius Naso, Metamorphosen B. XIII–XIV, 1986, 244–245.   JO.S.

Heruli Seafaring East Germanic tribe [1], which at the beginning of the 3rd cent. AD was allegedly driven out of Scandinavia by the Danes and split into East and West Heruli. The latter attacked the Romans at the Lower Rhine in 287, were defeated and repeatedly attacked Roman territory from the Dutch-Frisian coast to southern Spain (esp. 456/459). Threatened by the → Franci, they made an effort in 476 to gain the friendship of the → Visigoths. At the beginning of the 6th cent. they are no longer attested.

From their home by the Sea of Azov, the much stronger East H. advanced in 267 with a fleet through the Hellespont, laying waste to Athens [2], as far as the Peloponnese, but they were beaten by Gallienus by the River Nessus. Claudius II succeeded in 269 in gaining a victory over the 'Goths' at Naissus [3; 4]. In the middle of the 4th cent. the Ostrogoth → Ermanaric brought them into his power [5. 46]. Later they were subjugated by the Huns, who they defeated at the River Nedao in about 454 in alliance with an anti-Hun 'coalition'. Settling presumably in the Carpathian Basin [6. 354–356], the H. found themselves under the leadership of → Odoacer in 471, whom they supported until 491. After that, they spread out into the Vienna Basin, where they were militarily important under Rodulf, the son-at-arms of Theoderic. They were crushingly defeated by the tributary Lombards (→ Langobardi) [7. 28–32; 8. 211f.] in about 508/9. While most of the surviving H. were taken into the eastern territory of the empire by Anastasius, were later settled near Singidunum by Justinian, and converted to Christianity (but see [9]), a small group migrated to Scandinavia with the royal family [10], from which those staying behind chose a new king for themselves (cf. [11]). Procop. Goth. 2,14f. presents a negatively distorted picture of them, yet a certain degree of brutality of the restless H., who are valued as mercenaries because of their courage and war skills, is well attested.

1 P. LAKATOS, Quellenbuch zur Gesch. der Heruler, 1978 2 G. E. WILSON, The Herulian Sack of Athens, A.D. 267, thesis Univ. Washington/Seattle 1971   3 E. KETTEN-HOFEN, Die Einfälle der Heruler ins Röm. Reich im 3. Jh. n. Chr., in: Klio 74, 1992, 291–313   4 T. KOTULA, Kaiser Claudius II und sein bellum Gothicum in den J. 269–270, 1994 (Polish and German summaries)   5 B. TÖNNIES, Die Amalertradition in den Quellen zur Gesch. der Ostgoten, 1989   6 J. TEJRAL, Probleme der Völkerwanderunsgzeit nördlich der mittleren Donau, in: W. MENGHIN (ed.), Germanen, Hunnen und Awaren, 1988, 351–367 7 W. MENGHIN, Die Langobarden, 1985   8 J. JARNUT, Die langobardische Herrschaft über Rugiland, in: R. BRA-TOŽ (ed.), Westillyricum und Nordostitalien in der spätröm. Zeit, 1996, 207–213   9 K. DÜWEL, s.v. Aria-nischen Kirchen, RGA 1, 403   10 K. ZIEGLER, s.v. Pro-kopios, RE 23, 454f.   11 N. WAGNER, Herulische Namenprobleme. Givrus, Datius und anderes, in: BN 16, 1981, 406–421.

A. ELLEGÅRD, Who were the Eruli?, in: Scandia 53, 1987, 5–34; J. GRUBER, s.v. Heruler, LMA 4, 2184f.   K.DI.

Hescanas Etruscan gentilicium of aristocratic families, especially in → Volsinii, known through the figured painted tomb of H. found there.
→ Etrusci, Etruria   F.PR.

Hesiodus (Ἡσίοδος; *Hēsíodos*): Hesiod.
A. PERSON   B. WORKS   C. LATER RECEPTION
D. TEXTUAL HISTORY

A. PERSON
The name H., perhaps from the Aeolic *Ϝᾶσι* (cf. ἥδομαι), adapted to the epic-Ionic form Ἡσι- and ὁδός, possibly alludes to his father's occupation of trader: 'He who rejoices about the roads (journeys?)' [14]. His father left Cyme in Aeolia due to financial difficulties, and settled in Ascra in Boeotia (Hes. Op. 635–640). Because of the division of the paternal inheritance H. took legal action against his brother Perses, who attempted to bribe the judges (Op. 35–39). When H. grazed his herds near Mount → Helicon, the Muses appeared to him and bestowed poetic talents on him, instructing him to celebrate the origin of the gods in verse (Theog. 22–34). H. took part in *agones* in Chalcis in Euboea, held by the sons of → Amphidamas in honour of their dead father, receiving a tripod as victory prize (Op. 650–659).

This permits a chronological placement: Plutarch reports of Amphidamas (Schol. vet. in Hesiodi opera et dies, 206, 2–3 PERTUSI) that he died during the Lelantine War between Chalcis and Eretria (in the final decades of the 8th cent. BC). From Op. 650–659 the tradition arose that H. and Homer took part in the *agon* for Amphidamas and consequently were contemporaries (→ Contest between Homer and Hesiod). The

thesis [3. 46–48] that H. lived before Homer (e.g. Ephoros, FGrH 70 F 101), which has recently been taken up again, is untenable. 1. H. assigns a didactic purpose to poetry. This typical characteristic of the Classical epoch cannot yet be found in Homer. 2. The works of H. show a unified character. The 'Theogony' deals with the origin of the physical world and the gods, the 'Catalogue of Women' with that of mankind, the 'Works and Days' with the position and role of mankind in the world. This choice of topics shows that H. is closer to the post-Homeric cyclical and the lyric poetry of → Stesichorus than to Homeric poetry. 3. Although H.'s poetic language essentially corresponds to epic, it lacks the mechanical features, and embellishing eptithets are fewer, the etymology of names and words is used more often. [17. 94–100; 6].

B. WORKS
Two ancient lists of works are recorded: Suda 2,592,20–22 ADLER and Pausanias 9,31,5. Preserved are the 'Theogony' (Θεογονία), the 'Works and Days' (Ἔργα καὶ ἡμέραι, *Opera et dies*) and the 'Shield' (Ἀσπίς, *Scutum*). Large fragments of the 'Catalogue of Women' (Γυναικῶν κατάλογος or Ἠοῖαι, *Catalogus* or *Ehoeae*) are found in papyri. The authenticity of the 'Theogony' and the 'Works and Days' is assured, but the greater part of the 'Shield' is not genuine. The authenticity of the 'Catalogue of Women' has been questioned, at least in recent times (cf. [22. 125–176]). It is difficult to judge the authenticity of other works attributed to H.

1. THEOGONY   2. CATALOGUE OF WOMEN
(EHOEAE)   3. WORKS AND DAYS   4. THE SHIELD
5. ADDITIONAL WORKS

1. THEOGONY
The 'Theogony' comprises 1,200 verses. Verses 1021–22 form the beginning of the proem of the 'Catalogue of Women'. The proem (vv. 1–115) consists of the tale of the encounter with the Muses (vv. 1–35), which does not conform with the tradition of Homeric poetry, of hymnographic elements (hymn to the Muses, vv. 36–103), and of other traditional elements such as the statement of the theme and the acclamation of the → Muses (v. 104–115). Then in v. 116 the representation of the different generations of the gods begins. At the beginning is → Chaos, then → Gaia, → Tartarus and → Eros follow with no genealogical connection between them. Gaia is the abode of the immortals, Tartarus is located underground, Eros is understood as the elemental procreative force (vv. 121–122). Chaos is not closely determined; it has been interpreted as the undefined formless state of the world [15].

In general, the beings of the first generations demonstrate a double physiognomy: one physical and one divine. Those of the later generations (vv. 886–917), however, personify intellectual properties or ethical principles: → Horae (vv. 901–906), → Charites (vv.

907–909), → Muses (vv. 915–917). The sequence of the generations provides the structure of the work. The relationship between parents (or father) and offspring varies: in the first generations of the gods it is characterized by similarity or contrast, elsewhere it is more complicated: cf. the descendants of Nyx (vv. 213–225) [7]. This relationship has completely levelled out by the final generations, e.g. in the generation of the Olympians, who all descend from Zeus (vv. 886–944). The episodes which describe the succession of the gods show parallels with the myths of the Near East [20]. They emphasize the sequence of the generations of the gods: Uranus is followed by Kronos, Kronos by Zeus. The seizure of power by Kronos, as also that of Zeus, happens through an act of violence (vv. 154–182, 413–500).

For very important figures the representation becomes somewhat more detailed, e.g. for Hecate (vv. 411–452), who is ascribed great power, or for Prometheus (vv. 521–616), who, by his quarrel with Zeus, provokes the sending of women and evil into the world. Two battles are described in detail: that of the final generation of the gods against the Titans, the sons of Uranus and Gaia (vv. 629–720), and that of Zeus against Typhoeus, the son of Gaia and Tartarus (vv. 820–868). The final section provides an enumeration of the connections of the gods to one another and the descendants arising from them (vv. 886–962). A renewed acclamation of the Muses (vv. 963–968) introduces a further catalogue of unions between goddesses and men (vv. 969–1018). Finally, a concluding formula (vv. 1019–1020) and the beginning of the 'Catalogue of Women' (vv. 1021–1022) follow. 'Theogony' and 'Catalogue of Women' were obviously considered as a whole. In archaic literature, works often had no clear ending (→ Poems, division of) [9. 25⁴⁹].

2. CATALOGUE OF WOMEN (EHOEAE)

The name Ēhoîai ('Hoîαι) derives from ἤ οἴη, 'or she who'. This wording, followed by the name of a female figure, introduces the genealogic sequences. The work tells of the origins of the various heroic lineages produced by the unions of gods and women. The sons of Prometheus (fr. 2–3) form the beginning, followed by the fates of their descendants, down to the Trojan War, which is instigated by Zeus in order to bring an end to the mingling of gods and humans (fr. 1,6–7). The work also tries to give the reasons for the differences between human races. Genealogies of individual heroes had been part of the content of the Homeric epic, but here they become the tool for the systemization of the whole mythic tradition. As in the 'Theogony' the genealogical structure of the 'Catalogue of Women' is interrupted by the narration of special events, for example the deeds of the daughters of Tyndareus, the rescue of Iphimede by Artemis (fr. 23a), the deification of Hercules (fr. 25), the catalogue of suitors of Helen shortly before the outbreak of the Trojan War (frs. 196–204).

3. WORKS AND DAYS

The 'Works and Days' (828 verses) introduces the most innovations in content and style into the tradition of the heroic epic. The proem is a call to the Muses to extol → Zeus as lord over human happiness and failure (vv. 1–8). In vv. 9–10, the poet calls on him to watch over the justice of men, while he himself takes on the task of reporting truths to his brother Perses. H. must therefore correct the image of → Eris drawn in Theog. 225 (vv. 11–26). She has two forms: a positive one that stimulates healthy competition, and a negative one that leads to envy and strife and keeps people away from their work. The compulsion to work and the presence of evil in the world are explained by H. as the consequences of the quarrel between Zeus and Prometheus (cf. Theog. 521–616). Zeus' punishments include sending the first woman (→ Pandora) and the ills associated with her (vv. 80–82). These are followed by the evils caused by the progressive moral decay of mankind; this section (vv. 106–201) is divided into the sequence of the five → periods (génē). Further evils arise through the misuse of power, which puts humans on the level of animals, whereas they should be following the law of → justice (vv. 202–285).

This first part is followed by advice for the correct behaviour toward other people or gods (vv. 286–382) and rules for agriculture. H. places this occupation above all others (vv. 383–617). H. had hardly any experience with sea trade (vv. 618–694). After a further series of advice (vv. 695–764), the 'Days' (Hēmérai, v. 765 to the end) give instruction about times favourable or to be avoided for everyday activities. The authenticity of this section, called into question on account of the petty taboos and the contradictory method of counting the days [10], has rightly been defended [4. 346–350], as it is about everyday religiosity. The chronological guidelines (not only for the counting of the days, but also sometimes for the individual times of day) cannot agree with the very generally held rules of a farmer's calendar. Verses 826–828 announce the transition to the Ornithomanteía (divination by birds), which Apollonius Rhodius did not consider to be genuine (Schol. vet. in Hesiodi opera et dies, 259. 3–5 PERTUSI).

4. THE SHIELD

Verses 1–56 (of 480) are from the 4th book of the 'Catalogue of Women'. The ehoie of Alcmene contained in it tells of her double union with Amphitryon and Zeus and the conception of Iphicles and Hercules. The section beginning with v. 57 (not genuine, as judged by Aristophanes of Byzantium according to his hypothesis) probably goes back to the first decades of the 6th cent. BC [1. 34]. He describes the duel between Heracles and Ares' son Cycnus, who robbed travellers on the way to the Delphic temple of Apollo. The most interesting and significant part of the work is represented by the description of Heracles' shield (v. 140–320), comparable to the shield description in Hom. Il. 18,478–608 (→ Ekphrasis).

5. ADDITIONAL WORKS

Of the titles listed in the Suda, large fragments of the *Melampodía* (Μελαμποδία, total of 3 books) survive, which deal with the famous seers Melampus, Calchas, and Mopsus (fr. 270–279), and of the 'Great Ehoiai' (Μεγάλαι Ἠοῖαι). Despite the fragments (fr. 246–262) little is known of this work.

C. LATER RECEPTION

The two most important innovations by H. compared to the literary tradition are his calling as a poet, understood as a ceremonial appointment on the part of the divine, and the role of the poet as a teacher, possessing privileged knowledge. This brings great responsibility, but also special prestige. The famous tale of H.'s consecration as poet provides a series of widespread metaphors and symbols for the description of the poet and his art. Every ancient poet who concerned himself with his own calling and art modelled himself on H. [13]. The 'Works and Days' became the epitome of didactic poetry (cf. → Vergilius, G. 2,176). Many widely spread topics in ancient literature have their origin in H., e.g. the longing for the Golden Age, the problems of theodicy, and the relationship between humanity and divinity in general. Since → Stesichorus, all (particularly Hellenistic [16]) poets who dealt with mythography were inspired by the 'Catalogue of Women'. Little has been handed down of the scholarly study of H., beginning with the Peripatetics [4. 63–71]: the corpora of scholia to the 'Theogony' and the 'Works and Days' show only a few traces of revision by the Alexandrian philologists. Not a single papyrus contains fragments of commentaries on H.'s works.

D. TEXTUAL HISTORY

A separation is already visible in the papyri in the 1st cent. BC between the 'Catalogue of Women' on the one hand and the 'Theogony', the 'Works and Days', and the 'Shield' on the other (cf. PMichigan inv. 6828) [3. 51]. The 'Catalogue of Women' was the best-known of H.'s works in Egypt. More than 50 independent papyrus fragments have survived. The mediaeval record is generally of poor quality. The three works of the Hesiodic corpus are not uniformly represented in the MSS: the 'Works and Days' appear more frequently. The oldest codices are the Parisinus suppl. gr. 663 (11th/12th cent.), which contains a part of the 'Theogony' and the 'Shield', and the Parisinus gr. 2771 (10th cent.) with the 'Works and Days'. The remaining significant MSS go back to the time between the 12th and 14th cents.

→ Aratus [4]; → Didactic poetry; → Theogony

EDITIONS: 1 C.F. RUSSO, Hesiodi Scutum, ²1965 2 F. SOLMSEN, Hesiodi Theogonia, Opera et Dies, Scutum. Fragmenta selecta ediderunt R. MERKELBACH et M.L. WEST, ³1990 3 M.L. WEST, Hesiod, Theogony, 1966 4 Id., Hesiod, Works and Days, 1978 5 R. MERKELBACH, M.L. WEST, Fragmenta Hesiodea, 1967. BIBLIOGRAPHY: 6 G. ARRIGHETTI, Poeti, eruditi e biografi, 1987, 22–36 7 Id., Notte e i suoi figli, in: R. PRE-

TAGOSTINI (ed.), Tradizione e innovazione nella cultura greca da Omero all'età ellenistica, 1993, 101–114 8 K. v. FRITZ et al., Hésiode et son influence (Entretiens 7), 1962 9 P. DRÄGER, Argo pasimelousa, 1993 10 H. FRÄNKEL, Wege und Formen frühgriech. Denkens, ³1968, 316–334 11 Id., Dichtung und Philosophie des frühen Griechentums, ³1969, 104–146 12 E. HEITSCH (ed.), Hesiod, 1966 13 A. KAMBYLIS, Die Dichterweihe und ihre Symbolik, 1965 14 M. MEIER-BRUGGER, Zu Hesiods Namen, in: Glotta 68, 1990, 62–67 15 R. MONDI, Χάος and the Hesiodic Cosmogony, in: HSPh 92, 1989, 1–4 16 H. REINSCH-WERNER, Callimachus Hesiodicus, 1976 17 I. SELLSCHOPP, Stilistische Unt. zu Hesiod, 1934 18 F. SOLMSEN, The 'Days' of Works and Days, in: Id., KS I, 1968, 22–49 19 Id., Hesiod and Aeschylus, 1949 20 P. WALCOT, Hesiod and the Near East, 1966 21 M. L. WEST, The Hesiodic Catalogue of Women, 1985 22 H. TROXLER, Sprache und Wortschatz Hesiods, 1964. A.GR.

Hesione (Ἡσιόνη; *Hēsiónē*).

[1] Oceanid, wife of → Prometheus (Aesch. PV 558).

[2] Wife of → Nauplius, mother of → Palamedes (Apollod. 2,23).

[3] Wife of → Atlas [2], mother of → Electra [3], progenitor through her grandson → Dardanus [1] of the Trojan royal house.

[4] Daughter of the Trojan king → Laomedon, who has to deliver her up to a sea monster after breaking an oath to Poseidon (Hellanicus FGrH 26b). → Heracles frees her (this motif overlaps with the → Andromeda myth) without receiving the promised reward. Therefore, he conquers Troy (Hom. Il. 5,638ff., Pind. I,6,26ff.), kills Laomedon, and awards H. to → Telamon, with whom she bears → Teucer (Apollod. 2,103f.; 136; 3,162). She is able to ransom her brother → Priamus with her veil (Apollod. 2,136). The legend was popular in literature and art (Soph. Aj. 1299ff.; Alexis fr. 88ff. PCG II; Ov. Met. 11,211ff., Hyg. Fab. 31; 89; Lycoph. 337; Eust. ad Hom. Il. 20,150ff.).

BIBLIOGRAPHY: G. WEICKER, s.v. H., RE 8, 1240–1242; J. H. OAKLEY, s.v. H., LIMC 8.1, 623 ILLUSTRATIONS: J. H. OAKLEY, s.v. H., LIMC 8.2, 386–389. R.HA.

Hesperia (Ἑσπερία; *Hespería*). Ancient name of Italia, characterized from the Greek view as 'land in the west' after the geographic location of the peninsula (Dion. Hal. Ant. Rom. 1,35,3). Judging from the → *Tabula Iliaca*, it was used by Stesichorus perhaps as early as the 6th cent. BC. Since then the name H. has continually been used in poetry (cf. Hor. Carm. 3,6,8). With increasing geographical knowledge, for the same reason, H. signified Spain (Suda s.v. Ἱσπανία), which was sometimes called H. *ultima* by way of distinction (cf. Hor. Carm. 36,4; Serv. Aen. 1,530).

S. EPPERLEIN, Zur Bedeutungsgesch. von Europa, H. und occidentalis, in: Philologus 115, 1971, 81–92. G.U.

Hesperides (Ἑσπερίδες; *Hesperídes*, Latin: *Hesperídes*). According to Hesiod (Theog. 215f.; 275), clear-voiced daughters of Night (→ Nyx), who guard the golden apples on the far side of Oceanus. Genealogy (parents: Nyx and Erebus, Atlas, or Hesperus; Phorcys and Ceto), number (three to seven) and names (Aegle, Erythea, Hesperethusa: Hes. fr. 360 M.-W.; Hespere, Erytheis, Aegle: Apoll. Rhod. 4,1427f.) vary in the ancient sources. The Garden of the H., where the dragon → Ladon guarded the tree with the golden apples, Ge/Gaia's wedding present to Hera (Pherecydes FGrH 3 F 16), was most often located on a mythical island (Stesich. S 8 SLG) in the extreme west (Hes. Theog. 275; Mimn. fr. 12 IEG) near → Atlas, the bearer of the heavens (Hes. Theog. 518), and endowed with paradisal features (Eur. Hipp. 742ff.), but also presumed to be in Libya (Diod. Sic. 4,26,2), in the Atlantic (Plin. HN 6,201), or in the land of the → Hyperborei (Apollod. 2,113). As the last of his twelve labours, → Heracles fetches the apples of the H., either with the help of Atlas (Pherecydes FGrH 3 F 17) or by killing the dragon himself (Panyassis, Heraclea EpGF F 10 = PEG I F 11; Soph. Trach. 1099f.; Eur. HF 394ff.). In Apollonius Rhodius (4,1396ff.), the → Argonauts, on their march through the Libyan desert the day after Heracles' deed, meet the grieving H., who change themselves into dust, trees, then back into women and show them a spring. For the H. in art cf. [1; 2], for reception [3].

1 I. McPhee, s.v. H., LIMC 5.1, 394–406   2 G. Kokkorou-Alewras, s.v. Herakles and the Hesperides, LIMC 5.1, 100–111   3 Hunger, Mythologie, s.v. H., 228ff.

                                         A.A.

Hesperius Decimius Hilarianus H., son of → Ausonius. One of those family members who profited from Ausonius' proximity to emperor → Gratianus [2]. In AD 376/7 documented as *proconsul Africae* and 377–380 as Praetorian Prefect in the West with varying jurisdiction. Corresponded with Symmachus (Epist. 1,75–88). Epist. 19/20 Mondin (= 16/18 Prete) by Ausonius are addressed to him. Probably a Christian [1]. PLRE 1,427f.

1 v. Haehling, 298f.   H.L.

Hesperus see → Planets

Hestia (Ἑστία; *Hestía*). Greek goddess of the → hearth. Like → Vesta, she is a personification closely connected to her subject and cannot be separated from the ritual role of the hearth in both public and private domains. The cultic worship of the hearth probably derives from notions originating in the Indo-European period [1].

The cult of H. is generally characterized by the fact that she is addressed first in every prayer and is the first to receive a donation in every sacrifice (Pind. Nem. 11,5; Eur. Phaeton fr. 781,35; Pl. Crat. 401a). In Olympia she received the first sacrifice while Zeus Olympios received the second (Paus. 5,14,5). She usually does not have a specific cult with her own temple (unlike Vesta in Rome). Rather, her cult centres are hearths in private houses and in the public buildings (prytaneia, council chambers). She is, however, documented in the epiclesis of Temenia, a fact which suggests the existence of a cult district for her (Erythrae, [2. 363]).

In the public sphere, the sacred centre of every Greek polis is the communal hearth in the → prytaneion, where the goddess is worshipped as H. Prytaneia. Pindar (Nem. 11,1, generalized by the schol.) emphasizes the central role of H. in the prytaneion for Tenedos. In Athens, on occasion of the → *synoikismos* of Attica, Theseus collected the hearths of the individual demes into the one public hearth in the Prytaneion on the Agora (Thuc. 2,15,2; Plut. Thes. 24,3). The cult of H. Prytaneia is well documented in inscriptions, also playing a role in the ephebeia, in that the ephebes devote their first sacrifice to her (cf. naming her first in the ephebic oath of Drerus, Syll.3 3463,15). In Paros at the hearth there was a statue of → Scopas, brought to Rome by Tiberius (Cass. Dio 55,9,6; Plin. HN 36,25; [3]). A number of epigrams from Imperial Ephesus attest to a cult of H., the 'eternal → fire' (*pŷr áphtharton*), to Artemis, Demeter and Kore, and So(si)polis ('protector of the city') [4]. As is the case for the Temple of Vesta in Rome, eternal fire is attested for several cities in Greece, as in the Prytaneion in Athens (Thuc. 2,15,2) and in Delphi (Plut. Numa 9,5; [5. 125–129]). Colonists took fire from the Prytaneion for their newly founded cities [4. 114–134] and those seeking shelter fled to its hearth. Aside from the Prytaneion, council chambers (*bouleutéria*) had fixed H. hearths and consequently she was also addressed with the epiclesis *Boulaîa*. This hearth as a focus of the political community must be regarded in the context of the hearth in archaic and Mycenaean royal palaces or in Cretan men's houses (*andreónes*; Ephor. FGrH 70 F 32 = Str. 10,4,20). H. will have received sacrifices at the beginning of all official occasions and sacrifices at the beginning of the month have been documented numerous times, matching her ritual role in beginnings [2. 166^{31}].

At the same time, the → hearth and its H. cult is the centre of the private house. In a floor plan which was antiquated for the Imperial period, it was located in the middle of the main room (Gal. De antidotibus, vol. 14,17 Kühn). It welcomed those seeking shelter, was the location of the rite of Amphidromia [6], in which the father introduces a new-born to the household (→ Birth) by carrying it round the hearth, and the place of sacrifices to H. in the family cult. Both rites were characterized by their strict limitation to the house and its inhabitants (proverb *Hestíai thyeîn*, Paroemiographi Graeci 1,201. 242,97; 2,423,35). Because of her role in the Amphidromia, H. occasionally bore the epiclesis Kourotrophos (Chalcis, Imperial period [7. no. 88]; EM s.v.).

H.'s myths reflect cultic facts. In keeping with her importance, H. belongs to the Olympian gods. She is the daughter of → Kronos and → Rhea and so sister of

→ Zeus and → Hera (Hes. Theog. 454; Pind. Nem. 11,2; the firstborn, H. Hom. ad Venerem 22). She remains a virgin, despite being courted by Poseidon and Apollo, and receives from Zeus the role of guardian and recipient of sacrifices 'in the middle of the house' (H. Hom. ad Venerem 22–30). Her virginity reflects the invariability of the cult rather than the role of the unmarried girl in her cult (a hypothetical role derived from that of the Roman Vestals).

1 G. NAGY, Six studies of sacral vocabulary relating to the fireplace, in: HSPh 78, 1974, 71–106   2 GRAF   3 R. MERKELBACH, Der Kult der H. im Prytaneion griech. Städte, in: ZPE 37, 1980, 77–92   4 BE 1967, no. 441   5 I. MALKIN, Rel. and Colonization in Ancient Greece, 1987   6 P. STENGEL, s.v. Amphidromia, RE 1, 1901f.   7 L. VIDMAN, Sylloge Inscriptionum Religionis Isiacae et Sarapicae, 1969.

L. GERNET, Sur le symbolisme politique. Le foyer commun, in: Id., Anthropologie de la Grèce antique, 1968 (1952); J.-P. VERNANT, H.-Hermès. Sur l'expression religieuse de l'espace et du mouvement chez les Grecs, in: Id., Mythe et pensée chez les Grecs 1, 1965, 124–170 (Ger. 1996).   F.G.

Hestiaea ('Εστιαία; *Hestiaía*). Attic *asty* deme of the Aegis phyle, with one *bouleutḗs*, given the road connexion with Ancyle (Harpocr. s.v. τριχέφαλον) presumably northeast of Athens at Cholargus.

TRAILL, Attica, 39, 70, 110 no. 55, table 2; Id., Demos and Trittys, 1986, 127.   H.LO.

Hestiaeus ('Εστιαῖος; *Hestiaîos*) from Perinthus (4th cent. BC), student of Plato (Philod. Academicorum index 6,2 after Timaeus; Diog. Laert. 3,46), who, according to Simplicius, together with Aristotle and Heraclides [15] Ponticus the Elder heard Plato's lectures 'On the Good' and also recorded them. According to Theophrastus' testimony (Metaphysica 11–13 = F 2 LASSERRE = Testimonium Platonicum 30 GAISER), H., like Xenocrates, also concerned himself to a certain extent with the derivation of the realms of being from the principles.
→ Academy

F. LASSERRE, De Léodamas de Thasos à Philippe d'Oponte. 1987, no. 9, p. 97–102, 311–316, 531–538 (coll. of and comm. on the fragments).   K.-H.S.

Hestiodorus ('Εστιόδωρος; *Hestiódōros*). Son of Aristoclides, Athenian *strategos*, besieged Potidaea from 432/1 BC accepting the city's capitulation in winter 430/29 (Thuc. 2,70,1). He died shortly afterwards in the battle for Spartolus (Thuc. 2,79).

DEVELIN, 1381; TRAILL, PAA 423910.   HA.BE.

Hesychius ('Ησύχιος; *Hēsýchios*).

[1] Alexandrian scholar, author of an alphabetically arranged lexicon, which has passed down to us numerous fragments (primarily of poetry), allows many text variants to be restored, and is of special significance to the study of ancient classical exegesis, of dialects, and of the history of the Greek language. The basis for dating him is the *Epistula ad Eulogium*, which introduces the lexicon: some scholars identify the addressee with → Eulogius Scholasticus (5th cent. AD), others, including LATTE [3], dispute this hypothesis, nevertheless the dating cannot be later than the 6th cent. The same *Epistula* declares that the main source of the work is the lexicon of → Diogenianus [2] of Heraclea or perhaps an adaptation of it (H. cites this not as 'All Kinds of Expressions', Παντοδαπὴ λέξις, but under the strange title Περιεργοπένητες: *Periergopénētes*). Furthermore H. states that he added glosses by → Aristarchus [4] of Samothrace, → Apion, and → Helodorus and proverbs and orthographic rules by Herodianus.

This lexicon has been handed down via the Codex Marcianus Graecus 622 (15th cent.) in a highly abridged and interpolated version in which there are remarkable errors and inconsistencies. In addition, the original readings are obscured by the corrections M. MUSURUS entered directly into the MS as he prepared it for the Aldina edition. As for the abridgements within the work, themselves resulting from the intention to condense diverse materials, it is noticeable in the Codex Marcianus that a large part of the quotations are missing, and that there is a too frequent tendency to simplify complex lexicographical structures, creating misunderstanding (this explains various anomalous glosses, in which the relationship between lemma and explanation is not that of simple synonymy; others, on the other hand, have their origins in special types of ancient exegesis, not in a supposed irrationality of the glosses). The interpolations, however, are indisputable: in particular, the H. of Marcianus is in all probability the result of a fusion of H.'s lexicon itself and that of Cyrillus. In addition it can be postulated that the glosses of pronounced Atticist content are attributable to interpolations. This also applies to those which concur with the D-scholia to Homer, to others taken from a commentary by Euripides, and – as R. BENTLEY has remarked – to those Biblical glosses which come from an *Onomasticum sacrum* and from Epiphanius's treatise *De metris et mensuris ad Sacra Scriptura spectantibus*. Even the Byzantine lexicographers who used H. were familiar with a version contaminated by Cyrillian glosses. On the other hand some families of Cyrillian codices are just interpolated from H.

EDITIONS: 1 J. A. ALBERTI (ed.), Hesychii lexicon, I–II, Lugduni Batavorum 1746–1766   2 M. SCHMIDT (ed.), Hesychii Alexandrini lexicon, I–V, Ienae 1858–1868   3 K. LATTE (rec. et emendavit), Hesychii Alexandrini lexicon, I–II (A-O), Hauniae 1953–1966.
BIBLIOGRAPHY: 4 A. v. BLUMENTHAL, Hesych-Studien, 1930   5 F. BOSSI, R. TOSI, Strutture lessicografiche greche, in: Bollettino dell'Istituto di Filologia greca dell'Uni-

versità di Padova, 5, 1979–1980, 7–20   6 E. DEGANI, Problemi di lessicografia greca, in: ibid. 4, 1977–1978, 135–146   7 K. LATTE, Neues zur klassischen Literatur aus Hesych, in: Mnemosyne s. III, 10, 1942, 81–96 (= KS, 667–679)   8 B. MARZULLO, La 'coppia contigua' in Esichio, in: Quaderni dell'Istituto di Filologia greca. Cagliari 3, 1968, 70–87   9 R. TOSI, Studi sulla tradizione indiretta dei classici greci, 1988.   R.T.

[2] A Jerusalem presbyter H. is documented by → Theophanes (p. 83,6 and 92,16 DE BOOR) and → Cyrillus of Scythopolis (p. 26,19f. SCHWARTZ) for the first third of the 5th cent. AD; he presumably died after 450 and was a monk. He wrote extensive commentaries on the OT, only some of which are currently edited satisfactorily and some not at all, and homilies, a great number of which are now available in a critical edition ([1] is significantly more critical than CPG 3, 257–267, certainly, as regards the authenticity of individual attributions; cf. also the menologion of Basilios, PG 117, 373). In addition, fragments of a Church history directed against → Nestorius have been preserved (CPG 3, 6582). In other respects too H.'s theology is associated with → Cyrillus of Alexandria without however adopting his Christological terminology. In a part of his commentary he offers an outline of biblical texts with very concise and somewhat allegorizing glosses next to them (e.g. in the commentary on Obadja, CPG 3, 6558). In Jerusalem in around 570 the 'pilgrim of Piacenza' visited a church dedicated to Hesychius (It. Ant. 27).

1 G. LOESCHKE, s.v. H. (13), RE 8, 1328–1330.

EDITIONS: CPG 3, 6550–6583; M. AUBINEAU (ed.), Les Homelies festales d'Hesychius de Jerusalem, 2 vols., 1978/1980 (Subsidia Hagiographica 59); C. RENOUX, C. MERCIER (ed.), Hesychius de Jerusalem, Homelies sur Job: Version armenienne, 1983 (Patrologia Orientalis 42/1–2).   C.M.

[3] H. of Jerusalem. Priest (presbyter) and exegete, died after AD 451. He was a 'teacher' (διδάσκαλος) and 'theologian' (θεολόγος) in → Jerusalem (→ Cyrillus of Scythopolis, Vita Euthymii 16,26), granted refuge to the fleeing → Eutyches [3], and is said to have protested in writing against the decisions of the Synod of → Calchedon in AD 451. In his Christology he opposed → Nestorius (→ Nestorianism), without adopting the terminology of → Cyrillus of Alexandria. His exegetic and homiletic works employ rich rhetorical stylistic devices. Some homilies, compiled at the same time as the 'Jerusalem Armenian Lectionary' are of significance for the 'Jerusalem Typicon'.

R. MENNES, H. van Jerusalem, 1971.   K.SA.

[4] H. Illustrius. Greek pagan chronicler from Miletus, died probably in about AD 530; it is unlikely he was still alive in 582 [1. 1322; 2. 924].

H. wrote a history of the world, which has not been preserved, in six books. As evidenced in the 'Library' of Photius (codex 69), book 1 covered the time from Belus, the mythical King of the Assyrians (on Belus/Baal [3. 1106]), upto the Trojan War, book 2 up to the founding of Rome, book 3 up to the founding of the Roman Republic, book 4 up to Caesar, book 5 up to the founding of Constantinople AD 330, book 6 up to the death of Anastasius I (AD 518).

Only three fragments from book 5 (FHG 4, 145f.) and two from book 6 are extant (ibid., 154f.). Under the title *Pátria* ('Local history') *katà Hēsýchion Illoústrion* (Pseudo-H.) there is an (abridged?) new edition of an excursus, probably originating in the 10th cent. (age of the only manuscript, Palat. gr. 398), which was added before book 6 of the historical work. Its subject is the history of ancient Byzantium before AD 330, which is mythologically modeled on the legend of Rome. A collection of texts on the local history of Constantinople, as a whole *Pátria Kōnstantinoupóleōs*, begins with Pseudo-H.

Furthermore, according to Photius H. is said to have written a sequel to his historical work, covering the period up to the first years of Justinian I. (ruled from 527).

Another work by H., a collection of short biographies of non-Christian Greek writers, the *Onomatológos è Pínax tôn en paideíai onomastôn*, was available to Photius (9th cent.) only in the form of an epitome, the details of which are handed down by the Suda (c. 1000) in an again abridged form. Only a few quotations from the original survive (discovery locations in [1. 1324]). The work edited in FHG 4, 155–177 *Perì tôn en paideía dialampsántōn sophôn* is incorrectly attributed to H.

1 H. SCHULTZ, s.v. H. (10), RE 8, 1322–1327   2 ODB 2, 924   3 H. BACHT, s.v. Baal, RAC 1, 1063–1113   4 PLRE 2, 555 (H.I. 14)   5 Hesychios, Tusculum-Lex. ed. by H. BUCHWALD, ³1982, 336f.
ON PSEUDO-H.:
EDITIONS: 6 TH. PREGER, Scriptores originum Constantinopolitanarum, 1, 1901, 1–18.
BIBLIOGRAPHY: 7 ODB 3, 1598   8 A. BERGER, Untersuchungen zu den Patria Konstantinupoleos, 1988   9 G. DAGRON, Constantinople imaginaire, 1984.   F.T.

Hetaerae

A. DEFINITION   B. HISTORY OF THE INSTITUTION OF THE HETAERAE

A. DEFINITION

Literally translated, the Greek term ἑταίρα (*hetaíra*) means 'female companion'. It was first used by Herodotus (2,134,1) to describe a Thracian woman named Rhodopis, who was sexually available to men and thus became rich. In scholarly research, *hetaerae* were therefore often identified with prostitutes, with a comment that their being named 'female companions' was euphemistic. DAVIDSON [1], on the other hand, stresses that, on the evidence of the sources, friendship was the basis of a relationship between a man and a *hetaíra*. In ancient texts, the *hetaíra* was clearly distinguished from the παλλακή (*pallaké*, concubine) and the πόρνη (*pórnē*, prostitute) on the one hand, and the legitimate spouse (γυνή, *gyné*) on the other (Dem. Or. 59,122; Amphis = Ath. 559a f.; Anaxilas = Ath. 572b).

B. HISTORY OF THE INSTITUTION OF THE HETAERAE

As early as in the lyric poetry of the archaic period, which was conceived for the aristocratic symposium (Mimnermus, › Theognis of Megara, → Anacreon [1]), women are mentioned with whom men have extramarital relations (Mimn. fr. 1 WEST). A generic term for these women, mentioned by name in some places (Anac. 346 PMG fr.1), and described in metaphor in others (Anac. 417 PMG), is lacking in lyric poetry. On Corinthian and Attic vase-paintings from the 6th cent. BC, women are also depicted as accompanying the men depicted at the symposium. Not until the 5th cent. BC was a generic term found with *hetaerae* (Hdt. 2,134,1; 2,135,5) for those women with whom men maintained extramarital, long-term erotic relationships, and the name was probably designed to indicate the idealistic value of such relationships. Moreover, prostitution and women engaged in prostitution in brothels and on the streets are rarely mentioned in the sources (Xen. Mem. 2,2,4) – in contrast to the partly very famous *hetaerae*.

Many *hetaerae* were slaves under the charge of a procurer or procuress (μαστροπός, *mastropós*). They were generally hired out for a fairly long period under a contractual arrangement (Dem. Or. 59,26). Many a man bought the slave he desired from her procurer and then set her free for her to live in his home with the status of a concubine. Other *hetaerae* were free women (And. 4,14; Xen. Mem. 3,11) – generally foreigners or women with the status of metics (→ Metoikoi). Lovers of *hetaerae* who were free women had to take care of their livelihood and provided them with clothes, jewellery, accommodation or slaves (Dem. Or. 59,35). Those who could afford it maintained relations with several *hetaerae* at the same time. As it represented a financial burden, associating with *hetaerae* could cause conflict within a man's family, as recorded by some court statements (Dem. Or. 36,45; 48,53ff.; cf. also Lys. 4). On the other hand, costly *hetaerae* were appropriate status symbols, to demonstrate their lover's wealth.

Hetaerae served as companions in particular at symposia (Dem. Or. 59,33f.; → Banquet) and municipal festivals (Dem. Or. 59,24). Quick-wittedness and literary education were regarded as the *hetaíra'* s 'special qualities (Ath. 13,582c-d), as well as having dancing and musical talents acquired in schools (Isoc. Or. 15,287). A large number of men, including politicians, orators, sculptors and philosophers, who had relations with *hetaerae* are known to us by name. Many anecdotes about the *hetaerae* of Hellenistic leaders were current already in antiquity. An important piece of evidence of the legal and social situation of *hetaerae* is the speech against → Neaera, who, together with other girls, had been brought up by Nicarete to earn money for her owner as a prostitute and was then sold several

times over, lived in Corinth and in Megara and finally returned to Athens, where she was brought to trial for passing herself off as an Athenian citizen (Dem. Or. 59).

On the *hetaerae* of the 4th cent. BC and the Hellenistic period, Athenaeus [3] offers comprehensive material (13,566e ff.) that makes it clear that the institution of the *hetaerae* in that period was a favourite theme of comedy. As historical sources for the Greek institution of the *hetaerae*, the fictitious 'conversations of *Hetaerae*' composed by Lucian in the 2nd cent AD, and the 'letters of *Hetaerae*' of Alciphron hold little value, as they are strongly coloured by the attitudes of the authors and the literary tradition.

→ Eroticism; → Prostitution; → Sexuality; → Woman

1 J. N. DAVIDSON, Courtesans and Fishcakes, The Consuming Passions of Classical Athens, 1997 2 M. F. KILMER, Greek Erotica, 1993 3 C. REINSBERG, Ehe, Hetärentum und Knabenliebe, 1989. E.HA.

Hetaireseos graphe (ἑταιρήσεως γραφή; *hetairéseōs graphḗ*). In Athens, popular charge to be brought before the → Thesmothetai against men who held a public office or appeared before the council or the public assembly as orators, in spite of their willingness to engage in homosexual intercourse for money (Aristoph. Plut. 153; Dem. Or. 22,23.29; Aeschin. 1,19f.; 1,29; 1,51; 1,72; 1,87). The law (Dem. Or. 22,21) allots capital punishment and is also directed against a father or guardian who has prostituted his son or ward. Non-citizens were not subject to this rule.

→ Prostitution

D. COHEN, Law, sexuality, and society, 1991 (review: G. THÜR, in: ZRG 114, 1997, 479f.). G.T.

Hetairia (ἑταιρία/*hetairía*, also ἑταιρεία/*hetaireía*).
[1] In Crete a sub-category of citizenry, with communal meals (*andreia* or *syssitia*: Aristot. Pol. 1272a 12ff.; Ath. 4,143a-b = Dosiadas FGrH 458 F 2) and a common cult of Zeus *Hetaireîos* (Hsch. s.v. ἑταιρεῖος/ *hetaireîos*), but neither an association of family members nor part of a phyle, as was the *hetairia* in Thera or Cyrene (ML 5, l. 16). Acceptance into the *hetairia* took place after those fit for military service had left the → *agélai* and it was a prerequisite for full citizenship. In Lyttos the *andreia* were financed partly by the polis' own resources, partly by taxes on the land-holdings of non-freemen and by a small contribution ($^1/_{10}$) of the members. The origin of the *hetaeria* is probably to be seen as a reaction to the exclusive symposia of the archaic period (Hybrias in Ath. 15,695f–696a), so that they were hardly relics of a pre-state stage of development but were intended to bring about a stronger integration of the upper class into the evolving community of the polis.

H.-J. GEHRKE, Gewalt und Gesetz, in: Klio 79, 1997, 23–68; M. LAVRENCIC, ANΔPEION, in: Tyche 3, 1988, 147–161; ST. LINK, Das griech. Kreta, 1994.

[2] From the 5th cent. BC, *hetairia* generally served as a term for exclusive 'clubs'. They no longer consisted solely of 'aristocrats', but ultimately go back to Homeric *hetairos*-groups [1. 127ff.], which were not organized according to families but constituted the core of the followers of more influential householders [2]: as a consequence of the institutionalization of the polis their function changed, as they were actively involved in the power struggles within the ruling classes.

In Athens, the scope of action for the *hetairiai*, which formed only small groups of people, was limited after Cleisthenes. The failed attempt by Thucydides, son of Melesius, to exploit the *hetairiai* politically against Pericles (Plut. Pericles 14) is exemplary. Because of the mutilation of the herms in 415, *hetairia* members in general came under suspicion of planning to overthrow democracy [3. 7ff.]. The *hetairiai* became a serious danger for the citizenry of Athens through its campaign of targeted terror before the oligarchic putsch of 411 (Thuc. 8,54,4) and the seizure of power by the Thirty ([Aristot.] Ath. Pol. 34,3; → Triakonta). Thucydides (3,82,4–6) considered the *hetairiai* to be at the spearhead of internal power struggles in many poleis in the Peloponnesian War.

In Thebes, around and after 400, two *hetairiai* formed larger groupings, comparable to the *staseis* (→ *stásis*) (Xen. Hell. 5,2,25), whose protagonists sought to dominate the Boeotian League (Hell. Oxy. 12,2ff.) [4. 173ff.].

1 CHR. ULF, Die homer. Ges., 1990   2 K.-W. WELWEI, Polisbildung, Hetairos-Gruppen und Hetairien, in: Gymnasium 99, 1992, 481–500   3 O. AURENCHE, Les groupes d'Alcibiade, de Léogoras et de Teucros, 1974   4 H.-J. GEHRKE, Stasis, 1985.

G. A. LEHMANN, Oligarchische Herrschaft im klass. Athen, 1997; E. STEIN-HÖLKESKAMP, Adelskultur und Polisges., 1989.   K.-W.WEL.

[3] In the Imperial period, *hetairia* denoted a professional association (Latin *collegium*) or a private club; in Byzantium, attested only from the early 9th cent. AD, a unit of the imperial bodyguard partly manned by foreigners, whose function has not been definitively explained. From around AD 750 the term also appears as a synonym of *f(r)atría* (φ(ρ)ατρία; *ph(r)atría*), in the sense of 'adherents, followers' who were gathered to increase one's personal power and/or to prepare for a revolt.

ODB 2, 925; H.-G. BECK, Byz. Gefolgschaftswesen, SBAW, 1965, H.5; N. OIKONOMIDÈS, Les listes de préséance byzantines des IXᵉ et Xᵉ siècles, 1972.   F.T.

Hetairoi *Hetairoi* (ἑταῖροι/*hetaîroi*, 'companions') constituted the king's retinue in Greek monarchies, even on the battlefield (e.g. Hom. Il. 1,179).

In the Classical period *hetairoi* were especially important in Macedonia: selected by the king himself, they made up his immediate entourage as his closest advisers and as the next generation of leaders. The king went to war at the head of their unit, which probably resulted in the original, military meaning of the term. *Hetairoi* (often supplemented by βασιλικοί, *basilikoí*) are attested for the Macedonian cavalry with certainty only with Alexander the Great. It is not clear whether already under Alexander I or II the → cavalry as a whole, or first only its aristocratic core, was named *hetairoi*, with the term then being extended to the whole troop. In any event, under Philip II and Alexander the Great the cavalry was expanded (from 600 to about 2,000 men) and reorganized several times. At the latest under Alexander it was divided into eight *ílai* (troops) with a required strength of *c.* 200 men, and after 328 BC (until 324 BC ?) into the same number of larger *hipparchiai*. The *ílē basilikḗ* (e.g. Arr. Anab. 3,8,1), later also called ἄγημα (*ágēma*; Arr. Anab. 4,24,1; 5,12,2), which was regarded as especially distinguished, had 300 men, and was led into battle by the king himself. After the Indian campaign, the *hetairoi* occasionally had their numbers built up by non-Macedonian horsemen. For a while the Diadochi preserved the name and organizational structure.

1 P. A. BRUNT, Alexander's Macedonian cavalry, in: JHS 83, 1963, 27–46   2 N. G. L. HAMMOND, The Macedonian State, 1989   3 HM 2, 408ff., 705ff.   4 M. LAUNEY, Recherches sur les armées hellénistiques, 1949, 362f.   5 W. W. TARN, Alexander the Great, 1948.   LE.BU.

Heteroclisis see → Inflection

Heuneburg Near Herbertingen-Hundersingen, in the district of Sigmaringen: fortified settlement of the late → Hallstatt culture (6th/5th cents. BC), situated on the upper Danube (ford?), with an open outer settlement and associated burial mounds, some richly fitted out. The H. is one of the most important centres of power (→ Prince's seat) of the earlier Hallstatt period in central Europe. Excavations took place in 1937/1938 primarily on the 'Hohmichele' burial mound, from 1950–1979 in the 'castle' and from 1977 in the outer settlement (see map).

The fortification of the Hallstatt period consists of several phases with different kinds of wood, stone and earth walls; one phase (1st half of the 6th cent. BC) is formed by a mud-brick wall with bastions placed in front, based on Mediterranean construction techniques. The inner area (*c.* 300 x 150 m), only partially exposed, was a densely built-up area during all phases, with demarcated lots, craftsmen's areas, etc., according to different concepts. No living area for the princes ('acropolis') has been found.

The wealth of finds reflects various local crafts (pottery with the potter's wheel, metalwork, bone sculptors and turners, etc.) and especially links to the Mediterranean (Attic black-figured ceramics, Massiliote amphorae, etc.). The unfortified outer settlement was positioned over a wide area in the north-west and the west in front of the castle. It comprised large farmsteads

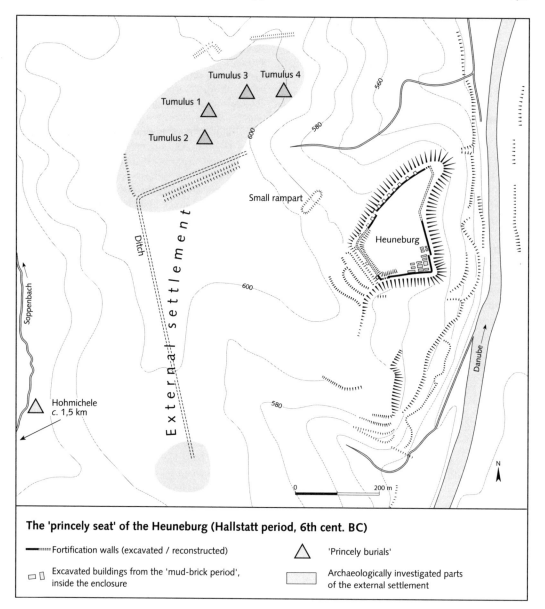

The 'princely seat' of the Heuneburg (Hallstatt period, 6th cent. BC)

━━▪▪▪▪ Fortification walls (excavated / reconstructed)

▢ ▯ Excavated buildings from the 'mud-brick period', inside the enclosure

△ 'Princely burials'

▭ Archaeologically investigated parts of the external settlement

and craft workshops of a similar type to those in the castle. In a late phase of the H. (end of the 6th cent. BC) at least parts of the outer settlement were abandoned and built over with large, opulent burial mounds, which are sometimes directly related to the farmsteads. The largest and most opulent burial mound, 'Hohmichele', is located *c.* 2 km west of the H. and contained several graves, partly robbed, some magnificently fitted out (→ Princely grave).

→ Bricks; → Crafts; → Fortifications; → Funerary architecture; → Lathe

W. KIMMIG et al. (ed.), H.-Studien, vol. 1, 1962 – vol. 10, 1996; Id., Die H. an der oberen Donau, ²1983; S. KURZ, Neue Ausgrabungen im Vorfeld der H., in: Arch. Ausgrabungen Baden-Württemberg 1995, 105–109.

MAPS: W. KIMMIG, Die H. an der oberen Donau, ²1983, fig. 34; S. KURZ, in: Arch. Ausgrabungen in Baden-Württemberg, 1995, 106, fig. 58.   V.P.

Hexakosioi see → Six Hundred

Hexapla see → Bible translations; → Origenes [2] B.

Hexas (ἑξᾶς; *hexâs*). Greek name for silver and *aes* coins from Sicily and (more rarely) southern Italy worth $^1/_6$ → *litra*; also called *dionkion*, Latin equivalent → *sextans*, since the coin system used there was based on 12 *unciae* to the *litra*. Value symbol: 2 dots. The extremely rare smallest silver coins (average weight 0.14 g) of this nominal are attested in Tarentum [5. 1117–1121], Acragas [2. 122], Himera [1. 30], Leontini [7. 1345],

Messana [7. 326], Segesta [1. 48] and Syracuse [3. 373]. Owing to the non-uniform standard of the bronze *litra*, the *aes* coins have greatly varying weights. Whereas in the 5th and 4th cents. BC they were on average *c.* 3.5 g in weight, in the 3rd and 2nd cents. weights of between 1.75 g and *c.* 18 g occur. Bronze *hexantes* were minted in Brundisium [8. 68] and by the Brettii [8. 185], in Aetna [7. 1162–1165], Acragas in round [7. 1047–1057] and conical forms [4. 113,22–36; 9. 120], Catane [7. 1278–1284], Centuripae [7. 1322–1326], Eryx with a value symbol of 2 rings [10. 583], Gela [7. 1334], Himera [4. 139,6–7; 6. 319], Menaeum [4. 146,22; 8. 357], Messana [9. 174], Segesta [9. 199] and Selinus [4. 168,24–28], on Lipara [6. 1087; 8. 550] and by the Mamertini [7. 420–422] and the Siculo-Punics [4. 195,1–8; 6. 516].

1 BMC Sicily, 1876   2 B.V. HEAD, Historia Numorum, 1910   3 E. BOEHRINGER, Die Münzen von Syrakus, 1929   4 E. GABRICI, La monetazione del bronzo nella Sicilia antica, 1927   5 O. RAVEL, Descriptive catalogue of the collection of Tarentine coins formed by M.P. Vlasto, 1947   6 SNG Copenhagen, 1942ff.   7 SNG, The Collection of the American Numismatic Society, 1969ff.   8 H.A. CAHN, L. MILDENBERG et al., Griech. Münzen aus Grossgriechenland und Sizilien – Antikenmuseum Basel und Sammlung Ludwig, 1988   9 P. STRAUSS, Collection Maurice Lafaille Monnaies grecques en bronze, 1990   10 SNG, The John Morcom Collection of Greek Bronze Coins, 1995.

K. REGLING, s.v. H, RE 8, 1387.   H.-J.S.

Hiarbas (Ἰάρβας; *Hiárbas*).
[1] H., Iarbas. Mythical African King of the Maxitani (Just. Epit. 18,6,1), son of Ammon and a nymph (Verg. Aen. 4,198). He unsuccessfully courted → Dido (Verg. Aen. 4,213ff.; Ov. Fast. 3,553f.), then captured Carthage after her death (Ov. Fast. 3,551f.).

A.M. GUILLEMIN, Comment Virgile construit un caractère. Iarbas, in: Humanités: revue d'enseignement secondaire et d'éducation 28, 1951, 20–22.   J.S.-A.

[2] Following the successes of Marius' followers, H. became king of East Numidia and → Hiempsal [2] was expelled in 87 BC. When the followers of → Cornelius [I 90] Sulla gained the upper hand in 83 BC, he was replaced once again by Hiempsal. H. was killed following → Pompeius' victory [1. 63f.] (Plut. Pompeius 12,4; Liv. per. 89).
→ Mauretania; → Numidia

1 M.-R. ALFÖLDI, Die Gesch. des numidischen Königreiches und seiner Nachfolger, in: H.G. HORN, C.B. RÜGER (ed.), Die Numidier, 1979, 43–74.   B.M.

Hiatus see → Prosody

Hiba (*Ibâs*) Bishop of → Edessa [2] († AD 28 October 457), where he, as teacher at the 'Persian School' and follower of Antiochene theology, translated the works

of → Theodorus of Mopsuestia, → Diodorus [14] of Tarsus, and Aristotle into Syrian. He was repeatedly attacked (i.e. accused of heresy and simony) and, as successor of the city bishop → Rabulas (Rabbula) in 436, was removed from office and exiled by the 'Robber Synod' of Ephesus (449) as a follower of → Nestorius, only to be reinstated at Chalcedon (451). Important is his letter from 433 addressed to the Persian Mari, the future archimandrite of the monastery of *akoímētoi* north of Constantinople [3], extant in Greek in the records of Chalcedon (CPG 6500: Acta Conciliorum Oecumenicorum II/1,3, 32–34): H. was anonymously convicted as a Nestorian in the 6th cent. (edict by Justinian in 544, Second Council of Constantinople in 553; the second of the so-called 'Three Chapters': [2]). His other works are lost, among them a commentary on the book of Proverbs, homilies and hymns.

1 G.G. BLUM (ed.), Rabbula von Edessa (CSCO 300), 1969, 196–205   2 A. GRILLMEIER, Jesus der Christus im Glauben der Kirche 2/2, 1989, 431–484   3 M. VAN ESBROECK, Who is Mari, the addressee of Ibas' Letter?, in: Journal of Theological Studies 38, 1987, 129–135.   J.RI.

Hibernia (Ireland).
A. ANCIENT KNOWLEDGE   B. TRADE   C. MIGRATIONS

A. ANCIENT KNOWLEDGE
Ancient geographers report little of the north-west coasts of Europe and the islands off this coast. The first knowledge regarding the island of Ireland, Ierne or H. was probably only obtained during the exploratory journey of Pytheas (*c.* 320 BC [1; 2]). Pytheas probably did not visit H. himself and his reports were only second-hand, but Strabo, Diodorus and Mela probably had access to his information (Str. 4,5,4; Diod. Sic. 5,32; Mela 3,6). Some elements of this tradition are pure fantasy (especially the horror stories complete with tales of cannibalism and sexual excesses). The geographical information for which Pytheas is the source, was more specific though not entirely free of errors. Strabo and Pomponius Mela report that H. is rectangular and lies to the north of → Britannia (Str. l.c.; Mela l.c.), which was repeated by Marinus and Ptolemy (Ptol. 1,6; 1,11,8). Caesar was better informed on the location of H. relative to Britannia, but he placed it too far south-west between Britannia and Hispania (Caes. B Gall. 5,13). Pomponius Mela reported the slow ripening of grain in H.'s climate; Solinus knew there were no snakes in Ireland (Solin. 22,3). Agrippa's map estimated the size of H. at 600 × 300 miles – a wild exaggeration. Mela miscalculated even more by equating the size of H. with that of Britannia. Caesar made an approximately accurate estimate: half the size of Britannia.
An important 1st-cent. AD source is Philemon (between AD 20 and 50), whose report was used by Pliny and who obtained at least part of his knowledge from merchants active in the northwest sea [1. 260f.]. When

Tacitus wrote his *Agricola*, H. was only little better known. According to him H. was smaller than Britannia, but larger than Sicilia; soil and climate were similar to those of Britannia (Tac. Agr. 24,2). The political and economic relationship to Britannia was not well developed. In AD 81 Agricola considered an invasion and conquest of the island but did not pursue the thought any further (Tac. Agr. 24,3). The knowledge collected to AD 100 about H. was summarized by Ptolemy in his *Geographia*; his main sources were Philemon and Marinus [1. 263–265]. His list of tribes, rivers and places is the most comprehensive for ancient Ireland: 16 tribes, 11 *póleis*, 15 river mouths and 6 ranges of hills are listed. It is risky to attempt locating his geographical information in the modern countryside, but admissible in some cases: Coriondi (Coraind?); Senos (Shannon?); Limnos (Lambay?).

B. TRADE

Considering that Ireland is so close to Britain, a certain amount of trade and other contacts should be expected. Finds of Roman origin have been made in Ireland, but not in large numbers [3]. They mostly consist of coins and pottery. In the 4th/early 5th cents. AD they are mostly precious metal objects that probably arrived as loot. Thus, the silver hoard of Ballinrees, Coleraine, was buried around AD 425 [4].

C. MIGRATIONS

In the late Roman period many raids were conducted from H. to Britannia. The northern part of H. was at that time held by the Scotti, who plundered the British coast before settling parts of west Scotland in the 5th cent. In one Irish raid on Britannia a young Briton, Patricius, was captured and taken to Ireland – he later became known as St. Patrick and converted many of the Irish to Christianity in the 1st half of the 5th cent. AD [5; 6].

1 J.J. TIERNEY, The Greek geographic tradition and Ptolemy's evidence for Irish geography, in: Proceedings of the Royal Irish Academy 76, 1976, 257–266 2 R.DION, Pytheas explorateur, in: Revue de Philologie 92, 1966, 191–216 3 J.D. BATESON, Roman Material from Ireland, in: Proceedings of the Royal Irish Academy 73, 1973, 21–97; 76, 1976, 171–180 4 J.S. PORTER, Recent Discovery of Roman Coins and other Articles near Coleraine, in: Ulster Journal of Archaeology 2, 1854, 182–187 5 R.P.C. HANSON, St. Patrick, 1968 6 D.DUMVILLE, St. Patrick, 1993.

C. THOMAS (ed.), The Iron Age in the Irish Sea Province, 1972. M.TO.

Hiberus

[1] (M. Antonius?) H. Imperial freedman, active in the financial administration of Egypt *c.* AD 26–28, perhaps in a similar position as the → *dioiketes* of later times (POxy. 3807; although he is not mentioned as *praefectus Aegypti* there). Tiberius appointed him in AD 32 as the prefect of Egypt for a few months after the death of

Vitrasius Pollio, but he died shortly after. The consul of AD 133, M. Antonius Hiberus, was supposedly his descendent (PIR² H 168; if the inscription AE 1975, 861 = [1] does not refer to him).

1 G. WAGNER, in: Bulletin de l'Institut Français d'Archeologie Orientale, 73, 1973, 183. W.E.

[2] see → Iberus

Hicesius Greek physician, head of an Erasistratean school in Smyrna, early 1st cent. BC (Str. 12,8,20); he wrote on → dietetics (Plin. HN 14,130; 20,35; 27,31), embryology (Tert. De anima 25) and toothache (Plin. HN 12,40). He was the inventor of a famous black plaster that 'helped with all types of wounds' (Gal. 13,787). Galen, who recorded four different recipes for this medication (13,780; 787; 810; 812) and cites the four authors (→ Andromachus [5] the Younger, → Heras, → Heraclides [27] and Statilius Criton), is puzzled by the differences, which are in fact so profound that no two recipes can be ascribed to the same source. V.N.

Hicetas (Ἱκέτας; *Hikétas*).
[1] Syracusan nobleman, friend of → Dion [I 1]. In the troubles after Dion's death in 353 BC he won the tyranny of Leontini. He initially supported the Syracusans in their struggle against → Dionysius [2] II. However, during his campaign against Syracuse in 346 he reached an understanding with Dionysius because of the approaching Carthaginians and supported his plea to the Corinthians for help. The superiority of the Carthaginians caused him to change sides by resuming the struggle against Dionysius and advising the Corinthians against a Sicilian expedition. In the battle against Dionysius II he even conquered Syracuse (with the exception of Ortygia) and kept it until Dionysius was finally expelled by → Timoleon in 343/2. After the Corinthians' landing, he fought Timoleon at the side of the Carthaginians, but after their retreat from Sicily *c.* 344 he made peace with him. When fighting between Timoleon and the Carthaginians erupted, he again joined the latter, but he was captured by Timoleon and executed after the Carthaginian defeat at the Crimissus in *c.* 340.

The continuous changing of sides by H. was due to his desire to play off the Corinthians and Carthaginians as the two external powers in Sicily against each other and to strengthen his position. Sources: Diod. Sic. (16,67–82) and Plutarch (Timoleon 1–33; a very hostile stance towards H., probably following Timaeus).

H. BERVE, Die Tyrannis bei den Griechen, 1967, 1, 275ff.; 2, 664ff.

[2] From *c.* 289/8 to 279 BC the ruler of Syracuse. In the troubles after the death of Agathocles [2], H. became the acting *strategos* of Syracuse in the struggle against → Menon of Segesta, who took the Italiot mercenaries of Agathocles into his service and besieged Syracuse with them. After initial successes, a Carthaginian intervention forced H. to accept an unfavourable peace and

the mercenaries (Diod. Sic. 21,16,6; 18,1ff.). He negotiated their withdrawal but they then founded the bandit state of the Mamertines in Messana. Later, H. successfully fought against Phintias of Acragas, but after a defeat against the Carthaginians, he was overthrown by Thoenon and Sosistratus, who called in → Pyrrhus and gave him the town (Diod. Sic. 22,2,1; 7,2–3).

H. BERVE, Die Tyrannis bei den Griechen, 1967, 1, 458ff.; 2, 732.   K.MEI.

[3] Pythagorean from Syracuse. Information regarding him is scant; he appears to have held the opinion – also attested for the Pythagorean → Ecphantus [2] of Syracuse (51,1 and 5 DK = Hippolytus, Refutationes 1,15 and Aetia 3,13,3) and for Heraclides Ponticus (fr. 104–110 WEHRLI) – that the earth rotates about its axis (or that of the universe), while other heavenly bodies stand still (Theophr. fr. 240 FHSG = Cic. Acad. 2,123; cf. Diog. Laert. 8,85); he also supposedly postulated a counter-earth (ἀντίχθων/antíchthōn; Aet. 3,9,2) – a theory otherwise ascribed to → Philolaus.
→ Heraclides Ponticus; → Pythagoras; → Pythagorean School

GUTHRIE, I, 327–329; W. BURKERT, Lore and Science in Ancient Pythagoreanism, 1972, 341; B.L. VAN DER WAERDEN, Die Pythagoreer, 1979, 462–464.   C.RI.

Hiempsal

[1] Together with his brother Adherbal [4] and cousin → Jugurtha heir to the rule of → Micipsa; tripartition of the kingdom. In 117 BC murdered on the orders of Jugurtha (Sall. Iug. 9,4; 11f.) [1. 59].
[2] Son of Gauda; the king of eastern Numidia; in 88 BC Marius' son fled to him. Pushed out in 87 by → Hiarbas but after the success of Sulla's followers in 83 again the ruler. In 63, Caesar supported → Masintha against H., who wrote a description of Numidia in Punic. [1. 63ff.] (Plut. Pompeius 12,4; Liv. per. 89).
→ Africa; → Mauretania; → Numidia

1 M.-R. ALFÖLDI, Die Geschichte des numidischen Königreiches und seiner Nachfolger, in: H.G. HORN, C.B. RÜGER (ed.), Die Numidier, 1979, 43–74.   B.M.

Hiera Kome, Hierocaesarea

(Ἱερὰ Κώμη; *Hierà Kṓmē*, Ἱεροχαισάρεια; *Hierokaisáreia*). Settlement in Lydia on the ancient Pergamon-Sardis road east of the → Hyllus near modern Sazova or Beyova. Hiera Kome (HK) developed around a sanctuary of → Anaetis; this cult, which was introduced under the Persians, was found throughout the Lydian Hermus valley and because of its strangeness (fire worship, Magi priests) was still commented upon by the Greeks in the 2nd cent. AD (Paus. 5,27,5ff.; 7,6,6). In 201 BC a victim of the invasion of Philip V (Pol. 16,1,8), the temple was again plundered in 156 BC by Prusias II (Pol. 32,27,11). By contrast, its inviolability (→ Asylon) was respected by

Seleucids and Attalids in the 3rd/2nd cents. (asylum guarantee of Attalus III: [1. 68]). Anaetis has appeared on coins since the Hellenistic period (BMC, Gr, Lydia, 102,1). Due to donations from the kings, the sanctuary possessed territory (boundary disputes with → Thyatira, cf. inscriptions of the 2nd/3rd cents. AD). No later than the 1st cent. BC, HK acquired an urban character. It was renamed to Hierocaesarea in gratitude for the 5-year tax relief granted by Tiberius after the earthquake in AD 17 (Tac. Ann. 2,47,3; ILS 156). The name *Hierocometae* (Plin. HN 5,126) became obsolete in the 1st cent. AD; the town name 'Hierocaesarea' appears on coins (under Nero). When all asylum rights were examined in AD 22, Hierocaesarea maintained its privilege (Tac. Ann. 3,62,3; Suet. Tib. 37,2).

1 WELLES.

L. BÜRCHNER, s.v. H.K., H., RE VIII 2, 1401f.; F. IMHOOF-BLUMER, Lydische Stadtmünzen, 1897, 5ff., 12f.; J. KEIL, A. v. PREMERSTEIN, Denkschr. der Akad. der Wiss. Wien 53,2, 1910, no. 18; MAGIE 2, 1019f.; ROBERT, Villes, 39, 84, 266.   H.KA.

Hierapolis

(Ἱεράπολις; *Hierápolis*).
[1] Important town in south-west Phrygia (as opposed to the town of same name in the 'Pentapolis' of central Phrygia) at the edge of the Lycus valley on the road in the Hermus valley from Sardis to Apamea, famous for its thermal springs whose water leaves white limestone terraces when evaporating; they gave the place its modern name Pamukkale ('cotton castle'). The water was used to dye wool: weaving and textile trade were the foundation of H.' wealth. The town was founded under the Seleucids and took its name from a cave that emitted lethal gases (Str. 13,4,14: *Plutónion*); on it the temple of Apollo Kareios, the town's patron deity, was built. His oracles are preserved in verse inscriptions and his epithet suggests a native deity that was equated with Apollo by the Greeks. H. was often struck by earthquakes; the earthquake in Nero's period provided the space for a huge building project under Domitian, while the theatre was reconstructed under the Severans (late 2nd/early 3rd cent. AD). A large necropolis with hundreds of sarcophagi and funerary buildings is preserved. In the quarries of Thiounta near H. a renowned marble was extracted. As the home of a large Jewish community, H. soon became a Christian centre; it was first an episcopal seat, then the metropolis of Phrygia Pacatiana. H. had several basilicas as well as being the location of the martyrdom of Philippus, the father of four prophetesses, who was soon equated to the apostle of the same name. Italian excavations have uncovered many monuments, sculptures and inscriptions since 1957.

T. RITTI, H., Scavi e Ricerche I. Fonti letterarie ed epigrafiche, 1985; BELKE/MERSICH, 268–272.   T.D.-B.

[2] see → Bambyce

[3] A town probably located on Crete's southern coast, only mentioned in Plin. HN 4,59, possibly identical with Hierapytna or perhaps only an epithet of Lebena [1].

1 P. FAURE, La Crète aux cent villes, in: Kretika Chronika 13, 1959, 200. H.SO.

[4] see → Castabala

Hierapytna ('Ιεράπυτνα; *Hierápytna*). Town on Crete, modern Ierapetra, at the narrowest point of the island between eastern and central Crete (Str. 10,4,3). In the Hellenistic period a significant political player as attested by several treaties primarily from the 2nd half of the 3rd cent. BC with other Cretan towns (Praesus, Itanus, Gortyn, Lyttus, Lato) [1]. There were links to powers outside Crete (Macedonia, Rhodes, Pergamum: Stv III 502; 551; Syll.³ 627). An aggressive territorial policy in eastern Crete, especially at the expense of Itanus, provoked a mediating intervention by the Romans in the 2nd cent. BC (Treaty of 112 BC [1. no. 57]). In 66 BC it was taken by Rome during the conquest of Crete (Cass. Dio 36,19,1f.). During the Imperial period an urban flourish (that has received little archaeological attention) with port facilities [2], theatre, amphitheatre, thermal baths and temples. In the Byzantine period a bishop's seat.

1 A. CHANIOTIS, Die Verträge zw. kretischen Poleis in der hell. Zeit, 1996, *passim* 2 K. LEHMANN-HARTLEBEN, Die antiken Hafenanlagen des Mittelmeeres, Klio Beih. 14, 1923, 201f.

M. GUARDUCCI, Inscriptiones Creticae 3, 1942, 18ff.; LAUFFER, Griechenland 268f.; I.F. SANDERS, Roman Crete, 1982, 139f. H.SO.

Hierarchy (Greek ἱεραρχία; *hierarchía*) Originally, the term meant 'sacred order'. The term hierarchy, which is not attested before late antiquity, was first defined in the late 5th cent. AD by the Neoplatonist (Pseudo-)Dionysius [54] Areopagites in his treatises *Perì tês ouranías hierarchías* and *Perì tês ekklēsiastikḗs hierarchías*: the hierarchy is a holy ranking that reflects divine beauty. All beings participate in God as the creator of the hierarchy and are ranked according to their participation in God. The hierarch is the man inspired by God, whose person is the pinnacle of the entire hierarchy subject to him. Precursors of this thought are found in Gnosticism and with the Church Fathers [3].

Pagan priesthoods lacked both the term hierarchy and the phenomenon. Even though a *hierárchēs* might function as a supervisor in some sanctuaries of the Greek world, there usually was only one priest for a sanctuary, to whom at most a few assistants were subject [2]. The highest authority in religious matters was with secular institutions, which referred particularly difficult problems to an oracle, especially the one in Delphi. There, → Apollo was the authority, not individual priests or the Pythia. In Rome the → *pontifex maximus* had certain powers of command over the Vestals and some other individual priests and colleges of priests. Their clear distinction in clothing, duration of office holding and cult resulted in a fragmentation of priestly power rather than a hierarchy. The decision-making powers under the Republic rested with the Senate [1]. In the Imperial period the ruler was the *pontifex maximus* and usually also a member of the four most respected priestly colleges (*amplissima collegia*), the → *pontifices*, → *augures*, → *quindecimviri sacris faciundis* and the → *septemviri epulonum*. This elevated the office of the *pontifex maximus* but did not constitute a proper hierarchy.

A change is indicated with the new religions of the Imperial period. There were seven degrees of initiation in the → Mithras cult. → Christianity developed the structure of → *episkopos* (bishop) – presbyter – deacon; late in the 2nd cent. the bishop of Rome's claim to primacy is first documented, but it only fully developed in the 5th cent.

Regarding military hierarchy, see → armies.

1 M. BEARD, Priesthood in the Roman Republic, in: M. BEARD, J. NORTH (ed.), Pagan Priests, 1990, 17–48 2 J.N. BREMMER, Götter, Mythen und Heiligtümer im antiken Griechenland, 1996, 31–33 3 G. O'DALY, s.v. Hierarchie, RAC 15, 41–73.

H. RAUSCH, s.v. Hierarchie, Geschichtliche Grundbegriffe III, 103–129. V.RO.

Hieratic Cursive form of the Egyptian → hieroglyphic script, both used alongside each other from their beginnings (*c.* 3000 BC) to the 3rd cent. AD. The cursive was especially used in administration, religion, literature, science, magic and for correspondence. Using black soot ink or red ochre ink, it was applied with a prepared rush stem (in the Roman period also with a reed pen) to papyrus, linen, leather, wood, stone, ceramics (shards), limestone slivers etc. It can also be found scratched or carved into stone (graffiti, steles) and other hard materials. Despite all its individual variations, the forms of the symbols and orthography of hieratic texts are very period specific. They permit dating according to phases of the Old, Middle and New Kingdoms as well as the Graeco-Roman period and even within them with more or less precision. During the 20th Dynasty differentiation of the Upper and Lower Egyptian scribal tradition is also possible. In the 7th cent. BC the hieratic script was displaced from daily use by a new cursive with a strongly deviating orthography, → demotic, and relegated to bibliographic and religious texts.
→ Egyptian; → DECIPHERMENT

G. MÖLLER, Hieratische Paläographie, 4 vol., 1936. J.OS.

Hierax ('Ιέραξ; *Hiérax*).
[1] H. of Antiochia, deserted Demetrius [7] I for Alexander [13] Balas (Diod. Sic. 33,3), and then deserted him in 146 BC for Ptolemy VI, whom he had pro-

claimed king by the Antiochenes (Diod. Sic. 32,9 c). He had a high position at the court and, as *strategos* (?) of Ptolemy VIII, he foiled the uprising of → Galestes, but then was eliminated by the king (Diod. Sic. 33,22; FGrH 87 F 4). PP 1/8,264; 2, 2163; 6, 17012.

[2] Sent by Ptolemy IX as commander in chief against the uprising in the Thebais in 88 BC; the revolt was put down by November.

> BENGTSON 3, 107; E. VAN 'T DACK et al., The Judaean-Syrian-Egyptian Conflict of 103–1 B.C., 1989, 147ff.; U. WILCKEN, Grundzüge und Chrestomathie der Papyruskunde, 1912. W.A.

[3] see → Pachomius

[4] Largely unknown philosopher, according to [1. 617 (= 79)] a representative of → Middle Platonism in the 2nd cent. AD. Author of a work (entitled 'On Justice'/ Περὶ δικαιοσύνης; *Perì dikaiosýnēs*?) from which Stobaeus quotes eight fragments. It examines several aspects of justice as part of a critical debate with the Stoa and the Peripatos.

> 1 K. PRAECHTER, H. der Platoniker, in: Hermes 41, 1906, 593–618 (= KS, 1973, 55–80).
>
> S. LILLA, Introduzione al Medio platonismo, 1992, 72f.
> M.BA. and M.-L.L.

[5] Neoplatonist of the 5th cent. AD. After the death of Hermias of Alexandria, his wife, the mother of Syranus, went to Athens with her sons Ammonius and Helodorus so they could attend the school of Proclus (Suda s.v. Αἰδεσία, 2,161,19–163,13 ADLER). Her friend H., the brother of Synesius (of Cyrene?) accompanied them (Damascius, Vita Isidori 79 and fr. 127 ZINTZEN) and also became a student of → Proclus (AD 412–485).
L.BR.

Hiereus see → Priests

Hierocaesarea see → Hiera Kome

Hierocles (Ἱεροκλῆς; *Hieroklês*).
[1] Carian mercenary leader of the 3rd cent. BC. In 287/6 together with Heraclides he foiled the attempt of Athenian democrats to take the Piraeus and the Munychia (Polyaenus, Strat. 5,17). Under → Antigonus [2] Gonatas, H. held the position of a Macedonian *phroúrarchos* ('commandant of a garrison') in Piraeus and repeatedly was host to the king. He was a friend of the leader of the Academy, Arcesilaus [5] (Diog. Laert. 4,39f.) and acquainted with Menedemus (Diog. Laert. 2,127).
→ Demetrius [2]

> W.S. FERGUSON, Hellenistic Athens, 1911 (repr. 1974), 150f.; 162; 234; HABICHT, 164. J.E.

[2] Greek rhetor about 100 BC from Alabanda in Caria. Together with his brother → Menecles (who was probably more significant, cf. Cic. Brut. 325) he was considered the main representative of → Asianism (Cic. Orat.

231); apart from the originality of the formulations, Cicero praised the artful parallelism in H.'s thought. The two brothers were very successful in their lifetimes; on Rhodes Menecles' students included famous authors such as Apollonius [5] and → Molon (Str. 14,2,13). H. seems to have closely co-operated with his brother (Cic. De or. 2,95). M.W.

[3] Stoic philosopher (2nd cent. AD). He lectured in Asia Minor and/or Athens and wrote treatises on ethics. One text ('Elements of Ethics') is preserved on papyrus, several dozen excerpts on pragmatic ethics are preserved in Stobaeus. They were taken from speeches on topics such as family relationships, marriage, the duties of citizens, household economy and religion. The 'Elements of Ethics' discusses theories of self-perception and → *oikeíōsis*. It takes the position that self-perception is the basis for self-possession. The text is also a source of stoic views of cognition and self-awareness, the nature of the soul and the 'self' as a complex relationship of the soul to the body. He sheds light on the problem of the reconciliation of the self-focussed tendencies of people (self-love, the natural desire for a proper development of one's virtue) with their social tendencies, which are the basis of virtues relating to others.

> H. v. ARNIM, W. SCHUBART, H.: Ethische Elementarlehre, 1906; G. BASTIANINI, A. A. LONG (ed.), H., in: Corpus dei papiri filosofici Greci e Latini I.1, 1992, 268–451; B. INWOOD, H.: Theory and argument in the second century AD, in: Oxford Studies in Ancient Philosophy 2, 1984, 151–183; A. A. LONG, H. on *oikeíōsis* and self-perception, in: Id., Stoic Studies, 1996; Id., Notes on H. apud Stobaeum, in: M. SERENA FUNGHI (ed.), Ὁδοὶ διζήσιος. Le vie della ricerca. Studi in onore di F. Adorno, 1996, 299–309; K. PRAECHTER, H. der Stoiker, 1901. B.I.

[4] He was considered a shameless slave of Carian origin and was a favourite of the emperor → Elagabalus [2]. He held great influence at the court and was able to obtain for his mother, a slave woman, an honorary position as a consular woman. He was to be appointed Caesar but was killed together with the emperor in the March of AD 222 (Cass. Dio 79(80),15,1; 21,1; S HA Elagabalus 6,5). PIR² H 172. T.F.

[5] **Sossianus H.** High official in the civil administration of the Tetrarch period (governor of Phoenicia, *vicarius*, governor of Bithynia and prefect of Egypt); because of his publishing activity and personal influence, he was a major inspiration behind the persecution of Christians in AD 303 (Lactant. De mort. pers. 16,4). His *Philalētés*, a Neoplatonic anti-Christian disputation is only known from its refutation in Eusebius' treatise 'Against Hierocles'.

> T.D. BARNES, Sossianus Hierocles and the Antecedents of the Great Persecution, in: HSPh 80, 1976, 239–259; M. FORRAT, Eusèbe de Césarée. Contre Hiéroclès, 1986 (SChr 333). B.BL.

[6] Educated jurist, author of the treatise 'On the Health of Horses'; wrongly considered the compiler of the *Hippiatriká*. His dates are unknown, but he worked after → Apsyrtus [2], whose work H. edited. For stylistic reasons it has been dated to before AD 500 or, more precisely, in the mid 4th cent. AD.

The work is dedicated to a Cassius who is not specified in more detail (and was wrongly equated with Cassianus Bassus), but who had supposedly asked H. to compile the work. It is divided into two bks. and represents a new version of the work of Apsyrtus in an improved style. It appears in fragments in the *Hippiatrica Berolinensia* and in a reconstructed version (apparently in the postscript of the latter work) in the illustrated MSS Leid. Voss. Q 50 and Paris. BN gr. 2244.

The second version was translated before the 14th cent. (with varying deformations of H.'s name) into Latin, Italian (illustrated text, using the names of Hippocrates and Damascenus) and the Sicilian dialect.
→ Hippiatrica; → Veterinary medicine   A.TO.

[7] **H. of Alexandria.** (5th cent. AD). Neoplatonic Greek philosopher, student of → Plutarchus of Athens. He taught in Alexandria and perhaps temporarily also in Constantinople, where he was persecuted because he was a pagan and sentenced to exile. We have a commentary by him on the anonymous 'Golden Poem of the Pythagoreans' and short fragments of his seven-book treatise 'On Premonition' preserved in the 'Library' of Photius (Cod. 214; 251). Contrary to an opinion long held by followers of K. PRAECHTER [1; 2; 4], H.'s philosophical system does not deviate from that of his time. H. did not refer back to Middle Platonist theories, especially those of the pagan → Origenes, nor did he accept Christian thought. Recent research [3; 5; 6] has come to the conclusion that H. was strongly influenced by the Neoplatonist Iamblichus through his teacher Plutarch and that his philosophy takes an intermediary position between → Iamblichus and → Proclus. The content of the 4th and 5th bks. of his treatise 'On Premonition', in which he attempts to demonstrate the agreement of the 'Chaldaean Oracle', Theurgy and the *Orphica* with Platonic teachings (Phot. Bibl. cod. 214,173a), also presupposes a degree of development in Neoplatonic philosophy that was only achieved with Iamblichus.

1 K. PRAECHTER, s.v. H. (18), RE 8, 1479–1487   2 TH. KOBUSCH, Studien zur Philos. des H. von Alexandrien, 1976   3 I. HADOT, Le problème du néoplatonisme alexandrin: Hiéroclès et Simplicius, 1978   4 N. AUJOULAT, Le néoplatonisme alexandrin: Hiéroclès d' Alexandrie, 1986   5 I. HADOT, Le démiurge comme principe dérivé dans le système ontologique d' Hiéroclès..., in: REG 103, 1990, 241–262   6 Id., À propos de la place ontologique du démiurge dans le système philosophique d' Hiéroclès le néoplatonicien. Dernière réponse à M. Aujoulat, in: REG 106, 1993, 430–459.   I.H.

[8] The otherwise unknown author of a work called *Synékdēmos* (συνέκδημος, 'travel companion'), an index of the 64 provinces (ἐπαρχίαι; *eparchíai*) and 923 (not 935, as stated in the title) towns (πόλεις; *póleis*) of the East Roman empire in the 6th cent. AD. It was perhaps based on a descriptive geographical work of the time of Theodosius II (cf. [1]), that was unsystematically continued by H. at the beginning of Justinian I's reign (AD 527–565) and transformed into a treatise on political statistics. It was used by → Constantinus [9] VII Porphyrogennetus for his early work *Perì tôn themátōn* (*De thematibus*).

1 JONES, Cities, 514–521.

PG 113, 141–156; KRUMBACHER I, 417; E. HONIGMANN, Le Synekdémos d'Hiéroklès, 1939 (edn., comm.); HUNGER, Literatur I, 531; II, 399.   K.BRO.

Hierodouloi (ἱερόδουλοι; *hieródouloi*, ἱεροὶ δοῦλοι; *hieroì doûloi*). Literally, 'temple slaves'; in ancient life they were, first, persons who (like land) were the property of a temple but not cultic personnel, second, persons who were donated as slaves (and often as cultic personnel) to the temple, and third, slaves who achieved partial or complete freedom through transfer to a deity (sacred → manumission). In modern terminology the holy prostitutes stand in the foreground (→ Prostitution), as attested in antiquity for the cult of Aphrodite in Corinth (Str. 8,6,20) and at the Eryx (Str. 6,2,6; Diod. Sic. 4,83 – in both cases referring to the past). However, in the sources on ancient religion the other functions are more important.

A large number of *hierodouloi* and large landholdings were characteristic of temple kingdoms in Asia Minor, such as that of Men (Str. 12,3,31; 12,8,14), and ecstatic male *hierodouloi* are mentioned for the Albani (Str. 11,4,7); in inscriptions they are called both *hierodouloi* and *hieroí/hierai*: They were assigned to a temple, tax free and could not be enslaved or sold. The institution dated back to the Hittites.

In Graeco-Roman Egypt, *hierodouloi* were legally free persons who were associated with a deity. This also continued a native custom. Some Mycenaean sanctuaries also possessed numerous 'slaves of the deity' (*teojo doero*) whose status was reminiscent of that of free persons. They were donated by the palace (Antiochus of Commagene in the 1st cent. BC still followed that custom, OGIS 383,161). In sacred manumission a slave was transferred from the possession of an individual to that of a deity without necessarily a mandatory service to the temple resulting in the process (→ *paramoné*).

P. DEBORD, L'esclavage sacré. Etat de question, in: Actes du colloque sur l'esclavage 1971, 1972, 135–150; Id., Aspects sociaux et économiques de la vie religieuse dans l'Anatolie gréco-romaine, 1982, 83–90; W. FAUTH, M.-B. v. STRUTZKY, s.v. Hierodulie, RAC 15, 73–82; R. SCHOLL, Hierodoulos im griech.-röm. Ägypten, in: Historia 34, 1985, 466–492; F. BÖMER, Untersuchungen über die Rel. der Sklaven in Griechenland und Rom 3, 1990.   F.G.

Hierogamou graphe see → Raptus

Hieroglyphic scripts
I. CRETE   II. ASIA MINOR

I. CRETE

A script that was formerly also described as 'pictographic' (but is still undeciphered) with many image-like symbols (human and animal body parts, plants, fruit, vessels, weapons, musical instruments, etc.) was created by the Minoan culture in Crete and especially used during the First Palace Period (1900–1700 BC). However, its origins are much older. The inspiration may have come from Egypt or the Levant, but the 'Anatolian hieroglyphs' are later. The evidence comes from 34 locations in Crete (main finding-places: Knossos and Mallia) but also from Cythera and Samothrace. So far, about 330 script-bearing objects are known (usually only a few symbols), among them more than 130 seals (made of stone or ivory); also clay pendants (*médaillons*) and prism-shaped lumps (*nodules*) with three or four sides (that often bear seal impressions) as well as brick-shaped 'ingots'. There are also short (one-word) inscriptions on vessels etc., but only a few tablets. The content is presumably usually profane, e.g., inventories of goods. The seals perhaps bear personal names or titles. The core of this script consists of almost 100 syllabic symbols; also, there are over 30 logograms as well as measure and number symbols (decimal system). The symbols were in part written in a careful and decorative manner (on seals) and in part in a hasty and cursive manner. In Middle Minoan III (17th cent.) the use of the Cretan hieroglyphic script (HS) overlaps with that of → Linear A; e.g., in Mallia and Knossos they existed side-by-side. Undoubtedly, there is a relationship between the two systems because many of their symbols resemble each other (and those of → Linear B).

A. J. EVANS, Scripta Minoa I, 1909; E. GRUMACH, Die kretischen Schriftsysteme, in: HdArch 1, 1969, 234–240; HEUBECK, 2–6; J.-P. OLIVIER, L. GODART, J.-CL. POURSAT, Corpus Hieroglyphicarum Inscriptionum Cretae, Études Crétoises 31, 1996 (fundamental, with extensive bibliography).   G.N.

II. ASIA MINOR
A. LUWIAN   B. URARTIAN

A. LUWIAN

The Luwian HS, which is primarily preserved on rock, orthostats, stelae and statues from Asia Minor and northern Syria (*c.* 15th-early 7th cents.) and was formerly, incorrectly known as the 'Hittite' HS for reasons of research history, is a genuine creation of the Luwians. It was specifically developed and used for writing the hieroglyphic Luwian dialect (→ Luwian; by convention named after the script), which belongs to the → Anatolian languages, although the HS was also used by the Hittites in the 15th–13th cents. on seals and in the 13th cent. for representational inscriptions (e.g.,

Boğazköy, Emirgazi, Yalburt/Ilgın). This is evident in the lack of the *e*-vowel (which Luwian did not possess in the 2nd millennium) and the acrophonically derived syllabic symbols; e.g., *u* (symbol: a cattle head, also serving as the logogram for BOS) presupposes ← *$uu̯a$- = Lycian *uwa*- 'cattle' < proto-Anatolian *$gu̯u̯ā́$- (< proto-Indo-European sing. acc. *$g^{u̯}ṓm$ < *$g^{u̯}óu̯-m̥$), also the specifically Luwian loss of *$*g$. The script alternated direction between left and right from line to line (*boustrophedon*). In the 2nd millennium it was still strongly pictographic, but in the 1st millennium it became increasingly abstract and linear as an adaptation to administrative use (cf. the few preserved letters and economic texts written on lead strips that are preserved in Assur and Kululu from the 8th cent.). Word separators were not in regular use. The system consists of a combination of logograms (now represented in Latin letters), which also functioned as determinatives and *c.* 80 syllabic symbols of type V (*a, i, u*), which in part only formed in the 1st millennium, CV (e.g., *ta, ti, tu*) and, to a lesser extent, CVCV (e.g., *tara/i*), among them homophone symbols identified by their frequency (e.g., *ta, tá, tà, ta$_4$, ta$_5$*). The graphic differentiation of syllable symbols after the *a*- and *i*-vowels in part only occurred early in the 1st millennium (e.g., *ịa : i, za : zi*), it never occurred in the case of *u̯a/i* and *ra/i* (always written with a ligature). Multiple meanings of Luwian hieroglyphs also result from some distinct oppositions not being described (e.g., tenuis/media, *nn/n*), through the graphically suppressed ante-consonant *n* and linguistically not covered *a*-vowel; in the 2nd millennium the increased use of logograms is accompanied by unwritten nominal/verbal endings. However, both phenomena, as is evident from the Ankarene silver bowl, which was published in 1996 (15th cent.; from → Karchemish?), with its largely syllabic inscription in which the endings are written out [1], are not characteristics of an as yet incompletely developed script. A relatively close, interpretative reading of Luwian hieroglyphs allows knowledge of morphology and word formation based on linguistic comparisons within Luwian; e.g., *á-za-tu [aztu]/á-ta-tu [adantu]* 'he shall/they shall eat', ASINUS*tara/i-ka-sa-ni-ịa-za [tarkasniịanz]* 'mules' (pl. dat.), *À-sú+ra/i*REGIO*-u̯a/i-na-ti*URBS *[Assurau̯annadi]* 'Assyrian' (abl.), AUDIRE-*MI-ma-ti-mi-i-sa [tummantimmis]* 'famous'. The Luwian HS, which in early 8th-cent. in Karchemish was simply called the 'urban script' in contrast to the 'Assyrian (cuneiform) script' and the (alphabetic) 'Phoenician' and 'Aramaic scripts' [2], was used at least temporarily and to a limited extent to represent → Urartaean [3]. However, in the 12th to 7th cents. it became a national means of expressing Luwian and asserted itself against cuneiform and alphabetic scripts. Its demise probably occurred primarily in the context of the political end of the Luwian states in Syria and Asia Minor at the hands of the Assyrians. For the most part, the Luwian HS, which has been known since the 18th cent., was deciphered in 1930–1950, but it only became possible in the 1970s through revised readings of a number of syllabic symbols (especially *i*, *i̯a*, *zi*, *za*; formerly read as *a*, *ā*, *i*, *ī*) to decisively demonstrate its suspected identity as Luwian. (s. also → Asia Minor, with a map showing the distribution of hieroglyphic inscriptions in the 12th–8th/7th cents.).

B. Urartaean

Apart from the Neo-Assyrian cuneiform, which was primarily used in Urartu, a HS is known from clay and metal vessels from Toprakkale (near Van), Karmir Blur, Kayalıdere and Bastām as well as on a single clay tablet (2 1/2 lines). The signs, which appear alone and in groups, are partially pictographs and partially abstract. Because the material is rather scant, only the logograms for the two volume measures *aqarqi* and *terusi* (according to the identical cuneiform inscription on the same tablet) have been deciphered.

→ Decipherment

1 J. D. Hawkins, A Hieroglyphic Luwian Inscription on a Silver Bowl in the Museum of Anatolian Civilizations, Ankara, in: Anadolu Medeniyetleri Müzesi, 1996, 7–24 2 F. Starke, Sprachen und Schriften in Karkamis, in: FS W. Röllig, 1997, 381–395 3 E. Laroche, Les hieroglyphes d'Altıtepe, in: Anadolu 15, 1971, 55–61.

Luwian: M. Marazzi, Il geroglifico anatolico, problemi di analisi e prospettive di ricerca, 1990; A. Mopurgo Davies, J. D. Hawkins, Il sistema grafico del luvio geroglifico, in: ASNP III/VIII 3, 1978, 755–782. Urartian: E. v. Schuler, s.v. Hieroglyphen, urartäisch, RLA 4, 400f.; M. Salvini, Gesch. und Kultur der Urartäer, 1995, 203–206. F.S.

Hieroglyphs The characters of Egyptian script in their detailed, non-cursive form, already in use before 3000 BC and in evidence until AD 394. The canon comprised *c.* 700 characters in more ancient times, some of which originated from the Hieratic cursives (→ Hieratic), and by the Graeco-Roman period reached *c.* 5,000 characters as a result of new formulations and in particular modifications. Texts are written in lines or columns, right-to-left or left-to-right. The direction of writing, especially on larger monuments such as temples or tombs, is often determined by orientation towards a symmetrical axis or a person represented.

The words are written in a combination of word and phonetic characters. The phonograms, which themselves in turn go back to word characters, reproduce only consonants (24 in the Old Kingdom, later, after changes in sound, fewer) – in characters of one, two, three or more consonants. Vowels are not taken into account and the 'weak' consonants j, w and alef only irregularly in the final position of the word. To reproduce foreign words and names, 'group writing' is already in use in the late Old Kingdom and then especially in the New Kingdom, in this case also for some Egyptian words and names. These also at least partially give expression to vowels. Of the word characters many are used independently as ideograms, often marked by an ideogram line (in feminines also with the ending t).

Many word characters are used in conjunction with preceding phonetic characters and so, as determinatives, identify certain semantic categories.

The texts are written in *scriptio continua*, but determinatives and ideogram lines also act as word separators. Only a small part of the vocabulary is written with phonetic characters only (in particular prepositions, prepositional adverbs and sentence particles, and also some substantives, adjectives and verbs).

The form of the characters and the orthography of the words remain strongly characterized by tradition, but over the millennia undergo many time-associated changes. The variance of the spelling of words is in part very broad, in other cases, often associated with the period, very restricted. Changes in sound are taken into account, if at all, with a time delay. In late antiquity knowledge of hieroglyphic script was lost (→ Horapollon).

→ Decipherment

H. G. Fischer, s.v. H., LÄ 2, 1189–1199; A. H. Gardiner, Egyptian Grammar, ³1957; Unité associée au C.N.R.S. 1068 (ed.), Valeurs phonétiques des signes hiéroglyphiques d'époque gréco-romaine, 4 vols., 1988–1996. J.OS.

Hieromancy, Hieroscopy see → Divination; → Sacrifices

Hieromnemones (ἱερομνήμονες; *hieromnḗmones*, singular *hieromnḗmōn*, ἱερομνήμων). Religious officials with wide-ranging duties. Aristot. Pol. 6,5, 1321b 35 counts them, together with *mnḗmones*, *epistátai* et al., as archives officers; Plut. Symp. 8,8,4 attests the title for the priests of → Poseidon Phytalmios in Leptis; this is an isolated instance. The copious epigraphical evidence shows that the *hieromnemones* in some places really were archivists, frequently organized festivals, conducted temple finances or looked after temple property; prominent *hieromnemones* were those of the Delphic amphictyony, who represented the individual member states (the duties in IG II² 1126). In some places, in Byzantium or Perinthus, for instance, the *hieromnemon* was the eponymous annual official; in other places *hieromnemones* remained in office for several years. They were normally organized in colleges; this and the religious bond are presumably the reason that *hieromnemones* sometimes appears as a translation of the Latin *pontifices* (Str. 5,3,2 or Dion. Hal. Ant. Rom. 8,55,3, for instance). *Hieromnemones* also rarely occur as functionaries in private cultural associations.

H. Hepding, s.v. H., RE 8, 1490–1496. F.G.

Hieron (Ἱέρων; *Hiérōn*).

[1] H. I. from Gela, → Deinomenid, brother of Gelon [1], born *c.* 540/530 BC. Married first a daughter of Nicocles of Syracuse (before 485), then of Anaxilaus of Rhegium (*c.* 480) and finally of Xenocrates, a brother of Theron of Acragas (*c.* 475). He was many times a victor in horse and chariot races in Delphi (482, 478, 470) and Olympia (476, 472, 468) [1. 208ff.]. Entrusted with the rulership of Gela by Gelon in 485, he succeeded the latter in 478 as tyrant of Syracuse. H. operated an expansionist foreign policy: in 477/6 he protected the Locrians against Anaxilaus [1] of Rhegium (schol. Pind. Pyth. 2,36), in c. 476 he helped Sybaris in the fight against Croton (Diod. Sic. 11,48,4) and in 474 he decisively defeated the Etruscans in the naval battle of Cyme (Pind. Pyth. 1,71–75; Diod. Sic. 11,51). In Sicily he founded the mercenary colony of Aetna in 475 (Diod. Sic. 11,49,1f.) and in 474 the town of Pithecusae on Ischia. In 472 he defeated Theron's son and successor Thrasydaeus of Acragas, who was contesting him over the hegemony of Sicily (Diod. Sic. 11,53,1–5). H. was a generous patron of art and culture. Those who spent time at his court included Simonides, Pindar, Bacchylides, Aeschylus and Epicharmus (on this [2]). H. died in 466/5 in Aetna and was given the honours of a hero there (Diod. Sic. 11,66,4). By contrast with the popular Gelon he was regarded as a despotic and repressive ruler (Diod. Sic. 11,67,2–4). Main source: Diod. Sic. 11,38,7–67,4 (predominantly from Timaeus, cf. [3. 44ff.]).

1 A. SCHENK GRAF VON STAUFFENBERG, Trinakria, 1963   2 D. A. SVARLIEN, Hieron and the Poets, thesis Univ. of Texas at Austin, 1991 (microfilm; summary in Dissertation Abstracts 52, 1991/92, 2541 A)   3 K. MEISTER, Die sizilische Gesch. bei Diodor, thesis 1967.

D. ASHERI, Sicily, in: CAH 5, ²1992, 147–170; H. BERVE, Die Tyrannis bei den Griechen 1, 1967, 148ff.; 2, 603ff.; G. MADDOLI, in: E. GABBA, G. VALLET (ed.), La Sicilia antica, vol. 2.1, 1980, 49ff.   K.MEI.

[2] H. II. of Syracuse, son of Hierocles (Syll.³ 427), born in 306 BC, first distinguished himself by bravery in the Carthaginian wars of → Pyrrhus in Sicily in c. 278–76. Faced with the Carthaginian threat to his home city, he set up a military monarchy in Syracuse in 275/74 with the aid of mercenaries and sections of the citizenry and was elected an authorized strategos (Pol. 1,8,1ff.; Paus. 6,12,2). He strengthened his position enormously by his marriage to Philistis, the daughter of an influential aristocrat (Pol., ibid.). After settlement of the Carthaginian war he first fought unsuccessfully in 271 against the Mamertines and then defeated them in 269 at Longanus and adopted the title of king: Basileùs Hiérōn (Syll.³ 427f.). In 264, at war again with the Mamertines outside Messana, he first allied himself to the Carthaginians (Pol. 1,11,7; Diod. Sic. 23,4,1), but soon, forced to retreat and besieged in Syracuse by the intervention of the Romans, concluded an alliance with the Romans that guaranteed him the rulership of Syracuse and parts of his east Sicilian area of influence (sources in StV III 479). H. kept doggedly to his pro-Roman line in both the First and the Second Punic War and supported the Romans repeatedly with money, troops and grain supplies. In c. 240 he elevated his son Gelon [2] to co-regent and gave him the title of king. Gelon died in 216/215

and H. himself the following year. During his long reign, which in titulature, dynastic order, court life and other representation has all the essential features of a Hellenistic monarchy, Syracuse experienced a final political, economic and cultural prosperity (H.'s building activity: cf. Cic. Verr. 2,4,118f.; Diod. Sic. 16,83,2. Effects of → Theocritus and → Archimedes [1] in Syracuse).

H. maintained close relations with the Ptolemies and made efforts to maintain harmony with the Greeks of his motherland. The lex Hieronica, which can be traced to him, regulated levy of the tithe in Sicily and the relationship between tenants and landowners. It was widely adopted by the Romans when they established the province of Sicily in 227 BC.

H. BERVE, König Hieron II., in: ABAW 47, 1959; Id., Die Tyrannis bei den Griechen, 1, 1967, 462ff.; 2, 733ff.; J. BRISCOE, in: CAH 8, ²1989, 44ff.; E. RAWSON, in: CAH 8, ²1989, 422ff.; A. SCHENK GRAF VON STAUFFENBERG, Hieron II. von Syrakus, 1933; H. H. SCULLARD, in: CAH 7,2, ²1989, 539ff.; G. DE SENSI SESTITO, Gerone II, 1977; Id., in: E. GABBA, G. VALLET (ed.), La Sicilia antica II 1, 1980, 343ff.   K.MEI.

[3] H. of Soli, helmsman (probably under → Nearchus) in → Alexander [4] the Great's fleet, in 324/3 BC, in connection with the plan for an attack on Arabia, was sent to circumnavigate the Arabian coast, but got only as far as the Strait of Hormuz (Arr. Anab. 7,20,7–10).

P. HÖGEMANN, Alexander der Große und Arabien, 1985, 91–93.   E.B.

[4] Son of Simus from Cos, where he acted as ἐπίτροπος (epítropos) to the children of Ptolemy VIII and Cleopatra III; between 124 and 116 BC he was honoured as τῶν πρώτων φίλων (tôn prótōn phílōn; → Court titles) for his services by Ptolemy VIII, Cleopatra II and III.

L. MOOREN, The Aulic Titulature in Ptolemaic Egypt, 1975, 207, no. 0383.   W.A.

Hieron oros (Ἱερὸν ὄρος; Hieròn óros).

[1] Holy mountain, name of a mountain range on the → Propontis, modern Tegirdağ. Religious centre of the → Thraci (Str. 7, fr. 55). The fortress of the Odrysae bearing the same name (Xen. An. 7,1,14) was situated there. Cotys I entrenched himself there in 362 BC at the time of the revolt of Miltocythes (Dem. Or. 23,104). Philip II conquered H. in 346 (Dem. Or. 9,15; Aeschin. Leg. 2,82f.; 3,73f.).

C. DANOV, Altthrakien, 1976, 122f.   I.v.B.

[2] Foothills on the south coast of the → Pontus Euxinus west of → Trapezus (Arr. Peripl. p. eux. 24), modern Fener Burnu, formerly Yeros Burnu), where according to Anon. Peripl. p. eux. 36, there was a city of the same name with a wharf.

OLSHAUSEN/BILLER/WAGNER, 135.   E.O.

Hieron Stoma ('Ιερὸν Στόμα; *Hieròn Stóma*). The most southerly branch of the Danube estuary (Str. 7,5,1; 8,6,1; Ptol. 3,10,2), also known by the name of → Peuce (Luc. 3,202; Plin. HN 4,79; Ptol. loc. cit.; Mart. 7,7,1; Amm. Marc. 22,8,46; Geogr. Rav. 4,5,13), in Scythia Minor, modern district of Tulcea in Romania. Of the seven branches of the estuary in the Danube delta the Hieron Stoma (HS) carried the largest amount of water into the sea. The HS was dedicated to St. George by the Christians and put under his protection; the name of the saint has survived beyond the Middle Ages into the modern period in the term for this branch of the Danube: Sfintu Gheorghe. In antiquity Peuce was also the name of an island in the Danube delta, probably north of HS.

→ Ister [2]

TIR L 35 Bucarest, 1969, 45, 57f. (with sources and literature). J.BU.

Hieronymus ('Ιερώνυμος; *Hierónymos*).
[1] Athenian, one of → Conon's representatives in his command over the Persian fleet in 395 BC (Diod. Sic. 14,81,4), campaigned for more expansive politics in Athens (Aristoph. Eccl. 201; Ephor. FGrH 70 F 73).

TRAILL, PAA 533930.

[2] Oecist from Mainalus in Arcadia at the founding of Megalopolis (→ Megale Polis) in 370 BC (Paus. 8,27,2), was one of the leading statesmen in Megalopolis and after 351 supported the policies of Philip II (Dem. Or. 18,295; 19,11). W.S.

[3] **H. of Syracuse.** born *c.* 230 BC, son of Gelon II and grandson of → Hieron [2] II. Succeeded the latter as king in 215 at the age of fifteen, initially under the control of fifteen guardians (Liv. 24,4). After the exposure of a conspiracy and execution of Thrason, who had pro-Roman views, the friends of the Carthaginians among his advisors gained increasing influence. By contrast with his predecessors, who had always been faithful to Rome, he therefore soon changed sides to the Carthaginians and allied himself with them to fight against Rome (cf. Stv III 529). According to Livy (24,26,1) he even planned a joint offensive against the Romans by Syracuse, Carthage and Egypt. However, in the summer of 214 he fell victim to a conspiracy. According to Polybius (7,7) the deeds and fate of H. were exaggerated and sensationalized in historiography.

H. BERVE, Die Tyrannis bei den Griechen, 1967, 1, 471ff.; 2, 735f.; G. DE SENSI SESTITO, in: E. GABBA, G. VALLET (ed.), La Sicilia antica II 1, 1980, 343ff. K.MEI.

[4] *Archisōmatophýlax* (→ Court titles), eponymous officer, *stratēgós* of Thebais (169/163 BC); his son Lysanias (PP 9,5189) was eponymous priest of the cult of kings in Ptolemais between 157 and 152 (on priestly offices held by his daughter see PP 9,5208.). PP 1/8,192.

E. VAN 'T DACK, Ptolemaica Selecta, 1988, 254, 269, 342. W.A.

[5] Tragedian and dithyramb poet of the 5th cent. BC; mocked by Aristophanes (Ach. 388) because of his superb thick head of hair. According to scholia (R Ald; cf. Suda α 676 and P Oxy. 6,856,27), in his inconsistently and unclearly constructed tragedies he used overly pathetic plots and frightening masks, though success with the public is attested for him; he is identified from the scholia (R; cf. Suda κ 1768) to Aristoph. Nub. 348–350 as the son of Xenophantus, who is ridiculed there because of his long, thick (body) hair and excessively lascivious pederasty. This equation is possibly supported by IG II² 1642, line 16 (mid 4th cent. BC), where a H. is mentioned as the son of Xenophantus and this is probably the same family (cf. PA 7556).

TrGF 31. F.P.

[6] **H. of Cardia.** Greek historiographer, born *c.* 360 BC. As a close friend of his fellow countryman → Eumenes [1] (Diod. Sic. 18,50,4 = FGrH 154 T3), in 320 BC he led a legation to Antipater [1] (Diod. Sic. loc. cit.) and after Eumenes' death in 316 remained as a high official at the headquarters of Antigonus [1] Monophthalmus (Diod. Sic. 19,44,3 = T 5). After his death in 301 he entered the service of Demetrius [2] Poliorcetes, who appointed him 'overseer and steward' of the Boeotian cities in 291 (Plut. Demetrius 39,4 = T 8). Finally he also had high standing with Antigonus [2] Gonatas (Paus. 1,9,8 = T 11). He died in full mental and physical health at the age of 104 (Agatharchidas of Cnidus FGrH 86 F 4).

The title of his historical work has been variously handed down as: 'Events after Alexander' (Suda s.v. H.), 'History of the Diadochi' (T 3), 'Historiae' (T 4–6). It began with Alexander's death in 323 BC (F 2) and went at least as far as the end of Pyrrhus in 272 BC. (F 15). H. opened the portrayal of Pyrrhus' wars in the west with an *archaiología* of Rome, according to Dionysius of Halicarnassus (Ant. 1,6,1) the first in Greek literature.

Only eighteen fragments of H.' work have been preserved, but he had lasting influence on the later tradition, especially Diodorus, bks. 18–20 (reservations more recently in [1. 194ff.]), Arrian, History of the Diadochi (FGrH 156) and also Plutarch, Lives of Eumenes, Demetrius and Pyrrhus. More recent research, especially [2] and [3], has therefore attempted to reconstruct and characterize H.'s work of history from Diodorus (cf. the excellent general assessment in [2. 1557f.]). The view of Pausanias (1,9,8) that H. judged the Diadochi kings, with the exception of Antigonus Gonatas, with bias and hostility, should accordingly be seen in relative terms; he does in fact prove to be 'a very reliable historian' (as in [3]). As a man of political practice H. had as little sympathy for the exaggerations of rhetorical historiographers as for the reports of 'mimetic' historiography, with their emphasis on sensationalism, and wrote in an unpretentious style without embellishments. FGrH 154.

1 F.Landucci Gattinoni, Duride di Samo, 1997
2 F.Jacoby, s.v. H. (10), RE 8, 1540–1560 = Griech.
Historiker, 1956, 245–256   3 J.Hornblower, Hieronymus of Cardia, 1981.

T.S. Brown, Hieronymus of Cardia, in: American Historical Review, 52, 1946, 684–696; R.Engel, Zum
Geschichtsbild des Hieronymos von Kardia, in: Athenaeum 50, 1972, 120–125; F.Landucci Gattinoni, Ieronimo e la storia dei diadochi, in: Invigilata Lucernis 3/4,
1981/82, 13–26; O.Lendle, Einführung in die griech.
Geschichtsschreibung, 1992, 190ff.; K.Meister, Die
griech. Geschichtsschreibung, 1990, 124ff.; I.L.Merker,
Diodorus Siculus and Hieronymus of Cardia, in: Ancient
History Bulletin 2, 1988, 90–93; K.-H.Richter, Untersuchungen zur hell. Historiographie, 1987, 33ff.; K.Ro-
sen, Political Documents in Hieronymus of Cardia (323–
302 B.C.), in: Acta Classica 10, 1967, 41–94.   K.MEI.

[7] H. of Rhodes. Peripatetic, lived around 290–230
BC. The majority of his fragments comes from writings
on ethics or the history of literature and culture, the
latter usually anecdotal. With his definition of the *telos*
as the absence of pain (*doloris vacuitas*, fr. 8–10) and a
work Περὶ ἐποχῆς ('On Suspension of Judgement', fr.
24) he consciously associated himself with the Hellenistic choice of subjects and we also learn that he believed
in, or at least discussed, a quasi-Atomist explanation of
sight (fr. 53). All the same, overall he seems to have
remained true to the Peripatetic tradition.
→ Aristotelianism

Fragments: Wehrli, Schule 10, 9–44; POxy. 3656.
Bibliography: F.Wehrli, in: GGPh², vol. 3, 575ff;
G.Arrighetti, Ieronimo di Rodi, Studi classici ed orien-
tali 2, 1955, 111–128.   H.G.

[8] Jerome
A. Overview B. Life C. Works D. Reception

A. Overview
The birth year of Eusebius H., as he called himself in
the Chron. praef., is disputed but assumed to fall between the years AD 331 and 348 (proponents of the
earlier dating follow the information given by Prosper
of Aquitaine, Epitoma chronicon MGH AA 9,451; 469;
the later dating is upheld by [1]). The location of his
place of birth, Stridon, is also disputed, H. himself describing it as lying on the frontier between Dalmatia
and Pannonia (Vir. ill. 135). H. died on 30 September
419/420 at Bethlehem.
    H. provides extensive documentation on the prob-
lems of allegiance affecting a Christian educated in the
traditional western manner. His mostly polemical involvement in intra-ecclesiastical disputes, owing much
to → Tertullian, is outstanding. In particular, and under
eastern influence, he made a case for an ascetic alignment in Christian life [2]. Of the four Latin → Church
Fathers, H. cannot be said to be the foremost theologian, but his was a personality of immense cultural
potency. His enormous authorial output, which continued throughout his life, is unparalleled, and it serves

equally as the main historical source for his own life [3].
Through his work as a translator and commentator, he
functioned as a mediator between Greek and Latin
Christianity [4]. During his sojourn in Syria, H. learned
Greek and Hebrew (epist. 125,12), thereby distinguishing himself from most western Christian authors.
Moreover, he influenced (indeed dominated) the later
attitude of Christianity towards the traditional Latin
literary culture of Antiquity [5]. In this he followed the
example of → Origenes, who had fulfilled this role on
behalf of Greek literature. Thus H. has been described
as a Christian humanist and a pioneer of the later re-
acquaintance of Western Europe with antiquity. In fact,
he exposed the problems of dealing with the traditional
literary legacy when he famously recounted a dream in
which he saw himself accused and punished before the
throne of God as *Ciceronianus ... non Christianus*
(epist. 22,30).

B. Life
    H. came from a Christian family which was evi-
dently wealthy, since after attending school in Stridon
he enjoyed a traditional literary education at Rome,
probably with the grammarian Aelius → Donatus [3],
whom he described as *praeceptor meus* ('my teacher')
(chron. for the year 354). While at Rome, he was also
baptized. His stay at the imperial court at Trier (Treves)
remained no more than an episode. H. seems to have
distanced himself quickly from an administrative
career. His decision to live the ascetic life led him first to
Aquileia around AD 373, then on a pilgrimage to Jerusalem. He next lived for three years as an anchorite in
the desert of Chalcis in Syria (*c.* 375–377). In 379 came
his ordination into the priesthood by Paulinus of Antioch, whom he accompanied to the Council of Constantinople in 381. From 382 he was once against in Rome
as secretary to Pope → Damasus, and while there he
became a leading light in a circle of ascetically minded
aristocratic Christians. After the death of Damasus in
384, H. was forced to leave Rome (385), going on to
Palestine, where from 386 he practised his ascetic ideals
with the help of Paula (the widow of a Roman aristocrat), her considerable fortune, and her daughter Eustochium. At Bethlehem he founded three cloisters for
women and one for men, and it was there, engaged entirely in his literary work, that he spent the second half
of his life, which was also his period of greatest productivity.

C. Works
    Among the earliest literary achievements of H. is the
Vita Pauli, the Life of Paul of Thebes, which probably
appeared before 381. It was of great literary quality and
came to have enormous influence in the West, like the
translation by → Evagrius [2] of the Life of Anthony
(→ Biography). Later (but probably still before 392)
followed the lives of Malchus and Hilarion [6]. During
his sojourn in Rome came the ascetic programmatic
tract *Adversus Helvidium de Mariae virginitate perpe-*

tua. H.'s most important literary accomplishment was the revision, commissioned by Pope Damasus, of older Latin translations of the NT based on Greek models. From 391–405 followed his independent translation of the OT from (variously) the Hebrew and Aramaic (Tobias, Judith) and from the Greek (Daniel, Esther). This collection would become canonical from the 13th to the mid-20th cents. under the name *Vulgate*. There are several editions of the psalms: the revision of the *Psalterium Romanum*, and the version of the psalms finally included in the *Vulgate*, which H. prepared following the *Hexapla* of Origenes. The latter of these revisions was named *Psalterium Gallicanum* owing to its widespread dissemination in Gaul. There exists also a *Psalterium iuxta Hebraeos*, which like the OT was translated from the Hebrew, but it did not achieve wide currency. The completion of this translation project, which he had begun while at Rome, was only possible once H. was permanently resident at Bethlehem. There are also many exegetic tracts which belong to this period, as well as the commentary on OT prophets (e.g. before 392 on the minor prophets Micha, Nahum, Habakuk, Zephania and Haggai), letters, 85 sermons, and the polemical pamphlets which H. wrote during the dispute which raged from 393 concerning the dogmatic legitimacy of certain teachings of → Origenes.

H. was strongly influenced by Origenes and had translated sermons by him, such as the homily on the Song of Songs. But now H. argued that Origenes should be denounced – opposing, among others, the friend of his youth → Rufinus Tyrannius. The break with Rufinus is attested particularly by the tract *Apologia contra Rufinum* in 3 vols. (402/3). There are also treatises directed against heretical movements (e.g. *Contra Pelagianos*) and – often unreasonably – against critics of the ascetic life. Thus in 393 H. took a moderate position with regard to marriage in the tract *Contra Iovinianum*. In 392/3, following the model of Suetonius, he wrote the Christian literary history *De viris illustribus*.

Of great importance was his translation of the 'Chronicle' of → Eusebius [7], which has otherwise come down to us only in an Armenian edition, and which H. supplemented for a western audience with more detail of cultural history and extended up to 378. It may well date from shortly after this; it developed into an indispensable instrument of Christian chronology. A unique source for cultural history and theology alike are the 154 letters, of which 26 are written to H. As a biographical witness they encompass H.' entire life, albeit with interruptions. Of particular importance, for example, are the letter *De optimo genere interpretandi* (epist. 57; [7]), which referred to the corresponding document by Cicero and formed a theoretical accompaniment to biblical translation, or the letter of 384 to Eustochium, to be interpreted as a treatise on virginity (epist. 22). In the last decade of his life he completed the commentaries on Isaiah (411) and Daniel (407), and the great commentary on Ezechiel and Jeremiah.

D. Reception

H.'s works reached a diverse audience. His monastic biographies became an important model, e.g. for the mediaeval hagiographical tradition (cf. the praef. of the *Vita Columbani* of Jonas of Bobbio, *c.* 641). The catalogue *De viris illustribus* received numerous updates. H.'s Chronicle was of fundamental importance for Christian → historiography. H.'s various commentaries were extensively cited and revised. The many pseudo-Hieronymian writings, too, reinforced his prominence. A dominant trait in H.'s reception is his interpretation as an archetypal ascetic and sage, an interpretation also evident in figurative depictions [8] (e.g. as 'St. Jerome in his Study' [9]). Well-regarded already in his lifetime, H. returned to favour after an interruption in the 6th and 7th cents., becoming one of the most widely copied authors in the Middle Ages. Great renown also came to H. during the Renaissance and the era of Humanism. Thus he was one of the authors most favoured by Erasmus. To the complete edition of the *Opera Hieronymi*, supervised by Erasmus and published by Froben of Basle in 1515, was prepended a Life of Jerome written by Erasmus himself. It is regarded as the first example of a critical historical engagement with the Church Father [10]. Of special importance is also the response to the dream, which served as a model for similar visions, e.g. in → Caesarius [4] of Arles, Odo of Cluny, Othlo of St. Emmeram in his *Liber visionum*, and Hermannus Contractus, and which is directly taken up by → Gregorius [4] of Tours in the first book of the *Libri miraculorum* and by Peter Abaelard.

1 D. Booth, The Chronology of Jerome's First Years, in: Phoenix 25, 1981, 237–259 2 P. Brown, Die Keuschheit der Engel, 1991, 372–394 (The Body and Society, 1988) 3 Ch. Favez, Saint Jérôme peint par lui-même (Collection Latomus 33), 1958 4 W. C. McDermott, Saint Jerome and Pagan Greek Literature, in: Vigiliae Christianae 36, 1982, 372–383 5 H. Hagendahl, Latin Fathers and the Classics, 1958, 89–328 6 M. Fuhrmann, Die Mönchsgeschichten des H., in: Entretiens 23, 1977, 41–89 7 G. J. M. Bartelink, Liber de optimo genere interpretandi (epist. 57), 1980 8 R. Jungblut, H.: Darstellung und Verehrung eines Kirchenvaters, thesis Tübingen 1967 9 O. Pächt, Zur Entstehung des "H. im Gehäus", in: Pantheon 21, 1963, 131–142 10 J. B. Maguire, Erasmus' Biographical Masterpiece: Hieronymi Stridonensis Vita, in: RQ 26, 1973, 265–273.

Editions: PL 22–30, Suppl. 2.; CCL 72–80 (not yet complete); Hilberg, CSEL 54–56, 1910–1918 (epist.); J. Labourt, 8 vols., 1949–1963 (Lat.-French); CSEL 88, 1981 (newly discovered Letters to Augustinus); E. Richardson, De viris illustribus, 1896; H. Quentin et al., Biblia Sacra iuxta Latinam vulgatam versionem, 1926ff. (Vulgata; not yet complete); J. Wordsworth, H. J. White, F. D. Sparks, 1889–1949; R. Helm, GCS 47, ²1986 (Chronicle); Overview: H. J. Frede, Kirchenschriftsteller-Verzeichnis und Sigel, 1954, 510–532. Transl.: BKV 15f. 18 (selection).

Bibliography: G. Grützmacher, H. (Stud. zur Geschichte der Theologie und der Kirche 6/10), 3 vols., 1901–1908; P. Jay, L'exégèse de s. Jérôme d'après son Commentaire sur Isaie, 1985; J. N. D. Kelly, Jerome,

1975; E.F. Rice jr., Saint Jerome in the Renaissance, 1985; K. Sugano, Das Rombild des H., 1983. U.E.

Hierophantes see → Mysteria

Hieropoioi see → Sacrifices

Hieros Gamos (ἱερὸς γάμος; *hieròs gámos*: sacred marriage).
I. Term II. Ancient Orient III. Greece

I. Term

A term which has attained great significance in modern research as the name for a ritual sexual union, since the emergence of the fertility paradigm in the 19th cent. (Mannhardt, Frazer). Based on the sexual intercourse between → Demeter and her mortal lover → Iasion 'in a thrice-ploughed field' recounted in the Homeric epic (Hom. Od. 5, 125–128; Hes. Theog. 969–971), which has been understood by analogy with north-European customs as the reflection of a sexual ritual for promoting agricultural and human fertility [1], analogous rites have been sought both in Greece and in the Ancient Orient. Whereas in the Ancient Orient such rites were regarded as proven in the cult of Inanna-Ištar-Astarte and the fertility paradigm was therefore retained until quite recently [2], only a few, disparate phenomena have remained in research on Greek religion after the rejection of this paradigm.

1 J.W. E. Mannhardt, Der Baumcultus der Germanen und ihrer Nachbarstämme, 1875, 480–488 2 S.N. Kramer, The Sacred Marriage Rite, 1969. F.G.

III. Ancient Orient

At first associated with the *hieros gamos* of Inanna (→ Ishtar), the city goddess of → Uruk, with the legendary ruler of the city, Dumuzi (→ Tammuz), performed as a cult, *hieros gamos* became the subject of numerous cult songs, confined to the period from the 21st to the 20th cent. BC. By contrast with the view, erroneously held in the wake of Frazer [2. 251f.], that this was a fertility rite, the union of goddess and ruler represents an ancient legitimization rite, revived by the rulers of the 3rd dynasty of Ur (→ Mesopotamia) and native to Uruk, at the beginning of the reign of a ruler [3]. These are not the same as the theogamies depicted in myths and mythologems, sometimes of cosmogonic relevance.

1 E. Matsushima, Texte accadien du rituel du marriage divin, 1985 2 J. Renger, s.v. h.g., RLA 4, 251–259 3 Id., s.v. Inthronisation, RLA 5, 128–136 4 W. H. Ph. Römer, Einige Überlegungen zur "Heiligen Hochzeit" nach altoriental. Texten (AOAT 211), 1982 5 P. Steinkeller, On Rulers, Priests and Sacred Marriage, in: K. Watanabe, (ed.), Priests and Officials in the Ancient Near East, 1998, 103–138 (with bibliography). J.RE.

III. Greece

Some local myths recount the marriage or the first sexual intercourse of the gods → Zeus and → Hera; the Homeric account of Hera's seduction of Zeus (*Diòs apátē*, Hom. Il. 14,159ff.) in the general view follows corresponding myths [1]. However, to associate these myths with sexual rites is very problematic. The sacrifice of a piglet for Zeus Heraios (LSCG Suppl. 1 A 20) and celebratory meals are attested for the Athenian festival of *theogamia* ('wedding of the gods', schol. Hes. Op. 780), which is probably identical to the Athenian festival called the 'sacred marriage of Zeus and Hera' [2]; the term *hieros gamos*, attested in Greek only in this context, seems to mean no more than a 'marriage relevant to the ritual' in the sense that a lively, sumptuous feast was justified by the corresponding myth. The festival was in the month of Gamelion; so it may have been the incentive for an increase in marriages. The Boeotian Daedala, in which a wedding procession with dolls took place, ending with their being burnt and a sacrificial festival in neighbouring cities, therefore have a clearly political function (Paus. 9,3,8), which fits in with the dual character of → Hera as goddess of *polis* and marriage. The Samian Toneia, which Varro (in Lactant. Div. inst. 1,17,8) calls a wedding, are a festival of release (with the untying of the otherwise bound cult image of venerable age), which in the typology is part of New Year's celebrations and again is associated with the marriage of the goddess only in myth [3].

Corresponding rites are supposed on the one hand in Crete and on the other in the Athenian Dionysus cult. The wedding of Zeus and Hera was 'imitated' in Crete (Diod. Sic. 5,72,4); the expression seems, however, to refer to nothing more than a lavish feast corresponding to the Athenian *theogamia*. In Athens at the festival of the → Anthesteria the wedding of the Basilinna (the wife of the chief religious officer, the Archon Basileus) to → Dionysus was performed in the Boukolion at the Agora; ancient witnesses use technical vocabulary ('give in marriage': Dem. Or. 59,63; *symmeîxis*, 'sexual act': Aristot. Ath. Pol. 3,5), and pictures on vases represent the Basilinna being led to the wedding by a → Satyr who is giving her away [4]. However, there is no information on the exact form of the ritual or the function; the ritually professed dissolution of the marriage of the Archon Basileus may belong to the onset of the Dionysian period of exception and its unregulated sexuality.

1 J.C. Bermejo Barrera, Zeus, Hera y el matrimonio sagrado, in: Quaderni di Storia 15, 1989, 133–156 2 Deubner, 177 n. 11 3 Graf, 93–96 4 A. Lezzi-Hafter, Anthesterien und H.G. Ein Choenbild des Methyse-Malers, in: Proc. of the 3rd Symposion on Ancient and Related Pottery, 1989, 325–334.

A. Klinz, H.G., 1933; Nilsson, GGR 1, 120–122; Burkert, 176–178; M. Cremer, H.G. im Orient und in Griechenland, in: ZPE 48, 1982, 283–290; A. Avagianou, Sacred Marriage in the Rituals of Greek Rel., 1991. F.G.

Hierosolyma see → Jerusalem

Hierosylia (ἱεροσυλία; *hierosylía*). In many Greek poleis 'temple robbery', removal from a sanctuary of objects consecrated to gods, which has been very broadly construed (e.g. also embezzlement of silver in state minting of coins, Syll.³ 530, Dyme in Achaea, soon after 190 BC. [2]). In Athens *hierosylia* was probably prosecuted in the 5th cent. by → *eisangelía*, later by a coming under the jurisdiction of the → thesmothetai ἱεροσυλίας γραφή (*hierosylías graphḗ*), involving the threat of the death penalty with denial of burial in Attica and financial ruin.

> 1 D. COHEN, Theft in Athenian Law, 1983, 93ff.
> 2 G. THÜR, G. STUMPF, Sechs Todesurteile und zwei plattierte Hemidrachmen aus Dyme, in: Tyche 4, 1989, 171–183.   G.T.

High treason see → Perduellio

Hiketeia (ἱκεσία, *hikesía*; ἱκετεία, *hiketeía*). With the ritual of *hiketeia* someone seeking protection (ἱκέτης, *hikétēs*) documents his status and requests help, often for acceptance in a new community. *Hiketeía* and *hikétēs* are derived from ἵκω, ἱκνέομαι, 'arrive' (cf. Hsch. s.v. ἱκέσθαι, ἱκετεῦσαι), and therefore the *hikétēs* is firstly the one who 'arrives'. As an institution of Greek sacral law, comparable with the stranger's right to hospitality (Hom. Od. 8,546f.; Hes. Op. 327f.; → Hospitality, → Aliens, position of) and closely associated with the establishment of the → asylia [7; 8] – since the Hellenistic period also part of state law –, the *hiketeia* represents an important counterbalance in the overall and interstate structure of power. The *hiketeia* is attested for the whole of Greek antiquity; the sources of the archaic and classical periods (especially epic and drama) are particularly informative about the details of the way the ritual was performed.

The attitude of the person pleading for protection seated by a hearth (Hom. Od. 7,153; Thuc. 1,136,3), altar (Hom. Od. 22,334f.; Aesch. Supp. 189f.; Thuc. 1,126,11) or image of a god (Aesch. Eum. 259) signifies his request; he is additionally marked out as a *hikétēs* by an olive branch, bound with wool and usually placed on the altar, the *hiketēría* (Aesch. Eum. 43–45; Soph. OT 3; Plut. Thes. 18,1; [1]; on the *hiketeia* branch before the public assembly: Aristot. Ath. Pol. 43,6; before the *boulḗ*: Dem. Or. 18,107). If the person asking for protection is turning directly to one person, he underlines his plea with → gestures with ritual connotations: as well as touching the chin and hands of the person being addressed, grasping his knee is of particular significance (Hom. Il. 1,498ff.; on the knee as the seat of the *vitalitas* or as an altar cf. Plin. HN 11,103; [4. 21f.; 5]). The function of contact with the divine sphere central to *hiketeia* is attested by Plutarch (Plut. Solon 12): those pleading for protection fasten a rope to the statue of Athena (cf. Hdt. 1,26). The binding power of *hiketeia* is based on the sanctity of all people or objects located on

holy ground (*asylía*). *Hikétai* were even regarded as 'sacred' and 'pure' (*hieroí* and *hagnoí*: Paus. 7,25,1). Their patron was Zeus Hikesios. The *hiketeia* could in principle be performed in any sanctuary, though, owing to their fixtures and position, certain temples became preferred places of refuge, in which the *hikétēs* sometimes stayed for fairly long periods [9. 95–97]. The *hiketeia* associated with the sanctuary was ideally followed by integration into the community in the form of 'personal' asylum granted by the state or else *metoikia* (→ *métoikoi*; cf. Aesch. Supp. 609ff.; [8. 44–47]). The religious protection of the *hiketeia* applied not only to those being innocently pursued, but also to criminals and even those guilty of blood crimes (cf. Hom. Il. 16,573f.; Hom. Od. 15,271ff.; critically: Eur. Ion 1314ff.; Tac. Ann. 3,60,1; *hiketeia* associated with cleansing: Orestes in Aesch. Eum.; Jason and Medeoe in Apoll. Rhd. 4,692ff.). Violence against *hikétai* was regarded as sacrilege (Pl. Leg. 730a; [6. 181–186]), cf. the rape of → Cassandra in front of the cult image of Athena, for instance (Alc. fr. 262,16–19 SLG) or the → Alcmaeonid curse (Thuc. 1,126f.). The petition for *hiketeia*, sometimes presented under threats (e.g. of suicide in the sanctuary), could lead to political conflict (war) (Aesch. Supp.; Eur. Heracl.).

The designation of the *mystes* as a *hikétēs* in the Underworld, attested on gold tablets, may be informative for an analogy worth considering of *hiketeia* and → initiation [3. 101] [10. 303f.: A2,6; cf. A3,6]. The uncertain status of the *hikétēs* is often also depicted in literary texts as a transition between life and death with ritual connotations.

→ Gestures; → Supplicatio

> 1 M. BLECH, Stud. zum Kranz bei den Griechen, 1982, 288–292 2 W. BURKERT, Die orientalisierende Epoche in der griech. Rel. und Lit., 1984, 68–72 3 J. GOULD, Hiketeia, in: JHS 93, 1973, 74–103 4 J. KOPPERSCHMIDT, Die H. als dramat. Form, 1967 5 R.B. ONIANS, The Origins of European Thought, 1951 (repr. 1988), 174–186 6 R. PARKER, Miasma, 1983 7 K.J. RIGSBY, Asylia, 1996 8 E. SCHLESINGER, Die griech. Asylie, 1933 9 U. SINN, Greek Sanctuaries as Places of Refuge, in: N. MARINATOS, R. HÄGG (ed.), Greek Sanctuaries, 1993, 88–109 10 G. ZUNTZ, Persephone, 1971.   S.G.

Hilaeira see → Leucippides

Hilarianus, Q. Iulius see → Iulius

Hilarius
[1] H. of Poitiers
A. BIOGRAPHY B. WORKS C. THEOLOGY

A. BIOGRAPHY
H. was probably born in Poitiers in the first quarter of the 4th cent. and baptized as an adult (De synodis 91). He became bishop of Poitiers before 356; H. is the first known bishop of this place, in which there cannot have been many Christians. In 356, at a synod in Bé-

ziers, H. was sent into exile in Asia Minor on the orders of the later emperor → Julianus [11]. Whereas formerly only a lengthy resistance activity against the line of ecclesiastical policy of the emperor → Constantius [2] II and his measures directed against → Athanasius were postulated as the reason for the synod's ruling, political suspicions in connection with the failed usurpation of → Silvanus or his partisanship with → Lucifer of Calaris [8], who was convicted of high treason, are now also surmised, though this is not certain. H. apparently spent his exile in Phrygia, yet took part in synods and corresponded with Gaulish bishops (De synodis 1f.). From 358 he became a consistent advocate of a theological re-orientation on the Nicene creed (AD 325) and tried to reconcile a specific eastern option of trinitarian theology (that of the Homoiousians) and the western opponents of the subordinationist imperial Church line of the emperor Constantius with one another, which ultimately foundered at the imperial synod of Seleucia/ Rimini. At the beginning of 360 H. returned to Gallia, possibly also because of news about the usurpation of Julian. Probably not until after the end of his exile, H. took up contact with → Martinus of Tours (Greg. Tur. Franc. 1,36; Ven. Fort. Vita Hilari 9 [33]; otherwise Sulp. Sev. Vita Martini 5,1) and attempted to repress the Homoean imperial Church theology in Gallia and northern Italy. He died in Poitiers in 367 or 368; fairly reliable information is extant only on the last ten years of his life.

B. Works

H. presented in particular exegetic commentaries and works on everyday questions of ecclesiastical politics: a commentary on St. Matthew's gospel created during the exile period is extant; in spite of a similar exegetic method there is no direct literary dependency on the St. Matthew commentary of → Origenes. Also handed down are *Tractatus super Psalmos* from the last years of his life (CPL 428); the corresponding works of Origen are used here. Some texts presumably go back to sermons. The *Tractatus in Iob* have been lost apart from fragments (CPL 429), likewise a NT work (CPL 432). Among the writings on everyday questions of ecclesiastical politics is a two-part collection, originally of commentaries, preserved only in parts, of documentary pieces on the history of the dispute over trinitarian theology (CPL 436; ed. [3]), which were perhaps posthumously combined into an *Opus historicum*. With his work *De synodis* (CPL 434) H. informed the Gaulish bishop colleagues about conditions in the Orient. The work *Contra Constantium* (CPL 461), not published until after the emperor's death, contains sharp polemics (Constantius as Antichrist: § 4–7) and is a reflection of H.'s disappointment over the failed attempt to make the monarch change his mind about his line of ecclesiastical politics, definitely not a manifesto for the 'division of state and Church'. H.'s main theological work, *De trinitate* (CPL 433), was possibly only subsequently extended to its present form of twelve bks. It starts with

the baptism command (Mt 28,19) and develops a biblically founded theology of the trinity, distinguishing between Arian and Marcellan concepts; the concept is in the tradition of Latin trinitarian theology (→ Tertullianus, → Novatianus), but also assimilates eastern concepts. Remnants from three hymns to Christ from a *Liber hymnorum* have been preserved (CPL 463).

C. Theology

At the centre of his theological interest are trinitarian theology and Christology: Father and Son form a unity (*unitas*), the Son exists independently, but his entire existence is a gift from the Father (De trinitate 8,20). The difference between them is based only on their mutual relationship: the Father begets, the Son is born. H. brought Greek trinitarian theology and exegesis to the west; in so doing he exerted a formative influence on subsequent generations. The *Vita* by → Venantius Fortunatus played a central role in the spread of his cult, especially in Gallia; it was created after the mid 6th cent.

EDITIONS: 1 J. DOIGNON, SChr 254/258, 1978/1979 (Comm. Mt.; CPL 430) 2 A. ZINGERLE, CSEL 22, 1891 (Tract. Ps.; CPL 428 [needs to be revised]) 3 A. FEDER, CSEL 65, 1916, 43–187 (Hist.; CPL 436) 4 PL 10, 479–546 (Syn.; CPL 434; forthcoming M. DURST, CSEL) 5 A. ROCHER, SChr 334, 1987 (Contra Const.; CPL 461) 6 P. SMULDERS, CCL 62/62A, 1979/1980 (Trin.; CPL 433) 7 A. FEDER, CSEL 65, 227–234 (Hymn.; CPL 463).
BIBLIOGRAPHY: 8 H. CH. BRENNECKE, H.v.P. und die Bischofsopposition gegen Konstantius II. (Patristische Texte und Studien 26), 1984 9 P. C. BURNS, The Christology of H. of P. Commentary on Matthew (Studia Ephemeridis Augustinianum 16), 1981 10 J. DOIGNON, H. de P. avant l'exil, 1971 11 Id., in: HLL 5, § 582 12 Id., s.v. H.v.P., RAC 15, 139–167 13 M. FIGURA, Das Kirchenverständnis des H.v.P. (Freiburger Theologische Studien 127), 1984 14 Hilaire et son temps, Actes du Colloque de Poitiers 29.9.–3.10.1968, 1969 15 P. SMULDERS, La doctrine trinitaire de Saint H., 1944 16 Id., H.v.P., in: M. GRESCHAT (ed.), Gestalten der Kirchengesch., vol. 1, 1984 (repr. 1993), 250–265 17 Id., H. of P.' Preface to his Opus historicum. Translation and Commentary (= Vigiliae Christianae Suppl. 29), 1995.   C.M.

[2] Bishop of Arles (429–449). His uncle Honoratus of Arles had founded a monastery around 410 on Lerinum (the island of Lérins off the coast of Cannes), which H. entered. Orientated towards Egyptian monasticism (Pachomius), Lerinum soon extended its influence over the whole of southern France and appointed numerous bishops. Honoratus became metropolitan of Arles in 424 and was followed by H., whose funeral oration to his uncle is extant. His pupil, Bishop Honoratus of Marseilles († after 492), reported on H.'s life. When H. tried to extend his pre-eminence in Gallia (deposing the metropolitan Celidonius of Besançon for infringements of Church discipline), Pope Leo I took away his rights as a metropolitan in 445, which Arles did not regain until 450.

EDITIONS: Honoratus, Vita Hilarii, PL 1219ff.; H., Vita Honorati, PL 50,1249ff.; H., epist. ad Eucherium, PL 50,1271.
BIBLIOGRAPHY: H. JEDIN (ed.), Hdb. der Kirchengesch. Bd II/1, 1973, 398f.; G. LANGGÄRTNER, Die Gallienpolitik der Päpste im 5. und 6. Jh. Eine Studie über den apostolischen Vikariat von Arles, 1964. RO.F.

Hilarodia see → Simodia

Hildericus, Hilderic Son of → Hunericus and Eudocia [2], the daughter of Valentinian III (Theoph. 5964; 6026), king of the Vandals in AD 523–530 who ended the anti-Catholic policies of his predecessors and attempted to come closer to Byzantium (he minted coins with the image of Justin I [1. 94]), while the relationship with the East Goths deteriorated considerably. The Vandal opposition under the leadership of → Gelimer therefore took advantage of a defeat of H.'s troops against Arabs in Byzacena to depose him and execute him in AD 533 (Procop. Vand. 3,9,1–26; 17,12; Iord. Get. 170), which Justinian (→ Iustinianus [1]) took as an excuse for his war against the Vandals.

1 W. HAHN, Moneta Imperii Byzantini 1, 1973.

PLRE 2, 564f.; CHR. COURTOIS, Les vandales et l'afrique, 1955, esp. 267ff.; H.-J. DIESNER, Das Vandalenreich, 1966, 94–97. M.MEI.

Hillel the elder, of Babylonian descent, lived at the time of → Herodes [1] the Great (end 1st cent. BC/beginning 1st cent. AD); pupil of the Pharisees Shemaya and Abtalion. H. was one of the most important 'rabbinic' authorities from the period before the destruction of the temple of → Jerusalem (AD 70). Tradition ascribes to him the seven rules of interpretation (*Middot*), strongly influenced by Greek rhetoric, as well as the introduction of the so-called prosbul: according to this a creditor could demand payment of his debt even after a sabbatical year (cf. Deut. 15,1–11). In rabbinic literature H. is balanced in stereotyped fashion against the strict rabbi Shammai, as he arbitrated less rigorously in Halachic questions (→ Halakhah) and in particular emphasized love of one's neighbour (cf. bShab 31a). In the depiction of his level-headed actions there is much in common with biographies of Hellenistic scholars.

N.N. GLATZER, Hillel. Repräsentant des klass. Judentums, 1966; G. STEMBERGER, Einl. in Talmud und Midrasch, 81992, 72; E. URBACH, The Sages, 1979, 579–593. B.E.

Himation see → Pallium

Himera (Ἱμέρα; *Himéra*). The settlers understood the non-Greek place name as ἡμέρα (*hēméra*, 'day') and made the cock their coat-of-arms (coins), also alluded to by Pind. Ol. 12,13. Apart from → Mylae, H. was the only ancient Greek colony on the north coast of Sicily, pushed way up towards Phoenician territory, founded,

starting from Zancle – 240 years before its destruction in 409, in other words in 649 BC (Diod. Sic. 13,62,4) – as an Ionian-Doric settlement (Thuc. 6,5,1). The prosperity of H. in the 6th/5th cents. is attested by its rich coin minting (HN 143–146). A votive inscription from Samos [1] attests battles around 500 BC against the Sicani. Called upon by the tyrant → Terillus, who was being threatened by → Theron of Acragas, the Carthaginians landed near H. in 480, but were beaten and annihilated by Theron in league with → Gelon [1] of Syracuse (Hdt. 7,165–167; Diod. Sic. 11,20–22). In the Peloponnesian War, H. remained faithful to Syracuse (Thuc. 3,115,1; 6,62,2; 7,1,1; 7,1,3; 7,58,2; Diod. Sic. 13,4,2; 13,7,6; 13,8,4; 13,12,4). In 409 H. fell victim to a great Carthaginian offensive and was totally destroyed in revenge for the role it had played in the battle of 480 (Diod. Sic. 11,59–62; Str. 6,2,6); the survivors were settled in the Carthaginian colony of Thermae Himeraeae (Diod. Sic. 13,79,8; 13,114,1).

The city [2; 3; 4; 5] developed both on the hill (upper city) and near the mouth of the river (lower city). Upper city: 1st phase (end 7th to end 6th cent. BC): individual houses; 2nd phase (end 6th/beginning 5th to end 5th cent. BC): isolated buildings arranged in a parallel scheme over the entire plateau. In the north-east region trapeziform *temenos* (2nd half 7th to end 5th cent. BC) with four sacred buildings. In the west of the *temenos* an agora (?). On the south side of the hill traces of walls. Lower city (defined by the existence of the river port): 1st phase (mid 7th to mid 6th cent.): scattered houses; 2nd phase (mid/end 6th to beginning 5th cent.): individual regular buildings. Doric Nike temple (480–470 BC). To the east of the river a quarter outside the city (6th cent. BC). Three necropolis areas in the west, north and south of the settlement. H.'s territory extended to approximately between Chephalodion and Thermae [6; 7].

1 G. MANGANARO, Una dedica di Samo rivolta non a Leukaspis, ma a Hera Thespis?, in: ZPE 101, 1994, 120–126 2 N. BONACASA, s.v. Imara, EAA² 3, 1995, 89–93 3 N. ALLEGRO, H. 1989–1993, in: Kokalos 39–40, II 2, 1993/4, 1119–1131 4 Id., Le fasi dell'abitato di H., in: H.P. ISLER et al. (ed.), Wohnbauforschung in Zentral- und Westsizilien, 1997, 65–80 5 S. VASSALLO, Indagini in un quartiere della città bassa di H., in: Ibid. 6 O. BELVEDERE, Prospezione archeologica nel territorio imerese (1986–1995), in: Ibid. 7 S. VASSALLO, Il territorio di H. in età arcaica, in: Kokalos 42, 1996, 199–223. GI.F.

Himeraeus (Ἱμεραῖος; *Himeraîos*). Son of Phanostratus of Phalerum, Athenian rhetor of the 4th cent. BC, brother of → Demetrius [4] of Phalerum, priest of Poseidon (Syll.³ 289,18); opponent of the Macedonians and counsel for the prosecution against Demosthenes in the trial of → Harpalus in 323 BC (Plut. Mor. 846C). After the defeat of Athens in the Lamian War in 322 BC, H. fled to Aegina, was sentenced to death in his absence on the orders of Demades, seized and executed by command of → Antipater [1] (Arr. FGrH 156 F 9 (13);

Lucian. Demosthenis Encomium 31; Plut. Demosthenes 28,4).

DAVIES, p. 108; DEVELIN, no. 1406; PA 7578; TRAILL, PPA 535130. J.E.

Himeras Name of two rivers in Sicily which, rising not far from one another in opposite directions on S. Salvatore (1910 m) near Polizzi (modern Imera Settentrionale, Imera Meridionale), were regarded as a single river and as the north-south central line of the island, although the eastern half of the island, thus divided, is almost twice as big as the western half. Evidence: Pol. 7,4,2; Liv. 24,6,7; Str. 6,2,1; Mela 2,119; Vitr. De arch. 8,3,7; Sil. Pun. 14,233. E.O.

Himerius
A. LIFE B. WORK C. CHARACTERISTICS

A. LIFE

From his own speeches and other sources (Lib., Eun. Vit. Soph. 14 (494), Suda) the following emerges: Greek rhetor from Prusias in Bithynia, c. AD 320 until after 383, son of the rhetor Aminias. After studying in Athens until the beginning of the 340s, H. first worked as a teacher of rhetoric in Constantinople (343–352). One of several journeys undertaken at this time took him to Nicomedia (around 350), where he lost to → Libanius in an oratory competition (Lib. Ep. 742,1F = 654W; Libanius' speech is extant, Decl. 46, but H.'s is not, Or. 53), another journey to Constantius [2] II in Sirmium (March 351). Sometime between 356 and 361 H. was a practising teacher in Athens, where he was obviously successful and had people in high positions as his pupils, e.g. → Basilius [1] of Caesarea, → Gregorius [3] of Nazianzus (Sozom. Hist. eccl. 6,17,1; Socr. 4,26,6) and for a brief time also the future emperor Julian (in the year 355: Greg. Naz. Or. 5,23); he also received Athenian citizenship. The increasing popularity of his Christian competitor → Prohaeresius persuaded H. to leave Athens. In Antioch he joined the emperor → Iulianus [11] and followed him until his death (363). Until 369 the further circumstances of his life are unknown; after that, perhaps occasioned by the death of Prohaeresius, he returned to Athens, where he stayed until he died. The fact that he remained an overt non-Christian (he was initiated into the cult of Mithras, Or. 41,1; cf. also Phot. 108b 42–109a 1) seems to have given him problems under Valens or Gratianus (Or. 46,1f.). A daughter and his gifted son both died before his own death (Or. 7f.).

B. WORK
The speeches by H. handed down come from several sources: 32 declamations, partly mutilated, are in the Cod. Par. Suppl. 352; Photius (107b 17–27 and 108a 4–b 27) names 72 titles; together with the material of further MSS (Oxon. Barocc. 131,3; Monac. 564) and more recent discoveries, (depending on the method of counting) 75 or 80 titles are known. No systematic arrangement within the corpus (perhaps going back to a selection made by H. himself or one of his pupils) is recognizable; it contains both *meletai* (→ *exercitatio*) on topical themes of the classical period and also occasional speeches on current events, such as the arrival or departure of important officials; several speeches deal with subjects connected with the running of schools (greeting and dismissal of pupils, disputes with rivals); there are → panegyrics to emperors and also eulogies to cities. In general H.'s non-political speeches remain within the confines of the subjects typical of the sophistic of late antiquity. The conventionality and avoidance of any precise details considerably impair the value of the sources of most of the speeches for the period and person of their author and those addressed (exception: Or. 7f.).

C. CHARACTERISTICS
H.' affected and extremely artificial style has recourse on the one hand to the model of the classical oratos, though on the other hand to a great extent to Plato and rhetoricians such as Aristides [3] and Polemon. The frequent appeals to the Muses, self-designation of the author as a poet and singer and also the very numerous quotations from Ionian and Aeolian poetry (Sappho, Alcaeus, Anacreon, Simonides) make it clear that H.' prose claims to compete with poetry. Carefully chosen words, artistic placing of commas and creating rhythms (merging into clauses determined by accent) and the frequency of Gorgianic figures reinforce the impression of mannerism. H. represents a trend in style which runs counter to the strict classicists (such as Libanius, in whose opinion H.' style does not obey Atticist rules, Epist. 742,1F), which, while being accorded much recognition (Eun.; Phot. 107b 27–108a 3), found no imitators.

EDITIONS: A. COLONNA, 1951 (also: N. TERZAGHI, in: GGA 208, 1954, 72–79).
BIBLIOGRAPHY: 1 T. D BARNES, H. and the Fourth Century, in: CPh 82, 1987, 206–225 2 N. BERNARDI, Un regard sur la vie étudiante à Athènes au milieu du IVᵉ s. après J.-C., in: REG 103, 1990, 79–94 3 E. BERTI, L'esemplare di Imerio letto da Fozio, in: Studi Classici Orientali 22, 1973, 111–114 4 G. CUFFARI, I riferimenti poetici di Imerio, Università di Palermo, Istituto di filologia greca. Quaderni 12, 1983 5 S. EITREM, L. AMUNDSEN, Fragments from the Speeches of H.P. Osl.inv.no. 1478, in: CeM 17, 1956, 23–30 6 H. GÄRTNER, s.v. H., RAC 15, 167–73 7 C. GALLAVOTTI, Echi di Alceo e di Menandro nei retori tardivi, in: RFIC 93, 1965, 135–146 8 A. GUIDA, Frammenti inediti, in: Prometheus 5, 1979, 193–216 9 T. HÄGG, Photios als Vermittler ant. Lit., 1975, 128f., 138f., 143–159 10 G. A. KENNEDY, Greek Rhetoric under Christian Emperors, 1983, 140–149 11 J. D. MEERWALDT, Epithalamica I: De H. Sapphus imitatore, in: Mnemosyne 4 Ser. 7, 1954, 19–38 12 NORDEN, Kunstprosa, 428–431 13 E. RICHTSTEIG, H. und Platon, Byz.-Neugriech. Jbb. 2, 1921, 1–32 14 K. WEITZMANN (ed.), Age of Spirituality, 1980, 53–73. M.W.

Himeros (Ἵμερος; *Hímeros*, 'desire'). The personification of affectionate longing. Together with → Eros [1], he accompanies Aphrodite (since Hes. Theog. 201); with the → Charites (the goddesses of 'grace'), he lives close to the Muses (Hes. Theog. 64, a poetological statement). Later he was firmly associated with Aphrodite and Eros, pictorially also with → Dionysus and → Pothos; he is indistinguishable iconographically from Eros and Pothos. A statue of H. by → Scopas used to stand in the temple of Aphrodite at Megara (Paus. 1,43,6).

> A. HERMARY, s.v. H., LIMC 5, 425f.; H. A. SHAPIRO, Personifications in Greek Art, 1993, 110–120.   F.G.

Himilkon (*[?]hmlkt = 'brother of Mlkt', Ἰμίλκων; *Imílkōn*).

[1] Carthaginian commander, son of a Hanno, great-grandson of the Magonid → Hamilcar [1] and a relation of → Hannibal [1], whom he accompanied to Sicily in 407 BC as (fleet?) *strategos* and after whose death H. took over the supreme command (Diod. Sic. 13,80; Iust. 19,2,7). H. besieged, conquered and destroyed → Acragas in 406/405, then → Gela and → Camarina, but soon after, in 405, failed in his siege of → Syracuse because of a plague among his army and concluded a peace treaty with → Dionysius [1] I (Diod. Sic. 13,86–88; 108–111; 114; StV 2,210) [1. 159–162; 2. 116–123; 3. 60f.; 4]. In the subsequent war of Carthage against Syracuse over the Greek cities in west and south Sicily H. was again dispatched in 397 BC as supreme commander; after the loss of → Motya, with the support of → Mago in 396 he quickly re-conquered the Carthaginian positions from Panormis and via Messana and Catana marched towards Syracuse, where after initial successes and some destruction of the city district, faced with another epidemic in the besieging army, H. had no choice but to (secretly?) withdraw his troops of citizens and sacrifice the rest of the army (Diod. Sic. 14,49; 55–57; 59f.; 62f.; 70–73; 75). In Carthage, though H. was not condemned because of the failure, he nevertheless committed suicide (Diod. Sic. 14,76) [1. 162–165; 2. 128–135; 3. 65–67].

[2] Commanded a Carthaginian army jointly with → Adherbal [1] in the year 307 BC against the Syracusan invasion troops under → Archagathus' [1] commander Eumachus and at → Tunes cut off → Agathocles' [2] advance into the interior (Diod. Sic. 20,59–61) [1. 166f.].

[3] As Carthaginian commandant of Lilybaeum and predecessor of → Geskon [3] in 250–241(?) BC skilfully defended the city against the Roman besiegers with the assistance of Hanno and → Carthalo (Pol. 1,42,7–43; 45; 48; 53,5; Diod. Sic. 24,1) [1. 167f.].

[4] Carthaginian commander in Sicily in 214–212 BC, close friend of → Hippocrates [8], with whom H. fought at Syracuse against the Roman consul M. → Claudius [I 11] Marcellus, after he had personally persuaded the Carthaginian government to adopt a more energetic policy towards Sicily and then by conquering → Acragas had brought the Siculi into renewed alliance. H. died during an epidemic in the besieged Syracuse (Liv. 24,35,3–39; 25,26) [1. 170f.; 2. 359f., 367–369].

[5] H. Phameas. (Pol. 36,8: *Hamilcar*; Liv. Per. 50: *Hamilco*; Eun. fr. 82: *Milkon*) [1. 22, n. 1300]. As a Carthaginian cavalry leader in the 3rd Punic War, H. caused the Romans continued losses in 149 BC at Lake Tunes by lightning attacks, until → Gulussa tracked him down and H. went over to the Romans with a strong contingent of cavalry (App. Lib. 100,471–101,473; 107,503–109,516; Diod. Sic. 32,17). Sent to Rome and richly rewarded there, H. returned to North Africa to support the Romans further (Pol. 36,8; App. Lib. 109,517f.) [1. 171f.].

[6] Legendary (?) Carthaginian seafarer, probably a contemporary of → Hanno [1]; first discoverer known by name of the coast of north-west Europe. Some reflections of the supposed report of his travels could be contained in → Avienus' *Ora maritima* (cf. Avien. 414) [2. 84,1]. H. reached his destination, the *exterae Europae* (Plin. HN 2,169), at the so-called Tin Islands, the Oestrumnids (Avien. 113) or the Cassiterites (cf. Hdt. 3,115), which are thought to be the Scilly Islands [1. 158; 2. 85,10]. There is disagreement about to what extent H. travelled on the official orders of Carthaginian authorities, to monopolize the tin and lead trade, for instance [2. 85], or whether this remarkable pioneering activity took place without goals of this kind [5. 1152; 6. 267].

> 1 GEUS   2 HUSS   3 L. M. HANS, Karthago und Sizilien, 1983   4 M. ZAHRNT, Die Verträge zwischen Dionysios I. und den Karthagern, in: ZPE 71, 1988, 209–228   5 H. TEIDLER, s.v. Himilkon (6), KlP 2, 1967   6 W. AMELING, Karthago, 1993.   L.-M.G.

Ḥimyar (Lat. *Homeritae*: Plin. HN 32,161). Arab tribe, attested epigraphically from about AD 100. The Ḥ. held the political hegemony in southern Arabia between AD 100 and 590. The centre of their kingdom was → Saphar (in Plin. HN 25,104: *Sapphar*) on the plateau south of modern Yarīm. From there the Ḥ. gradually conquered the ancient Southern Arabic kingdoms of → Qatabān, → Sabaʾ and → Ḥaḍramaut. In the mid-4th cent., Judaism and Christianity began to spread while simultaneously the attempts of the Sassanid and Byzantine empires to influence the Ḥ. kingdom increased (cf. → *Leges Homeritarum*). Repeated ruptures of the dam of Mārib (→ Mariaba) attest to a general decline starting in the 6th cent. In 597 South Arabia became a province of the Sassanid empire (→ Sassanids).

> K. SCHIPPMANN, Geschichte der Alt-Südarabischen Reiche, 1998, 60–73 (with bibliography).   I. T.-N.

Ḥimyaritic see → Ancient South Arabian

Hin Egyptian hollow measure for fluids and dry materials of $^1/_{10}$ *ḥq3t* (*hekat*) in the Old Kingdom or $^1/_{40}$ *jpt* (*oipe*) in the New Kingdom, corresponding to *c.* 0.48 l [3. 1201], with minimal differences upwards [1. 1644] and downwards [2. 1152]. The hin is the only remaining unit from the Demotic period, corroborated by extant measuring vessels. Its relations to the → artabe and → choinix are contentious [3. 1210]. Measuring vessels based on the hin have also been handed down from the New Kingdom: *mḥt* = 1 hin, *pg3* = $^1/_4$ hin, *mndqt* = 50 hin, which seem, however, not to have had generally binding calibration [3. 1202].

1 O. VIEDEBANTT, s.v. H., RE 8, 1644–1649   2 H. CHANTRAINE, s.v. H., KlP 2, 1152   3 W. HELCK, S. VLEMING, s.v. Maße u. Gewichte, LÄ 3, 1199–1214.   H.-J.S.

Hipana (῎Ιπανα; *Hípana*). Small Siculan town (Pol. 1,24,8–13; Diod. Sic.23,9, manuscript *Sittanan*), mentioned in connection with the battles of the first Punic war in 261–258 BC. Steph. Byz. (s.v. ῎Ι.) describes H. as a 'town in the entourage of Carthage' (πόλις περὶ Καρχηδόνα; *pólis perì Karchēdóna*). It was conquered with difficulty by the Romans in 258 BC. Its location on the Monte dei Cavalli near modern Prizzi is ensured by bronze coins with a bull (reverse) and legend ΙΠΑ (truncated), which were reminted using Punic models. Further finds: silver *lítrai* after an Agrigentinian pattern (obverse: eagle on capital, surrounded by the name of a tribe ῾Ιπανατᾶν), fragment of a *kerykeion*. Plin. HN 3,8,91 mentions *Hyppanenses* among the *stipendiarii* of Rome.

G. MANGANARO, Un Kerykeion perduto degli Hipanatai e la ubicazione di Hipana, in: Orbis Terrarum 3, 1997, 127–130, with pl. 1–7.   GI.MA.

Hippalektryon (῾Ιππαλεκτρυών; *Hippalektryón*, 'horse rooster'). Fantastic → monster, a combination of cock and horse. The earliest literary record is Aesch. Myrmidones fr. 134 RADT. The references in Aristophanes (Pax 1177; Av. 800; Ran. 932, as in Aesch. with the epithet *xouthós*, 'golden, yellow') are parodies of tragedies. In Hesychius and Photius s.v. and in the scholia to Aristophanes, the creature has a bird's head – this is the exact opposite of the archaeological findings (a cock's hindquarters with two cock's legs, front of a horse with two horse's legs). Very often, it is depicted as an animal used for riding. Records exist almost exclusively for Attica from the period between 560 and 470 BC. Related in a compositional way are monsters such as the 'panther cock' or the 'girl cock' [1. 432–433]. An Oriental origin is uncertain but always a reasonable assumption regarding monsters.

1 D. WILLIAMS, s.v. H., LIMC 5.1, 427–433.

FIGURE: Id., s.v. H., LIMC 5.2, 301–308.   JO.S.

Hippalus (῎Ιππαλος; *Híppalos*).
[1] Son of Sosus (?); father of the district commander Theomnestus (PP 1/8, 260; 3/9, 5147) and the athlophore Batra (PP 3/9, 5051). From 185–169 BC, priest of the royal cult in Ptolemais Hermou; documented in 182 and 173 as an eponymous officer; before November 176 (from 185?) ἀρχισωματοφύλαξ (*archisōmatophýlax*, 'arch-bodyguard') and first *stratēgós* of the Thebaid (court title dependent on reading of PLond VII 2188, 214); from November 176 until at least May 172 τῶν πρώτων φίλων (*tôn prốtōn phílōn*) and *epistratēgós* of the entire *chóra*.

J.D. THOMAS, The Epistrategos in Ptolemaic and Roman Egypt 1, 1975, 87ff., no. I; PP 1/8, 193; 2/8, 1919; 3/9, 5155.   W.A.

[2] Otherwise unknown Greek seafarer, who, according to Peripl. m.r. 57 (GGM I 298f.; → Periplus), discovered a direct sea route from Egypt and Arabia to India, made possible by the south-west monsoon; according to H. the wind was called ἵππαλος/*híppalos*. This name is also given by Plin. (HN 6,100; 6,104; in contrast [1]: written as *hyphalum*), who in 6,172 also uses it for, among other things, a range of foothills in Africa; Ptol. 4,7,41 knows of a H. Sea there. Since Str. (2,5,12; 17,1,13) among others describes this sea route as actively sailed recently, the discovery of H. can most probably be dated to the late 2nd or early 1st cent. BC.

1 S. MAZZARINO, Sul nome del vento "hipalus" in Plinio, in: Helikon 22/27, 1982/87, vii-xiv.

A. DIHLE, Ant. und Orient, 1984; A. TCHERNIA, Moussons et monnaies, in: Annales: Histoire, Sciences sociales 50, 1995, 991–1009; J. READE (ed.), The Indian Ocean in Antiquity, 1996.   K.BRO.

Hipparchia (῾Ιππαρχία; *Hipparchía*). Cynic philosopher from Maronea in Thrace (*floruit* 111th Olympiad = 336–333 BC), of a wealthy family, sister of the Cynic → Metrocles, and pupil of → Crates of Thebes. H. wanted to marry Crates and threatened suicide if her parents refused permission (Diog. Laert. 6,96). She lived the life of a Cynic and constantly accompanied Crates. She had sexual intercourse with him in public (designated as κυνογαμία; *kynogamía* 'marriage of dogs') to demonstrate her indifference (ἀδιαφορία; *adiaphoría*) to the act. She amazed → Theodorus of Cyrene by presenting him with a false conclusion which he did not know how to respond to. In this way she proved her abilities as a philosopher who preferred to use her time for intellectual education, rather than for working at the loom (Diog. Laert. 6,98). H., the only known woman Cynic philosopher, embodies a concept of marriage and sexuality in harmony with the denial of human culture and the return to nature extolled by the Cynics. Diog. Laert 96–98 mentions no works by H., but the Suda s.v. ῾Ιππαρχία recognizes the 'treatises of the philosophers' (Φιλοσόφων ὑποθέσεις; *Philosóphōn hypothéseis*), the 'lines of argumentation' (᾽Επιχειρήματα; *Epicheirémata*) and the 'formulations of questions' (Προτάσεις; *Protáseis*) which had been directed at Theodorus of Cyrene.

→ Cynic School; → Women philosophers

SSR II, 577–579; SSR V 1; L. PAQUET, Les cyniques grecs. Fragments et témoignages, ²1988, 113–115; A.J. MAL-HERBE, The Cynic epistles, 1977 (from Crates to H.: 53–89); J.M. GARCÍA GONZÁLEZ, Hiparquia, la de Maronea, filósofo cínico, in: Id., A.POCIÑA PÉREZ (ed.), Studia Graecolatina C. Sanmillán in memoriam dicata, 1988, 179–187; T.DORANDI, Figure femminili della filosofia antica, in: F. DE MARTINO (ed.), Rose di Pieria, 1991, 263–278, esp. 268–273. M.G.-C.

Hipparchus ("Ιππαρχος; *Hípparchos*).

[1] Second son of → Peisistratus and an Athenian woman. Together with his older brother → Hippias [1] and the younger Thessalus, H. assumed his inheritance (528/527 BC) after his father's death (Thuc. 6,55; [Aristot.] Ath. Pol. 18,1). In contrast to Hippias, H. exhibited no political profile. He dedicated himself to aristocratic social life and culture and invited, among others, → Anacreon [1] of Teos and → Simonides of Ceos to Athens (Pl. Hipp. 228b-d). After he was murdered by → Harmodius and → Aristogeiton [1] at the Panathenaea of 514 BC (Thuc. 6,54; 56; 59; [Aristot.] Ath. Pol. 18,2; → Tyrannicide), H. appeared as the epitome of a tyrant. As a result, tradition tended to the creation of legend early on; thus already Thucydides critically (1,20).

H. BERVE, Die Tyrannis bei den Griechen, 1967, 63ff., 554ff.; L. DE LIBERO, Die Archaische Tyrannis, 1996, 116ff.; K.-W. WELWEI, Athen, 1992, 247ff. B.P.

[2] Greek comic dramatist, assigned by the Suda to Old Comedy [1. test.]; however, the four extant titles 'The Saved' ('Ανασωζόμενοι), 'The Painter' (Ζωγράφος), 'Thais' (Θαίς), 'The Nocturnal Festival' (Παννυχίς, also the name of hetaerae) and the five extant fragments prove him to have been a practitioner of the New Comedy.

1 PCG V, 605–607. H.-G.NE.

[3] Pythagorean, whose historical authenticity is uncertain; he is sometimes confused with → Hippasus (Tert. Anim. 5,2; Macrob. In Somn. 1,14,19), sometimes with → Archippus (both 5th cent. BC) (Olympiodorus in Pl. Phd. 61d, p. 57,8f. WESTERINK, from schol. in Pl. Phd. 61d). Information derived from Iambl. VP 73 and 246, the main source of surviving documentation, and the forged letter of → Lysis to H. indicate that he was barred from the secret society due to publication of Pythagorean teachings (Clem. Al. Strom. 5,57,2f., in [1] related to Hippasus). Excerpts survive from a forged Neopythagorean 'On Euthymia' [2].

→ Pythagorean School

1 DIELS/KRANZ, I, 108 2 H. THESLEFF, The Pythagorean Texts of the Hellenistic Period, 1965, 89–91. C.RI.

[4] **H. of Stagira.** Student and executor (see Diog. Laert. 5,12) of Aristotle, author of a work 'What is the Masculine and the Feminine Among the Gods, and What is Marriage' (Τί τὸ ἄρρεν καὶ θῆλυ παρὰ θεοῖς καὶ τίς ὁ γάμος: Suda s.v.; for the problem of philosophical myth interpretation cf. Aristot. Metaph. 1000a 5ff.). He is probably not identical with the H. mentioned in → Theophrastus' will (Diog. Laert. 5,51ff.) as his business manager.

H.B. GOTTSCHALK, Notes on the Wills of the Peripatetic Scholarchs, in: Hermes 100, 1972, 318 n. 3, 331f. H.G.

[5] Hellenistic poet. Athenaeus (3,101a; 9,393c = SH 496–497) quotes four hexameters with culinary/gastronomical content from his 'Egyptian Iliad' (on the exquisiteness of *vulva eiecticia*, cf. Plin. HN 11,210), and against the Egyptian practice of plucking quail). For this reason, he has to be classified as a practitioner of epic-gastronomical poetry which parodied Homer.

→ Archestratus [2]; → Gastronomical poetry; → Matron of Pitane S.FO.

[6] **H. of Nicaea** in Bithynia, Greek astronomer and geographer. His observations (quoted by Ptolemy) of equinoxes occurred between 162 and 128 BC and appear to have been made predominantly on Rhodes. His works, which he compiled himself (Ptol. Syntaxis 3,1 p. 207,18: Άναγραφὴ τῶν ἰδίων συνταγμάτων), are based on especially exact observations and are characterized by an extremely severe scepticism for the theories of his predecessors as well as a dislike for everything hypothetical.

A. LOGIC B. ASTRONOMY C. GEOGRAPHY

A. LOGIC

According to Plutarch (Symp. 732f; De Stoicorum repugnatione 1047d), H. criticized the solution to a problem of combinatorics from → Chrysippus [1]. The allocation of algebraic works in Arabic sources is probably based on a mistake.

B. ASTRONOMY

The only extant work is a critical commentary to a (student?) Aeschrion (3 B) of a description of the heavens that → Aratus [4], according to → Eudoxus [1] of Cnidus, gave in his successful didactic poem *Phainómena* (Τῶν Ἀράτου καὶ Εὐδόξου Φαινομένων ἐξηγήσεως βιβλία τρία). In this, H. gives the geographical latitude of Athens (37°) as well as the simultaneous rising and setting (*synanatolaí* and *synkatadýseis*) of the extrazodiacal constellations with reference to the varying extent of the constellations and the different lengths of time in the rising of the ecliptic twelfths. The subsequent fixed star catalogue is based on the centre of the map of the world of → Eratosthenes, Rhodes (36°). Added to this is an index of prominent stars, on which the 24 equatorial hours can be read [2]. The calculations are based on a chord (sinusoidal) table like that created after H. by Ptol. Syntaxis 1,10f. According to Theon's commentary on *Sýntaxis* (1 p. 110 HALMA), H.

wrote a special treatise on the subject (Περὶ τῆς πραγματείας τῶν ἐν κύκλῳ εὐθεινῶν βιβλία ιβ'). This makes H. the creator of spherical trigonometry. Additional theoretical works (List: [3. 15f.]): on simultaneous risings and settings (ἡ τῶν συνανατολῶν πραγματεία and Περὶ τῆς τῶν ιβ' ζῳδίων ἀναφορᾶς), positions and distances of the of the sun and moon (Adrastus in Theon Smyrnaeus 197 H.: two bks. Περὶ μεγεθῶν καὶ ἀποστημάτων ἡλίου καὶ σελήνης), eclipses of the sun (Achilles, Commentarius in Arati relationes [4] p. 47,14), parallaxes (Ptol. Syntaxis 5,19 p. 450,21–451,5: at least 2 bks. of Παραλλακτικά), gravitation (Simpl. In Aristot. De cael. 1,8 p. 264,25–267,6 H.: Περὶ τῶν διὰ βαρύτητα κάτω φερομένων), precession of the equinoxes (Ptol. Syntaxis 7,2 p. 12,21 Περὶ τῆς μεταπτώσεως τῶν τροπικῶν καὶ ἰσημερινῶν σημείων), length of the solar year (Ptol. Syntaxis 3,1 p. 207,20: Περὶ τοῦ ἐνιαυσίου μεγέθους βιβλίον ἕν) and of a month (title derived from Gal: Περὶ μηνιαίνου χρόνου), the latitudinal movement of the moon (Περὶ τῆς κατὰ πλάτος μηνιαίας κινήσεως), calendrical leap months and days (Ptol. Syntaxis 3,1 p. 207,7: Περὶ ἐμβολίμων μηνῶν τε καὶ ἡμερῶν). Pappus Collectio 6,70–71 p. 554–556 Hu. also attests to a work on the size and distances of the sun and moon. His *parapegma* was used by → Ptolemy in the *Pháseis*. Finally, H. also made observations of the weather (Ael. NA 7,8). Occasional mentions in Vettius Valens (9,12,10), especially in the zodiacal geography (App. 3,14), are as doubtful as a *Prooímion* to Aratus. [4. 102,2 App. crit.].

The now lost stellar catalogue (Ptol. Syntaxis 7,1 p. 3,8 Αἱ περὶ τῶν ἀπλανῶν ἀναγραφαί, cf. Plin. HN 2,95) was based on the data of Eratosthenes' *Katasterismoí* and calculated with ecliptic co-ordinates. It assumes the use of precision instrumentation, the 'Hipparchic' → dioptra (Procl. Hypoth. 4,73.87) or a globe. Its extent is estimated to have had not more than 850 stars (the alleged number of 1080 stars [4. 128[13]] is probably wrong). Ptolemy expanded this and corrected it, taking precession into account. This was discovered in 128 (Ptol. Syntaxis 3,1) by H. during observations of Spica (α Vir) comparing calculations made by → Timocharis and Aristyllus 160 years before him, his most important scientific achievement. Ptolemy improved the value calculated by H., but set it too high himself at 1° in 100 years.

H. calculated the solar year with astonishing accuracy (with a deviation of only 6 minutes and 26 seconds) as well as the synodal month (deviation less than one second). Using the epicycle theory probably combined with the eccentricity theory of → Apollonius [13] of Perge, he calculated the anomaly of the sun's orbit (Ptol. Syntaxis 3,4 p. 233,1) and determined the moon's orbit (Ptol. Syntaxis 4,2 p. 270,19). He was thus able to improve upon → Callippus' work on leap months and days. While his calculation of the distance of the moon from the earth is rather exact, his calculation of the sun's distance from the earth is far less than the actual distance. Had he not been so sceptical of the heliocen-

tric system of → Aristarchus [3] of Samos, this system might have been accepted about 1,700 years earlier.

C. GEOGRAPHY

H. wrote three books 'Against the Geography of Eratosthenes of Cyrene' (Πρὸς τὴν Ἐρατοσθένους γεωγραφίαν). Most of the fragments have survived in the writings of → Strabo, who gladly takes the position of Eratosthenes [2] against H. Strabo's criticism of H., however, is only partially justified; H. contributes, with his superior astronomical knowledge, to substantial improvements on the subject [3]. He concentrates on the exact determination of the positioning of geographical units in cartography using the *klímata*. In bks. 1 and 2, H. criticizes the 'Sphragides' of Eratosthenes, and in bk. 3 offers his own, more exact method of triangulation in opposition. The especially difficult calculation of longitude he accomplished using eclipse charts. Higher accuracy would only have been possible using an international network, which during a time in which the museum at Alexandria had deteriorated was not possible. In calculating the circumference of the earth, he basically followed the principle of Eratosthenes, but took into account the longitudinal deviation of the Syene – Alexandria – Rhodes [5] line. Much space is devoted to the triangulation for the Near East and the approximate determination of the latitudes of India. H. disputed the assumption of Eratosthenes of a single world ocean and the possible existence of other continents. In this excessive criticism of Eratosthenes he prefers, if Strabo is correct, Homer as source.

→ Astronomy; → Eratosthenes [2]

1 K.-R. BIERMANN, J. MAU, Überprüfung einer frühen Anwendung der Kombinatorik in der Logik, in: Journ. of Symbolic Logic 23, 1958, 129–132   2 H. C. F. C. SCHELLERUP, Sur le chronomètre céleste d' H., in: Copernicus 1, 1881, 25–39   3 D. R. DICKS, The Geographical Fragments of H., 1960 (bibliogr., transl., comm.)   4 E. MAASS, Commentariorum in Aratum reliquiae, 1898   5 O. VIEDEBANTT, Eratosthenes, H., Poseidonios, in: Klio 14, 1915, 207–256.

EDITION OF THE COMM. ON ARATUS (GREEK-GERMAN): C. MANITIUS, 1894.
STAR CATALOGUE: F. BOLL, Die Sternkataloge des Hipparch und des Ptolemaios, in: Bibliotheca Mathematica, 3. F. 2, 1901, 185–195; E. MAASS (ed.), De magnitudine et positione <in>errantium stellarum, in: [4], 13–139; ST. WEINSTOCK, in: CCAG 9,1, 1951, 189f.
GEOGRAPHICAL FRAGMENTS: DICKS [3].
BIBLIOGRAPHY: A. REHM, s.v. H., RE 8, 1666–1681; H. VOGT, Versuch einer Wiederherstellung von Hipparchs Fixsternverzeichnis, in: Astronomische Nachr. 224, 1912, 17–32; E. HONIGMANN, Die sieben Klimata und die ΠΟΛΕΙΣ ΕΠΙΣΗΜΟΙ, 1929; O. BEKKER, Das mathematische Denken in der Ant., 1957; O. NEUGEBAUER, The Exact Sciences in Antiquity, [2]1957; Id., A History of Ancient Mathematical Astronomy, 1975, 274–298.   W.H.

[7] H., M. Antonius. Corinthian, who in 43 BC, as a freedman of M. Antonius [I 9], was a profiteer during the proscriptions (Plin. HN 35,200). At Actium (31), H.

quickly abandoned the man who had paved the way for his ascent (Plut. Antonius 67,10; 73,4). During the reign of Augustus, H. was *duumvir* in his hometown (RPC 1, no. 1134ff.).   T.FR.

Hipparinus (Ἱππαρῖνος; *Hipparînos*).
[1] Syracusan, father of → Dion [I 1], elected commander in 406/5 BC, together with → Dionysius [1] I. (Plut. Dion 3). Supported the coup of Dionysius and gave him his daughter Aristomache to wed (Aristot. Pol. 5,5,6). Praised by Plato (Ep. 8, 353b).

> H. BERVE, Die Tyrannis bei den Griechen, 1967, 1, 222f.; 2, 638f.

[2] Syracusan, son of Dionysius [1] and Aristomache, grandson of H. [1]. In 353 BC, he exiled Callippus, the murderer of Dion [I 1] (Diod. Sic. 16,36,5), and became ruler himself, but was murdered only two years later (Theopomp FGrH 115 F 186 with comm.). Plato's (Ep. 8, 356a) judgement of H. is not unfavourable.

> H. BERVE, Die Tyrannis bei den Griechen, 1967, 1, 273f.; 2, 662.

[3] Syracusan, son of Dion [I 1], probably outlived his father (Pl. Ep. 7, 324b; 8, 355e, 357c). Circumstances and date of his death are disputed.

> H. BERVE, Dion, in: AAWM, 1956, 77, 116f.   K.MEI.

Hipparis The bigger and northernmost of the two rivers that run into the south-west coast of Sicily near Camarina, modern Íppari (→ Oanis), praised by Pindar (Ol. 5,12) as benefactor of Camarina, depicted on city coins as a horned youth.

> J.B. CURBERA, Onomastic of River-Gods in Sicily, in: Philologus 142, 1998, 59f.   GI.MA. and E.O.

Hippasus (Ἵππασος; *Híppasos*). Name often used in epic texts for figures lacking any further characterization, particularly common in patronymic information about less important heroes. Esp. interesting in this context are [1] – [4]:
[1] Father of Actor, the Argonaut (Apoll. Rhod. 1,112; Hyg. Fab. 14).
[2] Father of → Charops [4] (Hom. Il. 11,426).
[3] Father of Hypsenor, killed by Deiphobus (Hom. Il. 13,411).
[4] Father of Apisaon, Prince of the Paeonians, killed by Lycomedes (Hom. Il. 17,387), son of Minyas' daughter Leucippe, torn to shreds by his mother in a Bacchic fury (Antoninus Liberalis 10,3).

> P. WATHELET, Dictionnaire des Troyens de l'Iliade, 1988, no. 165.   E.V.

[5] Important Pythagorean from the (early?) 5th cent. BC, from Metapontium (Aristot. Metaph. 984a 7; Iambl. VP 81; Diog. Laert. 8,84; however, Croton or Sybaris are named as his origin in Iambl. VP 81 and

267). H. can be regarded as the founder of the 'mathematical' faction of the → Pythagorean School (cf. Iambl. VP 88, 81 is inapplicable, and *De communi mathematica scientia* 25; [1. 193–197, 206f.]). The reproach that he betrayed the mathematical secret of the dodekaeder (Iambl. VP 88, cf. less importantly 247) must be understood in the context of the school's internal tensions between *akousmatikoí* and *mathēmatikoí* (cf. → Pythagorean School. Earlier attempts at interpreting the betrayal as the discovery and publicizing of mathematical irrationality are refuted convincingly by [1. 457–461]). It was also claimed that H. wrote a 'mystic *logos*' intended to slander Pythagoras (Heraclides Lembos FHG 3, S.170 = Diog. Laert. 8,7; cf. Apollonius in Iambl. VP 257 and 259; [2; 1. 207 n. 78]). However, according to Demetrius of Magnesia in Diog. Laert. 8,84, H. did not leave behind any writings at all). In Aristotle (Metaph. 984a 7), H. is named alongside Heraclitus as representative of the theory that posits fire as the original matter of the world (also Theophr. Doxographia physica fr. 225 FORTENBAUGH/HUBY/SHARPLES/GUTAS = Simpl. CAG 9, p.23). Furthermore, it is said that he took the soul to be 'fiery' (Aet. 4,3,4; Tert. De anima 5,2). H. is also seen as connected to the so-called 'harmonious means' (Iambl. in Nicomachi arithmetica introductio p. 100 PISTELLI; [1. 441f.]). The fact that H. is attributed with musical experiments using bronze disks of varying thickness or vessels filled to varying degrees allows the conclusion that he was familiar with the number relationships in basic consonance (Aristox. fr. 90 WEHRLI = Schol. in Pl. Phd. 108d; Theon of Smyrna p. 59f. HILLER; cf. also Boeth. De institutione musica 2,19; [1. 377f.; 3; 4]). The reference to numbers as a 'paradigm' and divine 'tool' in the creation of the world (Iambl. ibid. p. 10 PISTELLI) is probably spurious [1. 248f., 275 n. 176].
→ Pythagorean School

> 1 W. BURKERT, Lore and Science in Ancient Pythagoreanism, 1972 2 A. DELATTE, Études sur la littérature pythagoricienne, 1915, 10f. 3 A. IZZO, Musica e numero da Ippaso ad Archita, in: A. CAPIZZI, G. CASERTANO (ed.), Forme del sapere nei Presocratici, 1987, 139–145 4 G. COMOTTI, Pitagora, Ippaso, Laso e il metodo sperimentale, in: R. W. WALLACE, B. MACLACHLAN (ed.), Harmonia mundi, 1991, 20–29.
>
> DIELS/KRANZ, no. 18; M. TIMPANARO CARDINI (ed.), Pitagorici I, 1958, 78–105.   C.RI.

Hippe (Ἵππη; *Híppē*).
[1] Mistress of → Theseus (Hes. fr. 147 M-W = Ath. 13,557a). Her identification with Hippolyte (= Antiope, according to Cleidemus FGrH 323 F 18 = Plut. Theseus 27,13a) is reasonable considering the identification of Antiope with Hippo (Callim. H. 3,239; 266); furthermore, the name H. appears in the form of Hippo (Clem. Al. Strom. 1,73,4–5 and [1st Prologue l. 21]).
[2] Daughter of the centaur → Chiron (Hyg. Poet. Astr. 2,18) and of Chariclo (only in Ov. Met. 2,636), Aeolus' daughter with Melanippe, the wise (Hyg. Poet. Astr.

2,18; Eur. fr. 480–488 ²NAUCK). She was immortalized in the constellation of Equus upon her request while escaping from her father (Hyg. Poet. Astr. 2,18; (Ps.-) Eratosth. Katasterismos 18). According to Callimachus, she is transformed into a mare, because she did not adequately serve Artemis (Hyg. Poet. Astr. 2,18 = Callim. Fr. 569). A third version presented by Hyginus explains the transformation with the misuse of her prophetic powers, a version that corresponds to the representation in Ov. Met. 2,635–675. There, however, her name prior to the transformation is Ocyrhoe; according to Hyg. Poet. Astr. 2,18, her earlier name in Euripides was Thetis.

1 H. v. ARNIM, Supplementum Euripideum p. 25–28 (Μελανίππη ἡ σοφή), 1913.   JO.S.

Hippegos (ἱππηγός/hippēgós, ἱππαγωγός/hippagōgós, Latin hippago, hippagogus). Special ship for transporting horses for naval forces in antiquity (Persia: Hdt. 6,48; 6,95,1; Tyre: Arr. Anab. 2,19,1; Demetrius Poliorcetes: Diod. Sic. 20,83,1; Pergamum: Liv. 44,28,7; Rome: Pol. 1,27,9). In Athens old triremes were converted to hippegoi (e.g. B. Thuc. 2,56,2; IG II² 1628,466; 471); they carried 30 horses (Thuc. 6,43,2). Pliny (HN 7,209) wrongly attributes the invention of the hippegos to Samos or Athens (cf. Hdt. 6,48; 6,95,1). → Navies

O. HÖCKMANN, Antike Seefahrt, 1985, 69.   LE.BU.

Hippeis Initially the term hippeis (ἱππεῖς/hippeîs, 'rider') denoted warriors who went into battle on horseback. In view of the great importance of hoplite warfare (→ hoplítai) during the archaic and classical periods, the hippeis did not play a substantial military role; often → horses were used only for the way to the battlefield. One reason for this was the fact that many areas of Greece provided only limited possibility to raise large numbers of horses (Hom. Od. 4,601ff.; Pl. Leg. 625d; cf. also Str. 8,8,1). Significantly, in areas where the situation was more suitable, → cavalry was more important, as in Boeotia (Hdt. 9,68f.; Diod. Sic. 12,70), in Syracuse (Pind. Pyth. 2,1ff.; Diod. Sic. 13,112,3; Plut. Dion 42,1ff.; 44,2), in Euboea (Hdt. 5,77; Aristot. Pol. 4,3,1289b 39; 5,6,1306a 35f.; Aristot. Ath. Pol. 15,2; Plut. Pericles 23,4), in various poleis of Asia Minor (Xen. Ages. 1,23; Aristot. Pol. 4,3,1289b 39f.; Str. 14,1,28; Polyaenus, Strat. 7,2,2; Ael. VH 14,46; Ath. 14,624e; IK 5,151f.) and above all in Thessaly (Hdt. 5,63; Pl. Men. 70ab; Pl. Leg. 625d; Aristot. fr. 456 R.).

Especially with the ascent of the Macedonian monarchy starting with Philip II (359–336 BC) and due to his and his son Alexander the Great's method of battle using 'combined' troops, the cavalry acquired militarily decisive importance from time to time. Xenophon dedicated a separate work to cavalry, in which selecting appropriate horses, training the horses and riders as well as tactics in war are dealt with at length (Xen. Hipp.; cf. Mem. 3,3 → Horsemanship).

Because of the high costs and efforts of breeding and maintaining horses, the term hippeis became also a social category. Hippeis can be an honorary title for elite units of the infantry [3. 344]. The connection between wealth, aristocratic lifestyle and horse breeding is not least demonstrated by the preference of aristocrats and tyrants for the hippic agon (Theog. 549ff.; 983ff.; Aristoph. Nub. 14ff.; 60ff.; Thuc. 6,12,2; 15,3; 16,2; And. 4,25ff.; Isoc. Or. 7,45; 16,25; 32ff.; Xen. Ages. 1,23; Xen. Hell. 3,4,15; [3. 210f., 344f.]). For this reason, political theory saw a close link between the aristocratic-oligarchical constitutions and a strong presence of hippeis (Aristot. Pol. 4,3,1289b 35ff.; 4,13,1297b 16ff.; 6,7,1321a 6ff.).

The links between military and social or political organization are especially evident in Athens: in the Solonic class system (→ Solon) the hippeis form the second tax class of the timocratic constitution (Aristot. Ath. Pol. 7,3f.). From this class, the 1,000 hippeis were recruited, which, according to the → phyles, were organized into 10 squadrons each with one phylarch and commanded by two hipparchs (Aristot. Ath. Pol. 61,4f.). They had to undergo a review by the council. (Xen. Hipp. 1,9; Aristot. Ath. Pol. 49,2). To serve in the cavalry without such a review was forbidden (Lys. 14,4–10).

As shown in the frieze with the Panathenaean procession on the Parthenon, the hippeis played an important roll in the visual self-presentation of the polis of Athens (cf. also Xen. Hipp. 3). The hippeis often appeared with their horses on grave reliefs, like that of the Athenian Dexileus who fell in battle about 394 BC (Athens, Ceramicus; [8. 315]). Although the polis assumed part of the costs for maintenance, arms and equipment (according to Xen. Hipp. 1,19 nearly 40 talents a year in the early 4th cent. BC), only members of the upper class were able to serve as hippeis (cf. Xen. Hipp. 1,9). Consequently, they developed not only an *esprit de corps* commensurate to their position and an aristocratic lifestyle, but also appeared to have increasingly distanced themselves from the radical democracy, especially after they acquired merits during the defence of Attica during the Peloponnesian War (Aristoph. Ach. 5f.; 300f. and especially Equ. passim). At times they were also heavily involved in the tyranny of the 'Thirty' (404/3) (Xen. Hell. 3,1,4) and for some time afterwards were regarded as suspect or incriminated (Lys. 16,6ff.; 26,10). During the 4th cent. the hippeis increasingly lost their military importance in Athens.

1 J. K. ANDERSON, Ancient Greek Horsemanship, ²1971 2 G. R. BUGH, The Horsemen of Athens, 1988 3 BUSOLT/SWOBODA I 4 L. A. BURCKHARDT, Bürger und Soldaten, 1996 5 HASEBROEK, 78–81 6 I. G. SPENCE, The Cavalry of Classical Greece, 1993 7 E. STEIN-HÖLKESKAMP, Adelskultur und Polisgesellschaft, 1989, 110f. 8 TRAVLOS, Athen.   H.-J.G.

Hippemolgi see → Galactophagi

Hippias ('Ιππίας/Hippías, Ion. 'Ιππίης/Hippíēs).
[1] Eldest son of → Peisistratus from his first marriage to an Athenian woman. Together with his brothers → Hipparchus [1] and Thessalus he assumed his father's inheritance in 528/7 BC and continued his father's moderate politics (Thuc. 6,54–55; [Aristot.] Ath. Pol. 18,1), e.g. as archon in 526/7. However, when Hipparchus was murdered at the Panathenaea of 514 BC, H. disarmed the population, ordered torture and assassinations and sent many of his rivals into exile (Hdt. 5,62; Thuc. 6,59; [Aristot.] Ath. Pol. 19). The subsequent marriage of his daughter Archedice with Aeantides, son of the tyrant → Hippoclus of Lampsacus, who was friendly with the Persians, indicates a move to reconciliation with the Persians. From Delphi the Alcmaeonids, and → Cleisthenes, initiated the overthrow of the tyrant with the help of → Cleomenes I of Sparta. In 510 H. surrendered and went first to Sigeum, then, after an unsuccessful reconciliation with Cleomenes, to Lampsacus and Susa (Hdt. 5,63–4; 65; 91–4; 96; Thuc. 6,59; [Aristot.] Ath. Pol. 19). From there he set off to Greece with the Persian army and at → Marathon saw his hopes of returning to Athens shattered (Hdt. 6,102; 107–9; 121). The Peisistratids were thereafter outlaws throughout Greece (Thuc. 6,55).

H. BERVE, Die Tyrannis bei den Griechen, 1967, 63ff.; 554ff.; L. DE LIBERO, Die Archaische Tyrannis, 1996, 116ff.; TRAILL, PPA 537810; K.-W. WELWEI, Athen, 1992, 247ff.

[2] From Thessaly, leader of the Arcadian mercenaries whom the satrap Pissuthnes gave as protection to the pro-Persian party in Notion. In 427 BC H. was taken by surprise by Paches and killed after Notion was taken (Thuc. 3,34).   B.P.

[3] Macedonian, from Beroea, high-ranking officer of → Perseus in the 3rd Macedonian War (Liv. 42,51,4; 44,4,1; 7,8; cf. Pol. 18,10,1); in 168 BC he surrendered to L. → Aemilius [I 32] Paullus. As a high-ranking friend of the king, H. was sent to Q. → Marcius Philippus in Larissa (Liv. 42,39,7f.) in 172 BC and in the spring of 171 to the Senate in Rome (Pol. 27,6,1–3; cf. Liv. 42,48,1–3; App. Mac. 11,5–9). Another mission followed in 169/8 to → Genthius (Pol. 28,9,3; 29,3,1–3; Liv. 44,23,2). The identity of the Macedonian officer H. and the homonymous person(s) as envoys of Perseus is disputed [1. 156–159; 2. 113f.].

[4] Boeotian, Boeotarch in 187 BC (IG VII 2407; 2408; Pol. 22,4,12) [1. 156f.], in 174/3 he participated in the alliance with → Perseus; on the eve of the 3rd Macedonian War (172/1) exiled by radical pro-Romans and indicted, H. received Roman protection from hostile action against his person along with → Ismenias and → Neon in Chalcis (Pol. 27,1,11; 2,2f.) [3. 153f.; 157f.].

1 E. OLSHAUSEN, Prosopographie der hell. Königsgesandten, 1974   2 S. LE BOHEC, Les phíloi des rois Antigonides,

in: REG 98, 1985, 93–124   3 J. DEININGER, Der polit. Widerstand in Griechenland gegen Rom, 1971.   L.-M.G.

[5] Sophist from Elis, 'much younger' than Protagoras (Pl. Hp. mai. 382e), still active at the beginning of the 4th cent. BC, he survived Socrates (cf. Pl. Ap. 19e). Two Platonic dialogues, the Hippias maior and Hippias minor, bear his name; he also appears in the Protagoras (cf. 337c–338b) as well as in a dialogue in Xenophon (Mem. 4,4,5–25). He held public office as envoy of his city (see Pl. Hp. mai. 281a-c)

Ancient tradition attributes to him knowledge in very diverse subjects (arithmetic, astronomy, geometry, music, prosody, poetry, philology, rhetoric, 'archaeology', mnemonics and practical skills). Of his works, only a single fragment survived (Clem. Al. strom. 6,15) along with some titles of his works: 'Trojan Dialogue' (Philostr. VS 1,11,4, cf. Pl. Hp. mai. 286a-b), 'Names of Peoples' (B 2 DK) a list of Olympic champions (Plut. Numa 1) and a 'Collection' (Ath. 13,608f) of possibly different informations in historical sequence. H. is the inventor of the 'quadratrix', whose application Proclus (in Euclidem 272,3) explained not so much for the approximate squaring of a circle, than for dividing a right angle into three equal parts. He was also probably the first doxograph (→ Doxography) and before Plato and Aristotle saw the poet Homer (Oceanus and Tethys are the source of all things) as predecessor of Thales (all is water).

In the 20th cent. H. was assigned a historically important role in the development of political thinking [8; 10.] and was seen as the first to formulate theories about natural law as well as cosmopolitanism (cf. Pl. Prt. 337c-d: 'by nature the same is related to the same'; 'The law is the ruler of man'; Xen. Mem. 4,4).

→ Mathematics;   → Plato;   → Political philosophy; → Sophists

EDITIONS: 1 DK⁶ 86   2 M. UNTERSTEINER, I Sofisti, Testimonianze e frammenti III, 1954, 38–109 (complementing DK).
BIBLIOGRAPHY: 3 H. GOMPERZ, Sophistik und Rhet., 1912 (repr. 1965), 68–79   4 A. A. BJÖRNBO, s.v. H. (13), RE 8, 1707–1711   5 A. MOMIGLIANO, Lebensideale in der Sophistik (1930), in: C. J. CLASSEN (ed.), Sophistik, 1976, 465–477   6 W. NESTLE, Vom Mythos zum Logos, ²1942, repr. 1975, 360–371   7 B. SNELL, Die Nachr. über die Lehren des Thales und die Anfänge der griech. Philos.- und Literaturgesch. (1944), in: C. J. CLASSEN (ed.), Sophistik, 1976, 478–490   8 E. DUPRÉEL, Les sophistes, 1948, 185–393   9 C. J. CLASSEN, Bemerkungen zu zwei griech. "Philosophiehistorikern", in: Philologus 109, 1965, 175–178   10 M. UNTERSTEINER, I Sofisti, ²1967 (repr. 1996), XV   11 H. BLUM, Die ant. Mnemotechnik, 1969, 48–55   12 GUTHRIE, I 3 (The Sophists), 1971, 280–285   13 J. MANSFELD, Cratylus 402a-c: Plato or Hippias?, in: L. ROSSETTI (ed.), Atti del Symposium Heracliteum 1981, I, 1983, 43–55   14 J. BRUNSCHWIG, H. d'Élis, philosophe-ambassadeur, in: K. BOUDOURIS (ed.), The Sophistic Movement, 1984, 269–276.   MI.NA.

Hippiatrica (Τὰ ἱππιατρικά; *Tà Hippiatriká*). Greek texts about the medicine of solidungulates, collected – except for a few inedita – in the *Corpus Hippiatricorum Graecorum* (CHG) [1].

At least four cents. separate the hippological texts by Simon of Athens (5th/4th cents. BC), by Xenophon, and the few places where Aristotle treats the reproduction and the diseases of solidungulates (esp. Hist. an. 572a–577a, 604a–605a, 611a and 631a) from the first texts about horse medicine extant in Greek. The long gap in the Greek evidence is, to some extent, offset by Latin sources, in particular by Varro's agricultural treatise (2,6–8) which contains the first literary record for the term ἱππιατρός (*hippiatrós*, attested already by an inscription from Lamia, 130 BC; IG IX,2,65,9), and by Columella (6,27–38), who is one of Eumelus' sources and one of the oldest known authors for equine medicine in Greek language. There are many connections between the Greek works on equine medicine (c. 2nd/3rd to 5th cents. AD) and their Latin counterparts in the 4th and 5th cents. (*Ars veterinaria* by Pelagonius, → *Mulomedicina Chironis*, and *Digesta artis mulomedicinalis* by Vegetius), indicating that borrowings took place from both sides. The influence of the (lost) treatise by Mago the Carthaginian, who is cited frequently in these text, must not be underestimated.

Not a single important author is known from the Byzantine period, when the *Hippiatrika* had been collected. Four consecutive editions of these collections can be discerned. The first three can be distinguished by the topical arrangement of the excerpts from various authors. The (first) edition M, which comes closest to the original collection (MS Par. Gr. 2322, 11th cent.), essentially consists of seven authors who appear to be cited in alphabetical order: → Apsyrtus [2] of Clazomenae, → Anatolius [1] (who is probably identical to Vindanius (or Vindonius) Anatolius of Berytus, 4th or 5th cent., one of the compilers of the → *Geoponica*, 16 bks. dealing with horses among others), Eumelus, Theomnestus (of Magnesia, according to the Arabic translation from the mid 9th cent.), Hippocrates, the veterinarian, → Hierocles (a lawyer who limited himself to rewriting several works by Apsyrtus into more elegant prose), and → Pelagonius (whose treatise was originally written in Latin). The order of their excerpts had been modified in later times and further sources were added: texts by Tiberius and a collection entitled *Prognóseis kaì iáseis* ('Prognoses and Treatments') in the (second) edition B (represented by the illuminated MS *Berolinensis Gr.* 134 [*Phillippicus* 1538], 10th cent., with the addition of about ten MSS from the 14th–16th cents.; furthermore, excerpts from Iulius Africanus with interpolations from → Aelianus [2], prescriptions from human medicine and texts about equine medicine, among them those by Simon of Athens, in the (third) edition D (MSS *Cantab. Coll. Emmanuelis* III,3,19, 12th cent., and *Lond. Sloan.* 745, 13th cent.). In the fourth edition, two parts can be distinguished: the first comprises three bks. which contain one illustration per chapter in the two MSS Par. gr. 2244 and Voss. gr. Q. 50 (14th cent.). Bk. 1 and 2 present pieces by Hierocles taken from the *Hippiatrika* and arranged in book form (not the original work by Hierocles). Bk. 3 is an epitome of the *Hippiatrika*, designed as a comprehensive manual for equine medicine, existing in several revisions. The second (not illustrated) part of this fourth edition presents excerpts arranged in parts by authors (esp. Apsyrtus and Tiberius) and in parts by topic. The 3 bks. of the 'illuminated branch', as it was named by [2. 43], played a special role in the western Middle Ages: In addition to an illustrated translation into Italian, it was also translated into Latin and Sicilian (?).

The excerpts in the CHG contain little information about their respective authors who are consulted only in one or two places. It is certainly no accident that the contributions of Apsyrtus and Theomnestus, both veterinarians, were of particular importance: they reflect real practical experience and contain considerations about the cause of disease, a rare occurrence in this specialized literature intended to facilitate the diagnosis and treatment of disease in solidungulates.

→ Mulomedicina Chironis; → Veterinary medicine

1 E. ODER, K. HOPPE (ed.), Corpus Hippiatricorum Graecorum, 2 vols., 1924/1927   2 G. BJÖRCK, Apsyrtus, Julius Africanus et l'hippiatrie grecque, 1944   3 J.N. ADAMS, Pelagonius and Latin Veterinary Terminology in the Roman Empire, 1995   4 A.M. DOYEN-HIGUET, The Hippiatrica and Byzantine Veterinary Medicine, in: Dumbarton Oaks Papers 38, 1984, 111–120   5 K.-D. FISCHER, Ancient Veterinary Medicine. A survey of Greek and Latin sources and some recent scholarship, in: Medizinhist. Journal 23, 1988, 191–209   6 Y. POULLE-DRIEUX, L'hippiatrie dans l'Occident latin du XIIIe au XVe s., in: G. BEAUJOUAN et al., Médecine humaine et vétérinaire à la fin du Moyen Age, 1966   7 J. SCHÄFFER, K.-D. FISCHER, s.v. Tiermedizin, LMA 8, 774–780   8 M. ULLMANN, Die Medizin im Islam, HbdOr I, Supplement VI, I, 1970, 217–222.   A.D.-H.

Hippitas (Ἱππίτας; *Hippítas*). Confidant of the Spartan king Cleomenes III, whom he accompanied to Alexandria after the battle of Sellasia, where he had himself killed willingly after the latter's failed uprising against Ptolemy IV in 219 BC (Pol. 5,37,8; Plut. Cleomenes 37,6–13).   K.-W.WEL.

Hippo (Ἱππώ; *Hippó*).
[1] → Oceanid, perhaps the goddess of a 'horse well'.
[2] → Amazon (= Hippolyte, Callim. H. 3,239ff.; 266f.).
[3] Daughter of → Chiron (= Hippe), mistress of Hellen's son → Aeolus [1].
[4] Wet-nurse of Dionysus (= Hippa, Orph. H. 48; 49; Procl. in Pl. Ti. 124c).   RE.ZI.
[5] (Punic ʾpʾ?). A Phoenician or Punic foundation or re-foundation north-west of Utica, modern Bizerte. Sources: [Scyl.] 111, GGM I 89f. (Ἵππου ἄκρα (*Hippou ákra*), 'Horse's Fortress' [?]); Pol. 1,82,8; 88,2 (ἡ τῶν

Ἱππακριτῶν πόλις (*he tôn Hippakritôn pólis*, 'City of the Hippacritae'); Sall. Iug. 19,1 (*Hippo*); Diod. Sic. 20,55,3 (ἡ Ἵππου καλουμένη ἄκρα (*he Híppou kalouménē ákra*), 'the so-called Fortress of the Horse [?]'), cf. 57,6 (ἡ ὀνομαζομένη ἄκρα Ἵππου; *he onomazoménē ákra Híppou*, a different place); Plin. HN 5,23 (*Hippo Dirutus*); 6,212; 9,26 (*Hippo Diarrutus*); App. Lib. 30,128 (Ἱππών; *Hippṓn*); 110,520; 111,523 (Ἱππάγρετα; *Hippágreta*); Ptol. 4,3,6 (Ἱππὼν διάρρυτος; *Hippôn diárrhytos*); It. Ant. 21,4 (*Hippo Zaritus*); Sol. 27,7 (*Hippo Diarrhytos*). H. became *colonia* either under Caesar or Augustus (CIL VIII 1, 1206). Inscriptions: CIL VIII 1, 1206–1210, Suppl. 1, 14333–14335, Suppl. 4, 25417–25424.

W. HUSS, Die punischen Namen ..., in: Semitica 38, 1990, 171–174; S. LANCEL, E. LIPIŃSKI, s.v. Bizerte, DCPP, 74f. W.HU.

[6] **H. Regius.** (Punic '[*p*]'?). Phoenician or Punic foundation or re-foundation near the mouth of the river Seybouse, modern Hippo. In 205 BC, C. Laelius arrived in the harbour of H., thereby initiating the Roman invasion of Africa (Liv. 29,3,7; Pol. 12,1). After the end of the 2nd Punic War, H. became one of the royal seats of → Massinissa (*Hippo Regius*). Sources: Sil. Pun. 3,259; cf. Plin. HN 5,22; 6,212; Ptol. 4,3,5; It. Ant. 6,1; 42,4; 42,7f.; 44,4; Solin. 27,7. Following Caesar's victory at Thapsus (46 BC), the city became part of the new African province, its harbour the site of P. Sittius' victory over the Pompeian fleet (Bell. Afr. 96); *municipium* at first [1. 1, 109], then *colonia* (It. Ant. 20,3). It had a large harbour and an extended land area. Bishops have been mentioned beginning in 259. → Augustinus, the most important in the series of H.'s bishops, died there in AD 430. In 431, the city was captured by the Vandali, in 533, it was retaken by the East Romans, only to be occupied by Arabs in the mid 7th cent. Numerous monuments from the pre-Christian and Christian periods have survived. inscriptions: [1. 1–88].

1 Inscriptions latines de l'Algérie I.

S. DAHMANI, H. Regius, 1973; H.V. M. DENNIS, H. Regius, 1970 (= 1924); W. HUSS, Die punischen Namen ..., in: Semitica 38, 1990, 171–174; E. MAREC, Hippone la Royale, ²1954; K. VÖSSING, Unt. zur röm. Schule – Bildung – Schulbildung im Nordafrika der Kaiserzeit, 1991, 163–183. W.HU.

Hippobotai (ἱπποβόται; *hippobótai*). The *hippobotai* were the social elite in → Chalcis [1] on Euboea; the founding of Chalcidian → *apoikiai* in the 8th cent. BC is attributed to them (Str. 10,1,8). According to Aristotle, Chalcis was an equestrian oligarchy, whose power rested on its military supremacy (Aristot. Pol. 1289b 36–40); during the → Lelantine War, however, Chalcis could defeat the cavalry of Eretria only with the help of Thessaly (Plut. Mor. 760e-f; Str. 10,1,10; 10,1,12). However, based on other sources, it is doubtful that the → cavalry held any large military significance in the pe-

riod around 700 BC. Perhaps the *hippobotai* were heavily armed foot soldiers who rode to battle on horseback. When Athens defeated Chalcis around 507 BC, they settled 4,000 → *klerouchoi* on the land of the *hippobotai* (Hdt. 5,77; 6,100f.; cf. Ael. VH 6,1, if this does not refer to 445). After crushing the uprising of Chalcis in 445 BC, Athens exiled the *hippobotai* (Plut. Pericles 23,4; cf. Thuc. 1,114).

1 P. GREENHALGH, Early Greek Warfare, 1973, 90–93. R.O.

Hippobotus (Ἱππόβοτος; *Hippóbotos*). Hellenistic writer on the history of philosophy, place of activity unknown, cited 15 times in → Diogenes [17] Laertius, also in Clement of Alexandria, Porphyrius, Iamblichus, and the Suda, also named in POxy. 3656. The titles of two works are known: 'On the Schools of Philosophy' (Περὶ αἱρέσεων; *Perì hairéseōn*; Diog. Laert. 1,19; 2,88) and 'Lists of Philosophers' (Περὶ φιλοσόφων ἀναγραφή; *Perì philosóphōn anagraphé*, ibid. 1,41). In the first work H. states that there are nine 'schools of philosophy' (→ Hairesis). The 'Lists' suggests that he wrote at the end of the 3rd cent. BC, before → Sotion. Most of the H. citations in Diog. Laert. contain biographical details of individual philosophers and undoubtedly come from the second work. This probably belongs to the Succession Literature (→ Doxography).

EDITIONS: M. GIGANTE, Frammenti di Ippoboto, in: Omaggio a Piero Treves, 1983, 151–193 (see also PdP Suppl., 1985, 69).
BIBLIOGRAPHY: H. v. ARNIM, RE 8, 1722f.; J. MEJER, Diogenes Laërtius and his Hellenistic Background, 1978, 45, 69–72, 77; J. GLUCKER, Antiochus and the Late Academy, 1978, 176–180 (for later dating). D.T.R.

Hippocampus (Ἱππόκαμπος/*Hippókampos*, Latin *equus marinus*). The sea horse, which Paus. 2,1,9 defines as a 'horse, which is like a sea monster (κῆτος; *kêtos*) from the chest downwards' (cf. Serv. Georg. 4,387: in the first part a horse, changing into a fish in the last part). The *hippokampos* is not identical with the homonymous Mediterranean fish that is mentioned by Plin. HN 32,58 *et passim* as a remedy (e.g. the spotted seahorse, *hippocampus guttulatus* [1. 138]). Literary references are rare (e.g. Str. 8,7,2 [384]). According to Ael. NA 14,20 the stomach of a *hippokampos*, cooked and dissolved in wine, is a dangerous poison for the drinker.

In ancient art, on the other hand, the seahorse is found on Mycenaean gold tablets and gems, in archaic times very often as – often winged – riding animal for Poseidon or an old man of the sea (→ Halios geron). In the 5th cent. BC it appears rarely on coins and gems, more often in sculpture of the 4th cent. (figure group by → Scopas with Achilles, Thetis, Poseidon, and with Nereids sitting on dolphins, sea monsters or *hippokampoi*; cf. Plin. HN 36,26) and on mosaics and vases from Olynthus (before 346 BC) as well as from Lower Italy. On the northern frieze of the Hellenistic Pergamon Altar in Berlin, Poseidon's chariot is drawn by sea horses, and the base of the statue of Domitius Ahenobarbus in Munich (35–32 BC) is decorated with *hippokampoi*. The sea horse is also a frequent motif in Etruscan art, for example as the riding animal of a Nereid on vases and mirrors or on grave-stones and sarcophagi. In the Roman Imperial period, sea horses were often portrayed on sarcophagi or urns, among others, but also on frescoes and mosaics (for example, triumphal chariot of Neptunus and Amphitrite, drawn by four sea horses, from Utica/Tunisia, 3rd cent. AD [1. colour fig. 22]).

1 LEITNER   2 A. DRISS, Die Schätze des Nationalmuseums in Bardo, 1962.

LAMER, s.v. H., RE 8, 1748ff.; E. BOEHRINGER, Die Mz. von Syrakus, 1929, 84ff.; A. RUMPF, Die ant. Sarkophagreliefs 5,1: Die Meerwesen, 1939, 115ff.   C.HÜ.

Hippocleides (Ἱπποκλείδης; *Hippokleídēs*). Son of Teisander, Athenian from the family of the Philaids (→ Philaidai). Around 575 BC, he sought the hand in marriage of → Agariste [1], daughter of the tyrant → Cleisthenes of Sicyon, but was unsuccessful despite good prospects, losing out to the Alcmaeonid (→ Alcmaeonidae) → Megacles due to a social affront (Hdt. 6,126–130; Ath. 14,628d) [1]. During the archonship of H., the Panathenaea were established, probably in 566/5 BC [2. 57f.] (Pherecydes FGrH 3 F 2; Hellanicus FGrH 4 F 22).

1 E. STEIN-HÖLKESKAMP, Adelskultur und Polisgesellschaft, 1989, 118f.   2 P. E. CORBETT, The Burgon and Blaca Tombs, in: JHS 80, 1960, 52–60, esp. 57f.

DAVIES, 8429, II; DEVELIN, no. 1414; TRAILL, PPA 538230.   HA.BE.

Hippocles (Ἱπποκλῆς; *Hippoklês*). H. of Cyme on the island of Euboea, oikist ('founder') of the Italian Cyme together with Megasthenes of Chalcis. According to Strabo (5,4,4), the colony was named by mutual agreement after H.' hometown, but must be considered as a Chalcidian foundation.

J. BÉRARD, La colonisation grecque, 1957, 38f.   M.MEI.

Hippoclus (Ἵπποκλος; *Híppoklos*). H., (probably the first) tyrant of Lampsacus, was supported by the Persians and took part in the Scythian campaign of → Darius [1] I *c.* 513 BC (Hdt. 4,138). → Hippias [1] of Athens concluded a marriage alliance with him through the marriage of his daughter Archedice with H.' son and successor Aeantides, which at the same time meant a move in the direction of the Persians (Thuc. 6,59) and possibly was a reason for Sparta's intervention in Athens in 511/510 BC [1. 301].

→ Tyrannis

1 D. M. LEWIS, in: CAH 4, ²1988.

H. BERVE, Die Tyrannis bei den Griechen, 1967, 87; 570; L. DE LIBERO, Die archaische Tyrannis, 1996, 383.   J.CO.

Hippocoon (Ἱπποκόων; *Hippokóōn*). Son of → Oebalus and Bateia (Nicostrate: Schol. Eur. Or. 457), half-brother or brother of → Tyndareus, whom he drove out of Sparta. As a consequence of H.'s refusal along with the Hippocoontides to purify Heracles, or because they are allied with → Neleus, but above all, because they had struck Oeonus dead, → Heracles takes revenge on them (aition of Athena Axiopoinos) and reinstalls Tyndareus (Diod. Sic. 4,33,5f.; Paus. 3,1,4; 15,3–6; 19,7; Ps.-Apollod. 2,143; 3,123–125; as early as Alcm. fr. 3 CALAME [1; 2]). Paus. 3,14,6–7; 15,1 identifies the sons of H., who was a Spartan god of the Underworld [3], with several Spartan cult heroes.

1 C. CALAME, Les choeurs de jeunes filles en Grèce archaïque, 1977, vol. 2, 52ff.; 60f.   2 Id., Le récit généalogique spartiate: la représentation mythologique d'une organisation spatiale, in: Quaderni di storia 13, 1987, 43–91, esp. 63–65, abridged English version in: J. BREMMER, Interpretations of Greek Mythology, 1987, 153–186, esp. 170–172   3 S. WIDE, Lakonische Kulte, 1893, repr. 1973, 322f., cf. 18f.   4 H. W. STOLL, s.v. H. (1), Roscher I 2, 2677–2678.   T.H.

[2] Thracian ruler with Greek name, the cousin of → Rhesus, counsellor of the Thracians before Troy (Hom. Il. 10,518; cf. Tzetzes, Prooemium in Il. 794; [1; 2; 3]).

1 P. MATRANGA (ed.), Anecdota Graeca, vol. 1, 1850 (repr. 1971), 27   2 P. WATHELET, Dictionnaire des Troyens de l'Iliade, 1988, no. 172   3 Id., Les Troyens de l'Iliade. Mythe et Histoire, 1989, Index s. v. H.

[3] (Lat. *Hippocoon*). Otherwise unknown son of → Hyrtacus, companion of → Aeneas [1]; Verg. Aen. 5,492 and 503; [1].

1 M. PASCHALIS, Virgil's Aeneid. Semantic Relations and Proper Names, 1997, 194.   T. H.

Hippocrates (Ἱπποκράτης; *Hippokrátēs*).
[1] Father of → Peisistratus. H. is presumed to have come from Brauron, the later deme of Philaidai, and traced his ancestry back to Neleus (Hdt. 1,59; 5,65; Plut. Solon 10; 30).

TRAILL, PPA 538385.   B.P.

[2] Son of the Alcmaeonid (→ Alcmaeonids) → Megacles from Athens, born around 560 BC, H. was the brother of Cleisthenes, the father of → Megacles and Agariste [2] and thus the grandfather of → Pericles on his mother's side (Hdt. 6,131; [Aristot.] Ath. pol. 22,5).

DAVIES 9688, X; TRAILL, PPA 538485.

[3] Son of Ariphron of Athens, born before 450 BC, H. was a *strategos* in 426/5 (SEG 10,227, Z.3) and 424/3. During the attack on → Megara in 424 he succeeded, after a secret agreement with the local 'leaders of the

démos', in taking the port of → Nisaea (Thuc. 4,66–67). At the end of this year he fell in the battle against the Boeotians near the sanctuary of → Delium [1] (Thuc. 4,101).

DAVIES 11811, II.; TRAILL, PPA 538615. E.S.-H.

[4] Son of Pantares of Gela. H. took over the rulership of the city after the murder of his brother Cleander around 498 BC and, with the help of a Siceliot army of mercenaries and a cavalry, led by the aristocratic Geloan → Gelon [1], administered a territorial state that stretched from south to north through Sicily: he brought → Callipolis and → Naxos, Zancle and → Leontini under his control and turned them over to political friends. Out of fear that Anaxilaus of Rhegium would intervene, H. negotiated an amicable agreement with the Samians, who occupied Zancle in 493 while fleeing from the tyrant → Aeaces [2], according to which the Zanclaeans were abandoned to the Samians while H. got half of the city's effects and slaves as well as the landed property. He had Scythians from Cos, whom he probably installed in Zancle, brought to Inycus as the guilty party (Hdt. 6,23). Around 492/1 he besieged → Syracusae. An amicable agreement was achieved through the mediation of Corinth and Cercyra, according to which Syracusae had to cede H. Camarina (Hdt. 7,154; Thuc. 6,5; 3). H. fell in 491/490 outside the city of Hybla in the war against the Sicels (Hdt. 7,155).

D. ASHERI, in: CAH 4, ²1988, 757–766; H. BERVE, Die Tyrannis bei den Griechen, 1967, 137ff., 597f.; T. J. DUNBABIN, The Western Greeks, 1948, 106f. B.P.

[5] H. of Chios. Mathematician and astronomer from the 2nd half of the 5th cent. BC. According to Eudemus, H., who lived after Anaxagoras and Oenopides, wrote the first 'Elements' (Procl. in Eucl. 1,66,7–8 FRIEDLEIN). Iamblichus (De communi mathematica scientia 25, p.78,1 FESTA) mentions him, together with → Theodorus of Cyrene, as the most prominent representative of the mathematical sect of the Pythagoreans and thus makes him an elder contemporary of Socrates. As a businessman H. is supposed to have lost his fortune to swindlers or pirates (Aristot. Eth. Eud. 1247a 17–20; Plut. Solon 2; Philoponus in Aristot. Ph. p. 31,3–7 VITELLI). H. presumably obtained his knowledge of mathematics already on Chios. He lived in Athens later on and, together with Oenopides, contributed to Athens becoming the centre of mathematics in Greece.

H. dealt especially with the so-called 'classical problems' which were the subjects in mathematics at that time (duplication of the cube, trisecting the angle, squaring the circle); these are problems in which equations need to be solved which go beyond the quadratic. H. made his own contributions to the duplication of the cube and the squaring of the circle. Even though his writings have been lost, essential parts of the 'quadrature of the lunes' can be reconstructed [1]. They are considered to be the oldest extant coherent Greek texts on mathematics. Duplication of the cube ('Delian prob-

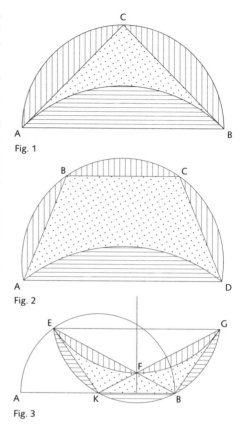

Fig. 1

Fig. 2

Fig. 3

lem') looks for the side of a cube whose volume is twice as big as that of a given cube. H. put this problem down to the problem of interpolating two mean proportionals x and y between two given lines a and $2a$ (Eutocius in Archim. De sphaera et cylindro, Archim. Op. 3, p. 88,17–23 HEIBERG; [9. 17–24]). This is correct because $x^3 = 2a^3$ follows from: $a{:}x = x{:}y = y{:}2a$. It is not known whether H. found a method for determining the two mean proportionals.

In the context of attempts to square the circle (that is, to construct a square that has the same area as a given circle), H. dealt with the problem of transforming lunes (that is, areas enclosed in arcs) into linear figures with the same surface area. H.'s text is passed on by Simplicius (in Aristot. Ph., p. 60,22–68,32 DIELS), who stated that he was quoting → Eudemus literally (for the reconstruction [1; 4; 9. 25–41]). First H. showed that circles act like the squares of their diametres and that this applies also to similar parts of a circle (sectors and segments). Then he observed chords whose squares act like small whole numbers (2:1, 3:1, 3:2). When similar segments of a circle are constructed over these chords and subtracted from each other, small lunes (μηνίσκοι/ *mēnískoi, lunulae*) remain as residual surface that can be squared because their surfaces are simple numerical ratios. In the simplest case (fig. 1) similar segments are drawn over the equilateral right triangle ABC (cut off from quarter circles); the outer arc is thus equal to the semicircle. According to the Pythagorean theorem $AB^2 = AC^2 + BC^2$, and since the segments act like the squares of their chords, then also segment AB = segment AC + segment BC. Since the lune ABC is formed by subtracting segment AB from triangle ABC and adding the segments AC and BC, lune and triangle have the same surface area.

In the 2nd case (fig. 2) the outer arc is larger than the semicircle, where AB = BC = CD and $AD^2 = 3\,AB^2$ apply. The segment over AD is thus three times as big as that over AB. As in the first case the sum of the smaller segments equals that of the larger segment.

In the 3rd case (fig. 3) the outer arc EKBG is smaller than a semicircle. The lune is made up of two arcs of which the outer one is divided into three, the inner one into two equal arcs, which surround the similar segments, where $EF^2 : EK^2 = 3:2$ applies. The linear figure, which is made up of five chords, has the same area as the lune, which accordingly can also be squared. The construction starts out from the semicircle over AB. The line EF is found by means of an insertion; this is the oldest known example of this kind of νεῦσις (*neûsis*) construction. – Finally H. squares another lune and a circle together. The whole design allows the assumption that thereby it was intended to prove that every lune can be squared; but this is not true because the proofs are not general.

H.'s squaring of the lune was known in the West in the 13th and 14th cents. in two versions [3]. The question which lunes can be squared elementarily has been discussed since the 18th cent., among others by D. BER-NOULLI and L. EULER, and it was finally solved in the 20th cent. (E. LANDAU, N. G. TSCHEBOTAREW, A. W. DORODNOW [11]).

The 'Elements', which H. supposedly was the first to author, possibly were an ordered compilation of what was known in the area of elemental geometry, in which everything was put down to certain basic principles. In this respect H. is a precursor of → Euclides [3]. The 'Elements' may have included theorems about angles and arcs, which H. uses as proven conditions for the squaring of the lune, as well as the Pythagorean theorem and the conclusion that the areas of circles correspond to the squares of their diametres.

H. is mentioned as an astronomer, for instance by Aristot. (Mete. 342b 36; 345b 9), with his explanation of the comets and the Milky Way, which is similar to the Pythagorean. The comet is regarded as a planet that can rarely be seen and the comet's tail as an optical illusion that is caused by spacial motion.
→ Duplication of the cube

EDITIONS: 1 F. RUDIO, Der Ber. des Simplicius über die Quadraturen des Antiphon und des H., 1907 2 M. TIM-PANARO CARDINI, Pitagorici. Testimonianze e frammenti, fasc. 2, 1962, 28–73 3 M. CLAGETT, The Quadratura circuli per lunulas, in: Id., Archimedes in the Middle Ages, vol. 1, 1964, 610–626.
BIBLIOGRAPHY: 4 O. BECKER, Zur Textgestaltung des eudemischen Ber. über die Quadratur der Möndchen durch H. von Chios, in: O. NEUGEBAUER et al. (ed.), Quel-len und Stud. zur Gesch. der Mathematik, Astronomie und Physik, B. 3, 1936, 411–419 5 O. BECKER, Das mathematische Denken der Ant., 1957, 15; 58–60; 75 6 A. A. BJÖRNBO, s.v. H. (14), RE 8, 1780–1801 7 I. BULMER-THOMAS, H. of Chios, in: GILLISPIE, vol. 6, 1972, 410–418 8 T. L. HEATH, History of Greek Mathematics, 1921, vol. 1, 183–202 9 W. KNORR, The Ancient Trad. of Geometric Problems, 1986 10 J. MAU, s.v. H. (7), KlP 2, 1967, 1165–1169 11 C. J. SCRIBA, Welche Kreismonde sind elementar quadrierbar? Die 2400jährige Gesch. eines Problems bis zur endgültigen Lösung in den Jahren 1933/1947, in: Mitt. der Mathematischen Ges. in Hamburg 11, 1988, 517–539 12 B. L. VAN DER WAER-DEN, Erwachende Wissenschaft, 1956, 216–224. M.F.

[6] H. of Cos, the physician.
A. LIFE B. IMAGES C. CORPUS HIPPOCRATICUM
D. LATER RECEPTION IN ANTIQUITY
A. LIFE B. IMAGES C. CORPUS HIPPOCRATICUM
D. HISTORY OF RECEPTION IN ANTIQUITY

A. LIFE
Little is known with certainty about the person apart from his early fame. His position as an excellent physician is evident from a reference in Plato (Prt. 311b-c) – his role in medicine is considered to be equal to the role of → Polyclitus and → Phidias in sculptured art; further, knowledge of his method, which started with the 'whole', by readers of the Phdr. (270c-e) is taken for granted. H.'s place of birth is confirmed by the reference in Protagoras, which also gives an indication of his lifetime: if his reputation had already been established at the time of the dialogue (*c.* 433 BC), it can be concluded that H., even if Plato is guilty of a slight anachronism, cannot have been born long after 460 BC, more likely before then. Aristotle's passing allusion to the contrast between H.'s small physical stature and his medical greatness (Pol. 1326a) illustrates how generally well known the physician had become up to the twenties of the 4th cent.

All later 'sources' on the life of H., that is the collection of documents (two speeches, one decree and 24 letters), which claims to refer directly to him, as well as the numerous reports – including a biographical tradition – about his deeds, writings and opinions [1], which start in the 3rd cent. BC and appear in increasing number in Greek and Roman literature of the Imperial period, lack any mentionable value as evidence. As soon as H.'s central position in the history of medicine was established and the writings of the *Corpus Hippocraticum* were compiled under his name in Alexandria, the prerequisites for elaborating his life and personality as appropriate for the founder of medicine were given. Even though research might really have been done in archives on Cos and might occasionally have brought actual facts to light, it is so difficult to separate facts from fiction in these 'sources' that their value by and large can only be judged as insignificant.

Hippocrates of Cos: Writings of the *Corpus Hippocraticum* (selection)

Abbreviation	Latin title	Greek title	English title
Acut.	De diaeta acutorum	*Perì diaítēs oxéōn*	On Regimen in Acute Diseases
Aër.	De aere, aquis, locis	*Perì aérōn, hydátōn, tópōn*	Airs, Waters, Places
Aff.	De affectionibus	*Perì pathôn*	On Affections
Alim.	De alimento	*Perì trophês*	On Nutriment
Anat.	De anatomia (De anatome)	*Perì anatomês*	On Anatomy
Aph.	Aphorismi	*Aphorismoí*	Aphorisms
Art.	De articulis	*Perì árthrōn ⟨embolês⟩*	On Joints
Carn.	De carnibus	*Perì sarkôn*	On Fleshes
Coac.	Coacae praecognitiones	*Kōakaì prognóseis*	Coan Prognoses
Cord.	De corde	*Perì kardíēs*	On the Heart
de Arte	De arte	*Perì téchnēs*	On the Art
Decent.	De decenti ornatu	*Perì euschēmosýnēs*	Decorum
Dent.	De dentitione	*Perì odontophyíēs*	On Dentition
Dieb. Judic.	De diebus iudicatoriis	*Perì krisímōn*	On Critical Days
Ep(ist).	Epistulae	*Epistolaí*	Letters
Epid. (1–7)	De morbis popularibus (med.: Epidemiarum 1.–7.)	*Epidēmiôn 1–7*	Epidemics
Fist.	De fistulis	*Perì syríngōn*	On Fistulae
Flat.	De flatibus	*Perì physôn*	On Breaths
Foet. Exsect.	De exsectione foetus	*Perì enkatatomês embrýou*	On the Excision of the Foetus
Fract.	De fracturis	*Perì agmôn*	On Fractures
Genit.	De genitura	*Perì gonês*	On Generation
Gland.	De glandulis	*Perì adénōn*	On Glands
Haem.	De haemorrhoidibus	*Perì haimorrhoḯdōn*	On Haemorrhoids
Hebd.	De hebdomadibus	*Perì hebdomádōn*	On Sevens
Hum.	De humoribus	*Perì chymôn*	On Humours
Int.	De internis affectionibus	*Perì tôn entòs pathôn*	On Internal Affections
Judic.	De iudicationibus	*Perì krisíōn*	On Crises
Jusj.	Iusiurandum	*Hórkos*	Oath
Liqu.	De liquidorum usu	*Perì hygrôn chrḗsios*	On the Use of Liquid
Loc. Hom.	De locis in homine	*Perì tópōn tôn katà án-thrōpon*	Places in Man
Medic.	De medico	*Perì iētroû*	On the Physician
Morb. (1–4)	De morbis	*Perì noúsōn*	On Diseases
Morb. Sacr.	De morbo sacro	*Perì hierês noúsou*	On the Sacred Disease
Mul. (1–3)	De muliebribus	*Gynaikeíōn 1–3*	On the Diseases of Women
Nat. Hom.	De natura hominis	*Perì phýsios anthrṓpou*	On the Nature of Man
Nat. Mul.	De natura muliebri	*Perì gynaikeíēs phýsios*	On the Nature of Woman
Nat. Puer.	De natura pueri	*Perì phýsios paidíou*	On the Nature of the Child
Oct.	De octimestri partu	*Perì oktaménou*	On the Eight-Months' Child
Off.	De officina medici	*Kat' iētreîon*	In the Surgery
Oss.	De ossium natura	*Perì ostéōn phýsios*	On the Nature of Bones
Praec.	Praeceptiones	*Parangelíai*	Precepts
Prog.	Praenotiones (Prognosticon)	*Prognōstikón*	Prognostic
Prorrh. (1–2)	Praedicta (Prorrheticon)	*Prorrhētikón*	Prorrhetic
Steril. (= Mul. 3)	De sterilibus	*Perì aphórōn è gynaikeíōn*	On Infertile Women
Superf.	De superfetatione	*Perì epikyḗsios*	On Superfoetation
Ulc.	De ulceribus	*Perì helkôn*	On Ulcers
VC	De capitis vulneribus (med.: De vulneribus capitis)	*Perì tôn en kephalêi trō-mátōn*	On Wounds in the Head
Vict. (1–3)	De victu	*Perì diaítēs*	Regimen
Vid. Ac.	De visu	*Perì ópsios*	On Eyesight
Virg.	De virginum morbis	*Perì partheníōn*	On the Diseases of Maidens
VM	De vetere medicina	*Perì archaíēs iētrikês*	On Ancient Medicine

The Latin title listed for each treatise is (one of) the title(s) used in antiquity. Where the standard abbreviation is based on the medieval title, the latter is also listed.

B. Images

In 1940 a Roman marble bust was found in Ostia (Mus. Ostiense, inv. no. 98; Helbig, vol. 4, no. 3036), which goes back to an original of the 2nd cent. BC. Both the finding place in the grave of the doctor Marcius Demetrius and the verse inscription on the column belonging to the bust, which can be interpreted as an allusion to the first Hippocratic aphorism, support the identification with H. Three different sorts of bronze coins that were minted in the early Imperial period on Cos show a bearded head or a figure with the inscription ΙΠ or ΙΠΠΟΚΡΑΤΗΣ (Bibliothèque nationale, Cabinet des médailles, no. 1273, 1274 = British Mus., Greek Coins, Caria, Cos, Rhodes etc., no. 215, 216; BN, no. 1246; Berlin, Staatliches Münzkabinett, Faustina II.).

C. Corpus Hippocraticum

1. General 2. Tradition 3. Overview of works 4. Medicine

1. General

The *Corpus Hippocraticum* (CH) most probably originated in Hellenistic Alexandria as the result of Ptolemaic diligence in collecting. Already before 200 BC → Bacchius [1] of Tanagra deals with 21 works in his Hippocratic glossary, while → Erotianus offers a list of *c.* 40 titles in the 1st cent. AD. Other ancient sources (mainly → Galen) mention about 10 further titles, so that about 12 works of the 62 titles mentioned in the index of the medieval MS Vaticanus gr. 276 remain without mention in antiquity. How this heterogeneous conglomerate, which obviously came from different authors who only had the Ionic dialect and some relationship to medicine in common, was finally ascribed to one author remains unclear. The only pre-Alexandrian quotation of a Hippocratic text can be found in Aristotle (Hist. an. 512b), where a longer passage from *Nat. Hom.* (for the abbreviation of the titles cf. the table) is ascribed to the physician → Polybus.

The critique of Hippocratic authenticity [2; 3] uses both outer and inner criteria. The above mentioned statement on H.'s methods in Phdr. serves as an outer point of reference; but the passage is so unspecific that until today no agreement has been achieved on the Hippocratic work that is supposed to correspond to this method. Secondly, the → Anonymus Londinensis, a papyrus from the 2nd cent. AD, which became known in 1892 and which goes back in part to Peripatetic school tradition, reports in detail on the opinions of H. in a longer treatise on pathological schools of thought (5,35–7,40). But this source too contains no certain references to concrete works by H. The third point of reference for the possible authenticity of certain works is the correspondence between individual statements and details from H.'s life as described in the biographical witnesses; but it is more likely that the biography was inspired by the works of the CH than that it has independent historical significance. The inner criteria of authenticity in the end all amount to an evaluation of the clinical or scientific achievement of the various works: works that correspond with the ideas of the respective physician or historian are reconsidered as originating from Cos or being authentically Hippocratic. Since this approach, which is used all too often in modern times, is conditioned by the times, it needs no further words [4].

Ordering the Hippocratic works according to schools of thought (in doing so mainly the two schools of Cos and of Cnidus can be distinguished), goes back to Galen who listed the main characteristics of two medical traditions contemporary with H. Consulting these and other sources, JOUANNA and GRENSEMANN have tried in recent times to work out clear-cut portraits of the competing schools, which could serve as assignment criteria; but these studies have not found any general agreement in spite of valuable findings towards understanding Hippocratic medicine [5; 6; 7; 8].

2. Tradition

The independent textual witnesses of CH comprise six medieval MSS, which each contain between four and about fifty of the works compiled in the CH: Laurentianus gr. 74,7 (9th cent.) = B; Marcianus gr. 269 (10th cent.) = M; Vindobonensis medicus gr. 4 (10th cent.) = Θ; Parisinus gr. 2253 (11th cent.) = A; Vaticanus gr. 276 (12th cent.) = V and in part Parisinus gr. 2141 (13th cent.) = I [9]. In addition a number of papyri offer smaller texts [10].

3. Overview of works

Since the *c.* seventy works of the CH are strongly divergent in form, scope, level of knowledge and theoretical perspectives, it is not possible to put up a general structure that could claim factual or historical validity. The following subdivision of selected works into six larger categories according to the literary genre serves purely practical purposes.

(a) Text-books (almost half of the CH), which can be assigned to the three special fields of internal medicine, surgery and gynaecology, each deal with more or less clear-cut groups of diseases or wounds. The five works from the field of inner medicine (*Aff.*; *Morb.* 1–3 [11] and *Int.*) show a common structure that consists in a series of independent chapters, which deal with a specific pathological condition, principally in the categories: name of the disease or main characteristic; symptoms and development; aetiology; prognosis; treatment. The order of the diseases within one work often go *a capite ad calcem*.

In the larger surgical books [12] (*Fract.*; *Art.* and *VC*) the most important fractures and sprains or wounds and their treatment are explained with great care and specialized knowledge, mostly in series of chapters that are each devoted to one type of injury. Smaller surgical works (*Haem.*; *Fist.*; *Liqu.*; *Vid. Ac.* and *Ulc.*) deal with various special fields.

The bks. *Mul.* 1–3, of which the third also bears the title *Steril.*, deal extensively with physiology, pathology and the treatment of the uterus including hyper- and amenorrhea, cancer, prolapsed uterus, sterility and pregnancy-related ailments [13]. An extensive part of these bks. consists of prescriptions, which are summarized in separate chapters (*Mul.* 1, 74–109; *Mul.* 2,185–212; *Steril.* 217–32).

(b) *Aph.*, the most widespread of all Hippocratic writings, which consists of 422 short statements in seven sections that cover all aspects of medicine, belongs to the collection of maxims. The two works *Coac.* and *Prorrh.* 1 [14] with 640 and 170 prognostic statements respectively, which are divided into areas with related contents, have a smaller scope. Two smaller works (*Dent.* and *Alim.* [15]), deal with the early care of children and with questions of nutrition and growth in 32 and 55 maxims respectively.

(c) A further quarter of the *CH* is devoted to monographic treatises with a clear objective. The works *Carn.* [16] and *Genit./Nat. Puer.* [17] describe a human being's origin from the meeting of the seeds of both parents until the formation of the individual parts of the body, and their functioning. In the work *Cord.* [18], which should probably be dated to the 3rd cent. BC because of its anatomical knowledge, the author gives a detailed description of the human heart in which he mentions heart valves and differentiates between arteries and veins.

Other monographs deal with questions of pathogenesis. *Nat. Hom.* proposes a system of four bodily fluids (blood, phlegm, yellow bile, black bile), according to which health is the even mixture and distribution of the fluids and illness is the disturbance of this balance. *Morb.* 4 [17] presents a similar system of four, but with water instead of black bile as the fourth fluid; *Vict.* [19] emphasizes the central contrast between fire and water in human nature and the necessity to keep the relationship between eating and physical exercise balanced; *Flat.* [20] derives all diseases from the air, which enters the body when breathing, eating, drinking or through wounds, while *Morb. sacr.* [21] explains the symptoms of epilepsy as the result of an interruption of the brain's supply with air caused by a vascular flow of phlegm. *VM* [22] presents a dietetic medicine based on experience, as the 'ancients' discovered, as opposed to the contemporary tendency to treat according to abstract factors like heat, cold, dryness and moistness. The details of a correct diet, above all the role of administering barley gruel, is the topic of the work *Acut.*, while *Prog.* [23] emphasizes the importance of a long series of signs on the patients as well as their excretions, which make general conclusions about the outcome of the disease independent of the diagnosis possible. The work *Aër.* [24] informs the itinerant physician about the significance of environmental factors like wind, water and geographical location for the health of the population, knowledge of which makes it easier for him to provide correct diagnoses and prognoses; in a second part the work offers a detailed comparison between Europeans and Asians, which is derived from the geographical peculiarities of both continents.

(d) A further group of theoretical works (for instance *Loc. hom.*, *Hum.*, *Acut.* [*spuria*]), which lacks structural cohesion – characteristic is rather heterogeneity with regard to form and contents, confusion or even contradiction – gives information about individual aspects of healing.

(e) Though they differ with regard to focus and elaboration, the bks. *Epid.* 1–7 [25] share the character of a collection of data gathered at the bedside, which consists mainly of individual case-studies and annual reports (*katastáseis*) about morbidity and mortality in relation to the weather in selected communities. *Epid.* 1 and 3 are more thoroughly elaborated than the remaining bks. on epidemics, they concentrate on feverish diseases and omit a clear indication of the diagnosis in the case-studies. *Epid.* 4, 5 and 7 offer exclusively medical histories, which vary greatly in content and size, while *Epid.* 2 and 6 [26] lack any inner order.

(f) Documents (for example the 'Oath' [27], speeches, letters [28]), whose historical value is difficult to assess, belong to the last group.

4. MEDICINE

The starting-point for Hippocratic physiology and pathology, which are the basis of the writings of the *CH* in spite of their divergences, is the implicit assumption, achieved by observation and experience [29], that the body consists of solid and liquid parts which affect each other in certain ways. The various body parts, insofar as they are visible from the outside or become visible through injuries, are anatomically (→ Anatomy) known and named; furthermore conclusions about the form and structure of the inner parts of the body are drawn from coincidental observations on animals. Every body part has a certain structure, which enables it more or less to attract and take in or to secrete bodily fluids – according to contemporary natural scientific conceptions. Fluid bodily substances are, apart from the various observable excretions and secretions, the two vital substances air and blood as well as hypothetical bodily fluids, mainly phlegm and bile, which become noticeable in an illness through observable changes in the body or in the patient's excretions [30]. A balanced mixture of the bodily fluids and the integrity of the solid structures are the basis of health; disease results from outward influences changing the quantity or temperature of the bodily fluids so much that they are brought out of balance. In this case phlegm and/or bile are set into motion, separate themselves from the blood and are attracted and absorbed by various parts of the body according to their structure, especially if these are heated up or dried out. If they get into the bloodstream they hinder the regular flow of blood and air in the vessels; if they deposit themselves in a certain part of the body they injure it and thus cause the various symptoms of the disease. On the other hand, inner or outer traumata of the solid parts of the body can be the cause of disease, which in turn has an effect on the motion of the fluids.

If the body wins the upper hand in the ensuing battle, then the harmful fluid, after it has become 'ripe' through a coction process promoted by fever, is excreted, the injury heals and the patient gets well. It is the physician's task to promote this natural healing process by strengthening the patient's body, or at least not weakening it, by giving or withholding food at the right time; on the other hand by actively intervening, be it through diet, medication or surgery, he influences the course of the disease directly with the goal of clearing up the disturbance by removing or diluting the harmful fluid, and/or restoring the natural structure of the body parts. The physician's clinical procedure progresses from the first examination of the patient, taking his whole life circumstances into account and investigating into his medical history, to diagnosis and prognosis and finally to treatment.

A series of deontological works as well as incidental remarks in the remaining works of the *CH* give information about the position of the Hippocratic physician in society. The three main characteristics of the physician's self-image based on these sources are, firstly, the conviction of the sole value of a rational procedure excluding all magical or religious considerations (*Morb. Sacr.*); secondly, the belief in the validity of theoretical knowledge and practical skill in spite of the lack of standard medical training and qualification approved by the state; thirdly, being conscious of the fact that the lack of public approval of the individual doctor makes it necessary for him to prove his competence and reliability with each individual case. This situation results in the special value that the Hippocratic physician places on his outward appearance and his behaviour, on his clarity and ability to convince in discussions, on his skill in surgical measures of all kinds and on his competence in predicting the course of a disease. These efforts to prove the existence of a professional ethos include also the writing of works like *Praec.* and *Decent.*, which contain explicit regulations for the practising physician, and presumably also the formulation of the 'Oath'. Medical training appears to have taken the form of personally following a master, as was common both with craftsmen and among Sophists.

D. HISTORY OF RECEPTION IN ANTIQUITY

Already in → Hellenism a lively occupation with the *CH* in the form of commentaries and glossaries had begun. → Herophilus is supposed to have written a refutation of the *Prognostikon* around 300, and his student → Bacchius [1] of Tanagra wrote a special dictionary of Hippocratic expressions. The first extant work that is based directly on a writing of the *CH* is the commentary with illustrations by → Apollonius [16] of Citium of 'On the joints', in which he attributes the epithet 'the most divine' to H. and calls him the physician *per se*. Among the Romans → Varro (Rust. 1,4,5) is the first to mention the deeds of H., while → Celsus [7] (Praef. 8) and → Scribonius Largus (Praef. 3; 5) in the 1st cent. AD grant H. as the author of the Hippocratic works a place as the founder of medicine.

In general the H. of the *CH* and the biographical tradition is mentioned and quoted by almost all medical writers, except the → Methodists, from the 1st cent. AD onwards to justify their own teaching opinions. The historically most important of these Hippocratics is Galen, who tries to do justice to his self-appointed role as the interpreter and defender of the great physician from Cos with a great wealth of historical and interpretative commentaries, propaganda works and a glossary [31]. Galen's H. achieved canonical validity when → Oribasius declared Galen's works as his preferred source for his medical compendia, 'because [Galen] endorsed H.'s principles and insights most exactly' (Collectionum Medicarum reliquiae 1, Praef.; [32]).

→ HIPPOCRATISM; → HIPPOCRATIC OATH

1 J. RUBIN, Hippocratic Lives and Legends, 1992, 1–93 2 H. DILLER, Stand und Aufgaben der Hippokratesforsch., in: Jb. 1959 der Akad. der Wissenschaften und der Lit., 271–287 3 G. E. R. LLOYD, Methods and Problems in Greek Science, 1991, 194–223 4 I. M. LONIE, Cos versus Cnidus and the Historians, in: History of Science 16, 1978, 42–92 5 W. D. SMITH, Galen on Coans and Cnidians, in: Bulletin of the History of Medicine 47, 1973, 569–585 6 J. JOUANNA, Hippocrate. Pour une archéologie de l'école de Cnide, 1974 7 H. GRENSEMANN, Knidische Medizin I–II, 1975/1987 8 A. THIVEL, Cnide et Cos?, 1981 9 A. RIVIER, Recherches sur la trad. manuscrite du traité Hippocratique 'De morbo sacro', 1962 10 MARGANNE 11 R. WITTERN, Die hippokratische Schrift De morbis I, 1974 12 J. E. PETREQUIN, Chirurgie d'Hippocrate, 1877/8 13 H. FASBENDER, Entwickelungslehre, Geburtshülfe und Gynäkologie in den hippokratischen Schriften, 1897 14 H. POLLACK, Textkritische Unt. zu der hippokratischen Schrift Prorrhetikos I, 1976 15 K. DEICHGRÄBER, Pseudhippokrates, Über die Nahrung, 1973 16 Id., Hippokrates, Über Entstehung und Aufbau des menschlichen Körpers, 1935 17 I. M. LONIE, The Hippocratic Treatises 'On Generation', 'On the Nature of the Child', 'Diseases IV', 1981 18 Id., The paradoxical Text 'On the Heart', in: Medical History 17, 1973, 1–34 19 R. JOLY Recherches sur le traité pseudo-hippocratique Du Régime, 1960 20 A. NELSON, Die hippokratische Schrift ΠΕΡΙ ΦΥΣΕΩΝ, 1909 21 H. GRENSEMANN, Die hippokratische Schrift 'Über die heilige Krankheit', 1968 22 A.-J. FESTUGIÈRE, Hippocrate. L'Ancienne Médecine, 1948 23 B. ALEXANDERSON, Die hippokratische Schrift Prognostikon, 1963 24 H. DILLER, Wanderarzt und Aitiologe, 1934 25 G. BAADER, R. WINAU (ed.), Die hippokratischen Epidemien, 1989 26 D. MANETTI, A. ROSELLI, Ippocrate Epidemie libro sesto, 1982 27 G. HARIG, J. KOLLESCH, Der hippokratische Eid, in: Philologus 122, 1978, 157–176 28 W. D. SMITH, Hippocrates. Pseudepigraphic Writings, 1990 29 L. BOURGEY, Observation et expérience chez les médecins de la Collection Hippocratique, 1953 30 E. SCHÖNER, Das Viererschema in der ant. Humoralpathologie, 1964, 15–58 31 W. D. SMITH, The Hippocratic Trad., 1979, 61–176 32 O. TEMKIN, Gesch. des Hippokratismus im ausgehenden Alt., in: Kyklos 4, 1932, 1–80.

EDITIONS: F. Z. ERMERINS, Hippocratis ... reliquiae, 3 vols., 1859–1864; J. L. HEIBERG et al., CMG I, 1927ff.; R. JOLY et al., Ed. Budé, 1967ff.; W. H. S. JONES et al., Loeb Classical Library, 1923ff.; H. KUEHLEWEIN, Hippocratis Opera, of which only 2 vols. appeared, 1894–1902; E. LITTRÉ, Œuvres complètes d'Hippocrate, 10 vols., 1839–1861.

CONCORDANCE/INDEX: J.H. KÜHN, U. FLEISCHER, Index Hippocraticus, 1986–1989; G. MALONEY, W. FROHN, Concordance des œuvres hippocratiques, 1984. BIBLIOGRAPHY: B. BRUNI CELLI, Bibliografía Hipocrática, 1984; S. BYL, Les dix dernières années (1983–1992) de la recherche hippocratique, in: Centre Jean-Palerne: Lettre d'informations 22, 1993, 1–39; G. FICHTNER, Corpus Hippocraticum. Verzeichnis der hippokratischen und pseudohippokratischen Schriften, ²1990; G. MALONEY, R. SAVOIE, Cinq cents ans de bibliogr. hippocratique, 1982.

OVERALL PRESENTATIONS: C. DAREMBERG, Œuvres choisies d'Hippocrate, ²1855; L. EDELSTEIN, s.v. H. (16), RE suppl. 6, 1290–1345; W. A. HEIDEL, Hippocratic medicine: its spirit and method, 1941; J. JOUANNA, Hippocrate, 1992 (with extensive bibliography); P. LAÍN ENTRALGO, La medicina Hipocrática, 1970; J. A. LÓPEZ FÉREZ (ed.), Tratados Hipocráticos. Actas del VIIe Colloque international hippocratique, 1992; V. NUTTON, Ancient Medicine, 2004; R. WITTERN, P. PELLEGRIN (ed.), Hippokratische Medizin und ant. Philos., Verh. des VIII. Internationalen Hippokrates-Kolloquiums, 1996.

P.PO. and BE.GU.

[7] from Sparta, defended Cnidus against the Athenians in 412 BC as the commander of a Peloponnesian squadron (Thuc. 8,35), as *epistoleús* ('vice commander') of the *naúarchos* ('fleet commander') Mindarus in 410 he took part in the battle near Cyzicus, in which Sparta suffered great losses (Thuc. 8,107; Xen. Hell. 1,1,23) and as harmost (→ *harmostaí*) he fell in 409 in Calchedon in the defence of the polis (Xen. Hell. 1,3,5f.; Diod. Sic. 13,66,2).

K.-W.WEL.

[8] Carthaginian of Syracusan descent, older brother of → Epicydes [2], together with whom, as the emissary of → Hannibal [4] in the 2nd Punic War in 214 BC, he negotiated the Syracusan-Carthaginian alliance (Pol. 7,2,3–5; Liv. 24,6,2); in the confusion after the death of → Hieronymus [3] the brothers had themselves elected *strategoi* (Liv. 24,27–32). After H. terminated negotiations with the Romans and M. → Claudius [I 11] Marcellus besieged Syracusae, he and → Himilkon [4] commanded the war (Liv. 24,33–35; Plut. Marcellus 14) and he finally fell victim to the epidemic in the Carthaginian army camp (Liv. 25,26,4–14).

HUSS, 350–360; 369.

L.-M.G.

Hippocrene (Ἱπποκρήνη; *Hippokrénē*, Ἵππου κρήνη; *Híppou krénē*, 'horse spring'; on the names, see [5. 1853]). A well, modern Kriopigadhi, below the eastern peak of the → Helicon to the west of the chapel of Agios Ilias which is built from ancient re-used architectural fragments [1. 186f.; 2. 239f.; 3. 97–99; 4. 621–624]. Documented as early as in Hes. Theog. 1ff. as a place of the Muses and poetic inspiration. From the Hellenistic period, the creation of the well was put

down to a kick from the hoof of → Pegasus [5. 1854ff.]. Sources: Str. 8,6,21; 9,2,25; Paus. 9,31,3f.; Prop. 3,3,1ff.; Ov. Fast. 5,7f., Met. 5,255ff.

1 V. L. ARAVANTINOS, Topographical and Archaeological Investigations on the Summit of Helicon, in: A. HURST, A. SCHACHTER (ed.), La montagne des Muses, 1996, 185–192   2 C. BURSIAN, Geogr. von Griechenland 1, 1862   3 H. H. ULRICHS, Reisen und Forschungen in Griechenland 2, 1863   4 H. G. LOLLING, Reisenotizen aus Griechenland (1876 and 1877), 1989   5 E. SITTIG, F. BÖLTE, s.v. H., RE VIII 2, 1853–1857.

P.F.

Hippodamas (Ἱπποδάμας; *Hippodámas*).
[1] Son of the river god → Achelous [2] and of Perimede, father of Euryte, brother of Orestes (Apollod. 1,52). In a different tradition, father of the Naiad → Perimele, the mistress of Achelous, who, after having been pushed into the sea by H., was transformed into one of the Echinades Islands by Poseidon (on the western coast of Acarnania) (Ov. Met. 8,573ff.).
[2] Name of Trojans: one H. is killed by Achilles (Hom. Il. 20,401), the other by Agamemnon (Hyg. Fab. 113); the third is the son of Priamus (Apollod. 3,152).   RE.ZI.
[3] Author of a hexametrical distich about the origin and the opposite nature of gods and men, handed down to us by Iambl. VP 82. According to Iamblichus, who claims that H. came from Salamis (or from Samos: conjecture by NAUCK), these verses were praised by Pythagoras.

Anth. Pal. Appendix III 17 COUGNY.

M.G.A.

Hippodamia (Ἱπποδάμεια/*Hippodámeia*, Ἱπποδάμη/*Hippodámē*, Latin Hippodamia).
[1] Daughter of king → Oenomaus of Pisa and Sterope (Paus. 5,10,6). Because an oracle prophesied his murder by the future son-in-law (Diod. Sic. 4,73,2), or because he himself desires H. (Hyg. Fab. 253), Oenomaus prevents H.'s marriage by challenging her many suitors (Hes. Cat. fr. 259a; Pind. Ol. 1,128; Paus. 6,21,10f.; Epimenides, FGrH 457 fr. 14) to a chariot race, during which he defeats and kills them. → Pelops, however, beats Oenomaus (Pind. Ol. 1,67–96) with the help of Pelops' chariot driver Myrsilus, who uses no nails or waxen nails on his master's axles (Pherecydes, FGrH 3 fr. 37a). Pelops marries H. and kills Myrsilus after he tried to rape H. (Pherecydes, FGrH 3 fr. 37b), or because he tries to withhold the reward promised to him (Paus. 8,14,11; Hyg. Fab. 84). The pair has many children (Pind. Ol. 1,144), among them → Atreus and → Thyestes. H. persuades them to kill her half-brother → Chrysippus [1]. When the deed is discovered, she flees or commits suicide (schol. Hom. Il. 2,105; cf. Pl. Crat. 395b; Paus. 6,20,7; Hyg. Fab. 85). The oldest surviving literary source is Pindar, who fails to mention Myrsilus' betrayal. Sophocles (TrGF IV fr. 471–477) and Euripides (TGF fr. 571–577) wrote an *Oenomaus*.

In Olympia, H. was venerated in a sanctuary called Hippodameion (Paus. 5,22,2; 6,20,7). According to

Paus. 5,16,4, she founded the festival of Hera – held every five years in Olympia – at which young unmarried women competed against each other in athletic competitions.   K.WA.

[2] Daughter of Butas (Diod. Sic. 4,70,3), of Adrastus (Hyg. Fab. 33,3) or of Atrax (Ov. Epist. 17,248). Wife of → Peirithous (Hom. Il. 2,742), mother of Polypoetes (Hom. Il. 2,40ff.; Ov. Met. 12, 210ff.; Apollod. epit. 1,21; Hyg. Fab. 33). She is the reason for which the battle between the → Centaurs and Lapiths erupted; → Eurytion [1].

[3] Wife of → Amyntor [2], mother of Phoenix. Since Amyntor turned away from H. because of Phthia (Apollod. 3,175) or Clytia (schol. Hom. Il. 9,448), H. incites her son to turn his father's mistress away from him, and he succeeds. He flees after being cursed and blinded by his enraged father (Hom. Il. 9,448ff.).

[4] According to schol. Hom. Il. 1,392, proper name of → Briseis.

[5] Maid of Penelope (Hom. Od. 18,182).

[6] Wife of Autonous. She is transformed into a bittern (Antoninus Liberalis 7).

M. PIPILI, s.v. H. (1), LIMC 5.1, 434–435; H. ZWICKER, s.v. H., RE 8, 1725–1730.   K.WA.

Hippodamus (Ἱππόδαμος; *Hippódamos*) of Miletus. Greek architect, town planner and author of writings on political theory; the 'Hippodamian system', which was erroneously named after him, a right-angled urban grid, was already known in archaic times in the colonies in the West and in Ionia (→ Insula; → Town planning). H.'s lifetime and period of activity is uncertain; the rebuilding of → Miletus (479 BC), which was destroyed in the Persian Wars, is connected to him as well as the building of the city facilities of → Piraeus (around 450 BC) and the urban concept of → Thurii (445/44 BC); the planning of the city of Rhodes (408), which was ascribed to him by Strabo (14,654), is probably fictitious.

The *hippodámeios trópos* ('in the style of H.'), which was praised as a novelty by Aristotle (Pol. H. 11,1330b 21) was more than a mere right-angled arrangement of streets. The construction of Piraeus, the only 'work' of H. that has been documented by a large number of sources, contains the first coherent concept for the utilization of land for a city, in which the → insula as a module within an orthogonal grid structured the entire settlement area; private homes, public areas for administration and economy as well as cult areas were separated from one another and at the same time connected in an orderly manner.

That H.'s plans intended a comprehensive, also politically anchored concept and not only the architectural structuring of a settlement area, can be concluded from only indirectly known writings, which have been mainly passed down fragmentarily by Aristotle (Pol. 1267b 24 – 1269a 29); at the same time this shows the broad spectrum of activity of an → architect of the clas-

sical period. Modern research has speculated about H.'s position on political theory; a 'radically democratic' H. has often been juxtaposed with an anti-democratic concept in the style of Plato's political utopia. Evaluations must take into account Aristotle's critically rejecting tone towards H.'s ideas as well as the fact that H. was active in Piraeus around the middle of the 5th cent. BC on behalf of Athens, both of which speak for more democratic tendencies in the Hippodamian concept. The debate on the writings of H. has at the same time also brought up the question of the relationship between urban planning and the political theory that conceives and legitimizes it, a problem area that has for generations remained focussed one-sidedly on the town-planning aspects.

P. BENVENUTI FALCIAI, Ippodamo di Mileto architetto e filosofo. Una ricostruzione filologica della personalità, 1982; A. BURNS, H. and the Planned City, in: Historia 25, 1976, 414–428; F. CASTAGNOLI, Ippodamo da Mileto e l'urbanistica a pianta ortogonale, 1956; H.-J. GEHRKE, Bemerkungen zu H. von Milet, in: Demokratie und Architektur. Der hippodamische Städtebau und die Entstehung der Demokratie, 1989, 58–63; W. HOEPFNER, E.L. SCHWANDNER, Haus und Stadt im klass. Griechenland, ²1994; H.R. MCCREDIE, Hippodamos of Miletos, in: Stud. Presented to G.M.A. Hanfmann, 1971, 95–100; I. HAUGSTED, H. fra Milet. Antikke graeske byplaner fra det 5. årh. f. Kr., 1978; CH. SCHUBERT, Land und Raum in der röm. Republik. Die Kunst des Teilens, 1996; J. SZIDAT, H. von Milet. Seine Rolle in Theorie und Praxis der griech. Stadtplanung, in: BJ 180, 1980, 31–44; CH. TRIEBEL-SCHUBERT, U. MUSS, H. von Milet. Staatstheoretiker oder Stadtplaner?, in: Hephaistos 5/6, 1983/4, 37–59; R.E. WYCHERLEY, H. and Rhodes, in: Historia 13, 1964, 135–139.   C.HÖ.

Hippodromos In Greek architecture *hippodromos* (ἱππόδρομος; *hippódromos*) denotes the racetrack for horses, which was a customary facility in the polis and the sanctuaries from the early 7th cent. (introduction of chariot races in Olympia in 680 BC). In archaic times the *hippodromos* was a first-rate place of aristocratic representation, where wealth could be demonstrated visibly before the public through the ownership and regular use of pure-bred race horses. The u-shaped facilities were surrounded by ranks for spectators and furnished with a starting and finishing device as well as a turning mark. The considerable dimensions (*c.* 250 × 600 m) made it usual to build the *hippodromos* outside of the sanctuaries. The hippodrome of Olympia, known only from the description of Pausanias (6,20f.), was located between the stadion and the Alpheius and has been almost completely buried by alluvial sand from the river; the *hippodromos* of Delphi was located far below the sanctuary of Apollo on the plains of Cirra. A *hippodromos* has been documented also for the sanctuaries of Nemea, Isthmia and Delos as well as for the cities of Athens, Sparta, Thebes and Mantinea. The dimensions of the facilities also made it necessary to dispense with architecturally planned structures – in contrast to the smaller → stadion. The Greek *hippodromoi* all remained ephemeral earth-ar-chitectures; sometimes, e.g. in Elis, chariot and horse races could even take place on the agora, which then was temporarily converted into a *hippodromos*.

A complicated architectural manifestation was first given to the *hippodromos* in the structure of the Roman → circus; to be distinguished from this is the *hippodromos* documented in Pliny's villa letters, among others, which should be seen more as a part of the garden of a Roman villa than as a race course.

> J. EBERT, Neues zum H. und den hippischen Konkurren-zen in Olympia, in: Nikephoros 2, 1989, 89–107; R. FÖRTSCH, Arch. Komm. zu den Villenbriefen des jün-geren Plinius, 1993, 78–80; M. VICKERS, The H. at Thes-saloniki, in: JRS 62, 1972, 25–32; H. WIEGARTZ, Zur Startanlage im H. von Olympia, in: Boreas 7, 1984, 41–78.
> C.HÖ.

Hippodromus M. Aurelius (?) H. Son of Olympiodo-rus. A sophist from Larissa in Thessaly, a student of → Chrestus from Byzantium, twice *agōnothétēs* of the Pythian Games (once in AD 193), in 209–213 he held the (probably imperial) chair in Athens [1]. He advised his student Philostratus of Lemnos at the Olympic Games in 213 (and afterwards refused to shame him through a speech of his own); he visited Smyrna in order to study with Megistias. Philostratus (Soph. 2,27) knows lyric *nómoi* and 30 speeches, praises H.'s memo-ry as well as the generosity with which he treated even his enemy Proclus.

→ Philostratus; → Second Sophistic

> 1 I. AVOTINS, The Holders of the Chairs of Rhetoric at Athens, in: HSPh 79, 1975, 323f.
> E.BO.

Hippolochus (Ἱππόλοχος; *Hippólochos*).
[1] Son of → Bellerophontes, father of the Lycian Prince → Glaucus [4] (Hom. Il. 6,206 et passim).
[2] Trojan, falls into Agamemnon's hands alongside his brother → Peisander. Agamemnon harshly rejects the ransom for the brothers by pointing to their father → Antimachus' [1] guilt and kills them both (Hom. Il. 11,122–148).

> P. WATHELET, Dictionnaire des Troyens de l'Iliade, 1988, no. 173f.
> MA.ST.

[3] In 218 BC during the fourth Syrian War, the Thes-salian H. went over to → Antiochus [5] III with 400 cavalrymen, defended the area of Samaria with 5,000 infantrymen, and, in 217, commanded *c.* 5,000 Greek mercenaries in the battle of Raphia (Pol. 5,70,11; 71,11; 79,9).

> M. LAUNEY, Recherches sur les armées hellénistiques, ²1987, 216.
> A.ME.

Hippology see → Cavalry

Hippolyte (Ἱππολύτη; *Hippolýtē*).
[1] → Amazon in the myth of Heracles and Theseus, daughter of → Ares and of Otrere. Heracles was order-ed by → Eurystheus to rob H. of the belt of Ares (Apoll. Rhod. 2,778ff.; 966ff.; Hyg. Fab. 30; Apollod. 2,98). According to some sources, he kills H. in the process (Eur. HF 407ff.). In conflicting versions of the myth of Theseus, H., → Antiope [2] or → Glauce [3] appear as the wife of Theseus (Isoc. Or. 12,193; Plut. Theseus 27,5,13). Theseus abducts H. and fathers → Hippolytus with her, or, he marries her following a peace agree-ment with the Amazons who had been fighting against Athens (Apollod. epit. 1,16). According to Plutarch, H. fights against the Amazons along with Theseus and is killed by → Molpadia. The heroine from Megara by the same name (Paus. 1,41,7) seems to be unconnected to the Amazons.

> BIBLIOGRAPHY: S. EITREM, s.v. H., RE VIII 2, 1863–1865.
> FIG.: P. DEVAMBEZ, A. KAUFFMANN-SAMARAS, s.v. Ama-zones, LIMC 1.2, 470–471, no. 233, 242.

[2] Daughter of → Dexamenus [1] (Diod. Sic. 4,33).
[3] Daughter of → Cretheus, wife of → Acastus, king of the Magnesians. She tries in vain to seduce → Peleus, then slanders him in front of her husband. Peleus esca-pes an attempt on his life and kills the royal pair (Pind. Nem. 4,54ff.; 5,26ff.).
> R.HA.

Hippolytus (Ἱππόλυτος; *Hippólytos*).
[1] Son of → Theseus and an Amazon (→ Antiope [2] or → Hippolyte). His mythical-literary image was shaped essentially through the H. dramas by Sophocles (*Pha-edra*, lost) and esp. by Euripides, the lost earlier *H. Kalyptómenos* ('The Veiled H.') and the extant *H. Ste-phanēphóros* ('The Garlanded H.'). The point of depar-ture for both authors is his stepmother → Phaedra's love for H., which he rejects, whereupon Phaedra ac-cuses him of sexually pursuing her. The enraged The-seus curses H., and in the end, Poseidon has his horses drag him to death. The differences between the two plays – of which *H. Kalyptómenos* can be recognized here and there in the echoes found in Ov. Epist. 4 and Seneca's *Phaedra* – must have existed in the characteri-zation of H. and Phaedra: The earlier play must have depicted Phaedra's erotic advances very directly (H. veiled himself out of shame, hence the title), while the later play presents H. as the single-minded admirer of the virgin → Artemis (for whom he picks a garland of flowers), thereby arousing the wrath of → Aphrodite. The plot is ultimately triggered by this conflict between the gods.

In other versions, H. is brought back to life by Ascle-pius (Apollod. 3,121, according to the archaic epic of *Naupaktiká*), then either emigrates to Italy to found the → Diana sanctuary of → Aricia (Paus. 2,27,3), brought as Virbius by Artemis to her sanctuary near Aricia (Verg. Aen. 7,761–783; Ov. Fast. 6,735–762), or is immortalized in the constellation of the Charioteer or Auriga (Eratosth. Katasterismoi 6; Paus. 2,32,1).

The myths can be regarded as an outgrowth of the cult of H. in Troezen and Athens. In Athens, H.'s tomb was located on the Acropolis near the sanctuary of Aphrodite ('at H.', Eur. Hipp. 31–33). A cult attested for a different location in Attica (IG I³ 255,7) is not definite, although the combination of tomb and temple is reminiscent of the common connection between hero cult and cult of the gods, esp. since the goddess is also referred to as 'Aphrodite in the Hippolyteion' (IG I³ 369,66). Of much greater importance was the cult in → Troezen which gave rise to the myth: H. owned a magnificent temenos – supposedly donated by Diomedes [1] – with its own temple, stadion, and two more temples of Apollo Epibaterios and Aphrodite Kataskopia ('the one gazing down', because Phaedra saw H. for the first time there). Furthermore, the myth was based on the tomb of Phaedra and a tumulus of H. (which the Troezenians did not acknowledge as a tomb in the time of Pausanias). H. had a priest and a yearly sacrificial festival with agon. Brides lamented for him and sacrificed their hair to him (Eur. Hipp. 1423–1430; Paus. 2,32,1–4); he, in turn, is claimed to have donated the temple of Artemis Lykeia (Paus. 1,31,4). One must assume that a cult existed in Sparta, where H. had a heroon next to that of Theseus (Paus. 3,12,9). → Virbius in the sanctuary of Diana of Aricia is identified with H., but no records exist for him prior to the identification. Even though horse sacrifices and the prohibition of horses in the sanctuary are explained with the circumstances of H.'s death, it is more likely that these rites in themselves were the cause for the identification (Callim. Fr. 190; Verg. Aen. 7,778–780; Ambr. De exhortatione virginitatis 3,5).

Due to the influence of the Euripidean tragedies, the myth of H. and Phaedra is often depicted in the visual arts beginning in the early Imperial period. The *Phaedra* by Seneca transmits the play to modern times, with the interest in H. diminishing in favour of Phaedra (RACINE; GLUCK). One of the rare exceptions is J.Ph. RAMEAU's opera *Hippolyte et Aricie* (1733).

W.FAUTH, H. und Phaidra, 1958/1959; W.BURKERT, Structure and History in Greek Mythology and Ritual, 1979, 111–118; P.LINANT DE BELLEFONDS, s.v. H. (1), LIMC 5, 445–464; C.MONTEPAONE, L'alsos/lucus, forma idealtipica artemidea. Il caso di Ippolito, in: O. DE CAZANOVE, J.SCHEID (ed.), Les bois sacrées, 1993, 69–78.
F.G.

[2] H. of Rome. Presbyter (head of a Christian community?) in Rome, Church author who wrote in Greek in the early 3rd cent. AD; a list of works was found in 1551 in an inscription on a cathedra (ICUR N.S. 7, 19933) as well as in Euseb. Hist. eccl. 6,22 and Jer. Vir. ill. 61. In the manuscript tradition, several works of exegetic, chronographic, heresiologic, apologetic, and legal (Church law) nature are attributed to H., among them the following:

1) Exegetic works to the OT, such as commentaries on the Song of Songs and Dan (CPG 1871, 1873), regarded as the oldest surviving Christian Bible commentaries. In a complementary relationship to these are:

2) *Refutatio omnium haeresium* in 10 bks. (CPG 1899), of which bk. 1 and bks. 4–10 have survived in different traditions. H. tries to achieve a 'refutation of all heresies' by tracing them back to non-Christian teachings. The heretical views are therefore of human rather than of godly origin, which makes them less reliable than Biblical texts. Today, the *Refutatio,* along with the *Stromata* by → Clemens [3] of Alexandria, is one of the most important sources for the lost early Christian works of Greek authors, however, the work is difficult to analyze due to H.'s unconventional methods [12; 15; 19. 511–524, 530].

3) Chronographical works, among them a → Chronicle (CPG 1896) and an inscriptionally transmitted Easter table (ICUR N.S. 7, 19934f.) for the years 222–333. If one considers the dating of both the monument and the shapes of the letters, the starting-point of the Easter table, and the fact that it could only have been used for a few years (cf. [19. 508–511]), one arrives at the conclusion that the inscription was carved into the base of the cathedra as early as in the Severan period ([9. 3; 11. 536, 538, 544f.], differently [19. 542]). It is therefore one of the oldest preserved Christian stone inscriptions in the West, its monumental character a testimony to the high degree of self-confidence of Roman Christians during the Severan period.

4) *Traditio apostolica* (CPG 1737): Church regulations, which must have emerged in the context of internal disputes within the community in Rome ([9. 398–457; 21. 398–402], differing: [19. 525; 20]). Based on his own understanding of his office, H. was the first in Christian tradition to draw a clear distinction between clerics and laymen [14. 98ff.] in his description of the offices in the Christian community (ch. 1–14, incl. a ritual for the inauguration of a bishop). H. creates a clerical hierarchy, positioning the bishop at the top as the only one to possess complete charisma (ch. 8). H. grants a special role only to confessors (ch. 9, cf., on the other hand, ch. 10–14). Also important are rules for Christian initiation (ch. 15–21 with a baptismal liturgy) as well as service and Christian life (ch. 22–42, esp. on communion).

Modern research is still debating questions about the unity of the work as well as H.'s position in the Roman Church (a recent comprehensive treatment by [9], cf. also [10; 16; 17; 18]; SCHOLTEN defends the unity of the author against the theory of P.NAUTIN, cf. [19. 501–504]). The work of H., the last western theologian to write in Greek was intensely mined in West and East alike, a fact that led to a complex textual tradition: There is ample documentation of excerpts and quotations, extensive revisions, translations into Near Eastern languages as well as texts falsely attributed to H. At first, and esp. in Rome, (evidence *i.a.* → Chronographer of 354, epigrams by → Damasus) H. was worshipped also as a martyr ([19. 534–549], cf. ibid. references to other martyrs by that name).

→ Heresy; → Heresiology; → Church regulations

EDITIONS: 1 CPG 1737, 1870–1925 2 A. KELLER, Translationes Patristicae Graecae et Latinae. Bibliographie der Übers. altchristlicher Quellen 1, 1997, 448–451. REFUTATIO: 3 P. WENDLAND, GCS 26, 1916 (Greek) 4 K. PREYSING, BKV 40, 1922 (Ger.) 5 M. MARCOVICH, Patristische Texte und Studien 25, 1986 (Greek). TRADITIO APOSTOLICA: 6 B. BOTTE, ⁵1989 (Lat./Greek-French) 7 B. BOTTE, W. GEERLINGS, Fontes Christiani 1, 1991 (Lat./Greek-Ger.) 8 G. DIX, H. CHADWICK, ³1992 (Lat./Greek-Engl.).
BIBLIOGRAPHY: 9 A. BRENT, Hippolytus and the Roman Church in the Third Century. Communities in tension before the emergence of a monarch-bishop (Vigiliae Christianae Suppl. 31), 1995 10 J. FRICKEL, Das Dunkel um Hippolyt von Rom. Ein Lösungsversuch. Die Schriften Elenchos und Contra Noëtum (Grazer theol. Stud. 13), 1988 11 M. GUARDUCCI, Epigrafia greca 4, 1978, 535–545 12 J. MANSFELD, Heresiography in Context. H.' Elenchos as a Source for Greek Philosophy (Philosophia Antiqua 56), 1992 13 M. MARCOVICH, s.v. H., TRE 15, 381–387 14 J. MARTIN, Die Genese des Amtspriestertums in der frühen Kirche, 1972 15 I. MÜLLER, Heterodoxy and Doxography in H.' Refutation of All Heresies, in: ANRW II 36.6, 1992, 4309–4374 16 Nuove Richerche su Ippolito (Studia Ephemeridis "Augustinianum" 30), 1989 17 Richerche su Ippolito (Studia Ephemeridis "Augustinianum" 13), 1977 18 V. SAXER, s.v. H., DHGE 24, 627–635 (bibliography up to 1993) 19 C. SCHOLTEN, s.v. H., RAC 15, 492–551 (bibliography up to 1991) 20 Id., C. SCHOLTEN, s.v. H., LThK³ 5, 147–149 21 E. WIRBELAUER, Die Nachfolgerbestimmung im röm. Bistum (3.–6. Jh.). Doppelwahlen und Absetzungen in ihrer herrschaftssoziologischen Bedeutung, in: Klio 76, 1994, 388–437; 77, 1995, 555f. E.W.

Hippomanes (ἱππομανές; *hippomanés*). Plant identified by Dioscorides 2,173 WELLMANN = 2,204 BERENDES as the caper (κάππαρις; *kápparis*), whose fruit was considered to be diuretic. According to Theoc. 2,48f. and Serv. Georg. 3,280 THILO in Arcadia it drove mares and foals mad. C.HÜ.

Hippomedon (Ἱππομέδων; *Hippomédōn*).
[1] One of the → Seven against Thebes, brother or nephew of → Adrastus [1], from Lerna, hero of gigantic size. In Aeschylus (Sept. 486ff.), he stands against Hyperbius at the Oncaean Gate, in Euripides (Phoen. 1113ff.; 119ff.), at the Ogygian Gate and at the head of the army. The motif on his shield is → Typhon or → Argus [II]. Euripides (Suppl. 881ff.) depicts him as a warrior limited to physical power. In Statius, he wins the discus competition (Thebes. 6,646ff.), is the first to cross the Asopus (7,424ff.), defends Tydeus' corpse, kills Crenaeus, the grandson of the river god Ismenus, only to find death in the water, overpowered by Thebans (9,86–539). CL.K.
[2] Lacedaemonian, son of Agesilaus [4], cousin of → Agis [4] IV, who fled from Sparta in c. 241 BC and became πάρεδρος (*párhedros*) in Alexandria,and σύμβουλος (*sýmboulos*) of Ptolemaeus III. Between 240 and 221, Ptolemaic *strategos* of the district of Hellespont and Thracia.

PP 6,14605; 15048; 16115; BENGTSON, 3, 178ff.; PH. GAUTHIER, ΕΞΑΓΩΓΗ ΣΙΤΟΥ, in: Historia 28, 1979, 76–89; S. SAHIN, Ehrendekret für H. aus Priapos, in: EA 4, 1984, 5–8. W.A.

Hippomenes (Ἱππομένης; *Hippoménēs*).
[1] Boeotian from Onchestus, son of → Megareus (Hyg. Fab. 185) or Ares (schol. Theoc. 3,40) and Merope (Hyg. Fab. 185). The foot race between H. and → Atalante was already known to Hesiod (fr. 74 M.-W.). The most comprehensive account can be found in Ov. Met. 10,560–707 [1]: Upon his request, Venus gives him three apples which Atalante picks up during the race, causing her to lose. H. fails to perform the thanks-offering; Venus entices H. and Atalante to defile the Temple of → Cybele by having sexual intercourse – as a consequence, they are transformed into lions (in Hyg. Fab. 185, it is the Temple of Jupiter Victor). H.'s grandfather by the same name is a son of Poseidon (Apollod. 3,210 WAGNER; in Paus. 1,39,5, Poseidon is the father of Megareus).
[2] Codrid, the fourth of the seven ten-year archonts (723/2–714/3 BC [2. 77–79]). He caught his daughter Leimone in the act of adultery, tied her to an unfed horse so that she was devoured by the hungry horse (the name of the girl might be derived from *limós*/'hunger') (Nicolaus from Damascus, FGrH 90 F 49; Heraclidis Lembi epit. 1 CHAMBERS; schol. Ov. Ib. 459; without names Aeschin. Or. 1,182).

1 F. BÖMER, P. Ovidius Naso, Metamorphosen B. X–XI, 1980, 188–190 2 P. J. RHODES, A Commentary on the Aristotelian Athenaion Politeia, 1981. JO.S.

Hippon (Ἵππων; *Híppōn*). Pythagorean natural philosopher, born c. 480–470 BC. Cratinus (38 A 2 DK) ridiculed H. in his comedy *Panóptai* (performed 435/431 BC). According to Aristoxenus H. was from Samos (38 A 1 DK) with the result that many include him in the Ionic school. All other sources connect H. with southern Italy (38 A 1; 3; 11 DK). H. carried on the line of Pythagorean natural history (physiology, embryology, botany) and Italian medicine (→ Alcmaeon [1], → Empedocles [4]). He wrote at least two works (38 A 11 DK), of which only one verbatim fragment survives. H.'s principle (rather 'moisture', *to hygrón*, than water) bears only a superficial resemblance to that of → Thales: H.'s teaching was oriented to physiology, not meteorology. It does not appear to have been very original (cf. Aristotle's poor opinion of H., 38 A 7; 10 DK), but H.'s idea, that health depended on the 'moisture' in an organism (38 A 11 DK), was groundbreaking in ancient medicine. The description of him as an atheist (38 A 4; 6; 8 DK) is late and misleading.

1 DIELS/KRANZ I, 385–389 (no. 38) 2 L. ZHMUD, Wissenschaft, Philosophie und Religion im frühen Pythagoreismus, 1997. L.ZH.

Hipponax (Ἱππῶναξ; *Hippônax*).
A. PERSON B. METRICS C. IAMBOI
D. RECEPTION

A. PERSON

H. was a poet of iambs (ἰαμβοποιός; *iambopoiós*) from Ephesus (cf. Callim. fr. 203,13). Based on the Marmor Parium 42, his life can be dated from *c.* 541/0 BC, Pliny (HN 36,11) mentions Ol. 60 = 540–537 BC.

B. METRICS

As opposed to → Archilochus and → Semonides, H. is not attributed with elegiac verses. In his *Íamboi*, he primarily (1–114a, 155–155b WEST) used choliambic trimeters (x – ˘ – x – ˘ – x – x) interspersed with occasional pure trimeters (e.g. 36,4; 42,4; 118a W.). Also occurring are trochaeic tetrameters, also 'lame', that is, ending in x x (120–127 W.); a single catalectic iambic tetrameter (119 W.) and perhaps one 'lame' version (177 W.); epodes that alternate between iambic trimeters and hemiepes (115; 116 W.) or iambic dimeters (117 W.); hexameters only rarely (only in parodies?) (128–129a W.).

C. IAMBOI

The primary target of the invectives is a certain Bupalus (cf. Callim. fr. 191,1–4; Philippus Anth. Pal. 7,405,3). According to Plin. HN 36,11 and Suda 2, 665,16, the cause lies in the fact that he and Athenis created an obscene statue of H. This statue supposedly incited H. to write his *Íamboi*, which, in turn, drove the two to commit suicide. Pliny rejects this view – similar cases of alleged suicides by targets of Archilochus shed further doubt on this transmission. While Athenis appears only once (70,11 W.), Bupalus is mentioned *c.* ten times, once as a sculptor (136 W.).

The opening of the first *Íambos* ('Oh Clazomenians, Bupalus killed ...', 1 W.) indicates a killing rather than a mocking sculpture; the poem seems to refer to an orgy incl. a feast, sex, and a brawl, in which H. was involved as was Bupalus with his mistress Arete.

Other *Íamboi* strongly criticize the painter Mimnes (28 W.) and a potter named Aeschylides (117,9 W.). The poem 115 W. severely curses a perfidious comrade (*hetaîros*; although the poem is attributed also to Archilochus: see [1]; for H.: [2; 3]; Hellenistic: [4]).

The invective, however, occupies no more room than the stories which often draw attention to H.'s own name (32,4; 36,2; 37; 79,9 and ?12; 117,4) and present him in a discrediting manner – as a poor man who begs Hermes for wealth (32–39 W.), as the victim of a humiliating treatment for impotence (92 W.), and as the shabby protagonist of an orgy following a scrap (104 W.). H.'s poems often tell of bizarre events with a focus on vividly depicted details that are often obscene. The speeches of the characters are interspersed with words borrowed from Lydian (e.g. 3 W., 92,1 W.), which were probably common in an Ephesus strongly influenced by Lydia. H.'s vituperation of himself and others was probably meant to entertain his audience rather than to cause uneasiness for his 'objects of attack'. H.'s target audience is difficult to identify based on the opening vocatives (ὦ Κλαζομένιοι: 1 W.; Μιμνῆ 28 W.; Ὤθηνι 70,11 W.; ὦ Σάνν' 118,1 W.) of his poems. Equally difficult to solve is the question whether H.'s position in society should be derived from his aristocratic name in *-anax* or from the audience of craftsmen and the stories about dirty adventures. Pliny's report about the sculptures by Bupalus and Athenis indicates that H. prefers to present real people over typified dramatic figures [5 W], although H.'s statements about himself might be entirely or largely fictitious (notice H.'s presumable introduction of Bupalus into an 'Odyssey', 74,1 W. with 77,2 and 4 W.).

D. RECEPTION

Aristophanes expects the Attic audience to recognize H. (Aristoph. Ran. 661) and the scrap with Bupalus (Aristoph. Lys. 361), while Diphilus expects the audience to enjoy his comedy in which Archilochus and H. are Sappho's lovers.

H. is the archaic iambographer who was imitated the most by → Phoenix, → Callimachus [6], and → Herodas (3rd cent. BC); epitaphs dedicated to him were written by Leonidas (Anth. Pal. 7,408), Theocritus (Anth. Pal. 13,3, in choliambs), Alcaeus from Messene (Anth. Pal. 7,536), and Philippus (Anth. Pal. 7,405, in trimeters). H.'s *Íamboi* appeared in at least 2 bks. Commentaries appeared as early as the 2nd cent. AD (POxy. 2176 = 118 W.) and were used by Athenaeus (Ath. 324a; 624b with Hipponax 118,12 W.). The lexicographers (Aristophanes [4] from Byzantium?; Erotian; Suetonius; Harpocration; Herodianus; Pollux; Phrynichus) and Athenaeus (15 quotations) went through H.'s poems searching for rare words and forms. Moralists largely ignored or scorned him (Clem. Al. Strom. 1,1 p. 3,11 STÄHLIN; Julian. Ep. 89b BIDEZ 300c-d). However, much of his work could be read (perhaps even in a complete edition) by Tzetzes in 12th-cent. Byzantium.

1 G.M. KIRKWOOD, The Authorship of the Strassburg Epodes, in: TAPhA 92, 1961, 267–282 2 G. PERROTTA, Il poeta degli epodi di Strasburgo, in: SIFC 15, 1938, 3–41 3 O. MASSON, in: REG 64, 1951, 427–442 4 C. DEL GRANDE, Note filologiche, 1942, 11–36 5 M.L. WEST, Studies in Greek Elegy and Iambus, 1974, 22–39, 140–149 6 A. ARDIZZONI, Callimaco "ipponatteo", in: Ann. della Facoltà di Lettere ... Cagliari 28, 1960, 3–16.

BIBLIOGRAPHY: D.E. GERBER, in: Lustrum 33, 1991, 108–128.

EDITIONS: E. DEGANI, Leipzig 1983; IEG; W. DE SOUSA MEDEIROS, Humanitas 13–14, 1961–1962 (with commentary); O. MASSON, 1962; A. FARINA, 1963.
BIBLIOGRAPHY: E. DEGANI, Studi su Ipponatte, 1984; C. MIRALLES, J. PÒRTULAS, The Poetry of H., 1988.

E.BO.

Hipponicus ('Ἱππόνικος; *Hippónikos*). Son of → Callias and → Elpinice, the (half)sister of → Cimon, rich Athenian (And. 1,130; Lys. 19,48) from the family of the Kerykes, in the office of *dadoûchos* in Eleusis like his father (→ Mysteria). As *stratēgós* in 427/6 BC, he led the successful campaign against the Tanagraeans alongside Eurymedon [4] (Thuc. 3,91,4f.; And. 1,115; Diod. Sic. 12,65,3ff.). He died shortly before 422. In her first marriage, his wife was married to → Pericles (Plut. Pericles 24,8, where it is falsely assumed that her first husband was H.), his daughter Hipparete married Alcibiades [3] (Isoc. Or. 16,31; Plut. Alc. 8). H.'s wealth and aristocratic demeanour aroused envy and mockery already during his lifetime (Eupolis fr. 20 and 156 PCG; Cratinus fr. 336 KOCK; And. 1,131; Ath. 5,218bc; 12,537b; Ael. VH 14,16).

PA 7658 with stemma 520; DAVIES 7826, IX.; TRAILL, PPA 538910. M.MEI.

Hipponous ('Ἱππόνοος; *Hippónoos*).
[1] According to schol. Hom. Il. 6,155 DINDORF, the old name of → Bellerophontes; schol. Hom. Il. 6,155 ERBSE offers the name of Leophontes (Λεωφόντης).
[2] Son of Adrastus [1] who deliberately threw himself on the pyre with him (Hyg. Fab. 242). The same motif can be found in the story about Capaneus' and Evadne's fate.
[3] With Astynome, H. fathered → Capaneus (Apollod. 3,63 WAGNER; Hyg. Fab. 70) and → Periboea (Apollod. 1,74 WAGNER). JO.S.

Hippopotamus *Hippopotamus amphibius* L., ὁ or ἡ ἵππος ποτάμιος/*híppos potámios*, literally 'river horse', Latin *hippopotam(i)us* or *equus fluvialis* (Ambr. Hexaemeron 5,1,4), *equus Nili* (Thomas of Cantimpré, Liber de natura rerum 6,19), known from the → Nile (Plin. HN 8,95 and 28,121), from west African rivers (Plin. HN 5,10) and from Palestine. That the animal was found in the Indus, as alleged by Onesicratus, was rejected by Str. 14,1,45 and Paus. 4,34,3. In Egypt, the hippopotamus was nearly extinct in late antiquity due to capture by Romans for animal fights (since 58 BC, the games of M. Aemilius [I 38] Scaurus, Plin. HN 8,96; see → *munus*; → *venatio*) and the → zoological garden of the emperors (e.g. Elagabalus [2]: S HA Heliogab. 28,3; Gordianus [3] III.: S HA Gord. 33,1).

Since the first mention of the hippopotamus in Herodotus 2,71 (after Hecataeus), actual observations made of its life on land and in water (Aristot. Hist. an. 7(8),2,589a 24–29; Ael. NA 11,37), its thick skin, huge canine teeth (Plin. HN 11,160), the blunt form of its head and even number of toes (cf. Aristot. Hist. an. 2,1,499b 10) were mixed with characteristics of horses, such as having a mane and tail and whinnying (ibid. 2,7,502a 9–15). It was also claimed that the hippopotamus walked backwards, as camouflage, after grazing on crops (Plin. HN 8,95; Ael. NA 5,53) and even self-bleeding (Plin. HN 8,96; 28,121) was alleged. The

hippopotamus supposedly behaved like → Oedipus, that is, devoured its own father (Ael. NA 7,1) and copulated with its mother. In Egypt, it was sometimes identified with the evil god Typhon/→ Seth, but was also regarded as tutelary god for pregnant women [1. 20 or 161]. As a pest that ate crops, it was trapped in pits and killed with harpoons (Diod. Sic. 1,35,8–10; fig. at [2. 957]). The skin of the hippopotamus served as material for shields and helmets (Plin. HN 8,95), was cut to make javelins (Hdt. 2,71; Plin. HN 11,227) and, in the form of ashes, was supposed to heal swollen glands (Plin. HN 28,121). Its fat was used as a means to treat cold fever (ibid.). Its blood was used by painters as a pigment (ibid.). Hippopotamus meat was regarded as difficult to digest (Diod. Sic. 1,35,10).

Starting with the grave relief of Sakkata [2] (c. 2650 BC) and into Roman times, the hippopotamus was often depicted on coins [3. pl. 4,21], in mosaics (among others → Nile Mosaic in Praeneste, modern Palestrina [4. pl. 13; 5. fig. 53]; Pompeii [6. fig. 57]; Piazza Armerina [6. pl. 27]; in north Africa, e.g. Leptis Magna [5. 114]), in wall paintings [7. fig. 57; 8. 371] and even in sculptures like the Vatican Nile Group [9. 129] with seven hippopotamuses or in a small bronze statue from Bingen [5. 115].

1 G. ROEDER, Die ägypt. Götterwelt, 1959 2 L. KLEBS, Die Reliefs des Alten Reiches, 1915 3 F. IMHOOF-BLUMER, O. KELLER, Tier- und Pflanzenbilder auf Mz. und Gemmen des klass. Alt., 1889, repr. 1972 4 G. GULLINI, I mosaici di Palestrina, 1956 5 TOYNBEE, Animals in Roman Life and Art, 1973 6 G. V. GENTILI, La villa erculia di Piazza Armerina: i mosaici figurati, 1959 7 KELLER, vol. 1, 158 8 K. SCHEFOLD, Die Wände Pompejis, 1957 9 W. AMELUNG, Die Sculpturen des vaticanischen Museums I, 1903.

A. STEIER, s.v. N., RE 17, 567–571; KELLER, vol. 1, 406f. C.HÜ.

Hippostratus ('Ἱππόστρατος; *Hippóstratos*).
[1] Son of Amarynceus who seduced → Periboea, daughter of Hipponous (Apollod. 1,74; Hes. fr. 12 M-W). J.S.-A.
[2] Nephew of → Attalus [1], brother of → Cleopatra, after whose death he was executed by → Alexander [4] the Great (cf. Iust. 11,5,1); not to be identified with other men by the same name.

BERVE 2, no. 390. E.B.

[3] H. Soter. One of the later Indo-Greek kings in Ghandhara (modern Pakistan) in the 1st cent. BC. Coins are the only evidence; Middle Indian Hipstrata.

BOPEARACHCHI 136f.,356–360. K.K.

[4] Author of a work in 7 vols. from probably the 3rd cent. BC about Sicilian genealogy (e.g. that of the Emmenidae), quoted by the scholia on Pindar and Theocritus as well as in the thaumasiographs. The fact that the dating by Olympiads is used indicates a familiarity with Timaeus. FGrH 568.

F. JACOBY, s.v. H. (7), RE 8, 1922. K.MEI.

Hippotae (Ἱππόται; *Hippótai*). Boeotian settlement (κώμη; *kṓmē*) between Thisbe and Coronea, probably identifiable with ancient remains near modern Koukoura on a high plateau on the eastern slope of the southern peak of Helicon, known as Paliaovouna. Thebes besieged and destroyed H. at an indeterminate time and divided the land between Thisbe and Coronea. Named in Plut. Mor. 775 A-B.

> A.R. BURN, Helikon in History, in: ABSA 44, 1949, 317f., 321; FOSSEY, 339; PRITCHETT 5, 156; A. SCHACHTER, Reconstructing Thespiai, in: A. HURST, A. SCHACHTER (ed.), La montagne des Muses, 1996, 104f.   P.F.

Hippotes (Ἱππότης; *Hippótēs*).
[1] The rarely mentioned father of → Aeolus [2]: Hom. Od. 10,2; 36; Apoll. Rhod. 4,778; 819; due to the confusion between Aeolus [1] and Aeolus [2], the son of Mimas (schol. Hom. Od. 10,2; Diod. Sic. 4,67,3).
[2] Son of → Phylas, grandson of Antiochus, great-grandson of Hercules, father of → Aletes [1] ([5. 7–10]; genealogical table [1; 4. 306 A 20]). In Naupactus H. kills the seer Carnus and is forced into exile for 10 years (Ps.-Apollod. 2,174–175; Oenomaus fr. 4 H. [2]: aition for the cult of Apollo Karneios [3; 4. 306] and two related rites [5]). Through H., Corinth is integrated into the aetiology of the distribution of power on the Peloponnese (→ Heraclidae) [4. 306].

> 1 C. PARADA, Genealogical Guide to Greek Mythology, 1993, table Heraclides 2 J. HAMMERSTAEDT, Die Orakelkritik des Kynikers Oenomaus, 1988, ad loc. 3 BURKERT, 357–358 4 F. PRINZ, Gründungsmythen und Sagenchronologie, 1979, 305–307 5 N. ROBERTSON, The Dorian Migration and Corinthian Ritual, in: CPh 75, 1980, 1–22.

[3] Son of → Creon, grandson of Lycaethus. In a version that differs from the vulgate one, H. takes Iason in and marries him to his daughter → Medea (schol. Eur. Med. 19). Following her escape, he demands her extradition from the Athenians (Diod. Sic. 4,55,5). According to Hyg. Fab. 27 (the content probably comes from Pacuvius, *Medus* [1]), Medus poses as H. in front of Perses.

> 1 A. ARCELLASCHI, Médée dans le théâtre latin d'Ennius à Sénèque, 1990, 102–103, 127–129, 148–149.   T.H.

Hippothoe (Ἱπποθόη/*Hippothóē*, 'the one as fast as a horse'). In [1] and [3], the name indicates a connection to Poseidon and the sea.
[1] → Nereid (Hes. Theog. 251; Apollod. 1,11).
[2] One of the daughters of → Pelias, who – deceived by → Medea's cunning – dismembered their father and boiled him in order to rejuvenate him (Apollod. 1,95; Hyg. Fab. 24).
[3] Daughter of → Mestor and → Lysidice, abducted by Poseidon, whom she bore → Taphius (Apollod. 2,50) or → Pterelaus (Herodorus FGrH 31 F 15). This abduction is used by Christian authors as a polemic example to warn against the anthropomorphism of the pagan gods (Arnob. 4,26; Firm. Mat. De errore profanarum religionum 12,3).   A.A.

Hippothontis (Ἱπποθοντίς; *Hippothontís*). Since Cleistenes' reform of the phyles, the 8th of 10 phyles of Attica; eponymous hero Hippothoon. At the time of the 10 phyles in the 4th cent. BC, the H. comprised 17 (6? *asty-*, 7? *paralia*, 4? *mesogeia-*) demes [1. 11f., 51f., 102] primarily around Eleusis and in north-west Attica; several are not located [1. map]. In 307/6 BC Coele and Oenoe (modern Myupolis) changed to the Demetrias, Auridae or Corydallus to the Antigonis, in 224/3 BC Oion Dekeleikon and Oenoe (from the Demetrias) to the Ptolemaïs. After the break-up of the Macedonian phyles in 201/o BC, Coele and Auridae or Corydallus returned to the H., Corydallus fell to the Attalis, Elaeus AD 127/8 to the Hadrianis [1. 11f., 27].

> 1 TRAILL, Attica, XVII, 11f., 21f., 24 no. 13, 26f., 32, 51f., 55, 57, 71, 82, 91, 102, 106, 134, table 8.

> P. J. BICKNELL, The City and Inland Trittyes of Phyle VIII H., in: Antichthon 7, 1973, 1–4; J. S. TRAILL, Demos and Trittys, 1986, 1ff., 16ff., 136ff.   H.LO.

Hippothoon (Ἱπποθόων; *Hippothóōn*).
[1] Second son of → Poseidon and → Alope (Hyg. Fab. 187; 252). As an infant abandoned by his grandfather → Cercyon and taken in by → Theseus; later king, probably in Eleusis (Hes. fr. 215 M-W; H. Hom. 2,153). This is further supported by the fact that H. was venerated there as a cult hero and phyle hero, as suggested by the Hippothoontion's location near Eleusis on the river Cephissus (Paus. 1,38,4).

> U. KRON, s.v. H., LIMC 5.1, 468–475.   J.S.-A.

[2] H./Hippothous (Ἱπποθόων/*Hippothóōn*; Ἱππόθοος/ *Hippóthoos*). In Stob. (3,589,13–590,1; 3,711,15ff.; 4,496,10ff.; 4,519,5f.; 4,652,4f.; 5,1023,9f; see also 4,546,22–547,2), several sententious trimeters are transmitted under the lemma Ἱπποθόου, /-θόωντος, /-θόου (*Hippothóou*, /-*thóōntos*, /-*thóou*) (some can also be found, for example, in → Menander's *Monosticha*), their attribution remaining partly uncertain. It is therefore questionable, whether H. is the name of a poet or the title of a play (cf. O. HENSE ad Stob. 3,589,13).   F.P.

Hippothous (Ἱππόθοος; *Hippóthoos*).
[1] Son of Priam (Hom. Il. 24,251).
[2] Son of the Pelasgian king → Lethus, son of Teuthamus, supplies the Trojans with Pelasgian reinforcements from Larisa (Hom. Il. 2,840ff.); killed by Telamonian Ajax in the fight over Patroclus' body (Hom. Il. 17,288ff.).
[3] Son of → Aleus [1] and Neaera, killed by his nephew → Telephus, whereupon his mother kills herself (Hyg. Fab. 243).
[4] Son of Cercyon, ruler in Arcadian Trapezus (Paus. 8,5,4); participates in the hunt for the Calydonian boar; depicted by → Scopas in the pediment of the temple of Athena at Tegea (Paus. 8,45,7).
[5] → Hippothoon [1] (Hyg. Fab. 187; 252).   RE.ZI.

Hippotomadae (Ἱπποτο/αμάδαι; *Hippoto/amádai*). Attic *asty*?-deme of the phyle Oeneis, from 307/6 BC until 201/200 BC of Demetrias, with one *bouleutés*. Location unknown.

E. MEYER, s.v. H., RE Suppl. 10, 325f.; TRAILL, Attica, 9, 19, 49, 62, 70, 110 no. 56, table 6, 12; Id., Demos and Trittys, 1986, 133. H.LO.

Hippotoxotai (ἱπποτοξόται; *hippotoxótai*). *Hippotoxotai* were mounted archers. The Scythians and Getae fought as *hippotoxotai* (Hdt. 4,46,3; Thuc. 2,96,1; Arr. Anab. 3,8,3). *Hippotoxotai* are documented for the Persian, Athenian, Macedonian and Hellenistic armies (Hdt. 9,49,2; Arr. Anab. 4,24,1; 5,12,2; 6,6,1; Diod. Sic. 20,113,4). During the Peloponnesian War, Athens had a squadron of 200 *hippotoxotai* (Thuc. 2,13,8); of these 20 served on the island of Melos, 30 in Sicily (Thuc. 5,84,1; 6,94,4), probably as skirmishers (Xen. Mem. 3,3,1). *Hippotoxotai* were citizens and possibly mercenaries; according to Lysias (15,6) they were not held in high esteem.

→ Cavalry

I. G. SPENCE, The Cavalry of Classical Greece, 1993, 56f., 217. LE.BU.

Hippus
[1] (Ἵππος/*Híppos* Str. 11,2,17; Steph. Byz. s.v. Αἶα; *Hippos* Plin. HN 6,13; Ἵππις/*Híppis* in Mocheresis Procop. Goth. 4,1,6); northern tributary of the → Phasis in → Colchis, the modern C'ḥeniscqali ('horse water') in West Georgia.

E. KIESSLING, s.v. H., RE 8, 1915–1918. A.P.-L.

[2] (ἡ Ἵππος/*hē Híppos*, Euseb. On. 22,21 Ἵππη/ *Híppē*; Aramaic *Sūsītā* 'mare'). Hellenistic-Byzantine city (region) east of Lake Genezareth. First named by Pliny (HN 5,71; 74) and Josephus (BI 1,156); possibly Seleucid foundation, later part of the → Decapolis (cf. coins), still flourishing in Byzantine times (with bishop); modern Qalʿat al-ḥiṣn, (Mt.) Susita (Israel); deserted settlement on steep mountain spur, wealth of ancient remains.

ABEL 2, 471f. M. AVI-YONAH, The Holy Land from the Persian to the Arab Conquests. A Historical Geography, 1966, 169f. H. BIETENHARD, Die Dekapolis von Pompeius bis Traian, in: ZPalV 79, 1963, 24–58 SCHÜRER 2, 130–132 G. SCHUMACHER, Der Dscholan, in: ZPalV 9, 1886, 327–334 (Plan T. VI) P. THOMSEN, Loca sancta 1, 1907, 73. CH.BU.

Hippys (Ἵππυς; *Híppys*) of Rhegium. Since [1], a much discussed and controversial author: According to the Suda s.v. = T 1, the oldest West Greek historian, alive during the Persian Wars of 480/479 BC. He wrote the following works: *Sikeliká* in 5 bks., *Ktísis Italías* ('Founding History of Italy'), *Chroniká* in 5 bks., *Argoliká* in 3 bks. Later, a certain Myes is claimed to have

epitomized the work. Due to the fact that the fragments are mostly mysterious (e.g. F 1–3 with the comm. of JACOBY) and that later authors such as Dionysius from Halicarnassus, Diodorus, Strabo, and Pausanias seem not to know H., [2] was the first to surmise that he may be a fraudulent author from the Hellenistic period – several researchers, among them [3], [4], and [5], concurred. However, Italian scholars, in particular G. DE SANCTIS, A. MOMIGLIANO, and E. MANNI (exact source references in [4. 8²³]) continue to believe in the early dating, regarding H. not only as the first West Greek historian, but also as an important source for Herodotus (7,153–156), Antiochus of Syracuse (FGrH 555), Thucydides (6,2–5), and Hellanicus of Lesbos (FGrH 323a). In actuality, H. had little influence on the transmission, even if the early dating were accurate. FGrH 554.

1 U. VON WILAMOWITZ, Hippys von Rhegion, in: Hermes 19, 1884, 442–452 2 F. JACOBY, FGrH III B 3 K. VON FRITZ, Die griech. Geschichtsschreibung, 1967, 1, 238f. 4 L. PEARSON, The Greek Historians of the West, 1987, 8–10 5 O. LENDLE, Einführung in die griech. Geschichtsschreibung, 1992, 210. K.MEI.

Hipta (Ἵππα; *Hípta*) Goddess of western Asia Minor, probably developed out of the old Anatolian Ḥepat, a form of the Great Goddess. Mentioned on inscriptions only in Lydia as *Mētēr H.* and apparently related to → Sabazius. In the Orphic myths, she appears as a wet-nurse, to whom Zeus hands the new-born Dionysus. On her head is a basket entwined with snakes (*líknon*) (Orph. fr. 199). She is addressed by the so-called Orphic hymns as the wet-nurse of Dionysus – son of Sabazius or the same – who resides on the Tmolus or the Ida Mountains (→ Orphism) (Orph. H. 48. 49). These hymns were used ritualistically in a city in western Asia Minor.

M. L. WEST, The Orphic Poems, 1983, 96. F.G.

Hira (Ἱρή/*Hiré*, Ἰρή/*Iré*, Εἶρα/*Eîra*). Mountain stronghold in the inaccessible ravined area in the south of the upper Neda on the northern border of Messenia, possibly on the 864 m high Hagios Athanasios near Kakaletri (traces of ancient fortifications). → Aristomenes [1] led the battle against the Spartans from here in 500–490/489 BC (Third Messenian War).

PHILIPPSON/KIRSTEN 3,2, 357; F. KIECHLE, Messenische Studien, 1959, 86ff. C.L. and E.O.

Hiram I King of Tyre (→ Tyrus) (*c.* 962–929 BC). The name is shortened from the Phoenician *Aḥīram* ('my brother is exalted'); known primarily for the trading expeditions sent as 'joint ventures' with King Solomon of Jerusalem to Ophir (India? East Africa? 1 Kg 9:26–28) and Tarshish (in the west of the Iberian peninsula, → Tartessus; 1 Kg 10:22, cf. Ez 27:12) [1. 251]. According to reliable surviving reports, including Josephus

(Ap. 1,109–121), he was an active urban builder in Tyre and erected new temples for → Astarte and → Melqart-Hercules, with whose special resurrection rites (ἔγερσις; *égersis*) he is also connected as founder [2. 223; 3. 326]. Significantly, in the ancient sources, H. is the only Phoenician city-king to undertake a foreign punitive expedition, probably against the Tyrian colony → Citium (Jos. Ant. Iud. 8,146; Ap. 1,119) [4. 615].

→ Solomon; → Tartessus

1 H. G. Niemeyer, Expansion et colonisation, in: V. Krings (ed.), La civilisation phénicienne et punique, in: HbdOr, 1. Abt., vol. 20, 1995, 247–267   2 G. Bunnens, L'histoire événementelle *partim* Orient, in: Ibid., 222–236   3 C. Bonnet, P. Xella, La religion, in: Ibid., 316–333   4 Cl. Baurain, A. Destrooper-Georgiades, Chypre, in: Ibid., 597–631.

E. Lipiński, s.v. H., DCPP, 218.   H.G.N.

Hirpini Samnite tribe in Samnium from *mons Taburnus* to the valleys of Volturnus, Calor, the upper Aufidus as far as *mons Vultur*. The name H. probably derives from that of the wolf (*hirpus*), holy to the H., which was said to have led the H. into their area of settlement from the north (Str. 5,4,12). During the Iron Age, they are represented by the Cairano culture and the Fossa culture of Caudium. The area of the H. encompassed Caudium, Malventum, Aeculanum, Romulea, Aquilonia [2] and Compsa, as well as the Abellinates, surnamed Protropi, and Marsi. In 313 BC, the Roman colony of Saticula was founded, after the victory over Pyrrhus in 268 BC, in the region of Malventum the colony of Beneventum was founded (Plin. HN 3,105), thereafter the main centre of the H. In 180 BC, 47,000 Ligurians were deported here (the so-called Baebiani and Corneliani). Major roads crossed the region: the extension of the *via Appia* from Capua to Tarentum, the *via Minucia* running along the Appennine, the *via Aurelia Aeclanensis*, the *via Traiana* from Beneventum to Brundisium and later the *via Herculia* through Lucania. In the year 130, the agrarian reform of the Gracchi was carried out here (ILS 25). After Italian regions were reorganized under Augustus, the area was part of the *regio II*. From here originates a *tabula alimentaria* of Trajan (ILS 6509). In late antiquity it was administered by the *consularis Campaniae*.

B. D'Agostino, Popoli e Civiltà dell'Italia Antica 2, 1974.   G.U.

Hirrius M. H. Fronto Neratius Pansa, PIR² N 56 → Neratius.   W.E.

Hirschfeld Painter Attic vase painter of the geometric period (late geometric I b, after 750 BC; → Geometric vase painting), named after Gustav Hirschfeld (1847–1897), who first described the main work excavated in 1870, the so-called Hirschfeld Krater (Athens, NM Inv. no. 990) [1; 2]. The Hirschfeld Painter (HP) and his workshop worked in the tradition of the → Dipylon Painter and had a preference for monumen-

tal kraters of which the eponymous krater and a further one in New York (MMA Inv. no. 14.130. 14) are especially important because of the → prothesis and → ekphora scenes depicted. The vases by the HP passed down to us show very extensive ornamentation: parallel lines, rows of dots, swastika motifs, maeanders as well as varnished stripes and circles are very common; in the figure style the head appears as a circle with a dot for the eye, and the chin and hair are also indicated as well as the breasts in women.

1 G. Hirschfeld, Vasi arcaici Ateniesi, in: Annali del Istituto 44, 1872, 142–144, no. 41   2 Monumenti inediti pubblicati dall'Instituto di Corrispondenza Archaeologica IX, 1872 pl.39/40.

J. N. Coldstream, Greek Geometric Pottery. A survey of ten local styles and their chronology, 1968, 41–44; G. Ahlberg, Prothesis and Ekphora in Greek Geometric Art, 1971, 220–224; R. Lullies, in: R. Lullies, W. Schiering (ed.), Archäologen-Porträts, 1988, 88–89; Th. Rombos, The Iconography of Attic Late Geometric II Pottery, 1988.   R.H.

Hirschlanden H.-Ditzingen, district of Ludwigsburg: finding-place of a stone statue of a warrior from the late → Hallstatt culture (6th/5th cents. BC). The 'Stele of H.', which is approximately life-size (extant H 1.50 m) and totally three-dimensional, represents the naked figure of a man with a conical hat or → helmet, mask (?), neck ring (→ Torques), → belt and a typical Hallstatt dagger. It was lying at the edge of the encirclement wall of a burial mound from the late Hallstatt culture that it originally crowned. Its design shows both Graeco-Etruscan and local Celtic elements.

→ Hochdorf; → Sculpture; → Statue

K. Bittel, S. Schieck, W. Kimmig, Die Kelten in Baden-Württemberg, 1981, esp. 87–95, 398–400; W. Kimmig, Eisenzeitl. Grabstelen in Mitteleuropa, in: Fundber. Baden-Württemberg 12, 1987, 251–297.   V.P.

Hirtia Sister of → Hirtius. In 46 BC she was evidently offered by her brother to Cicero as a possible wife after his divorce from Terentia. Cicero declined on the grounds that marriage and philosophy are incompatible (Hieron. Adversus Iovinianum 1,48), and married the young and rich Publilia. H. is probably alluded to in a letter written by Cicero (Att. 12,11) dated November 46 BC, in which he informs Atticus that he had never seen anything so ugly (*nihil vidi foedius*).

J. Kerschensteiner, Cicero und Hirtius, in: FS S. Laufer, vol. 2, 1986, 559–575.   W.W.

Hirtius, Aulus H.'s early career is shrouded in mystery. He probably served as a legate in Gallia from *c.* 54 (Cic. Fam. 16,27,1–2). He became a devoted follower of Caesar, to whom he owed his further advancement (Cic. Phil. 13,24). In 49 he accompanied Caesar to Spain, in 47 he stayed with him in Antioch; apart from that he defended Caesar's interests in Rome. The office of people's tribune in 48 is not certain. His introduction of a law aimed against the followers of Pompey (*rogatio Hirtia,* CIL I² 2,604), later to be abolished (Cic. Phil. 13,32), must fall into the year 46, when H. was praetor (MRR 2, 295); *pace* Cassius Dio (42,20,1). In 45, H. advanced to governor (proconsul?) of Gallia comata and Narbonensis (Cic. Att. 14,9,3). Probably in the same year he became augur and finally, in 43, still appointed by Caesar, he took up the office of consul (MRR 2, 334–336). After Caesar's death, faced with the unfamiliar situation of having to make decisions on his own, H. first showed reserve regarding politics and devoted himself to literary activity. When the conflict with Antonius [I 9] became obvious, Caesar's murderers even attempted to win his favour through the intervention of his friend Cicero. In the summer H. became so seriously ill, that he was not yet entirely recuperated when he entered his office on 1 January 43 (alongside C. → Vibius Pansa). Along with Pansa and Octavianus (→ Augustus), H. assumed the task of freeing D. → Iunius [I 12] Brutus, who had been besieged in Mutina since December. He succeeded in occupying Bononia and Forum Gallorum and defeating Antony in mid April, following Pansa's defeat in March. He fell at Mutina in another victorious encounter on 21 April. 'The glorious soldier's death', writes VON DER MÜHLL 1913 [1. 1961], 'relieved H. from a position of such difficulty that neither his talents nor his energy were equal to the task'; he thus summarizes in one sentence a view that was commonly held by researchers until the seventies.

H.'s importance for posterity lies in the literary realm. After having published a diatribe against Cato in 45 on behalf of Caesar and as a response to Cicero's laudatio, he wrote the eighth book of *De bello Gallico* probably in mid 44, thus filling the temporal gap (51–50) between Caesar's *Commentarii* on the Gaulic War and the Civil War. He was not able to realize his plan – the completion of which he had already announced in the preface in the form of a fictitious letter to Cornelius Balbus (praef. 2) – of describing also the wars up to the time of Caesar's death [2].

1 VON DER MÜHLL, s.v.a. Hirtius, RE 8,2, 1956–1962 2 S.A. PATZER, Aulus Hirtius als Redaktor des Corpus Caesarianum, in: WJA N.F. 19, 1993, 111–130.   w.w.

Hirtuleius, L. Probably quaestor in 86 or 85 BC (introduction of the dual accounting system for debts under the *lex Valeria,* Cic. Font. 2), 79–75 BC proquaestor of the renegade Q. → Sertorius in Spain and his most capable officer. In 79 he defeated the governor M. Domitius [I 11] Calvinus at the Anas, in 78 the proconsul of Gallia Transalpina, L. Manlius (MRR 2, 83; 87). In 76 he was defeated by Q. Caecilius [I 31] Metellus Pius near Ilerda and fell shortly afterwards together with his brother near Segontia at the Duero (Liv. p. 90f.; Sall. Hist. 2,31; 59M; Frontin. Str. 21,2 et passim; Flor. 2,10,6f.; Oros. 5,23,3–12 among others).

C. F. KONRAD, Plutarch's Sertorius, 1994, 131f.   K.-L.E.

Hispal(is, Spalis) Modern Seville. First mentioned as a base for Caesar's Spanish campaigns, but surely an ancient Iberian settlement; Phoenician origin has been assumed. H. belongs to the few cities that have retained their importance from antiquity until today. For antiquity this is attested by literary sources, inscriptions (CIL II Suppl. p. 1145f.) and coins [1]. Its importance is based on its geopolitically favourable location on the → Baetis estuary – even today H. is accessible for ocean ships – and its fertile environs. Most important dates: 45 BC promoted to *colonia Iulia Romula* by Caesar (Isid. Etym. 15,1,71; [2. 271]). In AD 428 conquered by the Vandali, in AD 441 by the Suebian king Rechila, was temporarily Byzantine [2. 411], in *c.* AD 567 conquered by the Visigoths under king Athanagild [2. 141f.]. H. played an important role as an episcopal see; a highlight was the metropolitan Leander (before AD 579 until *c.* AD 600 [2. 450]); in AD 590 the *Concilium Hispalense I,* in 619 or 620 the *Concilium Hispalense II* took place in H. [2. 217, 252]; from AD 712–1248 H. was under Arab rule.

1 A. VIVES, La mondeda hispánica 4, 1924   2 A. SCHULTEN (ed.), Fontes Hispaniae Antiquae 9, 1959.

TOVAR 2, 140–143; 3, 411.   P.B.

Hispallus Epithet ('Spaniard') of Cn. Cornelius [I 78] Scipio H. (cos. 176); taking the form of Hispanus with his son Cornelius [I 79].   K.-L.E.

Hispania, Iberia

I. GEOGRAPHY AND HISTORY   II. LANGUAGES III. SYSTEMS OF WRITING   IV. RELIGION   V. ARCHAEOLOGY   VI. INCORPORATION INTO THE ROMAN EMPIRE

I. GEOGRAPHY AND HISTORY
A. NAME   B. TOPOGRAPHY   C. ECONOMY D. POPULATION   E. ROMAN PERIOD   F. LATE ANTIQUITY AND BYZANTINE PERIOD

A. NAME
Since the 1st cent. AD, H. has referred more and more to the entire Iberian Peninsula. The name *Iberia* may only be attested since the time of the 2nd Punic War (218–201 BC; Liv. 21,2; Enn. Ann. 503), but it is the oldest of all, since it is derived from Phoenician *i-shephanním,* 'rabbit coast' (according to a new interpretation 'land of metal plates'). A further name was *Ophioussa* ('land of the snakes'; Avien. 148; 152; 172; 196), which was probably coined by the Phocaeans when they came into contact with some regions of the eastern and southern coast (Avien. 195; 199; cf. 156). *Ibéría* ('Iβηρία) originally only meant the areas settled by Iberians, later the entire country; *Keltiké* (Κελτική) probably always referred to the central plateau of the Iberian Peninsula which had been occupied by Celts. *Hesperia* was a poetic name for Italy, later also for Spain. For more about these names see [2].

B. Topography
1. General 2. Mountains 3. Rivers

1. General

The author of the ancient *Periplus*, whose text is contained in the *Ora maritima* of Avienus, already had a very exact idea of the peninsula's character. This knowledge was expanded for topography and ethnography; however, some geographical inaccuracies prevailed until the Middle Ages [2. vol. 1, 12–22]. The most important of the mountains, foothills and rivers known in antiquity are listed below.

2. Mountains

(*Montes*) *Pyrenaei*, *Pyrene*, Πυρηναῖα (*Pyrēnaîa*), present-day Pyrenees. Oldest mention in Avien. 472; 533; 555; 565. The city of Pyrene is probably eponymous. The western continuation of the → Pyrenaei are the Cantabrian Mountains, whose western parts were called *iuga Asturum* (Plin. HN 3,6). *Mons Vindius* is the mountainous region north of Villafranca del Bierzo, but the term is used more generally as well [4]. The Cordillera Central is called *Iuga Carpetana* (Plin. HN 3,6), the Iberian border range (today Cordillera Ibérica) is called *Idubeda* (Str. 3,4,10; 12; Ptol. 2,6,20). The *mons Caius* (present-day Moncayo; Mart. 1,49,5; 4,55,2) lies here. The *Vadavero* (Mart. 1,49,6) is probably the modern Sierra de Madero east of Numantia [3. vol. 8, 252], *Voberca* (Mart. 1,49,14) refers to modern Bubierca near Ateca on the Jalón, about 20 km west of Calatayud. The *mons Medullius* is mentioned for Galicia (Flor. Epit. 2,33,50; Oros. 6,21,7); its location is disputed [4. 146ff.]. The *montes Nerbasii* (Hydatius 71 = Chron. min. 2,20) are to be found in the area of Orense [2. vol. 1, 171]. In the south the *iuga Oretana* (Plin. HN 3,6, present-day Sierra Morena) are important, the *mons Argentarius* near Castulo at the source of the → Baetis (Avien. 291; Str. 3,2,11). *Orospéda* (Ὀροσπέδα, Str. 3,4,12; Ὀρτόσπεδα with Ptol. 2,6,20) are the mountains from the middle of the east coast to → Cartagena (correct determination [2. vol. 1, 191]). The *mons Silurus* (Avien. 433) is identical with the *mons Solorius* (Plin. HN 3,6), that is the Sierra Nevada. *Il(l)ípoula* (Ἰλ(λ)ίπουλα, Ptol. 2,4,12) is present-day Sierra de Ronda [2. vol. 1, 192].

Foothills of the east coast: *prominens Pyrenae*, *Pyrenae(um) iugum* (Avien. 533; 472; 565; evidence: [2. vol. 1, 178]). The *promunturium Ferrarium* (Mela 2,91) is identical with the *Tenébrion ákron* (Τενέβριον ἄκρον, Ptol. 2,6,16) or present-day Cabo de la Nao. The *iugum Trete* (Avien. 452) is identical with *promonturium* (= *pr.*) *Saturni* (Plin. HN 3,19) and the *Skombraría ákra* (Σκομβραρία ἄκρα, Ptol. 2,6,14), present-day Cabo Palos, the *iugum Veneris* (Avien. 437) with the *Xaridémou akrōtérion* (Χαριδήμου ἀκρωτήριον, Ptol. 2,4,7), present-day Cabo Gata.

Southern coast: *Calpe*, present-day Gibraltar (first mention in Avien. 344); *pr. Iunonis* (Mela 2,96; Plin. HN 3,7), present-day Cabo Trafalgar; *cautes sacra Saturni* (Avien. 215), present-day Cabo Sagres; the *pr.*

Sacrum (Str. 3,1,2; Mela 3,7; Plin. HN 2,242; 4,115) is identical with *iugum Cyneticum* (Avien. 201), present-day Cabo de São Vicente.

Western coast: The *pr. magnum* (Mela 3,7; Plin. HN 4,113) is identical with *pr. Olisiponense* (Plin. HN loc. cit.) and *pr. Ophiussae* (Avien. 172) as well as *mons Sacer* (Columella 6,27,7), present-day Cabo da Roca. Pliny (HN 4,113f.) confuses it with *pr. Artabrum*. The *pr. Nerium* (Str. 3,1,3; 3,3,5) is identical with *pr. Celticum* (Plin. HN 4,111; 115) and the *pr. Artabrum* (Plin. HN 2,242), modern Punta de Nariga west of La Coruña. Pliny (HN 4,113f.) confuses it with Cabo da Roca. The *iugum Aryium* (Avien. 160) is identical with *Lapatía* (Λαπατία), *Kórou ákron* (Κώρου ἄκρον) and *Tríleukon* (Τρίλευκον) (Ptol. 2,6,4), modern Cabo Ortegal.

Northern coast: The *iugum Veneris* (Avien. 158) is identical with *Oiassó ákron* (Οἰασσὼ ἄκρον, Ptol. 2,6,10), modern Cabo Higuer, the western part of the Pyrenaei [2. vol. 1, 246]. For more details on the shape of the coast see [2. vol. 1, 207–246, 268–293].

3. Rivers

East coast: *Anystus* (Avien. 547) is identical with the *Ticis* (Mela 2,89) – not to be confused with *Ticis*, modern Tech, or *Ticer* (Plin. HN 3,22) – probably also *Dilunus* (Sall. Hist. 3,6; [3. vol. 4, 232]), modern Muga; *Rubricatum* (Mela 2,90; Plin. HN 3,21), modern Llobregat; *Subi* (Plin. HN 3,21) is probably not identical with the Gaya, rather modern Riera de Riudecañes or Francoli near Tarragona [2. vol. 1, 306]. The *(H)iberus* (earliest mention by Cato; [3. vol. 3, 186]) is identical with *Íbēr* (Ἴβηρ, earliest mention by Pol. 2,13,7) and the *flumen Oleum* (Avien. 505), present-day Ebro. Left tributary: *Sicoris* (often mentioned, especially in Caes. B Civ.), modern Segre, with the *Cinga*, which is still called Cinga. Right tributary: *Salo*, present-day Jalón. *Tyrius* (Avien. 482) is identical with the *Turia* [3. vol. 4, 206, 213] and *Turis* (Ptol. 2,6,15), present-day Guadalaviar. *Sicanus* (Avien. 469) is the *Sucro* [3. vol. 4, 208f.; 5 88], present-day Júcar. *Tader* (Plin. HN 3,19) is identical with the *Taber* (Ptol. 2,6,14) and *Theodorus* (Avien. 456), present-day Segura. This probably refers to the *Iber* of the Hasdrubal contract (Pol. 3,21,1; 30,3; [6]).

Southern coast: *Menace* (Avien. 427 cf. 431) is identical with the *Maenuba* (Plin. HN 3,8), present-day Velez. *Chrysus* (Avien. 419) is the *Barbesula* (Plin. HN 3,8; Ptol. 2,4,7), present-day Guadiaro. The *Tartessus* (Avien. 225; 284; [3. vol. 12, 182]) is identical with the Baetis, present-day Guadalquivir. Left tributaries: *Singilis* (Plin. HN 3,10; 12), modern Genil, and *flumen Salsum* (Bell. Hisp. 7,1; 3), present-day Guadajoz. *Hiberus* (Avien. 248) is identical with *Luxia* (Plin. HN 3,7), present-day Río Tinto. *Anas* (Plin. HN 3,6), modern Guadiana.

Western coast: *Tagus* [2. vol. 1, 341ff.], present-day Tajo/Tejo; *Tagonius* (Plut. Sertorius 17), present-day Tajuña, right tributary of the Tajo; *Munda* (Str. 3,3,4; Plin. HN 4,115), present-day Mondego; *Durius*, present-day Duero/Douro; *Urbicus* (Hydatius 173 = Chron. min. 2,28; Chronici Caesaraugustani ad a. 458 = Chron. min. 2,222; cf. also Isid. Historia Gothorum 31 = Chron. min. 2,279; Iord. Get. 44), right tributary of the Astura, present-day Orbigo; *Limia* (Mela 3,10; Ptol. 2,6,1; Plin. HN 4,112), Greek Λιμαίας (*Limaías*, Str. 3,3,4; Plin. HN 4,115) is identical with the *Oblivio* (Sall. Hist. 3,44; Plin. HN 4,115), the Λήθης (*Léthēs*, Str. loc. cit., App. Hisp. 73), Βελιών (*Belión*, Str. loc. cit.) and the *Aeminius* (Plin. HN 4,115), present-day Lima; *Minius* [2. vol. 1, 354], Greek Βαῖνις (*Baînis*, Str. loc. cit.) or Βαίτης (*Baítēs*, App. Hisp. 73), modern Miño/Minho.

Northern coast: *Navia* (Plin. HN 4,111; Ptol. 2,6,4), present-day Navia; *Melsos* (Str. 3,4,20), modern Canero, but cf. [9. 590; 3. vol. 6, 267]; *Namnasa* (Mela 3,15), modern Nansa; *Nerva* (Ptol. 2,6,7), present-day Nervión near Bilbao; *Deva* (Mela 3,15; Ptol. 2,6,8), present-day Deva.

C. ECONOMY

The topography and vegetation of the peninsula determined its economical importance: the east and west coasts were very rich in vegetation (Str. 3,3,4; 3,4,16). Olives (above all in the Baetica; Str. 3,2,6), wheat (Str. 3,4,16) and wine were predominantly cultivated here. The cultivation of flax and the resulting production of linen were also important (Plin. HN 19,10). Cattle and horse breeding supplemented agricultural production. There was extensive fishing along the coasts; → Gades was known for tuna fishing (cf. its coat of arms). Metals were found mainly in the southern and northern border ranges (Huelva, Castulo), while there were few metals in the plateau region. In the south near Cartagena, silver (Str. 3,2,10) and lead were found (Str. 3,2,11), gold in northern Asturia (Plin. HN 33,78), silver (Str. 3,2,10) and iron in the Ebro Valley (Pol. 6,23 fr. 96) and in Cantabria (Plin. HN 34,149).

D. POPULATION

The Iberian Peninsula has been settled since the Lower Palaeolithic period and has experienced constant immigration. For this reason its ethnology presents countless problems. A difference must be made between the indigenous population and the immigrant groups, who came into the country temporarily as conquerors, colonists or traders, enticed by its rich metal deposits. Indigenous: the Iberians settled mainly along the eastern and southern coast. To this day they constitute the majority of the population ([5. 286ff.]; earliest mention in Avien. 250; 472; 480; 253; 613; [3. vol. 1², 188f.]). The fact that the Tartessians belong to the Iberians is no longer disputed.

→ Celts: they penetrated the area between 800 and 500 BC via the Pyrenaei and at times overran large parts of the peninsula. It is disputed whether they came in one wave or – more likely – in several. Sources, finds (Hallstatt culture) and countless place names and personal names attest to the significance of this immigration, which affected above all the north and the middle of the peninsula. Basques: they are first mentioned in the literature in the 1st cent. BC, but according to archaeological and linguistic characteristics they are a people of mysterious origins. Peoples who immigrated after the Celts: many finds prove that trade goods were already imported from the eastern Mediterranean in prehistoric times, but it cannot be determined if by direct means or through intermediaries, through the Cretans or seafarers. But the appearance of the Phoenicians in → Gades and in other places (cf. Almuñécar, Sexi, Toscanos) in the 8th cent. BC is confirmed by the sources. They founded trading posts which developed into cities in some places [7; 8]. The Phoenicians were followed by Greeks, especially the Phocaeans, who from *c.* 600 BC onwards were the first to set up trading posts and cities along the eastern and southern coast on their trips from Massalia to Tartessus [5; 6. 44ff.]. While Phoenicians and Greeks generally appeared as traders, the Carthaginians under → Hamilcar [3] Barkas in 237 BC came as conquerors. They relied on the old Phoenician settlements; → Acra Leuce was newly founded under Hamilcar and → Carthago Nova under Hasdrubal around 226 BC. Their cultural influence has often been underestimated [6]. The Romans entered H. in 218 BC. With the help of Iberian tribes they were able to drive the Carthaginians out by 206, but the complete subjugation of the peninsula was only completed under Augustus against the stubborn resistance of the Iberian, Celtiberian and Cantabrian population. H. was considered a *provincia pacata* from around 19 BC at the earliest.

E. ROMAN PERIOD

The country was divided into two (Ulterior, Citerior), later three provinces (Lusitania, Baetica, Tarraconensis). Romanization began in the aftermath. The old languages with the exception of → Basque disappeared, so that at the time of Strabo (2nd half of the 1st cent. BC) Baetica was considered to be one of the most Romanized provinces of the empire (Str. 3,2,15). Caesar and Augustus founded more colonies in H. than in other areas – 12 in Tarraconensis and 9 in Baetica. There were 23 indigenous cities which became Roman *municipia*, and 45 Latin communities.

The Roman culture manifests itself in many historical monuments such as theatres, amphitheatres, temples and aqueducts, for example in → Tarraco, → Augusta [2] Emerita and → Saguntum. Later incursions by other peoples starting in AD 255 changed little in the degree of Romanization. The Visigoths and the Suebi, entering from the 5th cent. onwards, comprised only a small warrior class, which was Romanized in the course of the 6th cent. [3. vol. 9, 195]. The Arabs, who arrived in the year 711, were only driven out of the country in the course of the Reconquista in 1492. The indigenous population consisted of tribes which probably had ethnological but less political significance and disappeared during the Roman rule. They consisted of clans (*gentilitas, gens, centuria*; [4. 58ff.]). But the cen-

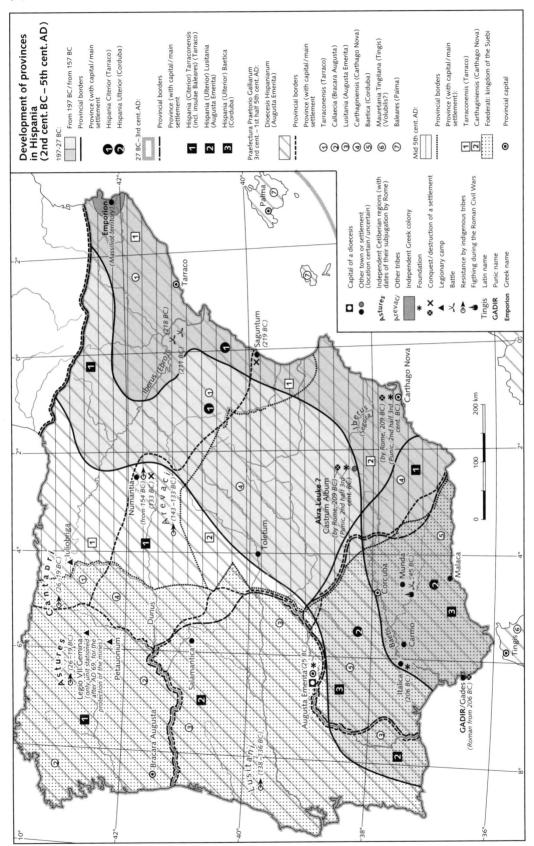

tral political unit was the city or the fortress, and the history of the country can be explained for the most part out of this fragmentation. On the Roman provinces especially see → Hispania Baetica, → Hispania Tarraconensis, → Lusitania.

1 M. ALMAGRO-GORBEA, Los Celtas: Hispania y Europa, 1993 2 SCHULTEN, Landeskunde 3 A. SCHULTEN (ed.), Fontes Hispaniae Antiquae, 1925ff. 4 F. J. LOMAS SALMONTE, Asturias prerromana y altoimperial, 1989 5 P. BARCELÓ, Aspekte der griech. Präsenz im westl. Mittelmeerraum, in: Tyche 3, 1988, 11ff. 6 Id., Die Grenzen des karthagischen Machtbereichs unter Hasdrubal, in: E. OLSHAUSEN, H. SONNABEND (ed.), Stuttgarter Kolloquium zur histor. Geogr. des Alt. 4. 1990 (Geographica Historica 7), 1994, 35–55 7 H. G. NIEMEYER, Auf der Suche nach Mainake, in: Historia 29, 1980, 165ff. 8 Id., Anno octogesimo post Troiam Cabotam... Tyria classis Gadis condidit? Polemische Gedanken zum Gründungsdatum von Gades (Cadiz), in: Hamburger Beitr. zur Arch. 8, 1981, 9ff. 9 A. SCHULTEN, s.v. Melsus, RE 15, 590

J. ALVAR, De Argantonio a los romanos, in: Historia 16, 1995; J. ARCE, El último siglo de la España romana: 284–409, 1982; P. BARCELÓ, Karthago und die Iber. Halbinsel vor den Barkiden, 1988; J. M. BLÁZQUEZ et al., Historia de España Antigua, 1978; J. L. LÓPEZ CASTRO, Hispania Poena, 1995; A. RUIZ, M. MOLINOS, Los Iberos, 1995.
                                                                        P.B.

F. LATE ANTIQUITY AND BYZANTINE PERIOD

The conquest of the Iberian Peninsula took place between 711 and 712 mainly by Berber troops and was the result of a more coincidental incursion as part of the great Islamic expansion towards Egypt and North Africa. After a short restless initial phase the → Umayyad prince 'Abd-ar-Raḥmān succeeded in stabilizing Islamic Spain, now called Al-Andalus, and in establishing an emirate (756–929) that was *de facto* independent of the → Abbasids in Baghdad. The apex of the Ibero-Islamic culture was the Umayyad caliphate (→ Caliph) in Córdoba (929–1030), whose dissolution was followed by a phase of political decentralization (1030–1086), which for the first time gave the Christian kingdoms in the north the opportunity to successfully reconquer larger territories. The Berber dynasty of the Almoravids (from 1086) and Almohads (from *c.* 1150) which followed could only sporadically withstand the Christian expansion ('Reconquista') successfully, and from the 13th cent. onwards Islamic Spain was reduced to the small kingdom of the Nasrids in Granada, which finally fell into the hands of the Catholic kings in 1492.

Characteristic of Al-Andalus was the special composition of its population and the linguistic situation associated with it. Thus the indigenous population consisted of a) Christians of Spanish-Roman and Visigothic origin who spoke a Romance dialect and used Latin as their written language – but it was replaced more and more by Arabic from the 9th cent. onward (= Mozarab, that is 'Arabicized' Christians), b) Jews, who mostly spoke the Romance as well as the Arab colloquial languages, but who also used Hebrew and eventually clas-

sical Arabic as their language of culture, c) a growing number of Spanish Muslim converts, who mostly kept the Romance colloquial as their spoken language but who did write classical Arabic. The ruling class was composed a) of Arab tribes who wrote and spoke Arabic, b) of Berber tribes who continued to speak Berber for a long time and c) slaves of European origins. These specific circumstances in communication created one of the most important basic conditions for a fruitful contact between the cultures on the Iberian Peninsula in the Islamic period.
→ SPAIN

R. ARIE, La España Musulmana, 1987; E. ASHTOR, The Jews of Moslem Spain, 1973; P. GUICHARD, Structures sociales "orientales" et "occidentales" dans l'Espagne musulmane, 1977; S. KH. JAYYUSSI, The Legacy of Muslim Spain, 2 vols., 1994; LEVI-PROVENÇAL, Histoire de l'Espagne Musulmane, 1950–1953; J. VERNET, Cultura hispanoárabe en Oriente y Occidente, 1987.   I.T.-N.

II. LANGUAGES

At least four different languages were spoken among the indigenous population of the Iberian Peninsula before Latinization. Epigraphic evidence for these – written mainly in a specific, 'ancient Hispanic' script – has been found along the Mediterranean coast, in the region of the Ebro, the interior region to the west of the latter, as well as in central and southern Portugal. The oldest of these date from the 4th cent. BC (possibly earlier in southern Portugal). For the north and northwest, personal and place names as well as names of divinities found on Imperial Latin inscriptions and in classical authors are our only sources for the language.

The language called 'Iberian', documented with relative homogeneity between Andalusia and southern France and in the central Ebro area, is probably not Indo-European. The very characteristic personal names are usually compounds, like Phoenician or Gallic full names. Grammar and vocabulary are still practically uninterpreted.

The language of the Celtiberian tribes, which belongs to the → Celtic languages, is known through epigraphic monuments from the upper Ebro, Tajo and Duero, but its interpretation is still in its fledgling stages. Several, clearly not yet definitive, attempts have been made at translating the most voluminous of these texts, of presumably juridical content, on a bronze tablet from Botorrita (province of Zaragoza). Parts of the inflection of nouns and verbs are clearly recognizable, e.g. in the *o*-stems nom. sing. *-os*, gen. sing. *-o*, dat. sing. *-ui*, acc. sing. *-om*, abl. sing. *-ud*, gen. pl. *-um*, dat. pl. *-ubos*; in the verb, third person sing. ind. *-ti*, third pl. ind. *-nti*, third person sing. imper. *-tud*.

Three inscriptions from central Portugal give evidence of a language referred to as 'Lusitanian', which has Celtic characteristics, but has also preserved the Indo-Germanic *p* in front of the vowel; it is considered – perhaps wrongly – an Indo-Germanic language of its own filiation. While the script of the southern Portu-

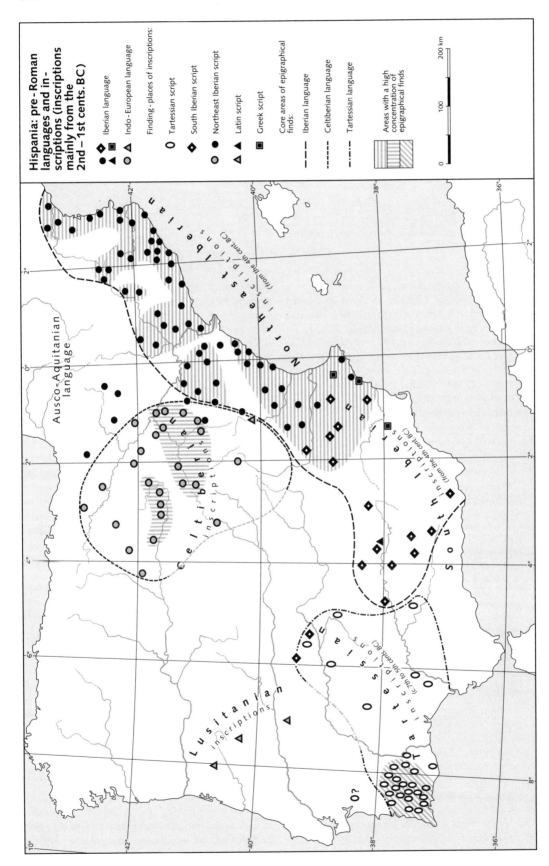

Hispania: pre-Roman languages and inscriptions (inscriptions mainly from the 2nd – 1st cents. BC)

Iberian language
Indo-European language

Finding-places of inscriptions:

Tartessian script
South Iberian script
Northeast Iberian script
Latin script
Greek script

Core areas of epigraphical finds:

Iberian language
Celtiberian language
Tartessian language

Areas with a high concentration of epigraphical finds

0   100   200 km

Northeast Iberian inscriptions (from the 4th cent. BC)

Ausco-Aquitanian language

Celtiberian inscriptions

South Iberian inscriptions (from the 4th cent. BC)

Lusitanian inscriptions

Tartessian inscriptions (7th to 5th cents. BC)

0?

The Northeast Iberian script (left to right)

			ka	ke	ki	ko	ku
a	Ρ R		Λ	⟨	⅄	Χ	⊙
e	Ε ⱶ						
i	Ν		ta	te	ti	to	tu
o	Η		Χ	⊘ ◇	Ψ	Ш	△
u	↑						
			ba	be	bi	bo	bu
s₁ ⧉ ꟽ s₂ (ś) Μ			⟨Ι	⅄⅄	Γ	✳	▯
r₁ ◁ ◖ r₂ (ŕ) φφ l ꞁ Λ							
n Ⲅ m (Celtiberian m, Iberian m when next to u) Ѱ Υ V							

guese 'Tartessian' inscriptions, stone monuments of a relatively stereotyped formula, has been deciphered with some certainty, albeit only recently, their language has not yet been identified convincingly. It is certain that it is not similar to Iberian, and presently promising attempts are being made to interpret it as a Celtic language. Personal names in the north-west and north demonstrate Celtic traits, but their relation to the languages of the Lusitanian and Celtiberian monuments can not be clearly defined.

Some names found on Latin inscriptions from Navarra reflect Aquitanian naming practices, which are well attested beyond the Pyrenees and are believed to be an early stage of → Basque, but their value as evidence is doubtful.

ED. (INSCR.): J. UNTERMANN (ed.), Monumenta Linguarum Hispanicarum I–IV, 1975–1997.
ON THE LANGUAGES: J. DE HOZ, La lengua y la escritura ibéricas, y las lenguas de los íberos, in: Lengua y cultura en la Hispania prerromana. Actas del V coloquio sobre lenguas y culturas prerromanas de la Península Ibérica, 1993, 635–666; D. E. EVANS, The identification of Continental Celtic with special reference to Hispano-Celtic, in: ibid., 563–608; J. UNTERMANN, Zum Stand der Deutung der "tartessischen" Inschriften, in: J. F. ESKA et al. (ed.), Hispano-Gallo-Brittonica. Essays in honour of D. Ellis Evans, 1995, 244–259; F. VILLAR, Estudios de Celtibérico y de toponimia prerromana, 1995. J.U.

III. SYSTEMS OF WRITING

On most epigraphic monuments, the pre-Roman languages of H. are represented by a specific, 'ancient Hispanic' script. It has three regional variants: the south-western or 'Tartessian' script, mainly in southern Portugal, the Southern Iberian, from Andalusia to the south of the province of Valencia and, by far the most common, the North-eastern Iberian script between Valencia and Béziers, and in the interior further east. The last-mentioned was deciphered by M. GÓMEZ-MORENO around 1920, and the other two are now

almost completely understood as well. The script is characterised by a system of 27 graphemes: five vowels, seven symbols for continuants (two each of nasals, vibrants and sibilants and one lateral) and 15 syllabic signs, which combine each of the three explosives (labial, dental, velar) respectively with one of the five vowels. These make no distinction between voiced and unvoiced, although, according to other sources, it did exist in the languages in question. When and where the script first took shape is not known with any certainty, but it is likely that it was created in the Andalusian region around 500 BC by a learned inventor taking his inspiration from the Greek and Phoenician alphabets, which he remodelled and expanded by a number of freely invented characters. An Ancient Hispanic alphabetic inscription of 27 letters, the first 14 of which (from α to υ) maintain exactly the sequence of their Greek model, has been found at Espanca (Castro Verde, Portugal).

J. A. CORREA, El signario de Espanca (Castro Verde) y la escritura tartesia, in: Lengua y cultura en la Hispania prerromana. Actas del V coloquio sobre lenguas y culturas prerromanas de la Península Ibérica, 1993, 521–562; J. DE HOZ, El origen oriental de las antiguas escrituras hispánicas ..., in: Estudos Orientais 1, 1990, 219–246; J. UNTERMANN, Monumenta Linguarum Hispanicarum III,1 1990, 132–149. J.U.

IV. RELIGION

As in other western European areas, religion on the Iberian Peninsula before Romanization is difficult to grasp. Apart from the few accounts by ancient authors (Strabo, Pliny), who focus almost exclusively the exceptional (divinatory human sacrifices: Str. 3,4,6; men and women dancing together: 3,4,7; myth of Habis: Just. 44,4,1), this moreover filtered through a Greek or Roman interpretation, there are archaeological, especially iconographical finds that are by their very nature difficult to interpret, and numerous inscriptions from the Roman period, which seldom contain more than the names of deities. The great variety of Iberian tribes and the varying onset of Romanization complicates matters further. At least for southern Spain the situation is exacerbated by the influence of the Tyrian colony of → Gades with its central cult of → Melqart, the intensive Punic colonization and the influence of the Greek colony of Emporion (where Str. 3,4,8 documents Artemis Ephesia), which affects the iconography in particular: indigenous cults could be behind Punic and Greek forms and names. While in the Punic cities of southern Spain the cult of the city god Melqart, but also probably that of → Tinnit (also attested epigraphically as Dea Caelestis) are especially well attested, the iconography reveals, as a particular feature of the indigenous cults, the dominance of female deities (Dama de Baza, probably also Dama de Elche) and the presence of a 'master of the horses' (cf. Str. 3,4,15 on wild horses).

Local cults and sanctuaries continue to exist after Romanization (description of a sanctuary near Cabo Sagres in southern Portugal in Str. 3,1,4f.). → Cave sanctuaries continuing pre-Roman cult sites have a certain significance. Inscriptions give evidence of a large variety of local theonyms (totalling over 300), which are most often expressed in → epicleses, while excavation finds confirm the Romanization of the architecture and the continued existence of the sanctuaries until late antiquity. The names of gods (in most cases attested only once) can often be interpreted as Indo-European, and their pantheon shows similarities to that of Gallia. (Likewise, the cult of – hot – springs is common to the Celtic area of both Iberia and Gallia.) Few theonyms are found outside their local boundaries (e.g. Endovellicus and Ataecina in Lusitania). In the Romanized cities they are joined by an abundance of official Roman cults (Capitoline Triad, esp. → Jupiter Optimus Maximus; → Ruler cult), but in many instances it is impossible to say whether a municipal cult continues a pre-Roman one. In this context, the cult of → Diana Maxima at Saguntum proves to be especially complex, since indigenous elements may have been blended with the Greek cult of the Ephesian Artemis. The Imperial period sees the arrival of Oriental cults, of which → Attis is very well attested in Baetica, and → Mithras all over the Iberian peninsula. The sanctuary of Melqart/→ Heracles at Gades takes up a special position: founded by colonists from Tyre, it achieves widespread fame in the course of the Hellenistic period. In Imperial times it remains, until the triumph of Christianity, one of the central sanctuaries of the western Mediterranean. From here, the cult of Melquart emanates into the entire Tartessian region. Hercules Gaditanus receives cult worship in all of Iberia and beyond.

SOURCES: J.M. BLAZQUEZ, Religiones primitivas de Hispania, I. Fuentes literarias y epigráficas, 1962; A.M. VÁZQUEZ, La religión romana en Hispania. Fuentes epigráficas, arqueológicas y numismáticas, 1982.
BIBLIOGRAPHY: A. GARCÍA Y BELLÍDO, Les religions orientales dans l'Espagne romaine, 1967; J.M. BLAZQUEZ, Diccionario de las religiones prerromanas de Hispania, 1975; J.D'ENCARNAÇÃO, Divinidades indigenas sob o dominio romano em Portugal, 1975; J.C. BERMEJO BARRERA (ed.), Mitología y mitos de la Hispania prerromana 1–2, 1986 and 1994; J.M. BLÁZQUEZ, Einheimische Religionen Hispaniens in der röm. Kaiserzeit, in: ANRW II 18.2, 164–275; J.MANGA, Die röm. Rel. in Hispanien während der Prinzipatszeit, in: ibid. 276–344; M.BENDALA GALÁN, Die oriental. Religionen Hispaniens in vorröm. und röm. Zeit, in: ibid., 345–408. F.G.

V. ARCHAEOLOGY

see → Pyrenean peninsula

VI. INCORPORATION INTO THE ROMAN EMPIRE

Rome had already demonstrated its interest in the Iberian peninsula before entering the 2nd → Punic War: in 226/25 BC in a treaty with Carthage, which demarcated their respective spheres of interest (Stv 2, no. 503), and through an alliance with → Saguntum (Pol. 3,30,1; 221 BC?). Right at the beginning of the war, the brothers Cn. Cornelius [I 77] Scipio (218 BC) and P. Cornelius [I 68] Scipio (217) landed in → Emporiae on the north-east Iberian coast. In the following years, they fought with varying success against the troops of the Carthaginians and their allies, defeated a Carthaginian fleet in 217 BC in the delta of the Iberus [1] (modern Ebro) (Pol. 3,95 f.; Liv. 22,19), operated together and separately in the eastern half of Iberia, and conquered Saguntum (Liv. 24,42,9–11) and → Castulo (Liv. 28,20,8–12) in 212; both were killed west of → Carthago Nova in 211 in two battles involving heavy losses (Liv. 25,34–36; cf. Pol. 9,22,3).

With the arrival of P. Cornelius [I 71] Scipio in the autumn of 210, the Roman campaigns received a new impetus: immediately in the following year, he conquered Carthago Nova (Pol. 10,9–17; Liv. 46,41–49); he celebrated victories at → Baecula on the upper → Baetis (modern Guadalquivir; Pol. 10,37–40; Liv. 27,17–20), in 208, and at → Ilipa (Pol. 11,20–24; Liv. 28,12,10–16) in 206, and finally drove the Carthaginians in the south-west back to → Gades (modern Cádiz). Mago [5] left the island with a few troops in order to join his brother Hannibal [4] in Italy; the city of Gades concluded a treaty with the Romans (Liv. 28,35–37; Stv 3, no. 541). Thus, there was no longer a Carthaginian army on the Iberian peninsula.

The area which was now nominally under Roman rule can be described as follows: a narrow coastal strip running from the north-east to the south-west from the eastern end of the Pyrenees [2] with an extension westwards up the Iberus, extending inland at the level of Carthago Nova and down the entire Baetis valley. Scipio's foundation of the veterans' colony → Italica on the lower course of the Baetis in 206 was intended as an enduring safeguard of the area in the south which was economically very valuable.

The organization of the occupied territory in H. was now opposed exclusively by indigenous forces, such as the Illergetes with their allies in the area between the Iberus and Pyrene (206: Liv. 29,2 f.), the → Edetani in the hinterland of Saguntum (200: Liv. 31,49,7), and the → Turdetani in the south-east (197: Liv. 33,21,7 f.). The establishment of a Roman province is generally dated to the consulate of M. Porcius → Cato [1] in 195 BC, who likewise had to put down the insurgency of the Turdetani and other tribes in the valley of the Iberus before he could devote himself purposefully and successfully to ordering the province (Liv. 34,8–21); Cato's sphere of influence encompassed the entire area claimed by Rome on the peninsula from → Corduba to the Iberus. The creation of two provinces, H. citerior (east coast with westward extension up the Iberus valley with its administrative centre in Carthago Nova) and H. ulterior (south-east coast and the valley of the Baetis in Andalusia with its administrative centre in Corduba, cf. Str. 3,4,19) was probably also Cato's doing; the two provinces were separated by the Saltus Castulonensis (modern Sierra Morena). However, the era of the provinces is calculated from as early as 206 onwards (cf. App. Hisp. 152), and in 197 the Senate had already increased the number of praetors' posts from four to six in order to entrust the leadership of the two provinces in H. each to one praetor (Liv. 32,27,6; 32,28,2; cf. Solin. 5,1).

In subsequent years, there were recurring isolated rebellions by native tribes which were countered by the various praetors in battles with heavy losses, without the country being brought any closer to pacification; cf. the Roman battles against the → Lusitani in 190/89 (Liv. 37,57,5 f.; 58,5). A milestone in this development was the praetorship or propraetorship of Ti. → Sempronius [I 15] Gracchus in 180/79 in H. citerior, who, after decisive victories over rebellious tribes in the central Iberian area, bound the pacified opponents into a workable treaty system (Liv. 40,44,4 f.; 40,47–50). The foundation of two cities by Gracchus, → Grac(c)uris and Iliturgis (near modern Mengíbar; [1]), can probably be seen as a form of dynastic self-representation in the Hellenistic manner.

Gradually, however, the ever stronger grip of the Roman public administration on the native environment, particularly on economic resources, became perceptible. Thus, understandably, several protracted wars were fought, sometimes in parallel, which had the most serious effects on the internal politics of Rome. These included the wars against the → Lusitani under → Viriatus (155–139) and two wars against the → Celtiberi, a constantly changing coalition of various tribes in the central Iberian region (153–151 and 143–133; → Numantia). The ambition of individual Roman politicians to win in H. the laurels for a → triumph (cf. the Roman defeat under Q. Fulvius [I 17] Nobilior in 153: App. Hisp. 45–47) had a catastrophic effect on the Roman social structure, since it led to ever greater weakening of manpower resources. However, even with the fall of Numantia, the series of revolts did not come to an end (cf. the battles of T. Didius [4] against the Celtiberian Arevaci in 97 BC: Sall. Hist. 1,88 M.; Liv. Per. 70).

The fact that Rome now exported over its disputes to H., as elsewhere in the world (cf. the wars against → Jugurtha in Africa, Mithridates [6] VI in Asia Minor, especially → Fimbria [I 6]), was bound to be all the more devastating for Roman rule in H.: in → Sertorius, the Roman popular and Lusitanian national ambitions clashed, which led to a dangerous war (80–72); the → Civil War from 49 to 45 was also fought in decisive phases in H. at Ilerda in 49 and Munda [1] in 45 BC (cf. the anonymous representation in the Bell. Hisp.). Only under Augustus, who had to conduct a lengthy war (26–19 BC) against the → Asturi and → Cantabri in northern H., was H. finally pacified. Previously, Augustus had already restructured H. as part of his reorganization of the Roman empire: the province H. citerior was extended considerably to the north-east and renamed H. Tarraconensis after the administrative centre Tarraco (seven *conventus*); H. ulterior was renamed H. Baetica (four *conventus*), and Lusitania (three *conventus*) was added to the peninsula as a third province.

The economic exploitation of the province by the Romans had begun as early as 206 BC. Especially profitable were the numerous iron, silver, and gold mines (cf. Posidonius in Str. 3,2,9): in the first seven years of Roman rule, 2,480 pounds of gold and 58,452 pounds of silver ended up in the → *aerarium* (Liv. 28,38,5; 31,20,7; 32,7,4). The many wars placed a heavy burden on the financial viability of the Roman state, but in return the military successes also brought in large amounts of booty (cf. → War booty). The economic exploitation of H. probably only began to be systematic about 170 BC. However, the economic strength of the country was not lastingly damaged, which is shown by the wealth of goods that were exported to Italy, for example (especially oil, wine; cf. Str. 3,2,6). Still, in particular, cases of unscrupulous exploitation of the inhabitants of the provinces in H. led to the first trials for → *repetundarum crimen* from 171 BC onward.

1 R. CONTRERAS DE LA PAZ, La conquista de Castulo por P. C. Escipión, in: Oretania 4, 1962, 125–137.

P. BARCELÓ, Das kantabrische Gebirge im Alt., in: E. OLSHAUSEN, H. SONNABEND (ed.), Gebirgsland als Lebensraum (Geographica Historica 8), 1996, 53–60; Id., Die Grenze des karthagischen Machtbereichs unter Hasdrubal: Zum sog. Ebro-Vertrag, in: Id., H. SONNABEND (ed.), Grenze und Grenzland (Geographica Historica 7), 1994, 35–55; G. V. SUMNER, Proconsuls and provinciae in Spain 218/7–196/5 B. C., in: Arethusa 3, 1970, 85–102; A. TRANOY, La Galice romaine, 1981; E. ARIÑO GIL, Centuriaciones Romanas en el valle medio del Ebro, 1986; G. K. TIPPS, The Rogum Scipionis and Gnaeus Scipio's Last Stand, in: CW 85.2, 1991, 81–90; J. DE ALARCÃO, Roman Portugal, 2 vols., 1988; L. VILLARONGA, Corpus Nummum Hispaniae Ante Augusti Aetatem, 1994; L. A. CURCHIN, Vici and pagi in Roman Spain, in: REA 87, 1985, 327–343; S. J. KEAY, Roman Spain, 1988; F. BELTRÁN LLORIS, F. MARCO SIMÓN (ed.), Atlas de Historia Antigua, 1987, no. 46 f.; T. BECHERT, Die Prov. des Röm. Reiches, 1999, 70 f. (bibliography). E. O.

Hispania Baetica, Hispania Ulterior The beginnings of the province Hispania Baetica (HB) are linked to Augustus' restructuring of the provinces in 27 BC (Cass. Dio 80,2). The earliest document naming HB is an inscription in the Forum Augustum in Rome (ILS 103). From the 2nd cent. AD, HB was named *Baetica Provincia* or *Hispania Baetica* (ILS 269). The borders of HB are the Anas (Guadiana) in the west, the Sierra Morena in the north, and the Atlantic and the Mediterranean in the south. The capital of this senatorial province was → Corduba.
→ Lusitania

> C. CASTILLO GARCIA, Städte und Personen der Baetica, in: ANRW II 3, 1975, 601–654; J. M. BLÁZQUEZ et al., Historia de España Antigua II, 1978; C. AMES, Unt. zu den Religion in der Baetica in röm. Zeit, thesis 1998.   P.B.

Hispania Tarraconensis, Hispania Citerior The province Hispania Tarraconensis (HT) was established by the administrative reorganization of the Iberian peninsula by Augustus in 27 BC (Cass. Dio 80,2). Initially it encompassed the northeastern half of Hispania and was the largest of the three Hispanic provinces. In the north it extended to the Atlantic and the Pyrenees, in the east the Mediterranean formed a natural border, including the Balearics, in the south it was bounded by Baetica, and in the west by Lusitania. As the number of provinces increased, HT was considerably reduced in size. In the Diocletian period it encompassed only about half of its original extent. Core regions were the Ebro valley and the northern section of the east coast. The provincial capital was → Tarraco.

> P. BOSCH-GIMPERA, Katalonien in der röm. Kaiserzeit, in: ANRW II 3, 1975, 572–600; J. M. BLÁZQUEZ et al., Historia de España Antigua II, 1978.   P.B.

> CARTOGRAPHY: J. ARCE et al. (ed.), Hispania Romana, exhibition catalogue Rome, 1997; J. M. BLÁZQUEZ, Hispanien unter den Antoninen und Severern, in: ANRW II 3, 1975, 452–522; P. BOSCH-GIMPERA, Katalonien in der röm. Kaiserzeit, in: ANRW II 3, 1975, 572–600; C. CASTILLO GARCIA, Städte und Personen der Baetica, in: ANRW II 3, 1975, 601–654; F. DIEGO SANTOS, Die Integration Nord- und Nordwestspaniens als röm. Prov. in der Reichspolitik des Augustus, in: ANRW II 3, 1975, 523–571; J. S. RICHARDSON, The Romans in Spain, 1996; A. TOVAR, J. M. BLÁZQUEZ MARTÍNEZ, Forsch.-Ber. zur Gesch. des röm. Hispanien, in: ANRW II 3, 1975, 428–451; W. TRILLMICH, Hispania Antiqua, 1993.

Hispellum Town in Umbria on a rise of Monte Subasio, modern Spello. Settled since the 7th cent. BC, connected to the *via Flaminia, municipium, Tribus Lemonia, Colonia Iulia* (possibly since the Second Triumvirate).The source of the → Clitumnus lay in the territory of H. (Plin. Ep. 8,8,6). Under Constantinus the town was *Colonia Flavia Constans* with a temple of the *Gens Flavia* and had the privilege of celebrating annually an Umbrian festival (ILS 705 of 333/337). Archaeology: remains of the city wall from the beginning of the

Augustan period with towers, monumental gates, amphitheatre, theatre, and Venus sanctuary.

> P. CAMERIERI et al., H., in: Atti dell'Accademia Properziana di Assisi, 1997.   G.U.

Histiaea (Ἱστίαια; *Histíaia*). City on the north coast of Euboea, still not identified, probably to be found near Xirochori, a settlement of Thessalian Hellopii and Perrhaebi. The territory of H. originally covered the entire north of Euboea (Dem. Or. 23,213) and was known for its wine (Hom. Il. 2,537). The temple of Artemis Proseoa in Artemisium was its main sanctuary. After the naval battle at Cape Artemisium, the Persians occupied and plundered H. (Hdt. 8,23f.; 66,1; Diod. Sic. 11,13,5). The city joined the → Delian League in 477 BC with a relatively small tribute (1,000 drachmas, ATL 1,274f.; 3,22; 197; 239; 267f.; 288). H. played a leading role on the Euboean uprising against Athens in 446 BC and after its defeat was more harshly punished than, for example, Chalcis or Eretria. The inhabitants were exiled for seizing an Athenian ship and murdering its crew. Some 2,000 Attic cleruchs were settled in Oreus, a deme of H.'s on the coast (near today's Molos). After the Peloponnesian War and the withdrawal of the cleruchs, the exiled inhabitants returned to H. from Thessaly. H. and Oreus merged, as documented by a communal wall; Oreus became established as the city's name. The period of independence of both places is recalled by the acropoleis of the lower and upper city (cf. Liv. 28,6,2; 31,46,9). In the Corinthian War H., like other cities of Euboea, sided with the enemies of the Spartans, who occupied H. until the city was liberated by the Athenians in 377 (Diod. Sic. 15,30,1ff.; Xen. Hell. 5,4,56f.). H. was a member of the 2nd → Athenian League from 371 to 357/6, except for interruptions caused by the alliance with Thebes and in 343–341 by the tyranny of Philistides who was supported by Philip II. In the Hellenistic period, H. was mostly under Macedonian rule. In 208 BC (Liv. 28,5,18ff.) and 199 BC (Liv. 31,46,6ff.) H. was conquered by the Romans and → Attalus [4] I of Pergamon, but declared free after 197 (Pol. 18,47,10; Liv. 33,34,10; 34,51,1). Widespread coin finds and many proxenies point to its great commercial and political importance in the Hellenistic period. By contrast, nothing is known from the Roman period: Pliny (HN 4,64) still mentions H., but Mela and later authors do not refer to it.

> C. BURSIAN, Geogr. von Griechenland 2, 1872, 82ff.; KODER/HILD, 1972; LAUFFER, Griechenland, 269f.; PHILIPPSON/KIRSTEN 1, 575ff.; T. W. JACOBSEN, s.v. H., PE, 396; A. PARADISSIS, Fortresses and castles of Greece 2, 1974, 107f.; L. ROBERT, Hellenica 11–12, 1960, 63ff.   H.KAL.

Histiaeus (Ἱστιαῖος; *Histiaîos*).

[1] Son of Lysagoras, tyrant of Miletus, spokesman for the Ionians on the Ister, urging to maintain the bridge for → Darius' [1] return from the Scythian campaign *c.*

513 BC with the argument that their → tyrannis depended on Darius (Hdt. 4,137). His disproportionately elaborate biography in Herodotus reveals two tendencies: he is the clever, ambitious hero without success; he is blamed for the negative course that the Ionian Revolt took [2. 486f.]. Darius rewarded H. with the rulership of Myrcinus in Thrace (Hdt. 5,11), and shortly thereafter summoned him to Susa as advisor (5,23f.); his place at Miletus was taken by → Aristagoras [3] (5,30). Supposedly the instigator of the Ionian Revolt by means of secret dispatches (5,35), he was sent by Darius to settle this dispute in 496 BC (5,106f.). After Aristagoras' death, however, H. pursued his own plans (6,1ff.). Without success, he sought a basis in Chios and Miletus. With 8 ships from Lesbos, he established himself in Byzantium (6,5). After the destruction of Miletus in 494 BC, H. attacked Chios (6,26) and Thasos, then withdrew to Lesbos from the Persian fleet (6,28). After landing in → Atarneus to replenish his supplies, he fell into Persian hands in 493 BC; the satrap → Artaphernes [2] had him crucified in Sardes and sent his head to Darius in Susa, who buried him with honour (6,29) [1. 102–105, 579–581; 3. 357–359, 364, 414–417].

[2] Son of Tymnes, hereditary ruler of Termera, settled in Caria with other pro-Persian 'tyrants' after the unsuccessful expedition against Naxos instigated by → Aristagoras [3] of Miletus at the start of the Ionian Revolt in 499 BC (Hdt. 5,37). At Salamis in 480 BC, Herodotus ranks him among the best-known leaders of the Persian fleet (7,98) [1. 121f., 590].
→ Ionian Revolt

1 H. BERVE, Die Tyrannis bei den Griechen, 1967 2 O. MURRAY, in: CAH 4, ²1988 3 L. DE LIBERO, Die archaische Tyrannis, 1996. J.CO.

Historium Coastal settlement of the Samnite Frentani, modern Vasto. Did probably not become a Roman *municipium* until after the Social War, *tribus Arnensis* (*quattuorviri*; incorrect in the Liber coloniarum 2, 260, 10f. L.: *colonia*). No autonomous bishopric. Byzantine base (Kastron Reunias) in the 6th and 7th cents.

M. BUONOCORE, H., in: Supplementa Italica 2, 1983, 97–144; A. R. STAFFA (ed.), Dall'antica Histonium al Castello del Vasto, 1995; A. R. STAFFA, Vasto (H.), in: EAA² Suppl. 5, 954f. M.BU.

Historia (Attic ἱστορία; *historía* and Ionian ἱστορίη; *historíē*). Technical term first used by Herodotus, based on the meaning of 'enquiry' (Hdt. 2,118), then evolving towards 'result of an enquiry' = 'knowledge' (Hdt. 1, pr.), finally with the meaning of 'written explanation of the enquiry', that is, in the case of Herodotus, (7,96) 'work of history'. This meaning (term for works of history) then remains constant throughout Greek literature (cf. Pol. 1,57,5) [1; 2].

In Latin, *historia* (in contrast to *fabula*) means 'history'/'historiography' in the narrower sense. Furthermore, records exist of attempts to determine the meaning of *historia* in contrast to *annales*: Verrius Flaccus (Gell. NA 5,18,1f.) postulates that the authors of *historiae* are eyewitnesses, similarly Serv. Aen. 1,373 [3] (cf. Isid. Orig. 1,44,4): *historia* is the representation of the time period which corresponds to the life of the author, while reports about previous time periods are *annales*. Gellius adheres to yet a different definition, which views *historia* as the generic term and *annales* as a strictly chronological work of history (5,18,3–7). In this context, he reviews Sempronius Asellio (fr. 1f.), who rejected *annales* — probably under the impression of Polybian ideas — in favour of *res gestae*, because *annales* could not point out any causal relationships between historical events.

There is no ancient evidence for further terminological differentiation (*historia* in the sense of historical monography) [4]. In the practice of historiography the position which was anonymously reported by Verrius/Gellius/Isidore seems to have established itself. The title *Historiae* is attested for the works by → Sallust and → Tacitus (Tert. Apol. 16), which correspond to the respective lifetimes of their authors [5]. As far as the work by → Coelius [I 1] Antipater is concerned, the records vary between *Annales* (Nonius) and *Historiae* [6].

1 K. KEUCK, H., thesis 1934 2 A. SEIFERT, H. im MA, in: Archiv f. Begriffsgeschichte 21, 1977, 226–284 3 D. B. DIETZ, H. in the Commentary of Servius, in: TAPhA 125, 1995, 61–97 4 G. PUCCIONI, Il problema della monografia storica latina, 1981 (see CR 32, 1982, 283) 5 R. P. OLIVER, The First Medicean Ms of Tacitus and the Titulature of Ancient Books, in: TAPhA 82, 1951, 232–261 6 W. HERRMANN, Die Historien des Coelius Antipater, 1979. MA.HO.

Historia acephala The *Historia acephala* (HA), also called *Historia Athanasii*, is one of the most important chronological sources for the life of the Alexandrian bishop → Athanasius. First edited in 1738 by F. S. MAFFEI, who gave it the name because of the poor condition of the surviving text, it is based on a single Latin manuscript of the 8th cent. The HA was probably written in AD 386 in celebration of the 40th anniversary of Athanasius' consecration as bishop. It offers a chronological history of the Alexandrian see from 346. The original Greek document was based on the episcopal files, but it underwent various editorial adaptations. The consular dates down to the death of Athanasius were added and passages on the Church history of Constantinople (1,4–7; 4,5f) and Antioch (2,7) were worked in between 385 and 412, together with a chronological appendix (5,14). At the beginning of the 5th cent., the HA was abridged and translated into Latin in Carthage. A critical edition with a French translation is provided by [1], an English one by [2]. A concordance is offered by [3. 233f.].

1 A. MARTIN (ed.), Histoire 'Acéphale' et Index Syriaque des lettres festales d'Athanase d'Alexandrie, 1985 2 PH. SCHAFF, H. WACE (ed.), Select Writings and Letters of Athanasius, Bishop of Alexandria, 1987 (repr.) 3 T.D. BARNES, Athanasius and Constantius, 1993. M.R.

Historia Apollonii regis Tyrii (HART) Latin → novel by an unknown author that tells of the journeys of Apollonius, King of Tyrus, up to the point when he is reunited with his wife, whom he had believed dead, and with his daughter Tarsia, and is reinstalled. The HART contains many Christian elements that are imbedded into a clearly pagan context without being completely integrated.

The reconstruction of the work's creation, its dating, and the textual structure are all contested. The oldest sources on the HART go back to the 6th cent. AD (Ven. Fort. carm. 6,8,5f.: AD 566–568; *De dubiis nominibus*, late 6th cent.). The fact that the HART (42–43) contains a few riddles which are also transmitted in the collection of the *Aenigmata Symphosii* (4th–5th cents. AD) does not facilitate the dating: It is possible that the riddles belong to a transmission used by both the author of the HART and by → Symphosius, or that they were inserted into the HART by whoever had made revisions to it in the 5th–6th cents.; even the very existence of the poet Symphosius has been questioned [1].

The HART is known to us through more than 100 MSS, which, however, transmit the text in different editions. The oldest of these recensions are the so-called RA and RB; RC is of particular importance because it contributes to the textual structure of RA and RB and because this version exerted much influence on the literature to follow. RA and RB were probably written in the 5th–6th cents. AD; RB depends on RA, but also draws directly on an even older version. The editor of RB seems to have modified the text of RA, the longer of the two versions: RB leans towards restoring a more 'classical' language as well as greater narrative coherence [2]. As far as the reconstruction of the older version is concerned, KORTEKAAS [1] views it as dependent on a pagan Greek novel from the 2nd–3rd cents. AD, of which RA and RB would be translation, revision, and epitome at the same time; SCHMELING [2], on the other hand, believes in a Latin novel from the 3rd cent. AD, which was Christianized in RA and RB. Two papyrus fragments of a novel (PSI 151; PMil. Vogliano 260) might belong to the Greek original of the HART [6; 7].

The HART shows the typical motifs of the Greek romantic novel, although the lovers are not the main focus of the story. It has been compared with the *Ephesiaká* by → Xenophon of Ephesus, with which it shares an unpretentious style and a story characterized by dryness, a story that in places presents contradictions and incoherent elements [8]. A network of references to the *Odyssey* might stem from the possibly Greek original [9]. A conspicuous characteristic of the HART is the focus on analogies between different figures and episodes (sometimes at the expense of narrative coherence); cf., for instance, the three storms that mark the life of Apollonius (11; 25; 39) [1. 125f.]; or the juxtaposition of the ruthless king Antiochus, who knowingly commits incest with his daughter, and the good king Apollonius, who unknowingly almost engages in incest with his daughter Tarsia [10].

The HART had a rich afterlife in the Middle Ages – the large number of transmitted copies and the many revisions and translations testify to this. Perhaps the most famous example of its popularity in later times is *Pericles, Prince of Tyre*, a play attributed to Shakespeare.

→ Novel

EDITIONS: 1 G. A. KORTEKAAS (ed.), Historia Apollonii Regis Tyri, 1984   2 G. SCHMELING (ed.), Historia Apollonii Regis Tyri, 1988.
BIBLIOGRAPHY: 3 F. MURRU, Aenigmata Symphosii ou Aenigmata Symposii?, in: Eos 68, 1980, 155–158 4 M. J. MUÑOZ JIMÉNEZ, Algunos aspectos de los «Aenigmata Symphosii», in: Emerita 55, 1987, 307–312 5 M. JANKA, Die Fassungen "RA" und "RB" der "Historia Apollonii Regis Tyri" im Vergleich, in: RhM 140, 1997, 168–187   6 R. KUSSL, Papyrusfragmente griech. Romane, 1991, 141–159   7 A. STRAMAGLIA, Prosimetria narrativa e «romanzo perduto», in: ZPE 92, 1992, 143–149   8 G. SCHMELING, Historia Apollonii Regis Tyri, in: Id., The Novel in the Ancient World, 1996, 534; 541–542 9 N. Holzberg, The 'Historia Apollonii regis Tyri' and the 'Odyssey', in: Groningen Colloquia on the Novel 3, 1990, 91–101   10 E. ROHDE, Der griech. Roman und seine Vorläufer, ³1914, 447   11 E. ARCHIBALD, Fathers and Kings in 'Apollonius of Tyre', in: M. M. MACKENZIE, C. ROUECHÉ (ed.), Images of Authority. Papers Presented to Joyce Reynolds on the Occasion of Her Seventieth Birthday, 1989, 33–34.   M.FU. and L.G.

Historia Augusta

A. WORK   B. DATE OF ORIGIN   C. THE QUESTION OF COMPOSITION   D. BIAS   E. SOURCES F. TRANSMISSION

A. WORK

Historia Augusta (HA) is the modern title of the *Scriptores historiae Augustae* (SHA), as CASAUBONUS in 1603, following the *Vita Taciti* (10,3), named the six otherwise unknown authors Aelius Spartianus, Iulius Capitolinus, Vulcacius Gallicanus, Aelius Lampridius, Trebellius Pollio and Flavius Vopiscus from Syracuse. They feature as the compilers of a collection of → biographies of Roman emperors, heirs apparent and usurpers from the time of Hadrian (AD 117–138) to Numerianus and Carinus (283–284/5). Some 30 biographies have survived; those of rulers between 244 and 253 have been lost, those of the Valeriani have survived only in fragmentary form, those of the Gallieni, not entirely. The beginning is probably missing, as the work probably sought to form a link with the imperial biographies of → Suetonius that it took as a model (SHA Max. Balb. 4,5; Prob. 2,7; Quatt. tyr. 1,1–2). Thus, the original title of the work is unknown; it was perhaps *vita principum* (SHA Tyr. Trig. 33,8; Aurel. 1,2; Prob. 2,7). The biographies up to 238 appear under the names of the first authors, those following under the names of Pollio and Vopiscus. 13 of the 21 biographies in the first group contain dedications to the emperors Diocletian and Constantine I. In the later *vitae*, Constantius I is referred to as still being alive (SHA Clod. 1,1; 3,1; Aurel. 44,5). That led to a conclusion that the work had to have originated from the Diocletianic-Constantinian period of between 293 and 330. Modern scholars use as their starting-point the astute critique of H. DESSAU, who in 1889 rejected the information contained in the *HA* itself and described it instead as the work of one single author from the end of the 4th cent. [6]. That suggestion provoked a debate, still raging today, about the work's date, its authorship, its purpose, bias and sources [10. 11–46]. Because of the vexed question of its authorship, the neutral term *HA* has gained acceptance.

B. DATE OF ORIGIN

Starting-points for a dating after 330 yield anachronisms of the most varied kind, allusions to events, figures and relationships from a later period and, in particular, traces of post-Constantine literature, such as the much discussed dependence of the Severus *vita* on the *Caesares* of Aurelius → Victor (SHA Sept. Sev. 17,5–19,3 and Aur. Vict. Caes. 20,1–30) written in 360/61. In recent decades, much discussion has taken place about the use of works by → Hieronymus, → Ammianus Marcellinus, → Claudianus [2] and from the 5th cent. Along with the *terminus post quem* of 360/61 [2], dating hypotheses for after 394/95 [7; 8] and after 405 [15] are also of significance. The assumption of a date of origin at the turn of the 4th to 5th cents. is widely held these days. The latest *terminus ante quem* is before 525, the year of the death of Q. Aurelius Memmius → Symmachus, who used the work (cf. Iord. Get. 15,83–88). As early as 1890 TH. MOMMSEN had developed a counter-thesis to that of DESSAU [14]. According to him, the foundation was laid in the Diocletianic-Constantinian period, collected around 330 and revised later, and this explains the anachronisms. This view has been taken up vigorously recently, especially by A. LIPPOLD [12; 13].

C. THE QUESTION OF COMPOSITION

Views on single or multiple authorship largely correspond to those espousing a late dating or the hypothesis of revision. Again, it was DESSAU, who first drew attention to the unusually large number of common features shared by the putative 6 authors. A great deal of research into language and style seems to have come up with pointers to a single author, though without having been able to remove all elements of doubt. Computer analysis has yielded variable results. Research in DESSAU's tradition has sought to identify the composer more accurately. W. HARTKE in 1940 argued for the younger Nicomachus → Flavianus [3] [7. 167f.], E. DE-MOUGEOT in 1953 for the historian Virius Nicomachus → Flavianus [2], cf. [5]. J. STRAUB and R. SYME have profiled the *scriptor* more closely as a philologist, antiquarian and grammarian [15; 16. 176–210]. There is a strong case for a biographer working on behalf of the aristocracy, perhaps an amanuensis of the Symmachi-Nicomachi [8. 412f.], with a great interest in the city prefecture of Rome and its office-bearers [10. 105–147]. The only one of the putative authors to make a personal appearance, Vopiscus, describes himself as the confidant of a city prefect, from whom he received the commission for an imperial *vita* (SHA Aurel. 1,1–2).

D. BIAS

An allegation of bias in the *HA* was first made in 1926 by N. H. BAYNES, who interpreted it as a work of propaganda for → Iulianus [5] Apostata [2]. 'Pagan historical apologia in Christian late antiquity', and indeed in the 5th cent., is according to STRAUB the objective of the biographical collection [15]. So far, however, there has been no successful demonstration of concrete intentions. In general, the history of the 2nd and 3rd cents. is perceived from the perspective of the non-Christian, senatorial aristocracy of the city of Rome, and the emperors are assessed in terms of their behaviour towards that class. Emperor → Severus Alexander is shown in a particularly idealized fashion in the longest *vita,* in contrast to his predecessor Elagabalus.

E. SOURCES

The historical value of the individual biographies varies. The *HA* provides good information along with obvious inventions and falsifications. The *vitae* of the generally accepted emperors from Hadrian to Caracalla contain reliable information, and in its structure the *vita Pii* shows the closest dependence on Suetonius. Up until the Severian period the work follows a reliable Latin source, probably the work of Marius Maximus, who wrote biographies from Trajan to Elagabalus and is quoted in 33 places. The work of an anonymous author is, however, suspected of being the main source [17. 30–53 with n. 1]. Of all the works quoted in the *HA,* only → Herodian's imperial history has survived. It served as the source for the biographies from Clodius Albinus to Maximus and Balbinus. → Dexippus' [2] chronicle was used for the *vitae* from Alexander to Claudius. The work of → Cassius [III 1] Dio is not named but was probably drawn on [11]. For the later 3rd cent. only → Eunapius and the → *Kaisergeschichte* were available. The biographies of the period of the soldier emperors and those of all the heirs apparent and the usurpers, the so-called secondary *vitae* [17. 54–77], are unreliable. Especially here, but not only in them, invention accumulates with references to the past (e.g. SHA Alex. 53,5–54,3) and also to the author's present (e.g. SHA Tac. 6,5). Through scattered miracle stories, short stories and anecdotes, parts of the *HA* come close to being novelistic. Of the *c.* 130 documentary inclusions only a Senate protocol is beyond suspicion (SHA Comm. 18f.). In spite of a declared striving for accuracy (SHA Tyr. Trig. 11,6f.), one of the so-called 'Thirty Tyrants' is pure invention (SHA Tyr. Trig. 33). The discrepancy between what is of some historical value and what is fictitious led MOMMSEN to call for a commentary – one that is the result of a co-operative international effort [cf. 3; 9], has been in print since 1991[12; 4; 18].

F. Transmission

The *HA* survived into the Middle Ages in only one copy that has since been lost but that was already then displaying the great lacuna. From that copy derive the MS families P and Σ. Cod. Palatinus Vaticanus 899 from the 9th cent. is the archetype for the 15 MSS of the family P, including Cod. Bambergensis of the 9th cent. The 5 codices of the family Σ go back to the 14th and 15th cents., as do also most of the P family. The ed. princeps, by Accursius, appeared in 1475 in Milan, the first separate publication, by I. Casaubonus, in 1603 in Paris.

1 T.D. Barnes, The Sources of the HA, 1978 2 N.H. Baynes, The HA. Its date and purpose, 1926 3 A.Al-földi, J.Straub, K.Rosen (ed.), Bonner Historia-Augusta-Colloquium (BHAC), 13 vols., 1964–1991 4 H.Brandt, Komm. zur Vita Maximi et Balbini, 1996 5 E.Demougeot, Flavius Vopiscus est-il Nicomaque Flavien?, in: AC 22, 1953, 361–382 6 H.Dessau, Über Zeit und Persönlichkeit der SHA, in: Hermes 24, 1889, 337–392 7 W.Hartke, Geschichte und Politik im spätantiken Rom, 1940 8 Id., Röm. Kinderkaiser, 1951 9 G.Bonamente, N.Duval, F.Paschoud et al., Historiae Augustae Colloquia (HAC), since 1991 10 K.-P.Johne, Kaiserbiographie und Senatsaristokratie, 1976 11 F.Kolb, Lit. Beziehungen zwischen Cassius Dio, Herodian und der HA, 1972 12 A.Lippold, Komm. zur Vita Maximini duo, 1991 13 Id., Die HA. Eine Sammlung röm. Kaiserbiographien aus der Zeit Konstantins, 1998 14 Th. Mommsen, Die SHA, in: Hermes 25, 1890, 228–292 (= Ges. Schriften, vol. 7, 1909, 302–362) 15 J. Straub, Heidnische Geschichtsapologetik in der christl. Spätantike, 1963 16 R. Syme, Ammianus and the HA, 1968 17 Id., Emperors and Biography, 1971 18 S. Walentowski, Komm. zur Vita des Antoninus Pius, 1998.

Editions: E.Hohl, Ch. Samberger, W.Seyfarth, 2 vols, ³/⁵1971 ; D.Magie, 3 vols., 1921–1932 (repr. 1960/61; with Engl. transl.); J.-P.Callu, R.Turcan et al., since 1992 (with French transl.).
German Translation: E.Hohl, J.Straub et al., 2 vols., 1976–1985.
Lexicon: C.Lessing, 1901–1906.   K.P.J.

Historia Monachorum Account, partly from secondary sources, of the journey that some Palestinian monks took to monastery centres in the Nile valley from the Thebaid to the Delta, composed *c.* AD 395 by one of the travellers, often transmitted together with the *Historia Lausiaca* of Palladius (*c.* 400) (DHGE 24, 681f.).

A.-J.Festugière, Historia Monachorum in Aegypto, 1961 (Ed.); Lat. Übers. des Rufinus von Aquileia: PL 21, 387–462.   F.T.

Historical epic Historical epic (HE), understood as a narrative depiction of events in the near or distant past, generally appears in Greek literature in three distinct forms: archaeological-ktistic (→ Ktisis-poems), historical-military and historical-encomiastic (the latter two mostly treat recent history, the historical-encomiastic concentrates on the figure of one single person).

In the archaic period, HE used the elegiac distich as its metre more frequently than the hexameter. This is perhaps because the distich was used as the recitative metre in the context of symposia more than the hexameter. The symposium might have functioned to foster recollection of events in public history just as much as the recollection of individual fates. This was the case at least for songs of limited scope; opportunities for declaiming longer elegiac poems (as for hexameters) were to be found instead at religious festivals or public celebrations.

It was in hexameters that those oldest works were composed that clearly treated remote 'history' in which mythological elements were either strong or the sole features (e.g. the *Korinthiaká* of → Eumelus, the *Naupáktia* from the 6th cent., the *Meropís*, about Cos, contemporary or Hellenistic, the genealogies of the Samians by Asius; see also → Aristeas). Composed in distichs, on the other hand, were another *Archaiología* of the Samians that was attributed to → Semonides of Amorgus and the oldest epic poems that (also or only) treat recent history: the *Politeîa* (*Eunomía*) of → Tyrtaeus, treating the first Messenian war, the *Smyrneḯs* of → Mimnermus, recalling the contemporary battle between the Smyrnaeans and Gyges (fr. 4 G.-P.; but perhaps the poem is also about the founding of Smyrna), → Simonides, who celebrates the battle of Plataeae and the naval battle of Artemisium. → Xenophanes wrote about both archaic history (the founding of Colophon) and the contemporary founding of the colony of Elea (in ἔπη/*épē*: hexameters or distichs), like → Panyassis, who recounted both the mythological origins of the Ionians and their colonization in pentameters (i.e. evidently in distichs). Also belonging to the middle of the 5th cent. BC is → Choerilus [1] from Samos: he was the first author known to have composed '*épē*' that were contemporary in material and large in scale, and he was one of the first to write historical-encomiastic poetry.

The Hellenistic period lacked sufficiently significant military undertakings that individual cities might have celebrated and claimed credit for. Here we have evidence of mythological *ktisis*-epics and depictions of more or less early regional history, fitting with the contemporary taste for aetiology (in most cases it cannot be established whether these were written in hexameters or pentameters), e.g. about Sparta or the Macedonians: → Phaestus; about Messenia and the Messenian wars: → Aeschylus [2] of Alexandria, → Rhianus; about the Argolid: → Lyceas of Argus, Telesarchus; about Elis, Achaea and Thessaly: Rhianus; about Thebes: → Menelaus of Aegae; about the Troad: → Hegemon of Alexandria (in the Troad); about Bithynia: Demosthenes of Bithynia; about Sicily: Polycritus/Polyclitus of Mende; about Palestine: → Theodotus; about Jerusalem: → Philo the Elder; about the battle at Leuctra in 371:

again → Hegemon of Alexandria; about the Marsian war: → Alexander [22] of Ephesus; about the Cimbrian war of Marius and the war of Lucullus against Mithridates: → Archias [7] of Antioch; about the battle of Philippi: Boethus of Tarsus; see also → Nicander. In the Hellenistic period, dactylic poetry on contemporary matters is generally encomiastic and devoted to individual rulers (much of it was probably not monumental epic, but poems of limited scope, cf. [8]): e.g. about Alexander the Great: Agis of Argus, → Anaximenes [2] of Lampsacus, → Choerilus [3] of Iasus, → Aeschrion of Mytilene; about Antiochus I Soter (or Antiochus III the Great): → Simonides of Magnesia; about Eumenes II and Attalus II: → Musaeus of Ephesus; about Cleopatra: → Theodorus; see also the large number of *fragmenta adespota* transmitted on papyri in SH.

Epic poetry on regional history disappeared in the Imperial period, and thereafter virtually only the encomiastic form flourished (see [14]).

EDITIONS: 1 PEG   2 GENTILI/PRATO I²-II,   3 E. HEITSCH, Die griech. Dichterfr. der röm. Kaiserzeit, I²-II, 1963–1964   4 SH   5 CollAlex.
BIBLIOGRAPHY: 6 S. BARBANTANI, L'elegia encomiastica in età ellenistica, thesis Urbino 1998   7 E. BOWIE, Early Greek Elegy, Symposium and Public Festival, in: JHS 106, 1986, 13–35   8 A. CAMERON, Callimachus and his Critics, 1995 (ch. X)   9 R. HÄUSSLER, Das historische Epos der Griechen und Römer bis Vergil, 1976 10 S. MAZZARINO, Il pensiero storico classico I, 1972 (ch. I)   11 W. R. MISGELD, Rhianos von Bene und das historische Epos im Hell., thesis Cologne 1968   12 W. RÖSLER, Mnemosyne in the *Symposium*, in: O. MURRAY (ed.), Sympotica, 1990, 230–237   13 T. VILJAMAA, Studies in Greek Encomiastic Poetry of the Early Byzantine Period, 1968   14 K. ZIEGLER, Das hell. Epos, ²1966.   M.FA.

Historical novel see → Novel

Historical reliefs Roman historical reliefs (HR) (→ Relief) are not images of real life. They poeticize historical events and invite generalizing interpretations. The genre originated early in the 1st cent. BC [1. 62]. It was probably inspired by panegyric paintings (→ Panegyrics) of Alexander [4] the Great [2], as well as, possibly, by the pillar (→ Pillar, monumental) taken by Aemilius [I 32] Paullus in Delphi [3]. The relief base of Sant' Omobono (*c.* 180 BC) is Pergamene in style ([4]; late date: [5]). The frescoes of the François Tomb [6] on the Esquiline (→ Esquiliae) [7] and the presentational images used in triumphs (→ Triumph [8]) constitute an Italic strand of the tradition. The HR was essential to Rome's process of finding an identity in the interface between → *mos maiorum* and Hellenism, which was initiated by Cato's [1] treatise *Origines* (between 170 and 149) [9].

The oldest preserved HR come from the Ara of Domitius (*c.* 80 BC) [1; 10]. In a tableau a → *census* is related there, the topic of which is the unification of Italy after the → Social Wars [3]. A multitude of legendary and historical scenes dominates the frieze of the

→ Basilica Aemilia [11; 12]. The attacks of Sextus Pompeius [I 5] are the subject of the reliefs of the tomb of Poplicola in Ostia [13]. Two reliefs showing ships [14. no. 198], the base of Falerii [1]/Civita Castellana and the frieze on the Porticus Octaviae (→ Porticus II) [14. no. 200] as well as the cameo from Boston, which commemorates the battle of Actium [15. 68], are also late Republican.

The major work of the Augustan period is the → Ara Pacis Augustae [15. 71, 121]. The inside of the enclosure's lower half represents a fence, the outside is a hedge. The processions above this should be perceived as walking along it: dedicatory reliefs of Greek families provided the inspiration for this composition [16]. The relief of armours of → Prima Porta and → Caesarea [1]/Cherchel glorify the empire of the divine Julians and the universal peace that was brought about by them [15. 69 f.]. The Hellenized elegance of a capital city is expressed in the tomb of the city's saviour Zoilus in → Aphrodisias [1] (cf. [17]) and Hellenistic pathos in the battle reliefs of the mausoleum of → Glanum (cf. [18]). However, the representation on an arch at Susa (Cottian Alps; 8 BC, dedicated by a vassal king) is entirely provincial [19]. The formation of an imperial iconography is illustrated on an altar of the *lares* in the Vatican [14. no. 223]. There are also triumphal and battle scenes from the temple of Apollo of Sosius [I 2] (20 BC) [20. 84–86, 118 f.].

The base of Puteoli is dated to AD 30 [15. 113–121]. It is an elaborated copy of a votive dedication by towns in Asia Minor to Tiberius (AD 19) in the city of Rome. The frieze from Paris with → *suovetaurilia* on two altars is also Tiberian [15. 105–113].

Important evidence for the 'royalization' of the concept of the Principate, which originated under Caligula is the fragment from Vienna of the earliest large Roman cameo (on Hellenistic precursors cf. the → Tazza Farnese [15. 85 f.]), which depicts the emperor with Roma and a double cornucopia (!) on a divine throne [15. 81]. The base of Sorento should also be mentioned in this context given its style and choice of scenes (imperial portraits are missing) ([14. no. 208]: Augustan).

HR from the time of Claudius [III 1] emphasize the dynasty; the Gemma Augustea and the silver cup of → Boscoreale are precursors [15. 59–63, 73–80] (cf. the imperial galeries [15. 79²³⁸] and the relief walls of the Sebasteion in Aphrodisias [1]; cf. [15. 28⁶¹⁻⁶³]). An onyx vessel depicts the birth of the emperor's only grandson (50/51 AD; name unknown; [15. 53 f., 56 f.]). The 'Actium' frieze from Budapest [21], the *ara* of the *vicomagistri* in Rome [20. 147, 164], the frieze of the provinces in the Valle-Medici collection (reworked under the Tetrarchs) [19. 197–201; 15. 73 f. with n. 227] and a fragment of an arch on the via Lata in Rome ([15. 73 f.] with bibliography) are also Claudian. The frequently discussed Ara Pietatis is a scholarly construct based on an error ([22]; by contrast [23]), and the Ara Gentis Iuliae is essentially the same [24; 5. 42⁶⁴; 25]. An altar for the gens Iulia is preserved from Carthage [26].

The *grand camée de France* must be ascribed to Nero (AD 59, Armenian victory; later recut for Constantine [1]) [15. 11–28]. Similarly, the relief of S. Vitale presumes the deification of Claudius [15. 35–41]. The Cancelleria reliefs refer to Armenia and the year 66 (reworked under Domitian and Nerva) [15. 125–139]. Galba and Vitellius also had Neronian art reworked [15. 38–41, 139 f.], while the tetrarchs later had the Valle-Medici temple reliefs altered [27]. From the Flavian period only the posthumous arch of Titus (cf. → Triumphal arch) [28] is recorded.

Trajan's period saw the rise of the colossal column with its circumcolumnar relief band (→ Monumental column; the Marcus, Theodosius and Arcadius column continue this type) [29; 30; 31]. Despite an abundance of images, identifiable locations and episodes the disposition is fundamentally determined by panegyric categories. It has been doubted that the great Trajanic frieze came from the forum of the emperor [32; 33]. The *optimus princeps* (alimentary donation, etc.) is the theme of the Beneventan arch (AD 114), which includes the first representation of the divine source of the emperor's power [34; 20. 264]. The Tropaeum Traiani in Dobrudja uses a coarser idiom dominated by military themes [35; 20. 264].

The Anaglypha Hadriani [20. 248–250, 265] emphasize continuity: alimentation and tax relief are at the centre; the Forum is represented with great detail. At the Arco di Portogallo [20. 253 f., 265], as it is now called, the apotheosis of → Sabina stands out. The eight tondi from a hunting-scene monument, which are model examples of the Renaissance of the Greek tradition during this period [36; 37], were incorporated into the Arch of Constantine [20. 251, 253, 265; 38] (→ Spolia).

Reliefs with depictions of provinces (cf. the representations of provinces in Aphrodisias [1]; [15. 28⁶¹⁻⁶³]) and trophies come from the temple of Divus Hadrianus [39]. The base of the posthumous column of Antoninus Pius [40; 20. 285–288, 314] is informative about imperial funerals because of its representation of funerary customs on the sides and of the apotheosis of the imperial couple on the front (→ Death II. H.). Here classicism and 'lay style' appear side-by-side. Themes of state craft are preserved in the reliefs of the arches of Marcus [2] Aurelius [42]. The most important Antonine monument in the east is the Parthian monument from Ephesus, while a long frieze from Seville with boats is only partly preserved [43; 15. 67].

The reliefs of the Arch of Severus on the Forum Romanum (AD 193) are badly damaged. Their themes are the campaigns of the emperor in the east [44; 20. 354]. Panegyrically more comprehensive is the arch of → Leptis Magna, which includes the entire imperial family [20. 340, 343, 354]. The first marriage of Caracalla played a special role on the Arch of the Argentarii; particularly instructive is the iconclastic destruction of the images of murdered members of the imperial family [20. 334–337, 354]. The arch of → Arausio/Orange has now also been dated to the (late) Severan period ([45; 20. 154, 164]: Tiberian).

After the Severans a gap appears that is probably not just matter of textual transmission, the Arch of Galerius in Thessaloniki [46; 47] (c. AD 304; → Palace IV. E.). Its panels deal with the emperor's career and the ideology of the → tetrarchy. The groups of emperors made of basalt emphasize solidarity in the college of rulers [20. 401–406, 428]; sacrifices and votives on the Five-Column Monument in Rome have the same purpose (AD 303) [20. 413–417, 428]. The collage-like style of the Arch of Constantine (AD 312–315) [20. 444–454, 464; 48] emphasizes an awareness of being on the threshold of a new era. In the scenes at the base of the Theodosius obelisk (setting up the obelisk, games; frontal style) a different world appears after AD 390 [49; 50]. Late antique pagan and Christian HR are found in ivory work [51].

→ Monumental Column;   → Propaganda;   → Relief; → Triumphal Arch

1 H. MEYER, Ein Denkmal des Consensus Civium, in: BCAR 95, 1993, 45–68   2 M. FUCHS, Aurea Aetas, in: JDAI 113, 1998, 91–108   3 M. FLASHAR, Delphische Forsch., in: Klio 78, 1996, 349–352   4 H. MEYER, Rom, Pergamon und Antiochos III. Zu den Siegesreliefs von Sant'Omobono, in: BCAR 94.1, 1991/92, 17–32; cf. vol. 95, 1993, 69 f.   5 CH. REUSSER, Der Fidestempel, 1993, 121–134   6 F. COARELLI, Le pitture della tomba François a Vulci, in: Dialoghi di Archeologia 1.2, 1983, 43–69; cf. 71–78   7 E. LA ROCCA, Fabio o Fannio, in: Dialoghi di Archeologia 2, 1984, 31–53   8 H. MEYER, Kunst und Geschichte, 1983, 86–107   9 M. BEARD, M. CRAWFORD, Rome in the Late Republic, 1985, 17   10 F. STILP, Mariage et suovetaurilia, 2001   11 P. KRÄNZLE, Der Fries der Basilica Aemilia, in: AntPl 23, 1994, 93–127   12 A. CARANDINI (ed.), Roma, 2000, 303–319; cf. 216 f.   13 F. ZEVI, Monumente e aspetti culturali di Ostia repubblicana, in: P. ZANKER (ed.), Hell. in Mittelit., 1976, 52–83   14 T. HÖLSCHER, in: Kaiser Augustus und die verlorene Republik, exhibition Berlin 1988   15 H. MEYER, Prunkkameen und Staatsdenkmäler röm. Kaiser, 2000   16 G. DESPINIS, in: B. GENTILI (ed.), Le orse di Brauron, 2002, 153–165   17 R. R. R. SMITH, The Monument of C. Iulius Zoilos, 1993   18 P. GROS, Le mausolée des Iulii, in: RA 1986, 65–80   19 S. DE MARIA, Gli archi onorari, 1988, 100 f., 329 f., no. 110   20 D. E. E. KLEINER, Roman Sculpture, 1992   21 H. PRÜCKNER, Das Budapester Actium-Relief, in: F. KRINZINGER (ed.), Forsch. und Funde, FS B. Neutsch, 1980, 357–366   22 G. M. KOEPPEL, Die 'Ara Pietatis Augustae': ein Geisterbau, in: MDAI(R) 89, 1982, 453–455   23 M. TORELLI, Typology and Structure, 1982, 63–88   24 E. LA ROCCA, Arcus et arae Claudii, in: V. M. STROCKA (ed.), Die Regierungszeit des Kaisers Claudius, 1994, 267–293   25 M. FLASHAR, review of CH. REUSSER, Der Fidestempel auf dem Kapitol und seine Ausstattung, in: Klio 78.1, 1996, 290–294   26 P. ZANKER, Augustus und die Macht der Bilder, 1987, 311   27 H. P. LAUBSCHER, Arcus Novus, 1976, 101 ff.   28 M. PFANNER, Der Titusbogen, 1983   29 F. COARELLI, La colonna traiana, 1999   30 S. MAFFEI, s. v. Columna Marci, LTUR I, 302–305   31 G. BECATTI, La colonna coclide istoriata, 1960   32 A. M. LEANDER TOUATI, The Great Trajanic Frieze, 1987   33 P. BARCELÒ, Una nuova interpretazione dell'arco di costantino, in: G. BONAMENTE (ed.), Costantino il Grande, vol. 1, 1983, 105–114   34 K. FITTSCHEN, Das Bildprogramm des Trajansbogens zu Benevent, in: AA

1972, 742–789 35 I.A. RICHMOND, Adamklissi, in: PBSR 35, 1967, 29–39 36 D.WILLERS, Hadrians panhellenisches Programm, 1990 37 H.MEYER, Der Obelisk des Antinoos, 1993, 151–183 38 Id., Antinoos, 1991, 218–221 39 M.C. CIPOLLONE, s. v. Hadrianus, Divus, LTUR 3, 7 f. 40 S.MAFFEI, s. v. Columna Antonini Pii, LTUR 1, 298–300 41 I.S. RYBERG, Panel Reliefs of Marcus, 1957 42 M.FUCHS, Staatsideologie und Herrscherpanegyrik, in: Jb. des Kunsthistor. Mus. Wien 4, 2001 43 G.KOEPPEL, A Historical Relief from Rome and Considerations on tensae and the pulvinas, in: Journ. of Roman Archaeology 12, 1999, 596–199 44 R.BRILLIANT, The Arch of Septimius, 1967 45 J.C. ANDERSON, The Date of the Arch, in: BJ 187, 1987, 159–192 46 H.MEYER, Die Reliefzyklen, in: JDAI 95, 1980, 374–444 47 W.RAECK, Tu fortiter, ille sapienter. Augusti und Caesares im Reliefschmuck des Galeriusbogens, in: H.-U.CAIN et al. (ed.), Beitr. zu Ikonographie und Hermeneutik. FS N. Himmelmann, 1989, 453–457 48 L.GIULIANI, Des Siegers Ansprache an das Volk. Zur polit. Brisanz der Frieserzählung am Constantinsbogen, in: CH. NEUMEISTER, W.RAECK (ed.), Rede und Redner, 2000, 269–287, with n. 1, 48 (bibliography) 49 B.KILLERICH, The Obelisk Base in Constantinople, 1998 50 U.RITZERFELD, 'OMNIA THEODOSIO CEDUNT SUBOLIQUE PERENNI'. Überlegungen zu Bildprogramm und Bed. des Theodosiusobelisken und seiner Basen in Konstantinopel, in: JbAC 44, 2001, 168–184 51 D.STUTZINGER (ed.), Spätant. und frühes Christentum, exhibition Frankfurt/M. 1983, no. 248 and 251.

G.M. KOEPPEL, Die histor. Reliefs der röm. Kaiserzeit, Teil 1–9, in: BJ 183, 1983 bis 192, 1992; P.E. J. DAVIES, Death and the Emperor, 2000; D.E. E. KLEINER, Roman Sculpture, 1992; H.MEYER, Prunkkameen und Staatsdenkmäler röm. Kaiser, 2000. H. ME.

Historiography

I. ANCIENT ORIENT   II. GREECE   III. ROME
IV. CHRISTIANITY

I. ANCIENT ORIENT
A. INTRODUCTION   B. MESOPOTAMIA
C. HITTITES   D. ISRAEL   E. EGYPT   F. IRAN

A. INTRODUCTION
Judged by the principles of modern historiography, this discipline did not exist in the Ancient Orient. Nevertheless, the past has been treated in the literature in various ways, which indicates that history was an essential source of political and religious identity in the Ancient Orient.

B. MESOPOTAMIA
Records with a historical orientation do not emerge until the middle of the 3rd millennium BC in the form of royal inscriptions of Lagaš. Deeds are reported for the sake of preserving the present for the future, only rarely referring to prior events [1. 15; 2. 24f.]. One historical tradition, which continued into the 1st millennium, emerged as a reaction to the fall of the empire of Akkad [1. 34–36]. At the same time a tradition of chronological texts emerged in Mesopotamia which had practical purposes (lists of dates) as well as a historical and ideological orientation [2]. In the same way the Assyrian list of kings legitimizes the notion of an eternal rulership of Assyrian royality through its linear view of history. The 1st-millennium 'Esagil Chronicle' is a reflection of the ideological and material interests of the temple sector. In addition to recording phenomena of the heavens and prices of goods, 'astronomical diaries' occasionally record political and other events [1. 29]. The texts of Mesopotamian historiography, to which the *Babylōniaká* by Berosus also belong, are part of a complex intertextual relationship often difficult to reconstruct [1. 27–33].

C. HITTITES
Although there is a lack of chronological texts, we do have historical reports full of nuance and detail, at times reaching back into the past for several generations, which have survived through legend traditions ('Zalpa Narrative'), in the annals of rulers (esp. those of Muršili II), and in contracts, decrees, and prayers [3]. The historical prologues tell of previous failed attempts at rebelling by treaty partners in order to show the hopelessness of future attempts, while the usurpers aim for justification by pointing to their divine assistance (apologia of Hattušili III) or to reports about the atrocities committed by their predecessors ('Edict of Telipinu'). In the plague prayers of Muršili II, where the cause of the epidemic is attributed to the sins of the fathers, history is treated as a semiotic process against a background of guilt [4. 236–248].

D. ISRAEL
The historiography of ancient Israel [5] is the result of a controversial long and complex editing process, the intermediate steps of which have not survived. The Deuteronomist history (Jos, Judg., 1–2 Sam, 1–2 Kgs) can be described as a great aetiology about the loss of land with which → Yahweh punishes his people for the repeated transgression of divine law and the Covenant [4. 249–255]. Based on this, the chronistic history (1–2 Chr, Ezra/Neh) emerged in the late Persian period within the clerical and scribal milieu of the Jerusalem Temple, a work which emphasises the continuity of the people of Israel beyond exile and includes a hidden → eschatology.

→ Berosus; → Genealogy

1 J.RENGER, Vergangenes Geschehen in der Textüberlieferung des alten Mesopotamiens, in: H.-J.GEHRKE, A.MÖLLER (ed.), Vergangenheit und Lebenswelt, 1996, 9–60 2 J.-J.GLASSNER, Chroniques Mésopotamiennes, 1993 3 H.A. HOFFNER, Histories and Historians of the Ancient Near East: The Hittites, in: Orientalia 49, 1980, 283–332 4 J.ASSMANN, Das kulturelle Gedächtnis, 1992 5 K.KOCH, s.v. Geschichte, G., TRE 12, 569–586.
E.FRA.

E. EGYPT

In Egypt, records were kept of the succession of kings and the main events of the year (e.g. buildings, endowments, wars, festivals) from earliest times, the original purpose probably being the naming and recording of individual years and their sequence. However, only two excerpts of any length of these often mentioned 'annals' have survived, in the form of inscriptions from the Old Kingdom (*c.* 2700–2190 BC). The king-lists with successions and lengths of reign (only fragments of a longer list and several partial revisions survive), probably excerpts from such annals, had practical as well as cultic purposes, as the reckoning of years began anew with each king. The work by → Manetho (3rd cent. BC) is also based on such annals and lists, as is (in principle) the division of Egyptian history into epochs. Beginning in the Middle Kingdom (*c.* 1990–1630 BC), notable events were (visibly) immortalized in inscriptions at sacred locations in which the event is always presented as a god-pleasing act accomplished by the king ('royal novellas'). The concrete information in them is taken from diaries kept by various institutions. Occurrences that contradict the Egyptian historical view of a state successfully governed by a good ruler, such as unrest, lost wars, or foreign rulerships, do not appear in contemporary accounts, except in retrospective as chaos overcome. Literary texts and (non-royal) biographical inscriptions contain historiographic information only as a background.

D. WILDUNG, J. V. BECKERATH, s.v. Geschichtsdarstellung, Geschichtsschreibung, LÄ 2, 564–568; D. REDFORD, Pharaonic King-Lists, Annals and Day-Books, 1986.   K.J.-W.

F. IRAN

Of special importance in the transmissions are the reports of deeds by rulers and others. They can be found in prominent places and often appear in connection with depictions or memorials – such as the inscription of → Bīsutūn (Darius [1] I) from the 6th cent. BC, the *res gestae* of the → Sassanid Šāpur I (→ Sapor; → Naqš-e Rostam, and → Narseh (→ Pāikūlī), as well as those of the Zoroastrian dignitary Kirdīr (Naqš-e Rostam, etc.) from the 3rd cent. AD. Parallel to these are royal inscriptions of timeless character from the Achaemenid period, also often with a text-image connection, which present stereotypical qualities of emperor and empire and demand the loyalty of the subjects.

While Christian and Manichaean Church historiography has been known for some time, the official view of the Iranian past was long transmitted only in oral form and was therefore subject to the rules of an oral communication of knowledge (projection into the past, 'organic' changes of transmission, loss of dates and names, etc.). The first authoritative record-keeping took place in the 'Book of Masters' (*Xwadāynāmag*) in the 6th cent. AD – later revised and continued numerous times – which presents the history of Iran from the mythical first kings to the reign of Husraw (→ Chosroes

[6]) II (7th cent.) in the form of a legendary cycle, incorporating the most varied genres of texts and seeking to teach as well as to entertain in the framework of Zoroastrian ideology and practice. It served, on the one hand, as a basis of viewing the Iranian past for the Persian-Arabic historiography of the early Islamic period, and, on the other, as a source for the great historical epics by other Persian writers such as Firdausī. In the late Sassanid period, other 'historical' works were created in Persian as well as foreign tradition (such as that of the → Alexander Romance).

H. SANCISI-WEERDENBURG, Political Concepts in Old-Persian Royal Inscriptions, in: K. RAAFLAUB (ed.), Anfänge politischen Denkens in der Antike, 1993, 145–163; M. SPRINGBERG-HINSEN, Die Zeit vor dem Islam in arabischen Universalgeschichten des 9. bis 12. Jahrhunderts, 1989; J. WIESEHÖFER, Das ant. Persien, 1994, s.v.; E. YARSHATER, Iranian National History, in: Cambridge History of Iran 3.1, 1983, 359–477.   J.W.

II. GREECE
A. ROOTS   B. CLASSICAL PERIOD   C. HELLENISTIC PERIOD   D. ROMAN IMPERIAL PERIOD
E. CHARACTERISTICS

A. ROOTS

Greek historiography is the result of a long historical development. Its roots and origins can be found 1. in the epics (Homer 8th cent. BC, Hesiod, the epic cycle) which contain numerous 'historical' elements, 2. in the expansion of the geographic and historical horizon due to the great wave of colonization (*c.* 750–550 BC.) and the numerous voyages of discovery (*c.* 650–450 BC), and 3. in the basic rationalist position that was conveyed to the Greeks by Ionian natural philosophers (→ Thales, → Anaximander, → Anaximenes [1]) beginning in the 6th cent..

B. CLASSICAL PERIOD

(*c.* 500–330 BC). Early in the 5th. cent. BC, → Hecataeus of Miletus created a 'map of the earth', a 'description of the earth' (with detailed geographical and ethnographic and occasionally historical information) as well as *Genealogíai*, in which he directed a rationalist critique of the traditional myths. For a long time, the 'logographers', → Charon [3] of Lampsacus (*Persiká*), the Lydian → Xanthus (*Lydiaká*), and Dionysius of Miletus ('Persian History after Darius'), were regarded as important predecessors of Herodotus. Modern research, however, usually dates them to the period following him. → Herodotus from Halicarnassus (*c.* 485–425), who referred to his work as *historíēs apódexis* ('exposition of the results of inquiry'), has been regarded as the 'father of historiography' since antiquity, because he excluded the mythical epoch, concentrated on 'human events', and, in the area of geography, replaced Hecataeus' constructions and speculations with the practice of inspecting things for himself ('autopsy') and empirical research. Inspired by Herodotus' work with its universally historical outlook centred around the → Persian Wars, many different specialized disciplines of history emerged, represented, among others, by the 'prolific' → Hellanicus, the first to write *Hellēniká*, a work about Greek history, also many 'barbaric' local stories, and by → Antiochus [19] of Syracuse, who founded western Greek historiography with his works *Sikeliká* and *Perì Italías*.

With his representation of the → Peloponnesian War, → Thucydides of Athens (*c.* 455–395) is regarded as the founder of the historical monograph, marking the beginning of critical historiography through his pursuit for historical truth. His unfinished work was continued by the Athenian → Xenophon, a highly diverse writer, by the anonymous author of *Hellēniká* from Oxyrhynchus, and by → Theopompus of Chios. While → Ctesias of Cnidus, a younger contemporary of Thucydides and the author of *Persiká*, is regarded as a predecessor of Hellenistic sensationalist history, western Greek historiography found its most important representative in → Philistus, an imitator of Thucydides and a contemporary of the two tyrants Dionysius [1] and [2]. In the mid–4th cent., Atthidography (→ *Atthís*) found outstanding representatives in → Cleidemus and → Androtion.

C. HELLENISTIC PERIOD

(*c.* 330–30). While the progress of historiography in the classical period is easily comprehensible and limited to a few authors, its development in the Hellenistic period is complicated and confusing. According to Dionysius [18] from Halicarnassus (comp. 4, 30), an entire day would not suffice to list all of the authors. In fact, the spectrum of historiography is characterized by an enormous wealth of production, variety of topics, and breadth of representation.

The following main trends can be identified, although they do not exist in any pure form since the authors began to mix them early on: 1. 'rhetorical' historiography, which was particularly interested in the stylistic composition of the work, the main representatives are → Ephorus of Cyme, → Theopompus of Chios (*c.* 378–320), and → Anaximenes [2] of Lampsacus, 2. 'tragic' historiography, which strove at *mímēsis* (μίμησις) i.e. realistic representation, but often degenerated into sensationalist history, the most important representatives being Duris of Samos (*c.* 340–270) and → Phylarchus of Athens, 3. 'pragmatic', i.e. historiography based on facts, as in its main representative, → Polybius of Megalopolis (*c.* 200–118), who emphasized an analysis of factual and causal relationships.

From a thematic point of view, the following authors must be mentioned above all: 1. the Alexander historians (e.g. → Callisthenes of Olynthus, → Chares [2] of Mytilene, → Ptolemaeus, the son of Lagus, and → Aristobulus [7] of Cassandria), 2. the historians of the Diadochi period (e.g. Hieronymus of Cardia (*c.* 360–260) and Duris of Samos), 3. local Greek historians (in immense number! → local history), among which the At-

thidographers played a special role (most importantly → Philochorus of Athens, *c.* 340–261) as did the western Greek historians (esp. important → Timaeus of Tauromenium, *c.* 350–260), 4. authors of works about foreign peoples and cultures, e.g. → Manetho on Egypt, Berosus on Babylonia, → Megasthenes (*c.* 300) on India, 5. authors on Rome, the new power in the west: among others, the Greeks → Philinus of Acragas (on the 1st Punic War), → Sosylus of Lacedaemon, and → Silenus of Caleacte (on the 2nd Punic War), and the Romans (writing in Greek) → Fabius Pictor, → Cincius [2] Alimentus (Roman history up to his own time, *c.* 200), 6. authors who treated the Roman rise to a great power from a universally historical perspective: Polybius of Megalopolis, → Posidonius of Rhodes, 7. universal historical compilations: mainly → Diodorus [18], whose 'Historical Library' published in *c.* 30 BC forms a type of melting pot as well as the final point of Hellenistic historiography.

D. ROMAN IMPERIAL PERIOD

(*c.* 30 BC–AD 600). Even in the early Principate after 30 BC, authors of universal historical compilations still dominated the field, e.g. → Strabo of Amasea, → Nicolaus of Damascus, → Timagenes of Alexandria (all late 1st cent. BC). → Dionysius [18] of Halicarnassus published his 'Roman Antiquities' in 7 BC. Numerous historians of the following two centuries from the east of the Imperium Romanum, came in close contact with the Romans and achieved high honours and ranks in the service of the emperor. Accordingly, the image they portrayed of Rome was a positive one, regarding Roman rulership as necessary and legitimate. Among others, this holds true for Flavius → Iosephus (*c.* AD 38–100, 'Jewish War', 'Jewish Archaeology. '), → Appianus of Alexandria (*c.* AD 95–165, a geographically structured Roman history) and his contemporary → Arrianus [2] of Nicomedia ('Anabasis of Alexander', 'History of the Diadochi'), → Cassius [III 1] Dio from Nicaea in Bithynia (*c.* AD 155–235): his comprehensive Roman history is the only coherent source for large periods in the early Imperial period and is also very important for the author's own time, and → Herodianus (*c.* 180–250), who wrote a history of emperors from 180–238. Little has survived from the later historians to the end of the western Roman Empire in 476. → Zosimus (early 6th cent.) was the last pagan representative of contemporary history, → Procopius of Caesarea in Judaea was the most important historiographer of the period of Justinian (527–65).

E. CHARACTERISTICS

There is a striking diversity of historiographical genres and breadth of the concept of history: universal history, historical monograph, *Hellēniká*, Greek local history, works on foreign peoples, and representations of epochs and personalities are only some of the many genres, containing information not only about political, diplomatic, and military events, but often considering questions of ethnography, geography, mythography, and the history of cultures and religions.

In addition the works are characterized by a skilful use of stylistic, dramatic, and compositional means. Most of these works are therefore important works of art and can be counted among the most elegant genres of literary prose. The historians knew how to present events in a dramatic and artistic way while simultaneously interpreting the underlying forces at work and creating an image representing the totality of events. Furthermore, Greek historiography presents history as an almost continuous whole, beginning with the period of the Persian wars, a kind of *historia perpetua*, since many authors continued the work of their predecessors both chronologically and thematically. Thucydides takes up where Herodotus stopped, Xenophon continues after Thucydides, Polybius after Timaeus, and Posidonius after Polybius.

There is also a strong interest in primary research. Although Greek historians usually referred to only one or two predecessors and quoted them uncritically (an 'unscholarly' practice according to modern understanding), their primary research was often superior to that of modern historians: they relied to a large degree on 'autopsy' and their own experiences, collected and examined the oral transmission, questioned eyewitnesses and sources, and visited the scenes of events in order to gather their information on the spot. The 'scientific' accomplishment of the Greek historians is therefore hardly inferior to that of modern researchers. The relevance of the Greek historiographers lies in the fact that the most important among them (such as Herodotus, Thucydides, Polybius) raised and discussed many methodological, theoretical, and ideological questions which have had influence up to modern times and are still intensely debated today.

SOURCES: F. JACOBY, Die Fragmente der Griech. Historiker (FGrH), 15 v., 1923ff. (largely replaces the earlier collection by C. and TH. MÜLLER, Fragmenta Historicorum Graecorum (FHG), 5 v., 1840–74, but incomplete.) BIBLIOGRAPHY: J.M. ALONSO-NUÑEZ (ed.), Griech. Geschichtsdenken und Geschichtsschreiber, 1991; N. AUSTIN, The Greek Historians, 1959; T.S. BROWN, The Greek Historians, 1973; K. VON FRITZ, Die griech. Geschichtsschreibung, v. 1, 1967; S. HORNBLOWER (ed.), Greek Historiography, 1994 (bibliography); Id., s.v. Historiography (Greek, Hellenistic), OCD ³1996 (bibliography); M. HOSE, Erneuerung der Vergangenheit. Die Historiker des Imperium Romanum von Florus bis Cassius Dio, 1994 (bibliography); F. JACOBY, Griech. Historiker, 1956; Id., Abhandlungen zur griech. Geschichtsschreibung, 1956; O. LENDLE, Einführung in die griech. Geschichtsschreibung, 1992 (bibliography); T.J. LUCE, The Greek Historians, 1997; S. MAZZARINO, Il pensiero storico classico, 2 v., 1966; K. MEISTER, Die griech. Geschichtsschreibung, 1990 (It. edition 1992) (bibliography); A. MOMIGLIANO, Primo-nono contributo alla storia degli studi classici e del mondo antico, 1955–1992; ED. SCHWARTZ, Griech. Geschichtsschreiber, 1959; H. STRASBURGER, Die Wesensbestimmung der Geschichte durch die antike Geschichtsschreibung, ³1975; G. WIRTH et al., s.v. Geschichtsschreibung, Kleines Lexikon des Hellenismus, ²1993 (bibliography).   K. MEI.

III. ROME
A. REPUBLIC   B. EARLY PRINCIPATE   C. SECOND CENTURY AD   D. LATE ANTIQUITY   E. LITERARY FORM

A. REPUBLIC

The first to make the history of Rome into a topic of Greek historiography is → Timaeus of Tauromenium (FGrHist 566, Gellius = Varro, T 9c [1. 294] virtually refers to him as Rome's historian), who includes Rome in his historical work about the Greek west [2]. Rome is also the topic of *ktisis*-literature, descriptions of the founding of cities. These beginnings are taken up by → Fabius Pictor (FGrHist 809), the father of Roman historiography. His work, written in Greek from a senatorial perspective (which is typical for Roman historiography overall), deals extensively with the history of the founding of Rome and with contemporary history, but treats the period in between (450–264 BC) only in summary (T 4a [4. 932–940]). Besides the intended effect on interior politics, it also aimed at presenting the genesis of Roman power to the Greek cultural area as the organic growth of a highly civilized old community [5. 119ff.]. Roman historiography was shaped by the latter [5. 120; 6]: Fabius Pictor's successors take up the connection between the moral greatness of Rome and its political and military success (→ Annalists). Cato's *Origines*, written in Latin, makes Romans the primary target audience: in as far as historiography touches on contemporary history, it is also an instrument of controversies in interior politics. After this Roman historians writing in Greek remain the exception until the Imperial period (Rutilius Rufus, FGrHist 815). Greek writers (writing in Greek) in the service of Roman politicians are more common (e.g. Theophanes of Mytilene). A new approach away from the annalistic form (cf. Cato HRR F 77, Sempronius Asellio HRR F 1/2 and Cic. De or. 2,53f.) can be found in the monograph by → Coelius [I 1] Antipater about the Second Punic War, in which the stylistic methods of Hellenistic historiography are used in a rhetorical and dramatic arrangement of the material (see II. C.). This new form is developed further by Cornelius → Sisenna. On the other hand, influenced by the pragmatic historiography of → Polybius, → Sempronius Asellio abstains from rhetoric-dramatic embellishments in the late 2nd cent.. This is not to say, however, that the annalistic form became obsolete after Coelius: it reaches a high point in the later → Annalists in the first half of the 1st cent., adopting stylistic means from Hellenistic historiography, albeit without reference to Polybius. We can therefore identify a conflict between the claim of authenticity on one hand and fiction on the other, a conflict that can be explained by the fact that these historians should be regarded as members of the Italian municipal aristocracy or the equestrian class, who, as clients of the Sullan aristocracy are now writing for a non-senatorial audience [8]. The fragmentary transmission of all of these works only seldom allows anything to be elicited from the combination of efforts at entertainment, moral education, and foreign and interior political propaganda.

B. Early Principate

The first texts, or parts of texts, we have are by Sallust (Iug., Catil.) and Livy. In these texts, the transformation of state and society is reflected in various ways. → Sallust's monographs of contemporary history from a senatorial perspective emphasize the pragmatic dimension in their imitation of Thucydides and aim for moral legitimacy through archaism, while his histories continue tradition in following Sisenna; the crisis of Rome finds expression in his basically pessimistic attitude. → Livy even confronts the question, a central one for those who follow him, of how to view the coming monarchic state. His presentation of Rome's history, *Ab urbe condita*, becomes canonical for early Roman history up to the end of the 1st cent. AD (cf. Quint. Inst. 10,1,102). Livy's non-senatorial perspective, which implicitly contrasts old Roman virtues with a problematic present and was easily integrated into the ductus of the Augustan restoration, required supplementary works from a senatorial perspective to cover the contemporary period. In a variety of approaches, these begin, for instance, with the Civil War (e.g. Pollio, → Cremutius Cordus, → Seneca the Elder), structure themselves according to the breaks important to the dynasty, and make judgements (cf. the remarks by Tac. Hist. 1,1; Ann. 1,1) or simply continue the material of predecessors (e.g. Aufidius Bassus, → Pliny the Elder) [9]. Aside from this type of senatorial historiography (→ Tacitus being the main preserved representative), which focuses on Rome around the central issue of the relationship between Princeps and Senate with an increasingly implicit questioning of this type of state (even if different answers existed) [10], there also exists an example of a thoroughly positive panegyrical evaluation of the Principate in the work of the equestrian → Velleius Paterculus. The more recent history is structured after the reigns of the emperors, a sign that the boundary between historiography and imperial → biography was beginning to fade. A special position is occupied by the *Historiae Philippicae* by → Pompeius Trogus, which combine a universal historical perspective with a focus on Rome.

C. Second century AD

Traditional senatorial historiography was unable to contend with the increasing integration of provincial elites into the state government in the 2nd cent. AD, esp. in view of the Senate's scepticism towards Hadrian and his politics [11]. A work by → Florus [1] based on Livy takes the changed situation into account by paying more attention to the provinces, whereas the work by → Granius Licinianus may have strengthened the traditional position [12]. Except for a description of the Parthian Wars (→ Fronto, *Principia Historiae*), historiography written in Latin is no longer prominent during the period of adoptive emperors. Greek historiography once more takes its place, though the conditions have changed: from → Posidonius to → Strabo, Rome had been a topic for Greek historians from an external point of view, but now the Greek world is part of the Imperium Romanum. The culture of the 2nd cent. is bilingual, and the task of historiography is to reconcile the regions of the empire with the past (see below II. D.). → Appianus of Egypt, from the group surrounding Fronto, writes a Roman history that strongly takes into account the provinces. The works by the senators Claudius Charax (FGrHist 103) and → Cassius [III 1] Dio represent a view of history which takes for granted the monarchy and the unity of the empire. In addition to this Greek senatorial historiography a Latin 'historiography' coexisted, which as a biographical form by → Suetonius reaches back past → Marius Maximus to the sources of the → Historia Augusta and was intended, above all, to entertain (→ Light reading).

D. Late antiquity

One of the consequences of the 3rd-cent. crisis in the empire was a breakdown of cultural traditions in the Latin West. At the end of the 3rd. cent., historiography was confronted with the task of conveying a basic knowledge of the past to the new elites [13]. Historiography is now the job of teachers (→ *grammaticus*) who rise to the highest rank. The works of this new epoch are characterized by brevity: in the mid 4th cent., Aurelius → Victor wrote a concise history of emperors (*Historiae abbreviatae*), which at the end of the cent. in combination with *Origo gentis Romanae, De viris illustribus urbis Romae* and *Epitome de Caesaribus* would form a brief yet complete history of Rome (Corpus Aurelianum) [14]. In addition breviaries appear by Eutropius and → Festus [4] Rufius, alongside short versions (*periochae*, → *epitomae*) of earlier historians such as the Pompeius-Trogus epitome by M. Iunianus → Iustinus, an expanded version of Livy's content tables (*periochae*) into a kind of independent text, and a new edition of Florus (division of the book, chapter titles, table of contents). The interest in emperors' biographies is unbroken, as is attested in the *Origo Constantini imperatoris* and the reconstructed → Kaisergeschichte, the → Historia Augusta being part of the same tradition. The literary ambitions of works serving the restoration of education are limited. Their purpose is didactic.

The consolidation of the senatorial class, once again the supporter of education and literature, results in a renascence in the occupation with the past, esp. the tensions surrounding Christianization: this encompasses the cultivation of tradition, as reflected, for instance, in the discussion of the Livy text in the circle around Nicomachus [15], in the reorientation of historiography from a senatorial perspective by Nicomachus → Flavianus [?] and → Ammianus Marcellinus (who takes up Tacitus' programme), in the Historia Augusta as an expression of the senatorial-pagan spirit [16], and in the history by → Symmacus attested by → Iordanes (Get. 15) and → Anecdoton Holderi. In these, we find the self-interpretation of a world in decline so characteristic of late antiquity [17; 18], evoking Rome's greatness as a time of cultural consciousness and imperial patriotism (e.g. Amm. Marc. 14,6,5) [13. 97; 19]. The end of the west Roman empire combined with the increasing Christianization of the upper class bring Roman historiography to an end. The catastrophic year of 410 is acknowledged by only one Christian Latin historiography (cf. [20]).

E. LITERARY FORM

In Rome historiography is a literary form. In contrast to specialized writing (→ Antiquarians) and to the → *Commentarii* [21], it becomes part of the culture industry in the late Republic, integrated into the practice of recitations (attested in Lib. Ep. 1063 also regarding Ammianus). The public expectations of this genre can be reconstructed from Cicero (Fam. 5,12) and Tacitus (Ann. 4,34 [22. 12]. These sources also serve to explain the difference from modern expectations of historiography (e.g., the general reluctance to cite documents *verbatim*, an exception being Marius Maximus HRR F 16).

Theoretical reflections about historiography and the role of the historian (for instance, his geographical limitations) have not survived [23. 302f.]. Instead, we often find criticisms of their predecessors (e.g. Tacitus [24]) as a way to implicitly define their own positions. Cic. Fam. 5,12 and Lucian's work *Quomodo sit historia conscribenda* are important sources for the contemplation of historiographical forms [25].

FRAGMENT: HRR.

1 K. HANELL, Zur Problematik der älteren röm. Geschichtsschreibung, in: Histoire et Historiens dans l'Antiquité, 1956, 147–184   2 F. W. WALBANK, Timaios und die westgriech. Sicht der Vergangenheit, 1992   3 B. W. FRIER, Libri Annales Pontificum Maximorum, 1979   4 D. TIMPE, Fabius Pictor und die Anfänge der röm. Historiographie, in: ANRW I 2, 928–969   5 A. ALFÖLDI, Das frühe Rom und die Latiner, 1977   6 J. v. UNGERN-STERNBERG, Überlegungen zur frühen röm. Überlieferung, in: G. VOGT-SPIRA (ed.), Stud. zur vorlit. Periode im frühen Rom, 1989, 11–27   7 N. ZEGERS, Wesen und Ursprung der tragischen Geschichtsschreibung, thesis 1959   8 D. TIMPE, Erwägungen zur jüngeren Annalistik, in: A&A; 25, 1979, 97–119   9 J. WILKES, Julio-Claudian Historians, in: CW 65, 1972, 177–203   10 D. TIMPE, G. und Prinzipat-Opposition, in: Entretiens 33, 1986, 65–102   11 P. STEINMETZ, Unt. zur röm. Lit. des 2. Jh. n. Chr., 1982   12 M. HOSE, Erneuerung der Vergangenheit, 1994   13 P. L. SCHMIDT, Zu den Epochen der spätant. lat. Lit., in: Philologus 132, 1988, 88–100   14 Id., Das Corpus Aurelianum und S. Aurelius Victor, RE Suppl. 15, 1583–1675   15 J. E. G. ZETZEL, Latin Textual Criticism in Antiquity, 1981   16 J. STRAUB, Historia Augusta, in: Regeneratio Imperii 2, 1986, 94–118   17 R. HERZOG, HLL § 500   18 K. ROSEN, Über heidnisches und christl. Gesch.-Denken in der Spätantike, 1982   19 M. FUHRMANN, Die Romidee in der Spätantike, in: Brechungen, 1982, 75–112, 215–231   20 R. C. BLOCKLEY, The fragmentary Classicising Historians of the later Roman Empire, 2 vols., 1981–83   21 D. AMBAGLIO, Fra hypomnemata e storiografia, in: Athenaeum 68, 1990, 503–8   22 A. J. WOODMAN, Rhetoric in classical historiography, 1988   23 O. LENDLE, Einführung in die griech. Geschichtsschreibung 1992   24 T. J. LUCE, Ancient views on the causes of bias in historical writing, in: CPh 84, 1989, 16–31   25 G. AVENARIUS, Lukians Schrift zur Geschichtsschreibung, 1956.   MA.HO.

IV. CHRISTIANITY
A. GREEK B. LATIN 1. FOUNDATIONS AND DEVELOPMENT 2. INDIVIDUAL WORKS 3. FORMAL PECULIARITIES 4. OUTLOOK

A. GREEK

The beginnings of an early historical description of the proclamation and expansion of the kingdom of God can be found in the NT (Lk 1:1–4; Acts 1:1–3). The fading of an expectation of nearness, combined with apologetic and catechetic trends, after AD 200 led to the creation of a Christian chronology. With Biblical models as a starting point, chronistic writings gradually emerge as an independent literary genre (→ Chronology). Furthermore, in the 3rd cent. the Church began to be viewed as a social institution within a pagan environment, a notion which yielded literary expression (including acts of martyrs, and *vitae*).

These different threads are brought together by → Eusebius [7] of Caesarea (died in 339). His work thus comprises the most varied historiographic genres (chronicle, *Vita Constantini*: biography, *De martyribus Palaestinae*: collection of acts of martyr). Innovative in both terminology and form [3. 755] is his 'Church History' (*Ekklēsiastikè historía*), which was finally completed after several intermediate editions, in 10 volumes. With this work, chronologically following secular history and rich in source material, the 'father of Church history' presents a detailed narrative (ἀφήγησιν: Euseb. Hist. eccl. 1,1,6) of the history of the People of God up to the time of → Constantinus [1] the Great, conceived as a history of salvation.

While the West makes do with translations, the Greek world produces several successors to Eusebius (overview with publication [3. 204–208]), such as, in the 5th cent., → Philostorgius, → Socrates Scholasticus, → Sozomenus, and → Theodoretus of Cyrrhus. Philostorgius focuses his history on the Arian controversies (→ Arianism) up to the year 425, whereas Socrates, striving for objectivity and balance [2. 243], writes a valuable Church history in 7 books, covering the period from 306 to 439. The latter, in turn, is the main source for Sozomenus, who presents the period from 324 to 422 in 9 bks., based on new documents. 'Superficially closest' [2. 38] to classical historiography was Theodoretus of Cyrrhus who wrote three important works of historiography: his anti-Arian apologetic Church history (5 books, covering the years 325–428), the *Historia religiosa* (history of monks), and the *Haereticarum fabularum compendium* (description of → heresies up to → Eutyches). Additional Church histories were written by, among others, → Gelasius of Cyzicus, → Zacharias Rhetor, → Evagrius Scholasticus (6 books covering the years 431–594), and Theodorus Lector, who in about 530 summarizes Socrates, Sozomenus, and Theodoretus into *Historia tripartita*, continuing it until 527. At the end of the 6th cent., → Iohannes of Ephesus (died *c.* 585) is the last of the independent Church historiographers under Byzantine rulership.

1 G.F. CHESNUT, The First Christian Histories, ²1986 2 H.LEPPIN, Von Constantin dem Großen zu Theodosius II., 1996   3 F.WINKELMANN, Kirchengeschichtswerke, in: Id., W.BRANDES (ed.), Quellen zur Gesch. des frühen Byzanz (4.–9. Jh.), 1990, 202–212 (edition)   4 Id., s.v. Historiographie, RAC 15, 724–765   5 M.WALLRAFF, Der Kirchenhistoriker Sokrates, 1997.   J.RI.

B. LATIN
1. FOUNDATIONS AND DEVELOPMENT

In Latin historiography in late antiquity there is a fundamental transformation of the existing genres and an institution of new forms. Christianity is of critical importance in this context, and so is its underlying orientation towards history. At first, the Latin tradition follows the Greek tradition which begins, in the 2nd half of the 2nd cent., with the acts of martyrs written with apologetic intent (→ Acta Sanctorum, → Martyrs), and from the last third of the 3rd cent. on with → chronicles. The beginning of Christian Latin endeavours regarding history is marked by the *Passio Perpetuae et Felicitatis*, which describes → Perpetua's martyr death and that of her servant Felicitas in Carthage in 202. However, a widespread production of Christian historiographical writings in Latin does not begin until the 4th cent. To begin with Greek translations were important. An early record is the translation of the chronicle by Hippolytus of Rome, which was then included in the → Chronographus of 381, a unifying collection of various basic historiographical forms such as lists of consuls and bishops. Also of great significance is Jerome's translation (381) of the 2nd book of the chronicle by Eusebius, the *Chronikoì kanónes*, and the Church history in 10 books, kept until 325 by Eusebius and translated by Rufinus of Aquileia (403), who himself continues it until 395. The lives of saints develop into a central historiographical genre beginning with the translation of the life of Antonius by Athanasius into Latin by Evagrius (an anonymous translation had previously existed).

On the whole, Latin Christian historiography develops its own dynamic. At the same time, older non-Christian endeavours are also continued, by authors such as Cornelius Nepos (chronicle), Pompeius Trogus (world history), or Sueton (lives). The work *De mortibus persecutorum*, written in 316–321 by Lactantius, which presents a somewhat negative collection of lives, occupies a special position in focusing on the persecutors of the Christians and their miserable ends. The collection of lives of 392/3, *De viris illustribus*, by Jerome

refers to the traditional form of biographically oriented literary historiography (Varro). Augustine can probably be regarded as the founder of the genre of → autobiography with his *Confessiones*, although at first there is no one to succeed him in Latin late antiquity, and the work itself shows parallels with the *Carmen de vita sua* by Gregory of Nazianzus (died 374). The specific political situation of the western Roman empire most affected by migrations is taken into account by folk history, which continues the ancient genre of *origo gentis*, expanding it in a Christian interpretation. Cassiodorus' (*c.* 490–583) history of the Goths *De origine actibusque Getarum* was the first work of this genre, whose relationship with the specifically Christian historiographic genres is difficult to determine and varies from one author to another.

2. INDIVIDUAL WORKS

With his chronicle, Jerome (→ Hieronymus) became the founder of the genre in the Latin west when he supplemented Eusebius' chronicle, which had a strong eastern balance, with events in the west. Many successors continued the chronicle, such as the Spaniard Hydatius (to 468) and Marcellinus Comes (to 534). Prosper Tiro of Aquitaine endeavoured to set his own emphasis by focusing on contemporary history (to 445/455). By doing so he exerted a decisive influence on later tradition, as is evident in the chronicles by Cassiodorus and Isidore of Seville. A special case separate from the works in Jerome's succession is the chronicle by the Gaul Sulpicius Severus (to 400). If less than in the East, Church history still prospered in the Latin world. In addition to Rufinus' translation of Eusebius, the *Historia ecclesiastica tripertita* particularly deserves mention. It is a Latin compilation of parts of the Church history by Socrates, Theodoretus, and Sozomenus, completed in Vivarium under the aegis of Cassiodorus in the 2nd half of the 6th cent.. Furthermore, there were locally oriented descriptions of persecutions such as those of the Catholic Christians in North Africa by the Arian Vandals in the *Historia persecutionis Africae provinciae* by Victor of Vita. The 7 books of the *Historia adversum paganos* by → Orosius stand alone as the first Christian universal history. They were written at the instigation of Augustine as a historiographical companion to *De civitate Dei*. Orosius interprets history as disaster, gradually changing for the better from the birth of Christ, and manifesting itself as the history of salvation.

In the Latin world, lives of saints (→ Biography) flourished enormously. The three lives of monks by Jerome already take on a special significance. Esp. influential are the collections of lives of Egyptian desert fathers quickly translated by Rufinus of Aquileia, the *Historia Lausiaca* and *Historia monachorum*. The *Vita Martini* (died 397) written during the saint's lifetime by Sulpicius Severus and the *Vita Severini* by Eugippius show a high literary level. The enormous blossoming of this genre, esp. in Gaul, is attested also in the 6th cent. in the *Libri miraculorum* in 8 books by Gregory of Tours and in the lives by Venantius Fortunatus, mostly dedicated to Gaulish bishops. In Italy, the *Dialogi de vita et miraculis patrum Italorum* (593/4) by Pope Gregory the Great deserve special attention. Also significant is the *Liber pontificalis*, a history of the papacy, written and revised continuously from the 6th cent. Beginning with Cassiodorus, ethnic history also develops. The collection by Fredegar (*Fredegar Chronicle*) in 6th cent. Franconia and the *Historia Britonum* originating in the 7th cent. endeavours to determine an *origo* by reference to the Trojans. The *Historia Francorum* by Gregory of Tours stands out in the 6th cent. Gregory introduces a new emphasis, as does the Anglo-Saxon Bede in his *Historia ecclesiastica gentis Anglorum* (731), by integrating many elements of universal Church history into a largely regional framework.

3. FORMAL PECULIARITIES

Although formal elements such as the insertion of speeches or excursuses and certain linguistic constructions hark back to non-Christian Latin historiography, certain peculiarities of Christian historiography are quite apparent. A new characteristic is the separation of *historia sacra*, which tells the story of salvation and its participants, and *historia profana*, which presents the traditional setting of historical events. Also among the peculiarities of Christian historiography are structural principles, such as the division of historical time into the duration of four empires underlying the chronicle of Sulpicius Severus according to the dream of Nebucadnezzar in the Book of Daniel (c. 2), and the adoption of six ages corresponding to the six days of Creation (Gen. 1) developed by Augustine and translated into a world chronology by Isidore of Seville. Another characteristic of Christian historiography is the expectation of the end of the world with the corresponding view of the future. In addition, we find a fundamentally new → date reckoning *ab orbe condito* used in parallel with the trusted chronology *ab urbe condita* or relating to olympiads, consulates, or local systems (→ Eras). It was only in the mid–6th cent. that Dionysius Exiguus determined the date of the birth of Christ as 754 *AUC*, creating a fixed point which would be accepted only slowly. An obvious additional characteristic is the universal quality, which is superimposed over ancient distinctions and structures and fundamentally places the history of mankind on a higher level than, for example, Roman history. In contrast to a strict observance of the rules of genre, Latin (as Greek) Christian historiography shows little formal rigidity, but tends to be unpretentious. Eusebius inserts documents into his church history, compilations are common, lists of bishops are combined with narrative texts. A further example is the mixture of genres, e.g. of Church and ethnic history by Gregory of Tours, which he combines with elements of a world chronology. The mostly mediaeval descriptions as *historia*, *annales*, or *chronica* are often chosen as a compromise owing to the indeterminacy of the genres.

4. OUTLOOK

Cassiodorus (Inst. 1,17,1) asserts the existence of a separate Christian Latin historiography. His canon becomes prescriptive from the Carolingian period and documents the change from the previous co-existence of traditional and Christian historiography. The image of 'antiquity' and the presentation of the past will now be determined by the Christian authors of the 4th–6th cents. for a long time to come.

→ HISTORIOGRAPHY

W. BERSCHIN, Biographie und Epochenstil im lat. MA, 2 vols., 1986–8; A.-D. VON DEN BRINCKEN, Stud. zur lat. Weltchronistik bis in das Zeitalter Ottos von Freising, 1957; A. EBENBAUER, Historiographie zwischen der Spätant. und dem Beginn volkssprachlicher G. im MA, in: Grundriß der romanischen Lit. des MA XI/1, 1986, 57–113; B. CROKE, A. EMMET (ed.), History and Historians in Late Antiquity, 1983; J. PH. GENE (ed.), L'Historiographie médiévale en Europe, 1991; H. HOFMANN, Die G., in: L. J. ENGELS, H. HOFMANN, NHL 4, 1997, 403–467; F. VITTINGHOFF, Zum gesch. Selbstverständnis der Spätant., in: HZ 198, 1964, 529–574; G. ZECCHINI, La storiografia cristiana Latina del IV secolo (Da Lattanzio ad Orosio), in: Id., Ricerche di storiografia Latina tardoantica, 1993, 7–28.   U.E.

Historiola ('Little story'). Modern term describing brief tales built into magic formulas, providing a mythic precedence for a magically effective treatment. Historiolas are already documented in Mesopotamian and ancient Egyptian → magic. In the Graeco-Egyptian → magic papyri (PGM), they provide references to both Greek (e.g. PGM XX) and Egyptian (e.g. PGM IV 1471) mythology, and to Christian legends in Christian rites. However, historiolas should not be understood as abridgments of well-known myths or as *ad hoc* inventions, rather the narrator understands them as proof of an all-embracing order into which he integrates his rite.

A. A. BARB, Antaura. The mermaid and the devil's grandmother, in: Journ. of the Warburg and Courtauld Institutes 29, 1966, 1–23; D. FRANKFURTER, Narrating power. The theory and practice of the magical historiola in ritual spells, in: M. MEYER, P. MIRECKI (ed.), Ancient Magic and Ritual Power, 1995, 457–476.   F.G.

Historis (Ἱστορίς; *Historís*). Daughter of the seer → Teiresias (hence the probable derivation from *Ϝιδ-*, 'to see, to know'). In the context of Theban statues of Pharmacides (= Moirai), Paus. 9,11,3 tells us that H. was able to outwit them like → Galinthias in Nicander. The epithet of Juno Historia (CIL XI 3573) can probably be traced back to H. [1].

1 M. RENARD, Iuno Historia, in: Latomus 12, 1953, 137–154.   T.H.

Histria, Histri Peninsula (4,437 km²) on the northern Adriatic between Tergeste and Tarsatica (Croatia/Slovenia). H. is derived from the Istri/Histri who already settled here in the 11th cent. BC (mentioned for the first time by Hecataeus, FGrH 1 F 91). Their settlements were on hills and on the coast (*gradine* or *castellieri*) and had monumental fortifications; there is evidence of cremations in clay urns. The development of the Histri between the Veneti in the north, the Iapodes in the north-east and the Liburni in the south and south-west can be traced back to the Roman conquest in the 2nd cent. BC. In the north (Tergeste region) the development of their culture was restricted by the Celtic Carni. There is evidence of imported Etruscan and Italian pottery (in the 7th cent., partly from Daunia; → Daunian vases), also of *situlae*, monumental stone sculptures from Nesactium showing archaic Greek southern Italian influence and from the area of Etruscan central Italy. In 221 BC Rome conducted its first military campaign against the Histri to stop their piracy, then probably in 181 BC at the time of the foundation of → Aquileia [1] which was opposed by the Histri. Rome conquered the Histrian kingdom in 178/7 (Liv. 41,10f.); in the process Mutila (possibly Medulin), Faveria (location not established) and Nesactium (modern Vizače) were destroyed.

The Histri were known in Rome as *gens inops* ('poor people', Liv. 41,11,8). They were settled close to Italy and to the Carni up to Pola (Str. 7,5,3); the coastal strip in which they settled was 1,300 stadia long. Histri is a collective term for several related tribes, e.g. the Menocaleni (location not established), the Fecusses (in the hinterland of Pola), and the Rundictes in the north. In the Late Republican period they were probably counted as part of the province of Illyricum, and at times probably also of Gallia Cisalpina. In 18/12 BC the eastern border of Italy was moved from the Formio to the Arsia (modern Raša) (*regio X*, later *Venetia et Histria*). The consequence of Romanization was an early municipalization; thus, → Tergeste and → Pola became *coloniae* under Caesar (*Pietas Iulia Pola*; the first *duumviri*: C. Cassius Longinus, L. Calpurnius Piso: InscrIt X 1,81). Parentium, initially a *municipium*, probably became a *colonia Iulia* under the subsequent Augustus, whilst → Nesactium finally became a *municipium* in the 1st half of the 1st cent. AD. The hinterland was far less urbanized; the centre was Piquentum (modern Buzet).

Commercial activities were stimulated by having Aquileia as a neighbour, as well as by numerous harbours, particularly Capris (modern Koper/Capodistria), Siparis (modern Šipar), Humagum (modern Umag), Neapolis (modern Novi Grad) and Ruginium (modern Rovinj). H. was very fertile (olive oil, wine). There is evidence of many large estates of emperors and senators, e.g. of Agrippa, Maecenas, the Statilii, Sergii, Cassii, Calpurnii, Laecanii, Calvii, Palpellii and Settidii. During the wars against the Marcomanni, the *praetentura Italiae et Alpium* was created, a defence system that encompassed the regions in northern Italy, southern Noricum and north-eastern H. to Tarsatica (including part of western Liburnia) with the towns of Albona (modern Labin), Flanona (modern Plomin) and Tarsatica. In the 4th cent. Christianity gained a foothold in H. and churches were built, particularly in Pola, Parentium (the Basilica of Euphrasius) and Nesactium. In the late Roman period, rulership over the H. changed fre-

quently (Odoacer 476–493, Ostrogoths 493–539, Byzantine emperors up to the invasion of the Lombards in AD 568). In the 7th–11th cents. the land was colonized by Slavs, while in the cities the Roman population was maintained. Inscriptions: InscrIt X 1 (Pola), 2 (Parentium), 3 (Histria septentrionalis), 4 (Tergeste).

S. GABROVEC, K. MIHOVILIĆ, Jadransko-zapadnobalkanska regija. Istarska grupa [The Adriatic, West-Balkan Region. The Istrian Group], in: Praistorija jugoslavenskih zemalja 5, 1987, 293–338; Š. MLAKAR, Istra u antici [Istria in Roman Times], 1962; A. DEGRASSI, Scritti vari di antichità I and II, 1962; III, 1967; IV, 1971; V. JURKIĆ, Priolg za sintezu povijesti Istre u rimko doba, in: Arheološka istraživanja u Istri i Hrvatskom primorju/Indagini archeologiche in Istria e nel litorale croato (Izdanja Hrvatskog arheološkog društva 11/1), 1987, 65–80; Id., Arheološka istraživanja u Istri [Archaeological Research in Istria] (Izdanja Hrvatskoj arheološkog društva 18), 1997; F. TASSAUX, L'implantation territoriale des grandes familles d'Istrie sous le Haut-Empire romain, in: Problemi storici e archeologici dell'Italia nordorientale e delle regioni limitrofe dalla preistoria al medioevo, 1983/4, 193–229; R. MATIJAŠIĆ, Ageri antičkih kolonija Pola i Parentium, 1988. M.Š.K.

Histria [2] see → Istria

Histrio

I. TERM   II. DEVELOPMENT FROM THE 3RD CENT. BC, SOCIAL POSITION   III. REQUIREMENTS OF THE HISTRIO   IV. MASKS AND COSTUMES

I. TERM

Term for the Roman actor. Livy (7,2: according to Varro) reports that after a plague epidemic in 364 BC, dancers (*ludiones*) with a flautist were called from Etruria in order to purify the city with a cultic ceremony. The local youth is said to have imitated their dances and added satirical verses until finally professional artists, for whom the Etruscan word *histrio* was used, developed this improvization further. → Livius Andronicus only had to add a fable to create the tragedy. This bold combination of Italian *ludi scaenici* and the Greek artistic drama contains a true core, for from then on the actors in literary drama were also called *histriones*, just like the dancers of the *pantomimus* in the Imperial period. With the same meaning as *histrio*, *scaenicus* (*see artifex*) was used from Cicero, however, *actor* is rare (Plaut. Bacch. 213).

II. DEVELOPMENT FROM THE 3RD CENT. BC, SOCIAL POSITION

As both the improvising *ludi scaenici* as well as literary tragedy and comedy reached Rome from outside, the actors were also foreigners, mostly Greeks. When Livius Andronicus first performed a tragedy in 240 BC based on the Greek model, he himself appeared as a *histrio*; but for Plautus that was already no longer the case. Writers and actors of the same rank had joined together with state approval to form a *collegium scri-*

barum histrionumque, and their meeting-place was the Temple of Minerva on the Aventine; but this *collegium* did not exist for long, perhaps because the reputation of the *histriones* did not keep pace with that of the writers. For a Roman citizen it was considered dishonourable and shameful (Nep. Praef. 5) to present oneself on stage; only slaves and freedmen were entitled to do so without discrimination. The general disdain for the *histriones* provides a remarkable contradiction to the fame and the social high esteem of individual 'stars' like Clodius → Aesopus or Q. → Roscius, to say nothing of pantomimes from the Imperial period. The fact that actors could also participate in the shaping of political opinion can be seen from the examples of the actor-writer D. → Laberius and the tragedian Diphilus (both 1st cent. BC); the former took aim at Caesar in 46 in an acting contest, whilst Diphilus used his appearance at the → Ludi Apollinares in 59 for provocative verses on the powerful position of Cn. Pompey (Cic. Att. 2,19,3; cf. Val. Max. 6,2,9). Despite respective laws the stage always held a great fascination so that even members of noble families did not shy away from acting as amateurs. The stage appearances of the emperor Nero as a cithara player and as a tragedian were a scandal that everyone accepted [1].

III. Requirements of the Histrio

The most important law for a *histrio* was to please the audience. Politically ambitious aediles as well as other officials in the function of *ludorum curatores* invested large sums to achieve popularity through the performances. They engaged a director (*actor*) who bought a play from the author, rehearsed it with his troop (*grex*) and took on the main role himself. T. Publilius Pellio did that for Plautus: he played Stichus (cf. the Didascalia, → Didaskaliai) and apparently Epidicus several times, but the latter representation displeased Plautus, and he fell out with him (Plaut. Bacch. 214f.). Terence did better with L. → Ambivius Turpio who gave his unwavering support to his innovative, cultivated style of comedy. The number of *histriones* in a troop was not subject to any restriction. For a comedy four or five speakers were usually required (i.e. more than the obligatory three of the Greeks: this shows great changes to the models), and in addition minor roles. Naturally individual *histriones* took on several roles (Plaut. Poen. 126), and in Plautus (Plaut. Asin.; Bacch.; Capt.) all recite an epilogue together, or one asks for applause for the entire troop as they step forward (*hunc gregem*, Plaut. Pseud. 1334).

Although the chorus hardly took a foothold in Roman drama, music was also of greatest importance (→ *canticum*). Therefore, all *histriones* had to be excellent singers and dancers. The comedies of Terence end in our editions (according to Hor. Ars P. 155 [2]) with the words: *cantor: plaudite* ('a singer: clap applause'); this description of the speaker probably also refers to an actor. The accompanying flautist (*tibicen*) was at the same time the composer. In *Stichus* it was Marcipor,

slave of Oppius (in Plaut. Stich. 755–765 he is included in the play), in Terence regularly Flaccus, slave of Claudius.

IV. Masks and costumes

The use of the → mask is contested. Only the improvized → Atellana was considered to be a masque from the start (*personata fabula*); that is why young Romans were allowed to devote themselves to this genre without social discrimination. The → mime, however, dispensed with it entirely. In literary drama the *histrio* appears to have initially only worn a wig (*galear*). Only after Terence is the mask mentioned: for comedy it is said to have been introduced by Cincius Faliscus or Roscius [4. 155, 164]. In Plaut. Epid. 725 the eponymous hero gets new clothes: shoes, shirt and coat (*socci, tunica, pallium*), and at the same time these everyday clothes describe the stage costume. The comedy genre of Plautus and Terence is named *fabula palliata* after the Greek coat (ἱμάτιον/*himátion*; Lat. *pallium*) (the later national Roman *fabula togata* is lost). Freeborn citizens, parasites and slaves wore the *pallium* without any distinction; the same applies to the light shoe (*soccus*) which could generally denote the comedy, just as the *cothurnus* (→ Cothurnus) was used as a general term for the tragedy (Hor. Ars P. 80). Whether the clothes had different colours depending on the type of role (Donat. De comoedia 8,6), cannot be deduced from the texts. On behalf of the aediles a lender of costumes and props (*choragus*) prepared what was desired for the head of the troop, especially for special disguises (Plaut. Curc. 4,1; Plaut. Persa 154–160; Plaut. Trin. 857f.) [3; 4].
→ Aesopus Clodius; → Ambivius Turpio; → Roscius, Q.

1 P.L. Schmidt, Nero und das Theater, in: J. Blänsdorf (ed.), Theater und Ges. im Imperium Romanum, 1990, 149–163   2 C.O. Brink, Horace on Poetry: The 'Ars Poetica' vol. 2, 1971, 231   3 G.E. Duckworth, The Nature of Roman Comedy, 1952, 88–94   4 M. Bieber, The History of the Greek and Roman Theater, 1961, ch. XI.

W. Beare, The Roman Stage, ³1964; J. Blänsdorf, Voraussetzungen und Entstehung der röm. Komödie, in: E. Lefèvre (ed.), Das röm. Drama, 1978, 92–134; M. Ducos, La condition des acteurs à Rome. Données juridiques et sociales, in: J. Blänsdorf (ed.), Theater und Ges. im Imperium Romanum, 1990, 19–33; Friedländer, vol. 2, 112–147; C. Garton, Personal Aspects of the Roman Theatre, 1972; H. Leppin, Histrionen, 1992; B. Zucchelli, Le denominazioni latine dell' attore, 1964.   H.-D.B.

Hittite

A. Tradition   B. History, characteristics

A. Tradition

The language, passed down to us in Babylonian cuneiform, of the Hittites who had political leadership in Asia Minor in the 2nd millennium BC (core area appr. the geographical region outlined by Halys/Kızıl İrmak, → Ḫattusa II), which they themselves called *Nesumnili-*

'Nesic', a derivative of the place name *Nēsa-* (= Old Assyrian *Kaneš*, near Kayseri; the modern term has its origin in the historical development of the discipline); at the same time the most important representative of the → Anatolian languages from the point of view of the scope and thematic diversity of its textual corpus as well as with regard to its philological grounding and analysis (since 1915). The textual tradition, predominantly from the capital city → Ḫattusa (Boğazköy/Boğazkale; excavations: 1906–1907, 1911–1912, 1931–1939, continuous since 1952, → Ḫattusa I), but also from Maşat, Kuşaklı, Ortaköy, Ugarit and Emar (→ Ḫattusa II, map), partly in contemporary transcripts from the 16th–13th cents., partly in more recent copies especially from the 13th cent. (main ed. [1; 2]) – it terminates abruptly with the end of the Hittite empire around 1200 BC – comprises historiographical texts on political themes, state contracts, diplomatic correspondence, administrative and technical literature (e.g. a constitution deed, laws, decrees, service directives, oaths of allegiance, deeds of donation of land, library catalogues, vocabularies, hippological and medical texts), wisdom literature, myths, as well as extensive religious literature (cult liturgy, prayers, oracles, omens, magic rituals, incantations) ([3], treated e.g. in series [4; 5]).

B. HISTORY, CHARACTERISTICS

From the point of view of the history of language, Hittite is classified into the language phases Old (16th cent.), Middle (beginning of the 15th – *c*. middle of the 14th cent.) and Neo-Hittite (middle of the 14th – end of the 13th cent.) which were essentially defined from the beginning of the 70s by using a textual chronology based on cuneiform palaeographical criteria (for cuneiform palaeography [6; 7], for dating methods [8]) and which regardless of the overall relatively short period of the tradition of Hittite (particularly in comparison with the other Anatolian languages), show an accelerated further linguistic development that affects all areas of grammar, especially morphology and stem formation of the noun and verb (e.g. reduction of the nominal content/expression paradigm, analogical reformation of the noun/verb stems) (e.g. [9]). The existence of this tendency from as early as before the 16th cent. is evident in view of the Hittite personal names and the appellatives of Old Assyrian secondary traditions from Asia Minor (18th cent.) which still show a range of characteristics that became obsolete in the later Old Hittite (e.g. productivity of the *e*-umlaut and of various suffixes of word formation, compounds of personal names) and can therefore be considered representatives of an 'early Old Hittite' language phase [10. 24¹²], but systematic investigations have not yet been carried out.

Nevertheless, as opposed to all other Anatolian languages, Hittite has preserved archaisms from the common Old Indo-European and Old Anatolian preliminary phase; e.g. still in Old Hittite: allative of *ă* (< *ō; cf. Greek ἄνω, κάτω), gen. pl. of *-an* (< *-om), enclitic possessive pronoun; further for instance: Old

Indo-European **e*, fientive, factitive and iterative verb of *-ess-*, *-aḫḫ-* or *-ske-*, differentiated stem formation in the *ḫḫi*-conjugation. On the other hand specific Hittite innovations are: assibilation **ti > zzi* (e.g. verb ending 3rd pres. sing. *-zzi*), *i*-prothesis before initial sound **sC°* (e.g. *isḫiul-* 'contract' : **sh₂i-* 'bind'), reduction or reformation of the motion suffix *-i-* for designating common gender (e.g. *dangui-/danguuai-* : cuneiform Luwian *tanku(i)-* 'dark' < **dʰéngᵘ-o-*). Although multilingualism was generally characteristic of Asia Minor in Hittite times and it was quite common especially at the royal court in Ḫattusa to deal with non-Anatolian languages like → Hattic, → Hurrite, → Akkadian (Babylonian), in contrast with earlier views, only the related → Luwian influenced Hittite vocabulary (nouns and verbs) to a noteworthy extent and indeed increasingly from the 16th–13th cents.; in particular Hurrite Luwian and Mycenaean proper nouns (e.g. **Etewoklewes-* > *Tauaglaua-*) in Hittite texts (from the 15th cent.) [11; 12] are based on Luwian mediation. Whilst several lexical and etymological dictionaries of Hittite that supplement each other are currently in the process of being published [13; 14; 15; 16], a presentation of the grammar appropriate to the Hittite language phases is still a desideratum (cf. [17]; orientation with regard to individual investigations, see [18; 19]).

→ Ḫattusa; → HITTITOLOGY

1 Keilschrifttexte aus Boghazköi (KBo), 1916ff. (so far 39 vols.)   2 Keilschrifturkunden aus Boghazköi (KUB), 1921–1990 (60 vols.)   3 E. LAROCHE, Catalogue des textes Hittites, 1971   4 Stud. zu den Boğazköy-Texten (StBoT), 1965ff.   5 Texte der Hethiter (THeth), 1971ff.   6 CHR. RÜSTER, StBoT 20, 1972   7 CHR. RÜSTER, E. NEU, StBoT 21, 1975   8 F. STARKE, StBoT 30, 1985, 21–27   9 N. OETTINGER, Stammbildung des hethit. Verbums, 1979   10 F. STARKE, Zur Herkunft von akkad. ta/urgumannu(m) "Dolmetscher", in: WO 24, 1993, 20–38   11 E. NEU, Zum Wortschatz des Hethit. ..., in: W. MEID (ed.), Stud. zum idg. Wortschatz, 1987, 167–188   12 F. STARKE, StBoT 31, 1990   13 J. FRIEDRICH, A. KAMMENHUBER, Hethit. WB, 1975ff.   14 H. G. GÜTERBOCK, H. A. HOFFNER, Chicago Hittite Dictionary, 1984ff.   15 J. PUHVEL, Hittite Etym. Dictionary, 1984ff.   16 J. TISCHLER, Hethit. etym. Glossar, 1977ff.   17 O. CARRUBA (ed.), Per una grammatica ittita, Stud. Mediterranea 7, 1992   18 Idg. Chronik (section "Anatolisch") in: Die Sprache   19 V. SOUČEK, J. SIEGELOVÁ, Systematische Bibliogr. der Hethitologie 1915–1995 (HbdOr), 3 vols., 1996.   F.S.

Hittite law

A. SOURCES B. CIVIL AND CRIMINAL LAW C. THE COURT SYSTEM D. RELATIONS TO OTHER ORIENTAL LAWS

A. SOURCES

1. The so-called Hittite laws 2. The Anitta text 3. The autobiography of Ḫattušilis I. 4. The 'Political Testament' of Ḫattušilis I. 5. Royal decrees 6. Court records. 7. Royal letters 8. Funerary rituals 9. So-called

deeds of donation of land 10. The field texts 11. The charters for individual vassals 12. The state contracts.

B. CIVIL AND CRIMINAL LAW

A body of laws, for which the name 'Hittite Laws' has come into use, primarily provides information (however, the term 'law' should be used guardedly, since the nature of the Hittite body of laws is unclear). The prologue known from the Mesopotamian rulers Urnammu, Lipit-Eštar and Ḥammurapi, in which the rulers introduced themselves by name, is missing. The place of discovery of the 'Laws' is the archive of the royal castle of Ḥattusa, the capital city of the Ḥatti empire; this could indicate a basic order – written down by virtue of a royal directive – for the administration of justice by the royal court as the supreme court, i.e. a constitution. The text is extant in numerous variants that point to a review undertaken at unknown intervals involving an adjustment in line with changed circumstances. The reform attributed to king Telibinu (15th cent. BC) is significant, which is evident from the depiction of the 'former' and the 'current' – milder – legal position within the individual paragraphs.

The Hittite body of law has been passed down to us in numerous clay tablet fragments that are more or less completely extant and that the Hittite scribes already described as '"If a man" tablet' and '"If a vine" tablet', each containing around 100 paragraphs by modern counting methods. Their structure follows the 'if/then' pattern and corresponds to that of the Mesopotamian omina and legal regulations.

Apart from some inconsistencies, the system of the two tablets takes as its starting-point, the principle of progress from the valuable to the less valuable legally protected right. The two tablets contain regulations for agriculture, viticulture and cattle-raising as well as for trades. At the beginning of the first tablet provisions for the protection of individual persons against attacks on their physical integrity are listed. Further regulations indicate that the family was organized patriarchally but also show that the Hittite wife had a more important position in comparison with the rest of the ancient Orient. 'Fief right' regulations follow. About another 40 paragraphs regulate the protection of agricultural property against theft and material damage. The second tablet links up with the first in content, but also contains price lists and finally provisions regarding sexual offences that today are part of criminal law (incest, rape, sodomy). *Leges erraticae* (legal principles with a system we cannot understand) show that the legal rules are not homogeneous. Murder is not mentioned because its punishment was probably left to the kinship law. This is documented by § 49 of the Telibinu decree: the king does not intervene in matters of the 'master of the blood' (of the blood avenger). Violations of laws in the civil law area are punished not just through compensation for damages in the actual sense but also through fines (these should probably be placed within the area of civil criminal law). Sometimes they considerably exceed the scope of compensation for damages.

According to the legal rules capital punishment is only seldom imposed, namely in cases which have a religious impact (rebellion against a judgement of the royal court, theft of sacred objects, sexual offences). Outside the above-mentioned sources on legal regulations, capital punishment is imposed for offences against the purity regulations in relation to the king and therefore only on the staff of the palace. In some regions they are replaced by banishment regulations that are to be heeded by the 'master of the vantage point', the border commander.

To date no documents regarding legal transactions in civil law have been found. Perhaps not clay tablets, otherwise common in the ancient Orient, but transitory wood was used for their recording (wax tablets?); this could be supported by the professional term 'wood tablet scribe' passed down in individual texts.

C. THE COURT SYSTEM

Aside from the royal court there was a lower jurisdiction. Among the diverse administrative duties of the 'internally (incorporated) countries' the border commander (the 'master of the vantage point') was also responsible for jurisdiction. The 'elders' (probably a relic from the time of the Older Empire, when jurisdiction was in the hands of local committees) assisted him. Detailed (though according to today's standards incomplete) court records from the 16th cent. BC document the swearing-in of witnesses and the judgements of gods in the form of the ordeal by water. Court judgements are not extant. Whoever questioned a decision had to expect capital punishment, which was also directed against the family in the case of a challenge of the judgement of the royal court. The king could take charge of legal procedures himself and summon the judges: if they did not comply with the summons immediately, they were under threat of punishment by blinding.

D. RELATIONS TO OTHER ORIENTAL LAWS

Factors of Hittite law that are reminiscent of other legal orders of the time arise from belonging to the ancient Oriental cultural circle and cannot be overlooked. Differences can be seen in the relatively lenient judgement of violations of the law: thus, capital punishment is just as rare as mutilation. Taking matters into one's own hands is hardly existent and talion not at all. Compensation for damages and fines are foregrounded.
→ Ḥattusa II; → State contracts; → HITTITOLOGY

HISTORY OF LAW: V. KOROŠEC, Keilschriften: HdbOr, 1st. div., suppl. vol. III), 1964, 177–219.
HITTITE LAWS: J. FRIEDRICH, Die hethit. Gesetze, 1959 (ed. princeps; repr. 1971); R. HAASE, Texte zum hethit. Recht. Eine Auswahl, 1985; Id., Beobachtungen zur hethit. Rechtssatzung nebst einem bibliogr. Anhang, 1995; H. A. HOFFNER, The Laws of the Hittites, 1997.
PROCEDURAL, CONSTITUTIONAL AND ADMINISTRATIVE LAW: ; G. BECKMAN, Hittite Diplomatic Texts, 1995; I. ENGNELL, Studies in Divine Kingship in the Ancient Near East, 1967, 52ff.; H. G. GÜTERBOCK, Authority and Law in the Ancient Orient, in: Journ. of the American

Oriental Society 17, 1954, 16–24; A. HAGENBUCHNER, Die Korrespondenz der Hethiter, 1989; I. HOFFMANN, Der Erlaß Telibinus, 1984; J. KLÍMA, La preuve dans le droit hittite, in: Recueils de la société Jean Bodin 17, 1965, 89–102; K. K. RIEMSCHNEIDER, Die hethit. Landschenkungsurkunden, in: MIO 6, 1958, 321–381; E. VON SCHULER, Hethit. Königserlässe als Quellen der Rechtsfindung und ihr Verhältnis zum kodifizierten Recht, in: FS J. Friedrich, 1959, 435–472; J. SIGELOVÁ, Hethit. Verwaltungspraxis im Lichte der Wirtschafts- und Inventardokumente, 1986; VL. SOUŠEK, Die hethit. Feldertexte, in: Archiv orientální 27, 1959, 5–43, 371–395; F. STARKE, s.v. Labarna, RLA 6, 404–408; R. WERNER, Hethit. Gerichtsprotokolle, 1967.

BIBLIOGRAPHY: R. HAASE, Hethit. Recht, in: J. GILISSEN (ed.), Bibliograph. Einführung in die Rechtsgesch. und Rechtsethnologie, 1967 (ch. A/3).   RI.H.

Hittites see → Ḫattusa

Hittite successor states see → Asia Minor

Hoard finds
I. CELTO-GERMANIC AREA   II. ITALY

I. CELTO-GERMANIC AREA
In central Europe from the Byzantine period onwards, hoard finds (HF; storage, treasure, safe-keeping, mass, hidden finds, etc.) primarily of metal objects (copper, bronze, iron, precious metals) are an important archaeological group of finds. The diversity of terms reflects the breadth of the discussion of the importance of the HF. The various contexts of the finds, e.g. solid ground, moors, rivers, special places (rocks, crevices, caves, transport routes, etc.), as well as in particular the composition of the objects (→ Jewellery, weapons, tools, surplus from casting, → ingots, fragmentary materials, new or damaged pieces) – which are used to find out the reasons for the depositing of the HF – are considered to be indicators of their functions. Two areas are foregrounded in the discussion; first, 'secular' HF that were meant to be recovered (hoarding of valuables, household treasures, possessions of traders or artisans, raw materials etc.) and second, 'ritual' HF which were not meant to be recovered (votive offerings, → sacrifices, cult treasures or treasures of the dead, etc.).

The existence of HF is concentrated in particular periods and is diverse. In the early Bronze Age (1st half of the 2nd millennium BC) in southern central Europe there are in particular HF with typical ingot shapes made of copper or bronze (ring ingots and bar ingots), whilst in the north there are more tools and jewellery in the HF. In the late Bronze Age (12th–8th cents. BC) initially scrap ore HF are common and then weapons (Armour, → Helmets etc.) and other prestige objects from rivers and moors and, especially in northern central Europe, bronze and gold vessels (Eberswalde). In the younger Celtic Iron Age (3rd–1st cents. BC) iron HF (weapons and devices as well as various ingot shapes)

and gold finds with coins and neck bands (→ Torques) are predominant. In the Imperial period (1st–4th cents. AD) in Germania there are numerous coin HF (hoards of valuables), as well as splendid Roman silver vessel HF (e.g. → Hildesheim silver hoard) and in particular HF from wells and moors (→ Thorsberg Moor), in which weapons, tools, etc. predominate. For the Middle Ages the most important HF are the cut silver finds in eastern and northern Europe whose function is more akin to that of money.

→ Celtic archaeology;   → Coins;   → Crafts;   → Cult; → Germanic archaeology; → Gold

H. GEISLINGER s.v. Depotfund, H., RGA 5, 320–338; A. and B. HÄNSEL (ed.), Gaben an die Götter – Schätze der Brz. Europas, 1997; S. HANSEN, Stud. zu den Metalldeponierungen während der älteren Urnenfelderzeit zwischen Rhône und Karpatenbecken, 1994; G. KURZ, Kelt. H.- und Gewässerfunde in Mitteleuropa, 1995; F. STEIN, Brz. H. in Süddeutschland, 1976; Id., Kat. der vorgesch. H. in Süddeutschland, 1979.   V.P.

II. ITALY
In Italy HF are attested from the Bronze Age onwards (e.g. on Lipari). Only very few of them should be regarded as deposits created in emergency situations, as in the case of enemy attacks or in cultic contexts. Rather, HF appear to be connected with the trading routes of copper ore and later of iron ore. This is vividly expressed by the term 'Road of the HF' (*via dei ripostigli*) which, with its collections of axes and 'bronze moulds', during the Bronze Age linked the rich ore deposits in the Colline Metallifere in Tuscany with the coast near Vulci (→ Volcae). In the subsequent period this link was extended to the ore deposits in the → Tolfa Mountains in present-day Latium and particularly to Elba (→ Ilva) (Proto-Villanova culture with quality metal vessels). These HF are mostly located close to the ancient roads outside the settlements and in their composition rather suggest a depositing of the goods for some time by traders or artisans along their trading routes (important finding-places: Ardea, Coste del Marano, Goluzzo, Piano di Tallone, Santa Marinella). The chronological framework includes the Iron-Bronze Age and the beginning of the Iron Age (11th–8th cents. BC) in the area of the → Villanova culture. The HF of San Francesco in Bologna occupies a special position. It comprises c. 14,800 bronzes that were placed together in a → pithos, among them are cut fragments, semifinished products, finished weapons, tools and traditional costume objects that, on the basis of their different dating (11th–7th cents. BC), can be regarded as provision stores of a bronze workshop within a settlement.

→ Etrusci, Etruria (with maps)

M. A. FUGAZZOLA DELPINO, Ripostigli "protovillanoviani" dell'Italia peninsulare, in: A. RADMILLI (ed.), Popoli e civiltà dell'Italia antica 4, 1975, 43–49, 57–60 M. CRISTOFANI, Economia e società, in: G. PUGLIESE CARRATELLI (ed.), Rasenna, 1986, 79–156, esp. 80–88 G. BARTOLONI, La cultura villanoviana, 1989.   C.KO.

Hochdorf Close to the south-west German town of Eberdingen-H., a levelled large grave mound was excavated in 1978–1979 that proved to be one of the few unrobbed Celtic → princely graves of the late → Hallstatt culture (2nd half of the 6th cent. BC) investigated in modern times. The hill was surrounded by a stone ring with a diameter of 57 m and originally had a height of c. 6 m. In the north there was a ramp-like access that led to the 2 m deep, central tomb chamber.

The chamber consisted of a double-walled block construction made of oak beams that was covered with c. 50 tons of pieces of rock. In the quadratic 4.7 × 4.7 tomb chamber an unusually tall (1.87 m) and powerful 40–50 year old man was buried with extremely rich, royal provisions. He lay with his personal belongings (birch bark hat, golden neck ring torques, golden arm band, belt, golden fibulas, dagger, quiver with arrows, toiletry items, clothing, etc.) on a large bronze settee similar to a sofa (*kline*). For the burial some of his equipment had been specially plated with gold (dagger, shoes, etc.). The 2.75 m long *kline*, worked richly in the local manner, decorated and moveable on anthropomorphic legs, is still unique.

The importance of the dead man is also confirmed by the burial offering of a four-wheeled wagon richly fitted with iron with a double-yoke harness as well as a considerable number of drinking and eating vessels. Nine horn-shaped drinking vessels and nine bronze plates were placed in the grave, in addition three bronze bowls and a large bronze pot (500 l) with three lion figures on it; in it were a gold plate dish and remains of a drink similar to → mead. The pot is a Magna Graecian import on which, however, a lion figure was finished locally. Hohenasperg, which is c. 10 km away, is under consideration as a princely seat pertaining to it.

→ Funerary architecture; → Glauberg; → Gold; → Heuneburg; → Hirschlanden; → Kline

J. BIEL, Ein Fürstengrabhügel der späten Hallstattzeit bei Eberdingen-H., in: Germania 60, 1982, 61–104 D. PLANCK (red.), Der Keltenfürst von H., 1985, 31–161. V.P.

Hodegon style Greek script of the 14th and first half of the 15th cent., named for the Hodegon monastery in Constantinople, a cursive, calligraphic, archaizing minuscule (→ Archaic script) with pronounced letter structure, relatively large body, a balanced contrast between large and small letters and some angular forms; the curved strokes occasionally are split at the ends. Usually, manuscripts produced in the Hodegon monastery are written on → parchment with a splendid layout. They were often written for the emperor and other important persons. This style was not just used in the East for liturgical and theological manuscripts but also in the West by important Renaissance copyists, even for profane authors up to the first half of the 17th cent. (cf. → Humanist script).

L. POLITIS, Eine Schreiberschule im Kloster τῶν Ὁδηγῶν, in: ByzZ 51, 1958, 17–36, 261–287; Id., Nouvelles données sur Joasaph, copiste du monastère des Hodèges, in: Illinois Classical Studies 7, 1982, 299–322. P. E.

Hodometron (ὁδόμετρον; *hodómetron*). Hero (Dioptra 34) and Vitruvius (10,9) describe a mechanical device for distance measurement on land in which a connection of endless screws and sprockets mounted on different levels, driven by a cart wheel, transmits each rotation of the wheel to a display system in a retarding manner (Hero: pointer; Vitruvius: falling balls). The *hodometron* was sufficient for one day trip and then had to be put back to the initial position. Vitruvius knew of a corresponding device for sea trips based on a bucket wheel.

A. G. DRACHMANN, The Mechanical Technology of Greek and Roman Antiquity, 1963, 157ff. E.O.

Hodopoioi (ὁδοποιοί; *hodopoioí*). The *hodopoioi* ('road masters') in Athens in the 4th cent. BC were an authority made up of 5 persons (perhaps appointed from phyles grouped as pairs) who were in charge of public slaves to keep the roads in a good condition ([Aristot.] Ath. Pol. 54,1). The assertion of Aeschines (Ctes. 25) that in the time of → Eubulus [1] the administrators of the *theorika* were *hodopoioí* can only mean that these officials supervised the *hodopoioi* or supplied them with the means but not that the authority had been abolished [2. 237f.].

1 BUSOLT/SWOBODA 2, 116 2 P. J. RHODES, The Athenian Boule, 1972. P.J.R.

Hoe Although grain was grown as usual through plough cultivation, hoeing made up a considerable part of the entire year's work (Columella 2,11; 2,12,1ff.); it was often the duty of chained slaves (*servi vincti*) and, in grain cultivation, was carried out in winter and for a second time in spring. The hoe was used here for various functions: instead of the plough it was utilized for breaking up the soil (κατεργασία/*katergasía*, *subigere*) in the garden, in fruit and wine cultivation, in fields close to towns, in tilling the fields of small farmers ('poor man's plough'; cf. re Apulia Varro, Rust. 1,29,2) or in the mountains. With the hoe, however, only small areas could be worked. In addition fertilizer or seeds were worked into the soil with the hoe. A further important task of the hoe was the production of fine topsoil particularly by breaking up the soil after ploughing (*occare*, → Harrow) and by loosening the earth (*sarire*). The hoe was also used to eliminate weeds (*purgare*, *runcare*).

For working the soil, a heavy hoe with a broad blade and long handle (μάκελλα/*mákella*, *ligo*, cf. Columella 2,15,5; a lighter form: *marra*, Columella 10,89) was used. For breaking up and turning the soil, and for clearing roots, the *dolabra*, a heavy, two-sided cross hoe or pickaxe hoe was used (Columella 2,2,28; already attested in Minoan times). There were also types of hoe that were suitable for various functions. The hoe with a smaller pointed blade (*sarculum*: Columella 2,11,1; 2,15,2; 2,17,4) was also utilized instead of the plough in the mountains (Plin. HN 18,178: *montanae gentes sarculis arant*) and for loosening the soil as well as for combating weeds in the field and garden (Plin. HN 18,241: *sarculo levi purgare*). The hoe with two prongs (δίκελλα/*díkella*, *bidens*) was used for the *subactio* in the vineyard (Columella 3,13,3; 4,5,1) and also for *pulveratio* and *ablaqueatio*; in addition the iron rake with several prongs was known (*rastrum*: Plin. HN 18,180). Today's double-sided, light garden hoe (with two prongs) is attested since late antiquity (perhaps under the term *ascia*).

→ Harrow

1 M.-C. AMOURETTI, Le pain et l'huile dans la Grèce antique, 1986, 93–100   2 G. COMET, Le paysan et son outil, 1992, 118–137   3 W. GAITZSCH, Werkzeug und Handwerk in Pompeji, in: AW 14, 1983, 3, 3–11   4 W. SCHIERING, Landwirtschaftliche Geräte, in: ArchHom 2, 1990, H 152–154   5 K. D. WHITE, Agricultural Implements of the Roman World, 1967, 36–68.   E.C.

Hoenius
[1] T.H. Severus. *Cos. ord.* in AD 141, possibly came from Umbria (PIR² H 189); perhaps related by blood to → Iuventius Celsus, *cos. II* in 129.

M. GAGGIOTTI, L. SENSI, in: EOS 2,237.

[2] T.H. Severus. Son of H. [1]. Patrician, *cos. suff.* in AD 170. PIR² H 190.   W.E.

Höyük also Hüyük. Turkish for hill, mostly used for old settlement sites that have been built up in a mound-like manner and, similar to Arabic → tell, a component in the name of many ruin sites.   H. J. N.

Hollow measures see → Measures of volume

Holofernes One of the most important characters in the book of → Judith, an apocryphal Jewish text that was probably written in the Maccabaean period and whose content is not considered historically certain. H., commander of → Nebucadnezzar, considers annihilating the Jews during a punitive expedition. This plan is thwarted by Judith (Hebrew 'Jewess') as she wins H.'s confidence, dines with him and then beheads him.

This main narrative strand in the book of Judith was taken up again on many occasions, for example in parallel tales in Midrash literature.

S. DUBNOW, Weltgesch. des jüdischen Volkes 2, 1925, 208f.; E. HAAG, Studien zum Buche Judith: seine theologische Bed. und lit. Eigenart, 1963; E. ZENGER, Das Buch Judit: histor. und legendarische Erzählungen, 1981.   Y.D.

Homarion (Ὁμάριον/*Homárion*, Ἁμάριον/*Hamárion*). Sanctuary of Zeus near Helice (Pol. 5,93,10 and Str. 8,7,3; 7,5; Syll.³ 490, [1]), centre of the Achaean League, after the destruction of Helice (373 BC) in the possession of Aegium. Its location cannot be pinpointed in spite of several finds of inscriptions north-west of Aegium [2; 3; 4; 5. 191–193]. Not to be confused with Homagyrion in Paus. 7,24,2. But cf. the Achaean sanctuary of Zeus Homarios in lower Italy (Pol. 2,39,6) [6].

1 A. AYMARD, Le Zeus fédéral achaien Hamarios-Homarios, in: Mélanges Navarre, 1935, 453–470   2 P. ASTRÖM, Ἁ βουλὰ τῶν Ἀχαιῶν. Une inscription d'Aigion, in: OpAth 2, 1955 (1956), 4–9   3 J. BINGEN, Inscriptions du Péloponnèse, in: BCH 77, 1953, 616–628   4 Id., Inscriptions d'Achaie, in: BCH 78, 1954, 402–407   5 A. STAVROPOULOS, Ἱστορία τῆς πόλεως Αἰγίου, 1954   6 M. OSANNA, Sull'ubicazione del santuario di Zeus Homarios in Magna Grecia, in: Dialoghi di archeologia 7, 1989, 55–63.

Y.L.

Homer see → Homerus

Homeric cups see → Relief ware

Homeric Hymns
I. GENRE AND PRESENTATION   II. CONTENT III. FUNCTION AND EFFECT

I. GENRE AND PRESENTATION
The term Homeric Hymns (HH) refers to thirty-three poems in dactylic hexameters, which have been preserved together with the hymns of → Callimachus [3], the Orphic hymns (→ Orphism), and the hymns of → Proclus [2], and are addressed to single Olympic deities or to a group of Olympic deities acting as a unity (text: [1; 2; 4; 8]). The length of the hymns addressed to → Apollo (H. Hom. 3), → Hermes (H. Hom. 4) and → Aphrodite (H. Hom. 6) is comparable to that of an individual book of Homer (*c.* 300–500 verses; → Homer [1]), the others are shorter, sometimes considerably so (e.g. H. Hom. 6 to Aphrodite: 21 verses; H. Hom. 7 to Dionysus: 59; H. Hom. 19 to Pan: 49). H. Hom. 2 to Demeter, which was discovered in 1777 in a Moscow stable, and significant fragments of an otherwise lost H. Hom. 1 to Dionysus, which was re-attributed by [7], have also survived.

Thucydides (3,104,4) quotes some preserved verses from the Apollo hymn (H. Hom. 3), a proem (*prooímion*) to Apollo. Also, the almost uniform formula at the end of the hymns (αὐτὰρ ἐγὼ καὶ σεῖο καὶ ἄλλης μνήσομ' ἀοιδῆς/'now I will think of you and another song') indicates that the hymns functioned as preludes to epic recitation by → rhapsodes at musical competitions [23. 22] and other festivals [10. 11] (cf. → Competitions, artistic; → Festivals; Feasts). Pind. Nem. 2,1–5 mentions the rhapsodes' custom of naming Zeus at the beginning of their performance during musical competitions at the Zeus sanctuary of Nemea [2] (→ Nemea [3]). Thus, the epics of → Hesiodus and (originally probably) of → Homerus [1] (cf. Lex Vindobonense 273 NAUCK; [19]) were preceded by hexametric invocations of the gods. Ps.-Plut. De musica 6,1133c summarizes the practice of the citharodes:

'After the worship of the gods (πρὸς τοὺς θεοὺς ἀφοσιω-σάμενοι), they (sc. the citharodes) turned immediately to the works of Homer and others'. [28] envisions two basic types of HH: one is short and used as a prelude in an informal presentation of heroic poetry, e.g. at → banquets, while the other is a longer, independent hymn, which could be a precursor – but is similar to the rhapsodies in competitive singing of Homer's → epic cycle. Of special interest is the record of a hexametric Apollo hymn with musical score from Epidaurus [26; 32].

It is not possible to distinguish with certainty between recited rhapsody and sung citharodic proem [10].

II. CONTENT

The HH reflect the tripartite structure also found in other hymns to the gods consisting of invocation, worship and prayer, with the central part of the longer HH being elaborated in conformity with the narrative rhapsodic genre [16]. The Apollo hymn (H. Hom. 3) covers the two major events in the god's history: his splendid birth on Delos – a topic that is repeatedly picked up by later Apollonian poetry (the Delphic paeans for Apollo with musical accompaniment) – and his triumphal entry into Delphi; this hymn consequently links → Apollo's [11] two major sites of action. The Demeter hymn (H. Hom. 2) describes the abduction of → Persephone/Kore by → Hades and the subsequent strike of her mother → Demeter, who no longer makes the crops ripen. Only after an annually recurring, limited liberation of her daughter from the realm of shadows has been arranged does Demeter initiate humanity into her rites (ὄργια/órgia) and end the famine [5. 21]. This tale, despite some discrepancies ([12], cf. [13]), is considered the founding myth of the → mystéria of → Eleusis, which were the largest Panhellenic cult of Athens. The Hermes hymn (H. Hom. 4) tells the story of → Hermes' birth, his invention of the lyre and theft of the cattle of his big brother Apollo. The humour and the jokes in this tale represent two attributes of the god Hermes. The Aphrodite hymn (H. Hom. 6) describes the subjugation of → Aphrodite by Zeus: she, like the other gods, must endure the hardships of a sexual union with a human. Zeus forces Aphrodite to bear the child of → Anchises with the telling name → Aeneas [1] (Torment) near Troy. The major HH outline the allocation of the spheres of action of individual Olympic gods since Zeus assumed power, which subsequently become canonical [27]. The extended narrative sequence of the long HH and the typical third-person style of the veneration [22] differentiate the rhapsodic hymns at a fundamental level from the lyric hymns, which are characterized by a second-person style and short narrative passages.

III. FUNCTION AND EFFECT

As a prelude to epic recitation, the longer HH are attributable to the flowering of Homeric rhapsody (7th –5th cent. BC). While Thucydides still ascribes the Apollo hymn to Homer, this authorship was already doubted in antiquity (Ath. 22b: 'Homer or one of the Homerids'; schol. Nic. Alexipharmaka 130: 'in the hymns attributed to Homer'). The study of linguistic characteristics (e.g. the disappearance of the → digamma) has provided sophisticated proof of a sub-epic diction [18. 4]. The original performance of the Apollo hymn may have been a celebration staged by the Samian ruler Polycrates [1] 522 BC (Pýthia and Délia) [4]. The Demeter hymn (Hom. h. 2; cf. v. 270 f.) can be readily linked with the construction of the → telestérion of Eleusis at the time of Solon [1] (early 6th cent. BC) [5]. The Aphrodite hymn (H. Hom. 5) has been linked (though this has been challenged) with the clan of the Aeneadae who settled in the Troas ([24], cf. [19]). Therefore, this hymn could be considered as part of an archaic aristocratic → court poetry. At least one hymn to → Ares (H. Hom. 8) can be dated from its astrological content to the 5th cent. AD [30].

The HH occupy a central position in the genre of epic Greek sacred poetry. → Orpheus, → Musaeus, → Pamphus and → Olen were considered legendary precursors. Callimachus [3], with his five literary and learned hymns, the later Orphic hymns (→ Orphism II. C.), and, in the 5th cent. AD, the philosophical and religious hymns of → Proclus [2] build on the model of the HH.

→ Agon; → Competitions, artistic ; → Homerus [1]; → Hymn I.; → Rhapsodes; → Hymn

1 T. W. ALLEN et al. (ed.), The Homeric Hymns, 1936 (with commentary)   2 F. CÁSSOLA (ed.), Inni Omerici, 1975 (with Italian transl.)   3 H. P. FOLEY, The Homeric Hymn to Demeter. Translation, Commentary and Interpretive Essays, 1994 (with Engl. transl. and commentary) 4 A. GEMOLL (ed.), Die Homerische Hymne, 1886 (with commentary)   5 N. J. RICHARDSON (ed.), The Homeric Hymn to Demeter, 1974 (with commentary) 6 A. WEIHER (ed.), H. H., 1986 (with German transl.) 7 M. L. WEST (ed.), The Fragmentary Homeric Hymn to Dionysos, in: ZPE 134, 2001, 1–11   8 G. ZANETTO (ed.), Inni Omerici, 1996 (Italian transl.) 9 A. ALONI, Prooimia, Hymnoi, Elio Aristide e i cugini bastardi, in: Quaderni Urbinati N. S. 4, 1980, 23–40   10 R. BÖHME, Das Prooimion. Eine Form sakraler Dichtung der Griechen, thesis Heidelberg 1937   11 W. BURKERT, Kynaithos, Polycrates and the Homeric Hymn to Apollo, in: G. W. BOWERSOCK et al. (ed.), Arktouros. FS B. M. W. Knox, 1979, 53–62 12 K. CLINTON, The Author of the Homeric Hymn to Demeter, in: Opuscula Atheniensia 16, 1986, 43–50 13 Id., Myth and Cult: The Iconography of the Eleusinian Mysteries, 1992   14 J. DANIELEWICZ, Hymni homerici minores quanam parte conscripti sint, in: Symbolae philologorum Posnanensium 1, 1973, 7–17   15 H. P. FOLEY, 1994 (see above [3])   16 D. FRÖHDER, Die dichterische Form der Homerischen Hymne untersucht am Typus der mittelgroßen Preislieder, 1994   17 A. HOEKSTRA, The Sub-Epic Stage of the Formulaic Tradition. Studies in the Homeric Hymns to Apollo, to Aphrodite and to Demeter, 1969   18 R. JANKO, Homer, Hesiod and the Hymns: Diachronic Development in Epic Diction, 1982   19 F. OSANN (ed.), Philemonis Grammatici qui supersunt: accedunt nonnulla Graeca..., 1821   20 R. PARKER, The Hymn to

Demeter and the Homeric Hymns, in: G&R 38, 1991, 1–17 21 C. PENGLASE, Greek Myths and Mesopotamia. Parallels and Influence in the Homeric Hymns and Hesiod, 1994 22 W. H. RACE, Style and Rhetoric in Pindar's Odes, 1990, ch. 4 23 R. VON SCHELIHA, Vom Wettkampf der Dichter. Der musische Agon bei den Griechen, 1987 24 P. M. SMITH, Nursling of Mortality. A Study of the Homeric Hymn to Aphrodite (Studien zur klass. Philol. 3), 1981 25 Id., Aineiadai as Patrons of Iliad XX and of the Homeric Hymn to Aphrodite, in: HSPh 85, 1981, 17–58 26 J. SOLOMON, The New Musical Fragment from Epidaurus, in: JHS 105, 1985, 168–171 27 J. STRAUSS CLAY, The Politics of Olympus. Form and Meaning in the Major Homeric Hymns, 1989 28 Id., The Homeric Hymns, in: I. MORRIS, B. POWELL (ed.), A New Companion to Homer, 1997, 489–507 29 M. H. VAN DER VALK, On the Arrangement of the Homeric Hymns, in: L'Antiquité Classique 45, 1976, 420–445 30 M. L. WEST, The Eighth Homeric Hymn and Proclus, in: CQ 64, 1970, 300–304 31 Id. (ed.), 2001 (s.o. [7]) 32 Id., The Singing of Hexameters: Evidence from Epidaurus, in: ZPE 63, 1986, 39–46.   W. D. F.

Homeric language

A. ARCHAIC CHARACTER B. DIALECTS C. LANGUAGE AND VERSE D. HETEROGENEITY E. TRADITION AND INFLUENCE

A. ARCHAIC CHARACTER

Because of the great age of the *Iliad* and *Odyssey*, Homeric language (HL) contains archaicisms that disappeared in an early stage in Greek and in later texts are attested usually only on the basis of imitation of Homer (see below E.): in the noun the instr. in -φι (ἶφι, ναῦφι; otherwise only in Mycenaean), Ζῆν' (accusative) 'Zeus' (in the verse end before a vowel) = Old Indian *dyā́m*, the suffix of ἀνδρο-μέος; in the verb, additional root presents (ἔδ-μεναι, στεῦ-ται) and aorists (ἔ-κτα-το, ὦρ-το), *nā* presents (δάμ-νη-μι), short-vowelled subjunctive (ἐρεί-ο-μεν, δαμάσσ-ε-ται), freer tmesis (ἄπο λοιγὸν ἀμῦναι, λίπω κάτα), unaugmented preterite forms (φέρε, ἴδεν; μὴ ἔνθεο as an injunctive). Older phonology is clearly evident in ἀέκων, φιλέει, νόος (Attic contracts ἄκων, φιλεῖ, νοῦς; φ. and ν. also in HL, see below D.). However, other such phonological phenomena have undergone changes in the pre-Homeric period and can only be detected in interruptions to the metre: θυγατέρα ἥν (⌣⌣⌣-?-) with position-making ἥν < *suā́m, ἀνδροτῆτα (-?⌣⌣⌣) obviously with ἀνδρο- < *anṛ-. The traces of the → 'digamma' in Homer also pertain here: κατὰ ἄστυ instead of older κατὰ Ϝάστυ.

The numerous epithets, some of which have semantically faded (ἀγέρωχος, ἀμιχθαλόεις, ἀτρύγετος, μέροψ, νῶροψ), as well as the formulaic but to some extent modifiable verse groups, verses and verse parts also point to preliminary phases in epic and indeed in oral poetry. Several constructions can be traced back to → Indo-European poetic language.

B. DIALECTS

HL cannot be classified as belonging to any clearly defined Greek dialect area. What is certain is a strong → Ionic component, particularly because of η < ā̆ also after e / i / r (νεηνίης, πρῆξις) and because of εω < ā̆ŏ (Πηλείδεω, πυλέων). Other manifestations, however, are not in keeping with the Ionic known to us; their classification and explanation is to some extent still controversial. Obviously HL contains characteristics from older Aeolian literature, e.g. πίσυρες with π- < *kʷ- (→ Gutturals), ἐρεβεννή with -εvv- < *-esn-, ἤμβροτε 'missed' with -ρο > *-ṛ-, genitive in -οιο such as ἠελίοιο, dative in -εσσι such as νήεσσι. The four last forms certainly show at the same time an Ionian η, and so are mixed forms adapted to Ionic.

Apart from Ionic and Aeolic, additional dialects have probably also contributed to HL.

C. LANGUAGE AND VERSE

It is no coincidence that certain forms that can hardly be fitted into the dactylic hexameter are absent from HL (κτημάτων ---); others have been artificially reshaped to suit the metre. The → metrical lengthening of a short vowel, visible in οὔνομα = ὄνομα, not visible in ἀνέρα (ā-), is merely an phonological device. Not always separated from this in scholarship is the analogical reshaping in favour of a long syllable (ἠνεμόεσσα from ἀνεμόεσσα, perhaps after ποδ-ήνεμος); purely metrical liberties like the filling of an arsis by a short final syllable (ἦλθες --? before vocative) must also be distinguished from this. A further device of HL is the elimination of a syllable within a word through synizesis: βουλέων (---) > βουλέων (--).

The artificial sounds αα, οω in ὁράασθαι, ὁρόων have a different genesis; they too show that HL has preliminary phases. In the verse there was initially regular ὁράεσθαι (⌣⌣⌣⌣⌣), ὁράων (⌣--). After contraction it was pronounced ὁρᾶσθαι, ὁρῶν. Through 'epic lengthening' (διέκτασις) of ā ω, the original syllable sequence requested for the verse was restored. The conversion of the accusative εὐρύοπα before Ζῆν' (see above A.) into an indeclinable so that it could occur in the same verse position also before Ζεῦ (vocative) or Ζεύς (nominative) would also appear to be artificial.

D. HETEROGENEITY

To sum up, HL has a relatively long prehistory, it bears traces of different times, different dialects and different poets who had a formative influence. As a result, it contains older and younger characteristics, Aeolic alongside Ionic elements, artificial and personal aspects as well as common elements. Thus, Homer had at his disposal synonymous forms with a varying sound structure whose different technique of application was welcome to him for use in the hexameter, e.g. for 'arose', archaic ὦρτο and younger ὤρετο with a different number of syllables, for 'four', Aeolic πίσυρες (⌣-- before a consonant) and Ionic τέσσαρες (-⌣⌣), for 'to see', the artificial ὁράασθαι (---=) and ὁρᾶσθαι (⌣--=) from ordinary language. Aeolic αἰ and Ionic εἰ 'if' are, for example, at least prosodically equivalent; in relation to plain-language ἄνδρα, ἀνέρα is on the one hand archaic (-ε-) and on the other hand artificial (ā-); artificial ὁράασθαι too is structurally older than ὁρᾶσθαι (see above C.). In view of these complicated circumstances, the determination of many an alternation in HL is understandably still a matter of contention (ὀμόσσαι / ὀμόσαι).

Scattered throughout Homeric works are conspicuous, mostly younger, singularities: μον-ωθείς (Il. 11,470); τέμ-νειν (Od. 3,175); νοῦς (Od. 10,240); ποντοπορ-ούσ-ης (Od. 11,11); Ὀδυσεύς (Gen.) (Od. 24,398) against the common: μουν-, ταμ-, νόος, -ευσ-, Ὀδυσ(σ)ῆος. Similarly strange and singular is e.g. βούλεται (subjunctive) (Il. 1,67).

E. TRADITION AND INFLUENCE
HL has been carefully passed down to us in the *Iliad* in particular. Even in small linguistic details not protected by the metre, the state of the tradition is usually uniform; e.g. the augment is written in δ'ἔκλυε (Il. 1,43) or ἐπέπλεον (Il. 1,312) where also unaugmented forms could have been used (*δὲ κλύε even with identical letters), as against unaugmented γε φάμεν (Il. 23,440). At the end of the verse, for example, -εν -ιν and -ε -ι alternate regularly depending on the subsequent sound; cf. also the firmly attested unique τέμνειν (see above D.). However, it is uncertain since when the text has had this traditional form. As accent particularities also belong to it, e.g. ἔνθά κεν, we can assume precise oral tradition of HL. We should therefore be cautious with regard to all earlier attempts to make HL even more ancient, e.g. through the introduction of γιγνώσκω for γῖν- or even of κατὰ Ϝάστυ for κατὰ ἄστυ. The final version of Homer can be credited with relatively young sounds like γίνωσκω (see end of section D. above) as well, and the 'digamma' Ϝ cannot be restored in many places for metrical reasons, and so probably no longer belonged to the final version.

HL was dominant in the Greek epic until late antiquity. From the outset it also influenced the remainder of Greek poetry, particularly the hexametric (elegy, epigram), but also lyric poetry and tragedy, and even to some extent prose: in the text of Herodotus there are even forms with metrical lengthening like οὔνομα. Furthermore HL influenced Latin from Ennius and through translations also modern languages: modern German *geflügelte Worte* can be traced back to Homeric ἔπεα πτερόεντα.

→ Aeolic (Lesbian); → Digamma; → Greek dialects; → Greek literary languages; → Indo-European poetic language; → Ionic; → Prosody

P. CHANTRAINE, Grammaire homérique vol. 1, ³1958, vol. 2, 1953; H. EBELING, Lex. Homericum, 1880–1885; B. FORSSMAN, Schichten in der homer. Sprache, in: J. LATACZ (ed.), Zweihundert Jahre Homerforschung (CollRau 2), 1991, 259–288 (with bibliography); A. GEHRING, Index Homericus, ²1970; J.P. HOLOKA, Homer, Oral Poetry Theory, in: J. LATACZ, see above, 456–481 (with bibliography); J. LA ROCHE, Die homer. Textkritik im Alterthum, 1866; LFE; J.R. TEBBEN, Concordantia Homerica, 1994ff.; J. UNTERMANN, Einf. in die Sprache Homers, 1987.   B.F.

Homeric philology see → Philology

Homeridai (Ὁμηρίδαι; *Homērídai*). Special group of → rhapsodes (first mentioned in Pind. Nem. 2,1, *c.* 485/480 BC) that is said, according to late sources (schol. ad loc. Harpocration s.v., among others), to have traced itself back biologically directly to → Homer [1] in the first generation and after that was considered to be the 'administrator of the legacy' of the Homeric epics. Located in: Chios; best-known representative: Cynaethus. Homeric associations by this name (admirers rather than rhapsodes: Pl. Ion 530d; Pl. Resp. 599e) are attested until the Hellenistic period [1. 87⁶].

1 SCHMID/STÄHLIN I 1, 157f.   2 H.T. WADE-GERY, The Poet of the Iliad, 1952, 19–21   3 W. BURKERT, Die Leistung eines Kreophylos, in: MH 29, 1972, 74–85   4 M. HASLAM, in: I. MORRIS, B. POWELL (ed.), A New Companion to Homer, 1997, 81.   J.L.

Homeritae see → Ḥimyar

Homerus
[1] Homer (Ὅμηρος/*Hómēros*, Lat. *Homērus*, French *Homère*, German *Homer*).

I. SHORT DEFINITION   II. PERSON, HOME, TIME, MILIEU OF ORIGIN   III. WORKS   IV. MATERIAL, LANGUAGE AND VERSE   V. ORALITY AND LITERACY   VI. TRADITION

I. SHORT DEFINITION
Homer is the first poet of the European cultural area of whom works of a major scope are completely extant (around 28,000 hexametric lines in the Greek language), which have been received continuously in all parts of the world influenced by European culture since they were composed *c.* 2,700 years ago and which have exerted evident as well as covert influence on cultural development until the present time [11; 39; 17. 274].

II. PERSON, HOME, TIME, MILIEU OF ORIGIN
A. IDENTITY AND NAME OF THE AUTHOR   B. HOME
C. TIME   D. MILIEU OF ORIGIN

A. IDENTITY AND NAME OF THE AUTHOR
As the genuine oeuvre (i.e. at least the *Iliad*, possibly also the *Odyssey*) was composed at a time (around 700 BC) that had only known writing (→ Alphabet) for a few decades and had not yet developed any textuality (hence also no documents, etc.) [18. ch. 1], we cannot count on contemporary information on the person of the author. The textuality probably first set in motion through the work of Homer [18. 26–29] attempted to fill this gap in information later through reconstruction;

the earliest phases of these attempts of reconstruction have been lost; we only have the final products that all date from the end of the Hellenistic and from the Roman Imperial periods, i.e. they are separated from the author by about 700 years and therefore cannot claim any authenticity: seven descriptions of his life (βίοι/*bíoi, vitae*) and one → 'contest between Homer and Hesiod' (*Certamen Homeri et Hesiodi*). Careful linguistic and content analyses of these narratives [38; 30; 33; 12; 34] compiled by WILAMOWITZ [1] have suggested that some of its key informations may go back to the 7th cent. (source: → Homeridai and → rhapsodes?): the Ionian name Ὅμηρος (*Hómēros*, attested for the first time indirectly and not with certainty in → Callinus test. 10 GENTILI-PRATO, around 650 BC, then with certainty in Xenophan. 21 B 10 and B 11,1 DK and Heraclitus 22 B 42, 56, 105 DK, both about the 2nd half of the 6th cent. BC, and in Sim. 564,4 PMG, around 500) is a common noun (used here as a personal name) (for the etymology: [7. s.v.]) which means 'guarantor', 'pledge' (e.g. Hdt. 8,94,3); the Aeolic form Ὅμαρος (*Hómāros*) is also attested in inscriptions as a man's name ([38. 372; 7. s.v.]; typologically similar names are *Próxeinos, Prýtanis, Synhístōr* etc., see [4. 513ff.]); the suspicion that the name could be a mere collective term for members of a singers' guild (as already in CURTIUS 1855 [8]; recently WEST [36. 217⁴³]) has no basis to date; it would be pointless to exchange the traditional name of the author, H., for another name (or even none at all) [5. 447].

B. HOME

The Ionic form of the name, the basic dialect (Ionic), as well as the extensive agreement in the biographical narrative information that the home of the author was Ionia (of the numerous towns that could have been Homer's birth-place – and later placed among the seven of them – most are Ionian), point to Ionia in Asia Minor as the country of origin of the author [38. 372; 18. 33f.]; other suggested regions – Oropus: [24]; Euboea: [25. 31] – have little evidence to support them because culture there was far less wide-spread. Nothing useful has been passed down to us concerning his genealogy.

C. TIME

Wide-ranging comparisons between the fundamental level of the cultural and social status reflected in the *Iliad* and the *Odyssey* with the individual phases of early Greek history reconstructed from modern archaeological, linguistic and historical knowledge suggest the 2nd half of the 8th cent. BC as the time when the author lived and created his works [29; 21. esp. 693; 13; 18. 74–90; 26. esp. 625]. Downward datings, primarily to the 7th cent. [6; 36] that argue their case on the basis of individual passages and certain objects have not asserted their position to date [25. 3f.].

D. MILIEU OF ORIGIN

The author is on such a high level from the point of view of thought, language, aesthetics, values and ethics, emotion and taste, and reflects so dominantly and at the same time so affirmatively the world view of an upper class that he must be placed on the highest rank of the hierarchy of singer-poets devised by BOWRA [5. 444–468] on the basis of a comparison between oral poetry from all peoples and times: As an → *aoidos* he probably either belonged to the nobility himself – like Achilles in Il. 9,186–188 – or lived constantly in their circles [18. 43–47].

III. WORKS

A. WORKS ATTRIBUTED TO HIM B. GENUINE WORKS 1. ILIAD 2. ODYSSEY

A. WORKS ATTRIBUTED TO HIM

Throughout antiquity the *Iliad* and the *Odyssey* were considered as genuine (for the already ancient hypothesis that only the *Iliad* was written by Homer see → Chorizontes). Numerous further works (some of which are also still available to us, with an asterisk in the catalogue below) were also transmitted in the name of H., but the Homeric philologists of antiquity already disputed his authorship fully or partly. In the → Suda lexicon of late antiquity the following are listed as 'attributed to him': → *Amazónia*, → *Iliás parva*, → *Nóstoi*, *Epikichlídes, Ethiépaktos* or *Íamboi* (unclear what is meant), *Batrachomachía* (meant: the → **Batrachomyomachía*), *Arachnomachía, Geranomachía, Kerameís*, → *Amphiaráou exélasis, Paígnia* ('frivolities, humorous poems'), → *Oichalías Hálōsis, Epithalámia, Kýklos* (meant: → **Epic Cycle*), *Hýmnoi* (meant: the → **Homeric Hymns*), → *Kýpria* (in other sources the → **Margítēs* is added). Ancient literary critics already disputed the authenticity of all these writings for reasons of style and quality (e.g. H.-*vita* no. 5 [1. 29, 19–22]). Modern Homeric philology has arrived at the same judgement (research report: [21. 821–831]).

B. GENUINE WORKS
1. ILIAD

A) SCOPE AND CLASSIFICATION

The work comprises (in [2]) 15,693 hexameters, divided up into 24 books or 'songs' (ῥαψ-ῳδίαι, *rhapsōidíai*, of between c. 450 and c. 900 verses each), corresponding to the 24 letters of the Greek standard alphabet since → Euclides [1]. The very designation – obviously ancient – of the units as *rhapsōidíai*, which refers to the → rhapsodes, makes it probable that the division as such was not first carried out by the Alexandrian philologists but had already developed early from natural 'performance units' [21. 839,15] (cf. the citation system already attested in Herodotus, 'H. in the *aristeia* of Diomedes': Hdt. 2,116) and was consolidated through the institutionalized recitation of works at the festival of the Panathenaea in Athens from the time of

Internal chronological structure of the Iliad

Day	Night	Number of verses	Section	Content
Day 1	–	41	1.12b – 52	Chryses prelude
Days 2-9	7 nights	1	1.53	Plague in the Achaean camp
Day 10	'pre-history' (21 days)	422	1.54 – 476	Quarrel; embassy to Chryses
Day 11	646 verses	16	1.477 – 492	Return of embassy / Wrath of Achilles
Days 12-20	8 nights	(1)	(1.493)	The gods visit the Aethiopes
Day 21and	following night	165	1.493 – 2.47	Thetis' appeal / Agamemnon's dream
Day 22		3,653	2.48 – 7.380 (almost 6 bks.)	'Testing' of the army (peîra)
				Catalogue
				Truce: decision of the war by single combat between Menelaus and Paris
	1st day of fighting (flashback)			Teichoskopia (view from the walls)
				Single combat Menelaus–Paris
				Breach of the truce (Pandarus)
				Diomedeia / homilia
				Single combat Hector–Ajax
Day 23		52	7.381 – 432	Truce / Burying of the dead
Day 24		50	7.433 – 482	Wall built by the Achaeans
Day 25 and	following night 2nd day of fighting	1,857	8.1 – 10.579 (almost 3 bks.)	Achaeans pushed back
				Trojans camping in the plain
				Embassy to Achilles (litaí)
				(Doloneia)
EPIC CORE (6 days)				Aristeia of Agamemnon
				Aristeia of Hector
13,444 verses		5,669		Wounding of the Achaean leaders
Day 26 and	following night 3rd day of fighting		11.1 – 18.617 (8 bks.)	Achilles sends Patroclus to Nestor
				Teichomachia (battle for the encampment wall)
				Incursion of the Trojans into the Achaean camp
				Battle by the ships
				Hera's seduction of Zeus (Diòs apátē)
		2,163		Patrokleia / Description of the shield
Day 27 and	following night		19.1 – 23.110a	Settling of the dispute (ménidos apórrhēsis)
	4th day of fighting	147	(almost 5 bks.)	Figthing resumes / Death of Hector
Day 28		662	23.110b – 227a	Funeral of Patroclus
Day 29 and	following night	9	23.227b – 24.21	Funeral games (âthla)
Days 30-40	10 nights	646	24.22 – 30	Maltreatment of Hector's corpse
Day 41 and	following night	105	24.31 – 676	Priam enters the Achaean camp
Day 42	post-narrative (24 days) 1,592 verses	3	24.677 – 781	Return of Hector's body
Days 43-50	7 nights	20	24.782 – 784	Truce / Gathering of firewood
Day 51			24.785 – 804	Hector's funeral

→ Hipparchus [1] (around 520) [37]; however, the canonization of the number 24 cannot have taken place until after 403 (setting of the number of letters by → Euclides [1]) so that the Vita Ps.-Plutarchea 2,4 ('*Iliad* and *Odyssey* are both divided up according to the number of letters, not by the poet himself but by the grammarians around Aristarchus') may have preserved something fundamentally correct (scholarly invention independent of the author).

b) Title

Ἰλιάς (*Iliás*, attested for the first time in Hdt. 2,116 (ἐν Ἰλιάδι), is a feminine adjective that Herodotus also puts with other substantives in an unterminologized manner (χώρη/*chórē* 5,94; γῆ/*gê* 5,122: 'Iliac country'; cf. Ἰλιὰς γυνή/*Iliàs gyné* Eur. Hel. 1114: 'Iliac woman'). The word to be supplemented here is ποίησις (*poíēsis*: 'Iliac poetry', 'poem with the theme of Ilius' (analogous titles: *Minyás, Dionysiás*, etc., with *i*-suffix: *Thēbaís, Aeneis*, etc.). As the provision of a title only becomes essential with growing textuality, the title cannot originate from the author himself (likewise [31. 24³]); the fact that this title is missing the central point (after all the theme is not Ilius, but the *mênis Achiléos*, the wrath of Achilles, Il. 1,1), is evident [32. 93⁵]; *Meniás* or *Achilléis* would be apt. The title will therefore have been given at a point in time before Herodotus that can no longer be determined, presumably by rhapsodes for the purposes of differentiation; it took up the foregrounded fact that the partial plot of the wrath of Achilles that forms the subject of the writing, is embedded in a framework plot that takes place before Ilius and in which Ilius is the issue (more precise information regarding this question: [19. 30–32]).

c) Content and composition

On a joint fleet expedition of an Achaean military alliance against Ilius (Troy), in the 9th year of the siege of the city, a dispute on basic principles arises between two Achaean noblemen, the supreme commander Agamemnon of Argos/Mycenae and the young Thessalian prince Achilles, who with his part of the army, the Myrmidons, is decisive for the fighting strength of the alliance. The dispute is about the correct interpretation of basic standards of the upper class that had been generally binding until then, such as honour, rank, dignity, willingness to give one's best for the general good etc. Achilles is so deeply humiliated by Agamemnon with regard to his honour and his claim to high rank that he feels compelled to leave the battle alliance. He is consumed by a deep wrath (*mênis Achiléos*) but does not go home; instead he hopes to achieve the restoration of the supra-personal norm, which had been violated by his personal humiliation, by way of seriously endangering the whole community which he expects to lead to the acknowledgement (= public apology) by Agamemnon of his wrongful action. He succeeds in winning his divine mother Thetis over to this radical plan and through her Zeus, the father of the gods.

Because of Zeus' support, the besieged Trojans make a successful sortie. When they – under their leader Hec-

tor, the son of the venerable Trojan king Priam – get as far as trying to set fire to the first ships of the Achaeans, the hoped-for effect actually occurs: Agamemnon recognizes his former blindness and makes a public apology. In the meantime, however, all those involved – not just the two adversaries but the whole alliance – have suffered such severe external and internal losses (Achilles himself has lost his beloved friend Patroclus) that all attempts at restitution come too late. Although Achilles re-engages in the battle, kills Hector and drives the Trojans back into the city so that the old state of affairs is outwardly not just restored but is even improved militarily, the community is weakened in its innermost core through the dispute, and the alliance that was once taken for granted has become problematic and made insecure in many ways.

This story is not an entertaining retelling of the 'Trojan War', but a reflection of the problems of the upper class of the 8th cent. in view of rapid economic and social re-structuring ('Renaissance of the 8th cent.') and of the general change in values associated with it: 'How should the upper class re-orientate itself in the new age?'. As a framework into which this story is embedded, the well-known Troy story (from the judgement of Paris and the abduction of Helen by Paris to the fall of Troy) is chosen. This technique is repeated in world literature a hundredfold (a well-known grand story is segmented, and in the segment a problem of the present is displayed – recapitulation of myth in literature, cf. for instance also the literature which draws upon the Bible); for the whole question [20. 12–18].

The plot of the *Iliad* comprises 51 days. For the plot, the temporal internal structure, the relationship between compression and expansion, between time narrated in an involved manner and time only summarized or just mentioned, etc., see the table 'Internal chronological structure of the *Iliad*').

The detailed composition becomes clear from the second table ('Structure of the *Iliad*'):

The dispute of the princes and the pleas of Achilles and Thetis take up one and a half books. From 2.484 the pleas of Achilles and Thetis as well as the related promise of Zeus are suspended for 5¹⁄₂ books (2² to 7) and instead the main events of the past 8 years (from the gathering of the fleet in Aulis to the capitulation offer of the Trojans *before* Achilles' withdrawal) are recapitulated (while the present-time plot – the wrath of Achilles – is repeatedly reminded of through 'recall passages'). In the 8th book the main line (the *mênis* plot) is taken up again and (bridging the later insertion of the 10th book, see [9]) is now developed swiftly towards the planned goal of the 1st book (extreme endangering of the Achaeans and apology of Agamemnon) in 19.67. Afterwards in 5¹⁄₂ books the resolution of the consequences of the *mênis* is narrated up to the killing of Hector by Achilles (22), the funeral games for Patroclus (23) and the conciliatory conclusion consisting in the release by Achilles of Hector's body to Priam, and Hector's burial in Troy 24).

Structure of the Iliad

Looking ahead = glimpses of the 'post-history' (fall of Troy)

1	2¹	2²	3	4	5	6	7	8	9	10	11-18	19	20	21	22	23	24
1st day of fighting in the epic								**2nd day of fighting in the epic = 1st day of fighting of the mênis plot ('Achilleis')**			**3rd day of fighting in the epic = 2nd day of fighting of the mênis plot ('Achilleis')**	**4th day of fighting in the epic = 3rd day of fighting of the mênis plot ('Achilleis')**					
Theme: Wrath of Achilles		(= compressed rendition of the fighting of the past 8 years) / Suspension of the narrative goal through retrospection						Battle cut short	Embassy to Achilles (litaí)	Doloneia (later)	(= 8 books = 1 third)	Renunciation of wrath (ménidos aporrhēsis) 67	'Aeneis' 67 (fulfilled!)	Battle by the rivers	Death of Hector (361)	Funeral games (âthla)	Ransoming of Hector
484		763ff.	509ff.	788	99	226											
mênis (v.1) Achilēéos (9th year of the war)	Thetis' appeal and Zeus' promise	Cata-logue of ships	Single combat Teicho-skopia Truce	Breach of truce epipolesis (visitation)	Greeks victorious (Dio-medeia)	Despair among Trojans (homilia)	Trojan offer of capitulation Building of the wall										
								Promise of Zeus			mênis						
								mênis						(death of Patroclus, avenged by the death of Hector; funeral games for Patroclus and funeral of Hector) / Resolution of the consequences of the mênis plot			

Looking backwards = glimpses of the 'pre-history': real narrative time (of the mênis plot) is implicitly suspended, but 'recalled' at intervals; cf. Odyssey 11.333-384.

In the main structure the narration has been composed as an obviously well-planned unity – without real overlaps, duplications, logical gaps and contradictions in the basic plan [18. 168f.]; lengthy passages and descriptions can well reflect the gradual reworking by the original author of his colossal work and need not be insertions by another hand [27. 209–211, 462–466, 533; 5. 483f.; 24. 234; 18. 168f.; 37]. The view that is gaining general acceptance is that the *Iliad* was written down and is the work of *one* great poet [37].

2. ODYSSEY

A) SIZE AND CLASSIFICATION

The work comprises (in [3]) 12,109 hexameters, divided up, as in the *Iliad*, into 24 books of *c*. 350 to *c*. 900 verses each. With regard to the origin of the division the same applies as for the *Iliad* (see above).

B) TITLE

Ὀδυσσείη/*Odysseíē* (later more commonly Ὀδύσσεια/*Odýsseia*) is attested for the first time in Hdt. 2,116 (ἐν Ὀδυσσείη). The title does not present any problems here: naming a work after the main hero is common from early on (*Hērakléïs* or *Hērakleía*, *Alkmaiōnís*, *Aithiopís*: poem on the Ethiopian king Memnon, etc.) and is factually accurate.

C) CONTENT AND COMPOSITION

After the conquest of Troy the Achaeans get into a dispute and travel separately and by different routes back to their homeland. Their adventures on the homeward journey (*nóstos*) formed the theme of a series of individual performances of the *aoidoi* (cf. Od. 1,325ff.), e.g. 'The Return Home of the Atreids', 'The Return Home of Nestor', 'The Return Home of Menelaus', etc.; later such individual performances were also compiled into an entire work called → *Nóstoi* ('Homeward Journeys'); the sole extant tale of homecoming is our *Odyssey* as a large-scale composition of one of these, the 'Return Home of Odysseus', probably made possible, like the *Iliad*, by the emergence of literacy.

The *Odyssey* tells of the critical last 40 days of the return home of the veteran of the Trojan War, Odysseus, to his home island of Ithaca and 'to his wife' (= Penelope; 1.13) in the 20th year (16.206 *et passim*) after he set out for Troy (10 years of Trojan War and 10 years of wanderings and of enforced stays, the last of which was brought about by the wrath of Poseidon, the god of the sea: 1,68–75). Of the 40 days of the plot, only 16 days and 8 nights are narrated, the rest is mentioned time; the prehistory, i.e. the almost 20 years before the plot starts, is integrated into the plot, in a manner that is similar to the *Iliad*, but technically more developed – through story flashbacks, particularly in the long first-person adventure-story told by Odysseus among the Phaeacians (books 6–12: so-called *Phaiakís*).

Plot after Odysseus' departure with 12 ships from Troy (books 9–12)

1. The land of the Cicones: destruction of the city of Ismarus. Battle with the Cicones of the surrounding area. Loss of 72 companions.

   Driven by the storm at Cape Malea (= southern tip of the Peloponnese) past the island of Cythera for 'nine days': departure from the real world, travel to the land of the sailor's yarns.

2. The land of the Lotophagi (= lotus eaters): by taking the lotus drug, the return home is almost forgotten.

3. The island of the Cyclopes (= one-eyed giants): the Cyclops Polyphemus (Πολύφημος, *Polýphēmos*, 'the much infamous'): locked up with 12 companions in the cave of the giant. 6 companions eaten by the Cyclops. The giant's only eye is gouged out with a sharpened olive tree stake heated red-hot. The 'No-one' trick. Escape from the cave entrance guarded by Polyphemus under the bellies of 3 sheep tied together. Provocation of the blind giant from onboard the ship. Polyphemus asks his father Poseidon to take revenge.

4. The floating island of the master of the winds Aeolus: gift of the bag of winds.

   Within sight of home, the foolish companions open the bag of wind: whirlwind carries the ships back to Aeolus. Curse of Aeolus on Odysseus.

5. The land of the Laestrygones (= giants): 11 ships destroyed by boulders thrown at them by the giants, the companions swimming in the water fished out and eaten. Only Odysseus' ship is still left.

6. The island of Aea with the sorceress Circe (daughter of the sun god Helios): 22 companions turned into pigs by Circe. Hermes gives Odysseus the antidote herb *moly* (μῶλυ, a wonder plant). Odysseus succumbs to Circe's attraction. Life of luxury for a year with Circe. At the departure Circe refers Odysseus to the seer Tiresias in the land of the dead.

7. The incantation of the dead on the other side of the ring stream of Oceanus: prophecy of Tiresias. Odysseus meets with his mother, with Agamemnon, Achilles, Patroclus, Ajax. He sees the judge of the dead Minos, the wrongdoers Tityus, Tantalus, Sisyphus; the benefactor Heracles.

   Return to Circe. Circe's warning about the Sirens, the Planctae, Scylla and Charybdis, the cattle of Helios.

8. The island of the Sirens: Odysseus escapes from the seduction of absolute knowledge by stuffing his ears with wax and having himself tied tightly to the mast.

9. Scylla and Charybdis (= sea whirlpool): loss of 6 companions.

10. Helios' island of Thrinacia: the hungry companions slaughter the forbidden cattle of Helios. Helios demands that Zeus take revenge. Zeus hits the ship with his lightning and all the companions drown. Odysseus, riding on the keel and mast, is the only survivor to come to Calypso in Ogygia.

The work is divided into two parts: 'Return Home before Reaching Ithaca' (1–12) and 'Return Home on Ithaca itself' (in the disguise of a beggar brought about by Athena, 13–24); the major emphasis is on the second part that tells of only 6 days in its 12 books. The 5th day of Odysseus' stay on Ithaca – the day of the decision with the climax of the recognition scene between Odysseus and Penelope – alone takes up 4 books (20–23) with 1,701 verses: the outward journey home (with the adventure story) is subordinated to the internal return

home (overcoming of alienation after 20 years of absence).

The centripetal main plot 'Return of the Father' dovetails with the centrifugal auxiliary plot 'Search of the Son (Telemachus) for His Father' (the 'Telemachia': books 3 and 4 plus a part of 15) which makes the son, who grew up fatherless, internally mature through encountering the *image* of his father in the memories of Odysseus' old companions-at-arms at Troy, Nestor in Pylus (book 3) and Menelaus in Sparta (book 4) – for the *real* meeting with his father (16th song). In detail, the structure is as follows:

The plot consists of 5 large plot elements:

Starting-point of action: meeting of the gods	Book
I. Ithaca before Odysseus' return	1 and 2
II. Telemachus' trip to Pylus and Sparta, so as to achieve certainty regarding the whereabouts of his father (I + II + Telemachus' return in book 15, are called 'Telemachia')	3 and 4
III. Odysseus' raft journey from Ogygia to Scheria	5
IV. Odysseus on Scheria among the Phaeacians (so-called 'Phaiakis'): Odysseus tells of his adventures from the fall of Troy to his arrival on Scheria	6 to 12
V. Odysseus on Ithaca	13 to 24

A basic structural division into two parts is clearly identifiable:

(A) 12 books preparation for the return home for all those involved (wife, son, domestic servants, suitors, people of Ithaca, the outside world of friendly noble houses; the gods; Odysseus himself),

(B) 12 books return within the homeland itself: reacquisition and securing of what was once owned as a matter of course.

IV. Subject-Matter

The material background of the *Iliad* is provided by the myth of → Troy whilst that of the *Odyssey* is provided by the myth of → Odysseus; both myths go back to the Mycenaean period (→ Mycenae) and were passed down from generation to generation between that time and the time of origin of both epics, the 8th cent., through the medium of the oral, improvizing hexametric performances of the → *aoidoi* (→ Epic II). For the language, see → Homeric language.

V. Orality and literacy

The myth of Troy and the myth of Odysseus were independent pieces in an immense reservoir of myths of heroes (e.g. the myths of the Argonauts, of Thebes and of Hercules) from which the *aoidoi* shaped their oral performances ever anew on request (this practice is reflected in the *Odyssey* itself e.g. 8.250–255 and 8.488–

498 [18. 42]). Prior to the introduction of the alphabet (around 800) these performances were unique recitations that were lost forever with the last word of the singer (→ Oral poetry; M. PARRY). Our *Iliad* and our *Odyssey* originated decades after the introduction of the alphabet and were most probably composed with the aid of writing, in any case however they were recorded by means of writing (whether they were dictated by the author or written down by himself remains an unanswered question; for the hypothesis of dictation e.g. JANKO [14. 37f.] following LORD [22], for a differentiated hypothesis of autography e.g. LATACZ [16. 12f.]) and were handed down. The writing down with the possibility of preliminary studies and planning [10] allowed for the creation of logically coherent and artfully composed thematizations of individual motifs that were taken from the narrative tradition to be expanded and deepened in diverse ways. The original myths, presumably linear narratives, were thus turned into reflections on questions of the writer's own time; they became established in the traditional area of storytelling and thus achieved a concentrated and condensed quality that ensured their survival [20].

VI. TRANSMISSION

With the transfer of a part of the traditional oral hexametric narrative tradition into the written tradition in the form of the two great epics, the *Iliad* and the *Odyssey*, the period of free improvization had in principle ended. Consequently, the former *aoidoi* (i.e. artists of improvization) now became rhapsodes (i.e. reciters of the *Iliad* and the *Odyssey*). As the autograph of the author did not have to be reproduced word for word because of the absence of copyright, the rhapsodes could undertake modifications depending on the circumstances of the recitation and their ambition for self-portrayal (additions, omissions, etc.). The general coherence of both plots suggests, however, that such modifications were limited to only a few passages and mostly to single verses or variants of formulas. The 10th book of the *Iliad*, the → Doloneia, is an exception.

The great popularity of both epics especially in Athens (depictions of scenes from the epics in Attic vase painting from before 600 [15]) led to their integration in the set programme of the Attic Panathenaea under Hipparchus (around 520): complete recitation by recitation ensembles every 4 years. Through this and through the introduction of the epics as compulsory reading into the educational programme for the Athenian upper class, Athens became formative for the further passing down of Homer; the Panathenaean recitations were probably based on a specific standard text. Nevertheless there was – as opposed to the Attic tragedians – no real 'state copy' of H. so that transmission (which after all did not only take place in Athens) remained basically inconsistent, as the H. citations in Plato, Aristotle and others show.

The philological academy of the Museion of Alexandria took up the 'national author' with great enthusiasm: the three most famous heads of the Museion library, → Zenodotus, → Aristophanes [4] of Byzantium and → Aristarchus [4] of Samothrace, critically analyzed the Homeric text and left behind traces of their work in the extant → scholia. From *c.* 150 BC the H. papyri offer a significantly more uniform text than previously (and our MSS of the Middle Ages deviate from it only to a small extent). This was probably the reaction of the book trade to Aristarchus' standardization of the Homeric text. The textual work of the three 'giants' was continued by the Alexandrian philologists → Aristonicus [5] and → Didymus [1] (under Augustus) and (besides others) by → Nicanor and → Herodianus (in the 2nd cent. AD). The work of these four philologists was compiled into a commentary (→ Four Men Commentary) which is the basis of the scholia in our MSS A and T. Despite this critical work on the text there was never a standardized uniform edition of H.; this is demonstrated by the around 2,000 H. papyri (3rd cent. BC – 7th cent. AD), which differ considerably in many (although not significant) details.

The codices of the Middle Ages commence in the 9th cent.; their exact number is still unknown (for the *Iliad* alone over 200 MSS and for the *Odyssey* well over 70 have been registered to date), and a collation of even just the known codices is far from being achieved. The *editio princeps* was produced in 1488 in Florence by Demetrios Chalkondyles on the basis of a MS now lost. Today's most widespread reading texts are [2] and [3]; a new Teubner edition of the *Iliad* by M. L. WEST is now completed [3a]. Since the compilation and collation of all H. MSS must remain a utopia, the Homeric philology of today assumes a vulgata whose lack of soundness is certainly known but which it nevertheless regards as an adequate working basis in view of the relatively few discrepancies in the H. MSS investigated to date.

→ Epic; → Homeric language; → ALLEGORESIS; → EPIC POETRY; → HOMERIC QUESTION

EDITIONS: 1 U. DE WILAMOWITZ-MOELLENDORFF, Vitae Homeri et Hesiodi in usum scholarum, 1915 et al. 2 D. B. MONRO, T. W. ALLEN (ed.), Homeri Opera, tom. I/ II (Ilias), 1902 et al. (Oxford Classical Texts)   3 P. VON DER MÜHLL (rec.), Homeri Odyssea, 1946 et al. (now Bibliotheca Teubneriana)   3a M. L. WEST (ed.) Homeri Ilias 1998/2000 (Bibliotheca Teubneriana).
BIBLIOGRAPHY :   4 F. BECHTEL, Die histor. PN des Griech. bis zur Kaiserzeit, 1917   5 C. M. BOWRA, Heroic Poetry, 1952   6 W. BURKERT, Das hunderttorige Theben, in: WS 89, 1976, 5–21   7 CHANTRAINE   8 G. CURTIUS, De nomine Homeri, 1855   9 G. DANEK, Studien zur Dolonie, 1988   10 A. DIHLE, Homer-Probleme, 1970 11 G. FINSLER, Homer in der Neuzeit von Dante bis Goethe, 1912   12 K. HELDMANN, Die Niederlage Homers im Dichterwettstreit mit Hesiod, 1982   13 R. JANKO, Homer, Hesiod and the Hymns, 1982   14 Id., The Iliad: A Commentary, vol. IV: bks. 13–16, 1992   15 R. KANNICHT, Poetry and Art, in: Classical Antiquity 1, 1982, 70–86   16 J. LATACZ, Hauptfunktionen des ant. Epos in Ant. und Moderne, in: AU 34(3), 1991, 8–17   17 Id., Hauptfunktionen ... (long edition, 1991), in: Id., Erschließung der Ant., 1994, 257–279   18 Id., Homer. His Art

and His World, 1996   19 Id., Achilleus (1995) ²1997
20 Id., Troia und Homer. Neue Erkenntnisse und neue
Perspektiven, in: Grazer Morgenländische Studien 4,
1997, 1–42   21 A. LESKY, s.v. H., RE Suppl. 11, 687–846
22 A. LORD, Homer's Originality: Oral Dictated Texts
(1953), in: Id., Epic Singers and Oral Tradition, 1991,
38–48   23 Id., The Singer of Tales, 1960   24 M. PETERS,
in: Die Sprache 33, 1987, 234ff.   25 B. POWELL, Homer
and Writing, in: I. MORRIS, B. POWELL (ed.), A New Companion to Homer, 1997, 3–32   26 K. RAAFLAUB, Homeric Society, in: ibid., 624–648   27 K. REINHARDT, Die Ilias
und ihr Dichter, 1961   28 W. SCHADEWALDT, Iliasstu-
dien (1938) ³1966 et al.   29 Id., Homer und sein Jh.
(1942), in: Id., Von Homers Welt und Werk, (1944)
³1959, 87–129   30 Id., Legende von Homer dem fahren-
den Sänger (1942), 1959   31 E. SCHMALZRIEDT, Περὶ φύ-
σεως. Zur Frühgesch. der Buchtitel, 1970   32 SCHMID/
STÄHLIN I   33 E. VOGT, Die Schrift vom Wettkampf
Homers und Hesiods, in: RhM 102, 1959, 193–221
34 Id., Homer – ein großer Schatten? Die Forschungen zur
Person Homers, in: J. LATACZ (ed.), Zweihundert Jahre
Homer-Forschung, 1991, 365–377   35 S. WEST, The
Transmission of the Text, in: A. HEUBECK, S. WEST, J. B.
HAINSWORTH, A Commentary on Homer's Odyssey, I,
1988, 33–48   36 M. L. WEST, The Date of the Iliad, in:
MH 52, 1995, 203–219   37 Id., Die Gesch. des Textes,
in: J. LATACZ et al., Homer, Ilias. Ein Gesamtkomm., I 2,
1999   38 U. v. WILAMOWITZ-MOELLENDORFF, Die Ilias
und H., in: Id., Die Ilias und Homer, 1916, 356–376
39 W. WIMMEL, Die Kultur holt uns ein. Die Bedeutung
der Textualität für das gesch. Werden, 1981.   J.L.

[2] **H. of Byzantium.** According to Suda o 253 (cf.
Tzetz. Chil. 12,399, v. 202), the son of Andromachus
and the poetess Myro (Suda μ 1464), grammarian and
tragedian, main period of activity 284/1–281/0 BC. H.
was a member of the tragic Pleiad (CAT A 5a,1 and b,6)
and a rival of Sositheus (TrGF 99; cf. Suda σ 860), he is
said to have written 45 (Suda o 253) or 57 (Tzetz. Vita
Lycophronis p. 4,30 SCH.) tragedies and an epic 'Eury-
pyleia' (Tzetz. Vita Hesiodi p. 49,25 WIL.); there are
reports of a statue in his honour in Byzantium (Anth.
Pal. 2,407ff.). He had the epithet *neós/neóteros* ('the
Younger'; cf. Tzetz. Vita Lycophronis, ibid.; Vita Hesiodi, ibid.). Timon (TrGF 112) is said, assisted him *i.a.* in
the writing of tragedies (Diog. Laert. 9,113). He is perhaps identical with the H. mentioned in DID A 3a, 66
who was victorious at the Dionysia (TrGF 109).

> METTE, 163; TrGF 98 and 109.   F.P.

Homicide
I. GENERAL   II. GREECE   III. ROME

I. GENERAL
In antiquity homicide is often not yet differentiated
from other crimes of killing (→ Killing, crimes of). In
many ancient laws the special reprehensibility or
danger of a behaviour that resulted in the death of another human being was not yet considered a reason for
a respective sanction. Thus, in the case of ancient Oriental laws, it would be inappropriate both with regard

to the term and the matter to speak of particular offences amounting to homicide within the framework of
crimes of killing.   H.N.

II. GREECE
In archaic Greece too the wilful killing (sometimes
defined in more detail) of a person was subsumed under
the wider objective offence of killing (φόνος, *phónos*).
According to the principle of liability, the perpetrator,
whether he had acted criminally or not, was subject to a
blood feud by the closest male relatives of the victim
(e.g. Hom. Il. 2,661; 13,694; 15,431; 16,572; 23,85;
[1. 6–13]). Homicide could be expiated through the private payment of a fine (blood money; ποινή, *poiné*:
Hom. Il. 18,498) (→ *aidesis*), but no longer in the
Athens of the 5th and 4th cents. BC. In classical Athens
the blood feud was replaced by the private lawsuit filed
by the relatives entitled to revenge (φόνου δίκη,
→ *phónou díkē*, there also on the other crimes involving
→ killing). Plato refined the principle of fault, taking as
his starting-point the positive law of Athens (Pl. Leg.
865a–874b, cf. [6. 217ff.]), however without impact on
the practice. The tradition regarding homicide in the
extra-Attic and Hellenistic sources is extremely incomplete. [7] is still not replaced, cf. [5. 151]; in general, see
[4] and [3]; special questions [2. no. 32, 86, 119], [8.
no. 7 and 8], [9. vol.1 no. 01, 02, 44, 56; vol.2, no. 2,
11, 78, 79].

> 1 M. GAGARIN, Drakon and Early Athenian Homicide
> Law, 1981   2 R. KOERNER, Inschr. Gesetzestexte der
> frühen griech. Polis, 1993   3 K. LATTE, s.v. M., RE 16,
> 278–289   4 R. MASCHKE, Die Willenslehre im griech.
> Recht, 1926   5 H.-A. RUPPRECHT, Kleine Einführung in
> die Papyruskunde, 1994   6 T. J. SAUNDERS, Plato's Penal
> Code, 1991   7 R. TAUBENSCHLAG, Das Strafrecht im
> Rechte der Papyri, 1916   8 IPArk   9 H. VAN EFFEN-
> TERRE, F. RUZÉ, Nomima, vol.1–2, 1994–1995.   G.T.

III. ROME
In Rome, however, a legal rule dating back to the
period of the monarchy (6th cent. BC) is said (cf. Fest.
221) to have defined → *parricidium* as a premeditated
deed with intent (*dolo sciens*). There the offence constitutes homicide, while crimes involving killing (including unintentional killing) were summarized as
→ *homicidium* from the 1st cent. AD onwards.   G.S.

Homicidium The Latin word *homicidium* ('homicide,
manslaughter', also 'unintentional killing') is not attested before Seneca the Elder (1st cent. BC) (*homicida* is
used three times in Cicero) and is still rarely used by the
jurists before AD 250, frequent however in the imperial
constitutions. Up till the late Republican period, the
term for wilful killing was → *parricidium*. A priestly
decree predating the 12 Tables (*c.* 450 BC) already determined that only the intentional perpetrator should
be a *parricida(s)*. According to ancient Roman law he
was subject to private revenge under the control of the
community. Before the assembled people, the uninten-

tional perpetrator had to offer to the *agnati* (→ *agnatio*) of the deceased a ram which they killed instead of the perpetrator. From the beginning of the 2nd cent. BC, private prosecution of the homicide gradually ran parallel to the prosecution *ex officio* which finally ousted it completely. The substantive law standards on which it is based will not have been different from those of the centre-piece of the *lex Cornelia de sicariis et veneficis* (81 BC) that firstly referred to being armed with criminal intent, and secondly referred to the wilful killing of a human being (including slaves) as well as the brewing of poison. The *lex Cornelia* remained in force with some changes until Justinian (6th cent. AD). From Hadrian (beginning of the 2nd cent. AD) the tendency to punish even negligent killing can be observed.

→ Homicide

W. KUNKEL, Unters. zur Entwicklung des röm. Kriminalverfahrens in vorsullanischer Zeit, 1962; Id., s.v. quaestio, RE 24, 720–786; A. VÖLKL, Die Verfolgung der Körperverletzung im frühen Röm. Recht, 1984, 98f.; WIEACKER, RRG, 246.   D.I.S.

Homilia see → Sermon

Homoioi

I. HOMOIOI IN ARISTOTLE   II. SPARTA

I. HOMOIOI IN ARISTOTLE

With the term *homoioi* (in Homer, in Ionian and in early Attic ὁμοῖοι/*homoîoi*, later ὅμοιοι/*hómoioi*, 'equal ones') Aristotle clearly describes, in a section regarding the prerequisites of political stability (Aristot. Pol. 1308a 11–13), an elite, i.e. a legally or socially defined ruling class that is clearly differentiated by birth or wealth. When many people belong to an elite of such kind, it represents, according to Aristotle, a type of people itself (ὥσπερ δῆμος ἤδη οἱ ὅμοιοι); it is then useful to involve, if possible, all *homoioi* in the government through a limitation of the time in office (Aristot. Pol. 1308a 13–17; cf. also 1332b 27–29).

II. SPARTA

As the word usage in Xenophon suggests (Hell. 3,3,4f.; Lac. 10,7; 13,1; 13,7; An. 4,6,14; cf. Aristot. Pol. 1306b 30, but perhaps an insertion), *homoioi* was one of the terms used to describe Spartan society. Further evidence for the use of the word in a figurative sense (Hdt. 7,234,2; Dem. Or. 20,107; cf. Isocr. Or. 7,61) confirms this. Obviously it was rather an unofficial synonym for Σπαρτιᾶται (→ *Spartiâtai*) – an expression that was used in official documents (SEG XI, 1204a, *c.* 600–550 BC) – and consequently denoted Spartan citizens with all the political and social rights. The corresponding term for the lower classes (ὑπομείονες, *hypomeíones*) appears only once in Xenophon (Hell. 3,3,5).

The term *homoioi* cannot be translated as 'the equal', for the Spartans were not ἴσοι (*ísoi*) nor did they call themselves so. They also were not ὁμοί (*homoí*,

'identical'), but *homoioi* – not equal in every respect but equal with regard to some decisive aspects. These included above all origin, education and way of life. Each of the *homoioi* had a Spartan father and (with the possible exception of the μόθακες, → *móthakes*) a Spartan mother. All of them, except the heirs to the throne from both royal families, had to pass the obligatory education (ἀγωγή, → *agōgḗ*). They wore the same clothes, ate the same food at communal meals (συσκάνια/*syskánia*, συσσίτια/*syssítia*) and fought together with the same equipment as → hoplites in the phalanx.

In reality, however, considerable inequalities existed for the *homoioi* in Sparta with regard to their social, political – and increasingly esp. – economic status. Consequently the word *homoioi* emphasized in an ideological manner – in a polis that was always intent on homogeneity and equality of its citizens both according to its self-image and in everyday life – what the Spartiates had in common, the aim probably being to disguise the growing differences. This is also strongly suggested by the fact that the term *homoioi* appeared in the 5th cent. BC, i.e. at a time in which the differences and inequalities actually tended to increase. It was precisely the factors that were actually meant to generate equality among the Spartiates, namely origin, education and way of life, that became the cause of this inequality. Some Spartiates, among them the kings, were aristocrats (Thuc. 5,16,2), whilst most of them belonged to the δᾶμος (*dâmos*, people). In the education system too a differentiation was made between those who were successful and those who failed and were even downgraded to the *hypomeíones*. Some Spartiates were extremely rich and hence in a position to devote themselves to horse racing or to even contribute wheat bread for communal meals (Xen. Lac. 5,3), whilst others were too poor to make the prescribed contribution of barley (Aristot. Pol. 1270a 30ff.). These disparities among the *homoioi* ultimately contributed to the destabilization of the famous Spartan κόσμος (*kósmos*).

→ Social structure; → Sparta

1 P. CARTLEDGE, Agesilaus and the Crisis of Sparta, 1987 2 Id., Hopliten und Helden: Spartas Beitrag zur Technik der antiken Kriegskunst, in: K. CHRIST (ed.), Sparta, 1986, 387–425, 470   3 K. CHRIST (ed.), Sparta, 1986   4 M. I. FINLEY, Sparta, in: K. CHRIST (ed.), Sparta, 1986, 327–350   5 S. HODKINSON, Social order and the conflict of values in Classical Sparta, in: Chiron 1983, 239–81 6 S. LINK, Der Kosmos Sparta: Recht und Sitte in klass. Zeit, 1994   7 M. NAFISSI, La nascita del Kosmos: Studi sulla storia e la società di Sparta, 1991   8 P. OLIVA, Sparta and her Social Problems, 1971   9 L. THOMMEN, Lakedaimonion Politeia, 1996.   P.C.

Homoioprophoron, Homoioteleuton see → Figures

Homole, Homolium (Ὁμόλη, Ὁμόλιον; *Homólē, Homólion*). Mountain at the northern end of the Thessalian → Ossa. At the outflow of the Peneius from the → Tempe Valley lay a town of the same name on the slope (not by the sea, Str. 9,5,22), attested to be above modern Omolion (formerly Laspochori). H. was the northernmost town of → Magnesia and so of Greece. H. overlooked the river crossing to lower Macedonia (Liv. 42,38,10; remains of a bridge about 1 km north of Omolion). Finds attest to settlement since ancient times. As the most important town of the Magnetae outside the Gulf of Pagasae, H. mostly sent to Delphi as envoy one of the *hieromnemones* (delegates to the Amphictyonic Council) of the tribe. As can be demonstrated from coins of the 3rd cent. (HN 296), H. avoided the → *synoikismos* of → Demetrias [1] in about 290 BC. In 172 negotiations took place at the Peneius bridge between Q. Marcius Philippus and Perseus (Liv. 42,39ff.). In the Byzantine period there was a hermitage above H.

> H. BIESANTZ, Die thessalischen Grabreliefs, 1965, 130f.; F. STÄHLIN, s.v. H. (1–2), RE 8, 2259ff.; Id., Das hellenistische Thessalien, 1924, 46 (sources); D. THEOCHARIS, in: AD 17, 1961/2,2, 17ff. and 20,2, 1965, 319 (excavation reports); TIB 1, 1976, 1973. HE.KR.

Homologia (ὁμολογία; *homología*), literally 'speaking the same way', describes in Greek colloquial language simple oral consent or agreement. In the legal sense *homologia* was soon also used for written agreements (→ *syngraphé*, → *synthéké*). The legal connection with the *homologia* originated, as can be seen in Athens, in the preliminary procedural concession of individual assertions of the opponent. In the preliminary procedure (→ *anákrisis*, see → *diaitétaí* [2]) the parties had the duty to answer each other's questions (Dem. Or. 46,10). Answering such a question in the affirmative, confirmed by witnesses, was decisive as *homologia* in the trial (see → *dikasterion*) (κυρία/*kyría*, Dem. Or. 42,122). The same effect was achieved by a *homologia* (Dem. Or. 56,2) before the proceedings, i.e. with no compulsion to give an answer (ἑκών/*hekón*, voluntarily). From the *homologia* as a mere 'agreement' it was therefore not possible to sue on the basis that there were indisputably conceded facts founded on liability. In the papyri of Egypt this legal condition continues. Frequently the text of a business document (especially those left with the → *agoranómoi*) and the → *cheirógraphon* is introduced with the clause that one or both parties 'admit to' or 'recognize', and this is why such a document is termed a *homologia* in accordance with its formulation. But even without this introduction the business partners themselves often describe a contractual document as a *homologia*.

The stipulation clause (→ *stipulatio*) common in the Roman form at the end of the document is described in Greek as ὁμολογεῖν (*homologeín*, to recognize), in the Babatha Archive (PYadin) from the Dead Sea by the beginning of the 2nd cent. AD, in Egypt only after the Constitutio Antoniniana in AD 212.

> H. J. WOLFF, Die Grundlagen des griech. Vertragsrechts, in: ZRG 74, 1957, 26–72; G. THÜR, Beweisführung vor den Schwurgerichtshöfen Athens, 1977, 152–158; H. A. RUPPRECHT, Einführung in die Papyruskunde, 1994, 113f. 138f. G.T.

Homo mensura maxim see → Protagoras

Homonoia (ὁμόνοια; *homónoia*). The word *homonoia* ('unity') was evidently reshaped in Athens's crisis of 411 BC (referred to in Thuc. 8,75,2; 93,3) as an exhortation of the democrats to internal cohesion (cf. Antiphon 87 B 44–71; Thrasymachus 85 B 1; Gorgias 82 B 8a DK).

Homonoia within the polis is from then on mostly based on socio-economic conflicts (antonym → *stásis*: Lys. 18,17–18), bilateral and trilateral *homonoia* (from the Hellenistic period) as well as border conflicts primarily in the rank disputes of Asia Minor in the Imperial period but also interest in economic relationships. Panhellenic *homonoia* develops in the 4th cent. first against the Persian, then the Macedonian threat, and again in the Chremonidean War against Antigonus Gonatas.

Instruments of harmonious regulation are primarily oaths, contracts, decisions, and the appeal to external arbitrators, and since Hellenistic times also to external judges (*homonoia* dikasts), later also to Roman courts. The cult of the political abstractum in particular which arose in the 4th cent., which includes the special cults of the '*homonoia* of the Hellenes' [1; 2] and of the Imperial *homonoia* (*Homonoia Sebasté*, → Concordia Augusta), has the function of swearing *homonoia* in all its forms.

> 1 R. ETIENNE, M. PIÉRART, Un décret du Koinon des Hellènes à Platées, in: BCH 99, 1975, 51–75   2 R. ETIENNE, Le Koinon des Hellènes à Platées, in: La Béotie antique, 1985, 259–263.
>
> P. R. FRANKE, Zu den Homonoia-Münzen Kleinasiens, in: Stuttgarter Kolloquium zur histor. Geogr. des Altertums. 1, 1980, 1987, 81–102; R. PERA, Homonoia sulle monete da Augusto agli Antonini, 1984; A. R. R. SHEPPARD, Homonoia in the Greek Cities of the Roman Empire, in: Ancient Society, 1984–86, 15–17; 229–252; G. THÉRIAULT, Le culte d'Homonoia dans les cités grecques, 1996. T.H.

Homo novus see → Novus homo

Homosexuality
I. DEFINITION II. GREECE III. ROME IV. CHRISTIANITY AND LATE ANTIQUITY

I. DEFINITION
The term homosexuality describing physical love directed towards a partner of the same sex is not ancient. It fails to describe typical ancient sexual life in that it asserts an individual characteristic. Sexual behaviour was, however, determined in antiquity less by individual inclinations than by social status as free or non-free, young or old, man or woman. The idea that sexuality related to a single sex was to a large extent alien to antiquity. In particular social circumstances, women as well as men could pursue their erotic interests in both sexes.

II. GREECE
A. FEMALE HOMOSEXUALITY B. MALE HOMOSEXUALITY

A. FEMALE HOMOSEXUALITY

Homoerotic encounters between women are described by the female poet → Sappho of Lesbos (c. 600 BC) (Sappho 1 LP/D) as a component of the education of young girls from aristocratic families in a circle headed by the poet herself, according to the view that knowledge could only be imparted through an emotional relationship between teachers and students. In the subsequent period 'Lesbian love' was considered to be a description of female homosexuality (Lucian. Dialogi meretricii 5). Alcman's choral ode poetry too alludes to homoerotic encounters among the women of Sparta in a paedagogical context (Alcm. 1 D). Later sources attest that young girls there, before they married, had as lovers older women who wished to impart their virtues and erotic experience and who were considered as role-models by the younger ones (Plut. Lycurgus 18,9; Ath. 602d-e). From the perspective of male authors homoerotic ambitions of women are mostly judged as being contrary to nature (παρὰ φύσιν) and as a sign of debauchery (Pl. Leg. 636c; Anth. Pal. 5,207). Artemidorus similarly counts physical love between women as among the sexual relationships which are 'against nature' (Artem. 1,80).

B. MALE HOMOSEXUALITY

There are more sources with regard to the erotic relationships amongst men, which were practised particularly in the form of paederasty in various poleis. Both men involved in the paederastic relationship had the status of free men but differed considerably with regard to their age. The active partner (ἐραστής; erastés) was older than 30 and in his relationship with the 12–18 year-old passive partner (ἐρώμενος; erómenos) took on the role of educator. In Sparta paederasty was structurally connected with the education of boys (Plut. Lycurgus 17f.; cf. Pl. Leg. 836b), in Thebes, too, male homosexuality was known (Plut. Pelopidas 19; cf. Pl. Symp. 182b). Wooing a boy was normally associated with gifts (Aristoph. Plut. 147ff.). The status of the sexual and the educational aspect of paederasty is weighted differently by scholars, being interpreted partly as 'erotically coloured mentoring' and partly as a sexual relationship disguised as educational. Anyone past the age of an erómenos who desired men, was mocked as effeminate (Aristoph. Thesm. 49f.; 97f.). Plato, who in the Symposium justifies the relationship between the lovers from the point of view of striving for the beautiful (Pl. Symp. 178c–179b) and describes the various forms of sexual desire with understanding (Symp. 191c–193c), also takes a critical point of view regarding male homosexuality in the Nómoi (Pl. Leg. 636c). With reference to nature and especially to the behaviour of animals, Plato supports the outlawing of male homosexuality in the polis he describes (Leg. 835b–842a). For homosexual intercourse between men there were also prostitutes who in Athens were forbidden from holding official positions and speaking in the Council or in the Assembly (Aeschin. Tim. 19f.).

In Greek black-figured and red-figured vase painting, male homosexuality is a central theme with very widespread direct depictions of wooed boys with gifts which have been given, often animals (cocks or hares).

III. ROME
A. FEMALE HOMOSEXUALITY B. MALE HOMOSEXUALITY

A. FEMALE HOMOSEXUALITY

Homosexual intercourse between women is extremely rare in the sources of the Roman period and the theme is always taken up from the male perspective and judged in a thoroughly negative manner (Mart. 1,90; 7,67). Laws relating to female homosexuality have not been passed down to us.

B. MALE HOMOSEXUALITY

The view represented in earlier research and suggested by Roman authors (Cic. Tusc. 4,70) that the erotic interest of the Romans in young men was due to the influence of Greek culture, is rejected in modern investigations. The comedies of Plautus show that it was common practice for Roman slave-owners to have sexual relations with their young slaves (pueri meriti). As in Greece, sexual encounters also took place in Rome between men of different ages; passions towards men who had outgrown youth (exoleti) were frowned upon (Sen. Ep. 47,7). In contrast to Greek paederasty, homosexual relationships with free-born men (ingenui) were rejected in Rome. Roman discourse on male homosexuality also does not predicate any educational intentions by the active partner. With marriage a relationship with a slave lover was supposed to come to an end (Catull. 61,141ff.); this appears however not always to have been the case. It was certainly possible for a slave-owner to have homoerotic relationships with several slaves at the same time. Sexual relationships with male prostitutes were also widespread in Rome. Like the Greeks, the Romans, too, differentiate analogously in regard to the status of the partners between active and passive sexual behaviour. The latter was indeed fitting for women but for a man it was considered to be an indication of unmanliness, the negative evaluation of which can be seen from the characterization of the men as mollis (soft) as well as from the pejorative terms borrowed from Greek – cinaedus and pathicus (Catull. 16).

Recent studies emphasize that the homoerotic verse of the late Republic and of the early Principate certainly reflects the behaviour of the authors and should not, as assumed earlier, be regarded as pure fiction. The reproach of sexual availability (impudicitia), particularly in conjunction with the assertion that someone had his sexual services paid for, has been shown to be a widespread topos of forensic rhetoric. Such accusations were rarely lacking in disputes between political opponents. Caesar, for example, was mocked both by his adversaries in the Senate and by his soldiers for an alleged sexual relationship with King Nicomedes of Bithynia (Suet. Jul. 49; Cass. Dio 43,20). Insinuations of this kind are particularly informative with regard to the moral concepts of society (Sall. Catil. 13; Cic. Cat. 2,23). Petronius openly takes up homosexuality as a theme in the *Satyricon* (Petron. 8ff.; 23; 79,9ff.; 114,7ff.). An important source on homosexuality in the Principate period are the epigrams by Martial (on female homosexuality: 1,90; 7,67; anal intercourse: 9,47; 9,57; 11,43; a wedding ritual with a homosexual background: 12,42). The satires of Juvenal show that male homosexuality in the period around AD 100 provided an opportunity for mockery; they criticize in particular the double standards of the social elite, whose members sought to hide their homosexuality behind a façade of ancient Roman virtues (Juv. 2; 9).

To what extent there were legal regulations regarding homosexual intercourse cannot be reconstructed precisely. Both the dating and the concrete conditions contained in the *lex Scantinia* mentioned in various texts (Cic. Fam. 8,12,3; Suet. Dom. 8,3; Juv. 2,44) are debatable. This law had come into force at the latest from the middle of the 1st cent. BC and made lewdness (*stuprum*) with underaged free-born persons liable to prosecution. A Roman citizen could initiate proceedings against anyone who had sexual relations with his slaves. Suetonius reports homosexual activities by almost all the *principes* (Suet. Tib. 43f.; Cal. 24,3; 36,1; Nero 28f.; Galba 22). In the *Historia Augusta* too, the homosexuality of *principes* is mentioned (Hadrianus: S HA Hadr. 11,7; 14,5ff.). Emperor Hadrian founded, at the place where his young lover → Antinous died, the city of Antinoupolis and set up a cult for him in Mantinea (Paus. 8,9,7f.; Amm. Marc. 22,16,2). The *lex Scantinia* remained valid, although applied only occasionally by the *principes* (Suet. Dom. 8,3), and was kept up to date in the course of time by the decreeing of further provisions.

IV. CHRISTIANITY AND LATE ANTIQUITY

The Old Testament recognizes God's likeness only in people who are joined together as man and wife (Gen 1,27; 2,18–24) and condemns sexual relationships between men 'as with a woman' (Lv 18,22; 20,13). In NT writings, too, homosexuality is rejected as against nature without reference to the OT. For Paul, homosexuality represented one of many possible misdemeanours that barred the sinner's entry into the kingdom of God (Rom 1,27; 1 Cor 6,9f.). The view represented by Christian authors like Clement of Alexandria (Clem. Al. strom. 2,23) that the sole purpose of desire was procreation is also to be found in pagan literature (Musonius Rufus 12). The Church Fathers always referred to the depraved nature of homosexuality (Aug. Ep. 211). In several synods of the 4th cent., Church punishments for homosexuals were stipulated. If clerics were accused of homosexuality they feared being deposed.

Among the Christian emperors the condemnation of homosexuality (especially of the passive partner) was introduced into different laws: a ruling in the Codex Theodosianus (9,7,6, AD 390) provided for the death penalty. There is a lack of sources for evaluating the application and effects of this regulation. In the 5th cent. Salvianus laments the fact that men in Carthage quite openly confess to their homosexual inclinations without having to fear punishment (Salv. Gub. 7,18). Emperor Justinian is considered to be a particularly relentless persecutor of homosexuality for religious reasons (527–565). His interpretation of the OT, recognizing a danger to all mankind in the revenge of God brought about by homosexuality, is still influential in the modern age.

→ Eroticism; → Hetaireseos graphe; → Paederasty; → Prostitution; → Sexuality; → Sexual roles

1 G. BLEIBTREU-EHRENBERG, Sexuelle Abartigkeit im Urteil der abendländischen Religions-, Geistes- und Rechtsgeschichte, 1970   2 E. CANTARELLA, Secondo natura, La bissessualità nel mondo antico, 1988 3 P. CARTLEDGE, The Politics of Spartan Pederasty, in: PCPhS 207, N.S. 27, 1981, 17–36   4 K. J. DOVER, Greek Homosexuality, 1978   5 D. M. HALPERIN, One Hundred Years of Homosexuality, 1988   6 K. HOHEISEL, s.v. Homosexuality, RAC 16, 289–364   7 G. KOCH-HARNACK, Erotische Symbole, 1989   8 Id., Knabenliebe und Tiergeschenke, 1983   9 W. KROLL, Röm. Erotik, in: Zschr. für Sexualwissenschaft und Sexualpolitik, 17, 1930, 145–178   10 E. MEYER-ZWIFFELHOFFER, Im Zeichen des Phallus, 1995   11 H. P. OBERMAYER, Martial und der Diskurs über männliche 'Homosexualität' in der Lit. der frühen Kaiserzeit (Classica Monacensia 18), 1998 12 H. PATZER, Die griech. Knabenliebe, 1982   13 C. REINSBERG, Ehe, Hetärentum und Knabenliebe, 1989 14 A. ROUSSELLE, Porneia: On Desire and the Body in Antiquity, 1983   15 J. M. SNYDER, Lesbian Desire in the Lyrics of Sappho, 1997   16 P. VEYNE, Homosexualität im antiken Rom, in: P. ARIÈS, A. BÉJIN (ed.), Western Sexuality, 1986   17 J. J. WINKLER, The Constraints of Desire, 1992.   E.HA.

Honestiores/Humiliores While in the early Principate period, Roman → penal law distinguished primarily between citizens and non-citizens and this was the criterion in terms of personal rights for the determination of punitive measures, from the end of the 2nd cent. AD social rank determined the treatment of individuals by the courts. The differentiation in punishments is linked in the legal texts and in modern research primarily with two terms, *honestiores* and *humiliores*. The *honestiores* were the members of the privileged classes (senators, *equites*, decurions, veterans); they were exempted from torture, dishonouring, forced labour, to a large extent also from the death penalty, and even in the case of capital offences were mostly punished only with exile, whereas the *humiliores* were subject to the full rigour of the law.

In the legal texts of the 2nd and 3rd cents. AD a large number of terms and descriptions are used to designate the *honestiores* and *humiliores*. For *honestiores* there are, e.g.: *honestiore loco natus, in aliquo honore positus, in aliqua dignitate positus, altior. Humiliores* are described, e.g., as *humiliore loco positus, qui humillimo loco est, plebeius, sordidior, tenuior*. As a universal concept the *honestiores/humiliores* terminology is first used in the *sententiae* of Pseudo-Paulus that originated in about AD 300. The Roman jurists offer no exact definition of the two groups: it was mostly left in court practice to the judges to decide who belonged to the *honestiores* and the *humiliores*. If the veterans were also counted among the *honestiores* even though they as a rule only had modest assets and so could not be considered to be among the wealthy classes, their privilege corresponding to that of the decurions (Marcianus, Dig. 49,18,3) can be explained by the great political importance of the Roman army.

The distinction between *honestiores* and *humiliores* is visibly expressed in the different punishments. The members of the privileged classes of the population received for the same crime a lesser penalty than the rest of the population: exile and if need be beheading instead of the harsher death penalties *(summa supplicia* were: crucifixion, burning, condemnation *ad bestias*), exemption from condemnation *ad metallum* (work in mines or quarries), or forced labour (*opus publicum*). The *lex Iulia de vi publica* of Augustus consolidated the protection of Roman citizens from floggings once again (Ulpian, Dig. 48,6,7). No later than the end of the 2nd cent. AD, corporal punishment had been enacted for the members of the lower classes of society: flogging with *fustes* (sticks; Cod. Just. 2,11(12),5 – AD 198; Callistratus, Dig. 48,19,28,2 and 5). Torture, originally limited by the court to slaves, was also a threat to the free-born poor from the 2nd cent. onwards. Especially frequently the jurists discuss the exemption of decurions from torture. As they were the lowest in rank by far in the hierarchy of the privileged social groups, their privileges were the most under threat (Paulus, Dig. 50,2,14). Towards the end of the 3rd cent., witnesses of low social origin could be tortured (Arcadius Charisius, Dig. 22,5,21,2). *Humiliores* tended to be kept in custody more than *honestiores*, who mostly escaped imprisonment before trial by putting up a guarantee (Ulpian, Dig. 48,3,1; 26,10,3,16). Before the court, both in criminal and in civil cases, greater weight was attributed to statements of witnesses from the upper classes (Callistratus, Dig. 22,5,3,pr.). A legal violation (*iniuria*) was considered to be especially serious if the perpetrator was a member of the lower classes and the victim was a senator or an *eques* (Ulpian, Dig. 47,10,35).

Although the members of the upper classes were always in a much better position before the court than the rest of the population, there was no clear differentiation between *honestiores* and *humiliores* until the 2nd cent. AD. The differentiation is closely connected with the enactment of the → *cognitio extra ordinem*: while the criminal laws of the late Republic had fixed a standard punishment regardless of the social status of the accused, the judge was completely free in the *cogni-*

tio extra ordinem to set the penalties and was not bound by statutorily predetermined punishments. The differentiation between the *honestiores* and *humiliores* initially developed in criminal practice and only entered into the legislation of the *principes*: Hadrian and Antoninus Pius were the first to set as a prerequisite the differentiation in criminal law between *honestiores* and *humiliores* (Callistratus, Dig. 47,21,2; Papinian, Dig. 48,5, 39(38),8).

The principle of determining punishment according to social rank was retained in late antiquity: while the members of the upper classes were penalized with fines, the poor received corporal punishment. Although the penalties which threatened the *humiliores* were like those prescribed for slaves (cf. Macer, Dig. 48,19,10, pr.), it should not be concluded that the differences in personal rights between slaves and the free-born poor had become blurred. In the legislation of late antiquity there is an observable tendency to differentiate again to a far greater extent between these two groups with regard to the penalty imposed.

1 ALFÖLDY, RG, 69–81 2 P. GARNSEY, Social Status and Legal Privilege in the Roman Empire, 1970 3 Id., Why Penalties Become Harsher: The Roman Case, Late Republic to Fourth Century Empire, in: Natural Law Forum 13, 1968, 141–162 4 J.-U. KRAUSE, Gefängnisse im Römischen Reich, 1996 5 R. RILINGER, Humiliores-Honestiores. Zu einer sozialen Dichotomie im Strafrecht der röm. Kaiserzeit, 1988.   J.K.

Honestus Epigrammarian from the 'Garland' of Philippus, under whose rare name Ὄνεστος (probably an assimilation of the Roman cognomen H.) – he is sometimes called *Korínthios* (cf. Anth. Pal. 9,216) and sometimes *Byzántios* (cf. ibid. 7,274) – ten mostly epideictic poems are extant, which often relate to Boeotia and are distinguished by antitheses and both lexically and phraseologically original coinings of words. It is almost certain he was the H. who wrote the epigrams which came to light in Thespiae, of which nine are dedicated to the Muses, one to Thamyris and one to a Σεβαστή (*Sebasté*), i.e. an *Augusta*, very probably Livia, the third wife of Augustus.

GA II 1, 268–279; 2, 301–309.   M.G.A.

Honey (μέλι: *méli*, Latin *mel*).
I. ANCIENT ORIENT   II. GREECE AND ITALY

I. ANCIENT ORIENT

In the ancient Orient and Egypt not always terminologically distinguished from types of syrup (date or fig). With a value of a shekel of silver for 1–2 litres (21st cent. BC), honey was one of the most valuable foods in Mesopotamia and was the entitlement particularly of the gods (sacrifices) and high officials. Literary tradition regards honey as a delicacy especially together with the highly regarded butter oil ('milk and honey').

H. A. HOFFNER, Alimenta Hethaeorum, 1974, 123; J. LE-
CLANT, s.v. Biene, LÄ 1, 1975, 786–789; D. T. POTTS,
Mesopotamian Civilization, 1997, 50.   R.K.E.

II. GREECE AND ITALY

Bee honey, a food widespread throughout the ancient world from prehistory, rose to become the most
important sweetener of antiquity because of its high
sugar content. Thyme honey was considered to be outstanding (Varro, Rust. 3,16,26); the best kinds came
from Attica, Sicily and from the Greek islands, and were
traded in the Mediterranean area (Plin. HN 11,32–33;
Dioscorides 2,101). Although keeping bees was part of
full farming operations (Cic. Cato 56) and the occupation of beekeeper had developed from this, the demand
for honey always exceeded the supply. Honey was
therefore one of the highly valued foods throughout the
whole of antiquity (Hes. Op. 233 on bees; Aristoph.
Pax 252–254; Ath. 4,36a). *Mel optimum* ('Top quality
honey') cost as much as the best olive oil at the beginning of the 4th cent. AD (Edictum Diocletiani 3,10; cf.
3,1a). The essential function of honey in cooking was
that of a sweetener (Apicius, Brevis pimentorum,
excerpta). Apicius adds honey to almost all sauces,
meat and fish courses, and vegetable dishes. In addition
honey was a substantial ingredient in pastries, sweet
dishes, and jams and was the basis of drinks like
→ mead and *mulsum*. Honey was also used as a preservative for fruit and meat (Columella 12,10,5; Apicius,
De re coquinaria 1,8 ANDRÉ).

Outside the kitchen, honey fulfilled important functions in medicine (Plin. HN 22,106): doctors drew upon
its anti-inflammatory (Theophr. Hist. pl. 9,11,3) and
strengthening effects (Dioscorides 2,104). Honey was
also used for cosmetic purposes, for instance as a preparation for hair loss and freckles (according to Plin. HN
25,18; Dioscorides 2,102). In cult, too, honey, regarded
as dew from heaven (Aristot. Hist. an. 5,553b 27–29)
and a gift of the gods (Verg. G. 4,1), was important; it
was sacrificed particularly in rites of passage, for instance on the occasion of death (cf. Hom. Il. 23,170;
Hom. Od. 10,519).

J. ANDRÉ, L'alimentation et la cuisine à Rome, ²1981;
O. BÖCHER, A. SALLINGER, s.v. Honey, RAC 16, 433–473;
A. DALBY, Siren Feasts. A History of Food and Gastrono-
my in Greece, 1996; G. LAFAYE, s.v. Mel, DS 3, 1701–
1706; M. SCHUSTER, s.v. Mel, RE 15, 364–384.   A.G.

Honorary inscriptions were used for public presentation of a person on the basis of special merits or a
general acknowledgement of his esteem. The honour
was always connected with a representation in statue
form of the honoured person, with the inscription at
the base of the statue. Honorary inscriptions (HI) were
accorded primarily to the emperor and his family, the
governor, high officials in the administration of the
empire, municipal officials, and priests, but also to private individuals. The honour was bestowed during the
lifetime of the honoured person but it was also pos-

sible after his death. Typical locations were the municipal forum and theatre, porticoes, temple entrance
halls, and public gardens. In Rome itself during the
Imperial period this form of sculptural representation
of the upper class became restricted more and more to
the private houses of the senators and *equites*, who
wanted to obviate a possible competitive situation
with the imperial house. Outside Rome, HI and honorary statues were among the typical features of public
places but they are also to be found in places that were
not generally accessible.

The textual formula contains the name and the
social position of the honoured person (mostly in the
dative or accusative), the name of the donor (e.g. the
Senate in Rome, provincial rural assemblies, municipal
council meetings, corporations, or private individuals),
and a closing formula (e.g. *statuam posuit* or *locus
datus decreto decurionum*). Latin HI often list the complete *cursus honorum* of the honoured person, a custom
also adopted in many Greek HI. If there was a concrete
reason for the honour (e.g. a special achievement/en-
dowment for a municipal community), this is mentioned in the inscription. But HI can also be kept extremely short and only record the name of the honoured
person without stating his social rank and any merits.
Detailed HI frequently mention the generous payment
of the costs by the honoured person himself. A special
case is represented by those HI in which the donor and
the honoured person are identical (for example a statue
inside a public building of the donor).

R. CAGNAT, Cours d'Epigraphie Latine, ⁴1914 (repr.
1964), 257–263; W. ECK, Ehrungen für Personen hohen
soziopolitischen Ranges im öffentlichen und privaten
Bereich, in: H. J. SCHALLES, H. v. HESBERG, P. ZANKER
(ed.), Die röm. Stadt im 2. Jh. n. Chr., 1992, 359–376;
G. KLAFFENBACH, Griech. Epigraphik, ²1966, 65–67;
E. MEYER, Einführung in die lateinische Epigraphik,
1973, 66–69; G. ZIMMER, Locus datus decreto decurionum, 1989.   ST.B.

Honoratus

[1] Official under Constantius [2] II. *consularis Syriae*
(before AD 353; Lib. Ep. 251), *comes Orientis* (353–
354; Amm. Marc. 14,1,3; 7,2; Lib. Ep. 386), *praefectus
praetorio Galliarum* (355/357; Lib. Ep. 386 FOER-
STER). From 359 to 361 he was the first *praefectus urbis
Constantinopolitanae* (Chron. min. 1,239 MOMMSEN)
and in this office he passed judgement on the heresy of
Aetius (Sozom. Hist. eccl. 4,23,3). PLRE 1, 438f. (H. 2).
[2] Son of the sophist and official Quirinus (Lib. Ep.
358; 359), in about AD 355 student of Libanius (Lib.
Ep. 405; 535). From 358 to 361 he was in the service of
the state, probably as a *notarius* (Lib. Ep. 358; 359 FO-
ERSTER). He is possibly identical to the *consularis Byza-
cii* of the same name attested for 368 (Cod. Just.
1,33,1). PLRE 1, 439 (H. 3 and 4).   W.P.

Honoria Iusta Grata H., western Roman empress. Daughter of → Constantius [6] III and of → Galla [3] Placidia, elder sister of → Valentinianus III, born in AD 417 or 418 (Olympiodorus fr. 34 FHG IV 65; Sozom. Hist. eccl. 9,16,2), probably became Augusta before 437 (ILS 817f.). She was forced to take a vow of eternal virginity, but in 449 was expelled from court because of an affair with her procurator and she became betrothed to a senator. She then asked → Attila, king of the Huns, for help and gave him a promise of marriage (Iord. Rom. 328; Iord. Get. 42,223f.; Iohannes Antiochenus fr. 199 FHG IV 613f.). When Attila's demand for her delivery and half of the western empire as a dowry was refused, he invaded Gaul in 451 with a large army (Prisc. fr. 15f. FHG IV 98f.; Chron. min. 1, 662, 139; 2, 79, 434 MOMMSEN).

> PLRE 2, 568f., 1308; J. B. BURY, Iusta Grata Honoria, in: JRS 9, 1919, 1–13; A. DEMANDT, Die Spätantike, 1989, 149, 154; ST. I. OOST, Galla Placidia Augusta, 1968; STEIN, Spätröm. Reihe, vol. 1, 494–498.   K.P.J.

Honorius

[1] Listed in [Aur. Vict.] Epit. Caes. 48,1 as father of the emperor Theodosius I, but may have been his grandfather. PLRE 1,441.

[2] Elder brother of Theodosius I, probably related to → Maria, whose daughter was → Serena; both were taken into the emperor's household. PLRE 1,441.   H.L.

[3] **Flavius H.** West Roman emperor AD 393–423, was born on 9 September AD 384 as the younger son of emperor → Theodosius I and Aelia Flavia Flacilla in Constantinople (Socr. 5,12,2). Already in 386, as *nobilissimus puer,* he took on the first of his 12 consulates (CIL XIV 231). In January 393 he was proclaimed Augustus (Socr. 5,25,8; Chron. min. 1, 298 MOMMSEN). Shortly before his death, Theodosius summoned him to Milan and handed him rule over the western part of the empire under the guardianship of → Stilicho (Ambr. Obit. Theod. 34f.; Claud. Carm. 7,151ff.; Zos. 4,59,1). The effective splitting of the empire in 17 January 395 between himself and his older brother → Arcadius was never reversed.

Unlike Theodosius and his predecessors, his sons and their successors no longer took part in military campaigns personally, but kept to palace-living as *principes clausi* (Sid. Apoll. Carm. 5,358). H. initially resided in Milan, then from 402 in Ravenna, which under his regime developed into the capital of the Western Empire. This residence he left almost only on trips to Rome, e.g. 403/4 (Claud. Carm. 28) and 407/8 (Cod. Theod. 16,2,38; 1,20,1). Throughout his life, the emperor remained under the influence of his commanders and advisers and seldom acted independently. Until 408 the young H. was controlled by the *magister utriusque militiae* Stilicho, who had himself called the emperor's *parens* (ILS 795) and in 398 married off his elder daughter Maria to him (Claud. Carm. 10) and, after her death, his younger daughter Thermantia (Zos. 5,28,1–3; 35,3). Both marriages were childless.

Under Stilicho's regency, tensions with the eastern part of the empire persisted. The attacks by the Gothic king → Alaricus [2] were repelled, in 398 → Gildo was defeated in Africa, in 406 → Radagaisus in Italy. It was not possible to avert the large-scale Germanic invasion over the Rhine into Gaul in 406 (Oros. 7,38; Greg. Tur. Franc. 2,9; Chron. min. 1, 299), nor in 407 the virtual abandonment of Britain. After Stilicho's murder in 408, Alaricus' Visigoths penetrated Italy and on 24 August 410 conquered Rome (Sozom. Hist. eccl. 9,9; Chron. min. 1, 300; 466). The plunder of the 'Eternal City' provoked violent controversy between pagan and Christian thinkers. Even after the death of his father-in-law, H. remained dependent on his advisers. In 408/9 the *magister officiorum* → Olympius conducted all political business, in 409/10 the *praefectus praetorio* → Iovius [2], in 411–21 the *patricius* → Constantius [6] III, who was finally elevated to the co-regency and who since 417 had been the husband of H.'s sister Galla [3] Placidia. Although the usurpation attempts by → Constantinus [3] III, → Attalus [11], → Iovinus [2] and → Heraclianus were all suppressed, further incursions by the Germans and other barbarians could no longer be checked. In 409–11 Vandals, Alani and Suebi invaded Spain, Visigoths, Franks, Burgundians and Alamanni invaded Gaul, and Huns invaded Pannonia (Sozom. Hist. eccl. 9,12f.; Oros. 7,40–43; Chron. min. 2,17f.). The formation of federate kingdoms began in 418 with the Visigoths in Aquitania (Chron. min. 1, 654; 2, 19).

The pious H., who in his early years had for a long time come under the influence of Bishop → Ambrosius of Milan, supported the Church and the privileges of the clergy (Cod. Theod. 16,2,29ff.). He had non-Christians attacked (Cod. Theod. 16,10,15ff.) just as vigorously as heretics, the Donatists in particular (Cod. Theod. 16,5,37ff.). In 404 gladiatorial games were abolished (Theod. Hist. eccl. 5,26), in 407 the Sibylline books were burned (Rut. Namat. 2,52–56). In 419 H. resolved a schism in favour of Pope Boniface (→ Bonifatius [2] I.). The emperor died of dropsy in August 423 (Socr. 7,22,20; Olympiodorus fr. 41 FHG IV 67). On his coins RIC 10, 1994, 123–37; 317–42; for the image on coins pl. 34–42; cf. [1].

> 1 R. DELBRUECK, Spätant. Kaiserportraits, 1933, 32, 96f., 206ff., 211ff.

> PLRE 1, 442 (H. 3); TH. S. BURNS, Barbarians within the Gates of Rome, 1994; A. CAMERON, Claudianus, 1970; A. DEMANDT, Die Spätantike, 1989, 137–150; E. DEMOUGEOT, De l'unité à la division de l'Empire Romain, 1951; v. HAEHLING, 593ff.; H. WOLFRAM, Die Goten, ³1990, 158–180.   K.P.J.

Honos Personification of honour. Ovid (Fast. 5,23ff.) is the only one to place H. in a genealogy as the husband of Reverentia and father of Maiestas. Apart from that H. plays a role mainly in the military sphere, where he represents honourable and virtuous conduct in situations of war and is closely connected to → Virtus. It is therefore not surprising that important military commanders dedicated temples to the deity, who is often represented with a spear and a cornucopia [1]. In 233 BC, Q. Fabius [30] Maximus Verrucosus erected a sanctuary to H. near the → Porta Capena, right next to the temple of Mars (Cic. Nat. D. 2,61). This was the starting-point of the → *transvectio equitum* (Aur. Vict. De viris illustribus 32). In 212 BC, it was decorated by M. Marcellus with spoils from the capture of Syracuse (Liv. 25,40,1ff.) and extended with a cella for Virtus (Liv. 27,25,7ff.; Plut. Marcellus 28; Val. Max. 1,1,8). The temple was still renovated by Vespasian (Plin. HN 35,120). C. Marius erected a temple to H. and Virtus with the spoils of the Cimbrian War (CIL XI 1831); its proportions were praised by Vitruvius (7 praef. 17). It was in this temple that the session of the Senate took place which gave Cicero permission to return from exile (Cic. Sest. 116).

H. was venerated from early on. A votive inscription in Old Latin from the area of Porta Collina (CIL I² 31) probably belonged to an ancient sanctuary of H. (cf. Cic. Leg. 2,58). According to Plutarch (Quaest. Rom. 266f), sacrifices to H. were not made with the head covered, as usual. In addition, female animals could be sacrificed to the male deity (CIL VI 2044 I 5). This indicates a cult in the Greek manner (*Graeco ritu*).

1 C. LOCHIN, s.v. H., LIMC 5.2, 341 no. 6; 10; 13.
B.SCH.

Hoopoe (ἔποψ/*épops*, named after its characteristic call *upupa* in Lat., Varro, Ling. 5,75; cf. Aristoph. Av. 57 ff., 227 and 260), common in the Mediterranean and the only European representative of the hoopoes (*Upupidae*). Paus. 10,4,8 and Plin. HN 10,86 describe its appearance, especially the impressive folding crest (Ov. Met. 6,672–674) and its long beak. Ael. NA 3,26 exaggerates the bird's uncleanliness (alleged use of faeces for nest building; cf. Aristot. Hist. an. 8(9),15, 616a 35 f.). Despite its beauty – which is never mentioned in ancient literature – the hoopoe had the reputation of a stinking bird because of its insect diet, which was often captured on animal dung (Plin. HN 10,86); it was considered an enemy of bees [1. 445]. People believed it capable of strange things – that it could transform into a → goshawk (Aeschyl. fr. 304 TGF; Gp. 15,1,22; cf. Plin. HN 10,86), that it had a miracle plant (ἀδίαντον/*adíanton*) with which it could open locks (Ael. NA 3,26; cf. 1,35; Aristoph. Av. 92), and that it predicted a good wine year when it called frequently (Horapollon 2,92). In Egypt is was worshipped because of its supposed concern for its aged parents (Ael. NA 10,16; Horapollon 1,55). The crest, which was interpreted as a crown, made it appear as transformed king (cf. the myth of → Tereus).

1 F. OLCK, s. v. Biene, RE 3, 431–450.

KELLER 2, 60–63; M. SCHUSTER, s. v. Wiedehopf, RE 8 A, 2108–2112; D'ARCY W. THOMPSON, A Glossary of Greek Birds, ²1936 (repr. 1966), 95–100.
C. HÜ.

Hopletes see → Iones

Hoplitai (Hoplites) The word ὁπλίτης (*hoplítēs*, pl. *hoplítai*) is derived from ὅπλον (*hóplon*, 'equipment, shield'; esp. in the pl. ὅπλα, *hópla* 'weapons') and describes heavily armed foot soldiers. Their bronze armament (panoply) consisted of a round shield of 0,9 m diameter with a vambrace (πόρπαξ, *pórpax*) in the centre and a handgrip (ἀντιλαβή, *antilabé*) at the edge, a helmet, a breastplate, greaves, which reached from the ankles to above the knees, a spear for thrusting as well as a short sword for close-quarters combat. There are archaeological records of weapons of this kind dating from the late 8th cent. BC, and the mode of combat associated with them is depicted on the Chigi Vase, a proto-Corinthian artefact (c. 650/640 BC.; Rome, VG); it can at least be assumed that the poet of the *Iliad* was already acquainted with these weapons.

Characteristic of the warfare of the time were the closed battle ranks (→ Phalanx), in which the warriors were arranged in a long line and with a depth of 8 or more men. They advanced together at a walking or running pace to the rhythm of the flute-players. What was decisive in the battle was the co-ordinated advance until its impact on the enemy, as well as the steadiness in the ensuing close combat. Since a hoplite covered the unprotected side of his neighbour with the left half of his shield, the greatest degree of dependability was imperative. At the same time a drifting off to the right occurred during the course of combat, towards the unprotected side (Thuc. 5,71,1), so that the enemy flank could also be attacked from there. The right wing was, consequently, the place for the elite units, and was regarded as a place of honour. A specific ethics of mutual solidarity was connected with this mode of combat, which related to the → polis (Tyrateus 6; 7; 8,11ff; 9,13ff. D.). This fighting strategy – together with the corresponding warrior ethos – was first developed in Sparta (7th cent. BC), then spread as especially successful and resulted in the important victories against the Persians (Marathon 490, Plataeae 479 BC). The phalanx only lost significance with the triumphant advance of the Macedonian tactics, which attributed more importance to the → cavalry (battle of Chaeronea 338 BC).

Since the warriors mainly had to equip themselves, the status of the hoplites required a certain economic position. Because of the size of armies in antiquity, hoplites were recruited not only from the nobility, but also from the ranks of affluent farmers, who then took on the aristocratic ideas and values. At the same time the mutual solidarity and allegiance to the polis were increasingly valued positively. For this reason the development of the polis was frequently linked to the simultaneous development of the hoplite phalanx. The opinions about this in modern research are controversial, but generally there can be no doubt that this mode of combat had an integrative effect in the sense of strengthening also the political solidarity.

The term *hoplitai* also had a social significance: those who served as *hoplitai* belonged to a socially elevated, middle class, between the → thetes (the dispossessed) and the aristocracy, who were well-to-do farmers; this is probably the term used by the third of the Solonic classes (the → Zeugitai). In various poleis this connection was formalized; a particular census that enabled or committed a person to serve as a hoplite also conferred certain political rights, for instance those of full citizenship or full political and civil rights (Aristot. Pol. 2,6,1265b 26ff.; 4,3,1291a 28ff.; 6,7,1321a 12f.); thus one speaks of a hoplite politeia, which in the political theory critical of democracy (Aristotle) was evaluated more positively. At the time of the oligarchical coup in Athens (411 BC) the introduction of such a constitution was planned (Thuc. 8,97,1; Aristot. Ath. Pol. 33,1), and in the year 322 BC such a structure seems to have become a reality. However, it is true that no alternative to democracy was constituted in Athens.

1 J.K. ANDERSON, Hoplites and Heresies, in: JHS 104, 1984, 152   2 P. CARTLEDGE, Hoplites and Heroes, in: JHS 97, 1977, 11–27   3 P. DUCREY, Guerre et guerriers dans la Grèce antique, 1985   4 H.-J. GEHRKE, Phokion, 1976, 90–93   5 Id., Stasis, 1985, 317f.   6 A.J. HOLLADAY, Hoplites and Heresies, in: JHS 102, 1982, 94–103   7 J. LATACZ, Kampfparänese, Kampfdarstellung und Kampfwirklichkeit in der Ilias, bei Kallinos und Tyrtaios, 1977   8 O. MURRAY, Early Greece, ²1993   9 J. SALMON, Political Hoplites?, in: JHS 97, 1977, 84–101   10 A.M. SNODGRASS, The Hoplite Reform and History, in: JHS 85, 1965, 110–122   11 P. SPAHN, Mittelschicht und Polisbildung, 1977.   H.-J.G.

Hoplites (Ὁπλίτης; *Hoplítēs*).

[1] Town north-east of Sparta (Pol. 16,16,2), possibly named ('warrior') after the archaic cult statue of Apollo in nearby Thornax.

F.W. WALBANK, A Historical Commentary on Polybius 2, 1967, 521.   Y.L.

[2] Small river in Boeotia, whose localization near Haliartus or Coronea was already disputed in antiquity; associated with an oracle on the death of Lysander (Plut. Lysander 29,3ff.; Mor. 408A-B).

F. BÖLTE, s.v. H. (2), RE 8, 2296f.; S. LAUFFER, Kopais 1, 1986, 80f.   P.F.

[3] see → Hoplitai

Hops (*Humulus lupulus* L., Family *Cannabinaceae*).

Hops often appear wild as creepers in central European alluvial forests. The cone-like fruit of the female plants are added to beer because of their aromatic and preservative bitter constituents. This is supposed to have been discovered by Finno-Ugric tribes, from whom this seasoning was adopted in western Europe in the 5th–7th cents. The first hop-garden (*humularium*) is proven in the abbey of St. Denis near Paris for 768 [1. 216]. The only ancient reference is in Pliny, who mentions *lupus salictarius* growing on willows as a delicacy (HN 21,86). The young shoots were consumed as vegetables, like → asparagus.

1 J. BECKMANN: Hopfen, in: Beyträge zur Gesch. der Erfindungen, vol. 5.2, 1803, 206–234.   C.HÜ.

Hor

An Egyptian from the district of → Sebennytus, a village scribe and perhaps also scribe for the district, he began a five-year journey in 173 BC, which he had been instructed to make by an oracle. → *Pastophóros* of Isis and from 167/6 priest (κάτοχος/*kátochos*?) at the ibis Sanctuary of Saqqara/Memphis, where he had an administrative position in the temple. His oracular prophesies delivered via dreams, were listened to even in the palace. Among other destinations he travelled from Alexandria to Sarapeum in 168, where he delivered an oracular prophesy in front of the king, directed against Antiochus IV, concerning the security of Alexandria and the dynasty. In 158 he wrote an encomium for the birthday (and expected visit) of Ptolemy VI. An archive of demotic, oracular communications has survived.

D. KESSLER, Die hl. Tiere und der König 1, 1989, 110ff.; J.D. RAY, The Archive of Hor, 1976; Id., Observations on the Archive of Hor, in: JEA 64, 1978, 113ff.   W.A.

Horace see Q. → Horatius [7] Flaccus

Horae (Ὧραι; *Hôrai*).

Divine beings governing cycles of time. Initially, there were three; later usually four (one Hora as goddess of youthful beauty: Pind. Nem. 8,1; series recapitulating 9 or 10 names: Hyg. Fab. 183), probably in connection with distinguishing a fourth season of the year (Alcm. fr. 12 CALAME; Hippoc. De aere aquis et locis 1. 10; Aristot. Gen. an. 784a 19). The appellative and the personification are at times barely distinguishable (e.g., Hom. Il. 21,450; Od. 10,469).

Like other grouped divinities, the H. often appear as attendants of Olympian gods, in particular of Demeter (H. Hom. 2,54; 192; 492), Apollo (SEG 33, 115, 13; Lycoph. 352; Anth. Pal. 9,525,25; [1]), Aphrodite and Dionysus.

Their various manifestations overlap partly. In the *Iliad* they are guardians of the gates of Olympus (5.749–751 = 8.393–395; 433–435); from Hesiod (Theog. 901–903), the H. → Eunomia, → Dike and → Eirene, daughters of → Zeus and → Themis, safeguarded the compliance with the human legal order – probably in connection with the notion of an inherent relationship between the observance of the law and the flourishing of nature (Hom. Il. 16,384–392; Hom. Od. 19,109–114). Additionally, from early on the H. were seen together with the → Charites as goddesses of adornment (Aphrodite: Hes. Op. 74–75; Cypria 1, fr. 4; H. Hom. 6, 5–13; Pandora: Hes. Op. 70–76) and were associated with spring (ibid.; Pind. fr. 75,14–15). The H. are also linked to birth (e.g., Aphrodite, Hermes), child-rearing (e.g., Pind. Pyth. 9,59–65: Aristaeus) and weddings (e.g.,

Peleus and Thetis, Dionysus and Ariadne), very likely due to the changing phases of life reflected in such situations.

In classical Athens, during a feast where meat is boiled rather than roasted, the H. are asked for moderate warmth and beneficial rain to foster growth (Philochorus FGrH 328 F 173). According to Pausanias (9,35,1–2), however, there seemed to have been only two H. → Karpo and → Thallo, while Auxo, together with Hegemone, was one of the → Charites (on this problem, see [2]). The names, however, indicate that they were goddesses of vegetation.

Evidence of a cult of the H. is attested not only in Attica (e.g., a sanctuary of the H. with an altar for Dionysus Orthos: Philochorus FGrH 328 F 5b; IG II/III²: 4877; [3; 4]), but also elsewhere, usually in connection with other gods (e.g., Opus, Olympia, Megalopolis, Argos, Cyrene). In the Hellenistic period, four H. marched in the procession of Ptolemy II Philadelphus [5].

Iconographically, the H., Charites and Nymphs are often indistinguishable (cf. Artem. 2,44), above all in the well-known mosaics and the sarcophagi of the Imperial period depicting the seasons. In [9], the three figures in the relief on the south-east corner of the → Ara Pacis are interpreted as H., and the main figure as Pax Augusta (= Eirene). The influence also persists in the presence of H. festivals in medieval calendars [8].

1 F. WILLIAMS, A Theophany in Theocritus, in: CQ 21, 1971, 142   2 CHR. HABICHT, Stud. zur Gesch. Athens in hell. Zeit, 1982, 87–90   3 FARNELL, Cults 5, 425 4 DEUBNER, 190f., 201   5 E. E. RICE, The Grand Procession of Ptolemy Philadelphus, 1983, 49–51; 57 6 M. PESSOA, Villa romaine de Rabaçal, Penela (Coimbra-Portugal): réalités et perspectives, in: Conimbriga 30, 1991, 109–119   7 J. ENGEMANN, Ein Missorium des Anastasius, FS für K. Wessel zum 70. Geburtstag, ed. by M. RESTLE, 1988, 103–115   8 G. COMET, Les calendriers médiévaux: une représentations du monde, in: Journal des Savants 1992, 35–98   9 N. TH. DE GRUMMOND, Pax Augusta and the Horae on the Ara Pacis Augustae, in: AJA 94, 1990, 663–677.

V. MACHAIRA, s.v. H., LIMC 5.1, 502–510; L. ABAD CASAL, s.v. H./Horae, LIMC 5.1, 510–538; CHR. BAUCH-HENSS-THÜRIEDL, Jahreszeiten, Kotinos, FS für E. Simon, 1992, 429–432; M. DUFKOVÁ, Noch zu Jahreszeiten-Sarkophagen, in: Listy filologické 115, 1992, 161–163; G. M. A. HANFMANN, The Season Sarcophagus in Dumbarton Oaks, 1951; A. JOLLES, s.v. H., RE 8, 2300–2313; P. KRANZ, Jahreszeiten-Sarkophage. Entwicklung und Ikonographie des Motivs der vier Jahreszeiten auf kaiserzeitlichen Sarkophagen und Sarkophagdeckeln, 1984; M. T. MARABINI MOEVS, Penteteris e le tre H. nella Pompè di Tolemeo Filadelfo, in: BA 72, 1987, 1–36; A. RAPP, s.v. H., ROSCHER 1.2, 2712–2731; M. SCHLEIERMACHER, Die Jahreszeitenfresken von Nida-Heddernheim, in: Kölner Jb. für Vor- und Frühgesch. 24, 1991, 213–218.   T.H.

Horapollo The Egyptian H., author of the *Hieroglyphiká*, possibly identical to H., the son of Asclepiades, came from a family of grammarians and philosophers from Phenebythis in Panopolites; was active in Alex-

andria around AD 500. H. is known, among other things, from the *vita* of the pupil of Proclus, → Isidorus [4], written by the Neoplatonist → Damascius, and from a Greek petition to an official of Phenebythis between 491 and 493 (pap. Cairo 67295).

The Greek text of the *Hieroglyphiká* is recorded in MSS of the 14th cent. and, according to its title, has been translated from the Egyptian by Philippus. An Egyptian (Coptic) original text cannot be assumed, however, on account of external circumstances and the language of the Greek text. In the first book of the work there are 70 → hieropglyphs, in the second 30, plus 89 imaginary signs, probably an addition by Philippus, and written according to the pattern: 'if you want to express an x, write a y'. This part is probably based on an Egyptian papyrus containing hieroglyphs, and reflects the expanded Graeco-Roman Egyptian range of meaning of individual characters. There follows a substantiation indicating the author's Neoplatonic background and his familiarity with ancient bestiaries. These allegorical and symbolical explanations created the idea of the hieroglyphs as mysterious images of condensed wisdom. They promoted the development of hieroglyphics and emblematics in humanist circles, which counter-acted the deciphering of the hieroglyphs until the modern era.

→ DECIPHERMENT; → EGYPTOLOGY

1 F. SBORDONE, Hori Apollinis Hieroglyphica, 1940 2 H.-J. THISSEN, Vom Bild zum Buchstaben – vom Buchstaben zum Bild. Von der Arbeit an H.s Hieroglyphika, 1998   3 E. WINTER, s.v. Hieroglyphen, RAC 15, 90–94. HE.FE.

Horatius Name of a patrician *gens* which had already died out in the 5th cent. BC. Later bearers of the name owe it to the provenance from the eponymous *tribus*. **[1] Horatii.** (Royal period). According to legend (Liv. 1,24–26; Dion. Hal. Ant. Rom. 3,13,4–22,10), under King Tullus → Hostilius [I 4], the conflict between Rome and → Alba Longa was decided by a fight between the Horatii triplets and the Curiatii triplets rather than a battle. After two brothers had fallen, the last H. overcame his opponent. On his return to Rome, H.'s sister recognized the cloak of her fiancé (one of the Curiatii) among the booty he brought; she lamented him and was killed by her brother as a warning not to take pity on an enemy. Condemned by the court as a murderer, he was set free after an appeal to the people, on the provision that he made atonement.   C.MÜ.
The expiatory sacrifice was customarily prepared on an altar beneath a beam, the Tigillum Sororium, stretched over the road at the *compitum Acilii*, near the Forum. The story is an *aition* for a series of ancient tumuli in Latium and for the ritual at the Tigillum Sororium, which conceals initiatory themes; the connection of *sororium* with *soror* ('sister') is folk etymology. Sources: Liv. 1,24–26; Dion. Hal. Ant. Rom. 3,13,4–22,10.

1 T. J. CORNELL, The Beginnings of Rome, 1995

H. J. ROSE, De religionibus antiquis questiunculae tres, in: Mnemosyne 53, 1925, 407–410; G. DUMÉZIL, Horace et les Curiaces, 1942; F. COARELLI, Il Foro Romano. Periodo Arcaico, 1983, 111–117; J. POUCET, Les origines de Rome, 1985, 219–221. F.G.

[2] **H., P.** Mentioned only by Dion. Hal. (Ant. Rom. 10,53,1; 56,2) as consul for 453 BC and *decemvir* in 451, probably due to confusion with a P. Curiatius. MRR 1, 43f.; 45f.

[3] **H. Barbatus, M.** Cognomen [Tu]rrin(us) ? (cf. Fasti feriarum Latinarum, CIL I², 56). In 449, after the end of the rule of the → *decemviri* [1], as *cos.* along with his colleague L. Valerius Potitus (MRR 1, 47) he completed the legislation of the *decemviri*, their former adversaries, by adding the last two law tables and setting up all 12 tables (→ *tabulae duodecim*) (Diod. Sic. 12,26,1; Liv. 3,57,10). The historicity of the *leges Valeriae Horatiae* ascribed to them (Liv. 3,55,3–7) is disputed as a possible backward projection of the results of the → struggle of the orders [1. 276–278; 2. 213–220]. As victor over the Sabines, H. is said to have been refused a triumph by the Senate, but was then granted one by the people (Liv. 3,57,9; 61,11–63; Dion. Hal. Ant. Rom. 11,48–50,1).

1 T. J. CORNELL, The Beginnings of Rome, 1995 2 D. FLACH, Die Gesetze der frühen römischen Republik, 1994.

[4] **H. Cocles.** Seen in Roman literary tradition as the epitome of old Roman *virtus*. The earliest account of the legend is given by Polybius (6,54): in the battle against the Etruscans led by → Porsenna as they stood outside Rome, H. defended the → *pons sublicius* against the attackers until the bridge was torn down behind him, then leapt into the water and lost his life. According to Livy (2,10,2–11), H. at first defended the bridge with two comrades, was able to rescue himself unscathed and received a series of honours. Ancient authors usually explain his cognomen *Cocles* ('the one-eyed') by saying that he had already lost an eye in an earlier battle.

[5] **H. Pulvillus, C.** Cos. 477 and 457 (MRR 1, 26f.; 41; Liv. 3,30,1 and Diod. Sic. 11,91,1 with the praenomen M. for the *cos.* 457). Based on the variation in the *praenomen*, the identification of the *cos.* of 477 with that of 457 is not completely certain. In 477, after the battle on the Cremera, H., who had been in battle with the Volscians, is said to have protected Rome against the Etruscans by his return (Liv. 2,51,1–3). During H.'s second consulate in 457, the number of people's tribunes was doubled to ten; he conquered Corbio himself in the war with the Aequi (Liv. 3,30; Dion. Hal. Ant. Rom. 10,28–30).

[6] **H. Pulvillus, M.** As representative of King Tarquinius at Ardea, he opposed the latter after his expulsion from Rome (Dion. Hal. Ant. Rom. 4,85). Polybius (3,22,1) names H. and L. Iunius [I 4] Brutus as first consuls of the Republic and places the first Roman-

Carthaginian treaty in their consulate. The remaining traditions identify H. as *cos. suff.* in 509 with his colleague P. Valerius Poplicola, with whom he held a second consulate (omitted by Livy) in 507 (MRR 1, 3; 6). On the basis of dedicatory inscription, H. was ascribed with the dedication of the Capitoline temple of Jupiter. The tradition is divided whether this occurred in his first or second consulate, and whether H. was acting as consul or pontifex (Cic. Dom. 139; Liv. 2,8,6–8; Dion. Hal. Ant. Rom. 5,35,3; Val. Max. 5,10,1; Sen. Dial. 6,13,1; Tac. Hist. 3,72,1f.; Plut. Poplicola 14). C.MÜ.

[7] **H. Flaccus, Q.** The poet Horace.
A. LIFE. B. WORKS C. IMPACT

A. LIFE

Ancient information about H. is comparatively abundant. He gives not a few accounts and hints in his works. Admittedly, one must be warned against considering this information, above all that contained in the lyric poetry, as definite data; they are poetic statements and must be regarded as such. In addition, there is information in the late antique scholia of → Porphyrius, Pseudo-Acro (→ Helenius Acro) and an indirectly handed-down *vita* of → Suetonius. The full name Q. Horatius Flaccus is connected to the *Carmen saeculare* (see below) in inscriptions; its elements also all appear in the poetry (*Quintus*: Sat. 2,6,37; *Horatius*: Epist. 1,14,5; Carm. 4,6,44; *Flaccus*: Epod. 15,12; Sat. 2,1,18). H. was born on 8 December 65 BC in Venosa/ Venusia (on the border between Lucania and Apulia) as the son of a freedman; he died on 27 November 8 BC.

Thanks to the care of his father, H. enjoyed an exceptional education, first in his home town (Epist. 2,1,70f.), afterwards in Rome in a circle of high-ranking classmates (Sat. 1,6,71–78; Epist. 2,2,41f.), finally as a student in Athens (Epist. 2,2,43–5). He was taught to constantly test himself through his father's example, but also to observe intensively and morally evaluate the life-style of others (Sat. 1,4,103–143). The location of his home town on the border aroused an uncertainty in H. regarding his tribal membership, and also led him to connect the fierceness of his character to this origin (Sat. 2,1,34ff.). After his years of education, he was caught up in the confusion of the civil wars (Epist. 2,2,46–48): Iunius [I 10] Brutus conferred an astonishingly high military command as *tribunus militum* on the student in Athens (Sat. 1,6,48). After the defeat at → Philippi, H. lost his entire paternal inheritance and earned his living working at the state treasury. Poverty, he says (Epist. 2,2,51f.), led him to making verses – a rather ironic statement as shown by the context.

Indeed, H.'s first poems were written in the 1st half of the 30s BC. They led him out of financial poverty through a series of encounters. The poets → Vergilius and → Varius became aware of him; through these new friends, he was recommended to → Maecenas (M.) and, through him, to Octavian, the later → Augustus. A first meeting with M. in the year 37 (Sat. 1,6,52–64) led, 9 months later, to H.'s acceptance into M.'s circle of friends; around 32, the latter gave him → Sabinum, a (modest, according to the view of the time) country estate in the Sabine mountains near Vicovaro, which was run by a manager, worked by five tenant families and served by eight slaves. H. thus had, along with a livelihood, a second home, which he esteemed highly and celebrated in pleasant colours (Sat. 2,6,1–15; 60–70; Epist. 1,16,5–16; Carm. 3,13). He did not give it up even when later, as the *Vita* reports, he received an extremely honourable offer of an influential position: Augustus himself wanted to have him as private secretary. His refusal, according to Suetonius, did not lead to any ill-feeling.

The 44-year-old H. describes himself as small in stature, portly, and with prematurely grey hair (Epist. 1,20,24; Epist. 1,7,26; Epist. 1,4,15; Vita). As a particular characteristic, he names his outbursts of anger (Epist. 1,20,25; Carm. 3,9,23; Sat. 2,3,323), which, however, never last long. Philosophically, H. belonged to the school of → Epicurus (Epist. 1,4,16); concepts from the → Stoa and the Cynic → diatribe occasionally left their mark on and were amalgamated into his work [25]. He died at the age of 57, two months after M. He named Augustus as his heir; the burial took place on the Esquiline.

B. WORKS
1. GRAECA 2. SATIRES 3. EPODES 4. ODES
5. CARMEN SAECULARE 6. EPISTLES AND ARS POETICA

1. GRAECA
The epigram Anth. Gr. 7,542 by a poet named Flaccus may be a poem by the young H. [18]. In any case, H. himself admits to having tried his hand, and later clearly distanced himself from his own Greek poetry (Sat. 1,10,39–43).

2. SATIRES
While H. followed a Greek model with → Archilochus in his epodes, written about the same time, he used a Roman form in the → 'Satires'. However, he clearly distanced himself, theoretically and practically, from → Lucilius. The title is *Sermones*, the two books were written around 41–35/3 and 35–30 respectively [22]. H. praised Lucilius for his candour, but criticized the all too careless style and the unrefined overproduction (Sat. 1,10; 1,4,8–13). However, he is fair enough to consider the time factor and to make the early epoch partly responsible for the deficits, not the author alone (1,10,64–69). Book 1 contains 10 pieces, book 2 only 8; the individual sizes alter between 35 (1,7) and 326 verses (2,3). They are dedicated to M. (1,1,1 and 1,6,1); Octavian receives honourable mention in 2,1,11 and 2,5,62–64. Both thus have their place at the start and at the beginning of the second half of the book [34]. The (perhaps) earliest satire (1,2) has fornication and adultery as its main theme (where at lines 69–71 even the penis has its say), the longest (2,3) five different forms

of madness (*insanire* 81), namely greed (82–160), ambition (160–223), luxury (224–246), being in love (247–280), superstition (281–297). Witchery is castigated (1,8); an underworld consultation of Teiresias attacks legacy-hunting (2,5). Besides the criticism of such bad habits, however, amicable scenes are also included, e.g. in the cheerful description of the trip to Brundisium (1,5). Traditional themes of satire such as *cena* (2,8) or *iter* (1,5; cf. Lucilius, *Iter Siculum*) appear repeatedly. A fable ('Town Mouse and Country Mouse') peacefully concludes the discourse on luxury and moderation, on unpleasant city life and peaceful rustic life (2,6). Another *tour de force* is the 'Bore' (1,9), in which a tiresome contemporary stops H. on the → *via Sacra* and asks for patronage from M.

3. EPODES
This book, also called 'Iambs' (→ Iambographers), and from the 30s as well, contains 17 poems, which all use iambic metres in different ways: the first 10 use iambic distichs (trimeter and dimeter), and at the end (17) is another purely iambic poem (trimeter); 11–16, on the other hand, combine various forms, sometimes iambic lines with hexameter (13–16), sometimes with the so-called elegiac iambs (11), sometimes (12) a purely dactylic verse form (hexameter and tetrameter [5; 16] also appears). This already addresses a first structural principle: a metrically based arrangement which also becomes apparent in the 'Odes'. Here again, as before in the 'Satires' and also later, poems are dedicated to M. (1, 2 and 4). The great patron is mentioned three more times, each time in accordance with the contents, in merriment (*iocose M.*, 3,20), in the joy of victory (*beate M.*, 9,4), in intimate closeness (*candide M.*, 14,5). Besides, in the opening poem, the courses of the lives of the high-ranking friend and his socially lower-placed protégé are contrasted; this sort of confrontational pattern of varying ways of life also returns in later works. In review, H. himself theoretically arranged the poetic program of his 'Iambs' (Epist. 1,19,19–25): he praised himself as the first (*princeps, primus*) to have brought iambs from Paros to Latium, and to have followed Archilochus in doing so – perhaps not in the actual themes and scolding by name, but in the verse form and the poetic impetus (*animus*). This marks a fundamental attitude of Augustan culture: connection to Greek patterns on the one hand, humanization of the archaic model on the other. At the same time, the choice of model broke free of the limited Hellenistic perspective of the → neoteric poets, thus embracing a fundamentally earlier, fresher past. This is also continued in the 'Odes'. Augustan 'Classicism' (as a kind of 'Renaissance') is beginning to emerge (→ Literature, Augustan; → Classicism).

4. ODES
In 23 BC, H. published 3 books of *Carmina* with a total of 88 lyric poems; a 4th book with 15 songs was published later, supposedly at the urging of Augustus, in around 15 or shortly thereafter. Earlier, in the summer of 17, the song for the celebration of a new

century (→ saeculum) was written as a commissioned work (see below). They were 'Aeolian' songs (Carm. 3,30,13; 4,3,12; Lesboum ... barbiton 1,1,34), which were oriented on poetic models such as → Alcaeus [4] (Carm. 2,13,27; 4,9,7) and → Sappho (Carm. 2,13,25) [41], and also adopted their metric forms. Besides their strophes, particularly those of → Asclepiades [1] were used as well; Pindar (→ Pindarus) was another model, or rather a counter-model (Carm. 4,2). The attention given to the early Greek period is significant; with the great gesture of these poems, H. distances himself from the daintiness of Hellenic poetry and its affected excesses and he becomes a 'Classic'. The poems are varied in their scale: two-strophe octets contrast with songs of more than 10 four-line verses; the Carmen saeculare comprises 76 vv., the 4th 'Roman ode' (3,4) 80. However, brevity is generally preferred.

Just as the 'Roman odes' at the beginning of book 3 form a solid block with only one metre [52], and the introductory poems of book 2 regularly switch between two metres, the first odes at the beginning of book 1 form a cycle (the so-called 'Parade odes') by introducing the verse forms newly developed by H. [39; 45]. H. defines (Ars P. 83–85) the themes of lyric poetry as follows: → hymnoi and → paeans to the gods and heroes, as well as → epinikia and → encomia, erotic and sympotic poetry, and finally (Carm. 4,2,21–24) → threnoi. These are rounded off by tributes to the ruler and his house, conversations with friends of different ranks, reflections and moral exhortations, thoughts on the transience of life and encouragement to enjoy it, exhortations to moderation, the true 'golden' mean (aurea mediocritas, Carm. 2,10,5). Private and political poems join together to form a broad panorama of poetic production (the 'Cleopatra Ode' Nunc est bibendum 1,37; the song to the → Bandusia spring 3,13; the exhortation carpe diem, 1,11 and the ode Integer vitae, 1,22). The most important are the so-called 'Roman odes' (3,1–6), where the poet turns to his people (Romane 3,6,2) and calls the young (virginibus puerisque canto 3,1,4) to the traditional values of the state, which he later summarizes as fides/pax/honos pudorque/virtus (Carm. saec. 57f.).

5. CARMEN SAECULARE

In 736 a.u.c. (= 17 BC), with reference to an oracle of the → Sibyl, Augustus held secular games (→ saeculum) after almost 2 centuries. The preparation committee, which he headed, commissioned H. with writing a cult song that would be performed on the Palatine by 27 (= 3×3×3) girls and boys from the nobility and repeated on the Capitol; it was rehearsed by the poet and possibly also accompanied by him (Carm. 4,3,29–44; cf. Epist. 2,1,132). The authorship is documented in an inscription (CIL VI,32323 = ILS no. 5050), and the text of the attestation can be seen in the cloister of the museum of the Diocletian Baths in Rome. The three-day festival began on the evening of May 31st; H.'s festival song was organized, in keeping with the number three, in 2×3×3 (Sapphic) verses with a final strophe as farewell.

In the first half Apollo appears as god of the sun at the beginning, and together with Diana as goddess of the moon at the end; thus they frame the chthonic deities, → Eileithyia, the Fates (→ Parcae) and → Tellus, who are called on in between. In the 2nd half, Rome's history is invoked. The conclusion in the final strophe is made by a variety of the → sphragis: the chorus speaks of its confident hope that the prayer will be heard. In contrast to the older positions ([14]: 'intellectual summary' of the celebration; [23]: its 'ideal image'), where the song appeared as an independent part of the celebration, [15] emphasizes and proves the unity of ritual and song.

6. EPISTLES AND ARS POETICA

Book 1: H. devoted himself once again to the minor hexametric form after 23 BC, possibly in part because of the unfavourable reception of his lyric poetry (Epist. 1,19,35–41). In the year 20, twenty poems (between 13 and 112 vv.) came out as the 1st book of letters, later followed by book 2. The introduction of the book, which is once again dedicated to M., emphasizes (1,1,10f.) that 'verses and all the rest of the trumpery' would now be put aside; attention would only be given to what is true and proper. Persons of all social status are addressed: the prince Tiberius (9), his patron M. (1; 19), his friend Lollius (2; 18), his poet friend Tibullus (4), and, on the other hand, the manager of his estate, who remains nameless (14), and even his own book (20). The contrasts between high and low, city and country, are discussed in the middle (9f.); also repeatedly the correct behaviour towards a patron (13; 17f.) and, on the other hand, maxims such as the detachment of nil admirari (6,1). A kind of ring composition is apparent: 1 and 19 are dedicated to M., 2 and 18 to Lollius. The sphragis of the closing letter (20) gives information about the person and circumstances of the author and his relation to the work. The balance of its diverse aspects between seriousness and cheerfulness make the book the 'most harmonious of all of the books of H.' ([23. 364]; similar [28; 29; 30]).

Book 2 and Ars poetica [31]: After two and a half decades of poetic production, at the end of his creative life H. discusses the theme which is dearest to him – poetry – in three longer poems (270, 216 and 476 vv.). Epist. 1, the first Horatian introductory poem dedicated to Augustus, contains, after the introductory praise of the ruler, a discussion with archaizing tendencies and, in the middle (vv. 126–138), praise of the poet in his position as pedagogue, priest and prophet of the community, followed by thoughts on the origin of Roman drama in the framework of rural festivals and its development under the influence of Greek theatre. The letter, a sort of report on the poetic state of the nation, leads to a self-definition of H. in his → recusatio because he cannot celebrate Augustus the way Virgil and Varius did in → epic. In Epist. 2 to Florus, to whom Epist. 1,3 had been dedicated, H. discusses the course of his education and his departure from lyric poetry; in the middle (vv. 109–125), the view turns to the rules for creating good poetry, in the last part to philosophy and its warnings against greed, ambition, anger, superstition, and fear of death. In the cheerful finale (vv. 213–216) the poet advises himself to fulfil his role as an ageing man properly. Practical philosophy and poetry, the two great fundamental ideas in the life of H., in his personal mould, are nowhere as clearly accessible as in the two books of letters.

→ Quintilian was the first to call the *Ars poetica* by that name (Inst., Praef. 2; 8,3,60); it is also known as *Ad Pisones*, 'To the Pisones', after the dedicatees. According to Porphyrio H. did 'not compile all, but the most important rules of → Neoptolemus of Parion in this book'. Fragments of the → Herculanean papyri have preserved part of a refutation of Neoptolemus by the Epicurean → Philodemus of Gadara, thus providing an indirect reference. Admittedly, the *Ars* is not a versified manual but a humane conversation with friends on a common theme. Nevertheless, the poetry–poet contrast appears to be taken up again in H.'s *Ars,* and to have influenced the structure. The contrast of *De arte poetica* (vv. 1–294) versus *De poeta* (vv. 295–end according to NORDEN) corresponds, to that between the aesthetics of work and the aesthetics of production and effect. Both major parts are devoted to a common question: how is it possible to create the perfect work of art? Out of the abundance of thoughts, in more modern terms, four should be emphasized. 1) The double purpose of poetry: it should connect the pleasant with the useful (vv. 343f.), as the poet wishes to be of use and amuse at the same time (vv. 333f.). 2) The significance of referring Roman poetry to Greek models (vv. 268f.). 3) The stress on caution in the production process, of constant revision, criticism and self-criticism (vv. 385–390). 4) Finally, the thoughts on the value and effectiveness of words, about new coinages and the revival of old words (vv. 47f.; vv. 240–243).

C. IMPACT

H. had already become a textbook author in antiquity; Quintilian accorded both the satirist (Inst. 10,1,94) and the lyric poet (10,1,96) great respect: he is *verbis felicissime audax,* 'of extremely successful boldness in the use of words'. → Petronius speaks of H.'s *curiosa felicitas,* the union of effort and happy success, NIETZSCHE of his 'solemn carelessness' ('Human, All Too Human' I,109). → Ovidius calls him *numerosus Horatius,* 'H. rich in rhythms' (Tr. 4,10,49). Christianity admired his form but distanced itself from his ideas: *Quid facit cum psalterio Horatius?* 'What does H. have to do with the psalter?' (Jer. Ep. 22,29). Only → Prudentius was able to solve the conflict by writing Christian songs in the strophes of H. Although a textual revision was made by → Mavortius (*cos.* 527) in the early 6th cent., H. was forgotten at the beginning of the Middle Ages [43].

New attention only set in during the → Carolingian Renaissance; this is also where the evidence of the textual record begins. The Roman breviary contains four → hymns in the metres of H., in which the Tegernsee

monk Metellus also composed odes to St. Quirinus in the 12th cent. DANTE includes H. ('Inferno' 4,94) in the illustrious group of the seven greatest poets with the epithet *satiro*: the satirical poet as *ethicus* is present in the Middle Ages, not the lyric poet, as Hugo VON TRIMBERG (d. 1313) confirms in his register of authors (2,66ff.). However, H. was rediscovered in the Renaissance and Baroque: PETRARCH modelled his 67 *epistole* on the letters of H.; humanists such as CELTIS and MELISSUS in the 16th cent., Jesuits such as BALDE and FABRICIUS in the 17th cent., wrote extensive song collections, following the Horatian pattern in metrics, verse form, word choice and way of thinking [46]. The first edition of 1470 has been followed by translations since 1535. Musical versions in the style of the so-called 'humanist odes' (choir compositions with transference of the syllable quantity in the length of the notes) by TRITONIUS, SENFL, HOFHAIMER appear; others, such as GLAREANUS and JUDENKÜNIG, counter them with rhythmless, monodic melodies. The path continues through various musical styles, from ORLANDO DI LASSO to Carl LOEWE, Peter CORNELIUS and Zoltán KODÁLY. H. also provides stimulus in the fine arts [51; 53]: in 1498, the Jacob LOCHER edition appeared in Strasbourg, illustrated with woodcuts; in 1607, 103 *emblemata* by Otto VAN VEEN, a student of Rubens, in Antwerp; in London in 1733, 229 copperplate engravings by John PINE; in the Parisian de luxe edition of 1799, 12 pictures by C. PERCIER/GIRARDOT.

Parodies have transplanted H.'s poems into, for instance, Bavarian or the Berlin underworld (MORGENSTERN), even into Yiddish. The image of H. has changed many times: from *ethicus* in the Middle Ages, to the lyrical model of the humanists, the Anacreontic poet of the Romantic era, to the political-patriotic poet in the 20th cent. Now the Hellenistic poet comes to the fore, now the national Roman poet. If the 'court poet' and 'imitator' is criticized by some, the philosopher is recognized by others; some admire the literary theorist, others celebrate the social critic. WIELAND, NIETZSCHE, BRECHT admired H.; Primo LEVI wrote a letter to him in the hereafter on 14 April 1985. The 2000th anniversary of his death in 1993 inspired a variety of events [27; 35; 44].

EDITIONS: 1 S. BORZSÁK, 1984 D.R. SHACKLETON-BAILEY, 1985 B. KYTZLER, 1992 (with transl.).
SCHOLIA: 2 A. HOLDER, O. KELLER (ed.), Scholia Antiqua in Q. Horatium Flaccum, 1894 (repr. 1979).
COMPLETE BIBLIOGRAPHY: 3 W. KISSEL, in: ANRW II 31.3, 1981, 1403–1558.
RESEARCH REPORTS: 4 E. DOBLHOFER, H. in der Forsch. seit 1957, 1992 5 A. SETAIOLI, Gli Epodi di Orazio nella critrica dal 1937 al 1972 (con un appendice fino al 1978), in: ANRW II 31.3, 1674–1788.
LEXICON: 6 D. BO, 1965/6.
CONCORDANCE: 7 I. ECHEGOYEN, 1990.
COMM.: 8 A. KIESSLING, R. HEINZE, ¹¹1964 9 H.P. SYNDIKUS, Die Lyrik des H., 2 vols., 1972/3 10 R.G.M. NISBET, M. HUBBARD, Odes I/II, 1970/78 11 C.O. BRINK, H. on Poetry, 3 vols., 1963–82.
BIBLIOGRAPHY: 12 R. ANCONA, Time and the Erotic in

H.'s Odes, 1995 13 D. ARMSTRONG, H., 1989
14 C. BECKER, Das Spätwerk des H., 1963 15 H. CAN-
CIK, Carmen und sacrificium, in: B. SEIDENSTICKER, R. FA-
BER (ed.), Wörter – Bilder – Töne. FS B. Kytzler, 1996,
99–113 16 R. W. CARRUBBA, The Epodes of H., 1969
17 N. E. COLLINGE, The structure of H.'s Odes, 1961
18 F. DELLA CORTE, Fra Statilio e Orazio, in: RFIC 101,
1973, 442–450 19 G. DAVIS, The Rhetoric of Horatian
Lyric, 1991 20 H. DETTMER, H.: A Study in Structure,
1983 21 J. DRAHEIM, G. WILLE, H.-Vertonungen vom
MA bis zur Gegenwart, 1985 22 K. FREUDENBURG, The
Walking Muse. H. on the Theory of Satire, 1993
23 E. FRAENKEL, H., 1963 (Engl. 1957) 24 O. GALL, Die
Bilder der horazischen Lyrik, 1981 25 O. GIGON, H. und
die Philos., in: Die ant. Philos. als Maßstab und Realität,
1977 26 T. HALTER, Vergil und H., 1970 27 S. J. HAR-
RISON (ed.), Homage to H., 1995 28 H. J. HIRTH, H., der
Dichter der Episteln, 1985 29 W. R. JOHNSON, H. and
the Dialectic of Freedom, 1993 30 R. S. KILPATRICK,
The Theory of Friendship, 1986 (Epist. 1) 31 Id., The
Poetry of Criticism, 1990 (Epist. 2) 32 B. KYTZLER, H.,
1996 33 E. LEFÈVRE, H. – Dichter im augusteischen
Rom, 1993 34 W. LUDWIG, Die Komposition der beiden
Satirenbücher des H., in: Poetica 2, 1968, 304–335
35 ID. (ed.), H. (Entretiens 39), 1993 36 R. LYNE, H.:
Behind the Public Poetry, 1995 37 D. MANKIN, H.'s
Epodes, 1995 38 D. MULROY, H.'s Odes and Epodes,
1994 39 F. H. MUTSCHLER, Beobachtungen zur
Gedichtanordnung in der ersten Odensammlung des H.,
in: RhM 117, 1974, 109–132 40 W. OTT, Metrische
Analysen zur Ars poetica, 1970 41 G. PASQUALI, Orazio
Lirico, 1920 (repr. 1964) 42 V. PÖSCHL, Horazische
Lyrik, 1991 43 M.-B. QUINT, Untersuchungen zur mit-
telalterlichen H.-Rezeption, 1988 44 N. RUDD (ed.), H.
2000, 1993 45 M. S. SANTIROCCO, Unity and Design in
H.'s Odes, 1986 46 E. SCHÄFER, Deutscher H., 1976
47 E. SIMON, H. und die Bildkunst seiner Zeit – ein Stil-
vergleich, in: Quaderni ticinesi di numismatica e antichità
classiche 23, 1994, 211–221 48 E. STEMPLINGER, Das
Fortleben der horazischen Lyrik seit der Renaissance,
1906 49 Id., H. im Urteil der Jahrhunderte, 1921
50 R. STORRS, C. TENNYSON, Ad Pyrrham, 1959 (154
translations into 25 languages of Carm. 1,5) 51 O. VAN
VEEN, Quinti Horati Flacci Emblemata, 1607 (repr. 1972)
52 C. WITKE, H.'s Roman Odes, 1983 53 P. VON ZEE-
SEN, Moralia Horatiana, 1656 (repr. 1963). B.KY.

Hordeonius

[1] M.H. Evidently the patrimonial procurator of Narbonensis under Tiberius (CIL VI 92 = 30690). Probably
the father of H. [2]; originating from Puteoli.

G. CAMODECA, in: EOS 2, 128f.

[2] M.H. Flaccus. Son of H. [1]. Cos. suff. in the
year AD 47 (AE 1988, 325; 1991, 474; [1]). In the
summer of 68, already as senex, he replaced Verginius
Rufus as legate of the army of Upper Germany. When
the troops refused to take the oath of allegiance to
Galba [2] on 1 January 69 in Moguntiacum, he did
nothing; he was possibly already in the know of → Vitellius' plans, which he followed publicly at the beginning of January. Left behind by Vitellius as legate of the
entire Rhine army, he was confronted with Vespasian's

proclamation and the Batavian rebellion under Civilis.
In Tacitus' report in the Histories, H. appears as insecure, weak and wavering in his loyalty. Yet this image of
him has perhaps been distorted later by Civilis and even
more by the Flavians out of self-interest. He made the
troops on the Rhine swear allegiance to Vespasian after
the defeat of Vitellius at Cremona. When, in the name
of Vespasian, he paid out to the troops a contribution
that Vitellius had sent, he was killed by the drunken
soldiers in the night. Tac. Hist. 1–4 passim.

1 G. CAMODECA, in: L. FRANCI DELL'ORTO (ed.), Ercolano
1738-1788, 1993, 525.

PIR² H 202; O. SCHMITT, in: BJ 193, 1993, 155ff. W.E.

Horeia, Horia see → Inland navigation

Hormisdas (Modern Persian Hormizd, Arab. Hurmuz;
Sassanids).
[1] H. I. Lat. Odomastes (HA Tyr. Trig. 2,2). Son of
→ Sapor I, on whose order he invaded Armenia. He was
in office there from c. AD 252 as Persian governor with
the title of Great King and succeeded his father after his
death (autumn 272) to the throne of Persia for c. one
year.
[2] H. II. Nephew of [1], king of Persia AD 302–309
(Agathias 4,25,1).
[3] Son of H. [2] II. When his elder brother, Adanarses,
was overthrown in 309 after a very short reign, H. was
also incarcerated. He was, however, able to escape by
means of his wife's trickery and, shortly before 324, fled
to Constantine the Great [1] (Zos. 2,27). Appointed
leader of a cavalry division by Constantine [2] II, he
served the latter in the war against Persia and accompanied the emperor to Rome in 357 (Amm. Marc.
16,10,16). In 363 he was in Antioch with the emperor
→ Iulianus [5] (Lib. Or. 18,258), who is said to have
considered making H. king of Persia in place of his
brother Sapor II (Lib. Ep. 1402 FOERSTER). H. then
took part in Julian's Persian War and rendered him
many services.
[4] Son of H. [3], appointed proconsul Asiae by the
usurper Procopius in 365. He fought bravely against
Valens (Amm. Marc. 26,8,12; Zos. 4,8,1). C. 380 he is
recorded as the commander of the emperor Theodosius
I (Zos. 4,30,5).
[5] H. III. Son (eldest?) of Yazdgird II and governor of
Sistan, he became Great King in 457 following the
death of his father. His younger brother Perozes rose
against him and, with the help of the → Hephthalitae,
succeeded in dethroning H. in 459.
[6] H. IV. Son and, from 579, successor to Chosroes
[5] I. Sources represent him as a socially-minded ruler,
who supported the poor, but fought against the Zoroastrian priesthood (→ Zoroastres) and the aristocracy.
The war against Byzantium that he inherited from his
father proceeded at first without tangible results. An
invasion by the Turks, who in 588 had advanced as far
as Balch and Herat, could be beaten back by the com-

mander → Wahram Tchobin. When, soon after, Wahram suffered a minor defeat by Byzantium in the Caucasus, he was dismissed by H. Thereupon the aristocratic general undertook an attempt to seize power, together with the military, the aristocracy and the priesthood, and marched to Ctesiphon. H. was overthrown in a palace revolution in the spring of 590 and was probably killed with the tacit approval of his son Chosroes [6] II.

[7] **H.V.** Great-grandson of H. [6] and grandson of Chosroes [6] II.; was proclaimed king by Persian troops in Nisibis and maintained his reign, without being universally recognized, from 631 to 632.

M. H. DODGEON, S. N. C. LIEU, The Roman Eastern Frontier and the Persian Wars AD 226–363, 1991; W. FELIX, Antike lit. Quellen zur Außenpolitik des Sāsānidenstaates, vol. 1, 1985; O. KLÍMA, Ruhm und Untergang des alten Iran, 1988; TH. NÖLDEKE, Geschichte der Perser und Araber zur Zeit der Sasaniden, repr. 1973; K. SCHIPPMANN, Grundzüge der Gesch. des sasanid. Reiches, 1990; M. SCHOTTKY, Dunkle Punkte in der armen. Königsliste, in: AMI 27, 1994, 223–235, esp. 232. M.SCH.

[8] Roman bishop and pope (AD 514–523) during the reign of → Theoderic. As successor to → Symmachus, H. succeeded within a few years in bringing about peace, both inside the Roman community (→ Symmachian Forgeries) as well as with regard to Byzantium (ending the so-called Acacian schism by the *Libellus fidei*, CPL 1684). Thanks to the extant correspondence in the → Collectio Avellana, his term of office belongs to the best documented phases of the Roman episcopacy in late antiquity. H. also succeeded in ensuring the collaboration of the most able expert in Church law of his time, → Dionysius [55] Exiguus, and promoted the spread of → Collectiones canonum, especially in Italy, Gaul and Spain. In general H. contributed significantly to the realization of the Leonian-Gelasian concept of the papacy as a universal rule. His son Silverius becomes one of his successors in 536/7.

→ Acacius [4]; → Leo (pope)

REGESTAE OVERVIEWS: JAFFÉ, [KALTENBRUNNER], 101–109 with no. 770–871; CPL 1683f.; H. J. FREDE, Kirchenschriftsteller. Verzeichnis und Sigel, ⁴1995, 550–554; A. KELLER, Translationes Patristicae Graecae et Latinae. Bibliogr. der Übers. altchristl. Quellen 1, 1997, 452f. EDITIONS OF LETTERS: A. THIEL, Epistolae Romanorum pontificum 1, 1867, 741–990 (largely outdated); O. GÜNTHER, CSEL 35, 1895–1898, no. 105–243. BIBLIOGRAPHY: G. PRINZING, s.v. H., LThK³ 5, 279f. (references to literature published before 1996); E. WIRBELAUER, Zwei Päpste in Rom. Der Konflikt zw. Laurentius und Symmachus (498–514). Stud. und Texte (Quellen und Forsch. zur Ant. Welt 16), 1993. E.W.

Hormus (Flavius) H. was Vespasian's freedman, who accompanied the Flavian troops during their advance into Italy and had great influence besides → Antonius [II 13] Primus (Tac. Hist. 3,12,3; 28,1). He was rewarded by the Senate with the equestrian rank on 1 January AD 70. Tac. Hist. 4,39,1; PIR² H 204. W.E.

Horned crown During the early dynastic period (middle of the 3rd millennium BC) the horned crown (HC) is developed in Mesopotamia in order to enable recognition of the divine character in anthropomorphic representations of gods. In the beginning it consists of a circlet or a simple cap, onto which a pair of cow's horns is fixed. The HC that developed in the following period, with horns tapering to points and having several pairs of inward-turned horns one on top of another, is represented until well into the 2nd millennium. Neo-Assyrian HC have either the form of a high domed helmet, or are cylindrical with a feathered end; late Babylonian gods wear, apart from archaized representations, *poloi* (tall, mostly cylindrical hats; → polos) without horns. Whilst the HC serves as the attribute of all divinities, it is (from the 12th cent. BC) a symbol restricted to the gods → Enlil, Anu and → Assur [2]. In neighbouring cultures horns are combined with independent crown forms. Cf. table.

R. M. BOEHMER, Die Entwicklung der H. von ihren Anfängen bis zum Ende der Akkad-Zeit, in: Berliner Jb. für Vor- und Frühgesch. 7, 1967, 273–291; Id., s.v. H., RLA 4, 431–434; U. SEIDL, Die babylon. Kudurru-Reliefs (OBO 87), 1989, 116f., 230; J. M. ASHER-GREVE, Reading the Horned Crown, in: AfO 42/43, 1995/96, 181–189. U.SE.

Horoi (ὅροι; *hóroi*). Boundary stones marking the boundaries (also called *horoi*) of political territories, temple districts and properties, public places and private land throughout the entire Greek world. They bore only the inscription *hóros*, sometimes with more precise additions, and were under the protection of Zeus Horios. Following inter-state arbitration in border disputes [4] and revision of leased temple land [8], commissions of ὁρισταί (*horistai*) often appeared to set the *horoi* in the site.

As the Greek *poleis* did not have a → land register, *horoi* also functioned as 'warning stones' to mark public mortgages on properties and houses. They were usually unworked limestone slabs bearing inscriptions by unpractised hands. Mortgage stones (→ Hypotheke, → Prasis epi lysei) served as security for loans, and to record when a guardian provided security for the value of a ward's fortune, or a husband for the value of a dowry (→ proix) by estimation (ἀποτίμημα; *apotímēma*) [6; 7]. *Horoi* were also set up to identify a property received as dowry or leasehold [1. 52f.]. The erection of *horoi* on the property of a condemned traitor had a degrading purpose (Plut. Vita X oratorum 834a; Antiphon).

1 D. BEHREND, Attische Pachturkunden, 1970 2 M. I. FINLEY, Studies in Land and Credit in Ancient Athens, n.d. (1951, ²1985) 3 A. R. W. HARRISON, The Law of Athens I, 1989, 257–279 4 K. HARTER-UIBOPUU, Das zwischenstaatliche Schiedsverfahren im Achäischen Koinon, 1998 5 F. PRINGSHEIM, Gesammelte Abh. II, 1961, 339–

Shapes of Ancient Oriental horned crowns: chronological and geographical distribution

368 6 H.J. WOLFF, Verpachtung von Mündelvermögen in Attika, in: FS H. Lewald, 1953, 201–208 7 Id., Das attische Apotimema, in: FS E. Rabel II, 1954, 293–333 8 A. UGUZZONI, F. GHINATTI, Le tavole greche di Eraclea, 1968. G.T.

Horologium see → Clocks

Horologium (Solare) Augusti The sundial with calendrical functions described by Pliny (HN 36,72f.), which was built on the Field of Mars in Rome (→ Roma) in the reign of Augustus and renovated many times in the 1st and 2nd cents. AD. The gnomon (→ Clocks) consisted of an obelisk which threw its shadow on to a paved area with a network of lines marked with bronze inlays. The reconstruction by [1] suggested as a result of various excavations and interpretations of the ancient and modern written records, assumed a complex dynastic monument (including the → Ara Pacis Augustae). It has been called into doubt by [3] who points out several errors in the mathematical and physical calculations.

1 E. BUCHNER, Die Sonnenuhr des Augustus, 1982 2 RICHARDSON, 190f. 3 M. SCHÜTZ, Zur Sonnenuhr des Augustus auf dem Marsfeld. Eine Auseinandersetzung mit E. Buchners Rekonstruktion ..., in: Gymnasium 97, 1990, 432–457. C.HÖ.

Horos see → Horoi

Horoscope
I. ANCIENT ORIENT II. GRAECO-ROMAN

I. ANCIENT ORIENT
Currently 32 horoscopes are known from Babylonia from the period 410 to 69 BC. They mostly begin with the date on which a child was born. This is followed by the positions of the moon, sun and planets in the sequence Jupiter, Venus, Mercury, Saturn, Mars. The positions are given relative to the signs of the zodiac, and sometimes the degree within a sign. Sometimes this is followed by further astronomical phenomena from the month or the year of birth. The positions are calculated and might come from the so-called almanacs. Only a few horoscopes contain predictions for the child's life. There are, however, omens, which provide predictions from the circumstances (incl. the astronomical ones) of the birth. Therefore horoscopes can be regarded as collections of symbols, with the respective predictions to be found in other tables.
→ Astrology; → Astronomy; → Divination

F. ROCHBERG-HALTON, Babylonian Horoscopes, in: Orientalia 58, 1989, 102–123. H.HU.

II. GRAECO-ROMAN
The c. nine Egyptian horoscopes (between 38 BC and AD 93) and 180 Greek horoscopes are recorded on stone, papyrus, as ostraca or graffiti, additionally in didactic poetry (in → Manetho as a sphragis in bk. 6) or in the texts of specialist literature (→ Vettius Valens, → Rhetorius, 'Palchos' = Abū Ma'šar). They refer to the births of individuals, the coronations of rulers, the founding or the consecration of cities or of whole countries to the *thema mundi* (Firm. Mathesis 3,1 according to Nechepso-Petosiris) and begin in 62 BC (the coronation horoscope of Antiochus of Commagene). We know, for example, the horoscopes of → Manetho, → Hadrianus [1] of Tyre and → Proclus. The standard work of [2] covers the period up to the year 621, for which → Stephanus Philosophus predicts the rule of Islam c. 150 years later. The first Arabic horoscope dates from 18 August 531. Numerous horoscopes are also known from Byzantine times. Firm., Mathesis 2,29,10–20, records the single extant Latin horoscope for Ceionius [7] Rufius Albinus (*13 March 303) and Mathesis 6,30,1–26 also offers a series of fictitious ideal horoscopes.
→ Astrology; → Firmicus Maternus; → HOROSCOPES

1 A. BOUCHÉ-LECLERCQ, L'astrologie grecque, 1899 2 O. NEUGEBAUER, H.B. VAN HOESEN, Greek Horoscopes, 1959 3 O. NEUGEBAUER, The Horoscope of Ceionius Rufius Albinus, in: AJPh 74, 1953, 418–420 4 T.D. BARNES, Two Senators under Constantine, in: JRS 55, 1975, 40–49. W.H.

Horrea
[1] see → Storehouses
[2] **H. Agrippina** see → Storehouses, see → Rome

Horsa see → Hengist and Horsa

Horse
I. INTRODUCTION II. RANGE AND DOMESTICATION OF WILD HORSES III. ANCIENT ORIENT IV. CLASSICAL ANTIQUITY

I. INTRODUCTION
The outstanding historical and cultural significance which has been attached to horses since the 2nd millennium BC – first to pull → war chariots, later primarily for riding – in the area of the ancient Orient and Graeco-Roman antiquity has meant that archaeologists in the last 100 years have focused on the (esp. early) history of the exploitation of this domestic animal far more than on that of all the others. Scientific discussion in the first half of the 20th cent. was heavily dominated by ethnological and sociological questions (even influenced, in part, by racial ideology) revolving largely around the (thoroughly overestimated) role of the horse in the spread of the → Indo-Europeans and the (supposed) introduction of horses and chariots to the ancient Orient by Indo-Aryans (for a literary overview of the history of research see [14. 78²⁶]). In recent decades, however, interdisciplinary research with a realistic approach has asserted itself, shedding new light on the history of the exploitation of horses through (re)evaluation of old and new finds.

II. Range and domestication of wild horses

Based on new osteo-archaeological research, it is certain today that the ranges of the four large wild equid groups, zebras, → donkeys, onagers and horses, in contrast to earlier scholarly opinion (e.g. [24. 254f.]), were not mutually exclusive geographically but clearly overlapped in the late Pleistocene (up to *c.* 12,000 years ago), and even in early historical times e.g. wild asses and onagers in Arabia and onagers and wild horses in Asia Minor were found living side by side [18; 21]. The (extinct) wild ancestor of domestic horses, *Equus ferus* BODDAERT 1785, was spread across broad areas of Europe and Asia. While Mongolian and other domestic horses of central Asia may be descended from their easternmost subspecies *Equus ferus przewalskii Poljakov* 1881, the European and western Asiatic domestic horse is obviously descended from several other (geographical) subspecies ([17. 122–124]).

Horse bones of the 5th/4th-millennia BC Sredniy Stog culture, found in the 1960s at Dereivka [2], were until quite recently taken as evidence for the steppe region north of the Black Sea being the exclusive area of origin of the domesticated horse, and the related hypothesis of horse-riding Indo-Europeans (e.g. [1]). However, the status of the Dereivka horse as a domestic animal is still unproved (for the supposed snaffle-gags of the Sredniy Stog culture cf. [5]). Also, the great chronological gap between the appearance of domestic horses in central and southwestern Europe and in the Near East (3rd/2nd millennia) rather suggests that they were wild. In fact, wherever there are sufficient wild horse populations, autochthonous domestication processes are generally to be expected. This is shown by detailed osteometric research on all previously documented horse bones from the Iberian peninsula, which makes the origin in the Bell-Beaker period of Spanish domestic horses from local wild horses likely [17. 125–133]. As central European domestic horses (Chamer culture group, 1st half of the 3rd millennium) were probably imported from the southeast [17. 139; 20. 558] and Bronze Age domestic horses of the Iberian peninsula show influences from the Near East, the southeast Europe/Asia Minor form of wild horse (provisionally referred to as *Equus ferus scythicus Radulesco* and *Samson* 1962), which is still not sufficiently documented, may be of particular significance. A special problem is posed here by Asia Minor, where wild horses have been demonstrated for the 4th millennium (Demircihüyük [21]; Altınova [4]), but there is then a hiatus in finds until the appearance of domestic horses in the Hittite period (2nd millennium). Their introduction by Hittites or Luwians (→ Hattusa II; → Luwian) is, in any case, disregarded because the speakers of the common ancient Anatolian prototype of the → Anatolian languages were certainly already in Asia Minor before the middle of the 3rd millennium.

Generally, in the question of early horse domestication, too little attention is still paid to the fact that evidence of domestic horses, which may initially have served only as a source of meat, as had hunted wild horses, does not in itself represent proof of their use for draught or riding. Even today, horses are not from the outset suited for this because of their overall anatomical construction, but first require thorough exercising, enabling them to maintain their balance in driving or riding. Without this they would become unusable in a very short time through wear and tear, particularly of the hocks. Driving and riding therefore require detailed knowledge of the physical structure and behaviour of horses (see also → Horsemanship). In fact these are only evidenced in the ancient Orient in the 2nd millennium BC, even if the domestication of horses appears to have been accomplished earlier in Europe according to modern understanding.

III. Ancient Orient
A. Oldest evidence of use of the horse (20th–17th cents.) B. Driving and riding in the 16th–12th cents. C. Breeding, keeping, horse medicine D. Significance in society and religion

A. Oldest evidence of use of the horse (20th–17th cents.)

In Mesopotamia, horses are occasionally mentioned, beginning in the Ur III period (about 2050 BC; Sumerian [ANŠE]sí-sí, loanword < old Akkadian *sisium*, later anše-kur-ra 'upland donkey'), but osteologically present only in the 2nd millennium; isolated bone finds dated earlier are doubtful with regard to dating as well as allocation to species [20. 560[19]]. The horse, certainly, did not play a significant role until the 16th/15th cents. particularly in Babylonia. This may be explained by the traditional use of the domesticated donkey, especially as a draught animal, since the 4th millennium. The common suggestion of waggon-pulling domesticated onagers is incorrect, because the onager can still not be tamed today [19]. The Sumerian-Akkadian equid terminology, including supposed domestic donkey-onager hybridization, [13] is in need of revision.

The situation is quite different in Hittite Asia Minor (→ Hattusa II), where in the earliest records (from the 20th/19th cents. BC), written in Old Assyrian, the horse appears as an already firmly integrated part of society. The military use of chariot teams is first documented for the end of the 18th cent. according to the Old Hittite 'Anitta' text (16th cent. copy), also indicated implicitly by the Old Assyrian court title *Rabi Sisê* (Great One of the Chariot Teams). In the Old Hittite law code, originating in the 18th cent., horses were differentiated into those in their first year of training (on the longe) (*saudist-*, 'one-year-old') and those in the first/second year of being broken in (*ịugas/dāịugas* 'of one/two yoke period(s)'), i.e. in the second/third year of training. This reveals a theoretically based (and today still valid) concept of a three-year-long basic training, which, for its part, requires long experience of handling horses [16. 23–29, 124f.]. Even if the idea of driving was adopted from Mesopotamia, this experience formed the crucial precondition for the development of the light two-wheeled chariot (carriable by only one person!) with axle at the rear and yoke saddle harness (cf. in general [9]), which, apart from older less precise representations in cylinder seals, is first demonstrable in its technically complete form on a 17th cent. Hittite relief fragment [3]. The oldest unquestionable evidence for the spoked wheel (20th/19th cents.) is also from Asia Minor (Kültepe, Acemhüyük) [11].

B. Driving and riding in the 16th–12th cents.

The use of chariot horses in military action, hunting, and for ceremonial purposes (parades, processions) was common in the entire ancient Orient by the end of the 16th cent. An example of this is Egypt, where the horse was still hardly known in the middle of the 17th cent. (Egyptian *śśm.t* 'horse' is a Semitic loanword), while driving skills had reached their peak soon after their adoption at the beginning of the 18th Dynasty (*c.* 1540 BC). This is reflected in the time of Ramses III (1187–1156) in particularly rich and varied recorded sources (textual and pictorial evidence [8; 15]; original chariots [10]; snaffle-bits and parts of harnesses [7]).

A deeper insight into the very high level of ancient Oriental driving skills is provided by the 'Sphinx Stela' of Amenhotep II (1426–1400), on which the theoretical and practical demands placed on horsemen (knowledge of horse's physique, intuition and empathy, etc.) are coherently formulated for the first time, as well as the Hittite instructions for training chariot horses, also from the 15th cent. (of these the best preserved is the 'Kikkuli' text in a 13th-cent. copy), which are devoted to special training goals [16]. These instructions, which are complemented by fragmentarily surviving Middle Assyrian instructions (13th cent.), offer not only the first systematic plans for training a living organism – a good thousand years before the scientific training treatises of the Greek gymnasts and doctors – but also make clear through their conceptualization (e.g. 'collecting' the horse) and expert methods of representation that the methodical foundations of Classical equestrianism (Xen. Eq.; modern European riding) had already been developed in the 1st half of the 2nd millennium BC (cf. → Horsemanship).

Riding, on the other hand, not unknown (e.g. couriers), was far less important than driving until the end of the 2nd millennium [9. 96f.]. All evidence before the 14th cent. is doubtful – particularly the cylinder-seal representations, none of which allows a definite identification of the species. Military riding, which took over the function of the chariot, can only be spoken of from the 9th/8th cents. BC onwards (→ Cavalry).

C. Breeding, keeping, horse medicine

There is comparatively little on record about horse breeding, which is often incorrectly emphasized in the secondary literature as a crucial prerequisite for driving and riding, failing to recognize the significance of the training of the horse. Only stallions were used for chariot teams. Breeding (as with training) began in the fourth year and breeding-mares and stallions were explicitly distinguished from the team horses [16. 27f.]. Middle Babylonian horse lists from Nippur and Nuzi provide information about colour and descent, although horse breeds and special breeding characteristics are never named. Southeastern Asia Minor and northern Syria were considered significant centres of horse breeding, as were → Urartu and northwestern Iran in the 1st millennium [9. 83, 112]. The value of a chariot horse, of course, depended primarily on its level of training.

The health of a horse was primarily maintained through proper keeping, care and feeding, which were generally considered very important [16. 146–148]. New insights into the demanding requirements for stabling and hygiene have been provided by the recently excavated royal stables of Ramses II (1279–1213) in Qantīr (in the Nile delta), which contained more than 400 stalls [7. VIII–XIX]. Continual medical care is documented in 14th/13th cent. Ugaritic and (1st millennium) Assyrian hippiatric texts, which are devoted to the treatment of illnesses of the stomach and intestines (colics) which occur frequently in horses [12].

D. Significance in society and religion

The fact that successful horse training requires mental engagement with the nature of the horse, and a large commitment of time and expense, and moreover represents an individual human achievement, necessarily limited the practice of driving to the cultured and wealthy upper class. However, an explicit class restriction is seen only in the sphere of influence of the Hurrian state of → Mittani (15th/14th cents.; for the early Indo-Aryan origin of the Hurrite-Akkadian word *marijannu* [23]) and in Egypt (here, for the military rather than the traditional bureaucracy). The recognition that equestrian principles (self-control, consistency, empathic sensitivity to the behaviour and reactions of another living creature) at the same time represent leadership qualities, made driving skills (just like archery with the composite bow; → Bow-shooting) an important component of the education of princes and the prerequisite for a political or military career in general [16. 136²⁹⁰]. Hittite and Egyptian envoys often bore the title of Charioteer or were identified as members of the chariot corps.

Horses had religious significance only in Asia Minor, where they were firmly integrated into myth (at least in Luwian-speaking → Kizzuwatna), cult (e.g. as a burnt offering performed only by kings), and royal funeral rituals (in connection with the originally Indo-European idea of the afterlife as pasture) [6]. Chariot racing, which can be inferred e.g. for Mittani only from personal names of early Indo-Aryan origin of the type Sattiuaza (< *sāti-vāja- 'having won the victory prize') or Abiratta (< *abhi-ratha- 'owning a superior chariot'), is also documented here, besides other sporting competitions, in a cultic connection [16. 127²⁶³]. The Quadriga of the → Sun God is first encountered in a Hittite prayer of the 15th cent., which is, however, in the old Babylonian tradition, so that the donkey(!) quadriga, demonstrated for the 1st half of the 3rd millennium in Mesopotamia, may have been the model [6. 85–87]. Outside Asia Minor, the horse has hardly found entry into religion. One peculiarity is represented by the white horses dedicated to the god Aššur and the moon god of Ḥarran (→ Moon deities) in Assyria in the 1st millennium BC (accordingly, in all likelihood, the horses dedicated to the sun by the kings of Judah at the Temple of Yahweh; 2 Kg 23:11) [23]. On the other hand, the widespread iconography of a goddess standing or riding on a horse (→ Anat/→ Astarte/Ašera) in Syria-Palestine and Egypt in the 14th/13th cents. may be linked to the protective horse goddesses of southeastern Asia Minor (Malija, Pirwa, Pirinkir) similar of nature [6. 81–82].

→ Domestication

1 D.W. Anthony, The Earliest Horseback Riders and Indo-European Origins, in: B. Hänsel, S. Zimmer (ed.), Die Indogermanen und das Pferd, 1994, 185–195   2 V. I. Bibikova, Appendixes 2 and 3, in: D.Y. Telegin (ed.), Dereivka, A Settlement and Cemetery of Copper Age Horse Keepers in the Middle Dnjepr, 1986, 135–186   3 K. Bittel, Fragment einer hethit. Reliefscherbe mit Wagendarstellung, in: S. Sahin (ed.), Stud. zur Rel. und Kultur Kleinasiens. FS F.K. Dörner, vol. 1, 1978, 179–182   4 J. Boessneck, A. von den Driesch, Pferd im 4./3. Jt. in Ostanatolien, in: Säugetierkundliche Mitt. 24, 1976, 81–87   5 U.L. Dietz, Zur Frage vorbronsezeitlichen Trensenknebel in Europa, in: Germania 70, 1992, 17–36   6 V. Haas, Das Pferd in der hethit. rel. Überl., in: B. Hänsel, S. Zimmer (ed.), Die Indogermanen und das Pferd, 1994, 77–90   7 A. Herold, Streitwagentechnologie in der Ramses-Stadt, 1999   8 U. Hofmann, Fuhrwesen und Pferdehaltung im Alten Ägypten, 1989   9 M.A. Littauer, J.H. Crouwel, Wheeled Vehicles and Ridden Animals in the Ancient Near East, 1979   10 Id., Chariots and Related Equipment from the Tomb of Tutʿankhamūn, 1985   11 Id., The Earliest Known Three-Dimensional Evidence for Spoked Wheels, in: AJA 90, 1986, 395–398   12 D. Pardee, Les Textes Hippiatriques, 1985   13 J.N. Postgate, The Equids of Sumer, Again, in: R.H. Meadow, H.-P. Uerpmann (ed.), Equids in the Ancient World (TAVO A 19/1), 1986, 194–206   14 P. Raulwing, Ein indoarischer Streitwagenterminus im Äg.?, in: Göttinger Miszellen 140, 1994, 71–79   15 C. Rommelaere, Les chevaux du Nouvel Empire égyptien, 1991   16 F. Starke, Ausbildung und Training von Streitwagen-Pferden, 1995   17 H.-P. Uerpmann, Die Domestikation des Pferdes im Chalkolithikum West- und Mitteleuropas, in: Madrider Mitt. 13, 1990, 109–153   18 Id., Equus africanus in Arabia, in: R.H. Meadow, H.-P. Uerpmann (ed.), Equids in the Ancient World (TAVO A 19/2), 1991, 19–33   19 A. von den Driesch, "Hausesel contra Hausonager", in: ZA 83, 1993, 258–267   20 Id., Ein Exkurs in die Frühgesch. des Haus-Pferdes, in: H. Gasche et al.

(ed.), Cinquante-deux réflexions sur le Proche-Orient ancien. FS L. de Meyer, 1994, 555–561   21 Id., J. Boessneck, Gesamtergebnisse an den Tierknochenfunden vom Demircihöyük, in: M. Korfmann (ed.), Demircihöyük, vol. 2, 1987, 52–66   22 E. Weidner, Weisse Pferde im Alten Orient, in: Bibliotheca Orientalis 9, 1952, 157–159   23 G. Wilhelm, s.v. Marijannu, RLA 7, 419–421   24 F. Zeuner, Gesch. der Haustiere, 1967.   F.S.

IV. Classical Antiquity

A. General   B. Ancient technical literature, breeding and keeping   C. Use by the military and in games   D. Economic use   E. The horse in art, myth, and literature

A. General

The significant role of horses in history has led historians to be more involved with horses and the history of their use and breeding than with any other domesticated animal. Small domesticated horses (with a height of c. 1.35 cm at the withers) are first documented in Greece around the year 2000, the smaller western breeds (approximately 1.25 cm) from the Bronze Age. A slight increase in horse size has been established for the Roman period; heights at the withers of as much as 1.4–1.5 m are documented for the 3rd cent., which is an indication of consistent selection of animals for breeding. The horses of Graeco-Roman antiquity are not comparable with modern horses, the product of centuries of breeding, and are more similar to modern ponies. Their speed and strength were highly esteemed and used in a variety of ways. The power output of a light horse (of 350 kg) was between 40 and 80 kg × m/s in a full working day. Theoretically a horse had approximately the same pulling-strength as an ox of the same weight, but was significantly faster. Of course, in view of the ancient harness, (→ Land transport) this is a relative statement, as the yoke corresponded better to the build of oxen than to that of horses.

B. Ancient technical literature, breeding and keeping

An extensive Greek and Roman technical literature dealt with horses, riding (→ Horsemanship), and horse breeding. Besides → Simon of Athens and → Xenophon, who wrote special works on the keeping of horses (περὶ ἱππικῆς; *perì hippikês*, ἱππαρχικός; *hipparchikós*), authors such as Aristotle [6], Theophrastus, Cato [1], Varro, Columella, Pliny, Palladius, and Vegetius dealt with this topic in detail in their treatises on zoology, agriculture (→ Agrarian writers) and military affairs (→ Military writers) and created the foundations for a true scientific hippology. The *Mulomedicina* by → Vegetius is one of the few surviving references to → veterinary medicine specializing in horses (ἱππιατρική; *hippiatrikē*). There was a canon of properties for an ideal military horse (ἵππος πολεμιστής; *híppos polemistés*; Latin *bellator equus*), parade horse (πομπικός; *pompikós*, λαμπρός; *lamprós*), and hunting horse (Latin *ven-*

ator equus). The qualities of a horse, natural or brought about by careful training, could be described with a refined vocabulary. The age was estimated based on the teeth and other indications (Xen. Eq. 1; 3; Aristot. Hist. an. 576a; Varro, Rust. 2,7,2; Plin. HN 11,168). Xenophon's observations are still valuable today for judging a horse. The names of horses often reflected their character or appearance, particularly their colour. White ones were much sought after. The horses of → Achilles were named Xanthus ('light reddish brown' or 'chestnut') and Balius ('dappled') (cf. Hom. Il. 19,400–424).

Many ancient names for individual horse breeds hint at their geographic origin, thus the Persians and Cappadocians famed as chariot horses, the large and noble Thessalians, the fast and tough Thracians and Epirotes, the Scythian horses (small, strong, and robust), the Libyans and Africans, which were fast learners and had great stamina, the swift Sicilians, the Venetians, Lucanians, Lusitanians, and the small Gallians (cf. Varro, Rust. 2,7,6).

Horses could be bred and kept on a stud-farm (ἱπποφόρβιον; *hippophórbion*; Latin *equitium*) or on private estates. Lengthy passages in Roman agrarian literature were devoted to horse breeding (Varro, Rust. 2,7; Verg. G. 3,72–156; Plin. HN 8,154–166; Columella 6,27–35). Great care was taken in selecting suitable animals for breeding (Verg. G. 3,72; Columella 3,9,5) and stalls were built in such a way that the animals would remain healthy (Vitr. De arch. 6,6,4; Columella 1,6,5; Pall. Agric. 1,21). Food consisted of a fodder mix of barley, oats, hay, clover, and lucerne, and a mixture of grains, grasses, and pulses known as → *farrago* (Varro, Rust. 1,31,5; 2,7,13). Besides the care of the mane, tail, and coat, great attention was given to strengthening the legs and hooves (Xen. Eq. 4; Veg. Mulomedicina 1,56; 2,55–58). The gelding (*cantherius*, Greek ἐκτομίας ἵππος; *ektomías híppos*) was used more frequently by the Roman world than by the Celts (Varro, Rust. 2,7,15; Plaut. Aul. 495). The horse was broken in by the owner or a horse trainer (ἱπποκόμος; *hippokómos*, Latin *equiso*), sometimes at the early age of two years. The principles used are still valid for modern horsemanship (Xen. Eq. 2,1–2; Varro, Rust. 2,7,13).

In Athens in about 400 BC, a horse cost approximately 12 minas (= 1200 drachmas; see → Prices; Lys. 8,10; Aristoph. Nub. 23). Exceptional horses were extremely expensive: 13 talents are supposed to have been paid for Bucephalus, the horse of Alexander [4] the Great, 100,000 sesterces for the horse of Cn. Seius, who was condemned to death in 44 BC by M. Antonius [I 9] (Plin. HN 8,154; Gell. NA 3,9,4).

C. USE BY THE MILITARY AND IN GAMES

Horses were used as riding and draught animals. The various possibilities for their use were concisely summarized by Varro: *Equi quod alii sunt ad rem militarem idonei, alii ad vecturam, alii ad admissuram, alii ad cursuram, non item sunt spectandi atque habendi*, 'Horses cannot all be regarded and treated in the same way, because horses are suitable for the different purposes of war, transportation, breeding, and racing' (Varro, Rust. 2,7,15). Horses were often ridden without a saddle or, as in Greece, with a cloth saddle blanket (*ephippium*, Hor. Epist. 1,14,43). In Rome, on the other hand, a saddle (*sella*) was often used. There were no stirrups, but spurs (μύωψ; *mýōps*, Latin *calcar*) and a complete bridle. A jointed bit was widely used in a variety of forms (χαλινός/*chalinós*, Latin *frenum*). In Rome horses were also shod.

No other animal had so strong a presence in all civil, military, and religious activities and in the arts as horses. The Homeric heroes used chariots pulled by two horses (→ Chariot) in aristocratic combat. The use of horses in the → cavalry was connected with the later development of the → *polis*. In Athens the establishment of the cavalry was ascribed to → Solon. Under Pericles [1] 1,000 riders were under the command of two *hípparchoi*. The rise of the cavalry to an important armed service, however, only dates to the time of Alexander [4] the Great.

From the time of Solon the → *hippeis* ('knights') were the respected second census class in Athens. In the Classical era, because their ownership was largely limited to aristocratic families, horses were symbols of nobility, wealth, and social prestige. This is also expressed in the choice of names in aristocratic families: many names allude to the horse through the element *hippos* (Hippias, Hipparchus: the sons of → Peisistratus, Hippocrates: brother of → Cleisthenes, Hipponicus: son of → Callias, → Philippus). In Rome the *ordo equester* (→ *equites Romani*) held an important position in the political system of the Republic and early Principate.

The appearance, symbolic significance, and beauty of horses connected them closely with great festivals, spectacles, and splendour, from the → Panathenaea to the triumphal processions (→ Triumph) of the *principes*. During the great festival of the Panathenaea in Athens, games, contests, and races were held, in which horses played an important role. In cavalry parades, the units performed certain manoeuvres at full gallop (Xen. Hipp. 3). The ceremonial funerary games in honour of → Patroclus were the literary beginning of horse racing in Greece (Hom. Il. 23,262–615), which enjoyed the highest reputation among the sporting competitions. In the pan-Hellenic Olympic, Pythian, Nemean, and Isthmian games (cf. → Olympia IV, → Pythia, → Nemea [3], → Isthmia), chariot races with teams of two and four as well as horse races were held in the hippodromes, which had a length of almost 400 m (→ hippodromos [1]). These races provoked not only incredible enthusiasm in the public but also enormous competitiveness between the participating cities. Victory meant an enviable honour. Sophocles gives a powerful depiction of such a chariot race (Soph. El. 698–756). → Pindar owed his literary fame in part to Pythian odes in which the winners of chariot races were praised (Pind. Pyth. 1f.; 4–7). The victorious horses were admired as much as their owners. → Cimon [1] had his horses, with which he won three times at the Olympic games, buried near his grave (Hdt. 6,103). Alcibiades [3] boasted of having sent seven four-horse teams to race in the Olympic Games in 416 BC (Thuc. 6,16,2; Plut. Alcibiades 11). In Acragas, grave monuments were erected to racehorses (Diod. Sic. 13,82,6; Plin. HN 8,155). Horses were also frequently ridden in hunting (→ Hunting); the characteristics of hunting-horses are described in detail by Oppianus (Opp. Kyn. 1,158–367).

D. Economic use

Horses were used less than → mules, → donkeys and → cattle. Nevertheless, their use in transportation should not be underestimated. The workhorse (Latin *caballus*, Greek καβάλλης; *kabállēs*) was often used, both with pack saddles and for passenger transport. The normal team consisted of a two-wheeled cart with a shaft between two horses harnessed to a double yoke. While horses and mules mostly pulled light carts, heavy loads were normally transported with the help of oxen. Like donkeys and mules, horses also served as pack-animals (Diod. Sic. 5,22,4; 5,38,5; for the types of carts, → land transport with fig.). Besides horses which were intended for economic use from the beginning, many old horses that had been written off had to end their lives performing the hardest and most thankless tasks (Apul. Met. 3,17; Anth. Gr. 9,19; 9,20; 9,21; 9,301).

There are countless reports of locomotion and → travelling in horse carts and on horseback, from Homer (Hom. Od. 3,478–495) to the price edict of Diocletian. Although there were no stirrups and the ancient saddle was not comparable with the modern one, long and difficult journeys were undertaken. Considerable distances could be covered in a short time: Cato [1] took only five days to go the about 550 km from Brundisium via Tarentum to Rome (Plut. Cato maior 14). A horse could usually cover a distance of 30–40 km a day if it was well treated (cf. Apul. Met. 1,2). Literature also mentions women on horseback (Ismene: Soph. OC 312ff.). During the Principate, horses and mules, either saddled or harnessed to carts, were also used for the → *cursus publicus*.

E. The horse in art, myth, and literature

Horses were the subject of numerous representations, from Geometric vases and monumental sculptures of the Classical Greek era to Roman equestrian statues and late ancient mosaics in North Africa. The horse was depicted both in its inherent beauty and in dramatic battle scenes. These works of art aroused enthusiasm in the patrons, artists, poets, and authors of antiquity, as later in the Renaissance. The sculptor → Strongylion was famous for his depictions of horses (Paus. 9,30,1). The bronze statue of a horse created by Lysippus [2] is praised in the poem Anth. Pal. 9,777. The two- and four-horse teams of the sculptor → Calamis were considered unsurpassed (Plin. HN 34,71).

Pausanias describes the attack of the Athenian cavalry at the battle of Mantinea painted by → Euphranor [1] in the stoa of Zeus Eleutherius in Athens (Paus. 1,3,4). In many cities in Greece there were statues of Castor and Pollux (→ Dioscuri) with horses (Argos: Paus. 2,22,5; Athens: Paus. 1,18,1). The artists had taken special care to observe and depict the gaits, especially the break into galop. The horses of → Pheidias from the → Parthenon, the horses on the east pediment of the temple of Zeus at → Olympia, the equestrian statue of Marcus [2] Aurelius on the Capitol (→ *capitolium*), and the horses of St Mark's in Venice can still be admired today.

Horses were ubiquitous in many Greek myths, and so were composite creatures such as the → Centaurs. → Theseus, for example, was linked to the → Amazons, the warlike women, inseparable from their horses, whose origin myth placed in the northeastern steppes between the Caucasus and central Asia – the region where the taming of horses began. Many gods and heroes, some descended from the gods, had horses. The sun god Helios drove a team of fiery horses, which → Phaeton did not know how to steer. It was said of → Athena that she invented chariots and reins. → Poseidon was said to have created horses and was considered the father of → Pegasus. In Athens, there were specific cults for Poseidon Hippios and Athena Hippia on the *Kolonos* [2] *hippios* ('horse hill'), where there were sanctuaries for these divinities. On the Mons Palatinus in Rome there was a cult of → Neptunus Equestris, founded by Evander [1] of Arcadia. Horse races were also held as part of the → *Consualia*, a festival connected with the harvest, and the animals themselves were crowned with wreaths.

The intelligence and loyalty of the horse was emphasized in numerous reports and anecdotes (Ath. 12,520c). In addition to the horses of Achilles, other famous horses are named in literature, for example Bucephalus, Alexander [4] the Great's horse, and Caesar's horse (Plin. HN 8,154f.). → Caligula had a magnificent stable built of marble, with an ivory manger, for his horse Incitatus, and is said to have intended to appoint it consul (Suet. Calig. 55,3). Probably the most beautiful ancient testimony to the attachment between human and horse is the funeral poem written by → Hadrianus to his hunting-horse Borysthenes [3. 446].

→ Cavalry; → Chariot; → Donkey; → Horsemanship; → Hunting; → Land transport; → Mule

1 J.K. Anderson, Ancient Greek Horsemanship, 1961 2 Id., Hunting in the Ancient World, 1985 3 J.W. and A.M. Duff (ed.), Minor Latin Poets, vol. 2, 1935 4 A. Hyland, Equus, The Horse in the Roman World, 1990 5 B. Kamminga, J. Cotterell, Mechanics of Pre-Industrial Technology, 1990, 193–233 6 S. Lepetz, L'animal dans la société gallo-romaine de la France du Nord, 1996 7 J. Peters, Röm. Tierhaltung und Tierzucht, 1998 8 G. Nobis, Zur Frage römerzeitlicher Hauspferde in Zentraleuropa, in: Zschr. für Säugetierkunde 38, 1973, 224–252 9 I.G. Sepence, The Cavalry of Classical Greece, 1993 10 Toynbee, Animals in Anti-

quity   11 P. Vigneron, Le cheval dans l'Antiquité grécoromaine, 1968   12 L. J. Worley, Hippeis: The
Cavalry of Ancient Greece, 1994.   G.R.

Horse head amphorae Large group of Attic black-figured belly amphorae with horse heads (head and neck)
in the image areas; first half of the 6th cent. BC. Apart
from a window-like image area without an ornamental
border on each side, the horse head amphorae (HHA)
are completely coated on the outside with black, glossy
clay. The horse heads that are directed towards the right
bear a halter and are represented with a flaming mane
according to proto-Attic convention – a stylization that
is preserved until the end of HHA around or after the
middle of the 6th cent. The emergence of the HHA was
related to the → Gorgo Painter. Of the over 100 HHA
the few large examples (height 50–60 cm) almost all
come from Attica and were probably made earlier than
the main quantity of smaller HHA (height 20–40 cm)
that were primarily exported, particularly to Etruria.
The stereotypical repetition of the horse head in its ancient design indicates a ritual use of the HHA. The controversial hypotheses regarding the function as a funerary vessel, prize amphora or symposium vessel are
mainly based on the significance of the horse as a
symbol of aristocracy as well as on its relations to the
hero cult and to Athena.
→ Amphora [1]; → Horse; → Vessels, vessel shapes (fig.
A)

M. G. Picozzi, Anfore attiche a protome equina, in: Studi
Miscellanei 18, 1971, 5–64; B. Kreuzer, Unt. zu den attischen P., in: BABesch 73, 1998, 95–114.   H.M.

Horsemanship

A. Introduction   B. 'Classical riding' according to Xenophon   C. The ancient Oriental principles

A. Introduction

Horsemanship refers to the riding style developed in
ancient times for military use of the → horse that has
remained dominant up to the present time for European
riding – the 'classical riding style'. It is distinguished
from other riding styles (that were only passed down or
arose in modern times) in that in the training of the
horse it is not satisfied with mere habituation but follows a systematic, gradually increased exercise programme that is based on strict observance of the physical (exterior) and mental (interior) predispositions of
the horse and is aimed at the training of a utilitarian
horse moving in perfect equilibrium that can fulfil the
requirements of the rider with rational use of strength
(and in the long term without damage to health; overview of the modern concept: [1]). Historically the term
horsemanship is most closely linked with → Xenophon's work 'On Horsemanship' (*Perì hippikês
<téchnés>*) that deals with the training of the military
horse (ἵππος πολεμιστήριος/*híppos polemistérios*, Xen.

Eq. 1,2). The treatise presents a fundamental theory of
horsemanship both methodologically and didactically
that apart from a few time-related details is still valid
today.

B. 'Classical riding' according to Xenophon

The claim formulated in Xen. Eq. 12,14 of not just
providing guidelines (*hypomnémata*) and practical
instructions for exercises (*meletémata*) but also imparting the theoretical fundamentals (*mathémata*) emerges
clearly already in the first section of the work (Xen. Eq.
1–3).

The core of the work is the advanced training of the
horse for use in war (Campaign School) and for parades
(*haute école*) (7–11). The Campaign School comprises
on the one hand the training on the riding track (ch. 7),
whose depiction at the same time paradigmatically
presents the structure of a riding lesson (mounting, sitting correctly, holding the reins, riding with the usual
gaits and on the different hooves, turns, parades,
change of tempo, dismounting *on* the riding track – a
modern counterpart e.g. [1. 316–339]) – and on the
other hand the training in open terrain (ch. 8): jumps,
jumping downwards, jumping ditches and riding
downhill. Most closely connected with these two types
of training (see e.g. [4. 1768]) are the comments on the
principles of horse education (8,9–12), providing help
and the conduct of the rider (ch. 9), as they show –
above and beyond the aspect of the communication between the human and the animal that is central to riding
(and vital in the case of use in war) – that practical
ability is not possible without theoretical knowledge.

In the first part of the *haute école*, the prerequisites
and principles are explained initially (10,1–14), with
fundamental importance being attributed above all to
the means of the training (rewards, informality and especially dispensing with overtaxing the animal; 10,12–
14). Even more significant than the succinct description
of the extraordinary gaits – piaffe (10,15) and passage
(10,16f.) – that does however contain all the essential
features (cf. [5. 56–59]) is their derivation from the
natural behaviour of the stallion when showing off
(10,4–5), as it makes it exemplarily clear that *haute
école* is not unnatural affectation but is based on exact
observation of nature. In addition it knocks the bottom
out of the critically devaluing assessment of the level
of ancient horsemanship (e.g. M. A. Littauer in
[3. 191]).

The second part (ch. 11) deals with the 'airs above
the ground'; here, too, it is not just the description of the
school jumps, the 'pesade' (raising of the forehand of
the horse in the most extreme assembly, systematically
building on the piaffe; 11,3) and the 'courbette' (11,3
and 11) developed from it, but also the presentation of
the training methods connected with it that characterize
horsemanship in particular. The training principle formulated in 11,6 – at the same time a key to understanding Xen. Eq. as well as horsemanship as such – is

famous (and still quoted today in almost every theory of riding because of its timeless topicality).

C. THE ANCIENT ORIENTAL PRINCIPLES

It is true that Xen. Eq. 1,1 explicitly places the author as a successor of → Simon of Athens (from whose treatise on 'Appearance and selection of horses' Xen. Eq. certainly fundamentally differs from the point of view of systematology and expertise [6. 9–15]), but regardless of the lifelong riding experience of Xenophon it was rather his encounter with Persian horsemen that had a decisive influence on him. Today this is considered all the more probable because ancient Oriental Persian military horsemanship was derived from chariot driving (see → Cavalry I) and almost all significant terms (e.g. 'handiness', obedience, collection) as well as principles of horsemanship (scheduled, gradually increased exercise programme, precise dosage of requirements, absence of coercion) are already attested for the training of chariot horses of the 2nd millennium BC, likewise for instance knowledge of the piaffe/passage and its use for the parade; cf. – also regarding the educational value of horsemanship for humans – [5] and → horse [III].

→ Cavalry; → Horse; → Riding; → Xenophon

1 K. ALBRECHT, Die Ausbildung des Dressur-Pf. bis zur Hohen Schule, in: P. THEIN (ed.), Hdb. Pferd, 1992, 306–342   2 J.K. ANDERSON, Ancient Greek Horsemanship, 1961   3 Id., Xenophon, 1974   4 H.R. BREITENBACH, s. v. Xenophon von Athen, RE 9 A 2, 1569–1928   5 F. STARKE, Ausbildung und Training von Streitwagenpferden, 1995   6 K. WIDDRA (ed.), Xenophon, Reitkunst (with German transl.), 1965.   F.S.

Horseshoe see → Land transport

Horsiesi Abbot general of the coenobitic association of monasteries founded by → Pachomius in Upper Egypt († after AD 386). Initially superior of the monastery in Šenesēt (Chenoboscium), H. was appointed by Abbot Petronius as his successor. After conflicts in the so-called poverty dispute, Theodorus took over the 'deputy leadership' [3. 527] for H. Later the latter again was head of the *koinōnía* ('community'), initially jointly with Theodorus, and on his own after Theodorus' death. As a spiritual testament he wrote the *Liber Orsiesii* (Latin translation by → Hieronymus, in 404; text and German trans. [2. 58–189]). In addition, letters, catechesis fragments as well as instructions for monks in Coptic (text and French trans. [1. 63–99]) are extant. In 1972 two additional letters were discovered (French trans. [4. 9–16]).

EDITIONS: 1 L. TH. LEFORT, Œuvres de S. Pachôme et de ses Disciples, 1956 (CSCO 159f.).
BIBLIOGRAPHY: 2 H. BACHT, Das Vermächtnis des Ursprungs. I, 1972   3 CH. JOEST, Pachom und Theodoros, in: Theologie und Philos. 68, 1993, 516–529   4 A. DE VOGÜÉ, Les nouvelles lettres d'Horsièse et de Théodore, in: Studia monastica 28, 1986, 7–50.   J.RI.

Horta (*Hortanum*, Plin. HN 3,52). Etruscan town on a volcanic mountain to the right of the Tiber, modern Orte; a place of commercial importance where several roads meet. Settled since the 6th cent. BC (necropolis of Le Piane), *municipium* after the → Social War [3], *tribus Stellatina* [1. 85]. Connected by a bridge with the *vicus* of the river port on the left bank of the river; recorded as *Castellum Amerinum* in the Tab. Peut. Remains of quays, warehouses, baths.

1 W. KUBITSCHEK, Imperium Romanum tributim discriptum, 1889.

G. NARDI, Le antichità di Orte 1–2, 1980; Id., Orte, in: EAA² 4, 1996, 132f.   G.U.

Hortarius King of the Alamanni, who, together with other Alamannic kings, was defeated by Julian's army at Strasbourg in AD 357 (Amm. Marc. 16,12,1). He surrendered in 358 (Amm. Marc. 17,10,5–9) and strove after a peaceful agreement both with the Romans and with the neighbouring Germanic tribes (Amm. Marc. 18,2,2; 13f.). PLRE 1, 444 (H.1).   W.P.

Hortensia Daughter of the famous orator Q. Hortensius [7] Hortalus. She is praised for having inherited the abilities of her father (Val. Max. 8,3,3; Quint. Inst. 1,1,6). In 42 BC, H. appeared successfully in the forum as a spokesman for prosperous Roman women against an exceptional war tax imposed by the triumvirs (App. B Civ. 4,135–146).

M. H. DETTENHOFER, Frauen in polit. Krisen, in: Id. (ed.), Reine Männersache?, 1994, 140f.   T.FR.

Hortensius Name of a Roman plebeian family, probably derived not from *hortus* but from the place names Hortense, Hortenses [1. 660; 2. 175; 177; 534]. The first definitely attested bearer of the name is H. [4], the most prominent member the orator II. [7]. Family tree: [3. 75].

1 WALDE/HOFMANN 1   2 SCHULZE   3 DRUMANN/GROEBE, vol. 3.

[1] H., L. As praetor in 170 BC commanded the fleet in the third Macedonian War (honours in Athens: IG II² 907, and Delos: IDélos III 461 Aa 83). He conquered Abdera, sold its population into slavery, and oppressed Chalcis, but had to rescind his orders by instruction of the Senate (Liv. 43,4,8–13; 7,5–8,7). In 155 one of a three-member legation to Attalus II and Prusias (Pol. 33,1,2).
[2] H., L. Fought successfully as Sulla's legate in the Battle of Chaeronea in 86 BC (MRR 2,56).
[3] H., L. or Q. Praetor, probably no later than 111 BC (good administration of Sicily, Cic. Verr. 2,3,42), perhaps identical with H. the consul, who was condemned in 108 before assuming office (MRR 1,541, n. 2).
[4] H., Q. Became dictator on the occasion of the last withdrawal of the plebs to the Ianiculum in 287 BC, and

passed a law declaring the decisions of the plebs (*plebiscita*) binding for the whole of the Roman people (Liv. Per. 11; Laelius Felix in Gell. NA 15,27,4; Plin. HN 16,37; Gai. Inst. 1,3 and others). The *lex Hortensia* facilitated legislation by the plebeian assembly under the leadership of the people's tribunes. It is therefore usually considered a sign of the integration of the tribunate into the state structure and a conclusion of the → class struggle, but may also have served the self-interests of the common people against the patrician-plebeian elite [1]. A law permitting trials on market days is also ascribed to H. (Granius Licinianus in Macrob. Sat. 1,16,30). He died in office.

> 1 K.-J. HÖLKESKAMP, Die Entstehung der Nobilität und der Funktionswandel des Volkstribunats: Die histor. Bed. der *lex Hortensia de plebiscitis*, in: AKG 70, 1988, 271–312. K.-L.E.

[5] H. (Hortalus), Q. (For the cognomen: Catull. 65,2). Son of Q. H. [7] Hortalus. During the fifties, led a lavish life among Rome's *jeunesse dorée*; in 51/50 BC (as quaestor? MRR 3,103) in Asia (Cic. Att. 6,3,9). A partisan of Caesar in the civil war, he took Ariminum by storm (Plut. Caesar 32,1; cf. Caes. B Civ. 1,8,1). In 49 he was entrusted by Caesar with the command of the fleet in the Tyrrhenian Sea (App. B Civ. 2,166), but failed in the Adriatic while relieving C. Antonius [I 3] (Oros. 6,15,8)], who was besieged on Curicta/Krk. Praetor in 45 (or earlier? MRR 3,103), afterwards as proconsul in Macedonia. After Caesar's death he changed his political orientation: H. surrendered the province, not to M. Antonius' brother C. Antonius, but to M. Iunius [I 10] Brutus, under whose supreme command he exercised proconsular authority in Macedonia until 42 (Cic. Phil. 10 passim; Plut. Brutus 25,2; Cass. Dio 47,21,4; Delian monument: ILS 9460). He had his prisoner C. Antonius executed. Captured at Philippi (autumn 42), H. was killed on the order of M. Antonius at the tomb of the latter's brother (Plut. Antonius 22,3; Brutus 28,1; cf. Liv. Per. 124; Vell. 2,71,2).

> M. H. DETTENHOFER, Perdita Iuventus, 1992, 18.

[6] (H.) Hortalus, M. Son of H. [5]. As part of Augustus' promotion of the continued existence of venerable *gentes* H. was generously provided with funds, allowing him to start a family. He was once again in precarious financial circumstances in AD 16, but Tiberius showed himself less amenable to his request for further subsidies (Suet. Tib. 47; Tac. Ann. 2,37f.). T.FR.

[7] H.L. f. Hortalus, Q. (114–50 BC). The most famous Roman orator until Cicero. His oratorical career began in the year 95 with the defence of some Africans before the consuls (Cic. De or. 3,229). In 86 he defended Cn. Pompeius, who protected him from the Sullan proscriptions. As the son of a consul, he opted politically for the aristocratic line [9. 764]. He married a sister of the Sullan Q. Lutatius Catulus (his second wife was Marcia, ex-wife of M. Cato). In 81 he prosecuted P. Quinctius: his first confrontation with the defender Cicero. In

the year 80 he was quaestor, in 75 aedile (outstanding games, grain supply: Cic. Verr. 2,3,215); in 72 praetor and in 69 consul. In the election year 70 H. took over the defence of his friend C. → Verres. He interrupted Cicero's prosecution in the *actio prima*, before the witnesses could be called (ibid., 2,1,71) and Verres went into exile. As in previous years H. remained in Rome instead of going to a province. Here he opposed the authorizations for Pompey [6. 50–52]. Cicero's consulate (63) brought H. and Cicero closer together; they now even acted together in court (defence of C. Rabirius, 63, L. Licinius Murena and P. Sulla 62). Thanks to Atticus' efforts [2. 91f.] the relationship even withstood the strains of Cicero's exile. In 53 the augur Hortensius successfully supported the cooptation of Cicero (as successor to the fallen P. Crassus, Cic. Brut. 1; Cic. Phil. 2,4; [2. 95]). In the conflict between Milo, who had killed the tribune Clodius [I 4], and Pompey H. took Milo's side and Cicero took on Milo's defence. In his final years H. defended M. Valerius Messalla (in 51) and Ap. Claudius (in 50) in bribery trials (*de ambitu*). H. died in 50 between the end of April and the beginning of June (for his death see Cic. Att. 6,6,2).

H. was active as an orator for 44 years (Cic. Brut. 229). The foremost of the Roman orators until the year of his consulate, he then gradually took second place to Cicero (ibid., 320). Cicero put this down to H.'s → Asianism, which better suited young orators than old ones (ibid., 325); see also [5. 97–100]. 25 speeches [1] are known and he also wrote a book on questions of rhetoric (*Quaestiones generaliter tracta<tae>*, Quint. Inst. 2,1,11; cf. [9. 764–766]) and poetry (Plin. Ep. 5,3,5; Varro, Ling. 8,14; 10,78). Rich to begin with, H. was increasingly attacked in his old age for excess, to which some anecdotes testify: he loved fish and is supposed to have 'watered' his plane-trees with wine (Macrob. Sat. 3,13,3). His clothing was always so carefully arranged that L. Torquatus mocked him with the name of a dancer, Dionysia (Gell. NA 1,5,3; [2. 98–102]). We owe the only direct quotation from H. to this episode.

> FRAGMENT: 1 ORF[4], 310–330.
> BIBLIOGRAPHY: 2 DRUMANN/GROEBE, 3,6, 78–102 3 A. E. DOUGLAS, M. Tulli Ciceronis Brutus, 1966 4 E. S. GRUEN, The Dolabellae and Sulla, in: AJPh 87, 1966, 385–399 5 G. KENNEDY, The Art of Rhetoric in the Roman World 300 BC-AD 300, 1972 6 E. S. GRUEN, The Last Generation of the Roman Republic, 1974 7 I. SHATZMAN, Senatorial Wealth and Roman Politics, 1975, 355f. 8 C. J. CLASSEN, Recht – Rhetorik – Politik, 1985 9 J.-M. DAVID, Le patronat judicaire au dernier siècle de la république romaine, 1992, 763–766. G.C.

Horti Agrippinae, Horti Caesaris see → Gardens; → Ianiculum; → Rome

Horticulture

I. Ancient Orient and Egypt II. Classical Antiquity

I. Ancient Orient and Egypt

In the kitchen gardens of the Middle East and Egypt fruit trees (principally apples, figs, pomegranates, but in Egypt also carob trees and jujube; → Pomiculture) were grown in so-called tiered cultivation in the shade provided by date palms, and below them → vegetables (especially onions and cucumber plants, pulses, leaf vegetables, such as cress, and also aromatic herbs, coriander, thyme, caraway and mint, for example). The date palms provided not only dates as the most important sweetener, but also raffia, palm leaves, leaf panicles and trunks for making mats, baskets, ropes and covering material for roofs. Date orchards not associated with a house were often leased in Mesopotamia. Contracts fixed the rent, which was paid in kind. Subsidiary products such as palm leaves, raffia, etc., were also included in this. Vineyards (→ Viticulture) existed in the mountainous regions of Assyria and Syria-Palestine and there were also olive plantations there.

→ Agriculture

1 F. Daumas, s.v. Früchte, Gemüse, LÄ 2, 344–348, 522–524   2 I. Gamer-Wallert, s.v. Palme, LÄ 4, 658–659   3 W. Helck, s.v. G., LÄ 2, 378–380   4 H. A. Hoffner, Alimenta hethaeorum, 1974, 95–112   5 N. Postgate (ed.), Bull. on Sumerian Agriculture 2, 1985; 3, 1987.

J.RE.

II. Classical Antiquity

A. General   B. Horticulture and nutrition
C. Methods of cultivation and irrigation
D. Dominion over nature and innovation
E. Horticulture as a discipline

A. General

In antiquity horticulture was an important branch of agriculture; the garden (κῆπος/*kêpos*, Lat. *hortus*) made an important contribution to human nutrition, by providing further vegetable products, in addition to the basic foodstuffs of → grain, → wine and oil, though it should be borne in mind that in antiquity pulses were categorized not as horticulture, but as crop growing (cf. already in Hom. Il. 13,588ff.). There were fundamental differences between growing crops, in particular growing grain, and horticulture in the methods of fertilization and cultivation and also with regard to irrigation.

B. Horticulture and nutrition

Horticulture normally offered a supplement to the main food (cf. Cic. Cato 56: one's own garden as a *succidia*, as a 'second side of bacon'), but for those of lesser social status horticulture had to replace the main food: Pliny's opinion that the garden was the field of the poor (*ager pauperis*) and → *macellum* of the plebs (Plin. HN 19,52), clearly shows the poverty which made the *hortus* the central source of food. The lower classes had

to resort increasingly to garden produce (Columella 10, praef. 2) and could in this way save on bread (Plin. HN 19,58; cf. also Apul. Met. 9,32ff.). The → fig was of the greatest significance, because it was both bread and vegetable; Cato reduced the bread ration of his slaves as soon as the figs were ripe (Cato Agr. 56). Pliny classified raw edible → vegetables, like lettuces, onions, cress, leeks, cucumbers, carrots and radishes, together as *acetaria*, their advantage being that no firewood was needed to prepare them (Plin. HN 19,58). Horticulture also guaranteed food in winter: pickled vegetables (sprouts, sticks of celery, carrots, asparagus, lettuce and endives, onions) and dried or preserved → fruit are mentioned in → Columella (Columella 12,6f.; 9f.), for instance. It was possible to store white cabbage, cabbage, turnips and onions. Both for the peasant who owned only *pauca iugera* and for the well-to-do, free food from one's own garden was something to aspire to and fitted in with the widespread desire for autonomy (Verg. G. 4,125–133; Hor. Epod. 2,47ff.; Columella 11,3,1). To the Greeks raw food was the food of philosophers (Diog. Laert. 6,58: Diogenes; 7,26: Zeno; 8,13: Pythagoras).

C. Methods of cultivation and irrigation

Donkey dung and pigeon droppings were preferred as → fertilizers, as was wood ash, which, like pigeon droppings, was at the same time used as a pesticide; compost was also used for fertilizing. This removed the need for fallow land, whereby in farming at least every other year about half the fields remained barren, though it was still necessary to cultivate the soil (fallow ploughing). This was intended to replace the regular fertilization which was impossible in crop growing. In gardens care was probably taken to alternate crops in individual beds during the year. This is demonstrated by the agriculture of Campania, which came close to horticulture with its seasonal sequences of crops (Plin. HN 18,191). In horticulture above all the dependancy of crop growing on autumn and winter rain was eliminated, which is why sowing normally took place in the autumn.

The choice of location was essential to the first basic condition of horticulture, the possibility of → irrigation, preferably by a watercourse, otherwise by digging a well, in the most unfavourable cases by cisterns (Columella 11,3,8ff.; cf. in general 1,5,1ff. and additionally Theophr. Caus. pl. 3,8,3f.; Plin. HN 19,60). From the Augustan period the improved water supply had also had a positive effect on horticulture. The great age of the most important horticultural technique, irrigation, is apparent in the old verbs ἄρδειν/*árdein* and Lat. *rigare* (cf. Hom. Il. 21,257ff.). So, in horticulture there was not only annual cultivation, but also the important aim of extending growing to the whole year. It was possible to achieve flowers that bloomed all year round (Theophr. Hist. pl. 6,8,2; Caus. pl. 1,13,12), early or late blooming by means of special watering, by planting at different depths or by repeated planting of a type of flower at monthly intervals. With → fruit there were early and late varieties and with vegetables there was a changeover to second sowings, as well as sowing at the usual main designated times (Theophr. Hist. pl. 7,1,2f.). Aristophanes had criticized this availability of many products contrary to the natural order of the year ('in the middle of winter') in the *Horai*, because of the temptation to greed and profligate expenditure; he said that Athens had been transformed into Egypt (fr. 581,1–11 PCG = Ath. 372bff.; cf. 653f.). In a vegetable calendar (Gp. 12,1) plants are sown in every month from January to December, even in August (endive, mangel, white cabbage). Many vegetables were therefore grown throughout the year, e.g. lettuce, carrots, radish, white turnips, garden rocket (used as a kind of spinach). If irrigation was impossible, it was recommended to store the moisture by digging over particularly deeply or by beds with a layer of tiles which sealed the ground below. Sunken gardens, which were up to a tier deeper than the surface of the earth, were probably rare.

In spite of the opportunities for irrigating and fertilizing horticultural land, the soil should already be fertile and easy to cultivate by nature (Columella 11,3,8; Plin. HN 17,36f.). The ideal position was on a plain at the foot of a mountain, which simplified the installation of irrigation systems. The earth was to dug over (Columella 10,45f.); the spade was therefore characteristic of horticulture. The quality of the horticultural land depended on intensive working over of the soil. Beds were typical of vegetable gardens (πρασιά/*prasiá*; *area, porca, pulvinus*), though they were not supposed to be too wide, as weeding was done by hand. The rule was to plant κατὰ γένος/*katà génos* (each variety separately), not ἀτάκτως/*atáktōs* (mixed up). However, there was the method of ἐπισπείρειν/*epispeírein*; *una serere, intermiscere* for combating pests: radishes and turnips were to be protected by vetches, cabbage by chickpeas or by mint, onions by *satureia* (summer savory), *brassica* by poppies, lettuce by garden rocket (Theophr. Hist. pl. 7,5,4; Plin. HN 19,107; 19,168; 19,179). Transplanting young plants (μεταφυτεύειν/*metaphyteúein; transferre*) was one of the customary methods of increasing the yield and preventing decay, used for cabbage, turnips, lettuce and other vegetable plants; it was regularly used for propagating seeds (Theophr. Hist. pl. 7,5,3).

Flowers were evidently at first assigned to the orchard, where they found shade and moisture in natural cushions of flowers in imitation of sacred groves and meadows; beds were laid in the gardens of villas and in commercial gardens. Until well into the Byzantine period, partly because of their economic importance, more or less the same flowers were preferred (roses, lilies, violets, crocuses, etc.; Theophr. Hist. pl. 6,6–8); they were used for cults, festivals and burials in the form of wreaths and garlands, and also scattered (not as bouquets). Already in Cato the suburban *villae* supplied *coronamenta* (flowers of all kinds for wreaths) and other requirements to the city (Cato Agr. 8,2; cf. Varro, Rust. 1,16,3: *violaria ac rosaria*). Flower gardens also acted as beekeeping land, where thyme also featured.

Gardens were typically fenced (cf. the etymologies of ὄρχατος/*órchatos* and *hortus*). Fencing often consisted of thorn hedges, as recommended in Columella (Columella 11,3,3ff.). Among the self-reliant an area of approximately 400 square metres would have covered the annual requirements of a family (*c.* 8–10 people).

D. DOMINION OVER NATURE AND INNOVATION

Whereas in farming the basic rule was to adapt prudently to the natural conditions of soil and climate, in horticulture there were already early attempts to overcome the limitations of nature by effort and ideas, and even to attempt the impossible. Even the simple gardener from Corycus in Virgil rebels against nature when, with pride in his early harvest, he ridicules the harvest times dictated by nature as too late (Verg. G. 4,127–138). This could result in criticism of horticulture if it was principally orientated towards the demand for expensive foods for the luxurious meals for guests of the rich (Columella 10, praef. 2; Plin. HN 19,52–56) or paid no heed to the order of nature.

Many opportunities for progress arose in horticulture as a result of new methods, the introduction of new types (Plin. HN 15,35ff.) and new varieties based on modification. Added to the early stock of fruit (apples, pears, figs, grapes) there were now sweet cherries, peaches, citrus fruits, apricots, quinces, pistachios and many others. Great pleasure was taken in experimenting, especially in grafting (grafting and budding: Columella 5,11; Plin. HN 17,99–122; 17,135–138). Only → viticulture bears any comparison with this development, while farming with its main products of → grain and pulses changed little throughout antiquity. In horticulture, on the other hand, there was a positive attitude to innovations (Plin. HN 15,35; 15,49); there were admittedly social considerations, as the refinement of products made them more expensive for poor people (Plin. HN 17,8; 19,53f.), but the innovations found social acceptance: new species were named after their inventor, 'as though he had achieved something significant in his life' (*tamquam ob egregium aliquod in vita factum*, Plin. HN 15,49). There were now, for instance, *appiana* (quinces; Plin. HN 15,49), *corelliana* (chestnuts; Plin. HN 17,122) and *caeciliana* (lettuce; Columella 11,3,26). If at any time no progress was achieved, this was regarded as an exception (*minimum in hac arbore ingenia profecerunt*, Plin. HN 15,97).

E. HORTICULTURE AS A DISCIPLINE

Already Homer knew of clever ancient gardeners, like Penelope's servant Dolius or Laertes, for instance (Hom. Od. 4,735–741; 24,219–247; 24,336–344). Yet the name of the profession κηπουρός (*kēpourós*) first appeared in the 5th/4th cents. BC, and then only rarely. Gardening books are first mentioned after Plato (Ps.-Pl. Min. 316e). They were apparently consistently incorporated into agricultural works. The authors of *Cepurica* mentioned by Pliny as the source writers for Book 19 of the *Naturalis Historia* are scarcely still attested (cf. Plin. HN 19,177: Sabinus Tiro). The most detailed sections on horticulture are found in agricultural literature: in Columella in bks. 10 and 11,3 (on supplies from the garden bk. 12; on the fruit garden 5,10–11), in Pliny (HN 14–15; 17 and 19), in Palladius in the rubrics *de hortis* and *de pomeris*, in Gp. 9–12 (olive tree, fruit, decorative trees and flowers, vegetables); to these are added the writings of → Theophrastus on plants. Gardening literature must also have dealt with the preservation of products (cf. Columella 12,4–10; 12,14–15; 12,44–50; 12,56). This was important for private supply, but also interesting economically for achieving good prices after the harvest.

→ Agricultural writers; → Agriculture; → Garden, Garden layouts; → Vegetable growing

1 J. ANDRÉ, Les noms de plantes dans la Rome antique, 1985   2 B. ANDREAE, "Am Birnbaum". Gärten und Parks im ant. Rom, in den Vesuvstädten und in Ostia, 1996   3 M. CARROLL-SPILLECKE (ed.), Der Garten von der Ant. bis zum MA, 1992   4 Id., ΚΗΠΟΣ, Der ant. griech. Garten, 1989   5 L. FARRAR, Gardens of Italy and the Western Provinces of the Roman Empire, 1996 (British Archaeological Reports International Ser. 650) 6 V. HEHN, Kulturpflanzen und Haustiere in ihrem Übergang aus Asien nach Griechenland und Italien, 1911 7 W. F. JASHEMSKI, The Gardens of Pompei, Herculaneum and the Villas Destroyed by Vesuvius, 2 vols., 1979/1993 8 J. KODER, Gemüse in Byzanz, 1993   9 R. OSBORNE, Classical Greek Gardens: Between Farm and Paradise, in: Garden History, 1992, 373–391   10 W. RICHTER, Die Landwirtschaft im homerischen Zeitalter, in: ArchHom 2 H, 1968, 123–127; 140–146   11 A. SARPAKI, The Palaeobotanical Approach. The Mediterranean Triad or is it a Quartet?, in: B. WELLS (ed.), Agriculture in Ancient Greece, 1992, 61–76   12 M. C. SHAW, The Aegean Garden, in: AJA 97, 1993, 661–685   13 WHITE, Farming.

E.C.

Hortona Frentanian coastal town (*regio IV Samnium*, Plin. HN 3,106), modern Ortona. Mentioned in connection with the Byzantine-Gothic War (AD 535–540) during the conquest of the coastal strip by the Byzantines (Marcellinus [14] Comes on the year 538); bishopric toward the end of the 6th cent.

M. BUONOCORE, G. FIRPO, Fonti latine e greche per la storia dell'Abruzzo antico 1, 1991, 528–537; A.R. STAFFA, Ortona, in: EAA² Suppl. 4, 1996, 133.   M.BU.

Horus The most important Egyptian hawk god, whose name (Egyptian *Ḥrw*, 'the remote') and form indicate his function as sky god. Any trace of his origins is lost in the mists of prehistory. The best-known H. god of historical times is H. Behedeti (*Bḥdtj*) from → Edfu in Upper Egypt, however, there is evidence of a Lower Egyptian origin. H. soon assimilated other hawk gods and was closely linked with the sun god. H. is also regarded as the morning sun; his name is an appellative in the sense of 'ruler/highest/sublime' (e.g. in Harachte, 'H. of the horizon'). Later the H. hawk is identified with

the heavens; his eyes are interpreted as the sun and the moon. Already on pyramid texts a form of H. is known as the morning star.

From early times, as king-god alongside → Seth, H. represented the divine kingship of both halves of the country. H. represented Lower Egypt within the symbol of the unity of the two lands, and Seth, as the god of Ombos, Upper Egypt. Other sources allocate rule over Egypt to H. and that over foreign lands to Seth. The king's throne is regarded as the throne of H., and the reigning king is regarded as the embodiment of H. on earth. This is documented, amongst other things, by the oldest of the five kings' names, the so-called H. name. H. and Seth, as a typical pair of gods of Egyptian mythology, represent numerous oppositions (home/abroad; sky/earth; rule/power through physical strength; order/disorder). The pyramid texts present early fragmentary indications of their disputes, in which, amongst other things, the eye of H. is either injured or stolen. The eye of H. – the sacrificial offering proper – is restored or returned, and thus life is guaranteed (through the continuity of the kingship, the provision for the gods and the dead, and the regeneration of the sun god). Various strands of tradition overlap in the mythical fragments concerning H. and Seth. A great or older H. (Haroeris) and an 'H. son of Isis' (Harsiese) exist side by side. According to one tradition, H. and Seth belong to the same generation, according to another Seth is the brother of → Osiris and → Isis and is thus the 'uncle' of H., whose hereditary right to the kingdom he disputes. Warrior aspects link both forms of H.

From the late NK the infant god 'H. the child' (Harpocrates) is attested, who enjoys special popularity with the people. He is the son of Isis and Osiris, the perfect child of a divine family, as well as youthful sun god and responsible for fertility and nourishment.

Genealogical and functional differentiations as well as new associations of gods, lead to the development of many independent forms of H. H. gods evidenced in local cults are differentiated partly through the emphasis on certain characteristics (e.g. the H. of Letopolis as a temporarily blind god and nocturnal sun god). H. is represented as a hawk, as a man with a hawk's head, or anthropomorphically; being a warrior, he can also take the form of a lion, sometimes with the head of a man. He was identified with, amongst others, → Apollo, → Hercules and → Eros [1]. He is attested in personal names until the Christian era.

→ Mandulis; → Rule; → Ruler

1 W. BRASHEAR, s.v. H., RAC 16, 574–597   2 J. G. GRIFFITHS, The Conflict of H. and Seth from Egyptian and Classical Sources, 1960   3 D. KURTH, Treffpunkt der Götter. Inschr. aus dem Tempel des H. von Edfu, ²1998 4 W. SCHENKEL, s.v. H., LÄ 3, 14–25.   HE.FE.

Hosidius

[1] **C.H. Geta.** Mint master, perhaps in the year 54 BC (MRR 2, 441); proscribed by the triumviri in 43, but rescued by his son; later struck from the proscription lists (App. B Civ. 4,171).

[2] [H.] Geta. Senator, whose fragmentary *cursus* probably belongs to the Augustan-Tiberian period because of the office of *quaesitor*. CIL IX 2844; PIR² H 215.

[3] C.H. Geta. Legionary legate during Claudius' Britannic campaign in the year AD 43; afterwards, he received *ornamenta triumphalia* although still a praetorian. ILS 971 probably refers to him; if so, he was admitted to the patricians by Claudius; later, he led a campaign against the Iberi. BIRLEY, 222ff.; PIR² H 217.

[4] Cn. H. Geta. Legate of Claudius in Mauretania; after his successes, the country was organized into two provinces. If AE 1997, 76 refers to him, he also took part in the Britannic campaign of Claudius. *Cos. suff.* from July-December AD 47.

> PIR² H 216; BIRLEY, 365; G. CAMODECA, in: Epigraphia. Actes...A. Degrassi, 1991, 70.

[5] M. Vitorius H. Geta. see → Vitorius

[6] Cn. H. Mauricus. Perhaps son of H. [4]. *Cos. suff.* in an unknown year, possibly in the Flavian period. PIR² H 220.

[7] C.H. Severus. Son of a Gnaeus, *tribus Claudia*. Equestrian from Sala in Mauretania Tingitana. After four equestrian *militiae,* he became *procurator ad census* in Britannia. Probably to be dated to the 2nd cent. AD. The citizenship of the family goes back to H. [4]. AE 1991, 1749; 1750.   W.E.

Hospes Cognomen in the Iulii and Vettii (→ Iulius, Vettius) families in the Imperial Fasti.

> DEGRASSI, FCIR 255.   K.-L.E.

Hospital

A. DEFINITION   B. TEMPLE MEDICINE
C. VALETUDINARIA   D. JEWISH HOSPITALS
E. EARLY CHRISTIANITY (UP TO AD 300)
F. EASTERN CHRISTIANITY IN THE 4TH CENT.
G. HOSPITALS IN THE LATIN WEST   H. HOSPITALS
IN THE EAST AFTER 400   I. INFLUENCE

A. DEFINITION

Hospital in the sense of public institutions for the medical care of exclusively sick people are not encountered before the 4th cent. AD, and even then the majority of terms used (Greek *xenón, xenodocheîon, ptōcheîon, gerontokomeîon,* Latin *xenon, xenodochium, ptochium, gerontocomium, valetudinarium;* 'guesthouse', 'pilgrims' hostel', 'poorhouse', 'old people's home', 'hospital') point to a diversity of functions, target groups and services that partly overlap with each other. Private houses for sick members of two narrowly defined groups, namely the slave *familia* and the army, have been mentioned since about 100 BC. Even earlier there may have been Jewish institutions that provided hospitality and care to fellow believers, especially pilgrims journeying to Jerusalem. A further extension of the definition of the hospital to all places where those in need stayed outside their home and their family circle

and could obtain care (Asclepieia, cf. → Asclepius; doctors' surgeries) is in danger of undervaluing the special developments within the Judaeo-Christian tradition [1].

B. TEMPLE MEDICINE

In the hope of being cured by a god, sick people in Egypt sought out countless temples, e.g. in → Memphis or Crocodilopolis. At the same time such temples with their priests who had a knowledge of healing were traditional reservoirs of medical knowledge [2]. In Classical Greece the temples of → Apollo and particularly → Asclepius had great power to draw sick people to them, some of whom stayed overnight at the sanctuary or even lived there for a relatively long time. According to later authors (e.g. Plin. HN 29,2), → Hippocrates [6] is said to have made full use of the temple records at the Asclepieum of → Cos as an important source of medical knowledge. In Roman times other sanctuaries like the one in Nodens (Lydney, England) or the one in the source region of the Seine attracted sick people seeking healing. In other places preparations were made at major festive events like the Olympic Games for the medical care of visitors.

C. VALETUDINARIA

Valetudinaria (infirmaries) are to be found from the 1st cent. BC on the estates of wealthy Romans, particularly at the imperial palaces in Rome. They offered sick members of the *familia* better food and care, although the landowner → Celsus [7] (De medicina, prooemium 65) despised the makeshift treatment given there. The *valetudinaria* owed their emergence to the increased prices on the slave market; their disappearance around AD 100 was probably connected with the decline in major *latifundia* managed predominantly by slaves, but could equally be explained through the history of tradition in that epigraphical information about slaves and freedmen at the imperial court becomes even more scanty from this period.

Institutions for sick members of the army appear initially only to have arisen *ad hoc* so that treatment was provided in tents put up on the battlefield or in allied towns. The change of function of the Roman army, which under Augustus operated far from every allied town and was later based on stationary forts and legionary fortresses (→ castra [I 1]) led to the building of special military hospitals. From about AD 5 (Aliso/?Haltern), rectangular hospitals were set up in legionary camps according to a carefully devised layout. They had small cubicles coming off a corridor that ran along three sides of the building and, if necessary, they could accommodate 10–20% of the legion. Minor hospitals were built in some auxiliary forts like Condercum (Benwell, England), Quintana (Künzing, Germany) and in the temporary siege camp at Hod Hill (southern England). In view of the fact that many hospitals were located in fortresses that lay miles away from the battle-front, they can hardly have been used within the framework of a triage system to care for seriously wounded soldiers (who would already have died while being transported), but rather to look after ill and injured soldiers. In military hospitals, which were under the supervision of an experienced administrative official, there were doctors on duty [3; 4].

D. Jewish hospitals

The Jewish commandment to care for one's suffering fellow believers also extended to providing accommodation for pilgrims going to Jerusalem and to providing medical assistance. Around AD 60 Theodotus, the son of Vettenus, built a large pilgrims' hostel in Jerusalem with numerous rooms and an adequate water supply [5]. In later times the rabbis traced this tradition of giving lodging and hospitality back to Abraham [6].

E. Early Christianity (up to AD 300)

Christianity extended the validity of these Jewish commandments to all people in need, whether they were sick, poor, lonely or needy. Deacons were ordered to distribute alms, and around 250 the Church in Rome had a fully developed system of assistance (Euseb. HE 7,22). Wealthy Christians and those in charge of the parishes within the scope of their missionary activities kept ready rooms in their houses for those in need, and later the → Manichaeans followed their lead in this (Aug. De moribus Manichaeorum 74). In 362 emperor → Iulianus [11] (Epist. 22) appealed to his pagan contemporaries to emulate this example of public charity bestowed upon everyone [7; 8].

F. Eastern Christianity in the 4th cent.

For the charitable activities of Christians there were initially no houses equipped specifically for this or dedicated especially to this purpose. The oldest known buildings of this kind were built by the bishop of Antioch Leontinus around AD 350 in → Antioch itself and in nearby → Daphne [4]. Several years later Eustathius [6] of Sebaste/Pontus who was bishop from 357 to 377 had a 'poorhouse' built in which those 'marked by disease' could find help. His friend → Basilius [1] the Great erected outside the city walls of Caesaria/Cappadocia 'almost a new city' in which sick people, lepers, poor people and travellers could be accommodated and find help [7]. Soon further hospital buildings followed in numerous towns along Christian pilgrimage routes, particularly in Jerusalem, Constantinople and Ephesus, where in 420 there was a hospital with more than 75 beds. Around 400, → Edessa [2] had a small hospital only for women [9]. Institutions like these were so well known that they could be used as a simile in a bishop's letter (Nilus of Ancyra, epist. 110, PG 79,248).

G. Hospitals in the Latin West

The founders of the first hospitals in the Christian-Latin world were influenced by developments in the Greek world. Fabiola, who founded a hospital in Rome around 397 (Jer. Ep. 77), as well as Pammachius, who built a hospital about a year later in nearby Portus (Jer. Ep. 66), were both members of a circle that → Hieronymus had gathered around himself, and both had travelled in the Holy Land. The eastern origin of the institution of the hospital was generally acknowledged as is shown by the use of the Latin word *xenodochium* derived from Greek, which remained common even in the subsequent centuries. Evidence for a spreading of hospital buildings, for instance in Augustonemetum (Clermond-Ferrand), is more scanty in the West than in the East but a chain of hostels had arisen by the 7th cent. along the pilgrimage roads [10]. Even if a monastery like → Cassiodorus' *Vivarium* in southern Italy (6th cent. AD) had therapeutic facilities and the plans of St. Gallen (820) provide for an extensive hospital complex, it remains unclear to what extent sickbays within the monastery walls served the needs of larger population groups outside the monastery. Hospital plans show a gradual development from one room within a bishop's palace to a separate autonomous building [11].

H. Hospitals in the East after 400

Hospitals were to be found everywhere in the Christianized Middle East. In the collections of the laws of the ancient Syrian Church, emphasis is repeatedly laid on the obligation of each individual parish to set up its own hospital, even if it is nothing more than a small room at the edge of the church square managed by an honest man who does not necessarily have to be a doctor. A town like Edessa, whose residents in AD 500 numbered 8,000 to 10,000, had at least three small hospitals, the capacity of which was supplemented in times of crisis by additional beds set up in public colonnades. In → Nisibis in c. 590 a hospital was built at the famous academy in order to protect students from robberies and insults when they went to the town 'for treatment' and in order to relieve their fellow students of the responsibility for their care [12]. In Egyptian → Antinoupolis a doctor's family managed its own hospital in 580 (PCairo Maspero 67151); however, we cannot always find indications that medical care was also guaranteed in the relevant facilities and numerous smaller institutions, e.g. in minor pilgrim locations in the Holy Land, offered care and assistance rather than medical treatment [7; 9]. In major cities hospitals could however grow into large institutions: the hospital of St. Sabas in Jerusalem had over 200 beds in 550, whilst the one of St. Sampson in Constantinople had almost double the number. There are also indications that there was increasing specialization: in Antioch and Constantinople women's and men's wards were created in large hospitals, and around 650 the hospital of St. Sampson in Constantinople had its own department for eye diseases and probably an additional one for surgical cases [7; 13].

I. Influence

The Islamic world followed the Christian model and built enormously large and complex hospitals in cities like Baghdad, Damascus or Cairo; these formed the centre of all social precautions in health care (including medical instruction) [14]. Similar developments, even if on a smaller scale, emerge in Constantinople, particularly in the royal foundation deed of the Pantocrator hospital from 1087; we cannot tell the extent to which people followed in practice the statutes stipulated there [15]. The Crusaders brought knowledge of the great hospitals in the East with them, particularly through the Hospitaller Order – whether this came from Constantinople or the Holy Land is unclear. Consequently, large hospital buildings were erected in Paris, Milan, Siena and Florence that were organized in a similar manner to those in the East [16]. At the same time the various forms of aid and support that had originated with the first Christian hospitals continued in small hospitals and foundations.

→ Hospital

1 G. Harig, Zum Problem 'Krankenhaus' in der Ant., in: Klio 53, 1971, 179–195 2 E. A. E. Reymond, A Medical Book from Crocodilopolis, 1976 3 J. C. Wilmanns, Der Sanitätsdienst im röm. Reich, 1995 4 R. Jackson, Doctors and Diseases in the Roman Empire, 1988 5 S. W. Baron, A Social and Religious History of the Jews, vol. 8, 1958 6 J. Preuss, Biblical and Talmudic Medicine, 1978 7 T. S. Miller, The Birth of the Hospital in the Byzantine Empire, ²1997 8 E. Kislinger, Kaiser Julian und die (christl.) Xenodocheia, in: W. Hörander et al. (ed.), Byzantios, FS Hunger, 1984, 171–184 9 K. Mentzou-Meimari, επαρχιακα ευαγη ιδρυματα μεχρι του τελος της εικονομαχιας, in: Byzantina 11, 1982, 244–308 10 T. Sternberg, Orientalium more secutus. Räume und Institutionen der Caritas des 5. bis 7. Jh. in Gallien, 1991 11 D. Jetter, Gesch. des Hospitals, vol. 1, 1966 12 N. Allan, Hospice to Hospital in the Near East: An Instance of Continuity and Change in Late Antiquity, in: BHM 1990, 446–462 13 T. S. Miller, The Sampson Hospital of Constantinople, in: ByzF 15, 1990, 101–135 14 M. W. Dols, The Origin of the Islamic Hospital: Myth and Reality, in: BHM 1987, 367–390 15 P. Gautier, Le typikon du Christ Sauveur Pantocrator, in: REByz 32, 1974 16 T. S. Miller, The Knights of Saint John and the Hospitals of the Latin West, in: Speculum 53, 1978, 709–733.

P. Horden, The Byzantine Welfare State: Image and Reality, in: Bulletin of the Society for the Social History of Medicine, 1985, 7–10; E. Kislinger, Der Pantokrator-Xenon, ein trügerisches Ideal, in: Jb. der österreich. Byzantinistik 37, 1987, 173–186; Id., Xenon und Nosokomeion – Hospitäler in Byzanz, in: Historia Hospitalium, 1986–1988, 1–10; U. Lindgren, Frühformen abendländischer Hospitäler im Lichte einiger Bedingungen ihrer Entstehung, in: Historia Hospitalium, 1977–78, 32–61; T. Meyer-Steineg, Krankenanstalten im griech.-röm. Alt., 1912; V. Nutton, L. I. Conrad, Jundishapur: From Myth to History (forthcoming); A. Philipsborn, Der Fortschritt in der Entwicklung des byz. K.-Wesens, in: ByzZ 54, 1961, 338–365; R. de Vaux, Les hôpitaux de Justinien à Jérusalem d'après les dernières fouilles, in: CRAI 1964, 202–207. V.N.

Hospitalitas Original meaning 'hospitality'. Militarily, *hospitalitas* means 'quartering, billeting'. Soldier and landlord were described as *hospes*, the latter also as *dominus* or *possessor*. The landlord was required to let the *hospes* have $^1/_3$ of his house, for *illustres* $^1/_2$, for lodging. Not every house could be turned into quarters by the *mensores* (*mediatores*). Senators, holders of high office, imperial and public civil servants were privileged, as were some tradesmen (Cod. Theod. 7,8,1f.; Cod. Iust. 12,41f. [3. 40–55]).

Hospitalitas is also encountered in the sources as a term in the settlement of *foederati* (i.e. barbarians) after AD 418. Among others [5], most recently [4], interpreted *hospitalitas* as a redistribution of land ownership according to the principles cited. [3] and [1] doubted whether the literal sense of the sources explained the form of the barbarian settlement. Among others, Cassiodorus (Var. 2,16), Ennodius (Epist. 9,23), Procopius (BG I [V], 1,4ff.; 28; Cod. Euricianus 276; 277; Lex Romana Burgundionum 54f.) provided an understanding of the distribution as a tax reform, which allocated a share of the taxes (*sortes*) to the barbarians, rather than property, and did not include any major expropriations [1; 2; 3 *passim*].

1 J. Durliat, Le salaire de la paix sociale dans les royaumes barbares, in: H. Wolfram, A. Schwarcz (ed.), Anerkennung und Integration, 1988, 21–73 2 Id., Cité, impôt et intégration des barbares, in: W. Pohl (ed.), Kingdoms of the Empire, 1997, 153–179 3 W. Goffart, Barbarians and Romans. A.D. 418–584, 1980 4 W. Liebeschütz, Cities, Taxes and the Accomodation of the Barbarians, in: W. Pohl (ed.), Kingdoms of the Empire, 1997, 135–141 5 F. Lot, Du régime de l'hospitalité, in: Revue belge de philologie et d'histoire 7, 1928, 975–1011. U.HE.

Hospitality
I. Ancient Orient and Egypt II. Iran III. Greece and Rome

I. Ancient Orient and Egypt

In Egypt and Mesopotamia, hospitality was not regarded as a value in itself, but generosity to the needy was seen in both cultures as an obligatory norm, in the sense of a communicative and vertical solidarity [1; 2].

According to Egyptian sources, strangers were treated with reserve, and late teachings (Ankh-Sheshonqi 21,24f.) speak of the loneliness of a person in a strange city where (s)he has no relatives. Rarely, letters contain admonitions to treat an announced guest with proper attention and not to be mean with food (Pap. Northumberland 1), or to receive an official on a tour of inspection with a gift (Pap. Berlin 13580, 15530)

For Mesopotamia, literary texts convey rules of hospitality, represented here among the gods and/or mythological heroes. A gift for the host is reciprocated on the occasion of a shared → banquet. This is also where ritualized combats (for accepting the stranger into the 'family') took place [1].

Besides family and businesses, tradesmen and couriers on journeys could make use of institutional bases [3].

1 J. J. Glassner, L'hospitalité en Mésopotamie ancienne, in: ZA 80, 1990, 60–75   2 J. Assmann, Ma'at, 1990   3 R. Westbrook, The Old Babylonian Term napṭarum, in: JCS 46, 1994, 41–46.   HE.FE.

II. Iran

Among the titles the Achaemenid Great Kings were wont to award, the *Orosángai*, i.e. the 'benefactors' ('Ορσάγγαι, Hdt. 8,85, < Median *varusanha-* 'widely famous'; often translated in Greek as εὐεργέται/*euergétai*), 'friends' (φίλοι/*phíloi*) and 'guest-friends' (ξένοι/*xénoi*) were the most significant; at the same time, they were connected with many and diverse privileges (and gifts). In the king-'benefactor' relationship, the initiative came from the latter, for whose service the ruler afterward showed his appreciation, while the king summoned into his presence as 'friends' (bearing in mind the differences in their ranks) those whom he had chosen for it, or who were entitled to it because of their descent. In contrast to this, hospitality – between king/satrap and *xénos* – was a relationship between equals, who had voluntarily created this bond of hospitality. For all three groups of those honoured, their names and privileges were recorded in the court, and their friendly relationship could be 'bequeathed' to descendants, → Privilegium.

P. Briant, Histoire de l'empire perse, 1996, 314–366; P. Calmeyer, Zur Darstellung von Standesunterschieden in Persepolis, in: AMI 24, 1991, 35–51; J. Wiesehöfer, Die "Freunde" und "Wohltäter" des Großkönigs, in: Studia Iranica 9, 1980, 7–21.   J.W.

III. Greece and Rome

(Greek ξεινίη/ξενία, *xeiníē/xenía*, Latin *hospitium*).
A. Definition   B. Findings

A. Definition

Judging the nature of ancient Graeco-Roman hospitality depends on whether it is considered from a moral, legal or political point of view. On the one hand, the idea that hospitality was of a purely altruistic character predominates in research, and is considered the quintessential expression of civilization [1; 2]; on the other hand, the view that hospitality pursued political and economic interests gained acceptance quite early. In this context, the reciprocal, i.e. contractual, character of hospitality is referred to, and it is ascribed a peace-keeping role in trade, as well as a function in political alliance [3; 4]. The reception of the gift theory of Marcel Mauss (→ Presents, Gifts) has thus brought about the interpretation of hospitality as an early form of contracts, and as a pre-state form of alliance [5]. Today, hospitality is counted among the forms of ritualized friendship with a political and military alliance function, without an *a priori* relation to a pre-state epoch [6; 7].

B. Findings

Hospitality is a topic frequently taken up in ancient literature and philosophy. The Homeric epic (cf. the Polyphemus episode in Hom. Od. 9,116–542) as well as Roman poetry (cf. the tale of Jupiter's reception by Philemon and Baucis in Ov. Met. 8,613–715) and the Byzantine novel [8] contain examples of proper behaviour of the host; philosophical and historical works inform about its political uses. While in Greek there was no distinction between stranger and guest – both were called ξένος, ξεῖνος or ξένη (*xénos, xeînos, xénē*) –, in Latin there was a strict conceptual separation between guest, *hospes/hospita*, and stranger. The latter was originally called *hostis*, which at the same time also means enemy (thus in the Law of the Twelve Tables: Lex XII 2,2; 3,7), later *peregrinus* (Cic. Off. 1,37; Varro, Ling. 5,3). The protection of the stranger was considered a divine commandment, watched over by Zeus Xenios (Hom. Od. 6,207; 9,270; Aesch. Ag. 60; Pl. Leg. 730a; Theodorus Prodromos, Rhodante 9,379) for the Greeks, and Jupiter Hospitalis (Ov. Met. 10,224; Verg. Aen. 1,731) for the Romans [9; 10; 11]. The ritual of *theoxénia* or *lectisternia*, the hosting of gods and heroes, was performed to honour them, as well as 'travelling' heroes such as Hercules or the Dioscuri, and *klinai* and tables with gifts were set up for the divine guests [12]. The threat to strangers is made clear by Plato, who castigated the endeavour of setting up houses on lonely roads in order to detain strangers there like prisoners and release them for ransom, rather than offering them hospitable gifts (*philiká xénia*) (Pl. Leg. 919a). The dishes for foreign guests, pilgrims to the oracles or ambassadors, who were received in the Prytaneion [13], were called ξεινήια/*xeinéia*, ξένια/*xénia* (Hom. Od. 4,33: ξεινήια ... φαγόντε; Hdt. 7,135; the fruits which strangers fetched from the fields for immediate consumption are so called in Pl. Leg. 845a). Where *xénia* were granted to passing armies or persons of high rank, they tended to bear the character of a tribute or duty (Hdt. 7,27–39; Hom. Od. 8,388–393). *Loca* (lodging), *lautia* (house and bathing articles) and → *munera* (silver and gold tableware) formed the components of Roman hospitality, which was offered to special ambassadors(Liv. 44,16,7; 28,39,19; CIL I² 588,8).

There were only a few inns (Greek ξενοδοχεῖον/*xenodocheîon*, Latin → *hospitium*). Accommodations and banqueting rooms were set up at central cult sites for festival envoys and pilgrims. In Roman cities, such as Pompeii, for example, there were at least three *hospitia*. On caravan routes, such as between Sardes in Lydia and Susa in Persia, travellers found rest stations (*stathmoí*) a day's journey (c. 30–40 km) apart (Hdt. 5,52–53) [14; 15]. High-ranking travellers mostly fell back on individual hospitality or were – like the Roman magistrates – quartered with dignitaries (Cic. Verr. 2,2,65). Maintaining hospitality was significant for political reputation. Respected Athenians like Cimon kept an open house and entertained both *xénoi* and deme members with great generosity (Plut. Cimon 10; Aristot. Ath. Pol. 27,3). For Xenophon, who was able to fall back on the support of guest-friends in his exile (Diog. Laert. 2,51–53), the maintenance of many *xénoi* was part of a good reputation (Xen. Oec. 2,5). Cicero valued having many *hospites*, which brought him gratitude (*gratia*) and help (*ops*) with foreign peoples (Off. 2,64). Hellenistic peristyle houses and Roman villas had numerous rooms for receiving and catering to guests (Vitr. De arch. 6,7,4; Cic. Off. 1,139).

Where the offer of hospitality led to a long-lasting relationship, special rituals were performed and commemorative gifts of varying symbolism exchanged. In the Homeric epic, bath, reclothing the guest and the presenting of gifts of clothes and drinking vessels were part of the ritual of hospitality, which led to the integration of the stranger into the domestic community and the local fellowship of the table and, hence, was performed by men and women (Hom. Od. 4,48–58; 8,430–432; 15,125–127; Xen. An. 7,3,16). The exchange of oaths (*hórkia*), handshakes (*dexiaí*) and gifts of weapons, which characterized hospitality in the classical era, bore a rather military character and served, like the armistice agreements (*spondaí*) and military alliances (*xénia kai symmachíai*) concluded between collectives, to ensure being spared (Hom. Il. 6,119–236; Xen. Hell. 4,1,29–40; Paus. 10,26,8) or supported in battle (Hdt. 7,165). In this context belongs the coinage of an independent Greek term for hospitality: ξεινοσύνη/*xeinosýnē* (first in Hom. Od. 21,35) and ξεινία/*xeinía* (since Herodotus), while in a different context it was also referred to by the term φιλία/*philía* (actually → friendship; Aristot. Eth. Nic. 8,12,1161b 11–17) [16; 17; 18]. Such hospitality could be in conflict with loyalty relationships which existed with one's own comrades-at-arms, and be interpreted as bribery (Thuc. 2,13,1–2; 5,59,5–60,6). This accusation was also made in the 4th cent. BC, when hospitality was used to obtain non-local resources, such as wood for shipbuilding or grain, during times of crisis (And. 2,11; Dem. Or. 19,114) [19; 20].

In Rome, a distinction was made between the *hospitium privatum*, concluded by individuals, and the *hospitium publicum*, granted by the Senate and people. The latter was received, for example, by the inhabitants of Caere as thanks for their support in the Gallic invasion of 390 BC (Liv. 5,50,3). The *hospitium privatum* had, in part, the character of a patronage relationship. From the 1st cent. BC, individual cities in the provinces sought a *hospes* in Rome as a patron who represented their interests (Cic. Verr. 2,2,110). The Marcelli, for example, held this function for Sicilian cities. Despite this conceptual separation between a *hospitium privatum* and a *hospitium publicum*, there was a closer connection on a political level. Personal hospitality relationships could lead to the foundation of alliances between communities (Liv. 1,45); Romans who were guest-friends of foreign rulers were used as ambassadors (Caes. B Gall. 1,47). Both forms were arranged with handshakes (Liv. 30,13,8; 13,11) and libations

(*sponsio*; Liv. 9,41,20). The exchange of *tesserae hospitales*, tokens of ivory, clay or metal in the form of clasped hands (Tac. Hist. 1,54; IG 14,279), also belongs in this context. This was also performed by guest-friends who had trade relations with one another (Plaut. Poen. 1039–1054). This is also true for the Greek σύμβολα/*sýmbola* (e.g. Hdt. 6,86,5), which served as identification in the context of → *proxenia* [21; 22].

→ Banquet; → Friendship; → Gifts; → Proxenia; → Travel

1 E. CURTIUS, Die G., in: Id., Alterthum und Gegenwart, ⁴1892, 203–218 2 L. J. BOLCHAZY, From Xenophobia to Altruism: Homeric and Roman Hospitality, in: Ancient World 1, 1978, 45–64 3 R. v. JHERING, Die Gastfreundschaft im Alterthum, in: Deutsche Rundschau 51, 1887, 357–397 4 T. MOMMSEN, Das röm. Gastrecht, in: HZ 1, 1859, 332–379 5 M. I. FINLEY, The World of Odysseus, 1954, ²1977 6 G. HERMAN, Ritualised Friendship and the Greek City, 1987, 10–40 7 J. PITT-RIVERS, The Law of Hospitality, in: Id., The Fate of Shecham, 1977, 94–112 8 R. E. HARDER,Diskurse über Gastlichkeit im Roman des Theodoros Prodromos, in: H. HOFMANN, M. ZIMMERMAN (ed.), Groningen Colloquia on the Novel VIII, 1997, 131–149 9 P. GAUTHIER, Notes sur l'étranger et hospitalité en Grèce et à Rome, in: AncSoc 3, 1972, 1–21 10 J. GAUDEMET, L'étranger dans le monde romain, in: Studii Clasice 7, 1965, 37–47 11 M. F. BASLEZ, L' étranger dans la Grèce antique, 1984 12 D. FLÜCKIGER-GUGGENHEIM, Göttliche Gäste, 1993 13 P. SCHMITT-PANTEL, La cité au banquet, 1992, 145–168 14 O. HILTBRUNNER, G. und Gasthaus in der Ant., in: H. C. PEYER (ed.), G. und Taverne, 1983, 1–20 15 C. BÖRKER, Festbankett und griech. Architektur, 1983 16 V. PEDRICK, The Hospitality of Noble Women in the Odyssey, in: Helios N.S. 15, 1988, 85–101 17 S. REECE, The Stranger's Welcome, 1993 18 B. WAGNER-HASEL, Die Macht der Kleider, 1994, ch. II/2 19 F. D. HARVEY, Dona Ferentes, in: P. A. CARTLEDGE (ed.), Crux, 1985, 76–117 20 G. HERMAN, Ritualised Friendship, 1987, 73–115 21 O. E. NYBAKKEN, The Moral Basis of Hospitium Privatum, in: CJ 41, 1945/6, 248–253 22 PH. GAUTHIER, Symbola, 1972, 62–104. B.W.-H.

Hospitium see → Hospitality

Hostia see → Immolatio, see Sacrifice

Hostilia *Vicus* in south-east Venetia on the Padus in the territory of Verona (Tac. Hist. 3,9), river port on the Ticinum – Ravenna route (*ab H. per Padum*, Tab. Peut. 4,5), modern Ostiglia. Beginning of the southern branch of the *via Claudia Augusta* (ILS 208, *Padana*). Mentioned in connection with the battles of AD 69 (Tac. Hist. 2,100). A special honey production was practised here (Plin. HN 21,73).

G. PAVIANI BUGANZA, Storia e topografia di Ostiglia, in: Atti e Memorie dell'Accademia Virgiliana di Mantova 39, 1971, 7–41; R. DE MARINIS, Villaggi e necropoli dell'età del Bronzo, 1987; Quaderni del Gruppo Archeologico Ostigliense, 1991ff. G.U.

Hostilia, Quarta Wife in her second marriage of C. Calpurnius [I 9] Piso (consul 180 BC), condemned for allegedly poisoning her husband in office in order to help to the consulate a son of her first marriage, Q. Fulvius [I 11] Flaccus (Liv. 40,37,5–7).   K.-L.E.

Hostilianus C. Valens H. Messius Quintus was the younger son of emperor → Decius [II 1] and Herennia Etruscilla. In September AD 250, he was named Caesar and *Princeps Iuventutis* (AE 1942/43, 55; ILS 518) and, after the death of his father in June 251, adopted by → Trebonianus Gallus and raised to Augustus (Zos. 1,25,1; RIC 4,3, 143ff.), probably to distract from the complicity of Trebonianus in the deaths of his father and brother. Shortly after, he died in Rome of the plague (Aur. Vict. Caes. 30,1; [Aur. Vict.] epit. Caes. 30; Eutr. 9,5) or, more likely, at the instigation of Trebonianus (Zos. 1,25,1).

PIR V 8; KIENAST, 207; M. PEACHIN, Roman Imperial Titulature and Chronology, 1990, 33f.; R. ZIEGLER, Aigeai, der Asklepioskult, das Kaiserhaus der Decier und das Christentum, in: Tyche 9, 1994, 187–212, esp. 188ff.   T.F.

Hostilius Old Latin family name, whose origin is unexplained; in inscriptions also *Hostillius* and *Hostilus* [1. 30; 175]. The great age of the name is shown by the third Roman king Tullus H. [4] and names such as *Curia Hostilia*, *Lares Hostilii* and the goddess *Hostilina*. In historical times, the family was Plebeian and, from the 2nd cent. BC, politically active, particularly in the Tubuli and Mancini branches; it died out at the end of the 1st cent. BC.

1 SCHULZE

[1] H. Praetor or people's tribune in the 2nd cent. BC (?), had a *lex Hostilia* passed, which allowed the plaintiff to be represented in court in theft trials.

KASER/HACKEL, RZ, ²1996, 63.

[2] H. (Tubulus?), C. Member of the three-man legation led by C. Popillius Laenas to Alexandria in the year 168 BC, which there obtained the immediate withdrawal of Antiochus [6] IV Epiphanes from Egypt. MRR 1, 430.   P.N.

[3] H., Hostus (or Hostius) Legendary grandfather of King Tullus H. [4], allegedly from the Alban colony Medullia, loyal supporter of → Romulus, fell in the Forum as Roman leader of the defence against the Sabines, who were attacking because of the kidnapping of their women, and was buried there. His wife was Hersilia (Liv. 1,12,3f.; Dion. Hal. Ant. Rom. 3,1,1–3). He is probably a complete fabrication of the older annalists.   K.-L.E.

[4] Tullus H. is the third king of Rome, after → Romulus and → Numa; according to tradition, he reigned 672–641 BC. His grandfather, Hostus H., a comrade-at-arms of Romulus, is supposedly buried in the Forum near the Lapis Niger. He owes the derivation of his name from *hostis* ('enemy') to his belligerent reputation, which made him 'more savage than Romulus' (Liv. 1,22,2). He is distinguished from Numa in that he is said to have begun the military rituals, especially the rites of the → *fetiales*. He fought against Fidenae, Veii and the Sabines, but above all he conquered and destroyed Rome's mother city → Alba Longa (the end of the war was the duel between the Horatii and Curiatii, → Horatius [1]) and settled the Albans on → mons Caelius, which he added to the city territory: that legitimated Rome's rule over all of Latium, the existence of Alban families in Rome, and the supervision of the Alban cults, including those of → Jupiter Latiaris on the *Albanus mons*. The Velia or the Caelius are generally regarded as his residence. Of the civic buildings, the first senate house (*curia Hostilia*), the *comitium*, and an enclosure (*saepta*) which surrounded those two are ascribed to him, which fits approximately chronologically with the archaeological finds (first paving of the *comitium* already in the 7th cent.?), but still does not provide any arguments for the historicity of H. He burned to death, together with his wife and children, in his house, either through an attack by his successor Ancus → Marcius, or because the house was struck by lightning because of religious sacrilege (which is told in various ways). Sources: Enn. Ann. 120–126; Cic. Rep. 2,31f.; Liv. 1,22–31; Dion. Hal. Ant. Rom. 3,1–35.

R. M. OGILVIE, A Commentary on Livy I–V, 1965, 105–125; F. COARELLI, Il Foro Romano. Periodo Arcaico, 1983, 121f.; J. POUCET, Les origines de Rome, 1985.   F.G.

[5] H., Tullus. People's tribune in 42 BC (MRR 2, 359; 3, 103). On the staff of M. Antonius [I 9] before Mutina; Cicero (Phil. 13,26) accuses H. of the attempted betrayal of his former general (D. Iunius [I 12] Brutus?).   T.FR.

[6] H. Cato, A. Held his offices together with his brother L.; 207 BC praetor (Sardinia), 201 decemvir for distribution of land seized in Apulia and Samnium, 190 legate under L. Cornelius [I 72] Scipio in the war against Antiochus [5] III. In 187, the brothers were accused of embezzlement in connection with the lawsuits against the Scipiones, A. was acquitted, L. condemned (Liv. 38,55,4–6; 58,1 after Valerius Antias).   K.-L.E.

[7] H. Mancinus, A. Praetor in 180 BC. As consul in 170, he was entrusted with the war against → Perseus of Macedon (MRR 1, 419f.), in which he first escaped an ambush in Epirus. He limited himself essentially to defensive measures, as well as strengthening Roman influence in Greece, and therefore produced no military decision; however, he restored military discipline and secured the co-operation of the allies (Liv. 44,1,5–8). Q. Marcius Philippus relieved him the following year.

[8] H. Mancinus, C. Son of [7], praetor about 148 BC. As consul in 137, he was allotted Hispania citerior and reinitiated the war against the Numantians (→ Numantia), after a peace treaty negotiated by Q. Pompeius failed in the Senate (MRR 1, 482). H. was repeatedly defeated, finally withdrew his troops, and was surrounded by the enemy, despite his numerical superior-

ity (Liv. Per. 56; App. Ib. 80; Vir. ill. 59,1–3). His capitulation in return for free passage (*foedus Mancinum*), which his quaestor Ti. → Sempronius Gracchus negotiated to a considerable extent, saved the lives of countless Romans, but was considered a disgrace in Rome and was rejected by the Senate (Cic. Har. resp. 43; Vell. Pat. 2,2,1; Plut. Ti. Gracchus 5–7). A decision of the people in 136 ordered him to be handed over to the Numantians, however they declined (Cic. Caecin. 98; Liv. Per. 56). After his return, he was expelled from the Senate (Cic. De or. 1,181), which he later returned to after again being elected praetor (Vir. ill. 59,4). His citizenship had earlier been confirmed by the people (Dig. 50,7,18).

[9] H. Mancinus, L. Received supreme command of the fleet in 148 BC as legate (MRR 1, 462 n. 3) in the 3rd Punic War, but was unsuccessful. In a failed attempt to take Carthage from the sea, he could only be rescued by the intervention of Scipio (App. Lib. 113–14; Plin. HN 35,23; Zon. 9,29). Consul in 145.

[10] H. Tubulus, C. *Praetor urbanus* in 209 BC. His *imperium* was renewed every year until 204. In the year 208, he occupied → Arretium as a precaution and demanded hostages (Liv. 27, 24,1–8). In 207, he was transferred to Taranto and later to Capua, where he remained until 204.

[11] H. Tubulus, L. Probably the grandson of H. [10]. In 142 BC, *praetor de sicariis* and thus one of the first chairmen of the standing tribunal for murder trials (MRR 1, 475); notorious until well into the 1st cent. BC for his corruption. In the year 141, he was subject to an extraordinary investigation [1]. He tried to avoid a judgement through voluntary exile, but was brought back and consequently took his life with poison (Ascon. 23 C).

1 ALEXANDER, 5. P.N.

Hostis Hostis originally referred to the foreigner (*peregrinus*), i.e. the enemy (*perduellis*) as well as the guest (*hospes*), as Cicero (Off. 1,37) correctly concludes from the provisions in the XII Tables (→ *tabulae duodecim*) (*aut status dies cum hoste*: 2,2; *adversus hostem aeterna auctoritas*: 6,4). At the same time they show that even a foreigner without → *commercium* could bring a lawsuit before the Roman magistrate. In the same way, with regard to the sphere of international relations, the older view that a 'permanent state of war' (MOMMSEN) or a 'natural hostility' (TÄUBLER) could only be reversed through a formal friendship treaty is refuted by the evidence of HEUSS that the relationship of → *amicitia* was 'a given fact by virtue of every type of peaceful intercourse between states'. The question of the possibility of a treaty that was purely for friendship certainly remains debatable according to ZIEGLER. An enemy in the legal sense – *iustus et legitimus hostis* (Cic. Off. 3,107) – could only be a state-organized polity with obligations of → *fides* (NÖRR) and *ius fetiale* (→ *fetiales*) and with whom a 'just war' (*bellum iustum*) could

be waged, otherwise one was dealing with pirates or robbers (Dig. 49,15,24).

In the crisis of the late Roman Republic the term *hostis* was applied to Roman citizens although within the Roman polity only the personal enemy (*inimicus*) was said to exist. The violent proceedings of Scipio Nascia→ against Tiberius Gracchus and his supporters in 133 BC, and the declaration of the state of emergency by the *senatusconsultum ultimum* in 121 BC against Gaius → Sempronius [I 11] Gracchus already implied reference of such kind to internal conflicts. Since 88 BC formal *hostis* declarations were repeatedly issued in states of threatened danger by a decision of the Senate against opponents outside the city area. Cicero, in the case of the imprisoned Catilinarians whose harm had already been neutralized in this way, in 63 BC went even further by attempting to eliminate the statutory protection of the Roman citizen from the → *coercitio* (*lex Sempronia de capite civis*) of the magistrate through the proposition of the automatic loss of citizenship in the case of hostile action against the polity. The extreme form of transforming citizens into *hostes* was achieved in the proscription lists of Sulla and of the Triumvirate of Antonius, Caesar (C. Octavius) and Lepidus (cf. also Flor. Ep. 2,16 for L. Antonius 41 BC).

1 S. ALBERT, Bellum iustum, 1980 2 J. BLEICKEN, Lex Publica, 1975, 473ff. 3 W. DAHLHEIM, Struktur und Entwicklung des röm. Völkerrechts im dritten und zweiten Jahrhundert v.Chr., 1968, 136f. 4 A. DRUMMOND, Law, Politics and Power. Sallust and the Execution of the Catilinarian Conspirators, 1995 5 C. HABICHT, Cicero der Politiker, 1990, 51 (on the concept of the *hostis domesticus*) 6 J. HELLEGOUARC'H, Le vocabulaire latin des relations et des partis politiques sous la république, 1972 7 A. HEUSS, Die völkerrechtlichen Grundlagen der röm. Außenpolitik in republikanischer Zeit, 1933, 46 8 M. KASER, Ius gentium, 1993 9 Id., K. HACKL, Das röm. Zivilprozeßrecht (HdbA 10.3.4), ²1996, 62, n. 15 10 W. KUNKEL, R. WITTMANN, Staatsordnung und Staatspraxis der röm. Republik, 2. Die Magistratur (HdbA 10.3.2.2), 1995, 238f. 11 M. MANTOVANI, Bellum iustum. Die Idee des gerechten Krieges in der röm. Kaiserzeit, 1990 12 MOMMSEN, Staatsrecht, vol. 3, 590ff. 13 D. NÖRR, Aspekte des röm. Völkerrechts. Die Bronzetafel von Alcántara (ABAW N.F. 101), 1989, esp. 102 14 E. TÄUBLER, Imperium Romanum 1, 1913 15 J.v. UNGERN-STERNBERG, Das Verfahren gegen die Catilinarier oder: Der vermiedene Prozeß, in: U. MANTHE, J.v. UNGERN-STERNBERG (ed.), Politische Prozesse in Rom, 1997, 85–99, esp. 93ff. 16 Id., Untersuchungen zum spätrepublikanischen Notstandsrecht. *Senatusconsultum ultimum* und *hostis*-Erklärung, 1970, 18ff.; 63ff. (with a list of the *hostis*-declarations: 116, n. 153) 17 F. VITTINGHOFF, Der Staatsfeind in der röm. Kaiserzeit, Untersuchungen zur "damnatio memoriae", 1936 18 WIEACKER, RRG, 266, n. 139 19 K.-H. ZIEGLER, Das Völkerrecht der röm. Republik, in: ANRW I 2, 68–114, esp. 87f. J.v.U.-S.

Hostius

[1] Wrote an → epic with the title *Bellum Histricum* in
at least 2 bks. of which 7 frs. are extant. It presumably
concerned the war waged in 129 BC by C. Sempronius
Tuditanus. The relationship between him and H. was
probably like that between → Ennius [1] and Fulvius
[15] Nobilior and the one between → Furius [I 7] Antias
and Lutatius Catulus; the epic was doubtless of the panegyric type as was common in Hellenistic writing. Prop.
3,20,8 mentions the *doctus avus* of a girl with whom he
had a relationship, and on the basis of the dubious
assumption that the girl was Cynthia, and that her real
name was Hostia, it has often been maintained that the
writer was her ancestor. That, however, is improbable.

> M. A. Vinchesi, Il Bellum Histricum di Ostio, in: V. Tan-
> doi (ed.), Disiecti Membra Poetae vol. 1, 1984, 35–59;
> Courtney, 52.   ED.C.

[2] H. Capito, Q. see → Capito [1]

Hostus Rare Latin *praenomen* of unknown origin (in
the sources commonly confused with Hostius), → Hostilius [3] and H. Lucretius Tricipitinus (consul in 429
BC)

> Salomies, 30f.   K.-L.E.

House

I. Near East and Egypt   II. Greece, Etruria,
Rome

I. Near East and Egypt

In the Near East, the residential ground plan was
usually of a rectangular shape containing multiple cells.
Clay bricks were the most important building material
in Mesopotamia, while stone was more frequently used
in Iran, Syria and Asia Minor. The typical Babylonian
residential house consists of rooms around a central
courtyard. It usually has only one entrance and a main
hall located to the south, directed away from the
midday sun. The Neo-Assyrian residence, on the other
hand, is divided into two parts – an outer courtyard
with utility rooms and an inner courtyard with living
quarters connected by a reception room. Sizes and furnishings of houses varied. Multi-storey houses also existed, but their existence is difficult to prove on the basis
of excavation finds. Since the same rooms were used for
different purposes, an example being different seasonal
needs, it is often impossible to clearly ascertain the function of the rooms. More recent studies in the area of
house research therefore increasingly focus on the
social organization of the residents (family structures)
and on differences in status, wherever applicable.

In Egypt, the house with courtyard and several
rooms made of clay brick was the most common type as
well. A strict division between rooms for public reception, the daily life of household members and the family's private sphere could already be found in the well-
equipped middle-class house. A central element in

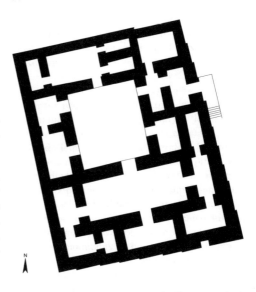

Babylon: late Babylonian domestic dwelling (ground-plan)

Amarna: house Q46/1, 18th Dynasty (ground-plan).

wealthier houses of the New Kingdom was a covered
middle room or columned hall. Adjacent to it were the
private quarters with bedroom, bathroom and toilet.
While country houses were free-standing with open
kitchen areas, stables and gardens, city houses were
built close together, occasionally multi-storey.

→ Architecture; → Construction technique

> D. Arnold, s.v. Haus, Lex. der ägypt. Baukunst, 1994,
> 99–102; C. Castel, Habitat urbain néo-assyrien et néo-
> babylonien, 1992; E. Heinrich, s.v. Haus, B. Arch. RLA
> 4, 1972–1975, 176–220; Id., Architektur von der alt- bis
> zur spätbabylon. Zeit, in: PropKg 14, 1975, 241–287;
> M. Krafeld-Daugherty, Wohnen im Alten Orient (Al-
> tertumskunde des Vorderen Orients 3), 1994; G. Leick,
> s.v. H., A Dictionary of Near Eastern Architecture, 1988,
> 95–100; P. A. Miglus, Das Wohngebiet von Assur
> (WVDOG 93), 1996; K. R. Veenhof (ed.), Houses and
> Households in Ancient Mesopotamia, 1996.   U.S.

II. Greece, Etruria, Rome
A. General   B. The Greek house   1. The
Pastas house   2. The Prostas house   3. The
hearth-room house   4. The peristyle house
5. Cost   C. Early Italic and Etruscan houses
D. Roman houses   1. The atrium house   2. Tenement blocks

A. General

In Greek, Roman and Etruscan culture, the house as
a building for use and protection, as a representative
object as well as a centre of domestic economy, is the
focus of the → family, and in Etruscan and Roman culture of religious activity, too (household gods and protective deities). Here the → private sphere and public
life intersect, insofar as the house constitutes, on the one
hand, an intimate place of withdrawal for the female
members of the household, and on the other, the framework for the man's social and (in Rome) professional
commitments. The form of the ancient house developed
from the 6th cent. BC at the latest, in both the Greek
and the Etrusco-Roman world, shows this ambivalence
by a striking combination of the partitioning-off
against the outside world (for instance by transferring
the → gynaikonitis to the upper floor, where it was inaccessible to strangers), with the construction of quasi-
public representational sections inside the house, e.g.
the → andrôn [4] for the symposium (→ Banquet) or the
→ atrium for receiving clients (→ cliens).

Every expansion of the spectrum of uses manifested
itself immediately in the architectural form through the
development of specific sections or rooms for the respective functions. As early as the turn of the first millennium BC, the hitherto prevalent and universally used
one-room building is ever more frequently replaced by
individualized architectures of several rooms, separa-
ting, as necessary, living quarters, utility, cult and representative spheres. Until the late 5th cent. BC, architectural display in houses remained strictly purpose-ori-
ented and therefore not very representational (buildings
made of mud bricks, rubble and wood on a fieldstone
socle prevailed, a fact which explains the generally bad
state of preservation and the resulting paucity of our
knowledge; cf. → Architecture). The situation changed
in the course of the 4th cent. BC: the withdrawal of
citizens into the private sphere, triggered by depolitici-
zation and by the decline of Greek polis society, found
expression in the rapid increase of luxury constructions, materials and décor in the architecture of houses;
typologically one cannot distinguish the Hellenistic
→ palace or the later Roman → villa, as luxurious, stately and representative forms of habitation, from the
house in general.

Within individual settlements, houses either formed
structurally interconnected agglomerations of rooms
(early post-Mycenaean and post-Minoan examples:
Dreros and Karphi on Crete; Zagora on Andros) or
were grouped into more or less densely developed scattered settlements (Antissa, Athens, Lefkandi, Ancient

Smyrna, Nichoria). Regular continuous development
over a larger surface only emerged in the context of the
foundation of Greek colonies in the late 8th and early
7th cents. BC – e.g. → Megara Hyblaea in Sicily (→ insula; → Town planning) – as well as in the extensive
urban structures in Etruria (→ Marzabotto, 6th cent.
BC). To what extent newly planned cities within the
Greek cultural sphere were built in standardized 'type
houses' (houses with the same, only slightly varied,
ground-plans and front elevations, built in rows) is a
matter of controversy; archaeological proof is habitually difficult to obtain, since it is never the original state
that can be reconstructed from the findings, but only
ever the result of numerous architectural alterations
over time. At least in the case of Piraeus, it appears that
the development of the equally-sized plots within an
insula was not centrally organized. A similar situation
can be observed in cities which were Etruscan and
Roman/Latin foundations (e.g. Cosa), where despite an
even division of the land, buildings were fairly individual.

Geological and geophysical conditions need to be
respected not only in the construction of a settlement,
but also in that of a house. Vitruvius' description (some
details of which are still being discussed by scholars) of
a Greek private house in bk. 6 of De architectura demonstrates sufficiently, details apart, the importance of
considering climatic conditions, positions of the sun
and cardinal directions, but also the relevance of incorporating potential problems of the infra-structure
(→ latrines; → Canals → Water supply); on making use
of solar energy, cf. also Xen. Mem. 3,8).

B. The Greek house

Although new finds and excavations in the last 20
years have significantly increased the number of monuments of residential architecture from the geometrical
period (10th–8th cents. BC) (as in Lefkandi, Nichoria,
Antissa/Lesbos, Zagora/Andros), the existence and the
quality of a building-typological tradition in the architecture of the Mycenaean-Minoan world is still under
discussion. The only house type that is clearly attested
(with some reservations) in its building-typological
continuity is the free-standing hearth-house (→ Megaron) found in a few late examples, for instance, in
Emporio/Chios (7th cent. BC). The most common type
in the geometric period are stretched-out houses with
apses (Athens, Thermus, Olympia) or oval houses,
rounded on the narrow sides (Old Smyrna), at times
subdivided into several sections (Antissa; → Apsis with
fig.), with a length of between 5 m (Old Smyrna) and
14 m (Nichoria), the only exception being the Toumba
building at Lefkandi with its total length of almost 45 m
(cf. → Temple). In addition, there are ante-houses and
rectangular houses, occasionally already internally divided into several rooms (Thorikos, Asine, Athens,
Tsikkalario) but lacking the axiality and symmetry of
contemporaneous Italic-Etruscan houses. So far, little is
known about the shape of these buildings of which only

small traces of the foundations and a few roof tiles from the 7th cent. BC have survived. The many extant clay models of houses do not serve as a firm basis for drawing conclusions about early Greek architecture as it was actually built. Beginning in the 7th cent. BC, the courtyard becomes the distinguishing element of the multi-tiered Greek house, giving rise to two basic types in the 5th and 6th cents. BC: the pastas house and the prostas house.

1. The Pastas house

The pastas house is an almost quadratic conglomerate oriented towards the south and the midday sun, usually with a two-storey living area accessible through a perpendicular, corridor-like entrance hall (*pastás*) open to the courtyard. The → andron [4], *xenon* (guest room), kitchen, *oikos* (living room), → baths, → *thalamoi* (bedrooms), and *tameion* (room for storing valuables) as well as the stairs to the upper floor with the → *gynaikonitis* are also accessible through the entrance hall. The courtyard is surrounded by single-level utility areas, storage rooms, workshops, and shops facing the street. In its early form, this type of house is found in Megara Hyblaea (where its development can be traced from the colonial single-room house of the 2nd half of the 8th cent. BC to the two-room house of the 7th cent. BC up to the archaic 'pastas house'). In its 'pure form', it can be found in the early houses of → Olynthus.

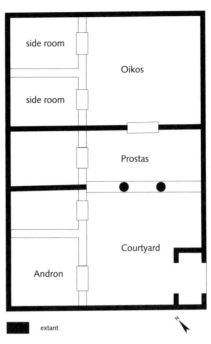

Piraeus: prostas house, 1st half 5th cent. BC (ground-plan)

Olynthus: pastas house, 1st half 4th cent. BC (ground-plan).

2. The Prostas house

The prostas house is most often understood as an elaboration of the one-room megaron house. Evidence of this derivation might be found in the prostas houses of Colophon (4th cent. BC), which structurally appear to continue in the tradition of older buildings, as well as in a megaron-type house near Ano Saphi/Boeotia. The long and rectangular conglomerate of rooms with a perpendicularly integrated courtyard reduces the corridor hall of the pastas house to an antechamber that only serves the *oikos* and is open to the courtyard; andron and antechamber have a separate entrance only accessible from the courtyard. The two-storey living area is

Ground floor

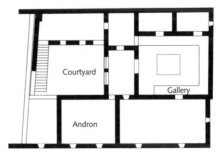

Upper floor

Orraon (Ammotopus): house 1, 4th cent. BC (ground and upper floors)

oriented towards the south as well; the single-level utility rooms are located on the opposite side of the courtyard, usually in separate buildings. The first example of a prostas house in its 'pure form' can be found in the newly conceived city of Piraeus (1st half of the 5th cent. BC; → Hippodamus of Miletus), then in Priene, Abdera, and in several other cities designed in the later 5th and 4th cents. BC.

3. THE HEARTH-ROOM HOUSE

It is unclear whether the hearth-room house of north-western Greece constitutes an independent type or another variation of the megaron house. The stone houses of Orraon/Ammotopos near Ambracia/Arta – extant to the base of the roof – (and possibly several analogous buildings in Cassope, all 4th cent. BC) reveal a two-story high, bright *oikos* with a central hearth accessible through a corridor that also connects to the courtyard, and an upper gallery with side rooms.

4. THE PERISTYLE HOUSE

The peristyle house is an innovation of the early 4th cent. BC and, at the same time, a clear indicator of a change in demands regarding house construction, furnishings (→ Incrustation; → Mosaic; → Wall paintings) and surroundings. The origin of the form is contested; on the one hand, the peristyle can be regarded as a change in the function of the courtyard – which originally belonged to the utility sphere – into a social space with interior columns (as suggested by the archaeologi-

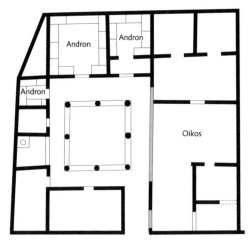

Eretria: so-called House of the Mosaics, 4th cent. BC (gound-plan)

cally well-documented findings in Polyanthus, where several pastas houses had been rebuilt into peristyle houses in the course of the 4th cent. BC); on the other hand, it is also possible to detect precursors in various banquet houses in sanctuaries (Argus, Troezen) or in other types of festival architecture such as the Pompeion on the Kerameikos in Athens, in which the placement of interior columns is difficult to explain in this sense. The house is characterized by the fact that different groups of rooms branch off from the peristyle. Early examples are several houses from → Eretria. The sizes of Hellenistic peristyle houses in Delos or in Pella (up to 2000 m² of floor space) had grown exorbitantly in comparison with houses from the classical period (size *c.*

300 m²). Some of those houses only differed from the palaces of Hellenistic emperors in terms of their size, their furnishings and their less exposed location – a difference of degree, not of principle.

5. COST

The building and maintenance costs of Greek houses varied strongly from place to place, at times even within one city. Inscriptions from Olynthus list a price range of 900 to 5,300 drachma; the average market value of a house must have amounted to 1,000 to 2,000 drachmas (with day's wages of 1 drachma). Up-to-date information about ownership and mortgages was kept in communal archives. Renting was always governed by contracts, and, as transmitted through inscriptions from Delos, relatively inexpensive (50 drachmae rent per year). Real-estate was often offered for rent or for sale without the door and the roof tiles; both elements were highly valuable, reusable, and thus counted as movable goods (→ Household equipment).

C. EARLY ITALIC AND ETRUSCAN HOUSES

The history of residential architecture in Etruscan culture began with one-room round or oval huts with hipped roofs and small canopies (e.g. huts on the Palatine in Rome, 8th cent. BC) or simple rectangular buildings of clay and wickerwork (S. Giovenale, 7th cent. BC), the structure of which has been reconstructed primarily based on house-shaped clay urns. These huts soon developed into more complex house types with various rooms and with building sections for different functions. The preserved extant remnants of foundations of the heavily built-up, orthogonally structured *insulae* of → Marzabotto (*c.* 500 BC) hardly allow any conclusions about the ground-plan organization of individual houses. However, Etruscan → funerary architecture reflects even the details of house construction. Extensive, representative aristocratic houses from the 6th cent. BC such as the 'Palace' of → Murlo (measurements *c.* 60 × 60 m) or the 'building F' at → Acquarossa reveal a division into three areas – living quarters, rooms for celebrations and banquets, rooms for sacral events – and great splendour in the furnishings (columned halls, richly painted terracotta coverings). These were the origins of the worship of house deities and protective gods which were to become so omnipresent in the later Roman house as an important aspect of domestic life. The Etruscan origin of Italic-Roman residential architecture is apparent in important houses in Rome, for example, in the *regia* at the Forum Romanum, built in the 4th cent. BC (not to be derived from the Greek megaron type), also in the → atrium widely used in Italic house construction beginning in the 4th cent. BC. The oldest known evidence of an atrium can be found in Etruscan houses on the Palatine in Rome as well as in the houses grouped around a central courtyard in Marzabotto (all 6th cent. BC).

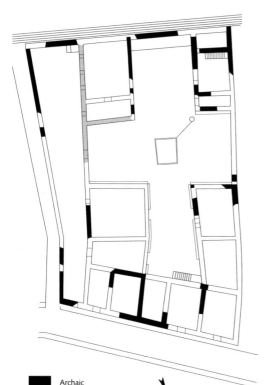

| Archaic |
| Post-archaic |
| Reconstruction |

0   4 m

Rome, Palatine: patrician house, late 6th cent. BC

D. ROMAN HOUSES
1. THE ATRIUM HOUSE

The atrium house is the most important Italic house type of Republican times. As a house type in Etruscan/Italic architecture, it appears initially not only as a private habitation (Rome, Palatine, 6th cent. BC), but also – in considerable size – as a public building (e.g. the *atrium publicum* on the forum at Cosa), its use spreading rapidly from the 4th cent. BC onwards. Its structure, a long rectangle, symmetrical along a central axis, with an open, variously shaped patio (→ *compluvium*; → *atrium*) in its centre, combines utility rooms (*tabernae*), living quarters, halls, corridors and a garden. A vestibule, often in two parts (→ *vestibulum*; *fauces*), leads in from the street side, passing between two or more utility rooms – accessible from the outside only and unconnected with the interior of the house – and reaches the atrium with the → *impluvium* (→ Cistern) in the middle. Adjacent to the atrium are the bedrooms *(cubicula)*; the rear part of the atrium consists of the *alae* (doorless side rooms, open to their full height, for various functions, e.g. as storage or dining rooms or as rooms for the images of the ancestors; → *ala* [1]) and the → *tablinum*, which in turn allows access to the garden *(hortus)*; the latter – a narrow space surrounded by high walls – is the last section in the back of the house. Not

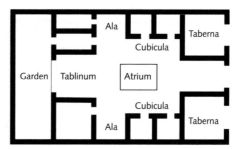

Schematic representation of an atrium house, 4th cent. BC (ground-plan).

all Italic houses were atrium houses: in Italic/Roman cities one can also find, up to the 1st cent. BC, a house type arranged in a comparatively asymmetrical way, which has neither atrium nor *tabernae* (and hence no utility sphere of any kind), but a number of *cubicula* around a roofed *tablinum* leading to a garden via the kitchen (Cosa).

The principle of the atrium house proved to be sufficiently flexible to satisfy higher requirements of representation. Especially by combining it with the peristyle, adopted from the architecture of Hellenistic house, large and prestigious constructions, as they are known, e.g. from Pompeii, were constructed from the 2nd cent. BC onwards. The *Casa dei capitelli figurati* uses the standard type of the atrium house, expanding it with a spacious garden peristyle in place of the garden. In the *Casa del Fauno* two atria have been fused with two peristyles (a living-space peristyle and a garden peristyle) to form an almost villa-like habitation which, however, still preserves the character of a city house that is made to fit into an *insula*. Finally, in Imperial Italy it is not unusual to find representational peristyle houses without an atrium (Ostia).

2. TENEMENT BLOCKS

Multi-storey multiple-family dwellings or blocks of flats, an important feature of the Roman city, can be found not only in metropolises, but, in a more modest guise, in provincial towns as well (multi-storey atrium houses at Herculaneum, in some cases refurbished specifically for lease, e.g. the *Casa sannitica* or the *Casa a graticcio*, where the atrium becomes a courtyard and the → *cenacula*, the rented second-floor flats, are accessible via a separate staircase). Particularly densely populated cities (Rome, Ostia, Puteoli) had high-rise buildings of up to six floors, built around a narrow courtyard. These were objects of speculation: usually built fast and cheaply by private firms, and covering an entire *insula*, often they did not conform to building regulations (→ Building law; cf. e.g. Juv. 3,188–310). On the ground floor they were surrounded by a *porticus* and furnished with shops, the first floor was a kind of *piano nobile*, with lower and more simply furnished floors above it; both quality and rent decreased from bottom to top. Partitions between flats were made of lightweight materials, and the individual floors were

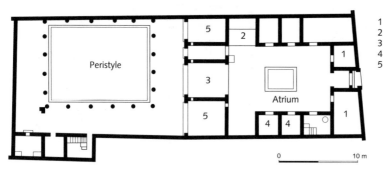

1 Taberna
2 Ala
3 Tablinum
4 Cubiculum
5 Triclinium

Pompeii: peristyle house,
Casa dei capitelli figurati,
2nd cent. BC (ground-plan)

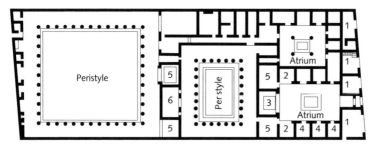

1 Taberna
2 Ala
3 Tablinum
4 Cubiculum
5 Triclinium
6 Exedra

Pompeii: house with
two peristyles,
Casa del Fauno,
2nd cent BC (ground-plan)

reached by stairs and crooked corridors. There was no
→ heating, no sanitation faciltities (cf. → Hygiene, personal; → *latrines*), and no kitchen. The handling of
open fires and portable stoves and braziers in the flats
often led to devastating fires. Luxurious living conditions tended to be rare in urban tenement blocks, and
the *Casa dei dipinti* at Ostia, with its generously built
flats, each covering several floors, was an exception,
although in general tenement blocks at Ostia did have a
higher standard than those of Rome's → *Subura*.

Several varieties of the courtyard or atrium house
(e.g. at Volubilis, often with a second courtyard, called
atriolum) can be found in urban contexts outside Italy
beside *insulae* (Augusta Raurica), which were densely
built up with modest two- or three-room houses. These
are generally not preserved beyond their foundations
and are therefore difficult to reconstruct insofar as their
layout and division by functions is concerned. The peristyle house was common throughout the entire empire:
for instance, richly furnished houses of several storeys
over irregular foundations with a central peristyle rose
along the Street of the Curetes at → Ephesus (2nd cent.
AD); in the north-western provinces, too, there were
numerous peristyle and courtyard houses, and in the
Gallo-Roman area as well as in Hispania one can observe an intermingling of traditional local and imported
forms.

E. AKURGAL, Alt-Smyrna I. Wohnschichten und Athena-
tempel, 1983; T. F. C. BLAGG, First-Century Roman
Houses in Gaul and Britain, 1990; E. BRÖDNER, Wohnen
in der Ant., 1989; V. J. BRUNO, R. T. SCOTT, Cosa 4. The
Houses, 1993; J. R. CLARKE, The Houses of Roman Italy,
100 B.C. – A.D. 250, 1991; M. CRISTOFANI (ed.), La
Grande Roma dei Tarquini, exhibition catalogue Rome,

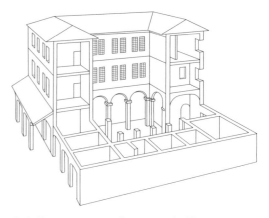

Ostia: Transverse section of a tenement building,
middle Imperial period

1990, 97–99; H. DRERUP, Griech. Baukunst in geom. Zeit,
ArchHom O, 1969; S. ELLIS, La casa, in: A. GUILLOU
(ed.), La civiltà bizantina, 1993, 167–226; K. FAGER-
STRÖM, Greek Iron Age Architecture, 1988; D. FUSARO,
Note di architettura domestica greca nel periodo tardo-
geometrico e arcaico, in: Dialoghi di archeologia 4, 1982,
5–30; H. VON HESBERG, Privatheit und Öffentlichkeit in
der frühhell. Hofarchitektur, in: W. HOEPFNER,
G. BRANDS (ed.), Basileia. Die Paläste der hell. Könige,
1996, 84–96; W. HOEPFNER, E. L. SCHWANDNER, Haus
und Stadt im klass. Griechenland, ²1994; W. HOEPFNER,
Zum Typus der Basileia und der königlichen Andro7nes, in:
W. HOEPFNER, G. BRANDS (ed.), Basileia. Die Paläste der
hell. Könige, 1996, 1–43; A. KALPAXIS, Früharcha. Baukunst in Griechenland und Kleinasien, 1976; M. KIDER-
LEN, Megale Oikia. Unt. zur Entwicklung aufwendiger

griech. Stadthausarchitektur von der Früharchaik bis ins 3. Jh. v.Ch., 1995; M.KREEB, Unt. zur figürlichen Ausstattung delischer Privathäuser, 1988; La casa urbana hispanorromana, conference Zaragoza (1988), 1991; C.LANG-AUINGER, Hanghaus 1 in Ephesos – Der Baubefund, FiE 8/3, 1996; F.LANG, Archa. Siedlungen in Griechenland, 1996, 78–117; H.LAUTER, Architektur des Hell., 1986, 223–227; H.MAEHLER, Häuser und ihre Bewohner im Fayum in der Kaiserzeit, in: G.GRIMM (ed.), Das röm.-byz. Ägypt., 1983, 119–137; A.G. McKAY, Röm. Häuser, Villen und Paläste, 1980; W.MÜLLER-WIENER, Griech. Bauwesen in der Ant., 1986, 176–179; Palast und Hütte. Beitr. zum Bauen und Wohnen im Alt. Conference Bonn (1979), 1982; F.PESANDO, Oikos e ktesis. La casa greca in età classica, 1987; F.PRAYON, Frühetr. Grabund Hausarchitektur (22. Ergh. MDAI(R)), 1975; J.RAEDER, Vitruv, De architectura VI 7 und die hell. Wohnungsund Palastarchitektur, in: Gymnasium 95, 1988, 316–368; K.REBER, Aedificia Graecorum. Zu Vitruvs Beschreibung des griech. Hauses, in: AA 1988, 653–666; TH. SCHATTNER, Griech. Hausmodelle. Unt. zur frühgriech. Architektur (15. Beih. MDAI(A)), 1990; S.SINOS, Die vorklass. Hausformen in der Ägäis, 1971; A. STREILY, Alt-Smyrna, Graben H: Zur griech. H.-Architektur des 9. und 8. Jh. v.Chr., in: Thetis 4, 1997, 63–84; A. WALLACE-HADRILL, Houses and Society in Pompeii and Herculaneum, 1994; E. WALTER-KARYDI, Die Nobilitierung des griech. Wohnhauses in der spätklass. Zeit, in: W. HOEPFNER, G.BRANDS (ed.), Basileia. Die Paläste der hell. Könige, 1996, 56–61; Wohnungsbau im Alt., conference Berlin (= DiskAB 3), 1978.   C.HÖ.

Household equipment

Household equipment (Greek τὰ ἔπιπλα/*tà épipla*, ἡ σκευή/*hē skeué*; Latin *supellex, instrumentum*). Household equipment (HE) comprises the objects that are needed in daily life and that constitute the majority of moveable belongings; this includes primarily → furniture, cooking utensils and kitchen crockery, lighting devices, → carpets, → blankets, and in a wider sense also → jewellery and → clothing, furthermore, according to current understanding, objects belonging to the sphere of immovables, e.g. the doors and roof tiles of the → house. In addition, those objects that constitute the autonomy of the Greek and Roman domestic economy should be considered as HE such as looms, weaving weights, weaving combs or hand presses and handmills (*trapetum*), → mortars and pestles for oil and grain and, also, in the extended sense farming and gardening equipment (collected e.g. in Anth. Pal. 6,297), not least also the slaves and servants needed for housekeeping. There are also kitchen utensils like cheese graters (κνῆστις/*knêstis*, Hom. Il. 11,640, or τυρόκνηστις/*tyróknêstis*, Aristoph. Vesp. 963, Av. 1579), frying pans, grills (*craticula*), saucepans, tripods for pots, the ἐσχάρα/*eschára* (flat pans), plates, serving plates (→ repositorium, → Table utensils), stirring spoons (→ rudis), ladles (κύαθος/*kýathos*, *simpulum*), salt cellars (ἁλία/*halía, concha, salinum*), pots, cutlery such as carving knives, forks and spoons (*ligula, cochlear*), boilers for → soap, → filters made of cloth, clay and other materials for straining oil, water, wine etc. and not least the storage vessels for wine, oil, flour, honey

etc., furthermore baskets and sacks for transporting food, clothes etc. In addition to the sumptuous metal vessels (cf. e.g. Juv. 12,43–48) that are known from tomb, hoard or settlement finds (finds of Boscoreale, Hildesheim, Kaiseraugst, and others), people also used clay dishes as → crockery, even in the higher social classes, for reasons of better taste (Vitr. De arch. 8,6,11, cf. Cic. Att. 6,1,13). As a matter of course, in all social classes wooden crockery, which has been preserved only rarely because of the transitory nature of the material, took a prominent place.

Additional HE objects were used for → lighting (candelabrum, lamps, torch holders etc.) or made life more comfortable such as rugs (e.g. Mart. 1,49,31), portable braziers (*foculus*) with the πνιγεύς (*pnigeús*), a lid that served to extinguish the flames, and with the *rutabulum* (poker); furthermore → cushions and pillows (which were filled with *plumae*, down feathers from geese or swans as well as with straw, hay, reeds or sea grass), covers made of linen, woollen materials or leather – and for going out – → litters and → umbrellas.

Implements for daily body care such as the bath tub (→ Baths) or portable (Anth. Pal. 11,74,7; Hor. Sat. 1,6, 109) toilets (ἀμίς/*amís, matella* for the men, σκάφιον/*skáphion, scaphium* for the women, Petron. Sat. 41,9; 47,5), or the λάσανον (*lásanon*) as a → chamber pot were also indispensable; for any cleaning that had to be done people used water and a sponge (Aristoph. Ran. 487) that could also be attached to a wooden stick (Mart. 12,48,7). People used to use the portable toilet at banquets as well as in the bedroom (Poll. 10,44). The slave who was summoned to bring the portable toilet by a snapping of the fingers (→ Gestures) was called *lasanophóros*. Lavatories that were installed as fixtures (ἄφοδος/*áphodos*, κοπρών/*koprón*, ἰπνός/ *ipnòs*, cf. Aristoph. Ach. 81; Poll. 10,44) were still rare in the 4th cent. BC (→ Latrines; see e.g. Syll.³ 1261,11, cf. Ath. 10,417d). Mart. 1,37 mentions a golden toilet. Also used for cleanliness were the bath tub (ἀσάμινθος/ *asáminthos, labrum, solium*), foot- and hand-washing basin (ποδανιπτήρ/*podaniptér*, λεκανίς/*lekanís, pelvis, gutturnium*), drying towels, → comb, → mirror, → scissors, tweezers, ear scoops, toothpicks, make-up jars etc. (→ Hygiene, personal), and not least the household's own → baths in the houses of the upper class.

To clean the house or HE, people had brooms (κάλλυντρον/*kállyntron*, κόρηθρον/*kórētron*, κόρημα/ *kórēma*, σάρωτρον/*sárōtron*, σάρον/*sáron, scopae*) for the floors made out of elm, tamarisk or myrtle twigs. In order to be better able to sweep away the rubbish that accumulated e.g. after downfalls of rain in the yard of the house or after banquets, people strewed the ground with wood shavings (Juv. 14,60–67; Hor. Sat. 2,4,81; Petron. Sat. 68); to clean furniture, the feather duster (→ *peniculus*) was used. People cleaned their shoes (Aristoph. Vesp. 600 [1] with a → sponge and oil. → Writing materials (→ Styluses, writing tablets, inkwells etc.) and various educational implements (scrolls, musical instruments) should also be regarded as HE. Romans attached the → *pluteus* (shelf, board) to the wall for busts, writing materials and other things. Toys for children (→ Children's games) are worthy of mention here. We should also add various cult implements (censers, → thymiaterion, altars, arula, sarcophagi, urns) for household and funerary worship.

HE also included working animals (horses, sheep, goats, fowl, etc.) as well as pets (snakes, foxes, dogs, crickets, hares, monkeys, domestic cats). Birds – kept in bird cages when they were not being played with or allowed to fly around the room – were very popular, particularly with the Romans (cf. Plin. Ep. 4,2); it is worth recollecting the sparrow or bullfinch of Lesbia (Catull. 2,3), the parrot of Corinna (Ov. Am. 2,6) or the talking starling of Britannicus and Nero (Plin. HN 10,120; Plut. Mor. 972f); in addition there were also owls and magpies and members of the cat family such as the lion, tiger and cheetah. Of practical importance were also domestic animals that were used for exterminating vermin, beetles or bedbugs (κόρις/*kóris*, cf. Aristoph. Ran. 114, [2]) in the house (e.g. herons, hedgehogs, cats). People rid themselves of mice with the help of traps, poison, cats or weasels. Bedbugs, lice (φθείρ/*phtheír*, head louse or clothes louse) or fleas (ψύλλος/*psýllos*) were combatted in various ways (cf. Plin. HN 33,17f.). Against flies (→ Fly) the fly-swat (*muscarium*, cf. Mart. 3,82,2) was used, or the mosquito net (ἀμφίβληστρον, *canopium*) at night. The lees of oil (Plin. HN 15,33) were effective against moths.

Lists recording the HE of a household in detail and showing the degree to which the objects were valued have been passed down to us in various ways, e.g. in the public auctions of the HE of → Alcibiades (414/3 BC; cf. ToD 80), the inheritance of Demosthenes (Dem. Or. 27,10, from which we can establish that the value of the HE was three times the value of the house); in the comedies of Aristophanes (e.g. Eccl. 730–747, cf. Plaut. Aul. 94f.) a wealth of objects are mentioned, likewise in the comedy fragments of Nicostratus (4th cent. BC) and in PLond. 3,191,15 (AD 113–117); further indications can be found from various → marriage contracts passed down to us. They reveal the extent of the various cushions, pillows, blankets, mats, towels, underclothes, covers, table utensils and metal implements (lights, kettles, mirrors etc.).

Depictions of accumulated HE are very common ([3], Attic grave relief, vases): e.g. vase images show women at the loom and performing other tasks, and there are also terracottas of women, children and men preparing food at the mortar, kneading dough, at baking ovens, at the grill, making weapons or tools [4] etc.; in addition numerous examples of real cooking ovens, pans, heating ovens, spits, firedogs, cutlery etc. have been preserved. The significance of HE objects can be seen from the fact that the bride received these (particularly clothing and jewellery) when she was led from her parents' home to that of the bridegroom, which applies equally to Greek and Roman → wedding customs (Eust. re Hom. Il. 24,29), and also from the custom of bringing one's hosts books, ointment vessels, blankets, belts and other items as gifts (Suet. Vesp. 19; schol. Juv. 6,203; Suet. Aug. 75; Mart. 7,53; Petron. Sat. 56,8; 60,4). Good information regarding the HE of the Roman house is provided not just by the literary sources but particularly by the numerous finds from the cities of Vesuvius and the tomb inventories of Italy and the northern provinces.

1 R. HURSCHMANN, Symposienszenen auf unterital. Vasen, 1985, pl. 22 A 34   2 V. M. STROCKA (ed.), Frühe Zeichner 1500 bis 500 v.Chr., Exhibition catalogue Freiburg, 1992, 74 no. 75   3 TRENDALL, Paestum, 84 no. 127 pl. 46 (and more)   4 B. A. SPARKES, L. TALCOTT, Pots and Pans of Classical Athens, 1958.

B. A. AULT, Classical houses and households: an architectural and artifactural case study from Halieis, Greece, 1994; F. BARATTE, Römisches Silbergeschirr in den gallischen und germanischen Provinzen, Limesmuseum Aalen 32, 1984; J. BOERSMA, Private latrines in Ostia: a case study, in: BABesch 71, 1996, 151–160; E. BRÖDNER, Wohnen in der Antike, 1989; G. BRUNS, Küchenwesen und Mahlzeiten, ArchHom Q, 1970; H. A. CAHN, A. KAUFMANN-HEINIMANN, Der spätröm. Silberschatz von Kaiseraugst, 1984; M. CREMEO, Venuskunkeln aus Kleinasien, in: AA 1996, 135f.; D. C. DRUMMOND, R. M. and J. J. JANSSEN, An ancient Egyptian rat trap, in: MDAI(K) 46, 1990, 90–98; L. FOXHALL, Household, gender and property in Classical Athens, in: CQ 39, 1989, 22–44; A. R. FURGER, Der Inhalt eines Geschirr- oder Vorratsschrankes aus dem 3. Jh. von Kaiseraugst-Schmidmatt, in: Jahresberichte aus Augst und Kaiseraugst 10, 1989, 213–268; W. GAITZSCH, Antike Korb- und Seilerwaren, 1986; J. F. GARDNER (ed.), The Roman Household. A Sourcebook, 1991; W. HILGERS, Lateinische Gefäßnamen, 31. Beih. BJ, 1969; D. W. HOBSON, House and Household in Roman Egypt, in: YClS 28, 1985, 211–229; H. J. KELLNER, G. ZAHLHAAS, Der Röm. Tempelschatz von Weißenburg in Bayern, 1993, 111–125; R. NEUDECKER, Die Pracht der Latrine, 1994; R. NOLL, Das Inventar des Dolichenusheiligtums von Mauer an der Url (Noricum), 1980; R. PETROVSKY, Studien zu röm. Bronzegefäßen mit Meisterstempeln, 1993; Pompeji wiederentdeckt, Exhibition Hamburg 1993, 1993; T. L. SHEAR JR., The Persian destruction of Athens, in: Hesperia 62, 1993, 429–480; B. A. SPARKES, The Greek kitchen, in: JHS 82, 1962, 121–137; D. B. THOMPSON, An ancient shopping center, 1971; TOYNBEE, Tierwelt; S. TREGGIARI, Jobs in the household of Livia, in: PBSR 43, 1975, 18–27; E. TRINKL, Ein Set aus Spindel, Spinnwirtel und Rocken aus einem Sarkophag in Ephesos, in: Österr. Jb. für Arch. 63, 1994, Beibl., 81–92; G. WICKERT-MICKNAT, Die Frau, ArchHom R, 1982, 38–80; M. VALLERIN, Pelvis estampillés de Bassit, in: Syria 71, 1994, 171–185.   R.H.

House tomb see → Funerary architecture C. 2.3

Housing conditions

I. General II. Physical basic conditions
III. Spatial separation of living functions
IV. Social and legal basic conditions

I. General

Unlike sojourn, residence designates a permanent or fairly long stay, and constitutes, along with protection against the weather, part of the basic needs and the functions essential to the biological preservation of the individual. In examining the housing conditions (HC) of Graeco-Roman antiquity, distinctions are made according to functions and basic conditions. The randomness of works handed down from antiquity, the way sources are focussed on the upper classes and Rome and the one-sidedness of the description of HC in literature, in particular satirical writings, all cause methodological problems.

II. Physical basic conditions

A. Architecture B. Position and infrastructure C. Fixtures

A. Architecture

The most important determinants of HC are the types of houses (→ House), differentiated by region, period and social class. In Greece, alongside the one-room house, there existed the → *pastas* house (with a hall in front of several rooms) and the *prostas* house (a narrow house with the hall in front of the living-room) and in the Hellenistic period the peristyle house (with a columned hall in the courtyard); additionally, further local forms (on Delos, for instance) are to be found. There is much critical discussion about typical houses (in Piraeus, in Priene and Olynthus, for example). Evidence of upper floors being rented out has been found in Delos, for instance. In many rural regions, such as Attica, tower farmsteads were common. The atrium house (*domus*: cf. Nep. Att. 13,2, for instance), the upper floor (→ *cenaculum*) of which was also sometimes rented out, was typical of the HC of the Roman upper classes in cities. The → garden as an inner garden in the peristylium (→ *peristýlion*) played a greater role than in Greek traditional housing. There were already three-storey tenements at the Forum Boarium in Rome (Liv. 21,62,3) by the late 3rd cent. BC; it is often possible to detect a social gradation from the lower floors to the top in housing blocks of this kind (→ *insula*). The extremely poor living conditions in the upper storeys are described in literary writings, in which the cramped conditions of the flats and the danger of collapse and fire are emphasized (Plut. Crassus 2; Tac. Ann. 4,64; 6,45; Juv. 3,190–222; Mart. 7,20; 12,32). Some of the poor population lived in residential commercial rooms (*taberna*: Tac. Hist. 1,86,2; Ascon. 37 C; Cassiod. 14,1,31; Dig. 50,16,183; *pergula*/mezzanine floor: Petron. Sat. 74,14). In the country the *villae* were temporary refuges of the upper classes; here too there were often ornamental gardens (Villa of Oplontis); at the same time the → *villa* was normally also the centre of properties used for agricultural purposes (Varro, Rust. 1,11; 1,13,6 f.; Columella 1,4,6–8). The *villa* was the world of active → leisure (*otium*) of the citizen involved in the community (descriptions of villas: Plin. Ep. 2,17; 3,19; 5,6; 9,7; Stat. Silv. 1,3; 2,2). There is also evidence of Roman types of houses in the provinces and they are a significant witness to → Romanization in Gaul, Germania, Britain and North Africa.

B. Position and infrastructure

In the city of Rome the upper classes already had their favourite locations, including, for instance, the area around the → Forum [III 8] Romanum and the → Mons Palatinus; the *plebs*, on the other hand, lived in the → subura (cf. → Roma III. with map 1 and 2). A change in residence was more than likely to have a political implication (Plut. C. Gracchus 12). Separation of poor and rich housing areas was not possible in → Pompeii (with map); superior houses went by the prestige of streets. Noise pollution due to traffic on the streets, by neighbours or public institutions reduced housing quality (cf. Sen. Ep. 56,1 ff.; Mart. 12,57; Juv. 3,232–238; → Noise). Roads and squares broadened the living space and were part of HC (e.g. Hor. Sat. 1,9,1 f.; Ov. Ars am. 1,67 ff.), although in ancient houses the side facing the road was characteristically closed. The possibility of access to various forms of → water supply was likewise a significant factor for the quality of living. Drainpipes or → latrines existed in many houses, though improper discharge could be a danger to passers-by in the road (Dig. 9,3,5 pr. 1; Juv. 3,268 f.). The landscape was often opened up by the building of a house (Herculaneum, Casa dei Cervi; Villa dei Papiri; Plin. Ep. 2,17,20 ff.; 5,6,37 ff.).

C. Fixtures

→ Wall painting, already attested for the 5th cent. BC (Plut. Alcibiades 16), was widespread from the Hellenistic period at the latest and not evidence of particular domestic luxury. The neutral fixtures of Greek and Roman homes were restrained and restricted to a few items of → furniture. Statues in wealthier houses were assembled according to aspects of content or shape (Herculaneum, Villa dei Papiri; Cic. Att. 1,8,2; 1,10,3; Petron. Sat. 29,6; Apul. Met. 2,4). The fixtures of the houses of the Roman upper classes had been augmented since the late Republic with expensive building materials and representative architectural elements (columns), which had previously been reserved for public or sacred buildings (Plin. HN 36,47 ff.; 36,109 ff.), so that luxury laws were discussed (Tac. Ann. 2,33,1 ff.; → luxury); there was social control of living conditions (Cic. Dom. 100; Vell. Pat. 2,14,3). Ensembles of fixtures have been preserved in Delos and the cities around Vesuvius. Comfort in houses was greatly dependent on weather conditions. Portable coal braziers normally served as → heating. Glazed → windows appeared in the middle of the 1st cent. BC (Sen. Ep. 90,25; Plin. Ep. 2,17,21);

finds in early private houses are rare (Settefinestre), though more frequent from the 2nd cent. AD. Oil lamps, often made of clay, were used for → lighting the rooms (→ Lamps).

III. SPATIAL SEPARATION OF LIVING FUNCTIONS

Spatial separation of the various living functions, such as cooking, heating, sleeping, hygiene, work, leisure, entertaining and representation was possible only to a limited extent in one-room houses, tower farmsteads and the flats of the large tenements. In Greek houses the central living area was the courtyard or → peristýlion, in Roman houses the → atrium. There was an enormous contrast between the living conditions of the ancient lower classes and those of the upper classes, especially evident in the difference between the *villae* with their large living areas and rooms for special purposes on the one hand and the cramped flats in the *insulae* on the other hand. Not all the functions of the rooms (such as → ándrôn [4], *cubiculum*, → *diaeta*, → *triclinium*, *tablinum*, *vestibulum* or → hearth) were structurally fixed, but were sometimes partly interchangeable by means of furnishing. Commercial activity took place even in superior houses; in particular the compartments facing the road or the upper floors were used for commercial purposes or let out. However, little is known of the density of occupation of ancient living units (Val. Max. 4,4,8; Plut. Aem. Paullus 5,6).

IV. SOCIAL AND LEGAL BASIC CONDITIONS

Spatial separation of social groups within the house was customary, but it was only in Greek houses that there was familial separation (on → *gynaikōnítis* cf. Lys. 1,9). Room division according to age was not customary in Rome. The houses of members of the Roman upper classes had to satisfy both private needs and public representation (e.g. → *salutatio*); they had graduated zones of public access. Representation appropriate to the social status was expected (Cic. Off. 1,138 ff.; Vitr. De arch. 6,5) and refusal to live in a representative way was regarded as inappropriate (Cic. Pis. 67; Apul. Met. 1,21). The religious components of the house cults (→ *imagines maiorum*, → *lararium*: Pol. 6,53; Plin. HN 35,6–8; Vitr. De arch. 6,3,6; Cic. Dom. 109) were also part of the living culture of antiquity.

It was possible to live under legal terms of ownership or renting (Dig. 9,3,9; → Tenancy IV.; → *locatio conductio*); renting is frequently attested in the sources for Rome and the cities of the Roman empire; rents were very high, particularly in Rome, from the 2nd cent. BC (Rome: Diod. Sic. 31,18,2; Vell. Pat. 2,10,1; Plut. Crassus 2; Cic. Cael. 17; Juv. 3,223–229; Gell. NA 15,1,2 f.; Pompeii: CIL IV 138 = ILS 6035; CIL IV 1136 = ILS 5723; Puteoli: Cic. Att. 14,9,1). Cicero owned several houses in Rome, which brought in 80,000 HS a year in rent in 44 BC (Cic. Att. 16,1,5; cf. 12,32,2). An attempt was made to improve living conditions by legal measures; Caesar carried through a rent decree (Cass. Dio 42,51,1; Suet. Iul. 38,2; criticism by Cicero: Cic. Off.

2,83), and Augustus limited the height of houses to 70 feet (Str. 5,3,7; cf. Suet. Aug. 89,2).

→ Emphyteusis; → Furniture; → Gardens; → Habitatio; → House (with fig.); → Household equipment; → Insula; → Tenancy; → Palace; → Villa (with fig.)

1 H. BLANCK, Einführung in das Privatleben der Griechen und Römer, 1976 2 J.-A. DICKMANN, Domus frequentata, 1999 3 E. J. DWYER, Pompeian Domestic Sculpture, 1982 4 B. W. FRIER, Landlords and Tenants in Imperial Rome, 1980 5 V. GASSNER, Die Kaufläden in Pompeii 1986 6 W. HOEPFNER (ed.), Geschichte des Wohnens, vol. 1, 1999 7 M. KREEB, Unt. zur figürlichen Ausstattung delischer Privathäuser, 1988 8 CH. KUNST (ed.), Röm. Wohn- und Lebenswelten, 2000 9 H. MIELSCH, Die röm. Villa, 1987 10 R. NEUDECKER, Die Skulpturenausstattung röm. Villen in It., 1988 11 A. OETTEL, Fundkontexte röm. Vesuvvillen im Gebiet um Pompeji, 1996 12 F. PIRSON, Mietwohnungen in Pompeji und Herkulaneum, 1999 13 M. TRÜMPER, Wohnen in Delos, 1998 14 Z. YAVETZ, The Living Conditions of the Urban Plebs in Republican Rome, in: Latomus 17, 1958, 500–517 15 A. WALLACE-HADRILL, Houses and Society in Pompeii and Herculaneum, 1994 16 P. ZANKER, Pompeji. Stadtbild und Wohngeschmack, 1995. T. M.

Hubris see → Hybris

Hulchnie Etruscan gentilicium of aristocratic families, especially in → Volsinii and → Tarquinii (Tomba dell' Orco), possibly synonymous with the Latin Fulginii.

F.PR.

Human dignity

A. GREEK-ROMAN   B. JEWISH-CHRISTIAN
C. MODERN

A. GREEK-ROMAN

While the term for human dignity (HD) was formed and transmitted through Stoic anthropology and ethics (→ Stoicism), the concept itself was very common and well-founded in Greek and Roman antiquity. → Cicero (Off. 1,30,106; autumn of 44 BC), in a comparison between animal and man, realizes 'what eminence and dignity lies in (our; sc. human) nature': *quae sit in natura <nostra –* em. TOUPIUS; *hominis* em. codex 14th cent., J. STURM, 1553 *i.a.> excellentia et dignitas*. This dignity is based on reason and the ability to freely make ethical decisions. (Universal) nature has superimposed this → 'person' (*persona* – mask, role) on man (Cic. Off. 1,30,107). This 'first persona' and the dignity resulting from it is common to all humans (*communis*). Other 'roles' determine the special qualities of the individual through predisposition (*propria natura*), historical situation (*casus et tempus*), and a person's own decision (*iudicium*). The source of the 1st bk. of Cicero's work 'On Duties', thus also the source of his theory of nature, reason, and personal dignity, is → Panaetius' lost treatise 'On Appropriate Actions' (*Perì kathēkóntōn*; probably 138/128 BC) [1].

Stoic theory of HD is universal; it argues philosophically rather than theologically. On the other hand, the metaphors (mask, role) and the term *dignitas* are culture-specific. In Cicero, 'dignity' is a concrete, visible quality of a person, of the Roman people, its government, the state. It bestows glory, it is radiant, and an ornament (*decus, decorum*). To reduce the collective dignity (*maiestatem minuere*) is a a serious offence. The word *dignitas* appears frequently in Cicero; the term 'dignity of (human) nature' only once.

B. Jewish-Christian

The Hebrew and the Greek Bible (cf. Ps. 8) show no record of the term HD. Only in the middle of the 4th cent. AD did western Christianity create a festival for the 'birth of the Lord', which, on the day of the winter solstice, celebrated God's 'incarnation' (*in-carnatio*). A prayer specific for this festival was created: 'Lord God, who miraculously created the dignity of human substance and miraculously rejuvenated it, give us ...' (*Deus qui humanae substantiae dignitatem mirabiliter condidisti et mirabilius reformasti: Da nobis ...*; Sacramentum Leonianum: collection *c.* 540, MS 7th cent.; PL 55, 146f.). This theory of HD is based on theological statements about creation, incarnation, and salvation. MSS of the 12th cent. attest to the adoption of the Christmas *oratio* into the fixed order of the mass (*ordo Missae;* → Missa) [2]. The mysteries of the Eucharist grant 'participation in the divinity' of God's son who had become human. The spread of the term in ancient and medieval Christian literature was rather limited in comparison to modern times (cf. Thomas Aquinas, Summa Theologica II II q. 64.2: *humana dignitas*).

C. Modern

Cicero's treatise on 'appropriate actions' was widely copied during the Renaissance: about 700 MSS in the 14th–15th cents ; first printed edition in Mainz in 1465; the first German translation was printed in 1488 in Augsburg, a richly illustrated edition by Johann Neuber (and Johann v. Schwarzenberg, died in 1528) was printed in Nürnberg in 1531. In the latter, the term *wyrde menschlicher Natur* appears for the first time in German literature. The term was used as a title in the 15th cent. (Gianozzo Manetti, *De dignitate et excellentia hominis*, 1452) and was added later to the oration which Giovanni Pico della Mirandola wanted to give in Rome in 1486 [3; 4; 5; 6].

The anthropology of Cicero (*De legibus; De natura deorum; De officiis*) played a large role in the development of an early modern law based on nature and reason by the Neo-Stoic philosophers, jurists, and politicians. Samuel Pufendorf (1632–1694), jurist and humanist, is the first to use the term HD in a legal context [4]. John Wise (1652–1725) refers to Pufendorf's work in the English translation of 1710 in order to legitimize the constitution of the churches in New England based on natural law and 'dignity of humane nature' [7]. In I. Kant's anthropology, the term HD

plays a subordinate role; Kant refers explicitly to the ancient Stoa [8; 9].

The central importance of the term only emerges with the modern theory of human rights. The formula 'freedom and HD' appears in anti-fascist texts (1943: Manifest of the National Committee 'Freies Deutschland'; principles of the Kreisau Circle). The preamble of the charter of the United Nations (26 June 1945) announces the 'belief in basic human rights, in dignity and worth of the human personality'; cf. the Universal Declaration of Human Rights (10 December 1948), preamble and article 1. It is not clear how far these declarations are related to each other or to older philosophical and legal traditions.
→ Humanitas; → Human rights

1 A.R. Dyck, A Commentary on Cicero, de Officiis, 1996, 17ff.   2 A. Ebner, Missale Romanum, 1896 (repr. 1957), 51, 300 and passim   3 Gian Francesco Pico, Bologna 1496 (editio princeps; new edn. with preface: Jacob Wimpfeling, Straßburg 1504)   4 H. Welzel, Die Naturrechtslehre Samuel Pufendorfs, PhD thesis Jena 1928, 1958 (repr. 1986)   5 G. Pico della Mirandola, Über die Würde des Menschen (trans. H.W. Rüssel), 1988   6 G. von der Gönna (ed.), G.F. Pico, Oratio de hominis dignitate (on the basis of the editio princeps), 1997   7 J. Wise, A Vindication of the Government of New-England Churches, 1717, ²1772 (repr. 1958), 67f. 8 H. Thomae (ed.), Immanuel Kant, Von der Würde des Menschen, 1941 (anthology)   9 C. Melches Gibert, Der Einfluß von Christian Garves Übersetzung Ciceros de officiis auf Kants Grundlegung zur Metaphysik der Sitten, 1994.

E. Bloch, Naturrecht und menschliche Würde, 1961; H. Cancik, Die Würde des Menschen ist unantastbar (1987), in: Id., Antik – Modern, 1998, 267–291; Id., Persona and Self in Stoic Philosophy, in: A. Baumgarten (ed.), Self, Soul and Body, 1998, 335–346; Ch. Enders, Die Menschenwürde in der Verfassungsordnung. Zur Dogmatik des Art. 1 GG, 1997; M. Forschner, Über das Handeln im Einklang mit der Natur, 1998; E. Picker, M. und Menschenleben, in: FS W. Flume, 1998, 155–263.
                                                        HU.C.

Humanistic scripts (Latin) The Italian humanists of the 15th cent. developed two new Latin scripts: (1) the script now commonly known as 'humanistic', which is rather formal, and (2) the so-called 'humanistic cursive'. (1) The former, known as 'antiqua', is basically a revived variant of the Carolingian → minuscule, which was introduced to Florence just before 1400 by Poggio Bracciolini (1380–1459) and Niccolò Niccoli (1364–1437). They named their model, the Carolingian minuscule, the 'antiqua' because they thought of it as a script from classical 'antiquity'. This term is currently used for the humanistic script *per se*. Already in the 1420s this script spread through all of Italy, in the middle of the 15th cent. also to Germany, England, France, the Netherlands, and Spain.

The 'antiqua' does not have a precisely identifiable model. Poggio's version presumably imitated the

Carolingian minuscule of the 11th and 12th cents. It is often differentiated from this model through shading and size ratios, but especially through graphic and codicological peculiarities that were taken over from the → Gothic script [2]. The antiqua acquired historical significance in 1465 when two German printers, Conrad SWEYNHEIM and Arnold PANNARTZ, used it in Subiaco (Italy) as the model for the later common Latin type.

(2) The humanistic cursive used in documents (also called 'humanistic chancellery script') and private scripts, as well as in representational codices, was developed by NICCOLI in the early 1420s. The script barely differentiates between thick and thin strokes, it normally slants to the right and is more angular than the antiqua. The letters *f* and the high *s* extend below the base line; letter parts are often executed in a continuous writing motion (e.g., for *m*). At the start of a particular letter (the upstroke) this script does not exhibit the loops that are normal for cursives, and in books the linkage of one letter to the next – except for certain → ligatures (*ct*, *et*, *st*) – is the exception rather than the rule. In the English language area, this script is called *italic* after its origin. The term *italica* is taken from the type set based on this script produced in 1501 by Aldus MANUTIUS; he eventually made the humanistic cursive the most commonly used script in European book printing. The humanistic round script exercised some influence on this cursive, but early Gothic and mixed type cursives were more important.

G. BATTELLI, Nomenclature des écritures humanistiques, in: Nomenclature des écritures livresques du IXe au XVIe siècle, 1954, 35–44; B. BISCHOFF, Latin Palaeography: antiquity and the middle ages, 1990, 145–149; L. E. BOYLE, Medieval Latin palaeography: a bibliographical introduction, 1984; A. C. DE LA MARE, The Handwriting of Italian Humanists, 1973; Id., Humanistic Script: The First Ten Years, in: F. KRAFFT, D. WUTTKE (ed.), Das Verhältnis der Humanisten zum Buch, 1977, 89–110; B. L. ULLMAN, The Origin and Development of Humanistic Script, 1960.
J. J. J.

Humanist script The Greek Script of the Humanist period of the 15th and 16th cents. reveals a continuation of older trends and styles. Aside from Otrantine script (→ South Italic script) which became rather insignificant even though it survived the Renaissance, other traditional types of script live on. Among the archaizing scripts was the so-called Hodegon style (14th cent.), used not only in eastern monasteries esp. for liturgical MSS, but also in the West by the leading copyists of the Renaissance such as Ioannes Rhosos, up to the 1st half of the 17th cent. At the same time a classicizing style developed beginning in the Palaeologi period, characterized by an overall balance but leaning slightly to the right, by careful separation between words and letters, much reduced ascenders and descenders, and small letters. This script was transferred to the West through the first MSS of classical authors brought from Constantinople by Italian Humanists and through Byzantine

copyists who fled to Italy, then continued to be used by many scholars and professional copyists of the 15th and 16th cents., although with varying results (e.g. Manuel Chrysoloras, Michael and Aristobulos Apostoles).

Many Greek and Italian scribes (such as Stephanos of Medeia, Demetrios Sgouropoulos) used a related style of script, although more affected and fluid and combined with several elements of → grease drop script. Similar, but with pronounced ascenders and descenders, are the scripts of Andronikos Kallistos, Demetrios Chalkondyles, Demetrios Moschos, and Zacharias Kallierges. This more cursive tendency can also be observed in many productive copyists of the 16th cent. (e.g. Camillo Zanetti). Several scribes, active primarily in Paris (the so-called 'grecs du roi'), developed a sweeping variant rich in ligatures and characterized by more flourishes and thicker ascenders (e.g. Ange Vergèce). In this context, one must also include the representatives of the so-called Baroque script: capital letters in sharp contrast to stunted small letters, flourishes and rolls, and pronounced ascenders and descenders characterize the script, crowded in appearance, of many 16th cent. professional scribes (esp. in Venice).

Italian Humanists often endeavour to imitate the script patterns of their Greek teachers, but their script reveals Latin writing habits. Usually, the result is a small, square script with a regular ductus, reduced ascenders and descenders, clear word and letter separations, with few abbreviations (e.g. Giovanni Aurispa, Lorenzo Valla, Poggio Braccioliny). Exceptions can be found in the individual traits of a few scholars such as Ciriaco of Ancona and Angelo Poliziano.
On Latin Humanist script: → Writing, styles of.

D. HARLFINGER, Zu griech. Kopisten und Schriftstilen des 15. und 16. Jh., in: La paléographie grecque et byzantine 1977, 327–341; P. ELEUTERI, P. CANART, Scrittura greca nell'Umanesimo italiano, 1991.
P. E.

Humanitas
A. DEFINITION B. LEVELS OF MEANING C. COMPLEMENTARY CHARACTER

A. DEFINITION
In *humanitas* as 'humanity' the following features emerge: 1. philanthropic respect, especially compassion (*misericordia*), 2. intelligent and tactful affability (*urbanitas*), 3. feeling for natural human solidarity (*sensus humanitatis*), 4. cultured humanity (*eruditio, doctrina*), 5. civilization (*cultus*). As early as Cicero's oration, *Pro Sex. Roscio* (84 BC) almost all shades of these can be found.

B. LEVELS OF MEANING
1. *Humanitas* as a donation to the needy (Greek *philanthropía*) became diversified to mean 'respect for the inferior', that was also rooted in ancient Roman tradition (particularly of *clementia*), through Greek influence in a wealth of related virtues: compassion, gentleness and a conciliatory nature, softness, goodwill, gen-

erosity etc. An element of *humanitas* is being sensitive to the needs and troubles of one's fellow human beings and behaving accordingly (Plin. Ep. 8,16,3). As a prerequisite for this there was the general consciousness of an imperfection common to all people, indicated not just by the vicissitudes of life, the recurrence of hopelessness and chance (Liv. 45,8,5f.) but also by errors and misdemeanours (Plin. Ep. 9,12,1; 8,22,1ff.), weaknesses and mortality (*condicio humana*). *Humanitas* was based on the adjective *humanus* in the initially predominant sense of 'fragile, frail' (Cic. Lael. 102). Accordingly, *humanitas* is a set topos of court speech as an appeal to the judges to show mercy for the defendant by taking into consideration extenuating circumstances in view of the vicissitudes of fortune and is already to be found in the Auctor ad Herennium (*c.* 84 BC). In another tradition (Hellenistic royal virtues), philanthropic *humanitas* is repeatedly emphasized by Cicero to those in the state who bear responsibility (commanders, magistrates) as concern for the welfare of those they rule over. Hardheartedness, arrogance and cruelty are the antitheses of *humanitas*.

2. *Humanitas* as urbanity characterized a refined, casual, obliging style and way of life, such as could be manifested among urban Romans in general, particularly however among their elites, in the conviviality of free time (*otium*) when they were relieved of their occupational and official duties (→ Leisure). It included cheerfulness (*hilaritas*), friendliness (*comitas*), affability (*facilitas, dexteritas*), kindness (*venustas, lepos, iucunditas*), refined wit (*facetiae*), elegance (*elegantia*), joking (*iocus*) and the like. This was linked with literary education, which Cicero considered to be decisively and particularly marked in the so-called → Scipionic circle (cf. Cic. Mur. 66; De or. 2,22; 154; Rep. 1,14ff.). *Urbanitas* gave it a special profile and arose strikingly from the connection between philanthropic and educated *humanitas* (e.g. in Cic. Fam. 11,27,6).

3. *Humanitas* as (in the sense of) the sharing of commonality by all people (*communis humanitas*) was explained particularly by Cicero in his philosophical writings (Cic. Fin. 3,62–65; Off. 1,50–56; see → *oikeíōsis*) following on from the Stoic theory of the natural, virtually organic community of the human race (*societas humani generis)* in which the individual must thoughtfully fit in. Protection of 'unity and commonality is even superior to striving for knowledge' (Off. 1,157). If one prefers one's own advantage over that of the common good, this attests to an 'atrocity that rejects all humanity' (Off. 1,62; 3,32), whilst *humanitas* by contrast – above and beyond all social, political and national borders – protects the life interests of all people, those of one's personal opponents (Quinct. 51) as well as those of subjugated peoples (Ad Q. fr. 1,1,27). The experiences of the civil wars of the 1st cent. BC meant that such *humanitas* was sorely missed (cf. Cic. S. Rosc. 154). Seneca, both concretely (Ep. 95,51; cf. Cic. Off. 1,51f.) and in general reiterated Cicero's views on *humanitas* (Epist. 5,4; 95,52).

4. *Humanitas* as perfected humanity was linked from 63 BC onwards with education (*doctrina*), again first by Cicero, adopting the Aristotelian-Stoic tradition that attributes excellent characteristics (*proprietas, praestantia*) to man in his reason. The 'arts' and 'studies' (*studia humanitatis*) typical of these qualities shape human rational nature into its perfect form (Cic. Arch. 4,15; Cic. De or. 3,58) and lead through their 'refinement' (Cic. Rep. 1,28) to actual humanity. In connection with *virtus*, it describes the elites.

The *humanitas* revealed through literary education became especially relevant for Cicero's ideal of a perfect orator (*in omni genere sermonis et humanitatis perfectum*; De or. 1,35; 1,71). Starting with leisure where as human culture there can be 'nothing more characteristic of *humanitas* than an elegant discourse that is coarse at no point' (De or. 1,32) right through to the organizing influence in public matters, rational speech (*ratio et oratio*, Off. 1,50) proves itself to be a humanizing power for social communication because it includes general knowledge, a wealth of ideas and a value orientation. Seneca denied *studia liberalia* a special significance for philanthropic *humanitas*, preferring in morality ancient Roman concepts of virtue like *simplicitas, modestia, clementia* (Ep. 88,30) instead. Pliny the Younger was able to see in *humanitas* again a combination of philosophical teaching and philanthropy (Ep. 1,10,2). Like Cicero he too regarded Greece as the home of true humanity and particularly of literary culture (Ep. 8,24,2; similarly Cic. Ad Q. Fr. 1,1,27). Gellius (13,17) erroneously considered the meaning of 'training and instruction in the good arts' as opposed to the 'vulgar' philanthropic meaning as the original one.

5. *Humanitas* as a civilization refinement of human life was connected with artistically designed vessels (Varro, Ling. 8,31), commercial wares of a higher standard of living (Caes. B Gall. 1,1,3), columned halls, baths and tasteful banquets (Tac. Agr. 21) (in the latter two cases also with the consequence of paralysizing the power of resistance of the subjugated).

C. COMPLEMENTARY CHARACTER

Humanitas was indeed always an important value concept but never a dominant one. In order to protect it in the social context from the suspicion of thoughtless openness, people liked to associate it with 'virtue' (*virtus*) and the ancient Roman values traditionally associated with it like incorruptibility, steadfastness, uprightness and similar virtues, just as in contrast it served to preserve these values from rigid application and to facilitate their pressure in a complementary sense (especially impressively documented in Cic. Mur. 65). The ideal – especially in Cicero (Mur. 66; Fam. 12,27) and Pliny the Younger (Ep. 4,3,2; 8,21,1; 9,9,2) – was considered to be a balance between the mixture of 'seriousness', *gravitas* (or 'strictness', *severitas*) and *humanitas* in the sense of friendliness and affability.

→ Scipionic circle; → HUMANISM

1 H. HAFFTER, Die röm. H., in: H. OPPERMANN (ed.), Röm. Wertbegriffe, 1967, 468–482   2 F. KLINGNER, Humanität und h., in: Id., Röm. Geisteswelt, ⁵1965, 704–746   3 W. SCHADEWALDT, H. Romana, in: ANRW 1 4, 1973, 43–62.   H.ST.

Human rights

A. INTRODUCTION   B. NATURAL LAW AND OTHER SPECULATIONS   C. NATIONAL   D. INTERNATIONAL   E. RECEPTION

A. INTRODUCTION

Ancient authors, inscriptions and institutions have standards that correspond to modern human rights (HR), as for instance the 'General Declaration of HR' by the United Nations (UN) on 10 December 1948. (The articles of each declaration are quoted below with their no. and 'UN §' placed in front of them; text of the HR declaration e.g. in [4. 775–782]). According to Tertullian (Ad Scapulam 2), 'It is the HR and innate decision-making power of each individual to worship what he believes in. ... It contradicts the nature of religion to enforce a religion' ... *Humani iuris et naturalis potestatis est unicuique, quid putaverit, colere ... nec religionis est cogere religionem*: here the HR to religious freedom (UN §18) is described as in the current sense as a *ius humanum* (not as the antithesis of *ius divinum*) and also proves the existence of the concept of 'HR' in ancient times (cf. Sen. Ben. 3,18,2). According to Ulpian (Dig. 1,1,4), following the *ius naturale* slavery is not justified, as all people are born free (cf. UN §§ 1; 4); but according to the corresponding right of peoples (*ius gentium*) slavery was generally widespread and was considered legitimate.

Hence HR in antiquity can be distinguished according to legal force and area of validity: 1) HR on the basis of philosophical and theological speculation (natural law) that are unwritten, eternal and valid everywhere and that come from the gods or from nature, reason or the dignity of the human being. 2) International basic rights, for instance of the Athenians or Romans, e.g. the right to private ownership of assets and the protection of same, to a fair court hearing or to political representation (UN §§ 17; 10; 21). Particularly in the international field, state power and the rights of the individual to freedom collided (e.g. 'unjust' use of power by tyrants, emperors, persecutors of Christians), which in antiquity as well as in modern history drove people to develop concrete ideas about the rights of those threatened or of victims to defend themselves. 3) HR in the international area that concern the relationships with foreigners, e.g. with war opponents or → barbarians and the corresponding rights of various states or peoples. As their starting-point, these take infringements of HR e.g. through slavery or exposure of children, not by the state but by society. The anthropology of rights, as can be seen from Ulpian (see above), touches on the problem of the universal validity of HR in another way than theories concerning natural laws do. As a whole,

HR have as their prerequisite the experience of injustice committed by state power or tolerated in society.

B. NATURAL LAW AND OTHER SPECULATIONS

Homer calls Zeus the 'Father of gods and of men' (Hom. Od. 18,137) which does not refer to family descent but to his patriarchal power. → Epictetus [2] (Dissertationes 1,3) on the other hand linked up with this the Stoic idea of the kinship of all people as children of Zeus and the obligation of fraternity (UN § 1) as members of a large family. → Sophocles' Antigone (Soph. Ant. 449–55) justifies her resistance to unjust state power by the 'unwritten, unchangeable, eternal right of the gods'. Cicero (Cic. Rep. 3,22) defines the (Stoic) natural law as law that is divine, in keeping with the rational world order, universally applicable and revealed in the human conscience, a law that no state is allowed to change.

Early Christianity deepens the concept of the dignity of man (UN § 1) with the teaching that he is made in the image of his creator and that Christ became man [2. 280–283].

C. NATIONAL

The Athenians swore in their ancient ephebic oath only to obey those orders and future laws that were decreed 'rationally' (*émphronos*) (TOD 204, 12; 14) [7. 34f.], which justifies political resistance, for instance to a tyrant (UN § Preamble). → Solon's measures contain various HR: the freedom of assembly and association (Sol. fr. 76a RUSCHENBUSCH; UN § 20); equal rights for the aristocracy and the non-aristocracy (fr. 36, 18–20 WEST; UN § 7); political representation for all citizens in the election of officials and in people's courts (Aristot. Ath. Pol. 7,3; UN § 21); protection of honour from slander (fr. 32 R.; UN § 12) and of human dignity by a law that permitted the killing of a criminal but forbade his abuse (fr. 16 R.; UN § 5). Solon in particular was probably the first to formulate the limitation on state power based on law and justice (fr. 36,16 WEST: βίην τε καὶ δίκην συναρμόσας/*bíēn te kaì díkēn synarmósas*, 'power and law tied together as one', cf. UN § Pr.).

In concentrated form → Pericles' funeral speech in Thucydides [7. 36–38] contains modern HR: political representation of all citizens (2,37,1; UN § 21); tolerance towards private structuring of one's own life (2,37,2; UN § 12, cf. § 26,2); recovery from work (2,38; UN § 24); freedom of information (2,39,1; UN § 19); participation in cultural life (2,40,1; UN § 27); broad education in keeping with a person's aptitudes (2,41,1; UN § 26,2). Despite its reference to male citizens, this idealized description of the Athenian state of mind, society and convictions provides insights into the basic needs of the refined individual in his community. In the Roman Republic the citizen was to a large extent guaranteed freedom, the right to life and to freedom from harm, political representation, equality before the law and freedom of assembly and of membership of associations (UN §§ 1; 3; 21; 7; 20); this served as a model for modern state theoreticians [3. 97–112].

D. INTERNATIONAL

Although the Trojans waged a (mythical) war against the Greeks, Homer does not discriminate against them (UN § 2); the same applies to the depiction of the Persians under Xerxes in Aeschylus ('Persians') and Herodotus. The duty to honour foreigners (as early as Hom. Od. 14,56–58) is one of the unwritten commands of general validity of the Hellenes; they are attested on several occasions from the time of Aeschylus (Aesch. Eum. 269–272) onwards [8. 629]. A further 'Law of the Hellenes' forbids the killing of an enemy who surrenders (Thuc. 3,58,3; Eur. Heracl. 961–966; 1009–1011, UN § 3). After the battle of Plataeae the commander → Pausanias rejected as barbaric the proposal to violate the corpse of the Persian Mardonius (Hdt. 9,79) – even though the latter had done this to the fallen Spartan king → Leonidas [1] – probably because it would have degraded the deceased (cf. UN § 5). Another Spartan king, Agesilaus [2], asked his soldiers not to take revenge on → prisoners of war but to treat them 'as human beings' (Xen. Ages. 1,21, similarly Rhet. Her. 4,16,23), which in addition to political calculation concerning the conclusion of a peace treaty indicates ideas of human dignity on the part of army leaders. Democritus (68 B 245 DK) and Cicero (Cic. Off. 3,5,22) formulated the principle, valid for most legal regulations, that the legitimate striving for freedom, power and wealth of the one is limited by the same demands of the other, which also applies to HR (UN § 29,2).

E. RECEPTION

Ancient HR reached the state theoreticians of the Middle Ages and of modern times [1; 2; 5; 6] through the theories of natural law, the Church Fathers, Roman law and the classical authors.
→ Justice; → Humanitas; → Human dignity; → HUMAN RIGHTS

1 O. BEHRENDS, M. DIESSELHORST (ed.), Libertas. Grundrechtliche und rechtsstaatliche Gewährungen in Ant. und Gegenwart. Symposion aus Anlaß des 80. Geburtstages von F. Wieacker, 1991   2 H. CANCIK, Die Würde des Menschen ist unantastbar, in: H. FUNKE (ed.), Trad. und Utopie, 1987, 73–107 (repr. in: Id., Antik – Modern, 1998, 267–291; quotes according to this later edition)   3 M. FUHRMANN, Grundrechte im Strafprozeß der röm. Republik und ihr Widerhall im 18. und 19. Jh., in: [1], 97–112   4 G. ALFREDSON, A. Eide (ed.), The Universal Declaration of Human Rights, 1999   5 H. JONES (ed.), Le monde antique et les droits de l'homme, 1998   6 G. OESTREICH, Gesch. der Menschenrechte und Grundfreiheiten im Umriß, ²1978   7 P. SIEWERT, Zur Frage der Universalität der Menschenrechte bei ant. Autoren, in: L. AIGNER FORESTI et al. (ed.), L'ecumenismo politico nella coscienza dell' Occidente, 1998, 31–42   8 G. TÈNÈKIDÈS, La cité d'Athènes et les droits de l'homme, in: F. MATSCHER, H. PETZOLD (ed.), Protecting Human Rights: The European Dimension: Studies in Honor of G.J. Wiarda, 1988, 605–637.   P. SI.

Human sacrifices

I. HISTORY OF THE CONCEPT AND ITS SUBSEQUENT INFLUENCE   II. OLD TESTAMENT AND SYRIA/PALESTINE   III. CLASSICAL ANTIQUITY

I. HISTORY OF THE CONCEPT AND ITS SUBSEQUENT INFLUENCE
A. CONCEPT   B. USAGE   C. SUBSEQUENT INFLUENCE

A. CONCEPT

Human sacrifice (HS) is a form of killing considered lawful, similar to killing in pursuit of war, capital punishment, or a blood feud. It is, however, limited to the performance of offering rites that (a) are universally accepted in the respective religion and culture and (b) are conducted in a fashion similar to the sacrificial killing of other creatures. Killing in the context of other lawful rituals, such as the cult of the dead (→ Gladiator) or the → devotio in battle, does not constitute HS. Scholars have disagreed over the status of a controversial borderline case (see below): the killing of humans in the context of the purifying expiation of omens (→ Divination; procuratio; → prodigium; → Expiatory rites). Deliberate, unlawful killing in the course of rituals that are not universally accepted (→ Magic; sorcery, foretelling the future) is considered manslaughter or, if applicable, (ritual) murder. It is essential to draw a distinction between these offences because the expression HS evolved, and became common parlance, within the context of western Christianity. The accounts of missionaries and ethnologists reporting so-called cannibalism in American and African cultures, as well as the vivid imagined scenes in the art, literature and mythology of the Greeks, Romans, and Etruscans, helped to turn the expression HS into a loaded cipher of the horrendum et fascinosum.

B. USAGE

Both the scholarly and the common usage of the term HS share the ambiguities of the concept → sacrifice. With the Graeco-Roman injunction against HS, the ceasing of the practice in Judaism, and the eventual end of Celtic, Germanic and Slavic sacrifices, the terminology of sacrifice was 'freed' from its moorings. A new sacrificial language emerged: (technical) terms became generalized, acquired metaphorical meaning, and turned vague. The most significant factor is the doctrine of the 'abolition' of all sacrifice in the sacrifice of Jesus on the cross (Hebr 9,11–14; 24–26; Aug. Trin. 4,14,19) as it is commemorated and represented in the Eucharist. Theological, ethical, social, and political elements combined to form a complex of ideas that effaces the historical facts as much as it does the discourses of antiquity – above all, the ancient critique of 'bloody sacrifice' that was formulated in part as its rejection (Graeco-Roman culture), and in part as its spiritualization (Hebrew Bible). Since then, any taking of human life – capital punishment, tyrannicide, purported or actual ritual murder (with or without anthropophagy), the death of a soldier, the extermination of the Jews, may be described – in protest or by way of legitimation – as HS (cf. the Holocaust). From everyday language to art and scholarship, the notions transmitted by Christianity have been projected back onto antiquity. This process gives rise to paganisms that compete with Christian concepts. Legitimation by means of sacralization continues to persist in everyday language [5; 6; 7]; and in religious studies it is rather seldom reflected upon [3. 68ff.]. Modern discourses of HS oscillate between fascination, outrage, and provocation. For that reason the question of the historical factuality of HS must necessarily be preceded by a clarification of the concept and a critical, historical examination of the attitudes of our sources [1. 222ff.; 8; 10; 11].

C. Subsequent Influence

The metaphor of human sacrifice has had a rich history. In SHAKESPEARE's play, the murderer of Caesar conceives of himself and his co-conspirators as 'sacrificers, not butchers' (*Julius Caesar*, II.i.166). In his plea against capital punishment, the jurist Cesare BECCARIA (1738–1794) describes the condemned as a 'sacrificial victim' (*vittima*) meant as an 'offering' (*sacrificio*) to the 'insatiable idols of despotism' [2]. Such pathos is due to the Christian polemic against 'pagan' sacrifice. At the same time, even in the 20th cent., Christian theologians continued to justify the claim of capital punishment's 'expiatory power' on the basis of Christ's sacrifice, thus implicitly affirming HS [4]. NIETZSCHE calls for HS 'for the betterment of the species' while simultaneously rejecting the self-sacrifice 'conceded' in Christianity [12. vol. 13, 218ff.; 469–471].

The names Isaac and → Iphigenia denote perhaps the best-known discursive paradigms of HS. In the modern era, these paradigms have been transmitted through 'great texts' – the Bible (Gn 22) and GOETHE (rather than → Euripides). The rejection of HS is represented as a purer form of worship (the 'binding of Isaac' in Judaic theology) [9] or as the victory of humanity (GOETHE, *Iphigenie auf Tauris*, 1787). Gerhart HAUPTMANN constructs an archaicized, dark and bloodthirsty antiquity: the rescued Iphigenia 'sacrifices her own life' by plunging from the top of the Phaedriades (*Iphigenie in Delphi*, 1941). The reception of Euripides rooted in NIETZSCHE takes no account of the fact that his characters may speak of sacrificial rites, but nonetheless recognize the driving forces as murder and revenge. This is in contrast to Christa WOLF's Cassandra: 'It was said that he (sc. Agamemnon) had to sacrifice her (sc. Iphigenia). That was not what I wanted to hear, but words like "murder" or "butchering" are of course unknown to murderers and butchers' [13. 68].

1 G. BAUDY, Der kannibalische Hirte, in: A. KECK et al. (ed.), Verschlungene Grenzen. Anthropophagie in Literatur und Kulturwissenschaft, 1999, 221–242   2 C. BECCARIA, Dei delitti e delle pene, 1764 (²1774)   3 W. BURKERT, Kulte des Altertums. Biolog. Grundlagen der Rel., 1998   4 H. CANCIK, Christentum und Todesstrafe, in:

H. v. STIETENCRON (ed.) Angst und Gewalt, 1979, 213–242   5 H. CANCIK-LINDEMAIER, Opferphantasien. Zur imaginären Antike der Jahrhundertwende in Deutschland und Österreich, in: AU 30.3, 1987, 90–104   6 Id., Opfer. Religionswissenschaftliche Bemerkungen zur Nutzbarkeit eines religiösen Ausdrucks, in: H.-J. ALTHAUS et al. (ed.), Der Krieg in den Köpfen, 1989, 109–120   7 Id., s.v. Eucharistie, HrwG 2, 347–356   8 J. DREXLER, Die Illusion des Opfers, 1993   9 J. EBACH, Theodizee, in: Id., Gott im Wort, 1997, 1–25   10 P. HASSLER, Menschenopfer bei den Azteken? Eine quellen- und ideologiekritische Studie, 1992   11 A. HENRICHS, Human Sacrifice in Greek Rel., in: Le sacrifice dans l'antiquité (Entretiens sur l'Antiquité Classique 27), 1981, 195–235   12 F. NIETZSCHE, Sämtliche Werke. Krit. Studienausgabe, 1980   13 CHR. WOLFF, Kassandra, 1983.   H.C.-L.

II. Old Testament and Syria/Palestine

HS in the Old Testament should not be understood in connection with the cult of → Moloch; rather, they appear in the text only in the case of extreme emergencies. The surrender of children to the conquerors shown on Egyptian reliefs commemorating the conquering of Canaanite cities should not be interpreted as HS, but as a sign of tribute and loyalty. Judging by the manner of their literary and paradigmatic representation, the few instances of the sacrifice of children in the Old Testament – 2 Kgs. 3:27 (Meša); Judg. 11:30ff. (Jephthah's daughter); Gn 22:1ff. (Abraham's son Isaac) – do not support the acceptance of HS. The redemption of the first-born (Ex 13:13; 34:20; Nm 3:45; 18:15) belongs within a different context. The existence of HS as a form of building sacrifice in Palestine has not been demonstrated.

→ Sacrifice

W. ZWICKEL, s.v. Menschenopfer, Neues Bibel Lexikon 2, 1995, 765–766.   TH.PO.

III. Classical Antiquity
A. General   B. Greek   C. Roman   D. Celtic

A. General

In accordance with the ancient sources, the concept of HS in the following shall only be applied to such rituals in which a human being is offered to a deity in the same manner as a sacrificial animal (→ Sacrifice). This is meant to counteract the modern tendency to level the concept by applying it to any kind of ritual killing. It should also distinguish HS from other acts such as, for instance, the Roman *sacratio* (the delivery of a human being into the possession of a god) or execution (see I. above). However, it makes little sense to attempt a general theory of HS. Like all sacrificial customs, the modalities of HS (ritual slaughter, burial, burning, suffocation or drowning, preservation and exhibition of the remains) differ among the individual ancient cultures. A sacrificial feast is usually not a part of HS. If such an occasion does arise, it serves as an illustration of the abnormalities of the described action and its participants; it occurs in conspiracies (Diod. Sic. 22,5,1; Sall. Catil. 22,1f.; Plut. Cicero 10,4; Cass. Dio 37,30,3; [1]) or among bandits (Ach. Tat. 3,15).

In antiquity, HS were often attributed to other groups – usually, to one's opponents: Carthaginians (Plin. HN 7,16; 36,39; Min. Fel. 30,1), Celts (see below), Germans (Tac. Germ. 9,1; 39,2), → 'Barbarians', political agitators (see above), Jews (Jos. Ap. 2,92–96; 2,121), Christians (Min. Fel. 9,5; Euseb. Hist. eccl. 5,1,26; cf. Plin. Ep. 10,96,7) [2]. HS (*puruṣamedha*) was documented already in Vedic literature. At the same time, however, this literature describes an evolutionary history of sacrifice from HS, through animal and vegetable sacrifice, to spiritual self-sacrifice [3]. In view of this tradition, scholarship has frequently denied the incidence of HS in the advanced cultures of the ancient world, relegating it either to an earlier period or to a barbaric neighbouring culture. Ancient reports of HS are given a symbolic meaning that either affirms or problematizes the cultural standards of the respective speaker against the negative background of HS – even when, in certain cases, the literary source or archaeological find allows for a contrary interpretation. Thus, in the Old Testament, we find – aside from testimony about the *ḥerem* (killing prisoners of war) – that the description (and critique) of the sacrifice of children or the first-born in times of danger (sources: see above II) is placed within narrative contexts that possibly polemicize against an existing practice of HS [4; 5. 52f.]. Similarly, the child graves of the *tofet* in Carthage (as in other Punic and Phoenician cities of the Mediterranean region) have been interpreted not as sacrificial sites but rather as children's cemeteries, despite the fact that the inscriptions of the *tofet* may refer to sacrifice ([5. 53–56], with bibliography) and the Carthaginians were reputed to have performed other HS (see above).

B. Greek

In classical scholarship, the occurrence of HS in Greek religion is frequently denied, transposed to an earlier period of Greek prehistory, relegated to the symbolic framework of initiation rites (→ Initiation) [6], or ascribed to 'Barbarians'. An example of the latter are the HS for the Taurian → Artemis (Hdt. 4,103,1; Eur. IT; Min. Fel. 30,1), although she appears as thoroughly 'Greek' in the sources. Indeed, in the literary, historiographical, and mythological sources, there is often talk of the Greek gods Zeus, Kore and Persephone, Athena, Artemis, Ares, Poseidon and Amphitrite and the Nereids, or of heroes such as Patroclus and Achilles, demanding HS. The god of → Delphi, Apollo (→ Oracles), in particular, prescribes human sacrifice to mortals as a possible way out of a crisis. In these texts the gods are mostly incensed over some insult on the part of mortals and demand not the usual animal sacrifice, but rather the sacrifice of a being most dear to those humans – above all (but not exclusively) young girls and boys who are, in addition, well-born. These HS are portrayed neither as a relapse into a cruel prehistory nor as

a violation of proper piety; rather, they are seen as a necessary and particularly effective sacrifice in emergencies and ascribed an entirely positive value (sources: [7]). In these texts, therefore, HS is not simply a negative component in a discourse over Greek culture and religion. This is also reflected in the representation of mythological HS (e.g. → Polyxene) in Greek art or in Etruscan grave painting [8], even if no simple correspondence exists between artistic representation and cult reality.

C. Roman

In Rome, the HS that Jupiter supposedly demanded in vain of → Numa Pompilius (Ov. Fast. 3,329–357; Plut. Numa 15,5–10), was seen as an un-Roman ritual practice (*minime Romanum sacrum*: Liv. 22,57,6). It was forbidden in 97 BC (Plin. HN 30,3,12). However, starting from 228 BC onwards (Plut. Marcellus 3,3f.; Zon. 8,20; Oros. 4,13,3) the Romans repeatedly celebrated (216 BC: Liv. 22,57,2–6; 114/3 BC: Plut. Quaest. Rom. 83) a rite that apparently continued up to the time of Pliny the Elder (HN 28,12). This was a public ritual dictated in times of great danger by the → *Sibyllini Libri* and understood as out of the ordinary, during which two pairs of Greeks and Gauls were buried alive at the Forum Boarium. The interpretation of this ritual as HS is controversial (discussion: [5. 41–46; 9; 10]), but is supported in the literary sources (sacrificial terminology: *sacrificium, hostiae*, θύειν/*thýein*). The two pairs were possibly offered to the *di* → *inferi* as a *pars pro toto* of the enemy. The future Augustus supposedly also carried out an unusual form of HS on his opponents (41 BC: Suet. Aug. 15; Cass. Dio 48,14,4).

D. Celtic

The HS described in ancient sources as a sign of the otherness of the Celts and the Germans (see above) also pose a problem for scholarship. The various evidence of Celtic HS has been interpreted as a form of 'punishment' or 'execution' [11. 132f.]. However, the reports of HS (Caes. B Gall. 6,16f.; Luc. 1,444–446; Str. 4,4,5; Diod. Sic. 5,31,3f.) may possibly be supported by the newer archaeological findings in the Celtic shrines of Picardy and Champagne, and in burial shafts throughout Celtic Europe ([12] with bibliography). The connection to HS has, in many cases, not been definitively resolved. Nonetheless, the possibility remains that among the Celts, no less than in other ancient cultures, HS was not merely a hypothetical contrast with the norm. Rather, it was a real ritual act that, though it was unusual, was seen as necessary under certain specific circumstances.

→ Cannibalism; → Expiatory rites; → Sacrifice

1 G. Marasco, Sacrifici umani e cospirazioni politiche, in: Sileno 7, 1981, 167–178   2 J. Rives, Human Sacrifice among Pagans and Christians, in: JRS 85, 1995, 65–85   3 Ch. Malamoud, Modèle et réplique. Remarques sur le paradigme du sacrifice humain dans l'Inde védique, in: Archiv für Religionsgesch. 1.1, 1999, 27–40   4 Th. Römer, Le sacrifice humain en Juda et Israël, in: ibid. [3],

17–26   5 C. GROTTANELLI, Ideologie del sacrificio umano: Roma e Cartagine, in: ibid. [3], 41–59   6 P. BONNECHÈRE, Le sacrifice humain en Grèce ancienne, 1994   7 S. GEORGOUDI, À propos du sacrifice humain en Grèce ancienne, in: Archiv für Religionsgesch. 1.1, 1999, 61–82   8 D. STEUERNAGEL, Menschenopfer und Mord am Altar. Griech. Mythen in etr. Gräbern, 1998   9 A. M. ECKSTEIN, Human Sacrifice and Fear of Military Disaster in Republican Rome, in: AJAH 7, 1982 (1985), 69–95   10 D. BRIQUEL, Des propositions nouvelles sur le rituel d'ensevelissement de Grecs et de Gaulois au Forum Boarium, in: REL 59, 1981, 30–37   11 J. L. BRUNAUX, Les religions gauloises. Rituels celtiques de la Gaule indépendante, 1996   12 F. MARCO-SIMÓN, Sacrificios humanos en la Céltica antigua, in: Archiv für Religionsgesch. 1.1, 1999, 1–15.

A. HENRICHS, Human Sacrifice in Greek Rel.: Three Case Studies, in: J. RUDHARDT, O. REVERDIN (ed.), Le sacrifice dans l'antiquité, 1981, 195–242; D. D. HUGHES, Human Sacrifice in Ancient Greece, 1991; F. SCHWENN, Die Menschenopfer bei den Griechen und Römern (RGVV 15,3), 1915.   J.S.

Humbaba see → Gilgamesh, → Gilgamesh Epic

Humiliores see → Honestiores

Humoral theory The idea that physical health was connected with bodily fluids was widespread. Mucus is already mentioned in ancient Egyptian medicine, and also in Babylonian medicine particular attention was paid to the quantity and colour of bodily fluids. The Greeks regarded → *ichór* of the gods, blood (αἷμα; *haîma*) in humans and sap (χυμός; *chymós*) in plants as the bearers of life. These fluids (χυμοί/*chymoí*, Latin *humores*) could also become dangerous in excess. Two humours, phlegm (φλέγμα; *phlégma*) and bile (χόλος; *chólos* or χολή; *cholé*), are already represented as hazardous in early Greek writing (Archilochus, fr. 96 DIEHL; Hipponax, fr. 51 DIEHL). In numerous texts of the *Corpus Hippocraticum* (→ Hippocrates [6]) disease is explained as an excess (more rarely as a lack) of such humours: in *De morbo sacro* mucus causes → epilepsy, bile causes madness (*manía*; → Mental illness C.). According to other Hippocratic texts (e.g. *De affectionibus* and *De victu*), the body is in a permanent fluctuating balance and secretes a series of fluids like pus (πύον; *pýon*), urine (οὖρον; *oûron*) and sweat (ἱδρώς; *hidrós*); cf. *De humoribus*; [1]. Even if a bodily humour, e.g. blood, is regarded as fundamentally useful, it can sometimes cause damage, particularly when it is changed by other substances. Then it also has to be removed either in a natural manner (as in menstruation or a nose bleed) or by the doctor (by purging or bloodletting; → Phlebotomy).

The four main humours are a later development deriving from the qualitatively interpreted theory of the four elements of → Empedocles [1] [2]. The author of *De morbis 4* understands by cardinal humours phlegm (φλέγμα; *phlégma*), blood (αἷμα; *haîma*), bile (χολή;

cholé) and water (ὕδωρ; *hýdor*), with each bodily humour having its own source in the body. The author of *De natura hominis*, Polybus [6] (about 410 BC), was the first to replace water by black bile (χολὴ μέλαινα; *cholè mélaina*; → Melancholia) and to develop the theory of the four humours into a complex pattern in which the four humours were equated with the four seasons, four ages of life and four qualities (cold, hot, dry, wet). The seasonal relationship to individual diseases and the homoeostatic tendencies of the body gave this theory its empirical basis. The clarity of this pattern gave it plausibility, not least because it could easily be extended to further areas that influence the well-being of the body. In this way, the astrologer → Antiochus [23] (about AD 180) linked the four bodily humours with the four cardinal points in the heavens (north, east, south and west) and attributed to each of them three constellations. Later authors, particularly in the Middle Ages, constructed even more curious correlations [3].

The apparently natural cycle of humoral occurrences was the precondition for the advocates of humoral theory (HT) to make prognoses and where possible to be able confidently to steer the course of a disease. Before the 1st cent. AD, HT was viewed as Hippocratic theory *par excellence* to such an extent that the → Anonymus Londiniensis (6,43) vehemently objected to Aristotle attributing to Hippocrates a theory that contradicted it. → Galen based his entire medical theory on the four-humour theory even though he was thoroughly aware of several inconsistencies in this theory (cf. *In Hippocratis De natura hominis commentarii*: CMG V,9,1) and he preferred to speak of changes in qualities rather than changes in the humours or elements [4]. Other doctors on the other hand rejected Hippocratic HT (e.g. the → Methodists) or continued to relate the term 'humour' (χυμός; *chymós*) to a whole series of bodily fluids whose harmful effects on the body could be explained without seeing in them constitutive basic substances of the body [5]. In late antiquity the Galenic model certainly already played the leading part so that for the adherents of HT there was no longer any alternative to the HT developed in *De natura hominis* (→ Temperaments).

→ MEDICINE

1 I. M. LONIE, The Hippocratic Treatises 'On Generation', 'On the Nature of the Child', 'Diseases IV', 1981, 54–62 (comm.)   2 J. JOUANNA, Hippocrate, 1992, 442–452   3 E. SCHÖNER, Das Viererschema in der ant. Humoralpathologie, 1964   4 I. W. MÜLLER, Humoralmedizin: physiologische, pathologische und therapeutische Grundlagen der galenistischen Heilkunst, 1993   5 W. D. SMITH, Erasistratus' Dietetic Medicine, in: BHM 56, 1982, 364–369.

C. M. BROOKS, Humors, Hormones and Neurosecretions, 1962; H. FLASHAR, Melancholie und Melancholiker, 1966; R. KLIBANSKY, E. PANOWSKY, F. SAXL, Saturn und Melancholie, 1990; V. NUTTON, Ancient Medicine, 2004.   V.N.

Humour see → Joke; → Philogelos

Hunericus, Huneric Eldest son of → Geisericus and his successor in AD 477–484. King of the Vandals (*rex Vandalorum et Alanorum*; Victor Vitensis 2,1). H. was first married to a daughter of the Visigoth king Theodoric I (Iord. Get. 184), and from 456 to Eudocia [2], the daughter of Valentinian III (Procop. Vand. 3,5,6), a marriage that was probably decided upon when H. was staying with him as a hostage, in order to ensure adherence to the treaty of 442 between the Romans and the Vandals (Procop. Vand. 3,4,13). H. sought a compromise with eastern Rome only at the beginning of his reign (Malchus fr. 13 FHG 4,120f.); from 482 he waged a bloody campaign of persecution against the Catholics (Victor Vitensis 2f.). He was unable to prevent the Moorish tribes from breaking free from the Vandal kingdom (Procop. Vand. 3,8), and even his policy aimed at strengthening the kingdom failed despite harsh measures against opposing nobles: his successor to the throne was not his son → Hildericus but → Gunthamundus (Iord. Get. 170).

PLRE 2,572f.; CHR. COURTOIS, Les vandales et l'Afrique, 1955, esp. 262ff.; H.-J. DIESNER, Das Vandalenreich, 1966, 75ff.   M.MEI.

Hunger see → Malnutrition

Hunimundus

[1] *Dux*, later *rex* of the Danubian Suebi, after a foray into Dalmatia defeated and 'adopted' in *c.* AD 465 by the king of the Goths Thiudimer. Mobilized a multi-tribe war coalition against the Goths also supported by eastern Rome but was defeated by them in *c.* 469 (Iord. Get. 273–279). Probably identical to the pillager of Batavis (Eugippius, Vita Severini 22,4) of the same name. PLRE 2, 574 (H. 2).

H. WOLFRAM, Die Goten, ³1990, 264ff.   P.KE.

[2] **H. the Younger.** King of the Ostrogoths, son of → Ermanaric, father of Thorismud (Iord. Get. 250; [1. 255f.]), from the younger Amal line, successor of Vinitharius. H. is probably not identical to H., the father of → Gesimund (see in this regard [2. 574]; different in [3. 27f.]).

1 H. WOLFRAM, Die Goten, ³1990 2 PLRE 2,573, H. 1
3 P. HEATHER, Goths and Romans 332–489, 1991, 27, 57, 240 4 B. TÖNNIES, Die Amalertrad. in den Quellen zur Gesch. der Ostgoten, 1989, 43.   ME.STR.

Hunni (Οὖννοι; *Oûnnoi*, Χοῦννοι; *Choûnnoi*), the Huns.
A. HISTORY B. CULTURE

A. HISTORY
Nomadic people, origin debatable. In all probability they came from central Asia shortly after the time of Christ. As Χοῦννοι (*Choûnnoi*) first mentioned in Ptol.

3,5,25 between → Bastarnae and Roxolani (additional later localizations in Amm. Marc. 2,1; Iord. Get. 36f.). Some of the Hunnic tribes moved to the Caucasus region; from the eastern Hunnic branch, several states emerged (Hephthalitae, Avares, Chazars and Protobulgarians). Around AD 376 Hunnic tribes crossed the Volga, vanquished the Alani and the Ostrogoth kingdom of → Ermanaric and destroyed the Visigoth army of → Athanaric (Amm. Marc. 31,2,13). They established a kingdom in the subjugated area, from which they launched attacks from AD 395 onwards on the Caucasus and the lower Danube areas. From there they advanced westward around 400. The army led by Khan Uldin supported Rome in Vlachia against Gaenas (400) and → Stilicho against → Radagaisus (405); in 408 it invaded Thrace (Oros. 7,37; Zos. 5,22; Sozom. Hist. eccl. 9,5). Between 402 and 404 they drove the Burgundiones and the Vandali from the Vistula and Oder, so triggering a chain reaction of tribal migrations. After the death of Arcadius they turned from 408 onwards against the eastern Romans, capturing fortresses and occupying Castra Martis south of the Danube. Only in 412 was a peace treaty made between Khan Karaton and Byzantium. In 422 the H. again invaded Thrace. In 424 Khan Rua moved his residence to the plain east of the Theiss. Khan Bleda, who followed him, and Attila made a treaty with eastern Rome in 435 at Margus (Moesia) which ensured the H. many political and economic privileges. In 440/1 Bleda conquered Moesia prima and Pannonia secunda. His brother Attila helped him on the eastern flank and captured Ratiaria the next year. Together they defeated the eastern Roman army of Aspar (→ Ardabur [2]). The First Peace of Anatolius in 443 brought very great wealth to the Hunnic state. The Hunnic empire, organized according to tribes and centrally controlled, encompassed the areas from the modern Ukraine to the Danube and stretched in the west to the Rhine. A system of vassal kings held the empire together. From Rua an attempt was made to unite the many tribes of the H. right through to the northern forest zone. The peak of Hunnic power was during the reign of → Attila (434–453). In 447 he advanced with Germanic allies to the Balkan peninsula and occupied Moesia prima and Dacia ripensis. After the Second Peace of Anatolius in 450, in which he dispensed with his conquests south of the Danube, he advanced with Germanic allies against Gaul and northern Italy. In the summer of 451 he was defeated by the united fighting strength of Aetius on the Catalaunian Fields (→ Campi Catalauni) and had to retreat to the right-hand side of the Rhine (Iord. Get. 194–218). This was the beginning of the decline of the Hunnic empire. In 452 the Huns still succeeded in capturing → Aquileia [1] and advancing to Milan but the attack by emperor Marcianus on Attila's heartland on the Danube forced him to turn around. After his death battles for the throne began, which were exploited by the Gepidae, Rugi, Suebi and Sarmatae, who had been subjugated by the H. Under Attila's sons Ellak and Dengitzik, who both died in 454 at the battle on the Nedao in Pannonia against Germanic tribes, the Hunnic empire fell apart in Europe. Many of the H. became mercenaries in the eastern Roman army and later also in the Germanic army, whilst others were settled in Dacia ripensis. On both sides of the Dnjepr, H. also settled whose ruler after 494 was probably Attila's youngest son Hernac (Iord. Get. 259ff.). From there the last attested incursion of the H. under Zeno was launched (Evagrius, Historia ecclesiae 3,2).

B. Culture

The H. achieved their historical importance because they triggered the Great Migration of Peoples. Because of their fast mounted archers, they had very great combat strength for their campaigns of conquest. Specimens of 'golden bows' covered with sheet-gold are well known as symbols of power from the Hunnic princes' tombs. Their language, conclusions about which can only be drawn from names, was Old Altaic and was closely related to Old Turkish. Only very little is known about the H. and their culture since they are generally negatively represented in ancient literature as a 'barbaric and wild' people (Iord. Get. 123) and the archaeological evidence only scantily aids our understanding. Elements of nomadic and warrior life were obviously prevalent, and major aspects of their life were hunting and animal husbandry. Sassanid influences are attested towards the end of the 4th cent. The most important sources are: Priscus of Panion; Constantinus Porphyrogennetus, Excerpta de legationibus; Iord. Get.; Amm. Marc. 31,2; Zos. 4,20.

F. ALTHEIM, Gesch. der Hunnen 1–5, 1959–1962; O. J. MAENCHEN-HELFEN, Die Welt der Hunnen, 1978; A. ALFÖLDY, Funde aus der Hunnenzeit und ihre ethnische Sonderung, 1932; E. A. THOMPSON, A History of Attila and the Huns, 1948; J. WERNER, Beitr. zur Arch. des Attilareiches, 1956.   I.v.B.

Huns see → Hunni

Hunsrück-Eifel culture Special group from the Celtic Iron Age in the western highlands area between Luxembourg, the Rhine, the high Eifel and the Nahe Valley. The Hunsrück Eifel culture (HEC) is part of both the late → Hallstatt culture and the early → La Tène culture (6th to the middle of the 3rd cent. BC). It is primarily characterized by continuously attested burial mound fields with body burials. Additional peculiarities are special pottery shapes as well as its own grave furnishings (a lot of ring jewellery, few fibulae, frequent lance burial gifts etc.). In the course of the HEC, especially in the 5th/4th cents. BC, a group of → princes' burials develops which is distinguished by rich gold jewellery, Graeco-Etruscan imports, swords and chariots as burial gifts (particularly two-wheeled war chariots) (e.g. Schwarzenbach, → Waldalgesheim).

Settlements for the HEC are known only in isolated cases as fortified elevated castles, none of which has been able to be classified to date as a → prince's seat.

The reasons for the development of this group are often seen as related to the local iron deposits. The HEC obviously has an important role in the development of the La Tène culture.
→ Iron; → Celtic archaeology; → Wagon

A. HAFFNER, Die westl. H., 1976; Id., A. MIRON (ed.), Studien zur Eisenzeit im Hunsrück-Nahe-Raum, 1991; H.-E. Joachim, Die H. am Mittelrhein, 1968.   V.P.

Hunting
I. ANCIENT ORIENT   II. CLASSICAL ANTIQUITY

I. ANCIENT ORIENT

Archaeological finds attest to battues with traps in the Middle East from the 7th millennium BC onwards. On the other hand, there is only a little cuneiform evidence of the occupation of the hunter, e.g. in the → Gilgamesh Epic (TUAT 3. 676, I iii 9ff.). Wild cattle, wild goats, wild donkeys, gazelles, lions, → elephants and many other animals were hunted. As hunting weapons, people used traps, nets and snares as well as bows and arrows, throwing-sticks, lances, swords and daggers, and mastiffs and greyhounds were used as hunting dogs. Pictorial representations of hunting are to be found from the beginning of the 3rd millennium BC particularly on Mesopotamian → cylinder seals.

As early as the 3rd millennium hunting was regarded as the sport of kings. Assyrian texts report – in the context of campaigns – royal hunts from Tiglatpilesar I (1114–1076 BC) onwards on foot or in chariots. Preferred hunting areas were the valley of the Euphrates and the bordering steppe. From Assurnasirpal II (883–859 BC) onwards there are depictions of these hunts and the subsequent hunt sacrifices on the → reliefs in Assyrian palaces as well. The art of → Urartu adopted the motif of the royal hunt. Under → Sargon II (722–705 BC) the hunt was first depicted in a courtly environment. It, like the military battle, attested to the power of the ruler; the animals suffered the same fate as the enemies: death or captivity. Parallel to this, Egyptian royal dogma also promoted the lion hunt as a ritual elevation of the ruler. → Assurbanipal's (668–627 BC) lion hunts – on foot, on horseback, from chariots or from a ship – took place in his own hunting-parks with animals brought in for the purpose. The lions appeared to be regarded as a symbol of the threat to Assyria. The link between the royal hunts and the ritual protection of the cultural heartland and the herds also becomes clear in the inscriptions and reliefs of the Assyrian kings. → Achaemenids and → Sassanids (Taq-i Bustan) adopted the tradition of the fenced or walled game reserve (→ Paradeisos).

H. ALTENMUELLER, s.v. J., LÄ 3, 221–233, esp. 221; J.K. ANDERSON, Hunting in the Ancient World, 1985; H.D. GALTER, Paradies und Palmentod, in: W. SCHOLZ (ed.), Der oriental. Mensch und seine Beziehungen zur Umwelt, 1989, 237–253; W. HEIMPEL, L. TRÜMPELMANN, s.v. J., RLA 5, 234–238; S.W. HELMS, A. PETTS, The Desert "Kites" of Badiyat esh-Sham and North Arabia, in: Paléorient 13, 1987, 41–67; U. MAGEN, Assyr. Königsdarstellungen, 1986, 29–36.   HA.G.

II. CLASSICAL ANTIQUITY

In early Greek literature and in myth hunting was initially regarded as the defence from animals that cause harm to human beings; the heroic killing of the dangerous animal was often represented pictorially on vases and reliefs and is central to literary testimonials. In this way → Hercules kills the Nemean lion and catches the Erymanthian boar (Apollod. 2,5,1; 2,5,4). Also famous was the hunt of → Meleager for a boar that, sent by → Artemis, destroyed the fields around Calydon (Hom. Il. 9,533–549; cf. Apollod. 1,8,3; Ov. Met. 8,273–424; pictorial representation: François Vase, Florence AM, BEAZLEY, ABV 76,1; BEAZLEY, Paralipomena 29). This view is still discernible in Plato: in his version of the Prometheus myth the wild animals are threatening to exterminate the weaker humans; 'war on animals' is clearly declared here (τὸν τῶν θηρίων πόλεμον; Pl. Prt. 322b; cf. also Anth. Gr. 6,168). Undoubtedly hunting was also used for providing food (Hom. Od. 9,152–162: goats; 10,156–184: deer; cf. Verg. Aen. 1,180–213). Bows and arrows as well as the spear are mentioned as the hunter's weapons. The hunt itself is depicted dramatically in the epic (Hom. Od. 19,428–458). In the archaic period Attic vase painting shows a large number of hunting scenes, among these being groups of riders hunting deer and wild pigs (for instance black-figured hydria, London BM, BEAZLEY, ABV 266,4). In Athens, hunting was part of the aristocratic lifestyle (Aristoph. Vesp. 1194–1204) and was part of the way of life of the Spartans (Xen. Lac. pol. 4,7).

More comprehensive information on hunting in the 4th cent. BC, the equipment of the hunters, the dogs and the game can be found in a piece of writing by Xenophon (Κυνηγετικός, Kynēgetikós). For the hunt, nets were used into which the game was driven, (Xen. Cyn. 2,3–9; 6,5–10; 10,19), and mantraps were also set (9,11–19); the selection and breeding of dogs suitable for hunting is treated in detail (3f.; 7). Of central importance was the hunt for hares (5f.), deer and wild pigs (9f.), whilst the hunt for lions, leopards or bears is only mentioned briefly (11). Xenophon sees the value of hunting in the fact that it ensures a healthy body, good eyesight and hearing and in this way physically prepares the hunter for all war service duties; Xenophon sums up by stating that hunters become στρατιῶταί τε ἀγαθοὶ καὶ στρατηγοί, good soldiers and commanders (Xen. Cyn. 12,1–9; cf. Xen. Lac. pol. 4,7). Similar ideas on hunting are also to be found in the Kyroupaideía (Xen. Cyr. 1,2,10; 1,6,28; 6,2,5; 8,1,34); hunting serves here explicitly as a model for the mode of action in war (Xen. Cyr. 2,4,25). Plato, who sets up a systematology of the various types of hunting including also the hunt for humans, rejects fishing (→ Fishing) and bird-catching, as they require neither effort nor bravery, and only considers hunting with horses and dogs for land animals to be honourable (Pl. Leg. 823a–824a).

A new epoch in the history of hunting began with Alexander the Great and the Hellenistic kings; for Alexander, who drew upon both Macedonian and Persian traditions, hunting on horseback and particularly the lion hunt was a royal activity whose function was to legitimate his rule (Plut. Alexander 40; Arr. Anab. 4,13,2). As the → Alexander Sarcophagus from Sidon (Istanbul, AM) with its battle and hunting-scenes shows, the depiction of overcoming wild animals was part of the pictorial representation of the Hellenistic rulers from the late 4th cent. BC onwards.

In the Roman upper class the interest in hunting appears to have been awakened only through the encounter with Hellenistic culture; in this way P. Scipio Aemilianus had become an enthusiastic hunter after 169 BC in Macedonia and after his return to Italy together with Polybius he dedicated himself intensively to hunting (Pol. 31,29). In the farming milieu, the winter was used for hunting (Verg. G. 1,307–310; cf. also the idyllic description of the life of the hunter in Dion. Chrys. 7,10–80). Hunting was certainly rejected too (Sall. Catil. 4,1), but for senators of the early Principate period it was probably not uncommon to go hunting when staying in the country (Plin. Ep. 1,6); this is also supported by the comment by Pliny about the stock of game on his estates in Etruria (frequens ibi et varia venatio: Plin. Ep. 5,6,7).

Of considerable importance for the Principate was the fact that even the principes dedicated themselves increasingly to hunting. This initially applies to Trajan, who was praised by Pliny because he did not kill animals in captivity but tracked down the game in the forests himself (Plin. Pan. 81). Hadrian is said to have killed several lions with his own hands but also suffered injuries in hunting (S HA Hadr. 26,3; cf. Cass. Dio 69,10,2). On the 'Hadrianic roundels' that were later put up on the Arch of Constantine, the princeps is depicted hunting a bear, a boar and a lion, with the sacrifice scenes creating the link with myth and religion. Befitting this inclination of the principes, several works on hunting were written from the 2nd cent., e.g. by Arrianus (Kynēgetikós) and by Oppianus (early 3rd cent.), whose Kynēgetiká written in hexameters, in contrast to Xenophon's treatise, now also give greater attention to hunting on horseback and the hunt for lions (Opp. Kyn. 1,158–367; 4,77–211). The Latin Cynegetica of Nemesianus (late 3rd cent.) have also been passed down in fragmentary form. The lion-hunt sarcophagi of the 3rd cent. are a testimonial to the fact that hunting-scenes were a preferred pictorial theme in the art of late antiquity as well.

1 J.K. ANDERSON, Hunting in the Ancient Greek World, 1985 2 A. DEMANDT, Das Privatleben der röm. Kaiser, 1996, 146ff. 3 J.-L. DURAND, A. SCHNAPP, Schlachtopfer und rituelle Jagd, in: C. BÉRARD et al. (ed.), Die Bilderwelt der Griechen, 1985, 73–99 4 R. LANE FOX, Ancient Hunting: From Homer to Polybios, in: G. SHIPLEY, J. SALMON (ed.), Human Landscapes in Classical Antiquity, 1996, 119–153.   H.SCHN.

Hunt Painter The main master of → Laconian vase painting, who worked about 560–540 BC and painted in particular cups as well as → hydriai; typical are his paintings on the inside of kylikes with tondo-shaped pictorial detail. Named after images of a (mythical?) boar hunt (kylix Paris, LV, E 670 and the fragment Leipzig T 302/Florence 85118), the Hunt Painter (HP) otherwise prefers battle, dance and banqueting images, as well as, among mythological subjects, the labours of Heracles. A common filling and subsidiary motif are birds and fish. The careful and decorative painting style of the HP had a sustained influence on vase painting in Sparta. The approximately 80 works attributed to him come primarily from Samos, Sparta and Italy.

> P. Settimi, Il pittore della caccia, in: Studi sulla ceramica laconica: atti del seminario; Perugia, 23–24 febr. 1981, 1986, 33–44; E. Simon, Die griech. Vasen, ²1981, pl. 36; C. M. Stibbe, Lakon. Vasenmaler des 6. Jh. v.Chr., 1972, 121–150, 280–285; Id., Das andere Sparta, 1996, 175–178.   M.ST.

Hurrian Ancient Oriental language, written in Babylonian and Ugaritic cuneiform script, widespread in eastern Anatolia, Upper Mesopotamia and northern Syria during the late 3rd and above all the 2nd millennium BC. Among the Hurrian texts known until now are letters, myths, spells, prayers, rituals, omens, wisdom texts and lexical lists. → Urartian is closely related; it is written in Assyrian cuneiform script and was used above all for royal inscriptions in eastern Anatolia and NW Iran from c. 820 until 600 BC. H. is an agglutinative and ergative language, which used suffixes only in a strict sequential order. Nouns have two numbers (singular, plural), but no grammatical gender. So far at least 11 cases have been observed. The verb of the → Mittani dialect has three tenses, the dialect of the tablets from → Ḫattuša and other older texts apparently have aspects and kind of action. In addition there is a complex system of non-indicative forms.

> F. W. Bush, A Grammar of the Hurrian Language, 1964; I. M. Diakonoff, Hurrisch und Urartäisch, 1971. GE.W.

Hurrians Old Oriental language group that has been documented from Akkadian times (around 2200 BC). The ancestors of the H. probably lived in the early 3rd millennium BC in eastern Anatolia. The H. came into the field of vision of the advanced cultures of the Ancient Orient through the expansion of the Mesopotamian empires (prisoners of war, payments of tribute; Hurrian incantations around 1750 BC). The H. poured into the northern part of the 'Fertile Crescent' especially during the course of the collapse of the Mesopotamian empires. City states under Hurrian rulers in Upper Mesopotamia and Assyria (Urkeš) have been attested from the late Akkadian period. The H. spread out towards the west at the beginning of the 2nd millennium. A Hurrian written culture developed in northern Syria already before the middle of the 2nd millennium,

combining ancient Hurrian traditions with long-established Syrian ones and influencing Hittite (→ Ḫattuša) culture from about 1400 BC. In the 16th cent. BC a H. kingdom arose in Upper Mesopotamia (→ Mittani), which reached from the Mediterranean to the Zagrus around 1400. In the 16th cent. its history was marked by the dispute with the Old Hittite Empire, in the 15th cent. by the conflict with Egypt and in the 14th cent. by the repulsion of Hittite and Assyrian efforts to expand, which were probably the reason for the peaceful agreement with Egypt (→ Amarna letters). Around 1335 Mittani was conquered by Hittites and Assyrians and afterwards continued to exist only as a residual state (Hanigalbat) that quickly lost any importance. The Hurrian language disappeared for the most part, but survived in parts of eastern Anatolia probably into the 7th cent. BC.
→ Hurrian

> G. Wilhelm, The Hurrians, 1989.   GE.W.

Hurrite see → Hurrian

Hurrites see → Hurrians

Husbandry (Animal)
I. Ancient Orient II. Egypt III. Greece
IV. Rome VI. Incorporation into the Roman Empire III. The unification of Italy by Rome

I. Ancient Orient

In the Ancient Orient and Egypt animal husbandry was always systemically linked with agricultural production (farming), insofar as both were mutually dependent and together formed the basis for society's subsistence. That view was given expression (i.a.) in the Sumerian polemical poem 'Mother ewe and grain' [1].

In Mesopotamia the basis of animal husbandry was mainly the keeping of herds of → sheep and to a lesser extent of → goats, which were collectively termed 'domestic livestock' (Sumerian u₈.udu-ḫia; Akkadian ṣēnu). Sheep were primarily producers of → wool as raw material for the → production of textiles, as well as of milk and meat; they also served as sacrificial animals. Goat's hair was important for tent manufacture, especially in the nomadic zone. Sheep-breeding to produce valuable high-quality wool is attested for Mesopotamia from the end of the 4th millennium BC [25]. The texts display a sharply differentiated terminology in respect of the breed, age and gender of the animals.

The system of managing herds, particularly with a view to increasing herd size, is evident in documents from the beginning of the third millennium [13. 190], from the 21st to the 18th cents. BC. On those calculations, at the end of each yearly period a shepherd was expected to hand over 80 lambs per 100 ewes, at an expected birth rate of one lamb in a twelve-month period – a mortality rate of 20% ([7; 13]; for cattle

[8. 139–144]). If the mortality rate was less than 20%, the shepherd could take the surplus animals into his own herd, but he bore the loss if the rate was higher. In the 1st millennium BC the rate was somewhat lower. Bodies of dead animals were collected by skinners, primarily for the skins and sinews that could be obtained from them. The duties and obligations of a shepherd were recorded in the lawbook of → Ḥammurapi (§§ 57 f.), especially his responsibilities in looking after newly sown grainfields. His supervision was mainly intended to help stimulate stronger growth in the young plants. As well, the grazing by the animals ensured an otherwise unavailable fertilization of the fields.

In both Mesopotamia and Egypt → cattle were bred primarily for the plough. Training them to work in yokes of four (especially in Mesopotamia) was the essential for optimal grain cultivation on the large estates (between 50 and 200 hectares in size) of institutional household [12] (→ Oikos economy).

In Mesopotamia's centralized economy under the 3rd dynasty of Ur (21st cent. BC) livestock levies, generated predominantly in the borderlands of the northern East Tigris area, were conducted partly in fact, partly only on paper, at a central cattleyard near → Nippur. The annual average amounted to c. 70,000 animals [18]. The tax calculation was based on a ratio of cattle to sheep of 1:10.

Insofar as breeding took place on cultivated land, it had to compete with arable farming for its grazing pastures. This is especially true of the raising of cattle, which (unlike sheep that could graze in areas of steppes) were dependent on cultivated land for adequate supplies of green fodder [14].

As well as the raising of sheep, goats and cattle, → donkeys and mules were especially important as transport animals for long-distance trade (→ Commerce I.). The → horse played no role in Mesopotamian animal husbandry, and breeding of → pigs and poultry-breeding (especially ducks and geese; → Breeding, of small domestic animals) played only a minor role. Poultry-breeding is attested, mainly from the Neo-Babylonian period (6th/5th cents. BC), in texts from Uruk [16].

Only a little information is available about animal husbandry in the Levant and Anatolia. The texts from → Ebla (24th cent. BC), which mention extensive herds of sheep and the textile production associated with them [11], are an exception. The story of Jacob [1] and Laban constitutes an observation on the problems of breeding in herds (Gn 29 f.).

The importance and high esteem enjoyed by the shepherd is reflected in the use of the term 'shepherd' in the title(s) given to Mesopotamian rulers [17. 244–250, 441–446]. In the OT it was an epithet of → Yahweh (e.g. Ps 23), in the NT Jesus is described as the 'Good Shepherd' (John 10,11 ff.).

II. EGYPT

Raising and breeding cattle was the focus of animal husbandry in Egypt and from the Middle Kingdom was the subject of numerous pictorial representations in → Mastaba. Cattle were used both as working animals in → agriculture and as animals of choice for sacrifice and food. The key cattle-raising areas were Lower Egypt and the Nile delta, where sufficient green fodder was available. Herds were also enlarged by the inclusion of captured animals, mainly cattle from Nubia. The economic importance of cattle-raising is shown in the pattern of institutional structures (cf. → Palace, → Temple). Shepherds in Egypt were apparently also able to take surpluses into their own herds. The raising of sheep, goats and donkeys does not feature in the pictorial representations, and that reflects their rather unimportant role in Egyptian husbandry overall. Poultry-farming, in the form of using coops and fattening the birds, represented a significant branch of the Egyptian economy and was depicted graphically. Geese, in particular, were preferred animals of sacrifice.(→ Sacrifice II. B.).

As Egypt, unlike Mesopotamia, had no suitable grazing grounds available, apart from the narrow Nile valley that was used intensively for agriculture, large-scale sheep-breeding to meet textile needs was not possible. The main material used in textiles was → linen (flax).

→ Agriculture; → Breeding, of small domestic animals

1 B. ALSTER, H. I. J. VANSTIPHOUT, Lahar and Ashnan. Presentation and Analysis of a Sumerian Disputation, in: Acta Sumerologica 9, 1987, 1–43 2 P. BEHRENS, s. v. Geflügel, LÄ 2, 503–508 3 K. BUTZ, Konzentrationen wirtschaftlicher Macht im Königreich Larsa, in: WZKM 65/66, 1973/74, 1–58 4 W. HELCK, s. v. V., LÄ 6, 1986, 1036–1038 5 Id., s. v. Schwein, LÄ 5, 762–764 6 B. HRUŠKA, Herden für Götter und Könige. Schafe und Ziegen in der altsumer. Zeit, in: Altoriental. Forsch. 22, 1995, 73–83 7 F. R. KRAUS, Staatliche Viehhaltung im altbabylon. Larsa, 1966 8 H. J. NISSEN et al., Frühe Schrift und Techniken der Wirtschaftsverwaltung im alten Vorderen Orient, 1990 9 J. N. POSTGATE, Early Mesopotamia, 1992, 159–166 10 Id., M. A. POWELL (ed.), Domestic Animals of Mesopotamia I and II (= Bull. on Sumerian Agriculture 7/8), 1993/1995 11 J. RENGER, Überlegungen zur räumlichen Ausdehnung des Staates Ebla an Hand der agrarischen und viehwirtschaftlichen Gegebenheiten, in: Annali dell'Istituto Universitario Orientale di Napoli, Series Minor 27, 1986, 293–311 12 Id., Report on the Implications of Employing Draught Animals, in: Irrigation and Cultivation in Mesopotamia, Part II (Bull. on Sumerian Agriculture 5), 1990, 267–279 13 Id., Wirtschaft und Ges., in: B. HROUDA (ed.), Der Alte Orient, 1991, 187–215 14 Id., Landwirtschaftliche Nutzfläche, Einwohnerzahlen und Herdengröße, in: H. GASCHE et al. (ed.), FS L. de Meyer, 1994, 251–253 15 Id., Das Palastgeschäft in der altbabylon. Zeit, in: A. C. V. M. BONGENAAR (ed.), Interdependency of Institutions and Private Entrepreneurs, 2000, 153–183 16 M. SAN NICOLÒ, Materialien zur V. in den neubabylon. Tempeln I–III, in: Orientalia 17, 1948, 273–293; 18, 1949, 288–306; 20, 1951, 129–150 17 J.-M. SEUX, Épithètes royales akkadiennes et sumériennes, 1967 18 M. SIGRIST, Drehem, 1992 19 L. STÖRK, s. v. Rind, LÄ 5, 257–263 20 Id., s. v. Schaf, LÄ 5, 522–524 21 Id., s. v. Ziege, LÄ 6, 1400 f. 22 M. STEPIEN, Animal Husbandry in the Ancient Near

East. A Prosopographical Study of Third-Millennium Umma, 1996 23 K. SZARZYNSKA, Sheep Husbandry and Production of Wool, Garments and Cloths in Archaic Sumer, 2002 24 G. VAN DRIEL, Bones and the Mesopotamian State? Animal Husbandry in an Urban Context, in: Bibliotheca Orientalis 50, 1993, 545–563 (review of M. A. ZEDER, Feeding Cities. Specialized Animal Economy in the Ancient Near East, 1991) 25 H. WAETZOLDT, Unt. zur neusumer. Textilindustrie, 1972 26 F. ZEEB, die Palastwirtschaft in Altsyrien, 2001.   J. RE.

III. GREECE
A. GEOGRAPHIC CONDITIONS B. ANIMAL HUSBANDRY IN THE MYCENAEAN AND HOMERIC PERIODS C. THE FORMS OF ANIMAL HUSBANDRY D. ECONOMIC GOALS

A. GEOGRAPHIC CONDITIONS
Like most regions of the Mediterranean, the landscape of Greece, on the Aegean islands as well as the mainland, was not well suited to animal husbandry in antiquity. Sufficient quantities of → fodder were available only for a limited period of the year and were moreover strongly dependent on the winter and spring rainfall. Large herds could thus be maintained only if they were taken to places where there was adequate fodder available. As well, raising them or importing them made less economic sense than cultivating crops for human → nutrition. Consequently, meat was always only a by-product of animal husbandry. Nevertheless, since their → domestication in the Neolithic period (7th millennium BC), working animals had been indispensable for the ancient → economy.

There were several possible ways of keeping animals in the Mediterranean landscape. In some periods, as in the early modern era, → sheep and → goats, in particular, were driven in summer to the higher mountain regions where fodder was available for longer and in winter to the warmer lowland plains. In the process, the entire population of villages dependent on husbandry often accompanied the herds. Modern scholarship has intensively studied this nomadic pastoral economy (→ Transhumance) in Greece and Italy and has stressed that transhumance in the early modern era depended on the existence of markets and the opportunity to move freely with the herds over long distances. These two conditions were not always met in the world of the Greek poleis. An account of shepherds from Corinth and Thebes meeting in the mountain region (Soph. OT 1133–1139) nevertheless attests to the existence of a nomadic pastoral economy in classical Greece.

B. ANIMAL HUSBANDRY IN THE MYCENAEAN AND HOMERIC PERIODS
The impressive numbers of sheep that were kept in the late Bronze Age for the rulers of → Knos(s)os do not indicate the existence of large herds in the palace economy, for they may also reflect popular tribute to the rulers. Even this example shows that political, social and economic factors, and not just geographic conditions, dictated the forms of husbandry.

As Homer often mentions banquets of Greek heroes and herds of cattle kept some distance from their noble owners' seat of residence (Hom. Od. 14,100–108; cf. Il. 15,630–636; 16,352–355), earlier scholarship sometimes assumed that Greece's → economy in the early Iron Age was predominantly dependent on animal husbandry. That view cannot be sustained, because in the Homeric period → grain was undoubtedly the staple food for the majority of the population, who usually only ate meat in connection with social and religious activities such as festivals and → sacrifices (→ Meat, consumption of). It is likely, however, that the ratio of animals to humans in regions with relatively low population density was higher than later on in regions with a higher population density. In the archaic period, conflicts occasionally developed in these conditions because the large herds of livestock of wealthy aristocrats claimed large areas for grazing (Megara: Aristot. Pol. 1305a).

C. THE FORMS OF ANIMAL HUSBANDRY
Particularly the boundaries between poleis or between demes (→ dēmos [2]) in larger poleis seem to have been favoured for keeping livestock, and this could lead to conflicts. Herds were, however, also kept close to settlements. In any event they moved between local pastoral areas. That was the case in Thessaly during the Neolithic period and is assumed to have been also the case in Attica during the Classical period. Modern scholars are divided as to the degree to which animal husbandry was integrated into → agriculture as a whole. Thus, [6] espouses the view that herds with their shepherds were regarded as independent property in addition to the farm and estates (cf. Isaeus 6,33) and were not necessarily kept on the owner's property, while [5] assumes that on a large number of rural properties there existed a balanced system of agriculture, encompassing → grain, → wine and trees as well as a small number of working animals. These two forms of keeping livestock may have existed at different times and in different regions. Archaeological surveys show that in some areas during the Hellenistic period small farm holdings were displaced by larger estates on which fairly large herds grazed.

In many poleis there were probably a number of rich citizens who owned large herds and provided sacrificial animals for the larger festivals (→ Sacrifice). In Hellenistic Orchomenus a foreigner was granted grazing rights for 220 cattle and horses and 1,000 sheep and goats (IG VII 3171; SEG 27, 63). By contrast, herds of more than 100 sheep or goats are not attested in Attica.

D. ECONOMIC GOALS
The breeding and keeping of → horses, → donkeys, → cattle, → sheep, → goats and → pigs need to be considered separately. Horses belonged to the lifestyle of the social elite and were of little economic value. Don-

keys and mules were valued as draught animals; the latter were also used for ploughing. Cattle served mainly as working animals for ploughing and transporting loads (Pl. Resp. 370e), but were also killed in sacrifice and provided a large portion of the meat that was consumed in *poleis* in public religious festivals. The demand for ox-hides for → leather could not be met in Athens through slaughter. Cow's milk – unlike → milk from sheep and goats – was not very important for the population in ancient Greece. Sheep were kept mainly for their → wool, the most important raw material for the → production of textiles,; even goat's hair was used for a variety of purposes. Sheep and goats were also important sacrificial animals; lambs and kids that were not selected for breeding made up a significant proportion of meat for consumption, and they were the animals most frequently sacrificed at non-*polis* levels. They were sacrificed at private festivals along with pigs, which were kept solely for their meat.

The differing purposes of husbandry led also to different techniques of animal-breeding and of choice in breeding animal. Castrated animals, like oxen, were valuable working animals (→ Castration of animals). Wethers provided better wool and were sacrificed mainly to male deities. Piglets from litters that were too large to be nurtured by the sow were slaughtered at minor sacrifices. That was possibly also the case because relatively few boars were used for breeding. Animal bones found at excavations of settlements often afford information on the age and sex of animals and allow us to draw conclusions about the methods and goals of animal husbandry in those regions and periods. → Agriculture; → Cattle; → Fodder; → Economy; → Goat; → Meat, consumption of; → Nutrition; → Sacrifice; → Sheep; → Stables, keeping of animals in

1 A. BURFORD, Land and Labor in the Greek World, 1993, 144–159   2 H. GRASSL, Zur Geschichte des Viehhandels im klass. Griechenland, in: MBAH 4, 1985, 77–88 3 P. HALSTEAD, Pastoralism or Household Herding? Problems of Scale and Specialization in Early Greek Animal Husbandry, in: World Archaeology 28, 1996, 20–42 4 V. D. HANSON, The Other Greeks. The Family Farm and the Agrarian Roots of Western Civilization, 1995 5 S. HODKINSON, Animal Husbandry in the Greek Polis, in: WHITTAKER, 35–74   6 ISAGER/SKYDSGAARD, 89–93; 99–107   7 M. H. JAMESON, Sacrifice and Animal Husbandry, in: WHITTAKER, 87–119   8 M. H. JAMESON et al., A Greek Countryside: The Southern Argolid from Prehistory to the Present Day, 1994, 285–301   9 J. T. KILLEN, The Linear B Tablets and the Mycenaean Economy, in: A. MORPURGO DAVIES, Y. DUHOUX (ed.), Linear B: A 1984 Survey, 1985, 241–305   10 R. OSBORNE, Classical Landscape with Figures, 1987   11 W. RICHTER, Die Landwirtschaft im homerischen Zeitalter, (ArchHom 2 H), 1968, 44–53   12 WHITTAKER.   MI. JA.

IV. ROME
A. GENERAL   B. WORKING ANIMALS   C. PRODUCE FROM ANIMAL HUSBANDRY   D. FORMS OF ANIMAL HUSBANDRY

A. GENERAL
For the production of foodstuffs in the Roman empire, animal husbandry was relatively less important than the cultivation of → grain, → wine and → vegetables and the production of olive oil (→ Oils for cooking). The core territory of the Roman empire was heavily populated, so arable land was needed principally to feed the population. Clear-cut competition arose between use of the land for cultivation and for pasture. Under these conditions intensive animal husbandry developed mainly in remote and lightly settled regions, such as in mountains or border provinces. However, livestock breeding had an important function for the Roman → economy, inasmuch as working animals were indispensable for → agriculture and as a means of transport, and beyond that, sheep-breeding provided → wool, the most important raw material for the production of → textiles.

In literary texts, and particularly in specialist literature on agriculture (→ Agrarian writers), animal husbandry was nevertheless accorded high esteem (Cic. Off. 2,89; Varro, Rust. 2,1,1–11; Columella 6 praef.), with profit named explicitly as its goal (Varro, Rust. 2,1,11).

B. WORKING ANIMALS
In pre-industrial agrarian society working animals, as a source of energy, represented, the most important supplement to human muscle power (→ Energy). They were employed primarily as draught animals in → agriculture and in → land transport. With a yoked team of oxen a farmer could – with less physical exertion on his part – work about three times more land than he could without using animals. That again involved the necessity of acquiring the → fodder for the oxen. As poor farmers needed their land entirely for feeding their families, they were obliged to do the hard work of tilling their fields themselves. In these circumstances owning an yoke of oxen was the most important feature distinguishing small farmers and well-to-do farmers. Columella begins his description of working animals with the observation that the ox was more deserving of esteem than all other and was the 'most hard-working helper in agriculture' (*laboriosissimus adhuc hominis socius in agricultura*: Columella 6 praef. 7). Along with oxen, the → donkey, used in many different ways as a beast of burden and as a plough animal, and the mule should also be mentioned. The → horse played an especially important role in the military domain.

C. PRODUCE FROM ANIMAL HUSBANDRY
Produce from animal husbandry, in Roman as in most societies, helped with human → nutrition. Especially the descriptions of banquets of the upper classes

(→ Banquet) are evidence that large amounts of meat were consumed. As good pastoral land was rare in the Mediterranean and as considerable amounts of calories were lost in the transition from plant fodder to meat and relatively little meat was produced per hectare, meat was correspondingly dear and remained for most of the population a luxury item beyond their means (cf. → Meat, consumption of). Pork in particular played an important dietary role; → pigs were easy to keep as they found fodder in the woods and also ate scraps. → Milk for the production of → cheese came mainly from → goats but also from → sheep, while in this respect cattle-raising was not very important. Milk was brought to market in the form of hard cheese; soft cheese and fresh milk were delivered from farms close to the towns. Highly valued fine → wool, the most important product from sheep-breeding, was produced for urban markets.

D. FORMS OF ANIMAL HUSBANDRY

On their intensively cultivated land, partly also on fallow land, small farmers kept a few sheep or goats. Larger herds could be kept either in close association with cultivation of → grain or else in the form of nomadic pastoral farming (→ Transhumance) in remote regions. Thus, in Italy large herds were driven up into the mountain regions in summer and in winter were put to graze in the plains of southern Italy (Varro, Rust. 2,2,9; 2,5,11; 3,17,9). The shepherds were mostly slaves who accompanied the animals on their migrations and protected them from wild animals and rustling. The overseers were expected to have some knowledge of writing as a prerequisite for using → veterinary medicine and for keeping accounts (Varro, Rust. 2,10,10).

Husbandry required large areas of land for extensive production. Thus, keeping oxen for ploughing and keeping animals for meat and milk production seem to have been restricted to rather large estates. Large herds of sheep were to be found mainly in northern and southern Italy in areas of low population density. There are indications that in some regions of Italy after the 2nd → Punic War small farmers were displaced from their properties because of the expansion of pastoral farming. As well, large estate owners from Italy engaged in husbandry in grand style (→ Large estates) in the provinces, for example in Sicily or in Epirus. Varro offers some data on the usual size of herds: 50–100 goats, 100–150 pigs and 100–120 cattle kept in one herd (Varro, Rust. 2,3,10; 2,4,22; 2,5,18). People had clear views on the appearance and qualities of individual types of domestic animal, and by careful selection of the male animals efforts were made to improve the quality of the animals being bred and their produce.
→ Agriculture; → Cattle; → Donkey; → Goat; → Horse; → Meat, consumption of; → Nutrition; → Mule; → Pig; → Sheep

1 C. CLARK, M. HASWELL, The Economics of Subsistence Agriculture, ⁴1970   2 H. FORBES, European Agriculture

Viewed Bottom-Side Upwards: Fodder- and Forage-Provision in a Traditional Greek Community, in: Environmental Archaeology 1, 1998, 19–34   3 P. HALSTEAD, Land Use in Postglacial Greece: Cultural Causes and Environmental Effects, in: P. HALSTEAD, C. FREDERICK (ed.), Landscape and Land Use in Postglacial Greece, 2000, 110–128   4 W. JONGMAN, Wool and the Textile Industry of Roman Italy, in: E. LO CASCIO (ed.), Mercati permanenti e mercati periodici nel mondo romano, 2000, 187–197   5 S. PAYNE, Kill-off Patterns in Sheep and Goats: The Mandibles from Asvan Kale, in: AS 23, 1973, 281–303   6 J. PETERS, Röm. Tierhaltung und Tierzucht, 1998   7 G. WALDHERR, Ant. Transhumanz im Mediterran. Ein Überblick, in: P. HERZ, G. WALDHERR (ed.), Landwirtschaft im Imperium Romanum 2001, 331–357   8 WHITE, Farming   9 WHITTAKER.   W. J.

Hussain (Ḥusain). Grandson of the Prophet → Muhammad (Muḥammad), son of his daughter → Fatima (Fāṭima) and cousin of → Ali ('Alī). Third → Imām of the → Shiites. After the death of the → Caliph → Mu'āwiya he was forced by members of his father's party to take over power from the → Umayyads, and was killed by their troops at Kerbela ('Irāq) in 680. His martyr's death is remembered by the Shiites annually in passion plays, his supporters' failure to succour him is atoned for in processions of flagellators.

H. HALM, Der schiitische Islam, 1994; Id., Shiism, 1991; L. VECCIA VAGLIERI, Ḥusayn b. 'Alī b. Abī Ṭālib, EI 3, 607a–615b.   H. SCHÖ.

Huwawa see → Gilgamesh epic

Hyacinthides (Ὑακινθίδες; *Hyakinthídes*). Name of a group of Athenian goddesses, in whose honour a yearly sacrificial festival with maiden dances was held, and who received wineless offerings prior to an army's march into battle. The mythical reason for these rites can be found in the legend that the H. had been sacrificed by → Erechtheus in order to fend off an invasion. Their names and number vary; certain names indicate a relationship to Artemis (who in Sparta received sacrifices prior to a battle). They may also be called simply Parthenoi, 'girls', or Erechtheides, and are usually regarded as Erechtheus' daughters, having received their name from being sacrificed on a hill named Hyacinthus. In a later opinion, probably based on the homonymy with → Hyacinthus [1] of Amyclae, he is supposed to be the father (presenting the double problem that Spartan women save Athens and that Hyacinthus usually dies as an ephebe). The myth follows a common scheme [2].

Sources: the Erechtheus tradition (Euripides, Erechtheus fr. 65,65–98 [1]; Phanodemus, FGrH 325 F 4; Philochorus, FGrH 328 F 12; Dem. Or. 60,27); the Hyacinthus tradition (Apollod. 3,212; Hyg. Fab. 128).

1 C. AUSTIN, Nova Fragmenta Euripidea, 1968
2 W. BURKERT, Homo necans, 1972, 76–80.   F. G.

Hyacinthus (Ύάκινθος; *Hyákinthos*). Hero whose tomb and cult are located in → Amyclae [1] near Sparta, but whose festival, the Hyacinthia, and the name of the month connected to it (*hyakínthios*, Cretan *bakínthios/wakínthios* [1]) is known in many Doric cities. The widespread familiarity with H. indicates the hero's ancient, supra-regional significance. The name must be pre-Greek due to the suffix -*nth*-. Although the Amyclaean sanctuary is pre-Doric, it can be traced only from the late Mycenaean period [1].

In the myth, H. is either the son of local hero Amyclas and the Lapith Diomede (Hes. fr. 171; Apollod. 3,116) or of the muse Clio (→ Cleio), whom Aphrodite joins in anger with → Pierus, son of Magnes (Apollod. 1,16). His brothers are Argalus and Cynortes (Paus. 3,1,3; Apollod. 3,116f.), his sister is Polyboea, who died young (Paus. 3,19,4). A dominant role of H. is that of the homoerotic beloved of either the singer → Thamyris, who thereby invented the practice (Apollod. 1,16), or, in the more common version, of → Apollo, who accidentally kills him when he throws a discus (Ov. Met. 10,162–219). Occasionally, it is said that it was → Zephyrus, Apollo's unsuccessful rival for H., who aimed the discus at H. (Paus. 3,19,5). In memory of his beloved, Apollo founded the Amyclaean cult with his annual festival of the Hyacinthia (Eur. Hel. 1469–1474) and lets the hyacinth grow from his blood (see below H. [2]), inscribing its petals with the mournful *AIAI*. This version of young H.'s death makes the Attic myth impossible according to which he was the father of the → Hyacinthides. This is the reason for an entirely different transmission detached from H.

The Amyclaean festival of the Hyacinthia connects H. and Apollo, the main occupant of the sanctuary, in the much documented parallels between god and hero: H. was buried below Appollo's altar-like throne with an archaic image of the god – armed and equipped with a lance and bow (Paus. 3,19,1–5). It is the main Spartan festival in the month of Hekatombaion, named after the great number of sacrifices, during which Sparta did not fight any wars (description: Polycrates, FGrH 588 F 1 [2]). The festival lasted for three days. The first was devoted esp. to H.; some of the customs that deviated from the Greek norm were explained with the mourning for H., who received a sacrifice for the dead on his altar on the 'throne' prior to the main sacrifice to Apollo (Paus. 3,19,3). The middle day was the most important, with a procession from Sparta to Amyclae (*pompa*, Ov. Met. 10,219) and with musical and agonistic performances by boys and young men as well as a banquet for slaves and foreigners [3]. The young women (*parthénoi*) rode on the wagons of the procession, the women offered a new robe to Apollo (Paus. 3,16,2); also attested are night-time dances of women and girls (Eur. Hel. 1468). At some point, the armour of Timomachus, who captured Amyclae for Sparta, was paraded as well (Aristot. fr. 532). Altogether, the festival's purpose was to give Sparta an opportunity for self-representation as did the Panathenaea for Athens [4].

In other Doric cities, there are few indications of H. except for the name of the month. The Spartan colony of Thera celebrated the Hyacinthia; in the Spartan colony of Tarentum, a tomb of H. or even of Apollo was shown, located east of the city (Pol. 8,28); one must presume the same cult constellation as in Amyclae. In Cnidus, Artemis appeared in inscriptions as *Hyakinthotróphos* and had a festival of Hyacinthotrophia, suggesting a myth in which she raises young H. (SGDI 3501; 3502; 3512).

Iconographically, H. is always depicted as a young man, except for the representation on the Amyclaean throne (Paus. 3,19,4; see → Amyclae).

1 W. BURKERT, Resep-Figuren, Apollon und Amyklai und die "Erfindung" des Opfers auf Cypern: Zur Religionsgesch. der "Dunklen Jh.", in: Grazer Beiträge 4, 1975, 51–79 2 SAMUEL, Index s.v. 3 NILSSON, Feste, 129–140 4 L. BRUIT, The Meal at the Hyakinthia. Ritual Consumption and Offering, in: O. MURRAY (ed.), Sympotica, 1990, 162–174 5 P. BRULÉ, Fêtes grecques. Périodicité et initiation. Hyakinthies et Panathénées, in: A. MOREAU (ed.), L'initiation. Actes du colloque international, 1992, 19–38.

M. J. MELLINK, H., 1943; B. C. DIETRICH, The Dorian Hyacinthia, in: Kadmos, 14, 1975, 133–142; L. VILLARD, F. VILLARD, s.v. H., LIMC 5, 546–550; M. PETTERSSON, Cults of Apollo at Sparta. The Hyakinthia, the Gymnopaidia and the Karneia, 1992. F.G.

Hyades (Ύάδες/*Hyádes*; *Hyas* only since Statius, otherwise *Suculae*, according to Plin. HN 18,247, the popular name is *sidus Parilicium*). Constellation in the head of Taurus, found – due to the fact that Taurus rises in reverse – at the end of the sign in the neighbourhood of Orion and the → Pleiades (the H. are mentioned along with the latter as early as Hom. Il. 18,486 on the shield of Achilles). Their name is derived from ὗς (*hŷs*; 'pig'; 'piglet') or from ὕειν (*hýein*; 'to rain'; 'rain sign') or from the shape of the letter Y as an image of a bull's head. The number of the H. varies between two and seven. The brightest star of the first size (α Tau, modern Aldebaran) was named ὁ λαμπρὸς τῶν Ὑάδων Simon., according to Ptol. Apotelesmata 1,9,3 Λαμπαύρας/*Lampaúras* (Λαμπαδίας varia lectio). It is one of the six reddish (ὑπόκιρροι) stars and is located, according to Ptol. Syntaxis 7,5 directly opposite of Antares (α Sco), which is also reddish. These two stars therefore belong to the four 'royal stars' (*stellae regales*, Firm. Mat. Mathesis 6,2). Due to its reddish colour, the constellation was assigned to the planet Mars (Ptol. Apotelesmata 1,9,3), with the later addition of Venus by Rhetorius (cf. already Manil. 4,151). The early setting of the H. in mid November announces the start of the ploughing season (Hes. Op. 614–617). Furthermore, the H. were regarded as signs of storm and rain. According to Teucer (anonymous, Anon. De stellis fixis 1,2,2), the H. promise βροχὰς ὑδραγωγούς, περιχύτας, according to Manil. (5,118, after that, Firm. Mat. Mathesis 8,6,6), they represent rebellious people and swineherds.

Hesiodus (fr. 291 MERKELBACH/WEST in schol. Arat. 172 p. 166,7 MARTIN) names the following individual H.: Phaisyle, Coronis, Cle(e)ia, Phaio, Eudore, or differently, Pherecydes in Hyg. Poet. Astr. 2,21 l.824 VIRÉ: Ambrosia, Eudora, Pedile, Coronis, Polyxo, Phyto, Thyone (in a few different versions; additional variations in [2. 2620]). Eratosthenes (Katasterismoi 14) and poets know them as daughters of → Atlas and sisters of the → Pleiades and of → Hyas (Musaeus) or as daughters of Hyas (Alexander), of Erechtheus (Euripides), of Cadmus (Myrtilus), of Lamus (Nonnus), or of Oceanus (schol. Germ.). They are regarded as nymphs and wet-nurses of young Dionysus, who was worshipped on Naxos and in Dodona as Ὕης (Hyḗs). As companions of the mature god, they were forced to throw themselves into the sea. Philochorus (fr. 31) reports that sacrifices were made to the H. and Dionysus together in Athens.

→ Pleiades

1 F. BOLL, Ant. Beobachtungen farbiger Sterne, 1916
2 W. GUNDEL, s.v. H., RE 8, 2615–2624   3 A. LE BOEUFFLE, Les noms latins d'astres et de constellations, 1977, 155–159, 207f.   4 W. HÜBNER, Grade und Gradbezirke der Tierkreiszeichen, 1995.   W.H.

Hyagnis Mythical musician from Celaenae in Phrygia, 'inventor' of the aulos, said to have introduced the Phrygian mode (harmonía) as well as nómoi of Cybele and of Pan (Aristox. fr. 78; Marmor Parium 10); named together with → Marsyas and → Olympus (Pseudo-Plut. Mus. 1132f; Anon. Bellermanni 28).
→ Musical instruments II (aulos)   F.Z.

Hyakinthia see → Hyacinthus

Hyakinthos (ὑάκινθος; hyákinthos). The name of the plant hyákinthos with its pre-Greek suffix [1. 510] denotes several flowers with clusters of crimson (blue, but also red) blossoms. Due to its natural realism, archaic Greek literature allows definite identifications: The hyákinthos growing wild in the mountains mentioned by Homer (Il. 14,348) and Sappho (105b VOIGT) is the squill, Scillabifolia L., an odourless plant of the lily family up to 20 cm tall with blue flowers that can cover large areas with intense colour on some mountain ranges in Southern Europe and Asia Minor, usually along with other geophytes such as crocuses. The 'Odyssey', however, mentions Hyacinthus orientalis L., which was described by Dioscorides (4,62 WELLMANN = 4,63 BERENDES): also with blue flowers, it grew wild originally only in Cilicia and Syria – a garden hyacinth which must have been imported to Greece early and cultivated there. In Hom. Od. 6,231 and 23,158, Odysseus' locks of hair are compared superbly with the backwardly curling perigone tips of the grape-like blossom clusters. The hyákinthos' pleasant smell is first mentioned in the Cypria (4,3 DAVIES); Theognis 537 places it on a level with the rose as a fine cultivated plant; Attic comedy was very familiar with it. Theophrastus (Hist. Pl.

6,8,1f.) distinguishes between the wild plant growing on mountains and the plant grown artificially from bulbs. The latter is found again and again in later Greek and Roman literature as a garden plant whose possession bespeaks wealth (e.g. Catull. 61,91–93; Longus 4,2,6).

In the late 4th cent. BC, we find the first connection between the flower and the hero → Hyacinthus – loved and accidentally killed by Apollo – in Palaephatus 46 (MythGr III 2, p. 68). The initial letters of his name were thought to be recognisable in the backwards curled perigone tips. Beginning with Euphorion (40 POWELL), the flower created from the blood of Ajax was named hyákinthos: On its petals, one can read the first two letters of his name, which, at the same time, represent a mournful sound (AIAI).

In antiquity, hyákinthos referred to pink-flowering gladiolus such as Gladiolus italicus Mill. (Iridaceae) as well as blue-flowering oriental knight's spur Consolida orientalis (Gay) Schröd. (synonymous with Delphinium ajacis L., Ranunculaceae) and related species, the dark veins of the petals indeed showing the letters. In later antiquity, the symbolic and mythic significance of hyákinthos gradually pushed aside the knowledge of the real plant, giving rise to an imaginary poetic plant – a botanical monster – to personify the tragic death of the two heroes (Ov. Met. 10,164–166; 206–216; cf. Plin. HN 21,66).

1 SCHWYZER, Gramm.

S. AMIGUES, H. – Fleur mythique et plantes réelles, in: REG 105, 1992, 19–36.   B.HE.

Hyampolis (Ὑάμπολις; Hyámpolis). City of eastern → Phocis, modern Bogdanou on the plateau of Kalapodi. In antiquity, it was the main access from northern Greece into the Cephisus valley (Hdt. 8,28; Paus. 10,1,11) through Thermopylae and the plains of Opus. The acropolis of H. is located on a hill where the passage leading to the plains of Exarchus joins the valley (→ Abae, distance c. 2,5 km), crossed by the road to Orchomenus. The name is derived etymologically from Hyántōn pólis (Paus. 10,35,5; Str. 9,2,3; 9,3,15); mentioned in the catalogue of ships (Hom. Il. 2,519–523). H. was strategically important due to its location at the end of a border pass (like Abae) for the control of Phocis and the passage to southern and central Greece. Thessalian rule over Phocis came to an end with the Phocian victory at Cleonae. In 480 BC, H. was pillaged by the Persians (Hdt. 8,33–35), in 395, plundered by the Boeotians, in 371 by Iason of Pherae, to be raided again in the 3rd Sacred War (Hell. Oxy. 18(13),5; Xen. Hell. 6,4,27; Diod. Sic. 16,56), in 346, destroyed by Philip II (Paus. 10,3,1–2), in 196, stormed by Flamininus (Liv. 32,18,6).

Remnants of the city wall stem from the 4th cent. BC. The remnants of a classical temple (46 × 19 m) on a hill at the edge of the plain of Kalapodi, 5 km north of H., belong to the sanctuary of Artemis Elaphebolos, the main deity of H. (Paus. 10,35,7; Plin. HN 4,27), in whose honour the Elaphebolia were celebrated (IG IX, 1, 90; cf. Plut. De mulierum virtutibus 24b, Symp. 4,1,1 660d). Votive offerings and inscriptions allow the reconstruction of the sanctuary's history up to the geometric period, revealing the different building phases from the 9th cent. into classical times [1]: extensions in 575/550 BC; building of a classical temple, which was damaged in an earthquake in 426 BC, restored towards the end of the cent. H. was still inhabited during the Imperial period and the temple still visited; Byzantine tombs are located near the temple [2].

1 R. C. S. FELSCH, H. J. KIENAST, H. SCHULER, Apollon und Artemis oder Artemis und Apollon?, in: AA 1980, 30–123   2 R. C. S. FELSCH, Kalapodi, in: AA 1987, 1–99.

P. ELLINGER, La légende nationale phocidienne, 1993; J. M. FOSSEY, The Ancient Topography of Eastern Phokis, 1986, 72–76; P. SIEWERT, Inschr. aus dem Heiligtum von H. bei Kalapodi, in: AA 1987, 681–687.   G.D.R.

Hyantes (Ὕαντες; *Hýantes*). Old, non-Greek tribe in Boeotia, expelled by the Phoenicians under Cadmus, founders of Hyas or → Hyampolis in eastern Phocis (schol. Pind. Ol. 6,148; schol. Apoll. Rhod. 3,1242; Str. 7,7,1; 9,2,3; Paus. 10,35,5).

G. HUXLEY, Aetolian H. in Phrynichus, in: GRBS 27, 1986, 235ff.   HE.KA.

Hyas (Ὕας; *Hýas*). Son of → Atlas [2] and → Aethra, killed when hunting in Libya. Several of his sisters died of grief, whereupon Zeus placed them in the sky as a constellation (→ Hyades) (Timaeus FGrH 566 F 91; Hyg. Poet. Astr. 2,21; Fab. 192; Ov. Fast. 5,170–182).

E. SIEBERT, s.v. H., LIMC 5.1, 550f.   HE.KA.

Hybadae (Ὑβάδαι; *Hybádai*). Attic *mesogeia*(?) deme of the phyle Leontis, with two (one) → *bouleutaí*. Location unknown.

E. MEYER, s.v. H., RE Suppl. 10, 327; TRAILL, Attica, 6, 18, 46, 62, 69, 110 no. 57, table 4; Id., Demos and Trittys, 1986, 131.   H.LO.

Hybanda (Ὑβάνδα; *Hybánda*). Former island in the → Icarian Sea (Plin. HN 2,91), modern Özbaşı 13.5 km south of Söke, which rises about 70 m above the → Maiandrou pedion. The Maeander [2], 1 km southeast of Özbaşı, today follows the ancient coast line. The extent of Hybandis, the *chóra* of H., is uncertain. In the east it extended to the river Hybandus (modern Kargın Çayı), which a peace agreement fixed in 185/80 BC as the boundary between Miletus [2] and Magnesia [2] [1; 2].

1 P. HERRMANN, Neue Urkunden zur Geschichte von Milet im 2. Jh. v. Chr., in: MDAI(Ist) 15, 1965, 94 with n. 66   2 Id., Inschr. von Milet (Milet 6.1), 1996, 182 f. (no. 148, l. 30).   H. LO.

Hybla (Ὕβλα; *Hýbla*).
[1] H. Megale/Heraea. (Ὕ. Μεγάλη; *H. Megálē*, Ἡραία; *Hēraía*). The existence of H. is indisputable (differing: [6]), but the location of the city near Ragusa (on Sicily) is not clearly determined. Hippocrates, the ruler of H., died during the siege by the Siculans in 491 BC (Hdt. 7,155,1). H. had three bronze coin emissions with the legend Ὕβλας Μεγάλας, their circulation was limited to a small area (around Ragusa, Modica, Vizzini). Of great importance is the list of the *theorodokoi* of Delphi, in which Ὕβλας appears after Camarina and before Hergetion. Somewhat ambiguous is Nonnus, Dion. 13,311–313. Cf. It. Ant. 89; Paus. 5,23 ('larger').

1 G. MANGANARO, Alla ricerca di poleis mikrai della Sicilia centro-orientale, in: Orbis Terrarum 2, 1996, 130 with no. 12   2 Id., Un Kerykeion perduto degli Hipanatai e la ubicazione di Hipana, in: Orbis Terrarum 3, 1997, 128 with no. 11.   3 BTCGI 14, 1996, 538ff.   4 BTCGI 8, 1990, 220f.   5 R. J. A. WILSON, Sicily under the Roman Empire, 1990   6 E. MANNI, Geografia fisica e politica della Sicilia ant. (Testimonia Siciliae antiqua 1,1), Kokalos Suppl. 4, 1981, 184–186   7 S. NICITA, Dossier Ibla, Prov. Reg. Ragusa, 1997.

[2] H. Geleatis/Gereatis. (Ὕ. Γελεᾶτις; *Hý. Geleâtis*, Thuc. 6,62,5; Γερεᾶτις; *Gereâtis*, Paus. 5,23,6: 'Settlement of the Catanaei'). City on Sicily near Poternò at Inessa-Aetna (modern Civita). The Athenians devastated H. and H. [1] in 414 BC (Thuc. 6,94,3; 63,2). According to Paus. 5,23, H. was home to a sanctuary for the goddess Hyblaea with priests who were dream interpreters (cf. FGrH 556 F 57). H. is said to have dedicated a statue of Zeus holding a sceptre at Olympia during the archaic period. Hyblaea was an Aphrodite (probably the figure with a bird on her extended hand which is depicted on the reverse of Catanian bronze coins from the 2nd cent. BC), called *Venus Victrix Hyblensis* in a votive inscription (CIL X 2,7013), worshipped in the → *pervigilium Veneris*.

R. J. A. WILSON, Sicily under the Roman Empire, 1990, 410 no. 79; BTCGI 13, 1994, 383ff.; BTCGI 8, 1990, 226f.

[3] A third city by this name never existed. Its existence was falsely deduced from Steph. Byz. s.v. Ὕ., who had contaminated various geographical and historiographical traditions by adding the epithet οἱ Μεγαρεῖς Ὑβλαῖοι κληθέντες ('the so-called Megarian Hyblaeans') after the name of the Siculan king Hyblon (Ὕβλων, Thuc. 6,4,1) in an effort to distinguish Megara in the north of Syracuse from the Greek mother town by the same name.   GI.MA.

Hybreas (Ὑβρέας; *Hybréas*). Greek orator and politician of the 1st cent. BC from Mylasa in Caria. He came from a simple background (Str. 14,2,24 = 659) but was fortunate enough to be taught by the rhetor Diotrephes in Antioch. After returning to his hometown, he acquired influence and wealth, becoming the most powerful man in Mylasa following the death of his rival

Euthydemus. He occupied the office of → *agoranomos* among others (ibid.). In the disputes following the murder of Caesar, H. was on the side of the Triumviri, but, in 41, rejected M. Antonius' [I 9] tribute demands in the role of spokesman for the cities of Asia Minor (Plut. Antonius 24,7f.). One year later, he was forced to flee from Labienus to Rhodes, but returned to Mylasa the following year in order to rebuild it (Str. 14,2,24 = 660). During his lifetime, H. achieved great fame as a rhetor (Str. 13,4,5 = 630; Jer. Chron. on the year 32 BC), which explains why several anecdotes refer to him (cf. Str. 14,2,24 = 659f.; Val. Max. 9,14). The few samples transmitted by Seneca (e.g. Controv. 1,2,23; 2,5,20; 9,1,12; 9,6,16) are models of the Asianic style (→ Asianism). Sen. Suas. 7,14 also knows H.'s son by the same name as a rhetor and advocate in the province of Asia.
M.W.

Hybrias (Ὑβρίας; *Hybrías*). At the end of a collection of scholia, Ath. 695f adds a poem by H. of Crete, which 'many consider to be a scholion' [1]. H. boasts of being the master of the public slaves (δεσπότας μνοΐας) and of earning a living as a soldier. The poem was formerly assumed to be a war song by a Doric nobleman, now is commonly regarded as the boasting of a man who comes from the class that he now rules [2]. A reference to the Persian Great King suggests the middle of the 6th cent. BC as *terminus post quem*. The two stanzas consist primarily of trochees, choriambs, and glyconics; the dialect shows Doric traces.
→ Work songs

1 PMG 909 2 D. L. PAGE, The Song of H. the Cretan, in: PCPhS 191, 1965, 62–65.
E.R.

Hybrid coins Coins on which obverse and reverse do not belong together. Hybrid coins (HC) were sometimes created by mistake, when the personnel of a mint combined the minting stamps of two different emissions (quinar, Rome, AD 261, obverse Gallienus, reverse Salonina, see [1]), other times when the stamp of a previous ruler was continued to be used by his successor (reverse of Aemilianus under Gallienus, [2]). The latter coins would constitute official HC. In times of inflation with large production of coins, HC appear quite frequently, as is evident in the antoniniani of → Gallienus that were minted during his single rule (AD 261–268). In the latter case, the reason was a lack or even a complete absence of any control over coinage.

A not insignificant part of HC are → counterfeit coins, produced with copies of original stamps or with stolen stamps.

1 GÖBL II, 141 no. 304 2 C. BRENOT, M. CHRISTOL, Un antoninianus de Gallien au revers d'Émilien, Bulletin de la Société Française de Numismatique, 1976, 84f.

GÖBL I, 55, 222; SCHRÖTTER, s.v. Zwittermünzen, 761f.
GE.S.

Hybris (ὕβρις; *hýbris*). Ethical term for a behaviour that is deliberately dishonouring, including humiliating bodily infringements such as rape (authoritative definition: Aristotle Rh. 1378 b; Latin *superbia*). Etymologically, *hybris* is probably derived from Hittite *huwap-*: 'to abuse', the noun being **huwappar* > **huppar* [1]. Positive opposites: → *aidós*, → *díkē*, → *eunomía*, → *sōphrosýnē*.
I. GENERAL II. LEGAL

I. GENERAL
In early Greek literature, *hybris* appears within the much varied terminological chain of *ólbos* – *kóros* – *hýbris* – *átē* ('wealth' – 'fullness' – 'arrogance' – 'ruin'; e.g. Aesch. Ag. 750–771). However, there is no indication that it was used appellatively in metaphorical contexts as a clear and unambiguous personification (e.g. Hes. Op. 213–218; Sol. fr. 6,3–4 IEG; Aesch. Pers. 821; Pind. Ol. 13,10; IIdt. 8,77; iconographical use beginning only in the 3rd cent. AD, in the vicinity of early Christian art [4]). There is also no evidence of a cult, an example being Cicero's (Leg. 2,11,28) misunderstanding of *líthoi hýbreōs kai anaideías* ('the stones of *hybris* and of shamelessness' describing the positions of defendants and accusers on the Areopagus).

1 O. SZEMERÉNYI, The Origins of the Greek Lexicon: ex oriente lux, in: JHS 94, 1974, 154 2 D. L. CAIRNS, Aidôs. The Psychology and Ethics of Honour and Shame in Ancient Greek Literature, 1993 3 M. L. WEST (ed.), Hesiod, Works & Days, 1978, on v. 213 4 H. A. SHAPIRO, Personifications in Greek Art. The Representation of Abstract Concepts 600–400 B.C., 1993, 41 with n. 29.

N. R. E. FISHER, H. A Study in the Values of Honour and Shame in Ancient Greece, 1992 (extensive bibliography); E. H. LOEB, s.v. H. (1), LIMC 5.1, 551–553; J. PROCOPÉ, s.v. Hochmut, RAC 15, 795–858.
T.H.

II. LEGAL
Dem. Or. 21,47 transmits a law outlining the wide range of circumstances that point to *hybris* as an offence against the state which must be prosecuted with a written complaint (→ *graphé*): 'Whoever physically offends or commits a crime against a child, a woman or a man, be they free or slaves...'. As in the → *asébeia*, it is a regulation which allowed the jury (→ *dikastérion*) much leeway in deciding on a judgement. The offender had to have violated the bodily integrity of the victim in a spirit aiming to humiliate the victim and to elevate himself, as in the case of sexual attacks. If a victim was simply hit, the victim was allowed only to prosecute on his own through the private → *aikeías díkē*. The fact that every citizen could stand up for a victim of hybris through popular complaint made the γραφὴ ὕβρεως (*graphé hýbreōs*) an effective instrument in controlling equality in Athenian society. The complaint had to be brought to the → *thesmothetai*, the estimated fine (→ *timētòs agón*) had to be paid to the state. The plaintiff thus had nothing to gain in a material sense, instead,

was forced to pay 1,000 drachmai if he dropped the complaint or if he received fewer than one fifth of the judges' votes.

A. R. W. HARRISON, The Law of Athens II, 1997; D. CO-HEN, Law, Violence and Community in Classical Athens, 1995.   G.T.

Hydarnes (Old Persian *Vidṛna*, Elamite *Miturna*, *Mitarna*). Common personal name which appears in the Persepolis tablets for several persons of different social class. Ctesias mentions *passim* marriages between Hydarnids and the royal family. Important bearers of the name are the following:
[1] H., son of Bagabigna, helper of Darius [1] [2. DB 4.84] against (Pseudo) Bardiya [2] (→ Gaumāta), who defeated the rebellious Medes in 522 BC [2. DB 2.19, 21]; according to Hdt. 3,70, he was a co-conspirator, brought into the plot by Aspathines, against (Pseudo-) → Smerdis. Ctesias' Idernes might be the only correct name in his list of Darius' seven allies (FGrH 680 F 13.16). H. was active in Media during the reign of Darius [1], probably as satrap [3. PF 1483; 4. 84]. This fact renders impossible that he acted simultaneously in Thrace, thus also the identification with H. [2] mentioned by Hdt. 6,133 [3. PF 1363, 2055].
[2] Persian, active in Thrace according to Hdt. 6,133, not identical – as is falsely stated in the literature [4. 84] – with H. [1] who, at that time, was probably acting as satrap in Media [3. PF 1363,2055].
[3] Son of H. [1]. As *stratēgós*, he received Sperthias and Bulis in Sardis; commanded the elite corps of the 10,000 'Immortals' in 480 BC, and led them on the way shown by Ephialtes at → Thermopylae (Hdt. 7,215).
[4] Father of Tissaphernes.
[5] Commander at the time of Darius III.

1 BRIANT, 607 2 R. KENT, Old Persian, 1953, 208 (on familial relationships of the Hydarnids) 3 R. T. HAL-LOCK, Persepolis Fortification Tablets, 1969 4 D. LEWIS, Sparta and Persia 1977.   A.KU. and H.S.-W.

Hydaspes (Ὑδάσπης; *Hydáspēs*; Βιδάσπης; *Bidáspēs* in Ptol.), probably from Old Indian, Old Indo-Aryan *Vitastā* (apparently through Iranian mediation); one of the main rivers of the Punjab, modern Jhelum in Pakistan – it rises in the western Himalayas and flows into the → Acesines [2]. At a place on its left shore that can no longer be identified, Alexander fought against → Porus after having traversed the river during a heavy monsoon rain. After the battle, the twin cities of → Nicaea and → Bucephala were founded (Arr. Anab. 5,9–19; 29; Diod. Sic. 17,87–89; 95; Curt. 8,13f.; 9,3). Following Alexander's return from the → Hyphasis, the river fleet was built there; the campaign then moved further downriver to the Acesines and the → Indus. The H. was so well known from the Alexander story that the name could be used in Roman literature as a synonym for all of India (e.g. Hor. Carm. 1,22,8).

K. KARTTUNEN, India and the Hellenistic World, 1997, Index s.v. H.   K.K.

Hydatius
[1] (**Ydacius**) Bishop of Emerita (Merida/Spain), died before 392. Vehement opponent of → Priscillianus, against whom he had called the synod of Saragossa in 380. H. achieved the latter's conviction, later (385) his execution by the emperor Maximus. His harshness against the Priscillianists, fuelled by personal resentments, was condemned by several bishops (→ Martinus of Tours, → Ambrosius, → Siricius) and led to his removal in 388.

Sulpicius Severus, Chronica II, 46–51, CSEL 1,99–105; Priscillianus, Liber ad Damasum, CSEL 18,34–43; A. FRANZEN, s.v. Priscillianismus, LThK² 8, 769–771; J. MARTIN, s.v. Priscillian, LThK² 8, 768–769; O. SEECK, s.v. H. (1), RE 9, 39f.

[2] Writer of a chronicle, born *c.* 394 in Limia (Xinzo de Limia/north-west Spain), in 427, bishop of (probably) Aquae Sextiae (Aix-en-Provence), died after 468. As an adolescent, he made the acquaintance of → Hieronymus on a voyage to Palestine. The *Chronica* later written by H. take up the chronicle by Jerome (broken off in 378) and continue it until 468. They are the most important source for the history of Spain in the 5th cent. The *Fasti*, compiled from several sources, present a list of consulates of Constantinople from the late 3rd cent. up to 468.

Chronica: PL 74,701–750; Fasti: MGH AA IX, 197–247; O. SEECK, s.v. H. (2), RE 9, 40–43.   RO.F.

Hydra
[1] (Ὕδρα; *Hýdra*, 'water snake'). A monster, born of the monsters → Typhon and → Echidna ('snake') and raised by → Hera out of anger at Zeus. It lives at the spring of → Amymone in the swamps of Lerna, stealing cattle and humans until it is finally killed by → Heracles (Hes. Theog. 313–318; Diod. Sic. 4,11,5f.; Apollod. 2,77–80; Hyg. Fab. 30) despite the help of a crab sent to its aid by Hera. This killing constitutes Heracles' second deed in the canonical sequence. His lion's fur protects Heracles against the H.'s poison, which he uses to make his arrows deadly. A centaur hit by Heracles flees to the Elean river Anigrus, where the poison gives the river a foul smell (Paus. 5,5,9). Beginning with its earliest image, the H. has been depicted as many-headed (Boeotian fibula *c.* 700 BC [1]). In literature, this image was first adopted by → Peisander of Rhodes, an epic writer from the mid–7th cent. (Paus. 2,37,4). However, the number of heads varies (usually there are nine, but at times as many as fifty, Verg. Aen. 6,576, or a hundred, Eur. HF 1190) and they can grow back. But → Iolaus scorches them all except for the ninth and immortal head, which he buries under a rock (visible along the road from Lerna to Elaeus, Apollod. 2,80). In the legends about stars, the H. (as the constellation H.) as well as the crab (as the constellation Cancer) are immortal-

ized as stars (Eratosth. Katasterismoi 11.13.16; Hyg. Poet. Astr. 2,23).

Beginning with orientalizing art, Heracles' fight against the H. has often been represented in the visual arts. The fight itself reveals the adoption of several Near Eastern themes – present in the story of the hero's fight against a monstrous snake as well as in the specific iconography; examples are the fight of → Ninurta against a seven-headed snake, → Baal's fight against a sea monster (Tiamat, Leviathan), and the Hittite narrative about the snake Iluyankas [2; 3]. The allegorical interpretation of the story usually refers to the draining of the Lernaean swamp by Heracles, who is a bringer of culture (Serv. Aen. 6,287) – a notion still accepted by modern research.

1 K. SCHEFOLD, Frühgriech. Sagenbilder, 1964, fig. 6a 2 J. FONTENROSE, Python. A Study of Delphic Mythology, 1959   3 M. L. WEST, The East Face of Helicon. West Asiatic Elements in Greek Poetry and Myth, 1997, 461.

G. KOKKOROU-ALEWAS, s.v. Herakles IVC, LIMC 5.1, 34–43.   F.G.

[2] Lake in the west of Aetolia, also referred to as → Conope and (as today) → Lysimachea (Str. 10,2,22; Ov. Met. 7,371–373; Antonius Liberalis 12).

C. ANTONETTI, Les Étoliens, 1990; F. BÖLTE, s.v. H., RE 9, 50–52.   D.S.

Hydraletes see → Mill

Hydraotes ('Υδραώτης/Hydraótēs in Arr., 'Υάρωτις/ Hyárōtis in Str., Hiarotis in Curt. is based on a Middle Indian form for Old Indian Airāvatī/Irāwatī, probably passed down through Iranian and following Greek ὕδωρ/hýdōr); one of the main rivers of the Punjab, modern Rāvī in Pakistan; originates in the western Himalayas, flows into the → Acesines [2] (Chenāb) and became known to the Greeks through Alexander's campaign.

E. KIESSLING, s.v. Hyarotis, RE 9, 23f.   K.K.

Hydrargyrum see → Mercury

Hydraulis see → Musical instruments

Hydrea ('Υδρέα; Hydréa). Island on the eastern coast of the Argolian Acte, rocky, not very fertile, settled already in the Mycenaean period, modern Hydra; belonged first to → Hermione, then to Troezen. References: Hdt. 3,59; Paus. 2,34,9; Steph. Byz. s.v. H.; Inscriptions: SEG 1, 79f.; 17, 172–177.

N. PHARAKLAS, Έρμιονίς, 1972.   Y.L.

Hydria (ἡ ὑδρία; hē hydría). Water jug with three handles and a narrow mouth, as it is described in the inscription of the Troilus scene on the Clitias Krater (Florence, MA). The form occurs already in Early Helladic

ceramics and on Mycenaean clay tablets from → Pylos (called ka-ti). The older rounded form was replaced in the 6th cent. BC, now in bronze and silver as well, by the elongated shoulder hydria and a bit later by the kalpis with continuous profile (→ Vessels fig. B 11–12). Very slender hydriae still existed in the 4th cent. BC and into the Hellenistic period; in the Imperial Roman period hydriae were no longer in use. Hydriae were used mainly at springs and wellhouses (→ Wells), but not at wells where the water was drawn up. Their use was even illustrated in pictures, especially on Attic hydriae. The horizontal pair of handles served to help lift the full hydria, the vertical handle helped carry the empty vessel and tilt it. Women carried them with pads, the τύλη (týlē), on their heads, men generally on their shoulders. Coarse ceramic and bronze hydriae, not the painted fine ceramics, were used to carry water daily. In keeping with the importance of water as a life-preserving and purifying element as well as for mixing with wine, the hydria took on numerous cultic functions, including ceremonial hydrophoria. Hydriae are also attested as prizes for victories, votive offerings, burial gifts, bridal gifts and as vessels for the ashes of the dead.

E. DIEHL, Die H. Formgesch. und Verwendung im Kult des Alt., 1964; E. MANAKIDOU, Athenerinnen in sf. Brunnenhausszenen, in: Hephaistos 11/12, 1992/93, 51–91; C. ROLLEY, Hydries de Bronze dans le Péloponnèse du Nord, in: BCH 87, 1963, 459–484.   I.S.

Hydromanteia see → Divination

Hydruntum

I. BRONZE AGE UNTIL IMPERIAL PERIOD   II. BYZANTINE PERIOD

I. BRONZE AGE UNTIL IMPERIAL PERIOD

A harbour town on the Iapygian coast (supposed to have been founded by Cretans, Steph. Byz. s.v. Βίεννος), c. 70 km south of → Brundisium in the area between Adriatic and Ionian Sea (Liv. 36,21,5; Plin. HN 3,100; CIL X 1795; Ps.-Scyl. 14; 27; Str. 6,3,4), where the crossing to Greece is the shortest (Plin. HN 3,100f.; cf. Cic. Att. 15,21,3; but Luc. 5,375: avius Hydrus [1]), modern Otranto. H. played an important role in the Bronze (Mycenaean finds) [2; 3] and Iron Age (settlement remains of the 9th/8th cents. BC, oldest Euboean, Corinthian, but also Albanian ceramic imports in Italy) [2; 4; 5], in the archaic period [5; 6], but especially in late antiquity and the Byzantine period (Cassiod. Var. 1,2; Procop. Vand. 1,1; Procop. Goth. 1,15) [2; 8]. It was fortified in the 4th/3rd cents. [7]. In the Imperial period the municipium was an important sea and land station of the via Appia Traiana (It. Ant. 119; 323; 329; It. Marit. 489; 497; 521; It. Burd. 609; Tab. Peut. 6f.) [1; 2; 8].

1 F. D'ANDRIA, D. MORESCHINI, s.v. Otranto, BTCGI 13, 1994, 127–142 (sources and bibliography until 1993) 2 F. D'ANDRIA, s.v. Otranto, EAA² Suppl. 2, 148–150 3 M. A. ORLANDO, L'età del Bronzo recente e finale a

Otranto, in: Studi di Antichità 4, 1983, 67–118
4 F. D'ANDRIA, Salento arcaico, 1979, 18–24   5 Id. (ed.),
Archeologia dei Messapi, 1990, 21–48   6 G. SEMERARO,
Otranto dal 6. secolo a.C. all'età ellenistica, in: Studi di
Antichità 4, 1983, 125–212   7 F. D'ANDRIA, Otranto, in:
Studi di Antichità 8,2, 1996, 189–206   8 D. MICHAE-
LIDES et al. (ed.), Excavations at Otranto, I–II, 1992.

M.L.

II. BYZANTINE PERIOD

The harbour of H. attained great importance from
the 6th cent. for the Byzantines as a landing place for
military campaigns in Italy at → Brundisium's expense.
From the 9th–11th cents. all known Byzantine expeditions passed through this bridgehead, until H. was
finally conquered by the Normans in the year 1068 and
now conversely became the starting-point for voyages
to the East (also in the Crusades). Its military importance is also attested to through the presence of a tribunus (in the year 599, Greg. Epist. 9,201; 206 NOR-
BERG) and the establishment of a duchy (ducatus) in the
8th and 9th cents., but after 876 Bari became the capital
of the → Theme of Langobardia. The diocese H. has
only been attested from 595 (Greg. M. Epist. 6,21;
9,170; 201; 11,57 NORBERG); in the 9th cent. (soon
after 876?) it became an autocephalic archdiocese, 968
the metropolis of its own church province. H. remained
one of the centres of Greek culture in southern Italy
after the departure of the Byzantines as well, a fact
which is attested by important church buildings and a
diverse culture of books and learning.

T.S. BROWN, D. KINNEY, s.v. Otranto, ODB 3, 1541;
G. CAVALLO, Libri greci e resistenza etnica in Terra
d'Otranto, in: G. CAVALLO (ed.), Libri e lettori nel mondo
bizantino. Guida storica e critica, 1982, 155–178, 223–
227; N. KAMP, s.v. Otranto, LMA 6, 1592 (bibliography
before 1993); S. PALESE, s.v. Otranto, LThK³ 7, 1217;
J. WEISS, s.v. H., RE 9, 87.

E.W.

Hydrussa (Ὑδροῦσσα/*Hydroûssa*; also Ὑδρόεσσα/
Hydróessa, Ὑδροῦσα/*Hydroûsa*, Ὕδρουσα/*Hýdrousa*;
'rich in water'). The name of numerous islands, the one
in Attica was off the coast of → Aexone according to
Str. 9,1,21. However, the name does not fit any of the
rocky islands off the western coast of Attica.

L. BÜRCHNER, s.v. H., RE 9, 79; W. KOLBE, s.v. H., RE 9,
87.

H.LO.

Hyena (ὕαινα; *hýaina*, from ὗς/*hýs*, 'pig'). First mention in Hdt. 4,192; γλάνος/*glános* (Aristot. Hist. an.
7(8),594a 31); κ(ο)ροκόττας/*k(o)rokóttas*, first in Ctesias fragment 87 M. and Agatharchides, Periplus maris
rubri 39. Latin *hyaena* and *c(o)rocotta(s)* in Plin. HN
8,72 and 107; post-Classical *belua* (*belva*) (S HA Gord.
33,1). It was probably not just the more common
striped hyena (*Hyaena striata* in the Middle East and
Africa) that was known but according to Opp. Kyn.
3,288 (Περὶ στικτῆσιν ὑαίναις) also the spotted hyena
(*Hyaena Crocuta crocuta* in Africa). It was erroneously

considered to be the product of a cross between a male
wolf and a female dog or a male dog and a female wolf
(Plin. ibid.; Ctesias ibid.; Diod. Sic. 3,35,10). The appearance of the hyena is described by Aristotle, who
probably saw it himself (Hist. an. 6,32,579b 15–29;
7(8),5,594a 31–b 5), and by Pliny (HN 8,105f.): it has
the coloration and size of a wolf, and a horse-like mane
which is however thicker, harder and runs over the entire backbone – and which with its rigidity (Plin. HN
8,105) prevents the turning of the neck (Plin. ibid.) – as
well as eyes with many variations of colour and expression.

Ancient literature mentions numerous strange notions. Aristotle (Hist. an. 6,32,579b 16–29; Gen. An.
3,6,757a 2–13) and Diodorus (32,12,2) already counter the widespread superstition that the hyena was her-
maphroditic and changed its sex every year (still in Ov.
Met. 15,409f.; Ael. NA 1,25; Physiologos 24) with the
argument of an anatomical distinctive feature; female
animals could in addition seldom be captured and
examined more closely. The hyena was said to be the
only animal that even dug up dead bodies. Their teeth
could break any bone (Diod. Sic. 3,35,10). Additional
oddities: it was said to imitate the vomiting of a human
being (to lure dogs) as well as calling out people's names
(Diod. Sic. 3,35 with doubts about it; Plin. HN 8,105;
Ael. NA 7,22) and it causes other animals to stay trans-
fixed by touching them with a paw or with its shadow
(Plin. HN 8,106; Ael. NA 6,14; Gp. 15,1,12; variant:
ibid. 15,1,10) or silences the dogs pursuing it. All these
motifs were passed down to the Middle Ages particularly by Pliny and Solinus 27,23–26 (cf. Thomas of Cantimpré 4,53 [1. 138f.]).

The body parts of the hyena were frequently used for
magical and organotherapeutic purposes (Plin. HN
28,92–106), for instance the skin for headache or the
teeth for toothache. Reclothing the sowing vessel with a
hyena pelt was thought to cause the grain to go up (Co
lumella 2,9,9 = Pall. Agric. 10,3,1) and, carried around
the land, to prevent hail damage (ibid. 1,35,14). Its top
cervical vertebra (the atlas) supposedly led to reconciliation between disputing parties (Luc. 6,672; Plin.
HN 28,99). The precious stone *hyaenia*, taken from its
eyes, was said to predict the future (Plin. HN 37,168;
Isid. Orig. 16,15,25) when laid under the tongue of a
human being. As a dream image, the hyena announce
sexually abnormal beings.

Hyenas were actually presented to the Romans for
the first time under the Roman emperors Antoninus
Pius (S HA Antoninus Pius 3,10,9), Alexander Severus
(Cass. Dio 77,1,3) and Philippus (S HA Gord. 33,1),
here with 10 specimens from the menagerie of Gordianus III. On mosaics the hyena is seldom depicted, e.g. on
one from Praeneste [2] and the striped hyena on the
so-called Worcester Hunt from Antioch on the Orontes
[3. 364, fig. 151 according to 4. 382].

1 H. BOESE (ed.), Thomas Cantimpratensis, Liber de
natura rerum, 1973   2 H. BESIG, s.v. H., RE Suppl. 8,
1248f.   3 D. LEVI, Antioch Mosaic Pavements I, 1947
4 TOYNBEE.

C.HÜ.

Hyettus ('Υηττός; *Hyēttós*). A city in Boeotia north of the Copais, northeast of Orchomenus, east of modern Loutsi; localized by inscriptions for Septimius Severus and Caracalla (IG VII 2833f.). Settled at least from the archaic to the Byzantine periods, bishop's seat in the 5th and 6th cents. AD. Numerous remains, rich epigraphical material (IG VII and [1]). Member of the Boeotian League, provided two Boeotarchs in the 5th/4th cents. BC together with Orchomenus (Hell. Oxy. 19,3,390: 'Υσιαῖοι/ *Hysiaîoi*). Hercules sanctuary with healing cult (Paus. 9,24,3; 36,6f.; [2. 2f.]). Traces of iron ore mining.

1 R. ETIENNE, D. KNOEPFLER, Hyettos de Béotie et la chronologie des archontes fédéraux entre 250 et 171 avant J.-C., 1976   2 SCHACHTER 2.

O. DAVIES, Roman Mines in Europe, 1935, 246; FOSSEY, 257–261; LAUFFER, Griechenland, s.v. H.; N. D. PAPACHATZIS, Παυσανίου Ἑλλάδος περιήγησις 5, ²1981, 163–166.
M.FE.

Hygiaeon ('Υγιαίων; *Hygiaíōn*). Ruler of the Kingdom of the Bosporus (→ Regnum Bosporanum), c. 220–200 BC. Successor of → Leucon II, but not as king, rather as *árchōn*, also portrayed without a royal diadem. Maybe not a Spartocid. On brick stamps and coins ἄρχοντος 'Υγιαίοντος.

V. F. GAIDUKEVIČ, Das Bosporan. Reich, 1971, 93, 95.
I.v.B.

Hygieia ('Υγίεια; *Hygíeia*). Personification of health and one of the daughters of → Asclepius and → Epione (along with → Aceso, Iaso and Panacea); she has no independent mythology. While her sisters incorporate various forms of healing in their names (Greek *iáomai*, *akéomai*), H. is the personification of 'health' itself. As such, by the late 5th cent. BC she began to displace the rest of her family, at least in cultic significance (Aristid. 38,22). In cult worship, she is usually the only one invoked together with Asclepius and may also receive dedications for cures on her own. H. is represented on votive reliefs as the sole female companion of Asclepius. Later tradition even makes her his wife (Orph. H. 67). The oldest representation is a group with H. and Asclepius in Olympia dedicated by Micythus of Rhegium (before 450 BC, Paus. 5,26,2). H. had a notable cult in Titane, where she was worshipped in an Asclepeum founded by → Machaon's son Alexanor and offered sacrifices of hair that completely covered her image. The age of the cult is unclear, but the statue of Asclepius is archaic (Paus. 2,11,6). On the Athenian Acropolis, the image of H. stood next to that of Athena H. The cult of the latter is documented in inscriptions from the late 6th cent. BC, and is thus clearly older than the cult of Asclepius (and with it, of H.), which was introduced in 421/20 BC. Later authors link the statue of Athena H., but not the introduction of the cult, with → Pericles (Plut. Pericles 13). Next to personification, H. as epiclesis of Athena represents an alternative (and older) form of entrusting a divinity with the protection of health.

H. SOBEL, H. Die Göttin der Gesundheit, 1990; F. CROISSANT, s.v. H., LIMC 5, 554–572; H. A. SHAPIRO, Personifications in Greek Art, 1993, 125–131.
F.G.

Hygiene, personal
A. GENERAL B. HEAD C. BODY D. LOWER BODY

A. GENERAL
In antiquity clean and regularly changed → clothes were part of physical well-being, as were washing or bathing followed by anointing the body with regular or perfumed olive oil and other fragrant oils (→ Cosmetics), the latter being also used out of health reasons. Peoples or people who were dirty or unkempt were bound to be disagreeable to the Greek and Roman sense of cleanliness (Hor. Sat. 1,2,27; 1,4,92), as well as those who used unusual or strange methods of washing, for example the Celtiberians, who supposedly cleaned their bodies and teeth with urine (Diod. Sic. 5,33,5; Catull. 37,20 and 39,17–21).

B. HEAD
Washing and anointing one's hair (cf. Hom. Od. 15,331f.; Archil. fr. 26 D) was popular and done often; some vase-paintings show women kneeling while water is poured over their hair from a hydria (for instance the pelike, Athens, NM 1472 [1. pl. 38,1]). Dental hygiene was considered to be appropriate to maintain the teeth and for good breath. Someone with black or dirty teeth was considered to be 'repulsive' (cf. Theophr. Char. 19); the Romans cleaned their teeth every morning and used, among other things, pulverised pumice to do this (Plin. HN 36,156). Preparations for dental hygiene (*dentifricia*) were available in various compositions (Plin. HN 28,178–194); the doctor Pythicus of the 1st cent. AD wrote a book about the production of these powders. Lozenges were sucked to improve one's breath (Hor. Sat. 1,2,27; 1,4,92, Plin. HN 33,93, cf. Mart. 1,87), according to Plin. HN 28,190 butter also took away bad breath. There were toothpicks (*dentiscalpium*) made of mastic wood. Ears were either washed or people used special ear scoops. Toothpicks and ear scoops (*auriscalpium*, Mart. 14,23) made of valuable materials are extant mainly from the Imperial period [2].

C. BODY
For those who did not avail themselves of the public bathing facilities (→ Thermal baths, → Baths), there was – as attested by Attic and lower Italian vase pictures – the well house for cleaning the body, or the hip-high *louterion* (→ Labrum); occasionally people also stepped into a large vessel in order to wash. Along with that they also used bathing facilities in the home. Homer (Od. 3,468 *et passim*: *asáminthos*) already mentions

bathtubs. One could bathe sitting down or had water poured over one's body (cf. H. Hom. Demeter 50); sponges were used to clean the body (first mention of the bathing sponge: Hom. Il. 18,414) or to mop up the water. The water was enriched with purifying bicarbonate of soda, soda or the like. Representations of an adult male sitting in a bathtub are not all too common (e.g. [3. pl. 1,1; 3,8; 4,10 and 11]). Olive oil was mostly used to keep the skin soft and supple (cf. Hes. Op. 515–519). The refined tastes of the Roman Imperial period led to unbelievable methods, of which bathing in donkey's milk (Plin. HN 28,183) is the best-known (more at e.g. Plin. HN 28,183–188). Pumice or moist bread dough, which was left on the face overnight and washed off with donkey's milk in the morning, was used on wrinkles, marks or calluses (Juv. 6,461). There were even preparations available for freckles.

D. LOWER BODY

After relieving oneself one used a sponge (Aristoph. Ran. 480–490, cf. Aristoph. Ach. 846; in Mart. 12,48 it is fastened to a staff and hung in the latrine, cf. Sen. Ep. 70,20) or a rag; using a stone or garlic (e.g. bowl, Boston, MFA, Inv. 08.31b, [4. pl. 11,2]; Aristoph. Plut. 816f.) was also possible. Legs and feet were washed over a *podaniptér*, Latin *pelvis* (Pl. Symp. 17a; Plut. Phocion 20; Hdt. 2,172f.), where one could also wash the hair and hands (Ath. 9,409e). In distinguished homes slaves cleaned their masters' feet (cf. Hom. Od. 19,343ff.). This included trimming the toenails at the start of a symposium (Petron. Sat. 31,2f.); otherwise one could have finger- and toenails trimmed and cleaned by the → barber or in the baths by the house personnel.

→ Comb; → Cosmetics; → Perirrhanterion; → Pins; → Razor; → Soap; → Sponge; → Thermal baths

1 K. SCHEFOLD, Unt. zu den Kertscher Vasen, 1934 2 M. MARTIN, in: A. KAUFMANN-HEINIMANN, H. A. CAHN, Der spätröm. Silberschatz von Kaiseraugst, 1984, 122–132 3 R. GINOUVÈS, Balaneutikè. Recherches sur le bain dans l'antiquité grecque, 1962 4 E. VERMEULE, Some Erotica in Boston, in: AK 12, 1969.

S. LASER, Medizin und Körperpflege (ArchHom 3,2=S), 1983, 135–188; M. MARTIN, Röm. und frühma. Zahnstocher, in: Germania 54, 1976, 456–460; E. RIHA et al., Röm. Toilettgerät und medizinische Instrumente aus Augst und Kaiseraugst (Forsch. in Augst 6), 1986; R. NEUDECKER, Die Pracht der Latrine, 1994; M. VALLERIN, Pelvis estamillés de Bassit, in: Syria 71, 1994, 171ff.; G. WÖHRLE, K. und körperliche Sauberkeit als Merkmale sozialer Differenziertheit in den homer. Epen, in: Gymnasium 103, 1996, 151–165.   R.H.

Hyginus, C. Iulius

I. LIFE AND WORK II. HYGINUS AS AGRARIAN WRITER

I. LIFE AND WORK

a) A philologist and polymath of the Augustan era from Spain or Alexandria; a freedman of Augustus who served as the prefect of the Palatine library after 28 BC while simultaneously engaging in extensive teaching activities (for biography, cf. Suet. Gram. 20). Nevertheless, he had to be supported his whole life by Clodius [II 6] Licinus and died in poverty. Ov. Tr. 3,14 is addressed to him. His substantial œuvre includes works of philology (comm. to the *Propempticon Pollionis* of → Helvius [I 3] Cinna; discussion of selected passages of → Vergilius, cf. [5. 51–67]), history (Exempla, cf. [9. 63ff.]; *De familiis Troianis*, cf. [6]; on Italian cities; *De proprietatibus deorum; De dis penatibus*) and agriculture (*De agricultura; De apibus*). Numerous fragments have survived. Of his collection of political biographies, *De viris illustribus*, which contained 9 vols. of 21 *vitae* each, the book *De excellentibus ducibus exterarum gentium* has been preserved. Handed down anonymously, it is today attributed predominantly to Cornelius → Nepos (cf. [7. 1645ff.]). This important early Augustan historical source was largely displaced by → Livy. On its further influence (eulogies of the Forum of Augustus; → Valerius Maximus; → Ampelius, HLL § 530; the *Viri illustres* of late antiquity, HLL § 532.3) cf. [7. 1636ff., 1647ff. and stemma 1654; 8. 1,52ff.; 2,9ff.]. On the exempla in Valerius Maximus as well as in Frontinus, see [9].

b) Probably by the same author [10. xxxiff.] is a handbook of astronomy and mythology in 4 vols. (vols. 1 and 4: astronomical explanations; vols. 2 and 3: legends and catalogues of the stars). An introduction to → Aratus by → Eratosthenes served as the source [2]. Numerous manuscripts (including illustrated ones) from the 9th cent. onwards demonstrate the popularity of the text in the Middle Ages.

c) Based on this attribution, (cf. Hyg. Poet. Astr. 2,12: *De quo in primo libro Genealogiarum scripsimus*) another mythological handbook may be reunited with its original author and title: the *Genealogiae* (*Fabulae* in later sources). It comprises a) genealogical trees of gods and heroes and b) 277 short narratives and lists with mythological content, which predominate after no. 221. Roman influence played only a very small role in the adaptation of the Greek mythographical sources. However, in the wake of numerous revisions and interpolations, the original form of the surviving Latin text is not always ascertainable. Some portions of the Greek version of the *Hygini Genealogia* in CGL 3,56–69 [18. 172ff.] may be attributed to the text of the MS (*c.* AD 900) on which the first edition [17] is based. Only fragments from this MS have been discovered.

FOR A)
FRAGMENTS: 1 GRF 525–537   2 HRR 2, p. 72–77
3 R. REITZENSTEIN, De scriptoribus rei rusticae librorum

deperditis, 1884, 18ff.; 53f.

BIBLIOGRAPHY: 4 P.V.D. WOESTIJNE, Hyginiana, 1930
5 S.TIMPANARO, Per la storia della filologia virgiliana
antica, 1986, 51–67   6 P.TOOHEY, Varro, H. and
Horace, in: Arethusa 17, 1984, 5–28   7 P.L. SCHMIDT,
s.v. H., RE Suppl. 15, 1978, 1644–1659   8 J.FUGMANN,
Königszeit und Frühe Rep. in der Schrift De viris illustribus, 2 vols., 1990/1997   9 A.KLOTZ, Stud. zu Valerius
Maximus, 1942.

FOR b)

EDITIONS: 10 A.BOEUFFLE, 1983 (with French transl.)
11 G.VIRÉ, 1992.

BIBLIOGRAPHY: 12 M.CHIABÒ, L.ROBERTI, Index verborum, 1990   13 W.HÜBNER, Nachlese zu H., in:
Hermes 113, 1985, 208–224   14 G.VIRÉ, La transmission du De astronomia, in: Revue de l'histoire du texte 11,
1981, 159–276   15 Id., Informatique et classement des
manuscrits. Essai méthodologique sur le De astronomia
d'H., 1986   16 Id., Le texte du De astronomia, in:
Latomus 51, 1992, 843–856.

FOR c)

EDITIONS: 17 J.MICYLLUS, 1535   18 H.I. ROSE, ²1963
19 P.K. MARSHALL, 1993 (with bibliography)   20 J.-
Y. BORIAUD, H. Mythographus, 1997.

BIBLIOGRAPHY: 21 H.MATAKIEWICZ, De Hygino
mythographo, in: Eos 34, 1932/33, 93–110
22 J.SCHWARTZ, Ps.-Hesiodeia, 1960, 297–314
23 C.DESMEDT, Fabulae Hygini, in: RBPh 48, 1970, 26–
35 and Bollettino di Studi Latini 3, 1973, 26–34   24 A.B.
BREEN, The 'Fabulae Hygini' reappraised, 1991.   P.L.S.

II. HYGINUS AS AGRARIAN WRITER

H. was highly regarded as an → agrarian writer, as is
made clear by his inclusion in the list of earlier agro-
nomists in → Columella (Columella 1,1,13). Pliny cites
him as a source for books 10–21 of the Naturalis Historia. Columella, who often refers to H. by name, describes him as a paedagogus of agriculture and praises him
as an author together with Virgil and → Celsus [7] (Columella 9,2,1). As the citations in Columella and Pliny
demonstrate, H. addressed all the branches of agriculture (Columella 3,11,8: soil quality in viticulture; Columella 11,2,83: keeping of oxen; Columella 11,3,62:
cultivation of root vegetables; Plin. HN 13,134: clover;
Plin. HN 16,230: wooden tools; Plin. HN 18,232:
wine). The book on → apiculture (Liber de apibus,
Columella 9,13,8) was particularly famous. Columella
follows it in many aspects of his own account. H., who
analyzed the writings of other authors extensively (Columella 9,2,1; 9,13,8 on Aristomachus), devoted
lengthy passages to the mythical origins of apiculture.
This was criticized by Columella on the grounds that
such portrayals were of little use to the farmer (Columella 9,2,2–5). His description of bee-keeping seems to
have been characterized by the precision of the instructions (Columella 9,14,1; 9,14,18).

1 W.RICHTER (ed.), L. Iunius Columella, Zwölf Bücher
über Landwirtschaft, vol. 3, 1983, 586; 619.   H.SCHN.

Hykkara (Ὕκκαρα; Hýkkara). Sicanian town in the
northwest of → Sicily; a few remains near the sea north
of modern Carini (compare the two place names), west
of Palermo. H. was conquered in 415 BC by the Athenians who were allied to Segesta [1] and its inhabitants
were enslaved (→ Peloponnesian War D.). The hetaera
Lais [2] was among the captives (Plut. Alcibiades 39;
Ath. 13,588c).   GI. MA.

E. O.

Hyksos (Egyptian Ḥqꜣ.w-ḫꜣs.wt, 'Rulers of foreign
lands'; Greek Ὑκσώς/Hyksós) Rulers of foreign peoples
are sporadically named H. from the late Old Kingdom
onwards: the Turin Royal Canon assigns this term to a
dynasty of six kings of foreign origin (15th Dynasty, c.
1650–1540 BC) in the 2nd intermediate period, whose
first representatives bore this title themselves before
fully adopting the Egyptian royal titulature later on.
Josephus (Ap. 1,14,82ff.), based on → Manetho, incorrectly applies the term, and with an inexact etymology,
to the people from whom these kings were descended.
Against the background of an (archaeologically provable) prolonged Canaanite infiltration in the eastern
Delta beginning in the 13th Dynasty, a line of Asiatic
invaders succeeded in forcibly seizing power in Egypt
(according to Manetho, and quite plausibly) during a
period of dynastic weakness after the Middle Kingdom.
Starting from their capital Avaris (Tall aḍ-Ḍabʿa) in the
eastern Delta, the H. succeeded in building a significant
kingdom, which in the north probably covered southern Canaan and in the south included, at least temporarily, the south of Upper Egypt as far as al-Ǧabalain.
The ethnic background of the H. continues to be a subject of controversy; in opposition to HELCK's [1. 95]
thesis of a → Hurrian origin, a west Semitic origin is
predominantly accepted today. Archaeologically, the
carriers of the H. rule can be assigned to the Syro-Pale-
stinian Middle Bronze II culture. Their progressive adaptation to Egyptian culture is evident, the usurpation
of older monuments by the H. is widespread. Under the
penultimate H. king, Apophis, members of the native
17th Dynasty, who had been able to hold out in southern Upper Egypt, took up the battle against the foreign
rule, which ended with the victory of Ahmose and the
founding of the New Kingdom (about 1540 BC). The
period of H. rule left deep marks on the Egyptian cultural inventory – for example, the introduction of the
horse, war chariot and scimitar – but above all in the
political consciousness of Egypt, as it is expressed in
political-ideological texts.

→ Egypt

1 M.BIETAK, s.v. H., LÄ 3, 93–103   2 Id., Avaris. The
Capital of the H., 1996   3 K.S.B. RYHOLT, The Political
Situation in Egypt During the Second Intermediate Period,
1997, 118–150.   S.S.

Hylaea (Ὑλαία; Hylaía). Forested area, east of the
Borysthenes (Hdt. 4,17; 19; Ps.-Scymn. 844f.) between
the Kinburn peninsula and Skadovska in the steppes of

the lower Dniester, belonging to → Olbia. In the archaic and classical eras, it was significant for → Scythians and Greek colonists. The Scythian name for H. was Abika (Steph. Byz. s.v. Ὑ.). H. played a large role in Scythian mythology (cf. Hdt. 4,9; 76). A large production and trade centre with docks, probably from the 6th/5th cents. BC, has been discovered (Jagorlyckoe poselenie).

J. G. VINOGRADOV, Olbia, 1981, 14–18.   I.v.B.

Hylaeus (Ὑλαῖος/*Hylaîos*, 'Man of the woods'). → Centaur, depicted in battle against the Lapiths (Verg. G. 2,457) on the François Vase (6th cent. BC); slain by Theseus (Serv. Aen. 8,294), Hercules (Hor. Carm. 2,12,6) or → Atalante (Apollod. 3,106; Callim. H. 3,221), whom he pursued together with Rhoeicus.
RE.ZI.

Hylas (Ὕλας; *Hýlas*). Son of → Theiodamas (Apollod. 1,117; Apoll. Rhod. 1,1212f.) and Menodice (Hyg. Fab. 14,11); local hero of → Cius. In a quarrel over food (for his son: Callim. Fr. 24), → Heracles kills Theiodamas (Apollod. 2,153; Apoll. Rhod. 1,1212–1219, where Heracles seeks a pretext for war against the Dryopians).

Furthermore, according to Apollod. 1,117; Apoll. Rhod. 1,1153–1283, Heracles takes H. with him as his lover on the journey of the → Argonauts. In Mysia, H. is kidnapped by nymphs while fetching water (transformed into an echo, Nicander fr. 48; Antoninus Liberalis 26); during the search by Heracles and → Polyphemus, who had heard H. scream, the Argonauts depart on the same evening, without noticing their absence. Hercules uses hostages to oblige the Mysians to search for H.

Depending on Apollodorus and Apollonius Rhodius (omitting Polyphemus): Theoc. 13 [1. 177f.], Prop. 1,20 (where → Calais and Zetes chase H. with kisses), as well as Val. Fl. 3,481ff. (3,182ff. *aristeia* of H.), where Juno carries out an attack on H., the Argonauts only depart after six days of deliberation and H. appears to Heracles in a dream at Jupiter's instigation [2. 47ff.]. Proponents of a rationalistic interpretation have H. fall from the ship or into the spring and drown [3. 112].

The H. myth forms the *aition* for a local ritual practice, related to that of the Mariandynian vegetation demon → Bormus [3. 113f.; 4. 429f.; 5. 35f.; 6. 58f., 218]: The natives sacrifice to H. at the spring and roam through the woods, while the priest calls H. three times and the echo answers (Str. 12,4,3). For this reason, Ὕλαν κραυγάζειν (*Hýlan kraugázein*) is proverbial for a futile search [3. 113]. H. in art: [3. 113; 7].

1 U. v. WILAMOWITZ-MOELLENDORFF, Die Textgesch. der griech. Bukoliker, 1905   2 J. ADAMIETZ, Zur Komposition der Argonautica des Valerius Flaccus, 1976   3 E. SITTIG, s.v. H. (1), RE 9, 110–115   4 NILSSON, Feste   5 P. KRETSCHMER, Mythische Namen, in: Glotta 14, 1925, 33–36   6 M. ALEXIOU, The Ritual Element in Greek Tradition, 1974   7 J. OAKLEY, s.v. H., LIMC 5.1, 574–579.   P.D.

Hyle (Ὕλη; *Hýlē*).
[1] Place in Boeotia (Hom. Il. 2,500; cf. Str. 9,2,26; Steph. Byz. s.v.). According to Hom. Il. 5,707ff. (with Paus. 9,38,7; Str. 9,2,27), H. is on the Copais, according to Str. 9,2,20, on the → Hylice (see also Stat. Theb. 7,267f.). Attempts by WALLACE and KNAUSS [3. 82f.; 2. 243–278] to identify it with one of the prehistoric settlement locations between the former Copais and the modern Hylike equate H. with the prehistoric settlement remains in the city area of Akraiphia, while FOSSEY [1. 225–229, 235–243] looks for H. between the modern lakes Paralimni and Hylike near Oungra (with a successor settlement farther south near Klimatariai).

1 FOSSEY   2 J. KNAUSS, Die Melioration des Kopaisbekkens durch die Minyer im 2. Jt. v.Chr., 1987   3 P. W. WALLACE, Strabo's Description of Boiotia, 1979.   P.F.

[2] Term in natural philosophy, see → Matter

Hylice (Ὑλικὴ λίμνη; *Hylikḕ límnē*). Boeotian lake west of the Copais, north of Thebes (Str. 9,2,20). Probably the lake formerly called Likeri, and H. again today [2. 494f.; 3. 81f.]. Referring to Nicander (Theriaka 887ff.), FOSSEY [1. 225–229] identifies H. with the more northerly modern Lake Paralimni, usually equated with the ancient Trephia.

1 FOSSEY   2 PHILIPPSON/KIRSTEN 1,2   3 P. W. WALLACE, Strabo's Description of Boiotia, 1979.   P.F.

Hylli (Ὕλλοι; *Hýlloi*). Illyrian tribe, first mentioned in the 4th cent. BC among the *bárbaroi* (Scyl. 22); other spellings *Hylleîs* (Steph. Byz. s.v. Ὑλλεῖς) and *Hyllaîoi* (Ὑλλαῖοι, Ptol. 2,16,5). Their settlement area has been located approximately between the rivers Titius (modern Krka) and Nestus (modern Cetina). Like other smaller Illyrian tribes, the H. were absorbed by the → Dalmatae after the 4th cent. BC, so that, in the Roman period, only the designation of the coast south of Šibenik as the peninsula *Hyllica/Hyllis* (Plin. HN 3,141; Scymn. 405) recalled the H. A connection between the Illyrian H. and the Doric phyle Hylleis cannot be proven [1].

1 G. NEUMANN, s.v. H., KlP 2, 1266.

M. FLUSS, s.v. H., RE Suppl. 6, 115–117; J. WILKES, The Illyrians, 1992.   D.S.

Hyllus (Ὕλλος; *Hýllos*).
[1] Son of → Heracles and → Deianira; brother of Macaria. Ctesippus, Glenos and Oneites (Hes. fr. 25,19 M-W; Apollod. 2,165 WAGNER) or Gleneus and Odites (Diod. Sic. 4,37,1) have been named as his brothers and Euaichme (Hes. fr. 251b M-W) as his daughter. Heracles asks him to burn his body on a pyre on Mount Oeta and to marry Iole (Soph. Trach. 1179–1258; (Ps.-)Sen. Hercules Oetaeus 1481–1491). After his father's death, he and the other Heraclidae flee from → Eurystheus –

first to Ceyx, the king of Trachis (Apollod. 2,167 WAG-NER), and then to Athens, led by Iolaus and accompanied by the aged Alcmene (Eur. Heracl. 1–47). There, they are taken in by Theseus (Paus. 1,32,6; Diod. Sic. 4,57,6) or his son Demophon (Eur. Heracl. 115–122; Antoninus Liberalis 33 = Pherecydes FGrH 3 F 84). The Athenians defend the Heraclidae in a battle against Eurystheus, during which the latter is killed on the Scironian Rock (by H.'s own hand: Apollod. 2,168 WAGNER; by Iolaus: Paus. 1,44,10; captured by Iolaus and executed later on Alcmene's command: Eur. Heracl. 859–863 and 928–1052). To ensure the successful outcome of the battle, → Macaria had to willingly sacrifice her life (Eur. Heracl. 408–601; Paus. 1,32,6). The Heraclidae then invade the Peloponnese, but have to withdraw soon after (Apollod. 2,169–170 WAGNER).

An oracle prophesies successful reconquest 'after the third fruit' (τὸν τρίτον καρπόν), which H. interprets as 'three years'. Victory is decided at the Isthmus by means of a duel between H. and the Tegean king, Echemus (Hdt. 9,26; Diod. Sic. 4,58,1–5), during which H. dies. The subsequent fifty- or hundred-year-long truce is broken by the Heraclidae. However, it is not until the third generation that they achieve victory, under Aristodemus, the great-grandson of H. (Hdt. 6,52), for that is in fact what 'after the third fruit' meant (Apollod. 2,172 WAGNER).

H. is the eponym of the Spartan Hyllaeans; his adoption by the Spartan king Aegimius (Str. 9,4,10) points to this interpretation. H.'s grave was shown at Megara. A heroon was located in Athens, near the Olympeum (Paus. 1,41,2).
→ Heraclidae

M. SCHMIDT, s.v. H., LIMC 5.1, 579–582.

[2] Son of → Heracles and the Corcyraean Naiad Melite; eponym of the Illyrian Hyllaeans. According to Apoll. Rhod. 4,522–551, he leaves Corcyra, which is ruled by Nausithous, and settles with his companions on the north-east coast of the Adriatic. Here, he is killed by the Mentores, a people located between the Liburnians and the Hylleans. JO.S.

[3] A gem-cutter of the Roman Imperial period, son of → Dioscorides [8]. Corresponding signatures exist on carnelian intaglios: with barbarian head (Florence, MA), classical head of Apollo (St. Petersburg, HR), frontal, comic mask (fr., Paris, CM), Triton and Nereid (Boston, MFA), and striding lion (Nicosia, Arch. Mus.); as well as on chalcedony: with sculptural image of Theseus (lost) and decorated sacrificial animal (Paris, CM). His signature on the sardonyx cameo with satyr (Berlin, SM) demonstrates that H. explored this technique as well. Further, the Divus Augustus cameo in Cologne has also been attributed to him [1. 31ff. n. 221 pl. 10, 58–61].
→ Gem cutting

1 E. ZWIERLEIN-DIEHL, Der Divus-Augustus-Kameo in Köln, in: Kölner Jb. für Vor- und Frühgesch. 17, 1980, 12–53.

O. NEVEROV, Master H. and the Sculptures on the Apollo Temple on the Palatine, in: Soobščenija Gosudarstvennogo ordena Lenina Ermituža 36, 1973, 43–47; ZAZOFF, AG, 317f. n. 71ff., pl. 92,4–93,2. S.MI.

[4] Northern tributary of the → Hermus in Lydia, modern Kum Çayı ('sand river'); its estuary region is located north-east of → Magnesia on the Sipylus. In antiquity, the river was rich in fish. Later, it was called *Phrygius* (Str. 13,4,5; *Phryx*, in Plin. HN 5,119). It is cited by that name, together with the Hermus, as the route taken by Roman troops before the battle of Magnesia in 190 BC (Liv. 37,37,9f.; App. Syr. 30). Another river H. (modern Demirci Çayı), stemming like the latter from the Temnus (modern Simav Dağları), flows into the Hermus north-east of Sardes. Here, where the plain is rich in water (Hdt. 1,80), Croesus was defeated by Cyrus in 547 BC and forced back to Sardes. The landscape north-east of Salihli has been significantly altered by the Demirköprü Dam.

K. BURESCH, Aus Lydien, 1898, map; W. M. CALDER, G. E. BEAN, A Classical map of Asia Minor, 1958; MAGIE 2, 783f. H.KA.

Hymenaeus (Ὑμέναιος; *Hyménaios*). God of marriage ceremonies or a wedding song (Sappho: ὑμήναος; *hyménaos*, Callimachus: ὑμήναιος; *hyménaios*).
[1] Greek god of weddings whose name derives from the Greek word for wedding hymn, *hyménaios*. The etymology is unclear. H. is a relatively late creation: he first appears as a personification of the wedding hymn in Pindar (fr. 128c) and Euripides (Tro. 310; 314). In the innovative choral lyrics of the 4th cent. BC, he appears to have been a favoured motif [1. 56]. Nonetheless, he is not cited as a legitimate wedding god before Catullus (61) and Seneca (Med. 67). A graffito in Dura Europus even names Hymenaioi in the plural, analogously to the Muses, Satyrs, and other groupings (SEG 17,772).

The various genealogies testify to the background of the wedding hymn: H. is usually represented as the son of a Muse, but can also be the son of the musician Apollo or of → Magnes [1. 55; 2. 583]. Interestingly, he also appears as the son of the god → Dionysus (Sen. Med. 110; Serv. Aen. 4,127), who also takes on the epithet *hymenéios* in the *Anthologia Palatina* (9,524,21). Indeed, in later representations, H. is given Dionysian traits [3]. The origin of this genealogy is clearly attributable to the cheerful sphere of the Dionysian world. There is no known cult of H., and his mythology is limited to a few details.

Serv. Aen. 4,99 tells how one day an Athenian named H. and a group of maidens on their way to Eleusis are captured by pirates. H., who is nearly indistinguishable from the girls due to his beauty, kills the pirates and marries one of the girls, whom he loves. Following this adventure, the Athenians begin to call upon H. during their wedding ceremonies. The motifs of H.'s victory over pirates and his girlish appearance suggest a strong influence of Homeric Dionysiac hymns (which is further evidence of the connection between H. and Dionysus in late antiquity). In the 1st cent. AD, Cornelius Balbus reports (in Serv. Aen. 4,127) that H. died during the wedding of Dionysus and Althaea, at which he sang. Apparently, the god of the wedding was not meant to be older than the bride and groom. The myth of the god's death goes back at least to the Hellenistic period: Apollodorus (FGrH 244 F 139) mentions that in the Orphic sources (fr. 40 KERN) H. is resurrected by Asclepius. The name H. was very common among Roman slaves and freedmen [4. vol. 1, 522f.; vol. 3, 1369].

1 A. HENRICHS, Ein neues Likymniosfragment bei Philodem, in: ZPE 57, 1984, 53–57   2 P. LINANT DE BELLE-FONDS, s.v. H., LIMC 4.1, 583–585   3 Id., Hyménaios: une iconographie contestée, in: MEFRA 103, 1991, 197–212   4 H. SOLIN, Die griech. Personennamen in Rom, vol. 1–3, 1982.   J.B.

[2] see → Hymenaios

Hymenaios (Ὑμέναιος; *Hyménaios*). Wedding song (cf. → Hymenaeus)
I. GREEK   II. LATIN

I. GREEK
A. ETYMOLOGY   B. HYMÉNAIOS AND EPITHALAMIUM   C. FORMULAS

A. ETYMOLOGY
The meaning of *hyménaios* is shared by ὑμήν (*hymén*), as it is usually found in the cry Ὑμὴν ὦ Ὑμέναιε [1. vol. 2,361]. The origin of the word ὑμήν is disputed: some claim its origin is pre-Greek and not Indo-European [2]; others maintain it is Greek, and synonymous with *hymén* = membrane, i.e. the hymen, although this meaning first appears in later authors [3. 964–965]. DIEHL, who assumes a connection with the Latin *suo*, sees a further link with ὕμνος (*hýmnos*, → Hymn), which is also derived from 'sewing, weaving' [4. 90]. Pindar and Sophocles presuppose a link between Ὑμέναιος and ὕμνος (Pind. fr. 128c; Soph. Ant. 813–816).

B. HYMÉNAIOS AND EPITHALAMIUM
The *hyménaios* as song is first mentioned in Hom. Il. 18,491–496, where it is part of the procession that accompanies the bride. It could also be sung when the wedding was announced (Eur. Hel. 1433–1435) or by the guests at the wedding feast, which usually took place at the bride's house (Hom. Od. 4,17).

Singing before the door of the bridal chamber on the night of the marriage's consummation is often called *epithalámios/-ion*. However, this usage is Alexandrian. The term *hyménaios* became established as the name for all forms of nuptial song, and it is difficult to assign the *epithalámia* of → Sappho to any specific point during the wedding ceremony [5. 116–126]. The longest surviving fragment by Sappho (44 VOIGT [6]) describes

how Hector brings Andromache to Troy. This poem is generally regarded as a wedding song, although there is no indication of the actual occasion [7. 102–109]. The title of Theoc. 18, a *hyménaios* sung by maidens outside the bridal chamber of Menelaus and Helena, has been given as *epithalámios*. The wedding hymn was often a jocular and suggestive affair: Much as Sappho's *epithalámia* (110 (a) V.), Theoc. 18 contains harmless mockery. Some have sought to discover obscenity in Sappho 111 V. [8].

C. FORMULAS
The wedding song supposedly began with the words ἐκκόρει κόρει κορώνας or ἐκκορὶ κορὶ κορώνη (881 PMG). This has been understood variously as obscenities or invocations of fertility and faithfulness, though it was probably just a meaningless string of syllables [9. 92–96]. A song meant for the morning after the wedding has survived in fragmentary form in Sappho's 30 V. It is apparent from Aeschyl. TrGF III 43 that the morning song contained the formula σὺν κόροις τε καὶ κόραις, which many have linked to ἐκκορὶ κορὶ κορώνη. But it is much more likely that these words refer to the composition of the chorus singing the song, which was made up of youths and maidens, friends of the bride and groom.

1 A. S. F. GOW, Theocritus, 1965   2 R. MUTH, "H." und "Epithalamion", in: WS 67, 1954, 5–45   3 FRISK II   4 E. DIEHL, "... fuerunt ante Homerum poetae", in: RhM 89, 1940, 81–114   5 D. L. PAGE, Sappho and Alcaeus, 1955   6 E.-M. VOIGT, Sappho et Alcaeus, 1971   7 E. CONTIADES-TSITSONI, H. und Epithalamion, 1990   8 G. S. KIRK, A Fragment of Sappho Reinterpreted, in: CQ n.s. 13, 1963, 51f.   9 G. LAMBIN, La chanson grecque dans l'antiquité, 1992.   E.R.

II. LATIN
The *hymenaeus* was not a component of the Roman nuptial ritual, and its relation to the literary *epithalamium* was minor. Where wedding processions contain glyconic refrains in which the god H. is invoked [1], it is clearly a case of imitating a Greek original (cf. Plaut. Cas. 798–854 with Aristoph. Av. 1720–1765; Pax 1316–1357). There are quotations of glyconic epithalamia by → Licinius Calvus (FPL ³1995, 211f.) and Ticidas (FPL 226), as well as by → Catullus (61). The latter is a poem for Manlius Torquatus and Iunia Aurunculeia, and leads the procession by torchlight from the house of the bride to that of the groom. During this *deductio*, → Fescennine verses are sung, demonstrating a strong Italic influence. The normal metre for the Latin nuptial poem is, however, the hexameter. Calvus uses it. Additionally, Catull. 62 is not bound to a specific wedding or particular place: The greater part of the poem is comprised of a *carmen amoebaeum* between two choruses, one made up of youths and the other of maidens. Catull. 64, an → epyllion on the wedding of Peleus and Thetis, contains an epithalamium that was sung by the Fates at those nuptials (323–381). Stat. Silv.

1,2 is a wedding song written in hexameters. Some verses from the epithalamium of emperor Gallienus have survived (FPL 378f.). The → Cento nuptialis (Lib. 18 PRETE = Lib. 17 LOEB) of Ausonius strings together some Virgilian verses into a narrative of a wedding. → Claudianus [2] also wrote some dactylic epithalamia for the wedding of Honorius and Maria, as well as for Palladius and Celerina; additionally, he composed Fescennine verses for the former.

Christian authors such as Dracontius, Ennodius, Sidonius Apollinaris and Venantius Fortunatus make use of the metaphorical language and mythology of the earlier poets in their epithalamia.

> FPL ³1995; A. D'ERRICO, L'epitalamio nella letteratura latina, dal fescennino nuziale al c. 62 di Catullo, in: Annali della Facoltà di Lettere e Filosofia dell' università di Napoli 5, 1955, 73–93; R. MUTH, H. und Epithalamion, in: WS 67, 1954, 5–45.   E.R.

Hymettus (Ὑμηττός; *Hymēttós*, name pre-Greek [17]). Mountain in Attica, modern Imittos, earlier Trelovuni, Turkish Deli Dağ (height 1027 m). H., which is mostly deforested today, consists of Triassic limestone, micaceous slate, marble and other metamorphites [19]. It isolates the *pedíon* of Athens in the south-east from the Attic *mesógaia*. From the defile between Pentelicon and H. near Stavro in the north it stretches over 22 km to the Saronic Gulf by Cape Zoster in the south [14]. The gorge of Pirnari separates the northern 'great H.' (μέγας Ὑ./*mégas H.*) from the southern 'waterless H.' (ἄνυδρος Ὑ./*lánydros H.*; Theophr. De signis tempestatum 1,20). Several ancient paths led over the H. [8. 135]. The → Ilis(s)us rises from the north-west slope of the H. The (upper) blue-grey Hymettian marble (μάρμαρος ... Ὑμεττίας, Str. 9,1,23) was used in sculpture from the early archaic period and preferred in architecture (Asclepieum, Dionysus Theatre, Attalus Stoa) from the 4th cent. BC [21]. The ancient quarries lie in the western part of the H. [11; 15. 25ff.; 21. 191].

Around the H., which was never explored systematically (what was known by 1971 in [18]), were numerous demes (→ Demos [2]) in → Attica, *hóros* inscriptions of some are preserved [4; 10; 20]. Aerial photographs show extended ancient terrace cultures [1] in southern H. near Aexone (modern Glyphada). Deforestation is attested by Plato (Critias 111c) already in the classical period, → apiculture still in the Imperial period by Pausanias (1,32,1). The → honey was famous (Hor. Carm. 2,6,15; Plin. HN 11,32; Str. 9,1,23) [5].

The cult of Zeus Hymettios (Paus. 1,32,2), obviously identical to that of Epakrios (EM s.v. ἐπάκριος Ζεύς) [8. 138; 3. 610, 624 (E 60)], is to be located on the summit, that of Zeus Ombrios (Paus. 1,32,2) near the chapel of the prophet Elijah above Koropi ([8. 139; 12; 15. 32], otherwise [9; 21. 191 figs. 246–248]). The 'H.-Tower' [12; 16] is not a signalling tower but maybe rather the cult site of Apollo Proopsios (Paus. 1,32,2; on further cult sites of Apollo [8. 139]). The Kaisariani monastery occupies the site of an Aphrodite sanctuary with a spring that promoted fertility [8. 139f.; 19. 807; 21. 192]. The grotto of the Nymphs of Vari (Synes. Epist. 136; [21. 447 fig. 581–586; 23. 90ff.]) lies on the south-eastern slope of the H. in Anagyrus, at the north-eastern summit there is a Pan cave [23. 175ff.]. According to VANDERPOOL [22] it is identical to the cave at Men. Dys. 407ff. in Paeania (modern Liopesi). A puzzle are a 'dragon house' on the western slope [2. 189ff.; 21. 191] and a defensive installation [13] on the ridge of the 'great H.'. In the Byzantine period numerous churches and monasteries were built on the H. [6; 21. 192].

1 J. BRADFORD, Fieldwork on Aerial Discoveries in Attica and Rhodes, in: Antiquaries Journal 36, 1956, 172–180 2 J. CARPENTER, D. BOYD, Dragon Houses: Euboia, Attika, Ikaria, in: AJA 81, 1977, 179–215 3 G. DAUX, La grande démarchie, in: BCH 87, 1963, 603–634 4 H. R. GOETTE, Neue att. Felsinschr., in: Klio 76, 1994, 120–134 5 J. E. JONES, Hives and Honey of H., in: Archaeology 29, 1976, 80–91 6 KIRSTEN/KRAIKER, 203ff. 7 U. KNIGGE, Eine prähistor. Siedlung am H., in: AA 1977, 137–141 8 W. KOLBE, s.v. H., RE 9, 135–140 9 M. K. LANGDON, A Sanctuary of Zeus on Mount H., in: Hesperia Suppl. 16, 1976 10 Id., Hymettiana I, in: Hesperia 54, 1985, 257–270 11 Id., Hymettiana II. An ancient Quarry on Mount H., in: AJA 92, 1988, 75–83 12 H. LOHMANN, Atene, 1993, 234 13 J. R. MCCREDIE, Fortified Military Camps in Attica, in: Hesperia Suppl. 11, 1966, 48ff. 14 E. MEYER, s.v. Zoster (1), RE 10A, 848–853 15 A. MILCHHÖFER, Karten von Attika. Text II, 1883 16 M. H. MUNN, The Defense of Attica, 1993, Index s.v. H. tower 17 G. NEUMANN, s.v. Vorgriech. Sprachen, KlP 5, 1336 18 M. PETROPOLAKOU, E. PENTAZOS, Ἀττική (Ancient Greek Cities 21), 1973, 101–111, 142–152 (grid squares X7–Y3 and X7–Y4) 19 PHILIPPSON/ KIRSTEN 1, 802–814 20 J. S. TRAILL, Demos and Trittys, 1986 21 TRAVLOS, Attika 22 E. VANDERPOOL, Pan in Paiania, in: AJA 71, 1967, 309–311 23 J. M. WICKENS, The Archaeology and History of Cave Use in Attica 2, 1986.   H.LO.

Hymn
I. THE GREEK HYMNOS   II. THE LATIN HYMNUS
III. THE CHRISTIAN HYMN   IV. THE BYZANTINE HYMN

I. THE GREEK HYMNOS
A. CULT HYMNS   B. LITERARY HYMNS   C. ISIS ARETALOGIES

A. CULT HYMNS
Although Greek *hýmnos* (ὕμνος) in the early stage generally means 'song', with an epic song or Pindaric → epinikion being equally called 'hymn', the specification of the term as 'song for a god' is found at the latest in the 5th/4th cents. BC (Pl. Resp. 10,607a: ὕμνους θεοῖς καὶ ἐγκώμια τοῖς ἀγαθοῖς: 'Hymns for gods and praise for outstanding people'; Pl. Leg. 700b 1–2: εὐχαὶ πρὸς θεούς, ὄνομα δὲ ὕμνοι ἐπεκαλοῦντο) [1]. *Hymnos* becomes the general term for 'religious song', to which belong forms of song allocated to individual cults e.g.

the → paean or the → dithyrambos (cf. Didymus [1] of Alexandria in Orion 155–6 STURZ; Proclus in Phot. Bibl. 320 a9–17 HENRY). *Hymnos* describes both what is sung – i.e. the words and the melody – and the recital of the song itself: a cult community sings to the accompaniment of the aulos or kithara around the altar – or on the way to the altar – a poem addressed to one or several deities that together with other cult activities (e.g. sacrifices, the offering of wine, prayer) should be regarded as a component of the worship of the god. The song is intended to draw the deity's attention to the worship of the people and to propitiate him. Out of this purpose, a typical form has emerged, recognizable from the earliest sources at our disposal and one which is to be found – allowing for differences in emphasis – in almost all cultures and literary genres:

(1) first the hymn addresses the deity (deities) by mentioning the name, appellation, genealogy and favourite dwellings of the god (*invocatio*); as the hymn is a form of communication, we can understand this opening as an oral 'address' for the message to follow, designating the deity addressed as precisely as possible. (2) Next various reasons are listed by the person making the request showing why this deity in particular is able to fulfil his wishes; the predication of divine attributes as analyzed by E. NORDEN ensues: participles, relative clauses, whole narratives are arranged next to each other either in second-person style or in third-person style in order to describe and praise divine power (*pars epica, aretalogia, sanctio* [2]). (3) After this preparation the request is made (*precatio*) – whether this be very general ('Lord, give your worshippers well-being') or specific ('Lord, save us from this plague').

The *Iliad* already mentions various types of hymns to the gods: paeans to Apollo to banish the plague (Hom. Il. 1,472–4); the *linos* – a harvest thanksgiving song (ibid. 18,570); girls' choruses for Artemis (ibid. 16,183). Lyricists like → Pindarus, → Bacchylides, → Simonides composed a large number of different cult songs that were collected separately by their Alexandrian editors but that with the exception of some papyrus finds (paeans and dithyrambs by Pindar and Bacchylides) are lost: → paean, → prosodion, → nomos, → dithyrambos, adonidion, iobakchos and *hyporchema* belong, according to the ancient classification of Proclus, to the hymns that exclusively praise gods; → partheneion, → daphnephorikon, tripodephorikon, oschophorikon and euktikon belong to those that praise both gods and men (Procl. Chrestomathy, summary in Photius Bibl.).

With their respective characteristic content, type of melody, dance and sound, these cult songs were for the most part allocated to specific gods or festivals; among these, the *dithyrambos* in honour of Dionysus with its rather turbulent manner of recital and the paean that praised Apollo (in particular) in a rather solid style, occupied a special place that can be partly reconstructed through the extant remnants [3; 4]. From the late classical/Hellenistic period there are frequent finds of

genuine cult hymns that have been passed down to us through inscriptions (paeans, *prosodia*, hymns); from Delphi we have the hymns of the Corinthian Aristonous (→ Aristonus [4]) to Apollo and Hestia; the two famous paeans (in the creto-paeonic metre: -˘-) and *prosodia* to Apollo with a musical or melodic score by → Athenaeus [7] and → Limenius. From Epidaurus anonymous hymns are extant to the mother of the gods, Pan, all gods, a paean to Asclepius in the Ionian metre (˘˘˘-) by → Isyllus, and → Ariphron's paean to Hygieia. The hymn of the Curetes found near Palaikastro in eastern Crete to 'the greatest kouros' (= the youthful Zeus) rightly attracted a great deal of attention at the beginning of the 20th cent. in J. E. HARRISON among others [5].

B. LITERARY HYMNS

Apart from the cult hymns (mostly lost), a number of literary hymns has been passed down to us whose formal features are adapted to the respective literary genre to which they belong [6]. The hexametric 'Homeric' hymns, among these the four 'great' ones to Demeter, Apollo, Hermes and Aphrodite, certainly are not by Homer, but stand firmly in the tradition of the epic art of recitation of the 7th and 6th cents. (→ Epic). They represent an opening song (*prooímion*) of the → rhapsode with which he wanted to ensure the goodwill of gods listening to him before his own contribution to the Homeric competition [7]. Various hymnic poems and fragments by → Alcaeus [4], → Sappho, → Anacreon [1] and → Ibycus should probably like the Homeric hymns be regarded as opening pieces of their citharodic recital (at the festival or symposium) [8]. To these belong the two famous odes to Aphrodite by Sappho (fragments 1 and 2). From the Hellenistic period come several distinctly literary poems that are classified by the authors with an archaizing intention as belonging to the genre 'hymns to the gods': the hymns of → Callimachus continue the narrative tradition of the Homeric hymn or that of the citharodic prooemium in order to report erudite details from the life and cult of Zeus, Artemis, Leto (Delos hymn), Apollo, Athena (in elegiac distichs) and Demeter, with 2, 5 and 6 using a mimetic narrative technique that gives the impression that the cult activity described is taking place at the moment of narration [9]. Two laments for 'Adonis' – one at the end of Theocritus' 15th poem, the other by → Bion [2] of Smyrna (main period of creativity c. 100 BC; ed.: [10]) – attest to the deliberate promotion of Oriental cults by the Ptolemaic ruling house in Alexandria (cf. Theocr. 15,106–111).

From the 4th cent. BC on a series of hymnic poems to abstract or personified concepts is composed commencing with the hymn to Arete (Virtue) by → Aristotle, which he wrote in honour of his late friend Hermeias in the dactylic-epitritic metre, and Ariphron's paean to Hygieia (Health); this type becomes increasingly important in subsequent years. There are hymns to Tyche (Good fortune), the Moirae (Fate), Mnemosyne (Memory), later also a hymn to Rome by → Melinno (SH 541). The traditional figure of Zeus is radically changed in the Zeus hymn of the Stoic → Cleanthes (331–232 BC) into the *arché* (principle) that is inherent in the cosmos. Related to these are natural-philosophy poems of → Mesomedes (Hadrianic period), e.g. to Physis (Nature), the Adriatic or the Sun, as well as the poems of the Neoplatonist → Proclus (5th cent. AD). Common to these works is the striving to clothe moral concepts or natural philosophical concepts in the dignity of hieratic forms of address from ancient tradition.

C. ISIS ARETALOGIES

Sub-literary but nonetheless of great interest are a number of magical hymns that were found in the → magic papyri of late Hellenism (30 BC – AD 600) that come from Egypt [11]. They are mainly hexametric poems that invoke the gods (Apollo, Hermes, Selene, Hecate) by repeatedly calling for them to come and support the practitioner of magic. The syncretism of these texts links Egyptian, Syrian and partially also Christian elements with the names of the Greek pantheon. The so-called Isis aretalogies – written in prose with the exception of the text from Andros (cf. [12]) – prove the entry of this Egyptian goddess from Memphis into official Greek cult; → Isis is assimilated with various Greek goddesses – preferably Artemis, as well as with Aphrodite or Demeter – in a similarly syncretistic spirit. The 'Orphic Hymns' (→ Orphism) belong, according to scholarly opinion, to the worship of a god by a community of practising 'Orphics' in Asia Minor in the 3rd cent. AD [13; 14].

1 K. THRAEDE, s.v. H. (1), RAC 16, 916f.; 922–924.
2 E. NORDEN, Agnostos Theos, 1913, 143–176
3 L. KÄPPEL, Paian, Studien zur Gesch. einer Gattung, 1992 4 B. ZIMMERMANN, Dithyrambos, Gesch. einer Gattung (Hypomnemata vol. 98), 1992 5 J. E. HARRISON, Themis, A study of the social origins of Greek religion, 1911 6 W. D. FURLEY, Types of Greek Hymns, in: Eos 81, 1993, 21–41 7 R. BÖHME, Das Prooimion. Eine Form sakraler Dichtung der Griechen, thesis Heidelberg 1937 8 J. DANIELEWICZ, De elementis hymnicis in Sapphus Alcaei Anacreontisque carminibus obviis quaestiones selectae, in: Eos 62, 1974, 23–33 9 W. ALBERT, Das mimetische Gedicht in der Antike. Gesch. und Typologie von den Anfängen bis in die augusteische Zeit (Beiträge zur Klass. Philol. 190), 1988 10 M. FANTUZZI, Bionis Smyrnaei 'Adonidis epitaphium', 1985 11 PGM 2, 237ff. 12 W. PEEK, Der Isis-Hymnus von Andros und verwandte Texte, 1930 13 W. QUANDT, Orphei Hymni, 1962 14 A. N. ATHANASSAKIS, The Orphic Hymns, 1988.

J. M. BREMER, Greek Hymns, in: H. S. VERSNEL, E. T. VAN STRATEN (ed.), Faith, Hope and Worship, 1981, 193–215; W. FURLEY, Praise and persuasion in Greek hymns, in: JHS 115, 1995, 29–46; W. BURKERT, Griech. Hymnoi in: W. BURKERT, F. STOLZ (ed.), Hymnen der Alten Welt im Kulturvergleich (Orbis Biblicus et Orientalis 131), 1994, 9–17; A. C. CASSIO, G. CERRI, L'inno tra rituale e letteratura nel mondo antico, in: Atti di un colloquio Napoli 21–24 ottobre 1991, 1991; CID III; M. LATTKE, Hymnus. Materialien zu einer Gesch. der ant. Hymnologie (NT et

Orbis antiquus 19), 1991; P. MAAS, Epidaurische Hymnen, 1933.   W.D.F.

II. THE LATIN HYMNUS
A. DEFINITION OF THE TERM B. THE HYMN IN PAGAN ROMAN LITERATURE

A. DEFINITION OF THE TERM

In Latin the oldest certain evidence for the term *hymnus* comes from the 2nd cent. AD (Apul.; Sen. fr. 88 is uncertain); as late as the 7th cent. it was considered as a foreign word (Isid. Orig. 1,39,17: *hymni autem ex graeco in latinum 'laudes' interpretantur*). As a literary genre however – in poetry (in various metres) and prose – the hymn was known at an early time and was both used (Catullus 34) and described (Hor. Carm. 4,2,13: 'to extol gods or kings'; Hor. Ars P. 83), but in most cases they will probably have been based on Greek models. The conceptual difference between the hymn as praise for a god and the *laudes* for humans occurs late (Porph. Hor. Epist. 2,1,134 counts the hymn as among the *carmina quibus dii placantur*, 'songs with which gods are made gracious'), but is in fact observed at no time (especially in the literary hymns). Characteristics of form as well as content go back to the Greek hymns [3]: address, predication, mostly in the anaphoric familiar form of the second person and often as a polyptoton (*tu/ad te/a te/per te/nec sine te*; also in the third-person or first-person style), polyonymy (e.g. Catull. 34,21f.: *sis quocumque tibi placet sancta nomine*), relative style, formulae indicating omnipotence (e.g. Lucr. 1,31: *tu sola potes*), aretalogy with naming of the cult centres, genealogy and enumeration of the power areas, epiphany descriptions (e.g. Tiberianus, Carm. 4,5f.: *quem maxima tellus intremit*; Apul. Met. 11,25: *tuam maiestatem tremescunt aves*), prayer, sometimes with reference to previous assistance (hypomnesis; cf. Catull. 34,23: *antique ut solita es, bona sospites ope gentem*). These hymnic *topoi* are to be found individually or also in combination in other literary genres as well (see B. below) and also in → parodies of hymns. Hymnic elements also contain simple → prayers, cult songs, → curses, eulogies to various addressees etc. Often the boundaries between hymns and other literary genres are fluid and a clear allocation to the hymnic genre is difficult. In case of doubt it is necessary to limit oneself to the diagnosis of the hymnic phrases and motifs [5. 922–924].

B. THE HYMN IN PAGAN ROMAN LITERATURE

A Roman hymnic tradition is tangible in the cult songs (→ Carmen Arvale; → Carmen Saliare). The literary hymns on the other hand are inspired by Greek forms even when clad in Roman cult and scenery, and the same applies too to the 'Salian priests' song' Verg. Aen. 8,293–302. Catullus' hymn to Diana in glyconeic strophes (Carm. 34) supposed to be sung by a chorus of girls and boys is constructed almost like a model: it shows almost all of the above-mentioned hymnic elements and evokes the idea of a choral lyrical performance in a cult framework. Despite the final plea for the welfare of the *Romuli gens* it is in all probability (*pace* [3. 166]) a matter of literary fiction and stylization according to Greek models. In the same way the lyrical poems shaped as hymns by → Horatius – with the exception of the *Carmen saeculare* – are not meant for a cult occasion, allowing the hymnic form to become more flexible and be used more freely: aside from the hymns to the gods in the conventional style (Carm. 1,10 to Mercury; 1,12 to a collective group of gods; 1,21 to Diana and Apollo; 1,30 to Venus; 1,35 to Fortuna; 2,19 and 3,25 to Bacchus; 3,18 to Faunus), he has hymns to his lyre (1,32), to the Bandusia spring (3,13) and to a wine tankard (3,21); moreover 3,4 (to the Muses with depiction of gigantomachy) and 3,22 (dedication of a pine to Diana) make use of the formal repertory of the hymn. The separation from the cult function also eases the incorporation of motifs originally alien to the genre, e.g. current political events (as in Hor. Carm. 1,21; 1,35; 3,4), and the change in function of the hymnic form (3,21 is a birthday poem for Messalla). In this way, Propertius also uses a hymn to Bacchus to express the agonies of *servitium amoris* (3,17). Ovid fashions two entries in the *Fasti* as hymn to Mercury (5,663–692) and to Augustus (2,119–144).

On occasion hymns are embedded in the text of another literary genre: hymns to Venus in Lucr. 1,1–43 and to Bacchus in Verg. G. 2,1–8 serve as prooemia; a hymn to Apollo is to be found in Stat. Theb. 1,696–720. Built into a prose narrative are hymns to Priapus in Petron. Sat. 133 (in hexameters), to Hymenaeus in Mart. Cap. 1,1 (elegiac distichs), two prose hymns to Isis in Apul. Met. 11,2 and 25 (cf. the Isis aretalogy in the first-person style ibid. 5). From the Imperial period come two lyrical prayers in hymnic form: Caesius Bassus, FPL 2 (to Bacchus, ithyphallic) and Septimius Serenus, FPL 23 (to Ianus, choriambic). The hymnic stylistic features are now used partly to excess (e.g. Anth. Lat. 385,38–60 with a 23-fold anaphoric invocation of Sol). Representative of late antiquity are not just the Christian hymnody (see III. below) but also philosophical (Neoplatonic) hymns (Tiberianus Carm. 4, with an ethopoieia of Plato, and Boeth. Cons. 3 Carm. 9 to the one who guides the universe; see III. below).

Frequently individual elements of the hymn are used in a context that is alien to the genre e.g. in the invocation of the Muses in Enn. Ann. 1,1, in the epithalamium of Catullus 61,46–75 (to Hymenaeus), in an invective of Catullus 36,11–17 (to Venus), in the personification of the *Patria* in Cic. Catil. 1,18 [4], in the prooemium Tusc. 5,5 (to philosophy), in descriptions of festivals Tib. 1,7 and 2,1 (to Osiris or Bacchus). Ovid exploits the formal repertory especially in the Met. [1]: In 4,11–17 with a list of Bacchus epicleses (topos of polyonymy), in 5,341–345 with a Ceres aretalogy; every now and then Ovid uses hymnic self-aretalogy (first-person and relative style) in boastful orations of a god towards a mortal (1,515–524: Apollo to Daphne;

1,589–597: Jupiter to Io; 4,226–228: Sol to Leucothoe; etc.). Plin. HN 2,154–159 describes the physical qualities of the earth with reference to the hymn. → *Pervigilium Veneris* is also hymnically stylized. Following the Greek model, Seneca gives certain passages of the tragic choral songs hymnic form [6. 178]. Hymnic elements are also to be found in encomia for humans (cf. e.g. Lucr. 3,1–30: to Epicurus; Verg. G. 1,24–42; 3,26–36; Aen. 6,791–807: to Augustus).

The hymn as a genre and the hymnic style are also repeatedly parodied [1; 2], e.g. Hor. Carm. 3,21 (to the wine tankard); Anth. Lat. 682 (to Pan); Mart. 5,24 (to the gladiator Hermes with a parody of the hymn to Hermes Trismegistus) [6]; Maximianus Elegiae 5,87–104 (to the penis, *mentula*); CE 1504 (to Priapus); Priap. 85 (first-person aretalogy of Priapus).
→ Prayer; → Song

1 T. Fuhrer, Der Götterh. als Prahlrede, in: Hermes 126, 1998, 1–12   2 H. Kleinknecht, Die Gebetsparodie in der Ant., 1937   3 E. Norden, Agnostos Theos, 1913   4 C. Ratkowitsch, Ein 'H.' in Ciceros erster Catilinaria, in: WS 15, 1981, 157–167   5 K. Thraede, s.v. H. I, RAC 16, 915–946   6 R. Wünsch, s.v. H., RE 9, 140–183.
T.FU.

III. The Christian hymn
A. Definition of the term   B. Greek   C. Latin
D. Middle Ages and early modern period

A. Definition of the term
In the LXX, partly in the NT and in early Christian literature, the terms ὕμνος (*hýmnos*), ψαλμός (*psalmós*) and ᾠδή (*ōidé*) and Latin *psalmus, hymnus, canticum/ carmen* are mostly used without distinction for all possible types of thanksgiving and songs of praise in (rhythmic) prose or poetry. In this way 'here too the academic definition of a "genre" fails', and for late antiquity a 'general mixture of genres' has to be expected [9. 918 and 940]. Common to the texts described as hymns are features regarding content (praise, thanksgiving, possible request) as well as formal features like the invocation of God (acclamation), predication and participle style, doxology (corresponding to the aretalogy in the pagan hymn). From the 3rd cent., Greek and Latin hymns frequently have alphabetical acrostics which is why they are called → abecedarii. Hymnic elements can also appear as parts of a → prayer or other textual locations. In principle we should differentiate between liturgical (→ Song) and literary hymns. A clear separation is, however, by no means always possible.

B. Greek
As several psalms from the OT can be called hymn [1. 97–121], the term can also be used for a series of NT texts: the (partly pre-Pauline) hymns to Christ in prose in the letters of St. Paul (especially Phil 2:6–11; Hebr 1:3; Col 1:15–20) and the hymnic songs in Luke (1:46–55: Magnificat; 1:68–79: Benedictus; 2:29–32: Nunc dimittis) and others [2]. Plin. Ep. 10,96,7 reports

hymnic songs of Bithynian Christians; 1 Clem. 59,3–61,3 quotes a prayer of praise of such kind. → Ignatius [1] of Antioch (beginning of the 2nd cent.) inserts in his letter to the Ephesians 19,1–3 his 'Star hymn'. The 24 odes of Solomon (early 2nd cent.?) can be regarded as hymns. Hymns and psalms also play an important part in Christian → Gnosticism [1. 254–260]. The Greek (primarily oral) hymnic output of the first cent. is however lost for the most part or only extant in fragments in later citations or on papyrus (partly with notation) [1. 261f.; 275]. The Syrian hymnic tradition is also worthy of mention (→ Bardesanes, → Aphrahat and others) [1].

From the end of the 2nd cent. there arose, apart from the liturgical hymnic tradition, also (purely literary?) hymns in classical lyrical metres: Clemens [3] of Alexandria closes his *Paidagōgós* (around AD 190) with a hymn to Christ (3,12,101,3 in lyrical anapaests; Platonizing epitheta in the predication). Pagan forms are also seen in the 'Evening hymn' φῶς ἱλαρόν (*Phôs hilarón*) (2nd or 3rd cent.) that has kept its place to the present time in Byzantine liturgy. Methodius (3rd/4th cents.) also places a hymn to Christ (*abecedarius* in iambic strophes with a refrain) at the end of his *Symposium*; here we find versification based on word accent, which becomes increasingly common from the 3rd cent. onwards, next to quantitative metre. Among the poems of → Gregorius [3] of Nazianzus (4th cent.) are hymns in various metres (among these anacreontics); the philosophical hymn ὦ πάντων ἐπέκεινα (*ô pántōn epékeina*, Carm. 1,1,29) is famous. Gregory often refers back to the formal repertory of the pagan hymns. → Synesius of Cyrene (4th/5th cents.) wrote nine (Neoplatonic Christian) hymns in Doric dialect and in various lyrical metres, some of which were remote from the standard form [4].

C. LATIN

In the Latin West too liturgical practice is the starting-point of a history of form (the *Gloria in excelsis* is considered to be the oldest known hymn in the Latin language). From the 4th cent. the principle of the χρῆσις (*chrêsis*) of pagan forms became effective also for hymnic poetry. The first poet of the Latin hymn that we know of is → Hilarius [1] of Poitiers, of whose *Liber hymnorum* (written around 360) fragments of 3 hymns in classical metres have been passed down. The theological (anti-Arian) content, the length and the artificial language made these hymns unsuitable for church singing. From → Marius Victorinus 3 hymns (*De trinitate*) in psalmodic prose are extant; the *Te Deum* is attributed to → Nicetas of Remesiana. But it is → Ambrosius who is considered to be the 'Father of Latin hymnic poetry' [3]. What is new is that he wrote hymns especially for communal singing in a uniform and simple form (8 four-line strophes in iambic dimeters) and with an anti-Arian tendency (→ Arianism). The reason for this Church-political function of the Ambrosian hymns is probably to be found in the pressures against the church

of Milan emanating from the Arian empress → Justina. The first explicit 'Battle Hymns' are, however, the anti-Donatistic abecedarius of → Augustinus (*psalmus contra partem Donati*) in 16-syllabic metre and the anti-Arian *Psalmus abecedarius* of → Fulgentius [2] of Ruspe (5th cent.). The success of the 'Ambrosian' strophe (cf. Aug. Conf. 9,7,15) already led at that time to numerous imitations (of *c.* 40 Ambrosian hymns, 14 are considered to be genuine), and particularly in the Middle Ages it became the dominant form of hymnic poetry.

The (partly excessively long) hymns of → Prudentius are certainly not solely intended for the liturgy, perhaps they are even meant as poetry purely for reading purposes (*pace* [10]). The collection *Cathemerinon* puts together hymns for the hours of the day or for certain days of the liturgical year; the cycle *Peristephanon* contains hymns to the martyrs. Both books of poems are structured according to a carefully thought out plan. By using (*i.a.*) complicated lyrical (Horatian) strophes and an artificial language, Prudentius turns his hymns into high poetry. Comparable is Paulinus of Nola's Carm. 6, a hymn to John the Baptist.

Also in the 4th cent. belong the hymns of → Ausonius (Ephem. 3) and of → Claudianus [2] (Carmina minora 32), whose form owes much to pagan hymnic tradition but whose content are clearly Christian. From the 5th cent. there are again many hymns that are anonymous or whose authorship is uncertain. Worthy of mention are the two hymns of → Sedulius (5th cent.), the 12 hymns of → Ennodius (5th/6th cents., primarily in the Ambrosian tradition), 2 hymns of Flavius (6th cent.). → Venantius Fortunatus (6th cent.) in his hymns links up again with the Roman lyric; of his two cross hymns the famous *Pange lingua gloriosi* is in the tradition of Prud. Cathemerinon 9.

D. MIDDLE AGES AND EARLY MODERN PERIOD

The hymnic form continued to develop independently, both outside and inside the liturgy (in the prayer of the hours) in the various regions of the Latin West [7; 8]: particularly in France (Chilperich [2]; Theodulf of Orléans; Fulbert of Chartres; Marbod of Rennes; Balderich of Bourgueil; hymn to Mary of Bernard of Cluny), Italy (school of Monte Cassino; Petrus Damiani), Spain (under the influence of Prudentius; hymns of the Mozarabic liturgy), Ireland (St. Patrick hymn; Bangor Antiphonary), England (Aethelwald; Beda; Alkuin; Stephen Langtons' *Veni Sancte Spiritus*) and Germany (Hrabanus Maurus; Walahfrid Strabo; Lupus of Ferrières; Gottschalk the Saxon). Various forms of metric or rhythmic songs (since the early Middle Ages also for multiple voices) as well as songs of praise in rhythmic prose are also designated as hymns. The popular hymn form abecedarius was maintained right through to the German of the 17th cent. People repeatedly took up the classical metres: Hildebert of Lavardin wrote a non-liturgical hymn in 200 strophes. Abaelard wrote a hymnic collection for the monastery of Heloïse with 20 different strophe forms. Aside from other liturgical forms, the tropes (glosses for liturgical songs) and sequences (texts to melody that were originally sung to the final 'a' of the alleluja) were also described as hymns (Notker Balbulus; rhyme sequences of the schools of St. Victor and Notre-Dame; Hildegard of Bingen). The Latin hymnic poetry reached its high point in the course of the establishment of new orders in the 13th cent. by Thomas Aquinas, Thomas of Celano, who is considered to be the author of *Dies Irae*, and Jacopone da Todi, to whom is attributed the *Stabat Mater*.

The early Christian hymns were repeatedly furnished with different melodies [10] from the early Middle Ages and particularly in Humanism. The hymnic song retained its importance in the Protestant church service (German reworkings, especially by Martin LUTHER). In Humanism various poets used the hymnic form for their own (non-liturgical) Latin poetry (Mathias FUNCK, Sebastian BRANT, Jakob WIMPFELING, Rudolf AGRICOLA, and others).

→ Liturgy; → Prayer; → Song; → HYMN

1 M. LATTKE, Hymnus, 1991   2 R. DEICHGRÄBER, Gottesh. und Christush. in der frühen Christenheit, 1967 3 J. FONTAINE, Ambroise de Milan. Hymnes, 1992 4 J. GRUBER, H. STROHM, Synesios von Kyrene. Hymnen, 1991   5 M. KILEY, Prayer from Alexander to Constantine, 1997   6 E. NORDEN, Agnostos Theos   7 J. SZÖVÉRFFY, Die Annalen der lat. H.-Dichtung, 2 vols., 1964/5 8 Id., Latin Hymns, 1989   9 K. THRAEDE, s.v. H. I, RAC 16, 1994, 915–946   10 G. WILLE, Musica Romana, 1967.   T.FU.

IV. THE BYZANTINE HYMN

In the Byzantine period all liturgical songs are initially described as hymns but later this only applies to those with non-Biblical texts. The use of ancient quantifying metres ends with Synesius and Gregorius [2] of Nyssa. From the 5th cent. the *kontakion* arose under the influence of spoken language and according to Syrian models – from the point of view of form it was a versified sermon consisting of a prooimion (introduction) and numerous rhythmically parallel strophes that are held together by a refrain and usualy by an *acrostichis*. The most important representative of the genre in the 6th cent. is Romanos Melodos. From the practice of singing not just the psalm but also the nine Biblical odes in the matins, the canon develops from the end of the 7th cent., gradually ousting the *kontakion*. The canon consists of nine, later mostly only eight short *kontakia* with a few strophes that paraphrase the Biblical odes or refer to the festival of the day. In the 8th cent. important poets of canons are Andreas [2] of Crete and John [33] of Damascus, in the 9th cent. Josephus [9] of Thessalonica and the hymnographs Joseph and Cosmas. Apart from the canons, minor forms like the *sticheron* (→ Syntomon) and *troparion* continued to be used. The composition of hymns for the liturgy ends with a few exceptions in the 11th cent.

→ Andreas [2] of Crete; → Canon; → Gregorius [2] of Nyssa; → Iohannes [33] of Damascus; → Kontakion; → Romanos Melodos; → Synesius; → Troparion

W. CHRIST, M. PARANIKAS, Anthologia graeca carminum christianorum, 1871; E. FOLLIERI, Initia hymnorum ecclesiae graecae, 1960–1966; E. WELLESZ, A History of Byzantine Music and Hymnography, 1961; K. MITSAKIS, Βυζαντινὴ ὑμνογραφία, 1971.   AL.B.

Hyoskyamos see → Henbane

Hypallage see → Figures

Hypallagma (ὑπάλλαγμα; *Hypállagma*). Literally 'exchange', a credit security law in Roman Egypt stipulated through contractual clauses. Unlike the → *hypothḗkē*, the H. guaranteed the creditor no proprietary rights over securities in the possession of the debtor, as a rule a piece of real estate, but only required the debtor to keep ready certain objects to satisfy the creditor by way of enforcement. Contracts contained no forfeiture clause, but the debtor, as with the *hypothḗkē*, was subject to certain restrictions in respect of disposal of the objects in his possession.
→ Debt

A. B. SCHWARZ, Hypothek und H., 1911; H.-A. RUPPRECHT, Einführung in die Papyruskunde, 1994, 134; Id., Die dinglichen Sicherungsrechte nach der Praxis der Papyri, in: FS H. Ankum II, 1995, 425–436, esp. 428f.   G.T.

Hypanis (Ὕπανις; *Hýpanis*).
[1] River in the Ukraine (modern Bug). According to Hdt. 4,47,52 it flows from west to east, next to → Ister (Danube) and → Tyras (Dniestr) the third of the Scythian rivers that flows to the Pontus. Further sources: Hdt. 4,17,18; Skymni periegesis V. 804 (= GGM 1,229); Str. 2,107; 7, 298; 306, Ptol. 3,5,2; Anonymi periplus Ponti Euxini 60 (= GGM 1,417); Steph. Byz. s.v. → Borysthenes; Mela 2,6; Plin. HN 4,83f.
[2] Modern Kuban, which rises in the northern Caucasus and which flows into the Black Sea near the ancient Phanagorea (modern region of Sennaya).
[3] see → Hyphasis

E. KIESSLING, s.v. H., RE 9, 210ff.   B.B. and H.T.

Hyparchia (ὑπαρχία; *hyparchía*). Hellenistic term for 'sub-district' of a satrapy, predominantly in the → Seleucid kingdom. In the *hyparchia* of Eriza (Asia Minor), as attested by OGIS 1,238, the 'governor' (*hýparchos*, ὕπαρχος) was directly subordinate to the satrap of Caria (OGIS 1,224); in this way there was no intermediate authority here between the two functionaries [1. 176]. The reference may, however, also originate from the Attalid era, though in this case conclusions could be drawn about the Seleucid administration, in which a *hýparchos* (OGIS 1,225) as administrator of a *hyparchia*, to be differentiated from the → *eparchía*, probably also assumed military duties [2. 93].

The *hyparchia* is also documented in the 1st half of the 3rd cent. BC in Ptolemaic ruled 'Syria and Phoenicia' (SB V 8008) and in the Parthian era in Media Atropatene and Mesopotamia [3. 28, 30; 4. 4]. A transposition of the term *hyparchia* to Indian circumstances can be inferred from Arrian (Ind. 12,7).

1 K. BRODERSEN, Appians Abriß der Seleukidengesch., 1989   2 B. BAR-KOCHVA, The Seleucid Army, 1976   3 E. H. MINNS, Parchments of the Parthian Period, in: JHS 35, 1915, 22–65   4 M. ROSTOVTZEFF, C. B. WELLS, A Parchment Contract of Loan from Dura-Europos on the Euphrates, in: YClS 2, 1931, 1–78.

BENGTSON, 2, 22ff.; D. MUSTI, in: CAH 7,1,²1984, 184ff.
K.-W.WEL.

Hypata (Ὑπάτα; *Hypáta*). Capital of the Aenianes (HN 296), not shown to have existed before the 5th or beginning of the 4th cent. BC, situated on a terrace cut off by ravines above the Spercheus valley on the northern slope of Mount Oete (→ Oetaei, Oete), modern Hypate. The fates of city and tribe largely coincide (references [1; 2; 3]), Macedonian rule began around 344, and following the interlude of the Lamian War, the rule was replaced by the Aetolian League from *c*. 273. In the year 191 → Acilius [I 10] ravaged the territory of H. (Liv. 36,14,15; 16,5). In 189 Roman-Aetolian negotiations took place there (Pol. 20,9f.; 21,4f.). After the peace agreement H. was the only Aetolian post north of the Oete. With the re-establishment of the Aenian League by Rome in 168 the resurgence of H. began. The future Augustus united the tribe with Thessaly around 30 BC. As early as the 1st cent. AD at least one family in H. possessed Roman citizenship, in the 2nd cent. H. appears to be the most important Thessalian city. Under Hadrian the governor of Macedonia fixed the border between H. and Lamia (ILS 5947a, and [4. 199]). From the 3rd cent. there was a bishop in H. Justinian had the fortifications renewed (Procop. Aed. 4,2,16). In the 10th cent. H. was metropolis as Neae Patrae, possibly after a resettlement following temporary devastation at the time of the migration of the slavs.

1 E. MEYER, s.v. H, KlP 2, 1271f.   2 F. STÄHLIN, s.v. H., RE 9, 236ff.   3 Id., Das hellen. Thessalien, 1924, 220ff.   4 W. ECK, Jahres- und Provinzialfasten der senatorischen Statthalter von 69/70 bis 138/9, in: Chiron 13, 1983, 143ff.

J. A. O. LARSEN, A Thessalian Family under the Principate, in: CPh 48, 1953, 86ff.; P. LAZARIDIS, in: AD 16,2, 1960, 166 and 27,2; 1972, 390; 28,2, 1973, 321 (excavation report); P. PANTOS, in: G. D. DELOPOULOU (ed.), 1. Συνέδριο Φθιωτικών Ερευνών (1. Synédrio Phthiōtikón Erevnón), 1990, 74ff. (situation report on the Hellenistic-Roman city); P. PANTOS, in: BCH 119, 1990, 772 (excavation report); TIB 1, 1976, 223ff.
HE.KR.

Hypatia (Ὑπατία; *Hypatía*) Neoplatonic philosopher at Alexandria [2] (died in AD 415), daughter of the philosopher (best known as a mathematician) → Theon of Alexandria. She provided the edition of the *Almagest*

by Ptolemaeus [65] I (from book III), which was placed before Theon's commentary [1]. She wrote commentaries (now lost) on → Diophantus [4], on the 'Conics' of → Apollonius [13] of Perge and on the 'Handy Tables' of Ptolemy (Suda I.4,664–646 ADLER). The (presumably private) lessons she gave in philosophy, which included mathematics, were highly successful. Although her teaching consisted of the usual commentaries on the works of Plato, Aristotle or other philosophers, they created a stir because a woman taught them. Her moral strictness was likewise admired. A trait of Cynic shamelessness has been seen in the fact that she showed a pupil who was in love with her her underwear stained with menstrual blood, but this may equally be seen as an example of Plotinic influence (Suda I.4,664–646 ADLER) [3]. In her Neoplatonic thinking, like her pupil → Synesius, she may have owed more to Plotinus and Porphyry than to Iamblichus. Seven letters (10; 15; 16; 46; 81; 124; 154 GARYZA) from Synesius to H. have survived, in which he describes her as his mother, sister, teacher and benefactor. H. was lynched by the Christian rabble of Alexandria. The rabble-rousing propaganda of the city's bishop, Cyrillus I, against the city prefect Orestes, who was known to be a friend of H. (Socrates Hist. eccl. 7,13–15), should be regarded as at least indirectly to blame.

Because of dramatic circumstances of her life in the confrontation between paganism and Christianity, her impact was already great in late antiquity, but it became particularly so in the anti-religious atmosphere of the Enlightenment [4]. The novel 'H.' (London 1853) by Charles Kingsley (1819–1876) made H. widely known. In modern times, a periodical of feminist philosophy, founded in 1986, is named after her.
→ Women philosophers

1 A. CAMERON, Isidore of Miletus and H.: On the Editing of Mathematical Texts, in: GRBS 31, 1990, 103–127   2 M. DZIELSKA, H. of Alexandria, 1995   3 D. SHANZER, Merely a Cynic Gesture?, in: RFIC 113, 1985, 61–66   4 CH. LACOMBRADE, s.v. H., RAC 16, 965.
P.HA.

Hypatius

[1] Student of → Libanius, from whom he received letters (Lib. Ep. 137; 157; 158). In AD 360/361 he was *consularis Palaestinae primae* (Lib. Ep. 156; 159). PLRE 1, 447 (H.us 1).
W.P.

[2] Flavius H. Brother of empress → Eusebia. Together with his brother Fl. Eusebius he was consul in AD 359 (Amm. Marc. 18,1,1). In 363 he was possibly *vicarius urbis Romae* (Cod. Theod. 3,5,8). He was sentenced along with his brother in a trial for high treason in 371, but amnestied soon thereafter (Amm. Marc. 29,2,9–16). In 379 he was *praefectus urbis Romae* (Cod. Theod. 11,36,26), in 382/383 *praefectus praetorio Italiae et Illyrici* (Cod. Theod. e.g. 11,16,15; 6,26,3.). Ammianus praised his noble character (29,2,16). Libanius dedicated a eulogy to him (cf. Lib. Or. 1,179–181). PLRE 1, 448 (H.us 2 and 4).
W.P.

[3] *Praefectus Augustalis* in AD 383, and perhaps again in 392 (Cod. Theod. 12,6,17; 11,36,31). The Potamius, documented in this office at the same time as he, seems to have relinquished his position to him for a short time [1. 166–168]. PLRE 1, 448 (H.us 3).

1 C. VANDERSLEYEN, Chronologie des préfets d'Egypte de 284 à 395, 1962.　　　　K.G.-A.

[4] Son of Secundinus and Caesaria, a sister of emperor → Anastasius [1] I., died AD 532, eastern Roman general and usurper. After he had assumed the office of consul in 500, in 503 he fought unsuccessfully as *magister militum praesentalis* against the Persians and in Thrace. In 513 he was dispatched by emperor Anastasius with an army against the usurper Vitalianus, and became his prisoner, but in 514 the emperor bought his release. From *c.* 516 he was *magister militum per Orientem*, and by 526 at the latest received the → court title πατρίκιος (*patríkios*). After unsuccessful negotiations and battles with the Persians he was relieved by → Belisarius in 529. During the Nika Revolt (January 532) he was elevated to emperor by a group of senators with the participation of the people of Constantinople in opposition to → Iustinianus [1] I on 17 January, but was executed after the uprising failed on 19 January. ODB 2, 962f.; PLRE 2, 577–581 (H.us 6).　　　F.T.

Hypatodorus (Ὑπατόδωρος; *Hypatódōros*). Bronze sculptor from Thebes, worked in the middle of the 5th cent. BC. In Delphi, H., together with Aristogiton, created the 'Seven Against Thebes', as well as, according to an extant signature, the votive for a Boeotian. The former was erected by the Argives as a victory votive after the battle of Oenoe (around 460 BC) (Paus. 10,10,3–4). Its base was identified at the beginning of the Sacred Way. H.'s bronze statue of Athena in Aliphera in Arcadia, the base of which was discovered, was famous for its size and beauty (Paus. 8,26,7). Polybius (4,78,3–5) indicates that the artist, whom he however refers to as Hecatodorus, worked together with someone called Sostratus. A H. dated 372–369 BC by Pliny (HN 34,50) is either a later artist of the same name or has been erroneously identified.

> H.BRUNN, Gesch. der griech. Künstler, 1, 1857, 293–295; G.DAUX, Pausanias à Delphes, 1936, 89–90; LOEWY, no. 101; J.MARCADÉ, Recueil des signatures de sculpteurs grecs, 1, 1953, 8; 38; H.POMTOW, Stud. zu den Weihgeschenken und der Topographie von Delphi 3, in: Klio 8, 1908, 187–205; A.K. ORLANDOS, Η αρκαδική Αλίφειρα και τα μνημεία της, 1967–68, 125–132; OVERBECK, no. 1569; 1570–73 (sources); C.VATIN, Monuments votifs de Delphes, 1991, 139–148.　　　R.N.

Hypatos The Republican office of consul (Greek ὕπατος, *hýpatos*) apparently continued under Augustus and his successors, but *de facto*, until AD 541, only as an honorary title, that after 541 was reserved exclusively for the ruling (east Roman) emperor (until the 7th cent.). As early as from the 7th cent. *hypatos* is documented on Byzantine seals as a → court title, that no longer has anything in common with the old office of consul. It is a relatively lowly rank according to the catalogues of ranks of the 9th and 10th cents. and is subordinate to the titles ἀνθύπατος (*anthýpatos*, proconsul) and δισύπατος (*dishýpatos*, twice consul). From the 11th cent. renowned scholars and teachers are occasionally given the title ὕπατος τῶν φιλοσόφων (*hýpatos tôn philosóphōn*).

> ODB 2, 963f.; N. OIKONOMIDÈS, Les listes de préséance byzantines des Iᵉ et Xᵉ siècles, 1972.　　　F.T.

Hypatus (Ὕπατος; *Hýpatos*). Located above Glisas, modern Sagmatas, southern ridge of Mt. Messapion in Boeotia, on which there was probably a shrine to Zeus Hypatos (Paus 9,13,3) on the site of the monastery (with many ancient re-used stones).

> FOSSEY, 223–225; H.G. LOLLING, Reisenotizen aus Griechenland (1876 and 1877), 1989, 506f.; N.D. PAPACHATZIS, Παυσανίου Ελλάδος Περιήγησις 5, ²1981, 122–125.　　　P.F.

Hyperakria see → Diakria

Hyperbolus (Ὑπέρβολος; *Hypérbolos*). Athenian statesman (411 BC) from the deme Perithoedae. Contrary to the accusations levelled against him he was Athenian by birth. He seems to have acquired his wealth from the fabrication or sale of lamps (cf. Aristoph. Equ. 1315). Both Aristophanes (e.g. Equ. 1304) and Thucydides (8,73,3) describe him as 'common' (*mochthērós*). As a → demagogue in the style of Cleon he strove for a leading position after Cleon's death in 422 BC and was a member of the council in 421/420 (Plato Comicus 166f. CAF = 182 PCG; cf. IG I³ 82). According to Plutarch, in the hope of being able to remove Alcibiades or Nicias he applied for an → ostracism, but was himself ostracized, as the two of them united against him (Plut. Alcibiades 13; Nicias 11; cf. Plut. Aristides 7,3–4). H. was the last victim of an ostracism. The date is disputed, but it must be in 415 or one to two years earlier. In 411 H. was murdered on Samos by the Athenian oligarchs (Thuc. 8,73,3).

> PA 13910; DAVIES 517; LGPN 2, s.v. H. (5); W.R. CONNOR, The New Politicians of Fifth-Century Athens, 1971; P.J. RHODES, The Ostracism of Hyperbolus, in: R.Osborne (ed.), Ritual, Finance, Politics. FS D. Lewis, 1994, 85–98; E.VANDERPOOL, in: Semple Lectures 2, 1966–1970, 215–270, 242f. with fig. 32, 64f.　　　P.J.R.

Hyperborei (Ὑπερβόρε(ι)οι; *Hyperbóre(i)oi*). The Hyperboreans, a mythical people imagined as living at the edge of the world (Pind. Isthm. 6,23) 'beyond the North Wind (Boreas)' (thus ancient etymology, which is considered uncertain today [1]). The H. share with other marginal peoples (such as the Ethiopians, their southern counterpart), traits of the ideal concept of a paradisical existence in proximity to the gods, in a country favoured by climate [2; 3; 4]. By their relation to → Apollo, the H. are closely connected with the most important centres of his cult, Delphi and Delos.

Beside the earliest evidence for the H., Hes. Cat. fr. 150,21 M-W, they feature in a paean by Alcaeus (fr. 307c V.), which celebrates Apollo's sojourn with the H. and his return to Delphi on a chariot drawn by swans: following a well-known pattern, the god's → epiphany is represented as his arrival from a foreign land [5. 230]. The concept of the country of the H. being accessible 'neither by ship nor on foot' (Pind. Pyth. 10,29), and only to gods or heroes (cf. the legend of the flight of the Hyperborean → Abaris), appears in Pindar – where Perseus visits the sacrifices, accompanied by music, for Apollo held by the H., who are exempt from illness and old age (Pind. Pyth. 10,29ff.; on the sacrifice of donkeys, cf. Callim. fr. 186,10; 492) and Heracles brings the olive tree to Olympia from their country (Pind. Ol. 3) – as well as in Bacchyl. 3,58–62, where Apollo carries off the pious → Croesus to the land of the H. from his pyre. In the latter case the image of 'Hyperborean bliss' (Aesch. Cho. 373), probably influenced by Orphic and Pythagorean teachings, converges with the eschatological ideas about the Islands of the Blessed (→ Makaron Nesoi) and about → Elysium [6].

The most detailed account about the H., shaped by cautious scepticism, is furnished by Hdt. 4,32–36, who cites the Delian tradition (cf. IG II 813): every year the H. send offerings bound in straw, handed on from people to people, to → Delos; originally the tribute for → Eileithyia was brought there personally by two Hyperborean maidens, Hyperoche and Laodice – on whose tomb (sêma) by the sanctuary of Artemis Delian girls and boys have been dedicating offerings of their hair ever since – together with five companions (perpherées). Even earlier Arge (→ Hekaerge) and → Opis were said to have come; they were buried in another tomb, the so-called thêkê, and were appealed to in a hymn by → Olen [5. 92f., 311; 7]. The route which the offerings took, described in a similar form also at Callim. Hymn. 4,278ff. (cf. fr. 186) and Paus. 1,31,2, has given rise to ancient and modern speculations about the identity of the H., whom → Aristeas [1] of Proconnesus considered as the northern neighbours of the → Arimaspi, Issedones and Scythians (Hdt. 4,13). In Hellenistic times, the H. became a utopian model (→ Hecataeus of Abdera), and later they turned into a symbol of the far north, losing any other significance.

1 FRISK, s.v. H., vol. 2, 967   2 B. GATZ, Weltalter, goldene Zeit und sinnverwandte Vorstellungen, 1967, 189–200   3 J. FERGUSON, Utopias of the Classical World, 1975, 16–22   4 J. S. ROMM, The Edges of the Earth in Ancient Thought, 1992, 60–67   5 BURKERT   6 E. KRUMMEN, Pyrsos Hymnon: festliche Gegenwart und mythisch-rituelle Trad. als Voraussetzung einer Pindarinterpretation, 1990, 255–263   7 W. SALE, The Hyperborean Maidens on Delos, in: Harvard Theological Review 54, 1961, 75–89.

O. CRUSIUS, s.v. H., ROSCHER 1.2, 2805–2835; H. DAEBRITZ, s.v. H., RE 9, 258–279; H. M. WERHAHN, s.v. H.,

RAC 16, 967–986; PH. ZAPHIROPOULOU, s.v. H., LIMC 8.1, 641–643.   A.A.

Hyperechius Gem-cutter of the Imperial Roman period (Antonine/1st cent.). Signed red jasper with Socrates bust (Berlin, SM) and yellow jasper (a variety of stone typical of the late Imperial period) with a lion (Boston, MFA).

→ Gem-cutting

ZAZOFF, AG, 322, n. 106, pl. 96,4;5.   S.MI.

Hypereides (Ὑπερείδης; *Hypereídēs*). Attic orator, son of Glaucippus, from the deme Collytus, born 390/89 BC (since he was *diaitetes* in 330/29 and thus 60 years old, IG II 941), died in 322 BC.

A. LIFE B. WORKS C. CHARACTERISTICS AND THE JUDGEMENT OF ANTIQUITY

A. LIFE

Of the rich biographical tradition of antiquity (Hermippus, Dionysius of Halicarnassus, Caicilius) all that has been preserved are the *Vita* in Ps.-Plutarch (Mor. 848d–850b) and short notes in Athenaeus, Photius (495b–496a) and in the Suda; in addition there is usable biographical information in H.' extant speeches and epigraphical testimonies.

H. came from a wealthy family (houses in Athens and Piraeus, estates in Eleusis; tombs in front of the Hippades Gate) and in 340 and 339 he performed three extensive → liturgies (*trierarchiai*, choregia; however, others are not documented). Although he did not need the money, he also was active as a → logograph in private court cases throughout his entire life. Sources describe him as a pupil of both → Isocrates and → Plato, but only the influence of the former is clearly evident in his philosophy and style. Otherwise there are anecdotes and racy stories about his private life (his preference for culinary delights, affairs with Phryne and other hetaerae).

Following his political emergence on the side of the group around → Timotheus (court cases against Aristophon 362 and Autocles c. 360) H. appears to have concentrated solely on logography in the next 17 years, where he became a specialist for smaller private court cases and *synegoria* in particular (support for a party to a court case by an outsider). True to the line taken by → Demosthenes [2] and against → Eubulus [1] H. operated in the years prior to the battle of Chaeronea (→ *eisangelía* against Philocrates 343, representing Athenian interests before the Delphian Amphictyony 343/2 and on Chios and Rhodes 341; allegiance with Thebes in the autumn of 339). He did not take part in the battle of Chaeronea, as he was a *bouleutes*, however, after the defeat he organized the resistance by every possible means (including freeing slaves), which proved to be superfluous given Philip's restraint following his victory, but brought H. a → *paranomia* charge by Aristogeiton due to the liberation of the slaves and the naturalization of the metics (cf. Ps.-Plut. Mor. 849a 1–4), from which he was acquitted. Even after Philip's death (336) and during the Alexander campaign H. remained steadfastly anti-Macedonian. The estrangement between him and Demosthenes, which probably began with the controversy around Chares and the mercenaries at Taenarum (shortly before 324), led, via differences of opinion on Alexander's decree on the deification of his person and the repatriation of all expatriates, to an open break in conjunction with the Harpalus affair: as one of the prosecutors H. achieved the imposition of a large fine on Demosthenes, who avoided it by fleeing (January 323). In the rebellion against Macedonian rule that followed Alexander's death (June 323) H. was the spokesman (funeral oration for the fallen, 323/2). Following the victory of the Macedonians at Crannon (September 322) H. avoided the demanded extradition by fleeing like Demosthenes, however he was captured in October of the same year by emissaries of Antipater [1], probably on Aegina, and died a cruel death.

B. Works

According to Ps.-Plutarch, in antiquity 77 speeches by H. were available, of which 52 were considered genuine. We have 71 titles (partly with some fragments), among which only one is classified as belonging to the epideictic genre (→ Epideixis), 15 to the symbouleutic genre, and all others to the judicial genre. According to the Humanist Brassicanus there was supposedly a MS of H. in the library of the Hungarian king in the 16th cent., but this is open to question nowadays. Great parts of four scrolls came to light when papyrus finds were published in five stages between 1848 and 1892. They contain the conclusion to the oration against Phidippides (probably shortly before Philip's death in 336; paranomia charge), the conclusion of the oration for Lycophron (333; inheritance dispute), the oration for Euxenippus (330; eisangelia), complete but for a few gaps, the oration against Athenogenes (after 330; dispute about a contract of sale), extensive sections of the oration against Demosthenes (323) and most of the Epitáphios (323/2). All that is extant, therefore, originates from the last 14 years of H.'s life.

C. Characteristics and the judgement of antiquity

As far as a judgement is possible on this still meagre basis, H. is distinguished by his art of ethopoeia, equal to → Lysias, and by his vivid descriptions (→ Ekphrasis). He avoids obvious rhetorical embellishment and conveys the impression of natural simplicity. His argumentation is skilful, the structure clear and based on the subject. His language incorporates words from everyday life and borrowings from comedy, occasionally also neologisms or words used in a new meaning. His humour is almost ubiquitous, oscillating between fine irony and biting sarcasm. On the other hand there are no polemical 'hits below the belt' of the kind used by Demosthenes or Aeschines (this may, however, be a result of the condition in which the texts have been handed down). The Epitáphios, with its heightened pathos and diction influenced by Isocrates and Gorgias, is a different genre.

The literary criticism of antiquity generally places H. second to Demosthenes for his eloquence, in some respects he is even ranked above Demosthenes (in heuresis, Dion. Hal. De imitatione 5,6; in the number and variety of his merits, Ps.-Longinus, Περὶ ὕψους 34) and as a model worthy of emulation (Dion. Chrys. 18,11). The less positive judgement of Hermogenes (ibid. 2,382) is as much a peripheral phenomenon as the political-moral condemnation of H. due to his attacks on Demosthenes (Lucian Demosthenis Encomium 31).

EDITIONS: C. JENSEN, 1917 (repr. 1963); G. COLIN, 1946; J. O. BURTT, 1954; M. MARZI, P. LEONE, E. MALCOVATI, 1977.
COMMENTARIES: V. DE FALCO, 1947 (Euxenippos and Athenogenes); A. N. OIKONOMIDES, 1958 (Euxenippos); G. SCHIASSI, 1959 (Epitáphios).
RESEARCH REPORT: G. BARTOLINI, Iperide. Rassegna di problemi e di studi (1912–1970) (Proagones studi 13), 1977.
BIBLIOGRAPHY: J. ENGELS, Studien zur polit. Biographie des H., 1989.
FOR PARTICULAR ORATIONS: G. BARTOLINI, I papiri e le edizioni dell' orazione di Iperide Contro Demostene, in: A&R; 17, 1972, 103–113; L. BRACCESI, L'epitafio di Iperide come fonte storica, in: Athenaeum 48, 1970, 276–301; S. SALOMONE, Originalità dell' epitafio Iperideo, in: A&R; 22, 1977, 15–25; Id., Osservazioni sull'orazione Iperidea "Per Licofrone", in: Maia n.s. 25, 1973, 55–63.
M.W.

Hyperion (Ὑπερίων; *Hyperíōn*; on the etymology [1]). In the tradition of Hesiod one of the → Titans, who with his sister Theia fathers the gods of light Helios (→ Sol), → Selene and → Eos (Hes. Theog. 134; 371–374; Apollod. 1,2,8). Opinions are divided on his participation in the → titanomachy (schol. Hom. Il. 14,274 DINDORF contra Serv. Aen. 6,580). In Homer, however, H. is an epithet (Hom. Od. 1,8) as well as an independent term for Helios (Hom. Il. 19,398, but especially in Roman poetry: e.g. Ov. Met. 8,565; Stat. Theb. 3,35). H. is the title of an epistolary novel by J.Ch. HÖLDERLIN (1797–1799), in which H., whose name is meaningful as a metaphor for light, is a fighter in the Greek war of independence.

1 O. JESSEN, s.v. H., RE 9, 287   2 A. KOSSATZ-DEISSMANN, s.v. H., LIMC 5.1, 587–588.   C.W.

Hypermestra (also Hypermnestra; Ὑπερμήστρα; *Hyperméstra*, Ὑπερμνήστρα; *Hypermnéstra*).
[1] Daughter of → Danaus, wife of → Lynceus (or Lyrceus). The only daughter of Danaus who, against her father's orders, did not kill her husband in their wedding night (Pind. Nem. 10,6; Aesch. PV 866; Apollod.

2,1,5). She spares him because she loves him (Aesch. PV 865–868; schol. Pind. Pyth. 9,195b; cf. Hor. Carm. 3,11,33–52) or because he does not touch her (Apollod. 2,1,5; cf. Ov. Epist. 14,64). H. is put on trial by Danaus, but is acquitted with the help of Aphrodite (Paus. 2,20,7), which scene presumably was portrayed in the 'Danaids' of Aeschylus (TrGF III fr. 43–46). For this reason H. dedicates a statue of Aphrodite Nikephoros in the temple of Apollo (Paus. 2,19,6) and founds a sanctuary for Artemis Peitho (Paus. 2,21,1). According to another version, Lynceus kills Danaus and his remaining daughters, becomes king of Argus and fathers → Abas [1] with H. (schol. Eur. Hec. 886; Paus. 2,16,1f.). This makes the pair the progenitors of the Argive heroes (cf. Paus. 10,10,5).

[2] Heroine, whose grave in Argis is shown to be next to H. [1], daughter of → Thestius, wife of → Oicles, mother of → Amphiaraus (Paus. 2,21,2; Diod. Sic. 4,68,5; Apollod. 1,7,7; Hyg. Fab. 73).

[3] Daughter of → Erysichthon at Antoninus Liberalis 17, otherwise called Mestra.

G. BERGER-DOER, s.v. H., LIMC 5.1, 588–590; O. JESSEN, s.v. H., RE 9, 289–292; CH. ROHWEDER, Macht und Gedeihen: Eine polit. Interpretation der Hiketiden des Aischylos, 1998. K.WA.

Hyperocha Literally 'surplus' (τὰ ὑπέροχα, *tà hypérocha*, or ἡ ὑπεροχή, *hē hyperochē*), technically it designates the extra value by which the value of the secured object exceeds the amount of the secured debt, Latin *superfluum*. As the Greek pledge is to be understood strictly as a lapsed pledge (cf. → *hypothēkē*), it necessitated special contractual or judicial regulations if the extra value was intended to serve as security for a further creditor or return to the security debtor following sale of the security. Multiple mortgaging is documented from Athens as early as the 4th cent. BC (cf. → *hypothēkē*), however the term *hyperocha* was not used there. *Hyperocha* appears for the first time in the so-called grain decree from Samos (Syll.³ 976, l. 66; around 260 BC), where the sale of securities is prescribed [3. 87; 5]. Logically the debtor is personally responsible there also for the deficit not covered by the security. With reference to *hyperocha* and the deficit (ἐλλεῖπον, *elleîpon*) in the papyri see [2. 134]; cf. also SB 18,13167, l. 25f. (Alexandria?, middle of the 2nd cent. AD), where instead of *hyperocha* an additional revenue (πλεόνασμα, *pleónasma*) is compared with the deficit [4. 243]. For surplus in Roman law see → *pignus*.

1 A. MANIGK, s.v. H., RE 9, 292–321, esp. 306ff.   2 H.-A. RUPPRECHT, Einführung in die Papyruskunde, 1994   3 G. THÜR, H. KOCH, Prozeßrechtlicher Komm. zum "Getreidegesetz" aus Samos, Anzeiger der Oesterr. Akad. der Wiss. 118, 1981, 61–88   4 G. THÜR, Hypotheken-Urkunden eines Seedarlehens, in: Tyche 2, 1987, 229–245   5 ST. TRACY, The Date of the Grain Decree from Samos, in: Chiron 20, 1990, 97–100. G.T.

Hyperochus (Ὑπέροχος; *Hypérochos*) from the Lower Italian Cyme, period unknown (according to JACOBY, commentary on H., FGrH 576) 3rd cent. BC at the earliest, 2nd cent. AD at the latest). Author of a local history of Cyme (*Kymaiká*), of which only 3 fragments are extant. K.MEI.

Hypeuthynos (ὑπεύθυνος; *hypeúthynos*) is used in the penal provisions of Greek decrees to mean 'liable, owing' (context: payment of monetary fines, e.g. IPArk 11,37), in Athens specifically for 'accountable'. Every Athenian holding an office had to submit to an accountability process when his term had expired (εὔθυναι, → *eúthynai*) before the completion of which he could not leave the country or dispose of his assets. In the Egyptian papyri, *hypeuthynos* simply means 'required to make payment'.

A. R. W. HARRISON, The Law of Athens 2, 1971, 208–211; IPArk. G.T.

Hyphaeresis see → Sandhi

Hyphasis (H. in Arr., → Hypanis in Str., Diod. Sic. and Dionys. Per., Hypasis in Curt. and Plin. HN, Bipasis in Ptol.; all of them possibly passed down from Old Indian *Vipāśā*- through Iranian); one of the five main rivers of the Punjab, modern Satlağ/Beas. At the upper reaches (modern Beas) was the point from which Alexander returned to the → Hydaspes. Thus the Satlağ (→ Zaradrus of Ptol.), which lies further to the east, remained unknown for the most part to the Alexander historians, and also the lower course, which both have in common, as far as the → Acesines [2] was considered to be the H. In the 2nd cent. AD Ptolemy, with somewhat further-reaching geographical knowledge, correctly recognized the Bipasis to be a tributary of the Zaradrus.

E. KIESSLING, s.v. H., RE 9, 230–236. K.K.

Hyphen see → Punctuation

Hypius (Ὕπιος; *Hýpios*).

[1] (*Hyp(p)ius*). River, modern Melen Çayı, which flows from Lake Daphnusis (modern Efteni Gölü) to the Black Sea; the upper reaches of the H. are identical to the Küçük Melen Çayı (differently [1]).

[2] (*Hypius mons*). Mountains north of → Prusias on the H. (Plin. HN 5,148; differently [1]).

1 L. ROBERT, A travers l'Asie Mineure, 1980, 11–106.

K. BELKE, Paphlagonien und Honorias, 1996, 217f.; W. RUGE, s.v. H., RE 9, 322f. K.ST.

Hypnus see → Somnus

Hypoboles graphe (ὑποβολῆς γραφή; *hypobolês graphé*). Civil suit against a person who was passed off as the child of a citizen. Such false children, usually bought as slaves, are frequently mentioned in Attic court speeches and → comedies: childless women attempted to consolidate their position in the household in this manner, but *hypoboles graphe* is only known from the *Lexica Segueriana* V [2]. The penalty for being a false child was being sold into slavery.

1 I. BEKKER (ed.), Anecdota Graeca I, 1814/1865, 311
2 LIPSIUS, 417.	G.T.

Hypocaustum see → Heating

Hypogaeum Collective term for underground architecture. In modern terms hypogaeum is mainly a part of → funerary architecture, in which case hypogaeum refers to architecture below the earth's surface and not that which is built above ground and then covered with earth in the sense of the tumulus with a tomb chamber inside; moreover heroa, which are closely related to tombs in character (e.g. that of → Calydon) as well as structures for special cult facilities (e.g. the nekromanteion of → Ephyra [3]) or, from the Roman period, the Mithraeum of → Capua/S. Maria Capua Vetere) appear as hypogaea.

The hypogaeum appeared more and more often from the 2nd half of the 4th cent. BC in the Greek cul-

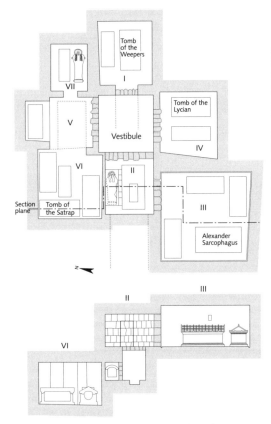

Royal necropolis of Sidon: hypogaeum A, late 6th cent.–late 4th cent.BC (ground-plan and cross-section).
(The Roman numerals refer to the chambers.)

tural sphere as well as in the neighbouring cultures of the Thracians or the indigenous cultures of southern Italy (Apulia; hypogaeum of Paestum, → Posidonia); a derivation of the numerous Alexandrian hypogaea from older Egyptian-Byzantine models (royal city of Sidon, cf. fig.) is under discussion, but would hardly be an explanation of the phenomenon on the whole. The hypogaeum, which was at times expanded to form → catacombs, played an important role as a burial and cult site in early Christian architecture and thus marks the emergence of the first cemeterial churches.

H. ALON EL-ATTA, The Relations between the Egyptian Tombs and the Alexandrine H., in: Études et travaux 16, 1992, 11–19; A. BARBET et al., L'hypogée paléochrétien des Orants à Constanta, in: MEFRA 108, 1996, 105–158; W. A. DASZEWSKI, The Origins of the Hellenistic H. in Alexandria, in: FS E. Winter, 1994, 51–68; U. KRON, Zum H. von Paestum, in: JDAI 86, 1971, 117–148; J. L. LAMBOLEY, Les hypogées indigènes apuliens, in: MEFRA 94, 1982, 91–194; L. REEKMANS, Spätröm. H., in: O. FELD (ed.), FS F.W. Deichmann, 1986, 11–37.	C.HÖ.

Hypokrites (ὑποκριτής; *hypokritḗs*).
I. CONCEPT II. DEVELOPMENT IN ATHENS
III. DUTIES (INCLUDING SUPERNUMERARIES)
IV. DEVELOPMENT OUTSIDE ATHENS FROM THE
4TH CENT. BC V. MASKS AND COSTUMES

I. CONCEPT
The underlying verb ὑποκρίνομαι (*hypokrínomai*) means in Homer 'to make a decision upon request', 'to interpret' (on omens: Hom. Il. 12,228 or dreams: Hom. Od. 19,535; 555) or 'to answer' (Hom. Od. 2,111). The basic meaning of the noun *hypokrites*, which is first attested in the 5th cent. BC, was thus postulated now as 'answerer' (to questions of the director of the chorus), now as 'interpreter' (of the myth which the chorus performed). It refers to the speaker who appeared opposite the singers of the chorus of the tragedy or comedy and made a dialogue possible, thus to the actor in all forms of drama.

II. DEVELOPMENT IN ATHENS
The first *hypokritai* were the tragedians themselves: from → Thespis (TrGF 1,49: DID D1) to → Aeschylus the poet was also the composer, director and actor. Aeschylus introduced a second speaker next to himself, the names Cleander and Mynniscus are mentioned by the Vita Aeschyli 15 (TrGF III, Testimonium A 1). → Sophocles refrained from taking the main part himself; he increased the number of speakers to three, thus aiming at professional performance and in this way founded the profession of the *hypokrites*, who enjoyed the same status as the poet. The number of the *hypokritai* stayed at three, it guaranteed equal opportunity in the competition. The 'first', or main, *hypokrites* (→ Protagonistes) got the main part, the two others (→ Deuteragonistes, → Tritagonistes) had to play a wealth of roles – men as well as women. The distribu-

tion of one role on various speakers was avoided at first (cf. however Theseus in Soph. OC 551–667, 887–1043), but it was a common practice for Menander. Comedy, which held onto improvisation longer, submitted later to the restriction to three *hypokritai* – occasionally already in → Cratinus (PCG IV Cratinus, Testimonia 19).

III. Duties (including supernumeraries)
In the course of the development of drama the dialogues continue to increase at the price of the chorus. For this reason the *hypokrites* was required to have, above all, perfect voice control. In a tragic tetralogy he had to embody completely different persons consecutively: now arguing, now declaiming to the accompaniment of the aulos, from the time of Sophocles also in song. The arias or monodies, which were performed on the stage (τὰ ἀπὸ τῆς σκηνῆς, *tà apò tês skēnês*, Aristot. Poet. 12,1452b 18) were divided into strophes at first, in the late work of Euripides, however, they were *durchkomponiert*, i.e. with no strophic structure (Eur. Or. 1369–1502: the Phrygian's aria) [1]. Lively acting and gesticulating, skilful singing and linguistic virtuosity were required above all by Old Comedy. Gradually the audience became just as interested in the actor as it was in his role. For this reason, around 449 BC, an agon of the tragic protagonists was set up at the Dionysia, a little later one for the comic ones at the Lenaea. The star cult was born. From now on the competing poets got their protagonist by drawing lots (Hsch. N 286), the two other *hypokritai* were chosen by them in their role as directors [2. 93–95]. The state paid the wages, only the supernumeraries (κωφὰ πρόσωπα, *kōphà prósōpa*) were paid by the → *choregos* as an additional service (παραχορήγημα, *parachorḗgēma*). There were two groups of supernumeraries: actors of roles in the plot who are sometimes or always mute since none of the three *hypokritai* is available (e.g. Ismene in Soph. OC 1096–1689; Pylades throughout in Aesch. Cho.; Soph. El.; Eur. El.), and supernumeraries in the actual sense of the word (guards, servants, children) [3]. Whether the mute women's roles in Aristophanes, like Opora and Theoria in 'Peace', were played by men or not (schol. Aristoph. Pax 849 mentions prostitutes) is disputed.

IV. Development outside Athens from the 4th cent. BC
Performances in the theatres of Attic communities (Piraeus, Thoricus, Icarium) and, since 386 BC reruns in the city → Dionysia as well, furthered the building of repertories. As new theatres were built in the entire Greek-speaking world, some *hypokritai* obtained fame and riches for themselves through a lively touring business: Callippides, Neoptolemus, Polus and Theodorus in tragedy, Lycon and Satyrus in comedy. As protagonists they formed their own ensembles and played pieces in which they shone [4]. While the stars stood in the centre of public interest, as honorary decrees and many anecdotes attest, the life of the other *hypokritai* (if

we can believe what Demosthenes reports about → Aeschines [2], cf. [5]) was difficult and lacklustre. This did not preclude that Aeschines could later gain great fame as a politician and orator. In Hellenism the Attic profession of the *hypokrites* had become a Panhellenic one; at that time all of the Dionysian artists (→ Technitai) in Athens, on the Isthmus and in Nemea, in Ionia and on the Hellespont joined together in guilds. These guaranteed legal protection and privileges to the travelling troupes and maintained the artistic standard of the performances as long as complete dramas were still performed rather than virtuoso musical and dancing solo performances.

V. Masks and Costumes
The → mask, which was closely linked to the cult of → Dionysus [I. C. 7.], allowed the *hypokrites* to disappear behind the figure that he embodied. Masks made it easier for him to take on female roles as well and to change roles quickly. The masks, which were identical for tragedy and satyr-play, were restrained in expression in the classical period, marked by ever greater emotion from the end of 4th cent.; conversely the comedy masks gradually lost their originally grotesque and demonic character and became more natural.

Costumes of the tragic *hypokrites* do not appear to have deviated much from everyday clothing according to the scarce pictorial sources [2. 177–231; 6] (→ Clothing, → Chiton, → Peplos); at the end of the 5th cent., however, there is evidence of a resplendent tragedy-costume: an ankle-length, richly decorated, oriental-style, sleeved garment possibly of Dionysian origin; the aulos actor also wore this. As a stage shoe (→ Cothurnus) he wore a soft close-fitting laced boot, well suited for walking and dancing; only in late Hellenism did this change to the high stilted shoe. – The *hypokrites* of Old Comedy appeared with stark sensuality: stomach and backside were grotesquely padded, and over a tight tricot he wore a ridiculously short chiton, with a phallus dangling from underneath it. The typical woman's dress was a long saffron yellow chiton. In the course of the 4th cent., analogous to the mask, the costume of the *hypokrites* in comedy also became more subdued. A list of costumes and a catalogue of masks for the New Comedy is passed down by Poll. 4,118–120; 133–154 [7].

→ Lycon; → Neoptolemus; → Polus; → Theodorus

1 W. BARNER, Die Monodie, in: W. JENS (ed.), Die Bauformen der griech. Trag., 1971, 277–320   2 A. PICKARD-CAMBRIDGE, The Dramatic Festivals of Athens, ²1968, 126–176   3 D. P. STANLEY-PORTER, Mute Actors in the Tragedies of Euripides, in: BICS 20, 1973, 68–93   4 P. E. EASTERLING, From Repertoire to Canon, in: Id. (ed.), The Cambridge Companion to Greek Tragedy, 1997, 211–227   5 H. WANKEL, Demosthenes. Rede für Ktesiphon über den Kranz, 1976, zu §180 und §262   6 B. A. TRENDALL, T. B. L. WEBSTER, Illustrations of Greek Drama, 1971   7 T. B. L. WEBSTER, J. R. GREEN, A. SEEBERG, Monuments Illustrating New Comedy vol. 1, ³1995, 1–51.

M. Bieber, The History of Greek and Roman Theater, ²1961; H.-D. Blume, Einführung in das ant. Theaterwesen, ³1991, 77–106; P. Ghiron-Bistagne, Recherches sur les acteurs dans la Grèce antique, 1976; A. Lesky, Hypokrites (1955), in: W. Kraus (ed.), Gesammelte Schriften, 1966, 239–246; J. B. O'Connor, Chapters in the History of Actors and Acting in Ancient Greece, 1908 (Suppl.: I. Parenti, in: Dioniso 35, 1961, 5–29); F. Poland, s.v. Technitai, RE 5, 2473–2558; K. Schneider, s.v. H., RE Suppl. 8, 187–232; B. Zucchelli, Ὑποκριτής. Origine e storia del termine (Pubblicazioni dell'Istituto di Filologia Classica dell' università di Genova 15), 1962.   H.-D.B.

Hypomeiones (οἱ ὑπομείονες/*hoi hypomeíones*, literally: the 'lesser ones'). In the context of the conspiracy of → Kinadon in 398 BC, the *hypomeiones* are named along with the → helots, the → *neodamṓdeis* and the → *períoikoi* as a group of Spartans with limited rights (Xen. Hell. 3,3,6). This was probably not a technical term but rather a collective designation for former → *Spartiátai*, who for various reasons and in different ways had fewer rights than the → *hómoioi*: cowardice in battle (cf. → *trésantes*) caused the *hypomeiones* to be socially stigmatized, and loss of wealth or failure in the → *agōgḗ* could even result in the loss of full Spartan citizenship.
→ Sparta III.

S. Link, Der Kosmos Sparta, 1994, 21–25.   M. MEI.

Hypomnema (ὑπόμνημα; *hypómnēma*, more rarely ὑπομνηματισμός; *hypomnēmatismós*; Latin *commentarius* or more rarely *commentarium*). The word *Hypomnema* (from the root of μιμνήσκω; *mimnḗskō*, 'to remember') has the abstract basic meaning 'memory', presence in the memory or call/support for the memory (in this sense it already appears in Thuc. 2,44,2 and in Isocrates, Demosthenes, Xenophon etc.), however, in the course of time it takes on a large number of different connotations and nuances, especially the widespread (concrete) meaning 'mention, reference', also in the literal meaning (e.g. Thuc. 4,126,1), 'notice, memory aid, record' to designate a written *memorandum* of a private or public nature: economic catalogues, accounts, lists of persons or things, legal records, also formal documents e.g. petitions or protocols [3; 16]. Examples of this usage are found above all in papyrus documents. At least from the Alexandrian period onwards the word also designates the official registers, i.e. the archives of courts and public authorities (for which the term *ephemerídes* is also used). The Latin equivalent *commentarius* covers all meanings of the Greek word – including the designation of official archives (of priests' colleges, e.g. the → *commentarii pontificum*, or of magistrates or state institutions, e.g. the *commentarii Senatus*; the *commentarii principis* were the archives of the emperors); the term *acta* was also used in the Imperial period.
Hypomnema can assume the meaning 'note, record to aid memory' with reference to various occasions and situations of a private nature, e.g. *list of* keywords for a

speech, lecture notes or records of newly acquired knowledge, teaching material etc. For example, 'to write notes' (ὑπομνήματα γράφειν) is used in Pl. Plt. 295c for a doctor or a teacher, who leaves behind written records for the sick or their pupils; in Pl. Phdr. 276d *hypomnḗmata* are written notes to help one's own memory against the forgetfulness that accompanies old age, i.e. a kind of personal diary. The connotation 'note of a private nature' justifies the use of the word *hypomnema* in the sense of a certain piece of writing not intended for dissemination to the public, in contrast to a published work. The use of the term in the sense of 'draft, outline' to prepare a work still to be elaborated also has this basis in historiography and philosophy. In historiography it is well documented, according to one theory the historian first had to prepare a rough outline of facts, a *hypomnema*, that was then developed rhetorically.

The connotation 'memorable things' easily leads to the meaning 'discussion, representation, treatise' of various kinds (except oration and dialogue), henceforth as a book that has actually been completed and published. We have examples with reference to works with historical (e.g. Pol. 1,1,1), geographical (e.g. Ptol. Geographica 1,6,2), medical (e.g. often in → Galenus), philosophical (Diog. Laert. 4,4 defines a part of the works of Speusippus as *hypomnema* compared with his dialogues) and rhetorical (Ps.-Longinus De Sublimitate 44,12) content or with reference to works of mixed content, such as the *Sýmmikta hypomnḗmata* of → Aristoxenus or the *Hypomnḗmata* of → Callimachus. The definition *hypomnema* is used in the special sense also for autobiographical writings and recollections of great men: Pol. 2,40,4 mentions the *hypomnēmatismoí* of the statesman Aratus of Sicyon (other examples found in FGrH 227–238). However, it is difficult to say whether and when the term was attributable to the author and really was the title of the work or a secondary designation of genre, attributable to → indirect tradition.

From the Hellenistic period onwards the term *hypomnema* is used to designate a running exegetic commentary on literary texts that was written on a separate scroll from the commented text and was generally extensive in scope: this is one of the characteristic products of the scholarly philological work of the Alexandrian grammarians (together with the text edition, *ékdosis*), that made a lasting impact with → Aristarchus [4] of Samothrace (c. 215 – 144? BC) In this case the *hypomnema* is the opposite of the *sýngramma*, that designates a monographic treatise (see e.g. Galen, Comm. on Hippocrates, De acutorum morborum victu 15,515 K.; Scholia Il. 2,111). The originals of these writings have been lost; the diverse bulk of the scholarly material has been handed down by the scholiastic and erudite collections of the Byzantines. Only through papyrus findings are we familiar with significant remains of *hypomnḗmata*. They are normally subdivided according to the lemma–exegesis model, that follows the annotated text, and they exhibit various interests and contents, from the simple glossographic explanation of individual words to the explanation of philological, exegetic, antiquarian or mythographical problems; from language and word usage, rhetorical figures, stylistic observations, proverbs, anecdotes and biographical questions to aesthetic and moral judgements on the work and eventually to → allegoresis. Often erudite-doxographic accumulation prevails, not infrequently in a shortened and brachylogical redaction. Extant examples of extensive commentaries from the Imperial period are the medically oriented annotations of → Galenus (his commentaries on philosophical themes have been lost) and those of → Alexander [26] of Aphrodisias on Aristotle; countless commentaries on Aristotle and Plato of late antiquity are also extant. → Commentarii

> G. ARRIGHETTI, Poeti, eruditi e biografi. Momenti della riflessione dei Greci sulla letteratura, 1987, 161–231; G. AVENARIUS, Lukians Schrift zur Geschichtsschreibung, 1956, 85–104; E. BICKERMANN, Beiträge zur ant. Urkundengesch., in: APF 9, 1930, 164ff.; F. BÖMER, Der Commentarius, in: Hermes 81, 1953, 215–250; M. DEL FABBRO, Il commentario nella tradizione papiracea, in: Studia Papyrologica 18, 1979, 69–132; ENTRETIENS XL, 1994,; FGrH 227–238; K. MCNAMEE, Sigla and Select Marginalia in Greek Literary Papyri, 1992; G. MISCH, Gesch. der Autobiographie, I 1, ³1949, 209ff.; F. MONTANARI, Filologia omerica antica nei papiri, Proc. of the XVIII Congress of Papyrology at Athens, Athenai, Greek Papyrological Soc., 1988, 337–344; Id., Zenodotus, Aristarchus and the Ekdosis of Homer, in: G. W. MOST, Editing Texts – Texte edieren (Aporemata 2), 1998, 1–21; PFEIFFER, KP I; J. RÜPKE, Wer las Caesars bella als commentarii?, in: Gymnasium 99, 1992, 201–226; E. G. TURNER, Greek Papyri. An Introduction, ²1980, 63–126; E. ZIEBARTH, s.v. H., RE Suppl. 7, 281–82. F.M.

Hypomosia (ὑπωμοσία; hypōmosía). In Athens there were two types of sworn statements: 1. in the court proceeding one party could apply in person or through a representative for sojournment (Dem. Or. 48,25f.; schol. Dem. Or. 21,84) if there was significant cause, such as travel or funerary duties. The opponent was able to dispute this with a ἀντωμοσία (antōmosía, counter-oath).

2. If an application was deliberated in the council (→ boulḗ) or the popular assembly (→ ekklēsía), every citizen was able to declare through a hypomosia that he would bring a suit against the applicant because of the resolution's contrariness to law (→ paranómōn graphḗ) or the law's inappropriateness. This caused the vote or, if it had already taken place, the effectiveness of the resolution to be suspended until the court of assizes decided.

> A. R. W. HARRISON, The Law of Athens 2, 1971, 155; H. J. WOLFF, "Normenkontrolle" und Gesetzesbegriff in der att. Demokratie, 1970. G.T.

Hyporchema (ὑπόρχημα; hypórchēma). Old Greek choral lyric that was originally associated with the weapon dance. The word hyporchema is first documented in Pl. Ion 534c, where it is cited along with forms of poetry. → Thaletas of Gortyn (7th cent. BC) was the first to compose hyporchḗmata to accompany the weapon dances of the → Curetes (schol. Pind. Pyth. 2,127). As warrior dances were more elaborate and mimetic than other choral dances, a soloist probably sang (Ath. 1,15d-e). Thaletas probably brought the hyporchema to Sparta, where, together with Xenodamus of Cythera, he was responsible for the second re-organizing of music for the State: both also composed → paeans (Plut. De musica 1134b-c). The longest extant fragment of an hyporchema stems from → Pratinas of Phleius (Ath. 14,617c-f), presumably from a satyr play: it emphasizes the association with Dionysus and subordinates music to song. Hyporchemata may perhaps have played a role in drama: some commentators claim to see hyporchemata in passages such as Soph. Aj. 693ff. and Trach. 205ff. [1. 342]. The quotations in Plut. Mor. 747a–748d were attributed to → Simonides [2. 399–401] and Pindar [3. 100–102]. The nature of the → Kastoreion in Pind. Pyth. 2,69 is especially problematic: the scholion calls it a hyporchema and cites the opening verses with the statement that the Dioscuri were associated with warrior dances. Others assert that this Kastoreion is in fact the epinikion [4. 96–101]. The attributions to Bacchylides are sometimes based on the fact that the Cretan metre is predominantly used, and that is supposedly characteristic of the hyporchema [5. 90–91] and an indication of its Cretan origin.

> 1 E. DIEHL, s.v. H., RE 9, 338–343   2 TH. BERGK, Poetae lyrici Graeci III, ⁴1882   3 H. MAEHLER, Pindari Carmina II, 1989   4 G. W. MOST, The Measures of Praise, 1985   5 B. SNELL, H. MAEHLER, Bacchylidis carmina cum fragmentis, ¹⁰1970. E.R.

Hyporon Town in Bruttium (bronze coins around 300 BC: HN 105), probably identical to Hipporum in It. Ant. 115.

> NISSEN 2, 949. E.O.

Hyposkenion see → Theatre

Hypostasis

[1] see → Word formation

[2] (ὑπόστασις/hypóstasis; substantia, subsistentia). In late antiquity – through the influence of Neoplatonism and in the disputes of the 4th cent. AD around the essence of the Trinity – hypostasis went from an ambiguous term, not precisely defined by any school (cf. Socr. 3,7), to one of the most important terms of philosophical and theological thinking (doctrine of the Trinity, Christology).

The term hypostasis first appears in medical-scientific texts (→ Hippocrates, → Aristotle [6]) and describes the settling of solid substances from liquid (e.g. in urine), but also the substance becoming evident itself ('sediment', 'precipitate') [1. 24–26]. The philosophical meaning ('lasting survival', 'reality', 'existence'), first tangible in the 2nd cent. BC in → Ocellus and → Demetrius [21] Lakon, picks up here. Despite attempts to credit the introduction of *hypostasis* as a philosophical term to the Old Stoa, it appears – as well as in the later Stoa – to not have played any role there at all [2]. The Hellenistic philosophers use *hypostasis* as a more emphatic term for 'existence'. Occasionally, *hypostasis* even appears interchangeable with οὐσία (*ousía*). In the 1st cent. AD *substantia* arises as a Latin trans., which soon however also expresses *ousía*. Therefore, in the 4th cent. AD *subsistentia* is coined by Marius Victorinus to make a differentiation, but it does not become generally accepted.

Although the Neoplatonic *hypostasis* doctrine goes back to Plotinus, according to which the Mind emerges from the One by → emanation and from this the Soul emerges, he does not yet apply the term *hypostasis* to this. → Porphyrius is the first to describe the One, the Mind and the Soul in the title of Plot. Enneades 5,1 (Περὶ τῶν τριῶν ἀρχικῶν ὑποστάσεων) as *hypostasis*; Plotinus, on the other hand, speaks of *phýseis*.

In the Christian Trinitarian discussion, the first to describe God the Father, Son and Holy Ghost as *hypostasis* was → Origenes; for him, however, *hypostasis* is still interchangeable with *ousía*; he does not yet understand this to be 'individual existence' in the sense of 'person' [3]. The Arian dispute (→ Arianism) triggered controversies, how unity and Trinity were to be thought of in God. During this, the term *hypostasis* was used to describe the inner-Trinitarian relationship (μία οὐσία, τρεῖς ὑποστάσεις, 'one substance, three *hypostaseis*'). Differing from Neoplatonic concepts, the *hypostaseis* in the Trinity, however, are of equal rank; the idea of ranking has been given up.

In the beginning, no differentiation was made between *hypostasis* and Nature (*phýsis*) in Christology, until finally the Council of Chalcedon (in 451) defined that both natures (divine and human) come together in one person and one *hypostasis*.

1 H.Dörrie, Ὑπόστασις. Wort- und Bedeutungsgesch., 1955 (also in: Id., Platonica minora, 1976, 12–69) 2 J.Hammerstaedt, Das Aufkommen der philos. H.bedeutung, in: JbAC 35, 1992, 7–11   3 Id., Der trinitarische Gebrauch des H.begriffs bei Origenes, in: JbAC 34, 1991, 12–20   4 Id., RAC 16, 986–1035   5 F.Romano, D.P. Taormina (ed.), Hyparxis e hypostasis nel neoplatonismo, 1994   6 R.Witt, Ὑπόστασις, in: Amicitiae corolla ... J.R. Harris, 1933, 319–343.   S.M.-S.

Hypostigme, Hypoteleia see → Punctuation

Hypotheke (ὑποθήκη; *hypothḗkē*).
[1] Legal
A. Greek law   B. Graeco-Egyptian law
C. Roman law

A. Greek law
The *hypotheke* (ὑποθήκη = deposit, literally 'place under') is encountered in Attic law as an encumbrance upon property, houses, businesses, as security on loan provisions. Stones of *hypotheke* (→ *hóroi*) specified the mortgaged encumbrance. The *hypotheke* was an institution found throughout Greece, but outside Attica the designation of the mortgaged property by the *hóroi* is found only on a few Aegean islands. The *hypotheke* was enforced by foreclosure. This is shown by the clauses stipulating forfeiture to the creditor found on many *hóroi*, e.g. [1. no. 1]. The *hypotheke* was also subject to compensation; the debtor assumed liability for the 'deficit' (ἐλλεῖπον; *elleîpon*). The encumbered object (the *hypotheke*) remained in the ownership of the debtor, whereas the security (ἐνέχυρον; *enéchyron*) passed to the possession of the creditor. In some places, a legal ban on amortization and sub-hypothecation applied to the *hypotheke*; e.g. at → Gortyn (Gortyn Law Inscription 10,25). In Athens, for example, a creditor could appeal against further injunctions (κωλύειν συμβάλλειν/ *kōlýein symbállein*; recollection in Cod. Iust. 8,44,24 dating from AD 294). In the case of → maritime loans, it was customary to forbid sub-hypothecation (ἐπιδανείζειν; *epidaneízein*) (Dem. Or. 35,11).

B. Graeco-Egyptian law
The Graeco-Egyptian *hypotheke* too was enforced by foreclosure. In the event of default, the creditor was entitled to seize property and possessions (κρατεῖν καὶ κυριεύειν/*krateîn kaì kyrieúein*, etc.). It was regarded as sufficient merely to refer to the general rules of the law of the *hypotheke*, linked to the initiation of the debtor's personal liability for the deficit (FIRA III no. 119 dating from AD 143/4). The otherwise widespread injunction forbidding alienation to the debtor is absent from documents written by the Romans in Egypt. Its legality was disputed by Roman jurists: Marcianus allowed it (Dig. 20,5,7,2), as did Justinian and Byzantine jurisprudence. Hypothecations from Roman times anticipate the later 'Gordian Pledge' (→ *pignus Gordianum*). The *hypotheke* is similar to the → *ōnḗ en pístei* (ὠνὴ ἐν πίστει, assigned transfer of security), which corresponds to the ancient Greek → *prâsis epí lýsei* (πρᾶσις ἐπὶ λύσει, sale on redemption). The → *hypállagma* (literally: exchange) is to be distinguished from the *hypotheke*.

C. Roman law
The word *hypotheca* is first encountered as a loanword in Cicero (Fam. 13,56,2) referring to a Greek foreclosure *hypotheca*. Queries to Roman jurists from the eastern provinces use the expressions *hypothḗkē* and *hypotíthesthai* (Scaevola Dig. 20,1,34,1; 17,1,60,4). They furthered the adoption of the word

hypotheca into the professional legal language of the Romans. The first demonstrable usage in a legal text is in Julian (Dig. 41,3,33,4) in the 2nd cent. AD. Thereafter it is commonly used by Gaius and Marcian, less often by other jurists.

By *hypotheca* the Romans meant the Roman → pledge law, which, however, was not subject to foreclosure. '*Hypotheca*' *proprie* described pledge law without possession (Ulp. Dig. 13,7,9,1). However, the expression is often used in a context incorporating the possession (e.g. in the title of monographs by Gaius and Marcianus), just as the word → *pignus* is also used to imply a hypothecary law, there having been no meaningful distinction between this and the actual transfer of possession of the thing pledged (Marcianus Dig. 20,1,5,1; Inst. Iust. 4,6,7). In both cases, the creditor was protected by the pledge action *in rem* (*actio Serviana*), and in both cases the creditor had the right of sale (*ius distrahendi*) when the security was subject to exploitation because the debt matured.

1 M. FINLEY, Studies in Land and Credit in Ancient Athens 500–200 B.C. The Horos-Inscriptions, n.d. (1951), ²1985.

A. BISCARDI, Appunti sulle garanzie reali in diritto romano, 1976, 150–156, 218–254; HONSELL/MAYER-MALY/SELB, 196 with n. 10, 203–206; KASER, RPR I, 459 with n. 8, 463–473; II, 312–321; H.-A. RUPPRECHT, Einführung in die Papyruskunde, 1944, 134f.; Id., Die dinglichen Sicherungsrechte nach der Praxis der Papyri, in: FS H. Ankum II, 1995, 425–436; TAUBENSCHLAG, 271–291.

D.SCH.

[2] Rhetoric, see → Gnome [2]

Hypothesis (ὑπόθεσις; *hypóthesis*). Introduction, summary.
A. HISTORY OF LITERATURE B. RHETORIC

A. HISTORY OF LITERATURE
Three types can be distinguished in tragedy: 1. The *hypothéseis* of → Aristophanes [4] of Byzantium found in the Peripatetic tradition (→ Dicaearchus fr. 78 WEHRLI); they contain a brief summary, point to the treatment of the same material by another tragedian, name the setting, the identity of the chorus and the speaker of the prologue and give further information on the play's performance (dating, title of the author's other pieces performed at the same time, competitors and placing in the agon, → choregos). Sometimes, a critical aesthetic acknowledgement follows. The *Pínakes* of → Callimachus and the → *Didaskalíai* of Aristotle probably represent the sources of these. A complete *hypothesis* of this type is not preserved. 2. The *hypothéseis* connected above all with Euripides, ordered alphabetically and partially composed in verse form. They name the first verse of the piece and contain a summary composed in the preterite; nameless *dramatis personae* are identified. Probably as a mythological compendium, they are thought as a replacement for the actual texts and not as introductory information. They

are likely to stem from the 1st cent. BC. 3. Certain *hypothéseis* were written on the basis of the second type in the Byzantine period (13th/14th cents.: Demetrios Triklinios, Manuel Moschopoulos) for school instruction.

The *hypothéseis* placed before comedies correspond to the pattern of those for tragedies. The *hypothéseis* of type 1 appear to go back to Aristophanes [4] of Byzantium. They were reworked by → Symmachus and contain more didascalic information than the corresponding tragic *hypothéseis*. In addition there are more comprehensive summaries (type 2, cf. POxy. 663 of → Cratinus' *Dionysaléxandros*, PCG IV, p. 140), of → Menander probably also in alphabetical order (POxy. 1235 to *Hiéraia* and *Ímbrioi*), and (type 3) Byzantine *hypothéseis* composed with moralizing, didactic intent (e.g. *hypothesis* II to Aristophanes' *Birds*). More often than for tragedy, *hypothéseis* appear written in even number of verses (10 or 12), whose attribution to Aristophanes of Byzantium – perhaps with the exception of Aristophanes' *Thesmophoriazousae* – is doubtful.

Hypothéseis of non-dramatic texts are preserved for Pindar (probably by → Didymus [1]), Ps.-Hesiod's *Aspís*, Theocritus (by → Artemidorus [4] of Tyana and his son → Theon), Apollonius [2] Rhodius, Lycophron and for the orators Isocrates, Isaeus, Antiphon, Andocides and Lycurgus. For the speeches of Demosthenes there are *hypothéseis* by → Libanius that were used as introductions to the publications in the Byzantine period.

B. RHETORIC
In → rhetoric the term *hypóthesis* refers to a special case (*quaestio specialis*) in contrast to a general question (*thésis*). The *hypothesis* is treated systematically by → Hermagoras of Temnus.
→ Argumentum

N. DUNBAR (ed., comm.), Aristophanes, Birds, 1995, 31–37; PFEIFFER, KP I, 238–242; E. PÖHLMANN, Einführung in die Überlieferungsgesch. und in die Textkritik der ant. Lit. I, 1994, 33f.; L. RADERMACHER (ed.), Aristophanes' Frösche, 1967, 74–85; G. ZUNTZ, The political plays of Euripides, 1954, 129ff.

B.Z.

Hypsaeus In the Republican period, a cognomen (inscriptionally also *Ypsaeus*) probably of Greek origin in the family of the → Plautii.

K.-L.E.

Hypsas ("Ὕψας; *Hýpsas*).
[1] A river in the west of → Sicily, the modern Belice. Its source rivers originate close to the north coast and flow into the sea 31 km below the confluence of the two largest branches (Belice Sinistro, Belice Destro) and 4 km east of Selinus [4] (in Plin. HN 3,90 erroneously located west of Selinus). The personification of the H. is depicted on the coins of Selinus as a sacrificing youth (5th cent. BC, HN 168).

J. B. CURBERA, Onomastic of River-Gods in Sicily, in: Philologus 142, 1998, 55.

[2] A river in the south of → Sicily, that flows by → Acragas to the west and after receiving the river Acragas (modern San Biagio), which flows by the town to the east, enters the sea (cf. Pol. 9,27,5; Ptol. 3,4,3), modern Drago (upper course) or Sant' Anna (lower course).   GI. MA. and E. O.

Hypseus (Ὑψεύς; *Hypseús*). King of the Thessalian → Lapithae (Pind. Pyth. 9,13–31; according to schol. ad loc. based on a *Ehoie* of Hes. fr. 215 M-W), born in the Thessalian Pindus mountains as a son of the river god → Peneius and of the naiad → Creusa (a daughter of Oceanus and of Gaia), or daughter of Philyra (schol. Pind. Pyth. 9,27); father of → Cyrene and Alcaea (schol. Pind. Pyth. 9,31), whom he fathers with Chlidanope; also father of Themisto (Apollod. 1,84; Hyg. Fab. 1).
                                                                    J.S.-A.

Hypsicles (Ὑψικλῆς; *Hypsiklês*). Hellenistic mathematician and astronomer. From the introduction to book 14 of Euclid's 'Elements' written by him, it follows that H. lived in Alexandria around 175 BC.

It is attested by MSS that he composed what later was added as book 14 to the 'Elements' of → Euclides [3] (ed. [1]). Like bk. 13 it deals with the inscribing of regular bodies into a sphere and was thought of as an explanation to a lost work of → Apollonius [13] about dodecahedra and icosahedra. H. shows that the planes that form an icosahedron and dodecahedron inscribed into the same sphere are circumscribed by the same circle. He further proves that surfaces and volumes of dodecahedron and icosahedron relate to each other like the edge of the cube inscribed in the same sphere does to the edge of the icosahedron. The supposition – based on Arabic tradition – that H. also contributed to the so-called bk. 15 of the 'Elements' is unlikely.

A short and presumedly incomplete treatise about the times the stars rise is also preserved (*Anaphorikós*, Ἀναφορικός; ed. [2; 3]). It is the earliest known Greek work in which the → ecliptic (probably after the Babylonian model) is divided into 360 degrees. H. provides a procedure to calculate the times which the different signs and degrees of the ecliptic need for their rising and setting. His method is not based on an exact calculation but rather on a rough approximation. He assumes that the duration of the longest day for Alexandria amounts to 210 temporal degrees, and assumes (incorrectly) that the rising times of the signs from Aries to Virgo form an ascending arithmetical progression, and from Libra to Pisces a descending arithmetical progression. For his calculations he uses auxiliary propostions on arithmetical progression. Despite the false assumption that the length of a day increases and decreases in a monotone fashion, he achieves results that are sufficient for practical applications (e.g. in astrology). Written in the style of Euclid, the text is mathematically correct; from an astronomical point of view it represents an interesting link between Babylonian and Hellenistic science: since H. did not yet have access to the trigonometric re-

sources of Ptolemy to calculate the rising and setting times exactly, he used approximations by means of arithmetical progressions, i.e. linear peak functions, with whose help the Babylonians calculated their ephemerides. – As one of the 'middle books' that was meant to be read after the study of Euclid in preparation of → Ptolemaeus' 'Almagest', the *Anaphorikós* was translated into Arabic in the 9th cent. (ed. [3]) and from there into Latin in the 12th cent. by Gerard of Cremona (*Liber Esculei de ascensionibus*; ed. [2]).

H.'s familiarity with arithmetical progressions and series is also attested by → Diophantus [4], who mentions that H. determined the value of any polygonal number (→ Gnomon [3]) (De polygonis numeris, p. 470,27 TANNERY).

EDITIONS: 1 J. L. HEIBERG, Hypsiclis liber, sive Elementorum liber XIV qui fertur, 1888 (= Euclidis opera omnia, vol. 5; Greek-Lat.)   2 K. MANITIUS, Des H. Schrift Anaphorikos nach Überl. und Inhalt kritisch behandelt, Programm Gymnasium Dresden, 1888 (Greek text and Latin transl. by Gerard of Cremona)   3 V. DE FALCO, M. KRAUSE (ed.), H.: Die Aufgangszeiten der Gestirne, in: AAWG, 3rd series, no. 62, 1966 (Greek-German with schol., Arab. transl. and comm.).
BIBLIOGRAPHY: 4 A. A. BJÖRNBO, s.v. H. (2), RE 9, 427–433   5 I. BULMER-THOMAS, H. of Alexandria, in: GILLISPIE, vol. 6, 1972, 616f.   6 T. L. HEATH, History of Greek Mathematics, 1921, vol. 1, 84; 419f.; vol. 2, 192; 213–218; 515   7 J. MAU, s.v. H., KlP 2, 1967, 1289f.
8 SEZGIN, vol. 5, 143–145; vol. 6, 80   9 B. L. VAN DER WAERDEN, Erwachende Wissenschaft, 1956, 445–448.
                                                                    M.F.

Hypsicrates (Ὑψικράτης; *Hypsikrátēs*) of Amisus. Historian and grammarian who lived to be 92 years old ([Lucian] Macrob. 22). The few fragments of his historical work point to the period of Caesar or Augustus (end of the 1st cent. BC). He also wrote about Homer, whom he viewed as a contemporary of Hesiod, and gave etymologies of Greek and Latin words that Varro rejected. In so doing, he derived Latin vocabulary from the Greek. FGrH 190.

R. GIOMINI, Ipsicrate, in: Maia 8, 1956, 49–55.   K. MEI.

Hypsipyle see → Iason; → Lemnian women; → Thoas

Hypsistos (ὕψιστος; *hýpsistos*, 'the highest') can be conferred as an adjective on every god, but, since later Hellenism, is above all the epigraphically attested epiclesis of → Zeus as mountain god or high god, and the name of a god (*theòs hýpsistos*) who can be identical to Zeus H., but can also indicate the Jewish or Christian God; a distinct differentiation is often difficult. A complete study of the material which has grown enormously since the first analyses, and which L. ROBERT has announced on numerous occasions, has still not appeared [1].

Zeus is consistently identified as the highest god; the adjective *hýpatos* is documented since the *Iliad*, since

Pindar (Pind. Nem. 1,60; 11,2) the adjective *hypsistos*, and this, not only for Zeus as highest god of all but also specifically as mountain god (Soph. Trach. 1091: cult on Mount Oeta); in cultic use, the mountain god Zeus carries the epiclesis *hýpatos* [2. 875f.] more frequently than *hýpsistos*. The inscriptional evidence for *hýpsistos* (Zeus and *theós*) is distributed over various areas:

1. Zeus as god of the Macedonian kingship is attested with the epiclesis H. since mid-Hellenism; the inscriptions stem from the royal cities of Edessa and Aegae as well as from other cities in Macedonia. Such dedications repeat themselves in a few towns of the Greek motherland, but their relationship to Macedonia is not totally verifiable. In Thebes there was a temple in the vicinity of a city gate named after it (Paus. 9,8,15), in Corinth the altars of Zeus Chthonios, the god of the depths of the earth, and his counterpart Zeus H., the god of the highest heavens, stood next to each other, and in Olympia there were several altars of Zeus H. (Paus. 2,2,8; 5,15,5).

2. From the early Imperial period onwards we find numerous inscriptions in Asia Minor that for the most part refer to a *theòs hýpsistos*, especially in the Pontus region, in Lycia, and in Phrygia. At least a portion of these inscriptions can describe one of the local high gods (analogously the local mother goddess appears as *hypsístē*). Occasionally the epiclesis is bestowed on → Helios as the highest visible god. Other texts, especially from the border region of Phrygia and Lydia, are the result of special religious development in one region of Anatolia that in the Imperial period distinguishes itself by religious innovation. This is true above all in those cases where a mediator figure (*theòs ángelos, tò theîon angelikón, tò theîon epiphanés*) [3] is added to a *theos hypsistos* as the highest god, without this being recognizable as Jewish or Christian; rather it reflects the tendency also visible in the philosophical/theological speculation of the Imperial period to move the highest god out of direct human reach.

3. In the Middle East numerous local Baalim (→ Baal), especially when they are gods located high above the earth, are addressed in an → *interpretatio graeca* as Zeus H. [2. 886–888]; therefore, a large number of such dedications are preserved from places like → Palmyra. This radiates out into the Aegean, e.g. when on Delos Zeus on Cynthus is called H. or when on Calymnos Zeus H., Hera Ourania (Tanit) and Poseidon Asphaleios are thanked for salvation from an earthquake ([4], under Antoninus Pius).

4. In the Septuagint, Jewish Hellenistic literature and (more rarely) the NT, but also in the Graeco-Egyptian → magic papyri, the Jewish god is addressed as *theòs hýpsistos*; outside of the Septuagint, the form often proves to be a description used by non-Jews [5]. It is also found in Jewish and Christian inscriptions of the Imperial period, especially in Asia Minor, where large Jewish, and later also Christian, diaspora congregations existed since the period of the Diadochi; the two inscriptions of Rheneia, for example, which call on

Theos H., 'the lord of the winds and of all flesh', as avenger in a murder case are Jewish (Syll.³ 1181).

These various groups cannot be clearly distinguished from one another in cultic reality: in view of the evidence of the concept one must expect the interaction of various spontaneously formed groups. In research the derivation from the Jewish (and after that Christian) word usage dominated. This is probably overdrawn insofar as Jewish and Christian citings are positively identifiable only when the context enables the classification; a differentiation between Zeus H. and Theos H. is likewise not verifiable in every instance when one considers that in several places official inscriptions tend to address Zeus H., but private dedications Theos H., and therefore Theos H. can be the private version of Zeus H. But just as important from the point of view of the history of religion as the clean division of groups is the fact that in the Imperial period and especially in Asia Minor the different religious groups used the name or the epiclesis H. to express a henotheistic or monotheistic religious ideal, in which pagan, Jewish and Christian traditions could converge and in this way distance themselves from the official polis religion. It is characteristic that the cults of (Zeus or Theos) H. were very often constituted as private cult organizations with joint banquets, at which the individual could find social and religious identity (i.e. Egypt PLond. 2710 [6]; Thessalonica IG X 2 no. 68–71, late 1st cent. AD; Miletus OGIS 755f. [7]), that Zeus or Theos H. was addressed as → Soter and 'helper in need' (Thessalonica IG X 2 no. 67, rescue from distress by a dream) and connected with salvation cults, in which private religious requests were especially clearly reflected: i.e. in Athens on the Pnyx [8], in Cos (together with → Asclepius and → Hygieia [9]) or in the Syro-Phoenician region (Ešmun [6. 62f.]). Therefore, it is not surprising that the Christians of Asia Minor actively and polemically distance themselves from splinter groups such as the Cappadocian Hypsistarioi or Hypsistianoi (Greg. Naz. or. 18,5; cf. Greg. Nyss. Contra Eunomium 38 [10]).

1 C. COLPE, A. LÖW, s.v. H. (Theos), RAC 16, 1036–1056 2 A. B. COOK, Zeus. A Study in Ancient Rel. 2: Zeus God of the Dark Sky, 1925 3 L. ROBERT, Reliefs votifs et cultes d'Anatolie, in: Anatolia 3, 1958, 112–120 (Opera Minora Selecta 1, 411–419) 4 M. SEGRE, Tituli Calymnii, in: ASAA 6/7, 1944/45, 31 no. XXXIII 5 M. SIMON, Theos H., in: Ex orbe religionum. Studia Geo Widengren, 1972, 1, 372–385 6 C. ROBERTS, TH. C. SKEAT, A. D. NOCK, The Gild of Zeus H., in: Harvard Theological Revue 29, 1936, 39–88 7 L. ROBERT, in: CRAI 1968, 594f. (Opera Minora Selecta 5, 610f.) 8 B. FORSÉN, The Sanctuary of Zeus H. and the Assembly Place of the Pnyx, in: Hesperia 62, 1993, 507–521 9 M. SEGRE, Iscrizioni di Cos, 1994, EV 127 10 M. SIMON, s.v. Gottesfürchtiger, RAC 11, 1068–1070. F.G.

Hypso (Ὑψώ; *Hypsó*). According to Val. Flacc. 1,365ff., mother of the Argonaut twins → Deucalion and → Amphion from Pella; the version at Apoll. Rhod. 1,176 gives a different account, naming Asterion (in place of Deucalion) and Amphion from Pellene as the sons of Hyperasius.   J.S.-A.

Hyrax see → Rock hyrax

Hyrcania ('Υρκανία; *Hyrkanía* < old Persian *varkāna-*, 'Wolf's Land'; middle Persian *gurgān*). Historically and geographically important region of Iran (inhabitants: 'Υρκάνιοι, 'Υρκανοί, *Hyrcani*) on the south-east corner of the Caspian Sea (Hecataeus FGrH 1 F 291: 'Υρκανίη θάλασσα); it is shielded in the south and south-east by the eastern wing of the Elburz mountains and opens up to the north-east to the Aralo-Caspian steppe. It was favoured climatically as well as naturally by the precipitation raining down on the north side of the Elburz (Plin. HN 31,43), numerous smaller stretches of water and the larger rivers Sarnius (modern Atrek) and Maxeras (modern Rōd-i Gurgān), which both flow into the Caspian Sea. Apollodorus of Artemita (Str. 11,7,1ff.) and Ptolemy (6,9) characterize H. as fertile, rich in animal life (cf. also Ael. NA 7,38; 16,10 on the dogs trained for war and hunting and Curt. 3,2,6 on the Hyrcanian cavalry) and densely settled. Among the cities, the Achaemenid satrapal residence city Zadracarta, later Syrinx and Tambrax stood out (not localized exactly even today). According to Arrian (Anab. 3,23,1), the most important overland road from Ecbatana to Bactra did not lead through H., but rather a royal road appropriate for carts and retinue branched off in Parthia toward Zadracarta and led over the Elburz mountains.

Probably annexed under Cyrus the Great to the Achaemenid Empire, H. rebelled (together with Parthia) without success in 521 BC against Darius I [4. DB 2,92ff.]. In 480 BC, the Hyrcanians fought in the army of Xerxes in Persian equipment (Hdt. 7,62). Under Darius III, → Phratapherenes acted as satrap of Parthia and H. (Arr. Anab. 3,23,4) and as such commanded the Parthians, Hyrcanians and Tapurians in the battle at Gaugamela in 331 BC (Arr. Anab. 3,8,4). Together with his sons, he went over to Alexander after the death of Darius before Zadracarta, and shortly thereafter received back from the former the satrapy.

A curious piece of information at Polybius (10,28,3) attests not only to Achaemenid irrigation systems in H., but also to royal privileges for those village communities maintaining them. Under Seleucus I, H. became a Seleucid satrapy (App. Syr. 57; between 311 and 304 BC); Greek administration is attested epigraphically (SEG 20,325) and Greek settlements are attested literarily (e.g. in → Syrinx: Pol. 10,31,5, where a 'palace', βασίλειον was also located). Some time before the eastern campaign of Antiochus III, H. fell temporarily to the Parthians (Iust. 41,4,8), but likely not finally until the beginning of the 2nd cent. BC.

In the Parthian period (from the 2nd cent. BC on), H. appears as the summer residence of the kings (Str. 16,1,16) and as exile location of the Seleucid ruler Demetrius II (Iust. 36,1,6; 38,9,3–9). Isidore of Charax indicates in his itinerarium (*Mansiones Persica* 14) that

H.'s expansion amounted to 60 *schoinoi* and mentions eleven settlements with caravanserais there; at Ptol. 6,9,2–8 thirteen Hyrcanian towns are mentioned by name, of which none could be reliably located to this day, however. If, contrary to popular belief, the Parthian king Artabanus II was not of Hyrcanian origin after all [7. 63–78], his successor and foster-son Gotarzes II [8. 445], who had his power base there (Tac. Ann. 11,8–10), certainly was. A revolt in H. – under the son Vardanes I? (according to [7. 118f.], otherwise [3. 77]) – kept the Parthian king → Vologaises I in the 50s of the 1st cent. AD from a successful conduct of the war against the Romans in Armenia (Tac. Ann. 13,37,5; 14,25,1f.; 15,1,1; 15,2,4); during the course of this uprising the Hyrcanians also sent envoys to Rome who sought an alliance (*societas*) that would be contractually agreed on (Tac. Ann. 14,25,2). Supposedly, at the beginning of the 60s it came to a compromise between Hyrcanians and Parthians, according to which the former again returned to submission under the Arsacid king; nothing speaks for a separate Hyrcanian kingdom allied with Rome [9. 18–20] [3. 88].

The problem of defending H. against attacks and raids from the steppe existed for the Iranian kings already from the Achaemenid period [6]. This was also the purpose of the imposing 'Alexander Wall' north of the Gurgān river, being over 180 km long and having around 40 castles. Supposedly built in the (late?) Parthian period [6. 240f.], it was probably completely restored in the Sassanid period. Arsacid period settlement remains are also verifiable in H. [5], however, as a rule neither exactly dateable nor identifiable with towns of the parallel written records. The threat from the northeast also remained in existence in the Sassanid period, in which H. (Gurgān) formed a province (*šahr*), whose functionaries to some extent are attested by their seals [2. 50,84]. From Yazdgird II (438–457) on we hear repeatedly of military operations of the kings to fend off nomadic groups and peoples. Gurgān was counted among the regions in which Christian deportees were settled; Christian witnesses speak of a diocese 'imprisonment/deportation of Gurgān' at the beginning of the 5th cent. [1. vol.4. 382–384]; from the middle of the 7th cent. even a Jacobite diocese is attested in Gurgān [1. vol.5. 332–334].

→ Parthians; → Sassanids

1 J.M. FIEY, Communautés syriaques en Iran et Irak, 1979   2 R.GYSELEN, La géographie administrative de l'Empire sassanide, 1989   3 M.HEIL, Die oriental. Außenpolitik des Kaisers Nero, 1997   4 R.G. KENT, Old Persian, 1953   5 M.Y. KIANI, Parthian Sites in H., 1982   6 M.J. OLBRYCHT, Parthia et ulteriores gentes, 1998   7 M.SCHOTTKY, Parther, Meder und Hyrkanier, in: AMI N.F. 24, 1991, 61–134   8 Id., Quellen zur Gesch. von Media Atropatene und H. in parth. Zeit, in: J.WIESEHÖFER (ed.), Das Partherreich, 1998, 435–472   9 W. SCHUR, Die Orientpolitik des Kaisers Nero, 1923.   J.W.

Hyrcanus Epithet of Jews, after → Hyrcania on the Caspian Sea, introduced by repatriates from the diaspora there.

[1] Son of the Ptolemaic general tax leaseholder of Coile Syria and Phoenicia, Josephus, from the Jewish magnate family of the Tobiads. After the conquest of Ptolemaic Syria by → Antiochus [5] III in the year 200 BC he retreated to Trans-Jordan, where his grandfather Tobias had founded the family's position of power as commander of the Jewish military settlers. H. presumably kept a pro-Ptolemaic position and was able to assert himself in a predominantly independent position until → Antiochus [6] IV brought his rulership to an end and he took his own life (c. 170 BC). The palace in → 'Irāq al-Amīr was probably his residence in Trans-Jordan. H. and his father are the main figures of the so-called 'Tobiad Romance', written out by Flavius Josephus (Ant. Iud. 12,154–236), a narration in the style of Hellenistic biography.

E. BIKERMAN, The Jews in the Greek Age, 1988, 231–234; M. HENGEL, Judentum und Hell., ²1973, 486–503.

[2] **Iohannes H.** Jewish high priest from the house of the → Hasmoneans in 135–104 BC, who was forced by → Antiochus [9] VII Sidetes after a war lasting several years to accept the Seleucid suzerainty (131–30 BC). Probably due to Roman diplomatic intervention (the dating of the documents in question at Josephus, Ant. Iud. 13, 260–265 and 14, 247–255, however is in dispute), H. kept Ioppe and other towns outside of Judaea in exchange for payment of tributes. In 130–29, H. had to follow military orders under Antiochus VII during his Parthian campaign. After his defeat and death, H. extracted profit from the defeat of the Seleucid kingdom, conquered areas in eastern Jordan, → Samaria, where he destroyed the city and the schismatic temple of the Samaritans without → Antiochus [11] IX being able to prevent this, and he won Scythopolis and Idumaea, where he Judaized the population. In the interior he came into conflict with the → Pharisaei (sources: Jos. BI 1,54–69; Ant. Iud. 13,230–300).

SCHÜRER 1, 200–215.

[3] **Iohannes H. II.** followed his father → Alexander [16] Iannaeus as high priest in 76 BC, and after the death of his mother → Alexandra Salome in 67 BC as king. In a quarrel with his brother → Aristobulus [2] II he won the aid of → Aretas [3] III by virtue of the mediation of the Idumaean → Antipater [4] and by Pompey's decision in 63 BC he received the high priest's office and rulership over the considerably reduced Hasmonean kingdom. In 57 BC the secular rulership was withdrawn from him, but he received it back through Caesar, to whom Antipater had given military aid in Alexandria, in a territorially enlarged framework with the title of 'ethnarch and Roman ally'. During the Parthian invasion in the year 40, H. was made ineligible for the office of high priest by having his ears cut off. Called back by King → Herodes [1] from imprisonment, he was exe-

cuted in 31–30 BC on the latter's orders (sources: Jos. BI 1,199–273; Ant. Iud. 14,80–369).

SCHÜRER 1, 267–280.

[4] Son of → Herodes of Chalcis and of Berenice, born before AD 48. H. did not emerge politically due to the preference given his half-brother → Aristobulus [6] (Jos. BI 2,221; Ant. Iud. 20,104). K.BR.

Hyria (Ὑρία; *Hyría*). Boeotian town on the → Euripus near Aulis and Chalia, mentioned in the Homeric catalogue of ships. Hometown of Lycus, Nycteus, Orion, Euphemus and Antiope. Dependent on Thebes in the classical period, from the Hellenistic period on Tanagra; the localization north of modern Paralia Avlidas (formerly Dhramesi) or on a hill called Tseloneri (also Glypha) on the west side of the Euripus Bay across from Chalcis remains uncertain. References: Hom. Il. 2,496; Hes. fr. 181; 253 WEST; Str. 8,6,17; 9,2,12; 9,2,21; Plin. HN 4,26; Apollod. 3,5,5; Nonnus, Dion. 13,96ff.; Steph. Byz. s.v. Ὑ., s.v. Χαλία).

S.C. BAKHUIZEN, Salganeus and the Fortification on its Mountains, 1970, 16f., 145–147; FOSSEY, 75f.; LAUFFER, Griechenland, 234f., 509.; P.W. WALLACE, Strabo's Description of Boiotia, 1979, 52f. P.F.

Hyrie (Ὑρίη; *Hyríē*). Aetolian nymph. After her son Cycnus' leap from the cliff, she dissolves into tears with grief and becomes the lake that is named after her (Ov. Met. 7,371ff.). At Antoninus Liberalis 12 she is called (according to Nicander and Areus of Laconia) Thyria; when Cycnus, her and Apollo's son, throws himself into the Lake of Canope, she follows him; Apollo transforms both of them into swans.

F. BÖMER, P. Ovidius Naso, Metamorphosen, B. VI–VII, 1976, 292. RE.ZI.

Hyrieus (Ὑριεύς; *Hyrieús*). Son of → Poseidon and → Alcyone [1], founder of the Boeotian town → Hyria. → Trophonius and Agamedes build him a treasury, but such that they can secretly steal from it; a story follows this which varies the tale of the master thief (Hdt. 2,121) (Paus. 9,27,5–7). The story of how H. comes by his son Orion is often told: Zeus and Apollo visit the childless widower, and in thanks for his hospitality (he slaughters his only cow for them) they urinate into the skin of the beast; from this is created the child Orion (wordplay on *oureîn*, 'urinate'; in detail Ov. Fast. 5,495–536; first documented Pind. fr. 73, special role of Hermes: Hyg. Fab. 195). F.G.

Hyrnetho (Ὑρνηθώ; *Hyrnēthó*). Eponym of the Argive phyle Hyrnathioi; sanctuaries in Argus and Epidaurus. Daughter of → Temenus and wife of the Heraclid → Deiphontes. H. was killed by her brothers because she took her husband's side in a family quarrel (Paus. 2,28,3–7). RE.ZI.

Hyrtacus (῞Υρταχος; *Hýrtakos*). Named in the Trojan allies' catalogue of the *Iliad* as father of Asius, who was the ruler over Arisbe at the Hellespont (Hom. Il. 2,835–839). H. himself only appears in Asius' patronymic information; his name is possibly to be connected with a Cretan town by the name of Hyrtacina. A hero of the same name appears in Virgil's *Aeneid* as the father of Nisus (Verg. Aen. 9,176f.).

KAMPTZ, 313f.; P. WATHELET, Dictionnaire des Troyens de l'Iliade, 1988, no. 325. E.V.

Hysiae (῾Υσίαι; *Hysíai*). Boeotian town on the northern slope of the → Cithaeron east of Plataeae, west of Erythrae (Eur. Bacch. 751; Thuc. 3,24,2; Paus. 9,1,6), *c.* 2 km east of modern Erythres (formerly Kriekouki) near the church of Pantanassa. Before the battle of Plataeae in 479 BC, the Persian encampment on the Asopus stretched from Erythrae through H. to Plataeae, whereas the Greek army initially took up a position near Erythrae, then moved via H. to the sanctuary of Demeter there (Hdt. 9,15,3; 25,3; Plut. Aristides 11,6). H. was considered to be an *apoikía* of Hyria founded by Nycteus (Str. 9,2,12; Steph. Byz. s.v. ῾Υ., s.v. ῾Υρία). From 519 BC it and Plataeae belonged to Athens (Hdt. 5,74,2; 6,108,6 with Thuc. 3,68,5), and H. with the other towns south of the Asopus fell to Thebes by 447 (Hell. Oxy. 19,3,391 confuses H. with → Hyettus). In Roman times H. with its sanctuary to Apollo and spring oracle lay in ruins (Paus. 9,2,1).

FOSSEY, 112–115; LAUFFER, Griechenland, 274f.; MÜLLER, 499; N.D. PAPACHATZIS, Παυσανίου Ελλάδος Περιήγησις 5, ²1981, 24–30; PRITCHETT 1, 104–106; 3, 74–77; 5, 101–103; SCHACHTER 1, 49, 152–154; P.W. WALLACE, Strabo's Description of Boiotia, 1979, 54f. P.F.

Hyspaosines (Greek ῾Υσπαοσίνης/*Hyspaosínēs*, Σπασίνης/*Spasínēs*, Πασίνης/*Pasínēs*; Latin *Spaosines*, cuneiform *Aspasine*, name of Iranian origin). Son of Sagdo(do)nacus, founder of a dynasty of independent local rulers in the → Characene, according to Pliny (HN 6,139) king (*rex*) of the Arabs, who were indeed mentioned in the cuneiform texts of his time but not in connection with him. In *c.* 165 BC appointed by Antiochus IV as administrator of Eparchia on the Red Sea, he succeeded, in conjunction with the passing of control of southern Mesopotamia from the Seleucids to the Arsacids (141 BC), in achieving full independence (royal title). His minting of coins begins about this time and from 138/7 [1. 168–171 et passim] he is also mentioned in cuneiform texts. Babylon was under his rule for a short time (in spring 127, but he was probably repelled in the same year [1. 254f.]). Aside from the disputes with the Arsacids there were also military conflicts with → Elymais. After a short illness he died – according to tradition – in old age (perhaps as a prisoner? [1. 274f.]) on 11 June 124 and his successor was a son who was a minor [1. 282f.]. Minting did not end until 121/20 [2. 91].

1 A. J. SACHS, H. HUNGER, Astronomical Diaries 3, 1996 2 S. A. NODELMAN, A Preliminary History of Charakene, in: Berytus 13, 1959/60, 85–91. J.OE.

Hystaspes (῾Υστάσπης; *Hystáspēs*, ancient Persian/Avestian *Vi/ištāspa-*, 'with untied horses (for the race)'). Name of various Iranian personalities.

[1] As *kauui-* (Kavi, prince) the decisive patron of Zarathustra (→ Zoroaster [4. 13,100]); son of Auruuaṭ.aspa-, husband of Hutaosā. In the Graeco-Roman world oft-used and quoted 'Oracles', which were concerned with the last things, went around under his name; cf. most recently [1. 376–381].

[2] Son of Arsames (ancient Persian *Aršāma-*), grandson of Ariaramnes (*Ariyāramna-*), father of → Darius I, in 521 BC. he put down a Parthian-Hyrcanian rebellion in two battles in Parthia after his son ascended to the throne (TUAT 1, 436 §§ 35f.).

[3] Son of Darius [1] I and Atossa, governor of Bactria and Sogdiana (Hdt. 7,64).

[4] Son of → Xerxes I (and Amastris?), who at the time of his father's murder (465 BC) was supposed to have been staying in his satrapy Bactria (Diod. Sic. 11,69,2) and later was supposed to have rebelled in vain against his brother and the new Great King → Artaxerxes [1] I (Ctes. FGrH 688 F 14: but there 'another Artabanus' is mentioned [2. 581–588]).

[5] Relative (*propinquus*) of Darius III and married to the daughter of Bisthanes, a granddaughter of Artaxerxes Ochus; Darius gave him a high military command (Curt. 6,2,7) and in the year 324 Alexander entrusted H. with the leadership of the oriental part of the *agema* of the companion cavalry (Arr. Anab. 7,6,5).

[6] According to Xen. Cyr. 2,2,2–5 *et passim*, friend and commander of Cyrus the Great, among others in Asia Minor (Hystaspas).

1 M. BOYCE, F. GRENET, A Hist. of Zoroastrianism, vol. 3, 1991 2 BRIANT, Index s.v. H. 3 R. G. KENT, Old Persian, 1953 4 W. W. MALANDRA, The Fravaši Yašt, 1971. J.W.

Hysteria The noun 'hysteria' does not occur in the classical period. But the womb (ὑστέρα, *hystéra*) was considered to be the physical cause of a range of physical and emotional impairments to health, which went from headaches to grinding of the teeth, loss of voice and breathlessness to an actual fit. The non-appearance of the menses, tiredness, undernourishment, sexual abstinence and abnormal lightness or dryness of the womb made this organ, as was believed, wander around in the body (cf. e.g. Hippoc. Mul. 1,7 = 8,32 L.). According to the teaching of Hippocratic → gynaecology, older women were more endangered since their womb was supposed to be lighter (Mul. 1,7 = 8,32 L.); Aretaeus, however, thought that younger women are more likely to be affected since their way of life and understanding of the world 'wanders around' (ῥεμβώδης/*rhembódes*, De causis et symptomatibus morborum 2,11 = CMG 2,34,5). The Hippocratic authors differentiate between a whole range of health impairments according to the different body parts where the wandering uterus stopped on its journey (Mul. 2,123–131 = 8,266–278 L.): If the womb travels towards the liver searching for moisture it could interrupt the flow of breath through the body; if it wanders towards the ribs it causes coughing attacks, a stitch in the side and the feeling as if a ball were in one's side. Plato (Ti. 91a-d) describes the womb as a living being, which, if it remains unfertilized, wanders through the body, blocks passages and in this way can cause disease. In the Hellenistic period medicine knew of a disease called ὑστερικὴ πνίξ/*hysterikè pníx*, 'suffocation of or through the womb'.

The discovery of the ligaments that hold the uterus in the stomach cavity by Herophilus (fr. 114 VON STADEN) in no way led to this disease entity being abandoned. Instead all sorts of explanations were offered on how the uterus could affect other organs of the body without actually reaching them as a wandering womb. → Aretaeus spoke of a 'sympathy' between the womb and the organs in the cranium and claimed that the ligaments are especially elastic, so that the uterus can still move about freely (De causis et symptomatibus morborum 4,11 = CMG 2,81,31). Galen (De loc. aff. 6,5 = 8,420–424; 432 KÜHN) differentiated between a choking fit that was caused by female retention of semen and one caused by the non-appearance of the menses; the former was considered to be the more dangerous since its effect on the body was like a poisoning. The

treatment for an attack supposedly caused by the womb consisted of measures likely to be suitable for bringing the apparently dead patient back to life; this included special preparations that could make the patient sneeze (e.g. Hippoc. Aph. 5,35 = 4,544 LITTRÉ), which included mustard (Plin. HN 20,87,238). In especially difficult cases, before beginning the therapy, the patient was first examined to see if she was still alive; for this purpose a feather or a scrap of wool was held under her nose or a bowl of water was set on her chest. Applying a vile-smelling substance to her nose was to help force the womb down: garlic, rupture wort and castoreum were commonly used. The person applying the treatment wrapped bandages around the patient's body (Mul. 2,127 = 8,272 L.) or used his hands (Diocles of Carystus, in: Soranus, Gynaecia 3.4.29 = CMG 4,112, 18–23) to force the womb to return to its proper place. In the context of Galenic medicine, bloodletting at the ankle was considered to be salutary. Marriage and pregnancy were, however, widely believed to be the best prophylactic for the morbid wandering of the womb.
→ Gynaecology; → Hippocrates (with table of works and abbreviations); → Woman

H. KING, Once Upon a Text: Hysteria from Hippocrates, in: S. GILMAN et al., Hysteria Beyond Freud, 1993, 3–90.

H.K.

Hysteron proteron see → Figures

I

I (linguistics)

A. Phonology B. Origins of the i-sounds; development

A. Phonology

The tenth letter of the Greek → alphabet had the following sounds: 1. vocalic (syllabic) ĭ in δίκη, τίς, 2. vocalic ī in ἴς 'strength', 3. consonantal (non-syllabic.) i̯, the latter applies to short diphthongs (ai̯; early classical ei̯; oi̯), long diphthongs (āi̯; ēi̯; ōi̯) as well as after vocalic i (non-phonemic): αἴθω, δείκνυμι, οἰνή, τοῖο; χώραι dat., τιμῆι, ἀγρῶι, ἠῶιος; Pamphylian δια [5. 312].

I had a similar value in Latin: 1. ĭ in dictus, quis, 2. ī in uīs 'strength', fīo, 3. i̯ in Old Latin aide accusative 'temple', ex-deicendum, oino accusative 'one'; as δια Latin inscription Fabiius; with that 4. initial i̯- in iecur, iocus (bisyllabic forms), 5. -i̯i- in forms like ai(i)o, ei(i)us (bisyllabic, with positionally long first syllable); aiio is a form used also by Cicero [2. 127; 6. 124].

The variant i longa is not recognized as a separate letter but it is well attested in inscriptions [1; 2. 13f.], notably for ī (FELICI), i̯ (IVSSV, EIIVS), ii (EIIVS), ii̯ (PIETAS).

B. Origins of the i-sounds; development

i̯ and ĭ were allophones in proto-Indo-European, e.g. in the root *dei̯k / dik 'show' (→ Ablaut); the change is preserved in δείκ-νυμι/δίκ-η as well as in Old Latin -deic-endum /dic-tus.

Initial i̯- has been inherited in Latin iecur (cf. Old Indian yákr̥t 'liver'), it was also present in older Mycenaean: jo-qi relative pronoun (cf. Old Indian yát 'which'), from this Homeric ὅτ-τι. In contrast, ī was probably marginal in proto-Indo-European; more common is ī < iə (→ laryngeal), which is probably to be assumed in the root noun *uī-s 'power' < *uiə-s as well; somewhat differently fīo < *bhūi-i̯ō < *bhuə-i̯ō [4. 108]. Dat. πόλῑ is the result of contraction (< *-ii). Not original is the antevocalic i-diphthong: τοῖο < *tosi̯o; aiio < *agi̯ō, eiius < *esi̯o-s, maiior < *magi̯ōs. Long diphthongs like in ἀγρῶι originated through (in part pre-proto-Greek) contraction (-ῶι < *-o-ei̯, with dat. ending). Apart from ĭ (dictus, quis) and ī (shortened e.g. in fīerem), Latin ĭ can have further origins: In an unstressed position it can have developed from other short vowels (ce-cid-ī, col-lig-o, per-fring-o; ag-it), in stressed position through assimilation (ni-sī); in medius (tri-syllabic) it goes back to i̯ (Old Indian mádhya-); in fac-i-lis it has been inserted ('anaptyxis').

Vocalic ĭ and ī remain constant in ancient Greek and Latin for the most part. In contrast ai̯ ei̯ oi̯ eventually become monophthongs in both languages; e.g. Old Latin oino- > classical Latin ūno-; deik- > Greek Latin dēk- > dīk- (classical Latin dīc-ere). In this way <EI> can be the sign for /ī/ (τειμη, feilia). By contrast the long diphthongs āi̯ ēi̯ ōi̯ (only in Greek) lose the i̯ in the Hellenistic era: ἀγρῶι > ἀγρω, in the Middle Ages ἀγρῷ again, with silent 'iota subscriptum' [3. 814].

In the originally quite vocalic sound i̯ of iocus, mai(i)or a fricative sound develops in late antiquity (It. gioco, maggiore).

→ E (linguistics); → Itacism; → J (linguistics); → Pronunciation

1 P. Flobert, Le témoignage épigraphique des apices et des I longae, in: G. Calboli (ed.), Latin vulgaire – latin tardif II, 1990, 101–110 2 Leumann 3 LSJ 4 H. Rix, Südpiken. kduíú, in: HS-ZVS 107, 1994, 105–122 5 Schwyzer, Gramm. 6 Sommer/Pfister.

ThlL VII 1,1–4. B.F.

Iabadiou (Ἰαβαδίου; *Iabadíou*; Old Indic *Yavadvīpa*, modern Java or Sumatra). Large island in south-east Asia (Ptol. 7,2,29). The identification is still disputed but Ptolemy knew that the name meant 'Island of Barley' (Old Indic, *yava*, barley). Supposedly it was rich in gold and its capital was called Argyre.

A. Herrmann, s.v. I. nesos, RE 9, 1175–77. K.K.

Iacchus (Ἴακχος; *Íakchos*). One of the deities of the Mysteries of → Eleusis [1]. I. is the personification of the ecstatic cultic cry (*íakchos*, onomatopoetic) by the participants in the Mysteries during their procession from Athens to the Eleusinian sanctuary where they underwent initiation into the mysteries (Hdt. 8,65; Aristoph. Ran. 316–353). His image, which was kept in a temple of Demeter, Kore and I. by the Pompeion at the Sacred Gate (Paus. 1,2,4, probably identical with the Iaccheion Plut. Aristides 27,4), was carried ahead of this procession by the *iakchagōgós* ('leader of I.'): The procession is therefore referred to as 'leading out I.' (e.g. Plut. Themistocles 15,1; Alcibiades 34,4). Attic inscriptions describe the escort, which the ephebes provide for the procession as the 'escort of I.' (e.g. IG II 2 1028,10). His attribute is the torch in the light of which participants arrived at Eleusis (Aristoph. Ran. 340–353, cf. Paus. 1,2,4) and ecstatic dance is his characteristic (Aristoph. Ran. 316–353; Str. 10,3,10). This reflects the ecstatic experiences of the participants in the Mysteries on their long march (24 km), which they completed on the last of three fasting days. Since Soph. Ant. 1152 and Eur. Ion 1074–1077 I. has therefore been identified in the literature with → Dionysus (cf. Str. 10,3,10); identification with a cultic cry of the Eleusinian *dadoûchos* (schol. Aristoph. Ran. 479) occurred in a later period.

The iconography of I. is disputed because no labelled vase image is preserved. The Eleusinian images represent two young men in *ependytes*, Thracian boots and (often) with torches. One of them is often considered to be I., but he could also be Dionysus I. who is frequently depicted in an Eleusinian context.

→ Mysteries

F. Graf, Eleusis und die orphische Dichtung Athens, 1974, 40–59; E. Kearns, The Heroes of Attica, 1989, 170f.; E. Simon, s.v. I., LIMC 5, 612–614; K. Clinton, Myth and Cult. The Iconography of the Eleusinian Mysteries, 1992, ch. 2f.   F.G.

Iacobus Psychrestus Physician, the son of Hesychius of Damascus, changed his residence in the early 6th cent. AD in order to join his father's medical practice in Constantinople. He treated emperor Leo, whereupon he became a → *comes* and → *archiatros* (Chron. pasch. 8254a; Malalas, Chronographia 370 Dindorf; Photius, Bibliotheca 344A). As a pagan philosopher who was honoured in Athens and Constantinople with statues, he ordered the rich to help the poor. The latter he incidentally treated without charging a fee. His nickname is derived from a new radical cure with cold baths that were supposed to reduce physical tensions and psychological, especially monetary worries.   V.N.

Iactus The technical term in Roman law for 'jettison', the unloading of goods at sea from a ship in distress. The so-called *lex Rhodia de iactu* held that in these cases a community of endangerment of all involved existed: between the damaged party, the mariner (*nauta*) and the owners of the salvaged load. In fact, this *lex* was a customary law throughout the Hellenistic world. Specifically, the damaged party could demand his share of compensation from the mariner in a service contract suit (*actio locati*), while the mariner could in turn demand a compensation from the other owners of goods in the *actio conducti*. As 'general average' or loss at sea the Romano-Hellenistic regulation of *iactus* has been part of European maritime law since the MA, first in the Mediterranean but later also in the Atlantic and in the North and Baltic Seas.

G. Wesener, Von der Lex Rhodia de iactu zum § 1043 ABGB, in: J. Bärmann, H. Lutter (ed.), Recht und Wirtschaft in Gesch. und Gegenwart: FS J. Bärmann, 1975, 31–51.   G.S.

Iader (τὰ Διάδωρα; *tà Diádōra*). Liburnian foundation of the Iron Age, later the most important city of Liburnia in the province of Dalmatia, modern Zadar (Italian Zara) in Croatia (Mela 2,57; Plin. HN 3,140 *colonia Iader*, cf. 141; 152; It. Ant. 272,1f.; cf. 496,7; 497,2; CIL III 2925). The inhabitants (*Iadertini*) fought with Caesar against Pompey (Bell. Alex. 42).

I. probably became a Roman *colonia* (*colonia Iulia*; earlier documented as a *conventus civium Romanorum*) under Caesar. Traces of centuriation on the territory of the *colonia* (including the island of Ugljan). Augustus (as the *parens coloniae*) donated the city wall and towers (CIL III 13264; 2907). The careers of municipal magistrates such as C. Vetidius Maximus (*eques, pontifex, duumvir, duumvir quinquennalis*, patron of the city: CIL III 2932; *ordo Iadestinus* CIL III 2919) are documented. The imperial cult is also attested (Cossutia, *flaminica divae Faustinae* [1]). Rich architecture:

forum (cf. CIL III 2922) with *capitolium, nymphaeum, basilicae* (Augustan, Severian) and other buildings (numerous spoliae in the church of St. Donatus), baths, arches, rich necropolis and *villae rusticae* in the environs. I. was an early Christian centre (church of St. Thomas, 5th cent., church of St. Peter, later St. Anastasia): the bishops Felix (late 4th cent.) and Andrew (1st half of the 6th cent.) are attested.

1 Inscriptiones Latinae Iugoslaviae 210.

M. Suić, Zadar u starom vijeku [Zadar in antiquity], 1981.   M.Š.K.

Iaitia (Ἰαιτία; *Iaitía*). Town in Sicily (Diod. Sic. 22,10,4; 23,18; Steph. Byz. s. v. I.; cf. HN 148), probably identical to → Ietae.   Gi. F.

Ialemus (Ἰάλεμος; *Iálemos*). Son of → Apollo and the Muse → Calliope, thus the brother of several mythical singers: → Hymenaus, → Linus, → Orpheus (schol. Eur. Rhes. 985). Just as Hymenaus is a personification of the wedding song and Linus of the dirge, so I. is the personification of those dirges that, poetically, are called *iálemoi*. The myth explains this either with I.'s early death which gives cause for lament (as for Linus) (Pind. fr. 139,8), or with I.'s invention of the dirge. He is occasionally identified with Linus (Schol. Eur. Or. 1390).   F.G.

Iallius M.I.M. f. Volt(inia tribu) Bassus Fabius Valerianus. Senator, who originated from Alba Helviorum in Narbonensis. In AD 156–159 he was in charge of Pannonia inferior as praetorian governor (AE 1976, 542; RMD II 102; 103). *Cos. suff.* shortly thereafter; *curator operum publicorum* in 161; consular governor of Moesia inferior; then *comes Augustorum* during the Parthian War. At the end of his career he was consular governor of Pannonia superior, where he made peace with invading Germanic tribes (Cass. Dio 71,3,1; PIR² J 4).

Kolb, Bauverwaltung, 1993, 213f.; J. Fitz, Die Verwaltung Pannoniens..., II, 1993, 488ff.   W.E.

Ialmenus (Ἰάλμενος; *Iálmenos*). Son of → Ares and → Astyoche. Along with his twin brother → Ascalaphus [2], he led the Minyan contingent at Troy (Hom. Il. 2, 511), and is therefore also mentioned as a suitor of → Helen (Apollod. 3,130). After the capture of Troy, he makes his home in the Crimean region with Minyan settlers (Pherecydes, FGrH 3 F 143; Str. 9,2,42). Like his brother, I. was probably a figure of pre-Iliadic myth.

W. Kullmann, Die Quellen der Ilias, 1960, 70f.; Kamptz, 252.   E.V.

Ialysus (Ἰάλυσος; *Iálysos*). City on the north coast of the island of Rhodes; with → Lindus and → Camirus one of the three ancient cities of Rhodes. Situated c.

15 km south-west of Rhodes city, on the western slope of the 267 m-high mountain Filerimos (ancient name *Achaía*, Diod. Sic. 5,57,6; Ath. 8,360e), which functions as the acropolis of I. Settlement and necropolis from the Mycenaean period at the present-day village of Trianda. The Heraclid → Tlepolemus was named as the legendary founder (Hom. Il. 2,653–656; Pind. Ol. 7). Together with Lindus, Camirus, Cos, Cnidus and Halicarnassus, I. was a member of the Dorian Hexapolis (Hdt. 1,144). For 591 BC a mercenary from I. is documented in Egyptian Abu Simbel [1]. The lyricist Timocreon, banished on suspicion of Medism (treasonable co-operation with the Persians) at the beginning of the 5th cent. BC, came from I. At this time, I. possessed an extensive territory: 11 demes are documented, also the island of Syme (Ath. 7,296c) and parts of the mainland Peraea [2].

In the 5th cent. BC I. belonged to the → Delian League with tribute payments of between 5 and 10 talents (ATL 1,290f.; 3,185, 191 A.26, 213, 242, 349). In 412/1 BC the Spartans convinced I., along with Lindus and Camirus, to break away from Athens (Thuc. 8,44,2). In 408 BC → Dorieus [2] from I., son of the Olympic champion Diagoras, initiated a → *synoikismos* with Lindus and Camirus, from which the new polis of Rhodes emerged. I. continued to exist thereafter as a settlement with a village character (Str. 14,2,12). Apart from necropoleis (documented up to the classical period) other archaeological remains on the acropolis are a temple to Athena Ialysia (with pre-existing building from the 6th cent. BC; it was in turn replaced by a Christian basilica) and a Doric well-house from the 4th cent. BC.

1 A. BERNAND, O. MASSON, Les inscriptions grecques d'Abou Simbel, in: REG 70, 1957, 1–46 2 P. M. FRASER, G. E. BEAN, The Rhodian Peraea and Islands, 1954, 8of.

Fr. HILLER VON GÄRTRINGEN, Die Demen der rhodischen Städte III: Jalysos, in: MDAI(A) 42, 1917, 179ff.; LAUFFER, Griechenland, 275f.   H.SO.

Iambe (Ἰάμβη; *Iámbē*). Maid in the house of → Celeus, where → Demeter, mourning her abducted daughter Persephone, accepts nothing but a simple chair, which I. offers to her (H. Hom. 2,192–197; reverse ritual related to *thrónōsis*, placing the initiant on a foot stool [1]). I. makes Demeter laugh with her cheeky jokes and provocative insults, thus improving her mood (H. Hom. 2,202–204, cf. SH 680,51ff.). This reflects the cultic practice of *aischrologia* (ritual insult). Evidently, there is a connection between the mythical figure of I. and the literary genre of the Iambus (→ Iambographers), even if the direction of the relationship is as unclear as the etymology.

1 W. BURKERT, Homo necans, 1972, 294–297.

N. RICHARDSON, The Homeric Hymn to Demeter, 1974, 213–223; CH. G. BROWN, Iambos, in: D. E. GERBER (ed.), A Companion to the Greek Lyric Poets, 1997, 16–25 (with bibliography).   RE.N.

Iambia (Ἰαμβία κώμη; *Iambía kṓmē*). Port town on the western coast of the Arabian peninsula, according to Ptolemy belonging to the territory of the Arsae (Ἄρσαι, Ptol. 6,7,3). I. is probably also identical with the island of Iambe, which, according to Plin. HN 6,168, lies off Berenice but is otherwise unknown. While the history of I. during the Hellenistic and Roman-Byzantine periods is largely unknown, the town achieved some importance under the Arab name of Yanbuʿ al-baḥr as the port of Medina (Ἰάθριππα; Iáthrippa/Yaṯrib), especially for pilgrim traffic.

→ Berenice [9]; → Erythra thalatta; → Yaṯrīb

J. TKAČ, s.v. I., RE 9, 636–639; S. E. SIDEBOTHAM, Roman Economic Policy in the Erythra Thalassa, 1986.   J.P.

Iambics see → Metre; → Iambographers

Iambic shortening see → Phonetics

Iamblichus (Ἰάμβλιχος; *Iámblichos*). Personal name (regarding the form cf. [1]).
[1] I., Syro-Arab ruler, probably identical with Phylarchus I of Arethusa and Emesa who was mentioned by Cicero (Fam. 15,1; 2). He was executed in 31 BC outside Actium in the army of Anthony. In AD 20 Augustus returned Emesa to his homonymous son (Cass. Dio 50,13,7; 51,2,2; cf. Str. 16,753).

1 SCHÜRER 1, 234f., 25.   H.G.G.

[2] Neoplatonist of the 3rd/4th cents. AD
A. PERSON   B. WORKS   C. PHILOSOPHY   D. LATER RECEPTION

A. PERSON
I. probably lived between AD 240 and 325 and died at the age of 85. He was born in Chalcis in the province of Syria Coele (probably Chalcis ad Belum, modern Qinnasrīn). His name is a transliteration of the Syrian or Aramaic *ya-mliku*, 'he is king' or 'may he be king'. Almost nothing is known of his parents. Anatolius was his first teacher, followed by → Porphyrius (Eun. Vit. soph. 5,1,2). He supposedly founded a school in Apamea in Syria (Ps.-Julian. Ep. 40 HERTLEIN = 184 BIDEZ-CUMONT; Lib. Ep. 1389 FÖRSTER; Or. 52,21 FÖRSTER) or, less likely, in Daphne, a suburb of Antioch (Malalas, Chronographia 12,312,11–12). His best-known student was Sopater. Because the latter was executed on the order of the emperor Constantine, I. was succeeded first by → Aedesius [1], who later settled in Pergamum, then by → Eustathius [2] (Eun. Vit. soph. 6,4,5–7). Other students were → Theodoros of Asine and → Dexippus [4].

B. WORKS
The chronological order of his works cannot be determined with accuracy. The most important appears to be a work on Pythagoreanism consisting of ten books. Of the four preserved books the first, which was prob-

ably an introduction, is a 'Life of Pythagoras' (Περὶ τοῦ Πυθαγορικοῦ βίου; *Perì toû Pythagorikoû bíou*). It is followed by a 'Call for Philosophy' (Λόγος προτρεπτικὸς ἐπὶ φιλοσοφίαν; *Lógos protreptikòs epì philosophían*), a treatise 'On General Mathematical Science' (Περὶ τῆς κοινῆς μαθηματικῆς ἐπιστήμης; *Perì tês koinês mathēmatikês epistémês*) and a commentary 'On the Introduction to the Arithmetic by Nicomachus' (Περὶ τῆς Νικομάχου ἀριθμητικῆς εἰσαγωγῆς; *Perì tês Nikoumáchou arithmētikês eisagogês*). The lost books treat physics, ethics, theology, geometry, music and astronomy. In Psellus excerpts from books 5–7 are found (cf. D. O'MEARA's edition of both fragments 'On Numbers in Nature '/Περὶ τοῦ φυσικοῦ ἀριθμοῦ (*Perì toû physikoû arithmoû*) book 5 and 'On Ethical and Theological Arithmetic'/Περὶ τῆς ἠθικῆς ἀριθμητικῆς καὶ τῆς θεολογικῆς (*Perì tês ēthikês arithmētikês kaì tês theologikês*) book 6 and 7]). 'The Theology of Arithmetic' (Τὰ θεολογούμενα τῆς ἀριθμητικῆς; *Tà theologoúmena tês arithmētikês*) is a compilation of excerpts from the work of same title by Nicomachus of Gerasa and a work by Anatolius (probably the teacher of I.) 'On the Decade and the Numbers Contained Therein' (Περὶ δεκάδος καὶ τῶν ἐντὸς αὐτῆς ἀριθμῶν; *Perì dekádos kaì tôn entòs autês arithmōn*).

I.'s most original work is his answer to → Porphyrius' 'Letter to Anebon', which carries the manuscript title 'Answer of the Teacher of Abammon to the Letter of Porphyrius to Anebon and Resolution of the Difficulties It Contains' (Ἀβάμμωνος διδασκάλου πρὸς τὴν Πορφυρίου πρὸς Ἀνεβὼ ἐπιστολὴν ἀπόκρισις καὶ τῶν ἐν αὐτῇ ἀπορημάτων λύσεις). This treatise in ten books supports 'true' → theurgy quoting Chaldean and Egyptian wisdom.

Stobaeus' work contains large fragments of the treatise 'On the Soul' (Περὶ ψυχῆς; *Perì psychês*), which discuss the nature, powers and migrations of the soul in a body and independent from it, and in which I. engages with the positions of some contemporary and earlier philosophers. Also preserved are fragments of a treatise in 28 books 'On the Chaldaean Oracles' (Περὶ τῆς τελειοτάτης Χαλδαϊκῆς θεολογίας; *Perì tês teleiotátēs Chaldaïkês theologías*) and the treatise 'On the Gods' (Περὶ θεῶν; *Perì theôn*), which is the basis of two speeches by the emperor Julian (Or. 4 and 5) and of Synesius' 'On the Gods and the Universe'.

Stobaeus' work also contains fragments of 19 letters by I. to eleven different recipients, among them his teacher Anatolius and his students Sopater, Dexippus and Eustathius. The letter to Macedonius on fate is of particular philosophical interest.

In his commentary technique I. appears to have developed the theory that any dialogue ought to deal with exactly one topic (Elias, In Aristot. Cat. 131,10–15 BUSSE), which constitutes the definite focus for everything else (σκοπός, *skopós*; Anon. prolegomena § 26,13–44 WESTERINK). The order of the Platonic dialogues was established by I. and probably also used by him for teaching. It was adopted by all later Neoplatonists. By way of the three traditional fields of philosophy – ethics (*Alcibiades 1, Gorgias, Phaedon*), logic (*Cratylus, Theaetetus*) and physics (*Sophistes, Politicus*) – the student reaches the most elevated philosophical discipline, theology (*Phaedrus, Symposium*), and the most elevated purpose of theology, Good itself (*Philebus*). The *Timaeus* and *Parmenides* conclude the series with a summary of the entire Platonic teachings in physics and theology.

A considerable number of fragments of a *Timaeus* commentary and several fragments each of a *Parmenides* and a *Phaedrus* commentary are preserved. Further, there are notes on specific exegetic questions in sections of the *Alcibiades 1, Phaedon* and *Philebus*. In a scholion on the *Sophistes* there is an allusion to the focus (*skopós*) that I. attributed to this dialogue. I.'s interpretation of the hypotheses of the *Parmenides*, which, in the opinion of the → Neoplatonists, discusses the organization of first principles, stands alone. For the purpose of assigning the bearers of theurgy (archangels, angels, demons and heroes), which he calls 'higher beings', a high rank in the hierarchy of the gods, he elevated the entire divine hierarchy by one level. Since he was forced to assume an unmentionable god outside the hypotheses of the *Parmenides*, he goes even beyond the framework of this dialogue. This important interpretive problem was later taken up by → Damascius.

I. probably wrote a commentary on Aristotle's *Categoriae* and *Analytica priora*. This is less certain for *De interpretatione* and *De caelo*, even though in his commentary on *De interpretatione* Stephanus of Alexandria quotes I.'s notes on specific questions of interpretation, and in his commentary on *De caelo*, Simplicius quotes his opinion on the *skopós* of the treatise.

C. PHILOSOPHY

I.'s philosophical system is essentially a refinement of Plotinus' system, but is based on an independent interpretation that is heavily influenced by Neopythagoreanism and the Chaldaean Oracles (→ *Oracula Chaldaïca*). I. assumes that above the One (Damascius, De principiis § 43, vol. II, 1. 1–9 WESTERINK-COMBÈS) an 'entirely inexpressible' (πάντῃ ἄρρητος; *pántēi árrētos*) principle exists. Between the One and the intelligible, the two principles of the limited (πέρας; *péras*) and the unlimited (ἄπειρον; *ápeiron*) exist. Thus, the 'One Being' (ἕν ὄν; *hén ón*) that stands at the summit of the intelligible triad, is a blend (μικτόν; *miktón*) of these two principles (Damascius De principiis § 50f.). With this view, I. may have prepared the ground for the Henad theory, which plays an important role in later Neoplatonism.

The realm of the One is followed by that of Being, i.e. that of the Intelligible and the Intellectual. According to Procl. In Pl. Ti. I 308.17f., I. assumes seven triads: three triads of intelligible deities, the first of which is that of the One Being (ἕν ὄν; *hén ón*), three triads of intelligible and intellectual deities and a triad of intellectual deities. The latter include Kronos, Rhea and Zeus, whom the

Neoplatonists consider the demiurge. Whether this representation is accurate is doubtful because Proclus (In Pl. Ti. I 307.14–308.17) cites it to show that I. expresses himself too imprecisely in a discussion with Porphyry when he refers to the entire intelligible world as the demiurge.

The realm of the soul follows, meaning the soul as hypostasis as well as other types of souls. With respect to individual souls, I. differs on one fundamental point from Plotinus and Porphyry: he refutes the thesis that a higher part of the soul remains on the level of the intelligible world, instead he believes that the soul unites completely with the body. A consequence of this notion, which is equivalent to the Aristotelian, is that salvation of the soul must necessarily come from elsewhere. The conflict between Porphyry and I. regarding this problem intensified. While Porphyry remained loyal to Plotinian rationalism, I. gave priority to theurgy over philosophy. He considered theurgy to be an intellectual movement with the help of which one directly approaches the gods through exactly defined rites to achieve unification of the soul with the gods. That is why he attributed such great significance to the 'Chaldaean Oracles'.

As far as nature is concerned, I. is less optimistic about the abilities of intellect than is Plotinus. Nevertheless, he is of the opinion that fate only has power over the lower (non-rational) soul and that the higher soul can free itself of its influence through the practice of theurgy.

Matter, finally, which may go back to the dyad in the realm of the One (Procl. in Pl. Ti. I 77.24–78.12) is to be considered that which differentiates the *lógoi* (Procl. In Pl. Ti. I 87.6–15). The *lógoi* are the manifestations of forms in the soul and in the sensual.

D. LATER RECEPTION

I. had a defining influence on the philosophers of the Neoplatonist school of Athens, especially on → Proclus and → Damascius.

EDD.: L. DEUBNER, Iamblichi De vita Pythagorica liber, 1937 (corr. ed. by U. KLEIN, 1975); É. DES PLACES, Protreptikos, texte et traduction, 1989; N. FESTA, De communi Mathematica Scientia, 1891 (corr. ed. by U. KLEIN, 1975); H. PISTELLI, In Nicomachi Arithmeticam Introductionem liber, 1894 (corr. ed. by U. KLEIN 1975); D. O'MEARA, Pythagoras revived, 1989, App. I: The excerpts from Iamblichus' On Pythagoreanism V–VII in Psellus: text, translation and notes; V. DE FALCO, Theologoumena Arithmeticae, 1922 (corr. ed. by U. KLEIN, 1975); B.D. LARSEN, Jamblique de Chalcis, Exégète philosophe, thesis Aarhus, with App.: Testimonia et fragmenta exegetica; J.M. DILLON, Iamblichi Chalcidensis In Platonis Dialogos commentariorum fragmenta, ed. with translation and commentary (Philosophia Antiqua 23), 1973; De anima, trad. A.J. FESTUGIÈRE, in: La révélation d'Hermès Trismégiste III, 1953, App. I.
BIBLIOGRAPHY: J.M. DILLON, Iamblichus of Chalcis (c. 240–325 A.D.), in: ANRW II 36.2, 862–909; H. BLUMENTHAL, E.G. CLARK (ed.), The Divine Iamblichus. Philosopher and Man of Gods, 1993.   L.BR.

[3] Author of the 'Babylonian Tales' (Βαβυλωνιακά; *Babylōniaká*). According to Schol. Phot. Cod.94, he was a Syrian, who had learned the language, culture and tales of Babylonia from a tutor, but had only learnt Greek and rhetoric as the king's scribe. However, this biography appears to be designed to lend historical authenticity to a novel rich in fantastic inventions. The autobiographical information inserted into the work by I. himself also seems unreliable: he claims to be a Babylonian magus with a Greek education who had predicted the outcome of Lucius Verus' war against the Parthian king → Vologaeses III (AD 166: *terminus post quem*), i.e. as a figure from a novel.

Only the summary of Photius, a few quotes in the Suda and three large fragments are preserved of the 'Babylonian Tales'. The novel, which is divided into 16 books according to Photius and 35 or 39 according to the Suda, deals with the betrothed couple Rhodanes and Sinonis who are being pursued by the Babylonian king Garmos and with their parallel experiences, which are always highly exaggerated (crucifixions, torture, cannibalism, executions: the tone is reminiscent of the *Phoinikiká* of → Lollianus). Many misunderstandings that underlie the plot are due to the physical resemblance of Rhodanes with the twins Tigris and Euphrates, and of that of Sinonis with her rival Kore: I. uses the *doppelganger*-motif in the same confounding function of the dominant logic as it will later be used in the narrative literature of the Baroque period and in Romantic fantastic tales. Also, the novel at times appears to break with the readers' expectations: the heroine, who marries another out of jealousy (and not necessity like the female protagonist of → Chariton), is depicted as unusually cruel and barbaric while her look-alike makes a more positive impression. The boundary between illusion and reality is continuously blurred by an almost paroxystic use of topoi (e.g. confusion of persons, apparent death, disguise and unexpected exchange of roles). MERKELBACH's [1] theory that a novel of the → Mithraic mysteries is hidden underneath this plot is unconvincing because this religion had seven stages of initiation but the novel contains no trace of an ascending hierarchy.

The Photius edition of 1601 and the Latin translation of Andreas SCHOTT of 1606 resulted in a certain afterlife of the novel in Baroque literature, especially in song XIV of the 'Adone' by Gianbattista MARINO (1623) and the 'Histoire africaine de Cléomède et Sophonisbe' by François GERZAN (1627–28).
→ Novel

1 R. MERKELBACH, Roman und Mysterium in der Ant., 1962   2 U. SCHNEIDER-MENZEL, Jamblichos' "Babylonische Gesch.", in: F. ALTHEIM, Lit. und Ges. im ausgehenden Alt. I, 1948   3 E. HABRICH (ed.), I. Babyloniaka, 1960   4 R. BECK, Soteriology, the mysteries, and the ancient novel, in: U. BIANCHI, M.J. VERMASEREN, La soteriologia dei culti orientali nell'impero romano, 1982   5 S. STEPHENS, Fragments of Lost Novels, in: G. SCHMELING, The Novel in the Ancient World, 1996   6 G. SANDY, The Heritage of the Ancient Novel in France and Great Britain, in: ibid.   M.FU. and L.G.

Iambographers
A. ARCHAIC AND CLASSICAL POETS B. TERM AND
METRICS C. TOPICS D. CIRCUMSTANCES OF RECITATION AND TARGETS E. POST-CLASSICAL IAMBOS

A. ARCHAIC AND CLASSICAL POETS
Among archaic Greek poets, → Archilochus, → Semonides and → Hipponax were regarded as the earliest authors of iambics (*iamboi*), followed by → Ananius and, later in the 5th century BC, → Hermippus [1]. The term *iambopoioí* is found not before the Byzantine lexica.

B. TERM AND METRICS
ἴαμβος (*iambos*) seems, although its earliest use (Archil. 215 W) is not decisive, initially to identify a type of poem defined by content (cf. Pl. Leg. 935e) rather than by metre (cf. Hdt. 1,12 ἐν ἰάμβῳ τριμέτρῳ, where probably τριμέτρῳ alone specifies metre).

Poets later termed *iambográphoi* ('I.') mostly used (iambic) trimeters and (trochaic) tetrameters, e.g. Ananius and Hermippus; but Epicharmus (fr. 88 KAIBEL) assigned an anapaestic line to *iamboi* of Aristoxenus of Selinus; a trimeter and hemiepes of Anacreon (5 iamb W) are ascribed to an iambos by EM and Et. gen.; and Alexandrians included among *iamboi* of Archilochus and Hipponax epodes (some asynartetic) as well as trimeters and tetrameters. The trimeter alone, however, is used in the surviving iambic fragments of the third of the canonical I., Semonides, and (in its choliambic form) predominates in Hipponax.

C. TOPICS
This predominance was presumably the basis for the metrical name *iambeíon*, coined before Kritias 4,4 W (? c. 420 BC; next Aristoph. Ran. 1204) and explained by Aristoteles (Poet. 1448b 33) as 'because in this metre they abused (ἰάμβιζον) each other'. This also shows that Aristoteles saw abuse as a mark of *iamboi* (cf. ὡς Ἀρχίλοχος ψέγει Rh. 1418 b 27): a definition of *iambos* as 'a poem of abuse intended to entertain an audience and/or embarrass a victim' matches both the Homeric hymn to Demeter's name → Iambe for the old woman whose jesting abuse (Χλεύης ... παρασκώπτουσ' 202–3) made Demeter laugh and many of our surviving fragments. In these obscenity (*aischrología*) is also common, but neither its ritual association with Dionysos and Demeter nor the name Iambe prove the ritual origins claimed for *iambos* by many and argued by WEST still to be the context of Archilochus' *iamboi* ([6], cf. [7], contra [8]). Fragments also preserve purportedly autobiographical narrative, some military (Archil. 88–113 W in tetrameters), some sexual, occasionally devoid of abuse (Hipponax 92 W) or obscenity (Archil. 196A W) or, it seems, either (Archil. 23–24 W, 48 W); abuse whose target is generic (Semonides 7 W, Susarion 1 W, against women) or remote (Hermippus 4 W on Herakleia); reflection similar to elegy (Semonides 1 W), sometimes focussed on food (id. 22–3 W; Ananius 5 W; Hermippus

2 W) or sympotic games (Hermippus 7 W). Either, then, *iamboi* admitted (whether *ab initio* or once developed by individual poets) more than abuse, or Alexandrian editions of I. included poems which their poets did not conceive as *iamboi*.

To be sure trimeters and tetrameters are used more widely by poets not later classed as I.: perhaps by Mimnermus (cf. 11a W) and certainly (for more closely argued political self-defence than in his elegies) by → Solon [1], as well as in drama, literary and inscribed epigram, and the → *Margites*.

D. CIRCUMSTANCES OF RECITATION AND TARGETS
Frequent address to named individuals (e.g. Archil. 48, 88, 96, 105, 124, 131, 168, 172, ?175 W, probably 124 W, 196 W; Hipponax 28 W, 70,11 W) sometimes in a sympotic context (Archil. 124 W; Semonides 22 W) counts against WEST's view of the genre as dramatic and points to the symposion as a primary context of performance (cf. the σκώπτειν, 'to poke fun' of Adespota elegiaca 27,6 W, not however necessarily iambic), though some poems address either an unnamed individual (Semonides 1 W ὦ παῖ); an individual unlikely to be present, whether named (Archil. 172 W: Lykambes) or unnamed (id. 188 W); or a broader group (Archil. 121 W ὦ ... πολῖται; Hipponax 1 W ὦ Κλαζομένιοι; Susarion 1 W ἀκούετε λεώι). Performance in a more public context is first firmly attested in the fourth century BC (Aristot. Pol. 1336b 20–2 θεαταί, 'spectators'; Lysanias 'in performances'; perhaps Clearchus ap. Ath. 620c of Archilochus' poems – not necessarily *iamboi* – performed 'in theatres') and in a festival only in Mnesiepes' third-century BC biography of Archilochus (251 W). Recitative performance accompanied by the *aulós* is attested for tetrameters by Xen. Symp. 6,3; Theocr. Epigr. 14 may imply that Archilochus' *iamboi* were sung; Ps.-Plut. De musica 1141a reports a tradition (φασί) that Arch. introduced both singing of iambic metres and their recitation to stringed accompaniment; and Phillis ap. Ath. 636b claimed that the *iambyke* and *klepsiambos* accompanied these respective types of performance. Perhaps typically tetrameters and epodes were sung, trimeters recited [9], but certainty is elusive [10].

E. POST-CLASSICAL *iambos*
Some later iambics retain features of archaic *iamboi*. Around 200 BC → Alcaeus [6] of Messene apparently used *iamboi* to attack Ephorus' plagiarisms (Porphyrius ap. Euseb. Praep. evang. 10,3,23 [11. 8]) and Hermeias of Curium choliambics to attack Stoics (Ath. 563d = CollAlex p. 237).

Criticism, fable and personal addressees persist early in the third century BC in the moralising choliambic *iamboi* of → Phoenix [4] (CollAlex pp. 231–236) and Parmenon (ibid. pp. 237f.). The genre developed by → Callimachus [3] in his book of thirteen *Íamboi*, which opened with a poem in which a revenant Hipponax speaks, and crossed Hipponax' Ionic dialect and sometimes diction with Archilochean metres and themes progressively less iambic. About the same time → Herodas used choliambics and sometimes 'low' iambic themes (prostitution in 1 and 2, dildoes in 6) for his dramatic mimiambs (imitated by Arrius Antoninus c. 100 AD: Plin. Ep. 4,3) and → Machon retained the humour and scurrility of *íamboi* in his trimeter *Chreíai* ('Anecdotes'). Late in the third century invective may have marked the choliambics of → Cercidas [3], but only one line survives (CollAlex fr. 14 p. 213). Much more remains of his *Meliamboi* that presented the critical reflections of *íamboi* in lyric metres. Choliambics were used in the first century AD by → Babrius, developing *íamboi*'s use of fable, for two books of Aesopic fables entitled *Mythíamboi*, and in the fourth by → Gregorius [3] of Nazianzus for paraenetic invective and self-defence.

But much poetry is iambic only in metre. Choliambics were used already in the late fourth century by → Aischrion for an epigram and for mythical narrative (SH fr. 5); and in the third by Asklepiades (SH fr. 216f.) and by → Apollonius [2] Rhodius for his *Kanobos*, perhaps a foundation narrative; and later in the Alexander Romance and even for epitaphs (GVI 722, *c.* 117 AD). Trimeters were used for epigrams at all periods and in the fourth and third century BC by philosophers and moralists: → Chares [3], → Crantor, → Crates [4], → Zeno [2], → Cleanthes [2], the *sententiae* of → Menander [4] and → Epicharmus. In the second century BC → Apollodorus' [7] *Chroniká* began a tradition of didactic poems in trimeters followed by (Ps.-)→ Scymnus [2], → Damokrates, → Dionysius [26] and others. In the late empire they were used for hymns, encomia, narrative poetry and prologues to hexameter poems.

In the second century BC Eratosthenes' teacher → Lysanias [2] of Cyrene wrote *On Iambic Poets* (Περὶ ἰαμβοποιῶν) in more than one book (Ath. 620c), and the early I. were trawled by metricians and (for rare words or forms) lexicographers.

→ Invective

BIBLIOGRAPHY: 1 D. E. GERBER, Early Greek Elegy and Iambus 1921–1989, in: Lustrum 33, 1991, 9–18.
EDITIONS: 2 IEG 1² and 2² 3 COLLALEX 4 SH 5 A. D. KNOX, Herodes, Cercidas and the Greek Choliambic poets, 1929.
LITERATURE: 6 M. L. WEST, Stud. in Greek Elegy and Iambus, 1974, 22–39 7 G. NAGY, The Best of the Achaeans, 1979, 243–252 8 C. CAREY, Archilochus and Lycambes, in: CQ n.s. 36, 1986, 63–65 9 A. M. DALE, Stichos and Stanza, in: CQ n.s. 56, 1963, 46–60 10 K. BARTOL, Greek Elegy and Iambus, 1993, 61–65 11 GA 1.2. 12 A. CAVARZERE, A. BARCHIESI, A. ALONI (ed.), Iambic Ideas, 2001.　　　E.BO.

Iambulus (Ἰαμβοῦλος; *Iamboûlos*). In his library of world history (2,55–60), → Diodorus [18] Siculus mentions a merchant I., who, while on a voyage in Arabia, was carried off to a blissful island by Ethiopians, who thereby practised a purification ritual that was more than 20 generations old. The description of the island (which might be Sri Lanka) contains all the characteristics of an ancient utopia: an ideal climate, unusual fertility and a communist social structure. There are paradoxical elements as well: The inhabitants have a (literally) split tongue, enabling them to conduct two conversations at the same time. After seven years on the island, I. is exiled from it due to an unspecified offence and he returns to Greece via India and Persia.

The novel available to Diodorus must have been carefully composed, and was given credit for this even in Lucian's satirical pastiche of the 'True Story' (1,3). ROHDE had labelled the work (as he did for *Hierà anagraphé* by → Euhemerus) a utopian novel, but this is no longer uncontested today because it is difficult to determine how far Diodorus had altered the original structure to allow more space for political description, and what kind of relationship existed between the narrative part (including the return trip) and the theoretical part.
→ Novel; → Utopia

E. ROHDE, Der griech. Roman und seine Vorläufer, ²1914; W. W. EHLERS, "Mit dem Südwestmonsun nach Ceylon": Eine Interpretation der Iambul-Exzerpte Diodors, in: WJA 11, 1985, 73–84; B. KYTZLER, Zum utopischen Roman der klass. Ant., in: Groningen Colloquia on the Novel 1, 1988, 7–16; N. HOLZBERG, Novel-like Works of Extended Prose Fiction II, in: G. SCHMELING (ed.), The Novel in the Ancient World, 1996.　　M.FU.

Iamus (Ἴαμος; *Íamos*). Forefather of the Elean family of seers named Iamidai, who were active in Olympia alongside the → Clytidae (Hdt. 9,33) up to the fall of the sanctuary. They usually read prophecies in the flames of the sacrificial fire (cf. Pind. Ol. 8,2f.), but Thrasybulus invented divination from the intestines of dogs (Paus. 6,2,4). Their prophecies were also expressed in detailed oracles (*lógia*) (Paus. 3,11,6). They were closely connected to Sparta (where the tomb of the Iamidai was located, Paus. 3,12,8), although their service to Messene (Paus. 4,16,1) and Mantinea (Paus. 10,5,8) is also attested.

I. is the son of → Apollo and → Evadne, daughter of Poseidon and Pitane, the Spartan local heroine. The mother gives birth to the child while fetching water, abandons it among violets (*ía*, thus the name), and snakes nourish it with honey. At Apollo's behest, → Aepytus [1] raises the child. As an adult, I. begs Poseidon and Apollo for an office and Apollo grants him the power of prophecy (Pind. Ol. 6,28–72).

H. HEPDING, s.v. I., RE 9, 685–689; H. W. PARKE, The Oracles of Zeus, 1967, 174–178; E. SIMON, s.v. I., LIMC 5, 614f.　　　F.G.

Ianiculum One of the seven hills of Rome (→ Roma), located on the right bank of the Tiber and already during the Republican period connected to the → Campus Martius by four bridges. Because of its military significance, the I. was incorporated into the *ager Romanus* at an early date (Cass. Dio 37,27,3 – 37,28,1). The name I. probably refers to a cultic site of Ianus. In the later Republic this hill, which was traversed by the *via Aurelia* was the location of several large → gardens (*horti Agrippinae; horti Caesaris*).

P. LIVERANI, s.v. I., LTUR 3, 1996, 89f. (sources); RICHARDSON, 205f.   C.HÖ.

Ianira ('Ιάνειρα; *Iáneira*, 'virility'). → Nereid (Hom. Il. 18,47; Apollod. 1,12) or → Oceanid (Hes. Theog. 356), one of Persephone's playmates (H. Hom. 2,421).

RE.ZI.

Ianitor see → Wedding customs and rituals

Iannes and Iambres (Iamnes and Mambres). The pseudepigraphic names of Iannes and Iambres are based on Ex 7,8ff. and was widely received: the two unnamed Egyptian magicians who appear in *Exodus* as opponents of → Moses and Aaron, are referred to as Iannes and Iambres (the spelling varies depending on whether the source is Greek, Latin or Hebrew) in Jewish, Greek and Roman texts, the NT and other Christian documents. The Iannes and Iambres material was also treated in Rabbinic and Targumic (Targum Ps.-Jonathan) literature.

A. PIETERSMA (ed.), The Apocryphon of Jannes and Jambres, the magicians, 1994; SCHÜRER 3, 781–783.   Y.D.

Ianthe ('Ιάνθη; *Iánthē*, 'violet blossom'). Daughter of → Oceanus and → Tethys (Hes. Theog. 349; Hyg. Fab. praef. 6; Paus. 4,30,4); playmate of → Persephone (H. Hom. 2,418).   J.S.-A.

Ianuarius Nepotianus Revisor of the collection of exempla by → Valerius Maximus for rhetoric instruction, probably from the 4th cent. AD (based on linguistic arguments [1]). While the original organization was maintained, there were stylistic revisions and additions – partially from Cicero (cf. 7,3; 9,24 etc.). A more complete copy of the excerpt, which has survived in the *Codex unicus* (*Vaticanus Latinus* 1321, s. XIV) only up to Val. Max. 3,2,7, was used still by Landolfus Sagax (*c*.1000).

1 F. BUECHELER, Kleine Schriften 3, 1930, 331–335 (¹1906)   2 D. M. SCHULLIAN, I. Nepotianus, in: F. E. CRANZ, P. O. KRISTELLER (ed.), Catalogus translationum et commentariorum 5, 1984, 251f.   3 M. IHM, Zu Valerius Maximus und I. Nepotianus, in: RhM 49, 1894, 254.

EDITIONS: C. KEMPF, Valerius Maximus, 1888, XVIIf., 592–624; H. DROYSEN, Nachträge, in: Hermes 13, 1878, 122–132.   P.L.S.

Ianus The Roman god of passage in a topographical, temporal and figurative sense. His name is derived from *ianua* ('passage, gate') and is connected with → Ianiculum. The name refers to the god as well as to the cultically relevant gates connected to him. Iconographical representations begin in the Republican period, depicting I. usually with two faces, occasionally with four (*bifrons, quadrifrons*).

A. CULT CENTRES   B. MYTH   C. CULT   D. REPRESENTATIONS

A. CULT CENTRES

His cult is almost exclusively public and political, only two private dedications to him are extant. Two old altars of I. in Rome are attested in the literature: one of them on the Ianiculum, the location of his royal palace (Varro in Aug. Civ. 7,4; Ov. Fast. 1,245f.), a second one on Mons Oppius at the so-called Tigillum Sororium, a wooden beam spanning the road commemorating the myth of the Horatii and Curiatii (→ Horatius), together with an altar of → Iuno Sororia. There, I. carried the epiclesis Curiatus (Liv. 1,26,13; Dion. Hal. Ant. Rom. 3,22,7f.) and received a sacrifice on 1 October. The cult has to do with rites of passage of puberty, which originally had to be performed by the young → *nobiles*. → Cornelius [II 19] Labeo interprets the epithet Curiatus, which is connected to the *curia* < *co-viria*, originally a type of organization for men, in the sense of 'protector of noblemen' (Lydus, Mens. 4,1) [1].

The most important cult building was the I. Geminus at the Forum Romanum (the exact location is still unclear [2]), a double gate, originally probably made of wood with bronze fittings, rebuilt entirely from bronze in the Augustan period and turned into a kind of shrine for the archaic bronze statue of I. which had a height of over 2 meters (description: Procop. Goth. 5 (1) 25,20f.; coin images [3]). It had one door to the east and one to the west, the directions into which the bearded faces of the statue gazed. The statue itself, one of the oldest in Rome (Plin. HN 34,33; attested in the 2nd cent. BC by the annalist L. → Calpurnius [III 1] Piso (fr. 9 HRR)), held a key and a staff (Ov. Fast. 1,99). Under Augustus (then also under Nero and more often in the Imperial period), the double doors were shut during periods of peace in the entire empire – a rite which was derived from Numa (Piso, fr. 9 HRR; Liv. 1,19,2), was first attested for the year 235 BC (Varro, Ling. 5,165), and was used by Augustus as an important ritual expression of his politics of peace (cf. Verg. Aen. 1,293–297). Beginning with the Augustan renewal, I. carried the epiclesis Quirinus (linguistically also related to *curia*) (R. Gest. div. Aug. 2,42; Suet. Aug. 22; [4. 421–424]), which ancient interpreters traced back to his martial (or peace-bringing) function (Macrob. Sat. 1,9,16) and which was translated accordingly with the name of the Greek god of war → Enyalius (Plut. Quaest. Rom. 25, cf. Lydus, Mens. 4,1: *prómachos*). Used in the prayer of the *flamen Cerialis* are the epicleses Patulcius ('opener') and Clusivius ('closer'), which also relate to this rite (Ov. Fast. 1,129f., Macrob. Sat. 1,9,16; [4. 416–420]). Domitia moved the cult into a new sanctuary on the → Forum Transitorium.

I.'s actual temple was located on the Forum Holitorium at the Theatre of Marcellus in Rome. It had been vowed by M. Duilius in the naval battle of Mylae (260 BC), restored by Augustus and re-dedicated by Tiberius who moved the day of foundation from 17 August to 18 October. It was probably this temple, which contained twelve altars that M. Terentius Varro (Macrob. Sat. 1,9,16) and Fonteius [I 9] (Lydus, Mens. 2,2) related to the twelve months.

B. Myth

The myth makes I. into the ancestral king of Latium who rules over the → Aborigines and who welcomes to his palace on the Ianiculum → Saturnus, the god who had fled to the west to bring agriculture and thereby also civilization to Latium (Macrob. Sat. 1,7,19–22): The topic of passages is thus projected onto the absolute beginning of Rome's history, and I. is marked as an authentically Roman deity without a Greek correspondence. A myth told only by Ov. Fast. 6,101–168 turns I. into the lover of Carna, the goddess of the door hinge. This playful if obvious connection (probably an Ovidian invention) is the aition for the Roman custom of hanging a hawthorn rod on the door, to keep the child-snatching Striges away from the house [5].

C. Cult

In Roman cult, I. plays a customary role in ritual beginnings. At each sacrifice, he receives the preparatory sacrifice of wine or incense (Cic. Nat. D. 2,67; Ov. Fast. 1, 171f.; examples, for instance, Cato Agr. 134. 141; Liv. 8,9,6; [6]) and he is invoked at the beginning of each sacrifice, Vesta at the end [7]. For this reason, Gavius [I 2] Bassus, the antiquarian, regards him as the god of the air, who transports prayers from humans to the gods (Lydus, Mens. 2,2). The antiquity and the comprehensive significance of his cult is suggested by his invocation in the song of the Salii (→ Carmen Saliare) (Varro, Ling. 7,27: *divom deus*, 'god of gods'; cf. Macrob. Sat. 1,9,14). Ancient opinions agreed that the first month of the year is dedicated to I. (doubts: [8]), even though the main sacrifice of 1 January on the Capitol is given to Jupiter Optimus Maximus (Ov. Fast. 1,79f.) and no trace of I. can be found in the festival of Calendae Ianuariae [9]. However, *ludi* are celebrated for him on 7 January and he receives the first *agonium* of the year on 9 January (Ov. Fast. 1,317f.). Records indicate only later that he received a sacrifice on the first day of every month, carrying the epithet Iunonius since the kalends are dedicated to → Juno (Macrob. Sat. 1,9,16, allegorised in Lydus, Mens. 4,1).

D. Representations

I. has always been depicted with two heads, on the archaic bronze statue of I. Geminus as well as on the front side of the old → as (middle and late Republic), the back of which was decorated with a ship's prow [10]. Ov. Fast. 1,229–254 interprets this from the myth of I. and Saturn. Modern research at times regards the two-headedness as a heraldic adaptation of Greek minting. Even if this is the case, the image expresses more: the fundamental function of the god of beginnings and passages, from which even his companions Antevorta and Postvorta were constructed (Macrob. Sat. 1,7,20). Furthermore, there probably is a connection to the Etruscan god Culsan, also two-headed [11; 12]. The attribute of the staff marks I. as a figure of authority (*I. pater* in the prayer in Cato Agr. 134), that of the key as a god of entrances. The notion that his fingers express the number of days in a year, 365, is an allegory that is only reasonable after Caesar's calendar reform, which turns the god of the first month into the god of the year in general (Plin. HN 34,44; Macrob. Sat. 1,9,10). Ov. Fast. 1,101–114 goes even further by turning I. into the cosmologically first god (Chaos), regarding his double faces as an indication for his being without form.

1 H. J. Rose, De religionibus antiquis quaestiunculae tres, in: Mnemosyne 53, 1925, 407–410   2 E. Tortoria, s.v. I. Geminus, LTUR 4, 92f.   3 RRC I 487 no. 478f.; II 739   4 G. Capdeville, Les épithètes culturels de Janus, in: MEFRA 85, 1973, 395–436   5 C. M. McDonough, Carna, Proca and the Strix on the Kalends of June, in: TAPhA 127, 1997, 315–344   6 J. Cels-Saint-Hilaire, Auguste, Diane et Hercule. A propos d'une inscription de Tibur, in: M.-M. Mactoux, E. Geny (ed.): Mélanges P. Lévêcque 6, 1992, 45–71   7 Latte, 134   8 RRC II 718   9 Latte, 134f.   10 F. Graf, Kalendae Ianuariae, in: Id. (ed.), Ansichten griech. Rituale. Geburtstagssymposium für W. Burkert, 1998, 199–216   11 E. Simon, Culsu, Culsans und Ianus, in: Id., Schriften zur etr. und ital. Kunst und Rel., 1996, 41–53 (1989)   12 I. Krauskopf, Culsan und Culsá, in: R. Altheim-Stiehl, M. Rosenbach (ed.), Beiträge zur altital. Geistesgesch. FS Gerhard Radke, 1986, 156–163.

G. Wissowa, Rel. und Kultus der Römer, ²1912, 103–113; L. A. Holland, Janus and the Bridge, 1961; M. Guarducci, I.Geminus, in: Id., Scritti scelti sulla religione greca e romana e sul cristianesimo, 1983, 165–179 (1966); R. Schilling, Janus. Le dieu introducteur, le dieu des passages, in: Id., Rites, cultes, dieux de Rome, 1979, 220–262 (1960); R. Turcan, Janus à l'époque impériale, in: ANRW II 17.1, 374–402; E. Simon, s.v. I., LIMC 5, 618–623.   F.G.

Iao see → Yahweh

Iapetus (Ἰαπετός; *Iapetós*). The etymology is uncertain, perhaps 'the one hurled down' (on ἰάπτειν; *iáptein*, 'to hurl' [1]). The often postulated connection to OT Japheth, the third son of Noah (Gen. 5,32 *et passim*), cannot be proven [2; 3]. I. is the titan who was hurled by Zeus into Tartarus along with → Kronos (Hom. Il.

8,479). Son of → Gaia and → Uranus (Hes. Theog.
134). He fathered the sons → Atlas [2], → Menoetius,
→ Prometheus and Epimetheus with the Oceanid Clymene (Hes. Theog. 507-511). Among others, Asia
(Apollod. 1,8; Lycoph. 1283) and Themis (Aesch. PV
18) are also referred to as his wives. He plays a role in
myth only in connection with his sons, the Iapetids (cf.
Ov. Met. 1,82). He was worshipped in cult only occasionally (on Imbros: IG XII 8,74). In the visual arts, I.
might be depicted on the south frieze of the Pergamon
altar (1st half of the 2nd cent. BC) [4].

1 FRISK 1, 705   2 M.L. WEST, Hesiod. Theogony
(comm.), 1966, 202-203   3 W. BURKERT, The Orientalizing Revolution, 1992, 177   4 E. SIMON, s.v. I., LIMC
5.1, 623-624, no. 1.

GRAF, 81-82.   R.B.

Iapis Son of → Iasus and favourite of Apollo. The god
wants to grant him the gift of prophecy, of playing the
lyre and of accurate archery, but I. asks him for the art
of healing instead so that he can save his father's life.
With the help of Venus, he heals Aeneas' wounds (Verg.
Aen. 12,391ff.; Serv. Aen. 12,391 (Iapyx); Macrob. Sat.
5,15,12).   RE.ZI.

Iapodes Indo-European people attested since the
9th/8th cents. BC, often erroneously classified as Illyrians, settled in Lika, the Karst plains of Gacko, Ličko,
Krbavsko (western Croatia), on the Una near Bihać
(western Bosnia) and Notranjska (Inner Carniolia/Slo-
venia). Administratively, they were part of the *conventus Scardonitanus* of the province of → Illyricum, later
Dalmatia. The Zrmanja and Velebit mountains separated them from the → Liburni in the south. These they
fought in the 3rd cent. BC with temporary success for
access to the sea at the Bay of Kvarner. In the north they
bordered on the Colapiani along the Colapis (= Kolpa/
Kupa), in the west their territory extended to the Ocra
Pass below the Nanos in the hinterland of Tergeste,
which they often raided (cf. Caes. B Gall. 8,24,3; App.
Ill. 18; 52 BC). The la Tène culture did not really affect
them (as opposed to Str. 7,5,2, who claimed they had
been Celticized). The I. were fundamentally hostile to
the Romans but seem to have reached an understanding
with Rome before 171 BC because they complained to
the Senate about the injustice of C. Cassius Longinus'
attack on them. C. Sempronius Tuditanus campaigned
against them in 129 BC. In 35/4 BC they were finally
subjected by the later Augustus (App. Ill. 18-21; Cass.
Dio 49,35), who took their fortifications Monetium (=
Brinje), Avendo (= Crkvina near Brlog), Arupium (=
Prozor) and Terponus (= Gornji Modruš), and destroyed their central town of Metulum (= located above
Viničica near Ogulin). These centres of the I. continued
into the Roman period as urban communities; Metulum even achieved the status of a *municipium* (cf. CIL
III 10060).

R. DRECHSLER-BIŽIĆ, Japodska grupa [The Iapodic cul-
ture group], in: Praistorija jugoslavenskih zemalja 5,
1987, 391-441; S. GRABOVEC, Notranjska grupa [The
Inner Crainian culture group], in: Ibid., 151-177; M. ŠA-
ŠEL KOS, A Historical Outline of the Region between
Aquileia, the Adriatic, and Sirmium in Cassius Dio and
Herodian, 1986, 128-145.   M.Š.K.

Iapyges, Iapygia People and region in the extreme
south-east of Italy (modern Puglia). First mentioned by
Hecataeus (FGrH 1 F 86f.) together with the unidentified settlements of *Eleútioi* (Ἐλεύτιοι), *Peukaíoi*
(Πευκαῖοι, possibly equivalent to Πευκέτιοι; *Peukétioi*)
and the *pólis Chandánē* (πόλις Χανδάνη). Hecataeus
(loc. cit.) may also mean the I. with 'town in Italia'
(πόλις ἐν τῆι Ἰταλίαι; *pólis en tēi Italíai*). According to
Hdt. 4,99 the peninsula south of the isthmus between
Tarentum and Brundisium was the acroterium of I.
[7. 170-172]. Antiochus (FGrH 555 F 12) draws the
border between Italy and I. near Metapontum (cf. F 3b;
Aristot. Pol. 7,9,2) and considers Tarentum part of the
I.'s territory (F 3a), while Scyl. 14 also includes Heraclea and Metapontum in I. (from Lucania to the Garganus). According to Strabo (6,3,1; 5) I., also called
Messapia, is simply the peninsula south of the isthmus
between Tarentum and Brundisium [8. 47f.]. I. is
mostly, and perhaps originally [4], associated with
Cape Leuca (Ἄκρα Ἰαπυγίας; *Ákra Iapygías*; cf. Thuc.
6,30,1; Scyl. 27; Aristot. Mir. 97; Diod. Sic. 13,3,3; Str.
2,5,20; Plin. HN 3,100). In Greek sources I. usually
means the entire population of south-east Italy (Hdt.
4,99; Scymn. 363) including the Messapii, Peucetii and
Dauni (Pol. 3,88; Str. 6,3,2), but especially the southern
Messapii, against whom the Greek colonists of Tarentum fought (founding oracle in Antiochus, FGrH 555 F
13; Diod. Sic. 8,21, cf. Hdt. 7,170) [8; 10]. Only Pol.
2,24,10 differentiates the I. from the Messapii.

Usually, tradition ascribes to the I. origins in Crete
during the Minoan period [4; 8; 11]. Hdt. 7,170 knew
of a landing of Cretans in I. (founding of Hyrie – Uria or
more likely Veretum, cf. Str. 6,3,2 – and other *poleis*)
and their renaming as *Iépyges Messápioi* (Ἰήπυγες Μεσ-
σάπιοι, cf. Conon, FGrH 26 F 1,25; Ath. 12,522f.). According to Str. 6,3,2 (cf. 6,3,6) and Sol. 2,7 the I. are
descended from Iapyx (→ Iapis), a son of Daedalus.
Nicander (in Antoninus Liberalis, Metamorphosis 31)
attributes Arcadian and Illyrian origins to the I. and
descent from Iapyx, the son of Lycaon. According to
Hellanicus of Lesbos (FGrH 4 F 79) the I. drove the
Ausonii out of Italy, which may agree with Ephoros'
reference to *Iapýgōn ákrai* in the area of Croton
(Ἰαπύγων ἄκραι, FGrH 70 F 140).

The wars of Tarentum against the I. in the late archaic period are well documented: the conquest of the town
of Carbina (Clearchus in Ath. 12,522 e-f) and of other
poleis (Hdt. 7,170); the victories over the Messapii, the
Peucetii and Opis, the king of the I. (Paus. 10,10,6;
13,10); the bloody defeat inflicted upon Tarentum in
470 (Hdt. 7,170; Aristot. Pol. 5,2,8; Diod. Sic. 11,52).

In 413 BC the Iapygian-Messapian prince Artas provided the Athenians with auxiliaries for the war against Syracuse (Thuc. 7,33,4; 57,11). Towards the end of the 4th cent. the I. were drawn into the wars between Rome and the Samnites (Diod. Sic. 20,35; 80). Early in the 3rd cent. Agathocles [2] formed an alliance with the I. and the Peucetii (Diod. Sic. 21, fr. 4).

Aristot. Mir. 97 recounts Hercules legends in I.; native myths are recorded by Antoninus Liberalis (Metamorphoses 31,3; cf. Ov. Met. 14,514–526). The assumption of an Illyrian descent of the I. [2; 4; 6; 7. 75–84] and their language, which is probably that of the 'Messapian inscriptions', cannot be proven [7. 107–110; 8; 11]. Archaeological sources document important cultural developments in I. from the 8th cent. onwards with a progressive differentiation between the Messapii in the south, the Dauni in the north and the Peucetii in the centre and their interaction with the Greeks [5; 6; 7; 8; 9].

1 NISSEN 1, 539–542   2 G. SUSINI, Fonti per la storia greca e romana del Salento, 1962   3 G. NENCI, Il βάρβαρος πόλεμος tra Taranto e gli Iapigi, in: ASNP III, 6, 1976, 719–738   4 Id., Per una definizione della Ἰαπυγία, in: ASNP III, 8, 1978, 43–58   5 F. D'ANDRIA, Greci e indigeni in Iapigia, in: Forme di contatto ... Atti Convegno Cortona, 1983, 287–305   6 E. DE JULIIS, Gli Iapigi, 1988   7 M. CONGEDO (ed.), Salento Porta d'Italia. Atti del convegno di Lecce 1986, 1989   8 M. LOMBARDO, I Messapi, in: A. STAZIO (ed.), Atti XXX Convegno sulla Magna Grecia, 1991, 35–109   9 D. YNTEMA, The Matt-Painted Pottery of Southern Italy, 1990   10 M. LOMBARDO, I Messapi e la Messapia nelle fonti letterarie greche e latine, 1992   11 Id., La Puglia prima dei Greci, in: P. BRONI (ed.), La Puglia prima della colonizzazione, 1997, 15–37.
M.L.

Iasdius

[1] L. I. Aemilianus Honoratianus Postumus. Son of I. [2]. *Frater Arvalis* AD 240–241. CIL VI 41225.

SCHEID, Collège 464ff.

[2] L.? I. Domitianus. Entered the Senate as *homo novus*. After being a praetor he commanded two legions, became *curator viae Aemiliae* and simultaneously *praefectus alimentorum*. Was praetorian governor and suffect consul between about AD 215 and 225. Subsequently, consular legate of Germania inferior or Pannonia inferior, then legate of the Tres Daciae (before 235), CIL VI 1428 = 31651 + 31805 = 41225; PISO, FPD I 192ff.
W.E.

Iasion ('Ιασίων; *Iasíōn*, also Ἰάσιος; *Iásios* and Ἴασος; *Íasos*). An adolescent hero from the realm of agricultural mysteries. According to a tradition from Crete, I. fathers → Plutus (personification of a wealth of grain) with → Demeter on a thrice ploughed fallow field; for this, Zeus kills him with lightning (Hom. Od. 5,125–128; Hes. Theog. 969–974; cf. schol. Theoc. 3,49–51d; Ov. Am. 3,10,25ff.). The myth explains the emergence of agriculture after the flood (schol. Hom. Od. 5,125).

Older research suspected the myth to be based on customs intended to renew the fertility of soil through sympathetic agricultural magic [1; 2]. A more appropriate interpretation, however, regards the myth as a reflection of rural prenuptial rites of initiation, which synchronize the transition into adult life with the new beginning of the agricultural year. I.'s death by lightning might be the mythical aition of a mystic consecration, which conveyed a double legitimacy to agriculture and the conception of children.

Based on these considerations, I. was able to be identified with the Samothracian Eëtion ('Ηετίων; *Ēetíōn*), brother of → Dardanus and → Harmonia, a mystic hero whom Zeus strikes dead with lightning after the flood because he had embraced a cult image (Hellanicus of Lesbos, FGrH 4 F 23; Str. 7,49 [50]; Apollod. 3,138) or a 'phantom' (Conon, FGrH 26 F 1, 21) of Demeter driven by sexual desire. According to an alternative version, I. introduces the mystic consecration shown to him by Zeus on → Samothrace (Diod. Sic. 5,48,4). This was a rite of initiation, in which the gift of seeds (ibid. 5,49,1 and 4) served, on the one hand, as an introduction into the life of farming (*pace* [3]) and, on the other hand, granted a symbolic licence for the conception of children.

A further story according to which Dardanus kills his brother I. and then leaves Samothrace in order to found a city in Asia Minor at the foot of the Ida (Serv. Aen. 3,167; Mythographici Vaticani 1,135) evokes the myth of the Corybantes and → Cabiri (cf. Clem. Al. strom. 19,1–4) [4]. Again, it can be interpreted as the aition of a custom analogous to the gardens of Adonis, that is, a *cista mystica* (→ Adonis) used in rites of puberty common in many regions.

Since I. was regarded as a parallel figure to the Eleusinian agricultural hero → Triptolemus, he was recognized at the side of the latter in the zodiacal sign of Gemini (Hyg. Poet. Astr. 2,22). Wandering myths connected the figure I. to more distant cult traditions, which let him reach Samothrace, together with Dardanus, from Arcadia (Dion. Hal. Ant. Rom. 1,61) or Etruria (Verg. Aen. 3,167–171 with Serv. ad loc.).

1 W. MANNHARDT, Myth. Forsch., 1884, 238ff. 2 NILSSON, GGR, 121, 462   3 A. AVAGIANOU, Sacred Marriage in the Rituals of Greek Religion, 1991, 165ff. 4 BURKERT, 177, 424f.

W. GUNDEL, s.v. I., RE 9, 752–758; B. HEMBERG, Die Kabiren, 1950, 89ff.; E. SIMON, s.v. I., LIMC 5.1, 627–628.
G.B.

Iaso see → Hygieia

Iason ('Ιάσων; *Iásōn*).

[1] Thessalian hero from → Iolcus, leader of the → Argonauts, participant in the Calydonian Hunt (Apollod. 1,68), son of → Aeson [1] and Polymela (Hes. Cat. 38–40; Apollod. 1,107) or → Alcimede (Pherecydes 3 F 104 FGrH; Apoll. Rhod. 1,47); brother of → Promachus

(Apollod. 1,143); with → Hypsipyle, he fathered → Euneus [1] (Hom. Il. 7,468) and Nebrophonos (Apollod. 1,115), and with → Medea, he fathered Medeus (Hes. Theog. 1001), → Mermerus [3] and Pheres (Apollod. 1,146).

Having been raised by → Chiron (Hes. Cat. 40), I. lives in Iolcus with Aeson without any rights to the throne (Hes. Theog. 997; Apollod. 1,107), while Pelias rules rightfully as the oldest son of → Tyro and Poseidon. At the time of → Cretheus' death, Pelias had been warned by the oracle – due to his animosity to Hera – of a one-shoed man (Apollod. 1,92) [1. 112ff.; 2. 132ff.]. When I. is revealed to be that man after wading through the Anaurus, Pelias orders him to fetch the Golden Fleece from → Aea, a task which he had promised Hera to do. With Hera's help (Hom. Od. 12,72). I. undertakes the journey of the Argonauts, which brings Medea to Iolcus as Hera's avenger against Pelias (Pherecydes 3 F 105 FGrH; Apollod. 1,107–109 [1. 12ff.]). Only in Pindarus (Pind. Pyth. 4,106–108) does I. have claims to the throne, because Pelias had pushed Aeson, the oldest legitimate son of Cretheus, from the throne. Aside from the Delphic Oracle of the one-shoed man, which I. fulfilled upon his return from an exile of 20 years with Chiron (ibid. 71–120), Pelias had a dream vision of Phrixus; on the basis of this vision and on the Delphic prophecy, he orders I. to appease the underworldly anger directed at the Aeolidae by bringing home the soul of Phrixus that had passed into the Golden Fleece, in exchange for the promise of handing back the rulership (ibid. 158–167 [1. 150ff.; 3]). In Apollonius Rhodius, it is the Pindaric dream vision of Phrixus that leads to the Delphic Oracle (Apoll. Rhod. 1,5–17) and I., Hera's friend (3,60–75), must travel to Colchis under orders of Pelias, the rightful ruler who disdains Hera (1,14), in order to expiate the wrath of Zeus caused by the Scythian tree burial (3,200–209) of Phrixus (2,1192–1195; 3,336–339 [1. 93ff.]). I.'s thirst for glory presents a danger to Pelias, the rightful ruler (Diod. Sic. 4,40; Val. Fl. 1,22–62), causing the latter to send I. off without an oracle [1. 328ff.]. After the building of the → Argo, the voyage of the Argonauts begins under the guidance of I., who, beforehand, had questioned the oracle of Dodona (Apollod. 1,110; Val. Fl. 1,544; 3,299) or Delphi (Apoll. Rhod. 1,412–414; Val. Fl. 3,299; 617f.; cf. Hdt. 4,179 [1. 336ff.]).

During the adventures on the voyage out (→ Argonauts), I. appears prominently in Lemnos as Hypsipyle's lover (Apollod. 1,114f.; Apoll. Rhod. 1,774–908ff.; Val. Fl. 2,72ff.; → Lemnian women), among the → Doliones as → Cyzicus' battle opponent (Apoll. Rhod. 1,1030–1034; Val. Fl. 3,239ff.), and on the island of Ares during the encounter with the sons of Phrixus, an episode invented by Apollonius Rhodius (2,1093ff. [1. 326f.]). In Aea (Colchis), → Aeetes stipulates that the Fleece will only be released in return for yoking the bulls, ploughing, sawing the teeth of the dragon of → Cadmus [1] (Pherecydes 3 F 22 FGrH), and defeating the → Gegeneis [2] ([2. 137; 4. 450ff.]; in Pindarus

(Pind. Pyth. 4,232–237), only yoking and ploughing is required [1. 182ff., 191[140]]; in Valerius Flaccus (5,541ff.) also assistance in the war against Aeetes' brother Perses). I. fulfils these demands with the help (ointment/herbs) and the advice (throwing a rock amid the Gegeneis) of Medea, who, with Aphrodite's intervention, falls in love with I. and to whom I. had promised marriage. Aeetes' refusal to give up the Fleece wins I. the right to steal it with Medea's help and to defend himself against his pursuers (even by killing Apsyrtus) (Apollod. 1,127–133; Pind. Pyth. 4,211ff.; Apoll. Rhod. 3,482–502; 4,410ff.; Val. Fl. 7,58ff.). The marriage between I. and Medea ([5. 197ff.] on the → Cypselus chest, Paus. 5,18,3) takes place in Iolcus (Hes. Theog. 997–999) or already in Colchis (Antimachus fr. 75), Byzantium (Dionysius Scytobrachion fr. 31 RUSTEN), in Cercyra/Drepane (Timaeus 566 F 87 FGrH; Apollod. 1,138; Apoll. Rhod. 4,1128ff.) or in Peuce (Val. Fl. 8,217ff.).

After handing over the Fleece and dedicating the Argo at the Isthmus (Apollod. 1,143f.; Diod. Sic. 4,53,2), I. avenges his parents' suicide and his brother's murder by Pelias with the help of Medea (Apollod. 1,143f.; Diod. Sic. 4,50; Val. Fl. 1,700ff.). I. is then (following the dragon fight: Lycoph. 1315 [5. 160]) rejuvenated by Medea (Simon. fr. 548 PMG; Pherecydes 3 F 113 FGrH [2. 137]).

After participating in the funeral games for Pelias (wrestling match with → Peleus on the Cypselus chest, Paus. 5,17,10), I. and Medea – driven out of Iolcus by Acastus – go to Corinth (Apollod. 1,144f.). According to Diod. Sic. 4,53, I. does so of his own free will after installing Acastus as ruler. According to Eumelus (fr. 5 PEG), I. rules there thanks to Medea, whom the Corinthians had brought from Iolcus as the daughter of Aeetes, the Corinthian, in order to grant her the rulership; I. returns to Iolcus after his estrangement from Medea. According to Naupactus (fr. 9 PEG), I. emigrates from Iolcus to Corcyra after Pelias' death; according to Apollod. (244 F 180a FGrH), he and Medea settle in Thesprotian → Ephyra; according to Justin (42,2,12f.), I. returns with Medea and her son Medos to Colchis, reinstalls Aeetes and enlarges the empire through military campaigns. When I. wants to marry → Glauce after 10 years in Corinth, Medea kills Glauce and her father but also her own children with I., Mermerus and Phere (Apollod. 1,145; Diod. Sic. 4,54f.). Along with Peleus and the → Dioscuri, I. destroys Iolcus under Acastus (Pherecydes 3 F 62 FGrH; Apollod. 3,173). Death of I.: not in Colchis through dragons [3] but he is struck dead by a beam of the Argo (Eur. Med. 1386f. with schol.); suicide (Diod. Sic. 4,55,1) by hanging (Neophron fr. 3 TGF) or by drinking the blood of a bull (Apollonius Sophista 156,18); burning with his bride (Hyg. Fab. 25,3).

The only telos of I.'s existence is the journey of the Argonauts, which I. undertakes originally as a representative of the cult of Hera in the interior of Thessaly opposite the newly emerging worship of Poseidon among the coast dwellers represented by Pelias [1. 136ff.]. In the end, I. is the leader of a communal undertaking, he is shaped after Aeneas [6. 237ff.], who in turn reflects traits of I. as portrayed in Euripides' *Medea* ([7. 13ff.] cf. Sen. Med. [8. 371ff.]) as well as those of the Alexandrian passive, realistic 'anti hero' of Apoll. Rhod. [4. 215; 9; 10. 210f.] (cf. Goethe, Faust II, 7373f.).

The ancient (schol. Pind. Pyth. 4,211a) and modern derivation of the name from ἰάομαι (*iáomai* 'to heal'; I. as healing god [11. 759; 12]) is neither confirmed nor justified [5. 244], a non-Greek origin is possible [13. 156, 373]. I. in art: [14; 16. 39ff.].

1 P. DRÄGER, Argo pasimelousa, I, 1993 2 A. MOREAU, Le Mythe de Jason et Médée, 1994 3 P. DRÄGER, 'Abbruchsformel' und Jona-Motiv in Pind. 4. Pyth. Ode, in: WJA 21, 1996/97, 1–7 4 R. HUNTER, Short on Heroics, in: CQ 38, 1988, 436–453 5 U. v. WILAMOWITZ-MOELLENDORFF, Hell. Dichtung, II, ²1962 6 E. BURCK, Die 'Argonautica' des Valerius Flaccus, in: Id. (ed.), Das röm. Epos, 1979, 208–253 7 A. BURNETT, Medea and the Tragedy of Revenge, in: CPh 68, 1973, 1–24 8 K. v. FRITZ, Die Entwicklung der I.-Medea-Sage und die Medea des Euripides, in: Ant. und mod. Trag., 1962, 322–429 9 G. LAWALL, Apollonius' Argonautica, in: YClS 19, 1966, 121–169 10 J. J. CLAUSS, The Best of the Argonauts, 1993 11 O. JESSEN, s.v. I. (1), RE 9, 759–771 12 LFE s.v. I. 13 KAMPTZ 14 J. NEILS, s.v. I., LIMC 5.1, 629–738 15 M. VOJATZI, Frühe Argonautenbilder, 1982.   P.D.

[2] Tyrant of → Pherae in Thessaly in the early 4th cent. The prototype of the younger → tyrannis in the homeland who was not satisfied with rulership of the city, comparable to Dionysius [1] I of Syracuse. He claimed that he would have to go hungry if he were not a tyrant (Aristot. Pol. 1277a 24). Tradition attributes to him the acumen of a sophist and a Thucydidian sense for power politics, characterizing him as a capable commander who successfully combined charisma and rationality (Xen. Hell. 6,1; 4). He is said to have coined the phrase that 'it is inevitable that those should act unjustly in small matters who wish to act justly in great matters' (Plut. Mor. 817f; Aristot. Rh. 1373a 26). Unlike Dionysius, however, in terms of his politics he could rely on the tradition of the Thessalian League.

The nature of I.'s connection to → Lycophron [2], founder of the Tyrannis in Pherae, is unclear – he succeeded Lycophron after his death in 390 BC either as his son or son-in-law. The first thing that is firmly documented is Polydamas of Pharsalus' unsuccessful plea for help from Sparta against him in 375 (Xen. Hell. 6,1). After Polydamas yielded, I. won all of → Thessaly and was voted → *tagós* (ταγός), the highest military commander in the league. He enlarged the basis of his power – 6,000 devoted mercenaries – by the contingent from the Thessalian League, which he changed to the following numbers: 20,000 hoplites, countless peltastai, and 8,000 cavalry, plus payments of tribute from the perioikoi. Allied with Macedon, Thebes and prob-

ably Athens as well, he nevertheless negotiated the safe withdrawal of the defeated Spartan contingent following the battle at Leuctra of 371, a move clearly serving his own interest (Xen. Hell. 6,4,20–26). About to demonstrate his power and glory at the Pythian games at Delphi in 370, he was murdered because he was perceived as a threat to Thebes; the conspirators were celebrated in many cities as tyrannicides (→ Tyrannicide) (cf. Xen. Hell. 6,4,31f.; Diod. Sic. 15,60,5). According to our sources, I. had still bigger plans: the building of a fleet, hegemony over Greece, a Panhellenic campaign against Persia (Xen. Hell. 6,1,8–12; Isoc. Or. 5,119f.; Diod. Sic. 15,60,1; Val. Max. 9,10, ext. 2).

H. BERVE, Die Tyrannis bei den Griechen, 1967, 285–290, 668–670; B. HELLY, L'état thessalien, 1995, 240–256, 334f., 345–353; J. MANDEL, Jason, the Tyrant of Pherae, tagus of Thessaly, in: Rivista storica dell'Antichità 10, 1980, 47–77; C. TUPLIN, The Failings of Empire, 1993, 117–121, 180f., 207–213.   J.CO.

[3] I. of Cyrene. Jewish-hellenistic historian, whose only known work – a history of the Maccabaean revolt (175–161 BC; → Iudas [2] Makkabaeus) in five bks. – has not survived. It formed the basis for the second book of Maccabees (2 Macc 2,23; [1.1 71f.; 4]). I. apparently relied on eyewitness reports and must therefore have lived in the mid–2nd. cent. BC. On the relations between 1 Macc and 2 Macc and I.'s work, its sources and documents used, cf. [1. 177; 5. 531f.].

1 CH. HABICHT, Das zweite Makkabäerbuch (JSHRZ I,3), 1976 2 M. HENGEL, Judentum und Hellenismus, 1969, 176–183 3 B. NIESE, Kritik der beiden Makkabäerbücher, 1900 4 R. PFEIFFER, History of New Testament Times, 1949, 506–518 5 SCHÜRER I, 19; 3/1, 531–537 6 M. E. STONE (ed.), Jewish Writings of the Second Temple Period, Apocrypha, Pseudepigrapha, Qumran Sectarian Writings, Philo, Josephus, 1984, 176–183.   I.WA.

[4] I. of Argus. According to the Suda s.v., I. was younger than Plutarchus and must therefore be dated into the 2nd cent. AD. Author of the work *On Greece* in 4 bks. This text should not be confused with the *Bíos tēs Helládos*, whose author was probably Iason from Nysa. Instead, it is an outline of the events up to the capture of Athens by Antipater in 322 BC, becoming very detailed in the last part. FGrH 94.   K.MEI.

[5] Sculptor from 2nd-cent. AD Athens. He signed a personification of the Odyssey in the form of a woman with an armour that depicts scenes from the Odyssey. This sculpture along with another personifying the Iliad formed a group that was probably displayed in the Pantaenus Library in Athens.

LOEWY, no. 329; K. STEMMER, Unt. zur Typologie, Chronologie und Ikonographie der Panzerstatuen, 1978, 115–116; H. A. THOMPSON, The Athenian Agora, vol. 14: The Agora of Athens, 1972, 115.   R.N.

Iasus (Ἴασος/Ἰάσιος; *Íasos/Iásios*).

[1] Kings of Argus: a) son of Argus and Evadne, father of Agenor (Apollod. 2,3), b) son of Argus and Ismene, father of → Io (ibid. 2,5), c) son of Triopas, bother of Agenor, father of Io (Paus. 2,16,1).

[2] Arcadian, son of Lycurgus and Cleophile, brother of Ancaeus, Epochus, and Amphidamas, husband of Minyas' daughter Clymene, father of → Atalante (Hes. Theog. 1288; Callim. H. 3,216; Apollod. 3,105; 109).

[3] Leader of the Athenians at Troy, killed by Aeneas (Hom. Il. 15,332, 337.). The patronym Iasides is carried by the following kings: Amphion of Orchomenus (Hom. Od. 11,283), Dmetor of Cypris (17,443), Iapyx (Verg. Aen. 5,843), Palinurus (12,391). *Iason Argos* (Hom. Od. 18,246) is a region of uncertain determination [1]; according to [2], the name refers to the 'land of Ionians'.

[4] One of the → Daktyloi Idaioi ('Tom Thumb': goblin of a forge, belonging to the great goddess Cybele) along with Heracles, Paionaeus, Epimedes, Idas, who are regarded as the participants in the first race in Olympia (Paus. 5,7,6).

1 B. MADER, s.v. Iason, LFE, 2, 1109   2 ED. MEYER, Forsch. zur Alten Gesch. I, 1892.   RE.ZI.

[5] (Ἰασός; *Iasós*). Carian harbour town in the northern corner of the Gulf of I. (modern Güllük körfezi) on a small, rocky island (a peninsula since the Roman Imperial period), modern Asın Kalesi across from Kuren. The legendary foundation coming from Argus (Pol. 16,12,1f.) points to the late Mycenaean period; the Greek settlers asserted themselves against the native Carians only with the aid of Miletus. I. was of Ionian character (the language of inscriptions) and largely shared in Caria's history: It was first under Lydian, from 546 BC under Persian rule; joined the → Delian League in the mid–5th cent., was plundered in 412 by the Spartan fleet as a city 'of old wealth' (Thuc. 8,28) and handed over to Tissaphernes; destroyed in 405 by Lysander, the men killed, the women and children enslaved (Diod. Sic. 13,104,7). After 387/6 I. belonged to the satrapy of → Hecatomnus. In 367/6, it imposed lifelong exile with confiscation of property on the fugitive conspirators against → Maussollus (Syll.³ 169). It was captured by → Alexander [4] the Great in 334. The brothers Gorgus and Minnion, citizens of I., succeeded in persuading Alexander to give back the 'little sea' (a fishing bay near I.) in 333/323 and contributed greatly to the repatriation of fugitives from Samos in 322/1 [1. vol. 1, 30; 1. vol. 2, T 50]. In the late 4th cent., I. was claimed by → Antigonus [1] I (Diod. Sic. 19,7); from 309/306, it was allied with Ptolemy I [1. vol. 1, 2f.]; under Macedonian rule probably from 227/220 on [2. 16, 20]. I. became free in 189/8 after the withdrawal of Philip V's garrison in 197/6 (Pol. 18,2,3; 8,9; 44,4; Liv. 32,33,7) and of that of the advancing garrison of Antiochus [5] III (Liv. 37,17,3–7). In 190 refugees from I. persuaded Rome to abstain from invading their home (Liv. 377,5–8). In 129 BC the city was integrated into the Roman province of Asia and plundered by pirates in AD 85 with Sulla's consent (App. Mith. 63).

The residents made a living from trade and fishing (Str. 14,2,21). I. is the home of → Choerilus [3], the court poet of Alexander the Great, and of → Diodorus [4], philosopher and dialectician. I. had a small Jewish community and was bishop's seat in the 4th cent. (Not. Episc. 1,340; 3,295; 8,392; 9,302; 10,409; 13,259).

Italian excavations (since 1960) indicate a certain degree of wealth in the Hellenistic and Imperial periods. Arch. remains: tombs from the Sub-Mycenaean and Geometric periods under the agora over Bronze Age masonry; city wall with towers and gates (4th cent. BC and Hellenistic); a Hellenistic-Roman theatre on the terraced eastern slope of the city mountain. Residential quarters, *villae* on the southern slope, occasionally with wall decorations and floor mosaics (1st–2nd cent.); a propylaion and a sanctuary of Demeter-Kore. A *bouleuterion* (AD 128 and 138) at the Hellenistic-Roman agora, next to it a sanctuary for the main goddess Artemis Astias, a Zeus-Megistos temple near the eastern gate to the outer harbour. In the northern and eastern part of I. are four early Byzantine basilicas (6th cent. and later), one within the agora, which had replaced a martyrium (5th cent.) and was succeeded by a church of reduced size (11th cent.); a further basilica can be found on the mainland. I. was still heavily fortified in the 10th/11th cents.: Byzantine barrier fortress on the isthmus, fortress on the acropolis hill, moles to protect the inner harbour, the ruin of a Byzantine harbour tower on its eastern side.

A monumental Roman heroon (2nd cent. AD) and part of an aqueduct (Balık Pazarı, 'fish market') are located inland of the isthmus, an extensive military installation with a Hellenistic land wall 2,5 km in length is located to the north-west of Kuren; Hellenistic-Roman tombs are to the south beyond the western harbour bay. The buildings of I., esp. the city wall and the theatre, fell victim to systematic despoliation in the 19th cent.

1 W. BLÜMEL, Die Inschr. von I. 1–2 (IK 28), 1985
2 H. BENGTSON, Die Inschr. von Labranda und die Politik des Antigonos Doson, in: SBAW 1971, 3.

G. E. BEAN, M. COOK, The Carian Coast III, in: ABSA 52, 1957, 100ff.; G. E. BEAN, Kleinasien 3, 1974, 71–84; F. BERTI, V. GRAZIANO, I. [guide book], 1994; L. BÜRCHNER, s.v. I. (15), RE 9, 786–790; C. CROWTHER, I. in the (early) second century B.C., I–II, in: BICS 36, 1989, 136ff.; 37, 1990, 143ff.; G. JOST, I. in Karien, thesis Hamburg, 1935; D. LEVI, G. PUGLIESE CARATELLI, Le due prime campagne di scavo a I. (1960–61). Nuove iscrizione di I., in: ASAA 39/40, 1961/2, 505–571; 573–632 (and following, exc. reports); Id. et al., I. Studi su I. di Caria, in: BA Suppl. 31/2, 1986 (with bibliography XI–XIII); W. KOENIGS, Westtürkei, 1991, 230ff.; MAGIE 2, 906f.; W. RADT, Siedlungen und Bauten auf der Halbinsel von Halikarnassos, unter spez. Berücksichtigung der archa. Epoche, in: MDAI(Ist) suppl. 3, 1970, 208ff.; H. H. SCHMITT, Antiochos d.Gr., 1964, 243, 247.   H.KA.

Iathrippa see → Yaṯrīb

Iatraleiptes Masseur, a profession that seems to have become fashionable in the 1st cent. AD (e.g. CIL 6,9476) but the linking of medicine and gymnastics extends as far back as Herodicus [1] of Selymbria (5th cent. BC). Trimalchio was treated by three *aliptae* (Petron. Sat. 28). Pliny considers this entire branch of medicine a form of quackery (HN 29,4–5). Vespasian however guaranteed all who practiced this art various privileges (FIRA 1,77) and Pliny the Younger managed to persuade Trajan to confer Roman (and Alexandrian) citizenship to his Egyptian *iatraleiptes* Harpocrates, who he believed had cured him from a serious illness (Epistulae 10,5–7,10). V.N.

Iatrocles (Ἰατροκλῆς; *Iatroklês*).
[1] Athenian, fled in 411 BC after the pro-democratic uprising of the Athenian fleet off Samos with the trierarch → Eratosthenes [1] and others, when the fleet was operating in the Hellespont, to Athens, where he supported the oligarchy (Lys. 12,42).

TRAILL, PAA 531050. W.S.

[2] Son of Pasiphon, in 348 BC captured by → Philippus II during the conquest of → Olynthus but then released (Aeschin. Leg. 15–16); twice in 347/46 an Athenian delegate sent to negotiate the peace of → Philocrates of 346 (Aeschin. Leg. 20 and 126; Dem. Or. 19,197f.).

DEVELIN no. 1443; PA 7442. J.E.

[3] Mentioned repeatedly in → Athenaeus [3] (2nd/3rd cents.) as the author of a bread and/or pastry bakery book (Ἀρτοποιικόν, *Artopoiikón*, only 326e; Περὶ πλακούντων, *Perì plakoúntōn*). His biographical dates cannot be determined. The references in Ath. 646a and 647b include the title of the pastry book; two notes in-between without a title are presumably taken from the same work. The information refers to the names of pastries: *teuthís* (squid) 326e; κριμνίτης πλακοῦς (*krimnítēs plakoûs*), a barley cake 646a; παῖσον (*paîson*), a small pastry from the island of Cos 646f. A pastry made of wheat and honey is mentioned in 647b under the keyword 'shells' or 'snails' (cf. 114a). It was awarded as 'prize' to the person who held up best during a feast (*pyramís, pyramýs*: cf. Aristoph. Equ. 277; Thesm. 94). The ingredients in 646b suggest a kind of cheese cake on a wheat dough base with a topping of water, honey, sesame and quark cheese. G.BI.

Iatromaia ('birth-helper', 'midwife'). Midwifery was usually practiced by women but was not exclusively in their hands. A Parian inscription, for example, records two male birth-helpers (IG 12,5,199) and the preserved treatises on midwifery address a male readership. *Iatromaia* as an occupational name appears in two Roman inscriptions of the 3rd and 4th cents. AD (CIL 6,9477f.); in one, a Valeria Verecunda is named as the 'first *iatromaia* in her region', an epithet that seems to refer to the quality of her work rather than a position in a *collegium*.
→ Midwife V.N.

Iatromathematics
A. DEFINITION B. SOURCES C. HISTORY OF SCIENCE D. RECEPTION

A. DEFINITION
Iatromathēmatiká (Herm. 1,387,1 IDELER) or *nosoúntōn perignostiká ek tês mathēmatikês epistḗmēs* (ibid. 1,430,2–3) etc. is the term for the medical implications of astrology, i.e. the recognition of a nosological predisposition of patients or a prognosis of current illnesses, connected with prevention or therapy, depending on the case.

B. SOURCES
The books on which iatromathematics is based are the alleged revelations of → Hermes, who was possibly assisted by Asclepius. These revelations are recorded in two *corpora*: one under the name of Hermes, which is extant in two versions (Herm. 1,387–396, 430–440 I.), and another by king → Nechepso who was aided by the priest → Petosiris [9; 1]. These texts indeed appear to have originated in the Greek milieu in Egypt (Ptol. Apotelesmatika 1,3,12), perhaps beginning in the 2nd cent. BC, and continued to develop into the 2nd cent. AD through accretion, while at the same time an anonymous production also flourished.

More information on iatromathematics is found in surveys of astrology that originated not much later than these *corpora* and are more or less detailed than these. They include (in a probable chronological sequence): → Manilius 2,453–465, 4,701–710; → Dorotheus [5] of Sidon 5,37–41 PINGREE; → Ptolemaeus, Tetrabiblos 3.12; → Sextus Empiricus, Adversus mathematicos 5,21f.; Vettius Valens, Anthologiae 2,37 (=2,36 PINGREE); → Firmicus Maternus 2,24; 4,22,1–2; [Galen], Prognostica de decubitu (19,529–573) [2]; and the pseudo-Ptolemaic *Karpós* (8; 19–21).

C. HISTORY OF SCIENCE
In the context of a theory of the equivalency of the micro- and macrocosm (the human body and the universe) and – more precisely – in the context of the astrological theory of an equivalency of body parts and internal organs with the zodiac symbols and planets, the twelve (Olympian) gods and the countries of the *oikoumene*, as well as in association with the flowering of magic, these techniques, whose origin has been attributed to the Egyptians since antiquity (Ptol. Tetrabiblos 1,3 = 30,20–32,22 ROBB.), appear to have developed in Greek Egypt during the Hellenistic period.

The recognition of the nosological predisposition is based on the principle of *melothesia*, i.e. an equivalency of the micro-/macrocosm type of body parts and internal organs with zodiac symbols [7; 8]. These in turn were more or less related to the planets based on Greek astrology (zodiaco-planetary *melothesia*) or the decans (zodiaco-decanic *melothesia*) based on Egyptian astrology (the equivalencies were variable; an example in [4. 27]). Starting with the patient's birth horoscope (genethliology) the influences affecting the signs and through them the equivalent body parts or organs had to be recognized to arrive at an early diagnosis in the manner of predictive medicine.

The prognosis of current illness was established by relating the phases assigned to the illness to various astronomical phases: the phases of the moon, its planetary conjunctions and the astral influences to which it is exposed according to its phases. Certain hours, days, months and years were considered dangerous or even lethal (*klimaktéres*). They were initially calculated in a simple mathematical manner and then more elaborately determined by the influence of the planets and fixed stars on the birth horoscope.

This diagnostic phase was followed by another, interventionist or preventative therapeutic phase that could take several forms: the *melothesia* resulted in advice on prevention and, as in the prognosis of illnesses, it could lead to interventions for therapeutic purposes that were based on the principle of cosmic sympathies and consisted of the administration of medicine. This approach involved two opposite strategies: filling up the influence period of the sign that was responsible for the diseased body part or organ (homeopathy; *corpus* of Hermes Trismegistus) or antagonistic administration with the aim of triggering a reaction to the negative influences (allopathy, *corpus* of Nechepso and Petosiris).

The principle of *klimaktéres* was also inverted and used to determine the most favourable time for therapeutic or surgical intervention according to the more general astrological system of the *katarchaí*.

The principle of cosmic sympathy included prescriptions that required absolute compliance during therapy and even extended into magic in the strict sense, especially since another form of therapy consisted of attempting to exercise a direct influence on the planets, stars and other phenomena behind the illness.

D. Reception

This discipline spread from the Greek milieu in Egypt across the entire Mediterranean region, was cultivated in Rome and continued in Byzantium and the West, where the treatises of Hermes Trismegistus were translated into Latin some time after the 6th cent. (ed.: [5]). Iatromathematics was passed on to the Arab world from Byzantium and translated there, whereupon it underwent an extraordinary development [6]. The same can also be said of the Western Middle Ages, particularly as this discipline and the rest of astrology were Christianized, and of the Renaissance, which revitalized it to a significant degree [10].

1 F. BOLL, Excerpta ex Nechepsone et Petosiride de Solis et Lunae defectionibus, in: CCAG 7, 1908, 129–151
2 F. CUMONT, Les »Prognostica de decubitu« attribués à Galien, in: BIBR 15, 1935, 119–131   3 A. DELATTE, Herbarius, ³1961   4 H. G. GUNDEL, Zodiakos, 1992 5 W. GUNDEL, Neue astrologische Texte des Hermes Trismegistos, 1936   6 F. KLEIN-FRANKE, Iatromathematics in Islam, 1984   7 O. NEUGEBAUER, Melothesia and Dodecatemoria, in: Studia biblica et orientalia 3, Oriens antiquus, Analecta Biblica 12, 1959, 270–275   8 A. OLIVIERI, Melotesia planetaria greca, in: Memorie e Rendiconti dell' Accademia di Architettura, Lettere e Arti di Napoli 5, 1936, 21–580   9 E. RIESS, Nechepsonis et Petosiridis fragmenta magica, in: Phil. Suppl. 6, 1891–1893, 325–394   10 L. Welker, Das iatromathematische Corpus, 1988.

CCAG, 11 vols., 1898–1934; S. FAZZO, Un'arte inconfutabile: la difesa dell'astrologia nella Tetrabiblos di Tolomeo, in: Rivista critica di storia della filosofia 46, 1991, 213–244; W. HÜBNER, Eine unbeachtete zodiakale Melothesie bei Vettius Valens, in: RhM N.F. 120, 1977, 247–254 (with bibliography); Id., Manilius als Astrologe und Dichter, in: ANRW II 32,1, 1984, 126–320; A. J. FESTUGIÈRE, La révélation d'Hermès Trismégiste, ²1950, 1; H. G. GUNDEL, Weltbild und Astrologie in den griech. Zauberpap., 1968; W. GUNDEL, H. G. GUNDEL, Astrologumena, 1966.   A.TO.

Iatros (Greek ἰατρός; *iatrós*, 'physician').
[1] Physician, → Medicine.
[2] Epiclesis of → Apollo as healing god, esp. common in the Ionian east and the Greek colonies along the western coast of the Black Sea. In Olbia, Apollo I. has replaced the Milesian Apollo Delphinios from the Hellenistic period. This form of Apollo was adopted as Apollo Medicus in early Republican Rome.
[3] Functional name and title of four Attic healing heroes. The (few and late) texts also present their proper names: Amphilochus (Athens near the Agora), Aristomachus (Marathon), Oresinius (Eleusis), Aristomachus (Rhamnus; also identified with → Amphiaraus). The inscriptions almost always use the functional titles: the respective worshippers were only interested in the healing power; a mythology, where applicable, was secondary.

E. KEARNS, The Heroes of Attica, 1989, 171f.   F.G.

Iatrosophistes Originally meaning a teacher of medicine (esp. in Alexandria), *iatrosophistes* could later refer to any experienced practitioner (*medicus sapientissimus*, Corpus Glossatorum Latinorum 3,600,32 GOETZ), either in orthodox medicine (e.g. → Agnellus, In Galeni De sectis commentarium 33) or in the magical arts of healing (Ps.-Callisthenes, Vita Alexandri 1,3) [1]. Contrary to the emendation by VON ARNIM in Dion. Chrys. 33,6, the term was probably not coined before the late 4th cent. AD (Epiphanius, Adversus haereses 56,10; Cassius Felix, De medicina 182; Fulg. Mythologiae 3,7). It is often used sarcastically by Christian authors (e.g. *Vita Archelai*, PG 10,12) and levelled at opponents of medicine, e.g. against → Gesius (Suda, s.v. Gesius). The first teacher to be given the title *iatro-*

sophistes was → Magnus of Nisibis, who was active around AD 360 (Palladas, Anth. Pal. 11,281, but only in one lemma). Magnus was know for his gifts of oratory and his talent for teaching: the Galenic tradition attached great value to the dual role of the physician as philosopher and practitioner. At the beginning of the 6th cent., the *iatrosophistaí* were regarded as the leading physicians, at least in Alexandria.

1 A. GRILLI, I., in: RIL 122, 1988, 125–128   2 J. M. DUFFY, Byzantine medicine in the sixth and seventh centuries, in: Dumbarton Oaks Papers 38, 1984, 22–25.
V.N.

Iavolenus

[1] **C.I. Calvinus Geminius Kapito Cornelius Pollio Squilla Q. Vulkacius Scuppidius Verus.** Senator, who had a prolonged praetorian career under Hadrian and Antoninus Pius, ending as governor in Lusitania, proconsul in Baetica and *consul suffectus*. ILS 1060; PIR[2] J 13.
W.E.

[2] **C. Octavius Tidius Tossianus L.I. Priscus.** Jurist, successor of Caelius Sabinus (→ Arulenus [1]) and predecessor of → Fulvius [II 2] Aburnius Valens as head of the Sabinian School (Dig. 1,2,2,53, → Law schools), was a member of the *consilium* of Trajan and probably also of that of Hadrian, was town magistrate (*cos. suff.* AD 86) and governor in Upper Germania, Syria and Africa [1]. He thus embodied the type of jurist common from the time of Vespasian who was a member of the imperial bureaucracy of justice [5. 165ff]. He wrote a collection of questions and responses, *Epistulae* (14 bks; see [2]), and critical commentaries on the legal writings: *Ex Cassio* on the *Ius civile* by → Cassius [II 14] Longinus (15 bks.; see [3]), *Ex Plautio* on the collection of questions by → Plautius (5 bks.) and on the *Posteriora* by → Antistius [II 3] Labeo (10 bks.; see [4]). True to both his casuistic inclination and the tradition of the Sabinian School (Dig. 50,17,1) I. considered 'definitions' (in the sense of all abstract legal clauses) to be 'dangerous' (Dig. 50,17,202) and in his commentaries he falsified many such 'definitions' of earlier jurisprudence. I. was a teacher of Salvius → Iulianus [5] (Dig. 40,2,5).

1 PIR IV, 1952–1956, 108p.   2 B. ECKARDT, Iavoleni epistulae, 1978   3 U. MANTHE, Die libri ex Cassio des I. Priscus, 1982   4 D. MANTOVANI, Sull'origine dei libri posteriores di Labeone, in: Labeo 34, 1988, 271–322   5 R. A. BAUMAN, Lawyers and Politics in the Early Roman Empire, 1989.
T.G.

Iaxartes River in western Central Asia, modern Syr Darya, 2,860 km long; rises at the Taedyk pass in the eastern Altai Mountains. After flowing northwards for a short distance it takes in the Naryn River, which originates not far from Lake Issyk-Kul, then enters the plains of Kazakhstan south-west of Tashkent (where it becomes navigable) and flows into the → Aral Sea (Amm. Marc. 23,6,59). The indigenous Scythians called the I. Silis or Orxantes, Alexander the Great called it Tanais (Plin. HN 6,49; Arr. Anab. 3,30–7–8 *et passim*, but also I. Arr. Anab. 7,16,3 among others), in view of the European Tanais (today Don) where Scythians also lived; Pers. Yaḫšart. According to Ptolemy (6,12,1) the I. fell into the area of Sogdiana, but it actually only touches on the northern part.

A. HERRMANN, s.v. I., RE 9, 1181–1189.   B.B. and H.T.

Iazyges, Iazuges (Ἰάζυγες; *Iázyges*). Iranian-Sarmatian tribe, first documented around the birth of Christ. They probably settled from the 3rd cent. BC at the earliest on the → Maeotis east of the Tanais in the area of the Roxolani (Ptol. 3,7; Amm. Marc. 22,8,31). In the 1st cent. BC a branch of the I. turned towards the southwest, crossed the Carpathians and settled on the plains between the lower Danube and the Tibiscus (later the province of Pannonia; cf. Ov. Pont. 4,7,9; Tr. 2,191; Ἰάζυγες μετανάσται/*Iázyges metanástai* with a list of the Iazygian cities, Ptol. 7,1f.; Str. 7,2,4; Plin. HN 4,12,80). Tacitus mentions *principes* and *eques* (Ann. 12,29; Hist. 3,5). From the time of Domitian the I. are known as constant enemies of Rome: from AD 166–180 on they repeatedly invaded the Roman Empire across the Danube together with Langobardi, Marcomanni and Sarmatae; Diocletian campaigned against the I. and Sarmatae in 292, Galerius in 294 (Eutr. 9,25; Aur. Vict. 39,43), likewise Maximinus Thrax, Gordianus III, Gallienus, Aurelianus, Probus and Carus.

J. HARMATTA, Studies on the History of the Sarmatians, 1950, 3ff.; A. MÓCSY, Pannonia and Upper Moesia, 1974; M. ROSTOVTZEFF, Iranians and Greeks in South Russia, 1922, 113ff., passim; Id., The Sarmatae and Parthians, in: CAH 11, 1936, 91ff.   I.v.B.

Ibas see → Hiba

Iberia

[1] (Ἰβηρία; *Ibēría*, Str. 11,3,1–6; Ptol. 5,10,1–2; Georgian K'art'li, Parthian Virčan, Armenian Virkʿ). Country in the centre of southern Caucasia, bordering on the Greater → Caucasus in the north, the Likh Range in the west which runs north-south from the Greater to the Lesser Caucasus, the Kura-Aras Lowland in the east and the Lesser Caucasus in the south, especially the southern and western frontiers being fluid; approximately modern eastern Georgia. Until the end of the 5th cent. AD, the capital was → Mestleta along with → Harmozice at the confluence of the → Cyrus and → Aragus Rivers, since then it has been Tbilisi ('warm springs'), downstream on the Cyrus. In the Achaemenid period it was in the sphere of Persian cultural influence, but politically independent (Plut. Alexander 34,7); in Hellenistic times it was sometimes dependant on the Seleucids, later on the Parthians.

According to the Georgian narrative compiled in the 9th/10th cents. AD → Pharnabazus founded the kingdom of I. *c.* 290/80 BC [6. 70ff.]. After a prosperous period in the 3rd cent. it lost territory in the 2nd/

1st cents. BC, especially to → Armenia maior under
→ Tigranes the Great. According to Strabo 11,3, I. is a
populous country with beautiful cities, developed crafts
and agriculture. Pompey's oriental campaign (66/65
BC), brought I. into Rome's circle of influence (App.
Mith. 101ff.; Plut. Pompey 34); since then it cleverly
manoeuvred between Parthians and Romans, who both
saw the country as a vassal state. With the reorganization of the provinces under the Flavians, I. came more
strongly into the Roman sphere; inscriptions transmit
the fortification of the walls of Mtskheta by Vespasian
in AD 75 [1. 214] in connection with the securing of the
passes of the Caucasus against the northern steppe
tribes. The visit to Rome of king → Pharasmanes of I. at
the time of Antoninus Pius (Fasti Ost. [6]; Cass. Dio
70,2,1) is considered the high point in Ibero-Roman
relations. The pressure from the east grew again with
the Sassanid rise to power; in the inscription of → Paikuli (before 298), I. is associated with the countries that
pay tribute to the Persian king [5. H15,03]. In 298 it
was brought back under Roman sovereignty; in 370
split up between Rome and Persia (Amm. Marc.
27,12,16–18). In Procopius the Iberians have always
been Persian subjects (BP 1,12,3); around 455–510/18
king Vakhtang Gorgasal ('Wolf's head'; → Gurgenes)
ruled. In the Lazian War, I. was an area of Persian deployment; in 579/80 the Persians removed the monarchy with the approval of the Iberian aristocracy; the
public administration of the de facto Persian province
was managed by representatives of the Iberian aristocracy.

The worship of astral deities has been documented,
also → Mazdaism (early Hellenistic fire temple of
Cixiagora) and → Mithras cult; Christianity was already officially introduced in 337 or 356. Excavations
attest to a developed metropolitan culture in the Hellenistic, and above all in the Roman period; during the
latter a distinctive Romanization of the until then Ira-
nian-influenced upper class can be determined.

1 A.I. BOLTUNOVA, Quelques notes sur l'inscription de
Vespasian trouvée à Mtskhetha, in: Klio 53, 1971, 213–
222   2 D.BRAUND, Georgia in Antiquity, 1995
3 O.LORDKIPANIDSE, Archäologie in Georgien, 1991,
146–176   4 Id., H.BRAKMAN, s.v. I., RAC 17, 12–106
5 E.HUMBACH, P.O. SKJAERVO, The Sassanian Inscription of Paikuli, 1983   6 H.NESSELHAUF, Ein neues Fr.
der Fasten von Ostia, in: Athenaeum 36,1958, 219–28
7 G.PÄTSCH, Das Leben Kartlis, 1985.   A.P.-L.

[2] see → Hispania

Iberian see → Hispania

Iberian archaeology see → Pyrenean peninsula

Iberians (Ἴβηροι/Íbēroi, Ἴβηρες/Íbēres). I. and Iberia
(Ἰβηρία/Ibēría), as terms for the inhabitants and country of East Georgia, occur only in Graeco-Roman and
Byzantine sources; possibly etymologically related to
virkʿ (Armenian) or Sáspeires (Σάσπειρες, Hdt. 4,37;

40) [1. 146]. Iberia was bordered in the north by → Sar-
matia, in the west by → Colchis, in the south by Greater
Armenia (→ Armenia) and in the east by → Albania [1]
(Ptol. 5,10,1f.).

→ ARMENIA; → Georgia, Georgians; → Georgian

1 O.LORDKIPANIDSE, Archäologie in Georgien (Quellen
und Forschungen zur prähistorischen provinzialrömi-
schen Archäologie 5), 1991.   K.SA.

Iberus (Hiberus). Name of two Spanish rivers, derived
from the people of the same name, not – as ancient
scholars (Plin. HN 3,21; Just. Epit. 44,1,2) believed –
the other way around [1. 307–315].
[1] Modern Ebro. All sources agree that the ancient I.,
with its tributaries, corresponds almost completely to
the modern Ebro. The single difference: the ancient river was navigable (Plin. I IN 3,21) as far as Vareia (modern Varea, east of Logroño), today only as far as Tor-
tosa (other, newer views contradict this identification,
including [2]). A mysterious ancient name of the I. was
Oleum (Avien. 505; attempted explanation in [1. 307–
315]).
[2] Modern Rio Tinto (Avien. 248). For this [1. 336].
Later name: Luxia (Plin. HN 3,7).

1 SCHULTEN, Landeskunde 1, ²1974   2 P.BARCELÓ, Die
Grenzen des karthagischen Machtbereichs unter Hasdrubal, in: E.OLSHAUSEN, H.SONNABEND (ed.), Stuttgarter
Kolloquium zur histor. Geogr. des Alt. 4 (1990, Geographica Historica 7), 1994, 35–55.   P.B.

Ibex The ibex (Capra ibex L.), which belongs to the
genus of goats, lives in the high mountains of Europe
(Alps, Pyrenees) and in Palestine. It was not known to
the Greeks; the Romans mention it as ibex only since
Pliny (HN 8,214). Where Isidore (Orig. 12,1,17) got
the nonsensical claim that the ibex would throw themselves from the peaks when enemies approached and
catch themselves unharmed by their horns is unknown.
Mass capture and use in arena fights is recorded for the
emperors Gordianus (SHA Gord. 3,7) and Probus
(SHA Probus 19). A coin [1. pl. 3,13] and many gems
(e.g. [1. pl. 18,22–23]) show the ibex, impressive because of its long horns, which could grow to 1m.

1 F.IMHOOF-BLUMER, O.KELLER, Tier- und Pflanzenbilder auf Mz. und Gemmen des klass. Alt., 1889 (repr.
1972).

KELLER 1,299–301; A.STEIER, s. v. S., RE 3 A, 2238–
2241.   C.HÜ.

Ibis (Egyptian hbj > Greek ἶβις; ibis).
I. EGYPT II. GREECE AND ROME

I. EGYPT
The ibis was considered a sacred bird (Hdt. 2, 65;
67; 75 and other ancient writers) in Egypt, where three
species were found. Above all, the 'Sacred ibis' (Thres-
kiornis aethiopicus) was worshipped as the holy animal

of → Thot, god of the moon and writing, and often represented. Ibis burials are known starting in the New Kingdom; in the Late Period, there were breeding colonies and animal cemeteries with mummified ibises everywhere in Egypt, particularly extensive in the chief cult centres of Thot.

D. KESSLER, Die heiligen Tiere und der König, 1989; A.-P. ZIVIE, s.v. I., LÄ 3, 115–121.   K.J.-W.

II. GREECE AND ROME

The Romans knew the ibis only from Egypt (Plin. HN 8,97): the dark one (i.e. the Glossy Ibis, *Plegadis falcinellus Kaup*) only from Pelusium, and the white one from everywhere (Plin. HN 10,87, according to Aristot. Hist. an. 8(9),27,617b 27–31) as a snake eater (Plin. HN 10,75). The story of its alleged self-purging with its curved beak was passed on to the Middle Ages via Isid. Orig. 12,7,33. The Bald or Hermit Ibis or Waldrapp (*Geronticus eremita L.*), which used to nest in the Alps, was first mentioned by Plin. HN 10,134. → Stork

J.-C. SAVIGNY, Histoire naturelle et mythologique de l'Ibis, 1805.   C.HÜ.

Ibycus (Ἴβυκος; *Íbykos*), born in Rhegium in the 6th cent. BC, the second important poet of Magna Graecia after → Stesichorus. He came to Samos in the 54th Olympiad (564–561 BC) (Suda: 'when Polycrates, the tyrant's father, ruled there', should probably be corrected to Πολυκράτους, which would result in more common Greek, and would then say – in accordance with Hdt. 3,39, who names Aeaces as the father: 'when the father of the tyrant Polycrates ruled there'). Eusebius' dating differs from this in stating that I. was famous in the years of the 61st Olympiad (536–533 BC) [1. 206–220], but this can hardly be accepted as true.

The 48 lines of the fr. 1 PMGF [2] written on papyrus are generally attributed to I. and addressed to Polycrates. It is reasonable to regard them as a song of praise to the beauty of the young man and future tyrant, written upon the poet's arrival at the same court, where → Anacreon [1] later achieved fame with his erotic poetry. Since the poem is written in the form of triads, it was formerly regarded as choral lyrics, but this improbable [3]. Following an artful *praeteritio* on Trojan themes, I. introduces the characters of Cyanippus and Zeuxippus, who do not play a role in the Homeric account of the Trojan War, and therefore must be taken from a transmission other than the usual epic one [4]. The poem goes on to state that the glory of the addressee depends on the reputation of the court poet. With this self-presentation and the use of mythological examples for the purpose of praise, I. is an important precursor to the later celebratory verses and in particular to the → epinikion. It is claimed that I. had told the story of the rape of Ganymede and Tithonus in a poem dedicated to a Gorgias (289a PMGF).

The Alexandrians organized the poems of I. into seven bks. and included him into their canon of nine lyrical poets. The sparse extant fragments reveal a consistently artful style with a large number of epithets. The language has epic, Doric, and Aeolic elements, the metre is often dactylic.

The poems 286 and 287 PMGF (possibly completely extant) belong to the most beautiful examples of Greek lyric poetry that have been transmitted. They are carefully composed pieces of erotic poetry, similar to each other [5. 323–326]. This is probably the reason why the Suda refers to I. as ἐρωτομανέστατος περὶ μειράκια, 'madly in love with boys' (TB1 PMGF; cf. Cic. Tusc. 4,71 = TB2 PMGF). As for Stesichorus, I.'s mythology was regarded as extremely unconventional, esp. in his erotic stories: for I., Idomeneus is the lover of Helena (297 PMGF), Achilles marries Medea in the Elysian Fields (291 PMGF), Menelaus, overwhelmed by Helena's beauty, drops his sword (296 PMGF). It is generally assumed that I. (just like Stesichorus) wrote narrative poems, his attribution with certain poems such as Ἆθλα ἐπὶ Πελίᾳ (Stesichorus, 179(i) PMGF) is therefore uncertain. He used topics such as Hercules, Meleager, and the Argonauts. However, the sparsity of records makes it impossible to determine how he treated these subjects, nor is it possible to justify the commonly accepted division of his work into an early Italian period of narrative poetry in the style of Stesichorus and into a Samian period of erotic verses.

According to a legend, I. was killed by robbers, whose crime was brought to light by cranes (TA5–11 PMGF). The story is famously retold in Schiller's ballad *Die Kraniche des Ibykus*.

1 L. WOODBURY, Ibycus and Polycrates, in: Phoenix 39, 1985, 193–220   2 PMGF, p. 235–305   3 M. DAVIES, Monody, choral lyric, and the tyranny of the hand-book, in: CQ, n.s. 38, 1988, 55   4 E. CINGANO, Tra epos e storia, in: ZPE 79, 1989, 27–38   5 H. FRÄNKEL, Dichtung und Philos. des frühen Griechentums, ²1962.   E.R.

Icarian Sea (Ἰκάριος πόντος; *Ikários póntos*). Southeastern part of the Aegean Sea, from Samos to Mykonos (Plin. HN 4,51) respectively from Icarus, with Corassiae (Corseae, modern Fourni) and Samos, via Patmos, Leros and Kalymnos to Kos (Str. 10,5,13). References: Hom. Il. 2,145 (Ἰκάριος πόντος); Sen. Hercules Oetaeus 694; Auson. epist. 23 (*Icarius pontus*); Ov. Fast. 4,283; 566; Plin. HN 4,68; 6,215 (*Icarium*); Hdt. 6,96; Str. 2,5,21; Ptol. 5,2,1–6; 17,2; Diod. Sic. 4,77,6 (Ἰκάριον πέλαγος); Claud. in Eutropium 2,265 (*Icarium pelagus*).

The Icarian Sea (IS) breaks on the coasts of the lands of western Asia Minor: Ionia, Caria, Doris; in the north, it comes to Teos, Lebedos, Colophon (harbour Notion), the mouth of the Caystrus, Ephesus, Cape Trogilion on Mycale, the mouth of the Maeander (Ptol. loc. cit.). Subdivisions of the IS are the Latmian Gulf (largely silted up in the Middle Ages, modern Lake Bafa as remnant), with the cities of Miletus, Myus and Heraclea

Latmus, to the south connecting with the bays of Iasus and Bargylia and the Ceramic Gulf, with Halicarnassus, Ceramus, Idyma, Cedreae. Feared in navigation were the numerous rocks (Hor. Carm. 3,7,21; Theaetetus, Anth. Pal. 7,499) and the stormy Etesian winds (*Icarii fluctus*, Hor. Carm. 1,1,15); its name is derived from the island Icarus (Icaria) (Str. 10,5,13; Plin. HN 4,68).

L. Bürchner, s.v. I.M., RE 9, 972f.; C. Bursian, Geogr. von Griechenland 2, 1872, 351 n. 2. H.KA.

Icarium (Ἰκάριον/*Ikárion*; Ἰκαρία/*Ikária* only Steph. Byz. s.v. Ἰ.).
[1] Attic *mesogeia* deme of the phyle Aegeis, from 307/6 to 201 of Antigonis, after 200 BC of Attalis, on the north-east slope of mount → Pentelicon (modern Dioniso). Only one deme named I. is recorded [7. 115 no. 16]. With five (six) *bouleutaí*, medium-sized, but (through cult business?) prosperous [9. 160 n. 77, 163]. In 1888/9, the Dionysus sanctuary [9. 221] with one of the oldest theatres in Attica [2; 3; 8] and archaic cult image of Dionysus (IG I³ 254, IG II² 2851 [5; 9. 215]) was uncovered [1; 8]. The tragic poet → Thespis came from I. Dramatic agons are cited in IG I³ 254 (2nd half of the 5th cent. BC). For the cult of the eponymous hero Icarius see [3; 6], for that of Apollo Pythius see [4]. Inscriptions.: IG I³ 253f.; IG II² 1178f., 2851, 3094f., 3098f., 4976; SEG 22, 44 no. 17.

1 W.R. Biers, T.D. Boyd, I. in Attica, 1888–1981, in: Hesperia 52, 1982, 1–18 2 H.R. Goette, Griech. Theaterbau der Klassik, in: E. Pöhlmann (ed.), Stud. zur Bühnendichtung und zum Theaterbau der Ant., 1995, 10f., fig. 1a and 1b 3 F. Kolb, Agora und Theater, 1981, 70ff. 4 E. Meyer, s.v. Pythion (5), RE 24, 561f. 5 I.B. Romano, The Archaic Statue of Dionysos from I., in: Hesperia 51, 1982, 398–409 6 A. Shapiro, Art and Cult under the Tyrants in Athens, 1989, 95f. 7 Traill, Attica, 7, 15, 33, 41, 59, 67, 83, 110 no. 58, 115 no. 16, table 2, 11, 14 8 Travlos, Attika, 85ff. fig. 96–100 9 Whitehead, Index s.v. I. H.LO.

[2] see → Icarius

Icarius (Ἰκάριος; *Ikários*).
[1] Attic hero, whose cult (probably in the deme Icaria) is recorded as early as the 5th cent. (IG I³ 253, 6.9); sacrifices to him, his daughter → Erigone [1] and their dog are mentioned by Ael. NA 7,28. His myth is known in various facets since the 'Erigone' of Eratosthenes, which has survived only in fragments (Hyg. Poet. Astr. 2,4; Apollod. 3,192f., etc.). The god → Dionysus comes to I., is fed by him, and gives him the first wine as thanks. When I. serves this to his neighbours undiluted, they become drunk; once again sober, they slay him as a poisoner. His dog, Maera, leads his daughter, → Erigone, to the body; Erigone buries him and hangs herself out of grief. Dionysus returns and teaches the mixing of wine with water; Zeus places I. in the heavens as Bootes, Erigone as Virgo, and Maera as Sirius (dog star, Procyon).

The cult of I. is older than Eratosthenes. His tale uses common themes (visit by a divine guest, hanging of the girl) for a series of *aitia*: besides the legend about the stars stand the introduction of wine and its mixing with water, the cultic worship of I., the custom of → *askoliasmos*, jumping on a greased wineskin (Hyg. Poet. Astr. 2,4), and the ritual of the → Aiora on the third day of the Anthesteria, for which the hanging of Erigone is an aition.
[2] Father of → Penelope. The 'Odyssee' hardly gives him shape. Later he is located in Sparta with a variety of genealogies, and it is told that he only reluctantly let his daughter go with Odysseus (Paus. 3,10,10f.).

D. Flückiger-Guggenheim, Göttliche Gäste. Die Einkehr von Göttern und Heroen in der griech. Myth., 1984, esp. 108–116; E. Kearns, The Heroes of Attica, 1989, 172; D. Gondicas, s.v. I., LIMC 5, 645–647; A. Rosokoki, Die Erigone des Eratosthenes. Eine komm. Ausgabe der Frg., 1995. F.G.

Icarus (Ἰκαρος; *Íkaros*).
[1] Son of → Daedalus [1]. Held captive on Crete by → Minos, Daedalus builds a pair of wings each for himself and I., which they use to escape Minos. However, I., despite the warnings of his father, comes too close to the sun; this melts the wax in his wings, he crashes near the island of → Icarus [2]/Icaria and drowns. Daedalus (or Hercules, Apollod. 2,132) buries him; the island and the sea around it are named after I.

The well-known version of the story is formulated in Ov. Met. 8,183–235 (cf. Apollod. Epitome 1,12f.); a Pompeiian fresco is from about the same time. It is difficult to make out what earlier tales were like: first, but recognizable only in outline, is the myth in Attic tragedy (since Aesch. Pers. 890; the lost 'Cretans' of Euripides were important), and whether the version, recorded since the 4th cent., that the Icarian Sea takes its name from I. falling from his father's ship and drowning (Menecrates of Xanthus, FGrH 769 F 1) precedes the tale of the flight or rather rationalizes it (cf. Diod. Sic. 4,77,6; Paus. 9,11,2), is unclear; the oldest pictorial representation (an Attic black-figured *skyphos* from about 600) shows only Daedalus. Despite the aetiology which clearly points to the island Icarus/Icaria and the Icarian Sea, I. probably first belonged in the Attic Icaria (→ Icarius), which neighboured the deme Daedalidae; Daedalus himself is an Athenian, son of Metion (Pherecydes FGrH 3 F 146).

In post-classical moralizing, I. is the image of youthful overestimation of one's abilities (Natalis Comes), since the Renaissance and particularly the 19th cent. a symbol for the dangers of technology overestimating itself, often also optimistically turned into the image of the heights of technology.

F. Bömer, P. Ovidius Naso, Metamorphosen, Buch VIII–IX, 1977, 66–70; J.E. Nyenhuis, s.v. Daidalos et I., LIMC 2, 313–321, esp. 316–319. F.G.

[2] **I., Icaria** (Ἴκαρος, Ἰκαρία; *Íkaros, Ikaría*). 257 km²
rocky island, stretching 40 km from east to west and
rising to 1041 m, off the coast of Asia Minor, with three
large Milesian colonies: the capital Oine (near the modern Kampos) on the north coast, Thermae (modern
Therma) on the south-east coast, and Drakanon on the
eastern cape of the same name. Ancient and Byzantine
remains are found primarily near Kampos, but also at
Therma (remains of the old bath complex; the hill
Kastro was the acropolis). The foundations of a temple,
which belonged to the sanctuary of Artemis Tauropo-
los, were uncovered on the west coast [1]. According to
legend, I. is named after Icarus, who is buried here and
whose tomb could still be seen in Roman times. Oine
and Thermae were members of the → Delian League,
with a tribute of 4,000–8,000 and 3,000 drachmae respectively (ATL 1,282f.; 360f.; 490; 528; 2,86; 3,190;
204). I. belonged to Samos, probably since the
2nd cent. BC; Thermae appears to have gone by the
name of Asklepieis at that time (Str. 10,5,13; 14,1,6;
14,1,19; HN 602). Above Oine lay the medieval settlement, with the partially preserved church Hagia Irini
from the 11th cent. The island, which was called Nika-
ria in the Middle Ages, was a place of exile, a Frankish
barony from 1204, then a Genoese possession and dependent on Chios. In 1481, I. fell to the Knights of Rhodes, and finally to the Turks in 1523. The centuries-long
pirate plague is recalled by the fortified pirate shelters,
which were sunk into the earth almost to their roofs.

1 U. JANTZEN, Arch. Funde vom Sommer 1937 bis
Sommer 1938. Griechenland, in: AA 53, 1938, 581–583
(L. POLITIS).

K. HOPF, Veneto-byz. Analekten, in: SAWW 32, 1859,
144ff.; LAUFFER, Griechenland, 277f.; I. LEHMANN, Ägäi-
sche Wanderungen, 1985; J. MELAS, Istoria tis nisu I., 2
vol., 1955–1958; G. B. MONTANARI, s.v. I., PE 406; PHI-
LIPPSON/KIRSTEN 4, 269ff.; H. W. PLEKET, The hot
springs at Icaria, in: Mnemosyne 13, 1960, 240f.; L. ROSS,
Reisen auf den Inseln des ägäischen Meeres 2, 1843,
156ff.   H. KAL.

Icauna Left side-arm of the river Seine, modern Yonne,
also the name of the river goddess (CIL XIII 2921: *dea
Icauna*, votive inscriptions from Autessiodurum; Vita
S. Germani 12, late 5th cent. AD: *flumen Ycaunense*).
                                                             Y. L.

Iccius Ruler of the → Remi (*primus civitatis*), allied
with Rome since 57 BC; in the same year, as he was in
command of Bibrax, he held the city against an assault
by the Belgae until the arrival of assistance from Rome
(Caes. B Gall. 2,3,1; 6,4; 7,1).
→ Caesar   W. W.

Iccus see → Olympic champions

Icelus Full name (Ser. Sulpicius) I. Marcianus. Freedman of → Galba [2], who had remained behind in Rome
during Galba's governorship in Tarraconensis. Impri-

soned by Nero following Galba's acclamation; freed
after Nero's death, he rushed to Spain in only seven
days to bring Galba the news. He received the gold ring
of the equestrian order from Galba and probably the
restitutio natalium. He exerted great influence on
Galba, allegedly was able to dominate him – although
this opinion is more likely to be a reflection of social
prejudice in the sources. Tacitus speaks of his cruelty
and greed (Hist. 1,37,5; 2,95,3). After Galba's death he
was executed by Otho.

PIR² I 16; DEMOUGIN, Prosopographie, 546f.   W. E.

Icelus see → Morpheus

Iceni Celtic tribe in the area of Norfolk and Suffolk
(south-eastern England). First mentioned under the
name Cenimagni as one of the tribes that submitted to
Caesar in AD 54 (Caes. B Gall. 5,21,1). At the time of
the conquest of Britain by Claudius (AD 43), they were
prepared to accept the alliance with Rome. In AD 47
they rebelled and were subjugated, however, they retained the status of a client kingdom (Tac. Ann. 12,31).
After the death of their King Prasutagus c. AD 59, their
entire territory was incorporated into the Roman administration, not only the half that Prasutagus had
bequeathed to Nero. → Boudicca, his widow, and her
daughters, led the I. to join the revolt of the Trinovantes
against Rome in AD 60–61 (Tac. Ann. 14,31–38;
[1. 70–74]). Under Boudicca's leadership the I. and
their allies destroyed the *colonia* in → Camulodunum
and the two towns → Verulamium and → Londinium.
The uprisings were quelled by Suetonius Paullinus. The
I. were organized into a *civitas* with Venta Icenorum as
administrative centre (nowadays, Caister-by-Nor-
wich).

1 S. S. FRERE, Britannia, ³1987.

G. WEBSTER, Boudicca, 1978.   M. TO.

Ichana (Ἴχανα; *Íchana*). Settlement on Sicily, fell under
the rule of Syracusae (Steph. Byz. s.v. I.). Evidence: handle of a bronze *kerykeion*, with the inscription
Ἰχανινοδαμοσιον; silver *hēmílitron* (obverse horned
head, personification of a river, to its right on some
impressions ΣΙΧΑ, on the reverse the bow of a ship with
the legend ΝΙΚΑ, datable to the end of the 5th cent. BC;
I., therefore, celebrated a naval victory); in a Siculan
inscription from Herbessus is ΘΙΚΑΝΑ.

G. MANGANARO, in: JNG 33, 1984, 31–33; Id., Alla
ricerca di poleis mikrai della Sicilia centro-orientale, in:
Orbis Terrarum 2, 1996, 140–141; Id., Modi dell'alfabe-
tizzazione in Sicilia, in: Medit. Ant. I, 1998, 22f.   GI.MA.

Ichara (Ἴχαρα; *Ichára*, modern Failaka). Island in the
Persian Gulf, on the east coast of Arabia. The island,
mentioned in Ptolemy (6,7,47 N), is today generally
regarded as a variant of → Icarus. While the identification fluctuated between Failaka, Kharg and Qaru for a

long time, the equation of Icarus (and thus Ichara?) with Failaka has meanwhile been confirmed by inscriptions. According to Arrian (Anab. 7,20,2–3), the island received its name from Alexander, after an island in the Aegean. However, the name probably goes back to a sanctuary É-KARA, which is recorded in Assyrian and Aramaic sources.

D. T. POTTS, The Arabian Gulf in Antiquity I, 1990, 349; II, 1990, 179–196; J. TKAČ, s.v. I., RE 9, 821–829. H.J.N.

Ichnae ("Ιχναι; *Ichnai*). Fortified settlement on the Balissus (Balīḫ); according to → Isidorus of Charax, situated between Alagma and → Nicephorium (Isidorus of Charax 1 SCHOFF; Plut. Crassus 25,17; Cass. Dio 40,12,2). Supposedly a Macedonian foundation; despite a similarity to Greek place names, the name may be identical with the old Babylonian Aḫūnā [1. 6]. → Licinius Crassus won a skirmish near I. in 54 BC against the Parthian satrap Silaces. Publius, the son of Crassus, was advised to flee to the Roman-friendly I. The old equation [2] with the modern toponym Ḥnez is doubtful.

1 B. GRONEBERG, Répertoire Géographique des Textes Cunéiformes, 3, 1980   2 F. H. WEISSBACH, s.v. I., RE 9, 830. K.KE.

Ichneumon Egyptian mongoose (*Herpestes ichneumon*, first mentioned under the name ἰχνεύμων by Aristot. Hist. an. 6,35,580a 25, but also ἰχνευτής/-ήρ; *ichneutés/-ḗr*), viverrid with dog-like feeding habits, in Egypt and, according to Vitr. De arch. 8,2,7, also in Morocco. The ichneumon stays mostly in the reeds and likes to raid poultry farms. In Egypt, it was known as the ferocious enemy of the crocodile, into whose open jaws it was said to creep and kill by consumption of its entrails (Str. 17,812; Diod. Sic. 1,87; Opp. Kyn. 3,407–432; Ael. NA 8,25; 10,47; Plin. HN 8,90; Plut. De sollertia animalium 10 = Mor. 966d). As *enhydros,* it entered the Latin literature of the Middle Ages (including as *ydros* in Thomas of Cantimpré 8,21 [1. 283f.]) through Isid. Orig. 12,2,36. Moreover, in Egypt, the ichneumon fought against the viper ἀσπίς, protected by a layer of mud (Theophr. in Aristot. 8(9),6, 612a 15–20; Nic. Ther. 190ff.; Str. ibid.; Plin. HN 8,88; Ael. NA 3,22; cf. mosaic from Pompeii [2. 81 and fig. 33]). It was sacred to → Leto and → Eileithyia, and it was particularly worshipped in Heracleopolis, even buried in honour (Hdt. 2,67; Str. 17,812; Ael. NA 10,47; Cic. Nat. D. 1,101). Pliny (HN 29,68) mentions its fat as a magical snake repellent of dubious value. In the Hadrianic period, the ichneumon adorned a bronze coin from Panopolis as a symbol of Egypt [3. pl. 1,25] as well as several ancient seal stones [3. pl. 16,5 and 6 and *passim*].

1 H. BOESE (ed.), Thomas Cantimpratensis, Liber de natura rerum, 1973   2 TOYNBEE, Tierwelt   3 F. IMHOOF-BLUMER, O. KELLER, Tier- und Pflanzenbilder, 1889, repr. 1972.

H. GOSSEN, s.v. I., RE Suppl. 8,233. C.HÜ.

Ichor (ἰχώρ; *ichōr*). The word has been connected to the Aramaic or Hebrew root meaning 'dignity', 'splendour', with possible etymological overlap of the Sumerian root meaning 'blood' and the Akkadian root meaning 'to pour'.

In Homer (Il. 5,340; cf. 416), the word denotes the lifeblood of the gods as opposed to regular blood that is produced by eating bread and drinking wine. *Ichor* also appears in Aeschylus (Ag. 1479f., 458 BC), where the word denotes a fluid which is discharged from wounds that will not close. In the 4th cent., it is more common and denotes pathogenic fluids and thin blood, i.e. perhaps blood serum; in this meaning it is applied to other fluids, from bile to milk. No later than 395 BC, it denoted any physiological fluid, without diagnostic value, and maintained this meaning, but had to be more closely identified for precise information about its nature, and could therefore designate any pathological secretion caused by arbitrary pathogenic mechanisms.

A.TO.

Ichthyas (Ἰχθύας; *Ichthýas*). Pupil of Euclides [2] of Megara, 4th cent. BC, member of the → Megarian School; eponymous character in a dialogue of → Diogenes [14] of Sinope. I. is usually identified with the man called in the MSS Icthydias or Ychtyas, who lost his life in an uprising against his home town (Megara?) (Tert. Apol. 46,16).

1 K. DÖRING, Die Megariker, 1972, 15, 91–94, 100–101   2 SSR II H. K.D.

Ichthyes (Pisces) see → Constellations

Ichthyocentaur see → Triton

Ichthyophagi (Ἰχθυοφάγοι/*Ichthyophágoi*, 'fish-eaters'). Collective ethnographic term for coastal peoples who primarily live on fish. As a Utopian people residing at the ends of the then-known world, the I. are described as models of justice, but sometimes also as animal-like, living on a low civilizational level (Agatharchides of Cnidus, De Mari Erythro, fr. 31–49 = GGM I, 129–141). Most frequently mentioned are the Ethiopian I. on the Red Sea, whom Herodotus reports as having been sent (in vain) by → Cambyses [2] to spy on the Ethiopeans, who are described in Utopian images as well (Hdt. 3,19–25).
→ Utopia

O. LONGO, I mangiatori di pesci, in: Materiali e discussioni per l'analisi dei testi classici 18, 1987, 9–55; J. S. ROMM, The Edges of the Earth in Ancient Thought, 1992, 38–40. R.B.

Ichthys/Fish

[1] Fish (Greek ἰχθύς/*ichthýs*; Latin *piscis*) was a common food in Greece and Rome, certain fishes in Rome were even considered a luxury food. This explains the Greek curiosity about neighbouring cul-

tures such as Egypt or Syria, where conspicuous food prohibitions were observed and generalized (priests in Egypt: Hdt. 2,37; Plut. De Is. et Os. 7, 353b; Plut. Symp. 8,8,2; Syria: Ov. Fast. 2,473f.; Porph. De abstinentia 2,61 etc.) that probably relate to the worship of fish in these cultures (Egypt: Str. 17,1,40, cf. PSI 8 no. 901; Syria from Xen. An. 1,4,9, to an extreme: Clem. Al. Protreptikos 2,39,9). This is particularly true for the Syrian goddess Atargatis at her main cult site Hierapolis (Lucian De Dea Syria 14) as well as in other places throughout Syria and the Mediterranean world (Smyrna LSAM 17; Delos LSCG Suppl. 54).

In Greece and in Rome, fishes are rarely sacrificed (generalizing: Plut. Symp. 8,8,3). The consumption of certain fishes is prohibited to certain priests or in certain cults, for instance, the red mullet (*tríglē*) for the *mystai* in Eleusis (Plut. Mor. 983f; Ael. NA 9,51) or for the Hera priestesses in Argus (Ael. NA 9,51), all fish for the priests of Poseidon in Leptis (Plut. Symp. 8,8,4). Similarly, the Pythagoreans follow a rule prohibiting the eating of certain or all fishes (Plut. Symp. 8,8,1–3). The rarity of fish sacrifices can be explained with the rarity of sacrifices of non-domestic animals in general. It is telling that fishes are sacrificed either to the ocean god Poseidon or to marginal deities such as Pan or Priapus. In the context of the widespread consumption of fish, the fish taboo must be understood as a ritual distinction of certain persons.

Fish already appears very frequently in old Christian iconography, both within larger scenes and alone; the latter representation is found on the walls of catacombs (to express affiliation to Christianity), or as an apotropaic sign above front doors, on gravestones, amulets, and rings. The NT already introduces a symbolic link between fish and the individual believers through Peter as 'fisher of men' (Mt 4,19), a link which soon finds literary expression (as in the list of images in Clem. Al. Paidagogos 3,101,3). Tertullian (De baptismo 1) is the first to relate this imagery – the Christians are *pisciculi* ('little fish') – with the Greek word *ichthŷs*. It is an acronym formed from the initials of *Iēsoûs Christòs Theoû Hyiòs Sōtér* ('Jesus Christ, Son of God, Saviour') and can be traced inscriptionally to about the same time as Tertullian and in the *Oracula Sibyllina* (8,217–250), thus reaching back to the 2nd cent. It appears in other ancient Christian literature as well and has various allegorical interpretations, for instance, that Christ could live human mortality as a fish in the sea (Aug. Civ. 18,23). In view of the complex state of records, the question must remain unanswered whether it was the acronym or the interpretation of the NT that gave rise to Christian fish symbolism. In any case, the two influences have mutually reinforced each other from early on.

F. J. DÖLGER, I., 5 vols., 1910–1943; J. ENGEMANN, s.v. Fisch, RAC 7, 959–1097.   F.G.

[2] Cape on the Elian west coast of the Peloponnese, modern Katakolo (Thuc. 2,25,4; Xen. Hell. 6,2,31).

PHILIPPSON/KIRSTEN 3, 345.   C.L. and E.O.

Icilius Name of a plebeian family, that probably already died out in the 4th cent. BC, according to the tradition known for its anti-patrician stance (Liv. 4,54,4).

[1] I., L. People's tribune in 456, 455, 449 BC (MRR 1,42; 48). In 456 he is said to have carried through the *lex de Aventino publicando*, which allocated the Aventine to the *plebs* (Liv. 3,31,1; 32,7; Dion. Hal. Ant. Rom. 10,31,2–32,5); as the fiancé of → Verginia he bravely resisted the despotism of the decemvir Appius Claudius [I 5] (Liv. 3,44,3; 45,4–46,8; 48,7–49,3; Dion. Hal. Ant. Rom. 11,28,2; 31,3–5; 38,2) and was subsequently spokesman for the *plebs* in the 2nd → *secessio* (449) (Liv. 3,51,7–10; 53,2f.). Furthermore it is assumed that the consuls Valerius and Horatius obtained a triumph by plebiscite through his endeavours (Liv. 3,63,8–11).

[2] I., L. As people's tribune proposed an agrarian law in 412 BC (Liv. 4,52,1–3). In 409 he was probably one of the three I. among the tribunes who carried through the occupancy of three of the four quaestor positions by plebeians and for 408 the election of consular tribunes (Liv. 4,54–56,3). The latter was significant in that consular tribunes were elected instead of consuls up to the Licinic-Sextic Laws in 367, with the exception of the years 393 and 392.

[3] I., Sp. According to Dion. Hal. (Ant. Rom. 6,88,4, here as elsewhere in Dion. incorrectly referred to as Sicinius or Sicilius due to confusion or corruption of the text) he was one of the envoys of the plebeians following their withdrawal to the *mons sacer* (Sacred Mount) As people's tribune in 492 BC, he is said to have introduced a law through which the disruption of plebeian assemblies became punishable (Dion. Hal. Ant. Rom. 7,17,4f.; 10,31,1). However, this law should possibly be dated to the year 470, for which the first full lists of people's tribunes are available (Calpurnius Piso fr. 23 HRR [= Liv. 2,58,1f.]; Diod. Sic. 11,68,8) and which also contain the name I. MRR 1,31.   C.MÜ.

Iconium (Ἰκόνιον; *Ikónion*, modern Konya). The most important city in Lycaonia developed out of a prehistoric settlement inhabited by the Phrygians (8th cent. BC); only in Xen. An. 1,2,19 is it mentioned as easternmost city of Phrygia, at the crossroads of major trading and military routes. In 25 BC, I. became part of the new province of Galatia along with the other possessions of King → Amyntas [9]. As early as the reign of Augustus the municipal area was divided between the Greek *pólis* and the colony founded by him; the colony was re-established under Hadrian [1. 51–59; 75–90]. Following proselytization by the apostle Paul (Acts 14,1–5,28; 16,1–5) there was a rapid growth of the Christian community [2. 773f.]; bishops are recorded from the beginning of the 3rd cent. (Euseb. Hist. eccl. 6,19,17f.). In 260 I. was conquered by the Sassanids. Under Diocletian it became part of the new province of Pisidia, around 370–372 it was the political and ecclesiastical metropolis of the new province Lycaonia. In the late 7th cent. it was a city of the theme Anatolikon; in 723 it was captured by the Arabs for the first time [3. 176–178].

1 H. V. AULOCK, Mz. und Städte Lykaoniens, 1976 2 A. V. HARNACK, Die Mission und Ausbreitung des Christentums in den ersten drei Jh., ⁴1924   3 BELKE 4 F. PRAYON, A. M. WITTKE, Kleinasien vom 12. bis 6. Jh. v. Chr., TAVO B 82, 1994.   K.BE.

Iconoclasm see → Constantinus [7] V.; → Leon III; → Syrian dynasty

Icorigium Roman road-station (It. Ant. 373,1: *Egorigio*; Tab. Peut. 3,1) where the Trier – Cologne road crossed the Kyll, modern Jünkerath. From the 1st cent. AD long-houses were built close to each other on both sides of the road, with the narrow side facing the street. Destroyed during the German invasions of the 3rd cent., protected in the late Constantinian period by a circular fortification (135 m diameter) with 13 round towers and two gatehouses. The defensive complex resembles those in → Beda and → Noviomagus. I. was abandoned toward the end of the 4th cent. Funerary reliefs reused for building show scenes typical for the Mosel region from the everyday lives of the inhabitants.

H. KOETHE, Straßendorf und Kastell bei Jünkerath, in: Trierer Zschr. Beih. 11, 1936, 50–106; W. BINSFELD, Jünkerath, in: Führer vor- und frühgesch. Denkmäler 33, 1977, 300–304; H. CÜPPERS, Jünkerath, in: Id. (ed.), Die Römer in Rheinland-Pfalz, 1990, 403–405.   RA.WI.

Icos ('Ἴκος; *Íkós*). Island, 62 km² in size, in the northern Sporades, modern Hallonesos (also Chelidromia or Chilidromia); member of the → Delian League with a tribute of 1,500 drachmae, likewise of the → Athenian League. After the conclusion of peace between the Athenians and Philippus II in 338, the island came under Macedonian suzerainty; in Athenian possession from 42 BC to the late Roman Imperial period. After the fall of Constantinople, I. was under Venetian influence; after 1537 under Turkish influence. Having suffered severe damage in the War of Independence, I. was incorporated into the Kingdom of Greece in 1830. Remains of the ancient city have survived on the southeast side near Kokkinokastro (remains of walls from the 4th cent. BC). A shipwreck (middle of the 12th cent. AD) with full cargo was found and recovered in 1970 near the island of Pelagos north of I.

C. BURSIAN, Geogr. von Griechenland 2, 1868–1872, 389; PHILIPPSON/KIRSTEN 4, 47ff.; KODER/HILD, 147; LAUFFER, Griechenland, 256.   H.KAL.

Icosium ('Ἰκόσιον; *Ikósion*, Punic *ʾj ksm*, 'island of the owls'?). Phoenician or Punic foundation in the later Mauretania Caesariensis, modern Algiers. References: Mela 1,31; Plin. HN 5,20; Ptol. 4,2,6; It. Ant. 15,5; Sol. 25,17 (with incorrect etymology); Amm. Marc. 29,5,16 (with allusion to this etymology); Geogr. Rav. 40,44; 88,12. A roman veterans' colony was founded at I. dur-

ing the reign of → Juba II (Plin. HN 3,19; 5,20). Under Vespasian, the city became a *colonia Latina* (CIL VIII Suppl. 3, 20853). A hoard of 158 coins from the period *c.* 150–50 BC was found in its territory [1]. Inscriptions: CIL VIII 2, 9256–9268; Suppl. 3, 20852f.

1 M. THOMPSON, O. MØRKHOLM, C. M. CRAY, (ed.), An Inventory of Greek Coin Hoards, 1973, 2303.

S. LANCEL, E. LIPIŃSKI, s.v. I., DCPP, 226.   W.HU.

Icovellauna Local Celtic goddess related to water by name and by the place of discovery. Four small plates of bronze or marble as well as remnants of an altar with dedications to Dea I. were uncovered inside (CIL XIII, 1.2, 4296–4298) and outside (CIL XIII, 1.2, 4294f.) of an octagonal well building in Sablon near Metz-Divodurum. The fact that a single marble plate for Dea I. was found in Trier, Altbachtal (CIL XIII, 1.2, 3644) does not refute the merely local significance of the goddess in the region of the → Mediomatrici.

W. BINSFELD et al., Kat. der röm. Steindenkmäler des Rhein. Landesmus. Trier, 1988, 55ff.; J. DE VRIES, Kelt. Rel., 1961, 115; J. B. KEUNE, s.v. I., RE 12, 856f.; Id., Sablon in röm. Zeit, in: Jb. der Ges. für lothring. Gesch. und Altertumskunde, 1903, 365ff.; F. MOELLER, Ein Nymphaeum in Sablon bei Metz, in: Westdt. Zschr. 2, 1883, 249ff.   M.E.

Ictinus ('Ἰκτῖνος; *Iktînos*). Architect of the classical period. His greatest achievement is considered to be the Athenian → Parthenon (Str. 9,395–396; Paus. 8,41,9), erected 447–438 BC, which he designed apparently together with → Callicrates (Plut. Pericles 13,7), whose contribution has been emphasized more strongly recently [1]). With the otherwise unknown Carpon he is reputed to have composed a book about the Parthenon (Vitr. 7 praef. 12). Tradition has repeatedly mentioned I. as the architect of the Telesterion in → Eleusis, built about 440 BC (Str. 9,395; Vitr. 7 Praef. 16), for the design of which others have also been made responsible (Plut. Pericles 13). In addition, he designed the temple of Apollo, begun after 429 BC near Phigalia (Paus. 8,41,8–9), the beauty of which is particularly renowned. The Odeum of Pericles in Athens is ascribed to him on more general grounds [2]. A late source probably going back to Varro (Auson. Mos. 309) groups him with the most significant architects, a distinction confirmed by the building works associated with his name.

Among other achievements, the Parthenon distinguishes I. as an architect who possessed outstanding technical competence, as well as exceptional artistic creativity. This is demonstrated in his ability to deal with the difficulties inherent in the pre-existing structure, as well as with the consistently proportioned design of the Parthenon throughout, and with a newly thematized understanding of interior spaces [3]. This characterizes the incomplete design for the hall of the Telesterion in Eleusis [4; 5] and the temple of Apollo near Phigalia, completed subsequently. Its innovative cella is shown to be a splendidly decorated chamber [6; 7; 8], for whose elaborate spatial design the Corinthian capital was apparently created. The structures and designs of I. started new developments in architecture, the consequences of which had a major impact on the subsequent period.

1 B. WESENBERG, Wer erbaute den Parthenon?, in: MDAI(A) 97, 1982, 99–125   2 A. L. ROBBIN, The Odeion of Pericles: Some Observations on its History, Form and Function, 1979   3 G. GRUBEN, Die Tempel der Griechen, ³1980, 163–178   4 A. CORSO, Gli architetti del telesterion di Eleusi nell' età di Pericle, in: Atti. Istituto veneto di scienze, lettere ed arti 140, 1981/82, 199–215   5 TRAVLOS, Attika, 94–95   6 A. MALLWITZ, Cella und Adyton des Apollontempels in Bassae, in: MDAI(A) 77, 1962, 140–177   7 G. ROUX, L'architecture de l'Argolide aux IVe et IIIe siècles avant J.-C., 1961, 21–56   8 CH. HOFFKES-BRUKKER, A. MALLWITZ, Der Bassaefries, 1975, 24–37.

E. FABRICIUS, s.v. I., RE 19,995f.; H. KNELL, I.: Baumeister des Parthenon und des Apollontempels von Phigalia-Bassae?, in: JDAI 63, 1968, 100–117; R. MARTIN, L'atelier Ictinos-Callicratès au temple de Bassae, in: BCH 100, 1976, 427–442; W. MÜLLER, Architekten in der Welt der Ant., 1989, 165–170; H. SVENSON-EVERS, Die griech. Architekten archa. und klass. Zeit, 1996, 157–211; C. WEICKERT, s.v. I., in: U. THIEME, U. BECKER, Allg. Lex. der bildenden Künstler 18, 560–566; F. E. WINTER, Trad. and Innovation in Doric Design 3. The Work of I., in: AJA 84, 1980, 399–416.   H. KN.

Ida (Ἴδη, Ἰδαῖον ὄρος; *Ídē*, *Idaîon hóros*).

[1] Highest mountain range in Crete, modern Psiloritis, with the peak Timios Stavros (2,456 m). Still heavily forested in antiquity (cf. the name I. = 'wooded mountains'), predominantly with cypresses (Eur. Hipp. 1253; Theophr. Hist. pl. 3,2,6; 4,1,3; Plin. HN 16,142). Used early on for mining metals (FGrH 239,11; Diod. Sic. 5,64,5) and agriculture (Theophr. De ventis, fr. 5,13 WIMMER; [1]). The cave considered the birthplace of Zeus – on the east slope of the Ida massif, on the edge of the Nida plateau – was worshipped in particular (Diod. Sic. 5,70,2; 4; Str. 10,4,8; Mela 2,113; Paus. 5,7,6; Arat. 31ff.; Pind. Ol. 5,42; Diog. Laert. 8,13; Porph. Vita Pythagorae 17). Here numerous votive gifts have been found, especially from the archaic era, including the so-called Idaean Bronzes from the 8th/7th cents. BC.

1 A. CHANIOTIS, Die kret. Berge als Wirtschaftsraum, in: E. OLSHAUSEN, H. SONNABEND (ed.), Stuttgarter Kolloquium zur Histor. Geogr. des Alt. 5 (1993), 1996, 255–266.

P. FAURE, Noms de montagnes crétoises (L'Association G. Budé, Lettres d'Humanistes 24), 1965, 426–446; LAUFFER, Griechenland, 277; R. F. WILLETTS, Cretan Cults and Festivals, 1962, 143f., 239ff.   H. SO.

[2] Mountain range in the southern Troad (modern Kazdağları), located through Homer (Il. 2,824; 4,103; 8,170; 8,410; 12,19ff.; 14,283ff.; cf. Str. 13,1,5). One

of its western foothills is Cape Lecton; to the north-east, it stretches as far as Zelia; in the south, it reaches the sea near Antandrus and Gargara. I. is rich in springs (Hom. Il. 8,47; 14,157; 283ff.); among the rivers arising in the region are Aesepus, Granicus, Simois and Scamander (Hom. Il. 12,19ff.). Ida's wealth of forests was of great significance for shipbuilding (Thuc. 4,52; Str. 13,1,51) and thus, important for Pergamum, although it was impassable in winter and made the land route to the west coast of the Troad more difficult. → Cybele and → Zeus were worshipped on the highest peak of I. (Hom. Il. 8,48). Idaea is the name of a nymph, the wife of the river god Scamander, mother of Teucer, the first king of Troy (Apollod. 3,139; Diod. Sic. 4,75), while Idaeus is the son of Dardanus and Chryse and is supposed to have introduced the cult of Cybele in the Ida mountains (Dion. Hal. Ant. Rom. 1,61; 1,68; Paus. 8,44,5).
→ Aesepus; → Granicus; → Idaea [2]; → Idaeus [2];
→ Simois; → Scamandrus; → Teucer

L. BÜRCHNER, s.v. I., RE 17, 862–864; J. M. COOK, The Troad, 1973, 443; W. LEAF, Strabo on the Troad, 1973, 352; A. PHILIPPSON, Petermanns geogr. Mitt., Ergh. 167 1910, 104; J. STAUBER, Die Bucht von Adramytteion 1 (IK 50), 1996, 362.   E. SCH.

Ida (Ἴδη; *Ídē*, Lat. Ida).

[1] Eponymous nymph of the → Ida mountains [2] in the Troad (Ps.-Plut. 13,3 = GGM 2,652), in Vergil (A. 9,177), mother of → Nisus, and a huntress; image with caption on the coins of Scamandria and Scepsis [1].

[2] Eponymous nymph of the Cretan → Ida [1], daughter of Melisseus/Melissus or of Corybas, mother of the → Daktyloi Idaioi by Dactylus (schol. Apoll. Rhod. 1,1129) or Zeus (Stesimbrotus FGrH 107 F 12). According to other sources, wife of Lycastus and mother of Minos, Rhadamanthys, and Sarpedon (Socrates of Argus FGrH 310 F 1; cf. Diod. Sic. 4,60,2f.); wet-nurse of Zeus along with her sister → Adrastea (Orph. Fr. 105; Apollod. 1,5; Plut. Symp. 3,8,657e; Paus. 8,47,3: image at the altar of Athena Alea in Tegea [2]).

1 CH. PAPAGEORGIADOU, s.v. I. (2), LIMC 5.1, 643 2 Id., s.v. I. (1), ibid., 642f.   A. A.

Idaea (Ἰδαία; *Idaía*).

[1] One of many epithets of the mother of gods (→ Cybele), named after her cult on the Phrygian → Ida [2] (e.g. Eur. Or. 1453; Str. 10,469).   C. W.
[2] Nymph of Ida [2] in Phrygia, wife of the river god Scamander, mother of → Teucer, the first king in the Troad, after whom the people of the Teucri are named (Apollod. 3,139; Diod. Sic. 4,75).
[3] Daughter of Dardanus, great-granddaughter of [2], second wife of → Phineus. She denounces her stepchildren Plexippus and Pandium to her husband. The latter blinds his sons only to be punished for this by the Argonauts (Soph. Ant. 966ff.; Apollod. 3,200; Diod. Sic. 4,43f.).

[4] Nymph, who gives birth to the → Sibyl Herophile in a grotto near Erythrae, the father being the shepherd Theodorus (Paus. 10,12,3f.).   RE.ZI.

Idaeus ('Ιδαῖος; *Idaîos*).

[1] Epithet of → Zeus from the Ida on Crete (Eur. fr. 472 TGF; Inscr. Creticae 1,12,1) or near Troy (Hom. Il. 24,291; Verg. Aen. 7,139; in Celaenae: Plut. Mor. 306e f.) and of → Heracles as Daktylos I. and founder of the Olympic Games (Paus. 5,7,6ff.; 8,31,3; also in Elis and Erythrae: Paus. 6,23,3; 9,27,8).   AN.W.

[2] Son of Chryse and → Dardanus [1] with whom he emigrates from Arcadia across Samothrace to the → Ida mountains [2], which are said to be named after I. There he installs the cult of the mother of gods (Dion. Hal. Ant. Rom. 1,61).

[3] Name of two Trojans in the *Iliad*: a) Herald: brings → Priamus to the duel between Paris and Menelaus with sacrificial animals (3,245ff.); presents the Greeks with Paris' offer of compromise (7,372ff.); accompanies Priam to the Greek army for the release of Hector's body (bk.. 24). b) Son of → Dares [1], a priest of Hephaestus, who saves I. in the battle against → Diomedes (5,9–24).

P. WATHELET, Dictionnaire des Troyens de l'Iliade 1, 1988, 598–601.   RE.N.

[4] I. of Rhodes. Epic poet who 'doubled' Homer's poetry by adding an additional verse to each original one (Suda II, 608,12–14 = SH 502); also the author of *Rhodiaká* in 3,000 verses.

FGrH 533 F 10.   S.FO.

Idaioi Daktyloi see → Daktyloi Idaioi

Idalium ('Ιδάλιον; *Idálion*). Mentioned in Assyrian inscriptions of 672 BC, a Graeco-Phoenician city in the interior of Cyprus, known to ancient literature as a principal seat of the cult of Aphrodite (Theocr. 15,100; Verg. Aen. 1,681; 692). Inhabited since the late Bronze Age. Ruins close to modern Dhali, between Larnaka and Nicosia, with two acropoleis, a city wall, house remains and necropoleis [1]. In the sanctuaries of Anat-Athena, Rešef-Apollo and Aphrodite, Greek, Phoenician and Cypro-syllabic inscriptions, as well as numerous sculptures were found (CIS I 88–94; [2; 3; 4]). Coinage [5]. From the end of the 5th cent. BC, part of the kingdom of → Citium. In Ptolemaic times, establishment of the ruler cult, Nymphaeum in the northerly situated cave of Kafizin [6]; in Pliny's time (HN 5,130) apparently abandoned.

1 V. KARAGEORGHIS, R.P. CHARLES, P. DUCOS, Excavations in the Necropolis of I., 1963, in: RDAC 1964, 28–113 2 MASSON, 233–257 3 O. MASSON, Kypriaka, Le sanctuaire d'Apollon a Idalion, in: BCH 92, 1968, 386–402 4 R. SENFF, Das Apollonheiligtum von I. (Studies in Mediterranean Archaeology 94), 1993 5 G. HILL, BMC, Gr Cyprus XLVIII–LIII, 24–28 6 T.B. MITFORD, The Nymphaeum of Kafizin (Kadmos Suppl. 2), 1980.

E. OBERHUMMER, s.v. I., RE 9, 867–872; M. OHNE-FALSCH-RICHTER, Kypros, die Bibel und Homer, 1893, passim; L.E. STAGER, A.M. WALKER et al., American expedition to I.: Cyprus. First Preliminary Report. Seasons of 1971 and 1972, 1974; Id. et al., American expedition to I., Cyprus 1973–1980, 1989.   R.SE.

Idas ("Ιδας; *Idas*). Son of → Aphareus [1], king of Messene, and brother of → Lynceus. The Messenian pair of brothers is juxtaposed with the Spartan pair of brothers of the → Dioscuri as Apharetidai, reflecting the rivalries and disputes between Sparta and Messene. I. is characterized throughout as superhumanly strong (since Hom. Il. 9, 556) and quarrelsome, and is also regarded as son of Poseidon (Apollod. 3,117). While courting → Marpessa, the daughter of the river god Evenus at the same time as Apollo, I. threatens the god with his bow (Hom. Il. 9,556–560). Marpessa is either abducted by Apollo (Paus. 5,18,2, on the Cypselus Chest), or by I. with the aid of a winged wagon which he had received from Poseidon (Apollod. 1,60). When Zeus makes Marpessa choose between the god and the hero, she chooses the hero so that she will not be left in old age by the eternally young god. (Apollod. 1,60f.).

Both brothers take part in the activities of the Calydonian Hunt (Meleager is I.'s son in law, Hom. Il. 9,556f.) and the voyage of the → Argonauts (Apoll. Rhod. 1,151). Both die in the battle against the Dioscuri, of which there are differing accounts. According to Theoc. 22,137–213, the Dioscuri abduct the daughters of → Leucippus, who had been promised to the Apharetidai. In the single combat at the tomb of Aphareus between Castor and Lynceus, the latter falls, but when I. tries to intervene contrary to the rules, Zeus strikes him dead with lightning. Otherwise, cattle theft is the cause: According to Pind. Nem. 10,60–72, I. and Castor have an argument about a herd, and in the ensuing fight at the tomb of Aphareus, I., Lynceus, and Castor all die, I. again killed by Zeus. In Apollod. 3,134–137, the deadly fight ensues after all four of them steal a herd of cattle and I. cheats the Dioscuri when dividing the shares. The fact that such differing accounts all take place at Aphareus' tomb and that I. is always struck dead by lightning suggests the existence of three tombs of which one was viewed as a lightning mark.

C. SCHWANZAR, s.v. Apharetidai, LIMC 1, 877f.   F.G.

Ideas, theory of The modern (19th cent.) term for part of → Plato's ontology. Whenever there are many perceptible things of the same kind, there is an imperceptible 'model', conceivable only in thought, that explains the nature of the 'copies' and accounts for their existence. Plato calls this model the 'idea' (ἰδέα/*idéa*, synonymous with εἶδος/*eîdos*). The idea does not come into being and is eternal, immutable, uniform and indivisible, outside space and time; it is what it is, without qualification and ambiguity. (Pl. Symp. 211a; Pl. Phd.

247c *et passim*). It is at once that which is fully recognizable and that which is actually real, the general and at the same time the ideal paradigm of individual things, and ultimately also their 'cause' (αἰτία/*aitía*). The connection between thing and idea is described through concepts such as 'participation', 'presence' and 'community' (μέθεξις, παρουσία, κοινωνία Pl. Phd. 100c-d; discussed aporetically Pl. Parm. 130b ff.). On the necessity of the theory of ideas: Pl. Phd. 96a–102a; Resp. 474b–480a.

There is a strict correspondence between the ways in which things are known and the ontologically separate classes of objects (about what can be perceived, only 'opinion', *dóxa*, is possible and about ideas only 'knowledge', *epistémē*, : Pl. Resp. 477b ff.; 511e; 534a; Pl. Ti. 51d-e), which to modern criticism constitutes the real Achilles' heel of the theory of ideas. Recognition of the idea is the precondition and foundation of all correct decisions in ethics, politics, the sciences and technology. The 'divine' world of ideas contains 'parts' of unequal rank (Resp. 485b), and is a well-ordered (ibid. 500c), organic whole, enjoying life (Soph. 248e) and reason: as the 'perfect form of life' (παντελὲς ζῷον, Tim. 30c-31b) it is the all-embracing model of the cosmos, whose perfection and bliss (ibid. 34b) reflect the corresponding features of its model. The highest dialectical concepts, (*mégista génē*), amongst them existence, movement, repose, sameness and diversity (Pl. Soph. 254c-d), permit an approach to the pinnacle of the world of ideas, the idea of the Good, which makes possible all knowing and being, and 'which itself stands beyond being' (ἐπέκεινα τῆς οὐσίας, Resp. 509b 9). The recognition of ideas is seen as a 'view' (θέα, θεᾶσθαι) that is 'suddenly' revealed at the end of an 'ascent' (Resp. 518d; Symp. 210e–212a; Phdr. 247a ff.).

According to Aristotle (Metaph. A 6; MN), the theory of ideas was part of a more comprehensive theory in which all things are derived from two principles, the One (identical with the good: ibid. 1091b 14) and the Indefinite Duality (→ Dyad). The numbers (as ideas) are the first product of the limitation of the dyad by the One, the remaining ideas follow, then the topics of mathematics as a separate realm of existence, then the apprehensible world. Aristotle criticizes the idea of the Dialogues (ibid. A 9) just as sharply as the theory of numbers as ideas of oral philosophy (ibid. MN). In his own conception the *eîdos* remains that which is fully recognizable and truly real, although not as a transcendent idea (εἶδος χωριστόν), but as an immanent form of the individual thing.

In Hellenism, the theory of ideas met with incomprehension and ridicule. In Middle Platonism the ideas were understood predominantly as the thoughts of God; at the same time, attempts were made to link the Aristotelian position with the Platonic: the immanent *eîdos* was said to explain the thing perceived by the senses, the transcendental idea the true essence. Philo of Alexandria, who was strongly influenced by Middle Platonism, conceived the cosmos of ideas as the creator's building plan (Phil. De opificio mundi 16; 19) drawn up before the creation of the world. → Plotinus was concerned amongst other things with the problem of deriving the world of ideas from the One, linking the precepts of Aristotle with the key sentences of the Dialogues (amongst others Plot. Enneades 6,7 Πῶς τὸ πλῆθος τῶν ἰδεῶν ὑπέστη; 6,6 Περὶ ἀριθμῶν). Christian writers initially rejected the theory of ideas (Justin. Dial. 2,6; Tert. De anima 18; 23,5f.; 24), but from the 3rd cent. increasingly accepted it [6. 238ff.]: the ideas, as with Philo, are created by God before the world, (Clem. Al. strom. 5,93,5; Mar. Vict. Adversus Arium 4,5), or had always been present in the mind of God (Aug. Diversae quaestiones 46,2).

→ PLATONISM

1 L. ROBIN, La théorie platonicienne des idées et des nombres d'après Aristote, 1908   2 P. NATORP, Platos I., ²1922   3 D. ROSS, Plato's Theory of Ideas, 1951   4 A. GRAESER, Platons I., 1975   5 H. J. KRÄMER, Dialettica e definizione del Bene in Platone, 1989   6 M. BALTES, s.v. Idee (Ideenlehre), RAC 17, 213–246.   T.A.S.

Idicra Place in Numidia south of Milev–Cuicul line, the modern Azziz-ben-Tellis (It. Ant. 28,4). Two inscriptions tell of a tariff of sacrifices for the cult of African gods (CIL VIII 1, 8246f.); further inscriptions: CIL VIII 1, 8243–8266. In the 4th and 5th cents. I. was an episcopal see (Optatus 2,18, p. 53,4; 19, p. 54,14; Notitia episcopatuum Numidiae 16ᵃ).

AAAlg, sheet 17, no. 214.   W.HU.

Idios Logos (Ἴδιος λόγος; *Ídios lógos*). The *idios logos* (IL) was set up under → Ptolemaeus VI as a 'special account' (first documented 5.1.162 BC, [1]). Almost all revenues from the sale of state property, especially abandoned or confiscated estates (ἀδέσποτα, γῆ ἐν ὑπολόγῳ /*adéspota, gê en hypológōi*) were paid into this account; by the 1st cent. BC at the latest there was an office πρὸς τῷ ἰδίῳ λόγῳ (*pròs tôi idíōi lógōi*) responsible for the administration of the land confiscated in favour of the IL and for reselling it (account management and administration had previously been βασιλικόν (*basilikón*, 'kings' property'); the IL was perhaps set up to separate the increasing number of irregular revenues from the regular revenues in the accounts.

Administration and sale of *adéspota* and other government possessions and investigation of any related queries and the corresponding jurisdiction were the most important function of the office of the IL also in the Augustan period (there was no longer an account for the IL, the revenues were posted under δημόσιον, *dēmósion*, 'public property'). From here the responsibility of the IL for all inheritance matters developed, as documented in the 2nd cent. AD, eventually also for questions of status under civil law. Initially responsible for the *bona caducum* (→ *caducum*), the IL later also took charge of the confiscation of the *Bona damnatorum*. It not only sold land but also leased it. In Roman times priesthoods were also sold by the IL and thus it also collected the related fees and forfeits; the IL therefore also had jurisdiction in such cases. Extant is a code of regulations attributable to Augustus, that contains addenda up to the year AD 161, the so-called 'Gnomon of the IL' (BGU v 1, 1210; POxy. 3014). In the Roman period the IL came under the jurisdiction of an equestrian *procurator* (*ducenarius*); the last holders of this office are documented among the Severi (beginning of the 3rd cent. AD).

1 L. MITTHEIS, U. WILCKEN, Grundzüge und Chrestomathie der Papyruskunde, vol. 1, 1912 (repr. 1962), 162 2 W. UXKULL-GYLLENBAND, Der Gnomon des I.L.; Komm. (BGU 5,2), 1934 3 S. RICCOBONO, Il Gnomon dell'Idios Logos, 1950 4 P. R. SWARNEY, The Ptolemaic and Roman Idios Logos, 1970 5 O. MONTEVECCHI, L'amministrazione dell' Egitto sotto i Giulio-Claudi, in: ANRW II 10, 1, 413–471, esp. 432ff. W.A.

Idiotes (ἰδιώτης; *idiótēs*). The term *idiotes* designated a private individual who did not hold any office and did not participate in political life; in the military field *idiotes* was a term commonly used by historians for the simple soldier as compared to those holding command (Xen. An. 1,3,11; 3,2,32; Pol. 5,60,3; Diod. Sic. 19,4,3). In the list of men from the Ptolemaic Egyptian army the simple soldier is designated as *idiotes* (e.g. P Hib. 1,30,21). LE.BU.

Idistaviso Site of a battle between Teutons under → Arminius and Romans under → Germanicus. The latter had led his troops over the sea to the river Ems and further on land via the river Weser in the summer of AD 16. The Romans won the battle in the I. plain (*campus*) between the Weser and hilly terrain (Tac. Ann. 2,16,1) I. cannot be localized but is generally assumed to be in the surroundings of Porta Westfalica.

B. RAPPAPORT, s.v. I., RE 9, 903–905; E. KOESTERMANN, Die Feldzüge des Germanicus, in: Historia 6, 1957, 429–479, esp. 425-455. RA.WI.

Idmon (Ἴδμων; *Ídmōn*).
[1] Son of → Asteria [2] (daughter of the Thessalian → Lapith Coronus) and of Apollo (Val. Fl. 1,228ff.), father of → Thestor, grandfather of → Calchas (Pherecydes, FGrH 3 F 108.). The Argive → Abas [1] is named as his human 'father' (Apoll. Rhod. 1,139ff.; Orph. A. 187ff.; Hyg. Fab. 14,11). As a seer with a telling name ('the one who knows'), what is apparently the original version of the myth of → Argonauts he takes part in the expedition despite his foreknowledge that he will die during the journey. He dies either from a boar's bite in the country of the Mariandynians (Apollod. 1,126; Apoll. Rhod. 2,815ff.; in Sen. Med. 652f., his death is mistaken for → Mopsus' death from a snake bite in Lybia) or from disease (Val. Fl. 5,1ff.). The Megareans and Boeotians founded the city of Heraclea at his tomb (Herodorus of Heraclea, FGrH 31 F 51; according to F

53, he may have died there on the return voyage). The (later) epic has him arrive at Colchis, where he plays an important role in the escape of the Argonauts (Naupactica F 5–7 PEG I, perhaps Eumelus F 19 PEG I).
[2] Crimson dyer from Colophon, father of → Arachne, Ov. Met. 6,8.

U. VON WILAMOWITZ, Hell. Dichtung II, ²1962, 237f. n. 4; P. DRÄGER, Argo pasimelousa, I, 1993, 348 n. 38. P.D.

Idols see → Cult image

Idomenae (Ἰδομεναί/*Idomenaí*, Lat. *Idomene*, *Eidomene*). Town in the Amphaxitis region of Macedonia, on the road from Thessalonica to the Danube (Str. 8,8,5; Tab. Peut. 8,1), perhaps near the modern Marvinci. I. is already documented in the 5th cent. BC (Thuc. 2,100,3); in the 3rd cent. BC, it was visited by Delphic *theōroí* ('sacred envoys') [1] and was still known in the 6th cent. AD (Hierocles, Synekdemos 639,5).

1 BCH 45, 1921, 17 Z. 68.

F. PAPAZOGLOU, Les villes de Macédoine, 1988, 177. MA.ER.

Idomeneus (Ἰδομενεύς; *Idomeneús*).
[1] Son of → Deucalion, grandson of → Minos; the name is indirectly attested as early as in Linear B [1]. I. is one of → Helena's suitors (today fr. 204,56ff. M-W) and a guest of Menelaus (Hom. Il. 3,230–233). He commands the rather large Cretan contingent (80 ships) in the Trojan campaign, assisted by his loyal follower → Meriones (Hom. Il. 2,645–652); he is the oldest Greek at Troy after Nestor, still fit for action (*aristeia* in Il. 13); I. belongs to the inner circle of Greek army leaders, but does not have a 'speaking role' in their debates. The account that I. kills a Lydian by the name of Phaestus (= Cretan city name) (Hom. Il. 5,43–47) is probably based merely on name association [2] rather than indicating a connection to a local legend about a war between cities [3].

According to Hom. Od. 3,191f., I. returns safely home; according to another version (Serv. Aen. 3,121), he promised Poseidon in a storm to sacrifice the first living being he encounters upon his safe return, which turns out to be his son (a common theme in fairy tales [4]). I. is henceforth driven from the throne and flees to southern Italy (Serv. Aen. 3,400f.; 11,264).

In the 'Odyssey', I. is usually the object of Odysseus' deceptive speeches: As a 'Cretan', Odysseus claims to have killed I.'s son Orsilochus (13,256–270) and then to have marched to Troy with I. as an army leader of equal standing (14,229–238); towards Penelope, Odysseus claims to be I.'s younger brother (19,181–202).

Later sources further expand the picture of I.: Dictys Cretensis – in following Odysseus' deceptive speeches – claims to have been I.'s companion, having been ordered by him to keep a war diary (p. 2,9–11 EISENHUT).

Quintus of Smyrna adds, for instance, that I. wins Achilles' team of horses without a fight during the funeral games for the latter (4,284ff.) and that he was in the wooden horse (12,320). In a scene adapted from the judgement of → Paris (Ps.- Athenodorus in Phot. 150a-b), the defeated Medea punishes the family of I. – that is, the (proverbially deceitful) Cretans – with the obligation of always having to lie henceforth.

1 DMic, s.v. i-do-me-ne-ja 1,272   2 G. S. KIRK, The Iliad 2, 1990, 58   3 W. KULLMANN, Die Quellen der Ilias, 1960, 104   4 M. L. WEST, The East Face of Helicon, 1997, 441–442.   RE.N.

[2] Epicurean, born in Lampsacus c. 325 BC. Encounters → Epicurus during his stay in Lampsacus in 310/309 BC. Following his return to Athens, I. leads the → Epicurean School in Lampsacus. He stays close to his teacher through a lively exchange of letters and participates in his disputes with competing schools of philosophy. Of his works, four excerpts from letters as well as parts of a book 'on the Socratics' are extant. The identity with I. [3] is subject to debates.

A. ANGELI, I frammenti di Idomeneo di Lampsaco, in: CE 11, 1981, 41–101; Id., L'opera 'Sui demagoghi in Atene' di Idomeneo, in: Vichiana 10, 1981, 5–16.   T.D.

[3] I. of Lampsacus. c. 350–270 BC, perhaps a Peripatetic, active as a politician in his native city. Author of three biographical works: 1. 'On the Socratics', from this, a fragment in Diogenes Laertius (2,20) about the Socratic Aeschines. 2. 'On leaders of the people' (Perì demagōgôn in at least 2 bks., used by Plutarchus and Athenaeus. 3. 'History of Samothrace'; composed in the form of a peripatetic biography, it contained a collection of anecdotes and scandals, the latter probably intended to defame political opponents. Perhaps identical with I. [2].

FRAGMENTS: H. USENER, Epicurea 128–38; FGrH 338 F 1–18.
EDITIONS: A. ANGELI, Bolletino del Centro internazionale per lo studio dei Papiri Ercolanesi (Cronache Ercolanesi), 1981, 41–101 (with vita).   K.MEI.

Idrias ('Ἰδριάς; Idriás). Mountainous region in Caria with the Marsyas valley east of Mylasa (Hdt. 5,118; Str. 14,5,23), with the like-named Carian city. Its allegedly older name, Chrysaoris (Steph. Byz. s.v. I.; s.v. Chrysaoris), is also attributed to the city of Stratoniceia and its countryside (Paus. 5,21,10), probably in the sense that I. lay in an area where the villages had joined together in the Carian league of Chrysaoreis around the sanctuary of Zeus Chrysaoreus; the city of Stratoniceia, founded in the 1st half of the 3rd cent. BC, lay in the vicinity of both I. and the league sanctuary (Str. 14,2,25), in the Chrysaoris region.

L. BÜRCHNER, s.v. I., RE 9, 912; MAGIE 2, 1031f.; H. OPPERMANN, Zeus Panamaros (RGVV 19,3), 1924, 9ff.; L. ROBERT, Ét. Anatoliennes, 1937, 571 n. 2.   H.KA.

Idrieus (Hidrieus; Ἰδριεύς/Hidrieús); son of → Hecatomnus and younger brother of → Maussolus, together with his sister and wife Ada satrap of Caria between 351 and 344. In the 340s I. helped Artaxerxes III to put down the Cypriot uprising against Persia and provided Evagoras II and Phocion of Athens with ships and troops (Diod. Sic. 16,42,6f.). He was honoured in Ionic Erythrae as euergetes ('benefactor') and proxenos ('guest/friend of the state'), (SEG 31,969); dedication to I. in → Labraunda (Labraunda 16) and Amyzon (OGIS 235). I. and Ada are also documented in Sinuri. He died a natural death in 344/3 (Diod. Sic. 16,69,1; Str. 14,2,17).

S. HORNBLOWER, Mausolus, 1982, Index s.v.; F. G. MAIER, Cyprus and Phoenicia, in: CAH² 6, 1994, 329f.; L. ROBERT, Le sanctuaire de Sinuri, 1, 1945, 94ff.; Id., Fouilles d'Amyzon, 1983, 93ff.; S. RUZICKA, Politics of a Persian Dyn., 1992, Index s.v.   J.W.

Idumaea see → Edom

Idus see → Calendar; → Month (Roman)

Idyia ('Ἰδυῖα/Idyîa, also Εἰδυῖα/Eidyîa, 'the knowing one'). → Oceanid (Hes. Theog. 352), wife of → Aeëtes, mother of → Medea (Hes. Theog. 960; Soph. fr. 546 TrGF; Apoll. Rhod. 3,243; Lycoph. 1024; Cic. Nat. D. 3,48; Ov. Epist. 17,232; Apollod. 1,129; Hyg. Fab. 25) and of → Chalciope [2], only in Tzetz. Lycoph. 798, 1024, mother of → Apsyrtus [1] as well.   A.A.

Idyll see → Bucolics, see → Eidyllion

Idyma (Ἴδυμα; Ídyma). Ancient Carian settlement (Ptol. 5,2,15; Steph. Byz. s.v. I.) on the eastern end of the gulf of Ceramus near Gökova, 4 km inland near İskele, by the river Idymus. Coins (from the 6th cent. BC onwards) showing a head of Pan and from the Hellenistic period with a Rhodian Apollo and fig leaf are preserved. In the mid-5th cent. BC I. was a member of the → Delian League and was ruled by Pactyes. In the 3rd/2nd cents. I. belonged to the Rhodian Peraea, was occupied in 201 by Philip V, probably reconquered by the Rhodian Nicagoras in 197 and still belonged to Rhodes after 167 BC. I. formed a federation of communities with neighbouring towns (→ Koinón). Archaeology: building remains and parts of a ring wall on the high acropolis, rock tombs in a necropolis, in part with Ionic temple façades (4th cent. BC).

G. E. BEAN, J. M. COOK, The Carian Coast 3, in: ABSA 52, 1957, 68ff.; P. M. FRASER, G. E. BEAN, The Rhodian Peraea and Islands, 1954, 71f.; F. IMHOOF-BLUMER, Kleinasiatische Münzen, 1901/2, 137; MAGIE 2, 879; 1030; E. MEYER, s.v. Peraia, RE 19, 566ff.; L. ROBERT, Études Anatoliennes, 1937, 472ff.   H.KA.

Idyrus see → Pamphylia

Ientaculum see → Meals

Ietae (Ἰεταί; *Ietaí*). Sicilian town near San Giuseppe Iato and San Cipirello on Monte Iato (852 m), 30 km south-west of Palermo (→ Sicily with map). The site was settled from the 8th cent. BC by the → Elymi or → Sicani; about 550 BC, construction of a temple to Aphrodite which was renovated in the 4th cent., and destroyed in AD 50. In the Hellenistic era, among other things, a theatre, an agora with stoa, bouleuterion, podium temple, and living quarters (mosaics, paintings) were built; only a few remains from the Roman Imperial period are extant; also, there are traces of a fortification. I. was in the Carthaginian sphere of influence, after 254 a *civitas decumana*. In 1246, I. now called Giato, was destroyed by Frederick II.

Literary references: Steph. Byz. s.v. I.; Cic. Verr. 2,3,103; Diod. Sic. 22,10,4; 23,18,5; Plin. HN 3,91; Plut. Timoleon 30,6.

BTCGI 12, 1992, 368–375; K. DALCHER, Das Peristylhaus 1 von Iaitas, 1994; H.P. ILSER, Monte Iato, 1991; Id., Glandes. Schleudergeschosse aus der Grabung auf dem Monte Iato, in: AA 1994, 239–254. E.O.

Ietragoras (Ἰητραγόρας/*Iētragóras*, Ἰητραγόρης/*Iētragórēs*) of Miletus, was assigned by the rebellious Ionians in 499 BC with waylaying the Persian fleet returning from Naxos and capturing the pro-Persian tyrants on the ships (Hdt. 5,36f.).

U. WALTER, Herodot und die Ursachen des Ionischen Aufstandes, in: Historia 42, 1993, 257–278. E.S.-H.

Iezdegerd see → Yazdgird

Ifriqiya see → Africa

Igel Column see → Monumental columns

Igilgili (Punic *'j glgl*[*t*]?, 'Skull Island'?). Phoenician or Punic foundation located in the later → Mauretania Sitifensis – west of the mouth of the Ampsaga – modern Djidjelli. Attested to Plin. HN 5,20; Ptol. 4,2,11; It. Ant. 39,7; 40,5; Tab. Peut. 3,1; Amm. Marc. 29,5,5; Notitia episcopatuum Mauretaniae Sitifensis 4ª; Anon. Geographia 40 (GGM II 505); Geogr. Rav. 40,22; 88,20; Guido p. 132,29. Augustus (?) elevated I. to a *colonia*. Inscriptions: CIL VIII 2, 8367–8373, 10330–10333; Suppl. 3, 20211–20213.

S. LANCEL, s.v. I., DCPP, 228; P. SALAMA, s.v. Djidjelli, EB, 2469–2476; L. TEUTSCH, Das Städtewesen in Nordafrika, 1962, 194. W.HU.

Igilium Island in the *mare Tyrrhenum*, off the *promonturium Argentarium*, modern Giglio. Settled since the Neolithic, I. belonged to the territory of the *colonia* of → Cosa and in 49 BC was part of the property of the Domitii, who equipped a fleet against Massilia there

(Caes. B Civ. 1,34,3). Regarding maritime traffic cf. the *corpus codicariorum* (CIL XI 2643). Due to its remoteness and dense forests, I. was used as a refuge by the Romans in the time of Alarich [2] (Rut. Namat. 1,325). Archaeology: a splendid *villa* near the port, another near Campese; Etruscan and Roman remains in nearby waters.

R. BRONSON, G. UGGERI, Isola del Giglio, in: SE 38, 1970, 201–214; L. CORSI, s.v. Giglio, BTCGI 7, 123–132. G.U.

Ignatius (Ἰγνάτιος; *Ignátios*).
[1] Bishop of Antioch, martyr, ranks as an Apostolic Father (→ Apostolic Fathers).
A. BIOGRAPHY B. LETTERS C. THEOLOGY

A. BIOGRAPHY
The person and work of I. cannot be separated from each other because the only certain biographical information is extant in the corpus of letters ascribed to him. Therefore, the position taken in the 'Ignatian debate', i.e. in the discussion over the unity and genuineness of the preserved letters (see [4], with response [5; 6]), also determines the image of the historical I., his works and his theology. Other indicators only have a subordinate significance: → Eusebius [7] of Caesarea writes that I. was the second bishop of Antioch after Evodius (Euseb. Hist. eccl. 3,22,1) and, after being taken to Rome as a prisoner, suffered martyrdom under the emperor Trajan (AD 98–117; Euseb. Hist. eccl. 3,36,3). The literary works of I. were collected at an early date (cf. Polyc. 13,2). For example, Eusebius was familiar with seven letters that I. wrote while travelling to Rome; four were written in Smyrna and three in the Troad (Euseb. Hist. eccl. 3,36,5–15).

B. LETTERS
The corpus of letters is extant in three versions. Apart from a short version of three letters preserved in Syriac, a *recensio longior* is preserved that includes six letters in addition to the seven mentioned in Eusebius. They are derived from an intermediate version whose content agrees with Eusebius. Since the late 19th cent. the seven letters of the intermediate version are considered authentic writings [3. 65] of I. from the early 2nd cent. Internal and external reasons (textual tradition, style etc.) have repeatedly generated doubt about the genuineness of the Ignatiana (cf. [9. 285–292]), most recently by R. M. HÜBNER [4].

C. THEOLOGY
Decisive for I.'s understanding of community is unity, which manifests itself on various levels (ἕνωσις/*hénōsis*, ἑνότης/*henótēs*, Ign. epist. ad Magnesios 1,2; 13,2 et passim; καθολικὴ ἐκκλησία/*katholikḕ ekklēsía*, Ign. Epist. ad Smyrnaeos 8,2). It is evident in the triad of offices advised by him (bishop/presbyter/deacon) with the bishop's office, which he describes in monarchical terms, being at the head. The assurance of salvation by

Christ to the community occurs during the celebration of the Eucharist (φάρμακον ἀθανασίας/*phármakon athanasías*, Ign. Epist. ad Ephesios 20,2). The eschatology of I. is characterized by his deep longing for martyrdom. Editions: on *Epistulae VII genuinae* (CPG 1025) see e.g. [1. 109–225], on *Epistulae interpolatae et epistulae suppositiciae* (CPG 1026) see [2. 83–269].

EDITIONS: 1 J.A. FISCHER, Die Apostolischen Väter, ⁹1986   2 F.X. FUNK, F.DIEKAMP, Patres Apostolici II, 1913.
BIBLIOGRAPHY: 3 M.GÜNTHER, Einleitung in die Apostolischen Väter, 1997, 64–75, 122f.   4 R.M. HÜBNER, Thesen zur Echtheit und Datierung der sieben Letters des I., in: Zschr. für ant. Christentum 1, 1997, 44–72   5 A.LINDEMANN, Antwort auf die 'Thesen zur Echtheit und Datierung der sieben Briefe des I. von Antiochien', in: ibid., 185–194   6 G.SCHÖLLGEN, Die Ignatianen als pseudepigraph. Briefcorpus, in: Zschr. für ant. Christentum 2, 1998, 16–25   7 CH. MUNIER, Où en est la question d'I.?, in: ANRW II 27.1, 359–484 (bibliogr. 360–376)   8 H.PAULSEN, s.v. I., RAC 17, 933–953   9 W.R. SCHOEDEL, Polycarp of Smyrna and I., in: ANRW II 27.1, 272–358.   J.RI.

[2] I. Magister. Deacon and *skeuophylax* in Constantinople (784–815), then metropolitan of Nicaea (died after 845). The works preserved under his name often cause problems of attribution because of conflicting homonyms (cf. [1]). The lost works include iambic verses against Thomas the Rebel (cf. Suda ι 84 ADLER). I. wrote *vitae* of the patriarchs Tarasius [2] and Nicephorus [3], an anacreontic poem on the premature death of his student Paulus [4], a iambic dialogue on original sin [5], a iambic-tetrastichic abbreviated version of Aesopic fables [6], iambic aphorisms of religious content in alphabetic order [7] and a poem on the rich man and Lazarus the poor [8]. He also wrote a few funerary epigrams (Anth. Pal. 15,29–31) that are classicistic in style and word selection though not devoid of faulty metrics (presumably it was I. who gave new respect to the elegiac distich after two centuries of neglect). Perhaps the two hexameters with subsequent pentameter (Anth. Pal. 15,39) in which he claimed the credit for bringing back to light 'the grammar that had been hidden in a sea of forgetfulness' were also his.

1 W.WOLSKA-CONUS, De quibusdam Ignatiis, in: Travaux et mémoires ... Byz. 4, 1970, 329–360   2 I.A. HEIKEL, in: Acta Societatis Scientiae Fennicae 17, 1889, 395–423   3 PG 100, 41–160   4 Matranga II 664–667   5 J.BOISSONADE, Anecdota Graeca 1, 1962, 436–444   6 C.F. MÜLLER, O.CRUSIUS, Babrii fabulae Aesopeae, 1897, 264–285   7 ID., in: RhM 46, 1891, 320–322   8 L.STERNBACH, in: Eos 4, 1897, 151–154   A.CAMERON, The Greek Anthology from Meleager to Planudes, 1993, 308, 331–333.

[3] Head of the chancellery in Constantinople, author of an epigram consisting of two iambic trimeters (Anth. Pal. 1,109). It celebrates the restoration of the renowned church of the Panagia of Blachernae (near the Gate of Selymbria) built by Justinian. Verse 2 seems to indicate that renovations took place under the joint rule of → Basilius [5] I and his two sons Constantinus and Leo (the epigram therefore was written *c.* 870–879).

A. CAMERON, The Greek Anthology from Meleager to Planudes, 1993, 151.   M.G.A.

Ignorantia An old Roman legal rule deals with *ignorantia*, also *ignoratio* (ignorance). According to Paulus (3rd cent. AD, Dig. 22,6,9 pr.) it reads: *iuris ignorantia nocet, facti vero ignorantia non nocet* ('ignorance of the law is harmful, but not ignorance of the facts'). The preferred term since the Middle Ages is *error*. For the Romans *error* and *ignorantia* were probably synonymous. Error in law neither prevents responsibility for individual behaviour (under criminal and civil law), nor the effectiveness of the → *consensus* in legal transactions *inter vivos* or in declarations about legal transactions in case of death. However, the *ignorantia facti* usually results, same as the error of fact, in excusability of behaviour and in repudiation of the legal declaration. Wills were of course frequently read with a favourable interpretation (→ *interpretatio*). An error in name (*error in nomine*) was generally regarded as irrelevant (Ulp. Dig. 18,1,9,1). In the Middle Ages this gave rise to the rule *falsa demonstratio non nocet* ('a false or mistaken description does not vitiate').

HONSELL/MAYER-MALY/SELB, 122–126; J.G. WOLF, Error im röm. Vertragsrecht, 1961; L.WINKEL, Error iuris nocet, German 1985 (Orig. thesis Amsterdam 1983).   G.S.

Iguvinian Tables see → Tabulae Iguvinae

Iguvium Town in Umbria on a hill in the upper valley of the Tiber, controlled an important traffic route linking the Tyrrhenian and Adriatic coasts via the Pass of Scheggia (63 m), modern Gubbio. Minted its own coins (*IKVVINI*, *IKVVINS* [1. 140–152]). After 268 BC it was *civitas foederata* (Cic. Balb. 47). In 167 BC the Illyrian king Genthius was interned here (Liv. 45,43,9). After the Social War it was *municipium, tribus Clustumina*. Pompey's base in the Civil War; occupied by Caesar (Caes. B Civ. 1,12,1). Under Augustus, I. was moved to the plain at the foot of Mount Ingino with reorganized urban structures. The fact that the *via Flaminia* now bypassed I. was the cause of its downfall. Remains: a theatre in the SW of I. (1st cent. AD), residential buildings, necropoleis, kilns, large temple on the edge of the territory of I. (in Monteleto).

In 1444, the famous → *Tabulae Iguvinae* were discovered near the theatre, seven large bronze tablets of varying sizes, some with inscriptions in the Umbrian language on both sides, partly running right-to-left in the Umbrian alphabet (240/150 BC), and partly left-to-right in the Latin alphabet (150/89 BC). They contain instructions for religious ceremonies of the *collegium* of the *fratres Atiedii*, with extensive information about institutions, ceremonies, cults (Jupiter, Pomonus,

Vesuna), about the *gens Petronia*, topography and language.

> 1 F. CATALLI, Monetazione preromana in Umbria, in: Antichità Umbre, catalogo di Perugia, 1989.

> J. W. POULTNEY, The Br. Tables of I. (TAPhA 18), 1959; G. DEVOTO, Tabulae Iguvinae, ³1962; A. PFIFFIG, Religio Iguvina, 1964; A. L. PROSDOCIMI, Le Tavole Iguvine, 1984; M. CIPOLLONE, Gubbio, in: NSA 38f., 1984f., 95–167; C. MALONE, S. STODDART, Territory, Time and State, 1994; P. MICALIZZI, Storia dell'architettura e dell'urbanistica di Gubbio, 1988; D. MANCONI, Gubbio, EAA, Suppl. 2,2, 895–897; A. ANCILLOTTI, R. CERVI, Le tavole di Gubbio e la civiltà degli Umbri, 1996.   G.U.

Ikrion see → Shipbuilding; → Theatre

Ilai see → Cavalry

Ilerda Ancient Iberian city on the Sicoris (modern Segre), modern Lérida (loss of the Iberian prefix *I*). Remains are mostly found above the modern city. Inscriptions: CIL II Suppl. p. 1146. Possibly already mentioned in Avien. 475. I. repeatedly played a role in Roman military history, especially in Caesar's battles with Pompey's legates. Augustus raised I. to the status of *municipium* (coins, Plin. HN 3,24). It is still mentioned several times in Ausonius (e.g. commemoratio professorum Burdigalensium 23,10; epist. 29,59 PEIPER), and in conciliar records it regularly appears as a Visigothic diocese [2]. SCHULTEN [1] assumes a second, even older town by the name of I.

> 1 SCHULTEN, Landeskunde 1, 309   2 J. D. MANSI (ed.), Sacrorum conciliorum collectio IX–XII.

> A. SCHULTEN (ed.), Fontes Hispaniae Antiquae 1, 1925, 3–9 (Indices); R. P. MERCE, Datos arqueológicos ilerd., in: Ilerda 2, 1952, 99–110; 12, 1954, 201–218; J. B. KEUNE, s.v. I., RE Suppl. 3, 1207–1210; TOVAR 3, 212, 420f.; A. VIVES, La moneda hispánica 2, 1924, 52ff.; 4, 1924, 43f.   P.B.

Ilergetes Iberian tribe around → Ilerda in the modern province of Huesca. The I. are often mentioned in the context of the Second Punic War. They initially supported the Carthaginians, were defeated by the Romans in 205 BC (Liv. 29,3) and later became *socii* (Liv. 34,11). Mentioned in Str. 3,4,10 and Plin. HN 3,21, but not later.

> A. SCHULTEN (ed.), Fontes Hispaniae Antiquae 3, 1935, 232; TOVAR 3, 1989, 46f.; SCHULTEN, Landeskunde 1, ²1974, 309; A. VIVES, La moneda hispánica 2, 1924, 52.   P.B.

Ilex see → Oak

Ilia see → Rhea Silvia

Ilias see → Homerus [1]

Ilias Latina BAEHRENS attributed the name to a Latin poem that abbreviates Homer's *Iliad* to 1,070 hexameters. It is quoted by → Lactantius [2] Placidus in regard to Stat. Theb. 6,114 (121) under the name of Homerus, which also appears in the titles of most of the early medieval MSS. Later it is attributed to Pindarus for unknown reasons. The only other trace of the *I.L.* from antiquity is the imitation by → Dracontius [3]. The prologue (= Il. 1,1–7) offers the acrostic ITALICPS, the (non-Homeric) epilogue SCQIPSIT. The latter can easily be amended into SCRIPSIT, the former might be a deliberately incorrect form of ITALICUS [1]. Differences in style and metre prohibit an identification with → Silius [II 5] Italicus. The rubricator (now identified as J. Cuspinianus [2. 31]) of a later and worthless MS uses the title *Bebii Italici poetae clarissimi Epithome* ... [2. tav. vi]. The identity of the name with the one taken from the acrostic (discovered not before the 19th cent.) indicated that Cuspinianus might have drawn on an unknown source independent of manuscript tradition. In the 20th cent. a → Baebius [II 7] Italicus appeared as *cos.* of the year AD 90, whose career as it is known today began under Vespasian (PIR² B 17). However, the identification remains uncertain.

Style and metre do not provide a firm basis for dating. The shortening of *-o* is avoided, but this is probably based on an artificial theory rather than habit [3]. Verses 899–902 probably refer to the deification of Augustus (although this has been questioned), but could have been written at any time [2. 52, n. 103]. The obvious echoes of Seneca's tragedies exclude a pre-Neronian dating. A much later dating is impossible due to the classicist style and metre. One argument for its dating into the Neronian period is the possibility that v. 261f. was added to the Homeric narrative as an allusion to Nero's *Troica*.

There is a marked unevenness in the length of the individual sections of the adaptation. The first eight bks. of the *Iliad* take up ²⁄₃ of the *I.L.*, while bks.13 and 17 are covered in only 5 and 3 lines respectively. This inconsistency shows that the author did not see himself as epitomator, although his work served just precisely purpose in the Middle Ages, when *epitomai* (→ Epitome) were common scholarly texts. In the epilogue, the author claims authorship of the material. This claim is supposed by a number of deviations from the Homeric narrative [2. 81ff.; 4. 60ff.]. There are, for instance, nine similes, of which only four have counterparts in Homer [2. 117]. The description of the shield (862ff.) has expressly non-Homeric characteristics. Vergil and Ovid have strongly influenced the style of the *I.L.* The work follows the translation of the *Iliad* by → Matius [3] to some extent (cf. [5]).

> 1 E. COURTNEY, Greek and Latin Acrostichs, in: Philologus 134, 1990, 12f.   2 G. BROCCIA, Prolegomeni all' 'Omero Latino', 1992   3 D. ARMSTRONG, Stylistics and the date of Calpurnius Siculus, in: Philologus 130, 1986, 130–35   4 M. SCAFFAI, Baebii Italici I.L., 1982   5 COURTNEY, 100f.   ED.C.

Ilias parva (Ἰλιὰς μικρά/*Iliàs mikrá*, the 'Little Iliad').
Lost part of the → Epic cycle. Except for short summaries in the *Chrestomathia* by → Proclus [2], the epitome by → Apollodorus [7], and a few testimonia, only seven direct quotations with a total of 26 hexameters [1; 2; 3. 95] are available for reconstruction and dating. According to Proclus, the work comprises 4 bks., the starting point apparently (in this, Proclus agrees with Aristot. Poet. 1459a 37–b 7 [4. 2411]) being the *Hóplōn krísis* (the decision on who deserves Achilles' armour). The opus must therefore have followed immediately after the → *Aithiopís* (which ended with Achilles' death and burial). According to Proclus, the story goes as follows (abbreviated): instead of → Ajax [1], Odysseus receives Achilles' armour; Ajax goes mad and (in the belief that he is taking revenge against the Atrides) he slaughters the captured cattle of the Achaeans. Once lucid again, he kills himself out of shame and disgrace. Odysseus seizes → Helenus [1], who reveals that Troy can only be captured by → Philoctetes; Diomedes fetches Philoctetes from Lemnos, → Machaon heals him, and Philoctetes kills Paris. Helena falls to → Deiphobus. Odysseus gets Achilles' son → Neoptolemus [1] from Scyros, who kills Troy's new helper → Eurypylus [2]. Now follows the story of the Wooden Horse up to its entrance into Troy and the celebratory banquet of the Trojans. According to Aristot. Poet. 1459a 37, the work continued up to the departure of the Achaeans after the capture of the city (see → Iliupersis). Homer, → Cinaethon and (late) a → Lesches were among those mentioned as authors (→ Epic cycle). The material is old, but the work was created no earlier than the 6th cent. BC [3. 100].
→ Epic cycle (with additional literature).

EDITIONS: 1 PEG   2 EpGr.
BIBLIOGRAPHY: 3 M. DAVIES, The Date of the Epic Cycle, in: Glotta 67, 1989, 89–100   4 A. RZACH, s.v. Kyklos, RE 11, 2410–2422   5 E. BETHE, Homer. Dichtung und Sage II 2.4 ('Der Troische Epenkreis'), 1929, 245–261.   J.L.

Iliberis

[1] I., Iliberri. Iberian town, probably near Granada in the Sierra de Elvira. Mentioned in Plin. HN 3,10 and Ptol. 2,4,9. Diocese in the Christian era, site of the *concilium Eliberitanum* (AD 306 ?) [1]. Often mentioned on coins and in inscriptions, here several times as *municipium Florentinum* (e.g. CIL II 1572; 2070). After the Arab invasion, the town appears to have steadily declined and the population to have moved to Garnatha, modern Granada. Inscriptions: CIL II p. 285ff., Suppl. p. 1146.

1 A. SCHULTEN et al. (ed.), Fontes Hispaniae Antiquae 8/9, 1959/1947.

J.B. KEUNE, s.v. I., RE Suppl. 3, 1210–1215; TOVAR 1, 137f.; A. VIVES, La moneda hispánica 2, 1924, 162.   P.B.

[2] Iberian town north of the Pyrenaei (→ Pyrenean peninsula), near the Mediterranean, modern Elne on the river of the same name, modern Tech. I. is first mentioned in 218 BC as a station on Hannibal's march to Italy (Liv. 21,24,1; 3; 5); derelict at the time of Pliny (HN 3,32), the town was undoubtedly rebuilt by Constantinus I and named after his mother Helena (hence Elne). Emperor Constantinus died in I. in 350 (Zos. 2,42,5; Oros. 7,29,7). Diocese since the 7th cent. [1; 2].

1 A. SCHULTEN (ed.), Fontes Hispaniae Antiquae 8, 69; 9, 319   2 J. B. KEUNE, s.v. I. (2), RE Suppl. 3, 1215.   P.B.

Ilici Ancient Iberian town, in late antiquity Elece, modern Elche. It is assumed that Hamilcar [3] Barka died here in 228 BC; however, this must be corrected in favour of Helice (Elche de la Sierra) [2. 11f.]. In the Roman era, I. was *colonia immunis* (Plin. HN 3,19). In its harbour the fleet of Maiorianus was destroyed by Vandali in AD 460 [3. 81f.]. In the Visigothic period, I. is often mentioned as a diocese [3. 449]. The ancient site lay somewhat closer to the sea on a hill, La Alcudia. Excavations testify to its significance. Elche became famous primarily for one find, the marble sculpture 'la Dama de Elche' [1]. Inscriptions: CIL II p. 479; Suppl. p. 1146f.
→ Pyrenean peninsula

1 A. GARCÍA Y BELLIDO, La Dama de Elche, 1943
2 A. SCHULTEN (ed.), Fontes Hispaniae Antiquae 3, 1935
3 Id. (ed.), Fontes Hispaniae Antiquae 9, 1947.

J.B. KEUNE, s.v. I., RE Suppl. 3, 1217–1221; TOVAR 3, ²1974, 198ff.; A. VIVES, La moneda hispánica 4, 1924, 39ff.   P.B.

Ilienses Ancient (Mela 2,123) Sardinian tribe; besides the Corsi, the only one not subjugated by Rome (Paus. 10,17,8f.). Pliny (HN 3,85) names three non-urbanized peoples under the heading *provinciae*, among them the I. Livy recalls the victorious campaigns of 181 BC (Liv. 40,34,12ff.) and 178–176 (Liv. 41,6,5ff.; 12,4ff.). The location of their settlements is doubtful – possibly from Marghine in the north (cf. the inscriptions on the nuraghes of Aidu Entos *Ili(ensium) iur(a))* to Ogliastra in the south (Flor. Epit. 1,22,35, mention of I. in connection with the *montes Insani* located between Dorgali and Baunei).

P. MELONI, Sardegna romana, 1990, 75ff., 229ff.; L. GASPERINI, La scritta latina del nuraghe Aidu Entos, in: M. BONELLO LAI (ed.), Sardinia Antiqua. Studi in onore di P. Meloni, 1992, 303ff.   P.M.

Ilione (Ἰλιόνη; *Ilíónē*). Oldest daughter of → Priamus and → Hecabe, wife of Polymestor, the Thracian (Verg. Aen. 1,653f. mentions her sceptre which Aeneas brings from Ilion; cf. Hyg. Fab. 90). She raises her youngest brother → Polydorus along with her and Polymestor's son → Deipylus. After the end of the Trojan War, Agamemnon induces Polymestor to kill Polydorus. He unknowingly kills his own son, since I. had passed Deipylus off as her brother. The real Polydorus then instigates I. to kill her husband. After the deed, I. commits suicide (Hyg. Fab. 109; cf. 240; 243, 254; Serv. Aen. 1,653). Pacuvius wrote the tragedy *Iliona* [1] (cf. Hor. Sat. 2,3,60).

1 I. D'ANNA, M. Pacuvii Fragmenta, 1967, 109–115, fr. 221–250.

S. EITREM, s.v. I., RE 11, 1066.   K.WA.

Ilioneus (Ἰλιονεύς; *Ilioneús*). Trojan warrior, son of a farmer by the name of Phorbas who was very wealthy due to his close connection to → Hermes; killed in battle by → Peneleus, the Minyaean prince (Hom. Il. 14,487–507). Virgil uses this name for the oldest leader of the Trojan refugees (A. 1,521 et passim).

P. WATHELET, Dictionnaire des Troyens de l'Iliade, 1988, no. 161.   E.V.

Ilipa Modern Alcalá del Río (from the Arabic for 'river fortification') on the right bank of the → Baetis. The name and town are Iberian [1. 1221]. I. was important for navigation (Str. 3,2,3; CIL II 1085), but also because of nearby silver mines (Str. l.c.), agriculture and fishing (coins), which earned it the epithet *Magna* (Ptol. 2,4,10; Plin. HN 3,11?). P. Cornelius Scipio defeated the Carthaginians near I. in 206 BC. I. was mentioned as a diocese in the Visigothic period [2. 216].

1 J. B. KEUNE, s.v. I. (1), RE Suppl. 3, 1221–1225   2 A. SCHULTEN (ed.), Fontes Hispaniae Antiquae 9, 1947.

A. SCHULTEN (ed.), Fontes Hispaniae Antiquae, 1925ff., esp. vol. 2, 5–9; Id., Forsch. in Spanien I/2, 1940, 113ff.; ID., Landeskunde 1, 489; TOVAR 2, 162f.; A. VIVES, La moneda hispánica 3, 1924, 87ff.   P.B.

Ilipula There were several towns with this name in the province of → Hispania Baetica [3. 1225]. Often they are difficult to distinguish from *Ilipa, Ilipla, Elepla, Elipla* [1]. Only the most important are briefly listed here.
[1] I. **Magna** (Ptol. 2,4,9) or I. Laus (*Iulia*?, Plin. HN 3,10). Location unknown.
[2] I. **Minor** (Plin. HN 3,12; CIL II 1469f.), modern Repla, south of Osuna.
[3] I., Ilipla ([2]; Ptol. 2,410). Between → Baetis and Anas, modern Niebla. The ruins of the old town are mostly from the Arabic period but finds date back to the 7th cent. BC.
[4] Mountains to the south of the → Baetis (Ptol. 2,4,12), probably the modern Sierra de Ronda.

1 A. SCHULTEN (ed.), Fontes Hispaniae Antiquae 9, 1947, 12, 446   2 A. VIVES, La moneda hispánica 3, 1924, 81   3 J. B. KEUNE, s.v. I. (2–5), RE Suppl. 3, 1225f.

J. P. DROOP, Excavations at Niebla, in: AAA 12, 1925, 175–206; SCHULTEN, Landeskunde 1, 192; TOVAR 1, 129, 139.   P.B.

Ilis(s)us (Ἰλισός/*Ilisós*, Ἰλισσός/*Ilissós*). One of the two main rivers of the plain of Athens (Str. 9,1,24), the other being the → Cephis(s)us [2]. Having its source on the north-western slope of the → Hymettus it turned towards the southwest at the southern edge of Athens (today completely built over and as in antiquity seasonal). It is disputed whether the I. emptied itself into the sea at Phalerum or into the Cephisus north of Piraeus [2. 164 fig. 213]. The Eridanus (Paus. 1,19,5) was a tributary of the I. The stadium of Athens and several temples were located on the I. [2. 112, 278, 289ff. fig. 379]. Bridges across the I.: [2. 498 fig. 155, 630, 634]. The Kallirhoe arose on an island in the I. below the Olympeion [2. 114, 204 fig. 154, 268]. A decree (IG I³ 1257) prohibited the tanners on the I. from polluting the river [1. 257f.; 2. 340f. fig. 442]. The cult of the I.: IG I³ 369e l. 89, 383 l. 206.

› Atheis (with map)

1 H. LIND, Neues aus Kydathen, in: MH 42, 1985, 249–261   2 TRAVLOS, Athen, Index s.v. I.

W. JUDEICH, Top. von Athen, ²1931, 48; W. KOLBE, s.v. I., RE 9, 1067f.; PHILIPPSON/KIRSTEN 1, 877, 889, 899ff., 922, 1001.   H.LO.

Ilium, Ilius see → Troy

Iliupersis (Ἰλίου πέρσις/*Ilíou pérsis*, 'The destruction of Ilius [= Troy]'). Lost part of an epic of the → Epic cycle; except for brief summary of its contents in the *chrestomathia* by → Proclus and in the epitome by → Apollodorus [7] of Athens and some testimonies there is only one literal quotation with eight hexameters [1; 2; 3. 96] available for reconstruction and dating. According to Proclus it consisted of two books, beginning with the discussions of the Trojans standing around the Wooden Horse in Troy (cf. Verg. Aen. 2,31–249). The *Iliupersis* thus takes up after the → Ilias parva [5. 214]. The further course of the narrative according to Proclus (abbreviated and in part added to or modified from Apollodorus): decision to sacrifice the horse to Athene, joyful celebration, → Laocoon episode, emigration of Aeneas, Sinon episode (Sinon's beacon), return of the fleet from Tenedos, battle in the streets of Troy, the Achaeans set Troy on fire and sacrifice Polyxena at the grave of Achilles, Neoptolemus kills Astyanax, distribution of the spoils of war, departure of the Greeks (Athene sends a sea storm, decimation and dispersion of the Greek fleet: probably a note added later [5. 214³]). Aristot. Poet. 1459a 37–b. 7 is familiar with 'Iliupersis, departure, Sinon and the Trojan women' (i.e. distribution of the booty) as parts of the *Iliás mikrá*. *Iliupérsis* was therefore probably only a separate title for the last part of the *Iliás mikrá*; differences in details between the contents of the *Iliás mikrá* and the *Iliupersis* are the responsibility of the referees from antiquity ([5. 218–225]; for a different hypothesis: → Aethiopis). The author is usually specified as → Arctinus, Aristot. ibid.

speaks only of 'the author of the Little Iliad'. For the dating see → Ilias parva.
→ Epic cycle (with additional literature).

EDITIONS: 1 PEG   2 EpGr.
BIBLIOGRAPHY: 3 M. DAVIES, The Date of the Epic Cycle, in: Glotta 67, 1989, 89–100   4 A. RZACH, s.v. Kyklos, RE 11, 2405–2410   5 E. BETHE, Homer. Dichtung und Sage II 2.4 ('Der Troische Epenkreis'), ²1929.
                                                                    J.L.

Iliupersis Painter Apulian vase painter of the second quarter of the 4th cent. BC, named after a volute crater in London (BM Inv. F 160 [1. 193 no. 8]) with the image of the → Iliupersis. The Iliupersis Painter (IP) belongs to those creatively engaged vase painters who produced pioneering innovations for the development of later → Apulian vase painting; among these are the introduction of burial scenes (→ Naiscus vases), additionally the fluting of vessels on their lower sections and the decoration of the handles on volute craters with round medallions, which he adorned with appliqués in the shape of heads or figures, either painted or in relief, and finally the head of a woman arising from the calyx between tendrils. The IP depicted mythic and Dionysian scenes, as well as genre-specific scenes with Erotes, men and women. As a result of his work, the volute crater has become one of the most important objects for the display of Apulian vase painting.
→ Baltimore Painter; → Darius Painter

1 TRENDALL/CAMBITOGLOU.

K. SCHAUENBURG, Zu Werken des Iliupersismalers und seines Umkreises in einer Privatsammlung, in: N. BASGELEN, M. LUGAL (ed.), FS J. Inan, 1989, 511–515; Id., Diesseits und Jenseits in der ital. Grabkunst, in: JÖAI 64, 1995, Beiblatt, 57; TRENDALL/CAMBITOGLOU, Suppl. I, 1983, 25–26; Id., Suppl. II, 1991, 43–48.   R.H.

Illus (Ἴλλος/*Íllos* or Ἰλλοῦς/*Illoûs*). Isaurian, high-ranking official and general in the East Roman Empire. In February AD 474, together with → Verina, widow of → Leo(n) [4], he supported the elevation of his compatriot → Zeno to the position of emperor, but as early as 475 he joined forces with Verina and the usurper → Basiliscus. After the defeat of Basiliscus in 476 he soon sided with Zeno again and in 477 became *magister officiorum* and *patricius*. At his instigation Verina, who together with Epinicus [2] had attempted to get rid of I. in 478, was exiled to Isauria. After escaping another assault in 480/81, Zeno appointed I. to the position of *magister utriusque militiae per Orientem* in 481, but because I. had arrested Zeno's brother Longinus and did not want to release him, Zeno clashed with I. and dismissed him again in 483. Although he professed to be a Chalcedonian Christian, I. was devoted to the pagan writer and magician → Pamprepius of Panopolis, who in 484 prophesized good chances for his renewed attempt to depose Zeno. As a result, I. joined with Verina, whom he had released in the meantime, and declared general Leontius anti-emperor at Tarsus on 19 July; however, before the year was over both Leontius and I. were defeated by Zeno's general Iohannes and came under siege while at the Isaurian fortress of Papyrios. There, Leontius and I. imposed the death penalty on Pamprepius because of his false prognosis, but were executed themselves on Zeno's order after the fortress was captured in 488.

ODB 2, 986; PLRE 2, 586–590; STEIN, Spätröm. R. 1, 535–539; Histoire du Bas-Empire 2, 8–31.   F.T.

Illustration see → Book illustration

Illustris vir As early as the Roman Republican period the word *illustris* – like the words *clarus, spectabilis* or *egregius* – can indicate a high social rank. In the *ordo dignitatum* of late antiquity, however, *illustris, illustrissimus* was especially applied to the highest level of office holders and dignitaries (Not. Dign. Or. 2–15 and Occ. 2–13; Cod. Theod. 6,7; 9,1; 14,1; Cod. Iust. 12,8,2; Greek adaptation: *illoústrios* Nov. Iust. 13,3; 15,1). Similarly, if it was usual to give all members of the senatorial class the title of *clari* or *clarissimi* up until the 4th cent. AD, it gradually became a custom thereafter to distinguish between senatorial holders of high and highest court and imperial offices, senatorial provincial administrators and senators in the imperial service on a non-career basis (Cod. Theod. 6,4,12). At the end of this development an order of courtly titles, later adopted into the Cod. Iust. (12,8,1, *lex* of 440/1) was introduced by Valentinian I. In it the titles of rank *spectabiles* and *illustres* (Cod. Theod. 11,30,31; 7,6,1), in use since the middle of the 4th cent – if not exclusively, were thenceforth strictly separated from those of merely senatorial rank.

According to this order, those in the *illustres* class were further distinguished: *illustres* by virtue of their office (*in actu*), as well as the *vacantes* and the *honorarii* (Cod. Iust. 12,8,2). Included among the *illustres in actu*, possibly in part from an even earlier date, were e.g. the consuls (in the late antique form of office), the *praefectus urbi*, the *praefecti praetorio*, the *magistri militum*, the *praepositus sacri cubiculi*, the *quaestor palatii*, the *magister officiorum*, the *comes sacrarum largitionum*, the *comes sacri patrimonii* and the *comites domesticorum*.

Until the 6th cent. the right to vote in the Senate was limited to those holding office and to the increasingly large number of honorary *illustres viri* (*qui a patriciis et consulibus usque ad omnes illustres viros descendunt, ... soli in senatu sententiam dicere possunt* – Dig. 1,9,12,1, a quote from Ulpian referring to the period of its drafting). Among those included among the *illustres* on an honorary basis as early as in the time of Theodosius I (died AD 395) was the Jewish Patriarch (Cod. Theod. 16,8,8 of 392); even Christian bishops were able to receive this rank.

The title brought with it exemption from *munera sordida* (→ munus, *munera*) and other burdens (e.g. Cod. Theod. 7,8,16; 11,16,23), as well as the grant of privileges in both civil and criminal law and a number of other honours (Cod. Iust. 12,1,16f.). In principle these privileges extended also to women (Cod. Theod. 2,1,7; Cod. Iust. 12,1,13).

→ Comes; → Court titles

A. CHASTAGNOL, Le sénat romain à l'époque impériale, 1992, 293–324; JONES, LRE 528–536; H. LÖHKEN, Ordo Dignitatum, 1982, 112–147. C.G.

Illyrian emperors Term applied to a group of Roman rulers whose feature in common was the fact that they came from Illyrian territory, more broadly the area between the Adriatic and the lower Danube. The sequence already begins with → Decius [II 1] (AD 249–251) but essentially includes the emperors → Claudius [III 2] Gothicus, → Aurelianus [2], → Probus, → Diocletianus, → Maximianus, and → Constantinus [1] I. Even in antiquity these rulers were credited with having little education but they were acknowledged as being experienced in military service and well suited to state administration (Aur. Vict. Caes. 39,26). In general they owed their rise to their military enterprise and, through internal reforms and foreign policy successes, they made a major contribution to remedying the crisis of the 3rd cent. Their origin in provinces that had long been Romanized but only weakly Christianized also explains why some of them (Decius, Diocletian, Maximianus) systematically persecuted Christians throughout the Empire. T.F.

Illyrian Wars The name Illyrian Wars (IW) is given to two wars conducted by Rome in → Illyricum in 229 to 228 and in 219 BC. The First Illyrian War of 229–228 was waged against → Teuta, widow of Agron [3], who after the latter's death (in 231?) continued his politics of expansion (230: annexation of Phoenice, and treaties with Epirus and Acarnania). In 229, when she had reached far south beyond the Straits of Ortranto, and laid siege to Corcyra, Epidamnos, and Apollonia [1], and also defeated a fleet of Achaeans and Aetolians off the island of Paxos, Rome dispatched 200 ships and a large army under the command of both consuls (Pol. 1,11,2 and 7). The sight of these forces alone was enough to cause Teuta to retreat (Pol. 2,11,9; App. Ill. 7). In the peace treaty concluded in the spring of 228, control of Teuta's territories was partly handed over to her stepson Pinnes, partly to → Demetrius of Pharus. Illyrian war ships were forbidden to sail beyond Lissus (*c.* 50 km north of Epidamnos).

The Second Illyrian War (219 BC) was waged against Demetrius of Pharus, who after his marriage to Triteuta, mother of Pinnes, had gained influence in the latter's territories. He pursued increasingly independent politics, including extensive pirate voyages as far as into the Aegean (220) (→ Piracy). In 219, a Roman fleet was dispatched again under the leadership of both consuls; it captured Demetrius' fortresses (Dimale, Pharos), and forced him to flee (to Philippus [7] V of Macedonia). Pinnes was confirmed as ruler, and, as after the first Illyrian War, Rome completely withdrew all of its army.

The importance of the IW within the Roman expansion to the east is controversial. Even to ancient authors, Rome's reasons for reaching beyond the Adriatic were not clear (cf. App. Ill. 6). → Polybius' [2] (2,2,1 f.) view, that Rome had thus taken its first step towards conquering Greece, leads one to suspect that Rome sought deliberate expansion in the IW (e.g. [1]), at least in the second war ([2. 75]; cf. [3. 61]). However, from the complete withdrawal of all Roman troops it may be concluded that both wars were predominantly conducted against the piracy originating from the Illyrian coast, and had the sole target of securing the sea routes between Greece and the Greek towns of southern Italy ([4. 359–373; 5. 85–94]) which were under Roman control since the war against → Pyrrhus [3] (280–275).

→ Macedonian Wars; → Parthini; → Piracy; → Teuta

1 E. BADIAN, Notes on Roman Policy in Illyria (230–201 B. C.), in: Id., Stud. in Greek and Roman History, 1964, 1–33 2 D. VOLLMER, Symploke, 1990, 48–83 3 H. BELLEN, Grundzüge der röm. Geschichte, ²1995 4 E. S. GRUEN, The Hellenistic World and the Coming of Rome, vol. 2, 1984 5 R.M ERRINGTON, Rome and Greece to 205 B.C., in: CAH 8, ²1989, 85–94. W. ED.

Illyricum (also *Hilluricum*, *Hillyricum*, *Illuricum*). The first Roman province on the eastern Adriatic coast, in 167 BC organized as a Roman territory, formerly part of the Illyrian kingdom.

A. STATE OF RESEARCH B. PRE-ROMAN HISTORY
C. ROMAN PROVINCE D. POST-PROVINCIAL
PERIOD E. CULTURE

A. STATE OF RESEARCH
Understanding of the term I. varies. The discussion on the 'Illyrian question' reached its climax with Panillyrianism, which saw the Illyrians as the bearers of the Urnfield culture (cf. the publications of H. KRAHE, but whose conclusions have since been thoroughly revised). From the beginning to the collapse of the Illyrian kingdom the Illyrians allied with various tribes of common or similar heritage and language. Only their personal and geographical names remained; it is not certain whether the Illyrian languages belonged to the Centum or the Satem group (→ Centum language, → Satem language); when denoting a language, therefore, the term 'Illyrian' too is no longer tenable; at best, the adjectives 'Illyrian', pre-Celtic or indigenous are used. The onomastic studies by KATIČIĆ are important; they attempt to establish the boundaries between various onomastic regions, including those Illyrian names that are attested for the south-eastern regions of the Adriatic coast and its hinterland – only these can justifiably be called Illyr-

ian. A central research problem is the question of an Illyrian proto-tribe (cf. *Illyrii proprie dicti*, Plin. HN 3,144; Mela 2,56; cf. also the legend of → Cadmus [1] and Harmonia) because from the beginning the word 'Illyrians' is used in the sense of a tribal league by ancient authors. According to Plin. loc. cit. they must be localized in the *conventus* of Narona between Epidaurus and Lissus, where the first contacts were made between Greek traders and/or explorers on the one hand and residents of the region, which afterwards was known as Illyris/Illyria, on the other hand. But the Illyrians were hardly known in the Greek world because Greek colonization of the eastern Adriatic coast started only in a very limited area (Epidamnos/Dyrrhachium, Apollonia) or late (e.g. Issa, Pharus).

B. Pre-Roman history

The earliest mention of the Illyrians are with Hecat. (FGrH 1 F 98–101, cf. 93–97) and Hdt. (1,196; 4,49); most of the details about Illyrian tribes can be found in the Periplus by Ps.-Scyl. (*c.* 330 BC, GGM 1,26ff.) and Ps.-Scymn. (2nd cent. BC, GGM 1,211ff.). According to Ps.-Scyl. their territory is supposed to have reached from the Enchelei to the → Chaones (northern Epirus). Of the peoples living in the interior only the → Autariatae are called Illyrian. In the area of these Illyrian tribes an Illyrian kingdom constituted itself in southern I. (5th cent. BC), whose best-known representatives are found in the final, the Ardiaeian dynasty of Agron (son of Pleuratus) and Teuta. Its name became eponymous for many neighbouring tribes which were only loosely connected to them. The earlier dynasties (with Bardylis, Grabos, Cleitus, Glaucias) are mainly known through their disputes with the Macedonians ever since they invaded Macedonia c. 393 BC; their earlier contacts are not documented, but later they were generally enemies of the Macedonians.

The protectorate established by Rome after the fall of Genthius in 167 BC over part of the Illyrian territory (part of the territory of the Parthini and → Atintani south of Lissus in the hinterland of Dyrrhachium, cf. Liv. 45,26,15) was called *Illyrís* in Greek, *Illyria* in Latin. After the defeat of Perseus in 168 it was included in the *provincia Macedonia* as 4th *merís*. This protectorate was probably the source of the Roman idea of I. All subsequent Roman conquests, first of the remainder of the Illyrian kingdom, then of the northern coastal areas and the Dalmatian hinterland, were gradually added to Illyris/Illyria. For administrative purposes, numerous tribes and peoples who had no ethnic ties to the Illyrians (→ Liburni, → Histria), were counted as belonging to I. and called Illyrian, because they lived in I. Greek and Latin authors of the time after the establishment of the I. protectorate in the 2nd cent. BC (from which the province of I. originated in the 1st cent. BC), who mentioned Illyris/Illyria and/or I. and Illyrians, did so only with regard to the administrative organization of the Balkan or in a geographical sense because the northwestern part of the peninsula belonged mainly to I. Ac-

cording to Strabo, *Illyrís* was a country that stretched from the upper regions of the Adriatic down to the Rhyzonian Gulf and the country of the Ardiaei, between the sea and the Pannonian peoples (7,5,3; cf. App. Ill. 1; Cass. Dio 12; Zon. 8,19,8). The Romans conducted their military campaigns mainly from their bases on the Italian coast of the Adriatic. The Roman army also operated from → Gallia Cisalpina; these attacks were aimed at various tribes and peoples who later entered the province of I., above all the Histri, who were already subjugated in 177 BC. In general the entire territory south of the Formio was known as I.; under Augustus, probably in 18/12 BC, Histria was allotted to Italy and along with Venetia it was incorporated into the 10th region.

C. Roman province

It is impossible to give an exact date for the establishment of the province of I.: according to Th. Mommsen the province was most likely established by Sulla (CIL III p. 279). Caesar was probably the first to give I. a vice governor who was responsible for this province alone (Vatinius 45–43), because Caesar himself ruled both the provinces of Gallia and I. since 58 BC. The senatorial province of I. included large parts of the later province of Dalmatia and parts of Pannonia. After the Pannonian-Dalmatian rebellion in AD 9 I. was probably divided into *I. superius* and *I. inferius* (cf. ILS 938). When the provinces of Dalmatia and Pannonia were formed out of I. under Vespasianus, neither of the newly formed provinces retained its old name. Under Augustus the name I. no longer had anything to do with the original Illyrian territory in southern Dalmatia, referring instead to the entire northern and central Balkans (cf. Suet. Tib. 16,4). I. comprised a territory larger than Pannonia and Dalmatia together, probably also the areas that were conquered by the proconsuls of Macedonia in the 2nd/1st cents., and it was more or less identical to the future province of Moesia. The name I. was now used for other administrative units, for example for the customs territories (*publicum portorii Illyrici*) which comprised the largest part of Raetia to the Pontus Euxinus (App. Ill. 6).

D. Post-provincial period

The term I. was presumably the only one available with the range of meaning that was necessary even to cover remotely the areas in question; it is certain that it paved the way for the usage of late antiquity when under Septimius Severus 'Illyrian' denoted the army stationed in the Balkans and later several emperors who came from the region. From Diocletianus onwards I. was more or less identical with the regions of the *publicum portorii Illyrici*; for in the Pannonian Balkans three dioceses within the new territorial administrative structure of the empire were established (Pannonia, Moesia, Thracia): they were counted as part of I., one of four prefectures established by Constantinus. In the *Notitia dignitatum* (*c.* AD 395), however, the prefectures of I.

(*Illyricum orientale*) comprises the dioceses Macedonia (with Greece) and Dacia, while the diocese I. (*Illyricum occidentale*) is counted with the prefecture of Italia, along with the two provinces of Noricum, the four provinces of Pannonia and Dalmatia, but without Praevalitana (→ Diocletianus, map).

E. Culture

Almost nothing is known about the Illyrian language (→ Balkans, languages, with map); in Hesychius only one word is defined as Illyrian, while over 100 are deemed Macedonian. There are great onomastic and cultural differences between the individual peoples in I. Some reached a more advanced stage of development; the differing degrees of civilization was especially pronounced between the coastal peoples and the tribes in the interior. Romanisation, its dominance varying from region to region, provided the chief common denominator.

G. Zippel, Die röm. Herrschaft in Illyrien bis auf Augustus, 1877; H. Krahe, Lexikon altillyr. PN, 1929; Id., Die Sprache der Illyrier 1: Die Quellen, 1955; M. Suić, Istočna Jadranska obala u Pseudo Skilakovu Periplu [The Eastern Adriatic Coast in Pseudo-Scylax's Periplus], in: Rad Jugoslavenske akademije znanosti i umjetnosti 306, 1955, 121–186; A. Mayer, Die Sprache der alten Illyrier 1, 1957; 2, 1959; F. Papazoglou, Les origines et la destinée de l'état illyrien, in: Historia 14, 1965, 143–179; R. Katičić, Ancient Languages of the Balkans 1, 1976; H. Parzinger, Archäologisches zur Frage der Illyrier, in: BRGK 72, 1991, 205–246; J. Wilkes, The Illyrians, 1992; M. Šašel Kos, Cadmus and Harmonia in Illyria, in: Arheološki vestnik 44, 1993, 113–136.   M.Š.K.

Ilorci Iberian town in the area of the upper → Baetis, with the tomb of one of the two Scipios who fell in 211 BC, probably Cn. Scipio (Plin. HN 3,25). The equation of I. with the modern Lorca (province of Murcia) is disputed. CIL II p. 476.

A. Schulten (ed.), Fontes Hispaniae Antiquae 3, 1935, 91; J. B. Keune, s.v. I., RE Suppl. 3, 1229; G. Alföldy, Röm. Städtewesen auf der neukastilischen Hochebene, 1981, 38.   P.B.

Iluraton (Ἰλούρατον; *Iloúraton*). Graeco-Scythian settlement north of the Curubas lake in the interior of modern Kerč, *c.* 17 km from Panticapaeum. Traces of settlement since the Neolithic; founded in the middle of the 1st cent. AD. The results of the excavations are representative for other inland settlements in the Bosporan kingdom of the Roman period: I. was naturally and artificially well fortified. The inhabitants were military peasants who engaged in agriculture and livestock breeding, Hellenized descendants of the Scythians: way of life, religious beliefs and cults were primarily Scythian, their native language was Greek. Destroyed by the Goths in AD 266–268.

V. F. Gaidukevič, Ilurat, in: Materialy instituta arheologii 85, 1958, 9–148; Id., Das Bosporan. Reich, 1971, 409f.   I.v.B.

Ilurcavones (Ilercavones). An Iberian tribe around Dertosa, on the lower Ebro. They submitted to the Romans in 218 BC (Liv. 21,60,3; for later times cf. also Liv. 22,21,6; Caes. B Civ. 1,60,2; Ptol. 2,6,16; Plin. HN 3,21).

A. Schulten (ed.), Fontes Hispaniae Antiquae 4–8, 1925ff. (Index); Tovar 3, 34f.   P.B.

Il(l)urco Iberian town in the province of → Hispania Baetica, modern Pinos Puente near Illora la Vieja west of Granada (Plin. HN 3,10). Its location is certain from inscriptions (CIL II p. 284; Suppl. p. 1147). Coins [1. 107f.; 2. 1234].

1 A. Vives, La moneda hispánica 3, 1924   2 J. B. Keune, s.v. I., RE Suppl. 3, 1233–1235.

Tovar 1, 136; 3, 163ff.   P.B.

Ilus (Ἶλος; *Îlos*).

[1] *Heros eponymos* and founder of Ilios/Ilium (→ Troy); son of → Tros, father of → Laomedon (Hom. Il. 20,231ff.; → Dardanidae). His tomb is mentioned in the *Iliad* (11,166 et passim) as a fixed topographical point in the plain of Troy. The fullest account of the foundation legend is offered by Apollod. 3,140ff.; a coin of the emperor Caracalla from Ilium shows I. sacrificing before the → Palladion, which he received from Zeus at the founding of the city, according to Apollodorus.

[2] According to Verg. Aen. 1,267f. original name of Aeneas' son → Iulus/Ascanius, through whom the *gens Iulia* traced itself back to the Trojan ruling dynasty and to Aphrodite [1. 317ff.].

1 G. Binder, Der brauchbare Held: Aeneas, in: H.-J. Horn, H. Walter (ed.), Die Allegorese des ant. Mythos, 1997, 311–330.

R. Vollkommer, s.v. I., LIMC 5.1, 650; P. Wathelet, Dictionnaire des Troyens de l'Iliade, 1988, no. 162.

MA.ST.

Ilva Island in the *mare Tyrrhenum*, off the coast of Populonia (Αἰθάλη; *Aithálē*, Αἰθαλία; *Aithalía*: Hecat. FGrH 1 F 59; Ps.-Scyl. 6), modern Elba. The *limēn Argôios* (λιμὴν Ἀργῷος) is supposed to have been founded by the → Argonauts (Str. 5,2,6; others trace the name back to the white colour of the beach). Settled since the Neolithic. I. was famous for its iron mines, which had been exploited since Etruscan times (smelting slag on Pithecussae and at Populonia). In 453 BC, I. was briefly occupied by Syracusae (Diod. Sic. 11,88,4f.). There are fortifications at Monte Castello and Castiglione San Martino, a sanctuary at Monte Serra, splendid Roman *villae* in Grotte di Portoferraio and Cavo di Rio Marina; numerous shipwrecks in the waters around the island.

V. Mellini, Memorie storiche dell'isola d'Elba, 1965; M. Zecchini, Gli Etruschi all'isola d'Elba, 1978; Id.,

L'isola d'Elba, 1982; L. Corsi, s.v. Elba, BTCGI 7, 127–146.

                     G.U.

Ilvates Ligurian tribe between Appenninus, Placentia and Regium. Rebellion against Rome in 200 BC under Punic leadership (Liv. 31,10,2), subjugated in 197 BC (Liv. 32,29,7; 31,4). Possibly identical with the Eleiates of the *Fasti Triumphales*.

Fontes Ligurum et Liguriae antiquae, 1976, s.v. I.   L.S.A.

Imachara (Ἰμάχαρα; *Imáchara*). Small town in Sicily (Cic. Verr. 2,3,47; Plin. HN 3,91; Ptol. 3,4,12,3; preserved are kerykeion, IG XIV 589, litrai in two versions). The identification with the excavation site near Nissoria is conceivable. There was a river in the area of I. (reverse of the litra).

E. Manni, Geografia fisica e politica della Sicilia antica (Testimonia Siciliae antiqua 1,1), Kokalos Suppl. 4, 1981, 190; R. J. A. Wilson, Sicily under the Roman Empire, 145, 378 no. 14; S. Cataldi, s.v. I., BTCGI 8, 238–247; G. Manganaro, Alla ricerca di poleis mikrai della Sicilia centro-orientale, in: Orbis Terrarum 2, 1996, 144 no. 74.   GI.MA.

Image I (εἰκών/*eikón*, εἴδωλον/*eídōlon*, Latin *imago*). The Greek word for image (εἰκών; *eikón*) first of all denotes works of art (τέχνῃ εἰκόνες/*téchnēi eikónes*: statues, paintings), but also natural images (φύσει εἰκόνες/*phýsei eikónes*: silhouettes and reflections). Plato uses the concept of 'image' in conjunction with the concept of 'participation' (μέθεξις; *méthexis*) to describe the relationship between ideas and sensual objects. In *Timaios* the demiurge creates the sensible world as the image of the ideas, which serve as models (παραδείγματα; *paradeígmata*). In contrast to later developments (Philo, Plotinus), Plato contends that there are no εἰκόνες (*eikónes*) in the intelligible world.

To obviate a misinterpretation of 'emanation', Plotinus uses the image to describe the relationship of the hypostaseis but in so doing he substitutes the τέχνῃ εἰκών (*téchnēi eikón*) of the Platonic demiurge for φύσει εἰκών (*phýsei eikón*), the reflection (Plot. Enneads 5,8,12,12–20; 6,4,10). The last reflection is matter which does not appear itself, but which conveys its nonexistence to the image appearing on it. (Enn. 3,6,13 f.)

To explain perception and thought, the Atomists expounded a theory of images, according to which groups of atoms constantly detach themselves from the surface of objects (εἴδωλα/*eídōla*, *simulacra*) and reach the soul through the sense organs. (Lucr. 4,34 ff.).

A. H. Armstrong, Platonic Mirrors, in: Eranos-Jb. 55, 1988, 147–181; W. Beierwaltes, Denken des Einen, 1985; L. Cardullo, Il linguaggio del simbolo in Proclo, 1985; F.-W. Eltester, Eikon im NT, 1958; H. Merki, Ὁμοίωσις θεῷ, 1952; E. Moutsopoulos, Sur la notion d'EIDOLON chez Proclus, in: Mélanges J. Trouillard, 1981, 265–274; H. Willms, EIKΩN, 1937.   S.M.-S.

Image II The concept of image common in the western world of ideas has its origin in Greece, especially in the writings of → Plato and of → Aristotle, but modern and ancient views appear to deviate considerably from each other (cf. also → Art; → Art, theory of). Neither with regard to the concept of image nor concerning the terminology applied in antiquity relating to image is there a comprehensive investigation although attempts have been made to formulate a Greek basic idea of image [1]. In the process, individual concepts like εἴδωλον (*eídōlon*), εἰκών (*eikón*) [2; 3], κολοσσός (*kolossós*) [4; 5], → ξόανον (*xóanon*) [6], σῆμα (*sêma*) [21] were analysed. Indeed it appears as if the concept from the time of → Simonides encompassed both the visual and the verbal (ὁ λόγος τῶν πραγμάτων εἰκών ἐστιν: fr. 190 B Bergk⁴), but the visual component became particularly important because of the close link in Greek thought between ἰδεῖν (*ideîn*, 'to see') and εἰδέναι (*eidénai*, 'to know') [7. 27].

The debate about the visual aspect of image was dominated by the link made by Plato and Aristotle with → mimesis and by the rejection of the fine arts encountered primarily in Plato [8. 31–58]. The concept of mimesis, which for a long time was understood as 'imitation', experienced a significant re-evaluation through the analysis of the pre-Platonic meaning [9–12]. The associations that were linked in the 5th cent. BC with related concepts appear to be related to the acting of actors, but perhaps already in Aeschylus (TrGF 3, fr. 78a, 364) [10. 78] and certainly at the time of Xenophon (Mem. 3,10,1–8) [1. 134], mimesis was also understood as covering pictorial representations. Plato counted poetry, drama, music, painting and sculpture as mimetic arts; he condemned mimesis as deviating from truth, misleading and corrupting for society. The *locus classicus* is the comparison between the three couches (Resp. 596e–598d): the one in 'nature', the one created by a carpenter and the depiction by an artist who, copying only the external manifestation of the second, is another step further away from 'nature'. The image therefore stands between being and not-being; its plausibility is dependent upon the similarity with the model (Soph. 240a-b). Plato's rejection of the fine arts was often regarded as a central component of his world of ideas. His view is however not consistent in this point, for his attitude to painting changes from gradual acceptance to radical rejection [13; 14]. The reason for this change remains unclear. Plato's statements cannot be convincingly related to contemporary art practice. His contradictory final conclusions therefore reflect less the loss of relevant art works. Rather they make it appear possible that his views on the visual arts should be regarded as a reflection of epistemological standpoints [14] and of certain polemical contexts.

Aristotle (Poet. 1447a–1448b) appears to incorporate the fine arts in the category of mimesis; therefore an image would be defined through the method of its creation, through the object that is copied and probably through the manner of the imitation. Aristotle too considers the image in addition as a trigger of moral effects: young people should consider works by → Polygnotus, who represented human beings as better than they are, and not images by → Pauson, who showed them as worse (Pol. 1340a 33–40; Poet. 1448a 5–6). It would appear that it was only from the 2nd cent. BC that mere power of imagination [1. 160] eclipsed the mimetic tie between a model and an image, and indeed in the wake of a further development of the Hellenistic theory of φαντασία (*phantasía*) [8. 52–55; 15].

Image is in addition an explicit theme in ancient texts that are concerned with the use, origin and development of image in cult operation [6; 16]. From ancient time the Greeks regarded their images of the gods as a specific feature of their culture. Their individuality and the power of representation attributed to them were not questioned until Hellenism when more intensive contacts with Jewish iconoclastic thought triggered debates about the received Greek world of images. Early Christian resistance to pagan customs led to a remarkable extent to iconoclastic polemics and image justification, with the history of the origin and creation of the images being an important argument. Aniconic representations were understood here either as a stage preceding figural presentation that must in principle be separated from it, or on the other hand as a process in whose course conceptional and artistic ability gradually developed into iconic representation. This late classical discourse in which the Jewish-Christian perception of Greek cultural practice and Greek theories on the development of the artistic skills that belong to civilization influenced each other reciprocally, addresses expressly the goals as well as the possibilities of pictorial representations. Although there is neither archaeological nor other evidence to substantiate the history of pictorial representation as it is described in the ancient texts, modern research was greatly influenced by this, as theories that free-standing sculpture originated from the representation of gods referred to these texts. This narrowed down the general question of the role of images in Greek religion to the category of the 'cult statue' to which a special position in relation to other image genres was attributed.

Testimonials to acts of worship with images provide a further clue to the ancient concept of image. Activities like the dressing, bathing or public presentation of icons as well as the hostile acts against icons passed down to us on many occasions support the assumption of a relationship between model and image bordering on identity [6; 17; 18; 19].

Sources regarding the Roman concept of image are rare. However, the considerable influence of Greek image presentation is clear, as e.g. Varro's statements about aniconic worship of images in early Rome (cf. Aug. Civ. 4,31) show [20]. When seen as a whole, Roman imagery is strongly marked by the Greek tradition. Because of this, specifically Roman imagery appears to be asserted particularly in the practice and ter-

minology of portrait art (→ Portrait), e.g. in the creation of ancestors' images [21].

→ Image; → Ideas, theory of; → Iconoclasm; → Mimesis; → Perception, theories of; → AESTHETICS

1 J.-P. VERNANT, Image et apparence dans la théorie platonicienne de la mimêsis, in: Journal de Psychologie 72, 1975, 133–160   2 S. SAÏD, Deux noms de l'image en grec ancien: idole et icône, in: CRAI, 1987, 309–330   3 J.-P. VERNANT, Figuration et image, in: Métis 5, 1990, 225–238   4 E. BENVENISTE, Le sens du mot κολοσσός et les noms grecs de la statue, in: RPh 6, 1932, 118–135   5 J. DUCAT, Fonctions de la statue dans la Grèce archaïque: *kouros* et *kolossos*, in: BCH 100, 1976, 239–251   6 A. A. DONOHUE, Xoana and the Origins of Greek Sculpture, 1988   7 B. SNELL, Die Entdeckung des Geistes, ⁵1980   8 J. J. POLLITT, The Ancient View of Greek Art, 1974   9 H. KOLLER, Die Mimesis in der Ant., 1954   10 G. F. ELSE, 'Imitation' in the Fifth Century, in: CPh 53, 1958, 73–90   11 G. SÖRBOM, Mimesis and Art, 1966   12 E. C. KEULS, Plato and Greek Painting, 1978   13 B. SCHWEITZER, Platon und die bildende Kunst der Griechen, 1953   14 N. DEMAND, Plato and the Painters, in: Phoenix 29, 1975, 1–20   15 G. WATSON, The Concept of 'Phantasia' from the Late Hellenistic Period to Early Neoplatonism, ANRW II 36.7, 4765–4810   16 C. CLERC, Les théories relatives au culte des images chez les auteurs grecs du IIᵉ siècle après J.-C., 1915   17 D. METZLER, Bilderstürme und Bilderfeindlichkeit in der Ant., in: M. WARNKE (ed.), Bildersturm, 1973, 14–29, 142–150   18 A. SCHNAPP, Why did the Greeks need Images?, in: J. CHRISTIANSEN, T. MELANDER (ed.), Ancient Greek and Related Pottery, 1988, 568–574   19 H. HOFFMANN, Why did the Greeks need Imagery?, in: Hephaistos 9, 1988, 143–162   20 P. BOYANCÉ, Les pénates et l'ancienne religion romaine, in: REA 54, 1952, 109–115   21 J. D. BRECKENRIDGE, Origins of Roman Republican Portraiture, ANRW I 4,826–854   22 H. G. NIEMEYER, Sémata. Über den Sinn griech. Standbilder, 1996, 12–31.

A.A.D./V.S.

Imaginarius (literally: 'imaginary') in Roman law the term for a legal transaction which expressed something other than what the parties actually intended. The most graphic example is the → *mancipatio nummo uno*, a transfer against, and by payment of, a merely symbolic copper coin (*aes*). Its outward appearance was that of a cash purchase; its actual effect, however, was to enable transfer for any purpose, it could thus be 'abstract' – an *imaginaria venditio* (Gai. Inst. 1,113). In early Roman law, surety meant subjugation to the power of seizure vested in the creditor. Release (*solutio*) also required a formal transaction. If the debt was just paid, release from surety was only achieved through an *imaginaria solutio*, again scales were symbolically struck with a coin (→ *libripens*). The *imaginaria solutio* later took on the form of a waiver of an existing debt. In addition to this very old legitimate use of legal forms for new purposes, from the 2nd or 3rd cent. AD onwards the *imaginaria venditio*, for example, also describes a transaction that is disapproved of, a mere fictitious transaction effected to conceal an illicit act (e.g. gift between marriage partners) (e.g. Paul. Dig. 18,1,55).

HONSELL/MAYER-MALY/SELB, 100f.; A. BERGER, s.v. Imaginarius, RE 9, 1094-1097.   G.S.

Imagines maiorum
A. TERM   B. FUNCTION   C. IMPACT ON OTHER REPRESENTATIONAL FORMS

A. TERM

Although *imago* essentially means any image, frequently even portrait busts of various materials, *imagines maiorum* (often just *imagines*) primarily designates the wax images (thus also *cerae*: Ov. Am. 1,8,65; Juv. 8,19) of the → ancestors, which were kept in the → atrium of distinguished Roman homes. An interpretation of Cicero (Verr. 2,5,36 *ius imaginis ad memoriam posteritatemque prodendae*) with MOMMSEN [7. 442-4] that such images only existed for curule magistrates is not certain (critical [3. 108; 9. 32f.]). The custom was considered old, existing since at least the 3rd cent. BC, and was described in detail by Polybius (6,53,4-10). Because there are no archaeological finds, it remains unclear whether they were face or (more likely) whole-body masks, and whether they were cast from a living person (thus, at least [5. 2³⁸]) or as death masks, or rather were freely modelled without a plaster mould.

B. FUNCTION

The images, which were created by *fictores* (Serv. Aen. 8,654) and were true-to-life representations of the deceased, were individually kept in cabinets (Pol. 6,53,4; Plin. HN 35,6), which were opened on feast-days (Pol. 6,53,6; *imagines aperire* is a technical term from Cic. Sull. 88 to SHA Tac. 19,6) and were crowned with laurels on special occasions (Cic. Mur. 88). However, there is not the slightest indication for a cultic worship of the *imagines maiorum* (IM) [1. 115-7]. The images were assigned *tituli* (Hor. Sat. 1,6,17; Val. Max. 5,8,3), which mentioned the names and offices, sometimes also the deeds, of the person represented (esp. Liv. 10,7,11; for the probable development of the *tituli* [5. 180-84]) and sometimes also contained exaggerations or inventions (Liv. 8,40,4-5). The IM kept the achievements and fame of the family impressed on the minds of subsequent generations, and served as an incentive to perform similar deeds (Sall. Iug. 4,5f.; more in [6]).

The most important function of the IM was, according to Pliny (HN 35,6), their use at the → burial (D. 2) of their descendants. The magisterial ancestors of the deceased, represented by persons who wore the masks with the features of the ancestors along with the robes of office to which they were entitled, accompanied the funeral procession (on carts: Pol. 6,53,8; later probably carried on biers) to the Forum and took their place in front of the *rostra* (→ Rostrum) on their → *sellae curules*, in order to hear the funeral oration (→ *laudatio funebris*), at the end of which their deeds were also listed with praise. This was not only a firm incentive for the younger listeners (Pol. 6,54,3), but also a powerful demonstration of the fame of one's *gens* in front of the entire citizenry (further interpretations e.g. in [4; 5]).

The participation of the IM in the funeral procession remained customary even in the Imperial period. At the burials of prominent *privati*, the images of related families were often carried along (e.g. Tac. Ann. 3,76,2), at imperial burials even those of arbitrary greats from Roman history (e.g. Cass. Dio 56,34,2). The deified members of the imperial house were not included, because they were not considered deceased. The participation of the IM in the funeral processions of certain condemned criminals (Caesar's assassins: Tac. Ann. 3,76,2; M. → Scribonius Libo Drusus: Tac. Ann. 2,32,1; Cn. → Calpurnius [II 16] Piso: *SC de Cn. Pisone patre* 76-82) was expressly forbidden. The participation of the ancestors in the funeral procession is no longer recorded for late antiquity, however, there continued to be IM in distinguished houses [5. 264-269].

C. IMPACT ON OTHER REPRESENTATIONAL FORMS

Because no IM have survived, their effect on portraiture in other media is difficult to prove. From about 60 BC onwards, realistic images of the ancestors of the mint masters are found on Roman coins, whose IM could have served as models (RRC 437,1-4; 439,1; 450,3; 455,1; 494,26-31: on this [10]). Highly debated is the relationship of Republican portrait sculpture (→ Portraiture) to the IM; even if the frequent assumption held earlier, that realistic portraits derived from death masks, is, for the most part, rejected today ([2]; against the differing position of [3] e.g. [8. 30f.]), a connection with (freely modelled) IM cannot be excluded.

1 F. BÖMER, Ahnenbild und Ahnenglaube im alten Rom, 1943, 104-123   2 F. BROMMER, Zu den röm. Ahnenbildern, in: MDAI(R) 60/61, 1953/54, 163-171 (= Röm. Porträts, 19/4, 336-348)   3 H. DRERUP, Totenmaske und Ahnenbild bei den Römern, in: MDAI(R) 87, 1980, 81-129   4 E. FLAIG, Die Pompa Funebris, in: O.G. OEXLE (ed.), Memoria als Kultur, 1995, 115-148   5 H.I. FLOWER, Ancestor Masks and Aristocratic Power in Roman Culture, 1996 (extensive bibliography)   6 G. LAHUSEN, Zur Funktion und Rezeption des röm. Ahnenbildes, in: MDAI(R) 92, 1985, 261-289   7 MOMMSEN, Staatsrecht 1, 442-447   8 R.R.R. SMITH, Greeks, Foreigners and Roman Republican Portraits, in: JRS 71, 1981, 24-38   9 A.N. ZADOKS-JOSEPHUS JITTA, Ancestral Portraiture in Rome and the Art of the Last Century of the Republic, 1932   10 H. ZEHNACKER, Moneta, 1973, 994-1007.   W.K.

Imaginiferi, Imaginifarii
The *imaginifer* was a soldier who, at least at festivals, carried an image (*imago*) of the *princeps* (Veg. Mil. 2,6; 2,7; Jos. Ant. Iud. 18,55); the *imaginiferi* certainly did not have any specifically military duties. There was an *imaginifer* in each legion, though he did not necessarily belong to the first cohort (→ *cohors*) (CIL III 2553: 3rd cohort). According to Vegetius (Mil. 2,7), *imaginiferi* also occurred in other units. *Imaginiferi* are attested in inscriptions for the *co-*

hortes urbanae and the → *vigiles* in Rome and for the legions and the units of the → *auxilia* (*alae, cohortes* and *numeri*), but not for the Praetorians. There is a pictorial representation of an *imaginifer* on the funerary relief of Genialis, holding the *imago* attached to a long pole in his right hand (Landesmuseum Mainz inv. no. p. 509; ILS 9167). The *imagines* are probably not identical to the images on the *signa* (→ Ensigns/Standards). It is unclear whether the army honoured only the reigning *princeps* in this way or also some of his predecessors. After Constantine I there were probably no longer any *imaginiferi* in the Roman army.

1 DOMASZEWSKI, 69   2 DOMASZEWSKI/DOBSON, 43
3 M. DURRY, Cohortes prétoriennes, ²1968, 206   4 R. O. FINK, Roman Military Records on Papyrus, 1971
5 G. WALSER, Röm. Inschrift-Kunst, 1988, 228f.   Y.L.B.

Imam (Arab. *imām*, in general 'conductor, leader'). 1. conductor of prayer, i.e. prayer-leader in the mosque, 2. leader of the community of all Muslims in succession to the prophet → Mohammed (Muḥammad), i.e. religious and political head. The schools of law and lines of belief evidently have different views about qualifications, investiture and offices/duties of the imam. Among the → Sunnites: defender of faith, (religious) law and justice. The imam following on from the four → Caliphs, who had direct links to Mohammed, were increasingly worldly rulers. Among the Twelve and other → Shiites: the qualities of the infallible imam – apart from communicating revelations – are prophetic. The twelfth imam, 'hidden' since the end of the 9th cent., is expected to return as Mahdī (a kind of → Messiah).

W. MADELUNG, s.v. Imāma, EI 3, 1163b–1169b.
H.SCHÖ.

Imaon Greek name of the Himalaya, old Indian Himavān, → Emodus.   K.K.

Imbrasus (Ἴμβρασος; *Ímbrasos*). River on Samos (Plin. HN 5,135), in ancient times also referred to as Parthenius (Str. 10,2,17), near the temple of Hera, modern Imvrasos. Ancient tradition holds that Hera was born under the *lygos* tree (chaste-tree) on the shore of the I. (Paus. 7,4,4; Apoll. Rhod. 1,187), a legend which repeatedly gave rise to cultic activities in the water of the I.

E. BUSCHOR, I., in: MDAI(A) 68, 1953 (1956), 1–10; H. J. KIENAST, Zum heiligen Baum der Hera auf Samos, in: MDAI(A) 106, 1991, 71–80; G. SHIPLEY, A History of Samos 800–188 B.C., 1987, 280.   H.SO.

Imbrius (Ἴμβριος; *Ímbrios*). Son of Mentor from Pedaeum. Married to Priamus' daughter Medesicaste, he lived at his father-in-law's house from the beginning of the Trojan War. He was killed in the battle for the ships of → Teucer (Hom. Il. 13,170ff.; Paus. 10,25,9).
C.W.

Imbros (Ἴμβρος; *Ímbros*, modern Turkish *Imroz adası*). Island in the northern Sporades at the southern exit of the Hellespont, 30 km long, 13 km wide, 225 square km in area, hill country rising to 597 m. The city of I., modern Kastro, was to the east of the north coast; remains of the city walls. Pelasgi or Tyrrheni are named as original inhabitants. Probably owing to Miltiades, I. became Athenian around 500 BC and remained so into the Imperial period (Hdt. 6,41; 104; Thuc. 7,57,2; Xen. Hell. 5,1,31). I. appears in the → Delian League with sums of tribute of between 3,300 drachmas and one talent (ATL 1, 292f.; 3, 289f.). Evidence: Hom. Il. 13,33; 14,281; Scyl. 67; IG XII 8 no. 46–149, pp.. 2ff. Suppl. p. 148; HN 261f.

K. FREDRICH, s.v. I., RE 9, 1105–1107; Id., I., in: MDAI(A) 33, 1908, 81ff.; E. OBERHUMMER, I., in: Beitr. zur alten Gesch. FS für H. Kiepert, 1898, 81ff.   H.KAL.

Imitatio see → Intertextuality; → Mimesis

Immaradus (Ἰμμάραδος/*Immárados*, Ἴσμαρος/*Ísmaros*). Eleusinian, son of → Eumolpus. Either alone or alongside his father, I. leads a Thracian army against the Athenians only to be killed in this 'Eleusinian War' by → Erechtheus (Apollod. 3,202). The duel was represented in a bronze group by → Myron on the Acropolis of Athens (Paus. 1,5,2).   RE.ZI.

Immiscere, se (*alicui rei*, 'to become involved in something'). A *suus heres* (immediate heir, → Succession, law of III A) could not effectively disclaim a legal or testamentary legacy according to → *ius civile* (*semel heres semper heres*), but if he declared the disclaimer before the praetor, he was treated by the praetor as if he had not become the heir (→ *abstentio*). However, if he had once behaved outwardly like an heir (*se immiscere*), he lost the → *beneficium abstinendi*. *Se immiscere* further designates the start of the discharge of other transactions. Only from the 4th cent. AD has *se immiscere* taken on the meaning of 'to interfere without authority' or 'to commit punishable acts' (differently [1]).

1 A. BERGER, s.v. I. se, RE 9, 1107–1112   2 KASER, RPR I, 715.   U.M.

Immolatio is the Latin term for the event of sacrifice, the sacrificial act, in contrast to the sacrificial offering (fruit, bread, wine) or the sacrificial animal (*hostia*). Sacrifice was one of the simplest ways to express oneself towards a deity in the private and state cult of Rome. The Latin expression *immolatio* describes this act; original meaning: sprinkling the sacrificial animal with salted sacrificial spelt (*immolare* = sprinkle with sacrificial meal, *mola salsa*; cf. Fest. 124 L.; Fest. 97 L. s.v. *immolare*; Serv. Aen. 10,541). *Immolatio* therefore denotes the act of purification before the actual killing. The term shows that the Romans saw the essence of the sacrifice not in the slaying, but in the offering, the dedication of the sacrificial animals; its extension to the killing of the animal only occurred later.

The *immolatio* served a variety of goals: increasing the strength of the gods through the offering (*mactare*), requesting a favour (Cato Agr. 139; 141), thanks, appeasement of an angry god, atonement for improper conduct towards a deity. A sacrifice was carried out before every act of state and political interest: at the assumption of office by officials (consuls, censors); before acts of war (departure for war, → *Lustratio*, → *Suovetaurilia*); from the time of Augustus before Senate meetings (burnt offering; Suet. Aug. 35; Cass. Dio 54,30,1); as well as, for example, at festivals of the gods, temple anniversaries or redemption of vows. A distinction must be made between bloodless and bloody sacrifices. The former chiefly took place in the home cult; because the original religion and gods were, for a large part, borrowed from the ancient farming calendar, primarily agricultural goods (fruits of the field, herd animals) were sacrificed here. To a particular extent, this included the first-fruit offerings (*primitiae*) as thanks for a good harvest. Because of their close relationship to the domestic environment, the offerings were frequently a share from the dining table, i.e. the meals that were offered to the household gods (→ *lares*, → *penates*). Likewise, this included incense-burning that gave the gods the pleasant aroma of certain plants (incense, spices), or fruits and other solid gifts (bread, cakes) were burned on the altar. Libations (wine, must, milk) could be performed alone or as preliminary offering before any other sacrifice. A prerequisite was, in any case, the suitability of the offerings for sacrifice, especially their flawlessness.

Bloody offerings, i.e. animal sacrifices, predominated in the state cult. Pigs, cattle and sheep were sacrificed above all. Besides being spotless, the animals had to meet certain criteria (age, gender, colour; Plin. HN 8,183). The *immolatio* was performed according to a fixed ritual. Many different acts were part of an animal sacrifice, which are well documented by both the ancient written sources and archaeology: a) Beginning of the sacrificial event: *probatio hostiae* or *victimae* (cf. Plin. HN 8,138; Cic. Leg. agr. 2,93), the examination of the animal for its suitability for sacrifice (represented in a statuette group in the Vatican, where a *pontifex minor* examines a bull for its fertility [1]). b) Decoration of the animal(s) with ribbons (→ *infulae*) or garlands of flowers. The horns of cattle were wrapped or had gilded frames (*frontale*) set between them. Cattle and pigs had a richly decorated ornamental band (*dorsualis*) laid across their back (cf. rear reliefs of the so-called Anaglypha Traiani [2; 3]). c) Ceremonial procession to the place of sacrifice.

After introductory requests for quiet by a herald (Donat. ad Ter. An. 24), and prayers by the leader of the sacrifice, the actual act of sacrifice began: d) Purification of the people participating in the sacrifice by washing their hands with water from a flowing source. e) Dedication of the sacrificial animal (the actual *immo-latio*) as central act, in which *mola salsa* (and later also wine) is poured over its head. Also, the sacrificial knife (*culter*; cf. Serv. Aen. 12,173; Juv. 12,84) and other sacrificial offerings (e.g. cakes; Varro in Non. 114,17) were sprinkled with salted spelt. After removal of the decoration, the leader of the sacrifice drew an imaginary line from the forehead to the tail of the animal with the knife, the symbolic sacrifice (discussion of the significance: [4]). f) Slaughter: stunning of the animal with a blow from the sacrificial hammer (*malleus*) by the sacrificial butcher (*popa, victimarius*), cutting of the carotid artery with a knife; this concluded the actual sacrifice. g) Examination of the entrails (*extispicium*), through which the will of the gods was ascertained based on the entrails (*exta*). h) Cooking of the entrails and burning them on the altar as the portion for the deity (meal, feast for the god = *epulum*), preparation and eating of the edible meat by the participants in the sacrifice.

Places used for sacrifice were specially dedicated, either permanently (→ Sanctuaries), only temporarily (Field of Mars for lustration) or once (in the field during war); → Altar. Any ritually clean free citizen was allowed to perform a sacrifice: private or family sacrifices were performed by the *pater familias*, at state sacrifices the leader of the sacrifice (magistrate, priest) only performed the symbolic sacrifice (cf. e), whilst sacrificial butchers performed the actual slaughter.

→ Sacrifice

1 H. R. GOETTE, Kuh und Stier als Opfertier. Zur probatio victimae, in: Bullettino della Commissione archeologica comunale di Roma 91, 1986, 61–68   2 U. RÜDIGER, in: AntPl 12, 1973, 161ff.   3 G. M. KOEPPEL, Die histor. Reliefs der röm. Kaiserzeit. II: Stadtröm. Denkmäler unbekannter Zugehörigkeit aus flavischer Zeit, in: BJ 186, 1986, 20; 23f. fig. 3.   4 LATTE, 388 n. 1.

LATTE, 45f., 375–393; H. PETERSMANN, Zu einem altröm. Opferritual (Cato de agricultura c. 141), in: RhM 116, 1973, 238–255, here 243–246; A. V. SIEBERT, Instrumenta sacra, 1998; F. FLESS, Opferdiener und Kultmusiker auf stadtröm. histor. Reliefs, 1995.   A.V.S.

Immunitas The exemption of individual legal persons from the obligations to military service, public service and consent, Lat. *immunitas* (*... vacationem militiae munerisque ... immunitatem appellari*: Dig. 50,16,18; Greek *atéleia, aneisphoría, aleitourgeisía*: Dig. 27,1,6,2), can be based on legal, generally formulated non-inclusion of a circle to which they belong, or on a temporary or long-term personal dispensation (Dig. 50,6: *de iure immunitatis*; 50,5: *de vacatione et excusatione munerum*). Depending on the duties in question, the *immunitas personae* exempted from burdens which placed physical or intellectual demands on individuals, the *immunitas patrimonii* from duties imposed on fortunes and, thus, their respective owners. Despite these categories, the rules of exemption are very different in their details. Legal reasons for exemptions could include age, gender, class (e.g. senators, knights; in

Christian times also priests and monks), membership of corporations important to provisioning (e.g. the *navicularii*); among the reasons for dispensation: physical weakness, poverty, other public or generally useful professional demands (e.g. for professors, rhetors, doctors), or even special awarding of honours (e.g. deserved high office, veterans) or other rewards (e.g. for athletes, actors).

Besides the *immunitas* for individuals, there is – particularly frequent in the period of the Roman Republic and granted by the Senate – the exemption of entire communities, mostly based on an ancient Roman treaty right. Thus, for example, an *immunitas ipso iure* was held in Italy by the Roman → *coloniae*, and likewise – because of their autonomy – the Italic cities with the status of a *civitas foederata et libera*. On the other hand, Roman *coloniae* and other – also autonomous – cities in the provinces have *immunitas* only through special treaty concessions or sovereign awards (Tac. Ann. 2,47; Liv. 45,26,13f.). In the Imperial period, this type of release occurred through imperial edict or *epistula* (Dig. 27,1,17,1; ILS 423).

→ Liturgies; → Munus, Munera

F.F. ABBOTT, A.C. JOHNSON, Municipal Administration in the Roman Empire, 1926, 504 (repr. 1968); JONES, LRE 535f., 734–737; MOMMSEN, Staatsrecht 3, 224–244.
C.G.

Impasto Modern technical term for a type of pottery of the Villanovan, Etruscan and Lazian cultures (→ Etrusci II. archaeology), designating vessels made of badly burned, uncleaned clay. Impasto is largely shaped by hand and not with a → potter's wheel. Typical vessels of the Villanovan period are biconical urns for ashes, amphorae and bowls. In the orientalizing period new forms appeared in Etruria, borrowed from the Greek and Phoenician repertoire and often associated with drinking wine. They are associated with the emergence of the aristocratic symposium. Variations of impasto, especially *impasto rosso* appear at the same time. The thin-walled 'buccheroid' impasto marks the transition to → bucchero. Though its distribution is generally narrowly confined to the northern and central Apennine peninsula, impasto pottery is sometimes found even at far distant locations, like Carthage, for instance [1].

1 H.G. NIEMEYER, R.F. DOCTER, Die Grabung unter dem Decumanus Maximus von Karthago. Vorber. über die Kampagnen 1986–1991, in: MDAI(R) 100, 1993, 227–229, fig. 11,e, pl. 58,3.

A. RATHJE, A Banquet Service from the Latin City of Ficana, in: Analecta Romana Instituti Danici 12, 1983, 7–29; R.D. DE PUMA, Etruscan Tomb-Groups, 1986, 8–10.
R.D.

Impedimenta Two Latin words, *impedimenta* and *sarcina*, were used to describe the baggage train that accompanied the Roman legions. *Impedimenta* referred to the heavy packs containing the supplies and equipment of the entire legion. They were transported by pack animals (Pol. 6,27; 6,40; Liv. 28,45; Caes. B Gall. 5,31,6). These packs held tents, the officers' belongings, hand mills for the grain, food supplies, weapons, and after a victory, → war booty and money. Originally, the word *impedimenta* was used only in reference to things. However, as language evolved, it also began to refer to people and animals – to the sick and the injured, even to the women and children who accompanied the legions on their march; pack animals as well as, for example, the carts necessary to transport the injured were also included (SHA Alex. Sev. 47,2–3). The *impedimenta* did not only have an important material value, but also a psychological one; to protect the baggage train, especially during a battle, the field commanders had to set up sentries.

The *calones* were responsible for the *impedimenta* both during the march and while in camp (Veg. Mil. 3,6; cf. Caes. B Gall. 6,36,3; Suet. Cal. 51,2). Normally, the *calones* were unarmed and only under exceptional circumstances fought in battles (Liv. 27,18,12; Caes. B Gall. 2,24,2). Occasionally, they were sent out to collect supplies for the troops (Tac. Hist. 3,20,3).

The term *sarcina* primarily referred to the packs of individual soldiers, to their tools, but especially their → weapons and their provisions (Jos. BI 3,93ff.; Veg. Mil. 1,19; 2,23). During training marches, food supplies sufficient for three days were taken along; during military campaigns, enough for 17 days (Jos. BI 3,95; SHA Alex. Sev. 47,1). In order to lighten the *impedimenta* and to increase the mobility of his army, Marius [I 1] ordered that each soldier carry his own *sarcina*, instead of having the pack animals carry it (Frontin. Str. 4,1,7: *vasa* and *cibaria*). The soldiers, therefore, began referring to themselves as the *muli Mariani*, 'mules of Marius'. Overall, according to ancient authors, these packs weighed between 30 to 50 kg per soldier. For very fast marches, the men might be temporarily relieved of their packs: the *miles* was then *expeditus* (Bell. Afr. 75).

1 N. FUENTES, The Mule of a Soldier, in: Journal of the Roman Military Equipment Studies 2, 1991, 65–99
2 F. STOLLE, Der röm. Legionär und sein Gepäck (mulus marianus), 1914, 67f.
Y.L.B.

Imperator Old Latin *induperator*; Greek στρατηγός (*stratēgós*), from Sulla onwards, however, αὐτοκράτωρ (*autokrátōr*); also transcribed ἰμπεράτωρ (*imperátōr*). General term for the supreme military commander of Roman or foreign origin.

A. REPUBLIC   B. PRINCIPATE   C. IMPERIAL PERIOD FROM THE 3RD CENTURY

A. REPUBLIC
Imperator was not a title of office. However, holders of the imperium used this expression from the 2nd cent. BC in decrees and dedications, primarily outside of Rome and Italy, instead of the regular name for the

office or function, which was only relevant for Rome, such as (pro)consul or (pro)praetor (CIL I² 614: *L. Aimilius L.f. inpeirator decreivit*, 189 BC; I² 2951a: *iudicium addeixit C. Valerius C.f. Flaccus imperator*, 'Tabula Contrebiensis', 87 BC). In the late Republican period, this non-technical use also found its way into official announcements (CIL I² 593, *lex Iulia municipalis*). The Roman soldiery can be assumed to have addressed their commanders with *imperator*.

Outwardly not distinguished from this general function of the term is its use as an honorary title. The salutation as *imperator* by his own soldiers after a successful battle allowed the holder of the imperium to place this address after his name as a title. The custom of the imperatorial acclamation is first recorded in the literature for the year 209 BC (Pol. 10,40,2–5; Liv. 27,19, 3–6; its historicity is disputed). Definite epigraphic and numismatic evidence exists for the 1st cent. BC, when it became customary with Sulla to record the number of these acclamations. The origins of the soldierly salutation (Hellenistic or genuinely Roman) and its significance (recognition, confirmation of a commander's qualities) are not certain. The greeting as *imperator* by the soldiers was not a basis for any legal claims.

The Senate could agree to such an acclamation and grant a triumph for the victorious commander. However, they could also refuse it. From the 60s of the 1st cent. BC, the Senate also granted the title of *imperator* for successful generals, independent of any soldierly acclamation (Cic. Pis. 44). The title of *imperator* was assumed for the time of the → *imperium* as a visible sign of *virtus*. With the crossing of the → pomerium, the *imperium* was lost and the title of *imperator* was given up. The triumphator, however, could call himself *imperator* in Rome for one day (thus for example CIL I² 626). From Sulla onwards, it became usual to document the iteration of the imperatorial acclamations in the title (e.g. RRC 359: *L. Sulla imper. iterum*; CIL XI 2104: *Cn. Pompeio Cn. f. Magno imper. iter.*).

From the 70s of the 1st cent. BC onwards it became increasingly frequent for the titulature not only to contain the title *imperator* but also current and former offices held. The first known evidence is an inscription from Oropus for the consul of the year 79 BC, P. Servilius Vatia Isauricus: ὕπατον, αὐτοκράτορα (*hýpaton, autokrátora*, IG VII 244, around 75 BC). The position of the *imperator* varied in the individual titulatures (e.g. CIL VI 1316: *cos. imp. iter.*; CIL IX 5837: *imp. cos. ter*). Caesar finally introduced the permanent use after 49 BC. *Imperator* no longer stood for one single victory, but for the military authority of its bearer. Counting thus became redundant, and the title was then also used in Rome. *Imperator*, however, did probably not yet become a component of Caesar's name (so, however, Suet. Iul. 76; Cass. Dio 43,44,2), even if it could outwardly take the place of the cognomen (CIL I² 788: *C. Caesare imp.*; but in the same way also AE 1991, 168: *Q. Scipio imp.*; generally [5]).

In the triumvirate, the titulature of the three rulers of Rome showed strict equality until about 39 BC. No later than 38 BC, however, the title of *imperator* was utilized in new ways in the power struggle between the individual potentates. C. Iulius Caesar (Octavianus) now replaced the inherited *praenomen* with *imperator*, and added the cognomen *Caesar* as a new gentilicium. The positive associations that these two names elicited were to be connected with his person alone. Characteristic for Octavian's titulature was the use of *imperator* both as a name and a title (e.g. CIL V 526: *Imp. Caesari divi f. imp. V*). In 29 BC, the Senate officially sanctioned the *praenomen imperatoris* of the now sole ruler, and in 27 BC decided on the honorary name 'Augustus', so that Octavian could call himself, as in the Republican *tria nomina*, 'Imperator Caesar Augustus' [9]. The purely military power the princeps drew upon was now expressed only in his name and in the recorded number of salutations.

B. PRINCIPATE

While a certain inflation of the title of *imperator* occurred in the time of the triumvirate [10], in the early Principate a deliberate restriction of the *titulum imperii* (Ov. Fast. 4,675f.) to the ruler and the male members of his family gradually set in. In 27 BC, Q. Iunius Blaesus was the last commander to be allowed to accept the imperatorial acclamation of his soldiers without being a member of the Imperial family (Tac. Ann. 3,74). In Rome, Augustus exercised restraint in using the name of *imperator* after 27 BC. His successors Tiberius, Gaius and Claudius did completely without the *praenomen imperatoris*, in view of the propagated *res publica restituta*. Nero, on the other hand, used it again, if only occasionally. Only with Vespasian did *imperator* finally become a fixed component of the ruler's name. As Augustus once did, this Princeps again placed the cognomen *Caesar* after the *praenomen imperatoris*. This combination quickly gained acceptance with his successors [8]. In the 2nd cent. AD, *imperator* in this word combination developed into a title under Marcus Aurelius and L. Verus. *Imperator* was now placed together with *Caesar* in front of the actual name of the emperor (e.g. AE 1992, 1184: *Imperator Caesar M. Aurelius Antoninus Augustus*; Greek AE 1993, 1554). The imperial titulature was now composed of the word pair *imperator* and *Caesar*, the name of the ruler, and of honorary and official titles. Until the end of the Principate in the 3rd cent. AD, this form was maintained over time, a lengthy list of epithets and triumphal as well as official titles was added. In the literary tradition, *imperator* became increasingly common as a non-titular term for 'emperor' from the 2nd cent. AD onwards.

C. IMPERIAL PERIOD FROM THE 3RD CENTURY

Towards the end of the 3rd cent., the meaning of Imperatorial acclamation finally changed. Not based on a concrete victory, but rather independent thereof, the *salutatio* of the army now took place every year.

This annual proclamation of the emperor as *imperator* outwardly served only to count the years of his reign. Also, in the 3rd cent., the raising to emperor by the army replaced the traditional transfer of power by the Senate, which was losing influence at the time. Legitimate rule was now solely based on military acclamation. *Imperator* was now the correct term for the emperor [6]. Even though *dominus noster* (*d.n.*) gradually gained acceptance as a title in the Dominate [8], *imperator* was still used as an appellative until the end of antiquity.

1 R. COMBÈS, Imperator, 1966   2 J. DEININGER, Von der Republik zur Monarchie, in: ANRW 1,1, 982–997   3 CHR. GIZEWSKI, Zur Normativität und Struktur der Verfassungsverhältnisse in der späteren röm. Kaiserzeit, 1988   4 D. KIENAST, Imperator, in: ZRG 78, 1961, 403–421   5 J. LINDERSKI, Q. Scipio Imperator, in: Imperium sine fine, 1996, 145–185   6 F. DE MARTINO, Storia della costituzione romana, 4.1, ²1974, 212ff.; 5, ²1975, 241f.   7 D. MCFAYDEN, The History of the Title Imperator under the Roman Empire, thesis 1922   8 D. A. MUSCA, Le denominazioni del principe nei documenti epigrafici romani, 1979   9 SYME, RP 1, 361–377   10 L. SCHUMACHER, Die imperatorischen Akklamationen der Triumvirn und die auspicia des Augustus, in: Historia 34, 1985, 191–222.   L.d.L.

Imperial aramaic see → Official Aramaic

Imperial family, women of the In contrast to the Republic, the Roman Empire, not constituted as an Imperial monarchy, brought no new legal opportunities for political influence by the women of the Imperial house. The Imperial women were never able to exercise power in their own right. However, due to their proximity to the centre of power, they gained influence through their husbands, brothers and, above all, sons (in the 1st cent., particularly → Agrippina [3] the Younger). With weak or under-age rulers (→ Emperors, child) they could in fact act in their place.

For a long time, → Augustus remained authoritative for the roles and positions of the Imperial women; his victory over a Hellenistic-Oriental queen, → Cleopatra [II 12], and his chief Roman rival M. Antonius [I 9], who had supposedly become 'degenerate' because of her, was part of the *realpolitik* and ideological foundations of his rule. Although Augustus propagated the *mores maiorum* (→ Mos maiorum) of the Republic, his sister and his wife received honours and honorary rights quite early. In 35 BC, he granted → Octavia [2] and → Livia [2] statues, as well as the right to manage their own affairs without a legal guardian, and to enjoy the same security and inviolability as the people's tribunes (*sacrosanctitas*) (Cass. Dio 49,38,1). In 9 BC, the *ius (trium) liberorum* was granted to Livia only (Cass. Dio 55,2,5ff.; → ius E. 2). The dynastic structure of the → Principate became increasingly clear: while the marriages of his 'heiress and daughter' → Iulia [6] to Marcellus, Agrippa and Tiberius still corresponded to the model of connections between aristocrats of the Repub-

lic, the granting of the title of Augusta to Livia, her adoption into the Iulian family (through the testament of Augustus: e.g., Tac. Ann. 1,8,1), as well as her appointment as priestess of the Divus Augustus (senate resolution: Cass. Dio 56,46,1) were new steps that were supposed to support the standing of her son Tiberius as successor. In AD 42, Livia's grandson Claudius [III 1] arranged for her consecration (Diva Iulia Augusta; → *consecratio*) on the anniversary of her marriage to Augustus, in order to emphasize his familial roots and to gain legitimation thereby.

As with the emperors themselves, a significant portion of the monarchization of Imperial women took place within the cultic/charismatic sphere. Following the Hellenistic model and starting in the Augustan age, the women of the *domus Augusta* – particularly in the Greek east, but also in Italy and the western provinces – were assimilated to female divinities already during their lifetime and identified with them (among them, cultic personifications such as Fortuna, Salus, Pietas, Concordia, Fecunditas) and, if dynastic considerations called for it, they were consecrated after their death by the Senate at the request of the emperor (Iulia [13] Drusilla, Livia, → Poppaea [2], Claudia [II 2] Neronis, → Flavia [2] Domitilla, Iulia Titi, Ulpia → Marciana, → Plotina, → Matidia [1] the Elder, Vibia → Sabina, → Faustina [2], → Faustina [3], → Iulia [12] Domna, → Iulia [17] Maesa, → Lollia [1] Paulina, Mariniana). Like Hellenistic queens, the Imperial women appeared as portrait busts on eastern coins (in Alexandria [1] and other cities), on Roman coins (with the exception of Octavia under M. Antonius [I 9]) only from Agrippina [3] the Younger onwards (starting in AD 50). Also in Hellenistic tradition, cities and settlements were named for Imperial women (Liviopolis, Iulias, Colonia Agrippinensis, Plotinopolis, Marcianopolis, Colonia Marciana Traiana Thamugadi, Faustinopolis, etc.; in late antiquity: Helenopolis, Eudoxias, Theodoropolis, etc.).

Like male members of the dynasty, Imperial women had, as it were, a universal presence with regard to name and image: statues, historical reliefs, dedicated buildings, coins and gems; public prayers and sacrifices; celebrations of their → birthdays, weddings and births; recording of familial events in official calendars such as, for example, the acta of the → Arvales fratres, → Fasti Ostienses, → Feriale Duranum. In the 2nd cent. (see also → Adoptive emperors), such honours further increased in order to strengthen the dynastic basis of the emperors: thus, a temple was built in Rome for Hadrian's mother-in-law Matidia, and Faustina [3] received the title of Augusta already under her father Antoninus [1] Pius and, under her husband Marcus Aurelius, the title *mater castrorum* for her presence in camp. In the Severan dynasty (193–235; → Septimius [II 7] Severus), which put a strong emphasis on continuity, this increased to a (partially unofficial) adulatory titulature (*mater castrorum et senatus et patriae*) – an expression of both the need for support from the military and a general intensification of the imperial self-representation (continued in the 3rd cent.: Otacilia Severa, Herennia Etruscilla, Ulpia Severina, Magna Urbica, Galeria Valeria).

In the Tetrarchy (turn of the 3rd to the 4th cent., → *tetrarches*), women played no role in aiding dynastic legitimation, and marriage connections served merely to consolidate the reciprocal relationships between the rulers. Imperial women only received new dynastic significance in the Valentinian-Theodosian dynasty (4th and 5th cents.: Galla [2], → Galla [3] Placidia, Licinia → Eudoxia [2], → Aelia [4] Eudoxia, → Pulcheria [2]). The varying origin of the Imperial women in late antiquity, some of whom came from the lowest classes (→ Helena [2], → Theodora [1]) or were even of Germanic descent (Aelia [4] Eudoxia, → Verina, Euphemia [2]), is considered a sign of the social permeability of the time.

Politically effective activity by the Imperial women is recorded or assumed many times in the Principate and late antiquity; however, the information is often difficult to evaluate, because the records vacillate between the extremes of traditional expectations (above all in eulogies) and a negative view in the literary sources (love of extravagance, immorality including the insinuation of incest, intrigues, involvement in conspiracies up to and including high treason, poisoning). Because of their fundamental dynastic significance, Imperial women frequently appear in the literary tradition as 'emperor-makers' (e.g. Livia, Agrippina [3] the Younger, Plotina, Iulia [17] Maesa), in order to ridicule the respective male rulers (most often their sons). The Imperial support of Christianity established a new, partly also politically relevant, sphere of activity for Imperial women; more strongly than in earlier cents., they appeared as founders (e.g. Helena [2]). Notable is their exertion of influence in times of religious strife, e.g. → Iustina against Ambrosius; Aelia [4] Eudoxia against Iohannes [4] Chrysostomos; Theodora, almost a co-regent of Iustinianus [1] I. (Zon. 14,6,1), in favour of the Monophysites. → Eudokia [1] was exemplary in her asceticism and piety, Pulcheria in transmitting Christian moral ethics (virginity) to female role models.

A. DEMANDT, Das Privatleben der röm. Kaiser, ²1998; U. HAHN, Die Frauen des röm. Kaiserhauses und ihre Ehrungen im griech. Osten, 1994; L. JAMES, Women, Men and Eunuchs, 1997; RAEPSAET-CHARLIER; W. SCHULLER, Frauen in der röm. Geschichte, 1987; H. TEMPORINI – GRÄFIN VITZTHUM, Frauen und Politik im ant. Rom, in: P. KNEISSL (ed.), Imperium Romanum. FS Karl Christ, 1998, 705–732.   H.T.-V.

Imperial period see → Dominatus; → Periods, division into; → Princeps; → Principate

Imperios(s)us Roman cognomen, designating excessive personal harshness, in the Republican period in the Manlii family (→ Manlius) in the 4th cent. BC.

KAJANTO, Cognomina, 266.   K.-L.E.

Imperium In the broader sense the general military power of command of any (also non-Roman) commander; in the narrow sense, the military command of the highest officials in Rome (consul, praetor, dictator, *magister equitum*).

In the early Republic *imperium* is a partial aspect of the Roman power of office (*auspicium*). No later than the end of the 4th cent. BC do foreign policy conflicts with neighbours lead to the emphasis and stress on the military competence of the upper officials (*auspicium imperiumque*: Plaut. Amph. 192; 196). Finally in the late Republic, *imperium* denotes the overall power of office, i.e. it now stands for the unity of military and civil magisterial power [1]. This so-called 'total *imperium*' therefore belongs – other than earlier researchers saw it [2] – in a later phase of Roman constitutional development, and not in the regal period or the early Republic [3]. The civil, and above all jurisdictional authority of the higher officials thus does not derive from *imperium* [4]. The holders of *imperium* are elected by the Roman people in the original military assembly (→ *comitia centuriata*). At the same time they also receive the right to consult the gods (auspices). However, they have to have their military competence (*auspicia militaria*) confirmed after taking office by a law (so-called *lex curiata de imperio*) in the curial assembly (*comitia curiata*). This law is a relic of an earlier time, when the elections of the highest officials still took place in this public assembly [1].

The external symbols of the power of office of the Roman magistrates *cum imperio* are the lictors, who precede them with bundles of rods (*fasces*), to which the axe is added outside of Rome as a symbol of sovereignty. The number of *fasces* depends on the rank of the officials (dictator: 24, consul: 12, praetor: 6) [5]. The lictors implement the police power (→ *coercitio*) of the *imperium* holder. To protect Roman citizens from the arbitrary use of power, this *coercitio* was limited from 300 BC onwards by the legislation of *provocatio* [6]. Like all officials, *imperium* holders are also subject to various control mechanisms which express themselves in legal principles: the principle of annuity and collegiality, the ban on the continuation and iteration of the office, as well as the plurality of offices [7]. In contrast to lower officials, the higher-ranking have the right of veto (*ius intercessionis*, → *intercessio*). Within this frame of reference, their power of office is therefore characterized as *potestas* (*maior* as opposed to *minor*) [1].

In the Republic one fundamental task of the magistrates *cum imperio* is the primarily military but also increasingly administrative activity in the areas outside the city (*militiae*). Because the assignments could hardly be managed by the incumbent *imperium* holders due to the increasing distances between the areas of office, new official positions were created from the middle of the 3rd cent. BC (*praetor peregrinus*, praetors for the newly established provinces of Sicilia, Sardinia et Corsica, Hispania citerior and Hispania ulterior) [1]. Preferred, however, was the extension of official power beyond the regular year of office (*prorogatio imperii*), which was practiced from 327/26 and, as a rule, had to be passed by the Senate and people. The former magistrates are now, 'in place of a consul' (*pro consule*) or 'in place of a praetor' (*pro praetore*), promagistrates (→ Promagistratus) and still for the most part active as military commanders in the areas outside the cities. They are subordinate to the regular higher officials of the same rank. Their job is of varying duration and depends on their assignment. Independently of this, their proconsular or propraetorian *imperium* ends with the crossing of the Roman city boundary (*pomerium*). Promagistrates who are granted a triumph in Rome therefore receive the *imperium* in the *domi* area for a day through a special resolution of the people ([4. 15–21]; fundamental [8]).

From the time of Cornelius [I 90] Sulla there is a geographical separation of the magisterial areas of responsibility. The *imperium* holders now have to serve out their regular year of office in Rome itself (*domi*). Then follows an additional year as promagistrate in the region outside the city (*militiae*), i.e. as a governor in the Roman provinces [9]. The higher officials do not, however, lose their *imperium militiae* through this separation. The military power of command still applies in the years between 80 and 49 BC [9; 10]. Through a *senatus consultum* in the year 53 and a *lex Pompeia* in the year 52, magistracies and promagistracies are separated from each other by a 5–year interval. The promagistracy now loses the character of an extended power of office, and the proconsular and propraetorian *imperia* are thus, in effect, detached from the regular higher office.

This development reaches its conclusion with Augustus. Senior officials under the Principate no longer hold the *de facto* military command [9]. This loss of substance thus leads Roman jurists to the construction of an *imperium merum* and an *imperium mixtum* in the 3rd cent. AD. These terms refer, as regards content, to the magisterial jurisdiction which is seen as a fundamental element of the power of office of the higher magistrates whose authority is limited to civil matters (Dig. 2,1,3f.; Dig. 1,21,5,1; 50,1,26) [4. 27f.].

The proconsular *imperium* of the triumvirs and the *princeps* goes back to the extraordinary commands of the late Republic. The unresolved problems of a large area of rule, but also the political ambition of the leading aristocrats of Rome, forces the transfer of such *imperia extraordinaria* or *infinita* to individuals, who mostly hold a cross-province military authority as promagistrates or *privati* of proconsular rank (Cn. Pompeius, C. Iulius Caesar). This extraordinary power in the *militiae* area competes with the *imperium* of the individual provincial governors, and is not an *imperium maius*. Advances for conferring such a higher command (57 and 43 BC; Cic. Att. 4,1,7; Cic. Phil. 11,30) are not successful [9]. Only in the Principate does the *imperium maius* turn up in the sense of a *potestas maior* with

regard to the proconsuls [11]. During the civil wars the triumvirate (43–33 BC), as a special power besides the consulate, then combines the proconsular power of command which governs several provinces, with magisterial authorities within the *pomerium,* on the basis of the *lex Titia.* The Sullan separation of the areas of office, *domi* and *militiae,* is set aside with this arrangement [12].

The *imperium consulare* or *proconsulare* (thus first in Val. Max. 6,9,7; 8,1, Amb. 2) is, besides the *tribunicia potestas,* the legal basis of the Principate. It stands for the absolute power of command of the ruler over the legions, and his sole power over the most important provinces. From 23 BC onwards a privilege validates this *imperium* within the city of Rome as well (Cass. Dio 53,32,5). This power is conferred on the new ruler by the Senate. The day of the bestowal, or later also the day of being elevated by the army, is regarded as the day of coming to power (*dies imperii*). The *imperium proconsulare* is not included in the imperial titulature. Until the reigns of Nero and Trajan, the *princeps* does not call himself 'proconsul'. Military power is recognizable only in the use of the *praenomen imperatoris* and the listing of the imperatorial acclamations. The individual authorities, rights and privileges of the *princeps* fuse to form a unified monarchical power (*imperatoria potestas*) early on. This development is already clear in the so-called appointment law of Vespasian, the *lex de imperio Vespasiani,* of the year AD 69 ([13]; cf. CIL VI 930). In the 3rd cent. AD, with the disempowerment of the Senate, the transfer of *imperium,* i.e. the imperial power and with it the legitimization by this committee, lost significance. Its place was taken by the acclamation to → *imperator* by the army [14].

Besides its military and constitutional significance one use of *imperium* in a spatial sense already appears in the Republic, *imperium Romanum.*
→ IMPERATOR

1 J. BLEICKEN, Zum Begriff der röm. Amtsgewalt, 1981   2 MOMMSEN, Staatsrecht 1, 22ff., 116ff.   3 A. HEUSS, Gedanken und Vermutungen zur frühen röm. Regierungsgewalt, 1982 (= Gesammelte Schriften 2, 1995, 908–985)   4 W. KUNKEL, Die Magistratur, 1995   5 TH. SCHÄFER, Imperii insignia, 1989   6 J. MARTIN, Die Provokation in der klass. und späten Republik, in: Hermes 98, 1970, 72–96   7 J. BLEICKEN, Die Verfassung der röm. Republik, ⁷1995   8 W. F. JASHEMSKI, The Origins and History of the Proconsular and Propraetorian Imperium to 27 B.C., 1950   9 J. BLEICKEN, Imperium consulare/proconsulare, in: FS A. Heuß 1993, 117–133   10 A. GIOVANNINI, Consulare imperium, 1983, 83ff.   11 W. ECK, A. CABALLOS, F. FERNANDEZ, Das senatus consultum de Cn. Pisone patre, 1996   12 J. BLEICKEN, Zwischen Republik und Principat, 1990   13 P. A. BRUNT, Lex de imperio Vespasiani, in: JRS 67, 1977, 95–116   14 F. DE MARTINO, Storia della costituzione romana, 4.1, ²1974, 460ff.; 5, ²1975, 228ff.   L.d.L.

Imperium Romanum see → Roman Empire

Impluvium The water basin in the → atrium of the Roman house in which rainwater from the → compluvium, the opening of the atrium, was collected and which was often part of a → cistern.

> E. M. Evans, The Atrium Complex in the Houses of Pompeii, 1980; R. Förtsch, Arch. Komm. zu den Villenbriefen des jüngeren Plinius, 1993, 30f.　　　　　　C.HÖ.

Imports / Exports The core of the debate triggered by M. I. Finley [1] on the ancient economy deals with the quantitative and qualitative classification of trade and → commerce within the entire scheme of the ancient economy. Clearly, more modern economic historical research is interested above all in the cities and their position in the ancient economy. The cities were designated as consumer cities by the 'primitivists' and 'neo-primitivists' in imitation of Max Weber. This perspective could be based above all on the comprehensive grain imports to Athens and Rome.

In contrast to this, many texts indicate that ancient cities not only imported but also exported goods. Imports and exports are mentioned together in political theory. This is true even for the ideal polis as described by Plato (Pl. Resp. 370e–371b; cf. Pl. Leg. 847b-d; Aristot. Pol. 1257a 31–34; 1327a 25–27). Access to the sea and a favourably situated harbour (→ Harbours, Docks) held great importance for the imports, but also for exports and the export-oriented city production.

Already in the 8th and 7th cents. BC, Corinth exported ceramics to Italy and to the Black Sea coast; the favourable location of Corinth supported transit trade and imports equally. By the 5th and 4th cents. BC, Athens had also developed not only as the most important commerce centre in the eastern Mediterranean region but also as a production centre. Athens exported ceramics in significant quantities to regions outside Greece from the late archaic period. The coats (Xen. Mem. 2,7,6) manufactured in Megara were surely likewise earmarked for exports. There developed a significant and sophisticated specialization in → crafts (Xen. Cyr. 8,2,5) simultaneously with the growing export opportunities. Alexandria was instrumental among the cities that exported crafted products; Strabo, who describes this city as the 'greatest trading place in the world' (μέγιστον ἐμπόριον τῆς οἰκουμένης), states emphatically that the exports were in greater volume than the imports (Str. 17,1,7; 17,1,13; cf. Cic. Rab. Post. 40). Furthermore, smaller cities in Egypt also produced exports for the foreign markets; this holds true also for textile production in → Oxyrhynchus, whose trade and communication extended beyond Egypt.

Not even Rome in the Principate period can be described as exclusively an import or consumer city; the funeral inscriptions alone (cf. esp. CIL VI) document more than 200 trades and professions. Roman bronze products reached Britain; similarly, clay lamps with relief decoration from the city of Rome were traded in the 1st cent. AD throughout the entire Mediterranean area; likewise, imported raw materials such as papyrus in the *officina* of Fannius (Plin. HN 13,75) were processed in Rome and at least to some extent exported. Many cities in the Roman empire are known as production centres of wares found in wide distribution, for instance, → Capua with the bronze vessels of L. Ansius Epaphroditus and of P. Cipius Polybius. Nonetheless, it must be conceded that due to the condition of the sources it is not possible to put together anything close to an exact balance of trade for ancient cities.

→ Economy

1 Finley, Ancient Economy　2 P. M. Fraser, Ptolemaic Alexandria, 1972　3 F. Kolb, Rom. Die Geschichte der Stadt in der Ant., 1995, 464–507　4 J. Kunow, Die capuanischen Bronzegefäßhersteller L. Ansius Epaphroditus und P. Cipius Polybius, in: BJ 185, 1985, 215–242　5 P. v. Minnen, The Volume of Oxyrhynchos Textile Trade, in: MBAH 5,2, 1986, 88–95　6 L. Neesen, Demiurgoi und Artifices, 1989　7 H. Parkins, C. Smith, Trade, Traders and the Ancient City, 1998　8 Rostovtzeff, Roman Empire　9 I. Scheibler, Griechische Töpferkunst, 1983, 150–186.　　　　　H.-J.D.

Impulse (ὁρμή/*hormé*; Lat. *appetitus, impetus*). *Hormé*, initially meaning 'quick movement, outbreak, attack' or 'new beginning' (cf. Hom. Il. 4, 466; Hdt. 1,11, 23; Pl. Ti. 27c 2), stands for psychological drives, wishes, impulses or tendencies. These are out of the individuals's control and can be directed at rational or irrational goals alike. Thus, → Plato [1] repeatedly uses *hormé* for rational inclinations (e.g. Pl. Phlb. 57d 1; Pl. Resp. 611e 4; cf. Pl. Ep. 7,325e 1), including also the more godlike impulse towards philosophy (*h. theiotéra*: Pl. Phdr. 279a 9; cf. Pl. Prm. 130b 1; 135d 2 f.). In Plato's theory of → pleasure, on the other hand, *hormé* denotes an irrational longing (Pl. Phlb. 35c-d). Aristotle understands *hormé* as a natural impulse, the restraint of which is a form of violence (Aristot. An. post. 95a 1; Aristot. Metaph. 1015a 27 ff.; 1023a 9 ff.; 1072b 12). He therefore speaks of a natural impulse (*physikè hormé*; Aristot. Mag. mor. 1,34,24; cf. 2,3,12 f.) towards → virtue, and similarly of a general inclination towards political association (Aristot. Pol. 1253a 29).

In → Epicurus, *hormé* has the technical sense of impulse of movement (Diog. Laert. 10,115,3 and 6). Arius [1] Didymus provides an overview over the complex theory of drives in → Stoicism (in Stob. 9–9a,86 f. Wachsmuth). He states that the Stoics distinguished five types of *hormaí* (partly rational, partly irrational) and two forms of *aphormaí* (for interpretation cf. [3. 224 ff.]). From Chrysippus [2] the Stoics sought to show that the primal drive (*prótē h.*) – i. e. the earliest impulse to occur in a person's life – is aimed at self-preservation (57a-f Long-Sedley). In human beings, however, reason also functions as creator of drives (*technítēs hormês*, Diog. Laert. 7,86). As early as Zeno of Citium, the concept of impulse is used in defining → affects (as an excessive impulse, *h. pleonázousa*, SVF I 205–207; cf. III 378; 389).

Cicero translates *hormé* as *appetitio animi* (Cic. Fin. 3,23; 5,17); Augustine uses *impetus* and *appetitus actionis* (Aug. Civ. 19,4; CCL 48, p. 665, 56–61). In his arguments against the Stoics, he raises the question whether it is appropriate to include impulses amongst the primary good features of Nature (*prima naturae bona*), when it could generate, for example, the wretched movements and actions of a madman. In the Middle Ages, the concept of a positive natural instinct is developed further, within the framework of the tradition of natural law (cf. [2]).

→ Desire; → Oikeiosis; → Pleasure

1 G. BERTRAM, s. v. ὁρμή etc.: ThWB 5, 1954, 468–475 2 R. A. GREENE, Instinct of Nature: Natural Law, Synderesis, and the Moral Sense, in: Journ. of the History of Ideas 58, 1997, 173–198 3 B. INWOOD, Ethics and Human Action in Early Stoicism, 1985 4 A. PREUS, Intention and Impulse in Aristotle and the Stoics, in: Apeiron 15, 1981, 48–58. C. HO.

Imuthes

[1] see → Petobastis IV

[2] (Imhotep; Egyptian *Jj-m-Ḥtp*; Greek Ἰμούθης/ *Imoúthēs*). Documented in contemporary inscriptions and papyri at the beginning of the 3rd Dynasty (around 2650 BC) under → Djoser and Sechemchet as the highest ranking official, senior demesne administrator and high priest of → Heliopolis, perhaps also in the (cult?) role of senior sculptor and site manager. In light of later tradition, he is attributed with an authoritative role in the building of the pyramid district of Djoser, of the first great stone structure; his grave is presumed to be in northern Saqqara. Already in the New Kingdom, I. was viewed as a great wise man and patron of scribes; from the Saitic period (7th–6th cents. BC), he enjoyed divine veneration as the son of the god Ptah first in Memphis. The image type associated with this cult shows him as a scribe enthroned on a block-shaped seat who is unrolling a roll of papyrus on his lap. In the Ptolemaic period his cult (equated with → Asclepius) also spreads to other cult locations of the land.

D. WILDUNG, s.v. I., LÄ 2, 145–148; Id., Imhotep und Amenhotep, 1977. S.S.

Ina

("Ίνα or "Ἰνα; *Hína/Ína*). Town on the southern tip of Sicily between → Motyca and → Pachynus (Ptol. 3,4,15). It is impossible to define its location more exactly. According to Cicero (Verr. 2,3,103), this *civitas decumana*, too, was ruined by → Verres during his propraetorship in 73/71 BC. GI. MA.
E. O.

Inachus

("Ίναχος; *Ínachos*; etymology unresolved).

[1] Son of → Oceanus and of → Tethys, who gave the main river of → Argus [II] and of → Argolis their names (schol. Eur. Or. 932). First king of Argus (Acusilaus,

FGrH 2 F 23c) and progenitor of the Argive kings and heroes ('Inachids': Eur. IA 1088). In the argument between Poseidon and Hera about Argus, I. decides in favour of the goddess and introduces her cult, which causes Poseidon to dry up his river (Paus. 2,15,4–5). I.'s wife is either his sister Argeia (Hyg. Fab. 143; 145) or the Oceanid Melia (Apollod. 2,1). As the father of → Io (Aesch. PV 589–590; 705; Hdt. 1,1; Callim. H. 3,254; Apollod. 2,5), I. is, however, scarcely attested in her iconography [1]. Named as further children are the following: Phoroneus, Aegialeus (Apollod. 2,1), Pelasgus (schol. Apoll. Rhod. 1,580), Argus (Asclepiades of Tragilus, FGrH 12 F 16), Phegeus (schol. Eur. Or. 932), Mycenae (Paus. 2,16,3). Sophocles named a satyr play after I. (TrGF IV F 269a–295a).

1 St. E. KATAKIS, s.v. I., LIMC 5.1, 653–654. R.B.

[2] Main river of the plain of Argus, rises in Lyrceum north of Artemisium (Malevo), flows east past Argus into the Gulf of Nauplia at Nea Kios. Already in antiquity it often had no water. Greek mythology raised the river to the progenitor of the Argive kings (Steph. Byz. s.v. Λάκμων; Str. 6,2,4; 7,5,8; 7,8; 8,6,7f.; Hecat. FGrH 1 F 102; Paus. 2,15,4f.; 18,3; 25,3; 8,6,6).

R. BALADIÉ, Le Péloponnèse de Strabon, 1980, 69–72; P. LEVI (tr.), Pausanias. Guide to Greece, vol. II. Southern Greece, 1984, 384 and n. Y.L.

Inanna City goddess of → Uruk, etymologized as the 'Queen of Heaven'. She is represented by symbols from the 2nd half of the 4th millennium (looped reed bundles, in the 1st millennium also a star), and by inscriptions from *c.* 3200 BC. She is the goddess of the planet Venus, unmarried, and representing the power of sexuality; she also has martial features. Mesopotamian mythology equates her with → Ištar; as such she appears in the Ninevite recension of the → Gilgamesh Epic as well as in the myth of 'Ishtar's descent into the Underworld'. → Hieros Gamos; → Tammuz; → Venus; Ishtar

F. BRUSCHWEILER, La déesse triomphante et vaincue dans la cosmologie sumérienne, 1987; U. SEIDL, C. WILCKE, s. v. I., RLA 5, 74–89. J. RE.

Inaros (Ἰνάρως; *Inárōs*). Libyan king, son of → Psammetichus, called on the Egyptians in 460 BC to revolt against the Persians. The Athenians called by I. to the aid of the Egyptians, participated in the initially successful enterprise and surrounded → Memphis. This siege was drawn out over years. Not until 456 did the Persians send an army to Memphis that surrounded the Athenians on the island of → Prosopis. But it was not until an arm of the Nile was laid dry that they were finally forced to burn their ships and surrender. I. was captured due to betrayal and was later crucified (Thuc. 1,104; 109f.; Hdt. 3,12; 7,7).

P. J. RHODES, in: CAH V², 1992, 54ff. E.S.-H.

Inauguratio In the actual sense 'the beginning', cf. also *inaugurare*: 'employ auguries', 'question divinatory birds'; 'consecrate'.

In Roman religious law, *inauguratio* is the priestly inauguration into office that has been applied from historically tangible time only for the → *flamines maiores* (*Dialis*: Gai. Inst. 1,130; 3,114; Liv. 27,8,4; 41,28,7; *Martialis*: Liv. 29,38,6; 45,15,10; Macrob. Sat. 3,13,11), the → *rex sacrorum* (Labeo at Gell. NA 15,27,1; Liv. 40,42,8) and the → *augures* (Liv. 27,36,5; 30,26,10; 33,44,3; Cic. Brut. 1; Suet. Calig. 12,1), but not for the other priests (*pontifices*, *Vestales*). In a special ceremony before the *comitia curiata/centuriata*, the agreement of Jupiter for the inauguration of the new priest was requested. The original thought was the transfer of the consecrating *augures'* inherent power to the office of the new priest; but this no longer has any relevance in historical time. The formula spoken for this was secret and was always passed on to the succeeding *augures* (Fest. 14 L.); it is even questionable whether the formula or wording given at Liv. 1,18,9 for the *inauguratio* of Numa Pompilius is authentic. During the act, which was performed by the *pontifices*, the inaugurating priest stood to the left of the new priest and touched his head with his right hand.

F. RICHTER, s.v. I., RE 9, 1220ff. LATTE, 141; 403ff. B. GLADIGOW, Condicio und I.: Ein Beitrag zur röm. Sakralverfassung, in: Hermes 98, 1970, 369–379. A.V.S.

Inaures see → Ear ornaments

Incantatio see → Magic

Incendium Latin 'fire', also 'arson'. As an emergency situation having numerous meanings: exonerating for the borrower upon the destruction of the performance items (in addition to destruction/*ruina*, and shipwreck/*naufragium*, a typical example for *force majeure*/ → *vis maior*; Dig. 2,13,6,9), intensifying liability (safekeeping/*depositum*, Dig. 16,3,1,1, robbery/*rapina*, Dig. 47,9) and in some cases justifying damage (Ulp. Dig. 9,2,49,1).

The Law of the Twelve Tables (8,10) already provided the death penalty for wilful arson. Later, the deed fell under the *lex Cornelia de sicariis et veneficis* (Marcianus Dig. 48,8,1 pr.), and also under the *lex Iulia de vi privata* (Marcianus Dig. 48,6,5 pr.). Whether the special treatment mentioned by Gaius (Dig. 47,9,9) in the case of negligence already belonged to the Law of the Twelve Tables is in dispute; the → *lex Aquilia* in any case is applicable. The punishments are later differentiated depending on the location, items and persons; the *praefecti urbi* and *praefecti vigilum* (Ulp. Dig. 1,15,5) have jurisdiction.

VIR III, 675–678, s.v. i., incendiarius; U. BRASIELLO, La repressione penale nel diritto romano, 1937, 205ff.; MOMMSEN, Strafrecht, 840f. C.E.

Incense (λίβανος; *líbanos*, λιβανωτός; *libanótós* as a Semitic loan-word, Lat. *tus*). Especially frankincense, the resin from bushes of the *Boswellia* species (e.g. *B. Carteri*), burnt for its aromatic smell. The actual appearance of the bushes was unknown in Graeco-Roman antiquity (cf. Plin. HN 12,55–57). These bushes also grew in India and the coast of Somalia, but the Greeks only knew them from Arabia (Theophr. Hist. pl. 9,4,2; Plin. HN 12,51). In the eastern Mediterranean, incense was used for cathartic and apotropaic purposes. The Egyptians, like Assyrians, Babylonians, Cretans, and Persians, used it in their religious cults and at funerals. In Palestine, frankincense itself was the sacrifice (Dt 2:30) or given as a precious gift (Mt 2:11).

Like the Arabs, Greeks, too, burned incense in many of their cults and → mysteries. → Pythagoras [2] advocated its use as an oblation, a notion rejected by Plato (Leg. 8,847b-c). Greeks also used incense at weddings (Sappho 44,30) and symposia (Xenoph. 1,7). The use as a cleansing sacrifice was rare in Greece (exception: schol. Aeschin. 1,23). In Rome, incense played a part in sacrifices, in the cult of the dead, and the emperor cult. In Christianity, despite initial rejection (cf. Cod. Theod. 16, 10,12), its use prevailed as a fumigant at the start of mass, as well as at funerals and processions.

Occasionally, grains of frankincense formed part of medical prescriptions (e.g. Cato Agr. 70,19; Plin. HN 25,131). Vase paintings frequently depict the burning of incense. The incense trade (Plin. HN 12,54: by the → Minaei in Arabia; cf. Theophr. Hist. pl. 9,4,6 and Plin. ibid. 12,63) was important (→ Incense Road). Several grades of quality were distinguished, as well as adulterations (Plin. ibid. 12,65). The *libanōtrís* apparently served both as incense box and burner.

R. PFISTER, s.v. Rauchopfer, RE 1 A, 267–286; W. W. MÜLLER, s.v. W., RE Suppl. 15, 700–777. C. HÜ.

Incense offering see → Sacrifice

Incense Road Overland trade route between the → incense growing areas in the south of the Arabian peninsula (Zufār) and the trading places in the Mediterranean (→ Gaza) and in the Persian Gulf (→ Gerrha). The beginning of the incense trade possibly dates back to the early part of the 1st millennium BC; written sources only exist for the Graeco-Roman period. The incense was transported on dromedaries, whose domestication (possibly in the 3rd millennium BC) was the prerequisite for any long-distance trade across the desert regions of Arabia. Important staging posts on the Incense Road (IR) were Qāniʾ, Sabwa, Mārib, Qarnāwu, Nagrān, Tabāla, → Yaṯrib, Dedān, → Petra; in Nagrān, a route branched off to Gerrha. The incense trade reached its peak in the 1st and 2nd cents. AD and began to decline after the 4th cent. The IR was initially under the control of the southern Arabian kingdom of → Sabaʾ, later – between the 4th and the end of the 2nd cent. BC – under that of the kingdom of Maʿīn (→ Minaei). From the 2nd cent. BC to the 1st cent. AD, the northern part of the IR led through Nabataean territory (→ Nabataei, Nabataeans). → Leuce Come [2] was an important reloading point there. The discovery of the → monsoon winds resulted in sea trade across the Red Sea increasing in importance from the end of the 2nd cent. BC onwards. Important ports were Okēlis and Muza on the Bāb al-Mandab and also → Berenice [9] and → Myos Hormos in Egypt, from where shipments were taken to Coptus, and then up the Nile to Alexandria [1].

→ India, trade with (with map)

W. W. MÜLLER, s. v. Weihrauch, RE Suppl. 15, 700–777; B. VOGT, Im Reich der Düfte: Weihrauch und Weihrauch-Handel in und um das Glückliche Arabien herum, in: W. DAUM et al., Im Land der Königin von Saba, 1999, 205–222.   K. BA.

Incensus ('not appraised') is one who neglects to have his property assessed by the censor in Rome (→ census: Dig. 1,2,2,17) and therefore, due to the non-determination of which voter class he belongs to and his military service obligation, it is possible he cannot be called in for his fundamental civic duties. *Incensus* is punishable by death in accordance with a legendary law of Servius Tullius (Liv. 1,44,1). In the Republican period the consequence of an omitted tax declaration can be the confiscation of property and being sold into slavery (Cic. Caecin. 99; Val. Max. 6,3; 4; Suet. Aug. 24.; Gai. Inst. 1,160). But this depends on the circumstances of the individual case, especially on the presence of fraud against the public at large or forgery. The normal consequence could have been the valuation conducted *ex officio* on a citizen known by name, which like today was done at his expense and therefore was sufficient as sanction.

→ Census

MOMMSEN, Staatsrecht 2 (3), 367, 434; 3 (3), 548.   C.G.

Incest see → Incestus

Incestus (also *incestum*, 'impure'; from *in* and *castus*). *Incestus* comes from the realm of religious prohibitions (*nefas*, see → *fas*); in particular, *incestus* is the violation of the chastity precept by a Vestal, who was punished by the pontifical college. She herself was buried alive, and her accomplice was whipped to death by the *pontifex maximus* (Liv. 22,57,3; Plin. Ep. 4,11).

Beyond the *fas*, *incestus* is the sexual joining between close kin and those related by marriage and is closely connected to the respective marriage prohibition that is traceable to the *veteres mores* ('ancient customs') (Paul. Dig. 23,2,39,1); the origin from the *fas* is perceptible in the expression *incestae et nefariae nuptiae* ('incestuous and religiously forbidden marriage', Gai. Inst. 1,59,64) as also in the direct reference to the *fas* (Marcianus Dig. 48,18,5). Originally recorded is the straight line, siblings and half-siblings, in their entirety up to the sixth degree. According to Ulp. (5,6), in the 3rd cent.

AD, the ban reaches to the fourth degree, apart from the exception effected by a *senatus consultum* of Claudius in a personal matter for the marriage between uncle and daughter of a brother (Tac. Ann. 12,5–6; Gai. Inst. 1,62). In any case, in the 2nd cent. AD those related by marriage were also effected (Gai. Inst. 1,63). From the end of the 3rd cent. AD legislative measures pile up leading to intensification: Diocletian (Coll. 6,4; Cod. Iust. 5,4,17), Constantius II (Cod. Theod. 3,12,1.2 with an emphasis regarding marriage with a sister-in-law), Theodosius I (Cod. Iust. 5,5,5), Arcadius (Cod. Theod. 3,12,3), Theodosius II (Cod. Theod. 3,12,4), Zeno (Cod. Iust. 5,5,9). The purpose was the repulsion of (fairly common) marriages between close kin; the categories of *incestus iure gentium* and *incestus iure civili* (Paul. Dig. 23,2,68; → *ius*) could also be connected. A marriage that was against the law was void, the children considered illegitimate without right of inheritance, and the right of the partners to set up a will and/or inherit was limited. Support for these children (so in Nov. 12,3 from 535) was eliminated in 539 (Nov. 89,15).

Prosecution (despite general formulation at Cic. Leg. 2,22), probably only for the Vestals, was the responsibility of the pontifical college, legal measures were the exception, punishments were in general imposed by the house court [2. 31]. *Incestus* was punished with capital punishment (throwing down from the rock: Tac. Ann. 6,19; Quint. Inst. 7,8,3), later replaced regularly by deportation, finally with asset penalties (Cod. Theod. 3,12,3). Nov. 12 regulates the punishments anew. In contrast to older opinion, the → *lex Iulia de adulteriis* appears to have captured *incestus* not only in competition with adultery (→ *adulterium*)[2]. Special regulations are concerned with the partly more lenient punishment of the woman, the taking into consideration of ignorance of the law, and the interrogation of slaves.

1 A. GUARINO, Studi sull' "incestum", in: ZRG 63, 1943, 175–267   2 L. SCHUMACHER, Servus Index, 1982, 13ff., 175ff.   3 Y. THOMAS, Mariages endogamiques à Rome. Patrimoine, pouvoir et parenté depuis l'époque archaique, in: Révue historique de droit français et étranger 58, 1980, 345–382.

P. BONTE (ed.), Épouser au plus proche, Inceste, prohibitions et stratégies matrimoniales autour de la Méditerranée, 1994.   C.E.

Incitaria Ships' mooring (It. Maritimum 499) on the *promonturium Argentarium* in Etruria, modern Porto Santo Stefano. The place name is to be interpreted as '*in cetaria*' and therefore denotes a fishing-port for tuna fish.

R. BRONSON, G. UGGERI, Isola del Giglio, in: SE 38, 1970, 208f.   G.U.

Inclination Modern technical term of archaeological construction research; what is described here is the noticeable slight inwards pitch of the → columns in the outer column circle in some Doric peripteral temples of the classical period (e.g. → Parthenon); together with the → entasis, the increased diameter of the corner columns and the → curvature, it is one element of the → optical refinements in Greek column construction.

D. MERTENS, Der Tempel von Segesta und die dor. Tempelbaukunst des griech. Westens in klass. Zeit, 1984, 255 s.v. Säulenneigung; W. MÜLLER-WIENER, Griech. Bauwesen der Ant., 1986, 136f.; E. RANKIN, Geometry Enlivened. Interpreting the Refinements of the Greek Doric Temple, in: Acta classica 29, 1986, 29–41.   C.HÖ.

Incrustation Wall decoration with a structure imitating architecture misleadingly described in Vitruvius (7,5) as stucco facing in the sense of the 1st Pompeian style (→ Stucco; → Wall paintings); as an archaeological technical term incrustation (from Latin → crustae sc. marmoreae, Greek πλάκωσις/plákōsis) in contrast describes solely the interior facing of walls of lesser material with marble slabs (however, the relationship of this 'genuine' incrustation to the 1st Pompeian style which imitates incrustation and therefore is frequently also called incrustation style continues to be unclear). The information handed down by Pliny (HN 36,48), that a certain Mamurra was the first to face walls with crustae in 60 BC, is apocryphal: the technique can be proven on various occasions in the Greek cultural area from the archaic period (Delos), becoming increasingly prevalent probably from the 4th cent. BC (Palace of Maussollus in Halicarnassus, Plin. HN 36,47; Vitr. De arch. 2,8,10). In Hellenistic Alexandria it becomes widespread; here, however, it was at first a surrogate that concealed the lack of marble, or was the result of high-speed construction [3. 229].

Incrustations are seldom preserved from their early period; they consisted not only of flat marble slabs, but could also include cornices, pilasters and architraves and in this way be fitted together into entire illusory architectures. The individual elements were attached to the wall with mortar, most of the time also with clamps and dowels [1. 286]. In the Republican period incrustations, as ideal facing elements of the newly developed cement-and-brick method of building (→ Construction technique), became a major component of Roman architecture and then quickly a means of representation. They could be decorated with elaborately ornamented → intarsia and figured inlay work of colourful stone and are to be allocated to the late Republican phenomenon of marble luxury [2. 13f.; 34]; Mamurra, cited above, could have been a pioneer here, as he was possibly the first to have this type of construction luxury carried out in a private house.

Incrustations can be found from the first years AD on all representative public architecture of the Roman empire, such as on basilicas, baths and theatres; in addition there were numerous examples on private houses of the rich and on imperial palaces. In late antique architecture incrustations form an element that is just as universal (i.a. the palace-villa of Stobi) as in early Chris-tian church construction (Rome: Santa Sabina, 5th cent. AD; Ravenna: San Vitale, 6th cent.; Constantinople: → Hagia Sophia, 6th cent.).

A post-classical revival of the incrustation technique occurred under the Cosmati in Rome (12th–14th cents.) and on various structures of the proto-Renaissance of northern Italy [4]. On ancient incrustation outside the genre of architecture → crustae; → Intarsia.

1 O. DEUBNER, s.v. I., RE Suppl. 7, 285–293   2 H. DRE-RUP, Zum Ausstattungsluxus in der röm. Architektur, ²1981   3 W. HOEPFNER, E. L. SCHWANDNER, Haus und Stadt im klass. Griechenland, ²1994   4 E. HUSTON, The Cosmati, 1951.

A. ANDREOU, Griech. Wanddekorationen, 1988; W. DRACK, Zum Farbenspiel röm. Marmor- und I.-Imitationen, in: Von Farbe und Farben, FS A. Knoepfli, 1980, 31–36; A. KLEINERT, Die I. der Hagia Sophia, 1979; B. WESENBERG, Certae rationes picturarum, in: MarbWPr 1975/6, 23–43.   C.HÖ.

Incubation (from the Latin incubare; Greek ἐγκοι-μᾶσθαι/enkoimâsthai, 'to sleep in a temple'). The term for a method, practised in many religions, for receiving revelations: the sleep in a sacred place, during which the superhuman occupant of the place appears, gives information and advice (even in the comic fracture of Aristoph. Plut. 698–747 Asclepius himself appears). In Graeco-Roman antiquity, just as in Byzantine Christianity, incubation was particularly practised in the → healing cults, above all in the cults of → Asclepius and → Isis, but also, for example, of → Amphiaraus at Oropus, of → Hemithea of Castabus, in the Daunian cult of → Calchas on the Monte Gargano (Str. 6,3,9), or of Podalirius (Lycoph. Alexandra 1050); in Byzantine churches it continued into the modern era [1; 2]. Because access to divine knowledge is desired in many situations in life, incubation, even with Asclepius – at least according to reports in the stories of miracles from → Epidaurus – is not restricted to healing illnesses [3]. Rather, incubation is a ritual means through which every individual can come directly into contact with the deity and not through the mediation of a priest (Philostr. VA 1,7); that is why personal, and often intimate, problems, particularly illnesses, are prevalent. While incubation is mostly embedded in an institutional framework through the place (sanctuary) and the preparatory rites, the Graeco-Egyptian → magic papyri, with their rites for dream sendings which occur in private bedrooms outside of an institutional context, take the individualization a decisive step further.

The ritual of incubation is complex; details are missing for most cults; most informative is a sacred law from the Asclepium of Pergamum (LSAM 14, cf. [4]); a burlesque description of incubation in the Asclepium in the Piraeus is given in Aristoph. Plut. 653–747. The incubation space itself (enkoimētérion or ádyton) is a special room in the sanctuary, which is often separated by gender (Amphiaraion, Asklepieia), and is enclosed at least well enough so as to ward off prying eyes. People sleep here on beds of twigs (*stibádes*) or on the hide of a sacrificial animal (Amphiaraion, Paus. 1,34,5), not on a bed, wearing a wreath and a special robe without a belt or rings. Access is granted only after purification rituals (in the Piraeus, after a bath in the sea: Aristoph. Plut. 656-658; preliminary sacrifices to a large number of gods in the Amphiaraion: Paus. 1,34,5), specific sacrifices immediately before entering the room (cakes for Asclepius and his circle at Pergamum, a ram for Amphiaraus, Calchas, Podalirius), but also after a sacrifice to → Mnemosyne, in order to preserve the memory of the dream (Pergamum). This underscores the extraordinariness of the experience: a wreath is worn at a sacrifice and symposium, *stibádes* were used in the rites of Dionysus and Demeter. After the night, one pays the fees due to the temple (in Oropus, money was thrown into the sacred spring, Paus. 1,34,4) and discusses the dream with the priests of the sanctuary (Aristid. Hieroi Logoi).

1 F. R. TROMBLEY, Hellenic Rel. and Christianization c. 370-529, 1993, vol. 1, 165-168; vol. 2, 5-15 2 P. MARAVAL, Lieux saints et pèlerinages d'Orient, 1985, 224-229 3 L. R. LiDONNICI, The Epidaurian Miracle Inscriptions. Text, Translation and Commentary, 1995 4 C. VELIGIANNI, Lex sacra aus Amphipolis, in: ZPE 100, 1994, 391-405.

L. DEUBNER, De incubatione capita quattuor, 1900; E. ROOS, De incubatione ritu per ludibrium apud Aristophanem detorto, OpAth 3, 1960, 55-93; M. F. G. PARMENTIER, Incubatie in de antieke hagiografie, in: A. HILHORST (ed.), De heiligenverering in de eerste eeuwen van het christendom, 1988, 27-40; F. GRAF, Heiligtum und Ritual. Das Beispiel der griech.-röm. Asklepieia, in: O. REVERDIN, B. GRANGE (ed.), Le sanctuaire grec (Entretiens sur l'antiquité classique 37), 1992, 159-199; P. ATHANASSIADI, Dreams, Theurgy and Freelance Divination. The Testimony of Iamblichus, in: JRS 83, 1993, 115-130.
F.G.

Incubus or Incubo (derived from the Latin *incubare*, 'to lie on something') denotes in late Latin both the sender of nightmares, who corresponds to the Greek Ephialtes (→ Aloads), and the nightmare he causes. As goblin and bringer of obscene dreams, *incubus* is equated with, e.g., → Faunus or, more precisely, the so-called *Faunus ficarius* ('Faunus of the fig trees'; Isid. Orig. 8,11,103-104) [1], with → Inuus and → Silvanus (Serv. Aen. 6,775). Christian authors have particularly stressed the lust of the *incubi* for intercourse with women (Aug. Civ. 15,23,108). It was believed that plants or other remedies (Plin. HN 25,4,29; 30,10,84) protected against their influence. Petron. Sat. 38 indicates a function of the *incubus* as a guardian of treasures. *Incubus* as well as *succubus* (from the Latin *succumbere*, 'to lie under something') survive in medieval demonology [2].

1 W. OTTO, s.v. Faunus, RE 6, 2060 2 D. MÜLLER, s.v. I. und Succubus, Enzyklopädie des Märchens 7, 113-117.
FR.P.

Incusi (hammered coins) Coins minted in lower Italy (Sybaris, Croton, Caulonia, Metapontum, Tarentum, Louse, Siris-Pyxus, Posidonia, Velia, Rhegium, and others) c. 550-440 BC, where on the reverse, the image of the obverse appears as a depression. This is a conscious effort to produce a view of the rear, not merely a duplication. Its meaning is debated. On the one hand, purely technical reasons are suggested; i.e. with hammerstruck coins, one attempted to strike clean, precisely centred coins. Others assume a philosophical context, usually in connection with the teachings of Pythagoras, according to which the whole world is built on antitheses. But Pythagoras cannot be regarded as the inventor of hammer-forged coins. Due to the minting technique, the blanks of hammer-forged coins are large and thin. During the late phase, an incuse second coin image appears; in the 430s, *incusi* minting is abandoned.

L. BREGLIA, La coniazione incusi, Annali dell' Istituto Italiano di Numismatica 1956, 23-37; G. GORINI, La monetazione i., 1975; A. JOHNSTON, in: S. P. NOE, The Coinage of Metapontum, 1984, 36-46; N. F. PARISE, Struttura e funzione delle monetazioni arcaiche de Magna Grecia, in: Atti del XII. convegno di studi sulla Magna Grecia, 1975, 87-124; W. SCHWABACHER, Zur Prägetechnik und Deutung der Inkuse Münzen, Actes Congrès International de Numismatique, Rom 1961, 1965, 107-116.
DI.K.

Index
[1] From Latin *dicere, in-dicere* 'to report'; informer, person providing information, traitor (Cic. Clu. 21; Cic. Verr. 2,5,161; Cic. Mur. 49), register, short summary of content (Cic. De or. 2,61: Paul. Dig. 22,4,2; Quint. Inst. 10,1,57); index finger (*digitus index*, Cic. Att. 13,46,1).

Persons making reports came from the lower social classes who mostly had neither the right nor the means to file a suit themselves. Eques acting as informers were denigrated by the term *index* (Cic. Att. 2,24,2); frequently the combination of *testis* (witness) and *index* (Juv. 10,69f.) is to be found; an incriminating statement by an unfree person is called *potestas indicandi* ('possibility for reporting') (Cic. Clu. 187). Despite the ban in the *Index Cornelia de falsis*, people later made also use of reporting by a *servus index* against the owner (*contra dominum*) for the purpose of betrayal, compulsion, defamation (for instance in the trial of Octavia, wife of Nero, according to the *Index Iulia de adulteriis*), or in the case of fiscal offences (particularly under Caligula, whose so-called *Index de servis indicibus* [ROTONDI, 467] did, in fact, interfere with the sanctity of private). If the *index* himself was involved in the misdeed (cf. Ulp. Dig. 48,18,1,26), at a later time he was granted immunity from prosecution in the case of individual offences under certain preconditions (cf. Liv. 8,18; 39,19; Cod. Just. 9,8,5,7). Sometimes the *index* also received a reward (cf. for instance Ulp. Dig. 47,10,5,1; 29,5,3,13-15; Modestinus Dig. 37,14,9,1).

In Amm. Marc. 29,1,41 legal works have been passed down to us in book form that were called *indices iuris*. As a literary genre *index* appears particularly in the Byzantine period. Justinian (Const. Deo auctore § 12) permitted revisions of his *Digesta* only in the form of word-for-word Greek translations (κατὰ πόδα; *katà póda*), of collections of parallel passages (παράτιτλα; *parátitla*) and of summaries that had to be adapted strictly to the wording of the individual fragments (*indices*). The authors of such *indices* to the *Digesta* were Theophilus, Dorotheus, Stephanus and Cyrillus. The so-called *index Florentinus* that today is named after its finding place, the Florentine digest MS, goes back to Const. Tanta/Δέδωχεν § 20, where Justinian orders the compilation of a register of all authors and writings included in the *Digesta*.

ThlL VII 1, 1140–1156, s.v. i., indicium, indicare; A. BERGER, Studies in the Basilica, in: Bull. dell'ist. di diritto Romano 55/56, 1952, 65–184; M. KASER, s.v. testimonium, RE 5A, 1047f.; MOMMSEN, Strafrecht 195, 504f.; SCHULZ, 404; L. SCHUMACHER, Servus I., 1982; WENGER, 578f., 681f.; F. WIEACKER, Textstufen klass. Juristen, 1960, 106. FR.R.

[2] see → Scrolls

India

I. NAME II. EARLY RELATIONSHIPS III. ALEXANDER'S CAMPAIGN AND HELLENISM IV. ROMAN IMPERIAL PERIOD V. LATE ANTIQUITY

I. NAME

Old Indian *Sindhu* as the name for the Indus river, is attested (with Iranian *h*) as *Hindu* in the ancient Persian inscriptions; from this came Greek Ἰνδός (*Indos*; with the Ionian loss of *h*) for the river and then Ἰνδική (*Indiké*) for the country. The Latin terms are Indus and India.

II. EARLY RELATIONSHIPS

Whilst relationships between north-western I. and Mesopotamia go back to the 3rd millennium BC, I. became known in Greece only in the late 6th cent. through Scylax (FGrH 709), who visited north-western I. himself in the service of Darius [1]. The later authors Hecataeus, Herodotus and Ctesias used information from Persia without having seen the countries themselves. The fantastic and exaggerated reports in Hdt. and especially Ctesia can often be shown to be modelled on Indian legends [2. 157ff.]. Despite his occasional sharp criticism, Aristotle to a large extent still relied on Ctesias in his few statements. During this period I. belonged to the realm of ethnographic legend, a country on the margins of the world with completely different conditions from Greece and other known countries. The geographical position was also unclear; I. was often considered to be the neighbouring country of Ethiopia. The true origin of the few Indian animals (e.g., chicken and peacock) and products (cinnamon and pepper) that had already reached Greece at that time remained largely unidentified.

III. ALEXANDER'S CAMPAIGN AND HELLENISM

Through Alexander's campaign, I. first became known more accurately to the Greeks. The Indus valley, which had already belonged to the Achaemenid empire in former times, was reconquered by → Alexander [4]. After the subjugation of the upper Indus valley, the Madeconians advanced through the Pañjab to → Hyphasis (modern Sutlej), went down the → Hydaspes (modern Jilam) and the Indus and conquered the lower Indus valley right through to the sea. As the furthest and most remarkable of Alexander's conquests, I. was treated in detail in many Alexander tales. The authors repeatedly cited for I. in antiquity were Aristobulus, Onesicritus, Nearchus and Cleitarchus with important details about contemporary history, ethnography and natural history. The emphasis was on the north-west (modern Pakistan) primarily conquered by Alexander; people were able to report very little about the area beyond the Hyphasis. The lost works of these early → Alexander historians are for the most part known only through Arrianus (Anab. and Ind.), Diodorus, Curtius Rufus and Strabo.

Shortly after his death Alexander's Indian satrapies became a centre of the revolt by Candragupta Maurya (→ Sandracottus) who soon incorporated large parts of northern I. into his new Maurya empire. A failed attempt by → Seleucus to reconquer the Indian satrapies ended with an agreement between him and Candragupta that allotted to the latter not only the actual Indian satrapies but also Gedrosia, Arachosia and Paropamisadae. Seleucus received 500 war elephants that became an important weapon in the subsequent Diadochi wars. Lively diplomatic relationships between the two empires lasted at least until the time of → Aśoka, the grandson of Candragupta. → Megasthenes, the envoy of Seleucus I Nicator at the Maurya court in → Palimbothra, wrote a detailed and much-quoted monograph (FGrH 715) on the country with a description of the Maurya empire and of the Ganges valley. (Unfortunately we learn very little from the *Indiká* of Daemachus.) In the north-west of the Maurya empire a Greek population was preserved (probably in settlements founded by Alexander), and Aśoka had his royal edicts engraved there in Greek as well (and also Aramaic).

The foundation of their own empires in Parthia and Bactria (→ Graeco-Bactria) around the middle of the 3rd cent. separated the Seleucids from I., although Antiochus III reached the Indian border regions once again. At the beginning of the 2nd cent. BC the Bactrian Greeks under Demetrius [10] and Menander conquered north-western I. The → Indo-Greeks soon formed several small states, and when their place was finally taken by the Parthians, Sakas and Indo-Scythians, no one in the west was interested: large parts of their history have to be reconstructed almost exclusively from coin finds. The most lasting influence is considered to be the later Greco-Buddhist art (so-called Gandhāra art).

IV. ROMAN IMPERIAL PERIOD

The most important connection between I. and the west was now the lively sea trade between I. and Egypt (partly also Mesopotamia) that is known both from the west (Indian ivory statuette in Pompeii, Brāhmī inscription in Egypt) and the east (Hellenistic-Roman ceramics, lamps and glassware, large quantities of Roman coins especially in southern I.). Among those of other sites the finds of → Arikamedu are especially famous. In literature Strabo, Pliny, Ptolemy and especially the *Periplus maris rubri* are the most important sources. This trade probably began as early as the 2nd cent. BC when the monopoly of the southern Arabian intermediary traders was broken by direct trade between I. and Ptolemaic Egypt; up to the time of Augustus the turnover was certainly modest. The most important harbours in I. were Barabara at the mouth of the Indus, → Barygaza and → Calliena, and in the south → Muziris and → Nelcynda; the goods were transported by land from Muziris on the Kerala coast to Tamilnadu.

The land route through Parthia to north-western I. played a lesser role. Most luxury goods like perfumes, healing remedies and spices, pearls, ivory and precious stones were imported from I. and exchanged for textile goods, wine, glass and corals, frequently also for silver and gold coins. The distribution and composition of the coin finds provides important clues to the history of the trade [3]. Greek papyri from Egypt and classical Tamil poetry as well as archaeological material [4] attest to Greek traders who stayed in southern I. In the 1st cent. AD, Greek ships mostly visited only the west coast, but later the east coast and → Taprobane (Sri Lanka), more rarely even south-east Asia, were reached from time to time as well. Indian ships, too, took part in this long-distance trade. Indian goods were available in the harbours of southern Arabia and eastern Africa. The literature mentions several Indian delegations and a Taprobanian delegation who visited Augustus, Claudius and later emperors.

The literary image of I. in the west remained almost unchanged and the early Alexander historians with Megasthenes continued to be the main sources [1. 32–36]. Thus, e.g., Strabo's paragraph on I. (15,1), one of the most important ancient descriptions of I., is completely dependent on these; this applies also to Arrianus who wrote his *Indiká* as an appendix to his Alexander history. Only in the area of geography were there new insights taken into consideration: Pliny (bk. 6), the author of *Periplus maris rubri* and Ptolemy (bk. 7) used new information from seafarers. Particularly in the *Periplus maris rubri* the precise details about harbours and trade on the Indian west coast are clearly first-hand accounts. Only with Ptolemy, who (following the lost work by Marinus) received part of his information from a certain Alexander, were people given a more accurate knowledge of the east coast and of south-east Asia.

For the informed reader nevertheless, I. always remained a country extremely far away that could moreover not always be distinguished from Ethiopia; a land of many natural wonders (among these valuable trading goods), of naked ascetics and still also of the gold-digging ants of Herodotus. The Indian naked ascetics or → Gymnosophists whom Alexander had met in Taxila, and among these particularly Calanus who followed Alexander and then burnt himself to death, were repeatedly mentioned with amazement in the literature. Philostratus dedicated two books to the visit of Apollonius to the Indian Brahmans (Philostr. VA. 3 and 4). Another popular theme, originally part of the history of Alexander, were the supposed I. campaigns of Hercules and especially of → Dionysus. The latter was often depicted with Indian animals such as tigers and leopards, and epic poets like → Dionysius [27] and → Nonnus described his I. campaign. The fact that the natural world of I., about which the Alexander historians had reported in such detail, still charmed the readers is evident from the animal books of Pliny and Aelianus.

V. LATE ANTIQUITY

The Christian mission in I. began perhaps with Bartholomaeus in the 2nd cent. AD [1. 37–39]; it was not until the 5th cent. that Thomas, originally the apostle of Edessa and Parthia, was also entrusted with the Indian mission. While trade gradually fell into the hands of the Axumites (→ Axum) and other intermediaries, there was, however, also direct contact between the Mediterranean world and I. The travel report by Scholastikos of Thebes is extant in Ps.-Palladius, and Christian writers like Clemens Alexandrinus could often report new things about I. The Syrian → Bardesanes supposedly wrote *Indiká* (FGrH 719). The old traditions of the Gymnosophists also remained popular with writers who were interested in asceticism. Some matters were probably also imparted through the Manichaeans (→ Mani). In the 6th cent. → Cosmas [2] Indikopleustes in his *Christian Topography* conveyed the first-hand reports from I. and Sri Lanka.

Whilst some authors still provided genuine (and even new) knowledge from I., it was increasingly confused with Ethiopia in literature, a mistake that has its roots in the earliest Greek and ancient Oriental sources. In the various reviews of the → Alexander Romance and in the fictitious letter of Alexander to Aristotle, I. was treated entirely as a place of legend. In Christian literature, I. was mixed up with ideas of paradise and the → Ganges (or Indus) was identified with Phison, the river of paradise. According to Cosmas, knowledge of I. in Byzantium was mostly and in the Latin west exclusively dependent upon the ancient sources [5; 6].
→ India, trade with (with map); → INDIA

1 A. DIHLE, s.v. I., RAC 18, 1–56   2 K. KARTTUNEN, I. in Early Greek Lit., 1989   3 P. J. TURNER, Roman Coins from I., 1989   4 V. BEGLEY, R. D. DE PUMA (ed.), Rome and I. The Ancient Sea Trade, 1991   5 N. V. PIGULEWSKAJA, Byzanz auf den Wegen nach Indien. Aus der Geschichte des byz. Handels mit dem Orient vom 4. bis 6. Jh., 1969   6 H. GREGOR, Das Indienbild des Abendlandes (bis zum Ende des 13. Jh.), 1964.

J. ANDRÉ, J. FILLIOZAT, L'Inde vue de Rome. Textes latins de l'Antiquité relatifs à l'Inde, 1986; B. BRELOER, F. BÖMER, Fontes historiae religionum Indicarum, 1939; R. M. CIMINO (ed.), Ancient Rome and I. Commercial and Cultural Contacts between the Roman World and I., 1994; P. DAFFINÀ, Le relazioni tra Roma e l'I. alla luce delle più recenti indagini. Conferenze Istituto Italiano per il Medio ed Estremo Oriente, 1995; A. DIHLE, Ant. und Orient. Gesammelte Aufsätze (SHAW Supplements vol. 2), 1984 (edited by V. PÖSCHL, H. PETERSMANN) ; Id., Indien und die hell.-röm. Welt (Literaturbericht), in: Geographia antiqua 1, 1992, 151–159; K. KARTTUNEN, Graeco-Indica. A survey of Recent Work, in: Arctos 20, 1986, 73–86; Id., Graeco-Indica 2, in: Topoi 3, 1993, 391–400; Id., I. and the Hellenistic World, 1997; F. F. SCHWARZ, Neue Perspektiven in den griech.-ind. Beziehungen, in: OLZ 67, 1972, 5–26; J. SEDLAR, I. and the Greek World, 1980.
K.K.

India, trade with As early as Herodotus, information about → India was compiled and a colourful picture was drawn of the morals and dietary habits of the Indians as well as the way in which they extracted gold (Hdt. 3,97–106), but it was not until the campaign of Alexander that Greece developed any sustained interest in India (Arr. Ind.; Diod. Sic. 2,35–42; Str. 15,1; Plin. HN 6,56–106). Extensive and regular trade in the early Hellenistic period hardly existed, although trading contacts may have led through the Graeco-Bactrian area. With the opening up of the monsoon routes towards the end of the 2nd cent. BC from the Red Sea to the region of the mouth of the → Indus [1] and to the coast of Malabar, regular maritime trade started between Ptolemaic Egypt and India (Str. 2,3,4; Peripl. m.r. 57; → Periplous). → Palmyra began to play an increasingly important role during this period with the organization of the → caravan trade between India and the Mediterranean. During this time, above all, luxury goods were imported from India whilst diverse ceramics from the Mediterranean, for instance, reached even the interior of India.

Undoubtedly intensive trading relationships existed in the time of the early Principate (1st/2nd cents. AD) between the Graeco-Roman and the Indian world. Sri Lanka and the Indo-Chinese region had already been included in this trade. In the Augustan period, according to Strabo, 120 ships already sailed every year from Myos Hormos on the Red Sea to India (Str. 2,5,12; cf. 17,1,13; 17,1,45). According to Pliny, there were three shipping routes: from Syagron, a promonotory on the southern coast of Arabia (modern Ras Fartak), to Patale at the mouth of the Indus, then from Syagron to Zigeros (Melizeigara, south of Bombay) and finally from Okelis (on the Bab el-Mandeb) to Muziris (on the coast of Malabar, modern Cranganore; Plin. HN 6,100; 6,101; 6,104; cf. Peripl. m.r. 57). From Myos Hormos the goods were transported by camel to Coptus on the Nile and then on to Alexandria (Str. 17,1,45; Plin. HN 6,102f.). The caravan trade via Palmyra was now fully organized and became more signifi-

cant; the Palmyrenian traders maintained trading stations in Seleucea, Babylon, Vologesias and Spasinu Charax.

From the beginning of the Principate, trade relations with the southern Indian region were more intensive than with the central and northern Indian regions, as is attested both by the impressive finds of Roman coins from the Augustan period onwards and the *Periplus maris Erythraei*. In Sri Lanka, too, numerous coins were found. Pliny put the blame for the exports of money and precious metals on the women's demands for luxury goods and criticized it because of the economic consequences: according to Pliny, 100 million sesterces were spent every year on goods from India, China and Arabia (Plin. HN 12,84; cf. 6,101; 21,11); Aristides on the other hand praised the Indian imports as an example of goods being brought to Rome from all over the world (Aristid. 26,12). Indeed, luxury products (→ Spices, → Silk, → Ivory) primarily came to Rome from the far East; in return, agricultural products (oil, olives, grain, wine) and textiles were exported. Moreover, archaeological finds in India have proven that there was considerable import of Roman ceramics, metal and glass products. The papyrus Vindob. G 40822 from the 2nd cent. AD, a sales contract drawn up in Muziris and Alexandria, is a testimony to these trading relationships. As only a small circle of purchasers could pay the high prices resulting from long transportation routes and the fiscal fees imposed, the volume of the trade with India should not be overestimated; the trading balance was by no means even. The customs duty on the *mare rubrum* (→ Erythrá thálatta) were collected by tax farmers on behalf of the *fiscus* (Plin. HN 6,84).

The trade with India was much affected by the crisis of the 3rd cent. AD. From AD 224 onwards, the Palmyrenian trading stations on the Persian Gulf came under Sassanid souvereignty, and Palmyra – the short-lived centre of a subsidiary empire – was destroyed by the Romans in AD 272; in Egypt unrest and military battles occurred by the end of the 3rd cent. With the consolidation of the Imperium Romanum under Diocletianus and Constantinus I (end of the 2nd to the beginning of the 3rd cent. AD) trade relations with southern India and Sri Lanka were restored, although to a lesser extent (Amm. Marc. 14,3,3). An edict of AD 356 or 352 (Cod. Theod. 9,23,1) that completely banned the export of money probably restricted the trade with India.

→ Commerce

1 V. BEGLEY, Ceramic Evidence for Pre-Periplus Trade on the Indian Coasts, in: V. BEGLEY, R. D. DE PUMA (ed.), Rome and India. The Ancient Sea Trade, 1991, 157–196 2 L. CASSON, The Periplus Maris Erythraei, 1989 3 A. DIHLE, Antike und Orient, 1984 4 Id., Die entdeckungsgeschichtlichen Voraussetzungen des Indienhandels der röm. Kaiserzeit, in: ANRW II 9.2, 546–580 (= Id., Antike und Orient, 1984, 118–152) 5 R. DREXHAGE, Untersuchungen zum röm. Osthandel, 1988 6 A. H. M. JONES, Asian Trade in Antiquity, in: Id., Economy, 140–150 7 K. KARTTUNEN, Early Roman Trade with South

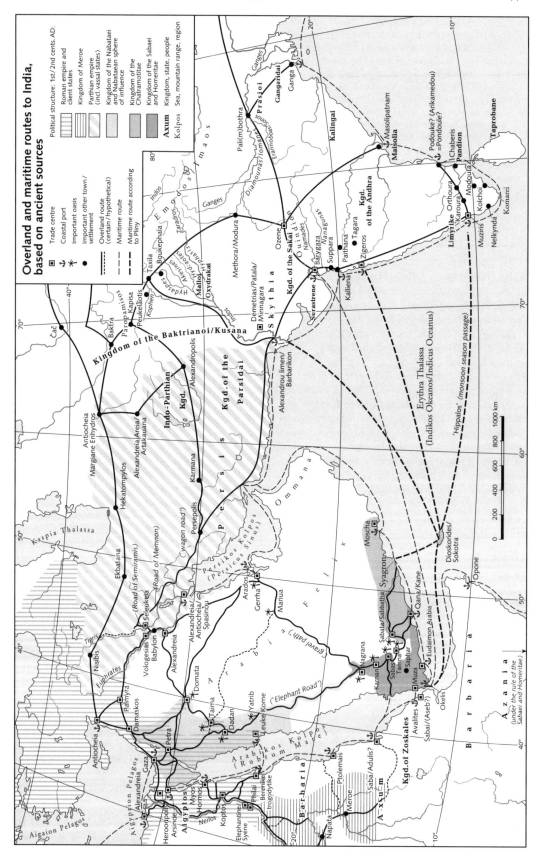

Overland and maritime routes to India, based on ancient sources

Political structure: 1st/2nd cents. AD:

Roman empire and client states

Kingdom of Meroe

Parthian empire (incl. vassal states)

Kingdom of the Nabataei and Nabataean sphere of influence

Kingdom of the Chatramotitae

Kingdom of the Sabaei and Homeritae

Axum Kingdom, state, people

Kolpos Sea, mountain range, region

Trade centre

Coastal port

Important oasis

Important other town / settlement

Overland route (certain / hypothetical)

Maritime route

Maritime route according to Pliny

India, in: Arctos 29, 1995, 81–91　8 J.I. MILLER, The Spice Trade of the Roman Empire, 1969　9 ROSTOV-TZEFF, Roman Empire, 94–97　10 P. J. TURNER, Roman Coins from India, 1989　11 R. WALBURG, Ant. Münzen aus Sri Lanka (Ceylon). Die Bedeutung röm. Münzen und ihrer Nachahmungen für den Geldumlauf auf Ceylon, in: Studien zu Fundmünzen der Antike 3, 1985, 27–260.

H.-J.D.

MAPS: L. CASSON, The Periplus Maris Erythraei, 1989; P. HÖGEMANN et al., Nordostafrika und Arabische Halb-insel. Staaten und Kulturen (4.–1. Jh. v.Chr.), TAVO B V 22, 1987; I. PILL-RADEMACHER et al., Vorderer Orient. Römer und Parther (14–138 n.Chr.), TAVO B V 8, 1988; H. WALDMANN, Die hell. Staatenwelt im 3. Jh. v.Chr., TAVO B V 3, 1983.

Indian Ocean The modern Indian Ocean (IO) was mostly known to the Greeks as → *Erythrá thálatta* [1] which actually only referred to the western part. With the increase in geographical knowledge, *Erythrá thá-latta* was also used for the entire ocean (e.g. Peripl. m.r.) that was otherwise called the Indian Sea ('Ἰνδικὸν πέλα-γος/*Indikòn pélagos*, Ptol. 7,1,1; 7,2,1) or IO ('Ἰνδικὸς ὠκεανός/*Indikòs ōkeanós*, Agathemerus 2,4; *Oceanus Indicus*, Mela 1,9, Sen. Q Nat. 4,2,4). With the large gulfs (Sinus Gangeticus, Sabaracus and Perimulicus) it formed the southern boundary of India according to the ancient authors. In the east the → Magnus Sinus stretched to the coast of the Sinai (China). According to Marinus (in Ptol. 7,3,6 and others), this ocean was a closed sea with a land link between East Asia and Africa, an idea that also seems to have been prevalent in the Ancient Orient where the name Meluḥḥa, used in the 3rd millennium BC for the → Indus cultures, was transferred in the 1st millennium to Ethiopia.
→ Hippalus; → India, trade with (with map); → Sacha-lites

J. READE, The Indian Ocean in Antiquity, 1996.　K.K.

Indibilis ('Ανδοβάλης; *Andobáles*). Tribal prince of the → Ilergetes; he and his brother → Mandonius were *omnis Hispaniae principes* (Liv. 27,17,3); As an ally of the Carthaginians in the 2nd Punic War, I. was captured by the Romans in 218 BC (Pol. 3,76,6f.), and in 211 was involved in the victory of → Hasdrubal [3] and → Mago over P. → Cornelius [I 68] Scipio (Liv. 25,34,6–9) [1. 319]. After reprisals on the part of → Hasdrubal [5] and courted by P. → Cornelius [I 71] Scipio, he went over to the Romans (Pol. 9,11; 10,18; 35,6–8; 40,1–6; Liv. 26,49; 27,17; 19,1–7). Having once again turned against the Romans from a military defeat (Pol. 11,29–33; Liv. 28,24–34,11; App. Ib. 37,147f.), he incited the Ausetanians and Sedetanians against the Romans after the retreat of Scipio and his troops [1. 409⁴⁹]. He died in 205 in the battle against L. → Cornelius [I 36] Lentulus and L. → Manlius Acidi-nus, to whom his brother Mandonius was then deliv-ered for execution (Liv. 29,1,19–3,5; Diod. Sic. 26,22; App. Ib. 38,156f.).

1 J. SEIBERT, Hannibal, 1993.　L.-M.G.

Indictio Originally 'levy, tax' (Dig. 19,1,13,6; Cod. Just. 1,51,11 and 12,52,3), from the 4th cent. AD also a term in chronology and from the 6th cent. solely used as a term in chronology.

In the Imperial period *Indictiones temporariae* were extraordinary duties on grain. In 287 emperor → Di-ocletianus introduced an annual tax census that in each case involved a five-year assessment. It was initially called ἐπιγραφή (*epigraphé*), and after 297 also *indictio* (ἰνδικτίων, *indiktíōn*). A 15–year tax cycle was intro-duced in 314, retroactively effective as of September 312. This was not, as has widely been assumed, done by → Constantinus [II 4] I, but (according to [5]) by → Li-cinius [1] in Nicomedia, who set as the first day of the *indictio* year the 23rd of September (the birthday of the emperor Augustus, widespread beginning of the year in Asia Minor). It was not until the 5th cent. (between 452 and 459), the original significance of this date having been forgotten, that the beginning of the *indictio* year was moved to the 1st of September, which made cal-culations easier [5. 193–202].

The *indictio* system was already being used in the 4th. cent. (first in a law of 356, Cod. Theod. 12,12,2) when it became customary to refer to a year by indica-ting its position in the relevant 15–year cycle. In this way, the year from September 312 to September 313, for example, is regarded as the 'first *indictio*' and the following year as the 'second *indictio*' etc.; in Septem-ber 327 counting begins anew etc. The detail 'in the x *indictio*' therefore indicates only the year x in any 15–year cycle from 312 onwards but not the cycle to which reference is being made. This is the disadvantage of this dating system for the historian.

The *indictio* (in Greek also ἐπινέμησις/*epinémēsis*) was made compulsory by → Justinian [1] I in 537 (Nov. 47) for the dating of all public documents. Until the late period of the eastern Roman empire, documents were dated by stating the *indictio*. In the west the use of either this so-called *indictio Graeca* or other *indictio* systems varied with time and place.
→ Time reckoning

1 P.-J. SCHALLER, s.v. Indiktion, LMA 5, 405f.　2 ODB 2, 993　3 O. SEECK, s.v. I., RE 9, 1327–1332　4 R.S. BAGNALL, K. A. WARP, The Chronological Systems of Byz-antine Egypt, 1978　5 V. GRUMEL, La chronologie, 1958, 192–206.　F.T.

Indiction see → Chronography

Indiges (Plural: *indigetes*) refers to a deity or a group of deities whose identity was interpreted in different ways already in antiquity (Serv. Aen. 12,794). The etymology is also disputed: the hypothesis most widely supported today is the one according to which *indiges* like → Indigitamenta are considered to be derived from *indigitare* < **end-ag-itare* [1] ('to invoke'; Fest. 101 L.: *indigitanto imprecanto*), with *indiges*, its sense passive, meaning 'invoked' (**indag-et-*) [2. 59].

Near Lavinium on the river Numicus a cult dedicated to Jupiter Indiges (Liv. 1,2,6) or Sol Indiges (Plin. HN 3,56) [3] is attested. It is later equated with that of Aeneas Indiges [2. 67f.], with Aeneas being worshipped as Pater Indiges (Dion. Hal. Ant. Rom. 1,64,5: πατὴρ θεὸς χθόνιος; *patèr theòs chthónios*) or identified with Jupiter Indiges (Serv. Aen. 1,259). The epithet *indiges* is applied to Aeneas after his deification (Verg. Aen. 12,794; Gell. NA 2,16,8–9). On the Quirinal there was a temple to → Sol Indiges whose birthday was celebrated on the 9th of August [4]. The *indiges*, in whose honour the agonalia were celebrated on the 11th of December [5], can be identified with Sol Indiges on the basis of Lydus, Mens. 4,155, according to whom Helios is honoured with this festival. Besides Lavinium and Rome the *dii indigetes* are also attested for Arpinum (CIL X 1, 5779), and according to Serv. Aen. 7,678, for Praeneste. On several occasions, the *dii indigetes* are mentioned alongside other gods (by Verg. G. 1,498; Ov. Met. 15,861; Claud. De bello Gildonico 15,131). In the prayer spoken by the consul Decius Mus before his self-sacrifice (*devotio*) (Liv. 8,9,6), the *dii indigetes* are invoked after the *novensides*. [6] uses this to distinguish the *indigetes* as indigenous (*indigenae*) gods from more recent arrivals. This interpretation has however not become the accepted view; neither has that of [7. 78ff.], according to which *indiges* means 'progenitor'.

1 ERNOUT/MEILLET, s.v. aio   2 R. SCHILLING, Le culte de l'indiges à Lavinium, in: REL 57, 1979, 49–68   3 Enea nel Lazio. Archeologia e mito (exhibition catalogue), 1981, 167ff.   4 InscrIt. 13,2,493   5 Ibid., 13,2,535–537   6 G. WISSOWA, Gesammelte Abh. zur röm. Rel.- und Stadtgesch., 1904, 175–191   7 C. KOCH, Gestirnverehrung im alten Italien, 1933.

S. BORZSÁK, Zur Indigetes-Frage, in: Hermes 78, 1943, 245–257; LATTE, 43ff.; B. LIOU-GILLE, Cultes 'héroïques' romains, 1980, 99ff.; RADKE, 149ff.; S. WEINSTOCK, s.v. Novensides di, RE 17, 1185–1189.   R.SCH.

Indigitamenta For the etymology, see → Indiges. According to WISSOWA, the word *indigitamenta* refers to collections of invocation phrases with which Roman priests turn to deities on different occasions and which are kept secret by the state because of their compelling authority [1; 2]. With reference to Varro (Antiquitates 14, fr. 87 CARDAUNS), however, the *indigitamenta* are frequently regarded as lists of deities that belong to the pontifical books. Many of these gods, so-called 'special gods or gods of the moment', have a limited role which is mostly expressed by their name: e.g. Paventia, named after the sudden fear suffered by children (Aug. Civ. 4,11,161), or Iterduca and Domiduca, who are responsible for guidance on the way and towards home (Aug. Civ. 7,3,276). The pre-deistic theory, according to which *indigitamenta* represent the first stage in the per-

sonification of the gods [3; 4], should be refuted; rather, they must be understood as subordinate deities who act in the service of higher deities as if they belonged to their *familia* [5]. They have neither priests nor cults of their own. Rarely are they mentioned in prayers to other gods, like the twelve gods passed down to us by Fabius Pictor and Varro (by Serv. Georg. 1,21; Aug. Civ. 4,8) who are invoked during the sacrifice to → Ceres (*sacrum Cereale*) [6], and those who are named by the → Arvales fratres during the expiatory sacrifice for the removal of a tree from the *lucus* (grove) of → Dea Dia (CIL VI 2099: Adolenda, Conmolenda, Deferunda; 21107a: Adolenda, Coinquenda) [7].

The works that contained direct information about the *indigitamenta*, e.g. Varro's *Antiquitates rerum divinarum*, whose primary source is the *Libri iuris pontificii* of → Fabius [I 34] Pictor, and also the book dedicated to Caesar *De indigitamentis* by → Granius [I 3] Flaccus (Censorinus, DN de die natali 3,2), have not been passed down to us. Some fragments of them, however, were handed down by Christian authors, particularly by Augustine (Civ., esp. bks. 4; 6; 7), for whom these works served as the basis for their criticism of the polytheism of pagan religion.

1 G. WISSOWA, Rel. und Kultus der Römer, ²1912, 37; 397; 513   2 Id., Gesammelte Abh. zur röm. Rel.- und Stadtgesch. 1904, 304ff.   3 L. DEUBNER, Altröm. Rel., in: Die Ant. 2, 1926, 61–78   4 H. USENER, Götternamen (1896), 1948, 301ff.   5 DUMÉZIL, 50ff.   6 J. BAYET, Croyances et rites dans la Rome antique, 1977, 181ff. 7 LATTE, 54.

C. KOCH, Gestirnverehrung im alten Italien, 1933, 78ff.   R.SCH.

Indirect tradition → Manuscripts, whether ancient (→ Papyrus) or medieval, are the basic source for our editions of ancient texts, but editors frequently need to take account also of evidence provided by the indirect or secondary tradition. This evidence may be classified as follows.

A. TRANSLATIONS   B. TEXTUAL QUOTATIONS
C. LITERARY QUOTATIONS

A. TRANSLATIONS

Many Greek texts, mainly philosophical or scientific, were translated into Latin (or one or more Oriental languages) in late antiquity or the early Middle Ages. Though the exemplars used by the translators were not in all cases older than the earliest witnesses to the direct tradition, and not all translators were equal to their task, the translations are often valuable. On the other hand translation of Latin into Greek was rare; the best examples are the versions by Planudes of some of the works of Ovid (*Metamorphoses*, published by J. BOISSONADE [1]; the *Heroides*, printed in A. PALMER's posthumous edition [2], with a new ed. by M. PAPATHOMOPOULOS [3]; the love poetry, published in [4]); editors have attached considerable weight to these in the past, but it is now clear that the manuscripts from which they derive were not of great value (see [5; 6]). From antiquity itself we have Catullus' versions of Sappho (fr. 31 LOBEL-PAGE/VOIGT = Catull. 51) and Callimachus, *Coma Berenices* (fr. 110 Pf. = Catull. 66), as well as Cicero's various translations of tragic passages.

B. TEXTUAL QUOTATIONS

Quotations, normally anonymous, may be found written on ancient artefacts other than papyrus or parchment. These are relatively rare, the main examples being graffiti from Pompeii. The most striking case is provided by CIL 4,1950, which gives a superior text of Propertius 3.16.13–14 (most recently: [7]). The writers of such material naturally felt free to adapt original texts, and to combine excerpts from more than one work; thus another Pompeian graffito *(CIL* 4,1520) reworks Propertius 1,1,5 into *candida (donec* Prop.) *me docuit nigras (castas* Prop.) *odisse puellas,* and adds a corrupt version of another hexameter, for us Ov. Am. 3,11,35 (part of a couplet excised by Heinsius): *odero, si potero; sed (si* Ovid) *non inuitus amabo.* A rarer case is the statue of Socrates which has on it a quotation from *Crit.* 46b 4–6; editors accept the variant it offers.

C. LITERARY QUOTATIONS

Much the most numerous and important indirect source is the use in one author of quotations from another. Often these are earlier than any witness of the direct tradition, and where the two disagree it is tempting (and will often be right) to prefer the older variant. But it is not safe to do so in all cases, because ancient and medieval writers were less likely to verify, the accuracy of their quotations; the *uolumen* form of book did not make for easy reference, and precise location by chapter and verse was almost unknown; authors relied on well-stocked but unreliable memories. However, when the secondary tradition has a variant at the point which the quotation was specifically designed to illustrate, the quoting author is less likely to be in error. Even here caution is required, as a famous example illustrates: Vergil, Ecl. 4,62–3. Quintilian quoted this (Inst. 9,3,8), and his manuscripts read *cui non risere parentes,/ nec deus hunc mensa, dea nec dignata cubili est* like those of Vergil himself. But the Context (on change of number), and the ensuing comment (*ex illis enim 'qui non risere' hic quem non dignata*), show that Quintilian himself read *qui.* As *ridere* with the accusative means 'to laugh at', not 'to smile for', this hardly fits with *parentes* (but for attempts to take it so, see [8]); most editors therefore accept Schrader's *parenti,* and suppose that the MSS of Quintilian have been doubly corrupted from those of Vergil. However, G.P. GOOLD [10] has produced a number of arguments against the modern vulgate *qui ... parenti,* and it may be that Quintilian's reading was a matter of faulty judgement rather than an uncorrupted text. There is an enormous variety of purposes for which quotations are made: from the lemmata of scholia, through the technical citations of grammarians and metricians, and the appeal to an earlier writer's authority, to creative reworking.

1. SCHOLIA   2. GRAMMARIANS AND METRISTS 3. REWORKING OF THE MODEL

1. SCHOLIA

Scholia are normally transmitted alongside the texts on which they comment, so they are not as independent as one would wish, but they can be useful in giving specific judgements on textual discrepancies already current in antiquity (even if modern editors rarely feel limited by their judgements), and occasionally in preserving material that the main tradition omits (cf. [11] for the *Aeneid,* and, more generally for the IT of Vergil: [12; 13]). For a discussion of ancient variants see, e.g., schol. Aristoph. Thesm. 162.

2. GRAMMARIANS AND METRISTS

Grammarians and lexicographers have transmissions that are more independent, and they usually have a particular oddity in mind which they confirm, leaving little room for editorial hesitation. Thus Charisius (KEIL 1,107,27–8) confirms the feminine *demissae ... sertae,* the reading of the oldest Propertian MS (N) at 2,33,37, against the neuter of the rest; and discussions of the conjugation of *necto* by Diomedes (KEIL 1,369,21) and Priscian (KEIL 2,536,7–15) show that at Prop. 3,8,37 we should read *nexisti retia lecto,* not the transmitted banalisation *tendisti* (itself of course anomalous). Such authors are usually conscientious in recording the source of their quotations, but errors do occur: thus Diomedes attributes the words *nexisti retia lecto* to 'Maecenas'. As quotations come in fists omission may often have led to such slips. In some cases the number of citations can be great enough for scholars to have built up a useful set of fragments from works for which there is no direct transmission. A signal example of this is Callimachus' *Hecale*: A. HECKER [14] deduced with extraordinary insight that not only the attributed but also the unattributed hexameter quotations given by the → Suda were (unless otherwise known) to be assigned to this lost poem. Subsequently the discovery of papyri has provided a direct tradition for some parts of the poem, and demonstrated the basic truth of his judgement.

Metricians regularly cite the first lines of poems and of books (and all scholars tend to refer more often to the books and poems early in a sequence), and so the pattern of citations informs discussions of the division of poems (→ poems, division of) and books: see also [16]. The attention paid to Catullus 1 is a fair example of the general point: verses from this 10–line poem are cited for metre (repeatedly), in a discussion of ancient book production (Isid. 6,12,3), and to introduce prefaces of Ausonius (1,4,1) and the elder Pliny (HN praef. 1, with an acknowledged change of word order – itself corrupted in transmission – to produce a spondaic rather than an iambic opening for verse 4).

3. REWORKING OF THE MODEL

A more concerted form of creative reworking is the → cento, in which a new poem is wrought through the reassembling of the *disiecta membra* of an earlier poem. Though the quotations are often accurate, they are not as useful to the editor as they might be, because Homer and Vergil are the normal source for the cento, and these texts are already preserved in ancient traditions. Ausonius' *Cento nuptialis* (on which see [17]) in its 131 lines does nothing more than add its support to one group of Vergilian MSS against another at places where they divide; at the same time, however, the Vergilian tradition functions as an indirect witness to Ausonius' text. More significant is the contribution the medieval play *Christus patiens* makes to our texts of Euripides' *Bacchae*, especially in helping to fill some of the great lacuna after verse 1329. Cento sets out to reproduce exactly the wording of the verses used; parodies, too, can stay very close to originals (cf. Eur. Hel. 570 in Aristoph. Thesm. 910, and other passages of paratragedy in Thesm.; Catullus 4 in [Verg.] Catal. 10); and even vaguer use of models may provide important indirect testimony. Following the majority of ninth-century MSS, editors give the text of Verg. G. 1,513 as *addunt in spatia*, although this is extremely hard to construe, and although the two antique MSS extant here (R and M) omit the *in*, and M together with some later MSS has *spatio*. The MSS of Quintilian, who quotes the verses at Inst. 8,3,78, divide between *in spatio* and *in spatia*; but, as we have already seen and as this in itself indicates, Quintilian's MSS were contaminated by readings from the direct Vergilian tradition. One might therefore have some sympathy with PULBROOK's bold conjecture *inuadunt spatia* [18], but if that is right, the corruption had apparently become established in the Vergilian tradition before Silius Italicus wrote 16,373 *in spatia* (or -o) *addebant*. Thus, too, those who follow WEST [19] in believing Soph. OT 1278–9 are due to → interpolation have to assume that the addition is antique, for the verses are paraphrased at Sen. Oed. 978–9. Sometimes the argument runs from model to quotation: at Ov. Am. 1,15,25 J.C. MCKEOWN follows the 1502 Aldine edition in reading *Tityrus et* segetes *Aeneiaque arma legentur* in preference to the transmitted *fruges*, on the grounds that this restores the allusion to Verg. G. 1,1 (*Quid faciat laetas segetes*) to match the echoes of Ecl. l,1 and Aen. 1,1 [20]; but the substitution of a synonym is effective variation, and we might see an allusion to Ecl. 10,76 (*nocent et frugibus umbrae*) where Vergil, in closing one work alludes to the next. But this is simply to illustrate that the boundaries of 'IT' are not fixed.

→ Author's variants; → TEXTUAL TRADITION

1 J. BOISSONADE (ed.), Metamorphoses, Paris 1822   2 A. PALMER (ed.), Heroides, Oxford 1898, pp.161–274   3 M. PAPATHOMOPOULOS (ed.), Heroides, 1976   4 P.E. EASTERLING, E.J. KENNEY, Ovidiana graeca (PCPhS suppl. 1), 1965 (love poetry)   5 R.J. TARRANT, in: L.D. REYNOLDS (ed.), Text and Transmission, 1983, 281, n. 20   6 E.J. KENNEY, in: Hermes 91, 1963, 214–216   7 J.L. BUTRICA, in: CQ 47, 1997, 181–182   8 TH. BIRT, in: Berliner Philologische Wochenschrift 1918, 186–192   9 R.G.M. NISBET, Collected papers, 1985, 73, n. 135   10 G.P. GOOLD, A skullcracker in Virgil, in: I. VASLEF, H. BUSCHHAUSEN (ed.), Classica et Mediaevalia: studies in honor of Joseph Szöv%/erffy, 1986, 67–76   11 R.A.B. MYNORS (ed.), P. Vergili Maronis Opera, 1969, p. xii   12 S. TIMPANARO, Per la storia della filologia virgiliana antica, 1986   13 M.L. DELRIGO, Testo virgiliano e tradizione indiretta. Le varianti probiane, 1987   14 A. HEKKER, Commentationum Callimachearum capita duo, 1842, 79–148   15 A.S. HOLLIS (ed.), Callimachus, Hecale, 1990, 41–44   16 J.L. BUTRICA, in: Illinois Classical Studies 21, 1996, 94–96   17 R.P.H. GREEN, The Works of Ausonius, 1991, 518–526   18 M. PULBROOK, in: Hermathena 120, 1976, 39–40   19 M.L. WEST, in: BICS 25, 1978, 121   20 J.C. MCKEOWN (ed.), Ovid, Amores, 1989 (commentary ad loc.)

S. TIMPANARO, Alcuni casi controversi di tradizione indiretta, in: Maia 22, 1990, 351–359; L.D. REYNOLDS, N.G. WILSON, Scribes and Scholars, ³1991, 219–221.

S.H. and N.W.

Indo-Aryan languages The Indo-Aryan languages (IL) comprise the majority of those → Indo-European languages that have been spoken on the Indian sub-continent since the immigration from the north-west in the 2nd millennium BC. Together with the → Iranian languages, they form the Indo-Iranian branch of this family of languages. Old Indo-Aryan (less precise: Old Indian) begins just before 1200 BC with Vedic and continues in Sanskrit [1. 16–48]. As an ancient and early-attested Indo-European language, it has many correspondences with Latin and particularly also with Greek that are not just formal; therefore it is also of the utmost importance for the reconstruction of the Indo-European basic language: cf. the noun (or pronoun) endings in the singular of *-o*-stems

	Proto-Indo-Eur.	Old Indo-Ar.	Homeric	Old Lat.
nom.	*-os	-as	-ος	-os
acc.	*-om	-am	-ον	-om
gen.	*-osio	-asya	-οιο	-osio

With reference to Greek, the following features of the older Vedic are especially worthy of emphasis: free musical word stress (→ Accent) as well as formal and functional opposition between augmented and non-augmented preterite forms (indicative as the mode of reporting: injunctive as the mode of mentioning) [2], cf. in the present tense stem

	Proto-Indo-Eur.	Indo-Ar.	Homeric
1st sg.	*b ʰér-o-m	bhár-a-m	φέρ-ο-ν
	*é-b ʰer-o-m	á-bhar-a-m	ἔ-φερ-ο-ν
2nd	*b ʰér-e-s	bhár-a-s	φέρ-ε-ς
	*é-b ʰer-e-s	á-bhar-a-s	ἔ-φερ-ε-ς
3rd	*b ʰér-e-t	bhár-a-t	φέρ-ε
	*é-b ʰer-e-t	á-bhar-a-t	ἔ-φερ-ε

Furthermore, in the period of Middle Indo-Aryan slight mutual loan relationships exist between the IL and particularly Greek, for example in proper names (e.g. *Milinda-* from Greek Μένανδϱος/*Ménandros* or Σανδϱόϰοττος/*Sandrókottos* from Indo-Aryan *Candragupta-*) or in the case of specialized terms: cf. *khalīna-* 'snaffle' from Greek χαλινός (*chalinós*) or σάϰχαϱ(-ι, -ον)/*sákchar (-i, -ou)* 'sugar' (borrowed into Latin as *saccharum*) from Pāli *sakkharā-* 'sand sugar' < Old Indo-Aryan *śárkarā-* 'gravel, scree, grit' [3. 155f.]. → Greek; → Latin

1 H. BECHERT, G. VON SIMSON (ed.), Einführung in die Indologie, ²1993   2 K. HOFFMANN, Der Injunktiv im Veda, 1967   3 SCHWYZER, Gramm.   R.P.

Indo-European languages

A. GENERAL, DEFINITION   B. REPRESENTATIVES
C. STOCK OF SOUNDS AND FORMS   D. COMMON
PROTO-LANGUAGE

A. GENERAL, DEFINITION

Since the beginning of the 19th cent. primarily outside the German language area (cf. French *langues indoeuropéennes* but German *Indogermanische Sprachen*) the common term for a group of related languages which in antiquity and in the Middle Ages stretched in a line running from the southeast to the northwest from India to Europe. This area of distribution gave its name to a family of ancient and recently attested, as well as extinct and still living languages. The Indo-European languages (IL) consequently cover not only a wide geographical area but also span a long period of time.

B. REPRESENTATIVES

The IL are essentially divided up into ten language branches (in each case with information about the length of attestation of the language's own sources): (1) *Indo-Iranian*, comprising the → Indo-Aryan languages (Old Indo-Aryan from c. 1200 BC, beginning with Vedic, continued in Sanscrit) and the → Iranian languages (Old Iranian with Old Persian from the 6th cent. BC and Avestan from the 1st half of the 1st millennium BC), (2) → *Anatolian languages* (→ Asia Minor, languages) with the oldest evidence of an Indo-European language, including → Hittite (from the 18th cent. BC), (3) → *Greek*, beginning with → Mycenaean (about 1400–1200 BC), continuous tradition from the 2nd half of the 8th cent. BC with alphabetic evidence, (4) *Italic* (→ Italy, languages) from c. 500 BC onwards, dividing into the Oscan-Umbrian and Latino-Faliscan groups (→ Oscan-Umbrian, → Latin), (5) → *Germanic* languages, dividing into Eastern Germanic with → Gothic (end of the 4th cent. AD), Northern Germanic with the Scandinavian languages (since the 3rd cent. AD), and Western Germanic, including Old High German, from AD 700, (6) → *Celtic languages* with two distinct features: Island Celtic (Britain, Ireland) from AD 400 and Mainland Celtic (Gaul, Spain, northern Italy) from the 2nd cent. BC, (7) *Balto-Slavonic*, consisting of the → Slavonic languages (from the 9th cent. AD with three groupings: Eastern Slavonic e.g.

Russian, Southern Slavonic including Bulgarian and Serbo-Croat, and Western Slavonic) and the → Baltic languages (Lithuanian, Latvian, Old Prussian, from the 14th cent. AD), (8) → *Armenian* from the 5th cent. AD onwards, (9) → *Tocharian* (in western China, Tarim Basin: 6th–8th cents. AD) with two dialects: A or Eastern Tocharian and B or Western Tocharian, and (10) → *Albanian* from the 15th cent. AD. Added to this are also (11) several languages from the ancient Mediterranean which are only known or have been deduced from a few, partly uncertainly interpreted testimonies (inscriptions, proper names, glosses, loan words) and whose relationship with (1)–(10) cannot be exactly determined: e.g. → Macedonian, → Messapic, → Phrygian.

C. STOCK OF SOUNDS AND FORMS

The fact that the IL belong together is demonstrated by the traceability to a common extinct proto-language: proto-Indo-European. From the interplay between the individual derivative languages, it is possible, as a result of the circumstance that a sound system will generally change regularly in accordance with phonetic laws, to derive the following phoneme inventory for proto-Indo-European:

I. Vowels:

1. short:	e	a	o
2. long:	$\bar{e}$	$\bar{a}$	$\bar{o}$

II. Resonants

I Semivowels

a) vocalic:	i	u
(rarely long:)	$\bar{i}$	$\bar{u}$)
b) consonantal:	$\underset{\cdot}{i}$	$\underset{\cdot}{u}$

II Liquids

a) vocalic:	$\underset{\cdot}{l}$	$\underset{\cdot}{r}$
b) consonantal:	l	r

III nasals

a) vocalic:	$\underset{\cdot}{m}$	$\underset{\cdot}{n}$
b) consonantal:	m	n

III Laryngeals h_1 h_3

IV. Consonants

1) Labials	p	b	b^h
2) Dentals	t	d	d^h
3) Velars	k	g	g^h
4) Palatals	$\acute{k}$	$\acute{g}$	$\acute{g}^h$
5) Labiovelars	k^w	g^w	g^{wh}

V Sibilants s z

The following can be established as characteristics of the Indo-European sound system: quantitative and qualitative → ablaut in the sonants, vocalic or consonantal realization of the resonants, formation of short or long diphthongs through a combination of sonants and resonants, three → laryngeals, and division of consonants according to the type of articulation into unvoiced (*tenues*), voiced (*mediae*) and voiced-aspirated (*mediae aspiratae*) sounds. In all IL, for the → gutturals the deduced triple (velar, palatal, labiovelar) of the proto-language is reduced to two by the convergence of

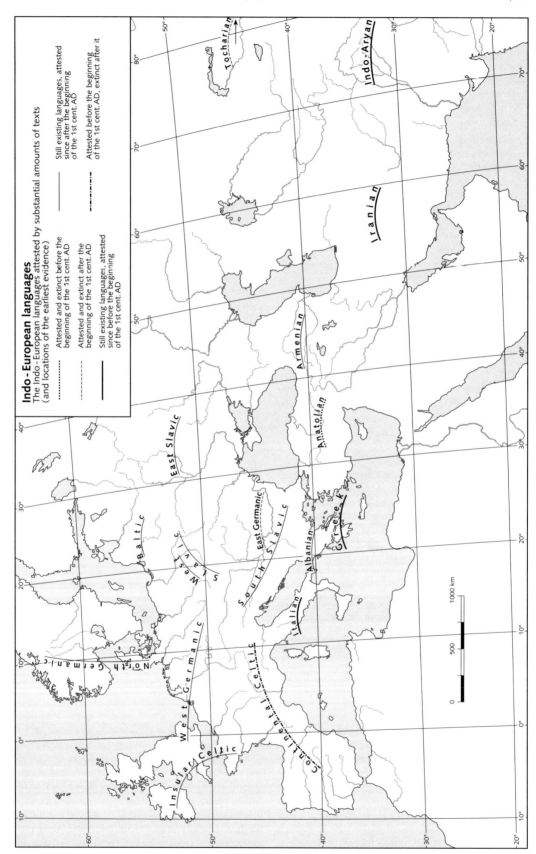

Indo-European languages
The Indo-European languages attested by substantial amounts of texts
(and locations of the earliest evidence)

··········· Attested and extinct before the
beginning of the 1st cent. AD

– – – – – Attested and extinct after the
beginning of the 1st cent. AD

———— Still existing languages, attested
since before the beginning
of the 1st cent. AD

———— Still existing languages, attested
since after the beginning
of the 1st cent. AD

–·–·–·– Attested before the beginning
of the 1st cent. AD, extinct after it

either the palatal or the labiovelar with the velar. Languages are divided into → *centum* (i.e. labiovelar) languages and → *satem* (i.e. palatal) languages according to the Latin or Avestan words for 100:

Centum languages		Satem languages	
Latin	*centum*	Avestan	*satə*
Greek	ἑκατόν	Old Indic	*śatám*
Old Irish	*cét*	Old Church Slavonic	*sŭto*
Gothic	*hund*	Lithuanian	*šim̃tas*
Tocharian A	*känt*	Latvian	*sìmts*

This feature allows for a division into eastern and western IL without this classification implying very much. By no means more meaningful is the criterion of the corresponding names for bodies of water in Europe, which used to be seen as a basis for the → Ancient European languages.

From the sound system and the evidence of individual languages, the stock of forms in the IL can often be determined in detail. Thus, the continuants of the following languages

Old Indic	*ásti*	:	*sánti*
Young Avestan	*asti*	:	*həṇti*
Old Persian	*astiy*	:	*haⁿti*
Hittite	*ešzi*	:	*ašanzi*
Greek	ἐστί	:	/ehensi/ (Mycenaean)
Oscan-Umbrian	*est*	:	*sent*

together with other languages, enable reconstruction of the proto-Indo-European forms $*h_1és\text{-}ti$ 'he/she/it is' and $*h_1s\text{-}énti$ 'they are'. By comparing languages, a class of present-tense stem formation (athematic root present) with a particular inflectional characteristic (→ Ablaut in the root syllable) and a series of endings (primary 3rd person endings $*\text{-}ti$ in he singular, $*\text{-}énti$ in the plural) can also be established.

D. Common proto-language

Because of the broad base of material from the Indo-European daughter languages, the common Indo-European proto-language can be deduced both lexically (and hence phonetically and morphologically) and syntactically. Furthermore, stylistic features (including particular word combinations) justify the postulation of → Indo-European poetics. The establishment of the facts and associated historical questions of the proto-language is one of the tasks of the study of Indo-European. Thanks to its research, it is possible to draw conclusions, based on the vocabulary assumed for the basic language, about real conditions among the speakers of proto-Indo-European, for instance about their way of life and social structure (→ Indo-Europeans).

→ Study of Indo-European

R. S. P. Beekes, Comparative Indo-European Linguistics, 1995; Brugmann/Delbrück; W. Cowgill, Indogermanische Gramm. I,1: Einl., 1986; Pokorny; O. Szemerényi, Einführung in die vergleichende Sprachwiss., ⁴1990.
R.P.

Indo-European poetics Indo-European poetics (IP) refers to phrases, largely corresponding etymologically, found in the oldest writings in various Indo-European languages, particularly Greek and Indo-Iranian. An example is Greek κλέος ἄφθιτον (*kléos áphthiton*) in Homer and Old Indian *ákṣitam śrávas*, both meaning 'immortal fame'. The fact that in Old Indian *ákṣitam* appears only in this connection supports the view that the phrase is very old. In this way it is possible to reconstruct IP $*kléu̯os\ ṇg^{wh}d^hitom$. Additional formulas from the same content area, for example Greek κλέα ἀνδρῶν (*kléa andrôn*) in Homer and Old Indian *śrávo...nṛṇám*, both of which literally mean 'fame of men' but in fact mean 'famous deeds of heroes', confirm the hypothesis. Also the existence of poetry itself is confirmed indirectly by formulas, as poets can be called ἐπέων τέκτονες (*epéōn téktones*) 'word carpenters' in Greek, and in Old Indian it is *vácāṁsi...takṣam* 'I will carpenter words'. Additional formulas obviously come from hymns or prayers, others, not in the narrower sense in poetic language, come from proverbial wisdom, mythical tradition and the like, in verse or prose.

Meillet has also shown that the eleven-syllable verse of the Aeolian poet Sappho corresponds to the Old Indian *triṣṭubh* verse of the same number of syllables even in the distribution of long and short syllables in the second half of the verse. Even if the latter property of Old Iranian poetry is not shared, the eleven-syllable verse is found here too, so that syllable-counting metre can be attributed to IP.

→ Homeric language; → Indo-Europeans; → Indo-European languages; → Metrics

R. Schmitt, Dichtung und Dichtersprache in indogermanischer Zeit, 1967 Id., (ed.), Indogermanische Dichtersprache, 1968 C. Watkins, How to Kill a Dragon. Aspects of Indo-European Poetics, 1995. N.O.

Indo-Europeans

A. Definition, general, methods B. Ancient homeland and spreading C. Material and spiritual culture

A. Definition, general, methods

I. refers to both the carriers of individual → Indo-European languages and those of reconstructed proto-Indo-European (proto-Indo-European basic language) or for instance of proto-Greek. The proof provided at the beginning of the 19th cent. of the linguistic affinity has given rise to the question who the speakers of the basic language were. With this new concept, the postulate was introduced into prehistory that a people with a characteristic culture should be sought. But the definition of an ethnos does not depend exclusively on the language factor. We should not form opinions about the racial composition of the original people. Because of different methods in the (pre)historic fields, indispensable interdisciplinary research is made more difficult. Linguistics determines the premises [1] by reconstructing elements of the proto-Indo-European vocabulary and, where applicable, interpreting them etymological-ly, arranging them according to areas of meaning or attempting to define their meaning more precisely through reciprocal semantic references. The procedure by which conclusions are drawn from a proto-language vocabulary regarding living conditions and the environ-ment of the speakers is called 'linguistic palaeontology'. The Indo-European 'Altertumskunde' which traces common cultural traditions back to prehistoric sources cannot be clearly distinguished from this: texts are vehi-cles for transporting content that has been handed down. Critics object that in principle the possibility of polygenesis or secondary spread of cultural achieve-ments and their designations always exists. In this way the discussion has not yet attained any exact determi-nation of space and time. We are unable to ascertain the existence of ancient loan words in proto-Indo-Euro-pean that could uncover prehistoric contacts.

B. Ancient homeland and spreading

Aside from linguistic palaeontology, the historical distribution allows us to draw conclusions about the prehistoric seats. The appearance at the beginning of the 2nd millennium of I. in Asia Minor (→ Anatolian languages), which was not itself the original homeland (incorrect [2]), directs the search towards neighbouring regions. A wide-area localization appears justifiable in the southern Russian and the Ukrainian regions al-though there are not enough grounds for a strict dem-arcation from neighbouring areas. The areas mentioned allow us to reconstruct the distribution. Gradual migra-tions producing dialect continua alternated with expan-sive migrations, which interrupted communication (models: 'wave theory' versus 'geneaological theory'). As Greek and languages close to it like → Macedonian should [3. 244f.] be placed side by side with → Phrygian and → Armenian when undertaking linguistic classifi-cation, the original homeland of this group could be the area between the Balkans and Asia Minor. It is highly probable that the distribution region of the prehistoric 'Graeco-Armenians' lay north of the Black Sea, not far from the point of origin of the proto-I. Another split resulted, through north-western migration in the 2nd millennium BC, in an epicentre in Central and Eastern Europe that corresponds with a modified concept of → Ancient European. From thence followed the settle-ment of European fringe territories, i.e. of the west by the Celts and of Italy by the Italic peoples, after they broke free from their association with the Celts. The driving forces behind the prehistoric spread are hard to determine. Presumably the proto-I. consisted of a rela-tively large population that had probably grown be-cause of the favourable natural conditions, utilizing multiple achievements in the process. In the search for other areas, they pushed back or subjugated foreign tribes until they attained the distribution known from the historical period.

C. Material and spiritual culture

The criteria for the chronological classification of the proto-I. (end of the Neolithic, c. 3rd millennium) arise from questions about the technical achievements. Aside from the ceramics still produced without a pot-ter's wheel, the metals known to them were *$(h_2)áies$- 'bronze, copper' (Old Indian áyas-, Latin aes) and *$h_2ar\hat{g}ntóm$ 'silver' (Old Indian rajatám, Latin argen-tum), but there is a lack of significant words from the sphere of the manufacture or working of metals. With regard to material foundations, there are dietary terms which can provide some information about the world in which the I. lived. Aside from agriculture and stock farming, the menu was enriched through hunting and fishing. The domesticated animals included dogs, horses, cattle, sheep, pigs and goats. Words for 'milk', 'to milk', 'wool', 'to spin', 'to weave' suggest that they refer to domesticated species of the animals mentioned. Reconstructible vocabulary for the plough and cart (wheel, shaft etc.) indicates the use of horses and/or cat-tle as draught animals. The fauna also included, among other animals, the eagle, bear, beaver, bee, fox, hare, crane and wolf. The reconstruction of legal, social or political concepts or the conditions allocated to these remains a difficult task. The views of Dumézil (against these in detail [4]) that the Indo-European society and its reflection in mythology was marked by a functional tripartite division are considered incorrect. Traces of comparable ritual practices and religious ideas can be established. A pantheon of natural and celestial deities is assumed (Greek → Eos, Latin Aurora). The epiclesis 'father' of the highest god 'day (sky)' (Latin Diespi-ter / → Juppiter, Greek → Zeus) shows, with the devel-opment of a system of kinship names, a patriarchal family structure. Despite uncertainties concerning the methodology, the material and spiritual culture of the proto-I. or of the ethnic groups that were already for-ming in the prehistoric period remain legitimate sub-jects of research. It is certainly relevant to know the extent to which institutions, traditions and customs were inherited from the prehistoric period, organically developed or introduced from elsewhere. As Greek and Latin are not all that closely related within the Indo-European language family the correspondences in vo-cabulary must either go back to the prehistoric period or be based on borrowings in the historical period.

→ Indo-European languages; → Indo-European poet-ics; → Linguistic affinity; → Indo-European studies

1 W. Dressler, Methodische Vorfragen bei der Bestim-mung der 'Urheimat', in: Sprache 11, 1965, 25–60 2 C. Renfrew, Archaeology and Language, 1987 3 G. Klingenschmitt, Die Verwandtschaftsverhältnisse der indogermanischen Sprachen, in: J. E. Rasmussen (ed.), In honorem H. Pedersen, 1994, 235–251 4 B. Schlerath, Georges Dumézil und die Rekonstruk-tion der indogermanischen Kultur, in: Kratylos 40, 1995, 1–48; 41, 1996, 1–67.

E. Benveniste, Indoeuropäische Institutionen, 1993 (French 1969); T. V. Gamkrelidze, V. V. Ivanov, Indo-European and the Indo-Europeans, 1995; B. Hänsel,

S. ZIMMER (ed.), Die Indogermanen und das Pferd, 1994;
W. MEID, Arch. und Sprachwissenschaft, 1989; A. SCHE-
RER (ed.), Die Urheimat der Indogermanen, 1968; S. ZIM-
MER, Ursprache, Urvolk und Indogermanisierung, 1990.
JOURNAL: The Journal of Indo-European Studies.   D.ST.

Indo-Greeks The Greeks of Hellenistic Bactria
(→ Graeco-Bactria), who conquered southeastern
Afghanistan (Paropamisadae and Arachosia) and
northwestern India (modern Pakistan) in the 2nd cent.
BC. After the first and most important kings (→ Demetrius [10] and Menander) the kingdom disintegrated
into several parts whose numerous rulers (almost 40)
are mostly attested only by coins. The I. held on until
the 1st cent. BC or even the 1st cent. AD, when territories were conquered by the → Parthians and the central Asian Sakas and Indo-Scythians. Their influence on
India and central Asia remained limited, but the Hellenistic formulaic idiom of subsequent Buddhist Gandhāra
art derives ultimately from them.

BOPEARACHCHI; K. NARAIN, The Indo-Greeks, 1957.
                                                        K.K.

Indo-Scythians (in Chinese sources *Yuèzhī*) originally a
Central Asian people, which migrated west in the 2nd
cent. BC. The I. conquered → Graeco-Bactria and later
moved to India, where they founded the powerful
→ Kushan dynasty (→ Kanishka). Their Indian kingdom is called Indo-Scythia by Ptolemy and others.
→ Scythians

J. E. VAN LOHUIZEN-DE LEEUW, The Scythian Period,
1949.   K.K.

Indulgentia The technical term from the beginning of
the 3rd cent. AD for a criminal law pardon by the
Roman emperor (e.g. Cod. Just. 9,23,5 of the year 225).
However there had long been pardons in Rome. They
could happen during criminal proceedings (e.g. Mod.
Dig. 48,16,17) as well as after them in order to lift the
sanction imposed, and even before the initiation of any
prosecution. In this way, Julius Caesar ordered the people's tribune M. Antonius to arrange a plebiscite to
pardon those condemned according to Pompey's law
on electoral fraud (→ *ambitus*) (Caes. B Civ. 3,1,4; Cic.
Phil. 2,98). From this form of pardon, traditional in the
period after Sulla, the connection with legislative power
becomes clear. The *indulgentia* granted to an individual
by the emperor therefore still appears among his legislative powers in Inst. Just. (1,2,6). The *indulgentia* differs here from the mere cessation of the proceedings (cf.
→ *abolitio*) that could also be decreed by the judge, but
fits in with the Greek → *amnēstía* allowed by law. Before the 3rd cent. AD, *indulgentia* was probably called
after its legal consequence, a → *restitutio*. It means in
general that those pardoned were fully restored to their
earlier legal position but no confiscated means were
returned (cf. Cod. Just. 9,51,2: reimbursement only by
special → *beneficium*). In the case of a mass pardon

(*indulgentia communis* or *generalis*), on the contrary,
the incidental consequence of the loss of honour (→ *infamia*) continued. Aside from the strict legal meaning,
indulgentia refers to the quality of mercy generally attributed to the emperor as the content of any measures
bestowing favour.

W. WALDSTEIN, Unt. zum röm. Begnadigungsrecht, 1964;
J. GAUDEMET, Indulgentia principis, 1962.   G.S.

Indus (Ἰνδός; *Indós*).
[1] The River Indus. Probably from Old Indian *Sindhu*
(for the etymology cf. → India); the Indian name is
better attested as *Sindus* in Plin. HN 6,71, than Σίνθος;
Sínthos in Peripl. m.r. 38; 40 and as Σίνδων/Σίνθων;
Síndōn/Sínthōn in Ptol. 7,1,2 (here a branch of the
delta). According to general Greek opinion (with the
exception of → Megasthenes), the I. is the largest river
in India, known to the Greeks since the end of the 6th
cent. BC (Scylax in Hdt. 4,44). The lower reaches for
instance downstream from the confluence with the River Kabul and the delta were explored by → Scylax and
later by Alexander the Great. The true source in western
Tibet remained unknown; it was believed that the
source of the river was not far from where it broke
through into the plain. The great significance of the I.
for nature and the economy of the river plain was correctly recognized by the Alexander historians and natural scientists, and the river was compared to the Nile.
Like the latter, the I. was also important as a communications and trading route; → Patala and → Barabara
in the delta were important trading ports.

1 K. KARTTUNEN, The Name of India, in: Cracow Indolo-
gical Stud. 1, 1995, 151–163   2 O. WECKER, s.v. I. (1), RE
9, 1369–73.   K.K.

[2] Lycian river in the border area of Caria, modern
Dalaman, in the upper reaches of the Koca or the Mor-
zon. It has its source in the mountains in the north of
Cibyratis (on Mount Eşler 2254 m), and is described by
Plin. HN 5,103 as exceptionally full of water, as it takes
up 60 perennial tributaries and over 100 mountain
streams in its course. The fort of Thabusion lay on the I.
(Liv. 38,14,2).

G. WINKLER, R. KÖNIG (ed.), C. Plinius Secundus. Naturalis Historiae Libri XXXVII, vol. 5, 1993, 220 (comm.).
                                                        E.O.

Indus Culture Prehistoric high culture in the 3rd millennium in northwestern South Asia, from Punjab to
Baluchistan and Gujarat, with Harappa and Mohenjo-
Daro as the most likely important centres. There was
lively overseas trade (a harbour was excavated at
Lothal in Gujarat) with Makan (modern Oman),
→ Dilmun (modern Bahrain), the island of Failaka
(now part of Kuwait) and Mesopotamia [1. 107ff.].
The famous Indus script is only attested in the form of
very short seal legends; the language on which it was
based is probably, although this is unconfirmed, a form
of Proto-Dravidian [2].

1 J. READE (ed.), The Indian Ocean in Antiquity, 1996
2 A. PARPOLA, Deciphering the Indus Script, 1994. K.K.

Industria *Oppidum* (*regio IX*, Plin. HN 3,49; from 124/3 BC?) close to the Ligurian Bodincomagus (Plin. HN 3,122), *municipium* (*tribus Pollia*), modern Monteu da Po. Sanctuary of Isis and Serapis (Hadrianic period), road, *insula*. CIL V 7468; 7469; Suppl. Italica, XII 1994, 41–61.

> Fontes Ligurum et Liguriae antiquae, 1976, s.v. Bodincomagus, Industria; E. ZANDA et al., Studi su Industria, in: Quaderni Soprintendenza Archeologica Piemonte 11, 1993, 29–97; E. ZANDA, Il santuario isiaco di Industria, in: E. A. ARSLAN (ed.), Iside, 1997, 352–357. L.S.A.

Indutiae As opposed to a mere pause in a battle (*quies a proeliis*), *indutiae* in martial and international law means an agreed truce (*cessatio pugnae pacticia*: Gell. NA 1,25,8) or the agreement on which it is based (*pactio indutiarum*). The historicity of *indutiae* valid beyond the year of office of the commander and ending a war for from 2 to 100 years, according to annalistic tradition like peace treaties, is contentious [2. 43f.]. The Roman international law which developed recognizes only the contractually agreed, deferred interruption of military action [2. 45] in continued war (Gell. NA 1,25,4; cf. Dig. 49,15,19,1). The deferment from one day to several months was functional, so as e.g. to bury the fallen, initiate negotiations and capitulation or to ratify a *foedus* after the conclusion of a preliminary peace. In late antiquity, *indutiae* serve as, among other things, short-term treaties to end a war [3. 73f.].

> 1 MARTINO, SCR 2,63ff.   2 K.-H. ZIEGLER, Kriegsverträge im ant. röm. Recht, in: ZRG 102, 1985, 40–90   3 Id., Völkerrechtsgesch., 1994. P.KE.

Indutiomarus
[1] Celtic compound name from *-marus* 'great' [1. 96–98]. Leader of a delegation of the → Allobroges, who accused M. → Fonteius [I 2] in 69 BC in *repetundae* proceedings (→ Repetundarum Crimen). Cicero defended him, evidently with success (*Pro M. Fonteio*) [2. 83–104].

> 1 EVANS   2 B. KREMER, Das Bild der Kelten bis in augusteische Zeit, 1994.

[2] Prince of the → Treveri, father-in-law and opponent of → Cingetorix [1]. In 54 BC he was involved in the uprising under → Ambiorix, but after Caesar advanced he initially had to stop the siege of → Labienus in the territory of the Treveri. I. fell in battle in 53 during a renewed attack, but his followers maintained control in the tribe and were also able to enlist German support (Caes. Gall 5,53; 55–58; 6,2; Flor. 1,45; Cass. Dio 40,11; Oros. 6,10,10).

> H. HEINEN, Trier und das Trevererland in röm. Zeit, 1985, 23–25. W.SP.

Inessa (Ἴνησσα; *Ínēssa*). Siculian city on the southern slope of Mount Etna (→ Aetne [1]) between Catana and Centoripae, occupied, after the death of Hieron I in 461 BC, by the settlers driven out of Catana, renamed Aetne [2], with the consecration of Hieron as Founder (οἰκιστής; oikistḗs, Diod. Sic. 11,76,3; Str. 6,2,3; Steph. Byz. s.v. I.; cf. Thuc. 3,103,1; 6,94,3). Should be identified with Città in Santa Maria di Licodia rather than Poira.

> G. MANGANARO, La caduta dei Diomenidi e il Politikon nomisma in Sicilia nella prima metà del V sec.a.C., in: Annali dell'Istituto Italiano di Numismatica 21/2, 1974/5, 35 no. 89; Id., Metoikismos, in: ASNP 20, 1990, 394 no. 18; R. J. A. WILSON, Sicily under the Roman Empire, 1990, 410 no. 79; M. MASSA, BTCGI 8, 286–293. GI.MA.

Infamia (from *infamis*, *in-* and *fama*) infamy, in the narrower sense a diminishing of legal position through loss of honour. Older sources prefer *ignominia*, especially for the consequences of a reprimand from the → censor (*nota censoria*, Cic. Rep. 4,6,6). *Infamia* is the direct consequence of some behaviours and activities (e.g. as an actor, debtor in bankruptcy proceedings, dishonourably discharged soldier), of some sentences in a public criminal proceeding (*iudicium publicum*), in a civil case for *actiones famosae* (→ *actio*), including wilful damage (*dolus*) and breach of trust (*fiducia*). *Infamia* means exclusion from office, from the jury service and role of prosecutor and limits the authority to make application and be representative in a civil action. *Infamia* developed from the time of Constantine the Great into a special punishment of dishonour.

> M. KASER, K. HACKL, Die röm. Zivilprozeßordnung, ²1997, 207f.; M. KASER, Infamia und ignominia in den röm. Rechtsquellen, in: ZRG 73, 1956, 220–278. C.E.

Infection see → Transmission of disease

Inferi Etymologically related to *infra* ('below'), *Inferi* is a collective term for all the gods of the Underworld (→ Manes). It corresponds to the Greek terms *katachthónioi* and *hypochthónioi*. The *Dii Inferi* are contrasted to the gods above the earth (*Dii Superi* CIL IX 5813) or the gods of the heavens (*Dii Caelestes*) and the earth (*Dii Terrestres*) (e.g. in a declaration of war by the → Fetiales: Liv. 1,32,9). In the cult, their Underworld nature is characterized by the way in which the sacrifice is offered to them: it is thrown on the ground (Fest. 27 L.; 440 L.) (Serv. Aen. 6,244) [1]. The point of contact between the world above and the world below is the → *mundus*, a pit understood as the altar of the *Dii inferi* (Serv. Aen. 3,134) or as the gate to the Underworld (Cato in Macrob. Sat. 1,16,18). Metonymically, *inferi* also refers to the Underworld whose most detailed description in Latin literature is in the 6th book of Vergil's *Aeneid* [2; 3]. Taking as its starting-point the two NT passages 1 Petr 3,19f.; 4,6, early Christianity develops the view of the descent of Christ after his resurrection into the Underworld as an article of Christian faith that was also adopted into creeds such as the Apostolic Creed (*descendit ad inferos/inferna*). The descent of Christ and his sermon to the dead are understood as the completion of his act of redemption and open the way to salvation for everybody [4. 182–189].

→ Afterlife, concepts of; → Underworld

1 J. Scheid, Romulus et ses frères, 1990, 587ff. 2 E. Norden, P. Vergilius Maro. Aeneis B. 6, ²1916 3 J. Amat, Songes et visions. L'au-delà d'après la littérature latine tardive, 1985 4 N. Brox, Der erste Petrusbrief, 1979.

G. Binder (ed.), Tod und Jenseits im Altertum, 1991; H.-J. Drexhage, J. Sünskes Thompson (ed.), Bestattung und Jenseits in der griech.-röm. Ant., 1994; H. Vorgrimler, Geschichte der Hölle, 1994. R.SCH.

Infibulation

(κρίκωσις; *kríkōsis*, κρικοῦσθαι; *krikoûsthai*, *infibulare*). Placement of a ring (κρίκος; *kríkos*) or a *fibula*, minor surgery on the penis described by Celsus (7,25,2) and by Oribasius (50,11). The operation entailed tightening a thread through perforations in the foreskin until it would close no farther. A ring (or *fibula*) was then attached to prevent exposure of the glans. In some cases at least, it could be removed.

Celsus considers the operation to be much more frequently useless than necessary and sees behind it health motives and an attempt to preserve the voice in pre-adolescent boys. Pliny views it as a chastity belt (cf. Mart. 11,75) in fairly widespread use, as it is reported until the time of Tertullian (De corona 24).

J. Jüthner, s.v. I., RE 9, 2543–2548. A.TO.

Infinity

Although the infinite (ἄπειρον/ *ápeiron*, Lat. *infinitum*) can be encountered in many early thinkers (Anaximander, Pythagoreanism, Democritus [1], Anaxagoras), the concept as such is only made a true theme of philosophy [2] beginning with Zeno of Elea and Aristotle [6]. The concept signified, on the one hand, infinite extension, e.g. of the universe (thus, Epic. epist. ad Herodotum 41–44; Lat. version in Lucr. 1,958–967) or emptiness [1. 125–141; 2. 321–335], and on the other hand, the divisibility of physical or mathematical quantities [3. 321–418]. One of the reasons for the assumption of a truly existent infinity was, according to Aristot. Ph. 3,4,203b 18–20, the claim that the principle of being is inexhaustible. In Anaximander, for instance, the Unlimited (*ápeiron*) is something eternal and inexhaustible from which the definite and limited world (*kósmos*) originated. Although Aristotle rejected this argument in favour of the idea of a permanent cosmic cycle (ibid. 3,8,208a 8–11), it appears again in → Neoplatonism (now for formal rather than material causes). Plotinus calls his highest metaphysical principle, the One, infinite, because its ability (*dýnamis*) of emanation is inexhaustible (e.g. 5,5,10,21–23; → Emanation). Augustine (Epist. 118,24) gives similar reasons for the

idea of the infinity of God. Both in Plotinus (5,5,11,1–5) and in Greek and Latin Patristics (e.g. Gregorius [2] of Nyssa, De vita Moysis 2,236; Hilarius of Poitiers, De Trinitate 2,6), the notion of God's infinity is likewise substantiated by the observation that God is not enclosed or limited by anything, or that He transcends all human thought (Min. Fel. 18,8); [4].

Zeno of Elea expounded the problems of the concept of infinite divisibility (particularly in the first two paradoxes of motion, 29 A 25 and 26 DK) [5]. Is it possible that limited substance contains an infinite amount of parts? If so, should not the substance (as a sum of an infinite amount of parts, each of which has a certain measure of expansion in itself) be infinitely large itself? Aristotle was the first to deal with such questions – and with the concept of infinity itself – philosophically. He thinks infinity can be found in three areas only (Aristot. Ph. 3,4–8): time is infinite; the – for their part limited – substances are infinitely divisible; and the sequence of numbers has no end. However, this infinity is not actual, but merely *potential*: infinity is not that outside of which there is nothing more, but rather that outside of which there still is something (Aristot. Ph. 3,6,206b 33). A limited body, therefore, does not really consist of an infinite number of parts; the sequence of numbers does not end in a truly infinite number (for each number is *per definitionem* countable, ibid. 3,5,204b 7–10), and neither does time consist of an actual infinite amount of days, because the past portions of time no longer exist (ibid. 3,6,206a 25–b 3).

With regard to the divisibility of the continuum, the leading Stoic Chrysippus [2] probably defended a position comparable to Aristotle: the division of a substance may be infinite, but in reality it never reaches infinity (SVF II, 482). Epicurus, on the other hand, denied any form of infinite divisibility, both in physics, where he considered the atom as the smallest indivisible unit (→ Atomism), and in theoretical mathematics, where he assumed theoretically indivisible minimum quantities (Epicurus Epist. ad Herodotum 56–59) – a view in stark contrast to the basic principles of → mathematics. In late antiquity, Aristotelian finitism played an important role in the debate concerning the eternity of the world [6]. In his defence of the idea of Creation, the Christian Neoplatonist Iohannes → Philoponus uses one Aristotelian thesis – that there is in reality no actual infinity – against another: the thesis that the world is eternal and thus has no beginning. In the latter case, the number of past days would actually be infinite. His opponent → Simplicius objected that the number of past days does not constitute an actual infinity in the Aristotelian sense precisely because these days no longer exist in any relevant sense (Simpl. in Aristot. Ph. 506, 3–18).

→ Cosmology; → Number; → Space; → Time, concepts of

1 R. Sorabji, Matter, Space and Motion, 1988 2 K. A. Algra, Concepts of Space in Greek Thought, 1995 3 R. Sorabji, Time, Creation and the Continuum, 1983 4 L. Sweeney, Divine Infinity in Greek and Medieval

Thought, 1992 5 W. C. SALMON (ed.), Zeno's Paradoxes, 1970 6 R. SORABJI, Infinity and the Creation, in: Id. (ed.), Philoponus and the Rejection of Aristotelian Science, 1987.   K. AL.

Inflation see → Devaluation of money

Inflection Blanket term for all types of differences between forms corresponding to a given stem (lemma). Inflection comprises declension of noun forms (substantive, adjective, and pronoun) and conjugation of verb forms. In the case of inflection various methods come to light that can be classified roughly as affixal and inflectional methods proper. In the Indo-European languages of antiquity, as well as in the modern age, both are represented equally.

Affixal methods comprise prefixes (elements placed before), suffixes (elements placed after) and infixes (inserted elements). We can regard the following as prefix components of verb inflection, e.g. the augment of the Greek verb, the *ge-* in the German participle (e.g. *geschrieben*) or, as a special case, reduplicative elements like Greek λε- in λέ-λοιπα (*lé-loipa*) or *pe-* in Latin *pe-perī*; verbal prefixes like Greek περι- (*peri-*) or Latin *per-* are on the contrary not a means of inflection but of → word formation, as new independent stem words are formed. All kinds of endings, which in the Indo-European languages express the noun categories of case, number and (partly) gender and the verb categories of person, number and (partly) tense, mood and voice (*genus verbi*) can be considered as suffix elements, which count as inflection. In this way, e.g. the ending -α in a Greek noun form like πόδα (*póda*) 'foot' designates at the same time accusative case and singular number, the ending -α in a verb form like λέλοιπα (*léloipa*), 'I have left' simultaneously shows 1st person, singular, and (together with reduplication and root ablaut, see below) perfect, indicative and active. Above and beyond this, various verb stem formation suffixes encountered in older Indo-European languages should be regarded as inflection, e.g. the present stem suffix -νῡ- in Greek ζεύγ-νυ-μι (*zeúg-ny-mi*) 'I connect' as opposed to the aorist stem suffix -σ- in ἔζευξα (ἔ-ζευγ-σ-α; *é-zeug-s-a*) 'I connected' or the Latin -ē- of the present stem in *pend-ē-s* 'you hang' as opposed to the perfect characterized by reduplication and special endings, *pe-pend-istī* 'you have hung'. Such suffixes can on many occasions also occur in combination, as in the case of the Latin imperfect *pend-ē-bā-s* 'you hung' that contains the imperfect suffix -*bā*- as well as the present stem suffix -*ē*-. In the case of suffixes, the distinction between inflectional, i.e. related to forms, and derivative validity, i.e. related to derivatives, is also not always easy. The Greek suffix -ε- (< *-εj-) in φοβέω (*phobéō*) 'I frighten, scare away' should e.g. be regarded as a derivative which (together with stem ablaut, see below) represents the secondary formation of a causative ('I cause to flee') from the basic φέβομαι (*phébomai*) 'I flee'. Latin verbs like *mon-ē-re* 'to admonish' (in fact 'to make to pon-

der', for *me-min-ī* < **me-men-*) or *noc-ē-re* 'to damage' (in fact 'to make go under') are based on a corresponding derivation process. Infixes occur only occasionally in the Indo-European languages. If we regard as root the element which to a certain extent constitutes the common denominator for all forms that can be created from a word, then, strictly speaking, only those components which are inserted into the root in inflection should be called infixes. The -*n*-element which occurs in all old Indo-European languages and which occurs in the formation of present stems e.g. in Latin (*re*)-*li-n-qu-ō* 'I leave', as opposed to perfect (*re*)-*līqu-ī* 'I have left' (root -*liqu-* < proto-Indo-European **-lik^w-*, Greek -λιπ-), can be termed an infix inherited from the proto-language. In Latin this infix is often transferred secondarily from the present stem to other stems, e.g. in *fingō* 'I form' < perfect *fīnxī* (but participle *fictus*; root -*fig-* < proto-Indo-European **-d^hig^h-*) and *iungō* 'I bind' > perfect *iūnxī* and > participle *iūnctus*. The uninfixed root -*iug-* (< proto-Indo-European **-iug-*, → Greek -ζυγ-; -*zyg-*) can be seen in the noun *iugum* 'yoke' (< proto-Indo-European **iug-o-m*, > Greek ζυγόν; *zygón*).

Such inflectional means are comparable to the affixal forming elements in which internal word elements are transformed (internal inflection). In the Indo-European languages, this primarily concerns a systematic vowel change called → ablaut, which was characteristic in ancient times of noun and verb inflection as well as derivation. One phenomenon represented as ablaut is e.g. the ascertainable change in the root vowel between Greek λείπ-ω; *leípō* (present) 'I leave' and λέ-λοιπ-α; *léloipa* (perfect) 'I have left' (-ε- versus -ο- as a gradation), which in addition is lost completely in forms like the aorist ἔ-λιπ-ον (*élipon*) 'I left' ('zero-grade' endings). A comparable ablaut pattern is shown within the stem formation suffix by the declension paradigm of words like Greek πατήρ; *patér* 'father', where beside the long grade in the nominative singular (-η-; -ē-) the full grade (-ε-; -e-) in the accusative singular πατέρα (*patéra*) and the zero grade occur in forms like the genitive singular πατρός; *patrós*, in addition in the derivation the long ablaut grade (-ω-; -ō-) in the nominative singular εὐπάτωρ (*eupátōr*) 'aristocratic, (descended) from a good father' and the 'ablaut full grade' (-ο-; -o-) in the accusative singular εὐπάτορα (*eupátora*). Through sound changes (→ Linguistic change) and by the effect of → analogy, original ablaut relationships in individual Indo-European languages have in many cases been distorted or eliminated. In this way, in the Latin present (*re*)-*linqu-ō* and perfect (*re*)-*līqu-ī* from the original change between the zero grade (**-li-n-k^w-*) and the full ablaut grade (**-loik^w-*), a secondary ablaut of -*i*- and -*ī*- arose, as **-oi-* developed into -*ī*-. In the accusative *patrem* of Latin *pater* 'father' the original full grade (**pa₂tér-m̥* > Greek πατέρα; *patéra*) was displaced by analogy by the zero grade.

Depending on which formation methods they prefer, human languages can be divided up into different types.

The Indo-European languages, which, as shown, use all conceivable elements alongside each other, as inflectional languages, can be compared with e.g. the agglutinative languages, among which (primarily suffix) elements occur each with a clear reference to a functional category (cf. e.g. Turkish *ev* 'house', *ev-im* 'my house', *ev-im-de* 'in my house', *ev-ler* 'houses', *ev-ler-im* 'my houses', *ev-ler-im-de* 'in my houses'). Sometimes the term inflection is used in a limited sense only for those grammatical formation methods in which a clear allocation of sound elements to individual functional categories is not possible in contrast to the agglutinative methods of the type presented (for the Greek ending -α in λέλοιπα see above) [1].

→ Ablaut;   → Analogy [2];   → Linguistic change; → Word formation

1 RIX, HGG, 109f.

GREEK: KÜHNER/BLASS, § 94–324; SCHWYZER, Gramm., 415–817.
LATIN: KÜHNER/HOLZWEISSIG, § 55–208; LEUMANN, 258–624; F. NEUE, C. WAGENER, Formenlehre der lat. Sprache, 4 vols., ³1892–1905; SOMMER, 314–618.   J.G.

Informers see → Secret police; → Espionage

Infrastructure
I. GENERAL   II. ENGINEERING   III. MANAGEMENT
IV. ASSESSMENT   V. BRONZE AGE   VI. GREECE
AND HELLENISM   VII. ROME

I. GENERAL
The modern term infrastructure refers to the structures and arrangements which create the material prerequisites for the social processes of production and exchange. This definition, under which for antiquity the systems of transport and communications infrastructure (roads, bridges, harbours) can be subsumed, emphasizes the economic function of infrastructure. It goes without saying that infrastructure also served military purposes. It is also meaningful to regard as infrastructure systems for the supply of drinking-water used to improve the quality of life (*utilitas, salubritas, securitas, voluptas*; 'utility', 'hygiene', 'safety', 'pleasure'), for which economic rationality played a subordinate role. The idea, present in Roman literature, that certain buildings served the public good (*ad usum rei publicae pertinent*, Cic. Off. 2,60; cf. Frontin. Aq. 1: *salubritas* and *securitas*) corresponds fairly exactly with the modern concept of infrastructure. In Vitruvius' theory of architecture public buildings are classified into three groups: buildings for defence (*defensio*), for worship of the gods (*religio*) and for general use (*opportunitas*; Vitr. 1,3,1; cf. 5,12,7); capital is therefore earmarked for the building of harbours and aqueducts (Vitr. 5,12; 8,5f.).
The construction of infrastructure was closely related to the process of urbanization, in which in the late archaic period on many occasions tyrants took the ini-

tiative. In founding cities, Hellenistic kings took the opportunity of appearing as benefactors (→ Euergetes; euergetism) by this. In Rome, the drainage canal (Cloaca Maxima), which may have been laid out on an Etruscan model, belongs to the early period of urban formation. In the Roman Republic, infrastructure buildings were the subject of competition among the aristocracy (Frontin. Aq. 5; 7), later they were part of the public self-representation of the *princeps* (R. Gest. div. Aug. 20; cf. also numerous milestones, building inscriptions, and coins) and a central area of competition for prestige between the cities. The fact that despite growing demand after 126 BC (Aqua Tepula), no new aqueduct to Rome was built, and the lack of maintenance of the existing aqueducts, although their benefit for the common good was not disputed (Frontin. Aq. 9; 76), also mirrored the inability and refusal to act of the political elite in the late Republic. Conversely, the initiatives and measures of M. Vipsanius → Agrippa [1] were directed primarily at building new roads, harbours, and aqueducts. The Imperium Romanum as an empire of cities depended on a transport network infrastructure and aqueducts (→ Water pipes) to supply the population centres from distant sources. Because of the high costs (sporadic data from the Principate period tells us about 340,000 HS/km for a road and 2 million HS/km for an aqueduct), already in antiquity infrastructure buildings could be financed only by the community or rulers, often with generous private donations for individual building or repairs (Philostr. VS 548). In constructing and maintaining roads the owners of neighbouring properties were consulted, particularly in the provinces. We should not underestimate for this epoch the aesthetic and representational dimension of infrastructure, which was also an expression of civilization and mastery over nature (Aristid. 26,182f.).

II. ENGINEERING
The planning and construction of infrastructure required a high technical competency on the part of the architects. Mountains were tunnelled through from both sides, which in the case of the → Eupalinus Tunnel on Samos (6th cent. BC; Hdt. 3,60) was successful at the first attempt, but not in the case of Saldae (Mauretania Caesariensis) around AD 150 when the *princeps* first had to dispatch a → *mensor* serving in the army to bring the construction of a tunnel to a conclusion with *patientia, virtus*, and *spes* ('patience', 'vigour', 'hope') (ILS 5795). Even today we are impressed by the levelling of Roman aqueducts with their extremely gradual descent (Caicus aqueduct in Pergamum: 31 cm/km; Nîmes: 34 cm/km) as well as the planning and construction of such aqueducts as the Pont du Gard, but there was also costly faulty planning leading to bankruptcy or greatly increased investment (Plin. Ep. 10,37f.). The building of road bridges over rivers at heights of over 25 m (Narni: 30 m; Alcántara: 48 m) with spans of over 20 m (Narni: 32,1 m; Alcántara: 28,5 m) was also one of the technically significant achievements. The → har-

bours at Puteoli and Ostia were also erected with great engineering outlay.

The systematic interconnection and hierarchization of a total of *c.* 500 km of the aqueducts for the water supply of Rome (*aquae*) achieved in the Imperial period, to guarantee supply in the event of partial failures, was of great importance (Frontin. Aq. 87; 92). Reservoirs were used to balance supply and demand.

III. MANAGEMENT

Building infrastructure made great demands not only on engineering and organizational skills and considerable resources of materials and manpower but also on efficient management and constant supervision for their permanent operation. This applied particularly to the water supply. From the 4th cent. BC, municipal officials (*agoranomoi, astynomoi*) in many places supervised the relevant installations or there were special commissioners such as the ἐπιμελητὴς τῶν κρηνῶν; *epimelētès tôn krēnôn* ('surveyor of wells'; Aristot. Ath. Pol. 43,1) in Athens. In Imperial Rome they had their counterpart in the high-ranking *curatores* (*curatores viarum, curatores aquarum*; → Cura [2]). M. Agrippa ensured an ordered administration of above-average professionalism in the area of municipal water supply for Rome (Frontin. Aq. 98), for which after his death a legal basis was created by a number of Senate resolutions (Frontin. Aq. 99ff.; 104; 106; 108). The subsequent tendency to centralize and regulate was further intensified through selective intervention in the local administration in order to correct faulty planning. The high priority of infrastructure is demonstrated by the fact that an owner who made difficulties (*difficilior possessor*) could be forced to sell a property which was needed (Frontin. Aq. 128,1). In the course of the 2nd cent. AD, major infrastructure projects funded by public means were generally subject to approval. In late antiquity governors themselves ordered new buildings or repairs.

IV. ASSESSMENT

Utilitary buildings were often rated extremely highly in ancient literature (Str. 5,3,8; Dion. Hal. Ant. Rom. 3,67,5; Anth. Gr. 7,379; 9,708; Plin. HN 36,104ff.; Frontin. Aq. 1; 16; Cassiod. Var. 7,6). The architects boasted of their achievements in infrastructure, for instance Mandrocles of Samos (Hdt. 4,88), Lacer, who built the bridge at Alcántara (ILS 287b), and Nonius Datus who surveyed the tunnel for the waterworks for Saldae (ILS 5795).

V. BRONZE AGE

Bronze Age infrastructure shows the close connection between infrastructure and the centralization of power. Examples are the road network on Crete and the paved roads with bridges and side walls on two parallel routes out of Mycenae, probably built for war-chariots. A road network has been demonstrated for Messenia, Phocis, and Boeotia. In Cnossus there were water conduits made of clay pipes. Significant Mycenaean constructions were a conduit to Thebes hewn into rock, a dike at Tiryns and the complex water regulation and drainage system on Lake Copais in Boeotia.

VI. GREECE AND HELLENISM

The mostly small poleis did not have the resources to build major infrastructure communications. A network of paved roads with simple bridges can however be demonstrated for some districts in the Classical period. Routes important for the civic community were constructed at greater expense, e.g. the Sacred Road between Athens and Eleusis. On the Isthmus of Corinth, the late-antique *diolkos*, a paved road, was used to transport shipping loads between the Aegean and the Corinthian Gulf. The cities founded by Alexander the Great and the Hellenistic kings expanded the road network of the Persian period, particularly in the Seleucid kingdom. Harbour structures were used primarily for trade and supplying the populace. Where natural circumstances did not suffice, by the late archaic period artificial harbours were being created by building moles out into the sea (Samos, Eretria). In Alexandria, two docks were dug out artificially (Str. 17,1,6–10).

In the late archaic period in some larger poleis (Samos, Athens, Megara), the existing water supply was supplemented by springs, wells, cisterns, and filtration galleries through underground channels. From the Classical period these are known for Aegina, Corinth, Acragas, and Syracuse. The contemporary perception of the pipeline to Athens, probably begun under Hippias (before 510 BC), which was almost 8 km long to the distribution point, appears in numerous depictions of well-houses on Attic vase paintings. However, most cities received a supply of flowing water only in the Principate, when this became part of the standard inventory of a polis (Paus. 10,4,1). The fact that attention was also paid to the functional suitability of private storage facilities is shown by the Pergamum *astynomos* inscription (OGIS 483).

VII. ROME

The first city-wide infrastructure in Rome is traditionally linked to Ap. → Claudius [I 2] Caecus (*aqua Appia, via Appia*). The public thorough-fares (*viae publicae*) were initially used primarily for the military and political penetration into conquered territories, but in the Imperial period civilian needs (trade, travel) predominated at least in Italy. Goods traffic between centres and their surrounding countryside was facilitated by the regional networks of the *viae vicinales*. The *principes* considerably improved the communications infrastructure, neglected in the late Republic, with new buildings, repairs, and continuity of administration. In the case of large undertakings such as the extension of the port of → Ostia under Claudius, technical innovation (poured mortar), enormous financial resources, and political will were combined (Cass. Dio 60,11,1–5). Under Trajan, projects with the accent on utility and functionality dominated the imperial building programme. Roman infrastructure was actually *magnitu-dinis imperii Romani praecipuum indicium* ('outstanding evidence of the greatness of the Imperium Romanum', Frontin. Aq. 119). As infrastructure do not tend to become superfluous as a result of drastic political or radical cultural changes, their deterioration in late antiquity signified a drastic loss of welfare services and was an indication of the decline of the administration. This applied especially to the water supply, whereas some main long-distance roads and bridges survived well beyound the end of the Imperium Romanum in the West (but cf. Rut. Namat. 37ff.). In any case the ruins of ancient infrastructure has held a great fascination up to modern times, which is expressed in the etchings of G. PIRANESI as well as in the paintings of H. ROBERT and in a large number of texts, such as the description of the Pont du Gard in ROUSSEAU.

→ Roads and bridges, onstruction of, → Transport and communications, → INFRASTRUCTURE

1 R. CHEVALLIER, Roman Roads, 1976   2 D. P. CROUCH, Water Management in Ancient Greek Cities, 1993   3 W. ECK, Die staatliche Organisation Italiens in der hohen Kaiserzeit, 1979, 25–87   4 Id., Die Wasserversorgung im röm. Reich, in: Id., Die Verwaltung des röm. Reiches in der hohen Kaiserzeit 1, 1995, 179–252   5 FRONTINUS-GESELLSCHAFT (ed.), Die Wasserversorgung ant. Städte, 1987   6 Id. (ed.), Die Wasserversorgung ant. Städte, 1988   7 Id. (ed.), Wasserversorgung im ant. Rom, 1982   8 A. NÜNNERICH-ASMUS, Straßen, Brücken und Bögen als Zeichen röm. Herrschaftsanspruchs, in: W. TRILLMICH (ed.), Hispania Antiqua. Denkmäler der Römerzeit, 1993, 121–157   9 H. SCHNEIDER, Die Gaben des Prometheus, in: W. KÖNIG (ed.), Propyläen Technikgeschichte 1, 1991, 267–297   10 Id., Infrastruktur und polit. Legitimation im frühen Prinzipat, in: Opus 5, 1986, 23–51   11 Id., Einführung in die ant. Technikgeschichte, 1992, 171–193   12 H. CHR. SCHNEIDER, Altstraßenforschung, 1982   13 R. TÖLLE KASTENBEIN, Ant. Wasserkultur, 1990   14 Id., Das archa. Wasserleitungsnetz für Athen, 1994   15 Y. TSEDAKIS et al., Les routes minoennes, in: BCH 113, 1989, 43–75; 114, 1990, 43–65.

U.WAL.

Infula (Woollen) band with various uses. Together with garlands, the *infulae* are the most commonly used items of decoration in Roman worship: on sacrificial animals, sacred buildings, sometimes also altars (Fest. 100 L.). They are also used to decorate houses on the occasion of a wedding (Luc. 2,355; Plin. HN 29,30; Serv. Aen. 4,458). As a component of priestly vestments (head band [1]), the *infula* is a diadem-like band from the ends of which tassels (*vittae*) hang down on both sides, sometimes of red and white threads, sometimes subdivided into individual segments (*astragalos* band) (Isid. Orig. 19,31,6). Vestals wear them constantly as a head covering (cf. Vestal bust, Florence, UF [2]; Cancelleria Relief B, Rome, MV [3]). Frequently the term *vitta* is used as a synonym for *infula* (primarily in poetic language). There is however a difference between them: *infula* is the band, *vitta* the tassel on the end.

1 H. FREIER, Caput velare, 1965, 71–75   2 H. JUCKER, Bildnisbüste einer Vestalin, in: RhM 68, 1961, 93–113 pl. 28–29   3 G. M. KOEPPEL, Die historischen Reliefs der röm. Kaiserzeit. II: Stadtröm. Denkmäler unbekannter Zugehörigkeit aus flavischer Zeit, in: BJ 184, 1984, 31 no. 8.

H. DRAGENDORFF, Die Amtstracht der Vestalinnen, in: RhM 51, 1896, 281–302; H. FREIER, Caput velare, 1965; B. I. SCHOLZ, Untersuchungen zur Tracht der röm. matrona, 1992, 123f. with n. 233; A. V. SIEBERT, Quellenanalytische Bemerkungen zu Haartracht und Kopfschmuck röm. Priesterinnen, in: Boreas 18, 1995, 77–92.

A.V.S.

Ingaevones A mythological Germanic tribal group attested probably as early as in Pytheas of Massilia (Plin. HN 37,35 DETLEFSEN with conjecture) (Plin. HN 4,96; 99; Tac. Germ. 2,2; → Herminones), which, although the closest to reality of the three Mannus groups, merely functioned as a fictitious blanket term for Cimbri, Teutoni, and Chauci.

D. TIMPE, Romano-Germanica, 1995, esp. 20–24.   K.DI.

In Genesin ad Leonem papam (204 hexameters), falsely ascribed in the MSS to → Hilarius of Poitiers, is dedicated to Pope Leo I (440–461). After a hymnic introduction, the largest part of the poem tells the creation story; a short conclusion reports the fall of man, the flood, and the prospects for redemption. The portrayal of nature shows the influence of → Lucretius, → Vergilius (esp. *Georgica*) and the cosmogony in Ov. Met. 1. → Biblical poetry

EDITIONS: R. PEIPER, CSEL 23, 231–239.   M.RO.

Ingenuus

[1] Governor of Pannonia and Moesia, proclaimed emperor rather than → Gallienus in AD 260 by the Moesian legions after → Valerianus was captured by the Persians and the Sarmatians threatened to invade (S HA Tyr. Trig. 9,1; Aur. Vict. Caes. 33,2; Zon. 12,24, p. 143 D). Gallienus' cavalry leader → Aureolus defeated him at Mursa near Sirmium. I. lost his life while fleeing (Zon. loc. cit..; Aur. Vict. Caes. 32,2; Eutr. 9,8,1; Oros. 7,22,10; Chron. min. 1, 521,45 MOMMSEN).

PIR² I 23; PLRE 1, 457 (I. 1); B. BLECKMANN, Die Reichskrise des 3. Jh., 1991, 226ff.; J. FITZ, I. et Régalien, 1966; KIENAST², 223.   T.F.

[2] Originally the → *patricii* were called *ingenui* (Cincius in Fest. p. 277), but no later than in the Imperial period, the principle applied that free-born people were designated *ingenui*: *ingenui sunt qui liberi nati sunt* (Gai. Inst. 1,11), but in cases of doubt the decisive factor was that the mother was free. In the 2nd cent. BC, marriages between *ingenui* and *iiberti* (→ Freedmen and -women) were apparently still forbidden, but after the Augustan *lex Papia Poppaea* they were allowed,

except for senators (as in [1. 429ff.] supported by the case of Fecennia Hispala in the Bacchanalia scandal, Liv. 39,19,3–5; contradicted by a large part of modern research, e.g. [2. 82ff.] with reference to Dig. 23,2,23). The literature of civil law does not differentiate further among *ingenui* who are compared to the *libertini* (a *libertinus* is originally the son of a *libertus*. When these were later regarded as *ingenui*, the terms *libertus* and *libertinus* became synonymous). In constitutional law, however, those who had a free-born father and a free grandfather are contrasted with the normal *ingenuus* (Suet. Claud. 24,1f.; Plin. HN 33,32). Free birth was the prerequisite for holding municipal and priestly offices. However, if a person wished to be accepted into the equestrian class and consequently also into the Senate, he would have to prove that he was *ingenuus* 'to a higher degree' (MOMMSEN). In exceptional cases, the sons of *liberti*, made *ingenuus* by the emperor, were increasingly accepted into the Senate.

1 MOMMSEN, Staatsrecht 3.1   2 S. TREGGIARI, Roman Freedmen during the Republic, 1969   3 B. KÜBLER, s.v. Ingenuus, RE 9, 1544–1552   4 KASER, RPR 1, 118, 296   5 G. VITUCCI, s.v. libertus, RUGGIERO 4, 1957, 925f., H.GA.

Ingots
I. EASTERN MEDITERRANEAN, GREECE, AND ROME
II. CENTRAL EUROPE IN EARLY HISTORICAL TIMES

I. EASTERN MEDITERRANEAN, GREECE, AND ROME

Unworked metal of various weights cast into various shapes which has served since the Bronze Age as raw material for further processing or as a pre-monetary method of payment. From earliest times gold, silver, and electrum occur in the eastern Mediterranean as crude lumps, small round ingots (perhaps crucible remnants), and round or shaped bars with division notches. Alloyed bronze, tin, and particularly copper appear as crude lumps, round ingots, flat slabs and brick- or bun-shaped ingots from which come the four-handled oxhide ingots (*Keftiu* ingots) in the middle of the 2nd millennium BC [3]. The early ingots bear engraved or stamped markings similar to writing which designate the place of production or the owner [3. 13ff.; 2]. From the ancient period stamps indicate the quality and the quantity of the ingots [6]. From the 1st millennium BC iron occurs in pancake shapes (cf. the πελανοί; *pelanoí* of the Spartans) and ingots pointed at both ends, and lead as brick or round ingots. An ingot found in Haltern shows engraved letters designating the weight CCIII pounds (in fact only 64 kg) and, with L XIX, the 19th Legion [5].

The use of ingots as money is mentioned e.g. in the *Iliad* (23,851) and for Britain by Caesar (Gall. 5,12) [1. 979f.]. The development of unshaped raw metal of a monetary nature into coins can easily be followed in Italy. After scrap metal (*aes rude*) follows rectangularly shaped standardized *aes signatum*, and finally cast round coins (*aes grave*). In late antiquity, gold and silver ingots with die-like markings were given to the soldiers as *donativum* in a disc or double axe shape. They weigh about 1–3 Roman pounds [6; 4. 71ff.; 7. 327f.].

→ Aes grave, → Aes rude, → Aes signatum, → Donativum, → Elektron, → Libra

1 REGLING, s.v. Geld, RE 7, 970–984   2 H.G. BUCHHOLZ, Der Kupferhandel des 2. vorchristl. Jt. im Spiegel der Schriftforsch., in: Minoica, FS J. Sundwall, 92–115   3 H.G. BUCHHOLZ, Keftiu-B. und Erzhandel im zweiten vorchristl. Jt., in: PrZ 37, 1959, 1–40   4 J.W. SALOMONSON, Zwei spätröm. Gedenk-Silber-B. mit eingestempelten Inschr. in Leiden, in: Oudheidkundige Meded. Rijksmus. Leiden 42, 1961, 63–77   5 S. VON SCHNURBEIN, Ein Blei-Barren der 19. Legion aus dem Hauptlager von Haltern, in: Germania 49, 1971, 132–136   6 H. WILLERS, s.v. Barren, RGA 2, 70f.   7 H.A. CAHN, Der spätröm. Silberschatz von Kaiseraugst, 1984.

H. WILLERS, Röm. Silber-Barren mit Stempeln, in: NZ 30, 1898, 211–235; Id., Nochmal die Silber-Barren nebst COMOB, in: NZ 31, 1899, 35–50; Id., Röm. Silber-Barren aus dem Britischen Mus., in: NZ 1899, 369–386; C. ARNOLD-BIUCCHI, L. BEER-TOBEY, N.M. WAGGONER, A Greek Archaic Silver Hoard from Selinus, ANSMusN 33, 1988, 1–35.   A.M.

II. CENTRAL EUROPE IN EARLY HISTORICAL TIMES

In the Celtic Iron Age iron ingots predominate. Only occasionally are there ingots of different metals. For iron ingots there are two shapes mainly distributed in the area of late Hallstatt and La Tène cultures (→ Hallstatt culture):

1. ingots pointed at both ends, often of parts of differing qualities welded together,

2. sword-shaped ingots. The former are demonstrable from the 6th cent. BC, also in the region of the more recent Lusatian (Lausitz) culture, and occur as late as the Roman Imperial period and in Roman camps. The latter date primarily from the period of the *oppida* (→ Oppidum) of the 2nd/1st cent. BC. Both ingot shapes were primarily raw material for further working in Celtic smithies. Frequently they appear in dumps close to large settlements or iron-ore centres, as shown by e.g. the finds at Schwanberg (Franconia) or at Kalteiche in Siegerland. They also occur however as votive finds in rivers and bogs. In the British Isles sword-shaped ingots, called *taleae ferreae* (Caes. B Gall. 5,12), are very common and were also means of payment. No generally valid standardization according to shape or weight can be demonstrated for iron ingots. Germanic cultures are not known to have had their own ingot shapes.

→ Iron, → Hallstatt culture, → Sacrifices, → Raw materials

H. WILLERS, s.v. Barren, RGA 2, 60–70; S. SIEVERS, Die Kleinfunde der Heuneburg, 1984, 73–74; K. PESCHEL, Ein Barren-Fund der Latènezeit vom Schwanberg im Steigerwald, in: Ber. der Bayerischen Bodendenkmalpflege 30/31, 1989/90 (1994), 137–178.   V.P.

Inguiomerus Respected aristocrat of the Cherusci tribe initially friendly to Rome, brother of → Segimerus, who with his nephew → Arminius later waged war on → Germanicus [2] (Tac. Ann. 1,60,1). Badly wounded in the futile attempt, against the advice of Arminius, to storm the camp of Aulus → Caecina [II 8] Severus (Tac. Ann. 1,68), I. fled from the battle at → Idistaviso (Tac. Ann. 2,17,5) and remained without success at the Angrivarian Wall (Tac. Ann. 2,21,2). As he no longer wished to obey his nephew Arminius, he went over in AD 17 with a band of followers (*cum manu clientium*) to the side of his opponent, the king of the Marcomanni → Maroboduus, as a result of which, after the defection of the Semnones and Lombards from Maroboduus, the power relationship between the rivals becomes balanced again (Tac. Ann. 2,45).

A. BECKER, Rom und die Chatten, 1992; D. TIMPE, Der Triumph des Germanicus, 1968.   V.L.

Inheritance, division of Greek law → *datetai*. In early Roman law, co-heirs formed a joint ownership community *ercto non cito* ('without division undertaken' [2]; each co-heir was authorized to dispose alone over estate property. The division occurred by consent or by the → *legis actio per arbitri postulationem* (Gai. Inst. 4,17a); the → *arbiter* divided the individual estate assets and where applicable likewise ordered equalization payments. Since the pre-Classical period, the community of co-heirs was regarded as a community of owners holding undivided shares in the property, in which each could indeed dispose over his share but not over individual assets; the division occurred through the → *actio familiae erciscundae*, with division orders of the testator being taken into consideration.
→ Succession, law of III F; → Fideicommissum

1 KASER, RPR I, 99f., 727f.   2 H.L. W. NELSON, Zur Terminologie der röm. Erbschaftsteilung, in: Glotta 44, 1966, 41–60.   U.M.

Inheritance, laws of see → Succession, laws of

Ininthimaeus (Ἰνινθίμαιος; *Ininthímaios*). Bosporan king, *c.* AD 234–239 of the dynasty of the Tiberii Iulii. Like his emblem, his name is also Sarmatian. Attested on coins and in inscriptions (including IOSPE 2, 334, 433).

V.F. GAIDUKEVIĆ, Das Bosporanische Reich, 1971, 458; A.N. ZOGRAPH, Ancient Coinage, 1977, II, 333.   I.v.B.

Initial (from Latin *initium*, 'beginning'). The emphasized initial letter of a passage of text. The history of the western initial begins in late antiquity. The *Codex Virgilius Augusteus* (5th cent. AD; Rome, Bibliotheca Vaticana, Vat. Latin 3256) is the oldest manuscript to have well-developed initials [2. 51–56]: separated from the writing, outlined with a circle and lines, and filled in with geometrical decorations ('filling ornaments' [1. 135, 153–161]).

In the 1st half of the 6th cent. in the area around Ravenna the zoomorphic initial then develops: the strokes and curves of the letter are replaced by zoomorphic motifs ('substitution ornaments' [1. 135, 161–180]). The zoomorphic initial first spreads to the British Isles and then to Merovingian and western Gothic scriptoria (7th and 8th cents.). At first the ornamental repertoire comprises only stylized fish and birds ('fish-and-bird letters' [2. 60–63]); later the representation of the animals becomes more vivid.

Anthropomorphic substitute ornaments are found from the late 8th cent. on. Figure initials, in which the body of the letter is made up of an interplay of animal or human figures, plants, and other objects, represent whole scenes of narrative content which can also relate to the text. The living beings can merge into one another in fluid transition (by the principle of kaleidoscopic metamorphosis) [3. 53]. Figure and kaleidoscopic initials do not develop further in the Carolingian and Ottonian period because of the programmatic recourse to Classical antiquity, and their history does not continue until the beginning of the 12th cent. Polymorphism puts at risk the readability of the letter (the mixing of script, decoration, and image is foreign to the Classical norm). Carolingian and Ottonian book illustration keeps the spheres of ornament and script strictly separate: the geometric form of the initial is clearly discernible. Two-dimensionally presented phytomorphic filling and edging ornaments (among which the Classical acanthus ornament predominates) gain acceptance as embellishment.

In the heyday of the Romanesque style two types of initial develop. 1. The 'inhabited initial' that is developed in the British Isles (10th–11th cents.): the body and the interior space of the letter are filled with three-dimensionally fashioned tendrils in which figural representations are depicted. This initial spreads throughout continental Europe and flourishes especially in northwestern France in the 11th cent., particularly in the numerous Norman centres. 2. The 'historiated initial': the body of the letter serves as a frame for an image linked as a rule with the text; the clear form of the letter is not impaired by ornaments. Preliminary phases of this initial can be found by the 8th cent. in several figure-filled initials of insular book illustration and it itself flourishes from the 12th to the 15th cent.

Initials are part of the complex decorative system of differentiated ornament typologies which corresponds to the hierarchical subdivision of the text. To this also belong rather standardized initials, e.g. the filigree initial (first in France in the 13th cent.) and simple two-dimensional colour initials. The hallmarks of humanistic initial ornamentation (15th cent.) are facet initials, letters with bodies shaped three-dimensionally, and initials with white vine leaf tendrils on a coloured background.
→ Book illustration

1 C. NORDENFALK, Die spätant. Zierbuchstaben, 1970
2 Id., Studies in the History of Book Illumination, 1992
3 O. PÄCHT, Buchmalerei des MA, 1984, 45–95.

J. J. G. ALEXANDER, The Decorated Letter, 1978; S. MAD-
DALO, s.v. Iniziale, Enciclopedia dell'arte medievale 7,
375–386.   G.d.F.

Initiation

A. GENERAL   B. RITES FOR ADOLESCENTS
C. STATE OF RESEARCH

A. GENERAL

Initiation refers a) in a perspective limited to Greek
and Roman religion, to ritual inauguration into a mystery cult, b) in additional ethnological and socio-an-
thropological terminology, to the complex of rites with
which in ancient society adolescents of both sexes are
accepted into the society of adults (in German scholarship formerly referred to also as puberty ceremony). For
the former function, corresponding ancient terminology exists (Greek μύησις; *myēsis*, more rarely
τελετή;*teletē*, Latin *initia* n.pl.), but not for the latter.
This does not exclude the possibility that corresponding
rites existed, corresponding to the assumption of social
anthropology that they are common to almost all societies, but lexicographical findings show that ancient
society knew ethnological initiation only as transformations and adaptations to their social structures. Here
these rites are a subgroup of the very wide category of
rites of passage [1]. The transformations include the
rites of the initiation cults (→ Mysteries), which are the
basis for the existence of the *mystai* [2]. Under no circumstances are they limited to adolescents (but in Eleusis a remnant is probably preserved in the initiation of
the παῖς ἀφ᾽ ἑστίας/*paîs aph' hestías*, a boy initiated at
the expense of the Athenian state).

B. RITES FOR ADOLESCENTS

In the rites and myths concerning adolescents, the
sexes have to be distinguished. For young men the cults
of → Apollo (the eternally young god), → Hermes, and
→ Heracles are especially relevant. It can be taken for
certain that the institutions of the ancient Cretan cities
in the area of young warriors and men's houses
(*andreónes*) are formally and functionally closely
linked with initiation (*locus classicus*: Ephoros FGrH
70 F 149). The servile role of boys in the *andreónes*,
particularly the induction of aristocratic young men
into the world of adult warriors through a period in the
open air characterized by homoerotic cohabitation
with adult men and hunting together, has clear ethnographical parallels. This applies similarly to the Spartan
→ *agoge* that was certainly transformed to a great
extent in the interest of militarizing the Spartan state.
Likewise in the institutions centred on the Athenian
→ *ephebeia* forms can be found that are connected phe-
nomenologically with initiation. Here the almost insoluble problem arises as to how they could have looked
prior to the reform of the *ephebeia* in the 4th cent. [3].

In any case, the aetiological myth of the → Apaturia, a
festival which, according to common Attic and Ionian
attestation, goes back to before the time of the Ionian
Migration (Hdt. 1,47), reflects initiatory themes [4],
[5]. A similar problem is presented by the mythology of
→ Theseus, who in some respects is the mythological
model of Attic ephebes, whose myths were however
greatly reshaped in the late ancient period [6].

In the initiation of girls, numerous myths and cults in
which dancing by girls in sanctuaries (especially of
→ Artemis and → Hera) outside the towns played a part
were connected with initiation [7]. Particularly well researched is Athens where on the one hand the cult of
Artemis of Brauron and on the other the rites of the
→ *arrhephoroi* in the cult of Athena Polias [8] can be
understood against this background. Generally it can
be assumed that in most Greek city states the initiation
rites had lost their general validity and were restricted
to the aristocratic upper class with regard to their gen-
erality (Crete) or individual representatives (boy and
girl priests, *arrhephoroi*). In this way they became an
instrument of aristocratic representation, which is also
evident in the Attic *ephebeia* from Hellenistic times as
the introduction of members of the upper class into the
traditions of the city.

With regard to the research done in respect of Greek
religion, analogous rites have also been shown in Rome
(for instance among the → Salii or the rites in the *Tigillum Sororium*, Liv. 1,26,13). In view of the relatively
late attestation (archaeological from the Middle
Republic, literary from the Late Republic and the early
Imperial period), these rites will have been transformed
to a much greater extent [9].

In the Christian ritual, initiations continue to exist
functionally and formally, and in older research the
connection with the rites of the Mysteries was discussed
[10]. → Baptism can certainly be regarded as an initiation ritual which accepts individuals (in ancient Christendom as adults) into a new community and changes
their status in this world and the next. The initiation
into the orders of monks, in which for instance ideas of
death and rebirth were also ritually played out were
much more strongly shaped [11]. Finally little attention
is still paid to the fact that even many saints' lives (e.g.
Athanasius, Vita Antonii Eremitae) appear in their narrative structure like stories of initiation.

C. STATE OF RESEARCH

The research regarding rites of initiation in antiquity
emerged from the research of the Cambridge School
into myth and ritual. It owes its decisive impetus to Jane
Ellen HARRISON, who in her 'Prolegomena to the Study
of Greek Religion' (1903) clearly showed with the help
of ethnological findings the connection between the
Curetes hymn of Palaikastro and the rites reflected in it.
In 'Couroi et Courètes' (1939), DURKHEIM's pupil
Henri JEANMAIRE expanded this into a study of the relevant myths and rites in the Doric societies of Crete and
Sparta as well as in other Greek towns (Aetolia,

Athens). He regarded the Greek phenomena as the historical continuation of ethnological rites (and sought to justify them with recourse to the culture group theory of Leo FROBENIUS). Finally, Angelo BRELICH in the (never finished) synthesis 'Paides e Parthenoi' (1968) deepened the approach. While these works have as a whole conclusively proved the theory of a transformation of ethnological initiation into Graeco-Roman rites and myths, a large number of recent works is marred by the effective equating of initiation rites with rites of passage (with which they share a three-phase basic structure). In detail it is certainly difficult, particularly in the case of myths, to go beyond the determination of this basic structure.

→ INITIATION

1 A. VAN GENNEP, Les rites de passage, 1909   2 W. BURKERT, Ant. Mysterien. Funktion und Gehalt, 1990 3 C. PÉLÉKIDES, Histoire de l'éphébie attique, 1962 4 P. VIDAL-NAQUET, Le chasseur noir et l'origine de l'éphébie athénienne, in: Annales. Economies, Sociétés, Civilisations 23, 1968, 947–964   5 Id., Retour au chasseur noir, in: J.-P. VERNANT, P. VIDAL-NAQUET, La Grèce ancienne. vol. 3: Rites de passage et transgressions, 1992, 215–251 (1989)   6 C. CALAME, Thésée et l'imaginaire athénien. Légende et culte en Grèce antique, 1990   7 Id., Les choeurs de jeunes filles en Grèce archaïque. 1: Morphologie, fonction religieuse et sociale, 1977   8 P. BRULÉ, La fille d'Athènes. La religion des filles à Athènes à l'époque classique, 1987   9 M. TORELLI, Lavinio e Roma. Riti Iniziatici e Matrimonio tra Archeologia e Storia, 1984 10 D. H. WIENS, Mystery concepts in primitive Christianity and its environment, in: ANRW II 23.2, 1248–1284 11 V. SAXER, Les rites de l'initiation chrétienne du IIᵉ au VIᵉ siècle. Esquisse historique et signification d'après leurs principaux témoins, 1988.

B. LINCOLN, Emerging From the Chrysalis. Studies in Rituals of Women's Initiation, 1981; C. SOURVINOU-INWOOD, Studies in Girls' Transitions. Aspects of the Arkteia and Age Representation in Attic Iconography, 1988; K. DOWDEN, Death and the Maiden. Girls' Initiation Rites in Greek Mythology, 1989; A. MOREAU (ed.), L'initiation. Actes du colloque international de Montpellier 11–14 avril 1991, 1992; F. GRAF, Initiationsriten in der ant. Mittelmeerwelt, in: AU 36,2, 1993, 29–40; J. N. BREMMER, Greek Religion, 1994, 44–48; S. I. JOHNSTON, Restless Dead, 1999, ch. 6.   F.G.

In iure cessio The *in iure cessio* of Roman law is an act of the transfer of a right in the form of a fictitious trial, the → *legis actio sacramento in rem*. It is – like the → *mancipatio* – not dependent on the existence of a cause in law (*causa*), e.g. of a purchase agreement, but rather is 'abstract'. The *in iure cessio* is concerned with items in which Quiritic ownership is possible (e.g. not provincial plots of land), and is only available to Roman citizens (Gai. Inst. 2,65). Some rights, like the → *ususfructus*, can only be transferred by *in iure cessio* (Gai. Inst. 2,30). The buyer takes up the matter before a Roman magistrate (→ praetor) and for example speaks the words *Hunc ego hominem ex iure Quiritium meum esse aio* ('I maintain that this slave is mine

according to the right of the Roman citizens'). The seller remained silent, whereupon the praetor or the provincial governor (Gai. Inst. 2,24) awards the matter to the buyer. Already in the time of Gaius in the 2nd cent. AD (Gai. Inst. 2,25) the *in iure cessio* is avoided as being too awkward. Justinianic law is no longer familiar with it.

HONSELL/MAYER-MALY/SELB, 104–106; KASER, RPR I 40, 48f., 134, 415; II 50, 274f.; M. KASER, K. HACKL, Das röm. Zivilprozeßrecht, ²1997, 42, 72 n. 18, 94 n. 34, 187.   D.SCH.

Iniuria On the one hand, a generic term for unlawful behaviour in general and for illegality and fault in respect of the → *lex Aquilia*, and on the other hand the term for an offence including wilful physical injury and insult to honour. The Twelve Tables provided retaliation in kind (→ *talio*) for serious cases of *iniuria*. This was not applicable in the case of agreement over damages (→ *pactum*). In less serious cases there were only fines which in general ultimately supplanted the *talio*. The amount of the fines varied with the seriousness of the deed and the social status of the victim (Gai. Inst. 3,225). Some forms of *iniuria* were also prosecuted in criminal law in the Imperial period.

→ Culpa; → Delictum; → Dolus

M. BALZARINI, De iniuria extra ordinem statui, 1983; MOMMSEN, Strafrecht, 784 – 808; F. RABER, Grundlagen klass. Injurienansprüche, 1969; A. VÖLKL, Die Verfolgung der Körperverletzung im frühen Röm. Recht, 1984; R. ZIMMERMANN, The Law of Obligations, 1990, 1050– 1062.   R.GA.

Ink In antiquity, ink took its name from its colour: μέλαν (*mélan*, literally 'black'), Lat. *atramentum* (from *ater*, 'black'). In the late-antique Latin period and later in the Byzantine period, the terms *ónkauston* or respectively Lat. *encaustum* ('burnt in') became prevalent. The Latin term *tincta* ('bedewed', 'dipped') only appears in the Middle Ages [1. 23 ff.]. References to ink and its production are found in Vitr. De arch. 7,10; Dioscorides 5,162 WELLMANN; Plin. HN 35,41. In the Middle Ages, ink production became the topic of a specialized technical literature [1. 31 ff.] based on these references, with such treatises as e.g. *Schedula diversarum artium* by Theophilus Presbyter (11th/12th cents.), the majority, however, being anonymous [1. 144 ff.]. From medieval times, ink was made from soot (mixed with any binding agent as well as an additional ingredient, e.g. wine or water) and from gallium (made from tannic acids with the addition of copper or iron sulphate, water, and a binding agent). Only recently have the ingredients of medieval ink been examined in a laboratory [2; 3; 4]. It was common practice to write the title and *incipit* in red ink (→ Rubrication) made from processed cinnabar or minium (themselves derivatives from mercury and lead). Byzantine emperors signed their documents (→ *subscriptio*) in purple ink made from snail secretions (Cod. Iust. 1,23,6; → Purple) [5].

From antiquity, the text of purple codices is written in gold or silver ink [6; 7].

→ Book; → Codex; → Writing materials

1 M. ZERDOUN BAT-YEHOUDA, Les encres noires au moyen âge, 1983 2 P. CANART et al., Recherches sur la composition des encres ... au XIᵉ siècle, in: M. MANIACI, P. F. MUNAFÒ (ed.), Ancient and Medieval Book Materials and Techniques, vol. 2, 1993, 29–56 3 P. DEL CARMINE et al., Particle-Induced X-Ray-Emission with an External Beam, in: [2], 7–27 4 M. BICCHIERI et al., Raman and Pixe Analysis of Salerno Exultet, in: Quinio 2, 2000, 233–240 5 O. LONGO (ed.), La porpora. Realtà e immaginario di un colore simbolico, 1998 6 D. V. THOMPSON, The Materials and Techniques of Medieval Painting, 1956 7 V. TROST, Gold- und Silbertinten, 1991.
S. MA.

Inland duties see → Toll

Inland navigation Inland navigation (IN) refers here to the regional and supraregional transportation of people and goods on rivers and lakes; this does not include the local use of boats, for instance for fishing, or of ferries. The significance of IN in antiquity results from the fact that the transportation of goods by ship was considerably more cost-effective than land transport with pack animals or by cart. For late antiquity a cost relationship between land transport, IN and overseas shipping that is extremely unfavourable for land transport is attested through the tariffs of the Price Edict of → Diocletianus. Furthermore we should take into consideration that land transport relied on a network of ways and roads that was hard to construct, whilst IN could use rivers or lakes as natural infrastructure. The options of IN were certainly limited in antiquity because there were only a few navigable rivers in the Mediterranean area and many rivers also carried very little water during the summer.

Ships were already used in prehistoric times. During the late Palaeolithic, boats made of animal skins were used on lakes and rivers. When forests began to grow after the Würm Ice Age, people learnt how to build dugout canoes that, from the Mesolithic Age onwards, became the most important type of boat. It is still the basis for (Celtic?) types of river or lake vessels of the Principate period. For the civilizations of Mesopotamia and Egypt rivers were the most important traffic routes that were of prime importance both for the control of the country and for the exchange of goods. The types of ships depended on local conditions (reed boats on the Euphrates/Tigris and in the early period on the Nile). Numerous written sources and pictorial representations attest to shipping on the Nile; a description of the ships that were used in the 5th cent. BC on the Euphrates and the Nile is provided by Herodotus (1,194; 2,96).

In Greece IN was probably restricted essentially to Lake Copais and to the rivers of Ionia and Macedonia. In the 5th cent. BC Greek freighters (ὁλκάδες; holkádes) used the lower Danube. In Italy at least the Tiber and the Po were used from prehistoric times onwards. For the large city of Rome, which already imported grain during the Republic, the Tiber was the main link with the sea port of Ostia (Portus). In the 6th cent. AD the grain barges (caudicariae) were towed up the Tiber and, with the current, floated back empty to the sea port (Procop. Goth. 1,26,10). At the same time the Tiber also had an important function for the transportation of agricultural products from Etruria to Rome (Plin. Ep. 5,6,11f.; cf. in addition Cato Agr. 1,3); IN is attested in Italy also for the region of the Pomptine Marshes (Hor. Sat. 1,5,13–23; Str. 5,3,6).

In the provinces IN was highly developed on the Rhine, the Moselle, the Maas, on the rivers of Gaul, the Alpine lakes and the Danube, as well as on the Nile. Navigation on the Rhine reached as far as the Nehalennia sanctuary near Collijnsplaat (votive stones for a good journey), where the transfer to seagoing vessels took place. For the development of Gaul by the Romans the fact that the land had good IN routes was decisive – a fact emphasized by Strabo on many occasions (4,1,2; 4,1,11; 4,1,14); in the province of Baetica, IN on the Baetis was advantageous for the transportation of agricultural products (Str. 3,2,3f.). Shipping on the Moselle in late antiquity is mentioned in Ausonius (Mos. 39–47). The ships were towed upstream with the sailors mostly pulling the boats themselves, as several funerary reliefs show. Ships in the north-western provinces often had a rudder that was firmly attached to the sternpost and thus differed considerably from the ships in the Mediterranean. Individual inland sailors are known from their gravestones, for example Blussus of Mainz (CIL XIII 7067). The sailors of individual rivers or river systems formed associations (corpora) that could cooperate with the annona; thus, e.g., the corpus n(autarum) Rhodanicor(um) et Arar(icorum) is epigraphically attested (CIL XIII 1695). IN was used for the transportation of food (grain, salt, wine), building materials (bricks, stone; wood was probably floated), metals, textiles, clay and glass vessels, as well as for travelling. Wharves and granaries (horrea) were built in harbours. In the literature, a series of plans to build canals in order to facilitate the transportation of goods is mentioned (Saône-Moselle: Tac. Ann. 13,53; Puteoli-Rome: Tac. Ann. 15,42). The arguments for canal building of such kind are discussed in detail by Pliny (Ep. 10,41; 10,61).

From the Augustan period onwards naval fleets were stationed at the borders of the Imperium Romanum; they were stationed on the big rivers and on the lakes of the Alpine foothills. These units secured the border along Rhine and Danube; they remained in place even when the Limes was moved to the other side of the rivers; they were then used primarily for the transportation of building materials and for supplying the troops. In the 3rd cent. AD these naval units gained new importance, now primarily providing fast transportation for the troops (for the Rhine fleet cf. Amm. Marc. 17,1,4; 18,2,12). The Danube fleet, too, still existed in late antiquity (Cod. Theod. 7,17). Naval ports on the Rhine,

Danube and Save are known through finds. Military IN ended in the west with the Germanic conquest, and in the east, on the Danube, with the Bulgarian-Slavic occupation.

→ Land transport

1 Actes du Colloque "Du Léman à l'Océan", Caesarodunum 10, 1975 2 L. CASSON, Harbour and River Boats of Ancient Rome, in: JRS 55, 1965, 31–39 3 G. CHIC GARCÍA, La navegación por el Guadalquivir entre Córdoba y Sevilla, 1990 4 A. DEMAN, Réflexions sur la navigation fluviale dans l'antiquité romaine, in: T. HACKENS, P. MARCHETTI (ed.), Histoire économique de l'antiquité, 1987, 79–106 5 H. G. FRENZ, Bildliche Darstellungen zur Schiffahrt röm. Zeit an Rhein und Tiber, in: G. RUPPRECHT (ed.), Die Mainzer Römerschiffe, ²1982, 78–95 6 O. HÖCKMANN, Röm. Schiffsverbände und die Verteidigung der Rheingrenze in der Spätant., in: JRGZ 33, 1986, 369–416 7 JONES, LRE, 841–844 8 I. PEKÁRY, Vorarbeiten zum Corpus der hell.-röm. Schiffsdarstellungen II: Die Schiffstypen der Römer, Teil B: Die Flußschiffe, in: Boreas 8, 1985, 11–126 9 WHITE, Technology, 227–229. O.H.

Inn

I. ANCIENT ORIENT II. CLASSICAL ANTIQUITY

I. ANCIENT ORIENT

So far, evidence of inns comes mainly from Mesopotamia. There the inn was usually also the place where – outside institutional households – → beer was brewed. Inns normally served beer, with only one mention of the operator of a → wine tavern (ancient Babylonian period, 17th cent. BC; [3]). The running of an inn by a landlord or landlady or a hot-food stall by a cook was registered and licensed by royal edict in the ancient Babylonian period [5. 85]. Both had to pay a regular tax in silver to the palace. According to § 108 of the Law-code of Ḥammurabi (TUAT 1, 55) the landlady was obliged to accept barley from her customers as payment for beer. The penalty for contravention of this or deceptive manipulation was capital punishment. It was also a criminal offence to hide people at an inn.

Inns were visited by men and women, even by married couples together. Omens indicate dissipated behaviour (urinating, sleeping with another man's wife) [1]. A brothel might be attached to an inn (Middle Assyrian Book of Law § 14: TUAT 1, 82; [3; 4. 389⁸]; → Prostitution I.). Priestly women were forbidden to visit taverns on pain of capital punishment (Codex Ḥammurabi § 110: TUAT 1,55). The word aštammu (Sumerian éš.dam) for inn or tavern (attested from the 2nd half of the 2nd millennium BC) was also used to designate temples to the goddess → Ishtar. Various writings speak of people talking and playing games together at the inn. Going to the inn is also required as a symbol of re-entry into society in Babylonian cleansing rituals [4]. The inn also acted as an economic institution, as the village moneylender [5. 86].

Inns outside Mesopotamia are attested so far only from → Alalaḫ, which can certainly be taken as representative of other places in Syria. There is no corresponding information from Egypt so far.

1 Chicago Assyrian Dictionary, vol. A/2, 1968, 473 f., s. v. aštammu 2 Ibid., vol. K, 1971, 206, s. v. karānu, bīt karāni 3 Ibid., vol. S, 1984, 5–9, s. v. sābû 4 S. M. MAUL, Der Kneipenbesuch als Heilverfahren, in: D. CHARPIN, F. JOANNÈS (ed.), La circulation des biens, des personnes et des idées dans le Proche-Orient ancien, 1992, 389–396 5 J. RENGER, Patterns of Non-Institutional Trade and Non-Commercial Exchange in Ancient Mesopotamia at the Beginning of the Second Mill. B. C., in: A. ARCHI (ed.), Circulation of Goods in Non-Palatial Context, 1984, 31–123. J. RE.

II. CLASSICAL ANTIQUITY

A. ORIGIN B. PUBLIC HOSTELS C. COMMERCIAL HOSTELS D. INN E. SERVING STAFF

A. ORIGIN

In the eyes of the upper classes inns were places where fundamental societal standards were constantly contravened. Literary tradition therefore mentions them only occasionally and normally gives a very negative view of them; there is no cohesive ancient illustration on the subject. The social function and significance of inns for the lower classes can be surmised above all from the archaeological finds particularly in → Pompeii, → Herculaneum and → Ostia.

For poorer travellers only winter accommodation is attested from the archaic period: beggars and poor people slept in the smithy or in the λέσχη/→ léschē – evidently a kind of public hostel (Hes. Op. 493–494; Hom. Od. 18,329). Members of the upper classes, on the other hand, when → travelling used the private → hospitality (ξενία/xenía; Lat. hospitio) based on → kinship in the widest sense, personal recommendations or professional common ground. Being catered for by a host (ξένος/xénos; Lat. hospes) was considered the best type of travel accommodation in antiquity and the only kind acceptable to members of the upper classes. Guest rooms are attested in Greek private houses from the 5th cent. BC onwards (Diod. Sic. 13,83,1–4) and in the Roman period they were very comfortably and luxuriously equipped. Members of the Roman upper classes like Cicero also owned private accommodation (deversorium) on the frequently used routes between their various villas (→ villa). Visiting inns, which apparently developed as a consequence of increasing travel activity in the classical and, in particular, in the Hellenistic period, was, on the other hand, regarded up until late antiquity as not compatible with the status of a person in a high position [1. 449–454, 459–461]. The reproach of seeking out inns for pleasure was used from the 1st cent. BC onwards to discredit members of the Roman upper classes, such as M. Antonius [I 9] or, later, principes such as Nero [1], Commodus, Elagabalus [2] or Gallienus [6. 93 f.; 7. 80 f.]. Privately run bars and inns remained the preserve of merchants, traders, sailors and members of the lower classes.

B. Public hostels

By the 5th cent. BC it was no longer possible for all the pilgrims, visitors of *agones*, artists and ambassadors to receive accommodation from private hosts. While ambassadors and foreign athletes were invited to the prytany (→ *prytaneîon*), where they normally received a single, very simple meal, ordinary travellers slept in tents. The problem of catering for travellers became a subject for discussion in the 4th cent. BC: while Plato [1] thinks it necessary to put travellers in barracks and keep them under the strictest surveillance in the dock area (Pl. Leg. 952d–953b), Xenophon [2] recommends setting up a public hostel system with separate accommodation for traders and merchants in the ports and at the markets, and for other travellers at other places in the *polis* (Xen. Vect. 3,12). Up to the 2nd cent. BC simple public accommodation (ἑστιατήριον/*hestiatérion*; κατάλυμα/*katályma*; ξενών/*xenón*) was provided in many Greek sanctuaries; the porticoes were also used for sleeping. However, this hostel system remained rudimentary in the Greek cultural sphere [1. 454–456]. The Roman → *cursus publicus* created a hostel system for magistrats, civil servants and military officers on official journeys; for instance, Nero had hostels built in Thrace (CIL III 6123 = ILS 231); however, this system was never widespread, so that private hospitality or public inns still had to be used as well [1. 458 f.].

C. Commercial hostels

Inns where, as in modern hotels, drinks, food and overnight facilities are offered, are in literary evidence in Athens from the 5th cent. BC: Aristophanes [3] describes a simple hostel (πανδοκεῖον/*pandokeîon*), run by two women and their two maids, where guests were served bread, sausage, garlic, salt meat and cheese, and rooms were available for guests on the upper floor (Aristoph. Ran. 549–578). Larger hostels were evidently called καταγώγιον/*katagógion*, whereas a κατάλυσις/ *katálysis* also provided room for mounts and draught animals [1. 457].

In the Roman period a distinction was made between hostels for travellers (*caupona*, or, if its respectability is to be emphasized, *hospitium*) and an inn with facilities for accommodating mounts and draught animals (*stabulum*) [6. 1–28]. Both types are archaeologically attested in Pompeii: they were near the city gates – in particular the Porta di Stabia and the Porta di Ercolano – and in *regio* VII to the east of the Forum. In general *cauponae* had a saloon with a brick bar, a dining room and lockable guest rooms in a residential wing, which also had separate access to the road; *stabula* additionally had an open courtyard with a drinking trough, stable and a separate entrance. *Cauponae* in the towns were generally adjacent to brothels, whereas the *cauponae* in the surrounding countryside were considered respectable [6. 31–34; 7. 78–81]; they were frequently located at important road junctions [1. 457 f., 465 f.]. The *caupona* belonging to Euxinus in Pompeii even had its own vineyard for his private use [5. 40–43].

From remaining evidence it is impossible to form a general opinion on prices. The quality of *cauponae* was very variable. It was possible – and sometimes recommendable – to have meals prepared by one's own slave or to bring one's own food and have it cooked by the landlord, and to sleep in one's own bedding [6. 98–120].

D. Inn

In Greece people who traded in food often ran inns where meals and drinks were sold (καπηλεῖον/ *kapēleîon*) as a secondary occupation. But it was the archaeological finds in Pompeii, Herculaneum and Ostia that first gave us a more precise understanding of Roman public houses (*popina* or *taberna*, only in Plautus *thermipolium*). They were lit at night by a lamp and had a brick bar in the saloon, shelves for crockery and a stove for preparing warm meals and drinks. They were very common in ancient cities and probably had no fixed opening times, so that they also stayed open late at night [6. 36–73; 7. 78 f.]. The excavations in Pompeii show an almost even distribution of *popinae* throughout the city – with the exception of the wealthy residential quarter: members of the upper classes owed it to their status to eat in their own homes or with families of friends. The spatial separation allowed them to keep their distance and to avoid any nuisance caused by the *popinae* staying open so late at night [7. 81–83]. For members of the lower classes, who often had no cooking facilities in their homes (→ Housing conditions), *popinae* were extremely important: this was the only place where they could enjoy warm meals and drinks [6. 54–56]. In the literature that has been handed down, on the other hand, with its inherent upper-class bias, inns are only places for outsiders to stay: they were a meeting-place for drinkers, gamblers, slaves, gladiators, thieves, gravediggers, hangmen, muleteers and sailors; fights and gambling were common, and guests could get in touch with prostitutes here (cf. → Prostitution) [1. 457 f.; 7. 70].

Apart from wine and warm water for mixing (*calida* or *calda*), *popinae* sold fresh and cooked meat, smoked products, liver, eggs, pastries, cheese, onions, plums, chestnuts, apples, berries, grapes and cucumbers. This range of foods was greatly restricted by the emperors Tiberius, Claudius, Nero and Vespasian through edicts. The → wine sold in *popinae* probably came predominantly from local production, though there is evidence of imported wines from Greece in Pompeii [6. 99–108].

E. Serving staff

It was quite possible for members of the upper classes to be owners of inns in Pompeii [6. 80], but all those working in them were held in contempt: landlords were regarded as wine-adulterators, cheats and sources of the latest gossip and were also associated with the handling of stolen goods and murder with robbery and poisoning. Landladies were regarded as either bickering old women or seductive procuresses. The staff were equated with prostitutes, so they were not legally protected against → rape. Landlords were exempt from military service, but from the end of the 4th cent. AD had their own → collegium [1]. The reservations and prejudices against landlords and inns were adopted by the Christian Church [1. 456–458; 6. 80–97], which created its own institution for looking after travellers with the → xenodocheîon.

→ Travel

1 J.M. ANDRÉ, M.-F. BASLEZ, Voyager dans l'antiquité, 1993 2 A. HUG, s. v. Καπηλεῖον, RE 10.2, 1888 f. 3 Id., s. v. Καταγώγιον, RE 10.2, 2459–2461 4 Id., s. v. Πανδοκεῖον, RE 18.3, 520–529 5 W. F. JASHEMSKI, The Caupona of Euxinus at Pompeii, in: Archaeology 20, 1967, 36–44 6 T. KLEBERG, Hôtels, restaurants et cabarets dans l'antiquité romaine. Études historiques et philologiques, 1957 7 R. LAURENCE, Roman Pompeii. Space and Society, 1994 8 A. MAU, s. v. Caupona, RE 3.2, 1806–1808 9 K. SCHNEIDER, s. v. Taberna, RE 4 A, 1870 f. 10 H. SCHROFF, s. v. Thermipolium, RE 5 A, 2394 f. 11 A. TCHERNIA, Il vino: produzione e commercio, in: F. ZEVI (ed.), Pompei 79. Raccolta di studi per il decimonono centenario dell' eruzione vesuviana, 1984, 87–96. M. DR.

Innocentius I Pope 402–417 born in Alba near Rome, son of Anastasius (pope 399–402). As Siricius (384–399) before him, he attempted to tie the western bishops to the Apostolic see. He used the following arguments: the bishop of Rome is *caput et apex episcopatus* (Epist. 37,1); all bishops of Italy, Gaul and Spain owe their installation to him (Epist. 25,2); all more important cases have to be submitted to him for decision (Epist. 2,3). With his decretalia, I. aimed to establish a more uniform church discipline in the western half of the empire. His attempts even to claim authority at Constantinople (e.g., his advocacy for the exiled Iohannes Chrysostomos) failed. With Augustinus' support, I. opposed the Donatists and Pelagians.

Innocentius, Briefe und Dekrete: PL 20,463–612; 84,639–674; M.-R. GREEN, Pope Innocent I., 1973; H. JEDIN (ed.), Hdb. der Kirchengesch. vol. II/1, 1973, 265–268. RO.F.

Ino (Ἰνώ; *Inṓ*). Daughter of → Cadmus [1] and → Harmonia, generally taken to be the second (first: schol. Hom. Il. 7,86 BEKKER according to Philostephanus and Eust. ad locum; schol. Lycoph. 22) wife of → Athamas in Thebes [2] (the first being → Nephele [1]). She is the mother of Learchus and → Melicertes. Envy of her stepchildren → Phrixus and → Helle prompted her to develop a cunning plan. She talked the women of the country into roasting the seed grains, thus causing a severe famine. She bribed the envoys sent by Athamas to Delphi to tell the king that the infertility of the land could only be reversed by offering Phrixus as a sacrifice. After Phrixus and his sister had been carried away by the ram sent by Nephele, Athamas succumbed to madness and, in the mistaken belief that he was out hunting, he killed his eldest son Learchus with arrows. I. fled and flung herself from a cliff into the sea together with her younger son Melicertes. From then on, she was cultically venerated as → Leucothea or respectively as → Mater Matuta. Melicertes became Palaemon (in Hom. Od. 5,333–353; 5,458–462; Apollod. 1,80–84; Paus. 1,44,7 f.; Hyg. Fab. 2; cf. Aristid. 3,25–28, p. 42–46 DINDORF). In a different version, → Hera was angry with Athamas and I., because they had taken in → Dionysus after the death of I.'s sister → Semele, and struck them both with a madness which led to their deaths (Eur. Med. 1282–1289; Apollod. 3,28 f.; Ov. Met. 4,416–562; Ov. Fast. 6,481–562 with an expanded version; further details in: Nonnus, Dion. 9,49–138; 9,243–10,138; Hyg. Fab. 1; 4). The story of I. has also been adapted in the eponymous tragedies by Euripides [1] (TGF F 398–423, p. 482–490 N²; cf. Hyg. Fab. 4) and Livius [III 1] Andronicus (TRF, p. 4 f.).

1 S. EITREM, s. v. Leukothea (1), RE 12, 2293–2306 2 A. NERCESSIAN, s. v. I., LIMC 5.1, 657–661 (with bibliography). SI. A.

Ino [2] see → Leucothea

Inquilinus The tenant (*conductor*) of a dwelling, not necessarily of low social position. In Roman law the *inquilinus* is bound to the landlord (*locator*) by a consensual contract (→ locatio conductio), on the basis of which he is entitled to use the dwelling. Roman jurists use *inquilinus* as a technical term in order to have a selective name specifically for the tenant of a dwelling within the far more comprehensive contract type of *locatio conductio* (in modern law also leasehold, service and work contract).

The *inquilinus* is distinguished by Roman jurists from *colonus* (→ colonatus), the leaseholder of an estate, who is also entitled to collection of fruits and benefits. The *inquilinus*, on the other hand, is entitled to an → interdictum de migrando against confiscation of fixtures and fittings by the landlord.

B. FRIER, Landlords and Tenants in Imperial Rome, 1980; T. MAYER-MALY, Locatio Conductio. Eine Unt. zum klass. röm. Recht, 1956; W. SCHEIDEL, Grundpacht und Lohnarbeit in der Landwirtschaft des röm. Italien, 1994; P. PANITSCHEK, Der spätant. Kolonat: Ein Substitut für die "Halbfreiheit" peregriner Rechtssetzungen?, in: ZRG 107, 1990, 137–154. N.F.

Inscriptio Technical term for the listing of sources at the beginning of the fragments of the digests (→ Digesta) and of the constitutions in the *Codex Iustinianus* (→ Codex II C). The *Digesta* list the author from the Classical period (e.g. Ulpian), his work (e.g. *ad edictum* = edict commentary), and the number of the 'book' (e.g. *libro quinto* for 5th bk.); the Codex Iustinianus – as already the Codex Theodosianus – lists the emperor who enacted the respective constitution and the addressee. The *inscriptiones* in the *Digesta* were the most important sources for reconstructing the classical legal

texts from the 1st cent. BC up to the middle of the 3rd cent. AD (still exemplary today [1]).
→ Constitutiones

1 O. LENEL, Palingenesia iuris civilis, 1889, repr. 1960.
G.S.

Inscription Painter Leading master of early → Chalcidian vase painting, working around 560–540 BC, who painted chiefly amphorae, hydriae and craters. The Inscription Painter (IP) is named for his inscribing of names on his mythological images. Preferred among these are the legends of Troy [1. 118–140], then come Bellerophon [1. 114–117], Perseus [1. 113] or the combat between Zeus and Typhon [1. 84–85]; twice the combat between Hercules and Geryoneus is found [1. 90–96]. Besides myths (approximately the half of all Chalcidian mythological images come from the hand of the IP), satyrs and maenads, horsemen and animal friezes are attested, often ordered in heraldic manner around a botanical ornament. The style of the IP is of a powerful malleability, his images cover large areas. The approximately 50 vases attributed to the IP have been found chiefly at Vulci and Reggio di Calabria.

1 J. KECK, Studien zur Rezeption fremder Einflüsse in der chalkid. Keramik, 1988.

M. IOZZO, La ceramica "calcidese", 1994, 15–31; E. SIMON, Die griech. Vasen, ²1981, pl. 18f., 39f. M.ST.

Inscriptions
I. ANCIENT ORIENT II. GREEK III. LATIN

I. ANCIENT ORIENT
A. GENERAL B. MESOPOTAMIA, ASIA MINOR, SYRIA/PALESTINE C. EGYPT

A. GENERAL
In the more restricted sense, inscriptions are texts – usually of monumental character – that, because of their function, are intended to last, as well as texts that are written on other-than-usual writing materials, e.g. clay tablets, → papyrus, → ostraka, etc. Inscriptions are closely tied to other texts by commonalities of writing, form and content. Therefore, despite specific research efforts, ancient oriental epigraphy has not developed as an independent sub-discipline – with the exception of the Hebraic/Aramaic tradition of the 1st millennium, where inscriptions, ostraka, etc., stand alongside the OT.

B. MESOPOTAMIA, ASIA MINOR, SYRIA/PALESTINE
Inscriptions originate above all from the region of cuneiform writing, but – to a lesser extent – they derive also from those cultures that employed alphabetical writing. Inscriptions are commissioned by the sovereign, and in rare instances by officials for the area of their jurisdiction, or by private persons (e.g. seal inscriptions, dedicatory inscriptions, funerary inscriptions).

Inscription carriers are made of baked clay, stone, metal (usually bronze) or bone; inscriptions are rarely found in painting or brick glazing; wood is not preserved. From the beginning of the 3rd millennium BC, inscriptions in Mesopotamia are often associated with figurative representations (statues or reliefs). Inscriptions are found on consecrated offerings, and on objects of daily life, such as weights, seals, vessels and weapons. Mesopotamian building inscriptions are often handed down in duplicate, on identical and also non-identical inscription carriers (e.g. bricks, clay nails, cylinders, stone/metal plates, figurines). Moreover, brick stamps allowed a mass replication of inscriptions. Building inscriptions were often laid down in depositories in the foundation, or were walled up between the bricks. Apart from those on stone construction parts (e.g. door-hinge stones, thresholds, wall orthostats), inscriptions on visible building parts are encountered only in exceptional cases in mud-brick architecture.

In inscriptions the → cuneiform script is written in representative, standardized, and archaicizing characters, and always engraved on the surface. Often with Luwian hieroglyphs (→ Luwian; → Hieroglyphic scripts, Asia Minor), less frequently with alphabetical scripts (Phoenician, Aramaic, Ancient Southern Arabian; → Alphabet), the characters are sublimely elaborated in stone relief. → Ancient Persian cuneiform is used exclusively in Achaemenid inscriptions. Inscriptions are usually written in the national language(s) (→ Bilingual inscriptions, trilinguals), or in languages with high cultural prestige.

A classification of inscriptions can be achieved on the basis of textual function. The simpler forms (1., 2.) are in each case implied in the succeeding forms: 1. Identifying inscriptions: the text refers to the client (name, title, of the ruler), owner and/or the object, or that which is depicted on the relief. 2. Reporting inscriptions: actions of the ruler are referred to (constructions, war reports – important above all in Neo-Assyrian and Achaemenid, also in Phoenician, Hebrew, and Aramaic inscriptions). 3. Dedicatory inscriptions are concerned with objects or constructions – in Babylonia the most frequently occurring form of inscriptions. 4. Declarative inscriptions establish legal conditions; specifically, this concerns steles with legal norms (late 3rd to early 2nd millennium; → Hammurapi, → Legal texts in cuneiform), document stones concerning land transactions or privileges (3rd millennium, 2nd half of the 2nd millennium until 7th cent.) and → international treaties. 5. Appellative inscriptions: here, the supplicant speaks in the text itself to an addressee, i.e., within the framework of other forms of inscriptions, to the deity (→ Prayer) or to a descendant (blessing and curse formulas; → Curse); amulets and magical figurines are addressed to demons. Building and dedicatory inscriptions serve their intended purpose without needing to be read (aloud) or seen; visible monumental inscriptions are not necessarily even legible (→ Bisutun).

→ DECIPHERMENT; → Historiography

> R.BORGER, Hdb. der Keilschriftlit., 1967–1975; CIS; Corpus Inscriptionum Iranicarum, 1985ff.; J.NAVEH, Early History of the Alphabet, 1982; Royal Inscriptions of Mesopotamia, 1987ff.; TUAT.   WA.SA.

C. EGYPT

Egyptian inscriptions were carved into writing materials, worked out of them, written down with ink or pigment, or are inlaid using other materials. Stone, wood, metal, clay, stucco, cardboard, cloth, and faience are most commonly attested. Among the items written upon were architectural components, items of equipment for religious, secular, and sepulchral structures, burial objects, votive offerings, and objects of everyday life (clay vessels, seals, amulets).

Typical scripts for inscriptions are → hieroglyphs (from the early period), less frequently → hieratic (inscriptions, graffiti) and, from the 2nd half of the 1st millennium BC in → demotic. From the time of the NK onwards, hieroglyphic inscriptions are primarily written in archaicizing language. Inscriptions of the 1st millennium BC to a certain extent combine differing linguistic form(s) and scripts [5]. In the case of Egyptian inscriptions, the aspect of publication is of lesser significance, rather, what is striven for is the eternal magical efficacy of the textual contents [2]. Hieroglyphic inscriptions in part develop the potency of representations. The details of their placement (location, alignment) are determined by rules that change in the course of time [4].

A textual division of the extensive literature comprised of inscriptions is problematic. Three different groups – not clearly separable from one another – can be distinguished: 1. Annotations, headings and lists (identifying and explanatory data concerning representations, summaries of properties, origins, and contents, lists of sacrifices, and calendars of festivals); 2. Historio-biographical texts (→ Autobiographies of private persons, reports of royal deeds and edicts); 3. Religious texts (devotional formulas, hymns, prayers, ritual texts, funerary texts, etc.). Due to their origin from a funerary and temple-related context, and through their claim to eternal duration, most inscriptions have religious connotations.

→ Bilingual inscriptions; → DECIPHERMENT; → Historiography; → Trilinguals

> 1 Annual Egyptological Bibliography, 1948ff.   2 J.ASS-MANN, Sprachbezug und Weltbezug der Hieroglyphen-schrift, in: Id., Stein und Zeit, ²1995, 76–92 (esp. 86–88)   3 A.FARID, Fünf demot. Stelen, 1995   4 H.G. FISCHER, L'écriture et l'art de l'Égypte ancienne, 1986   5 J.HORN, s.v. Bilingue, Trilingue, LÄ 7, 1–8   6 J.KAHL et al., Die I. der 3. Dyn., 1995   7 B.PORTER, R.L.B. MOSS, Topographical Bibliography, ²1960ff.   8 Textes et langages de l'Égypte pharaonique, vols. 2 and 3, 1972.   HE.FE.

II. GREEK

A. GENERAL   B. IMPORTANCE   C. TECHNIQUES
D. SCRIPT   E. CONTENT   F. DATING   G. HISTORY
OF GREEK EPIGRAPHY

A. GENERAL

Inscriptions written in Greek letters are the object of Greek → EPIGRAPHY (ἐπιγραφή, *epigraphē*: 'inscription'). Special areas of study are Greek texts written in non-Greek → script (→ Linear B, → Cypriot syllabic script [26]). Their spatial spread corresponds to that of the Greek language; focal points are the Greek mainland and the eastern Mediterranean area, with the greatest number being furnished by Athens (approximately 18,000). The most ancient inscriptions are from the 8th cent. BC (Nestor Cup); the lower time limit cannot be exactly ascertained, and in the corpora is generally set in the time of Justinian (6th cent. AD). Later inscriptions belong to Byzantine epigraphy. As writing materials, stone and metal are most commonly used, and, more rarely, wood. For inscriptions on ceramics (vase inscriptions, → Ostraka), there are special collections. → NUMISMATICS is concerned with inscriptions on coins, and → PAPYROLOGY with inscriptions on papyri.

B. IMPORTANCE

Inscriptions are primary sources; they supplement, illustrate, and correct extant writings and ancient authors. Each inscription is an original. Found primarily in fragmentary form, they are very much in need of complementation and interpretation. To this end, what is needed – along with a knowledge of epigraphical parallels – is autopsy (personal inspection) of inscriptions, or of the → squeeze. The influx of new Greek inscriptions continues undiminished: *c.* 1,000 new finds are published annually. On the other hand, the stock of inscriptions cited by ancient writers is exhausted. [35; 36].

C. TECHNIQUES

As a rule, inscriptions are carved or punched into metal, chiselled in stone and laid out with pigment (red, blue). The quality and quantity of inscriptions are dependent on the types of stones available (in Attica Pentelic and Eleusinian marble). Metal plates (partly with nail holes) are particularly widespread on the Peloponnese. Small lead plates – rolled up – are preferred for curses. Silver and gold are extremely rare (in Roman times there are gold-plated bronze letters, *litterae auratae*).

The most ancient inscriptions [27] run from right to left (left-running), while longer texts are alternately left-running and right-running in boustrophedon (βουστροφεδόν; → Writing, direction of); in Attica letters are placed exactly underneath one another, vertically and horizontally (στοιχεδόν, *stoichedón*, 5th–3rd cent. BC [28]). There is no space between the words (*scriptio continua*); in earliest times, punctuation is arbitrary, but in the Imperial period it can be found occasionally, following the Roman model; then also abbreviations.

D. SCRIPT

The Greek → script was developed from the Phoenician in the 10th cent. BC (?). The archaic → alphabets show different regional characteristics [28], and their chronology is a matter of controversy; their spread does not correspond to that of the dialects [8]. From the 4th cent. BC onwards, the professional scribes of official inscriptions can be recognized from their specific characteristics [29]. Further standardization of the script occurring parallel to the formation of → Koiné involved adornment (thickened and split stems, so-called apices) and coarsening; in the Imperial period cursive and uncial forms appear, and later angular forms and ligatures (→ Ligature/Cursive writing).

E. CONTENT

The content and purpose of inscriptions are highly diverse, such as: Funerary inscriptions (most frequently) with the name of the deceased and a greeting on funerary steles (with relief), columns and altars. Special forms include funerary poems (funerary epigrams) [14; 15]; dedicatory inscriptions to the gods, often on the dedicated object, and frequently donated after a victory in a sporting or artistic agon (→ Competition) [16]; honorary inscriptions, above all as signatures on statues, appear more frequently only from the 4th cent. BC, and in Roman times in great abundance; sculptors' inscriptions in which the artist refers to himself [17; 18]; decrees (with different formulas in the individual poleis) with the decisions of the entire community or sections of it, as well as associations [31]. In this instance, the majority are honorary decrees for citizens of other city-states, kings, Roman magistrates, to whom honorary citizenship (→ proxenía) is granted; manumission documents for emancipated slaves, (→ Manumission), often carried out as a fictitious sale to a deity, and documented in that deity's temple (especially in Delphi and northern Greece); border and mortgage stones (→ hóroi [32]); laws and regulations concerning civil, public [19], and religious matters [20], even the codification of established law [33]; religious texts, hymns (with music) [34]; letters of kings [22] and Roman emperors [23]; building inscriptions, settlements of accounts, inventories of cult-related utensils; lists and catalogues of objects (for example, on the ships of the Athenian fleet) and persons (e.g. of eponymous officials and priests); international documents (asylia decrees [24], international treaties [25], legal records).

F. DATING

For the most part, one must rely exclusively upon the form of the letters. These allow for dating that is accurate to within one century of the actual date; scepticism is called for where more exact time frames are specified. Internal clues, moreover, are content, language, formulas and prosopographic relations. Not infrequently dating is possible on the basis of eponymous officials (→ Eponyms in chronology). Lists of eponyms – which differ from polis to polis – are preserved in fragmentary form or can be reconstructed: for the Athenian archons (480–301, referred to in Diodorus Siculus, and thereafter in inscriptions, but controversial as to details [37]), for the archons of Delos (326–168) and of Delphi [38] as well as the stephanephoroi in Miletus (525–259 [39]). From the time of the → Diadochi, there is also dating by reigning years of the king, and later according to → eras [40]: of the Seleucid (from 312), Macedonian (from 148), Sullan (from 85), and the Actian or Imperial era (from 32 BC).

G. HISTORY OF GREEK EPIGRAPHY

There were ancient collections of inscriptions, but they are no longer extant (→ Philochorus, → Craterus, → Polemon of Ilium). Greek inscriptions were first collected again by CYRIACUS OF ANCONA (AD 1391 to after 1455). The corpora of the 16th–18th cents. were compilations of scattered copies made by travellers in Greece and the Orient; in addition, a few pieces ended up in museums. In 1815, A. BÖCKH (1785–1867) founded the Corpus Inscriptionum Graecarum (CIG) at the Prussian Academy of Sciences. During the period of 1828–1859, all inscriptions collected into four volumes, in geographical order, with commentaries. With the independence of Greece (1832), and the inception of systematic excavations, there was a dramatic increase in material. In 1902, U. v. WILAMOWITZ-MOELLENDORFF combined the principle of autopsy with that of completeness, and at the same time restricted the designation 'Inscriptiones Graecae' (IG) to Greece, Italy and the Aegean islands [1]. Concomitantly with this, there came into existence a multitude of corpora of the most diverse quality. The resulting confusion is still increasing, and is reflected in epigraphical databases, which moreover only seek to include already-published inscriptions (the most comprehensive of these is the 1998 CD ROM #7 of the Packard Humanities Institute). All the more important for research, therefore, is the treatment of new publications released every year in the Bulletin épigraphique (BE), the REG (reviews) and in the Supplementum Epigraphicum Graecum (SEG, patchy since 1923, complete since 1976, with texts and indices). In any event, technical progress cannot take the place of the admittedly time-consuming, but necessary process of autopsy; moreover, the safeguarding of the ever-expanding stocks of inscriptions in museums becomes a problem. Extensive collections are to be found in Athens (Epigraphic Museum, EM), London, Paris and Berlin; the 'Inscriptiones Graecae' at the Academy in Berlin possesses the largest epigraphical archive.

→ EPIGRAPHY; → INSCRIPTIONS

CORPORA: 1 IG, 15 vols. (presently 45 fascicles, partly in 2nd and 3rd eds.) 2 TAM, 6 vols. 3 IK, 52 vols.
COLLECTIONS: 4 Syll.³, 4 vols., 1915–24 5 OGIS, 2 vols. 1903–05 6 TOD, 2 vols., 1933–48 7 ML, 1969.

8 SGDI, 4 vols., 1884–1915.
TRANSL.: 9 R. Meiggs, D. Lewis, A Selection of Greek Historical Inscriptions, 1969.
BIBLIOGRAPHY: 10 Guide de l'épigraphiste, 1986 (with suppl. 1993)
MANUALS: 11 W. LARFELD, Hdb. der griech. Epigraphik, 3 vols., 1902–07 12 M. GUARDUCCI, Epigrafia greca, 4 vols., 1967–78 13 G. KLAFFENBACH, Griech. Epigraphik, ²1966.
THEMATIC CORPORA: 14 CEG, 2 vols., 1983–89 15 GVI, 1955 16 L. MORETTI, Iscrizioni agonistiche greche, 1953 17 E. LOEWY, I. griech. Bildhauer, 1885 18 J. MARCADÉ, Recueil des signatures des sculpteurs grecs, 1953–57 19 R. KOERNER, Inschr. Gesetzestexte der frühen griech. Polis, 1993 20 LSCG, 1969 21 LSAM, 1955 22 WELLES, 1934 23 OLIVER, 1989 24 K. RIGSBY, Asylia. Territorial Inviolability in the Hellenistic World, 1996 25 StV, vol. 2–3, 1962–69 26 MASSON, 1961 27 LSAG, ²1990 28 R. P. AUSTIN, The Stoichedon Style in Greek Inscriptions, 1938 29 ST. V. TRACY, Attic Letter-Cutters of 229 to 86 BC, 1990 30 A. KIRCHHOFF, Studien zur Gesch. des griech. Alphabets, ⁴1887 31 P. J. RHODES, The Decrees of the Greek States, 1997 32 M. I. FINLEY, Studies in Land and Credit in Ancient Athens 500–200 BC, 1951 33 R. F. WILLETTS, The Law Code of Gortyn, 1967 34 M. L. WEST, Ancient Greek Music, 1992 35 C. MEYER, Die Urkunden im Geschichtswerk des Thukydides, 1955 36 CH. HABICHT, Pausanias und seine 'Beschreibung Griechenlands', 1985 37 B. D. MERITT, The Athenian Year, 1961 38 G. DAUX, Chronologie delphique, 1943 39 IMilet I 3, no. 122–123 40 W. LESCHHORN, Antike Ären, 1993. K.H.

III. LATIN
A. GENERAL B. HISTORY C. TRADITION D. PRODUCTION E. DEVELOPMENT OF LATIN EPIGRAPHY

A. GENERAL
By inscriptions (Latin *titulus*, rarely *inscriptio*) in the narrower sense of the word, one understands communications recorded in stone or metal, and intended to last. Election-calls or proclamations (for example, in Pompeii) that were painted on wood, or on walls, were not created with a view to duration. Belonging to this class of sources, in a wider sense of the word, are the producer's marks on ceramics and bricks ('stamps'), glass and metal objects – which are often designated as brief inscriptions or *instrumentum domesticum* – as well as name graffiti on ceramics, and these together could be at least as large in numbers as stone inscriptions [1; 2]. The foregoing inscriptions are usually written in capital letters (*capitalis*, → Capital scripts) [3]. In Petronius (58,7), Hermerus says of himself: *lapidarias litteras scio*. We also know of the draft of an inscription on papyrus that is written in monumental *capitalis* [4. 13]. Dispatch marks painted by brush on amphoras, as well as communications on ceramics shards (Bou N'Djem), and also documents written on wooden tablets with ink (as, for example, those from Vindolanda) are written in lower-case letters (→ Minuscule).

In contrast to papyri – which are closely related in terms of source – inscriptions are extant from the whole of the Roman Empire, in the eastern portions of which the few Latin inscriptions are complemented by contemporary Greek inscriptions.

Inscriptions amplify our source material for areas that are only sparsely dealt with in the literary tradition: social and economic history, and religions, as well as the organization of the empire outside of the capital city. Occasionally, they also constitute the primary sources in parallel with the reports of the historians: the → *Senatus consultum de Bacchanalibus*, the → *Monumentum Ancyranum*, the → *Senatus consultum de Pisone patre* and the Tablet of Lyons (*Tabula Lugudunensis*), the Price Edict of Diocletian (→ *Edictum* [3] *Diocletiani*).

B. HISTORY
At the end of the 8th cent. BC the Etruscans took over their script from the Greeks in Cumae – with only minor changes. From there it pressed forward into wider areas of Italy from the middle of the 7th cent., to the Venetians around Este, to the Umbrians, and to the Adriatic coast of central Italy (the inscriptions of the warrior of Capestrano from the 7th cent.). In the 6th cent. the Romans also adopted the script, although with fresh loans from the Greeks (B, D and X do not exist in the Etruscan alphabet). Z was deleted by Ap. Claudius [I 2] in 312; in the middle of the 3rd cent., there appeared in its place in the alphabet the media G (C with a stroke). Y and Z were (re-)introduced in the 1st cent. for the writing of Greek names. The attempt of the emperor Claudius to introduce three new Roman letters was unsuccessful, even though in the opinion of, for example, Quintilian the fund of Roman letters was no longer suited to the pronunciation of the time, and so the alphabet of the time of Cicero remains the one we use to this day (Prisc. 2,15 GL).

The oldest extant Latin inscriptions are found on the *fibula Praenestina* (CIL I²,3 = ILLRP 1) from the 7th cent. BC – whose genuineness is a matter of controversy (doubts in [5]; [6] disagrees) – and the → *Lapis niger* → from the Forum Romanum, a cult charter from the end of the 6th cent. BC. The first treaty with the Carthaginians (507?) and the Law of the Twelve Tables (451/50, → *tabulae duodecim*) were published on bronze plates, while the → *Foedus Cassianum* of 486 was published on a bronze column. Not until around the middle of the 4th cent. does the number of → votive inscriptions – and still later that of → funerary inscriptions – begin slowly to increase. Roughly 3,000 inscriptions derive from the five centuries of the Republic, while 300,000 are from the Imperial period. From the middle of the 3rd cent. AD there follows a rapid decline, with only a negligible resurgence in the 4th cent.

C. TRADITION
Of the formerly many millions of inscriptions intended to last, those written upon stone are the ones

that are chiefly extant, while those inscribed on especially valuable material (e.g. gold and silver) are the fewest in quantity. Of the more than 300,000 Roman stone inscriptions discovered so far (with an annual increase of about 1,000), funerary inscriptions represent by far the largest group. Of the remainder, dedicatory inscriptions to gods and to the emperors can be said to constitute the main share, then building inscriptions, and donor inscriptions, etc. The traditional ordering of inscriptions – as adopted from the CIL, through the ILS, and extending down to many modern corpora – begins with the Republican inscriptions, then leads through dedications to the gods, emperor inscriptions, those concerning senators, *equites*, and the military, *tituli municipales* and funerary inscriptions, and finally to the ubiquitously abundant fragments. Inscriptions of ephemeral significance – such as council-session minutes, lists of members, etc., which were usually published on whitened wooden tablets (the *tabulae dealbatae*) – are almost completely missing, as are – with the exception of Pompeii – election summons [7]. The local distribution is extremely various. Up to now, Rome itself has provided about a third of all Latin inscriptions discovered thus far, Latin North Africa approximately 50,000, and the German-Gaulic region around 25,000. Among single cities, Pompeii – with approximately 10,000 inscriptions (only 800 of them on stone) – would have to be regarded as the best-known; for medium-sized cities such as Cologne or Italica (near Seville), even as few as 500 to 1,000 stone inscriptions constitute a good source-basis. The number of inscriptions handed down – whether they remained extant, were used as building material, sold, or burned to make lime – depends decisively on the later history of the city, and therefore is hardly susceptible to generalization.

D. Production

Little is known of the activities of the workshops (*officinae lapidariae*). It is probable that they usually received the draft written in cursive script, which could be a source of transmission errors. Some stonecutters (*lapicidae*) could not read, while others may have composed texts (according to sample books?) for clients who could not write. The arrangement of the inscriptions on the stone (*ordinatio*) included the division of the writing field, the measurement and pre-sketching of lines and letters, and the planning of abbreviations, which cut costs and could hide a lack of linguistic ability (Gell. NA 10,1). *Capitalis* (*quadrata* or *rustica*, also the slimmer *actuaria*,) was usually selected as the script; only occasionally – with brief inscriptions or graffiti – is the → cursive script used. In order to make them more clearly visible, the letters of stone inscriptions were filled with minium (red), while those on bronze were filled with ceruse (white). In the case of extremely expensive inscriptions – for example the dedication of the Colosseum – there were bronze letters carved into the surface or embossed, and these were often gold-plated (*inscriptiones caelatae*) [8].

Christians also wrote inscriptions, albeit – for understandable reasons – at first only funerary inscriptions; these differed very little from pagan inscriptions, except in terms of symbols and many formulas. From the time of Constantine I, building inscriptions for basilicas are also encountered, the first being that for a church in Castellum Tingitanum in 324 [9], and *elogia* (→ *elogium* [1]) for popes and martyrs, with those composed by Pope Damasus (→ Epigrammata Damasiana) and produced by → Filocalus (ILCV 963 and [10]) being of particularly high quality.

Only in few instances is the dating of inscriptions directly possible through references to eponyms, i.e., by the naming of consuls, or through a *tribunicia potestas* of the emperor, or the like. Indirect criteria are – in decreasing order of precision – the mention of historically-known occurrences or situations (wars, emperors, and details of history of people or military units), style and formulas (for example the superlatives of later times), the form of the letters, the types of stone used, as well as ornamentation and illustrations on the material inscribed. For this reason among others, the publication of inscriptions should never take place – as it used to be done in the past – without an exact description of the entire monument.

E. Development of Latin Epigraphy

The first collections of Latin inscriptions (especially those from Rome) – from which the so-called Codex Einsidlensis of roughly AD 800 obtained a portion of its material – seem to have been already in existence during late antiquity. After centuries during which the Roman monumental script could no longer even be read, there follow from the end of the 14th cent. increasingly comprehensive and precise collections, among which those of Cyriacus of Ancona, – and later those of Ligorius, Alciatus and Pighius – had a wide-reaching effect. After precursors in the 18th cent., such as Scipione MAFFEI and Bartolomeo BORGHESI, → EPIGRAPHY as an academic discipline began in 1845 with the appearance of the Corpus Inscriptionum Latinarum (CIL) of the Prussian Academy of Sciences, in which Theodor MOMMSEN – along with a series of co-workers – published virtually all of the Latin inscriptions that were known at that time, in accordance with the principles of completeness and autopsy (personal examination). This work was published in Latin, and thus circumvented the problem of national corpora in the national language, which even then was a virulent problem; for these national-language corpora, in the second half of the 20th cent., seemed to claim the field for themselves, which resulted in ever-increasing obscurity. Therefore, the new edition of the CIL has returned to Latin as the language of publication.

On the other hand, epigraphical databases are now emerging in many different places, in ways that are hardly co-ordinated and only of limited compatibility; it is one of the most important tasks of the future, in terms of research policy, to co-ordinate these efforts, and to place the results on the Internet in a corpus of inscriptions that is based on universal give and take. The language employed then will probably no longer be Latin.

→ EPIGRAPHY; → INSCRIPTIONS

1 M. ORMOS (ed.), Instrumenta Latina Inscripta, Specimina Nova VII.1, 1992   2 W. V. HARRIS (ed.), The Inscribed Economy, Journal of Roman Archeology, Suppl. 6, 1993   3 G. SUSINI, The Roman Stonecutter, 1973   4 L. KEPPIE, Understanding Roman inscriptions, 1991   5 M. GUARDUCCI, La cosidetta Fibula Praenestina: elementi nuovi, in: Memorie della Classe di Scienze morali e storiche dell' Accademia dei Lincei, VIII 28, 1984, 127ff. 6 A. E. GORDON, The Inscribed Fibula Praenestina: Problems of Authenticity, 1975   7 W. ECK, Inschriften auf Holz, in: Imperium Romanum (FS K. Christ), 1998, 203–217   8 G. ALFÖLDY, Eine Bauinschrift aus dem Kolosseum, in: ZPE 109, 1995, 195–226   9 L. LESCHI, Atti del IV Congr. Internazionale di Archeologia Cristiana I, 149ff.   10 C. M. KAUFMANN, Hdb. der altchristl. Epigraphik, 1917, 327f.

CORPORA AND COLLECTIONS: Corpus Inscriptionum Latinarum (CIL; by now more than 60 folio volumes, parly in 2nd ed.; for its structure E. MEYER (see below), 131ff.); H. DESSAU (ed.), Inscriptiones Latinae Selectae (ILS; thematic selection); L'Année Épigraphique (AE; yearly publication).
BIBLIOGRAPHIES: J. BÉRARD et al., Guide de l'épigraphiste. Bibliographie choisie des épigraphies antiques et médiévales, ²1989.
MANUALS AND BIBLIOGRAPHIES: R. CAGNAT, Cours d'épigraphie latine, ⁴1910; I. CALABI LIMENTANI, Epigrafia latina, ⁴1991; A. E. GORDON, Illustrated Introduction to Latin Epigraphy, 1983; E. MEYER, Einführung in die lat. Epigraphik, ³1991.   H.GA.

Inscription style

Inscription style refers to the script of the oldest Greek literary → papyri and papyrus documents (c. 4th–3rd cents. BC); it is a → majuscule which imitates the style of contemporaneous inscriptions. Records are, for instance, the papyrus of the *Persians* by → Timotheus of Miletus [3], the papyrus from Derveni [1], the so-called lament of Artemisia [4], and few other papyri from Saccara and Hibeh [2]. The inscriptional character is revealed in the bilinear, rigid, uniform and heavy strokes: in the forms of E (in four strokes), of Z (two horizontal strokes connected by one vertical stroke), of Θ (a circle with a dot in the middle), of M (in four separate lines), of the angular Σ, of Ξ (in three parallel strokes) and of Ω, in the archaic form typical of inscriptions. In the course of the 3rd cent. BC which saw a wider spread of script, the inscriptional style developed into softer forms, and a faster cursive hand (→ Writing, styles of III.) began to distinguish itself from the book hand.

1 S. G. KAPSOMENOS, Ὁ ὀρφικὸς πάπυρος τῆς Θεσσαλονίκης, in: AD 19, 1964, 17–25   2 E. G. TURNER, Ptolemaic Bookhands and Lille Stesichorus, in: Scrittura e Civiltà 4, 1980, 26–27   3 U. VON WILAMOWITZ-MOELLENDORFF (ed.), Timotheos, die Perser, aus einem Papyrus von Abusir, 1903 (Faksimile: Der Timotheos-Papyrus gefunden bei Abusir am 1. Februar 1902, 1903)

4 U. WILCKEN, Urkunden der Ptolemäerzeit, I, 1927, 97–104.

E. CRISCI, Scrivere greco fuori d'Egitto (Papyrologica Florentina XXVII), 1996, 9–15; E. G. TURNER, Ptolemaic Bookhands and Lille Stesichorus, in: Scrittura e Civiltà 4, 1980, 19–40.   G.M.

Insects

This class of animals was first named by Aristotle (Hist. an. 1,1,487a 32–34; 4,1,523b 13–15) for the notches (ἐντομαί/*entomaí*) on their ventral side or on both the ventral and dorsal sides ἔντομα/*éntoma* (sc. ζῷα; *zôa*), from which the modern term 'entomology' and the German word '*Kerbtier*' (notched animal) are derived. The other most important characteristics listed by Aristotle are: insects do not breathe in air (Hist. an. 1,1,487a 30–32; 4,9,535b 5; obviously he was not familiar with the tracheal system, which differs from the respiratory system of higher animals), are bloodless (ἄναιμα/*ánaima*, Hist. an. 1,6,490b 14) and often have many feet (πολύποδες/*polýpodes*, ibid. 490b 15). The three pairs of legs, which are considered decisive in modern systematics (hence the modern name Hexapoda for this class) are only mentioned by Aristotle in Part. an. 4,6,683b 2f. for the hopping insects (→ Grasshoppers and → Fleas). Varro (Rust. 3,16,5) suspects a link between the hexagonal honeycomb and the six legs of bees. The wings (cf. Aristot. Hist. an. 4,7,532a 19–26) may always be present (e.g. → Bee, μέλιττα/*mélitta*; (dung?) → Beetle, μηλολόνθη/*mēlolónthē*; → Wasp, σφήξ/*sphéx*) or only temporarily (in → Ants, μύρμηκες/*mýrnēkes*, and fireflies (= → Glow-worm?), πυγολαμπίδες/*pygolampídes*, ibid. 4,1,523b 20f.). Their body, which according to modern knowledge is encased in a rigid chitin coat, has no bones but is self-supporting (ibid. 523b 15–17; 4,7, 532b 1–3). Errors, such as the classification of the permanently wingless centipede (σκολόπενδρα/*skolópendra*, ibid. 523b 18) as an insect (and not in a class of its own, the Myriopoda), are understandable given the taxonomic difficulties. The partially sexual, partially parthenogenetic reproduction with several developmental stages begins, according to Aristotle, with maggots (σκώληξ/*skólēx*, Hist. an. 5,1,539b 11; 5,19,552a 21 = *vermiculus* in Plin. HN 10,190) in bees, wasps, → flies and → horse flies, but with caterpillars in other insects (κάμπη/*kámpē*; main source: Aristot. Gen. an. 3,9,758a 29– b 759a 7), which after the motionless pupae stage (χρυσαλλίς; *chrysallís*) are transformed into adult insects (ζῷον ἐπιτελεσθέν/ *zôion epitelesthén*, e.g. Gen. an. 3,9,758b 26f.; metamorphosis).

The 'mating flight' of the queen bee (in Aristotle βασιλεύς/*basileús*, 'king'; he believed this animal to be male) with the drones (κηφῆναι; *kēphênai*), which die afterwards, was never observed by Aristotle. Hence, after considerable doubts (ἀπορία/*aporía*, Gen. an. 3,10,759a 8–b 31), he has worker bees who have both male (sting!) and female characteristics produce the drones by parthenogenesis. He also often suspects asexual genesis from other materials, e.g. Hist. an.

5,19,552a 15 from couch grass (ἀγρῶστις; *agróstis*) in the case of 'sheep lice' (κρότωνες; *krótōnes*).

Pliny (HN 11,1ff.) borrows the term *insecta* from Aristotle (Hist. an. 4,1, s.o.) along with many other details. Yet he explicitly contradicts the supposed lack of respiration and the lack of a voice (HN 11,5–7). However, there was much that Pliny also did not understand. For example, Virgil (Georg. 4,284f.) claims that bees are generated from putrid cattle blood. Pliny makes reference to this (HN 11,70) and expands this peculiar theory, which is based on insufficient observation, to include wasps (*vespae*) arising from horse flesh (Servius Georg. 4,286: from donkeys) and hornets (*crabrones*) and drones from the flesh of mules (*muli*; cf. also Nic. Ther. 740f.; Archelaus in Varro, Rust. 3,16,4; cf. ibid. 2,5,5; Ov. Fast. 1,377f.; Met. 15,364–366; Ael. NA 1,28 and 2,57) as well as that of other animals (Isid. Orig. 11,4,3 and 12,8,2). In the Middle Ages asexual generation was considered characteristic of the insects now renamed *vermes* ('worms'; no later than Isid. Orig. 12,5,1–19), and usually fought as annoying parasites.
→ Bedbug;   → Cicada;   → Cricket;   → Cockroach;
→ Lepidoptera; → Louse; → Mosquito

1 KELLER 2,395–460.   C.HÜ.

Insteius Name of a Roman *gens*, more frequently attested from the late Republic, though rooted in the early period of Rome as indicated by a street name, the *vicus Instei(an)us* on the southern peak of the Quirinal, the *collis Latiaris* (Varro, Ling. 5,52; Liv. 24,10,8).
I. REPUBLIC II. IMPERIAL PERIOD

I. REPUBLIC
[I 1] I., L. Served in the → Social War [3] in 89 BC under Cn. Pompeius Strabo outside Asculum (ILLRP 515); probably identical with the legate who fought on → Sertorius' side in Spain in 76 (Liv. 91, fr. 22: here also a C.I. as *praefectus equitum*, a brother of L.I.?). MRR 3,104.
[I 2] I., M. People's tribune in 42 BC (MRR 2,359). During the War of → Mutina (43) on the side of M. Antonius [I 9], scorned by Cicero (Phil. 13,26). At Actium (31), I. operated at the centre of Anthony's fleet (Plut. Antonius 65,1; MRR 3,104: as *praefectus classis*?).
[I 3] I. Cato A leader of the Italians in the → Social War [3] (from 90 BC onwards); only attested in Velleius (2,16,1) and probably mistaken for P. → Vettius [I 6] Scato (cf. App. B Civ. 1,181).   T.FR.

II. IMPERIAL PERIOD
[II 1] M.I. Bithynicus Senator from Volcei in Lower Italy [1]; *cos. suff.* AD 162. He may be identical with the *frater Arvalis* in 186–187 [2].

1 G. CAMODECA, in: EOS 2, 154f.   2 SCHEID, Collège, 102   3 PIR² I 30.

[II 2] I. Capito Centurion in the Syrian army who was put in charge of taking over Parthian hostages by Ummidius Quadratus; under → Domitius [II 11] Corbulo he was *praefectus castrorum*. PIR² I 31.
[II 3] Q.I. Celer Cos. *suff.* in the Hadrianic period, perhaps in AD 128 (AE 1973, 36). CIL XIV 2924 and Dig. 26,5,12,1 probably refer to him; later he became a consular governor; if he is also the one named in RMD II 90, he was legate of Germania superior in AD 130.

ECK, Statthalter, 54.   W.E.

Institor *Institor* is the term for the person appointed by a business owner to conduct a commercial or business transaction that is part of an ongoing business activity (comparable to a senior employee or manager) (cf. Ulp. Dig. 14,3,3). Persons of either gender, both those subject to authority (slaves and free persons) as well as those not subject to authority could be appointed as *institores* (cf. Dig. 14,3,7). The business owner was liable for obligations towards third parties into which the *institor* had entered while conducting business ('entrepreneur'). This was based on the 'dependent' *actio institoria*, which the contract partner of the *institor* could initiate against the business owner (cf. Dig. 14,3; Cod. Iust. 4,25; Gai. Inst. 4,71). An *actio ad exemplum institoriae actionis* that expands institorial liability to transactions of the → *procurator*, which were formerly not included among the *institor's* activities, originated with Papinianus (Dig. 14,3,19 pr.). General direct deputization of free persons was unknown to Roman law.
→ Actio (*adiecticiae qualitatis*)

J. AUBERT, Business Managers in Ancient Rome. A Social and Economic Study of Institores, 200 BC-AD 250, 1994; N. BENKE, Zu Papinians actio ad exemplum institoriae actionis, in: ZRG 105, 1988, 592–633; HONSELL/MAYER-MALY/SELB, 380f.; KASER, RPR I, 606 ff; vol. 2, ²1975, 103ff.; A. WACKE, Die adjektizischen Klagen im Überblick, in: ZRG 111, 1994, 280–362.   V.T.H.

Institutiones The Roman jurists were probably the first who derived *institutiones* as a title for elementary textbooks from the term *institutio* (teaching course) in the 2nd cent. The significance of this Roman genre for European legal history extends far beyond what one might expect of ancient introductory didactic works: when the work of codifying Roman juristic law in the form of the → *Digesta* had advanced to a point that their success seemed certain, in AD 533 emperor Justinian commissioned his minister of justice → Tribonianus as well as the Byzantine law teachers → Theopilus [7] and → Dorotheus [10] to compile a students' manual with legislative validity on the law of the *Digesta*. Thus the *Institutiones* gained a unique authority, which has remained unchallenged in the teaching of law at western European universities since the 12th cent. The *institutio* thus developed from a term for a literary legislative form to a synonym for the fundamental institutions of (Roman) law per se.

Justinian states explicitly (Const. *Imperatoriam* § 6) that these *Institutiones* in significant sections are based on the homonymous work by → Gaius [2] from the mid-2nd cent. AD. While the works of the jurists that provided material for the *Digesta* are almost all lost, the *Institutiones* of Gaius are the only work of a classical jurist that is almost preserved in its entirety. Since their rediscovery in 1816 in the cathedral library of Verona the *Institutiones* by Gaius have become almost as important for the reconstruction of classical Roman law and its development in the context of the Republican process as Justinian's *Institutiones* for academic legal teaching and the 'system' of common law since the High Middle Ages.

The system of Gaius' *Institutiones* and, therefore, also Justinian's is still the foundation of modern civil law systems. It differentiates *personae* (personal and family law), *res* (material law and law of succession, in part also law of obligations) and *actiones* (procedural law and again parts of the law of obligations). Systematization was carried into the details. An example is the subdivision into consensual, real, formal and literal contracts (→ *contractus*). With this comprehensive systematic approach, the surviving *Institutiones* of legal literature, probably as much as their largely lost parallels by other authors (e.g. → Florentinus [3], → Pomponius [III 3], → Ulpianus), stand in the tradition of the Hellenistic textbooks (→ Isagoge).

O. BEHREND, R. KNÜTEL, B. KUPISCH, H. H. SEILER, Corpus Iuris Civilis, Text und Übersetzung I: Institutionen, ²1997 (with annotations 273–298). G.S.

Instrumentum The term *instrumentum* (an object that has been 'erected' or 'set up') has widely differing meanings in Roman legal terminology: 1. in the Imperial period, especially in late antiquity, *instrumentum* was the document recorded by a document writer (→ *Tabellio*) concerning a civil legal transaction or (as *instrumentum publicum*) by an authority regarding a private or public matter. The *instrumentum publicum* and the *instrumentum* of the document writer, which was attested as authentic by three witnesses and also by the *tabellio* in writing, had full status as proof in court in late antiquity unless proven to be a forgery. A particularly important application of the private *instrumenta* was the promise of a dowry (→ *Dos*). The *instrumenta dotalium* replaced the former conventional → *dictio dotis* and its abstract-binding declaration in the form of the → *stipulatio* in late antiquity. Its establishment also strongly indicated an awareness of marriage (*affectio maritalis*; → Marriage III).

2. Usually in the compound *instrumentum fundi*, this term designates accessories, especially as pertaining to an agricultural property. There, it comprises all agricultural implements and storage facilities (Cato Agr. 1,5; Columella 1,8; 15,3). Most jurists understood the *instrumentum* in a more broadly sense, e.g., inclusive of all the working slaves belonging to the business (→ Household equipment). The term had practical significance in the interpretation of legal transactions in which sales, wills and leases included accessories (*cum instrumento*). An entire title in the Digesta is devoted to this issue in the context of wills as the apparently most important field of application (Dig. 33,7). In the early 3rd cent. AD Ulpian still mentioned a proposed decision of Q. → Mucius Scaevola in the 1st cent. BC that differentiated between a slave who was temporarily allotted to an estate (in that case not an *instrumentum*) or was specifically kept there on a permanent basis (in that case an *instrumentum*; Dig. 28,5,35,3). But even without mention of the *instrumentum*, an interpretation could indicate that depending on their typical use the accessories were included in a legal transaction. In this sense, decisions were made e.g. in leases, but not in wills.

KASER, RPR II, 677ff. A. STEINWENTER, Fundus cum instrumento, 1942. G.S.

Insubres Powerful Celtic people (Pol. 2,17,4; Str. 5,1,6; according to Liv. 5,34,9 the district of the Haedui), of a simple lifestyle (Pol. loc. cit.), in Upper Italy to the east of the Salassi (Ptol. 3,1,34) and Libici (Ptol. 3,1,36) and west of the → Cenomanni [3] (Ptol. 3,1,33; Pol. 2,17,4; Str. 5,1,9) and the river Clusius (Κλούσιος, Pol. 2,32,4) with their main settlement at Mediolan(i)um (Liv. 5,34,9; Plin. HN 3,124; Str. 5,1,6). Other towns of the Insubres (Ptol. 3,1,33): Comum, Ticinum (Cic. Fam. 15,16,1), Novaria, Acerae (Pol. 2,24,4f.), Victumulae (Liv. 21,45,3). The Insubres fought against Rome in 225 BC (Pol. 2,22–35; at Telamon), and again in 223 (Pol. 2,32f.) and in 222 (Pol. 2,34; at → Clastidium). They joined Hannibal (Liv. 21,39,1) and remained allies of the Carthaginians until 203 (Liv. 30,18,1). In subsequent years they continued to form the core of the Celtic resistance against Rome but were defeated in 197 (Liv. 33,23,4), 196 (33,37,10) and in 194 (34,46,1; Cic. Balb. 32; triumphs: CIL 1², p. 47f.). The jurist T. Catius (Cic. Fam. 15,16,1) and the comedian Statius Caecilius (Jer. Chron. 1838) were Insubres; according to Tac. Ann. 11,23,3 the Insubres also provided senators. → Gallia Cisalpina

C. PEYRE, La Cisalpine gauloise du IIIᵉ au Iᵉʳ siècle avant J.-C., 1979. Y.L. and G.RA.

Insula Modern technical term in urban studies derived from Latin *insula* ('island', 'residence') that in → town planning describes an area surrounded on all sides by streets and marked for development because of this structure. *Insulae* are not exclusively the products of comprehensive town planning. Within an orthogonal street grid they are usually rectangular or trapezoid, and rarely square, but the cut-out section of the irregular street system of a 'grown' town is also called an insula (e.g. in Delos or parts of Pompeii).

In Greek town planning the insula as the result of an orthogonal or pseudo-orthogonal division of the settlement area into strips is first to be found in the context of the early colonial towns of the West. The town facilities of Megara Hyblaea in Sicily are considered to be the earliest example; already in the 8th cent. BC a grid of streets that partly ran parallel, and partly crossed each other covered large parts of the area within the walled town. Presumably, this practise served to distribute land in equal shares to the colonists and corresponded with similar grids of the chora outside the town, which nowadays can only rarely be reconstructed (cf. especially → Metapont).

In the context of the first comprehensive conceptions of Greek town planning, usually associated with the town built by → Hippodamus of Miletus in → Piraeus near Athens, the insula was the nucleus of a concept of land development. As is still evident in Priene, it formed a module within the superordinate planning grid that covered the entire town area with proportionally balanced areas through addition or division that also defined the public and religious spheres of the town. While the insula was created in the Greek colonial towns during the archaic and early classical period for the purpose of a just division of the land, the hypotheses by [5] regarding the standard size of the insula in urban planning of the 5th and 4th cents., regarding the uniform house types built on them and the related idea of an equation of democracy, isonomia and equality of property have not passed uncontradicted from an archaeological and historical perspective. Probably, however, the insula system consisting of several houses resulted in the residential building being oriented towards a sun-lit court such as a pastas, peristyle or atrium (→ House).

The insula of the Roman town fits into the concept of appropriating and dividing land (centuriatio; → Limitation) that was originally handled as a sacred, later rather as a pragmatic act of power; the municipal structure, which is divided into insulae, has its point of origin at the crossing of the → cardo and the → decumanus in the centre of the town and, therefore, corresponds with the superordinate concept of land development of the traditional military camp on the one hand and to Greek urban planning of the 5th and 4th cents. BC, at least in its essentials, on the other hand. Parts of this concept were borrowed from the Etruscan rites connected with town foundation and the structuring of settlements. Already in Etruria we find an orthogonal plan with insulae that, as the product of a ritual act of foundation, is aligned with Decumanus and Cardo (e.g. in Marzabotto, 6th. cent. BC). The insulae were densely built up, sometimes in centres of conurbation such as Rome or Ostia with multi-storey tenements; in country towns such as Pompeii the often spacious town houses had a maximum of two storeys, with stores towards the street but otherwise separated from the outside world by high, windowless walls.

In numerous Latin literary sources insula also refers to a single block of tenements, as opposed to the *domus*, the stately home; these houses were mostly rented out to the poor (*insularii*) and were usually administered by a slave (*servus insularius*).

1 D. ASHERI, Distribuzioni di terre nell'antica Grecia, 1966   2 T. BOYD, M. JAMESON, Urban and Rural Land Division in Ancient Greece, in: Hesperia 50, 1981, 327–342   3 K.-V. v. EICKSTEDT, Beitr. zur Top. des ant. Piräus, 1991   4 B. FEHR, Kosmos und Chreia. Der Sieg der reinen über die praktische Vernunft in der griech. Stadtarchitektur des 4. Jh. v.Chr., in: Hephaistos 2, 1980, 155–185   5 W. HOEPFNER, E. L. SCHWANDNER, Haus und Stadt im klass. Griechenland, ²1994   6 F. LANG, Archa. Siedlungen in Griechenland, 1996, 58–63   7 TH. LORENZ, Röm. Städte, 1987   8 D. MERTENS, E. GRECO, Urban Planning in Magna Grecia, in: G. PUGLIESE CARATELLI (ed.), The Western Greeks, 1996, 243–262   9 F. PRAYON, Die Etrusker, 1996, 85–89   10 CH. SCHUBERT, Land und Raum in der röm. Republik. Die Kunst des Teilens, 1996.   C.HÖ.

Insula Columbaria Island in the *mare Tyrrhenum* near Ilva (Plin. HN 3,81). G.U.

Insulae Aegates An archipelago between Lilybaeum and Carthage (modern Favignana and Levanza). In 250 BC the Carthaginian fleet anchored here when called to aid by Lilybaeum (Pol. 1,44,2). In 241 BC the naval battle between C. Lutatius Catulus and Hanno (Pol. 1,60,4ff.), which decided the First Punic War, took place within sight of Favignana [1. 248f.].

1 HUSS.

R. J. A. WILSON, Sicily under the Roman Empire, 1990, 228, 393 no. 179; G. PURPURA, in: SicA 15/48, 1982, 56f.; 18/57–58, 1985, 59–86; A. M. FALLICO, Sicilia: XII. Favignana e Marettimo (Isole Egadi), in: NSA 23, 1969, 321. GI.MA.

Insulae fortunatae see → Makaron Nesoi

Insulae Gorgades Unlocated archipelago mentioned by Pliny (HN 6,200; Mela 3,99: *Dorcades*), who refers to → Xenophon [8] of Lampsacus (location of the island two days' journey from the African west coast; name derived from the Gorgons who once lived there) and → Hanno [1] (characterization of the inhabitants as savages; their women are said to have hairy skin). In Hanno's report, which is available in a much altered form (Peripl. 18, GGM 1,1–14), the women of the Insulae Gorgades are called *Goríllai* (Γορίλλαι, possibly a misspelling of the Greek translation for *Gorgades*).

S. GSELL, Histoire ancienne de l'Afrique du Nord 1, ³1921, 499ff.; K. BAYER, in: G. WINKLER, R. KÖNIG (ed.), C. Plinius Secundus, Naturalis historiae libri XXXVII, vol. 5, 1993, 360–363 (bibliography). E.O.

Intaglio see → Gem cutting

Intaphernes (Old Persian *Vindafarna*, Elamite *Mindaparna*). Supporter of Darius I in the conspiracy against (Pseudo-)Bardiya [2] (→ Gaumata) [1. DB 3.84] in 522 BC. He crushed the second Babylonian rebellion [1. DB 83–91]. Herodotus (3,118–119) tells of an alleged uprising of I. for which his entire family was exterminated; only the brother of his wife was spared at her pleading (a parallel to Sophocles' *Antigone*).

1 R. G. Kent, Old Persian, 1953 2 M. Mayrhofer, Onomastica Persepolitana, 1973, 8.1078 3 H. Sancisi-Weerdenburg, 'Exit Atossa', in: A. Cameron, A. Kuhrt, Images of Women in Antiquity, 1983, 32ff.

A. KU. and H. S.-W.

Intarabus (Entarabus). Celtic deity only attested in inscriptions (CIL VIII, 3632, 4128), worshipped in the territory of the Treveri (Trier, Germany). The inscriptions speak of buildings dedicated to Intarabus (*porticus*, *aedes*, *fanum*, *simulacrum*), which indicates the deity's popularity. In CIL VIII, 3653 I. is given the epithet Mars.

RE.ZI.

Intarsia
I. Ancient Orient II. Classical archaeology

I. Ancient Orient
In Middle Eastern archaeology intarsia is the term for the laying of decorative elements of different materials onto or into a substratum. To achieve better colour contrasts, combinations of different materials, especially coloured stones, shells, bones, ivory, metals, ceramics, glass and silicate were used; the most common substrata were stone, metal, wood and clay/ceramics. The binder was usually bitumen. The oldest examples of intarsia were found in the preceramic Neolithic of Palestine (c. 8000 BC; e.g. gypsum-coated human skulls with shell inlays in the eye sockets from Jericho). From the late 4th millennium BC onwards intarsia are often found on stone vessels, in portable art (e.g. seals), on sculptures, as wall decoration, on luxury goods (so-called standard and game board of Ur), on Egyptian mummy masks. A special form of intarsia related to buildings are wall decorations in the form of cone mosaics (e.g. Uruk, late 4th millennium).

R.W.

II. Classical archaeology
In classical archaeology intarsia are pieces of inlaid work not only of wood but also of such diverse materials as poured glass, alabaster, amber, ivory, tortoise shell, gold leaf and coloured marble with wood, metal and stone plates as substrata. Intarsia are found in a wide variety of genres in the arts and crafts. Intarsia were most common on → furniture (especially on → clines), but board games, musical instruments and other implements could also serve as substrata. Not much has been preserved but there are literary descriptions and vase paintings. The inlays were sawed, cut or poured and then fixed on the substratum with a binder (bitumen, pitch, various resins); the whole was finally uniformly polished. Intarsia could be ornamental decoration (→ Ornaments), but could also consist of figurative scenes or even entire sequences of images.

Intarsia originated no later than the 3rd millennium BC in the Middle East and are found, though infrequently, in the Minoan culture of Crete; from post-Mycenaean Greece to the classical period they were part of imported luxury art from the 'East' with an ambivalently assessed colourful ornamental wealth of images. Intarsia from Greek workshops became frequent only after the 4th cent. BC; in the Hellenistic period and the Imperium Romanum they became common property in a diversity of forms among the wealthy elite. Inlaid work in many forms and techniques was particularly wide-spread on early Christian portable art, such as devotionalia and liturgical instruments.

→ Mosaics in their various technical executions must essentially be classified as intarsia, especially those using the *opus sectile* technique (cf. also → Pavimentum). On intarsia in architectural contexts (wall covering): → Incrustation.

H. S. Baker, Furniture in the Ancient World, 1966; E. Bielefeld, Eine Patene aus dem frz. Krönungsschatz. Ein Versuch zur Kleinkunst des 4. Jh. n. Chr., in: Gymnasium 79, 1972, 395–445; F. Guidobaldi, L'intarsio marmoreo nella decorazione pavimentale e parietale di età romana, in: E. Dolci, Il marmo nella civiltà romana, 1990, 55–67; H. Kyrieleis, Throne und Klinen (24. Ergh. JDAI), 1969; H. Mielsch, Buntmarmore aus Rom im Antikenmus. Berlin, 1985; H. W. Müller, Koptische Glasintarsien mit figürlichen Darstellungen aus Antinoe, Mittelägypten, in: Pantheon 20, 1962, 13–18; G. M. A. Richter, The Furniture of the Greeks, Etruscans and Romans, 1966, 122–126; R. L. Scranton, Glass Pictures from the Sea, in: Archaeology 20, 1967, 163–173.

C.HÖ.

Intellect In Homer the intellect is embodied in Athena at the divine level and in Odysseus at the human level – this doubling is also later preserved in the concept of the *nous* (νοῦς/*noûs*: spirit, reason) as (a) divine substance and (b) human cognition. In pre-Socratic philosophy it is the force guiding the world in → Xenophanes [1] (21 B 23–25 DK) and especially in → Anaxagoras [2], for whom the divine *nous* recognizes, orders and rules everything (59 B 12 DK). Anaxagoras also emphasizes the special status of humans who live the intellectual life (59 A 29–30 DK). Plato continues the speculation about *nous*: he develops the → theory of ideas based on his dissatisfaction with the Anaxagorean form (Pl. Phd. 97b ff.). The world of ideas itself has the nature of intellect because it has *nous* (Pl. Soph. 248e f.). The → Demiourgos [3] who shapes the visible world is often considered a divine intellect [3]. He constructs the world as a living being gifted with intellect (ζῷον ἔννουν/*zôion énnoun*, Pl. Ti. 30b). The divinity of the inner-cosmic gods is based on their mode of being as intellect (Pl. Phdr. 249c). The gods partake in the *nous* as does that rare type of human (Pl. Ti. 51e) who is 'beloved of the gods' (θεοφιλής; *theophilés*) due to his alignment with the world of ideas (Pl. Symp. 212a), i.e. the philosopher who is capable of the cognition of ideas. The idea of what is good ranks above that of the intellect (ibid. 508e 3–509a 7, here *epistémē* ('science') means the same as *nous* 508c 1; 511d 4). That god 'is either intellect or something beyond intellect' (ἢ νοῦς ἐστὶν ἢ ἐπέκεινά τι τοῦ νοῦ; *è noûs estìn è epékeina ti toû noû*) was considered by Aristotle in *On Prayer* fr. 1 Rose. Otherwise, Aristotle considers the intellect that thinks itself as the highest principle on which the world depends (Metaph. 12,7,1072a 19–19,1075a 10). At the same time, the *nous* is the (externally entering: Aristot. Gen. an. 736b 28) divine in humans that makes an exhilarating theoretical lifestyle and immortality possible (ἀθανατίζειν/ *athanatízein*; Eth. Nic. 10,1177b 26–1178a 2).

Stoics demanded that humans be completely ruled by the intellect; here, too, the agreement between the human use of reason and divine reasonableness of the world is the guiding idea. Human reason is 'divine' (SVF I 40,5; II 307,24), the (firy) reason of the cosmos is god (ibid. I 42,7); 'God, *nous* and *heimarménē* are one' (I 28,22). Aristotelianism, especially through the interpretation of the *nous politikós* (cf. Aristot. An. 3,5,430a 10–25) by Alexander of Aphrodisias (An. 81,24ff.; 888,22ff.; 106,19ff.) had a lasting effect on all later and especially medieval discussions. Middle and Neo-Platonism, following Plato's *Timaeus*, emphasized the function of the intellect as the cause of the world and continued the speculation initiated by Plato (Charm. 166a ff.) and Aristotle (Metaph. 12,9) on the reflectiveness of the *nous* (on Numenius s. [5]). Plotinus repeatedly explained the *nous* as the second → *hypóstasis* of his system, especially with respect to its origin from the source ('overflow' of the One and 'return') and its structure (duality of the one who thinks and that which is thought and their unity in the course of thinking, 'all together' (ὁμοῦ πάντα; *homoû pánta*), as persistent mutual interpenetration and connection of all contents with everything (Plot. Enneades 5 and 6 passim). → Proclus' [2] philosophy of the intellect attempts to demonstrate the triadic structure of the *nous* (staying – going out – return: μονή - πρόοδος - ἐπιστροφή/*moné* – *próhodos* – *epistrophé*) as the comprehensive structural principle of the intelligible (and indirectly the sensible) world. Among Latin Christian authors, Marius Victorinus understood god in Neo-Platonic fashion as surpassing the intellect (Adversus Arium 3,7,15–17), while Augustine in *De trinitate* (B. 10, 14,15) attempted to demonstrate that human intellect (*mens humana*) as a reflection of the divine intellect had a 'trinitarian' structure.

1 W. Jaeger, Die Theologie der frühen griech. Denker, 1953   2 H. J. Krämer, Der Ursprung der Geistmetaphysik, ²1967   3 G. Reale, Zu einer neuen Interpretation Platons, 1993   4 K. Oehler, Subjektivität und Selbstbewußtsein in der Ant., 1997   5 J. Halfwassen, Geist und Selbstbewußtsein. Studien zu Plotin und Numenios (AAWM), 1994   6 Th. A. Szlezák, Platon und Aristoteles in der Nuslehre Plotins, 1979   7 W. Beierwaltes, Proklos. Grundzüge seiner Metaphysik, ²1979

8 P. Moraux, Alexandre d'Aphrodise, exégète de la noétique d'Aristote, 1942.   T.A.S.

Intentio The petition that determined the object of the dispute (which might have to be proven; Gai. Inst. 4,41) in the formula characteristic of the Roman formulary procedure (→ *formula*). In the case of a declaratory action, this formula is limited to the *intentio* (Gai. Inst. 4,44), while suits for obligations were differentiated depending on whether the object was a *certum* (i.e. a particular sum, object or quantity of goods) or an *incertum* (i.e. *quidquid dare facere oportet*, 'everything that someone is required to pay'). In the latter case, the *intentio* was used to give precision to the petition by supplementing it with a preceding reference to the facts of the case (→ *demonstratio*). This differentiation is also significant for the 'legal consequence' of the formula, the → *condemnatio* (sentence): in suits for an *incertum* the judge must determine the extent of payment demanded by *bona* → *fides*, while this was the plaintiff's task in suits for a *certum*. Lack of precision in the petition described by the *intentio* was penalized by the → *pluspetitio* (loss of the proceeding due to an excessive demand; Gai. Inst. 4,54). However, it should be noted that the *intentio* could essentially be interpreted in a manner (at least in the opinion of Iulianus and Paulus) that would let the suit proceed (Dig. 34,5,12; 50,17,172,1). However, the two variants of the obligation suit had in common that the petition expressed in the *intentio* corresponded with the obligation requirement of the *condemnatio* if the plaintiff won – in that case he became the creditor of this obligation. There are a few exceptions to this that amount to an antiquated form of the derivative action: in the *actio Rutiliana* the *bonorum emptor* (person acquiring goods) was not named in the *intentio* but instead the beneficiary of the *condemnatio* (Gai. Inst. 4,35).

M. Kaser, K. Hackl, Das röm. Zivilprozeßrecht, ²1997, 311–314; W. Selb, Formeln mit unbestimmter I. Iuris, vol. I, 1974.   C.PA.

Interamna

[1] (*Interamna Nahars*, CIL XI 4213; ethnic designation *Interamnates Nartes*, CIL VI 140). Town in Umbria, modern Terni. The place name refers to its location on the confluence of the Nera (Umbrian *Nahar* [1], Latin *Nar*) and the Serra (which had a different course in antiquity). Settlement phases of the 10th– 7th cents. are attested in Pentima and in San Pietro in Campo. A 7th cent. settlement in the town's Clai district appears to confirm the tradition that Interamna was founded in 672 BC (cf. CIL XI 4170: 704 years since the foundation = AD 32). *Municipium, tribus Clustumina*. Disputes with → Reate, which suffered damage from flooding by the Nar in 54 BC (Cic. Att. 4,15,5) and AD 15 (Tac. Ann. 1,79), are known. Archaeology: remains of Roman walls beneath the public park; remains of the *cardo*, the *decumanus maximus*

and the theatre; near the walls in the south-west an am-phitheatre of the Tiberian period; *villa* under the church San Salvatore; 6th cent. sanctuary at Monte Torre Maggiore. Inscriptions: CIL XI 4170–4344.

1 G. DEVOTO, Il nome Naharko, in: SE 33, 1965, 369–377.

E. ROSSI-PASSAVANTI, I. Nahars, 1932; P. RINALDI, Materiali per il museo archeologico di Terni, 1985; L. BONOMI PONZI, Terni, in: EAA² 5, 1997, 674–677.

[2] Interamna Lirenas, Interamna Sucasina A town near Casinum on a small elevation on the left bank of the Liris at modern Termini near Pignataro Interamna; inhabited by Aurunci, Volsci and Samnites from the 7th cent. BC onwards. From 312 BC a Latin colony (Liv. 9,28,8; Diod. Sic. 19,105,5; Vell. Pat. 1,14,4), received the epithet *Lirenas* (CIL X 4960) but also *Sucasina* (Plin. HN 3,64), *regio I*. It refused to provide support against Hannibal and was punished by Rome as a result (Liv. 27,9,8). From 90 *municipium*, *tribus Teretina* (Cic. Phil. 2,105; CIL X 4860). Inscription: CIL X 5331–5365.

M. CAGIANO DE AZEVEDO, I. Lirenas vel Sucasina, 1947; G. LENA, I.L., in: Quaderni del Museo Civico di Pontecorvo 2, 1982, 57–75; E. M. BERANGER, I.L., in: EAA² 3, 1995, 115f.   G.U.

[3] Interamna Praetuttiorum Town of the Praetuttii (Ptol. 5,1,58) at the confluence of the Tordino and the Vezzola, modern Teramo (the name *Interamnia* is inappropriate). The *conciliabulum civium Romanorum* was founded in 268 BC, when the Praetutii were granted the *civitas optimo iure* (*VIII viri*, ILS 5666 from the early Augustan age); the *Interamnates* or *Interamnites Praetuttiani* were enrolled in the *tribus Velina*. After the Social War, Interamna became a *municipium*, then a Sullan *colonia* with *praetores* and *II viri*; the coexistence of the *municipes* and *coloni* is attested by inscriptions up to the 2nd cent. AD.

A. MIGLIORATI, Municipes et coloni, in: Archeologia classica 28, 1976, 242–246; J. B. DE SMET, Interamnia Praetuttiorum (Teramo) et le problème des communautés à statut juridique double, in: Acta archaeologica Lovaniensia 38/9, 1989/1990, 63–74; P. SOMMELLA, Teramo, in: EAA² Suppl. 5, 1997, 665f.; M. BUONOCORE, Un' inedita testimonianza di munificentia femminile a Teramo, in: Athenaeum 86, 1998, 463–467.   M.BU.

Interamnium Road station in the Sybaris valley in Lucania (Tab. Peut. 7,1; Geogr. Rav. 4,34).

NISSEN 2, 918.   E.O.

Interaspiration see → Punctuation

Interaxial space see → Spacing, interaxial

Intercalation see → Calendar

Intercessio

I. CONSTITUTIONAL LAW II. CIVIL LAW

I. CONSTITUTIONAL LAW

In Roman Republican constitutional law, the *intercessio* (from *intercedere* = to step in-between) denoted a veto against magisterial decrees (→ *Decretum*), against Senate resolutions (→ *Senatus consultum*) and against → rogations of all types presented to the various people's assemblies. It rendered decrees ineffective unless an *intercessio* was unlawful, as for example in the case of magisterial court decrees during an ongoing legal proceeding. Senate resolutions were reduced to mere recommendations (→ *auctoritas*) and rogations became void if the people had not yet decided on them. This right to veto was held a) by every officeholder with respect to a colleague of equal rank, b) by every officeholder with respect to officeholders of lower rank, c) by every officeholder with respect to Senate resolutions unless they had been co-authored by higher ranking Senate members, d) every people's tribune with respect to all officeholders (except dictators), to all Senate resolutions and all rogations presented to the people's assembly. The *intercessio* may be assumed to have arisen at the end of the monarchy as a result of a separation of powers among colleagues. However, in the class struggles of the 5th cent., it also became an important tool of the people's tribunes for protecting the *plebs* against excesses of the magistrates. In general it was a means of controlling the government and the administration in the interest of those harmed by them because on their request it could be used by all magistrates in this manner. The Latin municipalities also had an *intercessio*, although they did not have tribunes.

MOMMSEN, Staatsrecht, 266–292.   C.G.

II. CIVIL LAW

In civil law the *intercessio* was an 'intervention' by assuming a debt in the interest of a third party, e.g., through surety, coliability, assuming the third party debt through → *novatio*, taking out a loan for another person and providing collateral security (→ *pignus*) for a third party debt.

Under Augustus and with the edicts of Claudius, an *intercessio* of wives for their husbands was supposedly forbidden (Ulp. Dig. 16,1,2 pr.). With the SC *Velleianum* (which was passed between AD 41 and 65), women were generally barred from the *intercessio* (Paul. Dig. 16,1,1; Ulp. Dig. 16,1,2,1). A woman sued because of an *intercessio* was able to object (→ *exceptio*, SC *Velleiani*). There is a rich casuistry regarding the extent of the prohibition of the *intercessio* (cf. Dig. 16,1; Cod. Iust. 4,29).

→ Surety

HONSELL/MAYER-MALY/SELB, 292–294; D. MEDICUS, Zur Gesch. des Senatus consultum Velleianum, 1957; J. BEAUCAMP, Le statut de la femme à Byzance I, 1990, 54–78; R. ZIMMERMANN, The Law of Obligations, 1990, 145–152.   F.ME.

Intercisa

[1] Military camp, toll station and civilian settlement near the limes of Pannonia inferior on the Aquincum – – Altinum – Mursa road (It. Ant. 245,3; Not. Dign. Occ. 33,25f.; 38), modern Dunaújváros, district of Fejér in Hungary. This fortification, which was originally made of wood and earth, was probably built by the *ala I Augusta Ituraeorum sagittariorum* in the late Flavian period. A military base of the *ala I Flavia Augusta Britannica* (AD 105-106), the *ala I Tungrorum Frontoniana* (until 118/9) and the *ala I Thracum veteranorum sagittariorum*. The *cohors milliaria Hemesenorum* was stationed in the later stone camp (176 × 205 m) after the Marcommani Wars. At that time there was significant construction activity inside and outside the camp. The *cuneus equitum Dalmatarum, cuneus equitum Constantianorum* and *equites sagittarii* are attested there from the late 3rd cent. In the camp and in the environs of the settlement, building remains, watchtowers, *villae*, milestones, graves, numerous inscriptions and two coin hoards have been found. Intercisa was still inhabited in the 5th cent.

> L. BARKÓCSI (ed.), Intercisa, 2 vols., 1954/1957; TIR L 34 Budapest, 1968, 66ff. (with sources and bibliography); J. FITZ (ed.), Der röm. Limes in Ungarn, 1976, 101ff.
> J.BU.

[2] Road station on the *via Flaminia* between Forum Sempronii and Pitinum Mergens near Gola del Furlo, named after a 37 m tunnel that Vespasian had built in AD 77 (CIL XI 6106; Claud. Carm. 281; 502; hence also the place name Petra Pertusa or Pertunsa Petra, Aur. Vict. Caes. 9,10, and Furlo). In the Gothic War a Byzantine military base (on the year 538 cf. Procop. Goth. 2,11,2; 10-13; on 552 cf. 4,28,13).

> NISSEN 2, 383; T. ASHBY, R. A. L. FELL, The via Flaminia, in: JRS 11, 1921, 125-190.
> G.U.

Intercisi dies see → Fasti

Intercolumnium see → Spacing, interaxial; → Column

Interdictum A command of the → praetor or provincial governor based on his → *imperium* (e.g. Iulianus, Dig. 43,8,7) for the purpose of quickly ending disputes, especially over → *possessio* (possession) and *quasi possessio* (Gai. Inst. 4,139). It always touched upon public interests. First signs of *interdicta* are found in Plautus (Stich. 696; 748-750; Asin. 504-509), Terence (Eun. 319f.) and the *lex Agraria* of 111 BC (l. 18); Cic. De or. 1,10,41 alludes to it.

Interdicta are partly orders, e.g. *exhibeas* (upon presentation) or *restituas* (upon restitution), hence *interdicta exhibitoria, restitutoria* (also *decreta*), and in part prohibitions (*interdicta prohibitoria*, also simply *interdicta*), e.g. *vim fieri veto* (prohibitions of force). Force could not be exercised against a 'rightful' owner but it could be exercised against a 'wrongful' owner (*interdictum uti possidetis* for real estate, *interdictum utrubi* for movables, respectively with the option of a defence of wrongful possession). Further examples: prohibiting a landlord from preventing a tenant about to move from removing unencumbered objects (*interdictum de migrando*); prohibition *ne quid in loco sacro fiat* (disturbance of a consecrated site, all this in Gai. Inst. 4,139f.).

Interdicta aim at (first-time) acquisition, preservation and recovery of property (*interdictum adipiscendae, retinendae, reciperandae possessionis causa conparata*; Gai. Inst. 4,143). For example, the *interdictum quorum bonorum* of the *bonorum possessor* ('praetorian possessor', Gai. Inst. 4,144) was used for acquisition, also the *interdictum Salvianum* of the land lessor for the lessee's surety for the rent (Gai. Inst. 4,147). The *interdicum uti possidetis* and *utrubi* served to maintain a possessory position. They also prepared the dispute over ownership by assigning roles to the parties (Gai. Inst. 4,148-153). The *interdictum unde vi* ('due to force', was used for the reacquisition of possession; with *duo genera causarum*, two types of causes, already recognized by the 'forefathers', *maiores*, Cic. pro Caec. 30,86) as well as the *interdictum de vi armata* (on armed force), the latter being without the defence of wrongful possession. *Interdicta* were either directed at one party or at both (*interdicta simplicia, duplicia*): the *interdicta exhibitoria* and *restitutoria* only against one party; the *interdicta prohibitoria* could be directed against one or both, the *interdictum de migrando* against one, also, the *interdictum ne quid in loco sacro fiat*, but the *interdictum uti possidetis* and *interdictum utrubi* were directed against both parties (Gai. Inst. 4,157-160).

The wording of the *interdictum* contained its preconditions, which the magistrate only cursorily checked. Whether they really are present and there has been or is action contrary to the *interdictum* is at that point still uncertain. Possibly, the proceeding will be continued based on formulas by the praetor before the judge (→ *iudex*, → *recuperatores*). It may end with a penalty (*poena*) for the violator (thus, always in the proceeding with penal provisions, *per sponsionem*, according to the *interdicta prohibitoria*, Gai. Inst. 4,141) or with acquittal or sentencing (thus in the proceeding with procedural formula for payment in kind, *formula arbitraria*, according to the *interdicta exhibitoria* and *restitutoria*, Gai. Inst. 4,162-164). The proceeding *per sponsionem* supplements compensation suits: the *iudicium Cascellianum sive secutorium* and the *iudicium de re restituenda vel exhibenda* (Gai. Inst. 4,165, 166a, 169). The *interdictum secundarium* is employed against a refusal to co-operate in the proceeding (Gai. Inst. 4,170).

In the late Republic protection against violent interference in possessions was strengthened. The *interdictum de vi armata* already protected the wrongful possessor (see above). In 76 BC, the praetor M. Lucullus introduced a criminal suit for cases of damage caused by an armed group or a mob (Cic. Tull. 3,7–5,11; 13,31). A *lex Iulia de vi armata* of Augustus threatened criminal penalties against private self-help (Mod. Dig. 48,7,8; Inst. Iust. 4,15,6); a decree of Marcus Aurelius even ordered that the perpetrator would lose existing claims (Callimachus Dig. 4,2,13 = 48,7,7).

From the post-classical period (from the mid–3rd cent.) the *interdicta* merged into the *actiones* (→ *actio*). The most important *interdictum unde vi* is obtained in a civil suit and called a 'preliminary proceeding' (*actio momentaria*) or such. Constantine abolished the defence of wrongful possession in 319 (Cod. Theod. 9,10,3). Under Constantine the criminalization of violent acts continued (Cod. Theod. 9,10,1 = Cod. Iust. 9,12,6; Cod. Theod. 9,10,2); thus, an owner using tactics of self-help lost his property to the *fiscus* (Cod. Theod. 9,10,3). Justinian retained this post-classical innovation and linked criminal prosecution with the interdict proceeding (Cod. Iust. 9,12,7; Inst. Iust. 4,15,6). The proceeding now becomes the *actio* of the general civil procedure (Inst. Iust. 4,15 pr.; 8).

> A. BERGER, s.v. I., RE 9, 1609–1707; HONSELL/MAYER-MALY/SELB, 551–553; KASER, RPR I 396–400, 472, 740; II 256–261; M. KASER, K. HACKL, Das röm. Zivilprozeßrecht, ²1997, 408–421, 637f.; O. LENEL, Das Edictum perpetuum, 1927 (repr. 1974), 446–500 (Tit. XLIII De interdictis); WIEACKER, RRG, 249–251.   D.SCH.

Interesse In Roman law, in cases of infringement of contract the *interesse*, compensation of damage, was often measured according to the interest of the claimant in its being properly complied with (*quod eius interest*). In evaluating this, Roman jurists resorted neither to stringent guidelines nor to a schematic comparison of assets (so-called differential method), but estimated the *interesse* according to the specific circumstances of the case. These included, for example, the value of the matter not accomplished, the loss in value of a defective object, the disadvantages caused by the default, the costs of any covering transaction, loss of profit or indirect damages. Evaluation of damages according to ch. 3 of the → *lex Aquilia* was also based on the *interesse*.
→ Damnum

> HONSELL/MAYER-MALY/SELB, 224–228; R. ZIMMERMANN, The Law of Obligations, 1990, 824–833, 961f.   R.GA.

Interest
I. ANCIENT ORIENT AND EGYPT II. CLASSICAL ANTIQUITY

I. ANCIENT ORIENT AND EGYPT
The early Mesopotamian documents (24th–21st cents. BC) that refer to → loans and advances from institutional bodies to private individuals allow us to surmise that interest was calculated, though without our being able to make any observations about the rates of interest. Instead of being made to pay interest, the debtor was often obliged to undertake agricultural

work for the creditor [10. 117]. In the Early Babylonian period (19th–17th cents. BC) a sharp distinction was drawn between loans of grain ($33\frac{1}{3}$%) and loans of silver (20%). This is evident from loan documents and legal books (Codex Ešnunna or Codex Hammurapi: TUAT 1, 34 f. §§ 18, 20 f. or 53, § 70) [8. 98–144]. Letters of Old Assyrian traders (20th cent. BC) talk of compound interest. Likewise, collections of mathematical problems (→ Mathematics) contain formulae for calculating compound interest. There is no Neo-Babylonian documentary evidence relating to loans of grain. The usual interest rate for loans of silver continued to be 20%. Admittedly, other rates of interest can occasionally be found in Neo-Babylonian loan documents: 5%, 10%, 12,5%, 13 $\frac{1}{3}$%, 16 $\frac{2}{3}$% on the one hand, and 25%, 30%, 40%, 60% on the other [6. 20, n. 43a; 11. 234 f.]. The documents do not indicate what special circumstances might have led to rates of interest departing from the 20% norm. A letter from → Ugarit justifies an interest-free loan because lender and borrower both belong to the same (high) social class [5. 19 RS 15.11, l. 23]. A similar approach is taken in the OT in stating that interest can be charged to a foreigner but not one's brother (i. e. another Israelite; Lev 25:36 f.; Dt 23:20). The much-debated issue as to whether interest rates of 20% or 33 $\frac{1}{3}$% are to be regarded as 'usury' can be resolved by referring to ethnographic data showing that interest rates even under neighbourly reciprocal circumstances can amount to 50% [7. 190 f., 195].

For Egypt only an extremely small number of textual documents relating to loans are available – mostly from the craftsmen's settlement of Dair al-Madīna. Its inhabitants conducted their commercial transactions with one another on the basis of → reciprocity. The question of whether, and to what extent, interest was paid, in the sense of adding to the amount of a loan – as is well attested in ethnological parallels [7. 191 f., 195] – remains unanswered. As far as we can discern from the documentation, no interest was charged, exceptions aside, in the New Kingdom.
→ Economy; → Loan

> 1 E. BLEIBERG, Loans, Credit and Interest in Ancient Egypt, in: M. HUDSON, M. VAN DE MIEROOP (ed.), Debt and Economic Renewal in the Ancient Near East, 2002, 257–276 2 Chicago Assyrian Dictionary, vol. H., 1956, s. v. hubullu A2. 3 Ibid., vol. Ṣ, 1962, 158–163 s. v. ṣibtu A 4 M. VAN DE MIEROOP, A History of Near Eastern Debt, in: s. [1], 59–94 5 J. NOUGAYROL, Mission de Ras Shamra, vol. 6, 1970 6 H. PETSCHOW, Neubabylon. Pfandrecht, 1956 7 J. RENGER, On Economic Structures in Ancient Mesopotamia, in: Orientalia 63, 1994, 157–208, esp. 194 f. 8 A. SKAIST, The Old Babylonian Loan Contract, 1994 9 P. STEINKELLER, The Renting of Fields in Early Mesopotamia and the Development of the Concept of 'Interest' in Sumerian, in: Journ. of the Economic and Social History of the Orient 24, 1981, 133–145 10 Id., Money Lending Practices in Ur III Babylonia, in: s. [1], 109–137 11 C. WUNSCH, Debt, Interest, Pledge and Forfeiture in the Neo-Babylonian and Early Achaemenid Period: The Evidence from Private Archives, in: s. [1], 221–255.   J. RE.

II. CLASSICAL ANTIQUITY
A. GREECE B. ROME C. LATE ANTIQUITY AND CHRISTIANITY

A. GREECE

The question of how many loans (→ Loan) were subject to interest (τόκος/*tókos*) and how many went interest-free is of importance for assessing cash transactions and the economical function of → money in classical Greece. For Athens, in particular, the frequency of interest-free loans has been stressed. Such loans conformed to the tradition of → reciprocity, were granted especially to relatives, friends and → neighbours, and helped cement social bonds. Most of the loans mentioned by Attic orators did not involve any charging of interest [9], although interest-bearing loans were still frequently attested. In various property transactions quite large cash payments were made using loans issued with interest (Lys. 32,15; Isaeus 11,42; Dem. Or. 27,9). Two categories of interest were distinguished, namely interest on → *fenus nauticum* and interest on standard land-based transactions (cf. Dem. Or. 33,3: οὔτε ναυτικοῦ οὔτ᾽ ἐγγείου; cf. → *nautikòn dáneion*). In the 4th cent. BC the general interest rate hovered around 15% for example, while the interest rate for *fenus nauticum* was substantially higher. Thus, in a *fenus nauticum* contract quoted by Demosthenes an interest rate of 22.5% had been settled on (Dem. Or. 35,10). It is still unclear whether professional bankers (→ Banks) paid interest on funds deposited with them; many bank deposits appear not to have borne interest; in some cases an interest rate of 10% was applied [5].

The Greeks calculated interest payments in *drachmai* (→ *drachmḗ* [1]) or *oboloi* (→ *obolós*) per *mina* (→ *mina*; 100 *drachmai*) per month. Accordingly, one *drachme* corresponded to an interest rate of 1% per month (cf. e.g. Isaeus 11,42: 9 *oboloi* = 1,5 %; Dem. Or. 27,9: 1 *drachmoi*; cf. → *dáneion*). The interest was regarded as income created by money itself; for this reason, Aristotle [6] rejected loans of money for interest as being contrary to Nature (παρὰ φύσιν/*parà phýsin*; Aristot. Pol. 1258b).

As in the Near East, temples and sanctuaries in the Greek world lent money for interest (→ Temple economy). In the 5th and 4th cents. BC, they charged interest at 6–10%, an interest rate lower than that charged by the → banks (12–18% per annum). Between the 5th and 2nd cents., BC the interest rate for loans between private individuals dropped to 8–12%, then to 6–10 %. In Ptolemaic Egypt, by contrast, the interest rate was 24% and dropped to 12% in Egypt only in the Roman period (cf. I. above).

B. ROME

Throughout Roman history interest rates (*faenus/ fenus*; *usura*) were repeatedly a political issue and subject of legislation. In his account of the debt crisis of AD 33 (Tac. Ann. 6,16), Tacitus [1] goes into the detail of regulations on interest in the Roman Republic: the Law

of Twelve Tables (→ *tabulae duodecim*) prohibited the charging of interest at a rate higher than the *faenus unciarium*; according to modern research [11], that probably involved a rate of 100 % (one twelfth per month). During the debt crisis between 350 and 340 BC a *faenus semiunciarium* was initially introduced, that is a rate of 50% per annum; finally, the *lex Genucia* in 342 BC banned the charging of interest altogether (Liv. 7,42,1). At the beginning of the 2nd cent. BC, however, lending money with interest became legal once again. From that time, drawing on the Greek model, the Romans calculated interest monthly, with the interest rate expressed as a percentage; an interest rate of 12% was described as *centesimae usurae* (that is, as interest of 1% per month).

In 51 BC the Senate limited the interest rate to 12% per annum (Cic. Att. 5,21,13). In the late Republic the high rates of interest on loans to the provinces and people living in the provinces developed into a problem. Charging of compound interest, in particular, could significantly increase the level of → debts. This was especially true of the province of Asia where the debt burden had more than doubled within a few years after 80 BC. Licinius [I 26] Lucullus lightened the financial burden of indebted cities by reducing interest payments (Plut. Lucullus 20,3). The people's tribune C. Cornelius [I 2] (67 BC), who sought to put an end to this deplorable state of affairs, voiced his concern that the provinces would be drained by usurious rates of interest (*exhauriri provincias usuris*, Ascon. 57 f. C; cf. → *publicani*). The situation is graphically illustrated by the case of M. Iunius [I 10] Brutus, who after 58 BC lent money to the city of Salamis on Cyprus at an interest rate of 48 % (Cic. Att. 5,21,10–12; 6,1,5–8; 6,2,7–9; 6,3,5).

It is unclear whether limiting the interest rate to 12% was endorsed by Augustus and whether there was an overall interest rate ceiling in the Principate. Loans (→ Loan) with interest were not forbidden in the Roman empire but the interest rate in some provinces such as Egypt was limited to 12% per annum. In Roman law, ἀνατοκισμός/*anatokismós* (compound interest) was forbidden (cf. → Anatokismos). Normally, interest rates could legally range from 4 to 12%; in the *Historia Augusta* an interest rate of 4% is termed *minimae usurae* (SHA Antoninus Pius 2,8). Other than in cases of usury, the interest rate of 12% was almost never exceeded.

Quite distinct regional differences in interest rates are discernible. For provinces, the interest rate could be fixed by edict (Ulp. Dig. 17,1,10,3; 26,7,7,10). Furthermore there were regional economic fluctuations: in the view of the Roman jurist Gaius [2], the interest rate depended on individual loan applications (Gai. Dig. 13,4,3). The interest rate could certainly also be entirely stable because of local traditions and it was then less dependent on economic fluctuations (Scaevola Dig. 33,1,21 pr.).

For the Late Republic and the Civil War period, serious fluctuations of interest rates in Italy are attested that have their origin, however, less in economic causes than in political and military developments: thus, the interest rate dropped from 12 to 4% when after the battle of Actium [1], the royal treasury of Egypt was brought to Rome and a large amount of money was put into circulation (Cass. Dio 51, 21,5; Suet. Aug. 41,1). By contrast, interest rate fluctuations in Italy during the Principate were not marked, and the rates that are mentioned are generally low (5 to 6% p.a.). Thus, in calculating the return from viticulture (→ Wine), Columella works on the basis of an interest rate of 6% on the amount borrowed, and Pliny also puts the return from one → endowment at 6% (Columella 3,3,9; Plin. Ep. 7,18).

The theory has often been advanced that interest was rather low (4–6 %) in the western Mediterranean, higher (8–9 %) in the Greek East, and extremely high (12 %) in Egypt. The source material for Egypt is quite good. Differences between East and West seem, on closer investigation, not to have been so clearly marked. In Africa four institutions offered an interest rate of 5–6 %, whereas a fifth offered a rate of 12%.

C. Late antiquity and Christianity

Towards the end of the 4th cent., the maximum permissible rate was set at 1 % per month (*usurae centesimae*), that is 12 % per annum; the authorities intervened to prevent that rate being exceeded (Cod. Theod. 2,33,2; AD 386). Special conditions applied to senators: after Severus [2] Alexander they were unable to charge more than 6 % per annum (0,5 % per month) (SHA Alex. 26,3); in 405 the highest interest rate that senators could charge was again set at 6 % (Cod. Theod. 2,33,4).

The Christian position on interest was of decisive importance for developments in late antiquity. There were already individual passages in the OT that forbade taking from the poor, whether in the form of money or foodstuffs (Ex 22:25; Lev 25:37). As well, other passages prohibited loans with interest to members of one's own people (Dt 23:19–20). In the Gospels there is only one explicit reference to interest, in the parable about the talents (Lc 19:23; Mt 25:27), but interest is in no way criticized there. In the period around 250, Cyprianus [2] was critical of bishops said to have enriched themselves, before the persecution under Decius [II 1], by charging interest on loans (Cypr. De lapsis 6). Both Basilius [1] and Gregorius [2] of Nyssa criticized usurers; Ambrosius devoted a text to the problem of interest (Basil. Homilia in psalmum 14,5; Greg. Nyss. contra usurarios; Ambr. de Tobia).

Several Councils forbade clerics from charging interest at all, on pain of excommunication, as, the Council of Elvira (between 295 and 306), of Arles (314), of Nicaea (325) and the Councils of Carthage (between 345 and 348, as well as in 397). Nevertheless, in the 4th cent. the Church did not forbid lay people from charging interest altogether.

→ Banks; → Daneion; → Debts; → Fenus nauticus; → Loan; → Money, money economy

1 J. Andreau, Banking and Business in the Roman World, 1999 2 Id., La vie financière dans le monde romain, 1987 3 Ch. T. Barlow, Bankers, Moneylenders and Interest Rates in the Roman Republic, 1978 4 G. Billeter, Geschichte des Zinsfusses im griech.-röm. Alt. bis auf Justinian, 1898 5 R. Bogaert, Banques et Banquiers dans les cités grecques, 1968 6 Id., Les origines antiques de la banque de dépôt, 1966 7 E. E. Cohen, Athenian Economy and Society. A Banking Perspective, 1992 8 A. Gara, Aspetti di economia monetaria dell'Egitto romano, in: ANRW II 10.1, 1988, 912–951 9 Millett 10 S. Mrozek, Faenus. Studien zu Z.-Problemen zur Zeit des Prinzipats, 2001 11 H. Zehnacker, Unciarium fenus (Tacite, Annales 6,16), in: Mélanges de littérature et d'épigraphie latines, d'histoire ancienne et d'archéologie. FS P. Wuilleumier, 1980, 353–362.   J. A.

International law

I. Overview II. Regulations governing peace
III. Law of war IV. Diplomatic exchanges
and laws governing foreigners V. The
theory of international law

I. Overview

International law (IL) was established as a field in its own right during the early modern period (especially by Hugo Grotius, 1583–1645). The term → *ius* (A.2.) *gentium*, which originated in Roman law, established itself as its name. However, in antiquity this term did not mean IL but those concepts of → law in general that were assumed to be common to all peoples. This also included principles that belong to IL in its narrow sense such as the inviolability of diplomatic representatives (Dig. 50,7,18). Antiquity did not have a term for IL *per se*. However, ancient cultures were familiar with IL as a concept, or at least its 'classical' themes: the law of war (if only in parts), peace, alliances and the law of delegations. Also touching upon IL are regulations concerning interaction with foreigners (→ Aliens, the position of).

II. Regulations governing peace

The most important instrument of ancient IL was the international treaty (→ International treaties). In the Ancient Orient, treaties from as far back as the 3rd millennium BC have been preserved. Particularly well known is the peace treaty between Ramses [2] II of Egypt and the Hittite king Ḫattusili II (formerly III), probably from 1259 BC, of which a copy is displayed at the UN head quarters in New York (→ Qadesh). This treaty was sworn by each party by its gods, i.e. violation of the treaty was subject to a divine curse. Therefore, the parties concluding the treaty followed the basic pattern of antiquity, which was also evident in Roman treaties of state. A similar continuity with the peace of Ramses is evident in the mutual address of the participating rulers and kings as 'brothers', which recurs in the diplomatic interaction, e.g., of the Roman emperor Constantine [1] the Great (early 4th cent. AD) with the Sassanid king. These fraternization formulas not only occur at the highest level of statecraft but also in the lower ranks of → diplomacy. In the spirit of an agreement they denote mutual recognition and accreditation – to use modern terms. Not all international treaties were based on the partners' equality. Many are treaties with dependent states, e.g. in the external relations of the Hittite empire (→ Hattusa). Greek treaties of alliance during the classical period (6th–4th cent. BC) often also had the structure of a hegemonic → symmachía, and an essential part of many Roman treaties was the subjugation of the external community as a treaty partner under the → maiestas (A.) ('superior power') of Rome (cf. also → foedus; → pax). Going even further than these agreements, the → deditio, a capitulation agreement, even resulted in the surrender of statehood. In the Roman perception this was not an international treaty because it deprived one partner of its quality as a state. However, as a → treaty, even the deditio constituted duties of the annexing state, i.e. Rome.

The political culture of Greece, with its city states, was fertile ground for the development of arbitration tribunals among states. In earlier ancient agreements they apparently did not occur and in Roman politics they played no significant role. Therefore, the practice of → arbitration (see also → diaitētaí) among Greek poleis stands out as 'an impressive symbol of an advanced legal culture' [1. 37].

III. Law of war

The ancient → law of war was to a greater extent a state law and ideology of rulership than a treaty. Legal rules of warfare or for combating 'war crimes' (a modern term) did not exist. Therefore, it was more of a political matter of fact than a legal rule that the population of the defeated state, with its possessions and its persons, was part of the → spoils. The only legal interest was the distribution of the spoils among the victors (cf. → War, consequences of).

According to internal rules, particular formalities and even material requirements had to be fulfilled before beginning a war. This is indicated in a requirement in the OT (Dt 20) that before starting belligerent actions a peace offer must be made. Especially in Rome, war was made dependent on the prior participation of the priests: only a war that was begun with the proper ritual actions of the → fetiales was a 'legitimate' and legal war. From this original meaning of bellum iustum, the first steps towards a concept of a just war conducted for legitimate objectives were developed in the political philosophy of → Cicero. This also made the bellum iustum a rule for communities of states and peoples (cf. also → War guilt, problem of). Special war agreements also developed at an early point, e.g. regarding prisoner exchanges, free withdrawal and especially armistices and truces (→ Law of war). Evidence of armistices is found in the Iliad (Hom. Il. 7,394 f.; 7,408 f.). Both Greek (→ ekecheiría) and Latin (→ indutiae) had a term for a truce.

IV. Diplomatic exchanges and laws governing foreigners

Delegates stood at the centre of ancient diplomatic contacts. However, they were not permanent representatives of their states or rulers at the seat of the foreign government, but were only authorized and sent as the occasion demanded. Testimonials of diplomatic correspondence between rulers or officials, including foreign delegates, are already preserved from the Ancient Orient, which typically use the address 'brother'. Usually, high-ranking persons were used for occasional delegations. However, messengers and heralds (→ kḗryx [2]), who only delivered the message of their polis, were also used, especially in the diplomacy of ancient Greece. They enjoyed the special protection of the gods and were considered inviolable. This rule, together with the also religiously-based special protection of the fetiales as the original delegates and heralds of the Roman state, is possibly the source of the Roman legal principle that delegates (→ legatus) were 'inviolable and sacred' (sanctus). From this, Isidore [9] of Seville (Isid. Orig. 5,6) in the 7th cent. AD derived legatorum non violandorum religio ('the religious duty of the delegate's inviolability') as an example of a principle of IL. This immunity of heralds and delegates touches upon the special protection that aliens in general enjoyed in antiquity; this is evident, e.g. in the OT (Ex 22: 23; Dt 24:27).

The Greek laws governing foreigners (→ Aliens, the position of) appear retroactively as a special subdivision of IL. They included the → proxenía as a precursor of embassies, the → asylía (cf. also → ásylon), the isopoliteía (comparable to modern freedom of residency) and legal aid agreements (symbolaí), which not only granted asylum and freedom of residence but also legal protection in case these laws were violated or the necessity to sue for private claims arose. Similar phenomena can be observed in Rome with the recognized hospitality of the hospitium publicum (→ Hospitality III.) the amicus populi Romani ('friend of the Roman people') and the legal protection for foreigners (peregrini) before the → praetor peregrinus according to the → ius (A.2.) gentium. The emperors of late antiquity built upon this (e.g. Cod. Iust. 4,64,4 protection of commerce between subjects of the Sassanid and Roman empires).

V. The theory of international law

Although antiquity did not produce a dogmatic or a philosophical theory of IL, in those spheres that may be considered parts of IL, legal values were practised that have become part of general considerations in legal theory and philosophy. Thus, all ancient cultures considered → treaties binding. Although treaty violation was initially considered a religious infraction, a secular understanding later developed in Greece and Rome regarding the practical wisdom and philosophical appropriateness of Faith (Greek → pístis, Latin → fides) that agreements would be kept. Together with the stoic concept of one humanity (→ Human dignity; → Human rights), this type of thought caused Roman authors such as Cicero and Livy in the 1st cent. BC to view international relationships on a theoretical level that early modern thinkers could use as a level for 'natural and IL'.

→ Agraphoi nomoi; → Aliens, the position of; → Amphiktyonia; → Diplomacy; → Fides; → Hostis; → Human rights; → International treaties; → Law of war; → Pistis; → Praeda

1 K.-H. ZIEGLER, Völkerrechtsgeschichte, 1994.

C. BALDUS, Regelhafte Vertragsauslegung nach Parteirollen im klass. röm. Recht und in der mod. Völkerrechtswissenschaft, vol. 1, 1998; DULCKEIT/SCHWARZ/WALDSTEIN, 138–143; M. KASER, Ius gentium, 1993; D. NÖRR, Aspekte des röm. V. Die Bronzetafel von Alcántara, 1989; Id., Die Fides im röm. V., 1991; H. STEIGER, Vom V. der Christenheit zum Weltbürgerrecht, in: P.-J. HEINIG et al. (ed.), Reich, Regionen und Europa in MA und Neuzeit. FS P. Moraw, 2000, 171 ff.; W. GRAF VITZTHUM, V., ²2001, 49 ff.; A. WATSON, International Law in Archaic Rome, 1993; A. ZACK, Studien zum "Röm. V." ..., 2001; K.-H. ZIEGLER, Zum V. in der röm. Antike, in: M. SCHERMAIER et al. (ed.), Iurisprudentia universalis, FS Th. Mayer-Maly, 2002, 933–944.   G. S.

International treaties

I. GENERAL   II. ANCIENT ORIENT   III. HITTITES
IV. GREECE   V. ROME

I. GENERAL

International treaties (IT) are official and binding agreements under international law between two or more subjects of international law, which are legally binding for the entire citizenship in question. They were stipulated orally or in writing; they took the form of unilateral, bi- or multilateral agreements, and always implied the recognition of the other party under international law. IT were often the result of preliminary negotiations; they required ratification by the 'sovereign' or the appropriate constitutional body (citizens' assembly, council/senate, monarch/emperor), were ratified through solemn oaths, and, where appropriate, endorsed by sacrifices. In general, they were published and archived centrally. IT were either valid for a stipulated period of time or for 'eternity' – treaties entered into with monarchs were generally valid only for the duration of their rule. Regarding their content, IT regulated the relations or the status quo between states, they contain demands for one-sided or mutual contributions, requirements for certain actions (or their omission) – also in relation to third parties –, and, where appropriate, imposed sanctions for non-compliance.   P. KE.

II. ANCIENT ORIENT

Even though the application of the concept of international law to the relations and conflicts between the states of the ancient Near East remains controversial, some cuneiform script texts from Mesopotamia and Syria can be taken as IT (or respectively as draft copies of such treaties). Alongside actual contractual agreements, these also include – for their content as well as for legal reasons – oaths of loyalty [1. 123–126] (cf. [2]). Formal characteristics of IT were: seals, introductory formula, the actual clauses of the contract – objectively or subjectively formulated or styled in form of an oath –, and also curse formulas [3. 234]. In view of the (royal) parties to a treaty, a distinction can be made between treaties amongst equal partners and vassalage treaties.

The earliest known examples are a treaty, dating from the 24th/23rd cents. BC, between the ruler of Ebla (located to the northwest of Syria) and the king of a city state (Abar-QA) [4], and a treaty, in the Elamite language, between → Narām-Sîn of Akkad (2260–2223 BC) and an Elamite ruler [5]. Other IT between equals, as well as vassalage treaties, date from the Old Babylonian/Old Assyrian period (19th/18th cents.) [6–9], and from the second half of the 2nd millennium BC (Alalaḫ and Ugarit) [3. 239–241]. These IT dealt, among other things, with the extradition of fugitives, the treatment of natives or traders of one contract party within the territory of the other, as well as the avengement of crimes against the above groups. The extant Neo-Assyrian IT from the 9th–7th cents. BC [10], together with references to such treaties in other sources [11. 184–185], prove that bilateral agreements between states and the contractual underpinning of declarations of loyalty constituted an important part of Assyrian rule. Their purpose was to safeguard the territory of the empire and its trade requirements, to regulate the obligations resulting from alliances as well as the provision of assistance, and also to ensure dependance and loyalty towards the Assyrian king. The latter was the case in the safeguarding of the succession to the throne, as initiated by → Asarhaddon in 672 BC [10. 28–58]. IT in Aramaic are also extant (8th cent. BC: TUAT 1, 1983, 178 189).

Apart from a treaty by Ramses [2] II with the Hittite king Ḫattusili II of 1259 (for the content see → Qadesh), recorded on a temple wall, no other Egyptian IT are known. The reason for this is that as yet no Egyptian state archives have been found.

1 B. KIENAST, Mündlichkeit und Schriftlichkeit im keilschriftlichen Rechtswesen, in: Zschr. für Altoriental. und Biblische Rechtsgesch. 2, 1996, 114–130   2 F. STARKE, Zur urkundlichen Charakterisierung neuassyrischer Treueide, in: s. [1], 1, 1995, 70–82   3 B. KIENAST, Der Vertrag Ebla-Assur in rechtshistor. Sicht, in: Heidelberger Studien zum Alten Orient 2, 1988, 231–243   4 D. O. EDZARD, Der Vertrag von Ebla mit A-bar-QA, in: P. FRONZAROLI (ed.), Literature and Literary Language at Ebla, 1992, 187–217   5 W. HINZ, Elams Vertrag mit Narām-Sîn von Akkade, in: ZA 58, 1967, 66–96   6 WU YUHONG, The Treaty between Shadlash (Sumu-Numhim) and Neribtum (Hammi-Dushur), in: Journ. of Ancient Civilizations 9, 1994, 124–136   7 D. CHARPIN, Un traité entre Zimri-Lim de Mari et Ibâl-pî-El II d'Ešnunna, in: D. CHARPIN (ed.), Marchands, diplomates et empereurs. FS P. Garelli, 1991, 139–166   8 F. JOANNÈS, Le traité de vassalité d'Atamrum d'Andarig envers Zimri-Lim de Mari, in: s. [7], 167–177   9 J. EIDEM, An Old Assyrian Treaty from Tell Leilan, in: s.

[7], 185–207 10 S. PARPOLA, K. WATANABE, Neo-Assyrian Treaties and Loyalty Oaths, 1988 11 S. PARPOLA, Neo-Assyrian Treaties from the Royal Archives of Nineveh, in: JCS 39, 1987, 161–189. H. N.

III. HITTITES

The more than 40 Hittite IT, generally preserved in several archive copies (15th–13th cent. BC), not only represent by far the most extensive corpus of IT from the Ancient Orient, but also occupy an outstanding place because of their diction, which is polished, precise and highly sensitive to political psychology, and which is rooted in the highly developed Hittite thinking on politics and constitutional law. All of these IT were bilateral ones under international law. Some of them concerned bilateral agreements between equal partners (e.g. the treaty with → Kizzuwatna, 15th cent.; Hittite-Egyptian peace treaty of 1259, → Qadesh). Most of them, however, were treaties regulating – in line with the federal structure of the Hittite empire (14th–13th cents. BC) – the admittance of new states into this empire. The content of these treaties was harmonized in the case of the northern Syrian and Arzawan member states (→ Karchemish; → Mirā), which were tied into a closer political unity. Their usual modern description as 'vassalage treaties' is misleading inasmuch as the admittance only resulted in the loss of certain sovereign rights (esp. in respect of foreign policies), whereas otherwise the kings of the member states were involved in the fundamental political decisions of the empire because of their acceptance into the Hittite royal dynasty.

Formally, all IT follow the same pattern: (a) preamble, (b) contract stipulations, (c) list of oath gods, (d) formulaic curses and blessings. In all membership treaties, the extensive preamble, about a quarter of the entire document, covers the history leading up to the conclusion of the treaty, setting out its historical and political preconditions. Within Asia Minor, these treaties were concluded in → Hittite; for treaties with states outside of Asia Minor, the text of the treaty was translated into → Akkadian. Even though the treaties were drawn up in the name of the Hittite great king, they originated from the country of → Hattusa, i.e. the empire. Accordingly, the treaties obliged the new members to loyalty not only to the great king, but also and particularly to the empire itself.

→ Hattusa II

G. BECKMAN, Hittite Diplomatic Texts, 1996; V. KOROŠEC, Hethitische S., 1938. F. S.

IV. GREECE

The legal foundation of Greek IT is closely interwoven with religious and socio-cultural practices as well as with the → ágraphoi nómoi. Genesis and development of law between states reflect the need to regulate relations between the emerging citizen states in the Archaic period [1. 126–128]. Of central importance to the development of supra-regional formulas for legal texts and documents were the Panhellenic sanctuaries ('Amphictyonic oath': Stv II 104; → amphiktyonía) and the intensive peer policy interaction, albeit without ever developing into systematic international law ([2; 3]; too static: [4]).

As a rule, exploratory talks were conducted by authorized envoys (→ kéryx [2]; → presbeía, présbeis). Following the assent by the relevant constitutional body [5. 1252 f.], the treaty was concluded by a ceremony of oaths and sacrifices (oaths sworn by officials, oath takers, or the citizenry as a whole, [6. 342 f.]). The display of the documents on the → agorá and in supraregional sanctuaries underlined the principle that the treaties should be public to all, as well as the desire to bestow religious authority upon IT. In the Hellenistic period, the exclusive right of the citizen states to enter into treaties was increasingly usurped by the (large) monarchies, which in some instances denied the poleis this right altogether.

The subjects of IT reflect the broad range of relations between states: treaties of friendship, legal assistance, and asylum [7], as well as arbitration treaties to settle disputes (in the Hellenistic period formalized as → synthḗkē [8. 3–33]); furthermore, bilateral treaties between warring parties (spondaí, standardized in the 5th cent.: [3. 123–154]). Particular especially to the Hellenistic period was the collective, generally mutual, granting of citizenship (→ isopoliteía; [9]) as well as treaties regulating the political merger of communities (→ sympoliteía; [10]), in which in some instances the smaller parties laid down the dissolution of their state as an independent unity (so-called incorporating sympolity), [11. 37]).

The most prominent type of Greek international treaty is the → symmachía. This was originally a bilateral contract for the conduct of war (called → epimachía if exclusively defensive in nature), with clauses specifying friend and foe [12. 298–307]. The symmachía, however, was increasingly supplemented with special clauses (stipulation of services to be provided, naming of the enemy, and territorial clauses; cf. [13]). However, the principle of bilaterality was retained even in the 'hegemonic symmaches', because the various parties were contractually linked to the dominating power only, but not to each other [14]. Limitations to the period of validity of a peace treaty (5, 10, 30, 50 years), found even in early documents, did not imply that war was to be resumed automatically upon its expiry [15]. Such clauses of limitation presuppose a developed legal understanding, and in particular a will to be legally bound for a limited period of time [16. 276–281]. Usually, alliances were entered into with a limitation to 100 years (3 generations, meaning, however, for 'eternity'; already explicitly so in the 6th cent.: Stv II 120). The oath sworn at the founding of the → Athenian League likewise implied an alliance unlimited in time (Aristot. Ath. Pol. 23,5). A special case was the multilateral framework of treaties constituting the 'Common

Peace', which claimed to be legally binding for all Greek states (→ *koinḗ eirḗnē*).

→ Agraphoi nomoi; → Athenian League; → Ceryx [2]; → Isopoliteia; → Koine Eirene; → Symmachia

1 V. EHRENBERG, Der Staat der Griechen, ²1965 2 E. BICKERMAN, Bemerkungen über das Völkerrecht im klass. Griechenland (1950), in: F. GSCHNITZER (ed.), Zur griech. Staatskunde, 1969, 474–502   3 E. BALTRUSCH, Symmachie und Spondai, 1994   4 P. KLOSE, Die völkerrechtliche Ordnung der hell. Staatenwelt in der Zeit von 280 bis 168 v. Chr., 1972   5 BUSOLT/SWOBODA 2 6 A. HEUSS, Abschluß und Beurkundung des griech. und röm. Staatsvertrages (1934), in: Id., Gesammelte Schriften, vol. 1, 1995, 340–419   7 W. ZIEGLER, Symbolai und Asylia, 1975   8 S. L. AGER, Interstate Arbitrations in the Greek World, 337–90 BC, 1996   9 W. GAWANTKA, Isopolitie, 1975   10 A. GIOVANNINI, Unt. über die Natur und die Anf. der bundesstaatlichen Sympolitie in Griechenland, 1971   11 H. H. SCHMITT, Überlegungen zur Sympolitie, in: Symposium 1993, 35–44   12 G. E. M. DE STE. CROIX, The Origins of the Peloponnesian War, 1972 13 F. GSCHNITZER, Ein neuer spartanischer S., 1978 14 V. MARTIN, La vie internationale dans la Grèce des cités, 1940   15 A. GRAEBER, Friedensvorstellung und Friedensbegriff bei den Griechen, in: ZRG 109, 1992, 116–161   16 F. J. F. NIETO, Die Abänderungsklausel in den griech. S. der klass. Zeit, in: Symposium 1979, 273–286.
                                                                    HA. BE.

V. ROME

The Roman state knew of three formulas for the conclusion of IT, each of them based on → *fides*, which was considered sacred and therefore inviolabe ([8]). These were: 1. the fetial → *foedus*, rooted in the Italic [12] tradition. It was concluded by → *fetiales* during a pig sacrifice and under self-cursing [1. 171–180; 13. 70–74; 9. 111–117]. 2. The solemn magisterial *foedus*, which replaced the fetial treaty at the start of Roman expansion overseas. In principle, this treaty was of eternal duration. It was characterized by mutual declarations, sacrifices, oaths. It was written down and made public on the Capitol [11. 44–132; 3; 4. 175–215]. 3. The → *sponsio*, a verbal contract resulting from questions and answers. This was usually a preliminary contract entered into by Roman generals. It required ratification by the Senate. Later, the emperors, who had unlimited authority to conclude any treaty, assumed control of all international affairs [13. 93 f.; 4. 176–183; 14. 48 f.].

While IT implied the existence of state → hospitality (*hospitium publicum*) to regulate diplomatic missions ([5]; → *legatio*), its guarantee remained an act of international law [13. 86]. From a strictly legal point of view, 'war treaties' such as → *pactio* and → *indutiae* were not IT in the strict sense of the word, and neither was the → *deditio* [1. 20–25; 4. 141–153], whose legal consequence – the dissolution of a subject of international law – Rome could unilaterally repeal (see → *restitutio*; [1. 69–82; 4. 154–174]). The relations of the thus restituted state with Rome could on occasion be shaped by unilateral and obligatory IT. The hypothesis that *deditio* and international treaties merged into one in the Imperial period was unconvincing [4. 138 f.], especially as both institutions still existed in late antiquity [10].

Rome entered into IT on an equal footing (*foedus aequum*) or an unequal one (*foedus iniquum*); in the latter case, a clause demanded the recognition of Roman → *maiestas* or the subordination to Rome in respect of foreign affairs [1. 119; 11. 63 f.; 13. 92 f.]. The heterogeneous requirements of Roman foreign policy preclude the modern assumption of set formulations. Still, all IT have integral constituents: the treaty partners are specified, as well as the treaty's subject and period [11. 47; 3]. The relation laid down at the beginning of the treaty (→ *amicitia*, → *pax*, → *societas*) as defined in the introduction, and the subsequent specification of its nature make it possible to distinguish different categories, e.g. peace treaties and/or treaties of alliance, treaties regarding spheres of interest [6], trade rights, and so on. As Rome avoided multilateral IT, even the system of → *socii* (Roman confederation) in Italy was no more than a total of bilateral IT. Rome had no need for pure friendship treaties, as every peaceful official contact brought about *amicitia* [2. 12–18; 1. 136–158; 15. 12]. *Clientela* treaties are a scholarly fiction ([13. 93; 4]; cf. [7]). Special clauses dealt with protective measures (→ *obses*, disarmament, → *transfuga*, 'defectors'), settlement of the → consequences of war (return of prisoners of war, reparations, evacuations of territories), frontier outlines, conflicts (clauses concerning neutrality, disarmament, demilitarization, and a ban on war), tributes and many more [11. 66–98; 4. 216–265], and also with modifications of a treaty.

1 W. DAHLHEIM, Struktur und Entwicklung des röm. Völkerrechts im 3. und 2. Jh. v. Chr., 1968   2 A. HEUSS, Die völkerrechtlichen Grundlagen der röm. Außenpolitik in republikanischer Zeit, 1933   3 Id., Abschluß und Beurkundung des griech. und röm. Staatsvertrages (1934), in: Id., Gesammelte Schriften, vol. 1, 1995, 340–419 4 P. KEHNE, Formen röm. Außenpolitik in der Kaiserzeit, thesis Hannover 1989   5 Id., s. v. Gesandtschaften, RGA 11, 1998, 457–461   6 Id., s. v. Interessensphären, in: H. SONNABEND (ed.), Mensch und Landschaft in der Ant., 1999, 234–236   7 Id., s. v. Klientelrandstaaten, RGA 17, 2001, 11–13   8 D. NÖRR, Die fides im röm. Völkerrecht, 1991   9 J. RÜPKE, Domi militiae, 1990   10 R. SCHULZ, Die Entwicklung des röm. Völkerrechts im 4. und 5. Jh., 1993 11 E. TÄUBLER, Imperium Romanum vol. 1, 1913 (repr. 1964)   12 A. WATSON, International Law in Archaic Rome, 1993   13 K.-H. ZIEGLER, Das Völkerrecht der röm. Republik, in: ANRW I 2, 1972, 68–114   14 Id., Völkerrechtsgesch., 1994   15 E. BADIAN, Foreign Clientelae, 1958.

COLLECTIONS OF GREEK AND ROMAN INTERNATIONAL TREATIES: Stv, vol. 2 and 3; R. K. SHERK (ed.), Roman Documents from the Greek East, 1969; W. G. GREWE (ed.), Fontes Historiae Iuris Gentium, vol. 1, 1995; A. CHANIOTIS, Die Verträge zw. kretischen Poleis in der hell. Zeit, 1996, 179–451; K. BRODERSEN et al. (ed.), Histor. griech. Inschr. in transl., vol. 3, 1999.   P. KE.

Interpolation Interpolation is generally understood as any effect on the text that is not due to purely mechanical causes but was undertaken consciously (or less consciously) by scribes or readers, especially the addition of external text, but also the alteration of individual words (cf. however [5]). Omission or deletion of parts of the text by scribes are other forms of interpolation.

Interpolation is a frequent phenomenon in the study of texts. TARRANT proposes three categories of interpolation in the sense of adding material: collaboration (or 'imitation'), emendation (i.e. replacing a corrupt text) and annotation (divided into 'glosses', 'commentaries' and 'quotations') [13]. Readers embellished the text, theatrical performers added their refinements to an established work. Readers noticed mistakes (or what they perceived as mistakes) in metre, grammar, style or line of thought and tried to improve them. Textual passages that encountered disapproval were censored (especially omissions occurred here as a result). If sections of a text were repeated, the extent of the repetition was enlarged ('Konkordanzinterpolation'). Commentaries, glosses or parallel passages were inserted into the text in a later phase. Specialized literature in particular was regarded as a living text; every generation adapted the contents to meet its needs or enlarged it (e.g. → Euclides' 'Theories of the Elements'; cf. → Editions, second).

The reference to Athens in the Homeric catalogue of ships (Hom. Il. 2,546ff.) was already a problem for ancient scholars, and the citizens of Megara accused the Athenians of having altered the text of lines 557–558. In general, the eccentric ('wild') Homeric papyri from the Ptolemaic period offer a large number of additional verses that do not reappear in the later tradition ([15]; general [1]).

Actors and producers had been revising tragic texts from the 4th cent. BC onwards (for example, the much discussed passage in Soph. Aj. 1028–1039; on Sophocles in general [6], on Euripides [9]). Explanatory glosses were often inserted into the tragic text (in e.g. Aesch. Ag. 549 the MS F has τυράννων/*tyránnōn*, a gloss on κοιράνων/*koiránōn*, which Triclinius had restored). The so-called 'Binneninterpolation' (probably textual insertions starting and ending within a verse) occurs surprisingly frequently: in Soph. OC 1321f. this is evident because the suspect words are missing in an important branch of transmission. In comedy texts, on the other hand, probably fewer interpolations have been made: cf. however the confusion at the end of Aristophanes' 'Frogs', where the disjointed variants suggest an addition on the part of the author himself (→ Author's variants). O. ZWIERLEIN has attempted to demonstrate an extensive interpolation in the transmitted text of Plautus ([19] and in later publications).

In prose texts, by contrast, additions and alterations are generally harder to identify, especially in authors with a wordy style (informative discussion of an especially complicated text in [10]; for Latin texts see also the Petronius-eds. of [11] and the comments by [12]).

In prose and poetry alike we have to reckon that ancient or medieval readers altered or improved the transmitted textual variant – the result *i.a.* of rhetorically-oriented training [6; 17]. That applies to Latin poetry as well, as TARRANT notes: the texts that are especially 'susceptible' to addenda are of a 'rhetorical' character – Ovid, Seneca's tragedies and Juvenal ([14] with a short introductory outline of the 'hunt' after interpolations). Especially for Juvenal, an extensive interpolation has been ascertained [16] after lengthy discussion [3; 7; 8; 12]. Hexameters were more subject to interpolation than lyrical verses, though individual readers evidently did try their hand at more difficult metres as well (cf. Hor. Carm. 3,11,17–20 and 4,8; Catull. 61,92–96, omitted by [4]).

Familiarity with Vergilian poetry led to frequent concordance-interpolation (e.g. Verg. Aen. 3,230: the repetition of 1,311 was prompted by the fact that the last words of 1,310 *sed rupe cavata* also appear in 3,229). Especially half-lines in the *Aeneid* were often completed: the words *de collo fistula pendet* (Verg. Aen. 3,661) would be a fine addition to the portrayal of Polyphemus as a figure in the Theocritean pastoral, if they were not absent from the majuscule-MSS. On the other hand, editors maintain the text of Verg. Aen. 11,309 in its entirety, despite the abnormal rhythm of *ponite* before *spes* (BURGESS and PORSON deleted the last eight words).

Christian faith and knowledge on the part of readers led, hardly surprisingly, to the river Iardanos (Hom. Il. 7,135) being changed into Jordan in the A-schol. to this passage. Cases of censorship also arose – albeit rather infrequently – from this mental attitude [18]. Thus, the Propertius-MSS display a range of relatively minor but typical cases of textual corruption that are probably due to prudery on part of a scribe or reader: in Prop. 2,31,3, the epithet *Poenis* (in medieval MSS mostly written as *penis*) is missing in the MSS F and L dependent on Petrarch's lost copy; in Prop. 4,4,47, PALMER'S *potabitur* is the best substitute for *pugnabitur*, which makes no sense in the context.

1 M. J. APTHORP, The Manuscript Evidence for I. in Homer, 1980   2 W. V. CLAUSEN (ed.), A. Persi Flacci et D. Iuni Iuvenalis Saturae, 1959   3 E. COURTNEY, The interpolations in Iuvenal, in: BICS 22, 1975, 147–162   4 B. GEORG, Catullus 61.90–6, in: CQ 46, 1996, 302–304   5 H. C. GÜNTHER, Quaestiones Propertianae, 1997, 96   6 Id., Exercitationes Sophocleae, 1997   7 G. JACHMANN, Studien zu Juvenal (Nachr. der Akad. der Wiss. in Göttingen, philol.-histor. Kl.), 1943, 187–266   8 U. KNOCHE (ed.), D. Iunius Iuvenalis, Satirae, 1950   9 D. J. MASTRONARDE (ed.), Euripides, Phoenissae, 1994, 39–49   10 K. MAURER, I. in Thucydides, 1995   11 K. MÜLLER (ed.), Petronius, 1983   12 R. G. M. NISBET, in: JRS 52, 1962, 227–238 (review and discussion of [2] and [11]; = Id., Collected Papers, 1995, 16–28, cf. also 283–284   13 R. J. TARRANT, Towards a typology of i. in Latin poetry, in: TAPhA 117, 1987, 281–298   14 Id., The reader as author: collaborative i. in Latin poetry, in: J. N. GRANT (ed.), Editing Greek and Latin Texts, 1989, 121–162, here: 158–162   15 S. R. WEST, The Ptolemaic papyri of

Homer, 1969, 12–13   16 J. WILLIS (ed.), D. Iuni Iuvenalis Saturae selectae, 1997   17 N. G. WILSON, Variant
readings with poor support in the manuscript tradition,
in: Révue d'histoire des textes 17, 1987, 1–13 (esp. 8ff.)
18 Id., Scholars of Byzantium, ²1996, 12–18, 276
19 O. ZWIERLEIN, Zur Kritik und Exegese des Plautus I
(AAWM 4), 1990.   N.W. and S.H.

Interpolation, critique of

In Roman legal history cri-
tique of interpolation specifically refers to the examination of the transmitted version of the texts of the *Corpus
Iuris* for falsifications compared with the original. This
is of particular relevance to the fragments from the writings of the classical jurists (1st cent. BC – 3rd cent. AD)
in the → *Digesta*, but also to the → *Institutiones* in comparison to their models and even to the older imperial
pronouncements collected in the → *Codex Iustinianus*.
With regard to the Digesta, emperor Justinian himself
had already given an express instruction in his petition
to the law commission from the year 530 (Const. Deo
auctore §§ 4/10) to 'cleanse' the texts, namely, to omit
obsolete legal institutions or replace them with modern
equivalents, to incorporate Justinian's own new legislation, to condense cases and rules or clothe them in general principles and to eliminate controversy among
jurists so that out of a wider context for debate, only a
single interpretation remained in each case. The principal task of critique of interpolation is to trace these
variations to the models in the digesta texts. Critique of
interpolation is also necessary to elaborate those variations in the text that inevitably arose due to the length
of the period of transmission between the development
of the original works, particularly in the 2nd and at the
start of the 3rd cent. AD, and their use in the *Corpus
Iuris*. This type of text corruption is also to be observed
on occasion in the few collections and individual works
outside the *Corpus Iuris* that have come down to us,
particularly the → *Institutiones* of → Gaius [2].

Since → HUMANISM, critique of interpolation itself
has been, particularly in → LEGAL HISTORY (ROMAN
LAW STUDIES) from the end of the 19th cent. on, an
important part of the history of reception and the history of Roman legal science. Nowadays, the 'genealogy'
of the text is reconstructible in a succession of collections and works with the aid of precise, and in some cases
computer-aided analyses (so-called stemmatic research); this has resulted in critique of interpolation becoming considerably more sophisticated. On the other
hand, from a modern perspective, the index of interpolation ([1], cf. [2]) published from 1929–1935
represents a wealth of astute objective criticism of the
content of the texts rather than a methodically sound
critique of interpolation. Extant tradition is again
examined in a very conservative manner in some cases
(representative [3]). A supremely sophisticated histori-
cal-philological awareness of method (cf. esp. [4])
means that critique of interpolation will always be relevant to the analysis of the historical sources of Roman
law.

→ INTERPOLATION, ANALYSIS OF

1 E. LEVY (ed.), Index interpolationum quae in Iustiniani
Digestis inesse dicuntur I, 1929, II, 1931, III 1935, Suppl.
I, 1929   2 G. BRUGGINI (ed.), Index Interpolationum
quae in Iustiniani Codice inesse dicuntur, 1969
3 M. KASER, Zur Methodik der röm. Rechtsquellen-
forsch., 1974   4 WIEACKER, RRG, 154–182.   G.S.

Interpretatio

I. LAW   II. RELIGION

I. LAW
A. CONCEPT   B. INTERPRETATIO AND LAW
C. INTERPRETATIO AS A SOURCE OF THE LAW
D. METHODS   E. INTERPRETATIO OF LEGAL TRANS-
ACTIONS   F. THE BAN ON INTERPRETATION IN LATE
ANTIQUITY

A. CONCEPT
Interpretatio is interpretation, not only of texts but
also of oral declarations and other matters of legal
import. The topos of simple truth requiring no mediator (Petron. Sat. 107,15) does not apply to the specialist
knowledge of astrologers (cf. → Divination), philologists (on both: Cic. Div. 1,34; 2,92) and jurists (Cic.
Leg. 2,59). At the end of the Republic, the words *interpres* ('interpreter') and *interpretari* ('to interpret') become conflated into the abstract *interpretatio* [3. 8off.,
91ff.]; this is already true of legal interpretation in the
case of the kings (Cic. Rep. 5,3) and the priests (Dig.
1,2,2,6), then in secular jurisprudence (Cic. De or.
1,199) and interpretation by judges (Cic. Clu. 146), and
finally by the *praetor* (Dig. 46,5,9). In the first Roman
legal commentary, the *Tripertita* of Sex. → Aelius [I 11]
Petus Catus (*c.* 200 BC), the text of the Law of the
Twelve Tables is followed by its *interpretatio*. Apart
from *interpretatio iuris*, there is also *interpretatio
legum, edicti* or *senatus consulti*. According to Pomponius (Dig. 1,2,2,12), however, the *interpretatio prudentium* is 'in reality' identical with *ius civile*, which is
created *sine scripto* (in unwritten form; Dig. 1,2,2,5).

B. INTERPRETATIO AND LAW
Modern conceptions of scientific interpretation have
obscured the political role of Roman *interpretatio* as a
substitute for legislation. Already in Rome 'knowledge
of the law' also embraced 'the sense and purpose of the
law' (*legum vis ac potestas*, Dig. 1,3,17). The concept
clara non sunt interpretanda ('that which is clear requires no interpretation') was as yet unknown: as even
'self-evident' edicts (Dig. 25,4,1,11) required *interpretatio*, *verborum interpretatio* (*interpretatio* of words)
became the very stuff of commentaries of edicts (Dig.
12,1,1 pr.).

In view of the slight role played by legislation, legal
changes under the Principate were effected mainly by
changes in interpretation, relying on juridical logic with
its precedent-based mindset. Between legal certainty
and fairness, there was room only for gradual development of law by means of interpretation of interpreta-

tion, conditional upon the continued validity of old law: *minime sunt mutanda, quae interpretationem certam semper habuerunt* ('by no means must those things be changed that have always had a solid interpretation', Dig. 1,3,23). Established law, too, was adjusted only in small stages: *optima legum interpres consuetudo* ('the best *interpretatio* of the law is custom', Dig. 1,3,37). Of course in arcane legal criticism the historical legislator took second place to the 'rational' impulse. The means used to this end were not only interpretation 'according to the sense' (*ex sententia*), but also reinterpretation of texts by so-called 'identifying interpretation', giving new content to old terms with the aid of *intellegitur, videtur* ('by which is understood') or *continetur* ('this comprises') [2. 42ff.]: the effect of such *interpretatio* growing alongside the text [7. 287] was to blend the letter and the spirit into one.

C. Interpretatio as a source of the law

Juridical *interpretatio*, which typically provides the people with its law in the form of → *responsa* (opinions) (Cic. Leg. 1,14: *interpretari et responsitare*; cf. Dig. 34,1,20,1), depends on its own formalized authority and specific methods. The interpretive authority of the → *pontifices* derived from their priesthood, that of late Republican jurisprudence from its honorary status (→ *iuris prudentia*), and under the Principate from the → *auctoritas principis*. But the *interpretatio* did not become fully valid until it received the assent of the interpretorial body [8. 81ff.], expressed as a *plerisque respondetur* ('is approved by the majority') or *placet/placuit* ('is recognized'). This body is referred to in Roman catalogues of legal sources: Pomponius' *interpretatio*, Gaius' (Inst. 1,2) *responsa* and Papinian's (Dig. 1,1,7 pr.) *auctoritas prudentium*.

D. Methods

Contrary to rhetorical allusion [2. 22ff.; 6. 669ff.], juridical *interpretatio* turned not on the historical legislator, but on the 'rational' legal impetus (Dig. 1,3,18). Thus, sometimes displaced by *cognitio* (insight) (Cic. Off. 2,65), it methodically followed the autonomous canon of rules of juridical logic, seeking on the basis of individual cases to 'improve' the law by conclusions based on analogy, magnitude, reversal and absurdity. The goal claimed by the jurists of the Principate is to make established law more precise (Dig. 1,3,11 *certius statuere*, 'define more precisely'), to support it on a continuous basis (Dig. 35,1,64,1 *adiuvari*), to add it (Dig. 1,3,13 *suppleri*), to extend it 'to similar cases' (*ad similia*, Dig. 1,3,12) and to perfect it (Dig. 23,5,4 *plenius* or Dig. 1,4,3 *plenissime interpretari*). *Interpretatio* embraces analogy (Gai. Inst. 1,165) as well as restriction (Dig. 50,16,120 *interpretatione coangustatum*).

Interpretive freedom is attested by the formula *aliter interpretantibus* (Dig. 18,1,77; 18,1,80 pr.; 34,2,39 pr.), by which an alternative *interpretatio* is quashed owing to its unacceptable consequences. Outcomes are approached by means of many value-related adjectives

(such as *durior, severa* for severity, *benignior, humanior* for mildness). *Interpretatio* serves to balance disadvantage (Dig. 13,5,17 *aequum est succurri reo ... iusta interpretatio*, 'it is just to help the accused by means of correct *interpretatio*'); penal law is interpreted so as to be *benignius* ('more benign') to the accused (cf. Dig. 50,17,155,2), manumissions interpreted so as to favour freedom (e.g. Dig. 40,5,24,10: *favor libertatis suadet, ut interpretemur*, 'the primacy of freedom advises us towards *interpretatio*'). Interpretation in favour of the ward is called *propter utilitatem benignior* (Gai. Inst. 3,109) or *pro favore pupillorum latior interpretatio facta* (Dig. 22,1,1,3).

The creativity already typical of ancient Roman semantic interpretation is attested by the modelling after legal transactions of priestly jurisprudence [6. 330ff., 581ff.]. Against this background, Q. → Mucius Pontifex decries the 'perversion' of *scripta simplicium* ('the writings of simple men') by *interpretatio disertorum* (*interpretatio* by eloquent minds, Cic. Brut. 196), Cicero the pettifogging *interpretatio malitiosa*, which turns the *summum ius* ('summit of justice') into *summa iniuria* ('summit of injustice') (Off. 1,33).

E. Interpretatio of legal transactions

Legal transactions were in principle treated in the same way as established law [6. 330, 580] – namely in contradistinction to so-called conclusive practice (Dig. 23,3,30; 28,4,2; cf. [4. 260, 269f.]) – as a normative text in the area of tension between what is said and what is meant. Although recourse to *voluntas* ('intent') in preference to *opinio singulorum* ('single opinion', Dig. 33,10,7,1f.) – as opposed to *communis usus* ('general usage') – was possible here (cf. [4. 253, 256; 6. 653f., 672f.]), even in this respect what one could call interpretive formalism was not entirely superseded until the end of the Principate [1. 34ff., 92ff., 155ff.; 6. 581]. Even in wills, unambiguous wording was paramount (Dig. 32,29 pr. *verborum interpretatio*). It was in the interpretation of affairs between living individuals (Dig. 50,16,125 *ad id quod actum est interpretationem redigendam*: 'to extend *interpretatio* to real actions'), with its obligation to preserve trust, that the burden of responsibility was placed firmly upon the shoulders of the individual making a declaration [4. 264]: an obscure *pactum* was interpreted as being *contra venditorem* ('against the interests of the seller', Dig. 50,17,172 pr.), the stipulation *contra stipulatorem* ('against the interests of the promisee', Dig. 45,1,38,18) or *secundum promissorem* ('favouring the promisor', Dig. 45,1,99 pr.).

F. The ban on interpretation in late antiquity

Because of the great significance of *interpretatio*, law during the Principate is termed jurists' law [6. 495ff.]. Within its purlieu, even the *princeps* was only an interpretor of the law [5. 379ff.], who followed the majority voice of the interpretive body [7. 149ff.] and intervened in private law only in isolated cases [7. 168f.]. But late antiquity sees the primacy of the imperial patronate over *interpretatio*, in an interpretive monopoly: from the time of Diocletian (from AD 284), the finding of law by interpretive means was displaced by the determination of law by supreme authority [1. 362f.]. In late antiquity, officials tended to 'defer' (*venerari*) to imperial law rather than interpret it (Symmachus, Relat. 30,4; cf. [5. 389, 403]). The *Interpretationes* to the → *Codex Theodosianus* and the *Pauli Sententiae* (→ Iulius [IV 16] Paulus) are of Visigoth origin (→ *Lex Romana Visigothorum*). Constantine the Great forbade *interpretatio*, 'mediating' as it did between the law and justice (*interposita interpretatio*, Cod. Theod. 1,2,3; cf. [5. 392f., 404]); Marcianus relies only on *imperatoria interpretatio* (Nov. Marciana 4 pr.; cf. [8. 163f.]); Justinian regards the interpretors of law as a source of dissension, and forbids *legum interpretationes* (Const. Tanta § 21) as *perversiones* [3. 98; 5. 405f.]: only what was called the authentic interpretation of the law by the emperor as sole 'creator and interpretor of laws' (*tam conditor quam interpres legum*, Cod. Iust. 1,14,12,5) was permitted.

1 SCHULZ   2 U. WESEL, Rhet. Statuslehre und die Gesetzesauslegung der röm. Juristen, 1967   3 M. FUHRMANN, I., in: Sympotica F. Wieacker, 1970, 80–110   4 P. VOCI, Interpretazione del negozio giuridico, Enciclopedia del Diritto 22, 1972, 252–277   5 J. GAUDEMET, Études de droit romain I, 1979, 375–409   6 Wieacker, RRG   7 M. BRETONE, Storia del diritto romano, 1987   8 F. GALLO, Interpretazione e formazione consuetudinaria del diritto, ²1993.   T.G.

II. RELIGION

Interpretatio graeca/interpretatio romana is the identification of a foreign divinity with a member of the indigenous pantheon, widespread in the Graeco-Roman world. The term *interpretatio romana* is attested in antiquity in association with Germanic gods in Tacitus' *Germania* (ch. 43). By analogy, the expression *interpretatio graeca* is used as modern technical term for the Greek phenomenon. The (little researched) phenomenon is originally a sign of the natural interrelationships between polytheistic systems; it is used secondarily in determining the origins of gods and as an expression of henotheistic tendencies.

In its true form, the *interpretatio graeca/interpretatio romana* treats theonyms as appellatives, thus translating a god's name from the foreign language into the vernacular; by analogy, in bilingual texts human names can be translated from one language into another (Lydian Bakivalis = Greek *Dionysíklēs*). This is already attested by Ancient Oriental Sumerian-Akkadian god lists, which belong in the lexicographical tradition of Ancient Oriental literate cultures. The same phenomenon must be assumed to have occurred in Greek by the adoption from the beginning of Near Eastern myths and mythological motifs into the mythology of the gods; the Hesiodic myth of succession suggests the iden-

tification of → Uranus with Anu, → Cronus with Enki (or with the Hittite Kumarbi), → Zeus with → Marduk (or with the Hittite weather god). *Interpretatio graeca* then becomes explicit in Herodotus, who systematically uses Greek names even for non-Greek gods [1], on rare occasions using the foreign name as an → epiclesis (Zeus Belos in Babylon, Hdt. 1,181,2). Exceptions are possible not only when a divinity does not have an equivalent (such as Janus in Greek, the Persian Mithras in the Graeco-Roman west), but also when the divinity in question is known by its indigenous name beyond its original locality, whether due to its significance, to the cult's original adherents' having transported it beyond their borders, or to the fact that under its indigenous name it acquires an additional meaning. Thus Herodotus uses the names Isis and Osiris, although he acknowledges that they are translated as Demeter and Dionysus (Hdt. 2,59,2, cf. 2,42,2); in Athens, the Thracian divinity → Bendis usually retains her indigenous name, in spite of her *interpretatio graeca* as Artemis, and the mysteries of → Isis, widely known from the Hellenistic period, build upon the exotic flavour lent by the retention of the name, as later do those of → Mithras.

In the course of the Hellenization/Romanization of the ancient Mediterranean world, *interpretatio graeca/interpretatio romana* extends its scope in that local indigenous divinities are given Greek or Latin names, even in the cult and even by local worshippers, as is shown by bilingual inscriptions from Lydia and Lycia. Local peculiarities are picked up by differentiation through epicleses; this is true of Hellenized Anatolia as well as Romanized Gaul [2]. Conversely, even the *interpretatio graeca/interpretatio romana* of a divinity of the politically dominant power is attested in the terms of the conquered people, as in the case of a sacral statute for the Persian cult, written in Greek, from the period of the Persian occupation of Sardis, in which the reference throughout is to Zeus [3].

The causes for the use of a particular *interpretatio* are by no means uniform, and cannot always easily be established, as is shown by a comparison of Herodotus' identifications with the corresponding divinities; in each case there is a selection of individual aspects of the ritual, occasionally also of the myth. Under the pressure of a dominant religious culture, local peculiarities not taken up in the *interpretatio* may in course of time decline or even disappear, as happened with most of the Roman and probably also countless Celtic gods. Habituation to the *interpretatio* also leads to situations where in Greek or Latin texts the indigenous name is used in such a specialized way as regularly to cause interpretors great problems; this is shown with particular clarity in the multitude of scholia to the catalogue of Celtic gods with human sacrifice in Luc. 1,445 [4].

Herodotus also attests the first extension of the *interpretatio graeca* to embrace a hypothesis involving the diffusion of rites and gods' names: according to him, almost all the names of the Greek gods as well as their rites came from the Egyptians to the → Pelasgians and thence to the Greeks (Hdt. 2,50–52). Such a derivation persists in sections of the tradition into late antiquity, when Iamblichus derives the 'true' names of the gods, as used in magical and theurgical ritual, from Egyptian and Assyrian, the languages closest to the gods (Iambl. Myst. 7,4).

Consequence of such a hypothesis of diffusion leads, in an important theological development, to the beginnings of henotheism [5]. If the names can be translated, then behind the various names must be one sole divine essence. The hypothesis has been developed to a particular extent for the cult of → Isis; in the course of her expansion during the Hellenistic and Imperial periods, she became an all-embracing goddess, in cult and theology given the epiclesis Polyonymos ('many-named') or Myrionymos ('ten-thousand-named'); in a long list, Apul. Met. 11,4 equates her with numerous other goddesses (cf. also Simpl. In Aristotelis Physica, CAG 9, 641,33).

Interpretatio graeca/interpretatio romana is therefore a phenomenon of linguistic concept. It may have its effect on iconography: the iconography of the foreign divinity may displace that of the indigenous one or create it from scratch – thus the Etruscan and Roman divinities almost exclusively adopt the iconography of their Greek parallels. Conversely, in spite of adoption, value may be ascribed to the retention of indigenous attributes; this is particularly true in the case of Gaulish divinities.

1 W. Burkert, Herodot über die Namen der Götter: Polytheismus als histor. Problem, in: MH 42, 1985, 121–132 2 G. Wissowa, Interpretatio Romana, in: ARW 19, 1918, 1–49 3 L. Robert, Une nouvelle inscription grecque de Sardes. Règlement de l'autorité perse relatif au culte de Zeus, in: CRAI 1975, 306–330 4 F. Graf, Menschenopfer in der Burgerbibliothek. Anmerkungen zum Götterkatalog der "Commenta Bernensia" zu Lucan 1,445, in: Arch. der Schweiz 14, 1991, 136–143 5 H. S. Versnel, Inconsistencies in Greek and Roman Rel., vol. 1: Ter Unus. Isis, Dionysos, Hermes. Three Studies in Henotheism, 1990. F.G.

Interregnum see → Interrex

Interrex (literally 'interim king'). The Roman official who had to conduct the election of a *suffectus* when someone holding the highest office became incapacitated. The word and the non-collegial nature of the office suggest that it has its origins in the period of kings (Liv. 1,17,12; Cic. Rep. 2,12,23; Plut. Numa 2). In the Republic the *interrex* intervened when the supreme office became vacant with the death of both consuls (*interregnum*) and substitute elections had to be held that for consuls would normally be held by a consul who was still in office. This is primarily based on the assumption that only consuls could conduct the auspication at which the gods gave their approval to the election process. Without a consul, however, the qualification to conduct an auspication remained with those who are at least qualified to assume the consulate. In the early period these were the patrician senators of the Senate. Even later, when plebeians were able to be appointed to the consulate, the qualification to revive the consular auspices remained with the patrician senators. Thus on a vacancy the auspices returned, as it were, to the Senate (*auspicia ad patres redierant*, Liv. 1,32,1; Cic. Leg. 3,4,9), whose task it then was to create an executive from its ranks that, 'after conducting the auspices' (*auspicato*) could take charge of the organisation of the suffect-elections of consuls. To this end, the patrician senators appointed one of their number as *interrex*, who after five days in office named someone else who likewise ruled for five days, and so on until the consular elections were completed. These elections were held after clearing away all constitutional obstacles as quickly as possible. The first *interrex*, however, could not conduct them, probably because, as the first in the chain of *interreges*, he was elected without auspication. The notion that the (patrician) Senate is the original source of the highest official power, to whom the initiative of appointing officials returned when dealing with the highest magistrature, is probably to be seen as reflecting the executive's strong dependence on the Senate. The last *interrex* held office in 52 BC. However, the possibility of an interregnum was still considered in 43 BC.

By analogy with Rome, the municipalities also had *interreges* on vacancy of the highest municipal office. Augustus replaced them with prefects.

→ Magistratus

A. Heuss, in: ZRG 64, 1944, 79ff.; Mommsen, Staatsrecht 1 (3), 647–661; P. Willems, Le Sénat de la république romaine, 1885 (2), 2, 10ff. (List of *i.*). C.G.

Interrogatio Generally refers to questioning before the court and has a narrower technical meaning in the Roman criminal procedure of the → *iudicium publicum* as *interrogatio legibus* and as *interrogatio in iure* in civil procedure. The former refers to the question put to the defendant, whether he pleaded guilty; it was occasionally used in the sources of the late Roman Republic to denote the indictment by the → *quaestio*. The latter, the questioning of the defendant before the court magistrate, was a means for the plaintiff to clarify liability as the proper party, hence whether he really had the correct plaintiff before him. A separate Digest title (Dig. 11,1) was devoted to the *interrogatio in iure*, which has a specific meaning in the case of an action against the heir and in the case of a noxal action. For the latter, it was necessary to ensure that the defendant had the wrongdoer in his legal and physical control, and for the former, whether and to what extent he claimed to be the heir. If the defendant answered incorrectly, it then fell to be determined whether this gave rise to the impression of a liability which did not actually exist or did not exist to such a great degree, and he was tried by separate *actiones interrogatoriae*, which feigned the correctness of the wrong answer. However, if he denied, wholly or in part, his liability which did actually exist, and the plaintiff was able to prove this, it brought him disadvantages which generally consisted of increased liability.

M. KASER, K. HACKL, Das röm. Zivilprozeßrecht, ²1997, 251ff.; M. LEMOSSE, Actiones interrogatoriae, in: Labeo 34, 1988, 7–17.   A. VÖ.

Intertextuality
A. CONCEPT B. INTERTEXTUALITY AND CLASSICAL PHILOLOGY C. AESTHETIC POTENTIAL OF PRODUCTION AND RECEPTION

A. CONCEPT
In the 1960s, criticism of the work-immanent interpretation of literary texts as closed systems was voiced in the aesthetics of reception of H. R. JAUSS and in intertextuality as shaped by the semiotician JULIA KRISTEVA. KRISTEVA was influenced by Mikhail BAKHTIN's concept of the literary text as an open system: no text originates in a socio-historical vacuum; even at the very moment of its production it represents a dialogue with other literary and non-literary texts and is at the same time the (fragmented) processing of social reality. KRISTEVA radicalized this position; she replaced the traditional interpretation of the text as a closed system with one single fixed meaning with the notion of the text as an intertext: at the very moment of its production every text is already a mosaic of various other texts and quotations. It therefore represents no static entity but is a process of continuous productivity, in the course of which other (pre-)texts are absorbed and transformed, overlap and penetrate each other. The influence of the pre-texts on the text results in its production per se – and thus ultimately in permanent semantic change [9]. In expanding BAKHTIN's position, KRISTEVA not only opened up the immanent concept of the text – every cultural system, every extra-literary structure and finally society as a whole was defined as 'text', which penetrates the intertext –, but she also replaced the author, omnipotent in traditional textual analysis, with the subjectless productivity of texts (the influence of the structural concept of Marxist-oriented social theory is quite obvious here): the sign in the text, released from its referential significate, communicates with other signs in a potentially infinite process of intertextual communication without being bound to the intentionality of the subject/author.

B. INTERTEXTUALITY AND CLASSICAL PHILOLOGY
KRISTEVA's program of the universal intertext was continued in deconstructionism. At the same time, in critical dialogue with this universalistic approach and taking into account the needs of philologists, the text-analytical method of a specific intertextuality was formulated, which described the conscious, intended and marked relations between a text and literary pre-texts. This descriptive concept of intertextuality not only negates the opening up of the concept of the text but at the same time retains the notion of authorial intentionality. It is important that in distinguishing between an intertextuality of an aesthetics of production and an intertextuality of an aesthetic of reception, the relative openness of the literary text's capacity to generate meaning is maintained: not all intertextual relations intended by the author have to be realized by the recipient for a direct understanding of the text, just as the recipient, on the basis of previous textual experiences establishes intertextual relations not provided or intended by the author. In practice, intertextuality promised to offer a refined methodology for describing the relations between literary texts [3; 7; 14], but the instruments of textual analysis were sufficiently well-known from traditional philological work (adaptation, allusion, imitation, parody, travesty, translation, quotation), frequently dispensing with the perspective of the textual dialogue with extra-literary systems that was central for KRISTEVA [6; 12].

The intention of the author and the unity of the transmitted text have not lost their appeal for classical philologists. Here, intertextuality mostly in its restricted text-analytical form, is employed in analyzing the use of Greek precursors and models in Latin literature. The concept of intertextuality can also be used to demonstrate the explicit or implicit references by Latin authors to their Roman predecessors as the history of genres: for example, the line of succession Ennius – Lucretius – Virgil – Ovid – Lucan – Statius (→ Epic). The compatibility of the concept of intertextuality with the vocabulary of traditional philological work (allusion, influence, imitatio, afterlife, source criticism) has, however, caused many a critic to question the novelty value of intertextuality applied to ancient texts.

C. AESTHETIC POTENTIAL OF PRODUCTION AND RECEPTION
This gradual levelling of the concept of intertextuality was to be countered by recalling the aesthetical potential of its production and reception. By drawing on the concept of μίμησις (→ mímēsis) /imitatio in antiquity and the Renaissance, traditional philology studies allusions and parallels from the perspective of the imitation of canonical models. As the history of ancient literature has shown, this classicist concept of literature frequently leads to an implicit or open devaluation of the imitators as epigones. By contrast, intertextuality can analyze the production of a text as an adaptation – either an affirmative or a subversive-negating one, and as a re-evaluation of available literary traditions in a new socio-political context: for example, Virgil's reinterpretation of the Homeric heroes and the epic tradition against the background of Augustan society [1; 10]; or the intertextual collage of the very different textual variations in Seneca's Apocolocyntosis [2]; or the adaptation of the Virgilian tradition by Ovid and the

authors of the so-called 'Silver Age' of Latin Literature, not for the purpose of *imitatio* of a literary canon but as a means of critically calling into question that very tradition. [8].

At the same time, intertextuality problematizes reception. In the classical tradition of the focus on the work and its author it is acknowledged that the text has an aesthetic autonomy. The purpose of interpretation is to reconstruct its intention. Complementarily, the appeal of JAUSS' aesthetics of reception can be explained by its attempt to reconstruct a historically concrete horizon of a reader's expectations. However, just as the author's intention is not directly accessible to the reader, the notion of a homogeneous horizon of expectations of a historically tangible readership remains heuristically elusive [11; 13]. Thus, the text as intertext remains the key category for analysis, as the accumulation and processing of earlier textual experiences and expectations that are not entirely controlled by the author nor the reader. The maximum requirement of a universal and subjectless intertext has not proved productive in practice. Nevertheless, the concept of intertextuality, with its idea of the text as productivity, has the potential to replace the static concepts of traditional literary criticism with a dynamic aesthetics of production and aesthetics of reception, which also takes into account findings from the psychology of production and reading.

1 A. BARCHIESI, La traccia del modello, 1984　2 J. BLÄNS-DORF, Senecas *Apocolocyntosis* und die Intertextualitäts-Theorie, in: Poetica 18, 1986, 1–26　3 U. BROICH, M. PFISTER, I., 1985, 1–58　4 G. B. CONTE, Memoria dei poeti e sistema letterario, ²1985　5 Id., A. BARCHIESI, Imitazione e arte allusiva, in: Id. (ed.), Lo spazio letterario di Roma antica, 1989, 1, 81–114　6 O. ETTE, I., in: Romanist. Zeitschr. f. Lit.-Gesch. 9, 1985, 497–522　7 J. HELBIG, I. und Markierung, 1996　8 S. HINDS, Allusion and Intertext. Dynamics of appropriation in Roman poetry, 1998　9 J. KRISTEVA, Séméiotiké, 1969　10 R. O. A. M. LYNE, Further voices in Vergil's Aeneid, 1987　11 Id., Vergil's Aeneid: subversion by intertextuality, in: G&R; 41, 1994, 187–204　12 H.-P. MAI, Bypassing intertextuality, in: H. F. PLETT (ed.), Intertextuality, 1991, 30–59　13 R. R. NAUTA, Historicizing reading: the aesthetics of reception and Horace's 'Soracte Ode', in: I. DE JONG, J. P. SULLIVAN (ed.), Modern critical theory and Classical literature, 1994, 207–230　14 H. F. PLETT, Intertextualities, in: Id. (ed.), Intertextuality, 1991, 3–29.

A.BEN.

Intestabilis In Roman law, legally incapable of being a witness (*testis*). The Inst. Iust. (2,10,6) lists as *intestabiles*: women, minors, slaves, the dumb, the deaf, the mentally ill, legally incapacitated wastrels and those who had been declared *improbus* (dishonourable) and *intestabilis* by a special law. Legal arrangements of this kind result, for example, (according to Ulp. Dig. 47,10,5,9) from the *lex Cornelia de iniuriis* against authors or distributors of articles with offensive content or (according to Cassius Dig. 1,9,2) from the *lex Iulia* *de repetundis* against those removed from the Senate owing to lack of morality. The Law of the Twelve Tablets (c. 450 BC) already associated *intestabilis* with the incapacity to make a → *testamentum* (Gell. NA 15,13,11).

G.S.

Intestatus A person who died without leaving a valid testament. Under Roman *ius civile* the estate of the deceased firstly devolved upon the → *sui heredes*, or else upon the agnatic relatives of the next degree (*agnati proximi*). According to the Law of the Twelve Tables (5th cent. AD), *sui* became *heredes* in the case of succession, *agnati* only acquired property (*familia*, XII 5.4) and became successors through → *usucapio*; in classical Roman law (1st–3rd cent. AD) agnates became successors through → *aditio hereditatis*. From the 2nd cent. BC on, agnatic relatives in the female line from the 3rd degree down had no right of succession (→ *lex Voconia*). If all *agnati proximi* disclaimed, more distant relatives were not called; the estate simply devolved upon the *gens* relatives. The law of succession of the *gentiles* was still alive in the 1st cent. BC (Suet. Caes. 1,1; Cic. De or. 1,39,176), but then died out (Gai. Inst. 3,17). The intestate succession of a freedman devolved upon his *sui*, or else upon the *patronus* and his agnatic descendants. → Latini Iuniani did not succeed since upon their death they were again regarded as slaves (Gai. Inst. 3,56).

In the late Republic the praetor created a new order of succession which partially superseded the civil law (→ *bonorum possessio*). He called (1) the *sui heredes* together with the emancipated children who had left the agnatic system by virtue of their emancipation (*liberi*), (2) the civil heirs by succession (*legitimi*: *sui* and *agnati*), (3) the blood relatives up to the 6th degree and the children of *sobrini* (great grandchildren descending from the same great-grandparents, → *cognati*), (4) the *patronus* and the descendants of the *patronus* (*familia patroni*) as well as (5) the *patronus* of a *patronus* who had himself been freed and his children and parents (*patronus patroni*), (6) the spouses (*vir et uxor*), (7) the cognates of the *patronus* (*cognati manumissoris*). Application periods were in force for each class; someone who had missed the application in a class could make it in another class to which he was called (*sui* e.g. in the classes of the *liberi*, *legitimi* and *cognati*).

The *lex Papia* (AD 9) gave a patron of a wealthy freedman as well as a patroness and daughter of a patron with *ius liberorum* (child privileges) a civil right of succession in addition to the *sui* of a freedman (Gai. Inst. 3,42; 46; 50). The SC *Tertullianum* (under Hadrian) gave a mother (who, if she was → *manus*-free, did not have a civil right of succession) with *ius liberorum* the civil right of succession after her children; the SC *Orfitianum* (AD 178) gave the children a civil right of succession after their mother. Caduciary entitlement (→ *caducum*) did not encroach upon intestate succession. An heir by intestate succession could only be burdened with entailed estates.

The classical law of intestate succession was repealed by amending statutes by Nov. 118 and 127 (AD 543, 548) in favour of cognate succession which prevailed in German common law (until 1889).

→ Agnatio; → Cognatio; → Consanguinei; → Succession, law of III. C.

1 HONSELL/MAYER-MALY/SELB, 442ff.   2 KASER, RPR I, 95ff.; 695ff.; II, 497ff.   3 H. L. W. NELSON, U. MANTHE, Gai Institutiones III 1–87, 1992, 51ff., 214ff.   4 P. VOCI, Diritto ereditario romano II, ²1963, 3ff.   5 A. WATSON, The Law of Succession in the Later Roman Republic, 1971, 175ff.   U.M.

Intoxicating substances
I. DEFINITION II. ALCOHOL
III. PHARMACEUTICALS AND ANAESTHETICS
IV. CULTIC AND RITUAL USE

I. DEFINITION
Intoxicating substances are natural drugs (e.g. henbane) or agents created through technical modification (e.g. alcohol). In antiquity they were almost always derived from plants and their psychotropic effect on the central nervous system ranged from slightly stimulating, causing optical or acoustic hallucinations, libido-enhancing sensations and ecstatic states to a complete loss of consciousness and senses. The physical and psychic form of the enhanced emotional state depends on the nature and dose of the agent used but also on the consumer's constitution and in part on external, situational and cultural circumstances. The use of intoxicants can be demonstrated since the prehistoric period and is found in virtually all cultures.

II. ALCOHOL
The pure agent alcohol (Arabic, originally 'antimon [powder]') was unknown in antiquity. The earliest known alcoholic intoxicant is → mead, a brew made from honey and water to which additional ingredients were added in later periods (cf. Columella 12,12; Plin. HN 14,113 f.). Since the late 4th millennium → ale of different varieties (the basic ingredient was usually barley malt, generally brewed without hops) became popular in the Ancient Orient [12]. It was not able to establish itself throughout Greece, where it had been known since about 700 BC (ζῦθος/zýthos); the same happened in Rome (zythum, cer(e)visia).

→ Wine (Greek οἶνος/oínos < Ϝοῖνος = Latin vinum), pressed from the grape (Vitis vinifera), was already enjoyed in the Mycenaean period, as is evident from → Linear B tablets and finds of drinking vessels. It was usually diluted with water (Latin dilutum, as opposed to merum, 'undiluted wine'). It was the most important intoxicant in antiquity (daily drug, basic foodstuff). There were no high-alcohol beverages due to an absence of suitable distillation procedures. Ethanol, which was formed during fermentation – quality wine had an alcohol content of up to 16% – reduced inhibitions and usually had a euphoric effect: for example,

Odysseus advised the Greeks not to go into battle sober (Hom. Il. 19,155–170). However, the drowsiness-causing effect of heavy consumption is evident in Odysseus' fight with the cyclops → Polyphemus, to whom he gave undiluted wine (Hom. Od. 9,345–374). The positive effect of moderate alcohol consumption was often described (e.g. Thgn. 1,475–498; Hor. Carm. 1,38; 2,19). During the first half of the 4th cent. BC the literary (sub-)genera of the 'symposium' (συμπόσιον, 'drinking-bout', cf. Plato [1], Xenophon; → Symposium literature) established itself. It ultimately is based on the positive stimulating effect of communal alcohol consumption by men and provided a framework for the discussion of a broad range of topics.

The proverb that wine reveals truth stems from Alcaeus, a writer of drinking-poetry (Alc. 66d, cf. Hor. Sat. 1,4,89 and the medieval in vino veritas). The implied danger of a loss of inhibitions due to excessive wine use has been written about since the earliest times (Hom. Od. 16,292–294). → Pittacus of Mytilene passed a law in the 6th cent. BC that violence in a drunken state was to be punished more harshly than in a sober state (Aristot. Pol. 2,1274b 13 with critical attitude). A discussion of the problem of addiction is found at the latest in the Attic → comedy. It closely links psychological and physical dependency to intoxicant consumption. Although the accusation of excess wine consumption against women in Aristoph. Thesm. 735–738 is unjustified in practice, it shows that there was an awareness of the problem. In fact, the heavy wine consumption of Aristophanes' rival Cratinus was even a literary subject: after allusions (Aristoph. Equ. 525–536), → Cratinus [1] appeared in a self-deprecating manner in his piece Pytínē as a frail and drunken old man (fr. 181–199 EDMONDS). The Peripatetic school (→ Peripatos) intensively discussed the topic of intoxication and its consequences (Aristot. Pr. 3).

Latin differentiates temporary drunkenness (ebrietas) from habitual drinking (ebriositas, cf. Cic. Tusc. 4,27). According to modern estimates, the per capita wine consumption of the average urban Roman male was 0.8–1 l per day [25. 91] and the number of literary mentions suggest that alcoholism [9. 24] was more common among the Romans than the Greeks (Plin. HN 14,137–148; Cic. Phil. 2,62 and 101: reproach of furiosa vinolentia ('excessive wine consumption') against Marcus Antonius [I 9]; see Sen. Ep. 83,25; Porcius [I 7] Cato Uticensis allegedly also tended towards (over-) abundant alcohol consumption (cf. Mart. 2,89; Plut. Cato Minor 6). Nevertheless, there are relevant examples on the Greek side as well, including Alexander [4] the Great, who killed his friend Clitus while drunk (Curt. 8,1,51 f.). A well-developed long-distance trade (→ Commerce, with map) underpinned the wine supply throughout the entire Roman empire. The wine trade was a significant economic factor with large revenues.

Wines, especially fruit wines, were usually used as dietetic drugs against various ailments (Hippoc. De affectionibus 52; Cels. De medicina 3,6,17; Plin. HN

14,100), Dioscorides even administered wine against snake venom (5,11 WELLMANN). Since wine also was often the solvent for other medication (e.g., Cels. ibid. 5,20,4) wine consumption during illness could be high.

III. PHARMACEUTICALS AND ANAESTHETICS

A few intoxicants, some quite potent, were among the large number of pharmaceuticals known in antiquity. → Poppy (Greek μήκων/*mḗkōn*) is the oldest and has been found in prehistoric contexts in Europe (post settlements on Swiss lakes). In the Ancient Orient it is encountered in Assyrian texts [6; 7], the Egyptians were already familiar with it in 1600 BC (Papyrus Ebers) [3. 19; 14. 3 f.]; the Egyptians possibly also used the → lotus (*Nymphaea* sp.) as an intoxicant [4. 12]. The analgesic that Helen mixes into the heroes' wine (Hom. Od. 4,219–229) has been identified as a poppy extract [3. 20]. As is evident from a statue of the 'Poppy Goddess' dating to 1500 BC [6; 14. 4], raw opium, which is obtained by incising the seed capsules of the opium poppy (*Papaver somniferum*) and then drying the milky juice (on harvesting, cf. Dioscorides 4,64 WELLMANN), was already used in the Minoan period. It contains more than 35 alkaloids; morphine, the main active ingredient, has an analgesic, sedative-hypnotic and respiration-depressing effect (cf. e.g. the sleeping agent of Dioscorides 4,63 WELLMANN) [23. 175–179]. Opium was an important medication of the Hippocratic school. The intoxicants opium and wine were major items in the ingredient list of theriac, which was still used in the early 18th cent. (Gal. De antidotis 2,1,2). For the most part, there are no warnings against a chronic use of opium in ancient literature.

Occasionally, intoxicants were used as aphrodisiacs or because of the pleasantness of the intoxicating effect (Dioscorides 4,73 WELLMANN).

In major surgical interventions (→ Surgery), intoxicants were used as anaesthetics (Dioscorides 4,75 WELLMANN). Apart from wine and poppy, → henbane (*Hyoscyamus* sp.), which was already known in Mesopotamia, was used. Its major alkaloids scopolamine and hyoscyamine initially produce visions that are followed by a strong sleepiness. Mandrake was often used as an anaesthetic, occasionally also → hemlock (*Conium maculatum*). They were supplemented by other herbs such as darnel rye grass or bearded darnel (*Lolium temulentum*). They were administered in an infusion or, especially in late antiquity and the Middle Ages, as sleep sponges (*spongia somnifera*) soaked in intoxicants that were placed on the mouth and nose of the patient. A controllable, routine anaesthesia with the principal task of inducing analgesia, eliminating consciousness and defensive reflexes as well as muscle relaxation, was not possible due to fluctuating concentrations of active ingredients and the falsification of ingredients: the effect fluctuated between ineffectiveness and lethal poisoning. The toxicity of these intoxicants was known; for example, Celsus De med. (5,27,12b) prescribed wine mead and donkey's milk as an antidote to henbane (also Scribonius Largus 181).

IV. CULTIC AND RITUAL USE

The use of intoxicants in a cultic and ritual context for the purpose of inducing ecstasy, visions etc. appears logical but is disputed in specific cases, e.g. the question if fly agaric (*Amanita muscaria*) was indeed used together with wine in the cult of → Dionysus (who was considered ecstatic: μαινόμενος/*mainómenos*, Hom. Il. 6,132) and the Eleusinian → Mysteries [22. 58; 11. 632]. The significance of poppy in the cult of → Demeter, although it is an attribute of the goddess as a fertility symbol, is uncertain. It is also unknown what caused the prophetic enrapture of the → Pythia [1] in the Delphic → oracle. The vapours arising there are ruled out as intoxicants. The extent to which intoxicants were used to artificially induce dreams at temple incubations (→ Incubation) is also obscure [18. 99].

Christianity symbolically elevated wine from an everyday drink to a sacred drug (1 Cor 11,28–30); → Paulus [2] clearly rejects intoxication (e.g. Gal 5,21; cf. Aug. Conf. 6,2). However, the Church Fathers did not outright condemn intoxication; thus Isid. Orig. 17,9,30f. mentions the pain-reducing effect of poppy and opium as well as a mixture of mandrake rind and wine.

→ Beverages; → Cult; → Poisons; → Pharmacology; → Viticulture

1 R.S. ATKINSON, T.B. BOULTON (ed.), The History of Anaesthesia, 1987   2 J.BERENDES, Die Pharmazie bei den alten Kulturvölkern, vol. 2, 1891 (repr. 1965) 3 L.BRAND, Illustrierte Gesch. der Anästhesie, 1997, 1–36 4 W.A. EMBODEN, Narcotic Plants. ... Their Origins and Uses, 1979   5 G.JÜTTNER, s. v. Alkohol, LMA 1, 416f. 6 P.G. KRITIKOS, S.N. PAPADAKI, The History of the Poppy and of Opium and Their Expansion in Antiquity in the Eastern Mediterranean, in: Bull. on Narcotics 19, 1967.3, 17ff.; 1967.4, 5ff.   7 A.D. KRIKORIAN, Were the Opium Poppy and Opium Known in the Ancient Near East?, in: JHB 8, 1975, 95–114   8 F.-J.KUHLEN, s. v. R., LMA 7, 479f.   9 J.O. LEIBOWITZ, Studies in the History of Alcoholism, II: Acute Alcoholism in Ancient Greek and Roman Medicine, in: British Journal of Addiction to Alcohol & Other Drugs 1967, 62–86   10 L.MILANO (ed.), Drinking in Ancient Societies, 1994   11 C.RÄTSCH, Enzyklopädie der psychoaktiven Pflanzen, ²1998 12 W.RÖLLIG, Das Bier im alten Mesopotamien, 1970 13 E.M. RUPRECHTSBERGER (ed.), Bier im Alt., 1992 14 H.SCHADEWALDT, Zur Gesch. einiger Rauschdrogen, in: Materia medica Nordmark 24.1–2, 1972, 1–31 15 H.SCHELENZ, Gesch. der Pharmazie, 1904 (repr. 1962) 16 A.SCHMIDT, Drogen und Drogenhandel im Alt., ²1927 17 W.SCHMIDTBAUER, J.VOM SCHEID, Hdb. der Rauschdrogen, ⁶1981   18 R.SCHMITZ, Gesch. der Pharmazie, vol. 1, 1998   19 Id., F. J.KUHLEN, Schmerz- und Betäubungsmittel vor 1600, in: Pharmazie in unserer Zeit 18, 1989, 10–19   20 C.SELTMAN, Wine in the Ancient World, 1957   21 W. VON SODEN, Trunkenheit im Babylon.-Assyr. Schrifttum, in: A.BURGMANN (ed.), Al-bahit. FS J. Henninger 1976, 317–324   22 G.VÖLGER (ed.), Rausch und Realität: Drogen im Kulturvergleich, vol. 1, 1981   23 H.WAGNER, Pharmazeutische Biologie 2: Drogen und ihre Inhaltsstoffe, ⁵1993   24 K.-W. WEEBER, Alkoholismus, in: Id., Alltag im Alten Rom, 1995   25 Id., Die Weinkultur der Römer, 1993.   CH.S.

Intrigue (τὸ μηχάνημα, τὸ τέχνημα; *tò mēchánēma, tò téchnēma*). Already Hom. Od., bks. 19–24 shows the close link between recognition scenes (→ Anagnorisis) and intrigue that is typical of Attic tragedy. *Locus classicus* is Aesch. Cho. Intrigue is missing from almost none of Euripides' plays, so that Aristoph. Thesm. 94 can rightly call him the 'master of the intrigue play'. Euripides composes *anagnórisis*-intrigue dramas especially in his later work. After the recognition, rescue is effected by an intrigue (e.g. Eur. IT 1017ff.; Eur. Hel. 1034ff.). In *Ion* there is a playful reversal: the first (false) *anagnórisis* does not set a rescue in motion but rather the murder of the protagonist. In 'Thesmophoriazousai' Aristophanes parodies this type of tragedy in form and content. Under the influence of Euripides, the authors of the New Comedy (→ Menander, → Plautus, → Terence) develop intrigue as a plot-determining element (cf. the stereotype of the *servus fallax*, the intriguing servant), which makes its way from comedy to the novel as well.
→ Novel

> TH. PAULSEN, Inszenierung des Schicksals, 1992, 172–192; F. SOLMSEN, Zur Gestaltung des Intriguenmotivs in den Tragödien des Sophokles und Euripides, in: E. R. SCHWINGE (ed.), Euripides, 1968, 326–344.   B.Z.

Inula see → Helenium

Inuus Along with → Pales, the Roman tutelary god of cattle herds (Arnob. 3,23); because of the Rutulian cult centre *Castrum Inui* (Verg. Aen. 6,775 and Serv. ad loc.) probably of Old Latin origin. According to Servius, the name is derived from *inire* ('to mount') (Serv. loc. cit.). I. was widely identified with → Pan or → Faunus (Liv. 1,5,2; Serv. loc. cit.; Prob. in Verg. G. 1,10,16; Macrob. Sat. 1,22,2). According to Livy, the → Lupercalia were held in honour of I. (Liv. loc. cit.).   J.S.-A.

Invective Attested as a concept (*invectiva oratio*) from the 4th cent. AD, invective is not sharply defined. Before a wide or restricted public audience, by means of a generally valid canon of values, it seeks to discriminate seriously against or destroy an opponent (possibly indicated indirectly only; through whatever means it employs for the purpose, see → Satire). In a tradition going back to Plato, ψόγος (*psógos*, reproach) forms a contrast with ἔπαινος (*épainos*, praise), encomium and hymn; but, according to Pl. Leg. 934d–936b, in keeping with the theory's instructional aspect, seriously running down or ridiculing someone is not allowed: praise and reproach affirm the code of values and have a pedagogical function (Leg. 829c-e). Praise and reproach are developed as a fixed pair of opposites in rhetoric and are classified as *genos epideiktikon* (*genus demonstrativum/laudativum*) (Aristot. Rh. 1358b 12f.); the definition of the *psógos* (the *vituperatio*) is achieved by forming a contrast with that of the *épainos* (the *laus*) (ibid. 1368a 33–37). Both elements are retained in rhetorical theory, even as the reproach is developed on its

own, particularly in the context of the *progymnasmata*. In terms of a definition for invective it is particularly unsatisfactory that neither the concrete intentionality of the invective is covered nor the special form of identification intended for the audience taken into account. In the case of invective, the listener/reader takes on also the function of the judge. A fixed inventory of defamation is evident [4. 358ff.; 13. 245ff.; 10. 81].

In the Latin domain (for the Greek, see the → iambographers, → satirical (mocking) poems, but also the Old → Comedy and the Attic orators), poetical invective, along with prose invective, is highly developed (*in tam maledica civitate*, Cic. Cael. 38), with a politically conditioned climax in the 1st cent. BC. Elements of invective can be found from early on, not only with the orators (Cato Censorinus 213, Scipio Aemilianus 17, C. Gracchus 43; 58, in each case ⁴ORF), but in all literary genres with an effect on the public (plays, epigrams, satires). In this context → Lucilius occupies a special position. C. Licinius Calvus and → Catullus (*c*. 29; 57 *i.a.*; the social and political implications become increasingly clearer [12; 14]) address defamatory poems to Caesar and Pompey (Suet. Iul. 73; cf. also 49 and COURTNEY 210), M. → Furius [I 9] Bibaculus against Augustus (Tac. Ann. 4,34,4). Catullus, Bibaculus and Horace are mentioned in the same breath by Quint. Inst. 10,1,96, and together with Archilochus, Hipponax and Lucilius by Diomedes [4] (Ars gramm. 1,485). Invective reached its peak with Cicero's orations (see also M. Caelius Rufus 17 ⁴ORF against C. Antonius), which takes account of rhetorical theory in describing a whole life in a derogatory manner [4. 14ff.]. Quint. Inst. 3,7 emphasizes in particular the non-extant speeches against competitors for the consulate, C. Antonius and Catilina, and *In Clodium et Curionem* as well as the *Pisoniana*. After the grammarians of the 4th cent. AD and in the MSS, the Catiline orations were called *invectiones/invectivae*. The *Pisoniana* (for the conventional anti-Epicurean elements [1]) and the (ps.-?)Sallustian Cicero-invectives became exemplary models.

The output of invectives continued in the Imperial period and not infrequently led to death or exile (Tac. Ann. 6,39; 14,48ff.; Suet. Dom. 8,3). A revival of the invective, according to the model Octavian – Antony, conditioned by the power struggles, is discernible under Julian (cf. however also the religiously conditioned 'Orations' in Greg. Naz. or. 4f. against Julian [5. 18ff.]) (Amm. Marc. 21,10,7f.; cf. 22,14,2f.). The integration of the invective into the 'secondary' → epic, with emotional involvement on the part of the narrator, is significant: Claudian's *In Eutropium* and *In Rufinum* are the most important examples. Christian polemical literature, too, is indebted to invective in the way it links ideological-group-specific and personal defamations (e.g. → *Carmen ad quendam senatorem*, → *Carmen contra paganos*), likewise Jerome, who does not spare even his fellow believers (see also Sid. Apoll. Epist. 2,1; cf. 1,11). Derogatory and defamatory poetry was extraordinarily widespread not only in the Middle Ages – including the anthologies; defamatory writings are to be found in any period (evident in the case of Thomas BERNHARD [16]), but especially in the 16th cent. (pamphlet, pasquil).

→ SATIRE

1 PH. DELACY, Cicero's invective against Piso, in: TAPhA 72, 1941, 49–58   2 S. GOZZOLI, La In Pisonem di Cicerone, in: Athenaeum 78, 1990, 451–463   3 J. A. HOLLAR, The traditions of satire and invective in Catullus, thesis Washington Univ. 1972   4 S. KOSTER, Die I. in der griech. und röm. Lit., 1980   5 A. KURMANN, Gregor v. Nazianz, Oratio 4 gegen Julian, 1988   6 H. L. LEVY, Claudian's In Rufinum and the rhetorical ψόγος, in: TAPhA 77, 1946, 57–65   7 J. F. LONG, Claudian's In Eutropium, 1996   8 N. W. MERRILL, Cicero and early Roman invective, thesis Cincinnati, 1975   9 R. G. M. NISBET, M. Tulli Ciceronis in L. Calpurnium Pisonem oratio, 1961, esp. 192ff.   10 U. SCHINDEL, Die I. gegen Cicero und die Theorie der Tadelrede, in: Nachrichten der Akademie der Wiss. in Göttingen, Phil.-Histor. Klasse, 1980, 77–92   11 K. SCOTT, The political propaganda of 40–33 B.C., in: Memories of the American Academy in Rome 11, 1933, 7–49   12 M. B. SKINNER, Parasites and strange bedfellows. A study in Catullus' political imagery, in: Ramus 8, 1979, 137–152   13 W. SÜSS, Ethos, 1910   14 W. J. TATUM, Catullus 79, in: Papers of the Leeds International Latin Seminar 7, 1993, 31–45   15 G. BEBERMEYER, s.v. Schmähschrift (Streitschrift), Reallexikon der dt. Lit.-Gesch. 3, ²1977, 665–678   16 F. VAN INGEN, Thomas Bernhards Holzfällen oder die Kunst der I., in: Amsterdamer Beitr. zur neueren Germanistik 36, 1993, 257–282.

W.-L.L.

Inventio (εὕρεσις, *heúresis*: invention, finding sc. of ideas). In the system of rhetoric, *inventio* denotes the first of five production stages in the compositon of a speech (→ *partes orationis*; apart from *inventio*, → *dispositio*, → *elocutio*, → *memoria*, → *pronuntiatio*). Within the separation of verbal realization (*verba*) and ideas (*res*), which permeates all rhetoric in antiquity and counteracts this quintuple division, the *inventio* together with the *dispositio*, to which it is inseparably linked, belong to the *res* that are conceded a peculiarly concrete status. The *inventio* serves the purpose of finding ideas that are suited to the subject (*aptum*); a disproportion between unimportant *materia* and the effort of argumentation may exist. The use of arguments is not restricted to certain persons, but they should be oriented towards probability and credibility and should ideally be controlled by the ethos of the orator. In antiquity *inventio* is not viewed as an autonomous act of creation as in modern poetic theories where, following a semantic shift, *inventio* denotes the power of imagination per se. Rather, *inventio* is interpreted as the finding through memory (in analogy to the Platonic concept of knowledge). According to this view, the ideas appropriate for a speech already exist in the soul as a store of knowledge of opinions and culturally determined patterns of cognition and perception (*copia rerum*). A good orator has to (re-)acquire that knowledge by means of

in-depth study and, using a memory technique (Cic. Inv. 1,69), has to keep that knowledge in mind and activate it through permanent repetition. Memory is imagined as a space, where in its various parts (Lat. *loci*, Greek *tópoi*) the individual ideas are distributed.

The *inventio* is the complete cognitive penetration of the speech's subject, which is viewed as a construct of typical possibilities. Their specific composition is not obvious at first sight, but has to be found. Apart from person, subject and time etc. (e.g. Quint. Inst. 5,8,4), the *inventio* is also oriented towards questions regarding the relationship of concepts (Cic. Inv. 1,41ff. *adiunctum*: after comparison, opposition, deduction and induction). The hypothesis which shapes the individual case is derived from the wealth of events and situations (*materia*). This raises the question about the → status of the case that is dealt with. Quintilian (Inst. 5,10,20f.) compares the *inventio* to the hunt in which a good huntsman always knows beforehand where to find the game. Using appropriate search categories (→ Topics) the ideas concealed in the *loci* are recalled. For the sake of practical usage, Roman rhetoric simplifies the dialectic and very complicated search categories of Aristotle's pertinent topics and establishes a division based on patterns of argumentation that are related to subjects and people: while Cicero (Inv. passim) believes the number of places in which to find ideas to be limited, because every individual case can be traced back to a general one, Quintilian postulates that what is specific must be learned from the case itself, and that there are arguments that search models cover only vaguely or not at all. Sometimes one has to follow nature rather than art (Quint. Inst. 5,10,103). The fact that ideas are preconceived does by no means exclude originality (*ingenium*) on the part of the individual orator.

The purpose of the *inventio* is the 'finding' and rough pre-sorting of ideas, the persuasiveness and suitability of which are already examined at this point. At the same time, the *inventio* is already oriented towards those parts of the speech (→ *partes orationis*: → *exordium, narratio*, → *argumentatio, peroratio*) that are assigned a particular function in the argumentation and among which the arguments are distributed. Working out the details of the structure of the ideas is left to the *dispositio*. Artificial as the position of the *inventio* may be in the context of rhetoric, on closer inspection it turns out to consist in fundamental *modi* of mental productivity and solving of problems.

1 K.-H. GÖTTERT, Einführung in die Rhet., ²1991, 26f.   2 M. HEATH, I., in: S. E. PORTER (ed.), Handbook of Classical Rhet. in the Hell. Period 330 B.C-A.D. 400, 1997, 89–119   3 J. MARTIN, Ant. Rhet., 1972, 13–51   4 G. UEDING, Klass. Rhet., 1995, 55–65.   C.W.

Invictus ('the undefeated', 'invincible'). Epithet of Roman emperors since → Commodus. Already in the Republican period, this epithet was occasionally bestowed on victorious military leaders (e.g. → Cornelius [I 71] Scipio), It is known that → Traianus [1] bore the

Greek epithet ἀνίκητος/*aníkētos* (of the same meaning). Commodus was the first to turn it into a permanent imperial epithet; this must be understood in the context of his veneration of → Hercules. Only with the Severans (→ Severan dynasty) did *Invictus* lose this connotation and referred to the triumphancy of the emperor, occasionally also *Invictissimus* is found. The title was not yet linked to the cult of → Sol (D.) Invictus (this only developed in the course of the 3rd cent.). At the time of the Tetrarchs (→ Tetrarches IV.), the epithet → *Victor* [3] became more common, but *Invictus* (generally as *Invictissimus*) is retained as a *cognomen* to at least Iustinus [4] II (ILS 833).

S. WEINSTOCK, Victor and Invictus, in: Harvard Theological Review 50, 1957, 211–247; P. KNEISSL, Die Siegestitulatur der röm. Kaiser, 1969. K. G.-A.

Invocatio see → Muse, acclamation of the

Inycon (Ἴνυκον; *Ínykon*). Place in Sicily (Hsch. s.v. Ἰνυκῖνος οἶνος; Steph. Byz. s.v. I.), whose wine was famous. → Charax identifies I. with Camicus, the residence of Cocalus (FGrH 103 F 58). → Hippocrates [4] of Gela held Scythes of Cos and Pythogenes captive in I., before they successfully escaped to Himera (Hdt. 6,23f.). The sophist Hippias is said to have owned more than twenty mines near the 'small village of I.' (Pl. Hp. mai. 282e). I. can be located between Selinus and Acragas, possibly near Camicus (modern S. Angelo Muxaro).

M. MASSA, BTCGI 8, 1990, 303–308; E. MANNI, Geografia fisica et politica della Sicilia antica (Testimonia Siciliae antiqua 1,1), Kokalos Suppl. 4, 1981, 192. GI.MA.

Io (Ἰώ; *Ió*). Daughter of → Inachus, king of Argus (Aesch. PV 589f.; Bacchyl. 19,18 et al.), or of → Peiren (or Peras or Peirasus), king of Tyrins (Hes. Cat. fr. 124), and Melia (Johannes Antiochenus FHG IV 544 fr. 14). Zeus falls in love with her and seduces her in the form of a bull. Out of jealousy, Hera transforms I. into a cow (Aesch. Supp. 299). According to Hes. Cat. fr. 124, I. is transformed by Zeus himself only after their affair in order to deceive Hera (so also Apollod. 2,1,3). According to Aesch. PV 645–686, I. is driven out of the house by her father because of oracles, and is transformed even before her encounter with Zeus. Zeus sweares a false oath to Hera that he has not slept with I., and as a gift presents her with the white cow into which I. has been transformed (Hes. Cat. 124; cf. Aesch. PV 589–592). Hera locks the cow into a grove and has her guarded by the giant → Argus [I 5] (Soph. El. 4f.; Acusilaus FGrH 2 F 26f.; Apollod.). However, Hermes kills Argus on Zeus's orders and frees I. (Aesch. Supp. 305; Bacchyl. 19,25–33; Apollod. 2,1,3). Hera then sends a horsefly that pursues the insane I. (Aesch. PV 589). According to Aesch. PV 567–573, the horsefly is the shade of the dead Argus (cf. Ov. Met. 1,725–727). I. wanders

through northern Greece, the Ionian Sea, which is said to be named after her (Aesch. PV 839–841), as well as the Bosporus (Aesch. PV 733). Travelling through Scythia and Asia, I. reaches Egypt (Aesch. Supp. 540–573; Prom. 707–735; 790–815; 829–847). There she is transformed back into human form by Zeus through the touch of his hand or through his breathing on her, and gives birth to Epaphos, from whom are descended *i.a.* Libye (or Libya) and → Danaos, the father of the Danaids (Aesch. Supp. 313ff.; PV 848–858; Bacchyl. 19,39–43 et al.).

The earliest sources of the myth of I. are epics from the 7th cent.: *Aegimius* (Hes. fr. 294; 296), *Danais* (EpGF p. 141) and *Phoronis* (EpGF p. 153–155). On them are based accounts by historians (Acusilaus FGrH 2 fr. 26f.; Pherecydes FGrH 3 fr. 67; Hdt. 1,1; 2,41; 3,27), as also the treatment of the material by lyric poets and dramatists (Pind. Nem. 4,35; Bacchyl. 19; Aesch. Supp. 291–315; PV 561–900; Soph. Inachus TrGF IV fr. 269a; Eur. Phoen. 247f.; 676–681; 828; IT 394). The title *Io* is attested for two comedies (Sannyrium, CAF I 795 fr. 10–11; Platonius, De differentia comoediarum, CAF I 615 fr. 55). Because of the myth's geographic dimension and because Herodotus identifies I. with Isis, Middle Eastern and Egyptian influence has been assumed. The location in Argus, the link with the cult of Hera and the parallel to the myth of → Proitides are important for the ritual background. [1].

1 W. BURKERT, Homo Necans, 1972, 181–189.

M. v. ALBRECHT, Die Erzählung von I. bei Ovid und Valerius Flaccus, in: WJA, N.S. 3, 1977, 139–148; K. DOWDEN, Death and the Maiden, 1989, 117–145; S. EITREM, s.v. I., RE 9, 1732–1743; N. ICARD-GIAROLIA, s.v. I. (1), LIMC 5.1, 661–665 (with bibliography); F. WEHRLI, I., Dichtung und Kultlegende, in: H. HOMMEL (ed.), Wege zu Aischylos, vol. 2, 1974, 136–148. K.WA.

Iobaritae (Ἰωβαρῖται; *Iōbarîtai*, Ἰοβαρῖται; *Iobarîtai*). Ethnic group in southern Arabia; only mentioned in Ptol. 6,7,24 as neighbours of the Sachalitae (→ Sachalites).

J. TKAČ, s.v. I., RE 9, 1832–1837. J.RE.

Iobates (Ἰοβάτης/*Iobátēs*, 'who strides along powerfully'). King of Lydia (anonymous in Hom. Il. 6,155–197), to whom Proetus sends → Bellerophontes with the 'Uriah letter' (Apollod. 2,30ff.; Hyg. Fab. 57; cf. Plut. Mor. 248a-d). Father of → Stheneboea and Philonoe. An homonymous tragedy by Sophocles has been transmitted in fragmentary form (TrGF IV 297–299); Euripides wrote a *Stheneboea* (TGF p.567).

T. R. BRYCE, The Lycians in Literary and Epigraphic Sources I, 1986, 16–20; 209. RE.ZI.

Iocaste (Ἰοκάστη/*Iokástē*, in older sources also Ἐπικάστη/Epicaste). Daughter of → Menoeceus, sister of → Creon, wife of → Laius, mother and later wife of

→ Oedipus. In spite of the negative oracle of Apollo in Delphi, Laius fathers Oedipus with I. After his birth, Oedipus is abandoned, later kills his father and, after solving the puzzle of the → Sphinx, marries his mother. In the older sources, the gods reveal the incest (Hom. Od. 11, 271–280), whereupon I. kills herself. Here, I. usually has two sons (Phrastor, Laonytos), who are killed in the war with the Minyae. Oedipus fathers his children (→ Eteocles [1], → Polyneices, → Antigone [3], → Ismene [1]) with his second wife → Euryganeia, I.'s sister (Pherecydes, FGrH 3 F 95; Peisander, FGrH 16 F 10; Epimenides, FGrH 457 F 13; Paus. 9,5,10f.). The tragedians are the first to make I. the mother of Oedipus' children (Aesch. Sept. 926ff.; Soph. OT); in Sophocles she hangs herself after the incest is revealed (OT 1235ff.), while later sources show her as a mediator in the war between Eteocles and Polyneices; her failure drives her to suicide (Eur. Phoen.; Hyg. Fab. 243; Stat. Theb. 7,470ff.; 11,315ff.; 642ff.).

BIBLIOGRAPHY: E. BETHE, s.v I., RE 8, 1841–1842; J. M. BREMER, A. M. VAN ERP TAALMAN KIP, S. R. SLINGS, Some Recently Found Greek Poems, 1987, 164–172; I. KRAUSKOPF, s.v. I., LIMC 5.1, 682–683.
ILLUSTRATIONS: I. KRAUSKOPF, s.v. I., LIMC 5.2, 458.
R.HA.

Iocheaira see → Artemis

Iodama (Ἰοδάμα; *Iodáma*). Local deity of Coronea (Boeotia), driven out by Athena. In mythology the daughter of → Itonus, granddaughter of → Amphictyon [2], priestess of Athena Itonia, who turned her to stone with the Gorgoneion (Paus. 9,34,2); in a different tradition mother of Thebe by Zeus, sister of Athena, killed by her out of jealousy (Simonides, FGrH 8 F 1). RE.ZI.

Iohannes (Ἰωάννης; *Iōánnēs*). Well-known persons *i.a.*: I. [1] the Evangelist, I. [4] Chrysostomos, bishop of Constantinople and Homilet, I. [18] Malalas, author of the world chronicle, I. [25] of Gaza, rhetor and poet, I. [33] of Damascus, the theologian, I. [39] Baptistes.

[1] I. the Evangelist
A. TRADITION AND CRITICISM B. THE EVIDENCE OF THE GOSPEL C. RECONSTRUCTION D. INFLUENCE

A. TRADITION AND CRITICISM
According to the inscriptions, the author of a → Gospel (Jo), of three letters and the Apocalypse in the NT is called I. (= J.; the name appears only in Apc. 1:1; 1:4; 1:9; 22:8). Since the end of the 2nd cent. (Iren. adversus haereses 3,1,1; Polycrates of Ephesus according to Euseb. Hist. eccl. 3,31,3; Clem. Al. according to Euseb. Hist. eccl. 6,14,7; Canon Muratori 9 LIETZMANN), he has been widely identified with the 'disciple of the Lord', the son of Zebedee and brother of James who ranked second after Peter among the disciples and in the early church (Mk 1:19; 9:22; Acts 3–4; Gal 2:9). He is said to have been exiled to Patmos under Domi-

tian (Tert. De praescriptione haereticorum 36,3; T Euseb. Hist. eccl. 3,18,1; cf. Apc. 1:9) and to have lived in Ephesus during the time of Trajan and to have completed his Gospel there (Iren. adversus haereses 2,22,5; Euseb. Hist. eccl. 3,23,3f.). According to another tradition (Papias, fr. 10 and 17 [13]), he was killed by Jews (as was his brother: Acts 12,2). This note was suppressed by the influential tradition about the author and therefore is more historically trustworthy [11. 88–91]. There are also many reasons of content (primarily the differences to the Synoptics in the selection of material and in diction) that stand in the way of the authorship of Jo by the son of Zebedee.

B. THE EVIDENCE OF THE GOSPEL
The problem of Jo's authorship is closely tied to the attribution of the three letters (1–3 Jo) and to the question of Jo's literary homogeneity. In contrast to the analysis of layers in older research [6; 2; on this 11; 10], the homogeneity of Jo has been reaffirmed recently [11; 20; 22]. However, it is a matter of dispute whether the editors that can be discerned in Jo 21:24 added only ch. 21 (thus [11; 19]) or also other shorter (Jo 5:28f.; 6:51c–58 etc.) and longer (ch. 15–17) passages [2; 18]. The extraordinary linguistic and stylistic homogeneity and independence of Jo [17; 11; 10. 429–445] suggests its linguistic and theological composition by one author and renders improbable longer supplements (except ch. 21). The assumed author is usually called the 'evangelist' (different [22]: the editor as the actual 'evangelist'). In 21:24, the editors identify the author with the 'disciple whom Jesus loved' who appears from the last supper onwards (13:23–25; 19:26f.; 20:2–10; 21:7.20–23) (1:40 and 18:15 are unclear) and who distinguishes himself before Peter through his greater closeness to Jesus. As the ideal disciple and witness he embodies Jo's claim of surpassing the older Gospels. Not to be dismissed as a mere literary fiction (against [14; 22]), he was a Christian teacher still known to the editors as well as to the addressees, regarded as one to uphold the tradition of the earliest time, but who was probably already dead at the time of Jo's publication (Jo 21:22f.). He left his work unfinished, to be supplemented carefully by students, furnished with an authentication (21,24f.), and then distributed [11].

C. RECONSTRUCTION
Most of the attempts to identify the 'disciple whom Jesus loved' with textual figures (e.g. Lazarus, Thomas) or other known persons (e.g. John Mark: Acts 12:12) are purely speculative [8. 72–85; 7. 127–224]. The most valuable reference can be found in Papias (fr. 5 [13]: Euseb. Hist. eccl. 3,39,4), who mentions another I. aside from the apostle, the 'presbyter' (Πρεσβύτερος; *Presbýteros*) I., whom he still has heard and whose traditions he is said to have recorded in his largely no longer extant work (Euseb. Hist. eccl. 3,39,7). This 'presbyter J.' can be related historically to the information on the author in 2 Jo 1:1 and 3 Jo 1:1. Thus, the

'presbyter' J. from Asia Minor would be the author of the two shorter letters [19; 21], or, more likely, the author of all three letters [11] who, as the head of a school, intervenes authoritatively in the conflict within the community connected to him. It is contested whether the letters should be related to the editorship of Jo [5; 12; 18] or whether they are part of its prehistory [11; 19; 21], in other words, how the author of the letters ought to be related to the evangelist. If Jo 15-17, which is thematically close to 1 Jo, cannot be separated from Jo as secondary additions, the later dating of the letters is questionable too, particularly since the conflict voiced in 1 Jo 2:18ff. is probably reflected also in Jo 6:60ff. et passim [19]. Consequently, it is more probable to identify the author of the letters with the head of a school who exerted essential influence on the communities connected to him and whose work gave rise to Jo, the evangelist [11].

On linguistic and theological grounds, Apc. was certainly written by another author, who was either an otherwise unknown prophet with the name of I., or an author who was still influenced by the school of the 'presbyter' and attributed his work to the I. known in Asia Minor after the latter's death [9].

The name I., the language and the received traditions regarding the places and interpretations suggest that I. was a Palestinian Jew (most likely from Jerusalem). His relationship to Jesus and to the early church, however, remains unclear. He might have come to Ephesus in the course of the Jewish War and been active there as a preacher and teacher from c. AD 70-100. His work was probably written over a long period of time and then published at the time of Trajan around the year 100 or shortly thereafter [19]. It shows that its author was a high-ranking theological thinker who led NT christology to its height.

D. INFLUENCE

The artfully preserved anonymity of the author in Jo prepared the way for the work's attribution to the apostle I. We find it not only in Irenaeus (→ Eireneaus, Irenaeus [2]), but already in the Valentinian Ptolemy (Epist. ad Floram: Epiphanius, Panarion 33,3,6 HOLL) in c. 150 [11. 38]. J. and the tradition connected with him were of fundamental importance for the church in Asia Minor (Polycrates of Ephesus according to Euseb. Hist. eccl. 5,24,7). Beginning with Origenes (in Ioannem, fr. 1), J. has the epithet 'the theologian' (ὁ θεόλογος; ho theólogos). Later legends paint his picture in great detail [1; 8].

1 W. BAUER, in: E. HENNECKE, W. SCHNEEMELCHER (ed.), Neutestamentliche Apokryphen II, ⁴1971, 24-27 2 J. BECKER, Das Evangelium nach J. I-II, ³1991 3 J. BEUTLER, s.v. J.-Evangelium, RAC 18, 646-670 4 F.-M. BRAUN, Jean le théologien I, 1959 5 R.E. BROWN, The Epistles of John, 1982 6 R. BULTMANN, s.v. Johannesevangelium, RGG³ III, 840-850 7 J.H. CHARLESWORTH, The Beloved Disciple, 1995 8 R.A. CULPEPPER, John, the Son of Zebedee, 1994 9 J. FREY, Erwägungen zum Verhältnis der Johannesapokalypse zu den übrigen Schriften im Corpus Johanneum, in: [11], 326-429 10 Id., Die johanneische Eschatologie I, 1997 11 M. HENGEL, Die johanneische Frage, 1993 12 H.-J. KLAUCK, Die Johannesbriefe, 1991 13 U.H. J. KÖRTNER, Papiasfragmente, in: Id., M. LEUTZSCH, Schriften des Urchristentums III, 1998, 3-103 14 J. KÜGLER, Der Jünger, den Jesus liebte, 1988 15 R. KYSAR, The Fourth Gospel. A Report on Recent Research, in: ANRW II 25.3, 2389-2480 16 K.H. RENGSTORF (ed.), J. und sein Evangelium, 1973 17 E. RUCKSTUHL, P. DSCHULNIGG, Stilkritik und Verfasserfrage im Johannesevangelium, 1991 18 R. SCHNACKENBURG, Das Johannesevangelium I-IV, 1965-1984 19 U. SCHNELLE, Einleitung in das NT, 1994 20 Id., Das Evangelium nach J., 1998 21 G. STRECKER, Die Johannesbriefe, 1989 22 H. THYEN, Noch einmal: Johannes 21 und "der Jünger, den Jesus liebte", FS Lars Hartman, 1995, 147-190.   J.FR.

[2] I. of Gischala (Hebr. Giš/Guš Ḥālāb). Gischala is regarded as the stronghold of Zelotism in Galilee at the time of the Jewish War, in which I. played a contested role as the spokesman of the Jewish insurgents against Rome. While he has been praised on the one hand for his vigour, courage, and intelligence (so for instance [1]), Iosephus [2] Flavius, his adversary, described him as an intriguer and hypocrite. I.'s main accomplishment was the reconstruction of the town Gischala, which had been destroyed by non-Jews prior to the Jewish War. Source: Jos. BI.

→ Bar Kochba; → Iosephus [2] Flavius; → Zelots

1 H. GRAETZ, Gesch. der Juden 3/2, 1906 2 SCHÜRER I, 490f., 496-498, 501-509.   Y.D.

[3] I. of Lycopolis. Hermit in the region of Lycus in the Thebais at the end of the 4th cent. AD. Many reports in ecclesiastical-historical and monastic literature say that he foretold emperor Theodosius I – when the latter had him questioned about the future – the victories over Maxentius in 388 and over Eugenius in 394 (Rufin. Historia ecclesiastica 11,19 and 32; Sozom. Hist. eccl. 6,28,1; 7,22,7-8; 7,29,1; Aug. Civ. 5,26; Aug. De cura pro mortuis gerenda 17,21; Historia Monachorum 1,1; Pall. Laus. 35 p. 101,1-15 BUTLER; Theod. Hist. eccl. 5,24,1f.; Iohannes Cassianus, Collationes 24,26; Chron. min. 1, 463,607 MOMMSEN; Claud. in Eutr. 1,312-316 and 2, praef. 37-40). The → Historia Monachorum (1,1-65) describes further scenes from I.'s life and presents the monk's Apophthegma. Texts that have occasionally been attributed to him are now attributed to the hermit Iohannes of Apamea (2nd half of the 5th cent.).

A.-J. FESTUGIÈRE (ed.), Historia Monachorum in Aegypto (Subsidia Hagiographica 34), 1961.   C.M.

[4] I. Chrysostomos Bishop of Constantinople (397-404); from the 6th cent. on, referred to as Chrysóstomos ('golden mouth'); most important homilete of the Greek Church.

A. LIFE B. WORKS (SELECTION) C. THEOLOGY

A. LIFE

Born in Antioch (probably in 349), I. got into contact with the Antiochene exegesis through his training in the Asceterium of → Diodorus [14] of Tarsus. He lived as an ascetic from 372 onwards, but – due to health problems – he returned to Antioch; he became deacon in 381 and priest in February of 386. Preaching was now his main task. In 397, he succeeded Nectarius as bishop of Constantinople. There, he gave special attention to pastoral and social problems (for instance, the founding of several hospices). Discontentment among the clergy, his advocacy for the so-called 'tall brothers' (Egyptian monks suspected of Origenism, → Origenes), as well as a conflict with the empress → Eudoxia [2] led to his deposition in the autumn of 403 in the so-called 'Synod of the Oak' [8. 211–227]. After ending his first temporary exile, he was permanently exiled on 8 June 404. I. died on 14 September 407 in Pontic Comana.

B. WORKS (SELECTION)

Comparable in number only to those by Augustinus, the works of I. fall into three groups: treatises, sermons and letters. Even as deacon he wrote his first treatises, such as the exhortatory work *Ad Theodorum lapsum* (CPG 4305). Directed towards → Gregorius [3] of Nazianz, he published the reformatory work *De sacerdotio* (CPG Suppl. 4316; dating uncertain, AD 385–391), in which he presents an ideal picture of priesthood. More than 700 sermons are regarded as authentic. His speeches, given on special occasions (celebrations of saints etc.), are regarded as a unique genre, for instance, the 'column homilies' (CPG Suppl. 4330), the baptismal catecheses (CPG Suppl. 4460–4472), as well as the 'Eight speeches against the Jews' (CPG 4327) directed against Judaizing Christians. 242 letters are filed under I.'s name, among them 17 letters of consolation to the deaconess Olympia. More than 1000 texts are known as Ps.-Chrysostomica.

C. THEOLOGY

Committed exegetically to the → Antiochene School with its ethical orientation, I. describes God's work of salvation, with the cross in the centre, as συγκατάβασις/ *synkatábasis* [7. 467f.]. Mainly practically oriented, I., who is reserved in matters of doctrine, emphasizes the social dimension of the Gospel. The early church and the monastic life are presented as exemplary. His goal was a newly formed society built upon Christian solidarity.

EDITIONS: 1 CPG 4305–5197 and CPG Suppl. ibid.
2 H. SAVILE, Eton 1610–1612 (complete edition)
3 MONTFAUCON PG 47–64 4 R. BRÄNDLE, V. JEGHER-BUCHER, J., Acht Reden gegen die Juden, 1995, 274–301 (survey of the edition/translation, according to CPG).
BIBLIOGRAPHY: 5 J. A. DE ALDAMA, Repertorium pseudochrysostomicum, 1965 6 CH. BAUR, Der hl. Johannes Chrysostomus und seine Zeit, 2 vols., 1929/1930

7 R. BRÄNDLE, V. JEGHER-BUCHER, s.v. Johannes Chrysostomus I., RAC 18, 426–503 (bibliography 495–503)
8 J. N. D. KELLY, Golden mouth, 1995 9 R. A. KRUPP, Shepherding the flock of God, 1991 10 J. H. LIEBESCHUETZ, Barbarians and bishops, 1990 11 K.-H. UTHEMANN, s.v. Johannes, Biographisch-Bibliogr. Kirchenlex. 3, 1992, 305–326 12 S. J. VOICU, s.v. Johannes Chrysostomos II. (Ps.-Chrysostomica), RAC 18, 503–515.
J. RI.

[5] *Tribunus et notarius*, went to Milan as an envoy of Theodosius in AD 394 (Paulinus of Milan, Vita S. Ambrosii 31). In 408, I. was *primicerius notariorum* and led a delegation to Alarich (Zos. 5,40,2). In 409, *magister officiorum* of the usurper Attalus [11] (Sozom. Hist. eccl. 9,8,3), but in 412–413 he was *praefectus praetorio Italiae* of Honorius (Cod. Theod. 13,11,13; 7,8,10). Possibly *praef. praet. Italiae* for a second time in 422 (Cod. Theod. 2,13,1). PLRE 1, 459 (I. 2).

[6] *Comes*, advisor of → Arcadius, alleged lover of empress → Aelia [4] Eudoxia and father of Theodosius II (Zos. 5,18,8). During the revolt of the Goths in AD 400, I. sought church asylum, but was handed over to Gaenas by Iohannes [4] Chrysostomos. In 404, *comes sacrarum largitionum* (Palladius Monachus, Dialogus de vita Ioannis Chrysostomi 3).

PLRE 2, 593f. (I. 1); AL. CAMERON, A Misidentified Homily of Chrysostom, in: Nottingham Mediaeval Studies, 32, 1988, 34–48; J. LIEBESCHUETZ, Friends and Enemies of John Chrysostom, in: A. MOFFAT (ed.), Maistor, 1984, 85–111.

[7] I. Primicerius. West Roman emperor in AD 423–425. After Honorius' [3] death on 15 August 423 and Theodosius' II failure to nominate a west Roman emperor, I. – formerly *primicerius notariorum* – was proclaimed Augustus in Rome on 20 November 423 (Socr. 7,23,3; Ann. Rav. sub anno 423; Olympiodorus FHG fr. 41; Chron. min. 1,470; 523; 658 MOMMSEN). The proclamation probably made on the Senate's decision. The troops stationed in Italy under Castinus, the *magister utriusque militiae,* followed I. as well (Chron. min. ibid.). Theodosius, on the other hand, refused recognition, had I.'s envoys arrested and sent into exile (Philostorgius 12,13; Socr. 7,23,4). Bonifatius, the *comes Africae,* stopped grain shipments to Rome, causing I. to arm an expeditionary force which, however, failed (Chron. min. 1,470). I.'s consulate in 425 was not recognized in the east. Probably in May 425, Aspar (Ardabur [2]) succeeded in capturing Ravenna; I. was arrested and executed (Procop. Vand. 1,3,7f.; Chron. min. 1,470). According to Nicephorus Callistus 14,7, he was a Goth, possibly an Arianist (Cod. Theod. 16,2,47). PLRE 2, 594f. (I. 6).

[8] *Comes rei privatae* c. AD 426–429 (Cod. Theod. 5,16,35), 429–431 *comes sacrarum largitionum*. At the Council of Ephesus (AD 431), he was active as Imperial mediator and was elevated to the office of *magisterium officiorum* (Acta conciliorum oecumenicorum 1,1,7, p.

74), for which he is attested until the year 433 (Cod. Theod. 7,8,15). He died before 450 (Nestorius, Liber Heracl. 306 NAU). PLRE 2, 596 (I. 12).   M.R.

[9] I. Stobaeus. see → Stobaeus

[10] I. of Scythopolis. Contemporary of → Iohannes [15] of Caesarea. Like the latter, he wrote an apology of the Council of Chalcedon in AD 451 (CPG 3, 6851) on the basis of neo-Chalcedonian theology. His scholia to the treatises of → Ps.-Dionysius [54] Areopagites (CPG 3, 6852; critical ed. by B.R. SUCHLA forthcoming) are transmitted from the early 6th cent. in the corresponding MSS and have had a profound influence on the reception of Dionysius' work into the present time.

> J. LEBON (ed.), Contra impium grammaticum, 1952, 202–204 (CSCO 94); L. PERRONE, La Chiesa di Palestina e le controversie cristologiche, 1980, 239–250; B.R. SUCHLA, Verteidigung eines platonischen Denkmodells einer christl. Welt (Nachr. der Akad. der Wiss. in Göttingen, Phil.-histor. Klasse 1), 1995.   C.M.

[11] I. I. Mandakuni. As archbishop in → Armenia (AD 478–490), he transferred his residence to Dvin/central Armenia in 484. I. is regarded as a reformer of Armenian Church regulations and liturgies and is venerated as a saint in the Armenian Church. His works were written in the classical Armenian written language (→ Armenian). Many of the homilies, hymns and canons attributed to him were actually by Ioannes of Mayragom and Iohannes of Odzun.

> K. SARKISSIAN, The Council of Chalcedon and the Armenian Church, ²1975, 186–195; R.W. THOMSON, A Bibliography of Classical Armenian Literature to 1500 A.D. (CCG 0,1), 1995, 224f. (bibliography).   K.SA.

[12] I. II., Bishop of Jerusalem. (died AD 10 January 417). In 387, as a young monk, I. was consecrated bishop. From 394 on, he was attacked by → Epiphanius [1] of Salamis and → Hieronymus for his alleged Origenism (so-called 'Apology of I.' in his defence, see CPG 3620). After Pelagius' arrival in Jerusalem and the recognition of his orthodoxy at the Synod of Diospolis (415), which I. chaired, I. became engaged in a friendly correspondence with Augustine. Several symbola are transmitted under I.'s name as well as several homilies, although the attribution of some of the latter is contested ([2. 411]; CPG Suppl. 3624–3626). I. is regarded as the author of the so-called mystagogical catecheses that were formerly attributed to his predecessor Cyrillus (CPG 3622). Lit. s. [1; 2].

[13] Bishop of Antioch. (AD 429–441/2). Raised along with → Theodorus of Mopsuestia and → Nestorius, I. supported the latter in his theological concerns. Having arrived too late at the Council of Ephesus (431), I. condemned → Cyrillus of Alexandria and the local bishop Memnon on a counter synod. In 432, on the emperor's intervention I. accepted Nestorius' condemnation and worked towards an agreement with his former opponents (union of 433). An extensive body of letters about the Nestorian controversy is extant (CPG 6301–6360). Bibliography see [3].

[14] I. Diacrinomenus. ('separatist'), Monophysite church historian (AD 6th cent). According to Photius (Phot. Bibl. 41), I. wrote an attractively composed church history in 10 vols. The first five vols. cover the time from the conflict over Nestorius (Council of Ephesus in 431) up to the reign of emperor Zeno (474–491). Written after 526 ([6. 69], so far mostly: 512–518), some fr. have survived with Byzantine historians.; fr. see [4], Bibliography see [5; 6].

> 1 E.A. CLARK, The Origenist Controversy, 1992, 132–137 2 K.-H. Uthemann, s.v. Johannes, Biographisch-Bibliogr. Kirchenlex. 3, 1992, 402–413 3 L.I. SCIPIONI, Nestorio e il concilio di Efeso, 1974, 195–299 4 G.C. HANSEN, Theodoros Anagnostes Kirchengeschichte, 1995 152–157 (GCS N.F. 3) 5 A. JÜLICHER, s.v. Johannes (46), RE 9, 1806 6 W.T. TREADGOLD, The Nature of the Bibliotheca of Photius, 1980, 69f.   J.RI.

[15] I. of Caesarea. The grammarian I., presbyter from Caesarea in Cappadocia (thus [2]), between AD 514 and 518 wrote an apology of the Synod of Chalcedon of which 44 quotations have survived in the work Contra impium grammaticum by Severus of Antioch. Several smaller writings have also been transmitted (CPG 3, 6855–6862). I. is an early representative of the so-called 'neo-Chalcedonian christology' intended to mediate between → Cyrillus of Alexandria and a christology that was regarded as 'Nestorian' (→ Nestorianism) by Cyrillus' followers. He coined the formula of the two 'enhypostatically united natures of Christ' [2. 53 Z. 118–120].

> 1 J. LEBON (ed.), Severi Antiocheni Liber contra impium grammaticum, 1952 (CSCO 111, 93, 101) 2 M. RICHARD (ed.), Iohannis Caesariensis Presbyteri et Grammatici Opera quae supersunt, 1977 (CCG 1) 3 A. GRILLMEIER, Jesus der Christus im Glauben der Kirche 2/2, 1989, 54.   C.M.

[16] Flavius I. 'the Cappadocian', from AD 531, praefectus praetorio per Orientem under emperor → Iustinianus [1]. Especially for financing Imperial wars, I. engaged in thrifty financial politics oriented towards high tax revenue, rendering him indispensable for the emperor yet unpopular among the people. As a consequence, he temporarily lost his office during the → Nika revolt (Jan. 532), but is attested to hold it again from Oct. 532. Contemporaneous historians also viewed him negatively, reproaching him for avarice and personal enrichment. Intrigues of the empress → Theodora led to his deposition and exile in 541. He was called back after her death in 548, only to die shortly afterwards in Constantinople.

> PLRE 3, 627–635 (I. 11); E. STEIN, Histoire du Bas-Empire 2, 879, Index, s.v. Jean de Cappadoce.   F.T.

[17] Nephew of the usurper → Vitalianus, AD 537–549 magister militum vacans in the war of emperor → Iustinianus [1] I against the Ostrogoths under → Belisarius

in Italia. In 545, he married Iustina, a daughter of → Germanus [1] (cousin of Iustinianus) in Constantinople. As *mag. mil. per Illyricum,* he spent the period from autumn 550 to 552 in Salona (Spalatum), from where he, alongside the *mag. mil.* Valerianus, gained a naval victory over the Goths in the summer of 551, on the coast of Italy near Sena Gallia. From 552 on, he fought under Narses in Italy, where he was mentioned for the last time in 553. PLRE 3, 652–661 (I. 46). F.T.

[18] I. Malalas. Author of the oldest preserved Byzantine world chronicle. Of Syrian origin (the name *Malalas* < Syr. *mallāl* means 'rhetor'), he was born in Antioch *c.* AD 490/500, where he was probably active as an administrative official, and died after 570. His chronicle of 18 bks. covers the history from the world's creation to the year 563. It is extant only in a single MS from the 11th cent., but a slightly shortened version as a comparison to the roughly contemporaneous and more complete translation into Old Church Slavonic shows. Originally, the work ended with the year 565, or perhaps as late as 574. The history of the Mediterranean peoples in antiquity is probably composed from sources which, although mostly named, appear to be secondary. Greek myths are presented as historical events, often in rationalised form. Antioch receives a privileged treatment and is presented in accordance with local sources. The author's preference for → Monophysitism is clearly noticeable. The last bk. about the reign of → Iustinianus [1] I (527–565) shows a different tendency: it places Constantinople into a more central position, it relies on contemporary sources, and perhaps the author's own experiences as well; in presenting the events it follows the official state propaganda while Monophysite tendencies are no longer so clearly apparent.

These differences have been explained either by the fact that I. lived in Constantinople from *c.* 530/540 where he may have adjusted his political views accordingly, or by the possibility that this part was written by a different author. The older assumption that the other author might be → Iohannes [28] III Scholastikos (565–577) of Constantinople, a patriarch from Antioch, is no longer supported today. The chronicle is clearly aimed at the tastes of a broader audience with its many anecdotes and miracle stories; for the most part, it lacks literary aspirations, its use of the contemporary vernacular making it highly important for the history of language. It strongly influenced the development of the entire genre, even in the west. Later Byzantine works such as the → *Chronicon Paschale* and → Theophanes used it as a source. It was translated into Slavic and Georgian.

L. DINDORF (ed.), Ioannis Malalae Chronographiae, 1831; A. SCHENK VON STAUFFENBERG, Die röm. Kaisergesch. bei Malalas, 1930; E. HÖRLING, Mythos und Pistis: Zur Deutung heidnischer Mythen in der christl. Weltchronik des Johannes Malalas, 1980; E. JEFFREYS, B. CROKE, R. SCOTT (ed.), Studies in John Malalas, 1990. AL.B.

[19] Philoponus. see → Philoponus
[20] I. Abba Biclarensis. Born in c. 540, died in c. 621. The Goth I., originally from Scallabis according to Isid. De viris illustribus 31, studied in Constantinople and after his return in c. 576 was interned in → Barcino because of his catholic faith (follower of the Chalcedonensis) together with the Arianic king Leovigild. Under king Reccared, he founded the monastery in Biclaro, Spain, in 586/7, and wrote a rule for it which is no longer extant. In 592 at the latest, I. became the bishop of Gerunda. In *c.* 590/1, he wrote a chronicle of the years 567–589, thus continuing the chronicle of → Victor Tonnunensis. With its concise style (thus Isidore) it is an important source for Byzantium and the Visigothic empire in the 6th cent.
→ Chronicle

EDITIONS: J. CAMPOS, Juan de Biclaro, 1960 (introd., comm.); TH. MOMMSEN, MGH AA XI, 1894, 207–220; K. B. WOLF, Conquerors and Chroniclers of Early Medieval Spain, 1990, 1–11, 61–80
BIBLIOGRAPHY: A. KOLLAUTZ, Orient und Okzident am Ausgang des 6. Jh., in: Byzantina 12, 1983, 464–506; S. TEILLET, Des Goths à la nation gothique, 1984, 421–455. JÖ.RI.

[21] I. from Antioch. Author's name linked to numerous fr. in Byzantine historical works. However, the texts can be attributed to at least two authors, the first of whom wrote in *c.* AD 520/530, the second in the 9th/10th cent. No biographical information exists about the older I., who is certainly not identical to → Iohannes [18] Malalas, nor to Iohannes I. (631–649), the Jacobitic patriarch of Antioch, as was formerly assumed at times. The work contains information about the late Roman and early Byzantine period not transmitted in any other work and served as a source i.a. for the collection of excerpts by → Constantine VII Porphyrogennetus and the chronicle by Iohannes → Zonaras (12th cent.).

FHG 4, 535–622; Suppl. FHG 5, 27–38; P. SOTIROUDIS, Unt. zum Geschichtswerk des Johannes von Antiocheia, 1989; ODB 2, 1062. AL.B.

[22] I. Diaconus. Author of an *Epistula ad Senarium* important for liturgical history, possibly identical to Pope I.I (523–526). Text [1. 170–179].
[23] I. Diaconus. Author of the catene commentary *Expositum in Heptateuchum* with textual fr. partly not transmitted elsewhere. He presupposes Victor of Capua (541–554) and might be identical to Pope I. III (561–574). Excerpts [2. 278–302] and [3. 165–176].

1 A. WILMART, Analecta Reginensia, Studi e testi 59, 1933 2 J. B. PITRA, Spicilegium Solesmense I, 1852 3 Id., Analecta sacra et classica I, 1888 4 CPL, no. 950–952 and register (bibliography). M.HE.

[24] **I. Alexandrinus.** → Iatrosophist and writer in Alexandria, active between AD 530 and 650. Although he refers to his teacher several times (CMG 11,1,4, p.12), no firm evidence supports the assumption that it was → Gesius. His transmitted work consists of a commentary on Galen's *De sectis* (his Latin version [1] shows great similarities to that of → Agnellus and is attributed to Gesius as well) and a commentary [2] – also translated into Latin – on the 6th bk. on epidemics by Hippocrates, some fr. of which have been transmitted in Greek [3]. Other Greek fr. of a commentary on *De natura pueri* by Hippocrates were first published by [4]. It is unlikely that an extensive medical compendium – in a MS in the Bibliothèque Nationale (Fond. gr. 2316) attributed to I., the Iatrosophist, in other MSS to I. Archiatros – was written by I. Alexandrinus, who, in Arabic medical texts, was confused also with Iohannes → Philoponus and the even more elusive I. Grammaticus [1]. His commentaries are typical examples of late Alexandrian scholarship: although strictly following Galen's interpretations of Hippocrates, I. is still capable of independent ideas based on his own practical experiences. In spite of his Christian name, he keeps all allusions to religion in his commentaries deliberately neutral.

1 C.D. PRITCHET (ed.), Iohannis Alexandrini commentaria in librum De Sectis Galeni, 1982 2 Id. (ed.), Iohannis Alexandrini commentaria in sextum librum Hippocratis Epidemiarum, 1975 3 J.M. DUFFY (ed.), CMG 11,1,4,25–107 4 Id., CMG 11,1,4,127–175.

O. TEMKIN, Gesch. des Hippokratismus im ausgehenden Alt., in: Kyklos 4, 1932, 66–71.   V.N.

[25] **I. of Gaza.** Greek rhetor and poet of the 6th cent. AD, author of Anacreontic occasional poetry [1; 3] and of a poetic → ekphrasis [2] about a dome painting in the winter spa of Antioch (before 526: [4]) which represented the cosmos in allegorical figures, transmitted between bk. 14 and 15 of the Anth. Pal. [5]. The poem, 2 bks. in hexameters, each with a iambic introduction, closely follows → Nonnus in style as well as metre [6].

EDITIONS: 1 T. BERGK, Poetae Lyrici Graeci 3, ⁴1882, 342–348 2 P. FRIEDLÄNDER, 1912.
BIBLIOGRAPHY: 3 R. GENTILE MESSINA, Note alle Anacreontee di Giovanni di Gaza, in: Studi di filologia bizantina 4, 1988, 33–39 4 A. CAMERON, On the date of J. of G., in: CQ 43, 1993, 348–351 5 C. CUPANE, Il κοσμικὸς πίναξ di Giovanni di Gaza, in: Jb. der österreich. Byzantinistik 28, 1979, 195–207 6 C. CAIAZZO, L'esametro di Giovanni di Gaza, in: Ταλαρίσκος. FS A. GARZYA, 1987, 243–252.   P.L.S.

[26] **I. of Ephesus.** (c. AD 507–c. 588). Syrian author, born near Amida, who became a monk early in his youth. He undertook many journeys, spent time in Constantinople on various occasions (which include a prison term under Iustinius [4] II). Although he belonged to the Syrian-Orthodox Church, Iustinianus commissioned him [1] (in c. AD 542) to convert the pagan population in the region surrounding Ephesus.

I. wrote two important works: 1) 'The Lives of the Oriental Saints': 58 short biographies of Syrian-Orthodox saints (men and women), primarily from the region of Amida. 2) a church history in three parts: the first part, from Iulius Caesar up to the year 449, is lost; the second, from 449 up to 571, is partially extant – interestingly, in the form of an insert into the chronicle by Zuqnīn from the 8th cent. (→ [Ps.-]Dionysius [23] of Tell-Maḥrē, → Joshua Stylites). The third part (up to 588) is extant.
→ Monophysitism

EDITIONS: 'The Lives of het Oriental Saints': E.W. BROOKS, Patrologia Orientalis 17–19, 1923f.; Church history: J.B. CHABOT, E.W. BROOKS R. HESPEL, CSCO Scr. Syri 53 and 213, 1933 and 1989 (part 2); W. WITAKOWSKI, 1996 (Engl. transl.); E.W. BROOKS, CSCO Scr. Syri 54f., 1935f. (part 3).
BIBLIOGRAPHY: A. D'YAKONOV, Ioann Yefesskiy, 1908; S.A. HARVEY, Asceticism and society in Crisis: John of Ephesus and the Lives of the Eastern Saints, 1990; L.M. WHITBY, John of Ephesus and the pagans, in: M. SALOMON (ed.), Paganism in the Later Roman Empire and in Byzantium, 1991, 111–131; J.J. VAN GINKEL, John of Ephesus. A Monophysite Historian in Sixth-Century Byzantium, thesis Groningen 1995.   S.BR.

[27] **I. IV. Nesteutes.** Patriarch of Constantinople (582–595). Due to his ascetic lifestyle – from whence the epithet 'the fasting' (νηστευτής/*nēstentḗs*, Latin *ieiunator*) – he had the reputation of a saint already during his lifetime and succeeded Eutychius in 582 as monk and cleric of the → Hagia Sophia. The popes Pelagius II and Gregorius [3] I, the Great, protested against the title used officially by I. from 587: οἰκουμενικὸς πατριάρχης (*oikoumenikòs patriárchēs*; 'ecumenical patriarch'). Byzantine tradition links several pseudepigraphical texts to I. (cf. [2. 423f.]; CPG 7555–7560), esp. on penitential discipline, i.a. the so-called *Protocanonarium* (penitential book, probably 9th/10th cent.; text: [1. 23–129]).

1 M. ARRANZ, I penitenziali bizantini, 1993 2 H.-G. BECK, Kirche und theologische Lit. im byz. Reich, ²1977, 423–425 3 D. STIERNON, s.v. Jean (129) le Jeuneur, in: Dictionnaire de Spiritualité 8, 1974, 586–589.
                                                                      J.RI.

[28] **I. Scholastikos.** Born as the son of a cleric in Antioch, I. was active first as *scholastikós* (jurist), then became (in c. AD 550) presbyter in Antioch, and finally, after working as *apokrisiarios* (ecclesiastical ambassador) for the Antiochan patriarch in Constantinople, became patriarch Iohannes III there in the year 565, and died in 577. I. wrote legal and theological texts (κατηχητικὸς λόγος/*katēchētikòs lógos*, attested in Photius, Bibl. cod. 75). However, only two works on ecclesiastical law are preserved (CPG 3, 7550/51): the oldest extant collection of the → *Canons* of church councils and provincial synods (along with the *Canones Apostolorum*) is his *Synagōgḗ kanónōn* (Συναγωγὴ κανόνων), which itself was based on a collection now lost; in addition, I. compiled a collection of texts rel-

evant for the church from the novellas by emperor → Iustinianus [1].

> V.N. BENEŠEVIČ (eEd.), Sinagogá v 50 Titulov i drugie juridičeskie sborniki Joanna Scholastika, 1914 (repr. 1972); E.SCHWARTZ, Die Kanonessammlungen der alten Reichskirche, in: Id., Gesammelte Schriften 4, 1960, 159–176; Id., Die Kanonessammlung des Johannes Scholastikos, SB der bayerischen Akad. der Wiss. (Phil.-histor. Klasse 6), 1933. C.M.

[29] I. Moschus. I. Eucrates, to be more exact. Son of Moschus, born shortly after AD 550 (perhaps in Damascus), monk in the monastery of Theodosius between Jerusalem and Bethlehem. He later entered the new Laura (monastic settlement) of Sabas, finally left Palestine after the Persian conquest in 614, and died in the spring of 619 (or 634) in Rome after extensive travels. His only work is the 'Spiritual Meadow' (*Leimṓn, Leimōnárion* or *Néos parádeisos, Pratum spirituale,* PG 87/3, 2852–3112; CPG 3, 7376). It was published by his student and travel companion → Sophronius, the later patriarch of Jerusalem (died in 638), and contains biographies, stories, and sayings of important contemporary monks, modelled after other stories about monks (such as the → *Historia monachorum*). I. defended the Council of Chalcedon in the midst of a monasticism that had always been critical of Chalcedon. The 'Meadow' is a unique source for such disputes and also for the time of crisis prior to the Persian invasion. It became one of the most popular books of the Byzantine Middle Ages.

> H. CHADWICK, John Moschus and his Friend Sophronius the Sophist, in: Journal of Theological Studies 25, 1974, 41–74; H. USENER, Der hl. Tychon, 1907, 83–107. C.M.

[30] I. Klimakos also referred to as Scholastikos or Sinaïtes (Κλῖμαξ/*Klîmax,* ὁ τῆς κλίμακος/*ho tês klímakos* and σχολαστικός/*scholastikós* or σιναΐτης/*sinaítēs*). A. LIFE B. WORK AND THEOLOGY

A. LIFE
I. was born c. AD 579 and died after 654. His epithet is based on his main work 'The Ladder of Paradise'. At the age of 16, he became a coenobite monk in St. Catharine's monastery on the Sinai under *i.a.* Anastasius [5] of Antioch and lived there as a hermit for 40 years after the latter's death. At the end of his life, he became abbot of the monastery on the Sinai.

B. WORK AND THEOLOGY
His main work 'The Ladder of Paradise' (Κλῖμαξ τοῦ παραδείσου, *Klîmax toû paradeísou*), which he wrote at the suggestion of his friend Iohannes of Raithu, attained normative status for the theory of mystagogical life. The work follows 'Jakob's Ladder' of the OT (Gen. 28) and presents the life of the mystic as an ascent to God over 30 steps (corresponding to the 30 years of Christ's hidden life). Depending primarily on → Evagrius [1] Ponticus and drawing on his own mystical experience,

I. offers monks a guide for obtaining 'calmness of the soul' (ἀπάθεια, *apátheia*) for the sanctification of their lives, which can only be achieved through an inner struggle with one's own affects (πάθη, *páthē*). This theme influenced the iconography, which presents the *páthē* as personified demons that snatch the mystic from the ladder at the end of which Christ awaits the ascending. The work finds its continuation in the so-called 'Handbook for the Abbot' (λόγος πρὸς τὸν ποιμένα; *lógos pròs tòn poiména*), which refers to an inquiry by I. of Raithu.

> EDITIONS: PG 88, 631–1210.
> BIBLIOGRAPHY: W. VÖLKER, Scala Paradisi, 1968; H.G. BECK, Kirche und theologische Lit., ³1989, 451f. K.SA.

[31] I. of Thessalonica. In the title of the story about the miracles of St. Demetrius of Thessalonica, *Miracula S. Demetrii,* I. is mentioned as its author and as a holy archbishop. He is probably identical with the abbot I. mentioned as already deceased in the second book of the same work who worked miracles and was the saviour of Thessalonica during a siege by the Slavs in the early 7th cent. AD. He was made the author of the text by a later editor and identified with the historical archbishop I. of → Thessalonica, attested for the year 680. The cult of St. Demetrius was originally at home in → Sirmium and, following the final loss of the city in AD 582, transferred to the city of Thessalonica, where Demetrius became the patron saint in the course of the 7th cent. The miracle story reflects this development by transferring several miracles originally connected to other persons onto Demetrius. In its final form, it was compiled in the 9th cent. from older material and, as a source, must therefore be interpreted with caution.

> P.LEMERLE, Les plus anciens recueils des miracles de Saint Démétrius, 2 vols., 1979–1981; P.SPECK, De miraculis Sancti Demetrii, qui Thessalonicam profugus venit, in: Varia IV, Poikila Byzantina 12, 1993, 255–532. AL.B.

[32] I. Eleemon, the Merciful. Born in Amathus on Cyprus, he was the Orthodox patriarch of Alexandria from AD 610; he fled to his homeland in 619 during the Persian conquest of Egypt, only to die soon thereafter. I. received the epithet Ἐλεήμων (*Eleémōn*; 'the merciful') due to his charitable work in Alexandria, where he founded several hospitals and looked after fugitives. I. is venerated as a saint in the Orthodox Church. His vita, written by Leontius of Neapolis, is extant; two further vitae by → Iohannes [29] Moschus and → Sophronius, however, are transmitted only in excerpts. → Leontius of Neapolis

> A.-J.FESTUGIÈRE, L.RYDÉN (ed.), Léontios de Néapolis, Vie de Syméon le Fou et Vie de Jean de Chypre, 1974, 257–637; ODB 2, 1058f. AL.B.

902

[33] I. of Damascus
A. LIFE B. WORK

A. LIFE

I. was born in AD 650 as the son of the wealthy Manṣūr family in → Damascus. Along with his adopted brother → Cosmas of Maiuma, he was educated according to the Hellenistic canon of studies. He resigned from his office of trust at the court of Caliph Yazīd (680–683) under ʿUmar II (717–720) when the status of Christians had deteriorated and he withdrew along with Cosmas to Mar Saba. There, he devoted himself to a contemplative life and wrote works intended to portray and defend orthodoxy. He was highly esteemed as an advisor in matters of church politics. Iohannes V of Jerusalem ordained him on the title of the Anastasis church in the holy city. During the iconographic controversy (→ Leo III, → Syrian dynasty), he developed a determined theology of the image which became decisive for the theology of icons. He also set the standard for ecclesiastical hymnic poetry (height of the → canon). The year of his death is not known; he was buried in Mar Saba. The Seventh Ecumenical Synod of → Nicaea (787) lifted the triple anathema which had been imposed on him by the Iconoclast Synod in Hiera (754).

B. WORK

His main work, the compilation *Pēgē gnóseōs* (Πηγὴ γνώσεως), dedicated to his brother Cosmas, deals with Greek-Roman philosophy and offers a detailed interpretation of the right faith in opposition to the heresies. In the 'Three Speeches to those who Decry Holy Images' (CPG 8045), he develops his theology of icons: the dialectical relationship between prototype and antitype corresponds to the distinction between the worship of the image (προσκύνησις, *proskýnēsis*) and the adoration of the deity (λατρεία, *latreía*). In the novel → ›Barlaam and Ioasaph‹, the legend of Buddha and Indian fables are interpreted in a Christian sense. Most of the MSS and the oldest vita (Arabic) lend support to I.'s authorship of the work.

EDITIONS: B. KOTTER (ed.), Die Schriften des J. von Damaskos I–V (Patristische Texte und Stud. 7, 12, 17, 22, 29), 1969–1986.
BIBLIOGRAPHY: R. VOLK, Urtext und Modifikationen des griech. Barlaam-Romans, in: ByzZ 86/7, 1993/4, 442–461; F. R. GAHBAUER, Die Anthropologie des Johannes von Damaskos, in: Theologie und Philos. 69, 1994, 1–21.
K.SA.

[34] I. of Nikiu. (died shortly after AD 700). Born during the Arabic conquest of Egypt (639–642), I. was active as bishop of the city of Nikiu, located on an island in the main western arm of the Nile in Lower Egypt. Installed as general supervisor of the monasteries in 696, he was deposed from this office soon thereafter due to his abuse of the office. A Monophysite (→ Monophysitism), he wrote a world chronicle, originally probably in Coptic [4. 1367] and extant only in a gar-

bled Ethiopian translation (early 17th cent.) based on an Arabic translation. Dependent on various sources (→ Iohannes [18] Malalas etc.), I. is a main witness – despite some gaps – to the political and ecclesiastical processes in Egypt between AD 580 and the Arabic conquest.

EDITIONS: 1 H. ZOTENBERG, Chronique de Jean, évêque de Nikiou. Texte éthiopien publiés et traduit, 1883 2 R. H. CHARLES, The chronicle of John, Bishop of Nikiu, 1916 (repr. 1980).
BIBLIOGRAPHY: 3 A. CARILE, Giovanni di Nikiu, cronista bizantino-copto del VII secolo, in: N. A. STRATOS (ed.), Byzantion: aphieroma ston Andrea N. Stratos 2, 1986, 353–398 4 P. M. FRASER, s.v. John of Nikiu, The Coptic Encyclopedia 5, 1991, 1366f.
J.RI.

[35] I. I. Tzimiskes. Byzantine emperor 969–976; an Armenian, born in *c.* AD 925; general under his uncle and predecessor → Nicephorus II, whom he murdered in December 969. I. defeated prince Svjatoslav of Kiev in 971, and in 972 and in 974–975, he fought successfully against the Egyptian Fatimides in Syria. ODB 2, 1045.
F.T.

[36] I. Philoponus. see → Philoponus
[37] I. Skylitzes. see → Skylitzes
[38] I. Mauropus. see → Mauropus
[39] I. the Baptist (Ἰωάννης ὁ βαπτιστής, Lat. I. Baptista). I., the son of a priest (sources: Jos. Ant. Iud. 18, 116–119; Gospels; Acts), began his activities as an apocalyptic prophet of penitence in *c.* AD 27–29 (Lc 3:1) on the river Jordan (→ Iordanes [2]) (in Mk 9:13, he is regarded as the returned → Elias [1]). His ascetic lifestyle (renunciation of marriage and alcohol) resembles that of priests and Nasiraeans (→ Nazirate; Num. 6,3), while his activities in the → desert is reminiscent of the desert prophets (Jos. Ant. Iud. 20,97 f.) and of the → Essenes; as opposed to the purification baths of the latter, I. practised a single → baptism as a sign of reversal (thus Jos.; Mt 3:2) or as a cleansing from sins (thus Mk 1:4; Lc 3:3). He admonished the people to observe the Torah (above all its rules regarding social ethics) [1]. I.'s protest against → Herodes [4] Antipas' marriage to his sister-in-law Herodias led to his decapitation in AD 35 (Mk 6:27; cf. → Salome [2]).

The Gospels present I. as a predecessor to → Jesus, placing emphasis in their narratives on the parallels to Jesus who was baptized by I. Both figures preach that the Kingdom of God is coming, have followers who are baptists (cf. Jo 4:1 f.), and suffer martyrdom. With I., the series of Biblical prophets comes tó an end (Mt 11:9) and the period of the → Messiah begins (Acts 1:22).
→ Prophets

1 E. LUPIERI, s. v. J. der Täufer, RGG⁴ 4, 2001, 514–517 2 H. STEGEMANN, Die Essener, Qumran, J. der Täufer und Jesus, 1993.
P. WI.

Iolaus (Ἰόλαος; *Iólaos*).
[1] Nephew of → Heracles, son of the latter's half-brother → Iphicles and the (shadowy) Automedusa. He accompanies Heracles on practically all his adventures (mainly as chariot driver), becomes the first Olympic champion (image in Olympia, Paus. 5,17,11), receives → Megara as wife from Heracles and finally kills → Eurystheus in Attica (Paus. 1,44,10, grave), for which he was specially rejuvenated for one day (Eur. Heracl. 843–863, perhaps following Aeschyl. fr. 361); he died either in Thebes (Pind. Ol. 9,80) or Sardis (Paus. 9,23,1). Consequently, I. has little mythical stature in his own right; nevertheless, after Heracles' death, he is said to have led colonists from Athens and Thespiai to Sardinia and to have built the Nuraghes (Diod. Sic. 4,29. 5,15; Paus. 7,2,2; Aristot. Mir. 100).

In cult as well, I. is generally linked to Heracles (Plut. Mor. 492c); where details are discernible, he appears specifically as a hero of young men. In Thebes he has a → *témenos* which was linked to a gymnasium and a stadium (Arr. Anab. 1,7,7; Paus. 9,23,1; horse races: Pind. Nem. 5,32; cult: Pind. P. 9,79) and contains his grave, which is also that of his grandfather → Amphitryon (Pind. Ol. 9,81); here Erastes and Eromenos sealed their bond of love (Aristot. fr. 97; Plut. Mor. 761de). He is so much incorporated into the great festival of the Heracleia that they are also called Iolaeia (schol. Pind. Ol. 7,53). Scholars generally assume that I. is the predecessor of Heracles in the Theban cult. Of greater importance is the fact that the coexistence of the heroes mirrors the rites of Theban young men. His cult in Agyrium on Sicily is more independent, with a sanctuary erected by Heracles on a lake by the city, where every year an important sacrificial feast took place and where the Ephebes sacrificed their hair. Although the emphasis on the rites of young men does also here fit in with the Theban findings, perhaps an older local cult has been transferred to I. (Diod. Sic. 4,24,4).

NILSSON, Feste 449f.; SCHACHTER 2, 17f.; 64f.; M. PIPILI, s.v. I., LIMC 5, 686–696. F.G.

[2] Commissioned by → Perdiccas with 200 men as the supreme cavalry commander at → Potidaea in 432 BC, but did not take part in the battle against the Athenians. Probably the father of → Antipater [1] (Thuc. 1,62f.; often misunderstood).

S. HORNBLOWER, Commentary on Thucydides 1, 1991, 165; J. SUNDWALL, s.v. Iolaos (4), RE 9, 1847. E.B.

[3] Son of → Antipater [1], grandson of I. [2], cup-bearer of → Alexander [4] the Great in the latter's last year; later the circle of → Olympias accused him of having poisoned Alexander (dismissed by Arr. Anab. 7,27,1f.; accepted e.g. by Diod. Sic. 17,118,1 and elaborated in the → Alexander Romance). In 322 BC he gave his sister → Nicaea to → Perdiccas as his bride (Arr. Anab. 21; Diod. Sic. 18,23,3). In 317 his grave was ostentatiously desecrated by Olympias (Diod. Sic. 19,11,8). E.B.

[4] Writer of comedies, only epigraphically attested [1. test.], who in 177 BC received second prize at the Dionysia.

PCG V, 608. H.-G.NE.

Iolaus fragment The name given to a work known only through a single papyrus fragment (POxy. 3010, beginning of the 2nd cent. AD). In it someone journeys to a certain Iolaus and delivers a speech in sotadic verses, claiming that he became a Gallus, i.e. a castrated adherent of Cybele [1. 57], and is omniscient. The papyrus breaks off with an Euripidean quotation (Eur. Or. 1155–7) about the value of friendship. The fragment's significance lies in its use of the → prosimetrum (the distinction between prose and verse is also graphically displayed) in a comic narrative; that is why people have suspected a link with the *Satyricon* of → Petronius. In any event, it attests to the existence of a realistic-comic novel among the Greeks (see also *Phoinikiká* of → Lollianus).

→ Novel

1 P. PARSONS, A Greek Satyricon?, in: BICS 18, 1971, 53–68 2 Ancient Greek Novels. The Fragments, ed. S. A. STEPHENS, J. J. WINKLER, 1995, 358–374. M.FU. and L.G.

Iolcus (Ἰωλκός; *Iōlkós*). Already named in the most ancient legends (Aeson, Alcestis, Argonautae, Jason, Neleus, Peleus, Pelias). Residence city at the northern exit of the Gulf of → Pagasae on the Anaurus (modern Xerias). A large settlement mound in the old city of Volos (Kastro Volo) bears witness to continuity of settlement at the latest since the early Bronze Age – many Mycenaean tombs, two palace complexes, a Doric temple (Artemis Iolkia). Large Mycenaean complexes near Dimini suggest that this may have been the site of the mythological place I. Pevkakia Magula (→ Nelea) on the coast near → Demetrias [1] comes into consideration possibly as a port at least of the Mycenaean I., as a result of finds, so it is possible that I. is a name for several associated settlement centres.

Tombs in and around Kastro Volo show that the place was prosperous in the Mycenaean and Imperial periods. Its decline at the beginning of the historical period is possibly explained by the silting up of the harbour and the founding of Pagasae as the port of the Thessalians (cf. the legend of Peleus). They offered I. to Hippias at the beginning of the 5th cent. (Hdt. 5,94,1). I. became incorporated into Demetrias [1] around 290 BC (Str. 9,5,15). In 169 BC the Roman fleet landed at I. and from there attacked Demetrias (Liv. 44,12,8; 13,4). In the Byzantine period it was an established bishop's seat. In the 14th cent. the city was called Golos (later Volos).

B. G. INTZESILOGLOU, Ιστορική τοπογραφία της περιοχής του κόλπου του Βόλου [Istoriкí topographía tis periochís tou kólpou tou Vólou], in: La Thessalie, Quinze années de recherches archéologiques 1975-1990, 1994, 31ff.;

K. LIAPIS, Το κάστρο του Βόλου μέσα στους αιώνες [To kástro tou Vólou mésa stous aiónes], 1991, 14ff.; PHI-LIPPSON/KIRSTEN 1, 154f.; F. STÄHLIN, s.v. I., RE 9, 1850ff. (there sources); Id., Das hellen. Thessalien, 1924, 62ff., 75f.; D. THEOCHARIS, I., Whence Sailed the Argonauts, in: Archaeology 11, 1958, 13ff.; TIB 1, 1976, 165f.

HE.KR.

Iole (Ἰόλη; *Iólē*). Daughter of → Eurytus [1], king of Oechalia, and Antioche (Hes. Cat. fr. 26,31a), sister of → Iphitus, who was murdered by Heracles (cf. Hom. Od. 21,11–41). Although Heracles wins I. in the archery contest arranged by Eurytus, the latter refuses to give him his daughter (Pherecydes FGrH 3 F 82a; Apollod. 2,6,1–3; Diod. Sic. 4,31,37). In revenge for the period of servitude with → Omphale imposed on him as retribution for the murder of Iphitus, Heracles destroys Oechalia and abducts I. as his mistress (Soph. Trach. 68–75; 254–260; 856–862; Bacchyl. 16). His wife → Deianira then kills Heracles with a poisoned tunic, which she had received from → Nessus and with the help of which she intends to win back her husband's love (Soph. Trach.). The dying Heracles gives I. to his son → Hyllus [1] as wife (Soph. Trach. 1219–1228). Heracles' courting of I. and the destruction of Oechalia were very likely part of the lost epic attributed to Creophilus of Samos, *Oichalías hálōsis* ('The Capture of Oechalia', EpGF, p. 149–153). A Corinthian crater (600–590 BC) shows Heracles, Eurytus, his sons and I., cf. [1]. In Sophocles and Bacchylides, Deianira's reaction to I.'s arrival is the focal point. Panyassis of Halicarnassus may also have recounted the myth in his *Heraclea*.

1 R. OLMOS, s.v. I. (1), LIMC 5.1, 700.

A. BECK, Der Empfang I.s, in: Hermes 81, 1953, 10–21; L. BERGSON, Herakles, Deianeira und I., in: RhM 136, 1993, 102–115.; S. EITREM, s.v. I., RE 9, 1847–1848.

K.WA.

Iomedes (Ἰομήδης; *Iomḗdes*). Otherwise unknown author of a grave inscription from the 2nd or 3rd cent. AD found at Nemra (Namarae Batanaeorum) in Syria (five partly damaged distichs). The poet, who calls himself 'master (*prýtanis*) of the Ausonian muse' (v. 10), celebrates in those lines his own forefathers, who once dedicated a memorial to Tyche in the same place. At the end (v. 9), he signs with his name (τήνδ' Ἰομήδης; *ténd' Iomḗdes*), which has been taken to be – because of its singularity – an intentional and witty alteration of 'Diomedes' [1].

1 EpGr 440   2 Anth. Pal. appendix II 665 COUGNY.

M.G.A.

Iomnium (Gr. Ἰόμνιον; *Iómnion* or Ἰόμνυον; *Iómnyon*). I. probably originated as a Phoenician or Punic trading post (as indicated by the letter I at the beginning of the name: *ʾj* = Punic 'island'), located in → Maure-

tania Caesariensis, near the modern Tigzirt (Algeria). Ptol. 4,2,8; It. Ant. 17,1; Tab. Peut. 2,2. Inscriptions: CIL VIII 2, 8995–9001; Suppl. 3, 20710–20728; AE 1994, 1898 f.; Rev. Africaine 58, 1914, 342–353. It became a *municipium* under Septimius [II 7] Severus. The Punic tradition continued to remain vibrant for a long time. In the Roman period, → Saturnus replaced → baal Hamon. In 411, the city was made an episcopal see (Acta concilii Carthaginiensis anno 411 habiti, cognitio 1, § 207). Remains: baths, temples, Christian basilica.

P. GAVAULT, Étude sur les ruines romaines de Tigzirt, 1897; AAAlg, sheet 6, no. 34 f.; M. LEGLAY, Saturne africain 2, 1966, 301 f.; P.-A. FÉVRIER, s. v. I., PE, 414.

W. HU.

Ion (Ἴων; *Íōn*).

[1] Eponymous hero of the Ionians (→ Iones). Several traditions of his ancestry emphasizing Athens' political primacy are extant. The earliest and most influential versions present I. as the son of → Xuthus and Creusa, thus as the grandson of → Hellen, progenitor of the Hellenes, and of the Athenian king → Erechtheus (Str. 8,383; Paus. 7,1,2). I.'s brother is Achaeus [1], progenitor of the Achaeans, his paternal uncles are → Aeolus [1] and → Dorus. With his wife → Helice, the daughter of the Peloponnese king Selinus, I. fathers the sons Geleon, Hoples, Argades and Aegicores, after whom the four primal Attic-Ionic phyles are named (Aristot. Ath. Pol. 41,2). Paus. 7,1,5 reports that I. came from the Peloponnese to the aid of the Athenians against the Eleusinians, only to die in the battle. Since Achaeans and Iones have the same father – Xuthus –, the two tribes are claimed to have a close relationship within the Greek tribal structure. However, the Iones on the islands and in Asia Minor were regarded as I.'s descendants not until much later (Vell. Pat. 1,4; Vitr. De arch. 6,1).

In another version of the genealogy, as it appears in the tragedy *I.* by Euripides and in Plato (Euthyd. 302c), the Athenian claim of leadership of the Greek mother country is ascertained even more clearly since any non-Athenian origin is eliminated (it is unclear in how far a tragedy by Sophocles with the same title deals with the same material): in contrast to his brothers Aeolus and Dorus, I. is presented as the son of the god → Apollo. Creusa had abandoned the son whom she had conceived from Apollo and born in secret in a cave immediately after his birth. Hermes, however, has I. raised in the temple of Apollo in Delphi where I. becomes the temple guardian. Creusa later marries king Xuthus, but the marriage remains childless at first. A visit at the oracle of Apollo in Delphi is meant to reveal the cause. After some complications, the *anagnórisis* between mother and son is finally achieved: Xuthus acknowledges I., who is commanded by Apollo to become the → eponym of the Ionians in Asia Minor (Eur. Ion 74; 1581–1588), as his son.

A cult from Samos is attested for I. and his sons. In East-Attic Potami, the tomb of I. (Paus. 1,31,3) was displayed, indicating a hero worship. Furthermore, I. is directly connected to the cult of → Apollo as *patrōiós* as it was practised in Athens, on Delos and in Asia Minor. The latter was identical to the Apollo Pythios and Hypoakraios who had a cave cult on the north-western slope of the Acropolis. There Creusa is said to have abandoned her son I.

1 W. A. OLDFATHER, s.v. I. (3), RE 9, 1857–1860
2 R. PARKER, Myths of Early Athens, in: J. BREMMER (ed.), Interpretations of Greek Mythology, 1987, 206–207
3 E. PRINZ, Gründungsmythen und Sagenchronologie, 1979, 356–370; 446–450   4 E. SIMON, s.v. I., LIMC 5.1, 702–704.   C.W.

[2] I. from Chios. *c.* 480–423/2 BC. He came to Athens as a young man (between 465–462, TrGF 19 T 4a). He is an exceptional figure among the literati of the 5th cent., since he worked with various genres – in prose as well as poetry. Callimachus in his Iambs expressly praises the variety of I.'s work (fr. 203,43ff. PFEIFFER). I. probably wrote ten tragic tetralogies, although only twelve plays were still known in Alexandria. His debut as a tragedian took place between 451 and 448. In the Dionysia of 428, he was defeated by → Euripides and → Iophon [2] (T 5), but for the same year a victory is attested in the agon of tragedies and dithyrambs (T 3). 68 fragments are extant, among them several from lyrical passages (F 10; F 14). 11 titles are known, among them the Satyr play *Omphálē* and the unique title *Méga Dráma* ('The Great Drama'). Ps.-Longinus (33,5) emphasizes that I. wrote flawless and elegant tragedies but that he lacked the poetic zest and inspiration found in authors like Sophocles. A note in the scholia stating that I. also wrote comedies refers probably to his Satyr plays (PCG V, p. 608).

As a lyrical poet, I. wrote dithyrambs, hymns and encomia (PMG 740–746). Aristoph. Pax 828ff. places I. into the context of the dithyrambics who were influenced by the New Music of the late 5th BC (cf. also → Cinesias in Aristoph. Av. 1372ff.). A hymn on the right moment (*kairós*) and an encomium on an otherwise unknown Scythiades are attested. Apparently the elegies that are attested (IEG II 26–32) belong to sympotic occasions. Fr. 27 was probably written for a symposium arranged by king → Archidamus [1] II of Sparta. It is impossible to decide whether the foundation story of Chios (*Chíou ktísis*) was also an elegy or a work of prose (FGrH 392).

Works of prose are certainly *Triagmós* and *Epidēmíai*: in *Triagmós*, I. offers an explanation of the world inspired by Pythagorean theory and based on the number three (36 bks 1 DK). The exact meaning of the title (triplicity, triathlon, division into three parts) is unclear. *Epidēmíai* ('travelogues') are the first memoirs in literary history. There, I. relates encounters with important figures of his time. Not only an important source for the biographies of I.'s contemporaries (fr. 5a BLUMENTHAL on Aeschylus' participation in the battle of Salamis), the work also offers details about their hab-

its and appearance (on Cimon fr. 2f. BLUMENTHAL, fr. 6 on Pericles, fr. 11 on Socrates) and is occasionally anecdotal in character (fr. 8 B. on Sophocles on Chios). → Dithyramb; → Historiography; → Tragedy; → Satyr play; → Pythagoreanism

A. v. BLUMENTHAL, Ion von Chios, 1939; B. GAULY et al. (ed.), Musa tragica, 1991, 64–81, 274f.; O. LENDLE, Einführung in die griech. Geschichtsschreibung, 1992, 28–32; A. LEURINI, Ionis Chii testimonia et fragmenta, 1992; M. L. WEST, Ion of Chios, in: BICS 32, 1985, 71–78.   B.Z.

[3] I. from Thessalonica, a high-ranking officer of → Perseus in the 3rd Macedonian War (Liv. 42,58,10). In 168 BC, he handed over Perseus' children to the Romans on Samothrace (Liv. 45,6,9; Plut. Aem. Paulus 26,6).   L.-M.G.

[4] Left tributary of the → Peneius that flows into it above the city of → Aeginium (Str. 7,7,9) in the Chassia mountains, modern Mourgani. The city of Oxyneia is located on its upper course.

L. DARMEZIN, Sites archéologiques et territoires du massiv des Chassia, in: Topographie antique et géographie historique en pays grec, 1992, 139–155; F. STÄHLIN, Das hellen. Thessalien, 1924, 114.   HE.KR.

Iones (Ἴωνες, Ionians). Name of a Greek tribe (older form *Iāwones*), first attested in a Cnossus text (B 164, l. 4) probably as the name of a foreign troop of warriors. Homer (Il. 13,685) applies the name to the Athenians, the Delphic hymn to Apollo (H. Hom. 5,147–155) refers to the Delphic festive gathering of the I., in the Amphiktyonia I. is the name of the tribe which is represented by Athens and the Euboean cities. In further sources of the archaic and classical periods I. in the narrower sense were the Greeks of Asia Minor from Phocaea and Smyrna (both previously on Aeolian territory) to Miletus along with the islands Chios and Samos off the coast, in the wider sense they were the inhabitants of all areas in which dialects of the Ionian-Attic group (→ Attic, → Ionic) were spoken from ancient times. Besides Ionia these were in Asia Minor the Cyclades without Cythnos and the Dorian arc of islands from Melos to Astypalaea, Euboea without the Dryopian cities Styra and Carystus, Oropus and finally Athens with its large area.

As a loose confederation of states the I. of Asia Minor preserved institutional relics of a tribal league of their early history until the Roman period. The fact that not only they, but with them all other I., were once a political unit is proven on the one hand by their closely related calendars (comparing them reveals a proto-Ionian festival and monthly calendar), on the other hand by the fact that in many Ionian cities identical phyle names have been attested. Thus the names of the four pre-Cleisthenian phyles of Athens, Aigikoreis, Argadeis, Geleontes and Hoplētes, show up in many Ionian cities; the cities of Asia Minor, in any case Miletus, Ephesus and Samos, had two additional phyles, Bōreis and Oinōpes. Thus much speaks for the fact that the I. were once a tribe in eastern central Greece, which could only prevail in Attica and Euboea in the course of the post-Mycenaean migrations, but the majority of which diverted via the Cyclades to Asia Minor and maintained a certain political entity there for a longer period of time (which explains the narrower sense of the name). From the early 1st millennium the name of the I. (in an older form *Jāwan*; earliest mention in cuneiform sources at the end of the 8th cent. BC, see [1]) was used widely in the Near East as the name for all Greeks; this can probably be traced back to the fact that, above all, I. (from Asia Minor and Euboea) carried on Greek trade with the Orient.

1 RLA 5, 150.

F. CASSOLA, La Ionia nel mondo miceneo, 1957; M. B. SAKELLARIOU, La migration grecque en Ionie, 1958; C. TRÜMPY, Unt. zu den altgriech. Monatsnamen und -folgen, 1997, 10–119.   F. GSCH.

Ionia (Ἰωνία; *Iōnía*, Ἰωνίη; *Iōníē*). West Anatolian countryside between Aeolis in the north, Lydia in the east, the Aegean in the west and Caria in the south; it includes the settlement area in Asia Minor of the → Iones, who moved in there in connection with the post-Mycenaean migration and since about 700 BC were amalgamated in the Panionian Amphiktyonia (cf. the descriptions of I. in Str. 14,1; Plin. HN 5,112–120) with the cities of (cf. Hdt. 1,142–148; Aesch. Pers. 771) Miletus, Myus, Priene, Ephesus, Colophon, Lebedus, Teus, Erythrae, Clazomenae, Symrna and Phocaea (the latter two originally Aeolian), which were close to the sea, as well as the islands of Samos and Chios (in other words excluding the Ionian Greeks on the Cyclades, Euboea, in Oropus and Attica). I. has never been a technical term in an administrative sense.

J. M. COOK, The Greeks in Ionia and the East, 1962.   E.O.

Ionian Revolt The Greek cities in → Ionia were compliant subjects of the Persians from 546/5 BC. Beginning with the further expansion of the Persian empire towards the west, the limitations to their trade as a result, increasing taxes and conscription led many cities to attach themselves in 499 to the initiator of the rebellions, → Aristagoras [2]. The latter had given up the tyranny in → Miletus, proclaimed → *isonomía* and secured military support from Athens and Eretria for the revolt. In 498 the Milesians and their allies attacked → Sardes and destroyed it. Thereupon, more cities on the Hellespont and in Caria joined the revolt. At the same time, the Greek cities on Cyprus revolted. The Persian counteroffensive began with the recapture of the island in 497. However, a severe setback in Caria, which at first stopped the Persian movements, followed their successes on the Hellespont and in the Propontis. Not until 494 were the Persians prepared for an attack on Miletus. Ineffective command structures, deficient cohesion and the flight of the Samians, who had been bribed by

the Persians, led to the defeat of the Ionian fleet in the sea battle near the island of → Lade. Miletus was then besieged and destroyed. The Persians punished the rebels with great severity and re-established their own rule over the coastal region and the islands.

The report of Herodotus (5,28–6,32), the only ancient source on the Ionian Revolt, is founded on local oral tradition. Herodotus downplays the achievements of the Ionians, emphasizes their lack of co-operative ability and fundamentally denies the attempt any chance at success. The existence of the *koinón*, a central institution for the co-ordination of the revolts, and the noteworthy early successes of the Ionians, however, demonstrate the one-sidedness of his judgement.

O. MURRAY, in: CAH 4, ²1988, 461–490; P. TOZZI, La rivolta ionica, 1978.   E. S.-H.

Ionians see → Iones

Ioniapolis (Ἰωνιάπολις; *Iōniápolis*). Milesian harbour town on the south bank of the former Latmian Gulf, modern Bafa Gölü. Material from the nearby marble quarries was shipped via this harbour to build the Temple of Apollo at → Didyma. Many Didymaean column drums within a settlement of late antiquity are preserved on the shore and in the water near Pınarcık Yayla (formerly Mersinet Iskelesi). The ancient harbour is assumed to have been further out to sea, as the water level has risen. The name is handed down in two Hellenistic inscriptions from Miletus [1] and a banishment document from Didyma.

1 IMilet I 3, 1914, no. 149 l. 45, no. 150 l. 103f.
2 IDidyma II, 1958, no. 40 l. 16.

A. PESCHLOW-BINDOKAT, I., in: Istanbuler Mitt. 27/8, 1977/8, 131–136; Id., in: JDAI 96, 1981, 186f.; Id., Der Latmos, 1996, 55–57, 59f.   A. PF

Ionic
I. PRE-CLASSICAL PERIOD TO THE KOINE
II. NEO-IONIC AND PONTIC

I. PRE-CLASSICAL PERIOD TO THE KOINE
Beginning in the pre-classical period, Ionic is attested in three main regions, from where it spread in the course of the second → colonization to the end of the Pontus and to Hispania: (1) West Ionic: Euboea (and Oropus) with colonies in Chalcidice (Olynthus), Lower Italy (Cyme, Pithekussa), and Sicily, (2) Ionic of the Cyclades: i.a. Ceos, Delos, Paros (and Thasos), Naxos (and Amorgos), (3) East Ionic: (Ionia and the offshore islands of Chios and Samos): i.a. Phocaea (including Massalia and its settlements in Emporiae in the northeast of Spain and Pech-Maho in the south of France), Smyrna, Clazomenae, Erythrae, Teos, Ephesus, Priene, Miletus, Halicarnassus. Archaic inscriptions are particularly instructive regarding Ionic, because it was strongly influenced or replaced by → Attic, regarded as

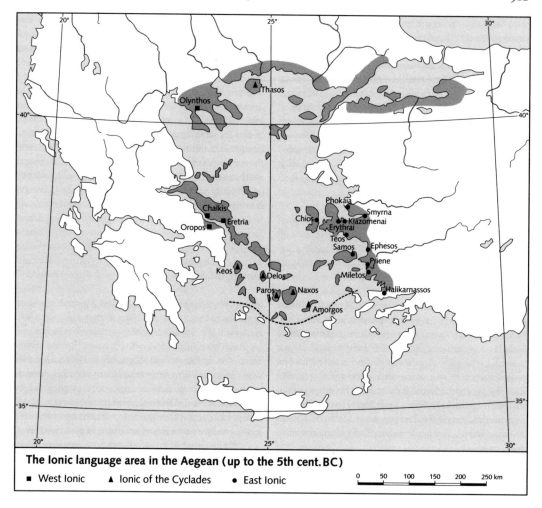

The Ionic language area in the Aegean (up to the 5th cent. BC)

■ West Ionic   ▲ Ionic of the Cyclades   ● East Ionic

0   50   100   150   200   250 km

the basis for *Koine*, from as early as the 2nd half of the 5th cent., rendering it difficult to trace authentic Ionic in non-archaic inscriptions. The literary Ionic, which essentially shaped the epic language and therefore all genres of poetic language and artistic prose (→ Greek literary languages), is rather artificial but offers insights into authentic Ionic vocabulary (e.g. in Hipponax).

Aside from (a) an East Greek component and (b) a number of analogies to Attic that clearly go back to an original unity ('Ionic-attic') at the turn of the 1st millennium BC, Ionic has (c) several distinctive characteristics distinguishing it from Attic.

(a): **-ti(-) > -si(-)*; *t$^{(h)}$*i̯* (τόσος type), **ts > s*; nominative plural οἱ, αἱ; 1st plural in -μεν; athematic infinitive in -ναι (but in Western Ionic sometimes -ν); ὅτε; ἄν; *g^u*ol-* 'to want'; πρῶτος; ἱερός (but Eastern Ionic ἱρός also); εἴκοσι '20'.

(b): **ā > ä̆*; metathesis **āo > eō* (with the so-called 'Attic' declension λεώς) and **ēa > eā*; early disappearance of **u̯*; *ny ephelkystikon*; ἡμεῖς, ὑμεῖς; 3rd singular ἦν 'was'; 3rd plural -σαν (ἔθε-σαν); πρός. Ionic has several other elements in common with Doric (**r̥ > ra* in the

context of C*r̥*C; *verba vocalia* in -άω, -έω; ἀπό; *ἐν-ς with accusative from which Ionian ἐς developed), esp. with the 'mild' form of Doric (*ē̦/ō̦* through compensatory lengthening and contraction, βουλή, τοῦ types).

(c): *ā̆ > ē̦* also following *e, i, r* (e.g. νέη, οἰκίη, χώρη); preservation of *ea, eo, eō* (but *eo > o* through *hyphaeresis* from the 5th cent., *eu* from the 4th cent., e.g. Θόκλος, θευπροπος = Θεόκλος, θεοπρόπος); genitive singular masculine of the type πολίτεω, -ω (East Ionic also -ευ); genitive singular of the i-stems in -ιος (but also in -εως, -εος); only **-ion-* in the comparative (μέζονα); thematic inflection in the reduplicated athematic present (type διδοῖ); aorist ἤνεικα; subjunctive in **-s-o/e-*; participle ἐών 'being'; ἤν (= ἐάν); τέσσε/αρες 'four'; ἱστίη (= ἑστία).

The geography of the Ionic dialect is made more difficult by the fact that the records from different cities (Miletus as the authoritative norm in East Ionic) and islands are incomplete in many ways, and that Attic forms often occur instead of true Ionic forms. Neither the fourfold grouping by Herodotus (1,142,3) nor the conventional, strictly geographical division in (1) West Ionic, (2) Ionic of the Cyclades, and (3) East Ionic does justice to the dialectal situation which emerges from the inscriptions. In many aspects, it is more appropriate to assume a (albeit incomplete) unity between (2) and (3) as opposed to (1), which is closer to Attic (*-rs-* > *-rr-*; ἐκεῖνος; χίλιοι '1000'), at times even closer to Boeotian (*$t^{(h)}$-i, *$k^{(h)}i$ [present in -ττω], *$t\underset{.}{u}$ > tt; ξένος; dative plural -αις, -οις) as against Ionic of the islands and East Ionic: *-rs-*; κεῖνος; χείλιοι; ss (-σσω); ξεῖνος; -η(ι)σι(ν), -οισι(ν). Typically West Ionic: *u*, not *ü* (φύϙνυς = Κύκνος); shortening of *-ēi*, *-ōi* to *-ei* (as in Attic), *-oi*; τουτα, τουτει, εντουθα (= ταῦτα, ταύτῃ, ἐνταῦθα); infinitive τιθεῖν, διδοῦν, εἶν (= τιθέναι, διδόναι, εἶναι); βόλομαι. Specific to Eretria: *-s(-)* > *-r(-)*. Typically East Ionic and Ionic of the Cyclades: <αο>, <εο> for *aṷ, eṷ* (αοτος, ταοτα, εο°, βασιλεος = αὐτός, ταῦτα, εὖ°, βασιλεύς), which indicates that *u was pronounced as *$ü$; γίνομαι. Exclusively East Ionic is → psilosis (hence the use of <H> for *ę* from *ā* < *$\bar{a}$ in the Milesian alphabet, which later became common); ὀκο- from *$\underset{.}{i}$o-k^{u}o- (e.g. οκοια for ὁποῖα); inflection of the type ἱέρεως, genitive -εω; ἑωυτο-, but also ἑαυ/οτο-; ἱρός, but also ἱερός (even within the same inscription). Predominantly in the north of Ionia (Phocaea and colonies, Chios, Smyrna, Erythrae), which was originally inhabited by Aeolian tribes (Hdt. 1,149–150), there are sporadic correspondences with Lesbian, possibly caused by substrata or adstrata: *-ons-* > *-ois-* (3rd plural -οισι, -ωισι from *-onti*, *-ōnti*); inflected numerals (e.g. τεσσ[ερ]α-κοντων); dative plural -αισιν; athematic inflection in the participle of the *verba vocalia* (διψαντ[ι in Emporiae); perhaps Ζιονυ[σιος] (Phocaea), ἀί and ἀί 'always'.

SAMPLES:

West Ionic: Cyme (7th cent.) Ταταιε̄ς ε̄μι λε̄ϙυθος · Ηος δ' αν με κλεφσει θυφλος εσται. – Eretria (411) εδοξεν τει βόληι · ... και σιτηριν ειναι και αυτωι και παι-ριν, οταν ε[π]ιδημεωριν και ατελεην και προεδριην ες τōς αγωνας: (c. 340) οπωρ αν τα Αρτεμιρια ... αγωμεν και θυωριν οι πλειστοι εδοξεν τει βουλει και τοι δημοι · τιθειν την πολιν αγωνα μουσικης ...

Ionic of the Cyclades: Naxos (7th–6th cents.: hex-ameter) Νικανδρη μ' ανεθε̄κεν Ηκηβολοι ιοχεαιρηι /ϙορη Δεινιδικηο του Ναησιο εΗσοχος αληον /Δεινομενεος δε κασιγνε̄τη ΦΗραΗσο δ' αλοχος ν[υν] (<η> = <H>!). Cor-responding to Νικανδρη μ' ἀνέθηκεν ἑκηβόλω ἰοχεαίρῃ /κούρη Δεινοδικεω τοῦ Ναξίου ἔξοχος ἀλλέων /Δεινομένεος δὲ κασιγνήτη Φράξου δ' ἄλοχος νῦν.

East Ionic: Miletus (6th cent.) Εοθρασο[ης] ... Λεω-δαμας Οναξο̄ πρυτ[α]νευοντες ανεθεσαν τῆκατηι. (c. 450) ην δε η πολι[ς ε]γκρατης γενηται, κατακτε̄ναι [αυτ]ο̄ς τōς επιμηνιος επ'ων αν λαφθεωσιν. (c. 344) ειναι δε ... τωι βουλομενωι εισαφιξιν ες Σαρδις ... κατα τα αοτα. – Chios (5th cent.) [οι πε]ντεκα[ιδεκ]α ες βōλη[ν εν]ει-καντων [εν] πεντ' ημερη[ι]σιν · τōς δε κηρυκας διαπεμ-ψαντες ες τας χωρας κη[ρ]υσσοντων και ... αποδεκνυντες την ημερην ην αν λαβωσιν και το πρηγμα προσκηρυσ-σοντων ο τι αν μελλη πρηξεσθαι. – Didyma (6th cent.) κα]θαιρεν και : τō : ιρεως : γι[νεσθαι – απο ιερηιο : κ[α]ι νεφρ[ον. – Pech-Maho (2nd half of the 5th cent.) και

κειν' ελαβεν εν τωι ποταμωι · τον αρραβων' ανεδωκα οκō τἀκατια ορμιζεται.

→ Aeolic (Lesbian); → Attic; → Greek dialects; → Greek literary languages; → Homeric language; → Psilosis

SOURCES (SELECTION): IG XI, 2–4; XII, 5; XII, 7; XII, 9; XII, Suppl.; IK 1–2; 11/1; 12; 15; 17/1; 17/3; 24/1; L. DU-BOIS, Inscriptions grecques dialectales de la Sicile, 1989 (1–20 Euboan colonies); Id., Inscriptions grecques dialec-tales de Grande Grèce I. Colonies eubéennes. Colonies ioniennes. Emporia, 1995; Id., Inscriptions grecques dia-lectales d'Olbia du Pont, 1996; J. POUILLOUX, M. LE-JEUNE, Une transaction commerciale ionienne au Ve siècle à Pech-Maho, in: CRAI 1988, 526–535; R. A. SANTIAGO, Epigrafía dialectal emporitana, in: E. CRESPO et al. (ed.), Dialectologica Graeca Miraflores, 1993, 281–295.

BIBLIOGRAPHY: M. DEL BARRIO, El dialecto de Eubea, thesis Madrid UCM 1987; BECHTEL, Dial.^{2} 3; CL. BRIXHE et al., Bulletin de dialectologie grecque, in: REG 98, 1985, 274–279; K. A. GARBRAH, A Grammar of the Ionic In-scriptions from Erythrae, 1978; P. HUALDE, Eolismos en Jonia: revisión de un problema de geografía intradialectal, in: Emerita 65, 1997, 221–256 (useful as a collection of examples); E. KNITL, Die Sprache der ion. Kykladen nach den inschr. Quellen, thesis Munich 1938; M. LEJEUNE, La dédicace de Νικάνδρη et l'écriture archaïque de Naxos, in: RPh 97, 1971, 209–215; A. LÓPEZ EIRE, Géographie intradialectale de l'ionien-attique, in: Verbum 10, 1987, 154–178; A. SCHERER, Zur Laut- und Formenlehre der milesischen Inschr., thesis Munich 1934; K. STÜBER, Zur dialektalen Einheit des Ostion., 1996; THUMB/SCHERER, 194–284, esp. 245–284.

CARTOGRAPHY: M. DEL BARRIO, El dialecto de Eubea, thesis Madrid UCM 1987; K. STÜBER, Zur dialektalen Einheit des Ostion., 1996; THUMB/SCHERER, 194–284, esp. 245–284.   J.G.-R.

II. NEO-IONIC AND PONTIC

As is the case for Tsaconian and the Modern Greek of Lower Italy, the question arises as to what extent the Pontic dialect of Modern Greek on the Black Sea Coast (threatened since the Greek-Turkish population ex-change in the 1920's) contains remnants preceding the *Koiné* or could even be described as a continuation of ancient Ionic. This question is particularly difficult to answer for the Pontic dialect, since later Attic and even more so the *Koiné* were strongly influenced by Ionic, so that the results of Koineization and the preservation of old dialects were often be identical. Altogether, Pontic presents itself as a particularly old dialect: the preser-vation of geminates as in the other border regions of the Modern Greek dialect area; the preservation of the original accent position in παιδία for what is in stand-ard Modern Greek (SMG) παιδιά, the preservation of <η> as /e/ as in νύφη for Old Greek νύμφη; the preser-vation of /o/ for example in Latin loanwords such as καρβώνιν, σαπώνιν as opposed to SMG καρβούνι, σαπούνι; the preservation of old meanings such as παιδεύω as 'educate' in contrast to SMG 'torment'. However, several characteristics of old Ionic have been preserved as well, such as the negation κιτ < Ionian οὐκί (Attic would be οὐχί; SMG has δέν < οὐδέν), final – η e.g. in αἴγειρη 'black poplar', the move of the aspiration such as in ἀχαντώνα for ἀκανθών as in Ionian βάθρακος in contrast to Attic βάτραχος or compensatory lengthening of the group *ολϜ in οῦλον instead of SMG ὅλος as in Ionian οῦλος in contrast to Attic ὅλος.

N. ANDRIOTIS, Lex. der Archaismen in den neugriech. Dial., 1974; N. KONTOSOPOULOS, Διάλεκτοι και ιδιώματα της νέας ελληνικής, 1981; J. NIEHOFF-PANAGIOTIDIS, Koine und Diglossie, 1995; D. E. OIKONOMIDIS, Γραμματική της ελληνικής διαλέκτου του Πόντου, 1958; A. PAPADOPOULOS, Ιστορική γραμματική της ποντικής διαλέκτου, 1955; A. SEMENOV, Der nordpontische Dialekt des Neugriech., in: Glotta 23, 1935, 91–107.   V.BI.

Ionic Migration see → Colonization

Ionicus of Sardis. Teacher and physician, who worked around AD 390. The son of a physician and a pupil of Zeno of Cyprus, he was well respected, particularly regarding his services to practical therapy, pharmacology, the art of bandaging, and surgery. In addition, he was a philosopher with particular gifts in medical prognostication as well as in fortunetelling (Eunapius, Vitae Philosophorum 499). Furthermore, he is reported to have distinguished himself as a well-known orator and poet, even though none of his works have survived.
                                                       V.N.

Ionidae (Ἰωνίδαι; *Iōnídai*). Attic Mesogea deme of the Aegeis phyle, sending two (one) *bouleutaí*. MEYER [1] localizes it near Charvati, SIEWERT [2] near Lutró, TRAILL [3; 4] near Draphi (?), and VANDERPOOL [5. 24ff.] near Vurva. Genealogical connections between its eponymous hero Ion and Gargettus (Paus. 6,22,7) might point to the deme's location in the general area of Charvati south of Pallene.

1 E. MEYER, s.v. I., RE Suppl. 10, 329   2 P. SIEWERT, Die Trittyen Attikas und die Heeresreform des Kleisthenes, 1982, 87 n. 2, 172ff.   3 TRAILL, Attica, 5, 15f., 41, 69, 110 no. 59, table 2   4 Id., Demos and Trittys, 1986, 127   5 E. VANDERPOOL, The location of the Attic deme Erchia, in: BCH 89, 1965, 21–26.   H.LO.

Ionios Kolpos (Ἰόνιος κόλπος), Adria (ὁ Ἀδρίας, *Mare Adriaticum* or *Supernum*), Ionian Sea. In contrast with the modern view, the Ionios Kolpos (IK) was seen by Hecataeus (FGrH 1 F 91f.) as starting from Istria, by Hellanicus (FGrH 4 F 4) from the mouth of the Spines. In the south the name is occasionally transferred to the Sicilian Sea (Mela 2,37; 48; 110). Originally, *Adria* only referred to the innermost corner of the Adriatic Sea at the mouth of the Po and the settlement area of the Veneti, from the name of whose town → Atria, the name Adria allegedly derived (Str. 5,1,8). In the 4th cent. BC, Adria and IK are used synonymously (Scyl. 14; 27). Later, the term Adria was extended to the waters beyond the Strait of Otranto (Ptol. 3,1,1; Paus. 5,25,3). Because of insufficient north-south routes in the Balkan peninsula, the IK was used from the Bronze Age as a trade route between Central Europe and Greece. From the 8th cent. BC, Greek seafarers and colonists opened up the IK, which became an important connection between Italy and Hellas. In late antiquity, it constituted the border between the West and the East Roman empire.

J. PARTSCH, s.v. Adria, RE 1, 417–419; W. M. MURRAY, s.v. Adriatic Sea, ³OCD, 14.   D.S.

Iophon (Ἰοφῶν; *Iophôn*)
[1] Son of → Peisistratus from his second marriage to the Argive Timonassa, the daughter of Gorgilus and widow of the → Cypselid Archinus of Ambracia. In contrast to his brother → Hegesistratus [1], only I.'s name has survived ([Aristot.] Ath. pol. 17,3; Plut. Cato maior 24,8; Hdt. 5,94f.).

L. DE LIBERO, Die Archaische Tyrannis, 1996, 88; Traill, PAA 537360.   B.P.

[2] Athenian tragedian (TrGF I 22), a son of → Sophocles and author of 50 plays (TrGF I T 1). The following titles are attested: *Achilleús*, *Télephos*, *Aktaiốn*, *Ilíou Pérsis*, *Dexamenós*, *Bákchai*, *Pentheús* (possibly a double title 'Bacchae and Pentheus'), a satyr play 'Satyrs singing to the *aulos*'; possible additions are titles which were probably wrongly attributed to → Cleophon (TrGF *77 T 1), such as *Amphiáraos*, *Ērigónē*, *Thyéstēs*, *Leúkippos*. A total of only five verses is extant. I. won at the Dionysia of 435 BC and in 428 came second after → Euripides and before → Ion. In comedies he was frequently mocked for not having his father's qualities or even for having his plays performed as his own (T 5a). → Satyrus reports in his life of Sophocles that I. had striven to have his father legally incapacitated because of senile dementia and that Sophocles countered by reciting from his 'Oedipus at Colonus'. It is likely that this story too had its origins in comedic mockery.

K. J. DOVER (ed., comm.), Aristophanes, Frogs, 1993, 199; B. GAULY et al. (ed.), Musa tragica, 1991, 88–93, 280f.   B.Z.

Iophossa (Ἰοφῶσσα; *Iophôssa*). According to Hesiod and Acusilaus another name of → Chalciope [2]. Daughter of Aeetes of Colchis and Idyia. Sister of Medea, wife of Phrixus, the father of her four sons (schol. Apoll. Rhod. 2,1122; 2,1149; Apollod. 1,83).
                                                       RE.ZI.

Ioppe (Egyptian *ypw*, Assyrian *yāpu*, *yappû*, Hebrew *yāpô* 'be beautiful'), Greek or Latin name for the modern Jaffa south of Tel Aviv. A place of settlement from the 2nd millennium BC to the Hellenistic-Roman period, I. is the only location in Palestine (→ Palaestina) of a Greek myth. It is in I. that Perseus rescued → Andromeda who had been left at the mercy of a sea-monster (Ov. Met. 4,772ff.). A comparable situation is found in the OT story of Jonah.

O. Keel, Orte und Landschaften der Bibel, 2, 1982, 12–28; J. Kaplan, H. R. Ritter-Kaplan, s.v. Jaffa, NEAEHL 2, 655–659.

R.L.

Iordanes

[1] Writer of the Justinian period (6th cent. AD), a German, probably of Gothic descent, grandson of Paria (secretary to the Prince of the Alani Candac), son of Alanoviamuth. Probably born in the late 5th cent. AD, I. also served as secretary to Cantac's nephew Gunthigis (Iord. Get. 265). Following his *conversio* (from Arianism to Orthodoxy?, from a secular to a clerical position?), in Constantinople in 551 (Iord. Rom. 4. 363; cf. Iord. Get. 104) he was asked by a friend named Vigilius (unlikely to be the contemporary pope of the same name) to write a history of suffering of the Roman world (Rom. 2). While working on that (Get. 1), he was approached by Castalius, a mutual friend, for an abbreviated version of → Cassiodorus' History of the Goths, which he worked into the *De summa temporum vel origine actibusque gentis Romanorum* (Rom. 4) and dedicated to Vigilius in *c.* 552.

His book *De summa temporum vel origine actibusque gentis Romanorum* (= Rom.) combines excerpts from the OT (8–61), from Jerome's chronicle (12–85; 256–314), from Florus and Festus (87–254), Eutropius (cf. [5]), and Orosius (255–318), as well as from Marcellinus Comes (315–384; also used in *De origine actibusque Getarum* (= Get.). However, the attempt by [4] to trace this 'mosaic of sources' to Memmius Symmachus' *Historia Romana* has failed (cf. [6]). In accordance with the Augustinian theology of history (→ Augustinus), the tenor of this work – in line with the express desire of the addressee and referring to his *conversio* (Rom. 4) – is to emphasize the *clades* and *casus* ('misfortunes' and 'changes of fortunes') of the history of the world (as a consequence of the history of Rome) for the period up to the Byzantine-Gothic war (AD 535–553, Rom. 368ff.).

De origine actibusque Getarum, a book he wrote in parallel, which microcosmically complements the history of the world, deals with the history of the Goths with particular emphasis on the Amal dynasty (→ Amali) until their catastrophic demise in AD 540. It is based on Cassiodorus' history of the Goths, which, however, I. only had access to for three days and so was not able to copy verbatim. He also supplemented it with other sources (Get. 2f., cf. [3. 234f.]). As [4] earlier, [7] also denies any individual input by I. (cf. however [8], [9. 25ff.], [11], [17. 38ff.], but against [16. 14ff.]). It is impossible to distinguish a pro-Gothic [7] or consistently pro-Justinian [9] tendency, or even any clear political tendency at all, in contrast to *De summa temporum*.

As a handy summary of Roman history, combined with the heroization of quasi-mythical people ('Gothicism', cf. [14]), this 'diptych' has enjoyed some success in the Middle Ages. Even modern historians (cf. [15]–[17], differently [10. 19ff.]) see the *Getica* as the main source for the history of the Goths.

Mommsen based his edition on the least 'classical' 'Class 1', mainly on Heidelberg, Pal. 921 (see VIII/IX; destroyed in a fire at Mommsen's house in 1880); the linguistically more standard 'Class 3' is now represented by the older Bobiensis Palermo, Archivio dello Stato, Cod. Basile (see VIII², Codices Latini Antiquiores Suppl. 1741). Only the future edition by Bradley (cf. [13]) promises a stemmatically balanced text, which should provide a new basis for any investigations of language and style.

1 N. Wagner, Getica, 1967   2 W. Suerbaum, Vom antiken zum frühmittelalterlichen Staatsbegriff, ³1977, 268–278, 380ff.   3 J. J. O'Donnell, The Aims of Jordanes, in: Historia 31, 1982, 223–240   4 W. Ensslin, Des Symmachus Historia Romana als Quelle für Jordanes, 1949   5 S. Ratti, Les Romana de Jordanès et le Bréviaire d'Eutrope, in: AC 65, 1996, 175–187   6 L. Várady, Jordanes-Studien, in: Chiron 6, 1976, 441–487   7 Momigliano 2, 207ff.   8 B. Croke, Cassiodorus and the Getica of Jordanes, in: CPh 82, 1987, 117–134   9 W. Goffart, The Narrators of Barbarian History, 1988, 20–111   10 Id., Two Notes on Germanic Antiquity Today, in: Traditio 50, 1995, 9–30   11 G. Zecchini, Ricerche di storiografia Latina tardoantica, 1993, 193–209   12 D. R. Bradley, The Getica of Jordanes, in: Hermes 121, 1993, 211–236   13 Id., Manuscript Evidence for the Text of the "Getica" of Jordanes, in: Hermes 123, 1995, 346–362, 490–503   14 J. Svennung, Zur Geschichte des Goticismus, 1967   15 S. Teillet, Des Goths à la nation gothique, 1984, 305–334   16 B. Tönnies, Die Amalertradition, 1989, 8–20   17 P. J. Heather, Goths and Romans, 1991, 1–67.

Editions: Th. Mommsen, 1882; F. Giunta, A. Grillone, 1991 (only Get.; bibliography XLI–XLVII).   P.L.S.

[2] The river Jordan, Hebrew *ha-Yardēn*, Greek ὁ Ἰωρδάνης; *ho Iōrdánēs*; Arabic *al-Urdunn* or *aš-Šarīʿat al-Kabīrah*, 'great watering place'. The etymology is controversial: possibly derived from Aramaic *RDY* or Hebrew *YRD* ('to flow'). Perennial body of water in the Syrian-African rift-valley with several sources. The Jordan flows through the now drained Lake Semechonitis (Buḥair al-Ḥūla, +70 m) and the Sea of Galilee (−208 m), is joined from the east by its tributaries Yarmuk and Jabbok, and flows into the Dead Sea (−395 m; → Asphaltitis limne). The valley between the Sea of Galilee and the Dead Sea has a subtropical climate, but south of the Jabbok, it is mainly desert apart from the oases. Because the river bed lies so low, irrigation farming is possible only from the lateral tributaries. Because of the climate, the valley never served as a communication link and the river was never navigable. Even for east-west traffic, it might have constituted an obstacle only during the spring floods; it more likely united the eastern and western regions into one economic unit. The common perception of the Jordan as the eastern border of the land promised to the people of Israel and its crossing as the beginning of the acquisition of additional lands presupposes the institution of the Assyrian province of Galʾad (*c.* 733 BC), and was

only recorded in border descriptions dating from the exile and post-exile periods (Num. 34:12; Ez 47:18).
→ Judah and Israel

K. BIEBERSTEIN, Josua – Jericho – Jordan, 1995.   K.B.

Ios (Ἴος; *Íos*). Sparsely fertile island of the southern Cyclades between Naxos and Thera, with an area of 103 km² and rising to 735 m (Pirgos). The eponymous town was located on the eastern side, near the modern main town. Few remains: the chief sanctuary of Apollo Pythios [2. 308f.; 311f.] is extant, also some prehistoric finds [1. 24], and the ruins of an ancient guard tower (Psaropyrgos). I. claims to be the home of → Homer and displays his tomb close to the northern tip of the island near the modern Plakoto (Paus. 10,24,2). In the 5th cent. BC, I. was a member of the → Delian League with an initial tribute of one talent, later reduced to half a talent (ATL 1, 288; 3, 33; 48; 198). Further documentary evidence: IG XII 5 no. 14 and 217 (copy of the Great Hymn to Isis); Scyl. 58; Str. 10,5,1; Stadiasmus maris magni 273; 284 (GGM I 497; 500); Ps.-Plut. Vita Homeri 3f. (= Aristot. fr. 76 R.); Steph. Byz. s.v. Ἴ.; Ptol. 3,14,23; IG XII 5 no. 1–23, Suppl. no. 167–176. I. minted coins showing Homer's head (HN 486).

1 D. FIMMEN, Kret.-myk. Kultur, ²1924   2 P. GRAINDOR, in: BCH 28, 1904.

L. BÜRCHNER, s.v. I., RE 9, 1930ff.; LAUFFER, Griechenland, 279; PHILIPPSON/KIRSTEN 4, 141ff.   H.KAL.

Iosephus (Ἰώσηπ(π)ος; *Iósēp(p)os*, Ἰώσηφ(ος); *Iósēph(os)*). From Hebrew *yosep yosipyah* 'may God add (further children)', a prevalent Jewish name in memory of the biblical patriarch Joseph (Gen. 35; 37–50), e.g. in the Herodian family.
[1] Uncle and brother-in-law of → Herod [1] the Great (Jos. Ant. Iud. 15,65; 81). He acted as his deputy for the duration of Herod's journey to M. → Antonius [I 9] in 34 BC. He became involved in the intrigues surrounding Queen → Mariamme, his wife Salome pressed charges for his adultery with Mariamme, and he was executed (Jos. BI 1,443; Jos. Ant. Iud. 15,87).
[2] Younger brother of Herod [1] the Great, acted as deputy when Herod travelled to Italy after the Parthian incursion in AD 40. He died in 38 in the fight against → Antigonus [5], the king and high priest installed by the Parthians (Jos. BI 1,266–323; Jos. Ant. Iud. 14,413–450 passim).
[3] Son of I. [2], husband of Herod's daughter Olympias (Jos. BI 1,562; Jos. Ant. Iud. 17,20), allied himself with Rome during the unrest after Herod's [1] death in 4 BC (Jos. BI 2,74; Jos. Ant. Iud. 17,294). His daughter Mariamme was married to the tetrarch → Herod [7] of Chalcis (Jos. BI 2,221; Jos. Ant. Iud. 18,134).   K.BR.

[4] I. Flavius
A. LIFE B. WORKS

A. LIFE
Jewish Hellenistic historian, born in Jerusalem in AD 37/8 (died in Rome presumably in AD 100). His family was part of the priestly aristocracy, but doubt is cast on his claim to kinship with the Hasmonaean dynasty (Vita 2). Even though as a priest, I. was closer to the religious party of the → Sadducees, he joined the → Pharisees (Vita 12; [22]). His native language was Aramaic, but he must have acquired his knowledge of Greek in his early youth. It is probable that he learned Latin only during his diplomatic mission to Rome (64–66), which resulted in the release of Jewish priests. In 66, he sided with the rebels rising against the Roman procurator → Gessius Florus and the Syrian governor Cestius Gallus and in the subsequent war, he assumed a leading position as general of the Galilean fortress → Iotapata (Jos. BI 2,568, Vita 29). However, there is dispute regarding his political and military role and his loyalty to John (→ Iohannes [2]) of Gischala and the Zealots [12. 181–231; 23. 144–173; 28. 231f.]. Contradictions also appear in his presentation of himself (Vita 28, Joseph BI 2,562–571). Following the capture of Iotapata by Vespasian in the spring of 67, I. was taken prisoner (Joseph BI 3,340–391). While in captivity, he prophesied Vespasian that he would accede to the imperial throne and he was freed after Vespasian was proclaimed emperor in 69. In 70 I. took part in Titus' capture of Jerusalem on Rome's side (BI 5). Living in Rome from AD 71, he was awarded Roman citizenship, an annual pension and estates.

B. WORKS
I.'s works survive complete. They are written in Greek; only for the *Bellum Iudaicum* is the existence of a (lost) original Aramaic version (*c.* AD 75) assumed. None of his works received a significant reception within Judaism, with the singular exception of the mediaeval Hebrew *Sepher* → *Josippon*.
Bellum Iudaicum: The Greek version of the *Bellum* (Περὶ τοῦ Ἰουδαϊκοῦ πολέμου; *Perì toû Ioudaïkoû polémou*) appeared between AD 79 and 81, and was mainly directed at the Hellenized educated elite of the Roman Empire. It deals with the developments leading up to the Jewish-Roman War up to the fall of the mountain fortress of Massadah. The apologetic tenor is unmistakable ([17. 198ff.], differently e.g. [23. 132ff.]), with the aim of blaming Jewish splinter parties for the uprising against Rome, thus exonerating the Jewish people and the aristocracy, as well as glorifying the Flavian emperors. I.'s sources were his own notes of the events of the war, the descriptions of the war by Vespasian and Titus, and the description of world history by → Nicolaus of Damascus [6. 392–419].
Antiquitates Iudaicae: 'Jewish Antiquities' (Ἰουδαϊκὴ ἀρχαιολογία; *Ioudaïkè archaiología*), probably published in 93/4 together with the *Vita*. In 20 volumes,

they describe Jewish history (Books 1–10: from the creation of the world to Persian rule, Books 11–20: from Alexander the Great to the Jewish-Roman War). Verifiable sources for the first half in particular are the Hebrew → Bible [14. 50–58] (Hebrew and Aramaic version and particularly the Septuagint [14. 97–115] and an unknown Greek translation [25. 773]), and those for the second half include Nicolaus of Damascus [14. 147–172], Polybius, Strabo, 1 Macc [14. 116–131], the → Letter of Aristeas [14. 97–115], and Jewish documents [24. 367–400] [11. 80ff.; 27. 256–283]. The documents and records used by I. are generally seen as authentic [11. 100]. The target audience of the *Antiquitates* should be assumed to be both educated Romans and Greeks, providing them with an insight into → Judaism, and Hellenized Jewish circles.

Vita Josephi: I.'s autobiography (Ἰωσήπου βίος; *Iōsḗpou bíos*) was first published in 93/4 as a supplement to the *Antiquitates* and is the first example of its genre. It is I.'s aim to justify his actions in the Jewish-Roman War and to display his competence as an author.

Contra Apionem: Central to I.'s book 'Against Apion' (Πρὸς Ἀπίωνα; *Pròs Apíōna*), published between 93/4 and 96 and known under that title since Jerome (Epist. 70,3), is the apologia of Judaism, even more clearly than in the *Antiquitates*. Prominence is given to the great age of the Jewish religion and its accordance with philosophical principles (Ap. 1,165; 2,145–286; [10. 220–232]).

EDITIONS: 1 B. NIESE, Flavii Josephi Opera, 7 vols., 1885–1895 2 S. A. NABER, Flavii Josephi Opera Omnia, 6 vols., 1888–1896.
TRANSLATIONS: 3 H. ST. J. THACKERAY, R. MARCUS, L. H. FELDMAN, Josephus, 9 vols., 1926–1965 4 O. MICHEL, O. BAUERNFEIND, Flavius Josephus: De Bello Judaico. Der jüd. Krieg, 3 vols., 1963–1982.
CONCORDANCES: 5 K. H. RENGSTORFF (ed.), A complete concordance to Flavius Josephus, 4 vols., 1973–1983.
BIBLIOGRAPHY: 6 L. H. FELDMAN, Josephus and Modern Scholarship (1957–1980), 1984 7 L. H. FELDMAN, Josephus. A Supplementary Bibliography, 1989 8 H. SCHRECKENBERG, Bibliogr. zu Flavius Josephus, 1968 9 Id., Bibliogr. zu Flavius Josephus. Suppl. mit Gesamtregister, 1979.
BIBLIOGRAPHY: 10 O. BETZ, K. HAACKER, M. HENGEL (ed.), Josephus-Studien: Unters. zu Josephus, dem ant. Judentum und dem NT, 1974 11 P. BILDE, Flavius Josephus between Jerusalem and Rome. His life, works and their importance, 1988 12 S. J. D. COHEN, Josephus in Galilee and Rome. His vita and development as a historian, 1979 13 L. H. FELDMAN, G. HATA (ed.), Josephus, Judaism, and Christianity, 1987 14 Id. (ed.), Josephus, the bible, and history, 1989 15 F. J. FOAKES JACKSON, Josephus and the Jews: The Religion and History of the Jews as Explained by Flavius Josephus, 1930 (repr. 1977) 16 C. GERBER, Die Heiligen Schriften des Judentums nach Flavius Josephus, in: M. HENGEL, H. LÖHR (ed.), Schriftauslegung im ant. Judentum und im Urchristentum, 1994, 91–113 17 M. GOODMAN, The Ruling Class of Judaea, 1987 18 M. HADAS-LEBEL, Flavius Josephus, le juif de

Rome, 1989 19 G. HÖLSCHER, Die Quellen des Josephus für die Zeit vom Exil bis zum jüd. Kriege, 1904 20 K.-S. KRIEGER, Geschichtsschreibung als Apologetik bei Flavius Josephus, 1994 21 R. LAQUER, Der jüd. Historiker Flavius Josephus, 1920 (repr. 1970) 22 S. MASON, Flavius Josephus on the Pharisees: A Composition-Critical Study, 1991 23 T. RAJAK, Josephus: the Historian and his Society, 1983 24 A. SCHALIT (ed.), Zur Josephus-Forschung, 1973 25 H. SCHRECKENBERG, s.v. Josephus (Flavius Josephus), RAC 18, 762–802 26 B. SCHRÖDER, Die "väterlichen Gesetze". Flavius Josephus als Vermittler von Halachah an Griechen und Römer, 1996 27 SCHÜRER 1, 43–63, 428–441, 485–496; 3/1, 186, 545f. 28 G. E. STERLING, Historiography and Self-Definition. Josephos, Luke-Acts and Apologetic Historiography, 1992 29 H. ST. J. THACKERAY, Josephus. The Man and the Historian, 1929 (repr. with introduction by S. SANDMEL, 1967). I.WA.

[5] I. of Thessalonica. Younger brother of Theodorus Studites, born AD 762, a monk from *c.* 780, from 798 in the Studium monastery in Constantinople, 807–809 Archbishop of Thessalonica, subsequently deposed and banished several times, died 832. After the Iconoclasm in 844 (→ Syrian dynasty), his remains were transferred to the Studium monastery in Constantinople. He was an author and important hymnodist of the Orthodox Church; poetry surviving under the name Iosephus is partly attributable to him, partly to the younger Iosephus, the hymnographer (*c.* 810 in Sicily – 886 in Constantinople).
→ Hymn; → Theodorus Studites

H.-G. BECK, Kirche und theolog. Lit. im byz. Reich, 1959, 50f. AL.B.

[6] I. Genesius. The conventional name of an anonymous Byzantine historical work on the period 813–886, written probably in the mid–10th cent. The name *Genesius* as that of the author is only mentioned in a postscript to an 11th cent. manuscript written by a much later hand. Identification with I. Genesius, mentioned by Iohannes Skylitzes as his predecessor, is possible but not provable. The name Genesius is of Armenian origin. Sources used in this book are Georgius Monachus, some other extant texts, and a lost chronicle, which was also used in the continuation to Theophanes' chronicle.
→ Georgius [5] Monachus; → Skylitzes; → Theophanes Continuatus

EDITIONS: A. LESMUELLER-WERNER, I. THURN (ed.), Iosephi Genesii regum libri quattuor, 1978.
TRANSLATIONS: A. LESMÜLLER-WERNER, Byzanz am Vorabend neuer Größe ... Die vier Bücher der Kaisergesch. des Ioseph Genesios, 1989. AL.B.

Iotacism see → Itacism

Iotapata (Ἰωτάπατα; *Iōtápata*, Ἰωταπάτη; *Iōtapátē*, Hebrew *Yodpat, Yotpat*), town in Lower Galilee 10 km north of → Sepphoris, modern Ḥirbat Šifāt. Archaeological finds indicate settlement from the late Bronze

Age [4], according to Rabbinic tradition (Mišna 'Arakin 9,6, it was a fortified town by the time of Joshua, possibly identical with the *yotbah* of 2 Kgs 21,19 [5]. In the Jewish war it was a centre of anti-Roman resistance under → Iosephus [4] (Jos. BI 3,141–288). It was captured in AD 67 by Vespasian after a siege lasting 47 days, and largely destroyed (ibid. 3,316–338). It continues to be mentioned into the 3rd cent. as a town with Jewish population (including the seat of one of the 24 priestly classes [2]) (cf. Babylonian Talmud Zebahim 110b; Me'ila 13 b).

1 SCHÜRER 1, 477, 490, 493   2 S. KLEIN, Beitr. zur Gesch. und Geogr. Galiläas, 1909, 50   3 G. DALMAN, Palästina-Jb. 8, 1912, 40–43   4 A. SAARISOLO, Journ. Palest. Orient Soc. 9, 1929, 37, 39   5 ABEL 2, 336   6 D. R. EDWARDS, M. AVIAM, D. ADAN BAYEWITZ, Yodefat 1992, in: Israel Exploration Journal 45, 1995, 191–197.
BE.SCH.

Iotape ('Ιοτάπη; *Iotápē*).
[1] Daughter of Antiochus [18] IV of Commagene. She was married to Alexander, the son of Tigranes, a descendant of Hero and for a short while king of Armenia. With the support of the Roman emperor Vespasian (= AD 79) her husband became king of a small territory in Cilicia and had coins minted with images of himself and his wife (Jos. Ant. Iud. 18, 139–141).

R. D. SULLIVAN, The Dynasty of Commagene, in: ANRW II 8, 1977, 794f.
A.ME.

[2] Coastal town in Cilicia Tracheia, the modern Aydap İskelesi, 8 km northwest of Selinus. Ptol. 5,7,2; Plin. HN 5,92; Hierocles 709,7.

1 HILD s.v. I.   2 E. ROSENBAUM, G. HUBER, S. ONURKAN, A Survey of Coastal Cities in Western Cilicia. Preliminary Report, 1967, 35ff. (with sketchmaps).
K.T.

Iotapianus I., who allegedly boasted of his descent from (Severus?) Alexander (Aur. Vict. Caes. 29,2), was proclaimed rival emperor to → Philippus Arabs in Cappadocia or Syria in AD 248/49 (Chron. min. 1, 521,38 MOMMSEN; Zos. 1,20,2; Aur. Vict. Caes. 29,2) and in September/October 249 he was killed by his soldiers (Zos. 1,21,2; RIC 4,3, 105).

PIR[2] I 49; KIENAST[2], 202; X. LORIOT, Les premières années de la grande crise du IIIe siècle, in: ANRW II 2, 1975, 657–797, esp. 794.
T.F.

Iota subscriptum see → Punctuation

Iovianus Flavius I. (Jovian), Roman emperor AD 363–364, born in Singidunum in 331, the son of the *Comes Domesticorum* Varronianus. His father-in-law was the *Magister Militum* Lucillianus, his wife was possibly called Charito (cf. Zon. 13,14). He served as *Protector Domesticus* under Constantius [2] II (Amm. Marc. 21,16,20), and under Julian [11] as *Primicerius Dome-*

sticorum (Amm. Marc. 25,5,4). The day after Julian's death in battle against the Persians, I. was proclaimed emperor on 27 June 363, while still on Persian territory. He ended the Persian War and agreed to the conditions offered by Sapor II for a 30-year peace, with the Romans renouncing all claims to territories beyond the Tigris as well as to the cities of Nisibis and Singara (Amm. Marc. 25,7,9–11; Zos. 3,30f.). In the eyes of his contemporaries this was an ignominious peace (Amm. Marc. 25,7,10; 13; Eutr. 10,17; Lib. Or. 18,278ff.). I., himself a Christian, revoked all of Julian's anti-Christian measures and recalled the exiled clergy (Theod. Hist. eccl. 4,2; Philostorgius 8,5; Sozom. Hist. eccl. 6,3). He later withdrew his initial measures against the adherents of the old pagan beliefs (closure of temples: Socr. 3,24,5), only sorcery and magic arts remaining forbidden (Them. Or. 5,70b). From Edessa I. marched via Antioch to Ancyra, where together with his son Varronianus he assumed the consulate 364. Themistius gave the celebratory address, which is extant (Or. 5). Only a short time later, on 17 February 364, I. died in Dadastana on the way to Constantinople (Socr. 3,26,5).

PLRE 1, 461 (I. 3); G. WIRTH, Jovian – Kaiser und Karikatur, in: Vivarium, FS Th. Klauser, 1984, 353–384.
W.P.

Iovinus
[1] **Flavius I.** In AD 361 *Magister Equitum* of → Iulianus [11] (Amm. Marc. 21,8,3; 22,3,1), in 363 *Mag. Mil. per Gallias* (Amm. Marc. 25,8,11; 10,6–17; 26,5,1–3). I. continued to hold these offices under Valentinianus and Valens. In 366 victory over the Alamanni on the upper Mosel (Amm. Marc. 27,2). He was consul in 367, and remained active in Gaul and Britain until 369. He was a Christian and built the church of Saint Agricola in Reims (CIL XIII 3256). PLRE 1, 462f. (F.I. 6).
K.G.-A.

[2] Gaulish usurper of AD 411–413, a descendant of the provincial aristocracy (Oros. 7,42,6), who was proclaimed rival emperor to → Honorius [3] with the support of king Guntiarius of the Burgundians, and king Goar of the Alani (Olympiodor fr. 17 FHG IV 61). With an army of Alani, Burgundians, Alamanni, and Franks, he captured Arelate (Greg. Tur. Franc. 2,9). Large tracts of Gaul fell to him and his coins were minted in Trier, Arelate and Lugdunum. He sought contact with king → Ataulfus of the Goths but came into conflict with him in 412, surrendering to him in 413. He was handed over to Honorius' [3] Gaulish *Praefectus*, and executed in Narbo (Olympiodor fr. 19 FHG IV 61; Sozom. Hist. eccl. 9,15,3; Iord. Get. 32,165; Chron. min. 1, 523, 654; 2, 18, 71 MOMMSEN). For his coins see RIC, 10, 1994, 152–54; 352–54, for his image on coins ibid., pl. 46.

PLRE 2, 621f. (I. 2); A. DEMANDT, Die Spätantike, 1989, 148; S. ELBERN, Usurpationen im spätröm. Reich, 1984; H. WOLFRAM, Die Goten, [3]1990, 168f.
K.P.J.

Iovis epulum Banquet in honour of → Jupiter (also included were Juno and Minerva: Val. Max. 2,1,2) on the Ides of November during the → Ludi plebeii, both events hosted by the plebeian aediles (see esp. Liv. 30,39,8). Imperial calendars [1] attest a Iovis epulum for the → Ludi Romani on the Ides of September.

At this festival, the senators assembled on the Capitol for a banquet. This bonding ritual (Gell. NA 12,8,2) could not be carried out in case of extreme conflict (Cass. Dio 39,30,4). It is comparable to the *Daps* banquet for Jupiter celebrated domestically prior to sowing millet, garlic and lentils (Cato Agr. 132).

→ Epulo, → Lectisternium

1 InscrIt 13,2,509; 530.

W.K. QUINN-SCHOFIELD, Observations upon the Ludi Plebeii, in: Latomus 26, 1967, 677–685. D.B.

Iovius

[1] Cognomen of Diocletian, → Tetrarchy. B.BL.
[2] Praetorian prefect under emperor → Honorius [3]. In 407, he was made *Praefectus Praetorio Illyrici* by Stilicho, in order to wrest this prefecture from the eastern empire, but remained dependent on the Gothic king → Alaricus [2] (Sozom. Hist. eccl. 8,25,3; 9,4,3; Zos. 5,48,2). In 409, he became *Praef. Praet. Italiae* and *Patricius* (Cod. Theod. 2,8,25; 16,5,47; Zos. 5,47,1). As the most influential adviser to the emperor, he headed the unsuccessful peace negotiations with Alaricus (Zos. 5,47–49; 51; Sozom. Hist. eccl. 9,7). In 410, he switched his allegiance to the usurper → Attalus [11] and was confirmed in his posts, but he then moved Alaric to depose Attalus (Olympiodor fr. 13 FHG IV 59f.; Zos. 6,8f.). He is possibly identical with the *comes* who destroyed pagan temples in Africa in 399 (Aug. Civ. 18,54) and who was the recipient of → Symmachus' letters 8,30; 50; 9,59.

PLRE 2, 622–24 (I. 2 and 3); V. HAEHLING, 314f., 471f.; STEIN, Spätröm. R. 1, 391–94. K.P.J.

Iphianassa (Ἰφιάνασσα; *Iphiánassa*).

[1] Daughter of → Proetus and → Stheneboea (Hes. fr. 129,16–24 M-W), cursed together with her sisters Lysippe and Iphinoe with madness owing to disrespect to the cult of Dionysus (Hes. fr. 131 M-W) or slander of Hera (Bacchyl. 11,40ff.). Finally, by sacrificing to Artemis Proteus makes her change Hera's mind. According to another version (Pherecydes, FGrH 3 F 114; Hdt. 9,34), the seer → Melampus heals the daughters after haggling for a long time over the reward. According to Diodorus (4,68) he is given I. in marriage (on the different versions [1. 196–202]).
[2] Daughter of → Agamemnon and → Clytaemnestra (Hom. Il. 9,145); I. represents or replaces → Iphigenia who is not mentioned in Homer (cf. [2]). According to the *Cypria* (fr. 24 BERNABÉ), they are sisters.

1 H.MAEHLER, Die Lieder des Bakchylides 1.2, 1982
2 A.HEUBECK, Zur neueren Homerforsch. (V), in: Gymnasium 71, 1964, 63. RE.N.

Iphianira (Ἰφιάνειρα; *Iphiáneira*).
Name of two different Greek heroines: of one, the daughter of the Argive king Megapenthes, the same story is told as of → Iphianassa [1] (Diod. Sic. 4,68,4); the other is the sister of → Amphiaraus (Diod. Sic. 4,68,5). C.W.

Iphicles (Ἰφικλῆς; *Iphiklês*, also Ἴφικλος; *Íphiklos*).
Son of → Alcmene and → Amphitryon, twin (half-) brother of → Heracles, for whose godlike powers he is used as a foil. In their cot he flees from the snakes, which Hercules strangles (Pherecydes FGrH 3 F 69). I. participates in the Calydonian Hunt and in Hercules' Trojan campaign (Diod. Sic. 4,49,3). With Automedusa, daughter of Alcathous, he fathers → Iolaus. After the battle against Erginus, Hercules is married to Creon's older daughter Megara, I. to the younger daughter. In his madness, Hercules also throws two of I.'s children into the fire (Apollod. 2,61ff.). I. falls in the battle against the sons of Hippocoon (Apollod. 2,145) or dies in Pheneus, where he is taken after suffering an injury in the battle against the Moliones and where he has a heroon (Paus. 8,14,9f.).

S.WOODFORD, s.v. I., LIMC 5.1., 734–737. C.W.

Iphiclus (Ἴφικλος; *Íphiklos*).
[1] Son of → Phylacus [1] (or of Cephalus: Paus. 10,29,6) and → Clymene [4], husband of Astyoche (or Diomede), father of → Podarces and → Protesilaus (Hom. Il. 2,704 f.; 13,698; Hom. Od. 11,289–297; 15,225–239). His father promised → Melampus [1] a large herd of cattle if he freed I. from his infertility, for which the sacrilege of the father was to blame (Paus. 4,36,3; Apollod. 1,98–102). The speed of I. was proverbial (Hom. Il. 23,636; Paus. 5,17,10).
[2] Son of → Thestius from Aetolian Pleuron, brother of → Althaea [1] and, thus, uncle of → Meleager [1]. He participated in the Calydonian Hunt and the journey of the Argonauts (→ Argonauts; Apollod. 1,67; 1,113; Apoll. Rhod. 1,201). CA. BI.
[3] see → Iphicles

Iphicrates (Ἰφικράτης; *Iphikrátēs*).
Son of Timotheus, an Athenian from Rhamnous, and an important general in the first half of the 4th cent. BC. In the Corinthian War, I. achieved prominence by creating a powerful corps of peltasts with which he operated in the Peloponnese between 393 and 390 and annihilated a Spartan → *mora* near Corinth (Xen. Hell. 4,5,11–18; Diod. Sic. 14,91,2; 15,44; Nep. Iphicrates 1). As commander he was victorious at the Hellespont against → Anaxibius in 389 BC (Xen. Hell. 4,8,34–39). Following the → King's peace (387/386 BC), I. entered the service of the Thracian king → Cotys, married his sister and was given the cities of Drys and Antissa (Dem. Or. 23,132). In 374/3, he served (once more on behalf of Athens) as a commander of mercenaries under the satrap → Pharnabazus in a campaign against the Egyptians (Diod. Sic. 15,41,1f.; 42,4f.; 43,1–6), but because of personal dif-

ferences with Pharnabazus he soon returned to Athens, where he was given several important commands: in 372 to the Ionian Sea, in 370/69 against → Epaminondas in the Peloponnese and from 369 against Amphipolis. When he was replaced by his domestic rival → Timotheus in 365, I. once again retreated to Thrace. During the → Social Wars (→ Social Wars [1]), he served again as commander (cf. IG II² 124) and made his peace with Timotheus. In 356–55, both were accused of high treason after the battle of Embata, but acquitted (Diod. Sic. 16,21,1–4; Nep. Iphicrates 3; cf. Lys. fr. 45–9). I. died soon after the trial.

→ Antalcidas; → Conon

> DAVIES, 7737; DEVELIN, 1449; J.HESKEL, The North Aegean Wars, 1997; L.KALLET, Iphikrates, Timotheos, and Athens, in: GRBS 24, 1983, 239–52; TRAILL, PAA 542925.   HA.BE.

Iphidamas (Ἰφιδάμας; *Iphidámas*). Figure from the Trojan epic cycle, son of → Antenor [1] and Theano. Raised by Cisseus, his maternal grandfather, in Percote in Thrace, he left his home against his wife's wishes in order to assist the Trojans. The slaying of I. and his brother → Coon by → Agamemnon, described in Hom. Il. 11,218–263, was also depicted on the → Cypselus chest (Paus. 5,19,4).

> I.ESPERMANN, Theano, Antenor und Antenoriden, 1980, 71–80; P.WATHELET, Dictionnaire des Troyens de l'Iliade, 1988, no. 180.   E.V.

Iphigenia (Ἰφιγένεια; *Iphigéneia*).
A. MYTH B. CULT C. AFTERLIFE'

A. MYTH
Daughter of → Agamemnon and → Clytaemnestra (Procl. Cypriorum enarratio, 55–62 EpGF S.32; Aesch. Ag.; but cf. Stesich. fr. 191 PMGF and Nicander fr. 58 = Antoninus Liberalis 27, where Theseus and Helena are her parents and Clytaemnestra merely adopts I.), sister of → Orestes, → Chrysothemis [2] and → Electra [4]. Although she was promised to marry Achilles [1], Agamemnon, on the advice of Calchas, sacrificed her to Artemis to allow the Greeks' departure for Troy, which had been delayed by an unnatural calm.

Aulis is most commonly referred to as the place of the sacrifice (Procl. loc. cit. 55; Eur. IA; Lucr. 1,84; Phanodemus fr. 10; 11 FHG, etc.), but Brauron (Euphorion fr. 91 CollAlex), Megara (where she had a grave: Paus. 1,43,1) and perhaps also Aegira and Hermione (where I. was worshipped: Paus. 7,26,5; 2,35,1f.) also lay claim to it. This suggests that I. may merely be one name of the archetypal dying girl who became better known than others because she found her way into the Panhellenic Myth at an early stage [1. ch. 2]. Other names: → Iphianassa (Lucr. 1,85; schol. Eur. Or. 22), Iphigone (Eur. El. 1023), Iphimede (Hes. Cat. fr. 23a, 17–26; cf. Iphimedea, who a sacrifice is documented for on a Linear B tablet from Pylos: PY 172 =

Tn 316; cf. also the story of girls from Brauron and Munichos (Suda s.v. Ἔμβαρός εἰμι and Ἄρκτος ἢ Βραυρωνίοις, [1. 20–22]).

As for the sacrifice, I. may be placed on a par with other girls sacrificed before a battle, e.g. Macaria [4. 57–63]. In some versions, Artemis rescues I. at the last moment by replacing her with a fawn, a bear, a bull, or an *eidolon* ('illusion') (Proc. loc. cit. 62; Eur. IT 28 and IA 1587; Phanodemus 325 F 14 FGrH; Nicander loc. cit.; Hes. Cat. fr. 23a). The escaped I. either becomes a goddess by the name of Orsilochia, Artemis Einodia or → Hecate (Nicander loc. cit.; Stesich. fr. 215 PMGF; Hes. Cat. fr. 23a, 17–26; cf. 23b = Paus. 1,43,1) or she becomes a priestess of Artemis in the land of the Taurians (Procl. loc. cit. 61), where it is among her duties to sacrifice all Greeks who arrive (Eur. IT 72ff.; cf. Hdt. 4,103).

I.'s story culminates in the arrival of her brother Orestes and his companion Pylades in the land of the Taurians. Just as I. is about to prepare them for the sacrifice comes the moment of recognition. The three flee to Greece and, at the behest of Athena, carry with them a statue of Artemis (Eur. IT; [5]). The myth is the aition for a number of Artemis cults in which a small ancient image was used (Artemis Orthia in Sparta, Phalekitis in Tyndaris and Diana Nemorensis in Aricia; [5]). Until her death I. remains priestess of Artemis in Brauron (Eur. IT 1462–1467; cf. Euphorion loc. cit.). According to other sources, she marries Achilles after her death and spends eternity with him in → Leuce, the 'White Island' paradise (Nicander loc. cit.). Tradition also shows connection with Achilles, where I. is lured to the site of her sacrifice by the pretence of marriage to Achilles (Procl. loc. cit. 59–60; Eur. IA 98–105).

B. CULT
Of all the cults connected with I. that of → Brauron is the best documented. According to Euripides (IT 1462–1467), the weaving of women dying in childbirth were to be presented to I. after their death as their *ágalma*, perhaps in contrast to Artemis who received the clothes of the surviving women (schol. Callim. H. 1,77). Temple records from Brauron have not yet been published, but this ritual may be reflected in the custom of sanctifying unfinished clothes at the Brauronion in Athens [6. 17–19]. This and the name Orsilochia ('cause of childbirth pain') and perhaps even the name I., which the Greeks of historic times understood as 'strong in childbirth' (cf. however [1. 46]), suggest a function as goddess of childbirth [2. ch. 6; 4. 27–28]. Her association with → Hecate [2. ch. 6], the goddess of childbirth and *kourotróphos,* indicates the same. In Brauron I. probably also served as a mythic archetype for young girls going through initiation rites at the threshold of their eligibility for marriage.

C. AFTERLIFE
Following the two tragedies of Euripides which presented I. in different stages of her life (sacrifice: IA, land

of the Taurians: IT), I.'s fate became the paradigm of the 'stranger' and served time and again as material for drama and opera, up until modern times. The most formative among these may well have been GOETHE's 'Iphigenia in Tauris' (1779), in which the heroine's yearning for Greece programmatically stands for the contemporary idealization and glorification of Greek antiquity.

1 K. DOWDEN, Death and the Maiden. Girls' Initiation Rites in Greek Mythology, 1989   2 S. I. JOHNSTON, Restless Dead, 1999   3 S. G. COLE, The Social Function of Rituals of Maturation: The Koureion and the Arkteia, in: ZPE 55, 1984, 233–244   4 E. KEARNS, The Heroes of Attica, in: BICS Suppl. 57, 1989   5 F. GRAF, Das Götterbild aus dem Taurerland, in: Ant. Welt 4, 1979, 33–41   6 T. LINDERS, Studies in the Treasure Records of Artemis Brauronia found in Athens, 1972   7 W. SALE, The Temple legends of the Arkteia, in: RhM N.S. 118, 1975, 265–284.

A. ATHANASIOS, Symbole sten historia tou hierou tes Brauronias Artemidos, 1990 (collection of sources); L. KAHIL et al., s.v. I., LIMC 5.1, 706–734; J. LARSON, Greek Heroine Cults, 1995.   S.I.J.

Iphimedea (Ἰφιμέδεια; Iphimédeia).

[1] Daughter of Triops, wife of Aloeus, lover of Poseidon, father of her children, the → Aloads Otus and Ephialtes (Hom. Od. 11,304; Pind. Pyth. 4,89; Apollod. 1,53; Hyg. Fab. 28). I. and her daughter Pancratis (Pancrato) play a part in the prehistory of Naxos (Diod. Sic. 5,50f.; Parthenius 19): the Aloads pursue the Thracians, who have abducted their mother and sister to Naxos, and free I., but Pancratis loses her life. Pausanias attests I.'s grave in Anthedon, a cult in Mylasa in Caria and a painting by Polygnotus in Delphi (Paus. 9,22,5; 10,28,8).
[2] see → Iphigenia.   C W

Iphinoe (Ἰφινόη; Iphinóē).
Name of various heroines in myth and cult: one was a daughter of the Megarian king → Alcathous [1] at whose grave girls offered libations and locks of hair before marriage (Paus. 1,43,3f.), another was a daughter of king → Proetus (Apollod. 2,29) who died when Melampus tried to cure her and her sisters of madness. She may have been honoured with rites during the Argive Agrigonia. (Hsch. s.v. Agrania).

W. BURKERT, Homo Necans, 1972, 189–200; K. DOWDEN, Death and the Maiden. Girls' Initiation Rites in Greek Mythology, 1989.   S.I.J.

Iphion
Greek painter from Corinth, whose name is known from two epigrams of praise from Anth. Pal. 9,757 and 13,17. His creative period, which can only be reconstructed from source criticism, is disputed, but presumably lay in the first half of the 5th cent. BC. Nothing is known of his work. Nevertheless, the Corinthian painters' school of this period enjoyed great esteem.

L. GUERRINI, s.v. I., EAA 4, 178; G. LIPPOLD, s.v. I., RE 9, 2023.   N.H.

Iphis (Ἶφις; Íphis).
Name of a series of minor heroes (genitive Ἴφιος; Íphios) and heroines (genitive Ἴφιδος; Íphidos). The ambivalence in sex is the basis for the story in Ov. Met. 9,666–797 of the change of sex of the daughter of Lygdus and Telethusa in Phaestus, which is a poetic transformation of the aitiology related by Antoninus Liberalis 17 after → Nicander for the ritual of Ekdysia in the cult of Leto at Phaestus, where the heroine is called Leucippe [1].

In addition, several Argive heroes, an Argonaut, a comrade of the Seven Against Thebes and a female slave of Patroclus bear this name. The story in Ov. Met. 14,698–761 originates from Antoninus Liberalis 39 (there the chief characters, after → Hermesianax of Colophon, are Arceophron and Arsinoe): the commoner I. is rejected by the noblewoman Anaxarete ('Ruler's Virtue', a meaningful name) and hangs himself at her door and when Anaxarete attempts to watch the funeral procession from her window she is turned to stone – the aition of a statue of Venus Prospiciens i.e. Aphrodite Parakyptousa [2].

1 D. LEITAO, The perils of Leucippus. Initiatory transvestism and male gender ideology in the Ekdysia at Phaistos, in: Classical Antiquity 14, 1995, 130–163   2 W. FAUTH, Aphrodite Parakyptusa. Untersuchungen zum Erscheinungsbild der vorderasiatischen Dea Prospiciens, Abh. Mainz 1966.   F.G.

Iphistiadae (Ἰφιστιάδαι; Iphistiádai).
Attic asty deme of the phyle Acamantis, providing one bouleutes. A plot of land owned by Plato was immediately adjacent in the south to the Herakleion of I. (Diog. Laert. 3,41), which according to a horos-inscription (IG II² 2611) is to be located 4 km southwest of Cephisia on the southwestern edge of the modern Iraklion (formerly Arakli) and which has retained its ancient name [1; 2; 3. 47]. An eponymous hero Iphistius is confirmed in Hesychius s.v. Ἶ. [4. 210].

1 G. KLAFFENBACH, Zwei neue Horossteine aus Attika, in: MDAI(A) 51, 1926, 21–25   2 P. SIEWERT, Die Trittyen Attikas und die Heeresreform des Kleisthenes 1982, 96   3 TRAILL, Attica, 47, 69, 110 no. 60, table 5   4 WHITEHEAD, 75 n. 37, 84, 207 n. 183, 210.   H.LO.

Iphitus (Ἴφιτος; Íphitos).
Son of → Eurytus [1] of Oechalia and Antiope (or Antioche) who was killed by Hercules because his father and brothers (except for I.: Apollod. 1,128) did not give Hercules → Iole as his wife, as had been promised to him as a prize for his winning at archery. The legend is told in Hom. Od. 21,14ff. (where the bow of Odysseus is a gift from I.), in the lost epic Oichalías hálōsis, and also in Soph. Trach. 225ff., Diod. Sic. 4,31,2ff. and Apollod. 2,127ff. According to another version, I. arrived at the stronghold of Tiryns searching for his mares, where Hercules lead

him on to the walls and threw him off a tower. For I. as Argonaut: Apoll. Rhod. 1,86.

R. OLMOS, s.v. I. (1), LIMC 5.1, 738–741.   C.W.

Iphthime ('Ιφθίμη; *Iphthímē*). Daughter of → Icarius (Hom. Od. 4,797) and possibly Asterodia, sister of → Penelope (schol. Hom. Od. 4,797); Athena sends I.'s image as a dream to comfort Penelope (Hom. Od. 4,799ff.).   J.S.-A.

Ipsus ("Ιψος; *Ípsos*). Town near the Turkish village of Çayırbağı (formerly Sipsin, retaining its ancient name) near Afyon in central Phrygia. Famous as the site of the battle in 301 BC in which → Lysimachus and → Seleucus put an end to the plans of → Antigonus [1] and his son Demetrius to retain the state created by Alexander the Great (Plut. Demetrius 29f.). I. has been located on a hill with Phrygian remains and Byzantine walls in the Caystrus plain. In the Hellenistic period, it was a city, but not confirmed as such for the Roman Imperial period, because I. was part of the large imperial estate *Regio Ipsina et Moeteana*, which comprised a part of central Phrygia with the marble quarries of Dokimeion and Soa. In the Byzantine period, I. is well attested as a city. It was the suffragan diocese of Synnada in Phrygia Salutaris, from the synod of Chalcedon in 451 until the 12th cent.

BELKE/MERSICH, 282.   T.D.-B.

Iran (Middle Persian *ērān*, genitive plural of *ēr*, in *Ērānšahr*, 'land of the → Aryans/Iranians' < Middle Persian *ēr*, Sassanid inscriptions and Pahlavī literature of the 9th cent. AD < Old Iranian **arya-*, Old Persian *ariya-*, Avestan *airya-*).

I. HISTORY OF THE TERM   II. GEOGRAPHY   III. HISTORY   IV. CULTURAL AND RELIGIOUS TRADITIONS

I. HISTORY OF THE TERM

Although *ariya-* in itself carries ethnical meaning (the Achaemenids referred to themselves as *ariya-* 'Aryan' or respectively *ariyaciça-*, respectively 'of Aryan descent'), the term I. (or respectively *Ērān-šahr*) as an ethical, religious, and political concept is an early Sassanid creation. Under Sapor I (AD 240–272), *Ērān* had been complemented by its opposite *Anērān*, e.g. in the title *Šāhān šāh Ērān ud Anērān* ('King of Kings of Ērān and Non-Ērān'). *Ērān* also became component of official titles or place names, for example the toponym *Ērān-xwarrah-Šābuhr* ('Glory of the Aryans of Sapor') documents the desire of the Sassanids to link the new concept of monarchy to a religious tradition, which is at the same time Zarathustrian, Kayanid, and Aryan (*Ērān xwarrah* < Avestan *airyaṇǝm xᵛarǝnō*). With the fall of the Sassanid empire also came the disappearance of I. as a political term. Islamic geographers and historiographers, and even the Persian epic poet Firdausī, use

it solely as a historicizing reference for the Sassanid empire. It reappeared as a political concept only in the empire of the Īl-Khāne (1265–1335). The replacement of the French term *Perse* by I. in all official contexts, as ordered by Reza Sha in 1934, has its roots in the power ideology of the Pahlavī dynasty.

II. GEOGRAPHY

For the ancient inhabitants of the region, I. did not only refer to the territory of the modern national state, but also included other regions inhabited by Iranians within the modern Afghanistan, Pakistan, Turkmenistan, Uzbekistan, Tajikistan, and Kyrgyzstan.

III. HISTORY

Five Iranian dynasties are prominent among those which ruled all or large parts of I. in the pre-Islamic period: a) the → Medes (early 7th to mid–6th cent. BC) with a territory probably extending from eastern I. to the Halys in Anatolia and with → Ecbatana as a/the centre, b) the → Achaemenids (559–330 BC) from → Iaxartes to southern Egypt/Nubia and from Thrace to the Indus with residences or royal centres in → Persepolis, Pasargadae, Ecbatana, Susa, Bactra (Bactria), Sardis and Babylon, c) the Arsacids (239/8 BC – AD 224; → Arsaces) from the Euphrates to eastern I. and from the borders with Parthia and Margiane to the Persian Gulf (with centres predominantly in → Nisa (Turkmenistan) and → Ctesiphon) and d) the Sassanids (AD 224–651) from eastern I. into Mesopotamia and from → Chorezmia to the Persian Gulf with chief cities → Istachr (Fars), → Merv (Turkmenistan) and Ctesiphon/al-Madāʾin. From the end of the 3rd cent. to *c.* 140 BC part of I. particularly the west were under Seleucid rule, whereas from *c.* 240 until *c.* 130 BC parts of eastern I. (Bactria) were controlled by Graeco-Bactrians, followed by the Sākā, the → Kushanians and the Indo-Parthians.

As the empires of the Achaemenids, → Parthians in which non-Iranian popularities lived and Sassanids all included regions, all Iranian dynasties were from the outset faced with the problem of how to deal with foreign languages, traditions and belief systems, and also with the political aspirations and activities of formerly independent peoples. The long duration of their rule over 'I. (and Non-I.)' is on the whole evidence of a careful and far-sighted and altogether successful policy of the kings in dealing with cultural, religious, and political minorities. Their religious policy is one of many indications in support of this thesis: dictates demanding religious unity were never used as means to secure the rule; on the contrary, the guiding principle was the patronage of faithful and reliable groups and communities and the punishment of disloyal ones. It was typical for pre-Islamic I. that it not only preserved its own traditions and customs (e.g. the Zoroastrian view of cosmic and secular events, the ideals of the ancient Iranian kingdoms, or the interest in an entertaining and simultaneously educational presentation of Iranian history), but also readily absorbed, blended in, transformed and passed on those of other cultures.

Crises in empire or rule were only partially the result of outside pressure by Greeks, Macedonians, and Romans in the west, steppe tribes in the north and east (cf. the traditionally substantial contrast between I. and Tūrān) and the Arabs in the south. At least equally important were problems and conflicts within the empire: tensions between the royal house and the land-owning aristocracy, the political ambitions of members of the ruling house and the high nobility as well as of sections of the population either undependable or suspected of disloyalty, but also at times epidemics, famines and social conflicts. It was possible for such domestic and external factors to combine, as e.g. during the great crisis of the Sassanid empire in the 5th cent. AD. Whereas the rule of the Achaemenids came to a rather sudden and unpredictable end with Alexander's victories (334–331 BC), not e.g. as the result of insoluble domestic problems, and the cause of the replacement of the Parthians by the Sassanids had more to do with Ardašīr's I political and military skills than with any weakness of the Arsacid rule, the end of Sassanid rule in 7th-cent. I. was due to a combination of external and internal factors: particularist interests of members of the high nobility, conflicts within the ruling house, the over-extension of Husrav's II forces in the fight against Byzantium, and finally the dissolution of the Lakhmid buffer state (→ Lakhmids) all favoured the advances of the Prophet's powerful armies against Mesopotamia and I.

IV. CULTURAL AND RELIGIOUS TRADITIONS

Achaemenids, Arsacids and Sassanids influenced I.'s cultural traditions in very different ways: whereas the latter two dynasties continued to live on the 'national history' which they themselves had compiled as Iranian kings *par excellence*, the Parthians were devalued by the same history to 'partial kings' – → Cyrus and his successors had to be rediscovered in modern times – and served as questionable 'ancestors' of rulers in need of legitimation.

Zoroastrianism (→ Zoroaster) very early became a minority religion even in I. and never gained the importance of Christianity, Judaism or Islam, even though Zoroaster's message had found admirers and followers throughout the ages.

In Europe, (early) modern travellers, decipherers of ancient scripts and archaeologists recaptured the testimonies of ancient I., and Iranists and historians redefined and re-evaluated the characteristics of the Iranian cultures.

→ Family; → Graeco-Bactria; → Historiography; → Hyrcania; → Woman

B. G. FRAGNER, Histor. Wurzeln neuzeitlicher iran. Identität, in: M. MACUCH et al. (ed.), Studia Semitica nec non Iranica Rudolpho Macuch dedicata, 1989, 79–100; Id., Der polit. Begriff "Iran" in der Neuzeit, in: G. GNOLI, A. PANAINO (ed.), First European Conference of Iranian Studies, 2, 1990, 365–376; G. GNOLI, The Idea of I., 1989; Id., I. als rel. Begriff im Mazdaismus, 1993; J. WIESEHÖFER, Das ant. Persien, 1994. J.W.

Iranian languages Iranian forms together with Indo-Aryan the Indo-Iranian branch of the Indo-European family of languages. It belongs to the Satem languages. Iranian split into a large number of individual languages which were in antiquity spread over a much larger area than today, from Hungary and the Ukraine in the west over Kazakstan and Chinese Turkestan in the east and as far as Baluchistan in the south. Two ancient Iranian languages are relatively well known: the Avestan of the sacred writings of the followers of → Zoroaster and – less extensively – the Old Persian of the Achaemenid Empire (→ Achaemenids, with map). Avestan consists of Old Avestan, also known as Gathic, and Young Avestan. The former comprises 17 hymns (Gāthās) and the liturgical text Yasna Haptaŋhāiti, attributed to the prophet Zoroaster himself and probably written by around 800 BC. In Young Avestan, it is mainly hymns and other prayers, as well as the sacred book of laws, the Videvdat, that have come down to us. These texts are at least two cents. later. Avestan was probably spoken in Ariana (→ Areia [1], today western Afghanistan) and died out at an early stage. The oldest Avestan MSS date only from the 13th cent. AD, and are also very corrupt, so that textual criticism assumes great importance. The archetype of the MSS has been dated by HOFFMANN to the 4th cent. AD, i.e. the Sassanid period. The Avestan script, unlike Pahlavi, from which it evolved, has vowel signs.

Old Persian inscriptions can be dated and located exactly, unlike Avestan. They are recorded in a cuneiform script designed especially for writing prestigious royal inscriptions in the Old Persian language and was probably invented c. 520 BC on the orders of King → Darius [1] the Great. Most of the inscriptions originate from him and his successor → Xerxes I (486–465), and were found chiefly in the capitals → Persepolis (in Persis) and → Susa as well as in → Bīsitūn west of Hamadān. In them the rulers record their deeds, and Darius' version partly agrees with information given by Herodotus. Old Persian is a southwest Iranian language, a precursor of Middle and Modern Persian. In northwest Iran, Median was spoken, which is known to us only through a few formulas borrowed into Old Persian and through names surviving in Old Persian, Greek and other languages.

In the classical languages, Old Iranian proper nouns such as e.g. Δαρεῖος (*Dareîos*), Lat. *Darius* < Old Persian *Dāraya-vau-š*, literally 'Preserve (*dāraya*) the Good (*vau*)!' have come down to us. From Median (cf. Avestan *pairi-daēza-*,'enclosure') Greek borrowed παράδεισος (*parádeisos*) 'walled animal park, park' later 'paradise'. Greek εὔξεινος πόντος (*eúxeinos póntos* in fact 'hospitable sea') as a term for the Black Sea is a → euphemism for πόντος ἄξεινος (*póntos áxeinos* 'inhospitable sea'), which in folk etymology may have been borrowed and re-interpreted from an Iranian name that meant 'dark-coloured sea': cf. Avestan *axšaēna-* 'dark-coloured'. The Greeks learnt the word κάνναβις (*kánnabis*) 'hemp' through contact with the Scythians, who settled in the Ukraine.

→ Avestan Script; → Indo-Aryan Languages; → Indo-European Languages; → Old Persian Cuneiform; → Satem Language

> K. HOFFMANN, Altiran., in: HbdOr, 1,4,1, 1958, 1–19 (= Id., Aufsätze zur Indoiranistik I, 1975, 58–76); K. HOFFMANN, B. FORSSMAN, Avest. Laut- und Flexionslehre, 1996, 31–38; W. BRANDENSTEIN, M. MAYRHOFER, Hdb. des Altpers., 1964; R. G. KENT, Old Persian, 1953; R. SCHMITT (ed.), Compendium linguarum Iranicarum, 1989.   N.O.

'Irāq al-Amīr (Araq al-Amir). The ruins of I. and Qaṣr al-ʿAbd are located in Wādī al-Sīr, to the west of present-day Amman. From Achaemenid times it was a domain of the → Tobiads (Neh. 2,10; 2,19; 3,33; 3,35). I. consists of two man-made cave galleries, about 300 m in length. Lying above on a plateau, the palace or monument structure with animal reliefs (Qaṣr al-ʿAbd) belonged to the fortification (βάρις) of Tyre of the Tobiad → Hyrcanus [1], founded in 181 BC (Jos. Ant. Iud. 12, 229–234).

> E. WILL, F. LARCHÉ et al., I.: Le château du Tobiade Hyrcan, 1991.   T.L.

Ireland see → Hibernia

Irenaeus see → Eirenaeus

Irenaeus Referendarius 6th-cent. AD poet of epigrams, author of three erotic epigrams that originate in the Cycle of Agathias: Anth. Pal. 5,249 (love with the haughty Rhodope is represented as the merging of soul and body); 5,251 (about an unnamed woman whose pride is not even broken by the evanescence of her beauty) and 253 (appeal to the coy Chrysilla to submit to Cypris' wishes). This last poem was imitated by Niketas Eugenianos.

> AL. and AV. CAMERON, The 'Cycle' of Agathias, in: JHS 86, 1966, 8.   M.G.A.

Irene (Εἰρήνη; *Eirénē*). Byzantine empress (AD 797–802; born in Athens *c.* 752, died on Lesbos in 803), from 768 wife of → Leon IV; after his death in 780 regent for her underage son → Constantinus [8] VI. The Council of Nicaea in 787, convened at her instigation and conducted by Tarasius, the patriarch of her choice, arrived at a moderate reconciliation of the Byzantine image controversy (→ Syrian dynasty) in favour of the cult of images. In 790 her son forced her to hand over power, but was deposed and blinded by her in 797. The supposition that she may have offered Charlemagne the imperial crown of the West is now supported by [1. 206f.]. In 802 she was deposed by the usurper → Nicephorus I.

> 1 R.-J. LILIE, Byzanz unter Eirene und Konstantin VI., 1996 2 P. SPECK, Kaiser Konstantin VI., 1978.   F.T.

Iria Ligurian *oppidum* and river (not of the Taurini, Ptol. 3,1,35 incorrect), *regio IX* (Plin. HN 3,49), *c.* 25 km before → Dertona (It. Ant. 288), modern Voghera. Forum probably dates from Augustan period; uncertain when it became *colonia Forum Iulium Iriensium* (CIL V 785; 7375). Pre-Roman remains, bridge on the *via Postumia* over the I.

> Fontes Ligurum et Liguriae antiquae, 1976, s.v. Forum Iulii Iriensium; P. TOZZI, Per la topografia di Forum Iuli Iriensium, in: Rendiconti Istituto Lombardo 109, 1975, 342–346.   L.S.A.

Iris (῏Ιρις; *Îris*, 'Rainbow')
[1] The deified rainbow. In Hesiod's genealogy (Hes. Theog. 266) she is the daughter of → Thaumas (cf. θαῦμα/*thaûma*, 'marvel') and → Electra [1] (cf. the shining metal electrum) and sister of the → Harpies, who flew as fast the wind. Her genealogy characterizes her: she herself is thought to be fast, and in Greek physics, the rainbow can produce winds. In mythological accounts, she is to a very great extent detached from her element, and has the function of a messenger of the gods (Hom. Il. 2,786 etc.), which she shares post-Homerically with → Hermes in such a way that she is assigned in particular to Hera. Only Roman poetry sometimes playfully recalls the underlying natural element. (Ov. Met. 11,589).

> A. KOSSATZ-DEISSMANN, s.v. I, LIMC 5, 741–760.   F.G.

[2] The aromatic roots of many varieties of iris that flower in rainbow colours (e.g. *I. florentina* and *germanica L.*) come mostly from the Balkans, from Libya and from Asia Minor. They were chopped up (Plin. HN 21,40–42; Dioscorides 1,1,1–3 WELLMANN = 1,1 BERENDES) or used in the form of oil (*oleum irinum*: Plin. HN. 15,30; Dioscorides 1,56 WELLMANN = 1,66 BERENDES) mostly to produce ointments (*unguenta*, Plin. HN 13,5). Externally, the iris was supposed (Plin. HN 21,140–144) amongst other things to cure boils on the head and dog-bites, internally (taken with honey) to be good for coughs and digestive complaints. When chewed, it cured halitosis and intoxication. Children who were teething or coughing were recommended to be bound up with it. Root and oil of iris could be added to the pitch used in barrels for storing wine (Plin. HN 14,128). Theophrastus (Hist. pl. 9,9,2, cf. De odoribus 24) mentions a perfume of iris obtained from the seed or rhizome. (ἴρινον μύρον; *írinon mýron*).   C.HÜ.

[3] (῏Ιρις; *Íris*). River in Pontus, modern Yeşil Irmak ('Green River'). It rises on the western slope of Köse Dağları, picking up the Scylax (modern Çekerek Irmaği) 12 km south of → Amasea and the Lycus (modern Kelkit Çay) *c.* 70 km north-east of Amasea before it flows with a *c.* 60 km-wide delta into the Black Sea after breaking through the north Anatolian coastal range. With these two tributaries, the I. is a distinctive feature

of the Pontian landscape, the heart of the Mithridatic kingdom.   E.O.

Irish-Scottish monks Irish monks who from the 7th cent. AD onwards went to the west coast of present Scotland, to Northumbria and on to the continent, to lead a life pleasing to God in → *peregrinatio*. Unlike the western monks on the continent they did not live by the rule of St → Benedict, but by the rule drawn up by St Columbanus the Elder around 600 in the form of a book of penitence. They also had a different way of calculating Easter, a different tonsure (tonsure of Jacob) and stressed penitence and asceticism, embodied not only in fasting and hardening of the body, but also in *peregrinatio*. This *peregrinatio* had great significance for the West, because by the preaching which went with it the monks spread and strengthened the Christian faith. They first went to the west coast of Scotland (St Columbanus the Elder to Iona at the beginning of the 7th cent.), then to Northumbria (Aidan starting out from Iona), Gallia (St Columbanus the Younger starting out from Bangor), Italy (622 Bobbio) and to Switzerland (Saint Gall); they preached among the Franks, the Alamanni, in Bavaria and in Bohemia. The *peregrinatio* usually led them into isolated areas, which meant that Aidan did not go into the Northumbrian royal city, but to Lindisfarne, where he founded a monastery. The Irish-Scottish monks (IM) generated great cultural activity in book illustration and script, which strongly influenced the development of insular scripts and had a long-lasting effect on the continent while retaining the insular features (e.g. in Saint Gall, St Emeram, Bobbio, Mainz, Fulda). Irish-Northumbrian monks were active at the court of Charlemagne (e.g. Alcuin, Dicuil, Dungal, Sedulius Scottus). IM came to the continent again in the 12th and 13th cents., where they founded the 'Scottish monasteries' (e.g. Würzburg, Regensburg, Vienna).

L. BIELER, Irland, Wegbereiter des Mittelalters, 1961; J. BLAIR, R. SHARPE, Pastoral Care before the Parish, 1992; H. LÖWE (ed.), Die Iren und Europa im früheren MA, 2 vols., 1982.   G. SP.

Irish script The Irish script is the most striking and independent development from the period between the Roman and Carolingian eras; although it originated in Ireland, it is often called 'insular' script because it soon became the main script for all of the British Isles. It includes two types (for the form of the letters cf. → Anglo-Saxon script): (1) the half-uncial (also called round uncial or majuscule), which probably originated in the 6th cent. AD. It died out in the 11th cent., but was still used in Gaelic MSS for certain purposes into the 15th cent. (2) The minuscule, which shows pointed forms, originated in the 7th cent. AD and was perfected in the 11th–12th cents. After the 13th cent., it was also only used for Gaelic texts; a modified form has survived in Ireland to this day.

1 B. BISCHOFF, Paläographie des röm. Alt. und des abendländischen MA, ²1986, 113–122   2 J. BATELY et al. (ed.),

A Paleographer's View: The Selected Writings of Julian Brown, 1993, 201–220   3 L. BIELER, Insular Palaeography. Present State and Problems, in: Scriptorium 3, 1949, 267–294   4 E. A. LOWE, Codices Latini Antiquiores, 11 vols. with suppl., 1934–1972, esp. vol. 2, x–xvi (2nd ed.: xiv–xx)   5 W. O'SULLIVAN, Insular Calligraphy. Current State and Problems, in: Peritia 4, 1985, 346–359.   J. J. J.

Iron

A.1 IRON AND IRON ORES   A.2 SMELTING TECHNOLOGY   A.3 METHODS OF MATERIAL ANALYSIS   B.1 ANCIENT ORIENT   B.2 GREECE   B.3 ITALY   B.4 CENTRAL EUROPE   C. IRON IN MYTH AND PHILOSOPHY

A.1 IRON AND IRON ORES

Since iron does not naturally occur in usable concentrations, it must be obtained by smelting iron ores. Previously, meteorite iron was occasionally worked to make tools and weapons. Iron obtained by smelting is differentiated with certainty from meteorite iron by its nickel content: meteorite iron usually has more than 5% nickel (values up to 10% are normal) while iron extracted from ores usually has less than 0.5% nickel. Various types of naturally occurring iron ore were the source of iron using metallurgical processes. They were noticeable because of their high weight, colour and shine. Therefore, most types of iron ore were already used at an early time for making iron. Common ores are the iron oxides magnetite (Fe_3O_4) and haematite (Fe_2O_3), the yellow iron hydrates and the iron oxide hydrates limonite, goethite, lepidocrocite (FeOOH), which lie over the primary iron ores as secondary, rust-like weathering products, as well as the related bog and meadow ores, the gold-glittering iron sulfides pyrrhotite (FeS), pyrite (FeS_2) and marcasite (FeS_2), more rarely the iron silicates chamosite and thuringite, and the iron carbonate siderite ($FeCO_3$). These ores all had to be smelted so that the metallic iron would be obtained in a reduction reaction.

Depending on the type of smelting, iron contains varying quantities of carbon, which significantly influences its properties. Iron types can be differentiated by metallographic methods based on the quantity and type of carbon inclusions. The iron used by early cultures was mostly a forged iron with a relatively low carbon content. In later periods, a cast iron with relatively high carbon content was produced through improved smelting processes. In it, carbon was incorporated into the iron in the form of graphite lamellae. Steel was produced through the enrichment of carbon in low-carbon iron and its reduction in high-carbon iron through oxidation. It incorporated the carbon as a ferric carbide. This made tempering the iron possible and improved its mechanical properties over the original material.

A.2 SMELTING TECHNOLOGY

Iron ore was reacted with charcoal at high temperatures, which created metallic iron, while the other ore components formed the slag or escaped as gases. Smelting was performed in furnaces that were sunk into the ground and covered with an earth layer in the early periods of iron-making. These bloomery furnaces developed into shaft furnaces through masonry on the pit walls that were initially less than a meter high but eventually were raised to several meters' height. The earliest forms of bloomery furnaces were pits in which iron ore mixed with charcoal and occasionally proper coal was introduced. By burning the coal, temperatures of about 1150°C were generated and metallic iron was produced and separated from the slag. The iron particles, which were still relatively small in the early phase of iron smelting, were embedded in the slag. By hammering the slag, the metal was separated from the glass-like silicate component and was then combined into larger aggregates. To produce the required high temperatures for smelting either bellows or natural drafts on slopes were used. Meteorite iron was generally worked by hammering in a cold state. The iron that was obtained in metallic form during the smelting process and by hammering the loop was worked by forging at high temperatures. For this purpose, the blank was heated until it was red hot and shaped into the right form on an anvil. Weapons such as arrowheads, sword blades and daggers as well as tools of all descriptions, such as hammers, axes, chisels, tongs and other ordinary implements, were made of iron.

Metallographic studies of finds from Cyprus, Palestine and Jordan demonstrate that steel-making through carburization of bloomery iron began in the 11th cent. BC in the eastern Mediterranean. A further development of smithing techniques was linked to the discovery of steel-making. Even before the 1st millennium BC, tempered iron was forged onto worn iron tools. This combination of iron parts by forging at red heat developed into the production of blades by forging together layers of iron sheets or alternating iron and steel sheets. Apart from increasing the hardness, a decorative effect was also achieved which reached a particular state of perfection in damascening. For creating plastic iron objects such as sword handles, drop forging has been used from the late La Tène period. Cast iron is formed in the smelting process from iron ores when an elevated temperature is maintained over longer periods of time, so that the iron can only take up small amounts of carbon. In the early bloomery process cast iron was only formed by accident. The earliest raw products made of cast iron are known from the Roman period: these are an unprocessed iron block and an iron bar. After the production of the iron objects, a more or less intensive reworking and ornamentation of their surface followed, which depended on the object's significance. Early iron objects of the Middle East, when iron, which was still rare, was expensive, were processed into jewellery and presentation weapons, and had surface applications such as leaf gold. Techniques of surface designing developed later: punching, engraving, etching, inlaying with metal wires, and intarsia, which achieved particu-

lar perfection in the blade production of the central European Iron Age.

A.3 METHODS OF MATERIAL ANALYSIS

In research on iron smelting techniques, material analyses on slags are performed on a large scale. Both chemical analysis and light-microscopic analysis provide information on the original material and the smelting technique. In the same way slags created during forging provide information on the nature of the processed iron and the processing technique. Studies on iron objects also emphasize chemical analysis and metallographic research. Technological information is provided by x-ray images. If sufficient sample material (iron enriched with carbon during smelting) is available, the age can be determined using the C14 method.

JO.R.

B.1 ANCIENT ORIENT

Individual iron objects of the 4th and 3rd millennia have been found in Anatolia and Mesopotamia. Their nickel content is about 10%, so their source was probably meteorite iron. Other iron objects were by-products of copper production. Slag finds of smelting sites extend back to the early 2nd millennium. Metallographic research shows that until the late 2nd millennium the technology of iron smelting had not been fully mastered yet in many places and iron of inferior quality was produced. Until the early 2nd millennium it remained relatively rare. It was a precious metal and the exchange of iron prestige objects had a special significance in the diplomatic exchange of gifts and ceremonial use. Although texts frequently mention iron, only about 35 iron objects from the period before 1200 BC have been published and a fair number of these do not withstand a critical examination. About 1200 BC a rapid spread of iron technology in the Middle East and the eastern Mediterranean can be observed with the number of iron finds in Iran (Tepe Giyan, Tepe Sialk, Susa), the Caucasus, Syria (Ra's Šamra) and Lebanon (Byblus) clearly increasing. In this period the technique of steel-making and the deliberate production of tempered steel objects spread widely. There is a lack of conclusive evidence that the Hittites and Philistines had special technical knowledge and a monopoly in iron, but knowledge of producing and processing iron appears to have spread in the late 2nd millennium from Palestine (Gæzær, Megiddo, Taʿānāk) to Egypt (Ṣaqqāra, Abu Ṣīr, Dahšūr, Thebes) and in the following centuries from there via the Sudan and the Sahara into Central and West Africa. In Cyprus and the central Mediterranean region an independent production and processing of iron is also recognizable in the early 1st millennium. An intensive iron trade is documented for the 1st half of the 1st millennium: in the palace of Sargon II in Ḥorsābād, 160 t of iron in pointed bars from about 720–705 BC were found.

JO.R. and R.W.

B.2 GREECE

The earliest iron finds in Mycenae are from the 14th cent. BC. However, an independent iron technology can only be demonstrated in Greece after the late 11th cent. from finds of slags and iron bars. It is certain that local ore was already smelted in this period. Iron was mostly made into swords and daggers before it also established itself as the preferred material for tools, especially in mining and stoneworking but eventually also in construction, e.g. for making iron brackets and pins.

Iron and iron processing are already found in early Greek literature. In the 'Iliad' among the booty of Achilles an iron disk is mentioned (Hom. Il. 23, 832ff.), and the technique of tempering iron by dipping it in water appears in a comparison in the 'Odyssee' (Hom. Od. 9,391ff.). Iron smelting is also found in Hesiod (Hes. Theog. 862ff.). Herodotus reports a smithy that was equipped with bellows and an anvil. The smith used an iron hammer for his work (Hdt. 1,68). According to Aristotle, the Greeks attempted to improve the quality of iron through repeated heating (Aristot. Mete. 383a32–383b5). Attic vase painting provides information on forge tools and the shape of smelting furnaces. Several images show a smith hammering red hot iron (black-figured amphora, Boston MFA; red-figured bowl, Berlin SM 1980,7; red-figured crater, Caltanisetta, BEAZLEY, Paralipomena 354,39); furnaces and tools are depicted true to detail on a black-figured oinochoe (London, BM, BEAZLEY, ABV 426,9).

B.3 ITALY

In Italy iron finds extend to the early 1st millennium BC. However, iron production on a significant scale was only developed by the Etruscans in the 4th cent. BC. The most important iron ore deposits were found on the island of Elba (Aristot. Mir. 93,837b). Initially, the ore was smelted on the island but later it was taken to Populonia on the mainland. There, about 2 million tons of slags are an impressive testimony to ancient iron smelting. In the Roman period iron from Elba was sold in bars to the smiths of Italy (Puteoli: Diod. Sic. 5,13,1–2). As finds of iron objects and smith's tools demonstrate, Roman iron processing was highly developed. In Roman society there was a high demand for iron or, rather, iron objects and tools. For example, a large quantity of iron was used for major buildings which required numerous brackets to hold natural stone (the Porta Nigra in Trier used about 10 t iron) and for equipping soldiers (about 38 t for a legion). Agricultural implements made of iron are well documented in archaeology, the agronomic literature and Pliny (Cato Agr. 135; Plin. HN 34,138).

Pliny dedicates a longer passage to iron (HN 34,138–155). He attributes the variable quality of iron mostly to the water used in tempering and emphasized that iron ore could be found almost anywhere. Of the iron ore deposits of the Roman empire, Spain (Str. 3,2,8; 3,4,6; Plin. HN 4,112; 34,144; Mart. 4,55; 12,18) and Noricum (Ov. Met. 14,712; Plin. HN 34,145; Rut.

Namat. 1,352) were renowned. In Italy, Populonia remained the centre of iron smelting (Str. 5,2,6). Smiths at work in the smithy are a common theme on Roman grave-stones in Italy with some reliefs showing the tools used by the smith in precise detail.

B.4 CENTRAL EUROPE

In Central Europe iron production and processing began in the 8th cent. BC with the Celts in the eastern Alps. In the 7th cent. the technology of iron production reached Bohemia and Poland, then the north German region, where numerous slag finds and bloomery furnaces are known from the 6th and 5th cents. Iron smelting in the region of the Franconian and Swabian escarpment with rich deposits of pea ore began somewhat later and reached the Siegerland in the 5th cent. In Sweden iron production began in the last centuries BC with the smelting of local swamp iron and reached a first climax in the early Middle Ages with the Vikings. The import of raw iron and finished iron products was always of great significance in Scandinavia. The earliest finds of iron objects in England date to the 7th cent. BC. The oldest smelting systems are also attested there from this period. In the early Middle Ages there were only few iron tools in Gaul and iron was rarely processed. The special emphasis on iron products in reports on raids and ecclesiastical buildings indicate the rarity of iron.

C. IRON IN MYTH AND PHILOSOPHY

The use of the adjective σιδήρεος (sidéreos, iron) in the meaning of 'merciless' in Homer (Hom. Il. 12,357; Hom. Od. 5,191; 23,172) reveals an ambivalent attitude towards iron, which is also expressed in the myth of the ages of man: Hesiod characterizes the age of iron as an age of worries, injustice, violence, perjury and envy (Hes. Op. 175–200). The myth of the ages cannot be taken as a statement on the development of metal working but rather the naming of the ages should be considered a metaphor. An explicitly critical attitude towards iron is found in Herodotus, who says that iron was invented to harm humans (Hdt. 1,68,4: ὡς ἐπὶ κακῷ ἀνθρώπου σίδηρος ἀνεύρηται). By contrast, iron appears in tragedy in the list of resources granted to humans by Prometheus (Aesch. PV 502). In Plato's theory of the development of civilization, early society, the age of δυναστεία (dynasteía), is characterized by a lack of iron and other metals as well as a lack of knowledge of metal working (Pl. Leg. 678cff.). Posidonius attributes the invention of iron tools to wise men (sapientes) and, thus, seems to consider metallurgy in a positive light (Sen. Ep. 90,11). Ovid describes the iron age based on Hesiod, but also creates a direct link between the discovery of iron and the permanent violence and greed of the people of this age. Hence metals are considered harmful: iamque nocens ferrum ... prodierat (Ov. Met. 1,141f.).

Pliny's assessment of iron is more nuanced. He considers it the best and worst means (Plin. HN 34,138:

optumo pessimoque vitae instrumento est), for it serves useful purposes such as agriculture and construction but also harmful ones such as war, murder and rapine. According to Pliny, the detrimental uses of iron should not be attributed to nature because iron as such is harmless (*innocens*).

→ Mining; → Metallurgy

1 BLÜMNER, Techn. 4, 67ff., 205ff., 340ff.   2 D. CLAUDE, Die Handwerker der Merowingerzeit nach den erzählenden und urkundlichen Quellen, in: H. JANKUHN (ed.), Das Handwerk in vor- und frühgeschichtlicher Zeit, AAWG, 3. Folge, 122, 1981, 204–266   3 H. F. CLEERE, Ironmaking, in: STRONG/BROWN, 127–141   4 Id., The Classification of Early Iron-Smelting Furnaces, in: The Antiquaries Journal 52, 1972, 8–23   5 H. H. COGHLAN, Notes on Prehistoric and Early Iron in the World, 1977   6 P. T. CRADDOCK, Early Metal Mining and Production, 1995   7 H. HAEFNER (ed.), Frühes Eisen in Europa, 1981   8 J. F. HEALY, Mining and Metallurgy in the Greek and Roman World, 1978   9 W. H. MANNING, Blacksmithing, in: STRONG/BROWN, 143–153   10 P. R. S. MOOREY, Ancient Mesopotamian Materials and Industries, 1994, 278–292   11 J. D. MUHLY, R. MADDIN, T. STECH and E. ÖZGEN, Iron in Anatolia and the Nature of the Hittite Iron Industry, in: AS 35, 1985, 67–84   12 R. PLEINER, Die Eisenverhüttung in der 'Germania Magna' zur römischen Kaiserzeit, BRGK 45, 1964, 11–86   13 J. RAMIN, La technique minière et métallurgique des Anciens, 1977   14 J. RIEDERER, Archäologie und Chemie, 1987, 142–149   15 R. F. TYLCOTE, A History of Metallurgy, 1976   16 T. A. WERTIME, J. D. MUHLY (ed.), The Coming of the Age of Iron, 1980   17 ZIMMER, no. 112–130.   JO.R.

Irony (Greek εἰρωνεία, *eirōneía*, orig. 'dissimulation', Lat. *simulatio, dissimulatio, illusio*).
I. RHETORIC II. PHILOSOPHY

I. RHETORIC

Like e.g. metaphor (→ Comparison), irony is classed in the rhetorical system among the tropes (→ Figures) (Rhet. Her. 4,46 assigns it to allegory). While metaphor works through the similarity between what is said and what is meant, irony is characterized by a relationship of contrast (*contrarium*) (Anaximen. Ars Rhetorica = [Arist.] Rh. Al. 21,1,1434a, 17f.; Quint. Inst. 8,6,54–56; Aquila Rhetor 7 p. 24,21f. H). Irony is context dependent, and, to avoid misunderstandings (*obscuritas*), must be reinforced by being signalled in the delivery (*pronuntiatio*). Verbal irony is the ironic use of individual words from the vocabulary of the opponent. Irony as a trope of thought appears in two forms: *simulatio*, in a way that either provokes or emphasizes its harmlessness, appropriates the opinion of the opponent, who ideally is led *ad absurdum* by his own words, whereas in *dissimulatio* one conceals one's own opinion by feigning ignorance (esp. with questions in the sense of Socratic inquiry, → Maieutic method), by being pointedly ambiguous or by playing down of one's own abilities and concerns (*detractio*). It can be the aim of both forms either to make the recipient understand the irony in an opposite sense, or in strategic irony deliberately to

maintain the state of misunderstanding, because the speaker does not (yet) wish ultimately or yet to reveal his opinion. (Cic. Brut. 292f. 298f). Ethics condemns strategic irony, and also its habitualized forms such as polite phrases. The opposite of *simulatio/dissimulatio* is frankness in speech (*sinceritas*), of which the means of expression in thought and language is *perspicuitas*.

C.W.

II. PHILOSOPHY

Expression of something by the opposite. *Eirōneía* [1. 381ff.] was originally seen negatively (Aristoph. Vesp. 174; Pl. Resp. 337a) as distorting by diminishing, associated with an intention of deceiving [2. 341ff.] (cf. Theophr. Char. 1 ad fin.). Aristotle sees distortion by understatement somewhat less negatively than by overstatement (Eth. Nic. 1127a 20–32). From time to time – surely with the figure of Socrates in mind [3. 29] – irony is also seen positively (Aspasius CAG 19, 54). In Plato, irony appears as a means of presentation in varied forms: to determine the action, to characterize people, to qualify opinions, and as self-mockery [4. 129ff.]. This irony is not to be confused with the irony of Romanticism as the expression of a fundamental cast of mind that qualifies everything. In Plato irony is not signalled where ideas are concerned. He uses irony as a means of presentation that can serve as an indication to the reader, but cannot make possible a solution of the problems addressed (*aporia*) [5. 1ff., 280ff.]. As with tragic irony, the addressee is the recipient, whose observations or the course of the conversation gain in additional meaning thanks to well-considered knowledge. [6. 87–90]. Irony is found in rhetoricians beginning with → Anaximenes [2] of Lampsacus. Tryphon of Alexandria distinguishes between irony aimed at oneself and irony aimed at another (De Tropis III 205,12 SPENGEL). Later rhetoricians distinguish between irony as a mental and as a verbal form [7. § 582–585, 902–904]. Cicero sees in irony a means of forensic examination, and claims it as a *modus vivendi* for himself (Brut. 292f.; 298f.). In early modern times, irony is important in narrative literature: irony serves Romanticism as an expression of the tensions of finite awareness and infinite truth (SCHLEGEL) [8. 23–36] and, as a 'new formulation' [9. 123] of Socratic irony, has influenced interpretations of Socrates and Plato (KIERKEGAARD, FRIEDLÄNDER).

→ IRONY

1 O. RIBBECK, Über den Begriff des Εἴρων, in: RhM 31, 1876, 381–400   2 W. BÜCHNER, Über den Begriff der Eironeia, in: Hermes 76, 1941, 339–358   3 G. VLASTOS, Socrates. Ironist and Moral Philosopher, 1991, 21–44   4 TH. A. SZLEZÁK, Platon lesen, 1993   5 M. ERLER, Der Sinn der Aporien in den Dialogen Platons, 1987   6 M. PFISTER, Das Drama, ⁵1988   7 LAUSBERG   8 W. BODER, Die sokratische Ironie in den platonischen Frühdialogen, 1973   9 E. BEHLER, Klass. Ironie, Romantische Ironie, Trag. Ironie, 1972.

B. ALLEMANN, s.v. Ironie, Fischer Lex. vol. 35/1 Lit. II/1, 1965, 305; S. KIERKEGAARD, Über den Begriff der I. mit

ständiger Rücksicht auf Sokrates, 1841; J. Martin, Ant.
Rhet. (HdbA 2.3), 1974, 262–264; H. Weinrich, s.v. Ironie, HWdPh 4, 578–582.   M.ER.

Irrigation
I. Near East and Egypt II. Greece and Rome

I. Near East and Egypt
Irrigation means the artificial provision of water to
fields in order to enable or intensify plant growth. It
supported cultivation in rain-fed regions (attested as
early as the 5th millennium BC in western Iran), but its
primary significance was in areas whose productivity
depended entirely on it, their own rainfall never being
sufficient, such as the Nile Valley and the middle and
lower reaches of the Euphrates and Tigris. In irrigation,
the entire surface to be irrigated was generally flooded
by damming, not only drenching the soil but also raising the water table. Water sources for irrigation were
large rivers, and also springs and mountain streams.
Drainage of surplus water was vital in order to remove
salts, which were concentrated in the dammed water by
evaporation and which, if left undrained would have
remained in the topsoil. As well as irrigation by damming, water was made available for gardens throughout the year by storage ponds and wells.
A. Near East B. Egypt

A. Near East
Apart from slope irrigation, employed in mountain
areas, in which water was diverted from mountain
streams to irrigate hillsides from channels running parallel to the slope, the characteristic form of irrigation in
the Near East was by use of an extensive system of
canals (→ Canal). The 'dendritic' pattern used here, in
which water was led into fields through smaller and
smaller channels, brought the risk of salting the soil,
since its design was intended to make the greatest possible use of the water. Drainage could only have been
achieved by means of a complementary system of channels, of which no indication exists. Salinity was therefore one of the gravest problems facing the Near East,
Babylonia in particular. A peculiarity of the Anatolian
and Iranian regions was irrigation by the use of qanats,
which tap a water-bearing layer on a hillside and drain
the water into an underground channel to convey it out
into the plains to irrigate large fields.

B. Egypt
Apart from the oases, the → Nile was the main
source of irrigation The regular widespread floods not
only drenched the soil and fertilized it by depositing a
layer of mud, but also drained salts off as they ebbed.
→ Euphrates; → Canals/Canal construction; → Garden
construction; → Nile; → Tigris

M. Stol, H. J. Nissen, s.v. Kanal(isation), RLA 5, 1980,
355–368; W. Schenkel, s.v. Be- und Entwässerung, LÄ 1,
1975, 775–782.   H.J.N.

II. Greece and Rome
The two most important areas of the Graeco-Roman
world in which agriculture was provided with water
from one or more rivers by artificial irrigation were
Mesopotamia (Babylonia) and Egypt. The low-lying
plain of Mesopotamia was irrigated by a network of
canals which received the spring floods of the Euphrates
and the Tigris. As these floods did not correspond exactly to the growth cycle of crops, the water often had to
be stored. The co-ordinated upkeep of the large dams
which allowed the rivers to flow in their natural courses
while allowing controlled use of the water required
strong central administration, for which the Seleucid
kings took responsibility. The maintenance of individual canal networks and the distribution of water to individual fields were normally organized at a local level.
The second vital task was to ensure drainage of the
fields, since the water, if allowed to stand too long,
caused salting, which rendered the soil barren.
    As the gradient of the Nile is slight, and the Nile
Valley south of Memphis is very narrow, the canal system in Egypt could be organized on a local level, independent of central political control. The role of the
pharaoh, later taken over by the Ptolemaic kings and, to
a certain extent, the Roman governors, consisted in securing the favour of the gods and delegating authority
to local officials. Most fields received water by a natural
system of irrigation, without the use of mechanical devices. Large canals brought Nile water to the villages,
then it was diverted into smaller and smaller channels.
A system of large and small dams controlled the distribution of the Nile water. The water with its load of Nile
mud was allowed to flow on to the flat fields, which
were enclosed by a circular dyke (περίχωμα, pe-
ríchōma). After about 40 days the standing water was
released either back into the canal or into a lower-lying
basin. Fortunately, the Egyptian climate allowed crop
cultivation to be synchronized with the Nile flood. The
irrigation system demanded constant maintenance
work: channels had to be cleared of vegetation, alluvial
sand and collapsed dams, dams had to be reinforced
and repaired. The maintenance of the larger channels
and dams was a communal task carried out under the
direction of local officials; landowners bore responsibility for the smaller channels and dams in their own
fields.
    The land the Nile flood did not reach had to be irri-
gated using water-raising equipment. This enabled
fields to be irrigated more than once a year, to achieve
more harvests, as long as enough water was available.
In Greek papyri, the expressions μηχανή (mēchané) and
ὄργανον (órganon) were used indiscriminately to denote any water-raising device. A bucket attached to a
pole (κηλώνειον; kēlóneion, Arabic šādūf) was always
the simplest mechanical device for raising water. During the Persian and Hellenistic epochs, the far more efficient man-driven Archimedean screw (κοχλίας; koch-
lías) and the animal-driven bucket-rimmed wheel
(Arabic sākīya) appeared, but neither seems to have

been widely used. As large estates capable of financing such investments grew during the Roman epoch, however, use of the *sākīya* became widespread. The appearance of the water-driven scoop-wheel (τύμπανον, *týmpanon*; Arabic *tābūt*) is to be seen in the same light, but its design restricted its use to the swiftly-flowing canals of the Faiyum. In spite of these technologies, irrigation in Egypt remained dependent on the annual floods, not least because of the nutrient-rich Nile mud. The rising of the Nile was carefully monitored at 'Nilometers', of which the most important were found below the first cataract (Phila, Elephantine) and at Memphis.

The artificial irrigation of meadows, orchards and vegetable gardens is occasionally attested for the other semi-arid regions of the Mediterranean, but artificial irrigation was so labour-intensive and costly that it mostly remained restricted to horticulture. For most regions of the Mediterranean world, the greatest problem was the irregularity of rainfall; it was necessary to use rainwater as efficiently as possible, and attempts in this direction were made using terracing and the construction of large cisterns. There were also a few areas in the Graeco-Roman world, notably the plains of Philippi and the Po, where agriculture depended on drainage of the land.

1 D. BONNEAU, Le fisc et le Nil, 1971   2 D. BONNEAU, Le régime administratif de l'eau du Nil dans l'Egypte grecque, romaine et byzantine, 1993   3 K. W. BUTZER, Early Hydraulic Civilization in Egypt, 1976   4 D. HILL, A History of Engineering in Classical and Medieval Times, 1984, 127–154   5 J. P. OLESON, Greek and Roman Mechanical Water-Lifting Devices, 1984   6 J. N. POSTGATE, Early Mesopotamia, 1992   7 T. SCHIØLER, Roman and Islamic Water-Lifting Wheels, 1973   8 M. SCHNEBEL, Die Landwirtschaft im hell. Ägypten, 1925, ch. 2.   D.R.

Irus (Ἶρος; *Îros*).
[1] Son of Actor from Opus, father of the Argonaut Eurytion, whom → Peleus accidentally killed during a hunt (Pind. Fr. 48). I. refused the sheep and cattle offered as atonement (Antoninus Liberalis 38).
[2] Derisive nickname (secondary masculine form of the name of the messenger to the gods → Iris: 'Mr Iris') for the beggar Arnaeus, because he ran errands for everyone (Hom. Od. 18,6f.). Greedy, presumptuous, but at the same time cowardly, I. tried to contest the position of the 'beggar' → Odysseus, but lost pitifully in a boxing match provoked by the suitors (18,1–116).   RE.N.

Isaac (from Hebrew *Yiṣḥāq*, 'he will laugh').
[1] Son of → Abraham [1] and Sarah, half-brother of → Ishmael (Gn 17ff.), father of Esau and → Jacob and the second o the patriarchs of Israel. The main event in I.'s life is the command issued by God to his father to sacrifice him. This sacrificial binding (Hebrew *aqedah*), by which God put Abraham's fidelity to the test, has been dealt with in detail in the Talmud and Midrash: unlike in the Biblical version, in many accounts in the → Haggadah the test was not by God but by Satan.

Here it is I. that calls on his father to sacrifice him to God. I. is also supposed to have asked Abraham to bind him tightly, so that he should not take fright at the sight of a sacrificial knife, escape and ruin the sacrifice. Another Midrash tells how I. announces to the arrogant Ishmael, who voluntarily had himself circumcised at the age of thirteen and looked down on I. because he had been unable to express any free will at the age of eight days when he was circumcised, that he will sacrifice himself to God. In the Biblical account I. goes blind in old age. Rabbinical literature links this loss of eyesight to the sacrificial binding: the tears of the angels present at this binding fell on I.'s eyes and they went blind. The idea prevailing in Muslim tradition is that it was Ishmael rather than Isaac that was sacrificed.
→ Circumcisio; → Rabbinical literature

A. AGUS, The binding of Isaac and Messiah: law, martyrdom and deliverance in early rabbinic religiosity, 1988; H. GAUBERT, Isaac et Jacob, les élus de Dieu, 1964; G. VERMES, Scripture and tradition in Judaism: Haggadic studies, 1983; W. ZUIDEMA, Isaak wird wieder geopfert, 1987.   Y.D.

[2] I. of Antioch. Almost 200 Syrian homilies (*memrē*, → Sermon) in I.'s name survive. By the 7th cent. three different authors called I. can be distinguished: I. of Amid (early 5th cent.), probably author of a → *memra* on Constantinople; I. 'the Great' of Edessa (but worked in Antioch; late 5th cent.), author of a *memrā* on a parrot, which sang the 'Trisagion', and also a further I. of Edessa from the early 6th cent.

EDITIONS: P. BEDJAN, 1903 (67 Memrē, text only); G. BICKELL, I–II, 1872/1877 (37 texts with Lat. trans.); C. MOSS, in: Zschr. für Semitistik 7, 1929, 298–306 (homily on Constantinople); S. KAZAN, in: Oriens Christianus 45, 1961, 298–306 (homily against Jews).
BIBLIOGRAPHY: A. BAUMSTARK, Gesch. der syr. Lit., 1922, 63–66; A. KLUGKIST, Pagane Bräuche in den Homilien des I. von Antiochia, in: Journ. of Semitic Studies 32, 1987, 279–313; M. VAN ESBROECK, The Memra on the Parrot by Isaac of Antioch, in: Journ. of Theological Studies N.S. 47, 1996, 464–476.

[3] I. of Nineveh. (I. Syrus). East Syrian author and monk of the late 7th cent., born in Qaṭar. After a short time as bishop of Nineveh (Mosul) he withdrew to be a hermit. He wrote comprehensive works on the spiritual life, preserved in two 'parts'. A Greek translation made in the monastery of Mar Saba (Palestine) of a large part of the 'First Part', consisting of 82 chapters, proved to be extremely influential both in the Greek and in translations of it (25 chapters were translated into Latin). The 'Second Part' comprises 42 chapters, including four versions of the *Kephalaia Gnostica*. The 'Book of Grace', also attributed to I., is possibly by his contemporary Šemʿōn dᵉ-Taibūṭeh.

EDITIONS:
FIRST PART: P. BEDJAN, 1909; A. J. WENSINCK, Mystic Treatises by Isaac of Nineveh, 1923 (repr. 1969; Engl. transl. from Syr.); N. THEOTOKES (ed.), 1770 (Greek; repr.

I. Spetsieris, 1895 and 1977); [D. Miller], The Ascetical Homilies of St. Isaac, 1984 (Engl. transl. from Greek); J. Touraille, 1981 (French transl. from Greek); PG 86.1, 811–886 (Lat.).
Second part: P. Bettiolo, Isacco di Ninive, Discorsi Spirituali, ²1990 (It. transl. of *Kephalaia Gnostica*); S. Brock, (CSCO Scr. Syri 224f.), 1995 (ch. 4–42, with Engl. transl.).
Bibliography: K. Treu, Remnants of a majuscule codex of I. Syrus from Damascus, in: TU 129, 1985, 114–120; Y. de Andia, Hesychia et contemplation chez Isaac le Syre, in: Collectanea Cisterciana 93, 1991, 20–48; S. P. Brock, Theoria in the writings of Isaac of Nineveh, in: Parole de l'Orient 20, 1995, 407–419; Dictionnaire de Spiritualité 7, 1971, 2041–2054.   S.BR.

Isadas ('Ισάδας; *Isádas*). Spartan, son of Phoebidas, proved himself in 362 BC at the defence of Sparta in battle against the forces of → Epaminondas (Plut. Agesilaus 34; Ael. VH. 6,3). In the writings of Polyaenos (2,9), who clearly confused the incursions of the Thebans of 370/69 and 362, erroneously given the name Isidas.   K.-W.WEL.

Isaeus ('Ισαῖος; *Isaîos*).

[1] Attic logographer from about the 1st half of the 4th cent. BC, son of Diagoras. Scant information about his life is offered in *vitae* in the MSS, Ps.-Plutarch (Mor. 839e-f), Harpocration, Suda and Photius (490a), all of which however depend on Dion. Hal. *De Isaeo* and Caecilius. The precise dates of his life are unknown; among the datable surviving speeches the earliest can be dated to about 389 and the latest to perhaps 344/3. Athens and Chalcis in Euboea are named as his birthplace. The fact that I. was in no way politically involved throughout his life, however, speaks for him having lived (as did → Lysias) as a metic in Athens. I. is said to have been a pupil of Lysias and teacher of → Demosthenes, which can be neither confirmed nor refuted, but nevertheless can be described as a chronologically obvious (and so easily invented) construction.

In antiquity 64 speeches by I. were known, of which 50 were considered genuine. We have 56 titles, ten speeches have survived complete, and one incomplete, as well as fragments, including a very extensive one, recorded by Dion. Hal. (Or. 12 in modern editions). All surviving speeches were written for trials dealing with inheritance disputes. They always involve the same core questions, namely the validity and status of testaments, as well as inheritance claims based on blood relationships as opposed to succession due to adoption. Furthermore, contrary points of view, depending on the interests of I.'s clients, are represented by subtle argumentations of profound legal expertise. A remark in Dion. Hal. De Isaeo 4,16, according to which the ingenuous respectability exhibited by I. concealed an especially crafty slyness, has had an effect on the way he is judged down to our century; only in newer works is the possibility considered that I. might for once have written a speech for what was in fact a legitimate position.

His final speeches are distinguished by clear, logical and perfectly comprehensible structure; the mostly plain style rises above the level of everyday speech by the avoidance of → hiatus and the use of metaphors and political and legal technical terms. Nothing is known of any kind of continuing influence by I., which is probably due to the highly specialized thematics of the majority of his speeches, which was of little interest to posterity. It is probably due to his being considered the teacher of the greatest of all orators that he was taken note of at all and his works handed down.

Editions: Th. Thalheim, 1903 (repr. 1963); P. Roussel, 1922; E. S. Forster, 1927 (repr. 1957).
Commentaries: W. Wyse, 1904.
Indices: W. A. Goligher, W. S. Maguiness, 1964; J. M. Denommé, 1968.
Bibliography: S. Avramović, Plaidoyer for Isaeus, or. IX, in: G. Nenci, G. Thür (ed.), Symposion 1988, 1990, 41–55; J. M. Denommé, Le choix des mots dans les discours d'I., in: Les études classiques 42, 1974, 127–148; J. M. Lawless, Law, argument and equity in the speeches of I., thesis Brown Univ., 1991; R. F. Wevers, I. Chronology, prosopography and social history, 1969.
On individual speeches: L. Huchthausen, Betrachtungen zur II. Rede des I., in: Klio 46, 1965, 241–262; N. Lewis, Pro Isaeo XI,50, in: AJPh 80, 1959, 162–168; W. E. Thompson, De Hagniae hereditate (Mnemosyne Suppl. 44), 1976; D. Welsh, Isaeus 9 and Astyphilus' last expedition, in: GRBS 32, 1991, 133–150.   M.W.

[2] Greek rhetor of the 1st and early 2nd cent. AD, who probably came from the extreme east of the empire (epithet 'the Assyrian'). What we know of him comes from two sources: besides anecdotal material (such as the complete transformation of I. from a hedonistic youth to an aescetic serious man), Philostr. (VS 1,20 = 512–514) provides the important information that I. rebuked his student → Dionysius [40] of Miletus, because he recited his declamations 'in a singsong' (ξὺν ὠιδῆι; *xỳn ōidêi*); I. himself strove for and achieved extreme brevity and precision of expression. This fits the description by Pliny, who had heard the by then 60–year-old I. himself (Ep. 2,3; cf. also Juv. 3,74), of his language as *Graecus immo Atticus*. I. may therefore have been an early representative of the blossoming Atticism. The two main sources contradict each other, however, in so far as Philostr. maintains that I. never improvised, while according to Pliny he spoke *semper ex tempore*. From inscriptions (IG 2/3² 3632 and 3709) we know that I. had a son of the same name whose daughter Isidote was a hierophant in Eleusis at the time of Marcus Aurelius and that the later emperor Hadrian was among those who heard I. speak.

P. Grimal, Deux figures de la correspondance de Pline, in: Latomus 14, 1955, 370–383.   M.W.

Isagoge
A. Definition B. Functions C. Formal elements D. Subjects E. Christianity

A. Definition
The term εἰσαγωγή (*eisagōgḗ* 'introduction') is first documented in book titles by the Stoics (Chrysippus, Περὶ τῆς εἰς τὰς ἀμφιβολίας εἰσαγωγῆς/'On the Introduction to the Ambiguities' among other logical topics, SVF II p. 6, 28; 30; p. 7, 15; 16; 28; 34; 35; Περὶ ἀγαθῶν καὶ κακῶν εἰσαγωγή SVF III p. 196, 34; Apollodorus [11] of Seleucia Εἰς τὰ δόγματα εἰσαγωγαί SVF III p. 259, 8–9; Posidonius Εἰσαγωγὴ περὶ λέξεως F 44 EDELSTEIN-KIDD). Documents from the Imperial period show that it was associated with a fixed genre: *isagogai* belong to the literature of textbooks and present the basics of a subject for beginners. Textbooks proper are distinguished from this by their completeness and professional means of presentation. In Latin the term appears as a foreign word (first occurrence: Gell. NA 14,7,2: Varro's *Commentarius* εἰσαγωγικός (*eisagōgikós*, 'introductory notes': see below B.3 and D.8), Latinized *isagoga*, later in translation *introductio*. In comparison, *institutio* can denote both an extensive instructional work (Quintilian) and an introductory text (see below D.8). The appearance of *isagogai* seems to be connected with the origin of a graduated system of instruction [10. 5]. This sets it apart from the older concept of the textbook. An isagogic instructional work could also serve non-professional educational interests, when an advanced level was not at all aspired to [4. 1454].

B. Functions
It is difficult to differentiate *isagogai* from other textbook forms. The ancient terminology is not fixed; words such as στοιχείωσις (*stoicheíōsis*, 'elementary book'), ἐγχειρίδιον (*encheirídion*, 'handbook') and others (see also D.7) occur as synonyms. Conversely, other types of works were also described as *isagogai*. Even formal elements are not uniform. Function is therefore recommended as the criterion ([4] and [1]). 1. The primary purpose can be seen to be to accompany oral elementary instruction. This explains texts with abstractly formulated concept diagrams which are barely understandable by themselves, but could be useful as written aids for orientation and mnemonics in teaching [1. 324f.] (example: Cleonides, see D.3 below). 2. Other *isagogai* are easy to read, clearly formulated in the style of an oral presentation (example: Cleomedes, see D.4 below). They could complement an introductory course or even replace one [1. 320f.]. The genres of encyclopaedias (→ Artes liberales, → Encyclopaedia) and compendiums border on this function. 3. The practical instructions for certain tasks, particularly administration belong in another context, that of pragmatism; potential users are those who do not have a specialized (legal, for example) education and are not seeking one. Varro's *isagoge* (see above) on the procedures of Senate meetings, which Pompey asked for at the beginning of his consulate (→ Technical literature) is typical.

C. Formal elements
In general, the goal is brevity and limitation to the essentials. The presentation is either clear, lively, vivid (see B.2 above) or dry, schematic, aimed at classifications (diaeresis) and abstract definition (see B.1 above). Collections of pure definitions: Ps.-Plat. Ὅροι; Ps.-Galen (see D.7 below). 3. Sometimes there is a salutation at the beginning: the teacher addresses the pupil or dedicatee. 4. There are dialogue forms, simplified to catechetical form. 5. The *isagogai* are sometimes directly connected to a larger textbook, for example, the first book of the Almagest by → Ptolemaeus or the prolegomena to Aristotle's commentaries (see D.1 below).

D. Subjects
The following is a concise overview of the material (more details in [10] and [11]).

1. Philosophy. This is where the title *isagoge* is first documented (see A. above and also → Galen, Εἰσαγωγὴ λογική, 'Introduction to Logic'?). Introductions to the study of Plato and Aristotle [7]: for Plato from → Alcinous [2] (or Albinus?) Εἰσαγωγὴ εἰς τοὺς Πλάτωνος διαλόγους ('Introduction to the Dialogues of Plato') [12. VII f.]; for individual dialogues from → Calcidius [10. 27–30]. An introduction to Aristotelian logic was written by → Porphyrius (Εἰσαγωγὴ εἰς τὰς Ἀριστοτέλους κατηγορίας, and a text in catechetical form Εἰς τὰς Ἀριστοτέλους κατηγορίας κατὰ πεῦσιν καὶ ἀπόκρισιν, 'On Aristotle's Categories in Question and Answer'); these, in turn, were provided with commentaries and introductions, expanded to general introductions to philosophy [10. 59–68]. Prolegomena to Aristotle: [2. 444–476; 10. 9–20; 12. 341–348].

2. Mathematics. To what extent the genre of the Στοιχεῖα (*Stoicheía*, Elements) belongs here is not clear. The works of → Euclides [3], in any case, go beyond the functions of an *isagoge*. → Nicomachus of Gerasa, Ἀριθμητικὴ εἰσαγωγή; → Heron of Alexandria, Εἰσαγωγαὶ τῶν στερεομετρουμένων ('Introductions to the Topics of Stereometry'); Ὅροι τῶν γεωμετρίας ὀνομάτων ('Definitions of Geometric Terms'); → Theon of Smyrna, Τὰ κατὰ τὸ μαθηματικὸν χρήσιμα εἰς τὴν Πλάτωνος ἀνάγνωσιν ('Useful Information for Reading Plato on Mathematics'). Neoplatonists also wrote mathematical introductions for the propaedeutics of their students.

3. Music. → Cleonides, Εἰσαγωγὴ ἁρμονική; → Nicomachus of Gerasa, Ἁρμονικὸν ἐγχειρίδιον; → Bacchius, Εἰσαγωγὴ τέχνης μουσικῆς (in catechetical form); → Alypius [3], Εἰσαγωγὴ μουσική.

4. Astronomy. → Geminus, Εἰσαγωγὴ εἰς τὰ φαινόμενα; → Cleomedes, Κυκλικὴ θεωρία μετεώρων (or Μετέωρα?) ('Cyclic Theory of Celestial Phenomena'); → Porphyrius, Εἰσαγωγὴ εἰς τὴν ἀποτελεσματικὴν τοῦ Πτολεμαίου (astrology).

5. Grammar. → Dionysius [17] Thrax, Τέχνη γραμματική (probably to be considered an *isagoge*, because it
is suitable to accompany elementary instruction as an
outline of abstract terminology). It remained the elementary textbook; in the 12th cent. the catechetical
form of the *Erōtḗmata* appeared (Moschopulos), which
predominated until the Humanists (more: [10. 30–46]).
Introductions to individual poets were probably added
in the Imperial period as *prolegomena* to the publications [10. 20–26; 7.43–57]. (The existence of an isagogic literature for poetics, such as E. NORDEN [9] assumed as the source for Horace's *Ars poetica*, is no
longer accepted today).

6. In rhetoric, → Cicero's *Partitiones oratoriae* (in
catechetical form) must be mentioned, later the *Prolegomena* to → Hermogenes.

7. Medicine. → Galen dedicated several instructional works and introductory works to beginners (listed in
De librorum ordine 19,54 KÜHN). They circulated
under titles such as ὑποτύπωσις, εἰσαγωγή, σύνοψις,
ὑφήγησις ('outline, introduction, overview, guide'). He
himself preferred to add τοῖς εἰσαγομένοις ('for beginners', De libris propriis 19,11 KÜHN) to the subject title.
Ps.-Galen, Ὅροι ἰατρικοί ('Medical Definitions') may
indicate older medical introductions [3. 179f.; 5]. Ps.-
Galen, Εἰσαγωγή ἢ ἰατρός, also in Latin adaptation (in
catechetical form) as Ps.-Soranus, *Quaestiones medi-
cinales*.

8. Jurisprudence. The literature of the → *Institutiones* belongs here, because it is intended for the lower
level of legal instruction [6]. Works with instructions
for office holders (*De officio proconsulis* etc., e.g. by
→ Ulpianus) are of the type mentioned under B.3. First
examples: Varro (see A. above), Q. Cicero, *Commen-
tariolum petitionis* ('Short Essay on Running for Office', more in [11. 876f.]).

E. CHRISTIANITY

1. Concise texts (e.g. creeds), used in baptismal
instruction, have isagogic features.

2. The concept of levels of instruction is found in
→ Clemens of Alexandria, who directed his Παιδαγω-
γός (*Paidagōgós*) to new converts ('children'). The higher level of 'teaching' (Διδάσκαλος; *Didáskalos*, 'teacher') was supposed to follow. Still clearer are the relationships in → Origenes, who organized two-tiered
teaching, in which he entrusted the introduction
(εἰσαγωγή; *eisagōgḗ*) of beginners to his helper Heraclas
(Euseb. Hist. eccl. 6,15). A corresponding text was
written by → Eusebius [7] of Caesarea (Καθόλου στοι-
χειώδης εἰσαγωγή, 'General Elementary Introduction').
His work *Praeparatio Evangelica/Demonstratio Evangelica* has two levels. The classification of the *Divinae
Institutiones* by → Lactantius is not entirely clear. This
follows the legal institutions (1,1,12), but connects
them with features of the *protreptikós* (→ Protreptics).
He does not appear to have considered a higher level of
scientific theology (as Origen did).

3. Texts for preparing Bible studies (cf. D.5: introduction to reading the poets): Jerome Epist. 53, → Ty-
conius *Liber Regularum*, → Augustinus *De Doctrina
Christiana* B. 1, → Hadrianus [2] Εἰσαγωγή εἰς τὰς θείας
γραφάς ('Introduction to the Holy Scriptures'), → Eu-
cherius [3] *Instructiones*, Iunilius *Instituta regularia
divinae legis*, → Cassiodorus *Institutiones* B. 1: *De
institutione divinarum litterarum* (for a retrospect on
this genre 1,10). The subject of 'isagogics' in modern
theology developed from this (TRE 9, 46of.). d) Practical instructions for holding Church offices can be
compared to the Roman texts *De Officio* (see B. 3
above, details [11. 888–897]).

1 M. ASPER, Zur Struktur und Funktion eisagogischer
Texte, in: W. KULLMANN et al. (ed.), Gattungen wiss. Lit.
in der Ant., 1998, 309–340   2 I. DÜRING, Aristotle in the
Ancient Biographical Tradition, 1957   3 M. FUHRMANN,
Das systematische Lehrbuch, 1960   4 Id., s.v. Isagogi-
sche Lit., KlP 2, 1453–1456   5 J. KOLLESCH, Zur Gesch.
des medizinischen Lehrbuchs in der Ant., in: R. BLASER,
H. BUESS (ed.), Aktuelle Probleme aus der Gesch. der
Medizin, 1966, 203–208   6 D. LIEBS, Rechtsschulen und
Rechtsunterricht im Prinzipat, in: ANRW II 15, 1976,
197–286, here: Das Aufkommen juristischer Elementar-
lit., 229–236   7 J. MANSFELD, Prolegomena: Questions
to be Settled before the Study of an Author, or a Text,
1994   8 L. MERCKLIN, Die isagogischen Schriften der
Römer, in: Philologus 4, 1849, 413–429   9 E. NORDEN,
Die Composition und Literaturgattung der horazischen
Epistula ad Pisones, in: Hermes 40, 1905, 481–528
10 M. PLEZIA, De commentariis isagogicis (Archiwum
filologiczne 23), 1949   11 K. TH. SCHÄFER, s.v. Eisagoge,
RAC 4, 862–904   12 L. G. WESTERINK, The Alexandrian
commentators and the introductions to their commentaries, in: R. SORABJI (ed.), Aristotle Transformed, 1990,
325–348   13 L. G. WESTERINK, J. TROUILLARD (ed.), Pro-
légomènes à la philos. de Platon, 1990.   H.GÖ.

Isagoras (Ἰσαγόρας; *Isagóras*).

[1] Son of Teisander, he fought → Cleisthenes for supreme power in Athens after the fall of the tyrants. The
conflict was initially between their *hetairiai* (→ Hetairia). It was only when I. was elected archon for the year
508/507 BC, that Cleisthenes was successful in winning
the support of the *démos*. I. too had to mobilize additional sources of power and in traditional aristocratic
manner had his guest → Cleomenes I of Sparta intervene in Attica and exile Cleisthenes and an additional
700 families. I.'s plan to dissolve the *boulé* and set up a
strictly oligarchic regime failed on account of the Council's resistance. Things went as far as a spontaneous
popular uprising. I. and the Spartan army were forced
to withdraw and his remaining supporters killed. A later attempt by Cleomenes to install I. as tyrant by military force remained unsuccessful and I. was subsequently condemned to death in his absence. (Hdt. 5,66;
70; 72–74; [Aristot.] Ath. Pol. 20; Schol. Aristoph. Lys.
274–281).

DEVELIN, 51; RHODES, 242ff.; E. STEIN-HÖLKESKAMP,
Adelskultur und Polisges., 1989, 154–167; TRAILL, PAA
539700.   E.S.-H.

[2] According to Philostr. VS 2,11 (p. 94f) KAYSER, I. was a tragic poet and pupil of the orator → Chrestus of Byzantium. His lifetime is estimated to c. the late 2nd cent. AD [1. 135,24].

1 F. SOLMSEN, s.v. Philostratos (9), RE 20, 135   2 TrGF 195.   F.P.

Isaiah (Hebrew Yəšāʿāhū, approximately 'God has saved'). Hebrew proper name, also the title of a biblical book, which on the one hand has I. himself as author and on the other an unknown prophet who has entered research as Deutero-I. There are also further parts neither by I. nor by Deutero-I., which are ascribed to Trito-I. The effect of the book as a whole is very heterogeneous. The first of the 'great prophets', son of Amos and descendant of Judah and Tamar, active in the 8th cent. BC. According to rabbinical legend, his ancestry can be traced to a royal line. I.'s universalistic prophecy (God as the only author of world history) is distinguished by its marked social thinking. Politically he argued for neutrality towards the great powers. In rabbinical tradition (e.g. Deut. rabba 2,3) I. is regarded without reservations, as the greatest prophet besides Moses.

→ Rabbinical literature

> H. BARTH, Die Jesaja Worte in der Josiazeit, 1977; J. BEKKER, Isaias, der Prophet und sein Buch, 1968; J. BEGRICH, Studien zu Deuterojesaja, 1963; J. CARLEBACH, Die drei großen Propheten Jesajas, Jirmija und Jecheskel, 1932 (repr. 1994); R. CLEMENTS, Isaiah and the deliverance of Jerusalem, 1980; C. EVANS, To see and not perceive: Isaiah 6.9–10 in early Jewish and Christian interpretation, 1989; H. HAAG, Der Gottesknecht bei Deuterojesaja, 1985; J. HIRSCH, Das Buch Jesaja, 1911; F. HUBER, Jahwe, Juda und die anderen Völker beim Propheten Jesaja, 1976; C. KUHL, Israels Propheten, 1956; D. MILLAR, Isaiah 24–27 and the origin of Apocalyptic, 1976; E. VINCENT, Studien zur lit. Eigenart und zur geistigen Heimat von Jesaja, ch. 40–55, 1977; H. WILDBERGER, Königsherrschaft Gottes, Jesaja 1–39, 1983.   Y.D.

Isara

[1] Left tributary of the Rhodanus, modern Isère, has its source in the → Alpes Graiae as a mountain stream (torrens: Plin. HN 3,33; maximum flumen: Cic. Fam. 10,15,3) and flows through the territory of the Allobroges. In 218 BC Hannibal marched upstream from the confluence of the I. and the Rhodanus (Pol. 3,49; Liv. 21,31). It was here that Q. Fabius Maximus beat the Arverni in 121 BC (Flor. Epit. 1,37,4). Further evidence: Str. 4,1,11; 2,3; 6,6; Ptol. 2,10,4; Cass. Dio 37,47.

> P. GUICHONNET (ed.), Histoire de la Savoie, 1973.   Y.L.

[2] Modern Oise, tributary of the Seine, mentioned on a milestone from Tongeren (CIL XIII 9158), in It. Ant. in 384 a staging post Briva Isarae, modern Pont-Oise.

> M. ROBLIN, Le terroir de l'Oise aux époques gallo-romaine et franque, 1978.   F.SCH.

[3] Tributary of the Danube in Raetia, modern Isar (Str. 4,6,9). Contrary to Strabo's opinion, it has its source in the same lake as the Ἀτησῖνος (Atesînos; modern Adige), which flows into the Adriatic. The name I. may be associated with the Raetian → Isarci or the Isarcus. Also cf. the Roman place name Iovisura (It. Ant. 259,5), the position of which can only be approximated.

> F. HAUG, s.v. Isar (3), RE 9, 2053; Id., s.v. Isarci, RE 9, 2053f.; U. PHILIPP, s.v. Isarcus, RE 9, 2054; TIR M 33, 1986, 46.   J.BU.

Isarci Raetian tribe in the Eisack valley in South Tyrol, subjugated by Augustus in the Alpine War (25–14 BC). The name is in the inscription on the Tropaeum Alpium from La Turbie.

> E. MEYER, Die röm. Schweiz, 1940, 70f., 80f., pl. I; Id., Tropaeum Alpium, RE Suppl. 11, 1269.   G.W.

Isauria, Isauri (Ἰσαυρία; Isauría, Ἴσαυροι; Ísauroi). Region in the south of Asia Minor between Pisidia, Lycaonia and Cilicia Tracheia, initially confined to the mountainous country in the Taurus around the two main settlements of Ísaura Palaiá (Ἴσαυρα παλαιά, modern Zengibar Kalesi) and Ísaura Néa (Ἴσαυρα νέα, modern Aydoğmuş, formerly Dorla) [1. 109ff.]. First mentioned in Diodorus (18,22): Ísaura (unclear which) was captured by Perdiccas in 322 BC. In the first Roman advance on Isauria. P. Servilius Vatia conquered Ísaura néa in 75 BC [2. 287ff., 1167ff.]. After the battle of Actium, I. passed to the Galatian king Amyntas, who had Ísaura palaiá extended and made into his residence (Str. 12,6,3). After his death in 25 BC it became part of the newly established province of Galatia [2. 453ff., 1303ff.]. Cass. Dio 55,28,3 mentions for AD 6 the beginning of revolts by the Isauri. From AD 138 I. formed part of the jointly administered eparcheíai Kilikía, I. and Lykaonía (OGIS 576). Under Probus (276–282), the Isaurian wars of late antiquity began with the revolt by Lydius (Zos. 1,69f.; according to SHA Prob. 16,4 under Palfuerius). At the beginning of the 4th cent. a province of I. was created, also comprising southern Lycaonia and Cilicia Tracheia [3. 34f.]. Initially under a praeses, about the middle of the 4th cent. I. was placed under a comes rei militaris per Isauriam et praeses (Not. Dign. Or. 29) and was given a garrison of firstly three and later two legions [3. 35; 4. 29ff.]. The Isauri carried out regular raids (Amm. Marc. 14,2; 19,13,1f.; 27,9,6f. on the years 354, 359 and 368 and also Zos. 4,20,1f.; 5,25 on the years 377 and 404). In about 370 the province of I. was made smaller and the north was annexed to the core Isaurian territory of the new province of Lycaonia [3. 37]. From the time of Theodosius II, Isauri were enlisted for army service and in 474 the Isaurian Tarasicodissas came to the imperial throne under the name of Zeno. He was able to hold on to the throne in long battles against the general Illos, who also came from I. [3. 40f.; 1. 116f.]. After Zeno's death in 491 the Isauri were removed from the army, finally subjugated by 498 in grievous battles and resettled in large numbers in Thrace [3. 41f.].

1 W.D. BURGESS, Isaurian names and the ethnic identity of the Isaurians, AncSoc 21, 1990, 109–121 2 MAGIE 3 HILD/ HELLENKEMPER 4 W.D. BURGESS, The Isaurians in the fifth century AD, thesis 1985 5 G.E. BEAN, T.B. MITFORD, Journeys in Rough Cilicia 1964–1968, 1970. K.T.

Isaurian emperors Byzantine dynasty from AD 717 to 802 (Leo III, Constantinus [7] V, Leo IV, Irene and Constantinus [8] VI). According to an unreliable source on its origin, its founder Leo III came from Isauria, but in fact, as has long been known, he came from Germanicaea in Syria. Nevertheless, the dynasty has regrettably – because there had been an Isaurian on the imperial throne in the person of emperor Zeno (474–91) – retained its traditional name. The first two representatives of the dynasty are said to be opponents of image worship (iconoclasts), yet [5] argues with good reason that Constantinus [7] V was definitely the first to have cult images removed from churches or whitewashed over with any consistency. In the view of more recent research the 'Isaurians' were not the important reformers as which a historiography influenced by the Enlightenment saw them. However, Leon III and Constantinus [7] V made contributions as defenders of the Empire against the Arabs and the Bulgars and also as legislators. The *Ecloga*/Ἐκλογή (→ Ecloge) was presented in 741 (according to recent dating) in their two names as a law code which selects and reformulates in an original manner the rules from the Justinian tradition of law relevant to everyday law in the 8th cent.

1 ODB 2, 1014f.; for the Ecloga: 1, 672f. 2 L. BURGMANN, Ecloga, 1983 3 R.-J. LILIE, Byzanz unter Eirene und Konstantin VI., 1996 4 I. ROCHOW, Kaiser Konstantin V., 1994 5 P. SPECK, Ich bin's nicht, Kaiser Konstantin ist es gewesen, 1990. F.T.

Isauricus Victory epithet ('Victor of the Isauri') of P. → Servilius Vatia (consul in 79 BC), bequeathed to his son P. Servilius I. (consul in 41). K.-L.E.

Isca Silurum Roman legionary camp set up *c.* AD 74 in Britannia, modern Caerleon (South Wales). The *legio II Augusta* was stationed there [1; 2]. In about AD 100 the fortifications were renewed in stone, followed by the internal buildings. An amphitheatre has been excavated outside the walls of the camp and likewise wharf constructions on the banks of the Usk [3; 4]. After 300 the garrison was reduced and in the 4th cent. completely withdrawn. From the 2nd cent. an extensive *vicus* developed.

1 G.C. BOON, I., ³1972 2 M.G. JARRETT, Legio II Augusta in Britain, in: Archaeologia Cambrensis 113, 1964, 47–63 3 R.E. M. WHEELER, T.V. WHEELER, The Roman Amphitheatre at Caerleon, in: Archaeologia 78,

1928, 111–218 4 J.D. ZIENKIEWICZ, The Legionary Fortress Baths at Caerleon, 1986.

R.J. BREWER, Caerleon-I.: The Roman Legionary Museum, 1987. M.TO.

Ischagoras (Ἰσχαγόρας; *Ischagóras*). Spartan, was unable, in 423 BC, to carry out his task of bringing reinforcements to → Brasidas in Thrace because of countermeasures by Perdiccas of Macedonia. He managed to reach the war zone there with a few companions, and with the aid of Brasidas had Spartans installed as commanders in some of the poleis (Thuc. 4,132). Having signed the Peace of Nicias in 421 and overseen the execution of its provisions in Thrace, in the same year he gave his oath for the alliance between Athens and Sparta, which was meant to last for 50 years. (Thuc. 5,19,2; 21; 24,1). K.-W.WEL.

Ischolaus (Ἰσχόλαος; *Ischólaos*). Spartan, fought in the Corinthian War against Chabrias in Thrace (Polyaen. Strat. 2,22), fell in battle in Scritis against the Arcadians during the winter of 370/69 BC (Xen. Hell. 6,5,24–26; Diod.Sic. 15,64,3f.). K.-W.WEL.

Ischys (Ἰσχύς; *Ischys*). Husband (Hes. Fr. 30) or lover of Apollo's lover → Coronis. Apollo, who learns of the relationship through a raven, interprets it as adultery (*adulterium*, Ov. Met. 2,545) and kills Coronis, who is pregnant with → Asclepius, but rescues the unborn child from the funeral pyre. (Pind. Pyth. 3,31–46; Apollod. 3,118). F.G.

Ishmael, Ishmaelites (personal name, from Hebrew *Yišmaʿel*, 'God hears'). Son of → Abraham [1] and Hagar (Gn 16,11). According to Gn 17:20 and Gn 25:15ff, the progenitor of the Ishmaelites fathered twelve tribes. In spite of their blood relationship, the Israelites regarded the supposedly freedom-loving and bellicose Ishmaelites as inferior, because I.'s mother had been an Egyptian maid and they had both been expelled by Abraham. The → Haggadah deals specifically with this expulsion in its many aspects. Particular attention is drawn to I.'s character: he appears as an idolater and brother-hater, who becomes ill from Sarah's evil eye. A change comes about when I. repents and starts to revere his brother → Isaac (Midraš ha-Gadhol 381). In → Islam, I. appears with the name Ishmail as a prophet. As Abraham's first-born he is the herald of a new religion known as Abrahamitic. According to tradition, Abraham is supposed to have erected the → Kaaba in → Mecca jointly with I.

L. GINZBERG, The legends of the Jews, vol. 1, vol. 5, 1968; J. LONGTON, Fils d'Abraham: panorama des communautés juives, chrétiennes et musulmanes, 1987; F. PETERS, Children of Abraham: Judaism, Christianity, Islam, 1982; S. STERN, Studies in early Ismailism, 1983. Y.D.

Ishtar The Semitic goddess I. is etymologically related to → Astarte (*Attarat*). Grammatically speaking, the name is masculine (cf. Western Semitic *Attar*). In southern Mesopotamia she was identified with Innana, the Sumerian city-goddess of → Uruk, and there is evidence of her being worshipped in that city into Achaemenid times. In northern Babylonia and Assyria figures of I. were venerated in numerous cities (I. of the cities → Akkad, → Arbela [1], → Nineveh) and to an extent identified with other goddesses. This is the explanation for the fact that in Mesopotamia this name, in the form Ištar(t)u, was used as the general term for *goddess*. I. (or Inanna), being a youthful figure, matrimonially connected to none of the gods of the pantheon, was viewed as the goddess of love, but also as the embodiment of warlike characteristics and furthermore in her astral manifestation she was worshipped as the Venus star. The connection of I.-Inanna to the ritual of the → Hieros Gamos is seen as critical in the Akkadian tradition.

F. BRUSCHWEILER, Inanna, 1987; C. WILCKE, U. SEIDL, s.v. Inanna, RLA 5, 74–88.   J.RE.

Ishtar Gate North main gate of → Babylon, a massive double-gateway, reinforced with towers, with gate rooms lying at right angles to each other and a tunnel-like passage about 46 m in length. The entire gate structure was covered with colourfully glazed tiles. Against a deep blue background there were geometrical ornaments, rosettes and depictions of animals (bulls, serpent-dragons) in high and low relief in varied colours. On the basis of inscribed brick stamps the Ishtar Gate (IG) can be dated to the second half of the reign of → Nebuchadnezzar II (604–562 BC). The naming of the gate after the goddess → Ishtar is similarly documented by inscriptions. The IG, together with the Procession Street, represented a total architectural complex, which comprised the architectural high point of the Babylonian New Year's procession (→ New Year's celebrations). The IG owed its size and magnificent decoration to this ceremonial function. A reconstruction can be found in the Museum of the Ancient Near East in Berlin.

R. KOLDEWEY, Das Ištar-Tor in Babylon, 1918; Id., Das wiedererstehende Babylon, ⁵1990, 43ff.; J. MARZAHN, Das Ištar-Tor von Babylon, 1994.   J.BÄ.

Ishuwa (Išuwa). Name of an Anatolian landscape in Hittite and Assyrian sources of the 15th to 9th cents. BC. I. was situated between the Euphrates and Tigris in the area of the Murat Su river, with the plain of Elazığ as its centre (Arsanias, modern Lake Keban).

I. is first mentioned in texts of the Hittite king Tudhaliya I/II (late 15th cent.); but even before, it was a bone of contention between the Hittite kingdom and the kingdom of → Mitanni in upper Mesopotamia. Texts of this period give the names of the elders of I.,

and report the flight of entire villages from I. Tudhaliya I/II conquered I.; Tudhaliya III lost it; his son Shuppiluliuma reconquered it in the middle of the 14th cent. Under Hittite rule I. had become a kingdom – by 1250 at the latest –, its sovereigns (Ari-šarruma, Ehli-šarruma) probably descended from the Hittite royal family. After the end of the Hittite kingdom (around 1190), the Assyrian King Tiglatpilesar I (1114–1077) conquered Enzata in the land of I. The last mention of I. is found in an inscription of Salmanassar III (858–824 BC).

H. KLENGEL, s.v. I., RLA 4, 214–216.   GE.W.

Isidorus (Ἰσίδωρος; *Isídōros*).

[1] Pirate captain who organized the Cilician pirates in the area around Crete, was besieged in 78 BC by P. Servilius Isauricus (Flor. 1,41,3), later entered the service of Mithridates and in 72 was defeated by Lucullus in the naval battle of Tenedos at the entrance to the Dardanelles (App. Mithr. 77, Memnon 42,2 = FHG 3,548) and killed (Plut. Lucullus 12.2).   ME.STR.

[2] **I. of Charax.** Geographer, certainly of the Augustan period (end of the 1st cent. BC). Nothing further is known of him personally. Handed down under his name: 1. fragment of a measurement of the *oikuménē* (parts in Plin. HN), 2. a small document 'Parthian Stations' (*Stathmoí Parthikoí*) – description and survey of the road from Zeugma on the Euphrates to Alexandria in Arachosia in the Parthian Kingdom, 3. fragment on pearl fishery in the Persian Gulf (in Ath. 3,93d = GGM 1,254), 4. claims about allegedly long-lived oriental kings (Ps.-Lucian. Macr. 15,15 = GGM 1, 256).

I. gives a summary of the discoveries of later Hellenism, basing himself on Eratosthenes' [2] measurement of the earth and thus providing the basis on which Pliny relies. Both latter works contain material extending to the period around 100 BC. Some attempt to solve the problems of dating which thus arise by assuming two authors with the same name.

→ Characene; → Charax Spasinu

F. H. WEISSBACH, s.v. I. (20), RE 9, 2064–2068; Trans.: W. H. SCHOFF, Parthian Stations by I. of Charax, 1914.
                    J.OE.

[3] Alexandrine Greek gymnasiarch, i.e. he belonged to a leading family of the city. In the disputes with the Jewish sector of the population in AD 38 he first used the *praefectus Aegypti* Avillius Flaccus for his purposes; later he incited the population against the prefect, whom he eventually also accused before Caligula in Rome. When in the late reign of Claudius he attempted to accuse King → Iulius [II 5] Agrippa II, he was himself condemned and executed. PIR² J 53.   W.E.

[4] Early Christian Gnostic (2nd half of the 2nd cent.) Domiciled in Alexandria, I. continued the teaching career of his father → Basileides [2] in the latter's spirit. Like his father, he selectively absorbed philosophical teaching material, above all of Platonic and Stoic prov-

enance, and related it – from the point of view of its pastoral use – to the Judaeo-Christian tradition. Differing strands of tradition, partially overlapping each other, make a clear differentiation between the views of Basileides and the other student circles around I. largely impossible (allocation of the fragments: [2. 326⁵]; according to LÖHR various student quotes are from I.). I. publishes – not before 160 [1. 291] – several independent monographs, only extant in a few fragments. In his writing *Perì prosphyoûs psychés* he speaks, in a platonizing sense, of two parts of the soul. Thus the passions given to the lower part of the soul as an appendage try to influence Man to evil. I.' *Ethiká* are probably the first treatise in the 2nd cent. about questions of practical Christian morality [2. 107²⁶] and opts, with 1 Cor 7,9, for marriage as *remedium concupiscentiae* in opposition to a rigid encratism. In his work *Toû prophétou Parchór exēgētiká*, he interprets the sayings of an otherwise unknown prophet Parchor and regards philosophy as the bearer of this earlier wisdom. Many of the themes addressed by Basileides and I. reappear later in → Clemens [3] of Alexandria and → Origenes.

1 A. HARNACK, Gesch. der altchristl. Lit. bis Eusebius, ²1958, vol. I/1, 157–161; vol. II/1, 290f.   2 W. A. LÖHR, Basilides und seine Schule, 1996 (collection and trans. of testimonia and fragments)   3 W. VÖLKER, Quellen zur Gesch. der christl. Gnosis, 1932, 38–44.   J.RI.

[5] Flavius Anthemius Isidorus. from Alexandria, was *proconsl Asiae* between AD 405 and 410, *praefectus urbis Constantinopolitanae* from 410 to 412 (Cod. Theod. 8,17,2; 15,1,50), *praefectus praetorio Illyrici* in 424 (Cod. Theod. 15,5,4), *praef. praet. Orientis* in 435–36 (Cod. Theod. 6,28,8; 12,1,192) and 436 *consul* (Acta conciliorum oecumenicorum 1,1,3 p. 67, 69). He died before 447 (Theod. Epist. 42; 47).

PLRE 2, 631–33 (Isidorus 9); V. HAEHLING, 86f.   K.P.J.

[6] I. of Pelusium. Clearly not the provost of a monastery (as the introduction in the → *Apophthegmata patrum* has it), rather a presbyter in Egyptian Pelusium (at least according to Severus of Antioch, Contra impium grammaticum 3,39 [1; 2]). He lived most probably between AD 360 and 435, probably studied in Alexandria and probably lived as a monk in Pelusium. I. left behind a wide-ranging body of 2,016 letters in a good style (CPG 3, 5557) as well as Apophthegmata (CPG 3, 5558), all else is lost. The letters use, among other things, fragments of the 'Hypotyposes' of → Clemens [3] of Alexandria; in addition, I. knows and quotes → Basilius [1] of Caesarea and → Gregorius [3] of Nazianzus. He was probably not, however, a direct student of → Iohannes [4] Chrysostomos (differently Nicephorus Callistus, Historia ecclesiastica 14,30,53). Theologically he followed the Alexandrine tradition (Epist. 4,99), used, however, the hermeneutical rules of the Antiochan exegeses (Epist. 4,117).

1 E. W. BROOKS (ed.), The Sixth Book of the Select Letters of Severus 2/2, 1904, 251   2 I. LEBON (ed.), Severi Anti-ocheni liber Contra impium grammaticum (CSCO 102), 1933, 183.

P. ÉVIEUX (ed.), Lettres 1: 1214–1413 (SChr 422), 1997; Id., Isidore de Péluse (Théologie Historique 99), 1995; A. M. RITTER, s.v. Isidore de Péluse, Dictionnaire de Spiritualite 7, 1971, 2097–2103; L. BAYER, Isidors von Pelusium klass. Bildung (Forsch. zur christl. Lit.- und Dogmengesch. 13/2), 1915.   C.M.

[7] Neoplatonist from Alexandria (5th cent. AD); son of Theodotes, whose brother Aegyptus was friends with → Hermeias [3] of Alexandria (Damascius Vita Isidori fr. 119 ZINTZEN). Pupil of → Heraïscus and of → Asclepiades (ibid. fr. 160 ZINTZEN), later, in Athens, of → Proclus (ibid. fr. 129–137 I.) and of → Marinus [1] (ibid. fr. 90 I.). After the death of Proclus (485), I. returned to Alexandria. In the first months of the Monophysite patriarchy of Athanasius II Keletes (489), he left the city and settled anew in Athens after an eight-months trip with → Damascius through Syria and Asia Minor (§§ 195–219 I.). After the death of Marinus he was elected Diadoch of the Academy (ibid. § 226 I.). His marriage with Domna produced a son, Proclus (fr. 339 I.). I. composed hymns (fr. 113 I.) as well as a letter to Marinus about the latter's interpretation of the hypotheses of Parmenides (fr. 245 I.). His students were Theodora (to whom Damascius' *Vita Isidori* is dedicated) and her sisters from the family of → Iamblichus, Dorus of Arabia and Damascius, whom he converted to philosophy and who became his biographer. I. was a declared opponent of Christianity (§ 38 I.; Zacharias' Vita Severi 16,22 KUGENER). He admired above all those philosophers who had achieved the ascent to the Divine: Plato, Iamblichus, Syrianus (fr. 77 I.) and Heraïscus, his only teacher (§ 37 I.). H. is, for Zacharias, manifestly a magician and trouble maker (Vita Severi 22), for Damascius, on the other hand, a true philosopher (Vita Isidori §§ 160; 164 I.).

EDITIONS: M.-A. KUGENER (ed.), Zacharie Rhéteur (ou: le Scholastique), Vita Severi, texte syriaque et traduction française (Patrologia Orientalis t. II/6, 1903; C. ZINTZEN (ed.), Damascius, Vita Isidori, 1967; R. ASMUS, Das Leben des Philosophen I., 1991 (Ger. trans.); Id., in: ByzZ 18, 1909, 424–480 und 19, 1910, 264–284.
BIBLIOGRAPHY: P. CHUVIN, Chronique des derniers païens, 1990, ²1991; M. TARDIEU, Les Paysages reliques. Routes et haltes syriennes d'Isidore à Simplicius, 1990; R. DONCEEL, M. SARTRE, Théandrios, dieu de Canatha, in: Electrum 1, 1997, 21–34.   MI.TA.

[8] Stobaeus (3,590,11f.; 5,731,2ff; cf. Men. 343 JAEKEL) has handed down five sententious trimeters under the lemma Ἰσιδώρου (cf. O. HENSE to Stob. 5,731,2).

TrGF 211.   F.P.

[9] Isidorus Bishop of Hispalis (Seville).

Theologian and encyclopaedic writer of the last phase of antiquity, born about 560, died in 636. His family belonged to an Hispano-Roman, confessionally orthodox leading social stratum; his older brothers, Leander and Fulgentius, were bishops as well. The family was driven out of Cartagena after 550 and lived in Seville, where I. succeeded his brother Leander as bishop in 599/600. The relations of the Catholic elite to the Visigoths had become normalized after the conversion of king Reccared in 589, and I. dedicated works to two Visigoth kings, Sisebut and Suinthila.

A. THEOLOGICAL AND ENCYCLOPAEDIC WRITINGS
B. MUSIC THEORY

A. THEOLOGICAL AND ENCYCLOPAEDIC WRITINGS

The two focal points of I.'s literary activity [1] are characterized by the labels 'Figure of Church History' [2] and 'Encyclopaedist' [3]. To the first category belong a number of exegetic, dogmatic and pastoral writings (especially noteworthy the synonyma *De lamentatione animae peccatricis* and *De origine officiorum*); to the second, that of secular education, belong grammatical (*Differentiae*), historical (*Chronica, De origine Gothorum, De viris illustribus*) and scientific works (*De natura rerum*). Here also belongs the comprehensive treatment of education, God and Man, which partially encompasses his previous work, constituted by the *Etymologiae* (vulgo *Origines*), which – left unfinished by I. – was edited for publication in 20 bks. by his friend Braulio [4]. In this work, bks. 1–4 of the Encyclopaedia treat the → *Artes liberales* (including Medicine), bks. 5–6 the Institutions of political-social and cultural life (justice and law, time, books and bibliographies, feast day calendars and divine service), bks. 7–8 God and the Church, bk. 9 social distinctions, bks. 11–12 biology (Man and animal), bks. 13–14 geography, bks. 15–20 town and country, war and games including materials, equipment, clothing and food. A satisfactory critical edition of his work does not yet exist (cf. [5]; on the arrangement of the MSS. [6]). This work of I. had the greatest impact and was fundamental for medieval education. I deserves to be studied for its systematic qualities, but also for its sources (e.g. → Cassiodorus, → Servius, → Solinus, older authors mostly cited indirectly, Church fathers cited more often by name) and also as the Christian answer to Pliny's *Naturalis historia* and Suetonius' *Pratum* [7], as well as the latter's frame of reference → Varro; in the question of the sources as well, it is possible to go beyond FONTAINE (1983) [8]. 'In any case I. appears everywhere as the man who selected received information critically, summarized it in a practical manner, and thus smoothed the way carefully and securely for the Middle Ages.' [9. 3]. → Encyclopaedia

1 C.H. LYNCH, P.GALINDO, San Braulio, 1950, 356ff. (Werkliste Braulios) 2 M.REYDELLET, I., in: M. GRESCHAT (ed.), Gestalten der Kirchengesch. 3, 1983, 47–57

3 C.CODOÑER, L'encyclopédisme, 1991, 19–35 4 W.PORZIG, Die Rezensionen der Etymologiae, in: Hermes 72, 1937, 129–170 5 U.SCHINDEL, Zur frühen Überl.-Gesch. der Etymologiae I.' von Sevilla, in: StM 3,29, 1988, 587–605 6 M.REYDELLET, La diffusion des Origines d'I. de Séville au haut moyen âge, in: MEFRA 78, 1966, 383–437, Stemma 437 7 P.L. SCHMIDT, in: HLL 4, 1997, 19ff. 8 U.SCHINDEL, Die Quelle von I.' 'rhet.' Figurenlehre, in: RhM 137, 1994, 374–382, here 375 n. 4 9 A.BORST, Das Bild der Gesch. in der Enzyklopädie I.', in: Deutsches Archiv für Erforschung des MA 22, 1966, 1–62.

EDITIONS: CPL 1186–1212; W.M. LINDSAY, 2 vols., 1911 (etym.); P.K. MARSHALL, 1983 (B. 2); M.REYDELLET, 1984 (B. 9); J.ANDRÉ, 1986 (B. 12; 17); M.RODRÍGUEZ-PANTOJA, 1995 (B. 19); C.CODOÑER, 1992 (Diff. 1); J.FONTAINE, 1960 (Nat. rer.); C.RODRÍGUEZ ALONSO, 1975 (Orig. Goth. Vand. Sueb.); T. MOMMSEN, MGH AA 11, 424–488 (Chronica); C.CODOÑER, 1964 (Vir. ill.).

BIBLIOGRAPHY: J.N. HILLGARTH, in: StM 24, 1983, 817–905 (1936-1975); A.FERREIRO, The Visigoths, 1988, 325–413.

BIBLIOGRAPHY: Miscellanea Isidoriana, 1936; M.C. DIAZ Y DIAZ (ed.), Isidoriana, 1961; Los Visigodos (Antiguedad y cristianismo 3), 1986, 303–413; L.HOLTZ (ed.), De Tertullien aux Mozarabes 2, 1992, 9–98; J.FONTAINE (ed.), L'Europe héritière de l'Espagne wisigothique, 1992, 195–283; J.MADOZ, San I. de S. Semblanza de su personalidad literaria, 1960; H.-J.DIESNER, I. von S. und seine Z., 1973; Id., I. von S. und das westgot. Spanien, 1978; J.FONTAINE, I. de S. et la culture classique dans l'Espagne Wisigothique 1–3, ²1983; Id., Tradition et actualité chez I., 1988; P.CAZIER, I. de S. et la naissance de l'Espagne catholique, 1994. P.L.S.

B. MUSIC THEORY

De musica (Orig. 3, 15–23), much read in the Middle Ages, gives instruction on elementary knowledge: *musica*, its discoverers and its power, its parts *harmonica, rhythmica, metrica* (18), its division into *harmonica* (20), *organica* (21), *rhythmica* (22) and its numbers (23). I. bases himself here certainly on → Cassiodorus and older sources. In the chapter *De officiis* (Orig. 6,19) liturgical-musical terms are explained. → Music III (Rome)

BIBLIOGRAPHY: 1 M.BERNHARD, Überl. und Fortleben der ant. lat. Musiktheorie im MA, in: GMth 3, 1990, 33–35 2 W.GURLITT, Zur Bed.-Gesch. von 'musicus' und 'cantor' bei I. von Sevilla, 1950 3 M.HUGLO, Les diagrammes d'harmonique interpolés dans les manuscrits hispaniques de la Musica Isidori, Scriptorium 48, 1994, 171–186 4 H.HÜSCHEN, Der Einfluß I. von Sevilla auf die Musikanschauung des MA, in: Miscellanea H. ANGLÉS, 1958–1961, B. 1, 397–406 5 O.STRUNK, Source Readings in Music History, 1950, 93–100 (Engl. transl. of orig. 3, 15–23) 6 G.WILLE, Musica Romana, 1967, 709–715. F.Z.

[10] I. Scholasticus. of Bolbythia (Bolbitine in Egypt?). Author (6th cent. AD) of an epigram from the 'Cycle' of Agathias. Fictional dedication of the henceforth useless bed, including blanket, to the beloved moon goddess Mēnē by the now completely grey-haired Endymion

(Anth. Pal. 6,58). Attribution of Anth. Pal. 9,11 should be rejected; cf. I. [11] of Aegeae.

AL. und AV. CAMERON, The 'Cycle' of Agathias, in: JHS 86, 1966, 8.   M.G.A.

[11] I. of Aegeae. Author of five elegant epigrams (four funeral and one epideictic), which show thematic links to the 'Garland' of Philippus: to Anth. Pal. 7, 280 (in iambic trimeters, as also the poem 7,293, in the case of which there is perhaps a real inscription) cf. Antiphilus, ibid. 7,175f. and Heraclides, ibid. 7,281; to Anth. Pal. 9,94 (a fisherman receives a hare caught by Polypenus) cf. Antiphilus, ibid. 9,14 and Bianor, ibid. 9,227. The attribution of a sixth epigram is doubtful (9,11: about the old motive of the blind man and the lame). It is attributed in the lemma to an I. (without ethnicon) or, alternatively, to Philippus of Thessalonica.

GA II 1, 432–435; II 2, 459–461.   M.G.A.

[12] – [13] The two architects handed down by Procop (Aed. 1,1,24; 50; 70; 2,3,7 and 2,8,16–18), related to each other and both from Miletus, successive architects of the → Hagia Sophia in Constantinople (6th cent. AD.).

H. KÄHLER, Die Hagia Sophia, 1967, 15–19.   C.HÖ.

Isigonus see → Paradoxographi

Isinda (Ἴσινδα; *Ísinda*).
[1] Central Lycian settlement near modern Belenli, Lycian name *isñt*. Polis identified by Steph. Byz. (s.v. Σινδία), which together with Simena and Apollonia was part of a sympolity around Aperlai. In the archaic and classical periods a dynastic seat with a walled acropolis. Three pillar tombs, one with reliefs (scenes of hunting, battle, music and wrestling) from the 2nd half of the 6th cent. BC, two rock tombs with Lycian inscriptions and sarcophagi, some of which are inscribed.

C. DELTOUR-LEVIE, Les Piliers funéraires de Lycie, 1982, 171ff.; M. ZIMMERMANN, Unt. zur histor. Landeskunde Zentrallykiens, 1992, 24f., 30ff.   KA.GE.

[2] Pisidian town west of Termessus, modern Kışlar near Korkuteli. First mentioned in connection with the campaign of Cn. Manlius Vulso in 189 BC (Pol. 21,35; Liv. 38,15,4), later probably for a time part of the Galatian kingdom of → Amyntas [9], then part of the province of Lycia-Pamphylia (-Pisidia). Relatively splendid late Hellenistic and Imperial coins preserved [1] with information on the era in the late 1st cent. BC [2] which cannot be interpreted with certainty. A 3rd-cent. AD claim of descent ('Iones') which is typical for the period and also appears on inscriptions. Late antique suffragan diocese of Perge.

1 AULOCK 1, 29–32, 76–101   2 W. LESCHHORN, Ant. Ären, 1993, 395–397.

W. RUGE, s.v. I. (3), RE 9, 2083.   P.W.

Isindus (Ἴσινδος; *Ísindos*, Ἴσινδα; *Ísinda*). Place name ocurring with these two name forms only in Steph. Byz. s.v. Isindos as a town in → Ionia.   E.O.

Isis
I. EGYPT   II. GREECE AND ROME

I. EGYPT
The origin, meaning of the name and original role of the Egyptian goddess I. are not entirely certain. There is much evidence to indicate a home in the 12th Egyptian district with its capital at Per-Hebit (*pr-ḥbjt*), Latin Iseum, modern *Bahbīt al-Ḥiǧāra*. The long-standing opinion that I. personifies the royal throne is based on the fact that her name was written with the image of a throne. However, the likely root of the name (*ȝst*) describes I. as 'one who has power to rule'. It is significant that she is included in the Osiris myth, in which several pairs of deities characterized by co-operation and tension (I./Osiris, I./Horus, Horus/Seth, Osiris/Horus, Osiris/Seth) produce a complex and in part contradictory whole. In the myth I. searches for and finds her dead husband → Osiris, conceives with him their son → Horus, buries Osiris and mourns him together with her sister → Nephthys, raises her son in hiding and intercedes with the gods for his rights. As the wife of Osiris and the mother of Horus, she becomes a mother and protector deity. In the 1st millennium BC, the image of I. as the nursing mother goddess with the Horus boy was very popular. She also appears at an early date as a mother goddess through her association with → Min (Horus) of Achmim. Together with Nephthys, → Neith and → Selcis, she is the protector of the sarcophagus. Her role as mother and nurse who effects birth and rebirth is significant. Identification with → Sothis also makes her the bringer of the Nile floods and the new year.

Mythical tales portray her wisdom and cunning. In Egyptian magical literature she often carries the epithet 'rich in magic'. I. appears anthropomorphically in a standing or seated posture, and theriomorphically as a female falcon, a serpent, a scorpion or a female hippopotamus. Numerous Egyptian cult sites and feasts demonstrate her outstanding role.
→ Healing deities; → Mandulis; → Philae; → Seth

J. BERGMAN, s.v. I., LÄ 3, 186–204; M. MÜNSTER, Unt. zur Göttin I., 1968; R. E. WITT, I. in the Ancient World, 1997.   R.GR.

II. GREECE AND ROME
A. GREECE   B. ITALY AND ROME   C. REACTIONS AGAINST THE ISIS CULT   D. ISIS AND THE DOMUS AUGUSTA   E. FESTIVALS AND PRIESTHOOD

A. GREECE
The Greeks knew the Egyptian gods before the Ptolemies and found similarities between the familiar Greek deities and the unfamiliar Egyptian ones (Hdt. 2.42ff.). For example, I. was equated with → Demeter.

Epithets of Isis

Apuleius, Metamorphoses 11,2		Aretalogy of Isis	Egyptian epithets
regina caeli	Queen of heaven		nbt pt (MK, NK) Mistress of heaven
Ceres alma	Nourishing Ceres	Ἐγώ εἰμι ἡ καρπὸν ἀνθρώποις εὑροῦσα.	
frugum parens originalis	Original mother of the fruits of the earth	It is I who have found the fruit of the earth for humans.	
caelestis Venus	Heavenly Venus	Ἐγὼ γυναῖκα καὶ ἄνδρα συνήγαγον.	ḥnwt ḥmwt Mistress of women
quae... sexuum	You who by giving birth to	I brought woman and man together.	(3rd cent. BC, Philae)
diversitatem generato	Amor have brought together	Ἐγὼ στέργεσθαι γυναῖκας ὑπὸ ἀνδρῶν ἠνάγκασα.	
Amore sociasti	the diversity of the sexes	I have made it so by force that women are loved by men.	
Phoebi soror...	Sister of Phoebus [= Diana]	Ἐγὼ γυναιξὶ δεχαμηνιαῖον βρέφος εἰς φῶς ἐξενεγκεῖν ἔταξα.	
partu fetarum medelis	having invigorated the child-	I have imposed it on women to bring forth a child	
lenientibus recreato	birth of pregnant women with soothing remedies	after ten months.	
Proserpina	[consort of Hades]	Ἐγώ εἰμι γυνὴ καὶ ἀδελφὴ Ὀσείριδος βασιλέως. I am the wife and the sister of Osiris the King.	snt nt Wsr Sister of Osiris
solis ambagibus	dispensing your uncertain light	Ἐγὼ ἡλίου καὶ σελήνης πορείαν συνεταξάμην.	
dispensans incerta	[the moon] according to the	I have ordered the course of sun and moon.	
lumina	course of the sun		
tu fortunam conlapsam	strengthen my fortune that	Ἐγὼ τὸ εἱμαρμένον νικῶ.	
adfirma	has fallen in ruins	I defeat destiny.	
tu saevis exanclatis	after I have endured cruel	Ἐμοῦ τὸ εἱμαρμένον ἀκούει.	
casibus pausam	misfortunes, give me rest	Destiny obeys me.	
pacemque tribue	and peace		

Apuleius, Metamorphoses 11,5

rerum naturae parens	Mother of all things in nature	Ἐγὼ ποταμῶν καὶ ἀνέμων καὶ θαλάσσης εἰμὶ κυρία.	
elementorum omnium	Mistress of all elements	I am the mistress of the rivers and the winds and the sea.	
domina		Ἐγὼ κεραυνοῦ κυρία εἰμί.	
		I am the mistress of thunder.	
		Ἐγὼ ὄμβρων εἰμὶ κυρία.	
		I am the mistress of the rainfalls.	
saeculorum progenies	Original offspring of		wrt šꜣt ḫpr
initialis	the centuries		The eldest, who began generation
summa numinum	Highest of the divinities		ḥnwt nṯrw nbw Mistress of all gods
regina manium	Queen of the Underworld		ḥnwt jmntt; ḥnwt ḏsr Mistress of the West; mistress of the necropolis
prima caelitum	First of the heavenly ones		
deorum dearumque	Appearance of the gods and		
facies uniformis	goddesses in one form		
		Εἶσις ἐγώ εἰμι ἡ τύραννος πάσης χώρας. I am Isis, the mistress of every land.	ḥnwt tꜣw nbw Mistress of all countries
		καὶ γράμματα εὗρον μετὰ Ἑρμοῦ τά τε ἱερὰ καὶ τὰ δημόσια. ...and I invented writing, both hieratic and demotic [script], together with Hermes.	ḥnwt mdwt nṯrw Mistress of the divine words [=hieroglyphs]
		Ἐγώ εἰμι Κρόνου θυγάτηρ πρεσβυτάτη. I am the eldest daughter of Kronos.	sꜣt Itm Daughter of Atum
		Ἐγώ εἰμι μήτηρ Ὥρου βασιλέως. I am the mother of Horus the King.	mwt Ḥrw (MK; NK) Mother of Horus
		Ἐγὼ παρεδρεύω τῇι τοῦ ἡλίου πορείᾳι. I take part in the course of the sun.	m ḥꜣt wjꜣ n Rꜥ The one who is placed in front in the bark of Re

The comparison is based on Apuleius (2nd cent. AD; [1; 5]). The most complete aretalogy of Isis [2; 3] to be preserved is that of the Cyme (Asia Minor) inscription (1st–2nd cent. AD), whose text presumably dates back to the 2nd cent. BC ([3.1f.]).

Unless marked otherwise, the Egyptian epithets ([4]) are documented for the New Kingdom (c. 1550–1070 BC). Some of the epithets juxtaposed here are world-for-word matches, while others only convey a comparable meaning.

M. HAA.

A decree of Piraeus (333 BC, SIRIS 1) shows that the first adherents of I. in Attica were Egyptians, who had economic connections with Attica. In the late 3rd cent. BC and generations after Ptolemy I Soter's selection of → Sarapis as the protector of the Macedonian pharaohs, the cult was established in Athens and its priests were Athenian citizens; the situation in Delos was similar. Early in the 3rd cent., Egyptians were priests of the cult, but they were succeeded by Delians and Athenians. In the 3rd and 2nd cents. the Egyptian deities had followers on islands and in port towns but also in the interior of Greece and Asia Minor. The least influence is evident in the Peloponnese [1]. The best information on the Egyptian deities outside Egypt is available from Delos. Merchants who went to this commercial centre of the Aegean also took the I. cult with them. The most important impulse in its spread was the conquest of Delos in 88 BC by Archelaus [4], a general of Mithridates VI of Pontus [2]. In the same way Egyptian gods arrived in Italy with returning Italian merchants.

B. Italy and Rome

As in the eastern Mediterranean, a more intensive reception of the I. cult began in Sicily, Sardinia and Italy with the Hellenistic period. Romanization was critical in all areas. In port towns (Puteoli, Pompeii and Ostia), I. was already well-established in 88 BC [3; 4; 5; 6]. The Iseum in Pompeii was built about the late 2nd cent. BC, the temple of the Alexandrian deities in Puteoli dates to 105 BC. With the forced return of Italian merchants, it was merely a matter of time for the I. cult to establish itself in Rome. Lucius Apuleius tells that the first *collegium pastophorum* in Rome was founded in the time of Sulla (Apul. Met. 11,30). An inscription (SIRIS 377), now unfortunately lost, makes a connection between Delos and Rome: it has been convincingly dated to the period 90 60 BC [7]. Sulla's time may have been favourable to the Egyptian cult [8], but it was not the unbound passions of the simple people that brought about its acceptance. Egyptian scenes and images such as I.'s head covering, sistra, uraei, obeliscs and lotus flowers were elements of the artistic repertoire. Control marks on coins are not the expression of a social revolution, but the artistic implementation of a (late Republican) cultural reality [9].

C. Reactions against the Isis cult

The reactions in Rome against the I. cult in the years 58, 53 and 48 BC (Tert. Ad nat. 1,10; Cass. Dio 40,47; 42,26) were of a political nature: the Senate increasingly considered itself deprived of power. One of its privileges was the approval and consequent introduction of foreign cults into the Roman system of religion. In this case it was self-affirmation and the safeguarding of its original authority that dictated the expulsion of the I. cult on a state-wide level. It is evident from the approval of an I. temple by the Second Triumvirate in 43 BC (Cass. Dio 47,15,4) [10] that I. did not simply vanish. Two later regulations (28 and 21 BC: Cass. Dio 53,2,4;

54,6,6) to prohibit the cult in Rome are seen as Augustan measures to secure the *mos maiorum* and indigenous gods. These provisions should be understood as control measures in social policy, especially given Augustus' still uncertain political position.

Tiberius' decree banishing Jews and I. worshippers from Rome (Tac. Ann. 2,85,5; Jos. Ant. Iud. 18,72; Suet. Tib. 36,1) may be considered a further attempt to preserve Roman morals, but was probably more closely linked to events in Egypt: Alexandria had the largest number of Jewish inhabitants in the Roman empire and I. was the most powerful of its city gods. Germanicus had had the grain stores opened and this triggered a famine in Rome (Tac. Ann. 2,67). The chosen successor of Augustus had visited Memphis without permission. The Memphite priests, guardians of the living and dead bulls of Apis, were able to elect and depose pharaohs. Removing I. followers and Jews from Rome publicly demonstrated the political power of the *princeps* and symbolized the restoration of order.

The option of declaring the I. cult a → *superstitio* disappeared with the consolidation of the Augustan state model and the concept of Egypt as an integral part of the Imperium Romanum. At the end of the reign of Gaius Caligula or early in that of Claudius the I. cult became a *sacrum publicum*, a public cult [11].

D. Isis and the Domus Augusta

The association of I. with the *domus Augusta* occurred during the reign of → Vespasian. He was proclaimed emperor in Alexandria. He spent the night before the *triumphus* with Titus in Rome's Iseum Campense (Jos. BI 7,123f.). A variant of this statement of piety towards the Alexandrine deities may be seen in Domitian's renovations of several I. sanctuaries. → Hadrian's interest in Egypt may be associated with the death of → Antinous [2]. Also, Hadrian was a Philhellene (Alexandria possessed the most extraordinary libraries of the Ancient World and could be considered the repository of Greek culture). Hadrian's reign brought about an increasing interest in Egyptian and Egyptianizing objects, as Domitian's had, [12; 13]. Inscriptions for the benefit of the *domus Augusta*, especially in the name of Sarapis, emerged in the Danubian provinces after the victory of Marcus Aurelius over the Quadi and were dedicated by his generals [14]. The reason appears to have been the rain miracle brought about by the *hierogrammateus* Arnouphis in the battle against the Quadi (Cass. Dio 71,8). This unintentional and unconscious implementation of the Pharaonic and Ptolemaic ideology was completed under the Severi.

E. Festivals and priesthood

Two large festivals associated with I. are known: the public *navigium Isidis*, 'Ship of I.' (→ *ploiaphésia*, 'I.'s Sea Voyage') on 5 March (Apul. Met. 11,8–17) and the *inventio* (*heuresis*) *Osiridis* ('Finding of Osiris') from 28 October to 3 November. Both were closely associated with the myth of I. and → Osiris. The spring festival, which coincided with the recommencement of maritime shipping, recalls I.'s voyage to Byblus to find Osiris. Apuleius draws a colourful picture of its procession (Apul. Met. 8,17). The other with its progression from sorrow to joy recalls the end of I.'s search with the finding of the dismembered corpse of Osiris, putting it together and reviving him. By contrast the mystery rites are, by their very nature, difficult to fathom. Apuleius (Met. 11) draws an extensive picture of the preparatory (dream command of initiation, ritual bath, fasting, clothing in a linen robe) and concluding rites (clothing with the twelve – cosmic? – robes, presentation to the community), but merely circumscribes the decisive nocturnal ritual as the voyage to the Beyond and encounter with Death and the gods. In any case, it fits into contemporary mystery rites.

A cult association probably had five *antistites*, priests or *pastophori* (*hierophoroi*), who ranked below the *sacerdos* in the hierarchy. They wore different insignia in processions (Apul. Met. 11,10). A *sacerdos* (man or woman) held this position for at least one year but sometimes for a lifetime. The lower priesthood and officialdom were generally lifelong positions. In inscriptions, temple guardians, *neokoroi* and *zakoroi*, who may also have helped at sacrifices, occur. The *pastophori* (statue bearers) recorded in the west and the Imperial period were equated with *hierophoroi* or *hagiophoroi*. Greeks in the Egypt translated the title of the highest priest as *prophḗtēs*. There are very few references for this outside Egypt and it appears that a *prophetes* is identical with a *pastophorus*. After the *prophetes*, the *stolistḗs* ('dresser') had the highest rank among Egyptian I. priests; there were *stolistai* in Athens only during the 2nd and 3rd cents. AD. An *ornatrix fani* ('sanctuary decorator') is attested only once in the west (SIRIS 731). The *scriba* (*grammateús*, *hierogrammateús*, 'scribe'; Apul. Met. 11,17) is below the *stolistes* in the Egyptian priestly hierarchy but, like astrologers (*hōroskópoi*, *hōrológoi*) and singers (*hymnōdoí*), is not attested outside Egypt. *Therapeutaí* (*cultores*) were cult adherents without rank or function. The *naúarchos* (*triḗrarchos*, *hieronaútēs*, *naubátēs*), known only from inscriptions of the Imperial period [15], was not a priest but a cult member and officiator of the *ploiaphesia*. It should generally be noted that priests and functionaries of cult associations (lay persons) could bear the same designations. Not every dedicator or addressee of an inscription was an initiate of the cult. Most personal inscriptions are *ex voto* and most official ones (e.g. *pro salute imperatoris*) are political in nature.

I. temples (*Isea*) are generally located outside the *pomeria* ('city boundary') in the Roman period and in water-rich areas (marsh, port, near a river or important water source) [16]. *Isea* were not oriented towards roads and public squares like Greek and Roman temples. Also, the *cella* (*naós*) of an *Iseum* opened only inwards. The temple was the site of initiation. The temple doors were opened and closed with a morning and an afternoon ceremony. Sacrifices were offered during these ceremonies. It is uncertain if this cult really demanded three initiation rituals of its initiates (Apul. Met. 21ff.). As in other → mysteries, the preparations required purification and abstinence. The *mýstēs* then experienced a ritual death and in this way found a new life. Unlike in the public cults there was no status difference in the I. religion. The different I. aretalogies underline the creative forces of this henotheistic goddess 'with a thousand names' (*myriónyma* or *-mos*) who was in a cosmic association with Sothis (Sirius) [17].

In all aspects of the cult, myth and image of I., the Egyptian elements predominate; part of the attraction must have been the eroticism. It reached beyond antiquity: the iconography of Mary with her child is inconceivable without that of I. with Horus. In the early modern period, Athanasius KIRCHNER in particular picked up on the mysteriosophic approaches of the I. mysteries; they have become part of common culture through the artistic transformation of MOZART's *Magic Flute*.

1 F. DUNAND, Le culte d'I. dans le bassin oriental de la Méditerranée, 1973   2 M. MALAISE, La diffusion des cultes Égyptiens dans les provinces européennes de l'empire romain, in: ANRW II 17.3, 1615–1691   3 L. ROSS TAYLOR, The Cults of Ostia, vol. 2, 1985   4 M. FLORIANI SQUARCIAPINO, I culti orientali ad Ostia, 1962   5 V. TRAN TAM TINH, Essai sur le culte d'I. in Pompei, 1964   6 Id., Le culte de divinités orientales en Campanie, 1972   7 F. COARELLI, Iside Capitolina, Clodio e i mercanti di schiavi, in: Studi e materiali dell'Instituto di Archelogia Università di Palermo 6, 1984, 461–475   8 L. VIDMAN, I. und Sarapis bei den Griechen und Römern, 1970   9 S. TAKACS, I. and Sarapis in the Roman World, 1995   10 K. LEMBKE, Das Iseum Campense in Rom, 1994   11 A. BARRETT, Caligula, 1989, 220–221   12 R. TURCAN, Les cultes orientaux, 1989, 77–127   13 A. ROULLET, The Egyptian and Egyptianizing Monuments of Imperial Rome, 1972   14 I. TÓTH, Marcus Aurelius' Miracle of the Rain and the Egyptian Cults in the Danube Region, in: Studia Aegyptiaca 2, 1976, 101–113   15 C. MAYSTRE, Les grands prêtres de Ptah Memphis, 1992   16 R. WILD, Water in the Cultic Worship of I. and Sarapis, 1981   17 M. TOTTI, Ausgewählte Texte der I.- und Sarapis-Rel., 1985   18 L. Vidman (ed.), Sylloge inscriptionum religionis Isiacae et Sarapiacae (SIRIS), 1969.

J. GWYN GRIFFITHS, Apuleius of Madauros, The I.-Book, 1975.   S.TA.

MAPS: 1 J. GWYN GRIFFITHS, Apuleius of Madauros, The Isis-Book (Metamorphoses, Book XI), EPRO 39, 1975   2 J. BERGMAN, Ich bin Isis. Stud. zum memphitischen Hintergrund der griech. Isis-Aretalogien, 1968   3 D. MÜLLER, Ägypten und die griech. Isis-Aretalogien, 1961   4 M. MÜNSTER, Unt. zur Göttin Isis. Vom AR bis zum Ende des NR, 1968   5 R. HELM, Apuleius, Metamorphosen (Latin and German), 5 1961.   M.HAA.

Islam (islām).

I. Definition II. History III. Western Image of Islam and Islamic Studies

I. Definition

Islam, 'complete, unreserved submission, devotion to God', agent noun *muslim*; both terms are Koranic. The most recent of the three monotheistic world religions, with today more than a billion adherents.

II. History

A. Origin B. Distribution C. Religion and law D. Orthodoxy and sects

A. Origin

In the predominantly nomadic society of 7th cent. Arabia, a number of gods and goddesses, most of them tribal and local deities, were worshipped. A tendency towards → monotheism (Allāh = '*the* God') developed, in the transition to a settled way of life during the lifetime of the Prophet → Muhammad (about 570–632). This was due to the influence of the Christian denominations that had been present in the Arabian peninsula (northern borderlands) for decades, as well as of Judaism. Retrospectively, the pre-Islamic period is called the *ğāhiliyya*, which means 'ignorance' (i.e. regarding the 'true' religion). Muhammad considered himself the recipient and transmitter of the divine revelation, the → Koran, which was written down and edited after his death (→ Utman).

B. Distribution

Revelations of an eschatological content and an orientation towards the life beyond motivated the first adherents of the Prophet (especially after the → Hejira) and the community of the faithful after his death. With the campaigns of conquest (first the four 'righteous' → caliphs, then the Umayyads), Islam experienced a rapid territorial expansion: conquests from the mid–7th cent.: Arabian peninsula, Syria-Palestine, Egypt, 'Iraq, Iran, early 8th cent.: North Africa, Spain (until the fall of Granada in 1492); Transoxania, north-western India, 11th cent.: Asia Minor; 14th cent.: penetration into south-eastern Europe. The initially positive and tolerant attitude towards Jews and Christians, as adherents of the other two major revealed religions based on the same 'Holy Scriptures', prevented forced conversions of these minorities, who were guaranteed protection in return for payment of a poll tax. In the modern period Islam is still mainly restricted to Africa and Asia. Migrations of labourers in the 2nd half of the 20th cent. resulted in the formation of large Muslim communities in Europe and America.

C. Religion and law

In Islam, which considers itself the last revealed religion after those of the other 'Peoples of the Book', all areas of human life, whether pertaining to the individual or the (religious and political) community of the faithful (*umma*), are regulated. Islam comprises faith and devotion to a creator god, as well as obedience to religious law. Islamic legal sciences regulate the duties of a Muslim in all respects. The religious writings are the foundation: the Koran and 'tradition' (*ḥadīt*, i.e. the tradition of the words and deeds of the Prophet and his closest companions as the standard of behaviour). The religious duties of Muslims are formulated as the five 'Pillars' of Islam: 1. The confession of faith, 'I believe that there is no god but Allah (= the one God) and that Muhammad is the prophet of God', emphasizes the monotheistic character (omnipotent creator god). 2. The ritual prayer towards Mecca (for a short time initially towards → Jerusalem, → Kaaba), said five times a day after the ritual washing. On Friday noon, prayer takes place in the mosque. 3. The legal alms tax is distributed among those in need. 4. Fasting from sunrise to sunset during the month of Ramadan, i.e. abstinence from food, drink, smoking and sexual intercourse. 5. The pilgrimage to Mecca should be made by every Muslim at least once in his lifetime, depending on his means.

However, only a declaration of intent makes a subsequent act valid in the sense of religious law. A religious duty (attested in the Koran) is 'Holy War' (jihad, literally 'effort', 'exertion on the divine path') for defending and spreading Islam, which promises a combatant merit in the afterlife and makes a fallen warrior a martyr.

D. Orthodoxy and sects

An Arabian-Iranian Islamic culture flourished under the → 'Abbasids, reaching its climax in the 10th cent. Increased translation activity from the 8th cent. promoted the reception of the ancient heritage and discussion of Hellenistic thought, especially in the areas of medicine, natural science and philosophy (e.g. reception of Aristotle, → Textual history), and this in turn exercised an influence on the discussion of theological questions (→ Kalam) as well as the formation and shaping of Islamic mysticism (→ Sufism). Religious and political movements in opposition to orthodoxy formed at an early time. This resulted in the formation of the main sects of the faith, the → Sunnites (more than four fifths of all Muslims) and the → Shiites. In the 8th/9th cents. four Sunni law schools formed: the Ḥanafites, Mālikites, Šāfiʿites and Hanbalites, each of which adopted slightly modified interpretations of the law.

III. Western image of Islam and Islamic studies

After a long phase of unfamiliarity and ignorance, a more active consideration of Islam began at the time of the Crusades. It was reflected in writing in the first Latin translations of Arabic scientific, medical and philosophical texts, as well as the → Koran. Nevertheless, polemics, misunderstandings and a lack of factual knowledge prevailed, strengthened in the 15th cent. by reorientation in the West towards the Greek and

Roman heritage and an exaltation of the native tradition. The shared ancient heritage and exchanges aroused interest only in the modern period. Objective and critical Islamic studies began during the Enlightenment. Late in the 19th cent., text editions, analysis and criticism of sources, the foundations of which were laid by the founder of Arabic philology, Johann Jakob REISKE (1716–1774), provided information for numerous biographies of the Prophet and later for Koranic studies. Since then, Islamic studies, now established in universities for more than a century, have expanded in scope beyond the purely religious context into a multidisciplinary field.

→ Judaism; → Textual history; → ARABIC-ISLAMIC CULTURAL REGION (ANDALUSIA)

C. CAHEN, Der Islam I (Fischer Weltgesch. 14), 1995; W. ENDE, U. STEINBACH (ed.), Der Islam in der Gegenwart, 1996; G. ENDRESS, Der Islam. Eine Einführung in seine Gesch., ²1991; G. E. VON GRUNEBAUM, Studien zum Kulturbild und Selbstverständnis des Islams, 1969; B. LEWIS (ed.), The World of Islam. Faith, People, Culture, 1976; E. W. SAID, Orientalism, 1979; A. SCHIMMEL et al., Der Islam III, 1990; D. WAINES, An Introduction to Islam, 1995; W. M. WATT, A. T. WELCH, Der Islam I, 1980; Id., M. MARMURA, Der Islam II, 1985.   H. SCHÖ.

Island (ἡ νῆσος/hē nêsos, Lat. *insula*). The large number of islands and their location in the centre of the geographic field of vision, the Mediterranean, highlighted the significance of islands in antiquity. In literature, they are terminologically clearly distinguished from the mainland (ἤπειρος/épeiros, Lat. *continens*) and treated under their own headings (cf. above all Diodorus [18] Book 5 in the *Nēsiotikḗ*, but also Mela 2,97–126; 3,46–58; Dionys. Per. 447–619 and Plin. HN 3,76–94; 3,151 f.; 4,51–74; 5,128–140). It was thought that the whole earth was an island around which → Oceanus flowed (Dionys. Per. 1–7; Aristot. Mund. 392b 20 ff.; Str. 1,1,7 f. and similarly Cic. Rep. 6,21). In ancient literature, islands were of particular interest as isolated locations for → utopias (cf. Plato's utopia of Atlantis : Pl. Ti. 24e–25e) and for their origins (Str. 1,3,10 on Sicilia; Plin. HN 4,12,63 on Euboea and Plin. HN 4,62 on Ceos).

However in reality islands, particularly in the → Mare Nostrum (Mediterranean), were hardly isolated locations, because most could be seen and reached either from the mainland or the next island. Only their function as places of exile (thus, e.g. → Pandateria: Tac. Ann. 1,53,1; Suet. Tib. 53,2; → Gyarus: Juv. 1,73; Tac. Ann. 3,68,2; cf. → exilium, → deportatio, → relegatio) or retreat (Tiberius on → Capreae: Tac. Ann. 4,67; Suet. Tib. 40) was special.

Nevertheless, there were characteristics which effectively distinguished islands from the mainland, such as their clear external boundaries. Above all, these could have economic consequences, because the scarcity of resources (cf. for Corsica Sen. Dial. 12,9,1) led island dwellers to enter into external trade relations and there-

by increased their trading activities. The characteristics of islands had political consequences, where the coastline was seen as the → border and, for example, a → synoikismós was restricted to the island (cf. the island poleis Cos and Rhodes which resulted from *synoikismós*) or a uniform insular → minting as developed (e.g. on Cos already before the *synoikismós*) [1]. Even with the existence of several poleis, the inhabitants identified with the island, thus Sappho (fr. 106) and Alcaeus [4] (fr. 129 f.) with Lesbos. Only islands close to the mainland also offered the opportunity of gaining possessions there (→ Peraea). In exceptional cases, islands were able to extend their sphere of influence to command of the sea (Crete: Aristot. Pol. 1271b 32–40; Thuc. 1,4; Diod. Sic. 5,78,3; Samos: Str. 14,1,16; Thuc. 1,13; Rhodes: Str. 14,2,5). They were, however, mostly the objects of foreign rule (even the League of the → Nesiotai [2] of 313 BC was mostly ruled by foreigners).

If an island had ships, it could only be captured with difficulty (on the strategic advantages of an island: Thuc. 1,93; 1,143; Flor. Epit. 1,33,3 f. compares Hispania to an island, Str. 6,4,1 It.), but if it lost its ships, it was that much easier to dominate. Clearly → navigation had greater significance for islands than for the mainland, which is why almost all island capitals are located on the coast, and islanders were considered the best sailors (e.g. the Rhodioi in Pol. 1,46 f.). The intensification of outside contacts through → commerce or foreign rule was often the cause of an ethnic mixing of the population, with obvious consequences for religion and culture. Exclusive individual developments can only be identified in prehistoric times (Crete, Cyclades and Malta).

1 G. REGER, Islands with One Polis versus Islands with Several Poleis, in: M. H. HANSEN (ed.), The Polis as an Urban Centre and as a Political Community (Acts of the Copenhagen Polis Centre 4), 1997, 450–492.

J. F. CHERRY et al. (ed.), Landscape Archaeology as Longterm History, 1991; R. ÉTIENNE, Ténos II., 1990; W. ORTH, I., in: H. SONNABEND (ed.), Mensch und Landschaft in der Ant., 1999, 231–234; F. PRONTERA, s. v. I., RAC 18, 312–328; C. RENFREW, M. WAGSTAFF (ed.), An Island Polity, 1982.   F. LE.

Isles of the Blessed see → Makaron Nesoi

Ismaris (Ἰσμαρίς; *Ismáris*). Lake near the Aegean coast between Maronea and the River Strymon (Hdt. 7,109) with a sanctuary of Maron (Str. 7, fr. 44), probably near modern Paguria.   I. v. B.

Ismarus (Ἴσμαρος; *Ísmaros*). Town located in Ciconia in south-eastern Thrace, near Maronea (Str. 7 fr. 44) or identical with it (schol. Hom. Od. 9,39f.). As an ally of Troy, I. was destroyed by Odysseus (Hom. Il. 2,846; schol. Hom. Od. 9,40). According to Archilochus, a well-known wine-growing area (Archil. fr. 2 W.). Later mentioned, e.g. in Verg. Aen. 10,381 and Prop. 3,12,25.

J. WIESNER, Die Thraker, 1963, 16f., 44.   J.S.-A.

Ismene (Ἰσμήνη; *Isménē*).

[1] Theban heroine, who because of her romantic connection with → Periclymenus incurs the wrath of Athene and is killed by → Tydeus (Mimn. Fr. 21 IEG; Pherecydes FGrH 3 F 95). In the 5th cent. BC she was integrated into the Oedipus myth by the tragedians: as the daughter of → Oedipus and → Jocasta or → Eurygane, as the sister of → Antigone [3], → Eteocles [1] and → Polynices, she survives with Antigone the attack of the Seven Against Thebes (Aeschyl. Sept. 861ff.; Soph. Ant.; OC). Sophocles presents her as a foil to Antigone, conforming closely to the social norm. According to Ion of Chios (fr. 740 PMG) she is burned together with Antigone by → Laodamas.

[2] Water nymph in Thebes, daughter of the river god Asopos, wife of → Argos [I 5], grandmother of → Io (Hes. fr. 294 M-W; Apollod. 2,6). It is likely that she was added only secondarily to the Argive genealogy, and should probably be associated with the heroine I. [1].

BIBLIOGRAPHY: G. BERGER-DOER, s.v. I. (2), LIMC 5.1, 799; E. BETHE, s.v. I., RE 8, 2135–2136; I. KRAUSKOPF, s.v. I. (1), LIMC 5.1, 796–797.

FIG.: I. KRAUSKOPF, s.v. I. (1), LIMC 5.2, 527.   R.HA.

Ismenias (Ἰσμηνίας; *Ismēnías* or Ἰσμηνίας; *Ismēnías*).

[1] Prominent Theban politician, famous for his wealth (Pl. Men. 90a). After the end of the Peloponnese War (431–404 BC), I., with → Androclidas, came to the fore as leaders of a Hetaeria which opposed the pro-Spartan politics of → Leontiades. The goals were to push back the Leontiades faction and to bring about a new orientation in international politics towards Athens (Hell. Oxy. 12,1f.; 13,1; Xen. Hell. 3,5,1–6) [1]. Under his rule, Thebes concluded an alliance with Athens in 395 BC and (supplied with Persian funds) became one of the chief protagonists of the anti-Spartan alliance in the → Corinthian War (Stv 2,223–5) [2]. When in 382 I. and Leontiades were both functioning as Theban polemarchs and I. again supported an anti-Spartan course in the Olynthus crisis, Leontiades led a coup with the help of the Spartan → Phoebidas (Xen. Hell. 5,2,27–31; Plut. Pel. 5; and others). I. was arrested, sentenced in a show trial before a special court of the Peloponnese Alliance for Persian sympathies (in the Corinthian War) and executed. (Xen. Hell. 5,2,35f.) [3].

1 H. BECK, Polis und Koinon, 1997, 231   2 P. FUNKE, Homonoia und Arche, 1980, 67–73   3 H.-J. GEHRKE, Stasis, 1985, 175–7.

M. COOK, Ancient Political Factions, in: TAPhA 118, 1988, 57–85; R. J. BUCK, Boiotia and the Boiotian League, 1994, 27ff.   HA.BE.

[2] Theban, son of I. [1]. Dispatched with → Pelopidas to Thessaly in 368 BC, to negotiate the independence of the Thessalonian cities with the tyrant → Alexander [15] of Pherae. The two Thebans were taken captive by Alexander and released only in 367 through the military intervention of → Epaminondas (Diod. Sic. 15,71,2–7; Plut. Pel. 27–29). Still in the same year, I. was sent (again with Pelopidas) on a legation to the Great King in Susa (Plut. Artaxerses 22,8; cf. Xen. Hell. 7,1,33–7; Plut. Pel. 30–1). In 340/39 he was the Boeotian *hieromnḗmōn* in the *synhédrion* of the Delphic → *amphiktyonía* (Syll.³ 243 D14) and shortly after that held the office of archonship of the Boeotian Alliance (SEG 3,333). His son received (clearly out of the highest respect for Pelopidas) the name Thettaliskos (Aristot. Rh. 1398b 5–8).

J. Buckler, The Theban Hegemony, 1980, 120–8, 135.   HA.BE.

[3] I. from Thebes. In 172 BC, his political opponents accused him, as the leader of the other party, of promoting an alliance between the Koinon of the Boeotians and → Perseus against the will of the Romans (Liv. 42,38,5; 43,9f.; between 174 and 172). I. was a proponent of keeping the Boeotian League (→ Boeotia) and was close to the pro-Macedonian grouping around Neon, Hippias and Dicetas ([1. 372; 377]: 'old Democrat'). As archon of the League in 173–172 (Liv. 42,43,9) he proposed going over completely to the Romans at the conference in Chalcis (Pol. 27,1f.; Liv. 42,44,1f.), although the Roman representatives demanded individual negotiations with the cities. He was forced to flee to the Romans to escape an attempt on his life. The advantage, hard-fought and maintained with difficulty by him and his followers Neon, Hippias and Dicetas in Thebes, could not be upheld. Thebes as well as all other Boeotian cities, other than Haliartus, Thisbe and Coronea, negotiated individually with the Roman representatives and the Senate: the League was dissolved. As soon as the Pro-Macedonians went to Chalcis, they were accused and imprisoned. Together with others, I. took his own life in prison (Pol. 27,2,9).

1 P. ROESCH, Études Béotiennes, 1982, 372–77   2 J. DEININGER, Der polit. Widerstand gegen Rom, 1971, 153–59   3 F. WALBANK, A Historical Commentary on Polybius, vol. 3., 1979, ad loc.   BO.D.

[4] 4th cent. BC Theban player and teacher of the *aulos* (Plut. Demetrios 1, 889b; Diog. Laert. 7,125), also a gem collector (Plin. HN 37,6). I. is said to have played as a prisoner for the Scythian king → Ateas, the latter being said to prefer to listen to horses neighing (Plut. Mor. 174f, 334b, 632c, 1095f).

→ Music II   F.Z.

[5] Greek painter from Chalcis, worked in the last quarter of the 4th cent. BC. According to Plutarch (Mor. 843e-f), a monumental panel in the Erechtheion in Athens is by him, showing the ancestors and family members of → Lycurgus. Whether the genealogical theme represented the merits of the Eteobuteades dynasty in the form of a family tree, as has been assumed by some scholars, must remain speculation.

G. LIPPOLD, s.v. I., RE 9, 2141; R. PINCELLI, s.v. I., EAA 4, 242; I. SCHEIBLER, Griech. Malerei der Ant., 1994, 160;

K. STÄHLER, Griech. Geschichtsbilder der klass. Zeit, 1992, 112.   N.H.

Ismenus (also *Hismenos*; Ἰσμηνός; *Ismēnós*, Ἰσμηνός; *Ismēnós*). Boeotian river with its source in → Thebes [1] near the Cadmeia. Outside the city it joined the → Dirce and flowed into the → Hylice. In poetry the I. is frequently mentioned. Apollo Ismenius was worshipped in the Ismenium south-east of the Cadmeia above the I. The river god I. gradually became part of the oracle cult of Apollo. A Geometrical temple in the Ismenium was destroyed by fire *c.* 700 BC and a second temple was erected in the 6th cent. In the 4th cent. a *peripteros* remained unfinished. Evidence in: Pind. Pyth. 11,7; Hdt. 1,52; 1,92; 5,59–61; Paus. 9,10,2–6; Str. 9,2,24.

1 S. SYMEONOGLOU, The Topography of Thebes, 1985, 302.

SCHACHTER 1, 77ff. (with other sources).   K.F.

Isocrates Logographer, teacher of rhetoric and publicist from Athens, Erchia deme, son of Theodoros and Hedyto, 436–338 BC.
A. BIOGRAPHY B. WORK C. IMPACT AND EVALUATION

A. BIOGRAPHY
The biographical tradition concerning I., which goes back to Hermippus, is essentially documented in Dion. Hal. De Isocrate 1, Ps.-Plut. Mor. 836e–839d, an anonymous Life in a few MSS, Phot. 486b–488a and a Suda article s.v. I. In addition, there are biographical details in I.'s own works, particularly in Or. 15. As the son of a wealthy flute maker, I. received an education fitting his social standing, → Prodicus, → Teisias and → Theramenes are named as his teachers. He was however most heavily influenced by → Gorgias, with whom he studied for several years in Thessaly. Closer contact with Socrates is unlikely. Financially ruined as a result of the Decelean War, I. was forced to make profitable use of the knowledge he had acquired. Thus, he worked as a logographer between *c.* 403 and the end of the 90s of the 4th cent. When he had once again earned a sound basis for economic independence in about 390, I. turned away from logography and opened a school of rhetoric in Athens. For the next 50 years, he was able, to concentrate on the one hand, on his teaching activities (famous pupils were → Timotheus, → Lycurgus, → Theopompus, → Ephoros, → Isaeus and → Theodectes) and, on the other hand, on writing speeches concerning the great political topics of the time and his ideas regarding education. He never delivered these speeches himself, because he felt that his constitution could not meet the demands on an orator (strength of voice, confidence in appearance); instead, they were read to larger or smaller audiences, and were also intended as templates for instruction and for private reading. I. married at an advanced age and adopted one of his wife's sons named Aphareus. I. kept himself apart from the political bustle of his home town, but he did fulfil the increasing duties that came with his wealth by taking on expensive liturgies. I. is supposed to have died not long after the battle of Chaeronea (August 338); whether he really starved himself intentionally is uncertain.

B. WORK
In the 1st cent. BC, there were 60 speeches under the name of I., of which 25 (Dion. Hal.) or 28 (Kaikilios) were considered genuine. By the Imperial period the corpus seems to have reduced itself to its modern scope, namely 21 speeches and 9 letters, probably including some which are false (Or. 1, Epist. 6 and 10).
1. LOGOGRAPHY 2. PHILOSOPHY 3. POLITICS 4. STYLE

1. LOGOGRAPHY
Six speeches from I.'s period as a logographer are preserved: Or. 21 (403/2), Or. 18 (402/1), Or. 20 (between 400 and 396), Or. 16 (probably 395/4), Or. 17 (between 393 and 391) and Or. 19 (391/0). Their wealth of general aphorisms commends them as promotional and educational material for the school. I. probably published these (and perhaps some more of his) court speeches himself (Dion. Hal. De Isocrate 18).

2. PHILOSOPHY
Of the speeches written after the founding of the school, some are concerned primarily or exclusively with I.'s independent design of an educational programme and its differentiation from those of rivals in the Sophistic (→ Alcidamas) and Socratic schools (→ Antisthenes, → Plato), namely: Or. 13 (*c.* 390), Or. 10 (between 390 and 380), Or. 11 (between 380 and 375), Or. 3, 2 and 9 (between 371 and 367), and Or. 15 (353). The basis of I.'s educational concept is an epistemological pessimism, which can be traced back to → Protagoras and → Gorgias, according to whom definite knowledge is not achievable and action must therefore be led by well-founded opinions and probability. At the centre of education is rhetorical schooling, because according to I.'s conviction, 'good speaking' and 'good thinking' are mutually dependent. Talent, instruction and practice are equally necessary for success. The goal is both the ability to formulate reasonable thoughts on important topics in appropriate forms and for the benefit of the listener, and the competence to behave accordingly, led by a healthy striving for fame, which is aware that it is bound by ethical requirements. With this concept, which he himself describes as *philosophia*, he clearly distinguishes himself from Socratic-Platonic optimism regarding the knowledge of virtue on the one hand, and from a rhetoric education limited to technique on the other. Conflicts with the representatives of both factions, particularly with Plato (whose opinion of I. is, however, still debated) was the result.

3. POLITICS
In the remaining speeches, his views on political topics came more to the fore: in Or. 4 'Panegyricus'

(finished in 380 after 10 years of work), I. first developed his concept of a Panhellenic campaign against the Persian empire. I. followed the short-lived supremacy of Thebes with disapproval (Or. 14 'Plataicus' of 373, Or. 6 'Archidamus' of 366). Or. 8 'On the Peace' (355) and Or. 7 'Areopagiticus' (355/4 or 358/7), which followed closely on one another, formulate the concept of a reorientation of Athenian foreign and domestic policies (renunciation of hegemonial ambitions, return to *patrios politeia*). I. reacted to the rise of Macedonia in Or. 5 'Philippus' (346) and Epist. 2 'To Philippus' (344). The last speech of I. (Or. 12 'Panathenaicus', 339) eludes concise summarization due to its diversity of topics and (in part still not satisfactorily explained) intellectual complexity. The politically most significant of the letters stem from the period between the beginning of 367 and autumn 338 (if Epist. 3 is genuine) and, besides those to Philipp, are addressed to the Syracusan ruler Dionysius (Epist. 1; 367), the sons of Jason of Pherae (Epist. 6; *c.* 358) and the Spartan king Archidamus (Epist. 9; 356). The authenticity of most is doubted, with more or less reason. The political thinking of I. is marked by a more cultural than ethnic Panhellenism, which considers the harmony of the *poleis* under preservation of their autonomy and proclaims the campaign to the east as a common goal. As one of its positive results, I. expected the elimination of social tension in Hellas, which he viewed with concern from a property owner's point of view. At first, he wanted to be sure that the unified leadership necessary for the war was in the hands of the traditional powers of Athens and Sparta, but from the 60s – probably impressed by the Theban expansion of power – he considered more and more the hegemony of a single ruler, finally that of Philippus. Nevertheless, I. did not become a monarchist, but remained a constitutional advocate of a limited democracy in the 'conservative' Attic tradition of Theramenes, Nicias or Cimon. However, he considered the form of the constitution to be secondary to the ethical make-up of those determining the policies. How strongly I. influenced real politics is debated; more seems to speak for a rather limited effect of his concepts on political practice than for the contrary.

4. STYLE

I. expresses his own linguistic and stylistic principles in several places: in choice of words, he strives for purity and precision, in sentence construction, harmony and balance (antitheses, parallelisms etc.). Gorgian figures are valued but used sparingly. I. wants his artistic prose to compete with poetry, and this is also indicated by his tendency to use rhythm and the increasingly strict avoidance of hiatus. The development of this unmistakable style can already be seen in the court speeches; the peak of its development was reached in the 'Panegyricus'.

C. IMPACT AND ASSESSMENT

I. was accepted into the canon of Attic orators, although according to ancient standards, he only fulfilled the first three of the five functions of an orator (*officia oratoris*). His influence on the education system in antiquity, as well as on its normative demands on artistic prose, can hardly be overestimated. His school, for example, shaped Hellenistic historiography to a great extent, flourished again in the → Second Sophistic, and after that had an effect on late antiquity and Byzantium. Occasionally expressed criticism of the monotony of the style of the Isocratic period (Dion. Hal. De Isocrate 13f.; 20) did nothing to change that. Even in Rome, by the time of → Cicero, and through him, the rhetorical and educational system of I. achieved a decisive validity, which it retained into the early modern period (Erasmus of Rotterdam). In the Renaissance, I. was esteemed as master of language and moral authority (particularly based on the probably false Or. 1 'To Demonicus'). In the 19th cent., in connection with the growing interest in Plato, an increasing number of voices declared I.'s philosophical thinking banal and superficial, his political concepts illusory. In the context of the German efforts for national unity, others believed they recognized a historical analogy in Hellas of the 4th cent. and correspondingly glorified I. as their pioneer. In more recent times, such notions have been adjusted; at the same time, new interest has arisen in a more accurate understanding of the I.'s philosophy and its position in the intellectual life of the 4th cent., and in the exceptional position, in terms of the aesthetics of reception of his 'speeches' written to be read (alone or to an audience) but not for oratorical delivery.

COMPLETE EDITIONS: G.B. NORLIN, L.VAN HOOK, 1928–45, 3 vols. (with Engl. transl.); G. MATHIEU, E. BRÉMOND, 1928–62, 4 vols. (with French transl.); J. CASTELLANOS VILA, 1971–91, 3 vols. (Or. 1–8, with Catalan transl.).

INDIVIDUAL SPEECHES: Or. 1: A. MORPURGO, 1960; Or. 2: F. SECK, 1965; Or. 2, 3: S. USHER, 1990; Or. 7: V. COSTA, 1983; Or. 10, 11, 13, 16, 18: R. FLACELIÈRE, 1961; Or. 13: S. CECCHI, 1959; Or. 15: K. TH. ARAPOPOULOS, 1958; Or. 18: E. CARLOTTI, in: Annali del Liceo classico G. Garibaldi di Palermo 3/4, 1966/67, 346–79; Or. 19: F. BRINDENSI, 1963.

TRANSLATIONS: M. MARZI, 1991, 2 vols. (Ital.); CHR. LEY-HUTTON, K. BRODERSEN, 1993–1997, 2 vols. (German).

INDEX: S. PREUSS, 1904 (repr. 1963).

SCHOLIA: W. DINDORF, 1852.

BIBLIOGRAPHY: E. ALEXIOU, Ruhm und Ehre, 1995; K. BARWICK, Das Problem der isokrateischen Techne, in: Philologus 107, 1963, 43–60 (also in: F. SECK (ed.), Isokrates (WdF 351), 1976, 275–95); BLASS 2,1ff.; K. BRINGMANN, Studien zu den polit. Ideen des I., 1965; P. CLOCHÉ, I. et son temps, 1963; N.D. DIMITRIADIS, Ἀνατομία τῆς ῥητορικῆς. Ἡ διαφωνία Πλάτωνος καὶ Ἰσοκράτους, 1983; W. EDER, Monarchie und Demokratie im 4. Jh. v.Chr. Die Rolle des Fürstenspiegels in der athenischen Demokratie, in: EDER, Demokratie, 153–173; H. ERBSE, Platons Urteil über I., in: Hermes 99, 1971, 183–97 (also in: F. SECK (ed.), Isokrates (WdF 351), 1976, 329–52); CH. EUCKEN, I. und seine Positionen in der Auseinandersetzung mit den zeitgenössischen Philosophen, 1983; P. FROLOV, Das Problem der Monarchie und der Tyrannis in der polit.

Publizistik des 4. Jh. v.Chr., in: E. Ch. Welskopf (ed.), Hellenische Poleis, vol. 1, 1974, 401–434; A. Fuks, Isocrates and the social-economic situation in Greece, in: Ancient Society 3, 1972, 17–44; G. Heilbrunn, I. on rhetoric and power, in: Hermes 103, 1975, 154–78; H. Kehl, Die Monarchie im polit. Denken des I., 1962; M. A. Levi, Isocrate, 1959; J. Lombard, Isocrate. Rhétorique et éducation, 1990; A. Masaracchia, Isocrate. Retorica e politica, 1995; G. Mathieu, Les idées politiques d'Isocrate, 1925 (repr. 1966); E. Mikkola, I., 1954; Norden, Kunstprosa 113ff.; S. Perlman, Panhellenism, the Polis, and Imperialism, in: Historia 15, 1976, 1–130; F. Pointner, Die Verfassungstheorie des I., thesis 1969; W. Steidle, Redekunst und Bildung bei I., in: Hermes 80, 1952, 257–96; Yun Lee Too, The rhetoric of identity in I., 1995; M. Tulli, Sul rapporto di Platone con I., in: Athenäum 68, 1990, 403–22; S. Usener, I., Platon und ihr Publikum, 1994; S. Usher, The style of I., in: BICS 20, 1973, 39–67; H. Wilms, Techne und Paideia bei Xenophon und I., 1995.
For individual speeches: Or. 1: B. Rosenkranz, Die Struktur der Ps.Isokrateischen Demonicea, in: Emerita 34, 1966, 95–129; Or. 4: E. Buchner, Der Panegyrikos des I., 1958; D. Gillis, I.' Panegyricus, in: WS 5, 1971, 52–73; C. W. Müller, Platon und der Panegyrikos des I., in: Philologus 135, 1991, 140–56; F. Seck, Die Komposition des 'Panegyrikos', in: Id., I. (WdF 351), 1976, 353–70; Or. 5: G. Dobesch, Der panhellenische Gedanke im 4. Jh. v. Chr. und der Philippos des I., 1968; D. Gillis, Isocrates, the Philippos, and the evening of democracy, in: Centro ricerche documentazione sull' antichità classica 8, 1976/7, 123–33; M. M. Markle, Support of Athenian intellectuals for Philipp, in: JHS 96, 1976, 80–99; Or. 7: M. Silvestrini, Terminologia politica isocratea II, in: Quaderni di storia 4, 1978, 169–83; Or. 8: J. Davidson, Isocrates against imperialism, in: Historia 39,1990,20–36; D. Gillis, The structure of arguments in Isocrates De pace, in: Philologus 114, 1970, 195–210; Or. 9: D. K. Mason, Studies in the Evagoras of Isocrates, thesis 1975; W. H. Race, Pindaric encomium and I.' Evagoras, in: TAPhA 117, 1987, 131–55; Or. 10: L. Braun, Die schöne Helena, wie Gorgias und I. sie sehen, in: Hermes 110, 1982, 158–74; G. Heilbrunn, The composition of Isocrates' Helen, in: TAPhA 107, 1977, 147–59; F. Parodi Scotti, Auctoritas del mito, in: Studi E. Corsini, 1994,79–90; Or. 11: S. Usener, I.' Busiris, in: W. Kullmann, J. Althoff, Vermittlung und Tradierung von Wissen in der griech Kultur, 1993, 247–62; Or. 12: M. Erler, Hilfe und Hintersinn, in: II. Symposium Platonicum, ed. L. Rosetti, 1992, 122–37; V. Gray, Images of Sparta, in: A. Powell, S. Hodkinson, The shadow of Sparta, 1994, 223–71; H.-O. Kroener, Dialog und Rede, in: A&A; 15, 1969, 102–121 (also in: F. Seck, I. (WdF 351), 1976, 296–328); C. Schäublin, Selbstinterpretation im Panathenaikos des I., in: MH 39, 1982, 165–78; Or. 13: M. Dixsaut, I. contre des sophistes sans sophistique, in: L. Brisson (ed.), Le plaisir de parler, 1986, 63–85; Or. 17: G. Thür, Komplexe Prozessführung dargestellt am Beispiel des Trapezitikos (I. 17), in: Symposion 1971, 1975, 157–88; Or. 18: J. H. Kuehn, Die Amnestie von 403 v.Chr. im Reflex der 18. I.-Rede, in: WS 80, 1967, 31–73.
Letters: R. N. Gaines, Isocrates, Ep. 6. 8, in: Hermes 118, 1990, 165–70; M. Marzi, Isocrate e Filippo II di Macedonia, in: A&R; 39, 1994, 1–10.   M.W.

Isodaites see → Pluto

Isogloss see → Dialect; → Linguistic affinity

Isonomia (ἰσονομία; isonomía). The concept of isonomia, (equality before the law) – along with other compounds formed with the element iso- ('equal') – seems to have played a significant role in political discourse in Greece during the late 6th and early 5th cents. BC. In the constitutional debate at the Persian Court, Herodotus uses isonomia to refer to democracy (3,80,6; 83,1), and in other places (3,142,3; 5,37,2) he employs isonomia to designate a constitutional government in contrast to one that is tyrannical (→ Tyrannis); in the latter sense he also uses the words isēgoría (equality of speech) and isokratía (equality of power) (5,78; 92a,1). For Thucydides, isonomia is a concept that one can apply to a solid oligarchy – established on broad foundation – as well as to a democracy. The → skolia (drinking songs) in honour of Harmodius and → Aristogeiton offer praise to them, not only because they killed the tyrant, but also because they brought isonomia to the Athenians (PMG 893–896): the word isonomia was probably used in the beginning as a means of drawing a contrast between interior political freedom and dependance on a tyrant; however, it may have been adopted by → Cleisthenes as a catchword for his reforms.

1 V. Ehrenberg, Origins of Democracy, in: Historia 1, 1950, 515–548   2 C. Meier, Die Entstehung des Polit. bei den Griechen, 1980, 281–284   3 M. Ostwald, Nomos and the Beginnings of the Athenian Democracy, 1969, esp. 96–136   4 K. A. Raaflaub, Einleitung und Bilanz, in: K. H. Kinzl (ed.), Demokratia, 1995, 49–51.
                                        P.J.R.

Isopoliteia (ἰσοπολιτεία; isopoliteía). The term isopoliteia (equal citizenship), was used from the 3rd cent. BC, (instead of → politeia) to denote the granting of citizenship by a Greek state to individual persons (e.g. IG V 2,11 = Syll.³ 501) or indeed chiefly to whole communities (e.g. IG V 2, 419 = Syll.³ 472). Modern research distinguishes between isopoliteia, the exchange of rights between states, which maintained their independence, and → sympoliteía, the merging of two or more states into a single state. The ancient linguistic usage is, however, more multifaceted. The Aetolian League used isopoliteia as a means to affiliate distant states; this isopoliteia was agreed either with the entire league or with an individual Aetolian city.

1 Busolt/Swoboda 225f., 1245, 1510–9   2 V. Ehrenberg, Der Staat der Griechen, ²1965, 319f.   3 J. A. O. Larsen, Greek Federal States, 1968, 202ff.   P.J.R.

Isoteleia (ἰσοτέλεια; isotéleia (equality of duties), i.e. of civic duties) was a privilege that a Greek state could bestow on non-citizens, if it wanted to raise them above the normal status of metics (→ métoikoi), but did not wish to grant them full citizenship. Since the isoteleia normally freed one from taxes and other burdens to which non-citizens were subject, the same status could be called either *isoteleia* or → *atéleia* (freedom from duties) (for example in Athens: IG II² 53: *atéleia*, 287: *isotéleia*). In Athens, *isotelés* could be added to a man's name as a designation to specify his status (i.e. [Demosth.] Or. 34, 18; 44; IG II² 791,51 in place of the deme-specification in a list of donors). *Isoteleia* was also granted by many other Greek states (i.e. Boeotia: Syll.³ 644, 30–31), often together with citizenship, in order to emphasize the complete equality of the receiver with the citizens (for example in Calchedon: Syll.³ 645, 71–72). In Ephesus in 86 BC the *isoteleís* can be found among the inhabitants to whom citizenship was offered, should they commit themselves in the fight against Mithridates VI of Pontus (Syll.³ 742, 44–48).

P.J.R.

Išōʿyahb III. Syrian author and patriarch of the eastern Church (AD 649–659), son of land owners. He became a monk at the monastery of Beṯ ʿAbē, subsequently he became bishop of Niniveh (Mosul) in 627 and metropolite of → Arbela [1] in 639; in 649 he was finally elected patriarch. A comprehensive collection of 106 letters supplies numerous pieces of information about the eastern Church in the transition period from the Sassanid to the Arabian rule. I. implemented extensive liturgical reforms, furthermore he wrote a work about the life of the martyr Išōʿsabrān.

> EDITIONS: R. DUVAL, CSCO Scr. Syri 11f., 1904f. (letters); J. B. CHABOT, in: Nouvelles archives des missions scientifiques et littéraires 7, 1897, 485–584 (life of Išhoʿsabran).
> BIBLIOGRAPHY: A. BAUMSTARK, Gesch. der syr. Lit., 1922, 197–200; J.-M. FIEY, Isho'yaw le Grand, in: Orientalia Christiana Periodica 35, 1969, 305–333; 36, 1970, 5–46; DHGE 150, 1995, 179–181.   S.BR.

Israel see → Judah and Israel; → Judaism

Issa (Ἴσσα; *Íssa*). Island and city off the Dalmatian coast, modern Vis, Croatia. The settlers who came from Syracuse to I. in the late 4th cent. BC (Scymn. 413f; Diod. Sic. 15,14,2) [3; 4] established colonies in their turn: Tragurium, Epetium and a settlement on Corcyra Melaina (SEG 43, 348) [3]. Elevated by Rome in 230/229 BC to a *civitas libera et foederata* [1. 100], in 167 BC I. was declared exempt from taxes. In 56 BC a legation from I. went to Caesar (SEG 43, 350). From the 1st cent. BC part of the administrative region of → Salona [1. 106f.], I. was incorporated into the province of → Illyricum. Coins: [2. 58–68; 4]. Inscriptions: SEG 31, 593–604; 35, 681–693; 40, 510–515; 42, 549; CEG 2, 662 [2; 3].

→ Epetium; → Corcyra Melaina; → Tragurium

> 1 G. ALFÖLDY, Bevölkerung und Ges. der röm. Prov. Dalmatien, 1965   2 J. BRUNŠMID, Die Inschr. und Mz. der griech. Städte Dalmatiens, 1898   3 P. M. FRASER, The Colonial Inscription of I., in: P. CABANES (ed.), L' Illyrie

méridionale et l'Épire, 1993, 167–174   4 P. VISONÀ, Colonization and Money Supply at I., in: Chiron 25, 1995, 55–59.

J. WILKES, The Illyrians, 1992.   D.S.

Issedones (Ἰσσηδόνες; *Issēdónes*, Ἰσσηδοί; *Issēdoí*, Ἐσσηδόνες; *Essēdónes*). A Scythian people of Asian origin. According to Herodotus (1,201; 4,13–26), they lived southeast of the Aral Sea; however, the heaviest population centres within the regions of their habitation lay in Central Asia. Ptolemy (6,16,5; 16,7; 8,24,3; 24,5 N) ascribes to them the cities of Ἰσσηδὼν Σκυθική (modern Kucha) and Ἰσσηδὼν Σηρική (modern Charqliq), which were located on the Silk Road in Chinese East Turkistan (Tarim Basin, Xinjiang), to the southwest of Lobnor.

→ Scythians   J.RE. and H.T.

Issorium (Ἰσσώριον; *Issórion*). Hill on the northern city border of Sparta, with a sanctuary to Artemis Issoria (Plut. Agesilaus 32,3; Polyaenus, Strat. 2,1,14; Nep. Agesilaus 6,2), possibly the heights known today as Klaraki.

> F. BÖLTE, s.v. Sparta, RE 3A, 1350ff.   C.L. and E.O.

Issus (Ἰσσός; *Issós*) City east of Cilicia Pedias between Amanides (Amanikai) and Ciliciae Pylae, today the settlement mound Yeşil Hüyük (formerly Kinet Hüyük), 2 km north-north-west of the mouth of the → Pinarus, where → Alexander [4] the Great defeated → Darius [3] III in 333 BC; later also called Nicopolis. In AD 194, Septimius Severus won a victory here over Pescennius Niger and had a triumphal arch known as a *kodrigai* (after *quadriga*) erected in Ciliciae Pylae to commemorate this. Nicopolis, conquered in AD 260 by the Sassanids (Res Gestae divi Saporis 30), flourished in the 9th/10th cents. as Ḥiṣn aṭ-Ṭīnāt, from where wood was exported from → Amanus to Syria and Egypt.

> F. HILD/H. HELLENKEMPER, 277f.   F.H.

Istachr (*Iṣṭaxr*, modern *Taxt-i Ṭāʾūs*). Site of ancient ruins located in Persis (Fārs) on the road from Iṣfahān to Shīrāz, at → Naqš-e Rostam; having been populated since prehistoric times, a fire sanctuary for → Anāhitā – according to Arabic tradition – was subsequently located there (archaeological investigations cannot prove this); Sāsān, the eponym of the → Sassanid Dynasty, is supposed to have been its priest. Inscriptions, finds of coins, seal legends, and literary accounts clearly show that I. was an important place politically, administratively, religiously, and cultically, as well as ideologically, a place that was taken by the Muslims only after heavy fighting. I. was the seat of a Nestorian bishop.

> M.-L. CHAUMONT, Le culte d'Anāhitā à Staxr, in: RHR 153, 1958, 154–175; J. M. FIEY, Communautés syriaques en Iran et Irak, 1979, Index s.v.; R. GYSELEN, La géogra-

phie administrative de l'empire sassanide, 1989; J.WIE-
SEHÖFER, Die "dunklen Jahrhunderte" der Persis, 1994,
Index s.v.   J.W.

Istaevones Mythological ancient tribe of the Germani
(Plin. HN 4,100; Tac. Germ. 2,2) with no concrete his-
torical base. According to Plin. l.c. they lived *proximi
Rheno* (near the Rhine).
→ Herminones   K.DI.

Ištar see → Ishtar

Ištar Gate see → Ishtar Gate

Ister, Istrus
[1] (ὁ Ἴστρος/*ho Ístros*; *Hister, Danuvius, Danubius*,
Δάνυβις; *Dánybis*, the modern Danube). According to
Apoll. Rhod. 4, the → Argonautae (with map of the
journey of the Argonauts) must have returned from the
Black Sea by way of the I. and its tributaries, in order to
reach the *mare Adriaticum*. Hdt. 4,33 is probably describing the same route that the → Hyperborei took
from Scythia to Dodona. The Greeks long knew primarily the lower reaches of the I. Hdt. 4,48f. describes
the I. as the most important of the rivers known to him
and located its sources in the land of the Celts. He
named many of its tributaries, among them the southern ones downstream from the Szava (Hdt. 2,33). It was
as a result of the campaign of → Darius [2] against the
Scythians in 512 BC that the lower reaches of the I.
became better known: the Ionians erected a pontoon
bridge over the I. upstream of the delta (Hdt. 4,89). The
Greek colonies on the Black Sea (especially Histria-
Istros, Tomis, Callatis) thrived on the trade that was
conducted in the lower valley of the river. The Macedonian kings Philip II and his son Alexander the Great
undertook campaigns through Thrace up to the right
bank of the I., without any lasting success in subjuga-
ting the Thracian population. Pol. 4,41f. mentions the I.
only in connection with the alluvial land in the delta
region.

Tiberius discovered the sources of the I. in 15 BC,
according to Str. 7,1,5 a day's march north of Lake
Constance. Str. l.c. differentiates between the section of
the I. from its source as far as the Iron Gate, and the
lower reaches of the I. In AD 45 Claudius annexed
Thrace and extended the province of Moesia as far as
the river mouth, which put Rome in a position, with
help from the provinces of Noricum, Pannonia and
Moesia, to control the course of the I. from source to
estuary. The I. was, nevertheless, an open frontier: Str.
7,3,10 reports on the settlement of 50,000 Getae from
the other side of the I. through Aelius [II 7] in Thrace
during the time of Augustus. Under Nero the legate of
Moesia, Plautius Silvanus, allowed 100,000 men and
women (Roxolani, Bastarnae) to cross the Danube; other crossings were more of a menace, e.g. that of the
Sarmatae in AD 67–69. Under Vespasianus a series of
camps along the I. were established, from which the

limes later arose. The *classis Moesica*, stationed in
→ Noviodunum at the west end of the delta, and the
classis Pannonica in Taurunum, near the confluence of
the I. and the Szava, secured the river frontier. Dacia
under → Decebalus represented a constant danger for
the Roman empire: in 101 Trajan began his campaign
against him, and his kingdom to the north of the I. became a Roman province in 106.

Towards the end of the 2nd cent. the Quadi and the
Marcomanni crossed the I.; they passed through Noricum and Pannonia in 167; in 174 Marcus Aurelius
fought against the Sarmatians, as a result of which the I.
regained its function as a frontier. From the middle of
the 3rd cent. an invasion by the Goths took place in
Greece and Asia Minor, against which only Constantinus was able to take action successfully in 332. After
375 the I. frontier could no longer withstand the Visigoths; Valens was defeated at the battle of Adrianopolis
in 378 and killed.

> J.WILKES, Les provinces danubiennes, in: Rome et l'inté-
> gration de l'Empire, 44 av. J.-C.–260 ap. J.-C. 2, in: Nou-
> velle Clio, 1998, LIII–LVII and 231–297.   PI.CA.

[2] Pupil of → Callimachus ('the Callimachean') of
uncertain origin wrote numerous texts, predominantly
of historical and antiquarian content, in Alexandria
with the aid of the library there, in about the middle of
the 3rd cent. BC. These texts have only survived in fragments and are cited primarily by Plutarch, Pausanias
and the lexicographers. His main work, a 'Compilation
of the Atthides' in at least 14 bks., rests for the most part
not on his own critical research, but contains a comparative compilation of written records on the history
of Athens and Attica. The *Argoliká* and the *Eliaká* in at
least 5 bks., should be thought of similarly. Further
texts concerned ancient Egypt (e.g. 'Egyptian settlements'), matters of religious history ('Manifestations of
Apollo', 'Manifestations of Hercules', 'Compilation of
the Cretan sacrifices') and biographical themes ('On
lyric poets'); yet others concerned grammatical or lexicographical problems ('Attic words', 'Miscellaneous',
'Unordered items'). In the 'Answers to Timeaus' he
reproached this historian for numerous errors and described him wittily, on account of his extreme polemics,
as *Epitímaios* ('calumniator'). FGrH 334 (with commentary).

> F.JACOBY, s.v. I., RE 9, 2270–2282 = Id., Griech. Histo-
> riker, 1956, 305–311; K.MEISTER, Die griech. Ge-
> schichtsschreibung, 1990, 130.   K.MEI.

Isthmia The Isthmia, held in the sanctuary of → Poseidon on the Isthmus of Corinth from 582 BC, belongs to
the → *períodos* (περίοδος, circulation) of the Panhellenic agons. Myths connect the founding of the Isthmic
Games with funeral games for the drowned Melicertes
(Paus. 2,1,3) or with Theseus (Plut. Thes. 11e) [1]. Archaeological finds for athletic competitions do not pre-

cede the 6th cent. BC [2. (jumping-weight); 1. 76 (chariot)]. As early as 229 BC, the Romans were permitted to take part in the Isthmia out of gratitude for the annihilation of pirates (Pol. 2,12,8). After the destruction of Corinth in 146 BC, the Isthmia took place for a while under the presidency of Sicyon.

The programme consisted of athletic, hippic and poetic disciplines, occasionally also of recitations and competitions in painting. A four-stadia long horse race (rarely attested elsewhere) was held here (perhaps in honour of Poseidon as patron of horses) [3]. An episode in Thucydides (8,9) touches on the festival peace of the Isthmia. The winners received wreaths, at first of pine branches, later of celery [4]. The Athenian winners of the competitions received 100 drachmas (Plut. Solon 91b; Diog. Laert. 1,55) from their native city, in contrast to the 500 drachmas awarded for an Olympic victory. Recently, small lead tablets inscribed with the names of athletes have come to light, with which judges delivered their decision in the question of arrangement into age groups [5; 6]. Of great importance is the starting-gate (*hysplex*) of the ancient stadium, still *in situ*, in the form of an isosceles triangle, which ensured that 16 runners started simultaneously. It was triggered by a centrally positioned starter by moving lengths of rope threaded through eyelets, thus causing the wooden starting-gates to fall [7]. In Hellenistic times, a new stadium was erected [7. 32f.]. The hippodrome is thought to have been approx. 2 km west of the sanctuary [8].

Among the famous athletes who participated at the Isthmia, Milon [9. no. 122] and Theogenes [9. no. 201; 2. no. 37] with 10 victories each deserve mention, but Cleitomachus [9. no. 584] also caused a sensation with three victories in combat sports in one day. Inscriptions pertaining to the games [10; 11] have been preserved on the spot, but no statues of victors.

1 E.R. GEBHARD, The Early Stadium at Isthmia and the Founding of the Isthmian Games, in: W. COULSON, H. KYRIELEIS (ed.), Proc. of an International Symposium on the Olympic Games, 5–9 September 1988, 1992, 73–79 2 J. EBERT, Epigramme auf Sieger an gymnischen und hippischen Agonen, 1972, no. 1 3 I. WEILER, Der Sport bei den Völkern der alten Welt, ²1988, 131 4 O. BRONEER, The Isthmian Victory Crown, in: AJA 66, 1962, 259–263 5 D.R. JORDAN, A.J.S. SPAWFORTH, A New Document from the Isthmian Games, in: Hesperia 51, 1982, 65–68 6 D.R. JORDAN, Inscribed Lead Tablets from the Games in the Sanctuary of Poseidon, in: Hesperia 63, 1994, 111–126 7 D.G. ROMANO, Athletics and Mathematics in Archaic Corinth: The Origins of the Greek Stadion, 1993, 24–33 8 E.R. GEBHARD, The Sanctuary of Poseidon on the Isthmus of Corinth and the Isthmian Games, in: O. TZACHOU-ALEXANDRI (ed.), Mind and Body, 1979, 82–88; esp. 87 9 L. MORETTI, Olympionikai, 1957 10 B.D. MERITT, Greek Inscriptions 1896–1927 (Corinth VIII, I) 1931, no. 14–18 11 J.H. KENT, The Inscriptions 1926–1950 (Corinth VIII, III) 1966, 28–31.

W. DECKER, Sport in der griech. Ant., 1995, 52–55; J.H. KRAUSE, Die Pythien, Nemeen und Isthmien, 1841, repr. 1975; K. SCHNEIDER, s.v. I., RE 9, 2248–2255.   W.D.

Isthmus (Ἰσθμός; *Isthmós*, ὁ (*ho*) or ἡ (*hē*)) means primarily any connecting link between two things (e.g. the neck, Pl. Ti. 69e); in a narrower sense, any strip of land between two seas, as i.e. the Thracian Chersonesus [1] (Hdt. 6,36), but especially the I. of Corinth (e.g. Hdt. 8,40; Thuc. 1,13,5; 108,2; 2,9,2; 10,3).

This I. corresponds to the fundamental definition in two respects – it links, on the one hand, the Corinthian Gulf with the Saronic Gulf, on the other hand, central Greece with the Peloponnese. The I. of Corinth is made up of strongly faulted layers of neogenic marl and sands with alluvial accretions, is without springs or streams and at its narrowest point is 6 km wide, up to 80 m high, and an area through which important traffic routes run (today car and train). Already in antiquity, several futile attempts were made to cut through the I. with a canal, e.g. by Periander (Diog. Laert. 1,7,99), Demetrius [2] Poliorcetes (Str. 1,3,11), Caesar (Plut. Caesar 58,4), Caligula (Suet. Calig. 21), Nero (Suet. Nero 19; the only plan to reach the construction phase, whose numerous traces however were covered by the building of the modern canal in 1881–1893) and Herodes Atticus (Philostr. VS 2,6). Instead, the → *diolkos*, a slipway laid in the beginning of the 6th cent. BC on which one could pull smaller ships from the western to the eastern gulf over the I., served as the means of moving ships (Thuc. 3,15,1; 8,7; 8,8,3; Aristoph. Thesm. 647f.; Pol. 4,19,7ff.; 5,101,4; Str. 8,2,1; Plin. HN. 4,10; Cass. Dio 51,5,2); it was in use until AD 883. Longer stretches of this *diolkos* have been uncovered at its western end [1. 2259f.; 2; 3; 4].

As early as the late Mycenaean period, the I. was closed off by a wall to prevent traffic from north to south (cf. Hdt. 9,26f.). Most famous is the fortification of 480 BC for defence against the Persians (Hdt. 8,40,2; 71; 9,7; Diod. Sic. 11,16,3), which was repeatedly renewed until modern times. What can still be seen today dates from the Justinianic period (Procop. Aed. 4,2,27f.; IG IV 204f.). South of the easterly end of the present-day canal, remains of the sanctuary of Poseidon (7th/5th cents. and later constructions) of Palaemon, theatre, stadium, baths and further buildings have been excavated (IG IV 203). In 390 BC → Agesilaus [2] occupied the sanctuary; on this occasion the temple went up in flames (Xen. Hell. 4,5,1ff.). During the Isthmic Games (→ Isthmia) in the stadium in 196 BC, the freedom of the Greek cities was proclaimed by T. Quinctius Flamininus (Pol. 18,46,4ff.; Liv. 33,32; Plut. Titus Quinctius Flamininus 10,3ff.; App. Mac. 9,4). There is evidence of intensive construction activity during Imperial times. (Str. 8,6,4; 6,22; Paus. 2,1,5–2,2; Plin. HN 4,9f.).

1 D. FIMMEN, s.v. I. (2), RE 9, 2256–2265 2 E. MEYER, s.v. Diolkos (2), RE Suppl. 11, 534 3 N.M. VERDELIS, Der Diolkos am I. von Korinth, in: MDAI(A) 71, 1956, 51ff.; 1958, 140ff. 4 G. RAEPSAET, M. TOLLEY, Le diolkos de l'Isthme à Corinthe, in: BCH 117/1, 1993, 233–261.

O. Broneer, s.v. Isthmia, PE, 417f.; Id., s.v. Isthmus of Corinth, PE, 418f.; B. v. Freyberg, Geologie des I. von Korinth, 1973; A. Philippson, Der I. von Korinth, in: Zschr. der Ges. für Erdkunde 25, 1890, 1ff.; Philippson/Kirsten 3, 71ff.   C.L. and E.O.

Istria (Ἴστρος/*Ístros*, Ἰστρίη/*Istríē*, Ἰστρόπολις/*Istrópolis*, *Histria*, *Histropolis*). Greek settlement on the western coast of the Black Sea to the south of the Danube estuary, the modern Caranasuf (Caranasif), in the district of Constanţa in Romania. I. was founded by Milesians in the last third of the 7th cent. BC. During the 6th cent. I. developed into a significant port engaged in busy trade with Miletus, Rhodes, Samos, Corinth and particularly Athens. In about 512 Darius I took I. on his Scythian campaign. The course of the Persian Wars had a strengthening effect on Athenian influence on the West Pontic cities. In the 5th cent. the city was extended on a grand scale. At the end of the 5th cent. silver coins were minted here. At that time the power of the Thracian Odrysae was increasing in the areas surrounding the city, and they were attempting to extend their influence to I. itself. From the beginning of the 4th cent. the Scythae were increasing in power in Scythia Minor; they were, however, soon to be exposed to increasing pressure from the Macedonians. Philip II actually defeated the Scythae, but had to refrain from the subjugation of the West Pontian cities. The Macedonians did not achieve this until Alexander and consolidated it under Lysimachus (Diod. Sic. 29,73). After the death of Lysimachus the West Pontic cities regained their independence. In 260 I. supported the most powerful West Pontic city of the time, Callatis, in its struggle against Byzantium. As a result I. was exposed to ever-increasing pressure from the surrounding indigenous tribes, who were also settling inside the city. In the 2nd cent. I. was attacked by the → Bastarnae. After the defeat of Mithridates VI, who had extended his influence as far as I., Roman power also made itself felt on the West Pontic coast after 72 BC. In about 50 BC the city suffered greatly under the attacks of the Dacian → Burebista, who for a short time held I. Little is known of the city's history under Roman rule. I. belonged to the league of West Pontic cities (κοινόν/*koinón*) and seems, from the beginning of the 3rd cent. AD, to have flourished again. The independent minting of coinage is still recorded under → Gordianus [3] III. In the middle of the 3rd cent. AD the city was pillaged by the Goths, and towards the end of the 6th cent. was destroyed by Avaro-Slavic tribes. The settlement was abandoned at the beginning of the 7th cent.

In the religious life of ancient I. the cults of Apollo, Zeus, Helius, Dionysus, Demeter, the Dioscuri, Cabiri and Hermes played a role. Remains of buildings (baths, basilica), city fortifications, roads and necropoleis are preserved, also numerous inscriptions and finds of coins.

C. Danoff, s.v. Pontos Euxeinos, RE Suppl. 9, 1082ff.; T. W. Blawatskaja, Westpontische Städte im 7.–1. Jh.

v.Chr., 1952 (Russian); D. M. Pippidi, Epigraph. Beitr. zur Gesch. Histrias in hell. und röm. Zeit, 1961; TIR L 35 Bucarest, 1969, 45f. (sources and bibliography).   J.BU.

Istros (Ἴστρος; *Ístros*). Island documented by Steph. Byz. s.v. I. with homonymous city at the promontory of Triopium (modern Deveboynu Burnu or Kırıyo Burnu) near Cnidus.   E.O.

Istrus see → Ister

Isus (Ἶσος; *Ísos*). Location uncertain, at the time of Strabo already a desolate area (ἴχνη πόλεως, Str. 9,2,14) near Anthedon in Boeotia. Vestiges at the north-east end of Lake Paralimni can probably be identified as I. ([1. 457f.; 2. 257–261], contrastingly [3. 62f.]).

1 F. Noack, Arne, in: MDAI(A) 19, 1894, 405–485 2 Fossey 3 P. W. Wallace, Strabo's Description of Boiotia 1979.   M.FE.

Isyllus (Ἴσυλλος; *Ísyllos*) from Epidaurus, son of Socrates. Around 300 BC, poet of a consecutive series of poems (in trochaic tetrametres, dactylic hexametres, ionics, elegiac distichs), extant as inscriptions, for the cult of → Asclepius of → Epidaurus (IG IV 1² 128 = [1. 380–383]). In these, I. creates on the one hand a specific Epidaurian mythology of Asclepius, which relocates the roots of the god to the healing sanctuary that had been of increasing importance since the 5th cent. BC. The traditional myth, on the other hand, is set in Thessalia (Coronis, the daughter of King Phlegyas of Tricca in Thessalia, gets pregnant by Apollo, cheats on the god and is killed by him. The child is rescued by the divine father and educated to become a doctor by the centaur Cheiron: thus H. Hom. 16; Pind. Pyth. 3 etc.). However, in I.'s work, Zeus gives the Muse Erato to Malus as his wife; their daughter Cleophema marries Phlegyas, who lives in Epidaurus; their daughter Aegle, called Coronis, is seduced by Apollo and gives birth to Asclepius in the sanctuary of Epidaurus. Thus the cult of Asclepius is closely tied to Epidaurus and to the local cult of Apollo Maleatas [2]. On the other hand, I. establishes a close political bond to Sparta: Apollo Maleatas is supposed to have saved Sparta from Philip of Macedonia. I.'s principal work, the → paean to Asclepius, exhibits structural similarities to the → Erythraean paean as well as to the paean of → Macedonius [1. 200–206; 382].

1 L. Käppel, Paian, 1992   2 R. A. Tomlinson, Epidauros, 1983, 13–15.

U. v. Wilamowitz-Moellendorff, I. von Epidauros (Philol. Unt. 9), 1886; E. J. and L. Edelstein, Asclepius, 2 vols., 1945.   L.K.

Itacism Itacism (coined after ἰωτακισμός; *iōtakismós*, from ἰωτακίζω (*iōtakízō*) < *ἰωτατίζω (*iōtatízō*), 'to pronounce like ἰῶτα, *iôta*') means in the first instance the 'pronunciation of the name of the letter ἦτα, êta, as ['ita]' and thus of the letter η as [i]. By this is meant 1) in a narrower sense the undifferentiated pronunciation of the letters or combinations of letters ει, η, ηι (ῃ), ι, οι, υ as [i], as came about in Greek towards the end of the 10th cent., 2) in a wider sense the pronunciation of all letters or certain combinations of letters (those mentioned apart from e.g. αι, αυ, ευ; γκ, μπ, ντ), as can be established for Greek at the time mentioned, and also which – except for peculiarities of dialect – continues to be the case, essentially unchanged, to the present day: the Byzantine and Modern Greek pronunciation.

The phonemic system underlying this pronunciation is the result of various changes determined by time, place and social status, which the phonemic system of Attic has undergone since the end of the classical period, and, which at the same time was accompanied by the loss of opposed quantities in the vowels, and by the replacement of the tonal oppositions by a dynamic stress.

Itacistic pronunciation, which Byzantine scholars brought to western Europe in the 15th cent., was adopted by most humanists, such as JOHANNES REUCHLIN (1455–1522) (hence Reuchlinian pronunciation), but was promoted particularly by PHILIP MELANCHTHON (1497–1560) and used in both Catholic and Protestant circles. It was opposed already at the end of the 15th cent., by, amongst others, ALDUS MANUTIUS THE ELDER (1448–1515), but primarily, in 1528, by ERASMUS OF ROTTERDAM (1469?–1536). He demanded the introduction of the pronunciation that could be approximately deduced for classical Greek, (etacism, since ἦτα should be pronounced as ['ɛ:ta] and η als [ɛ:]; Erasmusian pronunciation). It was disseminated by Calvinism, but has only prevailed over itacism since the beginning of the 19th cent. in learned linguistic usage, in teaching in Germany (starting in Leipzig and Berlin) and internationally thanks to the efforts of German 'neo-Humanists'.

E. DRERUP, Die Schulaussprache des Griech. von der Renaissance bis zur Gegenwart, 2 vols., 1930/1932; SCHWYZER, Gramm., esp. 174ff., 392ff.; E. H. STURTEVANT, The Pronunciation of Greek and Latin, 1940; A. MIRAMBEL, La langue grecque moderne, Description et analyse, 1959.
C.H.

Itala see → Bible translations; → Vulgate

Italia
I. GEOGRAPHY AND HISTORY   II. RELIGION
III. THE UNIFICATION OF ITALY BY ROME

I. GEOGRAPHY AND HISTORY
A. THE NAME AND ITS DEVELOPMENT   B. GEOGRAPHY   C. NATURAL PRODUCTS   D. PRE-ROMAN PEOPLES   E. ROMANIZATION   F. ITALIA FROM THE TIME OF AUGUSTUS   G. LATE ANTIQUITY AND BYZANTINE PERIOD

A. THE NAME AND ITS DEVELOPMENT

The name I. acquired its modern meaning during the Augustan period; it originally described the kingdom of the Oenotrian ruler Italus, comprising the Bruttian peninsula from Sila to Scylletium (Antiochus FGrH 555 F 5; according to Hecat. FGrH 1 F 41,51–53, Medma, Locris, Caulonia, and Krotalla were in I.). Hellanicus links I. with the term *vitulus* ('calf') and the legend of the calf of → Geryoneus which had run away from Hercules (Dion. Hal. Ant. Rom. 1,35); Timaeus associates the name with this region's wealth in cattle (Gell. NA 11,1; cf. Fest. 94 s.v. I.); for that reason, Italic communities minted coins bearing the image of a calf and the legend *Viteliu* during the → Social War [3] (90–88 BC). The spread of the name I. is linked to the Greek colonization and the Pythagorean School, having moved from → Croton to → Metapontum. During the 2nd half of the 5th cent. BC, the name I. referred to the part of the peninsula extending in the west up to the river → Laus (within the territory of the Opici), and in the east to the river Bradanus (within the territory of the → Iapyges)(Thuc. 7,33,4; Antiochus FGrH 555 F 3) [1; 2; 3]. In the 4th cent., it encompassed, with the Italiote League, also Tarentum and Posidonia (Dion. Hal. Ant. Rom. 1,73,4). Rome's treaty with Carthage in 306 guaranteed its predominant influence in I. By the 3rd cent., Greek authors demonstrate an understanding of I. as a geographical unity extending up to the Alps (Pol. 1,6,2; Str. 5,3,5; [4; 5]); however, I. still was a mixture of different peoples and languages, which, together with their institutions, Rome tried to standardize between the 3rd and 1st cents. BC. Cato saw the Alps as I.'s walls (fr. 85); his *Origines* deal with all peoples from the Alps to Sicily. However, as a political entity, I. only comprised the peninsula (up to the river → Aesis), whose inhabitants were granted Roman citizenship in 89 BC. In 81 BC, Sulla moved the border northwards to the rivers Arnus and Rubico. In 49, citizenship was extended to the Transpadani (Cass. Dio 41,36), but the province *Gallia Cisalpina* continued in existence until 43 BC (Cic. Phil. 3,4,5). From 42, I. extended from the river Varus to the Formio, and in the late Augustan period to the Arsia. That completed the political unity of this 'beautiful country, divided by the Apennine, enclosed by the sea and the Alps' (PETRARCA). The ethnic units are the *Itali* as opposed to the *Italiotai*, i.e. the Greek colonists, and the *Italici* as opposed to the Romans. In poetry, I. is described in archaizing terms: *Hesperia*,

Ausonia, Opicia, Oinotria (Hecataeus, Antiochus) [6]; *Saturnia tellus* is initially limited only to Latium.

B. Geography

With the exception of the Po valley, I. is essentially a mountainous region with small plains.

1) Volcanic features

Colli Albani, Pithecusa (eruption after the colonization, Timaeus FGrH 566 F 58), Vesuvius (eruption of AD 79), Etna, Stromboli; utilization of thermal springs. Frequent earthquakes, bradyseism, hydrographic changes, and changes in the coastline.

2) Mountain ranges

The Alpes, from west to east: Maritimae (with *tropaea Augusti* near Monaco and *mons Caenia*), Cottiae (*mons Vaesulus*; pass of *mons Matrona*), Graiae (Little St. Bernard Pass), Poeninae (Great St. Bernard Pass, Poeninus), Carnicae, Iuliae (*mons Ocra*). Appenninus, from north to south: *mons Auginus*; Tetrica, Fiscellus, Ceraunii, and Tifernus in Samnium; Taburnus, Voltur, Alburnus, Sila to the *promonturium* of Leucopetra.

3) Seas, coastlines, and islands

The *mare Adriaticum*, or, respectively, *Superum*, with *mons Garganus*; the *mare Ionium* with the *promonturium Iapygium*, the *sinus Cocynthum*, the *promonturium Zephyrium*, and the *fretum Siculum*; Sicily and the surrounding islands (Aeoliae or Lipareaeae; Aegusae or Aegates: Cossura, Melita, and Gaulos); the *mare Tyrrhenum, Tuscum* or *Inferum* with the *sinus Terinaeus, sinus Laus, sinus Paestanus*, the *promonturium Minervae,* and the island of Capreae, the *sinus Puteolanus,* and the island of Aenaria; *sinus Formianus, sinus Amyclanus, promonturium Circei,* and the island of Pontia, *mons Argentarius,* and the islands of Igilium and Dianium, the *promonturium* of Populonia, the islands of Elba, Corsica, and Sardinia, the *mare Ligusticum* with *portus Lunae.*

4) Rivers flowing into the mare Adriaticum

The Padus, navigable from Turin to the sea, rises at *mons Vesulus* and is swollen by its left tributaries, rising from the Alpes: Duria minor, Stura, Orgus, Duria maior, Sesites, Ticinus, Lambrus, Addua, Sarius, Ollius (with Mella and Clesis), Mincius, Tartarus; its right tributaries rising in the Appenninus: Tanarus (with Stura), Trebia, Nure, Tarus, Parma, Incia, Secia, Scultenna, Rhenus, Idex, Silarus, Vatrenus. Venetian rivers of Alpine origin north of the Padus: Athesis (navigable), Meduacus, Plavis, Liquentia, Tiliaventus, Natiso, Isontius (with Frigidus), Formio, Ningus, Arsia. To the south of the Padus are these smaller rivers of Apennine origin: Rubico, Ariminus, Pisaurus, Metaurus, Aesis, Flusor, Cluentus, Tinna, Truentus, Vomanus, Aternus, Sagrus, Trinius, Tifernus, Frento, Aquilo, Cerbalus, Aufidus.

5) Rivers flowing into the mare Ionium

Galesus, Bradanus, Casuentus, Acalandrus, Aciris, Siris, Sybaris, Crathis, Trais, Naethus, Sagras.

6) Rivers flowing into the mare Tyrrhenum

Sabatus, Laus, Silarus (with Calor and Tanager), Sarnus, Volturnus (with Calor and Tamarus), Savo, Liris (with Trerus and Melpis), Amasenus, Astura, Numicius, Tiberis (navigable at least up to Castellum Amerinum; its tributaries are Anio, Cremera, Fabaris, Nar, Pallia, Clanis, and Tinia), Minio, Marta, Arminia, Albinia, Umbro, Caecina, Arnus (navigable), Auser, Macra; in Liguria the smaller rivers Entella, Tavia, Rutuba and Varus.

7) Lakes (lacus)

Within the Alps: Verbanus, Ceresius, Larius, Sebinus, Benacus. In Etruria: Trasimenus, Volsiniensis, Ciminius, Sabatinus. In Latium: the smaller lakes Regillus, Albanus, Nemorensis. Within the territory of the Marsi: Fucinus. Larger lagoons are the *VII maria* in Venetia. Presumably, malaria must have presented a major endemic phenomenon, preventing cultivation and settlement, cf. the interpretation of Graviscae, the Pomptine marshes (*paludes Pomptinae*), or Maremma (Plin. Ep. 5,6) [7].

C. Natural products

Some of the well-known natural products were marble from the Ligurian Alps within the territory of the Apuani, *pozzolana*, alum, and salt; agricultural produce, increased by cultivation, centuriation, and intensive farming methods (transition from wheat to olive farming and vineyards); cattle breeding, also transhumance, to supply markets and fairs. Literary sources describe the country as particularly fertile (Varro, Rust. 1,2,6; Verg. G. 2,136–176; Dion. Hal. Ant. Rom. 1,36f.; Str. 6,4,1; Plin. HN 3,39–42; 60; 37,13; 77) [8; 9].

D. Pre-Roman peoples

(Without consideration of the prehistoric cultures [10; 11; 12]). Irrespective of the great mobility linked to the custom of → *ver sacrum*, the following groups can be distinguished: the Ligures, widely spread across the western Alps, the northern Apenninus and Gallia Narbonensis; the Euganei and Veneti north of the Padus (centres in Ateste and Patavium with the Atestina culture and Venetic inscriptions); the → Etrusci, who had settled between the Tiberis and the Arnus, then advanced into Campania and Gallia Cisalpina (with original visual arts and a wealth of epigraphical material); the Umbri, formerly further along between the Padus and the Tiberis (the → *Tabulae Iguvinae* bear witness to their language), the Picentes in Picenum (stele of Novilara), the Falisci (→ Faliscan) around Mount Soracte; the Latini around *mons Albanus*, whose language (→ Latin) prevailed in the course of the Roman conquests; the Samnites (Sabini), Vestini, Paeligni, Marrucini, Aequi and Aequiculi, Marsi, Hernici, Carricini, Pentri, Hirpini in the mountainous interior, Ausones (Aurunci), Oinotres, Opici, furthermore the Osci in Campania (→ Oscan-Umbrian); the Lucani and Bruttii in the extreme south; the Iapyges (Hecataeus), Daunii, Peucetii, and Messapii of Illyrian origin (Messapic inscriptions, → Messapic) in Apulia. References such as *Megálē Hellás* (Μεγάλη Ἑλλάς) or → *Magna Graecia* reflect the colonization which began in the 8th cent.; the terms themselves, however, only seem to correspond to political tendencies of the 4th cent. [13; 14]. → Gallia Cisalpina developed in the course of the Celtic invasions of the 5th and 4th cents., but the term only prevailed with the setting up of the Roman province. In the valleys of the Alps, the Raeti represent the remainder of the Etruscan occupation.

E. ROMANIZATION

I. is the result of a process of Romanization of various peoples by means of alliances or conquests (cf. terms such as *socii, civitates sine suffragio,* or also *ager publicus populi Romani, coloniae maritimae* [15], and *Latinae*). The Romans brought about the construction of an efficient road network, → deportation of entire nations, the resettlement of mountain dwellers into the valleys and the relocation of settlements from the higher ground onto the plains, the phenomenon of large-scale urbanization and the reorganization of urban planning in the 2nd and 1st cents. BC, the granting of citizenship to the *municipia Italicorum,* the extension of citizenship to Gallia Cisalpina and Transalpina.

F. ITALIA FROM THE TIME OF AUGUSTUS

Augustus was the instigator of the *discriptio totius Italiae* in 11 *regiones,* based on the pre-Roman peoples and recorded on a map, progressing from south to north (with south at the top of the map), numbered consecutively (the names of the regions only prevailed later). For each region, a distinction was made between *coloniae* and *municipia,* in alphabetical order, possibly for practical reasons such as the archiving of census data, but without direct benefit to the administration (Plin. HN 3,46). For the legal administration, Hadrian introduced four *consulares,* however, from Marcus Aurelius to Aurelianus, there existed jurisdictional districts with judges [16; 17; 18]; there was only one single *corrector* in the whole of I. In AD 297, Diocletian started the process of provincializing I.; Rome was no longer the capital, I. one of 12 *dioeceses* of the empire, split into two *partes* (*annonaria* in the north, *suburbicaria* in the south) and 12 provinces: Venetia et Histria, Aemilia et Liguria, Alpes Cottiae, Flaminia et Picenum, Tuscia et Umbria, Campania et Samnium, Apulia et Calabria, Lucania et Bruttii, Corsica, Sardinia, Sicilia, Raetia. In the 4th cent., these changed into 17: Venetia et Histria, Aemilia, Liguria, Flaminia et Picenum annonarium, Alpes Cottiae, Raetia I, Raetia II, Tuscia et Umbria, Campania, Samnium, Apulia et Calabria, Lucania et Bruttii, Picenum suburbicarium, Valeria, Sardinia, Corsica, Sicilia.

Description of I. according to the Augustan regions:

Regio I: Latium et Campania from the Tiberis to the Silarus; a distinction is made between *Latium vetus* as far as the *promonturium Circei,* and *Latium adiectum* as far as *mons Massicus;* the main port was Puteoli, later followed by the military port of Misenum and the commercial port of Ostia; over time, Rome dominated over the other centres, many disappeared altogether; in Campania Cumae and Pithecusa on the opposite shore, the metropolis of Capua at the centre of an immensely wealthy region, whose centuriation was aligned to astronomical events; Nola, the ports of Neapolis and Salernum.

Regio II: Apulia, Calabria, Sallentini, Hirpini: they more or less comprised modern Apulia from the Tifernus to the Bradanus including the Sallentina peninsula and *mons Garganus;* in Daunia the colony of Luceria; in Hirpinum the colony of Beneventum; in Peucetia the ports of Barium and Egnathia, in the interior of the country Canusium and Venusia; in Calabria the metropolis of Taras-Tarentum and the colony of Brundisium, the end of the *via Appia* and the *via Traiana,* and also the port for the Orient.

Regio III: Lucani et Bruttii; modern Basilicata and Calabria from the Silarus to the Bradanus; the following Greek colonies on the *mare Tyrrhenum:* Posidonia-Paestum, Elea-Velia, Pyxus-Buxentum, Laos, Terina, Hipponion-Vibo Valentia, Medma; Rhegium on the *fretum Siculum,* and on the *mare Ionium* Locri, Caulonia, Croton, Crimisa, Sybaris-Thurii-Copia, Siris-Heraclea, Metapontum. The region declined in the Roman period, with the exception of Rhegium and Croton, and Potentia, Grumentum, Consentia in the interior of the country.

Regio IV: Samnites, Sabini, Marsi, Vestini, Paeligni, Marrucini, Frentani; in the Apenninus from the Tiberis to the Volturnus, along the *mare Adriaticum* from Salinus to the Tifernus; its ports were Ostia Aterni, Hortona, Histonium; Reate and Nursia were towns of the Sabini, Teate a town of the Marrucini, Corfinium a town of the Paeligni, Bovianum a town of the Pentri; in the land of the Aequiculi the colony of Alba Fucens on *lacus Fucinus.*

Regio V: Piceni et Praetuttii, along the *mare Adriaticum* from Aesis to Salinus, and in the interior of the country as far as the Appenninus (Tetrica, Fiscellus); the main port was Ancona, in the interior Auximum, Firmum, Asculum, and Interamna. End of the *via Salaria* and the *via Caecilia.*

Regio VI: Umbria et ager Gallicus; from Pisaurum to Aesis on the coast of the *mare Adriaticum,* and in the Appenninus from the Arnus to the Tiberis and the Nar; towns: Interamnia Nahars, Carsulae, Ameria, Spoletium, Camerinum, Sassina, and on Lake Pisaurum, Fanum Fortunae, and Sena Gallica.

Regio VII: Etruria; from the Macra to the Tiberis and as far as the Appenninus; its towns were Caere, Veii, Tarquinii, Volci, Volsinii, Rusellae, Vetulonia, Volaterrae, Clusium, Perusia, Cortona, and Faesulae;

some of them had fallen into ruin. Roman colonies near the ports of Cosa and Luna; Pisae, Florentia and Arretium on the Arnus, as well as Luca on the Auser as a colony under Latin law. Transversed by the *viae Cassia, Clodia*, and *Aurelia*.

Regio VIII: Gallia Cispadana, its name Aemilia was derived from the eponymous road, which crossed its entire length from Ariminum to Placentia, flanked by rich centuriated lands; from the Appenninus to the Padus. From the Etruscan period: Felsina, Spina, Marzabotto. Roman colonies were Ariminum, Placentia, and Bononia. Ravenna was the base of the *classis praetoria* from the time of Augustus, and an administrative centre since 403.

Regio IX: Liguria; from the Varus to the Macra, from the Appenninus to the Padus; its main port was Genoa; in the interior of the country Dertona, junction of the *via Postumia* and the *via Iulia Augusta*.

Regio X: Venetia, Carni et Histri; from the Padus to the Alpes, from the Ollius to the Arsia; in chronological order, its most important ports were: Adria, Altinum, and Aquileia; Verona and Tridentum on the Athesis; the colonies of Cremona and Hostilia on the Padus, Brixia on the Mella, Mantua on the Mincius, Patavium on the Meduacus. Extensive centuriated lands; roads across the Alpes (*via Iulia, via Claudia Augusta*), *fossae* in the *VII maria*.

Regio XI: Gallia Transpadana; from the Padus to the Alpes Graiae et Poeninae and the Ollius; main centres: Ticinum, Augusta Taurinorum, and Augusta Praetoria, and along the roads to Gallia Comum, Mediolanum, the latter administrative centre from AD 286 to 402.

Epigraphical evidence on I.: CIL I; IV; IX–XI; XIV; XV.

1 L. MATTEINI, L' I. nel Περὶ Ἰταλίας di Antioco, in: Helikon 18/9, 1978/9, 293–300   2 F. PRONTERA, Antioco di Siracusa, in: Geographia Antiqua 1, 1992, 109–136 3 C. CUSCUNÀ, Quale I. per Antioco?, in: Kokalos 41, 1995, 63–78   4 G. DE SANCTIS, Storia dei Romani 1, 1956, 111   5 E. LEPORE, L' I. nella formazione della comunità romano-italica, in: Klearchos 5, 1963, 89 6 M. AMERUOSO, La visualizzazione geografica di I., in: Miscellanea greca e romana 17, 1992, 65–131 7 P. FRACCARO, La malaria e la storia dell' I. antica, in: SE 2, 1929, 197ff.   8 TOYNBEE, Hannibal 2, 373f.   9 PH. DESY, Grec et Latin en 1991 et 1992, 1994   10 G. GIACOMELLI, Gli etnici dell' I. antica, 1960   11 M. CRISTOFANI, Etruschi e altre genti nell' I. preromana, 1996 12 R. PITTIONI, Italien. Urgeschichtliche Kulturen, RE Suppl. 9, 105–372   13 G. PUGLIESE CARRATELLI (ed.), Magna Grecia, 1985   14 D. MUSTI, Strabone e la Magna Grecia, 1988   15 E. T. SALMON, The coloniae maritimae, in: Athenaeum 41, 1968, 3–38   16 R. THOMSEN, The Italic Regions, 1947   17 M. CORBIER, Les circonscriptions judiciaires de l' I., in: MEFRA 85, 1973, 2 18 W. ECK, Die regionale Organisation ital. Iuridikate, in: ZPE 18, 1975, 155–166.

B. FLAVIO, I. illustrata, 1453 (Rome 1471) (first topographical reconstruction of ancient Italy); L. ALBERTI, Descrittione di tutta I., 1550; PH. CLUVERII, I. antiqua, 1624; L. HOLSTENII, Adnotationes ad Cluverium, 1666;

H. KIEPERT, A Manual of Ancient Geography, 1881, 209–256; K. J. BELOCH, Der ital. Bund, 1880; NISSEN; RUGGIERO; G. DE SANCTIS, Storia dei Romani, 1907–1923; 1956–1964; E. PAIS, Storia della colonizzazione di Roma antica, 1923; Id., Storia dell' I. antica, 1925; Carta archeologica d'I., 1927ff. (= Forma Italiae ser. 2); Forma Italiae, 1928ff.; G. DEVOTO, Gli antichi Italici, 1929; ESAR; J. WHATMOUGH, The Prae-Italic Dialects of I., 1933; Id., The Foundations of Roman I., 1937; B. PACE, Arte e civiltà della Sicilia antica, 1935–1949; E. WIKÉN, Die Kunde der Hellenen, 1937; SYME, RR; J. BÉRARD, La Colonisation grecque, 1941; T. J. DUNBABIN, The Western Greeks, 1948; E. SERENI, Comunità rurali nell' I. antica, 1955; P. FRACCARO, Opuscula, 1957; F. CASTAGNOLI, Le ricerche sui resti della centuriazione, 1958; EAA¹; EAA²; U. KAHRSTEDT, Die wirtschaftliche Lage Großgriechenlands in der Kaiserzeit, 1960; L. R. TAYLOR, The Voting Districts of the Roman Republic, 1960; A. DEGRASSI, Scritti vari di antichità, 1962–1971; G. SCHMIEDT, Atlante aerofotografico delle sedi umane in I., 1964ff.; A. H. TOYNBEE, Hannibal; E. T. SALMON, Roman Colonization under the Republic, 1969; G. A. MANSUELLI, Popoli e Civiltà dell' I. Antica, 1971ff.; P. A. BRUNT, Italian Manpower, 1971; W. V. HARRIS, Rome in Etruria and Umbria, 1971; ANRW II 11.2; H. GALSTERER, Herrschaft und Verwaltung im republikanischen I., 1976; C. NICOLET, Les structures de l' I. romaine, 1977; BTCGI; G. TIBILETTI, Storie locali dell' I. romana, 1978; W. ECK, Die staatliche Organisation Italiens, 1979; A. GIARDINA, A. SCHIAVONE, L' I., insediamenti e forme economiche, 1981; E. T. SALMON, The Making of Roman I., 1982; R. CHEVALLIER, La Romanisation de la Celtique du Pô, 1983; L. KEPPIE, Colonisation and Veteran Settlement in I., 1983; A. KEAVENEY, Rome, 1987; P. SOMMELLA, I. antica, l'urbanistica romana, 1988; F. M. AUSBÜTTEL, Die Verwaltung der Städte und Prov. im spätant. I., 1988; M. AMERUSO, Megale Hellas, 1996.   G.U.

G. LATE ANTIQUITY AND BYZANTINE PERIOD

After their invasion of I. (AD 488), the Ostrogoths captured → Ravenna; as a result, under → Theodoric, I. remained only formally under the suzerainty of the Roman emperor. Thus it had to be Justinian's (→ Iustinianus) declared aim as part of his policy of *restauratio* to return I. and particularly the prestigious city of Rome back to East Roman control. However, the lengthy and costly campaigns (until 555) under the command of → Belisarius and → Narses (described by → Procopius) only brought a temporary success, even though farreaching in its consequences [1. 20ff., 54ff.]: the Langobards invaded in 568, and the end of that cent. saw the settlement of → Slavs in Istria (→ Histria). Byzantium could only hold on to Venice and Ravenna with their respective territories, the coast of Istria, and southern I. (Campania, Apulia, Calabria, Lucania, and Sicily); the papacy recognized the suzerainty of Byzantium. This situation remained stable until about the middle of the 8th cent. [2]: Ravenna, the seat of the exarch (→ Exarchate), was only lost in 751. Byzantium transferred the ecclesiastical jurisdiction over the south to the patriarch of Constantinople; one of the consequences of this was that the pope began to lean towards the new power in the north, i.e. the kingdom of the Franks. The weakness of the Langobardic dukedoms in the south further contributed to the strengthening of Byzantium's presence there, including the imposition of the theme system (→ Theme). Thus, the geographical dichotomy was complete in about 800: the north was ruled by the Frankish king or respectively the German emperor, the south by Byzantium, with the independent Papal State in between. Only Venice remained nominally with Byzantium, as confirmed in the Peace of Aachen (812), the same peace in which Byzantium lost Istria. With the beginning of the conquest of Sicily [3] (completed in 902 with the fall of Taormina), a further factor came into play: the extreme south was now dominated by a Graeco-Latin-Arab mixed culture. The rest of southern I. remained Byzantine (before 969 → Katepanate), despite the attempts of the Ottonians to gain control over the entire *regnum Italiae* [4]. The fragile balance of powers in I. was only disrupted by the conquests and subsequent rebellion of G. Maniakes (1038–1042), which allowed the Normans, who aimed to bring together both Byzantine and Arab territories, to secure their conquests.

In both culture and language, the south thus remained an integral part of the Greek world, even beyond the 11th cent.; at the time of the iconoclasm (→ Syrian dynasty), numerous persecuted iconodulists fled to I. The monastic culture in southern I. remained a distinctive phenomenon (Neilos of Rossano, d. 1004). Only in recent decades has Byzantium's influence on the culture of southern I. been positively acknowledged [5; 6]: apart from the fine arts (with most of the monuments dating from the Hohenstaufen period) and book culture [7], the presence of Greeks, which continues to the present day, also needs mentioning [8]. The influence of the Byzantine culture on the Hohenstaufen empire was decisive. In Venice, Byzantine influence is at least on a par: there, too, the cultural influence far outlasted political rule (St Mark's Cathedral; Venetian *gondola* < κοντοῦρα). However, the most enduring fact was that as a result of the Byzantine-Frankish contrast, I. belonged for centuries to two, later three, cultural spheres; the effects of this are still evident today.

→ ITALY

1 R. HODGES, D. WHITEHOUSE, Mohammed, Charlemagne and the Origins of Europe. Archaeology and the Pirenne Thesis, 1983   2 P. CLASSEN, Karl der Große, das Papsttum und Byzanz, 1985   3 V. V. FALKENHAUSEN, La dominazione bizantina nell'Italia meridionale dal IX all XI secolo, 1967/1978   4 R. HIESTAND, Byzanz und das regnum italicum im 10. Jh., 1964   5 G. CAVALLO (ed.), Bizantini in Italia, 1982   6 W. BERSCHIN, Griech.-Lat. MA, 1980   7 G. CAVALLO, Libri e lettori nel mondo bizantino, 1982   8 G. ROHLFS, Grammatica storica dei dialetti italogreci (Calabria-Salerno), 1977.   J.N.

II. RELIGION

The Italian religions of the Bronze and early Iron Age are almost unknown. There is some evidence for a cult of the dead, some other cults in caves, also votive offerings in the form of bronze weapons found in rivers (northern I.), and clay horses and oxen inside settlements. The priestly offices date back to the period of Indo-European unity (cf. Latin *flamen* = Old Indo-Aryan *brahman*). The *rex* carried out priestly tasks; however, over time, the priestly offices became more differentiated and also increased in number. Archaeological and epigraphical evidence for Etruria and Latium shows an increase in religious activities from the 7th and 6th cents. BC, for the Sabelli, Umbri, and Veneti only from the 5th cent. BC. From the 7th cent. onwards, Italian cults show signs of increasing Hellenization: initially, Greek myths – esp. of → Odysseus and → Heracles – were assimilated mainly by the elite; this was followed by the equation of indigenous deities with Greek ones (e.g. Jupiter with Zeus, Minerva with Athena, Venus with Aphrodite); new deities were also introduced from the Greek pantheon (e.g. Heracles, the Dioscuri, Hermes). It is not always easy to discover the ancient Latin and Etruscan traits of deities for whom Greek iconography and mythology had been adopted (e.g. Ceres and the Etruscan Turan prior to their equation with Demeter and Aphrodite respectively). However, even for newly introduced deities, the original traits of the Greek deities underwent a process of interpretation in view of religious and socio-economic requirements. Thus Castor became the god of young Roman *equites*, and Heracles, too, was linked to local deities. Amongst the most important indigenous deities are the masters and mistresses of beasts, who were also *numina* of fertility or the Underworld, such as Faunus and Diana in Latium, Suri in Etruria, and a Venetian goddess equated with Artemis Aitolike. Furthermore, deities were venerated whose names were personifications, e.g. Ceres (goddess of growth), Liber (god-son), Venus (goddess of love's enchantment), Salus, Spes, Victoria, etc.

In the course of the 6th cent. BC, the first monumental temples were built in Etruria and Latium, with other regions following only later. The sacred groves with their right of asylum for men and beast continued to exist. Towns and cities organized their pantheon around city deities, who personified the highest of civic values: e.g. Jupiter in Rome, Juno Regina in Veii, Fortuna in Praeneste. In a similar manner, federations centred around federal cults, e.g. the Etruscan cities around the cult of Voltumna, and the Latini around Jupiter Latiaris and Diana. Other deities played an important role in initiation rites and marriage rites, especially Minerva and Venus in antithetical and complementary roles, but also Mars, Hercules, and Liber. From the 5th to the 1st cent., it was a widespread custom to present as votive offerings statuettes, depicting gods, humans, or parts of the human body, and demonstrating the search for *sanatio* (healing). *Sanatio* was not only sought from → healing deities in the stricter sense, such as Aesculapius or Apollo, but from all deities. Across the entire Italian peninsula, the practice of *auspicia* was prevalent in the public sector, as was the divination of *sortes* in private consultations. In Etruria and in Rome, the interpretation of prodigies and the liver of sacrificial animals was the domain of Etruscan → *haruspices*, who had developed a complex theory to this end.

RADKE; Italia omnium terrarum alumna, Antica madre 11, 1988; Italia omnium terrarum parens, Antica madre 12, 1989.   A.MAS.

III. THE UNIFICATION OF ITALY BY ROME

At the end of the 6th cent. BC, after the expulsion of the Etruscan kings (→ Porsenna), → Rome was just one of many communities within Italy. At the time, Italy was populated by numerous politically independent tribes and cities, all with different dialects or languages, and political structures (see above Italia I. D.; → Magna Graecia). Two-and-a-half centuries later, the land stretching from southern Italy (without the islands) to the Arnus and the Rubico in the north (to modern Pisa and Rimini) either belonged to Rome itself (→ *ager Romanus*, see Addenda to the whole work) or to its colonies (→ *coloniae*; → Latin law), or was allied to Rome by treaties (→ *foedus*; → *socii*; Roman confederation). The *ager Romanus* had its heartlands in central Italy and in the early 3rd cent. BC extended from the Tyrrhenian Sea to the Adriatic (cf. map in → Socii (Roman confederation)). With an area of *c.* 26,000 sq km, it made up about a fifth of the total area defined above, with another 5–6 % added by the territories of the Latin colonies (*c.* 7,000 sq km). The sizeable remainder was shared between separate communities which – in their majority subdued by Rome, but some after voluntary affiliation – were autonomous in their internal affairs and not subject to Roman taxation, but could not pursue an independent foreign policy, and were contractually obliged to provide military services for Rome.

Rome's dominant position in Italy was unexpected, considering its unfavourable initial conditions in the early years of the Republic, when it not only faced external threats, but was also torn internally (→ Struggle of the orders; → Rome I.D.2.). Rome's dominance was not the result of a continuous expansion; it was the military and organizational achievement mainly of the five decades between 326 (begin of the Second Samnite War; → Samnites IV) and 275 BC (victory over → Pyrrhus [3] and the Samnites at Maleventum/→ Beneventum). This success had become possible because Roman dominance in Latium had been secured (341–338; → Latin Wars), because its military power had increased after the integration of the Latin armies following the political reorganization of Latium (338 BC). Furthermore, it had become possible because of the political settlement of the struggle of the orders, which in 366 ended with the admission of plebeians to the consulate, and not least because of the primarily military ethics of achievement, which the patrician/plebeian → *nobiles* had gained in that struggle.

The military course of Roman expansion (for details on the wars see → Samnites IV; → Etrusci I.J.; → Umbri II.; → Pyrrhus [3]; → Taras [2] II) is inseparable from the attendant organizational measures to secure the gains. The stability of Roman rule in Italy in later times was founded on the latter. While the Second Samnite War (326–304) was still being fought, Rome instituted two new → *tribus* (Oufentina, Falerna) in Campania in 318, and in 314/13 founded five Latin colonies around Samnium, among them → Luceria, a military base at the rear of the Samnites and at the same time a sign of increased Roman involvement in the south. Lastly, Rome constructed the → *via Appia* from Rome to Capua in 312, not only a link to the newly instituted *tribus*, but also a military deployment route to the south. This was followed in 307 by the → *via Valeria* from Rome to the Abruzzi, to the north of the Samnites. After the conclusion of the war, which had been accompanied by successful fights against the Etruscans and the Umbrians (311–308), Rome increased its diplomatic and territorial security measures. In 304 Abruzzi tribes (Marsi, Paeligni and others) signed treaties with Rome (including their obligation to provide military support in the case of war), after Rome had completely wiped out the Aequi the same year. In the Abruzzi, the colonies of Sora, Alba Fucens (both in 303) and Carseoli (298) were founded (the latter already enrolled in the *tribus Aniensis*, established only in 299), while in Umbria the colony of Narnia was founded in 299. In the same year, the *tribus Teretina* was set up to close the gap between the *tribus Oufentina* and *Falerna*.

The Third Samnite War (298–290) started with the southern Italian Lucani issuing a request for Rome's assistance, after they had been attacked by the Samnites. Soon, however, it developed into a coalition of Samnites, Etruscans, Umbrians, and Gauls against Rome, nearly pushing Rome to the brink. The war could only be won with the aid of the troops of Rome's allies, who far outnumbered Roman legionaries in the decisive battle of → Sentinum.

It was only logical for Tarentum (→ Taras) to seek assistance from a Hellenistic monarch, Pyrrhus [3], when it came into conflict with Rome (280–272). This conflict had been long in coming following the foundation of the Latin colony of Venusia (291) in Tarentum's sphere of interest and Rome's military involvement in 285 in support of the Thurii (against the Lucani). But Pyrrhus could not prevail against Rome and the armies of its allies, whose numbers had grown considerably following the Third Samnite War. After that, Roman rule over all of Italy had only become a question of time; Tarentum was taken in 272, the resistance of the Samnites, Lucani, and Bruttii broken over the following decade, and Roman control strengthened through the foundation of further Latin colonies (Paestum in 273, Beneventum in 268, Aesernia in 263).

Meanwhile, Rome had also extended its influence to the Adriatic coast with the Latin colonies of Hadria (289), Castrum Novum (283), Ariminum (268), and

Firmum (264); furthermore, with the settlement of Roman citizens on the *ager Gallicus* (Sena Gallica), it had created an outpost against Gaulish attacks. The structure of Rome's rule in Italy remained largely stable, even during the war against → Hannibal [4] (→ Punic Wars), who had counted on the secession of Rome's allies, but had only found supporters in southern Italy. (After the war their territories were fenced in with Latin colonies). It was only the crude imbalance between the military contribution made by the allies to Rome's expansion in the Mediterranean, and the economic and political benefits, which Rome conceded to them, that led to the → Social War [3] (91–88). At the end of that war, all of Italy between Rhegium and the river Po was granted Roman citizenship.

Rome's achievement in this process of unification did not merely consist in reaching its military targets; it lay mainly in

(1) the ways Rome's relation with its affiliated states were shaped. This was not only based on (many different kinds of) treaties, but also on granting all soldiers a share in the spoils of war, and most of all on the personal relations between the Roman → *nobiles* and the Italian elite, which could rely on Rome's support should conflicts arise in their home communities. Thus, its members themselves became representatives of Roman interests;

(2) the consistent use of Latin colonies as a tool both to control and to Romanize (→ Romanization) their environment. For these communities, placed as they were in potentially hostile territory, had to develop a strong loyalty to Rome for their own protection;

(3) the development of the → infrastructure by building a network of → roads, which connected the territories of citizens, colonists, and allies alike Rome, thus enhancing an impression of a unified Italian territory.

A. AFZELIUS, Die röm. Eroberung It.s, 1942; E. BADIAN, Foreign Clientelae, 1958; K. J. BELOCH, Der Ital. Bund unter Roms Hegemonie, 1880; T. J. CORNELL, The Beginnings of Rome, 1995, 345–398; H. GALSTERER, Herrschaft und Verwaltung im republikanischen It., 1976; E. T. SALMON, The Making of Roman Italy, 1982; CH. SCHUBERT, Land und Raum in der röm. Republik, 1996, 88–105; H. RUDOLPH, Stadt und Staat im röm. Italien, 1935.   W. ED.

Italic see → Oscan-Umbrian

Italica City near Santiponce in the vicinity of Seville. Founded in 206 BC by P. Cornelius Scipio and settled with veterans (App. Hisp. 38) as a *vicus civium Romanorum* (CIL II 1119). From the time of Caesar, I. appears as a *municipium* (Bell. Alex. 52,4; coins), from the time of Hadrian (AD 117–138) as a *colonia* (Gell. NA 16,13,4; CIL II 1135; XI 2699; XII 1856). I. was the home of the emperors Trajan and Hadrian, but probably not that of the poet Silius Italicus. The *legio VII* (CIL II 1125f.) and the *cohors III Gallica* (CIL II 1127) were stationed in I. Judging by the archaeological

remains, in particular the large amphitheatre, I. was of importance, among other reasons, because of the export of oil (CIL XV 2631) and its quarries (CIL II 1131). In the Visigothic period, in 584, I. was significant as a fortress and as an episcopal see [1. 449]. The city fell into decline after AD 711 [2. 49ff.].

1 A. SCHULTEN (ed.), Fontes Hispaniae Antiquae 9, 1947 2 A. GARCÍA Y BELLIDO, Colonia Aelia Augusta Italica, 1960.

A. PARLADÉ, Excavaciones en el anfiteatro de Itálica, in: Memorias de la Junta Superior de Excavaciones y Antigüedades, 1920/1, no. 2, 1–7; 1921/2, no. 7, 1–6; 1923/4, no. 10; 1924/5, no. 11, 1–6; A. SCHULTEN, Forsch. in Spanien, in: AA 1940, I/2, 112f.; TOVAR 1, 1974, 163ff.; F. CHAVES TRISTÁN, Las monedas de Italica, 1973.   P.B.

Italic League see → Socii (Roman confederation)

Italicus Common Roman cognomen. Most famously the poet → Silius I.

KAJANTO, Cognomina, 180.   K.-L.E.

[1] Son of the Cheruscan → Flavus (the brother of → Arminius) and of a daughter of the Chatti leader Actumerus, born and raised in Rome. Because the quarrelling nobility demand I. as king of the → Cherusci, emperor → Claudius [III 1] installs this last offshoot of the *stirps regia* as king in AD 47 (Tac. Ann. 11,16); this shows the new development of Romano-Germanic relations since the Battle of the Teutoburg Forest. Driven out after internal struggles, reinstalled by the → Langobardi, I. is able to assert his rule (Ann. 11,17).

R. WOLTERS, Röm. Eroberung und Herrschaftsorganisation, 1990.   V.L.

[2] *Rex Sueborum*, probably son and successor of → Vangio; driven, together with → Sido, to join the civil war party of → Vespasianus in AD 69, for which he fought at → Betriacum (Tac. Hist. 3,5,1; 21,2). → Suebi   P.KE.

Italus (Ἴταλος; *Ítalos*). Important figure in the mythological-factual history of settlement and eponym of Italy (Dion. Hal. Ant. Rom. 1,35,1; Verg. Aen. 1,533; Steph. Byz. s.v. Ἰταλία). Aristotle ascribes to the king and legislator of the Oenotrians, the later Italici, (Antiochus, FGrH 555 F 5f.) the establishing of *syssitiae* and of agriculture (Aristot. Pol. 1329b 8–20; [1]). I. (Thuc. 6,2,4), or his son Sicelus (Philistus, FGrH 556 F 46), is also regarded as king of the Siculi, who had been expelled from Italy. As king of Sicily he is also supposed to have come to Latium; further identifications in Servius (A. 1,533).

1 G. HUXLEY, Antiochos on Italos, in: Φιλίας χάριν, FS Eugenio Manni, vol. 4, 1197–1204.   C.R.

Italy, alphabetic scripts

A. Introduction B. The Etruscans C. The
Latins D. The Faliscans E. The Venetics
(Lepontics, Raetics) F. The Umbrians
G. The Oscans H. Various

A. Introduction

The alphabet was imported to Italy by the Euboean
Greeks and adopted by the Etruscans in its entirety
(→ Alphabet, II. B.). The abecedary of Marsiliana d'Albegna (c. 700–650 BC; see table) corresponds to the
Italian prototype. The history of Italian writing can best
be read from the abecedaries (*I.1ff. in [1], thus also
quoted in the following). Apart from the scripts that
derive from the Etruscan alphabet, Greek ones can be
found in southern Italy (also in trading settlements further north and on imported goods) – among them the
supposed earliest Greek inscription, ευλιν (complete),
770 BC [2] –, further, Semitic scripts, e.g. on Sardinia
(→ Alphabet), on Ischia [3] and in Pyrgi [4].

B. The Etruscans

The Etruscans [5. 234f.] learned the alphabet in
unreduced form until after 600 BC (see also *I.4, *I.6
with syllable exercise ci ca cu ce vi va vu ve etc., *I.3),
but several characters were almost never used (in the
table, characters no. 2, 4, 15, 16; cf. the exercise!), or
(in southern Etruria) used as variants (no. 24), or in an
orthographic distribution (no. 3, 11, 19 [6. 15ff.]).
Then the number of characters was reduced: northern
and southern Etruria gave up characters no. 2, 4, 15,
16, 24, the north (= N) also no. 3 and 19 (see *II.5,
*III.21; *III.2, *III.19). The efforts concerning the
script are also reflected in the didactic measure of the
so-called syllabic punctuation [7]. A few decades after
this reform (in the south *II.5, s. tab., in the N *II.7,
*II.12, see table; see below E.) – soon after the middle of
the 6th cent. – a character 8 was added in the south (= S)
and N (in the S *III.2, in the N *III.1, see table) for/f/,
which was previously written HF or FH. Finally, probably still in the 5th cent., no. 11 and 19 were eliminated
in the S (*III.19., see table, shortly before, *III.20 probably soon after the reform). Thus, the alphabets acquired their final shapes (in the N e.g. *III.8b; in the S
e.g. *IV.1, see table, and *IV.6).

In the N and S, no. 18 and 21 were transposed from
early on [4. I 38f.]. In the S, the u-diphthongs were written with F (e.g. in the S avle, in the N aule)from c. 500
BC. From c. 400 onwards, C was increasingly used
instead of K in the N as well; but since it took the place
of K (no. 11; *IV.4, c. 200 BC, see table; [8. 54⁷³]), this
does not count as writing reform, but only as a special
case changing the shape of a letter.

C. The Latins

The Latin alphabet was derived from an unreduced
Etruscan alphabet (therefore still in the 7th cent.); a
Greek alphabet must have acted as a model for the pho-
netic values of B, D, O, X (but not for C, whose main

phonetic value/k/ proves the dependence on the Etruscan alphabet) [6. 20ff.]. We do not know exactly when
the transposition from FH/ HF to F for/f/ (and at the
same time from F to V for/w/) as well as the elimination
of no. 9, 15, 18, 25, 26 took place [6. 23ff., 32f.]. It was
only towards the middle of the 3rd cent. that for zeta
(no. 7, 'dead'; see table) a character G was substituted
for/g/ (by the teacher Sp. → Carvilius [2], a freedman,
probably of Greek origin [6. 324–333]). Y and Z were
added for Greek loan words and names in the late
1st cent. BC. The additional letters [9. 12 § 10] conceived by emperor → Claudius [III 1], however, were
unsuccessful. Alone of the scripts derived from the
Etruscan script, Latin took the step of writing from left
to right (probably soon after 500, after Greek fashion).

D. The Faliscans

The Faliscan alphabet [6. especially 37ff.] is also derived from the Etruscan alphabet, as is shown by the use
of no. 3 for/k/. It is most likely derived (early) via the
Latin alphabet, with which it shares the use of V for/w/
(and also the southern Etruscan-Latin-Faliscan archaic
orthographical distribution of no. 3, 11, 19 and later
the generalization of no. 3 for/k/, in Faliscan also in/
kʷ/, e.g. cuicto, Quintus). No abecedary has been found
until now, therefore we do not know if the dead letters
(no. 2, 6, 15, 18, 25, 26) were ever eliminated (the rare
use of no. 9 rather speaks against it) and if the special
letter ↑ (f) (no. 27) was appended or e.g. substituted for
no. 6 (in any case it attests to a reform); see table.

E. The Venetics (Lepontians, Raetians)

The Venetics took over a reduced northern Etruscan
alphabet, which did not yet include no. 8 (f), as is
shown by the use of FH for/f/ (therefore in the 1st half of
the 6th cent.). They added O (o). They wrote/b/ with
no. 25,/g/ with no. 26 and/d/ with no. 7 or 22. Small
local peculiarities arose secondarily. The sanctuary of
Fondo Baratela in Este has provided us with numerous
votive inscriptions with abecedaries (see table, Es 23
[10. 28, 195 no. 4a; 11. 97ff., 95–142]) and syllable
lists [10. 187–202; 11 passim]. Syllabic punctuation,
which was introduced secondarily from southern Etruria, became the orthographic standard in Venetic.

The Lepontic [12] and Raetic [13; 14] alphabets also
stem from the northern Etruscan alphabet, but no abecedaries have been found to date.

F. The Umbrians

An Umbrian abecedary has likewise yet to be found.
The fact that no. 16 (o), a character which would be
useful to the Umbrian language, is missing, suggests
that the reduced reform of the Etruscan alphabet was
already complete when the Umbrian alphabet was created. The (rare) use of no. 9 and 18 as graphic variants
for/t/ and/s/ indicates that no further reductions took
place (therefore at least no. 25 and 26 were probably
also learned as dead letters). It is not known which place
in the alphabet was occupied by the C, used in southern

Italy: alphabetic scripts

	West Greek = archaic Etruscan (*I.1 Marsiliana, c. 675–50) ←	Latin (Monteroni di Palo, late 4th cent.) →	Faliscan (no alphabetary; c. 4th cent.) ←	South Etruscan, reduced (*II.5 Gravisca, 1st half 6th cent.; with 8 *III.19 Nola, 1st half 5th cent.) ←	North Etruscan reduced (*II.12 Perugia, 2nd half 6th cent.) ←	Venetic (P=Padua, V=Vincenza, E=Este; Es 23, early 3rd cent.) ←	South Etruscan definitive (with 8; without K and Q) (*IV.1 Bomarzo, 3rd cent.) →	North Etruscan definitive (with 8; later occasionally with C instead of K) (*III.1 Magliano, 2nd half 6st cent.; *IV.4 Vetulonia, c. 200) ←	Umbrian (no alphabetary; Tab. Iguv.) ←	Oscan (with í and ú) (Pompeii, 1st cent.) ←
1	A	Λ	Я	A A	A	A	M	A A	A	A
2	8 † B	B		– –	–	–	–	– –		B /b/
3	/g/ ⌐ /k/	C /k/	⊃	[c])	–	–	⊂	– –		⟩ /g/
4	⟨ †	D	⟨	⟨	– –	–	–	– –		Я /d/
5	Ⅎ	E	Ⅎ	[e] Ⅎ	Ⅎ	Ⅎ	E	Ⅎ Ⅎ	Ⅎ	E
6	Ⅎ /w/	F /f/		[v] ⅃	⅃	Ⅎ	⅃	⅃ ⅃	⊃	⊂
7	I	I †	⊏	[z] ⊥	⊥	X (PV †, E /d/)	I	⊥ Ⅎ	⧣ /ts/	I /ts/
8	⊟	H	⊠	ḥ	⊟	⊟ ⫿	⊟	⊟ ⊖ Ø	Ø	⊟
9	⊗	–	⊙	O ⊗	⊙	P ⊙ (E, V) X /t/	O	⊙ O	⊙ /t/ (†)	⊙
10	I	I	I	I I	I	I	I	I I	I	I
11	⅄	K	⅄	⅄ ⊂	⅄	⅄	–	⊂ K	⅄ ⊂	⅄
12	⅃	⅃	⅃	⅃ ⅃	⅃	⅂	⅃	⅃ ⅃	⅃	⅃
13	M	M	M	M M	M	M	M	M M Λ	M Λ	M
14	Y	N	M	ṇ M	M	Y	M	Y H	M	H
15	† ⊞ †	–	–	– –	–	–	–	– –		–
16	O †	O	O	– –	–	–	–	– –		–
17	⌐	Γ	⌐	[p] ⌐	⌐	⌐	⌐	⌐ ⌐	⌐	Π
18	† M /ʃ/	–		[σ] ⋈	M /ś/	M	M /ʃ/	M M /ś/	M /s/ (†)	M /ts/
19	Φ	Q	Φ	[q] Ọ	–	–	–	– –		–
20	⌐	R	Я	[r] ⌐	⌐	⌐	D	⌐ ⌐	⌐	⌐
21	Ⅎ /s/	Ƨ	Ƨ	[s] ⟨	⟨ /ś/	⟨	⟨ /s/	Ƨ ⟨ /ś/	⟨ /s/	⟨
22	T	T	⊦	T T	T	X (PV /d/, E †)	T	⊦ ⅄	⊦ ⅄ /t/	T
23	Ⅎ	V	V /uw/	V V	V	Λ	V	V V	V	V
24	/ks/ X /s/(†)	+ /ks/	X	– –	–	–	–	– –		–
25	Φ	–		Φ ⊕	⊕	⬦ /b/	⊕	⊕ Φ	? †	–
26	Ψ	–		⅄ ↓	⅄	⅄ /g/	↓	⅄ [χ]	? †	–
27		↑ /f/		8 /f/		⬦ /o/	8 /f/	8 [f]	8 /f/	8 /f/
28+									9 /ř/	⊦ /í/
									ᚦ /ç/	V̇ /ú/
									B /b/	

Umbrian inscriptions, the two supplementary letters (of which the first must be very old), and B (probably added last); see table.

→ Iguvium; → Tabulae Iguvinae

G. THE OSCANS

In Campania, the Oscan language was originally written in the Etruscan alphabet (in part with syllabic punctuation). Presumably, it was the Samnians who, around 400, introduced the more suitable Oscan alphabet (because of the shapes of the letters no. 4 and 20, it was probably originally identical to the Umbrian alphabet) and reformed it (restitution of no. 2, 3, 4, doubtlessly following the Greek example; possible elimination of no. 18 at the same time). A clearly later [15] reform added two additional letters (around 300 BC). Several (incomplete) abecedaries have been found [16]; see table with synthesis.

H. VARIOUS

The stele of → Novilara (near Pisaurium) [17], the Negau helmet [18], and the → Messapian [19] and → Sicel [20] languages provide us with Italic alphabets which cannot be classified (and for the most part incomprehensible languages). South Picenian (→ Oscan-Umbrian) also belongs to the Italic languages.

1 M. PANDOLFINI, A. L. PROSDOCIMI, Alfabetari e insegnamento della scrittura in Etruria e nell'Italia antica, 1990, esp. 3–94   2 A. M. BIETTI SESTIERI, The Iron Age community of Osteria dell' Osa, 1992, 184f., 259 (bibliography)   3 G. BUCHNER, D. RIDGWAY, Pithekoussai I, 3 vols., 1993   4 ET, no. Cr 4.4   5 H. RIX, La scrittura e la lingua, in: M. CRISTOFANI (ed.), Gli Etruschi: una nuova immagine, 1993, 199–227   6 WACHTER   7 R. WACHTER, Die etr. und venet. Silbenpunktierung, in: MH 43, 1986, 111–126   8 Id., Zur Vorgesch. des griech. Alphabets, in: Kadmos 28, 1989, 19–78   9 LEUMANN 10 M. LEJEUNE, Manuel de la langue vénète, 1974 11 A. MARINETTI, Le tavolette alfabetiche di Este, in: [1], 95–142   12 PROSDOCIMI (esp. M. G. TIBILETTI BRUNO, Ligure, Leponzio e Gallo, 129–208)   13 M. G. TIBILETTI BRUNO, Camuno e dialetti retico e pararetico, in: [12], 209–255   14 E. RISCH, Die Räter als sprachliches Problem, in: Das Räterproblem in geschichtlicher, sprachlicher und arch. Sicht, 1984, 22–36   15 VETTER no. 117, 120, 128, 131   16 R. ANTONINI, Gli alfabetari oschi, in: [1], 143–153   17 M. DURANTE, Nord Piceno: La lingua delle iscrizioni di Novilara, in: [12], 393–400   18 A. L. PROSDOCIMI, L'iscrizione "germanica" sull'elmo B di Negau, in: [12], 381–392   19 O. PARLANGELI, C. SANTORO, Il Messapico, in: [12], 913–947   20 A. ZAMBONI, Il Siculo, in: [12], 949–1012.

M. PANDOLFINI, A. L. PROSDOCIMI (above [1]); M. CRISTOFANI, L'alfabeto etrusco, in: [12], 401–428.   R.WA.

Italy, languages of

A. GENERAL   B. GEOGRAPHICAL DISTRIBUTION
C. UPPER ITALY AND ETRURIA   D. THE ITALIC LANGUAGE GROUP   E. LOWER ITALY AND SICILY
F. CONCLUSION

A. GENERAL

Pre-Roman Italian shows an astonishing linguistic variety, which is definable in terms of at least four Indo-European branches, namely the Italic branch (→ Latin, → Faliscan, → Oscan-Umbrian, → Venetic), the Celtic branch (→ Celtic languages: → Lepontic, Gaulish), the Messapian branch (Illyric?), and the Greek branch (see stemma). Indo-European languages of (as yet) unknown assignment are Sicily's indigenous idioms (see below, end) as well as (presumably) the as yet undeciphered → Northern Picene [1]. Non-Indo-European groups are the Tyrrhenian – as attested by the → Raetic and the → Etruscan, – and the Semitic – as attested by Punic (approximately 170 inscriptions from archaic trade colonies of Sicily, Sardinia and Pyrgi/Cerveteri [2]). It is unclear to which group Camunic (approximately 70 inscriptions; 5th – 1st cents. BC) of Valcamonica [3] belongs. All in all, thanks to early alphabetization – which started before 700 in southern Etruria (Tarquinii, Caere/Cerveteri), had extended to the entire Etruscan-language area (including the Po Plain and Campania) by the 7th cent., and by the 6th cent. at the latest had reached the whole of Italy (→ Italy: alphabetical scripts) – approximately one and a half dozen languages (and other affiliated dialects) have been handed down to us directly in epigraphical testimonies. In the case of some others we know scarcely more than names, for instance, the Daunian (→ Daunia) or → Ligurian. Glosses and onomastic material [4; 5], which could serve as secondary sources for languages such as these – as also for languages that have been directly transmitted to us – usually have negligible informational content, and their linguistic affiliation is often problematic.

B. GEOGRAPHICAL DISTRIBUTION

The variegated language map of ancient Italy (see map) was a result of multiple, mutually overlapping migration movements. These are only occasionally discernible from historical sources, for example, the incursion of the Gauls into the Po Plain in the 6th to 4th cents. (Liv. 5,34), or the southward expansion of the Samnites (Str. 5,242). The immigration of the Italici should probably be assigned to the second millennium (see below, D.), possibly in two waves, one of which brought the Latins into the country, and the other of which brought the Sabellians (Oscan-Umbrian). However, migration movements for this period are not (yet) archaeologically demonstrable [6. 75f.]: the spread of the practice of cremation from the north around the middle of the 2nd millennium (a practice preferred by the Etruscans and Latins, while the Sabellians held to burial) does not necessarily point to a corresponding

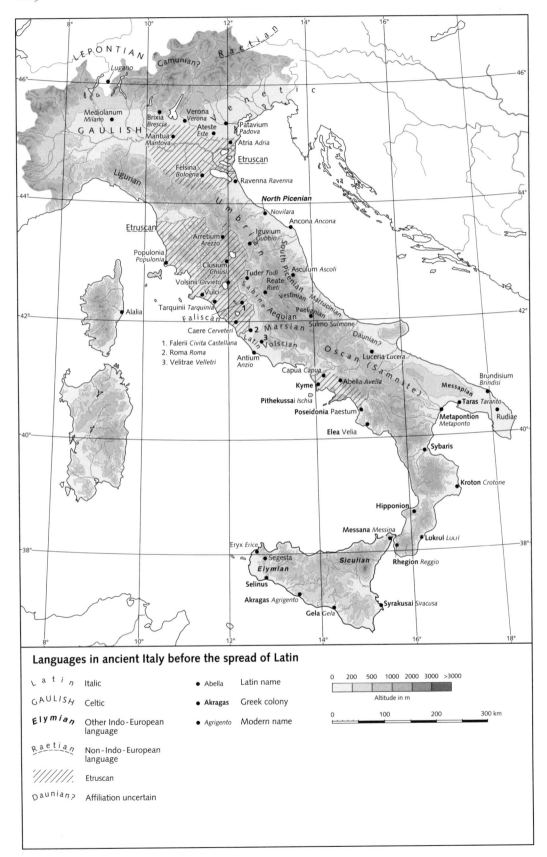

Languages in ancient Italy before the spread of Latin

L a t i n   Italic

GAULISH   Celtic

Elymian   Other Indo-European language

Raetian   Non-Indo-European language

/////   Etruscan

Daunian?   Affiliation uncertain

● Abella   Latin name

● **Akragas**   Greek colony

● *Agrigento*   Modern name

0   200   500   1000   2000   3000   >3000

Altitude in m

0   100   200   300 km

population movement. It was probably prior to the split into Latino-Faliscan and Oscan-Umbrian that Venetic split off (see below, D.). As indicated by the epigraphical legacy as well as by onomatology, the Etruscans penetrated from the Tyrrhenian coast into the inland regions that were previously populated by the Umbro-Sabinians and by the Latins in the south (which among other things caused the migration of the Volscians southward, cf. [7. 14, 48f.]); by the 7th cent., this process was largely complete. Single settlements of the → Villanova Culture there [6. 138, 149] are evidence of their encroachment upon the Po Plain and Campania as early as the 9th cent. For the question as to the origin of the Etruscan language, either autochthonous or introduced from outside (from the east) – the geographical relationship to its closest relative, Raetian, language remains a problem.

C. UPPER ITALY AND ETRURIA

Within a radius of 50 km around Lugano, Lepontic, a Celtic language, is attested to by the existence of approximately 100 inscriptions (6th–1st cents.) [8; 9; 10]; cf. *uvamokozis: plialeθu: uvltiauiopos: ariuonepos: siteš: tetu;* 'Uvamogostis Bl. established these seats for the Uvlt. Ar. (dat. pl.)', (Prestino, *c.* 500 BC). Since the time of the conquest of the Po Plain by the Gauls in the 4th cent., it has been a Gaulish language-area; the few inscriptions (3rd/2nd cents.), with the exception of the bilingual inscriptions of Todi, originate from the area bordering on the Lepontic on the left of the Po [11; 12].

Raetic, which is attested both in the north and south of the Brenner pass, as demonstrated by morphological and lexical similarities, is closely related to Etruscan; however it is not merely an Etruscan dialect [13; 14; 15]. By a total of just under 9,000 inscriptions, Etruscan is documented in Upper Italy (Felsina/Bologna, Adria, Spina, Mantua) from the 7th cent. and in Campania from that same period; moreover, it is documented from an even earlier period in its heartland in the western portion of central Italy.

D. THE ITALIC LANGUAGE GROUP

The unity of the Italic group, with its subgroups Latino-Faliscan and Oscan-Umbrian is demonstrated by commonalities, such a declension system which is very similar in both structure and content (with specific innovations, such as imperfect subjunctive), typical phonetic developments – like occurrence of the proto-Indo-European mediae aspiratae $d^h b^h g^{wh} g^h$ (at first as aspirants $d^h b^h g^{wh}$ as initial sounds becoming f, etc.), above all, however, by numerous identical modes of word-formation. An important difference, for instance, is the development of the labio-velar kw gw (> Latin *qu* u̯, Sabellic *p b*; cf. Latin *quis*, Oscan *pis).*

The eastern portion of central Italy is the zone of the Umbro-Sabinian dialects (→ Oscan-Umbrian), to which belong South Picenian (6th – 4th cents.), Sabinian (mainly glosses), Aequian (of the Aequiculi), Marsian (from the 4th cent.), also in the south Volscian

(Velitrae), and of the pre-Samnite (the pre-Oscan Italic of Campania; 6th/5th cents.) alongside Umbrian ('Paleo-Umbrian', from the 7th cent.). The heartland of the Oscan-speaking Samnites – whose idiom spread out over nearly the whole of southern Italy in the 5th cent. – lies eastward, as well as southward (see above, B.), and thus, besides pre-Samnite, eclipsed further Italic dialects (as shown for instance in [16], cf. [17]), as well as the closely related dialects of Paelignian, Vestinian and Marrucinian. The Latino-Faliscan group is represented, above all, by the Latin of the city of Rome and by Faliscan; the sparsely attested dialects of the Latin communities are distinguished from Latin in individual features..

Based on phonetic correspondencies – e.g. in the development of the proto-Indo-European mediae aspiratae – Venetic also belongs to the Italic branch (approximately 300 inscriptions from the 6th–1st cents. BC) in Venetia (chief locations: Este, Padua). However, inflectional divergences (for example, the verb endings *do-to*, *dona-s-an*: he gave, they gave a gift) indicate an early split [18; 19].

E. LOWER ITALY AND SICILY

The language of the → Messapians, who immigrated from Illyria, is attested by approximately 300 inscriptions in Apulia (6th–1st cents.) [20].

The ancient division of the indigenous population of Sicily into → Elymi (north-west), Sicani (west) and Siculi (east) is only supported to a certain extent by linguistic and epigraphical findings (generally, 7th–5th cents. BC). Findings relative to dative singular -ai < -āi, ō̦i (?), pl. -ib (< proto-Indo-European instrumental pl. -i-b^hi) suggest the Indo-European character of Elymite, as do *emi* 'I am', cf. [21] *]xsilai emi* 'I belong to -ksila.' Here, as with the other, probably also Indo-European idioms, for which → Sicel may legitimately be viewed as a unifying concept, closer connections to 'Italic' cannot be discovered. The dialect of the building inscriptions of Mendolito constitutes an exception in this regard [22], cf. *iam* 'eam', *teuto* ~Oscan *touto*, *verega* ~Oscan *vereiia*, *verehasio*, perfect-tense ending in *geped* ~Oscan *-ed*. ZAMBONI for example, offers Sicilian glosses and toponymical material ([23]; cf. also [21. comments 13; 24; 25; 26]).

F. CONCLUSION

In the aftermath of the → Social War of 90/89 BC, all Italians were granted citizenship rights, and this involved the use of Latin. Therefore, in the course of the 1st cent. BC at the latest, the abandoning of indigenous idioms in favour of Latin is everywhere to be observed; by around the turn of the century, this process had carried itself through to completion in nearly the whole of Italy [27]. Next to it, only the Greek spoken in southern Italy and Sicily could hold its own alongside Latin.
→ Celtic languages; → Daunia; → Elymite; → Etruscan; → Faliscan; → Greek; → Italia: alphabetical scripts; → Latin; → Lepontic; → Ligurian; → Messapian; → Oscan-Umbrian; → Raetic; → Sicel; → Venetian

Italy: languages and their interrelation

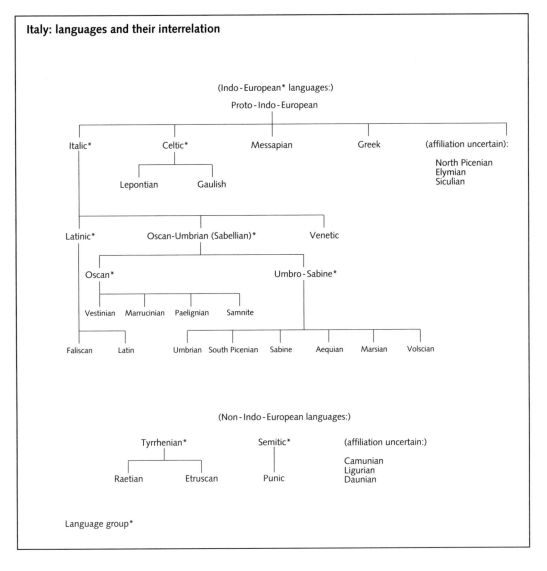

(Indo-European* languages:)
Proto-Indo-European

Italic*   Celtic*   Messapian   Greek   (affiliation uncertain):

North Picenian
Elymian
Siculian

Lepontian   Gaulish

Latinic*   Oscan-Umbrian (Sabellian)*   Venetic

Oscan*   Umbro-Sabine*

Vestinian   Marrucinian   Paelignian   Samnite

Faliscan   Latin   Umbrian   South Picenian   Sabine   Aequian   Marsian   Volscian

(Non-Indo-European languages:)

Tyrrhenian*   Semitic*   (affiliation uncertain:)

Camunian
Ligurian
Daunian

Raetian   Etruscan   Punic

Language group*

1 M. Durante, Nordpiceno, in: Prosdocimi, 393–400
2 S. Moscati, Le iscrizioni fenicio-puniche, in: Le Iscrizioni prelatine, 1979, 45–55   3 A. Mancini, Le iscrizioni della Valcamonica, in: Studi Urbinati di storia, filosofia e letteratura, Supplemento linguistico 2, 1980, 75–167
4 J. Untermann, Namenlandschaften im alten Oberit., in: BN 10, 1959, 74–108, 121–159; 11, 1960, 273–318; 12, 1961, 1–30   5 J. B. Pellegrini, Toponymi ed etnici ..., in: Prosdocimi, 79–127   6 M. Pallottino, Etruscologia, ⁷1985   7 I Volsci. Quaderni di Arch. Etrusco-Italica 20, 1992   8 M. Lejeune, Lepontica, 1971
9 F. Motta, Vues présentes sur le celtique cisalpin, in: Études Celtiques 29, 1992, 311–317   10 V. Daniele (ed.), Celti ed Etruschi nell'Italia centro-settentrionale dal V. secolo alla romanizzazione, 1987   11 P.-Y. Lambert, La langue Gauloise, ³1997   12 M. Lejeune, Recueil des Inscriptions Gauloises. 2,1: Textes Gallo-étrusques ..., 1988   13 S. Schumacher, Die rätischen Inschr. ..., 1992
14 Id., Sprachliche Gemeinsamkeiten zw. Rätisch und Etruskisch, in: Der Schlern 72, 1998, 90–114   15 H. Rix, Rätisch und Etruskisch, 1998   16 Vetter, no. 186f.

17 P. Poccetti, Per un' identità culturale dei Brettii, 1988, 89–124   18 M. Lejeune, Manuel de la langue vénète, 1974   19 G. Fogolari, A. L. Prosdocimi, I Veneti antichi, 1988   20 C. Santoro, Nuovi Studi Messapici, 3 vols., 1982–1984   21 L. Agostiniani, Le iscrizioni anelleniche di Sicilia, 1977, no. 312   22 M. Durante, Il Siculo e la sua documentazione, in: Kokalos 10/1, 1964/5, 440ff.   23 A. Zamboni, Il Siculo, in: Prosdocimi, 971ff.
24 L. Agostiniani, Epigrafia e linguistica anelleniche di Sicilia ..., in: Kokalos 26/7, 1980/1, 503ff.   25 R. van Compernolle, L'apporto dell'epigrafia e della linguistica anelleniche ..., in: Kokalos 39/40, 1993/4, 143ff.
26 U. Schmoll, Die vorgriech. Sprachen Siziliens, 1958
27 P. Bruun et al., Studies in the romanisation of Etruria, 1975.

Prosdocimi, passim; Le Iscrizioni prelatine. Atti dei Convegni Lincei 39, 1979; A. Morandi, Epigrafia Italica, 1982; M. Pallottino, Storia della prima Italia 1981 [English: A History of Earliest Italy, 1991].   GE.ME.

Itanus (Ἴτανος; *Ítanos*). Port in the extreme north-east of Crete, between two acropoleis, modern Erimupolis. Traces of settlement date as far back as the Minoan period. In the 7th cent. BC, Corobius, a purple fisher from I., allegedly led colonists from → Thera to → Cyrene (Hdt. 4,151). In the Hellenistic period, it served as the Aegean base of the Ptolemies [1]. In 112 BC, rivalries with → Hierapytna were mediated on Roman initiative [2. no. 57]. Few remains, amongst other things a Byzantine basilica.

1 S. SPYRIDAKIS, Ptolemaic I. and Hellenistic Crete, 1970 2 A. CHANIOTIS, Die Verträge zw. kret. Poleis in der hell. Zeit, 1996.

LAUFFER, Griechenland, 281f.; I. F. SANDERS, Roman Crete, 1982, 138.   H.SO.

Ithaca (Ἰθάκη; *Itháke*, Lat. *Ithaca*).
A. GEOGRAPHY B. HISTORY C. THE ITHACA QUESTION D. SOURCES

A. GEOGRAPHY
One of the central Ionian islands west of Greece, nowadays also known as Thiaki; it is 23 km long and *c.* 6 km wide, with a total area of *c.* 94 sq km, east of the island of → Cephallenia and separated from the latter by a 2–5 km wide sound. I. is divided into a larger northern half with Mt. Neriton (808 m), and a southern half with Mt. Merovigli (671 m); they are joined by a narrow isthmus (600 m wide) with Mt. Aetus (380 m). The steeply descending western side is little structured (bays at Mt. Aetus and the plain of Polis), whereas the east boasts good harbours, e.g. near modern Frikes and Kioni, as well in the bay of Molo in the north-east, leading in a south-easterly direction to the bay of Skinos and the excellent harbour of Vathy. The rocky and almost infertile island is nowadays almost deforested and covered with sparse phrygana and maquis vegetation.

B. HISTORY
Early settlement remains from the period around 2200 BC have been found on Mt. Pelikata; there, as in the nearby Tris Langadas (SH III A house, excavation report in [4]) and at Mt. Aetus (excavation report in [5]), Mycenaean findings were discovered; in spite of intensive searches, though, no palace has been found [17. 302]. As the style of the locally produced Proto-geometric pottery developed from the Sub-Mycenaean one, a continuity of settlement cannot be ruled out. From the 10th to the 8th cent., the most important settlement was that on the isthmus at Mt. Aetus (later known as → Alalcomenae [2]), in which evidence of at least two sanctuaries dating from the 10th/9th cents. has been found [5]. Finds of ceramics, bronze, ivory, amber, fibulae, needles etc. from the 9th–7th cents. BC point to seafarers from across the entire Aegean and Adriatic region [1]; presumably, the ports at the Aetus were an important staging-post en route from Greece to Italy [9]. In the north, the name Bay of Polis seems to

indicate the location of the chief settlement of I., but to date there have been no striking finds [4; 17]. The most important finding-place in the area is the grotto on the northern shore of the Bay of Polis, in which about 14 tripods dating from the 9th–8th cents. BC have been excavated (excavation report in [6; 2]). A late Hellenistic dedication to Odysseus, found in the grotto, leads to the assumption that from the (late) Mycenaean period it was the location of a → hero cult. However, the deities with the earliest verifiable cults were Athena and Hera ([7] *c.* 550 BC), and in Hellenistic times the Nymphs and Artemis. The reference to → Odysseus is predominantly a Hellenistic-Roman phenomenon from a period when epic reminiscences abounded everywhere on I.: there were Odysseia games [10], and an Odysseus cult (Helodorus 5,16,22; cf. coins); even I.'s constitution contained deliberate references to the conditions in the Homeric epics [3]. In later periods, I. plays no prominent role, but seems to have shared the fate of its neighbouring island of Cephallenia: membership of the Aetolian League in 226 BC (→ Aetolians, Aetolia, with map), declared *civitas libera* in 189, in the early Imperial period part of the province of → Achaia, later that of Epirus (Ptol. 3,13,9; Tab. Peut. 7,4; Hierocles, synecdoche 652,7) [12].

C. THE ITHACA QUESTION
Attempts have been made ever since antiquity to prove the historical I. as the model for the epic I. of the Odyssey (→ Homer) (Str. 10,2,10–16). Some features described in the Odyssey can really be found – albeit not in every detail – on the modern I. [15]: e.g. the port of Phorcys in the Bay of Vathy, the pigsties of Eumaeus and the rock of Corax on the elevated plain of Marathia. Other descriptions owe much to poetic imagination (e.g. Odysseus' palace) or the transposition of well-known geographical features of the Ionian islands to I. (similarities between Mt. Aenus on Cephallenia and Mt. → Neriton of the Odyssey; the grotto of the Nymphs has models both on I. and on Cephallenia). For that reason, the attempts to localize the I. of the Odyssey on Cephallenia, → Leucas, or → Corcyra are misleading. If there is an Ionian island at all to claim identity with the Homeric I., it would in the opinion of this author be modern Thiaki [11; 16]. It is impossible to decide on the current state of research whether in historical times there ever was a ruler by the name of Odysseus on I. (or Cephallenia) and whether his kingdom as described in Homer (Od. 9,21–26; Il. 631–637) ever existed [14].

D. SOURCES
Scyl. 34; Plut. De sera 12 (557C); Scymn. 466; Dion. Calliphontis 51f.; Dionys. Per. 495f.; Cic. De or. 1,196; Plin. HN 4,55; Mela 2,110; Porph. De antro Nymph.; Steph. Byz. s.v. Κροκύλειον. Coins: BMC, Gr (Peloponnese), 105–106; Inscriptions: SEG 38, 432; 43, 228 [8; 10; 13].

1 J.N. COLDSTREAM, Geometric Greece, 1977
2 W. COULSON, The "Protogeometric" from Polis reconsidered, in: ABSA 86, 1991, 42–64   3 O. GIGON, Aristotelis Opera 3, 1987, 645f. no. 68 fr. 509–514   4 ABSA 35, 1934–35, 1–44 (Pelikata); 47, 1952, 227–242 (Stavros); 68, 1973, 1–24 (Tris Langadas)   5 ABSA 33, 1932–33, 22–65; 40, 1939–40, 1–13; 43, 1948, 1–124; 48, 1953, 255–361; Praktika 1990, 271–278; 1992, 200–210; Ergon 1995, 63–67   6 ABSA 35, 1934–35, 45–73; 39, 1938–39, 1–51   7 LSAG 231, 234 no. 3   8 E. MEYER, s.v. I., KlP 2, 1487   9 C. MORGAN, Corinth, the Corinthian Gulf and Western Greece during the Eighth Century B.C., in: ABSA 83, 1988, 313–338   10 K. J. RIGSBY, Asylia, 1996, no. 86   11 W. SIEBERER, Zur Lokalisation des homer. I., in: Tyche 5, 1990, 149–164   12 SOUSTAL, Nikopolis, 168f.   13 D. STRAUCH, Aus der Arbeit am Inschr.-Corpus der Ion. Inseln: IG IX 1², 4, in: Chiron 27, 1997, 217–226   14 E. VISSER, Homer. Kat. der Schiffe, 1997, 574–598   15 A. J. B. WACE, F. H. STUBBINGS (ed.), A Companion to Homer, 1962, 398–421   16 H. WARNEKE, Die histor.-geogr. Lösung des I.-Problems, in: Orbis Terrarum 3, 1997, 77–99   17 H. WATERHOUSE, From Ithaca to the Odyssey, in: ABSA 91, 1996, 301–317.

H. BEISTER, s.v. I., in: LAUFFER, Griechenland, 282f.; J. PARTSCH, Kephallenia und I., Petermanns Mitt. Ergh. 98, 1890; PHILIPPSON/KIRSTEN 2, 491–502.   D.S.

Ithobalus ('Ιθόβαλος; Ithóbalos, Εἰθώβαλος; Eithóbalos and similar, Phoenician ʾittōbaʿal, Baʿal is with him). Name of various Phoenician princes.
[1] King of Byblus c. 1000 BC, known from his inscription on the sarcophagus of his father Aḥīrām (KAI no. 1).
[2] I. I of Tyre (and Sidon) Priest of Astarte and – as a result of rebellions – sixth successor of Hiram I (Jos. Ap. 1,123). Definitely identical with Ethbaal, father of Jezebel (1 Kgs 16,31) and contemporary of Ahab of Israel in the 9th cent. BC. According to Menander of Ephesus (Jos. Ant. Iud. 8,324), he is supposed to have founded → Botrys in Phoenicia and Auza in Libya.
[3] I. II of Tyre (ᴵTu-ba-il) appears c. 737 BC among the tributaries of → Tiglatpilesar III
[4] I. of Sidon (and Tyre?) 701 BC installed by → Sanherib (ᴵTu-ba-ʾa-lu [1]).

1 D. LUCKENBILL, The Annals of Sennacherib, 1924, 30, 47.

[5] I. III of Tyre. Was supposedly besieged for 13 years (from 587–574 BC) by → Nebuchadnezzar II (Jos. Ant. Iud. 10,228; Ap. 1,156).

H. J. KATZENSTEIN, The History of Tyre, 1973; M. WEIPPERT, Menahem von Israel und seine Zeitgenossen in einer Steleninschr. des assyr. Königs Tiglathpileser III. aus dem Iran, in: ZPalV 79, 1973, 46ff.; M. COGAN, Tyre and Tiglath-Pileser III, in: JCS 25, 1973, 97f.   W.R.

Ithome ('Ιθώμη; Ithómē).
[1] This chalk mountain (modern Vurkano), rising to 802 m and dominating the Messenian plain, together with Eua, its southern secondary summit (modern Hagios Vassilios), forms the natural acropolis for the entire region of Messenia, and its centre in legend and history. The lengthy siege of Mt. I. was the main topic of Myron of Priene's prose novel on the First Messenian War (Paus. 4,9–13). During the major uprising of the helots in 464 BC, the Messenians successfully maintained their position on the mountain for ten years (Hdt. 9,35,2; Thuc. 1,101–103; Diod. Sic. 11,64,4; 15,66,4; Plut. Cimon 17,2); after the liberation of Messenia, the capital Messene was built as one of Greece's strongest fortresses at the foot of Mt. I.: Paus. 4,26,6–27,8; 29,5; 31,4; 33,1f.; Diod. Sic. 15,66; Plut. Pel. 24,5; Arat. 50,2ff.; Pol. 7,12,3; Str. 8,4,1; 4,8; IG v 1, 1399. On its summit was a sanctuary of Zeus Ithomatas with a cult image by Ageladas (Paus. 4,33,1f.). Epigraphical evidence points to a festival named Ithōmaía: SEG 23,208,22f.; [1. 96, 9f.].

1 P. THEMELIS, Ausgrabungen in Messenia, in: Praktika 146, 1991 (1994).

E. MEYER, s.v. Messene, RE Suppl. 15, 149f.; W. K. PRITCHETT, Thucydides' Pentekontaetia and other Essays, 1995, 268–279.   Y.L.

[2] ('Ιθώμη; Ithómē, Θώμη; Thómē, Θαμαι; Thamai, Θούμαιον; Thoúmaion). Town in the Thessalian Hestiaiotis near modern Phanarion. At the end of the 5th cent. BC, it was included in the → synoikismos of Metropolis, together with Onthyrion and other places. Archaeology: remains of an ancient ashlar wall, medieval fort. Source references: Hom. Il. 2,129; Str. 9,5,17; Steph. Byz. s.v. I.

PHILIPPSON/KIRSTEN 1, 52ff., 291ff.; F. STÄHELIN, Das hell. Thessalien, 1924, 129; KODER/HILD, 237 s.v. Phanarion.   E.O.

Ithoria ('Ιθωρία; Ithōría). Fortified settlement in Aetolia, destroyed in 219 BC by Philip V (Pol. 4,64,9f.). Finds within the line of the Hellenistic walls on the left bank of the → Achelous [1] on the hilltop above the modern village of Hagios Ilias date from the Mycenaean to the early Roman periods.

S. BOMMELJÉ (ed.), Aetolia and the Aetolians, 1987, 74; PRITCHETT 7, 15f.; R. SCHEER, s.v. I., in: LAUFFER, Griechenland, 284.   D.S.

Itinerare
I. ANCIENT ORIENT   II. IMPERIUM ROMANUM

I. ANCIENT ORIENT
Some Mesopotamian texts come very close to later travel accounts. An Old Babylonian text describes in detail a 38-day journey from Babylonian Dūr-Apil-Sîn to North Syrian Emar [1], two Old Babylonian tablets a journey of more than 6 months from Babylonian Larsa to North Syria and back [2]. The Neo-Assyrian 'Zamua Itinerary' [5] includes the description of a 4-day trip through the → Zagrus mountains indicating exact travel distances.

Especially Neo-Assyrian reports of military campaigns from the 9th/8th cents. BC often contain longer passages mentioning daily stages. Brief notes about travel routes can frequently be found in administrative texts and on balance sheets from the late 3rd millennium BC, but also in Neo-Assyrian letters. Parts of the roads between Assur and the Old Assyrian trade colonies in Anatolia (→ Kaneš) can be traced back based on expense reports of the carriers.

Hittite texts reveal elements of itineraries only indirectly in oracle consultations pertaining to military campaigns or cultic excursions of the king or the cultic personnel. No real itineraries from Egypt have been preserved, but their existence can be deduced from information in the Papyrus Anastasi I (XVIII 7ff.; [4]). The Egyptian lists of place names and the toponym lists based on military campaigns often reveal their dependency on itineraries.

1 D. O. EDZARD, G. FRANTZ-SZABÓ, s.v. I., RLA 5, 216–220   2 A. GOETZE, An Old Babylonian Itinerary, in: JCS 7, 1953, 51–72   3 W. W. HALLO, The Road to Emar, in: JCS 18, 1963, 67–88   4 W. HELCK, s.v. I., LÄ 3, 206   5 L. LEVINE, K 4675+. The Zamua-Itinerary, in: State Archives of Assyria Bulletin 3, 1989, 75–92.   K.KE.

II. IMPERIUM ROMANUM
A. GENERAL INFORMATION   B. ROMAN ITINERARIA   C. CHRISTIAN ITINERARIA   D. ITINERARIA PICTA

A. GENERAL INFORMATION
Itineraria, road maps or 'travel guides' for the Roman empire that could serve civil as well as military purposes, handbooks, which listed directions of main roads with their turnoffs and adjacent settlements (rest stops). Important details included distances between individual settlements, nearby rivers, the nature of the respective landscape. In the civil sphere, such information was of particular importance to merchants and in Christian late antiquity to pilgrims. The function of *itineraria*, in military sense 'marching routes', is illustrated by Vegetius (Mil. 3,6,1; 4): 'Those who have dealt more intensely with warfare assure that the dangers encountered on the road are often greater than those in battle itself... First of all (the commander) must have complete road directories of all regions in which war is being waged, so that he can familiarize himself with the distances between places based not only on number of miles, but also on road conditions, and form an opinion about shortcuts, bypass possibilities, mountains and rivers on the basis of a reliable description; (the importance of knowledge of a place is so great) that more skilful commanders confirm to have had available to them road descriptions of the province, in which tasks needed to be performed, not only in written but also in visual form, so that it was possible to choose the intended route not only by means of reason but also based on pictorial evidence.'

The knowledge of geographical conditions was particularly indispensable in areas where an army moved in proximity of the enemy. Vegetius differentiates between *itineraria adnotata* (situations described verbally or general outlines) and *itineraria picta* (pictographic drawings), which he clearly prefers. It follows from Veg. l.c. that certain objective criteria need to be met in order to use the term *itineraria*. From this point of view, indications on milestones or signposts cannot be referred to as *itineraria*. Likewise, the predominantly literary-oriented travel accounts or memoirs cannot be considered *itineraria* in the word's proper sense. Such is the case of the so-called → *Itinerarium Alexandri*, whose author (around AD 340) wanted to present with his description of the Eastern campaigns of Alexander the Great and Trajan the experiences of those rulers to his emperor Constantius II, just on the onset of the Persian campaign.

B. ROMAN ITINERARIA
The core of all *itineraria*, regardless if *itineraria adnotata* or *itineraria picta*, consisted of the road network and its stations, with the respective distances listed in *milia passuum* ('miles'). The numbers were rounded off and represent a more or less approximate value. A special case of *itineraria* are the four silver cups discovered in Vicarello in the vicinity of *lacus Sabatinus*. On the cups, the connection between Gades and Rome is noted in the manner characteristic of the *itineraria* (CIL XI 3281; 3283f.; 32828). Furthermore, the term *itinerarium* (3281), resp. *intinerare* (3282, 3283), is mentioned specifically. However, despite all basic accordance in the representations found on the cups, the details also reveal differences. The three first named cups (CIL XI 3281–3283) show an internal connection. The fourth, mentioning neither *itinerarium* nor *itinerare* in its text, is apparently older (originating from before AD 333–337) and differs in its external form and representation from the other cups. To this date, no convincing explanation has been offered regarding the question of the paragon of this *itinerarium*. Another epigraphical *itinerarium* that has been recorded is the inscription of Autun, an *itinerarium* of the route Rome – Augustodunum from the 3rd cent. AD (CIL XIII 2681).

Among the *itineraria* recorded as manuscripts, the so-called *Itinerarium provinciarum Antonini Augusti* represents an important source for our knowledge of the topography of the Roman empire, even though some of its details contain inaccuracies, mistakes and other errors. However, these are not only to be attributed to the author himself, but also to the status of the models available to him as well as to the contemporary and later misrepresentations of such models. The representation follows a territorial principle, but without observing a consistent, systematic classification of the material. The work distinguishes between 17 main routes, while its horizon is limited by the borders of the Imperium. It is unlikely that the *Itinerarium provinciarum* should have served as an official handbook. In its extant form, the work originated in the beginnings of Diocletianic times and apparently goes back to a model dating from the reign of Caracalla. In the MSS, the *Itinerarium maritimum Antonini Augusti* is recorded along with it. This latter, smaller work lists mainly geographical distances, not travel times between the harbour towns and islands in the Mediterranean. It then enumerates and summarizes the islands from the Orcades in the north-west and further in eastern direction.

C. Christian Itineraria

The Christian pilgrim culture gave rise to numerous *itineraria*, some of which have been preserved. An early version of such an *itinerarium* appears to be the geographical handbook composed by → Eusebius [7] of Caesarea before 331 (GCS 11,1,1904; Latin version by Jerome, PL 23,903–976). From 333 dates the *Itinerarium Hierosolymitanum sive Burdigalense*, in which a Christian pilgrim describes his journey from Burdigala to Jerusalem and back via Rome to Mediolanum. It does not only contain information characteristic of the *itineraria* regarding stations along the route and the distances between them, but also points out sights, especially holy sites (PL 8,783–795). Jerome added an *itinerarium* to the consolatory letter to Eustochium, daughter of the deceased Paula: Paula's journey from Rome to Jerusalem (PL 22,881–883). Rich in detail is also the *Itinerarium Egeriae* (also *Peregrinatio Aetheriae*, originated 395–398 or 415–418, CSEL 89,37–101, → Peregrinatio ad loca sancta). Other Palestine pilgrims were the Archdeacon Theodosius (*Itinerarium de situ Terrae Sanctae*, around 525, CSEL 39,135–150), the Anonymus, who composed an *Itinerarium ad loca sancta* (erroneously identified with the martyr Antonius of Piacenza, between 560 and 570, CSEL 39,157–218). The bishop Arculf is author of an *Itinerarium de locis sanctis* (recorded by Adamnanus of Iona/Hy, dating from 674 or 685, PL 88,779–814).

D. Itineraria picta

An approximate idea of the manner of representation of the *itineraria picta* is offered by the *Tabula Peutingeriana*. It is the copy of a Roman road-map, which originated probably in the 2nd/3rd cents. AD and the original of which was edited later (in the 4th cent.?). A MS of this map from the 12th/13th cents. was discovered by Konrad Celtis, who handed it over to Augsburg alderman Konrad Peutinger in 1508. In 1737, it was acquired by the Viennese Court Library (Austrian National Library), where it is still preserved today. The map originally consisted of 12 segments, the first of which (Morocco, Spain, a great part of Britain and Ireland) has been lost. The 11 preserved segments map the ancient world all the way to India. In its extant form, the Peutinger Table is a strip of 6.82 m in length and 34 cm in width [1]. The *Cosmographia* of the *Anonymus (Geographus, Cosmographus) Ravennas* from the 7th/8th cents. seems to go back to a similar map [2; 3].
→ Catalogue

1 E. Weber, Tabula Peutingeriana. Codex Vindobonensis 324, 1976　　2 J. Schnetz, Ravennatis Anonymi Cosmographia et Guidonis Geographia, Itineraria Romana 2, 1940　　3 Id., Ravennas Anonymus, Nomina Germanica 10, 1951 (transl.).

K. Brodersen, Terra Cognita, 1993; O. Cuntz, I. Romana, 1, 1929; J. Schnetz, I. Romana 2, 1940; B. Kötting, Peregrinatio religiosa, 1950; W. Kubitschek, s.v. Itinerarien, RE 9, 2308–2363; K. Miller, I. Romana, 1916; Schanz/Hosius 4,1, 112–115.　　J.BU.

Itinerarium Alexandri Following the → Alexander Romance by → Iulius [IV 23] Valerius, Ambrosianus P 49 sup. records an anonymous, abbreviated version (*breviarium*, § 3) of the Alexander story under the title *Itinerarium Alexandri*, which is based on → Arrianus' [2] *Anabasis*, but also on Iulius Valerius' translation of (Ps.-)→ Callisthenes and other texts. The text is dedicated to → Constantius II and dated 340 (the emperor died in April) and promises, as an encouragement for the planned Parthian war, also a report of Trajan's Parthian campaign; however, the text ends with Alexander's journey to the Pillars of Hercules. The style is reminiscent of → Dictys and → Dares: simple, paratactical, mostly in the historic present tense, without the senile fussiness of Iulius Valerius, although it is pretentious and the *praefatio* is excessively rhetorical.

Editions: A. Mai, 1817; K. Müller, 1846 (in F. Dübner, Arrianus 2, 155–167); D. Volkmann, 1871 (with the new Wolfenbüttel fragment); H. J. Hausmann, I.A., unpublished doctoral thesis 1970.
Bibliography: R. Tabacco, Per una nuova ed. critica dell' I.A., in: Pubbl. Ist. Filol. Ling. Trad. class. di Torino, 1992, 1–23; R. Merkelbach, Die Quellen d. Alexanderromans, 1954, 179ff.; H. Tonnet, Le résumé et l'adoption de l'Anabase d'Arrien dans l' I.A., in: Revue d'Histoire des Textes 9, 1979, 243–254.　　KL.SA.

Itium, Itius portus Promontory and port of the Morini in Gallia → Belgica, starting-point of Caesar's fleet for the expeditions to Britain (Caes. B Gall. 4,21–23; 5,2). Caesar only mentions I. in the context of his second expedition of 54 BC; τὸ Ἴτιον in Str. 4,5,2 refers to the operation of the preceding year. The promontory (Ἴτιον ἄκρον, Ptol. 2,9,1) is to be located near Cap Gris-Nez rather than near Cap d'Albrech. Of the numerous theories regarding the exact location of this port (e.g. in Flanders or the Calaisis area), only two deserve serious consideration: the broad bay of the river Liane at Boulogne [1], the location of the later Roman ferry port, or – recently favoured – 20 km to the north of Boulogne, the area at Wissant-Sangatte [2; 3].
→ Gesoriacum

1 R. Delmaire, Civitas Morinorum, in: Latomus 33, 1974, 269–275　　2 R. Dion, Les campagnes de César en l'année 55, in: REL 41, 1963, 186–209　　3 A. Grisart, Portus Itius, 1986.　　F.SCH.

Iton (ὁ/ἡ Ἴτων; *ho/hē Ítōn*, Ἴτωνος; *Ítōnos*). One of the oldest Greek cities, within the Thessalian core territory of Tetras Thessaliotis (Str. 9,5,14) in the valley of the Curalios/Cuarius, a right tributary of the → Peneius. Within its territory was the Thessalian tribal sanctuary of Athena Itonia (Str. 9,5,17). Because of an erroneous distance given by Strabo (9,5,8), the city and its sanctuary were thought to be near → Halus (Achaea Phthiotis) [1; 2; 3], but excavations near modern Philia have verified their location *c.* 16 km south-east of Karditsa and *c.* 10 km upriver of → Cierium. The excavations produced shards, votive offerings, the remains of buildings ranging from the early Mycenaean to the Roman Imperial periods. The remains of an early Christian basilica point to a continuation of the cultic tradition.

I. is already mentioned in Homer's Catalogue of Ships in the *Iliad* (Il. 2,696). The sanctuary enjoyed supraregional esteem. Votive offerings and spoils of war were deposited there, amongst others in 274 BC by Pyrrhus following his victory over → Antigonus [2] Gonatas (Paus. 1,13,2; Plut. Pyrrhus 26,5); furthermore, it was used for the public display of decrees (e.g. Perseus' amnesty of 179 BC: Pol. 25,3). Cultic games and festive assemblies were held there. The Thessalian battle cry was 'Athena Itonia', and a month in the Thessalian calendar was named Itonios. From 196 BC, the image of the goddess appeared on the coins of the renewed Thessalian League (sources: [1; 2; 3]). The Boeotians, forced away from the Cuarius valley southwards by the Thessalians (→ Arne [2]), brought the cult of Athena Itonia with them to their historical seats. There is evidence of the cult elsewhere in Greece, too [1].

1 E. MEYER, s.v. I., KlP, 1492   2 F. STÄHLIN, s.v. I., RE 9, 2371ff.   3 Id., Das hellen. Thessalien, 1924, 175f.

H. W. CATLING, Archaeology in Greece, in: Archaeological Reports for 1982/3, 35 and 1983/4, 36; J.-C. DECOURT, La vallée de l'Enipeus en Thessalie, 1990, 154f.; C. HABICHT, Ambrakia und der thessal. Bund z.Z. des Perseuskrieges, in: V. MILOJČIĆ, D. THEOCHARIS, Demetrias 1, 1976, 175ff.; B. G. INTZESILOGLOU, (research report), in: AD 40,2, 1985, 197 (= Id., in: Programme, rapports et communications du Colloque international sur la Thessalie, 1990, 99f.); D. THEOCHARIS, (excavation report), in: AD 22,2, 1967, 296 (= Id., in: AAA 1, 1968, 240).   HE.KR.

Itonus (Ἴτωνος; *Ítōnos*). Father of → Boeotus (only in Diod. Sic. 4,67,7 his son); eponym of the town of → Iton, situated close to Coronea in Boeotia, with an important sanctuary of Athena Itonia [1]. The homonymous place and sanctuary in Thessaly (situated between Larisa and Pherae) is an important indication of the conquest and settlement of Boeotia, starting from the north, which allegedly began sixty years after the fall of Troy (Thuc. 1,12,3). I. is, however, mentioned as eponymous hero only in connection with Boeotian settlement.

1 SCHACHTER, 1, 117–127.

E. VISSER, Homers Katalog der Schiffe, 1997, 272; 665.
       E.V.

Ituraea (Ἰτουραία; *Itouraía*). Region named after an Arab tribe, whose eponym Jeṭūr (Hebrew *Y*ᵉ*ṭūr*) was regarded as a son of → Ishmael (Gn 25,15; 1 Chr 1,31). In the early Hellenistic period, the tribe is referred to as living east of the Jordan (1 Chr 5,19; Eupolemus in Euseb. Praep. evang. 9,30). However, it settled in the area of the Antilebanon, on the plains of Massya (modern Beqaʿ), and in the Lebanon itself. Infamous for their brigandry (Cic. Phil. 2,112), the Ituraeans raided → Byblus and Beirut (→ Berytus; Str. 16,2,18) from their fortified bases in the Lebanon, and → Damascus from Trachonitis (Jos. BI 1,398f; Ant. Iud. 15, 344).

Ptolemy, a son of Mennaeus (*c.* 85–40 BC), established a rulership in Chalcis (modern Anǧar?), encompassing Abilene in the east and in the south Paneas and Ulatha (Str. 16,2,10; Jos. Ant. Iud. 14,126). Having already been forced to pay tribute by Pompey in 63 BC (Jos. Ant. Iud. 14,39f), Lysanias, Ptolemy's son and heir to the throne, was executed in 36 or 34 BC at the orders of Antony, who then granted his territory to Cleopatra (Cass. Dio 49,32,5; Jos. BI 1,440; Ant. Iud. 15,92f.). In order to stabilize the region further, the colony of Heliopolis was set up in the Beqa valley (→ Baalbek), and the remaining territory given to loyal local dynasties prior to its incorporation into the Roman provincial structure: Lysanias' former territory around Paneas and Ulatha was leased to Zenodorus. Augustus initially transferred control over Trachonitis and then, following Zenodorus' death in *c.* 20 BC, over the entire region down to Galilee to → Herodes the Great (Jos. BI 1,398–400; Ant. Iud. 15,344; 359f.), after whose death it fell to his son Philippus (Lc 3,1; Jos. Ant. Iud. 17,319). Under Tiberius, the ruler of Abilene was another Lysanias (Lc 3,1); later Abilene came under the rule of the Herodians Agrippa I and II, together with the tetrarchy of Philippus (Jos. Ant. Iud. 18,237; 19,275; 20,138). The territory of the Ituraean Arabs – probably north of Heliopolis stretching to Laodicea – was granted by Caligula in AD 38 to a ruler by the name of Sohaemus (Cass. Dio 59,12,2). After the death of the latter (Tac. Ann. 12,23), it was incorporated into the province of Syria in AD 49. The core territory around Chalcis was ruled by Herod of Chalcis from AD 41–48 (Jos. Ant. Iud. 19,277), and was probably the last part to be incorporated into the Syrian province in *c.* AD 92.

G. SCHMITT, Zum Königreich Chalkis, in: ZPalV 98, 1982, 110–124; W. SCHOTTROFF, Die Ituräer, ibid., 125–152.   K.B.

Iturius *Cliens* of Iunia Silana, who in the year AD 55, after Agrippina's [3] first loss of power, raised an accusation against her. On the demand of Agrippina, he was banished by Nero; after her death in 59 he was allowed to return, Tac. Ann. 13,19; 21f.; 14,12,4; PIR² J 62.
       W.E.

Itylus (Ἴτυλος; *Ítylos*). Son of → Zethus and → Aedon (Hom. Od. 19,518; Pherecydes FHG 1,95); also traditionally said to be the son of → Procne, otherwise called Itys (Cat. 65,14).　　　　RE.ZI.

Itys (Ἴτυς; *Ítys*). Son of → Tereus and → Procne (differently: Antoninus Liberalis 11); I. (or Itylus: schol. Thuc. 2,29,3) was killed by his mother and presented to his father to eat (Apollod. 3,193ff.; Ov. Met. 6,424ff.); he was transformed into a pheasant (Serv. Ecl. 6,78). I. is the plaintive cry of the nightingale (Aesch. Ag. 1144; schol. Aristoph. Av. 212).　　　　AN.W.

Iucundus

[1] According to Jos. BI 1,527, one of the cavalry commanders, according to Jos. Ant. Iud. 16,314, one of the bodyguards, of → Herodes [1] the Great, I. was suspected of conspiring with Herod's son Alexander against the king, tortured and executed after a forced confession (AD 9).

[2] Officer of the Roman garrison in → Caesarea [2], attempted without success in AD 66 to put an end to the fighting there between Greeks and Jews (Jos. BI 2,291); possibly identical with the *praefectus alae* Aemilius I., referred to in Jos. BI 2,544, who fell in the year 66 during the course of his retreat from Jerusalem.　　K.BR.

[3] see → Terra sigillata

Iudaea see → Palaestina

Iudex Literally, 'one who dispenses justice', i.e. 'judge'. Usually, this means the individual judge in Roman law (*iudex privatus; iudex unus*) who in a separate stage of the proceeding that usually ended a legal dispute (*apud iudicem*) conducts the deliberation of the evidence and passes a judgement roughly suggested by the → praetor in the first proceeding stage (*in iure*, → *ius*). While the term *iudex* was already exchangeable with that of → arbiter at the time of the Law of the Twelve Tables (5th cent. BC), the → recuperatores and → centumviri constitute separate categories of judges who in the context of collegial courts had to decide on cases of greater public significance.

The judge was appointed by the praetor (→ *addicere* or *dare*) who adhered to the generally consensual choice of the parties or otherwise used a two-step elimination procedure: he was probably limited to those entered in the list of judges (*album iudicum selectorum*); in the formular procedure a choice of judges not on the list existed. Initially, only senators were entered into this list but, as a consequence of the dispute raised to a political level by the Gracchi, *equites* (at the latest with a *lex Aurelia* of 70 BC) also qualified. The prerequisite was Roman citizenship, a minimum age (30, from Augustus 25 years) and a minimum in wealth. Furthermore, the *iudex* had to be male (Dig. 50,17,2), free of certain ailments (Dig. 5,1,12,2), and was not allowed to hold magistracy. He administered justice in his private home (Vitr. De arch. 6,5,2), i.e. acted as a private per-

son. Nevertheless, assuming a judicial office was a public duty with few options available for being exempted (Dig. 50,5,13 pr.).

If the *iudex* did not know the law (this is the typical case), he would – at least in difficult cases – have a *consilium* of legal advisors present during deliberations. This was sensible because of a *culpa* (culpability) liability towards the damaged party (*lis sua facta*, a legal dispute that the judge has made his own, Dig. 5,1,15,1). Otherwise, the proceedings were probably conducted with more or less rhetorical pomposity because the actual judicial questions had more or less been dealt with when the trial programme was set (→ *editio*), so that essentially only the proof presented was disputed before the *iudex*.

With the gradual introduction of the cognition procedure (→ *cognitio*) during the Principate, the proceeding, which was divided into many jurisdictions (preparatory discussions of the parties, *in iure, apud iudicem*), was uniformized while the private *iudex* was replaced by a professional judge (*iudex datus* or *iudex pedaneus*).

J. KELLY, Studies in the Civil Judicature of the Roman Republic, 1976, 112; M. KASER, K. HACKL, Das röm. Zivilprozeßrecht, ²1997, 52, 192; F. LAMBERTI, Riflessioni in tema di "litem suam facere", in: Labeo 36, 1990, 218–266; W. SIMSHÄUSER, Iuridici und Municipalgerichtsbarkeit in Italien, 1973.　　C.PA.

Iudicatum Either the payment order pronounced in a civil law trial (Dig. 2,12,6: *iudicatum facere vel solvere*), or the entire judgement; the latter primarily in the expression *res iudicata*; e.g. Dig. 42,1,1: *res iudicata dicitur, quae finem controversiarum pronuntiatione iudicis accipit: quod vel condemnatione vel absolutione contingit* ('res iudicata is the end of the proceeding that has been brought about by the judgement, which is either sentencing or acquittal'). In the masculine form *iudicatus* means a sentenced person, e.g. Dig. 42,2,1: *confessus pro iudicato est* ('who confesses is considered sentenced').

A separate judication obligation arises from the awarding *iudicatum* (Gai. Inst. 3,180), which the defendant had to fulfil up to Justinian's reign (6th cent. AD) within 30 days (Lex XII tab. 3,1; this type of delay, which in German was called the *Paritionsfrist* in the 19th cent., is still encountered in modern enforcement law. The plaintiff must initiate an *actio iudicati* ('enforcement proceeding') if the defendant does not pay. The latter will either immediately recognize his payment obligation and smoothen the path to the enforcement proceeding or – risking a penalty (doubling of the disputed amount; Gai. Inst. 4,9) – dispute it (Dig. 5,1,75; 42,1,7).

A formal legal force only came about with the introduction of an appeal sequence, i.e. an → *appellatio* to the *princeps* (limited to a two- to three-day term: Dig. 49,4,1,5). By contrast, the binding force of the content of the judgement *inter partes* (material legal force) was always ensured since a fulfilment or the *exceptio rei iudicatae vel in iudicium deductae* (defence with a matter that has been judged or is pending) prevented a renewed enforcing of the plaintiff's petition.

H. ANKUM, Pap. D. 20.1.3. pr.: "res iudicata" and Full and Bonitary Ownership, in: Estudios en homenaje de Iglesias, 1988, 1121–1149; M. KASER, K. HACKL, Das röm. Zivilprozeßrecht, ²1997, 375, 384; D. MEDICUS, Zur Urteilsberichtigung in der actio iudicati des Formularprozesses, in: ZRG 81, 1964, 233–292.   C.PA.

Iudicium A central concept of Roman → procedural law, it appears in several different senses: in the wider sense for the whole process, in the narrower sense (esp. in the context of the *legis actio* and formulary procedure which are divided into different procedural stages) for the last stage which took place before the judge (→ *iudex*). Upon transition to the *cognitio* procedure (→ *cognitio*) and concomitant elimination of the procedural stages, *iudicium* then only referred to the whole process for which the word *processus* has been in habitual usage since the MA. Additional meanings of *iudicium* include intellectual power of judgement (Dig. 5,1,12,2; 40,2,25), an (ecclesiastical) dogma (Cod. Iust. 1,5,2,1) or testament as defined by the 'last will' (Dig. 10,2,20,3, *supremum iudicium*).

Iudicium in the narrower sense is chiefly found in judicial edicts and enactments in the form of the *iudicium dabo*. This gave expression to the fact that the magistrate charged with administering justice appointed an individual court for each case brought before him and instructed it to decide in accordance with the statement of issues determined by him, subject to fulfilment of the procedural requirements. Since the → *formula* in the formulary procedure contained the judicial proposal established by the parties (see → *iudex*) as well as the statement of issues, *iudicium* and *formula* could have the same meaning. Hence, *dare iudicium* meant that the magistrate accepted the formula the parties had negotiated or reached with his assistance. This conclusion (pronounced by the magistrate) of the procedural stage *in iure* was an act of state. Acceptance of the appointment of the court by the parties resulted in a → *litis contestatio* (joinder of issue). According to a *lex Iulia* by Augustus from the year 17 BC, the granting of a formula of this nature was called *iudicium legitimum* (in contrast to *iudicium imperio continens*, a *iudicium* bound to the term of office), if (1) a sole judge (*iudex*) was appointed in Rome itself or inside the first milestone, and if (2) the judge and both parties were Roman citizens (Gai. Inst. 4,104).

Iudicium also has the following more specific meanings: *iudicium calumniae*: this legal redress offered the defendant, as an alternative to an oath of calumny (*non calumniae causa agere*, 'not to bring a vexatious action'), the opportunity to defend himself (Gai. Inst. 4,174–179) against an improper action that had been brought, i.e. against one's better judgement (Dig. 5,1,10). If the defendant succeeded with it, the plaintiff

had to pay a penalty for non-observance of procedural requirements in the sum of (at least) one tenth of the amount sued for.

Iudicium contrarium: this can mean one of two things: (1) a specific variation of the aforementioned *iudicium calumniae* (Gai. Inst. 4,177). While it has been found to be a cross-action in the modern sense due to its indispensable connection with the approach to the action adopted by the other party, (2) the other meaning was assigned (at least in the classical period of Roman law (1st cent. BC–3rd cent. AD), Dig. 13,6,17,1) a substantive circumstance – namely, the existence of an incomplete bilateral legal transaction (→ gratuitous loan, → *depositum*, → *fiducia*, → *mandatum*, → *negotiorum gestio*, → *pignus*, → *tutela*). It is remarkable in that it only imposed a duty on one of the two parties, leaving the other with a mere entitlement. The obligated party could, however, some day also be liable for the reimbursement of expenses or compensatory damages for claims arising out of the activity it had assumed in a particular case, which then had to be enforced with the assistance of a *iudicium contrarium*, or alternatively *an actio contraria*.

Iudicium de moribus: an action abolished by Justinian in the year 533 (Cod. Iust. 5,17,11,2 b) which was brought by a husband against his ex-wife for a share in her dowry (→ *dos*) which had already been returned, provided his wife's moral lapses were to blame for the divorce.

Iudicium domesticum: this refers to the domestic court for private-law disputes and criminal offences which the → *pater familias* was able to hold over those in his control by virtue of his → *patria potestas*.

Iudicium privatum: this refers to judicial proceedings for private matters in contrast to the *iudicium publicum* (cf. → *ius*). In the course of Roman legal history, civil procedure passed through three phases which were not distinct completely from each other, but overlapped. What distinguished the first phase (legis actio procedure) and the second phase (formulary procedure) was their division into several stages: granting of judicial proceedings by a magistrate (praetor, aedile etc.) – *in iure* – as well as the subsequent hearing of evidence and rendition of judgment by a private judge (→ *iudex*, → *recuperatores*) *apud iudicem*. In the formulary procedure at least there was a further stage which preceded the procedure *in iure* and had to be recorded, namely communication between the parties themselves about the impending trial (→ *editio*). What distinguished the → *legis actiones* procedure was the correct recital by the parties of contentious allegations according to formulae consisting of specially prepared phrases. A *lex Aebutia* from the 2nd cent. BC limited the scope of application of this type of procedure, and the *lex Iulia* eliminated it almost entirely. The formulary procedure that prevailed instead demonstrated greater flexibility. The written formulae as provided in the edictal promises were capable of much more precise adaptation to the specific characteristics of the respective individual case

which found clear expression in the *bonae fidei iudicia*
(→ *fides*) in particular, but also in the granting of → *ex-
ceptiones*. The *cognitio* procedure used under the first
principes and which had definitively superseded its predecessors in AD 342, transferred the entire decision
about a case to a judge who had to clarify the factual
questions as well as the legal issues in integrated proceedings.

Iudicium publicum: this refers to classical Roman
criminal procedure which was reformed by the Augustan *lex Iulia iudiciorum publicorum*. It was initiated by
the 'indictment' of a citizen, → *delatio nominis* (Dig.
37,14,10), which was then followed by a trial before a
jury court presided over by a magistrate. Not all criminal offences were adjudged by *iudicium publicum*, but
in accordance with Dig. 48,1,1 only those which were
derived from the following laws: *Iulia maiestatis, Iulia
de adulteriis, Cornelia de sicariis et veneficis, Pompeia
parricidii, Iulia peculatus, Cornelia de testamentis,
Iulia de vi privata, Iulia de vi publica, Iulia ambitus,
Iulia repetundarum* and *Iulia de annona* (for procedure
cf. → *quaestio*).

Iudicium rescissorium: an action granted by the
praetor or provincial governor, in order to be able to
reverse objectionable juridical positions for the purposes of restitution to the previous condition (→ *restitutio in integrum*).

M. KASER, K. HACKL, Das röm. Zivilprozeßrecht, ²1997,
288; W. KUNKEL, Unt. zur Entwicklung des römischen
Kriminalverfahrens in vorsullanischer Zeit, 1962; M. LE-
MOSSE, Les deux régimes de l'instance "in iure", in: Labeo
37, 1991, 297–304; C. G. PAULUS, Die Beweisvereitelung
in der Struktur des dt. Zivilprozesses, in: Archiv für die
civilistische Praxis 197, 1997, 136–160, 151ff.; Y. THO-
MAS, Remarques sur la jurisdiction domestique à Rome,
in: J. ANDREAU, H. BRUNS (ed.), Parenté et stratégies fami-
liale dans l'antiquité romain, 1990, 449–474.   G.T.

Iuenna Roman settlement in Noricum, 23 miles from
→ Virunum in the direction of Celeia (Tab. Peut. 4,2),
modern Globasnitz in the Jaun Valley (Carinthia). Sanctuary of the Celtic god Iovenat on Mount Hemma,
developed into a Christian pilgrimage site from the 5th
cent..

F. GLASER, Die röm. Siedlung I. und die frühchristl. Kirchen am Hemmaberg, 1982.   H.GR.

Iugatio see → Capitatio-iugatio

Iugerum Latin name for a square measure comprising a
rectangle of 120 × 240 feet = 35,52 × 71,04 m =
2523 m² = ¹/₄ ha, made up of two squares (→ Actus [2])
[1. 84f.; 3. 9f.], according to Plin. HN 18,3,9 the area
which could be ploughed in one day by one yoke of
oxen, in a figurative sense a 'day's work'. Division according to the duodecimal system into 2 *actus*, 12 *unciae*, 288 → *scripula*, with 1 *scripulum* corresponding
to 100 square feet. A full calculation of the sub-units is

given by Columella 5,1,4–5,2,10 [2. 627]. Varro, Rust.
1,10,2 mentions → *heredium* (2 I.), *centuria* (200 I.)
and → *saltus* (800 I.) as multiples of the *iugerum*. Modifications of the norm are found in the Egyptian provincial system, where one *iugerum* corresponded to
2450 m² [1. 610]. In the Roman Imperial period also
used as a length measurement to indicate field lengths
[2. 629]. The sizes of the estates situated on the periphery of the Colonia Claudia Ara Agrippinensium aver-
aged between 3 and 10 *iugera* [4. 405–408].
→ Surface measures

1 F. HULTSCH, Griech. und röm. Metrologie, ²1882
2 ThlL VII   3 D. FLACH, Röm. Agrargesch. (HdbA III 9),
1990   4 W. GAITZSCH, Grundformen röm. Landsiedlun-
gen im Westen der CCAA, in: BJ 186, 1986, 397–427
5 H. CHANTRAINE, s.v. I., KlP 2, 1512   6 F. T. HINRICHS,
Die Gesch. der gromatischen Institutionen – Unt. zu Land-
verteilung, Landvermessung, Bodenverwaltung und
Bodenrecht im röm. Reich, 1974   7 U. HEIMBERG, Röm.
Landvermessung, 1977.   H.-J.S.

Iuglans or *iugulans*. Etymology according to Varro,
Ling. 5,102: *a Iove et glande appellata* ('named after
Jupiter and the acorn'; cf. Isid. Orig. 17,7,21 according
to Serv. Ecl. 8,29f. and Plin. HN 15,91, translated from
Διὸς βάλανος/*Diòs bálanos*, which otherwise designates the edible chestnut), the walnut (*Iuglans regia* L.).
Introduced into Italy from Persia on the Black Sea via
Greece (according to Pall. Agric. 2,15,14–19, sown
from the end of January onwards, according to Columella 5,10,14 in March), it was already known to
Theophrastus. He mentions that the καρύα ἡ Περσική/
karýa hē persikē ('Persian nut') sprouts from the side
branches (Hist. pl. 3,6,2). Varro (Rust. 1,67) recommends early harvesting of the *nux iuglans*: a large
number of big trees, he claims, make the soil of an estate
sterile (ibid. 1,16,6). Isidore says their shade and the
water dripping from the leaves is detrimental to the
growth of nearby trees (Orig. 17,7,21); Plin. HN 17,89
blames the *iuglans* for headaches in humans (cf. 15,87:
because of its strong smell). According to Isidore ibid.,
the walnut is supposed to remove the poison from suspicious herbs or mushrooms if mixed with them. According to Servius ibid., walnuts, which were dedicated
to Jupiter, were scattered at weddings as omens. Cicero
recounts (Tusc. 5,58) that the tyrant Dionysius of Syracuse, in fear of the shaving knife, made his daughters
singe off the hair of his head and his beard with glowing
walnuts.   C.HÜ.

Iugum

[1] *Iugum* ('yoke'), according to Varro Rust. 1,10,1,
was the name of a field measurement in Hispania ulterior equal to the value of the → *iugerum*. From the time
of Diocletian onwards, the *iugum* consisted of a virgate
of varying size, according to the quality of the land. In
Syria, therefore, one *iugum* comprised 5 *iugera* of vineyard, 20, 40, 60 iugera of agricultural land of declining
yield or 220 resp. 450 *perticae* (at 100 square feet each)

of oil-producing plantings (FIRA 2,795f.). Other measurements and classes are found in Palestine, Arabia and the islands, while the corresponding fiscal units in Egypt are based on the → aroura, in Africa on the *centuria* (at 200 iugera each), in Italy on the *millena*.
→ Capitatio-iugatio

> J. MARQUARDT, Röm. Staatsverwaltung, vol. 2, 1876 (Hdb. der röm. Alterthümer 5), 225ff.; A. H. M. JONES, The Later Roman Empire, 1964, 62ff.; 453ff.; 820.
>
> HE.C.

[2] see → Land transport

Iugum Cremonis Modern Mont Cramont on the route of the Little St Bernard Pass, over which, according to Coelius Antipater (HRR fr. 14 = Liv. 21,38,7), Hannibal crossed the Alps.   H.GR.

Iugurtha 160–104 BC; grandson of → Massinissa, son of → Mastanabal, who with → Micipsa and → Gulussa was joint ruler of Numidia. Brought up in the ways of war by Micipsa, in 134 BC he was sent to → Numantia as commander of the Numidian archers, slingers and elephants. Owing to his military achievements he enjoyed great popularity and had personal relations with the Roman elite, esp. with → Cornelius [I 70] Scipio Africanus; he learned the Latin language (Sall. Iug. 5,4–9,1; 101,6; App. Hisp. 387). At the personal recommendation of Scipio he was adopted by Micipsa; in 118 BC, after the death of Micipsa, he became joint ruler with Micipsa's younger (natural) sons → Adherbal [4] and → Hiempsal [1]. In the course of disputes over the division of the property, J. defeated Hiempsal and had him killed. Adherbal, expelled from the kingdom by J., turned to the Roman Senate (Sall. Iug. 8,2–11,9; Liv. Per. 62) [2. 59]. With the division of the kingdom, the fertile west fell to J., the east to Adherbal (Sall. Iug. 12–16) [2. 60]. In 112 BC J. made a new attack on Adherbal, who was killed at Cirta together with merchants from Italy (Sall. Iug. 20–27; Diod. Sic. 34/35,31; Liv. Per. 64) [3. 165ff.]; Roman declaration of war in spite of a delegation from J. (Sall. Iug. 27,1–28,2).

Owing to J.'s exerting his influence, the campaign of L. Calpurnius [I 1] Bestia lead in 111 to peace for low reparations and without J.'s personal surrender (Sall. Iug. 28,4–29,7) [1. 97ff.]. The peoples' tribune C. Memmius compelled J. to be summoned to Rome, where J. had the pretender → Massiva, son of Gulussa, killed by → Bomilcar [4]; J. and Bomilcar had to leave Rome (Sall. Iug. 30; 32–35; Diod. Sic. 34/35,35a; App. Num. 1) [1. 99ff.]. Sp. and Aulus Postumus Albinus made again war on J. (110 BC); J. was victorious at Suthul and forced the Romans to withdraw (Sall. Iug. 36–38) [1. 102ff.]. The *foedus* dictated by J. was not recognized by the Senate [1. 103]. Q. → Caecilius [I 30] Metellus (*cos.* 109) led the ensuing campaign and intensified armament and troop training (Sall. Iug. 39f.; 43–45; Cic. Brut. 127f.); he captured Vaga and defeated J. at the Muthul, but failed to control J. and his land (Sall. Iug. 46–69; Plut. Marius 8; App. Num. 3) [1. 103–109].

After fruitless negotiations for J.'s capitulation, Bomilcar carried out an assassination attempt on J.; eastern Numidia was occupied by Q. Caecilius Metellus. J., mobilizing the tribe of the Gaetuli against the Romans, allied himself with Bocchus of Mauretania; Metellus attempted to weaken the opposing alliance by means of negotiation (Sall. Iug. 62; 70–84). The legate → Marius criticized Metellus' conduct of war; in 107 Marius received the consulate and the supreme command against J. (Sall. Iug. 67,3; 69,4; 73,2; 84; 86; Plut. Mar. 7–9; Cic. Off. 3,79). Marius captured → Capsa, and was able to ward off attacks at Cirta and at the → Mulucha, but did not control the surrounding country (Sall. Iug. 87–101). Therefore, he negotiated with Bocchus for the surrender of J., which → Cornelius [I 90] Sulla achieved as *quaestor* in 105 (Plut. Marius 10,3–6; Sall. Iug. 103–109; 111–113; Liv. Per. 66; App. Num. 4f.; Diod. Sic. 34/35,39) [1. 113ff.]. In 104 BC, J. was carried along in Marius' triumphal procession, and was killed (Liv. Per. 67; Plut. Marius 12,3–6; Sall. Iug. 114,3). Bocchus played up his act of betrayal for propaganda purposes by portraying the surrender of J. to Sulla on the Capitol (cf. Plut. Sulla 6,1), and by portraying Sulla and his family on a signet ring and on coins [1. 115f.].
→ Numidia

> 1 H. W. RITTER, Rom und Numidien, 1987   2 M.-R. ALFÖLDI, Die Gesch. des numid. Königreiches und seiner Nachfolger, in: H. G. HORN, C. B. RÜGER (ed.), Die Numidier, 1979, 43–74   3 C. SAUMAGNE, La Numidie et Rome, 1966.   B.M.

Iulia

[1] Paternal aunt of C. Iulius → Caesar; between 115 and 109 BC, she married C. Marius, with whom she had a son named C. Marius (*cos.* 82; Plut. Marius 6,3; Plut. Caesar 1,1; Sall. Hist. 1,35 MAUR). There is almost no information regarding I.'s life. On the occasion of her death in 68, Caesar held a large funeral ceremony (Suet. Iul. 6,1; Plut. Caesar 5,1).
[2] Daughter of L. Iulius [I 5] Caesar and Fulvia (daughter of M. Fulvius Flaccus). From her first marriage to M. Antonius [I 8] Creticus, she had three sons, including the later triumvir M. Antony [I 9]. After 71 BC, she married P. Cornelius [I 56] Lentulus Sura. His execution as a Catilinarian in 63 BC does not appear to have discredited I. (Cic. Cat. 4,13). In the power struggle between Octavian and Antony, together with her daughter-in-law Fulvia [2], she supported Antonius (App. B Civ. 3,51,58), but unlike Fulvia, I. had a mediating and moderating influence. In 43, I. rescued her proscribed brother, L. Iulius [I 6] Caesar (Plut. Antonius 20,2; App. B Civ. 4,37), and supported Roman *matronae* against the taxation of their wealth (App. B Civ. 4,32). During the Perusian War (→ Augustus C.), she fled to Sextus Pompeius; in 40, she supported the treaty of Brundisium (Plut. Antonius 32; App. B Civ. 5,52; 63; Cass. Dio 48,15,2; 16,2). Plutarch (Antonius 2,1) describes I. as one of the 'best and most decorous' women of her time.

[3] Little-known (older) sister of C. Iulius → Caesar.

[4] The younger of Caesar's two sisters. It was probably her, not the elder I., who, in 61 BC, gave evidence with her mother Aurelia [1] in the Bona Dea trial (Suet. Iul. 74,2; schol. Bobiensia 89,26–28 ST). I. had two daughters with her husband M. Atius Balbus; through the elder, she was the grandmother of the later Augustus (Suet. Aug. 4,1), whose upbringing she supervised from about 58 until her death in 51. Her grandson delivered her funeral oration (Suet. Aug. 8,1; Quint. Inst. 12,6,1).

[5] Daughter of C. Iulius → Caesar and Cornelia [I 3], born between 83 and 76 BC [1. 19]. Caesar first betrothed her to Q. Servilius Caepio; to consolidate the so-called first triumvirate, however, he married her to Cn. Pompeius in April of 59 (Plut. Caesar 14,7; Suet. Iul. 21,1). Although politically motivated (Cic. Att. 2,17,1; Plut. Pompey 49,4; Gell. NA 4,10,5), the marriage was very happy (Plut. Pompey 53,1; Val. Max. 4,6,4). Following a miscarriage in the summer of 55, I. died in early Sept. 54 while giving birth to another child (Cic. Ad Q. Fr. 3,1,17,25; Plut. Pompey 53,5; Cass. Dio 39,64,1). At the insistence of the *plebs*, she was not buried on Pompey's estate of Albanum, but was given an honourable burial on the Field of Mars (Plut. Pompey 53,6; Suet. Iul. 84,1; Liv. epit. 106). Caesar honoured I. in 46 with funeral games (Plut. Caesar 55,4; Suet. Iul. 26,2). I.'s death was already connected in antiquity with the open outbreak of the power struggle between Caesar and Pompey (Luc. 1,111–120; Vell. Pat. 2,47,2; Flor. 2,13,13).

1 M. GELZER, Caesar, 6 1960.   H.S.

[6] Daughter of → Augustus and → Scribonia [1]. Born 39 BC, on the same day Octavian left Scribonia. From very early on, she became a factor in the dynastic politics of her father; hence her engagement to Antyllus, the son of Antony, in 37 on the occasion of the treaty of Tarentum. In 25, she married her cousin M. Claudius [II 42] Marcellus; because Augustus had fallen ill in Spain, Agrippa [1] performed the wedding. Following Marcellus' early death in 23 BC, Augustus married her to Agrippa [1] in 21. This marriage produced five children: Gaius Iulius [II 32] Caesar (b. 20), I. [7] (b. 19), Lucius Iulius [II 33] Caesar (b. 17), Agrippina [2] (b. 15), Agrippa [2] Postumus (b. 12, after the death of his father). She probably accompanied Agrippa to Gallia, definitely to the east. Many of the statues and accompanying inscriptions which refer to her most likely stem from these years [1]. They show that similar forms of reverence, also of a cultic nature, were applied to both the *princeps* and his daughter. On the *Ara Pacis*, she appears with Agrippa and their son Gaius Caesar.

After Agrippa's death, → Tiberius [1] had to marry I., on the orders of Augustus. That marriage produced a son, who soon died. The rift between the two was one of the reasons for Tiberius' self-exile in Rhodes. Political motives and the character of I. – who had grown up in an already 'monarchical' atmosphere, which had shaped her public appearance and behaviour, even toward Tiberius – may have also played a role. As a result, in 2 BC, she also came into conflict with Augustus, against whose marriage and decency legislation she scandalously 'demonstrated' in the Forum at night with young senators from influential families, by offering herself as a prostitute – at the very moment that Augustus was being declared *pater patriae*. Augustus indicted her before the Senate; she was banished to the island of Pandateria. In AD 3, Rhegium became her place of exile; her mother Scribonia accompanied her. After Augustus' death, Tiberius allegedly drove her to death in AD 14 by withdrawing all her funds. Augustus had forbidden her burial in his mausoleum. PIR² J 634.

1 U. HAHN, Die Frauen des röm. Kaiserhauses, 1994, 106ff.   2 P. SATTLER, Studien aus dem Gebiet der Alten Geschichte, 1962, 1ff.   3 J. LINDERSKI, in: ZPE 72, 1988, 181ff. = Id., Roman Questions, 1995, 375ff., 663ff. 4 R.A. BAUMAN, Women and Politics in Ancient Rome, 1992, 99ff.   5 R. SYME, AA, 90ff.

[7] (Vipsania) I. Daughter of M. Vipsanius Agrippa [1] and Iulia [6], granddaughter of Augustus, sister of Gaius and Lucius Caesar. Born c. 19 BC, she spent her childhood in Augustus' house. In 5/4 BC, she married Aemilius [II 13] Paullus. In AD 8, she was exiled for adultery (*adulterium*), her husband for crimes of → *maiestas*. The affair was connected with the struggle for power and succession within the family of Augustus. Augustus had her villa destroyed. A child born to her after she was exiled he had killed and he forbade her burial in his mausoleum. In 28, she died in exile, where → Livia [2] had supported her after Augustus' death. PIR² J 635.

R. SYME, History in Ovid, 1978, 209ff.; Id., AA, 115ff.

[8] Daughter of Drusus [II 1], the son of Tiberius, and → Livia [3] (PIR² L 303). Born c. AD 3. In 20, probably in the autumn, she married Nero Iulius [II 34] Caesar, the oldest son of Germanicus. She is said to have reported all of his remarks to her mother Livia, who in turn passed them on to Seianus (→ Aelius [II 19]), her lover, and thus to Tiberius. After the condemnation of Nero, it was not she but her mother who married Seianus (despite Cass. Dio 58,3,9; cf. [1]). In the year 33, she married Rubellius Blandus, an action Tacitus (Ann. 6,27,1) characterized as damaging the dignity of the *domus Augusta*. Under Claudius, she was killed at the instigation of Messalina. PIR² J 636.

1 J. BELLMORE, in: ZPE 109, 1995, 255ff.   W.E.

[9] I. Avita Mamaea. Younger daughter of Iulius [II 22] Avitus and I. [17] Maesa, married to the Syrian procurator Gessius Marcianus, mother of the later emperor M. Aurelius → Severus [2] Alexander (Cass. Dio 78(79),30,2f.; Dig. 1,9,12), whom she arranged to have brought up with great care (Hdn. 5,7,5; SHA Alex. Sev. 3,1–3).

Together with I. Maesa, and against the resistance of her rival sister I. [22] Soaemias, I. successfully supported the elevation of her son to the throne (Cass. Dio 79(80),19,2; 4; 20,1; Hdn. 5,7,3; 8,2f.). After the murder of → Elagabalus [2] in March AD 222, together with the *praefectus praetorio*, Ulpianus, and at first probably in agreement with her mother (Hdn. 5,8,10; 6,1,1–4), I. exercised considerable influence on the new, still youthful ruler [2. 205–212; 1. 138ff.]. Alexander appears to have granted I. a powerful lifelong position (Hdn. 6,1,5–10; SHA Alex. Sev. 14,7; 26,9; 60,2). She held the honorary title of *Augusta, mater Augusti (et castrorum et senatus atque patriae)* (CIL VIII 1406; II 3413; inscriptions and coins, see [3. 156–171, 282–295]). I. probably accompanied Alexander on the Persian campaign [3. 50–52], definitely on the German campaign in 235 to the Rhine, to Feldberg and Saalburg, where Alexander, perhaps on the advice of I., offered his enemy peace negotiations and the payment of tributes (Hdn. 6,7,9; Zon. 12,15). I. and Alexander were murdered by mutinous soldiers in March, 235 (Hdn. 6,9,1–8; SHA Alex. Sev. 59–61).

Christian sources in particular mention I.'s open-mindedness toward Christianity; she was in personal contact with → Origenes (Euseb. Hist. eccl. 6,21; Jer. Vir. ill. 8,93; Zon. 12,15); Herodian 6,1,8 (incorrectly) describes her as mean and greedy (see SHA Alex. Sev. 14,7). Portraits: [4. 924].

1 J. BABELON, Impératrices syriennes, 1957 2 F. GROSSO, Il papiro Oxy. 2565 e gli avvenimenti del 222–224, in: RAL 23, 1968, 205–220 3 E. KETTENHOFEN, Die syr. Augustae in der histor. Überlieferung, 1979 4 M. FLORIANI SQUARCIAPINO, s.v. Giulia Mamea, EAA 3, 924.
H.S.

[10] I. Balbilla. Companion of Sabina and the emperor Hadrian in Egypt, when they received the oracle of → Memnon on the 20th and 21st of November AD 130. Four of her epigrams, which document her stay, have been preserved on the left ankle and foot of the Colossus of Memnon [1. 80–98]. These elegiac distichs are written in archaic, primarily Aeolic, Greek with some epic elements and uncommon words. She claims to be the descendant of a Balbillus ὁ σοφός ('the Wise'; he is varyingly identified [2. 308–309]) on her mother's side, and of the kings of Antioch on her father's side.

1 A. and É. BERNAND, Les inscriptions grecques et latines du Colosse de Memnon, 1960 2 PIR IV, 3 3 A. SPAWFORTH, Balbilla, the Euclids and the Memorials for a Greek Magnate, in: ABSA 73, 1978, 249–260 4 A.R. BIRLEY, Hadrian, 1997, 250f.
E.R.

[11] I. Cornelia Paula. First wife of the emperor → Elagabalus [2], who had her elevated to Augusta, but separated from her after a short period (CIL X 4554; Cass. Dio 79(80), 9,1–3; Hdn. 5,6,1) [1. 376f.].

1 H. COHEN, Monnaies sous l'empire romain, repr. 1955, vol. 2.

[12] I. Domna. From Emesa in Syria, daughter of the priest of the sun, Bassianus. In AD 185, she married the later emperor → Septimius [II 7] Severus; in 186 and 189, she gave birth to their sons → Caracalla and → Geta [2] (SHA Sev. 3,8f.). I.'s influence on the emperor and his policies is difficult to assess [3. 10–62; 1.9ff.]. In 205, she was probably involved in the overthrow of the *praefectus praetorio* → Fulvius [II 10] Plautianus, who had worked against her (Cass. Dio 75 (76),15,6f.; Hdn. 3,11f.) [3. 10f.]. From 208 to 211, I. accompanied Severus on his campaign in Britain, as before in the Orient, which earned her the honorary title *mater castrorum* (CIL XII 4345; XIV 120). After Severus' death in 211, I. is said to have endeavoured to reconcile her estranged sons and to preserve the unity of the empire (Hdn. 4,3,1–9). In 212, however, Caracalla had Geta killed in her presence (Cass. Dio 77(78),2; Hdn. 4,4,3). Involved by Caracalla in the operation of the government as needed, I.s political role appears to have been essentially limited to that of adviser (Cass. Dio 77(78),10,4; 18,2f.); however, her ruling position is also attested through honorary titles such as *pia felix mater Augusti et senatus et patriae* [2. 200–219]. In 214, I. was staying in Nicomedia (Cass. Dio 77(78), 18,1–3), then in Antioch (Cass. Dio 78(79),4,2f.), where in 217, she learned of Caracalla's murder (Cass. Dio 78(79),23,1; Hdn. 4,13,8). Rebuked by → Macrinus, presumably for political agitation, I. died not much later, probably through suicide, and was buried in Rome (Cass. Dio 78(79),23,2–6; 24,1–3).

I. is not least famous as a well-educated, religiously interested [4. 228–237] woman, who surrounded herself with a circle of literary figures, namely → Philostratus [5], to whom she gave the incentive to write the *vita* of Apollonius [14] of Tyana (Philostr. VA 1,1,3), and → Philiscus [8] of Thessaly [3. 13–16]. Numerous epigraphic and numismatic sources, as well as portraits, which are not always beyond doubt, are preserved ([3. 75–143]; BMCRE 5, 27f., no. 156–170).

1 F. GHEDINI, Giulia Domna tra Oriente e Occidente, 1984 2 H.U. INSTINSKY, Studien zur Geschichte des Septimius Severus, in: Klio 35, 1942 3 E. KETTENHOFEN, Die syr. Augustae in der histor. Überlieferung, 1979 4 I. MUNDLE, Dea Caelestis in der Religionspolitik des Septimius Severus und der I. Domna, in: Historia 10, 1961, 228–237.
H.S.

[13] I. Drusilla. Daughter of Germanicus [2] and Agrippina [2]; born AD 15 or 16/17 in Germania. She grew up in the house of her grandmother Antonia [4]. In 33, she was married to L. Cassius [II 16] Longinus by Tiberius, in 38, to M. Aemilius [II 9] Lepidus. Her brother → Caligula bestowed on her the rights of a Vestal; she and her sisters were depicted on imperial coins in the guise of goddesses. Tributes to her, also in cultic form, are numerous throughout the empire. Caligula named her and her husband as his successors; he is also said to have presented her in public like a wife for a certain period; in addition, she was included in the *vota* of the state priests. She died on 10 June 38, and was buried in the Mausoleum Augusti; also in 38, she was consecrat-

ed as *diva*, though after Caligula's death, the consecration was probably annulled.

> PIR² J 664; P. HERZ, Diva Drusilla, in: Historia 30, 1981,
> 324ff.; U. HAHN, Die Frauen des röm. Kaiserhauses, 1994,
> 151ff.

[14] I. Drusilla. Daughter of Caligula and Milonia Caesonia; born AD 40. Her father named her for his favourite sister Iulia [13]. Immediately after her birth, she was
entrusted to the Roman state gods for protection. Murdered on 24 January 41 by members of the conspiracy
against Caligula. PIR² J 665; KIENAST², 86.

[15] I. Fadilla. Half-sister of the later Antoninus Pius;
her father was P. Iulius Lupus. Owner of *praedia* in the
area of Rome; her full name may have been I. Lupula
Arria Fadilla.

> PIR² J 667; A.R. BIRLEY, Marcus Aurelius, ²1987, 243;
> RAEPSAET-CHARLIER, no. 444.   W.E.

[16] see → Livilla

[17] I. Maesa. Married to Iulius [II 22] Avitus, with
whom she had two daughters, I. [22] Soaemias and I.
[9] Mamaea. She was a sister of I. [12] Domna, with
whom she lived at court until the death of → Caracalla
(Hdn. 5,3,2f.; 8,3; Cass. Dio 78(79),30,2f.). In AD 217,
→ Macrinus banished I. from Rome to her hometown
of Emesa (SHA Macrinus 9,1), where, allegedly also
with gifts of money to the soldiers (Hdn. 5,3,2; 11;
5,4,1f.), she helped bring about a situation in which the
legio III Gall. stationed there proclaimed her grandson
Bassianus-Elagabalus (→ Elagabalus [2]) emperor in
218 (Hdn. 5,3,8–12; Cass. Dio 78(79),31). In the decisive battle at Antioch, she is said to have morally
supported the troops against Macrinus (Cass. Dio
78(79),38,4).

I.'s important political role at the beginning of the
reign of Elagabalus and her powerful position as grandmother of the still young emperor are not in question
(this assessment borne out by the coin findings, cf.
BMCRE 5, pp. 539–542, no. 61–83); nevertheless, she
was probably not the all-dominating *grande dame* of
the imperial court often read into Herodian (5,5–8) by
researchers (see also Cass. Dio 79 (80),17,2; SHA
Heliogab. 12,3; 15,6) [3. 33–42]. I.'s unsuccessful criticism of Elagabalus is attested by several sources (Hdn.
5,5,3–6; Cass. Dio 79(80),15,4). Out of concern for the
state of the dynasty, I. then distanced herself from the
ever more unpopular Elagabalus in favour of her younger grandson Severus Alexander, the son of Mamaea
(Hdn. 5,7,1–3; 5,8,3f.; Cass. Dio 79(80),19,1–4). I.'s
influence after the accession of Alexander in 222 until
her death in 226 was probably not as great as Herodian
(5,8,10; 6,1,1–4) suggests [1. 276; 2. 207–210].

Inscriptions [3. 144–151] complement the literary
sources (portraits: [4. 924f.]).

> 1 A.R. BIRLEY, Septimius Severus, ²1988   2 F. GROSSO, Il
> papiro Oxy. 2565 e gli avvenimenti del 222–224, in: RAL
> 23, 1968, 205–220   3 E. KETTENHOFEN, Die syr. Augu-
> stae in der histor. Überlieferung, 1979   4 M. FLORIANI
> SQUARCIAPINO, s.v. Giulia Mesa, EAA 3, 924f.   H.S.

[18] I. Mettia Aurelia Helena. Wife of a senator of consular rank. AE 1994, 1730.

[19] I. Paulina. Daughter of Iulius [II 141] Servianus
and Domitia [10] Paulina; niece of Hadrian; married to
Pedanius Fuscus Salinator; her name is listed as the first
of the recipients of legacies in the will of Domitius Tullus.

> AE 1976, 77 = W. ECK, in: ZPE 30, 1978, 277ff.; A.R.
> BIRLEY, Hadrian, 1997, 309.

[20] I. Procilla. Wife of Iulius [II 70] Graecinus, mother
of Iulius [II 3] Agricola. She had great influence on her
son. In AD 69, she was murdered by Othonian troops in
Liguria, PIR² J 693.

[21] I. Proculina. Wife of the *cos. suff.* C. Aquillius [II 4]
Proculus.

> CIL X 1699 = G. CAMODECA, in: Puteoli 6, 1982, 62ff.
> RAEPSAET-CHARLIER, no. 456.   W.E.

[22] I. Soaemias (Bassiana) Older daughter of Iulius [II
22] Avitus and I. [17] Maesa, wife of Sex. Varius Marcellus from Syrian Apamea and mother of → Elagabalus
[2] (Cass. Dio 78(79),30,2; Hdn. 5,3,3). In AD 218, I.
helped secure the elevation of Elagabalus to the throne,
not least through her support in the battle of Antioch
(Cass. Dio 78(79),38,4; Hdn. 5,3,11f.).

As Augusta and *mater Augusti*, I. appears to have
been included by Elagabalus in his policy-making, but
the extent of her influence cannot be determined [2. 9–
14]. The image of the immoral wanton, who ruled the
emperor and officially interfered in state business
[1. 228–233], is, however, based to a considerable
extent on the *Historia Augusta*, which defamed the
reign of Elagabalus with the fiction of a bawdy regiment
of women (SHA Heliogab. 2,1f.; 4,1–4; 18,2f.; SHA
Macrinus 7,6; cf. Cass. Dio 79(80),6,2; 17,2) [3. 63–
69]. In contrast to her mother and her sister I. [9]
Mamaea, who, swayed by the increasing animosity
towards Elagabalus, turned to Mamaea's son Severus
Alexander, I. remained loyal to her son, until both were
murdered in 222 (Cass. Dio 79(80),20,1f.; Hdn. 5,8,8).

> 1 J. BABELON, Imperatrices syriennes, 1957   2 H.W.
> BENARIO, The Titulature of Julia Soaemias and Julia
> Mamaea, in: TAPhA 90, 1959, 9–14   3 E. KETTEN-
> HOFEN, Die syr. Augustae in der histor. Überlieferung,
> 1979   4 J. SÜNSKES-THOMPSON, Aufstände und Protest-
> aktionen im Imperium Romanum, 1990.   H.S.

[23] I. Tertulla. Daughter or sister of Iulius [II 48], wife
of Iulius [II 90].

[24] I. Valeria Marciana Crispinilla. *Clarissima femina*,
mother of L. Flavius Cleonaeus, Cn. Suellius Rufus
Marcianus, Flavia Polymnia Marciana and Flavia Crispinilla, who were all members of the senatorial class;
period of Antoninus Pius and Marcus Aurelius; buried
in Puteoli.

> G. CAMODECA, in: Puteoli 7/8, 1983/4, 79ff. = AE 1986,
> 155.   W.E.

Iuliacum Roman posting station (It. Ant. 375,8; 378,7; Tab. Peut. 2,5) in Germania inferior on the road from Cologne to Tongeren at the crossing of the Rur, the modern Jülich. Epigraphically attested is *[vic]ani [Iuliac]enses* on the base of a Jupiter column from the early 2nd cent. AD [1. 195 no. 196]. Bricks of the *legio VI Victrix*, a dedication by one of its soldiers (CIL XIII 7869), and a funerary relief confirm the presence of the military. I. was the central place of a fertile settlement landscape with many *villae rusticae*. In the early 4th cent., I. was fortified with a fourteen-cornered wall. It is still mentioned in Amm. Marc. 17,2,1 for AD 357.

1 H. NESSELHAUF, H. LIEB, Dritter Nachtrag zu CIL XIII, in: BRGK 40, 1959.

G. ALFÖLDY, Ein neuer Matronenaltar aus Jülich, in: Epigraphische Stud. 4, 1967, 1–25; P. J. THOLEN, I.-Jülich. Eine top. Stud., in: BJ 175, 1975, 231–255; C. B. RÜGER, P. NOELKE, K. GREWE, Jülich, in: H. G. HORN (ed.), Die Römer in Nordrhein-Westfalen, 1987, 447–452.   RA.WI.

Iulianus Epithet of many gentilicia [1]. Famous persons: the jurist Salvius I. [1]; the doctor I. [2]; the emperor I. [11], called 'Apostata'; the bishops I. [16] of Aeclanum and I. [21] of Toledo.

1 RE 10, 26, s.v. I. (25).

[1] L. Octavius Cornelius P. Salvius I. Aemilianus. Jurist, born about AD 100 in North Africa, died about AD 170; he was a student of → Iavolenus [2] Priscus (Dig. 40,2,5) and the last head of the Sabinian law school (Dig. 1,2,2,53). I., whose succession of offices is preserved in the inscription from Pupput, province of Africa (CIL VIII 24094; [2. 411ff.]), was praetor in AD 138 and consul in AD 148, served on the Imperial council of Hadrian and probably also that of Antoninus Pius, as well as that of the *divi fratres* L. Verus and Antoninus Pius [1; 4. 263ff.]. On the instruction of Hadrian, who particularly valued the legal competence of I. (the inscription from Pupput mentions the doubling of his quaestor's salary *propter insignem doctrinam*, 'due to his remarkable erudition'; cf. [2. 419f.; 4. 238, 256f.]), he carried out the final editing of the praetorian edict (→ Edictum [2] perpetuum; *Tanta* § 18; [3]) in AD 131. The editing of the edict was based on a survey of the → *Ius B*; I.'s only innovation was the so-called *nova clausula Iuliani*: division in two of the inheritance (*bonorum possessio*, → *bona*) between the emancipated son and the grandchildren of the testator who remained under the power of their grandfather (Dig. 37,8,3; [2. 424f.]). I. did not believe in the possibility of settling every legal dispute exclusively through the application of laws (Dig. 1,3,10f.) and recommended that the holder of jurisdiction close loopholes through analogy (Dig. 1,3,12). He wrote no commentary on the edict or the remaining sources of established law, but rather depended on the organizational structure of the edict (→ Digesta system) in dealing with actual or hypothetical legal cases.

I.'s *Digesta* (90 bks.; [2. 431ff.; 4. 231, 245]), which were published under Antoninus Pius after AD 150, are an example of abstract casuistry, which reduces legal cases to a few brief surveys. With his solutions inspired by → *aequitas* (justice) or *utilitas* (interests), I. smoothed over the traditional conflict between Sabinians and Proculians (→ Law schools). Although he very rarely used citations himself, he became the most cited jurist in later years [5. 105]. His digests, which were probably already annotated by → Iunius [III 4] Mauricianus and later → Ulpius [8] Marcellus, Cervidius → Scaevola [1] and → Iulius [IV 16] Paulus, were placed by Justinian's compilers – as the height of Roman jurisprudence – at the head of their index of the texts used for the → Digesta (*Index Florentinus*). I.'s smaller works [2. 434ff.] *Ex Minicio* (6 bks.) and *Ad Urseium Ferocem* (4 bks.) fall back on the Sabinian school tradition through little-known intermediaries. His early work, *De ambiguitatibus* (1 bk.), was dedicated to the clarification of 'uncertainties' in the interpretation of legal matters [2. 438f.]. In it, I. proved himself to be an expert in formal logic (Dig. 34,5,13), however, he later warned against the danger of its strict application (Dig. 50,17,65) and disregarded it with reference to the common good (Dig. 9,2,51,2), because not all law could be rationally explained (Dig. 1,3,15; Dig. 1,3,20; on this [5. 105]). Decisions by I. are also extensively recorded in the *Quaestiones* of his pupil Sex. → Caecilius [III 1] Africanus.

1 PIR III, 164ff.   2 E. BUND, Salvius I., Leben und Werk, in: ANRW II 15, 1976, 408–454   3 WIEACKER, RRG 468ff.   4 R. A. BAUMAN, Lawyers and Politics in the Early Roman Empire, 1989   5 D. LIEBS, Jurisprudenz, in: HLL 4, 1997, 83–217.   T.G.

[2] (Iulianos) Doctor of the Methodist school, active between AD 140 and 175; student of Apollonides of Cyprus, who, in turn, was a student of Olympicus (Gal. Methodus Medendi 1,7 = 10,53f. K.). He taught in Alexandria, where Galen followed him, even if only to find confirmation in his lessons of those nonsensical views which had been reported to him earlier. I. wrote a work 'On Mental and Physical Diseases' (Gal. Adversus Iulianum 3,1–7 = CMG 5,10,3, pp. 40–42), as well as a work with the title 'Philo', in which he set out the methods of the → Methodists. Whether the bitumen plaster, which is ascribed to I. in a lemma in Galen (De compositione medicamentorum 2,22 = 13,557 K.), was indeed his idea, or occurred in one of the two named works, cannot be said with certainty. I. also wrote an introduction to medicine, which underwent several revisions, because, thus Galen (Methodus Medendi 1,7 = 10,53 K.), its author was allegedly always dissatisfied with his own formulations. He also annotated the Hippocratic 'Aphorisms' in 48 bks. One passage from the 2nd bk. of this commentary offered Galen (Adversus Iulianum = CMG 5,10,3, pp. 33–70) a fitting opportunity to denounce I.'s alleged errors: I.'s writing is long-winded, distorted and unphilosophical, he does not remain faithful to → Hippocrates [6] and is not able to give a short and coherent answer to questions. As a Methodist, I. could never please Galen anyway, yet his interpretation of the 'Aphorisms' shows, at any rate, that in his day there were various patterns of interpretation, which differed considerably from a later Hippocratic tradition. V.N.

[3] In AD 197, → Septimius [II 7] Severus, after his victory over → Clodius [II 1] Albinus, forced the latter's follower I. to betray his partisans under torture, although he had earlier assured him of immunity (Cass. Dio 74,9,5). PIR² I 93. T.F.

[4] **I. the Chaldaean** and
[5] **I. the Theurgist** were father and son, who, according to ancient and Byzantine sources, introduced → theurgy; wrote down the → Oracula Chaldaica, which were supposedly dictated to them by → Hecate and → Apollo; and authored a variety of works on magic and philosophy. The father is said to have lived under Trajan; the son accompanied Marcus Aurelius on his campaigns and supposedly helped him by splitting a rock with magic, creating a mask which hurled lightning at the enemy, and summoning rain to save the army from dying of thirst; this rain miracle was claimed by a variety of religious groups for their miracle workers (Suda s.v. Ἰουλιανός, I 433 and 434; Psellus, Scripta Minora 1,446; Sozom. Hist. eccl. 1,18,7). According to another legend, the younger I. competed with → Apollonius [14] of Tyana and → Ap(p)uleius [III] to save Rome from a plague; I. brought the epidemic to a standstill with a single word, which made him the victor (Anastasius Sinaiticus, PG 89, 252ab). Both summoned the dead; the father is supposed to have summoned Plato's soul and introduced it to his son (Procl. In Platonis rem publicam 2,123,9; Psellus, De aurea catena Homeri 217,2–7).

R. Majercik, The Chaldean Oracles. Text, Translation, Commentary, 1989, 1–5; S.I. Johnston, Rising to the Occasion: Theurgic Ascent in its Cultural Milieu, in: P. Schaefer, H. Kippenberg (ed.), Envisioning Magic. A Princeton Seminar and Symposium, 1997, 165–194; G. Fowden, Pagan Versions of the Rain Miracle of AD 172, in: Historia 36, 1987, 83–95. S.I.J.

[6] **(Iulianos)** Greek grammarian and lexicographer of the 2nd cent. AD. According to Phot. (Bibl., cod. 150 [99a-b]), he wrote an alphabetic 'lexicon of the ten Attic orators' vocabulary' (Λεξικὸν τῶν παρὰ τοῖς δέκα ῥήτορσι λέξεων), which is said to have been of great use to those reading the orators, by virtue of its scope and wealth of citations, as well as its explanations of Attic legal terminology, and of historical references. Photius compares it to the analogous work of Valerius Diodorus (the son of the philosopher and grammarian Valerius Pollio, from the Hadrianic period).

L. Cohn, Griech. Lexikographie, in: Brugmann/Thumb, 696; A. Gudeman, s.v. I. (2), RE 10, 9–10; W. Schmid, s.v. Diodoros (46), RE 5, 708. F.M.

[7] **Imp. Caes. M.A. (Sabinus) I. Aug.** Alleged *corrector* in Venetia (Aur. Vict. Caes. 39,10) or *praef. praet.* of → Carinus (Zos. 1,73), who calls him Sabinus Iulianus. I. accepted the purple in Italy (after the death of Carus, Aur. Vict. Caes. 39,10 or only after the death of Numerianus in AD 284, Aur. Vict. Epit. Caes. 38,6), but was defeated at Verona by Carinus and killed (Aur. Vict. epit. Caes. 38,6; Zos. 1,73).

PIR² A 1538; PLRE 1, 474, no. 24; RIC 5,2, 181ff.; Kienast, ²1996, 263. A.B.

[8] **I. Nestor.** Under Caracalla (AD 211–217), leader, together with Ulpius Iulianus, of the → secret police and notorious for his machinations (Cass. Dio 78, 15,1). Despite their obvious incompetence, Caracalla's successor, Macrinus (217/18), appointed them both as praetorian prefects in 217; I. was killed in Syria by Elagabalus in AD 218 (Cass. Dio 79,3,4). PIR² I 99. T.F.

[9] Greek rhetor from Caesarea in Cappadocia, contemporary of the Neoplatonist → Aedesius [1], thus probably c. AD 275–340. He lived and taught in Athens for the majority of his life; our only significant source, Eunapius (VS 482–485), emphasizes that I. took first place by far among all contemporary rhetors. He therefore had numerous students, among them such famous names as Diophantus of Arabia, Epiphanius, Tuscianus, Hephaestion and Prohaeresius; he bequeathed his Athenian house, which Eunapius still saw there, to Prohaeresius. Eunapius describes, above all, a dispute conducted before the Roman proconsul between the followers of I. and those of → Apsines. The allocation of the six letters to Iamblichus (Cumont), handed down under the name of the emperor I. (but not from him), to this I. is unfounded. PLRE 1, I. 5 M.W.

[10] Maternal uncle of the emperor I. [11] (Amm. Marc. 23,1,4). He was first *praeses Phrygiae* (Lib. Ep. 764), then *praefectus Aegypti* (Sozom. Hist. eccl. 5,7,9). He professed the Christian faith, but was converted to the old religion by Julian (Philostorgius 7,10) and named *comes Orientis* (362–363; Cod. Theod. 12,1,51; Cod. Iust. 8,35,12; Amm. Marc. 23,1,4). In Antioch, he severely prosecuted the Christians and, among other things, had their churches closed (*Passio Artemii* 23 in Philostorgius p. 82, Bidez). He died in office (Philostorgius 7,10). He received letters from I. [5] (Julian. Ep. 28 and 80 Bidez-Cumont) and Libanius (Lib. Ep. 701; 725). PLRE 1,470f. (I. 12). W.P.

[11] **Fl. Claudius I.** The emperor Iulianus Apostata (Julian the Apostate)
A. Sources B. Youth C. The Caesar D. The Emperor

A. Sources

I.'s letters and speeches form the kind of basis for a biography that in antiquity is available only for Cicero and Augustinus. The Codex Theodosianus contains c. 45 extracts from the emperor's laws; in addition, coins and inscriptions are also extant [1]. First among the primary literary sources is the *Res gestae* of → Ammianus Marcellinus, who probably met the Caesar in Gallia and accompanied the emperor on his Persian campaign. → Libanius worked numerous personal reminiscences and information into the 'Epitaphios' (Lib. Or. 18; cf. Or. 17). Despite their panegyrics, the new year's speech of the consul Claudius Mamertinus from AD 362 (Pan. Lat. 3 [11]) and the speeches of Libanius to the emperor (Lib. Or. 12–15) contain important historical material. To a lesser extent, this is also true for the 7th speech of Himerius, the two speeches written by Gregorius of Nazianzus, I.'s schoolmate in Athens, against the apostate after his death (Greg. Naz. or. 4–5), as well as the *Carmina Nisibena* of the Syrian → Ephrem. Of later authors, the non-Christians Eunapius and Zosimus see I. in the most favourable light, while for the Church historians Rufinus, Socrates, Sozomenus, Philostorgius and Theodoretus, he remains the Apostate. Neutral outlines are offered by Aurelius Victor, the *Epitome de Caesaribus* and Eutropius.

B. YOUTH

I. was born in May/June of 331 or 332 [7. 448–454] at Constantinople. His father, Iulius Constantius, was a half-brother of Constantine the Great; his mother, Basilina, died a few months after his birth. I. and his older half-brother, Gallus, survived the massacre to which several relatives, including his father, fell victim six months after Constantinus' [1] death at Constantinople in 337. The Arian bishop → Eusebius [8] of Nicomedia took in the orphan at first, and then the Gothic eunuch → Mardonius [2], who introduced him to the Greek classics. About 343/44, the emperor Constantius II sent his cousins → Constantius [5] Gallus and I. to the Cappadocian domain of Macellum. There, both appeared in Christian services as lectors, and I. made extensive use of a neighbouring bishop's library. When the emperor named Gallus as Caesar at the end of 351, I. was also allowed to leave Macellum and continue his education in Constantinople, Nicomedia and Pergamum. In Ephesus, he stayed for some time with the Neoplatonist and theurgist Maximus. From a later, simplifying perspective, it has been assumed that the decisive push for I.'s apostasy from Christianity came from Maximus [8]. After Gallus' execution in 354, Constantius first summoned I. to Milan, but then allowed him to continue his philosophical studies in Athens. At the end of 355, he named I. Caesar for Gallia, which was threatened by Germans. His marriage to Helena [3], the emperor's sister, was supposed to ensure the loyalty of the Caesar, whom the empress Eusebia also supported.

C. THE CAESAR

At first, the *praefectus praetorio Galliarum* still supervised the Caesar to a certain degree. Yet, thanks to his tireless efforts and a good relationship with the troops, I. quickly gained in stature. By 356, he had already freed Cologne from Frankish occupation and subsequently went on joint operations along the upper Rhine with Constantius, who was stationed in Raetia.

In 357, he defeated a coalition of Alemanni under Chnodomar near Strasbourg and endeavoured to secure Gallia as far as the Rhine in 358/59. He used the winter months to study philosophy, and about 356 and 358 wrote two speeches on Constantius (Julian Or. 1; 3) and one on Eusebia (Julian Or. 2). When Constantius wanted to deploy units from Gallia against the Persians in 360, they refused and proclaimed the Caesar as Augustus in Paris. Apparently unwillingly, I. gave in; to what extent he had thought of an elevation himself is disputed [7. 409–447]. In vain, he attempted to win Constantius over to co-rulership, based on models offered by the imperial structure since Diocletian. In order to forestall an attack by the emperor, I. advanced along the Danube in April 361 as far as the pass of Succi, but withdrew to Naissus (modern Niš) to show his willingness to negotiate. There he learned that Constantius had died on 3 November in Mopsucrene in Asia Minor, after having confirmed him as his successor.

D. THE EMPEROR

I. first appeared in public as a follower of the old religion after Constantius' death. In 362/63, he wrote to the Alexandrians (Julian. Ep. 111) that he was now in the twelfth year of his path to the gods. Based on this personal testimony, a conversion at the age of twenty has often been assumed; with Libanius (Lib. Or. 18,19) and Ammianus (Amm. Marc. 22,5,1), its secrecy was explained as caution toward the distrustful Constantius. However, with the image of the path, I. was indicating a long religious development, which only led to ultimate conversion with the surprising political turn of events [8]. In Constantinople, I. sought to eliminate irregularities in public administration and justice through numerous laws. In order to strengthen the financial standing of the communities, he lowered taxes and abolished the exemption of clerics from the decurionate. He had temples restored and recalled Athanasius and other Catholic bishops from exile. But his hope that the old and new religions could live peacefully side by side remained illusory. Bloody riots ensued in some cities in the east. I.'s decrees, which strengthened the old religions, did not contribute to a reconciliation. His school edict, which barred Christian teachers from higher instruction, met with a lack of understanding, even from non-Christians. I. engaged in religious-philosophical propaganda in the literary speeches on the mother of the gods (Julian Or. 8) and Helius (Julian Or. 11), and in the pamphlets against the Cynics (Julian Or. 7; 9). In the apology *Contra Galilaeos*, which is preserved in fragments, he took up old accusations against Christianity. In the *Symposium*, written for the Saturnalia of 361, in which the Roman emperors argue over precedence before the gods, he allowed Marcus Aurelius to win (Julian Or. 10).

In the middle of 362, I. set out for Antioch to prepare for the war against Persia. He fell out with the Antiochians and answered them in the *Misopogon* (Julian Or. 7). He declined a peace offering from king Sapor II, and opened the war in March 363. As he advanced along the Euphrates, he met with only scattered resistance. However, Sapor's scorched-earth tactics proved effective when, despite a victory near Ctesiphon, I. could not conquer the city itself. He had to turn back, and because he had burned the transport fleet, which had been an impediment, it was difficult to supply the army, which increasingly suffered under Persian attacks. On 26 June, in a skirmish at Maranga on the Tigris, I. was struck by a spear and died a few hours later. He was buried in Tarsus. Soon thereafter, a discussion arose whether a Christian from his own ranks had thrown the spear, or whether the emperor had sought his own death in battle after the failure of his unnecessary undertaking [7. 455–507].

In the 4th and 5th cents., the name I. remained a symbol in the struggle between 'pagans' and Christians; afterwards, he was overtaken by legend, from which only modern historiography has sought to free him. But even in the 20th cent., the personality and the religious struggle of the Apostate held a fascination which went far beyond scholarly interest [6] and gave him an after-life that can only be compared to that of Alexander and Caesar.

EDITIONS: J. BIDEZ, F. CUMONT (ed.), Imperatoris Caesaris Flavii Claudii Iuliani epistulae, leges, poematia, fragmenta varia, 1922   J. BIDEZ et al. (ed.), L'empereur Julien. Oeuvres complètes, 1,1, 1932; ²1972; 1,2, 1924; ³1972; 2,1, 1963; 2,2, 1964   E. MASARACCHIA (ed.), Giuliano imperatore contra Galilaeos, 1990 (with transl.) B. K. WEIS (ed.), Julian. Briefe, Greek-German, 1973.
BIBLIOGRAPHY: 1 J. ARCE, Estudios sobre el emperador Fl.C. Juliano, 1984   2 P. ATHANASSIADI, Julian and Hellenism, ²1992   3 J. BIDEZ, La vie de l'empereur Julien, 1930, repr. 1965   4 J. BOUFFARTIGUE, L'empereur Julien et la culture de son temps, 1992   5 G. W. BOWERSOCK, Julian the Apostate, 1978   6 R. BRAUN, J. RICHER (ed.), L'empereur Julien. De l'histoire à la légende (331–1715), 1978; De la légende au mythe (de Voltaire à nos jours), 1981   7 R. KLEIN (ed.), Julian Apostata, 1978   8 K. ROSEN, Julians Weg vom Christentum zum Heidentum, in: JbAC 40, 1997, 126–146.   K.R.

[12] **Amnius Anicius I.** Was *proconsul Africae* around AD 300 (ILS 1220, Collatio Mosaicarum et Romanarum legum 15,3 MOMMSEN). The consulate which was granted to him by Constantine I in 322 (ILS 6111c) was not recognized by Licinius. From 13 November, 326 until 7 September 329, he was *praefectus urbis Romae* (Chron. min. 1,67; 68 MOMMSEN; Cod. Theod. 6,4,1f. etc.). He was the father of Amnius Anicius Paulinus iunior (*consul* 334) and possibly the son of Anicius Faustus (*consul II* 298). (PLRE 1,473f.: I. 23).
[13] **Iulius I.** Under Licinius, he was first *praefectus Aegypti* (AD 314), then *praefectus praetorio* from 315–324 (ILS 8938). Constantinus [1] praised his administration (Lib. Or. 18,9) and promoted him to consul in 325 (Socr. 1,13,13). He was the father of Basilina, the mother of the emperor I. [11] (Socr. 3,3,21). (PLRE 1,478: I. 35).

[14] Came from Tarsus, was (before AD 359) *praeses Phrygiae* (Lib. Ep. 1363). He was accepted into the senate of Constantinople in 359 (Lib. Ep. 40). In 361, he was *praeses Euphratensis* (Lib. Ep. 1363), and *censitor Bithyniae* (Lib. Ep. 1367) in 363. He received numerous letters from Libanius (Lib. Ep. 673; 678; 689 etc.). He is not identical (*pace* KlP 2, 1517, no. 8) with the like-named friend of Gregorius of Nazianzus, a Christian who was *peraequator* in Cappadocia around 374/375 (Greg. Naz. Or. 19; Epist. 67–69). (PLRE 1, 472: I. 17, cf. 471: I. 14).
[15] Came from Syria, was *consularis Phoenices* (Cod. Theod. 12,1,52) in AD 362, and *comes Orientis* (Cod. Iust. 1,4,1) in 364. He was educated (Lib. Ep. 668) and had a close relationship with Libanius (cf. Lib. Ep. 1296–1298). (PLRE 1,472: I. 15).   W.P.
[16] Born *c.* AD 385 in Apulia; as the son of a bishop, I. enjoyed a good education and married Titia, daughter of a bishop. Consecrated as deacon in 408, I. became bishop of Aeclanum in Campania in 416. While still a deacon, I. was invited, through his father Memorius, to visit → Augustinus in Hippo (Aug. Epist. 101). In 418, I. and eighteen other Italian bishops refused to sign the papal condemnation (*Epistola tractoria*) of → Pelagius [4]; I. supported Pelagius and his teachings with the *comes* Valerius and Pope Zosimus. Condemnation by pope and emperor (9 June, 419) followed promptly; excommunicated, I. lost his see and home and made his way to → Theodorus [I 25] of Mopsuestia in Cilicia. In 428/9, he stayed in Constantinople with bishop → Nestorius, who was ordered by Pope Coelestinus to endorse the condemnation of I. The Council of Ephesus (431) confirmed the condemnation of I. and his comrades. By that time I. had already been forced to leave Constantinople on imperial orders. His later fate is unclear: he may have sought rehabilitation in 439; he appears to have died before 455 (Gennadius, Vir. ill. 45).

The lasting influence of I. is based on his exegetic and polemic writings. From exile, he conducted his famous theological debate with Augustine (4 bks. to Turbantius; 8 bks. to Florus): I. defended the Pelagian position (emphasis on the justice of the Creator and the goodness of Creation, as well as the integrity of human free will, condemnation of Augustine's teaching of original sin and sexual desire as Manichaean) and thus forced Augustine to render more precisely his theology of grace and sin.

EDITIONS: CPL 773–777; L. DE CONINCK, M. J. D'HONT (ed.), CCL 88/88A; E. KALINKA, M. ZELZER (ed.), Augustinus contra Julianum, CSEL 85,1; PL 45, 1337–1608; 48, 509–526; Acta Conciliorum Oecumenicorum 1,5, 12–19.
BIBLIOGRAPHY: J. S. ALEXANDER, s.v. Julian von Aeclanum TRE 17, 441–443; F. NUVOLONE, A. SOLIGNAC, s.v. Pélage et Pélagianisme, Dictionnaire de Spiritualité XII,2, 2902–2908 (with additional literature); F. REFOULÉ, Julian d'Éclane, Théologien et philosophe, in: Recherches de science religieuse 52, 1964, 42–84; 233–247.   W.LÖ.

[17] **I. Pomerius.** see → Pomerius

[18] **I. of Halicarnassus.** Monophysite bishop and theologian; he was driven from his see by Justin I. In AD 518, together with → Severus [3] of Antioch, who had supported him in his dispute with the Patriarch Macedonius of Constantinople (496–511), he went into exile in Alexandria, where he died after 527. There, he fell out with Severus, because he taught the permanent incorruptibility of the body of Christ (while the other supported the incorruptibility of the body of Christ only after the Resurrection [3. 2/2, 25f.]); substantial fragments of his polemics against Severus have survived (CPG 3, 7125 and 7126). Thus, on one hand, I. became the head of the 'Aphthartodocetics' (Julianists or Phantasiasts), and on the other hand, a condemned heretic, splitting the 'Monophysite' movement, which was directed against the Council of Chalcedon (→ Monophysitism). A careful analysis of the positions can show that the dispute was over terminology rather than theology [3. 2/2, 111].

The Job commentary edited by D. Hagedorn [4], which has been attributed to a subordinating homoean theologian named I., is not by I. of Halicarnassus.

1 R. Draguet, Julien d'Halicarnasse et sa controverse avec Sévère d' Antioche sur l'incorruptibilité du corps du Christ, 1924   2 A. Sanda (ed.), Severi Antiulianistica, 1931   3 A. Grillmeier, Jesus der Christus im Glauben der Kirche 2/1, 1986; 2/2, 1989, 83–116   4 D. Hagedorn, Der Hiobkomm. des Arianers Julian (Patristische Texte und Studien 14), 1973.   C.M.

[19] **I. of Laodicea.** Astrological writer, born 26 October AD 497. His Ἐπίσκεψις ἀστρονομική (*Epískepsis astronomikḗ*) uses → Petosiris and → Ptolemaeus [65] (particularly the Meteorology Ap. 2,14); the *Katarchaí* also uses → Dorotheus [5]. I., for his part, is used by → Rhetorius, → Theophilus [8] of Edessa and Abū Ma'šar.

→ Astrology; → Meteorology

Fragments: F. Cumont (ed.), CCAG I, 1898, 134–139; IV, 1903, 99–103; VI, 1903, 80; VIII 4, 1921, 244–253; W. and H. G. Gundel, Astrologumena, 1966, 248–249; F. Cumont, P. Stoobant, La date où vivait l'astrologue Julien de Laodicée, in: Bull. de l'Académie Royale de Belgique, Classe des Lettres et des Sciences Morales et Politiques, 1903, 554–574.   W.H.

[20] Egyptian, epigrammatist of the 'Kyklos' of Agathias, very probably to be equated with the I. who, in AD 530/31, was praetorian prefect, involved in the politics of → Hypatius [4] (executed 532) and addressee of two funerary epigrams (Anth. Pal. 7,591f.). His approximately 70 poems (except for the erotic poem, ibid. 5,298, and the Anacreontic, ibid. 16,388, all are funerary or epideictic) take up traditional themes (and imitate, above all, → Antiphilus [3], → Antipater [8] of Sidon, → Leonidas [3] of Tarentum and → Posidippus [2]); personal inspiration is rare and can only be found in the poems addressed to contemporaries (cf. e.g.

Anth. Pal. 9,445; 9,661). This I. is probably identical with I. Scholastikos, the author of Anth. Pal. 9,481 (the contemptuous epithet *Metéōros* probably goes back to a confusion with the emperor I. Apostata).

Al. and Av. Cameron, The 'Cycle' of Agathias, in: JHS 86, 1966, 12–14; H. v. Schulte, Julian von Ägypten, 1990 (ed. with transl. and comm.).   M.G.A.

[21] **I. of Toledo.** born around 642, died 6 March 690. I. came from an originally Jewish family, which converted to Christianity; he was a student of archbishop → Eugenius [4] II, was named archbishop of Toledo in 680 and presided over the 12th–15th synods in Toledo (681–688). His extant works display great learning: *Prognosticon futuri saeculi* (systematic eschatology), *Apologeticum de tribus capitulis* (on the dispute of the Three Chapters), *De comprobatione sextae aetatis libri III* (apologetic work on the 6th age of the world), *Antikeimena libri II* (deals with contradictory passages in the Old and New Testaments), *Historia Wambae regis* (on the reign of the Visigothic king Wamba and the suppression of a rebellion by Paulus in Visigothic Gallia), *Epistula ad Modoenum* (on rhythmic and metric poetry), *Elogium Ildefonsi* (appendix to *De viris illustribus* by Ildefonso of Toledo) and a *Grammatica* (model: Donatus [3]). Lost or not identified are poems, letters, sermons, excerpts from Augustine and other theological writings.

→ Donatus

PL 96, 427–818 (Antikeimena lib. II)   2 CCL 115, I 3 Brunhölzl, vol. 1, 103–110; 523   4 L. Munzi, Il *De partibus orationis* di Giuliano di T., 1983   5 M. A. H. Maestre Yenes (ed.), Ars Juliani Toletani episcopi, 1973   6 S. Teillet, Des Goths à la nation gothique, 1984, 585–636.   JÖ.RI.

[22] **I. of Ascalon.** Called Ἀρχιτέκτων/*Architéktōn*. From his work on the customs and traditions in Palestine (probably from the Byzantine era), a section on the measurements of length, distance and acreage used there is extant.

F. Hultsch, Metrologicorum scriptorum reliquiae, vol. 1, 1864, 54f., 200f.; Id., Griech. und röm. Metrologie, ²1882, 437f., 597–601; O. Viedebantt, s.v. I. (10), RE 10, 17–19; Id., Forsch. zur Metrologie des Alt., 1917, 123ff.   M.F.

Iuliobriga (Celtic for 'castle of Iulius'; [1. 87]). Probably a foundation by Augustus dating from the Cantabrian campaign [2. 195]. Remains near the village of Retortillo, 3 km south of Reinosa, not far from the source of the Ebro. References: Plin. HN 3,21; 27; 4,111; Ptol. 2,6,50; Not. Dign. Occ. 42,30; CIL II Suppl. p. 1148.

1 Holder 2, 1919   2 A. Schulten, Los Cántabros y Astures, 1943.

A. García y Bellido, Excavaciones en Iuliobriga, in: Archivio español de arqueología 26, 1953, 193ff.; 29, 1956, 131ff.; A. Hernándes Morales, Juliobriga, 1946;

A. SCHULTEN, Forsch. in Spanien, in: AA 1940, I,2, 78f.
P.B.

Iulium Carnicum Venetic, later Celtic (→ Carni) settlement centre, probably constituted as a Roman *vicus* after the attack of the → Iapodes in 52 BC. *Municipium* since Augustus, *colonia* since Claudius. Location: on the road from Aquileia to Aguntum. Local Belenus cult. After its destruction, most likely by → Alaricus [2], the inhabitants moved to the hill of San Pietro, modern Zuglio. Archaeology: forum with *porticus*, *capitolium*, in the south a *basilica*; thermal baths; aqueduct; early Christian cemetery basilica.

P. M. MORO, I.C., 1956; G. BANDELLI, F. FONTANA (ed.), I.C., Convegno, Arta 1995, 1997.
G.U.

Iuliupolis (Ἰουλιούπολις; *Ioulioúpolis*). Originally Gordiou Kome, settlement in Galatia where the road from Nicaea to Ancyra crossed over the → Scopas (Procop. Aed. 5,4). Home of the dynast Cleon, who defected to Augustus in 31 BC. The settlement was named I. in his honour and extended to become a city (Str. 12,8,9; Plin. HN 5,143). After 25/4 BC it belonged to Bithynia (Plin. HN 5,149), from the time of Diocletian to the province of Galatia, then to Galatia I. Also called Basilaion (Basileon) in honour of Basilius I. A bishopric since the beginning of the 4th cent. Today for the most part flooded by the Sarıyar reservoir.

BELKE, 181f.; K. STROBEL, Die Galater, vol. 2, in print; W. WEISER, Röm. Stadtmz. aus Bithynia et Pontus, in: SNR 68, 1989, 67.
K.ST.

Iulius Name of an old patrician family, probably connected with the name of the god → Jupiter [1. 281; 2. 729]. The *gens* was one of the so-called 'Trojan families', who were said to have moved from Alba Longa to Rome under king Tullus Hostilius [I 4] (see below). The Iulii were prominent in the 5th and 4th cents. BC. Their connection to the family branch of the Caesares, which rose to prominence from the 3rd cent. and whose outstanding member was the dictator → Caesar (with family tree), is unclear. Caesar's adoptive son, later the emperor → Augustus, founded the → Julio-Claudian dynasty (family tree). Owing to the many manumissions and conferrals of citizenship under Caesar and the first emperor, the name I. itself became very widespread. From at least the 2nd half of the 2nd cent. BC, the Caesares traced their lineage back to the goddess → Venus via → Iulus (= Ascanius) the son of Aeneas and their origin to his foundation Alba Longa; the dictator Caesar attached particular importance to this (Liv. 1,30,2; Serv. Aen. 1,267; Verg. Aen. 1,288; Dion. Hal. Ant. Rom. 3,29,7; Suet. Iul. 6,1; Tac. Ann. 11,24,2; coins: RRC 258 and 320; summarized: [4. 5–18]). In 45 BC, the dictator even donned the official dress of the Alban kings (Cass. Dio 43,43,2). → Bovillae, on the site of Alba, was the seat of the family cult and games

(ILLRP 270: consecration of the *genteiles Iuliei* on Vediovis early 2nd cent. BC.; Dion. Hal. Ant. Rom. 1,70,4; Tac. Ann. 2,41,1; 15,23,3). There was an *ara gentis Iuliae* on the Capitol [5. 369ff.]; communal patronage of Ilium was hereditary (ILS 8770). Praenomina: → C., L., Sex. also Augustus, Agrippa, Caesar, Caligula, Drusus, Frontinus, Germanicus [2], Historia Augusta, Hyginus, Obsequens, Postumus, Severianus, Sohaemus, Solinus, Theodotus, Tiberius, Titianus.

1 SCHULZE   2 WALDE/HOFMANN I   3 F. MÜNZER, S.V. I., RE 10,1   4 ST. WEINSTOCK, Divus Julius, 1971 5 E. DE LA ROCCA, s.v. Gens Iulia, ara, LTUR 2.   K.-L.E.

I. REPUBLICAN ERA   II. IMPERIAL ERA   III. BISHOPS   IV. LITERARY FIGURES

I. REPUBLICAN ERA

[I 1] I., C. According to annalistic tradition, *cos.* 447 BC, *cos. iI* 435, III 434.; irrecoverable as a historical figure.

[I 2] I., C. Said to have attempted to have two patricians elected consuls (Liv. 7,21,9; 7,22,1) in 352 BC while he was dictator.

[I 3] I., Proculus. According to a widespread Roman legend, the apotheosized Romulus appeared to him as the god → Quirinus (Cic. Rep. 2, 20; Cic. Leg. 1, 3; Ov. Fast. 2, 499; Dion. Hal. Ant. Rom. 2,63, 2ff.; Liv. 1, 16, 5; Plut. Romulus 28, 1; Numa 2,3 etc.). This legend, already known to Cicero before Caesar's autocratic rule, was intended to draw a connection between the Iulii and the founder of Rome.

IULII CAESARES

[I 4] I. Caesar, C. Father of the dictator → Caesar, quaestor shortly after 100 BC, praetor around 92, then governor in Asia, died 85 in Pisae (InscrIt 13,3, no. 7; 75a; Plin. HN 7,181; Suet. Iul. 1,1). Married to Aurelia [1], brother-in-law of C. → Marius. MRR 2, 19²; 22.

[I 5] I. Caesar, L. Brother of I. [I 11]; with his relatives took part in the defeat of L. Appuleius [I 11] Saturninus (Cic. Rab. perd. 21), applied unsuccessfully for quaestorship, became praetor not later than 94 BC, then proconsul in Macedonia. As consul in 90 BC, he fought successfully in the → Social War [3] against the Samnites (App. B Civ. 1, 40–42; Liv. Per. 73 etc.), promulgated a law providing for the conferral of citizenship on loyal Latins and Italians, and thereby brought about an end of the war (Cic. Balb. 21; Gell. NA 4,4,3; App. B Civ. 1,49, cf. ILS 8888). As censor in 89 BC with P. Licinius Crassus, he began the process of dividing the new citizens among the tribus (MRR 2, 32). One of the most prominent victims of the Civil War, he was murdered with his brother by the Marians when they took Rome in 87.
K.-L.E.

[I 6] I. Caesar, L. Son of I. [I 5], uncle of the triumvir M. Antonius [I 9], quaestor in Asia 77 BC, praetor 67 (?) (MRR 2,89; 143; 575). As consul of 64, he initiated a Senate decree banning political associations (*collegia*

sublata sunt; Ascon. 7C). During the famous trial of the Catilinarians (→ Catilina) on 5 December 63, he demanded the death penalty for all prisoners (including his brother-in-law, Cic. Cat. 4,13). He became censor in 61 [1. 118ff.]. As such, he is mentioned in a statute concerning the exemption of Delos from public burdens (Roman Statutes 1, 1996, no. 22, l. 22). An honorary inscription from Ilion concerning exemption from property taxes (ILS 8770) probably also refers to him, rather than his father, as was hitherto assumed (MRR 3,110). From 52 to 49, he rendered service in the protection of Gallia Narbonensis as Caesar's legate (Caes. B Gall. 7,65,1). It is unclear whether he later transferred his allegiance to Pompey, like his son. Siding against his nephew Antonius following Caesar's death earned him second place after the brother of Lepidus on the triumvir's proscription list at the end of 43 BC (App. B Civ. 4,45). He was pardoned, but died soon afterwards.

1 CL. NICOLET, Insula sacra, 1980.

[I 7] I. Caesar, L. Son of I. [I 6]; early in 49 BC, he attempted to negotiate between his relative Caesar and Pompey. I. followed the latter, was commander of a small fleet in 48/47, and proquaestor with Cato in Africa in 47/46. As the victor of Thapsus, Caesar publicly pardoned him, only to have him assassinated in secret (Cass. Dio 43,12,3). W.W.

[I 8] I. Caesar, Sex. Legate in the east in 170 BC (Liv. 43,4,12–13). *Aed. cur.* 165, consul 157, the first of his family to ascend to the post (MRR 1, 446ff.). In 147 he led a mission to the Peloponnese to negotiate between the Spartans and the Achaeans (Pol. 38, 9–11; Cass. Dio fr. 72), after an earlier delegation under L. Aurelius [I 14] Orestes (*cos.* 157) had failed. MRR 1, 464. P.N.

[I 9] I. Caesar, Sex. Probably brother of [I 4], praetor no later than 94 BC, consul 91 (MRR 2, 20), in 90 BC he fought in the → Social War [3] and died of an illness during the siege of Asculum (in sources often confused with I. [I 5]; App. B Civ. 1,48; Liv. Per. 73). K.-L.E.

[I 10] I. Caesar, Sex. *Amicus et necessarius* of the future dictator Caesar (Bell. Alex. 66,1), on whose side he fought in Spain in 49 BC during the Civil War (Caes. B Civ. 2,20,7). Quaestor in 48, governor of Syria from July 47 BC with a legion. He was overthrown there in mid–46 BC by the Pompeian Q. Caecilius [I 5] Bassus and was murdered by his own troops. On the identity of the *flamen Quirinalis* of 58, Sex. I. Caesar (RE no. 152), see MRR 2,199. W.W.

[I 11] I. Caesar Strabo (Vopiscus), C. Brother of I. [I 5], uncle of I. [I 4], in 103 BC member of a commission for the implementation of the agricultural law of L. Appuleius [I 11] Saturninus, quaestor before 96, curule aedile 90, prior to 99 until his death in 87 (Cic. Brut. 305; InscrIt 13,3, no. 6; Ascon. 25C). In 88, he applied for the consulship of 87 in contravention of the *lex annalis*, thus ensnaring himself in the turmoil of the Civil War. He was killed in 87 with his brother by the Marians (Cic. Brut. 307).

J.-M. DAVID, Le patronate judiciaire au dernier siècle de la republique romaine, 1992, 728. K.-L.E.

I. was highly regarded as an orator and as a poet of tragedies by Asconius (Ascon. 26,28ff.) and to some extent also by Cicero. The unconventional titles of three tragedies: *Adrastus, Tecmesa and Teutras* (the latter two perhaps after Hellenistic models) and the two preserved fragments suggest a Hellenizing tendency (cf. Mar. Vict. ars gramm. 6,8,6–10); the fragment Isid. Orig. 4,12,7 (= KLOTZ 305) is probably the work of the dictator → Caesar (COURTNEY 187, otherwise [4. 35ff.]). As an orator, mainly his urbanity, cheerfulness and jocularity are attested, but also *lenitas sine nervis* (Cic. Brut. 177; cf. De or. 2,98; 3,30; Tusc. 5,55; Off. 1,133) in accordance with the tragedies. In De or. 2,216ff., Cicero has him represent the theory of wit and humour [5; 8]. As a young man, Caesar is said to have taken him as an oratorical role model (Suet. Iul. 55).

EDITIONS: 1 TRF ²1871, 227f.; ³1897, 263f.
2 A. KLOTZ, SRF 1 (= TF), 1953, 304f. 3 ORF ⁴1976, 272–275, 537f. (cf. [4]).
BIBLIOGRAPHY: 4 E. BICKEL, C. Caesar L. f. Persona in Ciceronis Dialogo de Oratore, in: RhM 100, 1957, 1–41 5 M. A. GRANT, The Ancient Rhetorical Theories of the Laughable, 1924 6 B. R. KATZ, C.S.'s Struggle for the Consulship – and More, in: RhM 120, 1977, 45–63 7 A. KEAVENEY, Sulla, Sulpicius and C.S., in: Latomus 38, 1979, 451–460 8 G. MONACO, Cicerone. Il trattato de ridiculis, 1964 9 O. RIBBECK, Die röm. Trag. im Zeitalter der Republik, 1875, 610–614 10 G. V. SUMNER, The Orators in Cicero's Brutus, 1973, 105f. W.-L.L.

[I 12] I. Calidus, L. Equestrian, proscribed because of his ownership of land in Africa in 43 BC, but spared thanks to the efforts of T. Pomponius Atticus. According to Nepos, a noted poet of his age (Nep. Att. 12,4). Possibly identical with the L. I., whom Cicero recommended in 56 to the governor of Africa, Q. Valerius Orca (Cic. Fam. 13,6,3). JÖ.F.

IULII IULLI

[I 13] I. Iullus, C. Consul in 482 BC (probably not identical to the consul of 489 of the same name); in 451 one of the decemvirs, according to tradition exemplary in his impartiality because he abstained from exercising the penal powers of his office (Cic. Rep. 2,61; Liv. 3,33,10). In 449, he is said to have been one of the emissaries of the Senate to the *plebs* who had marched to the Aventine (→ Secessio), negotiating fruitlessly for their return (Liv. 3,50,15).

[I 14] I. Iullus, C. Consular tribune in 408 and 405 BC (beginning of the siege of Veii, Liv. 4,61,2); censor in 393, died in 392 in an epidemic while in office. Because the Gauls overran Rome during this → lustrum, the death of a censor was thereafter regarded as an evil omen, and led to the resignation of the dead man's colleague (Liv. 5,31,6f.).

[I 15] I. Iullus, L. (C.?) Consular tribune in 438 BC, in 431 cavalry officer of the dictator A. → Postumius Tubertus, consul in 430 BC with L. Papirius Crassus and originator of a *lex Iulia Papiria de multarum aestimatione*, by which the livestock fines in the Laws of the

Twelve Tables were replaced by monetary fines (Cic. Rep. 2,60; Liv. 4,30,3). MRR 1, 58; 63f.

[I 16] I. Iullus, Vopiscus. Consul in 473 BC. According to annalistic tradition, his period of office saw civil unrest (Liv. 2,54,3f.; Dion. Hal. Ant. Rom. 9,37).

[I 17] I. Libo, L. Consul in 267 BC, conquered Brundisium with his colleague M. Atilius [I 21] Regulus and triumphed (MRR 1,200).

[I 18] I. Mento, C. (Praenomen in Liv. 4,26,2 incorrectly given as Cn.). As consul in 431 BC, he consecrated the temple of Apollo Medicus near the Circus Flaminius (Liv. 4,27, 1; 29,7).

[I 19] (I.) Salinator, L. Legate of Sertorius, → Livius Salinator, L.(?).   K.-L.E.

[I 20] I. Salvius, C. Freedman of Caesar and → apparitor (CIL XI 7804 = ILS 9039; [1. 155–157; 196]). Maintained contact with Cicero (cf. for instance Cic. Att. 9,7,1).

> 1 S. TREGGIARI, Roman Freedmen during the Late Republic, 1969.   JÖ.F.

II. IMPERIAL PERIOD

[II 1] (Ti.) I. Father of Claudius Etruscus, to whom Statius devoted Silvae 3.3, when I. died at the age of 90 in AD 92. Born in Smyrna, I. came to Rome as an imperial slave; he was freed under Tiberius, accompanied Caligula to Gaul, and attained a higher position as *libertus* under Claudius. Under Nero probably active in an eastern province, where he became acquainted with Vespasian. Took part in the latter's triumph in AD 71, promoted to a *rationibus*, he later reached equestrian rank. Banished for 7 years by Domitian; returned around 90. Married to one Etrusca, by whom he had two sons; related to the senator (Tettius) Iulianus. He is an example of a *libertus Augusti*, who was active in the service of a number of rulers (→ Freedmen).

> PIR² C 763; P. WEAVER, Familia Caesaris, 1972, 284ff.; J. K. EVANS, in: Historia 27, 1978, 102ff.; I. A. CARRADICE, Coinage and Finances in the Reign of Domitian, 1983, 157f.

[II 2] I. Africanus. Gaul from the tribe of the Santones; in AD 32 he was drawn into the aftermath of the conspiracy of → Seianus and condemned (Tac. Ann. 6,7,4). Probably father of the orator I. [IV 1] Africanus.

[II 3] Cn. I. Agricola. Born 13 June AD 40 in Forum Iulii in the Narbonensis, Tac. Agr. 44,1. Both his grandfathers had equestrian rank, his father L. Iulius [II 70 = IV 9] Graecinus was a senator, his mother was Iulia [20] Procilla. Educated at Massilia, he became military tribune under Suetonius Paullinus in Britannia. After his marriage to Domitia Decidiana, a senator's daughter, he became *quaestor* in Asia, probably in 63/64 (VOGEL-WEIDEMANN 441), people's tribune in 66 and praetor in 68. In 69 he quickly joined Vespasian, was entrusted with the levying of recruits and finally appointed legate of the *legio XX Valeria* in Britannia by Mucianus (Tac. Agr. 7,3). He returned to Rome in 73,

was accepted into patrician rank by Vespasian during the censorship and appointed praetorian imperial governor of Aquitania, where he stayed less than three years (Agr. 9,6). Probably suffect consul in 77; in the same year he married his daughter to Cornelius Tacitus. Then consular governor of Britannia for 7 years, probably 77–84 [2. 72ff.]. Tacitus portrays (Agr. 18–39) above all his military activities in Britannia, but also that he encouraged cultural development among the Britons. He advanced as far as Scotland, and was victorious in battle in 83 against Calgacus at Mons Graupius (Agr. 29–38). Honoured in Rome with a triumphal statue and the *ornamenta triumphalia* (Agr. 40,1), shortly afterwards recalled – after such an exceptionally long governorship this was in no way surprising. Domitian's reasons, as put forward by Tacitus, can therefore not be taken at face value as historically reliable. Retirement into a more private life, did not participate in the drawing of lots for a proconsulship in Africa or Asia (Agr. 42,1). He did not actively oppose Domitian. He died on 23 August 93 (Tac. Agr. 44,1).

> 1 SYME, Tacitus, I, 19ff.   2 BIRLEY   3 P. SALWAY, Roman Britain, 1981, 138ff.   4 M-TH. RAEPSAET-CHARLIER, in: ANRW II 33,3, 1807ff.

[II 4] I. Agrippa. Participated in the Pisonian conspiracy in AD 65; banished to one of the Aegean islands. PIR² J 127.   W.E.

[II 5] M. I. Agrippa II. Son of → Herodes [8] I. Agrippa, born AD 28, educated in Rome; owing to his youth, he was not appointed as his father's successor in AD 44, but in 50 he received the kingdom of his uncle → Herodes [7] of Chalcis together with the charge of the Temple of Jerusalem and the right to appoint its high priests. In Rome he promoted Jewish interests with the emperor Claudius: in 44 during a controversy surrounding high-priestly garb (Jos. Ant. Iud. 20,9–15) and in 52 during the trial of the Roman *procurator* Cumanus (Jos. Ant. Iud. 134–136). His entreaties on behalf of the Jewish diaspora in Alexandria caused him to be brought to trial before Claudius by Isidorus, the spokesman for the anti-Jewish movement there [1]. In 53 he was awarded the tetrarchies of → Philippus (Batanaea, Trachonitis, Gaulanitis) and → Lysanias (Abila) and other lands in Lebanon in place of Chalcis. Nero enlarged his kingdom with cities in Galilee and Peraea. As a Roman vassal (Φιλοκαῖσαρ; *Philokaîsar* and Φιλορωμαῖος; *Philorōmaíos*: OGIS 419f.; 424) he took part in the Parthian campaign of 54, and, after 66, in the suppression of the Jewish Revolt, the outbreak of which he had in vain attempted to prevent. Vespasian, whose ascent to the imperial throne he supported, extended his kingdom northwards (Tac. Hist. 2,81). I.'s death occurred in the year 92/3. His kingdom was annexed.

I. represented Jewish interests, but his primary loyalty was to Rome. He sponsored the building of temples and had the streets of Jerusalem paved with marble, but, like his father, he also supported the pagan Hellenistic cities, such as Berytus, where he financed the construction of theatres and annual performances. He regarded the Jewish religion with distant interest: in the conflict between Paul and the Sanhedrin he appeared as remote from fanaticism as from inner sympathy (Acts 25f.). He corresponded with → Iosephus about the latter's account of the Jewish Revolt (*vita* 364–366), which he attested as an accurate description. Sources: Jos. BI 2,220; Jos. Ant. Iud. 19,354–20,213; Vita 32–410 passim.

1 V. TCHERIKOVER, A. FUKS (ed.), Corpus Papyrorum Iudaicorum, 1957–1964, 156 a-c.

A. H. M. JONES, The Herods of Judaea, ²1967, 217–261; SCHÜRER, vol. 1, 471–483. K.BR.

[II 6] I. Alexander. Son of Tigranes VI and great-nephew of Tigranes V of Armenia, great-great-grandson of → Herodes [1] the Great and Archelaus [7] Sisines of Cappadocia (Jos. Ant. Iud. 18,5,4). He was married to Iotape, daughter of Antiochus IV of Commagene, and was thus brother-in-law to I. [II 11] and [II 76]. After the incorporation of the Commagenian kingdom (AD 72), Vespasian seems to have created a client kingdom, Cetis or Cietis, out of Commagenian possessions in Rough Cilicia (where Archelaus once had also ruled). Cetis encompassed the valley of the Calycadnus and the coast and for a few years was ruled by I. and Iotape. During this time, → Babrius may have dedicated the second book of his fables to one of their sons. The lands of the small kingdom were incorporated into the province of Cilicia, perhaps under Domitian, and I. became a member of the Roman Senate while keeping the title of king. His later fate and that of his family are evident from inscriptions. One son, C. I. Agrippa, who was *quaestor pro praetore* of Asia around the turn of the 1st/2nd cents., was honoured by the Ephesians who placed his statue in the theatre (OGIS 429). Years later (but before AD 109, see [4. 154]) I. Alexander himself must have attained the rank of consul: in an inscription from AD 117 at Ancyra, dedicated to C. Iulius Severus, the consular King Alexander is numbered among his relatives (OGIS 544 = IGR III 173 = [1. no. 105]). (PIR² A 500, cf. PIR² J 141).

1 E. BOSCH, Quellen zur Gesch. der Stadt Ankara im Alt., 1967, 122–130 2 R. D. SULLIVAN, The Dynasty of Commagene, in: ANRW II 8, 1977, 732–798; 794f. 3 Id., Papyri Reflecting the Eastern Dynastic Network, in: ANRW II 8, 1977, 908–939, 936–938 4 R. SYME, Reviews and Discussion, in: JRS 43, 1953, 148–161 5 HALFMANN, 141. M.SCH.

[II 7] Ti. I. Alexander, see → Alexander [18]
[II 8] C. I. Alexander Berenicianus. Perhaps son of I. [II 6]; probably also related to the royal house of Herod. Senator; took part in the Parthian War; *cos. suff.* AD 116; proconsul of Asia probably 132/3, PIR² J 141. HALFMANN, 141.
[II 9] Ti. I. Alexander Capito. Son of one Gaius, of the tribus Cornelia. Equestrian, became *procurator Achaiae* under Nerva and Trajan, under Trajan also *procu-*

rator Asiae (before AD 102). AE 1966, 445 = IEph III 684A; PFLAUM, Suppl. 27ff.
[II 10] C. I. Antiochus. see → Antiochus [18] W.E.
[II 11] C. I. Antiochus Epiphanes. Son of Antiochus [18] IV of Commagene and his sister and spouse Iotape, elder brother of I. [II 76] and brother-in-law to I. [II 6]. He had been engaged to → Drusilla, daughter of Agrippa I., but the planned marriage failed due to religious differences (Jos. Ant. Iud. 19,9,1; 20,7,1). In April AD 69, he fought for Otho against Vitellius (Tac. Hist. 2,25,2), and in May/June 70 for Titus before Jerusalem (Jos. BI 5,11,3). Coin records indicate that I. was made king shortly before the end of his father's kingdom. In early 72, L. Caesennius [3] Paetus, the legate of Syria, invaded Commagene on the pretext that Antiochus IV and I. were conspiring with the Parthians (*Bellum Commagenicum*). After an initially brave defence, I and his brother were forced to flee to the Parthians accompanied by only ten riders. On receiving a Roman extradition request, Vologaeses I. obtained for them the forgiveness of Vespasian (Jos. BI 7,7,1–3). The brothers were taken to Rome by C. Velius Rufus (ILS 9200) and they lived there with the standing of royalty. I.'s son was I. [II 12] Philopappus. PIR² I 150.

D. R. SEAR, Greek Imperial Coinage, 1982, 544, no. 5515–5519; R. D. SULLIVAN, The Dynasty of Commagene, in: ANRW II 8, 1977, 732–798, esp. 790–796. M.SCH.

[II 12] C. I. Antiochus Epiphanes Philopappus. Son of I. [II 11], brother of Iulia [10] Balbilla. He lived in Athens, where he held the position of archont. Received into the Senate by Trajan, he became *frater Arvalis* and *cos. suff.* in AD 109. In Athens, he erected a striking mausoleum for himself on the Hill of the Muses. Like his forefathers, he used the title *basileús* in Greek regions.

PIR² J 151; R. SULLIVAN, in: ANRW II 8, 1977, 796f.

[II 13] I. Apellas. Senator, to whom privileges were granted between AD 253 and 259 by an imperial letter (CIL III 412 = [1]). Descendant of the Pergamene Apellas mentioned in Aristid. or. 30.

1 W. ECK, in: Chiron 7, 1977, 367f. n. 53; 58 2 H. HALFMANN, in: EOS 2, 627. W.E.

[II 14] L. I. Apronius Maenius Pius Salamallianus. Of oriental origin (*Salām Allah* = 'Peace of God'), perhaps from a senatorial family, ascended a steep *cursus honorum*, partly under Severus Alexander (AD 222–235): *tribunus laticlavus* of the *legio X Gemina, adlectus inter quaestorios, praepositus actis senatus, aedilis curulis, praetor, legatus Augusti provinciae Belgicae, legatus* of the *legio I Adiutrix, legatus Augusti pro praetore provinciae Galatiae* in AD 222, *legatus Augusti pro praetore legionis III Augustae Severianae et provinciae Numidiae* around 224/225. He was nominated for the consulship for the year 226 or 227 (AE 1917/18,51; CII VIII 17639; 18270; 19131; AE 1942/43, 93).

PIR² I 161; G. BARBIERI, L'albo Senatorio, 1952, 214, no. 1065; E. BIRLEY, The Governors of Numidia, in: JRS 40,

1950, 60–68, esp. 64; LEUNISSEN (Konsuln), 185f.; R.K. SHERK, Legates of Galatia, 1951, 82f.; B.E. THOMASSON, Die Statthalter der röm. Provinzen Nordafrikas 2, 1960, 210f.; Id., Fasti Africani, 1996, 182f., no. 59.   TH.F.

[II 15] C. I. Aquila. Equestrian, *praefectus* of Egypt AD 10/11; kinship with I. [II 16] is possible.

PIR² J 165; DEMOUGIN, Prosopographie, 125.

[II 16] C. I. Aquila. Perhaps one of a family settled by Augustus in Amastris [4]. Equestrian, commanded a military expedition to the Crimea in AD 49 against Mithridates, who was trying to regain his kingdom. Honoured by Claudius for his success with the *ornamenta praetoria*. Procurator of Pontus-Bithynia in 58.

PIR² J 166; DEMOUGIN, Prosopographie, 443f.

[II 17] Ti. I. Aquila Polemaeanus. From Ephesus, son of I. [II 40], senator, *cos. suff.* AD 110. He caused the library in Ephesus, which was named after his father, to be built and decorated with statues; the building work was completed only after his death. IEph VII 2, 5101–5103, 7, 13, 14; PIR² J 168.   W.E.

[II 18] C. I. Asper. Cultured senator and excellent orator, held the office of suffect consul under Commodus (AD 180–192), was proconsul of the province of Africa in 200–201 or 204–205 and *cos. ord. II* together with his son C. I. Galerius Asper in 212; probably also *praefectus urbi* at the same time (CIL VIII 24585; ILS 355; Inscriptions of Roman Tripolitania, 1047). Initially honoured by Caracalla, then banished. Macrinus therefore appointed him to the position of proconsul of the province of Asia, but hindered him in the execution of his duties and sent a successor. Elagabalus allowed him to return to Rome (CIL VI 2003; 1063; Cass. Dio 77,5; 78,22; 79,4; Tert., Ad Scapulam 4,3).

PIR² I 182; G. BARBIERI, L'albo Senatorio, 1952, 69f., no. 285; LEUNISSEN (Konsuln), 216, 225; B.E. THOMASSON, Die Statthalter der röm. Provinzen Nordafrikas, 1960, 2, 106; Id., Fasti Africani, 1996, 80f., no. 107.   JÖ.F.

[II 19] C. I. Augurinus. Equestrian, attested as *praefectus* of the *ala Gallorum Petriana* in AD 56 in Mainz. He participated in the Pisonian conspiracy in 65 and was therefore banished.

PIR² J 187; DEMOUGIN, Prosopographie 473ff.

[II 20] I. Avitus. Young senator, quaestor in a province; he died during the homeward sea voyage. Probably from Gallia. Closely acquainted with Pliny the Younger, who sketches a highly complimentary picture of him (Plin. Ep. 2,6; 5,21; 6,6,6f.).

SYME, RP VI 219; PIR² J 189.

[II 21] C. I. Avitus. Perhaps a descendant of I. [II 20] or [II 97]. Praetorian governor of Lycia-Pamphylia AD 146/7–149; *cos. suff.* 149. PIR² J 191.   W.E.

[II 22] (C.) I. Avitus Alexianus. Grandson of C. I. [II 21] Avitus, the governor of Lycia and Pamphylia in the year

AD 148, husband of Iulia [17] Maesa, father of Iulia [9] Avita Mamaea and Iulia [22] Soaemias (Bassiana), thus grandfather of the emperors → Elagabalus [2] and → Severus Alexander. Having first completed the career path of the *eques*, he was accepted into senatorial rank, attained praetorship in 194, then become legionary legate of the *Legio IIII Flavia* around 195–6 and a suffect consul around 200. Later in his *cursus honorum* he was governor of the province of Raetia (around 196/197–199/200), twice *praefectus alimentorum* (212–214), governor of Dalmatia (around 214–215/216) and Asia (215–216 or 216–217), possibly also Cyprus (217). He acted as *comes* for the emperors Septimius Severus and Caracalla, and was *sodalis Titialis* (Cass. Dio 78,30; 79; 79,16; AE 1921, 64 = 1963, 42 = 1979, 450; AE 1962, 229).

PIR² I 190 and 192; LEUNISSEN (Konsuln), 159, 225, 240, 379.

[II 23] I. Aurelius Zenobius. Close relative of → Zenobia of Palmyra (but not her father); gave military support as a high-ranking commander to the governor of the province of Syria Phoenice, Rutilius Pudens Crispinus, in Severus Alexander's campaign against the Persians, AD 232 (IGR III 1033). PIR² I 196.   TH.F.

[II 24] I. Auspex. Gaul, of the ruling elite of the Remi; at a gathering of Gaulish tribes late in AD 70 he advised peace with Rome (Tac. Hist. 4,69). PIR² J 197.

[II 25] Q. I. Balbus. Senator. *Cos. suff.* in AD 85; proconsul of Asia 100–101 (or 101–102) [1]; Trajan wrote him a letter concerning the privileges of Aphrodisias [2]. His descendant was the consul of 129 of the same name. PIR² 199 and 200.

1 W. ECK, in: Chiron 12, 1982, 334f.   2 J. REYNOLDS, Aphrodisias and Rome, 1982, 113ff.   W.E.

[II 26] I. Basilianus. Follower of → Macrinus (AD 217/18), *praefectus Aegypti* from April 217 to April 218; supported in this office by the senator Marius Secundus (Cass. Dio 78(79),35,1; ILS 8919; [1. 123]). Designated for the post of *praefectus praetorio*, he fled to Italy following the fall of Macrinus, where he was arrested at Brundisium and executed at Nicomedia (Cass. Dio 78(79),35,2). PIR² I 201.

1 STEIN, Präfekten.

[II 27] I. Bassianus. Priest of Sol Elagabalus from Emesa, father of → Iulia [12] Domna and → Iulia [17] Maesa, thus grandfather of Caracalla, → Iulia [9] Avita Mamaea and → Iulia [22] Soaemias ([Aur. Vict.] Epit. Caes. 21,2; 23,2). PIR² I 202.   TH.F.

[II 28] C. I. Bassus. Senator; quaestor in Pontus-Bithynia under Vespasian; at that time accused in the Senate, but acquitted. Banished by Domitian, but recalled by Nerva. Proconsul of Pontus-Bithynia under Trajan, not later than AD 101–102, before Trajan received the title of Dacicus. Accused by the Bithynians in the Senate in the winter of 102–103 for *repetundae*, defended by Pliny the Younger. Only narrowly acquitted, he remained a member of the Senate. As Pliny (Ep. 4,9,22) spoke of his *senectus*, he must by then already have been around 60 years old (PIR² J 205). It cannot be known whether he was related to I. [II 120].

[II 29] C. I. Bassus. Praetorian legate of Dacia superior in AD 135; *cos. suff.* 139. He may have been a son of I. [II 120]

PIR² J 206; PISO, FPD, 1, 53f.

[II 30] I. Briganticus. Batavian, nephew of I. [II 43] Civilis. He defected to Vitellius as *praefectus* of a cavalry unit in AD 69, but later joined Vespasian, participating in the battles against his uncle Civilis; there he fell.

PIR² J 211; DEMOUGIN, Prosopographie, 580.

[II 31] Agrippa I. Caesar, see → Agrippa [2]

[II 32] C. I. Caesar. Eldest son of Agrippa [1] and Iulia [6], daughter of Augustus. Born. 20 BC, between 14 August and 13 September. Adopted by Augustus in 17 BC, together with his brother Lucius I. [II 33] Caesar; this at once made clear that they were one day to inherit his political position. Took part in public life from his early years. In 8 BC he accompanied Augustus to Gaul; the soldiers on the Rhine were granted a → *congiarium* in his name. Tensions with Tiberius became palpable. Following the latter's self-imposed exile to Rhodes in 6 BC, Gaius came still more strongly into the foreground. In 5 BC, Augustus, who was himself *cos. XII*, presented him personally to the people on his adoption of the *toga virilis*. The Senate designated him consul five years later; he was granted the right to take part in sessions of the Senate. Elected *princeps iuventutis* by the *equites*. Sent to the Danube with the army. In 1 BC marriage to Claudia Livia Iulia, daughter of Drusus [1] the Elder. Departed for the east with the *imperium proconsulare*; his *rector* was M. Lollius, with whom he soon fell out. Travelled to Greece and Asia Minor in 1 BC and AD 1. Commenced his consulship on Samos, travelled to Syria and Egypt; intervened in the ordering of the Nabataean kingdom. Diplomat. Negotiated with Phraates V, who was recognized as Parthian king. Appointed Ariobarzanes [8], then the latter's son Artavasdes [4] as king in Armenia. The consequence was a revolt by Addon; siege of Artagira; there, on 7 September AD 3, Gaius was wounded. Following the fall of the fortress he was for the first time acclaimed by the soldiers as *imperator*. Owing to his wounds, he requested of Augustus that he might be allowed to remain in Syria as a private citizen, but Augustus refused. Returned to Italy, died on 21 February AD 4 at Limyra in Lycia, where a cenotaph was erected in his honour. His ashes were placed in the mausoleum of Augustus.

Countless statues were erected to Gaius even during his lifetime; he was appointed magistrate in many cities. After his death a *porticus Iulia* was named after him in Rome; the *basilica Iulia* in the Forum Romanum was built by Augustus in his and his brother's name; a law

was introduced founding 10 destination centuries, named after Gaius and Lucius (cf. M.H. CRAWFORD, Roman Statutes I, 1996, 507ff.). A decree from Pisa in his honour is preserved (CIL XI 1421 = ILS 140). PIR² J 216.

1 J. GANZERT, Der Kenotaph für Gaius Caesar in Limyra, 1984 2 A.- K. MASSNER, Das röm. Herrscherbild, vol. 4, 1982, 53ff. 3 J. POLLINI, The Portraiture of Gaius and Lucius Caesar, 1987 4 H. V. HESBERG, S. PANCIERA, Das Mausoleum des Augustus, 1994, 98ff. 5 F. HURLET, Les collègues du prince sous Auguste et Tibère, 1997, 113–141, 573ff. 6 CIL VI 40322–40325.

[II 33] L. I. Caesar. Son of Agrippa [1] and Iulia [6], daughter of Augustus; brother of I. [II 32]. Born 17 BC between 14 June and 15 July [1]. Adopted by Augustus together with his brother Gaius shortly after birth, marking him out as a future 'heir' to Augustus' position. Educated with his brother by Augustus himself and presented to the public. Took the *toga virilis* in 2 BC, for which Augustus took the consulship for the last time. On the same occasion the Senate designated him as consul five years from that time; elected *princeps iuventutis* by the Roman *equites*; he was granted the right to take part in Senate sittings. All this took place in parallel with his brother's career. Together with Gaius he held games in Rome. Accepted into the College of Augurs. Engaged to Aemilia [4] Lepida. In AD 2 he was sent to Spain, to become familiar with the army. On 20 August of the same year he died in Massilia. The consuls arranged a → *iustitium* (CIL VI 895 = 31195 = 40360). His ashes were placed in the mausoleum of Augustus. On posthumous honours, see above under I. [II 32]. The elogium from Pisa which refers to him is in CIL XI 1420 = ILS 139. On honours during his lifetime PIR² J 222; [2].

1 S. PRIULI, in: Tituli 2, 1980, 47ff. 2 F. HURLET, Les collègues du prince sous Auguste et Tibère, 1997, 573ff.

[II 34] Nero I. Caesar. Eldest son of Germanicus [2] and Agrippina [2] maior. Born AD 6. At the triumph over Germania in AD 17 he was allowed to enter the city alongside his father on the triumphal chariot. When Germanicus went to the east he remained in Rome; in early AD 20 he received his mother, who was returning with the ashes of his dead father, in Terracina together with his siblings. He received the *toga virilis* on 7 June 20; at the same time Tiberius had a → *congiarium* distributed (VIDMAN, FO²: for the year 20; Tac. Ann. 3,29,1–3). At the end of the trial of Cn. Calpurnius [II 16] Piso [1] he was promoted as *iuvenis* ahead of his brothers in the Senate's thanksgiving. Recommended to the Senate by Tiberius, he was allowed the privilege of applying for the quaestorship five years before the legal age. After the death of Drusus [II 1] in AD 23, whose daughter Iulia [8] Nero had married in 21, he was the heir apparent to → Tiberius. Numerous priestly appointments, *quaestor* in 26. Increasing tensions with Tiberius, aggravated by → Seianus and his mother Agrippina. Following the death of Livia in 29, he was accused and condemned by Tiberius in the Senate; he was banished to the island of Pontia, where he died before 31 October. His brother → Caligula had his ashes buried in the *mausoleum Augusti* in AD 37. PIR² J 223.

> 1 W. ECK, A. CABALLOS, F. FERNÁNDEZ, Das senatus consultum de Cn. Pisone patre, 1996, 49, 112, 116, 246. 2 H. v. HESBERG, S. PANCIERA, Das Mausoleum des Augustus, 1994, 140f.   3 F. HURLET, Les collègues du prince..., 1997, 573ff.   4 Z. KISS, L'iconographie des princes Julio-Claudiens, 1975   5 FITTSCHEN/ZANKER, 1.

[II 35] L. I. Calenus. A Haeduan, probably an equestrian legionary tribune in the army of Vitellius; following its defeat in October AD 69, the Flavians sent him to Gaul as a messenger of victory.

> PIR² J 227; DEMOUGIN, Prosopographie, 562.

[II 36] C. I. Callistus. Sold into the household of Caligula as a slave, manumitted by him. His daughter Nymphidia was the emperor's lover. Although already in a position of great influence, he took part in conspiracies against Caligula, including the successful one of January AD 41. This gained him a position of extreme power with Claudius, under whom he occupied the position of a → libellis. This allowed him to establish many contacts and build up vast wealth. Pliny writes of a dining hall containing 30 marble pillars made of onyx (HN 36,60). He remained cautiously in the background when → Messalina was eliminated; and Claudius rejected the marriage candidate he had put to the emperor. However, his influence endured alongside that of → Narcissus and → Pallas, depending as it did above all upon his immediate proximity to the emperor. → Scribonius Largus dedicated his work to him, and Callistus presented it to Claudius. Probably died before Claudius. PIR² J 229.

[II 37] Ti. I. Candidus Caecilius Simplex. Senator, *frater Arvalis*, attested between 105 and 122; son of I. [II 38].

> SCHEID, Collège, 41f.

[II 38] Ti. I. Candidus Marius Celsus. From the province of Asia. Related to A. Marius Celsus, consul in the year AD 69. Probably entered the Senate in 69 or 70; *frater Arvalis* from no later than 72. Cos. suff. 86; consular legate of Galatia-Cappadocia c. 87/8–91/2. Cos. ord. II in 105, also *praefectus urbi* at around the same time. Died after 109. He was one of the most influential senators of Trajan's time. His sons were I. [II 37] and one Ti. I. Candidus.

> SCHEID, Collège, 5f. 39f., 41f.; W. ECK, s.v. I. (166), RE Suppl. 14, 207; PIR² J 241.

[II 39] I. Celer. *Quaestor pro praetore* of the province of Asia; wrote a letter to the magistrate of Aphrodisias.

> J. REYNOLDS, Aphrodisias and Rome, 1982, 179f.

[II 40] Ti. I. Celsus Polemaeanus. From Sardeis; later strong connections with Ephesus. He supported Vespa-sian in AD 69 as tribune of the *legio III Cyrenaica*. Entered the Senate; *legatus iuridicus* in Galatia-Cappadocia 79/80; after occupying several praetorian offices under Domitian cos. suff. in 92; *curator aedium sacrarum*; proconsul of Asia c. 105/6. On his death interred in a sarcophagus in the library in Ephesus, which had been erected by his son I. [II 17]. He and his *virtutes* are represented in images, including two equestrian statues. IEph VII 2, 5101–14; HALFMANN, 111f.; PIR² J 260.

[II 41] I. Cestillus. Equestrian; *procurator provinciae* of Mauretania Caesariensis in AD 221. AE 1985, 976; cf. Bulletin d'archéologie Algérienne, 7, 1977/9, 217ff.

[II 42] A. I. Charax. Descendant of A. Claudius [II 18] Charax from Pergamum. Probably also related to I. [II 119].

[II 43] I. Civilis. Batavian, of royal descent. Early military service as *praefectus cohortis*, probably under the terms of the → foedus between his tribe and Rome; he remained in this position for more than two decades. Falsely accused of rebellion at the end of Nero's reign, sent before Nero, but acquitted by Galba; his brother Claudius Paulus was executed. Tensions continued with parts of the army on the Rhine, although → Vitellius supported him. He joined Vespasian in the civil war between the latter and Vitellius, after Antonius [II 13] Primus had invited him to defect. His tribe and Batavian cohorts in the Roman army joined him. Allegedly the general break from Rome was already planned in AD 69; he called on other Gaulish tribes and Germani on the right bank of the Rhine to join the rebellion. Short-term successes: the Treveri joined the revolt, Castra Vetera was taken, and Colonia Agrippinensis was forced into an alliance. The rebellion never extended farther than to central Gaul. The *Imperium Galliarum*, which I. allegedly aimed to found, is more likely an aspect of Flavian historical falsification. Defeated and repelled by Petillius Cerialis; the report of Tacitus (Hist. 5,26,1) ends with talks between Civilis and Cerialis on a bridge over the River Nabalia. Nothing further is known of his fate.

→ Batavian Revolt

> PIR² J 264; H. HEINEN, Trier und das Trevererland in röm. Zeit, 1985, 70ff.; R. URBAN, Der "Bataveraufstand" und die Erhebung des Iulius Classicus, 1985.

[II 44] I. Classicus. Member of a prominent and wealthy family of the Treveri, which traced its lineage back to the Gaulish kings. Served as a cavalry officer in the Roman army; in AD 69 he commanded an *ala Treverorum* under Vitellius. He joined I. [II 43] Civilis only early in 70; took part in a meeting at Colonia Agrippinensis (Cologne), where he was forced to leave his daughter as a hostage to guarantee the keeping of treaties with other Gaulish tribes. Having received Roman standards, he allegedly had the defeated Roman troops swear allegiance to the *Imperium Galliarum*. His military resistance at Trier was broken by Petillius Cerialis. He and other aristocrats of his tribe finally fled to the

Germani on the right bank of the Rhine. The exact political aims of his revolt remain unclear.

→ Batavian Revolt

PIR² J 267; H. HEINEN, Trier und das Trevererland in röm. Zeit, 1985, 67ff.; R. URBAN, Der 'Bataveraufstand' und die Erhebung des Iulius Classicus, 1985.

[II 45] Ti. I. Clatius Severus. see Ti. → Oclatius Severus, cos. suff. c. AD 169–172.

[II 46] C. I. Commodus Orfitianus. Senator, legate of the legio I Adiutrix (AE 1976, 551); praetorian governor of Thracia c. AD 155–157; cos. suff. in September 157 (RMD III 170); curator operum publicorum 161; consular governor of Syria Palaestina not before 162 (CIL III 6645 and unpublished text from Caesarea); consular legate of Pannonia superior around 170. Whether, and if so, when he occupied an office in Africa, is uncertain.

PIR² J 271; THOMASSON, Fasti Africani, 152f.

[II 46a] I. Constitutus Praesidial procurator of the Alpes Graiae, more probably in the 2nd than in the 3rd cent. AD, because he still does not bear a title (AE 1998, 871).

[II 47] Q. I. Cordus. Proconsul of Cyprus in AD 65; legate of Aquitania 69, joined Otho; however, the province turned to Vitellius. He must have defected quickly to the Flavians, since he became cos. suff. in November 71 ([1]). He possibly came from Lusitania, as did Q. I. Cordus Iunius Mauricus.

1 G. CAMODECA, in: Epigrafia. Actes ... A. Degrassi, 1991, 57ff.

AE, 1972, 238; R. ETIENNE, in: EOS 2, 525f.; PIR² J 272.

[II 48] C. I. [—] Cornutus Tertullus. From Perge in Pamphylia; related to the family of Plancius Varus. Born before AD 45; probably entered the Senate under Nero; adlectio inter praetorios 73/74. Following a proconsulship in the Narbonensis, his career came to a standstill under Domitian; according to Pliny (Pan. Lat. 90), he withdrew voluntarily, because he rejected Domitian's politics. Praefectus Aerarii Saturni with Pliny the Younger in 97; likewise cos. suff. in 100; consular curator of the via Aemilia; legate for the census in Aquitania; succeeded the deceased Pliny as special legate in Pontus-Bithynia in 111; probably proconsul of Africa 116–117 (at the age of 75 or thereabouts). Linked to the Stoic opposition under Domitian; guardian of the daughter of Helvidius Priscus; petition against Publicius Priscus in 97. With Pliny prosecutor against Marius Priscus in 100. Buried at Tusculum. His daughter (or sister) Iulia [23] Tertulla was married to I. [II 90].

PIR² J 273. 706; SYME, RP, II, 478ff.; HALFMANN, 117.
W.E.

[II 49] see → Cottius [1]
[II 50] see → Cottius [2]
[II 50a] I. Crassipes Praetorian governor of Thrace in AD 138; suffect consul between 1 March and 1 November 140 ([1], also RMD II 58/95); consular legate of Moesia inferior under Antoninus [1] Pius (AE 1998, 1620; [2]).

1 K. DIETZ, Ein neues Militärdiplom aus Altegolfsheim. Lkr. Regensburg, in: Beiträge zur Arch. in der Oberpfalz 3, 1999, 254 f. 2 M. M. ROXAN, P. WEISS, Die Auxiliartruppen der Prov. Thracia. Neue Militärdiplome der Antoninenzeit, in: Chiron 28, 1998, 371–420.

[II 51] L. I. Crescens. Equestrian; primipilus of the legio II Traiana in Egypt, at the same time praefectus castrorum in AD 157 (AE 1955, 238); praefectus classis Misenatis in 166. CIL XVI 122; PFLAUM, Suppl., 46f.

[II 52] Ti. I. Eupator. see → Eupator

[II 53] C. I. Eurycles. see → Eurycles

[II 54] C. I. Eurycles Herculanus L. Vibullius Pius. From a highly illustrious Spartan family. He held various offices in Sparta, including those of patronómos and archiereús in the ruler cult. According to [1], perhaps born as late as Domitian's reign, then only brought into the Senate by Hadrian; his career appears to have ended with the command of the legio III (Gallica). IG VI 1172; PIR² J 302.

1 A. BIRLEY, in: ZPE 116, 1997, 237ff.

[II 55] Ti. I. Ferox. Probably a provincial senator. He initiated the decisive legal proceedings in the trial of Marius Priscus. Cos. suff. at the end of AD 99. curator alvei Tiberis from 101 to 103. Governor of a consular province before c. 111 (Plin. Ep. 10,87,3; [1]). Proconsul of Asia 116/117 (cf. [2]). Linked to Pliny the Younger. PIR² J 306.

1 W. ECK, in: Chiron 12, 1982, 346 A. 266; Chiron 13, 1983, 210 2 Id., in: Chiron 12, 1982, 361.

[II 56] C. I. Fl(avius) Proculus Quintillianus. Son of I. [II 121]. Cos. suff. around AD 235; proconsul Asiae 249/250.

D. H. FRENCH, in: EA 25, 1995, 95f.; PIR² J 502.

[II 57] I. Florus. Comes of Tiberius during the latter's diplomatic mission to the Middle East in 20 BC; linked to Horace. PIR² J 316.

[II 58] I. Florus. From an aristocratic family of the Treveri. He provoked a revolt in Gaul in AD 21 together with I. [II 126] Sacrovir; after its failure he first withdrew into hiding; later he committed suicide. Tac. Ann. 3,40; 42; PIR² J 315.

[II 59] I. Florus. Orator from Gaul in the Augustan-Tiberian period; he was related to I. Secundus (Quint. Inst. 10,3,12f.). PIR² J 317.

[II 60] I. Fronto. Tribune in the cohorts of the Vigiles, discharged by Galba [2], restored to the army by Otho. PIR² J 325.

[II 61] I. Fronto. Prefect of the fleet of Misenum in AD 129 (CIL XVI 74); unlikely to be identical with Fronto the praesidial procurator of Raetia in AD 116, cf. AE 1993, 1240.

[II 62] I. Fronto. Senator of consular rank; probably from Lycia. AE 1994, 1730.

[II 63] C. I. Fronto. Son of Iulia Polla, the sister of I. [II 119]. From Pergamum. Possibly identical with the senator (praetor or governor) under Trajan in Dig. 48,19,5. PIR² J 323; 326; HALFMANN, Senatoren, 137.

[II 63a] C. I. Fron[to] Praefect of an Italian fleet under Hadrian.

> W. ECK et al., Neue Militärdiplome für Truppen in Italien, in: ZPE 139, 2002, 198 ff.

[II 64] Q. Fl(avius) I. Fronto. Praetorian governor of Arabia in AD 181. AE 1991, 1585; PIR² J 327.

[II 65] Ti. I. Frugi. Senator. Praetorian governor of Lycia-Pamphylia AD 113–114. IGR III 739.

[II 66] Ti. I. Frugi. His *cursus* is known up to his proconsulate of Macedonia; probably son of I. [II 65]. PIR² J 329.

> W. ECK, s.v. I. (252), RE Suppl. 14, 209.

[II 67] Ti. I. Frugi. Proconsul of Lycia-Pamphylia from 161 to 169 (SEG 34, 1309/10 = S. ŞAHIN, IArykanda = IK vol. 48, 25a-d). It may be possible to relate CIL VI 31717 = Hisp. Ant. 3, 1973, 299ff. = 41125 to him, if the extrapolation *pro/[cos. Lyc. Pamph.]* in l. 2/3 can be accepted. This senator had a very long career, probably with some interruptions. He may have attained consulship, if CIL XVI 188 (dated to *c.* AD 177–190) and a further unpublished fragment refer to him. CIL VI 41125 and literature.

[II 68] P. I. Geminius Marcianus. From Cirta. His senatorial career up to consulship, is entirely known; leader of legionary vexillations in Cappadocia *c.* AD 161/2. Legate in Arabia from 162; *cos. suff. c.* 164–165. The date of his proconsulship in Macedonia is disputed [1]; proconsul of Asia *c.* 183–184. PIR² J 340.

> 1 P. LEUNISSEN, in: ZPE 89, 1991, 222f.

[II 69] C. I. Geminus Capellianus. Praetorian governor of Pannonia inferior in AD 159. (CIL XVI 112; RMD I, 61f. and III, 247, n. 61f); *cos.suff.* 161 or 162. RMD III, 177.

> W. ECK, D. ISAC, I. PISO, in: ZPE 100, 1994, 582ff.

[II 70] L. I. Graecinus. Father of Cn. I. [II 3] Agricola from Forum Iulii (Tac. Agr. 4,1); brought into the Senate under Tiberius, people's tribune and praetor (AE 1946, 94 = CIL VI 41069). Executed by Caligula in late AD 39 or early 40 for refusing to condemn Iunius Silanus (Tac. Agr. 4,1; Sen. Ben. 2,21,5). According to Columella (1,1,14), he wrote a work on viticulture in two volumes (cf. Plin. HN 14,33; 16,241; PIR² J 344). One M. Iulius L. f. Ani(ensi) Graecinus was either his brother or another son alongside Agricola (AE 1946, 94 = CIL VI 41069). On his literary work, see → I. [IV 9].

[II 71] (Ti. I.) Graptus. Freedman of Tiberius, lived into the Neronic period; he accused Faustus Cornelius Sulla in AD 58, *cos.* 52. His son may be named in CIL X 6638, col. 2. 1. PIR² J 347.

[II 72] I. Indus. From an aristocratic family of the Treveri; opponent of I. [II 58] Florus, whose troops he annihilated. The *ala Indiana Gallorum* was named after him. PIR² J 358; DEMOUGIN, Prosopographie 210.

[II 73] I. Ininthimaeus, see → Ininthimaeus

[II 74] Ti. I. Iulianus Alexander. Descendant of Ti. Iulius Alexander (→ Alexander [18]), perhaps his grandson. *Frater Arvalis* at least from AD 114. Praetorian governor of Arabia *c.* 123–126 [1], *cos. suff.* 126?, *curator aedium sacrarum* [2; 3].

> 1 N. LEWIS, The Documents from the Bar-Kokhba Period in the Cave of Letters, 1989, 51ff., no. 13–15   2 SCHEID, Collège, 44   3 KOLB, Bauverwaltung, 180ff.

[II 75] P. I. Iunianus Martialianus. Senator, whose career is known from quaestorship to the consulate. Finally governor of Numidia under Severus Alexander and *cos. suff.* PIR² J 369; THOMASSON, Fasti Africani, 1996, 182f.   W.E.

[II 76] I. Callinicus. Son of Antiochus [18] IV of Commagene, younger brother of I. [II 11]. Both tried to prevent the Roman conquest of Commagene (*Bellum Commagenicum*, AD 72), but were forced to flee to the Parthians when almost all their followers deserted them. Vologaeses I. supported the brothers' cause with Vespasian, who pardoned them and let them live in Rome with the standing of royalty (Jos. BI 7,7,2f.).

> D. R. SEAR, Greek Imperial Coinage, 1982, 544, no. 5515–5519; R. D. SULLIVAN, The Dynasty of Commagene, in: ANRW II 8, 1977, 732–798, 790–796.   M.SCH.

[II 77] I. Kallistos, see → I. [II 36] Callistus

[II 78] C. I. Laco. Son of C.I. [II 53] → Eurycles. He was a leading figure in Achaia and was dynast of Sparta after his father's death. His name appears on coins. Soon after the accession of Tiberius, he lost his friendship and thereby also his position of power in Sparta. Whether a *procurator Ti. Claudi Caesaris Augusti Germanici* (ICorinth VIII 2, no. 67) of the same name is identical with him or his son (cf. PIR² J 372) is disputed. His son was I. [II 136].

> G. W. BOWERSOCK, in: JRS 51, 1961, 112ff.; HALFMANN, 125ff.; A. R. BIRLEY, in: ZPE 116, 1997, 237ff.   W.E.

[II 79] I. Laetus. led the emperor → Septimius Severus to have → Tullius Crispinus, the praetorian prefect of Didius [II 6] Iulianus, killed, since he had been ordered to make an attempt on his life. He commanded the cavalry at the battle of Lugdunum (Lyon) against → Clodius [II 1] Albinus on 19 February AD 197, intervening late, but ensuring by his intervention the victory for Severus. Owing to his hesitation and the suspicion thereby aroused that he had sought power for himself, he was later executed by Septimius Severus (Hdn. 3,7,3–6; SHA Did. Iul. 7,4; 8,1; Cass. Dio 75(76),6,8). PIR² J 373.   JÖ.F.

[II 80] I. Lepidianus. Consular governor of Syria Palaestina in AD 186. RMD I 69.

[II 81] Q. I. Licin[ianus?] Senator; consular governor of the *tres Daciae* under Maximinus Thrax (? AD 237/8). AE 1983, 802; PISO, FPD, I, 201ff.

[II 82] Ti. I. Lupus. Praetorian tribune who killed Caesonia Milonia, the wife of Caligula, and her young daughter in January AD 41. Executed by Claudius. PIR² J 388.

[II 83] Ti. I. Lupus. *Prafectus Aegypti* in AD 73 [1]; named in one of the papyri of Masada.

> 1 G. BASTIANINI, in: ZPE 17, 1975, 275; ZPE 38, 1980, 78
> 2 H. G. COTTON, J. GEIGER, Masada 2, 1989, 62ff.

[II 84] Sex. I. Maior. From Nysa in Asia. Senator. Legate of the *legio III Augusta c.* AD 124–126; *cos. suff.* 126; consular governor of Moesia inferior *c.* 132–135, then also briefly in Syria. His son was I. [II 85].

> PIR² J 397 E. DĄBROWA, The Governors of Roman Syria, 1998, 97ff.

[II 85] Sex. I. Maior Antoninus Pythodorus. Son of I. [II 84]. Senator, had numerous buildings erected, mainly in Epidaurus and in his home city of Nysa. Acquainted with Aelius Aristides (→ Aristides [3]). PIR² J 398; HALFMANN, 171f.; 143f.

[II 86] I. Marcus. *Praefectus classis Augustae Alexandrinae* after AD 214. P Oxy. 3920.

[II 87] C. I. Marcus. Governor of Britannia in AD 213. PIR² J 405; BIRLEY, 166ff. W.E.

[II 88] I. Marinus. Of Arabian origin, from Trachonitis, he was the father of C. → I. [II 114] Priscus and the emperor → Philippus Arabs (AD 244–249), during whose reign he died and was deified (IGR I 1196; 1199; 1200; [1]). PIR² I 407.

> 1 H. COHEN, Monnaies sous l'empire romain, repr. 1955, 5, 180, no. 1. JÖ.F.

[II 89] L. I. Marinus. Senator. Proconsul of Pontus-Bithynia, probably *cos. suff.* in AD 93 (VIDMAN, FO² 44; 86); consular governor of Moesia inferior. PIR² J 401.

[II 90] L. I. Marinus Caecilius Simplex. Son of I. [II 89], married to Iulia [23] Tertulla, the daughter of I. [II 48]. His career up to consulship is entirely known; his last office were as legate of Lycia-Pamphylia AD 96/7–98/9, *proconsul Achaiae* 99/100, *cos. suff.* 101. SCHEID, COLLÈGE, 28f.; PIR² J 408.

[II 91] I. Martialis. Friend of the poet Martial, associated with him for 34 years. PIR² J 421. → I. [IV 11]. W.E.

[II 92] I. Martialis served as *evocatus* (→ evocati) in the bodyguard of → Caracalla, murdering him out of personal animosity on 8 April AD 217 on the way from Edessa to Carrhae, near the famous temple of the lunar goddess. Shortly afterwards, he was himself killed by the other bodyguards (Cass. Dio 78,5,3ff.; Hdn. 4,13). PIR² I 412. TH.F.

[II 93] M. I. Maximianus. Equestrian from Sagalassus. Imperial procurator, married to Flavia Severa (AE 1993, 1560); he is probably identical with the *epistrategos* of the Heptanomia in AD 118, who served from 137–139 as *iuridicus* in Egypt.

PIR² J 417; D. THOMAS, The Epistrategos in Ptolemaic and Roman Egypt 2, 1982, 187.

[II 94] C. I. Maximinus. *Cos. suff* before AD 208; governor of the *tres Daciae* 208–*c.* 210. PIR² J 419; PISO, FPD, I, 166ff.

[II 95] I. Maximus. Batavian, marched under the orders of I. [II 43] Civilis against the Roman army under Dillius Vocula. PIR² J 421.

[II 96] I. Maximus. Probably equestrian governor of Thracia from AD 270–275. AE 1978, 728 = IGBulg 5, 5637.

[II 97] T. I. Maximus Manlianus Brocchus Servilianus. Senator from Nemausus. Entered the Senate under Domitian, participated in Trajan's Dacian campaign as legionary legate; praetorian governor of Pannonia inferior AD 110; *cos. suff.* in 112. It is not certain whether he is identical with the consular Maximus killed by the Parthians.

> PIR² J 426; J. FITZ, Die Verwaltung Pannoniens, 2, 1993, 518f.

[II 97a] L. I. Messala Rutilianus Suffect consul on 11 August, probably in AD 192 (not 193), together with C. Aemilius Severus Cantabrinus ([1] and an unpublished dissertation, reference A. PANGERL). He may be identical to the Messalla Rutilianus of CIL XIV 3966.

> 1 B. PFERDEHIRT, Ein neues Militärdiplom für Pannonia inferior vom 11.8.193 n. Chr., in: Arch. Korrespondenzblatt 32, 2002, 247 ff.

[II 98] I. Naso. Friend of Pliny and Tacitus, brother of I. [II 20] Avitus. Applied for senatorial office. Probably from Gaul. SYME, RP, 6, 219; PIR² J 437.

[II 99] C. I. Nigrinus. Senator, probably from Lycia. AE 1994, 1730.

[II 100] C. I. Octavius Volusenna Rogatianus. Consular governor, probably of Pontus-Bithynia in AD 253. (ZPE 90, 1992, 199ff. = AE 1992, 1566); proconsul of Asia under Valerian, the year 254 is doubtful. CIL III 6094 = IEph VII 1, 3162.

[II 101] Ti. I. Optatus Pontianus. Imperial freedman; *procurator et praefectus classis* in Misenum, AD 52. PIR² J 443. W.E.

[II 102] C. I. Pacatianus. From Vienna (Vienne) in southern Gaul; followed an equestrian career, attaining the position of a cavalry prefect in AD 191/192, before being appointed procurator of the province of Osrhoene *c.* 195. Thereafter he commanded a legion with the epithet *Parthica* in Mesopotamia. In 197, as → Clodius [II 1] Albinus threatened to invade Italy, he administered the Cottian Alps as procurator. After 198 he was one of the *comites* of → Septimius Severus and his sons, later fulfilling the procuratorial administration of the province of Mauretania Tingitana. To this were later added the offices of *procurator ludi magni* and the governorship of the province of Mauretania Caesariensis. After this, around 215, he received a special military command in the east, during Caracalla's Parthian War.

Finally, around 216, he was prefect of the province of Mesopotamia (CIL III 865; XII 1856; VI 1642).

> PIR² I 444; PFLAUM, 605ff.; THOMASSON, Fasti Africani, 234f., no. 25.   TH.F.

[II 103] I. Paelignus. *Amicus* of Claudius [III 1]; *praefectus vigilum*; praesidial procurator of Cappadocia. His behaviour led to political complications. PIR² J 445; DEMOUGIN, Prosopographie 387.

[II 104] I. Paullus. Probably from Antioch in Pisidia; probably entered the Senate under the Flavians. AE 1960, 35; HALFMANN, 116.

[II 105] I. Pelago. Imperial freedman, who, on Nero's orders, had Rubellius Plautius killed in Asia. PIR² J 455.

[II 106] M. I. Philippus. see → Philippus Arabs   W.E.

[II 107] M. I. Severus Philippus. Son of → Philippus Arabs and → Marcia Otacilia Severa, born AD 237–238 ([Aur. Vict.] epit. Caes. 28,3). Elevated to Caesar and *princeps iuventutis* in July/August 244 (CIL III 8031), from July/August 247 he also had the title of Augustus, the supreme pontificate and the proconsulate (CIL VIII 8323, cf. 20139; XVI 152; 153). Following his father's death in September/October 249, he was murdered in the praetorian camp in Rome (Aur. Vict. Caes. 28,11; [Aur. Vict.] Epit. Caes. 28,3; Eutr. 9,3).

> MÜNZEN: H.COHEN, Monnaies sous l'empire romain, repr. 1955, 5, 159–178; RIC 4,3, 95ff. PIR² I 462; KIENAST², 200; X.LORIOT, Les premières années de la grande crise du IIIᵉ siècle, in: ANRW II 2, 1975, 657–797, esp. 791; M.PEACHIN, Roman Imperial Titulature and Chronology, 1990, 31; H.A. POHLSANDER, Did Decius Kill the Philippi?, in: Historia 31, 1982, 114–222, esp. 214ff.   TH.F.

[II 108] I. Pollio. Praetorian tribune; helped Nero poison Britannicus; later governor of Sardinia. PIR² J 473; DEMOUGIN, Prosopographie, 450f.

[II 109] (C. I.) Polybius. Freedman of Augustus; read the latter's will in the Senate, in September AD 14. PIR² J 475.

[II 110] A. I. Pompilius Piso. Senator whose career is preserved up to his appointment to the consulship. Legate of the *legio III Augusta* AD 176–177 or 177–179, at the same time *cos. designatus*.

> PIR² J 477   PISO, FPD, 1, 218ff.   THOMASSON, Fasti Africani, 1996, 161ff.

[II 111] Q. I. Potitus. Proconsul of Creta-Cyrenae under Antoninus Pius. AE 1974, 679.

[II 112] I. Priscianus. Equestrian. Procurator from AD 208 to 211, perhaps of Asia; father of I. [II 137]. IEph III 691 and 693 = ZPE 42, 1981, 246ff.

[II 113] I. Priscus. Equestrian, cohort prefect under Vitellius; appointed *praefectus praetorio*. Was meant to secure the Apennine passes against Flavian forces. After the conquest of Rome by the Flavians he committed suicide. PIR² J 487.   W.E.

[II 114] C. I. Priscus. Brother of the emperor → Philippus Arabs (AD 244–249). Began his career in state serv-ice as financial procurator of a number of provinces, however, of these only his office in Hispania citerior is known, and as deputy to governors, among others, of the provinces of Macedonia and Egypt, after he had been → *iuridicus* of Alexandria. Thereafter he administered the province of Mesopotamia as *praefectus*, in 242–243 was appointed to the post of *praefectus praetorio* and finally occupied the extraordinary post of a *rector orientis* during the reign of his brother (CIL III 14149,5; Zos. 1,19,2; IGR III 1033; 1201f.; CIL VI 1638). PIR² I 488.   TH.F.

[II 115] C. I. Proculianus. *Cos. suff.* in AD 179. RMD II 123.

[II 116] C. I. Proculus. Perhaps son of I. [II 124] and from Larinum. His career is preserved in CIL X 6658 = ILS 1040 and in a text from Larinum (cf. [1. 231]). Probably *quaestor* of Domitian and Nerva in AD 96, *ab actis* (*senatus*), *praetor* and legate of the *legio VI Ferrata* in Syria. Consul in 109. Legate for the census in Lugdunensis, perhaps as praetorian; *legatus Augusti pro praetore regionis Transpadanae*, either for the establishment of the *alimenta* or, more likely, only after 128 under Hadrian as one of the *consulares*; Fronto (Ad amicos 2,7,19 VAN DEN HOUT) must then refer to him. He may have been designated for a second consulship in 133, since the Larinum inscription refers to him in a later addendum as *cos. II.*; however, he apparently died before taking this office. PIR² J 497.

> 1 A.R. BIRLEY, in: ZPE 116, 1997, 229ff.

[II 117] C. I. Proculus. Equestrian; *iuridicus* in Egypt; financial procurator of Cappadocia et Cilicia under Nero. AE 1966, 472; DEMOUGIN, Prosopographie, 511f.

[II 118] L. I. Proculus. Praetorian governor of Dacia superior, perhaps under Antoninus Pius. AE 1967, 385; PISO, FPD, 1, 65f.

[II 119] C. Antius A. I. Quadratus. From Pergamum. Brought into the Senate by Vespasian; member of the *Arvales*. The praetorian career path led him to the governorship of Lycia-Pamphylia *c.* AD 89/90–92/93 [1]. *Cos. suff.* 94; governor of Syria *c.* 100–104; *cos. ord. II* 105; *proconsul Asiae c.* 109/110. *Euergetes* of Pergamum; established an agon in honour of Trajan. Countless statues were erected in his honour in Pergamum and Ephesus. Related to I. [II 120]. PIR² J 507.

> 1 W.ECK, in: Chiron 12, 1982, 316ff.   2 Id., in: ZPE 117, 1997, 107ff.   3 HALFMANN, 112ff.

[II 120] C. I. Quadratus Bassus. Probably from Pergamum. Related to I. [II 119]. His entire senatorial career is known from the inscription Pergamum VIII 3, 21. As legionary legate he took part in the first Dacian War; governor of Judaea AD 102/103–104/105; *cos. suff.* 105; took part in the second Dacian War, after which he was honoured with the *ornamenta triumphalia*. Governor of Cappadocia-Galatia; took part in the Parthian War; governor of Syria *c.* 115–117. Sent to Dacia again by Trajan to suppress a revolt; there he fell in battle.

Hadrian ordered his body to be brought to Asia, where a tomb was erected for him at the state's expense. PIR² J 508; HALFMANN, 119f.

[II 121] C. I. Quintillianus. Father of I. [II 56]. *Praefectus vigilum* AD 210/211. (PIR² J 511); probably *adlectus inter consulares*; consular governor of Moesia inferior *c.* 213–215

W. ECK, M. M. ROXAN, in: Archäologisches Korrespondenzblatt 28, 1998, 96ff.

[II 122] L. I. Romulus. *Cos. suff.* AD 152 (PIR² J 521); perhaps son of I. [II 116].

[II 123] M. I. Romulus. Equestrian. Brought into the Senate *inter tribunicios* by Claudius. Legionary legate, praetor; *proconsul extra sortem* in Macedonia; father of I. [II 124].

PIR² J 523; DEMOUGIN, Prosopographie, 367ff.; A. R. BIRLEY, in: ZPE 116, 1997, 233.

[II 124] M. I. Romulus. Son of I. [II 123]. Legate of the proconsul of Sardinia AD 68–69. ILS 5947; PIR² J 522.

[II 124a] L. I. S[·] Suffect consul AD 115 (AE 1949, 23). He cannot be identified with any known senator.

H. M. COTTON, W. ECK, P.MURABBA'AT 114 und die Anwesenheit röm. Truppen in den Höhlen des Wadi Murabba'at nach dem Bar Kochba Aufstand, in: ZPE 138, 2002, 173–183. W. E.

[II 125] I. Sabinus. From the aristocratic family of the Lingones. In AD 70 he joined I. [II 43] Civilis. After defeat at the hands of the Sequani his wife hid him for nine years. When he was discovered, Vespasian had him executed. PIR² J 535.

[II 126] I. Sacrovir. Haeduan; revolted against Rome with I. Florus in AD 21. Took up position in Augustodunum. After defeat at the hands of C. Silius he committed suicide. PIR² J 539.

[II 127] M. I. Sanctus Maximinus. Equestrian from Sagalassus, who reached the position of *iuridicus Alexandreae* (AE 1993, 1561). I. [II 93] was probably his son. W.E.

[II 128] see → Saturninus (Imperial usurper AD 281)

[II 129] P. I. Scapula Tertullus Priscus. was *cos. ord.* in AD 195 and *proconsul* of the province of Africa in 212–213 (CIL III 4407; 12802; 14507; VIII 24131; XIV 169; 4560). Tertullian directed his essay *Ad Scapulam* after the solar eclipse of 14 August 212 at him, because of I.'s assertive action against the Christians (Tert. Ad Scapulam 3,3f.).

PIR² I 557; LEUNISSEN (Konsuln), 217; B. E. THOMASSON, Die Statthalter der röm. Provinzen Nordafrikas 2, 1960, 112f.; Id., Fasti Africani, 1996, 83f., no. 113. TH.F.

[II 130] C. I. Septimius Castinus. Possibly from Africa, related to the imperial house of the Severans and had great influence over Caracalla. Around AD 194–195, he successively occupied the posts of military tribune in the legions *I Adiutrix* and *Macedonica*, was quaestor and people's tribune (around 200), *curator* of Aecla-

num (southern Italy), *curator* of the *via Salaria*, *iuridicus* of Apulia, Calabria, Lucania and Bruttium, later taking the proconsulship of the province of Creta and Cyrenae (around 204) and command of the *legio I Minervia* in Bonn (*c.* 205–207/208). Thereafter he commanded a special military unit composed of elements of the four legions stationed on the Rhine, the *XXX Ulpia Victrix, I Minervia, XXII Primigenia* and the *VIII Augusta*, which undertook action against *defectores et rebelles* (around 208). Following his praetorian governorship of the province of Pannonia inferior, he held the suffect consulship in 212 or 213. His last known office was from 214 as governor of the province of Dacia (CIL III 3480; 7638; 10360; 10471–73; XIII 7945; AE 1980, 755); from there he was recalled by Macrinus owing to his sympathy for the Severans (Cass. Dio 78,13,2). After that he lived in Bithynia, where Elagabalus had him killed (Cass. Dio 79,4,4ff.).

PIR² I 566; DEGRASSI, FCIR 60; FPD 178ff., no. 39; LEUNISSEN (Konsuln), 174, 239, 279, 328, 330, 337, 348, 363, 388, 403. TH.F.

[II 131] C. I. Severus. Descendant of the Galatian-Attalid royal house, from an extremely wealthy family of Ancyra. Brought into the Senate by Hadrian *inter tribunicios*. Legate of the *legio IV Scythica* in Syria AD 132–134, at the same time deputizing for the absent governor. Proconsul of Achaia, *praefectus aerarii Saturni, cos. suff.* 138 or 139. Legate of Germania inferior, *proconsul Asiae* probably 152–153. PIR² J 573; HALFMANN, 151f.

[II 132] Ser. I. Servianus. see → L.I. [II 141] Ursus Servianus

[II 133] Cn. Minicius Faustinus Sex. I. Severus. From Dalmatia. His senatorial career began under Trajan; he was also promoted by Hadrian. Praetorian legate of Dacia superior AD 120–126; *cos. suff.* 127; consular governor of Moesia inferior *c.* 129–131/2; then of Britannia 132–133. Hadrian sent him to Judaea as he was a capable general, to fight the → Bar Kochba Rebellion in 133 or 134, where, with the support of Publicius Marcellus and Haterius Nepos, he defeated the rebels in a long campaign up to the end of 135 or early 136, without any great battles. He is not mentioned in the Jewish sources, the Mishna or the Talmud. He was rewarded for his success with the *ornamenta triumphalia*, as were his fellow generals. It is assumed, following CIL III 2830 = ILS 1056, that he then served for a further short period as governor of Syria. However, Syria can also be taken to mean Syria Palaestina.

PIR² J 576; W. ECK, in: JRS 89, 1999, 76–89.

[II 134] C. I. Severus. Son of I. [II 131]. A swift senatorial career saw him in command of the *legio XXX Ulpia Victrix* in Germania inferior; *curator viae Appiae; cos. ord.* in AD 155. He was governor of Syria Palaestina *c.* 156–157. Possibly legate of Cappadocia under Marcus. PIR² J 574; HALFMANN, 81.

[II 135] C. I. Silvanus Melanio. Equestrian with a long procuratorial career, in northern Spain among other places, possibly including Asia (AE 1968, 229–231), if Asia was not his homeland. If Roman inscriptions of Britain I 1273 refers to him, his career may be dated to the period between c. AD 250 and 260.

> PIR² J 581; A.R. BIRLEY, in: ZPE 43, 1981, 13ff.; PFLAUM, Suppl., 67f.

[II 136] C. I. Spartiaticus. Son of I. [II 78]. In Corinth he took over several municipal offices and priesthoods. Brought into equestrian rank by Claudius, he became *tribunus militum* and later *procurator* of Nero and Agrippina (AE 1927, 2 = ICorinth VIII 2, no. 68). Honoured by numerous cities; later banished by Nero.

> PIR² J 587; A.R. BIRLEY, in: ZPE 116, 1997, 240ff.

[II 137] M. I. Sura. Equestrian military tribune, son of a procurator, early 3rd cent. AD (IEph III 691 and 693 = ZPE 42, 1981, 246ff.). Kin relation to [–] Iulianus Sura Magnus, *procos. Lyciae-Pamphyliae* and M. I. Sura Magnus Attalianus, who were probably father and son. PIR² J 101, 594.

[II 138] C. I. Tiro Gaetulicus. Senator, achieved the praetorship; friend of Sempronius Senecio, after whose death Tiro was accused of falsifying a codicil to his will. Plin. Ep. 6,31; PIR² J 603; PFLAUM, Suppl., 33ff.

[II 139] I. Tutor. Treverian; made *praefectus ripae* on the Rhine by Vitellius. Defected to I. [II 43] Civilis. Forced the *Colonia Agrippinensis* to join the rebellion. After the fall of Trier he retreated into Batavian territory. PIR² J 607; DEVIJVER J 133.

[II 140] L. I. Ursus. Probably from Narbonensis. *Praefectus annonae* (AE 1939, 60); *praefectus Aegypti* under Domitian (AE 1956, 57). Perhaps praetorian prefect. Linked with Iulia, daughter of Titus, and Domitia [6] Longina, the wife of Domitian. For a time his life was threatened by Domitian, however, then he was accepted into the Senate; *cos. suff.* AD 84. *Cos. suff. II* together with Trajan in March 98, as successor of I. Frontinus. Both had influenced Nerva at the adoption of Trajan in the autumn of 97. This is also evident from I.'s third consulship in 100, as successor of Trajan, again alongside Frontinus. He adopted I. [II 141] Ursus Servianus. PIR² J 630; SYME, RP, 4–7 *passim*.

[II 141] L. I. Ursus Servianus = Ser. I. Servianus. Born c. AD 47, possibly in Narbonensis. Adopted before AD 102 by L. I. [II 140] Ursus. Married to Domitia [10] Paulina, sister of the future emperor Hadrian earlier than 98. *Cos. suff.* in 90, consular governor of Germania superior from autumn 97; accompanied Trajan to the Danube in 98, governor of Pannonia. Probably took part in the first Dacian War. *Cos. ord. II* in 102 alongside Licinius Sura, thus evidently belonging to the innermost circle of Trajan's trusted followers. Pliny befriended him (Plin. Ep. 10,2). Domitius [II 25] Tullus charged him in his will with arranging his funeral; from this it is also evident that he had several children (CIL VI 10229). Influential with Hadrian; but Annius [II 16]

Verus was more powerful (cf. [1]). *Cos. III* not until 134. His daughter Iulia Paulina was married to Pedanius Fuscus Salinator, *cos.* 118. He wanted his nephew from this marriage, Pedanius Fuscus (born 113), a great-nephew of Hadrian, to succeed Hadrian; when Hadrian adopted Ceionius [3] Commodus, Servianus, by then 90 years of age, and his nephew acted against Hadrian. Fuscus was executed, Servianus probably forced to commit suicide. PIR² J 631.

> 1 E. CHAMPLIN, in: ZPE 60, 1985, 159ff.   2 A. BIRLEY, Hadrian, 1997, *passim*.

[II 142] I. Valens. see → Licinianus

[II 143] I. Valentinus. Treverian; he joined I. [II 43] Civilis and called the Gauls to war against Rome. After his capture executed by Petillius Cerialis. PIR² J 611.

[II 144] Cn. I. Verus. Son of I. [II 132] His senatorial career began under Hadrian; he attained the suffect consulship c. AD 151, after only two praetorian posts, the second of which was *praefectura aerarii Saturni*. Thereafter legate in Germania inferior, Britannia and finally Syria, not before 163. Took part in the reconscription of the *legiones II* and *III Italicae* in c. 165 (AE 1956, 123). Designated for a second consulate in 180, but died before.

> PIR² J 618; E. DĄBROWA, Governors of Roman Syria, 1998, 110ff.   W.E.

[II 145] C. I. Verus Maximus Caesar was the son of → Maximinus Thrax (AD 235–238) and Caecilia Paulina (?). Made Caesar and *princeps iuventutis* early in 236 by his father (Hdn. 8,4,9; SHA Max. Balb. 22,6; Aur. Vict. Caes. 25,2) and co-opted into the *Sodales Antonini* and the *Sodales Flaviales Titiales* (CIL VI 2001,19–20; 2009,21–23), he ruled alongside his father, bearing like him the honorific titles of *Germanicus maximus, Dacicus maximus* and *Sarmaticus maximus* (CIL II 4756; III 3708; 10639; RIC 4,2, S. 151ff., 154ff.). He and his father were killed by mutinying soldiers near Aquileia in 238; he suffered *damnatio memoriae* (Hdn. 8,5,9).

> PIR² I 620; KIENAST², 185.   TH.F.

[II 146] L. I. Vestinus. Equestrian from Vienna in Narbonensis. An intimate of Claudius [III 1], who praised him fulsomely in his speech on the *ius honorum* of the Gauls (CIL XIII 1668 = ILS 212 col. II). *Praefectus Aegypti* AD 60–62. [1]. Entrusted with the reconstruction of the Capitol by Vespasian in 70. I. [II 147] was his son. PIR² J 622.

> 1 G. BASTIANINI, in: ZPE 17, 1975, 273   2 DEMOUGIN, Prosopographie, no. 683.

[II 147] M. I. Vestinus Atticus. Son of I. [II 146]. Claudius spoke in AD 48 of the priestly offices conferred upon the sons of I. [II 146] Vestinus. Closely linked with Nero. *Cos. ord.* in 65. While I. was still consul, Nero forced him to slit his wrists. PIR² J 624.

[II 148] C. I. Victor. Governor of Arabia under two emperors; consul. AE 1989, 748 = Inscriptions de la Jordanie, 2, 25.

[II 149] C. I. Victor. Equestrian; deputized for a governor of Moesia inferior between AD 253 and 260. AE 1993, 1376.

[II 150] C. I. Vindex. Of an Aquitanian royal family; his father was already a Roman senator. Praetorian governorship of Lugdunensis not later than AD 67. Disillusioned with Nero and his regime, he organized a conspiracy involving numerous Gaulish tribes; only the Treverians and Lingones withheld their support. In Tarraconensis, he invited Galba to lead the rebellion. After Nero had at first ignored the insurgency, Verginius Rufus marched against it with three legions of the army of Germania superior. Allegedly, secret discussions were held between the two parties; however, the legions annihilated Vindex' troops and he committed suicide at Vesontio, PIR² J 628; the anonymous coins were minted not by him but by Galba [1].

1 P.-H. MARTIN, Die anonymen Münzen des J. 68, 1974.
W.E.

III. BISHOPS

[III 1] Pope, 337–352. Two Greek texts of his are preserved through → Athanasius. In them, I. rebukes the eastern bishops, for failing to bring the dispute concerning Athanasius and the see of Alexandria to Rome for a ruling. His attempt to reconcile the differences between the Arians and the Nicenes at the Synod of Serdica (Sofia) in 342 (or 343) failed: the eastern bishops excommunicated the bishop of Rome and his supporters; the western bishops replied in kind (→ Arianism).

Athanasios, Apologia contra Arianos 20–36; 49; 52–53 = PG 25,247ff.; Athanasios, Epistula de synodis 20, PG 26,681ff.; H. JEDIN (ed.), Hdb. der Kirchengesch. Bd II/1, 1973, 37–42.

[III 2] Q. I. Hilarianus. Lived in the second half of the 4th cent. AD. This bishop, who (presumably) resided in North Africa, was the author of two texts of AD 397: De ratione Paschae et mensis ('On the calculation of Eastertide') and De cursu temporum, a world history divided into six periods, of a thousand years each, in which the birth of Christ is dated to the year 5530 and the end of the world to AD 470.

De ratione Paschae et mensis, PL 13,1105–1114; K. FRICK (ed.), Chronica minora, 1892, 153–174 (De cursu temporum); B. KÖTTING, Endzeitprognosen zw. Lactantius und Augustinus, in: Histor. Jb. der Görres-Ges. 77, 1958, 129f.; K.-H. SCHWARTE, Die Vorgesch. der augustinischen Weltalterlehre, 1966, 169–176. RO.F.

IV. LITERARY FIGURES

[IV 1] I. Africanus. Orator of the 1st cent. AD, from Gaul (Quint. Inst. 8,5,15; on his father Tac. Ann. 6,7,4), contemporary and rival of Domitius [III 1] Afer (died AD 59). Quint. Inst. 10,1,118 singles out both from among the older generation of orators (cf. Tac. Dial.

15,3), however, he has a slightly lesser regard for the stylistically more modern I. (cf. Plin. Ep. 7,6,11): his powerful style is recognized (Quint. Inst. 12,10,11), but his pedantic choice of words is criticized, along with periodic sentence structure and an excessive use of metaphor. After the death of Agrippina in 59, he gave a congratulatory address to Nero (Quint. Inst. 8,5,15). His countryman I. Secundus wrote a biography of I. Africanus (Tac. Dial. 14,4).

FRAGMENTS: H. MEYER, ORF ²1842, 570ff.
BIBLIOGRAPHY: PIR² I 120; BARDON, 2,157f.; J. STROUX, Zu Quintilian, in: Philologus 91, 1936, 228f. (for 12,11,3). P.L.S.

[IV 1a] I. Africanus, S. see → Sextus Iulius Africanus
[IV 1b] I. Aquila Author of a work De disciplina Etrusca, who is known only from the index of authors in Pliny [1] the Elder (Plin. HN index 2 and 11).

PIR ²A 163. J. R.

[IV 2] I. (Gallus?) Aquila. Jurist, who wrote a book Responsa not before the time of the Severi [2] (early 2nd cent. AD) (extracts from it appear twice in Justinian's digests: [1]).

1 O. LENEL, Palingenesia Iuris civilis 1, 1889, 501f.
2 D. LIEBS, Jurisprudenz, in: HLL 4, 1997, 126f. T.G.

[IV 3] I. Atticus. Atticus is mentioned by → Columella (1st cent. AD) as one of his older contemporaries (Columella 1,1,14). He wrote a single-volume book (singularem librum) on viticulture (De vitibus? De cultura vitium?). REITZENSTEIN dated it prior to → Celsus [7], arguing that the latter had used it in his encyclopaedia; against him, SCHANZ/HOSIUS, BARDON and RICHTER argue the precedence of Celsus – probably wrongly. The fact that Columella predominantly writes of the two in the order Celsus et Atticus does not, in fact, confirm that Celsus was chronologically earlier: the only use of both names where chronology is explicitly a factor places Atticus first (Columella 3,17,4).

The importance of this respected author clearly lay in his technical praecepta (instructions); his economic rationes (calculations), on the other hand, are often criticized by Columella. A., like Celsus, belonged to a faction advocating moderate expenditure in viticulture (minor sumptus, compendium, cf. Columella 4,1,1; 4,2,3), which Columella and Graecinus opposed. His language and style appealed less to Columella; in contrast to his treatment of → I. [IV 9] Graecinus, he did not consider him worthy of a single verbatim quotation, despite referring to him frequently. Pliny names Atticus as the source of HN 14,15,17 (Plin. HN 1; cf. 17,90).
→ Agrarian writers; → Agriculture; → Viticulture

1 BARDON 2, 140ff. 2 PIR 4, no. 183
3 R. REITZENSTEIN, De scriptorum rei rusticae qui intercedunt inter Catonem et Columellam libris deperditis, thesis Berlin 1884, 27–30; 54 4 W. RICHTER (ed.), L. Iunius Columella, Zwölf Bücher über Landwirtschaft, vol. 3, 1983, 620 5 SCHANZ/HOSIUS 2, 791; 864 6 A. TCHERNIA, Le vin de l'Italie Romaine, 1986, 219 7 WHITE, Farming, 25. E.C.

[IV 4] I. Bassus, C. Latin rhetor of the Augustan-Tiberian period; known only from numerous references and quotations by Seneca the Elder, whose sons were among I.'s students (Sen. Controv. 10, pr. 12: *vos*), and from his funerary urn (ῥήτορος/*rhétoros*; IG 14,1675, here also the praenomen). In spite of his implicit and also explicit admiration, Seneca criticizes I. for imitating practical-forensic eloquence in declamatory teaching (Sen. Controv. 10, pr. 12; generally 3, pr. 1) – and shows thereby the deep division between the two spheres (although Seneca's position here is extreme: [3. 239]). Seneca's criticism of unnecessary harshness and vulgarity in his choice of words may also be connected to this (Sen. Controv. 1,2,21; 1,6,10f.; [3. 295; 190–197]). The assumption, based on the *cognomen*, that I. and the iambographer → Bassus [1] (PIR B² 82), the friend of the young Ovid and Propertius, are identical, is unfounded and chronologically improbable.

1 PIR I² 204   2 K. GEHRT, s.v. I. 122, RE 10,178–180 3 J. FAIRWEATHER, Seneca the Elder, 1981.   J.R.

[IV 5] I. Cerealis. Poet friend of → Martialis (Mart. 10,48,5; dedicatee of 11,52: cf. [1]) and of L. → Arruntius [II 12] Stella. Author of a *Gigantomachia* and of *Georgica*, reminiscent of Virgil's; both were common themes of his time. Otherwise unknown (see PIR² I 261). I. is equated to *Kereálios*, the author of the epigrams Anth. Pal. 11,129 (on a pretentious poet) and 144 (ironic on the use of uncommon words in declamations), and also – less likely however – with Velius Cerialis mentioned by Pliny (Ep. 2,19; 4,21).

1 N.M. KAY, Martial. Book XI. A Commentary, 1985, 180–185.

E. LIEBEN, s.v. I. (184), RE 10, 550; M. CITRONI, s.v. I.C., OCD, ³1996, 784–785.   S.FO.

[IV 6] I. Exuperantius. Grammarian of late antiquity, author of a *breviarium* on the history of the early Roman civil wars from the rise of Marius to Sertorius (109 to 71 BC). Sallust in particular ('Jugurtha'; 'Historiae') attested their grave historical inaccuracies and loose rhetorical style.

LEXICON: N. CRINITI, 1968.
EDITIONS: N. ZORZETTI, 1982.

[IV 7] Sex. I. Gabinianus. Famous rhetor and declaimer of the Flavian period (Tac. Dial. 26,8), from Gaul. Suetonius' biography (cf. grammar in index, before Quintilian) is lost, but cf. Jer. Chron. a.ABr. 2092 (AD 76), p. 188 H. and Comm. in Isaiam 8 pr.

R. HELM, Hieronymus' Zusätze in Eusebius' Chronik, 1929, 85.

[IV 8] I. Genitor. Rhetor of the 1st cent. AD, acquaintance and literary advisor of Pliny the Younger (cf. Plin. Ep. 7,30,4f.), who recommended him (ibid. 3,3,5–7) as a highly moral (cf. also 9,17) and conscientious teacher to → Corellia Hispulla. The letters 3,11; 7,30 and 9,17 are addressed to him.   P.L.S.

[IV 9] I. Graecinus, L. I., who came from Forum Iulii and initially belonged to the *ordo equester*, rose to be a senator. He was the father of the I. [II 3] Agricola much praised by Tacitus and ended his life as a victim of Caligula (Tac. Agr. 4,1; funeral inscription: BCAR 68, 1940, 178; see AE 1946, 94); on his political career, see I. [II 70]. His work on viticulture (*De vineis*; two volumes, Columella 1,1,14) arose in response and opposition to → Iulius Atticus. He could not exceed him in technical expertise, but much more in questions of economics. Pliny's view that I. had taken → Celsus [7] as a starting-point must be erroneous (Plin. HN 14,33). The great intellectual and linguistic impression made on Columella by the erudite, wise and stylistically skilful I. (Tac. Agr. 4,1; Columella 1,1,14: *facetius et eruditius*), can be seen in Columella's many, often *verbatim* references in his books on viticulture (Columella 3f.). This is particularly the case in the viticulture profitability model (Columella 3,3,4–11; cf. 4,3,1–6, unfortunately incompletely reproduced). His economic thinking revolved around *diligentia* (diligence) in the choice of soil (Columella 3,12,1), the handling of seedlings when planting and in maximizing yields. In this I. seems to have recommended small efficiently operating businesses (Columella 4,3,6). Pliny refers to him as a source for his HN 14–18, but rarely in the text.

→ Agrarian writers; → Agriculture; → Viticulture

1 J. ANDRÉ (ed.), Plin. nat. 14, 1958, 86, n. 1 on § 33 2 BARDON 2, 140ff.   3 F. MÜNZER, Beiträge zur Quellenkritik der Naturgeschichte des Plinius, 1897 (repr. 1988), 30f.   4 PIR 4, no. 344   5 R. REITZENSTEIN, De scriptorum rei rusticae qui intercedunt inter Catonem et Collumellam libris deperditis, thesis Berlin 1884, 41–44; 56 6 SCHANZ/HOSIUS 2, 724f.; 791; 864   7 A. TCHERNIA, Le vin de l'Italie Romaine, 1986, 198ff.; 209–221 8 WHITE, Farming, 25f.   E.C.

[IV 10] I. Honorius. Latin grammarian and teacher of rhetoric from the 4th/5th cents. AD. For teaching purposes, I. drew up a copy of the catalogue of names of a scarcely legible map of the world (ch. 1), which had been published by a pupil (ch. 51). He indexed it according to the points of the compass and geographical categories (countries, cities, rivers, peoples). The original version of this *Excerpta sphaerae* (Cosmographia = A in GLM), which Cassiodorus (Inst. 1,25,1) recommended to his monks for study, is only partly preserved in Par. Lat. 4808 (mid 6th cent.; [1. 5,550]). A revision from late antiquity (Cosmographia Iulii Caesaris = B), surviving in several MSS (from Verona, Cap. 2, around 600; [1. 4,477]) deletes the passages relating to I. and places at the beginning a probably apocryphal report of an imperial survey of the Caesarian Augustan period. Its expanded revision, after Orosius 1,2, probably also still from the 5th cent., presents the first part of the work identified since the 8th cent. (Vind. 181; [1. 10,1473]) and called *Cosmographia Aethici* since the 9th cent., which attempts a rhetorical stylization of the bare bones of the skeleton text.

1 E. A. Lowe (ed.), Codices Latini antiquiores, 1934ff.; Suppl. 1971.

EDITIONS: GLM, xix-xxix. xlvif. 21–55 (recension A and B), 71–103 (Aethicus); W. KUBITSCHEK, in: WS 7, 1885, 1–24; 278–303 (ch. on rivers).

BIBLIOGRAPHY: W. KUBITSCHEK, Kritische Beitr. zur Cosmographia des J.H., 2 vols., 1882f.; C. NICOLET, P. GAUTIER DALCHÉ, Les 'quatre sages' de Jules César, in: Journal des savants 1986, 157–218.

[IV 11] I. Martialis. One of the closest friends of the poet → Martialis (cf. Mart. 1,15; 11,80,5ff.; 12,34), who sent him bk. 3 (cf. 3,5), bk. 6 (cf. 6,1) and then the first seven bks. in a copy corrected by his own hand (cf. 7,17); the epigrams 5,20; 9,97 and 10,47 are also directed at Martial. He owned a villa in a glorious location (4,64, cf. 7,17) on the Clivus Cinna (modern Monte Mario) [3].

1 L. FRIEDLÄNDER (ed.), Martial, 1886, 174   2 PIR²
I 411   3 C. NEUMEISTER, Das ant. Rom, 1991, 215–221.
P.L.S.

[IV 12] I. Modestus. An educated freedman of Iulius → Hyginus, whose interest in grammar and ancient history he shared (Suet. Gram. 20,3). Probably active in the late Augustan and Tiberian periods, he wrote a monograph De feriis (Macrob. Sat. 1,4,7; 1,10,9; 1,16,28) and miscellanea in at least three volumes (Gell. NA 3,9,1, cf. praef. 9). The quotations in Quintilian, Charisius and Diomedes [1. fragments 3–8] may originate from the latter. It is uncertain whether the Modestus referred to in Mart. 10,21,1, Ps.-Acro, Vita Hor. 2 (1.3 KELLER) and the Virgil scholia (schol. Vat. Georg. 3,53; brevis expositio ad 1,170; 364; 378) is I. or another scholar, Aufidius Modestus.

1 GRF (add), 9–23   2 R. A. KASTER, Suetonius, De Grammaticis et Rhetoribus, 1995, 213f.   R.A.K.

[IV 13] I. Montanus. see → Montanus
[IV 14] I. Paris. Late antique epitomator of the 9 volumes of Exempla of → Valerius Maximus; the work is dedicated to one Licinius Cyriacus. The Exempla are reduced to pure information, so as to serve as a fund of rhetorical argumentation – unlike the original. The transmission is based on a Carolingian copy of a late antique version [1].

EDITIONS: 1 C. KEMPF, Valerius Maximus, 1888, xv-xviii; 473–587   2 R. FARANDA, Valerius Maximus, 1971, 756–1001.
BIBLIOGRAPHY: 3 G. BILLANOVICH, Dall' antica Ravenna alle biblioteche umanistiche, in: Annali dell'Università cattolica S. Cuore 1955–57, 73–107   4 D. M. SCHULLIAN, I.P., in: P. O. KRISTELLER et al. (ed.), Catalogus translationum et commentariorum, vol. 5, 1984, 253–255   5 P. L. SCHMIDT, in: HLL 5, § 534.1.

[IV 15] I. Paulus. Poet of the 2nd cent. AD, a member of the circle of → Gellius [6]; in the latter's Noctes Atticae (19,7,1) discussions take place on I. P.'s farm in the ager

Vaticanus. Described by Gellius (cf. e.g. 5,4,1) several times as doctissimus, I. P. comments at 1,22,9ff.; 16,10,9ff. on the semantics and etymology of particular phrases. He may be identical to the Paulus cited in Charisius, Gramm. p. 161,8ff.; 181,10ff.; 281,24ff.; 314,6.ff BARWICK, who commented on Coelius [I 1] Antipater and the fabulae togatae of Afranius [4].

K. SALLMANN, in: HLL 4, § 491.2.   P.L.S.

[IV 16] I. Paulus. Roman jurist of between c. AD 160 and 230 [1]. Probably a pupil of Cervidius → Scaevola (Dig. 23,3,56,3; Dig. 28,2,19), at times lawyer (on this [3. 1831f.]) and assessor of the Praetorian prefect → Papinianus (Dig. 12,1,40), also councillor under Septimius Severus and Caracalla. I. was banished by Elagabalus, but recalled to the → consilium by Alexander Severus [3. 1841; 8. 151]. As author of around 85 works (300 book rolls), I. was even more prolific than the second 'encyclopaedist' of his time, → Ulpianus. More excerpts of the latter's works were used in Justinian's → Digesta, nonetheless I.'s excerpts amounted to a sixth. I. also wrote one shorter (23 bks.) and one more comprehensive edict commentary (Ad edictum; 80 bks.; on this see [8. 155ff.]), law commentaries, Ad legem Iuliam et Papiam (10 bks.), Ad legem Aeliam Sentiam (3 bks.) and Ad legem Iuniam (2 bks.), monographs on financial law (De iure fisci; De censibus, each 2 bks.), civil law (De fideicommissis, 3 bks.), administrative law (De officio proconsulis, 2 bks.) and criminal law (De adulteriis, 3 bks.), casuistic works (Quaestiones, 26 bks.; on this [6]) and reports (Responsa, 23 bks. [2. 304f.]) as well as textbooks (Institutiones, 2 bks.), Regulae ('Rules of Law', 7 bks.) and Manualia ('Handbooks', 3 bks.; [2. 217ff.]). I. also compiled the only collection of annotated imperial judgements from the Principate, which was available to Justinian's editors in two editions, as Decreta (3 bks.) and the Imperiales sententiae in cognitionibus prolatae (6 bks.) [2. 181ff.; 8. 172]. I. wrote numerous other monographs in single volumes: annotations to laws and Senate decrees, also on individual issues of civil, procedural, criminal and administrative law. Some of his short monographs are only excerpts from the edict commentary [8. 156f.] or other duplicate editions [8.156f, 165, 169].

I. engaged with the entire tradition of jurisprudence: He wrote abstracts of the Digesta of → Alfenus [4] Varus (7 bks.) and the Pithana ('Arguments') of → Antistius [II 3] Labeo (8 bks.), commented on other jurists of the early Principate (Ad Plautium 18 bks., Ad Sabinum 16 bks., Ad Vitellium 4 bks., see [2. 261; 8. 152f.], and Ad Neratium 4 bks.) and annotated the Digesta of Salvius → Iulianus [1], the Responsa of his teacher C. Scaevola and the Quaestiones and Responsa of → Papinianus. In these commentaries, didactic exposition, interspersed with classifications, rules and definitions, often takes second place to polemics.

Because I. was one of the most popular jurists of late antiquity, updated 'summaries' of various juridical writings in his name were in circulation from the early

4th cent. onwards, e.g. (each 1 bk.) *Regulae, De poenis paganorum, De variis lectionibus* [5. 67, 71], *De cognitionibus* and *De poenis omnium legum* [8. 174]. The *Sententiae receptae ad filium* (*Sententiae Pauli*, 5 bks.), published at the end of the 3rd cent., is also considered likely to be pseudepigraphic; its spread in the West is attested by the Visigothic *Interpretationes* [4; 7]. Constantine the Great forbade the judicial use of the critical *Notae* on Papinian (Cod. Theod. 1,4,1; 9,43,1), but he confirmed the validity of all of I. Paulus' other writings, in particular the *Sententiae* (ibid. 1,4,2). The law governing → citations of 426 (ibid. 1,4,3), which incorporated I. in its posthumans judgement, confirmed the validity of the *Sententiae* and the invalidity of the *Notae*, whose use in digest compilation Justinian, however, permitted (Constitution *Deo auctore* § 6).

1 PIR II, 203f.   2 SCHULZ   3 H. T. KLAMI, Iulius Paulus, in: Sodalitas 4, 1984, 1829–1841   4 WIEACKER, RRG, 133, 150   5 D. LIEBS, Recht und Rechtslit., in: HLL 5, 1989, 55–73   6 J. SCHMIDT-OTT, Pauli Quaestiones. Eigenart und Textgesch. einer spätklass. Juristenschrift, 1993   7 D. LIEBS, Die pseudopaulinischen Sentenzen, in: ZRG 112, 1995, 151–171; ZRG 113, 1996, 132–242   8 Id., Jurisprudenz, in: HLL 4, 1997, 83–217.   T.G.

[IV 17] I. Pollux. (Ἰούλιος Πολυδεύκης; *Ioúlios Polydeúkēs*). Rhetor from Naucratis (Egypt), 2nd half of the 2nd cent. AD (each of the 10 bks. of his → *Onomastikón* is preceded by a dedication to the emperor Commodus), pupil of → Hadrianus [1] (a pupil of Herodes Atticus). He assumed the chair of rhetoric in Athens (not before 178) following a competition with his rival, the Atticist → Phrynichus. He was also famed for the beauty of his speech (cf. Philostr. VS 2,12); he died at the age of 58.

The Suda (π 1951) catalogues various works (which are not preserved): 'Conversations' (Διαλέξεις ἤτοι λαλιαί; *Dialéxeis ḗtoi laliai*), Μελέται/*Melétai*, 'Wedding Song for the emperor Commodus' (Εἰς Κόμοδον Καίσαρα Ἐπιθαλάμιον; *Eis Kómodon Kaísara Epithalámion*), 'Roman Speech' (Ῥωμαϊκὸς λόγος; *Romaïkós lógos*), 'The Salpinx Player or The Musical Contest' (Σαλπιγκτὴς ἢ ἀγὼν μουσικός; *Salpingtḕs è agòn mousikós*), 'Against Socrates' (Κατὰ Σωκράτους; *Katà Sōkrátous*), 'Against the Inhabitants of Sinope' (Κατὰ Σινωπέων; *Katà Sinópéōn*), Πανελλήνιον/*Panellénion*, Ἀρκαδικόν/*Arkadikón*.

Today the name of Pollux is associated primarily with the *Onomastikón*, the only work of Greek lexicography not to offer a series of lemmata and *interpretamenta*, but instead synonyms or concepts belonging to the same semantic field, arranged horizontally. Its importance lies in the fact that this arrangement was of great antiquity (it may have originated as early as the 2nd cent. BC, in the Middle East) and was certainly the most commonly used up to the Augustan period. Today the *Onomastikón*, however, is not preserved in its original version, but in an edited one (which is based on four families of codices, of which the *Ambrosianus* D 34

from the 10th/11th cents. is the oldest); it is based on an interpolated and abridged version, which was in the possession of Arethas of Caesarea (10th cent.) and was used by him.

Pollux was an Atticist (→ Atticism), but his very decision against the lexicographical and alphabetical structure in favour of an onomastic one – which was in fact less suitable for the presentation of precise rules – is evidence of a less rigourous, more descriptive turn of mind than the decisively prescriptive one of his rival → Phrynichus, the pupil of Aelius Aristides. I. inveighs directly against Phrynichus in bks. 8–10 with a reply to his criticism of 49 of the glosses recorded in books 1–7; above all, Pollux could not accept the narrow selection of authors which Phrynichus considered exemplary (for instance, there is a great difference in their respective attitudes to the New Comedy, especially Menander: Pollux deemed it linguistically inferior to the work of the authors of the Old Comedy, but nonetheless worthy) and did not hesitate to record words of literary Doric, Ionic and Aeolic (while explicitly rejecting words from everyday language). This willingness to compromise on lexicographical issues, and the resultant dispute with Phrynichus (which reached its climax in the matter of the occupation of the Athenian chair) brought him into conflict with various of his contemporaries (e.g. Chrestus and Athenodorus). → Lucianus also mocked him, esp. in Rhetorum praeceptor 24 (however, it is unlikely that the protagonist of his *Lexiphánes*, so fond of archaisms, represents Pollux). Although the followers of Phrynichus later regarded him as the ignoramus *par excellence*, there are references to him in the later lexicographical tradition which were not sufficiently acknowledged (e.g. in Hesychius, where various glosses are present with onomastic structure and materials closely related to those of Pollux).

Pollux used extremely disparate sources: in addition to the colossal lexicon of → Pamphilus, they include the *Onomastiká* of Gorgias and Eratosthenes (used above all in bk. 10, where Pollux defends himself against the attacks by Phrynichus concerning the description of various instruments), also Xenophon (Pollux in the section of bk. 5 on hunting), Aristophanes of Byzantium (several times, e.g. in bk. 2 on the terms for the ages of man, in bk. 3 on familiar and political onomatology, and in bk. 9 on children's jokes), perhaps Juba (in bk. 4), Rufus of Ephesus (in a section of bk. 2 dealing with parts of the body) and Epaphroditus.

The *Onomastikón* of Pollux not only provides information on many factual aspects of science and language (such as, in addition to those already mentioned, the theatre in bk. 4 and the constitution and institutions of the Athenian judiciary in bk. 8), but also, and mainly, constitutes a lexical repertory for many *loci classici*. Many citations are inexact and some are transformed into onomastic sequences (e.g. the case of Demosth. Olynth. 2,19 in Poll. 6,123), others show errors caused by the particular structure of the work (e.g. in 2,8, concepts may be ascribed to Thucydides which are not to be found there). On the other hand, Pollux offers many *variae lectiones* from antiquity and some indications for the attribution of works which, whether true or false, must be reasonably considered, e.g. the attribution of the pseudo-Xenophontic 'State of the Athenians' (Ἀθηναίων Πολιτεία; *Athēnaíōn Politeía*) to Critias (8,25), and perhaps that of the 'Margites' to Xenophanes (7,148).

→ Lexicography; → Onomastikon

> EDITIONS: E. BETHE, Pollucis Onomasticon, 3 vols., 1900–1937.
> BIBLIOGRAPHY: M. NÄCHSTER, De Pollucis et Phrynichii controversiis, thesis Leipzig 1908; E. BETHE, s.v. I. Pollux, RE 10, 773–779; R. TOSI, Studi sulla tradizione indiretta dei classici greci, 1988, 87–114.   R.T.

[IV 18] C. I. Polybius. see → Polybius

[IV 19] I. Romanus. Latin grammarian, lived probably in the 3rd cent. AD, since he cited → Ap(p)uleius [III] but certainly preceded → Charisius [3]. He is the author of a work entitled Ἀφορμαί (*Aphormaí*): the so-called 'materials' are probably to be understood in the sense of *Latinitatis*, 'pure Latin'. Only those parts are preserved which Charisius incorporated in his *Ars grammatica*. The work deals with parts of speech, case theory and orthography. Of the edition of Charisius by BARWICK, the following are attributable to I. R.: pp. 75,21–76,6; 145,21–27; 146,22–25; 149,21–187,6; 246,18–289,17; 296,14–297,28; 301,16–21; 307,17–311,2; 311,14–315,27. I. R., whom Charisius appears to have quoted *verbatim*, was not directly known in mediaeval times; wherever his name occurs, it is through the testimony of Charisius.

> J. TOLKIEHN, s.v. I. (434), RE 10,788f.; K. BARWICK, Remmius Palaemon und die röm. Ars grammatica, 1922, 63–66; 250; Id. (ed.), Charisius, 1925; P. L. SCHMIDT, in: HLL 4, § 439.1.   P.G.

[IV 20] I. Rufinianus. 3rd/4th cent. AD, author of a compiled guide to figures of speech, a continuation of the work of → Aquila [5] Romanus, adding a further 38 figures (some overlapping) (cf. p.38,1f. HALM), arranged alphabetically (on the title, see [7]). There are similarities above all to Quintilian. The examples are predominantly from Cicero's speeches and Virgil; only Latin authors are used. The work was preserved only in the Cod. Spirensis (sceptical [8]), lost (in the fire in the cathedral library of Speyer in 1689) but transcribed by Beatus RHENANUS (in Frobenius, Basel 1521). The tracts, *De schematis lexeos* (one excerpt in the Codex Casanat. 1086, 9th cent., see [6]) and *De schematis dianoeas*, also transmitted in the name of I. R., are not his.

> EDITIONS: HALM, p. 38–47 [48–62].
> BIBLIOGRAPHY: 1 G. BALLAIRA, Sulla trattazione dell'iperbole in Diomede, in: Grammatici latini d'età imperiale, 1976, 183–193, esp. 188ff. 2 A. GANTZ, De Aquilae Romani et J. R. exemplis, thesis 1909, 61ff. 3 B. GERTH, s.v. I. (437), RE 10, 790–793 4 M. C. LEFF, The Latin Stylistic Rhetorics of Antiquity, in: SM 40, 1973, 273–279, esp. 276f. 5 W. SCHÄFER, Quaestiones

rhetoricae, thesis 1913, 60ff. 6 U. SCHINDEL, J.R. – Zum Nutzen von Exzerptüberl., in: Voces 4, 1993, 55–66 7 Id., in: HLL 6, § 617.5.
TRANSMISSION: 8 M. WELSH, The Transmission of Aquila Romanus, in: CeM 28, 1967, 286–313, hier 288f.   W.-L.L.

[IV 21] I. Secundus. Roman orator of the 1st cent. AD, from Gaul, contemporary and friend of Quintilian (Inst. 10,3,12), *ab* → *epistulis* of Otho in AD 69 (Plut. Otho 9) and teacher of Tacitus (cf. the latter's verdict in Dial. 2), who considered him worthy of a role in the *Dialogus*. I. died relatively young (Quint. Inst. 10,1,120f.). In spite of his respect, Quintilian draws attention (12,10,11) to I.'s overly timid choice of words (10,3,12ff., cf. Tac. Dial. 2,1). I. also wrote a biography of his countryman → Iulius [IV 1] Africanus (Tac. Dial. 14,4).

> PIR² I 559; BARDON, 2,200; R. SYME, Tacitus, 1958, 104ff; 614f.; 800; HRR 2, CLXXXLf.

[IV 22] I. Caesar Strabo, see → I. [I 11]

[IV 23] I. Valerius Alexander Polemius. From Alexandria, author of a translation of the Greek → Alexander Romance (review a) of the mid–4th cent. AD (cf. [2]), dedicated to the emperor Constantius II, not to be confused with the *cos.* of 338. The rendering, which paraphrases and expands, on the whole adheres closely to the text of the original; its style, characterized by poetic expressions, archaisms and neologisms, is affected. It was used in the → *Itinerarium Alexandri* (AD 341–345, cf. [2]), probably also by I. The preservation of the complete text depends on a few MSS, some fragmentary. However, a medieval epitome was widely distributed; it was responsible to a considerable degree for the influence of the Alexander Romance.

> EDITIONS: M. ROSELLINI, 1993 Epitome: J. ZACHER, 1867.
> BIBLIOGRAPHY: 1 B. AXELSON, Kleine Schriften zur lat. Philol., 1987, 43–73 2 D. ROMANO, Giulio Valerio, 1974 3 R. MERKELBACH, Die Quellen des griech. Alexanderromans, ²1977, 91; 98f.; 101; 163f. 4 D. J. A. ROSS, Alexander Historiatus, ²1988, 9–27; 108ff. et passim 5 P. L. SCHMIDT, in: HLL 5, § 540.

[IV 24] I. Victor. Author of a textbook of rhetoric, datable to the end of the 4th cent. AD. An *Ars rhetorica*, the work is a complete description of the rhetorical system. Its organisational principles are the → *officia oratoris*, while under *inventio* it also considers → status theory and → *partes orationis*. At the end are miscellaneous non-systematic sections on training technique (*exercitatio*), conversation (*sermocinatio*) and letters. As far as the sources enumerated in titles and subscriptions – Hermagoras (on Roman intermediate positions), Cicero (Inv., De or., Or.), Quintilian, Aquilius, Marcomannus (also the source of Consultus Fortunatianus and Sulpicius Victor), Tatian – can be checked, I. compiled, but was original in his successful synthesis of system elements and their adaptation. Typical too is the account's orientation towards the concrete, its practical sense; the vocabulary shows clear late Latin characteristics. The work is completely transmitted only in Vat. Ottob. Lat. 1968 (12th cent.), also in excerpts (Par. Lat. 13955, 9th/10th cents.; Munich, Clm 14436, 12th cent.), all of which – along with the sections included by Alcuin in his 'Rhetoric' (Rhetores Latini minores 523–550) – are based on a single archetype of the insular tradition.

EDITIONS: R. GIOMINI, M.S. CELENTANO, Ars rhetorica, 1980.
BIBLIOGRAPHY: A. REUTER, Unt. zu ... Julius Victor ..., in: Hermes 28, 1893, 73–134   R. GIOMINI, M.S. CELENTANO, Ars rhetorica, v-xxxvii (with bibliography)   M.S. CELENTANO, Un galateo della conversazione, in: Vichiana 3, p. 1, 1990, 245–253 (on p. 99–103)   Id., La comunicazione epistolare ... nell'Ars rhetorica di Giolio Vittore, in: RFIC 122, 1994, 422–435 (on p. 105f.)   U. SCHINDEL, in: HLL 6, § 617.3.   P.L.S.

Iullus Name (also in manuscripts *Iulus*) of the son of Aeneas (→ Iulus); epithet in the family of the Iulii [I 13–16]; first name of I. Antonius [II 1].   K.-L.E.

Iulus In the tradition set by Virgil I. is the only son of → Aeneas and → Creusa of Troy, progenitor of the Roman *gens Iulia*; in Troy he is called Ilus, later Ascanius (Aen. 1,267f.). The name Ascanius for a (usually the eldest) son of Aeneas first appears after Homer (in Homer two confederates of the Trojans have this name, Hom. Il. 2,862 from Ascania in Phrygia; 13,790), both in founding legends (Hellanicus FGrH 4 F 31; Dion. Hal. Ant. Rom. 1,54,2), which rule out his arrival in Italy, as in the account of Aeneas' flight from Troy (Tabula Iliaca; Str. 13,1,53, perhaps after Sophocles, but cf. fr. 373). Because there are no supporting documents, the name of the child depicted as accompanying Aeneas with his father Anchises on Attic vases of the 6th cent. and later is not clear. Usually Aeneas and Ascanius arrive in Italy together, as also in Fabius Pictor [1. 394f.], but Ascanius may also reach Italy alone (Dion. Hal. Ant. Rom. 1,53,4). There he is the successor of Aeneas as ruler of Lavinium and founder of → Alba Longa (according to Dion. Hal. Ant. Rom. 1,65,1 he was first called Euryleon; Liv. 1,1,11 makes him the son of Aeneas and → Lavinia).

The name I. appears only in Cato (Orig. fr. 9), where this (significant) name is conferred on him after the killing of → Mezentius (as a kind of initiation) and in Liv. 1,3,2, where the possibility is mentioned of distinguishing the older Ascanius, the son of Creusa of Troy, who is also called I., from a younger one, the son of → Lavinia; after this the *gens Iulia* definitely took on the Trojan myth. In Roman epic tradition before Virgil Aeneas had either a son Romulus (Naev. fr. 25) or a daughter Silvia (Enn. in Serv. Aen. 6,777).

1 G. MANGANARO, Una biblioteca storica nel ginnasio di Tauromenion e il P. Oxy. 1241, in: PdP 158–159, 1979.

E. FLORES, s.v. Ascanio, EV 1, 353–366; E. PARIBENI, s.v. Askanios, LIMC 2, 860–863; M. PETRINI, The Child and the Hero. Coming of Age in Catullus and Vergil, 1997, 87–110.   F.G.

Iuncus Widespread Roman cognomen and family name ('rush') [1. 729; 2. 334].
[1] I., M. Praetor in 76 BC see → Iunius [I 22] I., M.

1 WALDE/HOFMANN 1   2 KAJANTO, Cognomina.   K.-L.E.

[2] I. Vergilianus. Senator, who was one of the circle of Messalina and Silius and knew of their marriage; executed in AD 48. His name was perhaps Iunius I. Vergilianus, PIR² J 712.   W.E.

Iunia
[1] Daughter of D. Iunius [I 30] Silanus and Servilia, the niece of Cato, wife of M. Aemilius [I 12] Lepidus (Cic. Phil. 13,8; Vell. Pat. 2,88,1). In 30 BC she was accused of knowing of her eldest son's attack on Octavian, but was acquitted (App. B Civ. 4,50).
[2] I. Tertia. (Suet. Iul. 50,2; Cic. Brut. 3,3; also known as I. Tertulla: Cic. Att. 14,202; 15,11,1), sister of I. [1], half-sister of M. Iunius [I 10] Brutus and wife of C. Cassius [I 10] (Plut. Brutus 7). She died in AD 22 and bequeathed her fortune to many distinguished people (Tac. Ann. 3,76). PIR² I 865.
[3] I. Caecilia. Daughter of Q. Caecilius [II 16], engaged to Nero Iulius [II 34] Caesar since AD 17 at the latest (Tac. Ann. 2,43,2 [1. 98]), probably died unmarried. She is interred in the mausoleum of Augustus (ILS 184).

1 R. SEAGER, Tiberius, 1972, 119   2 RAEPSAET-CHARLIER 464.

[4] I. Calvina. Daughter of M. → Iunius [II 41] and Aemilia Lepida (Suet. Vesp. 23,4), high-spirited wife of (Sen. Apocol. 8,2) L. Vitellius, *cos. suff.* in AD 48, whose father accused her in 48 of incest with her brother L. Iunius (Tac. Ann. 12,4,1). Banished in 49, recalled by Nero in 59 (Tac. Ann. 12,8,1; 14,12,3), she lived until near the end of the reign of Vespasian (Suet. Vesp. 23,4). In her honour ILS 6239.

PIR² I 856; B. LEVICK, Claudius, 1990, 71,78; CAH 10, ²1996, 240, 900; RAEPSAET-CHARLIER 469; VOGEL-WEIDEMANN 197f., 322.

[5] I. Claudia. (Tac. Ann. 6,20,1; 45,3), also Claudilla (Suet. Cal. 12,1–2). Daughter of M. Iunius [II 37] Silanus, married → Caligula in Antium in 33 AD (Cass. Dio 58,25,2; [1. 32,63], contrary to the account in Cass. Dio 59,8,7 not repudiated [1. 34]). Died in *c.* 37 in childbed. PIR² I 857.

1 A. A. BARRETT, Caligula, 1989   2 RAEPSAET-CHARLIER 470   3 VOGEL-WEIDEMANN 231f.

[6] Daughter of M. Iunius [II 37] ([1. 474; 2. 245], Tac. Ann. 11,12,2). In AD 47 her husband C. Silius divorced her because of Messalina. Because Agrippina [3], once a

friend of I., prevented T. Sextius Africanus from mar-
rying with I., I. wanted to slander her to Nero (Tac.
Ann. 13,19–22). She was exiled by him in 55, but reha-
bilitated in 59. She died (childless) on the return trip in
Tarentum (Tac. Ann. 13,19,2). PIR² I 864.

> 1 RAEPSAET-CHARLIER 474   2 CAH 10, ²1996
> 3 D. BALSDON, Die Frau in der röm. Antike, 1979, 115,
> 126, 133f.

[7] I. Torquata. Daughter of C. Iunius [II 31], still a
Vestal (CIL VI 2128 = ILS 4923) at 64 years of age, later
Vestalis maxima (CIL VI 2127; Tac. Ann. 3,69,6). In
her honour CIL VI 20788; 20852; Syll.³ 794. PIR²
I 866. RAEPSAET-CHARLIER, 475.   ME.STR.

Iunianus see → Iustinus [5]

Iunior Author of a dedicatory inscription (six distichs
under the heading Ἰουνίωρος; *Iouníōros*), in which a
statue of Aphrodite proclaims that it was erected in
Sinuessa (Campania) next to a temple with a view of the
sea: Eon (Ἠιῶν; *Ēiôn*, v. 3), the one performing the
dedication, introduces herself as a freedwoman of
Drusus (the Elder or the Younger?) and his wife (v. 4). It
cannot be proved that this poet is identical with Seneca's friend Lucilius Iunior or with the epigrammatist
→ Pompeius Macer Iunior.

> EpGr 810 = Anth. Pal. appendix I 199 COUGNY.   M.G.A.

Iuniores Under the centuriation system, which the
historiographical tradition ascribed to king Servius Tullius, the Roman people were divided into *classes* according to the wealth of individual citizens. It was simultaneously used for political and military purposes.
Each class consisted of two groups of citizens: the *iuniores* (men of 17–46 years), who had to perform military
service and fight where and whenever it was demanded
of them, whereas it was the duty of the *seniores* (men of
46–60 years) to defend the town itself against attacks
(Pol. 6,19,2; Liv. 1,43,1f.: *seniores ad urbis custodiam
ut praesto essent, iuvenes ut foris bella gererent*; Gell.
NA 10,28,1; Dion. Hal. Ant. Rom. 4,16f.).

In the 4th cent. AD, the term *iuniores* described
recruits of sufficient physical and intellectual ability
(Cod. Theod. 7,13,1, AD 353; Veg. Mil. 2,5). Also, in
the → *Notitia Dignitatum* certain units were described
as *iuniores*; they were probably formed from already
existing units and then supplemented with new recruits.
The older units were known as *seniores*; this applied,
e.g. to the *legiones Herculiani seniores* and the *Herculiani iuniores* as well as the *vexillationes* of the *Batavi
seniores* and *Batavi iuniores* cavalry units. This practice
was perhaps introduced by Valentinian I.
→ Armies

> 1 R. TOMLIN, Seniores-Iuniores in the Late-Roman Field
> Army, in: AJPh, 1972, 253–278.   J.CA.

Iunius Roman surname, derived from the name of the
goddess Iuno [1. 470; 2. 731]. The *gens* was plebeian;
the idea that this family originated from the patrician
founder of the Republic L. I. [I 4] Brutus (Cic. Att.
13,40,1), which was particularly propagated by the
murderers of Caesar, M. and D. I. Brutus [I 10 and 12],
was already a matter of controversy in ancient times
(Plut. Brutus 1,6–8). T. → Pomponius Atticus (Nep.
Att. 18,3) composed a family history at the request of
M. Brutus. This gens became politically important from
the 4th cent. BC with the lines of the Scaevae, Bubulci
and Perae. From the end of the 3rd cent., the Bruti and
Silani became dominant. The Bruti died out after the
murderers of Caesar were executed; the Silani, who derived their epithet from the Greek σιλανός (*silanós*, 'Silenus') (RRC 220; 337; [3. 535]), still belonged to the
leading families of senators in the 1st cent. AD. The
most important *praenomina*: D., L. and M.

> 1 SCHULZE   2 WALDE/HOFMANN 1   3 WALDE/HOF-
> MANN 2.   K.-L.E.

I. REPUBLICAN PERIOD   II. IMPERIAL PERIOD
III. LITERARILY ACTIVE PERSONS

I. REPUBLICAN PERIOD

[I 1] I., C. Aedile 75 BC (MRR, 2,100; cf. 158; 162). 74
leaders of the *quaestio de veneficiis*, accused of bribery
by the people's tribune L. Quinctius in the proceedings
against → Abbius Oppianicus, and sentenced while still
in office (Cic. Clu. 1; 55; 89–96; 108). The iudicium
Iunianum discredited Sulla's court reform, which fore-
saw only senators as jurors, and which was overturned
by the *lex Aurelia* of 70 BC.   JÖ.F.

[I 2] I., M. Praetor 67 BC (MRR 2.150 n. 3), led the
legal proceedings against D. Matrinius (Cic. Clu. 126).
                                                    P.N.

IUNIUS BRUTUS

[I 3] I. Brutus, D. Son of I. [I 14], 100 BC adversary of L.
Appuleius [I 11] Saturninus, supporter of Sulla, praetor
at the latest 80, insignificant as consul of 77 (MRR
2,88). Married to → Sempronia, who in 63 made his
house available for meeting with the emissaries of the
Allobroges (Sall. Catil. 40,5). Cicero (Brut. 175) characterized him as a highly cultured and successful forensic orator.

[I 4] I. Brutus, L. The founder of the Roman Republic.
The historicity of his person, as well as that of the entire
account concerning the decline of kingship is disputed;
some scholars view the story as an invention of the late
4th cent. BC, some see it as a good oral transmission.
According to the literary tradition (particularly, Liv.
1,56–2,7; Dion. Hal. Ant. Rom. 4,67 – 5,18; additional
sources MRR 1, 1–3), Brutus (B.) is the son of Tarqui-
nia, sister of king → Tarquinius Superbus. After father
and brother were murdered by the king, B. plays dumb
in order to escape the same fate (hence, the epithet B.,
the 'dumb'). Because of an evil omen, B. accompanies
the sons of Tarquinius to the Delphic oracle. He alone

interprets correctly the oracle's answer that the one will rule who is the first to kiss his mother upon his return, by kissing the earth of Italy. After the rape of → Lucretia by Sextus Tarquinius, the son of the king, B. can restrain himself no longer, but calls for the abolition of the kingship, and Tarquinius is overthrown: L. B. introduces 'freedom (*libertas*) and the consulate constitution (*consulatus*)' (Tac. Ann. 1,1,1).

B. and L. Tarquinius Collatinus become the first consuls (according to the Varronian chronology in 509 BC). B. introduces a series of further constitutional and religious innovations: the fetching in of auspices before assumption of the office of consul (Val. Maximum 4,4,1); the *lex curiata* as the basis of the consular *imperium* (Tac. Ann. 11,22); changes of the *fasces* between the consuls (Liv. 2,1,8); introduction of the sacrificial king (*rex sacrorum*); and expansion of the Senate (back) to 300 members, through acceptance of the *gentes minores*. When two of his sons conspire with the Tarquinians to overthrow the Republic, they are sentenced to death and executed in presence of their father. Brutus thereupon induces his colleague to abdicate (he is succeeded by P. → Valerius Poplicola), and manages to have all Tarquinians banished from Rome by law. He himself subsequently falls in a battle against the Etruscans in single combat with Aruns Tarquinius. He is first succeeded by Sp. Lucretius Tricipitinus, then by M. Horatius [6] Pulvillus (a singular transmission by Pol. 3,22,1 portrays him as a colleague of B., and dates the 1st Roman-Carthaginian treaty during his consulate).

The story of B. is a projection of the ideals of the Roman Republican aristocracy: the victorious struggle against monarchical domination, constitutional government, individual severity, and self-sacrifice for the fatherland. These ideals were revitalized during the crisis in the Republic that followed the murder of Caesar I. [I 10 and 12], and the anti-Imperial propaganda. The story of the decline of the monarchy, through the hubris of the king, was a powerful historical example that continued to exert an influence well into modern times. An old statue of B. stood on the Capitol, under the statues of the seven kings (Plut. Brutus 1,1). → Accius composed a tragedy *B.* (perhaps inspired by I. [I 14]), (TRF³ 328–331 = 237–239D). The famous bronze head (Rome, MC) is not authentic.
→ Porsenna

A. MASTROCINQUE, Lucio Giunio Bruto, 1988.

[I 5] **I. Brutus, L.** According to annalist tradition, as the people's tribune in 494 BC, he was the driving force behind the exodus of the plebeians from Rome (Dion. Hal. Ant. Rom. 6,70–81; 7,14–16); a later invention, based on I. [I 4].　　　　　　　　　　　　　K.-L.E.

[I 6] **I. Brutus, M.** The people's tribune of 195 BC. As *praetor urbanus et peregrinus* of 191 he consecrated the temple of the Great Mother on the Palatine, whereby the *Pseudolus* of → Plautus was presented (MRR 1, 353). From 189 to 188, he was a member of a 10–man commission to Asia Minor. As *cos.* in 178, at first he

fought against the Ligurians, and finally went to the aid of his colleague A. Manlius Vulso against the Istrians (Liv. 41,5,5; 9–12).　　　　　　　　　　　　　P.N.

[I 7] **I. Brutus, M.** Politically unimportant (curulian aedile 146 BC ?, praetor 140?), one of the founders of Roman jurisprudence, see I. [III 1]

[I 8] **I. Brutus, M.** As praetor in 88 BC, he was to stop L. Cornelius [I 90] Sulla on the march to Rome; in 87 he went over to the side of the Marians, and committed suicide in 82 during the battle against Cn. Pompey in Sicily (Liv. Per. 89; App. B Civ. 1,271).　　　　K.-L.E.

[I 9] **I. Brutus, M.** Spouse of → Servilia, father of the murderer of Caesar I. [I 10]; the people's tribune in 83 BC and founder of a colony in Capua [1]. In 78, after the transfer of Mutina, and while serving as legate of Aemilius [I 11] Lepidus in Gallia Cisalpina, he was killed under mysterious circumstances at the bidding of Cn. Pompeius (Plut. Pompeius 16).

1 P. B. HARVEY, Cicero, Consius and Capua, II: Cicero and M. Brutus' Colony, in: Athenaeum 60, 1982, 145–161.
　　　　　　　　　　　　　　　　　　　　W.W.

[I 10] **I. Brutus, M.** The murderer of Caesar, was born in about 85 BC. After the death of his father I. [I 9] in the year 78 the half-brother of his mother, M. → Porcius Cato, took charge of his education. In the year 59, Brutus (B.) – whose name became Q. Servilius Caepio Brutus after he was adopted by a relative of his mother [2. 975f.] – became involved in the Vettius affair (→ Caesar) but was freed from this unpleasant situation by Caesar, whose long-standing relationship with his mother → Servilia (cf. [4]) was the talk of the town (Cic. Att. 2,24,2–4). During the period 58–56, B. accompanied Cato, who had been placed in charge of the annexation of Cyprus. Through the correspondence of Cicero, various money transactions of B. from this period are known to us by chance; these shed light on the business practices of private persons of Rome in the provinces [6. 228–232]: B. granted loans to Cypriot cities in straitened circumstances, e.g. to Salamis, at an annual interest rate of 48 percent. In 53, after he had returned to Cyprus (Ps. Aur. Vict. Vir. ill. 82,3–4) as quaestor and attendant of his father-in-law Appius Claudius [I 24] Pulcher (the marriage with Claudia was probably in 54), the governor of Cilicia (53–51), he sought to collect outstanding payments by force; the transactions were condemned by Cicero, the successor to Claudius, (Cic. Att. 5,21,10–13; 6,1,3–7; 2,7–10; 3,5).

In Rome, B. at first stood against → Pompeius in 52 (Quint. Inst. 9,3,95), who was responsible for his father's death; after the assassination of Clodius [I 4], he wrote a pamphlet in favour of the murderer Milo (Ascon). 41C. The events surrounding this deed brought B. together with Cicero; in 51, however, a brief alienation occurred (by reason of the above-mentioned financial affair). In 49 B. was active as legate in Cilicia, and later in Macedonia. In the Civil War, he took the side of Pompey, which he had attacked before. After the decisive battle of Pharsalus (9 August 48 BC) he fled; however, Caesar pardoned the son of his mistress, and B. shifted from the circle of friends of Pompey into that of Caesar [2. 980f.]. Thereafter he worked for the latter in Asia Minor; in 46 Caesar handed over to him the administration of Gallia Cisalpina, in which office he remained until the spring of 45 (MRR 2, 301); in 44 he obtained the office of praetor (MRR 2, 321); in 41 Caesar placed him in prospect for the consulate. After his return from Gaul, B. had separated from Claudia, and contracted a second marriage with → Porcia. The wedding with the daughter of Cato and widow of Bibulus, like the nearly simultaneous publication of Cato's written encomium, was a sensational political event. (Porcia's father and first husband alike had remained until their deaths the most implacable opponents of Caesar.) Nevertheless B.'s break with Caesar did not take place until February 44, when the latter had himself nominated as dictator for life [2. 988].

Because of his reputation and his closeness to Caesar, I. along with → Cassius [I 10], [I 10] quickly assumed the leading role among the approximately 60 conspirators against the dictator. His motive (to save the Republic), which was born more out of misguided idealism than from political understanding, was glamourized later. The fact that, by his deed, he sacrificed his own secured career speaks for B. After Caesar's assassination on 15 March 44 (Plut. Brutus 7–18 with the facts leading up to it [2. 988ff.]), it became clear how inadequately the subsequent course of action had been thought through. B. quickly found himself on the defensive against M. → Antonius [I 9] as well as Octavianus (→ Augustus). In April he left the capital; in August Italy. In Greece, he gathered troops, secured himself Macedonia, as well as Illyria as his own power base, until the Senate finally legalized the action through an *imperium maius* over all provinces of the east (in common with Cassius, after the provinces of Creta et Cyrenae had been assigned to both of them for 43 by a. *s.c.* of September 44). After the reversal in Rome and the formation of the so-called 2nd Triumvirate between → Aemilius [I 12] Lepidus, Octavianus and Antony (27 November 43 BC) B. and Cassius in the east prepared for the decisive struggle. In two great battles (October/November 42) they were defeated by Antony at Philippi; I. committed suicide (Plut. Brutus 40–52). B. found a belated apotheosis in the French Revolution as the classic freedom-fighter *in tyrannos*. Nothing has been preserved of the multifaceted literary output of B. (philosophical and moral treatises, speeches, letters, poems, pamphlets).

1 M.H. DETTENHOFER, Perdita Iuventus, 1992
2 M. GELZER, s.v. Iunius (Brutus) (53), RE 19, 973–1020
3 K.M. GIRARDET, Die Rechtsstellung der Caesaratten-täter, in: Chiron 23, 1993, 207–232   4 F. MÜNZER, s.v. Servilia, RE 2A, 1818–1820   5 U. ORTMANN, Cicero, Brutus und Octavian, 1988   6 W. WILL, Julius Caesar, 1992.   W.W.

[I 11] I. Brutus, P. Curule aedile in 192 BC. Praetor in Etruria in the year 190, took over for L. Baebius [I 7] Hispania Ulterior in 189. MRR 1, 362.   P.N.

[I 12] I. Brutus Albinus, D. Son of D.I. [I 3] Brutus, adopted by Postumius Albinus. In the year 56 BC Brutus (B.) was prefect of the fleet sent by Caesar against the Veneti (Caes. B Gall. 3,11,5–16,4), in 52 he fought against → Vercingetorix (Caes. B Gall. 7,9,2; 87,1). He probably occupied the quaesture in 50 [1]. As legate, he commanded naval operations at the siege of Massilia in the year 49 (MRR 2, 267) and in 48 very likely directed (MRR 3, 112f.) coin-minting operations in Rome. The administration of Gallia Comata probably followed in 47 (or shortly thereafter), as well as 46 (MRR 3, 113), and the office of praetor in the 2nd half the year 45. Caesar appointed him as one of the heirs in his will of 13 September 45 (Suet. Iul. 83,2), placed Gallia Cisalpina under his control at the outset of 44, and designated him as consul for the period of his planned absence from 42 (App. B Civ. 3,408). B. however joined the conspirators and escorted the hesitant Caesar into the Senate session [2] on 15 March 44. In the beginning of April, B. went to his province. As he refused to relinquish his control over this province, M. → Antonius [I 9], – to whom it had been assigned from 1 June – laid siege to his army towards the end of December near Mutina (→ Mutina, War of / Bellum Mutinense). In April 43 B. was freed by the consuls → Hirtius and Vibius Pansa. As commander-in-chief of the consular troops, B. took up the struggle against the ostracized Mark Antony in Gallia Transalpina, however he was defeated without battle, when his co-commander → Munatius Plancus deserted to the side of Mark Antony in September, B. was killed as he fled towards Macedonia (MRR 2 328, 347).

1 G. V. SUMNER, The Lex Annalis under Caesar, in: Phoenix 25, 1971, 358f.   2 F. MÜNZER, s.v. Iunius (Brutus) (55a), RE Suppl. 5, 373–375.   W.W.

[I 13] I. Brutus Bubulcus, C. Consul I 291 BC, consul II 277, was victorious over Lucanians and Bruttians (InscrIt 13,1,73).

[I 14] I. Brutus Callaicus, D. Younger brother of I. [I 7], consul in 138 BC with P. Cornelius [I 84] Scipio Nasica Serapio; both were imprisoned briefly by the people's tribunes, because they did not want to allow any exceptions on levies (MRR 1,483). I. then fought against the Lusitanians in Spain, then and settled the supporters of → Viriatus there. As proconsul in 137, he defeated the Callaici; in 136, he helped his colleague L. Aemilius [I 17] Lepidus against the Vaccaeians; however (MRR 1, 487), both failed. After his return, he triumphed (winner-epithet), and built the Temple of Mars on the field of Mars (with statues of the → Scopas). In 129, as legate, he helped the consul C. Sempronius of Tuditanus in Illyria (Liv. Per. 59). In 121 he supported the consul L. Opimius in his struggle against the supporters of C. Sempronius Gracchus on the Aventine (Oros. 5,12,7). He was an augur, highly cultured in literature, and a patron of the poet → Accius (Cic. Arch. 27; Leg. 2,54; Brut. 107; Val. Max. 8,14,2). His son: I. [I 3].

[I 15] I. Brutus Damasippus, L. (in the sources usually only Damasippus). Marian, was defeated in 83 BC by Pompey in Picenum, when he attempted to prevent the unification of Pompey's troops with L. Cornelius [I 90]; in 82, as praetor (urbanus?) – on the orders of the consul C. → Marius – he had prominent members of the nobility – who still remained in Rome – brutally murdered, with the Pontifex Maximus Q. → Mucius Scaevola among the victims (Cic. Fam 9,21; Sall. Catil. 51,32; Hist. 1,77,7M; Liv. Per. 86; Vell. 2,26,2; App. B Civ. 1, 403 among others). Then, he attempted in vain to free Marius, who was under siege in Praeneste, fought against the Sullans in the battle of Porta Collina, was then seized and executed on the command of Sulla.

[I 16] I. Brutus Pera, D. After his death, the first gladiatorial contests in Rome were organized in his honour by his son I. [I 25].

[I 17] I. Brutus Scaeva, D. 339 BC magister equitum of the dictator Q. Publilius Philo, in 325 first consul of the Iunii with L. Furius [I 12] Camillus; 313 probably IIIvir for founding of the colony in Saticula in Samnium.

[I 18] I. Brutus Scaeva, D. Son of I. [I 17], legate in 293, consul 292 with Q. Fabius [I 26] Maximus Gurges, fought against the Faliscans. With his election as consul, the first decade of Livy comes to an end.

[I 19] I. Bubulcus Brutus, C. Consul I 317, II 313, III 311, was victorious over the Samnites in 311 (InscrIt 13,1,71), censor 307 with M. Valerius Maximus; commissioned the construction of the temple of → Salus, which, he had vowed, and consecrated as dictator in 302 (Liv. 10,1,8f.; Val. Max. 8,14,6; later minting of the gens: RRC 337,2). The details of his career are unclear.

HÖLKESKAMP, Index s.v. I.

[I 20] I. Congus (Gracchanus?), M. Roman antiquarian, characterized by Lucilius in 123 BC as a man of adequate educational attainments (Lucil. 595f.). Cicero knows him as an expert on history (Cic. De or. 1,256; Planc. 58); he was dead not long before 54 (Planc. ibid.). Frequently identified with him is a M. I., who composed a work on Roman constitutional law (De potestatibus) in at least 7 bks.; this work was dedicated to the father of T. → Pomponius (Cic. Leg. 3,49). He is also identified with I. Gracchanus, who acquired his epithet due to his friendship with C. → Sempronius Gracchus (cf. Plin. HN 33,36; Ulp. Dig. 1,13,1 pr); the pro-Gracchian tendency of the work is a matter of dispute.

FRAGMENTS: F.P. BREMER, Iurisprudentiae antehadrianae quae supersunt 1, 1896, 37–40
BIBLIOGRAPHY: C. CICHORIUS, Untersuchungen zu Lucilius, 1908, Index s.v. I.; B. ZUCCHELLI, Un antiquario romano contro la nobilitas, in: Stud. Urbinati (B) 49, 1975, 109–126.

[I 21] (I.) Damasippus. Art dealer, see Licinius Crassus Damasippus, L. (?)   K.-L.E.

[I 22] I. Iuncus, M. (on the name MRR 3,113.). Praetor in 76 BC, then in 75–74 governor with the proconsular imperium (MRR 2,98). After the death of Nicomedes – by the provisions of whose will → Bithynia had fallen to Rome – he established Bithynia as a province, and affiliated it with Asia. When Caesar – after being captured by pirates and later ransomed – demanded their punishment, he refused to do this for unknown reasons (Vell. 3,41,3; Plut. Caesar 2,6–7; Suet. Iul. 4).   W.W.

[I 23] I. Pennus, M. Praetor in Hispania Citerior 172 BC, in the year 167 with Q. Aelius [I 10] consul (MRR 1, 432); unsuccessful command against the Ligurians (Liv. 45,16,3; 17,6; 44,1). Consulted the Senate because of the legation from Rhodes (Liv. 45,20,4–10).

[I 24] I. Pennus, M. Son of I. [I 23]. In the year 126 BC, as the people's tribune, enacted a law that envisioned the expulsion of non-citizens from Rome, in order to weaken the support of C. → Sempronius Gracchus (MRR 1, 508). He died shortly after attaining the position of an aedile (Cic. Brut. 109).   P.N.

[I 25] I. Pera, D. In 266 BC, as consul, triumphed over the Sassinates, as well as over the Sallentines and Messapians; as censor in 253 he relinquished his office after the death of his colleague (MRR 1,201; 211). In 264, he held the first gladiatorial games in Rome in honour of his deceased father I. [I 16] (Liv. Per. 16; Val. Max. 2,4,7). The reports in Ausonius (Griphus 2,36f.) that these were fought by Thracians or with Thracian weaponry, are not reliable.   C.MÜ.

[I 26] I. Pera, M. Son of I. [I 25], fought against the Ligurians; consul in 230 BC, with his colleague M. Aemilius [I 4] Barbula; 225 censor with C. Claudius [I 4] Centho. After the defeat at Cannae in 216, he became dictator with the task of exacting further levies. In autumn of that year, he was stationed with the army in Campania, where Casilinum was nevertheless lost to → Hannibal (MRR 1,248).

[I 27] I. Pullus, L. Consul in 249 with P. Claudius [I 29] Pulcher. On the way from Syracusae to Lilybaeum, the fleet under his command was forced by the Carthaginians to land at Camarina, where it got destroyed by a storm (Pol. 1,52–54). Later this was attributed by I. – as well as by his colleague – to alleged contempt for the auspices (Cic. Nat. D. 2,7; Div. 1,20; 2,20; 71 among others). With the salvaged troops I. occupied Mount → Eryx, but then was either captured by the Carthaginians, or committed suicide (Pol. 1,55; Zon. 8,15)

IUNIUS SILANUS

[I 28] I. Silanus, D. 146 BC leader of a commission for the translation of the agricultural books of → Mago of Carthage (Plin. HN 18,22f.).   K.-L.E.

[I 29] I. Silanus, D. Son of T. Manlius Torquatus (cos. 165), adopted by I. [I 28] (Cic. Fin. 1,24); one of the earliest documented instances of the change of a patrician into a plebeian family. Praetor of Macedonia in

141 BC. After his return due to complaints about his administration condemned in the *consilium* of his own father. He committed suicide from grief.

MRR 1, 477; 3, 113; ALEXANDER 7.   P.N.

[I 30] I. Silanus, D. Born in about 107, aedile before 69, praetor before 66, Pontifex before 64 (MRR 2,127; 143, 182). Consul in 62 BC. He is known to posterity because of his appearance in the Senate session of 5 December 63, while the matter of punishment for the Catilinarians was being discussed. As designated consul (in the summer I. had won the election against → Catilina, among others), he was the first whom Cicero asked for his opinion concerning this issue; he pleaded for the highest penalty (*ultima poena*); the following speakers – among others 14 consuls – agreed. After Caesar's famous rebuttal, I. claimed that by *ultima poena* is meant lifelong imprisonment (Cic. Cat. 4,7; 11; Sall. Catil. 50–53,1; Suet. Iul. 14,1). I. was married to → Servilia, the mother of the later murderer of Caesar M. I. [I 10] Brutus. He died before 57.   w.w.

[I 31] I. Silanus, M. Occupied Naples in 216 BC before → Hannibal; 212/1 praetor in Etruria, 210–206 with the proconsular *imperium* (?, cf. MRR 3,113f.) together with P. Cornelius [I 71] Scipio in Spain, where he also achieved military successes in 207/6.

[I 32] I. Silanus, M. Perhaps mint master in 145 BC (RRC 220; probably not identical with the mint master of 116 or 115, cf. RRC 285), in 124 or 123 maybe the people's tribune who enacted a *lex de repetundis* as forerunner of the so-called *lex Acilia* (→ Acilius [I 12]) [1]. Praetor no later than 112, consul in 109, rescinded exemptions from military service (Ascon. 68C, in 108 was defeated by the Cimbri in Gallia Transalpina, MRR 1,545; 3, 114) for which defeat he was charged by Cn in 104. Domitius [I 4] Ahenobarbus, but was acquitted (Cic. Div. Caec. 67; Ascon. 80C).

1 M.H. CRAWFORD, Roman Statutes, 1, 1996, no. 1, l. 74.

[I 33] I. Silanus (Murena?), M. Quaestor in Asia at the beginning of the 1st cent. BC (IPriene 121; for dating and *cognomen* cf. MRR 3,114f.), 77 praetor, 76 proconsul in Asia, where he observed a solar phenomenon (Plin. HN 2,100). He brought an image of the painter → Nicias to Rome, which Augustus had displayed in the Curia (Plin. HN 35,27; 131).   K.-L.E.

[I 34] I. Silanus, M. As Caesar's legate in 53 BC, he recruited troops, since there was a threat of rebellion in Gallia (Caes. B Gall. 6,1,1).

[I 35] I. Silanus, M. In 43 BC military tribune of M. Aemilius [I 12] Lepidus, by whom he was of sent out to Mutina (the identification, however, is debatable; it may possibly have been a reference to I. [I 34], see MRR 3,115. In 34 or 33 he was quaestor *(pro consule)* in Greece. Taunted by Cleopatra (Plut. Antonius 59), he changed from Antony to Octavian at the right time. The latter appointed him as *collega* to consul in 25.   w.w.

II. IMPERIAL PERIOD

[II 1] D. I. Arabianus Socrates. Financial procurator in the province of Arabia under Severus Alexander. SEG 37, 1539.

[II 2] Q. I. Arulenus Rusticus. see → Arulenus [2]

[II 3] L. I. Aurelius Neratius Gallus Fulvius Macer. Praetorian governor of Thracia, then of Arabia, finally *cos. suff.*, presumably in the late Severian period [1]. The senator mentioned in CIL VI 1433 is his relative. PIR² J 732.

1 O. SALOMIES, in: ZPE 97, 1993, 253ff. = AE 1993, 432.

[II 4] I. Avitus. In close contact with Pliny the Younger. Military tribune under Iulius [II 141] Servianus in Upper Germany and Pannonia AD 97–99; quaestor around 105–106; died as *aedilis designatus*, probably after the middle of 108, since he is mentioned in the will of → Domitius [II 25] Tullus. PIR² J 731.

[II 5] I. Blaesus. Senatorial governor of the province of Lugdunensis in AD 69. Although he was allied to Vitellius, the latter had him murdered, supposedly because he considered him a competitor. Related to I. [II 6] and [II 7]. PIR² J 737.

[II 6] Q. I. Blaesus. Proconsul of Sicily, *cos. suff.* in AD 10. In AD 14 consular governor of Pannonia, where he at first could not put an end to the mutiny of the legions; he was successful in this only with the help of → Drusus [II 1] the Younger. In the years 21–23 proconsul of Africa, appointed by the Senate without drawing lots, supposedly because he was *avunculus* of Seianus. After his successes against the rebellious Tacfarinas, he was declared *imperator* by the soldiers; Tiberius awarded him *triumphalia ornamenta* (Tac. Ann. 3,32; 35; 58; 72; 74). After the death of Seianus, he was attacked by Tiberius, and presumably died shortly thereafter. PIR² J 738.

[II 7] Q. I. Blaesus. Son of I. [II 6]. He was military tribune under his father in Pannonia, in AD 22, probably legate of his father in Africa. *cos. suff.* in 28 (cf. to AE 1987, 163). Since Tiberius refused to grant him the office of a priest in the year 36, he killed himself, together with his brother (Tac. Ann. 6,40,2). PIR² J 739.

[II 8] Q. I. Calamus. *cos. suff.* AD 143, on 9 August, testified together with M. Valerius Iunianus (unpublished military diploma).

[II 9] M. I. Chilo. Probably patrimonial procurator of Pontus (-Bithynia), hardly governor; he brought king Mithridates to Rome in AD 49, who had been driven out of the Bosporan Kingdom; for this he was designated with the title *Ornamenta Consularia* by Claudius. Although accused of extortion, he remained in his position up to the Neronian period. PIR² J 744.

[II 10] M. II. Concessus Aemilianus. Referred to in the dossier from Tacina (AE 1989, 721 = SEG 37, 1186). Probably proconsul of the province of Lycia-Pamphylia in AD 213–214.

G. CAMODECA, in: Ostraka 3, 1994, 467ff. = AE 1994, 1725.

[II 11] I. [–]cus Gar[gilius?—]ntilianus. Senator in the 2nd half of the 2nd cent. AD. *IIIvir capitalis, quaestor,* [–], *praetor, Iuridicus per Aemiliam, curator* of Cirta (the first known in Africa), legate with the two legions, *praepositus* of a vexillation of the Britannic legions, legate of the *legio II Italica, sodalis Flavialis* and probably *consul.* A statue was erected in Rome in his honour on the recommendation of Commodus.

> G. L. GREGORI, in: ZPE 106, 1995, 269ff. = CIL VI 41127.

[II 12] C. I. Faustinus [Pl]a[ci?]dus Postumianus. Senator, probably of African origin. After long-term praetorship, governor of Lusitania, then of Belgica, *cos. suff. c.* AD 204; probably consular legate of Lower Moesia in about 205–207. PIR² J 751. Cf. I. [II 13].

[II 13] C. I. Faustinus Postumianus. Either a descendant of I. [II 12] or identical with him. *Cos. suff.,* consularis governor of Tarraconensis and of Britain. PIR² J 752; BIRLEY, 161ff.

[II 14] I. Gallio. Senator, probably of Spanish origin. AD 32 banished to Lesbos by order of Tiberius, then returned to Rome. Friends with Seneca Rhetor; adopted his son I. [II 15]. PIR² J 756.

[II 15] L. I. Gallio Annaeanus. Eldest son of Annaeus Seneca and Helvia [2], Brother of Annaeus → Seneca. Adopted by I. [II 14]. Entered the Senate at the latest under Caligula; praetor at the latest around AD 46; *Proconsul Achaea* 51–52 (THOMASSON, I, 191); in a letter Claudius calls him *amicus* (SEG 3, 389 = [1]). The Jews of Corinth raised an accusation against Paulus before him; however, he rejected these accusations (Acta apostolorum 18,12ff.). *Cos. suff.* with T. Cutius Ciltus in July/August 56. After the enforced suicide of his brother, he also appears to have died. PIR² J 757; CABALLOS, I, 171f.; for his declamations see I. [III 3].

> 1 L. BOFFO, Iscrizioni ... per lo studio della Bibbia, 1994, 247ff.

[II 16] I. Homullus. Probably the son of I. [II 17]. *Cos. suff.* under Hadrian, consular legate of the province of Tarraconensis. PIR² J 759; Alföldy, FH, 26ff.

[II 17] M. I. Homullus. *Cos. suff.* AD 102; participated in the legal proceedings against Iulius Bassus and Varenus Rufus; consular governor of Cappadocia in *c.* 111–114.

> W. ECK, in: Chiron 12, 1982, 351ff. PIR² J 760.

[II 18] I. Iunillus. *Vir perfectissimus,* equestrian governor of Mauretania Caesariensis; comes from Ureu in Africa.

> AE 1975, 862; W. ECK, s.v. I. (86a), RE Suppl. 15, 125.

[II 19] Q. I. Marullus. As consul designate he proposed to the Senate the execution of → Antistius [II 5]. His proposal was prevented by Paetus Thrasea (Tac. Ann. 14,48,2f.). *Cos. suff.* AD 62 with → Eprius Marcellus. PIR² J 769.

[II 20] I. Mauricus. Senator, brother of Q. Iunius → Arulenus [2] Rusticus. Even under Nero, he already belonged to the Senate's so-called philosophical opposition. In AD 70 he sought from Domitian the release of the names of the informers under Nero (Tac. Hist. 4,40,4). Banished during the late period of Domitian's reign, he returned under Nerva, and belonged to the latter's trusted inner circle; he was even associated with Trajan. Several letters of Pliny the Younger to him.

> PIR² J 771; SYME, RP, 7, 571ff.

[II 21] I. Maximus. As military tribune of the *legio III Gallica,* he brought to Rome news of the victory of Lucius Verus over the Parthians. He was honoured with the *dona Militaria,* and he was designated as *quaestor* in an unusual fashion; *quaestor provincia Asiae* (IEph III 811); if certain fragments of a Roman municipal inscription have reference to him, he received even further military assignments, probably rose all the way up to the consulate, and was honoured with statues in the Forum of Trajan at the behest of the emperor (CIL VI 41144). PIR² J 774.

[II 22] T. I. Montanus. *Cos. suff.* in AD 81. AE 1973, 500, from Alexandria in the Troad probably refers to him: his career ranged from the position of a *IIIvir monetalis* up to the consulate, but with only one a praetorian office, the proconsulate on Sicily. It remains unclear how that is to be interpreted.

> W. Eck, s.v. I. (105), RE Suppl. 15, 125f.; HALFMANN, Senatoren 103.

[II 23] Kanus I. Niger. *Cos. ord.* AD 138; his son must have been the homonymous governor of Upper Germania in the years 116 and 118 (unpublished military diploma). PIR² J 782f.

[II 24] I. Otho. Son of a senator of the same name, who had joined the Senate under Tiberius. As *tribunus plebis* in AD 37, the son interceded in the Senate against the granting of a prosecution award, which resulted in his death soon thereafter. PIR² J 788f.

[II 25] A. I. Rufinus. *Cos. ord.* in AD 153; around 169/170 proconsul of Asia, where he is attested in IEph III 665; IV 2433 and IGR IV 1363; his brother is I. [II 26]. PIR² J 806; 811 (the evidence from Asia refers to him, not to I. [II 26]). Father of Pomponia Triaria.

> W. ECK, in: FS D. Knibbe, 1999, 299–302.

[II 26] M. I. Rufinus Sabinianus. Brother of I. [II 25]. *Cos. ord.* AD 155; proconsul of Africa 172–173.

> CIL VIII 10844 M. KHANOUSSI, A. MASTINO, Uchi Maius 1, 1997, 173ff. PIR² J 811.

[II 27] I. Rusticus. Senator, who in AD 29, was the first person to hold the office of *ab actis senatus* (PIR² J 813); his descendants were probably I. [II 28] and Q. Iunius → Arulenus [2] Rusticus.

[II 28] Q. I. Rusticus. Son or grandson of Q. I. → Arulenus [2] Rusticus (cf. SYME, RP, 7, 584). *Cos. suff.* AD 133; *cos. II ord.* 162. City prefect under Marcus Aurelius and Verus. As attested by numerous findings, weights and measurements were first standardized in a comprehensive fashion under him. It was in his law court that the Christian trial against Iustinus was carried out. As a Stoic, he was the teacher of Marcus Aurelius, who speaks of him in *Eis heautón* (1,7). PIR² J 814.

IUNIUS SILANUS

[II 29] C. Appius I. Silanus. see → Appius [II 4]

[II 30] C. I. Silanus. *Cos. ord.* AD 17; genealogical ordering is uncertain. PIR² J 823; SYME, AA, 191.

[II 31] C. I. Silanus. Father of I. [II 32 and 33]. Was married to an Appia Claudia. PIR² J 824; RAEPSAET-CHARLIER, no. 214; SYME, AA, 193.

[II 32] C. I. Silanus. Son of I. [II 31], Brother of I. [II 33], Father of Appius [II 4]. *Flamen Martialis, consul ordinarius* AD 10. Proconsul of Asia 20–21. In the year 22 there was an accusation against him in the Senate by the province of Asia and several consularis (Tac. Ann. 3,66ff.). He was condemned on the basis of *saevitia* and *repetundae*, and banished to the island of Cythnus. Out of gratitude, the province of Asia erected a temple for Tiberius, Livia and the Senate (Tac. Ann. 4,15,3). PIR² J 825.

[II 33] D. I. Silanus. Son of I. [II 31], brother of I. [II 32 and 37]. Accused of adultery with Iulia, Augustus' granddaughter. He was forced to leave Rome in AD 8 – without conviction. In AD 20, under Tiberius, he was allowed to return, without however being permitted to hold political office (PIR² J 826); for his descendant SYME, AA, 194.

[II 34] L. I. Silanus. Brother of M.I. [II 37] Silanus. He attempted to attain the consulate in AD 21, however, his efforts were not successful. PIR² J 827; SYME, AA, 191.

[II 35] L. I. Silanus. Son of I. [II 33]. *Flamen Martialis,* probably in AD 22 in place of I. [II 32]. *Cos. suff.* in 26. AE 1987, 163.

[II 36] L. I. Silanus. Son of I. [II 41]; related to Augustus through his mother Aemilia Lepida (RAEPSAET-CHARLIER, no. 29). In AD 41 engaged by Claudius to his daughter. *Comes* in the Britannia campaign, provided with the triumphal insignia. Privileged to hold political office 5 years before the legally stipulated time. Praetor in 48, accused of adultery, pushed out of the Senate by the *censor* Vitellius; resignation from the praetor's office on 29 December. This is all supposed to have happened at the instigation of Agrippina. He committed suicide on the day of his wedding early in AD 49. PIR² J 829.

[II 37] M. I. Silanus. Brother of I. [II 32 and 33]. Closely allied with → Tiberius. *Frater Arvalis; cos. suff.* AD 15 together with Tiberius' son Drusus. Of great influence in the Senate, often the first one to be asked for his *sententia*. In 20 he was able to achieve the return of his brother I. [II 33]. In 22 he made a petition to no longer date by the order of the consuls but by the *tribunicia potestas* of the emperor, which Tiberius rejected (Tac. Ann. 3,57,1). His daughter Iunia [5] Claudilla was mar-

ried to Caligula, probably in 33, however, by the year 37 she had already died. Caligula forced him to commit suicide before 24 May 38. PIR² J 832; SYME, AA, 194ff.

[II 38] M. I. Silanus. Son of I. [II 41] and Aemilia Lepida; in this manner a blood relative of Augustus. Born in AD 14, before 19 August. *Frater Arvalis. Cos. ord.* 46 during the entire year. In 54 proconsul of Asia. Toward the end of 54 Agrippina had him murdered by the procurator P. → Celerius and the freedman Helius, because she feared his revenge for the death of his brother I. [II 36], (*prima novo principatu mors*, Tac. Ann. 13,1,1). PIR² J 833.

[II 39] D. I. Silanus Torquatus. Son of I. [II 41] and Aemilia Lepida. Brother of Iunia Lepida and Iunia Calvina. Patrician; held various priestly offices. Quaestor of Claudius, *cos. ord.* AD 53. Because of his kinship with Augustus he was suspicious of Nero, who in 64 forced him to open his arteries. PIR² J 837.

[II 40] L. I. Silanus Torquatus. Son of I. [II 38], Iunia Lepida was his aunt, and Torquatus was raised by her husband C. Cassius. He was *salius palatinus* from AD 60. In the wake of the Pisonian conspiracy, he was accused of incest with his aunt, since he was viewed as politically dangerous also due to his kinship to Augustus. He was murdered by a centurio in Bari. Under Nerva the knight Titinius Capito erected a statue in the Forum Romanum in his honour (Plin. Ep. 1,17). PIR² J 838.

[II 41] M. I. Silanus (Torquatus) He married Aemilia Lepida, the great-granddaughter of Augustus [1]. *Cos. ord.* AD 19. Proconsul of Africa under Tiberius or under Caligula; whether for 6 years is a matter of dispute [2; 3; 4]. His sons are I. [II 36, 38, 39]. PIR² J 839.

1 U. WEIDEMANN, in: AC 6, 1963, 138ff.   2 VOGEL-WEIDEMANN, 97ff.   3 THOMASSON, Fasti Africani, 32ff.   4 SYME, AA, 191f.

[II 42] C. I. Tiberianus. According to the reconstruction of [1] both *consules ordinarii* of 281 and 291 (*cos.II*) are to be separated. The *cos. II* of AD 291 was for the first time consul *circa* 265, then *cos. II* and simultaneously *praefectus urbi*; he was probably also the tribune of the *legio X Gemina* in the year 249 (CIL III 4558, cf. p. 2328). His homonymous son was *cos. ord.* 281, *proconsul Asia* in c. 295–296 (IEph II 305); he became *praefectus urbi* in 303–304 (cf. PIR² J 841; 843).

1 M. CHRISTOL, Essai sur l'évolution des carrières senatoriales, 1986, 204ff.

[II 42a] I. Valerianus Equestrian patrimonial procurator in Macedonia under Hadrian, probably before AD 137; named in an imperial letter (unpublished inscription from Apollonia Mygdonia; personal communication from G. SOURIS).   W. E.

[II 43] L. I. Q. Vibius Crispus. see → Vibius   W.E.

III. Persons active in literature

[III 1] I. Brutus, M. Jurist, praetor 140? BC, along with P. → Mucius Scaevola and M'. → Manilius 'founder' of Roman jurisprudence (Dig. 1,2,2,39; Cic. Off. 2,50; Cic. Brut. 130). He wrote a *De iure civili* in dialogue form (3 bks., probably not of a technical juridical nature), to which presumably 4 further bks. were added, with his → responsa, which were edited retaining the names of the parties involved (just as in *Porcius Cato Licinianus*) (Cic. De or. 2,142; Cic. Clu. 141).

FRAGMENTS : F.P. BREMER, Iurisprudentiae antehadrianae quae supersunt 1, 1896, 22–25.
BIBLIOGRAPHY : BAUMANN, LRRP, Index s.v. I.   WIE-ACKER, RRG, 542f., 572.   T.G. and W.W.

[III 2] I. Filagrius. Gallo-Roman grammarian of the 5th cent. AD, according to [8] identical with the Philagrius at Sid. Apoll. Carm. 7,156f. (cf. 24,90ff.). He worked in Milan at the time of Augustus Valentinianus III (425–455), to whom I.F. had dedicated his commentary on Virgil's *Bucolica* and *Georgica* (on the other hand [11]), which was largely based on → Donatus [3] ([6. 233ff.]; for his use of Servius [11]); the commentary on the *Aeneis* [4. 95] is lost (but cf. [5]). Excerpts from I.F. – in common with those from the explanations of → Gaudentius [6] and Titus Gallus – form the core of a compilation of scholia to Virgil Ecl. and Georg. Two recensions have been handed down, partly in several versions (review a: *Explanatio* 1 and 2, lemma comm. on Ecl. [1. 1–189]); *Brevis expositio*, the same on Georg. 1/2 [1. 191–320]; recension b, *Scholia Bernensia* on Ecl. and Georg. 1–4 [2]. Irish glosses – especially in a – and insular abbreviations point to an Irish archetype (of the 7th cent.).

EDITIONS (preliminary): 1 H. HAGEN (ed.), Servius 3,2, 1902   2 Id., Scholia Bernensia, 1867.
BIBLIOGRAPHY: 3 W. HERAEUS, Drei Fragmente, in: RhM 79, 1930, 391, n. 1   4 K. BARWICK, De I.F., in: Commentationes philologiae Ienenses 8,2, 1909, 57–123 5 H.J. THOMSON, A New Suppl. to the Berne Scholia, in: JPh 35, 1920, 257–286   6 G. FUNAIOLI, Esegesi Virgiliana antica, 1930   7 J.J. BREWER, An Analysis of the Berne Scholia, 1973   8 M. GEYMONAT, F. gallo-romano?, in: Atti convegno nazionale di studio su Virgilio, 1984, 171–174   9 Id., s.v. F., in: EV 2, 1985, 520f. 10 Id., D. DAINTREE, s.v. Scholia Bernensia, in: EV 4, 1988, 711–720   11 R.A. KASTER, Guardians of Language, 1988, 284f.

[III 3] I. Gallio. Famous declamator of the early Imperial period (cf. Sen. Controv. 10, pr. 13; Jer. Comm. in Isaiam 8 pr.) probably of Spanish origin (Stat. Silv. 2,7,32), which explains his friendship with Seneca the Elder, whose son Novatus, I. [II 15]) was adopted by I.G.; for his political fate, see also I. [II 14] G. Annaeanus. Ovid, too, was on friendly terms with him (Sen. Suas. 3,7) and extended condolences (Ov. Pont. 4,11) upon the death of his wife. In AD 32, I.G. fell into disfavour with Tiberius, was expelled from the Senate and harshly punished (Tac. Ann. 6,3; Cass. Dio 58,18).

The numerous references to him in Seneca the Elder (cf. particular Sen. Controv. 1,1; 2,3; 9,1. 4f; 10, 1f. 4) yield a good picture of I. G.'s declamations; he was especially skilful with *idiotismos*, i.e. a uniquely personal tone. (Sen. Controv. 7, pr. 5f). However, his sententious, pointed, richly metaphorical style (cf. Sen. Controv. 10,2,10; Sen. Suas. 5,8) sounds like a 'jingle of words' (*tinnitus*) to the classicist Messalla in Tac. Dial. 26,1. Neither the pamphlet against T. Labienus for Maecenas' favourite Bathyllus (Controv. 10, pr. 8) nor the rhetorical treatise mentioned by Quint. Inst. 3,1,21 are extant.

H. MEYER, ORF ²1842, 543f.; PIR² I 756; H. BORNEC-QUE, Les déclamations, 1902, 173–176; J. FAIRWEATHER, Seneca the Elder, 1981, esp. 277ff.   P.L.S.

[III 4] I. Mauricianus. Lawyer under Antoninus Pius (AD 2), wrote a commentary *Ad legem Iuliam et Papiam* (6 bks.; four direct citations in Justinian's → *Digesta*: [1]) and probably annotated the *Digesta* of Iulianus [11] [2]. The writing mentioned only in Dig. 2,13,3 *De poenis* is presumably a fragment of the commentary on *lex Iulia* [2].

1 O. LENEL, Palingenesia Iuris civilis I, 1889, 689ff.
2 D. LIEBS, Jurisprudenz, in: HLL 4, 1997, 143.   T.G.

[III 5] M. Iunius Nypsus. (or Nipsus) is mentioned in the *Corpus Agrimensorum* (→ Surveyors) as the author of three writings: *Fluminis Varatio* ('Measurement of a River') [1. 285f.], *Limitis Repositio* ('Restoration of a Limitation') [1. 286–295] and *Podism* ('Measuring by Feet') [1. 295–301]. Due to the unclarified tradition of the corpus, neither the assignments nor the datings of the works (AD 2 ?) are certain.

→ Surveyors

1 F. BLUME, K. LACHMANN, A. RUDORFF, Die Schriften der röm. Feldmesser, vol. 1, 1848 (repr. 1967).

J. BOUMA, Marcus Iunius Nypsus, 1993.   K.BRO.

[III 6] I. Otho. Declamator of the early Imperial period, at first operated an elementary school; he later rose as a favourite of → Seianus, and in AD 22, as praetor, brought an accusation against C. → Iunius [II 13] Silanus (Tac. Ann. 3,66). The description of his declamations in Sen. Controv. 2,1,33ff.; 37ff. characterize him as a master of insinuation; as *colores*, he had a predilection for the use of dreams (Sen. Controv. 7,7,15). His style, of which antitheses and alliterations are highly conspicuous features, and his sophistical points (cf. Controv. 7,3,5) were (often) criticized (Controv. 7,3,10; 10,5,25). Of his four bks. *Colores* (Controv. 1,3,11; 2,1,33) nothing remains extant.

PIR² I 788; H. BORNECQUE, Les déclamations, 1902, 176f.   P.L.S.

Iuno (Etruscan → Uni).
I. Cult and Myth II. Iconography

I. Cult and Myth

J. is an important Latin goddess and besides → Minerva the most significant goddess of the Roman pantheon; while myth makes her the wife of → Jupiter, according to the Greek model, in the cult – in spite of her association with Jupiter (and Minerva) in the Capitoline triad – she is a significant figure in her own right, embodying the same tensions as with → Hera.
A. Name B. Cult C. Temples of Juno
D. Identifications

A. Name

The name of J. is not related to that of Jupiter: the initial sound is always /i-/, never /di-/, and the /ū/ is monophthongal (*Iunone Loucinai Diovis castud facitud* CIL I 2 360, cf. 361) [1]. Ancient etymologies, followed by their modern counterparts, associate her with *iunior* and *iuventas*.

B. Cult

J. is primarily associated with two contrasting areas: the life of married women, esp. → birth, on the one hand, and the state, esp. its young warriors, on the other hand.
1. Juno and Women 2. Juno and warlike men
3. Juno and the Kalends

1. Juno and Women

As goddess of → birth, J. bears the transparent epithet Lucina, 'she who brings to the light' (= Lucifera: Cic. Nat. D. 2,68, *Héra phōsphóros*: Dion. Hal. Ant. Rom. 4,15,5; cf. Ov. Fast. 2,450 et passim.); she is attested as such throughout Latium (Varro, Ling. 5,69; cf. Norba CIL I 2 359f. 362, Pisaurium CIL I 2 371; J. Lucina Tuscolona at Capua l.c. 1581). In Rome, her grove lies at the summit of the Mons Cispius on the Esquiline, together with the temple consecrated by the *matronae* on 1 March 375 BC (Varro, Ling. 5,50; Fasti Praenestini on 1 March); in accordance with a law going back to king Servius → Tullius, a gold coin was offered here before every birth (Dion. Hal. Ant. Rom. 4,15,5). Nobody wearing a knot was allowed access to the sanctuary (Serv. Aen. 4,518); pregnant women had to wear their hair loose when praying to her (Ov. Fast. 4,257f.), so as not to complicate the birth. After the birth, during which the goddess was invoked, for a month a table was set up in the private house with gifts for J. Lucina (Tert. De anim. 39, cf. Plaut. Truc. 476; Varro, Ling. 5,69).

1 March, the foundation day of the temple of J. Lucina, is at the same time the day of the → Matronalia, on which a Roman husband would give presents to his wife, and both would pray for the continuation of the marriage (Dig. 34,1,38,8; cf. Porph. Hor. comm. and Helenius Acro on Hor. Carm. 3,8); Romulus founded the feast as an act of gratitude for the aid of women in

the war against the Sabines (Plut. Romulus 21,1,30f.). The feast day is nowhere associated with J., but the relationship suggests itself in view of the role of the *matronae* in the consecration of the temple of J. Lucina. It is true that J. is not so clearly the goddess of marriage as is the Greek → Hera, whose principal epithet is Teleia (from *télos* in the sense of marriage); all the same, a supposed law of Numa forbade concubines from touching the altar of J. (Fest. 248; Gell. NA 4,3,3). More important is her role in → wedding rituals, not only in literature and the figurative arts, but also in cult. An altar of J. Iuga (*quam putabant matrimonia iungere*, 'declared to be responsible for marriages') is attested in the Vicus Iugarius (Fest. 92), as is the epithet Iugalis (Serv. Aen. 4,16), and J. Cinxia ('of the girdle') supervises the loosening of the girdle on the wedding night (Fest. 55, cf. Mart. Cap. 2,149, who associates further aspects of the wedding feast with specific epithets of J.). → Livia, who was linked with J. by analogy with Augustus' association with Jupiter, is invoked as patroness in Graeco-Egyptian marriage contracts into the 2nd cent. AD. The story of the cult snake of J. at Lavinium, which refused food offered by girls who were no longer virgins, may also fit in here (Prop. 4,8,3–16, cf. Ael. NA 11,16).

As the goddess of women – of *matronae* as well as slaves – J. also appears behind the feast of → Capratinae Nonae, which has the character of a feast of dissolution before the beginning of the summer grain harvest; ancient etymologies that derive the names of the feast and the epithet from the wild fig-tree (*caprificus*) [2] are unreliable.

2. Juno and warlike men

On the other hand, there are the associations of J. with adolescent men; in Rome itself only traces may be detected. In the → curiae, the oldest groups of citizens capable of bearing arms, J. received a regular sacrifice, instituted by Titus Tatius; consequently she bore the epithet Curis (Fest. 56; Dion. Hal. Ant. Rom. 2,50,3). This epithet is inseparable from that of J. Quiritis or Curitis, who, was venerated in Rome on the Field of Mars (foundation day of the temple: 7 October) and in other Latin cities; the epithet is usually derived from the Sabine *curis* = 'lance' (Fest. 43; 55), but belongs to *curia* < *co-viria* and the warlike → Quirinus. At the → Lupercalia the running *luperci* used straps made from the skin of a sacrificial goat to whip the women and make them fertile, the skin being supposedly sacred to J. (Fest. 75f.; Ov. Fast. 2,425–453 does not mention it, but invokes J. Lucina).

Information from other cities in central Italy is clearer. In Lanuvium, J. was worshipped as Sispes, Sispita or Sospita (Fest. 462; inscriptions mostly have S(e)ispes), often with the addition of Mater Regina, which denotes her status as 'saviour' (Fest. s.v.); her image wore a goatskin with head and horns, together with a lance, a shield and pointed shoes (Cic. Nat. D. 1,82), thus depicting her as a warrior goddess who brings rescue at times of military need. In 194 BC, C.

Cornelius [I 11] Cethegus built her a temple also in Rome because of a vow made during the war with the Insubres (Liv. 32,30,20). J. Quiritis or Curitis (CIL XI 3125f.) was venerated at Falerii; she was the principal goddess of the city. At her feast, visited by Ovid (Ov. Am. 3,13), → suovetaurilia (white female cattle, calves, pigs and rams) were sacrificed; the goat was excluded, but was hunted by boys with spears in a ritual contest.

The goddess is derived from Argos (Cato fr. 47; Ov. Am. 3,13,31); taken in combination with the epithet, this indicates a character akin to the Argive Hera, as protector of young warriors [3]. At Tibur too, a J. Quiritis was worshipped, appearing in inscriptions also as Argeia (Serv. Aen. 1,17; CIL XIV 3556), without knowing of the cult; here too the epithet as well as the prayer to her cited in Servius, which mentions her shield, indicate an armed image and warlike character. Finally, the frequently attested J. Populona (Aesernia CIL IX 2630; Teanum Sidicinum CIL X 4780 etc.), who also had a temple in Rome (Macrob. Sat. 3,11,6; Populonia: Arnob. Adv. nat. 3,30), may be understood, at least originally, as the goddess of the *populus* in the sense of the military marching off.

More complex is J. Regina. Where she is the principal goddess of her city, as at Veii, Ardea and Lanuvium, this political function must be considered together with her role with regard to young warriors and the citizens' army. When, after the conquest of Veii in 392 BC, Furius [I 13] Camillus transfers her cult to Rome in a temple on the Aventine (Liv. 5,21,3; 22,7; 23,7; 31,3), the cult loses this comprehensive function; the same applies to the two other Republican temples of J. Regina, consecrated by M. Aemilius [I 10] Lepidus in 179 BC after a vow made during the Ligurian War (Liv. 39,2,11; 40,52,1ff.) and Q. Caecilius [I 27] Metellus Macedonicus on the occasion of his triumph in 146 BC (Vell. Pat. 1,11,3). As part of the Capitoline triad, J. Regina is entirely subordinate to Jupiter as mythical king of the gods, even if in the genesis of the triad her political role may have been significant.

J. Moneta (most probably 'she who warns', Cic. Div. 1,101; Isid. Orig. 16,18,8), whose temple on the Roman Arx, appr. on the site of the Church of Sta Maria in Aracaeli, was consecrated in 344 BC by Furius [I 12] Camillus (Liv. 7,28,4f.), must have had a political function too: at any rate the combination of the epithets J. Moneta Regina is thus best understood (CIL VI 362). The foundation day, the Kalends of June (dedicated to her and named after her), underlines the importance of the cult.

3. JUNO AND THE KALENDS

All Kalends are sacred to J., in contrast to the Ides, which are dedicated to Jupiter: in the monthly proclamation (*kalatio*) of the Nones she is invoked as J. Covella (Varro, Ling. 6,27) and receives a sacrifice in the *regia* (Macrob. Sat. 1,15,19); this is one of the few cultic links between J. and Jupiter (cf. also the sacrificial law CIL I2 362 [4]). In private cult she is in particular the protector of births; besides she is the protector of all

women, and (probably as a secondary development) a woman's individual J. corresponds to a man's individual → genius [5].

C. TEMPLES OF JUNO

While there are difficulties in attesting the temples in the city of Rome [6], the temple of J. Curitis at → Falerii [1], is attested at least through its votive offerings [7], and so is a large temple-complex of J. from the 2nd cent. BC at → Gabii, through excavations; the latter sanctuary had a theatre in front of the altar and the temple façade as well as a grove enclosed by a portico; the cult is not attested in literature [8].

D. IDENTIFICATIONS

In literature, J. largely continues the role of the Greek → Hera; but in Virgil's *Aeneid* she also becomes the opponent of Aeneas by her identification with the Punic → Tinnit (Caelestis), the principal goddess of → Carthage. Her political function disappears entirely behind that of the wife of the king of the gods and goddess of marriage (cf. Mart. Cap. 2,147–148). In physical allegory she is identical with Hera, being understood as a symbol of air (Cic. Div. 2,66; Macrob. Sat. 1,17,54). This is adopted in post-antique iconography.

1 LEUMANN, 362   2 J. N. BREMMER, The Nonae Capratinae, in: Id., N. M. HORSFALL, Roman Myth and Mythography, 1987, 76–88   3 H. LE BONNIEC, La fête de Junon au pays des Falisques, in: A. THILL (ed.), L'élégie romaine, 1980, 233–244   4 WACHTER, 460–463   5 J. RIVES, The "Iuno Feminae" in Roman Society, in: Echos du Monde Classique/Classical Views 36, 1992, 33–49   6 LTUR 3, 120–130   7 F. COARELLI, I santuari del Lazio in età repubblicana, 1987, 11–21.

W. F. OTTO, I. Beiträge zum Verständnisse der ältesten und wichtigsten Thatsachen ihres Kultes, in: Philologus 64, 1905, 161–223; G. WISSOWA, Religion und Kultus der Römer, ²1912, 181–191; G. DUMÉZIL, La religion romaine archaïque, 1974, 299–310; R. E. A. PALMER, Juno in Archaic Italy, in: Id., Roman Religion and Roman Empire. Five Essays, 1974, 3–56; G. DURY-MOYAERS, M. REDARD, Aperçu critique de travaux relatifs au culte de Junon, in: ANRW II 17.1, 142–188; J. CHAMPEAUX, Religion romaine et religion latine. Les cultes de Jupiter et Junon à Préneste, in: REL 60, 1982, 71–104; R. HÄUSSLER, Hera und Juno. Wandlungen und Beharrung einer Göttin, 1995.   F.G.

II. ICONOGRAPHY

It is of J. Regina, the goddess belonging to the Capitoline triad with Jupiter and Minerva and also venerated in some cities of Latium as their patron goddess, that probably most representations have survived: the statue in the left cella of the Capitoline temple of Jupiter Optimus Maximus in → Rome, only a few fragments of which have survived, is known from coins of the Imperial period. The goddess is dressed in a girdled → chiton, often with a cloak which may also cover her head; her typical attributes are *stephane*, sceptre and patera, frequently with a peacock in her vicinity. She is often depicted standing or enthroned with Jupiter and Minerva, cf. *i.a.* the marble relief in Kiel, mid–2nd cent. AD; bronze statuettes of the three enthroned divinities from Pompeii (Naples, MN, 1st cent. AD). Cult statues of the goddess have survived from various Capitolia of the Roman empire: e.g. colossal head from Pompeii (Naples, MN, 2nd quarter of 1st cent. BC), Alba Pompeia (Turin, Mus. Ant., early 1st cent. BC), Cumae (Imperial period; Naples, MN); cf. also the colossal head in Rome (CM, mid–2nd cent. BC). The J. statue in the Farnese collection (Naples, MN, Imperial period) is seen as a variant of the Hera of Ephesus; a colossal statue from Otricoli (Rome, MV, 2nd cent. AD) refers to the so-called Hera Borghese. Attribution of the colossal head of the J. Ludovisi with portrait traits (Rome, MN, Claudian) to a cult statue of J. is not certain (cf. also the portrait adaptations of the imperial family on cameos, coins and reliefs).

J. Regina Dolichena, cult consort of Jupiter → Dolichenus, the Romanized city god → Baal from Doliche in Syria, is shown standing with her characteristic attribute, a mirror, on the back of a hind or cow (besides Jupiter on a bull): her cult was widespread from the last quarter of the 1st cent. AD in Rome and the north-western provinces of the Roman empire (marble reliefs from the Aventine, 2nd half of the 2nd/beginning of the 3rd cent. AD). J. is depicted with various gods on the → four-god stones of the so-called Jupiter columns known esp. from Roman Germania. Numerous representations have survived of the Italian J. Sospita, armed with a lance and an octagonal shield: in chiton and goatskin, its head worn over her head in place of the horned helmet, and pointed shoes, often with a snake at her delicate feet: colossal statue in the Vatican (Sala Rotonda; Antonine), Etruscan bronze statuette (Florence, MA; beginning of the 5th cent. BC).

G. DURY-MOYAERS, Réflexion à propos de l'iconographie de Juno Sospita, in: R. ALTHEIM-STIEHL (ed.), Beiträge zur altital. Geistesgesch.: FS für G. RADKE, 1986, 83–101; E. LA ROCCA, s.v. Juno, LIMC V, 814–856 (with additional bibliography).   A.L.

Iuppiter
I. CULT AND MYTH   II. ICONOGRAPHY

I. CULT AND MYTH
J. (rarely *Iupiter*, archaic *Diovis*, Umbrian *Iupater*) is the supreme god of the Roman and Latin pantheon; while in iconography and myth he is identified completely with the Greek → Zeus, he exists in his own right in the cult.
A. ETYMOLOGY AND ORIGIN   B. FUNCTIONS, CULT SITES AND PRIESTS   C. FESTIVALS
D. INTERPRETATIO ROMANA

A. ETYMOLOGY AND ORIGIN
The derivation from *Dieu-pater*, i.e. Indo-European *dieu-/diu-* and the invoking *pater*, is undisputed; it connects him with Greek *Zeus* (*dieus*, vocative Ζεῦ

πάτερ) and Old Indo-Aryan *Dyaus*, and actually denotes the deity of the bright day sky (cf. Latin *dies*), indicating that this deity was already worshipped in an Indo-European stage of religion. However, the dissociation from the Indo-European basic meaning, the connection with the dark bad-weather sky and with kingship belong already to pre-Latin and pre-Greek times.

B. FUNCTIONS, CULT SITES AND PRIESTS
As the deity of the sky he is often worshipped on hills, but rarely on mountain peaks like Zeus. The highest sanctuary of J. in Latium lies on Mons Albanus (Monte Cavo), while the allocation of the sanctuary on top of the cliff of Terracina to J. Anxur(us) (cf. Verg. Aen. 7,799 with Serv. ad loc.) is hypothetical [1]; sanctuaries of J. are attested for several of the hills of Rome [2]. As the deity of the sky he is associated with lightning, the celestial sign of light (J. Fulmen Fulgur Tonans CIL XI 2.1 4172, frequently Fulgur or Fulminator in inscriptions; he has a sanctuary on the Field of Mars, with a sacrifice on October 7 [3]); this may also include the epiclesis Lucetius mentioned in the Carmen Saliare, in spite of the late antique derivation from *lux* ('light') (cf. Macrob. Sat. 1,15,14; [4. 114]). In recognition of his narrow escape from a stroke of lightning during the Cantabrian War, Augustus dedicated a temple on the capitol to J. Tonans in 22 BC [5]. J. is also a deity of rain, ritually invoked during dry season to provide water; the ritual was called *aquaelicium* and consisted of a procession with the *lapis manalis* ('rhyolite') (Fest. 2; Varro fr. Non. 547); another rain ritual in a (Campanian?) cult of J. (→ Nudipedalia, since the *matronae* conducting the ritual are barefooted) is described at Petron. Sat. 44,17f. Modern research also includes J. Elicius here, who had an altar on the Aventine dedicated to him by → Numa (Varro, Ling. 6,95; Liv. 1,20,5ff.); ancient aitia, however, consider him to be the god ritually called (*elicere*) by Numa to obtain a ritual against strokes of lightning (Ov. Fast. 3,327f., cf. Valerias Antias fr. 6 HRR; Greek etymology in Plut. Numa 15,9,70e).

More important is J. as the god of the → *augures* (Liv. 1,18,9), probably less as the deity of the heights, where the *auguracula* can be found, and of the open sky, where the bird oracles manifest themselves, but rather as guarantor of the order within which the events predicted by the oracles must happen: therefore, the *augures* are considered to be *interpretes Iovis Optimi Maximi* (Cic. Leg. 2,20). In the cult of → Fortuna of Praeneste, J. is attested as a boy (*puer*) (Cic. Div. 2,85) or as Fortuna's father (CIL I 2, 60 = VETTER 505); this obviously reflects the ambivalence of the cult goddess, who is both the goddess of birth and of the oracle; her divination is ultimately subordinate to J.'s plan.

A central aspect is the connection between J. and state (later, under Greek influence, also cosmic) order, which finds its best expression in the role of J. Optimus Maximus (= J.O.M.) in his temple on the Capitol. On his altar the civil servants assuming office offer white bulls, as a thanksgiving sacrifice for his aid in the past year, and they solemnly promise new bulls for the next year, if his aid continues (Ov. Fast. 1,79–86); the first sitting of the Senate in the temple follows. It is this altar where the commander sacrifices at his departure and vows to sacrifice for the victory; it is here that he then sacrifices as triumphator. On the day of the foundation of the temple, the Ides of October, a nail is driven into the side wall of the cella (Liv. 7,3,3ff.) to mark a new → *saeculum*. Many Roman colonies had a Capitolium with the cult of J.O.M. and the goddesses accompanying him, Juno and Minerva, as a replica of the cult in the city of Rome. The fact that the consecration of the great temple, started by the Tarquinii, coincides with the beginning of the Republic (Liv. 2,8,6), is therefore more than mere chance. The two → *ludi*, in which the *urbs Roma* represents itself politically, are likewise dedicated to J.: the old *ludi Romani*, whose main day, September 13, coincides with his *epulum* (→ *Iovis epulum*), the day of foundation of the Capitoline temple, just as the younger *ludi Plebei* coincide with the respective *epulum* on November 13, i.e. both Ides.

From the time of Augustus, the emperor is likened to J., especially in literary representations (beginnings in Horace, implemented in Ovid). The old relationship to the political man of power also lies behind J. Feretrius, to whom the commanders-in-chief dedicate the captured weapons of enemy leaders (*spolia opima*) (Fest. 202; the temple founded by Romulus, Liv. 1,10,5ff.); however, ancient scholarship also connects the epiclesis with the throwing (*ferire*) of lightning bolts as weapons in battles (Plut. Marcellus 8,2–10, 302bc). As the god who restores the steadfastness of the people's army in a situation of crisis in battle, he is called Stator in common Italian epiclesis (in aetiology, his temple on the Palatine goes back to Romulus, Liv. 1,12,6; however, it was only dedicated by M. Atilius Regulus 295 BC, Liv. 10,36,11; Q. Caecilius Metellus Macedonius built a second temple in 146 BC, Vitr. De arch. 3,2,5) [6]; as the god who brings victory to the army, he is Victor (foundation of the temple in 295 BC, Liv. 10,29,14; on the Quirinal [7]). In the Danube provinces during Imperial times, J. Propulsor is finally the god who keeps the invading barbarians at bay [8].

God of the league of all Latin cities is J. Latiaris in his sanctuary on the → Mons Albanus. According to tradition, an old grove existed on the mountain peak (Liv. 1,31,3); Tarquinius founded (or renewed) the cult and established the ritual of the common festival, the → Feriae Latinae, according to which each city had to contribute to the meal (Dion. Hal. Ant. Rom. 4,49) and received its share of the sacrificial bull (Varro, Ling. 6,25). At least in historical times, Latium's unity under the leadership of Rome was celebrated this way: Rome's senior civil servants had to participate, master of the sacrifice was usually a consul, and all of Latium held truce (Macrob. Sat. 1,16,17). Just as on the Capitol, a victorious commander could celebrate a → triumph, and although without the state's legitimation

(*sine publica auctoritate*, Liv. 42,21,7), it was valid nevertheless: thus, the sanctuary participates in the same tension between closeness and distance to Rome.

Part of the world's order are its borders. Inside the Capitoline temple, under an opening in the roof, the god → Terminus can be found in shape of a border-stone. The myth explains the intertwining of the cults with the impossibility to move the cult monument of the god Terminus when Tarquinius began building his temple (Cato Orig. 1 fr. 24 P.; Liv. 1,55,3f.); in any case, Terminus and the immovability of borders are therefore closely linked to J., which is why J. is sometimes referred to as Ter(minalis).

As guarantor of the state's order as well as of the political and social order, J. (like → Zeus Horkios) presides over oaths and alliances. The → *fetiales*, entrusted with alliances between states as well as with their dissolution for the purpose of war, retrieve staff and fire-stone (*silex*) in the sanctuary of J. Feretrius for the execution of the oath sacrifice (Fest. 81) and invoke J. in ritual prayer (Liv. 1,32,6f.), while the person taking the oath holds the *silex* in his hands (Pol. 3,25,6; Fest. 102). This is called *Iovem lapidem iurare*, 'to swear by the stone of J.' (Cic. Fam. 7,12,2; Gell. NA 1,21,4; *lapis* is not an epiclesis). Visually, J. can be represented as guarantor between the parties, i.e. as participant of the contract (relief on Trajan's arch in Benevento [9]). In the private sphere, he presides as J. Farreus (Gaius 1,112) over the → *confarreatio*, the most sacrilized form of a wedding. A further development to a figure in its own right represents Dius Fidius, who is often called upon in asseverations (Dion. Hal. Ant. Rom. 4,58,4; 9,60,8 characteristically calls him Zeus Pistios).

Priest of J. is the *flamen Dialis*, who, together with the → *flamines* of Mars and Quirinus, belongs to the *flamines maiores*; this grouping reflects old and close ritual connections between the three deities (e.g. in the prayer of the Fetiales, Pol. 3,25,6). Among the *flamines*, J.'s priest distinguishes himself by the great number of restrictions, which characterize his person as well as his wife (wedded to him in *confarreatio*), the *flaminica*; while some precepts – e.g. to refrain from riding, to not be permitted to see an army or to sleep in a strange bed for more than three nights – exclude him as the only priest from holding a high state office and could therefore be understood as a form of separation of powers, others – e.g. prohibitions regarding food – have been keenly discussed by scholars, although they also suggest a political interpretation (a list in Gell. NA 10,15; some in Plut. Quaest. Rom. 109–112; 289f–291b [10; 11]).

Rome also had various smaller sanctuaries of J. The main city temple is the temple of J.O.M. on the Capitol, which, according to tradition, Tarquinius Superbus began and consul M. Horatius Pulvillus consecrated in 509 BC (Liv. 2,8,6; inscription Dion. Hal. Ant. Rom. 5,35,3); a predecessor building can be assumed. The temple was one of the largest of its time [12. 96] and had a cult image in clay in Etruscan style (Plin. HN 35,157). In three cellae, J. was worshipped in the middle, Juno Regina to the left and Minerva to the right (Liv. 7,3,5); this Capitoline triad replaced the older triad of J., Mars and Quirinus. Its derivation from Etruria, given the absence of this triad there, is just as problematic [13; 14] as the direct derivation from Greece, where at least a collective cult of Zeus, Hera and Athena is attested in the Phokikon (the central sanctuary of the Phocians (Paus. 10,5,1; Hera sits to the right); the best explanation for the connection of the three deities is offered, of course, by Greek myth. The temple burnt down several times, e.g. in the turmoils of the Year of the Four Emperors (AD 69), but was reconstructed in full splendour each time.

C. FESTIVALS

Festivals dedicated to Jupiter, next to those of political unity mentioned above (ludi Romani and Plebei, feriae Latinae), are especially the wine festivals of the Vinalia (priora) on 23 April, of the Vinalia (rustica) on 19 August and the Meditrinalia of 11 October [15; 16]. The Vinalia rustica designated the beginning of the vintage, when the flamen Dialis cut the first grape and sacrificed a lamb to J. (Varro, Ling. 6,16; Varro, Rust. 1,1,6, however, associates them with Venus); the Meditrinalia, when the first fermented grape juice was tasted (Fest. 110), were, according to the Fasti Amiterni a festival of J.; on the Vinalia priora the new wine was tasted (Plin. HN 18,287) and the first offering made to J. (Fest. 57). The objective of all three festivals is the integration of wine, an ambivalent beverage, into J.'s well-ordered world, in order to free it from its harmfulness, because as the central liquid of the sacrifice, wine is indispensable to the proper relationship between humans and gods. With the exception of these festivals, the festivals of J. usually occur on the Ides; next to the ones mentioned above, this also applies to the ludi Capitolini (13 October), celebrated between the ludi Romani and ludi Plebei. They remember a victory over Veii and were established by Romulus (Plut. Romulus 33de) or Camillus (Liv. 5,31,4); most notable, however, are the signs of ritual inversion, which set them prominently apart from the preceding and subsequent ludi (Plut. l.c.).

The Ides, peak and point of reversal of the original moon year, are also holy to J. Every Ides, the flamen Dialis offered a lamb on the Capitoline altar (ovis Idulis, Fest. 93) (Ov. Fast. 1,587f.; Macrob. Sat. 1,15,16). This corresponds with the fact that the Kalends are holy to → Juno; the regina, wife of the rex sacrorum, sacrificed to her a lamb or a sow in the Regia, as did a pontifex in the Curia Calabra on the Capitol (Macrob. Sat. 1,15,19). While this latter sacrifice is linked to the function of the Kalends as 'proclamation day', the first sacrifice (to Juno, by a woman) is an inversion of the sacrifice on the Ides. This opposition still structures the month even after the termination of the lunar month (the ancient explanation from I., the god of light. Macrob. Sat. 1,15,14; [4. 114]).

D. INTERPRETATIO ROMANA

Early on, J. was equated with → Zeus; iconography and mythology of J. are, to a large extent, a product of this equation; he was also identified with the Etruscan → Tinia. In the common → interpretatio Romana, oriental supreme gods (especially J. → Dolichenus [17]) of the Imperial period as well as deities of the Celts appear under J.'s name and image. Of particular interest are the collosal columns of J. of the Germanic provinces, which depict a J. on a horse, riding down one of the Giants, on top of a column [18].

1 F. COARELLI, I santuari del Lazio in età repubblicana, 1987, 113–140   2 LATTE, 79–83   3 D. MANACORDA, s.v. I. Fulgor, LTUR 3, 136–138   4 G. WISSOWA, Rel. und Kultus der Römer, ²1912, 113–129   5 P. GROS, s.v. I. Tonans, LTUR 3, 159–160   6 A. VISCOGLIOSI, s.v. I. Stator, LTUR 3, 157–159   7 F. COARELLI, s.v. I. Victor, LTUR 3, 161   8 J. KOLENDO, Le culte de Juppiter Depulsor et les incursions des barbares, in: ANRW II 18.2, 1062–1076   9 M. BEARD, J. NORTH, S. PRICE, Religions of Rome, 1998, vol. 2, 27f.   10 A. BRELICH, Appunti sul flamen Dialis, in: Acta Classica 8, 1972, 17–21   11 F. GRAF, Plutarco e la religione romana, in: I. GALLO (ed.), Plutarco e la religione, 1996, 281–283   12 T. J. CORNELL, The Beginnings of Rome, 1996   13 L. BANTI, Il culto del cosidetto tempio di Apollo a Veii e il problema delle triadi etrusco-italiche, in: SE 17, 1943, 187–224   14 T. GANTZ, Divine Triads on an Archaic Etruscan Frieze Plaque from Poggio Civitate (Murlo), in: SE 39, 1971, 1–22   15 G. DUMÉZIL, Juppiter et les Vinalia, in: REL 39, 1961, 261–274   16 O. CAZENEUVE, Jupiter, Liber et le vin latin, in: RHR 205, 1988, 245–265   17 M. P. SPEIDEL, Jupiter Dolichenus. Der Himmelsgott auf dem Stier, 1980   18 G. BAUCHHENSS, P. NOLKE, Die Iuppitersäulen in den german. Provinzen, 1981.

J. RUFUS FEARS, The Cult of Jupiter and Roman Imperial Ideology, in: ANRW II 17.1, 3–141; C. KOCH, Der röm. Juppiter, 1937.   F.G.

II. ICONOGRAPHY

Of J. Optimus Maximus, the supreme state god of the Romans, several, mostly fragmentary, cult statues from groups of cult images of the Capitoline triad have been preserved, mainly from the provinces: colossal torso of a seated statue from Pompeii (Naples, MN, after 80 BC) and Cumae (Naples, MN, 2nd cent. AD), seated statue of Khamissa (Guelma/Algeria, beginning of 2nd cent. AD.), so-called J. Verospi (Rome, MV, 3rd cent. AD), and others. The Capitoline triad, with J. in its centre and → Juno and → Minerva to his sides, is often depicted on coins and reliefs; a set of bronze statuettes from Pompeii also shows J. with Juno and Minerva (Naples, MN, 1st cent. AD). The majority of representations show J. standing: reliefs, coin images, cameos and bronze statuettes (frequently from Lararium (→ Lararium). The standing J. is shown naked, often with a cloak draped over his left shoulder; the enthroned J. is represented half-naked, with bare chest, while the cloak covers the lower part of his body. J. appears mostly dignified and bearded; the raised left hand rests on the sceptre, in his right he holds the lightning bolts; further attributes are eagle and patera. J. is frequently associated with → Victoria, especially on coins and cameos of the Imperial period: he is crowned by the goddess of victory or holds a small image of her in his hand; Victoriae accompany him in representations of triumph, where J. is rendered in a quadriga (in analogy to the group on the roof of the Capitoline temple in Republican times). J. fighting with raised lightning bolts is shown by several coins and bronze statuettes.

The connection of Roman emperors and J. becomes apparent in numerous representations; they propagate him as J. Conservator, keeper of the Imperium and protector of the emperors and their politics: attica relief of Trajan's arch in Benevent (AD 114), relief on Trajan's Column in Rome (AD 113); numerous coin images; cf. also the ideal portraits of Roman emperors based on the standing or enthroned J.: portrait statue of Claudius (Vatican, Sala Rotonda); seated statue of Augustus (Rome, Mus. Torlonia); colossal seated statue of Constantine (fragment, Rome, Conservatory Palace) and many others.

On the so-called J. columns of the 1st to 3rd cents. AD, widespread in the north-western provinces of the Roman empire (→ Monumental column), J. is enthroned as ruler of the world, with a sceptre in his left hand, lightning bolts in his right (J. column in Mainz, AD 58–67). The cult of J. → Dolichenus, the Romanized city god → Baal of Doliche in Commagene, spread throughout the Roman empire due to Syrian soldiers and can be found in numerous representations: mostly standing on a bull, he is wearing a tiara or → a horned crown, as well as a cuirass and a Phrygian cap; he is armed with a sword, double-axe and with lightning bolts, sometimes crowned by Victoria (statuettes, reliefs and 'votive triangles').

F. CANCIANI, A. COSTANTINI, s.v. Zeus/Juppiter, LIMC 8, 421–470 (with additional bibliography); R. VOLLKOMMER, s.v. Zeus/Juppiter Dolichenus, LIMC 8, 471–478.   A.L.

Iura (Caes. B Gall. 1,2,3; 1,6,1; 1,8,1; *Iurensis, Iorensis,* Sidon. Apoll. Epist. 4,25,5; Greg. Tur. vit. patr. 1; *Iures,* Plin. HN 3,31; 4,105; 16,197; Ἰόρας/*Ióras,* Ἰουράσιος/*Iourásios,* Str. 4,3,4; 4,6,11; Ἰουρασσός/*Iourassós,* Ptol. 2,9,2; 2,9,10). Mountain chain, *c.* 250 km long and up to 70 km wide, stretching in an arch shape from the Rhône at the Lac du Bourget, in a northerly/north-easterly direction to Baden in Switzerland. According to Caesar and Strabo, it formed the frontier between the Helvetii and the Sequani; the Raurici settled in the north. The road leading through Vindonissa across the Swiss Midlands was connected to Gaulish territory by several Iura crossings: a) across the two Hauenstein Passes, b) by the road leading from Petinisca through the Taubenloch Gorge and the Pierre Pertuis, and c) by the crossings to Abiolica either by way

of the St. Croix and the Col des Etroits or the Col de Jougne.

A.-S. DE COHËN, M.-J. ROULIÈRE-LAMBERT (ed.), Dans le Jura gallo-romain. Lons-le-Saunier, Musée d'Archéologie, 13 avril–31 mai 1992, 1992; P. CURDY, G. KAENEL (ed.), L'Âge du Fer dans le Jura. Act. du 15ᵉ Colloque de l'Association Française pour l'Étude de l'Âge du Fer, Pontarlier et Yverdon-les-Bains 9–12 mai 1991, Cahiers d'Archéologie Romande 57, 1992; W. DRACK, R. FELLMANN, Die Römer in der Schweiz, 1988, 97f.; W. REBER, Zur Verkehrsgeographie der Pässe im östl. Jura, 1970.   F.SCH.

Iurgium A term in the Law of the Twelve Tables (*c.* 450 BC, → *Tabulae duodecim*). Its significance in legal history is still very disputed. *Iurgium* is a milder form of dispute than the litigation before court (→ *lis*); otherwise a general term for a dispute. It is conceivable that *iurgium* meant an out-of-court settlement, perhaps with the support of the *pontifices*. In the classical period (1st cent. BC – 3rd cent. AD) this form of resolution had long fallen out of use.

M. KASER, K. HACKL, Das röm. Zivilprozeßrecht, ²1997, 58).   G.S.

Iuridicus The term *iuridicus* ('person employed in law') appears in sources of the Roman Imperial period with very different meanings.

1. From Hadrian, perhaps even Vespasian, *iuridici provinciae*, more frequently called *legati iuridici,* appear in imperial provinces. They are representatives of the provincial governor's jurisdiction, sometimes for the whole province, sometimes only for districts. It is disputed whether the juridical powers of the *iuridicus* were merely derived from the governor (e.g. [1. 1149]) or were genuine imperial powers (as in [2]).

2. The *iuridicus Alexandriae* (δικαιοδότης/*dikaiodótēs*) certainly had his own mandate for dispensing justice in Egypt. He was the representative of the → *praefectus Aegypti.* He exercised the contentious and the voluntary jurisdiction in civil matters using a very free and formless cognition procedure (→ *cognitio*). He was appointed by the emperor with his own mandate independent of the *praefectus.*

3. *Iuridicus* was also the technical term for jurisdictional magistrates that were appointed of praetorial rank by the emperor for certain Italian districts after AD 163. Responsibility for the voluntary jurisdiction in the form of a → *legis actio* (Ulp. Dig. 1,20,1), for fideicommissary controversies (Scaevola Dig. 40,5,41,5), for the appointment of a guardian and disputes relating to urban council members (→ *decuriones*); for all cases see [3]. Furthermore, the *iuridicus* also probably was responsible for proper civil and criminal matters. As the replacement and successor of the conventional carriers of legal mandates, especially the praetor, the *iuridicus* probably also conducted the formulary procedure (→ *formula,* → *iudicium*) and over time also increasingly the free → *cognitio* which had no subdivision of the

proceeding. When it displaced the traditional civil procedure is disputed [4]. The *iuridici* disappeared as jurisdictional magistrats and administrators with the administrative reforms of Diocletian (about 300).

1 A.v. PREMERSTEIN, s.v. Legatus, RE 12, 1133–1149
2 MARTINO, SCR 4, 732 3 W.SIMSHÄUSER, Iuridici und Munizipalgerichtsbarkeit in Italien, 1973, 242f.
4 M.KASER, K.HACKL, Das röm. Zivilprozeßrecht, ²1997, 468 with n. 12.

G.FOTI TALAMANCA, Ricerche sul processo nell' Egitto greco-romano II.2, 1984; B.GALOTTA, Lo "iuridicus" e la sua "iurisdictio", in: Studi A. Biscardi 4, 1983, 441–444; M.PEACHIN, Iudex vice Caesaris, 1996, 56ff.   G.S.

Iuris consultus Preferred expression for the Roman specialized jurist aside from *iuris prudens, peritus, auctor* or *studiosus*. The *iuris consultus* is an authority 'consulted' about law and hence implicitly competent to answer [1. 25; 4. 554], 'experienced in statutory and customary law' (*legum et consuetudinis ... peritus*, Cic. De or. 1,212). For the designation *iuris consultus* (IC) neither the literary or the official work nor – in view of the private character of → legal instruction – a formal educational level was decisive but only consultation practice based on practical exercising of functions [3. 124, 149ff.; 4. 554ff.].

Both the indispensability of official experience and the free-of-charge consultation demanded of the IC a high social status and as a rule he was a member of the nobility, or from the last cent. of the Republic onwards also of the equestrian class [4. 595f.]. The consultation (*consuli*) in the Republic was standardized [4. 557ff.] as procedural (*agere*), business (*cavere*) and other legal advice (*respondere*) and was not only given to private individuals, magistrates and judges but also attorneys usually only trained in rhetoric (→ *advocatus*, → *causidicus, patronus* [1. 128f.]). In the 1st cent. AD, IC was probably the technical term for the bearers of the 'entitlement to give answer' (*ius respondendi*, Inst. Iust. 1,2,8; in this regard [2. 283f.; 5. 106ff., 121 in juristic questions) authorized by the *princeps*. Sen. Ep. 94,27 [1. 147] mentions the 'validity' of *iuris consultorum responsa*.

With the gradual fading in importance of the *responsum* as the legal source in favour of the imperial rescript, the title of IC also lost its narrow meaning (→ *iuris prudentia*) from the high Principate period onwards. In the provinces it was probably already at an early time related to any specialized jurist [2. 347f.; 6. 18ff.].

1 SCHULZ 2 KUNKEL 3 D.LIEBS, Nichtlit. röm. Juristen der Kaiserzeit, in: Symposion F.WIEACKER, 1980, 123–198 4 WIEACKER, RRG 5 A.MAGDELAIN, Ius, imperium, auctoritas. Études de droit romain, 1990 6 D.LIEBS, Röm. Jurisprudenz in Africa, 1993.   T.G.

Iurisdictio Literally 'speaking law'. Where *iurisdictio* was split into various stages of procedure (in particular *in iure, apud iudicem*), it means the sovereign powers conferred on a Roman court magistrate for observing judicial practice. This term was originally used for private judicial practice, but in the 2nd cent. AD it was also extended to criminal judicial practice and to the procedure of cognition (→ *cognitio*), in the context of which *iurisdictio* describes the official judicial competences as a whole – in other words also the authority to pass judgement, which was what in particular the court magistrate did not normally have. Instead, he had been charged only with the → *iudicium dare* (appointing the tribunal) and further decision had been reserved for the judge (→ *iudex*).

Equating *iurisdictio* with → *imperium* is also ruled out for the Republican and the classical periods of the Roman law; firstly because the curule aediles did not have any official power of this kind and otherwise because the *imperium* of the praetor comprised a whole range of powers (cf. the efforts to define them in Dig. 2,1,4; 50,1,26 pr.: *Ea quae magis imperii sunt quam iurisdictionis magistratus municipalis facere non posset*, 'The matters which belong more to the *imperium* than to the *iurisdictio* cannot be carried out by the municipal magistrates'). The main content of the *iurisdictio* is therefore appointing a tribunal to pass judgement (possibly by granting a proceeding formula, → *formula*), though it also allows the magistrate further measures for conducting proceedings, such as, for instance, restoring to the former state (→ *restitutio in integrum*, Dig. 4,4,16,5), an instruction on the legitimate ownership of an object or a collection of objects (*missio in possessionem, in bona*, Dig. 39,2,4,3; 43,4,1 pr.) or the enforcement of a stipulation (Dig. 39,2,1; 4,3; 7 pr.). Within certain limits the court magistrate could confer the powers described by the term *iurisdictio* by act of law individually or as a whole to other officials (*mandare, delegare*, Dig. 1,21,1 pr.); moreover, there were also similar conferrals by force of law, on the municipal magistrates by the praetor, for instance.

The present distinction between litigious and voluntary jurisdiction has its roots in the classical division between *iurisdictio contentiosa* and *iurisdictio voluntaria*. Among the latter are technical acts resulting from the *legis actio* procedure, such as, for instance, → *in iure cessio, manumissio vindicta*, → *emancipatio* or → *adoptio*.

Finally, *iurisdictio* can also be the expression of another – in modern terms – variant of functional competence. For instance, the → *praetor urbanus* is responsible for lawsuits (in other words he has appropriate *iurisdictio*) litigated between Roman citizens and the *praetor peregrinus* for those that have arisen between a citizen and a non-citizen or between non-citizens among themselves. Market jurisdiction in general is incumbent upon the → *aediles* – without consideration of citizenship. On the other hand this again reflects on the competence of municipal magistrates – for the citizens there (*cives* or *municipes*), whereas in the provinces the governor's competence corresponds to the place of residence (Dig. 50,16,190: *provinciales eos*

accipere debemus, qui in provincia domicilium habent,
'those who have their place of residence in a province
must be regarded by us as provincials'). Ambassadors
and certain other people (Dig. 5,1,2,3–6) were granted
a *ius domum revocandi*, i.e. a right to be legally prosecuted in their province (*privilegium fori*, → Forum II).

O. BEHRENDS, Die röm. Geschworenenverfassung, 1970;
Id., Der Zwölftafelprozeß, 1974; M. KASER, K. HACKL,
Das röm. Zivilprozeßrecht, ²1997, 183,244,528; G. NO-
CERA, Reddere ius, 1976; W. SIMSHÄUSER, Stadtröm. Ver-
fahrensrecht im Spiegel der lex Irnitana, in: ZRG 109,
1992, 163–208.   C.PA.

Iuris prudentia
A. CONCEPT AND FUNCTION   B. HISTORICAL DE-
VELOPMENT

A. CONCEPT AND FUNCTION

Iuris prudentia (IP), 'astuteness in the law', is the
most succint designation for the legal profession
(→ *iuris consultus*), which in antiquity formed an independent discipline only in Rome. In Rome *IP* did not
denote 'any professional preoccupation with the law'
[2. 1 f.], but only private jurisprudence. Legal practi-
tioners and magistrates were not *iuris prudentes*, but
were instructed by the latter either from case to case as
experts or as permanent assessors. For the relevance of
a mistake in a point of law (→ *ignorantia*) a clear
distinction was made between lay knowledge that was
personal or substantiated by inquiries and the superior,
authoritative *IP* [1. 1164]. The latter especially became
a source of law in private law [3. 33ff, 47f.; 5. 495ff.].
The founders of *IP*, M. → Iunius [II 1] Brutus, P.
→ Mucius Scaevola and M.' → Manilius were hence
those 'who founded the civil law ' (*qui fundaverunt ius
civile*, Dig. 1,2,2,39).

The autonomy of *IP* was based on a rigorous rejection of questions of fact, the determination of which in
the ordinary two-stage legal proceedings was (→ *ordo
iudiciorum*) incumbent upon the lay judge in the second
phase of the proceedings (*apud iudicem*): the jurist limited himself to the legal ruling [2. 52, 66; 5. 601, 667).
He therefore did not dispense justice, but an interpretative, daily 'amendment' (Pomp. Dig. 1,2,2,14: *in melius
produci*) of the law by selective reference to older
jurists. As late as the 3rd cent. AD, → Iulius [IV 16]
Paulus (Dig. 45,1,4,1) and → Ulpianus (Dig. 21,1,10,1)
cited → Porcius Cato Licinianus from the 2nd cent. BC.
However, even this conservative development of law
was itself dependent on the consensus of the legal community and the complete law in fact. Expressions like
hoc iure utimur ('we use this law'), *constat* ('it is established') or *placet* ('it is approved') used by the jurists
point to this.

B. HISTORICAL DEVELOPMENT

The pontifical college (→ *pontifex*) [5. 310ff.] that
was responsible for legal matters exercised an early *IP*
collectively and secretly. It was not until the 'laicization'

of jurisprudence by the first plebeian *pontifex maximus*
in BC 254, Ti. → Coruncanius, who was also the first to
render opinions publicly and in connection with
instruction in the law (Dig. 1,2,2,35 and 38; see [2. 13;
5. 528, 535]), that Roman jurisprudence with its *disputatio fori* (discussion of legal problems, Dig. 1,2,2,5;
see [1. 1163; 5. 564f.]) emerged from the anonymity of
the pontifical college. Profane jurisprudence initially remained a jurisprudence of dignitaries or of the aristocracy [2. 9, 26ff., 70ff.; 5. 528ff.]: its competence in legal
interpretation was based on its legitimate → *auctoritas*.

From the last cent. BC onwards *IP* recruited increasingly from the equestrian class in the course of a certain
social democratization and intellectual specialization
[5. 595f.; 6. 115f., 173f.]. The jurist lost his universal
competence as the sage who had still also been consulted on marriage, on land purchase and on cultivation of
the soil in the middle of the 2nd cent. BC (Cic. Off.
3,133; see [6. 119f.]), and became an expert on private
law. The tradition of pontifical jurisprudence [2. 47f.;
5. 549] died with Q. → Mucius Scaevola Pontifex (deceased 82 BC). After → Antistius [II 3] Labeo and
→ Ateius [6] Capito (Augustan era) no more works *De
iure pontificio* were written. At the end of the Republic,
IP instead established a systematic structure of the law
as a whole with definitions and rules, classifications and
systematizations by applying Hellenistic dialectics
[5. 630ff.]. Even if the opinions did not require substantiation (Sen. Ep. 94,27: *valent ... etiamsi ratio non red-
ditur* [2. 146f.]), rational argumentation was indispensable in legal discourse. This produced an avalanche-
like development of legal literature in the Principate,
and legal discourse no longer took place in the form of
the oral *disputatio fori*, but typically in the writings.

Concerned about the 'respect for the law' (Dig.
1,2,2,49), Augustus made use of jurisprudence with his
ius respondendi (privilege to give answer in juristic
questions).The *responsa prudentium* were defined as
the opinions of those 'who were permitted to lay down
the law' (*quibus permissum est iura condere*, Gai. Inst.
1,7). The jurists grouped around the upholders of the
ius respondendi and formed two allegiances – inconceivable under the conditions of the Republican
autonomy of dignitaries –, the → law schools of the
Sabinians and the Proculians. Given its equilibrium and
freedom to form juridical opinions, juridical law remained a 'controversial law' (*ius controversum*
[1. 1163; 3. 34ff.]), but it lost its relevance with the
gradual bureaucratization of jurisprudence. From
Vespasian onwards, jurists increasingly became members of the central judicial bureaucracy [2. 121ff.].
Hadrian ordered the final drafting of the praetorian
edict (→ *edictum [2] perpetuum*) and reorganized his
→ *consilium* as a judicial advisory body which was constituted by appointed salaried members and was concentrated in the hands of the *princeps* [2. 119, 131, 139,
146, 149f.]. Decentralized juridical production through
legal discourse gave way to the imperial ordinances in
the name of legal certainty, the *responsum* to the *re-*

scriptum. The two-stage legal procedure was displaced by the uniform public service procedure (→ *cognitio extra ordinem*), juridical training in the form of assistance by the advisory work by the assessor with the legal officials.

→ Gaius [2] (Inst. 1,80; 2,126; 2,195) with his *hoc iure utimur* no longer referred to the consensus of the jurists, but to the imperial constitutions. Nevertheless, not only → Iuventius [II 2] Celsus (Dig. 1,1,1 pr.) defined → *ius* as *ars boni et aequi* ('the science of what is good and just'), hence as juridical law, but → Ulpianus (Dig. 1,1,10,2) also defined *IP* as all-embracing 'wisdom': *divinarum et humanarum rerum notitia, iusti atque iniusti scientia* ('cognizance of divine and human affairs, knowledge of what is just and what is unjust' [2. 160; 6. 185, 230]), as already the jurists in the 3rd cent. BC knew *de omnibus divinis atque humanis rebus* ('about all divine and human affairs') (Cic. De or. 3,134 [5. 319, 535]). In view of the selective character of rescript legislation, *IP* of the 3rd cent. AD remained a necessary component of the legal order because it alone could ensure the integration of different legal layers and sources: the jurists completed the development of the old Roman *ius civile* initiated by the → *praetor peregrinus* (foreign praetor) in the late Republic to the universal law of the classical world [5. 474ff.]. However, the concept of juridical law as a 'technique of justice' became obsolete at the same time since a technique such as this required a consensus of purpose and values, hence social homogeneity.

The Dominate of late antiquity abandoned jurisprudence with its ultimate monopolization of legal production and administration by the emperor [2. 335ff.]. Jurisprudence, which was anonymous from now on, was restricted to the passing down of works from the Principate; its new production consisted of *epitomai*, florilegia and collections of the imperial legislation [4; 6. 241ff.]. The kernel of *IP*, legal interpretation and further training by the jurists (→ *interpretatio prudentium*), fell into disrepute. In view of the 'nationalization and ... churchification of jurisprudence' [4. 286], a *IP* certainly existed in late antiquity as 'any professional preoccupation with the law' [2. 1f.], but no longer as autonomous legal interpretation.

1 A. BERGER, s.v. Iurisprudentia, RE 10, 1159–1200 2 SCHULZ   3 M. KASER, Röm. Rechtsquellen und angewandte Juristenmethode, 1986   4 D. LIEBS, Jurisprudenz im spätant. Italien, 1987   5 WIEACKER, RRG 6 M. BRETONE, Gesch. des röm. Rechts, 1992.   T.G.

Ius

A. HISTORICAL OVERVIEW   B. IUS HONORARIUM C. IUS IN THE REPRESENTATION OF LAW   D. IUS AND CITIZENSHIP   E. IUS AND SUBJECTIVE RIGHTS

A. HISTORICAL OVERVIEW

1. IUS IN ANCIENT ROME   2. THE LAYERS OF *ius* IN ITS DEVELOPED STATE

1. IUS IN ANCIENT ROME

Ius, the Roman expression for law, went through considerable changes during the thousand-year history of the Roman state. *Ius* was originally the criterion by which the permitted exercise of liberty, particularly the legitimate exercise of power (over people and things) was distinguished from the disruptive exercise of force (*vis*). *Ius* in modern terminology was thus subjective law. It attested its legal character 'by observing a generally known and practised ritual' [1. 253] in the way it was exercised. This fundamental ritualistic trait survives at a later period in the precisely prescribed formulae of individual legal transactions and processes, e.g. in the *hanc rem meam esse aio* ('I maintain that this thing is mine') the action for the return of property (→ *vindicatio*) and transfer (originally by way of sale), including transfer of power (→ *mancipatio*). The ritual experts were the priests (→ *pontifex*), who advised on the relevant formulae for particular transactions and processes. But one historically significant peculiarity of Roman *ius* is precisely that from early times it was distinguished from divine law (→ *fas*). In early Roman history there is more of a 'division of labour' between the two categories of human activity: compliance with *ius* was the basis for legal probity; *fas* was the area of activity that was free of religious regulation. The bonds of community life were originally protected more by *fas* and by sanctions against *nefas*, its infringement, whereas *ius* 'was essentially restricted to ownership' [2. 52]. It is, however, true that the early → *legis actio sacramento* process embodied a link between the two ritual areas, in that the oath to be sworn by each party (→ *sacramentum*) drew the divinity invoked into the 'secular' legal arena.

With the Law of the Twelve Tables (→ Tabulae duodecim, *c.* 450 BC) at the latest, the meaning of *ius* changed: although the original meaning of 'subjective law' remained, it was restricted in that henceforth personal submission as a sanction for wrongdoing or by virtue of a definite process of arrest (→ *nexum*) ceased to be based on a right of power and became an 'immaterial' legal bond of → *obligatio*. Ritually based power was reinforced by being confirmed by judicial verdicts. The content of such verdicts became the *ius dicere*, or declaration by a → *iudex* that something was *ius* (→ *iuris dictio*). This inevitably happened on repeated occasions, and thereby according to customs and rules. *Ius* continued to be augmented by the accumulation of verdicts. Their quality as constituting law, however, which had to enjoy a minimum of social recognition in order to lay a claim to validity, threatened to collapse during the class struggles of the 5th cent. BC; because of this, *ius* needed to be reinforced and underpinned in the Law (→ *lex*) of the Twelve Tables (→ *Tabulae duodecim*). These became the embodiment of *ius*, or more precisely of *ius civile* as the objective law applying to all Roman citizens. Thus the development towards an autonomous secular order as the basis of *ius* came to a temporary conclusion. This henceforth objectively understood order of *ius* existing as it were above the individual was complemented by the traditional rights of power and the law founded on verdicts.

Both components of *ius* developed further with the decisive help of the priests: the exercise and transfer of private power by the invention of types of transaction borrowing from the old rituals; the proliferation of verdicts through the increased activity of the judicial magistrates, above all from 367 BC the → praetors. In a particular *in iure* procedure (here *ius* as a place of justice), the judicial magistrates gave judgement as to whether and upon what basis a trial could take place at all. This gave them the right to augment the *ius civile* with a *ius honorarium* (law by the magistrates) created by themselves. Finally, the *ius civile* itself, especially the Law of the Twelve Tables, acquired new content by being subject to → *interpretatio* on the part of the priests and secular jurists; in addition, legislating bodies amended the *ius civile* with further laws, of which the *lex Aquilia* (286 BC) achieved the greatest practical significance.

2. THE LAYERS OF *ius* IN ITS DEVELOPED STATE

The conceptual expansion of *ius* and its practical implementation were given vital impetus by the institution, probably in 242 BC, of a *praetor peregrinus*, at first responsible for cases between non-Romans, then (perhaps even from the beginning) also for those between them and Roman citizens. The *ius civile* could not be used for such mixed trials or for disputes that did not involve Roman citizens, as it applied only to *cives Romani*. But there was no invocation of the right of → *peregrini* to be tried at home, for the trial was carried out under Roman jurisdiction, and the Romans did not yet have any concept of 'international private law'. So the *praetor* referred to a particular, objective order of law, in many cases invented by himself: the 'common peoples' law' (*ius gentium*). According to later scholarly opinion, it comprises 'that which natural reason has ordained for all people' (*quod naturalis ratio inter omnes homines constituit*; Gai. Inst. 1,1; Inst. Iust. 1,2,1). Probably the most important concept within this *naturalis ratio* is maintaining one's pledge (→ *fides*), a peculiarly Roman judicial concept, by no means common to all people (nor to all peoples). Many institutions of the *ius gentium* were later taken over by the *praetor urbanus*, who had jurisdiction over Romans. They thus became part of the *ius honorarium*. Important institutions having arisen in this way, such as consensual contracts (→ *consensus*; → *contractus*), were then added to the *ius civile* as former *ius honorarium* during the early Imperial period (1st cent. AD). In this

way rules from the *ius gentium* could, over a long period of development, be 'promoted' into the *ius civile*.

The designation *ius* was the unifying bond between the multitude of different layers of law, sometimes complementing, sometimes overlapping each other. In this way, in the legal literature of the 2nd and 3rd cents. AD with their stronger systematizing tendencies and their admixture of (vulgar) philosophical considerations, *ius* in its own right was able to become a general term for 'law'. This is demonstrated by the generalizing definitions of *ius* in the → 'Digesta', e.g. Celsus' definition as *ars boni et aequi* ('art' of the good and equitable, Dig. 1,1,1) or Ulpian's rendering of the (prime) precept of *ius*: *honeste vivere, alterum non laedere, suum cuique tribuere* ('to live honourably, to harm no-one, to give everyone what is his', Dig. 1,1,10,1). But altogether much more important for the practice and development of Roman law than these theoretical exercises were the discourses of the literary active classical jurists of the late Republic and Principate (2nd cent. BC to 3rd cent. AD), directed as they were towards practical case solutions. The jurists of this period were to a large extent creative in the interpretation of the law. From the time of Augustus the most important among them were granted the right to give legal opinions backed by the → *auctoritas* of the emperor (*ius respondendi*). Gaius (Inst. 1,7) expressly and aptly describes the activities of these jurists as *ius condere* ('making law').

This led in late antiquity to yet another new meaning for the term *ius*: it now signified the law handed down (and in many cases also created) by the classical jurists. It was distinguished from the laws of the imperial constitutions, which were termed *leges*. The emperors of late antiquity strove to bring some order to this *ius*, and to compile it. The first of these goals was served by the repeated concern to compile a law governing → citations. The first to achieve both goals were Justinian and his legislator → Tribonianus, with the 'Digests' (AD 530–533), a much reduced (to *c.* 5 %) collection of the classical *ius*.

B. IUS HONORARIUM

The *ius* of the Romans is perhaps the most influential of all their bequests to the future Europe. As to the conditions that made this degree of influence possible, the *ius honorarium* (law by the magistrates) must always be considered the primary factor that gave Roman *ius* such a particular quality. Originally, this component of *ius* was not a source of law at all, but simply the prerogative of the magistrate, primarily that of the *praetor*, to apply *ius* to the cases appearing before him. But it was in those very cases that the ponderous nature of *ius* as derived from the laws (→ *lex*) became evident. For this reason, it was an important step in increasing the flexibility of *ius* when in 367 BC the praetors were granted a solid and decisive role in the constitution of the Roman courts, especially the civil court. A vital factor in determining the internal legitimation of the praetors' activities, their method and their effectiveness was the fact that they did not confront the existing *ius civile* in an antithetical spirit, but, as Aemilius → Papinianus (*c.* AD 200) aptly remarked by supporting, complementing or correcting (Dig. 1,1,7,1) – *adiuvandi vel supplendi vel corrigendi gratia.* A further factor, not to be overestimated, determining the reliability of the praetors' legislative endeavours was the separation of procedures: the entire case was not in the hands of the magistrate, but only the task of testing it for legal admissibility. The verdict that in fact emerged depended largely upon the evidence. But it was not the magistrate's function to find on that question, and this preserved his objectivity in face of the temptations of personally or politically opportune outcomes.

The separation of procedures remained continuously in place during the various stages in the development of procedural law in Rome under the influence of the *praetor*: it already applied to the oldest procedure, the → *legis actio*, as it did to the trial based on spoken formulae and to the procedure based on written formulae, which lasted into the high classical period. Although the *ius honorarium* developed in the context of actual case experience, this was not on the basis of each individual case, but by dint of extending and improving the formulae relating to particular actions, especially in the form of 'counterclaims' (→ *exceptio*), and indeed formally in the → *edictum* given by the individual office-holder. The edict, in constantly borrowing from the *status quo*, became ever more perfect – to the point where under the emperor Hadrian (*c.* AD 130) it was finally written down by Salvius → Iulianus [1] in the form of the *edictum perpetuum*. In formulating their edict the magistrates relied not on their own political competence, but on the expert knowledge of professional jurists, the best of whom worked in the praetor's *consilium* as a kind of 'expert advisory committee'.

Papinianus' description attributes the *ius honorarium* to the *utilitas publica* (common good). The conceptions of the *praetor* and the jurists of the *consilium* (→ *consilium*) in this regard had since the final period of the Republic also been coloured by theoretical conceptions derived from the philosophy of law, among which were Stoic thoughts on a *ius naturale* and the reflections set down by → Cicero in his political-philosophical masterworks (*De legibus, De officiis, De republica*). Often, the *ius gentium* (see above A.2.) under the jurisdiction of the *praetor peregrinus* constituted a forum for initial experiment, where new ideas were tested before being adopted in the formulae of the *ius honorarium*. In this process, the newer conceptions did not displace the institutions of the *ius civile*, but were set next to them in a supportive function; e.g. for 'property', beside the → *dominium* of the *ius civile* the *bonorum possessio* of the *ius honorarium*; beside the traditional form of transfer, the → *mancipatio*, the simpler → *traditio ex iusta causa*.

C. Ius in the representation of law
1. Ius as a term in legal tradition
2. Classifications in the academic tradition

1. Ius as a term in legal tradition

In the ancient representation of the history of law by Pomponius (Dig. 1,2,2) in the 2nd cent. AD, the legendary literary tradition of early Roman law is referred to by employing *ius* in association with the name of the particular author and collector. The earliest of this kind of collection named by Pomponius is the *ius Papirianum*. It is supposed to originate from a *pontifex maximus* → Papirius at the end of the Monarchy or the beginning of the Republic (*c.* 500 BC). Paulus (Dig. 50,16,144) mentions a commentary on the *ius Papirianum* by the religious writer → Granius [I 3] Flaccus from the 1st cent. BC. This *ius* is said to have contained the → *leges regiae* (old cult rules and religiously sanctioned legal precepts). We are probably speaking here of a forgery to favour the Papirii family in the 1st cent. AD. Of course this does not exclude the possibility that it contained original precepts from an earlier time [1. 307ff.].

Ius Flavianum is the name given by Pomponius to a collection of *dies fasti* (court calendar) and *actiones* (formulae for actions and legal transactions), said to have been compiled or at least published *c.* 300 BC by Gn. → Flavius [I 2], the scribe of Ap. → Claudius [I 2]. As this is supposed to have occurred at the period when spoken formulae were being used in the practice of law, it represented a considerable practical alleviation, and probably also a preparation for the later procedure using written formulae. It is, however, hardly possible to characterize Flavius' action as an act of rebellion against the priests as the administrators of arcane legal knowledge up to that point [1. 526f.; 3].

Procedural formulae together with the text of the Law of the Twelve Tables and an interpretation of it (→ *interpretatio*) may also have figured in the *ius Aelianum*, probably the first published specialist legal text of all. Owing to its presentation in three parts, it was also called *tripertita*. It was written by Sex. → Aelius [I 11] Petus Catus *c.* 200 BC. With this literary version of *ius* began the development of 'jurists' law' as a component of *ius* (see above A.1 at end).

2. Classifications in the academic tradition

Whereas *ius civile, ius honorarium* and *ius gentium* (see above A.) developed historically as layers of Roman law, other adjectivally described categories of *ius* arose from subsequent legal writings, which often contained theoretical reflections on the *ius* phenomenon. Such terms typically acquired their profile by means of dialectical juxtapositions. Probably the most general of these is that of *ius humanum* and *ius divinum* (human and divine law). *Ius divinum* is originally not to be identified with → *fas*, the concept of cult licence. In Cicero's philosophical reflection (cf. Cic. Part. or. 37), *ius divinum* denotes the law that comes from the gods, in contrast with *ius humanum*, which is formulated by people themselves. By extension, *ius divinum* came to refer to the objects of divine law (such as prayers, sacrifices, omens, divine truces) in contrast to the 'secular' affairs of *ius humanum*.

In this meaning, the term partly overlaps with *ius sacrum* (sacred law) and *ius pontificium* (priestly law). The latter is the province of the administrators and experts of the law applying to religious affairs. Just as the priests had originally monopolized the implementation of the laws through → *interpretatio* and through imparting formulae for actions and legal transactions, all the more did they have 'jurisdiction', and for a much longer time exclusively, over the observance of religious rites and the relations between people and gods. To this end, they provided *responsa* (opinions) to the city and its magistrates, and also to private individuals. Otherwise 'secular' jurists of the last cent. BC and the 1st cent. AD wrote texts on sacred law, evidently because of the similarity of the methods of the *ius pontificium* with those of secular law [1. 107f. with n. 135, 568f.]. In particular, the *ius sacrum* decided by means of → *confarreatio* the conditions for legal acts of religious relevance such as marriage, and by → *testamentum* stipulated who would succeed as head of a family; it also decreed the sanctions to be applied when the sacred law had been infringed against, the observance of religiously determined court sittings (→ *fasti*), or the aspects of a property that rendered it or part of it *res sacra*, and immune from the provisions of private law.

While the distinction between *ius divinum* and *ius humanum* at least had a solid place, according to circumstance, in the Roman legal consciousness, the juxtaposition of *ius aequum* and *ius strictum* (just and strict law) belongs only in academic literature. Thus Gai. Inst. 3,18ff. portrays the inheritance rule in the Law of the Twelve Tables as *strictum ius*, whose injustice (*iniquitas*) had been removed by the praetors. *Ius strictum* has a firm place in Justinian's legal language, e.g. Inst. Iust. 4,6,28: *actionum autem quaedam bonae fidei sunt, quaedam stricti iuris* ('many actions are such by good faith, many by strict law'). This is the academic summary of developments since the introduction of *bonae fidei iudicia* by the *praetor* in the late Republic. The philosophical root of *ius aequum* may be *ius naturale* ('natural *ius*') as treated by Roman literature in its reception of Stoic thinking since Cicero: *natura* as the basis of → *justice* and the standard for the assessment of laws (Leg. 1,43ff.). Ulpian (beginning of the 3rd cent. AD) considered *ius naturale* as the basis of practical jurisprudence, and in particular established its association with *ius gentium*.

Ius naturale and previously → *aequitas* (justice) were a favourite means in rhetoric to use valid, written law (*lex scripta*) by avoiding recourse to a superior 'unwritten law' (*ius non scriptum*) [4]. The jurists resisted this device down to the end of the classical period (3rd cent. AD). Their preferred method was careful adaptation from case to case by means of → *interpretatio*, and

by consensus between those jurists who expressed a view on the individual case in question.

In this historical process of categorization, the most influential juxtaposition is that of *ius publicum* and *ius privatum*, public and private law (Ulp. Dig. 1,1,1,2: *publicum ius est quod ad statum rei Romanae spectat, privatum quod ad singulorum utilitatem*, 'public law concerns the affairs of the Roman state, private law the interests of the individual'). This distinction was preceded in the Republican period by the designation of the legal actions of a free citizen as *ius privatum*, and that of the basic rules for living in common, including the fundamental principles for the handling of disputes between private individuals by the magistrates, as *ius publicum*. Of course the increasing power of the emperors, and their *de facto* defining monopoly in politically relevant matters, had as its consequence that jurists of the high and late antique period (1st–3rd cent. AD) scarcely concerned themselves with the *ius publicum*. Thus Ulpian's statement probably has above all a negative function: to state what is not the concern of *ius privatum* [5. 111ff.].

D. IUS AND CITIZENSHIP
1. IUS QUIRITIUM 2. IUS LATII 3. IUS ITALICUM

1. IUS QUIRITIUM
The various layers of the law (see above A.) demonstrate that, at least until the full development of the subservient state of late antiquity, *ius* was identified not by general equality before the law but by membership of an association of people with a particular statutory quality. *Ius civile* in this sense was not 'civil law', but rather 'the law of (Roman) citizens'. A point of paramount importance, therefore, in understanding the concept of *ius* in the Roman period is the individual's membership within the hierarchy of this association of people. This is normally understood as a question of 'citizenship' (or its absence). The oldest term for such membership is the *ius Quiritium*. This concept, which lacks an etymological explanation (→ *Quirites*), may best be understood in the formulae of legal actions for the assertion of private rights of power: *meum esse aio ex iure Quiritium* ('I maintain that this is my property according to the law of the *Quirites*'). It is not clear whether this merely represents the use of an alternative expression for *ius civile*, or whether it originally had a distinct meaning, e.g. as a particular *ius* applying to those who had private power rights (the *patres familias*). In Gai. Inst. 1,32c ff. in any case, the *ius Quiritium* is simply full Roman citizenship. As awareness of the importance of the *ius gentium* has grown, the preferred term for institutions of law that, by their own nature, go back solely to Roman tradition, and thus show no contact with the *ius gentium*, is *ius proprium Romanorum*.

2. IUS LATII
From the dissolution of the Latin League in 338 BC, the → *Latini*, a tribe related to the Romans, stood in three kinds of legal relationship to their Roman cousins:

insofar as their lands were Roman territory, their free inhabitants normally also had Roman citizenship, as was the rule in any case for military settlements founded by the Romans on Italian soil. Communities with *ius Latii*, on the other hand, were legally autonomous, enjoying their own legal order as citizens. But, through → *commercium* and → *conubium* with Romans, the free citizens of these communities also enjoyed legal equality with them in matters of commerce and marriage rights; they also had the *ius migrandi* ('freedom of domicile'), enabling them to migrate to Rome and be entered on the census list, thus achieving the status of a Roman citizen (*civis Romanus*) without having to abandon their original citizenship. Inhabitants of *coloniae Latinae* of course did not enjoy this right. There as in other Latin communities, however, the holding of a magistrature conferred Roman citizenship on the incumbent and his descendants (*ius civitatis per honorem adipiscendi*). In a third group of *municipia civium Romanorum* (semi-citizenship communities) with self-government, the free inhabitants possessed the formal trappings of Roman citizenship, but without *ius suffragii* (the suffrage), and in many cases even without *conubium*. With the granting of full citizenship to all free Italians after the Social War (89 BC), these distinctions became outdated in Italy. From then on until the → *constitutio Antoniniana* (AD 212), Rome, or the emperor, granted the *ius Latii* to communities and their inhabitants as a 'transitional stage in a process of prudential integration into full citizenship' [1. 369]. From the time of Hadrian, acquisition of citizenship by virtue of holding an honorary post was extended to council members (→ *decurio* [1]). Since Augustus many → freedmen also had the *ius Latii* as so-called → *Latini Iuniani*.

3. IUS ITALICUM

The term *ius Italicum* does not describe any status of citizenship, but perhaps the granting of privileges to communities outside Italy, by way of autonomy in their relations with provincial governors [cf. 6. 1242, 1248ff.], and a particular legal approach to provincial lands. This meaning of *ius Italicum* only made sense once all of Italy itself had gained equal status with the city of Rome, i.e. after 89 BC. Legal transactions and actions under the *ius civile*, even for Roman citizens, were available only for land located in *dominium ex iure Quiritium*. In the case of provincial lands this was generally not the case, as such lands were regarded as the property of the Roman state or of the emperor, so that private individuals could have only a material right of use and possession (*uti, frui, habere, possidere*) with regard to them. Digest 50,15, however, contains a long list of Roman colonies and other communities that were, themselves or their land, subject to the *ius Italicum*. Besides the possibility of using the rules of the *ius civile* in matters of property and usucapion (→ *usucapio*), land with *ius Italicum* may also have enjoyed complete exemption from taxation. This conclusion is indirectly derived from Paul. Dig. 50,15,8,7, and fits with the fact that these lands were not regarded as the property of the state.

E. IUS AND SUBJECTIVE RIGHTS

The probably original meaning of *ius* as subjective law (see above A.1.) remained intact throughout the entire development of Roman law. Thus in Roman legal language nearly all personal entitlements are also described as *ius*.

1. PERSONAL RIGHTS IN THE STATE AND IN PUBLIC ADMINISTRATION 2. PRIVATE ENTITLEMENTS

1. PERSONAL RIGHTS IN THE STATE AND IN PUBLIC ADMINISTRATION

Accordingly, the Romans call a multitude of 'public rights' *ius*. Among these are the various levels of citizenship (see above D.) as well as the *ius suffragii* (suffrage, see above D.2., see also → *suffragium*), the *ius migrandi* and the *ius provocationis* (right of appeal, → *provocatio*) of individual citizens sentenced by the magistrates (→ *coercitio*) to the public assembly. Access to honorary office, i.e. the passive suffrage, was called *ius honorum (petendorum)*. It was available only to those with active rights of suffrage. Restrictions applied to priests, for particular offences (e.g. electoral fraud, → *ambitus*), to criminals, the insolvent, and members of dishonourable professions (cf. → *infamia*). Moreover, patricians did not have the *ius honorum* with regard to the plebeian magistrature (people's tribunes, *aediles*). Until Sulla's time a condition of candidature was 10 years' military service. Also to be taken into consideration was a minimum age that differed from one office to another, and the need to comply with the → *cursus honorum* (chain of offices); cf. for all the above [7. 52–64].

Above all, the prerogatives of officeholders were referred to as *iura*: in accordance with the principle of collegiality and the rights of intervention of the people's tribunes they had the *ius intercedendi* (right of veto, → *intercessio* [1]). The tribunes (→ *tribunus*) had the monopoly right to summon the → *concilium plebis*, the *ius agendi cum plebe*, the consuls the *ius agendi cum populo* (summoning of the public assembly) and the *ius agendi cum senatu* (right to speak and make proposals in the Senate). Particular rights relating to the ordering of business applied to members of the Senate (→ *senatus*): *ius referendi* (the right to speak in a particular order), the emperor's *ius primae relationis* (right to speak first). For the fulfilment of their actual functions, the magistrates, above all the *praetor*, had the *ius edicendi* (→ *edictum* [1]). In relation to lower-ranking officeholders they had a *ius prohibendi* (right to forbid). As regards policing powers (→ *coercitio*), the magistrates had the *ius vocationis* (right of summons) and the *ius prensionis* (right of arrest).

2. PRIVATE ENTITLEMENTS

At the end of the Republic and in the Imperial period, the conception of *ius* as subjective law was no longer restricted to the original rights of power. Thus there were now also rights (→ *privilegium*) granted by the state or by the emperor; these were termed *ius singulare* (a right granted to the individual) as against the *ius commune* (general right). A particular manifestation of this conception is the *ius liberorum* (right on the grounds of the number of children) introduced under the marriage laws of Augustus: in general, there was a legal obligation to marry, but exceptions to the rule under the *ius liberorum* were men or women who had engendered or born three freeborn children. A woman with this *ius* required no guardian (→ *tutela*), and, as a mother, had a legal right of succession on the basis of the *SC Tertullianum* (2nd cent. AD).

Family-based legal authority is certainly one of the oldest legal conceptions. The strictest of all expressions of a subjective 'right' is the so-called *ius vitae necisque*, the right of life and death enjoyed by the *dominus* (master) and → *pater familias* over all members of the family and its slaves. This prerogative may from the beginning have been sacral, and then limited by the strictures of the censor. Already in early times its exercise was tied to the holding of a household trial. In late antiquity such killings were punishable. The rights of the person are, however, affected by the *ius postliminii* (right of return of prisoners of war, → *postliminium*) and the *ius anuli aurei* (right to the golden ring), an exclusive right of rank for the freeborn, which could, however, in special cases be granted to freedmen by the emperor. Property laws too are associated with prerogatives that were referred to as *ius*: thus the holder of an easement (→ *servitus*) or of a share in a property has a *ius prohibendi* (right of prohibition) against the (full) owner, who is also so entitled. If improvements have been made on items with other items, the person who has made the improvements has the right of a *ius tollendi* (right of removal), i.e. to take away his items (provided that the original items suffer no damage by such an operation). A subordinate secured creditor has a *ius offerendi et succedendi* (right to claim repayment and order of rank, → *pignus*) to the prior creditor. In isolated cases in late antiquity, the individual property right itself is augmented by being called *ius*. Thus the → *emphyteusis* (hereditary lease) is also called *ius perpetuum* (permanent right); there is also occasional talk of a *ius emphyteuticarium*.

→ Actio; → Citizenship; → Civitas (B.); → Formula; → Iudicium; → Lex; → Peregrini; → Quirites; → JUSTICE; → HISTORY OF LAW/ROMAN-LAW STUDIES

1 WIEACKER, RRG   2 DULCKEIT/SCHWARZ/WALDSTEIN   3 J.G. WOLF, Die lit. Überlieferung der Publikation der Fasten und Legisaktionen durch Gnaeus Flavius (Nachr. der Akad. der Wiss. Göttingen I 2), 1980   4 U. WESEL, Rhet. Statuslehre und Auslegung der Juristen, 1967   5 M. KASER, Der Privatrechtsakt in der röm. Rechtsquellenlehre, in: FS F.Wieacker, 1978, 90–114   6 A. V. PREMERSTEIN, s.v. Ius Italicum, RE 10, 1238–1253   7 W. KUNKEL, R. WITTMAN, Staatsordnung und Staatspraxis in der röm. Republik 2, 1995.

M. BRETONE, Storia del diritto romano, 1987; HONSELL/MAYER-MALY/SELB, 2–14, 22–29, 46f., 49–60; M. KA-SER, Das altröm. ius, 1949; KASER, RPR I, 24–39, 60ff., 194–214, 299, 320, 342, 437, 467f., 702; P. STEIN, Röm. Recht und Europa, Ger. 1996, 14–37; F. VITTINGHOFF, Röm. Stadtrechtsformen der Kaiserzeit, in: ZRG 68, 1951, 435–485, 465ff.   G.S.

Ius iurandum The oath to be sworn to Roman law (→ *ius*) or before the court (at the praetor or *iudex*). The older type of oath is probably the → *sacramentum*, which however, from the late Republic onwards with the dying out of the *legis actio sacramento*, essentially described the soldier's oath. The *ius iurandum* was sworn by → Jupiter, all the gods or by the → genius of the emperor. The magistrates swore the existing laws with a *ius iurandum in leges* within five days of taking up office, and magistrates stepping down usually also swore the legitimacy of their administration [1. 94ff., 253]. In order to guarantee that the laws were followed completely, laws enacted during their term in office likewise had to be sworn by the magistrates. No general oath of an official has been passed down to us for the Republican period [1. 95 with n. 152].

In Roman civil procedure, the oath of the parties is widespread. As a voluntary oath (*ius iurandum voluntarium*) in the proceedings before the praetor (*in iure*), it can be 'shifted' by each party to the respective other one (*ius iurandum deferri*). If the other party accepts, he can swear the oath (*ius iurandum dare*) or the 'deferrer' can agree to cancel the oath (*remittere*); then this is the equivalent of swearing an oath. In both cases, from a legal point of view, it is a statement of undisputed facts: if the plaintiff has shifted the oath to the defendant, the suit is considered now as unfounded; a new suit can only be admitted via the fact of the swearing of the oath or its cancelling and with the defence that the oath has been sworn (*exceptio iurisiurandi*). If the defendant has shifted the oath to the plaintiff, then only an *actio in factum* (suit for the facts of the case) regarding the content of the sworn or cancelled oath can still be given. If the oath is refused, the matter must be further heard by the praetor and *iudex*. This is different in the case of a suit regarding repayment of borrowed money (*actio certae creditae pecuniae*) and a small number of other suits if the plaintiff has, upon request by the defendant, paid the *ius iurandum calumniae* (oath that he is not suing for harassment): then the plaintiff can again shift the oath to the defendant and if the defendant now refuses the oath, the plaintiff can apply for (probably provisional) debt enforcement (*missio in bona*). The *ius iurandum calumniae* can also otherwise be requested in order to avoid improper litigation.

Further *iura iuranda* are used as proof, through interrogation of parties or witnesses, before the → *iudex*. The latter can also impose on the plaintiff a valuation oath (*ius iurandum in litem*) if the defendant has arbitrarily refused or wilfully obstructed the restoration of the object which is the subject of litigation. Perjury was, as such, originally not criminal but was subject to censorial reprimand. With the oath, however, a false testimony could be given so that it was a matter of a → *crimen falsi* or the person swearing the oath made himself liable to prosecution for high treason if he swore a false oath by the genius of the emperor (*crimen → laesae maiestatis*).

1 W. KUNKEL, R. WITTMANN, Staatsordnung und Staatspraxis der röm. Republik 2, 1995.

M. KASER, K. HACKL, Die röm. Zivilprozeßordnung, ²1997, 266ff., 284ff., 365ff. G.S.

Ius Latii see → Ius D.2.; → Latin law

Iussum (from *iubere*, to order). A unilateral declaration which acts as a legal command or authorization. In private law *iussum* is found in particular 1. as a direction by someone in authority to those under his authority (slaves or children of the house) to perform a specific legal act, e.g. to acquire something for him; 2. as authorization by the person in authority to a third person to conduct a particular transaction with someone under his authority at his expense (for which the person in authority takes responsibility by means of *actio quod iussu*); 3. at the → *delegatio* as authorization of the assignor to the assignee to perform a service to the receiver of the instruction at his expense; 4. generally as authorization of the indirect representative (e.g. in the case of a → *mandatum*), to conduct a transaction at the expense of the person represented; 5. in the law of succession as (principally testamentary) arrangement of the testator.
→ Pater familias

HEUMANN/SECKEL, s.v. *iubere*; KASER, RPR I, 262f., 265f., 608; II, 106, 415. F.ME.

Iustina Roman empress, married in a second marriage to → Valentinianus I, mother of Valentinianus II. Other children: Iusta, Grata, Galla [2]. She supported the Arian line of belief and is said to have backed the Milan ecclesiastical conflict with → Ambrosius of AD 385/86. This concerned the use of a church by the Arians, but it seems unlikely that she would have been able to pursue this alone [1. 170–173]. In any case this episode has resulted up to the present day in a negative image of I. among (ecclesiastical) historians. In 387 she fled with her children from the usurper Maximus to Thessalonica, where she married her daughter Galla to emperor → Theodosius I. She died sometime during the war against Maximus or at the latest shortly after victory over him (388). PLRE 1, 488–489.

1 N. B. MCLYNN, Ambrose of Milan, 1984. K.G.-A.

Iustinianopolis (Ἰουστινιανόπολις; *Ioustinianópolis*). Place on the peninsula of Miletus (→ Milesia), first mentioned in an inscription of the time of Justinian from the Sacred Way in → Didyma (unpublished). Possibly identical with Didyma, which, however, in Byzan-

tine sources always appears as *Tò Hierón* (Τὸ Ἱερόν, from this Turkish *Jeronda*), or with a deserted city discovered in 1995 on the Gulf of Akbük [1. 304f.].

1 H. LOHMANN, Survey in der Chora von Milet, in: AA 1997, 285–311. H.LO.

Iustinianus

[1] Flavius Iustinianus I. The Roman emperor Justinian (AD 527–565), born *c.* 482 of Thracian-Illyrian origins as the son of a farmer, with the Latin name Petrus Sabbatius in Bederiana by Tauresium, in the area of the city Iustiniana Prima, which he later built (probably identical with modern Caričin Grad, 45 km south of Niš; see [1. 1085]), died on 14 November 565 in Constantinople. He owed his rise to → Iustinus [1] I, his mother's brother. He trusted I. especially, who was serving as *candidatus* in the imperial palace guard when his uncle came to power in 518, adopted him and had him crowned in April 527 by the patriarch as Augustus and co-emperor, his wife → Theodora, a former actress, as Augusta. When he died on 1 August 527, I. became the sole ruler.

A. FOREIGN AFFAIRS   B. ADMINISTRATIVE REFORMS AND LEGAL CODICES   C. RELIGIOUS POLICY   D. BUILDING ACTIVITIES   E. SOURCES

A. FOREIGN AFFAIRS

During his 38-year rule I. tried to restore to its former power and size the Roman empire, whose former western provinces were in the hands of Germanic tribes from the 5th cent. (Franks, West and Ostrogoths, Vandals), and at the same time to protect its territory against every outside threat. In spite of efforts to resolve conflicts by diplomatic means, he pursued his goals in foreign policy above all by means of elaborate wars which were exclusively delegated to his generals, and in this way greatly overextended the resources of the empire in the long run.

At first he saw himself forced to intervene at the eastern border. The Lazian king at the eastern end of the Black Sea, since 468 a vassal of Sassanid Persia, had received baptism already in 522 in Constantinople and submitted to East Rome. Thus the Persians' access to the Black Sea was cut off and at the same time the block of Christian peoples in the Caucasus was strengthened, who saw in Byzantium their support against Persia. I. was able to temporarily settle the armed conflict (since 526) that had resulted from this in September 532 through an 'eternal peace'. He entered into a treaty with the Arabian Ghassanids in order to secure Syria's eastern borders.

The Balkans remained a constant hotbed of unrest because of the repeated raids by Hun and Slav, later also Avar, tribes, which I. neglected from time to time in order to reconquer territories of the former western part of the empire. His first goal was the Vandal kingdom, which had existed since AD 429 in north-west Africa. In spring of 533, the general → Belisarius was sent out against the insubordinate usurper → Gelimer; he was able to end the war victoriously in December 533 and restore the Vandal territory to the Roman empire in 534. Soon after that the military conflicts with the East Goths in Italy began, which lasted much longer. The conflict was sparked by the murder of → Amalasuntha, the daughter of → Theodoric the Great, who was friendly with Byzantium, by her cousin Theodahad (April 535), because he supported a policy of confrontation against East Rome. From June 535 Belisarius again led the armed conflict, first against Theodahad, who was soon deposed and killed by opponents among his own people, then against his successor → Vitigis. Since spring 538 the all too powerful Belisarius had to share the supreme command, after the will of the emperor, with the *praepositus sacri cubiculi* → Narses. The first phase of the war ended in May 540 with the taking of Ravenna by the imperial troops and the capture of King Vitigis.

Almost at the same time, in March of 540, Persia under Chosroes [5] I. broke the 'eternal peace' with a raid along the eastern front of the empire. This second war in the east ended 545 with a truce for five years, which could not, however, prevent unrest in the territory of the Lazi. A third Persian war from 550 ended finally with a peace treaty in 561.

In the west Totila, king of the Goths since autumn 541, gathered a new army and expanded his power over wide areas of Italy in the following years. It was only after his death in the summer of 552 that Narses could defeat the Goths finally in 553 and occupy all of Italy. The attempt (553–555) to expand eastern rule to Visigothic Spain was only successful in the extreme south of the country.

B. ADMINISTRATIVE REFORMS AND LEGAL CODICES

From the beginning I. tried to secure the empire internally as well, above all through his streamlined financial politics, reforms of the public administration and law, patronage of the orthodox state church and numerous building activities. But his zeal to reform also led to opposition, which vented itself already in his first years of rule (13–18 January 532) in the so-called → Nika revolt (thus called because of the victory cry of the rebels), a popular revolt probably steered by the senatorial opposition above all against the restrictive finance politics of the *praefectus praetorio* → Iohannes [16]; but it was put down through the intervention of Belisarius. A severe inner threat was also the plague of 542–543, which caused numerous deaths.

Probably the most important achievement of the emperor, which stood the test of time, was the compilation of the → Corpus iuris civilis. First, in February 528, he charged a commission to which the important lawyer → Tribonianus belonged, with collecting all imperial laws, which were promulgated as *Codex Iustinianus* for the first time in April 529, and in amended, final form in November 534. In November 533 the elementary treat-

ise → *Institutiones* became law, and in December 533 the codification of classical jurisprudence (→ *digesta*), which had been compiled from 530 under the leadership of Tribonianus. The laws made after November 534, the *Novellae*, were not sanctioned officially as I. had intended; they have only been passed down in private compilations.

C. RELIGION, POLICY OF

I. made efforts to restrict the influence of all non-Christian religions (pagans, Jews, Samaritans, Manichaeans) and 'heretical' confessions in order to support the state Church. But – probably under the influence of Theodora – after an initial confrontation (see also → Iustinius I) he sought a rapprochement with the → Monophysites, among other things by interceding for the pre-Chalcedonian Christology of the Alexandrians (Neo-Chalcedonianism) and the condemnation of the Antiochene theologians, which was sanctioned at the oecumenical council of Constantinople 553. But an agreement with the Monophysites failed to materialize.

D. BUILDING ACTIVITIES

→ Procopius reports in detail in his work *De aedificiis* about the lively building activities of I. in the entire empire, including numerous buildings to fortify the borders, above all in the east. Of the many sacred buildings of his time only the new buildings of the → Hagia Sophia (dedicated December 537, collapse of the dome 558, rededication 562) and the no longer extant Apostles' church (550) in Constantinople, San Vitale 547 and Sant' Apollinare in Classe 549 in Ravenna should be mentioned here.

E. SOURCES

Among the numerous contemporary sources on I. and his time, apart from the *Corpus iuris*, the historical works of Procopius and → Agathias as well as the last (18th) book of the Chronicle of → Iohannes [18] Malalas are mentioned; among the sources of the later period the Chronicle of → Theophanes (early 9th cent.) is especially to be mentioned.

1 ODB 2, 1083f.   2 PLRE 2, 645–648 (I. 7)   3 TRE 17, 478–486   4 R. BROWNING, J. and Theodora, ²1987 5 J. A. S. EVANS, The Age of J., 1996   6 C. MANGO, Byzantine Architecture, 1976, 97–160   7 G. PRINZING, Das Bild Justinians I. in der Überlieferung der Byzantiner, in: Fontes Minores 7, 1986, 1–99   8 RUBIN, 1–2 9 E. STEIN, Histoire du Bas-Empire 2, 1949, 275–845 10 F. TINNEFELD, Die frühbyz. Gesellschaft, 1977 11 L. WENGER, Die Quellen des röm. Rechts, 1953, 562–679.

[2] Son of → Germanus [1], East Roman general, first documented AD 550 in a responsible military mission in Dalmatia, 552 troop leader against the 'Sclaveni' in Illyricum, 572 *patricius*, 572–573 *magister militum per Armeniam*, 574/575–577 *mag. mil. per Orientem* under emperor → Tiberius in the Persian war, after initial successes unsuccessful, recalled 577 (ODB 2, 1083; PLRE 3, 744–747 [I. 3]).

[3] I. II. Byzantine emperor of the dynasty of Heraclius (→ Heraclius [7]), son of Constantinus IV; born around AD 668, ruled 685–695 and 705–711. I. called 692 the council in the *triklinos tou troullou* (hall of the dome) of the imperial palace, which took fundamental decisions in questions of discipline of the Orthodox Church. He had the image of the emperor moved to the reverse for the first time from the obverse of the *nómisma*, the Byzantine standard gold coin, and put the image of Christ in its place. Unpopular because of his rigourous administrative and financial measures, he was overthrown in 695 by the usurper → Leontius, who had his nose cut off. He first found refuge with the → Chazars; the khan of the Bulgars Tervel helped him regain his throne in 705. In 711 a new uprising broke out against him, and he was beheaded by an army officer on the orders of the usurper → Philippicus Bardanes near Damatrys in Bithynia.

> ODB 2, 1084f.; H. OHME, Das Concilium Quinisextum und seine Bischofsliste, 1990 (on the Trullanum).   F.T.

Iustinus

[1] I. I (AD 518–527), emperor of the Eastern Roman Empire, born a farmer's son around 450 in Bederiana (like → Iustinianus [1] I.), he came to Constantinople with → Leo I and was soon a member of the palace guard; under → Anastasius I he was *comes rei militaris* and from 515 *comes excubitorum*. In the dispute over the succession to Anastasius, who died without an heir, a majority in the Senate supported his candidacy and eventually he was also acclaimed by the army and the people, and was crowned on 10 July 518 by the patriarch. In contrast to his predecessors he resolutely supported the Christology of the Council of Chalcedon (451) and opposed → Monophysitism. He attempted the political exclusion of the supporters of Anastasius in the Senate. During the period of his reign there was much unrest amongst the population. In the final years before his death (1 August 518) his nephew, adopted son and successor, Iustinianus [1] I was already essentially ruling ODB 2, 1082; PLRE 2, 648–651 (I. 4).

[2] I. General of the Eastern Roman Empire, *magister militum per Illyricum* around AD 538, *mag. mil. vacans* 538/544–552, along with → Narses supported → Belisarius in the war against the Ostrogoths in Italy, where he is in evidence intermittently until 552. PLRE 3, 748f. (I. 2).

[3] I. Son of Germanus [1], brother of Iustinianus [2], general of the Eastern Roman Empire, born *c.* AD 525, fought against the Sclaveni in Illyricum 551–552, in Lazica from 554 and in the region bordering the Danube from 561. He was a promising candidate for emperor in 565 along with I. [2] II. Banished to Alexandria by the latter on his becoming emperor, he was murdered there – probably at the behest of I. PLRE 3, 750–754 (I. 4).

[4] I. II. Eastern Roman emperor (AD 565–578), born around 510–515 the son of Vigilantia, sister of → Iusti-

nianus [1] I., died October 578; married to Sophia, a niece of the empress → Theodora. From 552 *cura palatii* (→ Kouropalates) at the imperial court, practically his co-regent during the final years of Justinian, and after the latter's death in November 565 he asserted himself against his rival, I. [3], son of Germanus. The court poet → Corippus portrayed in a Latin poem an idealized version of the circumstances of the take-over of power. The period of his reign was clouded by the grave aftermath of his predecessor's wars of conquest. In 568 Italy, only recently seized from the Goths, was in great part conquered by the invading Lombards from Pannonia. In Spain the Visigoths won back some cities; the Avars broke through across the Danube; parts of North Africa were also lost. Moreover, by inept diplomacy, I. provoked a new and lengthy war with the Persians in 572. → Tiberius (II.), who, at the instigation of I.'s wife, was adopted by I. and in December 574 made Caesar (→ court title D.), carried out the business of government to a greater and greater extent in the final years on behalf of a mentally ill emperor.

> ODB 2, 1082f.; PLRE 3, 754–756 (I. 5); A. CAMERON (ed.), Flavius Cresconius Corippus, In laudem Iustini Augusti minoris, 1976; E. STEIN, Studien zur Geschichte des byz. Reiches, 1919; H. TURTLEDOVE, The Immediate Successors of Justinian, thesis 1977.   F.T.

[5] M. Iunian(i)us I. Compiler of an extract from the lost *Historiae Philippicae* of → Pompeius Trogus (*Epitome historiarum Philippicarum*). He does not strive for a uniform paraphrase: in the interests of *brevitas* the anecdotal and the exemplary are emphasized so that a kind of anthology of the corresponding, original extracts is given; concrete details (geographical digressions, chronology, prosopography etc.) are avoided. The work also remains close to the original linguistically; I.'s own additions (e.g. 41,4,8) are rare and may make up 10–15 % of the original. In contrast to earlier studies, which dated the *epitome* in the 2nd or 3rd cent. AD, according to the particular nature of the text as a breviarium, the relevance of the Persian theme, the sudden appearance of attestations by the Church Fathers around 400, and linguistic arguments, a plausible dating to around 390 has been suggested [1]. In late antiquity reliable traces of reception are rare. However, in the Middle Ages, Pompeius Trogus is replaced by I.

The tradition of the text, which so far has not been conclusively investigated, is rich and diverse: of over 230 surviving codices more than 30 can be ascribed to the early and high Middle Ages (8th–12th cents.). Two Italian families, γ (Monte Cassino) and π (Verona), are known only from the period of early Humanism; a third, also Italian (ι), had earlier connections to France; the last (τ) becomes, via the sphere of influence of the Carolingian court library and of the monastery of Lorsch respectively, the source of early reception in France and south west Germany. To the rich mediaeval and humanistic reception, I. is one of the most important sources of information on historical Greece and other texts relating to Alexander the Great, to which a continuous printing tradition corresponds up to the school editions of 19th cent.

1 SYME, RP 6, 358–371.

EDITIONS: F. RÜHL, 1886; O. SEEL, ²1972 (unsatisfactory); J. C. YARDLEY, W. HECKEL, 1997 (transl. and comm. of bks. 11 and 12).
BIBLIOGRAPHY: G. BILLANOVICH, La biblioteca di Pomposa, 1994, 181–212; L. FERRERO, Struttura e metodo dell' Epitome, 1957; G. FORNI, Valore storico e fonti di Pompeo Trogo, 1958; Id., M. G. ANGELI BERTINELLI, in: Pompeo Trogo come fonte di storia, in: ANRW II 30, 2, 1982, 1301–1312; H. HAGENDAHL, Orosius und I., 1941; F. RÜHL, Die Verbreitung des Justinus im MA, 1871; Id., Die Textquellen des Justinus, 1872; P. L. SCHMIDT, in: HLL 6, 637.3 (in preparation); W. SUERBAUM, Vom ant. zum frühma. Staatsbegriff, ³1977, 128–146, 368f.   P.L.S.

[6] Iustinus Martys. Philosopher and Christian martyr (died AD 165). Born in Flavia Neapolis/Palaestina, I. devoted himself, after acquaintance with other factions, to the middle Platonic school of philosophy. Admiration for the Christian martyrs and the OT prophets led to his conversion (Justin. Dial. 3–8). Then as a wandering priest clothed in the philosopher's robes he travelled around, spending his final years in Rome. I., who in 165 was executed by the prefect Rusticus, wrote numerous texts (cf. Euseb. Hist. eccl. 4,18,2–7; fr. among others CPG 1078–1089; CPG suppl. 1082–1084). Three extant works are original: the 'First' and 'Second Apologia' (150–155 or shortly after) and the 'Dialogue with the Jew Tryphon' (155–160). The 'Apologia' defends the Christians against the accusation of atheism and supports Christ's position as the son of God by means of documentary evidence from the OT. The concept of Christianity as the sole and true philosophy is connected with the oration of the *lógos spermatikós* borrowed from the Stoa, which assumes that seeds of truth are present in the reason of all men. Developed out of intensive contact with Judaism, I. writings promulgate a Christ who fulfils the OT promise of a Messiah [8. 428].

EDITIONS: 1 M. MARCOVICH, Iustini Martyris Apologiae pro Christianis, 1994 (Patristische Texte und Studien 38) 2 Id., Iustini Martyris Dialogus cum Tryphone, 1997 (Patristische Texte und Studien 47).
GERMAN TRANSLATIONS: 3 PH. HAEUSER, BKV 33 (Justin), 1917, 1–231 (Dial.) 4 G. RAUSCHEN, BKV 12 (Frühchristl. Apologeten 1), 1913, 65–155 (Apol.).
BIBLIOGRAPHY: 5 L. W. BARNARD, Justin Martyr, 1967 6 G. GIRGENTI, Giustino martire, 1995 7 E. R. GOODENOUGH, The Theology of Justin Martyr, 1923 8 O. SKARSAUNE, The Proof from Prophecy, 1987.   J.RI.

[7] The location and lifespan of the Gnostic I. are unknown (2nd/beginning 3rd cent. AD). An excerpt from his 'Book of Baruch' survives among Gnostic material in → Hippolytus' [2] *Refutatio* (5,23–27); numerous other texts (Hippolytus, Refutatio 5,23,2) have been lost. A doctrine of three principles exists: the Good One (God), the Father (Elohim) and the female Earth (Edem). Out of the union of Edem and Elohim arise 12 paternal and 12 maternal angels (all 24 together = Paradise), among them, in each case the third, Baruch and Naas. Elohim's angels create out of Edem mankind, which possesses *pneuma* (from Elohim) and soul (from Edem). Elohim departs from Edem and ascends to the Good One; the human *pneuma* is to follow him. The abandoned Edem allows the Evil One to arise through Naas, but Baruch assists the *pneuma*'s ascent (finally by Jesus' revelation).

→ Gnosis, Gnostics

J. J. BUCKLEY, Transcendence and Sexuality in 'The Book Baruch', in: HR 24, 1984/5, 328–344 (= Id., Female Fault and Fulfilment in Gnosticism, 1986, 3–19); E. HAENCHEN, Gott und Mensch, 1965, 298–334; M. MARCOVICH, Justin's Baruch, in: Id., Studies in Graeco-Roman Religions and Gnosticism, 1988, 93–119 (with bibliography); M. TARDIEU, Justin the Gnostic. A Syncretistic Mythology, in: M. BONNEFOY (ed.), Mythologies, 1991, vol. 2, 686–688.   J.HO.

Iustitium In Rome the suspension of judicial activity generally ordered by a magistrate (the highest present in Rome) with an edict and associated with further restrictions of transactions, e.g. the closure of the state treasury (→ *aerarium*, Cic. Har. resp. 55) or the stores in the Forum (Liv. 9,7,8). By the late Republic this order had to be preceded by a resolution of the Senate (Liv. 3,3,6). The *iustitium* was not solely an emergency measure but already in the Republican period could be caused by public mourning over a military defeat (Liv. 9,7,8) or the death of a prominent statesman.

W. KUNKEL, R. WITTMANN, Staatsordnung und Staatspraxis der röm. Republik, 2, 1995, 225ff.   G.S.

Iustus

[1] see → Pescennius

[2] I. of Tiberias. Jewish historian of the 1st cent. AD, wrote a 'Jewish War' (66–70/74), in which he dealt critically with the work of the same name by → Josephus [4] Flavius (this made Josephus write a retort in his autobiography: *Vita* 65), and a chronological-genealogical work on Jewish kings from Moses to → Iulius [II 5] Agrippa II. This work, which appears to have been available to the patriarch Photius (Bibl. cod. 33), bore the title *Perì Iudaíōn basiléōn en toîs stémmasin* and may have been part of a larger work which also treats non-Jewish subjects (see Diog. Laert. 2,41 = F 1). By necessity I. took part in the early stage of the great Jewish revolt just as Josephus did. Both left the rebel camp as soon as possible and later tried to blame each other for the outbreak of the revolt in Tiberias. FGrH 734.

SCHÜRER, 1, 34–37.   K.BR.

[3] Cousin of emperor → Iustinianus [1] I, brother of Germanus [1], supported the emperor in the → Nika revolt in AD 532 (Procop. Pers. 1,24,53), in 542–543 he was a commanding officer in the Persian War (2, 20, 20–28; 24, 15; 20; 25, 35) and died 544 (2, 28, 1).

PLRE 3 A, 758f. (I. 2); E. STEIN, Histoire du Bas-Empire 2, 454, 498–502.   K.P.J.

[4] Name of various physicians. Galen (Methodus medendi 14,19 = 10,1019 K.) describes a contemporary ophthalmologist named I., who was active around AD 180 and who is supposed to have healed some patients of purulent flux of the eyes by making them sit on a chair and then shaking their heads vigourously back and forth so that the pus could flow out and be shaken off. He may also have been the one to whom Galen dedicated *De partibus artis medicae* (ed. M. C. LYONS, CMG, Suppl. Orientale 2, 1969) since the art of couching cataracts is discussed in some detail in the 4th ch. of this writing. It is less likely that he was the husband of the lovesick patient whom Galen treated (De praecognitione 5 = 14,626 K.). He is presumably not identical to the I. who appears in the late Latin translation of Oribasius as the inventor of several clysters (→ Enemas) and to whom other remedies as they have been preserved in late Greek and Latin texts go back [1]. In some MSS the *Gynaecia* of → Vindicianus are attributed to I. (who is erroneously also called Accius I.).

1 E. WICKERSHEIMER, Le médecin Justus, contemporain de Galien et les écrits portants son nom, in: Actes du 10ᵉ Congrès International d'Histoire des Sciences, 1964, I, 525–530.   V.N.

Iuthungi ('offsprings, descendants'). One of the Germanic warrior communities living north of the Danube, identified by the Romans with the → Semnones [1; 2], defeated by the Romans (AE 1993, 1231; [5]) at Augsburg on 24/25 April AD 260 (unnecessary doubt over the date in [3], cf. [4]) on the way back from Italy. Annoyed at the absence of annual tributes, contrary to treaty and without a declaration of war, they advanced into Italy again in 270, but were overcome by Aurelianus 'at the crossing of the Danube' and after attacks in 271 at → Fanum Fortunae and → Ticinus were beaten (Dexippus fr. 6f.; [6]). Weakened as a result of the positioning of reserve troops (Not. Dign. Or. 22,31; 28,43), they were defeated by → Constantius [1] in 297 (Pan. Lat. 8[5]10,4) became a *pars Alamannorum*. They even ventured to besiege cities in 358 (Amm. Marc. 17,6,1f.; [7]) and were defeated by Valentinianus II. after invasions in 383/4 (Ambr. Epist. 18,21; 24,4,6–8; Zos. 4,35,5; Socrates 5,11,2) and by Aetius [2] in AD 430 (Sid. Apoll. Carm. 7,233–235; [8]).

1 T. STICKLER, I. sive Semnones, in: Bayerische Vorge-schichtsblätter 60, 1995, 231–249, esp. 233–239 2 P. LE ROUX, Armées, rhetorique et politique dans l'empire gal-lo-romain, in: ZPE 115, 1997, 181–290 3 I. KÖNIG, Die Postumus-Inschr. aus Augsburg, in: Historia 46, 1997, 341–354 4 M. JEHNE, Überlegungen zur Chronologie der J. 259 bis 261 n.Chr., in: Bayerische Vorgeschichts-blätter 61, 1996, 185–205 5 L. BAKKER, Raetien unter Postumus, in: Germania 71, 1993, 369–386 6 R. T. SAUNDERS, Aurelian's Two Iuthungian Wars, in: Historia

41, 1992, 311–327 7 G. E. THÜRY, Chronologische und numismatische Bemerkungen zu den Germaneneinfällen von '357', in: Bayerische Vorgeschichtsblätter 57, 1992, 305–310 8 R. SCHARF, Der Iuthungenfeldzug des Aetius, in: Tyche 9, 1994, 139–145.   K.DI.

Iuturna A Roman water nymph, whose name came to be associated with the Latin *iuvare* ('to help', 'to support') in popular etymology (Varro Ling. 5,71; Serv. Auct. Aen. 12,139). The ending –*turna* led to a connection with → Turnus, whose sister she was believed to be (Verg. Aen. 12,146). She is, however, also called Diurna (= the eternal, sc. Sources) (CIL VI 1, 3700). However, the etymology is still uncertain.

I. is one of the mistresses of → Jupiter, who made her a goddess and gave her rule over lakes and rivers (Verg. Aen. 12,139–141). The nymph Lara/Tacita disclosed to → Juno at her spring on the Forum Romanum that Jupiter was deceiving her with I. (Ov. Fast. 2,585). Nevertheless Juno and I. are allies in the *Aeneid*, in helping → Turnus: I. sends a false augural sign to the Rutulians, so that they take up the fight again (Verg. Aen. 12,244–265). Eventually she gives up trying to save her brother, when she sees the *dirum omen* sent by Jupiter (Verg. Aen. 12,869–886).

In Virgil, I. is the daughter of → Daunus [2] and Venilia (Verg. Aen. 10,76; however, Venilia as wife of Ianus: Ov. Met. 14,334); Arnobius (3,29), on the other hand, mentions another genealogy according to which I. is the daughter of → Volturnus and the wife of → Ianus, with whom she has as son Fontus, the god of springs. Only Serv. Aen. 12,139 mentions Lavinium as the dwelling place of I. (*iuxta Numicum fluvium*). In fact the cult of I. was located in Rome: I.'s small *lacus* was excavated at the temple of the Dioscuri in Rome. According the legend of the the the battle at Lake Regillus, the Dioscuri came of to Rome in order to water their horses at the spring of I. and to announce the victory of the Romans (Dion. Hal. Ant. Rom. 6,13; Ov. Fast. 1,707; Lactant. Div. inst. 2,7,9: Symmachus, Or. 1,95,3). A similar appearance of the → Dioscuri at the lake of I. is recorded for the battle at Pydna (AD 168) (Cic. Nat. D. 2,6; 3,11; 13; Val. Max. 1,8,1; Min. Fel. 7,3).

The lake of I. is a square pool which can be dated not before 117 BC in which statues of the Dioscuri have been found, which were probably dedicated after the victory of Pydna. The pool has the same orientation as the temple of the Dioscuri. Next to it traces of a small temple or sacellum have been found (cf. CIL VI 36806), and a *puteal* of the goddess (CIL VI 36807). Inscriptions of the *curatores aquarum* (CIL VI 4.3, 36951; 37121; 37133; AE, 1901, 175) and the base of a statuette of the *genius stationis aquarum* (CIL VI 4.3, 36781) originate from this area. The spring of I. was renowned for its healing powers (Varro Ling. 5,71; Prop. 3,22,26; Frontin. Aq. 4; Serv. Aen. 12,139; Stat. Silv. 4,5; 33–36). The water for sacrifices was also drawn from it (Serv. l.c.). During times of drought sacrifices were made (Serv. l.c.).

After the First Punic War, Lutatius Catulus dedicated a second temple to I. on the Campus Martius near the *statio aquarum* (on modern Largo Argentina). The *statio* at the Forum, however, was erected in the late Imperial period. Its consecration took place on 11 January (Ov. Fast. 1,463f.), the Iuturnalia (Fasti Antiates), and was celebrated by all who needed water for their work (Serv. Aen. 12,139).

→ Nymphs

F. COARELLI, L'area sacra di Largo Argentina, 1981, 42–46; A. ZIOLOWSKI, in: MEFRA 98, 1986, 625ff.; E.M. STEINBY, Lacus Iuturnae, 1989.   A.MAS.

Iuvavum (modern Salzburg). In the territory of the Alauni the developing Roman site of I. (etymology disputed) on the left bank of the Salzach replaced the Celtic hill settlements on the Rainberg, the Festungsberg and the Kapuzinerberg in the later years of Augustus' reign (beginning 1st cent. AD). I. was built at the junction of the northern road along the crest of the Alps from Bregenz (Brigantium) and the long distance road from Aquileia leading over the Radstädter Tauernpass, and was raised to the status of *municipium* by Claudius, achieving a certain affluence judging from archaeological finds of the 1st and 2nd cents. [1; 2; 3; 4]. I. had the largest territory of all the Noric cities, comprising the whole of the Chiemgau as far as the bend of the Inn as well as the regions of the Ambisontes and Alauni. Around the centre of the settlement, which expanded on the right bank of the Salzach, lay numerous *villae rusticae* either in the Salzach valley north of the Lueg Pass, around the Chiemsee or around I. itself. Previously favoured by Italian traders, I. suffered from the consequences of the war with the Marcomanni and also from the plague. While the centre of the settlement was rebuilt on a smaller scale, the land became increasingly deserted as a result of Alamannic depredations in the 3rd cent. From the time of Diocletian (c. 300), I. belonged to Noricum Ripense. Its valley settlements (including those of Cucullis/Kuchl) were increasingly abandoned in the 4th and 5th cents., and the population was resettled on the fortified hill terraces of the Nonnberg. Despite scant evidence of early Christianity [5], church services were widespread at I. at the time of Severinus. Although the Bavarians owned the Flachgau and the Saalfeld Basin in the 2nd half of the 6th cent., cohesive groups of Roman population remained in the southern Salzburg Basin until after AD 1000 [6].

1 N. HEGER, Die Skulpturen des Stadtgebietes von I., in: CSIR Österreich 3,1, 1975   2 W. JOBST, Röm. Mosaiken in Salzburg, 1982   3 H. LANGE, Röm. Terrakotten aus Salzburg, 1990   4 W. KOVACSOVICS, Neue arch. Unt. in der Stadt Salzburg, in: Pro Austria Romana 41, 1991, 30f. 5 E. BOSHOF, H. WOLFF (ed.), Das Christentum im bairischen Raum, 1994, 139   6 H. DOPSCH, s.v. Salzburg, LMA 7, 1331–1336.

N. HEGER, Salzburg zu röm. Zeit (Jahresschrift des Salzburger Mus. Carolino Augusteum 19), 1973 (1974); N. HEGER, s.v. I., RE Suppl. 13, 173–184; G. ALFÖLDY,

Noricum, 1974, 398 (index); H. DOPSCH (ed.), Gesch. Salzburgs. I: Vorgesch., Alt., MA 1, 1981.   K.DI.

Iuvenalia Tacitus reports that Nero 'introduced the festival days called the Iuvenalia, for which people signed up in droves. Neither nobility nor age nor the holding of public offices prevented anyone from climbing onto the stage, in order to perform in Greek or Latin, even with unmanly gestures and songs. To top it all, distinguished ladies learned indecent roles' (Tac. Ann. 14,15,1f.). The performances had a private character and took place in the palace or in the emperor's gardens before a relatively limited audience (Tac. Ann. 15,33,1). Suetonius uses the term *ludi iuvenales* and confirms that the emperor 'permitted even old consuls and elderly matrons as actors' (Suet. Nero 11,2). Dio Cassius gives a detailed report about the first I. in the year AD 59; among other things, it shows that the feast was meant to celebrate the fact that Nero was then shaved for the first time (Cass. Dio 61,19,1–3). The explanation for these strange events must undoubtedly, as [1] has remarked, be sought in the great freedom of action that was granted to the → *iuvenes* of Rome in the past and from which Nero profited. The excerpt from Dio Cassius explains the name of the feast as that of the 'young people'. The Iuvenalia are still attested to in inscriptions under Domitian (Cass. Dio 67,14,3) and Gordianus I (S HA Gord. 4,6) as well as outside Rome (in Ostia CIL 14,409; in Tusculum: CIL 14,2640; in Velitrae CIL 10,6555).

→ Youth; → Ludi

1 J.P. NÉRAUDAU, La jeunesse dans la littérature et les institutions de la Rome républicaine, 1979, 376.

J.A. HILD, s.v. Juvenalia, DS 3, 782; W. KROLL, s.v. Juvenalia, RE 10, 1355f.   G.F.

Iuvenalis, D. Iunius Juvenal, the last outstanding satirical poet of Rome, probably from Campanian Aquinum (cf. Juv. Sat. 3,318ff. and ILS 2926 = CIL 10,5382), contemporary of Tacitus; from Sat. 13,16f. and 15,27f., [1] deduces that he was born in AD 67. The silence of his poems concerning autobiographical detail – in contrast to → Horatius – and the fictitious nature of the *vitae* (no. 1 JAHN), which were not compiled until late antiquity, make any reconstruction of the details of his life circumstances impossible. The statement that I. was active as a reciter until his manhood years is credible; his friend (7,24) → Martialis calls him (Mart. 7,91 from the years 91/2) *facundus* ('eloquent'), and Sat. 1,1ff. presents an introduction to the recitation activities of the epoch. The publication of the first two bks. probably did not take place until the last years of Trajan's reign (cf. [1] and Sat. 6,407ff.; 1,49f. establishes 99/100 only as a *terminus post quem*), and I.'s main period of creativity was during the period of the rule of Hadrian, upon whom Juv. 7,1ff. sets great hope; in any case I. had an estate in Tivoli (11,65). Reports of his being exiled in old age are dubious; the satirist did perhaps not die until the time of Antoninus Pius.

16 satires (the last one passed down to us in a garbled form), divided up among 5 bks., are extant. Their subjects are primarily the corruption of morals (2. 6. 9) and the hypocrisy of contemporary municipal Roman (3) society, especially of the upper class (8), that is measured against the standard of an idealized ancient Rome. Bk. 1 ranges from programmatic satire to orgy satire 5 that is viewed from the perspective of the humiliated client. I.'s strength is shown here in precisely observed and epigrammatically presented detailed scenes, for instance in the famous 'Big-city satire' 3 or in his acquittal with the regime of Domitian in 4 that is presented as an epic parody. The unusually long 'Women's satire' 6 (= bk. 2) contrasts with the satirization of homoeroticism in 2. The 3rd bk. (the deplorable situation of the intellectual professions: 7; the decline of the nobility: 8; a second attack on homoeroticism: 9) remains on the satirical level of the first two bks, whilst in bk. 4 (10–12, the correct prayer, here the best-known, mostly incompletely quoted verse of I., 356: *orandum est, ut sit mens sana in corpore sano*; the simple life; the subject of legacy hunting) and bk. 5 (13–16, the bad conscience; the correct upbringing; religious fanaticism; the military) a milder, more philosophical tone prevails. Overall the stylization – especially marked at the beginning of the collection – of the protest within the genre satire is pushed forward in I., even if the sharpness of this tone is caused by his personal situation as a client (cf. 5. 7 and Mart. 12,18) (→ *cliens*). The means of expression of the *indignatio* ('indignation') presented in the programmatic satire 1 is not the irony of Horace but a pathos not toned down until the later pieces (from 10 onwards). The freedom of language that marks the claimed realism is traditional; the often used rhetorical figures, with a tendency to exaggerated aphorism, are also noticeable.

I.'s satires were not read very much in the archaizing epoch of the 2nd/3rd cents. In the context of a new interest in the literature of the Imperial period at the end of the 4th cent. the commented edition decisive for our tradition was created, which was not spared interpolations. The additional verses after 6,365ff. represent a special case. The late ancient archetype is represented in a purer form in a smaller MSS group and is again interpolated in a larger MS (F). The interest of the Middle Ages when the *ethicus* I. was a school author, is attested by several hundreds MSS and comm. Today the depreciation of I. as a 'rhetorical' poet since Romanticism makes way for a more just appreciation of his literary texts that are extremely artificial and at the same time socio-historically informative.
→ Satire

1 R. SYME, Tacitus, vol. 2, 1958, 499f.; 774f.

EDITIONS: O. JAHN, 1851 (with schol. vet. and Vitae); ID., F. BÜCHELER, F. LEO, ⁴1910; L. FRIEDLAENDER, 1895 (with commentary); A. E. HOUSMAN, ²1931; U. KNOCHE, 1950; W. C. CLAUSEN, ²1992; S. M. BRAUND, 1996 (s. 1–5, with comm.); J. WILLIS, 1997.
COMMENTARIES: E. COURTNEY, 1980.

SCHOLIA: P. WESSNER, 1931.; M. COFFEY, J. 1941–1961, in: Lustrum 8, 1963, 161–215; R. CUCCIOLI MELONI, Otto anni di studi giovenali (1969–1976), in: Bollettino di studi latini (Napoli) 7, 1977, 61–87; M. DE NONNO et al., s.v. I. in: G. CAVALLO (ed.), Lo spazio letterario di Roma antica 5, 1991, 452–455.
BIBLIOGRAPHY: G. HIGHET, J. the Satirist, 1954 (for the reception 179–232); J. ADAMIETZ, Unt. zu J., 1972; Id., J., in: Id., Die röm. Satire, 1986, 231–307; J. GÉRARD, J. et la réalité contemporaine, 1976; W. S. ANDERSON, Essays on Roman Satire, 1982, 197–486; J. FERGUSON, A Prosopography to the Poems of J., 1987; S. H. BRAUND, Beyond Anger, 1988 (Iuv. 7–9); ANRW II 33,1, 1989, 592–847 (various authors); M. COFFEY, Roman Satire, ²1989, 119–146; 277ff.; 286ff.; ALBRECHT, 806–820; J. DE DECKER, J. declamans, 1913; I. G. SCOTT, The Grand Style in the Satires of J., 1927; F. GAUGER, Zeitschilderung und Topik bei J., 1936; A. C. ROMANO, Irony in J., 1979; R. W. COLTON, J.'s Use of Martial's Epigrams, 1991; U. KNOCHE, Handschriftliche Grundlagen des J.-Textes, 1940; R. J. TARRANT, J., in: REYNOLDS, 200–203; B. MUNK OLSEN, L'étude des auteurs classiques latins aux XIe et XIIe siècles, vol. 1, 1982, 553–597; E. M. SANFORD, J., in: O. KRISTELLER (ed.), Catalogus translationum et commentariorum, 1, 1960, 175–238; 3, 1976, 432–445; B. LÖFSTEDT (ed.), Vier J.-Komm. aus dem 12. Jh., 1995.   P.L.S.

Iuvencus, C. Vettius Aquilinus Spanish presbyter of aristocratic origin whose Latin epic *Evangeliorum libri* was written under Constantinus [1] probably after 325 (cf. the epilogue 4,802–812 and Jer. Chron. 232 H. re AD 329; Vir. ill. 84,2; Epist. 70,5); a second, likewise hexametric work regarding the *Ordo sacramentorum* (Jer. Vir. ill. 84,1) is lost. – The biblical epic to the New Testament, framed by a prologue and an epilogue, describes the story of Christ's life in 4 bks. of Virgilian scope (i.e. an average of about 800 vv.) in the style of a Gospel harmony: the basis is Matthew, and in the infant narrative (1,1–306) Luke is added and in 2,101ff.; 637ff. and 4,306ff. three pericopes from John; aside from a Vetus Latina, the Greek original is also drawn upon. The Virgilizing versification of the respective biblical text generally follows the model faithfully; its Classicism can be related to the poetic paraphrase of the rhetorical school, and its biblical nature should be related to its edifying purpose that is aimed at the Christian community of the time. The content and form soon also brought the work general recognition and a wide reception; the numerous MSS from the 9th cent. in particular attest to its significance for Carolingian cultural reform.
→ Biblical poetry

EDITIONS: J. HUEMER, 1891.
INDEX: M. WACHT, 1990.
BIBLIOGRAPHY: N. HANSON, Textkritisches zu J., 1950; R. HERZOG, Die Bibelepik der lat. Spätant. 1, 1975; Id., in: HLL 5, § 561 (bibl.); M. FLIEGER, Interpretationen zum Bibeldichter J., 1993; R. FICHTNER, J. Taufe und Versuchung Jesu, 1994; W. RÖTTGER, Stud. zur Lichtmotivik bei I., 1996.   P.L.S.

Iuvenes (Iuventus) The term *iuvenes*, although also related to adults or non-junior teams, usually refers to the
Roman or Italian youth of military training or serving
age. The organizations of the *iuventutes* existing in the
late Republican period in Italy that were originally military and later rather paramilitary or pre-military were
revitalized by Augustus in the context of his reorganization of the aristocratic youth; later they had the character of an association. There is evidence of such → *collegia* in Italy (*collegia iuvenum*) and in the western
provinces (*collegia iuventutis*) particularly for the 2nd
and 3rd cents. AD, with the latter only having some
military significance; both had cultic practice in common, a fact that may also have brought about their end
after 350.
→ Youth

1 P. GINESTET, Les organisations de la jeunesse dans l'Occident romain, 1991   2 M. JACZYNOWSKA, Les associations da la jeunesse romaine sous le Haut-Empire, 1978
3 D. LADAGE, Collegia iuvenum – Ausbildung einer muni-
cipalen Elite?, in: Chiron 9, 1979, 319–347   4 J.-P. NE-
RAUDAU, La jeunesse dans la littérature et les institutions
de la Rome républicaine, 1979.   J.W.

Iuventia I. Maxima. Wife of C. Cassius Statilius [II 9]
Severus Hadrianus. She is probably identical with the
homonymous daughter of Lucius, attested in Berytus in
AE 1998, 1437. She may have originated from Syria,
like her husband.   W. E.

Iuventius Roman *cognomen* [1. 281; 482; 2. 735]. The
gens belonged to the municipal nobility of Tusculum,
came into Roman politics around 200 BC and with I. [I
6] achieved the sole consulate in the middle of the 2nd
cent. BC, to which they referred to also later (Cic.
Planc. 12, 15; 18f. and others; cf. Catull. 24,1–3). The
most important families were the Thalnae (also *Talnae*
in inscriptions) and the Laterenses.

1 SCHULZE   2 WALDE/HOFMANN 1.

I. REPUBLICAN PERIOD   II. IMPERIAL PERIOD

I. REPUBLICAN PERIOD

[I 1] According to fictitious family tradition, the first
curule aedile of the *plebs* at the end of the 4th cent. BC
(Cic. Planc. 58; cf. MRR 1,166).   K.-L.E.
[I 2] Little-known Roman comedy writer of the Republic, probably from the generation before Varro (cf. Ling.
7,65). In the citations that mention his name clearly
(Varro, Ling. 6,50; Gellius 18,12,2; Charisius, Gramm.
p.286,3f. B.), the titles of the plays are lacking; the allocation of an *Anagnorizomene*, quoted in Fest. p. 398L²,
that shows I. to be a poet of the *palliata*, is based on a
change by the transmitting Terence.

FRAGMENTS: CRF ³1898, 94ff.
BIBLIOGRAPHY: BARDON, 1,49f.   P.L.S.

[I 3] I. Laterensis, L. In 48 BC, after an assassination
attempt on the generally hated Q. Cassius [I 16] Longinus – whom Caesar had installed as propraetor in
Spain in 48 – he was proclaimed praetor by mutinous
legions and then executed by the recuperated Cassius
(Bell. Alex. 53,4f.; 54,1; 55,2).
[I 4] I. Laterensis, M. As quaestor he held games in
Praeneste in 64 or 63 BC, and was perhaps proquaestor
in Cyrene (MRR 3,116) afterwards. In 55 I. stood in
vain for the position of aedile and accused the more
successful Cn. → Plancius of bribery. Cicero's extant
speech for his defence (*Pro Cn. Plancio*) provides numerous details on I.'s life. In 51 he became praetor.
Under Caesar's patronage he obviously withdrew from
politics; I. was finally legate of → Aemilius [I 12] Lepidus in 43. He ended his futile efforts to contribute to the
rescue of the Republic by committing suicide (cf. Cic.
Fam. 10,23,4).
[I 5] I. (Thalna?) Boy from an aristocratic family, appears in homoerotic poems by Catullus (24; cf. 48; 81;
99) [1. 164–167]. Perhaps also mentioned in Cicero
(Attic. 13,28,4; 16,6,1).

1 H.P. SYNDIKUS, Catull, vol. 1, 1984.   W.W.

[I 6] I. Thalna, M. Son of I. [I 8]. As people's tribune, he
took legal action in 170 BC against C. Lucretius (praetor 171) for offences against the Greek allies. In 167, as
praetor peregrinus, he agitated for war against the Rhodians, but failed because of the intercession of the people's tribunes M. Antonius [I 9] and M. Pomponius
(MRR 1, 433). In 163 he was the first and also the only
member of his family to attain the consulate. His colleague was Ti. Sempronius Gracchus, likewise a plebeian (consul I in 177). Still in the same year I. waged
war successfully in Corsica, for which the Senate granted him a thanksgiving festival. When he heard news of it
during a sacrifice, he died a sudden death (Val. Max.
9,12,3; Plin. HN 7,182).   P.N.
[I 7] I. Thalna, P. Perhaps the mint master between 179
and 170 BC (RRC 161), praetor in 149, fell in battle in
148 as propraetor in Thessaly against the rebellious
Macedonian pretender to the throne → Andriscus [1]
(Liv. Per. 50 and Per. Oxyrhynchia 50; Flor. Epit.
1,30,4f.; Eutr. 4,13 and others; coins: [1]).

1 H. GÄBLER, Die ant. Münzen von Makedonia und Pai-
onia, vol. 1, 1906, 62f.   K.-L.E.

[I 8] I. Thalna, T. Probably the son of T.I. (Thalna?)
who fell in battle as military tribune in Gallia Transalpina in 197 BC, father of [I 6]. In 194 he became *praetor
peregrinus* (Liv. 34,42,4; 43,6). In 172 he, together with
Sex. Digitius and M. Caecilius, went to Apulia and
Calabria as legate to buy up grain for the war against
→ Perseus of Macedonia (Liv. 42,27,8).   P.N.

II. IMPERIAL PERIOD
[II 1] M. I. Caesianus. Senator. Legate of the *legio VIII
Augusta* in Argentorate in AD 186; later *cos. suff.* Re-
lated to I. [II 5], whose wife he honoured in Brixia.

PIR² J 879; J. WILLMANNS, in: Epigraph. Stud. 12, 1981, 46ff.   W.E.

[II 2] P. I. Celsus T. Aufidius Hoenius Severianus. [1]. Roman jurist of the 2nd cent. AD, son and student of P. Iuventius Celsus *pater* (Dig. 31,20) from whom he, together with → Neratius Priscus, took over the leadership of the Proculian → law school, he was conciliar of Hadrian, *cos. II* in AD 129 (Dig. 1,2,2,53) and later governor in Asia [4. 221ff., 263ff.]. As consul he influenced the *SC Iuventianum* (Dig. 5,3,20,6) that limited the liability of an owner of an inheritance acting in good faith – to which a claim had been laid (→ *caducum*) – to his enrichment [2].

I. was no more a commentator on statutory law than → Iulianus [1]: knowledge of laws meant for him not hairsplitting but was a reference to their 'sense and purpose' (Dig. 1,3,17, → Interpretatio). His earlier casuistic works *Quaestiones* (at least 12 bks.), *Epistulae* (11 bks.) and *Commentarii* (7 bks.) were collected by I. into the *Digesta* comprising 39 books [4. 264; 5. 248f.]. Only from this work extracts were made by the compilers of the Justinian → *Digesta*. I. formulated the definition of the → *ius* (Dig. 1,1,1 pr.) as *ars boni et aequi* ('art of the good and just') [3. 5ff.] that was decisive for the legal concept of the Roman jurists: jurisprudential 'technique of justice' (→ *iuris prudentia*). Accordingly he supported the interpretation [5. 254ff.) of laws according to the *voluntas legis* ('will of the law'), of last wills and testaments according to the *voluntas testantis* ('will of the testator') and of contracts according to the will of the silent party (*quod actum est*). Like → Iavolenus [2] and → Iulius [IV 16] Paulus, I., in contrast to the well-balanced Iulianus, is characterized by a markedly polemical style [5. 249ff.]. Typical of his method are modifications of the traditional legal dogmatism on the basis of justice (→ *aequitas*) [5. 252f.]: the so-called *condictio Iuventiana* (Dig. 12,1,32: in the active delegation, the recipient of a loan who is wrong about the person of the lender is liable to the 'true person making the payment') and the *purgatio morae* (Dig. 45,1,91,3: even in the case of strictly legal obligations, the debtor can 'settle' his arrear by making a later offer of payment). More rarely I. exercizes a systematizing jurisprudence (Dig. 12,1,1,1: *credendi generalis appellatio*, general term for providing a loan or being a creditor; in this regard [3. 192ff.]).

1 PIR² 4,366f.   2 KASER, RPR I, 739   3 P. CERAMI, La concezione celsina del ius, in: Annali del Seminario giuridico di Palermo 38, 1985, 5–250   4 R. A. BAUMAN, Lawyers and Politics in the Early Roman Empire, 1989   5 H. HAUSMANINGER, Publius I. Celsus, in: FS R.S. Summers, 1994, 245–264.   T.G.

[II 3] P. I. Celsus. Descendent of *cos. II* of AD 129, most likely his grandson (→ I. [II 2] Celsus). *Pontifex* in 155; Praetorian governor of Galatia 161–163 (THOMASSON I, 257). *Cos. ord.* 164. PIR² J 881.

[II 4] M. I. Rixa. *Eques*; praesidial procurator of Sardinia in the first half of the year AD 67; he was replaced by a proconsul (CIL X 7852 = ILS 5947; PIR² J 884). He comes from Transpadana, probably from Brixia.

[II 5] M. I. Secundus. From Brixia; *cos. suff.* perhaps at the end of the 2nd cent. AD; married to Postumia Paulla, inscriptions X 5, 1, 139; 140; 141; 143; 144; PIR² J 887; P 903.

[II 6] M. I. Secundus Rixa Postumius Pansa Valerianus ... Severus. Probably the son of I. [II 5]. His senatorial career led him to a praetorian proconsulate, to the governorship of Aquitania, to the consulate and to the *cura alvei Tiberis* (CIL V 4334/5 = InscrIt X 5, 1, 122f.); he can perhaps be dated to the middle of the 3rd cent. AD.

G. ALFÖLDY, in: EOS 2, 348; PIR² J 888.

[II 7] M. I. Surus Proculus. Related to I. [II 2, 4, 5]; came from Brixia. Praetorian governor of Noricum in AD 201; there he designated consul. PIR² J 889.   W.E.

Iuventus(-as) Roman goddess, personification of youth. The earliest evidence for the appellativum is *Iuventus* (3rd cent. BC [1. 154]), from the 1st cent. BC also *Iuventas*; *Iuventa*, however, is rare and late.

In Rome I. had cult centres on the Capitol and at the Circus Maximus: the integration of her *aedicula* ('chapel') inside the → *cella* of Minerva at the temple of Jupiter on the Capitol (Dion. Hal. Ant. Rom. 3,69,5) was interpreted as an indication of the older age of I. worship (cf. Liv. 5,54,7). For the history of the construction of her temple at the Circus Maximus cf. Liv. 36,36,5; Cass. Dio 54,19; R. Gest. div. Aug. 4,8. In the cult I. was associated with the rite of transition to the age when a boy became fit for military service (Dion. Hal. Ant. Rom. 4,15,5): the initiation ritual when putting on the *toga virilis* also included a monetary donation to I. on the part of the boys (*Iuventa novorum togatorum*: Tert. Ad nat. 2,11). The annual cult of I. at the beginning of the year was probably related to the → *iuvenes* (Fest. 92,24; Cic. Att. 1,18,3). Augustus also used the cult of I. for political-representative purposes: the conferment of the honorary title *principes iuventutis* on the day of the *toga virilis* was restricted to his grandsons and his adopted sons Gaius and Lucius (cf. [2. 465 no. 3]). The official equating of I. with → Hebe in 218 BC (Liv. 21,62,9) did not bring about a substitution: the Greek traits became an integrative partial aspect of the Roman goddess (cf. I.'s name as *Neótēs* in Greek sources).

1 WACHTER, 147; 153–154   2 E. SIMON, s.v. Hebe/I., LIMC 4.1, 464–467.

W. BERINGER, s.v. Princeps iuventutis, RE 22, 2296–2311; SIMON, GR, 118; 137.   HE.K.

Iversheim Roman centre of lime extraction in Germania inferior, modern Bad Münstereifel-I. on the Erft. The oldest finds go back to the 1st cent. AD. A complete lime kiln was excavated. Around AD 270 the plants were badly destroyed by the Franks, but were rebuilt soon afterwards. In the 4th cent. the operation of the kiln was abandoned. The area was for the most part under the control of the military. From the middle of the 2nd to the 3rd cent. a *vexillatio* of the *legio I Minervia* (CIL XIII 7943–7948) from Bonn was stationed there. From the 3rd cent. votive stones of members of the *legio XXX Ulpia victrix* from Xanten are attested (AE 1968, 390; 391; 394, cf. 393). The evidence of AE 1968 for the temporary presence of the *legio III Cyrenaica* in 392 or one of its vexillations in the last third of the 3rd cent. is doubtful.

> G. ALFÖLDY, Inschr. aus den Kalkbrennereien der niedergerman. Legionen in I., in: Epigraphische Stud. 5, 1968, 17–27; U. SCHILLINGER-HÄFELE, Vierter Nachtrag zu CIL XIII und zweiter Nachtrag zu Fr. Vollmer, Inscriptiones Baivariae Romanae, in: BRGK 58, 1977, 531–533 (no. 152–156); W. SÖLTER, Röm. Kalkbrennereien, 1970; Id., I., in: Führer vor- und frühgesch. Denkmäler 26, 1974, 169–177; Id., I., in: H. G. HORN (ed.), Die Römer in Nordrhein-Westfalen, 1987, 338–342.   RA.WI.

Ivory (ἐλέφας/*eléphas*, Latin *ebur*) was obtained from the tusks of African and Indian elephants, and like silk, amber, incense and pepper is one of those precious goods that had to be imported from areas outside the Roman empire; according to Pliny, ivory was the most valuable material supplied by land animals (Plin. HN 37,204). The price for ivory was extraordinarily high in the 1st cent. AD; nevertheless there was a shortage of ivory so that people began also to process the ordinary bones of the elephant (Plin. HN 8,7–8; 8,31). The hunting of elephants greatly decimated the herds in Africa; large tusks that according to Polybius had been used in Ethiopia as stakes for fences and posts in houses, at the time of Pliny only still existed in India. Ivory could be bought up as a trading commodity at the ports on the Red Sea and India (Peripl. m. Erythraei 3f.; 6; 10; 17; 49; 56). The centre of the ivory trade in Africa was the harbour town of Adulis on the Red Sea; the ivory was taken from the inland to the coast. According to Strabo, the ivory that was offered for sale in the ports of India primarily came from Ceylon (Str. 2,1,14).

> L. CASSON (ed.), The Periplus Maris Erythraei, 1989.
>   H.SCHN.

Ivory carvings
I. MIDDLE EAST AND PHOENICIA II. ETRURIA
III. GREECE AND ROME

I. MIDDLE EAST AND PHOENICIA

Ivory, i.e. tusks of the boar, the hippopotamus and particularly the (African as well as Asian) → elephant, was extremely popular from the Neolithic period onwards as a material in 'craftwork'. In the Bronze Age and the early Iron Age, the important workshops of the Syrian-Phoenician coastal towns and also of Egypt developed styles that were recognizably their own. Ivory carvings (IC) were widespread through intensive trade and almost always formed part of the tributes to the Assyrian kings. The repertoire comprised luxury goods of all kinds: jewellery, seals, linings of furniture made of wood/panels, vessels, reliefs and three-dimensional figurative representations. The methods of IC were to a large extent identical to those of wood carving: three-dimensional elaboration, flat engraving and linear cutting, perforated work (*ajouré*). Joints with other materials and for larger format objects were constructed by means of brackets, tongues, pins or binders such as asphalt. The surface could be colourfully inlaid, plated with gold, painted and stained. Important examples of IC come from Egypt (tomb of Thutankha'mun), from the royal palaces of Kalaḥ (Nimrud) and Niniveh, → Arslantaş, Megiddo, Samaria, Ḥasanlū and others, as well as from the royal tomb 79 of the necropolis of Salamis (Cyprus, end of the 8th cent. BC): among other things the throne and large parts of a bed of state with rich IC such as Homer (Od. 19,55ff. and *passim*) must have had in mind are preserved.

> R. D. BARNETT, Ancient Ivories in the Middle East and Adjacent Countries, in: Qedem 14, 1982, 1–99; S. M. CECCHINI, Ivoirerie, in: V. KRINGS (ed.), La civilisation phénicienne et punique, Hdb. der Orientalistik I 20, 1995, 516–526 (with bibliography); E. GUBEL, E. A. AUBET, M. F. BASLET, s.v. Ivories, DCPP, 233–237; V. KARAGEORGHIS, Die Elfenbein-Throne von Salamis auf Zypern, in: S. LASER, Hausrat, ArchHom II P, 99–103; Id., Excavations in the Necropolis of Salamis III, I–III, 1973/4 (= Salamis, vol. 5); P. R. S. MOOREY, Ancient Mesopotamian Materials and Industries, 1994, 115–127; I. J. WINTER, North Syria in the Early First Millenium B.C. With Special Reference to Ivory Carving, 1975 (thesis 1973).
>   R.W. and H.-G.N.

II. ETRURIA

Stimulated by imported pieces from the Middle East, especially northern Syria, significant IC developed in the 7th and 6th cents. BC in Etruria that comprised both statuettes ('Goddess' from Marsiliana d'Albegna) and relief work (Pyxis from Chiusi with Greek mythological motifs) and devices.

> M. E. AUBET, Los marfiles orientalizantes de Praeneste, 1971; Y. HULS, Ivoires d'Étrurie, 1957.   F.PR.

III. GREECE AND ROME

Processed ivory first reaches the Greek and Italian cultural area as a migratory gift and votive from the Oriental high cultures. Because of the expensive material, IC mostly remains limited to small-scale works of art, is combined with gold and other valuable materials and is primarily to be found in the sacred sphere and among the nobility. The material properties are favourable for a style of the finest linearity and relief differentiation and made IC a preferred medium of precious craftwork in late antiquity.

From Mycenaean princes' tombs come devices and a group of statuettes decorated with IC, and from Knossos comes a bull jumper. At the time of the 'Nimrud ivories' (9th–8th cents. BC) the first geometric IC arise in Greece, for instance the Polus goddesses from Dipylon (around 730 BC) that were found in a tomb together with eastern imported pieces. IC are even more widespread from the Orientalizing epoch onwards (7th to the middle of the 6th cent.), initially under the influence of the statuettes and relief work distributed by the Phoenicians throughout the entire Mediterranean, especially in Etruria and Latium (→ Etruscan archaeology, → Phoenician archaeology). In Ephesus, Miletus and Samos, statuettes are manufactured under the influence of Anatolia with inlay technique and already with clear Ionian characteristics. Through the link with Samos, Sparta becomes a leading manufacturer of reliefs from the late 7th to the middle of the 6th cent. (sanctuary of Artemis Orthyia). The description of the → Cypselus Chest of 600 BC provides information about the use of such reliefs. Round three-dimensional IC should be attributed to furniture, musical instruments or devices that were deposited as votives or burial objects. In the 6th cent. the chryselephantine technique starts to be used in Greece which results in large-scale idols with IC (horses of the Dioscuri of Dipoinos and Skyllis, Athena Alea of Endoios; → Gold-ivory technique). The numerous chryselephantine works of Classicism are only passed down in writing, and the most famous were the Athena and Zeus of → Phidias.

In the Hellenistic period the images of rulers join those of gods (family of Philippus of Leochares). In Rome this use of IC continues, for instance on the gates of the Palatine temple of Apollo, on thrones and state requisites. With the transfer of the prestige of the IC to civil sphere of the Imperial period, carvings in tooth and bone start to be created as a substitute in all media of craftwork for *klinai*, devices and dolls.

→ Sculptor, technique of

C. ALBIZZATI, EAA I, 1106–1141, s.v. avorio; A. CULTER, Five Lessons in Late Roman Ivory, in: Journal of Roman Archaeology 6, 1993, 167–192; J. FITTON (ed.), Ivory in Greece and the Eastern Mediterranean from the Bronze Age to the Hellenistic Period, 1990; FUCHS/FLOREN, 7–8; J. KOLLWITZ, RAC 4, 937–945, s.v. Elfenbein; O. KRZYSZKOWSKA, Ivory and the Related Materials, 1990; I. TOURNAVITOU, The Ivory Houses at Mycenae, The British School at Athens, Suppl. 24, 1995, 123–207.
R.N.

Ivy

I. BOTANICAL II. RELIGIOUS

I. BOTANICAL

Ivy (κισσός/kissós, ἕλιξ/hélix, Latin hedera) represents the only European genus of *Araliaceae*. English 'ivy' as well as German *Efeu* and *Eppich* (another word for ivy; → Celery) are derived from Old High German *ebihouui* or *eboue*. Because of confusion with the rock-rose mentioned in Theophrastus (κίσθος/kísthos, Hist. pl. 6,2,1), Pliny (HN 16,145) distinguishes between a male (*hedera mas*) and a somewhat smaller female form (*h. femina*). In his further statements on ivy, he also follows Theophrastus who in turn regards the ivy as

being represented by three forms, a white, a black and a coiled one (ἕλιξ/hélix) (Hist. pl. 3,18,6; likewise Dioscorides 2,179 [1. 248ff.] and 2,210 [2. 254f.]); in reality, however, these are only varieties of *Hedera helix L.* The officinal use is traced back to the assumed pungent, astringent and nerve-numbing effect, and can be used for instance for chronic headache and wound pain, as well as for dysentery. According to Theophr. Hist. pl. 3,18,9 and Plin. HN 16,151, ivy kills trees by withdrawing sap. The wreaths made from its foliage were above all dedicated to Dionysus (hence the epithets κισσεύς/kisseús, κισσοφόρος/kissophóros, κισσοστέφανος/kissostéphanos and others; [3. 85]) or to Bacchus (epithets *corymbifer* and *racemifer*) as well as to Apollo and the goddesses Aphrodite, Artemis and Athene. Dionysus is said to have freed → Cissus – who as his companion had an accident whilst jumping about frenetically – from his suffering by turning him into ivy (Nonn. Dion. 10,401ff.). Pausanias mentions a festival Κισσοτόμοι (*Kissotómoi*) for Hebe in Phleius (2,13,4) and an Ἀθηνᾶ Κισσαία (*Athēnâ Kissaía*) in Epidaurus (2,29,1). Ivy was a popular decorative motif in art from the Cretan-Mycenaean period onwards.

1 WELLMANN I 2 Berendes 3 H. BAUMANN, Die griech. Pflanzenwelt, 1982.
C.HÜ.

II. RELIGIOUS

In Greek and Roman religion ivy is firmly linked to → Dionysus and the deities identified with him (generally Plut. Symp. 3,1, 648B – 649F; → Sabazius ibid. 4,6, 671; cf. Demosth. 18,259f.; the 'God of the Jews', Plut. ibid; → Osiris with black ivy: PGM IV 172–176). Therefore the god carried the epicleses of Kisseus and similar ones. If maenads and satyrs are represented with ivy [1], the ivy leaf is a symbol of the Dionysian mysteries [2; 3]. In the rites of other gods (for instance Hera in Athens, Aphrodite in Thebes) ivy could be forbidden (Plut. Quaest. Rom. 112, 290 F).

Analogously ivy was associated in Rome with → Liber and the Liberalia (Varro, Ling. 6,14) – whilst the Flamen Dialis (→ Flamines) connected with the cult of Jupiter was not allowed to touch ivy or to use a road overhung by vine tendrils (Plut. Quaest. Rom. 112, 290E). The reason is hardly to be found in possible hallucinogenic properties of the ivy berries but rather in the extraordinary (evergreen, parasitic) nature of the plant.

1 J. KRAUSKOPF, E. SIMON, s.v. Mainades, LIMC 8.2, 524–550 2 F. GRAF, Dionysian and Orphic Eschatology. New texts and old questions, in: TH. H. CARPENTER, C. A. FARAONE (ed.), Masks of Dionysus, 1993, 239–258 3 M. W. DICKIE, The Dionysiac mysteries in Pella, in: ZPE 109, 1995, 81–86.
F.G.

Ixion (Ἰξίων; *Ixíōn*). Thessalian king and one of the great sinners being punished in the Underworld. According to Pindar, he is the first murderer of a relative (Pindar leaves the identity of the victim open, later – Pherecydes FGrH 3 F 51 – it is his father-in-law Eïoneus). When Zeus purifies him personally from the blood of murder (Aesch. Eum. 717f.) and takes him to himself, he wants to indecently assault Hera; but Zeus substitutes a cloud for her and I. fathers the first → Centaurs (understood etymologically and playfully as 'wind spearers' and related to the begetting of the offspring). As a punishment I. is bound to a fiery wheel that turns eternally (Pind. Ol. 2,21–48) – this is how he also appears in iconography. In later reports and images he is, like the other evildoers punished in the Underworld, chained to his wheel (Apoll. Rhod. 3,61), or (occasionally) together with the Lapith → Peirithous under a threatening overhanging rock at an unreachable, richly laid table (Verg. Aen. 6,601–607, but on the wheel: Verg. G. 4,484); he is also regarded as the father of Peirithous (Apollod. 1,68).

D. GIORDANO, s.v. Issione, EV 3, 31–33; C. LOCHIN, s.v. I., LIMC 5, 857–862.   F.G.

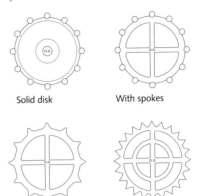

Solid disk   With spokes

Serrated (2 examples)

Shapes of *iynges* as seen in Attic and Lower Italian vase-painting, 5th–4th cents. BC

Iynx (ἴυγξ; *iynx*).

[1] Iynx ('sounding', cf. ἰύζω/*iýzō*) refers to 1. a bird, 2. a humming wheel used in magical rites, and 3. a demon in → theurgy who is associated with the origin of the world and mediates between humans and gods.

In myth the bird is transformed from a seductive nymph, the daughter of Echo or Peitho and perhaps → Pan (Callim. Fr. 685; Phot. and Suda, s.v. I.), or from a woman who competed with the Muses in singing (Nicander in Antoninus Liberalis 9).

The wheel and the bird were important in the Greek love-spell in myth and are associated with unhappy love and deceitful persuasion [1; 2]. In theurgy the wheel was used for soteriological rites; the *iynx* demon (first in the → *Oracula Chaldaica*) was developed from the Platonic idea of → Eros (Pl. Symp. 202e–203a) and identified by several theurgists with the Platonic Ideas [3. 90–110; 4. 68–85].

1 S. I. JOHNSTON, The Song of the I.: Magic and Rhetoric in Pythian 4, in: TAPhA 125, 1995, 177–206 2 V. PIRENNE-DELFORGE, L'Iynge dans le discours mythique et les procédures magiques, in: Kernos 6, 1993, 277–289 3 S. I. JOHNSTON, Hekate Soteira, 1990 4 F. CREMER, Die chaldäischen Orakel und Jamblich de Mysteriis, 1969.   S.I.J.

ILLUSTRATIONS: A. S. F. GOW, Iynx, Rhombos, Rhombus, Turbo, in: JHS 54, 1934, 1–13; G. NELSON, A Greek Votive Iynx-Wheel in Boston, in: AJA 44, 1940, 443–456; E. BÖHR, A Rare Bird on Greek Vases: The Wryneck, in: J. H. OAKLEY, W. D. E. COULSON, O. PALAGIA (ed.), Athenian Potters and Painters, Congr. Athens 1994, 1997, 109–123, esp. 116–120 with n. 49 (bibliography).   M.HAA.

[2] see → Wryneck

Iyrcae (Ἰύρκαι/*Iýrkai*, Hdt. 4,22; *Tyrcae*, Plin. HN 6,19; Mela, 1,116). Tribe of hunters east of Thyssagetae, east of Tanais, probably in the Ural region, in the plains of Kama, Vjatka, Belaja and Volga. The precise

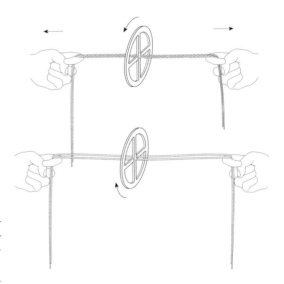

Handling of the *iynx*
By alternately tightening and loosening the thong, the wheel is made to turn one way and then the other.
       M. HAA.

localization and ethnic identification are debatable and cannot be determined on the basis of the sources. Russian research links the I. with the Ananino culture (8th–3rd cents. BC), of which burial mounds and fortified settlements are known and whose trading reached as far as the Caucasus.

J. HARMATTA, Quellenstud. zu den Skythika des Herodot, 1941; K. F. SMIRNOV, Die Skythen, 1966; S. I. RUDENKO, Kul'tura naselenija Gornogo Altaja v skivskoe vremja, 1953.   I.v.B.

Izala In Neo-Assyrian sources from the 9th cent. BC onwards, I. is a centre of viticulture, the mountainous area between → Harran, → Amida (modern Diyarbakır) and Mardin in north-eastern Mesopotamia. In Babylonian the toponym is also still used later. Darius I defeated (Old Persian *Izalā*, Elamite *Izzila*) the Armenians in I. (TUAT 1, 433 § 29,53). In AD 359, the *mons Izala* (Amm. Marc. 18,6,12; 19,9,4) was the scene of Roman battles against the Persians. In Syrian and Byzantine texts (Bar Hebraeus; Theophylaktes Simocatta: Ἰζάλας/*Izáles*) I. can also include the Mardin mountain range and Ṭūr ʿAbdīn.

L. DILLEMANN, Haute Mésopotamie Orientale et pays adjacents, 1962, 32–34; J. N. POSTGATE, s.v. I., RLA 5, 225f.; F. H. WEISSBACH, s.v. I., RE 10, 1390.   K.KE.

Izates (Ἰζάτης; *Izátēs*).
[1] I. I. King of → Adiabene until *c.* AD 30.
[2] I. II. Grandson of I. [1], king from *c.* AD 36. Some years later he took in his hard-pressed Parthian overlord Artabanus [5] II and organized the latter's return to the throne, for which he was rewarded with the territory of Nisibis and privileges. His fickle politics in the struggles for the succession after Artabanus' death can be most likely explained in that he was a follower of the latter's foster-son Gotarzes II. Thus I. refused to support Gotarzes' rival Vardanes in the conquest of Armenia around 43. In AD 49 he likewise feigned to follow the pretender Meherdates, called from Rome, only to leave him before the decisive battle and thereby to make the Gotarzes' victory possible. I. survived yet another conflict with Vologaeses I in 53, but died shortly thereafter.

M. SCHOTTKY, Parther, Meder und Hyrkanier, in: AMI 24, 1991, 61–134, esp. 83–117.   M.SCH.

J

J (linguistics) Already in antiquity there were attempts to render the different phonetic values of the Latin letter *I* with different characters. But in general the same character applied to syllabic sounds (*i*, *ī*) as well as to consonantal sounds (*i̯*, *i̯i̯*), a difficulty ancient grammarians were aware of [2. 2, 12–44]. Grammarians of early modern times, especially P.RAMUS (P.LA RAMÉE), made another attempt by first applying the purely graphic variant *J* to the consonantal sound [1. 12]. In this way *jam, jocus, jubeo, Julius, cujus* could be differentiated externally from *etiam, iaspis, io, Iulus, Latoius*. But unlike the similar differentiation between *V* and *U*, it did not find wide usage.
→ I (linguistics); → U (linguistics); → V (linguistics)

1 M.NIEDERMANN, Historische Lautlehre des Lat., 1953
2 ThlL VII 1.   B.F.

Jabne (Ἰάμνια; *Iámnia*). City, situated south of modern Tel Aviv. After the destruction of the Temple of Jerusalem in AD 70, it became the new centre in which Judaism reconstituted itself as rabbinic Judaism, initially under Rabbi Jochanan ben Zakkai and later under Gamaliel [2] II. A first formulation of the material which was later to be incorporated into the Mišna was undertaken here, whereby the aspect of an ordering of the religious life without temple cult and priests, as well as the setting up of a Jewish self-administration, played a special role. Following the failed Bar-Kochba uprising (AD 132–135; → Bar Kochba), the centre of Judaism moved to Galilee.

The hypothesis of a synod of Javne, at which the books belonging to the canon of the Hebrew → Bible were formally established in order to distinguish it from Christianity, is no longer accepted in recent research.

S.SAFRAI, Das Zeitalter der Mischna und des Talmuds (70–640), in: H.HILLEL BEN-SASSON (ed.), Geschichte des jüdischen Volkes, 1978 (repr. 1992), 377–469, esp. 391–405; P.SCHÄFER, Geschichte der Juden in der Antike, 1983, 151–155.   B.E.

Jackal This wild dog (*Canis aureus*), principally found in Africa, still occurs today in Eurasia from the Balkans eastwards. It hunts at night, often in packs, preying mainly on small mammals and birds, but it also eats carrion. An earlier theory that it, together with the wolf, was a progenitor of the domestic dog ([1]; cf. [2. 70–72]), has now been abandoned. The θώς/*thós*, as distinct from the → wolf, was well known to Aristotle (Hist. an. 2,17,507b 17: internal organs resemble those of the wolf; 6,35,580a 26–31: gives birth to two to four blind whelps; emphasis on small body height, its ability to jump and its speed; 8(9),1,610a 13 f.: enmity with the lion as a rival for food; 8(9),44,630a 9–17: little timidity and accustomed to humans, summer- and winter-coat are different). The jackal is probably the 'slug-

gish little wolf in Africa' (*inertes hos parvosque [sc. luporum] Africa ... gignunt*) mentioned in Plin. HN 8,80 [3. 158]. A Roman hunting mosaic from Carthage is said to show a jackal being pursued by a hunter and his dog [5. 14]. Another mosaic, on the floor of the late antique church of Cosmas and Damian in Syria (Gerasa, modern Ǧaraš), portrays a jackal in a rectangular field with birds and various mammals [6. drawing on 5. 280]. It also seems to be shown on coins [7. pl. 1,1] and gems [7. pl. 16,7 and 17,17].

1 K.LORENZ, So kam der Mensch auf den Hund, 1950
2 F.E.ZEUNER, Geschichte der Haustiere, 1967
3 LEITNER 4 M.A.MAHIOUBI, Une nouvelle mosaïque de chasse à Carthage, in: CRAI 1967, 263–278 with fig.
5 TOYNBEE, Tierwelt, 14 and 360   6 J.W.CROWFOOT, Early Churches in Palestine, 1941, 134, pl. 17   7 F.IMHOOF-BLUMER, O.KELLER, Tier- und Pflanzenbilder auf Mz. und Gemmen des klass. Alt., 1889 (repr. 1972).
                                                                C.HÜ.

Jackdaw The smallest species of crow. Pliny (HN 10,77) mentions this flocking bird of upper Italy, with its characteristic proverbial predilection for shiny objects like gold and coins, calling it *monedula* (*Coloeus monedula*, probably identical to κολοιός/*koloiós*, attested since Hom. Il. 16,583 and 17,755; atypical statements about the bird in Aristotle (Hist. an. 2,12,504a 19; 2,17,509a 1; 9(8),9,614b 5 and 9(8),24,b 16); common in Aristophanes ([1. 155; 2. 2. 109ff.]). In addition, Pliny knows the *graculus*, probably the Alpine chough (*Pyrrhocorax alpinus*, κορακίας/*korakías* in Aristot. Hist. an. 9(8),24,617b 16) or chough (*P. pyrrhocorax*; [3. 131]). Accordingly, in Ovid (Met. 7,465–68), Arne who commits treason for gold, is transformed into a jackdaw with black feet and feathers. Cic. Flac. 31 already alludes to its instinctive desire to steal, which is passed down to the Middle Ages by Isid. Orig. 12,7,35, as well as the etymology (*monedula quasi monetula*). According to Plin. HN 17,99, it is said to gather seeds in its hole and make them sprout. Dionysius [29] in 3,18 [4. 46f.] provides instructions on catching the jackdaw, a popular pet, and the → Jay, in snares laid out with olives as bait. Thomas of Cantimpré (5,89 [5. 216]) describes them for the first time as dark in coloration and delicate, with their capacity to imitate human language after training as a young bird, whilst Albertus Magnus (De animalibus 23,129; [6. 1504]) refers to the grey top of the head. The experimentalist in Thomas (and Albertus) maintains that it loves to be tickled on the head to stop its head itching, which is passed on to humans when they consume its meat.

1 D'ARCY W.THOMPSON, A Glossary of Greek Birds, ²1936, repr. 1966 2 KELLER 3 LEITNER 4 A.GARZYA (ed.), Dionysii Ixeuticon libri, 1963 5 H.BOESE (ed.), Thomas Cantimpratensis, Liber de natura rerum, ed.

1973   6 H. STADLER (ed.), Albertus Magnus, de animalibus, ed. II, 1920.   C.HÜ.

Jacob

[1] According to Gn 25:26 a person 'who holds the heel
(of Esau)'; otherwise the etymology of the word is
unsolved. The son of Isaac and Rebecca, third and most
outstanding patriarch apart from → Abraham [1] and
→ Isaac, as well as the father of the twelve tribes of
Israel, is named after his battle with the angel *Israel* ('he
who wrestles with god'). From the regal period
onwards, J. also served as a metaphor for the people of
Israel.

J., who – according to the traditional view – embodies virtuousness, truth and fear of God on one hand,
but on the other hand is also viewed as egotistical, even
cunning, is considered in his conduct to be a model for
the future history of the Jewish people, as well as the
personification of the people of Israel. One of the few
moral weaknesses of J. is seen in his preferential treatment of his son → Joseph. In several Haggadic sources
(→ Haggadah) the strong bond between J. and God is
already heralded in the period before his birth: when
Rebecca during her pregnancy went past a teaching
institution, J. moved; if she went past a heathen temple,
his twin brother Esau stirred. Whilst the Biblical story
of J. represents an independent narrative, in the Islamic
tradition the occurrence centred around J. is totally
embedded in the story of Joseph. J. – called *Israil* only
twice in the → Koran – is regarded there as a prophet
chosen by God.

> H. GAUBERT, Isaac et Jacob, les élus de Dieu, 1964;
> L. GINZBERG, The legend of the Jews 1, 1968; D. GOLD-
> STEIN, Jewish folklore and legend, 1980; A. PURY, Pro-
> messe divine et légende culturelle dans le cycle de Jacob,
> 1975.   Y.D.

[2] **J. Baradaeus.** (*Burdᵉ'ānā*). Syrian orthodox bishop
of Edessa, born in Tella, grew up in the monastery of
Phesilta (near Nisibis; *c.* AD 500–578). He lived for 15
years as the protégé of the empress → Theodora in Constantinople. In AD 542, when the Gassanid king asked
for a bishop, he was consecrated secretly. The members
of the Syrian Orthodox church were called Jacobites by
the supporters of the council of Chalcedon, because a
hierarchy directed against Chalcedon developed
through J.'s secretly implemented ordinations of
priests. → Iohannes [26] of Ephesus describes his life in
his collection of biographies, History of the Oriental
saints (ch. 49f.). Several letters and a creed are extant.
→ Monophysitism

> Patrologia Orientalis 18–19 (Biographie); H. G. KLEYN,
> J.B. de stichter der syrische Monophysitische Kerk, 1882;
> A. BAUMSTARK, Gesch. der syr. Lit., 1922, 174f.; E. HO-
> NIGMANN, Évêques et évêchés monophysites du VIᵉ siècle
> (CSCO Subs. 227), 1951, 157–177; D. BUNDY, J.B. The
> state of research, in: Le Muséon 91, 1978, 45–86.

[3] **J. of Sarug.** (Sᵉrūḡ). Syrian poet, died in AD 521.
Educated at the Persian school in Edessa, he became the
Syrian Orthodox suffragan bishop (chorepiscopus) in
the area of Sarug and in 519 bishop of Baṭnān-da-Sa-
rug. He wrote several hundred excellent verse homilies
(*memrē*), mostly on Biblical themes (*c.* 225 are
published), moreover six festival homilies in prose (*tur-
gāmē*), 43 letters, and two biographies of local saints
(unpublished). In addition, three *Anaphorai* and the
Maronite baptismal rite are attributed to him.

> EDITIONS:
> MEMRE: P. BEDJAN, I–V, 1905–1910 (only text);
> C. MOSS, in: Le Muséon 48, 1935, 87–112 (fragment);
> M. ALBERT, Patrologia Orientalis 38, 1976 ('Against the
> Jews'); W. STROTHMANN, Göttinger Orientforschungen
> 12, 1976 ('On the Apostle Thomas'); K. ALWAN, CSCO
> Scr. Syri 214f., 1989 ('On creation'); J. AMAR, Patrologia
> Orientalis 47, 1995 ('On Ephraem').
> PROSE HOMILIES: F. RILLIET, Patrologia Orientalis 43,
> 1986.
> LETTERS: J. OLINDER, CSCO Scr. Syri 57, 1937 (text
> only).
> BIBLIOGRAPHY: A. VÖÖBUS, Handschriftliche Überlie-
> ferung der Memre-Dichtung des J.v.S. I–IV CSCO Subs.
> 39f. and 60f., 1973 and 1980; W. CRAMER, Irrtum und
> Lüge. Zum Urteil des J.v.S., über Reste paganer Rel. und
> Kultur, in: JAC 23, 1980, 96–107; T. BOU MANSOUR, La
> Théologie de J. de S. I, 1993; T. KOLLAMPARAMPIL, J. of
> S.: Select Festal Homilies, 1997.
> BIBLIOGRAPHY: K. ALWAN, in: Parole de l'Orient 13,
> 1986, 313–383; Dictionnaire de spiritualité 8, 1974, 56–
> 60; TRE 16, 1987, 470–474.

[4] **J. of Edessa.** (*c.* AD 640–708). Syrian writer and
scholar, born near Antioch. After studying at the monastery of Kenneshre (on the Euphrates) and in Alexandria, he became Syrian Orthodox bishop of Edessa
around 684, but because of the careless attitude of the
priesthood towards the rules of the order, he soon gave
up his office. He first moved back to a monastery at
Kaisūm (near Samosata), and then to Tel 'Ada. Of the
large number of his works which are extant, the following are of particular interest: his commentary on the
Hexaemeron, scholia on the Old Testament, a large
number of letters about the most varied of topics, a
philosophical enchiridion, as well as numerous canonical books (mostly in question-answer style). His chronicle and grammar are only preserved in fragmentary
form. In addition, he revised older translations from
Greek, among these, translations of the homilies and
hymns of Severus, several books of the OT, various
liturgical texts, and perhaps also of the 'Categories' of
Aristotle. His own translations from Greek contain the
Testamentum Domini.

> EDITIONS: J. B. CHABOT, A. VASCHALDE, CSCO Scr. Syri
> 44 and 48, 1928 and 1932 (comm. on the Hexaemeron);
> A. MERX, Historia artis grammaticae apud Syros, 1889,
> 48–62, 73*–84* (grammar); E. W. BROOKS, CSCO Scr.
> Syri 5f., 1905 and 1907 (Chronicle); G. FURLANI (in: Ren-
> diconti della R. Accademia Nazionale dei Lincei (Cl. Sc.
> mor. 6:4), 1928, 222–249 (Encheiridion); K. GEORR,
> 1948 (transl. of Aristotle's 'Categoriae'); C. KAYSER, 1886

(German transl. of *Kanones*).

BIBLIOGRAPHY: E. J. REVELL, The Grammar of Jacob of E. ..., in: Parole de l'Orient 3, 1972, 365–374; Dictionnaire de spiritualité 8, 1974, 33–35; TRE 16, 1987, 468–470.   S.BR.

Jaffa see → Ioppe

Jargon see → Technical terminology

Jariri Prince regent of Karchemish, at the beginning of the 8th cent. BC, tutor of Kamani, the son of Astiruwa. Pictorial representation of J. with Kamani: CARCAMIS bk. 7. In his inscription in Luwian hieroglyphs (CARCAMIS A 6,2–3) (→ Hieroglyphic scripts (Asia Minor)), he boasts of being well known in foreign countries: in Egypt, Urartu, among the Lydians, Phrygians and Phoenicians, countries in which J. probably travelled. For in his second inscription (CARCAMIS A 15b, 4), in which he maintains that he can write four scripts (*SCRIBA-lalija*): hieroglyphic Luvian, Phoenician, Assyrian, and Aramaic, and speak 12 languages (*lalati-*), (diplomatic) journeys (*ḫarwatāḫid-*) are mentioned.
→ Karchemish

J. D. HAWKINS, Rulers of Karkamis 1986, 259–271; F. STARKE, Sprachen und Schriften in Karkamis, in: FS W. Röllig, 1997, 381–395.   PE.HÖ.

Jason see → Iason

Jastorf culture Term for culture groups of the pre-Roman Iron Age in North Germany (→ Germanic archaeology, with map), derived from the urnfields of Jastorf, in the district of Ülzen (Lower Saxony). The burial complexes and furnishings with jewellery, pottery, and occasionally also weapons and equipment, are typical of the Germanic Jastorf culture. It is the first iron-working culture in the nordic area.
→ Iron; → Jevenstedt

H-J. HÄSSLER (ed.), Ur-und Frühgesch. in Niedersachsen, 1991, 380; G. SCHWANTES, Die Urnenfriedhöfe in Niedersachsen I 2, 1911, 95–139.   V.P.

Javelin-throwing Outside the Graeco-Roman world, sporting use of the javelin (ἀκόντιον; *akóntion*, δόρυ; *dóry*, Lat. *iaculum*) is attested only for Etruria [1. 306–314]. In Homer (Hom. Il. 23,618–623; 629–637; 884–897: uncontested victory for Agamemnon; Hom. Od. 4,625–627; 8,229), javelin-throwing is still a separate discipline. Later on, it is almost only conducted as the third discipline in the framework of the → pentathlon. The sling-strap fastened onto the javelin (ἀγκύλη; *ankýlē*, Lat. *amentum*) increased the distance of the throw, the distance determining the winner. Deaths caused by javelin-throwing are occasionally mentioned (Plut. Pericles 36,5; Antiph. 2,1,1). Javelin-throwing is

a theme in Greek art [2. no. 158–161; 3. pl. 93–100]. Throwing at a target from a horse, as was done competitively at the → Panathenaea (IG II 444, 446, 965), helped improve accuracy for warfare and → hunting.
→ Sports

1 J.-P. THUILLIER, Les jeux athléthiques dans la civilisation étrusque, 1985   2 O. TZACHOU-ALEXANDRI (ed.), Mind and Body, 1989   3 J. JÜTHNER, F. BREIN, Die athletischen Leibesübungen der Griechen, vol. 2.1, 1968, 307–350.

I. WEILER (ed.), S., 1993.   W. D.

Jay (κίσσα/*kíssa* or κίττα/*kítta*, *Garrulus glandarius*). It was often confused in Greek with the → Magpie [1. 146] and, as *garrulus*, in the Middle Ages (among others in Isid. Orig. 12,7,45) with either the *graculus*, the Alpine chough (→ Jackdaw), or the rook (e.g. in Thomas of Cantimpré 5,62; [2. 209]). The colourful crow shows characteristic coloration and behaviour. Plin. HN 10,119 already admires the talkativeness of the related magpies and of the acorn eaters (*earum quae glande vescantur*). Aristot. Hist. an. 9(8),13,615b 19–23 describes the changeability of its voice, which can be trained to talk, its nest building and the burying of acorns it collects. Mart. 8,87 says it is frequently kept in cages as a fashionable ornamental bird. On wall paintings in Pompeii it is depicted twice [3. 113]. The colourful illustration [4. colour tablet II above = fig. 121,1] from the Viennese MS of AD 512 of the *Ixeutica* of Dionysius re 1,18 [5. 12f.], and its copy from the 15th cent. [4. colour tablet VIII,4 = fig. 130,11], are true to life.

1 D'ARCY W. THOMPSON, A glossary of Greek birds, ²1936 (repr. 1966)   2 H. BOESE (ed.), Thomas Cantimpratensis, Liber de natura rerum, 1973   3 KELLER II   4 Z. KÁDÁR, Survivals of Greek Zoological Illustrations in Byzantine Manuscripts, 1978   5 A. GARZYA (ed.), Dionysii Ixeuticon libri, 1963.   C.HÜ.

Jehuda ha-Nasi Most often simply called 'rabbi' or 'our holy rabbi', *c.* AD 175–217; son and successor of Simeon ben Gamaliel [2] II, the most important of the Jewish Patriarchs, under whose rule the office was at its most powerful. He was officially acknowledged by the Romans as the representative of Judaism and in addition acted as the head of the Sanhedrin (*Bēt Dīn*; → Synhedrion), being the highest authority in questions of teachings (*Ḥakham*). J. had at his disposal a solid financial basis, and maintained extensive trading relations and contacts with the → Diaspora, towards which he demonstrated his power, particularly through the determination of the calendar. The reference to J.'s descent from the house of → David likewise served to secure and legitimize his rule. J. moved the seat of the patriarchate from Uša (Lower Galilee, close to modern Haifa) to → Beth Shearim (from *c.* 175) and later – *c.* around 200 – to the more important → Sepphoris, which was strongly influenced by Graeco-Roman lifestyle and culture. The → Haggadah tells of good relationships between J. and the Severan imperial house. It is uncertain whether and in what form J. levied taxes. Rabbi J. is traditionally considered to be the editor of Mišna (→ Rabbinical literature).

M. JACOBS, Die Institution des jüd. Patriarchen. Eine quellen und traditionskritische Studie zur Gesch. des Judentums in der Spätant. (Texte und Stud. zum Antiken Judentum 52), 1995, 115ff., 124ff.; L.I. LEVINE, The Rabbinic Class of Roman Palestine in Late Antiquity, 1989, 33–37; S. SAFRAI, Das Zeitalter der Mischna und des Talmuds (70–640), in: H.H. BEN-SASSON (ed.), Gesch. des Jüd. Volkes, 1978 (repr. 1992), 377–469, here: 415–417; P. SCHÄFER, Gesch. der Juden in der Ant. Die Juden Palästinas von Alexander dem Großen bis zur arab. Eroberung, 1983, 182–184.   B.E.

Jellyfish (zoological: *Medusa*). The swimming reproductive form of polyp from the seanettle subspecies (*Cnidaria*) of zoophytes. Aristot. Hist. an. 4,6,531a 32-b 17 describes very well their stinging tentacles, the ἀκαλήφη/*akaléphē* sc. θαλασσία/*thalassía* 'stinging nettle' (nettle-jellyfish) or, synonymously, κνίδη/*knídē* (ibid. 5,16,548a 22–27) (The comic passages quoted by Ath. 3,90a-b mean by *akaléphē* not the jellyfish, but the stinging nettle). In Latin the *urtica marina* corresponds to the *knide* (Plin. HN 32,146). Aristotle classes jellyfish as molluscs without shells. Within the framework of the *scala naturae* in Aristot. Hist. an. 7(8),1,588b 20, they stand, with their fleshy bodies, at a transitional point between plants and animals. They spend their time partly clamped on stones and partly swimming around (Aristotle does not realize the alternation in generations here). Live food, e.g. small fish, is taken into the oral aperture – located in the middle of their underside – by means of the tentacles (cf. as well Plin. HN 9,147). Aristotle does not believe that food waste is excreted (Hist. an. 4,6,531b 8f.), but he does describe (Hist. an. 7(8),2,590a 29f.) a suitable opening on its upper side (cf. Plin. HN 9,147: *excrementa per summa tenui fistula reddi*, 'having expelled excreta on the upper side through a thin tube').

The smaller of the two subspecies mentioned by Aristotle (Hist. an. 4,6,531b 10f.) is said to be edible in winter. According to Plut. Mor. 670d, the Pythagoreans prohibited its consumption. According to Plin. HN 31,95 it was also used in fish broth (*allex*). Taken with wine, the *urtica marina* is also said to help alleviate urolithiasis (Plin. HN 9,102).

KELLER 2, 575f.   C.HÜ.

Jeremiah (Hebrew *Jirmᵉjāhū*). Personal name and title of the book of the Bible written by the author of the same name. In several Haggadic sources (→ Haggadah), the name of the second of the great prophets is linked with the destruction of → Jerusalem which took place during his lifetime. The possible meaning 'may God exalt' is uncertain. J. was probably born around

650 BC during the reign of king Jošija. J., in his capacity as a prophet, led a turbulent life between being held in high esteem and being rejected violently, right through to death threats on several occasions. His prophecy essentially shows two basic tendencies: 1) characteristic is the conviction that only a prophet of misfortune was a true prophet, 2) his individual prophecy distinguishes him strikingly from other prophets: the individual is prominent in his relationship with God; the internal conversion of every individual ultimately leads to the salvation of the entire people. J.'s influence shaped large parts of Haggadic literature.

J. BREUER, Das Buch Jirmejah, trans. and comm. by J. Breuer, 1914; G. BRUNET, Les lamentations contre Jérémie, 1968; J. CARLEBACH, Die drei großen Propheten Jesajas, Jirmija und Jecheskel, 1932 (repr. 1994); S. HERRMANN, J., 1986; B. HUWYLER, J. und die Völker: Untersuchungen zu den Völkersprüchen in Jeremia 46–49, 1997; N. ITTMANN, Die Konfessionen J.s, 1981; J. KASTEIN, Jeremias: der Bericht vom Schicksal einer Idee, 1938; C. KUHL, Israels Propheten, 1956; H. LAMPARTER, Prophet wider Willen, 1964; A. NÉHER, Jérémie, 1960; T. ODASHIMA, Heilsworte im J.-Buch, 1984; L. PRIJS, Die J.-Homilie Pesikta Rabbati ch. 26, 1966; S. SODERLUND, The Greek text of Jeremiah, 1985; C. WOLFF, J. im Frühjudentum und Urchristentum, 1976.   Y.D.

Jericho (Hebrew *Yᵉriḥō*; Greek Ἰεριχώ, Ἰεριχοῦς, Ἰεριχοῦς; Latin *Hierichô, Hierikoûs, Hierichoûs*; Arabian *ar-Rīḥā*; from western Semitic *yrḥ*, 'moon'?). Oasis with a wealth of palms, famous for dates and balsam (Str. 16,2,41; Pomp. Trog. 3,2–3; Plin. HN 13,44; Jos. BI 1,138; 4,452–475; Jos. Ant. Iud. 14,54; 15,96), 8 km west of the Jordan, 10 km north of the Dead Sea, 250 m below sea level, watered by the spring ʿAin as-Sulṭān on the north-western edge of the oasis. J. has been populated since the Natufian culture (9100–8500 BC), and in the pre-ceramic Neolithic Age (8500–6300) the town was surrounded by a protective wall; it was resettled in the ceramic Neolithic Age (6300–4500), in the late Chalcolithic Age (from 3500) and in the early Bronze Age II–III (3100–2250; solid clay tile city wall). During the transition from the Early to the Middle Bronze Age (2250–2000), there is evidence of only loose construction; in the Middle Bronze Age II (1800–1570) J. was an important town (surrounded by an 11 m high rampart). Around 1570 it was destroyed and there was a shortlived later settlement in the late Bronze Age II (1400–1350/25); it was only resettled between 1200 and 1000.

As the destruction of the city narrated in the Bible (Jos 2–6) must have occurred, according to the internal Biblical chronology, during the late Bronze Age interruption to settlement, it was initially interpreted as aetiology or as historicization of an annual Pesah-Matzot festival (→ Pesah), but recent investigations indicate purely literary narrative inventions, dating, at the earliest, the late 8th cent. BC, when the Jordan had become a frontier river and J. a border town; in a fictional colonization tale this could not have occurred without mention being made of a destruction.

For the Achaemenid period (5th/4th cents.), an unfortified settlement on the northern slope of the tell has been attested (Esr 2:34; Neh 3:2; 7:36). After involvement in the uprising against → Artaxerxes [3] III (344–343), some members of the population were deported (Caspian Sea, Babylonia). As early as the Hasmonaean period, a partly uncovered winter palace with garden and bath facilities (Ant. Iud. 15,54) was built south-west of the oasis (*Tulūl Abī l-ʿAlāʾiq*), which was expanded by → Herodes the Great (Jos. BI 1,407), who died in it (BI 1,659; 194), and renovated by → Archelaus [10] (Ant. Iud. 17,340), as well as a hippodrome (*Tall as-Samarat*; BI 1,659; 2,3), and an amphitheatre (unloc.; BI 1,666; Ant. Iud. 17,161; 194). For the civilian settlement, which can be assumed to have existed since the Hellenistic period in the area of the oasis, and for its late antique surrounding wall, there are hardly any archaeological finds, apart from three churches and a synagogue. Under Hišām Ibn ʿAbd al-Malik, the construction of a winter palace (*Ḫirbat al-Mafǧir*) was commenced, from AD 742, north of the oasis, but after the earthquake of 746 and the end of the Umayyad dynasty in 750, it was never completed.

K. M. KENYON et al., s.v. J., NEAEHL II, 674–697; K. BIEBERSTEIN, Josua – Jordan – J., 1995.   K.B.

Jerome see → Hieronymus

Jerusalem
I. NAME II. LOCATION AND HISTORY III. SITES IN THE SURROUNDING AREA

I. NAME
Hebrew *Yᵊrūšālēm*, presumably 'foundation of the (god) Šalēm', in the Masoretic texts (→ Masorah) always vocalized in the dual form *Yᵊrūšālayim*; Greek Ἰερουσαλήμ, Ἱεροσόλυμα; Latin *Ierusalem*, [*H*]*ierosolyma*), archaizing *Šālēm* (Gn 14:18; Ps 76:3) or *Yᵊbōs* (Judg 19:10–11; 1 Chr 11:4–5), under Hadrian renamed *Colonia Aelia Capitolina*, under Commodus renamed *Colonia Aelia Commodiana*, already in the early Islamic Period called *al-Quds*, 'the Holy One'.

II. LOCATION AND HISTORY
A. PRE-EXILIC PERIOD B. POST-EXILIC PERIOD

A. PRE-EXILIC PERIOD
J. lies a little to the east of the watershed of the West Jordanian hill country, overlooked by the Mount of Olives in the east, and a little to the south of a trade route that leads via → Jericho into the East Jordanian plateau along the border between the territories of the tribes of Benjamin and Judah (Jos 15:8; 18:16). Already at the end of the 4th millennium, an open settlement came into being on the narrow spur to the west of and above the Gihon (ʿAin al-Sitt Maryam), the only perennial spring within the settlement, but it was abandoned after a few decades. A new settlement founded around 1800

BC was soon fortified with a ring wall and may be mentioned already in Egyptian → apotropaic texts of the 12th Dynasty (19th cent. BC) as *ʾwšʾmm* [3. 53 no. e27 and e28, 58 no. f18], but certainly in the early 14th cent. in the letters of its ruler Abdi-Ḫepa to → Amenophis [4] IV as *ú-ru-sa-lim* [2. no. 285–290]. After J. was captured around 1000 BC by David and made the capitol of Israel and Judah (2 Sam 5:6–9; so the later, retrospective depictions), → Solomon built the temple of → Yahweh on a cultic site on the hilltop north of the City of David, and between it and the City of David, he built his palace and surrounded both with an expanded ring wall (1 Kgs 6–8). But the earliest archaeological finds from the area in question originate only from the 9th or 8th cents. BC. A new channel, part tunnel and part open channel, brought the water of the Gihon at the foot of the City of David to the south, irrigated the royal gardens in the Kidron Valley, and then flowed into a reservoir at the southern end of the city (*al-Birkat aš-Šamra*); Isaiah presumably referred to this stream when he mentioned the quietly flowing waters of Šiloaḥ (Is 8:6).

Apart from a double chamber grave on the Mount of Olives (16th–14th cents. BC), the earliest known necropolis with shaft graves, following Phoenician practice (10th–9th cents. BC), lay immediately west of the Solomonic upper city, west of the Tyropoeon Valley. Only the royal graves (at least until Ahaz (734/3–715/4 BC), deviating grave references in 2 Chr are construed tendentiously) were situated in the south-east of the City of David, but their identification with burial chambers found there is disputed. Although a new burial field with graves with Phrygian and Urartian parallels was built in the late 8th cent. opposite the City of David and east of the Kidron Valley, yet in recent diggings in the upper reaches of the Hinnom Valley west of the city, a new burial field was discovered, which was built in the 8th cent., and which, up until and into the Hellenistic period, moved gradually down the valley to the place where the latter meets the Kidron Valley. This is significant in terms of the history of religion, in that the Moloch cult (→ Moloch) was also practised there, which is less to be interpreted by analogy with Punic *mlk* sacrifices, but rather as worship of the god Mālik, known from → Ebla, → Mari, and → Ugarit, which gave the Hinnom Valley its chthonic connotations (Jer 7:26–35).

With the fall of the Aramaean kingdom of → Damascus in the year 733 and the northern kingdom of Israel in 722 BC, Judah came under direct pressure from Assyria: Hezekiah (725–697 BC), probably also in order to take in the refugees from the former northern kingdom, expanded the city wall towards the west and created a new upper city, both in the New City (Zeph 1:10; 2 Kgs 22:14) and in Maktesh (Zeph 1:11), which got its water from the upper pool (Pool of Bethesda or *Birkat Šammām al-Baṭraq*? Is 7:3; 36:2; 2 Kgs 18:17). He also routed the water from the Gihon Spring through a 533 m long tunnel into the city (KAI 189),

Map A: **Jerusalem from the Middle Bronze Age to the destruction by Nebuchadnezzar (1800 – 587 BC)**
Map B: **Jerusalem from the reconstruction in Achaemenid times to the destruction by Titus (520 BC – AD 70)**

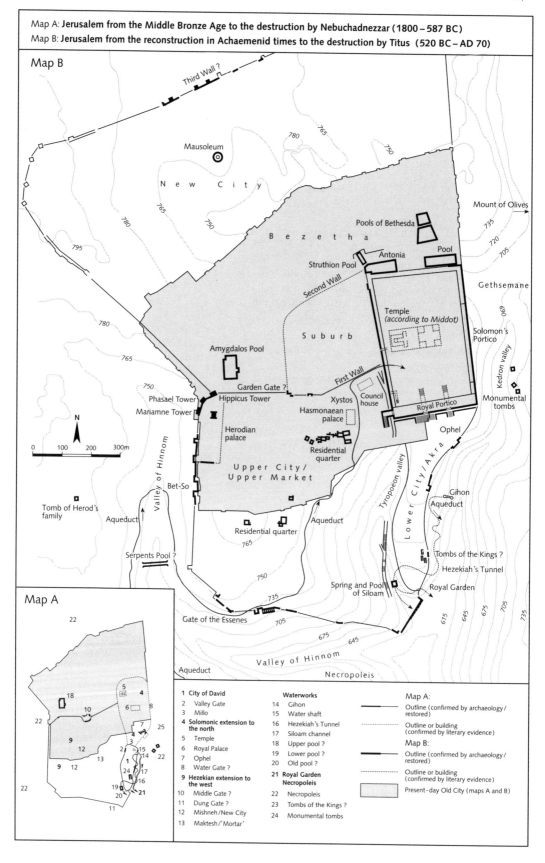

Map B

Third Wall ?

Mausoleum

New City

Mount of Olives

Pools of Bethesda

B e z e t h a

Antonia

Pool

Struthion Pool

Gethsemane

Second Wall

Temple
(according to Middot)

Solomon's
Portico

S u b u r b

Kedron valley

Amygdalos Pool

First Wall

Garden Gate ?

Monumental
tombs

Phasael Tower

Hippicus Tower

Xystos

Council
house

N

Mariamne Tower

Hasmonaean
palace

Royal Portico

Ophel

Herodian
palace

Residential
quarter

0   100   200   300m

Upper City /
Upper Market

Gihon

Bet-So

Aqueduct

Tomb of Herod's
family

Aqueduct

Residential quarter

Aqueduct

Tombs of the Kings ?

Hezekiah's Tunnel

Serpents Pool ?

Spring and Pool
of Siloam

Royal Garden

Gate of the Essenes

Aqueduct

Valley of Hinnom

Necropoleis

Map A

1 City of David	**Waterworks**	**Map A:**
2 Valley Gate	14 Gihon	——— Outline (confirmed by archaeology / restored)
3 Millo	15 Water shaft	
4 Solomonic extension to the north	16 Hezekiah's Tunnel	········· Outline or building (confirmed by literary evidence)
5 Temple	17 Siloam channel	**Map B:**
6 Royal Palace	18 Upper pool ?	——— Outline (confirmed by archaeology / restored)
7 Ophel	19 Lower pool ?	
8 Water Gate ?	20 Old pool ?	········· Outline or building (confirmed by literary evidence)
9 Hezekian extension to the west	**21** Royal Garden	Present-day Old City (maps A and B)
10 Middle Gate ?	**Necropoleis**	
11 Dung Gate ?	22 Necropoleis	
12 Mishneh /New City	23 Tombs of the Kings ?	
13 Maktesh / 'Mortar'	24 Monumental tombs	

closed off the spring which was outside of the city (2 Kgs 20:20; 2 Chr 32:3–4.30; Sir 48:47), and thus secured the city against an attack. This, perhaps, is why → Sanherib refrained from storming the city in 701 BC, after being paid tribute. Under the Babylonian ruler → Nebuchadnezzar II, King Jehoiachin, along with part of the Jewish upper class, was deported to Babylon (597 BC), and the city was taken in the year 587 by the Babylonian army after renewed attempts at autonomy, and after further deportations it was destroyed (2 Kgs 24–25).
→ Judah and Israel; → Judaism; → Palaestina → Yahweh

1 K. BIEBERSTEIN, H. BLOEDHORN, Jerusalem I–III, 1994 2 W. M. MORAN, The Amarna Letters, 1992 3 K. SETHE, Die Ächtung feindlicher Fürsten, Völker und Dinge auf altäg. Tonscherben des MR, 1926.   K.B.

B. Post-exilic Period

In the year 538 BC, the first of the deported Israelites returned to J. under the leadership of Šešbazzar. In 520–515, at the time of Zerubbabel and the priest Jošua, the temple was rebuilt under the aegis of the prophets Haggai and Zechariah, as well as under the critical opposition of the Trito-Isaian circles (Esr 1–6). In 445, → Judah was made a Persian province; Nehemiah restored the city walls to the size of the pre-Hezekian city (Neh 2–6; 12:27–43). In 175, the leadership under → Antiochus [6] IV. Epiphanes obtained permission to found a gymnasium, which prepared the establishment of a polis (1 Macc 1:33). In the year 168, the Seleucid occupation constructed the Akra as a stronghold at the ascent to the temple district (1 Macc 1:29–37), and in 167 the temple of Yahweh was dedicated to Zeus Olympius (1 Macc 1:54–61). After a three-and-a-half-year battle, the Orthodox opposition under → Judas Makkabaios reconquered the city in 164 BC and restored the orthodox Yahweh cult (1 Macc 4:36–61). In 141 Simon Makkabaios was able to capture the Akra and regain complete control (1 Macc 13:49–51). Under Iohannes → Hyrcanus [2] I (135–104) the Akra was torn down and the fortress Baris built north-west of the temple district (Jos. Ant. Iud. 18,91f.), which still served as a palace for → Aristobulus [2] II. (67–63 BC; Jos. BI 1,120–122). Presumably the city was expanded to the west only under his rulership (First Wall, Jos. BI 5,142–145), which gave it the same size as in the late pre-exilic period. Furthermore a new, not yet archaeologically determined palace was built in the new suburb (Jos. BI 1,142–144; 2,344; Ant. Iud. 14,58–63; 20,189–198); soon after, the city was expanded again to the north (Second Wall, Jos. BI 5,146; 158).

At the beginning of his rule, → Herodes [1] the Great (37–4 BC) secured the northern flank of the temple district by converting the Baris into the fort Antonia (Jos. BI 1,401; 5,238–245); in addition, in his 13th year he built a new palace for himself at the north-west corner of the city (Jos. BI 1,402; 5,161–183; Ant. Iud. 15,318), which also served as a residence for the Roman governors (Sabinus: Jos. BI 2,46; Jos. Ant. Iud. 17,257; Pontius Pilatus: Phil. legatio ad Gaium 299–306; Gessius Florus: Jos. BI 2,301). He replaced the temple of Yahweh from his 15th (Jos. BI 1,401) or 18th (Ant. Iud. 15,380) year onwards with a new one, whereby he expanded its temenos to the size still extant today (Jos. BI 5,184–237; Ant. Iud. 380–402). In the Tyropoeon Valley between the former Hasmonean royal palace and the temple grounds were the Xystus (Jos. BI 2,344; 4,581; 5,144; 6,191; 325; 377; Ant. Iud. 20,189) and the city hall (Jos. BI 5,144; 6,354), both archaeologically not attested. After an aborted attempt under → Herodes [8] Agrippa I (AD 41–44) to expand the city once again towards the north (Third Wall, Jos. BI 2,218f.; 5,146–160), the temple and the city were destroyed after a siege of several months by Titus in AD 70 because of the Jewish Revolt, and, except for a part of the western fortress, where the *legio X Fretensis* was stationed for its protection, it was razed to the ground (Jos. BI 5,67–7,5).

The 2nd Jewish Revolt under Šimon → Bar Kochba (132–135) started because of Hadrian's decision to re-establish J. as *Colonia Aelia Capitolina* and capitol of the province Palaestina, and to build a temple to Jupiter Capitolinus on the site of the temple of Yahweh (Cass. Dio 69,12,1–3), but the revolt did not encroach on the city. After the revolt was put down, the decision to build was modified and the Jupiter temple (Jer. Ep. 58,3) was built next to a temple of Aphrodite (Euseb. Vita Const. 3,26) west of the → *cardo*. In spite of an alleged ban to the contrary, but which was only circulated by Christian authors (Euseb. Hist. eccl. 4,6,3 et passim), a small Jewish community seems to have existed from the time of Severus. In contrast, the Jewish Christian community may only have existed until the time of the Bar Kochba revolt (Euseb. Hist. eccl. 4,5,1–4; 4,6,4; 5,12). The uninterrupted list of bishops passed down by Eusebius, of initially Jewish Christian (Euseb. Hist. eccl. 4,5,3) and later Gentile Christian (Hist. eccl. 5,12) bishops, was only constructed under Bishop Narcissus or his successor Alexander in order to secure apostolic authority in the controversy over the Easter festival (Hist. eccl. 5,22–25).

After the *legio X Fretensis* was transferred to Aila (Euseb. On. 6,17–20), the city was given a ring wall again under Diocletian. Constantine transformed it into a living Christian memorial: after the Council of Nicaea (325), a basilica was built in Bethlehem in memory of Christ becoming man, a church in memory of Christ's resurrection in the area of the temple grounds west of the *cardo*, and a basilica in memory of Christ's ascension into heaven (Euseb. Vita Const. 3,33–43) on the Mount of Olives, to which was added a rotunda already before AD 374 by a donor named Poimenia. After the Council of Constantinople (381), the Hagia Sion was built in memory of the descent of the Holy Spirit, and already before 391 the Gethsemane Church was built at the foot of the Mount of Olives. In spite of the fact that the city was made a patriarchy at

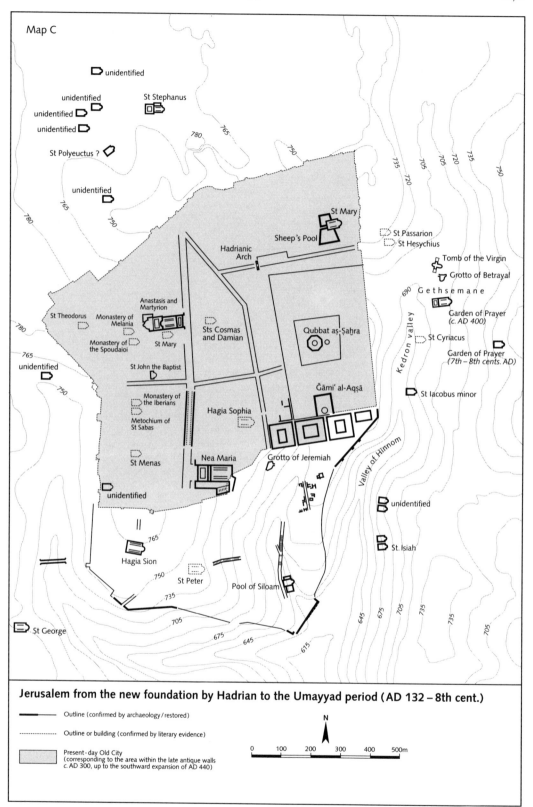

Map C

unidentified

unidentified
unidentified
unidentified

St Stephanus

St Polyeuctus ?

unidentified

St Mary

Sheep's Pool

Hadrianic
Arch

St Passarion
St Hesychius

Tomb of the Virgin
Grotto of Betrayal

Gethsemane

St Theodorus

Monastery of
Melania

Anastasis and
Martyrion

Sts Cosmas
and Damian

Qubbat aṣ-Ṣaḫra

Garden of Prayer
(c. AD 400)

St Cyriacus

Garden of Prayer
(7th – 8th cents. AD)

Monastery of
the Spoudaioi

St Mary

unidentified

St John the Baptist

Monastery of
the Iberians

Metochium of
St Sabas

Hagia Sophia

Ğāmiʿ al-Aqṣā

St Iacobus minor

Grotto of Jeremiah

St Menas

Nea Maria

unidentified

unidentified

St. Isiah

Hagia Sion

St Peter

Pool of Siloam

St George

Kedron valley

Valley of Hinnom

Jerusalem from the new foundation by Hadrian to the Umayyad period (AD 132 – 8th cent.)

———— Outline (confirmed by archaeology / restored)

------------- Outline or building (confirmed by literary evidence)

Present-day Old City
(corresponding to the area within the late antique walls
c. AD 300, up to the southward expansion of AD 440)

N

0   100   200   300   400   500m

the Council of Chalcedon (451), the monastic movement first sided with the anti-Chalcedonian opposition; the first mention of Mary's grave stems from the context of the resulting confusion. At about the same time the house of Caiphas (St. Peter) and the Praetorium of Pilate (Hagia Sophia) were marked with churches, and the city wall was expanded to the south by the empress → Eudocia [1]. The Nea Maria was completed under Iustinian (543) in the south of the city as the largest church with hospice (Procop. Aed. 5,6), not least to provide care for the streams of pilgrims. The destruction caused by the Sassanid raid (614) was cleared in a short time with Sassanid help. While the city returned to Byzantine control in 630 or 631, it had to open its gates to the Islamic army under the leadership of Ḫālid ibn Ṯābit al-Fahmī between 635 and 638. The churches remained untouched. A mosque (Ǧamiʿ al-Aqṣā) was built on the former location of the temple (al-Ḥaram al-Ašraf) as a continuation of the Jewish temple tradition. This was replaced with a stone building under Abd al-Malik and furnished with the Dome of the Rock, which was completed in the year 692 (Qubbat aṣ-Ṣaḫra).

→ JERUSALEM

K. BIEBERSTEIN, H. BLOEDHORN, J. I–III, 1994; Id., J. Baugeschichte, TAVO B IV 7, 1992; K. M. KENYON, Digging Up J., 1974; E. OTTO, J., 1980; Y. SHILOH, A. DE GROOT, D. T. ARIEL, Excavations at the City of David I–IV, 1980–1996; J. J. SIMONS, J. in the Old Testament, 1952; H. VINCENT, Jérusalem I, 1912; H. VINCENT, F.-M. ABEL, Jérusalem II, 1914–1926; L.-H. VINCENT, A.-M. STEVE, Jérusalem de l'Ancien Testament I–III, 1954–1956.   K.B.

III. SITES IN THE SURROUNDING AREA
A. GETHSEMANE   B. GOLGOTHA

A. GETHSEMANE

Gethsemane (Greek Γεθσημανεί, Lat. *Gethsēmaneí*, from Hebrew גתשמנים, 'oil press') is the name of an olive garden at the foot of the Mount of Olives east of J., which is only mentioned in the NT. According to Mk 14:26–53 (and parallel passages), it is the place where → Jesus and his disciples prayed, as well as the place where Jesus was arrested after his betrayal through → Judas [1] Iškariot. From the end of the 4th cent. onwards, a church structure has been described at this location (among others by the → *Peregrinatio ad loca sancta* of Egeria and by → Hieronymus) [1. 183–217; 2. 338–346; 3. 387–399].

B. GOLGOTHA

Golgotha (Greek Γολγοθᾶ, Lat. *Golgothâ*; either from Aramaic גולגנתא, 'stone circle', or גולגולתא, 'skull') is the site of executions north-west of J. (outside the city gates), where → Jesus was crucified (Mk 15:22 and parallel passages); it was incorporated into the city from the time of → Herodes [1] Agrippa (AD 41–44) due to expansion of the municipal area. Under → Constantinus [1] the Great, the site, which had been buried

by the restructuring of the city under Hadrian (AD 136), was excavated and honoured as a Christian place of pilgrimage (from AD 326). In 336 the Church of the Holy Sepulchre, where the G. rock lay in the so-called inner atrium, was consecrated. It was only from the time that the church was rebuilt under the crusaders (1140–1149), that the site of execution and the grave were located together under the same roof. The travel report of Egeria (→ *Peregrinatio ad loca sancta*, around AD 400) contains a description of the place and of the Jerusalem Liturgy, in which Golgotha has an important place. The first pictorial representation is found on the city map of J. in the Madaba mosaic (6th cent. AD) [1. 183–217; 2. 183–217; 3. 422–444].

1 K. BIEBERSTEIN, J. 2, 1994   2 G. DALMANN, Orte und Wege Jesu, ⁴1924   3 C. KOPP, Die hl. Stätten der Evangelien, 1959.   I.WA.

Jesters see → Entertainers

Jesus During the course of the historicist Enlightenment, the early Christian tradition of J. became the subject of an in-depth study of the sources. Next to the dogmatic unity of the divine and human nature of J. Christ, there appeared the question of the historical Jesus, which seeks the authentic historical figure of J. within the context of contemporary Judaism. At the same time however, the history of the research into the life of Jesus shows that reconstructing a historical J. depends not only on decisions regarding textual criticism, but is also subject to contemporary hermeneutical biases [3; 19]. Moreover, theologians differ in opinion about what the relative and relativizing historical statements regarding J. mean for the Christian-theological evaluation of his person. This is all the more pressing because historical research increasingly draws the figure of J. in the plurality of groups of contemporary Judaism, an impression especially conveyed by Jewish researchers [10; 11; 25].

At least three intensive phases of the research on Jesus can be distinguished after its beginnings in the 18th cent. [23. 21ff.]. The first one is characterized by the liberal Life-of-Jesus theology of the 19th cent. and the establishing of textual criticism. The second responds, in the fifties and sixties, to the theological irrelevance of the historical Jesus-question, as stated in dialectic theology, and, especially, by Rudolf BULTMANN, which, in turn, was a result of the failure of the historical optimism subscribed to by the Life-of-Jesus theology with regard to the reconstruction of a biography of J. This second phase is characterized by the attempt to develop criteria which allow to distinguish J. historically from Judaism as well as from early Christianity. The third phase began a little over ten years ago in the English-speaking world ('third quest') [26]. It is characterized by renewed textual criticism, and especially by the inclusion of non-canonical early Christian literature, by the self-evident integration of J. within the religious, social, and cultural context of contemporary Judaism, and by the integration of social-historical and cultural-anthropological methods that go along with it. Accordingly, a methodical pluralism emerges at the present time, shaped by the combination of literary-historical with religious-, social-, economic-historical and cultural-anthropological (including gender studies) questions.

A. Sources and their evaluation B. Jesus of Nazareth: Historical reconstruction C. Jesus Christ: Oldest Christology

A. Sources and their evaluation

J. himself has not left writings of any kind. Non-Christian antique testimonies are rare, so that the historical reconstruction must be based primarily upon texts from the NT and non-canonical early Christian texts [1; 2; 23. 35ff]. Those in turn need to be viewed from a critical, literary-historical perspective and to be evaluated within the context of the sources on Judaism in the land of Israel as well as within the context of early Christianity.

1. Non-Christian testimonies 2. Christian testimonies 3. Evaluation

1. Non-Christian testimonies

a. The Jewish historian Flavius → Iosephus mentions, around AD 93, in his 'Jewish Antiquities', in conjunction with the account of the execution of Jacobus (AD 62), that the latter was the brother of J. who is called Christus (Jos. Ant. Iud. 20,200). The epithet *Christus* clarifies the common name *Jesus* (as Col 4:11: J. who is called Iustus), and is unlikely to be an acknowledgement of J.'s Messianic significance by Josephus.

The authenticity of the *Testimonium Flavianum* in the same work is controversial (Jos. Ant. Iud. 18,63f.). Within its treatment of the tenure of → Pontius Pilatus, prefect of Judaea, it offers a brief and essentially Christian version of the life of J. This orientation along Christian lines has led to the opinion that the passage – especially as it interrupts a compositional unity – is a secondary Christian interpolation. Lately, however, it is increasingly supposed that the text was originally written by Josephus and was later edited in some way. But the question as to what exactly this original text may have been remains exceedingly hypothetical and controversial. The texts in the Old Russian version of the Jewish War which refer to J. are not included in the Greek version and are definitely spurious.

b. The Roman senator and epistolographer C. → Plinius Caecilius Secundus (Pliny the Younger) mentions trials against Christians, in his official correspondence with the emperor Trajan, as legate with special powers in the province of → Bithynia et Pontus (around AD 111/113) These stated, according to Pliny, that they gathered before sunrise on a specific day in order to alternately sing a song to Christ, as their god (*carmenque Christo quasi deo dicere secum invicem*, Plin. Ep.

10,96,7). Because Pliny, in the course of the advanced criminalization of Christians [22. 272ff.], considered being a Christian in itself a capital crime (*nomen ipsum*) and punished the refusal of renunciation with the death penalty, this statement should be understood as a defence by Christians trying to prove their harmlessness.

c. The Roman historian Cornelius → Tacitus mentions in his 'Annals' (c. AD 115/117), in conjunction with the description of the burning of Rome (AD 64) and Nero's blaming of the Christians, that this name derives from Christ, who was executed under Tiberius by the prefect Pontius Pilate (*auctor nominis eius Christus Tiberio imperitante per procuratorem Pontium Pilatum supplicio adfectus erat*, Tac. Ann. 15,44,3). His principal interest consists in the characterization of Christians as people who were hated for their misdeeds (*flagitia*), and of Christianity as a 'fatal superstition' (*exitiabilis superstitio*), emphasized by the fact that the originator of the name had been executed as a criminal by the Roman governor of Judaea. Where Tacitus found his information regarding *Christus* is uncertain.

d. The Roman writer C. → Suetonius Tranquillus mentions in his biographies of the emperors (around AD 120), that Claudius drove the Jews out of Rome, because, incited by Chrestus, they continued to disturb the peace (*Iudaeos impulsore Chresto assidue tumultuantes Roma expulit*, Suet. Claud. 25,4). Two things are remarkable here: 1. The displacement of i/e (→ Itacism), although not unusual, leads to certain associations due to the fact that *Chrestus* was a popular slavename. 2. Suetonius seems to assume that *Chrestus* himself is responsible for the unrest in Rome. The passage probably refers to an administrative measure of the emperor Claudius ('Edict of Claudius'), also mentioned in the Acts of the Apostles (18,2), where Jewish believers in Christ (such as the married couple → Aquila [4] and Priscilla in Acts 18:2) are expelled from Rome, because their missionary activities were causing unrest among the Roman Jews. The most plausible date for this is the year AD 49.

e. The chronographer → Iulius Africanus (around 170–240) mentions (cf. FGrH II B 1157), with reference to the 'third book of the Histories' by a certain Thallo (who composed, around AD 52, a world history in three volumes), the latter's interpretation of the darkness, which supposedly occurred all over the world during the crucifixion of J., as a natural solar eclipse. Iulius Africanus calls this illogical and insists on the miraculous character of the event because J. was crucified during the time of Passover, and therefore in the middle of the full moon of spring, which excludes a natural solar eclipse. If the reference is authentic, then it shows that Christian interpretations of the Passion met with opposition early on.

f. A Syrian MS in the British Museum (text in [1. 2ff.]), dated to the 7th cent. AD, contains the text of a letter that a Mara bar Sapion, claiming to be a Stoic philosopher, writes to his son from a Roman prison. He draws parallels between the executions of Socrates, a sculptor (!) Pythagoras and J., who is only referred to as the wise king of the Jews. All three deaths resulted in misfortune for their fellow countrymen, yet the executed men lived on in their teachings or in their work. The passage referring to J. interprets, in an adoption of Christian historical theology, the Jewish defeat in the first large revolt against Rome (AD 66–70), the killings of the Jews, and their expulsion into the → Diaspora, as punishment for J.'s execution. The title of 'king' also takes on Christian meaning, being already connected to the tradition of wisdom in the Gospel of John. He is considered to be living on, not in the resurrection, but in the laws that he (sc. the wise King of the Jews) passed. This also reflects the tradition of wisdom, as the letter shows earlier: 'The life of men, my son, leaves the world, their praise and their gifts last forever'. Because the letter creates the impression of having been composed shortly after AD 73, some scholars consider it the oldest non-Christian testimony (most recent [23. 84ff.]). Others date it to the second or third cents. The latter seems most plausible, especially because the parallels with → Socrates (and other philosophers) take up a motive that is not present until Christian apologetics. This raises questions about the entire letter being of Christian origin.

g. References to J. in rabbinical sources (→ Rabbinical literature, →) are rare and, with regard to their age, very controversial. The extensive examinations of Johann MAIER come to the conclusion that no passages referring to J. exist in texts from the Tannaitic Period, i.e. before AD 220, and that the Amoraic passages are to be traced back to later interpolations [13. 268ff.]. The name *Yeshu* or *Yeshua-ha-nozri* would have been added later, and certain rabbinical polemics against sorcery and seduction to idolatry would have had to be subsequently reinterpreted as to pertain to J. According to MAIER, this also applies to the figure of Ben-Stada/Ben-Pandera. In any case, the extensive polemics, contained in the folk book → *Toledot Jeshu*, of which numerous versions and variations existed, should be dated to medieval times. Some scholars, however, consider a Baraita to the Talmud treatise *Sanhedrin* (bSanh 43a) to be Tannaitic, according to which J. was accused before the Sanhedrin, stoned and finally hanged for sorcery and seduction (to apostasy), on the eve of Passover (approx. [11]). Most probably this is anti-Christian polemic and not a historically plausible testimony.

2. CHRISTIAN TESTIMONIES

a. The oldest canonical testimonies of J. are to be found in the letters (c. AD 50–60) of Paul, some claiming to derive from the Lord Himself, which may mean that they are considered to have been communicated to him via revelation (cf. 1 Thess 4:15–17; 1 Cor 7:10; 9:14; 11:23–25).

b. The most extensive canonical tradition is preserved in the → Gospels (c. AD 70–100), which form a separate Christian literary genre. Textual criticism, in the course of the first phase of the Life-of-Jesus research, has a principal preference for the historical reconstruction of the Synoptic Gospels (Mt, Mk, Lc) as opposed to the Gospel of John. The latter is distinguished from the others on the basis of a literary-historical Two-Source-Theory (i.e. two sources for the historical J.). This theory states that Mk is the oldest gospel, used by Mt and Lc, and that Mt and Lc are based on a second source, which is to be dated before AD 70 (and sometimes considered to be an oral tradition only). This is called the source of speeches or sayings (Q), because it consists mainly of sayings and speeches of J. The most important role for the reconstruction of the teachings of J. is attributed to this source. Some importance is also placed on the non-synoptic material, the so-called *Sondergut*, in Lc and Mt. Although Mk seems trustworthy because of its chronological-geographical outline of the life of Jesus, a literary, formal and editorial analysis shows this framework to be secondary. Due to the different editorial frameworks and older traditions, complexes of tradition or collections of different editorial or compositorial levels were assumed to lie behind these oldest literary sources. A diachronic literary and formal analysis has separated the traditional material of the synoptic Gospels into smaller units of maxims (sayings, analogies) and stories, which show characteristic formelements and stem, on a literary-sociological level, from the needs of early Christianity. This situation means that the deduction of a historical J. from the Gospels requires special criteria, because the diachronic analysis also leads to the traditions of the oldest congregations.

c. In the first two phases of the question of the historical J., non-canonical early Christian testimonies were paid attention to and collected under the term → *Agrapha*. But only due to the efforts of the representatives of the 'third quest' in the United States are they, for the first time, considered as equal, partly based on – controversial – early datings [12]. The following texts are of particular importance:

Papyrus Egerton 2: these are fragments from an unknown codex with a debate and miracle stories of J., which clearly reveal the influence of the canonical gospels and are unlikely to have originated any earlier than AD 150. POxy. 840: a sheet of parchment (!), found in Egypt in 1905, from a codex composed after 400, which contains variations of synoptic material (Mk 7; Mt 23). A 1st-cent. dating is uncertain.

Gospel of Thomas: a collection related to Q, containing 114 *logia* or sayings, discovered in 1945 in → Nag Hammadi and part of its library of Coptic writings (NHCod II/2). Greek fragments were already known from the Oxyrhynchus-Papyri (POxy. 1; 654; 655), which is why the Gospel of Thomas must have originated no later than AD 140. Given the convergence of about 50% of the *logia* with the material of the canonic gospels, it is disputed whether the Gospel of Thomas can be considered an independent testimony – as argued by the representatives of the 'third quest' in the United States – or merely a Gnostically emended and extended version of the synoptic tradition.

The Gospel of Peter: Greek fragments, mostly from the Passion of one of the Gospels, the narrator of which pretends to be Peter, found in 1886 in Upper Egypt. The MS is dated to the 8th/9th cents. It may have originated before AD 200 (due to parallel fragments in POxy. 2949 and 4009), but no earlier than c. AD 150. Whether the Gospel of Peter contains a very old 'Gospel of the Cross' (as in [7. 506ff.]) is extremely controversial. It is more plausible that it is based on the four canonical gospels.

Secret Gospel of Mark: a letter written by → Clement [3] of Alexandria, discovered by Morton SMITH in the monastery of Mar Saba near Jerusalem in 1958 (and edited later) contains a quote from a secret Gospel of Mark, which tells of the resurrection of a young man in → Bethania [1] (parallel to Mk 10:34) [21]. The MS has not been accessible since its discovery. Even in the event that the letter is genuine, the quote is unlikely to originate from a preliminary stage of the Gospel of Mark, but rather from a (Gnostic) revision of the latter (in variation of Jo 11) from the 2nd cent.

3. EVALUATION

The non-Christian testimonies are all reactions, in part very polemical, to the development of Christianity or its founder Christ, and already reflect Christian interpretations. Most weight should be attributed with regard to a historical reconstruction to the Tacitus passage, because it speaks for the historicity of J. as well as attesting the fact that he was tried and executed as a criminal in a Roman trial by the prefect of Judaea. Among Christian testimonies, and despite many tendencies to the contrary in present research, the canonical, especially the synoptic tradition, is still to be considered the historically richest and most reliable tradition, although the non-canonical tradition should be considered in individual cases as well. The diachronic analysis of canonical traditions does not allow, despite many assumptions to the contrary [15], direct conclusions about the historical J. Rather, a differentiated method is required, so that reconstructions always remain hypothetical. However, the extreme scepticism that opposes any reconstruction is not appropriate. Literary-historical, together with religious- and socio-historical methods can develop criteria which can place J. and his first followers ('Jesus movement') in the context of contemporary Judaism in the land of Israel as well as in the context of his impact on early Christianity [24]. Historical plausibility, however, is always determined not only by the decisions based on critical analysis of the sources, but also by the evaluation of the correspondence between these contexts and the differences between the two.

B. JESUS OF NAZARETH: HISTORICAL RECONSTRUCTION

1. ORIGIN AND FORMATIVE FORCES 2. BASIC TRAITS OF HIS DEEDS AND TEACHINGS 3. THE FATE OF JESUS

1. ORIGIN AND FORMATIVE FORCES

J. comes from a Jewish family, commonly considered Davidic (father Joseph, mother Maria or Mirjam; apart from his sisters, four brothers Mk 6:3 are mentioned by name, among them Jacobus, later of importance to the religious community of Jerusalem). The Greek name Ἰησοῦς/Iēsoûs is, in the LXX, a rendition of the Hebrew Yᵊhôšuaʿ ('JHWH helps') as well as of the later form Yēšuaʿ and was, until the 2nd cent. AD, common among Jews. Born perhaps before 4 BC (in the lifetime of Herod [1] the Great, if Mt 2/Lc 1:5 are historical; but this stands in contrast to the census under Quirinius in the province of Judaea mentioned in Lc 2:1, which did not take place before AD 6, more likely later), J. grew up in → Galilaea, in or near → Nazareth (Mk 6:1 his home town; therefore in the Gospels and elsewhere, in order to distinguish him from others with the same name, Ἰ. ὁ Ναζαρηνός/Nazarēnós or Ναζωραῖος/ Nazōraîos; also J. of Nazareth). → Aramaic was the colloquial language in Galilaea at the time of J.; → Hebrew was the holy language or the language of the religious doctrine, hence it can be assumed that J. had knowledge of Hebrew. Knowledge of Greek is improbable. Hebrew and knowledge of the Bible and of religious traditions were probably taught to Jesus by his father, like to so many other children (or maybe in school); further learning, as for example had by → Iosephus, who was a member of the priestly aristocracy, must be excluded. According to Mk 6:3, J. was, like his father, tektōn, i.e. a building craftsman (Mt 13:55), which classifies him socially as part of the underclass and economically as part of the relatively poor (pénētes), but not of the destitute (ptōchoí).

The character of → Judaism in the land of Israel was, at the time of J., shaped on the one hand by common institutions (temple, → Synagogue, house), convictions (→ Monotheism, chosenness, Torah) and practices (temple cult, circumcision, → Sabbath, Torah study, meal- and purity regulations), and, on the other hand, by a plurality of groups (→ Pharisees, → Sadducees, → Qumran-Essenes, prophetic-charismatic groups etc.). These groups interpreted the common characteristics of identity differently and controversially, also depending on their socio-economic position. J.'s Galilean context was part of this 'common Judaism' [16] and its pluralism. He was hardly the Hellenistic-urban type, rather conservative-Jewish and rural; the more markedly Hellenistic cities of Sepphoris and Tiberias, for example, are not places where J. was influential. Just as implausible, for the same reason, is J.'s characterization as a Jewish Cynic, who combined wisdom with magic [7. 119ff.; 553f.], or his designation as a marginal Jew [14]. The travelling activity connected with his public appearances (according to Lc 3:23 in his 30th year) is to be connected with the specific type of his movement, to be characterized in socio-religious terms as Charismatism [22. 171ff.; 23. 175ff.]. This character is typical of socio-economic crises and related crises of traditional beliefs and practices. J.'s most formative influence constituted the priest John the Baptist, who had created a messianic-prophetic penitence movement, following a biblical Moses-Elijah typology. His expectation of a radical final judgement, when only those symbolically cleansed of their sins by a baptism in the river Jordan would be saved (Mt 3:7ff./Lc 3:7ff.), adopts early Jewish-apocalyptic concepts. His ascetic lifestyle, together with a close discipleship, to which J. belonged, as well (according to Jo 3:22ff., J. even assisted the Baptist), points to mobilization of the masses and criticism of authority (Mk 6:17f.: criticism of the forbidden interfamily marriage of Herodes Antipas). All this reveals charismatic traits. Other influences on J., especially the Pharisean interpretation of the Torah, were most likely communicated by the broad effect of these groups, an effect that was particularly strong in the case of the Pharisees.

2. BASIC TRAITS OF HIS DEEDS AND TEACHINGS
J.'s public appearance – probably immediately after the martyrdom of the Baptist (Mk 1:14) – is associated with the manifestation of charismatic powers of healing (*dynámeis*: Mk 6:2. 5. 14 *et passim*), especially exorcisms (Mk 1:21ff. *et passim*), which are considered proof of his divinely legitimated mission and power (*exousía*: Mk 1:22 *et passim*). Insofar, J.'s proximity to thaumaturgical healers has rightly been emphasised, in recent times, against the stylization of J. as eschatological preacher predominant in Protestant research (as again recently [17]). Decisive is, however, that he unfolds these unusual powers in the context of a charismatic, itinerant, non-economic and non-family-oriented (probably also sexually ascetic) movement of close disciples and a wider range of followers, and that he prophetically and apocalyptically interprets them as a partial and contemporary presence of the Kingdom of God.

The Gospels connect J.'s appearance from the beginning on with the summoning of disciples as followers (Mk 1:16ff.), the core group may have come from the followers of the Baptist (Jo 1:35ff.). Many of them were fishermen from the northern shore of Lake Genezareth, and so from the lower class as well. Together with J. they formed a community of life and fate and participated in his charismatic healings (Mk 6:7ff.). This implies leaving their families – and for the duration also their wives – and living a vagabond's lifestyle in poverty, corresponding to the self-stigmatization of charismatic movements, as described in religious-sociological studies. If J. himself created a circle of twelve, then this would represent the eschatologically restored twelve tribes of Israel. A wider range of followers, most of whom remained sedentary, but who provided new followers as well, supported the immediate discipleship as

patrons; they also included women (Mk 15:40f.; Lc 8:2f.). Often, a women-friendly, emancipatory tendency of the Jesus movement is assumed. [18]. Its egalitarian traits, however, are primarily due to its charismatism.

With the keyword 'Kingdom of God' or 'God's Reign' (*basileía tou theoû*) J. accentuates in his preaching, and especially with allegories, the new situation in the eschatological drama as opposed to John. This apocalyptical horizon of J.'s Gospel has again been controversial as of late, particularly among representatives of the third quest, mainly due to the preference for the (Gnostic) Gospel of Thomas [4; 7], but not rightly so. For the inclusion of J.'s proclamation of the Kingdom of God into an apocalyptic context, particularly its association with his preaching of the Last Judgement, can hardly be considered a mere retrospective Christian interpretation. J. explains his charismatic healings as partial and contemporary presence of the apocalyptic Kingdom of God (Mt 12:28/Lc 11:20), which has come closer, but remains by and large in the future (Mt 6:11; Lc 11:2f. *et passim*). The keyword is prepared in the Bible, and otherwise only occurs in post-biblical Jewish writings. It obviously represents a symbol of a divine (ideal) reign, which can be actualized in times of crisis, in which the evil powers have been defeated and hardship and deprivation of any kind have been abolished. The destitute and needy, as well as the (orphaned) children, who are awarded God's Kingdom unconditionally (Lc 6:20f.; Mk 9:33ff.; 10:14f.), are considered the core of the eschatological collection of God's people. This shows J.'s claim to be the agent and enforcer of a Kingdom of God, destined to heal the Jewish society of poverty, economic and religious hardship. This corresponds to social-integrative behaviour as shown by his meals together with sinners and tax collectors (Mk 2:13ff.). In allegories (Lc 15:1ff.; Mt 20:1ff.) he defends this against criticism. Although starting points may be found here for the later spreading of the belief in Christ among non-Jews in the Mediterranean centres, these peoples appear in J.'s apocalyptical concept only marginally, not programmatically.

J. does not fundamentally question the institutions, basic beliefs or common practices of Judaism. Certainly there is criticism, such as of the events in the temple, connected possibly with prophecies of disaster and divine punishment (Mk 11:1ff.; 14:58). There is also a partially differing interpretation of the Torah, especially of the Sabbath → *Halakhah* (the Pharisean principle that mortal danger overrides the Sabbath is extended to the emergency of hunger: Mk 2:23ff. *et passim*), the right to divorce (similar to the Pharisean school of Shammai, divorce is only allowed in case of adultery: Mt 5:32 *et passim*) and the meal and purity regulations (ethical purity of the heart prevails over ritual purity: Mk 7:1ff.). Also radicalized, in accordance with the social-integrative trait of J.'s teachings, are the traditional commands of solidarity of Judaism (brotherly love, also towards the enemy, renunciation of violence,

duty to reconciliation, debt relief: Lc 6:20–49/Mt 5–7).
A discussion of the power-political and socio-economic
problems is missing, as is a criticism of the Jewish elite.
Rich people are criticized wholesale. Conflicts with
Pharisees, Sadducees and scholars are, when not retrojections from later Christian-Jewish conflicts, motivated by differing interpretations of basic beliefs and
practices of Judaism.

3. THE FATE OF JESUS

J.'s end in Jerusalem stands in the context of a traditional exercise in piety, the pilgrimage of Passover. The
representations of the Passion are, in part, contradictory, the assumptions regarding older traditions behind
them exceedingly hypothetical. It is more than likely
that tendentious retrojections from experiences of conflict in later times shape these representations, with
apologetical interests in the defence against Roman
criminalization of Christians being at play. The only
fact to be considered as certain is that J., in a Roman
trial, (→ coercitio), was judged and executed by crucifixion, as was usual for provincials, at the hands of the
prefect Pontius Pilate, present in Jerusalem because of
the pilgrimage festival, charged as rebel (robber) or
(bandit) anti-king (title on the Cross: 'King of the
Jews'). An antecedent Jewish process (before the → Synhedrion) must be excluded, any Jewish involvement,
even on a semi-official level, is unlikely [6; 8]. As for the
dating of the day of his death, the Gospels agree insofar
as they name the same day of the week (Friday). It is
contentious whether this was the eve of Passover (14th
Nisah, as in Jo 18:28; 19:31) or the first day of Passover
(15th Nisah, as in the synoptic gospels). The dating of
the year of death varies accordingly. It must have been
during the tenure of the prefect Pontius Pilate (AD 27–
34). The chronology of John suggests the year 30
(nowadays commonly considered as the year of his
death) or 33, the synoptic chronology AD 27 or 34
[23. 152ff.].

C. JESUS CHRIST: OLDEST CHRISTOLOGY

As an apocalyptic-charismatic movement, J.'s appearances claim a mission from beginning on: he has
been sent as the authorized executor of the apocalyptic
Reign of God. Accordingly, the keyword 'belief' in the
synoptic tradition is to be connected with the miracle
tradition: belief means to consider J. capable of the
charismatic healing powers, which he has as proof of
the coming of the apocalyptic Kingdom. J. possibly considered himself a prophet. He probably also expected
his own martyrdom, given the fate of his teacher, admittedly – if the tradition of the Lord's supper is authentic –
in connection with the expectation that his death would
play a part in the history of salvation, leading to the
establishment of the Kingdom of God amongst his followers (cf. 1 Cor 11:23ff.; Mk 14:22ff.; Mt 26:26ff.).
Not very likely but controversial is the question of
whether he understood himself as → Messiah/Anoin-
ted, in the sense of the expectation of an ideal ruler in
the Davidic line. There are many arguments in favour of

the fact that this interpretation was only applied to him
after his execution as King of the Jews, and only in connection with a series of other messianic expectations
(especially the one of a Son of Man).

Certainly historical is the fact that, soon after the
execution of J., numerous visionary experiences occurred among his disciples and followers (1 Xor
15,3ff.), which, because they were considered appearances from heaven, were interpreted to the effect that
the dead J. had been resurrected and taken-up to
Heaven. This interpretation is based upon the Jewish
theology of martyrdom. At the same time it unfolds the
apocalyptic self-image even further, insofar as it associates the ascent to heaven with the institution of the
position of a heavenly ruler as Son of God and → Kyrios
(Rom 1:3ff.). According to the oldest synoptic tradition, J. is also attributed the role of Son of Man, a heavenly figure, who is, according to Jewish apocalyptics
(Ethiopian Hen 37–71; 4 Ezra 13 adopting the metaphorical tradition of the Son of Man in Dan 7) the com-
municator of the apocalyptic judgement and of the salvation coming from heaven, as well as the leader of the
heavenly army (Ethiopian Hen 48,10; 52,4 also identifies him as the Messiah). It is controversial whether J.
himself referred or related to such a figure [23. 447ff.].
In any case, all titles applied to J. stand in the context of
a messianic-apocalyptic interpretation according to
which his earthly appearance and fate are part of an
apocalyptic initiative of Salvation by God, ending with
the early arrival of the resurrected J. as ruler. Accordingly, J. is integrated early on (Phil 2,6ff.) in an extensive conceptual framework, based on which he was sent
to earth for Salvation as the pre-existing Son of God,
then returned to heaven after his (expiatory) death,
where he stands by for the consummation as eschatological Judge, Saviour and Ruler. This Christological
development is connected, in religious-sociological
terms, with the depersonalization of the charisma in the
Jesus-movement and contains, at the same time, elements of universalization, which favoured its spreading to the urban centres of the Mediterranean.

→ Bible; → Christianity; → Gospels (literary forms);
→ Jerusalem; → Judaism

1 J.B. AUFHAUSER, Ant. J.-Zeugnisse (Kleine Texte 126),
³1925   2 F.F. BRUCE, J. and Christian origins outside the
New Testament, 1984   3 M.J. BORG, J. in Contemporary
Scholarship, 1994   4 Id., J. a new vision, 1987
5 C. BURCHARD, J. von Nazareth, in: J. BECKER (ed.), Die
Anfänge des Christentums, 1987, 12–58   6 C. COHN,
Der Prozeß und Tod J. aus jüdischer Sicht, 1997   7 J.D.
CROSSAN, The historical J., 1994   8 Id., Who Killed J.?,
Exposing the Roots of Anti-Semitism in the Gospel Story
of the Death of J., 1995   9 C.A. EVANS, Life of J. Re-
search. An Annotated Bibliography (New Testament
Tools and Studies 13), 1989   10 D. FLUSSER, J. in Selbst-
zeugnissen und Bilddokumenten, 1968   11 J. KLAUSNER,
J. von Nazareth, ²³1952   12 H. KOESTER, Ancient Chris-
tian Gospels. Their History and Development, 1990
13 J. MAIER, J. von Nazareth in der talmudischen Überl.,
1978   14 J.P. MEIER, A Marginal Jew. Rethinking the
Historical J., Vol. 1, 1991; Vol. 2, 1994   15 R. RIESNER, J.

als Lehrer. Eine Unt. zum Ursprung der Evangelien-Überl. (WUNT 2. Reihe 7), ⁴1993   16 E. P. SANDERS, Judaism. Practice and Belief 63 BCE – 66CE, 1992   17 Id., The historical figure of J., 1993   18 E. SCHÜSSLER-FIORENZA, Zu ihrem Gedächtnis ... Eine feministische Rekonstruktion der christl. Ursprünge, 1988   19 A. SCHWEITZER, Gesch. der Leben-Jesu-Forschung, ⁹1984   20 E. SCHWEIZER, J., das Gleichnis Gottes. Was wissen wir wirklich vom Leben J.?, 1995   21 M. SMITH, Auf der Suche nach dem histor. J, 1974   22 E. STEGEMANN, W. STEGEMANN, Urchristl. Sozialgesch. Die Anfänge im Judentum und die Christusgemeinden in der mediterranen Welt, ²1997   23 G. THEISSEN, A. MERZ, Der histor. J. Ein Lehrbuch, ²1997   24 G. THEISSEN, D. WINTER, Die Kriterienfrage in der Jesusforsch. (Novum testamentum et orbis antiquus 34), 1997   25 G. VERMES, J. der Jude, 1993   26 B. WITHERINGTON III, The J. Quest. The Third Search for the Jew of Nazareth, 1995.   E.STE.

Jeu see → Nag Hammadi

Jevenstedt in the county of Rendsburg (Schleswig-Holstein). Burial ground of the Germanic pre-Roman Iron Age (6th–4th cents. BC) furnished with painted pottery vessels and iron slag, which indicates a privileged position within the → Jastorf culture and points to early iron production through contacts with the → Hallstatt culture. The presence of iron ore and slag mounds in the area is known, but cannot definitely be assigned.

→ Germanic archaeology; → Iron

    H. HINGST, Jevenstedt, 1974.   V.P.

Jewellery Material and motifs indicate that jewellery in antiquity could be thought of as warding off evil or bringing luck. Not only men, women and children, but also idols wore jewellery. Jewellery was also often used as grave goods.
I. NEAR EAST   II. EGYPT   III. PHOENICIA
IV. CLASSICAL ANTIQUITY   V. CELTO-GERMANIC
REGION

I. NEAR EAST
    Beads made of shell and bone (later also wood) are again and again found in graves from the 7th/6th millennia BC. Gold and silver jewellery is known from the middle of the 3rd millennium BC from the Near East, sometimes with inlaid semiprecious stones, and in a great variety of forms (pearls, earrings, pendants, diadems, hair coils, rings) [20]. In this period, the granulation technique (see below IV), which had probably spread outwards from Mesopotamia, was already being used. Similarly sumptuous jewellery was found in → Troy (Layer II) [5]. Only at the beginning of the 2nd millennium BC did pendants exist in the form of praying goddesses [12th fig. 62]; from this time until the end of the ancient Near Eastern cultures, circular pendants with stars and rosettes [12. 140–149. fig. 108–109. 111–112], which can be associated with the god-

desses → Ishtar and → Astarte, were also widespread. In this context also belong the pendants widespread in the Levant, made of thin films of metal tapering downwards, with full or abbreviated representations of a naked goddess with an Egyptian hairstyle [12. 138–140. fig. 102–107]. Jewellery from the first half of the 1st millennium BC is known first and foremost from Neo-Assyrian reliefs [10. pl. 8–9]; besides earrings and chains, here, for the first time, animal head armrings appear [18. 50]. Very few items of jewellery from this period have been excavated so far [4]. They show i.a. the use of émail cloisonné [2]. In the following Persian period the neck ring was added as a new form of jewellery, influenced by the peoples of the steppes [18. 83–85]; Hellenistic and ancient Oriental elements were interwoven in the Arsacid period (Parthian period) [11. 282–285].
    From the 2nd millennium BC, jewellery production in the Levant was also orientated towards Egypt, while in the territory of Asia Minor separate traditions dominated. It is only in these western areas that fibulae (→ Needle) are attested in great numbers as part of the dress in the 1st millennium BC [16; 18. 229–231].

II. EGYPT
    Although jewellery of the highest quality, including some with figurative inlays, is already known from the Old Kingdom [19. fig. 8], the Middle Kingdom must be seen as the time when jewellery really flourished, as the works of this period are exceedingly fine [9. 668]. The ring was added as a new shape, perhaps influenced by Cretan tradition. The great variety of New Kingdom jewellery has become particularly well-known from the finds in the tomb of → Tutenchamun [3. pl. 75–86]. In the late period jewellery still shows signs of Egyptian tradition, whereas in the Ptolemaic epoch Greek influence clearly emerges.
    Apart from the usual forms, such as rings, bracelets and chains, must be mentioned in particular pectorals, mostly made in the cell technique [6; 7; 8]. These were popular from the Middle Kingdom onwards; often crowned by the winged sun or the magic eyes of Horus (Udjat), they depict heraldic scenes of gods. Equally typically Egyptian – and, unlike in Mesopotamia, very numerous – are pendants in the form of small figures of gods made of gold, but also of frit. The latter have been found in very large numbers. They were widespread in many countries of the ancient world, as were frit pendants in the form of hieroglyphs [13].
    The jewellery from → Meroë from the period around the birth of Christ, known because of its abundance of gold [17], while showing Egyptian elements, is nevertheless greatly interspersed by native tradition, sometimes supplemented with Hellenistic motifs and forms.

1 C. ANDREWS, Ancient Egyptian Jewellery, 1990   2 J. BOESE, U. RÜSS, s. v. Goldschmiedetechniken, RLA 3, 519–531   3 H. CARTER, The Tomb of Tutankhamun, vol. 2, 1927   4 M S. B. DAMERJI, Gräber assyr. Königinnen aus Nimrud, in: JRGZ 45, 1999 3–83   5 W. P. TOLSTIKOW, M. J. TREJSTER (ed.), Der Schatz aus Troja, Ausst.-Kat.

Moskau 1996/97 6 E. FEUCHT, Pektorale nicht königl. Personen, 1971 7 Id., s. v. Einlegearbeiten C., LÄ 1, 1208–1209 8 Id., s. v. Goldschmiedekunst, LÄ 2, 751–754 9 Id., s. v. Schmuck, LÄ 5, 668–670 (with extensive bibliography) 10 B. HROUDA, Die Kulturgesch. des assyr. Flachbildes, 1965 11 K. LIMPER, Uruk. Perlen, Ketten, Anhänger, 1988 12 K. R. MAXWELL-HYSLOP, Western Asiatic Jewellery c. 3000–612 B. C., 1971 13 C. MÜLLER-WINCKLER, Die äg. Objekt-Amulette, 1987 14 B. MUSCHE, Vorderasiat. Schmuck von den Anfängen bis zur Zeit der Achaemeniden (10.000–330 v. Chr.), 1992 15 Id., Vorderasiat. Schmuck zur Zeit der Arsakiden und der Sasaniden, 1988 16 F. PEDDE, Vorderasiat. Fibeln, 2000 17 K.-H. PRIESE, Das Gold von Meroe, Ausst.-Kat. Berlin 1992 18 E. REHM, Der Schmuck der Achämeniden, 1992 19 M. VILÍMKOVÁ, Altäg. Goldschmiedekunst, 1969 20 C. L. WOOLLEY, The Royal Cemetery (Ur Excavations vol. 2), 1934. E.RE.

III. PHOENICIA

The craft of jewellery-making was already blossoming in the Bronze Age in the region of the later Phoenician city states on the Syrian Levant coast. The jewellery from the royal tombs of the early 2nd millennium BC in → Byblus had been developed to the highest technical level and proves to be an amalgam of Mesopotamian and Egyptian influences. The late Bronze Age gold finds from the treasury (tomb construction?) of the palace complex of Kāmid el-Loz/Kumidi on the Beka'a plain (in the Phoenician hinterland) are evidence of the early development of the forms and features of Phoenician jewellery [1] characteristic of the 1st millennium BC, especially the decoration of surfaces with representational triangles made of granulation pearls and the type of diadem composed of rectangular and trapezoid sheets of metal in relief [2].

Phoenician jewellery, traded at the latest since the 9th cent. BC to Mediterranean aristocracies, led in the Aegean to the revival and in Etruria to the development of granulation and filigree techniques. From the 7th cent. BC, the most widespread items of jewellery, especially in the west, included disc, wine skin, spherical and leech pendants, rings with moving ring stone settings (for scarabs, among other things), as pendant earrings or worn in a necklace, the more complex of them decorated with granulation and filigree, or sometimes with inlays of gems or paste. Workshops can be identified with certainty in → Gades, → Carthage and → Tharrus.

Figurative decoration was usually orientated towards Egyptian models (winged sundisc, Horus falcon, Ureus snake, etc.); Phoenician jewellery had predominantly magic significance (amulet function). → Gem cutting

1 R. MIRON, Kamid el-Loz. Das Schatzhaus im Palastbereich. Die Funde, in: Saarbrücker Beitr. zur Altertumskunde 46, 1990, 45–61, pl. 1–10 2 H. G. NIEMEYER, Zw. Sichem und Aliseda: Bemerkungen zu einem orientalischen Schmucktypus und seiner Rezeption im Mittelmeerraum, in: E. ACQUARO (ed.), Alle soglie della classicità. FS S. Moscati, vol. 2, 1996, 881–887.

G. MARKOE, Phoenicians, 2000, 152–156; G. PISANO, Orfèvrerie, in: V. KRINGS (ed.), La civilisation phénicienne et punique (HbdOr I 20), 1995, 494–500; B. QUILLARD, Bijoux carthaginois, vol. 1: Les colliers, 1979; Id., Bijoux carthaginois, vol. 2: Porte-amulettes, sceaux-pendentifs, etc., 1987. H. G. N.

IV. CLASSICAL ANTIQUITY
A. INTRODUCTION B. MATERIALS C. TYPES
D. HISTORY E. TECHNIQUES

A. INTRODUCTION

The most important evidence for knowledge of ancient jewellery are the original finds from tombs, settlements and sanctuaries; added to this are finds from depositories or treasure-troves. They provide information on the diversity of shapes and types of ancient jewellery and also on technical changes and those dictated by fashion. Pictorial representations in vase painting, on statuary art works, wall paintings, mosaics, mummy portraits, coins, etc., together with the literary sources, complete the picture.

B. MATERIALS

Various materials were available for making jewellery in antiquity: → lead, → bronze, → iron, → elektron, → ivory, → glass (or glass pearls), → gold, → wood, bone, → pearls, clay and → silver, niello. There were also semiprecious stones and → precious stones (→ Gem cutting). The most prized precious metal was probably gold, which was found in almost all parts of the Mediterranean.

C. TYPES

Ancient forms of jewellery included necklaces (→ Neck ornaments), earrings and pendant earrings (→ Ear ornaments), bracelets and armrings (→ Bracelets), head jewellery (→ Diadem, → Wreath, hair jewellery), finger rings (→ Rings); in addition, special forms, such as amulets (→ Phylakterion), bullae, → crepundia and pectorals, in the wider sense also fibulae (→ Needle) and belt clasps, can be listed here; leg jewellery was represented by thigh bands (→ Periskelis) and ankle rings (e.g. Anth. Pal. 6,172; 206; 207 περισφύριον/perisphýrion, ἐπισφύριον/episphýrion). Body jewellery (τὸ περίαμμα/tò períamma, Lat. [ornamentum] mamilare) consisted of chains placed in a cross over the upper body, decorated with a large number of medallions.

Clothing jewellery was already very popular in the Mycenaean period (gold beads or thin gold leaves were in this case sewn on to garments). Individual finds from the archaic, late classical and Hellenistic periods suggest continuous popularity of this type of garment decoration (cf. Demosth. Meidias 22).

D. HISTORY
1. GREECE 2. ROME

1. GREECE

In the Aegean region jewellery finds from Troy (Layer II) and Crete are known from as early as the mid 3rd millennium BC, and from Aegina (London, BM) and the Thyreatis (→ Cynuria [1]; Berin, SM) from the 2nd millennium BC. Among the repertoire of forms are neck chains made of gold wire rings and pearls, diadems, hair jewellery, and ear and finger rings. The granulation and filigree techniques adopted from the Near East and Egypt were already appearing in Crete by the beginning of the 2nd millennium BC. Mycenaean jewellery, known principally from finds from the shaft-graves of → Mycenae (after 1600 BC, Athens, NM), is distinguished by austere ornamentation (spirals, concentric circles, rosettes) and a preference for symmetric-heraldic shapes. Materials used included gold, rock crystal, → amber, cornelian and → lapis lazuli.

After the decline of → Mycenaean culture Greek jewellery tended to be marked by simple shapes and sparing use of gold and other expensive materials. Bronze became the predominant working material. In the 8th cent. BC, through contacts with the Orient, the repertoire of representations was extended, in particular, plant and animal decoration, oriental motifs (sphinxes, griffins, winged horses) and human figures or mythological scenes now became popular, and gold became more common as a material. Jewellery from this and the archaic epochs is known from, among other places, sanctuaries (Samos, Olympia, Ephesus, Delphi); tomb finds are rarer (e.g. from Sindos, today in Thessalonica, Archaeological Mus.). A novelty of the classical period (5th and 4th cents. BC) was the extension of the technical repertoire: coloured → enamel appeared, and the filigree technique was used by preference. Additionally, animal and plant motifs, and also Aphrodite and Erotes figures were adopted to a greater extent into the pictorial repertoire. Finds from this period come principally from the outer zones of the Greek world (Rhodes, Cyprus, Black Sea area, Macedonia). In the Hellenistic period, the desire for polychromy becomes clear, expressed in the use of → precious stones (amethyst, rock crystal, beryl, garnet, cornelian, emerald, etc.). Colour effects were further achieved by coloured glass pastes.

2. ROME

Gold jewellery was already worn in the Roman Republic, as attested by a ban of the Law of the Twelve Tables (→ Tabulae duodecim 10,7) preventing gold being placed in tombs. The wearing of intricate and expensive jewellery was restricted in 215 BC by the Lex Oppia; the law decreed that no woman could own more than $^1/_2$ ounce of gold (13–14 g or three Roman gold coins), cf. Liv. 34,1 and Oppius [I 1]; the law was suspended in 195 BC, however. Nevertheless, there were constant complaints about the extravagant use of jewellery, which legislation tried to check (e.g. Suet. Iul.

43,1). The women of the Imperial household became particular targets for criticism in this respect (Plin. HN 9,117; cf. 33,40). The ladies of Roman society of the 1st cent. AD liked to wear bands or hair ornaments in their hair, rarely hair pins or a hair net; among the most popular items of jewellery were earrings and pendant earrings, but neck chains, several of which were sometimes worn at the same time, were also popular. Bracelets or armrings adorned wrists and upper arms, and women often wore identical versions on each arm. → Rings were initially customary only on the ring finger of the left hand, but as fashions changed, thumbs, index fingers and little fingers also became adorned with rings (Plin. HN 33,1; 24). Gem rings, which probably served as signet rings (→ Seal), were the most popular of rings. In general a preference for geometric patterns and shapes can be seen in Roman jewellery. The effect of the smooth metal surface which, by contrast with Etruscan and Hellenistic jewellery, was not broken up by granulation or similar techniques, was also favoured. In the course of the 1st, and even more in the course of the 2nd cent. AD, application of coloured stones to the smooth metal surface increased, and a further characteristic was the increased use of works of enamel.

At the end of the 2nd cent. AD, precious metal coins worked into chains, medallions and bracelets brought a new variation to the range of jewellery, which continued beyond late antiquity into the early Middle Ages. Likewise, at the end of the 2nd cent., a new decorative technique was introduced with the opus interrasile (see below E.), which gained significance in the 3rd and 4th cents. and reached its full glory principally in Byzantine jewellery.

E. TECHNIQUES

One of the first of the ancient techniques for designing jewellery was engraving, which was used in all periods. This was the carving out of the material (removal of filings) using a graving tool made of bronze or iron in order to apply a figurative or ornamental pattern. Equally as widespread as engraving was chasing: this involved beating decorative patterns into the surface of the metal with a hammer and chasing tool.

Enamel achieves its effect through its special variety of colours. Indented grooves were already present in the casting mould for items of jewellery, mostly cast of bronze (grooved enamel), or they were put in by chasing and engraving. The molten glass mass coloured with metal oxides was sealed into the indentations.

A setting was used to frame and hold a precious stone or a gem. It could have various shapes (e.g. round, oval, box-shaped), depending on the shape of the stone. Its upper edge was pressed down to hold the stone. Stones with holes bored through them could be pinned on or held by wires (later medieval madder setting).

Filigree (Lat. filum = thread; granum = corn) means decoration with gold or silver wire; the wire, could be applied as a round, notched or pearl wire or moulded into a separate item of jewellery in perforated work. A special effect was achieved by corded wire, created by torque (rotating) or twisting of one or more wires.

In granulation, very tiny particles of gold and silver were heated in charcoal dust, until they formed small balls (granules), which were then sorted according to size. They were then stuck to the surface to be decorated with organic lime; copper salt was applied and heated, causing reduction of the copper by means of the lime burning to form carbon. This produced a firm bond between the granulated metal and the metal base. Filigree and granulation are among the oldest techniques and are attested in Greek jewellery as early as the 3rd millennium BC (Trojan jewellery).

In repoussé, indentations were worked into the basic metal with a flat graving tool by digging in underneath it at the side, and filling in these indentations by hammering in different coloured soft leaves of metal (fine gold of silver). The method in the 'niello technique' (from *nigellum*, 'blackish') was different; the motif, predominantly engraved in silver, more rarely in gold, was filled with a metal paste (mainly consisting of lead and silver sulphide), which was dark grey to black, depending on the ratio of the mixture; after heating and grinding, this mass stood out impressively from the brightly shining metal background.

In the late 2nd cent. AD a new technique appeared. Great decorative effect was achieved with *opus interrasile* by ornamentally piercing sheet gold by perforating most of its surface using graving or chasing tools. The resulting mesh could be enriched with inset stones or pearls.

→ Bracelets; → Ear → Neck ornaments; ornaments; → Rings; → Torques

H. HOFFMANN, P. F. DAVIDSON, Greek Gold. Jewellery from the Age of Alexander, 1965; E. BIELEFELD, Schmuck (ArchHom I C), 1968; A. GREIFENHAGEN, Schmuck-Arbeiten in Edelmetall, vol. 1, 1970; vol. 2, 1975; B. PFEILER, Röm. Gold-Schmuck des 1. und 2. Jh. n. Chr. nach datierten Funden, 1970; I. BLANCK, Stud. zum griech. Hals-Schmuck der archa. und klass. Zeit, 1974; ST. G. MILLER, Two Groups of Thessalian Gold, 1979; R. HIGGINS, Greek and Roman Jewellery, ²1980; J. OGDEN, Jewellery of the Ancient World, 1982; T. HACKENS, R. WINKES (ed.), Gold Jewelry. Craft, Style and Meaning from Mycenae to Constantinopolis, 1983; E. M. DE JULIIS (ed.), Gli ori di Taranto in età ellenistica, Ausst. Milano 1984, Hamburg 1989; B. DEPPERTZ-LIPPITZ, Griech. Gold-Schmuck, 1985; M. PFROMMER, Unt. zur Chronologie früh- und hochhell. Gold-Schmuck (IstForsch. 37), 1990; F. FALK (ed.), Gold aus Griechenland. Schmuck und Kleinodien aus dem Benaki-Museum Athen, Ausst. Pforzheim 1992; L. PIRZIO STEFANELLI, L'oro dei Romani. Gioielli di età imperiale, 1992; C. REINHOLDT, Der Thyreatis-Hortfund in Berlin. Unt. zum vormyk. Edelmetall-Schmuck in Griechenland, in: MDAI(A) 108, 1993, 1–41; T. G. DAMM, B. SCHNEIDER, Gold-Schmuck der röm. Frau, Ausst. Köln 1993; D. WILLIAMS, J. OGDEN, Greek Gold. Jewellery of the Classical World, 1994; W. RUDOLPH, A Golden Legacy. Ancient Jewelry from the Burton Y. Berry Collection, Ausst. Bloomington 1995; M. EFFINGER, Minoischer Gold-Schmuck (British Archaeological Reports, International Series 646), 1996; A. BÖHME-SCHÖNBERGER, Kleidung und Schmuck in Rom und den Prov. (Schriften des Limesmuseums Aalen 50), 1997; K. DEMAKOPOULOU (ed.), Gods and Heroes of the European Bronze Age, Europe at the Time of Ulysses, 1999; M. A. GUGGISBERG, Der Goldschatz von Erstfeld. Ein kelt. Bilderzyklus zw. Mitteleuropa und dem Mittelmeerwelt, 2000; E. DESPINIS, ΑΡΧΑΙΑ ΧΡΥΣΑ ΚΟΣΜΗΜΑΤΑ, 1996.   R. H.

V. CELTO-GERMANIC REGION
see → Germanic archaeology

Jewish-Hellenistic Literature see → Literature

Jewish Wars Term for a series of violent conflicts between Jews and non-Jews in the eastern Mediterranean between the 2nd cent. BC and the 2nd cent. AD, beginning with the Maccabean revolt against the → Seleucids (→ Maccabees; → Judas [1] Maccabaeus). In the narrower sense, the three major Jewish revolts against Roman rule in the 1st and 2nd cents. AD.

I. THE 'JEWISH WAR' II. THE DIASPORA REVOLT III. THE BAR KOCHBA REVOLT IV. IMPACT

I. THE 'JEWISH WAR'
The best-known – thanks to the completely preserved works of the Jewish historian and contemporary → Iosephus [4] Flavius – conflict (AD 66–70) began in the spring/summer of 66 as a protest revolt against the Roman procurator of Iudaea, → Gessius Florus. He had taken a large sum of money from the Jewish temple treasury – in Jewish eyes a severe sacrilege (→ Temple III.) – probably to cover outstanding tax debts. The disturbances spread quickly and combined with local conflicts between the Jewish ethnical group and the non-Jewish neighbouring cities, as well as between Jews and non-Jews in those cities. The actual revolt began with the refusal to perform the daily sacrifice for the Emperor in the summer of 66. The governor of → Syria (with map), → Cestius [II 3] Gallus, attempted to gain control of Jerusalem in the autumn, but had to withdraw with heavy losses.

As a result, the command in Iudaea was transferred to → Vespasianus. In the course of the year 67, he subjugated Galilee in a series of sieges and brought the entire country, with the exception of Jerusalem and a few fortresses, back under Roman control by the end of 69, although the military operations on the Roman side were interrupted again and again because of the confusion after the downfall of → Nero [1] (→ Year of four emperors). On the Jewish side, serious battles broke out between several combating ideological and/or political power factions (most important leaders: → Simon [9] bar Giora and → Iohannes [2] of Gischala). Following its nearly five-month-long siege by Vespasianus' son → Titus [3] in the spring/summer of 70, the city was completely razed, the population massacred or enslaved, and the → temple (III.) burned down as a symbol of determined Jewish political and religious resistance. An epilogue was the storming of the Sicarii (→ Zealots) fortress → Masada in AD 73 or 74.

II. THE DIASPORA REVOLT

This revolt (AD 115–117) – difficult to track in the sources – probably broke out in close connection with the Parthian campaign of → Traianus [1] and the uprising of the population of Babylonia against the Roman conquerors. It included, above all, Cyrenaica, Egypt, and Cyprus; its spread to Judaea itself is disputed. Here, too, the Roman-Jewish battles were accompanied by bloody disputes between Jews and local non-Jews. The result was primarily the expulsion of the Jews from Cyprus and the collapse of the position of Judaism in Egypt, which had been important until then.

III. THE BAR KOCHBA REVOLT

The sources are also meagre here, although along with the fragments handed down from Graeco-Roman and Talmudic literature (→ Talmud) as well as the coinage of the rebels, documentary sources have recently come to light with the papyrus finds from the Dead Sea [1. 229]. The uprising (AD 132–135) included large parts of Judaea, perhaps also parts of the neighbouring areas settled by Jews (Galilee is unclear); it temporarily tied down a Roman military force composed of parts of 12–13 legions [2]. This time there was a leading figure with clearly Messianic pretensions, who was probably recognized by the majority of the Jewish population, (cf. → Messiah): → Bar Kochba ('Son of a Star'), titled *Nāsi' Yisra'ēl* ('Prince of Israel') on his coins. According to the papyrus finds, the rebels were tightly organized. Disputed in both sources and research is the question of exactly what chronological and logical connection the ban on circumcision by → Hadrianus and the re-founding of Jerusalem as the Roman *Colonia Aelia Capitolina* (cf. → *Coloniae*) has with the revolt (cause or effect?). The war resulted in heavy losses to the Jewish population through death and enslavement, and for the first time since about 100 BC the Jews were a minority in Palestine.

IV. IMPACT

Besides the destruction of the autonomous Jewish community in Judaea-Palestine and the radical demographic changes, the Jewish Wars also determined the character of the inner development of → Judaism to a considerable extent: the end of the temple cult and the deprivation of power and destruction of the priestly aristocracy ultimately prepared the way for the development of Rabbinic Judaism. Furthermore, particularly the catastrophe of AD 70 made an enduring impact on Jewish (and Christian) historical consciousness. In the Roman context, the radical nature of the Jewish revolts and their suppression is unparalleled in this period (→ Tolerance). Attempts to explain this in modern research range from the particular socio-economic and socio-political problems of Judaea to specific Jewish ideological conditions (apocalypticism, Messianism).

However, only the Bar Kochba revolt appears to have produced a religious Messiah figure clearly recognized by a majority.

→ Jerusalem; → Juda and Israel II.; → Judaism; → Palaestina; → Tolerance; → JUDAISM

1 H. M. COTTON et al., The Papyrology of the Roman Near East: A Survey, in: JRS 85, 1995, 214–235 2 W. ECK, The Bar Kokhba Revolt: The Roman Point of View, in: JRS 89, 1999, 76–89.

E. BALTRUSCH, Die Juden und das Röm. Reich, 2002; M. GOODMAN, The Ruling Class of Judaea: The Origins of the Jewish Revolt against Rome A. D. 66–70, 1987; M. HENGEL, Die Zeloten, ²1976; F. G. B. MILLAR, The Roman Near East, 1993; P. SCHÄFER, Der Bar Kokhba-Aufstand, 1981; SCHÜRER, vol. 1; E. M. SMALLWOOD, The Jews under Roman Rule, 1976. JÖ. GE.

Jezira, Sefer ha- (Hebrew 'Book of creation'). Attempt at a systematic description of the fundamental principles of the world order. This Hebrew text, comprising only a few pages and extant in three different recensions, was probably written between the 3rd and 6th cent. and thus is one of the oldest texts of Jewish esoteric writing. In the first part, the ten original numbers, and in the second part the twenty-two letters of the Hebrew alphabet are presented as elements of creation through whose combination God created the world 'on secret paths of wisdom'. Microcosm-macrocosm speculations that create links between the human body, the world of the stars, and the order of time play a significant role, especially in the explanations of letter-combinations that are said to be endowed with secret powers. Aside from early Jewish concepts of creation, ideas from late Hellenistic and late Neoplatonist → Number mysticism are also to be found. The work, with its often very opaque and obscure manner of expression, was the basis of numerous comm. from the early Middle Ages onwards.

J. DAN, The Ancient Jewish Mysticism, 1993, 198–211; L. GOLDSCHMIDT, Sepher Jezirah. Das Buch der Schöpfung, 1894 (repr. 1969); I. GRUENWALD, Some Critical Notes on the First Part of the Sēfer Yezīrā, in: Rev. des Études Juives 132, 1973, 475–528; J. MAIER, Die Kabbalah. Einführung – Klassische Texte – Erläuterungen, 1995, 38–43; PH. MERLAN, Zur Zahlenlehre im Platonismus und im Sefer Yezira, in: Journ. of the History of Philosophy 3, 1965, 167–181; G. SCHOLEM, Die jüd. Mystik in ihren Hauptströmungen, 1967, 81–84. B.E.

Job Central figure in the eponymous book of the Bible, one of the *K'tūbīm*, the writings, in the Hebrew canon. The etymology of the name leads us to an apparently Edomite word *Ayyab*, which can be translated approximately as 'penitent, convert'. The Hebrew *'Iyōb* suggests the word 'enemy' so that the name can also mean 'the one treated with hostility' (sc. by God). The Edomite J., whose fear of God is put to a hard test by God himself through the intervention of Satan, indeed complains about his fate, but always remains faithful and devoted to God and is rewarded by God for his sufferings towards the end of his life.

The idea of the suffering just man subsequently found its expression in post-Biblical literature; in the Talmud the person and biographical details of J. are certainly contentious – including the statement that J. never lived, and that he and his lot should only be regarded as a parable. J.'s path of suffering is described graphically in the → Haggadah; in his (religious) significance, he is, although not an Israelite, equated with the Patriarchs.

A. BERLINER, Zur Auslegung des Buches Ijob, 1913; R. EKKER, Die arab. Job-Übersetzung des Gaon Saadja ben Josef, 1962; G. FOHRER, Das Buch Hiob, 1963; N. GLATZER, The dimensions of Job, 1969; P. HUBER, Hiob, Dulder oder Rebell?, 1986; J. LÉVÊQUE, Job et son Dieu, 1970; A. KÜNZLI, Gotteskrise: Fragen zu Hiob, 1998; N. TUR-SINAI (TORCYNER), The book of Job, 1957; P. ZERAFA, The wisdom of God in the book of Job, 1978; J. ZIEGLER, Beiträge zum griech. Iob, 1985.   Y.D.

Job market With BOHANNAN and DALTON we can distinguish between the market a) as a place and b) as a price-regulating mechanism of supply and demand [1]. While a job market in the sense of b) did not develop in antiquity, work was available like other goods in the marketplace. It could either be bought permanently in the form of a slave, or temporarily 'lent' by a free wage-earner (Latin *locatio*; Menander Sam. 189–95; Plaut. Trin. 843 f; 853 f.). Conversely, everyone could offer his work at the market (Mt 20:1–16). In Athens, there was a special area of the agora (κολονος μίσθιος/kolonós místhios) where wage-earners (ἐργάτης, μισθωτής, θής; Latin *mercenarii*) offered their work (Schol. Aesch. I 125; Schol. Eur. I p. 411, 9–13; Schol. Aristoph. Av. 997; Etym. m., s. v. *Kolonós*; Harp./Suda s. v. *Kolonétas*; Poll. 7.32 ff.). This corresponded with the division of the agora into κύκλοι/kýkloi (rings) in which goods (σκευή/skeué) and slaves (σώματα/sómata) were sold (Hesych. s. v. κύκλοι/kykloi; Poll. 7.11). Specialized work could be found in the various areas within or close to the market, where certain trades were concentrated (e.g. cooks in so-called μαγειρεῖαι/mageireíai: Theophr. char. 6.9; Antiphanes fr. 203 KOCK II 98, smiths near the Hephaiston: Anecd. Bekk. 1,316,23, potters in the Keramaikos). As can be seen from the Greek building industry, specialized work was in short supply and the situation of unqualified workers was precarious because of the irregularity of jobs. Artisans had to be mobile and were recruited for special projects (temple construction, weapon production) from other cities. In this way the Epidaurians looked for workers from a large number of towns, so that they could carry out their temple building project [2]. On the other hand, construction work came to a standstill in times of war, not only because of a shortage of money, but also because of the lack of a workforce. Economically related wage fluctuations and competition between workers are not known, rather salaries were determined according to how much specialized knowledge and learnt skill a job required. Incentives were not provided through wages, but through privileges, legal protection and special honours [4].

1 P. BOHANNAN, W. DALTON, Markets in Africa, 1962, 1–10   2 A. M. BURFORD, The Economics of Greek Temple Building, in: PCPhS 11, 1965, 21–34   3 J. A. CROOK, Law and Life of Rome, 1967   4 P. H. DAVIS, The Delian Building Contracts, in: BCH 61, 1937, 119   5 A. FUKS, Kolonos Misthios. Labour Exchange in Classical Athens, in: Id., Social Conflict in Ancient Greece, 1984, 303–305   6 R. E. WYCHERLEY, The Market of Athens. Topography and Monuments, in: G&R; 3, 1956, 2–23.   S.v.R.

John see → Iohannes

Jokes (γελοῖον/geloîon; Lat. *dicacitas, facetiae, iocus, ridiculum, sal, urbanitas*; for terminology cf. [1. 754–757]).
A. JOKES IN EVERYDAY LIFE   B. THEORY OF THE JOKE

A. JOKES IN EVERYDAY LIFE
Like us, the ancients enjoyed telling a joke (for the joke culture of the Romans cf. [2; 3]). Jokes were also written down *risus gratia* (for enjoyment: Quint. Inst. 6,3,65). The only completely preserved ancient collection of jokes is written in Greek, the → *Philógelōs* (4th/5th cents. AD). From Plautus, we know that such collections existed long before, and that they were not confined to private entertainment, but also used almost professionally (Plaut. Stich. 400 f.; 454–457). So-called *scurrae* (Cic. Quinct. 11) and γελωτοποιοί/gelōtopoioí (Ath. 613d) could earn their living as → entertainers by telling jokes (Plaut. Stich. 218–232; Plaut. Capt. 482 f.; Mart. 6,44), especially at → banquets (cf. Ath. 614c; Plut. Symp. 629c; Hor. Sat. 2,8,21 f.; 2,8,80–85; Macrob. Sat. 1,1,2), but also, for example, at weddings (Catull. 61,126 f.). In the Imperial period, there was also the option of seeking employment as a court jester [4. 88 f.].

The jokes preserved in the *Philógelōs* mock, above all, *scholastikoí* (here in the sense of learned fools) and the inhabitants of certain cities (Abderites, Sidonians, Cumaeans); however, the thematic variety of ancient jokes was much larger. Greek and Latin primarily Greek and Latin → comedies, → satires and → epigrams (literary documents are collected in [5]) show that anything and anyone could become the butt of a joke, as do numerous anecdotes preserved in → Buntschriftstellerei and → biographies (for example, Diog. Laert. 6,20–81 on the Cynic → Diogenes [14]). A telling proverb said: *potius amicum quam dictum perdere* ('better to lose a friend than a punch-line': Quint. Inst. 6,3,28). Just as many jokes were made about slaves (Cic. De or. 2,248) or certain professions, such as doctors (Anth. Pal. 11,112–126; Mart. 1,30), as about political and cultural figures, such as when → Aristophanes [3] caricatured

Socrates in the 'Clouds' or Lucilius, in his satires, gossiped about the entire city (*urbem defricuit*: Hor. Sat. 1,10,4). Jokes could be based on erotic preferences (Hor. Sat. 1,2,28–72; Mart. 9,69 et *passim*), linguistic blunders (Catull. 84; Suet. Gram. 22,1), laziness (Philogelos 211–213 THIERFELDER; Anth. Pal. 11,276 f.), or on excess or lack of personal hygiene (Hor. Sat. 1,2,27; Anth. Pal. 11,241 f.). There were no inhibitions about making fun of physical anomalies (Cic. De or. 2,239; Mart. 1,19) – as in the → *grylloi* or → caricatures. During the → Saturnalia, a *dominus* would not be safe from the impertinence (*licentia*) of his slaves (Hor. Sat. 2,7), nor a commander from the jokes of his legionaries during a → triumphal procession (*ioci militares*: Liv. 5,49,7; Vell. Pat. 2,67,4; Suet. Iul. 49,4; 51; Mart. 1,4,3 f.; 7,8,7 f.).

There existed many collections of witty sayings by public figures. It is said that Caesar had several compilations made of such ἀποφθέγματα/*apophthégmata*, and that he could always tell a genuine Cicero from a false one (Cic. Fam. 9,16,4). Cicero's *dicta* (examples in Quint. Inst. 6,3,73–77; Cic. De or. 2,275; Plut. Mor. 205; cf. also [6]) were circulating in a three-volume edition (possibly edited by his secretary Tiro [1]: Quint. Inst. 6,3,5). Comparable collections existed from, for example, → Domitius [III 1] Afer (Quint. Inst. 6,3,42).

B. THEORY OF THE JOKE

Philosophy and rhetoric examined the *geloîon* or *ridiculum* scientifically and soberly. Plato [1] defined it as something unpleasant (πονηρία/*ponēría*), composed of a mixture of joy (ἡδονή/*hēdoné*) and grief (λύπη/*lýpē*; Pl. Phlb. 48a–50b). It was extensively treated by Aristotle [6] in that portion of the 'Poetics' which is lost today (cf. Aristot. Rh. 1372a 1 f.; 1419b 6 f.). He considered it a subtype of the nasty (αἰσχρόν/*aischrón*, Lat. *turpe*: Aristot. Poet. 1449a 33 f.) and thought it the intention (τέλος/*télos*) of comedy [cf. 7. 306 f.]. For him, laughing stemmed from the non-fulfilment of an expectation (Aristot. Rh. 1412a); it expressed surprise and deception (Aristot. Pr. 965a). Theophrastus even dedicated a whole book Περὶ γελοίου/*Perì geloíou* (not preserved) to the subject (Diog. Laert. 5,46), and Cicero (Cic. De or. 2,217) speaks vaguely of several Greek treatises *De ridiculis*.

Cicero developed a theory of the *ridiculum*, rooted in Peripatetic views (cf. [7. 309]), in the second book of *De oratore* (Cic. De or. 2,216–289), to which Quintilianus [1] later referred (Quint. Inst. 6,3): even if jokes defy any workable definition and useful classification, (Quint. Inst. 6,3,7; 6,3,35), an orator must train his witticisms as part of his education, in order to make judge and jury laugh at the right moment (Cic. De or. 2,236; cf. already Gorg. fr. 82 B 12 DK; Dem. Or. 23,206). It must be admitted, however, that the possibilities of *ars* in this case are limited (Quint. Inst. 6,3,11).

In antiquity, the primary distinction was between verbal jokes and physical jokes (Cic. De or. 2,248;

Quint. Inst. 6,3,22; Tractatus Coislinianus 3 = CGF 50–53). Verbal jokes would be, for instance, the play on a person's name – very popular at the time –, e.g. Cicero's *ius verrinum* ('Verres' law', but also 'pork broth': Cic. Verr. 2,1,121) or Trimalchio's *Carpe, Carpe*! (Petron. Sat. 36,5–8; cf. also the forced staging of a verbal joke in Petron. Sat. 41,6–8). Physical jokes include mimicking (Cic. De or. 2,242).

The material for jokes is found in the same *loci* which the → *inventio* cites for finding arguments (Cic. De or. 2,248–250; Quint. Inst. 6,3,65). Appropriateness (*aptum*) must be taken into consideration when joking (cf. Cic. De or. 2,221; Quint. Inst. 6,3,28) so as not to appear as a buffoon (*scurra*; Cic. De or. 2,247). *Scurrilitas* was to be avoided at all costs by orators (Cic. De or. 2,244; Cic. Orat. 88; Quint. Inst. 6,3,29; Tac. Dial. 22,5); indeed, in educated circles, *scurra* was almost considered a swear-word (Cic. Phil. 13,23).

→ Comedy; → Entertainer; → Satire

1 G. LUCK, s. v. Humor, RAC 16, 1994, 753–773 2 K.-W. WEEBER, s. v. W., in: Id., Alltag im Alten Rom, 1998, 408–410 3 G. VOGT-SPIRA, Das satirische Lachen der Römer und die Witzkultur der Oberschicht, in: S. JÄKEL (ed.), Laughter Down the Centuries, vol. 3, 1997, 117–129 4 FRIEDLÄNDER, vol. 1, ¹⁰1922 (repr. 1964) 5 K.-W. WEEBER, Humor in der Ant., 1991 6 W. G. SCHNEIDER, Vom Salz Ciceros. Zum polit. Witz, Schmäh und Sprachspiel bei Cicero, in: Gymnasium 107, 2000, 497–518 7 G. E. DUCKWORTH, The Nature of Roman Comedy, ³1965.

H. GREINER-MAI (ed.), Der verliebte Zyklop. Humor und Satire in der Ant., 1989; M.-L. DESCLOS (ed.), Le rire des Grecs. Anthropologie du rire en Grèce ancienne, 2000.
JA. and R. DA.

Joldelund in the district of North Friesland. A Germanic centre of iron production – surveyed in modern times – from the period of the late Roman Empire and early barbarian invasions (*c.* AD 350–450). In the area of a village settlement with several peasant farms, specialized smelting of bog iron ores that occur locally took place in several hundred bloomery furnaces that were found distributed over *c.* 8 hectares. The raw iron that was extracted was further worked on site at several smithing locations. The necessary charcoal was produced in J. in at least one proven charcoal burner's location.

→ Iron; → Germanic archaeology

S. BACKER et al., Frühgesch. Eisengewinnung und -verarbeitung am Kammberg bei J., in: M. MÜLLER-WILLE, D. HOFFMANN, Der Vergangenheit auf der Spur, 1992, 83–110; H. JÖNS, Frühe Eisengewinnung in J., Kr. Nordfriesland, 1997.
V. P.

Jonathan (from Hebrew *Yeho natan*, 'God gave'). Name of several biblical figures as well as post-biblical people, especially of rabbis from the 2nd and 3rd cents. AD. The most important biblical figures by this name are 1) J., the son of Gerschom, according to Judges

18:30 a priest of the tribe of Dan, and 2) J., the son of Saul, the first king of Israel (1 Sam 13 and 14). The son of Saul is considered to be one of the noblest characters in the Bible. His sincere and close friendship with → David [1], that was, however, not highly regarded by Saul, is the subject of Haggadic stories (→ Haggadah) that emphasize its selfless and impartial aspects, as opposed to friendships marked by material and utilitarian considerations.

K. BUDDE, Das Buch der Richter, 1897; Id., Die Bücher Samuel, 1902; W. DIETRICH, Die Samuelbücher, 1995; L. GINZBERG, The Legends of the Jews, 1968 (Index). Y.D.

Joppa see → Ioppe

Jordan see → Iordanes [2]

Joseph (Hebrew personal name, from the Hebrew verb stem *jasaf*, 'to add'). The biblical tradition of the J. story (Gn 30ff.), a novella-like didactic tale, shows in its core statement how the hidden workings of God are behind the fate of an individual: J., the favourite son of → Jacob and Rachel, father of Ephraim and Manasse, is sold by his brothers into slavery in Egypt. He works as the servant of the pharaoh, once he has cleared his name of the accusation that he had raped the wife of Potiphar.

The material of the J. story, that goes back among other things to Egyptian models, was used in many ways in the Jewish, Islamic and Christian tradition right through to the 20th cent. (e.g. by THOMAS MANN). In Jewish-Hellenistic literature, J. is represented as an originator of the Egyptian civilization; Philo describes him primarily as a statesman and politician. In the Midrašim (→ Rabbinical literature) and the → Haggadah, his piety and righteousness are accentuated instead. The cause of the sufferings of J. is seen to be that he was preferred by his father Jacob. The sale of J. by his jealous brothers and his deportation to Egypt in particular are the subject of imaginative and vivid embellishments in the Midraš. In the Koran (12th Sura), the J. story, that has central status in the Muslim tradition, is supplemented with details that are not to be found in the biblical model; a different weighting is accorded to, for example, the seduction scene in which J. indeed feels passionate longing for Potiphar's wife but – as a god-fearing man – resists this for the sake of Allah.

M. J. BIN-GORION, Die Sagen der Juden, 1935 and passim; H. DONNER, Die lit. Gestalt der alttestamentarischen Josephsgesch., 1976; L. GINZBERG, The Legends of the Jews 2, ⁹1969; 5, ⁸1968; D. GOLDSTEIN, Jewish Folklore and Legend, 1980; J. HOROVITZ, Die Josefserzählung, 1921; L. RUPPERT, Die Josephserzählung der Genesis, 1965; I. SCHAPIRO, Die haggadischen Elemente im erzählenden Teil des Korans, 1907. Y.D.

Joshua Stylites ('the pillar saint'). A Syrian chronicle that contains detailed information about the local history of Edessa for the years 495–507 (e.g. about the siege of Amida), and is embedded in the chronicle of Zuqnīn, also known as the 'Chronicle of → [Ps.-] Dionysius [23] of Tell-Maḥrē'. It is frequently attributed to I. Stylites. He is probably also rightly considered to be the author of the entire chronicle.

EDITIONS: J. B. CHABOT, CSCO Scr. Syri 43 and 66, 1927 and 1949; W. WRIGHT, 1882 (with Engl. transl.); J. WATT, The chronicle of pseudo-Joshua the Stylite (Engl. transl. and notes).
BIBLIOGRAPHY: W. WITAKOWSKI, The Syriac Chronicle of Ps.-Dionysius of Tel-Mahre, 1987. S.BR.

Jossipon This historical depiction of world events (from Adam to the destruction of the Jewish temple in Jerusalem by Titus in AD 70) was written in Hebrew, presumably in the 10th cent. in southern Italy. It is based on the works of → Iosephus [4] Flavius (*Antiquitates Judaicae, Bellum Judaicum, Contra Apionem*). Aside from the Latin version of the *Bellum* (so-called Latin Hegesippus, 4th cent. AD) diverse medieval chronicles can be established as the main models. At the centre are disputes between Rome and Israel. Medieval translations into Arabic, Ethiopian and Latin are extant; editio princeps: Mantua before 1480 (short Hebrew version); Constantinople 1510 (long Hebrew version).

EDITIONS: ; J. F. BREITHAUPT, Josephus Gorionides, sive Josephus Hebraicus, Latine Versus, 1707; H. HOMINER, Shearith Yisrael complete, the second volume of Josiphon, 1967, (introduction by A. J. WERTHEIMER).
BIBLIOGRAPHY: S. BOWMAN, "Yosippon" and Jewish Nationalism, in: Proceedings of the American Academy for Jewish Research 61, 1995, 23–51; D. FLUSSER, Der lat. Josephus und der hebr. Jossipon, in: O. BETZ et al. (ed.), Josephus-Studien, 1974, 122–132; H. SCHRECKENBERG, Rezeptionsgeschichtliche und textkritische Unters. zu Flavius Josephus, 1977, 48–53; SCHÜRER 1, 117f.; S. SHULAMIT, From Joseph son of Mathias to Joseph son of Gorion, in: Tarbiz 64, 1994/5, 51–63; S. ZEITLIN, Jossipon, in: Jewish Quarterly Review 53, 1953, 273–297. I.WA.

Juba (Ἰόβας; *Ióbas*, Ἰούβας; *Ioûbas*, Ἰόβα; *Ióba*).
[1] Born in c. 85 BC, died in 46 BC, king of Numidia, son and successor of Hiempsal. In 63 J. represented Numidian interests in Rome (Cic. Leg. agr. 2,59). In 62 he became the enemy of Caesar who protected → Masintha and pulled J.'s beard (Suet. Iul. 71; re his appearance [1; 2]). In 50 J. was already king, but not yet recognized by Rome [3. 126–128]. C. → Scribonius Curio demanded Numidia's annexation; the Senate rejected this but left J.'s status open. In the civil war, the king stood by Pompey. His enemy Curio landed near Utica on 19 June 49; J. and his general → Saburra enticed him into a trap and killed Curio along with a large part of his army (Caes. B Civ. 2,23–44). The remainder surrendered to the followers of Pompey, but J. had most of them executed. Pompey now recognized him as *rex*, whilst Caesar had him declared an enemy of the state and had J.'s enemies Bocchus [2] and Bogudes [2] of Mauretania

declared kings. After the battle of Pharsalus, the followers of Pompey gathered under Q. → Caecilius [I 32] Metellus Scipio in Africa; the sources tell of leadership demands by J. which were ended only with the arrival of Cato (Plut. Cato minor 57f.; Cass. Dio 42,57,1–4). The king was ready with large numbers of troops when Caesar landed in Africa at the end of 47, but withdrew with the bulk of his army when Bocchus and P. Sittius invaded Numidia (Bell. Afr. 25,2–5). Only Scipio's promise that he would receive the whole of Africa (Cass. Dio 43,4,6) is said to have induced him to return. After Caesar's victory at Thapsus, J. fled without his army to his empire, where the city of Zama, however, locked its gates to him in view of his utter defeat. In despair he sought death near Zama in single combat with Pompey's follower M. Petreius (cf. [4]). Caesar incorporated Numidia as the province Africa Nova (→ Africa 3) and still triumphed over J. in Rome in 46.

1 RICHTER, Portraits III, 280   2 J. MAZARD, Corpus nummorum Numidiae Mauretaniaeque, 1955, 49–52 3 H. W. RITTER, Rom und Numidien, 1987   4 W. C. MCDERMOTT, M. Petreius and Juba, in: Latomus 28, 1969, 858–862.

H. G. HORN, C. B. RÜGER (ed.), Die Numider (cat. Bonn, RLM), 1979.   JÖ.F.

[2] Born in *c.* 50 BC, probably died in AD 23. Son of J. [1], king of Mauretania and writer. J. was displayed in → Caesar's triumphal procession in 46 BC. He was raised close to Octavianus (→ Augustus) in the Hellenistic-Roman manner, and received citizenship through him (cf. PIR² I 65). However, he went to war with him in 32 (Avien., De ora maritima, 279; Cass. Dio 51,15,6). In 25 Augustus appointed J. as client king of Mauretania and allocated parts of Gaetulia to him ([1]; formerly it was concluded incorrectly from Cass. Dio 53,26,2 that he ruled Numidia before this [2]). In 20 BC J. married → Cleopatra Selene whose royal origin is also reflected in the name of their joint son and heir → Ptolemaeus [I 24]. The existence of a daughter, Drusilla, is uncertain.

J. followed the model of Augustus in the minting of coins [3]. His residence and cultural centre in the Hellenistic style was called Iol, now → Caesarea [1]; the status of → Volubilis as a second seat is debatable [4]. The Romanization of → Mauretania progressed rapidly under J.; as a source of income he developed the extraction of purple (Plin. HN 6,201; [5]). After several apparently peaceful years, Cossus → Cornelius [II 26] Lentulus had to combat an uprising of the Gaetulians against the king in AD 3–6; from AD 17 there followed the revolt under → Tacfarinas, that was not ended before J.'s death [6. 2386f.]. Cleopatra died late; thereafter J. was married for a short time to → Glaphyra [2], the daughter of → Archelaus [7] of Cappadocia.

J.'s literary work [6. 2388–2395] concentrates on ethnography: books about Assyria, Arabia (dedicated to Augustus' grandson C. Caesar), Africa (different from the other works drawn from his own experience)

are known. There are also a short outline of Roman history, a comparative moral history and natural history works (→ Elephant), and large compendia about the theatre, music and painting. J.'s sources are Berosus, Onesicritus, Punic authors, perhaps also Varro and Verrius Flaccus. Fragments of J.'s work are provided particularly by Pliny the Elder, as well as Plutarch, Athenaeus and others.

1 R. DESANGES, Les territoires gétules de Juba II, in: REA 66, 1964, 33–47   2 H. W. RITTER, Rom und Numidien, 1987, 137–142   3 J. MAZARD, Corpus nummorum Numidiae Mauretaniaeque, 1955, 71–121   4 H. GHAZI-BEN MAISSA, Volubilis et le problème de regia Jubae, in: L' Africa Romana 10, 1992, 243–261   5 J. GATTEFOSSÉ, La pourpre gétule, invention du roi Juba de Maurétanie, in: Hespéris 44, 1957, 329–334   6 F. JACOBY, s.v. Iuba 2, RE 9,2, 2384–2395.

EDITIONS: FGrH 275; PIR² I 65.
BIBLIOGRAPHY: H. G. HORN, C. B. RÜGER (ed.), Die Numider (cat. Bonn, RLM), 1979.   JÖ.F.

[3] Author of a work about metric theory in at least four, probably eight or more bks. (Rufin. Gramm. 6,561,11 K; Prisc. Gramm. 3,420,24 K). The only statement about J. is offered by → Marius Victorinus (→ Asmonius) Gramm. 6,94,6: 'Our Juba, who, following the models of Heliodor, is a leading authority among the metricians because of his erudition'. J. therefore followed the system, represented by Heliodorus and Hephaestion, of *métra prōtótypa* (→ Metre), which is confirmed by the extant fragments. The title of the work was perhaps *ars metrica* (*J. artigraphus* in Serv. Aen. 5,522); the period in which it was written is between → Heliodorus [6] and → Plotius Claudius Sacerdos (end of the 3rd cent.) who quotes him; it is uncertain whether J. cites the poet → Septimius Serenus (beginning of the 3rd cent.) [4. 63f.]. The work of J. was of considerable influence; according to → Terentianus Maurus, he is the Latin theoretician of metrics most commonly quoted by the later Latin grammarians. The verbatim excerpts in Rufin. gramm. 6,561ff provide an impression of his depiction, that also included Greek examples in detail.

EDITIONS: 1 O. HENSE, De I. artigrapho (= Acta Soc. Lipsiensis 4), 1875   2 See GL 7,602.
BIBLIOGRAPHY: 3 P. L. SCHMIDT, in: HLL, § 442.2 4 J.-W. BECK, Annianus, Septimius Serenus und ein vergessenes Fr., 1994.
PARTIAL INDEX: 5 P. R. DÍAZ Y DÍAZ, Varro, Bassus, I., ceteri antiquiores (= Scriptores Latini de re metrica. Concordantiae, vol. 7), 1990.   J.I.E.

Jubilees, Book of see → Liber Iubilaerorum, see Liber Antiquitatum Biblicarum

Judah and Israel

I. ANCIENT ORIENT II. HELLENISTIC AND LATE
ANTIQUE PERIOD

I. ANCIENT ORIENT
A. DEFINITION B. PRE-MONARCHIC PERIOD
C. MONARCHIC PERIOD D. POST-MONARCHIC PE-
RIOD

A. DEFINITION

Juda (= J.) and Israel (= I.) are names that, in the
course of history, have displayed geographical, political, ethnic and theological components. J. was initially
the name of a region in southern → Palaestina; later, it
referred to the fictitious founding hero of a tribe and
thus became the name of the tribe itself. J. became a
political construct with David's kingdom (10th cent.
BC). The name J. (in OT *yhwdh*, in Ancient Hebrew
texts outside the OT *yhd/yhwd*, Assyrian *ia-u/ʾu-da-
a-a*, Babylonian *ia-a-ḫu-du*) possibly means '→ Yahweh
is victorious/may He be victorious' (cf. Gn 49:9; Dt
33:7), in which case it would be related semantically to
the name I. ('God rules/may God rule'; cf. Gn 32:29;
Hos 12:4).

At the end of the 13th cent. BC, the name I.
(*jsʾr/jsirʾr*) is for the first time attested for an ethnic
group in the Middle Palestinian region on the 'Israel
Stele' of Pharaoh Merneptah (4,552). In Assyrian inscriptions of the 1st millennium BC *Sirʾilajja* appears
once next to *Ḫumri* or *Bīt Ḫumri* (Omri or House of
Omri) and *Samerina* (Samaria). The entity with the
name I. is ambiguous in biblical usage: as a personal
name it appears solely in the form of the later renaming
of the founding hero Jacob as I. (Gn 32:29). There, a
unified people of I. is already envisioned that is projected into the early period as a religious community by the
Books of Ex to Jdg, that are meant to represent the
pre-monarchic period. It is not until the time of the
kings (1st half of the 1st millennium BC) that I. becomes
an autonomous state alongside J. (1 Sam 17:52; 18:16).
After David and → Solomon, the northern state of I.
exists alongside the southern state of J. (1 Kg 12 – 2 Kg
17). Even in this period, I. can be identified beyond its
territorial boundaries by way of ethos (2 Sam 13:12)
and religion (Is. 5:19; 5:24), especially in the Prophets
(Hos 9:1 and passim). After the fall of the northern and
southern states (722 or 587/86 BC), I. becomes the
name for Yahweh's chosen people (Is. 41:8 and *passim*),
while only the name J. continues to be used as a political
term (Neh 2:7 and passim), surviving in its Aramaic
form *Jehud* as the name of a Persian province, and in the
form *Iudaia* into the Hellenistic period under the Ptolemies and → Seleucids.

B. PRE-MONARCHIC PERIOD

The biblical view of history for the period following
'prehistory' (Gn 1–11) is a conception that did not take
on its final form until after the collapse of I. and J. and
the loss of the land for part of the people. More recent
research voices doubts on the picture presented in the
OT [6. 68–73]: the narratives about the 'Fathers' Abraham, Isaac and Jacob contain no indications that are of
any use historically; they reflect social and cultural
situations from various epochs and regions of the Ancient Near East; their image of the 'God of our fathers'
('the God of X'/'the God of my father' et al.) is not an
indicator for a religious epoch, but an expression of
familiar piety unrelated to period [2. 146–148]. Above
all, in these narratives, the experiences and the hopes of
the exiled 'I.' (2nd half of the 1st millennium BC) are
projected onto individuals from a distant past. In spite
of the OT fundamental creed of the liberation of the
enslaved people (Ex 1:11) from Egypt (Hos 11:1; 13:4
et al.) there are extreme positions that contest the historicity of the Exodus or transform the liberation into an
exile [6. 52–68]. A more moderate view has a small
Exodus group (but cf. Ex 12:37f.) fleeing from Egypt
under → Moses, and, after the theophany of their libe-
rating god Yahweh and after desert wanderings, entering the Promised Land (Ex 3:8 et al.) [1. 68–104].

Seen historically, the origin of 'I.' was a complex
process. When *c.* 1200 BC the system of city states in
Syria-Palestine was to a large extent collapsing in connection with the migration of the Sea Peoples (→ Sea
peoples, migration of), the tribes of I. formed during the
transition from Bronze Age to the Iron Age in the mountain regions of Palestine. On the basis of their material
culture, which displays continuity (everyday objects)
and discontinuity (domestic architecture, layout of
settlements) between pre-Israelite-Canaanite culture
and identifiably Israelite culture, they formed from the
populations of Canaanite cities and from socially un-
integrated groups in the vicinity of cities (*Ḫapiru*), and
from nomads who lived at the edge of the cultivated
region in symbiosis with the urban population [2.104–
121]. Models of a peaceful infiltration or warlike invasion of nomads from the desert, or a revolution of
Ḫapiru, are false, as is the theory of a subsequent
→ Amphiktyonia covering the entire country, in analogy with Ancient Greek and Ancient Italian examples
[2. 121–128]. Early 'I.' was a leaderless society of
tribes, segmentary in that its components were scattered. It comprised groups based on fictional ties of relationship, living from agriculture and cattle-raising. As
a consequence of interfamilial political alliances this
society developed into a stratified tribal culture and
eventually into a confederation of tribes and a state.

C. MONARCHIC PERIOD

Political (→ Philistines), economic (collapse of international trade, overpopulation) and societal factors
(social complexity) at the beginning of the Iron Age
favoured individual forms of rule, the first of which is
chieftainship (Gideon: Jdg 6–8, Abimelech: Jdg 9), to
which the reign of Saul (1 Sam 8–31) belonged, and
strictly speaking even that of David in → Hebron (2
Sam 2:1–11) [5. 111]. While Saul's rule over the territory of the subsequent northern kingdom was limited (2

Sam 2:9), David (2 Sam 1–24) ruled at first in Hebron over J. (2 Sam 2:1–4), then also over I. (2 Sam 5:1–5), with → Jerusalem as its capital (2 Sam 5:6–12). The 40-year reign (1 Kg 2:11) of → David [1] (*c.*1000 BC) could be as much of an idealization as his foreign-policy successes (2 Sam 8; 10:1–11:1; 12,26–31). Apart from the peasants' levy, he also maintained a mercenary army (Cherethites and Pelethites: 2 Sam 8:18 et al.) and a bureaucracy (2 Sam 8:15–18; 20:23–26). David's son Solomon (1 Kg 1) became his successor through court intrigue. The dynastic principle was (later) sanctioned by court theology (2 Sam 7). The building of both temple and palace are ascribed to Solomon (1 Kg 1–11; 1 Kg 6–7), who is also supposed to have ruled for 40 years (1 Kg 11:42): however, no consistent constructional activity (1 Kg 9:15–19) has been attested archaeologically for his period.

The conflict between I. and J., which arose already under David in the revolt of his son Absalom (2 Sam 15–19, cf. 2 Sam 20), became acute under Solomon's son Rehoboam (926–910 BC), with escalating measures of forced labour (1 Kg 12). The outcome was a split between I. and J. Rehoboam became king over J. in Jerusalem, Jeroboam I. (927–907 BC) in Sichem over I. Unlike in the southern kingdom, where the dynastic principle continued throughout the monarchic period, in the northern kingdom Omri (882–871 BC) was the first to lay the foundations of a lasting dynasty; he made → Samaria the capital of the northern kingdom, but his political achievements (cf. 1 Kg 16:21–28) together with those of his son → Ahab (871–852 BC) are obfuscated by the portrayal of prophetic opposition (Yahweh against → Baal, 1 Kg 17–19; 21; 2 Kg 1; 2). In the 9th cent. Assyria became a permanent threat to I. In 853 BC, Ahab participated in an opposition directed against Salmanassar III (858–824) [4. 361]; in 842 Jehu, who founded a further dynasty (2 Kg 10:29–36), paid tribute to Salmanassar [4. 363], and in 738 Menahem (2 Kg 15:17–22) to Tiglatpilesar III (745–727 BC) [4. 371], under whom I. lost Gilead, Dor and Galilee. Soon after, the remaining rump state of Efraim became an Assyrian province; when the last Israelite king Hosea (732–722 BC) refused tribute payments, Salmanassar V (727–722 BC) conquered Samaria (2 Kg 17, cf. [4. 382f.]), thus bringing about the political end of the northern kingdom.

Contrary to the picture given by the books of Kings, J., which fought for the territorial borders during the period of Rehoboam's successors (e.g. 1 Kg 15,21f.), was politically and economically inferior to the northern kingdom of I. A comparable standard of town planning and cultural assets was achieved only a cent. later than in I. [9. 518–30]. In 701 the Assyrian → Sanherib (705–681 BC) conquered J., but not Jerusalem [4. 390], whose ruler Hezekiah (725–697 BC) is particularly revered (2 Kg 18–20), as is also Josiah (639–609 BC; 2 Kg 22–23) later, when Assyrian power had fallen into decline. The Babylonians succeeded the Assyrians, conquering J. with its capital Jerusalem in 587/6, and making it a province. Thus both part-kingdoms, I. with 19 kings in a history of 200 years, J. with 19 kings and 1 queen in a history of 350 years, had been extinguished as political entities.

D. POST-MONARCHIC PERIOD

During the Babylonian Exile, J. belonged to the province of Samaria; during the Persian period under → Nehemiah it became an autonomous province with Jerusalem as its capital. The Temple was rebuilt, and the literary and religious heritage of I. and J. collected and codified on the basis of the Torah (Gn-Dt). The fallen states were not revived in the texts; at most, the restoration of the rule of David took place in a multitude of messianic aspirations. 'In the attempt to define and delimit itself, which began in Persian times and ended with the closing of the Canon, this Israel ... outlined the »biblical Israel«: an utopia, since that time regarded by two religions, each with many denominations, as binding. It is an aspect of the history of effect and reception that since 1948 a state – and now a nation – of I. exists again' [5. 189].

→ Bethlehem

1 R. ALBERTZ, Religionsgesch. Israels in at. Zeit, 1992 2 V. FRITZ, Die Entstehung I. im 12. und 11. Jh. v.Chr., 1996   3 S. HERRMANN, Gesch. Israels in at. Zeit, ²1980 4 TUAT   5 E. A. KNAUF, Die Umwelt des AT, 1994 6 N. P. LEMCHE, Die Vorgesch. Israels, 1996   7 H. M. NIEMANN, Herrschaft, Königtum und Staat, 1993 8 TH. L. THOMPSON, Early History of the Israelite People, 1992   9 H. WEIPPERT, Palästina in vorhell. Zeit, 1988.

R.L.

II. HELLENISTIC AND LATE ANTIQUE PERIOD

Under the rule of Alexander the Great from 332 BC, I. first fell to the Ptolemies after his death, but at the beginning of the 2nd cent. BC passed into Seleucid possession along with the whole of → Palaestina. In I., the heartland of Jewish settlement, the Maccabean revolt (→ Iudas Maccabaeus) broke out as a reaction to measures of enforced Hellenization and the desecration of the Temple in Jerusalem in 167 BC by → Antiochus [6] IV Epiphanes (175–164 BC). In the aftermath, the → Hasmonaeans (with stemma) succeeded in establishing rule, initially over a territory restricted to I. From the time of Simon (142–135/4), the Hasmonaean sphere of influence began to extend beyond the borders of I., the term Judaea, going back to the Greek *Iudaía chóra* (Ἰουδαία χώρα) designating the Hasmonaean kingdom as well as the country in a narrower sense.

In 63 BC Pompey occupied → Jerusalem. After the dissolution of the Hasmonaean kingdom, I. together with Idumaea and parts of → Galilee, became a Roman vassal state. As an ally of Rome → Herod [1], after repelling the Parthian invasion in 37 BC, extended his rule to the whole of Palaestina. As a consequence of the division of the kingdom on the basis of the will of Herod, in AD 4, I. together with Idumaea and → Samaria passed to Herod's son → Archelaus [10]; in AD 6, however, the latter was banished by the emperor Augustus. I. came under direct Roman rule, becoming part of the procuratorial province of Judaea under the overall hegemony of the province of Syria. The First Jewish War (AD 66–70/74) eventually led to Judaea's transformation into an independent praetorial province and to the stationing of the *legio X Fretensis* in Jerusalem. Many Jewish settlements were devastated during the course of the war. Once the revolt had been suppressed, the land passed in great part to the emperor, who settled Roman veterans at Emmaus [3]. The destruction of the Temple (AD 70) brought about the refoundation of Judaism in the form of rabbinical Judaism. Still more far-reaching were the consequences of the Bar Kochba uprising (132–135, → Bar Kochba). Jerusalem became the Roman *colonia Aelia Capitolina*, and Jews were forbidden to enter the city and its environs, so that the centre of Judaism moved to Galilee. The economic structure of I., specializing in the production of wine or grain as conditions allowed and the raising of sheep, was largely destroyed. The Christianization of I. began under Constantine [1] the Great, who built numerous churches at Christian holy sites. C. AD 400 I. belonged to the newly founded province of Palaestina prima.

→ Jerusalem; → Judaism

H.-P. KUHNEN, Palästina in griech.-röm. Zeit, 1990; F. MILLAR, The Roman Near East, 1993; J. A. SOGGIN, Einf. in die Gesch. Israels und Judas, 1991; G. STEMBERGER, Juden und Christen im Heiligen Land, 1987.   J.P.

Judaic law

A. BIBLICAL LAW: THE TORAH   B. THE DEVELOPMENT OF THE TALMUD   C. OTHER SOURCES OF JUDAIC LAW

A. BIBLICAL LAW: THE TORAH

Not much can be established with regard to the historical beginnings of Judaic law (JL), which has persisted for 3,000 years and is still observed in many parts of the world. Many of its rules (e.g. concerning murder and theft) exist in all cultures, although their historical origin cannot be attested. Thus, the law in the Bible has characteristics in common with legal systems known from other cultures in the Ancient Near East. The question of overlappings is much disputed, and so far convincing links have not emerged. The Codex Hammurapi for instance, which was effective well into the 1st millennium BC, was an academic statute book. Hammurapi and the biblical law givers may have created theoretical constructs on the basis of the same intellectual attitude towards themes of special interest (e.g. waiving of debts every seven years, restoration of land to its original owner every 49 years).

Biblical statutes (the Book of the Covenant in Ex 20:22–23:19, the laws in Dt 12–26, and numerous rules in the books of Numbers and Leviticus) are ascribed to → Moses; only in exceptional cases God himself imparts rules (thus to Noah and his sons, Gn 9, the Decalogue in Ex 19 and Dt 5). In his statutes 'Moses' takes up problems of his own time (the oppression of his people in Egypt) and the time of his ancestors (Abraham's marriage to his half-sister), but also those of much later times (the appointment of a king in Israel). The editors of this legal material founded their own legal tradition; thus, the early history of this material is very difficult to extricate.

A notable aspect of biblical law is the fact that different legal sources were inserted into a narrated story in various places; this story covers the period until that point in time when Moses is awaiting his death and the people of Israel are absent to enter the land of Canaan. The anonymous authors who are responsible for this fusing of statutes and narrative turn Moses into a legendary figure judging past events in the history of his people (Genesis to Deuteronomy), and predicting future developments (Joshua to 2 Kings). Thus, the literary tradition in these books of the Bible contains the same themes as those dealt with in the statutes. When one works out the connections between the statutes and individual narratives, the content of the statutes, their language and their often confusing sequences can be explained: thus, for example, in the Decalogue the interdiction on murder is mentioned in close proximity to the command to honour one's parents, with the promise of a long life on earth (Hebrew 'the ground'), because here the focus is on Cain's murder of Abel, the consequence of which is that Cain may no longer cultivate the ground.

In the 5th cent. BC, the Israelites succeeded in returning from captivity in Babylon under the leadership of Ezra and Nehemiah. The Torah (the first five books of Moses) became the sacred constitution of the people returning home; this implied strict reforms. Although the Torah originally had no force of law, its rules are nevertheless given that force in later books of the Bible. Thus, the development of ancient Judaic (biblical) law reached its conclusion.

B. THE DEVELOPMENT OF THE TALMUD

The next great legal corpus is the Talmud. It displays an advanced stage of legal development, demonstrating that JL was a dynamic system that underwent momentous changes between 100 BC and AD 500 (extension of contractual liability beyond dishonesty to negligence; rules in accordance with scripture instead of mere examples as exegetical legal authority). The Talmud contains material from the 1st cent. BC onwards, but most of its legal rules date from the 2nd cent. AD onwards. There are two versions of the Talmud: the Jerusalem or Palestinian (*c.* AD 425) and the Babylonian (*c.* 475 AD).

Both versions of the Talmud comprise a commentary, the Gemara, on the Mishna and the Tosefta. The Mishna is a codification of JL in Hebrew, written down at the end of the 2nd cent. AD by Rabbi → Jehuda. The Tosefta contains additions to the Mishna by Rabbi Jehuda's student, Hiyya bar Abba. Characteristic of the

Mishna is its emphasis on the legal constructs of the → Tannaim (rabbis who lived between 50 BC and AD 200). The Gemara presents the opinions of the → Amoraim (rabbis who lived between AD 200 and 500). The Talmud, mainly written in Aramaic dialect and covering all areas of life, consists of often unresolved legal and extra-legal controversial issues. Its discursive and didactic intention is obvious.

The Talmud demonstrates that large parts of the JL developed independent of the content of the biblical sources. From the 2nd cent. BC, the Pharisees (→ Pharisaei; an educated class who devoted themselves above all to the study of law and religion) had particular influence on this development; their traditions are preserved by the Talmud. The → Sadducees, an influential class of old, land-owning families, opposed the views of the Pharisees. Their criticism that the Pharisees disregarded regulations of the Holy Scriptures caused → Hillel (1st cent. BC) to make comprehensive use of Hellenistic rules of interpretation in order to 'prove' that the Pharisees' treatment of the law could in fact be derived from biblical legal rules. Rabbi Ismail (2nd cent. AD) used 13 hermeneutic rules (Hebrew *middoth*, Aramaic *mekilātā*, Greek *kanónes*), to develop legal statutes from biblical commandments. Rabbi Eliezer ben Gelili later proposed 32 rules for the interpretation of all biblical texts. To this complex process of interpretation may be imputed the frequently felt difficulty in understanding the logic of the Talmudic mode of argumentation. Dogmas and legal statements either opposed to or new to the content of Holy Scriptures are nevertheless attributed to it (belief in the resurrection, baptism of converts, kinds of capital punishment, the payment of damages instead of talio).

C. Other sources of Judaic law

The Apocrypha, the translation of the Bible into Greek (the → Septuagint) and Aramaic (the → Targums), the documents from a Jewish military settlement under the Persians in Egypt (the law of the papyri of Elephantine, 5th cent. BC), from → Qumran (the Dead Sea Scrolls) and from Judaeo-Christian circles (NT) all contribute to our modern understanding of ancient JL between the biblical period and that of the Talmud. The commentaries on the Holy Scriptures by → Philo of Alexandria (20 BC to AD 40) and that on the legal (et al.) content of the Book of Exodus by rabbis of the 2nd cent. AD (the Mekhilta) provide significant insights. The Apocrypha, with little to say on JL as a whole, may reflect regional usage. The papyri from Elephantine display a tendency to include facets of alien law. The language of the Septuagint reveals a greater knowledge of legal terminology than previously recognized. Philo's allegorization of biblical law combines refined legal analysis with comprehensive intellectual goals. The Dead Sea Scrolls record the narrow but very vivid interests of sectarian groups. The Judaism of the NT is indispensable to our comprehension of the history of the terms and conventions of the Talmud. Noteworthy in all these sources is the constant modernization of the ancient law. Rules so far narrowly interpreted are generalized. Outmoded institutions are adjusted: Hillel's prosbul neutralizes the rule for the remission of debts every seven years (Dt 15:1–11), by enabling repayment of loans to be enforced even after the seventh year.

→ Rabbinical literature

C.M. CARMICHAEL, The Spirit of Biblical Law, 1996; D. DAUBE, Collected Works: Talmudic Law, ed. C.M. CARMICHAEL, 1992; W. SELB, Ant. Rechte im Mittelmeerraum, 1993, 157ff., 202ff.   C.M.C.

Judaism
A. GENERAL, TERMINOLOGY B. THE FOUNDATIONS OF JUDAISM C. JUDAISM FROM ALEXANDER THE GREAT TO AD 800

A. GENERAL, TERMINOLOGY

The term Judaism is derived from the Hebrew *Yehuda* (cf. the tribal name Juda, → Juda and Israel), whose etymology is not entirely certain. It denotes not only the Jewish religion, but also – and quite particularly so – the ethnic belonging to the Jewish people, which is not unproblematical from our modern view, as well as the people's entire cultural, political and philosophical milieu, in Ancient Israel and in the → Diaspora. A generally recognized, handy definition of Judaism is lacking to this day, since even within Judaism itself with its various tendencies – from ultra-orthodoxy to reform Judaism – no unified understanding of Judaism exists. The term can probably be best grasped through the → Halakha, the Jewish religious law. Here, the religious aspect is always combined with the idea of belonging to the Jewish people (which appears to have finally reached its climax in the foundation of the state of Israel). The term Judaism is especially problematic also with regard to the various groups within Judaism (Ashkenazim, Sephardim, Yemenites), which do not allow for a homogenous concept of *one* Jewish people.

B. THE FOUNDATIONS OF JUDAISM

Basic to a *religious* understanding of Judaism is a strictly monotheistic conception of God without a mediator between God and humanity like → Jesus or → Mohammed. The Torah (→ Pentateuch), given by God to the people of Israel, determines the entire life of a Jewish person through its commandments and prohibitions as well as its moral duties, with *zedaka*, justice as the highest moral duty. Although Judaism knows no dogmatic teachings, it knows regulations that were already set out in the Torah and later expanded, commented upon and – entirely in accordance with the Torah – supplemented (→ Talmud) in the Halakha: since God as creator is the centre of the world, He is to be honoured in gratitude and humility; thus, the entire Jewish year with its feasts is directed towards the sanctification and veneration of the Eternal. The highest Jewish holiday, *Yom Kippur*, requires of each individual that he/she do penance in a spirit of repentance and remorse. For humans with their inclination to evil (*jeṣær hā-rāʿ*), endowed by God with the free will to do good but also evil, sin continually, and it is only by repentance (*tᵉšubāh*) that they can save themselves from evil.

Alongside the individual's endowment with a free will, a further basic principle of Judaism is God's choosing the entire people of Israel (often misunderstood as an arrogant sense of superiority over other peoples). The sense of this choice lies in the fact that adherents of Judaism are obliged to strict compliance with the laws, especially with regard to the Covenant (*bᵉrīt*) that God entered into with Israel and which is sealed by the circumcision of every new-born boy at the age of eight days. Even the sufferings of the Jewish people as portrayed in the Bible may only adequately be understood against the background of this state of being chosen (for suffering).

Judaism knows no systematic theology, such as defined in Christianity; although there were (and are) attempts to systematize religious subject matters (cf. → Philo of Alexandria).

> F. BAUTZ (ED.), Geschichte der Juden von der biblischen Zeit bis zur Gegenwart, 1983; G. FOHRER, Gesch. Israels, 1982; J. MAIER, Gesch. des Judentums im Altertum, 1989; N. DE LANGE, Judaism, 1986; T. SCHWEER, Stichwort J., 1994; G. STEMBERGER, Die jüdische Religion, 1995.   Y.D.

C. JUDAISM FROM ALEXANDER THE GREAT TO AD 800

1. PROBLEMS AND HISTORY OF RESEARCH
2. EXTERNAL HISTORY   3. SITUATION AS REGARDS COMMUNICATION   4. HISTORY OF THOUGHT

1. PROBLEMS AND HISTORY OF RESEARCH

Jewish history and culture between → Alexander [4] the Great and the Middle Ages was for a long time discredited as 'intertestamental period' or 'Late Judaism'; these labels reflected a particular theological or historical position rather than doing justice to the subject [16]. Classical philology, however, had and still has a problem with Judaeo-Hellenistic literature (→ Literature): the part conceded to it within literary history is as a rule minimal in relation to its influence. Theology, on the other hand, is traditionally inclined to usurp Judaeo-Hellenistic culture *in toto* as a *praeparatio evangelica* [12; 13; 14]; Jewish Studies is a recent academic discipline, in which scholars can no longer be expected to have a classical education as a matter of course. Thus, only in recent years a real change has come about [38]. Jewish Studies and theology, classical philology and ancient history [6] are beginning to understand Judaeo-Hellenistic culture as a phenomenon *sui generis* on which → Christianity builds, but whose specifically Jewish character cannot be denied. The place of the Jews in the ancient world and their relationship with its culture was to mark the relationship between Jews, 'pagans', Christians and Muslims to this day (→ Anti-Semitism).

2. EXTERNAL HISTORY

After the conquest of Palestine by Alexander (332 BC), due to strategic considerations, Palestine belonged first (312–198 BC) to the kingdom of the Ptolemies, then that of the Seleucids (from 198 BC). Thus, until the loss of Babylon to the Parthians (160 BC; → Parthian Wars) these two kingdoms ruled over the two main centres of Judaism Politico-religious parties, sparkled off by the increased → Hellenization, formed groups round the opposing priestly families of the Oniads (of whom one, → Onias III, built a temple at → Leontopolis/Egypt with the permission of Ptolemy VI) and the → Tobiads. The attempt by Seleucus IV and especially Antiochus [6] IV (175–164) to Hellenize the Temple led to the resistance of traditional groups, and after its suppression to a national uprising, soon led by → Judas [1] Maccabaeus. His dynasty, the → Hasmonaeans, were in the same dilemma as their successors, the dynasty of → Herodes [1]: political survival in a Hellenistic environment required acculturation; this, however, caused the resistance of those traditional circles that had helped this dynasty to gain power, and upon whose support it was dependent. Successful in a certain sense as the foreign policy of the Hasmonaeans was (conquest and forced conversion of the Edomites to Judaism), internal opposition erupted in the civil war of the → Pharisaei against → Alexander [16] Jannaeus. Roman rule, clearly demonstrated by Pompey's Middle Eastern campaign (63), did not alter the basic constellation: the dynasty of Herod, loyal to the Romans, faced a quiet but growing opposition, which, after the direct take-over of Palestine by the Romans, erupted in the uprising of the → Zealots (AD 66). Not the Jewish War itself but its consequences (the destruction of the Second Temple and the extinction of the Temple service; payment of the Temple tax to the Roman treasury [→ *fiscus Iudaicus*]; disappearance of the office of High Priest and transfer of religious leadership to the rabbis) have been formative for Judaism to this day (synagogues replaced Temple service). Jewish reaction to the increase in Roman power was not uniform: it ranged from cooperation (Patriarch Juda I) to further, militarily unsuccessful uprisings (AD 115–117 under Trajan; 132–135 under Hadrian, → Bar Kochba). Antoninus Pius rescinded most of Hadrian's punitive measures; the leader of Palestinian Judaism, the Patriarch, resided first in Jamnia, then (from the 3rd cent.) in → Tiberias, and was leader of the Jewish self-government, which even included also jurisdiction affairs. The Severan dynasty (→ Severus) was well-disposed towards the Jewish community.

At first, Rome's transformation into a Christian state made things easier for the Jews under → Constantinus [1] the Great (partial lifting of the prohibition of settling in → Jerusalem), but already under → Constantius [2] II an inglorious series of legal restrictions against the Jews began (with the exception of → Iulianus [11], who even ordered the rebuilding of the Temple): prepared by the anti-Semitic polemic of the

Church, these restrictions range from Theodosius I and the Codex Theodosianus, to → Iustinianus, whose laws governing politics and legislation with regard to the Jews were to remain definitive for the next centuries.

The situation of the Babylonian community living first under Parthian then Sassanid rule was entirely different. Under an → Exilarch, who was obliged to be loyal to the Persian regime, the local theological schools, such as Sura and Pumbeditha, flourished to such an extent that even Palestine was put into the shade: thus, the Babylonian and not the Jerusalem → Talmud, has predominated (to this day). The Jewish magical bowls with inscriptions in Aramaic, found in great numbers, show that syncretic forms of religion existed alongside evolving rabbinical orthodoxy in ancient Mesopotamia. The fundamentally more tolerant attitude of the Persians eventually led to a situation in which the support of the Jews became a factor in Sassanid politics, as in the capture of Jerusalem (AD 614) and in the conflicts in Yemen (Dū Nuwās).

The Byzantine attitude towards the Jews remained characterized by Justinian's legislation, but the Arabian → Caliphs adopted the attitude of → Mohammed: Christianity and Judaism are legitimate religions of the possessors of the Book (*ahl al-kitāb*); proselytism is forbidden; both communities must pay a special tax and are obliged, through their leaders, to remain loyal to the Islamic ruler. This markedly more liberal attitude in comparison to the Byzantine, and the strong affinity between Judaism and → Islam, based especially on religious legislation and the basically horizontal rather than centralist/vertical structure of the religious elite, resulted in a revival of Jewish intellectual life under Islamic rule, especially in Spain, so that after the translation of the Torah by Saadja Gaon (from the Fajjum, born 882, died 942 in Sura / Babylonia) an adequate medium of expression was available even in Arabic.

In contrast to Islam, Jews under Byzantine rule led a marginal existence, although their situation can nevertheless be defined as better compared to that in medieval Western Europe. Attempts by Byzantine emperors such as → Heraclius [5] or Basil I to convert the Jews by force remained episodes. Hebrew works such as the 'Vision of Daniel' (*ḥ^azōn D.*) from the 10th cent. reflect the persecutions down to the time of → Constantinus Porphyrogenetus. In spite of immigration from Islamic lands (including Karaites from Babylon) and the association with the → Chazars, a distinct Judaeo-Byzantine identity developed during the Byzantine period: to the present day, these communities, called 'Romaniots' (from Ῥωμανία, Byzantium), contrast with the Spanish, Arabic and Ashkenazi communities and in cultural and linguistic respects they are the sole direct descendants of Hellenistic Judaism. Their non-Hebrew synagogal literature is written in modern Greek; their centre is the north-western Greek town of Jannina (near Chalcis). Although the line of tradition thus flows from the Hellenistic period down to the present day, research has left these communities virtually untouched.

3. SITUATION AS REGARDS COMMUNICATION

Analogous to the expansion of the Jewish communities across the entire Mediterranean, from the time of Alexander the linguistic situation of Judaism changed fundamentally: from the post-exilic period only the two immediately related idioms Hebrew and Aramaic prevailed in Palestine (Aramaic as the administrative language of the Middle East was increasingly widespread), but the presence of Jews in Hellenistic cities (above all Alexandria) and then also in the West (Rome) soon made knowledge of these languages an issue for educated people. The adoption of Greek as an oral and to some extent written medium of communication did not only create the condition for the rise of Hellenistic-Jewish literature (→ Literature), but, since the Torah was actualized through interpretive translations into Greek or Aramaic, it became an essential prerequisite for Jewish discourse on the written tradition: oral translation by the *meturgeman* was fixed in written form; such translations, however, are not necessarily literal, but range from slavish imitation of the Hebrew original to a free retelling (e.g. the *Targum šēnī* on Esther [8]). In this context, the later Christian adoption of the Septuagint simply represents a Greek Targum as the Torah. In spite of the increasing tendency in the Roman period for Hebrew to disappear as a spoken language, the rabbis in Palestine and Babylon preserved the language in its later form as well as Aramaic (as in the Babylonian Talmud); at this period both idioms are extensively enriched with Greek and Latin loan words (cf. [18]). Judaism in the diaspora, on the other hand, predominantly used Greek: → Philo had only a slight command of Hebrew, and Paul's mother-tongue was certainly Greek. It may therefore be assumed that circumstances during the Hellenistic period had already provided the basic constellation for Judaism to become a mediator between linguistic and cultural areas at a later period: educated Jews were as a rule bilingual. This is especially evident in the multilingual epitaphs in the capital city of Rome [26]. The predominance of Greek as a second language next to the representative Hebrew was not altered even by the existence of Jewish communities in the western half of the empire: the Jewish catacombs in Rome show a clear predominance of Greek. Yet it is very probable that a Judaeo-Latin literature did exist (e.g. the → *Collatio legum Mosaicarum et Romanarum*). It is a matter of dispute whether, owing to their distance from the Roman state, the Jews and later the Christians spoke a particular kind of Greek or Latin; this is of particular importance as Christian terminology was evidently shaped by the Greek and Latin terminology for Jewish monotheism and its organisation. The best answer seems to be that in spoken language the differences, if they existed, were only very slight: the vulgarisms of the inscriptions in the catacombs in Rome are not particularly 'Jewish'. Literary culture seems to present a different picture: it is in translated literature or other kinds of re-created original texts that the influence of the Hebrew original is most probable. It may in any case be said that the Latin Targums of the Greek-Jewish → Bible that may be supposed to lie behind the *Vetus Latina* have had a decisive formal and stylistic influence on European literature. As a result of the preference of rabbinical orthodoxy for Hebrew-Aramaic, Greek-Jewish literature became increasingly marginalized in late antiquity; the rise of Judaeo-Aramaic literature (Aramaic was rightly recognized as being similar to Hebrew) in the Islamic realm meant further losses. Thus, if research, insofar as it is supported by Protestant theology, did not restrict itself mainly to Judaeo-Hellenistic literature down to the end of the 1st century AD, the Greek literature of the Romaniots in Jannina and Chalcis would acquire increased significance as a living example of the Hellenistic tradition.

4. HISTORY OF THOUGHT

The basic problem for Jewish culture in the Hellenistic and Roman periods was the confrontation with the prevailing non-Jewish culture surrounding it; in this respect, no difference can at first be determined between it and other cultures of the eastern Mediterranean: each in their own manner either took on the challenge posed by the dominance of Hellenism or were threatened by assimilation (→ Hellenization). The essential difference was, of course, the monotheism of Judaism: a simple → *interpretatio Graeca* as in the case of the Egyptian or Babylonian gods was, if we disregard the efforts of Hellenistic circles around the High Priest Iason under → Antiochus [6] IV, not possible. Thus, the cultural development in the Hellenistic-Jewish context is entirely marked by this dilemma, on another level also experienced by rulers such as → Herod [1]: survival and expansion (proselytism) presupposed acculturation; but this could endanger the core of Jewish identity.

The most important document of this acculturation is the extant Hellenistic-Jewish literature: whether authors try to narrate Jewish history in terms of the categories of Hellenistic historiography (→ Iosephus [4] Flavius) or to formulate Jewish history of salvation by applying the terminology of Stoicism or Platonism (→ Philo of Alexandria), or even to bring the Exodus story into line with Hellenistic models as a tragedy (→ Ezechiel), in the background there is always the endeavour to preserve their own tradition and thus their identity by means of partial adoption. Thus, it makes no sense to separate the retelling of the Torah by Josephus or Philo from parallel texts of the rabbinical tradition: the specific Jewish tradition of the 'rewritten Bible', arising from the linguistic and historical need to reformulate tradition in order to preserve it. In fact, the two textual corpora complement each other: the rabbinical, written for the most part in Hebrew-Aramaic, and the 'Hellenizing' written in Greek. How small the line is between translation, reinterpretation and reformulation is demonstrated by the history of the Greek → Targum which the Church calls the 'Septuagint' (LXX): the numerous parts of the Greek Torah, either written or surviving only in Greek, have lived on to the present day as canonical of the Greek and Eastern Churches.

This 'multi-lingualism' of Judaism was made possible by its lack of a hierarchical and dogmatic structure which Islam was to inherit. Thus, the events surrounding the Jewish War and the Bar-Kochba uprising were indeed to weaken the Jewish-Hellenistic tradition, but not to extinguish it: although the LXX is eliminated from the Jewish tradition, Greek Targums continue to be created in antiquity (→ Symmachus; → Aquila [3]). Thus, although it is true that → rabbinic literature contains numerous allusions [21; 22] to classical languages and loan words from them, while recounting within its structure oral discussions typical of rabbinical academies [11], Hellenistic Judaism in the form of Romaniote Judaism has survived to the present day; only recently the (polemical) use of the LXX has been attested until the Ottoman period [19]. This is in line with the fact that, although in late antiquity Jewish literature flourished again in Hebrew and Aramaic (*Piyyūṭīm*), while other languages such as Greek and Latin became marginal, from the time of Saadja a new literary language arises in the Jewish-Arabic context; the Greek synagogue songs and Targumim of today's Romaniots, the oldest of which have their origins in the 12th cent., presuppose an older tradition.

The crucial research question thus remains that of the relationship of the Jews to their non-Jewish environment; an exemplary attempt to deal with this question, though limited to Rome, but also from an archaeological, historical, literary and linguistic perspective, was provided by [26]. But the surviving monuments in Rome already demonstrate the complexity of the problem; an expanding tendency in late antiquity to return to traditional values, to separation and the revival of the Hebrew language, is unquestionable; as a result, groups such as the Jewish Christians were marginalized. The great influence on the emerging Islam by isolated Jewish groups such as those on the Arabian Peninsula [15] is also evident. In a certain sense, Islam too may be regarded as an heir of the cultural community of late antiquity, which owes fundamental aspects to Judaism.

→ Jerusalem; → Juda and Israel; → Literature (Jewish); → JUDAISTICS; → JUDAISM

1 Z. ANKORI, Karaites in the Byzantine Empire: The Formative Years 970–1100, 1959   2 M. AVI-YONAH, The Jews under Roman and Byzantine Rule, 1984   3 D. R. G. BEATTIE, M. McNAMARA (ed.), The Aramaic Bible. Targums in their Historical Context, 1994   4 J. L. BERQUIST, Judaism in Persia's Shadow. A Social and Historical Approach, 1995   5 E. J. BICKERMAN, The Jews in the Greek Age, 1988   6 H. BOTERMANN, Das Judenedikt des Kaisers Claudius, 1996   7 A. DIEZ MACHO, El Targum. Introducción a las traducciones aramaicas de la Biblia, 1979   8 B. EGO, Targum Scheni zu Ester (TSAJ 54), 1996   9 L. H. FELDMAN, Jew and Gentile in the Ancient World. Attitudes and Interactions from Alexander to Justinian, 1993   10 R. FELDMEIER, U. HECKEL (ed.), Die Heiden, Christen und das Problem des Fremden, 1994   11 A. GOLDBERG, Der verschriftete Sprechakt als rabbinische Literatur, in: A. und A. ASSMANN, CHR. HARDMEIER (ed.), Schrift und Gedächtnis, 1983, 123–140   12 M. HENGEL, Die Zeloten, ²1976   13 Id., Judentum

und Hellenismus, ⁴1988   14 M. HENGEL, A. M. SCHWE-MER, Paul Between Damascus and Antioch, 1997   15 J. W. HIRSCHBERG, Jüd. und christl. Lehren im vor- und frühchristl. Arabien. Ein Beitrag zur Entstehungs-gesch. des Islams, 1939   16 C. HOFFMANN, Juden und Judentum im Werk dt. Althistoriker des 19. und 20. Jh., 1988   17 Italia Judaica. Atti del I. convegno internazio-nale, Bari 18.–22.5.1981, 1983   18 S. KRAUSS, Griech. und lat. Lehnwörter in Talmud, Midrasch und Targum, 2 vols., 1898/9   19 D. J. LASKER, S. STROUMSA, The Polem-ic of Nestor the Priest. With an Appendix by J. NIEHOFF-PANAGIOTIDIS, 2 vols., 1996   20 L. I. LEVINE, The Rab-binic Class of Roman Palestine in Late Antiquity, 1989   21 S. LIEBERMANN, Greek in Jewish Palestine, 1942   22 Id., Hellenism in Jewish Palestine, 1950   23 J. LIEU et al. (ed.), The Jews Among Pagans and Christians in the Roman Empire, 1992   24 A. LINDER, The Jews in Roman Imperial Legislation, 1987   25 M. J. MULDER (ed.), Mikra. Text, Translation, Reading and Interpretation of the Hebrew Bible in Ancient Judaism and Early Christian-ity, 1988   26 L. V. RUTGERS, The Jews in Late Ancient Rome. Evidence of Cultural Interaction in the Roman Diaspora, 1995   27 P. SCHÄFER (ed.), Stud. zur Gesch. und Theologie des rabbinischen Judentums, 1978   28 H. SCHRECKENBERG, Die christl. Adversos Judaeos Texte und ihr lit. und histor. Umfeld (1.–11. Jh.), 1982   29 SCHÜRER   30 S. SHAKED (ed.), Irano-Judaica: Studies relating to Jewish contacts with Persian culture through-out the ages, n.d.   31 J. STARR, The Jews in the Byzantine Empire. 641–1204, 1939   32 M. STERN, Greek and Latin Authors on Jews and Judaism, 3 vols., 1974–1984   33 G. STEMBERGER, Das klass. Judentum. Kultur und Gesch. der rabbinischen Zeit, 1979   34 Id., Einl. in Talmud und Midrasch, ⁸1992   35 H. L. STRACK, P. BIL-LERBECK, Komm. zum NT aus Talmud und Midrasch, 4 vols. and 2 index vols., 1926–1961   36 V. TSCHERI-KOVER, Hellenistic Civilisation and the Jews, 1959   37 Id., A. FUKS, Corpus Papyrorum Judaicarum, 3 vols., 1957–1964   38 G. VELTRI, Eine Tora für den König Tal-mai. Unters. zum Übersetzungsverhältnis in der jüd.-hell. und rabbinischen Lit., 1994   39 Id., Magie und Halakha: Ansätze zu einem empirischen Wissenschaftsbegriff im spätant. und frühma. Judentum, 1997   40 P. WEXLER, Three Heirs to a Judaeo-Latin Legacy: Judaeo-Ibero-Ro-mance, Yiddish and Rotwelsch, 1988   41 Th. WILLI, Juda-Jehud-Israel. Stud. zum Selbstverständnis des Juden-tums in pers. Zeit, 1995.   J.N.

Judas

[1] J. Maccabaeus. (The epithet probably from Hebrew *maqqaebaet*, 'the hammer', owing to military success). Third son of the priest Mattathias (→ Hasmonean), in 167/166 BC he took over leadership of the Jewish rebels who rose against the desecration of the Temple in Jeru-salem, the ban on the Jewish religion and the pressure of taxation under → Antiochus IV [6]. J. proved himself to be a master of guerrilla tactics and politics as well as a charismatic leader. His military success made Anti-ochus IV hold out the prospect of an amnesty and the restoration of the old religious order, under the condi-tion that the rebels should lay down their arms. J. thwarted the respective negotiations by recapturing Jerusalem, where the Jewish cult was resumed in

December 165 (the day of the reconsecration of the Temple, the 25th of Kislew, is remembered the feast of Chanukka), and by extending the war to encompass the rescue and resettlement of Jewish minorities. This caused → Lysias, the 'chancellor' of → Antiochus [7] V, to force peace with a large army: in the summer of 163, J. was defeated at Beth-Sacharja, the Jewish fortress of Beth-Zur was captured, and a High Priest named Alci-mus [4] was installed in Jerusalem with the agreement of the Hasidim, who broke off the alliance with J. J. went underground with his supporters. The uprising regained ground under the new Seleucid supreme lord → Demetrius [7] I. In March 161, J. defeated a Seleucid army under → Nicanor at Adasa (on the 13th of Adar, which as Nikanor day became a Jewish feast day), and by means of a delegation obtained an alliance with Rome. But Demetrius [7] I forestalled a Roman inter-vention. In April 160 J. suffered a crushing defeat through the Seleucid *strategos* → Bacchides, and fell in the battle. Sources: 1 and 2 Macc.

→ Jerusalem; → Judaism

1 SCHÜRER 1, 158–179   2 K. BRINGMANN, Hell. Reform und Religionsverfolgung in Judäa, 1983   3 B. BAR-KOCHVA, Judas Maccabaeus, 1989.   K.BR.

[2] J. Iscariot. Probably Hebrew *Iš kariot* or *keriot*, a man 'from Kariot' (in the territory of the tribe of Juda), one of → Jesus' twelve disciples. The figure of J. is dis-puted in the literature on the life of Jesus: he is supposed to have delivered Jesus to the authorities and then com-mitted suicide. But, in spite of several NT references, neither the figure of J. nor the act itself can be confirmed historically. Through the great (theological) signifi-cance acquired by J. in the Christian world, the name J. became synonymous with 'traitor'; more recent re-search (e.g. [2]) has it that the Jew J. committed the betrayal out of disillusionment when Jesus refused to organise an uprising against the Romans. Another, more Christian-orientated view understands J. as some-one who betrayed Jesus in the belief that his death would bring about the longed-for redemption. In post-biblical literature J. acquired great popularity, not least owing to the atrocious nature of his supposed deed.

1 C. COHN, Der Prozeß und Tod Jesu aus jüd. Sicht, 1997 2 D. FLUSSER, Die letzten Tage Jesu in Jerusalem, 1982 3 W. FRICKE, Standrechtlich gekreuzigt, 1986   4 W. JENS, Der Fall J., 1975   5 SCHÜRER   6 S. ZEITLIN, Who Cru-cified Jesus?, 1964.   Y.D.

Judge see → Dikastes; → Iudex

Judith (Ιουδιθ, *Iudith*, *Iudit*). The Book of J., which has come down to us only in Greek and (dependent on it) in Latin and belongs to the Apocrypha (→ Apocryphal lit-erature), goes back to a Hebrew original. In a politically and militarily difficult situation, with the inhabitants of the mountain city of Betylia besieged by Nebuchadnez-zar's commander → Holofernes, and consequently suf-fering from lack of water, Judith, a young, rich and pious widow, appears. After admonishing the people to trust in God, and after saying a prayer, she goes to the enemy's camp, where she claims that she has left her people and wishes to help Holofernes capture the city. After several days' stay in the camp of the enemy, during which she continues to live true to the law, she succeeds in beheading Holofernes' as he lies drunk after a banquet, whereupon the Israelites are able to defeat the weakened Assyrians. A hymn ascribes this triumph to God's intervention. In spite of the numerous details as to the location of the episode and the characters involved, the unhistorical nature of the story is obvious. Nebuchadnezzar is introduced as the king of the Assyrians, residing in → Niniveh; Holofernes was in fact the commander of the Persian king Artaxerxes [3] III. Thus, this narrative is a kind of historical novella, reminiscent of the story of Esther in the Septuagint (→ Esther): God appears as the Lord of history, who puts His people to the test but unmasks all military power and brings salvation to His people when they turn to Him in prayer. The Book of J. originated not before 150 BC, probably in Jerusalem. Especially the portrayal of J. at the banquet with Holofernes shows the influence of the Hellenistic → novel.

M. HELLMANN, Judit – eine Frau im Spannungsfeld von Autonomie und göttlicher Führung, 1992; E. ZENGER, Das Buch Judit (Jüd. Schriften aus hell.-röm. Zeit: Histor. und legendarische Erzählungen I/6), 1981; Id., s.v. J./Judithbuch, TRE 17, 404–408 (with further bibliography). B.E.

Jugglers see → Entertainers

Jugurtha, Julian, Juno, Jupiter etc. see → Iu-

Julio-Claudian dynasty This term describes the first five sole rulers of Rome (including their families) after the end of the Republic and the Civil Wars: Augustus, Tiberius, Caligula, Claudius [III 1], and Nero. If we begin Augustus' monarchical status with his victory at Actium (→ Actium) on 2 Sept. 31 BC, the dynasty's rule lasted almost 99 years, until the suicide of Nero on 9 (?) June, AD 68. It descends from four families (→ Augustus: stemma 'The Julio-Claudian dynasty'): the *familia Iulia, familia Octavia, familia Claudia* and *familia Domitia*. But in reality the dynasty unfolded almost exclusively by adoption, although as far as possible blood relatives were adopted: Augustus was Caesar's great-nephew through his sister Iulia [4]; Tiberius was Augustus' stepson; Caligula's father Germanicus [2] was the nephew of Tiberius and adopted by him; Claudius adopted his stepson L. Domitius Ahenobarbus (Nero). Only Claudius himself, brother of Germanicus, was not received into the family by adoption; but as Tiberius' nephew and Caligula's uncle he was a close relative. So he also took on the names Caesar Augustus, as all other *principes* of this dynasty, although they gradually lost the character of names and took on the significance of titles. The means of → adoption or of establishing fami-

ly relationships through marriage were also applied to individuals who later did not come to power, such as Agrippa [1], Gaius and Lucius Caesar (= Iulius [II 32] and [II 33]), Germanicus [2] and Aemilius [II 9] Lepidus (under Caligula).

The respective wives and daughters, too, played a decisive role in the family network, also with regard to adoptions and transferences of power: Augustus' daughter Iulia [6]; his wife Livia; Vipsania Agrippina [1], wife of Germanicus and mother of Caligula; Iulia Agrippina [3], daughter of Germanicus, sister of Caligula, wife of Claudius and mother of Nero. Family connections, mainly established by adoption, provided the solution to the problem of passing on the imperial *patrimonium*, which was by law private property. The fiction of inheritance within the family was still maintained even in Claudius' case; it ended only with Galba [2], and this meant also the end of the dynasty.

1 R. SYME, Augustan Aristocracy, 1986   2 H. BELLEN, in: ANRW II 1, 1964, 91ff.   3 F. HURLET, Les collègues du Prince sous Auguste et Tibère, 1997. W.E.

Juniper For the Greeks, the name κέδρος/*kédros* (→ *cedrus*) described, among other things, various species of juniper, such as the prickly juniper (also ὀξύκεδρος/*oxýkedros*: *Juniperus oxycedrus* L.) and the common juniper (*J. communis* L.) which grows in the higher mountains of Greece. The latter is also called κεδρίς; *kedrís* (Theophr. Hist. pl. 1,9,4; 1,10,6; 1,12,1), while ἄρκευθος/*árkeuthos* is thought to refer to the Phoenician juniper (*J. phoenicea*), whose berries only ripen in the second year (ibid. 1,9,3; 3,12,3 f.). Six species occur in Greece today, including the Syrian juniper (*J. drupacea*; [1. 33, colour photo 55]), which can barely be distinguished from cedars, the arborvitae (*Thuja* L.) and the savin (*J. sabina* L.). With the Romans, the juniper was called *iuniperus* (Varro, Rust. 1,8,4; Verg. Ecl. 7,53; Plin. HN 16,73; Isid. Orig. 17,7,35). To what extent the juniper (*kédros*) – and not the cedar – was actually used as building timber, for cosmetics, and as incense (cf. Hom. Od. 5,60) is uncertain. Pliny mentions juniper posts (HN 17,174), juniper berry wine (ibid. 14,112, cf. Dioscorides 5,36,2 WELLMANN = 5,46 BERENDES) and the diuretic effect of the berries (*arkeuthís*) used, among other things, to treat coughs, and pains in the chest, side and stomach (Plin. HN 24,54 f., cf. *árkeuthos* in Dioscorides 1,75 WELLMANN = 1,103 BERENDES).

1 H. BAUMANN, Die griech. Pflanzenwelt, 1982.

M. C. P. SCHMIDT, s. v. Ceder, RE 3, 1821–1826; H. O. LENZ, Botanik der alten Griechen und Römer, 1859 (repr. 1966), 355–362; J. MURR, Die Pflanzenwelt in der griech. Myth., 1890 (repr. 1969), 127–129. C. HÜ.

Justice/Right (δίκη/*díkē*, δικαιοσύνη/*dikaiosýnē*, τὸ δίκαιον/*díkaion*; *iustitia, aequitas*). 'Justice'/'right' is a relational term which identifies the fairness or reasonableness between two parameters. In Greek, on the other hand, the archaic word *díkē* (δίκη) goes back to the root *deik-* (δειϰ-) and means the way 'pointed out', the directive. This meaning still manifests itself in the earliest philosophical speculation on justice, in the poet Hesiod (around 700 BC): the jurisdiction of the kings (*díkē* as a judgement, used mainly in the plural) can be 'straight' (ἰθεῖα; *itheîa*), in other words just, or 'crooked' (σϰολιή; *skoliḗ*), in other words unjust (Theog. 86; Op. 248–266). Yet *díkē*, used in the singular, already in Hesiod takes on the meaning of the term 'justice', i.e. a measure of fairness. It is primarily a matter of fair allocation, which is personified and deified as → *Díkē* (Theog. 901–903). Violation of *díkē* is caused by lack of moderation (ὕβρις/*hýbris*) and violence (βία/*bía*) (Op. 213–247). In both areas justice is achieved if the traditional rights to status of the individual remain protected and if the social partner's sphere of rights is not violated by lack of moderation. This sphere of rights is already called *díkē* in Homer (Hom. Il. 19,118). There, it is linked to the 'honorary rank' (τιμή/*timḗ*) (Hom. Il. 1,510). In Hesiod the world of the gods is similarly organized: a just allocation of domination to the gods by Zeus consists of assigning honorary ranks (Hes. Op. 881–885). Violation of the sphere of rights happens, according to Hesiod's thinking, above all if violence is added to lack of moderation (βία; *bía*). Human beings are superior to all the animals according to Hesiod because they possess *díkē*, since they can resolve their conflicts by a judge's verdict instead of by violence (Hes. Op. 274–280).

The basic concepts implied in Hesiod's speculations on *díkē* of justice as a divine power which manifests itself in fair allocation and respect for the allocation were in part applied and in part given a different, deeper interpretation in the period following. In pre-Socratic thinking (6th and 5th cents. BC) the order of nature was subject to the verdict of *díkē* (Anaximander 2 B1 DK); in Heraclitus (22 B23 and B28 DK) and Parmenides (28 B8,14 DK) *dike* guards the truth.

On the other hand *díkē* appears in the → Sophistic as political justice (5th and 4th cents. BC). It is explained by Protagoras (Pl. Prt. 322a–324d) as the basis of state life, but dismissed by Antiphon as obedience to the law from the criterion of what is 'salutary by nature' (87 B 44 DK).

In classical Attic philosophy (5th and 4th cents. BC), on the other hand, justice becomes the attitude that distinguishes human beings as human beings. → Socrates supports the general Attic view of justice as obedience of the citizen to state laws: however, for the first time this obedience is removed from the area of external behaviour alone and rooted in moral personality (Pl. Crit. 49e–54d).

In Plato speculation about justice reaches its zenith, as the term (the idea) of the just refers to a universal principle of order of everything that exists. Justice is on the one hand the overall virtue of the individual soul and consists of rational control over oneself (Pl. Resp. 4,443c-e). On the other hand it is the constitutive aspect of the state, insofar as the *polis* is given its natural constitution solely by justice (Resp. 2,369a–4,428a; Leg. 6,756e–757d). The common denominator of the two ideas of justice (individual virtue – state order) is the concept of order (ϰόσμος/*kósmos*; τάξις/*táxis*; Pl. Grg. 503d–504d). A more precise definition of this order emerges by using the Pythagorean model of proportional or geometrical equality (ἰσότης γεωμετριϰή, τάξις ϰατὰ λόγον), which proves to be a uniting force in the realm of true being (Resp. 500b-c), the sensual cosmos (Pl. Grg. 507e–508a; Pl. Ti. 30c-d), the state (Pl. Leg. 6,756e–757a) and the soul (Pl. Resp. 4,443c-e).

Aristotle retracts this extension of the term justice and reduces justice to the realm of the state. By contrast with Plato, he clearly separates right (τὸ δίϰαιον/*to díkaion*; τὸ νόμιμον/*to nómimon*; Eth. Nic. 5,1130b 18–1131a 9; 1135a 6) and justice as a virtue among human beings (Eth. Nic. 5,1133b 18–1134a 6).

In the period following, i.e. via the Stoa to Cicero, and, following him, Ulpian (around AD 200), the word *dikaiosýnē* (διϰαιοσύνη) or *iustitia* designates the social virtue of human beings and is identified with distributive justice. Its definition in the ancient Academy (4th cent. BC) was already: 'justice is a firm attitude of will which gives to each his share according to his worth (ἀξία)' (ἕξις διανεμητιϰὴ τοῦ ϰατ' ἀξίαν ἑϰάστῳ; Pl. Def. 411d-e) and appears in Roman thought as the formula of the *suum cuique tribuere* (Cic. Inv. 2,53,160; Cic. Rep. 3,11,18; Cic. Leg. 1,6,19; Cic. Off. 1,5,15; Ulp. Dig. 1,1,10). This consistent tradition (up to Augustine and Thomas of Aquinus) is opposed in the pre-Christian era only by Epicurus (Kyriai Doxai 33–37); according to him justice originates from the calculation of a person's usefulness and is defined as 'not harming one another'. In the Platonic school from the time of the Principate onwards (1st cent. BC) justice counts as one of the low, social virtues which prepare for promotion to the intellectual virtues. Fundamental to the period following was, however, Cicero's adoption of the distributive justice of the *suum cuique* ('to each his own'). This formula ends up in the entire following western legal philosophy up to the current legal theory of John RAWLS.

→ JUSTICE

F. SENN, De la justice et du droit, 1927; A. VERDROSS-DROSSBERG, Abendländische Rechtsphilos., 1962; H. WELZEL, Naturrecht und materielle Gerechtigkeit, ⁴1990; A. NESCHKE, Platonisme politique et théorie du droit naturel, vol. 1: Platonisme politique dans l'antiquité (D'Hésiode à Proclus), 1995.   A. NE.

Addenda

Fat Fluid, semi-solid or solid material obtained from vegetable or animal cells, and of great importance to human → Nutrition as a source of energy and vehicle of flavour. In early antiquity → Butter, lard and suet predominated. Use of these animal fats subsequently remained at a high level in antiquity, especially in northern regions; in the Mediterranean region, olive oil eventually gained absolute pride of place. Although relatively expensive (CIL III 2, p. 827 3,1–3; 4,10–11; p. 828 4,49–50), olive oil was held in highest regard of all fats in the kitchen of classical antiquity (Ath. 4,169e; 170b; 173e-f). It was added to dry foods such as salad and raw → Vegetables, to sauces, desserts and cakes, and was also used for frying and conserving (Plin. HN 18,308; 19,143).

> J. ANDRÉ, L'alimentation et la cuisine à Rome, ²1981, 181–185; A. DALBY, Siren Feasts. A History of Food and Gastronomy in Greece, 1996; A. S. PEASE, s.v. Oleum (oil), RE 17, 2454–2474.   A.G.

Faustinupolis (Φαυστινούπολις; *Phaustinoúpolis, colonia Faustinopolitanorum*). Originally the village of Halala, 24 km south-east of Tyana; the modern Başmakcı. Here died in AD 176 → Faustina the Younger [3] (SHA Aur. 26,4; 9), for which M. Aurelius elevated F. to the status of *colonia*. Attested since 431 as a bishopric.

> M. H. BALLANCE, Derbe and F., in: AS 14, 1964, 139–145; R. P. HARPER, s.v. F., PE, 326; HILD/RESTLE, 258f.; T. DREW-BEAR, Inscriptions de Cappadoce, in: J. DESCOURTILS (ed.), De Anatolia Antiqua, 1991, 130–149; M. COINDOZ, Cappadoce méridionale, in: B. LE GUEN-POLLET, O. PELON, La Cappadoce méridionale, 1991, 83.   K.ST.

Fire, Greek A weapon of the Byzantine navy similar to a flame-thrower, first mentioned in the defence against the Arab attack on Constantinople in AD 674–678. Its mode of operation was successfully kept secret for several centuries. Presumably petroleum (extracted from natural sources) was heated in a pressure container, ejected with air pressure through a metal pipe and ignited. The flames continued to burn on the water and were hard to extinguish.
→ Callinicus [3]

> J. F. HALDON, M. BYRNE, A Possible Solution to the Problem of Greek Fire, in: ByzZ 70, 1977, 91–99; TH. KORRES, Ὑγρόν Πῦρ, 1985.   AL.B.

Frontier (ὅρος/*hóros*, μεθορία/*methoría*; Latin *finis, limes*).
I. SUBJECTIVE AND OBJECTIVE FRONTIER PERCEPTION II. THE FRONTIER AS CONTROL SYSTEM III. THE FRONTIER AS HABITAT IV. FRONTIER LINE AND FRONTIER AREA

I. SUBJECTIVE AND OBJECTIVE FRONTIER PERCEPTION

The earliest evidence for the perception of the topographical dimensions of frontier zones predates the concept of the state. In Greece, differences in burial rites, cults of the dead and of heroes and the territorial distribution of crafted goods since the Iron Age point to actions motivated socially and subjectively, defining ethnically coherent communities or peoples as distinct from others. As states arose, bringing territorial stability, the frontier became an objective instrument by which the territorial extent of a politically organized community was marked.

Other areas of concern are the conditions under which frontiers were drawn up, the measures taken to define and maintain frontier lines, the effects of the drawing up of frontiers upon the social, economic and political spheres (including the division of land, which came about as a result either of spontaneous agreement between neighbours on the use of frontier zones, or of interstate agreements and treaties). Lexical development in the semantic field of 'frontier', which followed a similar path in various spatial and temporal contexts (in Greece: *eschatiá, perioikís*; in Rome: *confinium, terminus, limes*), indicates the normative process in which peripheral regions were included.

II. THE FRONTIER AS CONTROL SYSTEM

One aspect of peripheral regions is their contacts with the external world, and in this capacity, frontier zones play a part in systems of international relations. In ancient Greece, social, political and economic points of contact primarily characterized neighbourly relations. Difficulties arose in creating conformity and balance between different social entities that were homogeneous in living conditions, language and religious traditions. The bilateral (rarely trilateral or multilateral) agreements documented in epigraphical evidence were clearly aimed at creating a system in which the division of the political space could be consciously and habitually accepted and recognized [1. 93–177]. The first border control devices were signs demarcating the frontier line on the ground, for which fixed natural objects (mountains, watercourses, peculiarities of the landscape such as outcrops, maquis, swamps and deserts) were used or, in their absence, man-made signs (*cippi* fixed in the ground (→ *cippus*), steles, cairns, or buildings, sacred or profane, already in existence before the drawing up of the frontier).

In large centralized kingdoms, the predominant concept was that of a frontier expanding constantly outwards (until it coincided with the → oikuménē); this was seen as the task of the ruling elite, and corresponded with their efforts to expand their own power. In ancient Egypt, the Pharaoh was 'Lord of the Earth to its frontier' and 'of that which is bounded by the course of the Sun', or the one who had laid out the frontier of Egypt 'where they live whom the Sun touches on its way'. The dynamics of the frontier are expressed in the texts of the New Kingdom: they confirm as the Pharaoh lays out the frontier in every place that it pleases him [2]. The ideology of a Roman Empire encompassing the world is manifest in the Latin formulations *Gentibus est aliis tellus data limite certo: Romanae spatium est urbis et orbis idem* ('To other peoples is given a land with fixed frontiers; to the Roman people, the extent of the city and that of the world are one and the same': Ov. Fast. 2,683 f) and *Imperium sine fine dedi* ('I [Jupiter] have given to them an Empire without frontiers': Verg. Aen. 1,279).

In the Persian empire, the geographical frontiers of the rule of the Great King were identical to the internal frontiers of the peoples and cities under royal authority; the public administration of the satraps failed to eradicate the lines of division which had their origins in the sense of ethnic identity of the peoples subservient to Persian rule or subject to Persian influence. In relation to the Greeks, the → Peace of Antalcidas (386 BC, Xen. Hell. 5,1,31) meant the universal recognition of royal power over the entire east of the *oikuménē*.

As a result of Greek → colonization groups with different social structures, political intentions and ways of seizing the land were brought into contact. According to time and circumstances, the results either favoured the process of integration or provoked disintegration, as is shown by the history of the Calabrian peninsula, where we find assimilated settlements with mythical founders (e.g. → Brundisium) on the one hand and antagonistic relations between Iapyges-Messapii and the Spartan colony of → Taras [2] on the other. As a result, the frontier was not only the preferred zone for contacts and trade between the Greek foundations and the indigenous population, but also an obstacle to processes of assimilation, and a defensive line for each group's own ethnic and cultural characteristics.

III. THE FRONTIER AS HABITAT

A frontier must predominantly be understood as a space which extends throughout and beyond the frontier established by political and legal action. In Egypt, Mesopotamia and ancient China, frontier areas defined ecologically and topographically were formed by deserts or dry steppes surrounding fertile, water-rich central plains, where settlements and primary economic activities were concentrated. In Greece, mountainous areas and hills were used as pasture and for timber harvesting, mostly with small-scale settlement. As in ancient China, contacts or exchanges between settled and

nomadic cultures could take place on the frontier. There were armed conflicts at frontiers; they could also, however, act as points of exchange for trade, as on the Limes (see below) and the polis frontier in Greece (Dem. Or. 23,37–39: *ephoría agorá*, 'frontier market'). This complex relationship, characterized by coexistence both peaceful and conflict-ladden, took shape both in the amphictyonic cults of some frontier regions (in which forms of limited, local trans-frontier solidarity among pastoral and agrarian communities arose) and in attempts by central authorities to expand the *chóra* (→ territorium) of the city. According to a law mentioned by Aristotle (Pol. 7,1330a), some states banned citizens living on the frontier from taking part in decisions concerning war with neighbouring states, as their private interests might prevent an unprejudiced judgement. Overall, there was a tendency to see the frontier as an autonomous economic system and independent living space. The recognition of territorial sovereignty led to the introduction of customs duties (→ Toll).

IV. FRONTIER LINE AND FRONTIER AREA

A frontier can be linear and marked with visible signs. It can arise as a unilateral decision, but more often as a result of an understanding between adjoining communities or states, to define their mutual territorial boundaries. The linearity of a frontier implies an assumption of its immovability; anyone damaging or destroying the visible signs of a frontier would have to expect state and sacral sanctions (Gaius [Dig. 10,1,13] cites a law of Solon; IG II² 1165,18 ff.). The frontiers were under the protection of divinities with the → epiclesis *Hórios* ('Protector of Frontiers'): in Greece these were above all Zeus (Dem. Or. 7,39; cf. Pl. Leg. 8,842e–843d) and Apollo (Paus. 2,35,2), also Demeter Thermasia (Paus. 2,34,6); in Rome it was → Terminus (Ov. Fast. 2,641; Liv. 1,55,3). In early Rome, the → pomerium separated the sacred inner precinct of the *auspicia urbana* (→ effatio) from the periphery, which did not have a clear definition. The ban originally placed on extending the *pomerium* was later lifted.

Frontier areas are zones recognized as extraterritorial by neighbouring states, on the grounds of established right or by agreements concerning the legal status of neutral zones (*chórai érēmoi, methória, methoríai, en methoríois*; Thuc. 2,18,2; 2,27,2; 2,98,1; 4,56,2; 4,91,1; 4,99,1; 4,128,2; 4,130,2; 5,3,5; 5,41,2; 5,54,1; 5,54,4; 8,10,3; 8,98,2; Suda s. v. Ἀπατήσει; Εὔβουλος; Κελαιναί; Μεθόριον; Σαραπίων; Σεβῆρος). In some cases, these areas were subject to shared rule, in order to share the use of their natural resources (*koinaí chórai*). Frontier areas lying between politically and militarily superior states were subject to the strategic considerations of the neighbouring powers. They were often the object of military attacks and annexation attempts, e.g. the small states of Triphylia and Acroreia in the mountains north of Elis [1] between Sparta and Elis [2] (Xen. Hell. 3,2,30; 4,2,16), Cynuria [1] or Thyreatis in the north of Cynuria between Sparta and Argus (Thuc.

2,27,2), Oropos between Athens and Boeotia (Paus. 1,34,1–4; 7,11,4–7,12,3; Str. 1,4,7; cf. Pl. Criti. 110e), Myus between Miletus [2] and Magnesia [3] (evidence in [1. no. 11]); the → Regnum Bosporanum similarly functioned as a buffer state shielding the Pontus against the aggressive political regime of the Mithridatids. Also to consider are regions, poleis and states which, owing to their particular geographical location, for example at the intersection of important roads, form transit areas; in Greece, Phocis and West and East Locris were a kind of corridor for mass migrations, trade routes and troop movements between northern and southern Greece (→ Migration, → Traffic).

The → Limes, originally a strip of land dividing the Roman Empire from territories outside, had two functions: one dynamic (as the front line in the military conquest of areas lying outside the Empire) and one static (as an enduring line of defense for the empire's frontier). Various activities corresponded to these two tasks, so that the Limes could, according to circumstances and local realities, be more aggressive or more defensive in nature. Over time, the Limes took on an increasingly military role, with fortification systems (→ burgus), walls and ditches; natural barriers such as massifs or watercourses, e.g. the Rhenus [2] (the Rhine) and the Istrus [1] (the Danube), reinforced with castella, were incorporated.

1 G. Daverio Rocchi, Frontiera e confini nella Grecia antica, 1988   2 E. Hornung, Zur geschichtlichen Rolle des Königs in der 18. Dynastie, in: MDAI(K), 15, 1957, 122–125.

S. De Atley, F. Findlow, Exploring the Limits: Frontiers and Boundaries in Prehistory, 1984; M. Liverani, Confine e frontiera nel Vicino Oriente del Tardo Bronzo, in: Scienze dell'Antichità, 2, 1988, 79–99; M. A. Levi, I nomadi alla frontiera, 1989; E. Olshausen, H. Sonnabend (ed.), Grenze und Grenzland (Geographica Historica 7), 1994; Y. Roman (ed.), La frontière, 1993; L. Braccesi, Grecità di frontiera, 1994; A. Rouselle (ed.), Frontières terrestres, frontières célestes dans l'antiquité, 1995; C. R. Whittaker, Frontiers of the Roman Empire, 1996; C. Ulf (ed.), Wege zur Genese griech. Identität, 1996; Confini e frontiera nella Grecità d'Occidente, Atti del XXXVII Convegno di Studi sulla Magna Grecia (Taranto 1997), 1999.   G. D. R.